OSL

OFFICIAL SCRABBLE® LISTS

OSL

OFFICIAL SCRABBLE® LISTS

Comprehensive lists, plus hints and strategies

Compiled by
Allan Simmons and Darryl Francis

Chambers

Scrabble® is a registered trade mark owned in the USA and
Canada by Milton Bradley Company, Massachusetts, in
Australia by Murfett Regency Pty Ltd, Victoria, and
elsewhere by J W Spear & Sons PLC, Enfield, England.

Published 1991 by W & R Chambers Ltd,
43–45 Annandale Street, Edinburgh EH7 4AZ

© W & R Chambers Ltd 1991

British Library Cataloguing in Publication Data

A catalogue record for this book is
available from the British Library

ISBN 0-550-19026-0

Printed in England by Clays Ltd, St Ives plc.

Preface

Scrabble® players already have the support of OSW (*Official Scrabble® Words*) in helping their games and minimizing their arguments. Now another ally is at hand – *Official Scrabble® Lists* (OSL) – which adds to the players' skills and strategies.

Based on OSW, and ultimately on *Chambers English Dictionary*, this vast collection of lists of words, specifically structured for most Scrabble situations, is the Scrabble player's ideal companion. As well as the lists, there are explanatory hints on such subtleties as Rack Balancing, Fours Feeding and Looking at Hooks.

OSL now takes its place along with OSW in ensuring that you enjoy making the most of every game of Scrabble.

Francis A Spear
Chairman
J W Spear & Sons PLC

Contents

Introduction

Official Scrabble Lists is a complete companion to *Official Scrabble Words* (OSW) itself hailed as the definitive authority for all Scrabble players. *Official Scrabble Lists* (OSL) is a unique and thorough collection derived from the wealth of words within OSW and categorized into sections according to usefulness and interest as recommended by two of the country's top Scrabble players. Whether you are a casual or regular Scrabble player, the lists are an invaluable aid, acting as a convenient vocabulary-building guide for the newcomer and a specialist reference for the more experienced.

The starter section serves as a quick introduction to an armoury of essential vocabulary, supplying all valid two, three and four-letter words plus complete lists of every high-scoring word containing J Q X or Z. There are lists to help players out of awkward situations: words with many consonants; words containing two B's, two C's, two F's etc.; words containing multiple A's, E's, I's, O's or U's. There is a section that concentrates on word endings and a section featuring some 200 specially selected combinations of letters unique to Scrabble playing, yielding thousands of likely seven and eight-letter 'bonus-scoring' words.

And then there's the specialist 'hook' section, detailing every possible single-letter extension of words from two to seven letters to form valid longer words. As well as 'everyday' examples such as BROAD to ABROAD and ABLE to TABLE there are fascinating novelties to be unearthed such as HOMELY to HOMELYN, HAROSET to CHAROSET, and common but often unthought of extensions such as FLAMING to FLAMINGO and UNFAIR to FUNFAIR. This particular section is a delight in itself.

Of course no Scrabble book is complete without anagrams. OSL is no exception, listing every valid

seven and eight-letter word according to its constituent letters arranged in alphabetical order. Here are thousands of anagrams at your fingertips, from the exotic KURSAAL/RUSKALA to the surprising CUSPATE/TEACUPS, and ready solutions for jumbles of letters such as HLPRSUU (SULPHUR of course) and AAAGMNR (what else but ANAGRAM!).

What more could the Scrabble-player want? How about advice on learning words and tips on strategic play? OSL provides the answer here too, with over twenty-five hints offering sound advice to help improve your vocabulary and revealing a few strategic secrets of success.

Official Scrabble Lists is the ultimate single-volume Scrabble players' ready-reckoner.

Allan Simmons

Hints

SECTION ONE

STARTER LISTS

Introduction

This section contains a variety of so-called 'starter lists'. There are the basic words – a complete listing of all valid two-letter, three-letter and four-letter words. There are lists of words with many vowels and words with many consonants – ammunition for helping you discard disproportionate numbers of vowels or consonants. There are lists of words with multiple numbers of the same vowel or same consonant – the awkward vowel dumps and the awkward consonant dumps. And there are complete lists of words up to eight letters long with a J, Q, X or Z. Each of the various lists is described in more detail in its accompanying introductory text.

BASIC WORDS

The following lists contain all the two-letter, three-letter and four-letter words. There are almost 6000 words in these three lists, and while it is not essential to know all of them, it will certainly help your game to know as many as possible.

There are 106 two-letter words listed here. Two-letter words can be considered as the backbone words of any Scrabble game. They are very important, not necessarily for the scores which they themselves achieve, but also for the scores of other words whose play they facilitate, either at the same time or later in a game.

The two-letter words provide a means of playing words parallel to other words already on the board, resolving surplus vowel problems (for example, AA, EE and OO), squeezing scores out of tight board situations, or opening the board for future scoring opportunities. Many of the two-letter words can have letters added before or after them, in order to make valid three-letter words – see the Hooks section for these.

Make a list of the two-letter words that you are not familiar with and try to introduce them into your games. You might find it additionally helpful to know what your words mean. It really can help to cement the words into your mind if you know roughly what they mean. But you will have to check *Chambers English Dictionary* for meanings. Top-flight Scrabble players will know *all* 106 of these words, and will also be able to define most of them!

There are just over 1000 three-letter words listed here. These are important as they provide a means of discarding unwanted letters, a means of squeezing scores out of difficult board situations, and a means of playing higher-scoring words (perhaps bonuses) by turning two-letter words into three-letter words. Try to familiarize yourself with some of those which are unknown to you, and see if you can play them in your games. Leading Scrabble players will be aware of most of the three-letter words and will be able to call on them when they are needed. But most of the top players will occasionally be uncertain of a three-letter specimen. For example, a Scrabble player may well recall FAY and FEY, but will be unsure of FOY, a player might know HAH and HOH, but will be uncertain about HEH and HUH.

There are approximately 4600 four-letter words here. Their importance is less than that of the two and three-letter words, but they do still provide a useful pool of words to dip into for scoring or rack balancing purposes.

2-LETTER WORDS

AA	AX	EE	GI	IS	MI	OE	OW	TA	WE
AD	AY	EF	GO	IT	MO	OF	OX	TE	WO
AE	BA	EH	GU	JO	MU	OH	OY	TI	XI
AH	BE	EL	HA	KA	MY	OI	PA	TO	YE
AI	BO	EM	HE	KO	NA	OM	PI	UG	YO
AM	BY	EN	HI	KY	NE	ON	PO	UM	YU
AN	CH	ER	HO	LA	NO	OO	RE	UN	ZO
AR	DA	ES	ID	LI	NU	OP	SH	UP	
AS	DI	EX	IF	LO	NY	OR	SI	UR	
AT	DO	FA	IN	MA	OB	OS	SO	US	
AW	EA	FY	IO	ME	OD	OU	ST	UT	

HINT _____

Two's Company

There are 106 two-letter words and they are all fundamental to the game. The importance of knowing all the two-letter words can't be emphasized enough. They are vital for parallel word play and maximizing scoring on tight boards and should be learnt off by heart. Write out the complete list over and over again. Play a few solo games allowing yourself to 'cheat' by referring to the list but don't rely on the lists for too long. If you don't exercise your memory you won't recall them during actual play.

HINT _____

Score or Strategy?

The highest-scoring move is not always the best play. Always consider lower-scoring alternatives that might be better for your strategy. A lower-scoring move might not give so many points away to your opponent, or might leave you with a better balance of letters on your rack, or might enable you to set yourself up for a good score the next turn. Losing 10 points one turn may provide an extra 20 points the following turn or, if your emphasis had been on rack balance rather than score, it may even yield a 50-point bonus play.

3-LETTER WORDS

AAS	BAH	CHI	DOR	EWT	GAY	HID	JIB	LES	MOD
ABA	BAM	CIG	DOS	EYE	GED	HIE	JIG	LET	MOE
ABB	BAN	CIT	DOT	FAB	GEE	HIM	JIZ	LEU	MOG
ABY	BAP	CLY	DOW	FAD	GEL	HIN	JOB	LEV	MOM
ACE	BAR	COB	DRY	FAG	GEM	HIP	JOE	LEW	MOO
ACT	BAS	COD	DSO	FAH	GEN	HIS	JOG	LEX	MOP
ADD	BAT	COG	DUB	FAN	GEO	HIT	JOR	LEY	MOR
ADO	BAY	COL	DUD	FAP	GET	HOA	JOT	LEZ	MOT
ADS	BED	CON	DUE	FAR	GEY	HOB	JOW	LIB	MOU
AFT	BEE	COO	DUG	FAS	GHI	HOC	JOY	LID	MOW
AGA	BEG	COP	DUN	FAT	GIB	HOD	JUD	LIE	MOY
AGE	BEL	COR	DUO	FAW	GID	HOE	JUG	LIG	MOZ
AGO	BEN	COS	DUP	FAX	GIE	HOG	JUS	LIN	MUD
AHA	BET	COT	DUX	FAY	GIF	HOH	JUT	LIP	MUG
AIA	BEY	COW	DYE	FED	GIG	HOI	KAE	LIS	MUM
AID	BEZ	COX	DZO	FEE	GIN	HON	KAI	LIT	MUN
AIL	BIB	COY	EAN	FEN	GIO	HOO	KAM	LOB	MUS
AIM	BID	COZ	EAR	FET	GIP	HOP	KAS	LOG	MUX
AIN	BIG	CRU	EAS	FEU	GIS	HOS	KAT	LOO	NAB
AIR	BIN	CRY	EAT	FEW	GIT	HOT	KAW	LOP	NAE
AIS	BIO	CUB	EAU	FEY	GJU	HOW	KAY	LOR	NAG
AIT	BIS	CUD	EBB	FEZ	GNU	HOX	KEA	LOS	NAM
AKE	BIT	CUE	ECH	FIB	GOA	HOY	KEB	LOT	NAN
ALA	BIZ	CUM	ECU	FID	GOB	HUB	KED	LOW	NAP
ALB	BOA	CUP	EDH	FIE	GOD	HUE	KEF	LOX	NAS
ALE	BOB	CUR	EEK	FIG	GOE	HUG	KEG	LOY	NAT
ALL	BOD	CUT	EEL	FIL	GOG	HUH	KEN	LUD	NAY
ALP	BOG	CUZ	EEN	FIN	GON	HUM	KEP	LUG	NEB
ALS	BOH	CWM	EFF	FIR	GOO	HUP	KET	LUM	NED
ALT	BOK	DAB	EFS	FIT	GOS	HUT	KEX	LUR	NEE
AMI	BON	DAD	EFT	FIX	GOT	HYE	KEY	LUX	NEF
AMP	BOO	DAG	EGG	FIZ	GOV	HYP	KID	LUZ	NEK
ANA	BOP	DAH	EGO	FLU	GOY	ICE	KIF	LYE	NEP
AND	BOR	DAK	EHS	FLY	GUB	ICH	KIN	LYM	NET
ANE	BOS	DAL	EIK	FOB	GUE	ICY	KIP	MAC	NEW
ANN	BOT	DAM	EKE	FOE	GUM	IDE	KIR	MAD	NIB
ANT	BOW	DAN	ELD	FOG	GUN	IDS	KIT	MAE	NID
ANY	BOX	DAP	ELF	FOH	GUP	IFF	KOA	MAG	NIE
APE	BOY	DAS	ELK	FON	GUR	IFS	KOB	MAK	NIL
APT	BRA	DAW	ELL	FOP	GUS	ILK	KON	MAL	NIM
ARC	BRO	DAY	ELM	FOR	GUT	ILL	KOP	MAM	NIP
ARE	BUB	DEB	ELS	FOU	GUY	IMP	KOS	MAN	NIS
ARK	BUD	DEE	ELT	FOX	GYM	INK	KOW	MAP	NIT
ARM	BUG	DEI	EME	FOY	GYP	INN	KYE	MAR	NIX
ARS	BUM	DEL	EMS	FRA	HAD	INS	LAB	MAS	NOB
ART	BUN	DEN	EMU	FRO	HAE	ION	LAC	MAT	NOD
ARY	BUR	DEW	END	FRY	HAG	IOS	LAD	MAW	NOG
ASH	BUS	DEY	ENE	FUB	HAH	IRE	LAG	MAX	NOH
ASK	BUT	DIB	ENG	FUD	HAJ	IRK	LAH	MAY	NOM
ASP	BUY	DID	ENS	FUG	HAM	ISH	LAM	MEL	NON
ASS	BYE	DIE	EON	FUM	HAN	ISM	LAP	MEN	NOR
ATE	BYS	DIG	ERA	FUN	HAP	ITA	LAR	MES	NOT
AUF	CAB	DIM	ERE	FUR	HAS	ITS	LAS	MET	NOW
AUK	CAD	DIN	ERF	GAB	HAT	IVY	LAT	MEU	NOY
AVA	CAM	DIP	ERG	GAD	HAW	JAB	LAV	MEW	NTH
AVE	CAN	DIT	ERK	GAE	HAY	JAG	LAW	MHO	NUB
AWA	CAP	DIV	ERN	GAG	HEM	JAK	LAX	MID	NUN
AWE	CAR	DOB	ERR	GAL	HEN	JAM	LAY	MIL	NUR
AWL	CAT	DOC	ERS	GAM	HEP	JAP	LEA	MIM	NUS
AWN	CAW	DOD	ESS	GAN	HER	JAR	LED	MIR	NUT
AXE	CAY	DOE	ETA	GAP	HES	JAW	LEE	MIS	NYE
AYE	CEE	DOG	ETH	GAR	HET	JAY	LEG	MIX	NYS
AYU	CEL	DOH	EUK	GAS	HEW	JEE	LEI	MIZ	OAF
BAA	CEP	DON	EVE	GAT	HEX	JET	LEK	MNA	OAK
BAD	CHA	DOO	EWE	GAU	HEY	JEU	LEP	MOA	OAR
BAG	CHE	DOP	EWK		HIC			MOB	

OAT	OWE	POH	REF	SAG	SOH	TEE	UEY	WAP	YEP
OBI	OWL	POI	REH	SAI	SOL	TEF	UFO	WAR	YES
OBS	OWN	POM	REM	SAL	SON	TEG	UGH	WAS	YET
OCA	OWT	POO	REN	SAM	SOP	TEG	UGS	WAT	YEW
OCH	OYE	POP	REP	SAN	SOS	TEL	ULE	WAW	YEX
ODA	OYS	POS	RES	SAP	SOT	TEN	UNI	WAX	YGO
ODD		POT	RET	SAR	SOU	TES	UNS	WAY	YIN
ODE	PAD	POW	REV	SAT	SOV	TEW	UPS	WEB	YIP
ODS	PAH	POX	REW	SAW	SOW	THE	URD	WED	YOB
OES	PAL	POZ	REX	SAX	SOX	THO	URE	WEE	YOD
OFF	PAM	PRE	RHO	SAY	SOY	THY	URN	WEM	YOK
OFT	PAN	PRO	RHY	SAZ	SPA	TIC	USE	WEN	YON
OHM	PAP	PRY	RIA	SEA	SPY	TID	UTE	WET	YOS
OHO	PAR	PSI	RIB	SEC	STY	TIE	UTS	WEX	YOU
OIK	PAS	PST	RID	SED	SUB	TIG	UTU	WEY	YOW
OIL	PAT	PUB	RIG	SEE	SUD	TIL	UVA	WHO	YUG
OKE	PAW	PUD	RIM	SEG	SUE	TIN		WHY	YUK
OLD	PAX	PUG	RIN	SEI	SUI	TIP		WIG	YUP
OLE	PAY	PUH	RIP	SEL	SUK	TIS	VAC	WIN	YUS
OLM	PEA	PUN	RIT	SEN	SUM	TIT	VAE	WIS	
OMS	PEC	PUP	RIZ	SET	SUN	TOD	VAS	WIT	
ONE	PED	PUR	ROB	SEW	SUP	TOE	VAT	WOE	ZAG
ONS	PEE	PUS	ROC	SEX	SUQ	TOG	VAU	WOG	ZAP
OOF	PEG	PUT	ROD	SEY	SUR	TOM	VEE	WOK	ZAX
OOH	PEN	PUY	ROE	SEZ	SUS	TON	VEG	WON	ZEA
OOM	PEP	PYE	ROK	SHE	SWY	TOO	VET	WOO	ZED
OON	PER	PYX	ROM	SHY	SYE	TOP	VEX	WOP	ZEE
OOP	PET		ROO	SIB		TOR	VIA	WOS	ZEK
OOR	PEW	QAT	ROT	SIC	TAB	TOT	VIE	WOT	ZHO
OOS	PHI	QUA	ROW	SIM	TAD	TOW	VIM	WOW	ZIG
OPE	PHO		RUB	SIN	TAE	TOY	VIN	WOX	ZIP
OPS	PIA	RAD	RUC	SIP	TAG	TRY	VIS	WRY	ZIT
OPT	PIC	RAG	RUD	SIR	TAI	TUB	VLY	WUD	ZIZ
ORB	PIE	RAH	RUE	SIS	TAJ	TUG	VOE	WYE	ZOA
ORC	PIG	RAJ	RUG	SIT	TAK	TUI	VOL	WYN	ZOO
ORD	PIN	RAM	RUM	SIX	TAM	TUM	VOR		ZOS
ORE	PIP	RAN	RUN	SKA	TAN	TUN	VOW		ZUZ
ORF	PIR	RAP	RUT	SKI	TAP	TUP	VOX		
ORS	PIS	RAS	RYA	SKY	TAR	TUT		XIS	
ORT	PIT	RAT	RYE	SLY	TAT	TWA	VUG		
OUK	PIU	RAW		SMA	TAU	TWO	VUM	YAH	
OUP	PIX	RAX		SOB	TAW	TYE		YAK	
OUR	PLY	RAY	SAB	SOC	TAX			YAM	
OUT	POA	RED	SAC	SOD	TEA	TYG	WAD	YAP	
OVA	POD	REE	SAD	SOG	TED		WAE	YAW	
			SAE		UDO		WAG	YEA	
					UDS		WAN	YEN	

HINT

Tackling the Threes

To the uninitiated the number of allowable three-letter words is quite daunting. However, if you ignore the everyday words the lists begin to become a little more manageable. Pay particular attention to those that can be made by extending two-letter words (see the Hooks section) and those containing tiles worth three points or more. Write out those you don't know and play a few solo games, going out of your way to play some of your newly learnt three-letter words. By actually playing the more obscure words on the board you will find that they soon begin to stick. Many players also find it helpful to know the definitions. These you will find in *Chambers English Dictionary*. Once you can picture what the words mean this too will help them become firmer in your memory.

HINT

Open Play

Most people play Scrabble to win, which is natural and should not be discouraged. However, if you are keen to improve your scoring power and vocabulary, try playing the occasional more open game. This will enable you to concentrate on strengthening your rack-balancing, bonus-spotting and hook-word skills. Here are a few tips on open play:

- Try to ensure vowels are next to premium squares to provide scoring opportunities for high-scoring consonants.
- Experiment with playing the first word to the left of the board to enable easier access to the otherwise awkward top left.
- Play conservatively and consider points per tile gained each move rather than points per move.
- Don't be afraid to open up the triple-word squares and equally don't think you have to take a triple-word square as soon as it is available.
- Change tiles if your rack gets imbalanced and the only moves available block the openings on the board.
- Whenever you get the opportunity start a game with a three-letter word consisting of vowel-consonant-vowel played centrally to open up all four areas of the board, eg ADO, EGO, IRE, OCA, UDO etc.

HINT

Knowing Non-Words

Much time can be wasted in a game when you have a promising-looking set of seven letters on your rack but can't remember whether they make a seven-letter word or not. Therefore it is also beneficial to be familiar with those common sets of seven letters that *don't* make a seven-letter word. Some examples are: ENRAISE, IRELAND, and TAILEND. Note that by forming 'non-words' with these racks they can be more easily recognized during play. Having armed yourself with a selection of non-words the next task is to learn the possible eight-letter plays so that you can be aware of possible bonus plays using available letters on the board. The IRELAND set makes eight-letter words with the letters B F G H N S. These words and those of the other non-words mentioned above can be readily unearthed from the Eight-Letter Anagram lists.

STARTER LISTS: Basic Words

4-LETTER WORDS

ABAC	AKIN	ARAK	AYUS	BEAM	BISH	BORA	BUNK	CART	CILL
ABAS	ALAE	ARAR	AZAN	BEAN	BISK	BORD	BUNS	CASA	CION
ABBA	ALAP	ARBA	AZYM	BEAR	BITE	BORE	BUNT	CASE	CIRE
ABBE	ALAR	ARCH		BEAT	BITO	BORN	BUOY	CASH	CIRL
ABBS	ALAS	ARCO	BAAS	BEAU	BITS	BORS	BURD	CASK	CIST
ABED	ALAY	ARCS	BABA	BECK	BITT	BORT	BURG	CAST	CITE
ABET	ALBE	AREA	BABE	BEDE	BLAB	BOSH	BURK	CATE	CITO
ABID	ALBS	ARED	BABU	BEDS	BLAD	BOSK	BURL	CATS	CITS
ABLE	ALEE	ARES	BABY	BEEF	BLAE	BOSS	BURN	CAUF	CITY
ABLY	ALES	ARET	BACH	BEEN	BLAG	BOTH	BURP	CAUK	CIVE
ABUT	ALEW	AREW	BACK	BEEP	BLAH	BOTS	BURR	CAUL	CLAD
ABYE	ALFA	ARIA	BADE	BEER	BLAT	BOTT	BURS	CAUM	CLAG
ACED	ALGA	ARID	BAEL	BEES	BLAY	BOUK	BURY	CAUP	CLAM
ACES	ALIT	ARIL	BAFF	BEET	BLEB	BOUN	BUSH	CAVE	CLAN
ACHE	ALLS	ARIS	BAFT	BEGO	BLED	BOUT	BUSK	CAVY	CLAP
ACHY	ALLY	ARKS	BAGS	BEGS	BLEE	BOWL	BUSS	CAWK	CLAT
ACID	ALMA	ARMS	BAHT	BEIN	BLET	BOWR	BUST	CAWS	CLAW
ACME	ALME	ARMY	BAIL	BELL	BLEW	BOWS	BUSY	CAYS	CLAY
ACNE	ALMS	ARNA	BAIT	BELS	BLEY	BOXY	BUTE	CEAS	CLEF
ACRE	ALOD	AROW	BAKE	BELT	BLIN	BOYG	BUTS	CECA	CLEG
ACTA	ALOE	ARSE	BALD	BEMA	BLIP	BOYO	BUTT	CEDE	CLEM
ACTS	ALOW	ARTS	BALE	BEND	BLOB	BOYS	BUYS	CEDI	CLEW
ACYL	ALPS	ARTY	BALK	BENE	BLOC	BRAD	BUZZ	CEES	CLIP
ADAW	ALSO	ARUM	BALL	BENI	BLOT	BRAE	BYES	CEIL	CLOD
ADDS	ALTO	ARVO	BALM	BENJ	BLOW	BRAG	BYKE	CELL	CLOG
ADIT	ALTS	ARYL	BALU	BENS	BLUB	BRAN	BYRE	CELS	CLOP
ADOS	ALUM	ASAR	BAMS	BENT	BLUE	BRAS	BYTE	CELT	CLOT
ADRY	AMAH	ASCI	BANC	BERE	BLUR	BRAT		CENT	CLOU
ADZE	AMBO	ASHY	BAND	BERG	BOAK	BRAW	CABA	CEPS	CLOW
AEON	AMEN	ASKS	BANE	BERK	BOAR	BRAY	CABS	CERE	CLOY
AERY	AMID	ASPS	BANG	BERM	BOAS	BRED	CADE	CERT	CLUB
AESC	AMIE	ATAP	BANI	BEST	BOAT	BREE	CADI	CESS	CLUE
AFAR	AMIR	ATOC	BANK	BETA	BOBA	BREN	CADS	CETE	COAL
AFFY	AMIS	ATOK	BANS	BETE	BOBS	BRER	CAFE	CHAD	COAT
AFRO	AMLA	ATOM	BANT	BETH	BOCK	BREW	CAFF	CHAI	COAX
AGAR	AMMO	ATOP	BAPS	BETS	BODE	BRIG	CAGE	CHAL	COBB
AGAS	AMPS	AUFS	BAPU	BEVY	BODS	BRIM	CAGY	CHAM	COBS
AGED	AMYL	AUKS	BARB	BEYS	BODY	BRIO	CAIN	CHAP	COCA
AGEE	ANAL	AULA	BARD	BHEL	BOFF	BRIT	CAKE	CHAR	COCH
AGEN	ANAN	AULD	BARE	BIAS	BOGS	BROD	CAKY	CHAS	COCK
AGES	ANAS	AUNT	BARF	BIBS	BOGY	BROG	CALF	CHAT	COCO
AGHA	ANCE	AURA	BARK	BICE	BOIL	BROO	CALK	CHAW	CODA
AGIN	ANDS	AUTO	BARM	BIDE	BOKE	BROS	CALL	CHAY	CODE
AGIO	ANES	AVAL	BARN	BIDS	BOKO	BROW	CALM	CHEF	CODS
AGMA	ANEW	AVAS	BARP	BIEN	BOKS	BRUT	CALP	CHER	COED
AGOG	ANIL	AVER	BARS	BIER	BOLD	BUAT	CALX	CHEW	COFF
AGON	ANKH	AVES	BASE	BIFF	BOLE	BUBA	CAME	CHEZ	COFT
AGUE	ANNA	AVID	BASH	BIGA	BOLL	BUBO	CAMP	CHIC	COGS
AHEM	ANNO	AVOW	BASK	BIGG	BOLO	BUBS	CAMS	CHID	COHO
AHOY	ANNS	AWAY	BASS	BIGS	BOLT	BUCK	CANE	CHIK	COIF
AIAS	ANOA	AWDL	BAST	BIKE	BOMA	BUDO	CANG	CHIN	COIL
AIDE	ANON	AWED	BATE	BILE	BOMB	BUDS	CANN	CHIP	COIN
AIDS	ANOW	AWES	BATH	BILK	BONA	BUFF	CANS	CHIS	COIR
AILS	ANTA	AWLS	BATS	BILL	BOND	BUFO	CANT	CHIT	COKE
AIMS	ANTE	AWNS	BATT	BIND	BONE	BUGS	CANY	CHIV	COKY
AINE	ANTI	AWNY	BAUD	BINE	BONG	BUHL	CAPA	CHOC	COLA
AIRN	ANTS	AWRY	BAUK	BING	BONK	BUIK	CAPE	CHOP	COLD
AIRS	ANUS	AXED	BAUR	BINK	BONY	BUKE	CAPO	CHOU	COLE
AIRT	APAY	AXEL	BAWD	BINS	BOOB	BULB	CAPS	CHOW	COLL
AIRY	APED	AXES	BAWL	BINT	BOOH	BULK	CARB	CHUB	COLS
AITS	APES	AXIL	BAWN	BIOG	BOOK	BULL	CARD	CHUG	COLT
AITU	APEX	AXIS	BAWR	BIOS	BOOM	BUMF	CARE	CHUM	COMA
AJAR	APOD	AXLE	BAYE	BIRD	BOON	BUMP	CARK	CHUT	COMB
AJEE	APSE	AXON	BAYS	BIRK	BOOR	BUMS	CARL	CIAO	COME
AKED	APTS	AYAH	BAYT	BIRL	BOOS	BUNA	CARP	CIDE	COMP
AKEE	AQUA	AYES	BEAD	BIRR	BOOT	BUND	CARR	CIEL	COMS
AKES		AYRE	BEAK	BISE	BOPS	BUNG	CARS	CIGS	COND

CONE	CULT	DEAD	DIRK	DOUT	DWAM	EMES	EYRE	FETS	FOBS
CONK	CUNT	DEAF	DIRL	DOVE	DYAD	EMEU	EYRY	FETT	FOCI
CONN	CUPS	DEAL	DIRT	DOWD	DYED	EMIR		FEUD	FOEN
CONS	CURB	DEAN	DISA	DOWF	DYER	EMIT	FACE	FEUS	FOES
CONY	CURD	DEAR	DISC	DOWL	DYES	EMMA	FACT	FEYS	FOGS
COOF	CURE	DEAW	DISH	DOWN	DYKE	EMUS	FADE	FIAR	FOGY
COOK	CURL	DEBS	DISK	DOWP	DYNE	EMYS	FADO	FIAT	FOHN
COOL	CURN	DEBT	DISS	DOWS	DZOS	ENDS	FADS	FIBS	FOIL
COOM	CURR	DECK	DITA	DOWT		ENES	FADY	FICO	FOIN
COON	CURS	DECO	DITE	DOXY	EACH	ENEW	FAFF	FIDS	FOLD
COOP	CURT	DEED	DITS	DOZE	EALE	ENGS	FAGS	FIEF	FOLK
COOS	CUSH	DEEM	DITT	DOZY	EANS	ENOW	FAHS	FIFE	FOND
COOT	CUSK	DEEN	DIVA	DRAB	EARD	ENVY	FAIK	FIGO	FONE
COPE	CUSP	DEEP	DIVE	DRAD	EARL	EOAN	FAIL	FIGS	FONS
COPS	CUSS	DEER	DIVI	DRAG	EARN	EONS	FAIN	FIKE	FONT
COPY	CUTE	DEES	DIVS	DRAM	EARS	EORL	FAIR	FIKY	FOOD
CORD	CUTS	DEEV	DIXI	DRAP	EASE	EPEE	FAIX	FILE	FOOL
CORE	CWMS	DEFT	DIXY	DRAT	EAST	EPHA	FAKE	FILL	FOOT
CORF	CYAN	DEFY	DOAB	DRAW	EASY	EPIC	FALL	FILM	FOPS
CORK	CYMA	DEID	DOAT	DRAY	EATH	EPOS	FALX	FILS	FORA
CORM	CYME	DEIL	DOBS	DREE	EATS	ERAS	FAME	FIND	FORD
CORN	CYST	DELE	DOCK	DREW	EAUS	ERED	FAND	FINE	FORE
CORS	CYTE	DELF	DOCS	DREY	EAUX	ERES	FANE	FINK	FORK
COSE	CZAR	DELI	DODO	DRIB	EBBS	ERGO	FANG	FINO	FORM
COSH		DELL	DODS	DRIP	EBON	ERGS	FANK	FINS	FORT
COSS	DABS	DELS	DOEN	DROP	ECAD	ERIC	FANS	FIRE	FOSS
COST	DACE	DEME	DOER	DROW	ECCE	ERKS	FARD	FIRK	FOUD
COSY	DADO	DEMO	DOES	DRUB	ECCO	ERNE	FARE	FIRM	FOUL
COTE	DADS	DEMY	DOFF	DRUG	ECHE	ERNS	FARL	FIRN	FOUR
COTH	DAFF	DENE	DOGE	DRUM	ECHO	ERRS	FARM	FIRS	FOUS
COTS	DAFT	DENS	DOGS	DSOS	ECHT	ERST	FARO	FISC	FOWL
COTT	DAGO	DENT	DOGY	DUAD	ECRU	ESKY	FARS	FISH	FOXY
COUP	DAGS	DENY	DOHS	DUAL	ECUS	ESNE	FART	FISK	FOYS
COUR	DAHL	DERE	DOIT	DUAN	EDDO	ESPY	FASH	FIST	FOZY
COVE	DAHS	DERM	DOJO	DUAR	EDDY	ESSE	FAST	FITS	FRAB
COWL	DAIS	DERN	DOLE	DUBS	EDGE	ETAS	FATE	FITT	FRAE
COWP	DAKS	DERV	DOLL	DUCE	EDGY	ETAT	FATS	FIVE	FRAP
COWS	DALE	DESK	DOLT	DUCK	EDHS	ETCH	FAUN	FIZZ	FRAS
COXA	DALI	DEUS	DOME	DUCT	EDIT	ETEN	FAUX	FLAB	FRAU
COXY	DALS	DEVA	DOMY	DUDE	EECH	ETHE	FAWN	FLAG	FRAY
COYS	DALT	DEWS	DONA	DUDS	EELS	ETHS	FAWS	FLAK	FREE
COZE	DAME	DEWY	DONE	DUED	EELY	ETNA	FAYS	FLAM	FRET
COZY	DAMN	DEYS	DONG	DUEL	EERY	ETUI	FAZE	FLAN	FRIG
CRAB	DAMP	DHAK	DONS	DUES	EEVN	EUGE	FEAL	FLAP	FRIS
CRAG	DAMS	DHAL	DOOB	DUET	EFFS	EUGH	FEAR	FLAT	FRIT
CRAM	DANG	DHOW	DOOK	DUFF	EFTS	EUKS	FEAT	FLAW	FRIZ
CRAN	DANK	DIAL	DOOL	DUGS	EGAD	EUOI	FECK	FLAX	FROG
CRAP	DANS	DIBS	DOOM	DUKE	EGAL	EURO	FEDS	FLAY	FROM
CRAW	DANT	DICE	DOOR	DULE	EGER	EVEN	FEED	FLEA	FROW
CREE	DAPS	DICH	DOOS	DULL	EGGS	EVER	FEEL	FLED	FUBS
CREW	DARE	DICK	DOPA	DULY	EGGY	EVES	FEER	FLEE	FUCI
CRIB	DARG	DICT	DOPE	DUMA	EGIS	EVET	FEES	FLEG	FUCK
CRIT	DARI	DIDO	DOPS	DUMB	EGMA	EVIL	FEET	FLEW	FUDS
CROC	DARK	DIEB	DOPY	DUMP	EGOS	EVOE	FEGS	FLEX	FUEL
CROP	DARN	DIED	DORM	DUNE	EHED	EWER	FEHM	FLEY	FUFF
CROW	DART	DIES	DORP	DUNG	EIKS	EWES	FEIS	FLIC	FUGS
CRUD	DASH	DIET	DORR	DUNK	EILD	EWKS	FELL	FLIP	FULL
CRUE	DATA	DIGS	DORS	DUNS	EINE	EWTS	FELT	FLIT	FUME
CRUS	DATE	DIKA	DORT	DUNT	EKED	EXAM	FEME	FLIX	FUMS
CRUX	DAUB	DIKE	DORY	DUOS	EKES	EXES	FEND	FLOE	FUMY
CUBE	DAUD	DILL	DOSE	DUPE	EKKA	EXIT	FENS	FLOG	FUND
CUBS	DAUR	DIME	DOSS	DUPS	ELAN	EXON	FENT	FLOP	FUNG
CUDS	DAUT	DIMS	DOST	DURA	ELDS	EXPO	FEOD	FLOR	FUNK
CUED	DAWD	DINE	DOTE	DURE	ELFS	EXUL	FERE	FLOW	FUNS
CUES	DAWK	DING	DOTH	DURN	ELKS	EYAS	FERM	FLUB	FURL
CUFF	DAWN	DINK	DOTS	DURO	ELLS	EYED	FERN	FLUE	FURR
CUIF	DAWS	DINS	DOTY	DUSH	ELMS	EYES	FESS	FLUS	FURS
CUIT	DAWT	DINT	DOUC	DUSK	ELMY	EYNE	FEST	FLUX	FURY
CULL	DAYS	DIPS	DOUP	DUST	ELSE	EYOT	FETA	FOAL	FUSC
CULM	DAZE	DIRE	DOUR	DUTY	ELTS	EYRA	FETE	FOAM	FUSE

STARTER LISTS: Basic Words

FUSS	GEES	GLUE	GROW	HAMS	HETS	HORS	IDLY		JEED	JUTS
FUST	GEIT	GLUG	GRUB	HAND	HEWN	HOSE	IDOL		JEEL	JYNX
FUZE	GELD	GLUM	GRUE	HANG	HEWS	HOSS	IDYL		JEEP	
FUZZ	GELS	GLUT	GRUM	HANK	HEYS	HOST	IFFY		JEER	KADE
FYKE	GELT	GNAR	GUAN	HAPS	HICK	HOTE	IGAD		JEES	KADI
FYLE	GEMS	GNAT	GUAR	HARD	HIDE	HOTS	IKAT		JEFF	KAED
FYRD	GENA	GNAW	GUBS	HARE	HIED	HOUF	IKON		JELL	KAES
	GENE	GNUS	GUCK	HARK	HIES	HOUR	ILEA		JERK	KAGO
GABS	GENS	GOAD	GUDE	HARL	HIGH	HOUT	ILEX		JESS	KAID
GABY	GENT	GOAF	GUES	HARM	HIKE	HOVE	ILIA		JEST	KAIE
GADE	GENU	GOAL	GUFF	HARN	HILA	HOWE	ILKA		JETE	KAIF
GADI	GEOS	GOAS	GUID	HARO	HILD	HOWF	ILKS		JETS	KAIL
GADS	GERE	GOAT	GULA	HARP	HILI	HOWK	ILLS		JEUX	KAIM
GAED	GERM	GOBO	GULE	HART	HILL	HOWL	ILLY		JIAO	KAIN
GAES	GEST	GOBS	GULF	HASH	HILT	HOWS	IMAM		JIBE	KAIS
GAFF	GETA	GOBY	GULL	HASK	HIND	HOYA	IMPI		JIBS	KAKA
GAGA	GETS	GODS	GULP	HASP	HING	HOYS	IMPS		JIFF	KAKI
GAGE	GEUM	GOEL	GULY	HAST	HINS	HUBS	INBY		JIGS	KALE
GAGS	GHAT	GOER	GUMP	HATE	HINT	HUCK	INCH		JILL	KALI
GAID	GHEE	GOES	GUMS	HATH	HIPS	HUED	INFO		JILT	KAME
GAIN	GHIS	GOEY	GUNK	HATS	HIPT	HUER	INGO		JIMP	KAMI
GAIR	GIBE	GOFF	GUNS	HAUD	HIRE	HUES	INIA		JINK	KANA
GAIT	GIBS	GOGO	GUPS	HAUL	HISH	HUFF	INKS		JINN	KANG
GAJO	GIDS	GOGS	GURL	HAUT	HISN	HUGE	INKY		JINX	KANS
GALA	GIED	GOLD	GURN	HAVE	HISS	HUGS	INLY		JIRD	KANT
GALE	GIEN	GOLE	GURS	HAWK	HIST	HUGY	INNS		JISM	KAON
GALL	GIES	GOLF	GURU	HAWM	HITS	HUIA	INRO		JIVE	KARA
GALS	GIFT	GOLP	GUSH	HAWS	HIVE	HULA	INTO		JIZZ	KART
GAMB	GIGA	GONE	GUST	HAYS	HIYA	HULE	IONS		JOBE	KATI
GAME	GIGS	GONG	GUTS	HAZE	HIZZ	HULK	IOTA		JOBS	KATS
GAMP	GILA	GONK	GUYS	HAZY	HOAR	HULL	IRES		JOCK	KAVA
GAMS	GILD	GONS	GYAL	HEAD	HOAS	HUMA	IRID		JOCO	KAWS
GAMY	GILL	GOOD	GYBE	HEAL	HOAX	HUMF	IRIS		JOES	KAYO
GANE	GILT	GOOF	GYMP	HEAP	HOBO	HUMP	IRKS		JOEY	KAYS
GANG	GIMP	GOOK	GYMS	HEAR	HOBS	HUMS	IRON		JOGS	KAZI
GANT	GING	GOOL	GYNY	HEAT	HOCK	HUNG	ISLE		JOHN	KEAS
GAOL	GINK	GOON	GYPS	HEBE	HODS	HUNK	ISMS		JOIN	KEBS
GAPE	GINN	GOOP	GYRE	HECH	HOED	HUNT	ISMY		JOKE	KECK
GAPO	GINS	GOOR	GYRI	HECK	HOER	HUPS	ITAS		JOKY	KEDS
GAPS	GIOS	GOOS	GYRO	HEED	HOES	HURL	ITCH		JOLE	KEEK
GARB	GIPS	GORE	GYTE	HEEL	HOGG	HURT	ITEM		JOLL	KEEL
GARE	GIRD	GORM	GYVE	HEFT	HOGH	HUSH	IWIS	JABS	JOLT	KEEN
GARS	GIRL	GORY		HEID	HOGS	HUSK	IXIA	JACK	JOMO	KEEP
GART	GIRN			HEIL	HOHS	HUSO		JADE	JOOK	KEFS
GASH	GIRO	GOSH	HAAF	HEIR	HOIK	HUSS		JAGS	JORS	KEGS
GASP	GIRR	GOUK	HAAR	HELD	HOKE	HUTS		JAIL	JOSH	KEIR
GAST	GIRT	GOUT	HACK	HELE	HOLD	HWYL		JAKE	JOSS	KELL
GATE	GISM	GOVS	HADE	HELL	HOLE	HYED		JAKS	JOTA	KELP
GATH	GIST	GOWD	HADJ	HELM	HOLM	HYEN		JAMB	JOTS	KELT
GATS	GITE	GOWF	HADS	HELP	HOLP	HYES		JAMS	JOUK	KEMB
GAUD	GITS	GOWK	HAEM	HEME	HOLS	HYKE		JANE	JOUR	KEMP
GAUM	GIVE	GOWL	HAET	HEMP	HOLT	HYLE		JANN	JOWL	KENS
GAUN	GIZZ	GOWN	HAFF	HEMS	HOLY	HYMN		JAPE	JOWS	KENT
GAUP	GJUS	GRAB	HAFT	HEND	HOME	HYPE		JAPS	JOYS	KEPI
GAUR	GLAD	GRAM	HAGG	HENS	HOMO	HYPO		JARK	JUBA	KEPS
GAUS	GLAM	GRAN	HAGS	HENT	HOMY	HYPS		JARL	JUBE	KEPT
GAVE	GLED	GRAT	HAIK	HEPS	HOND			JARS	JUDO	KERB
GAWD	GLEE	GRAY	HAIL	HEPT	HONE	IAMB		JASP	JUDS	KERF
GAWK	GLEG	GREE	HAIN	HERB	HONG	IBEX		JASY	JUDY	KERN
GAWP	GLEI	GREN	HAIR	HERD	HONK	IBIS		JATO	JUGA	KESH
GAYS	GLEN	GREW	HAJI	HERE	HONS	ICED		JAUP	JUGS	KEST
GAZE	GLEY	GREY	HAJJ	HERL	HOOD	ICER		JAWS	JUJU	KETA
GAZY	GLIA	GRID	HAKA	HERM	HOOF	ICES		JAYS	JUKE	KETS
GEAL	GLIB	GRIG	HAKE	HERN	HOOK	ICKY		JAZY	JUMP	KEYS
GEAN	GLID	GRIM	HALE	HERO	HOOP	ICON		JAZZ	JUNK	KHAN
GEAR	GLIM	GRIN	HALF	HERS	HOOT	IDEA		JEAN	JURA	KHAT
GEAT	GLIT	GRIP	HALL	HERY	HOPE	IDEE		JEAT	JURE	KHOR
GECK	GLOB	GRIS	HALM	HESP	HOPS	IDEM			JURY	KHUD
GEDS	GLOM	GRIT	HALO	HEST	HORE	IDES			JUST	KIBE
GEED	GLOW	GROG	HALT	HETE	HORN	IDLE			JUTE	KICK
		GROT	HAME							

KIDS	LABS	LEET	LITH	LUGS	MART	MILK	MORA	NANA	NODI
KIER	LACE	LEFT	LIVE	LUIT	MASE	MILL	MORE	NANS	NODS
KIFS	LACK	LEGS	LOAD	LUKE	MASH	MILO	MORN	NAOI	NOEL
KIKE	LACS	LEHR	LOAF	LULL	MASK	MILS	MORS	NAOS	NOES
KILD	LACY	LEIR	LOAM	LULU	MASS	MILT	MORT	NAPA	NOGS
KILL	LADE	LEIS	LOAN	LUMP	MAST	MIME	MOSE	NAPE	NOIL
KILN	LADS	LEKE	LOBE	LUMS	MASU	MINA	MOSS	NAPS	NOLE
KILO	LADY	LEKS	LOBI	LUNE	MATE	MIND	MOST	NARD	NOLL
KILP	LAER	LEME	LOBO	LUNG	MATH	MINE	MOTE	NARE	NOMA
KILT	LAGS	LEND	LOBS	LUNT	MATS	MING	MOTH	NARK	NOME
KINA	LAHS	LENG	LOCH	LURE	MATT	MINI	MOTS	NARY	NOMS
KIND	LAIC	LENO	LOCI	LURK	MATY	MINK	MOTT	NATS	NONE
KINE	LAID	LENS	LOCK	LURS	MAUD	MINO	MOUE	NAVE	NONG
KING	LAIK	LENT	LOCO	LUSH	MAUL	MINT	MOUP	NAVY	NOOK
KINK	LAIN	LEPS	LODE	LUSK	MAUN	MINX	MOUS	NAYS	NOON
KINO	LAIR	LERE	LOFT	LUST	MAWK	MINY	MOVE	NAZE	NOOP
KINS	LAKE	LESS	LOGE	LUTE	MAWR	MIRE	MOVY	NEAL	NOPE
KIPE	LAKH	LEST	LOGO	LUTZ	MAWS	MIRK	MOWA	NEAP	NORI
KIPP	LAKY	LETS	LOGS	LUXE	MAXI	MIRS	MOWN	NEAR	NORK
KIPS	LAMA	LEVA	LOID	LYAM	MAYA	MIRY	MOWS	NEAT	NORM
KIRI	LAMB	LEVE	LOIN	LYES	MAYS	MISE	MOXA	NEBS	NOSE
KIRK	LAME	LEVY	LOIR	LYME	MAZE	MISO	MOYA	NECK	NOSH
KIRN	LAMP	LEWD	LOKE	LYMS	MAZY	MISS	MOYL	NEDS	NOSY
KIRS	LAMS	LEYS	LOLL	LYNE	MEAD	MIST	MOYS	NEED	NOTE
KISH	LANA	LEZZ	LOMA	LYNX	MEAL	MITE	MOZE	NEEM	NOTT
KISS	LAND	LIAR	LOME	LYRE	MEAN	MITT	MOZZ	NEEP	NOUL
KIST	LANE	LIBS	LONE	LYSE	MEAT	MITY	MUCH	NEFS	NOUN
KITE	LANG	LICE	LONG	LYTE	MEED	MIXT	MUCK	NEIF	NOUP
KITH	LANK	LICH	LOOF		MEEK	MIXY	MUDS	NEKS	NOUS
KITS	LANT	LICK	LOOK	MAAR	MEER	MIZZ	MUFF	NEMN	NOUT
KIWI	LANX	LIDO	LOOM	MACE	MEET	MNAS	MUGS	NENE	NOVA
KNAG	LAPS	LIDS	LOON	MACK	MEIN	MOAN	MUID	NEON	NOWL
KNAP	LARD	LIED	LOOP	MACS	MELD	MOAS	MUIL	NEPS	NOWN
KNAR	LARE	LIEF	LOOR	MADE	MELL	MOAT	MUIR	NERD	NOWS
KNEE	LARK	LIEN	LOOS	MADS	MELS	MOBS	MULE	NESH	NOWT
KNEW	LARN	LIER	LOOT	MAGE	MELT	MOCK	MULL	NESS	NOWY
KNIT	LASE	LIES	LOPE	MAGG	MEMO	MODE	MUMM	NEST	NOYS
KNOB	LASH	LIEU	LOPS	MAGI	MEND	MODI	MUMP	NETE	NUBS
KNOP	LASS	LIFE	LORD	MAGS	MENE	MODS	MUMS	NETS	NUDE
KNOT	LAST	LIFT	LORE	MAID	MENG	MOES	MUON	NETT	NUKE
KNOW	LATE	LIGS	LORN	MAIK	MENT	MOGS	MURE	NEUK	NULL
KNUB	LATH	LIKE	LORY	MAIL	MENU	MOHR	MURK	NEUM	NUMB
KNUR	LATS	LILL	LOSE	MAIM	MEOW	MOIL	MURL	NEVE	NUNS
KNUT	LAUD	LILO	LOSH	MAIN	MERC	MOIT	MUSE	NEWS	NURD
KOAN	LAUF	LILT	LOSS	MAKE	MERE	MOKE	MUSH	NEWT	NURL
KOAS	LAVA	LILY	LOST	MAKO	MERI	MOKI	MUSK	NEXT	NURR
KOBS	LAVE	LIMA	LOTA	MAKS	MERK	MOKO	MUSS	NIBS	NURS
KOFF	LAVS	LIMB	LOTE	MALE	MERL	MOLD	MUST	NICE	NUTS
KOHL	LAWK	LIME	LOTH	MALI	MESA	MOLE	MUTE	NICK	NYAS
KOLA	LAWN	LIMN	LOTO	MALL	MESE	MOLL	MUTT	NIDE	NYED
KOLO	LAWS	LIMP	LOTS	MALM	MESH	MOLT	MYAL	NIDI	NYES
KOND	LAYS	LIMY	LOUD	MALS	MESS	MOLY	MYNA	NIDS	
KONK	LAZE	LIND	LOUN	MALT	METE	MOME	MYTH	NIED	OAFS
KONS	LAZY	LINE	LOUP	MAMA	MEUS	MOMS		NIEF	OAKS
KOOK	LEAD	LING	LOUR	MAMS	MEVE	MONA	NAAM	NIES	OAKY
KOPS	LEAF	LINK	LOUT	MANA	MEWL	MONG	NAAN	NIFE	OARS
KORA	LEAK	LINN	LOVE	MAND	MEWS	MONK	NABK	NIFF	OARY
KOSS	LEAL	LINO	LOWE	MANE	MEZE	MONO	NABS	NIGH	OAST
KOTO	LEAM	LINS	LOWN	MANS	MHOS	MONY	NACH	NILL	OATH
KOWS	LEAN	LINT	LOWS	MANY	MICA	MOOD	NADA	NILS	OATS
KRIS	LEAP	LINY	LOWT	MAPS	MICE	MOOI	NAFF	NIMS	OBEY
KSAR	LEAR	LION	LOYS	MARA	MICK	MOOL	NAGA	NINE	OBIA
KUDU	LEAS	LIPS	LUAU	MARC	MICO	MOON	NAGS	NIPS	OBIS
KUKU	LEAT	LIRA	LUCE	MARD	MIDI	MOOP	NAIF	NIRL	OBIT
KYAT	LECH	LIRE	LUCK	MARE	MIDS	MOOR	NAIK	NISI	OBOE
KYLE	LEED	LIRK	LUDO	MARG	MIEN	MOOS	NAIL	NITS	OBOL
KYND	LEEK	LISK	LUDS	MARK	MIFF	MOOT	NAIN	NIXY	OCAS
KYNE	LEEP	LISP	LUES	MARL	MIKE	MOPE	NALA	NOBS	OCHE
KYTE	LEER	LIST	LUFF	MARM	MILD	MOPS	NAME	NOCK	ODAL
	LEES	LITE	LUGE	MARS	MILE	MOPY	NAMS	NODE	ODAS

ODDS	ORTS	PASH	PHUT	POKY	PRYS	RACK	REHS	ROCH	RUNG
ODEA	ORYX	PASS	PIAS	POLE	PSIS	RACY	REIF	ROCK	RUNS
ODES	OSSA	PAST	PICA	POLK	PSST	RADE	REIK	ROCS	RUNT
ODIC	OTIC	PATE	PICE	POLL	PUBS	RADS	REIN	RODE	RURP
ODOR	OTTO	PATH	PICK	POLO	PUCE	RAFF	REIS	RODS	RUSA
ODSO	OUCH	PATS	PICS	POLT	PUCK	RAFT	REKE	ROED	RUSE
ODYL	OUKS	PAUA	PIED	POLY	PUDS	RAGA	RELY	ROES	RUSH
OFAY	OULK	PAUL	PIER	POME	PUER	RAGE	REMS	ROIL	RUSK
OFFS	OUPH	PAVE	PIES	POMP	PUFF	RAGG	REND	ROIN	RUST
OGAM	OUPS	PAWA	PIET	POMS	PUGH	RAGI	RENS	ROKE	RUTH
OGEE	OURN	PAWK	PIGS	POND	PUGS	RAGS	RENT	ROKS	RUTS
OGLE	OURS	PAWL	PIKA	PONE	PUIR	RAHS	RENY	ROKY	RYAL
OGRE	OUST	PAWN	PIKE	PONG	PUJA	RAID	REPP	ROLE	RYAS
OHMS	OUTS	PAWS	PILA	PONK	PUKE	RAIK	REPS	ROLL	RYES
OHOS	OUZO	PAYS	PILE	PONS	PULE	RAIL	REST	ROMA	RYFE
OIKS	OVAL	PEAG	PILI	PONY	PULK	RAIN	RETE	ROMP	RYKE
OILS	OVEN	PEAK	PILL	POOD	PULL	RAIT	RETS	RONE	RYND
OILY	OVER	PEAL	PIMP	POOF	PULP	RAJA	REVS	RONG	RYOT
OINT	OVUM	PEAN	PINA	POOH	PULU	RAKE	REWS	RONT	RYPE
OKAY	OWED	PEAR	PINE	POOK	PULY	RAKI	RHEA	ROOD	RYVE
OKES	OWER	PEAS	PING	POOL	PUMA	RALE	RHOS	ROOF	
OKRA	OWES	PEAT	PINK	POON	PUMP	RAMI	RHUS	ROOK	SABS
OLDS	OWLS	PEBA	PINS	POOP	PUMY	RAMP	RIAL	ROOM	SACK
OLDY	OWLY	PECH	PINT	POOR	PUNA	RAMS	RIAS	ROON	SACS
OLEO	OWNS	PECK	PINY	POOS	PUNK	RANA	RIBS	ROOP	SAFE
OLID	OWRE	PECS	PION	POOT	PUNS	RAND	RICE	ROOS	SAGA
OLIO	OWTS	PEDS	PIOY	POPE	PUNT	RANG	RICH	ROOT	SAGE
OLLA	OXEN	PEED	PIPA	POPS	PUNY	RANI	RICK	ROPE	SAGO
OLMS	OXER	PEEK	PIPE	PORE	PUPA	RANK	RICY	ROPY	SAGS
OLPE	OYER	PEEL	PIPI	PORK	PUPS	RANT	RIDE	RORE	SAGY
OMBU	OYES	PEEN	PIPS	PORN	PURE	RAPE	RIDS	RORT	SAIC
OMEN	OYEZ	PEEP	PIPY	PORT	PURI	RAPS	RIEL	RORY	SAID
OMER		PEER	PIRL	PORY	PURL	RAPT	RIEM	ROSE	SAIL
OMIT	PACA	PEES	PIRN	POSE	PURR	RARE	RIFE	ROST	SAIM
ONCE	PACE	PEGH	PIRS	POSH	PURS	RASE	RIFF	ROSY	SAIN
ONER	PACK	PEGS	PISE	POSS	PUSH	RASH	RIFT	ROTA	SAIR
ONES	PACO	PEIN	PISH	POST	PUSS	RASP	RIGG	ROTE	SAIS
ONLY	PACT	PEKE	PISS	POSY	PUTS	RAST	RIGS	ROTI	SAKE
ONST	PACY	PELA	PITA	POTE	PUTT	RATA	RILE	ROTL	SAKI
ONTO	PADS	PELE	PITH	POTS	PUTZ	RATE	RILL	ROTS	SALE
ONUS	PAGE	PELF	PITS	POTT	PUYS	RATH	RIMA	ROUE	SALP
ONYX	PAHS	PELL	PITY	POUF	PYAT	RATS	RIME	ROUL	SALS
OOFS	PAID	PELT	PIUM	POUK	PYES	RATU	RIMS	ROUM	SALT
OOHS	PAIK	PEND	PIXY	POUR	PYET	RAUN	RIMU	ROUP	SAME
OOMS	PAIL	PENE	PIZE	POUT	PYNE	RAVE	RIMY	ROUT	SAMP
OONS	PAIN	PENI	PLAN	POWN	PYOT	RAWN	RIND	ROUX	SAND
OONT	PAIR	PENK	PLAP	POWS	PYRE	RAWS	RINE	ROVE	SANE
OOPS	PAIS	PENS	PLAT	POXY	PYRO	RAYS	RING	ROWS	SANG
OOSE	PALE	PENT	PLAY	POZZ		RAZE	RINK	ROWT	SANK
OOSY	PALL	PEON	PLEA	PRAD	QADI	RAZZ	RINS	RUBE	SANS
OOZE	PALM	PEPO	PLEB	PRAM	QATS	READ	RIOT	RUBS	SAPS
OOZY	PALP	PEPS	PLED	PRAT	QUAD	REAK	RIPE	RUBY	SARD
OPAH	PALS	PERE	PLIE	PRAU	QUAG	REAL	RIPP	RUCK	SARI
OPAL	PALY	PERI	PLIM	PRAY	QUAT	REAM	RIPS	RUCS	SARK
OPED	PAMS	PERK	PLOD	PREE	QUAY	REAN	RIPT	RUDD	SARS
OPEN	PAND	PERM	PLOP	PREP	QUEP	REAP	RISE	RUDE	SASH
OPES	PANE	PERN	PLOT	PREX	QUEY	REAR	RISK	RUDS	SASS
OPTS	PANG	PERT	PLOW	PREY	QUID	RECK	RISP	RUED	SATE
OPUS	PANS	PERV	PLOY	PRIG	QUIM	REDD	RITE	RUES	SATI
ORAL	PANT	PESO	PLUG	PRIM	QUIN	REDE	RITS	RUFF	SAUL
ORBS	PAPA	PEST	PLUM	PROA	QUIP	REDO	RITT	RUGS	SAUT
ORBY	PAPE	PETS	PLUS	PROD	QUIT	REDS	RIVA	RUIN	SAVE
ORCS	PAPS	PEWS	POAS	PROF	QUIZ	REED	RIVE	RUKH	SAWN
ORDS	PARA	PHEW	POCK	PROG	QUOD	REEF	RIVO	RULE	SAWS
ORES	PARD	PHIS	POCO	PROM	QUOP	REEK	ROAD	RULY	SAYS
ORFE	PARE	PHIZ	PODS	PROO		REEL	ROAM	RUME	SCAB
ORFS	PARK	PHOH	POEM	PROP	RABI	REEN	ROAN	RUMP	SCAD
ORGY	PARR	PHON	POET	PROS	RACA	REES	ROAR	RUMS	SCAG
ORLE	PARS	PHOS	POIS	PROW	RACE	REFS	ROBE	RUND	SCAM
ORRA	PART	PHOT	POKE	PRUH	RACH	REFT	ROBS	RUNE	SCAN

SCAR	SHAW	SKEO	SOAP	SPIK	SWEE	TATH	THUG	TONG	TUFT
SCAT	SHAY	SKEP	SOAR	SPIN	SWIG	TATS	THUS	TONK	TUGS
SCAW	SHEA	SKER	SOBS	SPIT	SWIM	TATT	TIAR	TONS	TUIS
SCOG	SHED	SKEW	SOCK	SPIV	SWIZ	TATU	TICE	TONY	TULE
SCOT	SHES	SKID	SOCS	SPOT	SWOB	TAUS	TICH	TOOK	TUMP
SCOW	SHET	SKIM	SODA	SPRY	SWOP	TAUT	TICK	TOOL	TUMS
SCRY	SHEW	SKIN	SODS	SPUD	SWOT	TAWS	TICS	TOOM	TUNA
SCUD	SHIM	SKIO	SOFA	SPUE	SWUM	TAWT	TIDE	TOON	TUND
SCUG	SHIN	SKIP	SOFT	SPUN	SYBO	TAXA	TIDS	TOOT	TUNE
SCUL	SHIP	SKIS	SOGS	SPUR	SYCE	TAXI	TIDY	TOPE	TUNS
SCUM	SHIR	SKIT	SOHS	STAB	SYED	TEAD	TIED	TOPI	TUNY
SCUP	SHIT	SKOL	SOIL	STAG	SYEN	TEAK	TIER	TOPS	TUPS
SCUR	SHIV	SKRY	SOJA	STAP	SYES	TEAL	TIES	TORC	TURD
SCUT	SHOD	SKUA	SOKE	STAR	SYKE	TEAM	TIFF	TORE	TURF
SCYE	SHOE	SKUG	SOLA	STAW	SYNC	TEAR	TIFT	TORI	TURM
SEAL	SHOG	SKYR	SOLD	STAY	SYND	TEAS	TIGE	TORN	TURN
SEAM	SHOO	SLAB	SOLE	STED	SYNE	TEAT	TIGS	TORR	TUSH
SEAN	SHOP	SLAE	SOLI	STEM	SYPE	TECH	TIKA	TORS	TUSK
SEAR	SHOT	SLAG	SOLO	STEN		TEDS	TIKE	TORT	TUTS
SEAS	SHOW	SLAM	SOLS	STEP	TAAL	TEDY	TIKI	TOSE	TUTU
SEAT	SHUL	SLAP	SOMA	STET	TABS	TEED	TILE	TOSH	TUZZ
SECS	SHUN	SLAT	SOME	STEW	TABU	TEEL	TILL	TOSS	TWAE
SECT	SHUT	SLAW	SONE	STEY	TACE	TEEM	TILS	TOST	TWAL
SEED	SHWA	SLAY	SONG	STIE	TACH	TEEN	TILT	TOTE	TWAS
SEEK	SIAL	SLED	SONS	STIR	TACK	TEER	TIME	TOTS	TWAT
SEEL	SIBB	SLEE	SOOK	STOA	TACO	TEES	TIND	TOUK	TWAY
SEEM	SIBS	SLEW	SOOM	STOB	TACT	TEFF	TINE	TOUN	TWEE
SEEN	SICE	SLEY	SOON	STOP	TADS	TEFS	TING	TOUR	TWIG
SEEP	SICH	SLID	SOOP	STOT	TAED	TEGG	TINK	TOUT	TWIN
SEER	SICK	SLIM	SOOT	STOW	TAEL	TEGS	TINS	TOWN	TWIT
SEES	SICS	SLIP	SOPH	STUB	TAES	TEHR	TINT	TOWS	TWOS
SEGO	SIDA	SLIT	SOPS	STUD	TAGS	TEIL	TINY	TOWT	TYDE
SEGS	SIDE	SLOB	SORA	STUM	TAHA	TELA	TIPI	TOWY	TYED
SEIF	SIEN	SLOE	SORB	STUN	TAHR	TELD	TIPS	TOYS	TYES
SEIL	SIFT	SLOG	SORD	STYE	TAIL	TELL	TIPT	TOZE	TYGS
SEIS	SIGH	SLOP	SORE	SUBS	TAIS	TELS	TIRE	TRAD	TYKE
SEKT	SIGN	SLOT	SORI	SUCH	TAIT	TELT	TIRL	TRAM	TYMP
SELD	SIKA	SLOW	SORN	SUCK	TAKA	TEME	TIRO	TRAP	TYND
SELE	SIKE	SLUB	SORT	SUDD	TAKE	TEMP	TIRR	TRAY	TYNE
SELF	SILD	SLUE	SOSS	SUDS	TAKS	TEMS	TITE	TREE	TYPE
SELL	SILE	SLUG	SOTS	SUED	TAKY	TEND	TITI	TREF	TYPO
SELS	SILK	SLUM	SOUK	SUER	TALA	TENE	TITS	TREK	TYRE
SEME	SILL	SLUR	SOUL	SUES	TALC	TENS	TIZZ	TRET	TYRO
SEMI	SILO	SLUT	SOUM	SUET	TALE	TENT	TOAD	TREW	TYTE
SEND	SILT	SMEE	SOUP	SUIT	TALI	TERF	TOBY	TREY	TZAR
SENS	SIMA	SMEW	SOUR	SUKH	TALK	TERM	TOCO	TREZ	
SENT	SIMI	SMIR	SOUS	SUKS	TALL	TERN	TODS	TRIE	UDAL
SEPS	SIMP	SMIT	SOUT	SULK	TAME	TEST	TODY	TRIG	UDOS
SEPT	SIMS	SMOG	SOVS	SUMO	TAMP	TETE	TOED	TRIM	UEYS
SERA	SIND	SMUG	SOWF	SUMP	TAMS	TEWS	TOES	TRIN	UFOS
SERE	SINE	SMUR	SOWL	SUMS	TANA	TEXT	TOFF	TRIO	UGHS
SERF	SING	SMUT	SOWM	SUNG	TANE	THAE	TOFT	TRIP	UGLI
SERK	SINK	SNAB	SOWN	SUNK	TANG	THAN	TOFU	TROD	UGLY
SERR	SINS	SNAG	SOWP	SUNN	TANK	THAR	TOGA	TROG	ULES
SESE	SIPE	SNAP	SOWS	SUNS	TANS	THAT	TOGE	TRON	ULEX
SESS	SIPS	SNAR	SOYA	SUPS	TAPA	THAW	TOGS	TROT	ULNA
SETA	SIRE	SNEB	SOYS	SUQS	TAPE	THEE	TOHO	TROW	UMBO
SETS	SIRI	SNED	SPAE	SURA	TAPS	THEM	TOIL	TROY	UMPH
SETT	SIRS	SNEE	SPAN	SURD	TAPU	THEN	TOKE	TRUE	UNAU
SEWN	SISS	SNIB	SPAR	SURE	TARA	THEW	TOKO	TRUG	UNBE
SEWS	SIST	SNIG	SPAS	SURF	TARE	THEY	TOLA	TRYE	UNCE
SEXT	SITE	SNIP	SPAT	SUSS	TARN	THIG	TOLD	TRYP	UNCI
SEXY	SITH	SNOB	SPAW	SWAB	TARO	THIN	TOLE	TSAR	UNCO
SEYS	SITS	SNOD	SPAY	SWAD	TARP	THIR	TOLL	TUAN	UNDE
SHAD	SIZE	SNOG	SPEC	SWAG	TARS	THIS	TOLT	TUBA	UNDO
SHAG	SIZY	SNOT	SPED	SWAM	TART	THON	TOLU	TUBE	UNIS
SHAH	SKAS	SNOW	SPET	SWAN	TASH	THOU	TOMB	TUBS	UNIT
SHAM	SKAT	SNUB	SPEW	SWAP	TASK	THRO	TOME	TUCK	UNTO
SHAN	SKAW	SNUG	SPIC	SWAT	TASS	THRU	TOMS	TUFA	UPAS
SHAT	SKEG	SOAK	SPIE	SWAY	TATE	THUD	TONE	TUFF	UPBY

UPGO	VATS	VINY	WALE	WEBS	WHIP	WOKE	YANG	YINS	YURT
UPON	VAUS	VIOL	WALI	WEDS	WHIR	WOKS	YANK	YIPS	YWIS
UPSY	VAUT	VIRL	WALK	WEED	WHIT	WOLD	YAPP	YIRD	
URAO	VEAL	VISA	WALL	WEEK	WHIZ	WOLF	YAPS	YIRK	ZACK
URDE	VEER	VISE	WALY	WEEL	WHOA	WOMB	YARD	YITE	ZAGS
URDS	VEES	VITA	WAME	WEEM	WHOM	WONS	YARE	YLEM	ZANY
URDY	VEGA	VITE	WAND	WEEN	WHOP	WONT	YARN	YLKE	ZAPS
UREA	VEHM	VIVA	WANE	WEEP	WHOT	WOOD	YARR	YMPE	ZARF
URES	VEIL	VIVE	WANG	WEER	WHOW	WOOF	YATE	YMPT	ZATI
URGE	VEIN	VIVO	WANK	WEES	WICK	WOOL	YAUD	YOBS	ZEAL
URIC	VELA	VIZY	WANS	WEET	WIDE	WOON	YAUP	YOCK	ZEAS
URNS	VELD	VLEI	WANT	WEFT	WIEL	WOOS	YAWL	YODE	ZEBU
URUS	VELE	VOAR	WANY	WEID	WIFE	WOOT	YAWN	YOGA	ZEDS
URVA	VELL	VOES	WAPS	WEIL	WIGS	WOPS	YAWP	YOGH	ZEES
USED	VENA	VOID	WARD	WEIR	WILD	WORD	YAWS	YOGI	ZEIN
USER	VEND	VOLA	WARE	WEKA	WILE	WORE	YAWY	YOKE	ZEKS
USES	VENT	VOLE	WARK	WELD	WILI	WORK	YBET	YOKS	ZELS
UTAS	VERB	VOLS	WARM	WELK	WILL	WORM	YEAD	YOLD	ZERO
UTES	VERS	VOLT	WARN	WELL	WILT	WORN	YEAH	YOLK	ZEST
UTIS	VERT	VORS	WARP	WELT	WILY	WORT	YEAN	YOMP	ZETA
UTUS	VERY	VOTE	WARS	WEMB	WIMP	WOST	YEAR	YOND	ZEZE
UVAS	VEST	VOWS	WART	WEMS	WIND	WOTS	YEAS	YONI	ZHOS
UVEA	VETO	VRIL	WARY	WEND	WINE	WOVE	YEDE	YONT	ZIFF
	VETS	VUGS	WASE	WENS	WING	WOWF	YEED	YOOP	ZIGS
VACS	VIAE	VULN	WASH	WENT	WINK	WOWS	YEGG	YORE	ZILA
VADE	VIAL	VUMS	WASP	WEPT	WINN	WRAP	YELD	YORK	ZIMB
VAES	VIAS		WAST	WERE	WINO	WREN	YELK	YOUK	ZINC
VAGI	VIBE	WADD	WATE	WERT	WINS	WRIT	YELL	YOUR	ZING
VAIL	VIBS	WADE	WATS	WEST	WINY	WUDS	YELM	YOWE	ZIPS
VAIN	VICE	WADI	WATT	WETS	WIPE	WULL	YELP	YOWL	ZITS
VAIR	VIDE	WADS	WAUK	WEXE	WIRE	WYES	YELT	YOWS	ZIZZ
VALE	VIED	WADY	WAUL	WEYS	WIRY	WYND	YENS	YUAN	ZOBO
VALI	VIER	WAES	WAUR	WHAM	WISE	WYNN	YEPS	YUCA	ZOBU
VAMP	VIES	WAFF	WAVE	WHAP	WISH	WYNS	YERD	YUCK	ZOEA
VANE	VIEW	WAFT	WAVY	WHAT	WISP	WYTE	YERK	YUFT	ZOIC
VANG	VILD	WAGE	WAWE	WHEE	WIST		YESK	YUGA	ZONA
VANS	VILE	WAGS	WAWL	WHEN	WITE	XYST	YEST	YUGS	ZONE
VANT	VILL	WAID	WAWS	WHET	WITH		YETI	YUKE	ZOOM
VARA	VIMS	WAIF	WAXY	WHEW	WITS	YACK	YETT	YUKS	ZOON
VARE	VINA	WAIL	WAYS	WHEY	WIVE	YAFF	YEUK	YUKY	ZOOS
VARY	VINE	WAIN	WEAK	WHID	WOAD	YAKS	YEVE	YULE	ZULU
VASA	VINO	WAIT	WEAL	WHIG	WOCK	YALD	YEWS	YUMP	ZUPA
VASE	VINS	WAKE	WEAN	WHIM	WOES	YALE	YGOE	YUNX	ZURF
VAST	VINT	WALD	WEAR	WHIN	WOGS	YAMS	YILL	YUPS	ZYME

HINT

Fours Feeding

Very few top players are actually familiar with all the four-letter words. The ones they tend to concentrate on are those that are formed from three-letter words (see the Hooks section), those that contain the higher-scoring consonants, and those that are useful for sorting out those vowel problems. Work through the four-letter list and highlight those you don't know then play a solo game restricting yourself to just four-letter words as far as you are able. Initially consult the list whilst playing but also try to play from memory. After a while oddities such as BAPU, COFT, DHAL and EUOI become second nature to your game, and impress your opponents!

HINT

Managing the Big Four

It is rarely worth holding on to the J Q X or Z in the hope of a very high score later in the game unless you are aware of the letters you are likely to pick up and you are not sacrificing scores in the process. Generally, keeping the high score letters back will hinder future opportunities and rack balance. It is often wiser to score what you can rather than wait for something better. But if you are to hold on to any of the big four the X is probably the safest and most flexible simply because of the two-letter words playable. It is also the one your opponent is most likely to unwittingly provide a scoring opportunity for.

HINT

Suspicious Minds

Don't be suspicious of all your opponent's moves. It is often better to play to the strength of your own rack and think about your scoring potential than worry too much about whether your opponent's play is a set-up for a good score next turn. Even amongst top players there are few occasions when there is a deliberate setup play.

HINT

Tile Turnover

An additional consideration when deciding upon the best move is the number of tiles you use. Although other factors such as the score, the balance of the letters left on your rack, and the openness of the move, are just as important, the basic philosophy that using more tiles than your opponent increases your chances of getting any of the good tiles remaining in the bag cannot be completely ignored.

When faced with a choice of moves with a poor rack, more often than not the play using most tiles is the one to favour. The exception is when the only tiles remaining are the awkward tiles that you would rather avoid (eg the Q and the V's). Keeping track of the tiles played is advantageous in judging the value of a high turnover play but ultimately you are at the mercy of your own discretion.

LIGHT AND HEAVY WORDS

Light words are those with many vowels, excluding Y's. Light words are useful for discarding excessive vowels from one's rack, in an attempt to return to a more balanced rack. The numbers of vowels for words of varying lengths in these lists are given here:

> 2-letter words, 2 vowels (eg AE, OI)
> 3-letter words, 3 vowels (AIA, EAU)
> 4-letter words, 3 vowels or more (eg EUOI, IOTA)
> 5-letter words, 4 vowels (eg AUDIO, QUEUE)
> 6-letter words, 4 vowels or more (eg COOKIE, LEAGUE)
> 7-letter words, 5 vowels or more (eg ANAEMIA, EVACUEE)
> 8-letter words, 5 vowels or more (eg ALIENATE, ORATORIO)

In trying to recall words with many vowels, try to think of groups of two and three vowels which do occur together – for example, AE, EA, IA, IAE, IOU and OU.

Heavy words are those with many consonants. These are useful for discarding excessive consonants from one's rack, again in an attempt to return to a more balanced rack. The numbers of vowels for words of varying lengths in these lists are given here:

> 2-letter words, no vowels except Y (eg MY, SH)
> 3-letter words, no vowels except Y (eg FRY, NTH)
> 4-letter words, no vowels except Y (eg HYMN, YMPT)
> 5-letter words, no vowels except Y (eg CRWTH, NYMPH)
> 6-letter words, 1 vowel (eg CHINTZ, RHYTHM)

To avoid these lists ballooning in size, plurals ending in -S have been omitted. In trying to recall words with many consonants, try to home in on words with frequently occurring clumps of letters – for example, CH, GHT, NCH, PH, SCH, SCR, TCH and TH. Of course, there are many others apart from these.

LIGHT WORDS (Many Vowels)

2-letter words - 2 vowels

AA	AE	AI	EA	EE	IO	OE	OI	OO	OU

3-letter words - 3 vowels

AIA	EAU

4-letter words - 3 vowels or more

AEON	AITU	ANOA	BEAU	EMEU	EVOE	IOTA	MOUE	OLIO	URAO
AGEE	AJEE	AQUA	CIAO	EOAN	HUIA	IXIA	NAOI	OOSE	UREA
AGIO	AKEE	AREA	EALE	EPEE	IDEA	JIAO	OBIA	OOZE	UVEA
AGUE	ALAE	ARIA	EASE	ETUI	IDEE	KAIE	OBOE	OUZO	VIAE
AIAS	ALEE	AULA	EAUS	EUGE	ILEA	LIEU	ODEA	PAUA	ZOEA
AIDE	ALOE	AURA	EAUX	EUOI	ILIA	LUAU	OGEE	ROUE	
AINE	AMIE	AUTO	EINE	EURO	INIA	MOOI	OLEO	UNAU	

5-letter words - 4 vowels

ADIEU	AIDOI	AQUAE	AURAE	COOEE	OIDIA	OURIE	ZOOEA
AECIA	AINEE	AUDIO	AUREI	EERIE	OORIE	QUEUE	
AERIE	AIOLI	AULOI	AVOUE	IAIDO	OUIJA	ZOEAE	

6-letter words - 4 vowels or more

ABELIA	AMEBAE	AURATE	COOEED	EPUISE	HEAUME	LEIPOA	OOZIER	QUALIA	TIBIAE
ABULIA	AMELIA	AUREUS	COOEES	EQUATE	HEEZIE	LIAISE	OPAQUE	QUELEA	TOORIE
ACACIA	AMOEBA	AURORA	COOKIE	EQUINE	HOODOO	LOONIE	OPIATE	QUEUED	TOUPEE
ACAJOU	AMOOVE	AUROUS	COOLIE	EQUIPE	HOOPOE	MANOAO	OPIOID	QUEUES	TOUTIE
ACEDIA	ANEMIA	AUTEUR	COTEAU	ETOILE	HOOROO	MEALIE	ORARIA	QUINIE	UAKARI
ADAGIO	ANOMIE	AVAILE	COULEE	EUCAIN	IAIDOS	MEANIE	OREIDE	QUINOA	UBIQUE
ADIEUS	ANOXIA	AVENUE	COUPEE	EUOUAE	IDEAED	MEDIAE	ORIOLE	QUOOKE	UNEASE
ADIEUX	ANURIA	AVIATE	CURIAE	EUREKA	IDEATE	MEINIE	OROIDE	REALIA	UNIQUE
AECIUM	AOUDAD	AVOUES	DAIMIO	EURIPI	IGUANA	MILIEU	OTIOSE	REDIAE	URAEUS
AEDILE	APIECE	AVOURE	DAUTIE	EVOLUE	IODATE	MOUSIE	OUGLIE	REEKIE	UREDIA
AEMULE	APNOEA	AZALEA	DEARIE	EVOVAE	IODIDE	NAUSEA	OUIJAS	RESEAU	UREIDE
AERATE	APOGEE	AZIONE	DEAWIE	FAERIE	IODINE	NOOKIE	OURALI	ROADIE	UREMIA
AERIAL	APORIA	BAGUIO	DEEPIE	FAUNAE	IODISE	OAKIER	OURARI	ROARIE	UTOPIA
AERIER	ARAISE	BAILEE	DOOLIE	FEAGUE	IODIZE	OARAGE	OUREBI	ROOKIE	UVULAE
AERIES	ARALIA	BAILIE	DOUANE	FEERIE	IODOUS	OARIER	OURIER	ROUCOU	VAUDOO
AEROBE	AREOLA	BATEAU	EASIER	FOODIE	IOLITE	OCREAE	OUTAGE	SAIKEI	VOIDEE
AGAPAE	AREOLE	BAUERA	EATAGE	FOVEAE	IONISE	ODIOUS	OUTATE	SAIQUE	VOODOO
AGOUTA	ARIOSI	BEANIE	ECURIE	GATEAU	IONIUM	OEDEMA	OUTEAT	SAULIE	VOUDOU
AGOUTI	ARIOSO	BOOBOO	EELIER	GAUCIE	IONIZE	OEUVRE	OUTLIE	SEMEIA	WEEPIE
AGUISE	AROUSE	BOODIE	EERIER	GIAOUR	IONONE	OIDIUM	OUTVIE	SOAPIE	WOODIE
AGUIZE	ATAXIA	BOOGIE	EIDOLA	GOALIE	JEELIE	OILIER	OZAENA	SOIREE	ZOOEAE
AIKIDO	ATOCIA	BOOKIE	EKUELE	GOATEE	KAIKAI	OLEATE	PALEAE	SOOGEE	ZOOEAL
AIKONA	AUBADE	BOOTEE	ELUATE	GOOIER	KEELIE	OOIDAL	PEERIE	SOOGIE	ZOOEAS
AIOLIS	AUCUBA	BOUGIE	ELUVIA	GOOLIE	KIERIE	OOLITE	PEEWEE	SOUARI	ZOOZOO
AIRIER	AUDILE	BUREAU	EMEUTE	GOOROO	KOODOO	OOMIAC	PERAEA	TAENIA	
ALALIA	AUDIOS	CADEAU	EPAULE	GUINEA	KOOKIE	OOMIAK	PEREIA	TAUPIE	
ALEXIA	AUGITE	CAIQUE	EPEIRA	HAIKAI	LAESIE	OORIAL	PIUPIU	TEEHEE	
ALOGIA	AUMAIL	COAITA	EPIZOA	HAIQUE	LAMIAE	OORIER	POURIE	TEEPEE	
AMADOU	AUNTIE	COATEE	EPOPEE	HEARIE	LEAGUE	OOSIER	QUAERE	TENIAE	

7-letter words - 5 vowels or more

ABOULIA	ALIENEE	AREOLAE	AURORAE	EQUINIA	EUTEXIA	NOUVEAU	ROULEAU	ZOOECIA
AECIDIA	AMOEBAE	AUREATE	AUTOCUE	ETAERIO	EVACUEE	OLEARIA	SAOUARI	
AEOLIAN	ANAEMIA	AURELIA	CAMAIEU	EUCAINE	EXUVIAE	OOGONIA	SEQUOIA	
AEONIAN	AQUARIA	AUREOLA	DOULEIA	EULOGIA	IPOMOEA	OUABAIN	TAENIAE	
AIERIES	AQUEOUS	AUREOLE	EPUISEE	EUOUAES	MOINEAU	OUAKARI	URAEMIA	

8-letter words - 5 vowels or more

ABOIDEAU	AERONAUT	APOLOGIA	AURELIAS	AWEARIED	DOULEIAS	EQUALIZE	EUPHUIZE
ABOITEAU	AGACERIE	APOLOGUE	AUREOLAS	BANLIEUE	DUOLOGUE	EQUATION	EUROPIUM
ABOULIAS	AGIOTAGE	APOSITIA	AUREOLED	BAUHINIA	EARPIECE	EQUINIAS	EUTAXIES
ACADEMIA	AGOUTIES	AQUACADE	AUREOLES	BEAUTIED	EATERIES	EQUIPAGE	EUTAXITE
ACAUDATE	AGUACATE	AQUANAUT	AURICULA	BEAUTIES	EBIONISE	EQUISETA	EUTEXIAS
ACAULINE	AIGUILLE	AQUARIAN	AURIFIED	BEAUXITE	EBIONIZE	EQUITIES	EUXENITE
ACAULOSE	AKINESIA	AQUARIUM	AURIFIES	BOUDERIE	ECAUDATE	EQUIVOKE	EVACUATE
ACIERAGE	ALEURONE	AQUILINE	AUROREAN	BOUTIQUE	EDACIOUS	ERADIATE	EVACUEES
ACIERATE	ALIENAGE	ARACEOUS	AUTACOID	BOUZOUKI	EGOITIES	ERIONITE	EVALUATE
ACOEMETI	ALIENATE	ARANEOUS	AUTOCADE	CAESIOUS	EGOMANIA	ETAERIOS	EXAMINEE
ACTINIAE	ALIENEES	ARAPAIMA	AUTOCUES	CAMAIEUX	EMACIATE	ETIOLATE	EXEQUIAL
ACUITIES	ALLELUIA	AREOLATE	AUTOGIRO	CARIACOU	EMERAUDE	ETOURDIE	EXEQUIES
ACULEATE	ALOPECIA	ASEITIES	AUTOMATA	CAUSERIE	ENCAENIA	EUCAINES	EXIGUOUS
ADEQUATE	AMOEBOID	ASSEGAAI	AUTOMATE	CAUTIOUS	EOLIENNE	EULOGIES	EXIMIOUS
ADULARIA	ANAEMIAS	ATARAXIA	AUTOPSIA	CAVIARIE	EOLIPILE	EULOGISE	EXUVIATE
AECIDIUM	ANAEROBE	AUDIENCE	AUTOSOME	COENOBIA	EPICEDIA	EULOGIUM	FACETIAE
AEGIRINE	ANALOGUE	AUDITION	AUTUNITE	COOEEING	EPIGAEAL	EULOGIZE	FAUTEUIL
AEGIRITE	ANOREXIA	AUDITIVE	AUXILIAR	DAIQUIRI	EPIGAEAN	EUPEPSIA	FEATEOUS
AEGLOGUE	ANOUROUS	AUGURIES	AVIARIES	DETAINEE	EPIGEOUS	EUPHOBIA	FEATUOUS
AERATION	APIARIAN	AULARIAN	AVIATION	DIALOGUE	EPILOGUE	EUPHONIA	FILIOQUE
AEROFOIL	APIARIES	AUMAILED	AVIFAUNA	DIAPAUSE	EPOPOEIA	EUPHORIA	FOEDARIE
AEROLITE	APOGAEIC	AURELIAN	AVOISION	DOUANIER	EQUALISE	EUPHUISE	FORHOOIE

GAIETIES	INDUCIAE	MEIONITE	OITICICA	OUTHOUSE	POACEOUS	SAOUARIS	UNIONISE
GUAIACUM	INDUVIAE	METAIRIE	OLEARIAS	OUTVALUE	POULAINE	SAPUCAIA	UNIONIZE
HEMIOLIA	INFERIAE	METANOIA	OOGAMIES	OUTVOICE	QUEASIER	SEAQUAKE	URAEMIAS
HEMIOPIA	INITIATE	MEUNIERE	OOGAMOUS	OUVRIERE	QUEAZIER	SEQUELAE	URAEUSES
HETAERAE	IPOMOEAS	MILIARIA	OOGENIES	OVARIOLE	QUEENITE	SEQUOIAS	UREDINIA
HETAERIA	ISOLOGUE	MINUTIAE	OOGONIAL	OVARIOUS	QUEUEING	SQUEEGEE	USURIOUS
HETAIRAI	JALOUSIE	MOIETIES	OOGONIUM	PAENULAE	QUIETIVE	TAENIATE	UXORIOUS
HETAIRIA	JEALOUSE	MOINEAUS	OOLOGIES	PAEONIES	QUIETUDE	TAENIOID	VIRAEMIA
HOODOOED	KAIKAIED	NAUSEATE	ORAGIOUS	PAHOEHOE	QUILLAIA	TENUIOUS	VOODOOED
IDEALISE	LACINIAE	NAUSEOUS	ORATORIO	PARANOEA	RADIALIA	THIOUREA	VOUDOUED
IDEALIZE	LAUREATE	OBSEQUIE	OSIERIES	PARANOIA	REAROUSE	TOXAEMIA	ZABAIONE
IDEATION	MAIEUTIC	OCEANAUT	OUABAINS	PAROEMIA	RELEASEE	UBIETIES	ZOIATRIA
IDEATIVE	MAIOLICA	ODALIQUE	OUAKARIS	PAROUSIA	RETIARII	UINTAITE	ZOOECIUM
IDIOCIES	MAUVAISE	OEILLADE	OUISTITI	PEEKABOO	ROULEAUS	UNEASIER	ZOOGLOEA
INAURATE	MAUVEINE	OILERIES	OUTEATEN	PERIAGUA	ROULEAUX	UNIAXIAL	ZOONOMIA

HINT _____

Practising with Plates

A convenient way to practise Scrabble vocabulary whilst travelling by car is to find words from car number plates. There are a number of Scrabble games playable (if you're not the driver!):

- Find the shortest word containing the three letters of the number plate (ignoring the letter denoting the year).

- Look for seven-letter words by converting the numerals to letters thus (1=I, 2=Z, 3=E, 4=A, 5=S, 6=G, 7=T, 8=B, 9=G, 0=O) eg DGF 105H makes DOGFISH!

- Look for seven-letter words by taking the four letters and adding the letters A E I, or I E S, or similar, to give a good 'rack'.

HINT _____

Vowel Advice

Once you have more than two of any vowel on your rack it is all too easy to accumulate more because of the difficulty in sorting out the initial problem. Try the following exercise to become more familiar with those words that solve your multiple vowel imbalance.

Select three A's and then repeatedly pick up any four consonants and see how many A-words you can think of for the first move. Try to find the highest scoring first move and then consult the Awkward Vowel lists for added inspiration. Do not actually play words on the board but treat each fresh rack as if it were the first move. Repeat the exercise with the O's, I's and U's.

HINT

Valuing the S and Blank

The blank and the S are the most valuable tiles in the Scrabble set. Treat them as if they are worth a potential 50 points each. They are the ingredients of most seven and eight-letter bonus plays and as such should be used wisely. It is rarely worth playing an S for just a few extra points unless the move is essential for blocking the opponent in a game where winning is all important. A blank retained on the rack, even if not utilized in a bonus play, will provide that extra degree of flexibility of choice for endgame strategy.

HINT

ING Addiction

Every Scrabble player has retained ING on their rack at some time or another in the hope of getting an -ING bonus word. The usefulness of this strategy is frequently overrated amongst less experienced players. Although it is a common ending, unless you have the fortune to pick up the right letters for an -ING seven-letter word you will find the G more of a hindrance. Furthermore, if you religiously cling on to the ING you are severely limiting your choice of play for each move and are effectively playing with only four tiles. The advice is to avoid any ING addiction and concentrate on just keeping any subset of the letters RETAIN that you may have. This will be more fruitful.

HINT

Looking at Hooks

The two, three and four-letter hook words are probably the most important of the hook words. Try to learn a few useful ones at a time and attempt to introduce them into your game. An interesting exercise to assist is as follows:

Take each letter of the alphabet and find a two, three and four-letter word that takes that letter before or after as a hook to make a longer word. There may be none for some of the more awkward letters. This will give you a balanced variety of some 100 hook words to study.

Note that, for ruthless blocking strategies, the three and four-letter words that do not take hook letters before or after are just as important.

HEAVY WORDS (Many Consonants) except -S plurals

2-letter words - no vowels except Y

BY	CH	FY	KY	MY	NY	SH	ST

3-letter words - no vowels except Y

CLY	DRY	GYM	LYM	PLY	PYX	SKY	STY	TRY	WHY
CRY	FLY	GYP	NTH	PRY	RHY	SLY	SWY	TYG	WRY
CWM	FRY	HYP	NYS	PST	SHY	SPY	THY	VLY	WYN

4-letter words - no vowels except Y

CYST	GYNY	JYNX	LYNX	RYND	SKYR	SYND	TYND	XYST
FYRD	HWYL	KYND	MYTH	SCRY	SPRY	TRYP	WYND	YMPT
GYMP	HYMN	LYMS	PSST	SKRY	SYNC	TYMP	WYNN	

5-letter words - no vowels except Y

CHYND	DRYLY	GRYPT	GYPSY	LYNCH	PSYCH	SLYLY	THYMY	XYLYL
CRWTH	GHYLL	GYNNY	KYDST	MYRRH	PYGMY	SYLPH	TRYST	
CRYPT	GLYPH	GYPPY	LYMPH	NYMPH	SHYLY	SYNCH	WRYLY	

6-letter words - one vowel

BLANCH	CRANCH	FROWST	PRANCK	SCRIMP	SHTETL	SPHINX	STARCH	STRONG	THRIST
BLENCH	CRATCH	GLITCH	PROMPT	SCRIPT	SHTICK	SPIGHT	STENCH	STROWN	THRONG
BLIGHT	CROTCH	GROWTH	PUTSCH	SCROLL	SHTUCK	SPILTH	STITCH	STRUCK	THROWN
BLINTZ	CRUNCH	GRUMPH	RHYTHM	SCROWL	SHTUMM	SPLASH	STOWND	STRUNG	THRUSH
BLOTCH	CRUTCH	GRUTCH	SCARTH	SCRUFF	SKARTH	SPLENT	STRACK	STRUNT	THRUST
BORSCH	CULTCH	HIGHTH	SCATCH	SCRUMP	SKETCH	SPLIFF	STRAFF	SWARTH	THWACK
BRANCH	DIRNDL	KIRSCH	SCHELM	SCRUNT	SKLENT	SPLINT	STRAMP	SWATCH	THWART
BRIGHT	DRACHM	KITSCH	SCHISM	SCULPT	SKLIFF	SPLOSH	STRAND	SWITCH	TRENCH
BROWST	DRENCH	KLEPHT	SCHIST	SHLOCK	SKRIMP	SPRACK	STRASS	SWOWND	TWIGHT
BRUNCH	FLANCH	KNIGHT	SCHLEP	SHRANK	SKRUMP	SPRANG	STRATH	TCHICK	TWITCH
CATCHT	FLENCH	KNITCH	SCHORL	SHREWD	SLIGHT	SPRAWL	STRAWN	THATCH	WARMTH
CHINCH	FLETCH	KRANTZ	SCHTIK	SHRIFT	SMATCH	SPREDD	STRESS	THETCH	WHILST
CHINTZ	FLIGHT	KVETCH	SCHUSS	SHRILL	SMIGHT	SPRENT	STREWN	THIRST	WHISHT
CHRISM	FLINCH	LENGTH	SCLAFF	SHRIMP	SMIRCH	SPRING	STRICH	THRALL	WRENCH
CHURCH	FLITCH	MENSCH	SCLIFF	SHRINK	SMUTCH	SPRINT	STRICT	THRANG	WRETCH
CLATCH	FLYSCH	PHLEGM	SCORCH	SNATCH	SNITCH	SPRONG	STRIFT	THRASH	WRIGHT
CLENCH	FRATCH	PLANCH	SCOTCH	SHROFF	SPARTH	SPRUNG	STRING	THRAWN	
CLINCH	FRENCH	PLIGHT	SCOWTH	SHROWD	SPERST	SPRUSH	STROLL	THRESH	
CLUNCH	FRICHT	PLINTH	SCRAWL	SHRUNK	SPETCH	STANCH	STROMB	THRIFT	
CLUTCH	FRIGHT	PLONGD	SCRAWM	SHTCHI	SPETCH	STANCK	STROND	THRILL	

HINT

Fishing

It is rarely worth holding on to a set of letters hoping to pick up that one tile that will transform your rack into a wonderful high-scoring bonus word. However, if the six letters you are holding on to are likely to yield a bonus play with *many* of the tiles that you are likely to pick up (see Bonus Word Sets section) then 'fishing' could be strategically beneficial. Always consider the chances of actually getting the tile or tiles you hope for and balance this against any alternative scoring plays. Knowledge of the letter distribution and the most fruitful six-letter combinations is mandatory for timely 'fishing'.

HINT

Mind Your Changing

Since it is permissible to change any number of your letters instead of a turn during a game (unless there are fewer than seven tiles in the bag), it can be a wise decision to change some or all of your letters even if you can find a word to play on the board. You should consider changing when:

- You have an imbalance of vowels and consonants and the available dump words do not solve your rack problems, score very little, or provide too many scoring opportunities for your opponent.
- There are no scoring opportunities on the board and you don't wish to block your opponent with a low-scoring play.
- You have a Q with no U and none of the U-less Q words are playable.
- You have a promising six-letter combination that combines well with many other letters to make a seven-letter word but not with the seventh letter on your rack. Changing the odd letter in this situation is often not the best strategic move but the time for such a change may be ripe if you desperately need the bonus to catch up or there are no other worthwhile alternatives.

HINT

Bonus Hunting

Faced with a rack of seven letters in any order it is not always easy to spot even common seven-letter words. Moving the tiles around will often enable an otherwise hidden seven-letter word to come to light. But rather than frantic shuffling and reshuffling in the hope of inspiration a more organized approach is recommended. Form beginnings and endings with the letters on your rack and check the remaining tiles to see if they form a word with that beginning or ending. For example, with the rack EEFGLOR making the prefix FORE will lead you to FORELEG. With ACEORTV, the prefix OVER will inspire OVERACT. Similarly with the racks AINOORT, AGEINOS and AEFHLTU it may only be by forming the endings -TION, -ISE and -FUL that you will stumble across ORATION, AGONISE and HATEFUL respectively. Also, splitting your rack into two shorter words may enable you to spot an allowable compound word. For example, the unlikely ADEEESW yields SEA and WEED (SEAWEED) and AADORWY makes ROAD and WAY (ROADWAY).

AWKWARD VOWEL DUMPS

It is often a problem when you are faced with two of the same vowel on your rack, except perhaps when they are two E's; it can be a nightmare when you are confronted with more than two, especially if they are I's or U's. Playing just one of the multiple vowels does not always resolve the problem, and one can be faced with the same problem on subsequent turns. This of course does not help your game, so ideally the problem needs to be resolved in one turn. You should find the following lists of words containing multiple A's, E's, I's, O's or U's will greatly assist you in such situations.

The words in these lists can be summarized as follows:

A words:	4 letters, 2 A's	(eg AWAY, LAVA)
	5 letters, 3 A's	(eg ABACA, KAAMA)
	6 letters, 3 A's	(eg BANANA, BAZAAR)
E words:	4 letters, 3 E's	(EPEE)
	5 letters, 3 E's	(eg GEESE, MELEE)
	6 letters, 4 E's	(eg PEEWEE, TEEPEE)
I words:	4 letters, 2 I's	(eg IRIS, KIWI)
	5 letters, 2 I's	(eg ICING, RIGID)
	6 letters, 3 I's	(eg BIKINI, IRITIC)
O words:	5 letters, 3 O's	(OVOLO)
	6 letters, 3 O's or more	(eg COCOON, VOODOO)
U words:	4 letters, 2 U's	(eg GURU, LUAU)
	5 letters, 2 U's or more	(eg AUGUR, QUEUE)
	6 letters, 3 U's	(eg MUTUUM, UHURUS)

(Note that there is no list of four-letter words with 2 O's – it is not too difficult to play a couple of O's in a four-letter word. Think of all the words with a double-O in them to begin with.)

AWKWARD VOWEL DUMPS - A's

4-letter words - 2 A's

ABAC	AIAS	AMAH	ARAK	AVAL	DATA	LAMA	NADA	RACA	TANA
ABAS	AJAR	AMLA	ARAR	AVAS	GAGA	LANA	NAGA	RAGA	TAPA
ABBA	ALAE	ANAL	ARBA	AWAY	GALA	LAVA	NALA	RAJA	TARA
ACTA	ALAP	ANAN	AREA	AYAH	HAAF	MAAR	NANA	RANA	TAXA
ADAW	ALAR	ANAS	ARIA	AZAN	HAAR	MAMA	NAPA	RATA	VARA
AFAR	ALAS	ANNA	ARNA	BAAS	HAKA	MANA	PACA	SAGA	VASA
AGAR	ALAY	ANOA	ASAR	BABA	KAKA	MARA	PAPA	TAAL	
AGAS	ALFA	ANTA	ATAP	CABA	KANA	MAYA	PARA	TAHA	
AGHA	ALGA	APAY	AULA	CAPA	KARA	NAAM	PAUA	TAKA	
AGMA	ALMA	AQUA	AURA	CASA	KAVA	NAAN	PAWA	TALA	

5-letter words - 3 A's

ABACA	ABAYA	AFARA	ALAAP	ALAPA	ANANA	ARABA	ASANA	KAAMA

6-letter words - 3 A's

ABACAS	ALALIA	ANARAK	ARMADA	AZALEA	BAZAAR	JATAKA	KARAKA	PALAMA	SAMAAN
ABAYAS	ALAPAS	ANATTA	ASANAS	BAHADA	CABALA	KAAMAS	KATANA	PANADA	SAMARA
ACACIA	ALBATA	ARABAS	ATABAL	BAJADA	CABANA	KABALA	LABARA	PANAMA	SATARA
AFARAS	ALPACA	ARALIA	ATAMAN	BALATA	CANADA	KABAYA	MANANA	PAPAYA	TAMARA
AGAPAE	ANABAS	ARCANA	ATAXIA	BANANA	DAGABA	KAMALA	MARACA	PATACA	ZAPATA
ALAAPS	ANANAS	ARGALA	AVATAR	BATATA	JACANA	KANAKA	NAGANA	SALAAM	

AWKWARD VOWEL DUMPS - E's

4-letter words - 3 E's

EPEE

5-letter words - 3 E's

BELEE	EERIE	EMEER	EXEME	HEEZE	MELEE	PEECE	REEDE	TEHEE
BESEE	EEVEN	EPEES	FEESE	KEEVE	NEELE	PEEPE	REEVE	TEPEE
DEERE	ELPEE	ETWEE	FEEZE	LEESE	NEESE	PEEVE	SEMEE	WEEKE
DEEVE	EMCEE	EXEEM	GEESE	LEVEE	NEEZE	PEWEE	TEENE	WEETE

6-letter words - 4 E's

PEEWEE   TEEHEE   TEEPEE

AWKWARD VOWEL DUMPS - I's

4-letter words - 2 I's

DIVI	IBIS	INIA	IWIS	KIWI	NIDI	PIPI	TIKI	WILI
DIXI	ILIA	IRID	IXIA	MIDI	NISI	SIMI	TIPI	
HILI	IMPI	IRIS	KIRI	MINI	PILI	SIRI	TITI	

5-letter words - 2 I's

ACINI	CIRRI	IAMBI	IMINE	IONIC	LICHI	MINIS	PILIS	SIRIH	VIRID
AIDOI	CIVIC	ICIER	IMMIT	IRIDS	LICIT	MODII	PIPIS	SIRIS	VISIE
AIOLI	CIVIL	ICILY	IMMIX	ISSEI	LIKIN	NIHIL	PIPIT	TIBIA	VISIT
ALIBI	DIGIT	ICING	IMPIS	IVIED	LIMIT	NIMBI	PIRAI	TIKIS	VIVID
BIFID	DILLI	ICTIC	IMSHI	IVIES	LININ	NISEI	PIXIE	TIMID	VIZIR
BIKIE	DINIC	IDIOM	INDRI	IXIAS	LIPID	NITID	RADII	TIPIS	WILIS
BLINI	DIVIS	IDIOT	INFIX	JINNI	LIVID	NIXIE	RICIN	TITIS	ZIMBI
CEILI	DIXIE	ILIAC	INION	KILIM	MEDII	OBIIT	RIGID	TORII	
CHILI	FINIS	ILIUM	INTIL	KININ	MIDIS	OIDIA	RISHI	VIGIA	
CILIA	GENII	IMARI	INWIT	KIRIS	MIMIC	ORIBI	SIGIL	VIGIL	
CIPPI	IAIDO	IMIDE	IODIC	KIWIS	MINIM	PILEI	SIMIS	VILLI	

6-letter words - 3 I's

BIKINI   IRIDIC   IRITIC   IRITIS   MIRITI

AWKWARD VOWEL DUMPS - O's

5-letter words - 3 O's

OVOLO

6-letter words - 3 O's or more

BOOBOO	COROZO	FORHOO	GOOROO	HOOPOE	KOODOO	OOLONG	ROTOLO	ZOOZOO
COCOON	DOOCOT	GOOGOL	HOODOO	HOOROO	OOLOGY	ROCOCO	VOODOO	

AWKWARD VOWEL DUMPS - U's

4-letter words - 2 U's

GURU	KUDU	LUAU	PULU	UNAU	UTUS
JUJU	KUKU	LULU	TUTU	URUS	ZULU

5-letter words - 2 U's or more

AUGUR	DURUM	JUGUM	LUAUS	QUEUE	UNAUS	UNGUM	USURP	ZULUS
BUCHU	FUCUS	JUJUS	LULUS	QUIPU	UNCUS	UPRUN	USURY	
BUCKU	FUGUE	KUDUS	LUPUS	TUQUE	UNCUT	URUBU	UVULA	
BUNDU	GURUS	KUDZU	MUCUS	TUTUS	UNDUE	URUBU	VOULU	
BUSSU	HUMUS	KUKUS	PULUS	UHURU	UNDUG	USURE	WUSHU	

6-letter words - 3 U's

MUTUUM   UHURUS   URUBUS

HINT

Triple Tactics

Every player recognizes the need to avoid giving the opponent easy access to the triple-word squares. However it is important not to be obsessive about giving away triple-word scores. Playing a word out to the edge of the board such that the word covers the double-letter square between two triple-word squares with a low-scoring tile, does not make it that easy for the opponent to score highly from the triple-word square. In fact, it may force the opponent to use his best tiles to block your use of the triple-word square next turn.

HINT

Flashcards

A popular way of testing Scrabble vocabulary is a system called flashcards. Small index cards are used which have 'questions' on one side and the 'answer words' on the reverse. For example if you were using flashcards to learn two-letter words you may have on one card A=13, with the 13 two-letter words beginning with A on the reverse. On another card B=4, and another C=1, would reveal BA BE BO BY and CH on the reverse respectively. Whenever you get a moment you can quickly flick through the cards and test yourself. The system can be used for many categories such as five-vowelled seven-letter words, words containing J Q X Z and so on. A good use of flashcards is to log every seven-letter word played against you that you didn't know thus naturally building up your personal testing library.

HINT

Fighting Back

Don't trade off catching up with poor rack retention. A more balanced rack will enable a greater choice of strategic plays in subsequent turns. Initially concentrate on not slipping any further behind and be wary of scoring opportunities open only to yourself. Perhaps you have the last S or the last A for an (A)JAR hook, and so on. Try to keep the board open unless you can block and catch up in a single play. If your opponent is in front it is likely their rack is worsening whilst they are blocking. Keeping the board open and maintaining your rack balance will keep your hopes alive whereas playing too defensively will only assist your opponent to keep their lead.

HINT

Passing Thoughts

It is allowable to pass in Scrabble, that is, to not play a word or change any tiles. This is in effect what a player does at the end of the game if stuck with any unplayable tiles. However, it is rarely worth passing during the game in the hope that the opponent will give you that vital opening or letter you need.

An example of an occasion where passing may be of advantage is if you have a good rack such as TAILEND and it is your play first, or your opponent has just changed letters instead of playing first. Since TAILEND combines with one of the four vowels (A E O U) to make an eight-letter word (DENTALIA, ENTAILED or LINEATED, DELATION, UNTAILED), it is likely your opponent may give you a bonus play next turn.

HINT

Learn As You Play

Always have a scrap of paper with you other than the scoresheet. Jot down any promising racks you find yourself with, seven-letter words you played that might have anagrams, and any words you think of playing but are unsure of. After the game spend a few minutes with *Official Scrabble Lists* and check out your words and racks, noting any new discoveries. Going through this exercise after every game will gradually strengthen your vocabulary without too much effort.

AWKWARD CONSONANT DUMPS

The best way to describe the words in the following lists is this: words of three to five letters that contain at least two of any one of the following consonants – B, C, F, H, V, W and Y. (Purists should note that Y is referred to here as a consonant, regardless of whether it is acting as a vowel or a consonant in any individual word.) It is not too difficult usually to dump a single F or an H in an attempt to achieve a reasonable score and balance one's rack. It is more of a problem to dump two F's, two H's and so on. These lists should help with your awkward consonant racks.

The lists are arranged so that all the B words come together, then the C word, and so on. The three-letter B words come before the four-letter B words, which come before the five-letter words. Similarly for the other awkward consonants. Do note that there are no three-letter lists here for the letters C, V and Y, as there are no three-letter words having two C's, or two V's or two Y's.

AWKWARD CONSONANT DUMPS - B's

3-letter words - 2 B's

ABB	BIB	BOB	BUB	EBB

4-letter words - 2 B's

ABBA	BABA	BABY	BLAB	BLUB	BOMB	BUBO	COBB
ABBE	BABE	BARB	BLEB	BOBA	BOOB	BUBS	EBBS
ABBS	BABU	BIBS	BLOB	BOBS	BUBA	BULB	SIBB

5-letter words - 2 B's or more

ABBAS	BABUL	BIMBO	BOBAS	BUBAL	COBBS	FUBBY	KEBAB	RIBBY	YOBBO
ABBES	BABUS	BLABS	BOBBY	BUBAS	COBBY	GABBY	KEBOB	SIBBS	ZEBUB
ABBEY	BARBE	BLEBS	BOMBE	BUBBY	CUBBY	GOBBI	LOBBY	SLUBB	
ABBOT	BARBS	BLOBS	BOMBO	BULBS	CUBEB	GOBBO	MOBBY	SYBBE	
BABAS	BEBOP	BLUBS	BOMBS	BUMBO	DEBBY	HOBBY	NABOB	TABBY	
BABEL	BEROB	BLURB	BOOBS	BUSBY	DIBBS	HUBBY	NOBBY	TUBBY	
BABES	BIBLE	BOBAC	BOOBY	CABBY	DOBBY	KABAB	NUBBY	WEBBY	
BABOO	BILBO	BOBAK	BRIBE	CABOB	EBBED	KABOB	RABBI	YABBY	

AWKWARD CONSONANT DUMPS - C's

4-letter words - 2 C's

CECA	CHIC	CHOC	COCA	COCH	COCK	COCO	CROC	ECCE	ECCO

5-letter words - 2 C's or more

ACCOY	CACHE	CHACK	CHOCS	CLACK	COCCI	CONCH	CUBIC	CYCLO	SECCO
ACOCK	CACTI	CHACO	CHUCK	CLECK	COCCO	CONIC	CULCH	CYNIC	SUCCI
BACCA	CAECA	CHECK	CINCH	CLICK	COCKS	COUCH	CUMEC	ICTIC	TICCA
BACCO	CASCO	CHICA	CINCT	CLOCK	COCKY	CRACK	CURCH	MUCIC	YACCA
BACCY	CATCH	CHICH	CIRCA	CLUCK	COCOA	CRICK	CUSEC	OCCUR	YUCCA
BOCCA	CECUM	CHICK	CIRCS	COACH	COCOS	CROCK	CUTCH	RECCE	ZOCCO
CABOC	CERCI	CHICS	CISCO	COACT	COLIC	CROCS	CYCAD	RECCO	
CACAO	CHACE	CHOCK	CIVIC	COCAS	COMIC	CRUCK	CYCLE	RECCY	

AWKWARD CONSONANT DUMPS   -   F's

3-letter words - 2 F's

EFF	IFF	OFF

4-letter words - 2 F's or more

AFFY	CAFF	DUFF	FUFF	HUFF	LUFF	OFFS	TEFF	YAFF
BAFF	COFF	EFFS	GAFF	IFFY	MIFF	PUFF	TIFF	ZIFF
BIFF	CUFF	FAFF	GOFF	JEFF	MUFF	RAFF	TOFF	
BOFF	DAFF	FIEF	GUFF	JIFF	NAFF	RIFF	TUFF	
BUFF	DOFF	FIFE	HAFF	KOFF	NIFF	RUFF	WAFF	

5-letter words - 2 F's or more

AFFIX	BUFFS	DAFFY	FIFES	GOFFS	JEFFS	NIFFS	QUIFF	SKOFF	TIFFS
BAFFS	CAFFS	DOFFS	FIFTH	GRAFF	JIFFS	NIFFY	RAFFS	SNIFF	TOFFS
BAFFY	CHAFF	DRAFF	FIFTY	GRIFF	JIFFY	NYAFF	REFFO	SNUFF	TOFFY
BIFFS	CHUFF	DUFFS	FLAFF	GRUFF	KOFFS	OFFAL	RIFFS	SOWFF	TUFFE
BLUFF	CLIFF	EFFED	FLUFF	GUFFS	LUFFA	OFFED	RUFFE	SPIFF	TUFFS
BOFFS	CLOFF	FAFFS	FUFFS	HAFFS	LUFFS	OFFER	RUFFS	STAFF	WAFFS
BUFFA	COFFS	FEOFF	FUFFY	HOUFF	MIFFS	PLUFF	SCAFF	STIFF	WAUFF
BUFFE	CUFFO	FIEFS	GAFFE	HOWFF	MIFFY	PUFFS	SCOFF	STUFF	WHIFF
BUFFI	CUFFS	FIFED	GAFFS	HUFFS	MUFFS	PUFFY	SCUFF	TAFFY	YAFFS
BUFFO	DAFFS	FIFER	GLIFF	HUFFY	NAFFS	QUAFF	SKIFF	TEFFS	ZIFFS

AWKWARD CONSONANT DUMPS   -   H's

3-letter words - 2 H's

HAH	HOH	HUH

4-letter words - 2 H's

HASH	HATH	HECH	HIGH	HISH	HOGH	HOHS	HUSH	PHOH	SHAH

5-letter words - 2 H's

AHIGH	HANCH	HAUGH	HEUCH	HIGHT	HOGHS	HOTCH	HUSHY	SHAHS	THIGH
CHICH	HARSH	HEATH	HEUGH	HILCH	HOHED	HOUGH	HUTCH	SHASH	WHICH
EPHAH	HASHY	HECHT	HEWGH	HITCH	HOOCH	HUMPH	HYPHA	SHCHI	WHISH
HAITH	HATCH	HEIGH	HIGHS	HITHE	HOOSH	HUNCH	HYTHE	SHUSH	

AWKWARD CONSONANT DUMPS   -   V's

4-letter words - 2 V's

VIVA	VIVE	VIVO

5-letter words - 2 V's

BEVVY	CIVVY	NAVVY	VALVE	VERVE	VIVAT	VIVER	VIVID	VOLVE
BIVVY	DIVVY	SAVVY	VARVE	VIVAS	VIVDA	VIVES	VOLVA	VULVA

AWKWARD CONSONANT DUMPS   -   W's

3-letter words - 2 W's

WAW	WOW

4-letter words - 2 W's

WAWE	WAWL	WAWS	WHEW	WHOW	WOWF	WOWS

5-letter words - 2 W's

EWHOW	PAWAW	WAWES	WAWLS	WHEWS	WIDOW	WOWED	WOWEE	WRAWL

AWKWARD CONSONANT DUMPS - Y's

4-letter words - 2 Y's

EYRY	GYNY	YAWY	YUKY

5-letter words - 2 Y's

AZYGY	DOYLY	GYNNY	KYLEY	SKYEY	WRYLY	YAWEY	YIPPY	YUKKY
BYWAY	DRYLY	GYPPY	PYGMY	SLYLY	XYLYL	YAWNY	YOLKY	YUMMY
COYLY	DYKEY	GYPSY	SHYLY	THYMY	YABBY	YESTY	YUCKY	YUPPY

HINT

Rack Balancing

Always try to keep a balanced rack of vowels and consonants. The more balanced your rack the more choice of words you will have each turn and the more chance you will have of being able to play a bonus-scoring seven-letter word. It helps to be aware that there are 42 vowels to 56 consonants (and 2 blanks) in the Scrabble set. That's three vowels for every four consonants. Counting how many vowels and consonants already played at any stage of a game will serve as a useful guide as to the vowel/consonant distribution remaining in the bag. If there is a surplus of consonants left you might wish to counteract your likely consonant pickup by retaining vowels on your rack when you play, or vice versa.

See the Awkward Vowel Dumps list and the Light and Heavy Words list for some words that will help you keep a balanced rack.

HINT

Edging the Endgame

In a tight game where the scores are close there is an advantage in being the player to be the first to play out and finish the game, thus gaining any points remaining on the opponent's rack and depriving him of another scoring opportunity. Playing out first is often the difference between winning and losing. A handy tip, whenever you have the opportunity or choice near the end of a game, is to ensure there is a single tile in the bag after your turn. This means that, next turn, you have the first opportunity to play with no tiles remaining in the bag thus giving you an advantage in planning a two-move finish. There is further advantage if you have been keeping track of the tiles since you can then have the benefit of the endgame initiative knowing your opponent's exact tiles.

Combination Management

If you have one of the promising six-letter combinations given under the Bonus Sets section but unfortunately do not have an appropriate seventh letter to make a bonus word, or the bonus word you have does not fit on the board, then it is wiser not to be overly concerned about holding on to your useful six-letter combinations. Rather than just playing the one letter and hoping for a playable bonus word next turn, play two or three tiles. This will probably enable you to score more whilst still retaining the makings of a bonus word. The skill is in making sure you play off the right letters.

For example, with OILERS and an F on your rack there is no bonus word. Rather than just play the F, in the hope of picking a B for BOILERS or a U for LOUSIER perhaps, it is better to play IF or OF. The retention of OLERS or ILERS with a vowel pickup next turn is likely to produce another good six-letter combination such as AILERS, OILERS or RELIES, and hopefully an obliging seventh letter to make a bonus play. If it doesn't, well at least you've scored some points meanwhile.

Unusual Clues

In browsing through the Anagram section you will find an abundance of unusual seven and eight-letter words. Some of these are more useful than others depending on their constituent letters. Those consisting of just the one and two-point Scrabble tiles (ie A D E G I L N O R S T U) are more likely to appear on your rack and are the ones to concentrate on. A good way to remember these words is by making up a non-existent anagram that you are more likely to form on your rack and that will act as an aide-mémoire. For example, the likely rack ELNOSTU yields the bonus word LENTOUS which may best be recalled as the anagram of the non-existent OUTLENS. Similarly, SEERING makes GREISEN and LOOTIER makes TROOLIE. Both SEERING and LOOTIER are not actual words but merely the clues to GREISEN and TROOLIE. Where there is a more common anagram of an unusual word then this naturally serves as a clue, eg OUTLINE gives ELUTION and AGAINST gives GITANAS.

HIGH SCORERS

The following lists contain all the words of length two to eight letters which contain any of the four high-scoring letters J, Q, X and Z. While most Scrabble players know the obvious words, such as JUDGE, QUEEN, EXALT and ZEROS, how many know the more obscure POOJA, SQUEG, SIXTE and NIZAM?

Knowing these words will enable you to be more adventurous when it comes to grabbing the odd triple-word-score square for 50-odd points – or perhaps playing a bonus word with six single-point letters and a high-scoring letter, such as NAARTJE, LASQUES, ANOXIAS and LAIRIZE, or even playing a bonus word using a letter on the board with words such as INJURANT, EQUITANT, XENURINE and LAZURITE.

If a word contains two of these four high-scoring letters (such as JAZZY, JYNX, QUIZ and ZOOTAXY), then it will appear in two places.

J-WORDS

J - 2-letter words

JO

J - 3-letter words

GJU	JAG	JAP	JAY	JEU	JIZ	JOG	JOW	JUG	RAJ
HAJ	JAK	JAR	JEE	JIB	JOB	JOR	JOY	JUS	TAJ
JAB	JAM	JAW	JET	JIG	JOE	JOT	JUD	JUT	

J - 4-letter words

AJAR	JADE	JARK	JEAN	JEST	JIMP	JOCO	JOMO	JOYS	JUNK
AJEE	JAGS	JARL	JEAT	JETE	JINK	JOES	JOOK	JUBA	JURA
BENJ	JAIL	JARS	JEED	JETS	JINN	JOEY	JORS	JUBE	JURE
DOJO	JAKE	JASP	JEEL	JEUX	JINX	JOGS	JOSH	JUDO	JURY
GAJO	JAKS	JASY	JEEP	JIAO	JIRD	JOHN	JOSS	JUDS	JUST
GJUS	JAMB	JATO	JEER	JIBE	JISM	JOIN	JOTA	JUDY	JUTE
HADJ	JAMS	JAUP	JEES	JIBS	JIVE	JOKE	JOTS	JUGA	JUTS
HAJI	JANE	JAWS	JEFF	JIFF	JIZZ	JOKY	JOUK	JUGS	JYNX
HAJJ	JANN	JAYS	JELL	JIGS	JOBE	JOLE	JOUR	JUJU	PUJA
JABS	JAPE	JAZY	JERK	JILL	JOBS	JOLL	JOWL	JUKE	RAJA
JACK	JAPS	JAZZ	JESS	JILT	JOCK	JOLT	JOWS	JUMP	SOJA

J - 5-letter words

AFLAJ	GADJE	JAGER	JAPED	JEANS	JERKS	JIFFY	JIVES	JOLED	JOURS
AJWAN	GAJOS	JAGGY	JAPES	JEATS	JERKY	JIGOT	JOBED	JOLES	JOUST
BAJAN	GANJA	JAGIR	JARKS	JEBEL	JERRY	JIHAD	JOBES	JOLLS	JOWAR
BAJRA	GAUJE	JAILS	JARLS	JEELS	JESTS	JILLS	JOCKO	JOLLY	JOWED
BAJRI	HADJI	JAKES	JARTA	JEELY	JESUS	JILTS	JOCKS	JOLTS	JOWLS
BANJO	HAJES	JALAP	JARUL	JEEPS	JETES	JIMMY	JODEL	JOLTY	JOYED
BIJOU	HAJIS	JAMBE	JASEY	JEERS	JETON	JIMPY	JOEYS	JOMOS	JUBAS
BUNJE	HAJJI	JAMBO	JASPE	JEFFS	JETTY	JINGO	JOHNS	JONTY	JUBES
BUNJY	HEJAB	JAMBS	JASPS	JEHAD	JEUNE	JINKS	JOINS	JOOKS	JUDAS
CAJUN	HEJRA	JAMBU	JATOS	JELAB	JEWEL	JINNI	JOINT	JORAM	JUDGE
DJINN	HIJRA	JAMES	JAUNT	JELLO	JHALA	JINNS	JOIST	JORUM	JUDOS
DOJOS	HODJA	JAMMY	JAUPS	JELLS	JIAOS	JIRDS	JOKED	JOTAS	JUGAL
EJECT	JABOT	JANES	JAVEL	JELLY	JIBED	JIRGA	JOKER	JOTUN	JUGUM
ENJOY	JACKS	JANNS	JAWAN	JEMMY	JIBER	JISMS	JOKES	JOUGS	JUICE
FALAJ	JADED	JANTY	JAWED	JENNY	JIBES	JIVED	JOKEY	JOUKS	JUICY
FJORD	JADES	JAPAN	JAZZY	JERID	JIFFS	JIVER	JOKOL	JOULE	JUJUS

JUKED	JUMBY	JUNKY	JURAT	KHOJA	NINJA	PUJAS	REJON	TAJES
JUKES	JUMPS	JUNTA	JUROR	KOPJE	OBJET	RAJAH	SAJOU	THUJA
JULEP	JUMPY	JUNTO	JUSTS	LAPJE	OJIME	RAJAS	SHOJI	UPJET
JUMAR	JUNCO	JUPON	JUTES	MAJOR	OUIJA	RAJES	SOJAS	YOJAN
JUMBO	JUNKS	JURAL	JUTTY	MUJIK	POOJA	REJIG	SUJEE	ZANJA

J - 6-letter words

ABJECT	EVEJAR	JACKET	JAPPED	JEHADS	JIBING	JOCKOS	JOUKED	JUMBAL	LAPJES
ABJURE	FINJAN	JACKSY	JARFUL	JEJUNA	JIGGED	JOCOSE	JOULED	JUMBIE	MAJORS
ACAJOU	FJORDS	JADERY	JARGON	JEJUNE	JIGGER	JOCUND	JOULES	JUMBLE	MASJID
ADJOIN	FRIJOL	JADING	JAROOL	JELABS	JIGGLE	JODELS	JOUNCE	JUMBLY	MOUJIK
ADJURE	GADJES	JADISH	JARRAH	JELLED	JIGJIG	JOGGED	JOURNO	JUMBOS	MUJIKS
ADJUST	GANJAS	JAEGER	JARRED	JELLOS	JIGOTS	JOGGER	JOUSTS	JUMPED	NINJAS
AJOWAN	GARJAN	JAGERS	JARTAS	JEMIMA	JIGSAW	JOGGLE	JOVIAL	JUMPER	OBJECT
AJWANS	GAUJES	JAGGED	JARULS	JENNET	JIHADS	JOHNNY	JOWARI	JUNCOS	OBJETS
BAJADA	GIDJEE	JAGGER	JARVEY	JERBIL	JILGIE	JOINED	JOWARS	JUNCUS	OBJURE
BAJANS	GURJUN	JAGHIR	JARVIE	JERBOA	JILLET	JOINER	JOWING	JUNGLE	OJIMES
BAJRAS	HADJES	JAGIRS	JASEYS	JEREED	JILTED	JOINTS	JOWLED	JUNGLI	OUIJAS
BAJREE	HADJIS	JAGUAR	JASIES	JERIDS	JIMINY	JOISTS	JOWLER	JUNGLY	OUTJET
BAJRIS	HAJJES	JAILED	JASPER	JERKED	JIMJAM	JOJOBA	JOYFUL	JUNIOR	OUTJUT
BANJAX	HAJJIS	JAILER	JASPES	JERKER	JIMPER	JOKERS	JOYING	JUNKED	PAJOCK
BANJOS	HANJAR	JAILOR	JASPIS	JERKIN	JIMPLY	JOKIER	JOYOUS	JUNKER	POOJAH
BEJADE	HEJABS	JALAPS	JATAKA	JERQUE	JINGAL	JOKING	JUBATE	JUNKET	POOJAS
BEJANT	HEJIRA	JALOPY	JAUNCE	JERSEY	JINGLE	JOLING	JUBBAH	JUNKIE	POPJOY
BENJES	HEJRAS	JAMBEE	JAUNSE	JESSED	JINGLY	JOLLED	JUDDER	JUNTAS	RAJAHS
BHAJAN	HIJACK	JAMBER	JAUNTS	JESSES	JINKED	JOLTED	JUDGED	JUNTOS	REJECT
BIJOUX	HIJRAH	JAMBES	JAUNTY	JESSIE	JINKER	JOLTER	JUDGES	JUPATI	REJIGS
BUNJEE	HIJRAS	JAMBOK	JAUPED	JESTED	JINNEE	JOOKED	JUDIES	JUPONS	REJOIN
BUNJES	HOBJOB	JAMBOS	JAVELS	JESTEE	JINXED	JORAMS	JUDOGI	JURANT	SAJOUS
BUNJIE	HODJAS	JAMBUL	JAWANS	JESTER	JINXES	JORDAN	JUDOKA	JURATS	SANJAK
CAJOLE	INJECT	JAMBUS	JAWARI	JETONS	JIRBLE	JORUMS	JUGALS	JURIES	SEJANT
COJOIN	INJURE	JAMJAR	JAWBOX	JETSAM	JIRGAS	JOSEPH	JUGATE	JURIST	SHOJIS
CONJEE	INJURY	JAMMED	JAWING	JETSOM	JISSOM	JOSHED	JUGFUL	JURORS	SOOJEY
DEEJAY	JABBED	JAMMER	JAZIES	JETSON	JITNEY	JOSHER	JUGGED	JUSTED	SUJEES
DEJECT	JABBER	JAMPAN	JAZZED	JETTED	JITTER	JOSHES	JUGGLE	JUSTER	SWARAJ
DJEBEL	JABBLE	JAMPOT	JAZZES	JETTON	JIVERS	JOSKIN	JUICED	JUSTLE	THUJAS
DJINNI	JABERS	JANGLE	JEBELS	JEWELS	JIVING	JOSSER	JUICER	JUSTLY	TINAJA
DONJON	JABIRU	JANGLY	JEEING	JEZAIL	JIZZES	JOSSES	JUICES	JUTTED	UNJUST
EJECTA	JABOTS	JANKER	JEELED	JHALAS	JOANNA	JOSTLE	JUJUBE	JYMOLD	UPJETS
EJECTS	JACANA	JANSKY	JEELIE	JIBBAH	JOBBED	JOTTED	JUKING	JYNXES	YOJANA
ENJAMB	JACENT	JANTEE	JEERED	JIBBED	JOBBER	JOTTER	JULEPS	KHODJA	YOJANS
ENJOIN	JACKAL	JAPANS	JEERER	JIBBER	JOBING	JOTUNN	JUMARS	KHOJAS	ZANJAS
ENJOYS	JACKED	JAPING	JEFFED	JIBERS	JOCKEY	JOTUNS	JUMART	KOPJES	

J - 7-letter words

ABJECTS	BEJADES	DEJEUNE	HIJACKS	JACKETS	JALAPIC	JAMPOTS	JASPERY	JEELIED
ABJOINT	BEJANTS	DISJECT	HIJINKS	JACKING	JALAPIN	JANGLED	JATAKAS	JEELIES
ABJURED	BEJEWEL	DISJOIN	HIJRAHS	JACKMAN	JALOPPY	JANGLER	JAUNCED	JEELING
ABJURER	BHAJANS	DISJUNE	HOBJOBS	JACKMEN	JALOUSE	JANGLES	JAUNCES	JEEPERS
ABJURES	BONJOUR	DJEBELS	INJECTS	JACKPOT	JAMADAR	JANITOR	JAUNSED	JEEPNEY
ACAJOUS	BRINJAL	DJIBBAH	INJELLY	JACKSIE	JAMBEAU	JANIZAR	JAUNSES	JEERERS
ADJOINS	BUNJEES	DONJONS	INJOINT	JACOBUS	JAMBEES	JANNOCK	JAUNTED	JEERING
ADJOINT	BUNJIES	EJECTED	INJUNCT	JACONET	JAMBERS	JANTIER	JAUNTIE	JEFFING
ADJOURN	CAJEPUT	EJECTOR	INJURED	JACUZZI	JAMBEUX	JANTIES	JAUPING	JEJUNUM
ADJUDGE	CAJOLED	ENJAMBS	INJURER	JADEDLY	JAMBIER	JAPPING	JAVELIN	JELLABA
ADJUNCT	CAJOLER	ENJOINS	INJURES	JADEITE	JAMBIYA	JARFULS	JAWARIS	JELLIED
ADJURED	CAJOLES	ENJOYED	JABBERS	JAEGERS	JAMBOKS	JARGONS	JAWBONE	JELLIES
ADJURES	CAJUPUT	ENJOYER	JABBING	JAGGERS	JAMBONE	JARGOON	JAWFALL	JELLIFY
ADJUSTS	COJOINS	EVEJARS	JABBLED	JAGGERY	JAMBOOL	JARKMAN	JAWHOLE	JELLING
AJOWANS	CONJECT	FINJANS	JABBLES	JAGGIER	JAMBULS	JARKMEN	JAWINGS	JEMADAR
AJUTAGE	CONJEED	FRIJOLE	JABIRUS	JAGGING	JAMDANI	JAROOLS	JAYWALK	JEMIDAR
ALFORJA	CONJEES	GARJANS	JACAMAR	JAGHIRE	JAMESES	JARRAHS	JAZZIER	JEMIMAS
AZULEJO	CONJOIN	GIDJEES	JACANAS	JAGHIRS	JAMJARS	JARRING	JAZZILY	JEMMIER
BAJADAS	CONJURE	GOUJONS	JACCHUS	JAGUARS	JAMMERS	JARVEYS	JAZZING	JEMMIES
BAJREES	CONJURY	GURJUNS	JACINTH	JAILERS	JAMMIER	JARVIES	JAZZMAN	JENNETS
BANJOES	DEEJAYS	HANDJAR	JACKALS	JAILING	JAMMING	JASMINE	JAZZMEN	JENNIES
BASENJI	DEJECTA	HANJARS	JACKASS	JAILORS	JAMPANI	JASPERS	JEALOUS	JEOFAIL
BEJADED	DEJECTS	HEJIRAS	JACKDAW	JAKESES	JAMPANS	JASPERS	JEALOUS	JEOPARD

JERBILS	JEWELRY	JINGLES	JOINERS	JOSSERS	JUDOKAS	JUNIORS	KHANJAR	PERJURY
JERBOAS	JEWFISH	JINGLET	JOINERY	JOSTLED	JUGFULS	JUNIPER	KHODJAS	POOJAHS
JEREEDS	JEZAILS	JINGOES	JOINING	JOSTLES	JUGGING	JUNKERS	KILLJOY	POPJOYS
JERKERS	JIBBAHS	JINJILI	JOINTED	JOTTERS	JUGGINS	JUNKETS	MAJESTY	PREJINK
JERKIER	JIBBERS	JINKERS	JOINTER	JOTTING	JUGGLED	JUNKIER	MAJORAT	PROJECT
JERKIES	JIBBING	JINKING	JOINTLY	JOTUNNS	JUGGLER	JUNKIES	MAJORED	PYJAMAS
JERKING	JIFFIES	JINXING	JOISTED	JOUKERY	JUGGLES	JUNKING	MANJACK	REJECTS
JERKINS	JIGAJIG	JIRBLED	JOJOBAS	JOUKING	JUGULAR	JUNKMAN	MASJIDS	REJOICE
JERQUED	JIGAJOG	JIRBLES	JOKIEST	JOULING	JUICERS	JUNKMEN	MISJOIN	REJOINS
JERQUER	JIGGERS	JISSOMS	JOLLIED	JOUNCED	JUICIER	JUPATIS	MOUJIKS	REJONEO
JERQUES	JIGGING	JITNEYS	JOLLIER	JOUNCES	JUICING	JURALLY	MUDEJAR	REJONES
JERRIES	JIGGISH	JITTERS	JOLLIES	JOURNAL	JUJUBES	JURANTS	MUNTJAC	REJOURN
JERSEYS	JIGGLED	JITTERY	JOLLIFY	JOURNEY	JUMARTS	JURIDIC	MUNTJAK	REJUDGE
JESSAMY	JIGGLES	JOANNAS	JOLLILY	JOURNOS	JUMBALS	JURISTS	NAARTJE	SANJAKS
JESSANT	JIGJIGS	JOANNES	JOLLING	JOUSTED	JUMBIES	JURYMAN	NARTJIE	SAPAJOU
JESSIES	JIGSAWN	JOBBERS	JOLLITY	JOUSTER	JUMBLED	JURYMEN	OBJECTS	SEJEANT
JESTEES	JIGSAWS	JOBBERY	JOLTERS	JOWARIS	JUMBLER	JUSSIVE	OBJURED	SJAMBOK
JESTERS	JILGIES	JOBBING	JOLTIER	JOWLERS	JUMBLES	JUSTEST	OBJURES	SKYJACK
JESTFUL	JILLETS	JOBLESS	JOLTING	JOWLING	JUMBUCK	JUSTICE	OUTJEST	SOJOURN
JESTING	JILTING	JOCKEYS	JONQUIL	JOYANCE	JUMELLE	JUSTIFY	OUTJETS	SOOJEYS
JETFOIL	JIMJAMS	JOCULAR	JONTIES	JOYLESS	JUMPERS	JUSTING	OUTJUMP	SUBJECT
JETSAMS	JIMMIED	JOGGERS	JOOKERY	JUBBAHS	JUMPIER	JUSTLED	OUTJUTS	SUBJOIN
JETSOMS	JIMMIES	JOGGING	JOOKING	JUBILEE	JUMPILY	JUSTLES	OVERJOY	TINAJAS
JETSONS	JIMPEST	JOGGLED	JORDANS	JUDASES	JUMPING	JUTTIED	PAJAMAS	TRAJECT
JETTIER	JIMPIER	JOGGLES	JOSEPHS	JUDDERS	JUNCATE	JUTTIES	PAJOCKE	UNJADED
JETTIES	JINGALS	JOGTROT	JOSHERS	JUDGING	JUNCOES	JUTTING	PAJOCKS	UNJOINT
JETTING	JINGLED	JOHNNIE	JOSHING	JUDOGIS	JUNGLES	JUVENAL	PERJINK	YOJANAS
JETTONS	JINGLER	JOINDER	JOSKINS	JUDOIST	JUNGLIS	KAJAWAH	PERJURE	ZANJERO

J - 8-letter words

ABJECTED	CARJACOU	HANDJARS	JAMBEAUX	JAUNTING	JETPLANE	JODELLED	JUDICIAL
ABJECTLY	COJOINED	HIGHJACK	JAMBIERS	JAVELINS	JETTIEST	JODHPURS	JUDOISTS
ABJOINTS	CONJECTS	HIJACKED	JAMBIYAH	JAWBONED	JETTISON	JOGGINGS	JUGGLERS
ABJURERS	CONJOINS	HIJACKER	JAMBIYAS	JAWBONES	JEWELLED	JOGGLING	JUGGLERY
ABJURING	CONJOINT	INJECTED	JAMBOLAN	JAWBOXES	JEWELLER	JOGTROTS	JUGGLING
ADJACENT	CONJUGAL	INJECTOR	JAMBONES	JAWFALLS	JIBBERED	JOHANNES	JUGULARS
ADJOINED	CONJUNCT	INJOINTS	JAMBOOLS	JAWHOLES	JIBBINGS	JOHNNIES	JUGULATE
ADJOINTS	CONJURED	INJUNCTS	JAMBOREE	JAYWALKS	JICKAJOG	JOINDERS	JUICIEST
ADJOURNS	CONJURER	INJURANT	JAMDANIS	JAZERANT	JIGAJIGS	JOININGS	JULIENNE
ADJUDGED	CONJURES	INJURERS	JAMMIEST	JAZZIEST	JIGAJOGS	JOINTERS	JUMARRED
ADJUDGES	CONJUROR	INJURIES	JAMPANEE	JEALOUSE	JIGGERED	JOINTING	JUMBLERS
ADJUNCTS	CRACKJAW	INJURING	JAMPANIS	JEALOUSY	JIGGINGS	JOINTURE	JUMBLIER
ADJURING	CUNJEVOI	JABBERED	JANGLERS	JEANETTE	JIGGLING	JOISTING	JUMBLING
ADJUSTED	DEEJAYED	JABBERER	JANGLIER	JEELYING	JIGSAWED	JOKESOME	JUMBOISE
ADJUSTER	DEJECTED	JABBLING	JANGLING	JEEPNEYS	JILLAROO	JOKINGLY	JUMBOIZE
ADJUSTOR	DEJEUNER	JACAMARS	JANITORS	JEERINGS	JIMCRACK	JOLLIEST	JUMBUCKS
ADJUTAGE	DEJEUNES	JACINTHS	JANITRIX	JEJUNELY	JIMMYING	JOLLYING	JUMELLES
ADJUTANT	DEMIJOHN	JACKAROO	JANIZARS	JEJUNITY	JIMPIEST	JOLTHEAD	JUMPIEST
ADJUVANT	DISJECTS	JACKBOOT	JANIZARY	JELLABAS	JIMPNESS	JOLTIEST	JUNCATES
AJUTAGES	DISJOINS	JACKDAWS	JANNOCKS	JELLYING	JINGBANG	JONCANOE	JUNCTION
ALFORJAS	DISJOINT	JACKEROO	JANSKIES	JELUTONG	JINGLERS	JONGLEUR	JUNCTURE
AZULEJOS	DISJUNCT	JACKETED	JANTIEST	JEMADARS	JINGLETS	JONQUILS	JUNCUSES
BANJAXED	DISJUNES	JACKPOTS	JAPANNED	JEMIDARS	JINGLIER	JORDELOO	JUNGLIER
BANJAXES	DJELLABA	JACKSIES	JAPANNER	JEMMIEST	JINGLING	JOSTLING	JUNIPERS
BANJOIST	DJIBBAHS	JACONETS	JAPONICA	JEOFAILS	JINGOISH	JOTTINGS	JUNKANOO
BASENJIS	EJECTING	JACQUARD	JARARACA	JEOPARDS	JINGOISM	JOUNCING	JUNKETED
BEJABERS	EJECTION	JACULATE	JARARAKA	JEOPARDY	JINGOIST	JOURNALS	JUNKIEST
BEJADING	EJECTIVE	JADEITES	JARGONED	JEREMIAD	JINJILIS	JOURNEYS	JURATORY
BEJESUIT	EJECTORS	JADERIES	JARGOONS	JERKIEST	JIRBLING	JOUSTERS	JURISTIC
BEJEWELS	ENJAMBED	JAGGEDLY	JAROSITE	JERKINGS	JIRKINET	JOUSTING	JURYMAST
BENJAMIN	ENJOINED	JAGGIEST	JARRINGS	JEROBOAM	JITTERED	JOVIALLY	JUSSIVES
BIJWONER	ENJOINER	JAGHIRES	JASMINES	JERQUERS	JOBATION	JOYANCES	JUSTICER
BRINJALS	ENJOYERS	JALAPINS	JASPISES	JERQUING	JOBBINGS	JOYFULLY	JUSTICES
CAJEPUTS	ENJOYING	JALOPIES	JAUNCING	JERRICAN	JOCKETTE	JOYOUSLY	JUSTLING
CAJOLERS	FLAPJACK	JALOUSED	JAUNDICE	JERRYCAN	JOCKEYED	JUBILANT	JUSTNESS
CAJOLERY	FORJUDGE	JALOUSES	JAUNSING	JESTBOOK	JOCOROUS	JUBILATE	JUTTYING
CAJOLING	FRABJOUS	JALOUSIE	JAUNTIER	JESTINGS	JOCOSELY	JUBILEES	JUVENALS
CAJUPUTS	FRIJOLES	JAMADARS	JAUNTIES	JETFOILS	JOCOSITY	JUDDERED	JUVENILE
CARCAJOU	GOUJEERS		JAUNTILY	JETLINER	JOCUNDLY	JUDGMENT	KABELJOU

KAJAWAHS	MAJORING	NIGHTJAR	PEJORATE	PYJAMAED	REJOICER	SJAMBOKS	TRAJECTS
KHANJARS	MAJORITY	NONJUROR	PERJURED	QUILLAJA	REJOICES	SKIPJACK	UNJOINTS
KILLJOYS	MANJACKS	OBJECTED	PERJURER	RAJASHIP	REJOINED	SKYJACKS	UNJOYFUL
KINKAJOU	MARJORAM	OBJECTOR	PERJURES	READJUST	REJONEOS	SLAPJACK	UNJOYOUS
KOMITAJI	MISJOINS	OBJURING	POPINJAY	REJECTED	REJOURNS	SOJOURNS	UNJUSTER
LOGJUICE	MISJUDGE	OUTJESTS	POPJOYED	REJECTER	REJUDGED	STICKJAW	UNJUSTLY
MAHARAJA	MUNTJACS	OUTJUMPS	PREJUDGE	REJECTOR	REJUDGES	SUBJECTS	UPJETTED
MAJESTIC	MUNTJAKS	OVERJOYS	PROJECTS	REJIGGED	SAPAJOUS	SUBJOINS	VERJUICE
MAJOLICA	NAARTJES	OVERJUMP	PULSEJET	REJIGGER	SCRAMJET	SUCURUJU	WHIPJACK
MAJORATS	NARTJIES	PAJOCKES	PULSOJET	REJOICED	SERJEANT	SWARAJES	ZANJEROS

Q-WORDS

Q - 3-letter words

QAT   QUA   SUQ

Q - 4-letter words

AQUA	QATS	QUAG	QUAY	QUEY	QUIM	QUIP	QUIZ	QUOP
QADI	QUAD	QUAT	QUEP	QUID	QUIN	QUIT	QUOD	SUQS

Q - 5-letter words

AQUAE	QIBLA	QUALE	QUAYS	QUEST	QUILL	QUIPU	QUOIF	QUYTE	SQUIT
AQUAS	QUACK	QUALM	QUEAN	QUEUE	QUILT	QUIRE	QUOIN	ROQUE	TALAQ
BURQA	QUADS	QUANT	QUEEN	QUEYN	QUIMS	QUIRK	QUOIT	SQUAB	TOQUE
EQUAL	QUAFF	QUARK	QUEER	QUEYS	QUINA	QUIRT	QUOLL	SQUAD	TUQUE
EQUIP	QUAGS	QUART	QUELL	QUICH	QUINE	QUIST	QUONK	SQUAT	
MAQUI	QUAIL	QUASH	QUEME	QUICK	QUINS	QUITE	QUOPS	SQUAW	
PIQUE	QUAIR	QUASI	QUENA	QUIDS	QUINT	QUITS	QUOTA	SQUEG	
QADIS	QUAKE	QUATS	QUERN	QUIET	QUIPO	QUOAD	QUOTE	SQUIB	
QANAT	QUAKY	QUAYD	QUERY	QUIFF	QUIPS	QUODS	QUOTH	SQUID	

Q - 6-letter words

ACQUIT	EQUANT	OPAQUE	QUAINT	QUEACH	QUEUED	QUINTA	QUOITS	SACQUE	SQUIDS
ASQUAT	EQUATE	PIQUED	QUAIRS	QUEANS	QUEUES	QUINTE	QUOKKA	SAIQUE	SQUIER
BARQUE	EQUINE	PIQUES	QUAKED	QUEASY	QUEYNS	QUINTS	QUOLLS	SEQUEL	SQUIFF
BASQUE	EQUIPE	PIQUET	QUAKES	QUEAZY	QUICHE	QUINZE	QUONKS	SEQUIN	SQUILL
BISQUE	EQUIPS	PLAQUE	QUALIA	QUEENS	QUICKS	QUIPOS	QUOOKE	SQUABS	SQUINT
BURQAS	EQUITY	PULQUE	QUALMS	QUEERS	QUIDAM	QUIPUS	QUORUM	SQUADS	SQUINY
CAIQUE	EXEQUY	QANATS	QUALMY	QUEEST	QUIETS	QUIRED	QUOTAS	SQUAIL	SQUIRE
CALQUE	FAQUIR	QIBLAS	QUANGO	QUEINT	QUIFFS	QUIRES	QUOTED	SQUALL	SQUIRM
CASQUE	HAIQUE	QIGONG	QUANTA	QUELCH	QUIGHT	QUIRKS	QUOTER	SQUAMA	SQUIRR
CHEQUE	JERQUE	QINTAR	QUANTS	QUELEA	QUILLS	QUIRKY	QUOTES	SQUAME	SQUIRT
CHEQUY	LASQUE	QUACKS	QUARKS	QUELLS	QUILTS	QUIRTS	QUOTHA	SQUARE	SQUISH
CINQUE	LIQUID	QUAERE	QUARRY	QUEMED	QUINAS	QUISTS	QUOTUM	SQUASH	SQUITS
CIRQUE	LIQUOR	QUAFFS	QUARTE	QUEMES	QUINCE	QUITCH	QUYTED	SQUATS	TALAQS
CLAQUE	LOQUAT	QUAGGA	QUARTO	QUENAS	QUINES	QUITED	QUYTES	SQUAWK	TOQUES
CLIQUE	MANQUE	QUAGGY	QUARTS	QUENCH	QUINIC	QUITES	QWERTY	SQUAWS	TORQUE
CLIQUY	MAQUIS	QUAHOG	QUARTZ	QUERNS	QUINIE	QUIVER	REQUIT	SQUEAK	TUQUES
CLOQUE	MARQUE	QUAICH	QUASAR	QUESTS	QUINOA	QUOIFS	RISQUE	SQUEAL	UBIQUE
COQUET	MASQUE	QUAIGH	QUATCH	QUETCH	QUINOL	QUOINS	ROQUES	SQUEGS	UNIQUE
EQUALS	MOSQUE	QUAILS	QUAVER	QUETHE	QUINSY	QUOIST	ROQUET	SQUIBS	

Q - 7-letter words

ACQUEST	AQUAVIT	BEZIQUE	CHARQUI	CONQUER	EQUALLY	FAQUIRS	JERQUES	LOQUATS
ACQUIRE	AQUEOUS	BISQUES	CHEQUER	COQUETS	EQUANTS	GRECQUE	JONQUIL	MACAQUE
ACQUIST	AQUIFER	BOUQUET	CHEQUES	COQUITO	EQUATED	HAIQUES	KUMQUAT	MADOQUA
ACQUITE	AQUIVER	BRIQUET	CINQUES	CROQUET	EQUATES	INQILAB	LACQUER	MARQUEE
ACQUITS	ASQUINT	BRUSQUE	CIRQUES	CROQUIS	EQUATOR	INQUERE	LACQUEY	MARQUES
ALFAQUI	BANQUET	CACIQUE	CLAQUES	CUMQUAT	EQUERRY	INQUEST	LASQUES	MARQUIS
ALIQUOT	BAROQUE	CAIQUES	CLIQUES	DOCQUET	EQUINAL	INQUIET	LIQUATE	MASQUER
ANTIQUE	BARQUES	CALQUED	CLIQUEY	ENQUIRE	EQUINIA	INQUIRE	LIQUEFY	MASQUES
AQUAFER	BASQUED	CALQUES	CLOQUES	ENQUIRY	EQUINOX	INQUIRY	LIQUEUR	MESQUIN
AQUARIA	BASQUES	CASQUES	COEQUAL	EQUABLE	EQUIPES	JERQUED	LIQUIDS	MESQUIT
AQUATIC	BEQUEST	CAZIQUE	COMIQUE	EQUABLY	ESQUIRE	JERQUER	LIQUORS	MOSQUES

OBLIQUE	QUAGGAS	QUASHED	QUETHES	QUILLON	QUITTED	RACQUET	SQUAILS	SQUINNY
OBLOQUY	QUAHAUG	QUASHEE	QUETSCH	QUILTED	QUITTER	RELIQUE	SQUALID	SQUINTS
OBSEQUY	QUAHOGS	QUASHES	QUETZAL	QUILTER	QUITTOR	REPIQUE	SQUALLS	SQUIRED
OPAQUED	QUAICHS	QUASHIE	QUEUING	QUINARY	QUIVERS	REQUERE	SQUALLY	SQUIRES
OPAQUER	QUAIGHS	QUASSIA	QUEYNIE	QUINATE	QUIVERY	REQUEST	SQUALOR	SQUIRMS
OPAQUES	QUAILED	QUAVERS	QUIBBLE	QUINCES	QUIZZED	REQUIEM	SQUAMAE	SQUIRMY
PARQUET	QUAKIER	QUAVERY	QUIBLIN	QUINCHE	QUIZZER	REQUIRE	SQUAMES	SQUIRRS
PERIQUE	QUAKING	QUAYAGE	QUICHED	QUINIES	QUIZZES	REQUITE	SQUARED	SQUIRTS
PICQUET	QUALIFY	QUEACHY	QUICHES	QUININE	QUODDED	REQUITS	SQUARER	SQUISHY
PIQUANT	QUALITY	QUEECHY	QUICKEN	QUINNAT	QUODLIN	REQUOTE	SQUARES	SQUITCH
PIQUETS	QUAMASH	QUEENED	QUICKER	QUINOAS	QUOIFED	RISQUES	SQUASHY	SUBAQUA
PIQUING	QUANGOS	QUEENLY	QUICKIE	QUINOLS	QUOINED	ROCQUET	SQUATTY	TEQUILA
PLAQUES	QUANNET	QUEERED	QUICKLY	QUINONE	QUOISTS	ROQUETS	SQUAWKS	TORQUED
PREQUEL	QUANTAL	QUEERER	QUIDAMS	QUINTAL	QUOITED	RORQUAL	SQUAWKY	TORQUES
PULQUES	QUANTED	QUEERLY	QUIDDIT	QUINTAN	QUOITER	SACQUES	SQUEAKS	TSADDIQ
QIGONGS	QUANTIC	QUEESTS	QUIDDLE	QUINTAS	QUOKKAS	SAIQUES	SQUEAKY	TZADDIQ
QINTARS	QUANTUM	QUELEAS	QUIESCE	QUINTES	QUONDAM	SEQUELA	SQUEALS	UNEQUAL
QUACKED	QUARREL	QUELLED	QUIETED	QUINTET	QUONKED	SEQUELS	SQUEEZE	UNIQUER
QUACKLE	QUARTAN	QUELLER	QUIETEN	QUINTIC	QUOPPED	SEQUENT	SQUEEZY	UNIQUES
QUADDED	QUARTER	QUEMING	QUIETER	QUINZES	QUORATE	SEQUINS	SQUELCH	UNQUEEN
QUADRAT	QUARTES	QUERIED	QUIETLY	QUIPPED	QUORUMS	SEQUOIA	SQUIDGE	UNQUIET
QUADRIC	QUARTET	QUERIES	QUIETUS	QUIRING	QUOTERS	SILIQUA	SQUIDGY	UNQUOTE
QUAERED	QUARTIC	QUERIST	QUIGHTS	QUIRKED	QUOTING	SILIQUE	SQUIERS	VAQUERO
QUAERES	QUARTOS	QUESTED	QUILLAI	QUIRTED	QUOTUMS	SQUABBY	SQUIFFY	
QUAFFED	QUARTZY	QUESTER	QUILLED	QUITING	QUYTING	SQUACCO	SQUILLS	
QUAFFER	QUASARS	QUESTOR	QUILLET	QUITTAL	QWERTYS	SQUADDY	SQUINCH	

Q - 8-letter words

ACQUAINT	CACIQUES	EQUATION	LIQUATES	PETANQUE	QUANTISE	QUEERITY	QUIETENS
ACQUESTS	CALQUING	EQUATORS	LIQUESCE	PHYSIQUE	QUANTITY	QUELCHED	QUIETERS
ACQUIGHT	CAZIQUES	EQUINIAS	LIQUEURS	PICQUETS	QUANTIZE	QUELCHES	QUIETEST
ACQUIRAL	CHARQUIS	EQUINITY	LIQUIDLY	PIQUANCY	QUANTONG	QUELLERS	QUIETING
ACQUIRED	CHEQUERS	EQUIPAGE	LIQUIDUS	PIQUETED	QUARRELS	QUELLING	QUIETISM
ACQUIRES	CHEQUIER	EQUIPPED	LIQUORED	PRATIQUE	QUARRIED	QUENCHED	QUIETIST
ACQUISTS	CINQUAIN	EQUISETA	LOQUITUR	PREQUELS	QUARRIER	QUENCHER	QUIETIVE
ACQUITES	CLAQUEUR	EQUITANT	LUSTIQUE	QALAMDAN	QUARRIES	QUENCHES	QUIETUDE
ADEQUACY	CLINIQUE	EQUITIES	MACAQUES	QUACKERY	QUARTANS	QUENELLE	QUIGHTED
ADEQUATE	CLIQUIER	EQUIVOKE	MADOQUAS	QUACKING	QUARTERN	QUERISTS	QUILLAIA
ALFAQUIS	CLIQUISH	ESQUIRES	MAQUETTE	QUACKLED	QUARTERS	QUERYING	QUILLAIS
ALIQUANT	CLIQUISM	ESQUISSE	MAROQUIN	QUACKLES	QUARTETS	QUESTANT	QUILLAJA
ANTIQUED	COEQUALS	EXEQUIAL	MARQUEES	QUADDING	QUARTETT	QUESTERS	QUILLETS
ANTIQUES	COLLOQUE	EXEQUIES	MARQUESS	QUADRANS	QUARTICS	QUESTING	QUILLING
APPLIQUE	COLLOQUY	FILIOQUE	MARQUISE	QUADRANT	QUARTIER	QUESTION	QUILLMAN
AQUACADE	COMIQUES	FREQUENT	MASQUERS	QUADRATE	QUARTILE	QUESTORS	QUILLMEN
AQUAFERS	CONQUERS	GRECQUES	MESQUINE	QUADRATS	QUARTZES	QUETCHED	QUILLONS
AQUALUNG	CONQUEST	HAQUETON	MESQUITE	QUADRIGA	QUASHEES	QUETCHES	QUILTERS
AQUANAUT	COQUETRY	HENEQUEN	MESQUITS	QUADROON	QUASHIES	QUETHING	QUILTING
AQUARIAN	COQUETTE	HENEQUIN	MISQUOTE	QUAESTOR	QUASHING	QUETZALS	QUINCHED
AQUARIST	COQUILLA	HENIQUIN	MOQUETTE	QUAFFERS	QUASSIAS	QUEUEING	QUINCHES
AQUARIUM	COQUILLE	ILLIQUID	MOSQUITO	QUAFFING	QUATCHED	QUEUINGS	QUINCUNX
AQUATICS	COQUITOS	INEQUITY	MUQADDAM	QUAGGIER	QUATCHES	QUEYNIES	QUINELLA
AQUATINT	COTQUEAN	INIQUITY	MUSQUASH	QUAGMIRE	QUATORZE	QUIBBLED	QUININES
AQUAVITS	CRITIQUE	INQILABS	MYSTIQUE	QUAGMIRY	QUATRAIN	QUIBBLER	QUINNATS
AQUEDUCT	CROQUETS	INQUERED	NARQUOIS	QUAHAUGS	QUAVERED	QUIBBLES	QUINONES
AQUIFERS	CUMQUATS	INQUERES	OBLIQUED	QUAILING	QUAVERER	QUIBLINS	QUINSIED
AQUILINE	DAIQUIRI	INQUESTS	OBLIQUER	QUAINTER	QUAYAGES	QUICHING	QUINSIES
ARQUEBUS	DETRAQUE	INQUIETS	OBLIQUES	QUAINTLY	QUAYSIDE	QUICKENS	QUINTAIN
BANQUETS	DISQUIET	INQUIRED	OBLIQUID	QUAKIEST	QUEACHES	QUICKEST	QUINTALS
BAROQUES	DOCQUETS	INQUIRER	OBSEQUIE	QUAKINGS	QUEASIER	QUICKIES	QUINTETS
BASQUINE	ELOQUENT	INQUIRES	ODALIQUE	QUALMIER	QUEASILY	QUICKSET	QUINTETT
BEQUEATH	EMBUSQUE	JACQUARD	OLDSQUAW	QUALMING	QUEAZIER	QUIDDANY	QUINTILE
BEQUESTS	ENQUIRED	JERQUERS	OPAQUELY	QUALMISH	QUEENDOM	QUIDDITS	QUIPPING
BEZIQUES	ENQUIRER	JERQUING	OPAQUEST	QUANDANG	QUEENING	QUIDDITY	QUIPPISH
BLANQUET	ENQUIRES	JONQUILS	OPAQUING	QUANDARY	QUEENITE	QUIDDLED	QUIPSTER
BOUQUETS	EQUALISE	KUMQUATS	PARAQUAT	QUANDONG	QUEENLET	QUIDDLER	QUIRKIER
BOUTIQUE	EQUALITY	LACQUERS	PAROQUET	QUANNETS	QUEERDOM	QUIDDLES	QUIRKING
BRELOQUE	EQUALIZE	LACQUEYS	PARQUETS	QUANTICS	QUEEREST	QUIDNUNC	QUIRKISH
BRIQUETS	EQUALLED	LIQUABLE	PERIQUES	QUANTIFY	QUEERING	QUIESCED	QUIRTING
BRUSQUER	EQUATING	LIQUATED	PERRUQUE	QUANTING	QUEERISH	QUIESCES	QUISLING

QUITCHED	QUONKING	REQUIRES	SQUABASH	SQUARERS	SQUEEDGE	SQUINTER	TRUQUAGE
QUITCHES	QUOPPING	REQUITAL	SQUABBED	SQUAREST	SQUEEGEE	SQUIRAGE	TRUQUEUR
QUITTALS	QUOTABLE	REQUITED	SQUABBER	SQUARING	SQUEEZED	SQUIREEN	TSADDIQS
QUITTERS	QUOTABLY	REQUITER	SQUABBLE	SQUARISH	SQUEEZER	SQUIRELY	TZADDIQS
QUITTING	QUOTIENT	REQUITES	SQUACCOS	SQUARSON	SQUEEZES	SQUIRESS	UBIQUITY
QUITTORS	QWERTIES	REQUOTED	SQUADRON	SQUASHED	SQUEGGED	SQUIRING	UMQUHILE
QUIVERED	RACQUETS	REQUOTES	SQUAILED	SQUASHER	SQUEGGER	SQUIRMED	UNEQUALS
QUIXOTIC	RAMEQUIN	REQUOYLE	SQUAILER	SQUASHES	SQUELCHY	SQUIRRED	UNIQUELY
QUIXOTRY	RELIQUES	ROCQUETS	SQUALLED	SQUATTED	SQUIBBED	SQUIRREL	UNIQUEST
QUIZZERS	REMARQUE	ROQUETED	SQUALLER	SQUATTER	SQUIDDED	SQUIRTED	UNQUEENS
QUIZZERY	REPIQUED	ROQUETTE	SQUALOID	SQUATTLE	SQUIDGED	SQUIRTER	UNQUIETS
QUIZZIFY	REPIQUES	RORQUALS	SQUALORS	SQUAWKED	SQUIDGES	SQUISHED	UNQUOTED
QUIZZING	REQUERED	SEAQUAKE	SQUAMATE	SQUAWKER	SQUIFFER	SQUISHES	UNQUOTES
QUODDING	REQUERES	SEQUELAE	SQUAMOSE	SQUAWMAN	SQUIGGLE	SUBEQUAL	VANQUISH
QUODLINS	REQUESTS	SEQUENCE	SQUAMOUS	SQUAWMEN	SQUIGGLY	SURQUEDY	VAQUEROS
QUOIFING	REQUIEMS	SEQUENTS	SQUAMULA	SQUEAKED	SQUILGEE	TEQUILAS	VEHMIQUE
QUOINING	REQUIGHT	SEQUOIAS	SQUAMULE	SQUEAKER	SQUINIED	TEQUILLA	VERQUERE
QUOITERS	REQUIRED	SILIQUAS	SQUANDER	SQUEALED	SQUINIES	TORQUATE	VERQUIRE
QUOITING	REQUIRER	SILIQUES	SQUARELY	SQUEALER	SQUINTED	TRANQUIL	

X-WORDS

X - 2-letter words

AX	EX	OX	XI

X - 3-letter words

AXE	FAX	HOX	LOX	MUX	POX	SAX	TAX	WEX	ZAX
BOX	FIX	KEX	LUX	NIX	PYX	SEX	VEX	WOX	
COX	FOX	LAX	MAX	PAX	RAX	SIX	VOX	XIS	
DUX	HEX	LEX	MIX	PIX	REX	SOX	WAX	YEX	

X - 4-letter words

APEX	AXON	DIXI	EXON	FLEX	IXIA	MAXI	ONYX	ROUX	WAXY
AXED	BOXY	DIXY	EXPO	FLIX	JEUX	MINX	ORYX	SEXT	WEXE
AXEL	CALX	DOXY	EXUL	FLUX	JINX	MIXT	OXEN	SEXY	XYST
AXES	COAX	EAUX	FAIX	FOXY	JYNX	MIXY	OXER	TAXA	YUNX
AXIL	COXA	EXAM	FALX	HOAX	LANX	MOXA	PIXY	TAXI	
AXIS	COXY	EXES	FAUX	IBEX	LUXE	NEXT	POXY	TEXT	
AXLE	CRUX	EXIT	FLAX	ILEX	LYNX	NIXY	PREX	ULEX	

X - 5-letter words

ADDAX	BOXER	DUXES	EXPEL	HOXED	MAXES	OXTER	REMEX	TELEX	WEXED
ADMIX	BOXES	EMBOX	EXPOS	HOXES	MAXIM	PANAX	SALIX	TEXAS	WEXES
AFFIX	BRAXY	ENFIX	EXTOL	HYRAX	MAXIS	PAXES	SAXES	TEXTS	WOXEN
ANNEX	BUXOM	EPOXY	EXTRA	IMMIX	MIXED	PHLOX	SEXED	TOXIC	XEBEC
ATAXY	CALIX	EXACT	EXUDE	INDEX	MIXEN	PIXEL	SEXER	TOXIN	XENIA
AUXIN	CALYX	EXALT	EXULS	INFIX	MIXER	PIXES	SEXES	UNBOX	XENON
AXELS	CAREX	EXAMS	EXULT	IXIAS	MIXES	PIXIE	SEXTS	UNFIX	XERIC
AXIAL	CAXON	EXCEL	EXURB	IXTLE	MOXAS	PODEX	SILEX	UNSEX	XYLEM
AXILE	CHOUX	EXEAT	FAXED	KEXES	MOXIE	POXED	SIXER	UNTAX	XYLIC
AXILS	CIMEX	EXEEM	FAXES	KYLIX	MUREX	POXES	SIXES	VARIX	XYLOL
AXING	CODEX	EXEME	FIXED	LATEX	MUXED	PREXY	SIXTE	VEXED	XYLYL
AXIOM	COXAE	EXERT	FIXER	LAXER	MUXES	PROXY	SIXTH	VEXER	XYSTI
AXLES	COXAL	EXIES	FIXES	LAXES	NEXUS	PYXED	SIXTY	VEXES	XYSTS
AXOID	COXED	EXILE	FLAXY	LAXLY	NIXES	PYXES	SOREX	VIBEX	YEXED
AXONS	COXES	EXINE	FOXED	LEXES	NIXIE	PYXIS	TAXED	VITEX	YEXES
BEAUX	CULEX	EXIST	FOXES	LEXIS	NOXAL	RADIX	TAXER	VIXEN	ZAXES
BOLIX	CYLIX	EXITS	HELIX	LIMAX	OXERS	RAXED	TAXES	WAXED	
BORAX	DESEX	EXODE	HEXAD	LOXES	OXIDE	RAXES	TAXIS	WAXEN	
BOXED	DIXIE	EXONS	HEXED	LUXES	OXIME	REDOX	TAXON	WAXER	
BOXEN	DRUXY	EXPAT	HEXES	MALAX	OXLIP	RELAX	TAXOR	WAXES	

X - 6-letter words

ADIEUX	CARFOX	ELIXIR	EXODES	EXUDES	HEXOSE	MENINX	PIXELS	SEXTON	VORTEX
AFFLUX	CAUDEX	EUTAXY	EXODIC	EXULTS	HOAXED	MINXES	PIXIES	SEXUAL	WAXERS
ALEXIA	CAXONS	EXACTS	EXODUS	EXURBS	HOAXER	MIXENS	PLEXOR	SIXERS	WAXIER
ALEXIC	CERVIX	EXALTS	EXOGEN	FAXING	HOAXES	MIXERS	PLEXUS	SIXTES	WAXING
ALEXIN	CHENIX	EXAMEN	EXOMIS	FIXATE	HOXING	MIXIER	POLLEX	SIXTHS	WEXING
ANNEXE	CLIMAX	EXARCH	EXONYM	FIXERS	IBEXES	MIXING	POXIER	SMILAX	WRAXLE
ANOXIA	COAXED	EXCAMB	EXOPOD	FIXING	ICEBOX	MOXIES	POXING	SPADIX	XEBECS
ANOXIC	COAXER	EXCEED	EXOTIC	FIXITY	ILEXES	MUXING	PRAXES	SPHINX	XENIAL
APEXES	COAXES	EXCELS	EXPAND	FIXIVE	IMBREX	MYXOMA	PRAXIS	STORAX	XENIAS
ATAXIA	COCCYX	EXCEPT	EXPATS	FIXURE	IMPLEX	NEXTLY	PREFIX	STYRAX	XENIUM
ATAXIC	COMMIX	EXCESS	EXPECT	FLAXEN	INFLUX	NIXIES	PREMIX	SUFFIX	XENONS
ATWIXT	CONFIX	EXCIDE	EXPELS	FLAXES	IXTLES	ONYXES	PREXES	SURTAX	XEROMA
AUXINS	CONVEX	EXCISE	EXPEND	FLEXED	JAWBOX	OREXIS	PROLIX	SYNTAX	XOANON
AXILLA	CORTEX	EXCITE	EXPERT	FLEXES	JINXED	ORIFEX	PTYXES	SYRINX	XYLEMS
AXIOMS	COWPOX	EXCUSE	EXPIRE	FLEXOR	JINXES	ORYXES	PTYXIS	TAXERS	XYLENE
AXISES	COXIER	EXEATS	EXPIRY	FLIXED	JYNXES	OUTBOX	PYXING	TAXIED	XYLOID
AXOIDS	COXING	EXEDRA	EXPORT	FLIXES	KLAXON	OUTFOX	RAXING	TAXIES	XYLOLS
BANJAX	CRUXES	EXEEMS	EXPOSE	FLUXED	LARNAX	OXALIC	REFLEX	TAXING	XYLOMA
BAXTER	DEFLEX	EXEMED	EXPUGN	FLUXES	LARYNX	OXALIS	REFLUX	TAXMAN	XYLOSE
BIAXAL	DEIXES	EXEMES	EXSECT	FORFEX	LAXEST	OXGANG	RHEXES	TAXMEN	XYLYLS
BIJOUX	DEIXIS	EXEMPT	EXSERT	FORNIX	LAXISM	OXGATE	RHEXIS	TAXORS	XYSTER
BOLLIX	DENTEX	EXEQUY	EXTANT	FOXIER	LAXIST	OXHEAD	SAXAUL	TETTIX	XYSTOI
BOMBAX	DEXTER	EXERTS	EXTASY	FOXING	LAXITY	OXIDES	SAXONY	THORAX	XYSTOS
BONXIE	DIAXON	EXEUNT	EXTEND	FRUTEX	LEXEME	OXIMES	SCOLEX	TOXINS	XYSTUS
BOXCAR	DIOXAN	EXHALE	EXTENT	GALAXY	LUMMOX	OXLAND	SEXERS	TOXOID	YEXING
BOXERS	DIOXIN	EXHORT	EXTERN	HALLUX	LUXATE	OXLIPS	SEXFID	TUTRIX	YUNXES
BOXFUL	DIPLEX	EXHUME	EXTINE	HATBOX	LUXURY	OXSLIP	SEXIER	TUXEDO	
BOXIER	DIXIES	EXILED	EXTIRP	HAYBOX	LYNXES	OXTAIL	SEXING	ULEXES	
BOXING	DOGFOX	EXILES	EXTOLD	HEXACT	MAGNOX	OXTERS	SEXISM	UNISEX	
BOYAUX	DOXIES	EXILIC	EXTOLS	HEXADS	MATRIX	OXYGEN	SEXIST	VERTEX	
CALXES	DUPLEX	EXINES	EXTORT	HEXANE	MAXIMA	OXYMEL	SEXPOT	VEXERS	
CARANX	EARWAX	EXISTS	EXTRAS	HEXENE	MAXIMS	PAXWAX	SEXTAN	VEXING	
CARFAX	EFFLUX	EXITED	EXUDED	HEXING	MAXIXE	PINXIT	SEXTET	VIXENS	

X - 7-letter words

ABAXIAL	AXINITE	CONTEXT	EXALTED	EXECUTE	EXOPODS	EXSERTS	FLEXING	HYRAXES
ABRAXAS	AXOLOTL	COTEAUX	EXAMENS	EXEDRAE	EXORDIA	EXTATIC	FLEXION	IMMIXED
ADAXIAL	BATEAUX	COXCOMB	EXAMINE	EXEEMED	EXOTICA	EXTENDS	FLEXORS	IMMIXES
ADDAXES	BAUXITE	COXIEST	EXAMPLE	EXEGETE	EXOTICS	EXTENSE	FLEXURE	INDEXED
ADMIXED	BAXTERS	CURTAXE	EXARATE	EXEMING	EXPANDS	EXTENTS	FLIXING	INDEXER
ADMIXES	BEESWAX	DESEXED	EXARCHS	EXEMPLA	EXPANSE	EXTERNE	FLUMMOX	INDEXES
AFFIXED	BETWIXT	DESEXES	EXARCHY	EXEMPLE	EXPECTS	EXTERNS	FLUXING	INEXACT
AFFIXES	BIAXIAL	DEXTERS	EXCAMBS	EXEMPTS	EXPENDS	EXTINCT	FLUXION	INFIXED
ALEXIAS	BOLIXES	DEXTRAL	EXCEEDS	EXERGUE	EXPENSE	EXTINES	FLUXIVE	INFIXES
ALEXINS	BONXIES	DEXTRAN	EXCEPTS	EXERTED	EXPERTS	EXTIRPS	FOXHOLE	INVEXED
ANNEXED	BORAXES	DEXTRIN	EXCERPT	EXHALED	EXPIATE	EXTORTS	FOXIEST	JAMBEUX
ANNEXES	BOSTRYX	DIAXONS	EXCHEAT	EXHALES	EXPIRED	EXTRACT	FOXINGS	JINXING
ANOREXY	BOXCARS	DIOXANE	EXCIDED	EXHAUST	EXPIRES	EXTRAIT	FOXSHIP	KLAXONS
ANOXIAS	BOXFULS	DIOXANS	EXCIDES	EXHEDRA	EXPLAIN	EXTREAT	FOXTROT	LATEXES
ANTEFIX	BOXIEST	DIOXIDE	EXCISED	EXHIBIT	EXPLANT	EXTREME	GATEAUX	LAXATOR
ANTHRAX	BOXINGS	DIOXINS	EXCISES	EXHORTS	EXPLODE	EXTRUDE	GEARBOX	LAXISMS
ANXIETY	BOXROOM	DRUXIER	EXCITED	EXHUMED	EXPLOIT	EXUDATE	HELIXES	LAXISTS
ANXIOUS	BOXWOOD	ELIXIRS	EXCITER	EXHUMER	EXPLORE	EXUDING	HEXACTS	LEXEMES
APOPLEX	BRAXIES	EMBOXED	EXCITES	EXHUMES	EXPORTS	EXULTED	HEXADIC	LEXICAL
APRAXIA	BRUXISM	EMBOXES	EXCITON	EXIGENT	EXPOSAL	EXURBAN	HEXAGON	LEXICON
APTERYX	BUREAUX	ENFIXED	EXCITOR	EXILIAN	EXPOSED	EXURBIA	HEXANES	LEXISES
ASEXUAL	BUXOMER	ENFIXES	EXCLAIM	EXILING	EXPOSER	EXUVIAE	HEXAPLA	LOXYGEN
ASPHYXY	CACHEXY	EPAXIAL	EXCLAVE	EXILITY	EXPOSES	EXUVIAL	HEXAPOD	LUXATED
ATARAXY	CADEAUX	EPITAXY	EXCLUDE	EXISTED	EXPOUND	FIXABLE	HEXARCH	LUXATES
ATAXIAS	CALIXES	EPOXIDE	EXCRETA	EXITING	EXPRESS	FIXATED	HEXENES	MALAXED
ATAXIES	CALYXES	EPOXIES	EXCRETE	EXOCARP	EXPUGNS	FIXATES	HEXINGS	MALAXES
AUXESES	CHOENIX	EQUINOX	EXCUDIT	EXODERM	EXPULSE	FIXEDLY	HEXOSES	MAXILLA
AUXESIS	COAXERS	EUTEXIA	EXCURSE	EXODIST	EXPUNCT	FIXINGS	HOAXERS	MAXIMAL
AUXETIC	COAXIAL	EXACTED	EXCUSAL	EXOGAMY	EXPUNGE	FIXTURE	HOAXING	MAXIMIN
AXIALLY	COAXING	EXACTER	EXCUSED	EXOGENS	EXPURGE	FIXURES	HYDROXY	MAXIMUM
AXILLAE	COMPLEX	EXACTLY	EXCUSER	EXOMION	EXSCIND	FLAXIER	HYPOXIA	MAXIXES
AXILLAR	CONFLUX	EXACTOR	EXCUSES	EXONYMS	EXSECTS	FLEXILE	HYPOXIC	

MAXWELL	OXHEADS	PHALANX	PYXIDIA	SEXTETS	TAXICAB	TRIAXON	VITEXES	XEROTIC
MILIEUX	OXIDANT	PHARYNX	REANNEX	SEXTETT	TAXIING	TRIPLEX	VITRAUX	XIPHOID
MIXABLE	OXIDASE	PHLOXES	RECTRIX	SEXTILE	TAXIMAN	TUXEDOS	VIXENLY	XOANONS
MIXEDLY	OXIDATE	PHOENIX	RELAXED	SEXTONS	TAXIMEN	UNBOXED	WAXBILL	XYLENES
MIXIEST	OXIDISE	PICKAXE	RELAXES	SEXTUOR	TAXINGS	UNBOXES	WAXIEST	XYLENOL
MIXTION	OXIDIZE	PLANXTY	RELAXIN	SILEXES	TAXIWAY	UNFIXED	WAXINGS	XYLITOL
MIXTURE	OXLANDS	PLEXORS	RESEAUX	SIMPLEX	TAXYING	UNFIXES	WAXWING	XYLOGEN
MONAXON	OXONIUM	PLEXURE	SALPINX	SIXAINE	TECTRIX	UNMIXED	WAXWORK	XYLOMAS
MUREXES	OXSLIPS	PODEXES	SAXAULS	SIXFOLD	TELETEX	UNSEXED	WRAXLED	XYLONIC
NARTHEX	OXTAILS	POSTFIX	SAXHORN	SIXTEEN	TELEXED	UNSEXES	WRAXLES	XYLOSES
NEXUSES	OXTERED	POXIEST	SEEDBOX	SIXTHLY	TELEXES	UNTAXED	XANTHIC	XYSTERS
NOXIOUS	OXYGENS	PRETEXT	SEXFOIL	SIXTIES	TEXASES	UNTAXES	XANTHIN	ZEUXITE
ORATRIX	OXYMELS	PREXIES	SEXIEST	SOAPBOX	TEXTILE	UNVEXED	XERAFIN	ZOOTAXY
OVERTAX	OXYTONE	PRINCOX	SEXISMS	SOREXES	TEXTUAL	UXORIAL	XERARCH	
OXALATE	PANAXES	PROXIES	SEXISTS	SUBTEXT	TEXTURE	VAUDOUX	XERASIA	
OXAZINE	PANCHAX	PROXIMO	SEXLESS	SYNAXES	TOOLBOX	VEXEDLY	XEROMAS	
OXBLOOD	PARADOX	PYREXIA	SEXPOTS	SYNAXIS	TORTRIX	VEXILLA	XEROSES	
OXGANGS	PAXIUBA	PYREXIC	SEXTANS	TAXABLE	TOXICAL	VEXINGS	XEROSIS	
OXGATES	PERPLEX	PYXIDES	SEXTANT	TAXABLY	TOXOIDS	VICTRIX	XEROTES	

X - 8-letter words

ADMIXING	CARBOXYL	DUPLEXES	EXCITONS	EXHUMERS	EXPERTED	EXTIRPED	GEOTAXES
AFFIXING	CARFAXES	DUXELLES	EXCITORS	EXHUMING	EXPERTLY	EXTOLLED	GEOTAXIS
AFFLUXES	CARFOXES	DYSLEXIA	EXCLAIMS	EXIGEANT	EXPIABLE	EXTOLLER	GIAMBEUX
ANNEXING	CARNIFEX	DYSLEXIC	EXCLAVES	EXIGENCE	EXPIATED	EXTORTED	GLORYBOX
ANNEXION	CATHEXES	EARTHWAX	EXCLUDED	EXIGENCY	EXPIATES	EXTRACTS	GLOXINIA
ANNEXURE	CATHEXIS	EARWAXES	EXCLUDEE	EXIGENTS	EXPIATOR	EXTRADOS	HARUSPEX
ANOREXIA	CAUDEXES	EFFLUXES	EXCLUDES	EXIGIBLE	EXPIRANT	EXTRAITS	HATBOXES
ANOREXIC	CERVIXES	EMBOXING	EXCRETED	EXIGUITY	EXPIRIES	EXTREATS	HAYBOXES
ANTEFIXA	CHATEAUX	ENDEIXES	EXCRETES	EXIGUOUS	EXPIRING	EXTREMER	HERITRIX
ANTHELIX	CHENIXES	ENDEIXIS	EXCUBANT	EXIMIOUS	EXPLAINS	EXTREMES	HEXAFOIL
APOMIXES	CICATRIX	ENFIXING	EXCURSED	EXISTENT	EXPLANTS	EXTRORSE	HEXAGLOT
APOMIXIS	CLACKBOX	EPICALYX	EXCURSES	EXISTING	EXPLICIT	EXTRUDED	HEXAGONS
APOPLEXY	CLIMAXED	EPOXIDES	EXCURSUS	EXITANCE	EXPLODED	EXTRUDER	HEXAGRAM
APPENDIX	CLIMAXES	EUTAXIES	EXCUSALS	EXOCARPS	EXPLODER	EXTRUDES	HEXAPLAR
APRAXIAS	COMMIXED	EUTAXITE	EXCUSERS	EXOCRINE	EXPLODES	EXUDATES	HEXAPLAS
APYREXIA	COMMIXES	EUTEXIAS	EXCUSING	EXODERMS	EXPLOITS	EXULTANT	HEXAPODS
ASPHYXIA	CONFIXED	EUXENITE	EXCUSIVE	EXODISTS	EXPLORED	EXULTING	HEXAPODY
ATARAXIA	CONFIXES	EXACTERS	EXECRATE	EXODUSES	EXPLORER	EXURBIAS	HEXYLENE
ATARAXIC	CONTEXTS	EXACTEST	EXECUTED	EXOERGIC	EXPLORES	EXUVIATE	HYDROXYL
AUXETICS	CONVEXED	EXACTING	EXECUTER	EXOGAMIC	EXPONENT	FABLIAUX	HYPOXIAS
AUXILIAR	CONVEXES	EXACTION	EXECUTES	EXOMIONS	EXPORTED	FIXATING	ICEBOXES
AVIATRIX	CONVEXLY	EXACTORS	EXECUTOR	EXOMISES	EXPORTER	FIXATION	IMMIXING
AXILLARY	CORTEXES	EXALTING	EXECUTRY	EXOPHAGY	EXPOSALS	FIXATIVE	IMPLEXES
AXINITES	COWPOXES	EXAMINED	EXEEMING	EXOPLASM	EXPOSERS	FIXATURE	INDEXERS
AXIOLOGY	COXALGIA	EXAMINEE	EXEGESES	EXORABLE	EXPOSING	FIXITIES	INDEXING
AXOLOTLS	COXCOMBS	EXAMINER	EXEGESIS	EXORCISE	EXPOSURE	FIXTURES	INEXPERT
AXOPLASM	COXINESS	EXAMINES	EXEGETES	EXORCISM	EXPOUNDS	FLAXIEST	INFIXING
BANDEAUX	COXSWAIN	EXAMPLAR	EXEGETIC	EXORCIST	EXPRESSO	FLEXIBLE	INFLEXED
BANJAXED	CREATRIX	EXAMPLED	EXEMPLAR	EXORCIZE	EXPUGNED	FLEXIBLY	INFLUXES
BANJAXES	CRUCIFIX	EXAMPLES	EXEMPLES	EXORDIAL	EXPULSED	FLEXIONS	INTERMIX
BANXRING	CURATRIX	EXANTHEM	EXEMPLUM	EXORDIUM	EXPULSES	FLEXUOSE	INTERREX
BAUXITES	CURTAXES	EXCAMBED	EXEMPTED	EXOSMOSE	EXPUNCTS	FLEXUOUS	INTERSEX
BAUXITIC	DEFLEXED	EXCAVATE	EXEQUIAL	EXOSPORE	EXPUNGED	FLEXURAL	JAMBEAUX
BEAUXITE	DEFLEXES	EXCEEDED	EXEQUIES	EXOTERIC	EXPUNGER	FLEXURES	JANITRIX
BERCEAUX	DENTEXES	EXCELLED	EXERCISE	EXOTOXIC	EXPUNGES	FLUXIONS	JAWBOXES
BICONVEX	DESEXING	EXCEPTED	EXERGUAL	EXOTOXIN	EXPURGED	FORFEXES	LARYNXES
BISEXUAL	DETOXIFY	EXCEPTOR	EXERGUES	EXPANDED	EXPURGES	FORNIXES	LAXATIVE
BOLLIXES	DEXTRANS	EXCERPTA	EXERTING	EXPANDER	EXSCINDS	FOXBERRY	LAXATORS
BOMBAXES	DEXTRINE	EXCERPTS	EXERTION	EXPANDOR	EXSECTED	FOXGLOVE	LAXITIES
BOXINESS	DEXTRINS	EXCESSES	EXERTIVE	EXPANSES	EXSERTED	FOXHOLES	LEXICONS
BOXROOMS	DEXTROSE	EXCHANGE	EXHALANT	EXPECTED	EXTASIES	FOXHOUND	LEXIGRAM
BOXWOODS	DEXTROUS	EXCHEATS	EXHALING	EXPECTER	EXTENDED	FOXINESS	LIXIVIAL
BRUXISMS	DIOXANES	EXCIDING	EXHAUSTS	EXPEDITE	EXTENDER	FOXSHARK	LIXIVIUM
BUXOMEST	DIOXIDES	EXCISING	EXHEDRAE	EXPELLED	EXTENSOR	FOXSHIPS	LOXYGENS
CACHEXIA	DISANNEX	EXCISION	EXHIBITS	EXPELLEE	EXTERIOR	FOXTROTS	LUMMOXES
CACODOXY	DOGFOXES	EXCITANT	EXHORTED	EXPENDED	EXTERNAL	GALAXIES	LUXATING
CACOMIXL	DOXOLOGY	EXCITERS	EXHORTER	EXPENDER	EXTERNAT	GENETRIX	LUXATION
CAMAIEUX	DRUXIEST	EXCITING	EXHUMATE	EXPENSES	EXTERNES	GENITRIX	LUXMETER

LUXURIES	ORIFEXES	PARADOXY	QUIXOTIC	SIXAINES	TAXIARCH	TUTRIXES	XANTHOMA
LUXURIST	ORTHODOX	PARALLAX	QUIXOTRY	SIXPENCE	TAXICABS	TUXEDOES	XANTHOUS
MAGNOXES	OUTBOXED	PAROXYSM	REFLEXED	SIXPENNY	TAXIWAYS	UNBOXING	XENOGAMY
MALAXAGE	OUTBOXES	PAXIUBAS	REFLEXES	SIXSCORE	TAXONOMY	UNFIXING	XENOLITH
MALAXATE	OUTFOXED	PAXWAXES	REFLEXLY	SIXTEENS	TEGUEXIN	UNFIXITY	XENOPHYA
MALAXING	OUTFOXES	PEROXIDE	REFLUXED	SIXTIETH	TELETEXT	UNIAXIAL	XENOTIME
MANTEAUX	OXALATES	PHORMINX	REFLUXES	SMALLPOX	TELEXING	UNSEXING	XENURINE
MATCHBOX	OXALISES	PICKAXES	RELAXANT	SMILAXES	TETRAXON	UNSEXIST	XERAFINS
MATRIXES	OXAZINES	PLATEAUX	RELAXING	SNUFFBOX	TETTIXES	UNSEXUAL	XERANSES
MAXILLAE	OXBLOODS	PLEXURES	RELAXINS	SPARAXIS	TEXTBOOK	UNTAXING	XERANSIS
MAXIMINS	OXIDANTS	PLEXUSES	RHEXISES	SPHINXES	TEXTILES	UXORIOUS	XERANTIC
MAXIMISE	OXIDASES	POLYAXON	RONDEAUX	SPINIFEX	TEXTUARY	VEXATION	XERAPHIM
MAXIMIST	OXIDATED	PONCEAUX	ROULEAUX	SPINTEXT	TEXTURAL	VEXATORY	XERASIAS
MAXIMIZE	OXIDATES	PONTIFEX	SARDONYX	STORAXES	TEXTURED	VEXILLUM	XYLENOLS
MAXWELLS	OXIDISED	POXVIRUS	SAXATILE	STYRAXES	TEXTURES	VEXINGLY	XYLITOLS
MIREPOIX	OXIDISER	PREFIXED	SAXHORNS	SUBOXIDE	THORAXES	VIDEOTEX	XYLOCARP
MIXTIONS	OXIDISES	PREFIXES	SAXONIES	SUBTEXTS	THYROXIN	VIXENISH	XYLOGENS
MIXTURES	OXIDIZED	PREMIXED	SAXONITE	SUFFIXAL	TOADFLAX	VORTEXES	XYLOIDIN
MONAXIAL	OXIDIZER	PREMIXES	SEXFOILS	SUFFIXED	TOXAEMIA	WAXBERRY	XYLOLOGY
MONAXONS	OXIDIZES	PRETEXTS	SEXINESS	SUFFIXES	TOXAEMIC	WAXBILLS	XYLONITE
MONOXIDE	OXIMETER	PROLIXLY	SEXOLOGY	SUPERTAX	TOXICANT	WAXINESS	XYSTOSES
MORCEAUX	OXONIUMS	PROXIMAL	SEXTANTS	SURTAXED	TOXICITY	WAXWINGS	XYSTUSES
MYXEDEMA	OXTERING	PTYXISES	SEXTETTE	SURTAXES	TOXOCARA	WAXWORKS	ZEUXITES
MYXOMATA	OXYMORON	PYREXIAL	SEXTETTS	SYNTAXES	TRACTRIX	WRAXLING	ZOOTOXIN
NALOXONE	OXYTOCIC	PYREXIAS	SEXTILES	SYNTEXIS	TRANSFIX	XANTHATE	
NEXTNESS	OXYTOCIN	PYROXENE	SEXTOLET	SYRINXES	TRIAXIAL	XANTHEIN	
NITROXYL	OXYTONES	PYROXYLE	SEXTUORS	TABLEAUX	TRIAXONS	XANTHENE	
OPOPANAX	PANMIXIA	PYXIDIUM	SEXTUPLE	TAXATION	TRIOXIDE	XANTHINE	
OREXISES	PANMIXIS	QUINCUNX	SEXUALLY	TAXATIVE	TRUMEAUX	XANTHINS	

Z-WORDS

Z - 2-letter words

ZO

Z - 3-letter words

BEZ	DZO	LEZ	POZ	ZAG	ZED	ZHO	ZIZ	ZUZ
BIZ	FEZ	LUZ	RIZ	ZAP	ZEE	ZIG	ZOA	
COZ	FIZ	MIZ	SAZ	ZAX	ZEK	ZIP	ZOO	
CUZ	JIZ	MOZ	SEZ	ZEA	ZEL	ZIT	ZOS	

Z - 4-letter words

ADZE	DZOS	HAZY	MAZY	PIZE	TREZ	ZEAL	ZEZE	ZOBO	ZURF
AZAN	FAZE	HIZZ	MEZE	POZZ	TUZZ	ZEAS	ZHOS	ZOBU	ZYME
AZYM	FIZZ	JAZY	MIZZ	PUTZ	TZAR	ZEBU	ZIFF	ZOEA	
BUZZ	FOZY	JAZZ	MOZE	QUIZ	VIZY	ZEDS	ZIGS	ZOIC	
CHEZ	FRIZ	JIZZ	MOZZ	RAZE	WHIZ	ZEES	ZILA	ZONA	
COZE	FUZE	KAZI	NAZE	RAZZ	ZACK	ZEIN	ZIMB	ZONE	
COZY	FUZZ	LAZE	OOZE	SIZE	ZAGS	ZEKS	ZINC	ZOOM	
CZAR	GAZE	LAZY	OOZY	SIZY	ZANY	ZELS	ZING	ZOON	
DAZE	GAZY	LEZZ	OUZO	SWIZ	ZAPS	ZERO	ZIPS	ZOOS	
DOZE	GIZZ	LUTZ	OYEZ	TIZZ	ZARF	ZEST	ZITS	ZULU	
DOZY	HAZE	MAZE	PHIZ	TOZE	ZATI	ZETA	ZIZZ	ZUPA	

Z - 5-letter words

ABUZZ	AZOTE	BEZEL	BUZZY	CROZE	DOZER	FURZE	GAZER	GRAZE	HUZZA
ADZES	AZOTH	BEZES	BWAZI	CZARS	DOZES	FURZY	GAZES	GRIZE	HUZZY
AGAZE	AZURE	BLAZE	CEAZE	DARZI	FAZED	FUZEE	GAZON	HAMZA	IZARD
AIZLE	AZURN	BLITZ	CLOZE	DAZED	FAZES	FUZES	GAZOO	HAZED	IZZET
AMAZE	AZURY	BONZE	COLZA	DAZES	FEEZE	FUZZY	GHAZI	HAZEL	JAZZY
AVIZE	AZYGY	BOOZE	COZED	DIAZO	FIZZY	GAUZE	GIZMO	HAZER	KANZU
AVYZE	AZYME	BOOZY	COZEN	DIZEN	FIZZY	GAUZY	GLAZE	HAZES	KARZY
AZANS	AZYMS	BRAZE	COZES	DIZZY	FRIZE	GAZAL	GLAZY	HEEZE	KAZIS
AZIDE	BAIZE	BRIZE	CRAZE	DOZED	FRIZZ	GAZED	GLITZ	HERTZ	KAZOO
AZOIC	BAZAR	BUAZE	CRAZY	DOZEN	FROZE	GAZEL	GLOZE	HIZEN	KLUTZ

KRANZ	MAZUT	OUZOS	RITZY	TIZZY	WEIZE	ZATIS	ZIGAN	ZOBUS	ZOONS
KUDZU	MEZES	OZEKI	ROZET	TOAZE	WHIZZ	ZAXES	ZILAS	ZOCCO	ZOPPO
LAZAR	MEZZO	OZONE	ROZIT	TOPAZ	WINZE	ZEALS	ZILCH	ZOEAE	ZORIL
LAZED	MILTZ	PEAZE	SARZA	TOUZE	WIZEN	ZEBEC	ZIMBI	ZOEAL	ZORRO
LAZES	MIZEN	PEIZE	SAZES	TOWZE	WOOTZ	ZEBRA	ZIMBS	ZOEAS	ZOWIE
LAZZI	MIZES	PIEZO	SEAZE	TOZED	WOOZY	ZEBUB	ZINCO	ZOISM	ZULUS
LAZZO	MOTZA	PIZES	SEIZE	TOZES	ZABRA	ZEBUS	ZINCS	ZOIST	ZUPAN
LEAZE	MOZED	PIZZA	SENZA	TOZIE	ZACKS	ZEINS	ZINCY	ZOMBI	ZUPAS
LEZES	MOZES	PLAZA	SIZAR	TZARS	ZAIRE	ZERDA	ZINEB	ZONAE	ZURFS
LEZZY	MUZZY	POZZY	SIZED	ULZIE	ZAMAN	ZEROS	ZINGS	ZONAL	ZUZES
LOZEN	NAZES	PRIZE	SIZEL	UNZIP	ZAMBO	ZESTS	ZINGY	ZONDA	ZYGAL
MAIZE	NAZIR	PUZEL	SIZER	VEZIR	ZAMIA	ZESTY	ZINKE	ZONED	ZYGON
MATZA	NEEZE	PZAZZ	SIZES	VIZIR	ZANJA	ZETAS	ZINKY	ZONES	ZYMES
MATZO	NIZAM	RAZED	SPITZ	VIZOR	ZANTE	ZEZES	ZIPPY	ZOOEA	ZYMIC
MAZED	OOZED	RAZEE	TAZZA	WALTZ	ZANZE	ZHOMO	ZIZEL	ZOOID	
MAZER	OOZES	RAZES	TAZZE	WANZE	ZAPPY	ZIBET	ZLOTY	ZOOKS	
MAZES	OUZEL	RAZOR	TEAZE	WAZIR	ZARFS	ZIFFS	ZOBOS	ZOOMS	

Z - 6-letter words

ABLAZE	BLAZED	DAZING	FUZZLE	HUZOOR	MEZZOS	PUTZES	SNOOZE	WINZES	ZIGGED
ABRAZO	BLAZER	DAZZLE	GAUZES	HUZZAS	MIZENS	PUZELS	SOZZLE	WIZARD	ZIGZAG
AGAZED	BLAZES	DEFUZE	GAZALS	IODIZE	MIZZEN	PUZZEL	SOZZLY	WIZENS	ZILLAH
AGNIZE	BLAZON	DIAZOS	GAZEBO	IONIZE	MIZZES	PUZZLE	STANZA	WIZIER	ZIMBIS
AGRIZE	BLINTZ	DIZAIN	GAZELS	IZARDS	MIZZLE	QUARTZ	STANZE	WUZZLE	ZIMMER
AGRYZE	BLOWZE	DIZENS	GAZERS	IZZARD	MIZZLY	QUEAZY	STANZO	YAKUZA	ZINCED
AGUIZE	BLOWZY	DONZEL	GAZIER	IZZETS	MOTZAS	QUINZE	SUIVEZ	ZABETA	ZINCKY
AIZLES	BONZER	DORIZE	GAZING	JAZIES	MOZING	RANZEL	SYZYGY	ZABRAS	ZINCOS
ALTEZA	BONZES	DOZENS	GAZONS	JAZZED	MOZZES	RAZEED	TAZZAS	ZADDIK	ZINEBS
AMAZED	BOOZED	DOZERS	GAZOON	JAZZES	MOZZIE	RAZEES	TEAZED	ZAFFER	ZINGED
AMAZES	BOOZER	DOZIER	GAZOOS	JEZAIL	MOZZLE	RAZING	TEAZEL	ZAFFRE	ZINGEL
AMAZON	BOOZES	DOZING	GAZUMP	JIZZES	MUZHIK	RAZORS	TEAZES	ZAGGED	ZINKED
APOZEM	BOOZEY	DRAZEL	GEEZER	KAMEEZ	MUZZLE	RAZURE	TEAZLE	ZAMANG	ZINKES
ASSIZE	BORZOI	DZEREN	GHAZAL	KANZUS	MZUNGU	RAZZED	TENZON	ZAMANS	ZINNIA
AVIZED	BRAIZE	ECZEMA	GHAZEL	KAZOOS	NAZIRS	RAZZES	TIZWAS	ZAMBOS	ZIPPED
AVIZES	BRAZED	ENTREZ	GHAZIS	KIBITZ	NEEZED	RAZZIA	TIZZES	ZAMIAS	ZIPPER
AVYZED	BRAZEN	ENZIAN	GIZMOS	KRANTZ	NEEZES	RAZZLE	TOAZED	ZANDER	ZIPTOP
AVYZES	BRAZES	ENZONE	GIZZEN	KUDZUS	NIZAMS	RHIZIC	TOAZES	ZANIED	ZIRCON
AZALEA	BRAZIL	ENZYME	GIZZES	LAZARS	NOZZLE	RIZARD	TOLZEY	ZANIER	ZITHER
AZIDES	BREEZE	EPIZOA	GLAZED	LAZIER	NUZZER	RIZZAR	TOUZED	ZANIES	ZIZELS
AZIONE	BREEZY	ERSATZ	GLAZEN	LAZILY	NUZZLE	RIZZER	TOUZES	ZANJAS	ZIZZED
AZOLLA	BRIZES	EVZONE	GLAZER	LAZING	NYANZA	RIZZOR	TOUZLE	ZANTES	ZIZZES
AZONAL	BRONZE	FAZING	GLAZES	LEAZES	OOZIER	ROZETS	TOWZED	ZANZES	ZLOTYS
AZONIC	BRONZY	FEEZED	GLITZY	LEZZES	OOZILY	ROZITS	TOWZES	ZAPATA	ZOCCOS
AZOTES	BROUZE	FEEZES	GLOZED	LIZARD	OOZING	ROZZER	TOZIES	ZAPPED	ZODIAC
AZOTHS	BUAZES	FEZZED	GLOZES	LOZELL	OUZELS	SARZAS	TOZING	ZARAPE	ZOETIC
AZOTIC	BUZZED	FEZZES	GOZZAN	LOZENS	OYEZES	SAZHEN	TREZES	ZAREBA	ZOISMS
AZURES	BUZZER	FIZGIG	GRAZED	LUTZES	OZAENA	SAZZES	TUZZES	ZARIBA	ZOISTS
AZYMES	BUZZES	FIZZED	GRAZER	LUZERN	OZEKIS	SCAZON	TWEEZE	ZARNEC	ZOMBIE
BAIZED	BWAZIS	FIZZEN	GRAZES	LUZZES	OZONES	SCHIZO	ULZIES	ZEALOT	ZOMBIS
BAIZES	BYZANT	FIZZER	GRIZES	MAHZOR	PANZER	SCRUZE	UNZIPS	ZEBECK	ZONARY
BANZAI	CEAZED	FIZZES	GUIZER	MAIZES	PATZER	SEAZED	UPGAZE	ZEBECS	ZONATE
BAZAAR	CEAZES	FIZZLE	GUTZER	MATZAH	PAZAZZ	SEAZES	VEZIRS	ZEBRAS	ZONDAS
BAZARS	CHINTZ	FLOOZY	GUZZLE	MATZAS	PEAZED	SEIZED	VIZARD	ZEBUBS	ZONING
BAZAZZ	CIZERS	FOOZLE	HAMZAH	MATZOH	PEAZES	SEIZER	VIZIER	ZELANT	ZONKED
BEDAZE	COLZAS	FOZIER	HAMZAS	MATZOS	PEIZED	SEIZES	VIZIES	ZELOSO	ZONOID
BENZAL	COROZO	FRANZY	HAZARD	MATZOT	PEIZES	SEIZIN	VIZIRS	ZENANA	ZONULA
BENZIL	CORYZA	FRAZIL	HAZELS	MAZARD	PEZANT	SIZARS	VIZORS	ZENDIK	ZONULE
BENZOL	COZENS	FREEZE	HAZERS	MAZHBI	PHEEZE	SIZELS	VIZSLA	ZENITH	ZOOEAE
BENZYL	COZIER	FRENZY	HAZIER	MAZIER	PHIZOG	SIZERS	VIZZIE	ZEPHYR	ZOOEAL
BEZANT	COZIES	FRIEZE	HAZILY	MAZILY	PIAZZA	SIZIER	WANZED	ZERDAS	ZOOEAS
BEZAZZ	COZING	FRIZES	HAZING	MAZING	PIAZZI	SIZING	WANZES	ZEREBA	ZOOIDS
BEZELS	COZZES	FRIZZY	HEEZED	MAZOUT	PIZZAS	SIZZLE	WAZIRS	ZERIBA	ZOOMED
BEZOAR	CRAZED	FROWZY	HEEZES	MAZUMA	PLAZAS	SLEAZE	WEAZEN	ZEROED	ZOONAL
BEZZLE	CRAZES	FROZEN	HEEZIE	MAZUTS	PODZOL	SLEAZY	WEIZED	ZEROTH	ZOONIC
BIZAZZ	CROZES	FURZES	HIZENS	MEAZEL	PRIZED	SLEEZY	WEIZES	ZEUGMA	ZOOZOO
BIZONE	CUZZES	FUZEES	HIZZED	MEZAIL	PRIZER	SNAZZY	WEZAND	ZHOMOS	ZORILS
BIZZES	CZAPKA	FUZZED	HIZZES	MEZUZA	PRIZES	SNEEZE	WHEEZE	ZIBETS	ZORINO
BLAIZE	DARZIS	FUZZES	HOWZAT			SNEEZY	WHEEZY	ZIGANS	ZORROS

ZOSTER	ZUFOLI	ZUPANS	ZYGONS	ZYGOTE	ZYMITE	ZYMOME
ZOUNDS	ZUFOLO	ZYGOMA	ZYGOSE	ZYMASE	ZYMOID	ZYTHUM

Z - 7-letter words

ABRAZOS	BEZANTS	CRAZILY	FIZZENS	HAZARDS	MESTIZA	PUZZELS	SNOOZES	WANZING
ADONIZE	BEZIQUE	CRAZING	FIZZERS	HAZELLY	MESTIZO	PUZZLED	SNOOZLE	WEAZAND
AGNIZED	BEZOARS	CROZIER	FIZZGIG	HAZIEST	METAZOA	PUZZLER	SNUZZLE	WEAZENS
AGNIZES	BEZZLED	CYANIZE	FIZZIER	HAZINGS	MEZAILS	PUZZLES	SOZZLED	WEIZING
AGONIZE	BEZZLES	CZAPKAS	FIZZING	HEEZIES	MEZUZAH	PZAZZES	SOZZLES	WEZANDS
AGRIZED	BIZARRE	CZARDAS	FIZZLED	HEEZING	MILTZES	QUARTZY	SPITZES	WHAIZLE
AGRIZES	BIZONAL	CZARDOM	FIZZLES	HEROIZE	MITZVAH	QUETZAL	SPREAZE	WHEEZED
AGRYZED	BIZONES	CZARINA	FLOOZIE	HERTZES	MIZMAZE	QUINZES	SPREEZE	WHEEZES
AGRYZES	BLAZERS	CZARISM	FOOZLED	HIZZING	MIZZENS	QUIZZED	SPULZIE	WHEEZLE
AGUIZED	BLAZING	CZARIST	FOOZLER	HOATZIN	MIZZLED	QUIZZER	SQUEEZE	WHIZZED
AGUIZES	BLAZONS	DAMOZEL	FOOZLES	HORIZON	MIZZLES	QUIZZES	SQUEEZY	WHIZZER
ALCAZAR	BLINTZE	DAZEDLY	FORZATI	HUMBUZZ	MOZETTA	RANZELS	STANZAS	WHIZZES
ALCORZA	BLITZED	DAZZLED	FORZATO	HUZOORS	MOZZIES	RAZURES	STANZES	WIZARDS
ALFEREZ	BLITZES	DAZZLER	FOZIEST	HUZZAED	MOZZLES	RAZZIAS	STANZOS	WIZENED
ALIZARI	BLOWZED	DAZZLES	FRAZILS	HUZZIES	MUEZZIN	RAZZING	STARETZ	WIZIERS
ALTEZAS	BLOWZES	DEFROZE	FRAZZLE	ICONIZE	MUZHIKS	RAZZLES	STYLIZE	WOOTZES
ALTEZZA	BONANZA	DEFUZED	FREEZER	IDOLIZE	MUZZIER	REALIZE	SUBZERO	WOOZIER
AMAZING	BOOZERS	DEFUZES	FREEZES	IODIZED	MUZZILY	REFROZE	SUBZONE	WOOZILY
AMAZONS	BOOZIER	DENIZEN	FRIEZED	IODIZES	MUZZLED	REPRIZE	SWAZZLE	WRIZLED
ANALYZE	BOOZILY	DIALYZE	FRIEZES	IONIZED	MUZZLER	RESEIZE	SWIZZES	WUZZLED
ANODIZE	BOOZING	DIARIZE	FRIZING	IONIZER	MUZZLES	RHIZINE	SWIZZLE	WUZZLES
ANZIANI	BORAZON	DIAZOES	FRIZZED	IONIZES	MYTHIZE	RHIZOID	SWOZZLE	ZABETAS
APOZEMS	BORZOIS	DIZAINS	FRIZZES	IRIDIZE	MZUNGUS	RHIZOME	TAILZIE	ZABTIEH
APPRIZE	BRAIZES	DIZENED	FRIZZLE	IRONIZE	NEEZING	RHIZOPI	TEAZELS	ZADDIKS
ARABIZE	BRAZENS	DIZZARD	FRIZZLY	ITEMIZE	NOZZLES	RIOTIZE	TEAZING	ZAFFERS
ASSIZED	BRAZIER	DIZZIED	FURZIER	IZZARDS	NUZZERS	RITZIER	TEAZLED	ZAFFRES
ASSIZER	BRAZILS	DIZZIER	FUZZIER	JACUZZI	NUZZLED	RIZARDS	TEAZLES	ZAGGING
ASSIZES	BRAZING	DIZZIES	FUZZILY	JANIZAR	NUZZLES	RIZZARS	TENDENZ	ZAKUSKA
ATHEIZE	BREEZED	DIZZILY	FUZZING	JAZZIER	NYANZAS	RIZZART	TENZONS	ZAKUSKI
ATOMIZE	BREEZES	DOCKIZE	FUZZLED	JAZZILY	OBELIZE	RIZZERS	TIZZIES	ZAMANGS
AVIZING	BRITZKA	DONZELS	FUZZLES	JAZZING	ODZOOKS	RIZZORS	TOAZING	ZAMARRA
AVYZING	BRONZED	DORIZED	GALLIZE	JAZZMAN	OOZIEST	ROZELLE	TOLZEYS	ZAMARRO
AZALEAS	BRONZEN	DORIZES	GAUZIER	JAZZMEN	ORGANZA	ROZETED	TOPAZES	ZAMOUSE
AZIMUTH	BRONZES	DOZENED	GAZEBOS	JEZAILS	OUTSIZE	ROZITED	TOUZING	ZANDERS
AZIONES	BROUZES	DOZENTH	GAZEFUL	KARZIES	OXAZINE	ROZZERS	TOUZLED	ZANELLA
AZOLLAS	BRULZIE	DOZIEST	GAZELLE	KIBBUTZ	OXIDIZE	SAZERAC	TOUZLES	ZANIEST
AZOTISE	BUMBAZE	DOZINGS	GAZETTE	KLUTZES	OZAENAS	SAZHENS	TOWZING	ZANJERO
AZOTIZE	BUZZARD	DRAZELS	GAZIEST	KOLKHOZ	OZONISE	SCAZONS	TRAPEZE	ZANYING
AZOTOUS	BUZZERS	DRIZZLE	GAZOOKA	KRANZES	OZONIZE	SCHERZI	TRIZONE	ZANYISM
AZULEJO	BUZZIER	DRIZZLY	GAZOONS	KYANIZE	PALAZZI	SCHERZO	TUILZIE	ZAPPIER
AZUREAN	BUZZING	DZERENS	GAZUMPS	LAICIZE	PALAZZO	SCHIZOS	TWEEZED	ZAPPING
AZURINE	BYZANTS	EBONIZE	GEEZERS	LAIRIZE	PANZERS	SCHMELZ	TWEEZES	ZAPTIAH
AZURITE	CADENZA	ECHOIZE	GENIZAH	LAZARET	PARAZOA	SCRUZED	TWIZZLE	ZAPTIEH
AZYGIES	CALZONE	ECTOZOA	GHAZALS	LAZIEST	PATZERS	SCRUZES	TZADDIK	ZARAPES
AZYGOUS	CALZONI	ECZEMAS	GHAZELS	LEZZIES	PEAZING	SEAZING	TZADDIQ	ZAREBAS
AZYMITE	CANZONA	EGOTIZE	GIZZARD	LIONIZE	PECTIZE	SEIZERS	TZIGANY	ZAREEBA
AZYMOUS	CANZONE	ELEGIZE	GIZZENS	LIZARDS	PEIZING	SEIZING	TZIMMES	ZARIBAS
BAIZING	CANZONI	EMBLAZE	GLAZERS	LOZELLS	PEPTIZE	SEIZINS	UNFAZED	ZARNECS
BAPTIZE	CAPSIZE	ENDOZOA	GLAZIER	LOZENGE	PEZANTS	SEIZURE	UNFROZE	ZARNICH
BAZAARS	CAZIQUE	ENFROZE	GLAZING	LOZENGY	PHEAZAR	SELTZER	UNGAZED	ZEALANT
BAZOOKA	CEAZING	ENTOZOA	GLITZES	LUZERNS	PHEEZED	SHMOOZE	UNITIZE	ZEALFUL
BEDAZED	CHALAZA	ENZIANS	GLOZING	MACHZOR	PHEEZES	SHOWBIZ	UNSIZED	ZEALOTS
BEDAZES	CHINTZY	ENZONED	GOZZANS	MADZOON	PHIZOGS	SIAMEZE	UNZONED	ZEALOUS
BEDIZEN	CHORIZO	ENZONES	GRAZERS	MATZAHS	PHIZZES	SIZABLE	UPGAZED	ZEBECKS
BEMAZED	CITIZEN	ENZYMES	GRAZIER	MATZOON	PIAZZAS	SIZIEST	UPGAZES	ZEBRASS
BENZALS	COALIZE	ENZYMIC	GRAZING	MATZOTH	PIZZLES	SIZINGS	UTILIZE	ZEBRINE
BENZENE	COGNIZE	EPIZOAN	GRIZZLE	MAZARDS	PODZOLS	SIZZLED	VIZARDS	ZEBROID
BENZILS	COROZOS	EPIZOIC	GRIZZLY	MAZEFUL	POETIZE	SIZZLER	VIZIERS	ZEBRULA
BENZINE	CORYZAS	EPIZOON	GUEREZA	MAZHBIS	POLYZOA	SIZZLES	VIZORED	ZEBRULE
BENZOIC	COZENED	EVZONES	GUIZERS	MAZIEST	POZZIES	SLEAZES	VIZSLAS	ZEDOARY
BENZOIN	COZENER	FAHLERZ	GUTZERS	MAZOUTS	PRENZIE	SNEEZED	VIZZIED	ZELANTS
BENZOLE	COZIERS	FANZINE	GUZZLED	MAZUMAS	PRETZEL	SNEEZER	VIZZIES	ZEMSTVO
BENZOLS	COZIEST	FEEZING	GUZZLER	MAZURKA	PREZZIE	SNEEZES	WALTZED	ZENANAS
BENZOYL	CRAZIER	FILAZER	GUZZLES	MAZZARD	PRIZERS	SNOOZED	WALTZER	ZENDIKS
BENZYLS	CRAZIES	FIZGIGS	HAMZAHS	MEAZELS	PRIZING	SNOOZER	WALTZES	ZENITHS

ZEOLITE	ZIFFIUS	ZINCIFY	ZINKIER	ZIZZING	ZONULAS	ZOOLOGY	ZORILLE	ZYGOTIC
ZEPHYRS	ZIGANKA	ZINCING	ZINKIFY	ZOARIUM	ZONULES	ZOOMING	ZORILLO	ZYMASES
ZEREBAS	ZIGGING	ZINCITE	ZINKING	ZOCCOLO	ZONULET	ZOONITE	ZORINOS	ZYMITES
ZERIBAS	ZIGZAGS	ZINCKED	ZINNIAS	ZODIACS	ZOOECIA	ZOONOMY	ZOSTERS	ZYMOGEN
ZEROING	ZILCHES	ZINCODE	ZIPPERS	ZOEFORM	ZOOGAMY	ZOOPERY	ZUFFOLI	ZYMOMES
ZESTFUL	ZILLAHS	ZINCOID	ZIPPIER	ZOISITE	ZOOGENY	ZOOTAXY	ZUFFOLO	ZYMOSES
ZESTIER	ZILLION	ZINCOUS	ZIPPING	ZOMBIES	ZOOGONY	ZOOTOMY	ZYGOMAS	ZYMOSIS
ZETETIC	ZIMMERS	ZINGELS	ZIRCONS	ZONATED	ZOOIDAL	ZOOTYPE	ZYGOSES	ZYMOTIC
ZEUGMAS	ZIMOCCA	ZINGIER	ZITHERN	ZONINGS	ZOOLITE	ZOOZOOS	ZYGOSIS	ZYMURGY
ZEUXITE	ZINCIER	ZINGING	ZITHERS	ZONULAR	ZOOLITH	ZORGITE	ZYGOTES	ZYTHUMS

Z - 8-letter words

ADONIZED	BAROMETZ	CANONIZE	DIMERIZE	FANZINES	GRAZIERS	LAICIZED	MUZZIEST
ADONIZES	BARTIZAN	CANZONAS	DISPRIZE	FARADIZE	GRAZINGS	LAICIZES	MUZZLERS
AGNIZING	BAZAZZES	CANZONET	DISSEIZE	FEMINIZE	GRAZIOSO	LAIRIZED	MUZZLING
AGONIZED	BAZOOKAS	CAPONIZE	DIVINIZE	FILAZERS	GRIZZLED	LAIRIZES	MYTHIZED
AGONIZES	BEDAZING	CAPSIZAL	DIZENING	FINALIZE	GRIZZLER	LAZARETS	MYTHIZES
AGRIZING	BEDAZZLE	CAPSIZED	DIZZARDS	FIZZGIGS	GRIZZLES	LAZINESS	NASALIZE
AGRYZING	BEDIZENS	CAPSIZES	DIZZIEST	FIZZIEST	GUEREZAS	LAZULITE	NEBULIZE
AGUIZING	BENZENES	CATALYZE	DIZZYING	FIZZINGS	GUZZLERS	LAZURITE	NODALIZE
ALBITIZE	BENZINES	CAZIQUES	DOCKIZED	FIZZLING	GUZZLING	LEGALIZE	NOMADIZE
ALCAZARS	BENZOATE	CHALAZAE	DOCKIZES	FLOOZIES	HAZARDED	LIONIZED	NOTARIZE
ALCORZAS	BENZOINS	CHALAZAS	DORIZING	FLUIDIZE	HAZARDRY	LIONIZES	NOVELIZE
ALGUAZIL	BENZOLES	CHINTZES	DOUZEPER	FOCALIZE	HAZELNUT	LOCALIZE	NUZZLING
ALIZARIN	BENZOYLS	CHORIZOS	DOZENING	FOOZLERS	HAZINESS	LOGICIZE	OBELIZED
ALIZARIS	BEZAZZES	CHUTZPAH	DOZENTHS	FOOZLING	HEPATIZE	LOZENGED	OBELIZES
ALKALIZE	BEZIQUES	CITIZENS	DOZINESS	FORZANDI	HEROIZED	LOZENGES	OOZINESS
ALTEZZAS	BEZONIAN	CIVILIZE	DRIZZLED	FORZANDO	HEROIZES	LYSOZYME	OPALIZED
AMAZEDLY	BEZZLING	COALIZED	DRIZZLES	FORZATOS	HOACTZIN	MACARIZE	OPTIMIZE
AMORTIZE	BIZAZZES	COALIZES	DYNAMIZE	FOZINESS	HOATZINS	MADERIZE	ORGANIZE
ANALYZED	BIZCACHA	COENZYME	EBENEZER	FRANZIER	HOLOZOIC	MADZOONS	ORGANZAS
ANALYZER	BLAZONED	COGNIZED	EBIONIZE	FRAZZLED	HORIZONS	MAGAZINE	OUTPRIZE
ANALYZES	BLAZONER	COGNIZES	EBONIZED	FRAZZLES	HOWITZER	MAHZORIM	OUTSIZED
ANNALIZE	BLAZONRY	COLONIZE	EBONIZES	FREEZERS	HUMANIZE	MANZELLO	OUTSIZES
ANODIZED	BLINTZES	COZENAGE	ECHOIZED	FREEZING	HUZZAING	MARZIPAN	OVERSIZE
ANODIZES	BLITZING	COZENERS	ECHOIZES	FRENZIED	HYDROZOA	MATZOONS	OXAZINES
ANTICIZE	BLIZZARD	COZENING	ECTOZOAN	FRENZIES	ICONIZED	MAXIMIZE	OXIDIZED
APHETIZE	BLOWZIER	CRAZIEST	ECTOZOIC	FRIEZING	ICONIZES	MAZARINE	OXIDIZER
APHORIZE	BONANZAS	CREDENZA	ECTOZOON	FRIZZIER	IDEALIZE	MAZEMENT	OXIDIZES
APPETIZE	BOOZIEST	CREUTZER	EGOTIZED	FRIZZING	IDOLIZED	MAZINESS	OZONISED
APPRIZED	BORAZONS	CROZIERS	EGOTIZES	FRIZZLED	IDOLIZER	MAZURKAS	OZONISER
APPRIZER	BOTANIZE	CRUZEIRO	ELEGIZED	FRIZZLES	IDOLIZES	MAZZARDS	OZONISES
APPRIZES	BOUZOUKI	CURARIZE	ELEGIZES	FROWZIER	IMMUNIZE	MELODIZE	OZONIZED
ARABIZED	BOZZETTI	CUTINIZE	EMBEZZLE	FURZIEST	INFAMIZE	MEMORIZE	OZONIZER
ARABIZES	BOZZETTO	CYANIZED	EMBLAZED	FUZZIEST	IODIZING	MESPRIZE	OZONIZES
ARCHAIZE	BRAZENED	CYANIZES	EMBLAZES	FUZZLING	IONIZERS	MESTIZAS	PAGANIZE
ARMOZEEN	BRAZENLY	CZARDOMS	EMBLAZON	GADZOOKS	IONIZING	MESTIZOS	PAPALIZE
ARMOZINE	BRAZENRY	CZAREVNA	EMPERIZE	GALLIZED	IRIDIZED	METAZOAN	PARALYZE
ASSIZERS	BRAZIERS	CZARINAS	ENDOZOIC	GALLIZES	IRIDIZES	METAZOIC	PARAZOAN
ASSIZING	BREEZIER	CZARISMS	ENDOZOON	GARBANZO	IRONIZED	METAZOON	PARAZOON
ATHEIZED	BREEZILY	CZARISTS	ENERGIZE	GAUZIEST	IRONIZES	MEZEREON	PARTIZAN
ATHEIZES	BREEZING	CZARITZA	ENFREEZE	GAZEBOES	ITEMIZED	MEZEREUM	PAZAZZES
ATHETIZE	BRITZKAS	DAMOZELS	ENFROZEN	GAZELLES	ITEMIZES	MEZUZAHS	PECTIZED
ATMOLYZE	BRITZSKA	DAZZLERS	ENTOZOAL	GAZEMENT	JACUZZIS	MEZUZOTH	PECTIZES
ATOMIZED	BRONZIER	DAZZLING	ENTOZOIC	GAZETTED	JANIZARS	MINIMIZE	PENALIZE
ATOMIZER	BRONZIFY	DEFREEZE	ENTOZOON	GAZETTES	JANIZARY	MISPRIZE	PEPTIZED
ATOMIZES	BRONZING	DEFROZEN	ENZONING	GAZOGENE	JAZERANT	MITZVAHS	PEPTIZES
AUTOLYZE	BRONZITE	DEFUZING	ENZOOTIC	GAZOOKAS	JAZZIEST	MITZVOTH	PETUNTZE
AZIMUTHS	BRUILZIE	DEMONIZE	EPIZOANS	GAZPACHO	JUMBOIZE	MIZMAZES	PEZIZOID
AZOTISED	BRULZIES	DENAZIFY	EQUALIZE	GAZUMPED	KAMEEZES	MIZZLIER	PHEAZARS
AZOTISES	BULLDOZE	DENIZENS	ERGOTIZE	GENIZAHS	KAMIKAZE	MIZZLING	PHEEZING
AZOTIZED	BUMBAZED	DEPUTIZE	ERSATZES	GIZZARDS	KAZATZKA	MOBILIZE	PIAZZIAN
AZOTIZES	BUMBAZES	DIALYZED	ETERNIZE	GIZZENED	KIBITZED	MONAZITE	PIROZHKI
AZULEJOS	BUZZARDS	DIALYZER	ETHERIZE	GLAZIERS	KIBITZER	MONETIZE	PIZAZZES
AZURINES	BUZZIEST	DIALYZES	ETHICIZE	GLAZIEST	KIBITZES	MORALIZE	PIZZERIA
AZURITES	BUZZINGS	DIARIZED	EULOGIZE	GLAZINGS	KRANTZES	MOTORIZE	POETIZED
AZYMITES	CADENZAS	DIARIZES	EUPHUIZE	GLITZIER	KREUTZER	MOZETTAS	POETIZES
BAPTIZED	CALZONES	DIAZEPAM	EXORCIZE	GLOZINGS	KYANIZED	MOZZETTA	POLARIZE
BAPTIZES	CANALIZE	DIGITIZE	FABULIZE	GOLDSIZE	KYANIZES	MUEZZINS	POLEMIZE

POLONIZE	RIGIDIZE	SLEEZIER	SUZERAIN	UNITIZES	ZABAIONE	ZIGZAGGY	ZOOMETRY
POLYZOAN	RIOTIZES	SMORZATO	SWAZZLES	UNMUZZLE	ZABTIEHS	ZIKKURAT	ZOOMORPH
POLYZOIC	RITZIEST	SNAZZIER	SWIZZLED	UNPRIZED	ZADDIKIM	ZILLIONS	ZOONITES
POLYZOON	RIVALIZE	SNEEZERS	SWIZZLES	UNSEIZED	ZAMARRAS	ZIMOCCAS	ZOONITIC
PRETZELS	RIZZARED	SNEEZIER	SWOZZLES	UNVIZARD	ZAMARROS	ZINCIEST	ZOONOMIA
PREZZIES	RIZZARTS	SNEEZING	SYZYGIAL	UNZIPPED	ZAMBOMBA	ZINCITES	ZOONOMIC
PRIZABLE	RIZZERED	SNOOZERS	SYZYGIES	UPGAZING	ZAMINDAR	ZINCKIER	ZOONOSES
PROTOZOA	RIZZORED	SNOOZING	TAILZIES	URBANIZE	ZAMOUSES	ZINCKIFY	ZOONOSIS
PTYALIZE	ROBOTIZE	SNOOZLED	TEAZELED	UTILIZED	ZAMPOGNA	ZINCKING	ZOONOTIC
PUZZLERS	ROYALIZE	SNOOZLES	TEAZLING	UTILIZER	ZANELLAS	ZINCODES	ZOOPATHY
PUZZLING	ROZELLES	SNUZZLED	TERRAZZO	UTILIZES	ZANJEROS	ZINGIBER	ZOOPERAL
PYRITIZE	ROZETING	SNUZZLES	TERZETTA	VALORIZE	ZANYISMS	ZINGIEST	ZOOPHILE
PYROLYZE	ROZITING	SOBERIZE	TERZETTI	VAPORIZE	ZAPPIEST	ZINKIEST	ZOOPHILY
QUANTIZE	RURALIZE	SODOMIZE	TERZETTO	VELARIZE	ZAPTIAHS	ZIPPERED	ZOOPHYTE
QUARTZES	SAMIZDAT	SOLARIZE	TETANIZE	VITALIZE	ZAPTIEHS	ZIPPIEST	ZOOSCOPY
QUATORZE	SANITIZE	SOLECIZE	THEORIZE	VIZAMENT	ZARATITE	ZIRCONIA	ZOOSPERM
QUEAZIER	SARRAZIN	SOLONETZ	THIAZIDE	VIZARDED	ZAREEBAS	ZIRCONIC	ZOOSPORE
QUETZALS	SATIRIZE	SORORIZE	TIZWASES	VIZCACHA	ZARNICHS	ZITHERNS	ZOOTHOME
QUIZZERS	SAZERACS	SOZZLIER	TOPAZINE	VIZIRATE	ZARZUELA	ZOARIUMS	ZOOTOMIC
QUIZZERY	SCHERZOS	SOZZLING	TOTALIZE	VIZIRIAL	ZASTRUGA	ZOCCOLOS	ZOOTOXIN
QUIZZIFY	SCHIZOID	SPETSNAZ	TOUZLING	VIZORING	ZASTRUGI	ZODIACAL	ZOOTROPE
QUIZZING	SCHIZONT	SPETZNAZ	TRAPEZED	VOCALIZE	ZEALANTS	ZOETROPE	ZOOTYPES
RACEMIZE	SCHMALTZ	SPREAZED	TRAPEZES	VOWELIZE	ZEALLESS	ZOIATRIA	ZOOTYPIC
RAZEEING	SCHMOOZE	SPREAZES	TRAPEZIA	WALTZERS	ZEALOTRY	ZOISITES	ZOPILOTE
RAZMATAZ	SCRUZING	SPREEZED	TRIZONAL	WALTZING	ZEBRINNY	ZOMBIISM	ZORGITES
REALIZED	SEIZABLE	SPREEZES	TRIZONES	WEAZANDS	ZEBRULAS	ZOMBORUK	ZORILLES
REALIZER	SEIZINGS	SPRITZER	TUILZIED	WEAZENED	ZEBRULES	ZONATION	ZORILLOS
REALIZES	SEIZURES	SPRITZIG	TUILZIES	WHAIZLED	ZECCHINE	ZONELESS	ZUCCHINI
REFREEZE	SELTZERS	SPUILZIE	TUTORIZE	WHAIZLES	ZECCHINI	ZONULETS	ZUCHETTA
REFROZEN	SFORZATI	SPULZIED	TWEEZERS	WHEEZIER	ZECCHINO	ZOOBLAST	ZUCHETTO
REGULIZE	SFORZATO	SPULZIES	TWEEZING	WHEEZILY	ZEMINDAR	ZOOCHORE	ZUGZWANG
RENDZINA	SHMOOZED	SQUEEZED	TWIZZLED	WHEEZING	ZEMSTVOS	ZOOCHORY	ZYGAENID
REPRIZED	SHMOOZES	SQUEEZER	TWIZZLES	WHEEZLED	ZENITHAL	ZOOCYTIA	ZYGANTRA
REPRIZES	SIAMEZED	SQUEEZES	TZADDIKS	WHEEZLES	ZEOLITES	ZOOECIUM	ZYGODONT
RESEIZED	SIAMEZES	STANZAIC	TZADDIQS	WHIZZERS	ZEOLITIC	ZOOGENIC	ZYLONITE
RESEIZES	SIMILIZE	STANZOES	UNAMAZED	WHIZZING	ZEPPELIN	ZOOGLOEA	ZYMOGENS
RESINIZE	SINICIZE	STRELITZ	UNDAZZLE	WIZARDLY	ZERUMBET	ZOOGRAFT	ZYMOLOGY
RHIZINES	SIZEABLE	STYLIZED	UNFREEZE	WIZARDRY	ZESTIEST	ZOOLATER	ZYMOTICS
RHIZOBIA	SIZINESS	STYLIZES	UNFROZEN	WIZENING	ZETETICS	ZOOLATRY	
RHIZOIDS	SIZZLERS	SUBERIZE	UNGLAZED	WOMANIZE	ZEUXITES	ZOOLITES	
RHIZOMES	SIZZLING	SUBSIZAR	UNGRAZED	WOOZIEST	ZIBELINE	ZOOLITHS	
RHIZOPOD	SLEAZIER	SUBZONAL	UNIONIZE	WURTZITE	ZIGANKAS	ZOOLITIC	
RHIZOPUS	SLEAZILY	SUBZONES	UNITIZED	WUZZLING	ZIGGURAT	ZOOMANCY	

HINT

Q But No U

If you are not familiar with *Official Scrabble Words* you may be unaware that there are several words that contain Q with no U. These are all to be found in the Q lists but it is worth highlighting them separately. Write them down and learn them all. They are so vital in situations that would otherwise necessitate a change.

INQILAB, QADI, QALAMDAN, QANAT, QAT, QIBLA, QIGONG, QINTAR, QWERTY, TALAQ, TSADDIQ, TSADDIQIM, TZADDIQ, TZADDIQIM

Note that plural forms of these are also allowed except for TSADDIQIM and TZADDIQIM which are already plural. Also note BURQA, MUQADDAM and SUQ have a U but not after the Q.

HINT

Do-It-Yourself Six-Letter Sets

The 200 six-letter combinations in this book represent those most useful to the Scrabble player. There are many more combinations that are useful to study and, as is nearly always the case, compiling lists yourself not only helps you memorize the words but is also more interesting than simply learning from those readily provided. Try deriving your own six-letter combination lists based on names (SHEILA, ALBERT, etc) or fictitious words (INCORE, POSIER, etc) as mnemonics. The Anagram section will be your ideal hunting-ground for this exercise.

HINT

Learning The J Q X Z Words

If you have trouble remembering those useful words containg the J Q X or Z then try the following solo game as a learning exercise. Take the J X Z Q and one U out of the letter bag and put to one side. Take six letters at random from the letter bag and place on your rack. Then give yourself a couple of minutes with each of J Q X and Z to see how many different words you can make by combining them with the six letters on your rack. When playing with the Q, if you haven't also picked a U, utilize the U you you've put to one side. Make a note of the highest scoring play you found with each of J Q X and Z and then check with the lists in this book to see if there was anything you missed. Having completed the exercise with the first rack, play any word from your six letters on the board, keeping the J Q X Z and U to one side, and return any remaining letters to the bag. Select another six letters at random for the second turn. repeat the exercise with the fresh rack and so on.

HINT

Tile-Tracking

It is acceptable in tournament Scrabble to have a note of the letter distribution and to use it during play as a checklist of what letters are still to come. Most top players use this method to enable them to work out what tiles their opponents have at the end of the game. Such a checklist, when used skilfully, can also provide mid-game information about likely pickups and enable the right combination of tiles to be kept on the rack to give the greatest possibility of playing a bonus word. If you practise tile-tracking whilst playing you will soon find you are more aware of the letter distribution which in turn will assist you to maintain a balanced rack. Even if you don't track all the tiles, keeping a note of the vowels, the S's and blanks, the J Q X Z and the awkward consonants C V and K, will help improve your rack management.

SECTION TWO

ENDINGS

Introduction

Scrabble players naturally think about beginnings of words when they are looking for a play. Can I find a word beginning with BE- or DIS- or QU- or RE- or UN-? As a player becomes more adept, he or she will consider the more obvious endings, such as -ED and -ER and -IER and -ING, and even the humble -S.

The subsequent lists offer a variety of words arranged according to their endings rather than their beginnings. The first set of lists covers useful suffixes, and the second set of lists addresses words ending with the vowels A, I, O and U.

USEFUL SUFFIXES

The following sets of lists offer seven and eight-letter words ending with these suffixes:

-ABLE	-IBLE	-MAN
-AGE	-INGS	-MEN
-EST	-ISH	-OUS
-FUL	-LY	-TION

Those ending with -INGS, -LY and -EST should be especially useful. There are many times that Scrabble players ponder questions such as:

'I know HOSTING is a word, but does it take an S?'
'I know SULTRY is all right, but what about SULTRILY?'
'I know the adjective OARY, but is the superlative OARIEST acceptable?'

Familiarity with the lists here should provide instant answers to these and similar questions. In the case of the -EST words, where these are superlatives, it can be implied that the corresponding comparatives ending in -ER are also acceptable, eg OARIER.

There are naturally many other endings useful to the Scrabble player besides those listed here, -OID, -ISM and -IST for example. Those shown here are meant only as a selection. For easy compilation of lists of other endings consult *Chambers Back-Words*, which shows all words according to alphabetical sequence of endings.

WORDS ENDING IN -ABLE

7-letter words -ABLE

ACCABLE	CURABLE	EFFABLE	HATABLE	MIXABLE	PAYABLE	RULABLE	TAKABLE	VOLABLE
AFFABLE	DATABLE	EQUABLE	HIRABLE	MOVABLE	PLIABLE	SALABLE	TAMABLE	
AMIABLE	DISABLE	ERRABLE	LIKABLE	MUTABLE	POTABLE	SAVABLE	TAXABLE	
ASTABLE	DOWABLE	FADABLE	LIVABLE	NAMABLE	RATABLE	SAYABLE	TENABLE	
BATABLE	DUPABLE	FINABLE	LOSABLE	NOTABLE	RETABLE	SEEABLE	TRIABLE	
BUYABLE	DURABLE	FIXABLE	LOVABLE	PACABLE	RIDABLE	SIZABLE	TUNABLE	
CAPABLE	DYEABLE	FLYABLE	MAKABLE	PAPABLE	ROPABLE	SKIABLE	UNHABLE	
CITABLE	EATABLE	FRIABLE	MIRABLE	PARABLE	ROWABLE	SUEABLE	VOCABLE	

8-letter words -ABLE

ABATABLE	BOOKABLE	ERASABLE	GUIDABLE	ISSUABLE	MAILABLE	PINTABLE	RENTABLE
ADORABLE	CLUBABLE	EVADABLE	GULLABLE	KICKABLE	MAKEABLE	PITIABLE	REUSABLE
AMENABLE	COOKABLE	EVITABLE	GUSTABLE	KISSABLE	MISSABLE	PLACABLE	RIDEABLE
AMICABLE	CULPABLE	EXORABLE	HANGABLE	KNOWABLE	MOCKABLE	PLAYABLE	RINSABLE
AMUSABLE	CURBABLE	EXPIABLE	HATEABLE	LAPSABLE	MOOTABLE	PORTABLE	ROLLABLE
ARGUABLE	DAMNABLE	FELLABLE	HEALABLE	LAUDABLE	MOVEABLE	POSEABLE	ROPEABLE
AVOWABLE	DATEABLE	FILMABLE	HELPABLE	LEASABLE	NAMEABLE	POURABLE	RUINABLE
BAILABLE	DENIABLE	FISHABLE	HIREABLE	LETTABLE	OATHABLE	PRIZABLE	RUNNABLE
BANKABLE	DIGGABLE	FOLDABLE	HUGGABLE	LEVIABLE	OPENABLE	PROBABLE	SAILABLE
BEARABLE	DISHABLE	FORDABLE	HUMMABLE	LIFTABLE	OPERABLE	PROVABLE	SALEABLE
BEATABLE	DRAWABLE	FORMABLE	IMITABLE	LIKEABLE	OPINABLE	QUOTABLE	SALVABLE
BEDDABLE	DRIVABLE	FUNDABLE	INARABLE	LIQUABLE	PALPABLE	RAISABLE	SATIABLE
BIDDABLE	DUTIABLE	GAINABLE	INSTABLE	LIVEABLE	PANTABLE	RATEABLE	SCALABLE
BISTABLE	EDUCABLE	GETTABLE	INVIABLE	LOANABLE	PASSABLE	READABLE	SEIZABLE
BLAMABLE	ENVIABLE	GRADABLE	ISOLABLE	LOVEABLE	PECCABLE	RELIABLE	SELLABLE

SHAKABLE	SOLVABLE	SYLLABLE	TELLABLE	TRADABLE	VARIABLE	WARHABLE	WORKABLE
SHAPABLE	SORTABLE	TAKEABLE	TESTABLE	TUNEABLE	VIEWABLE	WASHABLE	WRITABLE
SINGABLE	SPARABLE	TALKABLE	TILLABLE	UNSTABLE	VIOLABLE	WEARABLE	
SIZEABLE	STATABLE	TAMEABLE	TILTABLE	UNUSABLE	VITIABLE	WELDABLE	
SMOKABLE	STORABLE	TANNABLE	TITHABLE	UNVIABLE	VOIDABLE	WILLABLE	
SOCIABLE	SUITABLE	TASTABLE	TOLLABLE	VALUABLE	WALKABLE	WINNABLE	

WORDS ENDING IN -AGE

7-letter words -AGE

ABUSAGE	BROKAGE	CRANAGE	GUNNAGE	MILEAGE	PLUSAGE	SACKAGE	TANKAGE	VINTAGE
ACREAGE	BUOYAGE	DISCAGE	HAULAGE	MINTAGE	PONDAGE	SALVAGE	TANNAGE	VITRAGE
AJUTAGE	BURGAGE	DOCKAGE	HERBAGE	MOCKAGE	PONTAGE	SAUSAGE	TEENAGE	VOLTAGE
AMENAGE	CABBAGE	DRAYAGE	HOSTAGE	MONTAGE	PORTAGE	SCAVAGE	TENTAGE	WAFTAGE
APANAGE	CARNAGE	DUNNAGE	KEELAGE	MOORAGE	POSTAGE	SCUTAGE	THANAGE	WAINAGE
ARRIAGE	CARTAGE	ESCUAGE	KIPPAGE	MOULAGE	POTTAGE	SEEPAGE	TILLAGE	WANTAGE
ASSUAGE	CENTAGE	ETALAGE	LAIRAGE	OUTRAGE	PRESAGE	SELVAGE	TOLLAGE	WASTAGE
ASSWAGE	COINAGE	FALDAGE	LASTAGE	OUVRAGE	PRIMAGE	SERFAGE	TONNAGE	WATTAGE
AULNAGE	COLLAGE	FARDAGE	LEAFAGE	PACKAGE	PRISAGE	SINKAGE	TRUCAGE	WEFTAGE
AVERAGE	COMPAGE	FLOTAGE	LEAKAGE	PANNAGE	PROPAGE	SOAKAGE	TUNNAGE	WINDAGE
BAGGAGE	CORDAGE	FLOWAGE	LIGNAGE	PASSAGE	QUAYAGE	SOCCAGE	UMBRAGE	WORDAGE
BANDAGE	CORKAGE	FOGGAGE	LINEAGE	PAYSAGE	RAMPAGE	SONDAGE	UPSTAGE	YARDAGE
BARRAGE	CORNAGE	FOLIAGE	LINKAGE	PEERAGE	REMUAGE	SPINAGE	VANTAGE	
BONDAGE	CORSAGE	FOOTAGE	LOCKAGE	PEONAGE	RESTAGE	STORAGE	VENDAGE	
BOSCAGE	COTTAGE	FULLAGE	LUGGAGE	PIERAGE	RIBCAGE	STOWAGE	VENTAGE	
BREWAGE	COURAGE	GARBAGE	MASSAGE	PILLAGE	ROOTAGE	SULLAGE	VIDUAGE	
BROCAGE	COWHAGE	GUIDAGE	MESSAGE	PLUMAGE	RUMMAGE	TALLAGE	VILLAGE	

8-letter words -AGE

ACCORAGE	BLOCKAGE	DIALLAGE	FRONDAGE	MALAXAGE	PUPILAGE	STEERAGE	TUTORAGE
ACIERAGE	BREAKAGE	DISUSAGE	FRONTAGE	MARITAGE	ROUGHAGE	STERNAGE	UMPIRAGE
ADJUTAGE	BROCKAGE	DRAINAGE	FROTTAGE	MARRIAGE	SABOTAGE	STILLAGE	VAULTAGE
AGIOTAGE	CABOTAGE	DRESSAGE	FRUITAGE	MESSUAGE	SEWERAGE	STOPPAGE	VAUNTAGE
ALIENAGE	CARRIAGE	DRIFTAGE	FUSELAGE	METAYAGE	SHORTAGE	STREWAGE	VERBIAGE
ALTARAGE	CARUCAGE	ENALLAGE	GRAINAGE	MISUSAGE	SLIPPAGE	STUMPAGE	VICARAGE
AMPERAGE	CHANTAGE	ENDAMAGE	GRILLAGE	MORTGAGE	SMALLAGE	SUBSTAGE	VICINAGE
APPANAGE	CHUMMAGE	ENSILAGE	GROUPAGE	MUCILAGE	SPILLAGE	SUFFRAGE	WAGONAGE
BADINAGE	CLEARAGE	ENVISAGE	GUARDAGE	OVERPAGE	SPOILAGE	TASSWAGE	WATERAGE
BARONAGE	CLEAVAGE	EQUIPAGE	HELOTAGE	PILOTAGE	SPOUSAGE	THIRLAGE	WEIGHAGE
BERTHAGE	CLOUDAGE	FERRIAGE	HERITAGE	PLANTAGE	SQUIRAGE	TRACKAGE	WHARFAGE
BEVERAGE	COVERAGE	FLOATAGE	LANGRAGE	PLUSSAGE	STAFFAGE	TRUCKAGE	WRAPPAGE
BIRDCAGE	COZENAGE	FOOTPAGE	LANGUAGE	POUNDAGE	STALLAGE	TRUQUAGE	WRECKAGE
BLINDAGE	CRIBBAGE	FRAUTAGE	LEVERAGE	PUCELAGE	STEARAGE	TUTELAGE	

WORDS ENDING IN -EST

7-letter words -EST

ACHIEST	BABIEST	CAMPEST	DANKEST	DOPIEST	EERIEST	FOXIEST	HAZIEST	JOKIEST
ACIDEST	BALDEST	CANIEST	DARKEST	DOTIEST	EGGIEST	FOZIEST	HEPPEST	JUSTEST
ACQUEST	BARGEST	CANTEST	DEADEST	DOUCEST	ELMIEST	FULLEST	HIGHEST	KEENEST
ACUTEST	BASSEST	CHICEST	DEAFEST	DOUREST	EVENEST	FUMIEST	HIPPEST	KINDEST
ADDREST	BEQUEST	CLOSEST	DEAREST	DOVIEST	FABBEST	GABFEST	HOKIEST	LACIEST
AERIEST	BIGGEST	COKIEST	DEEDEST	DOWIEST	FADIEST	GAINEST	HOLIEST	LAKIEST
AGILEST	BLATEST	COLDEST	DEEPEST	DOZIEST	FAINEST	GAMIEST	HOMIEST	LANGEST
AIRIEST	BLUIEST	CONFEST	DEFTEST	DROLEST	FAIREST	GAZIEST	HOTTEST	LANKEST
AMPLEST	BOLDEST	CONGEST	DEIDEST	DUFFEST	FALSEST	GLUIEST	ICKIEST	LARGEST
ANAPEST	BONIEST	CONTEST	DENSEST	DULLEST	FASTEST	GOLDEST	IFFIEST	LAZIEST
ARCHEST	BOSSEST	COOLEST	DEWIEST	DUMBEST	FATTEST	GOOIEST	IMPREST	LEANEST
ARIDEST	BOXIEST	COSIEST	DICIEST	DUNNEST	FELLEST	GORIEST	INANEST	LENGEST
ARTIEST	BRAVEST	COXIEST	DIKIEST	DUSKEST	FIKIEST	GOWDEST	INKIEST	LEWDEST
ASHIEST	BRAWEST	COZIEST	DIMMEST	DYKIEST	FIRMEST	GRAVEST	INLIEST	LIEFEST
AULDEST	BUSIEST	CRUDEST	DINKEST	EARNEST	FITTEST	GRAYEST	INQUEST	LIEVEST
AVIDEST	CAGIEST	CURTEST	DISGEST	EASIEST	FLUIEST	GREYEST	IRATEST	LIMIEST
AWAREST	CAKIEST	DAFTEST	DISNEST	EDGIEST	FONDEST	HARDEST	ISMIEST	LIMPEST
AWNIEST	CALMEST	DAMPEST	DOMIEST	EELIEST	FOULEST	HARVEST	JIMPEST	LINIEST

LITHEST	MIMMEST	NUMBEST	PINIEST	RATHEST	SAIREST	STEYEST	TRITEST	WAVIEST
LONGEST	MINIEST	OAKIEST	PINKEST	REALEST	SALTEST	SUAVEST	TUNIEST	WAXIEST
LOOSEST	MIRIEST	OARIEST	PIPIEST	REDDEST	SAMIEST	SUGGEST	UGLIEST	WEAKEST
LOTHEST	MIRKEST	OBESEST	POKIEST	REQUEST	SEAREST	TAKIEST	UNBLEST	WETTEST
LOUDEST	MITIEST	OILIEST	POOREST	RICHEST	SEXIEST	TALLEST	UNDREST	WHITEST
LOWSEST	MIXIEST	OORIEST	PORIEST	RICIEST	SICKEST	TANNEST	VAGUEST	WILDEST
LUSHEST	MOOTEST	OOSIEST	POSHEST	RIMIEST	SIZIEST	TARTEST	VAINEST	WILIEST
MADDEST	MOPIEST	OOZIEST	POXIEST	ROKIEST	SKEWEST	TAUTEST	VASTEST	WILLEST
MAINEST	MOTIEST	OPENEST	PRONEST	ROPIEST	SKYIEST	TEDIEST	VERIEST	WINIEST
MATIEST	MURKEST	ORBIEST	PROTEST	RORIEST	SLOWEST	TEMPEST	VINIEST	WIRIEST
MAUVEST	NAIFEST	OURIEST	PROWEST	ROSIEST	SNIDEST	TENSEST	VOGIEST	WOTTEST
MAZIEST	NAIVEST	OUTJEST	PUIREST	RUBIEST	SOFTEST	TERSEST	WALIEST	WOWFEST
MEANEST	NEAREST	OWLIEST	PULIEST	RULIEST	SOONEST	TIDIEST	WANIEST	YUKIEST
MEEKEST	NEATEST	OWRIEST	PUNIEST	RUMMEST	SOUREST	TINIEST	WANNEST	ZANIEST
MEETEST	NIGHEST	PACIEST	RACIEST	SADDEST	SPAREST	TONIEST	WARIEST	
MIDDEST	NOBLEST	PALIEST	RANKEST	SAGIEST	SPRYEST	TOOMEST	WARMEST	
MILDEST	NOSIEST	PERTEST	RASHEST	SAIDEST	STALEST	TOWIEST	WATTEST	

8-letter words -EST

ACERBEST	BOOZIEST	COMBIEST	DOTTIEST	FLAMIEST	GENTIEST	HEADIEST	KINKIEST
ACRIDEST	BOSKIEST	COMFIEST	DOTTLEST	FLARIEST	GENTLEST	HEADREST	KITTLEST
ADEPTEST	BOSSIEST	CONQUEST	DOWDIEST	FLASHEST	GIDDIEST	HEAPIEST	KOOKIEST
AFFOREST	BOUSIEST	COOMIEST	DOWNIEST	FLATTEST	GIRNIEST	HEAVIEST	LAIGHEST
ALCAHEST	BRAIDEST	COPSIEST	DRABBEST	FLAWIEST	GLADDEST	HEDGIEST	LAIRIEST
ALERTEST	BRAKIEST	CORKIEST	DREAREST	FLAXIEST	GLADIEST	HEFTIEST	LANKIEST
ALKAHEST	BRASHEST	CORNIEST	DROLLEST	FLEETEST	GLARIEST	HEMPIEST	LARDIEST
ANAPAEST	BRENTEST	COUTHEST	DRONIEST	FLIPPEST	GLAZIEST	HENNIEST	LARKIEST
ANGRIEST	BRIEFEST	CRANKEST	DRUNKEST	FLORIEST	GLEGGEST	HERBIEST	LATHIEST
ARBALEST	BRINIEST	CRAPIEST	DRUSIEST	FLUKIEST	GLIBBEST	HILLIEST	LAWNIEST
ARTSIEST	BRISKEST	CRASSEST	DRUXIEST	FLUSHEST	GLIDDEST	HIPPIEST	LEADIEST
ASTUTEST	BROADEST	CRAZIEST	DUCKIEST	FLUTIEST	GLUMMEST	HOARIEST	LEAFIEST
BAGGIEST	BROWNEST	CREPIEST	DUDDIEST	FOAMIEST	GOATIEST	HOARSEST	LEAKIEST
BALKIEST	BUDDIEST	CRISPEST	DULLIEST	FOGGIEST	GODLIEST	HOOKIEST	LEARIEST
BALMIEST	BULGIEST	CRONKEST	DUMMIEST	FOOTIEST	GOLDIEST	HOOLIEST	LEAVIEST
BANALEST	BULKIEST	CROOKEST	DUMPIEST	FOOTREST	GOODIEST	HOPPIEST	LEDGIEST
BANDIEST	BULLIEST	CROSSEST	DUNGIEST	FORKIEST	GOOFIEST	HORNIEST	LEERIEST
BARDIEST	BUMPIEST	CRUMPEST	DUNNIEST	FRAILEST	GOOPIEST	HORSIEST	LEGGIEST
BARGHEST	BUNTIEST	CURDIEST	DURGIEST	FRANKEST	GOOSIEST	HUFFIEST	LEISHEST
BARKIEST	BURLIEST	CURLIEST	DUSKIEST	FRESHEST	GORMIEST	HULKIEST	LICHTEST
BARMIEST	BURRIEST	CURNIEST	DUSTIEST	FROWIEST	GORSIEST	HULLIEST	LIGHTEST
BASSIEST	BUSHIEST	CURVIEST	EARLIEST	FUBBIEST	GOUTIEST	HUMANEST	LINGIEST
BATTIEST	BUSTIEST	CUSHIEST	EMONGEST	FUBSIEST	GRANDEST	HUMBLEST	LINTIEST
BAWDIEST	BUTCHEST	CUTTIEST	EMPTIEST	FUFFIEST	GRAPIEST	HUMIDEST	LIPPIEST
BEADIEST	BUXOMEST	DAFFIEST	ENFOREST	FUGGIEST	GREATEST	HUMPIEST	LITTLEST
BEAMIEST	BUZZIEST	DAMPIEST	EVILLEST	FUNKIEST	GREENEST	HUNKIEST	LIVIDEST
BEEFIEST	CADGIEST	DANDIEST	EXACTEST	FUNNIEST	GRIMIEST	HUSHIEST	LOAMIEST
BEERIEST	CALMIEST	DAUBIEST	FADDIEST	FURRIEST	GRIMMEST	HUSKIEST	LOATHEST
BENDIEST	CAMPIEST	DEBBIEST	FAINTEST	FURTHEST	GRITTEST	IMMODEST	LOFTIEST
BENTIEST	CANNIEST	DEEDIEST	FANCIEST	FURZIEST	GROSSEST	IMPUREST	LOOBIEST
BILGIEST	CANTIEST	DEFOREST	FARTHEST	FUSSIEST	GRUFFEST	INDIGEST	LOONIEST
BIRSIEST	CARNIEST	DEMUREST	FATTIEST	FUSTIEST	GRUMMEST	INEPTEST	LOOPIEST
BITSIEST	CATTIEST	DICKIEST	FEEBLEST	FUTILEST	GUCKIEST	INERTEST	LOSSIEST
BITTIEST	CAULDEST	DICTIEST	FEINTEST	FUZZIEST	GULFIEST	INSANEST	LOURIEST
BLACKEST	CHARIEST	DILLIEST	FENDIEST	GABBIEST	GUMMIEST	INTEREST	LOUSIEST
BLANDEST	CHASTEST	DINGIEST	FENNIEST	GAMMIEST	GUNGIEST	ITCHIEST	LOWLIEST
BLANKEST	CHEAPEST	DINKIEST	FERLIEST	GAPPIEST	GURLIEST	JAGGIEST	LUCIDEST
BLEAKEST	CHEWIEST	DIPPIEST	FERNIEST	GASPIEST	GUSHIEST	JAMMIEST	LUCKIEST
BLEAREST	CHIEFEST	DIRTIEST	FETIDEST	GASSIEST	GUSTIEST	JANTIEST	LUMMIEST
BLINDEST	CHILLEST	DISHIEST	FICKLEST	GAUCHEST	GUTSIEST	JAZZIEST	LUMPIEST
BLITHEST	CHOICEST	DIVINEST	FIERCEST	GAUCIEST	HAILIEST	JEMMIEST	LURIDEST
BLONDEST	CHOKIEST	DIZZIEST	FIERIEST	GAUDIEST	HAIRIEST	JERKIEST	LUSHIEST
BLOWIEST	CISSIEST	DOCILEST	FILMIEST	GAUMIEST	HAMMIEST	JETTIEST	LUSTIEST
BLUDIEST	CLAYIEST	DODDIEST	FINNIEST	GAUNTEST	HANDIEST	JIMPIEST	MALTIEST
BLUFFEST	CLEANEST	DODGIEST	FIRRIEST	GAUZIEST	HANGNEST	JOLLIEST	MANGIEST
BLUNTEST	CLEAREST	DOGGIEST	FISHIEST	GAWCIEST	HAPPIEST	JOLTIEST	MANIFEST
BOGGIEST	COALIEST	DOILTEST	FISTIEST	GAWKIEST	HARDIEST	JUICIEST	MANKIEST
BONNIEST	COARSEST	DONSIEST	FITLIEST	GAWSIEST	HARSHEST	JUMPIEST	MANLIEST
BOOKIEST	COBBIEST	DOOMIEST	FIZZIEST	GELIDEST	HASHIEST	JUNKIEST	MARDIEST
BOOKREST	COCKIEST	DORTIEST	FLAKIEST	GEMMIEST	HASTIEST	KEDGIEST	MARLIEST

MASHIEST	NETTIEST	PONGIEST	RITZIEST	SHORTEST	SPIRIEST	TEUCHEST	VIVIDEST
MASSIEST	NEWSIEST	POOFIEST	ROARIEST	SHOWIEST	SPRUCEST	TEUGHEST	VOGUIEST
MASTIEST	NIFFIEST	POOVIEST	ROCKIEST	SILKIEST	SPUMIEST	THAWIEST	VUGGIEST
MATUREST	NIFTIEST	PORKIEST	ROILIEST	SILLIEST	SQUAREST	THEWIEST	WACKIEST
MAWKIEST	NIMBLEST	PORTIEST	ROOFIEST	SILTIEST	STABLEST	THICKEST	WALLIEST
MEAGREST	NIPPIEST	POTTIEST	ROOMIEST	SIMPLEST	STAGIEST	THINNEST	WALTIEST
MEALIEST	NIRLIEST	POUTIEST	ROOPIEST	SINKIEST	STAIDEST	THYMIEST	WARBIEST
MEATIEST	NITTIEST	PRICIEST	ROOTIEST	SISSIEST	STARKEST	TICHIEST	WARTIEST
MERRIEST	NOBBIEST	PRIMMEST	RORTIEST	SKIEYEST	STEEPEST	TIDDIEST	WASHIEST
MESHIEST	NOISIEST	PRIVIEST	ROUGHEST	SKINTEST	STEEVEST	TIGHTEST	WASPIEST
MESSIEST	NOOKIEST	PROSIEST	ROUNDEST	SKIVIEST	STERNEST	TILLIEST	WEARIEST
MIFFIEST	NOUNIEST	PROUDEST	ROUPIEST	SLACKEST	STEWIEST	TIMIDEST	WEBBIEST
MIGHTEST	NUBBIEST	PUDGIEST	ROWDIEST	SLATIEST	STIEVEST	TINNIEST	WEEDIEST
MILKIEST	NUTTIEST	PUDSIEST	RUDDIEST	SLEEKEST	STIFFEST	TINTIEST	WEENIEST
MINGIEST	OBTUSEST	PUFFIEST	RUGGIEST	SLICKEST	STILLEST	TIPPIEST	WEEPIEST
MINTIEST	OFTENEST	PUGGIEST	RUMMIEST	SLIMIEST	STIVIEST	TIPSIEST	WEIRDEST
MINUTEST	OPAQUEST	PULPIEST	RUNNIEST	SLIMMEST	STONIEST	TIREDEST	WENNIEST
MIRKIEST	ORANGEST	PURPLEST	RUNTIEST	SLOPIEST	STOUTEST	TOFFIEST	WERSHEST
MIRLIEST	ORNATEST	PURSIEST	RUSHIEST	SLUGFEST	SUBTLEST	TOSHIEST	WHEYIEST
MISSIEST	OUNDIEST	PURTIEST	RUSTIEST	SMALLEST	SUDSIEST	TOSSIEST	WHINIEST
MISTIEST	OUTWREST	PUSHIEST	RUTTIEST	SMARTEST	SUETIEST	TOTTIEST	WHITIEST
MOISTEST	OVERKEST	QUAKIEST	SAGGIEST	SMOKIEST	SULKIEST	TOUGHEST	WIMPIEST
MOODIEST	PALLIEST	QUEEREST	SAILIEST	SMUGGEST	SUNNIEST	TOUSIEST	WINDIEST
MOONIEST	PALMIEST	QUICKEST	SALTIEST	SNAKIEST	SUPPLEST	TOUTIEST	WINGIEST
MOORIEST	PALSIEST	QUIETEST	SANDIEST	SNARIEST	SURFIEST	TOWNIEST	WISPIEST
MOPPIEST	PAPPIEST	RABIDEST	SAPPIEST	SNELLEST	SURGIEST	TOWSIEST	WITHIEST
MOROSEST	PARKIEST	RAGGIEST	SARKIEST	SNIPIEST	SURLIEST	TRIGGEST	WITTIEST
MOSSIEST	PASTIEST	RAINIEST	SASSIEST	SNOWIEST	SVELTEST	TRIMMEST	WONKIEST
MOTHIEST	PAWKIEST	RANDIEST	SAUCIEST	SNUGGEST	SWALIEST	TUBBIEST	WOODIEST
MOTLIEST	PEAKIEST	RANGIEST	SAVAGEST	SOAPIEST	SWANKEST	TUFTIEST	WOOFIEST
MOTTIEST	PEATIEST	RAPIDEST	SCALIEST	SOBEREST	SWEETEST	TURFIEST	WOOZIEST
MOUSIEST	PEERIEST	RASPIEST	SCANTEST	SODDIEST	SWELLEST	TUSKIEST	WORDIEST
MUCKIEST	PEPPIEST	RATTIEST	SCARCEST	SOGGIEST	SWIFTEST	TWINIEST	WORMIEST
MUDDIEST	PERKIEST	RAUCLEST	SCARIEST	SOILIEST	SWIPIEST	UNHONEST	WRONGEST
MUGGIEST	PESKIEST	READIEST	SEAMIEST	SOLIDEST	SWISHEST	UNIQUEST	YAWNIEST
MUMSIEST	PETTIEST	REAMIEST	SECUREST	SOMBREST	TACKIEST	UNPRIEST	YOLKIEST
MURKIEST	PHONIEST	REARREST	SEDATEST	SONGFEST	TALKFEST	UNRIPEST	YOUNGEST
MURLIEST	PICKIEST	REDDIEST	SEDGIEST	SONSIEST	TANGIEST	UNSAFEST	YUCKIEST
MUSHIEST	PIGGIEST	REEDIEST	SEEDIEST	SOOTHEST	TARDIEST	UNSUREST	YUKKIEST
MUSKIEST	PINKIEST	REEKIEST	SEELIEST	SOOTIEST	TARRIEST	UNTRUEST	YUMMIEST
MUSSIEST	PIPPIEST	REINVEST	SEEPIEST	SOPPIEST	TARTIEST	UNWISEST	ZAPPIEST
MUSTIEST	PITHIEST	REMOTEST	SEMPLEST	SORRIEST	TASTIEST	URBANEST	ZESTIEST
MUZZIEST	PLAINEST	RESTIEST	SERENEST	SOUNDEST	TATTIEST	UTTEREST	ZINCIEST
NAGGIEST	PLATIEST	RIBBIEST	SEVEREST	SOUPIEST	TAWNIEST	VAIRIEST	ZINGIEST
NAKEDEST	PLUMIEST	RICHTEST	SHADIEST	SPACIEST	TAWTIEST	VALIDEST	ZINKIEST
NAPPIEST	PLUMPEST	RIDGIEST	SHAKIEST	SPARSEST	TEARIEST	VAPIDEST	ZIPPIEST
NARKIEST	PLUSHEST	RIFTIEST	SHALIEST	SPEWIEST	TECHIEST	VASTIEST	
NASTIEST	POCKIEST	RIGHTEST	SHARPEST	SPICIEST	TEENIEST	VEALIEST	
NATTIEST	PODDIEST	RIGIDEST	SHEEREST	SPICKEST	TENTIEST	VEILIEST	
NEEDIEST	PODGIEST	RINDIEST	SHINIEST	SPIKIEST	TEPIDEST	VEINIEST	
NERVIEST	POLITEST	RISKIEST	SHOALEST	SPINIEST	TESTIEST	VIEWIEST	

WORDS ENDING IN -FUL

7-letter words -FUL

BALEFUL	DIREFUL	FOODFUL	HEEDFUL	LUSTFUL	PESTFUL	RISKFUL	SONGFUL	TUNEFUL
BANEFUL	DISHFUL	FRETFUL	HELPFUL	MASTFUL	PIPEFUL	ROOMFUL	SOULFUL	VIALFUL
BASHFUL	DOLEFUL	GAINFUL	HOPEFUL	MAZEFUL	PITHFUL	RUTHFUL	TACTFUL	WAILFUL
BODEFUL	DOOMFUL	GASHFUL	HORNFUL	MINDFUL	PITIFUL	SACKFUL	TALEFUL	WAKEFUL
BOOKFUL	DUREFUL	GAZEFUL	HURTFUL	MISTFUL	PLAYFUL	SARKFUL	TANKFUL	WAMEFUL
BRIMFUL	DUTIFUL	GLADFUL	JESTFUL	MOANFUL	PLOTFUL	SHIPFUL	TEARFUL	WILEFUL
CAREFUL	EASEFUL	GLEEFUL	LIFEFUL	MUSEFUL	POKEFUL	SHOPFUL	TEEMFUL	WISHFUL
CROPFUL	FATEFUL	GUSTFUL	LISTFUL	NEEDFUL	PREYFUL	SIGHFUL	TENTFUL	WISTFUL
DAREFUL	FEARFUL	HANDFUL	LOCKFUL	PAILFUL	PUSHFUL	SKEPFUL	TOILFUL	WORKFUL
DEEDFUL	FISHFUL	HARMFUL	LOOFFUL	PAINFUL	RAGEFUL	SKILFUL	TRAYFUL	ZEALFUL
DERNFUL	FISTFUL	HATEFUL	LUNGFUL	PALMFUL	RESTFUL	SKINFUL	TUBEFUL	ZESTFUL

8-letter words -FUL

APRONFUL	DOUBTFUL	GHASTFUL	MERCIFUL	PRESSFUL	SPADEFUL	TOOTHFUL	VAUNTFUL
AVAILFUL	DREADFUL	GLASSFUL	MIGHTFUL	PRIDEFUL	SPEEDFUL	TRADEFUL	VENGEFUL
BASINFUL	DREAMFUL	GLOOMFUL	MIRTHFUL	PURSEFUL	SPELLFUL	TRISTFUL	VOICEFUL
BELLYFUL	EVENTFUL	GRACEFUL	MOURNFUL	RIGHTFUL	SPITEFUL	TROTHFUL	WAGONFUL
BLAMEFUL	FAITHFUL	GRATEFUL	MOUTHFUL	SCENTFUL	SPOILFUL	TROUTFUL	WASTEFUL
BLISSFUL	FANCIFUL	GRIEFFUL	NIEVEFUL	SCOOPFUL	SPOONFUL	TRUNKFUL	WATCHFUL
BLUSHFUL	FAULTFUL	GROANFUL	NOISEFUL	SCORNFUL	SPORTFUL	TRUSTFUL	WEARIFUL
BOASTFUL	FEASTFUL	GUILEFUL	PAUSEFUL	SENSEFUL	STARTFUL	TRUTHFUL	WORTHFUL
CHARMFUL	FORCEFUL	HOUSEFUL	PEACEFUL	SHAMEFUL	STICKFUL	UDDERFUL	WRACKFUL
CHEERFUL	FOUNTFUL	LADLEFUL	PLAINFUL	SHELLFUL	STORMFUL	UNARTFUL	WRATHFUL
CHESTFUL	FRAUDFUL	LAUGHFUL	PLATEFUL	SLOTHFUL	SURGEFUL	UNJOYFUL	WREAKFUL
CRIMEFUL	FREAKFUL	LIGHTFUL	POUCHFUL	SMILEFUL	TABLEFUL	UNLAWFUL	WRECKFUL
DEARNFUL	FRISKFUL	LOATHFUL	POWERFUL	SNOOTFUL	TASTEFUL	UNUSEFUL	WRONGFUL
DEATHFUL	FRUITFUL	MENSEFUL	PRANKFUL	SOOTHFUL	THANKFUL	UNWILFUL	YOUTHFUL

WORDS ENDING IN -IBLE

7-letter words -IBLE

AUDIBLE	DELIBLE	DOCIBLE	FUSIBLE	LEGIBLE	PATIBLE	RIBIBLE	RISIBLE	VISIBLE

8-letter words -IBLE

CREDIBLE	ELUDIBLE	FEASIBLE	GULLIBLE	MISCIBLE	RINSIBLE	TANGIBLE	VENDIBLE
CRUCIBLE	EVASIBLE	FENCIBLE	HORRIBLE	PARTIBLE	RUNCIBLE	TENSIBLE	VINCIBLE
EDUCIBLE	EXIGIBLE	FLEXIBLE	INEDIBLE	PASSIBLE	SENSIBLE	TERRIBLE	
ELIGIBLE	FALLIBLE	FORCIBLE	MANDIBLE	POSSIBLE	SUASIBLE	THURIBLE	

WORDS ENDING IN -INGS

7-letter words -INGS

ACHINGS	CAKINGS	DRYINGS	GAPINGS	LAYINGS	NOSINGS	RAWINGS	SPAINGS	ULLINGS
ACTINGS	CANINGS	DYEINGS	GATINGS	LIKINGS	OFFINGS	RIDINGS	SPRINGS	UNKINGS
AGEINGS	CASINGS	EARINGS	GIVINGS	LIMINGS	OGLINGS	RISINGS	SPYINGS	UPPINGS
AIRINGS	CAVINGS	EATINGS	GORINGS	LININGS	ONDINGS	ROBINGS	STRINGS	URGINGS
ANTINGS	CAWINGS	EDGINGS	HAVINGS	LIVINGS	OUTINGS	RODINGS	TAKINGS	URNINGS
ARCINGS	CODINGS	ELDINGS	HAYINGS	LOBINGS	PAGINGS	ROPINGS	TAMINGS	VEXINGS
AWNINGS	COMINGS	ENDINGS	HAZINGS	LORINGS	PALINGS	ROVINGS	TAWINGS	VIKINGS
BAAINGS	COOINGS	ENRINGS	HEWINGS	LOSINGS	PARINGS	ROWINGS	TAXINGS	WADINGS
BAKINGS	COPINGS	ERRINGS	HEXINGS	LOVINGS	PAVINGS	RUEINGS	TIDINGS	WAKINGS
BESINGS	COVINGS	FACINGS	HIDINGS	LOWINGS	PAYINGS	RULINGS	TILINGS	WANINGS
BIDINGS	CRYINGS	FADINGS	HIRINGS	LUGINGS	PIPINGS	SAVINGS	TIMINGS	WAVINGS
BIKINGS	DARINGS	FILINGS	HOLINGS	LUTINGS	POLINGS	SAWINGS	TIRINGS	WAXINGS
BITINGS	DATINGS	FININGS	HOMINGS	MAKINGS	POSINGS	SAYINGS	TOLINGS	WIPINGS
BLUINGS	DICINGS	FIRINGS	INNINGS	MAYINGS	PRYINGS	SEEINGS	TOWINGS	WIRINGS
BODINGS	DIVINGS	FIXINGS	JAWINGS	MININGS	PULINGS	SEWINGS	TOYINGS	WONINGS
BONINGS	DONINGS	FLYINGS	LACINGS	MOWINGS	RACINGS	SIDINGS	TRYINGS	WOOINGS
BORINGS	DOPINGS	FOXINGS	LADINGS	MUSINGS	RAKINGS	SIZINGS	TUBINGS	YOKINGS
BOXINGS	DOTINGS	FRYINGS	LASINGS	NAMINGS	RATINGS	SKIINGS	TUNINGS	ZONINGS
BUSINGS	DOZINGS	GAMINGS	LAWINGS	NIDINGS	RAVINGS	SOWINGS	TYPINGS	

8-letter words -INGS

ABIDINGS	BANKINGS	BEGGINGS	BOILINGS	BUNTINGS	CARVINGS	COININGS	CURSINGS
AISLINGS	BANTINGS	BELTINGS	BOLTINGS	BURNINGS	CASTINGS	COLLINGS	CUTTINGS
AMBLINGS	BARRINGS	BENDINGS	BONDINGS	BUSKINGS	CATLINGS	COMBINGS	CYCLINGS
ANGLINGS	BASHINGS	BETTINGS	BOOKINGS	BUSSINGS	CEASINGS	CONNINGS	DAFFINGS
ARCKINGS	BASTINGS	BIASINGS	BOOMINGS	BUSTINGS	CEILINGS	CORDINGS	DAMPINGS
AWAKINGS	BATTINGS	BIDDINGS	BOWLINGS	BUZZINGS	CHASINGS	COWLINGS	DANCINGS
BACKINGS	BAWLINGS	BILLINGS	BREWINGS	BYGOINGS	CHIDINGS	CRAVINGS	DARLINGS
BAGGINGS	BEADINGS	BINDINGS	BRIMINGS	CABLINGS	CIELINGS	CUBBINGS	DARNINGS
BAITINGS	BEAMINGS	BIRDINGS	BROKINGS	CALLINGS	CLOSINGS	CULLINGS	DAUBINGS
BALKINGS	BEARINGS	BIRLINGS	BUCKINGS	CANTINGS	COAMINGS	CUNNINGS	DAWNINGS
BALLINGS	BEATINGS	BLUEINGS	BUDDINGS	CAPPINGS	COATINGS	CUPPINGS	DEALINGS
BANDINGS	BEDDINGS	BOATINGS	BUGGINGS	CARPINGS	CODLINGS	CURLINGS	DECKINGS

DEVLINGS	GAININGS	INBRINGS	MAIMINGS	PLATINGS	SAGGINGS	STEWINGS	UPSWINGS
DIGGINGS	GANGINGS	INGOINGS	MALTINGS	POLLINGS	SAILINGS	STONINGS	VAMPINGS
DILLINGS	GASPINGS	INKLINGS	MARKINGS	POSTINGS	SALTINGS	STOPINGS	VANNINGS
DIPPINGS	GASSINGS	INSWINGS	MARLINGS	POURINGS	SALVINGS	STOVINGS	VARYINGS
DISHINGS	GAUGINGS	IRONINGS	MASHINGS	POUTINGS	SANDINGS	STOWINGS	VEERINGS
DOATINGS	GEARINGS	JARRINGS	MATTINGS	PRATINGS	SAPLINGS	SUBBINGS	VEILINGS
DOCKINGS	GELDINGS	JEERINGS	MEANINGS	PRAYINGS	SARKINGS	SUCKINGS	VEININGS
DOGGINGS	GETTINGS	JERKINGS	MEETINGS	PRIMINGS	SCALINGS	SUITINGS	VENTINGS
DOPPINGS	GILDINGS	JESTINGS	MELTINGS	PROSINGS	SCORINGS	SUMMINGS	VERSINGS
DRAWINGS	GIRDINGS	JIBBINGS	MENDINGS	PRUNINGS	SCRYINGS	SURFINGS	VESTINGS
DUBBINGS	GLAZINGS	JIGGINGS	MERLINGS	PUDDINGS	SEALINGS	SURGINGS	VIEWINGS
DUCKINGS	GLIDINGS	JOBBINGS	MESHINGS	PUFFINGS	SEARINGS	SWALINGS	VOICINGS
DUFFINGS	GLOZINGS	JOGGINGS	MICHINGS	PUGGINGS	SEATINGS	SWAYINGS	VOIDINGS
DUNNINGS	GODLINGS	JOININGS	MILKINGS	PUNNINGS	SEEDINGS	SYNDINGS	WADDINGS
EANLINGS	GOLFINGS	JOTTINGS	MILLINGS	PURGINGS	SEELINGS	TABLINGS	WAFTINGS
EARNINGS	GOSLINGS	KARTINGS	MINCINGS	PURLINGS	SEEMINGS	TACKINGS	WAILINGS
EARRINGS	GRATINGS	KEELINGS	MINDINGS	PURRINGS	SEININGS	TAILINGS	WAITINGS
EASTINGS	GRAVINGS	KEENINGS	MISTINGS	PUTTINGS	SEIZINGS	TALKINGS	WALKINGS
EEVNINGS	GRAZINGS	KEEPINGS	MOCKINGS	PYONINGS	SENDINGS	TAMPINGS	WALLINGS
EILDINGS	GRICINGS	KEMPINGS	MOORINGS	QUAKINGS	SENSINGS	TANKINGS	WANTINGS
ENVYINGS	GROWINGS	KENNINGS	MOOTINGS	QUEUINGS	SERVINGS	TANLINGS	WARDINGS
ETCHINGS	GUIDINGS	KIDLINGS	MORLINGS	RACKINGS	SETTINGS	TANNINGS	WARLINGS
EVENINGS	GUMMINGS	KILLINGS	MORNINGS	RAGGINGS	SHADINGS	TAPPINGS	WARMINGS
FABLINGS	GUNNINGS	KIRKINGS	MOSLINGS	RAILINGS	SHAKINGS	TARRINGS	WARNINGS
FAGGINGS	HACKINGS	KITLINGS	MOUSINGS	RAISINGS	SHAPINGS	TASKINGS	WARPINGS
FAILINGS	HAININGS	KNIFINGS	MUGGINGS	RANKINGS	SHARINGS	TASTINGS	WASHINGS
FAIRINGS	HALLINGS	LAGGINGS	MUMMINGS	RAPPINGS	SHAVINGS	TATTINGS	WASTINGS
FALLINGS	HALTINGS	LALLINGS	MUNTINGS	RASPINGS	SHOEINGS	TEAMINGS	WAULINGS
FANNINGS	HANGINGS	LAMMINGS	NAILINGS	RATLINGS	SHORINGS	TEASINGS	WAWLINGS
FARCINGS	HARLINGS	LANDINGS	NECKINGS	RATTINGS	SHOWINGS	TELLINGS	WAXWINGS
FARDINGS	HARPINGS	LAPPINGS	NETTINGS	READINGS	SIBLINGS	TENTINGS	WEARINGS
FARMINGS	HASTINGS	LAPWINGS	NITHINGS	REDDINGS	SIFTINGS	TESTINGS	WEAVINGS
FASTINGS	HATTINGS	LASHINGS	NODDINGS	REDWINGS	SINDINGS	THAWINGS	WEBBINGS
FATLINGS	HAWKINGS	LASTINGS	NOGGINGS	REEDINGS	SINGINGS	TICKINGS	WEDDINGS
FAWNINGS	HEADINGS	LATHINGS	NOONINGS	REEFINGS	SINKINGS	TIFFINGS	WEDGINGS
FEEDINGS	HEALINGS	LEADINGS	NOTHINGS	REELINGS	SITTINGS	TILLINGS	WEEDINGS
FEELINGS	HEARINGS	LEANINGS	NULLINGS	RENNINGS	SKATINGS	TILTINGS	WEEPINGS
FEERINGS	HEATINGS	LEASINGS	NUTTINGS	REPPINGS	SKIVINGS	TINNINGS	WELDINGS
FELTINGS	HEAVINGS	LEAVINGS	OAKLINGS	RESTINGS	SLATINGS	TINTINGS	WELLINGS
FENCINGS	HEDGINGS	LEERINGS	ONGOINGS	RIBBINGS	SLICINGS	TIPPINGS	WESTINGS
FERNINGS	HEELINGS	LEGGINGS	OPENINGS	RIDGINGS	SLIDINGS	TITHINGS	WHALINGS
FEUDINGS	HELPINGS	LEKKINGS	OUTWINGS	RIFLINGS	SLOWINGS	TITLINGS	WHININGS
FILLINGS	HERLINGS	LEMMINGS	PACKINGS	RIGGINGS	SMILINGS	TOILINGS	WHITINGS
FINDINGS	HERRINGS	LENDINGS	PADDINGS	RIGLINGS	SMOKINGS	TOLLINGS	WIGGINGS
FIRRINGS	HIDLINGS	LETTINGS	PAIRINGS	RINGINGS	SNARINGS	TOOLINGS	WILDINGS
FISHINGS	HILDINGS	LICKINGS	PANNINGS	RINSINGS	SNIPINGS	TOPPINGS	WINCINGS
FITTINGS	HIPPINGS	LIGGINGS	PANTINGS	RIOTINGS	SNORINGS	TOSSINGS	WINDINGS
FIZZINGS	HIRLINGS	LIMPINGS	PARKINGS	RISPINGS	SOAKINGS	TOTTINGS	WINKINGS
FLUTINGS	HISSINGS	LISPINGS	PARSINGS	ROADINGS	SOARINGS	TOURINGS	WINNINGS
FLYTINGS	HOGGINGS	LISTINGS	PARTINGS	ROARINGS	SOBBINGS	TOUSINGS	WISHINGS
FOAMINGS	HOLDINGS	LOADINGS	PASSINGS	ROCKINGS	SOGGINGS	TRACINGS	WITLINGS
FOILINGS	HOPPINGS	LOAFINGS	PASTINGS	RODDINGS	SOILINGS	TRADINGS	WITTINGS
FOLDINGS	HORNINGS	LOANINGS	PAUSINGS	ROLLINGS	SOOPINGS	TUBBINGS	WOLFINGS
FOOLINGS	HORSINGS	LODGINGS	PECKINGS	ROOFINGS	SOPPINGS	TUFTINGS	WOLVINGS
FOOTINGS	HOSTINGS	LOGGINGS	PEELINGS	ROOTINGS	SORNINGS	TUGGINGS	WORDINGS
FOPLINGS	HOUSINGS	LONGINGS	PEGGINGS	ROUMINGS	SORTINGS	TUNNINGS	WORKINGS
FORGINGS	HOWLINGS	LOOKINGS	PELTINGS	ROUTINGS	SOSSINGS	TURFINGS	WRITINGS
FORMINGS	HUMMINGS	LOONINGS	PETTINGS	RUBBINGS	SOTTINGS	TURNINGS	YAWNINGS
FOWLINGS	HUNTINGS	LOOPINGS	PICKINGS	RUCHINGS	SOUMINGS	TWININGS	YELLINGS
FRAMINGS	HURLINGS	LOPPINGS	PIGGINGS	RUGGINGS	SOURINGS	UNBEINGS	YELPINGS
FRAYINGS	HUSKINGS	LORDINGS	PIGLINGS	RUININGS	SOUSINGS	UNDOINGS	YOWLINGS
FUCKINGS	HUSTINGS	LOURINGS	PINKINGS	RUNNINGS	SPACINGS	UNITINGS	
FUNDINGS	HUTTINGS	LUGEINGS	PINNINGS	RUSTINGS	SPILINGS	UNSLINGS	
FURRINGS	HYLDINGS	LURKINGS	PIONINGS	RUTTINGS	STAGINGS	UNTYINGS	
GADLINGS	IMAGINGS	MADLINGS	PITTINGS	SACKINGS	STARINGS	UPBRINGS	
GAFFINGS	INBEINGS	MAILINGS	PLACINGS	SACRINGS	STAYINGS	UPGOINGS	

WORDS ENDING IN -ISH

7-letter words -ISH

ABOLISH	CATFISH	DOVEISH	GAMPISH	HOTTISH	MOONISH	POORISH	SADDISH	VAMPISH
ALUMISH	CATTISH	DRONISH	GARFISH	HUFFISH	MOORISH	PRUDISH	SALTISH	VARNISH
ANGUISH	CHERISH	DULLISH	GARNISH	JEWFISH	MOREISH	PUBLISH	SELFISH	VOGUISH
BABYISH	CLAYISH	DUMPISH	GIRLISH	JIGGISH	MUGGISH	PUCKISH	SERFISH	WAGGISH
BADDISH	CODFISH	DUNNISH	GNOMISH	KERNISH	MUMPISH	PUGGISH	SICKISH	WAMPISH
BALDISH	COLDISH	DUSKISH	GOATISH	KNAVISH	MURKISH	PUPFISH	SLAVISH	WANNISH
BEAMISH	COLTISH	EVANISH	GOLDISH	LADYISH	NEBBISH	RAFFISH	SLOWISH	WASPISH
BEARISH	COOLISH	FADDISH	GOODISH	LARGISH	NICEISH	RAMMISH	SNAKISH	WEARISH
BEAUISH	COWFISH	FAIRISH	GREYISH	LARKISH	NOURISH	RATTISH	SNOWISH	WENNISH
BIGGISH	CUBBISH	FALSISH	GUARISH	LOMPISH	NUNNISH	REDDISH	SOFTISH	WETTISH
BLEMISH	CULTISH	FASTISH	GULLISH	LONGISH	OGREISH	REDFISH	SOTTISH	WHEYISH
BOARISH	CURRISH	FATTISH	HAGFISH	LOUDISH	OOFTISH	RELLISH	SOURISH	WHITISH
BOBBISH	DAMPISH	FENNISH	HAGGISH	LOUTISH	PARKISH	RIGGISH	STYLISH	WHORISH
BOOKISH	DANKISH	FILMISH	HARDISH	LUBFISH	PECKISH	ROGUISH	SWINISH	WILDISH
BOORISH	DARKISH	FINEISH	HASHISH	LUMPISH	PEEVISH	ROINISH	TARNISH	WIMPISH
BRINISH	DERVISH	FLEMISH	HAWKISH	LUSKISH	PETTISH	ROMPISH	TARTISH	WOLFISH
BRUTISH	DIMMISH	FOGYISH	HELLISH	MAIDISH	PIEDISH	ROOKISH	TIGRISH	WOLVISH
BUCKISH	DOGFISH	FOOLISH	HIGHISH	MANNISH	PIGGISH	ROYNISH	TOFFISH	WORDISH
BULLISH	DOGGISH	FOPPISH	HIPPISH	MAWKISH	PINFISH	RUBBISH	TONNISH	YOBBISH
BURNISH	DOLLISH	FULLISH	HOBBISH	MISSISH	PINKISH	RUMMISH	TOWNISH	
CADDISH	DOLTISH	FURBISH	HOGGISH	MOBBISH	PLANISH	RUNTISH	TUBBISH	
CARLISH	DONNISH	FURNISH	HORNISH	MONKISH	PLENISH	RUTTISH	TUBFISH	

8-letter words -ISH

ADMONISH	CLANNISH	DRUMFISH	GOLDFISH	POKERISH	SHEEPISH	STARFISH	TOLLDISH
ASTONISH	CLAPDISH	DWARFISH	GREENISH	PRANKISH	SHORTISH	STARTISH	TOUGHISH
BABELISH	CLERKISH	EMPERISH	GRUFFISH	PRIGGISH	SHREWISH	STEEPISH	TOVARISH
BAITFISH	CLIQUISH	ENRAVISH	IDIOTISH	PROUDISH	SKIRMISH	STIFFISH	TRICKISH
BLACKISH	CLODDISH	ESSAYISH	JINGOISH	PSEUDISH	SKITTISH	STILTISH	UNMODISH
BLANDISH	CLOWNISH	FAINTISH	KINGFISH	PUPPYISH	SLANGISH	STOCKISH	UNPOLISH
BLIMPISH	CLUBBISH	FEEBLISH	KNACKISH	PURPLISH	SLIMMISH	STOUTISH	VAGARISH
BLOCKISH	COALFISH	FEVERISH	LANGUISH	QUALMISH	SLUGGISH	SUMPHISH	VANQUISH
BLUEFISH	COARSISH	FIENDISH	LIGHTISH	QUEERISH	SLUTTISH	SWAINISH	VIGORISH
BLUNTISH	COMPLISH	FIFTYISH	LIVERISH	QUIPPISH	SMALLISH	SWEETISH	VIPERISH
BOARFISH	CRAWFISH	FLATFISH	LUMPFISH	QUIRKISH	SNAPPISH	SWELLISH	VIXENISH
BOOBYISH	CRAYFISH	FLATTISH	MILKFISH	ROSEFISH	SNEAKISH	SYLPHISH	WALLFISH
BRACKISH	CROSSISH	FLIRTISH	MONKFISH	ROUGHISH	SNOBBISH	THICKISH	WATERISH
BRAINISH	DANDYISH	FLOURISH	NANNYISH	ROUNDISH	SNUBBISH	THIEVISH	WEAKFISH
BRANDISH	DEALFISH	FORTYISH	NOHOWISH	ROWDYISH	SOLIDISH	THINNISH	WOMANISH
BRATTISH	DEMOLISH	FRAILISH	NOVELISH	SAINTISH	SORRYISH	TICKLISH	YOKELISH
BRISKISH	DEVILISH	FREAKISH	NYMPHISH	SANDYISH	SPARKISH	TIGERISH	YOUNGISH
BROADISH	DIMINISH	FRESHISH	OVERFISH	SCAMPISH	SPOFFISH	TIGHTISH	
BROWNISH	DOWDYISH	FRUMPISH	PAGANISH	SCARFISH	SPOOKISH	TILEFISH	
CAMELISH	DRABBISH	GHOULISH	PIPEFISH	SCOMFISH	SQUARISH	TINGLISH	
CHILDISH	DRAFFISH	GLUMPISH	PLAINISH	SCUMFISH	STABLISH	TOADFISH	
CHURLISH	DROLLISH	GOATFISH	PLUMPISH	SHARPISH	STANDISH	TOADYISH	

WORDS ENDING IN -LY

7-letter words -LY

ACUTELY	APISHLY	BLANDLY	BRIEFLY	CHIEFLY	CRAZILY	DENSELY	DURABLY	FADEDLY
AFFABLY	AUDIBLY	BLANKLY	BRISKLY	CHILDLY	CRINKLY	DIRTILY	DUSKILY	FAINTLY
AGILELY	AURALLY	BLEAKLY	BRISTLY	CIVILLY	CRISPLY	DISALLY	DUSTILY	FAIRILY
ALERTLY	AWFULLY	BLINDLY	BROADLY	CLEANLY	CROSSLY	DIZZILY	DYINGLY	FALSELY
ALONELY	AXIALLY	BLOWFLY	BUIRDLY	CLEARLY	CRUDELY	DOUCELY	EAGERLY	FATALLY
ALOOFLY	BAGGILY	BLUFFLY	BULKILY	CLERKLY	CRUELLY	DOWDILY	EARTHLY	FIERILY
AMIABLY	BAIRNLY	BLUNTLY	CANNILY	CLOSELY	CRUMBLY	DREADLY	ELDERLY	FIFTHLY
ANGERLY	BALMILY	BONNILY	CATTILY	COCKILY	DANDILY	DRIBBLY	EMPTILY	FINALLY
ANGRILY	BANALLY	BOOZILY	CAVALLY	CORNFLY	DAZEDLY	DRIZZLY	EQUABLY	FIREFLY
ANOMALY	BAWDILY	BOSSILY	CHARILY	COURTLY	DEARNLY	DROPFLY	EQUALLY	FIRSTLY
APETALY	BEAMILY	BRAMBLY	CHEAPLY	CRACKLY	DEATHLY	DUCALLY	ERECTLY	FIXEDLY
APHYLLY	BEASTLY	BRAVELY	CHEERLY	CRASSLY	DEEDILY	DUOPOLY	EXACTLY	FLEETLY

FLESHLY	GRISTLY	JUMPILY	MODALLY	PESKILY	RURALLY	SOBERLY	TARDILY	VAGUELY
FOAMILY	GRIZZLY	JURALLY	MOISTLY	PETTILY	RUSTILY	SOGGILY	TASTILY	VALIDLY
FOCALLY	GROSSLY	KNOBBLY	MONTHLY	PIOUSLY	SAINTLY	SOLIDLY	TATTILY	VAPIDLY
FOGGILY	GRUFFLY	KNUBBLY	MOODILY	PITHILY	SALABLY	SOOTHLY	TAXABLY	VENALLY
FRAILLY	GRUMBLY	LADYFLY	MORALLY	PLAINLY	SALTILY	SOOTILY	TENSELY	VERMILY
FRANKLY	GRYESLY	LARGELY	MOVABLY	PLIABLY	SAUCILY	SOPPILY	TENTHLY	VEXEDLY
FRECKLY	GRYSELY	LEGALLY	MUDDILY	PLUMPLY	SCANTLY	SORRILY	TEPIDLY	VISIBLY
FRESHLY	GYRALLY	LEGIBLY	MURKILY	PRICKLY	SCRAWLY	SOUNDLY	TERSELY	VITALLY
FRIARLY	HAMMILY	LICHTLY	MUSHILY	PRIMELY	SEEDILY	SPANGLY	TESTILY	VIVIDLY
FRITFLY	HANDILY	LICITLY	MUSKILY	PRIVILY	SHADILY	SPARELY	THICKLY	VIXENLY
FRIZZLY	HAPPILY	LIGHTLY	MUTABLY	PRONELY	SHAKILY	SPARKLY	THIRDLY	VOCALLY
FUGALLY	HARDILY	LITHELY	MUZZILY	PROSILY	SHAPELY	SPICILY	THISTLY	VOLUBLY
FUNNILY	HARSHLY	LOATHLY	NAIVELY	PROUDLY	SHARPLY	SPIKILY	THRILLY	VOWELLY
FUSSILY	HARTELY	LOCALLY	NAKEDLY	PUFFILY	SHEERLY	SPINDLY	TIGERLY	VYINGLY
FUSTILY	HASTILY	LOFTILY	NARGILY	PULPILY	SHINGLY	SPRAWLY	TIGHTLY	WEARILY
FUZZILY	HAZELLY	LOOBILY	NASALLY	QUEENLY	SHOGGLY	SQUALLY	TIMIDLY	WEEVILY
GAUDILY	HEADILY	LOOSELY	NASTILY	QUEERLY	SHOOGLY	STAGILY	TIPSILY	WEIRDLY
GAUNTLY	HEARTLY	LOUSILY	NATTILY	QUICKLY	SHORTLY	STAIDLY	TOSSILY	WHITELY
GELIDLY	HEAVILY	LOVERLY	NEEDILY	QUIETLY	SHOWILY	STALELY	TOTALLY	WIGHTLY
GHASTLY	HOARILY	LOWLILY	NIGHTLY	RABIDLY	SHRILLY	STARKLY	TOUGHLY	WINDILY
GHOSTLY	HUFFILY	LOYALLY	NINTHLY	RAPIDLY	SIGHTLY	STARTLY	TREACLY	WITTILY
GIANTLY	HUMANLY	LUCIDLY	NOBBILY	RATABLY	SILKILY	STATELY	TREMBLY	WOFULLY
GIDDILY	HUMIDLY	LUCKILY	NOISILY	READILY	SILLILY	STEEPLY	TRICKLY	WOMANLY
GODLILY	HUSKILY	LUMPILY	NOTABLY	REAPPLY	SIXTHLY	STERNLY	TRIFOLY	WOOZILY
GOOFILY	IDEALLY	LURIDLY	NOTEDLY	REGALLY	SLACKLY	STIFFLY	TRITELY	WORDILY
GOUTFLY	IGNOBLY	LUSTILY	NYMPHLY	RIGHTLY	SLANTLY	STONILY	TUMIDLY	WORLDLY
GRADELY	INANELY	LYINGLY	ORDERLY	RIGIDLY	SLEEKLY	STOUTLY	TUNABLY	WRIGGLY
GRANDLY	INAPTLY	MASCULY	OVERFLY	RISKILY	SLICKLY	STUBBLY	TWADDLY	WRINKLY
GRAVELY	INEPTLY	MERRILY	OVERPLY	ROCKILY	SLIMILY	STUMBLY	TWIDDLY	WRONGLY
GRAYFLY	INERTLY	MESALLY	OVERTLY	ROOMILY	SMARTLY	SUAVELY	UNAPTLY	YOUNGLY
GREATLY	INJELLY	MESSILY	PANOPLY	ROUGHLY	SMICKLY	SULKILY	UNFITLY	YOUTHLY
GREENLY	IRATELY	METALLY	PAPALLY	ROUNDLY	SMOKILY	SUNNILY	UNGODLY	
GREISLY	JADEDLY	MILKILY	PAWKILY	ROWDILY	SNAKILY	SURLILY	UNMANLY	
GRIESLY	JAZZILY	MISERLY	PEARTLY	ROYALLY	SNIDELY	SWEETLY	UNTRULY	
GRIMILY	JOINTLY	MISTILY	PENALLY	RUDDILY	SNOWILY	SWIFTLY	USUALLY	
GRISELY	JOLLILY	MIXEDLY	PERKILY	RUMMILY	SOAPILY	TACITLY	UTTERLY	

8-letter words -LY

ABJECTLY	BEGGARLY	CLEVERLY	DEUCEDLY	FATHERLY	FRUGALLY	HOPINGLY	LATTERLY
ABRUPTLY	BEHOVELY	CLOUDILY	DEVOUTLY	FAULTILY	FUTILELY	HORRIBLY	LAUDABLY
ABSENTLY	BENIGNLY	CLUMSILY	DIRECTLY	FEASIBLY	GAPINGLY	HORRIDLY	LAVISHLY
ABSURDLY	BESEEMLY	COARSELY	DISAPPLY	FELLOWLY	GARISHLY	HORSEFLY	LAWFULLY
ACTIVELY	BITCHILY	COGENTLY	DISMALLY	FERVIDLY	GENIALLY	HUMANELY	LAWYERLY
ACTUALLY	BITTERLY	COMMONLY	DISTALLY	FESTALLY	GIBINGLY	HUNGERLY	LEADENLY
ADORABLY	BLAMABLY	CONVEXLY	DIVERSLY	FEUDALLY	GIFTEDLY	HUNGRILY	LETHALLY
ADROITLY	BLITHELY	COOINGLY	DIVINELY	FIERCELY	GINGELLY	IMMANELY	LIMPIDLY
AERIALLY	BLOODILY	COUSINLY	DOCTORLY	FILIALLY	GINGERLY	IMPISHLY	LINEALLY
AGUISHLY	BOUNCILY	COVERTLY	DOGGEDLY	FILTHILY	GLASSILY	IMPURELY	LINEARLY
AMAZEDLY	BOYISHLY	COWARDLY	DORSALLY	FINITELY	GLOBALLY	INFIRMLY	LIQUIDLY
AMENABLY	BRASSILY	COYISHLY	DREAMILY	FITFULLY	GLOOMILY	INNATELY	LITHERLY
AMICABLY	BRAZENLY	CRABBILY	DREARILY	FLASHILY	GLOSSILY	INSANELY	LIVELILY
AMUSEDLY	BREEZILY	CRAFTILY	DROOPILY	FLEXIBLY	GOLDENLY	INTENTLY	LOBLOLLY
ANIMALLY	BRIGHTLY	CRANKILY	DROWSILY	FLIMSILY	GRAITHLY	INWARDLY	LOSINGLY
ANNUALLY	BROKENLY	CRAVENLY	EASTERLY	FLINTILY	GRAVELLY	IREFULLY	LOUCHELY
APICALLY	BRUTALLY	CREAKILY	EFFETELY	FLOPPILY	GREASILY	ISSUABLY	LOVELILY
ARCANELY	CANDIDLY	CREDIBLY	EIGHTHLY	FLORALLY	GREEDILY	JAGGEDLY	LOVINGLY
ARDENTLY	CARNALLY	CROAKILY	ELATEDLY	FLORIDLY	GREENFLY	JAUNTILY	LUBBERLY
ARGUABLY	CASUALLY	CROUSELY	ELIGIBLY	FLUENTLY	GRUMPILY	JEJUNELY	LUMBERLY
ARGUTELY	CATCHFLY	CRUSTILY	ENTIRELY	FORCEDLY	GUILTILY	JOCOSELY	LUMPENLY
ARRANTLY	CAUSALLY	CULPABLY	ENVIABLY	FORCIBLY	HEARTILY	JOCUNDLY	MAIDENLY
ARTFULLY	CHASTELY	CURSEDLY	EPICALLY	FORKEDLY	HEAVENLY	JOKINGLY	MALIGNLY
ASSEMBLY	CHEEKILY	DAINTILY	ERRANTLY	FORMALLY	HECTORLY	JOVIALLY	MANFULLY
ASTUTELY	CHEERILY	DAMNABLY	ERRINGLY	FORMERLY	HEROICLY	JOYFULLY	MANNERLY
AUGUSTLY	CHILLILY	DAPPERLY	EVANGELY	FOURTHLY	HIDDENLY	JOYOUSLY	MANUALLY
AVERSELY	CHIRPILY	DARINGLY	EXPERTLY	FRIENDLY	HITCHILY	KERNELLY	MARKEDLY
AVOWEDLY	CHOICELY	DECENTLY	FACIALLY	FRIGIDLY	HOARSELY	KINDLILY	MASTERLY
BADGERLY	CHORALLY	DEMISSLY	FACILELY	FRISKILY	HOLLOWLY	KNIGHTLY	MATRONLY
BEARABLY	CHURCHLY	DEMURELY	FALLIBLY	FROSTILY	HOMELILY	LABIALLY	MATURELY
BEASTILY	CLAMMILY	DENIABLY	FAMOUSLY	FROTHILY	HONESTLY	LATENTLY	MEAGRELY

MEDIALLY	PALLIDLY	QUEASILY	SCRIGGLY	SMUTTILY	STRAGGLY	TRYINGLY	UVULARLY
MELLOWLY	PALPABLY	QUOTABLY	SCRIMPLY	SNAPPILY	STRAITLY	TUNBELLY	VACANTLY
MENTALLY	PALTRILY	RACIALLY	SCURVILY	SNEAKILY	STRICTLY	TURBIDLY	VALUABLY
MESIALLY	PANDERLY	RADIALLY	SEAMANLY	SNIFFILY	STRONGLY	TURGIDLY	VARIABLY
MIGHTILY	PASSABLY	RAGGEDLY	SECONDLY	SNIVELLY	STUFFILY	UNCOMELY	VARIEDLY
MINUTELY	PASSIBLY	RAGINGLY	SECRETLY	SNOTTILY	STUMPILY	UNCOSTLY	VENDIBLY
MISAPPLY	PASTORLY	RAKISHLY	SECURELY	SOCIABLY	STUPIDLY	UNEASILY	VENIALLY
MODERNLY	PATCHILY	RANDOMLY	SEDATELY	SOCIALLY	STURDILY	UNEVENLY	VERBALLY
MODESTLY	PATENTLY	RASCALLY	SENILELY	SOLEMNLY	SUBTILLY	UNFAIRLY	VERNALLY
MODISHLY	PEDATELY	RATEABLY	SENSIBLY	SOMBRELY	SUDDENLY	UNGAINLY	VEXINGLY
MOLTENLY	PETTEDLY	RAVINGLY	SERENELY	SORDIDLY	SUITABLY	UNGENTLY	VIOLABLY
MOMENTLY	PITIABLY	READABLY	SERIALLY	SOUTERLY	SULLENLY	UNHOLILY	VIRGINLY
MONOPOLY	PLACABLY	RECENTLY	SEVERELY	SPARSELY	SULTRILY	UNHOMELY	VISUALLY
MOPINGLY	PLACIDLY	RECTALLY	SEXUALLY	SPEEDILY	SUMMERLY	UNIQUELY	VULGARLY
MOPISHLY	PLAGUILY	REFLEXLY	SHABBILY	SPIRALLY	SUPERBLY	UNITEDLY	WANTONLY
MORBIDLY	PLIANTLY	RELIABLY	SHAGGILY	SPONGILY	SUPINELY	UNJUSTLY	WEASELLY
MOROSELY	PLUCKILY	REMISSLY	SHAUCHLY	SPOOKILY	SYMPHILY	UNKINDLY	WEEVILLY
MORTALLY	PLURALLY	REMOTELY	SHIFTILY	SPOONILY	TAKINGLY	UNKINGLY	WESTERLY
MOTHERLY	POLITELY	RETRALLY	SHODDILY	SPORTILY	TANGIBLY	UNLIKELY	WHEEZILY
MOVEABLY	POPISHLY	RITUALLY	SHREWDLY	SPOTTILY	TARTARLY	UNLIVELY	WHIMSILY
MOVINGLY	PORTERLY	ROBUSTLY	SICKERLY	SPRITELY	TASSELLY	UNLORDLY	WICKEDLY
MULISHLY	POSINGLY	ROOTEDLY	SICKLILY	SPRUCELY	TAWDRILY	UNLOVELY	WILFULLY
MULTIPLY	POSSIBLY	ROTTENLY	SIGNALLY	SQUARELY	TENDERLY	UNMEETLY	WINGEDLY
MUSINGLY	POTENTLY	ROTUNDLY	SILENTLY	SQUIGGLY	TERRIBLY	UNREALLY	WINTERLY
MUTUALLY	PRETTILY	ROVINGLY	SILVERLY	SQUIRELY	TETCHILY	UNSAFELY	WITTOLLY
NARGHILY	PRIESTLY	RUEFULLY	SISTERLY	STANCHLY	THWARTLY	UNSEEMLY	WIZARDLY
NARGILLY	PRIMALLY	RUGGEDLY	SKIMPILY	STARRILY	TIMOUSLY	UNTIDILY	WOEFULLY
NARROWLY	PRINCELY	RUGOSELY	SLANGILY	STATEDLY	TINSELLY	UNTIMELY	WOODENLY
NATIVELY	PROBABLY	SACREDLY	SLEAZILY	STEADILY	TONISHLY	UNUSABLY	WOOINGLY
NOCENTLY	PROLIXLY	SAILORLY	SLEEPILY	STEAMILY	TORPIDLY	UNWARELY	WORTHILY
NORMALLY	PROMPTLY	SALEABLY	SLIGHTLY	STEEVELY	TOUCHILY	UNWARILY	WOUNDILY
OBTUSELY	PROPERLY	SAVAGELY	SLOPPILY	STICKILY	TOWARDLY	UNWIFELY	WRATHILY
OCCULTLY	PROVABLY	SAVINGLY	SLOVENLY	STIEVELY	TOYISHLY	UNWISELY	WRITERLY
OCULARLY	PRYINGLY	SAVOURLY	SMALMILY	STINGILY	TRASHILY	UPPISHLY	YEOMANLY
ODIOUSLY	PUBLICLY	SCANTILY	SMARMILY	STOCKILY	TREVALLY	UPWARDLY	YONDERLY
ONWARDLY	PULINGLY	SCARCELY	SMEARILY	STODGILY	TRIBALLY	URBANELY	YONGTHLY
OPAQUELY	PUTRIDLY	SCRAGGLY	SMOOTHLY	STOLIDLY	TRICKILY	URGENTLY	ZOOPHILY
ORNATELY	QUAINTLY	SCRIBBLY	SMUDGILY	STORMILY	TRUSTILY	USEFULLY	

WORDS ENDING IN -MAN

7-letter words -MAN

ARTSMAN	CASEMAN	FREEMAN	HOODMAN	LINKMAN	OARSMAN	REELMAN	SPAEMAN	WOODMAN
BASEMAN	CAVEMAN	FROGMAN	HOSEMAN	LOCKMAN	ODDSMAN	RINGMAN	SURFMAN	WOOLMAN
BATSMAN	CHAPMAN	GADSMAN	INHUMAN	LOCOMAN	OTTOMAN	ROADMAN	SWAGMAN	WORKMAN
BEADMAN	CLUBMAN	GLEEMAN	ISLEMAN	MAGSMAN	OVERMAN	RODSMAN	TAPSMAN	YARDMAN
BEDEMAN	COALMAN	GOODMAN	JACKMAN	MAILMAN	PACKMAN	SAGAMAN	TAXIMAN	YEGGMAN
BELLMAN	DAYSMAN	GOWNMAN	JARKMAN	MALTMAN	PASSMAN	SANDMAN	TOLLMAN	
BILLMAN	DECUMAN	GUDEMAN	JAZZMAN	MARKMAN	PEATMAN	SHIPMAN	TOOLMAN	
BIRDMAN	DRAYMAN	HANGMAN	JUNKMAN	MASHMAN	PIKEMAN	SHOPMAN	TOPSMAN	
BOATMAN	DUSTMAN	HANUMAN	JURYMAN	MILKMAN	POLLMAN	SHOWMAN	TRUEMAN	
BONDMAN	FACEMAN	HEADMAN	KEELMAN	MOBSMAN	PORTMAN	SICKMAN	TURFMAN	
BOOKMAN	FIREMAN	HELIMAN	KINSMAN	MOORMAN	POSTMAN	SNOWMAN	UNHUMAN	
BUSHMAN	FOOTMAN	HERDMAN	LANDMAN	MOOTMAN	RAFTMAN	SOKEMAN	UNWOMAN	
BYREMAN	FOREMAN	HIGHMAN	LINEMAN	NEWSMAN	RAILMAN	SONGMAN	WAKEMAN	

8-letter words -MAN

AIRWOMAN	BONDSMAN	CLASSMAN	FORGEMAN	HANDYMAN	HUNTSMAN	MARKSMAN	PLAIDMAN
ALDERMAN	BOTHYMAN	COACHMAN	FREEDMAN	HEADSMAN	ISLESMAN	MERESMAN	PLATEMAN
BAILSMAN	BRAKEMAN	CRAGSMAN	FRESHMAN	HELMSMAN	LANDSMAN	MERRYMAN	PREHUMAN
BANDSMAN	BRIDEMAN	DAIRYMAN	FRONTMAN	HENCHMAN	LEADSMAN	MOTORMAN	PRESSMAN
BANDYMAN	BRINKMAN	DALESMAN	FUGLEMAN	HERDSMAN	LIEGEMAN	NOBLEMAN	PROSEMAN
BANKSMAN	BUTTYMAN	DOOMSMAN	GANGSMAN	HIELAMAN	LINESMAN	OVERSMAN	PUNTSMAN
BARGEMAN	CHAIRMAN	DRAGOMAN	GAVELMAN	HOASTMAN	LOCKSMAN	PENWOMAN	QUILLMAN
BATWOMAN	CHESSMAN	DRAGSMAN	GLASSMAN	HOISTMAN	LODESMAN	PETERMAN	RAFTSMAN
BEADSMAN	CHOIRMAN	EARTHMAN	GOADSMAN	HORSEMAN	MADWOMAN	PITCHMAN	RAMPSMAN
BEDESMAN	CLANSMAN	FERRYMAN	GOWNSMAN	HOUSEMAN	MARCHMAN	PLACEMAN	RANCHMAN

REINSMAN	SEEDSMAN	SPACEMAN	STOREMAN	TACKSMAN	TRACKMAN	WATCHMAN
RIFLEMAN	SHAREMAN	SPADEMAN	STUNTMAN	TALESMAN	TREWSMAN	WATERMAN
RIVERMAN	SHEARMAN	SPEARMAN	SUBHUMAN	TALISMAN	TRIPEMAN	WEALSMAN
ROADSMAN	SHIREMAN	SQUAWMAN	SUPERMAN	TALLYMAN	TRUCHMAN	WHEELMAN
ROUTEMAN	SHOREMAN	STALLMAN	SWAGSMAN	TOWNSMAN	TRUCKMAN	WINCHMAN
SALESMAN	SIDESMAN	STOCKMAN	SWORDMAN	TOYWOMAN	UNDERMAN	WOODSMAN

WORDS ENDING IN -MEN

7-letter words -MEN

ABDOMEN	BONDMEN	DURAMEN	GUDEMEN	JUNKMEN	MASHMEN	PIKEMEN	SANDMEN	TAXIMEN
AGNOMEN	BOOKMEN	DUSTMEN	HANGMEN	JURYMEN	MILKMEN	POLLMEN	SHIPMEN	TOLLMEN
ALBUMEN	BUSHMEN	FACEMEN	HEADMEN	KEELMEN	MOBSMEN	PORTMEN	SHOPMEN	TOOLMEN
ARTSMEN	BYREMEN	FIREMEN	HELIMEN	KINSMEN	MOLIMEN	POSTMEN	SHOWMEN	TOPSMEN
BASEMEN	CACUMEN	FOOTMEN	HERDMEN	LANDMEN	MOORMEN	PUTAMEN	SICKMEN	TRUEMEN
BATSMEN	CASEMEN	FORAMEN	HIGHMEN	LINEMEN	MOOTMEN	RAFTMEN	SNOWMEN	TURFMEN
BEADMEN	CAVEMEN	FOREMEN	HILLMEN	LINKMEN	NEWSMEN	RAILMEN	SOKEMEN	VELAMEN
BEDEMEN	CERUMEN	FREEMEN	HOODMEN	LOCKMEN	OARSMEN	REELMEN	SONGMEN	WAKEMEN
BELLMEN	CHAPMEN	FROGMEN	HOSEMEN	LOCOMEN	ODDSMEN	REGIMEN	SPAEMEN	WOODMEN
BILLMEN	CLUBMEN	GADSMEN	ISLEMEN	MAGSMEN	OVERMEN	RINGMEN	SUDAMEN	WOOLMEN
BIRDMEN	COALMEN	GLEEMEN	JACKMEN	MAILMEN	PACKMEN	ROADMEN	SURFMEN	WORKMEN
BITUMEN	DAYSMEN	GOODMEN	JARKMEN	MALTMEN	PASSMEN	RODSMEN	SWAGMEN	YARDMEN
BOATMEN	DRAYMEN	GOWNMEN	JAZZMEN	MARKMEN	PEATMEN	SAGAMEN	TAPSMEN	YEGGMEN

8-letter words -MEN

AIRWOMEN	CHAIRMEN	FORGEMEN	HOASTMEN	MERRYMEN	RANCHMEN	SPECIMEN	TRIPEMEN
ALDERMEN	CHESSMEN	FREEDMEN	HOISTMEN	MOTORMEN	REINSMEN	SQUAWMEN	TRUCHMEN
BAILSMEN	CHOIRMEN	FRESHMEN	HORSEMEN	NOBLEMEN	RIFLEMEN	STALLMEN	TRUCKMEN
BANDSMEN	CLANSMEN	FRONTMEN	HOUSEMEN	OVERSMEN	RIVERMEN	STOCKMEN	UNDERMEN
BANDYMEN	CLASSMEN	FUGLEMEN	HUNTSMEN	PENWOMEN	ROADSMEN	STOREMEN	WATCHMEN
BANKSMEN	CLINAMEN	GANGSMEN	ISLESMEN	PETERMEN	ROUTEMEN	STUNTMEN	WATERMEN
BARGEMEN	COACHMEN	GAVELMEN	LANDSMEN	PITCHMEN	SALESMEN	SUPERMEN	WEALSMEN
BATWOMEN	COGNOMEN	GLASSMEN	LEADSMEN	PLACEMEN	SEEDSMEN	SWAGSMEN	WHEELMEN
BEADSMEN	CRAGSMEN	GOADSMEN	LIEGEMEN	PLAIDMEN	SHAREMEN	SWORDMEN	WINCHMEN
BEDESMEN	CYCLAMEN	GOWNSMEN	LINESMEN	PLATEMEN	SHEARMEN	TACKSMEN	WOODSMEN
BONDSMEN	DAIRYMEN	GRAVAMEN	LOCKSMEN	PRESSMEN	SHIREMEN	TALESMEN	
BOTHYMEN	DALESMEN	HANDYMEN	LODESMEN	PROSEMEN	SHOREMEN	TALLYMEN	
BRAKEMEN	DOOMSMEN	HEADSMEN	MADWOMEN	PUNTSMEN	SIDESMEN	TOWNSMEN	
BRIDEMEN	DRAGSMEN	HELMSMEN	MARCHMEN	QUILLMEN	SPACEMEN	TOYWOMEN	
BRINKMEN	EARTHMEN	HENCHMEN	MARKSMEN	RAFTSMEN	SPADEMEN	TRACKMEN	
BUTTYMEN	FERRYMEN	HERDSMEN	MERESMEN	RAMPSMEN	SPEARMEN	TREWSMEN	

WORDS ENDING IN -OUS

7-letter words -OUS

ACAJOUS	AZYMOUS	COPIOUS	FUNGOUS	IMPIOUS	OCHROUS	POMPOUS	SPINOUS	VEINOUS
ACEROUS	BADIOUS	CORIOUS	FURIOUS	INVIOUS	ODOROUS	PORTOUS	SPUMOUS	VICIOUS
ACETOUS	BILIOUS	CORMOUS	FUSCOUS	JEALOUS	OMINOUS	PULPOUS	SUCCOUS	VIDUOUS
ACINOUS	BIVIOUS	CUPROUS	GASEOUS	LENTOUS	ONEROUS	RAMEOUS	TALCOUS	VILLOUS
AGAMOUS	BRUMOUS	CURIOUS	GEALOUS	LEPROUS	ONYMOUS	RAUCOUS	TEDIOUS	VISCOUS
AMADOUS	BULBOUS	DEVIOUS	GIBBOUS	LIMBOUS	OPACOUS	RHODOUS	TENUOUS	VOUDOUS
AMOROUS	BURNOUS	DUBIOUS	GLEBOUS	LUTEOUS	OSMIOUS	RIOTOUS	TIMEOUS	ZEALOUS
ANUROUS	CACHOUS	DUTEOUS	GLOBOUS	NACROUS	OSSEOUS	ROUCOUS	TYPHOUS	ZINCOUS
ANXIOUS	CALLOUS	EMULOUS	GRUMOUS	NERVOUS	PAPPOUS	ROUTOUS	UBEROUS	
APODOUS	CARIOUS	ENVIOUS	GUMMOUS	NIMIOUS	PARLOUS	RUBIOUS	UMBROUS	
AQUEOUS	CASEOUS	ESTROUS	HEINOUS	NIOBOUS	PERLOUS	RUINOUS	URANOUS	
ARDUOUS	CEREOUS	FATUOUS	HERBOUS	NITROUS	PETROUS	SANIOUS	URINOUS	
ATHEOUS	CHYMOUS	FEATOUS	HIDEOUS	NIVEOUS	PICEOUS	SARCOUS	USUROUS	
ATOKOUS	CIRROUS	FERROUS	HUGEOUS	NOCUOUS	PILEOUS	SERIOUS	VACUOUS	
AZOTOUS	CITROUS	FIBROUS	HYDROUS	NOXIOUS	PITEOUS	SIMIOUS	VALGOUS	
AZYGOUS	CONGOUS	FULVOUS	IGNEOUS	OBVIOUS	PLUMOUS	SINUOUS	VARIOUS	

8-letter words -OUS

ACARPOUS	CERNUOUS	EXIGUOUS	GRIEVOUS	NEMOROUS	POPULOUS	SIBILOUS	TUBULOUS
ADUNCOUS	CHLOROUS	EXIMIOUS	GRISEOUS	NIDOROUS	PORTEOUS	SOMBROUS	TUMOROUS
AMBEROUS	CITREOUS	FABULOUS	GYPSEOUS	NODULOUS	PRECIOUS	SONOROUS	ULCEROUS
ANOUROUS	CORNEOUS	FACTIOUS	HALITOUS	NUBILOUS	PREVIOUS	SOPOROUS	UNCTUOUS
ANTICOUS	COUSCOUS	FASHIOUS	HUMOROUS	NUMEROUS	PYRITOUS	SPACIOUS	UNDULOUS
APHONOUS	COVETOUS	FASTUOUS	ICHOROUS	NUMINOUS	PYRRHOUS	SPECIOUS	UNJOYOUS
APHTHOUS	COVINOUS	FEATEOUS	INCUBOUS	OCHEROUS	RAMULOUS	SPERMOUS	USURIOUS
APTEROUS	CROCEOUS	FEATUOUS	INFAMOUS	OCHREOUS	RAVENOUS	SPURIOUS	UXORIOUS
ARACEOUS	CROUPOUS	FELONOUS	JOCOROUS	OESTROUS	RESINOUS	SQUAMOUS	VALOROUS
ARANEOUS	CUMBROUS	FERREOUS	KOUSKOUS	OOGAMOUS	RIGOROUS	STANNOUS	VANADOUS
ARBOROUS	CUPREOUS	FEVEROUS	LACTEOUS	ORAGIOUS	RUMOROUS	STOTIOUS	VAPOROUS
ASPEROUS	DARTROUS	FIDDIOUS	LEAPROUS	ORDUROUS	SABULOUS	STRATOUS	VENOMOUS
ASTOMOUS	DECOROUS	FLATUOUS	LIGNEOUS	ORGULOUS	SAPAJOUS	STRUMOUS	VENTROUS
ATROPOUS	DESIROUS	FLEXUOUS	LUMINOUS	OVARIOUS	SAPOROUS	STUDIOUS	VERTUOUS
BIBULOUS	DEXTROUS	FRABJOUS	LUSCIOUS	PABULOUS	SAVOROUS	SUBEROUS	VIGOROUS
BIGAMOUS	DIDYMOUS	GEMINOUS	LUSTROUS	PALUDOUS	SCABIOUS	SUDOROUS	VIPEROUS
BIMANOUS	DIGAMOUS	GEMMEOUS	MANITOUS	PAPULOUS	SCABROUS	TEMEROUS	VIRTUOUS
BIPAROUS	DIGYNOUS	GENEROUS	MARABOUS	PATULOUS	SCARIOUS	TENUIOUS	VITREOUS
CADUCOUS	DIMEROUS	GLABROUS	MELANOUS	PERILOUS	SCIOLOUS	THALLOUS	WAVEROUS
CAESIOUS	DIPNOOUS	GLAREOUS	MIASMOUS	PERVIOUS	SCLEROUS	TIMOROUS	WONDROUS
CANOROUS	DITOKOUS	GLAUCOUS	MUTICOUS	PETALOUS	SCORIOUS	TINAMOUS	WRONGOUS
CAPTIOUS	DOLOROUS	GLORIOUS	MUTINOUS	PLUMBOUS	SEDULOUS	TITANOUS	XANTHOUS
CARIBOUS	EDACIOUS	GOITROUS	NACREOUS	PLUVIOUS	SELENOUS	TORTIOUS	YTTRIOUS
CARNEOUS	ENORMOUS	GORGEOUS	NAUSEOUS	POACEOUS	SENSUOUS	TORTUOUS	
CAUTIOUS	EPIGEOUS	GRACIOUS	NEBULOUS	POLYPOUS	SEPALOUS	TUBEROUS	

WORDS ENDING IN -TION

7-letter words -TION

AMATION	CAPTION	DICTION	EMOTION	FICTION	MIXTION	PORTION	STATION	UNCTION
AUCTION	CAUTION	EDITION	EMPTION	LECTION	ORATION	RECTION	SUCTION	UNITION
BASTION	COCTION	ELATION	ENATION	MENTION	OVATION	RUCTION	TACTION	
CANTION	COITION	ELUTION	FACTION	MICTION	PACTION	SECTION	TUITION	

8-letter words -TION

ABLATION	COACTION	EGESTION	FRICTION	LAVATION	NEGATION	QUESTION	TRACTION
ABLUTION	COLATION	EJECTION	FRUITION	LEGATION	NIDATION	REACTION	VACATION
ABORTION	CONATION	ELECTION	FUNCTION	LENITION	NODATION	RELATION	VENATION
ADAPTION	CREATION	EMICTION	GELATION	LIBATION	NOLITION	REMOTION	VEXATION
ADDITION	DELATION	ENACTION	GUMPTION	LIGATION	NOTATION	ROGATION	VOCATION
ADNATION	DELETION	EQUATION	GYRATION	LIMATION	NOVATION	ROTATION	VOLITION
ADOPTION	DEMOTION	ERECTION	HALATION	LOBATION	NUDATION	SANCTION	VOLUTION
AERATION	DERATION	ERUPTION	HIMATION	LOCATION	NUTATION	SCONTION	ZONATION
AGNATION	DEVOTION	EVECTION	IDEATION	LOCUTION	OBLATION	SEDATION	
AMBITION	DILATION	EVICTION	IGNITION	LUNATION	PACATION	SEDITION	
AUDITION	DILUTION	EXACTION	ILLATION	LUXATION	PETITION	SOLATION	
AVIATION	DONATION	EXERTION	INACTION	MONITION	POSITION	SOLUTION	
BIBATION	DOTATION	FIXATION	INUSTION	MUNITION	POTATION	SORPTION	
CIBATION	DURATION	FLECTION	JOBATION	MUTATION	PUNITION	SUDATION	
CITATION	EDUCTION	FRACTION	JUNCTION	NATATION	PUPATION	TAXATION	

UNUSUAL VOWEL ENDINGS

Even when Scrabble players are thinking about the endings of words, they tend to concentrate on the 'obvious' endings – like -ATE, -ISE, -URE, -ED, -ER and -ENT. These tend to end with a fairly restricted group of letters – usually D, E, R, S and T. They do not naturally think of words ending with unusual letters. It takes some effort to start thinking about words ending in A, I, O and U. Yet these four letters make up 30% of the tiles in a Scrabble set. They will frequently appear on your rack, but familiarity with everyday English does not encourage you to think of these letters at the ends of words. They can be very useful for linking on to other letters on the board, making two-letter words which begin or end with A, I, O or U.

The following lists are ammunition for correcting that rather limiting view of word endings. Here are lists of all words of lengths two to eight which end with A, I, O and U.

WORDS ENDING IN -A

2-letter words ending in -A

AA	DA	FA	KA	MA	PA
BA	EA	HA	LA	NA	TA

3-letter words ending in -A

ABA	ANA	BRA	GOA	LEA	OVA	RIA	SPA	YEA
AGA	AVA	CHA	HOA	MNA	PEA	RYA	TEA	ZEA
AHA	AWA	ERA	ITA	MOA	PIA	SEA	TWA	ZOA
AIA	BAA	ETA	KEA	OCA	POA	SKA	UVA	
ALA	BOA	FRA	KOA	ODA	QUA	SMA	VIA	

4-letter words ending in -A

ABBA	BOBA	DONA	HILA	KINA	MOYA	PICA	RUSA	TANA	VITA
ACTA	BOMA	DOPA	HIYA	KOLA	MYNA	PIKA	SAGA	TAPA	VIVA
AGHA	BONA	DUMA	HOYA	KORA	NADA	PILA	SERA	TARA	VOLA
AGMA	BORA	DURA	HUIA	LAMA	NAGA	PINA	SETA	TAXA	WEKA
ALFA	BUBA	EGMA	HULA	LANA	NALA	PIPA	SHEA	TELA	WHOA
ALGA	BUNA	EKKA	HUMA	LAVA	NANA	PITA	SHWA	TIKA	YOGA
ALMA	CABA	EMMA	IDEA	LEVA	NAPA	PLEA	SIDA	TOGA	YUCA
AMLA	CAPA	EPHA	ILEA	LIMA	NOMA	PROA	SIKA	TOLA	YUGA
ANNA	CASA	ETNA	ILIA	LIRA	NOVA	PUJA	SIMA	TUBA	ZETA
ANOA	CECA	EYRA	ILKA	LOMA	OBIA	PUMA	SKUA	TUFA	ZILA
ANTA	COCA	FETA	INIA	LOTA	ODEA	PUNA	SODA	TUNA	ZOEA
AQUA	CODA	FLEA	IOTA	MAMA	OKRA	PUPA	SOFA	ULNA	ZONA
ARBA	COLA	FORA	IXIA	MANA	OLLA	RACA	SOJA	UREA	ZUPA
AREA	COMA	GAGA	JOTA	MARA	ORRA	RAGA	SOLA	URVA	
ARIA	COXA	GALA	JUBA	MAYA	OSSA	RAJA	SOMA	UVEA	
ARNA	CYMA	GENA	JUGA	MESA	PACA	RANA	SORA	VARA	
AULA	DATA	GETA	JURA	MICA	PAPA	RATA	SOYA	VASA	
AURA	DEVA	GIGA	KAKA	MINA	PARA	RHEA	STOA	VEGA	
BABA	DIKA	GILA	KANA	MONA	PAUA	RIMA	SURA	VELA	
BEMA	DISA	GLIA	KARA	MORA	PAWA	RIVA	TAHA	VENA	
BETA	DITA	GULA	KARA	MOWA	PEBA	ROMA	TAKA	VINA	
BIGA	DIVA	HAKA	KETA	MOXA	PELA	ROTA	TALA	VISA	

5-letter words ending in -A

ABACA	BURSA	DOUMA	HALFA	KRONA	MORIA	PELMA	RUPIA	STIPA	USNEA
ABAYA	BWANA	DOURA	HALMA	KURTA	MORRA	PELTA	RUSMA	STOLA	UVULA
ABUNA	CAECA	DOWNA	HALVA	KWELA	MOTZA	PENNA	SABRA	STOMA	VACUA
ADYTA	CALLA	DRAMA	HAMZA	LABDA	MOWRA	PHOCA	SACRA	STRIA	VARNA
AECIA	CALPA	DULIA	HAOMA	LABIA	MUDRA	PHYLA	SAIGA	STUPA	VEENA
AFARA	CANNA	DUMKA	HASTA	LABRA	MULGA	PICRA	SAKIA	SULFA	VESPA
AGILA	CARTA	DURRA	HEJRA	LAIKA	MURRA	PIETA	SALSA	SUMMA	VESTA
AGORA	CELLA	EDEMA	HENNA	LAMIA	MURVA	PILEA	SAMBA	SURRA	VIFDA
ALAPA	CERIA	ENEMA	HERMA	LARVA	MUSHA	PINNA	SANSA	SUTRA	VIGIA
ALDEA	CHARA	ENTIA	HEVEA	LAURA	MYOMA	PINTA	SARSA	SYLVA	VILLA
ALOHA	CHAYA	ERBIA	HIJRA	LAVRA	NABLA	PITTA	SARZA	TABLA	VINCA
ALPHA	CHEKA	ERICA	HODJA	LEMMA	NAIRA	PIZZA	SAUBA	TAFIA	VIOLA
ALULA	CHELA	ETYMA	HOLLA	LEPRA	NALLA	PLAYA	SAUNA	TAIGA	VIRGA
AMEBA	CHICA	EXTRA	HOOKA	LEPTA	NANNA	PLAZA	SCALA	TAIRA	VISTA
AMNIA	CHINA	FACIA	HOSTA	LIANA	NAPPA	PLICA	SCAPA	TALMA	VITTA
ANANA	CHUFA	FAUNA	HURRA	LIBRA	NERKA	POAKA	SCENA	TALPA	VIVDA
ANIMA	CILIA	FELLA	HUTIA	LIMMA	NINJA	PODIA	SCHWA	TANGA	VODKA
AORTA	CIRCA	FESTA	HUZZA	LINGA	NORIA	POLKA	SCOPA	TANKA	VOILA
APNEA	CNIDA	FETTA	HYDRA	LLAMA	NORMA	POOJA	SCUBA	TANNA	VOLTA
ARABA	COBIA	FETWA	HYENA	LOGIA	NUBIA	POOKA	SCUTA	TAPPA	VOLVA
ARECA	COBRA	FLORA	HYPHA	LONGA	NUCHA	POPPA	SELVA	TAYRA	VULVA
ARENA	COCOA	FLOTA	HYPNA	LOOFA	NULLA	PORTA	SENNA	TAZZA	WALLA
AROBA	COLZA	FOLIA	INFRA	LUBRA	NYALA	PRANA	SENSA	TENIA	WINNA
AROMA	COMMA	FONDA	INTRA	LUFFA	OCREA	PRESA	SENZA	TERRA	WONGA
ASANA	CONGA	FOSSA	INULA	LYSSA	OIDIA	PRIMA	SEPIA	TESLA	XENIA
ATRIA	CONIA	FOVEA	JARTA	LYTTA	OMASA	PSORA	SEPTA	TESTA	YACCA
BACCA	COPRA	FRENA	JHALA	MAFIA	OMEGA	PUCKA	SERRA	TETRA	YAKKA
BAJRA	CORIA	GALEA	JIRGA	MAGMA	OPERA	PUKKA	SESSA	THANA	YARFA
BALSA	COSTA	GAMBA	JUNTA	MAHUA	ORGIA	PULKA	SHAMA	THECA	YARTA
BANIA	COTTA	GAMMA	KAAMA	MAHWA	OSSIA	PUNKA	SHAYA	THEMA	YENTA
BARCA	CRENA	GANJA	KACHA	MALVA	OSTIA	QIBLA	SHEVA	THETA	YERBA
BASTA	CUPPA	GARDA	KALPA	MAMBA	OUIJA	QUENA	SHOLA	THUJA	YUCCA
BATTA	CURIA	GEMMA	KANGA	MAMMA	PACHA	QUINA	SIDHA	TIARA	ZABRA
BELGA	DACHA	GENOA	KAPPA	MANIA	PACTA	QUOTA	SIGLA	TIBIA	ZAMIA
BIGHA	DAGGA	GOMPA	KARMA	MANNA	PADMA	RASTA	SIGMA	TICCA	ZANJA
BIOTA	DARGA	GONIA	KASBA	MANTA	PAISA	REATA	SILVA	TINEA	ZEBRA
BOCCA	DELTA	GONNA	KHAYA	MARIA	PAKKA	RECTA	SOFTA	TONGA	ZERDA
BOHEA	DERMA	GOTTA	KHEDA	MASSA	PALEA	REDIA	SOPHA	TREFA	ZONDA
BRAVA	DICTA	GRAMA	KHOJA	MATZA	PALLA	REGMA	SOPRA	TREMA	ZOOEA
BUFFA	DIOTA	GROMA	KINDA	MEDIA	PAMPA	RENGA	SORDA	TRONA	
BULLA	DOGMA	GUANA	KOALA	MISSA	PANDA	REPLA	SORRA	TSUBA	
BUNIA	DOLIA	GUAVA	KOFTA	MOCHA	PANGA	RHYTA	SPICA	ULEMA	
BUNYA	DOLMA	GUMMA	KOKRA	MOLLA	PARKA	RIATA	SPINA	ULTRA	
BURKA	DONGA	GUSLA	KOPPA	MOMMA	PASHA	ROOSA	SPUTA	UMBRA	
BURQA	DORSA	GUTTA	KORMA	MOOLA	PASTA	RUMBA	STELA	URENA	

6-letter words ending in -A

ABELIA	AMRITA	ARROBA	BERTHA	CESURA	CONIMA	DAGOBA	ESPADA	FUNKIA	HEJIRA
ABOLLA	ANATTA	ASTHMA	BODEGA	CHACMA	CONTRA	DAHLIA	EUREKA	GALENA	HEMINA
ABULIA	ANCORA	ATAXIA	BOSHTA	CHAETA	COPITA	DATURA	EXEDRA	GARRYA	HERNIA
ACACIA	ANEMIA	ATOCIA	BREGMA	CHAKRA	COPULA	DHARMA	FACULA	GARUDA	HOLLOA
ACEDIA	ANGINA	AUCUBA	BROLGA	CHAPKA	CORNEA	DHARNA	FARINA	GEISHA	HOLMIA
AGENDA	ANGORA	AURORA	BUCKRA	CHARTA	CORNUA	DHURRA	FASCIA	GELADA	HYAENA
AGOUTA	ANOXIA	AXILLA	BUNNIA	CHATTA	CORONA	DUENNA	FAVELA	GENERA	HYDRIA
AHIMSA	ANTLIA	AZALEA	BURKHA	CHICHA	CORYZA	ECZEMA	FECULA	GENEVA	IGUANA
AIKONA	ANURIA	AZOLLA	CABALA	CHOREA	COSMEA	EGESTA	FEDORA	GITANA	IMPALA
ALALIA	APHTHA	BAHADA	CABANA	CHORIA	CRANIA	EIDOLA	FEMORA	GLIOMA	INDABA
ALBATA	APNOEA	BAJADA	CAFILA	CHROMA	CRISSA	EJECTA	FERULA	GLORIA	INDUNA
ALEXIA	APORIA	BALATA	CALTHA	CHUKKA	CRISTA	ELUVIA	FIBULA	GLOSSA	INFULA
ALISMA	ARALIA	BALBOA	CAMERA	CICADA	CRUSTA	ELYTRA	FIESTA	GOANNA	INSULA
ALOGIA	ARCANA	BANANA	CANADA	CICALA	CUBICA	EMPUSA	FOOTRA	GOPURA	INTIMA
ALPACA	AREOLA	BARYTA	CAPITA	CICUTA	CUESTA	ENIGMA	FOUSSA	GORGIA	INYALA
ALTEZA	ARGALA	BATATA	CARINA	CINEMA	CUPOLA	ENTERA	FOUTRA	GRAPPA	ISCHIA
ALUMNA	ARISTA	BAUERA	CASSIA	CLOACA	CURARA	EPEIRA	FRAENA	GUINEA	JACANA
AMELIA	ARMADA	BEFANA	CATENA	CLUSIA	CUTCHA	EPIZOA	FRISKA	HALLOA	JATAKA
AMENTA	ARNICA	BELUGA	CEDULA	COAITA	CZAPKA	EPOCHA	FRUSTA	HEBONA	JEJUNA
AMOEBA	AROLLA	BEMATA	CEMBRA	CONCHA	DAGABA	ERRATA	FULCRA	HEGIRA	JEMIMA

JERBOA	LABARA	MARINA	NEBULA	PATACA	PYEMIA	RUSSIA	SISTRA	TANTRA	VALUTA
JOANNA	LACUNA	MARKKA	NOCTUA	PATERA	PYURIA	SAHIBA	SITULA	TAPETA	VARROA
JOJOBA	LAGENA	MASULA	NOMINA	PATINA	QUAGGA	SALINA	SKOLIA	TARSIA	VEDUTA
JUDOKA	LAMBDA	MAUNNA	NOVENA	PAYOLA	QUALIA	SALIVA	SMEGMA	TEGULA	VELETA
KABALA	LAMINA	MAXIMA	NUMINA	PELOTA	QUANTA	SALVIA	SOLERA	TELEGA	VESICA
KABAYA	LATRIA	MAZUMA	NUTRIA	PERAEA	QUELEA	SAMARA	SONATA	TEPHRA	VICUNA
KACCHA	LEIPOA	MEDINA	NYANZA	PEREIA	QUINOA	SAMOSA	SOPHIA	TERATA	VIHARA
KAFILA	LIGULA	MEDUSA	OCHREA	PESETA	QUINTA	SAPOTA	SPIREA	TEREFA	VIMANA
KALMIA	LINGUA	MEGARA	OEDEMA	PESEWA	QUOKKA	SATARA	SQUAMA	TERTIA	VIZSLA
KAMALA	LIPOMA	MEZUZA	OMENTA	PESHWA	QUOTHA	SATYRA	STADDA	THANNA	VOMICA
KAMELA	LITHIA	MGANGA	OMERTA	PETARA	RADULA	SCHEMA	STADIA	THULIA	WHATNA
KAMILA	LOCHIA	MIASMA	ONYCHA	PHOBIA	RAFFIA	SCILLA	STANZA	TINAJA	WOMERA
KANAKA	LOGGIA	MIMOSA	OPTIMA	PIAZZA	RANULA	SCLERA	STATUA	TIPULA	XEROMA
KANGHA	LORCHA	MINIMA	ORARIA	PILULA	RAPHIA	SCORIA	STEMMA	TORANA	XYLOMA
KANTHA	LORICA	MODENA	ORBITA	PINETA	RAZZIA	SCOTIA	STIGMA	TORULA	YAKUZA
KARAKA	LUCUMA	MONERA	ORGANA	PIRANA	REALIA	SEMEIA	STIRRA	TOTARA	YARPHA
KATANA	LUMINA	MOORVA	OSCULA	PIRAYA	REDOWA	SENEGA	STRATA	TRAUMA	YOJANA
KERRIA	LUNULA	MORULA	OTTAVA	PITARA	REGINA	SEROSA	STRIGA	TRIVIA	YTTRIA
KGOTLA	LUSTRA	MOTUCA	OZAENA	PLANTA	REGULA	SHARIA	STROMA	TROIKA	ZABETA
KHANGA	MACOYA	MUCOSA	PAELLA	PLASMA	REMORA	SHEILA	STRUMA	TSAMBA	ZAPATA
KHODJA	MACULA	MUMMIA	PAGODA	PLEURA	REMUDA	SHERIA	SUBSEA	TUNDRA	ZAREBA
KHURTA	MAFFIA	MURENA	PAKEHA	PNEUMA	RESEDA	SHIKSA	SULPHA	ULTIMA	ZARIBA
KINEMA	MALTHA	MURRHA	PAKORA	POSADA	RETAMA	SHIRRA	SUNDRA	UNGULA	ZENANA
KORORA	MANANA	MUTUCA	PALAMA	PREMIA	RETINA	SIDDHA	SYLVIA	UREDIA	ZEREBA
KORUNA	MANILA	MYOPIA	PALLIA	PROTEA	RHUMBA	SIENNA	TABULA	UREMIA	ZERIBA
KUFIYA	MANTRA	MYXOMA	PANADA	PRUINA	ROSTRA	SIERRA	TAENIA	URTICA	ZEUGMA
KUMARA	MANTUA	NAGANA	PANAMA	PTERIA	ROSULA	SIESTA	TAHINA	UTOPIA	ZINNIA
KUTCHA	MANUKA	NATURA	PAPAYA	PULKHA	ROTULA	SIFAKA	TAMARA	VAGINA	ZONULA
KWACHA	MARACA	NAUSEA	PAPULA	PUNCTA	RUMINA	SILICA	TANKIA	VALETA	ZYGOMA

7-letter words ending in -A

ABOMASA	APHAGIA	BEGORRA	CASCARA	CURCUMA	EROTICA	GONDOLA	KATORGA	MAREMMA
ABOULIA	APHASIA	BERGAMA	CASSATA	CURIOSA	EULOGIA	GONIDIA	KEITLOA	MARGOSA
ACANTHA	APHELIA	BIODATA	CASSAVA	CURTANA	EUTEXIA	GORILLA	KERYGMA	MARIMBA
ACAPNIA	APHONIA	BIRETTA	CATALPA	CYATHIA	EXCRETA	GRANDMA	KHALIFA	MARKKAA
ACHARYA	APLASIA	BOMBORA	CATASTA	CZARINA	EXEMPLA	GRANDPA	KHEDIVA	MASCARA
ACTINIA	APRAXIA	BONANZA	CATAWBA	DATARIA	EXHEDRA	GUARANA	KIBITKA	MASTABA
ACUSHLA	APTERIA	BORONIA	CAVALLA	DECIDUA	EXORDIA	GUEREZA	KITHARA	MAXILLA
ADDENDA	AQUARIA	BOTTEGA	CEDILLA	DECURIA	EXOTICA	GUMMATA	KUCHCHA	MAZURKA
ADENOMA	ARABICA	BOURKHA	CELESTA	DEJECTA	EXURBIA	GUNNERA	LABELLA	MEDULLA
ADHARMA	ARAROBA	BRACCIA	CEMENTA	DELENDA	FALBALA	HARMALA	LACINIA	MELISMA
AECIDIA	ARGYRIA	BRAVURA	CHALAZA	DELIRIA	FALCULA	HELLOVA	LAMELLA	MESHUGA
AGRAPHA	ARIETTA	BRECCIA	CHECHIA	DIGAMMA	FARRUCA	HELLUVA	LAMPUKA	MESTIZA
ALAMEDA	ARMILLA	BRITSKA	CHIASMA	DILEMMA	FELUCCA	HEMIOLA	LANGAHA	METAZOA
ALCHERA	ASCIDIA	BRITZKA	CHIKARA	DILUVIA	FERMATA	HETAERA	LANTANA	MICELLA
ALCORZA	ASHRAMA	BRUHAHA	CHIMERA	DIORAMA	FIBROMA	HETAIRA	LASAGNA	MILITIA
ALFALFA	ASPIDIA	BUBINGA	CHOLERA	DIPLOMA	FILARIA	HEUREKA	LAVOLTA	MINEOLA
ALFORJA	ASTERIA	BUCCINA	CIBORIA	DOMATIA	FIMBRIA	HEXAPLA	LEMMATA	MINUTIA
ALGEBRA	ATALAYA	BULIMIA	CIMELIA	DOULEIA	FISTULA	HIDALGA	LEMPIRA	MOMENTA
ALGESIA	ATHLETA	CABBALA	CINEREA	DRACHMA	FLUTINA	HIMATIA	LEUCOMA	MONARDA
ALLUVIA	ATRESIA	CADENZA	CITHARA	DROSERA	FORLANA	HOSANNA	LINGULA	MONILIA
ALTEZZA	ATROPIA	CAESURA	CLARKIA	DUODENA	FORMULA	HYMENIA	LOBELIA	MORPHIA
ALTHAEA	AURELIA	CAFFILA	COCHLEA	DVANDVA	FOSSULA	HYPOGEA	LOCUSTA	MORRHUA
ALUMINA	AUREOLA	CALDERA	CODILLA	DYSPNEA	FOVEOLA	HYPOXIA	LOMENTA	MOUSAKA
AMANITA	BACCARA	CALUMBA	COMITIA	DYSURIA	FREESIA	IKEBANA	MADOQUA	MOZETTA
AMENTIA	BACLAVA	CAMPANA	CONARIA	ECHIDNA	FUCHSIA	IMPRESA	MADRASA	MUDIRIA
AMMONIA	BAKLAVA	CANASTA	CONIDIA	ECTHYMA	FURCULA	INDICIA	MADRONA	MULATTA
AMNESIA	BALISTA	CANDELA	COPAIBA	ECTOPIA	FURLANA	INDUSIA	MAGENTA	MURAENA
AMOROSA	BANDANA	CANDIDA	COPAIVA	ECTOZOA	GALABEA	INERTIA	MAGMATA	MUTANDA
AMPHORA	BANDORA	CANELLA	CORALLA	EMBLEMA	GALABIA	INFANTA	MAHATMA	MYALGIA
AMPULLA	BANDURA	CANNULA	CORDOBA	EMPORIA	GALANGA	INGESTA	MAHONIA	MYCELIA
ANAEMIA	BANKSIA	CANTATA	CORELLA	EMPYEMA	GALATEA	IPOMOEA	MALACIA	MYELOMA
ANESTRA	BARBOLA	CANTINA	COROLLA	ENCOMIA	GANGLIA	ISODOMA	MALARIA	MYRINGA
ANGIOMA	BARILLA	CANZONA	CORPORA	ENDOZOA	GAZOOKA	JAMBIYA	MAMILLA	NAPHTHA
ANNATTA	BASIDIA	CARAMBA	CORRIDA	ENEMATA	GENISTA	JELLABA	MANDALA	NEMESIA
ANONYMA	BATTUTA	CARANNA	COTINGA	ENTOZOA	GERBERA	KABBALA	MANDIRA	NEUROMA
ANOSMIA	BAZOOKA	CARAUNA	CREMONA	EPHEDRA	GLUCINA	KACHCHA	MANDOLA	NIGELLA
ANTENNA	BEFFANA	CARIAMA	CROTALA	EQUINIA	GOBURRA	KACHINA	MANDORA	NIRVANA
APEPSIA	BEGONIA	CARIOCA	CURACOA	EROTEMA	GODETIA	KANTELA	MANILLA	NOTANDA

NOTITIA	PANDORA	PISCINA	PYREXIA	RUBELLA	SERPULA	SUMATRA	TORMINA	VIATICA
NOUMENA	PANDURA	PITUITA	PYXIDIA	RUBEOLA	SESTINA	SYNOVIA	TRACHEA	VIDENDA
NOVALIA	PANOCHA	PLACITA	QUASSIA	RUELLIA	SHASTRA	SYRINGA	TREHALA	VIHUELA
NOVELLA	PAPILLA	PLANULA	RABANNA	RUSALKA	SHEHITA	TAFFETA	TRISULA	VINCULA
OCARINA	PAPRIKA	PLATINA	RAMENTA	SABELLA	SHICKSA	TAKAHEA	TSARINA	VIRANDA
OCTAPLA	PARATHA	PLECTRA	RATAFIA	SABURRA	SIGNORA	TALARIA	TUATARA	VISCERA
OLEARIA	PARAZOA	PLEROMA	REFUGIA	SACELLA	SILESIA	TAMASHA	TUTANIA	VIVARIA
OMMATEA	PAREIRA	PLUMULA	REGALIA	SAGITTA	SILIQUA	TAMBURA	TYMPANA	VOLUSPA
OMNIANA	PARELLA	PODAGRA	REGATTA	SAMBUCA	SILPHIA	TANAGRA	ULNARIA	WALLABA
ONDATRA	PARERGA	PODESTA	REGMATA	SANGRIA	SINOPIA	TANTARA	URAEMIA	WEIGELA
ONYCHIA	PARGANA	POLACCA	REPLICA	SARCOMA	SKIMMIA	TAPIOCA	URETHRA	WOOMERA
OOGONIA	PARTITA	POLENTA	RESIDUA	SARDANA	SOREDIA	TARTANA	VALONEA	WOORARA
OPUNTIA	PATAGIA	POLYNIA	RETSINA	SATSUMA	SPATULA	TAVERNA	VALONIA	XERASIA
ORGANZA	PATELLA	POLYNYA	RHODORA	SAVANNA	SPECTRA	TEDESCA	VALVULA	YAMULKA
OROPESA	PAVLOVA	POLYZOA	RHYTINA	SCAGLIA	SPECULA	TEGMINA	VANESSA	YESHIVA
OSMUNDA	PAXIUBA	POTASSA	RICKSHA	SCAPULA	SPICULA	TEMPERA	VANILLA	ZAKUSKA
OSTEOMA	PEISHWA	PRIMULA	RICOTTA	SCHISMA	SPIRAEA	TEMPURA	VARIOLA	ZAMARRA
OSTRACA	PELORIA	PRONOTA	RIVIERA	SCHOLIA	SPLENIA	TEQUILA	VASCULA	ZANELLA
OSTRAKA	PENTHIA	PROPYLA	ROBINIA	SCOPULA	SRADDHA	TEREBRA	VEDALIA	ZAREEBA
OTALGIA	PEREIRA	PTERYLA	ROBUSTA	SCOTOMA	STAMINA	TESSERA	VELARIA	ZEBRULA
OVERSEA	PERGOLA	PUDENDA	ROMAIKA	SCYBALA	STASIMA	THEMATA	VENTANA	ZIGANKA
PADELLA	PERIDIA	PUNALUA	ROMNEYA	SECRETA	STOMATA	THRIMSA	VERANDA	ZIMOCCA
PAENULA	PERSONA	PUPARIA	ROSACEA	SEDILIA	STRETTA	THRYMSA	VERBENA	ZOOECIA
PALABRA	PETUNIA	PUPUNHA	ROSALIA	SEQUELA	STRIATA	TILAPIA	VERRUCA	
PALMYRA	PINNULA	PURPURA	ROSELLA	SEQUOIA	SUBAQUA	TOCCATA	VERRUGA	
PALOOKA	PIRAGUA	PYAEMIA	ROSEOLA	SERIEMA	SUCCUBA	TOHEROA	VETTURA	
PANACEA	PIRANHA	PYGIDIA	ROTUNDA	SERINGA	SULTANA	TOMBOLA	VEXILLA	

8-letter words ending in -A

ABSCISSA	AUTOMATA	CASTELLA	DEMERARA	FIBRILLA	HYDROZOA	MANUBRIA	PARANOEA
ACADEMIA	AUTOPSIA	CATHEDRA	DENTALIA	FISTIANA	HYPALGIA	MARCELLA	PARANOIA
ACALEPHA	AVIFAUNA	CATHISMA	DENTARIA	FLABELLA	HYPOGAEA	MARCHESA	PARHELIA
ADESPOTA	BABUSHKA	CAVATINA	DIARRHEA	FLAGELLA	HYSTERIA	MARIPOSA	PAROEMIA
ADULARIA	BACTERIA	CERCARIA	DIASPORA	FLOTILLA	IMPLUVIA	MARSUPIA	PAROUSIA
ADYNAMIA	BALLISTA	CHARISMA	DIASTEMA	FORAMINA	INSIGNIA	MASSOOLA	PASHMINA
AGNOMINA	BANDANNA	CHIMAERA	DICENTRA	FUGHETTA	INSOMNIA	MATAMATA	PELLAGRA
AGRAPHIA	BARATHEA	CHINAMPA	DICHASIA	GALABIYA	INTARSIA	MELANOMA	PENUMBRA
AKINESIA	BARRANCA	CHINKARA	DIELYTRA	GALLABEA	ISABELLA	MENSTRUA	PERFECTA
ALGAROBA	BASILICA	CHIRAGRA	DIPLOPIA	GALLABIA	ISCHEMIA	MESHUGGA	PERIAGUA
ALIGARTA	BATTALIA	CHLOASMA	DJELLABA	GALTONIA	ISCHURIA	METANOIA	PETECHIA
ALLELUIA	BAUHINIA	CHURINGA	DULCIANA	GARDENIA	JAPONICA	MIASMATA	PHOTOPIA
ALOPECIA	BERGENIA	CHYLURIA	DYSCHROA	GASTRAEA	JARARACA	MILIARIA	PHYSALIA
AMBROSIA	BERYLLIA	CINCHONA	DYSLEXIA	GASTRULA	JARARAKA	MILTONIA	PIASSABA
AMYGDALA	BETHESDA	CLAUSTRA	DYSMELIA	GEMATRIA	KALYPTRA	MINNEOLA	PIASSAVA
ANACONDA	BISCACHA	CLAUSULA	DYSPNOEA	GEROPIGA	KARATEKA	MONSTERA	PIZZERIA
ANALECTA	BIZCACHA	CLITELLA	DYSTOPIA	GESNERIA	KATAKANA	MONTARIA	PLACENTA
ANAPHORA	BLASTEMA	CNIDARIA	ECCLESIA	GLABELLA	KAZATZKA	MOUSSAKA	PLANURIA
ANASARCA	BLASTULA	COCCIDIA	EFFLUVIA	GLAUCOMA	KHANSAMA	MOZZETTA	PLATANNA
ANATHEMA	BRANCHIA	COENOBIA	EGOMANIA	GLIOMATA	KINAKINA	MRIDANGA	PLATYSMA
ANGELICA	BRASSICA	COLCHICA	ENCAENIA	GLORIOSA	KRAMERIA	MYCETOMA	PLETHORA
ANOESTRA	BREGMATA	COLLEGIA	ENGRAMMA	GLOSSINA	LAVATERA	MYXEDEMA	POLLINIA
ANOREXIA	BRITZSKA	COLLYRIA	EPHEMERA	GLOXINIA	LECANORA	MYXOMATA	POLYGALA
ANTEFIXA	BROMELIA	CONFERVA	EPICEDIA	GLUMELLA	LIPOMATA	NAVICULA	POLYURIA
ANTHELIA	BRONCHIA	CONSULTA	EPITHEMA	GOLFIANA	LODICULA	NUBECULA	PREDELLA
ANTHEMIA	BROUHAHA	CONTINUA	EPOPOEIA	GUERILLA	LONICERA	NYMPHAEA	PRESCUTA
ANTISERA	BUDDLEIA	COQUILLA	EQUISETA	GURDWARA	LYMPHOMA	ODONTOMA	PRESIDIA
APOLOGIA	BURLETTA	COXALGIA	ERYTHEMA	GYMKHANA	MACAHUBA	OITICICA	PROFORMA
APOSITIA	CAATINGA	CREDENDA	ESTANCIA	GYMNASIA	MADRASSA	OMBRELLA	PROGERIA
APYREXIA	CACHEXIA	CREDENZA	ESTHESIA	HABANERA	MAGNESIA	OPERCULA	PROTOZOA
ARAPAIMA	CACHUCHA	CRIBELLA	EUPEPSIA	HACIENDA	MAGNOLIA	OPERETTA	PRUNELLA
ARAPONGA	CALDARIA	CRITERIA	EUPHOBIA	HAMARTIA	MAHARAJA	OPUSCULA	PRYTANEA
ARAPUNGA	CALISAYA	CROMORNA	EUPHONIA	HEARTPEA	MAIOLICA	ORCHELLA	PTERYGIA
ARBORETA	CALYPTRA	CUNABULA	EUPHORIA	HEMIOLIA	MAJOLICA	ORCHILLA	PUTAMINA
ASPHYXIA	CAMELLIA	CYMBIDIA	EXCERPTA	HEMIOPIA	MALVASIA	PALESTRA	PYCNIDIA
ASTHENIA	CAMPAGNA	CZAREVNA	FALDETTA	HERBARIA	MAMMILLA	PANDEMIA	QUADRIGA
ASTIGMIA	CAPITULA	CZARITZA	FANTASIA	HETAERIA	MANDIOCA	PANMIXIA	QUILLAIA
ATARAXIA	CAPYBARA	DECENNIA	FASCIOLA	HETAIRIA	MANDORLA	PANORAMA	QUILLAJA
ATHEROMA	CARACARA	DEMENTIA	FASCISTA	HOSPITIA	MANTILLA	PARABEMA	QUINELLA
AURICULA	CARNAUBA	DEMENTIA	FENESTRA	HYDREMIA	MANTISSA	PARABOLA	RACHILLA

```
RADIALIA  SCHEMATA  SHRADDHA  STOTINKA  SYNECHIA  TOXAEMIA  UREDINIA  VULSELLA
RAKSHASA  SCIATICA  SIDALCEA  STROBILA  SYNEDRIA  TOXOCARA  VACCINIA  WISTARIA
RAPHANIA  SCLEREMA  SIGNORIA  STROMATA  SYNTAGMA  TRACHOMA  VAGINULA  WISTERIA
REDDENDA  SCLEROMA  SILICULA  STRONTIA  SYSSITIA  TRAPEZIA  VALLONIA  XANTHOMA
RENDZINA  SCOLIOMA  SINFONIA  SUBCOSTA  TAKAMAKA  TRAUMATA  VELAMINA  XENOPHYA
RESINATA  SCOTOPIA  SONATINA  SUBPHYLA  TAMANDUA  TRICHINA  VELATURA  YARMULKA
RESPONSA  SCROFULA  SORBARIA  SUBPOENA  TAMBOURA  TRIDACNA  VENDETTA  YERSINIA
RETINULA  SCUTELLA  SPIRILLA  SUBTOPIA  TAPADERA  TRIFECTA  VERONICA  YTTERBIA
REWAREWA  SEMANTRA  SPORIDIA  SUBUCULA  TENTORIA  TRIFORIA  VERTEBRA  ZAMBOMBA
RHIZOBIA  SEMICOMA  SQUAMULA  SUBURBIA  TEQUILLA  TRILEMMA  VESICULA  ZAMPOGNA
RUTABAGA  SEMOLINA  STALAGMA  SUDAMINA  TERATOMA  TRIPUDIA  VESTIGIA  ZARZUELA
SACRARIA  SEMUNCIA  STAPELIA  SVASTIKA  TERRARIA  TRITONIA  VIBRISSA  ZASTRUGA
SALICETA  SENSILLA  STAROSTA  SWASTIKA  TERRELLA  TROCHLEA  VICTORIA  ZIRCONIA
SAPUCAIA  SEPTARIA  STEATOMA  SWEETPEA  TERZETTA  TROPARIA  VIEWDATA  ZOIATRIA
SARMENTA  SEPTLEVA  STEMMATA  SYMPODIA  TESSELLA  TSAREVNA  VIRAEMIA  ZOOCYTIA
SASARARA  SERENATA  STERIGMA  SYMPOSIA  TETRAPLA  TSARITSA  VIRTUOSA  ZOOGLOEA
SASTRUGA  SHAMIANA  STIGMATA  SYNANGIA  THERIACA  ULTIMATA  VISCACHA  ZOONOMIA
SAYONARA  SHECHITA  STOCCATA  SYNAPHEA  THIOUREA  UMBRELLA  VITICETA  ZUCHETTA
SCHAPSKA  SHIGELLA  STOMODEA  SYNCYTIA  TORTILLA  UNDERSEA  VIZCACHA  ZYGANTRA
```

WORDS ENDING IN -I

2-letter words ending in -I

```
AI    GI    LI    OI    SI    XI
DI    HI    MI    PI    TI
```

3-letter words ending in -I

```
AMI    DEI    HOI    LEI    PHI    PSI    SEI    SUI    TUI
CHI    GHI    KAI    OBI    POI    SAI    SKI    TAI    UNI
```

4-letter words ending in -I

```
ANTI    DELI    GYRI    KAZI    MERI    NODI    RAGI    SIMI    TOPI    WILI
ASCI    DIVI    HAJI    KEPI    MIDI    NORI    RAKI    SIRI    TORI    YETI
BANI    DIXI    HILI    KIRI    MINI    PENI    RAMI    SOLI    UGLI    YOGI
BENI    ETUI    IMPI    KIWI    MODI    PERI    RANI    SORI    UNCI    YONI
CADI    EUOI    KADI    LOBI    MOKI    PILI    ROTI    TALI    VAGI    ZATI
CEDI    FOCI    KAKI    LOCI    MOOI    PIPI    SAKI    TAXI    VALI
CHAI    FUCI    KALI    MAGI    NAOI    PURI    SARI    TIKI    VLEI
DALI    GADI    KAMI    MALI    NIDI    QADI    SATI    TIPI    WADI
DARI    GLEI    KATI    MAXI    NISI    RABI    SEMI    TITI    WALI
```

5-letter words ending in -I

```
ABACI   BASSI   COCCI   FERMI   INDRI   MAQUI   OZEKI   RECTI   SUSHI   URARI
ACARI   BENNI   CORGI   FRATI   ISSEI   MEDII   PAGRI   RISHI   SWAMI   UTERI
ACINI   BLINI   CORNI   FUNDI   JINNI   MODII   PALKI   SALMI   TANTI   VILLI
AGAMI   BRAVI   DARZI   FUNGI   KARRI   MOOLI   PALPI   SAMPI   TARSI   XYSTI
AGGRI   BUFFI   DHOBI   GARNI   KATTI   MUFTI   PAOLI   SCAPI   TEMPI   ZIMBI
AGUTI   BWAZI   DHOTI   GENII   KAURI   NAEVI   PARDI   SCUDI   TERAI   ZOMBI
AIDOI   CACTI   DILLI   GHAZI   KHADI   NIMBI   PARKI   SERAI   THAGI
AIOLI   CARDI   DUOMI   GOBBI   KHAKI   NISEI   PARTI   SHCHI   THOLI
ALIBI   CEILI   ELCHI   GUSLI   KUKRI   NOMOI   PERAI   SHOJI   TONDI
APPUI   CERCI   ELEMI   HADJI   LATHI   OBELI   PILEI   SOLDI   TOPHI
ARDRI   CHILI   ENNUI   HAJJI   LAZZI   OBOLI   PIRAI   SPAHI   TOPOI
ASSAI   CHOLI   ENVOI   HOURI   LENTI   OCULI   PUTTI   STOAI   TORII
AULOI   CIPPI   FARCI   IAMBI   LICHI   OKAPI   QUASI   STYLI   TRAGI
AUREI   CIRRI   FASCI   IMARI   LUNGI   ORIBI   RABBI   SUCCI   TUTTI
BAJRI   COATI   FASTI   IMSHI   LURGI   OVOLI   RADII   SULCI   URALI
```

6-letter words ending in -I

```
AGOUTI  ARGALI  AVANTI  BHISTI  BUKSHI  CHICHI  CUMULI  DEWANI  ECHINI  FLOCCI
ALKALI  ARGULI  BAILLI  BIKINI  BURITI  CHILLI  CURARI  DHOOTI  ELTCHI  GARDAI
ALUMNI  ARILLI  BANZAI  BOLETI  CALAMI  CHOWRI  CYATHI  DJINNI  EMBOLI  GELATI
ANNULI  ARIOSI  BHAKTI  BONSAI  CANTHI  CLYPEI  CYTISI  DROMOI  EPHEBI  GEMINI
ARCHEI  ASKARI  BHINDI  BORZOI  CESTUI  COLOBI  DECANI  DUETTI  EURIPI  GHARRI
```

GILGAI	JAWARI	LOBULI	MUNSHI	OURARI	RENVOI	SATORI	SOLIDI	THYRSI	YOGINI
GLUTEI	JOWARI	LOCULI	NAGARI	OUREBI	RHOMBI	SBIRRI	SONERI	TITOKI	ZUFOLI
GOMUTI	JUDOGI	MALLEI	NEROLI	PAPYRI	RUBATI	SCAMPI	SOUARI	TROCHI	
GRIGRI	JUNGLI	MANATI	NIELLI	PERITI	SACCOI	SCYPHI	STRATI	TROPHI	
GURAMI	JUPATI	MAULVI	NILGAI	PHALLI	SAFARI	SESELI	SUNDRI	TSOTSI	
HAIKAI	KABUKI	MAZHBI	NOSTOI	PITHOI	SAIKEI	SHALLI	TAHINI	TUMULI	
HAMULI	KAIKAI	MILADI	NUCLEI	PITURI	SAKKOI	SHTCHI	TAMARI	UAKARI	
HUMERI	KOWHAI	MIRITI	OCELLI	POLYPI	SALAMI	SHUFTI	TAPETI	UNCINI	
ILLUPI	KUMARI	MISHMI	OCTOPI	PUTELI	SALUKI	SIDDHI	TATAMI	WAKIKI	
INCAVI	LIMULI	MODULI	OCTROI	RAGINI	SANDHI	SIMPAI	THALLI	WAPITI	
INCUBI	LITCHI	MUESLI	OURALI	RAMULI	SANSEI	SMALTI	THOLOI	XYSTOI	

7-letter words ending in -I

ALFAQUI	BOUILLI	DAKOITI	GHILGAI	LAPILLI	OUSTITI	RHONCHI	SOPRANI	TSUNAMI
ALIZARI	BRONCHI	DASHEKI	GINGILI	LECYTHI	PACHISI	RHYTHMI	SORDINI	TYMPANI
ALVEOLI	CADUCEI	DASHIKI	GLUTAEI	MACRAMI	PADRONI	RILIEVI	SPLENII	URCEOLI
AMORINI	CALCULI	DEMENTI	GNOCCHI	MAESTRI	PALAZZI	RIPIENI	STAMNOI	VENTURI
ANESTRI	CALZONI	DENARII	GOURAMI	MAFIOSI	PECCAVI	SACCULI	STICHOI	VITELLI
ANZIANI	CANZONI	DIDAKAI	GRADINI	MARCONI	PENUCHI	SAIMIRI	STIMULI	WISTITI
APPALTI	CAVETTI	DIDAKEI	GUARANI	MARTINI	PINDARI	SAMURAI	STRETTI	WOORALI
ARCHAEI	CHAPATI	DIDICOI	HALLALI	MENISCI	PRELUDI	SAOUARI	SUCCUBI	WOURALI
ASSAGAI	CHARQUI	DOCHMII	HIBACHI	MODIOLI	PRONAOI	SARANGI	SUNDARI	ZAKUSKI
ASSEGAI	CHONDRI	EFFENDI	INTARSI	MOLOSSI	PULVINI	SASHIMI	SURCULI	ZUFFOLI
ASTATKI	CHORAGI	ELENCHI	JACUZZI	NAUPLII	QUILLAI	SCHERZI	SYLLABI	
BACCHII	CHOREGI	EMERITI	JAMDANI	NAUTILI	RABBONI	SECONDI	TERMINI	
BACILLI	CHUPATI	EPIGONI	JAMPANI	NONETTI	RAVIOLI	SENARII	THALAMI	
BAMBINI	CLARINI	ETOURDI	JINJILI	NUCELLI	REMBLAI	SERKALI	THROMBI	
BASENJI	COLIBRI	FAGOTTI	KACHERI	NURAGHI	REVERSI	SHIKARI	TIMPANI	
BILIMBI	COLOSSI	FORZATI	KAMICHI	ORIGAMI	RHIZOPI	SIGNORI	TONDINI	
BIRYANI	CRIMINI	FUMETTI	LAMPUKI	OUAKARI	RHOMBOI	SONDELI	TRIPOLI	

8-letter words ending in -I

ACOEMETI	BROCCOLI	COTHURNI	FEDELINI	LINGUINI	PASTRAMI	SASTRUGI	TEDESCHI	
ALBERGHI	CANCELLI	CUNJEVOI	FLOCCULI	LITERATI	PEPERONI	SCALDINI	TEOCALLI	
AMORETTI	CANTHARI	DAIQUIRI	FORZANDI	LUMBRICI	PERFECTI	SFORZATI	TERAKIHI	
ANOESTRI	CAPITANI	DECUBITI	FUNICULI	MACARONI	PERIBOLI	SHANGHAI	TERIYAKI	
ANTENATI	CAPRICCI	DIADOCHI	GINGLYMI	MAHARANI	PERRADII	SIGISBEI	TERZETTI	
ASSEGAAI	CASTRATI	DIDDICOI	GLADIOLI	MALLEOLI	PIROSHKI	SOFFIONI	UMBILICI	
BANDITTI	CHAPATTI	DIPTEROI	GRAFFITI	MARAVEDI	PIROZHKI	SOLFEGGI	UTRICULI	
BERIBERI	CHUPATTI	DIVIDIVI	HETAIRAI	MARCHESI	PRODROMI	STAPEDII	VIRTUOSI	
BIMBASHI	CICERONI	DRACHMAI	HYDROSKI	MARIACHI	PULVILLI	STOTINKI	ZASTRUGI	
BIRIYANI	CICISBEI	DUPONDII	KACHAHRI	MORBILLI	RENMINBI	STROBILI	ZECCHINI	
BONAMANI	CONCEPTI	DURUKULI	KOFTGARI	NARCISSI	RETIARII	SUKIYAKI	ZUCCHINI	
BOSTANGI	CONCETTI	DUUMVIRI	KOHLRABI	NUCLEOLI	RISPETTI	SUMOTORI		
BOUZOUKI	CONDUCTI	ESOPHAGI	KOMITAJI	OUISTITI	RYOTWARI	TAGLIONI		
BOZZETTI	CONFETTI	FASCISMI	LEKYTHOI	PARCHESI	SANNYASI	TANDOORI		
BRINDISI	CORNETTI	FASCISTI	LIBRETTI	PASTICCI	SARTORII	TARAKIHI		

WORDS ENDING IN -O

2-letter words ending in -O

BO	GO	IO	KO	MO	OO	SO	WO	ZO
DO	HO	JO	LO	NO	PO	TO	YO	

3-letter words ending in -O

ADO	BRO	DUO	GEO	LOO	PHO	ROO	UDO	YGO
AGO	COO	DZO	GIO	MHO	POO	THO	UFO	ZHO
BIO	DOO	EGO	GOO	MOO	PRO	TOO	WHO	ZOO
BOO	DSO	FRO	HOO	OHO	RHO	TWO	WOO	

4-letter words ending in -O

AFRO	ALTO	ANNO	AUTO	BOKO	BRIO	BUDO	CIAO	COHO	DECO
AGIO	AMBO	ARCO	BEGO	BOLO	BROO	BUFO	CITO	DADO	DEMO
ALSO	AMMO	ARVO	BITO	BOYO	BUBO	CAPO	COCO	DAGO	DIDO

DODO	FICO	HERO	JOCO	LILO	MINO	PEPO	SILO	TOHO	VETO
DOJO	FIGO	HOBO	JOMO	LINO	MISO	PESO	SKEO	TOKO	VINO
DURO	FINO	HOMO	JUDO	LOBO	MOKO	POCO	SKIO	TRIO	VIVO
ECCO	GAJO	HUSO	KAGO	LOCO	MONO	POLO	SOLO	TYPO	WINO
ECHO	GAPO	HYPO	KAYO	LOGO	ODSO	PROO	SUMO	TYRO	ZERO
EDDO	GIRO	INFO	KILO	LOTO	OLEO	PYRO	SYBO	UMBO	ZOBO
ERGO	GOBO	INGO	KINO	LUDO	OLIO	REDO	TACO	UNCO	
EURO	GOGO	INRO	KOLO	MAKO	ONTO	RIVO	TARO	UNDO	
EXPO	GYRO	INTO	KOTO	MEMO	OTTO	SAGO	THRO	UNTO	
FADO	HALO	JATO	LENO	MICO	OUZO	SEGO	TIRO	UPGO	
FARO	HARO	JIAO	LIDO	MILO	PACO	SHOO	TOCO	URAO	

5-letter words ending in -O

ADDIO	BUNCO	CUFFO	FORGO	HOLLO	LENTO	MUNGO	POTTO	SCHMO	VERSO
AGGRO	BUNKO	CURIO	FUERO	HOWSO	LIMBO	NAPOO	PRIMO	SCUDO	VIDEO
AMIGO	BUROO	CUTTO	GADSO	HULLO	LINGO	NEGRO	PROMO	SECCO	VIREO
AUDIO	BURRO	CYCLO	GARBO	HYDRO	LITHO	NGAIO	PULMO	SEGNO	VISTO
AVISO	CACAO	DANIO	GAZOO	IAIDO	LLANO	ORTHO	PUNTO	SERVO	VULGO
AWETO	CAMEO	DECKO	GECKO	IGAPO	LOTTO	OUTDO	PUTTO	SHAKO	WAHOO
BABOO	CANTO	DEKKO	GESSO	IGLOO	MACHO	OUTGO	QUIPO	SMOKO	WHOSO
BACCO	CARGO	DIAZO	GIPPO	IMAGO	MACRO	OVOLO	RADIO	SOCKO	YAHOO
BALOO	CASCO	DILDO	GISMO	INTRO	MAIKO	PANTO	RATIO	SOLDO	YARTO
BANCO	CELLO	DINGO	GIZMO	IROKO	MAMBO	PAOLO	RECCO	SORBO	YOBBO
BANJO	CENTO	DIPSO	GOBBO	JAMBO	MANGO	PAREO	RECTO	SORDO	ZAMBO
BASSO	CHACO	DISCO	GODSO	JELLO	MANTO	PASEO	REFFO	SORGO	ZHOMO
BASTO	CHIAO	DITTO	GOMBO	JINGO	MATLO	PATIO	REPRO	SPADO	ZINCO
BEANO	CHINO	DOGGO	GREGO	JOCKO	MATZO	PEDRO	RETRO	STYLO	ZOCCO
BILBO	CISCO	DSOBO	GUACO	JUMBO	MESTO	PESTO	RHINO	TABOO	ZOPPO
BIMBO	COCCO	DSOMO	GUANO	JUNCO	METRO	PHOTO	RODEO	TANGO	ZORRO
BINGO	COMBO	DUNNO	GUIRO	JUNTO	MEZZO	PIANO	RONDO	TANTO	
BOMBO	COMMO	DUOMO	GUMBO	KAZOO	MICRO	PIEZO	RONEO	TEMPO	
BONGO	COMPO	ESTRO	GUSTO	KEMBO	MISDO	PINGO	RUMBO	TIMBO	
BORGO	CONGO	FANGO	GYPPO	KENDO	MISGO	PINKO	SALTO	TONDO	
BRAVO	CONTO	FATSO	HALLO	KIMBO	MOLTO	PINTO	SALVO	TORSO	
BUCKO	CORNO	FIBRO	HELLO	LARGO	MORRO	POLIO	SAMBO	TURBO	
BUFFO	CORSO	FOLIO	HILLO	LASSO	MOTTO	PONGO	SANKO	TYPTO	
BUMBO	CREDO	FORDO	HIPPO	LAZZO	MUCRO	PORNO	SARGO	UREDO	

6-letter words ending in -O

ABRAZO	BOLERO	CRYPTO	FRANCO	GRINGO	MANOAO	PHYSIO	ROCOCO	STEREO	VIGORO
ADAGIO	BONITO	CUCKOO	FRESCO	GROTTO	MATICO	POMATO	ROTOLO	STINGO	VIRAGO
AIKIDO	BOOBOO	DAIMIO	FUGATO	HALLOO	MEDICO	POMELO	RUBATO	STUCCO	VOMITO
AKIMBO	BRONCO	DAYGLO	FUMADO	HERETO	MELANO	PONCHO	SAMFOO	STUDIO	VOODOO
ALBEDO	BUMALO	DOMINO	GABBRO	HOODOO	MERINO	POTATO	SANCHO	SUBITO	VORAGO
ALBINO	BURGOO	DORADO	GAUCHO	HOOROO	MIKADO	PRESTO	SAPEGO	TATTOO	WANDOO
ALBUGO	CALICO	DRONGO	GAZEBO	IGNARO	MODULO	PRONTO	SBIRRO	TENUTO	WEIRDO
ANATTO	CALIGO	DUELLO	GELATO	INCAVO	MORPHO	PSEUDO	SCHIZO	TERCIO	WHACKO
ANGICO	CAMSHO	DUETTO	GENTOO	INDIGO	NANDOO	PSYCHO	SCRUTO	TEREDO	WHATSO
APOLLO	CASINO	DYNAMO	GHERAO	JOURNO	NARDOO	PUEBLO	SHIPPO	THICKO	ZELOSO
ARIOSO	CATALO	EMBRYO	GHETTO	KAKAPO	NIELLO	PUMELO	SHIVOO	TOMATO	ZOOZOO
ARISTO	CHEAPO	ENHALO	GIGOLO	KIMONO	NUNCIO	PUNCTO	SISSOO	TORERO	ZORINO
ARROYO	CHEERO	ERINGO	GINGKO	KOODOO	NYMPHO	QUANGO	SKIDOO	TRILLO	ZUFOLO
BAGNIO	CHOCHO	ERYNGO	GINKGO	LANUGO	OCTAVO	QUARTO	SMALTO	TROPPO	
BAGUIO	CHROMO	ESCUDO	GITANO	LAVABO	OVERDO	QUBATO	SOLANO	TUPELO	
BAMBOO	CICERO	FASCIO	GIUSTO	LEGATO	OVERGO	RABATO	SOLITO	TURACO	
BARRIO	COLUGO	FIASCO	GOMBRO	LIBIDO	PALOLO	RANCHO	SORGHO	TUXEDO	
BISTRO	COMEDO	FINSKO	GOMUTO	LUCUMO	PARAMO	REBATO	SPEEDO	ULTIMO	
BLANCO	COROZO	FOREGO	GOOROO	MACACO	PEDALO	REGULO	STALKO	VAUDOO	
BLOTTO	CRAMBO	FORHOO	GORGIO	MANITO	PHYLLO	ROBALO	STANZO	VIBRIO	

7-letter words ending in -O

AGITATO	ANNATTO	AZULEJO	BOTARGO	BUFFALO	CANTICO	CHAMISO	CORANTO	DIABOLO
AILANTO	APPALTO	BAMBINO	BRACCIO	BUGABOO	CASSINO	CHEERIO	CORNUTO	EIGHTVO
ALBERGO	ARNOTTO	BAROCCO	BRASERO	BUMMALO	CATTALO	CHICANO	CRIOLLO	ELECTRO
ALLEGRO	ARRIERO	BARRICO	BRAVADO	BUSHIDO	CAVETTO	CHORIZO	CRUSADO	EMBARGO
AMORINO	ASINICO	BATTERO	BRONCHO	CALANDO	CEMBALO	CLARINO	CURACAO	ESPARTO
AMOROSO	AVOCADO	BEEFALO	BUDGERO	CALYPSO	CENTAVO	COQUITO	CYMBALO	ETAERIO

FAGOTTO	INFERNO	MORENDO	PASSADO	PORTICO	SAGUARO	SOPRANO	TORNADO	VOLPINO
FARRAGO	LENTIGO	MORISCO	PATRICO	POTOROO	SALTATO	SORDINO	TORPEDO	WENDIGO
FERRUGO	LLANERO	MOROCCO	PEDRERO	PRIMERO	SAMSHOO	SQUACCO	TOURACO	WHERESO
FINNSKO	LUMBAGO	MULATTO	PEEKABO	PRIVADO	SAPSAGO	STRETTO	TREMOLO	WHERETO
FORZATO	MADRONO	NATHEMO	PERSICO	PROVISO	SCALADO	SUBZERO	TROMINO	WINDIGO
FUMETTO	MAESTRO	NAVARHO	PIANINO	PROXIMO	SCHERZO	SUPREMO	TYMPANO	ZAMARRO
FURIOSO	MAFIOSO	NELUMBO	PICCOLO	PRURIGO	SCIOLTO	TANGELO	UNDERDO	ZANJERO
GAMBADO	MAGNETO	NONETTO	PIFFERO	REJONEO	SCORPIO	TEDESCO	UNDERGO	ZEMSTVO
GIOCOSO	MALICHO	OKIMONO	PIMENTO	RELIEVO	SECONDO	TENTIGO	VAQUERO	ZOCCOLO
GRADINO	MARCATO	OLOROSO	PINTADO	REVERSO	SENECIO	TESTUDO	VERISMO	ZORILLO
GUANACO	MEMENTO	OREGANO	PLACEBO	RIDOTTO	SERPIGO	THEORBO	VERTIGO	ZUFFOLO
HIDALGO	MESTIZO	PAISANO	PLENIPO	RILIEVO	SFUMATO	THERETO	VIBRATO	
HISTRIO	MISTICO	PAKAPOO	POINADO	RIPIENO	SHAKUDO	TIMPANO	VILIACO	
HORNITO	MOCKADO	PALAZZO	POMPANO	RISOTTO	SHAMPOO	TOBACCO	VILIAGO	
HUANACO	MONTERO	PAMPERO	POMPELO	RONDINO	SIROCCO	TOMBOLO	VIRANDO	
IMPASTO	MORELLO	PAPILIO	PORRIGO	ROSOLIO	SOLDADO	TONDINO	VOLCANO	

8-letter words ending in -O

ALFRESCO	CASTRATO	EXPRESSO	IMPETIGO	MANZELLO	PIMIENTO	SESTETTO	TUCOTUCO
AMORETTO	CAUDILLO	FALSETTO	INNUENDO	MARTELLO	PLUMBAGO	SFORZATO	TUCUTUCO
ARMIGERO	CHARNECO	FANDANGO	INTAGLIO	MODERATO	POIGNADO	SIGISBEO	TWELVEMO
ARPEGGIO	CHECHAKO	FASCISMO	INTARSIO	MONTANTO	POLITICO	SMORZATO	UMBRELLO
ASSIENTO	CICISBEO	FELLATIO	JACKAROO	MOSQUITO	PRELUDIO	SOMBRERO	VARGUENO
AUTOGIRO	COCKATOO	FINNESKO	JACKEROO	NEUTRINO	PRESIDIO	SPADILLO	VARLETTO
AUTOGYRO	COMMANDO	FINOCHIO	JILLAROO	OCOTILLO	PRUNELLO	SPICCATO	VERDELHO
BALLYHOO	CONCERTO	FLAMENCO	JORDELOO	ORATORIO	PULVILIO	STACCATO	VILLAGIO
BARBASCO	CONCETTO	FLAMINGO	JUNKANOO	OSTINATO	RANCHERO	STAMPEDO	VILLIAGO
BARGELLO	CONTANGO	FORZANDO	KAKEMONO	OTTAVINO	REDDENDO	STICCADO	VINDALOO
BARRANCO	CONTINUO	GALAPAGO	KANGAROO	PACHINKO	RENEGADO	STICCATO	VIRTUOSO
BESOGNIO	CONTORNO	GARBANZO	LENTANDO	PADERERO	RISOLUTO	STILETTO	VITILIGO
BONAMANO	CORAGGIO	GARDYLOO	LIBECCIO	PALAMINO	RISPETTO	STOCCADO	WALLAROO
BORACHIO	CORNETTO	GAZPACHO	LIBRETTO	PALISADO	RITENUTO	SUBIMAGO	WANDEROO
BORDELLO	COROCORO	GILLAROO	LITERATO	PALMETTO	ROSOGLIO	SUPPEAGO	ZECCHINO
BOZZETTO	CRUZEIRO	GRACIOSO	LOCOFOCO	PALOMINO	SALTANDO	TAPACOLO	ZUCHETTO
BUCKAROO	CURCULIO	GRAFFITO	MACHISMO	PARLANDO	SARGASSO	TAPACULO	
BUCKAYRO	DOLOROSO	GRAZIOSO	MAESTOSO	PATERERO	SCALDINO	TAPADERO	
BUCKEROO	DUETTINO	GUACHARO	MAKIMONO	PEDERERO	SCENARIO	TENEBRIO	
CACAFOGO	ESCALADO	HALLALOO	MALGRADO	PEEKABOO	SCIROCCO	TERRAZZO	
CAMISADO	ESCAPADO	HEREUNTO	MALLECHO	PEPERINO	SCORDATO	TERZETTO	
CAPITANO	ESPRESSO	HITHERTO	MAMELUCO	PERDENDO	SEICENTO	TRAPUNTO	
CAPUCCIO	ESPUMOSO	HUBBUBOO	MANCANDO	PERFECTO	SERAGLIO	TRECENTO	

WORDS ENDING IN -U

2-letter words ending in -U

GU	MU	NU	OU	YU

3-letter words ending in -U

AYU	ECU	FLU	GJU	LEU	PIU	UTU
CRU	EMU	FOU	GNU	MEU	SOU	VAU
EAU	FEU	GAU	JEU	MOU	TAU	YOU

4-letter words ending in -U

AITU	BEAU	EMEU	JUJU	LUAU	OMBU	RIMU	THOU	TUTU	ZULU
BABU	CHOU	FRAU	KUDU	LULU	PRAU	TABU	THRU	UNAU	
BALU	CLOU	GENU	KUKU	MASU	PULU	TAPU	TOFU	ZEBU	
BAPU	ECRU	GURU	LIEU	MENU	RATU	TATU	TOLU	ZOBU	

5-letter words ending in -U

ADIEU	BUCHU	CORNU	HOKKU	LASSU	PERDU	QUIPU	SNAFU	VERTU
BAYOU	BUCKU	COYPU	JAMBU	NANDU	PILAU	SADHU	TATOU	VIRTU
BIJOU	BUNDU	FICHU	KANZU	NOYAU	POILU	SAJOU	UHURU	VOULU
BOYAU	BUSSU	HAIKU	KUDZU	PAREU	PRAHU	SAMFU	URUBU	WUSHU

6-letter words ending in -U

ABATTU	BATEAU	CONGOU	GAGAKU	JABIRU	MZUNGU	PILLAU	SADDHU	TELEDU
ACAJOU	BUREAU	COTEAU	GATEAU	KIKUYU	NILGAU	PIUPIU	SAMSHU	VOUDOU
AMADOU	CACHOU	DETENU	GOMOKU	LANDAU	NOGAKU	RESEAU	SUBFEU	YNAMBU
APERCU	CADEAU	EPERDU	INGENU	MILIEU	ORMOLU	ROUCOU	TAMANU	

7-letter words ending in -U

BABASSU	BUNRAKU	CATTABU	FABLIAU	MARABOU	PARVENU	ROULEAU	TINAMOU
BANDEAU	CAMAIEU	CHANOYU	INCONNU	MOINEAU	PLATEAU	SAPAJOU	TONNEAU
BASBLEU	CARDECU	CHAPEAU	JAMBEAU	MORCEAU	PONCEAU	SEPPUKU	TRUMEAU
BEBEERU	CARIBOU	CHATEAU	MANITOU	NOUVEAU	PURLIEU	SHIATSU	
BERCEAU	CATECHU	CORBEAU	MANTEAU	NYLGHAU	RONDEAU	TABLEAU	

8-letter words ending in -U

ABOIDEAU	CARCAJOU	CARJACOU	FLAMBEAU	KABELJOU	PIRARUCU	SUCURUJU
ABOITEAU	CARIACOU	FELDGRAU	HAUSFRAU	KINKAJOU	PYENGADU	SURUCUCU

SECTION THREE

BONUS WORD SETS

Introduction

Since there is a 50-point bonus for playing all seven tiles at one turn, seven-letter words are an essential part of the Scrabble player's vocabulary. As seven tiles can also be played around an existing letter on the board, eight-letter words are also a key part of the Scrabble player's word knowledge. Any word which uses all seven of the letters on your rack is called a bonus word, or just plain bonus. Bonuses usually have seven or eight letters, but could have more. (In the USA and some other parts of the world, words which score a 50-point bonus are called 'bingos'.)

Some seven-letter words are more useful than others, simply because they are more likely to occur, given the distribution of letters in the Scrabble set. For this reason, it is an unnecessary task (and a painstakingly lengthy one!) to attempt to learn all of the seven-letter words. There are over 25,000 seven-letter words, yet it is much more worthwhile (and a lot easier!) to concentrate on some of the 20-25% that are going to be the most useful to you. Such seven-letter words can be arranged conveniently according to common six-letter groups of letters. Each group yields a list of seven-letter words that can be made by the addition of a single seventh letter. These are the '6-plus-1 lists' – six letters plus another one letter to make a variety of seven-letter words. The more different letters of the alphabet that a combination goes with, the higher its utility to the Scrabble player.

There are 200 such six-letter sets in the subsequent 6-plus-1 lists, representing the 200 most fruitful and most likely combinations, based on an algorithm of the probability of the six-letter set occurring and the number of different letters it combines with. The six-letter combinations are listed in alphabetical sequence with their respective position in the top 200 shown alongside. In each case, a mnemonic of the six-letter combination is also provided as an aide-mémoire. It is easier to recall that LADIES plus an O makes DEASOIL, rather than ADEILS plus an O.

These six-letter combinations simplify learning and should assist recollection during an actual game. If the concept is new to you, then just concentrate on two or three of the most fertile sets, such as AEINRT (RETAIN), AENRST (ANTERS) and EGINRS (INGERS). When the seven-letter words associated with these become familiar, move on and tackle other six-letter sets. On the other hand, you may want to expand on the 200 lists here. Just select a group of six letters *not* in the list of 200, and then use the seven-letter anagrams list in Section 5 to search for the seven-letter words which can be made by the addition of a single letter to your chosen group of six.

Eight-letter words also need to be in the Scrabble player's armoury. There will be many occasions when the seven letters on your rack can be added to a single letter already on the board, to make an eight-letter word. Perhaps the seven letters on your rack do not make a bonus word by themselves. Even if they do, perhaps the bonus word won't fit on the board anywhere. These are the occasions when you may need to think bigger – eight-letter words! Of course, the seven-letter word on your rack may go down on the board, but the potential eight-letter word might score quite a few more points. Sometimes an eight-letter word will score a lot more points, if it covers two triple-word-score squares – this is the 'nine-timer' which Scrabble players strive for in high-scoring games!

The eight-letter words are arranged here into the 200 most worthwhile six-letter groups – the same top 200 as used for the seven-letter words. Listed beneath each six-letter group are the two-letter combinations which can be added to create an eight-letter word. So, for example, ABEILS plus AL yields both ISABELLA and SAILABLE; ABEILS plus AR yields RAISABLE; and so on. These, then, are the '6-plus-2 lists'. If you don't feel able to tackle all 200 lists in one go, break them up into smaller groups. Begin by concentrating on the most fertile groups (AEIRST, AEINST, and AEINRS are the top three). Once you feel confident about these, move on to other groups. If your own favourite six-letter groups are not listed here, why not use the Eight Letter Anagrams list in Section 5 to create new 6-plus-2 lists?

7-LETTER SETS
from the top 200 6-letter combinations

ABDEIR 134
(ABRIDE)
C CARBIDE
D BRAIDED
E BEADIER
  BEARDIE
G ABRIDGE
  BRIGADE
L BRAILED
  RIDABLE
M EMBRAID
N BANDIER
  BRAINED
R BARDIER
  BRAIDER
  BRIARED
  RABIDER
S BRAISED
  DARBIES
T TRIBADE
U DAUBIER
W BAWDIER

ABEILS 188
(ISABEL)
A ABELIAS
D DISABLE
E BAILEES
F FAIBLES
I BAILIES
K SKIABLE
M EMBAILS
  LAMBIES
N LESBIAN
R BAILERS
S ABSEILS
  ISABELS
  LABISES
T ALBITES
  ASTILBE
  BESTIAL
  LIBATES
  STABILE
W BEWAILS
Y BAILEYS
Z SIZABLE

ABEORS 144
(ABORES)
B EARBOBS
E AEROBES
G BORAGES
I ISOBARE
J JERBOAS
L LABROSE
N BORANES
P SAPROBE
R BRASERO
T BOASTER
  BOATERS
  BORATES
  SORBATE
U AEROBUS
V BRAVOES
X BORAXES

Z BEZOARS

ABERST 122
(BREAST)
A ABREAST
B BARBETS
  RABBETS
  STABBER
D DABSTER
E BEATERS
  BERATES
  REBATES
G BARGEST
H BATHERS
  BERTHAS
  BREATHS
I BAITERS
L ALBERTS
  BATLERS
  BLASTER
  LABRETS
  STABLER
M TAMBERS
N BANTERS
O BOASTER
  BOATERS
  BORATES
  SORBATE
R BARRETS
  BARTERS
S BASTERS
  BESTARS
  BRASSET
  BREASTS
T BATTERS
  TABRETS
U ARBUTES
  SURBATE
V BRAVEST
W BRAWEST
  WABSTER
X BAXTERS
Y BARYTES
  BETRAYS

ACEILR 121
(LACIER)
B CALIBER
  CALIBRE
D DECRIAL
  RADICEL
  RADICLE
F FILACER
G GLACIER
  GRACILE
H CHARLIE
M CALMIER
  CLAIMER
  MIRACLE
  RECLAIM
N CARLINE
O CALORIE
  CARIOLE
  COALIER

  LORICAE
P CALIPER
  REPLICA
R CERRIAL
S CLARIES
  ECLAIRS
  SCALIER
T ARTICLE
  RECITAL
U AURICLE
V CALIVER
  CLAVIER
  VELARIC
Y CLAYIER

ACEINR 65
(CANIER)
A ACARINE
B CARBINE
D CAIRNED
  CARNIED
E CINEREA
F FANCIER
G GRECIAN
L CARLINE
M CARMINE
N CANNIER
P CAPRINE
R CARNIER
S ARSENIC
  CARNIES
  CERASIN
T CANTIER
  CERTAIN
  CRINATE
  NACRITE

ACEINS 119
(INCASE)
D CANDIES
  INCASED
F FANCIES
  FASCINE
  FIANCES
G CEASING
  INCAGES
H INCHASE
L ANCILES
  INLACES
  SANICLE
M AMNESIC
  CINEMAS
N CANINES
  NANCIES
O ACINOSE
P INSCAPE
  PINCASE
R ARSENIC
  CARNIES
  CERASIN
S CASEINS
  INCASES
T CANIEST
  CINEAST
U EUCAINS

V INCAVES
Y CYANISE

ACENRS 175
(CANERS)
C CANCERS
D DANCERS
E CAREENS
  CASERNE
  ENRACES
H CHENARS
  RANCHES
I ARSENIC
  CARNIES
  CERASIN
K CANKERS
L LANCERS
  RANCELS
N CANNERS
  SCANNER
O CARNOSE
  COARSEN
  CORNEAS
P PRANCES
S ANCRESS
  CASERNS
T CANTERS
  CARNETS
  NECTARS
  RECANTS
  SCANTER
  TANRECS
  TRANCES
U SURANCE
V CAVERNS
  CRAVENS
Y CARNEYS
  SCENARY
Z ZARNECS

ACENRT 96
(CANTER)
A CATERAN
D CANTRED
  TRANCED
E CRENATE
F CANTREF
H CHANTER
  TRANCHE
I CANTIER
  CERTAIN
  CRINATE
  NACRITE
L CENTRAL
O ENACTOR
S CANTERS
  CARNETS
  NECTARS
  RECANTS
  SCANTER
  TANRECS
  TRANCES
T TRANECT
U CENTAUR
  UNCRATE

  UNTRACE
Y ENCRATY
  NECTARY

ACENST 149
(STANCE)
A CATENAS
C ACCENTS
D DECANTS
  DESCANT
  SCANTED
E CETANES
  TENACES
H CHASTEN
  NATCHES
I CANIEST
  CINEAST
K NACKETS
L CANTLES
  CENTALS
  LANCETS
  SCANTLE
N NASCENT
O COSTEAN
  OCTANES
P CATNEPS
R CANTERS
  CARNETS
  NECTARS
  RECANTS
  SCANTER
  TANRECS
  TRANCES
S ASCENTS
  SECANTS
  STANCES
T CANTEST
U NUTCASE

ACEORS 103
(ORACES)
A ROSACEA
D SARCODE
E ACEROSE
G CARGOES
  CORSAGE
  SOCAGER
H CHOREAS
  ORACHES
  ROACHES
I ORACIES
  SCORIAE
L COALERS
  ESCOLAR
  ORACLES
M AMORCES
N CARNOSE
  COARSEN
  CORNEAS
R COARSER
S ROSACES
T COASTER
  COATERS
U ACEROUS
  CAROUSE

X COAXERS

ACEOST 146
(ACTOSE)
D COASTED
E ACETOSE
  COATEES
I SOCIATE
L ALECOST
  LACTOSE
  LOCATES
  SCATOLE
  TALCOSE
M COMATES
N COSTEAN
  OCTANES
P CAPOTES
  SCOPATE
  TOECAPS
R COASTER
  COATERS
T COSTATE
U ACETOUS
V AVOCETS
  OCTAVES

ACERST 141
(CATERS)
A ACATERS
D REDACTS
  SCARTED
E CERATES
  CREATES
  ECARTES
  SECRETA
H ARCHEST
  CHARETS
  CHASTER
  RATCHES
I CRISTAE
  RACIEST
  STEARIC
K RACKETS
  STACKER
  TACKERS
L CARTELS
  CLARETS
  SCARLET
  TARCELS
M MERCATS
N CANTERS
  CARNETS
  NECTARS
  RECANTS
  SCANTER
  TANRECS
  TRANCES
O COASTER
  COATERS
P CARPETS
  PRECAST
  SPECTRA
R CARTERS
  CRATERS
  TRACERS

```
S ACTRESS      N STEANED        RIDABLE      C CAIRNED      C CARDIES        TIRADES
  CASTERS      R DEAREST      C DECRIAL        CARNIED        RADICES      S DISSEAT
  RECASTS        DERATES        RADICEL      D DANDIER        SIDECAR        SAIDEST
T SCATTER        ESTRADE        RADICLE        DRAINED      E DEARIES      U DAUTIES
U ACTURES        REASTED      D DIEDRAL      F FRIANDE        READIES      V AVIDEST
  CAUTERS        SEDATER        DRAILED      G AREDING      F FRAISED        DATIVES
  CRUSTAE        STEARED      E LEADIER        DEARING      G AGRISED        VISTAED
  CURATES      S SEDATES      G GLADIER        DERAIGN      H SHADIER      W DAWTIES
Y SECTARY      T ESTATED        GLAIRED        EARDING      I DAIRIES        WAISTED
               U SAUTEED      I DELIRIA        GRADINE        DIARIES
ADEERS 70      W SWEATED        IRIDEAL        GRAINED        DIARISE      ADELNR  79
(SEARED)       Y YEASTED      L DALLIER        READING      K DAIKERS      (LANDER)
B DEBASER                       DIALLER      H HANDIER        DARKIES      A ADRENAL
  SABERED      ADEGLN 197       RALLIED      I DENARII      L DERAILS      B BLANDER
C CREASED      (DANGLE)       O DARIOLE      M ADERMIN        SIDERAL      D DANDLER
  DECARES      B BANGLED      P PEDRAIL        INARMED      M ADMIRES      E LEARNED
  SEARCED      C CANGLED        PREDIAL      O ANEROID        MARDIES      G DANGLER
D DEADERS        CLANGED      R LARDIER      P PARDINE        MISREAD        GNARLED
G DRAGEES      D DANGLED      S DERAILS      R DRAINER        SIDEARM      H HANDLER
  GREASED        GLADDEN        SIDERAL        RANDIER      N RANDIES      K RANKLED
H ADHERES      E GLEANED      T DILATER      S RANDIES        SANDIER      L LANDLER
  HEADERS      F FANGLED        TRAILED        SANDIER        SARDINE      M MANDREL
  HEARSED        FLANGED      V VALIDER        SARDINE      O ROADIES      O LADRONE
  SHEARED      I ALIGNED      Y READILY      T DETRAIN        SOREDIA      S DARNELS
I DEARIES        DEALING                       TRAINED      P ASPIRED        ENLARDS
  READIES        LEADING      ADEILS  33     U UNAIRED        DESPAIR        LANDERS
K SKEARED      J JANGLED      (LADIES)         URANIDE        DIAPERS        SLANDER
L ARLESED      M MANGLED      B DISABLE      V INVADER        PRAISED        SNARLED
  DEALERS      N ENDLANG      C SCAILED        RAVINED      R ARRIDES      U LAUNDER
  LEADERS      R DANGLER      D DAIDLES                       RAIDERS        LURDANE
  REDEALS        GNARLED        LADDIES      ADEINS  22     T ARIDEST        RUNDALE
M REMADES      S DANGLES      E AEDILES      (SANDIE)         ASTERID      Y DEARNLY
  REMEADS        GLANDES        DEISEAL      A NAIADES        ASTRIDE
  SMEARED        SLANGED      F DISLEAF      B BANDIES        DIASTER      ADELNS 137
N DEANERS      T TANGLED      G SILAGED      C CANDIES        DISRATE      (ANDLES)
  ENDEARS      U LANGUED      H HALIDES        INCASED        STAIDER      C CALENDS
O OREADES      W WANGLED      I DAILIES      D DANDIES        STAIRED        CANDLES
P PREASED                       LIAISED        SDAINED        TARDIES      D DANDLES
  SPEARED      ADEGNR 126       SEDILIA      E ANISEED        TIRADES      E LEADENS
R DREARES      (DANGER)       K SKAILED      G AGNISED      U RESIDUA      G DANGLES
  READERS      E ANGERED      L DALLIES      K KANDIES      V ADVISER        GLANDES
  REDSEAR        DERANGE        DISLEAL      L DENIALS        VARDIES        SLANGED
  REREADS        ENRAGED        LALDIES        SNAILED                     H HANDLES
S RESEDAS        GRANDEE        SALLIED      M DEMAINS      ADEIST  26       HANDSEL
T DEAREST        GRENADE      M MEDIALS        MAIDENS      (IDATES)       I DENIALS
  DERATES      I AREDING        MISDEAL        MEDIANS      B BASTIDE        SNAILED
  ESTRADE        DEARING        MISLEAD        MEDINAS      C ACIDEST      K KALENDS
  REASTED        DERAIGN      N DENIALS      O ADONISE        DACITES      O LOADENS
  SEDATER        EARDING        SNAILED        ANODISE      E IDEATES      R DARNELS
  STEARED        GRADINE      O DEASOIL        SODAINE      F DAFTIES        ENLARDS
V ADVERSE        GRAINED      P ALIPEDS      P PANDIES        FADIEST        LANDERS
W DRAWEES        READING        PAIDLES        PANSIED      G AGISTED        SLANDER
                 GNARLED        PALSIED        SPAINED      L DETAILS        SNARLED
ADEEST 85      L DANGLER      R DERAILS      R RANDIES        DILATES      S SENDALS
(SEATED)         GNARLED        SIDERAL        SANDIER      M MISDATE      T DENTALS
B BESTEAD      O GROANED      S AIDLESS        SARDINE      N DETAINS        SLANTED
  DEBATES      P PRANGED        DEASILS      S SDAINES        INSTEAD      U UNLADES
C TEDESCA      R GNARRED      T DETAILS      T DETAINS        SAINTED        UNLEADS
D DEADEST        GRANDER        DILATES        INSTEAD        SATINED
  SEDATED      S DANGERS      U AUDILES        SAINTED        STAINED      ADELRS  88
  STEADED        GANDERS        DEASIUL        SATINED      O IODATES      (ALDERS)
F DEAFEST        GARDENS      V DEVISAL        STAINED        TOADIES      B BEDRALS
  DEFASTE      T GRANTED      Y DIALYSE      V INVADES      R ARIDEST      C CRADLES
  DEFEATS      U ENGUARD        EYLIADS      W DEWANIS        ASTERID        SCALDER
  FEASTED        RAUNGED                                      ASTRIDE      D LADDERS
H HEADSET                     ADEINR   4     ADEIRS  12       DIASTER        RADDLES
I IDEATES      ADEILR  19     (RAINED)       (RAISED)         DISRATE        SADDLER
L DELATES      (RAILED)       A ARANEID      A ARAISED        STAIDER      E ARLESED
  STEALED      A RADIALE      B BANDIER      B BRAISED        STAIRED        DEALERS
M STEAMED      B BRAILED        BRAINED        DARBIES        TARDIES        LEADERS
```

```
  REDEALS          SLANDER        M TANDEMS          STANDER        K DISRANK          BREARES
F FARDELS          SNARLED        N STANDEN          STARNED        L ALDRINS        C CAREERS
G DARGLES        M MANREDS        O ASTONED        O DOATERS        M MANDIRS        D DREARES
H HARELDS          RANDEMS          DONATES          ROASTED        N INNARDS          READERS
  HERALDS          REMANDS          ONSTEAD          TORSADE        O INROADS          REDSEAR
I DERAILS        P PANDERS        P PEDANTS          TROADES          ORDAINS          REREADS
  SIDERAL        R DARNERS          PENTADS        P DEPARTS        T INDARTS        G GREASER
K DARKLES          ERRANDS        R ENDARTS          DRAPETS        U DURIANS        H HEARERS
M MEDLARS          SNARRED          STANDER          PETARDS          SUNDARI          REHEARS
N DARNELS        S SANDERS          STARNED        R DARTERS        W INWARDS          SHEARER
  ENLARDS          SARSDEN        T ATTENDS          DARTRES                         I REARISE
  LANDERS        T ENDARTS        U SAUNTED          RETARDS        AEELRS  72       M REAMERS
  SLANDER          STANDER          UNSATED          STARRED        (EALERS)         N EARNERS
  SNARLED          STARNED        V ADVENTS          TRADERS        C ALERCES        O REAROSE
O LOADERS        U ASUNDER        Y STAYNED        T STARTED          CEREALS        P REAPERS
  ORDEALS          DANSEUR                           TETRADS          RESCALE        R REARERS
  RELOADS          DAUNERS        ADEORS  48       V ADVERTS        D ARLESED        S ERASERS
P PEDLARS        W DAWNERS        (ADORES)           STARVED          DEALERS        T SERRATE
R LARDERS          WANDERS        C SARCODE        W STEWARD          LEADERS          TEARERS
S SARDELS          WARDENS        D DEODARS          STRAWED          REDEALS        U ERASURE
T DARTLES        Z ZANDERS        E OREADES          WRASTED        E RELEASE        V REAVERS
U LAUDERS                         F FEDORAS        Y STRAYED        G GALERES        W SWEARER
W WARSLED        ADENRU  64       I ROADIES                          REGALES          WEARERS
Z DRAZELS        (AUNDER)           SOREDIA        ADGINR 135       H HEALERS
               B UNBARED          L LOADERS        (RADING)         I REALISE        AEERST  20
ADELST 110     C DURANCE            ORDEALS        B BARDING        K LEAKERS        (EATERS)
(SALTED)           UNRACED          RELOADS          BRIGAND        M MEALERS        A AERATES
B BALDEST        D DAUNDER        M RADOMES        C CARDING        O AREOLES        B BEATERS
  BLASTED        E UNEARED        R ADORERS        E AREDING        P LEAPERS          BERATES
  STABLED        G ENGUARD          DROSERA          DEARING          PLEASER          REBATES
C CASTLED        H UNHEARD        T DOATERS          DERAIGN          RELAPSE        C CERATES
  SCLATED        I UNAIRED          ROASTED          EARDING          REPEALS          CREATES
D STADDLE          URANIDE          TORSADE          GRADINE        S ARLESES          ECARTES
E DELATES        K UNRAKED          TROADES          GRAINED          EARLESS          SECRETA
  STEALED        L LAUNDER        U AROUSED          READING          LEASERS        D DEAREST
I DETAILS          LURDANE        V SAVORED        F FARDING          RESALES          DERATES
  DILATES          RUNDALE        W REDOWAS        G GRADING          RESEALS          ESTRADE
K SKLATED        M DURAMEN                           NIGGARD          SEALERS          REASTED
  STALKED          MANURED        ADERST  49       I GRADINI        T ELATERS          SEDATER
L STALLED          MAUNDER        (DATERS)           RAIDING          REALEST          STEARED
N DENTALS          UNARMED        B DABSTER        L DARLING          RELATES        F AFREETS
  SLANTED        O RONDEAU        C REDACTS          LARDING          STEALER          FEASTER
O SALTOED        P UNPARED          SCARTED        M MRIDANG        U LEASURE        G ERGATES
P SPALTED        S ASUNDER        D ADDREST        N DARNING        V LAVEERS          RESTAGE
  STAPLED          DANSEUR        E DEAREST          NARDING          REVEALS        H AETHERS
R DARTLES          DAUNERS          DERATES          RANDING          SEVERAL          HEATERS
S DESALTS        T DAUNTER          ESTRADE        O ADORING        X RELAXES          REHEATS
T SLATTED          NATURED          REASTED          GRADINO        Y SEALERY        I AERIEST
U AULDEST          UNRATED          SEDATER          ROADING                           SERIATE
  SALUTED          UNTREAD          STEARED        P DRAPING        AEEPRT 142       K RETAKES
               Y UNREADY          F STRAFED        R DARRING        (REPEAT)           SAKERET
ADENRS  62                         H DEARTHS        S DARINGS        A PATERAE        L ELATERS
(ANDERS)         ADENST  36          HARDEST          GRADINS        D ADEPTER          REALEST
C DANCERS        (STANED)           HATREDS        T DARTING          PREDATE          RELATES
D DANDERS        A ANSATED          THREADS          TRADING          TAPERED          STEALER
E DEANERS        C DECANTS          TRASHED        U DAURING        H PREHEAT        M STEAMER
  ENDEARS          DESCANT        I ARIDEST        W DRAWING        I PEATIER          TEAMERS
F FARDENS          SCANTED          ASTERID          WARDING        K PERTAKE        N EARNEST
G DANGERS        E STEANED          ASTRIDE        Y YARDING        L PRELATE          EASTERN
  GANDERS        G STANGED          DIASTER                         M TEMPERA          NEAREST
  GARDENS        H HANDSET          DISRATE        ADINRS 105       O OPERATE        O ROSEATE
H HANDERS        I DETAINS          STAIDER        (DRAINS)         R TAPERER        P REPEATS
  HARDENS          INSTEAD          STAIRED        A RADIANS        S REPEATS        R SERRATE
I RANDIES          SAINTED          TARDIES        B RIBANDS        U EPURATE          TEARERS
  SANDIER          SATINED          TIRADES        E RANDIES        Y PEATERY        S RESEATS
  SARDINE          STAINED        K DARKEST          SANDIER        Z TRAPEZE          SAETERS
K DARKENS        K DANKEST          STARKED          SARDINE                           SEAREST
L DARNELS        L DENTALS        L DARTLES        F FRIANDS        AEERRS 162         SEATERS
  ENLARDS          SLANTED        M SMARTED        G DARINGS        (ERASER)           STEARES
  LANDERS                         N ENDARTS          GRADINS        B BEARERS          TEASERS
```

TESSERA	M GERMAIN	GLANCES	Z GLAZERS	GREATEN	GARTERS
T ESTREAT	MANGIER	D DANGLES		REAGENT	GRATERS
RESTATE	REAMING	GLANDES	**AEGLST 187**	F ENGRAFT	S STAGERS
U AUSTERE	N AGINNER	SLANGED	(GLATES)	I GRANITE	T TARGETS
W SWEATER	EARNING	F FANGLES	A AGELAST	INGRATE	V GRAVEST
	ENGRAIN	FLANGES	ALGATES	TANGIER	Y GRAYEST
AEGILN 55	GRANNIE	G LAGGENS	LASTAGE	TEARING	GYRATES
(EALING)	NEARING	I LEASING	B GABLETS	L TANGLER	STAGERY
C ANGELIC	O ORIGANE	LINAGES	E EAGLETS	TRANGLE	
ANGLICE	P REAPING	SEALING	LEGATES	M GARMENT	**AEHRST 169**
D ALIGNED	R ANGRIER	J JANGLES	TEAGLES	MARGENT	(HATERS)
DEALING	EARRING	L LEGLANS	TELEGAS	RAGMENT	B BATHERS
LEADING	GRAINER	M MANGELS	H HAGLETS	N REGNANT	BERTHAS
E LINEAGE	RANGIER	MANGLES	I AGILEST	P TREPANG	BREATHS
F FEALING	REARING	O ENGAOLS	AIGLETS	R GRANTER	C ARCHEST
FINAGLE	S ANGRIES	P SPANGLE	LIGATES	REGRANT	CHARETS
LEAFING	EARINGS	R ANGLERS	TAIGLES	S ARGENTS	CHASTER
G GEALING	ERASING	LARGENS	L GALLETS	GARNETS	RATCHES
LIGNAGE	GAINERS	S GLASSEN	N LANGEST	STRANGE	D DEARTHS
H HEALING	GRAINES	T LANGEST	TANGLES	U GAUNTER	HARDEST
K LEAKING	REGAINS	TANGLES	O LEGATOS		HATREDS
LINKAGE	REGINAS	U ANGELUS	R LARGEST	**AEGNST 115**	THREADS
L NIGELLA	SEARING	LAGUNES	T GESTALT	(TANGES)	TRASHED
M LEAMING	SERINGA	LANGUES	W TALWEGS	A AGNATES	E AETHERS
MEALING	T GRANITE	W WANGLES		D STANGED	HEATERS
N ANELING	INGRATE	Y LYNAGES	**AEGNRS 86**	E NEGATES	REHEATS
EANLING	TANGIER		(ANGERS)	H STENGAH	F FATHERS
LEANING	TEARING	**AEGLNT 118**	B BANGERS	I EASTING	SHAFTER
NEALING	V REAVING	(TANGLE)	GRABENS	EATINGS	G GATHERS
P LEAPING	VINEGAR	D TANGLED	D DANGERS	GAINEST	H HEARTHS
PEALING	W WEARING	E ELEGANT	GANDERS	GENISTA	I HASTIER
PLEAING		H ALENGTH	GARDENS	INGATES	SHERIAT
R ENGRAIL	**AEGLNR 91**	I ATINGLE	E ENRAGES	INGESTA	L HALTERS
LEARING	(ANGLER)	ELATING	G GANGERS	SEATING	HARSLET
NARGILE	A ALNAGER	GELATIN	GRANGES	TANGIES	LATHERS
REALIGN	B BRANGLE	GENITAL	NAGGERS	TEASING	SLATHER
REGINAL	C CLANGER	O TANGELO	H GNASHER	TSIGANE	THALERS
S LEASING	D DANGLER	R TANGLER	HANGERS	L LANGEST	M HAMSTER
LINAGES	GNARLED	TRANGLE	I ANGRIES	TANGLES	N ANTHERS
SEALING	E ENLARGE	S LANGEST	EARINGS	M MAGNETS	HARTENS
T ATINGLE	GENERAL	TANGLES	ERASING	N GANNETS	THENARS
ELATING	GLEANER	T GANTLET	GAINERS	R ARGENTS	O ASTHORE
GELATIN	G GANGREL	U LANGUET	GRAINES	GARNETS	HAROSET
GENITAL	I ENGRAIL	W TWANGLE	REGAINS	STRANGE	P SPARTHE
U LINGUAE	LEARING		REGINAS	T GESTANT	TEPHRAS
V LEAVING	NARGILE	**AEGLRS 167**	SEARING		THREAPS
Y ALEYING	REALIGN	(LAGERS)	SERINGA	**AEGRST 80**	S RASHEST
	REGINAL	A ALEGARS	L ANGLERS	(GATERS)	SHASTER
AEGINR 15	J JANGLER	LAAGERS	LARGENS	A AGRASTE	TRASHES
(EARING)	L LANGREL	B GARBLES	M ENGRAMS	B BARGEST	T HATTERS
B BEARING	M MANGLER	D DARGLES	GERMANS	E ERGATES	RATHEST
C GRECIAN	P GRAPNEL	E GALERES	MANGERS	RESTAGE	SHATTER
D AREDING	S ANGLERS	REGALES	O ONAGERS	G GAGSTER	THREATS
DEARING	LARGENS	F REFLAGS	ORANGES	GARGETS	V HARVEST
DERAIGN	T TANGLER	G GARGLES	P ENGRASP	STAGGER	THRAVES
EARDING	TRANGLE	LAGGERS	R GARNERS	TAGGERS	W THAWERS
GRADINE	U GRANULE	RAGGLES	RANGERS	H GATHERS	WREATHS
GRAINED	W WANGLER	I GRAILES	S SERANGS	I AGISTER	
READING	WRANGLE	K GRAKLES	T ARGENTS	GAITERS	**AEILMN 133**
E REGINAE	Y ANGERLY	M MALGRES	GARNETS	STAGIER	(MALINE)
F FEARING		N ANGLERS	STRANGE	STRIGAE	A LAMINAE
G GEARING	**AEGLNS 170**	LARGENS	U RAUNGES	TRIAGES	C MELANIC
NAGGIER	(ANGLES)	O GAOLERS	UNGEARS	L LARGEST	F FEMINAL
H HEARING	A ALNAGES	P GRAPLES	W GNAWERS	N ARGENTS	INFLAME
K REAKING	ANLAGES	S LARGESS		GARNETS	G LEAMING
L ENGRAIL	GALENAS	T LARGEST	**AEGNRT 54**	STRANGE	MEALING
LEARING	LAGENAS	V GRAVELS	(GANTER)	O ORGEATS	H HELIMAN
NARGILE	LASAGNE	VERGLAS	A TANAGER	STORAGE	L MANILLE
REALIGN	B BANGLES	Y ARGYLES	D GRANTED	P PARGETS	M MAILMEN
REGINAL	C CANGLES	GRAYLES	E GRANTEE	R GARRETS	N LINEMAN

```
      MELANIN          SAILERS          TALKIES     H HAEMINS          SAMPIRE          SEARING
O     MINEOLA          SERAILS        L TALLIES       HEMINAS     R   MARRIES          SERINGA
P     IMPANEL          SERIALS        N EASTLIN     J JASMINE         SIMARRE     H    ARSHINE
      MANIPLE        T REALIST          ELASTIN     K KINEMAS     S   MASSIER          HERNIAS
R     MANLIER          RETAILS          ENTAILS     L ISLEMAN     T   MAESTRI     I    SENARII
      MARLINE          SALTIER          SALIENT       MENIALS         MAISTER     K    SNAKIER
      MINERAL          SALTIRE          SLAINTE       SEMINAL         MASTIER     L    NAILERS
      RAILMEN          SLATIER          STANIEL     M MISNAME         MISRATE     M    MARINES
S     ISLEMAN        V REVISAL          TENAILS     O ANOMIES         SEMITAR          REMAINS
      MENIALS        W SWALIER        O ISOLATE     R MARINES         SMARTIE          SEMINAR
      SEMINAL          WAILERS        P APLITES       REMAINS     U   UREMIAS          SIRNAME
T     AILMENT                           PALIEST       SEMINAR     W   AWMRIES     N    INSANER
      ALIMENT      AEILRT  10           TALIPES       SIRNAME                          INSNARE
                    (RETAIL)          R REALIST     S INSEAMS     AEIMST  95      O    ERASION
AEILNT  11        B LIBRATE            RETAILS       SAMISEN      (MATIES)        P    RAPINES
 (ENTAIL)           TRIABLE            SALTIER     T INMATES     C   ACMITES     R    SIERRAN
A     ANTLIAE     C ARTICLE            SALTIRE       MAINEST         ETACISM          SNARIER
E     LINEATE       RECITAL            SLATIER       MANTIES         MICATES     S    ARSINES
F     INFLATE     D DILATER          U SITULAE       TAMINES         SEMATIC          SARNIES
G     ATINGLE       TRAILED          V ESTIVAL                   D   MISDATE     T    ANESTRI
      ELATING     E ATELIER          W WALIEST     AEIMNT  53    E   STEAMIE          NASTIER
      GELATIN       REALTIE          Y TAILYES      (INMATE)     G   GAMIEST          RATINES
      GENITAL     H LATHIER          Z LAZIEST     A AMENTIA         SIGMATE          RESIANT
M     AILMENT     L LITERAL                          ANIMATE     H   ATHEISM          RETAINS
      ALIMENT       TALLIER        AEIMNR  61      B AMBIENT     I   AMITIES          RETINAS
O     ELATION     M LAMITER         (REMAIN)       C EMICANT         ATIMIES          RETSINA
      TOENAIL       MALTIER        B MIRBANE         NEMATIC     K   MISTAKE          STAINER
P     PANTILE     N ENTRAIL        C CARMINE       D MEDIANT     M   MISMATE          STARNIE
R     ENTRAIL       LATRINE        D ADERMIN       E MATINEE         TAMMIES          STEARIN
      LATRINE       RATLINE          INARMED       G MINTAGE     N   INMATES     V    AVENIRS
      RATLINE       RELIANT        E REMANIE         TEAMING         MAINEST          RAVINES
      RELIANT       RETINAL        F FIREMAN         TEGMINA         MANTIES
      RETINAL       TRENAIL        G GERMAIN       I INTIMAE         TAMINES     AEINRT   1
      TRENAIL     P PLAITER          MANGIER         MINIATE     O   AMOSITE      (RETAIN)
S     EASTLIN       PLATIER          REAMING       L AILMENT         ATOMIES     B    ATEBRIN
      ELASTIN     R RETIRAL        H HARMINE         ALIMENT         ATOMISE     C    CANTIER
      ENTAILS       RETRIAL        K MANKIER       N MANNITE         OSMIATE          CERTAIN
      SALIENT       TRAILER          RAMEKIN       R MINARET     P   IMPASTE          CRINATE
      SLAINTE     S REALIST        L MANLIER         RAIMENT         PASTIME          NACRITE
      STANIEL       RETAILS          MARLINE       S INMATES     R   MAESTRI     D    DETRAIN
      TENAILS       SALTIER          MINERAL         MAINEST         MAISTER          TRAINED
U     ALUNITE       SALTIRE          RAILMEN         MANTIES         MASTIER     E    RETINAE
V     VENTAIL       SLATIER        O MORAINE         TAMINES         MISRATE          TRAINEE
                  T TERTIAL        R MARINER       X TAXIMEN         SEMITAR     F    FAINTER
AEILRS  16        U URALITE        S MARINES       Y AMENITY         SMARTIE          FENITAR
 (SAILER)         W WALTIER          REMAINS         ANYTIME     S   ASTEISM     G    GRANITE
A     AERIALS     Y IRATELY          SEMINAR                         SAMIEST          INGRATE
B     BAILERS       REALITY          SIRNAME       AEIMRS  112       SAMITES          TANGIER
C     CLARIES                      T MINARET        (ARMIES)         TAMISES          TEARING
      ECLAIRS     AEILST  24         RAIMENT       B AMBRIES     T   MATIEST     H    INEARTH
      SCALIER      (ALITES)        V VERMIAN       D ADMIRES         MATTIES     I    INERTIA
D     DERAILS     B ALBITES                          MARDIES     Z   MAZIEST     J    JANTIER
      SIDERAL       ASTILBE        AEIMNS  98        MISREAD         MESTIZA          NARTJIE
E     REALISE       BESTIAL         (MANIES)         SIDEARM                     K    KERATIN
G     GRAILES       LIBATES        A AMNESIA       E SEAMIER     AEINRS   6      L    ENTRAIL
H     HAILERS       STABILE          ANEMIAS         SERIEMA      (SARNIE)            LATRINE
      SHALIER     C ASTELIC        C AMNESIC       F MISFARE     C   ARSENIC          RATLINE
I     LAIRISE       ELASTIC          CINEMAS       G GISARME         CARNIES          RELIANT
      SAILIER       LACIEST        D DEMAINS         MAIGRES         CERASIN          RETINAL
J     JAILERS       LATICES          MAIDENS         MIRAGES     D   RANDIES          TRENAIL
K     SERKALI       SALICET          MEDIANS       H MASHIER         SANDIER     M    MINARET
L     RALLIES     D DETAILS          MEDINAS         MISHEAR         SARDINE          RAIMENT
M     MAILERS       DILATES        E MEANIES       L MAILERS     F   INFARES     N    ENTRAIN
      REALISM     G AGILEST          NEMESIA         REALISM     G   ANGRIES          TRANNIE
N     NAILERS       AIGLETS        F FAMINES       M RAMMIES         EARINGS     O    OTARINE
P     PALSIER       LIGATES          INFAMES       N MARINES         ERASING     P    PAINTER
      PARLIES       TAIGLES        G ENIGMAS         REMAINS         GAINERS          PERTAIN
R     RAILERS     H HALITES          GAMINES         SEMINAR         GRAINES          REPAINT
      RERAILS     I LAITIES          MEASING         SIRNAME         REGAINS     R    RETRAIN
S     AIRLESS     K LAKIEST          SEAMING       P IMPRESA         REGINAS          TERRAIN
```

```
  TRAINER      R ANESTRI      V PARVISE        TIRASSE        ATTIRES       AELNST  34
S ANESTRI        NASTIER      W WASPIER      T ARTIEST        IRATEST       (ANTLES)
  NASTIER        RATINES                       ARTISTE        STRIATE     A SEALANT
  RATINES        RESIANT      AEIRST   3       ATTIRES        TASTIER     C CANTLES
  RESIANT        RETAINS      (SATIRE)         IRATEST        TERTIAS       CENTALS
  RETAINS        RETINAS    A ARISTAE          STRIATE      T TATTIES       LANCETS
  RETINAS        RETSINA      ASTERIA          TASTIER      U SITUATE       SCANTLE
  RETSINA        STAINER      ATRESIA          TERTIAS      V STATIVE     D DENTALS
  STAINER        STARNIE    B BAITERS        V TAIVERS      W TWAITES       SLANTED
  STARNIE        STEARIN      BARITES          VASTIER      Y SATIETY     E ELANETS
  STEARIN      S ENTASIS    C CRISTAE        W WAISTER                      LEANEST
T INTREAT        NASTIES      RACIEST          WAITERS      AELNRS  63    G LANGEST
  ITERANT        SESTINA      STEARIC          WARIEST      (LANERS)        TANGLES
  NATTIER        TANSIES    D ARIDEST                     A ARSENAL       H HANTLES
  NITRATE        TISANES      ASTERID        AEIRTT  29   B BRANLES       I EASTLIN
  TARTINE      T INSTATE      ASTRIDE        (ATTIRE)       BRANSLE         ELASTIN
  TERTIAN        SATINET      DIASTER      A ARIETTA      C LANCERS         ENTAILS
U RUINATE      U AUNTIES      DISRATE      B BATTIER        RANCELS         SALIENT
  TAURINE        SINUATE      STAIDER        BIRETTA      D DARNELS         SLAINTE
  URANITE      V NAIVEST      STAIRED      C CATTIER        ENLARDS         STANIEL
  URINATE        NATIVES      TARDIES        CITRATE        LANDERS         TENAILS
W TAWNIER        VAINEST      TIRADES      D ATTIRED        SLANDER       K ANKLETS
  TINWARE      W AWNIEST    E AERIEST      E ARIETTE        SNARLED         ASKLENT
                 TAWNIES      SERIATE        ITERATE      F SALFERN         LANKEST
AEINST   2       WANIEST    F FAIREST      F FATTIER      G ANGLERS       M LAMENTS
(SATINE)         WANTIES    G AGISTER      L TERTIAL        LARGENS         MANTELS
A TAENIAS      Z ZANIEST      GAITERS      N INTREAT      I NAILERS         MANTLES
B BASINET                     STAGIER        ITERANT      K RANKLES       N STANNEL
  BESAINT      AEIPRS  75      STRIGAE        NATTIER      N ENSNARL       O ETALONS
  BESTAIN      (PRAISE)        TRIAGES        NITRATE        LANNERS       P PLANETS
C CANIEST    A SPIRAEA      H HASTIER        TARTINE      O ORLEANS         PLATENS
  CINEAST    C EPACRIS        SHERIAT        TERTIAN      P PLANERS       R ANTLERS
D DETAINS      SCRAPIE      I AIRIEST      P PARTITE        REPLANS         RENTALS
  INSTEAD      SPACIER        IRISATE      R RATTIER      R SNARLER         SALTERN
  SAINTED    D ASPIRED      K ARKITES        RETRAIT      S RANSELS         STERNAL
  SATINED      DESPAIR        KARITES        TARTIER      T ANTLERS       T LATTENS
  STAINED      DIAPERS      L REALIST      S ARTIEST        RENTALS         TALENTS
E ETESIAN      PRAISED        RETAILS        ARTISTE        SALTERN       U ELUANTS
F FAINEST    E APERIES        SALTIER        ATTIRES        STERNAL         UNLASTE
  NAIFEST      EPEIRAS        SALTIRE        IRATEST      Z RANZELS       V LEVANTS
G EASTING    G GASPIER        SLATIER        STRIATE                      Y STANYEL
  EATINGS      PRISAGE      M MAESTRI        TASTIER      AELNRT  28      Z ZELANTS
  GAINEST      SPAIRGE        MAISTER        TERTIAS      (ANTLER)
  GENISTA    H HARPIES        MASTIER      T ATTRITE      B BRANTLE       AELORS  42
  INGATES      SHARPIE        MISRATE        TATTIER      C CENTRAL       (ALORES)
  INGESTA    L PALSIER        SEMITAR        TITRATE      E ALTERNE       B LABROSE
  SEATING      PARLIES        SMARTIE      V TAIVERT        ENTERAL       C COALERS
  TANGIES    M IMPRESA      N ANESTRI      W TAWTIER        ETERNAL         ESCOLAR
  TEASING      SAMPIRE        NASTIER      X EXTRAIT      G TANGLER         ORACLES
  TSIGANE    N RAPINES        RATINES                       TRANGLE       D LOADERS
I ISATINE    O SOAPIER        RESIANT      AEISTT  83    H ENTHRAL         ORDEALS
J JANTIES    P APPRISE        RETAINS      (TASTIE)      I ENTRAIL         RELOADS
K INTAKES      SAPPIER        RETINAS      A SATIATE        LATRINE       E AREOLES
L EASTLIN    R PARRIES        RETSINA      B BATISTE        RATLINE       F LOAFERS
  ELASTIN      PRAISER        STAINER      C CATTIES        RELIANT         SAFROLE
  ENTAILS      RAPIERS        STARNIE        TIETACS        RETINAL       G GAOLERS
  SALIENT      REPAIRS        STEARIN      F FATTIES        TRENAIL       H SHOALER
  SLAINTE    S ASPIRES      O OARIEST      H ATHEIST      L ENTRALL       L ROSELLA
  STANIEL      PARESIS        OTARIES        STAITHE      N LANTERN       M MORALES
  TENAILS      PRAISES      P PARTIES      K TAKIEST      P PANTLER       N ORLEANS
M INMATES      SPIREAS        PASTIER      M MATIEST        PLANTER       O AEROSOL
  MAINEST    T PARTIES        PIASTRE        MATTIES        REPLANT         ROSEOLA
  MANTIES      PASTIER        PIRATES      N INSTATE      S ANTLERS       P PAROLES
  TAMINES      PIASTRE        PRATIES        SATINET        RENTALS         REPOSAL
N INANEST      PIRATES        TRAIPSE      O OSTIATE        SALTERN       S OARLESS
O ATONIES      PRATIES      R ARTSIER        TOASTIE        STERNAL         SOLERAS
P PANTIES      TRAIPSE        TARRIES      P PATTIES      T TRENTAL       T OESTRAL
  PATINES    U SPURIAE        TARSIER        TAPETIS      U NEUTRAL
  SAPIENT      UPRAISE      S SAIREST      R ARTIEST      V VENTRAL
  SPINATE                     SATIRES        ARTISTE
```

AELOST 46	SLATERS	P EMPARTS	G GRANTER	TRANSES	SORBATE
(SOLATE)	TARSELS	STAMPER	REGRANT	T NATTERS	C COASTER
B BOATELS	T RATTLES	TAMPERS	I RETRAIN	RATTENS	COATERS
OBLATES	SLATTER	R SMARTER	TERRAIN	U AUNTERS	D DOATERS
C ALECOST	STARLET	S MASTERS	TRAINER	NATURES	ROASTED
LACTOSE	STARTLE	STREAMS	O ORNATER	SAUNTER	TORSADE
LOCATES	TATLERS	T MATTERS	P PARTNER	V SERVANT	TROADES
SCATOLE	U SALUTER	SMATTER	S ERRANTS	TAVERNS	E ROSEATE
TALCOSE	V TRAVELS	U MATURES	RANTERS	VERSANT	G ORGEATS
D SALTOED	VARLETS	STRUMAE	T TRANTER	W STRAWEN	STORAGE
E OLEATES	VESTRAL	W WARMEST	Y TERNARY	WANTERS	H ASTHORE
G LEGATOS	W WASTREL	Y MASTERY		Y TRAYNES	HAROSET
H LOATHES	Y RAYLETS	MAYSTER	**AENRST 8**		I OARIEST
I ISOLATE		STREAMY	(ANTERS)	**AENRTT 71**	OTARIES
K SKATOLE	**AEMNST 168**		A ANESTRA	(NATTER)	L OESTRAL
M MALTOSE	(STAMEN)	**AENNST 152**	B BANTERS	A TARTANE	M AMORETS
N ETALONS	A NAMASTE	(ANNETS)	C CANTERS	C TRANECT	MAESTRO
P APOSTLE	B BATSMEN	A ANNATES	CARNETS	D TRANTED	OMERTAS
PELOTAS	D TANDEMS	C NASCENT	NECTARS	E ENTREAT	N ATONERS
R OESTRAL	E ENTAMES	D STANDEN	RECANTS	RATTEEN	SENATOR
V SOLVATE	MEANEST	E NEATENS	SCANTER	TERNATE	TREASON
Z ZEALOTS	G MAGNETS	F ENFANTS	TANRECS	I INTREAT	P ESPARTO
	H ANTHEMS	G GANNETS	TRANCES	ITERANT	PROTEAS
AELRST 38	HETMANS	I INANEST	D ENDARTS	NATTIER	SEAPORT
(ALTERS)	I INMATES	K KANTENS	STANDER	NITRATE	R ROASTER
B ALBERTS	MAINEST	L STANNEL	STARNED	TARTINE	T ROTATES
BATLERS	MANTIES	R TANNERS	E EARNEST	TERTIAN	TOASTER
BLASTER	TAMINES	T TANNEST	EASTERN	L TRENTAL	
LABRETS	L LAMENTS	TENANTS	NEAREST	N ENTRANT	**AEPRST 129**
STABLER	MANTELS	W WANNEST	G ARGENTS	P PATTERN	(PATERS)
C CARTELS	MANTLES		GARNETS	REPTANT	A PETARAS
CLARETS	O MANTOES	**AENPST 185**	STRANGE	R TRANTER	C CARPETS
SCARLET	P ENSTAMP	(PATENS)	H ANTHERS	S NATTERS	PRECAST
TARCELS	TAPSMEN	A ANAPEST	HARTENS	RATTENS	SPECTRA
D DARTLES	R ARTSMEN	PEASANT	THENARS	U TAUNTER	D DEPARTS
E ELATERS	MARTENS	C CATNEPS	I ANESTRI	Y NATTERY	DRAPETS
REALEST	SARMENT	D PEDANTS	NASTIER		PETARDS
RELATES	SMARTEN	PENTADS	RATINES	**AENSTT 116**	E REPEATS
STEALER	S STAMENS	E PENATES	RESIANT	(ATTENS)	G PARGETS
F FALTERS	U UNTAMES	PESANTE	RETAINS	B BATTENS	H SPARTHE
G LARGEST	UNTEAMS	I PANTIES	RETINAS	C CANTEST	TEPHRAS
H HALTERS	Y AMNESTY	PATINES	RETSINA	D ATTENDS	THREAPS
HARSLET		SAPIENT	STAINER	E NEATEST	I PARTIES
LATHERS	**AEMRST 124**	SPINATE	STARNIE	F FATTENS	PASTIER
SLATHER	(MATERS)	L PLANETS	STEARIN	G GESTANT	PIASTRE
THALERS	A AMEARST	PLATENS	K RANKEST	I INSTATE	PIRATES
I REALIST	RETAMAS	M ENSTAMP	STARKEN	SATINET	PRATIES
RETAILS	B TAMBERS	TAPSMEN	TANKERS	L LATTENS	TRAIPSE
SALTIER	C MERCATS	R ARPENTS	L ANTLERS	TALENTS	L PALTERS
SALTIRE	D SMARTED	ENTRAPS	RENTALS	N TANNEST	PLASTER
SLATIER	E STEAMER	PANTERS	SALTERN	TENANTS	PLATERS
K STALKER	TEAMERS	PARENTS	STERNAL	O ATTONES	PSALTER
TALKERS	H HAMSTER	PASTERN	M ARTSMEN	NOTATES	STAPLER
L STELLAR	I MAESTRI	PERSANT	MARTENS	P PATENTS	M EMPARTS
TELLARS	MAISTER	TREPANS	SARMENT	PATTENS	STAMPER
M ARMLETS	MASTIER	S APTNESS	SMARTEN	R NATTERS	TAMPERS
MARTELS	MISRATE	PATNESS	N TANNERS	RATTENS	N ARPENTS
N ANTLERS	SEMITAR	PESANTS	O ATONERS	T ATTENTS	ENTRAPS
RENTALS	SMARTIE	T PATENTS	SENATOR	U ATTUNES	PANTERS
SALTERN	K MARKETS	PATTENS	TREASON	NUTATES	PARENTS
STERNAL	L ARMLETS	U PEANUTS	P ARPENTS	TAUTENS	PASTERN
O OESTRAL	MARTELS	PESAUNT	ENTRAPS	TETANUS	PERSANT
P PALTERS	M STAMMER	W STEWPAN	PANTERS	UNSTATE	TREPANS
PLASTER	N ARTSMEN	Y SYNAPTE	PARENTS	X SEXTANT	O ESPARTO
PLATERS	MARTENS	Z PEZANTS	PASTERN		PROTEAS
PSALTER	SARMENT		PERSANT	**AEORST 13**	SEAPORT
STAPLER	SMARTEN	**AENRRT 87**	TREPANS	(ORATES)	P TAPPERS
S ARTLESS	O AMORETS	(RANTER)	R ERRANTS	B BOASTER	R PARTERS
LASTERS	MAESTRO	A NARRATE	RANTERS	BOATERS	PRATERS
SALTERS	OMERTAS	E TERRANE	S SARSNET	BORATES	S PASTERS

REPASTS
SPAREST
T PATTERS
SPATTER
TAPSTER
U PASTURE
UPRATES
UPSTARE
UPTEARS
Y YAPSTER
Z PATZERS

AERRST 138
(RATERS)
B BARRETS
BARTERS
C CARTERS
CRATERS
TRACERS
D DARTERS
DARTRES
RETARDS
STARRED
TRADERS
E SERRATE
TEARERS
F FRATERS
RAFTERS
G GARRETS
GARTERS
GRATERS
I ARTSIER
TARRIES
TARSIER
K STARKER
M SMARTER
N ERRANTS
RANTERS
O ROASTER
P PARTERS
PRATERS
S ARRESTS
RASTERS
STARERS
T RATTERS
RESTART
STARTER
Y STRAYER

AERSTT 97
(TASTER)
B BATTERS
TABRETS
C SCATTER
D STARTED
TETRADS
E ESTREAT
RESTATE
G TARGETS
H HATTERS
RATHEST
SHATTER
THREATS
I ARTIEST
ARTISTE
ATTIRES
IRATEST
STRIATE
TASTIER
TERTIAS

L RATTLES
SLATTER
STARLET
STARTLE
TATLERS
M MATTERS
SMATTER
N NATTERS
RATTENS
O ROTATES
TOASTER
P PATTERS
SPATTER
TAPSTER
R RATTERS
RESTART
STARTER
S ASTERTS
STARETS
STATERS
TASTERS
T STRETTA
TARTEST
TATTERS
U ASTUTER
STATURE
W SWATTER
TEWARTS
Y YATTERS
Z STARETZ

AERSTW 194
(WATERS)
A AWAREST
B BRAWEST
WABSTER
D STEWARD
STRAWED
WRASTED
E SWEATER
F FRETSAW
WAFTERS
H THAWERS
WREATHS
I WAISTER
WAITERS
WARIEST
L WASTREL
M WARMEST
N STRAWEN
WANTERS
S WASTERS
T SWATTER
TEWARTS
Y WASTERY

AGILNR 199
(RALING)
B BLARING
D DARLING
LARDING
E ENGRAIL
LEARING
NARGILE
REALIGN
REGINAL
F FLARING
G GLARING
H HARLING
I GLAIRIN

LAIRING
RAILING
K LARKING
M MARLING
N LARNING
P PARLING
T RATLING
W WARLING
Y ANGRILY
NARGILY
RAYLING

AGILNT 174
(LATING)
B TABLING
C CATLING
E ATINGLE
ELATING
GELATIN
GENITAL
F FATLING
H HALTING
LATHING
I TAILING
K TALKING
M MALTING
N TANLING
O ANTILOG
P PLATING
R RATLING
S ANGLIST
LASTING
SALTING
SLATING
STALING
Y GIANTLY

AGINRS 123
(GRAINS)
A NAGARIS
SANGRIA
SARANGI
B SABRING
C ARCINGS
RACINGS
SACRING
SCARING
D DARINGS
GRADINS
E ANGRIES
EARINGS
ERASING
GAINERS
GRAINES
REGAINS
REGINAS
SEARING
SERINGA
F FARSING
G SIRGANG
H GARNISH
RASHING
SHARING
I AIRINGS
ARISING
RAGINIS
RAISING
SAIRING
K RAKINGS
SARKING

M MARGINS
N SNARING
O IGNAROS
ORIGANS
SIGNORA
SOARING
P PARINGS
PARSING
RASPING
SPARING
T GASTRIN
RATINGS
STARING
V RAVINGS
W RAWINGS
Y SIGNARY
SYRINGA

AGINRT 69
(RATING)
C CARTING
CRATING
TRACING
D DARTING
TRADING
E GRANITE
INGRATE
TANGIER
TEARING
F FARTING
INGRAFT
RAFTING
G GRATING
TARGING
I AIRTING
RAITING
K KARTING
L RATLING
M MARTING
MIGRANT
N RANTING
O ORATING
ROATING
P PARTING
PRATING
TRAPING
R TARRING
S GASTRIN
RATINGS
STARING
T RATTING
Y GIANTRY

AGINST 108
(SATING)
A AGAINST
GITANAS
B BASTING
C ACTINGS
CASTING
D DATINGS
E EASTING
EATINGS
GAINEST
GENISTA
INGATES
INGESTA
SEATING
TANGIES
TEASING

TSIGANE
F FASTING
G GASTING
GATINGS
STAGING
H HASTING
TASHING
K SKATING
STAKING
TAKINGS
TASKING
L ANGLIST
LASTING
SALTING
SLATING
STALING
M MASTING
TAMINGS
N ANTINGS
STANING
O AGONIST
GITANOS
P PASTING
R GASTRIN
RATINGS
STARING
T STATING
TASTING
U SAUTING
V STAVING
W STAWING
TAWINGS
WASTING
X TAXINGS
Y STAYING

AINRST 40
(TRAINS)
A ANTIARS
ARTISAN
TSARINA
D INDARTS
E ANESTRI
NASTIER
RATINES
RESIANT
RETAINS
RETINAS
RETSINA
STAINER
STARNIE
STEARIN
G GASTRIN
RATINGS
STARING
H TARNISH
I INTARSI
L RATLINS
M MARTINS
O AROINTS
RATIONS
P SPIRANT
SPRAINT
Q QINTARS
S INSTARS
SANTIRS
STRAINS
T STRAINT
TRANSIT
U NUTRIAS

ANORST 60
(RATONS)
A TORANAS
B BARTONS
C CANTORS
CARTONS
CONTRAS
CRATONS
E ATONERS
SENATOR
TREASON
I AROINTS
RATIONS
L LATRONS
M MATRONS
TRANSOM
N NATRONS
O RATOONS
P PARTONS
PATRONS
TARPONS
T ATTORNS
RATTONS
ROTTANS
U ROUSANT
SANTOUR
Y AROYNTS

BEIRST 184
(TRIBES)
A BAITERS
BARITES
D BESTRID
BISTRED
E REBITES
F FIBSTER
H HERBIST
I BITSIER
K BRISKET
L BLISTER
BRISTLE
RIBLETS
M BETRIMS
TIMBERS
TIMBRES
O ORBIEST
S BESTIRS
BISTERS
BISTRES
T BITTERS
U BUSTIER
RUBIEST

CEINOS 109
(CONIES)
A ACINOSE
C CONCISE
D SECONDI
E SENECIO
G COGNISE
COIGNES
I ICONISE
K CONKIES
L CINEOLS
CONSEIL
INCLOSE
M INCOMES
MESONIC
N CONINES
R COINERS

CRINOSE	INSECTS	COARSEN	G SEDGIER	L DENTELS	SINGLED
CRONIES	Y INSECTY	CORNEAS	L RESILED	NESTLED	T GLINTED
ORCEINS		D CONDERS	M REMEIDS	M DEMENTS	TINGLED
ORCINES	**CEIORS 156**	CORSNED	REMISED	N DENNETS	U ELUDING
SERICON	(COSIER)	SCORNED	N DENIERS	STENNED	INDULGE
S CESSION	A ORACIES	E ENCORES	NEREIDS	O DENOTES	V DELVING
COSINES	SCORIAE	NECROSE	RESINED	R STERNED	DEVLING
T NOTICES	B CORBIES	F CONFERS	O OREIDES	TENDERS	W WELDING
SECTION	C CICEROS	G CONGERS	OSIERED	TENDRES	
V NOVICES	D DISCOER	I COINERS	P PREDIES	S DENSEST	**DEGINR 82**
	H HEROICS	CRINOSE	PRESIDE	T DETENTS	(RINGED)
CEINRS 183	L RECOILS	CRONIES	SPEIRED	STENTED	A AREDING
(INCERS)	N COINERS	ORCEINS	R DERRIES	U DETENUS	DEARING
A ARSENIC	CRINOSE	ORCINES	DESIRER	X EXTENDS	DERAIGN
CARNIES	CRONIES	SERICON	RESIDER		EARDING
CERASIN	ORCEINS	K CONKERS	SERRIED	**DEERST 151**	GRADINE
D CINDERS	ORCINES	RECKONS	S DESIRES	(RESTED)	GRAINED
DISCERN	SERICON	L CORNELS	RESIDES	A DEAREST	READING
RESCIND	P COPIERS	N CONNERS	T DIETERS	DERATES	B BREDING
E CERESIN	COPSIER	O CEROONS	REISTED	ESTRADE	C CRINGED
SCRIENE	PERSICO	P CREPONS	U RESIDUE	REASTED	D GRINDED
SINCERE	R CIRROSE	R CORNERS	UREIDES	SEDATER	REDDING
G CRINGES	CORRIES	SCORNER	V DERIVES	STEARED	E DREEING
H NICHERS	CROSIER	S CENSORS	DEVISER	C CRESTED	ENERGID
RICHENS	S COSIERS	T CONSTER	DIVERSE	D REDDEST	GREINED
I IRENICS	T EROTICS	CORNETS	REVISED	TEDDERS	REEDING
SERICIN	TERCIOS	CRONETS		E REESTED	REIGNED
SIRENIC	U SCOURIE	U ROUNCES	**DEENRS 92**	STEERED	F FRINGED
K NICKERS	V CORSIVE		(ENDERS)	I DIETERS	H HERDING
SNICKER	VOICERS	**DEEINR 43**	A DEANERS	REISTED	I DINGIER
M CREMSIN	W COWRIES	(DENIER)	ENDEARS	N STERNED	N GRINNED
MINCERS	SCOWRIE	B BENDIER	B BENDERS	TENDERS	RENDING
O COINERS	Z COZIERS	INBREED	C DECERNS	TENDRES	O ERODING
CRINOSE		C CEDRINE	SCERNED	O OERSTED	GROINED
CRONIES	**CEIRST 166**	E NEEDIER	D REDDENS	ROSETED	IGNORED
ORCEINS	(CITERS)	F DEFINER	E NEEDERS	TEREDOS	NEGROID
ORCINES	A CRISTAE	ENFIRED	SERENED	P PRESTED	REDOING
SERICON	RACIEST	FENDIER	SNEERED	S DESERTS	R GRINDER
P PINCERS	STEARIC	REFINED	F FENDERS	DESSERT	REGRIND
PRINCES	C CRETICS	G DREEING	G GENDERS	TRESSED	S DINGERS
S SCRINES	D CREDITS	ENERGID	H HERDENS	V STERVED	ENGIRDS
T CISTERN	DIRECTS	GREINED	I DENIERS	VERDETS	U DUNGIER
CRETINS	E CERITES	REEDING	NEREIDS	W STREWED	W REDWING
V CRIVENS	RECITES	REIGNED	RESINED	WRESTED	WRINGED
W WINCERS	TIERCES	H INHERED	L LENDERS	X DEXTERS	Y YERDING
	H CITHERS	L RELINED	SLENDER	Y DYESTER	
CEINST 196	ESTRICH	M ERMINED	M MENDERS		**DEGINS 154**
(INSECT)	RICHEST	O ORDINEE	O ENDORSE	**DEGILN 164**	(SINGED)
A CANIEST	I ERISTIC	P REPINED	P SPENDER	(DINGLE)	A AGNISED
CINEAST	RICIEST	RIPENED	R RENDERS	A ALIGNED	E SDEIGNE
E ENTICES	K RICKETS	R DERNIER	S REDNESS	DEALING	SEEDING
F INFECTS	STICKER	S DENIERS	SENDERS	LEADING	G EDGINGS
H ETHNICS	TICKERS	NEREIDS	T STERNED	B BINGLED	SNIGGED
STHENIC	L RELICTS	RESINED	TENDERS	E DELEING	I DINGIES
I INCITES	M CRETISM	U UREDINE	TENDRES	G GELDING	L DINGLES
J INJECTS	METRICS	W WIDENER	U ENDURES	GINGLED	ELDINGS
K SNICKET	N CISTERN	X INDEXER	ENSURED	NIGGLED	ENGILDS
TICKENS	CRETINS		V VENDERS	H HINDLEG	SINGLED
L CLIENTS	O EROTICS	**DEEIRS 58**	Z DZERENS	I EILDING	M SMIDGEN
LECTINS	TERCIOS	(RESIDE)		ELIDING	N ENDINGS
STENCIL	P TRICEPS	A DEARIES	**DEENST 111**	J JINGLED	SENDING
O NOTICES	T TRISECT	READIES	(NESTED)	M MEDLING	O DINGOES
SECTION	U CUITERS	B DERBIES	A STEANED	MELDING	R DINGERS
P INCEPTS	CURIETS	C DECRIES	C DESCENT	MINGLED	ENGIRDS
INSPECT	ICTERUS	D DERIDES	SCENTED	N LENDING	S DESIGNS
PECTINS	W TWICERS	DESIRED	D STENDED	O GLENOID	T NIDGETS
PEINCTS		DIEDRES	E STEENED	P PINGLED	STEDING
R CISTERN	**CENORS 172**	RESIDED	I DESTINE	S DINGLES	STINGED
CRETINS	(CONERS)	E SEEDIER	ENDITES	ELDINGS	U GUNDIES
S INCESTS	A CARNOSE	F DEFIERS	STEINED	ENGILDS	SUEDING

W SWINDGE	INDORSE	INSTEAD	VOIDERS	SORTIED	B BORDELS
SWINGED	ROSINED	SAINTED	W DOWRIES	STEROID	C SCOLDER
Y DINGEYS	SORDINE	SATINED	ROWDIES	STORIED	E RESOLED
DYEINGS	S ONSIDES	STAINED	WEIRDOS	TRIODES	F FOLDERS
DEILNS 120	T DITONES	B BIDENTS	Z DORIZES	P SPIRTED	G LODGERS
(INDLES)	STONIED	D DISTEND	**DEIOST 35**	STRIPED	H HOLDERS
A DENIALS	**DEINRS 51**	E DESTINE	(ODITES)	R STIRRED	I SOLDIER
SNAILED	(DINERS)	ENDITES	A IODATES	S DISSERT	SOLIDER
D DINDLES	A RANDIES	STEINED	TOADIES	STRIDES	M SMOLDER
SLIDDEN	SANDIER	F SNIFTED	C CESTOID	U DUSTIER	N RONDELS
E ENISLED	SARDINE	G NIDGETS	COTISED	REDUITS	P POLDERS
ENSILED	B BINDERS	STEDING	D TODDIES	STUDIER	S DORSELS
LINSEED	REBINDS	STINGED	F FOISTED	V DIVERTS	RODLESS
G DINGLES	C CINDERS	I INDITES	H HOISTED	STRIVED	SOLDERS
ELDINGS	DISCERN	TINEIDS	J JOISTED	VERDITS	T DROLEST
ENGILDS	RESCIND	K DINKEST	M DOMIEST	**DEIRSU 143**	OLDSTER
SINGLED	E DENIERS	KINDEST	MODISTE	(URDIES)	STRODLE
I INISLED	NEREIDS	L DENTILS	MOISTED	A RESIDUA	W WELDORS
K KINDLES	RESINED	M MINDSET	N DITONES	B BRUISED	Y YODLERS
M MILDENS	F FINDERS	N DENTINS	STONIED	BURDIES	**DELORT 100**
N DINNLES	FRIENDS	INDENTS	O OSTEOID	C CRUISED	(DOLTER)
LINDENS	G DINGERS	INTENDS	P DEPOSIT	DISCURE	A DELATOR
O INDOLES	ENGIRDS	O DITONES	DOPIEST	D RUDDIES	LEOTARD
SONDELI	H HINDERS	STONIED	PODITES	E RESIDUE	D TODDLER
P SPELDIN	SHRINED	P STIPEND	POSITED	UREIDES	I DOILTER
SPINDLE	I INSIDER	R TINDERS	SOPITED	G GUIDERS	L TROLLED
SPLINED	K KINREDS	S DISNEST	TOPSIDE	H HURDIES	N ENTROLD
T DENTILS	REDSKIN	DISSENT	R EDITORS	K DUIKERS	O ROOTLED
W SWINDLE	M MINDERS	SNIDEST	ROISTED	DUSKIER	P DROPLET
WINDLES	REMINDS	T DENTIST	ROSITED	N INSURED	S DROLEST
Y SNIDELY	N DINNERS	DISTENT	SORTIED	P PUDSIER	OLDSTER
DEILRT 73	O DONSIER	STINTED	STEROID	SIRUPED	STRODLE
(TRIDLE)	INDORSE	U DISTUNE	STORIED	Q SQUIRED	T DOTTLER
A DILATER	ROSINED	DUNITES	TRIODES	R DRUSIER	DOTTREL
TRAILED	SORDINE	Y DENSITY	T DOTIEST	DURRIES	U TROULED
B DRIBLET	P PINDERS	DESTINY	STOITED	S DISEURS	**DENORU 99**
D TIDDLER	T TINDERS	**DEIORS 27**	U OUTSIDE	SUDSIER	(UNDOER)
E RETILED	U INSURED	(ORIDES)	TEDIOUS	T DUSTIER	A RONDEAU
F FLIRTED	W REWINDS	A ROADIES	V DOVIEST	REDUITS	B BOUNDER
TRIFLED	WINDERS	SOREDIA	W DOWIEST	STUDIER	REBOUND
H THIRLED	**DEINRU 52**	B BORIDES	X EXODIST	**DELNOS 181**	UNROBED
K KIRTLED	(RUINED)	DISROBE	Z DOZIEST	(OLDENS)	D REDOUND
L TRILLED	A UNAIRED	C DISCOER	**DEIRST 57**	A LOADENS	ROUNDED
N TENDRIL	URANIDE	D DORISED	(STRIDE)	B BLONDES	UNDERDO
TRINDLE	C INDUCER	SODDIER	A ARIDEST	BOLDENS	F FOUNDER
O DOILTER	D UNDRIED	E OREIDES	ASTERID	D NODDLES	REFOUND
P TRIPLED	E UREDINE	OSIERED	ASTRIDE	F ENFOLDS	G GUERDON
U DILUTER	F UNFIRED	L SOLDIER	DIASTER	FONDLES	UNDERGO
W TWIRLED	G DUNGIER	SOLIDER	DISRATE	G DONGLES	UNGORED
DEINOS 41	H UNHIRED	M MISDOER	STAIDER	GOLDENS	I DOURINE
(ONSIDE)	I URIDINE	MOIDERS	STAIRED	I INDOLES	OUNDIER
A ADONISE	J INJURED	N DONSIER	TARDIES	SONDELI	L LOUNDER
ANODISE	M UNRIMED	INDORSE	TIRADES	M DOLMENS	ROUNDEL
SODAINE	N DUNNIER	ROSINED	B BESTRID	O NOODLES	ROUNDLE
C SECONDI	INURNED	SORDINE	BISTRED	SNOOLED	M MOURNED
D NODDIES	O DOURINE	O OROIDES	C CREDITS	R RONDELS	N ENROUND
G DINGOES	OUNDIER	P PERIODS	DIRECTS	S OLDNESS	P POUNDER
H HOIDENS	S INSURED	S DORISES	E DIETERS	U LOUDENS	UNROPED
I IODINES	T INTRUDE	DOSSIER	REISTED	NODULES	R RONDURE
IONISED	TURDINE	T EDITORS	F FRISTED	NOUSLED	ROUNDER
L INDOLES	UNTIRED	ROISTED	H DITHERS	W DOWLNES	UNORDER
SONDELI	UNTRIDE	ROSITED	SHIRTED	Z DONZELS	S RESOUND
M MISDONE	UNTRIED	SORTIED	I DIRTIES	**DELORS 145**	SOUNDER
N ONDINES	W UNWIRED	STEROID	K SKIRTED	(OLDERS)	UNDOERS
P DISPONE	**DEINST 32**	STORIED	N TINDERS	A LOADERS	W REWOUND
SPINODE	(SINTED)	TRIODES	O EDITORS	ORDEALS	WOUNDER
R DONSIER	A DETAINS	V DEVISOR	ROISTED	RELOADS	
		DEVOIRS	ROSITED		
		VISORED			

DENOST 74
(STONED)
A ASTONED
  DONATES
  ONSTEAD
B OBTENDS
C DOCENTS
E DENOTES
F FONDEST
I DITONES
  STONIED
M ENDMOST
N STONNED
  TENDONS
O SNOOTED
  STOODEN
R RODENTS
  SNORTED
T SNOTTED
U DEUTONS
  SNOUTED

DENRSU 179
(UNDERS)
A ASUNDER
  DANSEUR
  DAUNERS
B BURDENS
D DUNDERS
E ENDURES
  ENSURED
F FUNDERS
  REFUNDS
G GERUNDS
H HURDENS
I INSURED
L LURDENS
  NURSLED
  RUNDLES
N UNDERNS
O RESOUND
  SOUNDER
  UNDOERS
P SPURNED
S SUNDERS
  UNDRESS
T RETUNDS
  UNDREST
U UNSURED

DEORST 50
(SORTED)
A DOATERS
  ROASTED
  TORSADE
  TROADES
B DEBTORS
E OERSTED
  ROSETED
  TEREDOS
F DEFROST
  FROSTED
G STODGER
H DEHORTS
  SHORTED
I EDITORS
  ROISTED
  ROSITED
  SORTIED
  STEROID

  STORIED
  TRIODES
K STROKED
L DROLEST
  OLDSTER
  STRODLE
M STORMED
N RODENTS
  SNORTED
O ROOSTED
P DEPORTS
  REDTOPS
  SPORTED
R DORTERS
  RODSTER
T DETORTS
U DETOURS
  DOUREST
  DOUTERS
  OUTREDS
  ROUSTED
W STROWED
Y DESTROY
  ROYSTED
  STROYED

DEOSTU 180
(OUSTED)
C CUSTODE
  DOUCEST
  DOUCETS
  SCOUTED
G DEGOUTS
H SHOUTED
  SOUTHED
I OUTSIDE
  TEDIOUS
J JOUSTED
L LOUDEST
  TOUSLED
M MOUSTED
  SMOUTED
N DEUTONS
  SNOUTED
O OUTDOES
P SPOUTED
R DETOURS
  DOUREST
  DOUTERS
  OUTREDS
  ROUSTED
T DUETTOS
  TESTUDO
U DUTEOUS
X TUXEDOS

EEILRS 90
(RELIES)
A REALISE
B BELIERS
D RESILED
E SEELIER
F FERLIES
  RELIEFS
G LEIGERS
  LIEGERS
H LEISHER
L LEISLER
N LIERNES

  RELINES
P REPLIES
  SPIELER
R RELIERS
S RESILES
T LEISTER
  RETILES
  STERILE
U LEISURE
V RELIVES
  REVILES
  SERVILE

EEILST 89
(ELITES)
C SECTILE
E EELIEST
F FELSITE
  LEFTIES
  LIEFEST
G ELEGIST
  ELEGITS
H SHELTIE
K KELTIES
  SLEEKIT
L TELLIES
M ELMIEST
N TENSILE
O ESTOILE
  ETOILES
P EPISTLE
  PELITES
R LEISTER
  RETILES
  STERILE
S TELESIS
  TIELESS
V LEVITES
  LIEVEST
X SEXTILE

EEIMNS 192
(EMINES)
A MEANIES
  NEMESIA
D DESMINE
E ENEMIES
G SEEMING
I MEINIES
L ISLEMEN
M IMMENSE
O SEMEION
R ERMINES
S INSEEMS
  MISSEEN
  NEMESIS
  SIEMENS
T MISWEEN
W MISWEEN
Y MEINEYS

EEINRT 7
(ENTIRE)
A RETINAE
  TRAINEE
B BENTIER
C ENTERIC
  ENTICER
E TEENIER
F FEINTER

G GENTIER
  INTEGER
  TEERING
  TREEING
H NEITHER
  THEREIN
I ERINITE
  NITERIE
K KERNITE
N INTERNE
P INEPTER
R INERTER
  REINTER
  RENTIER
  TERRINE
S ENTRIES
  NERITES
  TRENISE
T NETTIER
  TENTIER
U NEURITE
  RETINUE
  REUNITE
  UTERINE

EEIRRS 182
(ERRIES)
A REARISE
B BERRIES
D DERRIES
  DESIRER
  RESIDER
  SERRIED
F FERRIES
H HERRIES
J JERRIES
L RELIERS
M MERRIES
N RESINER
O ROSIERE
P PERRIES
  REPRISE
  RESPIRE
S SERRIES
  SIRREES
T ETRIERS
  REITERS
  RESTIER
  RETIRES
  TERRIES
V REIVERS
  REVERSI
  REVISER
  RIEVERS
W REWIRES

EEIRST 31
(ESTIER)
A AERIEST
  SERIATE
B REBITES
C CERITES
  RECITES
  TIERCES
D DIETERS
  REISTED
E EERIEST
H HEISTER

L LEISTER
  RETILES
  STERILE
M METIERS
  TREMIES
  TRISEME
N ENTIRES
  ENTRIES
  NERITES
  TRENISE
P RESPITE
R ETRIERS
  REITERS
  RESTIER
  RETIRES
  TERRIES
T TESTIER
U SUETIER
V RESTIVE
  SIEVERT
  STIEVER
  VERIEST
W STEWIER
Z ZESTIER

EELNST 161
(NESTLE)
A ELANETS
  LEANEST
D DENTELS
  NESTLED
E STELENE
G GENTLES
  LENGEST
I TENSILE
P PENTELS
R RELENTS
S NESTLES
T NETTLES
U ELUENTS
  UNSTEEL
Y ENSTYLE
  TENSELY

EELRST 157
(ELTERS)
A ELATERS
  REALEST
  RELATES
  STEALER
B BELTERS
  TREBLES
C TERCELS
F FELTERS
  REFLETS
G REGLETS
H SHELTER
I LEISTER
  RETILES
  STERILE
K KESTREL
  SKELTER
L RETELLS
  TELLERS
M SMELTER
N RELENTS
P PELTERS
  PETRELS

  RESPELT
  SPELTER
S STREELS
  TRESSEL
T LETTERS
  LETTRES
  SETTLER
  STERLET
  TRESTLE
V SVELTER
W SWELTER
  WELTERS
  WRESTLE
Y RESTYLE
  TERSELY
Z SELTZER

EENRST 56
(ENTERS)
A EARNEST
  EASTERN
  NEAREST
C CENTERS
  CENTRES
  TENRECS
D STERNED
  TENDERS
  TENDRES
E ENTREES
  RETENES
G GERENTS
  REGENTS
H THRENES
I ENTIRES
  ENTRIES
  NERITES
  TRENISE
L RELENTS
N RENNETS
  TENNERS
P PRESENT
  REPENTS
  SERPENT
R RENTERS
  STERNER
S NESTERS
  RESENTS
  STRENES
T TENTERS
  TESTERN
U NEUTERS
  RETUNES
  TENURES
  TUREENS
V VENTERS
  VENTRES
W WESTERN
X EXTERNS
Y STYRENE
  YESTERN

EERSTT 200
(ETTERS)
A ESTREAT
  RESTATE
B BETTERS
C TERCETS
E TEETERS
F FETTERS
G GETTERS

H TETHERS
I TESTIER
L LETTERS
  LETTRES
  SETTLER
  STERLET
  TRESTLE
N TENTERS
  TESTERN
O ROSETTE
P PERTEST
  PETTERS
R TERRETS
S SETTERS
  STREETS
  TERSEST
  TESTERS
T STRETTE
  TETTERS
U TRUSTEE
Y STREETY

EFIRST 191
(STRIFE)
A FAIREST
B FIBSTER
D FRISTED
F RESTIFF
  STIFFER
H SHIFTER
I FISTIER
K FRISKET
L FILTERS
  LIFTERS
  STIFLER
  TRIFLES
M FIRMEST
  FREMITS
N SNIFTER
O FOISTER
  FORTIES
S SIFTERS
  STRIFES
T FITTERS
  TITFERS
U FUSTIER
  SURFEIT
W SWIFTER

EGILNR 125
(LINGER)
A ENGRAIL
  LEARING
  NARGILE
  REALIGN
  REGINAL
C CLINGER
  CRINGLE
E LEERING
  REELING
F FLINGER
G NIGGLER
H HERLING
I LEIRING
  LINGIER
J JINGLER
M GREMLIN
  MERLING
  MINGLER
P PINGLER

S GIRNELS
  LINGERS
  SLINGER
T RINGLET
  TINGLER
  TRINGLE
Y RELYING

EGILNS 117
(SINGLE)
A LEASING
  LINAGES
  SEALING
B BINGLES
D DINGLES
  ELDINGS
  ENGILDS
  SINGLED
E LEESING
  SEELING
F SELFING
G GINGLES
  NIGGLES
  SNIGGLE
H SHINGLE
I SEILING
J JINGLES
K KINGLES
L LEGLINS
  LINGELS
  LINGLES
  SELLING
M MINGLES
N GINNELS
O ELOIGNS
  LEGIONS
  LINGOES
P PINGLES
  SPIGNEL
R GIRNELS
  LINGERS
  SLINGER
S SINGLES
T GLISTEN
  LESTING
  SINGLET
  TINGLES
U LUNGIES
  SLUEING
W SLEWING
  SWINGLE
Z ZINGELS

EGILNT 66
(TINGLE)
A ATINGLE
  ELATING
  GELATIN
  GENITAL
B BELTING
D GLINTED
  TINGLED
E GENTILE
F FELTING
H ENLIGHT
  LIGHTEN
I LIGNITE
J JINGLET
K KINGLET
L TELLING

M MELTING
O LENTIGO
P PELTING
R RINGLET
  TINGLER
  TRINGLE
S GLISTEN
  LESTING
  SINGLET
  TINGLES
T ETTLING
  LETTING
U ELUTING
W WELTING
  WINGLET

EGILOS 132
(LOGIES)
A GOALIES
B OBLIGES
E ELOGIES
L GOLLIES
M SEMILOG
N ELOIGNS
  LEGIONS
  LINGOES
O GOOLIES
  OLOGIES
R GLOIRES
  GLORIES
S GLIOSES
T ELOGIST
U OUGLIES

EGILRS 159
(LIGERS)
A GRAILES
B GERBILS
D GILDERS
  GIRDLES
  GLIDERS
  GRISLED
  LIDGERS
  RIDGELS
E LEIGERS
  LIEGERS
G LIGGERS
I GIRLIES
K KILERGS
L GRILLES
N GIRNELS
  LINGERS
  SLINGER
O GLOIRES
  GLORIES
S GRILSES
T GLISTER
  GRISTLE
U GUILERS
  LIGURES
  LURGIES
Y GREISLY
  GRIESLY
  GRISELY

EGILST 190
(LEGIST)
A AGILEST
  AIGLETS
  LIGATES

  TAIGLES
B GIBLETS
E ELEGIST
  ELEGITS
G GIGLETS
H SLEIGHT
L GILLETS
M GIMLETS
N GLISTEN
  LESTING
  SINGLET
  TINGLES
O ELOGIST
P PIGLETS
R GLISTER
  GRISTLE
S LEGISTS
U GLUIEST
  UGLIEST
Z GLITZES

EGINNR 178
(GINNER)
A AGINNER
  EARNING
  ENGRAIN
  GRANNIE
  NEARING
C CERNING
D GRINNED
  RENDING
E ENGINER
  INGENER
F FERNING
G GERNING
I REINING
K KERNING
M RINGMEN
N RENNING
R GRINNER
S ENRINGS
  GINNERS
T RENTING
  RINGENT
  TERNING
U ENURING
V NERVING
Y GINNERY
  RENYING

EGINOS 78
(INGOES)
A AGONIES
  AGONISE
B BIOGENS
C COGNISE
  COIGNES
D DINGOES
E SOIGNEE
H SHOEING
J JINGOES
L ELOIGNS
  LEGIONS
  LINGOES
M MISGONE
P EPIGONS
  PIGEONS
  PINGOES
R ERINGOS
  IGNORES

  REGIONS
  SIGNORE
U IGNEOUS
W INGOWES
  WIGEONS
Y ISOGENY

EGINRS 68
(SINGER)
A ANGRIES
  EARINGS
  ERASING
  GAINERS
  GRAINES
  REGAINS
  REGINAS
  SEARING
  SERINGA
B BINGERS
C CRINGES
D DINGERS
  ENGIRDS
E GREISEN
F FINGERS
  FRINGES
G GINGERS
  NIGGERS
  SNIGGER
L GIRNELS
  LINGERS
  SLINGER
M GERMINS
N ENRINGS
  GINNERS
O ERINGOS
  IGNORES
  REGIONS
  SIGNORE
P PERSING
  PINGERS
  SPRINGE
R ERRINGS
  RINGERS
  SERRING
S INGRESS
  RESIGNS
  SIGNERS
  SINGERS
T RESTING
  STINGER
U REUSING
  RUEINGS
  SIGNEUR
V SERVING
  VERSING
W SWINGER
  WINGERS
Y SYRINGE

EGINRT 39
(TINGER)
A GRANITE
  INGRATE
  TANGIER
  TEARING
E GENTIER
  INTEGER
  TEERING
  TREEING
H RIGHTEN

I IGNITER
  TIERING
  TIGRINE
L RINGLET
  TINGLER
  TRINGLE
M METRING
  TERMING
N RENTING
  RINGENT
  TERNING
O GENITOR
S RESTING
  STINGER
T GITTERN
  RETTING
U TRUEING
V VERTING
Y RETYING

EGINST 107
(ESTING)
A EASTING
  EATINGS
  GAINEST
  GENISTA
  INGATES
  INGESTA
  SEATING
  TANGIES
  TEASING
  TSIGANE
B BESTING
D NIDGETS
  STEDING
  STINGED
H NIGHEST
I IGNITES
J JESTING
K KESTING
L GLISTEN
  LESTING
  SINGLET
  TINGLES
M STEMING
  TEMSING
N NESTING
  SENTING
  TENSING
R RESTING
  STINGER
S INGESTS
  SIGNETS
T SETTING
  TESTING
U GUNITES
V VESTING
W STEWING
  TWINGES
  WESTING

EGNORS 155
(ONGERS)
A ONAGERS
  ORANGES
C CONGERS
E ENGORES
  NEGROES
I ERINGOS
  IGNORES

REGIONS	SHORTEN	**EILNOS 47**	TINKLES	B BETOILS	U LUSTIER	
SIGNORE	THRENOS	(OLINES)	L LENTILS	C CITOLES	RULIEST	
M MONGERS	THRONES	C CINEOLS	LINTELS	E ESTOILE	RUTILES	
MORGENS	O HOOTERS	CONSEIL	N LINNETS	ETOILES		
O ORGONES	SHOOTER	INCLOSE	O ENTOILS	G ELOGIST	**EILSTU 136**	
OROGENS	SOOTHER	D INDOLES	LIONETS	H EOLITHS	(UTILES)	
P SPONGER	P POTHERS	SONDELI	P PINTLES	HOLIEST	A SITULAE	
S ENGROSS	STROPHE	F OLEFINS	PLENIST	HOSTILE	B BLUIEST	
U SURGEON	THORPES	G ELOIGNS	R LINTERS	I IOLITES	SUBTILE	
V GOVERNS	R RHETORS	LEGIONS	SNIRTLE	OILIEST	D DILUTES	
Y ERYNGOS	ROTHERS	LINGOES	S ENLISTS	L OILLETS	F FLUIEST	
GROYNES	SHORTER	I ELISION	LISTENS	M MOTILES	G GLUIEST	
	S TOSHERS	ISOLINE	SILENTS	N ENTOILS	UGLIEST	
EHIRST 153	T HOTTERS	LIONISE	TINSELS	LIONETS	I UTILISE	
(ITHERS)	U SHOUTER	L LIONELS	U LUTEINS	O OOLITES	L TUILLES	
A HASTIER	SOUTHER	NIELLOS	UNTILES	OSTIOLE	N LUTEINS	
SHERIAT	W THROWES	M MOLINES	UTENSIL	STOOLIE	UNTILES	
B HERBIST	X EXHORTS	O LOONIES	V VENTILS	P PIOLETS	UTENSIL	
C CITHERS		P EPSILON	W WESTLIN	PISTOLE	O OUTLIES	
ESTRICH	**EIILST 139**	PINOLES	WINTLES	R LOITERS	P PULIEST	
RICHEST	(TILIES)	R NEROLIS		TOILERS	PUTELIS	
D DITHERS	A LAITIES	S ESLOINS	**EILORS 37**	T LITOTES	STIPULE	
SHIRTED	C ELICITS	INSOLES	(OILERS)	TOILETS	R LUSTIER	
E HEISTER	I ILEITIS	LESIONS	B BOILERS	U OUTLIES	RULIEST	
F SHIFTER	K KILTIES	LIONESS	REBOILS	V OLIVETS	RUTILES	
G SIGHTER	L ILLITES	T ENTOILS	C RECOILS	VIOLETS	T TITULES	
H HITHERS	M ELITISM	LIONETS	D SOLDIER	W OWLIEST		
I HIRSTIE	LIMIEST	U ELUSION	SOLIDER		**EIMNOS 131**	
L SLITHER	LIMITES		G GLOIRES	**EILRST 44**	(MONIES)	
M HERMITS	N INLIEST	**EILNRS 77**	GLORIES	(LITERS)	A ANOMIES	
MITHERS	LINIEST	(LINERS)	I SOILIER	A REALIST	C INCOMES	
O HERIOTS	LINTIES	A NAILERS	M MOILERS	RETAILS	MESONIC	
HOISTER	O IOLITES	B BERLINS	N NEROLIS	SALTIER	D MISDONE	
SHORTIE	P SPILITE	E LIERNES	O ORIOLES	SALTIRE	E SEMEION	
TOSHIER	R SILTIER	RELINES	P SLOPIER	SLATIER	G MISGONE	
P HIPSTER	T ELITIST	G GIRNELS	SPOILER	B BLISTER	L MOLINES	
T HITTERS	U UTILISE	LINGERS	R LORRIES	BRISTLE	O MOONIES	
TITHERS	W WILIEST	SLINGER	S LORISES	RIBLETS	NOISOME	
U HIRSUTE		I INLIERS	LOSSIER	C RELICTS	P IMPONES	
V THRIVES	**EIINRT 30**	K SLINKER	RISSOLE	E LEISTER	PEONISM	
W SWITHER	(INTIRE)	M LIMNERS	T LOITERS	RETILES	R MERINOS	
WITHERS	A INERTIA	MERLINS	TOILERS	STERILE	MERSION	
WRITHES	C CITRINE	O NEROLIS	U LOUSIER	F FILTERS	S EONISMS	
Z ZITHERS	CRINITE	P PILSNER	SOILURE	LIFTERS	T MOISTEN	
	INCITER	T LINTERS	V OLIVERS	STIFLER	W WINSOME	
EHORST 189	NERITIC	SNIRTLE	VIOLERS	TRIFLES		
(OTHERS)	D INDITER	V SILVERN		G GLISTER	**EIMNRS 177**	
A ASTHORE	E ERINITE		**EILORT 18**	GRISTLE	(MINERS)	
HAROSET	NITERIE	**EILNST 45**	(LOITER)	H SLITHER	A MARINES	
B BOSHTER	F NIFTIER	(INTLES)	B TRILOBE	I SILTIER	REMAINS	
BOTHERS	G IGNITER	A EASTLIN	C CORTILE	K KILTERS	SEMINAR	
C HECTORS	TIERING	ELASTIN	D DOILTER	KIRTLES	SIRNAME	
ROCHETS	TIGRINE	ENTAILS	E TROELIE	L RILLETS	C CREMSIN	
ROTCHES	H INHERIT	SALIENT	F LOFTIER	STILLER	MINCERS	
TOCHERS	L LINTIER	SLAINTE	TREFOIL	TILLERS	D MINDERS	
TORCHES	NITRILE	STANIEL	J JOLTIER	TRELLIS	REMINDS	
TROCHES	M INTERIM	TENAILS	M MOTLIER	M MILTERS	E ERMINES	
D DEHORTS	MINTIER	C CLIENTS	N RETINOL	N LINTERS	G GERMINS	
SHORTED	TERMINI	LECTINS	O TROOLIE	SNIRTLE	H MENHIRS	
F FOTHERS	N TINNIER	STENCIL	P POITREL	O LOITERS	K MERKINS	
I HERIOTS	T NITRITE	D DENTILS	POLITER	TOILERS	L LIMNERS	
HOISTER	NITTIER	E TENSILE	S LOITERS	P SPIRTLE	MERLINS	
SHORTIE	TINTIER	G GLISTEN	TOILERS	TRIPLES	M NIMMERS	
TOSHIER	V INVITER	LESTING	T TORTILE	S LISTERS	O MERINOS	
L HOLSTER	VITRINE	SINGLET	TRIOLET	T LITTERS	MERSION	
HOSTLER	W TWINIER	I INLIEST	U OUTLIER	SLITTER	T ENTRISM	
M MOTHERS		LINIEST		STILTER	MINSTER	
SMOTHER		LINTIES	**EILOST 21**	TESTRIL	MINTERS	
THERMOS		K LENTISK	(OILETS)	TILTERS	U MURINES	
N HORNETS			A ISOLATE	TITLERS	NEURISM	

V VERMINS	T METRIST	IGNORES	REPINES	CRETINS	TAURINE
	U MUSTIER	REGIONS	G PERSING	D TINDERS	URANITE
EIMOST 150	Y MISTERY	SIGNORE	PINGERS	E ENTIRES	URINATE
(SOMITE)	SMYTRIE	H HEROINS	SPRINGE	ENTRIES	B BUNTIER
A AMOSITE		INSHORE	I INSPIRE	NERITES	TRIBUNE
ATOMIES	**EINNST 113**	I IONISER	PIRNIES	TRENISE	TURBINE
ATOMISE	(SINNET)	IRONIES	SNIPIER	F SNIFTER	D INTRUDE
OSMIATE	A INANEST	IRONISE	SPINIER	G RESTING	TURDINE
D DOMIEST	D DENTINS	NOISIER	K PERKINS	STINGER	UNTIRED
MODISTE	INDENTS	J JOINERS	L PILSNER	K SKINTER	UNTRIDE
MOISTED	INTENDS	REJOINS	N PINNERS	STINKER	UNTRIED
F FOMITES	E INTENSE	L NEROLIS	SPINNER	TINKERS	E NEURITE
G EGOTISM	G NESTING	M MERINOS	O ORPINES	L LINTERS	RETINUE
H HOMIEST	SENTING	MERSION	PIONERS	SNIRTLE	REUNITE
L MOTILES	TENSING	O EROSION	PROINES	M ENTRISM	UTERINE
M TOMMIES	I INTINES	P ORPINES	P NIPPERS	MINSTER	G TRUEING
N MOISTEN	L LINNETS	PIONERS	SNIPPER	MINTERS	M MINUTER
P MOPIEST	O INTONES	PROINES	S SNIPERS	N INTERNS	O ROUTINE
OPTIMES	TENSION	R IRONERS	T NIPTERS	TINNERS	R RUNTIER
R EROTISM	P PINNETS	S ORNISES	PTERINS	O NORITES	S TRIUNES
MOISTER	SPINNET	SENIORS	U PRUINES	ORIENTS	UNITERS
MORTISE	TENPINS	SONERIS	PURINES	STONIER	T NUTTIER
TRISOME	R INTERNS	SONSIER	UPRISEN	TERSION	V UNRIVET
S MITOSES	TINNERS	T NORITES	Y INSPYRE	TRIONES	VENTURI
SOMITES	S SENNITS	ORIENTS		P NIPTERS	W UNWRITE
T MOTIEST	SINNETS	STONIER	**EINPST 148**	PTERINS	
TITMOSE	T INTENTS	TERSION	(INSTEP)	S INSERTS	**EINSTT 160**
U TIMEOUS	U TUNNIES	TRIONES	A PANTIES	SINTERS	(INTEST)
V MOTIVES	V INVENTS	V RENVOIS	PATINES	T ENTRIST	A INSTATE
Z MESTIZO		VERSION	SAPIENT	STINTER	SATINET
	EINOPS 130	W SNOWIER	SPINATE	TINTERS	D DENTIST
EIMRST 140	(PONIES)		C INCEPTS	U TRIUNES	DISTENT
(MITERS)	D DISPONE	**EINOST 14**	INSPECT	UNITERS	STINTED
A MAESTRI	SPINODE	(TONIES)	PECTINS	V INVERTS	G SETTING
MAISTER	E PEONIES	A ATONIES	PEINCTS	STRIVEN	TESTING
MASTIER	G EPIGONS	B BONIEST	D STIPEND	W TWINERS	I SITTINE
MISRATE	PIGEONS	EBONIST	E PENTISE	WINTERS	TINIEST
SEMITAR	PINGOES	C NOTICES	I PINIEST	Y SINTERY	K KITTENS
SMARTIE	H PHONIES	SECTION	PINITES		M MITTENS
B BETRIMS	I PIONIES	D DITONES	K PINKEST	**EINRTT 76**	SMITTEN
TIMBERS	K PINKOES	STONIED	L PINTLES	(TINTER)	N INTENTS
TIMBRES	L EPSILON	H HISTONE	PLENIST	A INTREAT	O TONIEST
C CRETISM	PINOLES	J JONTIES	M PIMENTS	ITERANT	TONITES
METRICS	M IMPONES	L ENTOILS	N PINNETS	NATTIER	P SPITTEN
E METIERS	PEONISM	LIONETS	SPINNET	NITRATE	R ENTRIST
TREMIES	N PENSION	M MOISTEN	TENPINS	TARTINE	STINTER
TRISEME	R ORPINES	N INTONES	O POINTES	TERTIAN	TINTERS
F FIRMEST	PIONERS	TENSION	PONTIES	B BITTERN	U TUNIEST
FREMITS	PROINES	O ISOTONE	P SNIPPET	C CITTERN	W ENTWIST
H HERMITS	S SPINOSE	P POINTES	R NIPTERS	D TRIDENT	Y TENSITY
MITHERS	T POINTES	PONTIES	PTERINS	E NETTIER	
I MIRIEST	PONTIES	R NORITES	S INSTEPS	TENTIER	**EINSTU 81**
MISTIER	W POWNIES	ORIENTS	SPINETS	G GITTERN	(UNITES)
RIMIEST	Y PIONEYS	STONIER	T SPITTEN	RETTING	A AUNTIES
K MIRKEST		TERSION	U PUNIEST	I NITRITE	SINUATE
L MILTERS	**EINORS 9**	TRIONES	PUNTIES	NITTIER	D DISTUNE
M MISTERM	(SENIOR)	S NOSIEST		TINTIER	DUNITES
N ENTRISM	A ERASION	SONTIES	**EINRST 17**	K KNITTER	G GUNITES
MINSTER	C COINERS	STONIES	(INTERS)	TRINKET	I UNITIES
MINTERS	CRINOSE	T TONIEST	A ANESTRI	O TRITONE	UNITISE
O EROTISM	CRONIES	TONITES	NASTIER	S ENTRIST	L LUTEINS
MOISTER	ORCEINS	W TOWNIES	RATINES	STINTER	UNTILES
MORTISE	ORCINES		RESIANT	TINTERS	UTENSIL
TRISOME	SERICON	**EINPRS 158**	RETAINS	U NUTTIER	M MINUETS
P IMPREST	D DONSIER	(PINERS)	RETINAS	W TWINTER	MINUTES
PERMITS	INDORSE	A RAPINES	RETSINA	WRITTEN	MISTUNE
R RETRIMS	ROSINED	C PINCERS	STAINER		MUNITES
TRIMERS	SORDINE	PRINCES	STARNIE	**EINRTU 25**	MUTINES
S MISTERS	G ERINGOS	D PINDERS	STEARIN	(TUNIER)	N TUNNIES
SMITERS		E EREPSIN	C CISTERN	A RUINATE	P PUNIEST

PUNTIES	TOILERS	O TOOTSIE	O RIOTERS	N INVERTS	U LUTEOUS
Q INQUEST	M EROTISM	P POTTIES	ROISTER	STRIVEN	V VOLUTES
QUINTES	MOISTER	TIPTOES	RORIEST	O TORSIVE	Z TOUZLES
R TRIUNES	MORTISE	R STOITER	R STIRRER	P PRIVETS	
UNITERS	TRISOME	T TOTTIES	S STIRRES	R STRIVER	**EMNOST 186**
S INTUSES	N NORITES	U TOUSTIE	T RITTERS	S STIVERS	(MONETS)
T TUNIEST	ORIENTS	W TOWIEST	TERRITS	STRIVES	A MANTOES
	STONIER		U RUSTIER	TREVISS	B ENTOMBS
EIOPST 101	TERSION	**EIPRST 147**	V STRIVER	VERISTS	D ENDMOST
(SOPITE)	TRIONES	(STRIPE)	W WRITERS	T TRIVETS	E TEMENOS
A ATOPIES	O OORIEST	A PARTIES		U VIRTUES	TONEMES
OPIATES	ROOTIES	PASTIER	**EIRSTT 104**		F FOMENTS
C POETICS	SOOTIER	PIASTRE	(SITTER)	**ELORST 67**	G EMONGST
D DEPOSIT	TOORIES	PIRATES	A ARTIEST	(TOLERS)	H MONETHS
DOPIEST	P PERIOST	PRATIES	ARTISTE	A OESTRAL	I MOISTEN
PODITES	PORIEST	TRAIPSE	ATTIRES	B BOLSTER	L LOMENTS
POSITED	REPOSIT	C TRICEPS	IRATEST	BOLTERS	MELTONS
SOPITED	RIPOSTE	D SPIRTED	STRIATE	LOBSTER	M MOMENTS
TOPSIDE	ROPIEST	STRIPED	TASTIER	C COLTERS	MONTEMS
E POETISE	R RIOTERS	E RESPITE	TERTIAS	CORSLET	O MOONSET
H ETHIOPS	ROISTER	H HIPSTER	B BITTERS	COSTREL	P POSTMEN
OPHITES	RORIEST	I PITIERS	C TRISECT	LECTORS	TOPSMEN
K POKIEST	S ROSIEST	TIPSIER	E TESTIER	D DROLEST	R MENTORS
L PIOLETS	SORITES	L SPIRTLE	F FITTERS	OLDSTER	MONSTER
PISTOLE	SORTIES	TRIPLES	TITFERS	STRODLE	MONTRES
M MOPIEST	STORIES	M IMPREST	H HITTERS	F FLORETS	S STEMSON
OPTIMES	TOSSIER	PERMITS	TITHERS	LOFTERS	U UNSMOTE
N POINTES	T STOITER	N NIPTERS	J JITTERS	H HOLSTER	Y ETYMONS
PONTIES	U OURIEST	PTERINS	K SKITTER	HOSTLER	
O ISOTOPE	TOUSIER	O PERIOST	L LITTERS	I LOITERS	**EMORST 198**
R PERIOST	V TORSIVE	PORIEST	SLITTER	TOILERS	(MOTERS)
PORIEST	W OWRIEST	REPOSIT	STILTER	J JOLTERS	A AMORETS
REPOSIT	TOWSIER	RIPOSTE	TESTRIL	L TOLLERS	MAESTRO
RIPOSTE		ROPIEST	TILTERS	N LENTORS	OMERTAS
ROPIEST	**EIORSV 127**	P TIPPERS	TITLERS	O LOOTERS	B BESTORM
S POSTIES	(VIROSE)	S ESPRITS	M METRIST	RETOOLS	MOBSTER
SEPIOST	A OVARIES	PERSIST	N ENTRIST	ROOTLES	D STORMED
SOPITES	C CORSIVE	PRIESTS	STINTER	TOOLERS	E METEORS
T POTTIES	VOICERS	SITREPS	TINTERS	P PETROLS	REMOTES
TIPTOES	D DEVISOR	SPRITES	O STOITER	S OSTLERS	G GROMETS
U PITEOUS	DEVOIRS	STIRPES	P PITTERS	STEROLS	H MOTHERS
X POXIEST	VISORED	STRIPES	SPITTER	TORSELS	SMOTHER
Y ISOTYPE	VOIDERS	TRIPSES	TIPSTER	T SETTLOR	THERMOS
	E EROSIVE	T PITTERS	R RITTERS	SLOTTER	I EROTISM
EIORST 5	I IVORIES	SPITTER	TERRITS	TOLTERS	MOISTER
(TORIES)	L OLIVERS	TIPSTER	S SITTERS	U ELUTORS	MORTISE
A OARIEST	VIOLERS	U PERITUS	T STRETTI	OUTLERS	TRISOME
OTARIES	M VERISMO	PUIREST	TITTERS	TROULES	N MENTORS
B ORBIEST	N RENVOIS	V PRIVETS	TRITEST	V REVOLTS	MONSTER
C EROTICS	VERSION	X EXTIRPS	U TERTIUS	W TROWELS	MONTRES
TERCIOS	R REVISOR	Y PYRITES	V TRIVETS	WORTLES	O MOOTERS
D EDITORS	S VIROSES	STRIPEY	W TWISTER		P TROMPES
ROISTED	T TORSIVE		WITTERS	**ELOSTU 173**	R TERMORS
ROSITED		**EIRRST 165**		(TOUSLE)	TREMORS
SORTIED	**EIOSTT 93**	(TRIERS)	**EIRSTV 163**	B BOLETUS	S MOSTERS
STEROID	(OTTIES)	A ARTSIER	(STRIVE)	D LOUDEST	U MOUTERS
STORIED	A OSTIATE	TARRIES	A TAIVERS	TOUSLED	OESTRUM
TRIODES	TOASTIE	TARSIER	VASTIER	F FOULEST	
F FOISTER	B BOTTIES	D STIRRED	D DIVERTS	I OUTLIES	**ENORST 23**
FORTIES	C COTTISE	E ETRIERS	STRIVED	L OUTSELL	(TONERS)
G GOITERS	D DOTIEST	REITERS	VERDITS	N LENTOUS	A ATONERS
GOITRES	STOITED	RESTIER	E RESTIVE	O OUTSOLE	SENATOR
GORIEST	G EGOTIST	RETIRES	SIEVERT	P TUPELOS	TREASON
H HERIOTS	H HOTTIES	RETRIES	STIEVER	R ELUTORS	B BRETONS
HOISTER	L LITOTES	TERRIES	VERIEST	OUTLERS	SORBENT
SHORTIE	TOILETS	K SKIRRET	G GRIVETS	S LOTUSES	C CONSTER
TOSHIER	M MOTIEST	SKIRTER	H THRIVES	SOLUTES	CORNETS
I RIOTISE	TITMOSE	STRIKER	I REVISIT	TOUSLES	CRONETS
K ROKIEST	N TONIEST	M RETRIMS	STIVIER	T OUTLETS	D RODENTS
L LOITERS	TONITES	TRIMERS	VISITER		SNORTED

H HORNETS
SHORTEN
THRENOS
THRONES
I NORITES
ORIENTS
STONIER
TERSION
TRIONES
K STONKER
STROKEN
TONKERS
L LENTORS
M MENTORS
MONSTER
MONTRES
N STONERN
O ENROOTS
P POSTERN
PRONEST
R SNORTER
S STONERS
TENSORS
T ROTTENS
SNOTTER
STENTOR
U TENOURS
TONSURE
Y TYRONES

ENOSTT 195
(ONTEST)
A ATTONES
NOTATES
C CONTEST
D SNOTTED
H SHOTTEN
I TONIEST
TONITES
J JETTONS
L TONLETS
O TESTOON
P POTENTS
R ROTTENS
SNOTTER
STENTOR
S OSTENTS
TESTONS
U STOUTEN

ENOSTU 94
(OUTENS)
A SOUTANE
C CONTUSE
ECONUTS
D DEUTONS
SNOUTED
G TONGUES
L LENTOUS
M UNSMOTE
N NEUSTON
O UNSOOTE
R TENOURS
TONSURE

S OUTNESS
TONUSES
T STOUTEN
U TENUOUS

ENRSTU 84
(TUNERS)
A AUNTERS
NATURES
SAUNTER
B BRUNETS
BUNTERS
BURNETS
BURSTEN
C ENCRUST
D RETUNDS
UNDREST
E NEUTERS
RETUNES
TENURES
TUREENS
G GUNTERS
GURNETS
SURGENT
H HUNTERS
SHUNTER
I TRIUNES
UNITERS
L RUNLETS
M MUNSTER
STERNUM
N RUNNETS
STUNNER
O TENOURS
TONSURE
P PUNSTER
PUNTERS
R RETURNS
TURNERS
S UNRESTS
T ENTRUST
NUTTERS

EOPRST 193
(POSTER)
A ESPARTO
PROTEAS
SEAPORT
B BESPORT
D DEPORTS
REDTOPS
SPORTED
F FORPETS
H POTHERS
STROPHE
THORPES
I PERIOST
PORIEST
REPOSIT
RIPOSTE
ROPIEST
L PETROLS
M TROMPES

N POSTERN
PRONEST
O POOREST
POOTERS
STOOPER
P STOPPER
TOPPERS
R PORTERS
REPORTS
SPORTER
S PORTESS
POSTERS
PRESTOS
REPOSTS
T POTTERS
PROTEST
SPOTTER
U PETROUS
POSTURE
POUTERS
PROTEUS
SEPTUOR
SPOUTER
TROUPES
W POWTERS
PROWEST
X EXPORTS

EORRST 106
(SORTER)
A ROASTER
C RECTORS
D DORTERS
RODSTER
E RESTORE
G GROSERT
H RHETORS
ROTHERS
SHORTER
I RIOTERS
ROISTER
RORIEST
K STROKER
M TERMORS
TREMORS
N SNORTER
O ROOSTER
ROOTERS
TOREROS
P PORTERS
REPORTS
SPORTER
R RORTERS
TERRORS
S RESORTS
ROSTERS
SORTERS
STORERS
T RETORTS
ROTTERS
TORRETS
U RETOURS
ROUSTER
ROUTERS

TOURERS
V TROVERS
W STROWER
Y ROYSTER

EORSTT 114
(OTTERS)
A ROTATES
TOASTER
B BETTORS
C COTTERS
D DETORTS
E ROSETTE
H HOTTERS
I STOITER
J JOTTERS
L SETTLOR
SLOTTER
TOLTERS
N ROTTENS
SNOTTER
STENTOR
O TOOTERS
P POTTERS
PROTEST
SPOTTER
R RETORTS
ROTTERS
TORRETS
T STOTTER
STRETTO
TOTTERS
U STOUTER
TOUTERS
W SWOTTER
X EXTORTS
Y ROSETTY

GILNOT 171
(TOLING)
A ANTILOG
B BILTONG
BOLTING
C COLTING
E LENTIGO
F LOFTING
H THOLING
I TOILING
J JOLTING
L TOLLING
M MOLTING
O LOOTING
TOOLING
P POLTING
S LINGOTS
TIGLONS
TOLINGS
T TOLTING
U LOUTING
W LOWTING

GINORS 128
(SIGNOR)
A IGNAROS

ORIGANS
SIGNORA
SOARING
B BORINGS
ROBINGS
SORBING
C SCORING
D RODINGS
E ERINGOS
IGNORES
REGIONS
SIGNORE
G GORINGS
GRINGOS
H HORSING
SHORING
I ORIGINS
SIGNIOR
SIGNORI
L LORINGS
M SMORING
N SNORING
SORNING
O ROOSING
P PROIGNS
PROSING
ROPINGS
S GRISONS
INGROSS
SIGNORS
T ROSTING
SORTING
STORING
TRIGONS
U ROUSING
SOURING
V ROVINGS
W ROWINGS
WORSING
Y ROSYING
SIGNORY

GINORT 102
(ROTING)
A ORATING
ROATING
D DORTING
E GENITOR
F FORTING
I RIOTING
K TROKING
O ROOTING
P PORTING
TROPING
S ROSTING
SORTING
STORING
TRIGONS
T ROTTING
U ROUTING
TOURING
W ROWTING
TROWING

GINOST 176
(OSTING)
A AGONIST
GITANOS
C COSTING
GNOSTIC
D DOTINGS
F SOFTING
H HOSTING
TOSHING
K STOKING
L LINGOTS
TIGLONS
TOLINGS
M GNOMIST
N STONING
O SOOTING
P POSTING
STOPING
R ROSTING
SORTING
STORING
TRIGONS
S STINGOS
TOSSING
T SOTTING
U OUSTING
OUTINGS
TOUSING
V STOVING
W STOWING
TOWINGS
TOWSING
Y TOYINGS

INORST 59
(TRIONS)
A AROINTS
RATIONS
B RIBSTON
C CISTRON
CITRONS
CORNIST
E NORITES
ORIENTS
STONIER
TERSION
TRIONES
F FORINTS
G ROSTING
SORTING
STORING
TRIGONS
H HORNIST
I IRONIST
L NOSTRIL
N INTRONS
O ISOTRON
TORSION
T TRITONS
U NITROUS
TURIONS

8-LETTER SETS
from the top 200 6-letter combinations

ABDEIR 134
(ABRIDE)
AD ABRAIDED
AS ARABISED
AZ ARABIZED
BR DRABBIER
BT RABBITED
CG BIRDCAGE
   CAGEBIRD
CL CALIBRED
CS ASCRIBED
· CARBIDES
DG ABRIDGED
   BRIGADED
DN BRANDIED
   RIBANDED
DR BRAIRDED
EL RIDEABLE
ES BEARDIES
ET EBRIATED
GN BEARDING
   BREADING
GR ABRIDGER
GS ABRIDGES
   BRIGADES
IT DIATRIBE
KM IMBARKED
LN BILANDER
LT LIBRATED
LV DRIVABLE
LY DIABLERY
MN BRIDEMAN
MO AMBEROID
MR IMBARRED
MS EMBRAIDS
NO DEBONAIR
NS BRANDIES
   BRANDISE
ST BARDIEST
   BRAIDEST
   RABIDEST
   TRIBADES
SW BAWDRIES
   DAWBRIES
TV VIBRATED

ABEILS 188
(ISABEL)
AL ISABELLA
   SAILABLE
AR RAISABLE
AT BALISTAE
   LABIATES
   SATIABLE
BH BABELISH
BM BABELISM
BR SLABBIER
BT BISTABLE
CM ALEMBICS
CO SOCIABLE
CR CALIBERS
   CALIBRES
DD DISABLED
DE ABSEILED
DH DISHABLE

DP PIEBALDS
DS DISABLES
EF FEASIBLE
EM BELAMIES
EV EVASIBLE
EZ SEIZABLE
   SIZEABLE
FG FILABEGS
FH FISHABLE
FR BARFLIES
FU FABULISE
FY FEASIBLY
GN SINGABLE
HR BLASHIER
IL BAILLIES
IR BISERIAL
IT ALBITISE
   SIBILATE
KN BLANKIES
KS KISSABLE
KT BALKIEST
LO ISOLABLE
   LOBELIAS
LR LIBERALS
LT BASTILLE
MN BAILSMEN
MR REMBLAIS
MS MISSABLE
MT BALMIEST
   TIMBALES
NP BIPLANES
NR RINSABLE
NS ALBINESS
   LESBIANS
NT INSTABLE
PS PASSIBLE
PT EPIBLAST
RT LIBRATES
ST ASTILBES
   BESTIALS
   STABILES
SU ISSUABLE
   SUASIBLE
TU SUITABLE
TY BEASTILY
UX BISEXUAL
VV BIVALVES

ABEORS 144
(ABORES)
AD SEABOARD
AT RABATOES
BD ABSORBED
BR ABSORBER
   REABSORB
CD BROCADES
CG BROCAGES
CH BROACHES
CI AEROBICS
CM CRAMBOES
CU CORBEAUS
DD ADSORBED
DN BANDORES
   BROADENS
DR BOARDERS

DT BROADEST
EN SEABORNE
ET REBATOES
FR FORBEARS
GK BROKAGES
   GROSBEAK
GO BARGOOSE
HT BATHORSE
IN BARONIES
IS ISOBARES
IT SABOTIER
KO ABROOKES
LT BLOATERS
   SORTABLE
   STORABLE
LU RUBEOLAS
LV ABSOLVER
MR EMBRASOR
MT BROMATES
MU AMBEROUS
NN BARONNES
NS BARONESS
NT BARONETS
PS SAPROBES
PT PROBATES
QU BAROQUES
RS BRASEROS
RT ARBORETS
   TABORERS
ST BOASTERS
   SORBATES
TT ABETTORS
   BATTEROS
   TABORETS
TU SABOTEUR

ABERST 122
(BREAST)
AC ABREACTS
   CABARETS
AL ARBALEST
AN ANTBEARS
· RATSBANE
AO RABATOES
AT RABATTES
   TABARETS
AU ABATURES
BD DRABBEST
   DRABBETS
BS STABBERS
CE ACERBEST
CH BRACHETS
CK BRACKETS
DE BETREADS
   BREASTED
   DEBATERS
DH BREADTHS
DI BARDIEST
   BRAIDEST
   RABIDEST
   TRIBADES
DN BANDSTER
DO BROADEST
DS DABSTERS
DU SURBATED

DW BEDSTRAW
DY DRYBEATS
EG ABSTERGE
EH BREATHES
   HARTBEES
EK BESTREAK
EL BLEAREST
   BLEATERS
   RETABLES
EO REBATOES
ER REBATERS
   TABRERES
   TEREBRAS
ET ABETTERS
EU SUBERATE
GH BARGHEST
GN BANGSTER
GS BARGESTS
HL BLATHERS
   HALBERTS
HO BATHORSE
HS BRASHEST
IK BARKIEST
   BRAKIEST
   BREASKIT
IL LIBRATES
IM BARMIEST
IN ATEBRINS
   BANISTER
IO SABOTIER
IR ARBITERS
   RAREBITS
IT BIRETTAS
IV VIBRATES
IW WARBIEST
IY BESTIARY
   SYBARITE
KY BASKETRY
LM LAMBERTS
LN BRANTLES
LO BLOATERS
   SORTABLE
   STORABLE
LS BLASTERS
   STABLERS
LT BATTLERS
   BLATTERS
   BRATTLES
LU BALUSTER
LW BLEWARTS
MO BROMATES
NO BARONETS
NU UNBRASTE
   URBANEST
OP PROBATES
OR ARBORETS
   TABORERS
OS BOASTERS
   SORBATES
OT ABETTORS
   BATTEROS
   TABORETS
OU SABOTEUR
SS BRASSETS
SU ABSTRUSE

   SURBATES
SW WABSTERS
TU ABUTTERS

ACEILR 121
(LACIER)
AT TAILRACE
AV CAVALIER
BB BARBICEL
BD CALIBRED
BK CRABLIKE
BL CRIBELLA
BO ALBICORE
   CABRIOLE
BS CALIBERS
   CALIBRES
CE CELERIAC
CL CLERICAL
CV CERVICAL
DF FRICADEL
DH HERALDIC
DP PLACIDER
DS DECRIALS
   RADICELS
   RADICLES
DT ARTICLED
DU AURICLED
   RADICULE
EH LEACHIER
EN CINEREAL
   RELIANCE
ES ESCALIER
EV RECEIVAL
FS FILACERS
GG CLAGGIER
GL ALLERGIC
GN CLEARING
GS GLACIERS
GV CLAVIGER
HK CHALKIER
   HACKLIER
HO HALICORE
   HEROICAL
HP PARHELIC
HS CHARLIES
IN IRENICAL
KT TALCKIER
KY CREAKILY
LM MICELLAR
   MILLRACE
LO ROCAILLE
LP CALLIPER
LV CAVILLER
MM CLAMMIER
MS CLAIMERS
   MIRACLES
   RECLAIMS
MT METRICAL
NN ENCRINAL
NO ACROLEIN
   CREOLIAN
   LONICERA
NS CARLINES
NT CLARINET

OR CARRIOLE
OS CALORIES
   CARIOLES
OT EROTICAL
   LORICATE
PS CALIPERS
   REPLICAS
   SPIRACLE
PT PARTICLE
   PRELATIC
PU PECULIAR
RT CLARTIER
RW CRAWLIER
SS CLASSIER
ST ALTRICES
   ARTICLES
   RECITALS
   SELICTAR
SU AURICLES
SV CALIVERS
   CLAVIERS
   VISCERAL
TT TRACTILE
TV VERTICAL
TY LITERACY

ACEINR 65
(CANIER)
AB CARABINE
AD CANARIED
   RADIANCE
AG CANAIGRE
AS CANARIES
AT CARINATE
AV VARIANCE
BS CARBINES
CH CHANCIER
   CHICANER
CN CANCRINE
DD CANDIDER
   RIDDANCE
DE DERACINE
DH INARCHED
DI ACRIDINE
DN CRANNIED
DR RANCIDER
DT CRINATED
   DICENTRA
EL CINEREAL
   RELIANCE
ES CINEREAS
   INCREASE
   RESIANCE
ET CENTIARE
   CREATINE
   INCREATE
   ITERANCE
FG REFACING
FS FANCIERS
FX CARNIFEX
GH REACHING
GK CREAKING
GL CLEARING
GM AMERCING
   CREAMING

GN ENRACING	DO DIOCESAN	PS INSCAPES	HS ARCHNESS	UNTRACED	AR CANASTER
GP CAPERING	OCEANIDS	PINCASES	HT CHANTERS	EI CENTIARE	CATERANS
PEARCING	DT DISTANCE	RS ARSENICS	SNATCHER	CREATINE	AT CANTATES
PREACING	DY CYANIDES	CERASINS	STANCHER	INCREASE	AY CYANATES
GS CREASING	CYANISED	RACINESS	TRANCHES	ITERANCE	BI CABINETS
GRECIANS	EF FAIENCES	RT CANISTER	HU RAUNCHES	EN ENTRANCE	CE ACESCENT
SEARCING	FIANCEES	CARNIEST	II RIANCIES	EO CAROTENE	CO COSECANT
GT CATERING	EG AGENCIES	NACRITES	IL CARLINES	EP PERCEANT	DH SNATCHED
CITRANGE	EL SALIENCE	SCANTIER	IM CARMINES	ER RECANTER	STANCHED
CREATING	EP SAPIENCE	ST CINEASTS	IN CRANNIES	RECREANT	DI DISTANCE
REACTING	ER CINEREAS	SCANTIES	IO SCENARIO	ES REASCENT	DL SCANTLED
HM CHAIRMEN	INCREASE	SU ISSUANCE	IS ARSENICS	SARCENET	DN SCANDENT
HS INARCHES	RESIANCE	SY CYANISES	CERASINS	EU ENACTURE	DP PANDECTS
HV VACHERIN	ET CINEASTE	TT CANTIEST	RACINESS	UNCREATE	DR CANTREDS
IL IRENICAL	EU EUCAINES	NICTATES	IT CANISTER	FP PENCRAFT	DS DESCANTS
IS RIANCIES	FN FINANCES	TV CISTVAEN	CARNIEST	FS CANTREFS	EG CENTAGES
JR JERRICAN	FR FANCIERS	VESICANT	NACRITES	GI CATERING	EI CINEASTE
KK KNACKIER	FS FASCINES	TY CYANITES	SCANTIER	CITRANGE	EL CLEANEST
KR CRANKIER	FT FANCIEST	YZ CYANIZES	KK KNACKERS	CREATING	LATENCES
LN ENCRINAL	GN ENCASING		KL CRANKLES	REACTING	EM CASEMENT
LO ACROLEIN	GO COINAGES	**ACENRS 175**	KP PRANCKES	HH ETHNARCH	EN CANTEENS
CREOLIAN	GP ESCAPING	(CANERS)	KT CRANKEST	HM MERCHANT	EO ACETONES
LONICERA	GR CREASING	AG CARNAGES	LN SCRANNEL	HO ANCHORET	ER REASCENT
LS CARLINES	GRECIANS	CRANAGES	LU LUCARNES	HP PENTARCH	SARCENET
LT CLARINET	SEARCING	AI CANARIES	MO CREMONAS	HS CHANTERS	FI FANCIEST
MO CORAMINE	GS CAGINESS	AP PANCREAS	ROMANCES	SNATCHER	FR CANTREFS
MS CARMINES	CEASINGS	AT CANASTER	NS SCANNERS	STANCHER	GO COGNATES
MU MANICURE	HH HAINCHES	CATERANS	OS COARSENS	TRANCHES	HI ASTHENIC
NS CRANNIES	HM MACHINES	BH BRANCHES	NARCOSES	HT TRANCHET	CHANTIES
OP APOCRINE	HN ENCHAINS	BI CARBINES	OT ANCESTOR	HU CHAUNTER	HL STANCHEL
CAPONIER	HR INARCHES	BK BRACKENS	ENACTORS	IL CLARINET	HM MANCHETS
PROCAINE	HS INCHASES	BU UNBRACES	SARCONET	IO ANORETIC	HN ENCHANTS
OS SCENARIO	HT ASTHENIC	CE CREANCES	SORTANCE	CREATION	HR CHANTERS
OT ANORETIC	CHANTIES	CH CHANCERS	OU CARNEOUS	REACTION	SNATCHER
CREATION	HY HYACINES	CHANCRES	NACREOUS	IS CANISTER	STANCHER
REACTION	SYNECHIA	CRANCHES	PR PRANCERS	CARNIEST	TRANCHES
OV VERONICA	IL SALICINE	CO CONACRES	PU ENCARPUS	NACRITES	HS CHASTENS
OX ANOREXIC	SILICANE	DE ASCENDER	PRAUNCES	SCANTIER	SNATCHES
RU CURARINE	IP PISCINAE	REASCEND	ST CRANTSES	IT INTERACT	STANCHES
RY CINERARY	IR RIANCIES	DO DRACONES	SU SURANCES	IV NAVICERT	HT ETCHANTS
SS ARSENICS	IT CANITIES	ENDOSARC	TT TRANECTS	IX XERANTIC	HU NAUTCHES
CERASINS	LM MESCALIN	DT CANTREDS	TRANSECT	KM TRACKMEN	UNCHASTE
RACINESS	LP CAPELINS	DU DURANCES	TU CENTAURS	KS CRANKEST	HY CHANTEYS
ST CANISTER	PANICLES	EE ENCREASE	RECUSANT	OO CORONATE	II CANITIES
CARNIEST	PELICANS	EG ENGRACES	UNCRATES	OP PORTANCE	IM SEMANTIC
NACRITES	LR CARLINES	EH ENARCHES	UNTRACES	OS ANCESTOR	IN ANCIENTS
SCANTIER	LS SANICLES	EI CINEREAS	TY ANCESTRY	ENACTORS	CANNIEST
TT INTERACT	LU AESCULIN	INCREASE		SARCONET	INSTANCE
TV NAVICERT	LUNACIES	RESIANCE	**ACENRT 96**	SORTANCE	IO ACONITES
TX XERANTIC	LY SALIENCY	EL CLEANERS	(CANTER)	OT CONTRATE	CANOEIST
VY VICENARY	MP PEMICANS	CLEANSER	AC CARCANET	OU COURANTE	IR CANISTER
	MR CARMINES	EM MENACERS	AI CARINATE	OUTRANCE	CARNIEST
ACEINS 119	MS AMNESICS	ES CASERNES	AL LACERANT	SS CRANTSES	NACRITES
(INCASE)	MT SEMANTIC	ET REASCENT	AS CANASTER	ST TRANECTS	SCANTIER
AD AIDANCES	MU SEMUNCIA	SARCENET	CATERANS	TRANSECT	IS CINEASTS
AL CANALISE	MY SYCAMINE	FI FANCIERS	AT REACTANT	SU CENTAURS	SCANTIES
AM AMNESIAC	NO CANONISE	FT CANTREFS	AY CATENARY	RECUSANT	IT CANTIEST
AR CANARIES	NP PINNACES	FU FURNACES	CO ACCENTOR	UNCRATES	NICTATES
AT ESTANCIA	NR CRANNIES	GH CHANGERS	DE CANTERED	UNTRACES	IV CISTVAEN
BR CARBINES	NT ANCIENTS	GI CREASING	CRENATED	SY ANCESTRY	VESICANT
BT CABINETS	CANNIEST	GRECIANS	DECANTER	TU TRUNCATE	IY CYANITES
CG ACCINGES	INSTANCE	SEARCING	NECTARED	UY CENTAURY	JO JACONETS
CH CHICANES	NU NUISANCE	GL CLANGERS	RECANTED	CYANURET	JU JUNCATES
CL CALCINES	NY CYANINES	GM CRAGSMEN	DI CRINATED		KM TACKSMEN
SCENICAL	OP CANOPIES	GO ACROGENS	DICENTRA	**ACENST 149**	KR CRANKEST
CO COCAINES	CAPONISE	CORNAGES	DO CARTONED	(STANCE)	LO LACTONES
CV VACCINES	PAEONICS	HI INARCHES	DS CANTREDS	AI ESTANCIA	LP CLAPNETS
DH ECHIDNAS	OR SCENARIO	HL CHARNELS	DU UNCARTED	AL ANALECTS	LS SCANTLES
INCHASED	OT ACONITES	HM ENCHARMS	UNCRATED	AM CAMSTANE	LT CANTLETS
DI SCIAENID	CANOEIST	HR RANCHERS	UNDERACT	AP PASTANCE	MO CAMSTONE

```
OP CAPSTONE      IL CALORIES      GN COGNATES      BH BRACHETS      IM CERAMIST      BL BEDERALS
OR ANCESTOR         CARIOLES      GR ESCARGOT      BK BRACKETS         MATRICES      BM EMBREADS
   ENACTORS      IN SCENARIO      GT COTTAGES      CE ACCRETES      IN CANISTER      BP BESPREAD
   SARCONET      IV COVARIES      HI TOISEACH      CH CATCHERS         CARNIEST      BS DEBASERS
   SORTANCE         VARICOSE      HL ESCHALOT         CRATCHES         NACRITES      BT BETREADS
OS COSTEANS      JL CAJOLERS      HR CHAROSET      CO ECTOSARC         SCANTIER         BREASTED
OT CONSTATE      KL EARLOCKS         THORACES      CR CARRECTS      IP CRAPIEST         DEBATERS
OV CENTAVOS      KR CROAKERS      HU CATHOUSE      CS SCARCEST         CRISPATE      CC ACCEDERS
PT PENTACTS      LL CORELLAS         SOUTACHE      DE CEDRATES         PICRATES      CE DECREASE
RS CRANTSES      LM CAROMELS      HY CHAYOTES      DH STARCHED         PRACTISE      CF DEFACERS
RT TRANECTS         SCLEROMA      IL ALOETICS      DI ACRIDEST      IR ERRATICS         FRESCADE
   TRANSECT      LP PARCLOSE         COALIEST      DN CANTREDS      IS SCARIEST      CH SEARCHED
RU CENTAURS         POLACRES         SOCIETAL      DO REDCOATS      IT CITRATES      CI DECIARES
   RECUSANT      LS ESCOLARS      IN ACONITES      DT DETRACTS         CRISTATE      CK SCREAKED
   UNCRATES         LACROSSE         CANOEIST      DU TRADUCES         SCATTIER      CL DECLARES
   UNTRACES      LT SECTORAL      IP ECTOPIAS      EH CHEATERS      IU SURICATE         RESCALED
RY ANCESTRY      LU CAROUSEL      IS SOCIATES         HECTARES      IZ CRAZIEST      CM SCREAMED
ST SCANTEST      LY CALOYERS      IT OSCITATE      EL CLEAREST      JM SCRAMJET      CN ASCENDER
SU NUTCASES         COARSELY      JN JACONETS         SCELERAT      JT TRAJECTS         REASCEND
SW NEWSCAST      MN CREMONAS      LL COLLATES         TREACLES      KL TACKLERS      CP ESCARPED
                    ROMANCES      LM CAMELOTS      EM CERAMETS      KN CRANKEST      CR SCAREDER
ACEORS 103       MP COMPARES         MOLECAST         CREMATES      KR TRACKERS      CS CARESSED
(ORACES)            COMPEARS      LN LACTONES         MEERCATS      KS STACKERS      CT CEDRATES
AS ROSACEAS         MESOCARP      LP POLECATS      EN REASCENT      KT RACKETTS      DG DEGRADES
AU ARACEOUS      MY SYCAMORE      LR SECTORAL         SARCENET      LO SECTORAL      DR DREADERS
BD BROCADES      NS COARSENS      LS ALECOSTS      EO CREASOTE      LP SCEPTRAL      DW SAWDERED
BG BROCAGES         NARCOSES         COATLESS      ER CATERERS         SPECTRAL      EG DEGREASE
BH BROACHES      NT ANCESTOR         LACTOSES         RETRACES      LS SCARLETS      EL RELEASED
BI AEROBICS         ENACTORS         SCATOLES         TERRACES      LT CLATTERS         RESEALED
BM CRAMBOES         SARCONET      LT CALOTTES      ES CATERESS         SCRATTLE      EN ENSEARED
BU CORBEAUS         SORTANCE      LU LACTEOUS         CERASTES      LU RAUCLEST         SERENADE
CH CAROCHES      NU CARNEOUS         LOCUSTAE      EU SECATEUR      MP CRAMPETS      ER ARREEDES
   COACHERS         NACREOUS         OSCULATE      EX EXACTERS      NO ANCESTOR      ET RESEATED
CL CORACLES      PP COPPERAS      LY ACOLYTES      FH FRATCHES         ENACTORS      FI FEDARIES
CN CONACRES      PX EXOCARPS      MN CAMSTONE      FN CANTREFS         SARCONET      FL FEDERALS
CS ARCCOSES      RT ACROTERS      MO COMATOSE      FO FORECAST         SORTANCE      FP PREFADES
CT ECTOSARC         CREATORS      NP CAPSTONE      FR REFRACTS      NS CRANTSES      FT DRAFTEES
CW CRACOWES         REACTORS      NR ANCESTOR      FU FACTURES      NT TRANECTS      GI DISAGREE
DG CORDAGES      RU CAROUSER         ENACTORS      GI AGRESTIC         TRANSECT      GN DERANGES
DI IDOCRASE      ST COARSEST         SARCONET      GO ESCARGOT      NU CENTAURS         GRANDEES
DM COMRADES         COASTERS         SORTANCE      GU TRUCAGES         RECUSANT         GRENADES
DN DRACONES      SU CAROUSES      NS COSTEANS      HH HATCHERS         UNCRATES      GP ASPERGED
   ENDOSARC      TT SECTATOR      NT CONSTATE      HI CHARIEST         UNTRACES         PRESAGED
DR CORRADES      TU OUTRACES      NV CENTAVOS         THERIACS      NY ANCESTRY      GR REGRADES
DS SARCODES      TV OVERACTS      PU OUTPACES      HL ARCHLETS      OR ACROTERS      GS DRESSAGE
DT REDCOATS         OVERCAST      RR ACROTERS      HM MATCHERS         CREATORS      GT RESTAGED
DU CAROUSED      TX EXACTORS         CREATORS      HN CHANTERS         REACTORS      GU GUARDEES
EL ESCAROLE                         REACTORS         SNATCHER      OS COARSEST      GW RAGWEEDS
EM RACEMOSE      ACEOST 146       RS COARSEST         STANCHER         COASTERS      HH REHASHED
ET CREASOTE      (ACTOSE)            COASTERS         TRANCHES      OT SECTATOR      HL ASHLERED
FF AFFORCES      AK OATCAKES      RT SECTATOR      HO CHAROSET      OU OUTRACES      HO SOREHEAD
FL ALFRESCO      AL CATALOES      RU OUTRACES         THORACES      OV OVERACTS      HP EPHEDRAS
FR FORECARS      AS SEACOAST      RV OVERACTS      HP CHAPTERS         OVERCAST         RESHAPED
FT FORECAST      BL OBSTACLE         OVERCAST         PATCHERS      OX EXACTORS      HR ADHERERS
FX CARFOXES      CD ACCOSTED      RX EXACTORS      HR CHARTERS      PU CAPTURES         REDSHARE
GK CORKAGES      CL CACOLETS      TU OUTCASTE         RECHARTS         PRESCUTA      HT HEADREST
GM SCARMOGE      CN COSECANT      UU AUTOCUES         STARCHER      QU RACQUETS      HW WASHERED
GN ACROGENS      CR ECTOSARC                      HS STARCHES      RT RETRACTS      IJ JADERIES
   CORNAGES      DH CATHODES      ACERST 141       HT CHATTERS      SS CRASSEST      IL REALISED
GO CARGOOSE      DK STOCKADE      (CATERS)            RATCHETS      ST SCATTERS         SIDEREAL
GS CORSAGES      DR COSTARED?     AB ABREACTS      HW WATCHERS      TT TETRACTS      IM MADERISE
   SOCAGERS      DT COSTATED         CABARETS      HY YACHTERS      TU CRUSTATE      IN ARSENIDE
GT ESCARGOT      EN ACETONES      AD CADASTRE      IL ALTRICES      TX EXTRACTS         DENARIES
GU COURAGES      ER CREASOTE      AF SEACRAFT         ARTICLES      TY SCATTERY         DRAISENE
HL CHOLERAS      ET ECOSTATE      AG CARTAGES         RECITALS      UX CURTAXES         NEARSIDE
   CHORALES      EV EVOCATES      AN CANASTER         SELICTAR                      IT READIEST
HP POACHERS      FP POSTFACE         CATERANS                      ADEERS 70           SERIATED
HR HORSECAR      FR FORECAST      AP CAPRATES                      (SEARED)            STEADIER
HT CHAROSET      FU OUTFACES      AT CASTRATE                      AP PASEARED      IV READVISE
   THORACES      GL CATELOGS      BE ACERBEST                      BI BEARDIES      KN KNEADERS
```

KT STREAKED
LL SARDELLE
LM DEMERSAL
   EMERALDS
LP PLEADERS
   RELAPSED
LT TREADLES
LV SLAVERED
LW LEEWARDS
LY DELAYERS
MN AMENDERS
   MEANDERS
   REAMENDS
MO SEADROME
MR DREAMERS
MT MASTERED
   STREAMED
MU MEASURED
NN ENSNARED
NO REASONED
NS DEARNESS
NU UNDERSEA
NW ANSWERED
OW OARWEEDS
PR SPREADER
PS ASPERSED
   PREASSED
   REPASSED
PT PREDATES
   REPASTED
   TRAPESED
PU PERSUADE
PV DEPRAVES
   PERVADES
PW PERSWADE
PZ SPREAZED
RT ARRESTED
   DREAREST
   RETREADS
   SERRATED
   TREADERS
RV ADVERSER
ST ASSERTED
   ESTRADES
TT ASTERTED
   RESTATED
TW DEWATERS
   TARWEEDS
   WASTERED
TY ESTRAYED

ADEEST 85
(SEATED)
AC ESTACADE
BD BEDSTEAD
   BESTADDE
BH BETHESDA
BI BEADIEST
   DIABETES
BN ABSENTED
BR BETREADS
   BREASTED
   DEBATERS
BS BASSETED
   BESTEADS
CH DETACHES
CP ASPECTED
CR CEDRATES
CU EDUCATES
DI STEADIED

DL DESALTED
DO DEODATES
EL TEASELED
ER RESEATED
FL DEFLATES
FN FASTENED
FR DRAFTEES
GO DOGEATES
GR RESTAGED
GT GESTATED
HH SHEATHED
HI ATHEISED
   HEADIEST
HN HASTENED
HR HEADREST
HS HEADSETS
IJ JADEITES
IL LEADIEST
IM MEDIATES
IN ANDESITE
IR READIEST
   SERIATED
IS STEADIES
IV DEVIATES
   SEDATIVE
KN NAKEDEST
KR STREAKED
LM MEDALETS
LO DESOLATE
LP PEDESTAL
LR TREADLES
LS DATELESS
LY SEDATELY
MN STAMENED
MP STAMPEDE
   STEPDAME
MR MASTERED
   STREAMED
MW MATWEEDS
NS ASSENTED
NU UNSEATED
PR PREDATES
   REPASTED
   TRAPESED
PS STAPEDES
PT ADEPTEST
RR ARRESTED
   DREAREST
   RETREADS
   SERRATED
   TREADERS
RS ASSERTED
   ESTRADES
RT ASTERTED
   RESTATED
RW DEWATERS
   TARWEEDS
   WASTERED
RY ESTRAYED
ST SEDATEST
TT ATTESTED
UX EXUDATES

ADEGLN 197
(DANGLE)
AH DANELAGH
AM MAGDALEN
AS SELADANG
BI BLINDAGE

BR BRANGLED
DE DANEGELD
DS GLADDENS
EO ENGAOLED
ER ENLARGED
   LARGENED
ET DANEGELT
FI FINAGLED
HI HEADLING
HO HEADLONG
II GLIADINE
IM MALIGNED
IO GALENOID
IP PLEADING
IR DEARLING
   DRAGLINE
IS DEALINGS
   LEADINGS
IT DELATING
IY DELAYING
LU GLANDULE
   UNGALLED
OY GONDELAY
PS SPANGLED
RS DANGLERS
   GLANDERS
RW WRANGLED
SS GLADNESS
TW TWANGLED
UZ UNGLAZED

ADEGNR 126
(DANGER)
AI AREADING
   DRAINAGE
   GARDENIA
AR ARRANGED
BI BEARDING
   BREADING
BL BRANGLED
BO BONDAGER
CE ENGRACED
CU UNGRACED
DE DANGERED
   DERANGED
   GARDENED
DI DREADING
DU UNGRADED
EE RENEGADE
EI REGAINED
EL ENLARGED
   LARGENED
EM GENDARME
EN ENDANGER
   ENRANGED
EO RENEGADO
ER GARDENER
   GARNERED
ES DERANGES
   GRANDEES
   GRENADES
EU DUNGAREE
   RENAGUED
   UNGEARED
EV ENGRAVED
FO FRONDAGE
HI ADHERING
   HEADRING
HT THRANGED
IK DAKERING

IL DEARLING
   DRAGLINE
IM DREAMING
   MARGINED
IO ORGANDIE
IR DREARING
IS DERAIGNS
   GRADINES
   READINGS
IT DERATING
   GRADIENT
   TREADING
IY DERAYING
   READYING
   YEARDING
JO JARGONED
LS DANGLERS
   GLANDERS
LW WRANGLED
MS DRAGSMEN
NO ANDROGEN
   DRAGONNE
OT DRAGONET
RU GRANDEUR
ST GRANDEST
SU ENGUARDS
UU UNARGUED
UZ UNGRAZED

ADEILR 19
(RAILED)
AH HEADRAIL
AP PRAEDIAL
AS SALARIED
BC CALIBRED
BE RIDEABLE
BN BILANDER
BT LIBRATED
BV DRIVABLE
BY DIABLERY
CF FRICADEL
CH HERALDIC
CP PLACIDER
CS DECRIALS
   RADICELS
   RADICLES
CT ARTICLED
CU AURICLED
   RADICULE
DE DEADLIER
   DERAILED
DH DIHEDRAL
DS DIEDRALS
EL REALLIED
EM REMEDIAL
EP PEDALIER
ER DERAILER
   RERAILED
ES REALISED
   SIDEREAL
ET RETAILED
EZ REALIZED
FI AIRFIELD
FN FILANDER
FO FORELAID
GL GRILLADE
GN DEARLING
   DRAGLINE
GS SLAIRGED
HN HARDLINE

IP PERIDIAL
IS LAIRISED
IZ LAIRIZED
LO ARILLODE
LP PALLIDER
LS DALLIERS
   DIALLERS
LV RIVALLED
MP IMPARLED
MY DREAMILY
NN INLANDER
NS ISLANDER
   SALIFIED
OS DARIOLES
   SOLIDARE
   SOREDIAL
OT IDOLATER
   TAILORED
OV OVERLAID
OX EXORDIAL
PS PEDRAILS
   PREDIALS
PT DIPTERAL
   TRIPEDAL
PU EPIDURAL
PV DEPRIVAL
RY DREARILY
ST DILATERS
   LARDIEST
SU RESIDUAL
SY DIALYSER
TT DETRITAL
TY DIELYTRA
VY VARIEDLY
YZ DIALYZER

ADEILS 33
(LADIES)
AC ALCAIDES
   SIDALCEA
AD ALIDADES
AM MALADIES
AP PALISADE
AR SALARIED
AS ASSAILED
AV VEDALIAS
BD DISABLED
BE ABSEILED
BH DISHABLE
BP PIEBALDS
BS DISABLES
CI LAICISED
CL CEDILLAS
CM CAMELIDS
   DECIMALS
   DECLAIMS
   MEDICALS
CO COALISED
CP DISPLACE
CR DECRIALS
   RADICELS
   RADICLES
CT CITADELS
   DIALECTS
DG GLADDIES
DN ISLANDED
DR DIEDRALS
DY DIALYSED
EH DEISHEAL
EI IDEALISE
EN DELAINES

ER REALISED
   SIDEREAL
ES DEISEALS
   IDEALESS
ET LEADIEST
EV DISLEAVE
EY EYELIADS
FG GADFLIES
   GASFIELD
FH DEALFISH
FI LADIFIES
   SALIFIED
FS DISLEAFS
FY LADYFIES
GL GALLISED
GN DEALINGS
   LEADINGS
GO GOLIASED
GR SLAIRGED
GS GLISSADE
GT GLADIEST
GV DISGAVEL
HP HELIPADS
HV LAVISHED
HW WHAISLED
IM IDEALISM
   MILADIES
IR LAIRISED
IT IDEALIST
KW SIDEWALK
LP ILLAPSED
   SPADILLE
LR DALLIERS
   DIALLERS
MM DILEMMAS
MO DAMOISEL
MP IMPLEADS
   MISPLEAD
MS MAIDLESS
   MISDEALS
   MISLEADS
MT MISDEALT
MY DYSMELIA
NN ANNELIDS
   LINDANES
NO NODALISE
NR ISLANDER
NU UNSAILED
NV ANDVILES
OP EPISODAL
   OPALISED
   SEPALOID
OR DARIOLES
   SOLIDARE
   SOREDIAL
OS ASSOILED
   DEASOILS
OT DIASTOLE
   ISOLATED
   SODALITE
   SOLIDATE
OU DOULEIAS
PR PEDRAILS
   PREDIALS
PS DESPISAL
PT TALIPEDS
QU SQUAILED
RT DILATERS
   LARDIEST
RU RESIDUAL

RY DIALYSER
SU DEASIULS
SV DEVISALS
SY DIALYSES
TV VALIDEST
TY DIASTYLE
   STEADILY
UV DISVALUE
XY DYSLEXIA
YZ DIALYZES

ADEINR 4
(RAINED)
AC CANARIED
   RADIANCE
AG AREADING
   DRAINAGE
   GARDENIA
AM MARINADE
AR DARRAINE
AS ARANEIDS
AT DENTARIA
BD BRANDIED
   RIBANDED
BG BEARDING
   BREADING
BL BILANDER
BM BRIDEMAN
BO DEBONAIR
BS BRANDIES
   BRANDISE
CD CANDIDER
   RIDDANCE
CE DERACINE
CH INARCHED
CI ACRIDINE
CN CRANNIED
CR RANCIDER
CT CRINATED
   DICENTRA
DG DREADING
DO ORDAINED
DT INDARTED
EF FREDAINE
EG REGAINED
EM REMAINED
EP PINDAREE
ES ARSENIDE
   DENARIES
   DRAISENE
   NEARSIDE
ET DETAINER
   RETAINED
FL FILANDER
FS FRIANDES
FU UNFAIRED
GH ADHERING
   HEADRING
GK DAKERING
GL DEARLING
   DRAGLINE
GM DREAMING
   MARGINED
GO ORGANDIE
GR DREARING
GS DERAIGNS
   GRADINES
   READINGS
GT DERATING
   GRADIENT

   TREADING
GY DERAYING
   READYING
   YEARDING
HL HARDLINE
HU UNHAIRED
IM MERIDIAN
IS DRAISINE
IT DAINTIER
IU UREDINIA
LN INLANDER
LS ISLANDER
MR MANRIDER
MS ADERMINS
   SIRNAMED
MY DAIRYMEN
MZ ZEMINDAR
NS INSNARED
NZ RENDZINA
OR ORDAINER
   REORDAIN
OS ANEROIDS
   DONARIES
OT AROINTED
   DERATION
   ORDINATE
   RATIONED
OU DOUANIER
PS SPRAINED
PT DIPTERAN
PU UNPAIRED
   UNREPAID
RS DRAINERS
   SERRANID
SS ARIDNESS
   SARDINES
ST DETRAINS
   RANDIEST
   STRAINED
SU DENARIUS
   UNRAISED
   URANIDES
SV INVADERS
   SANDIVER
SY SYNEDRIA
TT NITRATED
TU DATURINE
   INDURATE
   RUINATED
   URINATED
UV UNVARIED
VY VINEYARD

ADEINS 22
(SANDIE)
AC AIDANCES
AR ARANEIDS
BG BEADINGS
   DEBASING
BH BANISHED
BR BRANDIES
   BRANDISE
BT BANDIEST
BU UNBIASED
BW BEDAWINS
CH ECHIDNAS
   INCHASED
CI SCIAENID
CO DIOCESAN
   OCEANIDS

CT DISTANCE
CY CYANIDES
   CYANISED
DL ISLANDED
DO ADENOIDS
   ADONISED
   ANODISED
DT DANDIEST
EL DELAINES
EM DEMAINES
   INSEAMED
EN ADENINES
   ANDESINE
ER ARSENIDE
   DENARIES
   DRAISENE
   NEARSIDE
ES ANISEEDS
ET ANDESITE
FI SANIFIED
FR FRIANDES
GH HEADINGS
   SHEADING
GL DEALINGS
   LEADINGS
GO AGONISED
   DIAGNOSE
GR DERAIGNS
   GRADINES
   READINGS
GS ASSIGNED
GT SEDATING
   STEADING
GW WINDAGES
HK SKINHEAD
HO ADHESION
HP DEANSHIP
   PINHEADS
HS SHANDIES
HT HANDIEST
HV VANISHED
IN SANIDINE
IR DRAISINE
IT ADENITIS
   DAINTIES
KY KYANISED
LN ANNELIDS
   LINDANES
LO NODALISE
LR ISLANDER
LU UNSAILED
LV ANDVILES
MM MISNAMED
MO NOMADIES
   NOMADISE
MR ADERMINS
   SIRNAMED
MS SIDESMAN
MT MEDIANTS
MU MAUNDIES
MY DYNAMISE
NN NANDINES
NR INSNARED
NU UNSAINED
NX DISANNEX
OR ANEROIDS
OS ADONISES
   ANODISES
OT ASTONIED

   SEDATION
OX DIOXANES
OZ ADONIZES
   ANODIZES
PR SPRAINED
PT DEPAINTS
PV SPAVINED
RR DRAINERS
   SERRANID
RS ARIDNESS
   SARDINES
RT DETRAINS
   RANDIEST
   STRAINED
RU DENARIUS
   UNRAISED
   URANIDES
RV INVADERS
   SANDIVER
RY SYNEDRIA
ST SANDIEST
SW WINDASES
TT INSTATED
TU AUDIENTS
   SINUATED
TV DEVIANTS
TY DESYATIN

ADEIRS 12
(RAISED)
AB ARABISED
AF FARADISE
   SAFARIED
AL SALARIED
AN ARANEIDS
AP PARADISE
AT DATARIES
   RADIATES
BC ASCRIBED
   CARBIDES
BE BEADIERS
BG ABRIDGES
   BRIGADES
BM EMBRAIDS
BN BRANDIES
   BRANDISE
BT BARDIEST
   BRAIDEST
   RABIDEST
   TRIBADES
BW BAWDRIES
   DAWBRIES
CE DECIARES
CG DISGRACE
CH RACHIDES
CL DECRIALS
   RADICELS
   RADICLES
CO IDOCRASE
CP EPACRIDS
CS SIDECARS
CT ACRIDEST
CU DECURIAS
DG DISGRADE
DI DIARISED
DL DIEDRALS
DM DISARMED
   MISDREAD
DO ROADSIDE
DP DISPREAD

DT DISRATED
DW SIDEWARD
EF FEDARIES
EG DISAGREE
EJ JADERIES
EL REALISED
   SIDEREAL
EM MADERISE
EN ARSENIDE
   DENARIES
   DRAISENE
   NEARSIDE
ET READIEST
   SERIATED
   STEADIER
EV READVISE
FM MISFARED
FN FRIANDES
FO FORESAID
GH GARISHED
   HEADRIGS
GL SLAIRGED
GN DERAIGNS
   GRADINES
   READINGS
GP SPAIRGED
HM MISHEARD
HP RAPHIDES
HS RADISHES
HT HAIRSTED
   HARDIEST
HV RAVISHED
HW RAWHIDES
IL LAIRISED
IN DRAISINE
IP PRESIDIA
IS DIARISES
IT IRISATED
IZ DIARIZES
JM JEMIDARS
KT STRAIKED
LL DALLIERS
   DIALLERS
LN ISLANDER
LO DARIOLES
   SOLIDARE
   SOREDIAL
LP PEDRAILS
   PREDIALS
LT DILATERS
   LARDIEST
LU RESIDUAL
LY DIALYSER
MM MERMAIDS
MN ADERMINS
   SIRNAMED
MR ADMIRERS
   DISARMER
MS MISREADS
   SIDEARMS
MT MARDIEST
   MISRATED
   READMITS
NN INSNARED
NO ANEROIDS
   DONARIES
NP SPRAINED
NR DRAINERS
   SERRANID
NS ARIDNESS

   SARDINES
NT DETRAINS
   RANDIEST
   STRAINED
NU DENARIUS
   UNRAISED
   URANIDES
NV INVADERS
   SANDIVER
NY SYNEDRIA
OP DIASPORE
   PARODIES
OT ASTEROID
PP APPRISED
   DRAPPIES
PR DRAPIERS
PS DESPAIRS
PT RAPIDEST
   SPIRATED
PU UPRAISED
RW SWARDIER
ST ASTERIDS
   DIASTERS
   DISASTER
   DISRATES
SU RADIUSES
   SUDARIES
SV ADVISERS
TT STRAITED
   STRIATED
TW TAWDRIES

ADEIST 26
(IDATES)
AM DIASTEMA
AR DATARIES
   RADIATES
AS DIASTASE
AT SATIATED
BE BEADIEST
   DIABETES
BN BANDIEST
BP BAPTISED
BR BARDIEST
   BRAIDEST
   RABIDEST
   TRIBADES
BS BASTIDES
BU DAUBIEST
BW BAWDIEST
CG CADGIEST
CH SCAITHED
CL CITADELS
   DIALECTS
CN DISTANCE
CP SPICATED
CR ACRIDEST
CT DICTATES
DE STEADIED
DF FADDIEST
DM MISDATED
DN DANDIEST
DR DISRATED
EH ATHEISED
   HEADIEST
EJ JADEITES
EL LEADIEST
EM MEDIATES

```
EN ANDESITE      DISASTER      RUNDALES     RS SLANDERS      PREDIALS      IV VALIDEST
ER READIEST      DISRATES    TY ARDENTLY    RU LAUNDERS    IT DILATERS     IY DIASTYLE
   SERIATED   RT STRAITED   UY UNDERLAY       LURDANES       LARDIEST        STEADILY
   STEADIER      STRIATED                     RUNDALES    IU RESIDUAL     NU UNSALTED
ES STEADIES      TARDIEST   ADELNS 137     TU UNSALTED    IY DIALYSER     NW WETLANDS
EV DEVIATES   RW TAWDRIES    (ANDLES)      TW WETLANDS    KP SPARKLED     OP TADPOLES
   SEDATIVE   SS ASSISTED   AC CANDELAS                   LN LANDLERS     OR DELATORS
FF DAFFIEST      DISSEATS   AG SELADANG    ADELRS  88     LO ODALLERS        LEOTARDS
GL GLADIEST   ST DISTASTE   AM DALESMAN     (ALDERS)      LU UDALLERS        LODESTAR
GM SIGMATED      STAIDEST      LEADSMAN    AB BASELARD        LODESTAR     OV SOLVATED
GN SEDATING   TU SITUATED   AR ADRENALS    AC CALDERAS    MN MANDRELS     PT SPLATTED
   STEADING                 AT EASTLAND    AH ASHLARED    MO EARLDOMS     PU PULSATED
GO GODETIAS   ADELNR  79    AW DANELAWS    AI SALARIED    NO LADRONES     RT STARTLED
GU GAUDIEST   (LANDER)      AY ANALYSED    AN ADRENALS       SOLANDER     TY STATEDLY
HK SKAITHED   AC CALENDAR   BB SNABBLED    AP PARDALES    NP SPANDREL
HN HANDIEST      LANDRACE   BS BALDNESS    BB DABBLERS    NS SLANDERS     ADENRS  62
HP PITHEADS   AH ANHEDRAL   BT BLANDEST       DRABBLES    NU LAUNDERS     (ANDERS)
HR HAIRSTED   AK KALENDAR   CE CLEANSED    BD BLADDERS       LURDANES     AI ARANEIDS
   HARDIEST   AM ALDERMAN   CO CELADONS    BE BEDERALS       RUNDALES     AL ADRENALS
HS SHADIEST      MALANDER   CT SCANTLED    BG BELGARDS    OP LEOPARDS     AV VERANDAS
IL IDEALIST   AS ADRENALS   CU UNSCALED    BH HALBERDS    OS ROADLESS     BI BRANDIES
IN ADENITIS   BG BRANGLED   DG GLADDENS    BR DRABLERS    OT DELATORS        BRANDISE
   DAINTIES   BI BILANDER   DI ISLANDED    BU DURABLES       LEOTARDS     BO BANDORES
IP STAPEDII   BO BANDEROL   DR DANDLERS    CD CLADDERS       LODESTAR        BROADENS
IR IRISATED   BY BYLANDER   DU UNSADDLE    CE DECLARES    OU ROULADES     BR BRANDERS
KR STRAIKED   CE CALENDER   EE ENSEALED       RESCALED    PW SPRAWLED     BS DRABNESS
LM MISDEALT      ENCRADLE   EI DELAINES    CH CHALDERS    RU RUDERALS     BT BANDSTER
LO DIASTOLE   CH CHANDLER   EM DALESMEN    CI DECRIALS    RW DRAWLERS     CE ASCENDER
   ISOLATED   CK CRANKLED      EMENDALS       RADICELS    TT STARTLED        REASCEND
   SODALITE   CO COLANDER      LEADSMEN       RADICLES    ZZ DAZZLERS     CO DRACONES
   SOLIDATE   CY CALENDRY   EP DEPLANES    CS SCALDERS                       ENDOSARC
LP TALIPEDS   DE ENLARDED   EU UNLEASED    CW SCRAWLED    ADELST 110      CT CANTREDS
LR DILATERS   DS DANDLERS      UNSEALED    CY SACREDLY    (SALTED)        CU DURANCES
   LARDIEST   EG ENLARGED   EV ENSLAVED    DI DIEDRALS    AN EASTLAND     DL DANDLERS
LV VALIDEST      LARGENED   FF SNAFFLED    DN DANDLERS    AT SALTATED     DT STRANDED
LY DIASTYLE   EH REHANDLE   FL ELFLANDS    DP PADDLERS    AU ADULATES     DU DAUNDERS
   STEADILY   EM ALDERMEN   FN FENLANDS    DS SADDLERS    AY DAYTALES        SERENADE
MM MISMATED   EO OLEANDER   GI DEALINGS    DT STRADDLE    BN BLANDEST     EG DERANGES
MN MEDIANTS   ET ANTLERED      LEADINGS    DW DAWDLERS    BU SUBLATED        GRANDEES
MO ATOMISED   EV LAVENDER   GP SPANGLED       SWADDLER    CI CITADELS        GRENADES
MP DAMPIEST   FI FILANDER   GR DANGLERS    DY SADDLERY       DIALECTS     EI ARSENIDE
   IMPASTED   FO FORELAND      GLANDERS    EE RELEASED    CN SCANTLED        DENARIES
MR MARDIEST   FU DEARNFUL   GS GLADNESS       RESEALED    CU CAULDEST        DRAISENE
   MISRATED   GI DEARLING   HR HANDLERS    EF FEDERALS       SULCATED        NEARSIDE
   READMITS      DRAGLINE   HS HANDLESS    EH ASHLERED    DE DESALTED     EK KNEADERS
MS MISDATES   GS DANGLERS      HANDSELS    EI REALISED    DG GLADDEST     EM AMENDERS
MU TAEDIUMS      GLANDERS   HT SHETLAND       SIDEREAL    DR STRADDLE        MEANDERS
MY DAYTIMES   GW WRANGLED   HU UNHALSED    EL SARDELLE    DS STADDLES        REAMENDS
NO ASTONIED   HI HARDLINE      UNLASHED    EM DEMERSAL    DW TWADDLES     EN ENSNARED
   SEDATION   HS HANDLERS      UNSHALED       EMERALDS    EE TEASELED     EO REASONED
NP DEPAINTS   IN INLANDER   IN ANNELIDS    EP PLEADERS    EF DEFLATES     ES DEARNESS
NR DETRAINS   IS ISLANDER      LINDANES       RELAPSED    EI LEADIEST     EU UNDERSEA
   RANDIEST   KP PRANKLED   IO NODALISE    ET TREADLES    EM MEDALETS     EW ANSWERED
   STRAINED   LS LANDLERS   IR ISLANDER    EV SLAVERED    EO DESOLATE     FI FRIANDES
NS SANDIEST   MS MANDRELS   IU UNSAILED    EW LEEWARDS    EP PEDESTAL     GI DERAIGNS
NT INSTATED   OP PONDERAL   IV ANDVILES    EY DELAYERS    ER TREADLES        GRADINES
NU AUDIENTS   OS LADRONES   KU UNSLAKED    FP FELDSPAR    ES DATELESS        READINGS
   SINUATED      SOLANDER   LP SPENDALL    GG DRAGGLES    EY SEDATELY     GL DANGLERS
NV DEVIANTS   OU UNLOADER   LR LANDLERS    GI SLAIRGED    FU DEFAULTS        GLANDERS
NY DESYATIN      URODELAN   LS LANDLESS    GN DANGLERS       SULFATED     GM DRAGSMEN
OP DIOPTASE   OV OVERLAND   LW ELLWANDS       GLANDERS    GI GLADIEST     GT GRANDEST
OR ASTEROID      RONDAVEL      WALLSEND    HN HANDLERS    HN SHETLAND     GU ENGUARDS
OX OXIDATES   PS SPANDREL   MN LANDSMEN    II LAIRISED    II IDEALIST     HK REDSHANK
OZ AZOTISED   PU PENDULAR   MO LODESMAN    IL DALLIERS    IM MISDEALT     HL HANDLERS
PR RAPIDEST      UNDERLAP   MR MANDRELS       DIALLERS    IO DIASTOLE     HM HERDSMAN
   SPIRATED      UPLANDER   OR LADRONES    IN ISLANDER       ISOLATED     HS HARDNESS
   TRAIPSED   PY PANDERLY      SOLANDER    IO DARIOLES       SODALITE     HU UNSHARED
PV VAPIDEST   SS SLANDERS   OY YEALDONS       SOLIDARE       SOLIDATE     HW SWANHERD
RS ASTERIDS   SU LAUNDERS   PR SPANDREL       SOREDIAL    IP TALIPEDS     II DRAISINE
   DIASTERS      LURDANES   PY DYSPNEAL    IP PEDRAILS    IR DILATERS
                                                             LARDIEST
```

IL ISLANDER
IM ADERMINS
   SIRNAMED
IN INSNARED
IO ANEROIDS
   DONARIES
IP SPRAINED
IR DRAINERS
   SERRANID
IS ARIDNESS
   SARDINES
IT DETRAINS
   RANDIEST
   STRAINED
IU DENARIUS
   UNRAISED
   URANIDES
IV INVADERS
   SANDIVER
IY SYNEDRIA
KS DARKNESS
LL LANDLERS
LM MANDRELS
LO LADRONES
   SOLANDER
LP SPANDREL
LS SLANDERS
LU LAUNDERS
   LURDANES
   RUNDALES
MO RANSOMED
   ROADSMEN
MU DURAMENS
   MAUNDERS
   SURNAMED
OP OPERANDS
   PANDORES
OT TORNADES
PP PARPENDS
PR PARDNERS
PU UNSPARED
QU SQUANDER
RY REYNARDS
SS SARSDENS
ST STANDERS
SU DANSEURS
TU DAUNTERS
   TRANSUDE
   UNTREADS
TX DEXTRANS
UY UNDERSAY

ADENRU 64
(AUNDER)
BB UNBARBED
BC UNBRACED
BF FABURDEN
BK UNBARKED
BR UNBARRED
BT BREADNUT
   TURBANED
CF FURNACED
CG UNGRACED
CH RAUNCHED
CK UNRACKED
CP PRAUNCED
CS DURANCES
CT UNCARTED
   UNCRATED
   UNDERACT

UNTRACED
DD DEUDDARN
DE DAUNERED
DG UNGRADED
DO UNADORED
DP UNDRAPED
DS DAUNDERS
DT DRAUNTED
   UNTRADED
DW UNWARDED
EF UNFEARED
EG DUNGAREE
   RENAGUED
   UNGEARED
EN UNEARNED
EP UNREAPED
ES UNDERSEA
ET DENATURE
EV UNREAVED
FI UNFAIRED
FL DEARNFUL
FM UNFRAMED
GR GRANDEUR
GS ENGUARDS
GU UNARGUED
GZ UNGRAZED
HI UNHAIRED
HM UNHARMED
HS UNSHARED
HT UNTHREAD
II UREDINIA
IO DOUANIER
IP UNPAIRED
   UNREPAID
IS DENARIUS
   UNRAISED
   URANIDES
IT DATURINE
   INDURATE
   RUINATED
   URINATED
IV UNVARIED
KM UNMARKED
LO UNLOADER
   URODELAN
LP PENDULAR
   UNDERLAP
   UPLANDER
LS LAUNDERS
   LURDANES
   RUNDALES
LY UNDERLAY
MN MUNDANER
   UNDERMAN
MR UNDERARM
   UNMARRED
MS DURAMENS
   MAUNDERS
   SURNAMED
MT UNDREAMT
MW UNWARMED
NR UNDERRAN
NW UNWARNED
OX RONDEAUX
PS UNSPARED
PT DEPURANT
PW UNWARPED
PY UNDERPAY
QS SQUANDER
   UNPRAYED

RT UNTARRED
SS DANSEURS
ST DAUNTERS
   TRANSUDE
   UNTREADS
SY UNDERSAY
TT TRUANTED
WY UNDERWAY

ADENST 36
(STANED)
AK ASKANTED
AL EASTLAND
AM MANDATES
AN ANDANTES
BE ABSENTED
BI BANDIEST
BL BLANDEST
BR BANDSTER
CH SNATCHED
   STANCHED
CI DISTANCE
CL SCANTLED
CN SCANDENT
CP PANDECTS
CR CANTREDS
CS DESCANTS
DI DANDIEST
DR STRANDED
EF FASTENED
EH HASTENED
EI ANDESITE
EK NAKEDEST
EM STAMENED
ES ASSENTED
EU UNSEATED
FS DAFTNESS
GI SEDATING
   STEADING
GR GRANDEST
HI HANDIEST
HL SHETLAND
HS HANDSETS
II ADENITIS
   DAINTIES
IM MEDIANTS
IO ASTONIED
   SEDATION
IP DEPAINTS
IR DETRAINS
   RANDIEST
   STRAINED
IS SANDIEST
IT INSTATED
IU AUDIENTS
   SINUATED
IV DEVIANTS
IY DESYATIN
LU UNSALTED
LW WETLANDS
NP PENDANTS
NU ASTUNNED
OR TORNADES
OS ONSTEADS
RS STANDERS
RU DAUNTERS
   TRANSUDE
   UNTREADS
RX DEXTRANS
TU UNSTATED

UNTASTED
UW UNWASTED
UY UNSTAYED
   UNSTEADY

ADEORS 48
(ADORES)
AB SEABOARD
BB ABSORBED
BC BROCADES
BD ADSORBED
BN BANDORES
   BROADENS
BR BOARDERS
BT BROADEST
CG CORDAGES
CI IDOCRASE
CM COMRADES
CN DRACONES
   ENDOSARC
CR CORRADES
CS SARCODES
CT REDCOATS
CU CAROUSED
DD ADDORSED
DI ROADSIDE
EH SOREHEAD
EM SEADROME
EN REASONED
EW OARWEEDS
FI FORESAID
GM ORGASMED
GT GOADSTER
GW DOWAGERS
   WORDAGES
HK HARDOKES
HM HADROMES
HP RHAPSODE
HR HOARDERS
HW SHADOWER
IL DARIOLES
   SOLIDARE
   SOREDIAL
IN ANEROIDS
   DONARIES
IP DIASPORE
   PARODIES
IT ASTEROID
JP JEOPARDS
KM DARKSOME
LL ODALLERS
LM EARLDOMS
LN LADRONES
   SOLANDER
LP LEOPARDS
LS ROADLESS
LT DELATORS
   LEOTARDS
   LODESTAR
LU ROULADES
MN RANSOMED
   ROADSMEN
MT STROAMED
NP OPERANDS
   PANDORES
NT TORNADES
PR EARDROPS
PT ADOPTERS
   ASPORTED
   READOPTS

RS DROSERAS
RT ROADSTER
ST ASSORTED
   TORSADES
TU OUTDARES
TX EXTRADOS
UV SAVOURED
WY RODEWAYS

ADERST 49
(DATERS)
AC CADASTRE
AG GRADATES
AI DATARIES
   RADIATES
AP ADAPTERS
   READAPTS
AS ASSARTED
AT ASTARTED
AW EASTWARD
BB DRABBEST
   DRABBETS
BE BETREADS
   BREASTED
   DEBATERS
BH BREADTHS
BI BARDIEST
   BRAIDEST
   RABIDEST
   TRIBADES
BN BANDSTER
BO BROADEST
BS DABSTERS
BU SURBATED
BW BEDSTRAW
BY DRYBEATS
CE CEDRATES
CH STARCHED
CI ACRIDEST
CN CANTREDS
CO REDCOATS
CT DETRACTS
   SCRATTED
CU TRADUCES
DI DISRATED
DL STRADDLE
DN STRANDED
EE RESEATED
EF DRAFTEES
EG RESTAGED
EH HEADREST
EI READIEST
   SERIATED
   STEADIER
EK STREAKED
EL TREADLES
EM MASTERED
   STREAMED
EP PREDATES
   REPASTED
   TRAPESED
ER ARRESTED
   DREAREST
   RETREADS
   SERRATED
   TREADERS
ES ASSERTED
   ESTRADES
ET ASTERTED
   RESTATED

EW DEWATERS
   TARWEEDS
   WASTERED
EY ESTRAYED
FF STRAFFED
FR DRAFTERS
   REDRAFTS
GN GRANDEST
GO GOADSTER
GR DRAGSTER
HH THRASHED
HI HAIRSTED
   HARDIEST
HY HYDRATES
II IRISATED
IK STRAIKED
IL DILATERS
   LARDIEST
IM MARDIEST
   MISRATED
   READMITS
IN DETRAINS
   RANDIEST
   STRAINED
IO ASTEROID
IP RAPIDEST
   SPIRATED
   TRAIPSED
IS ASTERIDS
   DIASTERS
   DISASTER
   DISRATES
IT STRAITED
   STRIATED
   TARDIEST
IW TAWDRIES
JU ADJUSTER
   READJUST
LO DELATORS
   LEOTARDS
   LODESTAR
LT STARTLED
MO STROAMED
MP STRAMPED
NO TORNADES
NS STANDERS
NU DAUNTERS
   TRANSUDE
   UNTREADS
NX DEXTRANS
OP ADOPTERS
   ASPORTED
   READOPTS
OR ROADSTER
OS ASSORTED
   TORSADES
OU OUTDARES
OX EXTRADOS
PP STRAPPED
PU PASTURED
   UPSTARED
RT REDSTART
SW STEWARDS
TU STATURED
UX SURTAXED
WW WESTWARD

ADGINR 135
(RADING)
AB ABRADING

AC ARCADING
   CARANGID
   CARDIGAN
AE AREADING
   DRAINAGE
   GARDENIA
AM MRIDANGA
AP PARADING
AR DARRAIGN
AU GUARDIAN
AW AWARDING
BB DRABBING
BE BEARDING
   BREADING
BH HANGBIRD
BI BRAIDING
BL BARDLING
BN BRANDING
BO ABORDING
   BOARDING
BS BRIGANDS
CL CRADLING
DE DREADING
DL RADDLING
EE REGAINED
EH ADHERING
   HEADRING
EK DAKERING
EL DEARLING
   DRAGLINE
EM DREAMING
   MARGINED
EO ORGANDIE
ER DREARING
ES DERAIGNS
   GRADINES
   READINGS
ET DERATING
   GRADIENT
   TREADING
EY DERAYING
   READYING
   YEARDING
FS FARDINGS
FT DRAFTING
FW DWARFING
GG DRAGGING
GS NIGGARDS
GU GUARDING
HO HOARDING
HP HANDGRIP
IL DRAILING
IM ADMIRING
IN DRAINING
IO RADIOING
IR ARRIDING
IY DAIRYING
JU ADJURING
KL DARKLING
LS DARLINGS
LT DARTLING
LW DRAWLING
LY DARINGLY
MM DRAMMING
MS MRIDANGS
MY MARDYING
NO ADORNING
NS DARNINGS
NT DRANTING
OO RIGADOON

OS ROADINGS
PP DRAPPING
ST TRADINGS
SW DRAWINGS
   SWARDING
   WARDINGS
TY TARDYING

ADINRS 105
(DRAINS)
AE ARANEIDS
AL LANIARDS
AM MANDIRAS
AR DARRAINS
AT RADIANTS
AV VIRANDAS
BB RIBBANDS
BE BRANDIES
   BRANDISE
BG BRIGANDS
BH BRANDISH
CI ACRIDINS
CO SARDONIC
DO ANDROIDS
   DISADORN
EE ARSENIDE
   DENARIES
   DRAISENE
   NEARSIDE
EF FRIANDES
EG DERAIGNS
   GRADINES
   READINGS
EI DRAISINE
EL ISLANDER
EM ADERMINS
   SIRNAMED
EN INSNARED
EO ANEROIDS
   DONARIES
EP SPRAINED
ER DRAINERS
   SERRANID
ES ARIDNESS
ET DETRAINS
   RANDIEST
   STRAINED
EU DENARIUS
   UNRAISED
   URANIDES
EV INVADERS
   SANDIVER
EY SYNEDRIA
FG FARDINGS
FM FINDRAMS
FT INDRAFTS
GG NIGGARDS
GL DARLINGS
GM MRIDANGS
GN DARNINGS
GO ROADINGS
GT TRADINGS
GW DRAWINGS
   SWARDING
   WARDINGS
IP PINDARIS
IT DISTRAIN
KS DISRANKS
KT STINKARD

LM MANDRILS
LO ORDINALS
LP SPANDRIL
LU DIURNALS
MW MISDRAWN
MY MISANDRY
NO ANDIRONS
NY INNYARDS
OP PONIARDS
OR ORDINARS
OT INTRADOS
OU DINOSAUR
OV VIRANDOS
RT TRIDARNS
SU SUNDARIS

AEELRS 72
(EALERS)
AB ERASABLE
AT LAETARES
BD BEDERALS
BG BEAGLERS
BN ENABLERS
BP BEPEARLS
BT BLEAREST
   BLEATERS
   RETABLES
BU REUSABLE
BV BESLAVER
CD DECLARES
   RESCALED
CH RELACHES
CI ESCALIER
CM RECLAMES
   SCLEREMA
CN CLEANERS
   CLEANSER
CO ESCAROLE
CP PERCALES
   REPLACES
CR CLEARERS
CS CARELESS
   RESCALES
CT CLEAREST
   SCELERAT
   TREACLES
CV CLEAVERS
DE RELEASED
   RESEALED
DF FEDERALS
DH ASHLERED
DI REALISED
   SIDEREAL
DL SARDELLE
DM DEMERSAL
   EMERALDS
DP PLEADERS
   RELAPSED
DT TREADLES
DV SLAVERED
DW LEEWARDS
DY DELAYERS
EE RELEASEE
EF EELFARES
ER RELEASER
ES RELEASES
ET TEASELER
EW WEASELER
FI SERAFILE
FS FEARLESS

FT REFLATES
FW WELFARES
GG GREGALES
GI GASELIER
GL ALLEGERS
GN ENLARGES
   GENERALS
   GLEANERS
GP PEREGALS
GS EELGRASS
   GEARLESS
GU LEAGUERS
HI SHIRALEE
HO ARSEHOLE
HT HALTERES
   LEATHERS
HV HAVERELS
IL REALLIES
IM ALMERIES
   MEASLIER
IP ESPALIER
   PEARLIES
IR REALISER
IS REALISES
IT ATELIERS
   EARLIEST
   LEARIEST
   REALTIES
IV VELARISE
IY YEARLIES
IZ REALIZES
   SLEAZIER
LP PARELLES
MT LAMETERS
NR LEARNERS
NS REALNESS
NT ALTERNES
NV ENSLAVER
NW RENEWALS
OP PAROLEES
OR RELEASOR
OT OLEASTER
OU AUREOLES
PR PEARLERS
   RELAPSER
PS PLEASERS
   RELAPSES
PT PRELATES
PU PLEASURE
   SERPULAE
PV VESPERAL
QU SQUEALER
RT RELATERS
RV REVERSAL
   SLAVERER
ST STEALERS
   TEARLESS
   TESSERAL
SU LEASURES
SV SEVERALS
SW WARELESS
TT ALERTEST
TU RESALUTE
TY EASTERLY
UV REVALUES
VY AVERSELY

AEEPRT 142
(REPEAT)
AH HEARTPEA
AK PARAKEET
AN PARANETE
AS ASPERATE
   SEPARATE
CC ACCEPTER
CD CARPETED
CF PERFECTA
   PRAEFECT
CH ETHERCAP
CN PERCEANT
CT ETTERCAP
CU PERACUTE
CX EXCERPTA
DD DEPARTED
   PREDATED
DE REPEATED
DG PARGETED
DL PALTERED
DM EMPARTED
   TAMPERED
DN PARENTED
DO OPERATED
DR DEPARTER
DS PREDATES
   REPASTED
   TRAPESED
DT PATTERED
DU DEPURATE
   EPURATED
DZ TRAPEZED
EM PERMEATE
ER REPARTEE
   REPEATER
GR PARGETER
HS PREHEATS
   SPREATHE
IL PEARLITE
IN APERIENT
IS PETARIES
IV PERVIATE
JO PEJORATE
KN PERTAKEN
KS PERTAKES
LR PALTERER
LS PRELATES
LY PTERYLAE
MN PETERMAN
MR TAMPERER
MS TEMPERAS
MT ATTEMPER
OR PATERERO
OS OPERATES
OT OPERETTA
RR PARTERRE
RS TAPERERS
RT PATTERER
RU APERTURE
SS TRAPESES
SU EPURATES
   SUPERATE
SZ TRAPEZES

AEERRS 162
(ERASER)
AF SEAFARER

AN ARRASENE
BC REBRACES
BG GERBERAS
BK BREAKERS
BT REBATERS
   TABRERES
   TEREBRAS
BY SEABERRY
CD SCAREDER
CH REACHERS
   RESEARCH
   SEARCHER
CI CARIERES
   CREASIER
CL CLEARERS
CM CREAMERS
   SCREAMER
CP CAPERERS
CT CATERERS
   RETRACES
   TERRACES
CU ECRASEUR
DD DREADERS
DE ARREEDES
DG REGRADES
DH ADHERERS
   REDSHARE
DM DREAMERS
DP SPREADER
DT ARRESTED
   DREAREST
   RETREADS
   SERRATED
   TREADERS
DV ADVERSER
EH REHEARSE
EL RELEASER
ET ARRESTEE
FI RAREFIES
FM REFRAMES
FT FERRATES
GI GREASIER
GP ASPERGER
   PRESAGER
GS GREASERS
GT REGRATES
GW WAGERERS
HI HEARSIER
HP REPHRASE
HS SHEARERS
IK RAKERIES
IL REALISER
IM SMEARIER
IN REARISEN
IP PEREIRAS
   SPEARIER
IS REARISES
IT ARTERIES
   REASTIER
KT RETAKERS
KW WREAKERS
LN LEARNERS
LO RELEASOR
LP PEARLERS
   RELAPSER
LT RELATERS
LV REVERSAL
   SLAVERER

```
MT STREAMER        CREMATES           LEATHERS        EARNESTS          DRAGLINE     RT ALERTING
MU MEASURER        MEERCATS        HM ERATHEMS          SARSENET     DS DEALINGS        ALTERING
NO REASONER     CN REASCENT        HN HASTENER       NT ENTREATS        LEADINGS        INTEGRAL
NS RARENESS        SARCENET           HEARTENS          RATTEENS     DT DELATING        RELATING
NT TERRANES     CO CREASOTE        HP PREHEATS       NV AVENTRES     DY DELAYING        TANGLIER
NV RAVENERS     CR CATERERS          SPREATHE          VETERANS     EM LIEGEMAN        TRIANGLE
NW ANSWERER        RETRACES        HT THEATERS       OP OPERATES     ER ALGERINE     RX RELAXING
   REANSWER        TERRACES           THEATRES          PROTEASE     ES ENSILAGE     RY LAYERING
OU REAROUSE     CS CATERESS        HV THREAVES       OV OVEREATS        LINEAGES        RELAYING
OW SOWARREE        CERASTES        HW WEATHERS       PR TAPERERS     ET GALENITE        YEARLING
PP PAPERERS     CU SECATEUR           WREATHES       PS TRAPESES        GELATINE     SS GAINLESS
   PREPARES     CX EXACTERS        IL ATELIERS       PU EPURATES        LEGATINE        GLASSINE
   REPAPERS     DE RESEATED           EARLIEST          SUPERATE     EV INVEAGLE        LEASINGS
PT TAPERERS     DF DRAFTEES           LEARIEST       PZ TRAPEZES     FS FINAGLES        SEALINGS
RT ARRESTER     DG RESTAGED           REALTIES       RR ARRESTER     GG ALEGGING     ST EASTLING
   REARREST     DH HEADREST        IM EMIRATES          REARREST     GL ALLEGING        GELATINS
ST ASSERTER     DI READIEST           REAMIEST       RS ASSERTER     GM GLEAMING        GENITALS
   REASSERT        SERIATED           STEAMIER          REASSERT     GN GLEANING        STEALING
   SERRATES        STEADIER        IN ARSENITE          SERRATES     GR GANGLIER     SV LEAVINGS
   TERRASES     DK STREAKED           RESINATE          TERRASES        REGALING        SLEAVING
SU ERASURES     DL TREADLES           STEARINE       RT RETRATES     GS LIGNAGES     SW SWEALING
   REASSURE     DM MASTERED           TRAINEES          RETREATS     GT TEAGLING     TV VALETING
SW SWEARERS        STREAMED        IO ETAERIOS          TREATERS     GU LEAGUING     TX EXALTING
TT RETRATES     DP PREDATES        IP PETARIES       RU AUSTERER     HR NARGHILE     TZ TEAZLING
   RETREATS        REPASTED        IR ARTERIES          TREASURE     HS HEALINGS     UV VAGINULE
   TREATERS        TRAPESED           REASTIER       RV TRAVERSE     HT ATHELING
TU AUSTERER     DR ARRESTED        IS SERIATES       RW WATERERS     HX EXHALING
   TREASURE        DREAREST        IT ARIETTES       ST ESTREATS     IN ALIENING     AEGINR  15
TV TRAVERSE        RETREADS           ITERATES          RESTATES     IR GAINLIER       (EARING)
TW WATERERS        SERRATED           TEARIEST       SW SWEATERS     JR JANGLIER     AB ABEARING
VW WAVERERS        TREADERS           TREATIES       SZ ERSATZES     KS LINKAGES     AC CANAIGRE
                DS ASSERTED           TREATISE       TT ATTESTER     KW WEAKLING     AD DRAINAGE
                   ESTRADES        IV EVIRATES       TX EXTREATS     LS NIGELLAS        GARDENIA
AEERST  20      DT ASTERTED        IW SWEATIER                       LU LINGULAE     AF AFEARING
  (EATERS)      DW DEWATERS           TAWERIES       AEGILN  55      LY GENIALLY     AG GRAINAGE
AG STEARAGE        TARWEEDS           WEARIEST        (EALING)       MP EMPALING     AL REGALIAN
AH HETAERAS        WASTERED        IY YEASTIER       AB GAINABLE     MR GERMINAL     AN ANEARING
AL LAETARES     DY ESTRAYED        JN SERJEANT       AC ANGELICA        MALIGNER     AS ANGARIES
AN ARSENATE     EG ETAGERES        KM MEERKATS       AE ALIENAGE        MALINGER     AT AERATING
   SERENATA        STEERAGE        KO KERATOSE       AP PELAGIAN     MS MEASLING     BD BEARDING
AP ASPERATE     EI EATERIES           KREASOTE       AR REGALIAN     MT LIGAMENT        BREADING
   SEPARATE     EL TEASELER        KP PERTAKES       AT AGENTIAL     MU AEMULING     BE BERGENIA
AT STEARATE     EN SERENATE        KR RETAKERS          ALGINATE     MY YEALMING     BK BREAKING
BC ACERBEST     ER ARRESTEE           STREAKER       BC BELACING     NR LEARNING     BL BLEARING
BD BETREADS     ES TESSERAE        KS SAKERETS       BD BLINDAGE     NS EANLINGS     BM BREAMING
   BREASTED     FH FEATHERS        LM LAMETERS       BG BEAGLING        LEANINGS     BO ABORIGEN
   DEBATERS     FL REFLATES        LN ALTERNES       BM EMBALING     NT GANTLINE     BS BEARINGS
BG ABSTERGE     FN FASTENER        LO OLEASTER       BN ENABLING        LATENING        SABERING
BH BREATHES        FENESTRA        LP PRELATES       BR BLEARING     NU UNGENIAL     BT BERATING
   HARTBEES     FR FERRATES        LR RELATERS       BS SINGABLE     NW WEANLING        REBATING
BK BESTREAK     FS FEASTERS        LS STEALERS       BT BELATING     NY YEANLING     BW BEWARING
BL BLEAREST     FU FEATURES           TEARLESS          BLEATING     OR GERANIOL     BY BERAYING
   BLEATERS     GM GAMESTER           TESSERAL          TANGIBLE        REGIONAL     CF REFACING
   RETABLES        MEAGREST        LT ALERTEST       BY BELAYING     OS GASOLINE     CH REACHING
BO REBATOES     GN ESTRANGE        LU RESALUTE       CG CAGELING     OT GELATION     CK CREAKING
BR REBATERS        GRANTEES        LY EASTERLY          GLACEING        LEGATION     CL CLEARING
   TABRERES        GREATENS        MM AMMETERS       CH LEACHING     PR PEARLING     CM AMERCING
   TEREBRAS        REAGENTS           METAMERS       CN CLEANING     PS ELAPSING        CREAMING
BT ABETTERS        SEGREANT        MN REMANETS          ELANCING        PLEASING     CN ENRACING
BU SUBERATE        SERGEANT        MO EROTEMAS          ENLACING     PT PLEATING     CP CAPERING
CC ACCRETES        STERNAGE        MP TEMPERAS       CR CLEARING     RR GNARLIER        PEARCING
CD CEDRATES     GR REGRATES        MR STREAMER       CT CLEATING     RS ARLESING        PREACING
CH CHEATERS     GS RESTAGES        MS MASSETER       CV CLEAVING        ENGRAILS     CS CREASING
   HECTARES     GT GREATEST           SEAMSTER       DF FINAGLED        NARGILES        GRECIANS
   RECHATES     GU TREAGUES           STEAMERS       DH HEALDING        REALIGNS        SEARCING
   RECHEATS     GW STREWAGE        MT TEAMSTER       DI GLIADINE        SANGLIER     CT CATERING
   TEACHERS     HH HEATHERS        MY METAYERS       DM MALIGNED        SLANGIER        CITRANGE
CL CLEAREST     HI HEARTIES        NO RESONATE       DO GALENOID                        CREATING
   SCELERAT     HL HALTERES        NR TERRANES       DP PLEADING                        REACTING
   TREACLES                        NS ASSENTER       DR DEARLING
CM CERAMETS
```

```
DD DREADING      NARGILES     AEGLNR  91       WRANGLES     OT TANGELOS     TU GAUNTLET
DE REGAINED      REALIGNS     (ANGLER)      SY LARYNGES     PR GRAPNELS     UU UNGULATE
DH ADHERING      SANGLIER     AG LANGRAGE    UY GUNLAYER        SPANGLER
   HEADRING      SLANGIER     AI REGALIAN                       SPRANGLE     AEGLRS 167
DK DAKERING   LT ALERTING     AS ALNAGERS    AEGLNS 170     PS PANGLESS     (LAGERS)
DL DEARLING      ALTERING     AU AULNAGER    (ANGLES)          SPANGLES     AB ALGEBRAS
   DRAGLINE      INTEGRAL     BD BRANGLED    AD SELADANG    PT SPANGLET     AI GASALIER
DM DREAMING      RELATING     BI BLEARING    AM GAMELANS    RT STRANGLE        LAIRAGES
   MARGINED      TANGLIER     BS BRANGLES    AR ALNAGERS       TANGLERS        REGALIAS
DO ORGANDIE      TRIANGLE     CI CLEARING    AS LASAGNES       TRANGLES     AN ALNAGERS
DR DREARING   LX RELAXING     CS CLANGERS    AU AULNAGES    RU GRANULES     AR REALGARS
DS DERAIGNS   LY LAYERING     DE ENLARGED    BI SINGABLE    RW WANGLERS        RESALGAR
   GRADINES      RELAYING        LARGENED    BR BRANGLES       WRANGLES     AT AGRESTAL
   READINGS      YEARLING     DI DEARLING    CO CONGEALS    RY LARYNGES     BB GABBLERS
DT DERATING   MN ENARMING        DRAGLINE    CR CLANGERS    TT GANTLETS        GRABBLES
   GRADIENT      RENAMING     DS DANGLERS    DD GLADDENS    TU LANGUETS     BD BELGARDS
   TREADING   MP EMPARING        GLANDERS    DI DEALINGS    TW TWANGLES     BE BEAGLERS
DY DERAYING   MR REARMING     DW WRANGLED       LEADINGS    UW GUNWALES     BM GAMBLERS
   READYING   MS GERMAINS     EE GENERALE    DP SPANGLED                       GAMBRELS
   YEARDING      SMEARING     EI ALGERINE    DR DANGLERS    AEGLNT 118      BN BRANGLES
EG AGREEING   MT EMIGRANT     EL ALLERGEN       GLANDERS    (TANGLE)        BR GARBLERS
EI AEGIRINE   MU GERANIUM     EN ENLARGEN    DS GLADNESS    AI AGENTIAL     CH SCHLAGER
EL ALGERINE   NS AGINNERS     ER ENLARGER    EI ENSILAGE       ALGINATE     CI GLACIERS
EM GERMAINE      EARNINGS     ES ENLARGES       LINEAGES    AP PLANTAGE     CK GRACKLES
EP PERIGEAN      ENGRAINS        GENERALS    EM MELANGES    AU ANGULATE     CN CLANGERS
ER REGAINER      GRANNIES        GLEANERS    EO GASOLENE    BI BELATING     DG DRAGGLES
ES GESNERIA      GLEANERS     GI GANGLIER    ER ENLARGES       BLEATING     DI SLAIRGED
EZ RAZEEING   NV RAVENING        REGALING       GENERALS       TANGIBLE     DN DANGLERS
FH HANGFIRE   NY RENAYING     GS GANGRELS       GLEANERS    CI CLEATING        GLANDERS
FK FREAKING      YEARNING     HI NARGHILE    EV EVANGELS    DE DANEGELT     EG GREGALES
FW WAFERING   OS IGNAROES        NARGILEH    FI FINAGLES    DI DELATING     EI GASELIER
FY AREFYING      ORGANISE     II GAINLIER    FS FANGLESS    DW TWANGLED     EL ALLEGERS
GK KNAGGIER      ORIGANES     IJ JANGLIER    GI LIGNAGES    EI GALENITE     EN ENLARGES
GL GANGLIER   OZ ORGANIZE     IM GERMINAL    GR GANGRELS       GELATINE        GENERALS
   REGALING   PP PAPERING        MALIGNER    HI HEALINGS       LEGATINE        GLEANERS
GN ANGERING   PS PREASING        MALINGER       LEASHING    EN ENTANGLE     EP PEREGALS
   ENRAGING      SPEARING     IN LEARNING       SHEALING    EO ELONGATE     ES EELGRASS
GS GEARINGS   PT TAPERING     IO GERANIOL    HO HALOGENS    GI TEAGLING        GEARLESS
   GREASING   PY REPAYING        REGIONAL    IK LINKAGES    HI ATHELING        LARGESSE
   SNAGGIER   RS EARRINGS     IP PEARLING    IL NIGELLAS    IM LIGAMENT     EU LEAGUERS
GV GREAVING      GRAINERS     IR GNARLIER    IM MEASLING    IN GANTLINE     GH HAGGLERS
GW WAGERING   RV AVERRING     IS ARLESING    IN EANLINGS       LATENING     GI SLAGGIER
HL NARGHILE   SS REASSIGN        ENGRAILS       LEANINGS    IO GELATION     GN GANGRELS
   NARGILEH      SEARINGS        NARGILES    IO GASOLINE       LEGATION     GT STRAGGLE
HS HEARINGS      SERINGAS        REALIGNS    IP ELAPSING    IP PLEATING     HU LAUGHERS
   HEARSING   ST ANGRIEST        SANGLIER       PLEASING    IR ALERTING     IM GREMIALS
   SHEARING      ASTRINGE        SLANGIER    IR ARLESING       ALTERING        LAMIGERS
HT EARTHING      GANISTER     IT ALERTING       ENGRAILS       INTEGRAL        REGALISM
   HEARTING      GANTRIES        ALTERING       NARGILES       RELATING     IN ARLESING
HV HAVERING      GRANITES        INTEGRAL       REALIGNS       TANGLIER        ENGRAILS
IL GAINLIER      INGRATES        RELATING       SANGLIER       TRIANGLE        NARGILES
IM IMAGINER      RANGIEST        TANGLIER       SLANGIER    IS EASTLING        REALIGNS
   MIGRAINE      REASTING        TRIANGLE    IS GAINLESS       GELATINS        SANGLIER
IN ARGININE      STEARING     IX RELAXING       GLASSINE       GENITALS        SLANGIER
IR GRAINIER   SV VINEGARS     IY LAYERING       LEASINGS       STEALING     IO GASOLIER
JL JANGLIER   SW SWEARING        RELAYING       SEALINGS    IV VALETING        GIRASOLE
KM REMAKING      WEARINGS        YEARLING    IT EASTLING    IX EXALTING        SERAGLIO
KS SKEARING   SY RESAYING     JS JANGLERS       GELATINS    IZ TEAZLING     IS GLASSIER
KT RETAKING   TT ARETTING     LS LANGRELS       GENITALS    MU GUNMETAL     IT GLARIEST
KW WREAKING      TREATING     MS MANGLERS       STEALING    NP PLANGENT        REGALIST
LM GERMINAL   TV AVERTING     OY YEARLONG    IV LEAVINGS    NU UNTANGLE     IY GREASILY
   MALIGNER      TAVERING     PS GRAPNELS       SLEAVING    OP GANTLOPE     IZ GLAZIERS
   MALINGER      VINTAGER        SPANGLER    IW SWEALING    OS TANGELOS     JN JANGLERS
LN LEARNING   TW TWANGIER        SPRANGLE    JR JANGLERS    PS SPANGLET     LN LANGRELS
LO GERANIOL      WATERING     RW WRANGLER    LO ALLONGES    RS STRANGLE     LO ALLEGROS
   REGIONAL   VW WAVERING     ST STRANGLE    LP LANGSPEL       TANGLERS     MN MANGLERS
LP PEARLING   VY VINEGARY        TANGLERS    LR LANGRELS       TRANGLES     MO GOMERALS
LR GNARLIER   WY WEARYING        TRANGLES    MR MANGLERS    ST GANTLETS     MU MAULGRES
LS ARLESING                   SU GRANULES    MS GLASSMEN    SU LANGUETS     NP GRAPNELS
   ENGRAILS                   SW WANGLERS                   SW TWANGLES        SPANGLER
```

```
        SPRANGLE    UV VULGATES      ENGRAILS     BI BERATING        RAGSTONE        STEARING
NT STRANGLE                         NARGILES        REBATING     OT TETRAGON     IS EASTINGS
   TANGLERS    AEGNRS  86           REALIGNS     BS BANGSTER     OY NEGATORY        GENISTAS
   TRANGLES    (ANGERS)             SANGLIER     BU BURGANET     PS TREPANGS        GIANTESS
NU GRANULES    AC CARNAGES          SLANGIER     CI CATERING     RS GRANTERS        SEATINGS
NW WANGLERS       CRANAGES       IM GERMAINS        CITRANGE        REGRANTS        TEASINGS
   WRANGLES    AE SANGAREE       IN AGINNERS        CREATING        STRANGER        TSIGANES
NY LARYNGES    AI ANGARIES          EARNINGS        REACTING     SU STRAUNGE     IT ESTATING
OP PERGOLAS    AL ALNAGERS          ENGRAINS     DH THRANGED                         TANGIEST
OT LEGATORS    AM MANAGERS          GRANNIES     DI DERATING     AEGNST  115     IU SAUTEING
OU GLAREOUS    AR ARRANGES       IO IGNAROES        GRADIENT     (TANGES)        IV VINTAGES
PP GRAPPLES    AT STARAGEN          ORGANISE        TREADING     AH THANAGES     IW SWEATING
PU EARPLUGS       TANAGERS          ORIGANES     DO DRAGONET     AI SAGINATE     IY YEASTING
   GRAUPELS    BI BEARINGS       IP PREASING     DS GRANDEST     AK TANKAGES     LO TANGELOS
RU REGULARS       SABERING          SPEARING     EE GENERATE     AM MAGENTAS     LP SPANGLET
TU GAULTERS    BL BRANGLES       IR EARRINGS        RENEGATE        MAGNATES     LR STRANGLE
   GESTURAL    BT BANGSTER          GRAINERS        TEENAGER     AN TANNAGES        TANGLERS
   TRAGULES    CE ENGRACES       IS REASSIGN     EM AGREMENT     AP PAGEANTS        TRANGLES
               CH CHANGERS          SEARINGS     EN GENERANT     AR STARAGEN     LT GANTLETS
AEGLST  187    CI CREASING          SERINGAS     ER ETRANGER        TANAGERS     LU LANGUETS
(GLATES)          GRECIANS       IT ANGRIEST     ES ESTRANGE     AT STAGNATE     LW TWANGLES
AA GALATEAS       SEARCING          ASTRINGE        GRANTEES     AV VANTAGES     MO MAGNETOS
AE ETALAGES    CL CLANGERS          GANISTER        GREATENS     AW WANTAGES        MEGATONS
AL GALLATES    CM CRAGSMEN          GANTRIES        REAGENTS     BI BEATINGS        MONTAGES
   STALLAGE    CO ACROGENS          GRANITES        SEGREANT     BN BANTENGS     MR GARMENTS
   TALLAGES       CORNAGES          INGRATES        SERGEANT     BR BANGSTER        MARGENTS
AR AGRESTAL    DE DERANGES          RANGIEST        STERNAGE     BU SUBAGENT        RAGMENTS
AS AGELASTS       GRANDEES          REASTING     EU GAUNTREE     CE CENTAGES     MU AUGMENTS
   LASTAGES       GRENADES          STEARING     FM FRAGMENT     CO COGNATES        MUTAGENS
BU GUSTABLE    DI DERAIGNS       IV VINEGARS     FO FRONTAGE     DI SEDATING     NO TONNAGES
CI GELASTIC       GRADINES       IW SWEARING     FS ENGRAFTS     DR GRANDEST     NT TANGENTS
CO CATELOGS       READINGS          WEARINGS     GS GANGSTER     EF FANTEEGS     NU TUNNAGES
DD GLADDEST    DL DANGLERS       IY RESAYING     HI EARTHING     EI SAGENITE     OP PONTAGES
DI GLADIEST       GLANDERS       JL JANGLERS        HEARTING     ER ESTRANGE     OR ORANGEST
EE LEGATEES    DM DRAGSMEN       LL LANGRELS     IK RETAKING        GRANTEES        RAGSTONE
EI ELEGIAST    DT GRANDEST       LM MANGLERS     IL ALERTING        GREATENS     PR TREPANGS
EO SEGOLATE    DU ENGUARDS       LP GRAPNELS        ALTERING        REAGENTS     RR GRANTERS
ES GATELESS    EG ENGAGERS          SPANGLER        INTEGRAL        SEGREANT        REGRANTS
EV VEGETALS    EH SHAGREEN          SPRANGLE        RELATING        SERGEANT        STRANGER
FO FLOTAGES    EI GESNERIA       LT STRANGLE        TANGLIER        STERNAGE     RU STRAUNGE
GR STRAGGLE    EL ENLARGES          TANGLERS        TRIANGLE     ET TENTAGES     SS GASTNESS
HI LAIGHEST       GENERALS          TRANGLES     IM EMIGRANT     EV VENTAGES     TU GAUNTEST
HW THALWEGS       GLEANERS       LU GRANULES     IP TAPERING     FI FEASTING        TUTENAGS
IL LEGALIST    EM AGREMENS       LW WANGLERS     IS ANGRIEST     FR ENGRAFTS
   STILLAGE    EN ENRANGES       LY LARYNGES        ASTRINGE     GI NAGGIEST     AEGRST  80
   TILLAGES    ET ESTRANGE       MO MEGARONS        GANISTER     GR GANGSTER     (GATERS)
IN EASTLING       GRANTEES       MT GARMENTS        GANTRIES     HI GAHNITES     AA GASTRAEA
   GELATINS       GREATENS          MARGENTS        GRANITES        HEATINGS     AC CARTAGES
   GENITALS       REAGENTS          RAGMENTS        INGRATES     HN HANGNEST     AD GRADATES
   STEALING       SEGREANT       NU GUNNERAS        RANGIEST     HS STENGAHS     AE STEARAGE
IO OTALGIES       SERGEANT       OO OREGANOS        REASTING     IL EASTLING     AG AGGRATES
IR GLARIEST       STERNAGE       OR GROANERS        STEARING        GELATINS     AL AGRESTAL
   REGALIST    EU RENAGUES       OT ORANGEST     IT ARETTING        GENITALS     AN TANAGERS
IZ GLAZIEST    EV AVENGERS          RAGSTONE        TREATING        STEALING     AT REGATTAS
LO TOLLAGES       ENGRAVES       OW WAGONERS     IV AVERTING     IM MANGIEST     BE ABSTERGE
NO TANGELOS    FF ENGRAFFS       PS ENGRASPS        TAVERING        MINTAGES     BH BARGHEST
NP SPANGLET    FR GRANFERS       PT TREPANGS        VINTAGER        STEAMING     BN BANGSTER
NR STRANGLE    FT ENGRAFTS       RT GRANTERS     IW TWANGIER        TEAMINGS     BS BARGESTS
   TANGLERS    GI GEARINGS          REGRANTS        WATERING     IN ANTIGENS     CI AGRESTIC
   TRANGLES       GREASING          STRANGER     LS STRANGLE        GENTIANS     CO ESCARGOT
NT GANTLETS       SNAGGIER       TU STRAUNGE        TANGLERS        STEANING     CU TRUCAGES
NU LANGUETS    GL GANGRELS                          TRANGLES     IR ANGRIEST     DE RESTAGED
NW TWANGLES    GR GRANGERS       AEGNRT  54      MS GARMENTS        ASTRINGE     DN GRANDEST
OR LEGATORS    GT GANGSTER       (GANTER)           MARGENTS        GANISTER     DO GOADSTER
OV VOLTAGES    HI HEARINGS       AI AERATING        RAGMENTS        GANTRIES     DR DRAGSTER
RU GAULTERS       HEARSING       AS STARAGEN     MU ARGUMENT        GRANITES     EE ETAGERES
   GESTURAL       SHEARING          TANAGERS     NO NEGATRON        INGRATES        STEERAGE
   TRAGULES    HS GNASHERS       AU RUNAGATE     NP PREGNANT        RANGIEST     EM GAMESTER
ST GESTALTS    IK SKEARING                       NY GANNETRY        REASTING        MEAGREST
UU GLUTAEUS    IL ARLESING                       OS ORANGEST
```

EN ESTRANGE
    GRANTEES
    GREATENS
    REAGENTS
    SEGREANT
    SERGEANT
    STERNAGE
ER REGRATES
ES RESTAGES
ET GREATEST
EU TREAGUES
EW STREWAGE
FI FRIGATES
FN ENGRAFTS
FR GRAFTERS
GI RAGGIEST
GL STRAGGLE
GN GANGSTER
GS GAGSTERS
    STAGGERS
HO SHORTAGE
IL GLARIEST
    REGALIST
IM MAGISTER
    MIGRATES
    RAGTIMES
    STERIGMA
IN ANGRIEST
    ASTRINGE
    GANISTER
    GANTRIES
    GRANITES
    INGRATES
    RANGIEST
    REASTING
    STEARING
IP GRAPIEST
IS AGISTERS
IT STRIGATE
IV VIRGATES
    VITRAGES
LN STRANGLE
    TANGLERS
    TRANGLES
LO LEGATORS
LU GAULTERS
    GESTURAL
    TRAGULES
MN GARMENTS
    MARGENTS
    RAGMENTS
NO ORANGEST
    RAGSTONE
NP TREPANGS
NR GRANTERS
    REGRANTS
    STRANGER
NU STRAUNGE
OO ROOTAGES
OP PORTAGES
OR GARROTES
OS STORAGES
OT GAROTTES
OU OUTRAGES
TY STRATEGY
UU AUGUSTER

AEHRST 169
(HATERS)
AE HETAERAS

AL TREHALAS
BC BRACHETS
BD BREADTHS
BE BREATHES
    HARTBEES
BG BARGHEST
BL BLATHERS
    HALBERTS
BO BATHORSE
BS BRASHEST
CC CATCHERS
    CRATCHES
CD STARCHED
CE CHEATERS
    HECTARES
    RECHATES
    RECHEATS
    TEACHERS
CF FRATCHES
CH HATCHERS
CI CHARIEST
    THERIACS
CL ARCHLETS
CM MATCHERS
CN CHANTERS
    SNATCHER
    STANCHER
    TRANCHES
CO CHAROSET
    THORACES
CP CHAPTERS
    PATCHERS
CR CHARTERS
    RECHARTS
    STARCHER
CS STARCHES
CT CHATTERS
    RATCHETS
CW WATCHERS
CY YACHTERS
DE HEADREST
DH THRASHED
DI HAIRSTED
    HARDIEST
DY HYDRATES
EF FEATHERS
EH HEATHERS
EI HEARTIES
EL HALTERES
    LEATHERS
EM ERATHEMS
EN HASTENER
    HEARTENS
EP PREHEATS
    SPREATHE
ET THEATERS
    THEATRES
EV THREAVES
EW WEATHERS
    WREATHES
FL FARTHELS
FS SHAFTERS
FT FARTHEST
GO SHORTAGE
HO HAROSETH
HR THRASHER
HS HARSHEST
    THRASHES
II HAIRIEST
IN INEARTHS

IO HOARIEST
IR TRASHIER
IS SHERIATS
IW SWATHIER
    WATERISH
IY HYSTERIA
KN THANKERS
LM THERMALS
LN ENTHRALS
LO LOATHERS
LS HARSLETS
    SLATHERS
MP HAMPSTER
MS HAMSTERS
MU MAUTHERS
MW MAWTHERS
NP PANTHERS
NU HAUNTERS
    UNEARTHS
    UNHEARTS
    URETHANS
OO TOHEROAS
OS ASTHORES
    HAROSETS
    HOARSEST
OT RHEOSTAT
OX THORAXES
PS SHARPEST
    SPARTHES
RU URETHRAS
RY TRASHERY
SS SHASTERS
ST SHATTERS
SV HARVESTS
TY SHATTERY
UU HAUTEURS

AEILMN 133
(MALINE)
AC ANALCIME
    CALAMINE
AH HIELAMAN
AT ALAIMENT
    LAMINATE
AV VELAMINA
BD MANDIBLE
BG EMBALING
BS BAILSMEN
BT BAILMENT
CE CAMELINE
CH INCHMEAL
CI LIMACINE
CN CLINAMEN
CP MANCIPLE
CS MESCALIN
DE ENDEMIAL
DF INFLAMED
DG MALIGNED
DI LIMNAEID
DP PLAIDMEN
DU UNMAILED
DY MAIDENLY
EG LIEGEMAN
EM MELAMINE
ET MELANITE
FR INFLAMER
    RIFLEMAN
FS FLAMINES
    INFLAMES
    MISFALNE

FT FILAMENT
GG GLEAMING
GP EMPALING
GR GERMINAL
    MALIGNER
    MALINGER
GS MEASLING
GT LIGAMENT
GU AEMULING
GY YEALMING
HY HYMENIAL
IN MAINLINE
IS ALIENISM
LS MANILLES
MS MELANISM
MT IMMANTLE
MY IMMANELY
NO MINNEOLA
NP IMPANNEL
NS LINESMAN
    MELANINS
OS MINEOLAS
    SEMOLINA
PS IMPANELS
    MANIPLES
RS MARLINES
    MINERALS
RT TERMINAL
RU LEMURIAN
SS ISLESMAN
ST AILMENTS
    ALIMENTS
    MANLIEST

AEILNT 11
(ENTAIL)
AC ANALCITE
    LAITANCE
AD DENTALIA
AE ALIENATE
AG AGENTIAL
    ALGINATE
AH ANTHELIA
AM ALAIMENT
    LAMINATE
AP PALATINE
AT ANTLIATE
AV AVENTAIL
BD BIDENTAL
BG BELATING
    BLEATING
    TANGIBLE
BM BAILMENT
BP PINTABLE
BS INSTABLE
BV BIVALENT
CC CANTICLE
CG CLEATING
CH CHAINLET
    ETHNICAL
CL CLIENTAL
CP ICEPLANT
    PECTINAL
    PLANETIC
CR CLARINET
DE ENTAILED
    LINEATED
DF INFLATED
DG DELATING
DO DELATION

DP PANTILED
DU UNTAILED
DV DIVALENT
EG GALENITE
    GELATINE
    LEGATINE
EL TENAILLE
EM MELANITE
EP PETALINE
    TAPELINE
ER ELATERIN
    ENTAILER
    TREENAIL
EV ELVANITE
    VENTAILE
FM FILAMENT
FO OLEFIANT
FS INFLATES
GG TEAGLING
GH ATHELING
GM LIGAMENT
GN GANTLINE
    LATENING
GO GELATION
    LEGATION
GP PLEATING
GR ALERTING
    ALTERING
    INTEGRAL
    RELATING
    TANGLIER
    TRIANGLE
GS EASTLING
    GELATINS
    GENITALS
    STEALING
GV VALETING
GX EXALTING
GZ TEAZLING
HL THALLINE
HX ANTHELIX
HZ ZENITHAL
IK KALINITE
IR INERTIAL
IS ALIENIST
    LITANIES
KS LANKIEST
MM IMMANTLE
MR TERMINAL
MS AILMENTS
    ALIMENTS
    MANLIEST
NR INTERNAL
NY INNATELY
OP ANTIPOLE
OR ORIENTAL
    RELATION
OS ELATIONS
    INSOLATE
    TOENAILS
OT TONALITE
PR TRIPLANE
PS PANTILES
    PLAINEST
RS ENTRAILS
    LATRINES
    RATLINES
    TRENAILS
RT RATTLINE
RU RETINULA

    TENURIAL
RV INTERVAL
RY INTERLAY
SS EASTLINS
    ELASTINS
    SALIENTS
    STANIELS
SU ALUNITES
    INSULATE
SV VENTAILS
SW LAWNIEST
VY NATIVELY
    VENALITY

AEILRS 16
(SAILER)
AB RAISABLE
AD SALARIED
AG GASALIER
    LAIRAGES
    REGALIAS
AO OLEARIAS
AS SALARIES
AU AURELIAS
BB SLABBIER
BC CALIBERS
    CALIBRES
BF BARFLIES
BH BLASHIER
BI BISERIAL
BL LIBERALS
BM REMBLAIS
BN RINSABLE
BT LIBRATES
CD DECRIALS
    RADICELS
    RADICLES
CE ESCALIER
CF FILACERS
CG GLACIERS
CH CHARLIES
CM CLAIMERS
    MIRACLES
    RECLAIMS
CN CARLINES
CO CALORIES
    CARIOLES
CP CALIPERS
    REPLICAS
    SPIRACLE
CS CLASSIER
CT ALTRICES
    ARTICLES
    RECITALS
    SELICTAR
CU AURICLES
CV CALIVERS
    CLAVIERS
    VISCERAL
DD DIEDRALS
DE REALISED
    SIDEREAL
DG SLAIRGED
DI LAIRISED
DL DALLIERS
    DIALLERS
DN ISLANDER
DO DARIOLES
    SOLIDARE
    SOREDIAL

```
DP PEDRAILS      LS RAILLESS      AP PARIETAL      GY REGALITY      BL BASTILLE         FRAILEST
   PREDIALS      LT LITERALS      AR ARTERIAL      HO AEROLITH      BM BALMIEST      FU FISTULAE
DT DILATERS         TALLIERS      AV VARIETAL         LOATHIER         TIMBALES      FV FESTIVAL
   LARDIEST      LU RUELLIAS      BD LIBRATED      HY HEARTILY      BN INSTABLE      FW FLATWISE
DU RESIDUAL      LY SERIALLY      BE LIBERATE      IN INERTIAL      BP EPIBLAST         FLAWIEST
DY DIALYSER      MM SMALMIER      BP PARTIBLE      IP LIPARITE      BR LIBRATES      FX FLAXIEST
EF SERAFILE      MN MARLINES      BS LIBRATES      IS LAIRIEST      BS ASTILBES      GH LAIGHEST
EG GASELIER         MINERALS      BW WRITABLE      IT LITERATI         BESTIALS      GL LEGALIST
EH SHIRALEE      MO MORALISE      CD ARTICLED      KS LARKIEST         STABILES         STILLAGE
EL REALLIES      MP IMPEARLS      CK TALCKIER         STALKIER      BU SUITABLE         TILLAGES
EM ALMERIES         LEMPIRAS      CM METRICAL         STARLIKE      BY BEASTILY      GN EASTLING
   MEASLIER      MR LARMIERS      CN CLARINET      LS LITERALS      CC CALCITES         GELATINS
EP ESPALIER      MS REALISMS      CO EROTICAL      LU TAILLEUR      CD CITADELS         GENITALS
   PEARLIES      MT LAMITERS         LORICATE      MM TRILEMMA         DIALECTS         STEALING
ER REALISER         MARLIEST      CP PARTICLE      MN TERMINAL      CG GELASTIC      GO OTALGIES
ES REALISES      MY SMEARILY         PRELATIC      MS LAMITERS      CH ETHICALS      GR GLARIEST
ET ATELIERS      NO AILERONS      CR CLARTIER         MARLIEST      CI SILICATE         REGALIST
   EARLIEST         ALERIONS      CS ALTRICES      MT REMITTAL      CM CALMIEST      GZ GLAZIEST
   LEARIEST         ALIENORS         ARTICLES      NN INTERNAL         CLEMATIS      HI HAILIEST
   REALTIES      NP PEARLINS         RECITALS      NO ORIENTAL         CLIMATES      HS SHALIEST
EV VELARISE         PRALINES         SELICTAR         RELATION         METICALS      HT LATHIEST
EY YEARLIES      NR SNARLIER      CT TRACTILE      NP TRIPLANE      CO ALOETICS         LITHATES
EZ REALIZES      NS RAINLESS      CV VERTICAL      NS ENTRAILS         COALIEST      HY HYALITES
   SLEAZIER      NT ENTRAILS      CY LITERACY         LATRINES         SOCIETAL      IL TAILLIES
FH FLASHIER         LATRINES      DE RETAILED         RATLINES      CP PLICATES      IN ALIENIST
FO FORESAIL         RATLINES      DO IDOLATER         TRENAILS      CR ALTRICES         LITANIES
FT FLARIEST         TRENAILS         TAILORED      NT RATTLINE         ARTICLES      IR LAIRIEST
   FRAILEST      NU LUNARIES      DP DIPTERAL      NU RETINULA         RECITALS      IS SAILIEST
FU FAILURES      NV RAVELINS         TRIPEDAL         TENURIAL         SELICTAR      IV VITALISE
FV FAVRILES      NX RELAXINS      DS DILATERS      NV INTERVAL      CS ELASTICS      IX LAXITIES
FZ FILAZERS      NY INLAYERS         LARDIEST      NY INTERLAY         SALICETS      IZ TAILZIES
GG SLAGGIER         SNAILERY      DT DETRITAL      OP EPILATOR         SCALIEST      KN LANKIEST
GM GREMIALS      OP PELORIAS      DY DIELYTRA         PETIOLAR      CT LATTICES      KO KEITLOAS
   LAMIGERS         POLARISE      EF FRAILTEE      OS SOTERIAL      CY CLAYIEST      KR LARKIEST
   REGALISM      OS SOLARISE      EH ETHERIAL      OT LITERATO      DE LEADIEST         STALKIER
GN ARLESING      OT SOTERIAL      EM EREMITAL      PR PALTRIER      DG GLADIEST         STARLIKE
   ENGRAILS      OV OVERSAIL         MATERIEL      PS PILASTER      DI IDEALIST      LP PALLIEST
   NARGILES         VALORISE         REALTIME         PLAISTER      DM MISDEALT         PASTILLE
   REALIGNS         VARIOLES      EN ELATERIN         PLAITERS      DO DIASTOLE      LR LITERALS
   SANGLIER         VOLARIES         ENTAILER      QU QUARTILE         ISOLATED         TALLIERS
   SLANGIER      OY ROYALISE         TREENAIL         REQUITAL         SODALITE      LS TAILLESS
GO GASOLIER      OZ SOLARIZE      EO AEROLITE      RS RETIRALS         SOLIDATE      LW WALLIEST
   GIRASOLE      PP APPERILS      EP PEARLITE         RETRIALS      DP TALIPEDS      MN AILMENTS
   SERAGLIO      PR REPRISAL      ER RETAILER         TRAILERS      DR DILATERS         ALIMENTS
GS GLASSIER      PT PILASTER      ES ATELIERS      RY LITERARY         LARDIEST         MANLIEST
GT GLARIEST         PLAISTER         EARLIEST      SS REALISTS      DV VALIDEST      MO LOAMIEST
   REGALIST         PLAITERS         LEARIEST         SALTIERS      DY DIASTYLE      MP IMPLATES
GY GREASILY      PV PREVAILS         REALTIES         SALTIRES         STEADILY         PALMIEST
GZ GLAZIERS      PW SLIPWARE      ET LATERITE         SLAISTER      EF FEALTIES         PALMIEST
HN INHALERS      QU SQUAILER         LITERATE      ST TERTIALS         LEAFIEST         PETALISM
HO AIRHOLES      RT RETIRALS      EV LEVIRATE      SU URALITES      EG ELEGIAST         SEPTIMAL
   SHOALIER         RETRIALS         RELATIVE      TY ALTERITY      EK LEAKIEST      MR LAMITERS
HP PLASHIER         TRAILERS      FO FLOATIER      UZ LAZURITE      EL LEALTIES         MARLIEST
HS HAIRLESS      RU RURALISE      FS FLARIEST      VV TRIVALVE      EM MEALIEST      MT MALTIEST
HU HAULIERS      ST REALISTS         FRAILEST                      EP EPILATES         SMALTITE
HV LAVISHER         SALTIERS      FT FILTRATE      AEILST  24       ER ATELIERS      MU SIMULATE
   SHRIEVAL         SALTIRES         FILATURE      (ALITES)            EARLIEST      MY LAYTIMES
IL RAILLIES         SLAISTER      GH LITHARGE      AB BALISTAE         LEARIEST         STEAMILY
IN AIRLINES      SV REVISALS         THIRLAGE         LABIATES         REALTIES      NO ELATIONS
   SNAILIER         RIVALESS      GN ALERTING         SATIABLE      ES ASTELIES         INSOLATE
IS LAIRISES      TT TERTIALS         ALTERING      AC SALICETA      ET AILETTES         TOENAILS
IT LAIRIEST      TU URALITES         INTEGRAL      AP STAPELIA      EV ELATIVES      NP PANTILES
IV RIVALISE      VV REVIVALS         RELATING      AV AESTIVAL         LEAVIEST         PLAINEST
IZ LAIRIZES      VY VIRELAYS         TANGLIER         SALIVATE         VEALIEST      NR ENTRAILS
KS SERKALIS                          TRIANGLE      AX SAXATILE      FI FILIATES         LATRINES
KT LARKIEST      AEILRT  10       GS GLARIEST      BB BISTABLE      FK FLAKIEST         RATLINES
   STALKIER      (RETAIL)            REGALIST      BI ALBITISE      FM FLAMIEST         TRENAILS
   STARLIKE      AC TAILRACE      GT AGLITTER         SIBILATE      FN INFLATES      NS EASTLINS
KV KLAVIERS      AL ARILLATE      GU LIGATURE      BK BALKIEST      FO FOLIATES         ELASTINS
LR RALLIERS      AM MATERIAL                                       FR FLARIEST         SALIENTS
```

```
   STANIELS
NU ALUNITES
   INSULATE
NV VENTAILS
NW LAWNIEST
OP SPOLIATE
OR SOTERIAL
OS ISOLATES
OT TOTALISE
OV VIOLATES
PR PILASTER
   PLAISTER
   PLAITERS
PS PALSIEST
PT PLATIEST
PY PTYALISE
QU LIQUATES
   TEQUILAS
RR RETIRALS
   RETRIALS
   TRAILERS
RS REALISTS
   SALTIERS
   SALTIRES
   SLAISTER
RT TERTIALS
RU URALITES
ST SALTIEST
   SLATIEST
SW SWALIEST
TW WALTIEST
VY VILAYETS

AEIMNR 61
(REMAIN)
AD MARINADE
AP PEARMAIN
AT MARINATE
AZ MAZARINE
BD BRIDEMAN
BG BREAMING
BS MIRBANES
CG AMERCING
   CREAMING
CH CHAIRMEN
CO CORAMINE
CS CARMINES
CU MANICURE
DE REMAINED
DG DREAMING
   MARGINED
DI MERIDIAN
DR MANRIDER
DS ADERMINS
   SIRNAMED
DY DAIRYMEN
DZ ZEMINDAR
EG GERMAINE
ES REMANIES
EX EXAMINER
FL INFLAMER
   RIFLEMAN
GI IMAGINER
   MIGRAINE
GK REMAKING
GL GERMINAL
   MALIGNER
   MALINGER
GN ENARMING
   RENAMING
```


```
GP EMPARING
GR REARMING
GS GERMAINS
   SMEARING
GT EMIGRANT
GU GERANIUM
HS HARMINES
   SHIREMAN
KS RAMEKINS
LS MARLINES
   MINERALS
LT TERMINAL
LU LEMURIAN
NS REINSMAN
OS MORAINES
OW AIRWOMEN
OZ ARMOZINE
PT TRIPEMAN
QU RAMEQUIN
RS MARINERS
RV RIVERMAN
SS SEMINARS
   SIRNAMES
ST MINARETS
   RAIMENTS
SU ANEURISM
SY SEMINARY
TT MARTINET
TU RUMINATE
TW WARIMENT
TY TYRAMINE

AEIMNS 98
(MANIES)
AA ANAEMIAS
AC AMNESIAC
AG MAGNESIA
AS AMNESIAS
AT AMENTIAS
   ANIMATES
BG BEAMINGS
BL BAILSMEN
BR MIRBANES
   EMBASING
BT AMBIENTS
CH MACHINES
CL MESCALIN
CP PEMICANS
CR CARMINES
CS AMNESICS
CT SEMANTIC
CU SEMUNCIA
CY SYCAMINE
DE DEMAINES
   INSEAMED
DM MISNAMED
DO NOMADIES
   NOMADISE
DR ADERMINS
   SIRNAMED
DS SIDESMAN
DT MEDIANTS
DU MAUNDIES
DY DYNAMISE
ER REMANIES
ES NEMESIAS
ET MATINEES
   SEMINATE
EX EXAMINES
FI INFAMIES
```


```
   INFAMISE
FL FLAMINES
   INFLAMES
   MISFALNE
FT MANIFEST
GI IMAGINES
GL MEASLING
GN MEANINGS
GR GERMAINS
   SMEARING
GT MANGIEST
   MINTAGES
   STEAMING
   TEAMINGS
GV VEGANISM
HR HARMINES
   SHIREMAN
HS SHAMISEN
HU HUMANISE
IL ALIENISM
IT MINIATES
JS JASMINES
KR RAMEKINS
KT MANKIEST
   MISTAKEN
LL MANILLES
LM MELANISM
LN LINESMAN
   MELANINS
LO MINEOLAS
   SEMOLINA
LP IMPANELS
   MANIPLES
LR MARLINES
   MINERALS
LS ISLESMAN
LT AILMENTS
   ALIMENTS
   MANLIEST
MS MISNAMES
NR REINSMAN
NT MANNITES
OR MORAINES
OU MOINEAUS
OW WOMANISE
RR MARINERS
RS SEMINARS
   SIRNAMES
RT MINARETS
   RAIMENTS
RU ANEURISM
RY SAMISENS
SS SAMISENS
ST MANTISES
SU ANIMUSES
SZ MAZINESS
UV MAUVEINS
   MAUVINES

AEIMNT 53
(INMATE)
AD ANIMATED
   DIAMANTE
AH ANTHEMIA
   HAEMATIN
AL ALAIMENT
   LAMINATE
AO METANOIA
AP IMPANATE
AR MARINATE
```


```
AS AMENTIAS
   ANIMATES
BL BAILMENT
BS AMBIENTS
CG MAGNETIC
CS SEMANTIC
DE DEMENTIA
DI MINIATED
DO DOMINATE
   NEMATOID
DS MEDIANTS
DY DYNAMITE
EG GEMINATE
EL MELANITE
EM MEANTIME
ES MATINEES
   SEMINATE
FL FILAMENT
FS MANIFEST
GL LIGAMENT
GN ENTAMING
GR EMIGRANT
GS MANGIEST
   MINTAGES
   STEAMING
   TEAMINGS
HI THIAMINE
HU INHUMATE
IS MINIATES
IT INTIMATE
IU MINUTIAE
IV VITAMINE
KS MANKIEST
   MISTAKEN
LM IMMANTLE
LR TERMINAL
LS AILMENTS
   ALIMENTS
   MANLIEST
MN IMMANENT
MO AMMONITE
NO NOMINATE
NS MANNITES
OP PTOMAINE
OZ MONAZITE
PR TRIPEMAN
RS MINARETS
   RAIMENTS
RT MARTINET
RU RUMINATE
RW WARIMENT
RY TYRAMINE
SS MANTISES
TU MATUTINE
VZ VIZAMENT

AEIMRS 112
(ARMIES)
AC MACARISE
   MESARAIC
AU URAEMIAS
BD EMBRAIDS
BG GAMBIERS
BJ JAMBIERS
BL REMBLAIS
BN MIRBANES
BT BARMIEST
BU AUMBRIES
CC CERAMICS
CE RACEMISE
```


```
CG GRIMACES
CH CHASMIER
   CHIMERAS
   MARCHESI
CK KERAMICS
CL CLAIMERS
   MIRACLES
   RECLAIMS
CM RACEMISM
CN CARMINES
CT CERAMIST
   MATRICES
DD DISARMED
   MISDREAD
DE MADERISE
DF MISFARED
DH MISHEARD
DJ JEMIDARS
DM MERMAIDS
DN ADERMINS
   SIRNAMED
DR ADMIRERS
   DISARMER
DS MISREADS
   SIDEARMS
DT MARDIEST
   MISRATED
   READMITS
EG GAMESIER
EL ALMERIES
   MEASLIER
EN REMANIES
EP EMPAIRES
ER SMEARIER
ES SERIEMAS
ET EMIRATES
   REAMIEST
   STEAMIER
FI RAMIFIES
FR FIREARMS
FS MISFARES
GL GREMIALS
   LAMIGERS
   REGALISM
GN GERMAINS
   SMEARING
GO GORAMIES
GP EPIGRAMS
   PRIMAGES
GR ARMIGERS
GS GISARMES
GT MAGISTER
   MIGRATES
   RAGTIMES
   STERIGMA
HN HARMINES
   SHIREMAN
HP SAMPHIRE
   SERAPHIM
HR MARSHIER
HS MARISHES
   MISHEARS
IT AIRTIMES
   SERIATIM
KN RAMEKINS
KP RAMPIKES
LM SMALMIER
LN MARLINES
   MINERALS
LO MORALISE
```


```
LP IMPEARLS
   LEMPIRAS
LR LARMIERS
LS REALISMS
LT LAMITERS
   MARLIEST
LY SMEARILY
MP SPAMMIER
MR SMARMIER
MT MARMITES
NN REINSMAN
NO MORAINES
NR MARINERS
NS SEMINARS
   SIRNAMES
NT MINARETS
   RAIMENTS
NU ANEURISM
NY SEMINARY
OR ARMOIRES
   ARMORIES
OT AMORTISE
   ATOMISER
PR RAMPIRES
PS IMPRESAS
   SAMPIRES
PT PRIMATES
PV VAMPIRES
PW SWAMPIER
QU MARQUISE
RR MARRIERS
RS SIMARRES
ST ASTERISM
   MAISTERS
   MISRATES
   SEMITARS
   SMARTIES
SY EMISSARY
TT MISTREAT
   TERATISM
TU MURIATES
   SEMITAUR
TW WARTIMES
TX MATRIXES
TY SYMITARE
WW SWIMWEAR

AEIMST 95
(MATIES)
AD DIASTEMA
AM IMAMATES
AN AMENTIAS
   ANIMATES
BC BETACISM
BE BEAMIEST
BG MEGABITS
BH IMBATHES
BL BALMIEST
   TIMBALES
BN AMBIENTS
BR BARMIEST
CE EMICATES
CH MISTEACH
   TACHISME
CJ MAJESTIC
CL CALMIEST
   CLEMATIS
   CLIMATES
   METICALS
CN SEMANTIC
```

```
CP CAMPIEST
   CAMPSITE
CR CERAMIST
   MATRICES
CS ETACISMS
DD MISDATED
DE MEDIATES
DG SIGMATED
DL MISDEALT
DM MISMATED
DN MEDIANTS
DO ATOMISED
DP DAMPIEST
   IMPASTED
DR MARDIEST
   MISRATED
   READMITS
DS MISDATES
DU TAEDIUMS
DY DAYTIMES
EL MEALIEST
EN MATINEES
   SEMINATE
ER EMIRATES
   REAMIEST
   STEAMIER
ES SEAMIEST
   STEAMIES
ET ESTIMATE
   ETATISME
   MEATIEST
   TEATIMES
EW TEAMWISE
FL FLAMIEST
FN MANIFEST
FO FOAMIEST
GM GAMMIEST
GN MANGIEST
   MINTAGES
   STEAMING
   TEAMINGS
GP PIGMEATS
GR MAGISTER
   MIGRATES
   RAGTIMES
   STERIGMA
GS SIGMATES
GU GAUMIEST
HM HAMMIEST
HP MATESHIP
   SHIPMATE
HS THEISMS
   MASHIEST
   MATHESIS
IN MINIATES
IR AIRTIMES
   SERIATIM
IT IMITATES
JM JAMMIEST
KN MANKIEST
   MISTAKEN
KS MISTAKES
KW MAWKIEST
LN AILMENTS
   ALIMENTS
   MANLIEST
LO LOAMIEST
LP IMPLATES
   PALMIEST
   PALMIETS

   PETALISM
   SEPTIMAL
LR LAMITERS
   MARLIEST
LT MALTIEST
LU SIMULATE
LY LAYTIMES
MP PSAMMITE
MR MARMITES
MS MISMATES
NN MANNIEST
NR MINARETS
   RAIMENTS
NS MANTISES
OR AMORTISE
   ATOMISER
OS AMITOSES
   AMOSITES
   ATOMISES
OZ ATOMIZES
PR PRIMATES
PS IMPASTES
   PASTIMES
RS ASTERISM
   MAISTERS
   MISRATES
   SEMITARS
   SMARTIES
RT MISTREAT
   TERATISM
RU MURIATES
   SEMITAUR
RW WARTIMES
RX MATRIXES
RY SYMITARE
SS ASTEISMS
   MASSIEST
ST MASTIEST
   MISSTATE
SZ MESTIZAS
YZ AZYMITES

AEINRS   6
(SARNIE)
AC CANARIES
AD ARANEIDS
AG ANGARIES
AP PANARIES
AT ANTISERA
   ARTESIAN
   RESINATA
BC CARBINES
BD BRANDIES
   BRANDISE
BG BEARINGS
   SABERING
BI BINARIES
BK BEARSKIN
   INBREAKS
BL RINSABLE
BM MIRBANES
BO BARONIES
BT ATEBRINS
   BANISTER
BU ANBURIES
   URBANISE
CE CINEREAS

   INCREASE
   RESIANCE
CF FANCIERS
CG CREASING
   GRECIANS
CH INARCHES
CI RIANCIES
CL CARLINES
CM CARMINES
CN CRANNIES
CO SCENARIO
CS ARSENICS
   CERASINS
   RACINESS
CT CANISTER
   CARNIEST
   NACRITES
   SCANTIER
DE ARSENIDE
   DENARIES
   DRAISENE
   NEARSIDE
DF FRIANDES
DG DERAIGNS
   GRADINES
   READINGS
DI DRAISINE
DL ISLANDER
DM ADERMINS
   SIRNAMED
DN INSNARED
DO ANEROIDS
   DONARIES
DP SPRAINED
DR DRAINERS
   SERRANID
DS ARIDNESS
   SARDINES
DT DETRAINS
   RANDIEST
   STRAINED
DU DENARIUS
   UNRAISED
   URANIDES
DV INVADERS
   SANDIVER
DY SYNEDRIA
EG GESNERIA
EH INHEARSE
EK SNEAKIER
EM REMANIES
EN ANSERINE
EP NAPERIES
ER REARISEN
ES SENARIES
ET ARSENITE
   RESINATE
   STEARINE
   TRAINEES
EU UNEASIER
FO FARINOSE
FP FIREPANS
FR REFRAINS
FS FAIRNESS
   SANSERIF
FT FENITARS
FX XERAFINS
GG GEARINGS
   GREASING

   SNAGGIER
GH HEARINGS
   HEARSING
   SHEARING
GK SKEARING
GL ARLESING
   ENGRAILS
   NARGILES
   REALIGNS
   SANGLIER
   SLANGIER
GM GERMAINS
   SMEARING
GN AGINNERS
   EARNINGS
   ENGRAINS
   GRANNIES
GO IGNAROES
   ORGANISE
   ORIGANES
GP PREASING
   SPEARING
GR EARRINGS
   GRAINERS
GS REASSIGN
   SEARINGS
   SERINGAS
GT ANGRIEST
   ASTRINGE
   GANISTER
   GANTRIES
   GRANITES
   INGRATES
   RANGIEST
   REASTING
   STEARING
GV VINEGARS
GW SWEARING
   WEARINGS
GY RESAYING
HL INHALERS
HM HARMINES
   SHIREMAN
HP HEPARINS
   PARISHEN
   SERAPHIN
HR SHARNIER
HS ARSHINES
HT INEARTHS
HV ENRAVISH
   VANISHER
IK KAISERIN
IL AIRLINES
   SNAILIER
IN SIRENIAN
IS AIRINESS
IT INERTIAS
   RAINIEST
IY YERSINIA
JT NARTJIES
KM RAMEKINS
KT KERATINS
   NARKIEST
KW SWANKIER
LM MARLINES
   MINERALS
LO AILERONS
   ALERIONS
   ALIENORS
LP PEARLINS

   PRALINES
LR SNARLIER
LS RAINLESS
LT ENTRAILS
   LATRINES
   RATLINES
   TRENAILS
LU LUNARIES
LV RAVELINS
LX RELAXINS
LY INLAYERS
   SNAILERY
MN REINSMAN
MO MORAINES
MR MARINERS
MS SEMINARS
   SIRNAMES
MT MINARETS
   RAIMENTS
MU ANEURISM
MY SEMINARY
NO RAISONNE
NP PANNIERS
NS INSNARES
NT ENTRAINS
   TRANNIES
NU ANEURINS
   UNARISEN
NW SWANNIER
OS ERASIONS
OT ANOESTRI
   ARSONITE
   NOTARIES
   NOTARISE
   ROSINATE
OV AVERSION
PP SNAPPIER
PT PAINTERS
   PANTRIES
   PERTAINS
   PINASTER
   REPAINTS
PU UNPRAISE
RT RESTRAIN
   RETRAINS
   STRAINER
   TERRAINS
   TRAINERS
   TRANSIRE
ST RESIANTS
   RETSINAS
   SNARIEST
   STAINERS
   STARNIES
SU SENARIUS
SW WARINESS
SX XERANSIS
TT INTREATS
   NITRATES
   STRAITEN
   TARTINES
   TERTIANS
TU RUINATES
   URANITES
   URINATES
TW TINWARES
UV VAURIENS
UZ AZURINES
   SUZERAIN

VV VERVAINS
ZZ SNAZZIER

AEINRT   1
(RETAIN)
AB RABATINE
AC CARINATE
AD DENTARIA
AG AERATING
AM MARINATE
AO AERATION
AS ANTISERA
   ARTESIAN
   RESINATA
AT REATTAIN
AU INAURATE
BG BERATING
   REBATING
BO BARITONE
   OBTAINER
BS ATEBRINS
   BANISTER
BU URBANITE
CD CRINATED
   DICENTRA
CE CENTIARE
   CREATINE
   INCREATE
   ITERANCE
CG CATERING
   CITRANGE
   CREATING
   REACTING
CL CLARINET
CO ANORETIC
   CREATION
   REACTION
CS CANISTER
   CARNIEST
   NACRITES
   SCANTIER
CT INTERACT
CV NAVICERT
CX XERANTIC
DD INDARTED
DE DETAINER
   RETAINED
DG DERATING
   GRADIENT
DI DAINTIER
DO AROINTED
   DERATION
   ORDINATE
   RATIONED
DP DIPTERAN
DS DETRAINS
   RANDIEST
   STRAINED
DT NITRATED
DU DATURINE
   INDURATE
   RUINATED
   URINATED
EH ATHERINE
EK ANKERITE
   KREATINE
EL ELATERIN
   ENTAILER
   TREENAIL
```

```
EP APERIENT      NR INERRANT      BO BOTANIES      FN INFANTES         ALIMENTS         URANITES
ER RETAINER      NS ENTRAINS         BOTANISE      FR FENITARS         MANLIEST         URINATES
ES ARSENITE         TRANNIES         NIOBATES      FT FAINTEST      LO ELATIONS      RW TINWARES
   RESINATE      OP ATROPINE         OBEISANT      GG NAGGIEST         INSOLATE      SS SAINTESS
   STEARINE      OR ANTERIOR      BP BEPAINTS      GH GAHNITES         TOENAILS         SESTINAS
   TRAINEES      OS ANOESTRI      BR ATEBRINS         HEATINGS      LP PANTILES      ST INSTATES
FI FAINTIER         ARSONITE         BANISTER      GL EASTLING         PLAINEST         NASTIEST
FS FENITARS         NOTARIES      BS BASINETS         GELATINS      LR ENTRAILS         SATINETS
GH EARTHING         NOTARISE         BASSINET         GENITALS         LATRINES      TT NATTIEST
   HEARTING         ROSINATE         BESAINTS         STEALING         RATLINES      TV TASTEVIN
GK RETAKING      OT TENTORIA         BESTAINS      GM MANGIEST         TRENAILS      TW TAWNIEST
GL ALERTING      OZ NOTARIZE      BT TABINETS         MINTAGES      LS EASTLINS      WY YAWNIEST
   ALTERING      PR TERRAPIN      CD DISTANCE         STEAMING         ELASTINS
   INTEGRAL      PS PAINTERS      CE CINEASTE         TEAMINGS         SALIENTS      AEIPRS  75
   RELATING         PANTRIES      CF FANCIEST      GN ANTIGENS         STANIELS      (PRAISE)
   TANGLIER         PERTAINS      CH ASTHENIC         GENTIANS      LU ALUNITES      AC AIRSPACE
   TRIANGLE         PINASTER         CHANTIES         STEANING         INSULATE      AD PARADISE
GM EMIGRANT         REPAINTS      CI CANITIES      GR ANGRIEST      LV VENTAILS      AG IGARAPES
GP TAPERING      PT TRIPTANE      CM SEMANTIC         ASTRINGE      LW LAWNIEST      AI APIARIES
GS ANGRIEST      PU PAINTURE      CN ANCIENTS         GANISTER      MN MANNITES      AN PANARIES
   ASTRINGE      PX EXPIRANT         CANNIEST         GANTRIES      MR MINARETS      AP APPRAISE
   GANISTER      QU QUAINTER         INSTANCE         GRANITES         RAIMENTS      AR PAREIRAS
   GANTRIES      RS RESTRAIN      CO ACONITES         INGRATES      MS MANTISES      AS SPIRAEAS
   GRANITES         RETRAINS         CANOEIST         RANGIEST      NO ENATIONS      AT ASPIRATE
   INGRATES         STRAINER      CR CANISTER         REASTING      NP PANTINES         PARASITE
   RANGIEST         TERRAINS         CARNIEST         STEARING      NR ENTRAINS         SEPTARIA
   REASTING         TRAINERS         NACRITES      GS EASTINGS         TRANNIES      BE BEPRAISE
   STEARING         TRANSIRE         SCANTIER         GENISTAS      NS INSANEST      CC CAPRICES
GT ARETTING      RV VERATRIN      CS CINEASTS         GIANTESS      NT ANTIENTS      CD EPACRIDS
   TREATING      RW INTERWAR         SCANTIES         SEATINGS         STANNITE      CG SPAGERIC
GV AVERTING      SS RESIANTS      CT CANTIEST         TEASINGS      OP SAPONITE      CH CHARPIES
   TAVERING         RETSINAS         NICTATES         TSIGANES      OR ANOESTRI         PARCHESI
   VINTAGER         SNARIEST      CV CISTVAEN      GT ESTATING         ARSONITE         SERAPHIC
GW TWANGIER         STAINERS         VESICANT         TANGIEST         NOTARIES      CI PIRACIES
   WATERING         STARNIES      CY CYANITES      GU SAUTEING         NOTARISE      CK EARPICKS
HP PERIANTH         STEARINS      DD DANDIEST      GV VINTAGES         ROSINATE      CL CALIPERS
HS INEARTHS      ST INTREATS      DE ANDESITE      GW SWEATING      OS ASSIENTO         REPLICAS
HU HAURIENT         NITRATES      DG SEDATING      GY YEASTING      OV STOVAINE         SPIRACLE
HW TARWHINE         STRAITEN         STEADING      HP PENTHIAS      OX SAXONITE      CP EPICARPS
IL INERTIAL         TARTINES      DH HANDIEST         THESPIAN      PP NAPPIEST      CR PERISARC
IP PAINTIER         TERTIANS      DI ADENITIS      HR INEARTHS      PR PAINTERS      CS SCRAPIES
IS INERTIAS      SU RUINATES         DAINTIES      HS ANTHESIS         PANTRIES      CT CRAPIEST
   RAINIEST         URANITES      DM MEDIANTS         SHANTIES         PERTAINS         CRISPATE
JS NARTJIES         URINATES      DO ASTONIED      HT HESITANT         PINASTER         PICRATES
JU JAUNTIER      SW TINWARES         SEDATION      HW INSWATHE         REPAINTS         PRACTISE
KS KERATINS      TU TAINTURE      DP DEPAINTS      IK KAINITES      PT PATIENTS      DD DISPREAD
   NARKIEST                       DR DETRAINS      IL ALIENIST      PU PETUNIAS      DG SPAIRGED
KW KNITWEAR      AEINST   2          RANDIEST         LITANIES         SUPINATE      DH RAPHIDES
LM TERMINAL      (SATINE)            STRAINED      IM MINIATES      PY EPINASTY      DI PRESIDIA
LN INTERNAL      AB BASANITE      DS SANDIEST      IP PIANISTE      QU ANTIQUES      DL PEDRAILS
LO ORIENTAL      AC ESTANCIA      DT INSTATED      IR INERTIAS         QUANTISE         PREDIALS
   RELATION      AG SAGINATE      DU AUDIENTS         RAINIEST      RR RESTRAIN      DN SPRAINED
LP TRIPLANE      AH ASTHENIA         SINUATED      IS ISATINES         RETRAINS      DO DIASPORE
LS ENTRAILS      AM AMENTIAS      DV DEVIANTS         SANITIES         STRAINER         PARODIES
   LATRINES         ANIMATES      DY DESYATIN         SANITISE         TERRAINS      DP APPRISED
   RATLINES      AR ANTISERA      EG SAGENITE      IV VANITIES         TRAINERS         DRAPPIES
   TRENAILS         ARTESIAN      EM MATINEES      IX AXINITES         TRANSIRE      DR DRAPIERS
LT RATTLINE         RESINATA         SEMINATE      IZ SANITIZE      RS RESIANTS      DS DESPAIRS
LU RETINULA      AT ASTATINE      ER ARSENITE      JR NARTJIES         RETSINAS      DT RAPIDEST
   TENURIAL         SANITATE         RESINATE      JT JANTIEST         SNARIEST         SPIRATED
LV INTERVAL         TANAISTE         STEARINE      JU JAUNTIES         STAINERS         TRAIPSED
LY INTERLAY      AV SANATIVE         TRAINEES      KL LANKIEST         STARNIES      DU UPRAISED
MP TRIPEMAN      BC CABINETS      ET ANISETTE      KM MANKIEST         STEARINS      EG PIERAGES
MS MINARETS      BD BANDIEST         TETANIES         MISTAKEN      RT INTREATS      EL ESPALIER
   RAIMENTS      BE BETAINES         TETANISE      KR KERATINS         NITRATES         PEARLIES
MT MARTINET      BG BEATINGS      EV NAIVETES         NARKIEST         STRAITEN      EM EMPAIRES
MU RUMINATE      BH ABSINTHE      FG FEASTING      KS SNAKIEST         TARTINES      EN NAPERIES
MW WARIMENT      BK BEATNIKS      FI FAINITES      KV KISTVAEN         TERTIANS      ER PEREIRAS
MY TYRAMINE      BL INSTABLE      FL INFLATES      KY KYANITES      RU RUINATES         SPEARIER
NO INORNATE      BM AMBIENTS      FM MANIFEST      LM AILMENTS                       ET PETARIES
```

```
FF PIAFFERS
FN FIREPANS
GK GARPIKES
GM EPIGRAMS
   PRIMAGES
GN PREASING
   SPEARING
GS PRISAGES
   SPAIRGES
GT GRAPIEST
HL PLASHIER
HM SAMPHIRE
   SERAPHIM
HN HEPARINS
   PARISHEN
   SERAPHIN
HO APHORISE
HP PAPISHER
   SAPPHIRE
HR PHRASIER
HS PARISHES
   SHARPIES
IR PRAIRIES
IT PARITIES
IW PAIRWISE
KM RAMPIKES
KT PARKIEST
LM IMPEARLS
   LEMPIRAS
LN PEARLINS
   PRALINES
LO PELORIAS
   POLARISE
LP APPERILS
LR REPRISAL
LT PILASTER
   PLAISTER
   PLAITERS
LV PREVAILS
LW SLIPWARE
MM SPAMMIER
MR RAMPIRES
MS IMPRESAS
   SAMPIRES
MT PRIMATES
MV VAMPIRES
MW SWAMPIER
NN PANNIERS
NP SNAPPIER
NT PAINTERS
   PANTRIES
   PERTAINS
   PINASTER
   REPAINTS
NU UNPRAISE
OV VAPORISE
PS APPRISES
PT PERIAPTS
PZ APPRIZES
RS PRAISERS
RY SPRAYIER
ST PASTRIES
   PIASTRES
   RASPIEST
   TRAIPSES
SU UPRAISES
SV PARVISES
TV PRIVATES
TW WIRETAPS
TY ASPERITY
```


```
VY VESPIARY
XY PYREXIAS

AEIRST   3
(SATIRE)
AD DATARIES
   RADIATES
AN ANTISERA
   ARTESIAN
   RESINATA
AP ASPIRATE
   PARASITE
   SEPTARIA
AS ASTERIAS
   ATRESIAS
AT ARIETTAS
AV VARIATES
BD BARDIEST
   BRAIDEST
   RABIDEST
   TRIBADES
BK BARKIEST
   BRAKIEST
   BREASKIT
BL LIBRATES
BM BARMIEST
BN ATEBRINS
   BANISTER
BO SABOTIER
BR ARBITERS
   RAREBITS
BT BIRETTAS
BV VIBRATES
BW WARBIEST
BY BESTIARY
   SYBARITE
CD ACRIDEST
CG AGRESTIC
CH CHARIEST
   THERIACS
CL ALTRICES
   ARTICLES
   RECITALS
CM CERAMIST
   MATRICES
CN CANISTER
   CARNIEST
   NACRITES
   SCANTIER
CP CRAPIEST
   CRISPATE
   PICRATES
   PRACTISE
CR ERRATICS
CS SCARIEST
CT CITRATES
   CRISTATE
   SCATTIER
CU SURICATE
CZ CRAZIEST
DD DISRATED
DE READIEST
   SERIATED
   STEADIER
DH HAIRSTED
   HARDIEST
DI IRISATED
DK STRAIKED
```


```
DL DILATERS
   LARDIEST
DM MARDIEST
   MISRATED
   READMITS
DN DETRAINS
   RANDIEST
   STRAINED
DO ASTEROID
DP RAPIDEST
   SPIRATED
   TRAIPSED
DS ASTERIDS
   DIASTERS
   DISASTER
   DISRATES
DT STRAITED
   STRIATED
   TARDIEST
DW TAWDRIES
EE EATERIES
EH HEARTIES
EL ATELIERS
   EARLIEST
   LEARIEST
   REALTIES
EM EMIRATES
   REAMIEST
   STEAMIER
EN ARSENITE
   RESINATE
   STEARINE
   TRAINEES
EO ETAERIOS
EP PETARIES
ER ARTERIES
   REASTIER
ES SERIATES
   ITERATES
   TEARIEST
   TREATIES
   TREATISE
EV EVIRATES
EW SWEATIER
   TAWERIES
   WEARIEST
EY YEASTIER
FG FRIGATES
FI RATIFIES
FL FLARIEST
   FRAILEST
FN FENITARS
FR FRATRIES
GG RAGGIEST
GL GLARIEST
   REGALIST
GM MAGISTER
   MIGRATES
   RAGTIMES
   STERIGMA
GN ANGRIEST
   ASTRINGE
   GANISTER
   GANTRIES
   GRANITES
   INGRATES
   RANGIEST
   REASTING
   STEARING
```


```
GP GRAPIEST
GS AGISTERS
GT STRIGATE
GV VIRGATES
   VITRAGES
HI HAIRIEST
HN INEARTHS
HO HOARIEST
HR TRASHIER
HS SHERIATS
HW SWATHIER
   WATERISH
HY HYSTERIA
IL LAIRIEST
IM AIRTIMES
   SERIATIM
IN INERTIAS
   RAINIEST
IP PARITIES
IR RARITIES
IS IRISATES
   SATIRISE
IV VAIRIEST
IW WISTERIA
IZ SATIRIZE
JN NARTJIES
JO JAROSITE
KL LARKIEST
   STALKIER
   STARLIKE
KN KERATINS
   NARKIEST
KP PARKIEST
KS ASTERISK
   SARKIEST
LL LITERALS
   TALLIERS
LM LAMITERS
   MARLIEST
LN ENTRAILS
   LATRINES
   RATLINES
   TRENAILS
LO SOTERIAL
LP PILASTER
   PLAISTER
   PLAITERS
LR RETIRALS
   RETRIALS
   TRAILERS
LS REALISTS
   SALTIERS
   SALTIRES
   SLAISTER
LT TERTIALS
LU URALITES
MM MARMITES
MN MINARETS
   RAIMENTS
MO AMORTISE
   ATOMISER
MP PRIMATES
MS ASTERISM
   MAISTERS
   MISRATES
   SEMITARS
   SMARTIES
MT MISTREAT
   TERATISM
MU MURIATES
```


```
   SEMITAUR
MW WARTIMES
MX MATRIXES
MY SYMITARE
NN ENTRAINS
   TRANNIES
NO ANOESTRI
   ARSONITE
   NOTARIES
   NOTARISE
   ROSINATE
NP PAINTERS
   PANTRIES
   PERTAINS
   PINASTER
   REPAINTS
NR RESTRAIN
   RETRAINS
   STRAINER
   TERRAINS
   TRAINERS
   TRANSIRE
NS RESIANTS
   RETSINAS
   SNARIEST
   STAINERS
NT INTREATS
   NITRATES
   STRAITEN
   TARTINES
   TERTIANS
NU RUINATES
   URANITES
   URINATES
NW TINWARES
OR ROARIEST
   ROTARIES
OV VOTARIES
PP PERIAPTS
PS PASTRIES
   PIASTRES
   RASPIEST
   TRAIPSES
PV PRIVATES
PW WIRETAPS
PY ASPERITY
RR STARRIER
RS TARRIERS
RT RETRAITS
   STRAITER
   TARRIEST
RW STRAWIER
   SWARTIER
SS TIRASSES
ST ARTISTES
   ARTSIEST
   STRIATES
SV TRAVISES
SW WAISTERS
   WAITRESS
   WASTRIES
TT RATTIEST
   TARTIEST
   TITRATES
TW WARTIEST
TX EXTRAITS
UZ AZURITES
```


```
VY VESTIARY

AEIRTT   29
(ATTIRE)
AN REATTAIN
AP PATRIATE
AS ARIETTAS
   ARISTATE
AZ ZARATITE
BC BRATTICE
BE BATTERIE
BR BRATTIER
BS BIRETTAS
BY YTTERBIA
CD TETRACID
   TETRADIC
CF TRIFECTA
CH CHATTIER
   THEATRIC
CL TRACTILE
CM TREMATIC
CN INTERACT
CR RETRAICT
CS CITRATES
   CRISTATE
   SCATTIER
CU URTICATE
CV TRACTIVE
DE ITERATED
DL DETRITAL
DN NITRATED
DO TERATOID
DS STRIATED
   STRIATED
   TARDIEST
DT TITRATED
EG AIGRETTE
EL LATERITE
   LITERATE
ER RETRAITE
ES ARIETTES
   ITERATES
   TEARIEST
   TREATIES
   TREATISE
FL FILTRATE
GL AGLITTER
GN ARETTING
   TREATING
GS STRIGATE
HP THREAPIT
IL LITERATI
IR IRRITATE
IT TRITIATE
LM REMITTAL
LN RATTLINE
LO LITERATO
LS LITERATS
LY ALTERITY
MN MARTINET
MO AMORETTI
MS MISTREAT
   TERATISM
NO TENTORIA
NP TRIPTANE
NS INTREATS
   NITRATES
   STRAITEN
   TARTINES
   TERTIANS
```

NU TAINTURE	STEATITE	**AELNRS 63**	HP SHRAPNEL	ES ALTERNES	BY ABSENTLY
OV ROTATIVE	EV AVIETTES	(LANERS)	HT ENTHRALS	EV LEVANTER	CD SCANTLED
RS RETRAITS	ESTIVATE	AD ADRENALS	II AIRLINES	RELEVANT	CE CLEANEST
STRAITER	EVITATES	AG ALNAGERS	SNAILIER	EX EXTERNAL	LATENCES
TARRIEST	FN FAINTEST	AK LARNAKES	IM MARLINES	FU FLAUNTER	CH STANCHEL
RT RETRAITT	FT FATTIEST	AP PRENASAL	MINERALS	GI ALERTING	CO LACTONES
RY TERTIARY	GN ESTATING	AS ARSENALS	IO AILERONS	ALTERING	CP CLAPNETS
SS ARTISTES	TANGIEST	AY ANALYSER	ALERIONS	INTEGRAL	CS SCANTLES
ARTSIEST	GO GOATIEST	BE ENABLERS	ALIENORS	RELATING	CT CANTLETS
STRIATES	GR STRIGATE	BG BRANGLES	IP PEARLINS	TANGLIER	DH SHETLAND
ST RATTIEST	GS STAGIEST	BI RINSABLE	PRALINES	TRIANGLE	DU UNSALTED
TARTIEST	HL LATHIEST	BS BRANSLES	IR SNARLIER	GS STRANGLE	DW WETLANDS
TITRATES	LITHATES	BT BRANTLES	IS RAINLESS	TANGLERS	EE SELENATE
SW WARTIEST	HN HESITANT	BY BLARNEYS	IT ENTRAILS	TRANGLES	EK KANTELES
SX EXTRAITS	HS ATHEISTS	CE CLEANERS	LATRINES	HL ENTHRALL	EM MANTEELS
	HASTIEST	CLEANSER	RATLINES	HS ENTHRALS	TALESMEN
AEISTT 83	STAITHES	CG CLANGERS	TRENAILS	II INERTIAL	ER ALTERNES
(TASTIE)	HW THAWIEST	CH CHARNELS	IU LUNARIES	IM TERMINAL	ES LATENESS
AD SATIATED	THWAITES	CI CARLINES	IV RAVELINS	IN INTERNAL	EY ENTAYLES
AG AGITATES	IM IMITATES	CK CRANKLES	IX RELAXINS	IO ORIENTAL	FI INFLATES
AN ASTATINE	IV VITIATES	CN SCRANNEL	IY INLAYERS	RELATION	FS FLATNESS
SANITATE	JN JANTIEST	CU LUCARNES	SNAILERY	IP TRIPLANE	FT FLATTENS
TANAISTE	LM MALTIEST	DD DANDLERS	KP PRANKLES	IS ENTRAILS	GI EASTLING
AP APATITES	SMALTITE	DG DANGLERS	LO LLANEROS	LATRINES	GELATINS
AR ARIETTAS	LO TOTALISE	GLANDERS	MO ALMONERS	RATLINES	GENITALS
ARISTATE	LP PLATIEST	DH HANDLERS	MP LAMPERNS	TRENAILS	STEALING
AS SATIATES	LR TERTIALS	DI ISLANDER	MU MENSURAL	IT RATTLINE	GO TANGELOS
BN TABINETS	LS SALTIEST	DL LANDLERS	NUMERALS	IU RETINULA	GP SPANGLET
BR BIRETTAS	SLATIEST	DM MANDRELS	NP PLANNERS	TENURIAL	GR STRANGLE
BS BATISTES	LW WALTIEST	DO LADRONES	NS ENSNARLS	IV INTERVAL	TANGLERS
BT BATTIEST	MR MISTREAT	SOLANDER	NT LANTERNS	IY INTERLAY	TRANGLES
CC ECSTATIC	TERATISM	DP SPANDREL	NU UNLEARNS	NS LANTERNS	GT GANTLETS
CD DICTATES	MS MASTIEST	DS SLANDERS	OP PERSONAL	NU UNLEARNT	GU LANGUETS
CH CHATTIES	MISSTATE	DU LAUNDERS	OU ALEURONS	OT TETRONAL	GW TWANGLES
TACHISTE	NN ANTIENTS	LURDANES	OV VERONALS	TOLERANT	HO ETHANOLS
CK TACKIEST	STANNITE	RUNDALES	PT PANTLERS	OU OUTLEARN	HR ENTHRALS
TIETACKS	NP PATIENTS	EG ENLARGES	PLANTERS	OY ORNATELY	HS NATHLESS
CL LATTICES	NR INTREATS	GENERALS	REPLANTS	PS PANTLERS	HY NAYTHLES
CN CANTIEST	NITRATES	GLEANERS	PU PURSLANE	PLANTERS	II ALIENIST
NICTATES	STRAITEN	ER LEARNERS	SUPERNAL	REPLANTS	LITANIES
CO OSCITATE	TARTINES	ES REALNESS	RS SNARLERS	PY PLENARTY	IK LANKIEST
CR CITRATES	TERTIANS	ET ALTERNES	ST SALTERNS	RY ERRANTLY	IM AILMENTS
CRISTATE	NS INSTATES	EV ENSLAVER	TT SLATTERN	SS SALTERNS	ALIMENTS
SCATTIER	NASTIEST	EW RENEWALS	TRENTALS	ST SLATTERN	MANLIEST
CT CATTIEST	NT NATTIEST	FK FLANKERS	TU NEUTRALS	TRENTALS	IO ELATIONS
SATINETS	NV TASTEVIN	FO FARNESOL	TV VENTRALS	SU NEUTRALS	INSOLATE
CU EUSTATIC	NW TAWNIEST	FS SALFERNS	UV UNRAVELS	SV VENTRALS	TOENAILS
DN INSTATED	OS TOASTIES	FU FLANEURS	VY SYLVANER		IP PANTILES
DR STRAITED	PS PASTIEST	FUNERALS	XY LARYNXES	**AELNST 34**	PLAINEST
STRIATED	RR RETRAITS	GG GANGRELS		(ANTLES)	IR ENTRAILS
TARDIEST	STRAITER	GI ARLESING	**AELNRT 28**	AB BANALEST	LATRINES
DS DISTASTE	TARRIEST	ENGRAILS	(ANTLER)	AC ANALECTS	RATLINES
STAIDEST	RS ARTISTES	NARGILES	AC LACERANT	AD EASTLAND	TRENAILS
DU SITUATED	ARTSIEST	REALIGNS	AM MATERNAL	AK ALKANETS	IS EASTLINS
EH ATHETISE	STRIATES	SANGLIER	AP PARENTAL	KANTELAS	ELASTINS
HESITATE	RT RATTIEST	SLANGIER	PATERNAL	AM TALESMAN	SALIENTS
EL AILETTES	TARTIEST	GJ JANGLERS	PRENATAL	AP PLATANES	STANIELS
EM ESTIMATE	TITRATES	GL LANGRELS	AT ALTERANT	PLEASANT	IU ALUNITES
ETATISME	RW WARTIEST	GM MANGLERS	ALTERNAT	AS SEALANTS	INSULATE
MEATIEST	RX EXTRAITS	GP GRAPNELS	AX RELAXANT	AZ ZEALANTS	IV VENTAILS
TEATIMES	ST TASTIEST	SPANGLER	BE RENTABLE	BD BLANDEST	IW LAWNIEST
EN ANISETTE	SU SITUATES	SPRANGLE	BS BRANTLES	BI INSTABLE	LM STALLMEN
TETANIES	SV VASTIEST	GT STRANGLE	CI CLARINET	BK BLANKEST	LS TALLNESS
TETANISE	TT TATTIEST	TANGLERS	DE ANTLERED	BLANKETS	LT TALLENTS
EP PEATIEST	TU ATTUITES	TRANGLES	DY ARDENTLY	BL NETBALLS	MO SALMONET
ER ARIETTES	TW TAWTIEST	GU GRANULES	EH LEATHERN	BM SEMBLANT	MT MANTLETS
ITERATES		GW WANGLERS	EI ELATERIN	BO NEOBLAST	MU NUTMEALS
TEARIEST		WRANGLES	ENTAILER	NOTABLES	NR LANTERNS
TREATIES		GY LARYNGES	TREENAIL	BR BRANTLES	NS STANNELS
TREATISE		HI INHALERS	EN LANNERET	BU UNSTABLE	NU ANNULETS
ET ETATISTE					

OP LAPSTONE
   PLEONAST
   POLENTAS
OV VOLANTES
PR PANTLERS
   PLANTERS
   REPLANTS
PX EXPLANTS
RS SALTERNS
RT SLATTERN
   TRENTALS
RU NEUTRALS
RV VENTRALS
SS SALTNESS
SY STANYELS
UV ENVAULTS

AELORS 42
   (ALORES)
AI OLEARIAS
AU AUREOLAS
BT BLOATERS
   SORTABLE
   STORABLE
BU RUBEOLAS
BV ABSOLVER
CC CORACLES
CE ESCAROLE
CF ALFRESCO
CH CHOLERAS
   CHORALES
CI CALORIES
   CARIOLES
CJ CAJOLERS
CK EARLOCKS
CL CORELLAS
CM CAROMELS
   SCLEROMA
CP PARCLOSE
   POLACRES
CS ESCOLARS
   LACROSSE
CT SECTORAL
CU CAROUSEL
CY CALOYERS
   COARSELY
DI DARIOLES
   SOLIDARE
   SOREDIAL
DL ODALLERS
DM EARLDOMS
DN LADRONES
   SOLANDER
DP LEOPARDS
DS ROADLESS
DT DELATORS
   LEOTARDS
   LODESTAR
DU ROULADES
EH ARSEHOLE
EP PAROLEES
ER RELEASOR
ET OLEASTER
EU AUREOLES
FH FAHLORES
FI FORESAIL
FN FARNESOL
FS SAFROLES
FT FLOATERS
   FORESTAL

   REFLOATS
FU FUSAROLE
FY FORELAYS
GI GASOLIER
   GIRASOLE
   SERAGLIO
GL ALLEGROS
GM GOMERALS
GP PERGOLAS
GT LEGATORS
GU GLAREOUS
HI AIRHOLES
   SHOALIER
HM ARMHOLES
HT LOATHERS
HY HOARSELY
IM MORALISE
IN AILERONS
   ALERIONS
   ALIANORS
IP PELORIAS
   POLARISE
IS SOLARISE
IT SOTERIAL
IV OVERSAIL
   VALORISE
   VARIOLES
   VOLARIES
IY ROYALISE
IZ SOLARIZE
KW SALEWORK
KY ROKELAYS
LN LLANEROS
LP REPOSALL
LS ROSELLAS
LT REALLOTS
LV OVERALLS
LW SALLOWER
MN ALMONERS
MP PLEROMAS
MT MOLERATS
MU RAMULOSE
MV REMOVALS
NP PERSONAL
NU ALEURONS
NV VERONALS
OS AEROSOLS
   ROSEOLAS
PP PROLAPSE
   PROPALES
   SAPROPEL
PS REPOSALS
PT PETROSAL
   PROLATES
PU LEAPROUS
PV OVERLAPS
RT REALTORS
   RELATORS
TU ROSULATE
TV LEVATORS
TY ROYALETS
UU ROULEAUS
VY OVERLAYS

AELOST 46
   (SOLATE)
AC CATALOES
AM OATMEALS
AX OXALATES
BC OBSTACLE

BN NEOBLAST
   NOTABLES
BP POTABLES
BR BLOATERS
   SORTABLE
   STORABLE
BU ABSOLUTE
BW BESTOWAL
CC CACOLETS
CG CATELOGS
CH ESCHALOT
CI ALOETICS
   COALIEST
   SOCIETAL
CL COLLATES
CM CAMELOTS
   MOLECAST
CN LACTONES
CP POLECATS
CR SECTORAL
CS ALECOSTS
   COATLESS
   LACTOSES
   SCATOLES
CT CALOTTES
CU LACTEOUS
CY ACOLYTES
DE DESOLATE
DI DIASTOLE
   ISOLATED
   SODALITE
   SOLIDATE
DP TADPOLES
DR DELATORS
   LEOTARDS
   LODESTAR
DV SOLVATED
EG SEGOLATE
ER OLEASTER
FG FLOTAGES
FI FOLIATES
FL FLOATELS
FR FLOATERS
   FORESTAL
   REFLOATS
FT FALSETTO
GI OTALGIES
GL TOLLAGES
GN TANGELOS
GR LEGATORS
GV VOLTAGES
HN ETHANOLS
HR LOATHERS
HS SHOALEST
HT LOATHEST
IK KEITLOAS
IM LOAMIEST
IN ELATIONS
   INSOLATE
   TOENAILS
IP SPOLIATE
IR SOTERIAL
IS ISOLATES
IT TOTALISE
IV VIOLATES
KS SKATOLES
   STALKOES
LR REALLOTS

MN SALMONET
MR MOLERATS
MS MALTOSES
MT MATELOTS
MY ATMOLYSE
NP LAPSTONE
   PLEONAST
   POLENTAS
NV VOLANTES
PR PETROSAL
   PROLATES
PS APOSTLES
PT PALETOTS
PU OUTLEAPS
   PETALOUS
RR REALTORS
   RELATORS
RU ROSULATE
RV LEVATORS
RY ROYALETS
SV SOLVATES
SY ASYSTOLE
TU TOLUATES
UV OVULATES
UY AUTOLYSE

AELRST 38
   (ALTERS)
AB ARBALEST
AE LAETARES
AG AGRESTAL
AH TREHALAS
AL LATERALS
AP PALESTRA
AZ LAZARETS
BE BLEAREST
   BLEATERS
   RETABLES
BH BLATHERS
   HALBERTS
BI LIBRATES
BM LAMBERTS
BN BRANTLES
BO BLOATERS
   SORTABLE
   STORABLE
BS BLASTERS
   STABLERS
BT BATTLERS
   BLATTERS
   BRATTLES
BU BALUSTER
BW BLEWARTS
CE CLEAREST
   SCELERAT
   TREACLES
CH ARCHLETS
CI ALTRICES
   ARTICLES
   RECITALS
   SELICTAR
CK TACKLERS
CO SECTORAL
CP SCEPTRAL
   SPECTRAL
CS SCARLETS
CT CLATTERS
   SCRATTLE
CU RAUCLEST
DD STRADDLE

DE TREADLES
DI DILATERS
   LARDIEST
DO DELATORS
   LEOTARDS
   LODESTAR
DT STARTLED
EE TEASELER
EF REFLATES
EH HALTERES
   LEATHERS
EI ATELIERS
   EARLIEST
   LEARIEST
   REALTIES
EM LAMETERS
EN ALTERNES
EO OLEASTER
EP PRELATES
ER RELATERS
ES STEALERS
   TEARLESS
   TESSERAL
ET ALERTEST
EU RESALUTE
EY EASTERLY
FH FARTHELS
FI FLARIEST
   FRAILEST
FO FLOATERS
   FORESTAL
   REFLOATS
FT FATTRELS
   FLATTERS
FU REFUTALS
GG STRAGGLE
GI GLARIEST
   REGALIST
GN STRANGLE
   TANGLERS
   TRANGLES
GO LEGATORS
GU GAULTERS
   GESTURAL
   TRAGULES
HM THERMALS
HN ENTHRALS
HO LOATHERS
HS HARSLETS
   SLATHERS
II LAIRIEST
IK LARKIEST
   STALKIER
IL LITERALS
   TALLIERS
IM LAMITERS
   MARLIEST
IN ENTRAILS
   LATRINES
   RATLINES
   TRENAILS
IO SOTERIAL
IP PILASTER
   PLAISTER
   PLAITERS
IR RETIRALS
   RETRIALS
   TRAILERS
IS REALISTS

   SALTIERS
   SALTIRES
   SLAISTER
IT TERTIALS
IU URALITES
KP SPARKLET
KS STALKERS
LO REALLOTS
MM STRAMMEL
   TRAMMELS
MO MOLERATS
MP TRAMPLES
MT MALTSTER
   MARTLETS
MY MASTERLY
NN LANTERNS
NP PANTLERS
   PLANTERS
   REPLANTS
NS SALTERNS
NT SLATTERN
   TRENTALS
NU NEUTRALS
NV VENTRALS
OP PETROSAL
   PROLATES
OR REALTORS
   RELATORS
OU ROSULATE
OV LEVATORS
OY ROYALETS
PS PLASTERS
   PSALTERS
   STAPLERS
PT PARTLETS
   PLATTERS
   PRATTLES
   SPLATTER
   SPRATTLE
PU APLUSTRE
PY PLASTERY
   PSALTERY
RT RATTLERS
   STARTLER
RW TRAWLERS
SS STARLESS
ST SLATTERS
   STARLETS
   STARTLES
SU SALUTERS
SW WARTLESS
   WASTRELS
TT TARTLETS
   TATTLERS
TU LUSTRATE
   TUTELARS
TY SLATTERY
UV VAULTERS
   VESTURAL
WZ WALTZERS

AEMNST 168
   (STAMEN)
AC CAMSTANE
AD MANDATES
AE EMANATES
AG MAGENTAS
   MAGNATES
AI AMENTIAS

	ANIMATES	RV VARMENTS	IO AMORTISE	EP PENTANES	IR PAINTERS	ST TRANTERS

```
        ANIMATES      RV VARMENTS     IO AMORTISE     EP PENTANES     IR PAINTERS     ST TRANTERS
AL TALESMAN      RW TRANSMEW        ATOMISER     ES NEATNESS        PANTRIES
AR SARMENTA         TREWSMAN     IP PRIMATES     FI INFANTES        PERTAINS     AENRST    8
   SEMANTRA      WY WAYMENTS     IS ASTERISM     FU UNFASTEN        PINASTER     (ANTERS)
AS NAMASTES                         MAISTERS     GH HANGNEST        REPAINTS     AB ANTBEARS
AU MANTEAUS      AEMRST 124          MISRATES     GI ANTIGENS     IT PATIENTS        RATSBANE
BE BASEMENT      (MATERS)            SEMITARS        GENTIANS     IU PETUNIAS     AC CANASTER
BI AMBIENTS      AF FERMATAS         SMARTIES        STEANING        SUPINATE        CATERANS
BL SEMBLANT      AN SARMENTA     IT MISTREAT     GO TONNAGES     IY EPINASTY     AE ARSENATE
CE CASEMENT         SEMANTRA         TERATISM     GT TANGENTS     LO LAPSTONE        SERENATA
CH MANCHETS      AU MURIATES     IU MURIATES     GU TUNNAGES        PLEONAST     AG STARAGEN
CI SEMANTIC      BI BARMIEST         SEMITAUR     IM MANNITES        POLENTAS     AI ANTISERA
CK TACKSMEN      BL LAMBERTS     IW WARTIMES     IO ENATIONS     LR PANTLERS        ARTESIAN
CO CAMSTONE      BO BROMATES     IX MATRIXES     IP PANTINES        PLANTERS        RESINATA
DE STAMENED      CE CERAMETS     IY SYMITARE     IR ENTRAINS        REPLANTS     AJ NAARTJES
DI MEDIANTS         CREMATES     LM STRAMMEL        TRANNIES     LX EXPLANTS     AM SARMENTA
EE EASEMENT         MEERCATS         TRAMMELS     IS INSANEST     MS ENSTAMPS        SEMANTRA
EH METHANES      CH MATCHERS     LO MOLERATS     IT ANTIENTS        PASSMENT     AO ANOESTRA
EI MATINEES      CI CERAMIST     LP TRAMPLES        STANNITE     MY PAYMENTS     AR NARRATES
   SEMINATE         MATRICES     LT MALTSTER     LR LANTERNS     NN PENNANTS     AT TARTANES
EL MANTEELS      CJ SCRAMJET         MARTLETS     LS STANNELS     NO PENTOSAN     AV TAVERNAS
   TALESMEN      CP CRAMPETS     LY MASTERLY     LU ANNULETS     OO TEASPOON        TSAREVNA
ER REMANETS      DE MASTERED     MO MARMOSET     MR MANRENTS     OR OPERANTS     BD BANDSTER
ES TAMENESS         STREAMED     MS STAMMERS        REMNANTS        PRONATES     BG BANGSTER
EU MANSUETE      DI MARDIEST     NN MANRENTS     NP PENNANTS     PR PARPENTS     BI ATEBRINS
FI MANIFEST         MISRATED         REMNANTS     OP PENTOSAN     RR PARTNERS        BANISTER
FR RAFTSMEN         READMITS     NO MONSTERA     OR RESONANT     RS PASTERNS     BL BRANTLES
GI MANGIEST      DO STROAMED         STOREMAN     OU TONNEAUS     RT PATTERNS     BO BARONETS
   MINTAGES      DP STRAMPED     NS SARMENTS     QU QUANNETS        TRANSEPT     BU UNBRASTE
   STEAMING      EG GAMESTER         SMARTENS     RT ENTRANTS     RU PERSAUNT        URBANEST
   TEAMINGS         MEAGREST     NU ANESTRUM     RY TYRANNES     SU PESAUNTS     CD CANTREDS
GO MAGNETOS      EH ERATHEMS         MENSTRUA                    SW STEWPANS     CE REASCENT
   MEGATONS      EI EMIRATES         TRANSUME     AENPST 185      SY SYNAPTES        SARCENET
   MONTAGES         REAMIEST     NV VARMENTS     (PATENS)        SZ SPETSNAZ     CF CANTREFS
GR GARMENTS         STEAMIER     NW TRANSMEW     AA ANAPAEST     ZZ SPETZNAZ     CH CHANTERS
   MARGENTS      EK MEERKATS         TREWSMAN     AC PASTANCE                        SNATCHER
   RAGMENTS      EL LAMETERS     OR REARMOST     AG PAGEANTS     AENRRT 87          STANCHER
GU AUGMENTS      EM AMMETERS     OS MAESTROS     AH PHEASANT     (RANTER)           TRANCHES
   MUTAGENS         METAMERS     OV OVERMAST     AL PLATANES     AB ABERRANT     CI CANISTER
HO HOASTMEN      EN REMANETS     PR TRAMPERS        PLEASANT     AD NARRATED        CARNIEST
HU HUMANEST      EO EROTEMAS     PS STAMPERS     AS ANAPESTS     AS NARRATES        NACRITES
II MINIATES      EP TEMPERAS     PT TRAMPETS        PEASANTS     BE BANTERER        SCANTIER
IK MANKIEST      ER STREAMER     PU TEMPURAS     AT ANTEPAST     CE RECANTER     CK CRANKEST
   MISTAKEN      ES MASSETER        UPSTREAM     AY PEASANTY        RECREANT     CO ANCESTOR
IL AILMENTS         SEAMSTER     ST MATTRESS     BI BEPAINTS     DU UNTARRED        ENACTORS
   ALIMENTS         STEAMERS         SMARTEST     CD PANDECTS     EG ETRANGER        SARCONET
   MANLIEST      ET TEAMSTER         SMATTERS     CL CLAPNETS     EI RETAINER        SORTANCE
IN MANNITES      EY METAYERS     SY MAYSTERS     CO CAPSTONE     ES TERRANES     CS CRANTSES
IR MINARETS      FN RAFTSMEN     TU MATUREST     CT PENTACTS     EV TAVERNER     CT TRANECTS
   RAIMENTS      FO FOREMAST         TESTAMUR     DI DEPAINTS     FS TRANSFER        TRANSECT
IS MANTISES         FORMATES                     DN PENDANTS     GS GRANTERS     CU CENTAURS
LL STALLMEN      GI MAGISTER     AENNST 152      EH HEPTANES        REGRANTS        RECUSANT
LO SALMONET         MIGRATES     (ANNETS)           PHENATES        STRANGER        UNCRATES
LT MANTLETS         RAGTIMES     AD ANDANTES        STEPHANE     IN INERRANT        UNTRACES
LU NUTMEALS         STERIGMA     AG TANNAGES     EN PENTANES     IO ANTERIOR     CY ANCESTRY
NR MANRENTS      GN GARMENTS     AN ANTENNAS     GL SPANGLET     IP TERRAPIN     DD STRANDED
   REMNANTS         MARGENTS     AT STANNATE     GO PONTAGES     IS RESTRAIN     DG GRANDEST
OR MONSTERA         RAGMENTS        TANNATES     GR TREPANGS        RETRAINS     DI DETRAINS
   STOREMAN      HL THERMALS     AU NAUSEANT     HI PENTHIAS        STRAINER        RANDIEST
OU NOTAEUMS      HP HAMPSTER     AV VENTANAS        THESPIAN        TERRAINS        STRAINED
   OUTNAMES      HS HAMSTERS     BG BANTENGS     HO PHAETONS        TRAINERS     DO TORNADES
   SEAMOUNT      HU MAUTHERS     CD SCANDENT        PHONATES        TRANSIRE     DS STANDERS
PS ENSTAMPS      HW MAWTHERS     CE CANTEENS        STANHOPE     IV VERATRIN     DU DAUNTERS
   PASSMENT      II AIRTIMES     CH ENCHANTS     HR PANTHERS     IW INTERWAR        TRANSUDE
PY PAYMENTS      IL LAMITERS     CI ANCIENTS     II PIANISTE     LY ERRANTLY        UNTREADS
RS SARMENTS         MARLIEST        CANNIEST     IL PANTILES     OO RATOONER     DX DEXTRANS
   SMARTENS      IM MARMITES        INSTANCE        PLAINEST     OS ANTRORSE     EE SERENATE
RU ANESTRUM      IN MINARETS     DP PENDANTS     IN PANTINES     PS PARTNERS     EF FASTENER
   MENSTRUA         RAIMENTS     DU ASTUNNED     IO SAPONITE     QU QUARTERN        FENESTRA
   TRANSUME                      EO NEONATES     IP NAPPIEST     RY ERRANTRY
```

```
EG ESTRANGE    IM MINARETS    PR PARTNERS    OS ORNATEST    OR ORNATEST    DU OUTDARES
   GRANTEES       RAIMENTS    PS PASTERNS    OX TETRAXON    PR PATTERNS    DX EXTRADOS
   GREATENS    IN ENTRAINS    PT PATTERNS    OY ATTORNEY       TRANSEPT    EI ETAERIOS
   REAGENTS       TRANNIES       TRANSEPT    PS PATTERNS    QU QUESTANT    EK KERATOSE
   SEGREANT    IO ANOESTRI    PU PERSAUNT       TRANSEPT    RR TRANTERS       KREASOTE
   SERGEANT       ARSONITE    RT TRANTERS    RS TRANTERS    RS TARTNESS    EL OLEASTER
   STERNAGE       NOTARIES    SS SARSNETS    SS TARTNESS    RU TAUNTERS    EM EROTEMAS
EH HASTENER       NOTARISE    ST TARTNESS    SU TAUNTERS    SU TAUTNESS    EN RESONATE
   HEARTENS       ROSINATE    SU ANESTRUS                      UNSTATES    EP OPERATES
EI ARSENITE    IP PAINTERS       SAUNTERS    AENSTT 116     SX SEXTANTS       PROTEASE
   RESINATE       PANTRIES    SV SERVANTS    (ATTENS)                      EV OVEREATS
   STEARINE       PERTAINS       VERSANTS    AC CANTATES    AEORST  13     FF AFFOREST
   TRAINEES       PINASTER    TU TAUNTERS    AG STAGNATE    (ORATES)       FL FLOATERS
EJ SERJEANT       REPAINTS    UV VAUNTERS    AI ASTATINE    AB RABATOES       FORESTAL
EL ALTERNES    IR RESTRAIN    UW UNWATERS       SANITATE    AN ANOESTRA       REFLOATS
EM REMANETS       RETRAINS    WY STERNWAY       TANAISTE    AR AERATORS    FM FOREMAST
EO RESONATE       STRAINER                   AN STANNATE    AT AEROSTAT       FOREMOST
ER TERRANES       TERRAINS    AENRTT  71        TANNATES    BD BROADEST       FORMATES
ES ASSENTER       TRAINERS    (NATTER)       AP ANTEPAST    BE REBATOES    FP FOREPAST
   EARNESTS       TRANSIRE    AC REACTANT    AR TARTANES    BH BATHORSE    FW FORWASTE
   SARSENET    IS RESIANTS    AD TARTANED    BI TABINETS    BI SABOTIER       SOFTWARE
ET ENTREATS       RETSINAS    AI REATTAIN    CH ETCHANTS    BL BLOATERS    FY FORESTAY
   RATTEENS       SNARIEST    AL ALTERANT    CI CANTIEST       SORTABLE    GH SHORTAGE
EV AVENTRES       STAINERS       ALTERNAT       NICTATES       STORABLE    GL LEGATORS
   VETERANS       STARNIES    AM ATRAMENT    CL CANTLETS    BM BROMATES    GN ORANGEST
FG ENGRAFTS       STEARINS    AS TARTANES    CO CONSTATE    BN BARONETS       RAGSTONE
FI FENITARS    IT INTREATS    BO BETATRON    CP PENTACS     BP PROBATES    GO ROOTAGES
FK FRANKEST       NITRATES    CH TRANCHET    CR TRANECTS    BR ARBORETS    GP PORTAGES
FM RAFTSMEN       STRAITEN    CI INTERACT       TRANSECT       TABORERS    GR GARROTES
FR TRANSFER       TARTINES    CO CONTRATE    CS SCANTEST    BS BOASTERS    GS STORAGES
GG GANGSTER       TERTIANS    CS TRANECTS    DI INSTATED       SORBATES    GT GAROTTES
GI ANGRIEST    IU RUINATES       TRANSECT    DU UNSTATED    BT ABETTORS    GU OUTRAGES
   ASTRINGE       URANITES    CU TRUNCATE       UNTASTED       BATTEROS    HH HAROSETH
   GANISTER       URINATES    DE ATTENDER    EG TENTAGES       TABORETS    HI HOARIEST
   GANTRIES    IW TINWARES    DI NITRATED    EI ANISETTE    BU SABOTEUR    HL LOATHERS
   GRANITES    KS STARKENS    DO ATTORNED       TETANIES    CC ECTOSARC    HO TOHEROAS
   INGRATES    KZ KRANTZES    DU TRUANTED       TETANISE    CD REDCOATS    HS ASTHORES
   RANGIEST    LN LANTERNS    DY TYRANTED    ER ENTREATS    CE CREASOTE       HAROSETS
   REASTING    LP PANTLERS    EE ENTERATE       RATTEENS    CF FORECAST       HOARSEST
   STEARING       PLANTERS    EF FATTENER    EV NAVETTES    CG ESCARGOT    HT RHEOSTAT
GL STRANGLE       REPLANTS    EH HATERENT    FI FAINTEST    CH CHAROSET    HX THORAXES
   TANGLERS    LS SALTERNS       THREATEN    FL FLATTENS       THORACES    IJ JAROSITE
   TRANGLES    LT SLATTERN    ES ENTREATS    GI ESTATING    CL SECTORAL    IL SOTERIAL
GM GARMENTS       TRENTALS       RATTEENS       TANGIEST    CN ANCESTOR    IM AMORTISE
   MARGENTS    LU NEUTRALS    EV ANTEVERT    GN TANGENTS       ENACTORS       ATOMISER
   RAGMENTS    LV VENTRALS    EX EXTERNAT    GU GAUNTEST       SARCONET    IN ANOESTRI
GO ORANGEST    MN MANRENTS    EY ENTREATY       TUTENAGS       SORTANCE       ARSONITE
   RAGSTONE       REMNANTS    GI ARETTING    HI HESITANT    CR ACROTERS       NOTARIES
GP TREPANGS    MO MONSTERA       TREATING    HS THATNESS       CREATORS       NOTARISE
GR GRANTERS       STOREMAN    GO TETRAGON    IJ JANTIEST       REACTORS       ROSINATE
   REGRANTS    MS SARMENTS    IL RATTLINE    IN ANTIENTS    CS COARSEST    IR ROARIEST
   STRANGER       SMARTENS    IM MARTINET       STANNITE       COASTERS       ROTARIES
GU STRAUNGE    MU ANESTRUM    IO TENTORIA    IP PATIENTS    CT SECTATOR    IV VOTARIES
HI INEARTHS       MENSTRUA    IP TRIPTANE    IR INTREATS    CU OUTRACES    KV OVERTASK
HK THANKERS       TRANSUME    IS INTREATS       NITRATES    CV OVERACTS    LL REALLOTS
HL ENTHRALS    MV VARMENTS       NITRATES       STRAITEN       OVERCAST    LM MOLERATS
HP PANTHERS    MW TRANSMEW       STRAITEN       TARTINES    CX EXACTORS    LP PETROSAL
HU HAUNTERS       TREWSMAN       TARTINES       TERTIANS    DG GOADSTER       PROLATES
   UNEARTHS    NO RESONANT       TERTIANS    IS INSTATES    DI ASTEROID    LR REALTORS
   UNHEARTS    NT ENTRANTS    IU TAINTURE       NASTIEST    DL DELATORS       RELATORS
   URETHANS    NY TYRANNES    LO TETRONAL       SATINETS       LEOTARDS    LU ROSULATE
II INERTIAS    OP OPERANTS       TOLERANT    IT NATTIEST       LODESTAR    LV LEVATORS
   RAINIEST       PRONATES    LS SLATTERN    IV TASTEVIN    DM STROAMED    LY ROYALETS
IJ NARTJIES    OR ANTRORSE       TRENTALS    IW TAWNIEST    DN TORNADES    MM MARMOSET
IK KERATINS    OS ASSENTOR    MO MARTENOT    LL TALLENTS    DP ADOPTERS    MN MONSTERA
   NARKIEST       SENATORS    NS ENTRANTS    LM MANTLETS       ASPORTED       STOREMAN
IL ENTRAILS       TREASONS    NY TENANTRY    LR SLATTERN       READOPTS    MR REARMOST
   LATRINES    OT ORNATEST    OP PATENTOR       TRENTALS    DR ROADSTER    MS MAESTROS
   RATLINES    OV VENATORS                   NR ENTRANTS    DS ASSORTED    MV OVERMAST
   TRENAILS    PP PARPENTS                                      TORSADES    NN RESONANT
                                                                            NP OPERANTS
```

```
       PRONATES          ASPORTED             PRONATES     EF FERRATES          ASSORTER          ITERATES
NR ANTRORSE              READOPTS     NP PARPENTS          EG REGRATES          ORATRESS          TEARIEST
NS ASSENTOR        DP STRAPPED        NR PARTNERS          EI ARTERIES          ROASTERS          TREATIES
   SENATORS        DU PASTURED        NS PASTERNS             REASTIER       OT ROSTRATE          TREATISE
   TREASONS           UPSTARED        NT PATTERNS          EK RETAKERS        PP STRAPPER       EL ALERTEST
NT ORNATEST        EH PREHEATS           TRANSEPT             STREAKER          TRAPPERS       EM TEAMSTER
NV VENATORS           SPREATHE        NU PERSAUNT          EL RELATERS        PU PARTURES       EN ENTREATS
OR SORORATE        EI PETARIES        OR PRAETORS          EM STREAMER           RAPTURES          RATTEENS
PR PRAETORS        EK PERTAKES        OS ESPARTOS          EN TERRANES        QU QUARTERS       ER RETRATES
   PRORATES        EL PRELATES           PORTASES          EP TAPERERS        ST RESTARTS          RETREATS
PS ESPARTOS        EM TEMPERAS           PROTASES          ER ARRESTER           STARTERS          TREATERS
   PORTASES        EO OPERATES           SEAPORTS             REARREST        SU SERRATUS       ES ESTREATS
   PROTASES        ER TAPERERS        OT PROSTATE          ES ASSERTER        SY STRAYERS          RESTATES
   SEAPORTS        ES TRAPESES        OU APTEROUS             REASSERT        UY TREASURY       ET ATTESTER
PT PROSTATE        EU EPURATES        OV OVERPAST             SERRATES                          EX EXTREATS
PU APTEROUS           SUPERATE        PR STRAPPER             TERRASES       AERSTT  97         FH FARTHEST
PV OVERPAST        EZ TRAPEZES           TRAPPERS          ET RETRATES       (TASTER)           FL FATTRELS
QU EQUATORS        FO FOREPAST        QU PARQUETS             RETREATS        AB RABATTES          FLATTERS
   QUAESTOR        FS PRESSFAT        RU PARTURES             TREATERS        AC CASTRATE       GI STRIGATE
RR ARRESTOR        GI GRAPIEST           RAPTURES          EU AUSTERER        AD ASTARTED       GO GAROTTES
RS ASSERTOR        GN TREPANGS        SS SPARSEST             TREASURE        AE STEARATE       GY STRATEGY
   ASSORTER        GO PORTAGES           TRESPASS          EV TRAVERSE        AG REGATTAS       HO RHEOSTAT
   ORATRESS        HM HAMPSTER        ST SPATTERS          EW WATERERS        AI ARIETTAS       HS SHATTERS
   ROASTERS        HN PANTHERS           TAPSTERS          FG GRAFTERS           ARISTATE       HY SHATTERY
RT ROSTRATE        HS SHARPEST        SU PASTURES          FI FRATRIES        AN TARTANES       IL TERTIALS
ST STRATOSE           SPARTHES           UPSTARES          FN TRANSFER        AO AEROSTAT       IM MISTREAT
   TOASTERS        II PARITIES        SY YAPSTERS          GN GRANTERS        AR TARTARES          TERATISM
SV VOTARESS        IK PARKIEST        TU STUPRATE             REGRANTS        AU SATURATE       IN INTREATS
SX STORAXES        IL PILASTER        TY TAPESTRY          GO GARROTES        BE ABETTERS          NITRATES
TT ATTESTOR           PLAISTER        UX SUPERTAX          HH THRASHER        BI BIRETTAS       IR RETRAITS
   TESTATOR           PLAITERS                             HI TRASHIER        BL BATTLERS          STRAITER
TU OUTRATES        IM PRIMATES     AERRST 138              HU URETHRAS           BLATTERS          TARRIEST
   OUTSTARE        IN PAINTERS     (RATERS)                HY TRASHERY           BRATTLES       IS ARTISTES
UW OUTSWEAR           PANTRIES        AN NARRATES          II RARITIES        BO ABETTORS          ARTSIEST
   OUTWEARS           PERTAINS        AO AERATORS          IL RETIRALS           BATTEROS          STRIATES
VY OVERSTAY           PINASTER        AS TARRASES             RETRIALS           TABORETS       IT RATTIEST
                      REPAINTS        AT TARTARES             TRAILERS        BU ABUTTERS          TARTIEST
AEPRST 129         IP PERIAPTS        BE REBATERS          IN RESTRAIN        CD DETRACTS          TITRATES
(PATERS)           IS PASTRIES           TABRERES             RETRAINS           SCRATTED       IW WARTIEST
AC CAPRATES           PIASTRES           TEREBRAS             STRAINER        CH CHATTERS       IX EXTRAITS
AD ADAPTERS           RASPIEST        BI ARBITERS             TERRAINS           RATCHETS       KS STARKEST
   READAPTS           TRAIPSES           RAREBITS             TRAINERS        CI CITRATES       LM MALTSTER
AE ASPERATE        IV PRIVATES        BO ARBORETS             TRANSIRE           CRISTATE          MARTLETS
   SEPARATE        IW WIRETAPS        CC CARRECTS          IO ROARIEST        CJ TRAJECTS       LN SLATTERN
AI ASPIRATE        IY ASPERITY        CE CATERERS             ROTARIES        CK RACKETTS          TRENTALS
   PARASITE        KL SPARKLET           RETRACES          IR STARRIER        CL CLATTERS       LP PARTLETS
   SEPTARIA        LM TRAMPLES           TERRACES             TARRIERS           SCRATTLE          PLATTERS
AK PARTAKES        LN PANTLERS        CF REFRACTS          IS TARSIERS        CN TRANECTS          PRATTLES
AL PALESTRA           PLANTERS        CH CHARTERS          IT RETRAITS           TRANSECT          SPLATTER
AP PARAPETS           REPLANTS           RECHARTS             STRAITER        CO SECTATOR          SPRATTLE
BO PROBATES        LO PETROSAL           STARCHER             TARRIEST        CR RETRACTS       LR RATTLERS
CH CHAPTERS           PROLATES        CI ERRATICS          IW STRAWIER        CS SCATTERS          STARTLER
   PATCHERS        LS PLASTERS        CK TRACKERS             SWARTIER        CT TETRACTS       LS SLATTERS
CI CRAPIEST           PSALTERS        CO ACROTERS          KS STARKERS        CU CRUSTATE          STARLETS
   CRISPATE           STAPLERS           CREATORS          LO REALTORS        CX EXTRACTS          STARTLES
   PICRATES        LT PARTLETS           REACTORS             RELATORS        CY SCATTERY       LT TATTLERS
   PRACTISE           PLATTERS        CT RETRACTS          LT RATTLERS        DE ASTERTED          TATTLERS
CL SCEPTRAL           PRATTLES           STARTLER             STARTLER           RESTATED       LU LUSTRATE
   SPECTRAL           SPLATTER        DE ARRESTED          LW TRAWLERS        DI STRAITED          TUTELARS
CM CRAMPETS           SPRATTLE           DREAREST          MO REARMOST           STRIATED       LY SLATTERY
CU CAPTURES        LU APLUSTRE           RETREADS          MP TRAMPERS           TARDIEST       MP TRAMPETS
   PRESCUTA        LY PLASTERY           SERRATED          NO ANTRORSE        DL STARTLED       MS MATTRESS
DE PREDATES           PSALTERY           TREADERS          NP PARTNERS        DR REDSTART          SMARTEST
   REPASTED        MR TRAMPERS        DF DRAFTERS          NT TRANTERS        DU STATURED          SMATTERS
   TRAPESED        MS STAMPERS           REDRAFTS          OO SORORATE        EG GREATEST       MU MATUREST
DI RAPIDEST        MT TRAMPETS        DG DRAGSTER          OP PRAETORS        EH THEATERS          TESTAMUR
   SPIRATED        MU TEMPURAS        DO ROADSTER             PRORATES           THEATRES
   TRAIPSED           UPSTREAM        DT REDSTART          OR ARRESTOR        EI ARIETTES       NN ENTRANTS
DM STRAMPED        NO OPERANTS        EE ARRESTEE          OS ASSERTOR
DO ADOPTERS
```

NO ORNATEST	MN TRANSMEW	RELAYING	CT CLATTING	PS PLATINGS	GREASING
NP PATTERNS	TREWSMAN	YEARLING	CU CLAUTING	SPALTING	SNAGGIER
TRANSEPT	NU UNWATERS	FF RAFFLING	DE DELATING	STAPLING	EH HEARINGS
NR TRANTERS	NY STERNWAY	GG GARGLING	DI DILATING	PT PLATTING	HEARSING
NS TARTNESS	OU OUTSWEAR	RAGGLING	DR DARTLING	RS RATLINGS	SHEARING
NU TAUNTERS	OUTWEARS	GI GLAIRING	EE GALENITE	STARLING	EK SKEARING
OP PROSTATE	ST SWATTERS	GN GNARLING	GELATINE	RT RATTLING	EL ARLESING
OR ROSTRATE		GY GRAYLING	LEGATINE	RW TRAWLING	ENGRAILS
OS STRATOSE	**AGILNR 199**	RAGINGLY	EG TEAGLING	SS ANGLISTS	NARGILES
TOASTERS	(RALING)	HS HARLINGS	EH ATHELING	LASTINGS	REALIGNS
OT ATTESTOR	AE REGALIAN	RINGHALS	EM LIGAMENT	SALTINGS	SANGLIER
TESTATOR	AG GANGLIAR	HY NARGHILY	EN GANTLINE	SLATINGS	SLANGIER
OU OUTRATES	AK KRAALING	IO ORIGINAL	LATENING	ST SLATTING	EM GERMAINS
OUTSTARE	AM ALARMING	IS GLAIRINS	EO GELATION	SU SALUTING	SMEARING
PS SPATTERS	MARGINAL	RAILINGS	LEGATION	TT TATTLING	EN AGINNERS
TAPSTERS	AR LARRIGAN	IT RINGTAIL	EP PLEATING	TW WATTLING	EARNINGS
PU STUPRATE	BB RABBLING	TRAILING	ER ALERTING	UV VAULTING	ENGRAINS
PY TAPESTRY	BD BARDLING	IV VIRGINAL	ALTERING	UX LUXATING	GRANNIES
QU QUARTETS	BE BLEARING	KN RANKLING	INTEGRAL	WZ WALTZING	EO IGNAROES
SQUATTER	BG GARBLING	LU ALLURING	RELATING		ORGANISE
RS RESTARTS	BI BRAILING	LINGULAR	TANGLIER	**AGINRS 123**	ORIGANES
STARTERS	BM MARBLING	LY NARGILLY	TRIANGLE	(GRAINS)	EP PREASING
SU STATURES	RAMBLING	RALLYING	ES EASTLING	AB BARGAINS	SPEARING
SW SWATTERS	BO LABORING	MS MARLINGS	GELATINS	AE ANGARIES	ER EARRINGS
UV VETTURAS	BT BRATLING	NS SNARLING	GENITALS	AI ARAISING	GRAINERS
VY TRAVESTY	BW BRAWLING	OP PAROLING	STEALING	AR ARRAIGNS	ES REASSIGN
	WARBLING	OT TRIGONAL	EV VALETING	AS SANGRIAS	SEARINGS
AERSTW 194	CD CRADLING	PS SPARLING	EX EXALTING	SARANGIS	SERINGAS
(WATERS)	CE CLEARING	SPRINGAL	EZ TEAZLING	AY ARAYSING	ET ANGRIEST
AD EASTWARD	CO ORACLING	ST RATLINGS	FH FANLIGHT	BD BRIGANDS	ASTRINGE
BD BEDSTRAW	CT CLARTING	STARLING	FL FLATLING	BE BEARINGS	GANISTER
BI WARBIEST	CW CRAWLING	SU SINGULAR	FO FLOATING	SABERING	GANTRIES
BL BLEWARTS	DD RADDLING	SW WARLINGS	FS FATLINGS	BH BRASHING	GRANITES
BS WABSTERS	DE DEARLING	WARSLING	FT FLATTING	BI BRAISING	INGRATES
CH WATCHERS	DRAGLINE	TT RATTLING	FU FAULTING	BR BARRINGS	RANGIEST
DE DEWATERS	DI DRAILING	TW TRAWLING	GI LIGATING	BT BRASTING	REASTING
TARWEEDS	DK DARKLING	VY RAVINGLY	TAIGLING	CE CREASING	STEARING
WASTERED	DS DARLINGS	WW WRAWLING	GN GNATLING	GRECIANS	EV VINEGARS
DI TAWDRIES	DT DARTLING	WX WRAXLING	TANGLING	SEARCING	EW SWEARING
DS STEWARDS	DW DRAWLING		GO GLOATING	CF FARCINGS	WEARINGS
DW WESTWARD	DY DARINGLY	**AGILNT 174**	GOATLING	SCARFING	EY RESAYING
EG STREWAGE	EE ALGERINE	(LATING)	HL ALLNIGHT	CH CHAGRINS	FI FAIRINGS
EH WEATHERS	EG GANGLIER	AB ABLATING	HO LOATHING	CRASHING	FRAISING
WREATHES	REGALING	AE AGENTIAL	HS HALTINGS	CK ARCKINGS	FM FARMINGS
EI SWATHIER	EH NARGHILE	ALGINATE	LATHINGS	RACKINGS	FRAMINGS
TAWERIES	NARGILEH	AO GALTONIA	IO INTAGLIO	CP CARPINGS	FT INGRAFTS
WEARIEST	EI GAINLIER	AP PALATING	LIGATION	SCARPING	STRAFING
ER WATERERS	EJ JANGLIER	BE BELATING	TAGLIONI	SCRAPING	FW SWARFING
ES SWEATERS	EM GERMINAL	BLEATING	IP PLAITING	CR SCARRING	FY FRAYINGS
FO FORWASTE	MALIGNER	TANGIBLE	IR RINGTAIL	CS SACRINGS	GG RAGGINGS
SOFTWARE	MALINGER	BI LIBATING	TRAILING	CT SCARTING	GI AGRISING
FS FRETSAWS	EN LEARNING	BN BANTLING	IS TAILINGS	TRACINGS	GP GRASPING
FU WAFTURES	EO GERANIOL	BO BLOATING	IT LITIGANT	CU SCAURING	SPARGING
HI SWATHIER	REGIONAL	OBLIGANT	IV VIGILANT	CV CARVINGS	GS GRASSING
WATERISH	EP PEARLING	BR BRATLING	KS SKLATING	CRAVINGS	SIRGANGS
HM MAWTHERS	ER GNARLIER	BS BLASTING	STALKING	DE DERAIGNS	GT GRATINGS
II WISTERIA	ES ARLESING	STABLING	TALKINGS	GRADINES	GU SUGARING
IM WARTIMES	ENGRAILS	TABLINGS	KY TAKINGLY	READINGS	GV GRAVINGS
IN TINWARES	NARGILES	BT BATTLING	LS STALLING	DF FARDINGS	GZ GRAZINGS
IP WIRETAPS	REALIGNS	BLATTING	LY TALLYING	DG NIGGARDS	HK SHARKING
IR STRAWIER	SANGLIER	BY TANGIBLY	MN MANTLING	DL DARLINGS	HL HARLINGS
SWARTIER	SLANGIER	CE CLEATING	MS MALTINGS	DM MRIDANGS	RINGHALS
IS WAISTERS	ET ALERTING	CH LATCHING	NP PLANTING	DN DARNINGS	HP HARPINGS
WAITRESS	ALTERING	CK TACKLING	NS SLANTING	DO ROADINGS	PHRASING
WASTRIES	INTEGRAL	CN CANTLING	TANLINGS	DT TRADINGS	SHARPING
IT WARTIEST	RELATING	CO LOCATING	OP PLOATING	DW DRAWINGS	HS SHARINGS
LR TRAWLERS	TANGLIER	CR CLARTING	OR TRIGONAL	SWARDING	HT TRASHING
LS WARTLESS	TRIANGLE	CS CASTLING	OS ANTILOGS	WARDINGS	IL GLAIRINS
WASTRELS	EX RELAXING	CATLINGS	SALTOING	EE GESNERIA	RAILINGS
LZ WALTZERS	EY LAYERING	SCLATING	OY ANTILOGY	EG GEARINGS	IN INGRAINS

```
IO SIGNORIA     AGINRT  69      IK TRAIKING         TACKINGS     GS STAGINGS     RS GASTRINS
IP ASPIRING     (RATING)        IL RINGTAIL      CL CASTLING     HL HALTINGS        STARINGS
   PAIRINGS     AE AERATING        TRAILING         CATLINGS        LATHINGS     RT RATTINGS
   PRAISING     BE BERATING     IN TRAINING         SCLATING     HN TANGHINS        STARTING
IS RAISINGS        REBATING     IP PIRATING      CN CANTINGS     HO HOASTING     RV STARVING
JR JARRINGS     BL BRATLING     IT ATTIRING         SCANTING     HR TRASHING     RW STRAWING
KM MARKINGS     BO ABORTING     KS KARTINGS      CO AGNOSTIC     HS HASTINGS        WRASTING
KN RANKINGS        TABORING        STARKING         COASTING        STASHING     RY STRAYING
KP PARKINGS     BS BRASTING     LO TRIGONAL         COATINGS     HT HATTINGS     ST TASTINGS
   SPARKING     CE CATERING     LS RATLINGS         COTINGAS     HW SWATHING     SW WASTINGS
KS SARKINGS        CITRANGE        STARLING      CR SCARTING        THAWINGS     SY STAYINGS
KT KARTINGS        CREATING     LT RATTLING         TRACINGS     IL TAILINGS     TT TATTINGS
   STARKING        REACTING     LW TRAWLING      CS CASTINGS     IM GIANTISM     TW SWATTING
LM MARLINGS     CF CRAFTING     MP TRAMPING      CT SCATTING     IN SAINTING
LN SNARLING        FRACTING     MS MIGRANTS      DE SEDATING        SATINING     AINRST  40
LP SPARLING     CH CHARTING        SMARTING         STEADING        STAINING     (TRAINS)
   SPRINGAL     CI GRANITIC     MU MATURING      DN STANDING     IV VISTAING     AB ATABRINS
LT RATLINGS     CK TRACKING     NO IGNORANT      DO DOATINGS     IW WAITINGS        BARTISAN
   STARLING     CL CLARTING     NS STARNING      DR TRADINGS     KL SKLATING     AC ARCANIST
LU SINGULAR     CN TRANCING     NT TRANTING      DU ADUSTING        STALKING     AD RADIANTS
LW WARLINGS     CS SCARTING     NU NATURING         SUDATING        TALKINGS     AE ANTISERA
   WARSLING        TRACINGS     NY TRAYNING      EE SAGENITE     KN TANKINGS        ARTESIAN
MM SMARMING     CT TRACTING        TYRANING      EF FEASTING     KO GOATSKIN        RESINATA
MO ORGANISM     DE DERATING     OO ROGATION      EG NAGGIEST     KR KARTINGS     AI INTARSIA
MT MIGRANTS        GRADIENT     OS ORGANIST      EH GAHNITES        STARKING     AM TAMARINS
   SMARTING        TREADING        ROASTING         HEATINGS     KS SKATINGS     AP ASPIRANT
MW SWARMING     DF DRAFTING     OT ROTATING      EL EASTLING        TASKINGS        PARTISAN
   WARMINGS     DL DARTLING        TROATING         GELATINS     LL STALLING     AS ARTISANS
MY MYRINGAS     DN DRANTING     OV GRAVITON         GENITALS     LM MALTINGS        TSARINAS
NR SNARRING     DS TRADINGS     OY GYRATION         STEALING     LN SLANTING     AV VARIANTS
NS SNARINGS     DY TARDYING        ORGANITY      EM MANGIEST        TANLINGS     AY SANITARY
NT STARNING     EH EARTHING     PP TRAPPING         MINTAGES     LO ANTILOGS     BE ATEBRINS
NW WARNINGS        HEARTING     PS PARTINGS         STEAMING        SALTOING        BANISTER
OR GARRISON     EK RETAKING        PRATINGS         TEAMINGS     LP PLATINGS     BG BRASTING
   ROARINGS     EL ALERTING     PT PRATTING      EN ANTIGENS        SPALTING     BO TABORINS
OS ASSIGNOR        ALTERING     PU UPRATING         GENTIANS        STAPLING     CE CANISTER
   SIGNORAS        INTEGRAL     PY PARTYING         STEANING     LR RATLINGS        CARNIEST
   SOARINGS        RELATING     RS STARRING      ER ANGRIEST        STARLING        NACRITES
OT ORGANIST        TANGLIER        TARRINGS         ASTRINGE     LS ANGLISTS        SCANTIER
   ROASTING        TRIANGLE     RY TARRYING         GANISTER        LASTINGS     CF INFARCTS
OU AROUSING     EM EMIGRANT     SS GASTRINS         GANTRIES        SALTINGS        INFRACTS
OV SAVORING     EP TAPERING        STARINGS         GRANITES        SLATINGS     CG SCARTING
PP RAPPINGS     ES ANGRIEST     ST RATTINGS         INGRATES     LT SLATTING        TRACINGS
PR SPARRING        ASTRINGE        STARTING         RANGIEST     LU SALUTING     CO CANTORIS
PS PARSINGS        GANISTER     SV STARVING         REASTING     MP STAMPING        CAROTINS
   RASPINGS        GANTRIES     SW STRAWING         STEARING        TAMPINGS     CP CANTRIPS
PT PARTINGS        GRANITES        WRASTING      ES EASTINGS     MR MIGRANTS     CU CURTAINS
   PRATINGS        INGRATES     SY STRAYING         GENISTAS        SMARTING        SATURNIC
PW WARPINGS        RANGIEST                         GIANTESS     MT MATTINGS        TURACINS
PY PRAYINGS        REASTING     AGINST 108          SEATINGS     NN TANNINGS     DE DETRAINS
   SPRAYING        STEARING     (SATING)            TEASINGS     NO ASTONING        RANDIEST
QU SQUARING     ET ARETTING     AE SAGINATE         TSIGANES     NP PANTINGS        STRAINED
RT STARRING        TREATING     AS ASSIGNAT      ET ESTATING     NR STARNING     DF INDRAFTS
   TARRINGS     EV AVERTING     BB STABBING         TANGIEST     NU SAUNTING     DG TRADINGS
ST GASTRINS        TAVERING     BD DINGBATS      EU SAUTEING        UNSATING     DI DISTRAIN
   STARINGS        VINTAGER     BE BEATINGS      EV VINTAGES     NW WANTINGS     DK STINKARD
SU ASSURING     EW TWANGIER     BI BAITINGS      EW SWEATING     NY STAYNING     DO INTRADOS
SY SYRINGAS        WATERING     BL BLASTING      EY YEASTING     OR ORGANIST     DR TRIDARNS
TT RATTINGS     FG GRAFTING        STABLING      FF STAFFING        ROASTING     EE ARSENITE
   STARTING     FH FARTHING        TABLINGS      FH SHAFTING     OS AGONISTS        RESINATE
TV STARVING     FS INGRAFTS     BN BANTINGS      FL FATLINGS     OT TANGOIST        STEARINE
TW STRAWING        STRAFING     BO BOASTING      FR INGRAFTS        TOASTING        TRAINEES
   WRASTING     FU FIGURANT        BOATINGS         STRAFING     PP STAPPING     EF FENITARS
TY STRAYING     GN GRANTING        BOSTANGI      FS FASTINGS        TAPPINGS     EG ANGRIEST
VW SWARVING     GS GRATINGS     BR BRASTING      FW WAFTINGS     PR PARTINGS        ASTRINGE
VY VARYINGS     GY GYRATING     BS BASTINGS      GG STAGGING        PRATINGS        GANISTER
WY RINGWAYS     HJ NIGHTJAR     BT BATTINGS      GH GHASTING     PS PASTINGS        GANTRIES
                HS TRASHING     BW BATSWING      GI AGISTING     PT SPATTING        GRANITES
                HW THRAWING     CH SCATHING      GN STANGING     RR STARRING        INGRATES
                   WRATHING     CK STACKING      GR GRATINGS        TARRINGS        RANGIEST
```

```
   REASTING
   STEARING
EH INEARTHS
EI INERTIAS
   RAINIEST
EJ NARTJIES
EK KERATINS
   NARKIEST
EL ENTRAILS
   LATRINES
   RATLINES
   TRENAILS
EM MINARETS
   RAIMENTS
EN ENTRAINS
   TRANNIES
EO ANOESTRI
   ARSONITE
   NOTARIES
   NOTARISE
   ROSINATE
EP PAINTERS
   PANTRIES
   PERTAINS
   PINASTER
   REPAINTS
ER RESTRAIN
   RETRAINS
   STRAINER
   TERRAINS
   TRAINERS
   TRANSIRE
ES RESIANTS
   RETSINAS
   SNARIEST
   STAINERS
   STARNIES
   STEARINS
ET INTREATS
   NITRATES
   STRAITEN
   TARTINES
   TERTIANS
EU RUINATES
   URANITES
   URINATES
EW TINWARES
FG INGRAFTS
   STRAFING
FK RATFINKS
FX TRANSFIX
GG GRATINGS
GH TRASHING
GK KARTINGS
   STARKING
GL RATLINGS
   STARLING
GM MIGRANTS
   SMARTING
GN STARNING
GO ORGANIST
   ROASTING
GP PARTINGS
   PRATINGS
GR STARRING
   TARRINGS
GS GASTRINS
   STARINGS
GT RATTINGS
   STARTING

GV STARVING
GW STRAWING
   WRASTING
GY STRAYING
HL INTHRALS
HO TRAHISON
HP TRANSHIP
HY RHYTINAS
IM MARTINIS
IO INTARSIO
IV VITRAINS
JO JANITORS
KO SKIATRON
LT RATTLINS
LU LUNARIST
MT TRANSMIT
MU NATRIUMS
   NATURISM
MV VARMINTS
NT INTRANTS
NU INSURANT
NY TYRANNIS
OO ORATIONS
OP ATROPINS
OS ARSONIST
OT STRONTIA
OU SUTORIAN
OX TRIAXONS
PS SPIRANTS
   SPRAINTS
PU PURITANS
   UPTRAINS
ST STRAINTS
   TRANSITS
TU NATURIST
TY TANISTRY

ANORST 60
(RATONS)
AD ONDATRAS
AE ANOESTRA
AH ATHANORS
AY SANATORY
BE BARONETS
BI TABORINS
BY BARYTONS
CE ANCESTOR
   ENACTORS
   SARCONET
   SORTANCE
CH CHANTORS
CI CANTORIS
   CAROTINS
CO CARTOONS
   CORANTOS
   OSTRACON
CT CONTRAST
CU COURANTS
DE TORNADES
DI INTRADOS
DM DORMANTS
   MORDANTS
DO DONATORS
DU ROTUNDAS
DW SANDWORT
EE RESONATE
EG ORANGEST
   RAGSTONE
EI ANOESTRI
   ARSONITE

   NOTARIES
   NOTARISE
   ROSINATE
EM MONSTERA
EN RESONANT
EP OPERANTS
   PRONATES
ER ANTRORSE
ES ASSENTOR
   SENATORS
   TREASONS
ET ORNATEST
EV VENATORS
FF AFFRONTS
FL FRONTALS
FM FORMANTS
GH STAGHORN
GI ORGANIST
   ROASTING
GM ANGSTROM
GR GRANTORS
HI TRAHISON
HL ALTHORNS
II INTARSIO
IJ JANITORS
IK SKIATRON
IO ORATIONS
IP ATROPINS
IS ARSONIST
IT STRONTIA
IU SUTORIAN
IX TRIAXONS
KO OSTRAKON
KU OUTRANKS
LO ORTOLANS
LP PLASTRON
MS TRANSOMS
MU ROMAUNTS
NO SONORANT
OP PATROONS
OT ARNOTTOS
SU SANTOURS
VY SOVRANTY

BEIRST 184
(TRIBES)
AD BARDIEST
   BRAIDEST
   RABIDEST
   TRIBADES
AK BARKIEST
   BRAKIEST
   BREASKIT
AL LIBRATES
AM BARMIEST
AN ATEBRINS
   BANISTER
AO SABOTIER
AR ARBITERS
   RAREBITS
AT BIRETTAS
AV VIBRATES
AW WARBIEST
AY BESTIARY
   SYBARITE
BI RIBBIEST
BL STIBBLER
   TRIBBLES
BU STUBBIER

   SUBTRIBE
CH BRITCHES
CO BISECTOR
CU BRUCITES
DE BEDRITES
   BESTRIDE
DL BRISTLED
   DRIBLETS
DO DEBITORS
EE BEERIEST
EF BRIEFEST
EH HERBIEST
EU UBERTIES
FL FILBERTS
FS FIBSTERS
GL GILBERTS
HL BLITHERS
HR REBIRTHS
HS HERBISTS
IL TRILBIES
IN BRINIEST
IO ORBITIES
IS BIRSIEST
KS BRISKEST
   BRISKETS
LM TIMBRELS
LO STROBILE
   TRILOBES
LS BLISTERS
   BRISTLES
LT BRITTLES
   TRIBLETS
LU BURLIEST
   SUBTILER
LY BLISTERY
MU IMBRUTES
   RESUBMIT
   TERBIUMS
NO BORNITES
   RIBSTONE
NT BITTERNS
NU TRIBUNES
   TURBINES
OO ROBOTISE
OR ORBITERS
OY SOBRIETY
QU BRIQUETS
RU BURRIEST
SU BUSTIERS
TU TRIBUTES
TY TREYBITS

CEINOS 109
(CONIES)
AC COCAINES
AD DIOCESAN
   OCEANIDS
AG COINAGES
AN CANONISE
AP CANOPIES
   CAPONISE
   PAEONICS
AR SCENARIO
AT ACONITES
   CANOEIST
BL BINOCLES
BM COMBINES
CD CONCISED
CH CONCHIES
CN INSCONCE

CR CONCISER
   CORNICES
CS CONCISES
CT CONCEITS
DE CODEINES
DF CONFIDES
DG COGNISED
DH HEDONICS
DI DECISION
   ICONISED
DL INCLOSED
DO COOSINED
DR CONSIDER
DT DEONTICS
DU DOUCINES
DZ ZINCODES
EL CINEOLES
ES SENECIOS
ET SEICENTO
FN CONFINES
FR CONIFERS
   FORENSIC
   FORINSEC
   INFORCES
FX CONFIXES
GL ECLOSING
GS COGNISES
GZ COGNIZES
HL CHOLINES
HO COHESION
HP CHOPINES
HR CHORINES
HY HYOSCINE
IL ISOCLINE
   SILICONE
IN CONIINES
   OSCININE
IP EPINOSIC
IR RECISION
   SORICINE
IS ICONISES
IV INVOICES
IX EXCISION
IZ ICONIZES
LL LIONCELS
LO COLONIES
   COLONISE
LP PINOCLES
LR INCLOSER
   LICENSOR
LS CONSEILS
   INCLOSES
LT LECTIONS
LX LEXICONS
MN MECONINS
MR CREMOSIN
   INCOMERS
   SERMONIC
NR INCENSOR
NV CONNIVES
OT COONTIES
PR CONSPIRE
   INCORPSE
RR RESORCIN
RS NECROSIS
   SERICONS
RT CORNIEST
   RECTIONS
RU NOURICES

   ROUNCIES
SS CESSIONS
   COSINESS
ST SECTIONS
SX SECTIONS
TT CENTOIST
   STENOTIC
TU COUNTIES
TX EXCITONS
TY CYTOSINE
UV UNVOICES
VV CONVIVES

CEINRS 183
(INCERS)
AA CANARIES
AB CARBINES
AE CINEREAS
   INCREASE
AF FANCIERS
AG CREASING
   GRECIANS
   SEARCING
AH INARCHES
AI RIANCIES
AL CARLINES
AM CARMINES
AN CRANNIES
AO SCENARIO
AS ARSENICS
   CERASINS
   RACINESS
AT CANISTER
   CARNIEST
   NACRITES
   SCANTIER
BI INSCRIBE
BU BRUCINES
CO CONCISER
   CORNICES
DO CONSIDER
DP PRESCIND
DS DISCERNS
DU INDUCERS
EE CERESINE
EG CREESING
   GENERICS
EH ENRICHES
   INHERCES
EK SICKENER
EL LICENSER
   RECLINES
   SILENCER
EN INCENSER
ER SINCERER
ES CERESINS
   SCRIENES
ET CENTRIES
   ENTERICS
   ENTICERS
   SCIENTER
   SECRETIN
EU INSECURE
   SINECURE
FO CONIFERS
   FORENSIC
   FORINSEC
   INFORCES
```

```
GL CLINGERS
   CRINGLES
GN SCERNING
GR CRINGERS
GT CRESTING
GU RECUSING
   RESCUING
   SCUNGIER
   SECURING
GW SCREWING
GY SYNERGIC
HO CHORINES
HP PINCHERS
HS RICHNESS
HT CHRISTEN
   CITHERNS
   SNITCHER
IO RECISION
   SORICINE
IS SERICINS
IT CITRINES
   CRINITES
   INCITERS
IU INCISURE
   SCIURINE
KK KNICKERS
KL CLINKERS
   CRINKLES
KS SNICKERS
KT STRICKEN
KU UNSICKER
LO INCLOSER
   LICENSOR
MO CREMOSIN
   INCOMERS
   SERMONIC
MT CENTRISM
NO INCENSOR
OP CONSPIRE
   INCORPSE
OR RESORCIN
OS NECROSIS
   SERICONS
OT CORNIEST
   RECTIONS
OU NOURICES
   ROUNCIES
PS PRINCESS
ST CISTERNS
TT CENTRIST
   CITTERNS
TU CURNIEST
UV INCURVES
VV CRIVVENS

CEINST 196
(INSECT)
AA ESTANCIA
AB CABINETS
AD DISTANCE
AE CINEASTE
AF FANCIEST
AH ASTHENIC
   CHANTIES
AI CANITIES
AM SEMANTIC
AN ANCIENTS
   CANNIEST
   INSTANCE
AO ACONITES
```


```
   CANOEIST
AR CANISTER
   CARNIEST
   NACRITES
   SCANTIER
AS CINEASTS
   SCANTIES
AT CANTIEST
   NICTATES
AV CISTVAEN
   VESICANT
AY CYANITES
CH TECHNICS
CO CONCEITS
CY SYNECTIC
DH SNITCHED
DO DEONTICS
DY SYNDETIC
EG GENETICS
EH SITHENCE
EI NICETIES
EK NECKTIES
EM CENTIMES
EN NESCIENT
EO SEICENTO
EP PECTINES
ER CENTRIES
   ENTERICS
   ENTICERS
   SCIENTER
   SECRETIN
ES CENTESIS
FL INFLECTS
GH ETCHINGS
GN SCENTING
GR CRESTING
HI ICHNITES
HK KITCHENS
   KNITCHES
   THICKENS
HL LINCHETS
   TINCHELS
HR CHRISTEN
   CITHERNS
   SNITCHER
HS SNITCHES
HW WITCHENS
HZ CHINTZES
IK KINETICS
IN INSCIENT
IR CITRINES
   CRINITES
   INCITERS
IU CUTINISE
IY CYTISINE
   SYENITIC
IZ CITIZENS
   ZINCIEST
   ZINCITES
KR STRICKEN
KS SNICKETS
LO LECTIONS
LS STENCILS
LU CUTLINES
   TUNICLES
MR CENTRISM
OO COONTIES
OR CORNIEST
   RECTIONS
```


```
OS SECTIONS
OT CENTOIST
   STENOTIC
OU COUNTIES
OX EXCITONS
OY CYTOSINE
PS INSPECTS
PY PYCNITES
RS CISTERNS
RT CENTRIST
   CITTERNS
RU CURNIEST

CEIORS 156
(COSIER)
AB AEROBICS
AD IDOCRASE
AL CALORIES
   CARIOLES
AN SCENARIO
AV COVARIES
   VARICOSE
BH BRIOCHES
BL BRICOLES
   CORBEILS
BM CROMBIES
   MICROBES
BR CRIBROSE
BT BISECTOR
CK COCKSIER
CN CONCISER
   CORNICES
CT CORTICES
DL SCLEROID
DN CONSIDER
DO CORODIES
DS DISCOERS
DT CORDITES
DU DISCOURE
DV DISCOVER
DW CROWDIES
DY DECISORY
EH CHEERIOS
EJ REJOICES
ET COTERIES
   ESOTERIC
EX EXORCISE
FF OFFICERS
FI ORIFICES
FN CONIFERS
   FORENSIC
   FORINSEC
   INFORCES
FP FORCIPES
GG GEORGICS
   SCROGGIE
HM MORICHES
HN CHORINES
HO CHOOSIER
   ISOCHORE
HP SOPHERIC
HS CHORISES
   ORCHESIS
   ORCHISES
HT ROTCHIES
   THEORICS
HW CHOWRIES
IM ISOMERIC
IN RECISION
```


```
   SORICINE
IP IRISCOPE
KM OCKERISM
KR ROCKIERS
KT CORKIEST
   ROCKIEST
   STOCKIER
LL COLLIERS
   ORSELLIC
LN INCLOSER
   LICENSOR
LT CLOISTER
   COISTREL
   CORTILES
   COSTLIER
   CREOLIST
MN CREMOSIN
   INCOMERS
   SERMONIC
MP COMPRISE
MR MORRICES
MT MORTICES
MX EXORCISM
MY ISOCRYME
NN INCENSOR
NP CONSPIRE
   INCORPSE
NR RESORCIN
NS NECROSIS
   SERICONS
NT CORNIEST
   RECTIONS
NU NOURICES
   ROUNCIES
OP OPORICES
PP CROPPIES
PS PERSICOS
PT PERSICOT
PU PRECIOUS
RS CROSIERS
RU COURIERS
RZ CROZIERS
SU SCOURIES
SV CORSIVES
SW SCOWRIES
SX SIXSCORE
TT COTTIERS
TU CITREOUS
   OUTCRIES
TV EVICTORS
   VORTICES
TX EXCITORS
   EXORCIST
VY VICEROYS

CEIRST 166
(CITERS)
AD ACRIDEST
AG AGRESTIC
AH CHARIEST
   THERIACS
AL ALTRICES
   ARTICLES
   RECITALS
   SELICTAR
AM CERAMIST
   MATRICES
AN CANISTER
   CARNIEST
   NACRITES
```


```
   SCANTIER
AP CRAPIEST
   CRISPATE
   PICRATES
   PRACTISE
AR ERRATICS
AS SCARIEST
AT CITRATES
   CRISTATE
   SCATTIER
AU SURICATE
AZ CRAZIEST
BH BRITCHES
BO BISECTOR
BU BRUCITES
CI ICTERICS
CK CRICKETS
CL CIRCLETS
CO CORTICES
DE DISCREET
   DISCRETE
DH DITCHERS
DO CORDITES
DP PREDICTS
   SCRIPTED
DU CRUDITES
   CURDIEST
   CURTSIED
DV VERDICTS
EF FIERCEST
EH CHESTIER
   HERETICS
EI SERICITE
EL RETICLES
   SCLERITE
   TIERCELS
EN CENTRIES
   ENTERICS
   ENTICERS
   SCIENTER
   SECRETIN
EO COTERIES
   ESOTERIC
EP CREPIEST
   RECEIPTS
ER RECITERS
EU CERUSITE
   CUTESIER
   EUCRITES
EV VERTICES
EX EXCITERS
FU FRUTICES
GN CRESTING
GU SCUTIGER
HH HITCHERS
HI CHRISTIE
HN CHRISTEN
   CITHERNS
   SNITCHER
HO ROTCHIES
   THEORICS
HP PITCHERS
   SPITCHER
HS STRICHES
HT CHITTERS
   RICHTEST
   STITCHER
HY HYSTERIC
IK STICKIER
IM MERISTIC
```


```
   TRISEMIC
IN CITRINES
   CRINITES
   INCITERS
IP PICRITES
   PRICIEST
IT RECTITIS
IV VERISTIC
JU JUSTICER
KL STICKLER
   STRICKLE
   TICKLERS
   TRICKLES
KN STRICKEN
KO CORKIEST
   ROCKIEST
   STOCKIER
KP PRICKETS
KR TRICKERS
KS STICKERS
LO CLOISTER
   COISTREL
   CORTILES
   COSTLIER
   CREOLIST
LT CLITTERS
LU CURLIEST
   UTRICLES
MN CENTRISM
MO MORTICES
MS CRETISMS
NO CORNIEST
   RECTIONS
NS CISTERNS
NT CENTRIST
   CITTERNS
NU CURNIEST
OP PERSICOT
OT COTTIERS
OU CITREOUS
   OUTCRIES
OV EVICTORS
   VORTICES
OX EXCITORS
   EXORCIST
PR RESCRIPT
PS CRISPEST
PU CREPITUS
   CUPRITES
   PICTURES
   PIECRUST
RT CRITTERS
   RESTRICT
   STRICTER
RU CRUSTIER
   RECRUITS
ST TRISECTS
SU CITRUSES
   CURTSIES
   RICTUSES
SV VICTRESS
TU TUTRICES
UV CURVIEST
UY SECURITY

CENORS 172
(CONERS)
AC CONACRES
AD DRACONES
   ENDOSARC
```

AG ACROGENS	**MU** CONSUMER	REEDLING	BESTRIDE	**MP** DEMIREPS	**AS** DEARNESS
CORNAGES	MUCRONES	**GN** ENRINGED	**CD** DECIDERS	PREMISED	**AU** UNDERSEA
AI SCENARIO	**OR** CORONERS	**GS** DESIGNER	DESCRIED	SIMPERED	**AW** ANSWERED
AM CREMONAS	CROONERS	ENERGIDS	**CL** SCLEREID	**MS** DERMISES	**BI** INBREEDS
ROMANCES	**OT** CORONETS	REDESIGN	**CM** MISCREED	**MT** DEMERITS	**BL** BLENDERS
AS COARSENS	**OU** CORNEOUS	REEDINGS	**CP** PRECISED	DEMISTER	**BP** PREBENDS
NARCOSES	**PY** NECROPSY	RESIGNED	**CR** DECRIERS	DIMETERS	**CE** RECENSED
AT ANCESTOR	**QU** CONQUERS	**HR** HINDERER	**CS** DESCRIES	MISTERED	SCREENED
ENACTORS	**RS** SCORNERS	**HS** DRISHEEN	**CT** DISCREET	**NN** SINNERED	SECERNED
SARCONET	**RW** CROWNERS	**JO** REJOINED	DISCRETE	**NO** ORDINEES	**CH** DRENCHES
SORTANCE	**ST** CONSTERS	**KL** REKINDLE	**CU** DECURIES	**NT** INSERTED	**CK** REDNECKS
AU CARNEOUS	**TT** CORNETTS	**KS** DEERSKIN	**CV** DESCRIVE	RESIDENT	**CO** CENSORED
NACREOUS	**TU** CONSTRUE	**KT** TINKERED	SCRIEVED	SINTERED	NECROSED
BE OBSCENER	CORNUTES	**LU** UNDERLIE	SERVICED	TRENDIES	SECONDER
BU BOUNCERS	COUNTERS	**MO** DOMINEER	**DP** PRESIDED	**NU** UREDINES	**CU** CENSURED
CI CONCISER	RECOUNTS	**MR** REMINDER	**DR** DERIDERS	**NV** INVERSED	**DO** ENDORSED
CORNICES	TROUNCES	**MV** VERMINED	**DT** REDDIEST	**NW** WIDENERS	**DP** SPREDDEN
CN CONCERNS	**TV** CONVERTS	**NS** SINNERED	**DV** DIVERSED	**NX** INDEXERS	**DU** SUNDERED
CT CONCERTS	**TW** CROWNETS	**NT** INDENTER	**EM** REMEDIES	**OV** OVERSIDE	**EL** NEEDLERS
CW CONCREWS	**UU** CERNUOUS	INTENDER	**EP** SPEEDIER	**PR** REPRISED	**EO** ENDORSEE
DE CENSORED	**UV** UNCOVERS	INTERNED	**ES** DIERESES	RESPIRED	**ET** RESENTED
NECROSED	**UY** CYNOSURE	**NU** UNREINED	**ET** REEDIEST	**PS** DESPISER	**FI** DEFINERS
SECONDER		**NV** INNERVED	**EZ** RESEIZED	DISPERSE	**GI** DESIGNER
DH CHONDRES	**DEEINR 43**	**OS** ORDINEES	**FI** DEIFIERS	PRESIDES	ENERGIDS
DI CONSIDER	(DENIER)	**OT** ORIENTED	EDIFIERS	**PT** PRIESTED	REDESIGN
DS CORSNEDS	**AC** DERACINE	**PP** NIPPERED	FIRESIDE	RESPITED	REEDINGS
DW DECROWNS	**AF** FREDAINE	**QU** ENQUIRED	**FL** DEFILERS	**PU** DUPERIES	RESIGNED
EF ENFORCES	**AG** REGAINED	INQUERED	FIELDERS	**PV** DEPRIVES	**HI** DRISHEEN
EG COGENERS	**AM** REMAINED	**RT** INTERRED	**FN** DEFINERS	PREVISED	**HM** HERDSMEN
CONGREES	**AP** PINDAREE	TRENDIER	**FO** FORESIDE	**RS** DERRISES	**HP** PREHENDS
EL ENCLOSER	**AS** ARSENIDE	**RV** REDRIVEN	**GL** LEIDGERS	DESIRERS	**IK** DEERSKIN
ES NECROSES	DENARIES	**ST** INSERTED	**GN** DESIGNER	DRESSIER	**IN** SINNERED
EV CONSERVE	DRAISENE	RESIDENT	ENERGIDS	RESIDERS	**IO** ORDINEES
CONVERSE	NEARSIDE	SINTERED	REDESIGN	**RT** DESTRIER	**IT** INSERTED
EZ COZENERS	**AT** DETAINER	TRENDIES	REEDINGS	**RU** RUDERIES	RESIDENT
FI CONIFERS	RETAINED	**SU** UREDINES	RESIGNED	**RV** REDRIVES	SINTERED
FORENSIC	**BD** REBIDDEN	**SV** INVERSED	**GO** GEORDIES	**ST** EDITRESS	TRENDIES
FORINSEC	**BF** BEFRIEND	**SW** WIDENERS	**GT** DIGESTER	RESISTED	**IU** UREDINES
INFORCES	**BG** BREEDING	**SX** INDEXERS	ESTRIDGE	SISTERED	**IV** INVERSED
FU FROUNCES	**BM** BRIDEMEN	**TU** REUNITED	**GU** GUDESIRE	**SU** DIURESES	**IW** WIDENERS
GH GROSCHEN	**BS** INBREEDS	**TV** INVERTED	**GV** DIVERGES	REISSUED	**IX** INDEXERS
GS CONGRESS	**CG** RECEDING	**TW** WINTERED	**HK** SHREIKED	RESIDUES	**LP** RESPLEND
GU CONGRUES	**CH** ENRICHED	**TX** DEXTRINE	SHRIEKED	**SV** DEVISERS	**MO** SERMONED
SCROUNGE	INHERCED		**HL** RELISHED	DISSERVE	**NO** ENDERONS
GY CRYOGENS	NICHERED	**DEEIRS 58**	SHIELDER	DISSEVER	**OR** ENDORSER
HI CHORINES	RICHENED	(RESIDE)	**HN** DRISHEEN	DIVERSES	**OS** ENDORSES
HO COEHORNS	**CK** NICKERED	**AB** BEARDIES	**HO** HEROISED	**TT** TIREDEST	**OT** ERODENTS
SCHOONER	**CL** RECLINED	**AC** DECIARES	**HP** HESPERID	**TU** ERUDITES	**OW** ENDOWERS
HV CHEVRONS	**CM** ENDERMIC	**AF** FEDARIES	PERISHED	SURETIED	WORSENED
II RECISION	**CP** PINCERED	**AG** DISAGREE	**HR** REDSHIRE	**TW** WEIRDEST	**PP** PERPENDS
SORICINE	**DF** FRIENDED	**AJ** JADERIES	**HV** SHIVERED		**PS** SPENDERS
IL INCLOSER	**DG** ENRIDGED	**AL** REALISED	SHRIEVED	**DEENRS 92**	**PT** PRETENDS
LICENSOR	**DH** HINDERED	SIDEREAL	**IM** DIMERISE	(ENDERS)	**RU** ENDURERS
IM CREMOSIN	**DM** REMINDED	**AM** MADERISE	**IP** EPEIRIDS	**AC** ASCENDER	SUNDERER
INCOMERS	**DN** DINNERED	**AN** ARSENIDE	**IS** DIERESIS	REASCEND	**SU** RUDENESS
SERMONIC	**DT** DENDRITE	DENARIES	**IT** SIDERITE	**AE** ENSEARED	**TU** DENTURES
IN INCENSOR	**EF** FINEERED	DRAISENE	**IV** DERISIVE	SERENADE	SEDERUNT
IP CONSPIRE	REDEFINE	NEARSIDE	**IW** WEIRDIES	**AG** DERANGES	UNDERSET
INCORPSE	**EL** NEEDLIER	**AT** READIEST	**KN** DEERSKIN	GRANDEES	**UU** UNDERUSE
IR RESORCIN	**ER** REINDEER	SERIATED	**KU** DUKERIES	GRENADES	**UV** UNVERSED
IS NECROSIS	**FF** NIFFERED	STEADIER	**KV** SKIVERED	**AI** ARSENIDE	
SERICONS	**FG** FINGERED	**AV** READVISE	**LU** LEISURED	DENARIES	**DEENST 111**
IT CORNIEST	**FR** INFERRED	**BC** DESCRIBE	**LV** DELIVERS	DRAISENE	(NESTED)
RECTIONS	**FS** DEFINERS	ESCRIBED	DESILVER	NEARSIDE	**AB** ABSENTED
IU NOURICES	**FZ** FRENZIED	**BD** BIRDSEED	SILVERED	**AK** KNEADERS	**AF** FASTENED
ROUNCIES	**GG** GINGERED	DEBRIDES	SLIVERED	**AM** AMENDERS	**AH** HASTENED
JU CONJURES	NIGGERED	**BF** DEBRIEFS	**LW** WIELDERS	MEANDERS	**AI** ANDESITE
KK KNOCKERS	RENIGGED	**BK** KERBSIDE	**LY** YIELDERS	REAMENDS	**AK** NAKEDEST
KT CRONKEST	**GL** ENGIRDLE	**BN** INBREEDS	**MM** IMMERSED	**AN** ENSNARED	**AM** STAMENED
LO CONSOLER	LINGERED	**BT** BEDRITES	SIMMERED	**AO** REASONED	

```
AS ASSENTED    AK STREAKED       TRENDIES     DS SLEDDING       GRADIENT          DIAGNOSE
AU UNSEATED    AL TREADLES    IP PRIESTED     DU DELUDING       TREADING       AR DERAIGNS
BI BENDIEST    AM MASTERED       RESPITED        INDULGED    AY DERAYING          GRADINES
BL BENDLETS       STREAMED     IR DESTRIER        UNGILDED       READYING          READINGS
CH STENCHED    AP PREDATES    IS EDITRESS     EN NEEDLING       YEARDING       AS ASSIGNED
CS DESCENTS       REPASTED        RESISTED     EO ELOIGNED    BE BREEDING       AT SEDATING
CY ENCYSTED       TRAPESED        SISTERED        LEGIONED    CE RECEDING          STEADING
DI DESTINED    AR ARRESTED    IT TIREDEST     ER ENGIRDLE    CU REDUCING       AW WINDAGES
EF ENFESTED       DREAREST     IU ERUDITES        LINGERED    CY DECRYING       BD BEDDINGS
EI NEEDIEST       RETREADS        SURETIED        REEDLING    DE ENRIDGED       BN BENDINGS
ER RESENTED       SERRATED     IW WEIRDEST     ES SEEDLING    DG DREDGING       BO OBSIGNED
ET DETENTES       TREADERS     LU LUSTERED     ET DELETING    DI DERIDING       CE SECEDING
EU DETENUES    AS ASSERTED        RESULTED     FG FLEDGING    DL REDDLING       CK DECKINGS
EX DENTEXES       ESTRADES        ULSTERED     FI DEFILING    DS REDDINGS       CN SCENDING
FI FENDIEST    AT ASTERTED    LW LEWDSTER        FIELDING    DU UNGIRDED       CO COGNISED
   INFESTED       RESTATED        WRESTLED     FU INGULFED    EF FINGERED       CY DYSGENIC
FO SOFTENED    AW DEWATERS    LY RESTYLED     GG GLEDGING    EG GINGERED       DE DESIGNED
FS DEFTNESS       TARWEEDS     MO MODESTER     GP PLEDGING       NIGGERED          SDEIGNED
GI INGESTED       WASTERED     MP DEMPSTER     GS GELDINGS       RENIGGED       DH SHEDDING
   SIGNETED    AY ESTRAYED    MU DEMUREST        SLEDGING    EL ENGIRDLE       DL SLEDDING
   STEEDING    BI BEDRITES        MUSTERED        SNIGGLED       LINGERED       DN SNEDDING
HI DISTHENE       BESTRIDE     NO ERODENTS     GU DELUGING       REEDLING       DR REDDINGS
HU ENTHUSED    BO BESORTED    NP PRETENDS     HS HINDLEGS    EN ENRINGED       DT STEDDING
II DIETINES       BESTRODE     NU DENTURES        SHINGLED    ES DESIGNER       DW SWINGDED
IL ENLISTED    CE DECREETS        SEDERUNT     IR GRIDELIN       ENERGIDS          WEDDINGS
   LINTSEED       RESECTED        UNDERSET     IS EILDINGS       REDESIGN       EF FEEDINGS
   LISTENED       SECRETED        UNDESERT        SIDELING       READINGS       EL SEEDLING
IM DEMENTIS    CI DISCREET     OP POSTERED     IT DILIGENT       RESIGNED       EN ENSIGNED
   SEDIMENT       DISCRETE        REEDSTOP     IV DEVILING    GU UNRIGGED       EP SPEEDING
IN DENTINES    CO CORSETED        REPOSTED     IW WIELDING    IL GRIDELIN       ER DESIGNER
   DESINENT       ESCORTED     OR RESORTED     IY YIELDING    IN NIDERING          ENERGIDS
IP PENTISED       SECTORED        RESTORED     KU DUKELING    IS DESIRING          REDESIGN
IR INSERTED    CP SCEPTRED        ROSTERED     LU DUELLING       RESIDING          READINGS
   RESIDENT    DE DESERTED     OS OERSTEDS     LW DWELLING    IT DIRIGENT          RESIGNED
   SINTERED    DI REDDIEST     OT ROSETTED     NO OLDENING    IV DERIVING       ES DINGESES
   TRENDIES    DL TREDDLES        TETRODES     NS LENDINGS       VIRGINED          EDGINESS
IS DESTINES    DU DETRUDES     OX DEXTROSE     OP DIPLOGEN    IW WEIRDING          SDEIGNES
IT DINETTES    EF FESTERED     OY STOREYED     OS GLENOIDS    LU INDULGER          SEEDINGS
IU DETINUES    EG DETERGES     PU PERTUSED        SIDELONG    LY YELDRING       ET INGESTED
IV EVIDENTS    EI REEDIEST     SS DESSERTS     PS SPELDING    MU DEMURING          SIGNETED
   INVESTED    EK STREEKED        STRESSED     RU INDULGER    NT TRENDING          STEEDING
KL SKLENTED    EL DEERLETS     SU RUSSETED     RY YELDRING    NU ENDURING       EW WEEDINGS
LP SPLENTED       STREELED     SY DYESTERS     SU INDULGES       UNRINGED       EX DESEXING
LY ENSTYLED    EM DEEMSTER     UV VESTURED     SV DEVLINGS    OP PROIGNED       FU DEFUSING
NO SONNETED    EN RESENTED     UX EXTRUDES     SW SWINGLED    OR ORDERING          FEUDINGS
NP PENDENTS    EO STEREOED                        WELDINGS    OS NEGROIDS       GH HEDGINGS
NU UNNESTED    EP ESTREPED    DEGILN 164       WY WINGEDLY    OU GUERIDON       GL GELDINGS
OP PENTODES       PESTERED     (DINGLE)                       OV DOVERING          SLEDGING
OR ERODENTS    ER DESERTER    AB BLINDAGE     DEGINR  82     OW DOWERING          SNIGGLED
OS STENOSED    ET RESETTED    AF FINAGLED      (RINGED)      PS SPRINGED       GW WEDGINGS
PR PRETENDS       SETTERED    AH HEALDING     AA AREADING    PY PREDYING       HI DINGHIES
RU DENTURES       STREETED    AI GLIADINE        DRAINAGE    RS GRINDERS       HL HINDLEGS
   SEDERUNT    EV REVESTED    AM MALIGNED        GARDENIA       REGRINDS          SHINGLED
   UNDERSET    EW WESTERED    AO GALENOID     AB BEARDING    RY GRINDERY       HN SHENDING
   UNDESERT    EX EXSERTED    AP PLEADING        BREADING    SS DRESSING       IL EILDINGS
TU UNTESTED    FO DEFOREST    AR DEARLING     AD DREADING    ST STRINGED          SIDELING
                  FORESTED       DRAGLINE     AE REGAINED    SW REDWINGS       IM DEMISING
DEERST 151        FOSTERED    AS DEALINGS     AH ADHERING    SY SYNERGID       IN DESINING
(RESTED)       GI DIGESTER       LEADINGS        HEADRING       SYRINGED          SDEINING
AB BETREADS       ESTRIDGE    AT DELATING     AK DAKERING                     IO INDIGOES
   BREASTED    GU GESTURED    AY DELAYING     AL DEARLING    DEGINS 154       IR DESIRING
   DEBATERS    HH THRESHED    BE BLEEDING        DRAGLINE     (SINGED)           RESIDING
AC CEDRATES    II SIDERITE    BN BLENDING     AM DREAMING    AB BEADINGS          RINGSIDE
AE RESEATED    IM DEMERITS    BO IGNOBLED        MARGINED       DEBASING       IT DINGIEST
AF DRAFTEES       DEMISTER       INGLOBED     AO ORGANDIE    AH HEADINGS          INDIGEST
AG RESTAGED       DIMETERS    DE ENGILDED     AR DREARING       SHEADING       IV DEVISING
AH HEADREST       MISTERED    DH HEDDLING     AS DERAIGNS    AL DEALINGS       LN LENDINGS
AI READIEST    IN INSERTED    DM MEDDLING        GRADINES       LEADINGS       LO GLENOIDS
   SERIATED       RESIDENT    DP PEDDLING        READINGS    AO AGONISED          SIDELONG
   STEADIER       SINTERED    DR REDDLING     AT DERATING
```

```
LP SPELDING
LU INDULGES
LV DEVLINGS
LW SWINGLED
   WELDINGS
MN MENDINGS
MO SMIDGEON
MS SMIDGENS
NP SPENDING
NS SENDINGS
NT STENDING
NU UNSIGNED
NY DESYNING
OP DEPOSING
   DISPONGE
   PIDGEONS
OR NEGROIDS
OW WENDIGOS
   WIDGEONS
PR SPRINGED
PU DISPUNGE
RR GRINDERS
   REGRINDS
RS DRESSING
RT STRINGED
RW REDWINGS
RY SYNERGID
   SYRINGED
SU DINGUSES
SW SWINDGES
TU DUNGIEST

DEILNS 120
(INDLES)
AD ISLANDED
AE DELAINES
AG DEALINGS
   LEADINGS
AN ANNELIDS
   LINDANES
AO NODALISE
AR ISLANDER
AU UNSAILED
AV ANDVILES
BR BLINDERS
   BRINDLES
BT BLINDEST
CE DECLINES
   LICENSED
   SILENCED
CO INCLOSED
CU INCLUDES
   NUCLIDES
DG SLEDDING
DP SPINDLED
   SPLENDID
DW DWINDLES
   SWINDLED
EE SELENIDE
EG SEEDLING
EH ENSHIELD
EK SILKENED
EO ESLOINED
ES IDLENESS
   LINSEEDS
ET ENLISTED
   LINTSEED
   LISTENED
EY DYELINES
FF SNIFFLED

FI INFIDELS
   INFIELDS
FR FLINDERS
GG GELDINGS
   SLEDGING
   SNIGGLED
GH HINDLEGS
   SHINGLED
GI EILDINGS
   SIDELING
GN LENDINGS
GO GLENOIDS
   SIDELONG
GP SPELDING
GU INDULGES
GV DEVLINGS
GW SWINGLED
   WELDINGS
IK DISLIKEN
IO LIONISED
KR KINDLERS
KS KINDLESS
LW INDWELLS
MS MILDNESS
   MINDLESS
MU MUSLINED
OO SOLENOID
OR DISENROL
OS SONDELIS
OU DELUSION
   INSOULED
   UNSOILED
PR SPELDRIN
PS SPELDINS
PT SPLINTED
RS RINDLESS
RT SNIRTLED
   TENDRILS
   TRINDLES
RW SWINDLER
SV VILDNESS
SW SWINDLES
   WILDNESS
   WINDLESS
TU DILUENTS
   INSULTED
   UNLISTED

DEILRT 73
(TRIDLE)
AB LIBRATED
AC ARTICLED
AE RETAILED
AO IDOLATER
AP DIPTERAL
   TRIPEDAL
AS DILATERS
AT DETRITAL
AY DIELYTRA
BB DRIBBLET
BO TRILOBED
BS BRISTLED
   DRIBLETS
CE DERELICT
CH ELDRITCH
CK TRICKLED
CY DIRECTLY

DI TIDDLIER
DN TRINDLED
DS STRIDDLE
   TIDDLERS
DW TWIDDLER
EF FILTERED
EL TILLERED
   TREDILLE
EO DOLERITE
   LOITERED
ET LITTERED
   RETITLED
HL THRILLED
HW WRITHLED
IP TRIPLIED
IS REDISTIL
NS SNIRTLED
   TENDRILS
   TRINDLES
OS STOLIDER
PP TRIPPLED
SU DILUTERS
   LURIDEST
VY DEVILTRY

DEINOS 41
(ONSIDE)
AC DIOCESAN
   OCEANIDS
AD ADENOIDS
   ADONISED
   ANODISED
AG AGONISED
   DIAGNOSE
AH ADHESION
AL NODALISE
AM NOMADIES
   NOMADISE
AR ANEROIDS
   DONARIES
AS ADONISES
   ANODISES
AT ASTONIED
   SEDATION
AX DIOXANES
AZ ADONIZES
   ANODIZES
BE EBONISED
BG OBSIGNED
BO NOBODIES
BU BEDOUINS
CC CONCISED
CE CODEINES
CF CONFIDES
CG COGNISED
CH HEDONICS
CI DECISION
   ICONISED
CL INCLOSED
CO COOSINED
CR CONSIDER
CT DEONTICS
CU DOUCINES
CZ ZINCODES
DP DISPONED
DR INDORSED
DW DISENDOW
   DISOWNED
EL ESLOINED
EM DEMONISE

EP DISPONEE
ER ORDINEES
GI INDIGOES
GL GLENOIDS
   SIDELONG
GM SMIDGEON
GP DEPOSING
   DISPONGE
   PIDGEONS
GR NEGROIDS
GW WENDIGOS
   WIDGEONS
HM HEDONISM
HP DIPHONES
   SIPHONED
   SPHENOID
HR HORDEINS
HT HEDONIST
IL LIONISED
IM DOMINIES
IR DERISION
   IRONISED
   RESINOID
IT EDITIONS
   SEDITION
IV VISIONED
JR JOINDERS
LO SOLENOID
LR DISENROL
LS SONDELIS
LU DELUSION
   INSOULED
   UNSOILED
MM DEMONISM
MN MISDONNE
MO DOMINOES
   MONODIES
MT DEMONIST
NR ENDIRONS
OP POISONED
OZ OZONISED
PR DISPONER
   POINDERS
   PRISONED
PS DISPONES
   SPINODES
PU UNPOISED
RS INDORSES
   SORDINES
RT DRONIEST
RU DOURINES
   SOURDINE
RW WINDORES
   WINDROSE
ST SONDIEST
SV VOIDNESS
SZ DOZINESS
TU OUNDIEST
TW DOWNIEST

DEINRS 51
(DINERS)
AA ARANEIDS
AB BRANDIES
   BRANDISE
AE ARSENIDE
   DENARIES
   DRAISENE
   NEARSIDE
AF FRIANDES

AG DERAIGNS
   GRADINES
   READINGS
AI DRAISINE
AL ISLANDER
AM ADERMINS
   SIRNAMED
AN INSNARED
AO ANEROIDS
   DONARIES
AP SPRAINED
AR DRAINERS
   SERRANID
AS ARIDNESS
   SARDINES
AT DETRAINS
   RANDIEST
   STRAINED
AU DENARIUS
   UNRAISED
   URANIDES
AV INVADERS
   SANDIVER
AY SYNEDRIA
BE INBREEDS
BL BLINDERS
   BRINDLES
BU BURNSIDE
CO CONSIDER
CP PRESCIND
CS DISCERNS
   RESCINDS
CU INDUCERS
DG REDDINGS
DK KINDREDS
DO INDORSED
DT STRIDDEN
EF DEFINERS
EG DESIGNER
   ENERGIDS
   REDESIGN
   RESIGNED
EH DRISHEEN
EK DEERSKIN
EN SINNERED
EO ORDINEES
ET INSERTED
   RESIDENT
   SINTERED
   TRENDIES
EU UREDINES
EV INVERSED
EW WIDENERS
EX INDEXERS
FL FLINDERS
GI DESIRING
   RESIDING
   RINGSIDE
GO NEGROIDS
GP SPRINGED
GR GRINDERS
   REGRINDS
GS DRESSING
GT STRINGED
GW REDWINGS
GY SYNERGID
   SYRINGED
HO HORDEINS
IO DERISION

   IRONISED
   RESINOID
IP INSPIRED
IS INDRISES
   INSIDERS
IT DISINTER
   INDITERS
   NITRIDES
IU DISINURE
   URIDINES
IV DIVINERS
JO JOINDERS
KL KINDLERS
KR DRINKERS
KS REDSKINS
LO DISENROL
LP SPELDRIN
LS RINDLESS
LT SNIRTLED
   TENDRILS
   TRINDLES
LW SWINDLER
NO ENDIRONS
OP DISPONER
   POINDERS
   PRISONED
OS INDORSES
   SORDINES
OT DRONIEST
OU DOURINES
   SOURDINE
OW WINDORES
   WINDROSE
PT SPRINTED
PY INSPYRED
SU SUNDRIES
TT STRIDENT
TU INTRUDES
TX DEXTRINS

DEINRU 52
(RUINED)
AF UNFAIRED
AH UNHAIRED
AI UREDINIA
AO DOUANIER
AP UNPAIRED
   UNREPAID
AS DENARIUS
   UNRAISED
   URANIDES
AT DATURINE
   INDURATE
   RUINATED
   URINATED
AV UNVARIED
BB UNRIBBED
BD UNDERBID
BL UNBRIDLE
BS BURNSIDE
BT TURBINED
   UNDERBIT
BU UNBURIED
CG REDUCING
CO DECURION
CP UNPRICED
CR INCURRED
CS INDUCERS
```

```
CV INCURVED
DD UNDERDID
DG UNGIRDED
DL UNRIDDLE
DN UNRIDDEN
DT INTRUDED
EL UNDERLIE
EN UNREINED
EQ ENQUIRED
   INQUERED
ES UREDINES
ET REUNITED
FL UNRIFLED
   URNFIELD
FN REINFUND
   UNFRIEND
GG UNRIGGED
GL INDULGER
GM DEMURING
GN ENDURING
   UNRINGED
GO GUERIDON
IQ INQUIRED
IS DISINURE
   URIDINES
IT UNTIDIER
KN UNKINDER
LP UNDERLIP
MP UNPRIMED
MT RUDIMENT
NO UNIRONED
NP UNDERPIN
NU UNINURED
NV UNDRIVEN
OS DOURINES
   SOURDINE
PP UNRIPPED
PT TURNIPED
PZ UNPRIZED
RT INTRUDER
SS SUNDRIES
ST INTRUDES
TW UNDERWIT

DEINST   32
(SINTED)
AB BANDIEST
AC DISTANCE
AD DANDIEST
AE ANDESITE
AG SEDATING
   STEADING
AH HANDIEST
AI ADENITIS
   DAINTIES
AM MEDIANTS
AO ASTONIED
   SEDATION
AP DEPAINTS
AR DETRAINS
   RANDIEST
   STRAINED
AS SANDIEST
AT INSTATED
AU AUDIENTS
   SINUATED
AV DEVIANTS
AY DESYATIN
BE BENDIEST
BL BLINDEST

CH SNITCHED
CO DEONTICS
CY SYNDETIC
DE DESTINED
DG STEDDING
DR STRIDDEN
DS DISTENDS
DU DISTUNED
EE NEEDIEST
EF FENDIEST
   INFESTED
EG INGESTED
   SIGNETED
   STEEDING
EH DISTHENE
EI DIETINES
EL ENLISTED
   LINTSEED
   LISTENED
EM DEMENTIS
   SEDIMENT
EN DENTINES
   DESINENT
EP PENTISED
ER INSERTED
   RESIDENT
   SINTERED
   TRENDIES
ES DESTINES
ET DINETTES
EU DETINUES
   INVESTED
FU UNSIFTED
GI DINGIEST
   INDIGEST
GN STENDING
GR STRINGED
GU DUNGIEST
HO HEDONIST
IK DINKIEST
IO EDITIONS
   SEDITION
IR DISINTER
   INDITERS
   NITRIDES
   RINDIEST
IS INSISTED
   TIDINESS
IU DISUNITE
   NUDITIES
   UNITISED
IV DIVINEST
IW WINDIEST
LP SPLINTED
LR SNIRTLED
   TENDRILS
   TRINDLES
LU DILUENTS
   INSULTED
   UNLISTED
MO DEMONIST
MS MINDSETS
MU MISTUNED
NU DUNNIEST
   DUNNITES
OR DRONIEST
OS DONSIEST
OU OUNDIEST

OW DOWNIEST
PR SPRINTED
PS STIPENDS
QU SQUINTED
RT STRIDENT
   TRIDENTS
RU INTRUDES
RX DEXTRINS
SS DISNESTS
   DISSENTS
ST DENTISTS
SU DISTUNES
UU UNSUITED

DEIORS   27
(ORIDES)
AC IDOCRASE
AD ROADSIDE
AF FORESAID
AL DARIOLES
   SOLIDARE
   SOREDIAL
AN ANEROIDS
   DONARIES
AP DIASPORE
   PARODIES
AT ASTEROID
BD DISORBED
BF FIBROSED
BM BROMIDES
BR BROIDERS
BS DISROBES
BT DEBITORS
BV OVERBIDS
CL SCLEROID
CN CONSIDER
CO CORODIES
CS DISCOERS
CT CORDITES
CU DISCOURE
CV DISCOVER
   DIVORCES
CW CROWDIES
CY DECISORY
DH SHODDIER
DM DERMOIDS
DN INDORSED
DP DROPSIED
DR DISORDER
   SORDIDER
EF FORESIDE
EG GEORDIES
EH HEROISED
EN ORDINEES
EV OVERSIDE
FF OFFSIDER
FG FIREDOGS
FU FOUDRIES
GG DISGORGE
GN NEGROIDS
GO GOODSIRE
GT STODGIER
HM HEIRDOMS
HN HORDEINS
HP SPHEROID
HS DISHORSE
   HIDROSES
IL IDOLISER
IN DERISION
   IRONISED
   RESINOID
IP PRESIDIO
IT DIORITES
IX OXIDISER
JN JOINDERS
KS DROSKIES
LL DOLLIERS
LN DISENROL
LS SOLDIERS
LT STOLIDER
LY SOLDIERY
MO MOIDORES
MP PROMISED
MR MISORDER
   MORRISED
MS MISDOERS
MT MORTISED
MU DIMEROUS
   ERODIUMS
   SOREDIUM
NN ENDIRONS
NP DISPONER
   POINDERS
   PRISONED
NS INDORSES
   SORDINES
NT DRONIEST
NU DOURINES
   SOURDINE
NW WINDORES
   WINDROSE
OW WOODSIER
PS DISPOSER
   DROPSIES
PT DIOPTERS
   DIOPTRES
   DIPTEROS
   PERIDOTS
   PROTEIDS
   RIPOSTED
PV DISPROVE
   PROVIDES
PW DROPWISE
RS DROSSIER
RW DROWSIER
RY DERISORY
SS DOSSIERS
ST STEROIDS
SU DESIROUS
SV DEVISORS
TT DORTIEST
TU IODURETS
   OUTRIDES
   OUTSIDER
   SUITORED
TW ROWDIEST
   WORDIEST
WW WIDOWERS

DEIOST   35
(ODITES)
AG GODETIAS
AL DIASTOLE
   ISOLATED
   SODALITE
   SOLIDATE
AM ATOMISED
AN ASTONIED
   SEDATION
AP DIOPTASE
AR ASTEROID
AX OXIDATES
AZ AZOTISED
BR DEBITORS
CL DOCILEST
CM DOMESTIC
CN DEONTICS
CP DESPOTIC
CR CORDITES
CS CESTOIDS
CT COTTISED
DD DODDIEST
DG DODGIEST
DI ODDITIES
DP PODDIEST
DS SODDIEST
DW DOWDIEST
EG EGOTISED
EM TEDISOME
EP EPIDOTES
   POETISED
GG DOGGIEST
GL GODLIEST
   GOLDIEST
GO GOODIEST
GP PODGIEST
GR STODGIER
HN HEDONIST
HU HIDEOUTS
IN EDITIONS
   SEDITION
IR DIORITES
LM MELODIST
LR STOLIDER
LS SOLIDEST
LT DOILTEST
LU SOLITUDE
MM IMMODEST
MN DEMONIST
MO DOOMIEST
   MOODIEST
   SODOMITE
MR MORTISED
MS MODISTES
MT DEMOTIST
NR DRONIEST
NS DONSIEST
NU OUNDIEST
NW DOWNIEST
OW WOODSIER
PR DIOPTERS
   DIOPTRES
   DIPTEROS
   PERIDOTS
   PROTEIDS
   RIPOSTED
PS DEPOSITS
   TOPSIDES
RS STEROIDS
RT DORTIEST
RU IODURETS
   OUTRIDES
   OUTSIDER
   SUITORED
RW ROWDIEST
   WORDIEST
SU OUTSIDES
SX EXODISTS

TT DOTTIEST
UZ OUTSIZED

DEIRST   57
(STRIDE)
AA DATARIES
   RADIATES
AB BARDIEST
   BRAIDEST
   RABIDEST
   TRIBADES
AC ACRIDEST
AD DISRATED
AE READIEST
   SERIATED
   STEADIER
AH HAIRSTED
   HARDIEST
AI IRISATED
AK STRAIKED
AL DILATERS
   LARDIEST
AM MARDIEST
   MISRATED
   READMITS
AN DETRAINS
   RANDIEST
   STRAINED
AO ASTEROID
AP RAPIDEST
   SPIRATED
   TRAIPSED
AS ASTERIDS
   DIASTERS
   DISASTER
   DISRATES
AT STRAITED
   STRIATED
   TARDIEST
AW TAWDRIES
BE BEDRITES
   BESTRIDE
BL BRISTLED
   DRIBLETS
BO DEBITORS
CE DISCREET
   DISCRETE
CH DITCHERS
CO CORDITES
CP PREDICTS
   SCRIPTED
CU CRUDITES
   CURDIEST
   CURTSIED
CV VERDICTS
DE REDDIEST
DL STRIDDLE
   TIDDLERS
DN STRIDDEN
DU RUDDIEST
   STURDIED
EE REEDIEST
EG DIGESTER
   ESTRIDGE
EI SIDERITE
EM DEMERITS
   DEMISTER
   DIMETERS
   MISTERED
EN INSERTED
```

RESIDENT	STUDIERS	NT INTRUDES	SU LOUDNESS	ROUNDLES	UNDERDOG
SINTERED	STURDIES	OS DESIROUS	UU UNDULOSE	UNSOLDER	DL UNLORDED
TRENDIES	TU DETRITUS	OT IODURETS	UNSOULED	OS LORDOSES	DS REDOUNDS
EP PRIESTED	UX DRUXIEST	OUTRIDES	UV UNSOLVED	OV OVERSOLD	DT ROTUNDED
RESPITED		OUTSIDER		OW WOOLDERS	DW UNWORDED
ER DESTRIER	**DEIRSU 143**	SUITORED	**DELORS 145**	PP DROPPLES	ET DEUTERON
ES EDITRESS	(URDIES)	PS DISPURSE	(OLDERS)	PT DROPLETS	FG UNFORGED
RESISTED	AC DECURIAS	SUSPIRED	AI DARIOLES	PU POULDERS	FL FLOUNDER
SISTERED	AL RESIDUAL	PT DISPUTER	SOLIDARE	POULDRES	UNFOLDER
ET TIREDEST	AN DENARIUS	STUPIDER	SOREDIAL	ST OLDSTERS	FM UNFORMED
EU ERUDITES	UNRAISED	QR SQUIRRED	AL ODALLERS	STRODLES	FO UNROOFED
SURETIED	URANIDES	QT SQUIRTED	AM EARLDOMS	SW WORDLESS	FR FRONDEUR
EW WEIRDEST	AP UPRAISED	RT STURDIER	AN LADRONES	TT DOTTRELS	FS FOUNDERS
FR DRIFTERS	AS RADIUSES	ST DIESTRUS	SOLANDER	UY DELUSORY	REFOUNDS
GG STRIGGED	SUDARIES	DRUSIEST	AP LEOPARDS		FT FORTUNED
GI RIDGIEST	BL BUILDERS	STUDIERS	AS ROADLESS	**DELORT 100**	GG UNGORGED
RIGIDEST	REBUILDS	STURDIES	AT DELATORS	(DOLTER)	GI GUERIDON
GN STRINGED	BM IMBURSED	SY DYSURIES	LEOTARDS	AF DEFLATOR	GN GROUNDEN
GO STODGIER	BN BURNSIDE	TT DETRITUS	LODESTAR	AI IDOLATER	GR GROUNDER
GU DURGIEST	BS DISBURSE	TX DRUXIEST	AU ROULADES	TAILORED	REGROUND
HI DISHERIT	CD DISCURED	VV SURVIVED	BU BOULDERS	AP PROLATED	GS GUERDONS
HT THIRSTED	CE DECURIES		DOUBLERS	AS DELATORS	GT TRUDGEON
THRISTED	CN INDUCERS	**DELNOS 181**	BW BOWLDERS	LEOTARDS	GU UNROUGED
IL REDISTIL	CO DISCOURE	(OLDENS)	CE RECLOSED	LODESTAR	HO HONOURED
IN DISINTER	CR SCURRIED	AC CELADONS	CI SCLEROID	BI TRILOBED	HS ENSHROUD
INDITERS	CS DISCURES	AI NODALISE	CL SCROLLED	BU TROUBLED	UNHORSED
NITRIDES	CT CRUDITES	AM LODESMAN	CO CROODLES	CH CHORTLED	IN UNIRONED
RINDIEST	CURDIEST	AR LADRONES	DECOLORS	CU CLOTURED	IS DOURINES
IO DIORITES	DP SPUDDIER	SOLANDER	CS CORDLESS	DS STRODDLE	SOURDINE
IP RIPTIDES	DS DRUIDESS	AY YEALDONS	SCOLDERS	STRODLED	KW UNWORKED
SPIRITED	DT RUDDIEST	BS BOLDNESS	CU CLOSURED	TODDLERS	LL UNROLLED
IT DIRTIEST	STURDIED	BT BLONDEST	CW CLOWDERS	EI DOLERITE	LS LOUNDERS
TRITIDES	EG GUDESIRE	CE ENCLOSED	SCROWLED	LOITERED	NOURSLED
LN SNIRTLED	EK DUKERIES	CI INCLOSED	DE SOLDERED	EN REDOLENT	ROUNDELS
TENDRILS	EL LEISURED	CO CONDOLES	DO DOODLERS	EO RETOOLED	ROUNDLES
TRINDLES	EN UREDINES	CONSOLED	DP PLODDERS	ET DOTTEREL	UNSOLDER
LO STOLIDER	EP DUPERIES	CS COLDNESS	DT STRODDLE	TOLTERED	LT ROUNDLET
LU DILUTERS	ER RUDERIES	CU ENCLOUDS	STRODLED	EV REVOLTED	MO UNMOORED
LURIDEST	ES DIURESES	UNCLOSED	TODDLERS	EY DELETORY	MW UNWORMED
MO MORTISED	REISSUED	CY CONDYLES	EM REMODELS	FO FORETOLD	NS ENROUNDS
MP DIREMPTS	RESIDUES	SECONDLY	EP DEPLORES	IS STOLIDER	OT UNROOTED
NO DRONIEST	ET ERUDITES	EI ESLOINED	ER SOLDERER	LS DROLLEST	PS POUNDERS
NP SPRINTED	SURETIED	EK SLOKENED	EU URODELES	STROLLED	PV UNPROVED
NT STRIDENT	FF DIFFUSER	EM LODESMEN	EV RESOLVED	NU ROUNDLET	RS RONDURES
TRIDENTS	FO FOUDRIES	EO LOOSENED	FN FONDLERS	OY ROOTEDLY	ROUNDERS
NU INTRUDES	FS FISSURED	ES LESSONED	FORLENDS	PS DROPLETS	UNORDERS
NX DEXTRINS	GL GUILDERS	EU ENSOULED	FO FORSLOED	SS OLDSTERS	RT ROTUNDER
OP GUILDERS	SLUDGIER	EY ESLOYNED	FU FOUDLERS	ST DOTTRELS	RU ROUNDURE
DIOPTRES	GM SMUDGIER	FP PENFOLDS	GG DOGGRELS		SS DOURNESS
DIPTEROS	GT DURGIEST	FR FONDLERS	GP PLEDGORS	**DENORU 99**	RESOUNDS
PERIDOTS	HR DHURRIES	FORLENDS	HU SHOULDER	(UNDOER)	SOUNDERS
PROTEIDS	IN DISINURE	GI GLENOIDS	II IDOLISER	AD UNADORED	ST ROUNDEST
RIPOSTED	URIDINES	SIDELONG	IL DOLLIERS	AI DOUANIER	TONSURED
OS STEROIDS	IS DIURESIS	II LIONISED	IN DISENROL	AL UNLOADER	UNSORTED
OT DORTIEST	KP SPRUIKED	IO SOLENOID	IS SOLDIERS	URODELAN	SU UNROUSED
OU IODURETS	KR SKURRIED	IR DISENROL	IT STOLIDER	AX RONDEAUX	UNSOURED
OUTRIDES	LM MISRULED	IS SONDELIS	IU SOULDIER	BS BOUNDERS	SW WOUNDERS
OUTSIDER	LO SOULDIER	IU DELUSION	IY SOLDIERY	REBOUNDS	TT UNROTTED
SUITORED	LT DILUTERS	INSOULED	LP REDPOLLS	SUBORNED	TW UNDERTOW
OW ROWDIEST	LURIDEST	UNSOILED	LS LORDLESS	CD UNCORDED	
WORDIEST	MO DIMEROUS	MU UNSELDOM	LT DROLLEST	CF FROUNCED	**DENOST 74**
PP STRIPPED	ERODIUMS	OU NODULOSE	STROLLED	UNFORCED	(STONED)
PU DISPUTER	SOREDIUM	UNLOOSED	MS SMOLDERS	CG CONGRUED	AI ASTONIED
STUPIDER	MQ SQUIRMED	OZ SNOOZLED	MU MOULDERS	CI DECURION	SEDATION
QU SQUIRTED	MS SURMISED	PR SPLENDOR	REMOULDS	CJ CONJURED	AR TORNADES
RU STURDIER	MU RESIDUUM	RU LOUNDERS	SMOULDER	CK UNCORKED	AS ONSTEADS
SS DISSERTS	NO DOURINES	NOURSLED	NP SPLENDOR	CT CORNUTED	BL BLONDEST
DISTRESS	SOURDINE	ROUNDELS	NU LOUNDERS	TROUNCED	CI DEONTICS
SU DIESTRUS	NS SUNDRIES	ROUNDLES	NOURSLED	DG GROUNDED	CN CONTENDS
DRUSIEST		UNSOLDER	ROUNDELS		CO SECODONT

```
CU CONTUSED
DM ODDMENTS
DU STOUNDED
DW STOWNDED
EF SOFTENED
EN SONNETED
EP PENTODES
ER ERODENTS
ES STENOSED
GO STEGODON
HI HEDONIST
HZ DOZENTHS
II EDITIONS
   SEDITION
IM DEMONIST
IR DRONIEST
IS DONSIEST
IU OUNDIEST
IW DOWNIEST
MR MORDENTS
MU DEMOUNTS
   MUDSTONE
NR TENDRONS
OU DUOTONES
PR PORTENDS
   PROTENDS
PU OUTSPEND
   UNPOSTED
PW STEWPOND
RU ROUNDEST
   TONSURED
   UNSORTED
SU SOUNDEST
UW UNSTOWED

DENRSU 179
(UNDERS)
AC DURANCES
AD DAUNDERS
AE UNDERSEA
AG ENGUARDS
AH UNSHARED
AI DENARIUS
   UNRAISED
   URANIDES
AL LAUNDERS
   LURDANES
   RUNDALES
AM DURAMENS
   MAUNDERS
   SURNAMED
AP UNSPARED
AQ SQUANDER
AS DANSEURS
AT DAUNTERS
   TRANSUDE
   UNTREADS
AY UNDERSAY
BI BURNSIDE
BL BLUNDERS
BO BOUNDERS
   REBOUNDS
   SUBORNED
BU UNBRUSED
CE CENSURED
CH CHUNDERS
CI INDUCERS
CU UNCURSED
DE SUNDERED
DH HUNDREDS
```


```
DO REDOUNDS
EI UREDINES
ER ENDURERS
   SUNDERER
ES RUDENESS
ET DENTURES
   SEDERUNT
   UNDERSET
   UNDESERT
EU UNDERUSE
EV UNVERSED
FO FOUNDERS
   REFOUNDS
GO GUERDONS
GT TRUDGENS
HO ENSHROUD
HT THUNDERS
II DISINURE
   URIDINES
IO DOURINES
IS SUNDRIES
IT INTRUDES
KT DRUNKEST
KY UNDERSKY
LO LOUNDERS
   NOURSLED
   ROUNDELS
   ROUNDLES
   UNSOLDER
LP PLUNDERS
LT RUNDLETS
   TRUNDLES
NO ENROUNDS
OP POUNDERS
OR RONDURES
   ROUNDERS
   UNORDERS
OS DOURNESS
   RESOUNDS
   SOUNDERS
OT ROUNDEST
   TONSURED
   UNSORTED
OU UNROUSED
   UNSOURED
OW WOUNDERS
PT UPTRENDS
PU UNPURSED
TT STRUNTED

DEORST 50
(SORTED)
AB BROADEST
AC REDCOATS
AG GOADSTER
AI ASTEROID
AL DELATORS
   LEOTARDS
   LODESTAR
AM STROAMED
AN TORNADES
AP ADOPTERS
   ASPORTED
   READOPTS
AR ROADSTER
AS ASSORTED
   TORSADES
AU OUTDARES
```


```
AX EXTRADOS
BE BESORTED
   BESTRODE
BI DEBITORS
BU DOUBTERS
   OBTRUDES
   REDOUBTS
CE CORSETED
   ESCORTED
   SECTORED
CI CORDITES
CS DOCTRESS
CU EDUCTORS
   SEDUCTOR
DL STRODDLE
   STRODLED
   TODDLERS
EE STEREOED
EF DEFOREST
   FORESTED
   FOSTERED
EM MODESTER
EN ERODENTS
EP POSTERED
   REEDSTOP
   REPOSTED
ER RESORTED
   RESTORED
   ROSTERED
ES OERSTEDS
ET ROSETTED
   TETRODES
EX DEXTROSE
EY STOREYED
FS DEFROSTS
FW FROWSTED
GI STODGIER
GS STODGERS
GU DROGUETS
HP POTSHERD
HR REDSHORT
II DIORITES
IL STOLIDER
IM MORTISED
IN DRONIEST
IP DIOPTERS
   DIOPTRES
   DIPTEROS
   PERIDOTS
   PROTEIDS
   RIPOSTED
IS STEROIDS
IT DORTIEST
IU IODURETS
   OUTRIDES
   OUTSIDER
   SUITORED
IW ROWDIEST
   WORDIEST
LL DROLLEST
   STROLLED
LP DROPLETS
LS OLDSTERS
   STRODLES
LT DOTTRELS
MN MORDENTS
MO DOOMSTER
NN TENDRONS
NP PORTENDS
   PROTENDS
```


```
NU ROUNDEST
   TONSURED
   UNSORTED
OP DOORSTEP
   TORPEDOS
PP STROPPED
PU POSTURED
   PROUDEST
   SPROUTED
RS RODSTERS
SW WORSTEDS
SY DESTROYS
TU STROUTED
UU OUTDURES
UV OVERDUST
UX DEXTROUS

DEOSTU 180
(OUSTED)
AB BOUTADES
AR OUTDARES
AT OUTDATES
BL DOUBLETS
BR DOUBTERS
   OBTRUDES
   REDOUBTS
CC STUCCOED
CL LOCUSTED
CM COSTUMED
   CUSTOMED
CN CONTUSED
CQ DOCQUETS
CR EDUCTORS
   SEDUCTOR
CS CUSTODES
DN STOUNDED
EG OUTEDGES
EW OUTWEEDS
EX TUXEDOES
GR DROGUETS
HI HIDEOUTS
HS STOUSHED
IL SOLITUDE
IN OUNDIEST
IR IODURETS
   OUTRIDES
   OUTSIDER
   SUITORED
IS OUTSIDES
IZ OUTSIZED
LP POSTLUDE
MN DEMOUNTS
   MUDSTONE
MO OUTMODES
NO DUOTONES
NP OUTSPEND
   UNPOSTED
NR ROUNDEST
   TONSURED
   UNSORTED
NS SOUNDEST
NW UNSTOWED
PR POSTURED
   PROUDEST
   SPROUTED
RT STROUTED
RU OUTDURES
RV OVERDUST
RX DEXTROUS
ST TESTUDOS
```


```
EEILRS 90
(RELIES)
AC ESCALIER
AD REALISED
   SIDEREAL
AF SERAFILE
AG GASELIER
AH SHIRALEE
AL REALLIES
AM ALMERIES
   MEASLIER
AP ESPALIER
   PEARLIES
AR REALISER
AS REALISES
AT ATELIERS
   EARLIEST
   LEARIEST
   REALTIES
AV VELARISE
AY YEARLIES
AZ REALIZES
   SLEAZIER
BF BELFRIES
BN BERLINES
BU BLUESIER
CD SCLEREID
CE CELERIES
CG CLERGIES
CN LICENSER
   RECLINES
   SILENCER
CT RETICLES
   SCLERITE
   TIERCELS
CU CISELEUR
   CISELURE
CV VERSICLE
DF DEFILERS
   FIELDERS
DG LEIDGERS
DH RELISHED
   SHIELDER
DU LEISURED
DV DELIVERS
   DESILVER
   SILVERED
   SLIVERED
DW WIELDERS
DY YIELDERS
EK SKEELIER
   SLEEKIER
EM SEEMLIER
EP SLEEPIER
ET LEERIEST
   SLEETIER
   STEELIER
EV RELIEVES
EZ SLEEZIER
FH FLESHIER
   SHELFIER
FO FORELIES
FS FIRELESS
FT FERLIEST
FU FUSILEER
GN LEERINGS
   REELINGS
GU REGULISE
GV VELIGERS
```


```
HL HELLIERS
   SHELLIER
HS HEIRLESS
   RELISHES
HV SHELVIER
IO OILERIES
IT TILERIES
IV LIVERIES
KL SKELLIER
KO ROSELIKE
KT TRISKELE
LM SMELLIER
LO ORSEILLE
LS LEISLERS
LT TREILLES
MN ERMELINS
MT TERMLIES
MV VERMEILS
NO ELOINERS
NP PILSENER
NS REINLESS
NT LISTENER
   SILENTER
OP PELORIES
OT LITEROSE
   TROELIES
OV OVERLIES
   RELIEVOS
   VOLERIES
OW OWLERIES
PR REPLIERS
PS SPIELERS
PT EPISTLER
   PELTRIES
   PERLITES
   REPTILES
QU RELIQUES
RV RELIVERS
   REVILERS
ST LEISTERS
   RITELESS
   TIRELESS
SU LEISURES
SV SERVILES
SW WIRELESS
TT RETITLES

EEILST 89
(ELITES)
AD LEADIEST
AF FEALTIES
AG ELEGIAST
AK LEAKIEST
AL LEALTIES
AM MEALIEST
AP EPILATES
AR ATELIERS
   EARLIEST
   LEARIEST
   REALTIES
AS ASTELIES
AT AILETTES
AV ELATIVES
   LEAVIEST
   VEALIEST
BN STILBENE
   TENSIBLE
BT BETITLES
CR RETICLES
```

```
        SCLERITE    SW WITELESS        ENTAILER    HT THIRTEEN    BU REBURIES    QU REQUIRES
        TIERCELS    SX SEXTILES        TREENAIL    HW WHITENER    BV BREVIERS    RT RETIRERS
CT TELESTIC         TX TEXTILES     AP APERIENT    IO ERIONITE    CD DECRIERS       TERRIERS
   TESTICLE         VY STIEVELY     AR RETAINER    IS ERINITES    CH CHERRIES    ST TRESSIER
CU LEUCITES                         AS ARSENITE       NITERIES    CN SINCERER    SV REVERSIS
DG GELIDEST         EEIMNS 192         RESINATE    IT INTERTIE    CP PIERCERS       REVISERS
   LEDGIEST         (EMINES)           STEARINE       RETINITE       PRECISER    TV REVERIST
DN ENLISTED      AD DEMAINES           TRAINEES    JL JETLINER    CS CERRISES       RIVERETS
   LINTSEED           INSEAMED      BI BENITIER    KS KERNITES       CRESSIER       RIVETERS
   LISTENED      AR REMANIES       BO TENEBRIO    LS LISTENER    CT RECITERS    TW REWRITES
DP EPISTLED      AS NEMESIAS       BT REBITTEN       SILENTER    CW SCREWIER    VV REVIVERS
DS TIDELESS      AT MATINEES       CF FRENETIC    LY ENTIRELY    DD DERIDERS
DU DILUTEES         SEMINATE       CG ERECTING       LIENTERY    DH REDSHIRE    EEIRST 31
DV DEVILETS      AX EXAMINES          GENTRICE    MO TIMONEER    DP REPRISED    (ESTIER)
EN SELENITE      CD ENDEMICS       CI ICTERINE    MP TRIPEMEN       RESPIRED    AD READIEST
ER LEERIEST      CG MISCEGEN       CN INCENTRE    MR TERMINER    DS DERRISES       SERIATED
   SLEETIER      CP SPECIMEN       CO ERECTION    MU MUTINEER       DESIRERS       STEADIER
   STEELIER      CT CENTIMES          NEOTERIC    MV VIREMENT       DRESSIER    AE EATERIES
ES SEELIEST      DE INSEEMED       CP PRENTICE    NS INTENSER       RESIDERS    AH HEARTIES
EV TELEVISE      DH INMESHED       CS CENTRIES       INTERNES    DT DESTRIER    AL ATELIERS
FM FISTMELE      DM ENDEMISM          ENTERICS    NT RENITENT    DU RUDERIES       EARLIEST
FR FERLIEST      DO DEMONISE          ENTICERS    OR REORIENT    DV REDRIVES       LEARIEST
FS FELSITES      DS DESMINES          SCIENTER    OS SEROTINE    EK SKEERIER       REALTIES
GG LEGGIEST         SIDESMEN          SECRETIN    OT TENORITE    EM MISERERE    AM EMIRATES
GN GENTILES      DT DEMENTIS       CT RETICENT    OX EXERTION    EN SNEERIER       REAMIEST
   SLEETING         SEDIMENT       CU CEINTURE    PX INEXPERT    ET REESTIER       STEAMIER
   STEELING      ET EMETINES          ENURETIC    RS INSERTER       RETIREES    AN ARSENITE
GS ELEGISTS      FI FEMINISE       DD DENDRITE       REINSERT    EV REREVISE       RESINATE
HS LEISHEST      GI GEMINIES       DK TINKERED       REINTERS       REVERIES       STEARINE
   SHELTIES      GK SMEEKING       DN INDENTER       RENTIERS    FN REFINERS       TRAINEES
IN LENITIES      GN MENINGES          INTENDER       TERRINES    FT FERRITES    AO ETAERIOS
IR TILERIES      GR REGIMENS          INTERNED    RV INVERTER    GN RESIGNER    AP PETARIES
IV LEVITIES      GS SEEMINGS       DO ORIENTED    RX INTERREX    GT REGISTER    AR ARTERIES
   VEILIEST      GT MEETINGS       DR INTERRED    SS INTERESS    GV GRIEVERS       REASTIER
IW LEWISITE         STEEMING          TRENDIER       SENTRIES    HK SHRIEKER    AS SERIATES
KP PIKELETS      GU EUGENISM       DS INSERTED       TRENISES    HN ERRHINES    AT ARIETTES
   SPIKELET      HO HEMIONES          RESIDENT    ST INERTEST    HP PERISHER       ITERATES
KR TRISKELE      HR SHIREMEN          SINTERED       INTEREST       SPHERIER       TEARIEST
LM MELLITES      HS INMESHES          TRENDIES       STERNITE    HS SHERRIES       TREATIES
LR TREILLES      IT ENMITIES       DU REUNITED    SU ESURIENT    HW WHERRIES       TREATISE
LV EVILLEST      LN LINESMEN       DV INVERTED       NEURITES    IT REISTIER    AV EVIRATES
MO MESOLITE      LR ERMELINS       DW WINTERED       RETINUES    IV RIVIERES    AW SWEATIER
   MISLETOE      LS ISLESMEN       DX DEXTRINE       REUNITES    KS SKERRIES       TAWERIES
MP IMPLETES      LU SELENIUM       EN INTERNEE    SV NERVIEST    LP REPLIERS       WEARIEST
MR TERMLIES         SEMILUNE       ES ETERNISE       REINVEST    LV RELIVERS    AY YEASTIER
MS TIMELESS      MR IMMENSER          TEENSIER       SERVIENT       REVILERS    BD BEDRITES
NN LENIENTS      NO NOMINEES       ET REINETTE       SIRVENTE    MP PREMIERS       BESTRIDE
   SENTINEL      NR REINSMEN          TEENTIER    SX INTERSEX       REPRIMES    BE BEERIEST
NO NOSELITE      OP EPISEMON       EZ ETERNIZE    SY SERENITY       SIMPERER    BF BRIEFEST
NP PLENTIES      OR EMERSION       FS FERNIEST    TY ENTIRETY    MT MERRIEST    BH HERBIEST
NR LISTENER      OT MONETISE       GG GREETING       ETERNITY       TRIREMES    BU UBERTIES
   SILENTER         SEMITONE       GM METERING                   NP REPINERS    CD DISCREET
NT ENTITLES      PT SEPIMENT          REGIMENT    EEIRRS 182     NS RESINERS       DISCRETE
NV VEINLETS      QU MESQUINE       GN ENTERING    (ERRIES)       NT INSERTER    CF FIERCEST
OP PETIOLES      RV MINEVERS       GP PETERING    AC CARIERES       REINSERT    CH CHESTIER
OR LITEROSE      SW MISWEENS       GS GENTRIES       CREASIER       REINTERS       HERETICS
   TROELIES      TT MINETTES          INTEGERS    AF RAREFIES       RENTIERS    CI SERICITE
OS ESTOILES                           REESTING    AG GREASIER       TERRINES    CL RETICLES
OW OWELTIES      EEINRT 7             STEERING    AH HEARSIER    NU REINSURE       SCLERITE
OZ ZEOLITES      (ENTIRE)             STREIGNE    AK RAKERIES    NV VERNIERS       TIERCELS
PR EPISTLER      AC CENTIARE       GU GENITURE       SKEARIER    OP ROPERIES    CN CENTRIES
   PELTRIES         CREATINE       GV EVERTING    AL REALISER    OR ORRERIES       ENTERICS
   PERLITES         INCREATE       GW TWEERING    AM SMEARIER    OS ROSERIES       ENTICERS
   REPTILES         ITERANCE       GX EXERTING    AN REARISEN       ROSIERES       SCIENTER
PS EPISTLES      AD DETAINER          GENETRIX    AP PEREIRAS    PP PERSPIRE       SECRETIN
PY EPISTYLE         RETAINED       HN INHERENT       SPEARIER    PR PERRIERS    CO COTERIES
RS LEISTERS      AH ATHERINE       HO ETHERION    AS REARISES    PS REPRISES       ESOTERIC
   RITELESS      AK ANKERITE       HP NEPHRITE    AT ARTERIES       RESPIRES    CP CREPIEST
   TIRELESS         KREATINE          PREHNITE       REASTIER    PV REPRIVES       RECEIPTS
RT RETITLES      AL ELATERIN          TREPHINE    BB BERBERIS    PZ REPRIZES    CR RECITERS
```

CU CERUSITE	IN ERINITES	RW REWRITES	AC CLEAREST	IM TERMLIES	RATTEENS
CUTESIER	NITERIES	ST RESTIEST	SCELERAT	IN LISTENER	AV AVENTRES
EUCRITES	IR REISTIER	SU SURETIES	TREACLES	SILENTER	VETERANS
CV VERTICES	IV VERITIES	SV SIEVERTS	AD TREADLES	IO LITEROSE	BP BESPRENT
CX EXCITERS	JK JERKIEST	TREVISES	AE TEASELER	TROELIES	BT BRENTEST
DD REDDIEST	KL TRISKELE	VESTRIES	AF REFLATES	IP EPISTLER	BW BESTREWN
DE REEDIEST	KN KERNITES	VV VETIVERS	AH HALTERES	PELTRIES	CC CRESCENT
DG DIGESTER	KP PERKIEST	VY SEVERITY	LEATHERS	PERLITES	CH TRENCHES
ESTRIDGE	LL TREILLES		AI ATELIERS	REPTILES	CI CENTRIES
DI SIDERITE	LM TERMLIES	**EELNST 161**	EARLIEST	IS LEISTERS	ENTERICS
DM DEMERITS	LN LISTENER	(NESTLE)	LEARIEST	RITELESS	ENTICERS
DEMISTER	SILENTER	AC CLEANEST	REALTIES	TIRELESS	SCIENTER
DIMETERS	LO LITEROSE	LATENCES	AM LAMETERS	IT RETITLES	SECRETIN
MISTERED	TROELIES	AE SELENATE	AN ALTERNES	KS KESTRELS	CL LECTERNS
DN INSERTED	LP EPISTLER	AK KANTELES	AO OLEASTER	SKELTERS	CN CENTNERS
RESIDENT	PELTRIES	AM MANTEELS	AP PRELATES	LO SOLLERET	CU UNSECRET
SINTERED	PERLITES	TALESMEN	AR RELATERS	MO MOLESTER	DE RESENTED
TRENDIES	REPTILES	AR ALTERNES	AS STEALERS	MS SMELTERS	DI INSERTED
DP PRIESTED	LS LEISTERS	AS LATENESS	TEARLESS	MY SMELTERY	RESIDENT
RESPITED	RITELESS	AY ENTAYLES	TESSERAL	NO ENTRESOL	SINTERED
DR DESTRIER	TIRELESS	BD BENDLETS	AT ALERTEST	NT LETTERNS	TRENDIES
DS EDITRESS	LT RETITLES	BI STILBENE	AU RESALUTE	OT LORETTES	DO ERODENTS
RESISTED	MM MERISTEM	TENSIBLE	AY EASTERLY	OU RESOLUTE	DP PRETENDS
SISTERED	MIMESTER	CG NEGLECTS	BH BLETHERS	PS SPELTERS	DU DENTURES
DT TIREDEST	MISMETRE	CK NECKLETS	HERBLETS	PZ PRETZELS	SEDERUNT
DU ERUDITES	MO TIRESOME	CR LECTERNS	BM TREMBLES	RW WRESTLER	UNDERSET
SURETIED	MP EMPTIERS	CU ESCULENT	CE RESELECT	SS RESTLESS	EG GREENEST
DW WEIRDEST	MR MERRIEST	DI ENLISTED	CF REFLECTS	TRESSELS	EI ETERNISE
EH ETHERISE	TRIREMES	LINTSEED	CI RETICLES	ST SETTLERS	TEENSIER
SHEETIER	MS TRISEMES	LISTENED	SCLERITE	STERLETS	EM ENTREMES
EK REEKIEST	MT TERMITES	DK SKLENTED	TIERCELS	TRESTLES	EN ETRENNES
EL LEERIEST	MU EMERITUS	DP SPLENTED	CN LECTERNS	SW SWELTERS	EP PRETENSE
SLEETIER	NN INTENSER	DY ENSTYLED	CO CORSELET	WRESTLES	TERPENES
STEELIER	INTERNES	EI SELENITE	ELECTORS	SY RESTYLES	ER ENTERERS
EM EREMITES	NO SEROTINE	EM ELEMENTS	ELECTROS	TYRELESS	RESENTER
EN ETERNISE	NR INSERTER	FO FELSTONE	SELECTOR	SZ SELTZERS	TERREENS
TEENSIER	REINSERT	GI GENTILES	CP PLECTRES	WY WESTERLY	TERRENES
EP PEERIEST	REINTERS	SLEETING	PRELECTS		ES SERENEST
STEEPIER	RENTIERS	STEELING	CS LECTRESS	**EENRST 56**	EV EVENTERS
ER REESTIER	TERRINES	GT GENTLEST	CU LECTURES	(ENTERS)	EX EXTERNES
RETIREES	NS INTERESS	II LENITIES	CY SECRETLY	AA ARSENATE	EY YESTREEN
ES STEERIES	SENTRIES	IN LENIENTS	DD TREDDLES	SERENATA	FI FERNIEST
FI FEISTIER	TRENISES	SENTINEL	DE DEERLETS	AC REASCENT	FM FERMENTS
FERITIES	NT INERTEST	IO NOSELITE	STREELED	SARCENET	FO ENFOREST
FIERIEST	INTEREST	IP PLENTIES	DU LUSTERED	AE SERENATE	SOFTENER
FL FERLIEST	STERNITE	IR LISTENER	RESULTED	AF FASTENER	GH GREENTHS
FM FEMITERS	NU ESURIENT	SILENTER	ULSTERED	FENESTRA	GI GENTRIES
FN FERNIEST	NEURITES	IT ENTITLES	DW LEWDSTER	AG ESTRANGE	INTEGERS
FR FERRITES	RETINUES	IV VEINLETS	WRESTLED	GRANTEES	REESTING
FT FRISETTE	REUNITES	KO SKELETON	DY RESTYLED	GREATENS	STEERING
FY ESTERIFY	NV NERVIEST	LS SNELLEST	EI LEERIEST	REAGENTS	STREIGNE
GN GENTRIES	REINVEST	LU ENTELLUS	SLEETIER	SEGREANT	GO ESTROGEN
INTEGERS	SERVIENT	OR ENTRESOL	STEELIER	SERGEANT	HO HONESTER
REESTING	SIRVENTE	OS NOTELESS	EO SLOETREE	STERNAGE	II ERINITES
STEERING	NX INTERSEX	TONELESS	EP REPLETES	AH HASTENER	NITERIES
STREIGNE	NY SERENITY	OT NOTELETS	ES TREELESS	HEARTENS	IK KERNITES
GO ERGOTISE	OP POETRIES	OU TOLUENES	ET RESETTLE	AI ARSENITE	IL LISTENER
GP PRESTIGE	OS EROTESIS	RT LETTERNS	EV LEVERETS	RESINATE	SILENTER
GR REGISTER	PS RESPITES	SU TUNELESS	VERSELET	STEARINE	IN INTENSER
GT GRISETTE	PT PRETTIES	UNSTEELS	FI FERLIEST	TRAINEES	INTERNES
TERGITES	PY PERSEITY	SY ENSTYLES	FT FETTLERS	AJ SERJEANT	IO SEROTINE
HM ERETHISM	QU QUIETERS	TU LUNETTES	FU FLEURETS	AL ALTERNES	IR INSERTER
ETHERISM	REQUITES	UNSETTLE	HH THRESHEL	AM REMANETS	REINSERT
HO ISOTHERE	QW QWERTIES		HO HOSTELER	AO RESONATE	REINTERS
THEORIES	RR RETIRERS	**EELRST 157**	HP TELPHERS	AR TERRANES	RENTIERS
THEORISE	TERRIERS	(ELTERS)	HS SHELTERS	AS ASSENTER	TERRINES
HP TREESHIP	RS TRESSIER	AA LAETARES	HY SHELTERY	EARNESTS	IS INTERESS
HS HEISTERS	RV REVERIST	AB BLEAREST	II TILERIES	SARSENET	SENTRIES
HT ETHERIST	RIVERETS	BLEATERS	IK TRISKELE	AT ENTREATS	TRENISES
IL TILERIES	RIVETERS	RETABLES	IL TREILLES		

IT INERTEST	DI TIREDEST	IN SNIFTIER	YEARLING	SW NEWSGIRL	DW SWINGLED
INTEREST	DO ROSETTED	IP SPITFIRE	BM REMBLING	UV VELURING	WELDINGS
STERNITE	TETRODES	IR FIRRIEST	BO IGNOBLER		EF FEELINGS
IU ESURIENT	EL RESETTLE	IT RIFTIEST	BT TREBLING	**EGILNS 117**	EG NEGLIGES
NEURITES	ER RESETTER	KO FORKIEST	CI CLINGIER	(SINGLE)	EH HEELINGS
RETINUES	EW TWEETERS	KS FRISKETS	CK CLERKING	AB SINGABLE	SHEELING
REUNITES	FI FRISETTE	LO FLORIEST	RECKLING	AD DEALINGS	EK KEELINGS
IV NERVIEST	FL FETTLERS	TREFOILS	CS CLINGERS	LEADINGS	SLEEKING
REINVEST	GI GRISETTE	LR TRIFLERS	CRINGLES	AE ENSILAGE	EP PEELINGS
SERVIENT	TERGITES	LS RIFTLESS	CU RECULING	LINEAGES	SLEEPING
SIRVENTE	HI ETHERIST	STIFLERS	ULCERING	AF FINAGLES	SPEELING
IX INTERSEX	HW WHETTERS	LT FLITTERS	CY GLYCERIN	AG LIGNAGES	ER LEERINGS
IY SERENITY	IL RETITLES	LW FEWTRILS	DD REDDLING	AH HEALINGS	REELINGS
LO ENTRESOL	IM TERMITES	MU FREMITUS	DE ENGIRDLE	LEASHING	ES SEELINGS
LT LETTERNS	IN INERTEST	NS SNIFTERS	LINGERED	SHEALING	ET GENTILES
MO SERMONET	INTEREST	OO ROOFIEST	REEDLING	AK LINKAGES	SLEETING
STOREMEN	STERNITE	OP FIREPOTS	DI GRIDELIN	AL NIGELLAS	STEELING
MW TREWSMEN	IP PRETTIES	OR FROSTIER	DU INDULGER	AM MEASLING	EV SLEEVING
NO TENONERS	IS RESTIEST	ROTIFERS	DY YELDRING	AN EANLINGS	EW SWEELING
OO ROESTONE	LN LETTERNS	OS FOISTERS	EF FLEERING	LEANINGS	FH FLESHING
OP PROTENSE	LO LORETTES	OW FROWIEST	EG LEGERING	AO GASOLINE	FN FLENSING
OT ONSETTER	LS SETTLERS	RT FRITTERS	EI LINGERIE	AP ELAPSING	FR FLINGERS
OV OVERNETS	STERLETS	RU FRITURES	EO ELOIGNER	PLEASING	FT FELTINGS
OX EXTENSOR	TRESTLES	FRUITERS	ER LINGERER	AR ARLESING	GG LEGGINGS
PP PERPENTS	MO REMOTEST	FURRIEST	ES LEERINGS	ENGRAILS	GR NIGGLERS
PS PERTNESS	MP TEMPTERS	SU SURFEITS	REELINGS	NARGILES	SNIGGLER
PRESENTS	NO ONSETTER	SURFIEST	EU REGULINE	REALIGNS	GS SNIGGLES
SERPENTS	NP STREPENT	SW SWIFTERS	EV LEVERING	SANGLIER	GU LUGEINGS
PT STREPENT	NS STERNEST	TU TURFIEST	FO FLORIGEN	SLANGIER	HI SHEILING
PV PREVENTS	TESTERNS	TURFITES	FS FLINGERS	AS GAINLESS	SHIELING
RV RENVERST	OP TREETOPS	UX FIXTURES	FY FERLYING	GLASSINE	HL SHELLING
ST STERNEST	OS ROSETTES	UZ FURZIEST	GI NIGGLIER	LEASINGS	HP HELPINGS
TESTERNS	PU UPSETTER		GS NIGGLERS	SEALINGS	HR HERLINGS
SU TRUENESS	PX PRETEXTS	**EGILNR 125**	SNIGGLER	SNIGGLER	SHINGLER
SW WESTERNS	RU REUTTERS	(LINGER)	GY GINGERLY	AT EASTLING	HS SHINGLES
SY STYRENES	UTTERERS	AA REGALIAN	HI HIRELING	GELATINS	HT ENLIGHTS
UV VENTURES	SU TRUSTEES	AB BLEARING	HS HERLINGS	GENITALS	LIGHTENS
	TU UTTEREST	AC CLEARING	SHINGLER	STEALING	HV SHELVING
EERSTT 200	UX TEXTURES	AD DEARLING	IJ JINGLIER	AV LEAVINGS	HW WELSHING
(ETTERS)		DRAGLINE	IK KINGLIER	SLEAVING	IN ENISLING
AA STEARATE	**EFIRST 191**	AE ALGERINE	IN RELINING	SLEEVING	ENSILING
AB ABETTERS	(STRIFE)	AG GANGLIER	IO RELIGION	AW SWEALING	IP SPIELING
AD ASTERTED	AG FRIGATES	REGALING	IS RESILING	BM SEMBLING	IR RESILING
RESTATED	AI RATIFIES	AH NARGHILE	IT GIRTLINE	BO IGNOBLES	IT LIGNITES
AG GREATEST	AL FLARIEST	NARGILEH	RETILING	INGLOBES	LINGIEST
AH THEATERS	FRAILEST	AI GAINLIER	TINGLIER	BS BLESSING	IV VEILINGS
THEATRES	AN FENITARS	AJ JANGLIER	TIRELING	GLIBNESS	IW WISELING
AI ARIETTES	AR FRATRIES	AM GERMINAL	IV RELIVING	BT BELTINGS	JR JINGLERS
ITERATES	BE BRIEFEST	MALIGNER	REVILING	BU BLUEINGS	JT JINGLETS
TEARIEST	BL FILBERTS	MALINGER	JS JINGLERS	BULGINES	KK LEKKINGS
TREATIES	BS FIBSTERS	AN LEARNING	JU JUNGLIER	CI CEILINGS	KP SKELPING
TREATISE	CE FIERCEST	AO GERANIOL	MS GREMLINS	CIELINGS	KS KINGLESS
AL ALERTEST	CU FRUTICES	REGIONAL	MERLINGS	CO ECLOSING	KT KINGLETS
AM TEAMSTER	DR DRIFTERS	AP PEARLING	MINGLERS	CR CLINGERS	LM SMELLING
AN ENTREATS	EI FEISTIER	AR GNARLIER	MU RELUMING	CRINGLES	LN SNELLING
RATTEENS	FERITIES	AS ARLESING	OS RESOLING	CU LUCIGENS	LO LOGLINES
AR RETRATES	FIERIEST	ENGRAILS	OW LOWERING	CY GLYCINES	LP SPELLING
RETREATS	EL FERLIEST	NARGILES	PS PINGLERS	DD SLEDDING	LT STELLING
TREATERS	EM FEMITERS	REALIGNS	SPERLING	DE SEEDLING	TELLINGS
AS ESTREATS	EN FERNIEST	SANGLIER	SPRINGLE	DG GELDINGS	LW SWELLING
RESTATES	ER FERRITES	SLANGIER	PY REPLYING	SLEDGING	WELLINGS
AT ATTESTER	ET FRISETTE	AT ALERTING	RU RULERING	SNIGGLED	LY YELLINGS
AX EXTREATS	EY ESTERIFY	ALTERING	RY ERRINGLY	DH HINDLEGS	MM LEMMINGS
BE BESETTER	FO FORFEITS	INTEGRAL	SS RINGLESS	SHINGLED	MR GREMLINS
BN BRENTEST	FU STUFFIER	RELATING	SLINGERS	DI EILDINGS	MERLINGS
BU BURETTES	GH FIGHTERS	TANGLIER	ST LINGSTER	SIDELING	MINGLERS
CU CURETTES	FREIGHTS	TRIANGLE	RINGLETS	DN LENDINGS	MT MELTINGS
DE RESETTED	GR GRIFTERS	AX RELAXING	STERLING	DO GLENOIDS	SMELTING
SETTERED	HI SHIFTIER	AY LAYERING	TINGLERS	SIDELONG	MU LEGUMINS
STREETED	HS SHIFTERS	RELAYING	TRINGLES	DP SPELDING	
				DU INDULGES	
				DV DEVLINGS	

```
NT NESTLING      CI GENTILIC         GOLDIEST   HN HERLINGS      FU GULFIEST      EG GREENING
OR RESOLING      CU CULTIGEN      DZ GOLDSIZE      SHINGLER      HN ENLIGHTS         RENEGING
OU LIGNEOUS      DE DELETING      ES GELOSIES   HT LIGHTERS         LIGHTENS      EP PREENING
OW LONGWISE      DI DILIGENT      EU EULOGIES      RELIGHTS      HP PIGHTLES      ES ENGINERS
PR PINGLERS      EF FLEETING         EULOGISE      SLIGHTER      HR LIGHTERS         INGENERS
   SPERLING      EG GLEETING      FG SOLFEGGI   IN RESILING         RELIGHTS         SERENING
   SPRINGLE      ES GENTILES      GO GOOGLIES   IR GRISLIER         SLIGHTER         SNEERING
PS SPIGNELS         SLEETING      HU OUGHLIES   JN JINGLERS      HS SLEIGHTS      ET ENTERING
PT PELTINGS         STEELING      LN LOGLINES   MM GLIMMERS      HT LIGHTEST      EV ENERVING
   PESTLING      EW TWEELING      MR GOMERILS   MN GREMLINS      IM LEGITIMS      EW RENEWING
PY YELPINGS      EX TELEXING      MU ELOGIUMS         MERLINGS   IN LIGNITES      EY ENGINERY
RS RINGLESS      FS FELTINGS      NR RESOLING   MO GOMERILS         LINGIEST         RENEYING
   SLINGERS      FT FETTLING      NU LIGNEOUS   NO RESOLING      JN JINGLETS      FI ENFIRING
RT LINGSTER      GN GENTLING      NW LONGWISE   NP PINGLERS      KN KINGLETS         INFRINGE
   RINGLETS         GLENTING      OO OOLOGIES         SPERLING   LN STELLING         REFINING
   STERLING      HP PENLIGHT      OU ISOLOGUE         SPRINGLE      TELLINGS      FS FERNINGS
   TINGLERS      HS ENLIGHTS      RS GLOSSIER   NS RINGLESS      MN MELTINGS      GI GREINING
   TRINGLES         LIGHTENS      SS GLOSSIES         SLINGERS      SMELTING         REIGNING
RW NEWSGIRL      IR GIRTLINE      ST ELOGISTS   NT LINGSTER      NN NESTLING      GN GRENNING
SS SIGNLESS         RETILING      TU EULOGIST         RINGLETS   NP PELTINGS      GO ENGORING
ST GLISTENS         TINGLIER                           STERLING      PESTLING      HI INHERING
   SINGLETS         TIRELING   EGILRS 159               TINGLERS   NR LINGSTER      IL RELINING
SU UGLINESS      IS LIGNITES   (LIGERS)                 TRINGLES      RINGLETS      IP REPINING
SW SWINGLES         LINGIEST   AA GASALIER   NW NEWSGIRL         STERLING         RIPENING
   WINGLESS      JS JINGLETS      LAIRAGES   OS GLOSSIER         TINGLERS      IS RESINING
TT LETTINGS      KS KINGLETS      REGALIAS   PP GRIPPLES         TRINGLES      NS RENNINGS
   SETTLING      LS STELLING   AC GLACIERS   ST GLISTERS      NS GLISTENS      OO RONEOING
TW SWELTING         TELLINGS   AD SLAIRGED      GRISTLES         SINGLETS      OP REPONING
   WINGLETS      LU GLUTELIN   AE GASELIER   TT GLITTERS      NT LETTINGS      OT NITROGEN
UV EVULSING      MS MELTINGS   AG SLAGGIER   TU GURLIEST         SETTLING      OV VIGNERON
                    SMELTING   AM GREMIALS   UV VIRGULES      NW SWELTING      RS GRINNERS
EGILNT  66       NS NESTLING      LAMIGERS   ZZ GRIZZLES         WINGLETS      RU UNERRING
(TINGLE)         NT NETTLING      REGALISM                   OS ELOGISTS      ST STERNING
AA AGENTIAL      PS PELTINGS   AN ARLESING   EGILST 190       OU EULOGIST      SU ENSURING
   ALGINATE         PESTLING      ENGRAILS   (LEGIST)         RS GLISTERS      TU RETUNING
AB BELATING      PT PETTLING      NARGILES   AC GELASTIC         GRISTLES      TV VENTRING
   BLEATING      RS LINGSTER      REALIGNS   AD GLADIEST      RT GLITTERS
   TANGIBLE         RINGLETS      SANGLIER   AE ELEGIAST      RU GURLIEST      EGINOS  78
AC CLEATING         STERLING      SLANGIER   AH LAIGHEST                       (INGOES)
AD DELATING         TINGLERS   AO GASOLIER   AL LEGALIST      EGINNR 178       AB BEGONIAS
AE GALENITE         TRINGLES      GIRASOLE      STILLAGE      (GINNER)         AC COINAGES
   GELATINE      SS GLISTENS      SERAGLIO      TILLAGES      AA ANEARING      AD AGONISED
   LEGATINE      ST LETTINGS   AS GLASSIER   AN EASTLING      AC ENRACING         DIAGNOSE
AG TEAGLING         SETTLING   AT GLARIEST      GELATINS      AG ANGERING      AL GASOLINE
AH ATHELING      SW SWELTING      REGALIST      GENITALS         ENRAGING      AR IGNAROES
AM LIGAMENT         WINGLETS   AY GREASILY      STEALING      AI ARGININE         ORGANISE
AN GANTLINE      UX EXULTING   AZ GLAZIERS   AO OTALGIES      AL LEARNING         ORIGANES
   LATENING                   BB GRIBBLES   AR GLARIEST      AM ENARMING      AS AGONISES
AO GELATION      EGILOS 132    BT GILBERTS      REGALIST         RENAMING      AZ AGONIZES
   LEGATION      (LOGIES)      CE CLERGIES   AZ GLAZIEST      AS AGINNERS      BD OBSIGNED
AP PLEATING      AC CALIGOES   CG SCRIGGLE   BB GLIBBEST         EARNINGS      BL IGNOBLES
AR ALERTING      AD GOLIASED   CN CLINGERS   BI BILGIEST         ENGRAINS         INGLOBES
   ALTERING      AF FOLIAGES      CRINGLES   BN BELTINGS         GRANNIES      BO BESOGNIO
   INTEGRAL      AN GASOLINE   DD GRIDDLES   BR GILBERTS      AV RAVENING      BR SOBERING
   RELATING      AP SPOILAGE   DE LEIDGERS   BU BULGIEST      AY RENAYING      CD COGNISED
   TANGLIER      AR GASOLIER   DR GIRDLERS   CH GLITCHES         YEARNING      CL ECLOSING
   TRIANGLE         GIRASOLE   DU GUILDERS   DD GLIDDEST      BE BEGINNER      CS COGNISES
AS EASTLING         SERAGLIO      SLUDGIER   DE GELIDEST         BENIGNER      CZ COGNIZES
   GELATINS      AS GOLIASES   DW WERGILDS      LEDGIEST      BN BRENNING      DI INDIGOES
   GENITALS      AT OTALGIES   EN LEERINGS   DH DELIGHTS      BO ENROBING      DL GLENOIDS
   STEALING      BE OBLIGEES      REELINGS      SLIGHTED         RINGBONE         SIDELONG
AV VALETING      BN IGNOBLES   EU REGULISE   DO GODLIEST      CO ENCORING      DM SMIDGEON
AX EXALTING         INGLOBES   EV VELIGERS      GOLDIEST      CS SCERNING      DP DEPOSING
AZ TEAZLING      CI LOGICISE   FN FLINGERS   EG LEGGIEST      CT CENTRING         DISPONGE
BE BEETLING      CN ECLOSING   GG GIGGLERS   EN GENTILES      DE ENRINGED      DR NEGROIDS
BR TREBLING      DD DISLODGE   GH HIGGLERS      SLEETING      DI NIDERING      DW WENDIGOS
BS BELTINGS      DN GLENOIDS   GN NIGGLERS      STEELING      DT TRENDING         WIDGEONS
BT BLETTING         SIDELONG      SNIGGLER   ES ELEGISTS      DU ENDURING      EO OOGENIES
CE ELECTING      DT GODLIEST   GW WIGGLERS   FN FELTINGS         UNRINGED      EP EPIGONES
CH LETCHING                      WRIGGLES                   EE ENGINEER
```

```
ER ERINGOES
ET EGESTION
GK GINGKOES
   GINKGOES
HS SHOEINGS
HT HISTOGEN
HU GINHOUSE
IM IGNOMIES
IR SEIGNIOR
LL LOGLINES
LR RESOLING
LU LIGNEOUS
LW LONGWISE
MR NEGROISM
MT MITOGENS
MU GEMINOUS
MY MOSEYING
NP OPENINGS
PR PERIGONS
   REPOSING
   SPONGIER
PT PONGIEST
PX EXPOSING
PY POESYING
RR IGNORERS
RS SIGNORES
RT GENITORS
   ROSETING
RY SEIGNORY
TT TENTIGOS

EGINRS  68
(SINGER)
AA ANGARIES
AB BEARINGS
   SABERING
AC CREASING
   GRECIANS
   SEARCING
AD DERAIGNS
   GRADINES
   READINGS
AE GESNERIA
AG GEARINGS
   GREASING
   SNAGGIER
AH HEARINGS
   HEARSING
   SHEARING
AK SKEARING
AL ARLESING
   ENGRAILS
   NARGILES
   REALIGNS
   SANGLIER
   SLANGIER
AM GERMAINS
   SMEARING
AN AGINNERS
   EARNINGS
   ENGRAINS
   GRANNIES
AO IGNAROES
   ORGANISE
   ORIGANES
AP PREASING
   SPEARING
AR EARRINGS
   GRAINERS
AS REASSIGN

   SEARINGS
   SERINGAS
AT ANGRIEST
   ASTRINGE
   GANISTER
   GANTRIES
   GRANITES
   INGRATES
   RANGIEST
   REASTING
   STEARING
AV VINEGARS
AW SWEARING
   WEARINGS
AY RESAYING
BE BIGENERS
BO SOBERING
BR BRINGERS
BW BREWINGS
CE CREESING
   GENERICS
CL CLINGERS
   CRINGLES
CN SCERNING
CR CRINGERS
CT CRESTING
CU RECUSING
   RESCUING
   SCUNGIER
   SECURING
CW SCREWING
CY SYNERGIC
DD REDDINGS
DE DESIGNER
   ENERGIDS
   REDESIGN
   READINGS
   RESIGNED
DI DESIRING
   RESIDING
   RINGSIDE
DO NEGROIDS
DP SPRINGED
DR GRINDERS
   REGRINDS
DS DRESSING
DT STRINGED
DW REDWINGS
DY SYNERGID
   SYRINGED
EE ENERGIES
EF FEERINGS
   REEFINGS
EG GREESING
EH GREENISH
   SHEERING
EJ JEERINGS
EK KREESING
   SKEERING
EL LEERINGS
   REELINGS
EM REGIMENS
EN ENGINERS
   INGENERS
   SERENING
   SNEERING
EO ERINGOES
EP SPEERING
   SPREEING

ER RESIGNER
ES GREISENS
ET GENTRIES
   INTEGERS
   REESTING
   STEERING
   STREIGNE
EU SEIGNEUR
EV SEVERING
   VEERINGS
EW SEWERING
FH FRESHING
FL FLINGERS
FN FERNINGS
FU GUNFIRES
   REFUSING
FW SWERFING
GL NIGGLERS
   SNIGGLER
GS GRESSING
   SNIGGERS
HK GHERKINS
HL HERLINGS
   SHINGLER
HP SPHERING
HR HERRINGS
HT RIGHTENS
HU USHERING
HW SHREWING
   WHINGERS
IL RESILING
IM REMISING
IN RESINING
IO SEIGNIOR
IP SPEIRING
IT GIRNIEST
   IGNITERS
   REISTING
   STINGIER
   STRIGINE
IU SIGNIEUR
IV REVISING
IW RINGWISE
JK JERKINGS
JL JINGLERS
KR SKERRING
KU RESKUING
LM GREMLINS
   MERLINGS
   MINGLERS
LO RESOLING
LP PINGLERS
   SPERLING
   SPRINGLE
LS RINGLESS
   SLINGERS
LT LINGSTER
   RINGLETS
   STERLING
   TINGLERS
   TRINGLES
LW NEWSGIRL
MO NEGROISM
MP IMPREGNS
MS GRIMNESS
MU RESUMING
NN RENNINGS
NR GRINNERS
NT STERNING
NU ENSURING

OP PERIGONS
   REPOSING
   SPONGIER
OR IGNORERS
OS SIGNORES
OT GENITORS
   ROSETING
OY SEIGNORY
PP REPPINGS
PR SPERRING
   SPRINGER
PS PRESSING
   SPERSING
   SPRINGES
PT PRESTING
PU PERSUING
   PERUSING
   SUPERING
RT RESTRING
   RINGSTER
   STRINGER
RW WRINGERS
RY SERRYING
ST RESTINGS
   STINGERS
   TRESSING
   TRIGNESS
SV SERVINGS
   VERSINGS
SW SWINGERS
SY SYRINGES
TT GITTERNS
TV STERVING
TW STREWING
   WRESTING
VW SWERVING

EGINRT  39
(TINGER)
AA AERATING
AB BERATING
   REBATING
AC CATERING
   CITRANGE
   CREATING
   REACTING
AD DERATING
   GRADIENT
   TREADING
AH EARTHING
   HEARTING
AK RETAKING
AL ALERTING
   ALTERING
   INTEGRAL
   RELATING
   TANGLIER
   TRIANGLE
AM EMIGRANT
AP TAPERING
AS ANGRIEST
   ASTRINGE
   GANISTER
   GANTRIES
   GRANITES
   INGRATES
   RANGIEST
   REASTING
   STEARING
AT ARETTING

   TREATING
AV AVERTING
   TAVERING
   VINTAGER
AW TWANGIER
   WATERING
BH BERTHING
   BRIGHTEN
BI REBITING
BL TREBLING
CE ERECTING
   GENTRICE
CH RETCHING
CI RECITING
CK TRECKING
CN CENTRING
CO GERONTIC
CS CRESTING
CU ERUCTING
DI DIRIGENT
DN TRENDING
DS STRINGED
EG GREETING
EM METERING
   REGIMENT
EN ENTERING
EP PETERING
ES GENTRIES
   INTEGERS
   REESTING
   STEERING
   STREIGNE
EU GENITURE
EV EVERTING
EW TWEERING
EX EXERTING
   GENETRIX
FH FRIGHTEN
FT FRETTING
FU FEUTRING
   REFUTING
FY GENTRIFY
HI THINGIER
HO THROEING
HS RIGHTENS
HW WRETHING
IL GIRTLINE
   RETILING
   TINGLIER
   TIRELING
IM MERITING
   MITERING
IR RETIRING
IS GIRNIEST
   IGNITERS
   REISTING
   STINGIER
   STRIGINE
IU INTRIGUE
IV RIVETING
IX GENITRIX
KK TREKKING
LS LINGSTER
   RINGLETS
   STERLING
   TINGLERS
   TRINGLES
NO NITROGEN
NS STERNING
NU RETUNING

NV VENTRING
OS GENITORS
   ROSETING
OT OTTERING
OU OUTREIGN
   ROUTEING
OW TOWERING
OX OXTERING
OZ ROZETING
PS PRESTING
PU ERUPTING
   REPUTING
RS RESTRING
   RINGSTER
   STRINGER
RY RETRYING
SS RESTINGS
   STINGERS
   TRESSING
   TRIGNESS
ST GITTERNS
SV STERVING
SW STREWING
   WRESTING
TU UTTERING

EGINST  107
(ESTING)
AA SAGINATE
AB BEATINGS
AD SEDATING
   STEADING
AE SAGENITE
AF FEASTING
AG NAGGIEST
AH GAHNITES
   HEATINGS
AL EASTLING
   GELATINS
   GENITALS
   STEALING
AM MANGIEST
   MINTAGES
   STEAMING
   TEAMINGS
AN ANTIGENS
   GENTIANS
   STEANING
AR ANGRIEST
   ASTRINGE
   GANISTER
   GANTRIES
   GRANITES
   INGRATES
   RANGIEST
   REASTING
   STEARING
AS EASTINGS
   GENISTAS
   GIANTESS
   SEATINGS
   TEASINGS
   TSIGANES
AT ESTATING
   TANGIEST
AU SAUTEING
AV VINTAGES
AW SWEATING
AY YEASTING
BE BEIGNETS
```

BH BENIGHTS
BL BELTINGS
BT BETTINGS
CE GENETICS
CH ETCHINGS
CN SCENTING
CR CRESTING
DD STEDDING
DE INGESTED
   SIGNETED
   STEEDING
DI DINGIEST
   INDIGEST
DN STENDING
DR STRINGED
DU DUNGIEST
EG EGESTING
EH SEETHING
   SHEETING
EK SEETHING
EL GENTILES
   SLEETING
   STEELING
EM MEETINGS
   STEEMING
EN STEENING
EO EGESTION
EP STEEPING
ER GENTRIES
   INTEGERS
   REESTING
   STEERING
   STREIGNE
ET GENTIEST
EU EUGENIST
EV STEEVING
   VENTIGES
EW SWEETING
EX EXIGENTS
FL FELTINGS
FM FIGMENTS
GT GETTINGS
GU GUESTING
   GUNGIEST
HI HEISTING
   NIGHTIES
   THINGIES
HL ENLIGHTS
   LIGHTENS
HN SENNIGHT
HO HISTOGEN
HR RIGHTENS
HT SHETTING
   TIGHTENS
IL LIGNITES
   LINGIEST
IM MINGIEST
IN STEINING
IR GIRNIEST
   IGNITERS
   REISTING
   STINGIER
   STRIGINE
IW WINGIEST
IX EXISTING
IZ ZINGIEST
JL JINGLETS
JS JESTINGS
KL KINGLETS
LL STELLING

   TELLINGS
LM MELTINGS
   SMELTING
LN NESTLING
LP PELTINGS
   PESTLING
LR LINGSTER
   RINGLETS
   STERLING
   TINGLERS
   TRINGLES
LS GLISTENS
   SINGLETS
LT LETTINGS
   SETTLING
LW SWELTING
   WINGLETS
MM STEMMING
MO MITOGENS
MP PIGMENTS
NN STENNING
NR STERNING
NT NETTINGS
   STENTING
   TENTINGS
NV VENTINGS
OP PONGIEST
OR GENITORS
   ROSETING
OT TENTIGOS
PP STEPPING
PR PRESTING
PT PETTINGS
   SPETTING
QU QUESTING
RR RESTRING
   RINGSTER
   STRINGER
RS RESTINGS
   STINGERS
   TRESSING
   TRIGNESS
RT GITTERNS
RV STERVING
RW STREWING
   WRESTING
ST SETTINGS
   TESTINGS
SV VESTINGS
SW STEWINGS
   WESTINGS
TT STETTING

EGNORS 155
(ONGERS)
AC ACROGENS
   CORNAGES
AI IGNAROES
   ORGANISE
   ORIGANES
AM MEGARONS
AO OREGANOS
AR GROANERS
AT ORANGEST
   RAGSTONE
AW WAGONERS
BI SOBERING
BU BURGEONS
CE COGENERS
   CONGREES

CH GROSCHEN
CS CONGRESS
CU CONGRUES
   SCROUNGE
CY CRYOGENS
DI NEGROIDS
DO DRONGOES
DU GUERDONS
EG ENGORGES
EI ERINGOES
EK KEROGENS
ET ESTROGEN
EU GENEROUS
EY ERYNGOES
GT GONGSTER
HL LEGHORNS
HU ENROUGHS
   ROUGHENS
II SEIGNIOR
IL RESOLING
IM NEGROISM
IP PERIGONS
   REPOSING
   SPONGIER
IR IGNORERS
IS SIGNORES
IT GENITORS
   ROSETING
IY SEIGNORY
LM MONGRELS
LU LOUNGERS
MU MURGEONS
NT RONTGENS
PS SPONGERS
PY PYROGENS
RT STRONGER
RW WRONGERS
ST SONGSTER
SU SURGEONS
TU STURGEON
TW WRONGEST

EHIRST 153
(ITHERS)
AC CHARIEST
   THERIACS
AD HAIRSTED
   HARDIEST
AE HEARTIES
AI HAIRIEST
AN INEARTHS
AO HOARIEST
AR TRASHIER
AS SHERIATS
AW SWATHIER
   WATERISH
AY HYSTERIA
BC BRITCHES
BE HERBIEST
BL BLITHERS
BR REBIRTHS
BS HERBISTS
CD DITCHERS
CE CHESTIER
   HERETICS
CH HITCHERS
CI CHRISTIE
CN CHRISTEN
   CITHERNS
   SNITCHER

CO ROTCHIES
   THEORICS
CP PITCHERS
   SPITCHER
CS STRICHES
CT CHITTERS
   RICHTEST
   STITCHER
CY HYSTERIC
DI DISHERIT
DT THIRSTED
   THRISTED
EE ETHERISE
   SHEETIER
EM ERETHISM
   ETHERISM
EO ISOTHERE
   THEORIES
   THEORISE
EP TREESHIP
ES HEISTERS
ET ETHERIST
FG FIGHTERS
   FREIGHTS
FI SHIFTIER
FS SHIFTERS
GG THIGGERS
GI TIGERISH
GL LIGHTERS
   RELIGHTS
   SLIGHTER
GN RIGHTENS
GO GHOSTIER
GR RIGHTERS
GS SIGHTERS
GT RIGHTEST
   STREIGHT
HW WHITHERS
IN INHERITS
IR SHIRTIER
IT SHITTIER
   THIRTIES
KN RETHINKS
   THINKERS
LL THILLERS
LP PHILTERS
   PHILTRES
LS SLITHERS
   THRISSEL
LT THRISTLE
LU LUTHIERS
LW WHIRTLES
   WHISTLER
LY SLITHERY
MO ISOTHERM
   MOITHERS
MS SMITHERS
MY SMITHERY
NN THINNERS
NO HORNIEST
NZ ZITHERNS
OP TROPHIES
OR HERITORS
OS HOISTERS
   HORSIEST
   HOSTRIES
   SHORTIES
OT THEORIST
   THORITES
OU OUTHIRES

OV OVERHITS
OW WORTHIES
PS HIPSTERS
   THRIPSES
PW WHIPSTER
RT THIRSTER
RV THRIVERS
RW WHIRRETS
SU RUSHIEST
SW SWITHERS
TW WHITRETS
   WHITSTER
   WHITTERS

EHORST 189
(OTHERS)
AB BATHORSE
AC CHAROSET
   THORACES
AG SHORTAGE
AH HAROSETH
AI HOARIEST
AL LOATHERS
AO TOHEROAS
AS ASTHORES
   HAROSETS
   HOARSEST
AT RHEOSTAT
AX THORAXES
BC BOTCHERS
BL BROTHELS
BO THEORBOS
BR BROTHERS
BT BETROTHS
CC CROCHETS
   CROTCHES
CE TROCHEES
CI ROTCHIES
   THEORICS
CL CHORTLES
CO CHEROOTS
CP POTCHERS
CR TORCHERS
CU SCOUTHER
   TOUCHERS
CW SCOWTHER
DP POTSHERD
DR REDSHORT
EI ISOTHERE
   THEORIES
   THEORISE
EL HOSTELER
EM THEOREMS
EN HONESTER
FN FORHENTS
GI GHOSTIER
GU ROUGHEST
HU SHOUTHER
IM ISOTHERM
   MOITHERS
IN HORNIEST
IP TROPHIES
IR HERITORS
IS HOISTERS
   HORSIEST
   HOSTRIES
   SHORTIES
IT THEORIST
   THORITES
IU OUTHIRES

IV OVERHITS
IW WORTHIES
LN HORNLETS
LS HOLSTERS
   HOSTLERS
LT THROSTLE
LY HOSTELRY
MO SMOOTHER
MS SMOTHERS
MU MOUTHERS
MY SMOTHERY
NR NORTHERS
NS SHORTENS
NT THORNSET
NU SOUTHERN
OS ORTHOSES
   SHOOTERS
   SOOTHERS
OV OVERSHOT
PP PROPHETS
PS STROPHES
PU POUTHERS
PY TROPHESY
RW THROWERS
ST SHORTEST
SU SHOUTERS
   SOUTHERS
UY OUTHYRES

EIILST 139
(TILIES)
AB ALBITISE
   SIBILATE
AC SILICATE
AD IDEALIST
AF FILIATES
AH HAILIEST
AL TAILLIES
AN ALIENIST
   LITANIES
AR LAIRIEST
AS SAILIEST
AV VITALISE
AX LAXITIES
AZ TAILZIES
BG BILGIEST
BR TRILBIES
BT STILBITE
CC SCILICET
CF FELSITIC
DD TIDDLIES
DL DILLIEST
DM DELIMITS
   LIMITEDS
DR REDISTIL
DU UTILISED
DV LIVIDEST
EN LENITIES
ER TILERIES
EV LEVITIES
   VEILIEST
EW LEWISITE
FH TILEFISH
FM FILMIEST
FT FITLIEST
GM LEGITIMS
GN LIGNITES
   LINGIEST
HL HILLIEST
HT LITHITES

```
KM MILKIEST      ET INTERTIE      CH CHOLINES      TV NOVELIST      FF SNIFFLER      AS EASTLINS
KS SILKIEST         RETINITE      CI ISOCLINE         VIOLENTS      FG FLINGERS         ELASTINS
LN NIELLIST      FL FLINTIER         SILICONE      TW TOWLINES      GG NIGGLERS         SALIENTS
LR STILLIER         INFILTER      CL LIONCELS      UV EVULSION      GH HERLINGS         STANIELS
LS SILLIEST      FO NOTIFIER      CO COLONIES      VV INVOLVES         SHINGLER      AU ALUNITES
LT TILLIEST      FS SNIFTIER         COLONISE                      GI RESILING         INSULATE
   TILLITES      GH THINGIER         ECLOSION      EILNRS  77       GJ JINGLERS      AV VENTAILS
LW TWILLIES      GL GIRTLINE      CP PINOCLES      (LINERS)         GM GREMLINS      AW LAWNIEST
MP LIMEPITS         RETILING      CR INCLOSER      AB RINSABLE         MERLINGS      BD BLINDEST
MR LIMITERS         TINGLIER         LICENSOR      AC CARLINES         MINGLERS      BE STILBENE
   MIRLIEST         TIRELING      CS CONSEILS      AD ISLANDER      GO RESOLING         TENSIBLE
MS ELITISMS      GM MERITING         INCLOSES      AG ARLESING      GP PINGLERS      BG BELTINGS
   SLIMIEST         MITERING      CT LECTIONS         ENGRAILS         SPERLING      BM NIMBLEST
MT MISTITLE      GR RETIRING      CX LEXICONS         NARGILES         SPRINGLE      BZ BLINTZES
MY MYELITIS      GS GIRNIEST      DE ESLOINED         REALIGNS      GS RINGLESS      CF INFLECTS
NO ETIOLINS         IGNITERS      DG GLENOIDS         SANGLIER         SLINGERS      CH LINCHETS
NR NIRLIEST         REISTING         SIDELONG         SLANGIER      GT LINGSTER         TINCHELS
   NITRILES         STINGIER      DI LIONISED      AH INHALERS         RINGLETS      CO LECTIONS
NT LINTIEST         STRIGINE      DO SOLENOID      AI AIRLINES         STERLING      CS STENCILS
NY SENILITY      GU INTRIGUE      DR DISENROL         SNAILIER         TINGLERS      CU CUTLINES
OP PISOLITE      GV RIVETING      DS SONDELIS      AM MARLINES         TRINGLES         TUNICLES
   POLITIES      GX GENITRIX      DU DELUSION         MINERALS      GW NEWSGIRL      DE ENLISTED
OR ROILIEST      HR HIRRIENT         INSOULED      AO AILERONS      IK SLINKIER         LINTSEED
OS SOILIEST      HS INHERITS         UNSOILED         ALERIONS      IT NIRLIEST         LISTENED
PP LIPPIEST      JK JIRKINET      EF FELONIES         ALIENORS         NITRILES      DP SPLINTED
PR TRIPLIES      KL TINKLIER         OLEFINES      AP PEARLINS      KK KLINKERS      DR SNIRTLED
PS PITILESS      LS NIRLIEST      ER ELOINERS         PRALINES      KM KREMLINS         TENDRILS
   SPILITES         NITRILES      ET NOSELITE      AR SNARLIER      KP SPRINKLE         TRINDLES
PY PYELITIS      MO MINORITE      EV NOVELISE      AS RAINLESS      KS SLINKERS      DU DILUENTS
RT STILTIER      MS INTERIMS      FU NOISEFUL      AT ENTRAILS      KT LINKSTER         INSULTED
RU UTILISER         MINISTER      FX FLEXIONS         LATRINES         STRINKLE         UNLISTED
ST ELITISTS      MT INTERMIT      GL LOGLINES         RATLINES         TINKLERS      EE SELENITE
   SILTIEST      MX INTERMIX      GR RESOLING         TRENAILS      KW WINKLERS      EG GENTILES
SU ULITISES      NV INVERTIN      GU LIGNEOUS      AU LUNARIES         WRINKLES         SLEETING
   UTILISES      OP POINTIER      GW LONGWISE      AV RAVELINS      MT MINSTREL         STEELING
UY TUILYIES      OR INTERIOR      HL HELLIONS      AX RELAXINS      OP PROLINES      EI LENITIES
UZ TUILZIES      PS PRISTINE      HP PINHOLES      AY INLAYERS      OR LORINERS      EN LENIENTS
   UTILIZES      RW WINTRIER      HS HOLINESS         SNAILERY      OT RETINOLS         SENTINEL
                 SS SINISTER      HT NEOLITHS      BB NIBBLERS      PS PILSNERS      EO NOSELITE
EIINRT  30       ST NITRITES      HV NOVELISH      BD BLINDERS      PT SPLINTER      EP PLENTIES
(INTIRE)            STINTIER      IS ELISIONS         BRINDLES      PU PURLINES      ER LISTENER
AD DAINTIER      SU NEURITIS         ISOLINES      BE BERLINES      ST SNIRTLES         SILENTER
AF FAINTIER      SV INVITERS         LIONISES      BI RINSIBLE      TU INSULTER      ET ENTITLES
AL INERTIAL         VINTRIES      IT ETIOLINS      BK BLINKERS         LUSTRINE      EV VEINLETS
AP PAINTIER         VITRINES      IV OLIVINES      CE LICENSER      TY TINSELRY      FG FELTINGS
AS INERTIAS                       IZ LIONIZES         RECLINES                      GH ENLIGHTS
   RAINIEST      EILNOS  47       KM MOLESKIN         SILENCER      EILNST  45          LIGHTENS
BE BENITIER      (OLINES)         KW SNOWLIKE      CG CLINGERS      (INTLES)         GI LIGNITES
BG REBITING      AD NODALISE      LT STELLION         CRINGLES      AB INSTABLE         LINGIEST
BS BRINIEST      AG GASOLINE      MM MOLIMENS      CK CLINKERS      AF INFLATES      GJ JINGLETS
CD INDIRECT      AK KAOLINES      MU EMULSION         CRINKLES      AG EASTLING      GK KINGLETS
CE ICTERINE      AM MINEOLAS      MV NOVELISM      CO INCLOSER         GELATINS      GL STELLING
CG RECITING         SEMOLINA      NT INSOLENT         LICENSOR         GENITALS         TELLINGS
CN INTRINCE      AN SOLANINE      NW SNOWLINE      DF FLINDERS         STEALING      GM MELTINGS
CS CITRINES      AP OPALINES      OP POLONIES      DK KINDLERS      AI ALIENIST         SMELTING
   CRINITES      AR AILERONS         POLONISE      DO DISENROL         LITANIES      GN NESTLING
   INCITERS         ALERIONS      OT LOONIEST      DP SPELDRIN      AK LANKIEST      GP PELTINGS
CU NEURITIC         ALIENORS         OILSTONE      DS RINDLESS      AM AILMENTS         PESTLING
DD NITRIDED      AT ELATIONS      OV VIOLONES      DT SNIRTLED         ALIMENTS      GR LINGSTER
DG DIRIGENT         INSOLATE      PP PLENIPOS         TENDRILS         MANLIEST         RINGLETS
DM DIRIMENT         TOENAILS      PR PROLINES         TRINDLES      AO ELATIONS         STERLING
DP INTREPID      BC BINOCLES      PS EPSILONS      DW SWINDLER         INSOLATE         TINGLERS
DS DISINTER      BG IGNOBLES      PT POINTELS      EG LEERINGS         TOENAILS         TRINGLES
   INDITERS         INGLOBES      RR LORINERS         REELINGS      AP PANTILES      GS GLISTENS
   NITRIDES      BO OBELIONS      RT RETINOLS      EM ERMELINS         PLAINEST         SINGLETS
   RINDIEST      BP BONSPIEL      SU ELUSIONS      EO ELOINERS      AR ENTRAILS      GT LETTINGS
DU UNTIDIER      BW BOWLINES      SW LEWISSON      EP PILSENER         LATRINES         SETTLING
EO ERIONITE      CD INCLOSED      TU ELUTIONS      ES REINLESS         RATLINES      GW SWELTING
ES ERINITES      CE CINEOLES         OUTLINES      ET LISTENER         TRENAILS         WINGLETS
   NITERIES      CG ECLOSING                         SILENTER                      HO NEOLITHS
```

```
IL NIELLIST    BM EMBROILS    EILORT 18      COALIEST       JT JOLTIEST       RATLINES
IO ETIOLINS    BR BROILERS    (LOITER)       SOCIETAL       KY YOLKIEST       TRENAILS
IR NIRLIEST    BT STROBILE    AC EROTICAL    AD DIASTOLE    LM MELILOTS    AO SOTERIAL
   NITRILES       TRILOBES       LORICATE       ISOLATED    LN STELLION    AP PILASTER
IT LINTIEST    BW BLOWSIER    AD IDOLATER       SODALITE    LR TRILLOES       PLAISTER
IY SENILITY    CD SCLEROID       TAILORED       SOLIDATE       TROLLIES       PLAITERS
KR LINKSTER    CL COLLIERS    AE AEROLITE    AF FOLIATES    LS TOILLESS    AR RETIRALS
   STRINKLE       ORSELLIC    AF FLOATIER    AG OTALGIES    LW LOWLIEST       RETRIALS
   TINKLERS    CN INCLOSER    AH AEROLITH    AK KEITLOAS    MO TOILSOME       TRAILERS
KS LENTISKS       LICENSOR       LOATHIER    AM LOAMIEST    MP POLEMIST    AS REALISTS
KT KNITTLES    CT CLOISTER    AN ORIENTAL    AN ELATIONS    MT MOTLIEST       SALTIERS
KW TWINKLES       COISTREL       RELATION       INSOLATE    NN INSOLENT       SALTIRES
LO STELLION       CORTILES    AP EPILATOR       TOENAILS    NO LOONIEST       SLAISTER
LY SILENTLY       COSTLIER       PETIOLAR    AP SPOLIATE       OILSTONE    AT TERTIALS
   TINSELLY       CREOLIST    AS SOTERIAL    AR SOTERIAL    NP POINTELS    AU URALITES
MR MINSTREL    DI IDOLISER    AT LITERATO    AS ISOLATES    NR RETINOLS    BB STIBBLER
MU MUSLINET    DL DOLLIERS    BD TRILOBED    AT TOTALISE    NU ELUTIONS       TRIBBLES
NO INSOLENT    DN DISENROL    BS STROBILE    AV VIOLATES       OUTLINES    BD BRISTLED
OO LOONIEST    DS SOLDIERS       TRILOBES    BB BIBELOTS    NV NOVELIST       DRIBLETS
   OILSTONE    DT STOLIDER    BT BLOTTIER    BF BOTFLIES       VIOLENTS    BF FILBERTS
OP POINTELS    DU SOULDIER       LIBRETTO    BO LOOBIEST    NW TOWLINES    BG GILBERTS
OR RETINOLS    DY SOLDIERY    CH CHLORITE    BR STROBILE    OP LOOPIEST    BH BLITHERS
OU ELUTIONS    EF FORELIES       CLOTHIER       TRILOBES    OR TROOLIES    BI TRILBIES
   OUTLINES    EI OILERIES    CI ELICITOR    BW BLOWIEST    OS OSTIOLES    BM TIMBRELS
OV NOVELIST    EK ROSELIKE    CP PETROLIC    CD DOCILEST       STOOLIES    BO STROBILE
   VIOLENTS    EL ORSEILLE    CS CLOISTER    CN LECTIONS    OZ ZOOLITES       TRILOBES
OW TOWLINES    EN ELOINERS       COISTREL    CP TOECLIPS    PR POITRELS    BS BLISTERS
PR SPLINTER    EP PELORIES       CORTILES    CR CLOISTER    PS PISTOLES       BRISTLES
PS PLENISTS    ET LITEROSE       COSTLIER       COISTREL       PTILOSES    BT BRITTLES
RS SNIRTLES    EV OVERLIES       CREOLIST       CORTILES       SLOPIEST       TRIBLETS
RU INSULTER       RELIEVOS    CT CLOTTIER       COSTLIER    PT PISTOLET    BU BURLIEST
   LUSTRINE       VOLERIES    CY CRYOLITE       CREOLIST       PLOTTIES       SUBTILER
RY TINSELRY    EW OWLERIES    DE DOLERITE    CS SOLECIST       POLITEST    BY BLISTERY
ST TINTLESS    FJ FRIJOLES       LOITERED       SOLSTICE    PX EXPLOITS    CC CIRCLETS
SU UTENSILS    FK FOLKSIER    DS STOLIDER    DG GODLIEST    RT TRIOLETS    CE RETICLES
TU LUTENIST    FP PROFILES    EH HOTELIER       GOLDIEST    RU LOURIEST       SCLERITE
               FS FLOSSIER    EK LORIKEET    DM MELODIST       OUTLIERS       TIERCELS
EILORS 37      FT FLORIEST    EM MOTELIER    DR STOLIDER    SS LOSSIEST    CK STICKLER
(OILERS)          TREFOILS    ER LOITERER    DS SOLIDEST    SU LOUSIEST       STRICKLE
AA OLEARIAS    GM GOMERILS    ES LITEROSE    DT DOILIEST    TT STILETTO       TICKLERS
AC CALORIES    GN RESOLING       TROELIES    DU SOLITUDE    UV OUTLIVES       TRICKLES
   CARIOLES    GS GLOSSIER    FF FORELIFT    EM MESOLITE       SOLUTIVE    CO CLOISTER
AD DARIOLES    HP PILHORSE    FS FLORIEST       MISLETOE                      COISTREL
   SOLIDARE       POLISHER       TREFOILS    EN NOSELITE    EILRST 44         CORTILES
   SOREDIAL    HS SLOSHIER    FU FLUORITE    EP PETIOLES    (LITERS)          COSTLIER
AF FORESAIL    IT ROILIEST    GH REGOLITH    ER LITEROSE    AB LIBRATES       CREOLIST
AG GASOLIER    LT TRILLOES    HP HELIPORT       TROELIES    AC ALTRICES    CT CLITTERS
   GIRASOLE       TROLLIES    HY RHYOLITE       TREFOILS       ARTICLES    CU CURLIEST
   SERAGLIO    LZ ZORILLES    IS ROILIEST    ES ESTOILES       RECITALS       UTRICLES
AH AIRHOLES    MO SLOOMIER    IT TROILITE    EW OWELTIES       SELICTAR    DD STRIDDLE
   SHOALIER    MP IMPLORES    KO ROOTLIKE    EZ ZEOLITES    AD DILATERS       TIDDLERS
AM MORALISE       PELORISM    LS TRILLOES    FJ JETFOILS       LARDIEST    DI REDISTIL
AN AILERONS    MR LORIMERS       TROLLIES    FM FILEMOTS    AE ATELIERS    DN SNIRTLED
   ALERIONS    NP PROLINES    NR RITORNEL    FR FLORIEST       EARLIEST       TENDRILS
   ALIENORS    NR LORINERS    NS RETINOLS       TREFOILS       LEARIEST       TRINDLES
AP PELORIAS    NT RETINOLS    NT TROTLINE    FT LOFTIEST       REALTIES    DO STOLIDER
   POLARISE    OT TROOLIES    OS TROOLIES    FU OUTFLIES    AF FLARIEST    DU DILUTERS
AS SOLARISE    PP SLOPPIER    OV OVERTOIL    GS ELOGISTS       FRAILEST       LURIDEST
AT SOTERIAL    PS SPOILERS    PR PORTLIER    GU UGLOSIST    AG GLARIEST    EE LEERIEST
AV OVERSAIL    PT POITRELS    PS POITRELS    HM HELOTISM       REGALIST       SLEETIER
   VALORISE    PU PERILOUS    PW PILEWORT    HN NEOLITHS    AI LAIRIEST       STEELIER
   VARIOLES    PV OVERSLIP    RU ULTERIOR    HO HOOLIEST    AK LARKIEST    EF FERLIEST
   VOLARIES    SS RISSOLES    ST TRIOLETS    HP HELISTOP       STALKIER    EI TILERIES
AY ROYALISE    SU SOILURES    SU LOURIEST       HOPLITES       STARLIKE    EK TRISKELE
AZ SOLARIZE    TT TRIOLETS       OUTLIERS       ISOPLETH    AL LITERALS    EL TREILLES
BB SLOBBIER    TU LOURIEST    TY TOILETRY    IN ETIOLINS       LITORALS    EM TERMLIES
BC BRICOLES       OUTLIERS                   IP PISOLITE    AM LAMITERS    EN LISTENER
   CORBEILS    ZZ SOZZLIER    EILOST 21         POLITIES       MARLIEST       SILENTER
BH BOLSHIER                   (OILETS)       IR ROILIEST    AN ENTRAILS    EO LITEROSE
BL BROLLIES                   AC ALOETICS    IS SOILIEST       LATRINES       TROELIES
                                             JL JOLLIEST
```

```
EP EPISTLER      TRIPPLES   HR LUTHIERS      SEMITONE   CT CENTRISM   DM IMMODEST
   PELTRIES   PS SPIRTLES   HS LUSHIEST   FI FISNOMIE   EG REGIMENS   DN DEMONIST
   PERLITES   PT SPLITTER   HT THULITES      OMNIFIES   EH SHIREMEN   DO DOOMIEST
   REPTILES      TRIPLETS   IR UTILISER   FR ENSIFORM   EL ERMELINS      MOODIEST
ES LEISTERS   PY PRIESTLY   IS ULITISES      FERMIONS   EM IMMENSER      SODOMITE
   RITELESS      SPRITELY      UTILISES   GI IGNOMIES   EN REINSMEN   DR MORTISED
   TIRELESS   QU QUILTERS   IY TUILYIES   GR NEGROISM   EO EMERSION   DS MODISTES
ET RETITLES   RU SULTRIER   IZ TUILZIES   GT MITOGENS   EV MINEVERS   DT DEMOTIST
FO FLORIEST   RW TWIRLERS      UTILIZES   GU GEMINOUS   FO ENSIFORM   EI MOIETIES
   TREFOILS   SS STIRLESS   KS SULKIEST   GY MOSEYING      FERMIONS   EL MESOLITE
FR TRIFLERS   ST SLITTERS   LQ QUILLETS   HI HOMINIES   FS FIRMNESS      MISLETOE
FS RIFTLESS      STILTERS   LV VITELLUS   HT HOISTMEN   GI REMISING   EM SOMETIME
   STIFLERS      TESTRILS   MM LUMMIEST   HU HEMIONUS   GL GREMLINS   EN MONETISE
FT FLITTERS   SU SURLIEST   MN MUSLINET   IS EMISSION      MERLINGS      SEMITONE
FW FEWTRILS   SY SISTERLY   MP LUMPIEST      SIMONIES      MINGLERS   EP EPITOMES
GH LIGHTERS   TU SURTITLE      PLUMIEST   IV VISNOMIE   GO NEGROISM      EPSOMITE
   RELIGHTS   TW WRISTLET   MR MURLIEST   KL MOLESKIN   GP IMPREGNS   ER TIRESOME
   SLIGHTER   TZ STRELITZ   MS LITMUSES   KR MONIKERS   GS GRIMNESS   FL FILEMOTS
GN LINGSTER   UV RIVULETS   NO ELUTIONS   KT TOKENISM   GU RESUMING   FT OFTTIMES
   RINGLETS                    OUTLINES   KU MOUSEKIN   HP PHRENISM   GN MITOGENS
   STERLING   EILSTU 136    NR INSULTER   LM MOLIMENS   HU RHENIUMS   GR ERGOTISM
   TINGLERS   (UTILES)         LUSTRINE   LU EMULSION   IP PRIMINES      GORMIEST
   TRINGLES   AB SUITABLE   NS UTENSILS   LV NOVELISM   IS MIRINESS   GS EGOTISMS
GS GLISTERS   AF FISTULAE   NT LUTENIST   MR MISNOMER   IT INTERIMS   GW TWIGSOME
   GRISTLES   AM SIMULATE   OR LOURIEST   NT MENTIONS      MINISTER   HL HELOTISM
GT GLITTERS   AN ALUNITES      OUTLIERS   OP EMPOISON   IV MINIVERS   HN HOISTMEN
GU GURLIEST      INSULATE   OS LOUSIEST   OR IONOMERS   KL KREMLINS   HO SMOOTHIE
HL THILLERS   AQ LIQUATES   OV OUTLIVES      MOONRISE   KO MONIKERS   HR ISOTHERM
HP PHILTERS      TEQUILAS      SOLUTIVE   OS MONOSIES   LT MINSTREL      MOITHERS
   PHILTRES   AR URALITES   PP PULPIEST   OT EMOTIONS   MO MISNOMER   HT MOTHIEST
HS SLITHERS   BD BLUDIEST   PS STIPULES      MOONIEST   OO IONOMERS   IP OPTIMISE
   THRISSEL   BG BULGIEST   QR QUILTERS   OX EXOMIONS      MOONRISE   IY MOYITIES
HT THRISTLE   BK BULKIEST   QU LUSTIQUE   PS PEONISMS   OS MERSIONS   KN TOKENISM
HU LUTHIERS   BL BULLIEST   RR SULTRIER   PT EMPTIONS      MINORESS   KS SMOKIEST
HW WHIRTLES   BR BURLIEST   RS SURLIEST      NEPOTISM   OU MONSIEUR   LL MELILOTS
   WHISTLER      SUBTILER   RT SURTITLE      PIMENTOS   OW WINSOMER   LO TOILSOME
HY SLITHERY   BT SUBTILE    RV RIVULETS   RS MERSIONS   PS PRIMNESS   LP POLEMIST
IL STILLIER   CC CUTICLES   ST LUSTIEST      MINORESS   ST ENTRISMS   LT MOTLIEST
IM LIMITERS   CD DULCITES   SU LITUUSES   RU MONSIEUR      MINSTERS   MP METOPISM
   MIRLIEST      LUCIDEST                  RW WINSOMER      TRIMNESS   MT TOTEMISM
IN NIRLIEST   CE LEUCITES   EIMNOS 131    ST MOISTENS   SU NEURISMS   NN MENTIONS
   NITRILES   CK LUCKIEST   (MONIES)      TU MOUNTIES   TU TERMINUS   NO EMOTIONS
IO ROILIEST   CN CUTLINES   AD NOMADIES                  TY ENTRYISM      MOONIEST
IP TRIPLIES      TUNICLES      NOMADISE   EIMNRS 177       MISENTRY   NP EMPTIONS
IT STILTIER   CR CURLIEST   AL MINEOLAS   (MINERS)                       NEPOTISM
IU UTILISER      UTRICLES      SEMOLINA   AB MIRBANES   EIMOST 150       PIMENTOS
KN LINKSTER   CT CUTICLES   AR MORAINES   AC CARMINES   (SOMITE)      NS MOISTENS
   STRINKLE   DE DILUTEES   AU MOINEAUS   AD ADERMINS   AD ATOMISED   NU MOUNTIES
   TINKLERS   DI UTILISED   AW WOMANISE      SIRNAMED   AF FOAMIEST   OR MOORIEST
LO TRILLOES   DL DUELLIST   BC COMBINES   AE REMANIES   AL LOAMIEST      MOTORISE
   TROLLIES      DULLIEST   BI EBIONISM   AG GERMAINS   AR AMORTISE      ROOMIEST
LS STILLERS   DN DILUENTS   BR BROMINES      SMEARING      ATOMISER   PP MOPPIEST
LT TESTRILL      INSULTED   CN MECONINS   AH HARMINES   AS AMITOSES   PR IMPOSTER
MN MINSTREL      UNLISTED   CR CREMOSIN      SHIREMAN      AMOSITES   PY PEYOTISM
MU MURLIEST   DO SOLITUDE      INCOMERS   AK RAMEKINS      ATOMISES   QU MISQUOTE
MY LYMITERS   DP STIPULED      SERMONIC   AL MARLINES      OSMIATES   RR MORTISER
NO RETINOLS   DR DILUTERS   DE DEMONISE      MINERALS   AZ ATOMIZES      STORMIER
NP SPLINTER      LURIDEST   DG SMIDGEON   AN REINSMAN   BB BOMBSITE   RS EROTISMS
NS SNIRTLES   DY SEDULITY   DH HEDONISM   AO MORAINES   BC COMBIEST      MORTISES
NU INSULTER   FG GULFIEST   DI DOMINIES   AR MARINERS   BG MISBEGOT      TRISOMES
   LUSTRINE   FK FLUKIEST   DM DEMONISM   AS SEMINARS   CC COSMETIC   RT OMITTERS
NY TINSELRY   FO OUTFLIES   DN MISDONNE      SIRNAMES   CD DOMESTIC   RU MOISTURE
OO TROOLIES   FP SPITEFUL   DO DOMINOES   AT MINARETS   CF COMFIEST   RW MISWROTE
OP POITRELS   FT FLUTIEST      MONODIES      RAIMENTS   CI COMITIES      WORMIEST
OT TRIOLETS      FUTILEST   DT DEMONIST   AU ANEURISM      SEMIOTIC   RY ISOMETRY
OU LOURIEST   GO EULOGIST   EH HEMIONES   AY SEMINARY   CO COOMIEST   SS MOSSIEST
   OUTLIERS   GR GURLIEST   EN NOMINEES   BO BROMINES   CR MORTICES   ST MOISTEST
PP RIPPLETS   HK HULKIEST   EP EPISEMON   CO CREMOSIN   CV VICOMTES   SU MOUSIEST
   STIPPLER   HL HULLIEST   ER EMERSION      INCOMERS   DE TEDISOME   SZ MESTIZOS
   TIPPLERS   HP SULPHITE   ET MONETISE      SERMONIC   DL MELODIST   TT MOTTIEST
```

```
      TOTEMIST
TU TITMOUSE

EIMRST 140
(MITERS)
AB BARMIEST
AC CERAMIST
   MATRICES
AD MARDIEST
   MISRATED
   READMITS
AE EMIRATES
   REAMIEST
   STEAMIER
AG MAGISTER
   MIGRATES
   RAGTIMES
   STERIGMA
AI AIRTIMES
   SERIATIM
AL LAMITERS
   MARLIEST
AM MARMITES
AN MINARETS
   RAIMENTS
AO AMORTISE
   ATOMISER
AP PRIMATES
AS ASTERISM
   MAISTERS
   MISRATES
   SEMITARS
   SMARTIES
AT MISTREAT
   TERATISM
AU MURIATES
   SEMITAUR
AW WARTIMES
AX MATRIXES
AY SYMITARE
BL TIMBRELS
BU IMBRUTES
   RESUBMIT
   TERBIUMS
CI MERISTIC
   TRISEMIC
CN CENTRISM
CO MORTICES
CS CRETISMS
DE DEMERITS
   DEMISTER
   DIMETERS
   MISTERED
DO MORTISED
DP DIREMPTS
EE EREMITES
EF FEMITERS
EH ERETHISM
   ETHERISM
EL TERMLIES
EM MERISTEM
   MIMESTER
   MISMETRE
EO TIRESOME
EP EMPTIERS
ER MERRIEST
   TRIREMES
ES TRISEMES
ET TERMITES
EU EMERITUS
```

```
FU FREMITUS
GI GRIMIEST
   TIGERISM
GM GRIMMEST
GO ERGOTISM
   GORMIEST
HO ISOTHERM
   MOITHERS
HS SMITHERS
HY SMITHERY
IK MIRKIEST
IL LIMITERS
   MIRLIEST
IN INTERIMS
   MINISTER
IT METRITIS
IW MISWRITE
KU MURKIEST
LN MINSTREL
LU MURLIEST
LY LYMITERS
MP PRIMMEST
MR TRIMMERS
MS MISTERMS
MT TRIMMEST
MU RUMMIEST
NS ENTRISMS
   MINSTERS
   TRIMNESS
NU TERMINUS
NY ENTRYISM
   MISENTRY
OO MOORIEST
   MOTORISE
   ROOMIEST
OP IMPOSTER
OR MORTISER
   STORMIER
OS EROTISMS
   MORTISES
   TRISOMES
OT OMITTERS
OU MOISTURE
OW MISWROTE
   WORMIEST
OY ISOMETRY
PS IMPRESTS
PU IMPUREST
   IMPUTERS
   STUMPIER
SS MISTRESS
ST METRISTS
SY SMYTRIES
TU SMUTTIER
UV VITREUMS
UX MIXTURES

EINNST 113
(SINNET)
AC ANCIENTS
   CANNIEST
   INSTANCE
AF INFANTES
AG ANTIGENS
   GENTIANS
   STEANING
AM MANNITES
AO ENATIONS
AP PANTINES
AR ENTRAINS
```

```
   TRANNIES
AS INSANEST
AT ANTIENTS
   STANNITE
BO BONNIEST
CE NESCIENT
CG SCENTING
CI INSCIENT
DE DENTINES
   DESINENT
DG STENDING
DU DUNNIEST
   DUNNITES
EF FENNIEST
EG STEENING
EH HENNIEST
EI NINETIES
EL LENIENTS
   SENTINEL
ER INTENSER
   INTERNES
ES TENNISES
ET SENTIENT
EW ENTWINES
   WENNIEST
FI FINNIEST
FU FUNNIEST
GH SENNIGHT
GI STEINING
GL NESTLING
GN STENNING
GR STERNING
GT NETTINGS
   STENTING
   TENTINGS
GV VENTINGS
HR THINNERS
HS THINNESS
HT THINNEST
IS TININESS
IT TINNIEST
IW INTWINES
KO INKSTONE
LO INSOLENT
MO MENTIONS
OR INTONERS
   TERNIONS
OS TENSIONS
OT TINSTONE
   TONTINES
OU NOUNIEST
PR ENPRINTS
PS SPINNETS
RU RUNNIEST
   STURNINE
RV VINTNERS
SU SUNNIEST
UW UNTWINES

EINOPS 130
(PONIES)
AC CANOPIES
   CAPONISE
   PAEONICS
AE PAEONIES
AH APHONIES
AL OPALINES
AT SAPONITE
AZ EPIZOANS
BH HOPBINES
```

```
BL BONSPIEL
CH CHOPINES
CI EPINOSIC
CL PINOCLES
CR CONSPIRE
   INCORPSE
DD DISPONED
DE DISPONEE
DG DEPOSING
   DISPONGE
   PIDGEONS
DH DIPHONES
   SIPHONED
   SPHENOID
DO POISONED
DR DISPONER
   POINDERS
   PRISONED
DS DISPONES
   SPINODES
DU UNPOISED
EG EPIGONES
EM EPISEMON
ER ISOPRENE
   PIONEERS
FR FORPINES
GN OPENINGS
GR PERIGONS
   REPOSING
   SPONGIER
GT PONGIEST
GX EXPOSING
GY POESYING
HL PINHOLES
HT PHONIEST
   SIPHONET
IR RIPIENOS
IT SINOPITE
LO POLONIES
   POLONISE
LP PLENIPOS
LR PROLINES
LS EPSILONS
LT POINTELS
MO EMPOISON
MS PEONISMS
MT EMPTIONS
NS PENSIONS
OR POISONER
OS SPOONIES
PR POPERINS
   PROPINES
RR PRISONER
RS PORINESS
   PRESSION
   ROPINESS
RT POINTERS
   PROTEINS
   REPOINTS
RU PRUINOSE
RV OVERSPIN
   PROVINES
TT NEPOTIST

EINORS 9
(SENIOR)
AB BARONIES
```

```
AC SCENARIO
AD ANEROIDS
   DONARIES
AF FARINOSE
AG IGNAROES
   ORGANISE
   ORIGANES
AL AILERONS
   ALERIONS
   ALIENORS
AM MORAINES
AN RAISONNE
AS ERASIONS
AT ANOESTRI
   ARSONITE
   NOTARIES
   NOTARISE
   ROSINATE
AV AVERSION
BB SNOBBIER
BF BONFIRES
BG SOBERING
BI BRIONIES
BM BROMINES
BT BORNITES
   RIBSTONE
BW BROWNIES
BY BRYONIES
CC CONCISER
   CORNICES
CD CONSIDER
CF CONIFERS
   FORENSIC
   FORINSEC
   INFORCES
CH CHORINES
CI RECISION
   SORICINE
CL INCLOSER
   LICENSOR
CM CREMOSIN
   INCOMERS
   SERMONIC
CN INCENSOR
CP CONSPIRE
   INCORPSE
CR RESORCIN
CS NECROSIS
   SERICONS
CT CORNIEST
   RECTIONS
CU NOURICES
   ROUNCIES
DD INDORSED
DE ORDINEES
DG NEGROIDS
DH HORDEINS
DI DERISION
   IRONISED
   RESINOID
DJ JOINDERS
DL DISENROL
DN ENDIRONS
DP DISPONER
   POINDERS
   PRISONED
DS INDORSES
   SORDINES
DT DRONIEST
DU DOURINES
```

```
   SOURDINE
DW WINDORES
   WINDROSE
EG ERINGOES
EH HEROINES
EK KEROSINE
EL ELOINERS
EM EMERSION
EP ISOPRENE
   PIONEERS
ES ESSOINER
ET SEROTINE
EV EVERSION
FK FORESKIN
FM ENSIFORM
   FERMIONS
FN INFERNOS
FP FORPINES
FU REFUSION
FX FORNIXES
GI SEIGNIOR
GL RESOLING
GM NEGROISM
GP PERIGONS
   REPOSING
   SPONGIER
GR IGNORERS
GS SIGNORES
GT GENITORS
   ROSETING
GY SEIGNORY
HS HERISSON
HT HORNIEST
IP RIPIENOS
IS IONISERS
   IRONISES
IV REVISION
   VISIONER
IZ IONIZERS
   IRONIZES
JT JOINTERS
KM MONIKERS
KO ROOINEKS
LP PROLINES
LR LORINERS
LT RETINOLS
MM MISNOMER
MO IONOMERS
   MOONRISE
MS MERSIONS
   MINORESS
MU MONSIEUR
MW WINSOMER
NT INTONERS
   TERNIONS
NU REUNIONS
NV ENVIRONS
OP POISONER
   SPOONIER
OS EROSIONS
OT SNOOTIER
OZ OZONISER
PP POPERINS
   PROPINES
PR PRISONER
PS PORINESS
   PRESSION
   ROPINESS
PT POINTERS
   PROTEINS
```

REPOINTS	SEDITION	QU QUESTION	GH SPHERING	AN PANTINES	ARTESIAN
PU PRUINOSE	DM DEMONIST	RR INTRORSE	GI SPEIRING	AO SAPONITE	RESINATA
PV OVERSPIN	DR DRONIEST	SNORTIER	GL PINGLERS	AP NAPPIEST	AB ATEBRINS
PROVINES	DS DONSIEST	RS TERSIONS	SPERLING	AR PAINTERS	BANISTER
RT INTRORSE	DU OUNDIEST	RT SNOTTIER	SPRINGLE	PANTRIES	AC CANISTER
SNORTIER	DW DOWNIEST	TENORIST	GM IMPREGNS	PERTAINS	CARNIEST
SS ROSINESS	EG EGESTION	TRITONES	GO PERIGONS	PINASTER	NACRITES
ST TERSIONS	EL NOSELITE	RU ROUTINES	REPOSING	REPAINTS	SCANTIER
SU NEUROSIS	EM MONETISE	SNOUTIER	SPONGIER	AT PATIENTS	AD DETRAINS
RESINOUS	SEMITONE	RV INVESTOR	GP REPPINGS	AU PETUNIAS	RANDIEST
SV VERSIONS	ER SEROTINE	RY TYROSINE	GR SPERRING	SUPINATE	STRAINED
TT SNOTTIER	ES ESSONITE	RZ TRIZONES	SPRINGER	AY EPINASTY	AE ARSENITE
TENORIST	ET NOISETTE	SS SONSIEST	GS PRESSING	CE PECTINES	RESINATE
TRITONES	TEOSINTE	STENOSIS	SPERSING	PENTICES	STEARINE
TU ROUTINES	FI NOTIFIES	ST SNOTTIES	SPRINGES	CS INSPECTS	TRAINEES
SNOUTIER	GH HISTOGEN	STONIEST	GT PRESTING	CY PYCNITES	AF FENITARS
TV INVESTOR	GM MITOGENS	SW SNOWIEST	GU PERSUING	DE PENTISED	AG ANGRIEST
TY TYROSINE	GP PONGIEST	TT TOTIENTS	PERUSING	DL SPLINTED	ASTRINGE
TZ TRIZONES	GR GENITORS	TW TOWNIEST	SUPERING	DR SPRINTED	GANISTER
UV SOUVENIR	ROSETING	UU TENUIOUS	HM PHRENISM	DS STIPENDS	GANTRIES
	GT TENTIGOS	VY VENOSITY	HU PUNISHER	EG STEEPING	GRANITES
	HL NEOLITHS		IM PRIMINES	EL PLENTIES	INGRATES
EINOST 14	HM HOISTMEN	**EINPRS 158**	IO RIPIENOS	EM SEPIMENT	RANGIEST
(TONIES)	HP PHONIEST	(PINERS)	IP SNIPPIER	ES PENTISES	REASTING
AB BOTANIES	SIPHONET	AA PANARIES	IR INSPIRER	ET INEPTEST	STEARING
BOTANISE	HR HORNIEST	AD SPRAINED	IS INSPIRES	SPINETTE	AH INEARTHS
NIOBATES	HS HISTONES	AE NAPERIES	IT PRISTINE	GL PELTINGS	AI INERTIAS
OBEISANT	HU OUTSHINE	AF FIREPANS	JU JUNIPERS	PESTLING	RAINIEST
AC ACONITES	IL ETIOLINS	AG PREASING	KL SPRINKLE	GM PIGMENTS	AJ NARTJIES
CANOEIST	IP SINOPITE	SPEARING	KU SPUNKIER	GO PONGIEST	AK KERATINS
AD ASTONIED	IS NOISIEST	AH HEPARINS	LO PROLINES	GP STEPPING	NARKIEST
SEDATION	IV NOVITIES	PARISHEN	LS PILSNERS	GR PRESTING	AL ENTRAILS
AL ELATIONS	JR JOINTERS	SERAPHIN	LT SPLINTER	GT PETTINGS	LATRINES
INSOLATE	JT JETTISON	AL PEARLINS	LU PURLINES	SPETTING	RATLINES
TOENAILS	KM TOKENISM	PRALINES	MS PRIMNESS	HM SHIPMENT	TRENAILS
AN ENATIONS	KN INKSTONE	AN PANNIERS	NS SPINNERS	HO PHONIEST	AM MINARETS
AP SAPONITE	KO NOOKIEST	AP SNAPPIER	NT ENPRINTS	SIPHONET	RAIMENTS
AR ANOESTRI	KW WONKIEST	AT PAINTERS	NY SPINNERY	IK PINKIEST	AN ENTRAINS
ARSONITE	LL STELLION	PANTRIES	OO POISONER	IO SINOPITE	TRANNIES
NOTARIES	LN INSOLENT	PERTAINS	SPOONIER	IP NIPPIEST	AO ANOESTRI
NOTARISE	LO LOONIEST	PINASTER	OP POPERINS	IR PRISTINE	ARSONITE
ROSINATE	OILSTONE	REPAINTS	PROPINES	IS SNIPIEST	NOTARIES
AS ASSIENTO	LP POINTELS	AU UNPRAISE	OR PRISONER	SPINIEST	NOTARISE
ASTONIES	LR RETINOLS	BE PEBRINES	OS PORINESS	LO POINTELS	ROSINATE
AV STOVAINE	LU ELUTIONS	CD PRESCIND	PRESSION	LR SPLINTER	AP PAINTERS
AX SAXONITE	OUTLINES	CH PINCHERS	ROPINESS	LS PLENISTS	PANTRIES
BB NOBBIEST	LV NOVELIST	CO CONSPIRE	OT POINTERS	MO EMPTIONS	PERTAINS
BE BETONIES	VIOLENTS	INCORPSE	PROTEINS	NEPOTISM	PINASTER
EBONITES	LW TOWLINES	CS PRINCESS	REPOINTS	PIMENTOS	REPAINTS
BI NIOBITES	MN MENTIONS	DG SPRINGED	OU PRUINOSE	MS MISSPENT	AR RESTRAIN
BN BONNIEST	MO EMOTIONS	DI INSPIRED	OV OVERSPIN	NR ENPRINTS	RETRAINS
BR BORNITES	MOONIEST	DL SPELDRIN	PROVINES	NS SPINNETS	STRAINER
RIBSTONE	MP EMPTIONS	DO DISPONER	PS SNIPPERS	OR POINTERS	TERRAINS
BS EBONISTS	NEPOTISM	POINDERS	RT PRINTERS	PROTEINS	TRAINERS
BT BOTTINES	PIMENTOS	PRISONED	REPRINTS	REPOINTS	TRANSIRE
BU BOUNTIES	MS MOISTENS	DT SPRINTED	SPRINTER	OT NEPOTIST	AS RESIANTS
CC CONCEITS	MU MOUNTIES	DY INSPYRED	ST SPINSTER	PS SNIPPETS	RETSINAS
CD DEONTICS	NR INTONERS	EG SPEERING	SY INSPYRES	PY SNIPPETY	SNARIEST
CE SEICENTO	TERNIONS	SPREEING	TU UNPRIEST	RR PRINTERS	STAINERS
CL LECTIONS	NS TENSIONS	EH INSPHERE	UNRIPEST	REPRINTS	STARNIES
CO COONTIES	NT TINSTONE	EI PINERIES		SPRINTER	STEARINS
CR CORNIEST	TONTINES	EL PILSENER	**EINPST 148**	RS SPINSTER	AT INTREATS
RECTIONS	NU NOUNIEST	EO ISOPRENE	(INSTEP)	RU UNPRIEST	NITRATES
CS SECTIONS	OR SNOOTIER	PIONEERS	AB BEPAINTS	UNRIPEST	STRAITEN
CT CENTOIST	OS ISOTONES	ER REPINERS	AD DEPAINTS	TX SPINTEXT	TARTINES
STENOTIC	OZ ZOONITES	ES EREPSINS	AH PENTHIAS	TY TINTYPES	TERTIANS
CU COUNTIES	PR POINTERS	RIPENESS	THESPIAN		AU RUINATES
CX EXCITONS	PROTEINS	EU PENURIES	AI PIANISTE	**EINRST 17**	URANITES
CY CYTOSINE	REPOINTS	RESUPINE	AL PANTILES	(INTERS)	URINATES
DH HEDONIST	PT NEPOTIST	FO FORPINES	PLAINEST	AA ANTISERA	AW TINWARES
DI EDITIONS					

BONUS WORD SETS: 8-Letter Sets

BI BRINIEST
BO BORNITES
   RIBSTONE
BT BITTERNS
BU TRIBUNES
   TURBINES
CE CENTRIES
   ENTERICS
   ENTICERS
   SCIENTER
   SECRETIN
CG CRESTING
CH CHRISTEN
   CITHERNS
   SNITCHER
CI CITRINES
   CRINITES
   INCITERS
CK STRICKEN
CM CENTRISM
CO CORNIEST
   RECTIONS
CS CISTERNS
CT CENTRIST
   CITTERNS
CU CURNIEST
DD STRIDDEN
DE INSERTED
   RESIDENT
   SINTERED
   TRENDIES
DG STRINGED
DI DISINTER
   INDITERS
   NITRIDES
   RINDIEST
DL SNIRTLED
   TENDRILS
   TRINDLES
DO DRONIEST
DP SPRINTED
DT STRIDENT
   TRIDENTS
DU INTRUDES
DX DEXTRINS
EE ETERNISE
   TEENSIER
EF FERNIEST
EG GENTRIES
   INTEGERS
   REESTING
   STEERING
   STREIGNE
EI ERINITES
   NITERIES
EK KERNITES
EL LISTENER
   SILENTER
EN INTENSER
   INTERNES
EO SEROTINE
ER INSERTER
   REINSERT
   REINTERS
   RENTIERS
   TERRINES
ES INTERESS
   SENTRIES
   TRENISES
ET INERTEST

   INTEREST
   STERNITE
EU ESURIENT
   NEURITES
   RETINUES
   REUNITES
EV NERVIEST
   REINVEST
   SERVIENT
   SIRVENTE
EX INTERSEX
EY SERENITY
FI SNIFTIER
FS SNIFTERS
GH RIGHTENS
GI GIRNIEST
   IGNITERS
   REISTING
   STINGIER
   STRIGINE
GL LINGSTER
   RINGLETS
   STERLING
   TINGLERS
   TRINGLES
GN STERNING
GO GENITORS
   ROSETING
GP PRESTING
GR RESTRING
   RINGSTER
   STRINGER
GS RESTINGS
   STINGERS
   TRESSING
   TRIGNESS
GT GITTERNS
GV STERVING
GW STREWING
   WRESTING
HI INHERITS
HK RETHINKS
   THINKERS
HN THINNERS
HO HORNIEST
HZ ZITHERNS
IL NIRLIEST
   NITRILES
IM INTERIMS
   MINISTER
IP PRISTINE
IS SINISTER
IT NITRITES
   STINTIER
IU NEURITIS
IV INVITERS
   VINTRIES
   VITRINES
JO JOINTERS
KL LINKSTER
   STRINKLE
   TINKLERS
KS STINKERS
KT KNITTERS
   TRINKETS
LM MINSTREL
LO RETINOLS
LP SPLINTER
LS SNIRTLES
LU INSULTER

   LUSTRINE
LY TINSELRY
MS ENTRISMS
   MINSTERS
   TRIMNESS
MU TERMINUS
MY ENTRYISM
   MISENTRY
NO INTONERS
   TERNIONS
NP ENPRINTS
NU RUNNIEST
NV VINTNERS
OO SNOOTIER
OP POINTERS
   PROTEINS
   REPOINTS
OR INTRORSE
OS TERSIONS
   SNORTIER
OT SNOTTIER
   TENORIST
   TRITONES
OU ROUTINES
   SNOUTIER
OV INVESTOR
OY TYROSINE
OZ TRIZONES
PR PRINTERS
   REPRINTS
   SPRINTER
PS SPINSTER
PU UNPRIEST
   UNRIPEST
QU SQUINTER
SS INSTRESS
ST ENTRISTS
   STINTERS
TU RUNTIEST
TW TWINTERS
TY ENTRYIST
UV UNRIVETS
   VENTURIS
UW UNWRITES

EINRTT 76
(TINTER)
AA REATTAIN
AC INTERACT
AD NITRATED
AG ARETTING
   TREATING
AL RATTLINE
AM MARTINET
AO TENTORIA
AP TRIPTANE
AS INTREATS
   NITRATES
   STRAITEN
   TARTINES
   TERTIANS
AU TAINTURE
BE REBITTEN
BS BITTERNS
CE RETICENT
CO CONTRITE
   CORNETTI
CS CENTRIST
   CITTERNS

CU INTERCUT
   TINCTURE
DO INTORTED
DS STRIDENT
   TRIDENTS
EE REINETTE
   TEENTIER
EH THIRTEEN
EI INTERTIE
   RETINITE
EN RENITENT
EO TENORITE
ES INERTEST
   INTEREST
   STERNITE
EY ENTIRETY
   ETERNITY
FG FRETTING
FL FLITTERN
FU UNFITTER
GO OTTERING
GS GITTERNS
GU UTTERING
IM INTERMIT
IS NITRITES
   STINTIER
KO KNOTTIER
KS KNITTERS
   TRINKETS
LO TROTLINE
NO TONTINER
NU NUTRIENT
OS SNOTTIER
   TENORIST
   TRITONES
OU RITENUTO
PU INPUTTER
SS ENTRISTS
   STINTERS
SU RUNTIEST
SW TWINTERS
SY ENTRYIST

EINRTU 25
(TUNIER)
AA INAURATE
AB URBANITE
AD DATURINE
   INDURATE
   RUINATED
   URINATED
AH HAURIENT
AJ JAUNTIER
AL RETINULA
   TENURIAL
AM RUMINATE
AP PAINTURE
AQ QUAINTER
AS RUINATES
   URANITES
   URINATES
AT TAINTURE
BD TURBINED
   UNDERBIT
BS TRIBUNES
   TURBINES
CC CINCTURE
CE CEINTURE
   ENURETIC
CG ERUCTING

CH RUTHENIC
CI NEURITIC
CL LINCTURE
CO NEUROTIC
CS CURNIEST
CT INTERCUT
   TINCTURE
DD INTRUDED
DE REUNITED
DI UNTIDIER
DM RUDIMENT
DP TURNIPED
DR INTRUDER
DS INTRUDES
DW UNDERWIT
EG GENITURE
EM MUTINEER
ES ESURIENT
   NEURITES
   RETINUES
   REUNITES
FG FEUTRING
FT UNFITTER
GI INTRIGUE
GN RETUNING
GO OUTREIGN
   ROUTEING
GP ERUPTING
   REPUTING
GT UTTERING
IS NEURITIS
JO JOINTURE
KP TURNPIKE
LS INSULTER
   LUSTRINE
LV VIRULENT
MS TERMINUS
NO NEUTRINO
NS RUNNIEST
NT NUTRIENT
OP ERUPTION
OS ROUTINES
   SNOUTIER
OT RITENUTO
PR PRURIENT
PS UNPRIEST
   UNRIPEST
PT INPUTTER
QS SQUINTER
ST RUNTIEST
SV UNRIVETS
   VENTURIS
SW UNWRITES
UV UNVIRTUE

EINSTT 160
(INTEST)
AA ASTATINE
   SANITATE
   TANAISE
AB TABINETS
AC CANTIEST
   NICTATES
AD INSTATED
AE ANISETTE
   TETANIES
   TETANISE
AF FAINTEST

AG ESTATING
   TANGIEST
AH HESITANT
AJ JANTIEST
AN ANTIENTS
   STANNITE
AP PATIENTS
AR INTREATS
   NITRATES
   STRAITEN
   TARTINES
   TERTIANS
AS INSTATES
   NASTIEST
   SATINETS
AT NATTIEST
AV TASTEVIN
AW TAWNIEST
BE BENTIEST
BG BETTINGS
BI STIBNITE
BO BOTTINES
BR BITTERNS
BU BUNTIEST
CO CENTOIST
   STENOTIC
CR CENTRIST
   CITTERNS
DE DINETTES
DR STRIDENT
   TRIDENTS
DS DENTISTS
EE TEENIEST
EF FEINTEST
EG GENTIEST
EI ENTITIES
EL ENTITLES
EM MINETTES
EN SENTIENT
EO NOISETTE
EP INEPTEST
   SPINETTE
ER INERTEST
   INTEREST
   STERNITE
ET NETTIEST
EW TENTWISE
   TWENTIES
EX EXISTENT
FI NIFTIEST
FM FITMENTS
GG GETTINGS
GH SHETTING
   TIGHTENS
GL LETTINGS
   SETTLING
GN NETTINGS
   STENTING
   TENTINGS
GO TENTIGOS
GP PETTINGS
   SPETTING
GR GITTERNS
GS SETTINGS
   TESTINGS
GT STETTING
HN THINNEST
IL LINTIEST

```
IM MINTIEST
IN TINNIEST
IR NITRITES
   STINTIER
IT NITTIEST
   TINTIEST
IW TWINIEST
JO JETTISON
KL KNITTLES
KR KNITTERS
   TRINKETS
KS SKINTEST
LS TINTLESS
LU LUTENIST
MU MINUTEST
NO TINSTONE
   TONTINES
OP NEPOTIST
OR SNOTTIER
   TENORIST
   TRITONES
OS SNOTTIES
   STONIEST
OT TOTIENTS
OW TOWNIEST
PX SPINTEXT
PY TINTYPES
QU QUINTETS
RS ENTRISTS
   STINTERS
RU RUNTIEST
RW TWINTERS
RY ENTRYIST
SW ENTWISTS
TU NUTTIEST
TW TWITTENS

EINSTU 81
(UNITES)
AD AUDIENTS
   SINUATED
AG SAUTEING
AJ JAUNTIES
AL ALUNITES
   INSULATE
AP PETUNIAS
   SUPINATE
AQ ANTIQUES
   QUANTISE
AR RUINATES
   URANITES
   URINATES
BB NUBBIEST
BM BITUMENS
BO BOUNTIES
BR TRIBUNES
   TURBINES
BT BUNTIEST
CI CUTINISE
CL CUTLINES
   TUNICLES
CO COUNTIES
CR CURNIEST
DD DISTUNED
DE DETINUES
DF UNSIFTED
DG DUNGIEST
DI DISUNITE
   NUDITIES
   UNITISED
```

```
   UNTIDIES
DL DILUENTS
   INSULTED
   UNLISTED
DM MISTUNED
DN DUNNIEST
   DUNNITES
DO OUNDIEST
DQ SQUINTED
DR INTRUDES
DS DISTUNES
DU UNSUITED
EG EUGENIST
EQ QUIETENS
ER ESURIENT
FK FUNKIEST
FN FUNNIEST
GG GUESTING
   GUNGIEST
GQ QUESTING
HK HUNKIEST
HO OUTSHINE
IM MUTINIES
IQ INQUIETS
IR NEURITIS
IS UNITISES
IZ UNITIZES
JK JUNKIEST
LM MUSLINET
LO ELUTIONS
   OUTLINES
LR INSULTER
   LUSTRINE
LS UTENSILS
LT LUTENIST
MO MOUNTIES
MR TERMINUS
MS MISTUNES
MT MINUTEST
NO NOUNIEST
NR RUNNIEST
   STURNINE
NS SUNNIEST
NW UNTWINES
OQ QUESTION
OR ROUTINES
   SNOUTIER
OU TENUIOUS
PR UNPRIEST
   UNRIPEST
QR SQUINTER
QS INQUESTS
QT QUINTETS
QU UNIQUEST
   UNQUIETS
RT RUNTIEST
RV UNRIVETS
   VENTURIS
RW UNWRITES
SS SENSUIST
SW UNWISEST
SX UNSEXIST
TT NUTTIEST

EIOPST 101
(SOPITE)
AC ECTOPIAS
```

```
AD DIOPTASE
AL SPOLIATE
AN SAPONITE
AP APPOSITE
AS SOAPIEST
BY BIOTYPES
CD DESPOTIC
CE ECTOPIES
   PICOTEES
CH POSTICHE
   POTICHES
CK POCKIEST
CL TOECLIPS
CR PERSICOT
CS COPSIEST
DD PODDIEST
DE EPIDOTES
   POETISED
DG PODGIEST
DR DIOPTERS
   DIOPTRES
   DIPTEROS
   PERIDOTS
   PROTEIDS
   RIPOSTED
DS DEPOSITS
   TOPSIDES
EL PETIOLES
EM EPITOMES
   EPSOMITE
ER POETRIES
ES POETISES
EZ POETIZES
FO POOFIEST
FR FIREPOTS
GN PONGIEST
GO GOOPIEST
HL HELISTOP
   HOPLITES
   ISOPLETH
HN PHONIEST
   SIPHONET
HP HOPPIEST
   POETSHIP
HR TROPHIES
IL PISOLITE
   POLITIES
IM OPTIMISE
IN SINOPITE
IV POSITIVE
KR PORKIEST
LM POLEMIST
LN POINTELS
LO LOOPIEST
LR POITRELS
LS PISTOLES
   PTILOSES
   SLOPIEST
LT PISTOLET
   PLOTTIES
   POLITEST
LX EXPLOITS
MM METOPISM
MN EMPTIONS
   NEPOTISM
   PIMENTOS
MP MOPPIEST
MR IMPOSTER
MY PEYOTISM
NR POINTERS
```

```
   PROTEINS
   REPOINTS
NT NEPOTIST
OP OPPOSITE
OR PORTOISE
   ROOPIEST
OS ISOTOPES
OV POOVIEST
PS SOPPIEST
RR PIERROTS
   SPORTIER
RS PERIOSTS
   PROSIEST
   REPOSITS
   RIPOSTES
   TRIPOSES
RT PORTIEST
   RISPETTO
   SPOTTIER
RU ROUPIEST
   SPOUTIER
RV PIVOTERS
   SPORTIVE
SS SEPIOSTS
SU SOUPIEST
SY ISOTYPES
TT POTTIEST
TU POUTIEST
TY PEYOTIST
UW WIPEOUTS

EIORST 5
(TORIES)
AB SABOTIER
AD ASTEROID
AE ETAERIOS
AH HOARIEST
AJ JAROSITE
AL SOTERIAL
AM AMORTISE
   ATOMISER
AN ANOESTRI
   ARSONITE
   NOTARIES
   NOTARISE
   ROSINATE
AR ROARIEST
   ROTARIES
AV VOTARIES
BC BISECTOR
BD DEBITORS
BI ORBITIES
BL STROBILE
   TRILOBES
BN BORNITES
   RIBSTONE
BO ROBOTISE
BR ORBITERS
BY SOBRIETY
CC CORTICES
CD CORDITES
CE COTERIES
   ESOTERIC
CH ROTCHIES
   THEORICS
CK CORKIEST
   ROCKIEST
   STOCKIER
CL CLOISTER
   COISTREL
```

```
   CORTILES
   COSTLIER
   CREOLIST
CM MORTICES
CN CORNIEST
   RECTIONS
CP PERSICOT
CT COTTIERS
CU CITREOUS
   OUTCRIES
CV EVICTORS
   VORTICES
CX EXCITORS
   EXORCIST
DG STODGIER
DI DIORITES
DL STOLIDER
DM MORTISED
DN DRONIEST
DP DIOPTERS
   DIOPTRES
   DIPTEROS
   PERIDOTS
   PROTEIDS
   RIPOSTED
DS STEROIDS
DT DORTIEST
DU IODURETS
   OUTRIDES
   OUTSIDER
   SUITORED
DW ROWDIEST
   WORDIEST
EG ERGOTISE
EH ISOTHERE
   THEORIES
   THEORISE
EL LITEROSE
   TROELIES
EM TIRESOME
EN SEROTINE
EP POETRIES
ES EROTESIS
FF FORFEITS
FK FORKIEST
FL FLORIEST
   TREFOILS
FO ROOFIEST
FP FIREPOTS
FR FROSTIER
FS FOISTERS
FW FROWIEST
GH GHOSTIER
GM ERGOTISM
   GORMIEST
GN GENITORS
   ROSETING
GS GORSIEST
   STRIGOSE
GU GOUSTIER
GV VERTIGOS
GY OYSTRIGE
GZ ZORGITES
HM ISOTHERM
   MOITHERS
HN HORNIEST
HP TROPHIES
HR HERITORS
HS HOISTERS
```

```
   HORSIEST
   HOSTRIES
   SHORTIES
HT THEORIST
   THORITES
HU OUTHIRES
HV OVERHITS
HW WORTHIES
IL ROILIEST
IR RIOTRIES
IS RIOTISES
IZ RIOTIZES
JN JOINTERS
KP PORKIEST
LL TRILLOES
LN RETINOLS
LO TROOLIES
LP POITRELS
LT TRIOLETS
LU LOURIEST
   OUTLIERS
MO MOORIEST
   MOTORISE
   ROOMIEST
MP IMPOSTER
MR MORTISER
   STORMIER
MS EROTISMS
   MORTISES
   TRISOMES
MT OMITTERS
MU MOISTURE
MW MISWROTE
   WORMIEST
MY ISOMETRY
NN INTONERS
NO SNOOTIER
NP POINTERS
   PROTEINS
   REPOINTS
NR INTRORSE
   SNORTIER
NS TERSIONS
NT SNOTTIER
   TENORIST
   TRITONES
NU ROUTINES
   SNOUTIER
NV INVESTOR
NY TYROSINE
NZ TRIZONES
OP PORTOISE
   ROOPIEST
OT ROOTIEST
   TORTOISE
PR PIERROTS
   SPORTIER
PS PERIOSTS
   PROSIEST
   REPOSITS
   RIPOSTES
   TRIPOSES
PT PORTIEST
   RISPETTO
   SPOTTIER
PU ROUPIEST
   SPOUTIER
PV PIVOTERS
```

```
          SPORTIVE        VIPEROUS     OS SOOTIEST        SPIRITED        UNRIPEST     DF DRIFTERS
QU QUOITERS          RS REVISORS          TOOTSIES     DM DIREMPTS     OO PORTOISE     DU STURDIER
RR ERRORIST          RT SERVITOR       PR PORTIEST     DN SPRINTED        ROOPIEST     EE REESTIER
RS RESISTOR          RU OUVRIERS          RISPETTO     DO DIOPTERS     OR PIERROTS        RETIREES
   ROISTERS          RV REVIVORS          SPOTTIER        DIOPTRES     OS PERIOSTS     EF FERRITES
   SORRIEST          RY REVISORY       PT POTTIEST        DIPTEROS        PROSIEST     EG REGISTER
RT RORTIEST          TT VIRETOTS       PU POUTIEST        PERIDOTS        REPOSITS     EI REISTIER
RU STOURIER          TU VIRTUOSE       PY PEYOTIST        PROTEIDS        REPOSITS     EM MERRIEST
RV SERVITOR             VITREOUS       RR RORTIEST        RIPOSTED        RIPOSTES        TRIREMES
ST STOITERS             VOITURES       RS STOITERS     DP STRIPPED        TRIPOSES     EN INSERTER
SY SEROSITY                            RU TUTORISE     DU DISPUTER     OT PORTIEST        REINSERT
TU TUTORISE          EIOSTT  93        RV VIRETOTS        STUPIDER        RISPETTO        REINTERS
TV VIRETOTS          (OTTIES)          SS TOSSIEST     EE PEERIEST        SPOTTIER        RENTIERS
UV VIRTUOSE          AC OSCITATE       SU TOUSIEST        STEEPIER     OU ROUPIEST        TERRINES
   VITREOUS          AG GOATIEST       SW TOWSIEST     EG PRESTIGE        SPOUTIER     ER RETIRERS
   VOITURES          AL TOTALISE       TT TOTTIEST     EH TREESHIP     OV PIVOTERS     ES TRESSIER
                     AS TOASTIES       TU TOUTIEST     EK PERKIEST        SPORTIVE     EV REVERIST
EIORSV 127           BI BIOTITES                       EL EPISTLER     PR STRIPPER        RIVERETS
(VIROSE)             BN BOTTINES       EIPRST 147         PELTRIES        TRIPPERS        RIVETERS
AC COVARIES          CD COTTISED       (STRIPE)           PERLITES     PT TRIPPETS        REWRITES
   VARICOSE          CN CENTOIST       AA ASPIRATE        REPTILES     QU QUIPSTER     EW REWRITES
AG VIRAGOES             STENOTIC          PARASITE     EM EMPTIERS     RZ SPRITZER     FG GRIFTERS
AL OVERSAIL          CR COTTIERS          SEPTARIA     EO POETRIES     SS PERSISTS     FI FIRRIEST
   VALORISE          CS COTTISES       AC CRAPIEST     ES RESPITES     ST SPITTERS     FL TRIFLERS
   VARIOLES          DL DOILTEST          CRISPATE     ET PRETTIES        TIPSTERS     FO FROSTIER
   VOLARIES          DM DEMOTIST          PICRATES     EY PERSEITY     SU PURSIEST        ROTIFERS
AN AVERSION          DR DORTIEST          PRACTISE     FI SPITFIRE     TU PURTIEST     FT FRITTERS
AP VAPORISE          DT DOTTIEST       AD RAPIDEST     FO FIREPOTS        PUTTIERS     FU FRITURES
AS SAVORIES          EN NOISETTE          SPIRATED     GN PRESTING                        FRUITERS
AT VOTARIES             TEOSINTE          TRAIPSED     HL PHILTERS     EIRRST 165         FURRIEST
AW AVOWRIES          FF TOFFIEST       AE PETARIES        PHILTRES     (TRIERS)        GG TRIGGERS
BD OVERBIDS          FL LOFTIEST       AG GRAPIEST     HO TROPHIES     AB ARBITERS     GH RIGHTERS
CD DISCOVER          FM OFTTIMES       AI PARITIES     HS HIPSTERS        RAREBITS     GN RESTRING
   DIVORCES          FO FOOTIEST       AK PARKIEST        THRIPSES     AC ERRATICS        RINGSTER
CS CORSIVES          GH GOTHITES       AL PILASTER     HW WHIPSTER     AE ARTERIES        STRINGER
CT EVICTORS          GN TENTIGOS          PLAISTER     IL TRIPLIES        REASTIER     GT GRITTERS
   VORTICES          GS EGOTISTS          PLAITERS     IN PRISTINE     AF FRATRIES     GY REGISTRY
CY VICEROYS          GU GOUTIEST       AM PRIMATES     IR STRIPIER     AH TRASHIER     HI SHIRTIER
DE OVERSIDE          HM MOTHIEST       AN PAINTERS     IS SPIRIEST     AI RARITIES     HO HERITORS
DP DISPROVE          HR THEORIST          PANTRIES     IT RISPETTI     AL RETIRALS     HT THIRSTER
   PROVIDES             THORITES          PERTAINS     IU PURITIES        RETRIALS     HV THRIVERS
DS DEVISORS          HS TOSHIEST          PINASTER     IV PRIVIEST        TRAILERS     HW WHIRRETS
EL OVERLIES          IS OSTEITIS          REPAINTS     IY PYRITISE     AN RESTRAIN     IO RIOTRIES
   RELIEVOS             OTITISES       AP PERIAPTS     KO PORKIEST        RETRAINS     IP STRIPIER
   VOLERIES          JL JOLTIEST       AS PASTRIES     LN SPLINTER        STRAINER     IW WRISTIER
EN EVERSION          JN JETTISON          PIASTRES     LO POITRELS        TERRAINS     KS SKIRRETS
EW OVERWISE          LM MOTLIEST          RASPIEST     LP RIPPLETS        TRAINERS        SKIRTERS
EZ OVERSIZE          LP PISTOLET          TRAIPSES        STIPPLER        TRANSIRE        STRIKERS
FG FORGIVES             PLOTTIES       AV PRIVATES        TIPPLERS     AO ROARIEST     LU SULTRIER
FH OVERFISH             POLITEST       AW WIRETAPS        TRIPPLES        ROTARIES     LW TWIRLERS
GT VERTIGOS          LR TRIOLETS       AY ASPERITY     LS SPIRTLES     AR STARRIER     MM TRIMMERS
GU GRIEVOUS          LT STILETTO       CD PREDICTS     LT SPLITTER        TARRIERS     MO MORTISER
HT OVERHITS          MM TOTEMISM          SCRIPTED        TRIPLETS     AS TARSIERS        STORMIER
IN REVISION          MR OMITTERS       CE CREPIEST     LY PRIESTLY     AT RETRAITS     NO INTRORSE
   VISIONER          MS MOISTEST          RECEIPTS        SPRITELY        STRAITER        SNORTIER
KP OVERSKIP          MT MOTTIEST       CH PITCHERS     MM PRIMMEST     AW STRAWIER     NP PRINTERS
LP OVERSLIP             TOTEMIST          SPITCHER     MO IMPOSTER        SWARTIER        REPRINTS
MP IMPROVES          MU TITMOUSE       CI PICRITES     MS IMPRESTS     BH REBIRTHS        SPRINTER
MS VERISMOS          NN TINSTONE          PRICIEST     MU IMPUREST     BO ORBITERS     OP PIERROTS
MW OVERSWIM             TONTINES       CK PRICKETS        IMPUTERS     BU BURRIEST        SPORTIER
NN ENVIRONS          NP NEPOTIST       CO PERSICOT        STUMPIER     CE RECITERS     OR ERRORIST
NP OVERSPIN          NR SNOTTIER       CR RESCRIPT     NN ENPRINTS     CK TRICKERS     OS RESISTOR
   PROVINES             TENORIST       CS CRISPEST     NO POINTERS     CP RESCRIPT        ROISTERS
NS VERSIONS             TRITONES       CU CREPITUS        PROTEINS     CT CRITTERS        SORRIEST
NT INVESTOR          NS SNOTTIES          CUPRITES        REPOINTS        RESTRICT     OT RORTIEST
NU SOUVENIR          NT TOTIENTS          PICTURES     NR PRINTERS        STRICTER     OU STOURIER
PT PIVOTERS          NW TOWNIEST          PIECRUST        REPRINTS     CU CRUSTIER     OV SERVITOR
   SPORTIVE          OR ROOTIEST       DE PRIESTED        SPRINTER        RECRUITS     PP STRIPPER
PU PERVIOUS             TORTOISE          RESPITED     NS SPINSTER     DE DESTRIER        TRIPPERS
   PREVIOUS                            DI RIPTIDES     NU UNPRIEST                     PZ SPRITZER
```

QU SQUIRTER	TERGITES	OU TUTORISE	VOITURES	EL SOLLERET	CT CULOTTES
RS STIRRERS	EH ETHERIST	OV VIRETOTS	RS STRIVERS	EM MOLESTER	DI SOLITUDE
SV STRIVERS	EL RETITLES	PP TRIPPETS		EN ENTRESOL	DP POSTLUDE
TU TRUSTIER	EM TERMITES	PS SPITTERS	**ELORST 67**	ET LORETTES	EN TOLUENES
	EN INERTEST	TIPSTERS	(TOLERS)	EU RESOLUTE	EP EELPOUTS
EIRSTT 104	INTEREST	PU PURTIEST	AB BLOATERS	FG FROGLETS	OUTSLEEP
(SITTER)	STERNITE	PUTTIERS	SORTABLE	FI FLORIEST	ER RESOLUTE
AA ARIETTAS	EP PRETTIES	QU QUITTERS	STORABLE	TREFOILS	EV EVOLUTES
ARISTATE	ES RESTIEST	RU TRUSTIER	AC SECTORAL	FT FORTLETS	VELOUTES
AB BIRETTAS	FI RIFTIEST	SU RUSTIEST	AD DELATORS	FW FELWORTS	FI OUTFLIES
AC CITRATES	FL FLITTERS	TRUSTIES	LEOTARDS	HN HORNLETS	GI EULOGIST
CRISTATE	FR FRITTERS	SW TWISTERS	LODESTAR	HS HOLSTERS	IN ELUTIONS
SCATTIER	FU TURFIEST	TU RUTTIEST	AE OLEASTER	HOSTLERS	OUTLINES
AD STRAITED	TURFITES	TW TWITTERS	AF FLOATERS	HT THROSTLE	IR LOURIEST
STRIATED	GG TRIGGEST	UX TUTRIXES	FORESTAL	HY HOSTELRY	OUTLIERS
TARDIEST	GH RIGHTEST		REFLOATS	II ROILIEST	IS LOUSIEST
AE ARIETTES	STREIGHT	**EIRSTV 163**	AG LEGATORS	IL TRILLOES	IV OUTLIVES
ITERATES	GL GLITTERS	(STRIVE)	AH LOATHERS	TROLLIES	SOLUTIVE
TEARIEST	GN GITTERNS	AA VARIATES	AI SOTERIAL	IN RETINOLS	JP PULSOJET
TREATIES	GR GRITTERS	AB VIBRATES	AL REALLOTS	IO TROOLIES	LP POLLUTES
TREATISE	GT GRITTEST	AE EVIRATES	AM MOLERATS	IP POITRELS	LS OUTSELLS
AG STRIGATE	HI SHITTIER	AG VIRGATES	AP PETROSAL	IT TRIOLETS	LT OUTTELLS
AL TERTIALS	THIRTIES	VITRAGES	PROLATES	IU LOURIEST	LW OUTSWELL
AM MISTREAT	HL THRISTLE	AI VAIRIEST	AR REALTORS	OUTLIERS	OUTWELLS
TERATISM	HO THEORIST	AO VOTARIES	RELATORS	LP POLLSTER	NR TURNSOLE
AN INTREATS	THORITES	AP PRIVATES	AU ROSULATE	LR STROLLER	NZ ZONULETS
NITRATES	HR THIRSTER	AS TRAVISES	AV LEVATORS	TROLLERS	OR TORULOSE
STRAITEN	HW WHITRETS	AY VESTIARY	AY ROYALETS	LY TROLLEYS	OS OUTSOLES
TARTINES	WHITSTER	CD VERDICTS	BH BROTHELS	MM TROMMELS	PR PLOUTERS
TERTIANS	WHITTERS	CE VERTICES	BI STROBILE	MO TREMOLOS	POULTERS
AR RETRAITS	IL STILTIER	CI VERISTIC	TRILOBES	NU TURNSOLE	PT OUTSLEPT
STRAITER	IM METRITIS	CO EVICTORS	BS BOLSTERS	OS ROOTLESS	RY SOUTERLY
TARRIEST	IN NITRITES	VORTICES	LOBSTERS	OT ROOTLETS	UROSTYLE
AS ARTISTES	IP RISPETTI	CS VICTRESS	BT BLOTTERS	OU TORULOSE	
ARTSIEST	IU UTERITIS	CU CURVIEST	BOTTLERS	PT PLOTTERS	**EMNOST 186**
STRIATES	IW TWISTIER	EI VERITIES	BU BOULTERS	PU PLOUTERS	(MONETS)
AT RATTIEST	IZ RITZIEST	EN NERVIEST	TROUBLES	POULTERS	AC CAMSTONE
TARTIEST	KN KNITTERS	REINVEST	CE CORSELET	PW PLOWTERS	AG MAGNETOS
TITRATES	TRINKETS	SERVIENT	ELECTORS	PY PROSTYLE	MEGATONS
AW WARTIEST	KS SKITTERS	SIRVENTE	ELECTROS	PROTYLES	MONTAGES
AX EXTRAITS	LL TESTRILL	ER REVERIST	SELECTOR	ST SETTLORS	AH HOASTMEN
BL BRITTLES	LO TRIOLETS	RIVERETS	CH CHORTLES	SLOTTERS	AL SALMONET
TRIBLETS	LP SPLITTER	RIVETERS	CI CLOISTER	UY SOUTERLY	AR MONSTERA
BN BITTERNS	TRIPLETS	ES SIEVERTS	COISTREL	UROSTYLE	STOREMAN
BU TRIBUTES	LS SLITTERS	TREVISES	CORTILES		AU NOTAEUMS
BY TREYBITS	STILTERS	VESTRIES	COSTLIER	**ELOSTU 173**	OUTNAMES
CH CHITTERS	TESTRILS	EV VETIVERS	CREOLIST	(TOUSLE)	SEAMOUNT
RICHTEST	LU SURTITLE	EY SEVERITY	CS CORSLETS	AB ABSOLUTE	CK STOCKMEN
STITCHER	LW WRISTLET	GN STERVING	COSTRELS	AC LACTEOUS	CM COMMENTS
CI RECTITIS	LZ STRELITZ	GO VERTIGOS	CROSSLET	LOCUSTAE	CN CONTEMNS
CL CLITTERS	MM TRIMMEST	HO OVERHITS	CT CLOTTERS	OSCULATE	DD ODDMENTS
CN CENTRIST	MO OMITTERS	HR THRIVERS	CROTTLES	AP OUTLEAPS	DI DEMONIST
CITTERNS	MS METRISTS	IN INVITERS	CU CLOTURES	PETALOUS	DR MORDENTS
CO COTTIERS	MU SMUTTIER	VINTRIES	CLOUTERS	AR ROSULATE	DU DEMOUNTS
CR CRITTERS	NO SNOTTIER	VITRINES	COULTERS	AT TOLUATES	MUDSTONE
RESTRICT	TENORIST	IP PRIVIEST	CY COYSTREL	AV OVULATES	EG EMONGEST
STRICTER	TRITONES	IS REVISITS	DD STRODDLE	AY AUTOLYSE	GEMSTONE
CS TRISECTS	NS ENTRISTS	VISITERS	STRODLED	BD BOUBLETS	EI MONETISE
CU TUTRICES	STINTERS	LU RIVULETS	DI STOLIDER	BR BOULTERS	SEMITONE
DE TIREDEST	NU RUNTIEST	MU VITREUMS	DL DROLLEST	TROUBLES	EM MEMENTOS
DH THIRSTED	NW TWINTERS	NN VINTNERS	DP DROPLETS	BY OBTUSELY	ER SERMONET
THRISTED	NY ENTRYIST	NO INVESTOR	DS OLDSTERS	CD LOCUSTED	STOREMEN
DI DIRTIEST	OO ROOTIEST	NU UNRIVETS	STRODLES	CE ELOCUTES	GI MITOGENS
TRITIDES	TORTOISE	VENTURIS	TODDLERS	CH SELCOUTH	HI HOISTMEN
DN STRIDENT	OP PORTIEST	OP PIVOTERS	DT DOTTRELS	CN NOCTULES	HL MENTHOLS
TRIDENTS	RISPETTO	OR SERVITOR	EE SLOETREE	CP COUPLETS	HO SMOOTHEN
DO DORTIEST	SPOTTIER	OT VIRETOTS	EH HOSTELER	OCTUPLES	IK TOKENISM
DU DETRITUS	OR RORTIEST	OU VIRTUOSE	EI LITEROSE	CR CLOTURES	IN MENTIONS
EF FRISETTE	OS STOITERS	VITREOUS	TROELIES	CLOUTERS	IO EMOTIONS
EG GRISETTE				COULTERS	MOONIEST

IP EMPTIONS
   NEPOTISM
   PIMENTOS
IS MOISTENS
IU MOUNTIES
LO MOONLETS
MY METONYMS
NW TOWNSMEN
OP METOPONS
OR MESOTRON
   MONTEROS
OS MOONSETS
RS MONSTERS
RT SORTMENT
   TORMENTS
RU MONTURES
   MOUNTERS
   REMOUNTS
SS STEMSONS

EMORST 198
(MOTERS)
AB BROMATES
AD STROAMED
AE EROTEMAS
AF FOREMAST
   FORMATES
AI AMORTISE
   ATOMISER
AL MOLERATS
AM MARMOSET
AN MONSTERA
   STOREMAN
AR REARMOST
AS MAESTROS
AV OVERMAST
BS BESTORMS
   MOBSTERS
   SOMBREST
CI MORTICES
CP COMPTERS
CU COSTUMER
   CUSTOMER
DE MODESTER
DI MORTISED
DN MORDENTS
DO DOOMSTER
EE EROTEMES
   STEREOME
EH THEOREMS
EI TIRESOME
EL MOLESTER
EN SERMONET
   STOREMEN
ES SOMERSET
ET REMOTEST
EU TEMEROUS
FO FOREMOST
FP POMFRETS
GI ERGOTISM
   GORMIEST
GM GROMMETS
GU GOURMETS
HI ISOTHERM
   MOITHERS
HO SMOOTHER
HS SMOTHERS
HU MOUTHERS
HY SMOTHERY
IO MOORIEST

   MOTORISE
   ROOMIEST
IP IMPOSTER
IR MORTISER
   STORMIER
IS EROTISMS
   MORTISES
   TRISOMES
IT OMITTERS
IU MOISTURE
IW MISWROTE
   WORMIEST
IY ISOMETRY
LM TROMMELS
LO TREMOLOS
NO MESOTRON
   MONTEROS
NS MONSTERS
NT SORTMENT
   TORMENTS
NU MONTURES
   MOUNTERS
   REMOUNTS
OP PROMOTES
OS MOROSEST
SU OESTRUMS
   STRUMOSE

ENORST 23
(TONERS)
AA ANOESTRA
AB BARONETS
AC ANCESTOR
   ENACTORS
   SARCONET
   SORTANCE
AD TORNADES
AE RESONATE
AG ORANGEST
   RAGSTONE
AI ANOESTRI
   ARSONITE
   NOTARIES
   NOTARISE
   ROSINATE
AM MONSTERA
   STOREMAN
AN RESONANT
AP OPERANTS
   PRONATES
AR ANTRORSE
AS ASSENTOR
   SENATORS
   TREASONS
AT ORNATEST
AV VENATORS
BI BORNITES
   RIBSTONE
BS SORBENTS
BU RUBSTONE
BW BESTROWN
   BROWNEST
BY RENTBOYS
CC CONCERTS
CI CORNIEST
   RECTIONS
CK CRONKEST
CO CORONETS
CS CONSTERS
CT CORNETTS

CU CONSTRUE
   CORNUTES
   COUNTERS
   RECOUNTS
   TROUNCES
CV CONVERTS
CW CROWNETS
DE ERODENTS
DI DRONIEST
DM MORDENTS
DN TENDRONS
DP PORTENDS
   PROTENDS
DU ROUNDEST
   TONSURED
   UNSORTED
EF ENFOREST
   SOFTENER
EG ESTROGEN
EH HONESTER
EI SEROTINE
EL ENTRESOL
EM SERMONET
   STOREMEN
EN TENONERS
EO ROESTONE
EP PROTENSE
ET ONSETTER
EV OVERNETS
EX EXTENSOR
FH FORHENTS
FN FORNENST
FP FORSPENT
FR RENFORST
FU FORTUNES
GG GONGSTER
GI GENITORS
   ROSETING
GN RONTGENS
GR STRONGER
GS SONGSTER
GU STURGEON
GW WRONGEST
HI HORNIEST
HL HORNLETS
HR NORTHERS
HS SHORTENS
HT THORNSET
HU SOUTHERN
IJ JOINTERS
IL RETINOLS
IN INTONERS
   TERNIONS
IO SNOOTIER
IP POINTERS
   PROTEINS
   REPOINTS
IR INTRORSE
   SNORTIER
IS TERSIONS
IT SNOTTIER
   TENORIST
   TRITONES
IU ROUTINES
   SNOUTIER
IV INVESTOR
IY TYROSINE
IZ TRIZONES
KO STROOKEN
KS STONKERS

KT KNOTTERS
KW NETWORKS
LU TURNSOLE
MO MESOTRON
   MONTEROS
MS MONSTERS
MT SORTMENT
   TORMENTS
MU MONTURES
   MOUNTERS
   REMOUNTS
NS STERNSON
NU NEUTRONS
NY SONNETRY
PS POSTERNS
PT PORTENDS
RS SNORTERS
RT TORRENTS
ST SNOTTERS
   STENTORS
SU TONSURES
TU STENTOUR
TY SNOTTERY
UV VENTROUS
UY TOURNEYS

ENOSTT 195
(ONTEST)
AC CONSTATE
AR ORNATEST
BI BOTTINES
CI CENTOIST
   STENOTIC
CN CONTENTS
CR CORNETTS
CS CONTESTS
CX CONTEXTS
EF OFTENEST
EI NOISETTE
   TEOSINTE
EL NOTELETS
EN NONETTES
ER ONSETTER
FL FLETTONS
   FONTLETS
GI TENTIGOS
HR THORNSET
IJ JETTISON
IN TINSTONE
   TONTINES
IP NEPOTIST
IR SNOTTIER
   TENORIST
   TRITONES
IS SNOTTIES
   STONIEST
IT TOTIENTS
KR KNOTTERS
MR SORTMENT
   TORMENTS
NO NONETTOS
OP POTSTONE
OS TESTOONS
PR PORTENTS
PU OUTSPENT
RR TORRENTS
RS SNOTTERS
   STENTORS
RU STENTOUR

ENOSTU 94
(OUTENS)
AM NOTAEUMS
   OUTNAMES
   SEAMOUNT
AN TONNEAUS
AS SOUTANES
BI BOUNTIES
BR RUBSTONE
CD CONTUSED
CF CONFUTES
CI COUNTIES
CK UNSOCKET
CL NOCTULES
CP POUNCETS
CQ CONQUEST
CR CONSTRUE
   CORNUTES
   COUNTERS
   RECOUNTS
   TROUNCES
CS CONTUSES
   COUNTESS
DD STOUNDED
DI OUNDIEST
DM DEMOUNTS
   MUDSTONE
DO DUOTONES
DP OUTSPEND
   UNPOSTED
DR ROUNDEST
   TONSURED
   UNSORTED
DS SOUNDEST
DW UNSTOWED
EL TOLUENES
FR FORTUNES
GH TOUGHENS
GN GUNSTONE
GR STURGEON
GY YOUNGEST
HI OUTSHINE
HN UNHONEST
HO OUTSHONE
HR SOUTHERN
HU NUTHOUSE
IL ELUTIONS
   OUTLINES
IM MOUNTIES
IN NOUNIEST
IQ QUESTION
IR ROUTINES
   SNOUTIER
IU TENUIOUS
LR TURNSOLE
LZ ZONULETS
MR MONTURES
   MOUNTERS
   REMOUNTS
NR NEUTRONS
NS NEUSTONS
   SUNSTONE
PT OUTSPENT
QU UNQUOTES
RS TONSURES
RT STENTOUR
RV VENTROUS

ENRSTU 84
(TUNERS)
AB UNBRASTE
   URBANEST
AC CENTAURS
   RECUSANT
   UNCRATES
   UNTRACES
AD DAUNTERS
   TRANSUDE
   UNTREADS
AG STRAUNGE
AH HAUNTERS
   UNEARTHS
   UNHEARTS
   URETHANS
AI RUINATES
   URANITES
   URINATES
AL NEUTRALS
AM ANESTRUM
   MENSTRUA
   TRANSUME
AP PERSAUNT
AS ANESTRUS
   SAUNTERS
AT TAUNTERS
AV VAUNTERS
AW UNWATERS
BH BURTHENS
BI TRIBUNES
   TURBINES
BO RUBSTONE
CE UNSECRET
CH CHUNTERS
CI CURNIEST
CK STRUCKEN
CL LECTURNS
CM CENTRUMS
CO CONSTRUE
   CORNUTES
   COUNTERS
   RECOUNTS
   TROUNCES
CR CURRENTS
CS CURTNESS
   ENCRUSTS
DE DENTURES
   SEDERUNT
   UNDERSET
   UNDESERT
DG TRUDGENS
DH THUNDERS
DI INTRUDES
DK DRUNKEST
DL RUNDLEST
   TRUNDLES
DO ROUNDEST
   TONSURED
   UNSORTED
DP UPTRENDS
DT STRUNTED
EI ESURIENT
   NEURITES
   RETINUES
   REUNITES
ES TRUENESS

```
EV VENTURES
FO FORTUNES
GL GRUNTLES
GO STURGEON
GR GRUNTERS
   RESTRUNG
HL LUTHERNS
HO SOUTHERN
HS HUNTRESS
   SHUNTERS
II NEURITIS
IL INSULTER
   LUSTRINE
IM TERMINUS
IN RUNNIEST
   STURNINE
IO ROUTINES
   SNOUTIER
IP UNPRIEST
   UNRIPEST
IQ SQUINTER
IT RUNTIEST
IV UNRIVETS
   VENTURIS
IW UNWRITES
JU UNJUSTER
KY TURNKEYS
LO TURNSOLE
MO MONTURES
   MOUNTERS
   REMOUNTS
MS MUNSTERS
   STERNUMS
NO NEUTRONS
NS STUNNERS
OS TONSURES
OT STENTOUR
OV VENTROUS
OY TOURNEYS
PS PUNSTERS
RU NURTURES
ST ENTRUSTS
SU UNSUREST
TU UNTRUEST

EOPRST 193
(POSTER)
AB PROBATES
AD ADOPTERS
   ASPORTED
   READOPTS
AE OPERATES
   PROTEASE
AF FOREPAST
AG PORTAGES
AL PETROSAL
   PROLATES
AN OPERANTS
   PRONATES
AR PRAETORS
   PRORATES
AS ESPARTOS
   PORTASES
   PROTASES
   SEAPORTS
AT PROSTATE
AU APTEROUS
AV OVERPAST
BS BESPORTS
CH POTCHERS
```

```
CI PERSICOT
CJ PROJECTS
CK SPROCKET
CM COMPTERS
CP PROSPECT
CR PORRECTS
CT PROTECTS
CW SCREWTOP
DE POSTERED
   REEDSTOP
   REPOSTED
DH POTSHERD
DI DIOPTERS
   DIOPTRES
   DIPTEROS
   PERIDOTS
   PROTEIDS
   RIPOSTED
DL DROPLETS
DN PORTENDS
   PROTENDS
DO DOORSTEP
   TORPEDOS
DP STROPPED
DU POSTURED
   PROUDEST
   SPROUTED
EG PROTEGES
EI POETRIES
EN PROTENSE
ES PORTESSE
ET TREETOPS
EU OUTPEERS
EV OVERSTEP
EY SEROTYPE
FI FIREPOTS
FM POMFRETS
FN FORSPENT
FO FORETOPS
   POOFTERS
FU POUFTERS
HI TROPHIES
HP PROPHETS
HS STROPHES
HU POUTHERS
HY TROPHESY
IK PORKIEST
IL POITRELS
IM IMPOSTER
IN POINTERS
   PROTEINS
   REPOINTS
IO PORTOISE
   ROOPIEST
IR PIERROTS
   SPORTIER
IS PERIOSTS
   PROSIEST
   REPOSITS
   RIPOSTES
   TRIPOSES
IT PORTIEST
   RISPETTO
   SPOTTIER
IU ROUPIEST
   SPOUTIER
IV PIVOTERS
   SPORTIVE
KU UPSTROKE
LL POLLSTER
```

```
LT PLOTTERS
LU PLOUTERS
   POULTERS
LW PLOWTERS
LY PROSTYLE
   PROTYLES
MO PROMOTES
NS POSTERNS
NT PORTENTS
OR TROOPERS
OS STOOPERS
OU OUTROPES
   PORTEOUS
OV OVERPOST
   OVERTOPS
OW TOWROPES
PS STOPPERS
RS PORTRESS
   SPORTERS
RU POSTURER
   TROUPERS
ST PROTESTS
   SPOTTERS
SU POSTURES
   SEPTUORS
   SPOUTERS

EORRST 106
(SORTER)
AA AERATORS
AB ARBORETS
   TABORERS
AC ACROTERS
   CREATORS
   REACTORS
AD ROADSTER
AG GARROTES
AI ROARIEST
   ROTARIES
AL REALTORS
   RELATORS
AM REARMOST
AN ANTRORSE
AO SORORATE
AP PRAETORS
   PRORATES
AR ARRESTOR
AS ASSERTOR
   ASSORTER
   ORATRESS
   ROASTERS
AT ROSTRATE
BH BROTHERS
BI ORBITERS
BU ROBUSTER
CC CORRECTS
CE ERECTORS
CF CROFTERS
CH TORCHERS
CP PORRECTS
CY CORSETRY
DE RESORTED
   RESTORED
   ROSTERED
DH REDSHORT
DS RODSTERS
EF FORESTER
   FOSTERER
EG OSTREGER
ER RESORTER
```

```
   RESTORER
   RETRORSE
ES RESTORES
EU REROUTES
EX EXTRORSE
FI FROSTIER
   ROTIFERS
FN RENFORST
FS FORTRESS
FW FROWSTER
FY FORESTRY
GN STRONGER
GS GROSERTS
HI HERITORS
HN NORTHERS
HW THROWERS
II RIOTRIES
IM MORTISER
   STORMIER
IN INTRORSE
   SNORTIER
IP PIERROTS
   SPORTIER
IR ERRORIST
IS RESISTOR
   ROISTERS
   SORRIEST
IT RORTIEST
IU STOURIER
IV SERVITOR
KS STROKERS
LL STROLLER
   TROLLERS
NS SNORTERS
NT TORRENTS
OP TROOPERS
OS ROOSTERS
PS PORTRESS
   SPORTERS
PU POSTURER
   TROUPERS
SS STRESSOR
   TROSSERS
SU ROUSTERS
   TROUSERS
SW STROWERS
   TROWSERS
SY ROYSTERS
TT TROTTERS
TU TORTURES
   TROUTERS

EORSTT 114
(OTTERS)
AA AEROSTAT
AB ABETTORS
   BATTEROS
   TABORETS
AC SECTATOR
AG GAROTTES
AH RHEOSTAT
AN ORNATEST
AP PROSTATE
AR ROSTRATE
AS STRATOSE
   TOASTERS
AT ATTESTOR
   TESTATOR
AU OUTRATES
   OUTSTARE
```

```
BH BETROTHS
BL BLOTTERS
   BOTTLERS
CI COTTIERS
CL CLOTTERS
   CROTTLES
CN CORNETTS
CP PROTECTS
DE ROSETTED
   TETRODES
DI DORTIEST
DL DOTTRELS
DU STROUTED
EL LORETTES
EM REMOTEST
EN ONSETTER
EP TREETOPS
ES ROSETTES
FL FORTLETS
FO FOOTREST
GO GROTTOES
HI THEORIST
   THORITES
HL THROSTLE
HN THORNSET
HS SHORTEST
IL TRIOLETS
IM OMITTERS
IN SNOTTIER
   TENORIST
   TRITONES
IO ROOTIEST
   TORTOISE
IP PORTIEST
   RISPETTO
   SPOTTIER
IR RORTIEST
IS STOITERS
IU TUTORISE
IV VIRETOTS
KN KNOTTERS
LO ROOTLETS
LP PLOTTERS
LS SETTLORS
   SLOTTERS
MN SORTMENT
   TORMENTS
NP PORTENTS
NR TORRENTS
NS SNOTTERS
   STENTORS
NU STENTOUR
NY SNOTTERY
PS PROTESTS
   SPOTTERS
RT TROTTERS
RU TORTURES
   TROUTERS
ST STOTTERS
SU TUTORESS
SW SWOTTERS
UW OUTWREST

GILNOT 171
(TOLING)
AA GALTONIA
AB BLOATING
   OBLIGANT
AC LOCATING
AE GELATION
```

```
   LEGATION
AF FLOATING
AG GLOATING
   GOATLING
AH LOATHING
AI INTAGLIO
   LIGATION
   TAGLIONI
AP PLOATING
AR TRIGONAL
AS ANTILOGS
   SALTOING
AY ANTILOGY
BS BILTONGS
   BOLTINGS
BT BLOTTING
   BOTTLING
BU BOULTING
CH CLOTHING
CT CLOTTING
CU CLOUTING
DD TODDLING
FO FOOTLING
FS SOFTLING
FU FLOUTING
   OUTFLING
GG TOGGLING
GU GLOUTING
HS SLOTHING
IP PILOTING
IS TOILINGS
JS JOSTLING
LR TROLLING
LS TOLLINGS
MR MORTLING
MT MOTTLING
MU MOULTING
NW TOWNLING
OR ROOTLING
OS STOOLING
   TOOLINGS
OT TOOTLING
PP TOPPLING
PT PLOTTING
RU TROULING
ST SLOTTING
SU TOUSLING
UY OUTLYING
UZ TOUZLING

GINORS 128
(SIGNOR)
AD ROADINGS
AE IGNAROES
   ORGANISE
   ORIGANES
AI SIGNORIA
AM ORGANISM
AR GARRISON
AS ASSIGNOR
   SIGNORAS
   SOARINGS
AT ORGANIST
   ROASTING
AU AROUSING
AV SAVORING
BD SONGBIRD
BE SOBERING
BH BIGHORNS
```

```
BK BROKINGS      MU ROUMINGS         THROWING     EP PONGIEST        SIGNPOST        ROSETING
BM SOMBRING      NS SNORINGS         WORTHING     ER GENITORS        STOPINGS     EH HORNIEST
BW BROWSING         SORNINGS      IN IGNITRON        ROSETING     PT SPOTTING     EJ JOINTERS
CD CORDINGS      NT SNORTING      IS RIOTINGS     ET TENTIGOS     PU POUTINGS     EL RETINOLS
CK ROCKINGS      NU GRUNIONS         ROISTING     FI FOISTING        SPOUTING     EN INTONERS
CN SCORNING      OP SPOORING         ROSITING     FL SOFTLING     RS SORTINGS        TERNIONS
CP CORPSING      OT ROOSTING      IZ ROZITING     FO FOOTINGS     RU ROUSTING     EO SNOOTIER
CS CROSSING         ROOTINGS      KS STROKING     FR FROSTING        ROUTINGS     EP POINTERS
   SCORINGS      PS PROSINGS      LL TROLLING     GH GHOSTING        TOURINGS        PROTEINS
   SCORSING      PT SPORTING      LM MORTLING     GO STOOGING     RW STROWING        REPOINTS
CU COURSING      PU INGROUPS      LO ROOTLING     HI HOISTING        WORSTING     ER INTRORSE
   SCOURING         POURINGS      LU TROULING     HL SLOTHING     RY ROYSTING        SNORTIER
   SOURCING      ST SORTINGS      MO MOTORING     HN NOTHINGS        STORYING     ES TERSIONS
DD RODDINGS      SU SOURINGS      MS STORMING     HO SHOOTING        STROYING     ET SNOTTIER
DE NEGROIDS      TU ROUSTING      NS SNORTING        SOOTHING     SS TOSSINGS        TENORIST
DI DORISING         ROUTINGS      OP TROOPING     HR SHORTING     ST SOTTINGS        TRITONES
DL GIRLONDS         TOURINGS      OS ROOSTING     HS HOSTINGS     SU TOUSINGS     EU ROUTINES
   LORDINGS      TW STROWING         ROOTINGS     HT SHOTTING     SV STOVINGS        SNOUTIER
DW DROWSING         WORSTING      OW WROOTING        TONIGHTS     SW STOWINGS     EV INVESTOR
   SWORDING      TY ROYSTING      PS SPORTING     HU SHOUTING     TT STOTTING     EY TYROSINE
   WORDINGS         STORYING      PU TROUPING        SOUTHING        TOTTINGS     EZ TRIZONES
EE ERINGOES         STROYING      SS SORTINGS     HW SOWTHING     TW SWOTTING     FG FROSTING
EI SEIGNIOR                       SU ROUSTING     IJ JINGOIST     UW OUTSWING     GH SHORTING
EL RESOLING      GINORT 102          ROUTINGS        JOISTING        OUTWINGS     GI RIOTINGS
EM NEGROISM      (ROTING)            TOURINGS     IL TOILINGS                        ROISTING
EP PERIGONS      AB ABORTING      SW STROWING     IM MOISTING                        ROSITING
   REPOSING         TABORING         WORSTING     IP POSITING     INORST  59      GK STROKING
   SPONGIER      AL TRIGONAL      SY ROYSTING        SOPITING     (TRIONS)        GM STORMING
ER IGNORERS      AN IGNORANT         STORYING     IR RIOTINGS     AB TABORINS     GN SNORTING
ES SIGNORES      AO ROGATION         STROYING        ROISTING     AC CANTORIS     GO ROOSTING
ET GENITORS      AS ORGANIST      TT TROTTING        ROSITING        CAROTINS        ROOTINGS
   ROSETING         ROASTING      TU TROUTING     IT STOITING     AD INTRADOS     GP SPORTING
EY SEIGNORY      AT ROTATING         TUTORING     JL JOSTLING     AE ANOESTRI     GS SORTINGS
FF GRIFFONS         TROATING                      JT JOTTINGS        ARSONITE     GU ROUSTING
FG FORGINGS      AV GRAVITON      GINOST 176      JU JOUSTING        NOTARIES        ROUTINGS
FM FORMINGS      AY GYRATION      (OSTING)        KO STOOKING        NOTARISE        TOURINGS
FO ROOFINGS         ORGANITY      AB BOASTING     KP KINGPOST        ROSINATE     GW STROWING
FT FROSTING      BI ORBITING         BOATINGS     KR STROKING     AG ORGANIST        WORSTING
GP PROGGINS      CE GERONTIC         BOSTANGI     LL TOLLINGS        ROASTING     GY ROYSTING
GS GROSSING      CF CROFTING      AC AGNOSTIC     LO STOOLING     AH TRAHISON        STORYING
GU GROUSING      CH TORCHING         COASTING        TOOLINGS     AI INTARSIO        STROYING
GW GROWINGS      CI TRIGONIC         COATINGS     LT SLOTTING     AJ JANITORS
HN HORNINGS      CK TROCKING         COTINGAS     LU TOUSLING     AK SKIATRON     HI HISTRION
HS HORSINGS      CU COURTING      AD DOATINGS     MO MOOTINGS     AO ORATIONS     HN TINHORNS
   SHORINGS      EH THROEING      AH HOASTING        SMOOTING     AP ATROPINS     HO HORNITOS
HT SHORTING      EN NITROGEN      AK GOATSKIN     MP STOMPING     AS ARSONIST     HS HORNISTS
HV SHROVING      ES GENITORS      AL ANTILOGS     MR STORMING     AT STRONTIA     IS IRONISTS
HW SHROWING         ROSETING         SALTOING     MS GNOMISTS     AU SUTORIAN     IT INTROITS
IL LIGROINS      ET OTTERING      AN ASTONING     MU MOUSTING     AX TRIAXONS     KK KIRKTONS
IN IRONINGS      EU OUTREIGN      AR ORGANIST        SMOUTING     BE BORNITES     LS NOSTRILS
   ROSINING      EW TOWERING         ROASTING     NN STONNING        RIBSTONE     LU TORULINS
IS SIGNIORS      EX OXTERING      AS AGONISTS     NO SNOOTING     BO ISOBRONT     MO MONITORS
IT RIOTINGS      EZ ROZETING      AT TANGOIST     NR SNORTING     BS RIBSTONS        TROMINOS
   ROISTING      FH FROTHING         TOASTING     NS STONINGS     CE CORNIEST     MY TRIONYMS
   ROSITING      FN FRONTING      BL BILTONGS     NT SNOTTING        RECTIONS     NO NOTORNIS
IV VISORING      FS FROSTING         BOLTINGS     NU SNOUTING     CR TRICORNS     OP PORTIONS
KT STROKING      GG TROGGING      BO BOOSTING        STOUNING     CS CISTRONS        POSITRON
KW WORKINGS      GU GROUTING      CI COTISING     NY STONYING        CORNISTS        SORPTION
LL ROLLINGS      HN NORTHING      CK STOCKING     OP STOOPING     CT CONTRIST     OS ISOTRONS
LM MORLINGS         THORNING      CO SCOOTING     OR ROOSTING     CU RUCTIONS        TORSIONS
LU LOURINGS         THRONING      CU SCOUTING        ROOTINGS     DE DRONIEST     OY SONORITY
MN MORNINGS      HS SHORTING      DG STODGING     PP STOPPING     DO TORDIONS
MO MOORINGS      HT TROTHING      EE EGESTION        TOPPINGS     DU STURNOID
   SMOORING      HW INGROWTH      EH HISTOGEN     PR SPORTING        TURDIONS
MT STORMING                       EM MITOGENS     PS POSTINGS     EE SEROTINE
                                                                  EG GENITORS
```

SECTION FOUR

THE HOOKS

Introduction

Which two-letter words can be transformed into which
three-letter words by the addition of a single letter at either
the front or the end? An example is HI to CHI, GHI and PHI
(by adding a letter at the front of HI), and HIC, HID, HIE,
HIM, HIN, HIP, HIS and HIT (by adding a letter at the end).
Words which can add a letter at the front or back are called
hooks, as they provide places for other words to hook on to.
All the two-letter hooks such as these appear in the
following lists. Of course, it is also helpful to be able to see at
a glance which two-letter words *don't* add a letter at either
end. All these hooks (and non-hooks!) are shown in the
following lists.

Subsequent lists show all the three-letter and four-letter
words, along with their hooks and non-hooks.

For longer words, of five, six and seven letters, only actual
hooks are shown. Non-hooks have been omitted.

In actual play, it can be very useful to play a three-letter
word, (BAP, say), which has an obscure extension to four
letters (BAPU). If all the S's and blanks have already been
played, the chances are your opponent won't know BAPU,
so the opening will likely be safe until you want to put a U on
the end of BAP. One other particularly neat hook is PAYS to
PAYSD. Chances are that your opponent won't think to
extend PAYS by the addition of a D!

PART A: 2-letter word hooks
including all root words

AA	SAM	ASK	PAY	DAP	REF	LES	GUY	**ID**	FIT
BAA	TAM	ASP	RAY	DAS	TEF	MES	**HA**	AID	GIT
AAS	YAM	ASS	SAY	DAW	EFF	OES	AHA	BID	HIT
AD	AMI	**AT**	WAY	DAY	EFS	RES	CHA	DID	KIT
BAD	AMP	BAT	AYE	**DI**	EFT	TES	HAD	FID	LIT
CAD	**AN**	CAT	AYU	DIB	**EH**	YES	HAE	GID	NIT
DAD	BAN	EAT	**BA**	DID	REH	ESS	HAG	HID	PIT
FAD	CAN	FAT	ABA	DIE	EHS	**EX**	HAH	KID	RIT
GAD	DAN	GAT	BAA	DIG	**EL**	HEX	HAJ	LID	SIT
HAD	EAN	HAT	BAD	DIM	BEL	KEX	HAM	MID	TIT
LAD	FAN	KAT	BAG	DIN	CEL	LEX	HAN	NID	WIT
MAD	GAN	LAT	BAH	DIP	DEL	REX	HAP	RID	ZIT
PAD	HAN	MAT	BAM	DIT	EEL	SEX	HAS	TID	ITA
RAD	MAN	NAT	BAN	DIV	GEL	VEX	HAT	IDE	ITS
SAD	NAN	OAT	BAP	**DO**	MEL	WEX	HAW	IDS	**JO**
TAD	PAN	PAT	BAR	ADO	SEL	YEX	HAY	**IF**	JOB
WAD	RAN	QAT	BAS	UDO	TEL	**FA**	**HE**	GIF	JOE
ADD	SAN	RAT	BAT	DOB	ZEL	FAB	CHE	KIF	JOG
ADO	TAN	SAT	BAY	DOC	ELD	FAD	SHE	IFF	JOR
ADS	VAN	TAT	**BE**	DOD	ELF	FAG	THE	IFS	JOT
AE	WAN	VAT	BED	DOE	ELK	FAH	HEM	**IN**	JOW
GAE	ANA	WAT	BEE	DOG	ELL	FAN	HEN	AIN	JOY
HAE	AND	ATE	BEG	DOH	ELM	FAP	HEP	BIN	**KA**
KAE	ANE	**AW**	BEL	DON	ELS	FAR	HER	DIN	SKA
MAE	ANN	CAW	BEN	DOO	ELT	FAS	HES	FIN	KAE
NAE	ANT	DAW	BET	DOP	**EM**	FAT	HET	GIN	KAI
SAE	ANY	FAW	BEY	DOR	GEM	FAW	HEW	HIN	KAM
TAE	**AR**	HAW	BEZ	DOS	HEM	FAX	HEX	KIN	KAS
VAE	BAR	JAW	**BO**	DOT	REM	FAY	HEY	LIN	KAT
WAE	CAR	KAW	BOA	DOW	WEM	**FY**	**HI**	PIN	KAW
AH	EAR	LAW	BOB	**EA**	EME	**GI**	CHI	RIN	KAY
BAH	FAR	MAW	BOD	KEA	EMS	GIB	GHI	SIN	**KO**
DAH	GAR	PAW	BOG	LEA	EMU	GID	PHI	TIN	KOA
FAH	JAR	RAW	BOH	PEA	**EN**	GIE	HIC	VIN	KOB
HAH	LAR	SAW	BOK	SEA	BEN	GIF	HID	WIN	KON
LAH	MAR	TAW	BON	TEA	DEN	GIG	HIE	YIN	KOP
PAH	OAR	WAW	BOO	YEA	FEN	GIN	HIM	INK	KOS
RAH	PAR	YAW	BOP	ZEA	GEN	GIO	HIN	INN	KOW
YAH	SAR	AWA	BOR	EAN	HEN	GIP	HIP	INS	**KY**
AHA	TAR	AWE	BOS	EAR	KEN	GIS	HIS	**IO**	SKY
AI	WAR	AWL	BOT	EAS	MEN	GIT	HIT	BIO	KYE
KAI	ARC	AWN	BOW	EAT	PEN	**GO**	**HO**	GIO	**LA**
SAI	ARE	**AX**	BOX	EAU	REN	AGO	MHO	ION	ALA
TAI	ARK	FAX	BOY	**EE**	SEN	EGO	OHO	IOS	LAB
AIA	ARM	LAX	**BY**	BEE	TEN	YGO	PHO	**IS**	LAC
AID	ARS	MAX	ABY	CEE	WEN	GOA	RHO	AIS	LAD
AIL	ART	PAX	BYE	DEE	YEN	GOB	THO	BIS	LAG
AIM	ARY	RAX	BYS	FEE	END	GOD	WHO	GIS	LAH
AIN	**AS**	SAX	**CH**	GEE	ENE	GOE	ZHO	HIS	LAM
AIR	AAS	TAX	ECH	JEE	ENG	GOG	HOA	LIS	LAP
AIS	BAS	WAX	ICH	LEE	ENS	GON	HOB	MIS	LAR
AIT	DAS	ZAX	OCH	NEE	**ER**	GOO	HOC	NIS	LAS
AM	EAS	AXE	CHA	PEE	HER	GOS	HOD	PIS	LAT
BAM	FAS	**AY**	CHE	REE	PER	GOT	HOE	SIS	LAV
CAM	GAS	BAY	CHI	SEE	ERA	GOV	HOG	TIS	LAW
DAM	HAS	CAY	**DA**	TEE	ERE	GOY	HOH	VIS	LAX
GAM	KAS	DAY	ODA	VEE	ERF	**GU**	HOI	WIS	LAY
HAM	LAS	FAY	DAB	WEE	ERG	GUB	HON	XIS	**LI**
JAM	MAS	GAY	DAD	ZEE	ERK	GUE	HOO	ISH	LIB
KAM	NAS	HAY	DAG	EEK	ERN	GUM	HOP	ISM	LID
LAM	PAS	JAY	DAH	EEL	ERR	GUN	HOS	**IT**	LIE
MAM	RAS	KAY	DAK	EEN	ERS	GUP	HOT	AIT	LIG
NAM	VAS	LAY	DAL	**EF**	**ES**	GUR	HOW	BIT	LIN
PAM	WAS	MAY	DAM	KEF	HES	GUS	HOX	CIT	LIP
RAM	ASH	NAY	DAN	NEF		GUT	HOY	DIT	LIS

LIT	MUG	ROB	CON	VOR	BOY	REN	TEA	NUN	WET
LO	MUM	SOB	DON	ORB	COY	REP	TED	PUN	WEX
LOB	MUN	YOB	EON	ORC	FOY	RES	TEE	RUN	WEY
LOG	MUS	OBI	FON	ORD	GOY	RET	TEF	SUN	**WO**
LOO	MUX	OBS	GON	ORE	HOY	REV	TEG	TUN	TWO
LOP	**MY**	**OD**	HON	ORF	JOY	REW	TEL	UNI	WOE
LOR	**NA**	BOD	ION	ORS	LOY	REX	TEN	UNS	WOG
LOS	ANA	COD	KON	ORT	MOY	**SH**	TES	**UP**	WOK
LOT	MNA	DOD	NON	**OS**	NOY	ASH	TEW	CUP	WON
LOW	NAB	GOD	OON	BOS	SOY	ISH	**TI**	DUP	WOO
LOX	NAE	HOD	SON	COS	TOY	SHE	TIC	GUP	WOP
LOY	NAG	MOD	TON	DOS	OYE	SHY	TID	HUP	WOS
MA	NAM	NOD	WON	GOS	OYS	**SI**	TIE	OUP	WOT
SMA	NAN	POD	YON	HOS	**PA**	PSI	TIG	PUP	WOW
MAC	NAP	ROD	ONE	IOS	SPA	SIB	TIL	SUP	WOX
MAD	NAS	SOD	ONS	KOS	PAD	SIC	TIN	TUP	**XI**
MAE	NAT	TOD	**OO**	LOS	PAH	SIM	TIP	YUP	XIS
MAG	NAY	YOD	BOO	OOS	PAL	SIN	TIS	UPS	**YE**
MAK	**NE**	ODA	COO	POS	PAM	SIP	TIT	**UR**	AYE
MAL	ANE	ODD	DOO	SOS	PAN	SIR	**TO**	BUR	BYE
MAM	ENE	ODE	GOO	WOS	PAP	SIS	TOD	CUR	DYE
MAN	ONE	ODS	HOO	YOS	PAR	SIT	TOE	FUR	EYE
MAP	NEB	**OE**	LOO	ZOS	PAS	SIX	TOG	GUR	HYE
MAR	NED	DOE	MOO	**OU**	PAT	**SO**	TOM	LUR	KYE
MAS	NEE	FOE	POO	FOU	PAW	DSO	TON	NUR	LYE
MAT	NEF	GOE	ROO	MOU	PAX	SOB	TOO	OUR	NYE
MAW	NEK	HOE	TOO	SOU	PAY	SOC	TOP	PUR	OYE
MAX	NEP	JOE	WOO	YOU	**PI**	SOD	TOR	SUR	PYE
MAY	NET	MOE	ZOO	OUK	PIA	SOG	TOT	URD	RYE
ME	NEW	ROE	OOF	OUP	PIC	SOH	TOW	URE	SYE
EME	**NO**	TOE	OOH	OUR	PIE	SOL	TOY	URN	TYE
MEL	NOB	VOE	OOM	OUT	PIG	SON	**UG**	**US**	WYE
MEN	NOD	WOE	OON	**OW**	PIN	SOP	BUG	BUS	YEA
MES	NOG	OES	OOP	BOW	PIP	SOS	DUG	GUS	YEN
MET	NOH	**OF**	OOR	COW	PIR	SOT	FUG	JUS	YEP
MEU	NOM	OOF	OOS	DOW	PIS	SOU	HUG	MUS	YES
MEW	NON	OFF	**OP**	HOW	PIT	SOV	JUG	NUS	YET
MI	NOR	OFT	BOP	JOW	PIU	SOW	LUG	PUS	YEW
AMI	NOT	**OH**	COP	KOW	PIX	SOX	MUG	SUS	YEX
MID	NOW	BOH	DOP	LOW	**PO**	SOY	PUG	YUS	**YO**
MIL	NOY	DOH	FOP	MOW	POA	**ST**	RUG	USE	YOB
MIM	**NU**	FOH	HOP	NOW	POD	PST	TUG	**UT**	YOD
MIR	GNU	HOH	KOP	POW	POH	STY	VUG	BUT	YOK
MIS	NUB	NOH	LOP	ROW	POI	**TA**	YUG	CUT	YON
MIX	NUN	OOH	MOP	SOW	POM	ETA	UGH	GUT	YOS
MIZ	NUR	POH	OOP	TOW	POO	ITA	UGS	HUT	YOU
MO	NUS	SOH	POP	VOW	POP	TAB	**UM**	JUT	YOW
MOA	NUT	OHM	SOP	WOW	POS	TAD	BUM	NUT	**YU**
MOB	**NY**	OHO	TOP	YOW	POT	TAE	CUM	OUT	AYU
MOD	ANY	**OI**	WOP	OWE	POW	TAG	FUM	PUT	YUG
MOE	NYE	HOI	OPE	OWL	POX	TAI	GUM	RUT	YUK
MOG	NYS	POI	OPS	OWN	POZ	TAJ	HUM	TUT	YUP
MOM	**OB**	OIK	OPT	OWT	**RE**	TAK	LUM	UTE	YUS
MOO	BOB	OIL	**OR**	**OX**	ARE	TAM	MUM	UTS	**ZO**
MOP	COB	**OM**	BOR	BOX	ERE	TAN	RUM	UTU	DZO
MOR	DOB	MOM	COR	COX	IRE	TAP	SUM	**WE**	ZOA
MOT	FOB	NOM	DOR	FOX	ORE	TAR	TUM	AWE	ZOO
MOU	GOB	OOM	FOR	HOX	PRE	TAT	VUM	EWE	ZOS
MOW	HOB	POM	JOR	LOX	URE	TAU	**UN**	OWE	
MOY	JOB	ROM	LOR	POX	RED	TAW	BUN	WEB	
MOZ	KOB	TOM	MOR	SOX	REE	TAX	DUN	WED	
MU	LOB	OMS	NOR	VOX	REF	**TE**	FUN	WEE	
EMU	MOB	**ON**	OOR	WOX	REH	ATE	GUN	WEM	
MUD	NOB	BON	TOR	**OY**	REM	UTE	MUN	WEN	

PART A: 3-letter word hooks
including all root words

AAS	GAGE	AINE	TALE	**AND**	APTS	FART	WATE	**BAG**	BENI
BAAS	MAGE	**AIR**	VALE	BAND	**ARC**	GART	YATE	BAGS	BENJ
ABA	PAGE	FAIR	WALE	FAND	MARC	HART	**AUF**	**BAH**	BENS
BABA	RAGE	GAIR	YALE	HAND	ARCH	KART	CAUF	BAHT	BENT
CABA	SAGE	HAIR	ALEE	LAND	ARCO	MART	LAUF	**BAM**	**BET**
ABAC	WAGE	LAIR	ALES	MAND	ARCS	PART	AUFS	BAMS	ABET
ABAS	AGED	PAIR	ALEW	PAND	**ARE**	TART	**AUK**	**BAN**	YBET
ABB	AGEE	SAIR	**ALL**	RAND	BARE	WART	BAUK	BANC	BETA
ABBA	AGEN	VAIR	BALL	SAND	CARE	ARTS	CAUK	BAND	BETE
ABBE	AGES	AIRN	CALL	WAND	DARE	ARTY	WAUK	BANE	BETH
ABBS	**AGO**	AIRS	FALL	ANDS	FARE	**ARY**	AUKS	BANG	BETS
ABY	DAGO	AIRT	GALL	**ANE**	GARE	NARY	**AVA**	BANI	**BEY**
BABY	KAGO	AIRY	HALL	BANE	HARE	OARY	KAVA	BANK	OBEY
GABY	SAGO	**AIS**	MALL	CANE	LARE	VARY	LAVA	BANS	BEYS
ABYE	AGOG	DAIS	PALL	FANE	MARE	WARY	AVAL	BANT	**BEZ**
ACE	AGON	KAIS	TALL	GANE	NARE	ARYL	AVAS	**BAP**	**BIB**
DACE	**AHA**	PAIS	WALL	JANE	PARE	**ASH**	**AVE**	BAPS	BIBS
FACE	TAHA	SAIS	ALLS	LANE	RARE	BASH	CAVE	BAPU	**BID**
LACE	**AIA**	TAIS	ALLY	MANE	TARE	CASH	GAVE	**BAR**	ABID
MACE	AIAS	**AIT**	**ALP**	PANE	VARE	DASH	HAVE	BARB	BIDE
PACE	**AID**	BAIT	CALP	SANE	WARE	FASH	LAVE	BARD	BIDS
RACE	GAID	GAIT	PALP	TANE	YARE	GASH	NAVE	BARE	**BIG**
TACE	KAID	RAIT	SALP	VANE	AREA	HASH	PAVE	BARF	BIGA
ACED	LAID	TAIT	ALPS	WANE	ARED	LASH	RAVE	BARK	BIGG
ACES	MAID	WAIT	**ALS**	ANES	ARES	MASH	SAVE	BARM	BIGS
ACT	PAID	AITS	DALS	ANEW	ARET	PASH	WAVE	BARN	**BIN**
FACT	RAID	AITU	GALS	**ANN**	AREW	RASH	AVER	BARP	BIND
PACT	SAID	**AKE**	MALS	CANN	**ARK**	SASH	AVES	BARS	BINE
TACT	WAID	BAKE	PALS	JANN	BARK	TASH	**AWA**	**BAS**	BING
ACTA	AIDE	CAKE	SALS	ANNA	CARK	WASH	PAWA	ABAS	BINK
ACTS	AIDS	FAKE	ALSO	ANNO	DARK	ASHY	AWAY	BASE	BINS
ADD	**AIL**	HAKE	**ALT**	ANNS	HARK	**ASK**	**AWE**	BASH	BINT
WADD	BAIL	JAKE	DALT	**ANT**	JARK	BASK	WAWE	BASK	**BIO**
ADDS	FAIL	LAKE	HALT	BANT	LARK	CASK	AWED	BASS	BIOG
ADO	HAIL	MAKE	MALT	CANT	MARK	HASK	AWES	BAST	BIOS
DADO	JAIL	RAKE	SALT	DANT	NARK	MASK	**AWL**	**BAT**	**BIS**
FADO	KAIL	SAKE	ALTO	GANT	PARK	TASK	BAWL	BATE	IBIS
ADOS	MAIL	TAKE	ALTS	KANT	SARK	ASKS	PAWL	BATH	OBIS
ADS	NAIL	WAKE	**AMI**	LANT	WARK	**ASP**	WAWL	BATS	BISE
CADS	PAIL	AKED	KAMI	PANT	ARKS	GASP	YAWL	BATT	BISH
DADS	RAIL	AKEE	RAMI	RANT	**ARM**	HASP	AWLS	**BAY**	BISK
FADS	SAIL	AKES	AMID	VANT	BARM	JASP	**AWN**	BAYE	**BIT**
GADS	TAIL	**ALA**	AMIE	WANT	FARM	RASP	BAWN	BAYS	OBIT
HADS	VAIL	GALA	AMIR	ANTA	HARM	WASP	DAWN	BAYT	BITE
LADS	WAIL	NALA	AMIS	ANTE	MARM	ASPS	FAWN	**BED**	BITO
MADS	AILS	TALA	**AMP**	ANTI	WARM	**ASS**	LAWN	ABED	BITS
PADS	**AIM**	ALAE	CAMP	ANTS	ARMS	BASS	PAWN	BEDE	BITT
RADS	KAIM	ALAP	DAMP	**ANY**	ARMY	LASS	RAWN	BEDS	**BIZ**
TADS	MAIM	ALAR	GAMP	CANY	**ARS**	MASS	SAWN	**BEE**	**BOA**
WADS	SAIM	ALAS	LAMP	MANY	BARS	PASS	YAWN	BEEF	BOAK
AFT	AIMS	ALAY	RAMP	WANY	CARS	SASS	AWNS	BEEN	BOAR
BAFT	**AIN**	**ALB**	SAMP	ZANY	EARS	TASS	AWNY	BEEP	BOAS
DAFT	CAIN	ALBE	TAMP	**APE**	FARS	**ATE**	**AXE**	BEER	BOAT
HAFT	FAIN	ALBS	VAMP	CAPE	GARS	BATE	AXED	BEES	**BOB**
RAFT	GAIN	**ALE**	AMPS	GAPE	JARS	CATE	AXEL	BEET	BOBA
WAFT	HAIN	BALE	**ANA**	JAPE	MARS	DATE	AXES	**BEG**	BOBS
AGA	KAIN	DALE	KANA	NAPE	OARS	FATE	**AYE**	BEGO	**BOD**
GAGA	LAIN	EALE	LANA	PAPE	PARS	GATE	BAYE	BEGS	BODE
NAGA	MAIN	GALE	MANA	RAPE	SARS	HATE	AYES	**BEL**	BODS
RAGA	NAIN	HALE	NANA	TAPE	TARS	LATE	**AYU**	BELL	BODY
SAGA	PAIN	KALE	RANA	APED	WARS	MATE	AYUS	BELS	**BOG**
AGAR	RAIN	MALE	TANA	APES	ARSE	PATE	**BAA**	BELT	BOGS
AGAS	SAIN	PALE	ANAL	APEX	**ART**	RATE	BAAS	**BEN**	BOGY
AGE	VAIN	RALE	ANAN	**APT**	CART	SATE	**BAD**	BEND	**BOH**
CAGE	WAIN	SALE	ANAS	RAPT	DART	TATE	BADE	BENE	**BOK**

BOKE	BUGS	CARD	SCOG	SCRY	DAWK	DIVS	**DUD**	EASY	**REFS**
BOKO	**BUM**	CARE	COGS	**CUB**	DAWN	**DOB**	DUDE	**EAT**	**TEFS**
BOKS	BUMF	CARK	**COL**	CUBE	DAWS	DOBS	DUDS	BEAT	**EFT**
BON	BUMP	CARL	COLA	CUBS	DAWT	**DOC**	**DUE**	FEAT	DEFT
EBON	BUMS	CARP	COLD	**CUD**	**DAY**	DOCK	DUED	GEAT	HEFT
BONA	**BUN**	CARR	COLE	SCUD	DAYS	DOCS	DUEL	HEAT	LEFT
BOND	BUNA	CARS	COLL	CUDS	**DEB**	**DOD**	DUES	JEAT	REFT
BONE	BUND	CART	COLS	**CUE**	DEBS	DODO	DUET	LEAT	WEFT
BONG	BUNG	**CAT**	COLT	CUED	DEBT	DODS	**DUG**	MEAT	EFTS
BONK	BUNK	SCAT	**CON**	CUES	**DEE**	**DOE**	DUGS	NEAT	**EGG**
BONY	BUNS	CATE	ICON	**CUM**	IDEE	DOEN	**DUN**	PEAT	TEGG
BOO	BUNT	CATS	COND	SCUM	DEED	DOER	DUNE	SEAT	YEGG
BOOB	**BUR**	**CAW**	CONE	**CUP**	DEEM	DOES	DUNG	TEAT	EGGS
BOOH	BURD	SCAW	CONK	SCUP	DEEN	**DOG**	DUNK	EATH	EGGY
BOOK	BURG	CAWK	CONN	CUPS	DEEP	DOGE	DUNS	EATS	**EGO**
BOOM	BURK	CAWS	CONS	**CUR**	DEER	DOGS	DUNT	EAU	BEGO
BOON	BURL	**CAY**	CONY	SCUR	DEES	DOGY	**DUO**	BEAU	SEGO
BOOR	BURN	CAYS	**COO**	CURB	DEEV	**DOH**	DUOS	EAUS	EGOS
BOOS	BURP	**CEE**	COOF	CURD	**DEI**	DOHS	**DUP**	EAUX	**EHS**
BOOT	BURR	CEES	COOK	CURE	DEID	**DON**	DUPE	**EBB**	REHS
BOP	BURS	**CEL**	COOL	CURL	DEIL	DONA	DUPS	EBBS	**EIK**
BOPS	BURY	CELL	COOM	CURN	**DEL**	DONE	**DUX**	**ECH**	REIK
BOR	**BUS**	CELS	COON	CURR	DELE	DONG	**DYE**	EECH	EIKS
BORA	BUSH	CELT	COOP	CURS	DELF	DONS	DYED	HECH	**EKE**
BORD	BUSK	**CEP**	COOS	CURT	DELI	**DOO**	DYER	LECH	LEKE
BORE	BUSS	CEPS	COOT	**CUT**	DELL	DOOB	DYES	PECH	PEKE
BORN	BUST	**CHA**	**COP**	SCUT	DELS	DOOK	**DZO**	TECH	REKE
BORS	BUSY	CHAD	COPE	CUTE	**DEN**	DOOL	DZOS	ECHE	EKED
BORT	**BUT**	CHAI	COPS	CUTS	DENE	DOOM	**EAN**	ECHO	EKES
BOS	ABUT	CHAL	COPY	**CUZ**	DENS	DOOR	BEAN	ECHT	**ELD**
BOSH	BUTE	CHAM	**COR**	**CWM**	DENT	DOOS	DEAN	**ECU**	GELD
BOSK	BUTS	CHAP	CORD	CWMS	DENY	**DOP**	GEAN	ECUS	HELD
BOSS	BUTT	CHAR	CORE	**DAB**	**DEW**	DOPA	JEAN	**EDH**	MELD
BOT	**BUY**	CHAS	CORF	DABS	DEWS	DOPE	LEAN	EDHS	SELD
BOTH	BUYS	CHAT	CORK	**DAD**	DEWY	DOPS	MEAN	**EEK**	TELD
BOTS	**BYE**	CHAW	CORM	DADO	**DEY**	DOPY	PEAN	KEEK	VELD
BOTT	ABYE	CHAY	CORN	DADS	DEYS	**DOR**	REAN	LEEK	WELD
BOW	BYES	**CHE**	CORS	**DAG**	**DIB**	ODOR	SEAN	MEEK	YELD
BOWL	**BYS**	ACHE	**COS**	DAGO	DIBS	DORM	WEAN	PEEK	ELDS
BOWR	**CAB**	ECHE	COSE	DAGS	**DID**	DORP	YEAN	REEK	**ELF**
BOWS	SCAB	OCHE	COSH	**DAH**	DIDO	DORR	EANS	SEEK	DELF
BOX	CABA	CHEF	COSS	DAHL	**DIE**	DORS	**EAR**	WEEK	PELF
BOXY	CABS	CHER	COST	DAHS	DIEB	DORT	BEAR	**EEL**	SELF
BOY	**CAD**	CHEW	COSY	**DAK**	DIED	DORY	DEAR	FEEL	ELFS
BOYG	ECAD	CHEZ	**COT**	DAKS	DIES	**DOS**	FEAR	HEEL	**ELK**
BOYO	SCAD	**CHI**	SCOT	**DAL**	DIET	ADOS	GEAR	JEEL	WELK
BOYS	CADE	CHIC	COTE	ODAL	**DIG**	UDOS	HEAR	KEEL	YELK
BRA	CADI	CHID	COTH	UDAL	DIGS	DOSE	LEAR	PEEL	ELKS
BRAD	CADS	CHIK	COTS	DALE	**DIM**	DOSS	NEAR	REEL	**ELL**
BRAE	**CAM**	CHIN	COTT	DALI	DIME	DOST	PEAR	SEEL	BELL
BRAG	SCAM	CHIP	**COW**	DALS	DIMS	**DOT**	REAR	TEEL	CELL
BRAN	CAME	CHIS	SCOW	DALT	**DIN**	DOTE	SEAR	WEEL	DELL
BRAS	CAMP	CHIT	COWL	**DAM**	DINE	DOTH	TEAR	EELS	FELL
BRAT	CAMS	CHIV	COWP	DAME	DING	DOTS	WEAR	EELY	HELL
BRAW	**CAN**	**CIG**	COWS	DAMN	DINK	DOTY	YEAR	**EEN**	JELL
BRAY	SCAN	CIGS	**COX**	DAMP	DINS	**DOW**	EARD	BEEN	KELL
BRO	CANE	**CIT**	COXA	DAMS	DINT	DOWD	EARL	DEEN	MELL
BROD	CANG	CITE	COXY	**DAN**	**DIP**	DOWF	EARN	KEEN	PELL
BROG	CANN	CITO	**COY**	DANG	DIPS	DOWL	EARS	PEEN	SELL
BROO	CANS	CITS	COYS	DANK	**DIT**	DOWN	**EAS**	REEN	TELL
BROS	CANT	CITY	**COZ**	DANS	ADIT	DOWP	CEAS	SEEN	VELL
BROW	CANY	**CLY**	COZE	DANT	EDIT	DOWS	KEAS	TEEN	WELL
BUB	**CAP**	**COB**	COZY	**DAP**	DITA	DOWT	LEAS	WEEN	YELL
BUBA	CAPA	COBB	**CRU**	DAPS	DITE	**DRY**	PEAS	**EFF**	ELLS
BUBO	CAPE	COBS	ECRU	**DAS**	DITS	ADRY	SEAS	JEFF	**ELM**
BUBS	CAPO	**COD**	CRUD	ODAS	DITT	**DSO**	TEAS	TEFF	HELM
BUD	CAPS	CODA	CRUE	DASH	**DIV**	ODSO	YEAS	EFFS	YELM
BUDO	**CAR**	CODE	CRUS	**DAW**	DIVA	DSOS	ZEAS	**EFS**	ELMS
BUDS	SCAR	CODS	CRUX	ADAW	DIVE	**DUB**	EASE	KEFS	ELMY
BUG	CARB	**COG**	**CRY**	DAWD	DIVI	DUBS	EAST	NEFS	**ELS**

BELS	GENS	NESS	FATE	**FLY**	**GAD**	**GEM**	GOEY	HAGS	HERL
CELS	HENS	SESS	FATS	**FOB**	EGAD	GEMS	**GOG**	**HAH**	HERM
DELS	KENS	ESSE	**FAW**	FOBS	IGAD	**GEN**	AGOG	SHAH	HERN
EELS	LENS	**ETA**	FAWN	**FOE**	GADE	AGEN	GOGO	**HAJ**	HERO
GELS	PENS	BETA	FAWS	FOEN	GADI	GENA	GOGS	HAJI	HERS
MELS	RENS	FETA	**FAX**	FOES	GADS	GENE	**GON**	HAJJ	HERY
SELS	SENS	GETA	**FAY**	**FOG**	**GAE**	GENS	AGON	**HAM**	**HES**
TELS	TENS	KETA	OFAY	FOGS	GAED	GENT	GONE	CHAM	SHES
ZELS	WENS	SETA	FAYS	FOGY	GAES	GENU	GONG	SHAM	HESP
ELSE	YENS	ZETA	**FED**	**FOH**	**GAG**	**GEO**	GONK	WHAM	HEST
ELT	**EON**	ETAS	FEDS	FOHN	GAGA	GEOS	GONS	HAME	**HET**
BELT	AEON	ETAT	**FEE**	**FON**	GAGE	**GET**	**GOO**	HAMS	SHET
CELT	NEON	**ETH**	FEED	FOND	GAGS	GETA	GOOD	**HAN**	WHET
FELT	PEON	BETH	FEEL	FONE	**GAL**	GETS	GOOF	KHAN	HETE
GELT	EONS	ETHE	FEER	FONS	EGAL	**GEY**	GOOK	SHAN	HETS
KELT	**ERA**	ETHS	FEES	FONT	GALA	**GHI**	GOOL	THAN	**HEW**
MELT	SERA	**EUK**	FEET	**FOP**	GALE	GHIS	GOON	HAND	CHEW
PELT	ERAS	NEUK	**FEN**	FOPS	GALL	**GIB**	GOOP	HANG	PHEW
TELT	**ERE**	YEUK	FEND	**FOR**	GALS	GIBE	GOOR	HANK	SHEW
WELT	BERE	EUKS	FENS	FORA	**GAM**	GIBS	GOOS	**HAP**	THEW
YELT	CERE	**EVE**	FENT	FORD	OGAM	**GID**	**GOS**	CHAP	WHEW
ELTS	DERE	LEVE	**FET**	FORE	GAMB	GIDS	EGOS	WHAP	HEWN
EME	FERE	MEVE	FETA	FORK	GAME	**GIE**	GOSH	HAPS	HEWS
DEME	GERE	NEVE	FETE	FORM	GAMP	GIED	**GOT**	**HAS**	**HEX**
FEME	HERE	YEVE	FETS	FORT	GAMS	GIEN	**GOV**	CHAS	**HEY**
HEME	LERE	EVEN	FETT	**FOU**	GAMY	GIES	GOVS	HASH	THEY
LEME	MERE	EVER	**FEU**	FOUD	**GAN**	**GIF**	**GOY**	HASK	WHEY
SEME	PERE	EVES	FEUD	FOUL	GANE	GIFT	**GUB**	HASP	HEYS
TEME	SERE	EVET	FEUS	FOUR	GANG	**GIG**	GUBS	HAST	**HIC**
EMES	WERE	**EWE**	**FEW**	FOUS	GANT	GIGA	**GUE**	**HAT**	CHIC
EMEU	ERED	EWER	**FEY**	**FOX**	**GAP**	GIGS	AGUE	CHAT	HICK
EMS	ERES	EWES	FEYS	FOXY	GAPE	**GIN**	GUES	GHAT	**HID**
GEMS	**ERF**	**EWK**	**FEZ**	**FOY**	GAPO	AGIN	**GUM**	KHAT	CHID
HEMS	KERF	EWKS	**FIB**	FOYS	GAPS	GING	GUMP	SHAT	WHID
REMS	SERF	**EWT**	FIBS	**FRA**	**GAR**	GINK	GUMS	THAT	HIDE
TEMS	TERF	NEWT	**FID**	FRAB	AGAR	GINN	**GUN**	WHAT	**HIE**
WEMS	**ERG**	EWTS	FIDS	FRAE	GARB	GINS	GUNK	HATE	HIED
EMU	BERG	**EYE**	**FIE**	FRAP	GARE	**GIO**	GUNS	HATH	HIES
EMUS	ERGO	EYED	FIEF	FRAS	GARS	AGIO	**GUP**	HATS	**HIM**
END	ERGS	EYES	**FIG**	FRAU	GART	GIOS	GUPS	**HAW**	SHIM
BEND	**ERK**	**FAB**	FIGO	FRAY	**GAS**	**GIP**	**GUR**	CHAW	WHIM
FEND	BERK	**FAD**	FIGS	**FRO**	AGAS	GIPS	GURL	SHAW	**HIN**
HEND	JERK	FADE	**FIL**	AFRO	GASH	**GIS**	GURN	THAW	CHIN
LEND	MERK	FADO	FILE	FROG	GASP	EGIS	GURS	HAWK	SHIN
MEND	PERK	FADS	FILL	FROM	GAST	GISM	GURU	HAWM	THIN
PEND	SERK	FADY	FILM	FROW	**GAT**	GIST	**GUS**	HAWS	WHIN
REND	YERK	**FAG**	FILS	**FRY**	GATE	**GIT**	GUSH	**HAY**	HIND
SEND	ERKS	FAGS	**FIN**	**FUB**	GATH	GITE	GUST	CHAY	HING
TEND	**ERN**	**FAH**	FIND	FUBS	GATS	GITS	**GUT**	SHAY	HINS
VEND	DERN	FAHS	FINE	**FUD**	**GAU**	**GJU**	GUTS	HAYS	HINT
WEND	FERN	**FAN**	FINK	FUDS	GAUD	GJUS	**GUY**	**HEM**	**HIP**
ENDS	HERN	FAND	FINO	**FUG**	GAUM	GNU	GUYS	AHEM	CHIP
ENE	KERN	FANE	FINS	FUGS	GAUN	GNUS	**GYM**	THEM	SHIP
BENE	PERN	FANG	**FIR**	**FUM**	GAUP	**GOA**	GYMP	HEME	WHIP
DENE	TERN	FANK	FIRE	FUME	GAUR	GOAD	GYMS	HEMP	HIPS
GENE	ERNE	FANS	FIRK	FUMS	GAUS	GOAF	**GYP**	HEMS	HIPT
MENE	ERNS	**FAP**	FIRM	FUMY	**GAY**	GOAL	GYPS	**HEN**	**HIS**
NENE	**ERR**	**FAR**	FIRN	**FUN**	GAYS	GOAS	**HAD**	THEN	CHIS
PENE	SERR	AFAR	FIRS	FUND	**GED**	GOAT	CHAD	WHEN	GHIS
TENE	ERRS	FARD	**FIT**	FUNG	AGED	**GOB**	SHAD	HEND	PHIS
ENES	**ERS**	FARE	FITS	FUNK	GEDS	GOBO	HADE	HENS	THIS
ENEW	HERS	FARL	FITT	FUNS	**GEE**	GOBS	HADJ	HENT	HISH
ENG	VERS	FARM	**FIX**	**FUR**	AGEE	GOBY	HADS	**HEP**	HISN
LENG	ERST	FARO	**FIZ**	FURL	OGEE	**GOD**	**HAE**	HEPS	HISS
MENG	**ESS**	FARS	FIZZ	FURR	GEED	GODS	THAE	HEPT	HIST
ENGS	CESS	FART	**FLU**	FURS	GEES	**GOE**	HAEM	**HER**	**HIT**
ENS	FESS	**FAS**	FLUB	FURY	**GEL**	YGOE	HAET	CHER	CHIT
BENS	JESS	FASH	FLUE	**GAB**	GELD	GOEL	**HAG**	HERB	SHIT
DENS	LESS	FAST	FLUS	GABS	GELS	GOER	SHAG	HERD	WHIT
FENS	MESS	**FAT**	FLUX	GABY	GELT	GOES	HAGG	HERE	HITS

HOA	HOWE	CIDE	**INK**	KISH	JIZZ	**KEG**	LACE	FLAX	ALEW
WHOA	HOWF	HIDE	BINK	PISH	**JOB**	SKEG	LACK	**LAY**	BLEW
HOAR	HOWK	NIDE	DINK	WISH	JOBE	KEGS	LACS	ALAY	CLEW
HOAS	HOWL	RIDE	FINK	**ISM**	JOBS	**KEN**	LACY	BLAY	FLEW
HOAX	HOWS	SIDE	GINK	GISM	**JOE**	KENS	**LAD**	CLAY	SLEW
HOB	**HOX**	TIDE	JINK	JISM	JOES	KENT	BLAD	FLAY	LEWD
HOBO	**HOY**	VIDE	KINK	ISMS	JOEY	**KEP**	CLAD	PLAY	**LEX**
HOBS	AHOY	WIDE	LINK	ISMY	**JOG**	SKEP	GLAD	SLAY	FLEX
HOC	HOYA	IDEA	MINK	**ITA**	JOGS	KEPI	LADE	LAYS	ILEX
CHOC	HOYS	IDEE	PINK	DITA	**JOR**	KEPS	LADS	**LEA**	ULEX
HOCK	**HUB**	IDEM	RINK	PITA	JORS	KEPT	LADY	FLEA	**LEY**
HOD	CHUB	IDES	SINK	VITA	**JOT**	**KET**	**LAG**	ILEA	BLEY
SHOD	HUBS	**IDS**	TINK	ITAS	JOTA	KETA	BLAG	PLEA	FLEY
HODS	**HUE**	AIDS	WINK	**ITS**	JOTS	KETS	CLAG	LEAD	GLEY
HOE	HUED	BIDS	INKS	AITS	**JOW**	**KEX**	FLAG	LEAF	SLEY
SHOE	HUER	FIDS	INKY	BITS	JOWL	**KEY**	SLAG	LEAK	LEYS
HOED	HUES	GIDS	**INN**	CITS	JOWS	KEYS	LAGS	LEAL	**LEZ**
HOER	**HUG**	KIDS	GINN	DITS	**JOY**	**KID**	**LAH**	LEAM	LEZZ
HOES	CHUG	LIDS	JINN	FITS	JOYS	SKID	LAHS	LEAN	**LIB**
HOG	THUG	MIDS	LINN	GITS	**JUD**	KIDS	**LAM**	LEAP	GLIB
SHOG	HUGE	NIDS	WINN	HITS	JUDO	**KIF**	CLAM	LEAR	LIBS
HOGG	HUGS	RIDS	INNS	KITS	JUDS	KIFS	FLAM	LEAS	**LID**
HOGH	HUGY	TIDS	**INS**	NITS	JUDY	**KIN**	GLAM	LEAT	GLID
HOGS	**HUH**	**IFF**	BINS	PITS	**JUG**	AKIN	SLAM	**LED**	LIDO
HOH	**HUM**	BIFF	DINS	RITS	JUGA	SKIN	LAMA	BLED	LIDS
PHOH	CHUM	JIFF	FINS	SITS	JUGS	KINA	LAMB	FLED	**LIE**
HOHS	HUMA	MIFF	GINS	TITS	**JUS**	KIND	LAME	GLED	PLIE
HOI	HUMF	NIFF	HINS	WITS	GJUS	KINE	LAMP	PLED	LIED
HOIK	HUMP	RIFF	KINS	ZITS	JUST	KING	LAMS	SLED	LIEF
HON	HUMS	TIFF	LINS	**IVY**	**JUT**	KINK	**LAP**	**LEE**	LIEN
PHON	**HUP**	ZIFF	PINS	**JAB**	JUTE	KINO	ALAP	ALEE	LIER
THON	HUPS	IFFY	RINS	JABS	JUTS	KINS	CLAP	BLEE	LIES
HOND	**HUT**	**IFS**	SINS	**JAG**	**KAE**	**KIP**	FLAP	FLEE	LIEU
HONE	CHUT	KIFS	TINS	JAGS	KAED	SKIP	PLAP	GLEE	**LIG**
HONG	PHUT	**ILK**	VINS	**JAK**	KAES	KIPE	SLAP	SLEE	LIGS
HONK	SHUT	BILK	WINS	JAKE	**KAI**	KIPP	LAPS	LEED	**LIN**
HONS	HUTS	MILK	YINS	JAKS	KAID	KIPS	**LAR**	LEEK	BLIN
HOO	**HYE**	SILK	**ION**	**JAM**	KAIE	**KIR**	ALAR	LEEP	LIND
SHOO	HYED	ILKA	CION	JAMB	KAIF	KIRI	LARD	LEER	LINE
HOOD	HYEN	ILKS	LION	JAMS	KAIL	KIRK	LARE	LEES	LING
HOOF	HYES	**ILL**	PION	**JAP**	KAIM	KIRN	LARK	LEET	LINK
HOOK	**HYP**	BILL	IONS	JAPE	KAIN	KIRS	LARN	**LEG**	LINN
HOOP	HYPE	CILL	**IOS**	JAPS	KAIS	**KIT**	**LAS**	CLEG	LINO
HOOT	HYPO	DILL	BIOS	**JAR**	**KAM**	SKIT	ALAS	FLEG	LINS
HOP	HYPS	FILL	GIOS	AJAR	KAME	KITE	LASE	GLEG	LINT
CHOP	**ICE**	GILL	**IRE**	JARK	KAMI	KITH	LASH	LEGS	LINY
SHOP	BICE	HILL	CIRE	JARL	**KAS**	KITS	LASS	**LEI**	**LIP**
WHOP	DICE	JILL	DIRE	JARS	SKAS	**KOA**	LAST	GLEI	BLIP
HOPE	LICE	KILL	FIRE	**JAW**	**KAT**	KOAN	**LAT**	LEIR	CLIP
HOPS	MICE	LILL	HIRE	JAWS	IKAT	KOAS	BLAT	LEIS	FLIP
HOS	NICE	MILL	LIRE	**JAY**	SKAT	**KOB**	CLAT	**LEK**	SLIP
MHOS	PICE	NILL	MIRE	JAYS	KATI	KOBS	FLAT	LEKE	LIPS
OHOS	RICE	PILL	SIRE	**JEE**	KATS	**KON**	PLAT	LEKS	**LIS**
PHOS	SICE	RILL	TIRE	AJEE	**KAW**	IKON	SLAT	**LEP**	LISK
RHOS	TICE	SILL	WIRE	JEED	SKAW	KOND	LATE	LEPS	LISP
ZHOS	VICE	TILL	IRES	JEEL	KAWS	KONK	LATH	**LES**	LIST
HOSE	ICED	VILL	**IRK**	JEEP	**KAY**	KONS	LATS	ALES	**LIT**
HOSS	ICER	WILL	BIRK	JEER	OKAY	**KOP**	**LAV**	ULES	ALIT
HOST	ICES	YILL	DIRK	JEES	KAYO	KOPS	LAVA	LEST	FLIT
HOT	**ICH**	ILLS	FIRK	**JET**	KAYS	**KOS**	LAVE	**LET**	GLIT
PHOT	DICH	ILLY	KIRK	JETE	**KEA**	KOSS	LAVS	BLET	SLIT
SHOT	LICH	**IMP**	LIRK	JETS	KEAS	**KOW**	**LAW**	LETS	LITE
WHOT	RICH	GIMP	MIRK	**JEU**	**KEB**	KOWS	CLAW	**LEU**	LITH
HOTE	SICH	JIMP	YIRK	JEUX	KEBS	**KYE**	FLAW	**LEV**	**LOB**
HOTS	TICH	LIMP	IRKS	**JIB**	**KED**	**LAB**	SLAW	LEVA	BLOB
HOW	**ICY**	PIMP	**ISH**	JIBE	AKED	BLAB	LAWK	LEVE	GLOB
CHOW	RICY	SIMP	BISH	JIBS	EKED	FLAB	LAWN	LEVY	SLOB
DHOW	**IDE**	WIMP	DISH	**JIG**	KEDS	SLAB	LAWS	**LEW**	LOBE
SHOW	AIDE	IMPI	FISH	JIGS	**KEF**	LABS	**LAX**		
WHOW	BIDE	IMPS	HISH	**JIZ**	KEFS	**LAC**			

LOBI	SLUG	MARS	EMIR	MOYA	NEKS	NOTE	COBS	OFFS	OLMS
LOBO	LUGE	MART	SMIR	MOYL	NEP	NOTT	DOBS	OFT	OMS
LOBS	LUGS	MAS	MIRE	MOYS	NEPS	NOW	FOBS	COFT	COMS
LOG	LUM	MASE	MIRK	MOZ	NET	ANOW	GOBS	LOFT	MOMS
CLOG	ALUM	MASH	MIRS	MOZE	NETE	ENOW	HOBS	SOFT	NOMS
FLOG	GLUM	MASK	MIRY	MOZZ	NETS	KNOW	JOBS	TOFT	OOMS
SLOG	PLUM	MASS	MIS	MUD	NETT	SNOW	KOBS	OHM	POMS
LOGE	SLUM	MAST	AMIS	MUDS	NEW	NOWL	LOBS	OHMS	TOMS
LOGO	LUMP	MASU	MISE	MUG	ANEW	NOWN	MOBS	OHO	ONE
LOGS	LUMS	MAT	MISO	SMUG	ENEW	NOWS	NOBS	COHO	BONE
LOO	LUR	MATE	MISS	MUGS	KNEW	NOWT	ROBS	TOHO	CONE
LOOF	BLUR	MATH	MIST	MUM	NEWS	NOWY	SOBS	OHOS	DONE
LOOK	SLUR	MATS	MIX	MUMM	NEWT	NOY	YOBS	OIK	FONE
LOOM	LURE	MATT	MIXT	MUMP	NIB	NOYS	OCA	HOIK	GONE
LOON	LURK	MATY	MIXY	MUMS	SNIB	NTH	COCA	OIKS	HONE
LOOP	LURS	MAW	MIZ	MUN	NIBS	NUB	OCAS	OIL	LONE
LOOR	LUX	MAWK	MIZZ	MUS	NID	KNUB	OCH	BOIL	NONE
LOOS	FLUX	MAWR	MNA	EMUS	NIDE	SNUB	COCH	COIL	PONE
LOOT	LUXE	MAWS	MNAS	MUSE	NIDI	NUBS	LOCH	FOIL	RONE
LOP	LUZ	MAX	MOA	MUSH	NIDS	NUN	ROCH	MOIL	SONE
CLOP	LYE	MAXI	MOAN	MUSK	NIE	NUNS	OCHE	NOIL	TONE
FLOP	LYES	MAY	MOAS	MUSS	NIED	NUR	ODA	ROIL	ZONE
PLOP	LYM	MAYA	MOAT	MUST	NIEF	KNUR	CODA	SOIL	ONER
SLOP	LYME	MAYS	MOB	MUX	NIES	NURD	SODA	TOIL	ONES
LOPE	LYMS	MEL	MOBS	NAB	NIL	NURL	ODAL	OILS	ONS
LOPS	MAC	MELD	MOD	SNAB	ANIL	NURR	ODAS	OILY	CONS
LOR	MACE	MELL	MODE	NABK	NILL	NURS	ODD	OKE	DONS
FLOR	MACK	MELS	MODI	NABS	NILS	NUS	ODDS	BOKE	EONS
LORD	MACS	MELT	MODS	NAE	NIM	ANUS	ODE	COKE	FONS
LORE	MAD	MEN	MOE	NAG	NIMS	GNUS	BODE	HOKE	GONS
LORN	MADE	AMEN	MOES	KNAG	NIP	ONUS	CODE	JOKE	HONS
LORY	MADS	OMEN	MOG	SNAG	SNIP	NUT	LODE	LOKE	IONS
LOS	MAE	MEND	SMOG	NAGA	NIPS	KNUT	MODE	MOKE	KONS
LOSE	MAG	MENE	MOGS	NAGS	NIS	NUTS	NODE	POKE	OONS
LOSH	MAGE	MENG	MOM	NAM	UNIS	NYE	RODE	ROKE	PONS
LOSS	MAGG	MENT	MOME	NAME	NISI	NYED	YODE	SOKE	SONS
LOST	MAGI	MENU	MOMS	NAMS	NIT	NYES	ODEA	TOKE	TONS
LOT	MAGS	MES	MOO	NAN	KNIT	NYS	ODES	WOKE	WONS
BLOT	MAK	EMES	MOOD	ANAN	UNIT	OAF	ODS	YOKE	ONST
CLOT	MAKE	MESA	MOOI	NANA	NITS	GOAF	BODS	OKES	OOF
PLOT	MAKO	MESE	MOOL	NANS	NIX	LOAF	CODS	OLD	COOF
SLOT	MAKS	MESH	MOON	NAP	NIXY	OAFS	DODS	BOLD	GOOF
LOTA	MAL	MESS	MOOP	KNAP	NOB	OAK	GODS	COLD	HOOF
LOTE	MALE	MET	MOOR	SNAP	KNOB	BOAK	HODS	FOLD	LOOF
LOTH	MALI	METE	MOOS	NAPA	SNOB	SOAK	MODS	GOLD	POOF
LOTO	MALL	MEU	MOOT	NAPE	NOBS	OAKS	NODS	HOLD	ROOF
LOTS	MALM	EMEU	MOP	NAPS	NOD	OAKY	PODS	MOLD	WOOF
LOW	MALS	MEUS	MOPE	NAS	SNOD	OAR	RODS	SOLD	OOFS
ALOW	MALT	MEW	MOPS	ANAS	NODE	BOAR	SODS	TOLD	OOH
BLOW	MAM	SMEW	MOPY	MNAS	NODI	HOAR	TODS	WOLD	BOOH
CLOW	IMAM	MEWL	MOR	NAT	NODS	ROAR	ODSO	YOLD	POOH
FLOW	MAMA	MEWS	MORA	GNAT	NOG	SOAR	OES	OLDS	OOHS
GLOW	MAMS	MHO	MORE	NATS	SNOG	VOAR	DOES	OLDY	OOM
PLOW	MAN	MHOS	MORN	NAY	NOGS	OARS	FOES	BOLE	BOOM
SLOW	MANA	MID	MORS	NAYS	NOH	OARY	GOES	COLE	COOM
LOWE	MAND	AMID	MORT	NEB	NOM	OAT	HOES	DOLE	DOOM
LOWN	MANE	MIDI	MOT	SNEB	NOMA	BOAT	JOES	GOLE	LOOM
LOWS	MANS	MIDS	MOTE	NEBS	NOME	COAT	MOES	HOLE	ROOM
LOWT	MANY	MIL	MOTH	NED	NOMS	DOAT	NOES	JOLE	SOOM
LOX	MAP	MILD	MOTS	SNED	NON	GOAT	ROES	MOLE	TOOM
LOY	MAPS	MILE	MOTT	NEDS	ANON	MOAT	TOES	NOLE	ZOOM
CLOY	MAR	MILK	MOU	NEE	NONE	OATH	VOES	POLE	OOMS
PLOY	MARA	MILL	MOUE	KNEE	NONG	OATS	WOES	ROLE	OON
LOYS	MARC	MILO	MOUP	SNEE	NOR	OBI	OFF	SOLE	BOON
LUD	MARD	MILS	MOUS	NEED	NORI	LOBI	BOFF	TOLE	COON
LUDO	MARE	MILT	MOW	NEEM	NORK	OBIA	COFF	VOLE	GOON
LUDS	MARG	MIM	MOWA	NEEP	NORM	OBIS	DOFF	OLEO	LOON
LUG	MARK	MIME	MOWN	NEF	NOT	OBIT	GOFF	OLM	MOON
GLUG	MARL	MIR	MOWS	NEFS	KNOT	OBS	KOFF	HOLM	NOON
PLUG	MARM	AMIR	MOY	NEK	SNOT	BOBS	TOFF	HOLM	POON

ROON	ORBS	OUPS	**OYS**	PEAG	PICS	EPOS	PUTS	RASH	**RES**
SOON	ORBY	**OUR**	BOYS	PEAK	**PIE**	POSE	PUTT	RASP	ARES
TOON	**ORC**	COUR	COYS	PEAL	SPIE	POSH	PUTZ	RAST	ERES
WOON	TORC	DOUR	FOYS	PEAN	PIED	POSS	**PUY**	**RAT**	IRES
ZOON	ORCS	FOUR	HOYS	PEAR	PIER	POST	PUYS	BRAT	ORES
OONS	**ORD**	HOUR	JOYS	PEAS	PIES	POSY	**PYE**	DRAT	URES
OONT	BORD	JOUR	LOYS	PEAT	PIET	**POT**	PYES	GRAT	REST
OOP	CORD	LOUR	MOYS	**PEC**	**PIG**	SPOT	PYET	PRAT	**RET**
COOP	FORD	POUR	NOYS	SPEC	PIGS	POTE	**PYX**	RATA	ARET
GOOP	LORD	SOUR	SOYS	PECH	**PIN**	POTS	**QAT**	RATE	FRET
HOOP	SORD	TOUR	TOYS	PECK	SPIN	POTT	QATS	RATH	TRET
LOOP	WORD	YOUR	**PAD**	PECS	PINA	**POW**	**QUA**	RATS	RETE
MOOP	ORDS	OURN	PADS	**PED**	PINE	POWN	AQUA	RATU	RETS
NOOP	**ORE**	OURS	**PAH**	APED	PING	POWS	QUAD	**RAW**	**REV**
POOP	BORE	**OUT**	OPAH	OPED	PINK	**POX**	QUAG	BRAW	REVS
ROOP	CORE	BOUT	PAHS	SPED	PINS	POXY	QUAT	CRAW	**REW**
SOOP	FORE	DOUT	**PAL**	PEDS	PINT	**POZ**	QUAY	DRAW	AREW
YOOP	GORE	GOUT	OPAL	**PEE**	PINY	POZZ	**RAD**	RAWN	BREW
OOPS	HORE	HOUT	PALE	EPEE	**PIP**	**PRE**	BRAD	RAWS	CREW
OOR	LORE	LOUT	PALL	PEED	PIPA	PREE	DRAD	**RAX**	DREW
BOOR	MORE	NOUT	PALM	PEEK	PIPE	PREP	PRAD	**RAY**	GREW
DOOR	PORE	POUT	PALP	PEEL	PIPI	PREX	TRAD	BRAY	TREW
GOOR	RORE	ROUT	PALS	PEEN	PIPS	PREY	RADE	DRAY	REWS
LOOR	SORE	SOUT	PALY	PEEP	PIPY	**PRO**	RADS	FRAY	**REX**
MOOR	TORE	TOUT	**PAM**	PEER	**PIR**	PROA	**RAG**	GRAY	PREX
POOR	WORE	OUTS	PAMS	PEES	PIRL	PROD	BRAG	PRAY	**RHO**
OOS	YORE	**OVA**	**PAN**	**PEG**	PIRN	PROF	CRAG	TRAY	RHOS
BOOS	ORES	NOVA	SPAN	PEGH	PIRS	PROG	DRAG	RAYS	**RHY**
COOS	**ORF**	OVAL	PAND	PEGS	**PIS**	PROM	RAGA	**RED**	**RIA**
DOOS	CORF	**OWE**	PANE	**PEN**	PISE	PROO	RAGE	ARED	ARIA
GOOS	ORFE	HOWE	PANG	OPEN	PISH	PROP	RAGG	BRED	RIAL
LOOS	ORFS	LOWE	PANS	PEND	PISS	PROS	RAGI	ERED	RIAS
MOOS	**ORS**	YOWE	PANT	PENE	**PIT**	PROW	RAGS	REDD	**RIB**
POOS	BORS	OWED	**PAP**	PENI	SPIT	**PRY**	**RAH**	REDE	CRIB
ROOS	CORS	OWER	PAPA	PENK	PITA	SPRY	RAHS	REDO	DRIB
WOOS	DORS	OWES	PAPE	PENS	PITH	PRYS	**RAJ**	REDS	RIBS
ZOOS	HORS	**OWL**	PAPS	PENT	PITS	**PSI**	RAJA	**REE**	**RID**
OOSE	JORS	BOWL	**PAR**	PEP	PITY	PSIS	**RAM**	BREE	ARID
OOSY	MORS	COWL	SPAR	PEPO	**PIU**	**PST**	CRAM	CREE	GRID
OPE	TORS	DOWL	PARA	PEPS	PIUM	**PUB**	DRAM	DREE	IRID
COPE	VORS	FOWL	PARD	**PER**	**PIX**	PUBS	GRAM	FREE	RIDE
DOPE	**ORT**	GOWL	PARE	PERE	PIXY	**PUD**	PRAM	GREE	RIDS
HOPE	BORT	HOWL	PARK	PERI	**PLY**	SPUD	TRAM	PREE	**RIG**
LOPE	DORT	JOWL	PARR	PERK	**POA**	PUDS	RAMI	TREE	BRIG
MOPE	FORT	NOWL	PARS	PERM	POAS	**PUG**	RAMP	REED	FRIG
NOPE	MORT	SOWL	PART	PERN	**POD**	PUGH	RAMS	REEF	GRIG
POPE	PORT	YOWL	**PAS**	PERT	APOD	PUGS	**RAN**	REEK	PRIG
ROPE	RORT	OWLS	SPAS	PERV	PODS	**PUH**	BRAN	REEL	TRIG
TOPE	SORT	OWLY	UPAS	**PET**	**POH**	**PUN**	CRAN	REEN	RIGG
OPED	TORT	**OWN**	PASH	SPET	**POI**	SPUN	GRAN	REES	RIGS
OPEN	WORT	DOWN	PASS	PETS	POIS	PUNA	RANA	**REF**	**RIM**
OPES	ORTS	GOWN	PAST	**PEW**	**POM**	PUNK	RAND	TREF	BRIM
OPS	**OUK**	LOWN	**PAT**	SPEW	POME	PUNS	RANG	REFS	GRIM
BOPS	BOUK	MOWN	SPAT	PEWS	POMP	PUNT	RANI	REFT	PRIM
COPS	GOUK	NOWN	PATE	**PHI**	POMS	PUNY	RANK	**REH**	TRIM
DOPS	JOUK	POWN	PATH	PHIS	**POO**	**PUP**	RANT	REHS	RIMA
FOPS	POUK	SOWN	PATS	PHIZ	POOD	PUPA	**RAP**	**REM**	RIME
HOPS	SOUK	TOWN	**PAW**	**PHO**	POOF	PUPS	CRAP	REMS	RIMS
KOPS	TOUK	OWNS	SPAW	PHOH	POOH	**PUR**	DRAP	**REN**	RIMU
LOPS	YOUK	**OWT**	PAWA	PHON	POOK	SPUR	FRAP	BREN	RIMY
MOPS	OUKS	DOWT	PAWK	PHOS	POOL	PURE	TRAP	GREN	**RIN**
OOPS	**OUP**	LOWT	PAWL	PHOT	POON	PURI	WRAP	WREN	GRIN
POPS	COUP	NOWT	PAWN	**PIA**	POOP	PURL	RAPE	REND	TRIN
SOPS	DOUP	ROWT	PAWS	PIAS	POOR	PURR	RAPS	RENS	RIND
TOPS	LOUP	TOWT	**PAX**	**PIC**	POOS	PURS	RAPT	RENT	RINE
WOPS	MOUP	OWTS	**PAY**	EPIC	POOT	**PUS**	**RAS**	RENY	RING
OPT	NOUP	**OYE**	APAY	SPIC	**POP**	OPUS	BRAS	**REP**	RINK
OPTS	ROUP	OYER	SPAY	PICA	POPE	PUSH	ERAS	PREP	RINS
ORB	SOUP	OYES	PAYS	PICE	POPS	PUSS	FRAS	REPP	**RIP**
SORB	OUPH	OYEZ	**PEA**	PICK	**POS**	**PUT**	RASE	REPS	DRIP

GRIP	TROW	SAIS	SEND	SKIT	**SUB**	TANG	TEND	TOGE	TUPS
TRIP	ROWS	**SAL**	SENS	**SKY**	SUBS	TANK	TENE	TOGS	**TUT**
RIPE	ROWT	SALE	SENT	ESKY	**SUD**	TANS	TENS	**TOM**	TUTS
RIPP	**RUB**	SALP	**SET**	SKYR	SUDD	**TAP**	TENT	ATOM	TUTU
RIPS	DRUB	SALS	SETA	**SLY**	SUDS	ATAP	**TES**	TOMB	**TWA**
RIPT	GRUB	SALT	SETS	**SMA**	**SUE**	STAP	UTES	TOME	TWAE
RIT	RUBE	**SAM**	SETT	**SOB**	SUED	TAPA	TEST	TOMS	TWAL
BRIT	RUBS	SAME	**SEW**	SOBS	SUER	TAPE	**TEW**	**TON**	TWAS
CRIT	RUBY	SAMP	SEWN	**SOC**	SUES	TAPS	TEWS	TONE	TWAT
FRIT	**RUC**	**SAN**	SEWS	SOCK	SUET	TAPU	THE	TONG	TWAY
GRIT	RUCK	SAND	**SEX**	SOCS	**SUI**	**TAR**	**THE**	TONK	**TWO**
WRIT	RUCS	SANE	SEXT	**SOD**	SUIT	STAR	ETHE	TONS	TWOS
RITE	**RUD**	SANG	SEXY	SODA	**SUK**	TARA	THEE	TONY	**TYE**
RITS	CRUD	SANK	**SEY**	SODS	SUKH	TARE	THEM	**TOO**	STYE
RITT	RUDD	SANS	SEYS	**SOG**	SUKS	TARN	THEN	TOOK	TYED
RIZ	RUDE	**SAP**	**SEZ**	SOGS	**SUM**	TARO	THEW	TOOL	TYES
FRIZ	RUDS	SAPS	**SHE**	**SOH**	SUMO	TARP	THEY	TOOM	**TYG**
ROB	**RUE**	**SAR**	SHEA	SOHS	SUMP	TARS	**THO**	TOON	TYGS
ROBE	CRUE	ASAR	SHED	**SOL**	SUMS	TART	THON	TOOT	**UDO**
ROBS	GRUE	KSAR	SHES	SOLA	**SUN**	**TAT**	THOU	**TOP**	BUDO
ROC	TRUE	TSAR	SHET	SOLD	SUNG	TATE	**THY**	ATOP	JUDO
CROC	RUED	SARD	SHEW	SOLE	SUNK	TATH	**TIC**	STOP	LUDO
ROCH	RUES	SARI	**SHY**	SOLI	SUNN	TATS	OTIC	TOPE	UDOS
ROCK	**RUG**	SARK	ASHY	SOLO	SUNS	TATT	TICE	TOPI	**UDS**
ROCS	DRUG	SARS	**SIB**	SOLS	**SUP**	TATU	TICH	TOPS	BUDS
ROD	TRUG	**SAT**	SIBB	**SON**	SUPS	TAU	TICK	**TOR**	CUDS
BROD	RUGS	SATE	SIBS	SONE	**SUQ**	**TAU**	TICS	TORC	DUDS
PROD	**RUM**	SATI	**SIC**	SONG	SUQS	TAUS	**TID**	TORE	FUDS
TROD	ARUM	**SAW**	SICE	SONS	**SUR**	TAUT	TIDE	TORI	JUDS
RODE	DRUM	SAWN	SICH	**SOP**	SURA	**TAW**	TIDS	TORN	LUDS
RODS	GRUM	SAWS	SICK	SOPH	SURD	STAW	TIDY	TORR	MUDS
ROE	RUME	**SAX**	SICS	SOPS	SURE	TAWS	**TIE**	TORS	PUDS
ROED	RUMP	**SAY**	**SIM**	**SOS**	SURF	TAWT	STIE	TORT	RUDS
ROES	RUMS	SAYS	SIMA	DSOS	**SUS**	TAX	TIED	**TOT**	SUDS
ROK	**RUN**	**SAZ**	SIMI	SOSS	SUSS	TAXA	TIER	STOT	WUDS
ROKE	RUND	**SEA**	SIMP	**SOT**	**SWY**	TAXI	TIES	TOTE	**UEY**
ROKS	RUNE	SEAL	SIMS	SOTS	**SYE**	TAXI	**TIG**	TOTS	QUEY
ROKY	RUNG	SEAM	**SIN**	**SOU**	SYED	**TEA**	TIGE	**TOW**	UEYS
ROM	RUNS	SEAN	SIND	SOUK	SYEN	TEAD	TIGS	STOW	**UFO**
FROM	RUNT	SEAR	SINE	SOUL	SYES	TEAK	**TIL**	TOWN	BUFO
PROM	**RUT**	SEAS	SING	SOUM	**TAB**	TEAL	TILE	TOWS	UFOS
ROMA	BRUT	SEAT	SINK	SOUP	STAB	TEAM	TILL	TOWT	**UGH**
ROMP	RUTH	**SEC**	SINS	SOUR	TABS	TEAR	TILS	TOWY	EUGH
ROO	RUTS	SECS	**SIP**	SOUS	TABU	TEAS	TILT	**TOY**	PUGH
BROO	**RYA**	SECT	SIPE	SOUT	**TAD**	TEAT	**TIN**	TOYS	UGHS
PROO	RYAL	**SED**	SIPS	**SOV**	TADS	**TED**	TIND	**TRY**	**UGS**
ROOD	RYAS	USED	**SIR**	SOVS	**TAE**	STED	TINE	TRYE	BUGS
ROOF	**RYE**	**SEE**	SIRE	**SOW**	TAED	TEDS	TING	TRYP	DUGS
ROOK	TRYE	SEED	SIRI	SOWF	TAEL	TEDY	TINK	**TUB**	FUGS
ROOM	RYES	SEEK	SIRS	SOWL	TAES	**TEE**	TINS	STUB	HUGS
ROON	**SAB**	SEEL	**SIS**	SOWM	**TAG**	TEED	TINT	TUBA	JUGS
ROOP	SABS	SEEM	PSIS	SOWN	STAG	TEEL	TINY	TUBE	LUGS
ROOS	**SAC**	SEEN	SISS	SOWP	TAGS	TEEM	**TIP**	TUBS	MUGS
ROOT	SACK	SEEP	SIST	SOWS	**TAI**	TEEN	TIPI	**TUG**	PUGS
ROT	SACS	SEER	**SIT**	**SOX**	TAIL	TEER	TIPS	TUGS	RUGS
GROT	**SAD**	SEES	SITE	**SOY**	TAIS	TEES	TIPT	**TUI**	TUGS
TROT	**SAE**	**SEG**	SITH	SOYA	TAIT	**TEF**	**TIS**	ETUI	VUGS
ROTA	**SAG**	SEGO	SITS	SOYS	**TAJ**	TEFF	UTIS	TUIS	YUGS
ROTE	SAGA	SEGS	**SIX**	**SPA**	**TAK**	TEFS	**TIT**	**TUM**	**ULE**
ROTI	SAGE	**SEI**	**SKA**	SPAE	TAKA	**TEG**	TITE	STUM	DULE
ROTL	SAGO	SEIF	SKAS	SPAN	TAKE	TEGG	TITI	TUMP	GULE
ROTS	SAGS	SEIL	SKAT	SPAR	TAKS	TEGS	TITS	TUMS	HULE
ROW	SAGY	SEIS	SKAW	SPAS	TAKY	**TEL**	**TOD**	**TUN**	MULE
AROW	**SAI**	**SEL**	**SKI**	SPAT	**TAM**	TELA	TODS	STUN	PULE
BROW	SAIC	SELD	SKID	SPAW	TAME	TELD	TODY	TUNA	RULE
CROW	SAID	SELE	SKIM	SPAY	TAMP	TELL	**TOE**	TUND	TULE
DROW	SAIL	SELF	SKIN	**SPY**	TAMS	TELS	TOED	TUNE	YULE
FROW	SAIM	SELL	SKIO	ESPY	**TAN**	TELT	TOES	TUNS	ULES
GROW	SAIN	SELS	SKIP	**STY**	TANA	**TEN**	**TOG**	TUNY	ULEX
PROW	SAIR	**SEN**	SKIS	STYE	TANE	STEN	TOGA	**TUP**	**UNI**

UNIS	CURN	VANT	**VOE**	WAPS	WEEK	YWIS	**WYE**	OYES	YUKE
UNIT	DURN	**VAS**	EVOE	**WAR**	WEEL	WISE	WYES	PYES	YUKS
UNS	GURN	AVAS	VOES	WARD	WEEM	WISH	**WYN**	RYES	YUKY
BUNS	OURN	UVAS	**VOL**	WARE	WEEN	WISP	WYND	SYES	**YUP**
DUNS	TURN	VASA	VOLA	WARK	WEEP	WIST	WYNN	TYES	YUPS
FUNS	URNS	VASE	VOLE	WARM	WEER	**WIT**	WYNS	WYES	**YUS**
GUNS	**USE**	VAST	VOLS	WARN	WEES	TWIT	**XIS**	YESK	AYUS
NUNS	FUSE	**VAT**	VOLT	WARP	WEET	WITE	AXIS	YEST	**ZAG**
PUNS	MUSE	VATS	**VOR**	WARS	**WEM**	WITH	**YAH**	PYET	ZAGS
RUNS	RUSE	**VAU**	VORS	WART	WEMB	WITS	**YAK**	YETI	**ZAP**
SUNS	USED	VAUS	**VOW**	WARY	WEMS	**WOE**	YAKS	YETT	ZAPS
TUNS	USER	VAUT	AVOW	**WAS**	**WEN**	WOES	**YAM**	YEW	**ZAX**
UPS	USES	**VEE**	VOWS	TWAS	WEND	**WOG**	LYAM	YEWS	**ZEA**
CUPS	**UTE**	VEER	**VOX**	WASE	WENS	WOGS	YAMS	**YEX**	ZEAL
DUPS	BUTE	VEES	**VUG**	WASH	WENT	**WOK**	**YAP**	**YGO**	ZEAS
GUPS	CUTE	**VEG**	VUGS	WASP	**WET**	WOKE	YAPP	YGOE	**ZED**
HUPS	JUTE	VEGA	**VUM**	WAST	WETS	WOKS	YAPS	**YIN**	ZEDS
OUPS	LUTE	**VET**	OVUM	**WAT**	**WEX**	**WON**	**YAW**	YINS	**ZEE**
PUPS	MUTE	EVET	VUMS	SWAT	WEXE	WONS	YAWL	**YIP**	ZEES
SUPS	UTES	VETO	**WAD**	TWAT	**WEY**	WONT	YAWN	YIPS	**ZEK**
TUPS	**UTS**	VETS	SWAD	WATE	WEYS	**WOO**	YAWP	**YOB**	ZEKS
YUPS	BUTS	**VEX**	WADD	WATS	**WHO**	WOOD	YAWS	YOBS	**ZEL**
UPSY	CUTS	**VIA**	WADE	WATT	WHOA	WOOF	YAWY	**YOD**	ZELS
URD	GUTS	VIAE	WADI	**WAW**	WHOM	WOOL	**YEA**	YODE	**ZHO**
BURD	HUTS	VIAL	WADS	WAWE	WHOP	WOON	YEAD	**YOK**	ZHOS
CURD	JUTS	VIAS	WADY	WAWL	WHOT	WOOS	YEAH	YOKE	**ZIG**
NURD	NUTS	**VIE**	**WAE**	WAWS	WHOW	WOOT	YEAN	YOKS	ZIGS
SURD	OUTS	VIED	TWAE	**WAX**	**WHY**	**WOP**	YEAR	**YON**	**ZIP**
TURD	PUTS	VIER	WAES	WAXY	**WIG**	SWOP	YEAS	YOND	ZIPS
URDE	RUTS	VIES	**WAG**	**WAY**	SWIG	WOPS	**YEN**	YONI	**ZIT**
URDS	TUTS	VIEW	SWAG	AWAY	TWIG	**WOS**	HYEN	YONT	ZITS
URDY	**UTU**	**VIM**	WAGE	SWAY	WIGS	TWOS	SYEN	**YOS**	**ZIZ**
URE	TUTU	VIMS	WAGS	TWAY	**WIN**	WOST	YENS	**YOU**	ZIZZ
CURE	UTUS	**VIN**	**WAN**	WAYS	**WOT**	**YEP**	YOUK	**ZOA**
DURE	**UVA**	VINA	SWAN	**WEB**	WIND	SWOT	YEPS	YOUR	**ZOO**
JURE	UVAS	VINE	WAND	WEBS	WINE	WOTS	**YES**	**YOW**	ZOOM
LURE	**VAC**	VINO	WANE	**WED**	WING	WOW	AYES	YOWE	ZOON
MURE	VACS	VINS	WANG	AWED	WINK	WOWF	BYES	YOWL	ZOOS
PURE	**VAE**	VINT	WANK	OWED	WINN	WOWS	DYES	YOWS	**ZOS**
SURE	VAES	VINY	WANS	WEDS	WINO	**WOX**	EYES	**YUG**	DZOS
UREA	**VAN**	**VIS**	WANT	**WEE**	WINS	**WRY**	HYES	YUGA	**ZUZ**
URES	VANE	VISA	WANY	SWEE	WINY	AWRY	LYES	YUGS	
URN	VANG	VISE	**WAP**	TWEE	**WIS**	**WUD**	NYES	**YUK**	
BURN	VANS	**VLY**	SWAP	WEED	IWIS	WUDS			

PART A: 4-letter word hooks
including all root words

ABAC	ACMES	SAGES	**AIRS**	GALAS	HALMS	SAMPS	**ANOAS**	LARCH	PARKS
ABACA	**ACNE**	WAGES	FAIRS	NALAS	MALMS	TAMPS	**ANON**	MARCH	SARKS
ABACI	ACNES	**AGHA**	GAIRS	PALAS	PALMS	VAMPS	CANON	PARCH	WARKS
ABACK	**ACRE**	AGHAS	HAIRS	TALAS	**ALOD**	**AMYL**	FANON	**ARCO**	**ARMS**
ABACS	NACRE	**AGIN**	LAIRS	**ALAY**	ALODS	AMYLS	**ANOW**	**ARCS**	BARMS
ABAS	ACRED	AGING	PAIRS	PALAY	**ALOE**	**ANAL**	**ANTA**	MARCS	FARMS
BABAS	ACRES	**AGIO**	SAIRS	ALAYS	ALOED	BANAL	ANTAE	**AREA**	HARMS
CABAS	**ACTA**	AGIOS	VAIRS	**ALBE**	ALOES	CANAL	ANTAR	AREAD	MARMS
ABASE	PACTA	**AGMA**	**AIRT**	ALBEE	**ALOW**	FANAL	**ANTE**	AREAL	WARMS
ABASH	**ACTS**	MAGMA	AIRTS	**ALBS**	ALOWE	**ANAN**	ZANTE	AREAR	**ARMY**
ABASK	FACTS	AGMAS	**AIRY**	**ALEE**	**ALPS**	ANANA	ANTED	AREAS	BARMY
ABBA	PACTS	**AGOG**	DAIRY	**ALES**	CALPS	**ANAS**	ANTES	**ARED**	**ARNA**
ABBAS	TACTS	AGOGE	FAIRY	BALES	PALPS	KANAS	**ANTI**	BARED	VARNA
ABBE	**ACYL**	**AGON**	HAIRY	DALES	SALPS	LANAS	TANTI	CARED	ARNAS
ABBES	ACYLS	WAGON	LAIRY	EALES	**ALSO**	MANAS	ANTIC	DARED	**AROW**
ABBEY	**ADAW**	AGONE	VAIRY	GALES	**ALTO**	NANAS	ANTIS	EARED	**ARSE**
ABBS	ADAWS	AGONS	**AITS**	HALES	SALTO	RANAS	**ANTS**	FARED	CARSE
ABED	**ADDS**	AGONY	BAITS	KALES	ALTOS	TANAS	BANTS	HARED	FARSE
ABET	WADDS	**AGUE**	GAITS	MALES	**ALTS**	**ANCE**	CANTS	OARED	PARSE
ABETS	**ADIT**	AGUED	RAITS	PALES	DALTS	DANCE	DANTS	PARED	ARSES
ABID	ADITS	AGUES	TAITS	RALES	HALTS	HANCE	GANTS	SARED	**ARTS**
RABID	**ADOS**	**AHEM**	WAITS	SALES	MALTS	LANCE	KANTS	TARED	CARTS
TABID	DADOS	**AHOY**	**AITU**	TALES	SALTS	NANCE	LANTS	WARED	DARTS
ABIDE	FADOS	**AIAS**	AITUS	VALES	**ALUM**	PANCE	PANTS	AREDD	FARTS
ABLE	**ADRY**	**AIDE**	**AJAR**	WALES	ALUMS	RANCE	RANTS	AREDE	HARTS
CABLE	**ADZE**	WAIDE	**AJEE**	YALES	**AMAH**	**ANDS**	VANTS	**ARES**	KARTS
FABLE	ADZES	AIDED	**AKED**	**ALEW**	AMAHS	BANDS	WANTS	BARES	MARTS
GABLE	**AEON**	AIDER	BAKED	ALEWS	**AMBO**	FANDS	**ANUS**	CARES	PARTS
HABLE	PAEON	AIDES	CAKED	**ALFA**	JAMBO	HANDS	MANUS	DARES	TARTS
SABLE	AEONS	**AIDS**	FAKED	HALFA	MAMBO	LANDS	**APAY**	FARES	WARTS
TABLE	**AERY**	GAIDS	LAKED	ALFAS	SAMBO	PANDS	APAYD	HARES	ARTSY
ABLED	FAERY	KAIDS	NAKED	**ALGA**	ZAMBO	RANDS	APAYS	LARES	**ARTY**
ABLER	**AESC**	LAIDS	RAKED	ALGAE	AMBOS	SANDS	**APED**	MARES	PARTY
ABLES	**AFAR**	MAIDS	WAKED	ALGAL	**AMEN**	WANDS	CAPED	NARES	TARTY
ABLET	AFARA	RAIDS	**AKEE**	**ALIT**	SAMEN	**ANES**	GAPED	PARES	**ARUM**
ABLY	**AFFY**	SAIDS	RAKEE	**ALLS**	YAMEN	BANES	JAPED	TARES	GARUM
ABUT	BAFFY	**AILS**	AKEES	BALLS	AMEND	CANES	RAPED	VARES	LARUM
ABUTS	DAFFY	BAILS	**AKES**	CALLS	AMENE	FANES	TAPED	WARES	ARUMS
ABYE	TAFFY	FAILS	BAKES	FALLS	AMENS	JANES	**APES**	**ARET**	**ARVO**
ABYES	**AFRO**	HAILS	CAKES	GALLS	AMENT	LANES	CAPES	ARETE	ARVOS
ACED	AFROS	JAILS	FAKES	HALLS	**AMID**	MANES	GAPES	ARETS	**ARYL**
FACED	**AGAR**	KAILS	HAKES	MALLS	AMIDE	PANES	JAPES	ARETT	ARYLS
LACED	AGARS	MAILS	JAKES	PALLS	**AMIE**	VANES	NAPES	**AREW**	**ASAR**
MACED	**AGAS**	NAILS	LAKES	WALLS	AMIES	WANES	PAPES	**ARIA**	TASAR
PACED	NAGAS	PAILS	MAKES	**ALLY**	**AMIR**	**ANEW**	RAPES	MARIA	**ASCI**
RACED	RAGAS	RAILS	RAKES	BALLY	AMIRS	**ANIL**	TAPES	ARIAS	FASCI
ACES	SAGAS	SAILS	SAKES	DALLY	**AMIS**	ANILE	**APEX**	**ARID**	**ASHY**
DACES	AGAST	TAILS	TAKES	GALLY	CAMIS	ANILS	**APOD**	MARID	HASHY
FACES	**AGED**	VAILS	WAKES	PALLY	KAMIS	**ANKH**	APODE	**ARIL**	MASHY
LACES	CAGED	WAILS	**AKIN**	RALLY	RAMIS	ANKHS	APODS	ARILS	WASHY
MACES	GAGED	**AIMS**	LAKIN	SALLY	TAMIS	**ANNA**	**APSE**	**ARIS**	**ASKS**
PACES	PAGED	KAIMS	TAKIN	TALLY	AMISS	CANNA	LAPSE	DARIS	BASKS
RACES	RAGED	MAIMS	AKING	WALLY	**AMLA**	MANNA	APSES	SARIS	CASKS
TACES	WAGED	SAIMS	**ALAE**	ALLYL	AMLAS	NANNA	**APTS**	ARISE	HASKS
ACHE	**AGEE**	**AINE**	**ALAP**	**ALMA**	**AMMO**	TANNA	**AQUA**	ARISH	MASKS
CACHE	RAGEE	DAINE	JALAP	HALMA	AMMON	ANNAL	AQUAE	**ARKS**	TASKS
NACHE	**AGEN**	FAINE	ALAPA	TALMA	AMMOS	ANNAS	AQUAS	BARKS	**ASPS**
RACHE	AGENE	RAINE	ALAPS	ALMAH	**AMOK**	ANNAT	**ARAK**	CARKS	GASPS
TACHE	AGENT	SAINE	**ALAR**	ALMAS	**AMPS**	**ANNO**	ARAKS	DARKS	HASPS
ACHED	**AGES**	AINEE	MALAR	**ALME**	CAMPS	ANNOY	**ARAR**	HARKS	JASPS
ACHES	CAGES	**AIRN**	TALAR	ALMEH	DAMPS	**ANNS**	ARARS	JARKS	RASPS
ACHY	GAGES	BAIRN	ALARM	ALMES	GAMPS	BANNS	**ARBA**	LARKS	WASPS
ACID	MAGES	CAIRN	ALARY	**ALMS**	LAMPS	CANNS	ARBAS	MARKS	**ATAP**
ACIDS	PAGES	AIRNS	**ALAS**	BALMS	RAMPS	JANNS	**ARCH**	NARKS	ATAPS
ACME	RAGES		BALAS	CALMS		**ANOA**			

ATOC	AVID	AYAHS	BANDY	BATTS	BEING	BIGGY	BLATT	BOFF	ABORD
ATOCS	PAVID	AYES	BANE	BATTY	BELL	BIGS	BLAY	BOFFS	BORDE
ATOK	AVOW	BAYES	BANED	BAUD	BELLE	BIKE	BLAYS	BOGS	BORDS
ATOKE	AVOWS	AYRE	BANES	BAUDS	BELLS	BIKED	BLEB	BOGY	BORE
ATOKS	AWAY	AYRES	BANG	BAUK	BELLY	BIKER	BLEBS	BOIL	ABORE
ATOM	AWAYS	AYUS	OBANG	BAUKS	BELS	BIKES	BLED	ABOIL	YBORE
ATOMS	AWDL	BAAS	BANGS	BAUR	BELT	BILE	BLEE	BOILS	BORED
ATOMY	AWDLS	BABA	BANI	BAURS	BELTS	BILES	BLEED	BOKE	BOREE
ATOP	AWED	BABAS	BANIA	BAWD	BEMA	BILK	BLEEP	BOKED	BOREL
ATOPY	CAWED	BABE	BANK	BAWDS	BEMAD	BILKS	BLEES	BOKES	BORER
AUFS	DAWED	BABEL	BANKS	BAWDY	BEMAS	BILL	BLET	BOKO	BORES
LAUFS	HAWED	BABES	BANS	BAWL	BEND	BILLS	BLETS	BOKOS	BORN
AUKS	JAWED	BABU	BANT	BAWLS	BENDS	BILLY	BLEW	BOKS	BORNE
BAUKS	KAWED	BABUL	BANTS	BAWN	BENDY	BIND	BLEY	BOLD	BORS
CAUKS	LAWED	BABUS	BAPS	BAWNS	BENE	BINDS	BLEYS	BOLE	BORT
WAUKS	PAWED	BABY	BAPU	BAWR	BENES	BINE	BLIN	BOLES	ABORT
AULA	SAWED	BACH	BAPUS	BAWRS	BENET	BINES	BLIND	BOLL	BORTS
AULAS	TAWED	BACK	BARB	BAYE	BENI	BING	BLINI	BOLLS	BOSH
AULD	YAWED	ABACK	BARBE	BAYED	BENIS	BINGE	BLINK	BOLO	BOSK
CAULD	AWES	BACKS	BARBS	BAYES	BENJ	BINGO	BLINS	BOLOS	BOSKS
HAULD	WAWES	BADE	BARD	BAYS	BENS	BINGS	BLIP	BOLT	BOSKY
TAULD	AWLS	BAEL	BARDS	BAYT	BENT	BINK	BLIPS	BOLTS	BOSS
YAULD	BAWLS	BAELS	BARDY	BAYTS	BENTS	BINKS	BLOB	BOMA	BOSSY
AUNT	PAWLS	BAFF	BARE	BEAD	BENTY	BINS	BLOBS	BOMAS	BOTH
DAUNT	WAWLS	BAFFS	BARED	BEADS	BERE	BINT	BLOC	BOMB	BOTHY
GAUNT	YAWLS	BAFFY	BARER	BEADY	BERES	BINTS	BLOCK	BOMBE	BOTS
HAUNT	AWNS	BAFT	BARES	BEAK	BERET	BIOG	BLOCS	BOMBO	BOTT
JAUNT	BAWNS	BAFTS	BARF	BEAKS	BERG	BIOGS	BLOT	BOMBS	BOTTE
NAUNT	DAWNS	BAGS	BARFS	BEAM	BERGS	BIOS	BLOTS	BONA	BOTTS
SAUNT	FAWNS	BAHT	BARK	ABEAM	BERK	BIRD	BLOW	BOND	BOTTY
TAUNT	LAWNS	BAHTS	BARKS	BEAMS	BERKS	BIRDS	BLOWN	BONDS	BOUK
VAUNT	PAWNS	BAIL	BARKY	BEAMY	BERM	BIRK	BLOWS	BONE	BOUKS
AUNTS	RAWNS	BAILS	BARM	BEAN	BERMS	BIRKS	BLOWY	BONED	BOUN
AUNTY	YAWNS	BAIT	BARMS	BEANO	BEST	BIRL	BLUB	BONER	BOUND
AURA	AWNY	BAITS	BARMY	BEANS	BESTS	BIRLE	BLUBS	BONES	BOUNS
LAURA	LAWNY	BAKE	BARN	BEAR	BETA	BIRLS	BLUE	BONG	BOUT
AURAE	TAWNY	BAKED	BARNS	ABEAR	BETAS	BIRR	BLUED	BONGO	ABOUT
AURAL	YAWNY	BAKEN	BARP	BEARD	BETE	BIRRS	BLUER	BONGS	BOUTS
AURAS	AWRY	BAKER	BARPS	BEARE	BETED	BISE	BLUES	BONK	BOWL
AUTO	AXED	BAKES	BARS	BEARS	BETEL	BISES	BLUEY	BONKS	BOWLS
AUTOS	FAXED	BALD	BASE	BEAT	BETES	BISH	BLUR	BONY	BOWR
AVAL	RAXED	BALE	ABASE	BEATH	BETH	BISK	BLURB	EBONY	BOWRS
NAVAL	TAXED	BALED	BASED	BEATS	BETHS	BISKS	BLURS	BOOB	BOWS
AVALE	WAXED	BALER	BASER	BEAU	BETS	BITE	BLURT	BOOBY	BOWSE
AVAS	AXEL	BALES	BASES	BEAUT	BEVY	BITER	BOAK	BOOH	BOXY
KAVAS	AXELS	BALK	BASH	BEAUX	BEYS	BITES	BOAKS	BOOHS	BOYG
LAVAS	AXES	BALKS	ABASH	BECK	BHEL	BITO	BOAR	BOOK	BOYGS
AVAST	FAXES	BALKY	BASK	BECKE	BHELS	BITOS	BOARD	BOOKS	BOYO
AVER	LAXES	BALL	ABASK	BECKS	BIAS	BITS	BOARS	BOOKY	BOYOS
CAVER	MAXES	BALLS	BASKS	BEDE	OBIAS	BITT	BOART	BOOM	BOYS
HAVER	PAXES	BALLY	BASS	BEDEL	BICE	BITTE	BOAS	BOOMS	BRAD
LAVER	RAXES	BALM	BASSE	BEDES	BICES	BITTS	BOAST	BOON	BRADS
PAVER	SAXES	BALMS	BASSI	BEDEW	BIDE	BITTY	BOAT	BOONG	BRAE
RAVER	TAXES	BALMY	BASSO	BEDS	ABIDE	BLAB	BOATS	BOONS	BRAES
SAVER	WAXES	BALU	BASSY	BEEF	BIDED	BLABS	BOBA	BOOR	BRAG
TAVER	ZAXES	BALUS	BAST	BEEFS	BIDES	BLAD	BOBAC	BOORD	BRAGS
WAVER	AXIL	BAMS	BASTA	BEEFY	BIDET	BLADS	BOBAK	BOORS	BRAN
AVERS	AXILE	BANC	BASTE	BEEN	BIDS	BLAE	BOBAS	BOOS	BRAND
AVERT	AXILS	BANCO	BASTO	BEEP	BIEN	BLAER	BOBS	BOOSE	BRANK
AVES	AXIS	BANCS	BASTS	BEEPS	BIER	BLAES	BOCK	BOOST	BRANS
CAVES	MAXIS	BAND	BATE	BEER	BIERS	BLAG	BOCKS	BOOT	BRAS
EAVES	TAXIS	ABAND	ABATE	BEERS	BIFF	BLAGS	BODE	BOOTH	BRASH
HAVES	AXLE	BANDH	BATED	BEERY	BIFFS	BLAH	ABODE	BOOTS	BRASS
LAVES	AXLES	BANDS	BATES	BEES	BIGA	BLAHS	BODED	BOOTY	BRAST
NAVES	AXON		BATH	BEET	BIGAE	BLAT	BODES	BOPS	BRAT
OAVES	CAXON		BATHE	BEETS	BIGG	BLATE	BODS	BORA	BRATS
PAVES	TAXON		BATHS	BEGO	BIGGS	BLATS	BODY	BORAS	BRAW
RAVES	AXONS		BATS	BEGOT				BORAX	BRAWL
SAVES	AYAH		BATT	BEGS				BORD	BRAWN
WAVES	RAYAH		BATTA	BEIN					BRAWS

BRAY	BUIK	BUSSU	CALPS	CART	CERES	CHIT	CLAPS	CODAS	CONK
ABRAY	BUIKS	BUST	CALX	SCART	CERT	CHITS	CLAT	CODE	CONKS
BRAYS	BUKE	BUSTS	CAME	CARTA	CERTS	CHIV	ECLAT	CODED	CONKY
BRED	BUKES	BUSTY	CAMEL	CARTE	CESS	CHIVE	CLATS	CODES	CONN
BREDE	BULB	BUSY	CAMEO	CARTS	CESSE	CHIVS	CLAW	CODEX	CONNE
BREE	BULBS	BUTE	CAMES	CASA	CETE	CHIVY	CLAWS	CODS	CONNS
BREED	BULK	BUTES	CAMP	CASAS	CETES	CHOC	CLAY	COED	CONS
BREEM	BULKS	BUTS	SCAMP	CASE	CHAD	CHOCK	CLAYS	COEDS	ICONS
BREER	BULKY	ABUTS	CAMPS	CASED	CHADS	CHOCS	CLEF	ICONS	CONY
BREES	BULL	BUTT	CAMPY	CASES	CHAI	CHOP	CLEFS	COFF	COOF
BREN	BULLA	BUTTE	CAMS	CASH	CHAIN	CHOPS	CLEFT	COFFS	COOFS
BRENS	BULLS	BUTTS	SCAMS	CASK	CHAIR	CHOU	CLEG	COFT	COOK
BRENT	BULLY	BUTTY	CANE	CASKS	CHAIS	CHOUT	CLEGS	COGS	COOKS
BRER	BUMF	BUYS	CANED	CAST	CHAL	CHOUX	CLEM	SCOGS	COOKY
BRERE	BUMFS	BUZZ	CANEH	CASTE	CHALK	CHOW	CLEMS	COHO	COOL
BRERS	BUMP	ABUZZ	CANES	CASTS	CHALS	CHOWS	CLEW	COHOE	COOLS
BREW	BUMPH	BUZZY	CANG	CATE	CHAM	CHUB	CLEWS	COHOG	COOLY
BREWS	BUMPS	BYES	CANGS	CATER	CHAMP	CHUBS	CLIP	COHOS	COOM
BRIG	BUMPY	ABYES	CANN	CATES	CHAMS	CHUG	CLIPE	COIF	COOMB
BRIGS	BUMS	BYKE	CANNA	CATS	CHAP	CHUGS	CLIPS	COIFS	COOMS
BRIM	BUNA	BYKED	CANNS	SCATS	CHAPE	CHUM	CLIPT	COIL	COOMY
ABRIM	ABUNA	BYKES	CANNY	CAUF	CHAPS	CHUMP	CLOD	COILS	COON
BRIMS	BUNAS	BYRE	CANS	CAUK	CHAR	CHUMS	CLODS	COIN	COONS
BRIO	BUND	BYRES	SCANS	CAUL	CHARA	CHUT	CLOG	COINS	COOP
BRIOS	BUNDS	BYTE	CANST	CAULD	CHARD	CHUTE	CLOGS	COIR	SCOOP
BRIT	BUNDU	BYTES	CANT	CAULK	CHARE	CIAO	CLOP	COIRS	COOPS
BRITS	BUNG	CABA	SCANT	CAULS	CHARK	CIAOS	CLOPS	COKE	COOS
BROD	BUNGS	CABAL	CANTO	CAUM	CHARM	CIDE	CLOT	COKED	COOST
BRODS	BUNGY	CABAS	CANTS	CAUMS	CHARR	CIDED	CLOTE	COKES	COOT
BROG	BUNK	CABS	CANTY	CAUP	CHARS	CIDER	CLOTH	COKY	SCOOT
BROGH	BUNKO	SCABS	CANY	SCAUP	CHART	CIDES	CLOTS	COLA	COOTS
BROGS	BUNKS	CADE	CAPA	CAUPS	CHARY	CIEL	CLOU	COLAS	COPE
BROO	BUNS	CADES	SCAPA	CAVE	CHAS	CIELS	CLOUD	COLD	SCOPE
BROOD	BUNT	CADET	CAPAS	CAVED	CHASE	CIGS	CLOUR	ACOLD	COPED
BROOK	BUNTS	CADI	CAPE	CAVEL	CHASM	CILL	CLOUS	SCOLD	COPER
BROOL	BUNTY	CADIE	SCAPE	CAVER	CHAT	CILLS	CLOUT	COLDS	COPES
BROOM	BUOY	CADIS	CAPED	CAVES	CHATS	CION	CLOW	COLE	COPSE
BROOS	BUOYS	CADS	CAPER	CAVY	CHAW	SCION	CLOWN	COLES	COPSY
BROS	BURD	ECADS	CAPES	CAWK	CHAWS	CIONS	CLOWS	COLEY	COPY
BROSE	BURDS	SCADS	CAPO	CAWKS	CHAY	CIRE	CLOY	COLL	CORD
BROW	BURG	CAFE	CAPON	CAWS	CHAYA	CIRES	CLOYE	COLLS	CORDS
BROWN	BURGH	CAFES	CAPOS	SCAWS	CHAYS	CIRL	CLOYS	COLLY	CORE
BROWS	BURGS	CAFF	CAPOT	CAYS	CHEF	CIRLS	CLUB	COLS	SCORE
BRUT	BURK	SCAFF	CAPS	CEAS	CHEFS	CIST	CLUBS	COLT	CORED
BRUTE	BURKA	CAFFS	CARB	CEASE	CHER	CISTS	CLUE	COLTS	CORER
BUAT	BURKE	CAGE	CARBS	CECA	OCHER	CITE	CLUED	COMA	CORES
BUATS	BURKS	CAGED	CARD	CEDE	CHERE	CITED	CLUES	COMAE	CORF
BUBA	BURL	CAGES	CARDI	CEDED	CHERT	CITER	COAL	COMAL	CORK
BUBAL	BURLS	CAGEY	CARDS	CEDES	CHEW	CITES	COALS	COMAS	CORKS
BUBAS	BURLY	CAGY	CARDY	CEDI	CHEWS	CITO	COALY	COMB	CORKY
BUBO	BURN	CAIN	CARE	CEDIS	CHEWY	CITS	COAT	COMBE	CORM
BUBS	BURNS	CAINS	SCARE	CEES	CHEZ	CITY	COATE	COMBO	CORMS
BUCK	BURNT	CAKE	CARED	CEIL	CHIC	CIVE	COATI	COMBS	CORN
BUCKO	BURP	CAKED	CARER	CEILI	CHICA	CIVES	COATS	COMBY	ACORN
BUCKS	BURPS	CAKES	CARES	CEILS	CHICH	CIVET	COAX	COME	SCORN
BUCKU	BURR	CAKY	CARET	CELL	CHICK	CLAD	COBB	COMER	CORNI
BUDO	BURRO	CALF	CAREX	CELLA	CHICS	YCLAD	COBBS	COMES	CORNO
BUDOS	BURRS	CALFS	CARK	CELLO	CHID	CLADE	COBBY	COMET	CORNS
BUDS	BURRY	CALK	CARKS	CELLS	CHIDE	CLADS	COBS	COMP	CORNU
BUFF	BURS	CALKS	CARL	CELS	CHIK	CLAG	COCA	COMPO	CORNY
BUFFA	BURSA	CALL	CARLS	CELT	CHIKS	CLAGS	COCAS	COMPS	CORS
BUFFE	BURSE	SCALL	CARP	CELTS	CHIN	CLAM	COCH	COMPT	CORSE
BUFFI	BURST	CALLA	SCARP	CENT	CHINA	CLAME	COCK	COMS	CORSO
BUFFO	BURY	CALLS	CARPS	SCENT	CHINE	CLAMP	ACOCK	COND	COSE
BUFFS	BUSH	CALM	CARR	CENTO	CHINK	CLAMS	COCKS	YCOND	COSED
BUFO	BUSHY	CALMS	CARRS	CENTS	CHINO	CLAN	COCKY	CONE	COSES
BUFOS	BUSK	CALMY	CARRY	CEPS	CHINS	CLANG	COCO	SCONE	COSH
BUGS	BUSKS	CALP	CARS	CERE	CHIP	CLANK	COCOA	CONED	COSS
BUHL	BUSKY	SCALP	SCARS	CERED	CHIPS	CLANS	COCOS	CONES	COST
BUHLS	BUSS	CALPA	CARSE		CHIS	CLAP	CODA	CONEY	

COSTA	CRAPY	CULTS	DAHLS	DAWS	DEMES	DIKEY	DIXIE	DOPEY	DRAB
COSTE	CRAW	CUNT	DAHS	ADAWS	DEMO	DILL	DIXY	DOPS	DRABS
COSTS	SCRAW	CUNTS	DAIS	DAWT	DEMOB	DILLI	DOAB	DOPY	DRAD
COSY	CRAWL	CUPS	DAISY	DAWTS	DEMON	DILLS	DOABS	DORM	ADRAD
COTE	CRAWS	SCUPS	DAKS	DAYS	DEMOS	DILLY	DOAT	DORMS	YDRAD
COTED	CREE	CURB	DALE	ADAYS	DEMY	DIME	DOATS	DORMY	DRAG
COTES	SCREE	CURBS	DALES	DAZE	DENE	DIMER	DOBS	DORP	DRAGS
COTH	CREED	CURD	DALI	DAZED	DENES	DIMES	DOCK	DORPS	DRAM
COTHS	CREEK	CURDS	DALIS	DAZES	DENS	DIMS	DOCKS	DORR	DRAMA
COTS	CREEL	CURDY	DALS	DEAD	DENSE	DINE	DOCS	DORRS	DRAMS
SCOTS	CREEP	CURE	ODALS	DEADS	DENT	DINED	DODO	DORS	DRAP
COTT	CREES	CURED	UDALS	DEAF	DENTS	DINER	DODOS	ODORS	DRAPE
COTTA	CREW	CURER	DALT	DEAL	DENY	DINES	DODS	DORSA	DRAPS
COTTS	SCREW	CURES	DALTS	DEALS	DERE	DING	DOEN	DORSE	DRAT
COUP	CREWE	CURL	DAME	DEALT	DERED	DINGE	DOER	DORT	DRAW
SCOUP	CREWS	CURLS	DAMES	IDEAL	DERES	DINGO	DOERS	DORTS	DRAWL
COUPE	CRIB	CURLY	DAMN	DEAN	DERM	DINGS	DOES	DORTY	DRAWN
COUPS	CRIBS	CURN	DAMNS	DEANS	DERMA	DINGY	DOEST	DORY	DRAWS
COUR	CRIT	CURNS	DAMP	DEAR	DERMS	DINK	DOFF	DOSE	DRAY
SCOUR	CRITH	CURNY	DAMPS	DEARE	DERN	DINKS	DOFFS	DOSED	DRAYS
COURB	CRITS	CURR	DAMPY	DEARN	DERNS	DINKY	DOGE	DOSEH	DREE
COURD	CROC	CURRS	DAMS	DEARS	DERV	DINS	DOGES	DOSES	DREED
COURE	CROCK	CURRY	DANG	DEARY	DERVS	DINT	DOGS	DOSS	DREES
COURS	CROCS	CURS	DANGS	DEAW	DESK	DINTS	DOGY	DOST	DREW
COURT	CROP	SCURS	DANK	DEAWS	DESKS	DIPS	DOHS	DOTE	DREY
COVE	CROPS	CURSE	DANKS	DEAWY	DEUS	DIPSO	DOIT	DOTED	DREYS
COVED	CROW	CURST	DANS	DEBS	DEVA	DIRE	DOITS	DOTER	DRIB
COVEN	SCROW	CURT	DANT	DEBT	DEVAS	DIRER	DOJO	DOTES	DRIBS
COVER	CROWD	CUSH	DANTS	DEBTS	DEWS	DIRK	DOJOS	DOTH	DRIP
COVES	CROWN	CUSHY	DAPS	DECK	DEWY	DIRKE	DOLE	DOTS	DRIPS
COVET	CROWS	CUSK	DARE	DECKO	DEYS	DIRKS	DOLED	DOTY	DROP
COVEY	CRUD	CUSKS	DARED	DECKS	DHAK	DIRL	DOLES	DOUC	DROPS
COWL	CRUDE	CUSP	DARES	DECO	DHAKS	DIRLS	DOLL	DOUCE	DROW
SCOWL	CRUDS	CUSPS	DARG	DECOR	DHAL	DIRT	DOLLS	DOUCS	DROWN
COWLS	CRUDY	CUSS	DARGA	DECOY	DHALS	DIRTS	DOLLY	DOUP	DROWS
COWP	CRUE	CUTE	DARGS	DEED	DHOW	DIRTY	DOLT	DOUPS	DRUB
SCOWP	CRUEL	ACUTE	DARI	DEEDS	DHOWS	DISA	DOLTS	DOUR	DRUBS
COWPS	CRUES	SCUTE	DARIC	DEEDY	DIAL	DISAS	DOME	ODOUR	DRUG
COWS	CRUET	CUTER	DARIS	DEEM	DIALS	DISC	DOMED	DOUT	DRUGS
SCOWS	CRUS	CUTES	DARK	ADEEM	DIBS	DISCO	DOMES	DOUTS	DRUM
COXA	ECRUS	CUTEY	DARKS	DEEMS	DICE	DISCS	DOMY	DOVE	DRUMS
COXAE	CRUSE	CUTS	DARKY	DEEN	DICED	DISH	DONA	DOVED	DSOS
COXAL	CRUSH	SCUTS	DARN	DEENS	DICER	DISHY	DONAH	DOVER	ODSOS
COXY	CRUST	CWMS	DARNS	DEEP	DICES	DISK	DONAS	DOVES	DUAD
COYS	CRUSY	CYAN	DART	DEEPS	DICEY	DISKS	DONE	DOWD	DUADS
COZE	CRUX	CYANS	DARTS	DEER	DICH	DISS	DONEE	DOWDS	DUAL
COZED	CUBE	CYMA	DASH	DEERE	DICHT	DITA	DONG	DOWDY	DUALS
COZEN	CUBEB	CYMAR	DATA	DEES	DICK	DITAL	DONGA	DOWF	DUAN
COZES	CUBED	CYMAS	DATAL	DEEV	DICKS	DITAS	DONGS	DOWL	DUANS
COZY	CUBES	CYME	DATE	DEEVE	DICKY	DITE	DONS	DOWLE	DUAR
CRAB	CUBS	CYMES	DATED	DEEVS	DICT	DITED	DOOB	DOWLS	DUARS
SCRAB	SCUDS	CYST	DATER	DEFT	EDICT	DITES	DOOBS	DOWN	DUBS
CRABS	CUED	CYSTS	DATES	DEFY	DICTA	DITS	DOOK	ADOWN	DUCE
CRAG	CUES	CYTE	DAUB	DEID	DICTS	DITT	DOOKS	DOWNA	DUCES
SCRAG	CUFF	CYTES	DAUBE	DEIDS	ADITS	DITTO	DOOL	DOWNS	DUCK
CRAGS	SCUFF	CZAR	DAUBS	DEIL	EDITS	DITTS	DOOLE	DOWNY	DUCKS
CRAM	CUFFO	CZARS	DAUBY	DEILS	DIDO	DITTY	DOOLS	DOWP	DUCKY
SCRAM	CUFFS	DABS	DAUD	DELE	DIDOS	DIVA	DOOM	DOWPS	DUCT
CRAME	CUIF	DACE	DAUDS	DELED	DIEB	DIVAN	DOOMS	DOWS	DUCTS
CRAMP	CUIFS	DACES	DAUR	DELES	DIEBS	DIVAS	DOOMY	DOWSE	DUDE
CRAMS	CUIT	DADO	DAURS	DELF	DIED	DIVE	DOOR	DOWT	DUDES
CRAN	CUITS	DADOS	DAUT	DELFS	DIES	DIVED	DOORN	DOWTS	DUDS
SCRAN	CULL	DADS	DAUTS	DELFT	DIET	DIVER	DOORS	DOXY	DUED
CRANE	SCULL	DAFF	DAWD	DELI	DIETS	DIVES	DOOS	DOZE	DUEL
CRANK	CULLS	DAFFS	DAWDS	DELIS	DIGS	DIVI	DOPA	DOZED	DUELS
CRANS	CULLY	DAFFY	DAWK	DELL	DIKA	DIVIS	DOPAS	DOZEN	DUES
CRAP	CULM	DAFT	DAWKS	DELLS	DIKAS	DIVS	DOPE	DOZER	DUET
SCRAP	CULMS	DAGO	DAWN	DELS	DIKE	DIXI	DOPED	DOZES	DUETS
CRAPE	CULT	DAGS	DAWNS	DEME	DIKED		DOPER	DOZY	
CRAPS		DAHL			DIKER		DOPES		
					DIKES				

DUETT	DYNES	EASY	LEECH	VELDS	WENDS	MERKS	EURO	EYRY	FASTS
DUFF	DZOS	EATH	REECH	WELDS	ENES	PERKS	EUROS	FACE	FATE
DUFFS	EACH	BEATH	EELS	ELFS	BENES	SERKS	EVEN	FACED	FATED
DUGS	BEACH	DEATH	FEELS	DELFS	DENES	YERKS	EEVEN	FACER	FATES
DUKE	LEACH	HEATH	HEELS	PELFS	GENES	ERNE	SEVEN	FACES	FATS
DUKED	PEACH	MEATH	JEELS	SELFS	LENES	CERNE	YEVEN	FACET	FATSO
DUKES	REACH	NEATH	KEELS	ELKS	MENES	GERNE	EVENS	FACT	FAUN
DULE	TEACH	EATHE	PEELS	WELKS	NENES	KERNE	EVENT	FACTS	FAUNA
DULES	EALE	EATS	REELS	YELKS	PENES	TERNE	EVER	FADE	FAUNS
DULL	VEALE	BEATS	SEELS	ELLS	TENES	ERNED	BEVER	FADED	FAUX
DULLS	EALES	FEATS	TEELS	BELLS	ENEW	ERNES	FEVER	FADES	FAWN
DULLY	EANS	GEATS	WEELS	CELLS	RENEW	ERNS	LEVER	FADO	FAWNS
DULY	BEANS	HEATS	EELY	DELLS	ENEWS	DERNS	NEVER	FADOS	FAWS
DUMA	DEANS	JEATS	JEELY	FELLS	ENGS	FERNS	SEVER	FADS	FAYS
DUMAS	GEANS	LEATS	SEELY	HELLS	LENGS	HERNS	EVERT	FADY	OFAYS
DUMB	JEANS	MEATS	EERY	JELLS	MENGS	KERNS	EVERY	FAFF	FAZE
DUMBS	LEANS	PEATS	BEERY	KELLS	ENOW	PERNS	EVES	FAFFS	FAZED
DUMP	MEANS	SEATS	LEERY	MELLS	ENVY	TERNS	MEVES	FAGS	FAZES
DUMPS	PEANS	TEATS	PEERY	PELLS	SENVY	ERRS	NEVES	FAHS	FEAL
DUMPY	REANS	EAUS	VEERY	SELLS	EOAN	SERRS	YEVES	FAIK	FEALS
DUNE	SEANS	EAUX	EEVN	TELLS	EONS	ERST	EVET	FAIKS	FEAR
DUNES	WEANS	BEAUX	EEVNS	VELLS	AEONS	PERST	REVET	FAIL	FEARE
DUNG	YEANS	EBBS	EFFS	WELLS	NEONS	VERST	EVETS	FAILS	FEARS
DUNGS	EARD	EBON	JEFFS	YELLS	PEONS	ESKY	EVIL	FAIN	FEAT
DUNGY	BEARD	EBONS	TEFFS	ELMS	EORL	PESKY	DEVIL	FAINE	FEATS
DUNK	HEARD	EBONY	EFTS	HELMS	CEORL	ESNE	EVILS	FAINS	FECK
DUNKS	YEARD	ECAD	HEFTS	YELMS	EORLS	MESNE	EVOE	FAINT	FECKS
DUNS	EARDS	DECAD	LEFTS	ELMY	EPEE	ESPY	EWER	FAIR	FEDS
DUNSH	EARL	ECADS	WEFTS	ELSE	TEPEE	ESSE	FEWER	FAIRS	FEED
DUNT	PEARL	ECCE	EGAD	ELTS	EPEES	CESSE	HEWER	FAIRY	FEEDS
DUNTS	EARLS	RECCE	BEGAD	BELTS	EPHA	DESSE	NEWER	FAIX	FEEL
DUOS	EARLY	ECCO	EGAL	CELTS	EPHAH	FESSE	SEWER	FAKE	FEELS
DUPE	EARN	RECCO	LEGAL	DELTS	EPHAS	GESSE	EWES	FAKED	FEER
DUPED	DEARN	SECCO	REGAL	FELTS	EPIC	ESSES	EWEST	FAKER	FEERS
DUPER	LEARN	ECHE	EGER	GELTS	EPICS	ETAS	EWKS	FAKES	FEES
DUPES	YEARN	ECHED	LEGER	KELTS	EPOS	BETAS	EWTS	FALL	FEESE
DURA	EARNS	ECHES	EGERS	MELTS	PEPOS	FETAS	NEWTS	FALLS	FEET
DURAL	EARS	ECHO	EGGS	PELTS	ERAS	GETAS	EXAM	FALX	FEGS
DURAS	BEARS	ECHT	TEGGS	WELTS	TERAS	KETAS	EXAMS	FAME	FEHM
DURE	DEARS	FECHT	YEGGS	YELTS	ERASE	ZETAS	EXES	FAMED	FEHME
DURED	FEARS	HECHT	EGGY	EMES	ERED	ETAT	HEXES	FAMES	FEIS
DURES	GEARS	WECHT	LEGGY	DEMES	CERED	ETATS	KEXES	FAND	FELL
DURN	HEARS	ECRU	PEGGY	FEMES	DERED	ETCH	LEXES	FANDS	FELLA
DURNS	LEARS	ECRUS	EGIS	HEMES	LERED	FETCH	SEXES	FANE	FELLS
DURO	NEARS	ECUS	AEGIS	LEMES	MERED	KETCH	VEXES	FANES	FELLY
DUROS	PEARS	EDDO	EGMA	TEMES	SERED	LETCH	WEXES	FANG	FELT
DUROY	REARS	EDDY	REGMA	EMEU	ERES	RETCH	YEXES	FANGO	FELTS
DUSH	SEARS	NEDDY	EGMAS	EMEUS	BERES	VETCH	EXIT	FANGS	FEME
DUSK	TEARS	REDDY	EGOS	EMIR	CERES	ETEN	EXITS	FANK	FEMES
DUSKS	WEARS	TEDDY	SEGOS	EMIRS	DERES	ETENS	EXON	FANKS	FEND
DUSKY	YEARS	EDGE	EHED	EMIT	FERES	ETHE	EXONS	FANS	FENDS
DUST	EARST	KEDGE	EIKS	DEMIT	GERES	ETHER	EXPO	FARD	FENDY
ADUST	EASE	LEDGE	REIKS	REMIT	LERES	ETHS	EXPOS	FARDS	FENS
DUSTS	CEASE	SEDGE	EILD	EMITS	MERES	BETHS	EXUL	FARE	FENT
DUSTY	LEASE	WEDGE	EILDS	EMMA	PERES	METHS	EXULS	FARED	FENTS
DUTY	MEASE	EDGED	EINE	EMMAS	SERES	ETNA	EXULT	FARES	FEOD
DWAM	PEASE	EDGER	SEINE	EMUS	ERGO	ETNAS	EYAS	FARL	FEODS
DWAMS	SEASE	EDGES	EKED	EMYS	ERGOT	ETUI	EYED	FARLE	FERE
DYAD	TEASE	EDGY	REKED	ENDS	ERGS	ETUIS	FEYED	FARLS	YFERE
DYADS	EASED	HEDGY	EKES	BENDS	BERGS	EUGE	HEYED	FARM	FERER
DYED	EASEL	KEDGY	PEKES	FENDS	ERIC	EUGH	KEYED	FARMS	FERES
DYER	EASES	LEDGY	REKES	HENDS	SERIC	HEUGH	EYES	FARO	FERM
DYERS	EAST	SEDGY	EKKA	LENDS	XERIC	LEUGH	EYNE	FAROS	FERMI
DYES	BEAST	EDHS	EKKAS	MENDS	ERICA	TEUGH	EYOT	FARS	FERMS
DYKE	FEAST	EDIT	ELAN	PENDS	ERICK	EUGHS	EYOTS	FART	FERN
DYKED	LEAST	EDITS	ELAND	RENDS	ERICS	EUKS	EYRA	FARTS	FERNS
DYKES	REAST	EECH	ELANS	SENDS	ERKS	NEUKS	EYRAS	FASH	FERNY
DYKEY	YEAST	BEECH	ELDS	TENDS	BERKS	YEUKS	EYRE	FAST	FESS
DYNE	EASTS	KEECH	MELDS	VENDS	JERKS	EUOI	EYRES	FASTI	FESSE

FEST	FIRMS	FLIP	FORE	FUBS	GAFF	GASPY	GENAS	GIRDS	GLOBY
FESTA	FIRN	FLIPS	AFORE	FUBSY	GAFFE	GAST	GENE	GIRL	GLOM
FESTS	FIRNS	FLIT	FOREL	FUCI	GAFFS	AGAST	AGENE	GIRLS	GLOMS
FETA	FIRS	FLITE	FORES	FUCK	GAGA	GASTS	GENES	GIRLY	GLOW
FETAL	FIRST	FLITS	FORK	FUCKS	GAGE	GATE	GENET	GIRN	AGLOW
FETAS	FISC	FLITT	FORKS	FUDS	GAGED	AGATE	GENS	GIRNS	GLOWS
FETE	FISCS	FLIX	FORKY	FUEL	GAGES	GATED	GENT	GIRO	GLUE
FETED	FISH	FLOE	FORM	FUELS	GAGS	GATES	AGENT	GIRON	GLUED
FETES	FISHY	FLOES	FORME	FUFF	GAID	GATH	GENTS	GIROS	GLUER
FETS	FISK	FLOG	FORMS	FUFFS	GAIDS	GATHS	GENTY	GIRR	GLUES
FETT	FISKS	FLOGS	FORT	FUFFY	GAIN	GATS	GENU	GIRRS	GLUEY
FETTA	FIST	FLOP	FORTE	FUGS	AGAIN	GAUD	GENUS	GIRT	GLUG
FETTS	FISTS	FLOPS	FORTH	FULL	GAINS	GAUDS	GEOS	GIRTH	GLUGS
FEUD	FISTY	FLOR	FORTS	FULLS	GAIR	GAUDY	GERE	GIRTS	GLUM
FEUDS	FITS	FLORA	FORTY	FULLY	GAIRS	GAUM	GERES	GISM	GLUME
FEUS	FITT	FLORS	FOSS	FUME	GAIT	GAUMS	GERM	GISMO	GLUT
FEYS	FITTE	FLORY	FOSSA	FUMED	GAITS	GAUMY	GERMS	GISMS	GLUTS
FIAR	FITTS	FLOW	FOSSE	FUMES	GAITT	GAUN	GEST	GIST	GNAR
FIARS	FIVE	FLOWN	FOUD	FUMET	GAJO	GAUNT	GESTE	GISTS	GNARL
FIAT	FIVER	FLOWS	FOUDS	FUMS	GAJOS	GAUP	GESTS	GITE	GNARR
FIATS	FIVES	FLUB	FOUL	FUMY	GALA	GAUPS	GETA	GITES	GNARS
FIBS	FIZZ	FLUBS	AFOUL	FUND	GALAH	GAUR	GETAS	GITS	GNAT
FICO	FIZZY	FLUE	FOULE	FUNDI	GALAS	GAURS	GETS	GIVE	GNATS
FICOS	FLAB	FLUES	FOULS	FUNDS	GALE	GAUS	GEUM	GIVED	GNAW
FIDS	FLABS	FLUEY	FOUR	FUNG	GALEA	GAUSS	GEUMS	GIVEN	GNAWN
FIEF	FLAG	FLUS	FOURS	FUNGI	GALES	GAVE	GHAT	GIVER	GNAWS
FIEFS	OFLAG	FLUSH	FOUS	FUNGS	GALL	AGAVE	GHATS	GIVES	GNUS
FIFE	FLAGS	FLUX	FOWL	FUNK	GALLS	GAVEL	GHEE	GIZZ	GOAD
FIFED	FLAK	FOAL	FOWLS	FUNKS	GALLY	GAWD	GHEES	GJUS	GOADS
FIFER	FLAKE	FOALS	FOXY	FUNKY	GALS	GAWDS	GHIS	GLAD	GOAF
FIFES	FLAKS	FOAM	FOYS	FUNS	GAMB	GAWK	GIBE	GLADE	GOAFS
FIGO	FLAKY	FOAMS	FOZY	FURL	GAMBA	GAWKS	GIBED	GLADS	GOAL
FIGOS	FLAM	FOAMY	FRAB	FURLS	GAMBS	GAWKY	GIBEL	GLADY	GOALS
FIGS	FLAME	FOBS	FRABS	FURR	GAME	GAWP	GIBER	GLAM	GOAS
FIKE	FLAMM	FOCI	FRAE	FURRS	GAMED	GAWPS	GIBES	GLED	GOAT
FIKED	FLAMS	FOEN	FRAP	FURRY	GAMER	GAYS	GIBS	GLEDE	GOATS
FIKES	FLAMY	FOES	FRAPS	FURS	GAMES	GAZE	GIDS	GLEDS	GOATY
FIKY	FLAN	FOGS	FRAS	FURY	GAMP	AGAZE	GIED	GLEE	GOBO
FILE	FLANK	FOGY	FRASS	FUSC	GAMPS	GAZED	GIEN	AGLEE	GOBOS
FILED	FLANS	FOHN	FRAU	FUSE	GAMS	GAZEL	GIES	GLEED	GOBS
FILER	FLAP	FOHNS	FRAUD	FUSED	OGAMS	GAZER	GIFT	GLEEK	GOBY
FILES	FLAPS	FOIL	FRAUS	FUSEE	GANE	GAZES	GIFTS	GLEES	GODS
FILET	FLAT	FOILS	FRAY	FUSES	GANG	GAZY	GIGA	GLEET	GODSO
FILL	FLATS	FOIN	FRAYS	FUSS	GANGS	GEAL	GIGAS	GLEG	GOEL
FILLE	FLAW	FOINS	FREE	FUSSY	GANT	GEALS	GIGS	GLEI	GOELS
FILLS	FLAWN	FOLD	FREED	FUST	GANTS	GEAN	GILA	GLEIS	GOER
FILLY	FLAWS	FOLDS	FREER	FUSTS	GAOL	GEANS	AGILA	GLEN	GOERS
FILM	FLAWY	FOLK	FREES	FUSTY	GAOLS	GEAR	GILAS	GLENS	GOES
FILMS	FLAX	FOLKS	FREET	FUZE	GAPE	GEARE	GILD	GLENT	GOEY
FILMY	FLAXY	FOND	FRET	FUZEE	AGAPE	GEARS	GILDS	GLEY	GOFF
FILS	FLAY	FONDA	FRETS	FUZES	GAPED	GEAT	GILL	GLEYS	GOFFS
FIND	FLAYS	FONDS	FRIG	FUZZ	GAPER	GEATS	GILLS	GLIA	GOGO
FINDS	FLEA	FONE	FRIGS	FUZZY	GAPES	GECK	GILLY	GLIAL	GOGS
FINE	FLEAM	FONS	FRIS	FYKE	GAPO	GECKO	GILT	GLIAS	GOLD
FINED	FLEAS	FONT	FRISK	FYKED	IGAPO	GECKS	GILTS	GLIB	GOLDS
FINER	FLED	FONTS	FRIST	FYKES	GAPOS	GEDS	GIMP	GLIBS	GOLDY
FINES	FLEE	FOOD	FRIT	FYLE	GAPS	GEED	GIMPS	GLID	GOLE
FINK	FLEER	FOODS	AFRIT	FYLES	GARB	GEES	GING	GLIDE	GOLEM
FINKS	FLEES	FOOL	FRITH	FYRD	GARBE	GEIT	GINGS	GLIM	GOLES
FINO	FLEET	FOOLS	FRITS	FYRDS	GARBO	GEITS	GINK	GLIMS	GOLF
FINOS	FLEG	FOOT	FRIZ	GABS	GARBS	GELD	GINKS	GLIT	GOLFS
FINS	FLEGS	AFOOT	FRIZE	GABY	GARE	GELDS	GINN	GLITS	GOLP
FIRE	FLEW	FOOTS	FRIZZ	GADE	GARS	GELS	GINS	GLITZ	GOLPE
AFIRE	FLEWS	FOOTY	FROG	GADES	AGARS	GELT	GIOS	GLOB	GOLPS
FIRED	FLEX	FOPS	FROGS	GADI	GART	GELTS	AGIOS	GLOBE	GONE
FIRER	FLEY	FORA	FROM	GADIS	GARTH	GEMS	GIPS	GLOBS	AGONE
FIRES	FLEYS	FORAY	FROW	GADS	GASH	GENA	GIPSY		GONER
FIRK	FLIC	FORD	FROWN	GADSO	GASP	GENAL	GIRD		GONG
FIRKS	FLICK	FORDO	FROWS	GAED	GASPS				GONGS
FIRM	FLICS	FORDS	FROWY	GAES					GONK

GONKS	GREN	GULF	HADED	HAMES	HATE	HEATS	THERE	HILLO	SHOER
GONS	GRENS	GULFS	HADES	HAMS	HATED	HEBE	WHERE	HILLS	HOERS
AGONS	GREW	GULFY	HADJ	CHAMS	HATER	HEBEN	HERL	HILLY	HOES
GOOD	GREWS	GULL	HADJI	SHAMS	HATES	HEBES	HERLS	HILT	HOGG
AGOOD	GREY	GULLS	HADS	WHAMS	HATH	HECH	HERM	HILTS	HOGGS
GOODS	GREYS	GULLY	HAEM	HAND	HATS	HECHT	THERM	HIND	HOGH
GOODY	GRID	GULP	HAEMS	SHAND	CHATS	HECK	HERMA	AHIND	HOGHS
GOOF	GRIDE	GULPH	HAET	HANDS	GHATS	CHECK	HERMS	HINDS	HOGS
GOOFS	GRIDS	GULPS	HAETS	HANDY	KHATS	HECKS	HERN	HING	SHOGS
GOOFY	GRIG	GULY	HAFF	HANG	THATS	CHECKS	HERNS	EHING	HOHS
GOOK	GRIGS	GUMP	CHAFF	BHANG	WHATS	HEED	HERO	THING	HOIK
GOOKS	GRIM	GUMPS	HAFFS	PHANG	HAUD	THEED	HEROE	HINGE	HOIKS
GOOL	GRIME	GUMS	HAFT	WHANG	HAUDS	HEEDS	HERON	HINGS	HOKE
GOOLD	GRIMY	GUNK	CHAFT	HANGS	HAUL	HEEDY	HERONS	HINS	HOKED
GOOLS	GRIN	GUNKS	SHAFT	HANK	HAULD	HEEL	HERS	CHINS	HOKES
GOOLY	AGRIN	GUNS	HAFTS	CHANK	HAULS	SHEEL	HERSE	SHINS	HOKEY
GOON	GRIND	GUPS	HAGG	SHANK	HAULT	WHEEL	HERY	THINS	HOLD
GOONS	GRINS	GURL	HAGGS	THANK	HAUT	THEEL	HERYE	WHINS	AHOLD
GOOP	GRIP	GURLS	HAGS	HANKS	HAUTE	HEELS	HESP	HINT	HOLDS
GOOPS	GRIPE	GURLY	SHAGS	HANKY	HAVE	HEFT	HESPS	AHINT	HOLE
GOOPY	GRIPS	GURN	HAIK	HAPS	HAVEN	THEFT	HEST	HINTS	DHOLE
GOOR	GRIS	GURNS	HAIKS	CHAPS	HAVER	HEFTE	CHEST	HIPS	THOLE
GOORS	GRISE	GURS	HAIKU	SHAPS	HAVES	HEFTS	GHEST	CHIPS	WHOLE
GOOS	GRIST	GURU	HAIL	WHAPS	HAWK	HEFTY	HESTS	SHIPS	HOLED
GOOSE	GRISY	GURUS	HAILS	HARD	HAWKS	HEID	HETE	WHIPS	HOLES
GOOSY	GRIT	GUSH	HAILY	CHARD	HAWM	HEIDS	THETE	HIPT	HOLEY
GORE	GRITH	GUSHY	HAIN	SHARD	HAWMS	HEIL	HETES	WHIPT	HOLM
GORED	GRITS	GUST	CHAIN	HARDS	HAWS	HEIR	HETS	HIRE	HOLMS
GORES	GROG	GUSTO	HAINS	HARDY	CHAWS	HEIRS	SHETS	HIRED	HOLP
GORM	GROGS	GUSTS	HAIR	HARE	SHAWS	THEIR	WHETS	HIRER	HOLS
GORMS	GROT	GUSTY	CHAIR	CHARE	THAWS	HELD	HEWN	HIRES	HOLT
GORMY	GROTS	GUTS	HAIRS	PHARE	HAWSE	HELE	SHEWN	HISH	HOLTS
GORY	GROW	GUTSY	HAIRY	SHARE	HAWSER	HELED	HEWS	SHISH	HOLY
GOSH	GROWL	GUYS	HAJI	WHARE	HAYS	HELES	CHEWS	WHISH	HOME
GOUK	GROWN	GUYSE	HAJIS	HARED	CHAYS	HELL	SHEWS	HISN	HOMED
GOUKS	GROWS	GYAL	HAJJ	HAREM	SHAYS	SHELL	THEWS	HISS	HOMER
GOUT	GRUB	GYALS	HAJJI	HARES	HAZE	HELLO	WHEWS	WHISS	HOMERS
GOUTS	GRUBS	GYBE	HAKA	HARK	HAZED	HELLS	HEYS	HIST	HOMES
GOUTY	GRUE	GYBED	HAKAM	CHARK	HAZEL	HELM	WHEYS	WHIST	HOMEY
GOVS	GRUED	GYBES	HAKAS	SHARK	HAZER	WHELM	HICK	HISTS	HOMO
GOWD	GRUEL	GYMP	HAKE	HARKS	HAZES	HELMS	CHICK	HITS	ZHOMO
GOWDS	GRUES	GYMPS	SHAKE	HARL	HAZY	HELP	THICK	CHITS	HOMOS
GOWF	GRUM	GYMS	HAKES	HARLS	HEAD	WHELP	HICKS	SHITS	HOMY
GOWFS	GRUME	GYNY	HALAL	HARM	AHEAD	HELPS	HIDE	WHITS	HOND
GOWK	GRUMS	GYPS	HALALS	CHARM	HEADS	HEME	CHIDE	HIVE	HONDS
GOWKS	GUAN	GYPSY	HALE	HARMS	HEADY	THEME	HIDED	CHIVE	HONE
GOWL	GUANA	GYRE	SHALE	HARN	HEAL	HEMES	HIDES	SHIVE	OHONE
GOWLS	GUANO	GYRED	WHALE	SHARN	SHEAL	HEMP	HIED	HIVED	PHONE
GOWN	GUANS	GYRES	HALED	HARNS	WHEAL	HEMPS	SHIED	HIVER	RHONE
GOWNS	GUAR	GYRI	HALER	HARO	HEALD	HEMPY	HIES	HIVES	SHONE
GRAB	GUARD	GYRO	HALES	HAROS	HEALS	HEND	RHIES	HIYA	HONED
GRABS	GUARS	GYRON	HALF	HARP	HEAP	SHEND	SHIES	HIZZ	HONES
GRAM	GUBS	GYROS	HALFA	SHARP	AHEAP	HENDS	HIGH	WHIZZ	HONEY
GRAMA	GUCK	GYTE	HALL	HARPS	CHEAP	HENS	AHIGH	HOAR	HONG
GRAME	GUCKS	GYTES	SHALL	HARPY	HEAPS	THENS	THIGH	HOARD	THONG
GRAMS	GUCKY	GYVE	HALLO	HART	HEAPY	WHENS	HIGHS	HOARS	HONGS
GRAN	GUDE	GYVED	HALLS	CHART	HEAR	HENT	HIGHT	HOARY	HONK
GRAND	GUES	GYVES	HALM	HARTS	SHEAR	SHENT	HIKE	HOAS	HONKS
GRANS	AGUES	HAAF	SHALM	HASH	WHEAR	HENTS	HIKED	HOAST	HONKY
GRANT	GUEST	HAAFS	HALMA	SHASH	HEARD	HEPS	HIKER	HOAX	HONS
GRAT	GUFF	HAAR	HALMS	HASHY	HEARE	HEPT	HIKERS	HOBO	PHONS
GRATE	GUFFS	HAARS	HALO	HASK	HEARS	HERB	HIKES	HOBS	HOOD
GRAY	GUID	HACK	HALOS	HASKS	HEARSE	HERBS	HILA	HOCK	HOODS
GRAYS	GUIDE	CHACK	HALSE	HASP	HEART	HERBY	HILAR	CHOCK	HOOEY
GREE	GULA	SHACK	HALT	HASPS	HEARTH	HERD	HILD	SHOCK	HOOF
AGREE	GULAG	THACK	SHALT	HAST	HEARTS	SHERD	HILI	HOCKS	HOOFS
GREED	GULAR	WHACK	HALTS	GHAST	HEAT	HERDS	HILL	HODS	HOOK
GREEN	GULAS	HACKS	HAME	HASTA	CHEAT	HERE	CHILL	HOED	CHOOK
GREES	GULE	HADE	SHAME	HASTE	WHEAT	CHERE	SHILL	SHOED	SHOOK
GREET	GULES	SHADE	HAMED	HASTY	HEATH	SHERE	THILL	HOER	HOOKA

HOOKS	**HOWF**	HUNTS	PICKY	TILLS	**IONS**	**JADES**	**JIBE**	**JOTA**	KAKIS
HOOKY	HOWFF	**HUPS**	TICKY	VILLS	CIONS	**JAGS**	JIBED	JOTAS	**KALE**
HOOP	HOWFS	**HURL**	WICKY	WILLS	LIONS	JAIL	JIBER	**JOTS**	KALES
WHOOP	**HOWK**	CHURL	**ICON**	YILLS	PIONS	JAILS	JIBES	**JOUK**	**KALI**
HOOPS	HOWKS	HURLS	ICONS	**ILLY**	**IOTA**	**JAKE**	**JIBS**	JOUKS	KALIF
HOOT	**HOWL**	HURLY	**IDEA**	BILLY	BIOTA	JAKES	**JIFF**	JOUR	KALIS
SHOOT	THOWL	**HURT**	IDEAL	DILLY	DIOTA	**JAKS**	JIFFS	JOURS	**KAME**
WHOOT	HOWLS	HURTS	IDEAS	FILLY	IOTAS	**JAMB**	JIFFY	**JOWL**	KAMES
HOOTS	**HOWS**	HUSH	**IDEE**	GILLY	**IRES**	JAMBE	**JIGS**	JOWLS	**KAMI**
HOPE	CHOWS	SHUSH	IDEES	HILLY	CIRES	JAMBO	**JILL**	**JOWS**	KAMIK
SHOPE	DHOWS	HUSHY	**IDEM**	SILLY	FIRES	JAMBS	JILLS	**JOYS**	KAMIS
HOPED	SHOWS	HUSK	**IDES**	TILLY	HIRES	JAMBU	**JILT**	**JUBA**	**KANA**
HOPER	HOWSO	HUSKS	AIDES	WILLY	MIRES	**JAMS**	JILTS	JUBAS	KANAS
HOPES	**HOYA**	HUSKY	BIDES	**IMAM**	SIRES	JANE	**JIMP**	**JUBE**	**KANG**
HOPS	HOYAS	**HUSO**	CIDES	IMAMS	TIRES	JANES	JIMPY	JUBES	KANGA
CHOPS	**HOYS**	HUSOS	HIDES	**IMPI**	VIRES	JANN	**JINK**	**JUDO**	KANGS
SHOPS	**HUBS**	**HUSS**	NIDES	IMPIS	WIRES	JANNS	JINKS	JUDOS	**KANS**
WHOPS	CHUBS	HUSSY	RIDES	**IMPS**	**IRID**	JAPE	**JINN**	**JUDS**	**KANT**
HORE	**HUCK**	**HUTS**	SIDES	GIMPS	VIRID	JAPED	DJINN	**JUDY**	KANTS
CHORE	CHUCK	PHUTS	TIDES	LIMPS	IRIDS	JAPES	JINNI	**JUGA**	**KAON**
SHORE	SHUCK	SHUTS	WIDES	PIMPS	**IRIS**	JAPS	JINNS	**JUGAL**	KAONS
WHORE	HUCKS	**HWYL**	**IDLE**	SIMPS	KIRIS	**JARK**	**JINX**	**JUGS**	**KARA**
HORN	**HUED**	HWYLS	SIDLE	TIMPS	SIRIS	JARKS	**JIRD**	**JUJU**	KARAS
SHORN	**HUER**	**HYED**	IDLED	WIMPS	**IRKS**	JARL	JIRDS	JUJUS	**KARAT**
THORN	HUERS	**HYEN**	IDLER	**INBY**	BIRKS	JARLS	**JISM**	**JUKE**	**KART**
HORNS	**HUES**	HYENA	IDLES	INBYE	DIRKS	**JARS**	JISMS	JUKED	SKART
HORNY	**HUFF**	HYENS	**IDLY**	**INCH**	FIRKS	JASP	**JIVE**	JUKES	**KARTS**
HORS	CHUFF	**HYES**	**IDOL**	CINCH	KIRKS	JASPE	JIVED	**JUMP**	**KATI**
KHORS	HUFFS	**HYKE**	IDOLS	FINCH	LIRKS	JASPS	JIVER	JUMPS	KATIS
HORSE	HUFFY	HYKES	**IDYL**	LINCH	MIRKS	JASY	JIVES	**JUMPY**	**KATS**
HORST	**HUGE**	**HYLE**	IDYLL	PINCH	YIRKS	**JATO**	**JIZZ**	**JUNK**	IKATS
HORSY	HUGER	CHYLE	IDYLS	WINCH	**IRON**	JATOS	JOBE	JUNKS	SKATS
HOSE	**HUGS**	PHYLE	**IFFY**	**INFO**	GIRON	JAUP	JOBED	JUNKY	**KAVA**
CHOSE	CHUGS	HYLEG	JIFFY	INFOS	IRONS	JAUPS	JOBES	**JURA**	KAVAS
THOSE	THUGS	HYLES	MIFFY	**INGO**	IRONY	JAWS	**JOBS**	JURAL	**KAWS**
WHOSE	**HUGY**	**HYMN**	NIFFY	BINGO	**ISLE**	**JAYS**	**JOCK**	JURAT	SKAWS
HOSED	**HUIA**	HYMNS	**IGAD**	DINGO	AISLE	JAZY	JOCKO	**JURE**	**KAYO**
HOSEN	HUIAS	**HYPE**	**IKAT**	JINGO	LISLE	**JAZZ**	JOCKS	**JURY**	KAYOE
HOSES	**HULA**	HYPED	**IKATS**	LINGO	ISLED	JAZZY	**JOCO**	**JUST**	KAYOS
HOSS	HULAS	HYPER	**IKON**	PINGO	ISLES	JEAN	**JOES**	JUSTS	**KAYS**
HOST	**HULE**	HYPES	EIKON	INGOT	ISLET	JEANS	**JOEY**	**JUTE**	OKAYS
GHOST	HULES	**HYPO**	IKONS	**INIA**	**ISMS**	JEAT	JOEYS	JUTES	**KAZI**
HOSTA	**HULK**	HYPOS	**ILEA**	**INKS**	GISMS	JEATS	**JOGS**	**JUTS**	KAZIS
HOSTS	HULKS	**HYPS**	PILEA	BINKS	JISMS	**JEED**	**JOHN**	JYNX	**KEAS**
HOTE	HULKY	**IAMB**	ILEAC	DINKS	**ISMY**	**JEEL**	JOHNS	**KADE**	**KEBS**
SHOTE	**HULL**	IAMBI	**ILEX**	FINKS	**ITAS**	JEELS	**JOIN**	KADES	**KECK**
HOTEL	AHULL	IAMBS	SILEX	GINKS	DITAS	JEELY	JOINS	**KADI**	KECKS
HOTEN	HULLO	**IBEX**	**ILIA**	JINKS	PITAS	**JEEP**	**JOINT**	KADIS	**KEDS**
HOTS	HULLS	VIBEX	CILIA	KINKS	**ITCH**	JEEPS	**JOKE**	KAED	**KEEK**
PHOTS	HULLY	**IBIS**	ILIAC	LINKS	AITCH	**JEER**	JOKED	**KAES**	KEEKS
SHOTS	**HUMA**	**ICED**	**ILKA**	MINKS	BITCH	JEERS	JOKER	**KAGO**	**KEEL**
HOUF	HUMAN	DICED	**ILKS**	PINKS	DITCH	**JEES**	JOKES	KAGOS	KEELS
HOUFF	HUMAS	RICED	BILKS	RINKS	FITCH	**JEFF**	**JOKEY**	**KAID**	**KEEN**
HOUFS	**HUMF**	TICED	MILKS	SINKS	HITCH	JEFFS	**JOKY**	KAIDS	KEENS
HOUR	HUMFS	VICED	SILKS	TINKS	MITCH	**JELL**	**JOLE**	KAIE	**KEEP**
HOURI	**HUMP**	**ICER**	**ILLS**	WINKS	PITCH	JELLO	JOLED	KAIES	KEEPS
HOURS	CHUMP	DICER	BILLS	**INKY**	TITCH	JELLS	JOLES	**KAIF**	**KEFS**
HOUT	THUMP	NICER	CILLS	DINKY	WITCH	**JELLY**	**JOLL**	KAIFS	**KEGS**
CHOUT	HUMPH	RICER	DILLS	KINKY	**ITCHY**	**JERK**	JOLLS	**KAIL**	SKEGS
SHOUT	HUMPS	**ICERS**	FILLS	PINKY	**ITEM**	JERKS	**JOLLY**	SKAIL	**KEIR**
HOUTS	HUMPY	**ICES**	GILLS	SINKY	ITEMS	JERKY	**JOLT**	KAILS	KEIRS
HOVE	**HUMS**	BICES	HILLS	ZINKY	**IWIS**	**JESS**	JOLTS	**KAIM**	**KELL**
SHOVE	CHUMS	DICES	JILLS	**INLY**	KIWIS	**JEST**	JOLTY	KAIMS	KELLS
HOVED	**HUNG**	RICES	KILLS	**INNS**	**IXIA**	JESTS	**JOMO**	**KAIN**	KELLY
HOVEL	**HUNK**	SICES	LILLS	JINNS	IXIAS	JETE	JOMOS	KAING	**KELP**
HOVEN	CHUNK	TICES	MILLS	LINNS	**JABS**	JETES	**JOOK**	KAINS	SKELP
HOVER	HUNKS	VICES	NILLS	WINNS	JACK	**JETS**	JOOKS	**KAIS**	KELPS
HOVES	HUNKY	**ICKY**	PILLS	**INRO**	JACKS	JEUX	**JORS**	**KAKA**	KELPY
HOWE	**HUNT**	DICKY	RILLS	**INTO**	JADE	JIAO	**JOSH**	KAKAS	**KELT**
HOWES	SHUNT	MICKY	SILLS	PINTO	JADED	JIAOS	**JOSS**	**KAKI**	KELTS

KELTY, KEMB, KEMBO, KEMBS, KEMP, KEMPS, KEMPT, KENS, KENT, KENTS, KEPI, KEPIS, KEPS, SKEPS, KEPT, KERB, KERBS, KERF, KERFS, KERN, KERNE, KERNS, KESH, KEST, KESTS, KETA, KETAS, KETS, KEYS, KHAN, KHANS, KHAT, KHATS, KHOR, KHORS, KHUD, KHUDS, KIBE, KIBES, KICK, KICKS, KIDS, SKIDS, KIER, SKIER, KIERS, KIFS, KIKE, KIKES, KILD, KILL, SKILL, KILLS, KILN, KILNS, KILO, KILOS, KILP, KILPS, KILT, KILTS, KILTY, KINA, KINAS, KIND, KINDA, KINDS, KINE, KING, AKING

EKING, KINGS, KINK, SKINK, KINKS, KINKY, KINO, KINOS, KINS, SKINS, KIPE, KIPES, KIPP, KIPPS, KIPS, SKIPS, KIRI, KIRIS, KIRK, KIRKS, KIRN, KIRNS, KIRS, KISH, KISS, KIST, KISTS, KITE, KITED, KITES, KITH, KITHE, KITHS, KITS, SKITS, KIWI, KIWIS, KNAG, KNAGS, KNAP, KNAPS, KNAR, KNARL, KNARS, KNEE, KNEED, KNEEL, KNEES, KNEW, KNIT, KNITS, KNOB, KNOBS, KNOP, KNOPS, KNOT, KNOTS, KNOW, KNOWE, KNOWN, KNOWS, KNUB, KNUBS, KNUR, KNURL, KNURR, KNURS, KNUT, KNUTS

KOAN, KOANS, KOAS, KOBS, KOFF, SKOFF, KOFFS, KOHL, KOHLS, KOLA, KOLAS, KOLO, KOLOS, KOND, KONK, KONKS, KONS, IKONS, KOOK, KOOKS, KOOKY, KOPS, KORA, KORAS, KOSS, KOTO, KOTOS, KOTOW, KOWS, KRIS, KSAR, KSARS, KUDU, KUDUS, KUKU, KUKUS, KYAT, KYATS, KYLE, KYLES, KYLEY, KYND, KYNDE, KYNDS, KYNE, KYTE, KYTES, LABS, BLABS, FLABS, SLABS, LACE, GLACE, PLACE, LACED, LACES, LACET, LACEY, LACK, ALACK, BLACK, CLACK, FLACK, SLACK, LACKS, LACS, LACY, LADE

BLADE, CLADE, GLADE, SLADE, LADED, LADEN, LADES, LADS, BLADS, CLADS, GLADS, GLADY, LAER, BLAER, LAERS, LAGS, BLAGS, CLAGS, FLAGS, SLAGS, LAHS, BLAHS, LAIC, LAICS, LAID, PLAID, SLAID, LAIDS, LAIK, GLAIK, LAIKA, LAIKS, LAIN, BLAIN, PLAIN, SLAIN, LAIR, FLAIR, GLAIR, LAIRD, LAIRS, LAIRY, LAKE, FLAKE, SLAKE, LAKED, LAKER, LAKES, LAKH, LAKHS, LAKY, FLAKY, LAMA, LLAMA, LAMAS, LAMB, LAMBS, LAME, BLAME, CLAME, FLAME, LAMED, LAMER, LAMES, LAMP, LAMPS, LAMS, CLAMS

FLAMS, SLAMS, LANA, LANAS, LAND, ALAND, BLAND, ELAND, GLAND, LANDE, LANDS, LANE, PLANE, SLANE, LANES, LANG, ALANG, CLANG, KLANG, SLANG, LANK, BLANK, CLANK, FLANK, PLANK, LANKS, LANKY, LANT, PLANT, SLANT, LANTS, LANX, LAPS, ALAPS, CLAPS, FLAPS, PLAPS, SLAPS, LAPSE, LARD, LARDS, LARDY, LARE, BLARE, FLARE, GLARE, LARES, LARK, LARKS, LARKY, LARN, LARNS, LASE, BLASE, LASED, LASER, LASES, LASH, BLASH, CLASH, FLASH, PLASH, SLASH, LASS, CLASS, GLASS, LASSO, LASSU, LAST, BLAST

PLAST, LASTS, LATE, ALATE, BLATE, ELATE, PLATE, SLATE, LATED, LATEN, LATER, LATEX, LATH, LATHE, LATHI, LATHS, LATHY, LATS, BLATS, CLATS, SLATS, LAUD, BLAUD, LAUDS, LAUF, LAUFS, LAVA, LAVAS, LAVE, CLAVE, SLAVE, LAVED, LAVER, LAVES, LAVS, LAWK, LAWKS, LAWN, LAWNS, LAWNY, LAWS, CLAWS, FLAWS, SLAWS, LAYS, ALAYS, BLAYS, CLAYS, FLAYS, PLAYS, SLAYS, LAZE, BLAZE, GLAZE, LAZED, LAZES, LAZY, GLAZY, LEAD, PLEAD, LEADS, LEADY, LEAF, LEAFS, LEAFY, LEAK, BLEAK

LEAKS, LEAKY, LEAL, LEAM, FLEAM, GLEAM, LEAMS, LEAN, CLEAN, GLEAN, LEANS, LEANT, LEANY, LEAP, LEAPS, LEAPT, LEAR, BLEAR, CLEAR, LEARE, LEARN, LEARS, LEARY, LEAS, LEASE, LEAST, LEAT, BLEAT, CLEAT, PLEAT, LEATS, LECH, LEED, LEEK, CLEEK, GLEEK, SLEEK, LEEKS, LEEP, BLEEP, CLEEP, SLEEP, LEEPS, LEER, FLEER, SLEER, LEERS, LEERY, LEES, FLEES, GLEES, LEESE, LEET, FLEET, GLEET, SLEET, LEETS, LEFT, ALEFT, CLEFT, LEFTE, LEFTS, LEFTY, LEGS

CLEGS, FLEGS, LEHR, LEHRS, LEIR, LEIRS, LEIS, GLEIS, VLEIS, LEISH, LEKE, LEKS, LEME, LEMED, LEMEL, LEMES, LEND, BLEND, LENDS, LENG, LENGS, LENO, LENOS, LENS, GLENS, LENT, BLENT, GLENT, OLENT, LENTI, LENTO, LEPS, LERE, LERED, LERES, LESS, BLESS, LEST, BLEST, LESTS, LETS, BLETS, LEVA, LEVE, CLEVE, LEVEE, LEVEL, LEVER, LEVY, LEWD, LEYS, BLEYS, FLEYS, GLEYS, SLEYS, LEZZ, LEZZY, LIAR, LIARD, LIARS, LIART, LIBS, GLIBS, LICE, SLICE, LICH, LICHI, LICHT, LICK

CLICK, FLICK, SLICK, LICKS, LIDO, LIDOS, LIDS, LIED, CLIED, PLIED, LIEF, LIEFS, LIEN, LIENS, LIER, LIERS, LIES, CLIES, FLIES, PLIES, VLIES, LIEU, LIEUS, LIFE, LIFER, LIFT, LIFTS, CLIFT, GLIFT, LIGS, LIKE, ALIKE, GLIKE, YLIKE, LIKED, LIKEN, LIKER, LIKES, LILL, LILLS, LILO, LILOS, LILT, LILTS, LILY, SLILY, LIMA, LIMAS, LIMAX, LIMB, CLIMB, LIMBO, LIMBS, LIME, LIMED, LIMEN, LIMES, LIMEY, LIMN, LIMNS, LIMP, BLIMP, FLIMP, LIMPS

LIMY, BLIMY, SLIMY, LIND, BLIND, LINDS, LINE, ALINE, CLINE, LINED, LINEN, LINER, LINES, LINEY, LING, CLING, FLING, SLING, LINGA, LINGO, LINGS, LINGY, LINK, BLINK, CLINK, PLINK, SLINK, LINKS, LINN, LINNS, LINNY, LINO, LINOS, LINS, BLINS, LINT, CLINT, FLINT, GLINT, LINTS, LINTY, LINY, LION, LIONS, LIPS, BLIPS, CLIPS, FLIPS, SLIPS, LIRA, LIRAS, LIRE, LIRK, LIRKS, LISK, FLISK, GLISK, LISKS, LISP, LISPS, LIST, BLIST, LISTS, LITE, BLITE, ELITE, FLITE, LITED, LITER, LITES

LITH	**LOKE**	LOREL	LOWER	PLUMS	MACKS	**MARD**	MAYST	MERES	**MILOR**
LITHE	BLOKE	LORES	LOWES	SLUMS	**MACS**	MARDY	**MAZE**	**MERI**	MILOS
LITHO	CLOKE	**LORN**	LOWN	**LUNE**	**MADE**	**MARE**	AMAZE	MERIL	**MILS**
LITHS	LOKES	**LORY**	BLOWN	LUNES	**MADS**	MARES	MAZED	MERIS	**MILT**
LIVE	LOLL	FLORY	CLOWN	**LUNG**	**MAGE**	**MARG**	MAZER	MERIT	MILTS
ALIVE	LOLLS	GLORY	FLOWN	CLUNG	IMAGE	MARGE	MAZES	MERK	**MILTZ**
BLIVE	LOLLY	**LOSE**	LOWND	FLUNG	MAGES	MARGS	**MAZY**	MERKS	**MIME**
OLIVE	**LOMA**	CLOSE	LOWNE	SLUNG	**MAGG**	**MARK**	**MEAD**	**MERL**	MIMED
SLIVE	LOMAS	LOSED	LOWNS	LUNGE	MAGGS	MARKS	MEADS	MERLE	MIMER
LIVED	**LOME**	LOSEL	LOWS	LUNGI	**MAGI**	**MARL**	**MEAL**	MERLS	MIMES
LIVEN	LOMES	LOSEN	BLOWS	LUNGS	MAGIC	MARLE	MEALS	**MESA**	**MINA**
LIVER	**LONE**	LOSER	CLOWS	**LUNT**	MAGS	MARLS	MEALY	MESAL	MINAE
LIVES	ALONE	LOSES	FLOWS	BLUNT	**MAID**	MARLY	**MEAN**	MESAS	MINAR
LOAD	CLONE	**LOSH**	GLOWS	LUNTS	MAIDS	**MARM**	MEANE	**MESE**	MINAS
LOADS	LONER	FLOSH	PLOWS	**LURE**	**MAIK**	SMARM	MEANS	MESEL	**MIND**
LOAF	**LONG**	SLOSH	SLOWS	ALURE	SMAIK	MARMS	MEANT	MESES	MINDS
LOAFS	FLONG	**LOSS**	LOWSE	LURED	MAIKO	**MARS**	MEANY	**MESH**	**MINE**
LOAM	PLONG	LOSSY	**LOWT**	LURES	MAIKS	MARSH	**MEAT**	MESHY	AMINE
CLOAM	LONGA	**LOST**	LOWTS	**LURK**	**MAIL**	**MART**	MEATH	**MESS**	IMINE
LOAMS	LONGE	**LOTA**	**LOYS**	LURKS	MAILE	SMART	MEATS	MESSY	MINED
LOAMY	LONGS	FLOTA	CLOYS	**LURS**	MAILS	MARTS	MEATY	**METE**	MINER
LOAN	**LOOF**	LOTAH	PLOYS	**LUSH**	**MAIM**	**MASE**	**MEED**	METED	MINES
SLOAN	ALOOF	LOTAS	**LUAU**	BLUSH	MAIMS	MASED	MEEDS	METER	**MING**
LOANS	KLOOF	**LOTE**	LUAUS	FLUSH	**MAIN**	MASER	**MEEK**	METES	MINGS
LOBE	LOOFA	CLOTE	**LUCE**	PLUSH	AMAIN	MASES	SMEEK	**MEUS**	MINGY
GLOBE	LOOFS	FLOTE	LUCES	SLUSH	MAINS	**MASH**	**MEER**	EMEUS	**MINI**
LOBED	**LOOK**	LOTES	**LUCK**	LUSHY	**MAKE**	SMASH	AMEER	MEUSE	MINIM
LOBES	LOOKS	**LOTH**	CLUCK	**LUSK**	MAKER	MASHY	EMEER	**MEVE**	MINIS
LOBI	**LOOM**	CLOTH	PLUCK	LUSKS	MAKES	**MASK**	MEERS	MEVED	**MINK**
LOBO	BLOOM	SLOTH	LUCKS	**LUST**	**MAKO**	MASKS	**MEET**	MEVES	MINKE
LOBOS	GLOOM	**LOTO**	LUCKY	LUSTS	MAKOS	**MASS**	MEETS	**MEWL**	MINKS
LOBS	SLOOM	LOTOS	**LUDO**	LUSTY	**MAKS**	AMASS	**MEIN**	MEWLS	**MINO**
BLOBS	LOOMS	**LOTS**	LUDOS	**LUTE**	**MALE**	MASSA	MEINS	**MEWS**	MINOR
GLOBS	**LOON**	BLOTS	**LUDS**	ELUTE	MALES	MASSE	MEINT	SMEWS	MINOS
SLOBS	LOONS	CLOTS	**LUES**	FLUTE	**MALI**	MASSY	MEINY	**MEZE**	**MINT**
LOCH	LOONY	PLOTS	BLUES	LUTED	MALIC	**MAST**	**MELD**	MEZES	MINTS
LOCHS	**LOOP**	SLOTS	CLUES	LUTER	MALIS	MASTS	MELDS	**MHOS**	MINTY
LOCI	BLOOP	**LOUD**	FLUES	LUTES	**MALL**	MASTY	**MELL**	**MICA**	**MINX**
LOCK	CLOOP	ALOUD	GLUES	**LUTZ**	SMALL	**MASU**	MELLS	MICAS	MINY
BLOCK	SLOOP	CLOUD	SLUES	KLUTZ	MALLS	MASUS	**MELT**	**MICE**	**MIRE**
CLOCK	LOOPS	**LOUN**	**LUFF**	**LUXE**	**MALM**	**MATE**	MELTS	AMICE	MIRED
FLOCK	LOOPY	LOUND	BLUFF	LUXES	SMALM	AMATE	**MEMO**	**MICK**	MIRES
LOCKS	**LOOR**	LOUNS	FLUFF	LYAM	MALMS	MATED	MEMOS	MICKS	**MIRK**
LOCO	FLOOR	**LOUP**	PLUFF	LYAMS	**MALS**	MATER	**MEND**	MICKY	MIRKS
LOCOS	LOORD	LOUPE	LUFFA	**LYES**	**MALT**	MATES	AMEND	**MICO**	MIRKY
LODE	**LOOS**	LOUPS	LUFFS	**LYME**	SMALT	MATEY	EMEND	MICOS	**MIRS**
GLODE	LOOSE	**LOUR**	**LUGE**	LYMES	MALTS	**MATH**	MENDS	**MIDI**	AMIRS
LODEN	**LOOT**	LOURE	LUGED	**LYMS**	MALTY	AMEND	**MEND**?	MIDIS	EMIRS
LODES	CLOOT	LOURS	LUGES	**LYNE**	MAMA	EMEND	MENDS	**MIDS**	SMIRS
LOFT	SLOOT	LOURY	LUGS	LYNES	MAMAS	MATHS	MENE	MIDST	**MIRY**
ALOFT	LOOTS	**LOUT**	**LUGS**	**LYNX**	MAMS	AMEND	AMENE	MIEN	**MISE**
LOFTS	**LOPE**	CLOUT	GLUGS	LYRE	IMAMS	MATS	MENED	MIENS	MISER
LOFTY	ELOPE	FLOUT	PLUGS	**LYRE**?	**MANA**	MATES	MENES	**MIFF**	MISES
LOGE	SLOPE	GLOUT	SLUGS	LYRES	MANAS	**MATT**	MENE	MIFFS	**MISO**
ELOGE	LOPED	LOUTS	**LUIT**	**LYSE**	**MAND**	MATTE	AMENE	MIFFY	MISOS
LOGES	LOPER	**LOVE**	SLUIT	LYSED	**MANE**	**MATY**	MENED	**MIKE**	**MISS**
LOGO	LOPES	CLOVE	**LUKE**	LYSES	MANED	**MAUD**	MENES	MIKES	AMISS
LOGOS	LOPED	GLOVE	FLUKE	**LYTE**	MANEH	MAUDS	**MENT**	**MILD**	MISSA
LOGS	**LOPS**	SLOVE	**LULL**	LYTED	MANES	**MAUL**	AMENT	MILDS	MISSY
CLOGS	CLOPS	LOVED	LULLS	LYTES	MANET	MAULS	**MENU**	**MILE**	**MIST**
FLOGS	ELOPS	LOVER	LULU	LYTES	**MANS**	**MAUN**	MENUS	SMILE	MISTS
SLOGS	FLOPS	LOVES	LULUS	FLYTE	MANSE	MAUND	**MENG**	MILER	MISTY
LOID	SLOPS	LOVEY	**LUMP**	**MAAR**	**MANY**	**MAWK**	MENGE	MILES	**MITE**
SLOID	**LORD**	**LOWE**	CLUMP	MAARS	**MAPS**	MAWKS	MENGS	**MILK**	SMITE
LOIDS	LORDS	ALOWE	FLUMP	MACE	**MARA**	MAWKY	**MENT**	MILKS	MITER
LOIN	LORDY	LOWED	PLUMP	MACED	MARAH	**MAWR**	AMENT	MILKY	MITES
ELOIN	**LORE**		LUMPS	MACER	MARAS	MAWRS	MENE	**MILL**	**MITT**
LOINS	BLORE		LUMPY	MACES	**MARC**	MAWS	MERED	MILLE	MITTS
LOIR			**LUMS**	**MACK**	MARCH	**MAXI**	MEREL	MILLS	**MITY**
LOIRS			ALUMS	SMACK	MARCS	**MAYS**	MERER	**MILO**	

AMITY	MOODY	MOTTY	MURKS	**NANA**	NEONS	KNITS	**NOTT**	ROARS	ODYLE
MIXT	**MOOI**	**MOUE**	MURKY	ANANA	**NEPS**	UNITS	**NOUL**	SOARS	ODYLS
MIXY	**MOOL**	MOUES	**MURL**	NANAS	**NERD**	**NIXY**	NOULD	VOARS	**OFAY**
MIZZ	MOOLA	**MOUP**	MURLS	**NANS**	NERDS	**NOBS**	NOULE	GOARY	OFAYS
MNAS	MOOLI	MOUPS	MURLY	**NAOI**	**NESH**	KNOBS	NOULS	HOARY	**OFFS**
MOAN	MOOLS	**MOUS**	**MUSE**	**NAOS**	**NESS**	SNOBS	**NOUN**	ROARY	BOFFS
MOANS	MOOLY	SMOUS	AMUSE	**NAPA**	**NEST**	**NOCK**	NOUNS	BOAST	COFFS
MOAS	**MOON**	MOUSE	MUSED	NAPAS	NESTS	KNOCK	**NOUP**	COAST	DOFFS
MOAT	MOONS	MOUSED	MUSER	**NAPE**	**NETE**	NOCKS	NOUPS	HOAST	GOFFS
MOATS	MOONY	MOUSER	MUSES	NAPES	NETES	**NODE**	**NOUS**	LOAST	KOFFS
MOBS	**MOOP**	MOUSES	MUSET	**NAPS**	**NETS**	ANODE	**NOUT**	ROAST	TOFFS
MOCK	MOOPS	MOUSET	**MUSH**	KNAPS	**NETT**	NODES	**NODI**	TOAST	**OGAM**
SMOCK	**MOOR**	MOUST	MUSHA	SNAPS	NETTS	**NODS**	**NODS**	OASTS	OGAMS
MOCKS	SMOOR	MOUSY	MUSHY	**NARD**	NETTY	SNODS	SNOUT	LOATH	**OGEE**
MODE	MOORS	**MOVE**	**MUSK**	NARDS	**NEUK**	**NOEL**	TOAST	OATHS	OGEES
MODEL	MOORY	AMOVE	MUSKS	**NARE**	NEUKS	NOELS	**NOVA**	OATS	**OGLE**
MODEM	**MOOS**	EMOVE	MUSKY	SNARE	**NEUM**	**NOES**	NOVAE	BOATS	BOGLE
MODES	MOOSE	MOVED	**MUSS**	NARES	NEUME	**NOGS**	NOVAS	COATS	FOGLE
MODI	**MOOT**	MOVER	MUSSE	SNARK	NEUMS	SNOGS	**NOWN**	DOATS	OGLED
MODII	SMOOT	MOVES	MUSSY	**NARK**	**NEVE**	**NOIL**	**NOWL**	GOATS	OGLER
MODS	MOOTS	**MOVY**	MUST	NARKS	NEVEL	NOILS	NOWLS	MOATS	OGLES
MOES	**MOPE**	MOWA	MUSTH	NARKY	NEVER	**NOLE**	KNOWN	OBEY	**OGRE**
MOGS	MOPED	MOWAS	MUSTS	**NARY**	NEVES	NOLES	**NOWS**	OBEYS	OGRES
SMOGS	MOPER	**MOWN**	MUSTY	SNARY	**NEWS**	**NOLL**	**NOWT**	COBIA	**OHMS**
MOHR	MOPES	MOWS	**MUTE**	**NATS**	ENEWS	NOLLS	NOWTS	OBIA	OHOS
MOHRS	**MOPS**	**MOYL**	MUTED	GNATS	NEWSY	KNOLL	**NOWY**	OBIAS	COHOS
MOIL	MOPSY	MOYLE	MUTER	**NAVE**	**NEWT**	NOLLS	SNOWY	OBIS	TOHOS
MOILS	**MOPY**	MOYLS	MUTES	KNAVE	NEWTS	**NOMA**	**NOYS**	OBIT	**OIKS**
MOIT	**MORA**	**MOYS**	**MUTT**	NAVEL	**NIBS**	NOMAD	**NUBS**	OOBIT	HOIKS
MOITS	MORAL	**MOZE**	MUTTS	NAVES	SNIBS	NOMAS	**OBIS**	OBITS	**OILS**
MOKE	MORAS	MOZED	**MYAL**	NAVEW	**NICE**	**NOME**	KNUBS	OBOE	BOILS
SMOKE	MORAT	MOZES	MYALL	**NAVY**	NICER	GNOME	SNUBS	OBOES	COILS
MOKES	MORAY	**MOZZ**	**MYNA**	**NAYS**	**NICK**	NOMEN	**NUDE**	**OBOL**	FOILS
MOKI	**MORE**	**MUCH**	MYNAH	**NAZE**	NICKS	NOMES	NUDER	OBOLI	MOILS
MOKIS	SMORE	**MUCK**	MYNAS	NAZES	SNICK	**NOMS**	NUDES	OBOLS	NOILS
MOKO	MOREL	MUCKS	**MYTH**	**NEAL**	NICKS	**NONE**	**NUKE**	**OBOL**	ROILS
SMOKO	MORES	MUCKY	MYTHS	NEALS	**NIDE**	NONES	NUKED	OBOLS	SOILS
MOKOS	**MORN**	**MUDS**	**NAAM**	**NEAP**	SNIDE	NONET	NUKES	OCAS	TOILS
MOLD	MORNE	**MUFF**	NAAMS	SNEAP	NIDES	**NONG**	**NULL**	COCAS	**OILY**
MOLDS	MORNS	MUFFS	**NAAN**	NEAPS	**NIDI**	NONGS	NULLA	OCHE	DOILY
MOLE	**MORS**	MUFFS	NAANS	**NEAR**	**NIDS**	**NOOK**	NULLS	BOCHE	ROILY
MOLES	MORSE	**MUGS**	**NABK**	ANEAR	**NIED**	NOOKS	**NUMB**	OCHER	SOILY
MOLL	**MORT**	SMUGS	NABKS	NEARS	**NIEF**	NOOKY	NUMBS	OCHES	**OINT**
MOLLA	AMORT	**MUID**	**NABS**	**NEAT**	NIEFS	**NOOP**	**NUNS**	**ODAL**	JOINT
MOLLS	MORTS	MUIDS	SNABS	NEATH	**NIES**	NOOPS	**NURD**	MODAL	NOINT
MOLLY	**MOSE**	**MUIL**	**NACH**	**NEBS**	**NIFE**	SNOOK	NURDS	NODAL	POINT
MOLT	MOSED	MUILS	NACHE	SNEBS	NIFES	**NOOP**	**NURL**	PODAL	OINTS
SMOLT	MOSES	**MUIR**	**NADA**	**NECK**	**NIFF**	SNOOP	**NURL**	ODALS	**OKAY**
YMOLT	MOSEY	MUIRS	NADAS	NECKS	NIFFS	**NOPE**	NURLS	ODAS	OKAYS
MOLTO	**MOSS**	**MULE**	**NAFF**	SNECK	NIFFY	**NORI**	KNURR	CODAS	**OKES**
MOLTS	MOSSY	EMULE	NAFFS	**NEDS**	**NIFF**	NORIA	KNURR	SODAS	BOKES
MOLY	**MOST**	MULES	**NAGA**	SNEDS	NIFFY	NORIS	NURRS	**ODDS**	COKES
MOME	MOSTS	MULEY	NAGAS	**NEED**	**NIGH**	NORK	**NURS**	**ODEA**	HOKES
MOMES	**MOTE**	**MULL**	**NAGS**	KNEED	ANIGH	NORKS	KNURS	IODIC	JOKES
MOMS	EMOTE	MULLS	**NAGS**	SNEED	NIGHS	**NORM**	NURSE	SODIC	LOKES
MONA	SMOTE	**MUMM**	KNAGS	NEEDS	NIGHT	ENORM	**NUTS**	**ODOR**	MOKES
MONAD	MOTED	MUMMS	SNAGS	NEEDY	**NILL**	NORMA	KNUTS	ODORS	POKES
MONAL	MOTEL	MUMMY	**NAIF**	**NEEM**	NILLS	NORMS	**NYAS**	**ODSO**	ROKES
MONAS	MOTEN	**MUMP**	**NAIK**	NEEMS	**NILS**	**NOSE**	**NYED**	GODSO	SOKES
MONG	MOTES	MUMPS	NAIKS	**NEEP**	ANILS	NOSED	**NYES**	**ODSOS**	TOKES
AMONG	MOTET	**MUMS**	**NAIL**	NEEPS	**NIMS**	NOSER	**OAFS**	**ODIC**	YOKES
EMONG	MOTEY	MUMSY	NAILS	**NEFS**	**NINE**	NOSES	GOAFS	IODIC	**OKRA**
MONGS	**MOTH**	MUMSY	SNAIL	**NEIF**	NINES	NOSEY	LOAFS	SODIC	KOKRA
MONK	MOTHS	**MUON**	**NAIN**	NEIFS	**NIPS**	**NOSH**	**OAKS**	**ODOR**	OKRAS
MONKS	MOTHY	MUONS	**NALA**	**NEKS**	SNIPS	NOSY	BOAKS	ODORS	**OLDS**
MONO	**MOTS**	**MURE**	NALAS	**NEMN**	**NIRL**	**NOTE**	SOAKS	**ODSO**	COLDS
MONOS	**MOTT**	EMURE	**NAME**	NEMNS	NIRLS	NOTED	**OAKY**	GODSO	FOLDS
MONY	MOTTE	MURED	NAMED	**NENE**	NIRLY	NOTER	**OARS**	**ODSO**	GOLDS
MOOD	MOTTO	MURES	NAMER	NENES	**NISI**	NOTES	BOARS	ODSOS	HOLDS
MOODS	MOTTS	**MURK**	**NAMS**	NEON	**NITS**	NOTES	HOARS	**ODYL**	MOLDS

SOLDS	GOOFS	MOPED	SORTS	**OUZO**	OWRES	PALET	**PART**	PEARE	PENKS
WOLDS	HOOFS	OOPED	TORTS	OUZOS	**OWTS**	**PALL**	APART	PEARL	**PENS**
OLDY	LOOFS	ROPED	WORTS	**OVAL**	DOWTS	SPALL	SPART	PEARS	OPENS
GOLDY	POOFS	TOPED	ORYX	OVALS	LOWTS	PALLA	PARTI	PEART	**PENT**
OLEO	ROOFS	**OPEN**	OSSA	**OVEN**	NOWTS	PALLS	PARTS	**PEAS**	SPENT
OLEOS	WOOFS	OPENS	FOSSA	COVEN	ROWTS	PALLY	PARTY	PEASE	PENTS
OLID	OOHS	**OPES**	**OTIC**	HOVEN	TOWTS	PALM	**PASH**	**PEAT**	**PEON**
SOLID	BOOHS	COPES	LOTIC	WOVEN	**OXEN**	PALMS	PASHA	SPEAT	PEONS
OLIO	**OOMS**	DOPES	OTTO	OVENS	BOXEN	PALMY	PASHM	PEATS	PEONY
POLIO	BOOMS	HOPES	LOTTO	**OVER**	WOXEN	PALP	**PASS**	PEATY	**PEPO**
OLIOS	COOMS	LOPES	MOTTO	COVER	**OXER**	PALPI	PASSE	PEBA	PEPOS
OLLA	DOOMS	MOPES	POTTO	DOVER	BOXER	PALPS	**PAST**	PEBAS	**PEPS**
HOLLA	LOOMS	POPES	OTTOS	HOVER	OXERS	**PALS**	PASTA	**PECH**	**PERE**
MOLLA	ROOMS	ROPES	**OUCH**	LOVER	**OYER**	OPALS	PASTE	PECHS	PERES
OLLAS	SOOMS	TOPES	COUCH	MOVER	COYER	PALSY	PASTS	**PECK**	**PERI**
OLLAV	TOOMS	**OPTS**	MOUCH	ROVER	FOYER	**PALY**	PASTY	SPECK	PERIL
OLMS	ZOOMS	**OPUS**	POUCH	OVERS	TOYER	**PAMS**	**PATE**	PECKE	PERIS
HOLMS	**OONS**	MOPUS	TOUCH	OVERT	OYERS	**PAND**	SPATE	PECKS	**PERK**
OLPE	BOONS	**ORAL**	VOUCH	**OVUM**	**OYES**	PANDA	PATED	**PECS**	PERKS
GOLPE	COONS	CORAL	**OUKS**	**OWED**	OYEZ	PANDS	PATEN	SPECS	PERKY
OLPES	GOONS	GORAL	BOUKS	BOWED	**PACA**	PANDY	PATER	**PEDS**	**PERM**
OMBU	LOONS	HORAL	GOUKS	COWED	PACAS	**PANE**	PATES	**PEED**	SPERM
OMBUS	MOONS	LORAL	JOUKS	DOWED	**PACE**	SPANE	PATH	**PEEK**	PERMS
OMEN	NOONS	MORAL	POUKS	JOWED	APACE	PANED	PATHS	**PEEL**	**PERN**
NOMEN	POONS	PORAL	SOUKS	LOWED	SPACE	PANEL	PATS	PEELS	PERNS
WOMEN	ROONS	RORAL	TOUKS	MOWED	PACED	PANES	PATSY	**PEEN**	**PERT**
OMENS	TOONS	SORAL	YOUKS	NOWED	PACER	PANG	PAUA	PEENS	APERT
OMER	WOONS	ORALS	**OULK**	ROWED	PACES	SPANG	PAUAS	**PEEP**	PERTS
COMER	ZOONS	**ORBS**	OULKS	SOWED	PACEY	PANGA	PAUL	PEEPE	**PERV**
HOMER	**OONT**	SORBS	**OUPH**	TOWED	**PACK**	PANGS	SPAUL	PEEPS	PERVE
VOMER	OONTS	**ORBY**	OUPHE	VOWED	PACKS	**PANS**	PAULS	**PEER**	PERVS
OMERS	**OOPS**	FORBY	OUPHS	WOWED	**PACO**	SPANS	**PAVE**	SPEER	**PESO**
OMIT	COOPS	**ORCS**	**OUPS**	**OWER**	PACOS	PANSY	PAVED	PEERS	PESOS
VOMIT	GOOPS	TORCS	COUPS	BOWER	**PACT**	**PANT**	PAVEN	PEERY	**PEST**
OMITS	HOOPS	**ORDS**	DOUPS	COWER	EPACT	PANTO	PAVER	**PEES**	PESTO
ONCE	LOOPS	BORDS	LOUPS	DOWER	PACTA	PANTS	PAVES	EPEES	PESTS
BONCE	NOOPS	CORDS	MOUPS	LOWER	PACTS	**PAPA**	PAWA	**PEGH**	**PETS**
NONCE	POOPS	FORDS	NOUPS	MOWER	**PACY**	PAPAL	PAWAS	PEGHS	SPETS
PONCE	ROOPS	LORDS	ROUPS	POWER	SPACY	PAPAS	PAWAW	**PEGS**	**PEWS**
SONCE	SOOPS	SORDS	SOUPS	ROWER	**PADS**	PAPAW	**PAWK**	**PEIN**	SPEWS
ONCER	YOOPS	WORDS	**OURN**	SOWER	**PAGE**	**PAPE**	PAWKS	PEINS	**PHEW**
ONCES	**OOSE**	**ORES**	BOURN	TOWER	APAGE	PAPER	PAWKY	**PEKE**	**PHIS**
ONER	BOOSE	BORES	MOURN	**OWES**	PAGED	PAPES	**PAWL**	PEKES	**PHIZ**
BONER	GOOSE	CORES	YOURN	BOWES	PAGER	**PAPS**	SPAWL	**PELA**	**PHOH**
GONER	LOOSE	FORES	**OURS**	HOWES	PAGES	**PARA**	PAWLS	PELAS	**PHON**
LONER	MOOSE	GORES	COURS	LOWES	**PAHS**	PARAS	**PAWN**	**PELE**	PHONE
MONER	NOOSE	LORES	FOURS	YOWES	OPAHS	**PARD**	SPAWN	PELES	PHONS
ONERS	ROOSE	MORES	HOURS	**OWLS**	**PAID**	SPARD	PAWNS	**PELF**	PHONY
ONES	OOSES	PORES	JOURS	BOWLS	APAID	PARDI	**PAWS**	PELFS	**PHOS**
BONES	**OOSY**	SORES	LOURS	COWLS	**PAIK**	PARDS	SPAWS	**PELL**	**PHOT**
CONES	GOOSY	TORES	POURS	DOWLS	PAIKS	PARDY	**PAYS**	PELLS	PHOTO
HONES	**OOZE**	YORES	SOURS	FOWLS	**PAIL**	**PARE**	APAYS	**PELT**	PHOTS
NONES	BOOZE	**ORFE**	TOURS	GOWLS	PAILS	SPARE	PAYSD	SPELT	**PHUT**
PONES	OOZED	ORFES	YOURS	HOWLS	**PAIN**	PARED	**PEAG**	PELTA	PHUTS
RONES	OOZES	**ORFS**	**OUST**	JOWLS	SPAIN	PAREO	PEAGS	PELTS	**PIAS**
SONES	**OOZY**	**ORGY**	JOUST	NOWLS	PAINS	PARER	**PEAK**	**PEND**	**PICA**
TONES	BOOZY	PORGY	MOUST	SOWLS	PAINT	PARES	APEAK	SPEND	SPICA
ZONES	WOOZY	**ORLE**	ROUST	YOWLS	**PAIR**	PAREU	SPEAK	PENDS	PICAS
ONLY	**OPAH**	ORLES	OUSTS	**OWLY**	PAIRE	**PARK**	PEAKS	**PENE**	**PICE**
FONLY	OPAHS	**ORRA**	**OUTS**	LOWLY	PAIRS	SPARK	PEAKY	PENED	SPICE
ONST	**OPAL**	MORRA	BOUTS	**OWNS**	**PAIS**	PARKA	**PEAL**	PENES	**PICK**
ONTO	COPAL	SORRA	DOUTS	DOWNS	PAISA	PARKI	SPEAL	**PENI**	SPICK
CONTO	NOPAL	**ORTS**	GOUTS	GOWNS	PAISE	PARKS	PEALS	PENIE	PICKS
ONUS	OPALS	BORTS	HOUTS	LOWNS	**PALE**	PARKY	**PEAN**	PENIS	PICKY
BONUS	**OPED**	DORTS	LOUTS	POWNS	SPALE	**PARR**	SPEAN	**PENK**	**PICS**
TONUS	COPED	FORTS	POUTS	TOWNS	PALEA	PARRS	PEANS		EPICS
ONYX	DOPED	MORTS	ROUTS	**OWRE**	PALED	PARRY	**PEAR**		SPICS
OOFS	HOPED	PORTS	SOUTS	HOWRE	PALER	**PARS**	SPEAR		**PIED**
COOFS	LOPED	RORTS	TOUTS	POWRE	PALES	PARSE			SPIED

PIER PIERS PIERT **PIES** SPIES **PIET** PIETA PIETS PIETY **PIGS** **PIKA** PIKAS **PIKE** SPIKE PIKED PIKER PIKES **PILA** PILAU PILAW **PILE** SPILE PILEA PILED PILEI PILER PILES **PILI** PILIS **PILL** SPILL PILLS **PIMP** PIMPS **PINA** SPINA PINAS **PINE** OPINE SPINE PINED PINES PINEY **PING** APING OPING PINGO PINGS **PINK** SPINK PINKO PINKS PINKY **PINS** SPINS **PINT** PINTA PINTO PINTS **PINY** SPINY **PION** PIONS PIONY **PIOY** PIOYE PIOYS **PIPA** PIPAL PIPAS

PIPE PIPED PIPER PIPES **PIPI** PIPIS PIPIT **PIPS** **PIPY** **PIRL** PIRLS **PIRN** PIRNS **PIRS** **PISE** PISES **PISH** APISH **PISS** **PITA** PITAS **PITH** PITHS PITHY **PITS** SPITS **PITY** **PIUM** OPIUM PIUMS **PIXY** **PIZE** PIZES **PLAN** PLANE PLANK PLANS PLANT **PLAP** PLAPS **PLAT** SPLAT PLATE PLATS PLATY **PLAY** SPLAY UPLAY PLAYA PLAYS **PLEA** PLEAD PLEAS PLEAT **PLEB** PLEBS **PLED** UPLED **PLIE** PLIED PLIER PLIES **PLIM** PLIMS **PLOD** PLODS **PLOP** PLOPS **PLOT** PLOTS

PLOW PLOWS **PLOY** PLOYS **PLUG** PLUGS **PLUM** PLUMB PLUME PLUMP PLUMS PLUMY **PLUS** PLUSH **POAS** **POCK** POCKS POCKY **POCO** **PODS** APODS **POEM** POEMS **POET** POETS **POIS** POISE **POKE** SPOKE POKED POKER POKES **POKY** **POLE** POLED POLER POLES POLEY **POLK** POLKA POLKS **POLL** POLLS POLLY **POLO** POLOS **POLT** POLTS **POLY** POLYP POLYS **POME** POMES **POMP** POMPS **POMS** **POND** PONDS **PONE** PONES PONEY **PONG** PONGO PONGS PONGY **PONK** PONKS **PONS** **PONY** **POOD**

POODS **POOF** SPOOF POOFS POOFY **POOH** **POOK** SPOOK POOKA POOKS **POOL** SPOOL POOLS **POON** SPOON POONS **POOP** APOOP POOPS **POOR** SPOOR POORT POORTS POOS **POOT** POOTS **POPE** POPES POPS POPSY **PORE** SPORE PORED PORER PORES **PORK** PORKS PORKY **PORN** PORNO PORNS **PORT** APORT SPORT PORTA PORTS PORTY **PORY** **POSE** POSED POSER POSES **POSH** SPOSH **POSS** POSSE **POST** POSTS **POSY** **POTE** POTED POTES **POTS** SPOTS **POTT** POTTO POTTS **POTTY** **POUF** POUFS **POUK**

POUKE **POUKS** **POUR** POURS **POUT** SPOUT POUTS POUTY **POWN** POWND POWNS POWNY **POWS** **POXY** EPOXY **POZZ** POZZY **PRAD** SPRAD PRADS **PRAM** PRAMS **PRAT** SPRAT PRATE PRATS PRATY **PRAU** PRAUS **PRAY** PRAYS **PREE** PREED PREEN PREES **PREP** PREPS **PREX** PREXY **PREY** PREYS **PRIG** SPRIG PRIGS **PRIM** PRIMA PRIME PRIMO PRIMP PRIMS PRIMY **PROA** PROAS **PROD** SPROD PRODS **PROF** PROFS **PROG** SPROG PROGS **PROM** PROMO PROMS **PROO** PROOF **PROP** PROPS

PROS PROSE PROSY **PROW** PROWL PROWS **PRUH** **PRYS** PRYSE **PSIS** APSIS **PSST** **PUBS** **PUCE** PUCES **PUCK** PUCKA PUCKS **PUDS** SPUDS PUDSY **PUER** PUERS **PUFF** PUFFS PUFFY **PUGH** **PUGS** **PUIR** **PUJA** PUJAS **PUKE** PUKED PUKER PUKES **PULE** SPULE PULED PULER PULES **PULK** PULKA PULKS **PULL** PULLS **PULP** PULPS PULPY **PULU** PULUS **PULY** **PUMA** PUMAS **PUMP** PUMPS **PUMY** **PUNA** PUNAS **PUNK** SPUNK PUNKA PUNKS **PUNS** **PUNT** PUNTO PUNTS PUNTY **PUNY** **PUPA**

PUPAE PUPAL PUPAS **PUPS** **PURE** PURED PUREE PURER PURES **PURI** PURIM PURIN PURIS **PURL** PURLS **PURR** PURRS **PURS** PURSE PURSY **PUSH** PUSHY **PUSS** PUSSY **PUTS** **PUTT** PUTTI PUTTO PUTTS PUTTY **PUTZ** **PUYS** **PYAT** PYATS **PYES** **PYET** PYETS **PYNE** PYNED PYNES **PYOT** PYOTS **PYRE** PYRES **PYRO** PYROS **QADI** QADIS **QATS** **QUAD** SQUAD QUADS **QUAG** QUAGS **QUAT** SQUAT QUATS **QUAY** QUAYD QUAYS **QUEP** **QUEY** QUEYN QUEYS **QUID** SQUID QUIDS **QUIM**

QUIMS **QUIN** QUINA QUINE QUINS QUINT **QUIP** EQUIP QUIPO QUIPS QUIPU **QUIT** SQUIT QUITE QUITS **QUIZ** **QUOD** QUODS **QUOP** QUOPS **RABI** RABIC RABID RABIS **RACA** **RACE** RACED RACER RACES **RACH** RACHE **RACK** RACKS **RACY** **RADE** **RADS** BRADS **RAFF** RAFFS **RAFT** RAFTS **RAGA** RAGAS **RAGE** RAGED RAGEE RAGER RAGES

RAGG RAGGS RAGGY **RAGI** TRAGI RAGIS **RAGS** BRAGS CRAGS DRAGS **RAHS** **RAID** RAIDS **RAIK** RAIKS **RAIL** BRAIL DRAIL FRAIL GRAIL TRAIL RAILE RAILS **RAIN** BRAIN DRAIN GRAIN TRAIN RAINE RAINS RAINY **RAIT** KRAIT TRAIT RAITS **RAJA** RAJAH RAJAS **RAKE** RAKED RAKEE RAKES **RAKI** RAKIS **RALE** RALES **RAMI** RAMIE RAMIS **RAMP** RAMPS **RAMS** PRAMS TRAMS **RANA** RANAS **RAND** BRAND

GRAND **RANDS** **RANDY** **RANG** KRANG ORANG PRANG RANGE RANGY **RANI** **RANIS** **RANK** BRANK CRANK DRANK FRANK PRANK RANKE RANKS **RANT** DRANT GRANT ORANT TRANT **RANTS** **RAPE** CRAPE DRAPE GRAPE TRAPE **RAPED** **RAPER** **RAPES** **RAPS** CRAPS DRAPS FRAPS TRAPS WRAPS **RAPT** WRAPT YRAPT **RARE** CRARE **RARER** **RASE** ERASE PRASE **RASED** RASES **RASH** BRASH CRASH TRASH **RASP** GRASP RASPS **RASPY** **RAST** BRAST WRAST **RASTA** **RATA** RATAN RATAS **RATE** CRATE FRATE GRATE IRATE

ORATE	UREAL	REEST	ARIAS	TRILL	RISEN	RODES	CROOK	ROTS	GRUFF
PRATE	REALM	REFS	RIBS	RILLE	RISER	RODS	DROOK	GROTS	RUFFE
URATE	REALS	REFT	CRIBS	RILLS	RISES	BRODS	ROOKS	TROTS	RUFFS
WRATE	REAM	REHS	DRIBS	RIMA	RISK	PRODS	ROOKY	ROUE	RUGS
RATED	BREAM	REIF	RICE	PRIMA	BRISK	TRODS	ROOM	ROUES	DRUGS
RATEL	CREAM	PREIF	GRICE	RIMAE	FRISK	ROED	BROOM	ROUL	TRUGS
RATER	DREAM	REIFS	PRICE	RIME	RISKS	ROES	GROOM	PROUL	RUIN
RATES	REAME	REIFY	TRICE	CRIME	RISKY	ROIL	VROOM	ROULE	RUING
RATH	REAMS	REIK	RICED	GRIME	RISP	BROIL	ROOMS	ROULS	RUINS
WRATH	REAMY	REIKS	RICER	PRIME	CRISP	DROIL	ROOMY	ROUM	RUKH
RATHE	REAN	REIN	RICES	RIMED	RISPS	ROILS	ROON	ROUMS	RUKHS
RATHS	REANS	GREIN	RICEY	RIMER	RITE	ROILY	CROON	ROUP	RULE
RATS	REAP	REINS	RICH	RIMES	TRITE	ROIN	ROONS	CROUP	BRULE
BRATS	REAPS	REIS	RICHT	RIMS	URITE	GROIN	ROOP	GROUP	RULED
PRATS	REAR	REIST	RICK	BRIMS	WRITE	PROIN	DROOP	ROUPY	RULER
RATU	AREAR	REKE	BRICK	PRIMS	RITS	ROINS	TROOP	ROUPS	RULES
RATUS	DREAR	REKED	CRICK	TRIMS	BRITS	ROKE	ROOPS	ROUT	RULY
RAUN	REARM	REKES	ERICK	RIMU	CRITS	BROKE	ROOPY	CROUT	TRULY
RAUNS	REARS	RELY	PRICK	RIMUS	FRITS	PROKE	ROOS	GROUT	RUME
RAVE	RECK	REMS	TRICK	RIMY	GRITS	TROKE	BROOS	TROUT	BRUME
BRAVE	DRECK	REND	WRICK	GRIMY	WRITS	WROKE	ROOSA	ROUTE	GRUME
CRAVE	TRECK	TREND	RICKS	PRIMY	RITT	ROKED	ROOSE	ROUTH	RUMEN
DRAVE	WRECK	RENDS	RICY	RIND	RITTS	ROKER	ROOST	ROUTS	RUMES
GRAVE	RECKS	RENS	PRICY	GRIND	RIVA	ROKES	ROOT	ROUX	RUMP
TRAVE	REDD	BRENS	RIDE	RINDS	RIVAL	ROKS	WROOT	ROVE	CRUMP
RAVED	AREDD	GRENS	BRIDE	RINDY	RIVAS	ROKY	ROOTS	DROVE	FRUMP
RAVEL	REDDS	WRENS	GRIDE	RINE	RIVE	ROLE	ROOTY	GROVE	TRUMP
RAVEN	REDDY	RENT	PRIDE	BRINE	DRIVE	ROLES	ROPE	PROVE	RUMPS
RAVER	REDE	BRENT	TRIDE	CRINE	RIVED	ROLL	GROPE	TROVE	RUMS
RAVES	AREDE	DRENT	RIDER	TRINE	RIVEL	DROLL	TROPE	ROVED	ARUMS
RAWN	BREDE	PRENT	RIDES	URINE	RIVEN	PROLL	ROPED	ROVER	DRUMS
BRAWN	REDES	URENT	RIDS	RINES	RIVER	TROLL	ROPER	ROVES	RUND
DRAWN	REDO	YRENT	GRIDS	RING	RIVES	ROLLS	ROPES	ROWS	RUNDS
PRAWN	REDOS	RENTE	IRIDS	BRING	RIVET	ROMA	ROPEY	BROWS	RUNE
RAWNS	UREDO	RENTS	RIEL	ERING	RIVO	AROMA	ROPY	CROWS	PRUNE
RAWS	REDOX	RENY	ARIEL	WRING	RIVOS	GROMA	RORE	DROWS	RUNED
BRAWS	REDS	REPP	ORIEL	RINGS	ROAD	ROMAL	CRORE	FROWS	RUNES
CRAWS	REED	REPPS	RIELS	RINK	BROAD	ROMAN	FRORE	GROWS	RUNG
DRAWS	BREED	REPS	RIEM	BRINK	TROAD	ROMAS	PRORE	PROWS	WRUNG
RAYS	CREED	PREPS	RIEMS	DRINK	ROADS	ROMP	RORES	TROWS	RUNGS
BRAYS	DREED	REST	RIFE	PRINK	ROAM	TROMP	RORT	ROWT	RUNS
DRAYS	FREED	CREST	RIFER	RINKS	ROAMS	ROMPS	RORTS	ROWTH	RUNT
FRAYS	GREED	DREST	RIFF	RINS	ROAN	RONE	RORTY	ROWTS	BRUNT
GRAYS	PREED	PREST	GRIFF	GRINS	GROAN	CRONE	RORY	RUBE	GRUNT
PRAYS	TREED	WREST	RIFFS	TRINS	ROANS	DRONE	FRORY	RUBES	PRUNT
TRAYS	REEDE	RESTS	RIFT	RINSE	ROAR	GRONE	ROSE	RUBS	RUNTS
RAZE	REEDS	RESTY	DRIFT	RIOT	ROARS	KRONE	AROSE	DRUBS	RUNTY
BRAZE	REEDY	RETE	GRIFT	ARIOT	ROARY	PRONE	BROSE	GRUBS	RURP
CRAZE	REEF	ARETE	RIFTE	GRIOT	ROBE	TRONE	EROSE	RUBY	RURPS
GRAZE	REEFS	RETES	RIFTS	RIOTS	PROBE	RONEO	PROSE	RUCK	RUSA
RAZED	REEK	RETS	RIFTY	RIPE	ROBED	RONES	ROSED	CRUCK	RUSAS
RAZEE	CREEK	ARETS	RIGG	GRIPE	ROBES	RONG	ROSES	TRUCK	RUSE
RAZES	REEKS	FRETS	RIGGS	TRIPE	ROBS	PRONG	ROSET	RUCKS	CRUSE
RAZZ	REEKY	TRETS	RIGS	RIPED	ROCH	WRONG	ROST	RUCS	DRUSE
READ	REEL	REVS	BRIGS	RIPEN	BROCH	RONT	CROST	RUDD	RUSES
AREAD	CREEL	REWS	FRIGS	RIPER	ROCK	FRONT	FROST	RUDDS	RUSH
BREAD	REELS	BREWS	GRIGS	RIPES	BROCK	RONTE	ROSTS	RUDDY	BRUSH
DREAD	REEN	CREWS	PRIGS	RIPP	CROCK	RONTS	ROSY	RUDE	CRUSH
OREAD	GREEN	GREWS	TRIGS	RIPPS	FROCK	ROOD	PROSY	CRUDE	FRUSH
TREAD	PREEN	TREWS	RILE	RIPS	TROCK	BROOD	ROTA	PRUDE	RUSHY
READS	TREEN	RHEA	RILED	DRIPS	ROCKS	ROODS	ROTAL	RUDER	RUSK
READY	REENS	RHEAS	RILES	GRIPS	ROCKY	ROOF	ROTAS	RUDS	RUSKS
REAK	REES	RHOS	RILEY	TRIPS	ROCS	GROOF	ROTE	CRUDS	RUST
BREAK	BREES	RHUS	RILL	RIPT	CROCS	PROOF	WROTE	RUED	BRUST
CREAK	CREES	RIAL	BRILL	RISE	RODE	ROOFS	ROTED	TRUED	CRUST
FREAK	DREES	PRIAL	DRILL	ARISE	ERODE	ROOFY	ROTES	RUES	FRUST
WREAK	FREES	TRIAL	FRILL	BRISE	TRODE	ROOK	ROTI	CRUES	TRUST
REAKS	GREES	URIAL	GRILL	CRISE	RODED	BROOK	ROTIS	GRUES	RUSTS
REAL	PREES	RIALS	KRILL	GRISE	RODEO		ROTL	TRUES	RUSTY
AREAL	TREES	RIAS	PRILL	PRISE			ROTLS	RUFF	RUTH

TRUTH	SALPS	SCAG	SEAT	SERF	SHINY	SIFTS	SITES	SLAW	SMITE
RUTHS	SALS	SCAGS	SEATS	SERFS	SHIP	SIGH	SITH	SLAWS	SMITH
RUTS	SALSA	SCAM	SECS	SERK	SHIPS	SIGHS	SITHE	SLAY	SMITS
RYAL	SALSE	SCAMP	SECT	SERKS	SHIR	SIGHT	SITS	SLAYS	SMOG
RYALS	SALT	SCAMS	SECTS	SERR	SHIRE	SIGN	SIZE	SLED	SMOGS
RYAS	SALTO	SCAN	SEED	SERRA	SHIRK	SIGNS	SIZED	SLEDS	SMUG
RYES	SALTS	SCAND	SEEDS	SERRE	SHIRR	SIKA	SIZEL	SLEE	SMUGS
RYFE	SALTY	SCANS	SEEDY	SERRS	SHIRS	SIKAS	SIZER	SLEEK	SMUR
RYKE	SAME	SCANT	SEEK	SERRY	SHIRT	SIKE	SIZES	SLEEP	SMURS
GRYKE	YSAME	SCAR	SEEKS	SESE	SHIT	SIKES	SIZY	SLEER	SMUT
RYKED	SAMEL	SCARE	SEEL	SESEY	SHITE	SILD	SKAS	SLEET	SMUTS
RYKES	SAMEN	SCARF	SEELD	SESS	SHITS	SILDS	SKAT	SLEW	SNAB
RYND	SAMES	SCARP	SEELS	SESSA	SHIV	SILE	SKATE	SLEWS	SNABS
RYNDS	SAMEY	SCARS	SEELY	SETA	SHIVE	ESILE	SKATS	SLEY	SNAG
RYOT	SAMP	SCART	SEEM	SETAE	SHIVS	SILED	SKATT	SLEYS	SNAGS
RYOTS	SAMPI	SCARY	SEEMS	SETS	SHOD	SILEN	SKAW	SLID	SNAP
RYPE	SAMPS	SCAT	SEEN	SETT	SHOE	SILER	SKAWS	SLIDE	SNAPS
GRYPE	SAND	SCATH	SEEP	SETTS	SHOED	SILES	SKEG	SLIME	SNAR
RYPER	SANDS	SCATS	SEEPS	SEWN	SHOER	SILEX	SKEGS	SLIMS	SNARE
RYVE	SANDY	SCATT	SEEPY	SEWS	SHOES	SILK	SKEO	SLIMY	SNARK
RYVED	SANE	SCAW	SEER	SEXT	SHOG	SILKS	SKEOS	SLIP	SNARL
RYVES	SANER	SCAWS	SEERS	SEXTS	SHOGS	SILKY	SKEP	SLIPE	SNARS
SABS	SANG	SCOG	SEES	SEXY	SHOO	SILL	SKEPS	SLIPS	SNARY
SACK	SANGS	SCOGS	SEGO	SEYS	SHOOK	SILLS	SKER	SLIPT	SNEB
SACKS	SANK	SCOT	SEGOL	SHAD	SHOOL	SILLY	ASKER	SLIT	SNEBS
SACS	SANKO	ASCOT	SEGOS	SHADE	SHOON	SILO	ESKER	SLITS	SNED
SAFE	SANS	ESCOT	SEGS	SHADS	SHOOS	SILOS	SKERS	SLOB	SNEDS
SAFED	SANSA	SCOTS	SEIF	SHADY	SHOOT	SILT	SKEW	SLOBS	SNEE
SAFER	SAPS	SCOW	SEIFS	SHAG	SHOP	SILTS	ASKEW	SLOE	SNEED
SAFES	SARD	SCOWL	SEIL	SHAGS	SHOPE	SILTY	SKEWS	SLOES	SNEER
SAGA	SARDS	SCOWP	SEILS	SHAH	SHOPS	SIMA	SKID	SLOG	SNEES
SAGAS	SARI	SCOWS	SEIS	SHAHS	SHOT	SIMAR	SKIDS	SLOGS	SNIB
SAGE	SARIN	SCRY	SEISE	SHAM	SHOTE	SIMAS	SKIM	SLOP	SNIBS
USAGE	SARIS	SCUD	SEISM	SHAMA	SHOTS	SIMI	SKIMP	SLOPE	SNIG
SAGER	SARK	SCUDI	SEKT	SHAME	SHOTT	SIMIS	SKIMS	SLOPS	SNIGS
SAGES	SARKS	SCUDO	SEKTS	SHAMS	SHOW	SIMP	SKIN	SLOPY	SNIP
SAGO	SARKY	SCUDS	SELD	SHAN	SHOWN	SIMPS	SKINK	SLOT	SNIPE
SAGOS	SARS	SCUG	SELE	SHAND	SHOWS	SIMS	SKINS	SLOTH	SNIPS
SAGS	KSARS	SCUGS	SELES	SHANK	SHOWY	SIND	SKINT	SLOTS	SNIPY
SAGY	TSARS	SCUL	SELF	SHANS	SHUL	SINDS	SKIO	SLOW	SNOB
SAIC	SARSA	SCULK	SELFS	SHAT	SHULS	SINE	SKIOS	SLOWS	SNOBS
SAICE	SASH	SCULL	SELL	SHAW	SHUN	SINED	SKIP	SLUB	SNOD
SAICK	SASS	SCULP	SELLE	PSHAW	SHUNS	SINES	SKIPS	SLUBB	SNODS
SAICS	SASSE	SCULS	SELLS	SHAWL	SHUNT	SINEW	SKIS	SLUBS	SNOG
SAID	SASSY	SCUM	SELS	SHAWM	SHUT	SING	SKIT	SLUE	SNOGS
SAIDS	SATE	SCUMS	SEME	SHAWS	SHUTS	USING	SKITE	SLUED	SNOT
SAIL	SATED	SCUP	SEMEE	SHAY	SHWA	SINGE	SKITS	SLUES	SNOTS
SAILS	SATES	SCUPS	SEMEN	SHAYA	SHWAS	SINGS	SKOL	SLUG	SNOW
SAILY	SATI	SCUR	SEMI	SHAYS	SIAL	SINK	SKRY	SLUGS	SNOWK
SAIM	SATIN	SCURF	SEMIE	SHEA	SIALS	SINKS	SKUA	SLUM	SNOWS
SAIMS	SATIS	SCURS	SEMIS	SHEAF	SIBB	SINKY	SKUAS	SLUMP	SNOWY
SAIN	SAUL	SCUT	SEND	SHEAL	SIBBS	SINS	SKUG	SLUMS	SNUB
SAINE	SAULS	SCUTA	SENDS	SHEAR	SIBS	SIPE	SKUGS	SLUR	SNUBS
SAINS	SAULT	SCUTE	SENS	SHEAS	SICE	SIPED	SKYR	SLURB	SNUG
SAINT	SAUT	SCUTS	SENSA	SHED	SICES	SIPES	SKYRE	SLURP	SNUGS
SAIR	SAUTE	SCYE	SENSE	SHEDS	SICH	SIPS	SKYRS	SLURS	SOAK
SAIRS	SAUTED	SCYES	SENT	SHES	SICK	SIRE	SLAB	SLUT	SOAKS
SAIS	SAUTES	SEAL	SENTS	SHET	SICKS	SIRED	SLABS	SLUTS	SOAP
SAIST	SAUTS	SEALS	ASHES	ASHET	SICS	SIREN	SLAE	SMEE	SOAPS
SAKE	SAVE	SEAM	SEPS	SHETS	SIDA	SIRES	SLAES	SMEEK	SOAPY
SAKER	SAVED	SEAME	ISHES	SHEW	SIDAS	SIRI	SLAG	SMEES	SOAR
SAKES	SAVER	SEAMS	SEPT	SHEWN	SIDE	SIRIH	SLAGS	SMEW	SOARE
SAKI	SAVES	SEAMY	SEPTA	SHEWS	SIDED	SIRIS	SLAM	SMEWS	SOARS
SAKIA	SAVEY	SEAN	SEPTS	SHIM	SIDER	SIRS	SLAMS	SMIR	SOBS
SAKIS	SAWN	SEANS	SERA	SHIMS	SIDES	SISS	SLAP	SMIRK	SOCK
SALE	SAWS	SEAR	SERAC	SHIN	SIEN	SISSY	SLAPS	SMIRR	SOCKO
SALEP	SAYS	SEARE	SERAI	SHINE	SIENS	SIST	SLAT	SMIRS	SOCKS
SALES	SAYST	SEARS	SERAL	SHINS	SIENT	SISTS	SLATE	SMIT	SOCS
SALET	SCAB	SEAS	SERE		SIFT	SITE	SLATS		SODA
SALP	SCABS	SEASE	SERED			SITED	SLATY		SODAS
	SCAD		SERER						
	SCADS		SERES						

SODS	SORBS	SPASM	STAR	STUNT	SWAN	TACHE	TANK	TAXA	STEME
SOFA	SORD	SPAT	STARE	STYE	SWANG	TACK	STANK	TAXI	TEMED
SOFAR	SORDA	SPATE	STARK	STYED	SWANK	STACK	TANKA	TAXIS	TEMES
SOFAS	SORDO	SPATS	STARN	STYES	SWANS	TACKS	TANKS	TEAD	TEMP
SOFT	SORDS	SPAW	STARR	SUBS	SWAP	TACKY	TANS	TEADE	TEMPI
SOFTA	SORE	SPAWL	STARS	SUCH	SWAPS	TACO	TANSY	TEADS	TEMPO
SOFTS	SORED	SPAWN	START	SUCK	SWAPT	TACOS	TAPA	TEAK	TEMPS
SOFTY	SOREE	SPAWS	STAW	SUCKS	SWAT	TACT	TAPAS	TEAL	TEMPT
SOGS	SOREL	SPAY	STAWS	SUDD	SWATH	TACTS	TAPE	TEALS	TEMS
SOHS	SORER	SPAYD	STAY	SUDDS	SWATS	TADS	ETAPE	TEAM	ITEMS
SOIL	SORES	SPAYS	STAYS	SUDS	SWAY	TAED	TAPED	TEAMS	STEMS
SOILS	SOREX	SPEC	STED	SUDSY	ASWAY	TAEL	TAPEN	TEAR	TEMSE
SOILY	SORI	SPECK	STEDD	SUED	SWAYL	TAELS	TAPER	TEARS	TEND
SOJA	SORN	SPECS	STEDE	SUEDE	SWAYS	TAES	TAPES	TEARY	STEND
SOJAS	SORNS	SPED	STEDS	SUER	SWEE	TAGS	TAPET	TEAS	TENDS
SOKE	SORT	SPET	STEM	SUERS	SWEED	STAGS	TAPS	TEASE	TENE
SOKEN	SORTS	SPETS	STEME	SUES	SWEEL	TAHA	ATAPS	TEAT	CTENE
SOKES	SOSS	SPEW	STEMS	SUET	SWEEP	TAHAS	STAPS	TEATS	TENES
SOLA	SOTS	SPEWS	STEN	SUETS	SWEER	TAHR	TARA	TECH	TENET
SOLAH	SOUK	SPEWY	STEND	SUETY	SWEES	TAHRS	TARAS	TECHS	TENS
SOLAN	SOUKS	SPIC	STENS	SUIT	SWEET	TAIL	TARE	TECHY	ETENS
SOLAR	SOUL	ASPIC	STENT	SUITE	SWIG	TAILS	TARED	TEDS	STENS
SOLAS	SOULS	SPICA	STEP	SUITS	SWIGS	TAIS	TARES	TEDY	TENSE
SOLD	SOUM	SPICE	STEPS	SUKH	SWIM	TAISH	TARN	TEED	TENT
SOLDE	SOUMS	SPICK	STEPT	SUKHS	ASWIM	TAIT	TARNS	STEED	STENT
SOLDI	SOUP	SPICS	STET	SUKS	SWIMS	TAITS	STARN	TEEL	TENTH
SOLDO	SOUPS	SPICY	STETS	SULK	SWIZ	TAKA	TARO	STEEL	TENTS
SOLDS	SOUPY	SPIE	STEW	SULKS	SWOB	TAKAS	TAROC	TEELS	TENTY
SOLE	SOUR	SPIED	STEWS	SULKY	SWOBS	TAKE	TAROK	TEEM	TERF
SOLED	SOURS	SPIEL	STEWY	SUMO	SWOP	TAKEN	TAROS	STEEM	TERFE
SOLEN	SOUSE	SPIES	STEY	SUMOS	SWOPS	TAKER	TAROT	TEEMS	TERFS
SOLER	SOUT	SPIK	STIE	SUMP	SWOPT	TAKES	TARP	TEEN	TERM
SOLES	SOUTH	SPIKE	STIED	SUMPH	SWOT	TAKS	TARPS	STEEN	TERMS
SOLI	SOUTS	SPIKS	STIES	SUMPS	SWOTS	TAKY	TARS	TEEND	TERN
SOLID	SOVS	SPIKY	STIR	SUMS	SWUM	TALA	STARS	TEENE	STERN
SOLO	SOWF	SPIN	ASTIR	SUNG	SYBO	TALAK	TARSI	TEENS	TERNE
SOLOS	SOWFF	SPINA	STIRE	SUNK	SYBOE	TALAQ	TART	TEENY	TERNS
SOLS	SOWFS	SPINE	STIRK	SUNKS	SYBOW	TALAR	START	TEER	TEST
SOMA	SOWL	SPINK	STIRP	SUNN	SYCE	TALAS	TARTS	TEERS	TESTA
SOMAS	SOWLE	SPINS	STIRS	SUNNS	SYCEE	TALC	TARTY	TEES	TESTE
SOME	SOWLS	SPINY	STOA	SUNNY	SYCES	TALCS	TASH	TEFF	TESTS
SONE	SOWM	SPIT	STOAE	SUNS	SYED	TALE	STASH	TEFFS	TESTY
SONES	SOWMS	SPITE	STOAI	SUPS	SYEN	TALES	TASK	TEFS	TETE
SONG	SOWN	SPITS	STOAS	SUQS	SYENS	TALI	TASKS	TEGG	TETES
SONGS	SOWND	SPITZ	STOAT	SURA	SYES	TALK	TASS	TEGGS	TEWS
SONS	SOWNE	SPIV	STOB	SURAH	SYKE	TALKS	TASSE	TEGS	STEWS
SONSE	SOWP	SPIVS	STOBS	SURAL	SYKER	TALL	TATE	TEHR	TEXT
SONSY	SOWPS	SPOT	STOP	SURAS	SYKES	TALLY	ETATS	TEHRS	TEXTS
SOOK	SOWS	SPOTS	STOPE	SURAT	SYNC	TAME	TATH	TEIL	THAE
SOOKS	SOWSE	SPRY	STOPS	SURD	SYNCH	TAMED	TATHS	STEIL	THAN
SOOM	SOYA	SPUD	STOT	SURDS	SYNCS	TAMER	TATS	TEILS	THANA
SOOMS	SOYAS	SPUDS	STOTS	SURE	SYND	TAMES	TATT	TELA	THANE
SOON	SOYS	SPUE	STOW	SURED	SYNDS	TAMP	TATTS	STELA	THANK
SOOP	SPAE	SPUED	STOWN	SURER	SYNE	TAMPS	TATTY	TELAE	THAR
SOOPS	SPAED	SPUES	STOWS	SURES	SYNED	TAMS	TATU	TELD	THARS
SOOT	SPAER	SPUN	STUB	SURF	SYNES	TANA	TATUS	TELL	THAT
SOOTE	SPAES	SPUNK	STUBS	SURFS	SYPE	TANAS	TAUS	TELLS	THAW
SOOTH	SPAN	SPUR	STUD	SURFY	SYPED	TANE	TAUT	TELLY	THAWS
SOOTS	SPANE	SPURN	STUDS	SUSS	SYPES	TANG	TAUTS	TELS	THAWY
SOOTY	SPANG	SPURS	STUDY	SWAB	TAAL	TANGA	TAWS	TELT	THEE
SOPH	SPANK	SPURT	STUM	SWABS	TAALS	TANGO	TAWSE	TEME	THEED
SOPHA	SPANS	STAB	STUMM	SWAD	TABS	TANGS	TAWT		THEEK
SOPHS	SPAR	STABS	STUMP	SWADS	TABU	TANGY	TAWTS		THEES
SOPS	SPARD	STAG	STUMPS	SWAG	TABUN		TEME		THEM
SORA	SPARE	STAGE	STUMS	SWAGE	TABUS				THEMA
PSORA	SPARK	STAGS	STUN	SWAGS	TACE				THEME
SORAL	SPARS	STAGY	ASTUN	SWAM	TACES				THEN
SORAS	SPART	STAP	STUNG	SWAMI	TACET				THENS
SORB	SPAS	STAPH	STUNK	SWAMP	TACH				THEW
SORBO		STAPS	STUNS						THEWS

THEWY	STILE	**TOES**	**TOOM**	TOWSE	TROTH	TURDS	TZARS	ZUPAS	LUTES
THEY	UTILE	**TOFF**	TOOMS	TOWSY	TROTS	**TURF**	**UDAL**	**UPBY**	MUTES
THIG	TILED	TOFFS	**TOON**	TOWT	**TROW**	TURFS	UDALS	UPBYE	**UTIS**
THIGH	TILER	TOFFY	TOONS	TOWTS	STROW	TURFY	**UDOS**	**UPGO**	CUTIS
THIGS	TILES	**TOFT**	**TOOT**	TOWY	TROWS	**TURM**	BUDOS	**UPON**	**UTUS**
THIN	**TILL**	TOFTS	TOOTH	**TOYS**	**TROY**	TURME	JUDOS	JUPON	TUTUS
THINE	STILL	**TOFU**	TOOTS	**TOZE**	STROY	TURMS	KUDOS	YUPON	**UVAS**
THING	TILLS	TOFUS	**TOPE**	TOZED	TROYS	**TURN**	LUDOS	**UPSY**	**UVEA**
THINK	TILLY	**TOGA**	STOPE	TOZES	**TRUE**	TURNS	**UEYS**	**URAO**	UVEAL
THINS	**TILS**	TOGAS	TOPED	**TRAD**	TRUED	**TUSH**	QUEYS	URAOS	UVEAS
THIR	**TILT**	**TOGE**	TOPEE	STRAD	TRUER	**TUSK**	**UFOS**	**URDE**	**VACS**
THIRD	ATILT	TOGED	TOPEK	TRADE	TRUES	TUSKS	BUFOS	URDEE	**VADE**
THIRL	STILT	TOGES	TOPER	TRADS	**TRUG**	TUSKY	**UGHS**	**URDS**	EVADE
THIS	TILTH	**TOGS**	TOPES	**TRAM**	TRUGS	**TUTS**	EUGHS	BURDS	VADED
THON	TILTS	**TOHO**	**TOPI**	TRAMP	**TRYE**	**TUTU**	**UGLI**	CURDS	VADES
THONG	**TIME**	TOHOS	TOPIC	TRAMS	TRYER	TUTUS	UGLIS	HURDS	**VAES**
THOU	STIME	**TOIL**	TOPIS	**TRAP**	**TRYP**	TUZZ	**UGLY**	NURDS	**VAGI**
THOUS	TIMED	TOILE	**TOPS**	STRAP	TRYPS	**TWAE**	**ULES**	SURDS	**VAIL**
THRO	TIMER	TOILS	STOPS	TRAPE	**TSAR**	TWAES	DULES	TURDS	AVAIL
THROB	TIMES	**TOKE**	**TORC**	TRAPS	TSARS	**TWAL**	GULES	URDY	VAILS
THROE	**TIND**	ATOKE	TORCH	**TRAY**	**TUAN**	TWALS	HULES	CURDY	**VAIN**
THROW	TINDS	STOKE	TORCS	STRAY	TUANS	**TWAS**	MULES	UREA	**VAIR**
THRU	**TINE**	TOKED	**TORE**	TRAYS	**TUBA**	**TWAT**	PULES	UREAL	VAIRE
THRUM	TINEA	TOKEN	STORE	**TREE**	TUBAE	TWATS	RULES	UREAS	VAIRS
THUD	TINED	TOKES	TORES	TREED	TUBAL	**TWAY**	TULES	**URES**	VAIRY
THUDS	TINES	**TOKO**	**TORI**	TREEN	TUBAR	TWAYS	YULES	CURES	**VALE**
THUG	**TING**	TOKOS	TORIC	TREES	TUBAS	**TWEE**	ULEX	DURES	AVALE
THUGS	STING	**TOLA**	TORII	**TREF**	**TUBE**	ETWEE	CULEX	LURES	VALES
THUS	TINGE	STOLA	**TORN**	TREFA	TUBED	TWEED	**ULNA**	MURES	VALET
TIAR	TINGS	TOLAS	**TORR**	**TREK**	TUBER	TWEEL	ULNAE	PURES	**VALI**
TIARA	**TINK**	**TOLD**	TORRS	TREKS	TUBES	TWEER	ULNAR	SURES	VALID
TIARS	STINK	**TOLE**	**TORS**	**TRET**	**TUBS**	TWEET	**UMBO**	**URGE**	VALIS
TICE	TINKS	STOLE	TORSE	TRETS	STUBS	**TWIG**	BUMBO	GURGE	**VAMP**
TICED	**TINS**	TOLED	TORSK	**TREW**	**TUCK**	TWIGS	GUMBO	PURGE	VAMPS
TICES	**TINT**	TOLES	TORSO	STREW	STUCK	**TWIN**	JUMBO	SURGE	**VANE**
TICH	TINTS	**TOLL**	**TORT**	TREWS	TUCKS	TWINE	RUMBO	URGED	VANED
STICH	STINT	ATOLL	TORTE	**TREY**	**TUFA**	TWINK	UMBOS	URGER	VANES
TICHY	TINTY	TOLLS	TORTS	TREYS	TUFAS	TWINS	**UMPH**	URGES	**VANG**
TICK	**TINY**	**TOLT**	**TOSE**	**TREZ**	**TUFF**	TWINY	BUMPH	**URIC**	VANGS
STICK	**TIPI**	TOLTS	TOSED	**TRIE**	STUFF	**TWIT**	HUMPH	AURIC	**VANS**
TICKS	TIPIS	**TOLU**	TOSES	TRIED	TUFFE	TWITE	SUMPH	**URNS**	**VANT**
TICKY	**TIPS**	TOLUS	**TOSH**	TRIER	TUFFS	TWITS	**UNAU**	BURNS	VANTS
TICS	TIPSY	**TOMB**	TOSHY	TRIES	**TUFT**	**TWOS**	UNAUS	CURNS	AVANT
TIDE	**TIPT**	TOMBS	**TOSS**	**TRIG**	TUFTS	**TYDE**	**UNBE**	DURNS	**VARA**
TIDED	**TIRE**	**TOME**	TOSSY	TRIGS	TUFTY	TYED	UNBED	GURNS	VARAN
TIDES	STIRE	TOMES	**TOST**	STRIG	TUGS	STYED	**UNCE**	TURNS	VARAS
TIDS	TIRED	**TOMS**	YTOST	**TRIM**	TUIS	**TYES**	OUNCE	URUS	**VARE**
TIDY	TIRES	ATOMS	**TOTE**	TRIMS	ETUIS	STYES	PUNCE	GURUS	VAREC
TIED	**TIRL**	**TONE**	TOTED	**TRIN**	TUISM	**TYGS**	BUNCE	URVA	VARES
STIED	TIRLS	ATONE	TOTEM	TRINE	**TULE**	**TYKE**	DUNCE	MURVA	**VARY**
TIER	**TIRO**	STONE	TOTES	TRINS	TULES	TYKES	UNCES	URVAS	OVARY
TIERS	TIROS	TONED	**TOTS**	**TRIO**	**TUMP**	**TYMP**	**UNCI**	**USED**	**VASA**
TIES	**TIRR**	TONES	STOTS	TRIOR	STUMP	TYMPS	**UNCO**	BUSED	VASAL
STIES	TIRRS	TONEY	**TOUK**	TRIOS	TUMPS	**TYND**	BUNCO	FUSED	**VASE**
TIFF	**TITE**	**TONG**	TOUKS	**TRIP**	TUMPY	TYNDE	JUNCO	MUSED	VASES
STIFF	TITER	STONG	**TOUN**	ATRIP	**TUNA**	**TYNE**	UNCOS	**USER**	**VAST**
TIFFS	**TITI**	TONGA	STOUN	STRIP	TUNAS	TYNED	**UNDE**	MUSER	AVAST
TIFT	TITIS	TONGS	TOUNS	TRIPE	**TUND**	TYNES	UNDEE	USERS	VASTS
TIFTS	**TITS**	**TONK**	**TOUR**	TRIPS	TUNDS	**TYPE**	UNDER	**USES**	VASTY
TIGE	**TIZZ**	STONK	TOURS	**TROD**	**TUNE**	TYPED	UNDO	BUSES	**VATS**
TIGER	TIZZY	TONKS	**TOUT**	TRODE	TUNED	TYPES	**UNIS**	FUSES	**VAUS**
TIGES	**TOAD**	**TONS**	STOUT	TRODS	TUNER	**TYPO**	**UNIT**	MUSES	**VAUT**
TIGS	TOADS	**TONY**	TOUTS	**TROG**	TUNES	TYPOS	UNITE	PUSES	VAUTE
TIKA	TOADY	ATONY	**TOWN**	TROGS	**TUNS**	**TYRE**	UNITS	RUSES	VAUTS
TIKAS	**TOBY**	STONY	STOWN	**TRON**	STUNS	TYRED	UNITY	SUSES	**VEAL**
TIKE	**TOCO**	**TOOK**	TOWNS	TRONA	**TUNY**	TYRES	**UNTO**	**UTAS**	UVEAL
TIKES	TOCOS	STOOK	TOWNY	TRONC	**TUPS**	**TYRO**	JUNTO	**UTES**	VEALE
TIKI	**TODS**	**TOOL**	**TOWS**	TRONE	**TURD**	**TYTE**	PUNTO	BUTES	VEALS
TIKIS	**TODY**	STOOL	STOWS	TRONS		**TZAR**	**UPAS**	CUTES	VEALY
TILE	**TOED**	TOOLS		**TROT**			PUPAS	JUTES	**VEER**

VEERS	VIES	VOLED	DWALE	SWASH	WEENY	WHEEL	WIMP	WIVED	WRITE
VEERY	IVIES	VOLES	SWALE	WASHY	WEEP	WHEEN	WIMPS	WIVES	WRITS
VEES	VIEW	VOLET	WALED	WASP	SWEEP	WHEN	WIMPY	WOAD	WUDS
VEGA	VIEWS	VOLS	WALER	WASPS	WEEPS	WHENS	WIND	WOADS	WULL
VEGAN	VIEWY	VOLT	WALES	WASPY	WEEPY	WHET	WINDS	WOCK	WULLS
VEGAS	VILD	VOLTA	WALI	WAST	WEER	WHETS	WINDY	WOCKS	WYES
VEHM	VILDE	VOLTE	WALIS	WASTE	WEES	WHEW	WINE	WOES	WYND
VEHME	VILE	VOLTS	WALK	WASTS	SWEER	WHEWS	DWINE	WOGS	WYNDS
VEIL	VILER	VORS	WALKS	WATE	TWEER	WHEY	SWINE	WOKE	WYNN
VEILS	VILL	VOTE	WALL	WATER	SWEES	WHEYS	TWINE	AWOKE	WYNNS
VEILY	VILLA	VOTED	WALLA	WATS	WEEST	WHID	WINED	WOKEN	WYNS
VEIN	VILLI	VOTER	WALLS	WATT	WEET	WHIDS	WINES	WOKS	WYTE
VEINS	VILLS	VOTES	WALLY	SWATS	SWEET	WHIG	WINEY	WOLD	WYTED
VEINY	VIMS	VOWS	WALY	TWATS	TWEET	WHIGS	WING	WOLDS	WYTES
VELA	VINA	AVOWS	SWALY	WATTS	WEETE	WHIM	AWING	WOLF	XYST
VELAR	VINAL	VRIL	WAME	WAUK	WEFT	WHIMS	OWING	WOLFS	XYSTI
VELD	VINAS	VRILS	WAMED	WAUKS	WEFTE	WHIN	SWING	WOMB	XYSTS
VELDS	VINE	VUGS	WAMES	WAUL	WEFTS	WHINE	WINGE	WOMBS	YACK
VELDT	AVINE	VULN	WAND	WAULK	WEID	WHINS	WINGS	WOMBY	YACKS
VELE	OVINE	VULNS	WANDS	WAULS	WEIDS	WHINY	WINGY	WONS	YAFF
VELES	VINED	VUMS	WANE	WAUR	WEIL	WHIP	WINK	WONT	NYAFF
VELL	VINER	WADD	WANED	WAURS	WEILS	WHIPS	SWINK	WONTS	YAFFS
VELLS	VINES	WADDS	WANES	AWAVE	WEIR	WHIPT	TWINK	WOOD	YAKS
VENA	VINEW	WADDY	WANEY	WAVE	SWEIR	WHIR	WINKS	WOODS	YALD
VENAE	VINO	WADE	WANG	WAVED	WEIRD	WHIRL	WINN	WOODY	YALE
VENAL	VINOS	WADED	SWANG	WAVER	WEIRS	WHIRR	WINNA	WOOF	YALES
VEND	VINS	WADER	TWANG	WAVES	WEKA	WHIRS	WINNS	WOOFS	YAMS
VENDS	VINT	WADES	WANGS	WAVEY	WEKAS	WHIT	WINO	WOOFY	LYAMS
VENT	VINTS	WADI	WANK	WAVY	WELD	WHITE	WINOS	WOOL	YANG
EVENT	VINY	WADIS	SWANK	WAWE	WELDS	WHITS	WINS	WOOLD	KYANG
VENTS	VINYL	WADS	TWANK	WAWES	WELK	WHITY	TWINS	WOOLS	YANGS
VERB	VIOL	SWADS	WANKS	WAWL	WELKE	WHIZ	WINY	WOON	YANK
VERBS	VIOLA	WADY	WANS	WAWLS	WELKS	WHIZZ	TWINY	WOONS	YANKS
VERS	VIOLD	WAES	SWANS	WAWS	WELKT	WHOA	WIPE	WOOS	YAPP
AVERS	VIOLS	TWAES	WANT	WAXY	WELL	WHOM	SWIPE	WOOSH	YAPPS
OVERS	VIRL	WAFF	WANTS	WAYS	DWELL	WHOP	WIPED	WOOT	YAPS
VERSE	VIRLS	WAFFS	WANTY	AWAYS	SWELL	WHOPS	WIPER	WOOTZ	YARD
VERSO	VISA	WAFT	WANY	SWAYS	WELLS	WHOT	WIPES	WOPS	YARDS
VERST	VISAS	WAFTS	WAPS	TWAYS	WELLY	WHOW	WIRE	SWOPS	YARE
VERT	VISE	WAGE	SWAPS	WEAK	WELT	EWHOW	SWIRE	WORD	YARER
AVERT	VISED	WAGED	WARD	TWEAK	WELTS	WICK	TWIRE	SWORD	YARN
EVERT	VISES	WAGER	AWARD	WEAL	WEMB	WICKS	WIRED	WORDS	YARNS
OVERT	VITA	WAGES	SWARD	SWEAL	WEMBS	WICKY	WIRER	WORDY	YARR
VERTS	VITAE	WAGS	WARDS	WEALD	WEMS	WIDE	WIRES	WORE	YARRS
VERTU	VITAL	SWAGS	WARE	WEALS	WEND	WIDEN	WIRY	SWORE	YATE
VERY	VITE	WAID	AWARE	WEAN	WENDS	WIDER	WISE	WORK	YATES
EVERY	VITEX	WAIDE	SWARE	WEANS	WENS	WIDES	WISED	AWORK	YAUD
VEST	VIVA	WAIF	WARED	WEAR	WENT	WIEL	WISER	WORKS	YAUDS
VESTA	VIVAS	WAIFS	WARES	SWEAR	WENTS	WIELD	WISES	WORM	YAUP
VESTS	VIVAT	WAIFT	WARK	WEARS	WEPT	WIELS	WISH	WORMS	YAWL
VETO	VIVE	WAIL	WARKS	WEARY	WERE	WIFE	SWISH	WORMY	YAWLS
VETS	VIVER	WAILS	WARM	WEBS	WERT	WIGS	WISP	WORN	YAWN
EVETS	VIVES	WAIN	SWARM	WEDS	WEST	WILD	WISPS	SWORN	YAWNS
VIAE	VIVO	SWAIN	WARMS	WEED	EWEST	WILDS	WISPY	WORT	YAWNY
VIAL	VIZY	TWAIN	WARN	WEEDS	WESTS	WILE	WIST	WORTH	YAWP
VIALS	VLEI	WAINS	AWARN	WEEK	WETS	WILED	WISTS	WORTS	YAWPS
VIAS	VLEIS	WAIT	WARNS	WEEKE	WEXE	WILES	WITE	WOST	YAWS
VIBE	VOAR	AWAIT	WARP	WEEKS	WEXED	WILI	TWITE	WOTS	YAWY
VIBES	VOARS	WAITE	WARPS	WEEL	WEXES	WILIS	WITED	SWOTS	YBET
VIBEX	VOES	WAITS	WARS	WEELS	WEYS	WILL	WITES	WOVE	YEAD
VIBS	VOID	WAKE	WARST	WEEM	WHAM	SWILL	WITH	WOVEN	YEADS
VICE	AVOID	AWAKE	WART	WEEMS	WHAMS	TWILL	WITHE	WOWF	YEAH
VICED	OVOID	WAKED	SWART	WEEN	WHAP	WILLS	WITHS	WOWS	YEAN
VICES	VOIDS	WAKEN	WARTS	WEENS	WHAPS	WILLY	WITHY	WRAP	YEANS
VIDE	VOLA	WAKER	WARTY		WHAT	WILT	WITS	WRAPS	YEAR
VIDEO	VOLAE	WAKES	WARY		WHATS	TWILT	SWITS	WRAPT	YEARD
VIED	VOLAR	WALD	WASE		WHEE	WILTS	TWITS	WREN	YEARN
IVIED	VOLE	WALDS	WASES			TWILTS	WIVE	WRENS	YEARS
VIER		WALE	WASH			WILY		WRIT	YEAS
VIERS			AWASH						YEAST

YEDE	YEPS	YILLS	YOGAS	AYONT	YUCKS	ZACKS	ZEST	ZINGY	ZOOMS
YEDES	YERD	YINS	YOGH	YOOP	YUCKY	ZAGS	ZESTS	ZIPS	ZOON
YEED	YERDS	YIPS	YOGHS	YOOPS	YUFT	ZANY	ZESTY	ZITS	ZOONS
YEEDS	YERK	YIRD	YOGI	YORE	YUFTS	ZAPS	ZETA	ZIZZ	ZOOS
YEGG	YERKS	YIRDS	YOGIC	YORES	YUGA	ZARF	ZETAS	ZOBO	ZULU
YEGGS	YESK	YIRK	YOGIN	YORK	YUGAS	ZARFS	ZEZE	ZOBOS	ZULUS
YELD	YESKS	YIRKS	YOGIS	YORKS	YUGS	ZATI	ZEZES	ZOBU	ZUPA
GYELD	YEST	YITE	YOKE	YOUK	YUKE	ZATIS	ZHOS	ZOBUS	ZUPAN
YELK	YESTS	YITES	YOKED	YOUKS	YUKED	ZEAL	ZIFF	ZOEA	ZUPAS
YELKS	YESTY	YLEM	YOKEL	YOUR	YUKES	ZEALS	ZIFFS	ZOEAE	ZURF
YELL	YETI	XYLEM	YOKES	YOURN	YUKS	ZEAS	ZIGS	ZOEAL	ZURFS
YELLS	YETIS	YLEMS	YOKS	YOURS	YUKY	ZEBU	ZILA	ZOEAS	AZYME
YELM	YETT	YLKE	YOLD	YOURT	YULE	ZEBUB	ZILAS	ZOIC	ZYMES
YELMS	YETTS	YMPE	YOLK	YOWE	YULES	ZEBUS	ZIMB	AZOIC	
YELP	YEUK	YMPES	YOLKS	YOWES	YUMP	ZEDS	ZIMBI	ZONA	
AYELP	YEUKS	YMPT	YOLKY	YOWL	YUMPS	ZEES	ZIMBS	ZONAE	
YELPS	YEVE	YOBS	YOMP	YOWLS	YUNX	ZEIN	ZINC	ZONAL	
YELT	YEVEN	YOCK	YOMPS	YOWS	YUPS	ZEINS	ZINCO	ZONE	
YELTS	YEVES	YOCKS	YOND	YUAN	YURT	ZEKS	ZINCS	OZONE	
YENS	YEWS	YODE	YONI	YUCA	YURTS	ZELS	ZINCY	ZONED	
HYENS	YGOE	YODEL	YONIS	YUCAS	YWIS	ZERO	ZING	ZONES	
SYENS	YILL	YOGA	YONT	YUCK	ZACK	ZEROS	ZINGS	ZOOM	

PART B: 5-letter word hooks
extensible words only

ABACA	**ABRIN**	GADDER	AGAMIC	MAIDED	**ALAPS**	BALLOT	AMBANS	CAMPLE
ABACAS	ABRINS	LADDER	AGAMID	RAIDED	JALAPS	TALLOT	**AMBER**	SAMPLE
ABAND	**ABSEY**	MADDER	AGAMIS	**AIDER**	**ALARM**	**ALLOTS**	CAMBER	AMPLER
ABANDS	ABSEYS	PADDER	**AGATE**	RAIDER	ALARMS	**ALLOW**	JAMBER	**AMPLY**
ABASE	**ABSIT**	SADDER	AGATES	AIDERS	**ALARY**	BALLOW	LAMBER	DAMPLY
ABASED	ABSITS	ADDERS	**AGAVE**	**AIDOS**	SALARY	CALLOW	TAMBER	**AMPUL**
ABASES	**ABUNA**	**ADDIO**	AGAVES	IAIDOS	**ALATE**	FALLOW	AMBERS	AMPULE
ABATE	ABUNAS	ADDIOS	**AGAZE**	**AILED**	MALATE	GALLOW	AMBERY	AMPULS
ABATED	**ABUSE**	**ADDLE**	AGAZED	BAILED	PALATE	HALLOW	**AMBIT**	**AMRIT**
ABATES	ABUSED	DADDLE	**AGENE**	FAILED	ALATED	MALLOW	GAMBIT	AMRITA
ABAYA	ABUSER	FADDLE	SAGENE	HAILED	**ALAYS**	SALLOW	AMBITS	AMRITS
KABAYA	ABUSES	PADDLE	AGENES	JAILED	PALAYS	TALLOW	**AMBLE**	**AMUSE**
ABAYAS	**ABYSM**	RADDLE	**AGENT**	MAILED	**ALBUM**	WALLOW	GAMBLE	AMUSED
ABBES	ABYSMS	SADDLE	AGENTS	NAILED	ALBUMS	ALLOWS	HAMBLE	AMUSER
ABBESS	**ACARI**	WADDLE	**AGGER**	RAILED	**ALDEA**	**ALLOY**	RAMBLE	AMUSES
ABBEY	ACARID	ADDLED	DAGGER	SAILED	ALDEAS	ALLOYS	WAMBLE	**ANANA**
ABBEYS	**ACCOY**	ADDLES	GAGGER	TAILED	**ALDER**	**ALLYL**	AMBLED	BANANA
ABBOT	ACCOYS	**ADEEM**	JAGGER	VAILED	BALDER	ALLYLS	AMBLER	MANANA
ABBOTS	**ACHED**	ADEEMS	LAGGER	WAILED	**ALDERN**	**ALMAH**	AMBLES	ANANAS
ABCEE	BACHED	**ADEPT**	NAGGER	**AIMED**	ALDERS	ALMAHS	**AMBOS**	**ANCLE**
ABCEES	CACHED	ADEPTS	SAGGER	MAIMED	**ALEPH**	**ALMAS**	JAMBOS	ANCLES
ABEAR	**ACHES**	**ADIEU**	TAGGER	**AIOLI**	ALEPHS	HALMAS	MAMBOS	**ANEAR**
ABEARS	BACHES	ADIEUS	YAGGER	AIOLIS	**ALERT**	TALMAS	SAMBOS	ANEARS
ABELE	CACHES	ADIEUX	AGGERS	**AIRED**	ALERTS	**ALMEH**	ZAMBOS	**ANELE**
KABELE	LACHES	**ADIOS**	**AGGRO**	FAIRED	**ALEYE**	ALMEHS	**AMEBA**	ANELED
ABELES	NACHES	RADIOS	AGGROS	HAIRED	ALEYED	**ALMUG**	AMEBAE	ANELES
ABHOR	RACHES	**ADMIN**	**AGHAS**	LAIRED	ALEYES	ALMUGS	AMEBAS	**ANENT**
ABHORS	TACHES	ADMINS	AGHAST	PAIRED	**ALFAS**	**ALOED**	**AMEER**	MANENT
ABIDE	**ACING**	**ADMIT**	**AGILA**	SAIRED	HALFAS	HALOED	AMEERS	**ANGEL**
ABIDED	FACING	ADMITS	AGILAS	**AIRER**	**ALGIN**	**ALOES**	**AMEND**	MANGEL
ABIDES	LACING	**ADOBE**	**AGILE**	FAIRER	ALGINS	HALOES	AMENDE	ANGELS
ABIES	MACING	ADOBES	VAGILE	SAIRER	**ALGUM**	**ALOHA**	AMENDS	**ANGER**
BABIES	PACING	**ADOPT**	AGILER	AIRERS	ALGUMS	ALOHAS	**AMENE**	BANGER
GABIES	RACING	ADOPTS	**AGING**	**AIRNS**	**ALIBI**	**ALONG**	AMENED	DANGER
RABIES	**ACKEE**	**ADORE**	CAGING	BAIRNS	ALIBIS	KALONG	**AMENS**	GANGER
ABLED	HACKEE	ADORED	GAGING	CAIRNS	**ALIEN**	**ALPHA**	YAMENS	HANGER
CABLED	ACKEES	ADORER	PAGING	**AISLE**	ALIENS	ALPHAS	**AMENT**	LANGER
FABLED	**ACORN**	ADORES	RAGING	AISLED	**ALIGN**	**ALTAR**	LAMENT	MANGER
GABLED	ACORNS	**ADORN**	WAGING	AISLES	MALIGN	ALTARS	AMENTA	RANGER
SABLED	**ACRED**	ADORNS	AGINGS	**AIZLE**	ALIGNS	**ALTER**	AMENTS	ANGERS
TABLED	SACRED	**ADULT**	**AGIST**	AIZLES	**ALINE**	FALTER	**AMICE**	**ANGLE**
ABLER	**ACRES**	ADULTS	AGISTS	**AJWAN**	SALINE	HALTER	AMICES	BANGLE
FABLER	NACRES	**ADUST**	**AGLET**	AJWANS	VALINE	PALTER	**AMIDE**	CANGLE
ABLES	**ACTIN**	ADUSTS	EAGLET	**AKEES**	ALINED	SALTER	AMIDES	DANGLE
CABLES	ACTING	**ADVEW**	HAGLET	RAKEES	ALINES	**ALTERN**	**AMIES**	FANGLE
FABLES	ACTINS	ADVEWS	AGLETS	**AKENE**	**ALKYD**	ALTERS	RAMIES	JANGLE
GABLES	**ACTON**	**AEONS**	**AGMAS**	AKENES	ALKYDS	**ALTOS**	**AMIGO**	MANGLE
SABLES	ACTONS	PAEONS	MAGMAS	**AKING**	**ALKYL**	SALTOS	AMIGOS	TANGLE
TABLES	**ACTOR**	**AERIE**	**AGOGE**	BAKING	ALKYLS	**ALULA**	**AMINE**	WANGLE
ABLEST	FACTOR	FAERIE	AGOGES	CAKING	**ALLAY**	ALULAS	FAMINE	ANGLED
ABLET	ACTORS	**AERIER**	**AGONS**	FAKING	ALLAYS	**ALURE**	GAMINE	ANGLER
GABLET	**ACUTE**	AERIES	WAGONS	LAKING	**ALLEE**	ALURES	TAMINE	ANGLES
TABLET	ACUTER	**AFARA**	**AGORA**	MAKING	MALLEE	**ALWAY**	AMINES	**ANGST**
ABLETS	ACUTES	AFARAS	AGORAS	RAKING	SALLEE	ALWAYS	**AMMAN**	ANGSTS
ABODE	**ADAGE**	**AFEAR**	**AGREE**	TAKING	ALLEES	**AMASS**	AMMANS	**ANIGH**
ABODED	ADAGES	AFEARD	AGREED	WAKING	**ALLEL**	CAMASS	**AMMON**	ANIGHT
ABODES	**ADAPT**	AFEARS	AGREES	**AKKAS**	ALLELE	**AMATE**	GAMMON	**ANIMA**
ABORD	ADAPTS	**AFRIT**	**AGUED**	YAKKAS	ALLELS	HAMATE	MAMMON	ANIMAL
ABORDS	**ADDED**	AFRITS	VAGUED	**ALAAP**	**ALLEY**	RAMATE	AMMONS	ANIMAS
ABORT	DADDED	**AFTER**	**AGUES**	ALAAPS	GALLEY	**AMATED**	**AMOUR**	**ANIME**
ABORTS	GADDED	DAFTER	VAGUES	**ALANG**	VALLEY	AMATES	AMOURS	ANIMES
ABOUT	MADDED	RAFTER	**AGUTI**	LALANG	ALLEYS	**AMAZE**	**AMOVE**	**ANION**
ABOUTS	PADDED	WAFTER	AGUTIS	ALANGS	**ALLOD**	AMAZED	AMOVED	FANION
ABRAY	WADDED	AFTERS	**AIDED**	**ALAPA**	ALLODS	AMAZES	AMOVES	ANIONS
ABRAYS	**ADDER**	**AGAMI**	LAIDED	ALAPAS	**ALLOT**	**AMBAN**	**AMPLE**	**ANISE**

ANISES · **ANKER** · BANKER · CANKER · DANKER · HANKER · JANKER · LANKER · RANKER · TANKER · WANKER · YANKER · ANKERS · **ANKLE** · **FANKLE** · RANKLE · WANKLE · ANKLED · ANKLES · ANKLET · **ANNAL** · ANNALS · **ANNAS** · CANNAS · MANNAS · NANNAS · TANNAS · **ANNAT** · ANNATS · **ANNEX** · ANNEXE · **ANNOY** · ANNOYS · **ANNUL** · ANNULI · ANNULS · **ANODE** · ANODES · **ANTAR** · CANTAR · KANTAR · ANTARS · **ANTED** · BANTED · CANTED · DANTED · GANTED · KANTED · PANTED · RANTED · WANTED · **ANTES** · ZANTES · **ANTIC** · MANTIC · ANTICK · ANTICS · **ANTIS** · MANTIS · **ANTRE** · ANTRES · **ANVIL** · ANVILS · **AORTA** · AORTAL · AORTAS · **APERY** · NAPERY · PAPERY · **APHID**

APHIDS · **APHIS** · RAPHIS · **APING** · CAPING · GAPING · JAPING · RAPING · TAPING · **APIOL** · APIOLS · **APISH** · PAPISH · **APISM** · PAPISM · APISMS · **APNEA** · APNEAS · **APODE** · APODES · **APPAL** · APPALS · **APPAY** · APPAYD · APPAYS · **APPLE** · DAPPLE · APPLES · **APPUI** · APPUIS · **APPUY** · APPUYS · **APRON** · NAPRON · APRONS · **APSES** · LAPSES · **ARABA** · ARABAS · **ARAME** · ARAMES · **ARBOR** · HARBOR · ARBORS · **ARCED** · FARCED · **ARDEB** · ARDEBS · **ARDRI** · ARDRIS · **AREAD** · AREADS · **ARECA** · ARECAS · **AREDE** · AREDES · **AREFY** · RAREFY · **ARENA** · ARENAS · **ARETE** · ARETES · **ARETS** · CARETS · **ARETT** · ARETTS · **ARGAL** · ARGALA · ARGALI · **ARGAN**

ARGAND · ARGANS · **ARGIL** · ARGILS · **ARGOL** · ARGOLS · **ARGON** · JARGON · ARGONS · **ARGOT** · ARGOTS · **ARGUE** · ARGUED · ARGUER · ARGUES · **ARGUS** · SARGUS · **ARIEL** · ARIELS · **ARISE** · ARISEN · ARISES · **ARISH** · BARISH · GARISH · HARISH · MARISH · PARISH · **ARKED** · BARKED · CARKED · HARKED · LARKED · MARKED · NARKED · PARKED · **ARLES** · FARLES · MARLES · PARLES · **ARMED** · FARMED · HARMED · WARMED · **ARMET** · ARMETS · **ARMIL** · ARMILS · **ARMOR** · ARMORS · ARMORY · **ARNAS** · VARNAS · **ARNUT** · ARNUTS · **AROBA** · AROBAS · **AROID** · LAROID · AROIDS · **AROMA** · AROMAS · **ARRAH** · JARRAH · **ARRAS** · NARRAS · TARRAS · **ARRAY** · WARRAY · ARRAYS

ARRET · BARRET · GARRET · ARRETS · **ARRIS** · KARRIS · ARRISH · **ARROW** · BARROW · FARROW · HARROW · MARROW · NARROW · TARROW · YARROW · ARROWS · ARROWY · **ARSES** · CARSES · FARSES · PARSES · **ARSON** · PARSON · ARSONS · **ARTAL** · HARTAL · **ARTEL** · CARTEL · MARTEL · ARTELS · **ARTIC** · ARTICS · **ARUMS** · GARUMS · LARUMS · **ARVAL** · LARVAL · **ASANA** · ASANAS · **ASCOT** · MASCOT · ASCOTS · **ASHEN** · WASHEN · **ASHES** · BASHES · CASHES · DASHES · FASHES · GASHES · HASHES · LASHES · MASHES · PASHES · RASHES · SASHES · TASHES · WASHES · **ASHET** · ASHETS · **ASIDE** · ASIDES · **ASKED** · BASKED · CASKED · MASKED · TASKED · **ASKER** · MASKER · TASKER

ASKERS · **ASPEN** · ASPENS · **ASPER** · GASPER · JASPER · RASPER · ASPERS · **ASPIC** · ASPICK · ASPICS · **ASSAI** · ASSAIL · ASSAIS · **ASSAY** · ASSAYS · **ASSES** · BASSES · GASSES · LASSES · MASSES · PASSES · RASSES · SASSES · TASSES · **ASSESS** · **ASSET** · BASSET · TASSET · ASSETS · **ASSOT** · ASSOTS · ASSOTT · **ASTER** · BASTER · CASTER · EASTER · FASTER · LASTER · MASTER · PASTER · RASTER · TASTER · VASTER · WASTER · ASTERN · ASTERS · ASTERT · **ASTUN** · ASTUNS · **ATMAN** · BATMAN · VATMAN · ATMANS · **ATOKE** · ATOKES · **ATOLL** · ATOLLS · **ATONE** · ATONED · ATONER · ATONES · **ATRIA** · LATRIA · ATRIAL · **ATTAP** · ATTAPS · **ATTAR** · ATTARS · **ATTIC**

ATTICS · **AUDIO** · AUDIOS · **AUDIT** · AUDITS · **AUGER** · GAUGER · SAUGER · AUGERS · **AUGHT** · CAUGHT · HAUGHT · NAUGHT · RAUGHT · TAUGHT · WAUGHT · AUGHTS · **AUGUR** · AUGURS · AUGURY · DAUNTS · GAUNTS · HAUNTS · JAUNTS · NAUNTS · SAUNTS · TAUNTS · VAUNTS · **AUNTS** · **AUNTY** · JAUNTY · **AURAS** · LAURAS · **AURIC** · TAURIC · **AUXIN** · AUXINS · **AVAIL** · AVAILE · AVAILS · **AVALE** · AVALED · AVALES · **AVANT** · SAVANT · AVANTI · **AVENS** · HAVENS · PAVENS · RAVENS · **AVERS** · CAVERS · HAVERS · LAVERS · PAVERS · RAVERS · SAVERS · TAVERS · WAVERS · AVERSE · **AVERT** · TAVERT · AVERTS · **AVINE** · RAVINE · SAVINE · **AVION** · AVIONS

AVISE · PAVISE · AVISED · AVISES · **AVISO** · AVISOS · **AVIZE** · AVIZED · AVIZES · **AVOID** · AVOIDS · **AVOUE** · AVOUES · **AVYZE** · AVYZED · AVYZES · **AWAIT** · AWAITS · **AWAKE** · AWAKED · AWAKEN · AWAKES · **AWARD** · VAWARD · AWARDS · **AWARE** · AWARER · **AWARN** · AWARNS · **AWETO** · AWETOS · **AWFUL** · LAWFUL · **AWING** · CAWING · DAWING · HAWING · JAWING · KAWING · LAWING · PAWING · RAWING · SAWING · TAWING · YAWING · **AWNED** · DAWNED · FAWNED · PAWNED · YAWNED · **AWNER** · DAWNER · FAWNER · PAWNER · AWNERS · **AWOKE** · AWOKEN · **AXING** · FAXING · RAXING · TAXING · WAXING · **AXIOM** · AXIOMS · **AXOID** · AXOIDS · **AXONS** · CAXONS · **AYAHS** · RAYAHS

AYRIE · AYRIES · **AZIDE** · AZIDES · **AZOTE** · **AZOTH** · AZOTHS · **AZURE** · RAZURE · AZURES · **AZYME** · AZYMES · **BABEL** · BABELS · **BABOO** · BABOOS · **BABUL** · BABULS · **BACCA** · BACCAE · BACCAS · **BACCO** · BACCOS · **BACON** · BACONS · **BADGE** · BADGER · BADGES · **BAGEL** · BAGELS · **BAIRN** · BAIRNS · **BAIZE** · BAIZED · BAIZES · **BAJAN** · BAJANS · **BAJRA** · BAJRAS · **BAJRI** · BAJRIS · **BAKER** · BAKERS · BAKERY · **BALER** · BALERS · **BALOO** · BALOOS · **BALSA** · BALSAM · BALSAS · **BANCO** · BANCOS · **BANDH** · BANDHS · **BANDS** · ABANDS · **BANGS** · OBANGS · **BANIA** · BANIAN · BANIAS · **BANJO** · BANJOS · **BARBE** · BARBED · BARBEL · BARBER

BARBES · BARBET · **BARCA** · BARCAS · **BARES** · BAREST · **BARGE** · BARGED · BARGEE · BARGES · **BARON** · BARONS · BARONY · **BARRE** · BARRED · BARREL · BARREN · BARRES · BARRET · **BARYE** · BARYES · **BASAL** · BASALT · **BASAN** · BASANS · **BASED** · ABASED · **BASES** · ABASES · BASEST · **BASIC** · BASICS · **BASIL** · BASILS · **BASIN** · BASING · BASINS · **BASON** · BASONS · **BASSE** · BASSED · BASSER · BASSES · BASSET · **BASSO** · BASSOS · **BASTE** · BASTED · BASTER · BASTES · **BASTO** · BASTOS · **BATED** · ABATED · **BATES** · ABATES · **BATHE** · BATHED · BATHER · BATHES · **BATIK** · BATIKS · **BATON** · BATONS · **BATTA** · BATTAS · **BAULK** · BAULKS · **BAVIN** · BAVINS

BAYLE	BELEES	BIBLES	BLACK	BLITES	BODLE	BORNE	BRACED	BREVE
BAYLES	BELGA	BICES	BLACKS	BLOAT	BODLES	ABORNE	BRACER	BREVES
BAYOU	BELGAS	IBICES	BLADE	BLOATS	BOGAN	BORON	BRACES	BREVET
BAYOUS	BELIE	BIDED	BLADED	BLOCK	BOGANS	BORONS	BRACK	BRIAR
BAZAR	BELIED	ABIDED	BLADES	BLOCKS	BOGEY	BORTS	BRACKS	BRIARS
BAZARS	BELIEF	BIDES	BLAES	BLOCKY	BOGEYS	ABORTS	BRACT	BRIBE
BEACH	BELIER	ABIDES	BLAEST	BLOKE	BOGIE	BOSOM	BRACTS	BRIBED
BEACHY	BELIES	BIDET	BLAIN	BLOKES	BOGIES	BOSOMS	BRAID	BRIBER
BEANO	BELLE	BIDETS	BLAINS	BLOND	BOGLE	BOSOMY	ABRAID	BRIBES
BEANOS	BELLED	BIDON	BLAME	BLONDE	BOGLES	BOSON	BRAIDE	BRICK
BEARD	BELLES	BIDONS	BLAMED	BLONDS	BOHEA	BOSONS	BRAIDS	BRICKS
BEARDS	BEMAD	BIELD	BLAMES	BLOOD	BOHEAS	BOSUN	BRAIL	BRICKY
BEARE	BEMADS	BIELDS	BLAND	BLOODS	BOING	BOSUNS	BRAILS	BRIDE
BEARED	BEMUD	BIELDY	BLANDS	BLOODY	BOINGS	BOTCH	BRAIN	BRIDED
BEARER	BEMUDS	BIGHA	BLANK	BLOOM	BOINK	BOTCHY	BRAINS	BRIDES
BEARES	BENET	BIGHAS	BLANKS	ABLOOM	BOINKS	BOTEL	BRAINY	BRIEF
BEARS	BENETS	BIGHT	BLANKY	BLOOMS	BOLUS	BOTELS	BRAKE	BRIEFS
ABEARS	BENNE	BIGHTS	BLARE	BLOOMY	OBOLUS	BOTTE	BRAKED	BRIER
BEAST	BENNES	BIGOT	BLARED	BLOOP	BOMBE	BOTTED	BRAKES	BRIERS
BEASTS	BENNET	BIGOTS	BLARES	BLOOPS	BOMBED	BOTTES	BRAME	BRIERY
BEATH	BENNI	BIJOU	BLASH	BLORE	BOMBER	BOUGE	BRAMES	BRILL
BEATHS	BENNIS	BIJOUX	BLASHY	BLORES	BOMBES	BOUGED	BRAND	BRILLS
BEAUT	BEPAT	BIKER	BLAST	BLOWS	BOMBO	BOUGES	BRANDS	BRINE
BEAUTS	BEPATS	BIKERS	OBLAST	BLOWSE	BOMBOS	BOUGET	BRANDY	BRINED
BEAUTY	BERAY	BIKIE	BLASTS	BLOWSY	BONCE	BOUGH	BRANK	BRINES
BEBOP	BERAYS	BIKIES	BLATE	BLUDE	BONCES	BOUGHS	BRANKS	BRING
BEBOPS	BERET	BILBO	ABLATE	BLUDES	BONER	BOUGHT	BRANKY	BRINGS
BECKE	BERETS	BILBOS	OBLATE	BLUES	BONERS	BOULE	BRASH	BRINK
BECKED	BEROB	BILGE	BLATER	BLUEST	BONGO	BOULES	BRASHY	BRINKS
BECKES	BEROBS	BILGED	BLATT	BLUESY	BONGOS	BOULT	BRASS	BRISE
BECKET	BERTH	BILGES	BLATTS	BLUEY	BONIE	BOULTS	BRASSY	BRISES
BEDEL	BERTHA	BIMBO	BLAUD	BLUEYS	BONIER	BOUND	BRAST	BRISK
BEDELL	BERTHE	BIMBOS	BLAUDS	BLUFF	BONNE	ABOUND	BRASTS	BRISKS
BEDELS	BERTHS	BINGE	BLAZE	BLUFFS	BONNES	YBOUND	BRAVE	BRISKY
BEDEW	BERYL	BINGED	ABLAZE	BLUID	BONNET	BOUNDS	BRAVED	BRIZE
BEDEWS	BERYLS	BINGER	BLAZED	BLUIDS	BONZE	BOURD	BRAVER	BRIZES
BEDIM	BESEE	BINGES	BLAZER	BLUIDY	BONZER	BOURDS	BRAVES	BROAD
BEDIMS	BESEEM	BINGO	BLAZES	BLUNK	BONZES	BOURG	BRAVO	ABROAD
BEDYE	BESEEN	BINGOS	BLEAK	BLUNKS	BOOKS	BOURGS	BRAVOS	BROADS
BEDYED	BESEES	BIOME	BLEAKS	BLUNT	BOOKSY	BOURN	BRAWL	BROCH
BEDYES	BESET	BIOMES	BLEAKY	BLUNTS	BOONG	BOURNE	BRAWLS	BROCHE
BEFIT	BESETS	BIONT	BLEAR	BLURB	BOONGS	BOURNS	BRAWLY	BROCHS
BEFITS	BESIT	BIONTS	BLEARS	BLURBS	BOORD	BOUSE	BRAWN	BROCK
BEFOG	BESITS	BIOTA	BLEARY	BLURT	BOORDE	BOUSED	BRAWNS	BROCKS
BEFOGS	BESOM	BIOTAS	BLEAT	BLURTS	BOORDS	BOUSES	BRAWNY	BROGH
BEGAR	BESOMS	BIPED	BLEATS	BLUSH	BOOSE	BOUTS	BRAYS	BROGHS
BEGARS	BESOT	BIPEDS	BLEED	ABLUSH	BOOSED	ABOUTS	ABRAYS	BROIL
BEGEM	BESOTS	BIPOD	BLEEDS	BOARD	BOOSES	BOWAT	BRAZE	BROILS
BEGEMS	BETEL	BIPODS	BLEEP	ABOARD	BOOST	BOWATS	BRAZED	BROKE
BEGET	BETELS	BIRLE	BLEEPS	BOARDS	BOOSTS	BOWEL	BRAZEN	BROKED
BEGETS	BETID	BIRLED	BLEND	BOART	BOOTH	BOWELS	BRAZES	BROKEN
BEGIN	BETIDE	BIRLER	BLENDE	BOARTS	BOOTHS	BOWER	BREAD	BROKER
BEGINS	BETON	BIRLES	BLENDS	BOAST	BOOZE	BOWERS	BREADS	BROKES
BEGUM	BETONS	BIRSE	BLENT	BOASTS	BOOZED	BOWERY	BREAK	BROND
BEGUMS	BETONY	BIRSES	YBLENT	BOBAC	BOOZER	BOWET	BREAKS	BRONDS
BEGUN	BEVEL	BIRTH	BLEST	BOBACS	BOOZES	BOWETS	BREAM	BROOD
BEGUNK	BEVELS	BIRTHS	ABLEST	BOBAK	BOOZEY	BOWNE	BREAMS	BROODS
BEIGE	BEVER	BISES	BLETS	BOBAKS	BORDE	BOWNED	BREDE	BROODY
BEIGEL	BEVERS	IBISES	ABLETS	BOCCA	BORDEL	BOWNES	BREDED	BROOK
BEIGES	BEVUE	BISON	BLIMP	BOCCAS	BORDER	BOWSE	BREDES	BROOKS
BEING	BEVUES	BISONS	BLIMPS	BOCHE	BORDES	BOWSED	BREED	BROOL
BEINGS	BEWET	BITCH	BLIND	BOCHES	BORDS	BOWSER	BREEDS	BROOLS
BEKAH	BEWETS	BITCHY	BLINDS	BODED	ABORDS	BOWSES	BREER	BROOM
BEKAHS	BEWIG	BITER	BLINI	ABODED	BOREE	BOXER	BREERS	BROOMS
BELAH	BEWIGS	OBITER	BLINIS	BODES	BOREEN	BOXERS	BREES	BROOMY
BELAHS	BEZEL	BITERS	BLINK	ABODES	BOREES	BOYAR	BREESE	BROOS
BELAY	BEZELS	BITTE	BLINKS	BODGE	BORER	BOYARS	BRENT	BROOSE
BELAYS	BHANG	BITTED	BLINS	BODGED	BORERS	BOYAU	YBRENT	BROSE
BELEE	BHANGS	BITTEN	ABLINS	BODGER	BORGO	BOYAUX	BRERE	BROSES
BELEED	BIBLE	BITTER	BLITE	BODGES	BORGOS	BRACE	BRERES	BROTH

BROTHS	BUNIA	CABOB	CANOE	CARVEL	SCENTS	CHARTS	CHIMED	CHUMPS
BROWN	BUNIAS	CABOBS	CANOED	CARVEN	CEORL	CHASE	CHIMER	CHUNK
BROWNS	BUNJE	CABOC	CANOES	CARVER	CEORLS	CHASED	CHIMES	CHUNKS
BROWNY	BUNJEE	CABOCS	CANON	CARVES	CERGE	CHASER	CHIMP	CHUNKY
BROWS	BUNJES	CACAO	CANONS	CASCO	CERGES	CHASES	CHIMPS	CHURL
BROWSE	BUNKO	CACAOS	CANTO	CASCOS	CERIA	CHASM	CHINA	CHURLS
BROWST	BUNKOS	CACHE	CANTON	CASTE	CERIAS	CHASMS	CHINAR	CHURN
BRUIT	BUNYA	CACHED	CANTOR	CASTED	CERNE	CHASMY	CHINAS	CHURNS
BRUITS	BUNYAS	CACHES	CANTOS	CASTER	CERNED	CHAYA	CHINE	CHURR
BRUME	BURAN	CACHET	CANTS	CASTES	CERNES	CHAYAS	CHINED	CHURRS
BRUMES	BURANS	CADET	SCANTS	CATCH	SCERNE	CHEAP	CHINES	CHUSE
BRUNT	BURGH	CADETS	CANTY	CATCHT	CESSE	CHEAPO	CHINK	CHUSES
BRUNTS	BURGHS	CADGE	SCANTY	CATCHY	CESSED	CHEAPS	CHINKS	CHUTE
BRUSH	BURIN	CADGED	CAPAS	CATER	CESSER	CHEAPY	CHINKY	CHUTES
BRUSHY	BURINS	CADGER	SCAPAS	ACATER	CESSES	CHEAT	CHINO	CHYLE
BRUST	BURKA	CADGES	CAPED	CATERS	CETYL	CHEATS	CHINOS	CHYLES
BRUSTS	BURKAS	CADIE	SCAPED	CATES	ACETYL	CHECK	CHIRK	CHYME
BRUTE	BURKE	CADIES	CAPER	ACATES	CETYLS	CHECKS	CHIRKS	CHYMES
BRUTED	BURKED	CADRE	CAPERS	CATTY	ACETYLS	CHECKY	CHIRL	CIBOL
BRUTES	BURKES	CADRES	CAPES	SCATTY	CHACE	CHEEK	CHIRLS	CIBOLS
BUAZE	BUROO	CAECA	SCAPES	CAULD	CHACED	CHEEKS	CHIRM	CIDER
BUAZES	BUROOS	CAECAL	CAPLE	CAULDS	CHACES	CHEEKY	CHIRMS	CIDERS
BUBAL	BURQA	CAFFS	CAPLES	CAULK	CHACK	CHEEP	CHIRP	CIDERY
BUBALS	BURQAS	SCAFFS	CAPON	CAULKS	CHACKS	CHEEPS	CHIRPS	CIGAR
BUCHU	BURRO	CAGOT	CAPONS	CAUPS	CHACO	CHEER	CHIRPY	CIGARS
BUCHUS	BURROS	CAGOTS	CAPOT	SCAUPS	CHACOS	CHEERO	CHIRR	CIMAR
BUCKU	BURROW	CAIRD	CAPOTE	CAUSE	CHAFE	CHEERS	CHIRRS	CIMARS
BUCKUS	BURSA	CAIRDS	CAPOTS	CAUSED	CHAFED	CHEERY	CHIRT	CIONS
BUDGE	BURSAE	CAIRN	CAPUL	CAUSEN	CHAFER	CHEKA	CHIRTS	SCIONS
BUDGED	BURSAL	CAIRNS	CAPULS	CAUSER	CHAFES	CHEKAS	CHIVE	CIRCA
BUDGER	BURSAR	CALIF	CARAP	CAUSES	CHAFF	CHELA	CHIVED	CIRCAR
BUDGES	BURSE	CALIFS	CARAPS	CAUSEY	CHAFFS	CHELAE	CHIVES	CISCO
BUDGET	BURSES	CALLA	CARAT	CAVEL	CHAFFY	CHELAS	CHOCK	CISCOS
BUFFE	BURST	CALLAS	CARATS	CAVELS	CHAFT	CHERT	CHOCKS	CITAL
BUFFED	ABURST	CALLS	CARDI	CAVER	CHAFTS	CHERTS	CHOIR	CITALS
BUFFER	BURSTS	SCALLS	CARDIS	CAVERN	CHAIN	CHERTY	CHOIRS	CITER
BUFFET	BUSED	CALPA	CARED	CAVERS	CHAINS	CHEST	CHOKE	CITERS
BUGLE	ABUSED	CALPAC	SCARED	CAVIE	CHAIR	CHESTS	CHOKED	CITES
BUGLED	BUSES	CALPAS	CARER	CAVIER	CHAIRS	CHESTY	CHOKER	CITESS
BUGLER	ABUSES	CALPS	SCARER	CAVIES	CHAIS	CHICA	CHOKES	CIVET
BUGLES	BUSSU	SCALPS	CARERS	CAVIL	CHAISE	CHICAS	CHOKEY	CIVETS
BUGLET	BUSSUS	CALVE	CARES	CAVILS	CHALK	CHICH	CHOLI	CIVIC
BUILD	BUTTE	CALVED	SCARES	CAXON	CHALKS	CHICHA	CHOLIC	CIVICS
BUILDS	BUTTED	CALVER	CARESS	CAXONS	CHALKY	CHICHI	CHOLIS	CLACK
BUIST	BUTTER	CALVES	CARET	CEASE	CHAMP	CHICK	CHOMP	CLACKS
BUISTS	BUTTES	CAMAN	CARETS	CEASED	CHAMPS	CHICKS	CHOMPS	CLADE
BULGE	BUTYL	CAMANS	CAROB	CEASES	CHANK	CHIDE	CHOOK	CLADES
BULGED	BUTYLS	CAMAS	CAROBS	CEAZE	CHANKS	CHIDED	CHOOKS	CLAIM
BULGER	BUYER	CAMASH	CAROL	CEAZED	CHANT	CHIDER	CHOOM	CLAIMS
BULGES	BUYERS	CAMASS	CAROLS	CEAZES	CHANTS	CHIDES	CHOOMS	CLAME
BULLA	BWANA	CAMEL	CAROM	CEDAR	CHANTY	CHIEF	CHORD	CLAMES
BULLAE	BWANAS	SCAMEL	CAROMS	CEDARN	CHAPE	CHIEFS	CHORDS	CLAMP
BULLAS	BWAZI	CAMELS	CARPS	CEDARS	CHAPEL	CHIEL	CHORE	CLAMPS
BULSE	BWAZIS	CAMEO	SCARPS	CEILI	CHAPES	CHIELD	CHOREA	CLANG
BULSES	BYLAW	CAMEOS	CARRY	CEILIS	CHARA	CHIELS	CHOREE	CLANGS
BUMBO	BYLAWS	CAMES	SCARRY	CELLA	CHARAS	CHILD	CHORES	CLANK
BUMBOS	BYWAY	CAMESE	CARSE	CELLAE	CHARD	CHILDE	CHOSE	CLANKS
BUMPH	BYWAYS	CAMIS	CARSES	CELLAR	CHARDS	CHILDS	CHOSEN	CLART
BUMPHS	CABAL	CAMISE	CARTA	CELLO	CHARE	CHILE	CHOSES	CLARTS
BUNAS	CABALA	CAMPS	CARTAS	CELLOS	CHARED	CHILES	CHOUT	CLARTY
ABUNAS	CABALS	SCAMPS	CARTE	CELOM	CHARES	CHILI	CHOUTS	CLASP
BUNCE	CABBY	CANAL	ECARTE	CELOMS	CHARET	CHILIS	SCHOUT	CLASPS
BUNCED	SCABBY	CANALS	CARTED	CENSE	CHARK	CHILL	CHUCK	CLASS
BUNCES	CABER	CANEH	CARTEL	CENSED	CHARKS	CHILLI	CHUCKS	CLASSY
BUNCH	CABERS	CANEHS	CARTER	CENSER	CHARM	CHILLS	CHUFA	CLATS
BUNCHY	CABIN	CANID	CARTES	CENSES	CHARMS	CHILLY	CHUFAS	ECLATS
BUNCO	CABINS	CANIDS	CARTS	CENTO	CHARR	CHIMB	CHUFF	CLAUT
BUNCOS	CABLE	CANNA	SCARTS	CENTOS	CHARRS	CHIMBS	CHUFFS	CLAUTS
BUNDU	CABLED	CANNAE	CARVE	CENTS	CHARRY	CHIME	CHUFFY	CLAVE
BUNDUS	CABLES	CANNAS	CARVED		CHART		CHUMP	
					CHARTA			

SCLAVE	CLOSE	COCOA	CONGES	COSTAL	CRAIGS	CREESH	CROUPE	CURAT
CLAVER	ECLOSE	COCOAS	CONGO	COSTE	CRAKE	CREME	CROUPS	CURATE
CLAVES	CLOSED	CODON	CONGOS	COSTED	CRAKED	CREMES	CROUPY	CURATS
CLEAN	CLOSER	CODONS	CONGOU	COSTER	CRAKES	CRENA	CROUT	CURER
CLEANS	CLOSES	COFFS	CONIA	COSTES	CRAME	CRENAS	CROUTE	CURERS
CLEAR	CLOSET	SCOFFS	CONIAS	COTTA	CRAMES	CREPE	CROUTS	CURIA
CLEARS	CLOTE	COGIE	CONIC	COTTAR	CRAMP	CREPED	CROWD	CURIAE
CLEAT	CLOTES	COGIES	ICONIC	COTTAS	CRAMPS	CREPES	CROWDS	CURIAS
CLEATS	CLOTH	COGUE	CONICS	COUCH	CRAMPY	CRESS	CROWN	CURIE
CLECK	CLOTHE	COGUES	CONNE	COUCHE	CRAMS	CRESSY	CROWNS	CURIES
CLECKS	CLOTHS	COHOE	CONNED	COUGH	SCRAMS	CREST	CROWS	CURIET
CLEEK	CLOUD	COHOES	CONNER	COUGHS	CRANE	CRESTS	SCROWS	CURIO
CLEEKS	CLOUDS	COHOG	CONNES	COUNT	CRANED	CREWE	CROZE	CURIOS
CLEEP	CLOUDY	COHOGS	CONTE	COUNTS	CRANES	CREWED	CROZES	CURRY
CLEEPS	CLOUR	COIGN	CONTES	COUNTY	CRANK	CREWEL	CRUCK	SCURRY
CLEFT	CLOURS	COIGNE	CONTO	COUPE	CRANKS	CREWES	CRUCKS	CURSE
CLEFTS	CLOUT	COIGNS	CONTOS	COUPED	CRANKY	CREWS	CRUDE	CURSED
CLEPE	CLOUTS	COLDS	COOEE	COUPEE	CRANS	SCREWS	CRUDER	CURSER
CLEPED	CLOVE	SCOLDS	COOEED	COUPER	SCRANS	CRICK	CRUDES	CURSES
CLEPES	CLOVEN	COLEY	COOEES	COUPES	CRAPE	CRICKS	CRUEL	CURVE
CLERK	CLOVER	COLEYS	COOEY	COUPS	SCRAPE	CRICKY	CRUELS	CURVED
CLERKS	CLOVES	COLIC	COOEYS	SCOUPS	CRAPED	CRIED	CRUET	CURVES
CLEVE	CLOWN	COLICS	COOMB	COURB	CRAPES	CRIER	CRUETS	CURVET
CLEVER	CLOWNS	COLIN	COOMBS	COURBS	CRAPS	CRIERS	CRUMB	CURVY
CLEVES	CLOYE	COLINS	COOPS	COURE	SCRAPS	CRIES	CRUMBS	SCURVY
CLICK	CLOYED	COLON	SCOOPS	COURED	CRARE	CRIME	CRUMBY	CUSEC
CLICKS	CLOYES	COLONS	COOTS	COURES	CRARES	CRIMED	CRUMP	CUSECS
CLIFF	CLUCK	COLONY	SCOOTS	COURS	CRATE	CRIMES	SCRUMP	CUTCH
SCLIFF	CLUCKS	COLOR	COPAL	COURSE	CRATED	CRIMP	CRUMPS	SCUTCH
CLIFFS	CLUCKY	COLORS	COPALS	COURT	CRATER	SCRIMP	CRUMPY	CUTCHA
CLIFFY	CLUMP	COLZA	COPER	COURTS	CRATES	CRIMPS	CRUOR	CUTER
CLIFT	CLUMPS	COLZAS	COPERS	COUTH	CRAVE	CRIMPY	CRUORS	ACUTER
CLIFTS	CLUMPY	COMBE	COPES	COUTHY	CRAVED	CRINE	CRUSE	CUTES
CLIFTY	CLUNK	COMBED	SCOPES	COVEN	CRAVEN	SCRINE	CRUSES	ACUTES
CLIMB	CLUNKS	COMBER	COPRA	COVENS	CRAVER	CRINED	CRUSET	SCUTES
CLIMBS	CLYPE	COMBES	COPRAS	COVENT	CRAVES	CRINES	CRUST	CUTEST
CLIME	CLYPED	COMBO	COPSE	COVER	CRAWL	CRISE	CRUSTA	CUTESY
CLIMES	CLYPEI	COMBOS	COPSED	COVERS	ACRAWL	CRISES	CRUSTS	CUTEY
CLINE	CLYPES	COMER	COPSES	COVERT	SCRAWL	CRISP	CRUSTY	CUTEYS
CLINES	CNIDA	COMERS	CORAL	COVET	CRAWLS	CRISPS	CRUVE	CUTIE
CLING	CNIDAE	COMET	CORALS	COVETS	CRAWLY	CRISPY	CRUVES	CUTIES
CLINGS	COACH	COMETS	CORBE	COVEY	CRAWS	CRITH	CRWTH	CUTIN
CLINGY	COACHY	COMIC	CORBEL	COVEYS	SCRAWS	CRITHS	CRWTHS	CUTINS
CLINK	COACT	COMICS	CORBES	COVIN	CRAZE	CROAK	CRYPT	CUTTO
CLINKS	COACTS	COMMA	CORED	COVING	CRAZED	CROAKS	CRYPTO	CUTTOE
CLINT	COAPT	COMMAS	SCORED	COVINS	CRAZES	CROAKY	CRYPTS	CUVEE
CLINTS	COAPTS	COMMO	CORER	COWAN	CREAK	CROCK	CTENE	CUVEES
CLIPE	COARB	COMMON	CORERS	COWANS	SCREAK	CROCKS	CTENES	CYCAD
CLIPED	COARBS	COMMOS	CORES	COWER	CREAKS	CROFT	CUBEB	CYCADS
CLIPES	COAST	COMMOT	SCORES	COWERS	CREAKY	CROFTS	CUBEBS	CYCLE
CLOAK	COASTS	COMPO	CORGI	COWLS	CREAM	CROMB	CUBIC	CYCLED
CLOAKS	COATE	COMPOS	CORGIS	SCOWLS	SCREAM	CROMBS	CUBICA	CYCLER
CLOAM	COATED	COMPOT	CORIA	COWPS	CREAMS	CROME	CUBIT	CYCLES
CLOAMS	COATEE	COMPT	SCORIA	SCOWPS	CREAMY	CROMED	CUBITS	CYCLO
CLOCK	COATER	COMPTS	CORNS	COYPU	CREDO	CROMES	CUFFS	CYCLOS
CLOCKS	COATES	CONCH	ACORNS	COYPUS	CREDOS	CRONE	SCUFFS	CYDER
CLOFF	COATI	CONCHA	SCORNS	COZEN	CREED	CRONES	CULET	CYDERS
CLOFFS	COATIS	CONCHE	CORNU	COZENS	SCREED	CRONET	CULETS	CYMAR
CLOKE	COBIA	CONCHS	CORNUA	CRABS	CREEDS	CROOK	CULLS	CYMARS
CLOKED	COBIAS	CONCHY	CORPS	SCRABS	CREEK	CROOKS	SCULLS	CYNIC
CLOKES	COBLE	CONES	CORPSE	CRACK	CREEKS	CROON	CUMEC	CYNICS
CLONE	COBLES	SCONES	CORSE	CRACKS	CREEKY	CROONS	CUMECS	CYTON
CLONED	COBRA	CONEY	SCORSE	CRAFT	CREEL	CRORE	CUMIN	CYTONS
CLONES	COBRAS	CONEYS	CORSES	CRAFTS	CREELS	CRORES	CUMINS	DACHA
CLONK	COCCI	CONGA	CORSET	CRAFTY	CREEP	CROSS	CUPEL	DACHAS
CLONKS	COCCID	CONGAS	CORSO	CRAGS	CREEPS	ACROSS	CUPELS	DAGGA
CLOOP	COCCO	CONGE	CORSOS	SCRAGS	CREEPY	CROSSE	CUPID	DAGGAS
CLOOPS	COCCOS	CONGED	COSTA	CRAIG	CREES	CROUP	CUPIDS	DAINE
CLOOT	COCKS	CONGEE	COSTAE		SCREES		CUPPA	SDAINE
CLOOTS	COCKSY	CONGER			CREESE		CUPPAS	

DAINED	DEBELS	DEPOTS	DINGEY	DONUTS	DRAFFY	DROOK	DURUM	DEARTH
DAINES	DEBIT	DEPTH	DINIC	DOOLE	DRAFT	DROOKS	DURUMS	HEARTH
DAINT	DEBITS	DEPTHS	DINICS	DOOLES	DRAFTS	DROOL	DUSTS	EARTHS
DAINTY	DEBUG	DERAY	DIODE	DOORN	DRAIL	DROOLS	ADUSTS	EARTHY
DAKER	DEBUGS	DERAYS	DIODES	DOORNS	DRAILS	DROOP	DUVET	EASED
DAKERS	DEBUT	DERMA	DIOTA	DOORS	DRAIN	DROOPS	DUVETS	CEASED
DALLE	DEBUTS	DERMAL	DIOTAS	ADOORS	DRAINS	DROOPY	DWALE	LEASED
DALLES	DECAD	DERMAS	DIPSO	DOPER	DRAKE	DROPS	DWALES	MEASED
DAMAN	DECADE	DERTH	DIPSOS	DOPERS	DRAKES	DROPSY	DWALM	PEASED
DAMANS	DECADS	DERTHS	DIRGE	DORAD	DRAMA	DROSS	DWALMS	SEASED
DAMAR	DECAL	DESSE	DIRGES	DORADO	DRAMAS	DROSSY	DWARF	TEASED
DAMARS	DECALS	DESSES	DIRKE	DORADS	DRANT	DROUK	DWARFS	EASEL
DAMME	DECAY	DETER	DIRKED	DOREE	DRANTS	DROUKS	DWAUM	TEASEL
DAMMED	DECAYS	DETERS	DIRKES	DOREES	DRAPE	DROVE	DWAUMS	WEASEL
DAMMER	DECKO	DEUCE	DISCO	DORSA	DRAPED	DROVER	DWELL	EASELS
DANCE	DECKOS	DEUCED	DISCOS	DORSAL	DRAPER	DROVES	DWELLS	EASES
DANCED	DECOR	DEUCES	DISME	DORSE	DRAPES	DROWN	DWINE	CEASES
DANCER	DECORS	DEVEL	DISMES	DORSEL	DRAPET	DROWNS	DWINED	LEASES
DANCES	DECOY	DEVELS	DITAL	DORSER	DRAWL	DROWS	DWINES	MEASES
DANIO	DECOYS	DEVIL	DITALS	DORSES	DRAWLS	DROWSE	DYING	PEASES
DANIOS	DEEMS	DEVILS	DITED	DOSEH	DREAD	DROWSY	DYINGS	SEASES
DANTS	ADEEMS	DEVOT	EDITED	DOSEHS	ADREAD	DRUID	EAGER	TEASES
IDANTS	DEEVE	DEVOTE	DITTO	DOTER	DREADS	DRUIDS	EAGERS	EASLE
DARAF	DEEVED	DEVOTS	DITTOS	DOTERS	DREAM	DRUNK	EAGLE	EASLES
DARAFS	DEEVES	DEWAN	DIVAN	DOUAR	DREAMS	DRUNKS	BEAGLE	EASTS
DARGA	DEFAT	DEWANI	DIVANS	DOUARS	DREAMT	DRUPE	TEAGLE	BEASTS
DARGAS	DEFATS	DEWANS	DIVER	DOUBT	DREAMY	DRUPEL	EAGLES	FEASTS
DARIC	DEFER	DHOBI	DIVERS	DOUBTS	DREAR	DRUPES	EAGLET	HEASTS
DARICS	DEFERS	DHOBIS	DIVERT	DOUCE	DREARE	DRUSE	EAGRE	LEASTS
DARRE	DEGUM	DHOLE	DIVES	DOUCER	DREARS	DRUSES	EAGRES	REASTS
DARRED	DEGUMS	DHOLES	DIVEST	DOUCET	DREARY	MEAGRE	EALES	YEASTS
DARRES	DEIGN	DHOLL	DIVOT	DOUGH	DRECK	DRYAD	VEALES	EATEN
DARZI	DEIGNS	DHOLLS	DIVOTS	DOUGHS	DRECKS	DRYADS	EANED	BEATEN
DARZIS	DEISM	DHOTI	DIWAN	DOUGHT	DRERE	DRYER	BEANED	NEATEN
DATAL	DEISMS	DHOTIS	DIWANS	DOUGHY	DRERES	DRYERS	LEANED	EATER
DATALS	DEIST	DIAZO	DIXIE	DOUMA	DRESS	DSOBO	MEANED	BEATER
DATER	DEISTS	DIAZOS	DIXIES	DOUMAS	DRESSY	DSOBOS	PEANED	HEATER
DATERS	DEKKO	DICER	DIZEN	DOURA	DRIER	DSOMO	SEANED	NEATER
DAUBE	DEKKOS	DICERS	DIZENS	DOURAS	DRIERS	DSOMOS	WEANED	SEATER
DAUBED	DELAY	DICHT	DJINN	DOUSE	DRIES	DUCAT	YEANED	EATERS
DAUBER	DELAYS	DICHTS	DJINNI	DOUSED	DRIEST	DUCATS	EARDS	EATERY
DAUBES	DELFT	DICOT	DODGE	DOUSER	DRIFT	DUCES	BEARDS	EATHE
DAULT	DELFTS	DICOTS	DODGED	DOUSES	ADRIFT	EDUCES	HEARDS	MEATHE
DAULTS	DELPH	DICTS	DODGEM	DOVER	DRIFTS	DUCTS	YEARDS	EAVES
DAUNT	DELPHS	EDICTS	DODGER	DOVERS	DRIFTY	EDUCTS	EARED	DEAVES
DAUNTS	DELTA	DIENE	DODGES	DOVIE	DRILL	DUETT	BEARED	HEAVES
DAVIT	DELTAS	DIENES	DOGIE	DOVIER	DRILLS	DUETTI	DEARED	LEAVES
DAVITS	DELVE	DIGHT	DOGIES	DOWAR	DRINK	DUETTO	FEARED	REAVES
DAWED	DELVED	DIGHTS	DOGMA	DOWARS	DRINKS	DUETTS	GEARED	WEAVES
ADAWED	DELVER	DIGIT	DOGMAS	DOWEL	DRIVE	DULIA	LEARED	EBBED
DEALS	DELVES	DIGITS	DOING	DOWELS	DRIVEL	DULIAS	NEARED	KEBBED
IDEALS	DEMAN	DIKAS	DOINGS	DOWER	DRIVEN	DULSE	REARED	NEBBED
DEARE	DEMAND	DIKAST	DOLCE	DOWERS	DRIVER	DULSES	SEARED	WEBBED
DEARED	DEMANS	DIKER	DOLCES	DOWIE	DRIVES	DUNCE	WEARED	ECADS
DEARER	DEMIT	DIKERS	DOLMA	DOWIER	DROIL	DUNCES	EARLS	DECADS
DEARES	DEMITS	DILDO	DOLMAN	DOWLE	DROILS	DUOMO	PEARLS	ECHED
DEARN	DEMOB	DILDOE	DOLMAS	DOWLES	DROIT	DUOMOS	EARLY	EECHED
DEARNS	DEMOBS	DILDOS	DONAH	DOWSE	DROITS	DUPER	DEARLY	LECHED
DEATH	DEMON	DILLI	DONAHS	DOWSED	DROLE	DUPERS	NEARLY	PECHED
DEATHS	DEMONS	DILLIS	DONEE	DOWSER	DROLER	DUPLE	PEARLY	ECHES
DEATHY	DEMUR	DIMER	DONEES	DOWSES	DROLES	DUPLET	REARLY	EECHES
DEAVE	DEMURE	DIMERS	DONGA	DOWSET	DROLL	DUPLEX	YEARLY	LECHES
DEAVED	DEMURS	DINAR	DONGAS	DOYEN	DROLLS	DURAL	EARNS	ECLAT
DEAVES	DENAY	DINARS	DONNE	DOYENS	DROLLY	DURALS	DEARNS	ECLATS
DEBAG	DENAYS	DINER	DONNED	DOZEN	DROME	DURES	LEARNS	EDEMA
DEBAGS	DENIM	DINERS	DONNEE	DOZENS	DROMES	DURESS	YEARNS	OEDEMA
DEBAR	DENIMS	DINGE	DONNES	DOZER	DRONE	DUROY	EARST	EDEMAS
DEBARK	DENSE	DINGED	DONOR	DOZERS	DRONED	DUROYS	PEARST	EDGED
DEBARS	DENSER	DINGER	DONORS	DRAFF	DRONES	DURRA	EARTH	HEDGED
DEBEL	DEPOT	DINGES	DONUT	DRAFFS		DURRAS		

KEDGED	EIKONS	ELUTED	ENDED	EPHOD	ESCOT	ETUDE	EXISTS	FARCE
SEDGED	EISEL	ELUTES	BENDED	EPHODS	ESCOTS	ETUDES	EXODE	FARCED
WEDGED	EISELL	ELVAN	FENDED	EPHOR	ESILE	ETWEE	EXODES	FARCES
EDGER	EISELS	ELVANS	HENDED	EPHORS	RESILE	ETWEES	EXPAT	FARCI
HEDGER	EJECT	ELVER	MENDED	EPOCH	ESILES	EUGHS	EXPATS	FARCIN
KEDGER	DEJECT	DELVER	PENDED	EPOCHA	ESKAR	HEUGHS	EXPEL	FARLE
LEDGER	REJECT	ELVERS	SENDED	EPOCHS	ESKARS	EUKED	EXPELS	FARLES
EDGERS	EJECTA	ELVES	TENDED	EPODE	ESKER	YEUKED	EXPOS	FARSE
EDGES	EJECTS	DELVES	VENDED	EPODES	ESKERS	EUPAD	EXPOSE	FARSED
HEDGES	EKING	HELVES	WENDED	EPOPT	ESSAY	EUPADS	EXTOL	FARSES
KEDGES	REKING	PELVES	ENDEW	EPOPTS	ESSAYS	EUSOL	EXTOLD	FASCI
LEDGES	ELAND	SELVES	ENDEWS	EPRIS	ESSES	EUSOLS	EXTOLS	FASCIA
SEDGES	ELANDS	EMBAR	ENDOW	EPRISE	CESSES	EVADE	EXTRA	FASCIO
WEDGES	ELATE	EMBARK	ENDOWS	EQUAL	DESSES	EVADED	EXTRAS	FATSO
EDICT	BELATE	EMBARS	ENDUE	EQUALS	FESSES	EVADES	EXUDE	FATSOS
EDICTS	DELATE	EMBAY	VENDUE	EQUIP	GESSES	EVENS	EXUDED	FAULT
EDILE	RELATE	EMBAYS	ENDUED	EQUIPE	JESSES	EEVENS	EXUDES	FAULTS
AEDILE	VELATE	EMBED	ENDUES	EQUIPS	LESSES	SEVENS	EXULT	FAULTY
SEDILE	ELATED	KEMBED	ENEMA	ERASE	MESSES	EVENT	EXULTS	FAUNA
EDILES	ELATER	EMBEDS	ENEMAS	ERASED	NESSES	EVENTS	EXURB	FAUNAE
EDUCE	ELATES	EMBER	ENEWS	ERASER	SESSES	EVERT	EXURBS	FAUNAL
DEDUCE	ELBOW	MEMBER	RENEWS	ERASES	YESSES	REVERT	EYING	FAUNAS
REDUCE	ELBOWS	EMBERS	ENIAC	ERBIA	ESTER	EVERTS	FEYING	FAVEL
SEDUCE	ELCHI	EMBOG	ENIACS	ERBIAS	FESTER	EVERY	HEYING	FAVELA
EDUCED	ELCHIS	EMBOGS	ENJOY	ERECT	JESTER	REVERY	KEYING	FAVELL
EDUCES	ELDER	EMBOW	ENJOYS	ERECTS	NESTER	SEVERY	EYRIE	FAVOR
EDUCT	GELDER	EMBOWS	ENMEW	ERGON	PESTER	EVETS	EYRIES	FAVORS
DEDUCT	MELDER	EMBUS	ENMEWS	ERGONS	RESTER	REVETS	FABLE	FAYNE
EDUCTS	WELDER	EMBUSY	ENNUI	ERGOT	TESTER	EVICT	FABLED	FAYNED
EERIE	ELDERS	EMCEE	ENNUIS	ERGOTS	WESTER	EVICTS	FABLER	FAYNES
FEERIE	ELDIN	EMCEED	ENROL	ERICA	YESTER	EVILS	FABLES	FEARE
PEERIE	ELDING	EMCEES	ENROLL	ERICAS	ESTERS	DEVILS	FACER	FEARED
EERIER	ELDINS	EMEER	ENROLS	ERICK	ESTOC	EVITE	FACERS	FEARES
EEVEN	ELECT	EMEERS	ENSEW	ERICKS	ESTOCS	LEVITE	FACET	FEARS
EEVENS	SELECT	EMEND	ENSEWS	ERING	ESTOP	EVITED	FACETE	AFEARS
EFFED	ELECTS	EMENDS	ENSUE	CERING	ESTOPS	EVITES	FACETS	FEAST
JEFFED	ELEMI	EMITS	ENSUED	DERING	ESTRO	EVOKE	FACIA	FEASTS
REFFED	ELEMIS	DEMITS	ENSUES	LERING	ESTROS	REVOKE	FACIAL	FECHT
EGERS	ELFED	REMITS	ENTER	MERING	ETAGE	EVOKED	FACIAS	FECHTS
LEGERS	SELFED	EMMAS	CENTER	SERING	METAGE	EVOKES	FADGE	FEESE
EGEST	ELFIN	LEMMAS	RENTER	ERINGO	ETAGES	EWERS	FADGED	FEESED
REGEST	ELFING	EMMER	TENTER	ERNED	ETAPE	HEWERS	FADGES	FEESES
EGESTA	ELFINS	EMMERS	VENTER	CERNED	ETAPES	SEWERS	FAGOT	FEEZE
EGESTS	ELIAD	EMMET	ENTERA	GERNED	ETHAL	EWEST	FAGOTS	FEEZED
EGGAR	ELIADS	EMMETS	ENTERS	KERNED	LETHAL	FEWEST	FAINE	FEEZES
BEGGAR	ELIDE	EMMEW	ENTRY	TERNED	ETHALS	NEWEST	FAINED	FEIGN
SEGGAR	RELIDE	EMMEWS	CENTRY	ERNES	ETHER	EXACT	FAINER	FEIGNS
EGGARS	ELIDED	EMOTE	GENTRY	CERNES	AETHER	HEXACT	FAINES	FEINT
EGGED	ELIDES	DEMOTE	SENTRY	GERNES	HETHER	EXACTS	FAINT	FEINTS
BEGGED	ELITE	REMOTE	ENURE	KERNES	NETHER	EXALT	FAINTS	FELLA
LEGGED	PELITE	EMOTED	TENURE	TERNES	PETHER	EXALTS	FAINTY	FELLAH
PEGGED	ELITES	EMOTES	ENURED	ERODE	TETHER	EXCEL	FAITH	FELLAS
EGGER	ELOGE	EMOVE	ENURES	ERODED	WETHER	EXCELS	FAITHS	FELON
LEGGER	ELOGES	REMOVE	ENVOI	ERODES	ETHERS	EXEAT	FAKER	FELONS
EGGERS	ELOIN	EMOVED	RENVOI	ERRED	ETHIC	EXEATS	FAKERS	FELONY
EGGERY	ELOINS	EMOVES	ENVOIS	SERRED	ETHICS	EXEEM	FAKERY	FEMAL
EGRET	ELOPE	EMULE	ENVOY	ERROR	ETHYL	EXEEMS	FAKIR	FEMALE
REGRET	ELOPED	AEMULE	LENVOY	TERROR	METHYL	EXEME	FAKIRS	FEMALS
EGRETS	ELOPER	EMULED	RENVOY	ERRORS	ETHYLS	LEXEME	FALSE	FEMME
EIDER	ELOPES	EMULES	ENVOYS	ERSES	ETTIN	EXEMED	FALSED	FEMMES
DEIDER	ELPEE	EMURE	EORLS	HERSES	ETTINS	EXEMES	FALSER	FEMUR
EIDERS	ELPEES	DEMURE	CEORLS	MERSES	ETTLE	EXERT	FALSES	FEMURS
EIGHT	ELSIN	EMURED	EOSIN	PERSES	FETTLE	EXERTS	FANAL	FENCE
HEIGHT	ELSINS	EMURES	EOSINS	VERSES	KETTLE	EXILE	FANALS	FENCED
KEIGHT	ELUDE	ENACT	EPACT	ERUCT	METTLE	EXILED	FANGO	FENCER
WEIGHT	DELUDE	ENACTS	EPACTS	ERUCTS	NETTLE	EXILES	FANGOS	FENCES
EIGHTH	ELUDED	ENARM	EPEES	ERUPT	PETTLE	EXINE	FANON	FEOFF
EIGHTS	ELUDER	ENARMS	TEPEES	ERUPTS	SETTLE	EXINES	FANONS	FEOFFS
EIGHTY	ELUDES	ENATE	EPHAH	ERVEN	ETTLED	EXIST	FARAD	FERES
EIKON	ELUTE	SENATE	EPHAHS	VERVEN	ETTLES	SEXIST	FARADS	FEREST

FERMI	FIORDS	FLIMPS	**FLYER**	**FOUND**	FRISKS	FUROLS	IGAPOS	**GENIP**
FERMIS	**FIRER**	**FLING**	FLYERS	FOUNDS	FRISKY	**FUROR**	**GARBE**	GENIPS
FESSE	FIRERS	FLINGS	**FLYPE**	FOUNT	FRIST	FURORE	GARBED	**GENOA**
FESSES	**FIRST**	**FLINT**	FLYPED	FOUNTS	FRISTS	FURORS	GARBES	GENOAS
FESTA	FIRSTS	FLINTS	FLYPES	**FOUTH**	**FRITH**	**FURZE**	**GARBO**	**GENOM**
FESTAL	**FIRTH**	FLINTY	**FLYTE**	FOUTHS	FRITHS	FURZES	GARBOS	GENOME
FESTAS	FIRTHS	**FLIRT**	FLYTED	**FOVEA**	**FRITS**	**FUSEE**	**GARDA**	GENOMS
FETOR	**FITCH**	FLIRTS	FLYTES	FOVEAE	AFRITS	FUSEES	GARDAI	**GENRE**
FETORS	FITCHE	FLIRTY	**FOEHN**	FOVEAL	**FRIZE**	**FUSIL**	**GARRE**	GENRES
FETTA	FITCHES	**FLISK**	FOEHNS	**FOWTH**	FRIZES	FUSILE	GARRED	**GENTS**
FETTAS	FITCHY	FLISKS	**FOGEY**	FOWTHS	**FRIZZ**	FUSILS	GARRES	AGENTS
FETWA	**FITTE**	FLISKY	FOGEYS	**FOYER**	FRIZZY	**FUTON**	GARRET	**GEODE**
FETWAS	FITTED	**FLITE**	**FOGLE**	FOYERS	**FROCK**	FUTONS	**GARTH**	GEODES
FEUAR	FITTER	FLITED	FOGLES	**FOYLE**	FROCKS	**FUZEE**	GARTHS	**GEOID**
FEUARS	FITTES	FLITES	**FOIST**	FOYLED	**FROND**	FUZEES	**GARUM**	GEOIDS
FEVER	**FIVER**	**FLOAT**	FOISTS	FOYLES	FRONDS	**FYTTE**	GARUMS	**GERAH**
FEVERS	FIVERS	AFLOAT	**FOLIA**	**FOYNE**	**FRONT**	FYTTES	**GATES**	GERAHS
FIBER	**FIXER**	FLOATS	FOLIAR	FOYNED	AFRONT	**GABLE**	AGATES	**GERBE**
FIBERS	FIXERS	FLOATY	**FOLIE**	FOYNES	FRONTS	GABLED	**GAUGE**	GERBES
FIBRE	**FJORD**	**FLOCK**	FOLIES	**FRACT**	**FRORE**	GABLET	GAUGED	**GERLE**
FIBRED	FJORDS	FLOCKS	**FOLIO**	FRACTS	FROREN	**GADGE**	GAUGER	GERLES
FIBRES	**FLACK**	**FLONG**	FOLIOS	**FRAIL**	**FRORN**	GADGES	GAUGES	**GERNE**
FIBRO	FLACKS	FLONGS	**FOLKS**	FRAILS	FRORNE	GADGET	**GAUJE**	GERNED
FIBROS	**FLAFF**	**FLOOD**	FOLKSY	**FRAIM**	**FROST**	**GADSO**	GAUJES	GERNES
FICHE	FLAFFS	FLOODS	**FONDA**	FRAIMS	FROSTS	GADSOS	**GAULT**	**GESSE**
FICHES	**FLAGS**	**FLOOR**	FONDAS	**FRAME**	FROSTY	**GAFFE**	GAULTS	GESSED
FICHU	OFLAGS	FLOORS	**FORAY**	FRAMED	**FROTH**	GAFFED	**GAUNT**	GESSES
FICHUS	**FLAIL**	**FLORA**	FORAYS	FRAMER	FROTHS	GAFFER	GAUNTS	**GESTE**
FIDGE	FLAILS	FLORAE	**FORBY**	FRAMES	FROTHY	GAFFES	**GAUZE**	GESTES
FIDGED	**FLAIR**	FLORAL	FORBYE	**FRANC**	**FROWN**	**GAITT**	GAUZES	**GESTS**
FIDGES	FLAIRS	FLORAS	**FORCE**	FRANCO	FROWNS	GAITTS	**GAVEL**	EGESTS
FIDGET	**FLAKE**	**FLOSS**	FORCED	FRANCS	**FROWS**	**GALAH**	GAVELS	**GHAST**
FIELD	FLAKED	FLOSSY	FORCER	**FRANK**	FROWST	GALAHS	**GAYAL**	AGHAST
AFIELD	FLAKES	**FLOTA**	FORCES	FRANKS	FROWSY	**GALEA**	GAYALS	GHASTS
FIELDS	**FLAME**	FLOTAS	**FOREL**	**FRATE**	**FROZE**	GALEAS	**GAZAL**	**GHAUT**
FIEND	AFLAME	**FLOTE**	FORELS	FRATER	FROZEN	**GALLY**	GAZALS	GHAUTS
FIENDS	FLAMED	FLOTEL	**FORES**	**FRAUD**	**FRUIT**	EGALLY	**GAZED**	**GHAZI**
FIENT	FLAMEN	FLOTES	FOREST	FRAUDS	FRUITS	**GALOP**	AGAZED	GHAZIS
FIENTS	FLAMES	**FLOUR**	**FORGE**	**FREAK**	FRUITY	GALOPS	**GAZEL**	**GHOST**
FIERE	**FLAMM**	FLOURS	FORGED	FREAKS	**FRUMP**	**GALUT**	GAZELS	GHOSTS
FIERES	FLAMMS	FLOURY	FORGER	FREAKY	FRUMPS	GALUTH	**GAZER**	GHOSTY
FIFER	**FLANK**	**FLOUT**	FORGES	**FREER**	FRUMPY	GALUTS	GAZERS	**GHOUL**
FIFERS	FLANKS	FLOUTS	FORGET	FREERS	**FRUST**	**GAMBA**	**GAZON**	GHOULS
FIFTH	**FLARE**	**FLUFF**	**FORGO**	**FREES**	FRUSTA	GAMBAS	GAZONS	**GHYLL**
FIFTHS	FLARED	FLUFFS	FORGOT	FREEST	FRUSTS	**GAMES**	**GAZOO**	GHYLLS
FIGHT	FLARES	FLUFFY	**FORME**	**FREET**	**FRYER**	GAMEST	GAZOON	**GIANT**
FIGHTS	**FLASH**	**FLUID**	FORMED	AFREET	FRYERS	GAMESY	GAZOOS	GIANTS
FILER	FLASHY	FLUIDS	FORMER	FREETS	**FUDGE**	**GAMIC**	**GEARE**	**GIBEL**
FILERS	**FLASK**	**FLUKE**	FORMES	FREETY	FUDGED	AGAMIC	GEARED	GIBELS
FILET	FLASKS	FLUKED	**FORTE**	**FREIT**	FUDGES	OGAMIC	GEARES	**GIBER**
FILETS	**FLAWN**	FLUKES	FORTED	FREITS	**FUERO**	**GAMIN**	**GEBUR**	GIBERS
FILLE	FLAWNS	FLUKEY	FORTES	FREITY	FUEROS	GAMINE	GEBURS	**GIGOT**
FILLED	**FLEAM**	**FLUME**	**FORTH**	**FREMD**	**FUGIE**	GAMING	**GECKO**	GIGOTS
FILLER	FLEAMS	FLUMES	FORTHY	FREMDS	FUGIES	GAMINS	GECKOS	**GIGUE**
FILLES	**FLECK**	**FLUMP**	**FORUM**	**FREON**	**FUGLE**	**GAMMA**	**GEIST**	GIGUES
FILLET	FLECKS	FLUMPS	FORUMS	FREONS	FUGLED	GAMMAS	AGEIST	**GILAS**
FILTH	**FLEER**	**FLUNK**	**FOSSA**	**FRERE**	FUGLES	**GAMME**	GEISTS	AGILAS
FILTHS	FLEERS	FLUNKS	FOSSAE	FRERES	**FUGUE**	GAMMED	**GEMEL**	**GILET**
FILTHY	**FLEET**	FLUNKY	FOSSAS	**FRESH**	FUGUES	GAMMER	GEMELS	GILETS
FINAL	FLEETS	**FLUOR**	**FOSSE**	AFRESH	**FUMET**	GAMMES	**GEMMA**	**GIMME**
FINALE	**FLEME**	FLUORS	FOSSED	**FRIAR**	FUMETS	**GAMUT**	GEMMAE	GIMMER
FINALS	FLEMES	**FLURR**	FOSSES	FRIARS	**FUNDI**	GAMUTS	GEMMAN	GIMMES
FINER	**FLESH**	FLURRS	**FOUAT**	FRIARY	FUNDIS	**GANJA**	**GEMOT**	**GINGS**
FINERS	FLESHY	FLURRY	FOUATS	**FRIER**	**FURAL**	GANJAS	GEMOTS	AGINGS
FINERY	**FLICK**	**FLUSH**	**FOUET**	FRIERS	FURALS	**GAPER**	**GENES**	**GIPPO**
FINES	FLICKS	FLUSHY	FOUETS	**FRILL**	**FURAN**	GAPERS	AGENES	GIPPOS
FINEST	**FLIER**	**FLUTE**	**FOULE**	FRILLS	FURANE	GAPOS	**GENET**	**GIRON**
FINIS	FLIERS	FLUTED	FOULED	FRILLY	FURANS		GENETS	GIRONS
FINISH	**FLIES**	FLUTER	FOULER	**FRISK**	**FUROL**		**GENIE**	**GIRTH**
FIORD	**FLIMP**	FLUTES	FOULES	FRISKA	FUROLE		GENIES	GIRTHS

GISMO
GISMOS
GISTS
AGISTS
GIUST
GIUSTO
GIUSTS
GIVER
GIVERS
GIVES
OGIVES
GIZMO
GIZMOS
GLACE
GLACES
GLADE
GLADES
GLAIK
GLAIKS
GLAIR
GLAIRS
GLAIRY
GLAND
GLANDS
GLARE
GLARED
GLARES
GLASS
GLASSY
GLAUM
GLAUMS
GLAUR
GLAURS
GLAURY
GLAZE
GLAZED
GLAZEN
GLAZER
GLAZES
GLEAM
GLEAMS
GLEAMY
GLEAN
GLEANS
GLEBE
GLEBES
GLEDE
GLEDES
GLEED
GLEEDS
GLEEK
GLEEKS
GLEET
GLEETS
GLEETY
GLENT
GLENTS
GLIDE
GLIDED
GLIDER
GLIDES
GLIFF
GLIFFS
GLIFT
GLIFTS
GLIKE
GLIKES
GLINT
GLINTS
GLISK

GLISKS
GLITZ
GLITZY
GLOAT
GLOATS
GLOBE
GLOBED
GLOBES
GLOGG
GLOGGS
GLOOM
GLOOMS
GLOOMY
GLOSS
GLOSSA
GLOSSY
GLOUT
GLOUTS
GLOVE
GLOVED
GLOVER
GLOVES
GLOZE
GLOZED
GLOZES
GLUER
GLUERS
GLUME
GLUMES
GLUON
GLUONS
GLYPH
GLYPHS
GNARL
GNARLS
GNARLY
GNARR
GNARRS
GNOME
GNOMES
GODET
GODETS
GODSO
GODSON
GODSOS
GOFER
GOFERS
GOING
AGOING
GOINGS
GOLEM
GOLEMS
GOLPE
GOLPES
GOMBO
GOMBOS
GOMPA
GOMPAS
GONAD
GONADS
GONER
GONERS
GOOLD
GOOLDS
GOOSE
GOOSED
GOOSES
GOOSEY
GOPAK
GOPAKS

GORAL
GORALS
GORGE
GORGED
GORGES
GORGET
GORSE
GORSES
GOSSE
GOSSES
GOUGE
GOUGED
GOUGES
GOURD
GOURDE
GOURDS
GOURDY
GOUTY
AGOUTY
GOWAN
GOWANS
GOWANY
GRAAL
GRAALS
GRACE
GRACED
GRACES
GRADE
GRADED
GRADER
GRADES
GRAFF
GRAFFS
GRAFT
GRAFTS
GRAIL
GRAILE
GRAILS
GRAIN
GRAINE
GRAINS
GRAINY
GRAIP
GRAIPS
GRAMA
GRAMAS
GRAME
GRAMES
GRAND
GRANDE
GRANDS
GRANT
GRANTS
GRAPE
GRAPED
GRAPES
GRAPEY
GRAPH
GRAPHS
GRASP
GRASPS
GRASS
GRASSY
GRATE
GRATED
GRATER
GRATES
GRAVE
GRAVED
GRAVEL

GRAVEN
GRAVER
GRAVES
GRAZE
GRAZED
GRAZER
GRAZES
GREAT
GREATS
GREBE
GREBES
GRECE
GRECES
GREED
AGREED
GREEDS
GREEDY
GREEN
GREENS
GREENY
GREES
AGREES
GREESE
GREET
GREETE
GREETS
GREGE
GREGO
GREGOS
GREIN
GREINS
GRESE
GRESES
GREVE
GREVES
GRICE
GRICER
GRICES
GRIDE
GRIDED
GRIDES
GRIEF
GRIEFS
GRIFF
GRIFFE
GRIFFS
GRIFT
GRIFTS
GRIKE
GRIKES
GRILL
GRILLE
GRILLS
GRIME
GRIMED
GRIMES
GRIND
GRINDS
GRIOT
GRIOTS
GRIPE
GRIPED
GRIPER
GRIPES
GRISE
AGRISE
GRISED
GRISES
GRIST

GRISTS
GRITH
GRITHS
GRIZE
AGRIZE
GRIZES
GROAN
GROANS
GROAT
GROATS
GROIN
GROINS
GROMA
GROMAS
GRONE
GRONED
GRONES
GROOF
GROOFS
GROOM
GROOMS
GROPE
GROPED
GROPER
GROPES
GROUF
GROUFS
GROUP
GROUPS
GROUPY
GROUT
GROUTS
GROUTY
GROVE
GROVEL
GROVES
GROWL
GROWLS
GROWLY
GRUEL
GRUELS
GRUME
GRUMES
GRUNT
GRUNTS
GRYCE
GRYCES
GRYDE
GRYDED
GRYDES
GRYKE
GRYKES
GRYPE
GRYPES
GUACO
GUACOS
GUANA
GUANAS
GUANO
GUANOS
GUARD
GUARDS
GUAVA
GUAVAS
GUEST
GUESTS
GUIDE
GUIDED
GUIDER

GUIDES
GUILD
GUILDS
GUILE
GUILED
GUILER
GUILES
GUILT
GUILTS
GUILTY
GUIMP
GUIMPE
GUIMPS
GUIRO
GUIROS
GUISE
AGUISE
GUISED
GUISER
GUISES
GULAG
GULAGS
GULPH
GULPHS
GUMBO
GUMBOS
GUNGE
GUNGES
GURGE
GURGES
GUSLA
GUSLAR
GUSLAS
GUSLE
GUSLES
GUSLI
GUSLIS
GUSTO
GUSTOS
GUTTA
GUTTAE
GUTTAS
GUYLE
GUYLED
GUYLER
GUYLES
GUYOT
GUYOTS
GUYSE
GUYSES
GYELD
GYELDS
GYRON
GYRONS
GYROS
GYROSE
HABIT
HABITS
HACEK
HACEKS
HACKS
CHACKS
SHACKS
THACKS
WHACKS
HADED

SHADED
HADES
SHADES
HADJI
HADJIS
HAFFS
HAFTS
CHAFFS
CHAFTS
SHAFTS
HAICK
HAICKS
HAINS
CHAINS
CHAIRS
HAIRST
HAJJI
HAJJIS
HAKAM
HAKAMS
HAKES
SHAKES
HAKIM
HAKIMS
HALAL
HALALS
HALED
SHALED
WHALED
HALER
THALER
WHALER
HALERS
HALES
SHALES
WHALES
HALEST
HALFA
HALFAS
HALLO
HALLOA
HALLOO
HALLOS
HALLOW
HALMA
HALMAS
HALMS
SHALMS
HALSE
HALSED
HALSER
HALSES
HALVA
HALVAH
HALVAS
HALVE
HALVED
HALVER
HALVES
HAMAL
HAMALS
HAMED
SHAMED
HAMES
SHAMES
SHAMMY
HAMZA
HAMZAH

HAMZAS
HANAP
HANAPS
HANCE
HANCES
HANDS
SHANDS
HANDY
SHANDY
HANGS
BHANGS
PHANGS
WHANGS
HANKS
CHANKS
SHANKS
THANKS
HAOMA
HAOMAS
HAPPY
CHAPPY
HARAM
HARAMS
HARDS
CHARDS
SHARDS
HARED
CHARED
SHARED
HAREM
HAREMS
HARES
CHARES
PHARES
SHARES
WHARES
HARIM
HARIMS
HARKS
CHARKS
SHARKS
HARMS
CHARMS
HARNS
SHARNS
HAROS
PHAROS
HARPS
SHARPS
HARRY
CHARRY
GHARRY
HARTS
CHARTS
HASTE
CHASTE
HASTED
HASTEN
HASTES
HATCH
THATCH
HATER
HATERS
HAUGH
HAUGHS
HAULD
HAULDS
HAULM

HAULMS
HAULS
HAULST
HAUNT
CHAUNT
HAUNTS
HAUSE
HAUSED
HAUSES
HAVEN
SHAVEN
HAVENS
HAVER
SHAVER
HAVERS
HAVES
SHAVES
HAVOC
HAVOCS
HAWED
CHAWED
SHAWED
THAWED
HAWMS
SHAWMS
HAWSE
HAWSED
HAWSER
HAWSES
HAYLE
HAYLES
HAZEL
GHAZEL
HAZELS
HAZER
HAZERS
HEALD
HEALDS
HEALS
SHEALS
WHEALS
HEAPS
CHEAPS
HEAPY
CHEAPY
HEARD
HEARDS
HEARE
WHEARE
HEARER
HEARES
HEARS
SHEARS
HEARSE
HEARSY
HEART
HEARTH
HEARTS
HEARTY
HEAST
HEASTE
HEASTS
HEATH
SHEATH
HEATHS
HEATHY
HEATS
CHEATS
WHEATS
HEAVE

SHEAVE	SHERDS	WHINGE	**HOLES**	**HORNY**	**HUMPHS**	**ICHORS**	**IMBAR**	PINGLE
THEAVE	**HERMA**	HINGED	DHOLES	THORNY	**HUMPS**	**ICIER**	MIMBAR	SINGLE
HEAVED	HERMAE	HINGES	THOLES	**HORSE**	CHUMPS	DICIER	**IMBARK**	TINGLE
HEAVEN	**HERMS**	**HINGS**	WHOLES	AHORSE	THUMPS	RICIER	IMBARS	INGLES
HEAVER	THERMS	THINGS	**HOLLA**	HORSED	**HUMUS**	**ICING**	**IMBED**	**INGOT**
HEAVES	**HEROE**	**HINNY**	HOLLAS	HORSES	HUMUSY	DICING	LIMBED	LINGOT
HEBEN	HEROES	SHINNY	**HOLLO**	**HORST**	**HUNKS**	RICING	NIMBED	INGOTS
HEBENS	**HERON**	WHINNY	HOLLOA	HORSTS	CHUNKS	TICING	IMBEDS	**INION**
HECHT	HERONS	**HIPPO**	HOLLOS	**HOSEN**	**HUNKY**	VICING	**IMBUE**	MINION
HECHTS	**HERRY**	SHIPPO	HOLLOW	CHOSEN	CHUNKY	ICINGS	IMBUED	PINION
HECKS	CHERRY	HIPPOS	**HOLLY**	**HOSES**	**HUNTS**	**ICKER**	IMBUES	**INKED**
CHECKS	SHERRY	**HIPPY**	WHOLLY	CHOSES	SHUNTS	BICKER	**IMIDE**	DINKED
HEDGE	WHERRY	CHIPPY	**HOMER**	**HOSTA**	**HURLS**	DICKER	IMIDES	FINKED
HEDGED	**HERSE**	WHIPPY	HOMERS	HOSTAS	CHURLS	KICKER	**IMINE**	JINKED
HEDGER	HERSED	**HIRER**	**HOMME**	**HOSTS**	**HURRA**	LICKER	IMINES	KINKED
HEDGES	HERSES	HIRERS	HOMMES	GHOSTS	DHURRA	NICKER	**IMMEW**	LINKED
HEELS	**HERYE**	**HIRES**	**HOMOS**	**HOTEL**	HURRAH	PICKER	IMMEWS	PINKED
SHEELS	HERYED	SHIRES	ZHOMOS	HOTELS	HURRAS	RICKER	**IMMIT**	RINKED
WHEELS	HERYES	**HISTS**	**HONED**	**HOUFF**	HURRAY	SICKER	IMMITS	TINKED
HEEZE	**HESTS**	WHISTS	PHONED	HOUFFS	**HURST**	TICKER	**IMPED**	WINKED
PHEEZE	CHESTS	**HITCH**	**HONES**	**HOUGH**	HURSTS	WICKER	GIMPED	ZINKED
WHEEZE	**HETES**	HITCHY	PHONES	CHOUGH	**HUTIA**	YICKER	LIMPED	**INKER**
HEEZED	THETES	**HITHE**	RHONES	SHOUGH	HUTIAS	ICKERS	PIMPED	DINKER
HEEZES	**HEUCH**	HITHER	HONEST	THOUGH	**HUZZA**	**ICTAL**	IMPEDE	JINKER
HEFTE	SHEUCH	HITHES	**HONEY**	HOUGHS	HUZZAS	RICTAL	**IMPEL**	PINKER
HEFTED	HEUCHS	**HIVED**	PHONEY	**HOUND**	**HYDRA**	**ICTUS**	IMPELS	SINKER
HEFTS	**HEUGH**	CHIVED	HONEYS	HOUNDS	HYDRAS	RICTUS	**IMPIS**	TINKER
THEFTS	SHEUGH	**HIVER**	**HONGS**	**HOURI**	**HYDRO**	**IDANT**	IMPISH	WINKER
WHEFTS	WHEUGH	SHIVER	THONGS	HOURIS	HYDROS	AIDANT	**IMPLY**	INKERS
HEIGH	HEUGHS	HIVERS	**HONOR**	**HOUSE**	**HYENA**	**IDANTS**	DIMPLY	**INKLE**
HEIGHT	**HEVEA**	**HIVES**	HONORS	CHOUSE	HYENAS	**IDEAL**	JIMPLY	KINKLE
HEIRS	HEVEAS	CHIVES	**HOOEY**	HOUSED	**HYING**	IDEALS	PIMPLY	TINKLE
THEIRS	**HEWED**	SHIVES	PHOOEY	HOUSEL	SHYING	**IDIOM**	SIMPLY	WINKLE
HEIST	CHEWED	**HIZEN**	**HOOEYS**	HOUSES	**HYLEG**	IDIOMS	**IMPOT**	INKLED
THEIST	SHEWED	HIZENS	**HOOKA**	**HOUTS**	HYLEGS	**IDIOT**	IMPOTS	INKLES
HEISTS	THEWED	**HOARD**	HOOKAH	CHOUTS	**HYLES**	IDIOTS	**INANE**	**INLAY**
HEJAB	WHEWED	HOARDS	HOOKAS	SHOUTS	CHYLES	**IDLED**	INANER	INLAYS
HEJABS	**HEWER**	**HOARS**	**HOOKS**	**HOVED**	PHYLES	SIDLED	INANES	**INLET**
HEJRA	HEWERS	HOARSE	CHOOKS	SHOVED	**HYMEN**	**IDLER**	**INARM**	INLETS
HEJRAS	**HEXAD**	**HOAST**	SHOOKS	**HOVEL**	HYMENS	IDLERS	INARMS	**INNED**
HELLO	HEXADS	HOASTS	**HOOLY**	SHOVEL	**HYNDE**	**IDLES**	**INCLE**	BINNED
HELLOS	**HEXES**	**HOCKS**	DHOOLY	HOVELS	HYNDES	SIDLES	INCLES	DINNED
HELLS	RHEXES	CHOCKS	**HOOPS**	**HOVER**	**HYPER**	IDLEST	**INCUR**	FINNED
SHELLS	**HICKS**	SHOCKS	WHOOPS	SHOVER	HYPERS	**IDYLL**	INCURS	GINNED
HELMS	CHICKS	**HODJA**	**HOORD**	HOVERS	**HYPHA**	IDYLLS	**INCUS**	LINNED
WHELMS	THICKS	KHODJA	HOORDS	**HOVES**	HYPHAE	**IGAPO**	INCUSE	PINNED
HELOT	**HIDED**	HODJAS	**HOOSH**	SHOVES	HYPHAL	IGAPOS	**INDEW**	SINNED
HELOTS	CHIDED	**HOERS**	WHOOSH	**HOWFF**	**HYSON**	**IGLOO**	INDEWS	TINNED
HELPS	**HIDES**	SHOERS	**HOOTS**	HOWFFS	HYSONS	IGLOOS	**INDOL**	**INNER**
WHELPS	CHIDES	**HOGAN**	SHOOTS	**HOWLS**	**HYTHE**	**IHRAM**	INDOLE	DINNER
HELVE	**HIGHS**	HOGANS	WHOOTS	THOWLS	HYTHES	IHRAMS	INDOLS	FINNER
SHELVE	THIGHS	**HOGEN**	**HOOVE**	**HOWRE**	**IAIDO**	**IKONS**	**INDRI**	GINNER
HELVED	**HIGHT**	HOGENS	HOOVED	HOWRES	IAIDOS	EIKONS	INDRIS	PINNER
HELVES	HIGHTH	**HOICK**	HOOVEN	**HUBBY**	**IAMBI**	**ILEUM**	**INDUE**	SINNER
HEMES	HIGHTS	HOICKS	HOOVER	CHUBBY	IAMBIC	PILEUM	INDUED	TINNER
THEMES	**HIJRA**	**HOISE**	HOOVES	**HUCKS**	**ICERS**	**ILEUS**	INDUES	WINNER
HENCE	HIJRAH	HOISED	**HOPER**	CHUCKS	DICERS	PILEUS	**INFER**	INNERS
THENCE	HIJRAS	HOISES	HOPERS	SHUCKS	RICERS	**ILIUM**	INFERE	**INORB**
WHENCE	**HIKER**	**HOIST**	**HOPPY**	**HUFFS**	**ICHED**	CILIUM	INFERS	INORBS
HENDS	HIKERS	HOISTS	CHOPPY	CHUFFS	MICHED	**ILLTH**	**INGAN**	**INPUT**
SHENDS	**HILLO**	**HOKED**	SHOPPY	**HUFFY**	NICHED	ILLTHS	FINGAN	INPUTS
HENGE	HILLOS	CHOKED	**HORAL**	CHUFFY	RICHED	**IMAGE**	INGANS	**INSET**
HENGES	**HILLS**	**HOKES**	CHORAL	**HULLO**	**ICHES**	IMAGED	**INGLE**	INSETS
HENNA	CHILLS	CHOKES	**HORDE**	HULLOS	FICHES	IMAGES	BINGLE	**INTER**
HENNAS	SHILLS	**HOKEY**	HORDED	**HUMAN**	LICHES	**IMAGO**	DINGLE	LINTER
HENRY	THILLS	CHOKEY	HORDES	HUMANE	MICHES	IMAGOS	GINGLE	MINTER
HENRYS	**HILLY**	**HOKUM**	**HORME**	HUMANS	NICHES	**IMARI**	JINGLE	SINTER
HEPAR	CHILLY	HOKUMS	HORMES	**HUMOR**	RICHES	IMARIS	KINGLE	TINTER
HEPARS	WHILLY	**HOLED**	**HORNS**	HUMORS	TICHES	**IMAUM**	LINGLE	WINTER
HERDS	**HINGE**	THOLED	THORNS	**HUMPH**	**ICHOR**	IMAUMS	MINGLE	INTERN

INTERS	IXTLES	JINNI	SKAILS	SKELPS	KNACK	KRENG	LADLE	GLANDS
INTRO	IZARD	DJINNI	KALIF	KEMBO	KNACKS	KRENGS	LADLED	LANES
INTRON	LIZARD	JIRGA	KALIFS	KEMBOS	KNACKY	KRILL	LADLES	PLANES
INTROS	RIZARD	JIRGAS	KALPA	KENAF	KNARL	KRILLS	LAGAN	SLANES
INULA	VIZARD	JIVER	KALPAK	KENAFS	KNARLS	KRONE	LAGANS	LANKS
INULAS	WIZARD	JIVERS	KALPAS	KENDO	KNAVE	KRONEN	LAGER	BLANKS
INURE	IZARDS	JOCKO	KAMIK	KENDOS	KNAVES	KRONER	LAGERS	CLANKS
INURED	IZZET	JOCKOS	KAMIKS	KERNE	KNEAD	KUDZU	LAHAR	FLANKS
INURES	IZZETS	JODEL	KANEH	KERNED	KNEADS	KUDZUS	LAHARS	PLANKS
INURN	JABOT	JODELS	KANEHS	KERNEL	KNEEL	KUKRI	LAIDS	LANKY
INURNS	JABOTS	JOINT	KANGA	KERNES	KNEELS	KUKRIS	LAIGH	BLANKY
INWIT	JACKS	JOINTS	KANGAS	KERVE	KNELL	KULAK	LAIGHS	LANTS
INWITH	JACKSY	JOIST	KANZU	KERVED	KNELLS	KULAKS	LAIKA	PLANTS
INWITS	JAGER	JOISTS	KANZUS	KERVES	KNIFE	KULAN	LAIKAS	SLANTS
IONIC	JAGERS	JOKER	KAPOK	KESAR	KNIFED	KULANS	LAIKS	LAPEL
BIONIC	JAGIR	JOKERS	KAPOKS	KESARS	KNIFES	KURRE	GLAIKS	LAPELS
PIONIC	JAGIRS	JORAM	KAPPA	KETCH	KNIVE	KURRES	LAIRD	LAPJE
IOTAS	JALAP	JORAMS	KAPPAS	SKETCH	KNIVED	KURTA	LAIRDS	LAPJES
BIOTAS	JALAPS	JORUM	KAPUT	KEVEL	KNIVES	KURTAS	LAIRS	LAPSE
DIOTAS	JAMBE	JORUMS	KAPUTT	KEVELS	KNOCK	KUTCH	FLAIRS	ELAPSE
IRADE	JAMBEE	JOTUN	KARAT	KHADI	KNOCKS	KUTCHA	LAIRY	LAPSED
TIRADE	JAMBER	JOTUNN	KARATE	KHADIS	KNOLL	KWELA	GLAIRY	LAPSES
IRADES	JAMBES	JOTUNS	KARATS	KHAKI	KNOLLS	KWELAS	LAKED	LARES
IRATE	JAMBO	JOULE	KARMA	KHAKIS	KNOSP	KYANG	FLAKED	BLARES
PIRATE	JAMBOK	JOULED	KARMAS	KHAYA	KNOSPS	KYANGS	SLAKED	FLARES
IRATER	JAMBOS	JOULES	KARRI	KHAYAS	KNOUT	KYLEY	LAKER	GLARES
IRKED	JAMBU	JOUST	KARRIS	KHEDA	KNOUTS	KYLEYS	LAKERS	LARGE
DIRKED	JAMBUL	JOUSTS	KARST	KHEDAS	KNOWE	KYLIE	LAKES	LARGEN
FIRKED	JAMBUS	JOWAR	KARSTS	KHOJA	KNOWER	KYLIES	FLAKES	LARGER
KIRKED	JAPAN	JOWARI	KARTS	KHOJAS	KNOWES	KYLIN	SLAKES	LARGES
LIRKED	JAPANS	JOWARS	SKARTS	KIANG	KNURL	KYLINS	LAKIN	LARGO
YIRKED	JARTA	JUDGE	KASBA	KIANGS	KNURLS	KYLOE	LAKING	LARGOS
IROKO	JARTAS	JUDGED	KASBAH	KIDEL	KNURLY	KYLOES	LAKINS	LARUM
IROKOS	JARUL	JUDGES	KASBAS	KIDELS	KNURR	KYNDE	LAMAS	ALARUM
IRONS	JARULS	JUGAL	KATTI	KIERS	KNURRS	KYNDED	LLAMAS	LARUMS
GIRONS	JASEY	JUGALS	KATTIS	SKIERS	KOALA	KYNDES	LAMED	LARVA
ISHES	JASEYS	JUICE	KAUGH	KIEVE	KOALAS	KYTES	BLAMED	LARVAE
BISHES	JASPE	JUICED	KAUGHS	KIEVES	KOBAN	SKYTES	FLAMED	LARVAL
DISHES	JASPER	JUICER	KAURI	KIGHT	KOBANG	KYTHE	LAMES	LASER
FISHES	JASPES	JUICES	KAURIS	KIGHTS	KOBANS	KYTHED	BLAMES	FLASER
HISHES	JAUNT	JULEP	KAVAS	KILEY	KOFFS	KYTHES	CLAMES	LASERS
KISHES	JAUNTS	JULEPS	KAVASS	KILEYS	SKOFFS	LABDA	FLAMES	LASSO
PISHES	JAUNTY	JUMAR	KAYAK	KILIM	KOFTA	LABDAS	LAMEST	LASSOS
WISHES	JAVEL	JUMARS	KAYAKS	KILIMS	KOFTAS	LABEL	LAMIA	LASSU
ISLED	JAVELS	JUMART	KAYLE	KILLS	KOINE	LABELS	LAMIAE	LASSUS
AISLED	JAWAN	JUMBO	KAYLES	SKILLS	KOINES	LABIA	LAMIAS	LASTS
MISLED	JAWANS	JUMBOS	KAYOE	KIMBO	KOKRA	LABIAL	LAMMY	BLASTS
ISLES	JEBEL	JUNCO	KAYOED	AKIMBO	KOKRAS	LABOR	CLAMMY	LATCH
AISLES	DJEBEL	JUNCOS	KAYOES	KIMBOS	KOKUM	LABORS	LAMPS	CLATCH
LISLES	JEBELS	JUNTA	KAZOO	KINAS	KOKUMS	LACED	CLAMPS	LATED
ISLET	JEHAD	JUNTAS	KAZOOS	KINASE	KOPJE	PLACED	LANCE	ALATED
ISLETS	JEHADS	JUNTO	KEBAB	KININ	KOPJES	LACES	ELANCE	ELATED
ISSEI	JELAB	JUNTOS	KEBABS	KININS	KOPPA	GLACES	LANCED	PLATED
ISSEIS	JELABS	JUPON	KEBOB	KINKS	KOPPAS	PLACES	LANCER	SLATED
ISSUE	JELLO	JUPONS	KEBOBS	SKINKS	KORMA	LACET	LANCES	LATEN
TISSUE	JELLOS	JURAT	KECKS	KIOSK	KORMAS	PLACET	LANCET	PLATEN
ISSUED	JERID	JURATS	KECKSY	KIOSKS	KOTOW	LACETS	LANCH	LATENS
ISSUER	JERIDS	JUROR	KEDGE	KISAN	KOTOWS	LACKS	BLANCH	LATENT
ISSUES	JETON	JURORS	KEDGED	KISANS	KRAAL	BLACKS	FLANCH	LATER
ISTLE	JETONS	KAAMA	KEDGER	KITED	KRAALS	CLACKS	PLANCH	BLATER
MISTLE	JEWEL	KAAMAS	KEDGES	SKITED	KRAFT	PLACKS	LANDE	ELATER
ISTLES	JEWELS	KABAB	KEEVE	KITES	KRAFTS	SLACKS	LANDED	PLATER
ITCHY	JHALA	KABABS	KEEVES	SKITES	KRAIT	LADED	LANDER	SLATER
BITCHY	JHALAS	KABOB	KEFIR	KITHE	KRAITS	BLADED	LANDES	LATHE
FITCHY	JIBER	KABOBS	KEFIRS	KITHED	KRANG	LADES	LANDS	LATHED
HITCHY	JIBERS	KAHAL	KELIM	KITHES	KRANGS	BLADES	BLANDS	LATHEE
PITCHY	JIGOT	KAHALS	KELIMS	KLANG	KRANS	CLADES	ELANDS	LATHEN
IVIED	JIGOTS	KAIAK	KELLY	KLANGS	SKRANS	GLADES		LATHER
DIVIED	JIHAD	KAIAKS	SKELLY	KLOOF	KRAUT	SLADES		LATHES
IXTLE	JIHADS	KAILS	KELPS	KLOOFS	KRAUTS			LATHI

THE HOOKS – PART B: 5-Letter Words

LATHIS	CLEARS	**LEMELS**	**LICKS**	BLIMPS	**LIVEN**	LOIPES	LOSERS	GLOWER
LATKE	**LEARY**	**LEMES**	CLICKS	FLIMPS	SLIVEN	**LOKES**	**LOSES**	SLOWER
LATKES	BLEARY	FLEMES	FLICKS	**LINCH**	LIVENS	BLOKES	CLOSES	LOWERS
LAUCH	**LEASE**	**LEMMA**	SLICKS	CLINCH	**LIVER**	CLOKES	ULOSES	LOWERY
LAUCHS	PLEASE	LEMMAS	**LIEGE**	FLINCH	OLIVER	**LOLOG**	**LOSSY**	**LOWES**
LAUDS	LEASED	**LEMON**	LIEGER	**LINDS**	SLIVER	LOLOGS	FLOSSY	LOWEST
BLAUDS	LEASER	LEMONS	LIEGES	BLINDS	LIVERS	**LONER**	GLOSSY	**LOWLY**
LAUGH	LEASES	LEMONY	**LIENS**	**LINED**	LIVERY	LONERS	**LOTAH**	SLOWLY
LAUGHS	**LEAST**	**LEMUR**	ALIENS	ALINED	**LIVES**	**LONGA**	LOTAHS	**LOWND**
LAUGHY	**LEATS**	LEMURS	**LIERS**	**LINEN**	OLIVES	LONGAN	**LOTAS**	LOWNDS
LAUND	BLEATS	**LENDS**	FLIERS	LINENS	SLIVES	LONGAS	FLOTAS	**LOWNE**
LAUNDS	CLEATS	BLENDS	PLIERS	**LINER**	**LIVOR**	**LONGE**	**LOTES**	LOWNED
LAURA	PLEATS	**LENTI**	**LIEVE**	LINERS	LIVORS	PLONGE	CLOTES	LOWNES
LAURAS	**LEAVE**	LENTIC	LIEVER	**LINES**	**LIVRE**	LONGED	FLOTES	**LOWNS**
LAVED	CLEAVE	LENTIL	**LIFER**	ALINES	LIVRES	LONGER	**LOTTO**	CLOWNS
SLAVED	GLEAVE	**LENTO**	LIFERS	CLINES	**LLAMA**	LONGES	BLOTTO	**LOWSE**
LAVER	SLEAVE	LENTOR	**LIFTS**	**LINGA**	LLAMAS	**LONGS**	LOTTOS	BLOWSE
CLAVER	LEAVED	LENTOS	CLIFTS	LINGAM	**LLANO**	FLONGS	**LOUGH**	LOWSER
SLAVER	LEAVEN	**LEONE**	GLIFTS	LINGAS	LLANOS	PLONGS	CLOUGH	LOWSES
LAVERS	LEAVES	LEONES	**LIGAN**	**LINGO**	**LOAMS**	**LOOFA**	PLOUGH	**LOZEN**
LAVES	**LEAZE**	**LEPER**	LIGAND	LINGOT	CLOAMS	LOOFAH	SLOUGH	LOZENS
CLAVES	SLEAZE	LEPERS	LIGANS	**LINGS**	**LOANS**	LOOFAS	LOUGHS	**LUBRA**
SLAVES	LEAZES	**LEPRA**	**LIGER**	CLINGS	SLOANS	**LOOFS**	**LOUND**	LUBRAS
LAVRA	**LEDGE**	LEPRAS	LIGERS	FLINGS	**LOATH**	KLOOFS	LOUNDS	**LUCKS**
LAVRAS	FLEDGE	**LETCH**	**LIGGE**	SLINGS	LOATHE	**LOOKS**	**LOUPE**	CLUCKS
LAWED	GLEDGE	FLETCH	LIGGED	**LINGY**	LOATHY	PLOOKS	LOUPED	PLUCKS
CLAWED	PLEDGE	**LEUCH**	LIGGEN	CLINGY	**LOAVE**	**LOOMS**	LOUPEN	**LUCKY**
FLAWED	SLEDGE	CLEUCH	LIGGER	**LININ**	LOAVED	BLOOMS	LOUPES	CLUCKY
LAWNS	LEDGER	PLEUCH	LIGGES	LINING	LOAVES	GLOOMS	**LOURE**	PLUCKY
FLAWNS	LEDGES	**LEUGH**	**LIGHT**	LININS	**LOBBY**	SLOOMS	LOURED	**LUCRE**
LAXES	**LEDGY**	CLEUGH	ALIGHT	**LINKS**	SLOBBY	**LOOPS**	LOURES	LUCRES
FLAXES	FLEDGY	PLEUGH	BLIGHT	BLINKS	**LOBED**	BLOOPS	**LOURS**	**LUFFA**
LAXEST	**LEDUM**	**LEVEE**	FLIGHT	CLINKS	**LOBES**	CLOOPS	**LOURY**	LUFFAS
LAYER	LEDUMS	LEVEED	PLIGHT	PLINKS	GLOBES	SLOOPS	FLOURY	**LUFFS**
FLAYER	**LEEAR**	LEVEES	SLIGHT	SLINKS	**LOBOS**	**LOORD**	**LOUSE**	BLUFFS
PLAYER	LEEARS	**LEVEL**	LIGHTS	**LINTS**	LOBOSE	LOORDS	BLOUSE	FLUFFS
SLAYER	**LEECH**	LEVELS	**LIGNE**	CLINTS	**LOCAL**	**LOOSE**	FLOUSE	PLUFFS
LAYERS	FLEECH	**LEVER**	LIGNES	FLINTS	LOCALE	LOOSED	LOUSED	**LUMEN**
LAZAR	SLEECH	LEVERS	**LIKEN**	GLINTS	LOCALS	LOOSEN	LOUSES	LUMENS
LAZARS	**LEEKS**	**LEVIN**	LIKENS	**LINTY**	**LOCKS**	LOOSER	**LOUTS**	**LUMMY**
LAZED	CLEEKS	ALEVIN	**LIKER**	FLINTY	BLOCKS	LOOSES	CLOUTS	PLUMMY
BLAZED	GLEEKS	LEVINS	LIKERS	**LIPID**	CLOCKS	**LOOTS**	FLOUTS	SLUMMY
GLAZED	SLEEKS	**LEVIS**	**LIKES**	LIPIDE	FLOCKS	CLOOTS	GLOUTS	**LUMPS**
LAZES	**LEEPS**	CLEVIS	GLIKES	LIPIDS	**LOCUM**	SLOOTS	**LOVAT**	CLUMPS
BLAZES	BLEEPS	**LEXES**	**LIKIN**	**LIPPY**	LOCUMS	**LOPED**	LOVATS	FLUMPS
GLAZES	CLEEPS	FLEXES	LIKING	SLIPPY	**LOCUS**	ELOPED	**LOVED**	PLUMPS
LEACH	SLEEPS	ILEXES	LIKINS	**LISKS**	LOCUST	SLOPED	GLOVED	SLUMPS
BLEACH	**LEERS**	ULEXES	**LILAC**	FLISKS	**LODEN**	**LOPER**	**LOVER**	**LUMPY**
PLEACH	FLEERS	**LIANA**	LILACS	GLISKS	LODENS	ELOPER	CLOVER	CLUMPY
LEACHY	**LEESE**	LIANAS	**LIMAX**	LISLE	**LODGE**	LOPERS	GLOVER	GLUMPY
LEADS	LEESES	**LIANE**	CLIMAX	LISLES	LODGED	**LOPES**	PLOVER	PLUMPY
PLEADS	**LEETS**	LIANES	**LIMBO**	**LITED**	LODGER	ELOPES	LOVERS	SLUMPY
LEAKS	FLEETS	**LIANG**	LIMBOS	FLITED	LODGES	SLOPES	**LOVES**	**LUNAR**
BLEAKS	GLEETS	LIANGS	**LIMBS**	**LITER**	**LOGAN**	**LORAL**	CLOVES	LUNARS
LEAKY	SLEETS	**LIARD**	CLIMBS	LITERS	SLOGAN	FLORAL	GLOVES	**LUNARY**
BLEAKY	**LEFTS**	LIARDS	**LIMED**	**LITES**	LOGANS	**LORAN**	**LOVEY**	**LUNCH**
LEAMS	CLEFTS	**LIBEL**	SLIMED	BLITES	**LOGES**	LORANS	LOVEYS	CLUNCH
FLEAMS	**LEGER**	LIBELS	**LIMEN**	ELITES	ELOGES	**LOREL**	**LOWAN**	**LUNGE**
GLEAMS	LEGERS	**LIBER**	LIMENS	FLITES	**LOGIA**	LORELS	LOWANS	BLUNGE
LEANS	**LEGGE**	LIBERS	**LIMES**	**LITHE**	ALOGIA	**LORES**	**LOWED**	PLUNGE
CLEANS	ALEGGE	**LIBRA**	CLIMES	BLITHE	**LOGIC**	BLORES	BLOWED	LUNGED
GLEANS	LEGGED	LIBRAE	SLIMES	LITHED	LOGICS	**LORIC**	FLOWED	LUNGES
LEARE	LEGGER	LIBRAS	**LIMEY**	LITHER	**LOGIE**	LORICA	GLOWED	**LUNGI**
LEARED	LEGGES	**LICHI**	LIMEYS	LITHES	LOGIES	LORICS	PLOWED	LUNGIE
LEARES	**LEGIT**	LICHIS	**LIMIT**	**LITHO**	**LOIDS**	**LOSED**	SLOWED	LUNGIS
LEARN	ELEGIT	**LICHT**	LIMITS	LITHOS	SLOIDS	CLOSED	**LOWER**	**LUNTS**
LEARNS	**LEMAN**	LICHTS	**LIMMA**	**LITRE**	**LOINS**	**LOSEL**	BLOWER	BLUNTS
LEARNT	LEMANS	**LICIT**	LIMMAS	LITRES	ELOINS	LOSELS	FLOWER	**LUPIN**
LEARS	**LEMEL**	ELICIT	**LIMPS**	**LIVED**	**LOIPE**	**LOSER**		LUPINE
BLEARS				SLIVED		CLOSER		

LUPINS	MAFIAS	**MANORS**	**MAVIN**	MENSES	**MIDGES**	**SMITES**	**MOOLA**	**MOUCH**
LURES	**MAGES**	**MANSE**	MAVINS	**MEREL**	MIDGET	**MITRE**	MOOLAH	SMOUCH
ALURES	IMAGES	MANSES	MAXIM	MERELL	**MIDST**	MITRED	MOOLAS	**MOULD**
LURGI	**MAGIC**	**MANTA**	MAXIMA	MERELS	AMIDST	MITRES	**MOOLI**	MOULDS
LURGIS	MAGICS	MANTAS	MAXIMS	MERELY	MIDSTS	**MIXEN**	MOOLIS	MOULDY
LURRY	**MAGMA**	**MANTO**	MAYBE	**MERES**	**MIEVE**	MIXENS	**MOORS**	**MOULT**
FLURRY	MAGMAS	MANTOS	MAYBES	MEREST	MIEVED	**MIXER**	SMOORS	MOULTS
SLURRY	**MAGOT**	**MANUL**	MAYOR	**MERGE**	MIEVES	MIXERS	**MOOTS**	**MOUND**
LUSHY	MAGOTS	MANULS	MAYORS	MERGED	**MIGHT**	**MIZEN**	SMOOTS	MOUNDS
FLUSHY	**MAHOE**	**MAPLE**	MAZED	MERGER	SMIGHT	MIZENS	**MOOVE**	**MOUNT**
PLUSHY	MAHOES	MAPLES	AMAZED	MERGES	MIGHTS	**MNEME**	AMOOVE	MOUNTS
SLUSHY	**MAHUA**	**MAQUI**	MAZER	EMERGE	MIGHTY	MNEMES	MOOVED	MOUNTY
LUTED	MAHUAS	MAQUIS	MAZERS	**MERIL**	**MILER**	**MOBLE**	MOOVES	**MOURN**
ELUTED	**MAHWA**	**MARAH**	MAZES	MERILS	SMILER	MOBLED	**MOPED**	MOURNS
FLUTED	MAHWAS	MARAHS	AMAZES	**MERIS**	MILERS	MOBLES	MOPEDS	**MOUSE**
LUTER	**MAIKO**	**MARGE**	MAZUT	MERISM	**MILES**	**MOCHA**	**MOPER**	SMOUSE
FLUTER	MAIKOS	MARGES	MAZUTS	**MERIT**	SMILES	MOCHAS	MOPERS	MOUSED
LUTERS	**MAIKS**	**MARID**	**MEANE**	MERITS	**MILLE**	**MOCKS**	**MORAL**	MOUSER
LUTES	SMAIKS	MARIDS	MEANED	**MERLE**	MILLED	SMOCKS	AMORAL	MOUSES
ELUTES	**MAILE**	**MARLE**	MEANER	MERLES	MILLER	**MODEL**	MORALE	MOUSEY
FLUTES	MAILED	MARLED	MEANES	**MERSE**	MILLES	MODELS	MORALL	**MOUST**
LUXES	MAILER	MARLES	**MEARE**	MERSES	MILLET	**MODEM**	MORALS	MOUSTS
FLUXES	MAILES	**MARMS**	MEARES	**MESEL**	**MILOR**	MODEMS	**MORAS**	**MOUTH**
LYCEE	**MAIRE**	SMARMS	**MEASE**	MESELS	MILORD	**MODES**	MORASS	MOUTHS
LYCEES	MAIRES	**MAROR**	MEASED	**MESES**	MILORS	MODEST	**MORAT**	MOUTHY
LYING	**MAISE**	MARORS	MEASES	EMESES	**MIMER**	**MOGGY**	MORATS	**MOVED**
CLYING	MAISES	**MARSH**	MEATH	TMESES	MIMERS	SMOGGY	**MORAY**	AMOVED
FLYING	**MAIZE**	MARSHY	SMEATH	**MESON**	**MIMIC**	**MOGUL**	MORAYS	EMOVED
PLYING	MAIZES	**MARTS**	MEATHE	MESONS	MIMICS	MOGULS	**MOREL**	**MOVER**
LYINGS	**MAJOR**	SMARTS	MEATHS	**METAL**	**MINAR**	**MOHEL**	MORELS	MOVERS
LYMPH	MAJORS	**MASER**	**MEDAL**	METALS	MINARS	MOHELS	**MORES**	**MOVES**
LYMPHS	**MAKAR**	MASERS	MEDALS	**METER**	**MINCE**	**MOHUR**	SMORES	**MOVIE**
LYRIC	MAKARS	**MASON**	**MEDIA**	METERS	MINCED	MOHURS	**MORIA**	MOVIES
LYRICS	**MAKER**	MASONS	MEDIAE	**METIC**	MINCER	**MOIRE**	MORIAS	**MOWER**
LYSIN	MAKERS	**MASSA**	MEDIAL	EMETIC	MINCES	MOIRES	**MORNE**	MOWERS
LYSINE	**MALAR**	MASSAS	MEDIAN	METICS	**MINER**	**MOIST**	MORNED	**MOWRA**
LYSING	MALARS	**MASSE**	**MEDIC**	METIF	MINERS	MOISTS	MORNES	MOWRAS
LYSINS	**MALIC**	MASSED	MEDICK	METIFS	**MINES**	**MOKES**	**MORON**	**MOXIE**
LYSOL	MALICE	MASSES	MEDICO	**METOL**	AMINES	SMOKES	MORONS	MOXIES
LYSOLS	**MALIS**	**MATCH**	MEDICS	METOLS	IMINES	MOKOS	**MORPH**	**MOYLE**
LYSSA	MALIST	SMATCH	**MEDLE**	**METRE**	**MINIM**	SMOKOS	MORPHO	SMOYLE
LYSSAS	**MALLS**	**MATED**	MEDLED	METRED	MINIMA	**MOLAR**	MORPHS	MOYLED
LYTED	SMALLS	AMATED	MEDLES	METRES	MINIMS	MOLARS	**MORRA**	MOYLES
FLYTED	**MALMS**	**MATER**	MEDLEY	**METRO**	**MINIS**	**MOLES**	MORRAS	**MPRET**
LYTES	SMALMS	MATERS	**MEERS**	METROS	MINISH	MOLEST	**MORRO**	MPRETS
FLYTES	**MALTS**	**MATES**	AMEERS	**MEUSE**	**MINKE**	**MOLLA**	MORROS	**MUCIN**
LYTHE	SMALTS	AMATES	EMEERS	SMEUSE	MINKES	MOLLAH	MORROW	MUCINS
LYTHES	**MALVA**	**MATIN**	**MEITH**	MEUSED	**MINOR**	MOLLAS	**MORSE**	**MUCOR**
LYTTA	MALVAS	MATING	MEITHS	MEUSES	MINORS	MOLLS	MORSEL	MUCORS
LYTTAS	**MAMBA**	MATINS	**MELEE**	**MEZZO**	**MIRKS**	SMOLTS	MORSES	**MUCRO**
MACAW	MAMBAS	**MATLO**	MELEES	MEZZOS	**MIRKY**	**MOLTS**	**MOSEY**	MUCROS
MACAWS	**MAMBO**	MATLOS	**MELIC**	**MHORR**	SMIRKS	**MOMMA**	MOSEYS	**MUDIR**
MACER	MAMBOS	MATLOW	MELICS	MHORRS	MURKY	MOMMAS	**MOTED**	MUDIRS
MACERS	**MAMMA**	**MATTE**	**MELLS**	MIAOW	SMIRKY	**MONAD**	EMOTED	**MUDRA**
MACHO	MAMMAE	MATTED	SMELLS	MIAOWS	**MIRTH**	MONADS	**MOTEL**	MUDRAS
MACHOS	MAMMAL	MATTER	**MELON**	MIASM	MIRTHS	**MONAL**	MOTELS	**MUFTI**
MACKS	MAMMAS	MATTES	MELONS	MIASMA	**MISER**	MONALS	**MOTES**	MUFTIS
SMACKS	**MANEH**	**MATZA**	**MELTS**	MIASMS	MISERE	**MONER**	EMOTES	**MUIST**
MACLE	MANEHS	MATZAH	SMELTS	MIAUL	MISERS	MONERA	**MOTET**	MUISTS
MACLED	**MANGE**	MATZAS	**MENDS**	MIAULS	MISERY	MONERS	MOTETS	**MUJIK**
MACLES	MANGEL	**MATZO**	AMENDS	**MICHE**	**MISES**	**MONEY**	MOTETT	MUJIKS
MACRO	MANGER	MATZOH	EMENDS	MICHED	AMISES	MONEYS	**MOTIF**	**MULCT**
MACRON	MANGES	MATZOS	**MENED**	MICHER	**MISSA**	MONOS	MOTIFS	MULCTS
MACROS	MANGEY	MATZOT	AMENED	MICHES	MISSAL	MONOSY	**MOTOR**	**MULES**
MADAM	**MANIA**	**MAUND**	OMENED	**MICRO**	MISSAS	MONTE	MOTORS	EMULES
MADAME	MANIAC	MAUNDS	**MENGE**	MICRON	MISSAW	MONTEM	MOTORY	**MULEY**
MADAMS	MANIAS	MAUNDY	MENGED	MICROS	MISSAY	MONTES	**MOTTE**	MULEYS
MADGE	**MANNA**	**MAUVE**	MENGES	**MIDDY**	**MITER**	**MONTH**	MOTTES	
MADGES	MANNAS	MAUVER	**MENSE**	SMIDDY	SMITER	MONTHS	**MOTZA**	
MAFIA	**MANOR**	MAUVES	MENSED	**MIDGE**	MITERS	MOOCH	MOTZAS	
					MITES	SMOOCH		

MULGA	NADIRS	ANEARS	SNIFFS	NOOKS	NURSER	MOCKER	COILED	OMERS
MULGAS	NAEVE	NEATH	NIFFY	SNOOKS	NURSES	ROCKER	DOILED	COMERS
MULSE	NAEVES	ANEATH	SNIFFY	NOOPS	NYAFF	SOCKER	FOILED	HOMERS
MULSES	NAGGY	SNEATH	NIFTY	SNOOPS	NYAFFS	OCKERS	MOILED	VOMERS
MUNGO	KNAGGY	UNEATH	SNIFTY	NOOSE	NYALA	OCREA	ROILED	OMITS
MUNGOS	SNAGGY	NEBEK	NIGER	NOOSED	INYALA	OCREAE	SOILED	VOMITS
MURAL	NAGOR	NEBEKS	NIGERS	NOOSES	NYALAS	OCTAD	TOILED	OMLAH
MURALS	NAGORS	NEBEL	NIGHT	NOPAL	NYLON	OCTADS	OILER	OMLAHS
MURED	NAHAL	NEBELS	ANIGHT	NOPALS	NYLONS	OCTET	BOILER	OMRAH
EMURED	NAHALS	NECKS	KNIGHT	NORIA	NYMPH	OCTETS	MOILER	OMRAHS
MURES	NAIAD	SNECKS	NIGHTS	NORIAS	NYMPHO	OCTETT	TOILER	ONCER
EMURES	NAIADS	NEELD	NIGHTY	NORMA	NYMPHS	OCULI	OILERS	ONCERS
MURRA	NAILS	NEELDS	NIHIL	NORMAL	OAKEN	LOCULI	OILERY	ONCES
MURRAM	SNAILS	NEELE	NIHILS	NORMAN	SOAKEN	ODDER	OINTS	BONCES
MURRAS	NAIRA	NEELES	NINJA	NORMAS	OAKER	DODDER	JOINTS	NONCES
MURRAY	NAIRAS	NEESE	NINJAS	NORTH	SOAKER	FODDER	NOINTS	PONCES
MURRE	NAIVE	NEESED	NINON	NORTHS	OAKERS	NODDER	POINTS	SONCES
MURREN	NAIVER	NEESES	NINONS	NOSER	OAKUM	ODEON	OJIME	ONELY
MURRES	NAKED	NEEZE	NINTH	NOSERS	OAKUMS	ODEONS	OJIMES	LONELY
MURREY	SNAKED	NEEZED	NINTHS	NOSES	OARED	ODEUM	OKAPI	ONERS
MURRY	NAKER	NEEZES	NIPPY	ENOSES	HOARED	ODEUMS	OKAPIS	BONERS
SMURRY	NAKERS	SNEEZE	SNIPPY	GNOSES	ROARED	ODISM	OKRAS	GONERS
MURVA	NALLA	NEIGH	NISEI	NOSEY	SOARED	IODISM	KOKRAS	LONERS
MURVAS	NALLAH	NEIGHS	NISEIS	NOSEYS	OASTS	ODISMS	OLDEN	MONERS
MUSED	NALLAS	NEIVE	NISSE	NOTCH	BOASTS	ODIST	BOLDEN	ONION
AMUSED	NAMER	NEIVES	NISSES	NOTCHY	COASTS	CODIST	GOLDEN	GONION
MUSER	NAMERS	NELLY	NITON	NOTER	HOASTS	MODIST	HOLDEN	ONIONS
AMUSER	NANAS	SNELLY	NITONS	NOTERS	ROASTS	ODISTS	OLDENS	ONIONY
MUSERS	ANANAS	NEPER	NITRE	NOTUM	TOASTS	ODIUM	OLDER	ONNED
MUSES	NANCE	NEPERS	NITRES	NOTUMS	OAVES	PODIUM	BOLDER	CONNED
AMUSES	NANCES	NEPIT	NITRY	NOULD	LOAVES	SODIUM	COLDER	DONNED
MUSET	NANDU	NEPITS	NITRYL	NOULDE	OBANG	ODIUMS	FOLDER	FONNED
MUSETS	NANDUS	NERKA	NIXIE	NOULE	GOBANG	ODOUR	GOLDER	WONNED
MUSIC	NANNA	NERKAS	NIXIES	NOULES	KOBANG	ODOURS	HOLDER	ONSET
MUSICS	NANNAS	NERVE	NIZAM	NOVEL	OBANGS	ODSOS	POLDER	ONSETS
MUSIT	NAPOO	ENERVE	NIZAMS	NOVELS	OBEAH	GODSOS	SOLDER	OOBIT
MUSITS	NAPOOS	NERVED	NOBBY	NOVUM	OBEAHS	ODYLE	OLDIE	OOBITS
MUSSE	NAPPA	NERVER	KNOBBY	NOVUMS	OBESE	ODYLES	OLDIES	OOHED
MUSSED	NAPPAS	NERVES	SNOBBY	NOWAY	OBESER	OFFAL	OLEIN	BOOHED
MUSSEL	NAPPE	NEUME	NOBLE	NOWAYS	OBIAS	OFFALS	SOLEIN	OOMPH
MUSSES	NAPPED	NEUMES	NOBLER	NOWED	COBIAS	OFFED	OLEINS	OOMPHS
MUSTH	NAPPER	NEVEL	NOBLES	SNOWED	OBITS	BOFFED	OLENT	OOPED
MUSTHS	NAPPES	NEVELS	NOCKS	UNOWED	OOBITS	DOFFED	DOLENT	COOPED
MUTCH	NAPPY	NEWED	KNOCKS	NOYAU	OBJET	GOFFED	OLEUM	HOOPED
SMUTCH	SNAPPY	ENEWED	NODAL	NOYAUS	OBJETS	OFFER	OLEUMS	LOOPED
MUTES	NARES	NEWEL	ANODAL	NUBBY	OBOES	COFFER	OLIOS	MOOPED
MUTEST	SNARES	NEWELL	ENODAL	KNUBBY	GOBOES	DOFFER	FOLIOS	POOPED
MUTON	NARKS	NEWELS	NODES	SNUBBY	HOBOES	GOFFER	POLIOS	ROOPED
MUTONS	SNARKS	NGAIO	ANODES	NUBIA	OCCUR	OFFERS	OLIVE	SOOPED
MVULE	NASAL	NGAIOS	NOINT	NUBIAS	OCCURS	OFLAG	SOLIVE	OORIE
MVULES	NASALS	NICHE	ANOINT	NUCHA	OCEAN	OFLAGS	OLIVER	TOORIE
MYALL	NATCH	NICHED	NOINTS	NUCHAL	OCEANS	OFTEN	OLIVES	OORIER
MYALLS	SNATCH	NICHER	NOISE	NUCHAS	OCHER	SOFTEN	OLIVET	OOSES
MYNAH	NAUNT	NICHES	NOISED	NUDES	OCHERS	OGGIN	OLLAS	BOOSES
MYNAHS	NAUNTS	NICKS	NOISES	NUDEST	OCHERY	HOGGIN	HOLLAS	GOOSES
MYOMA	NAVEL	KNICKS	NOLLS	NUDGE	OCHES	NOGGIN	MOLLAS	LOOSES
MYOMAS	NAVELS	SNICKS	KNOLLS	NUDGED	BOCHES	OGGINS	OLLAV	NOOSES
MYOPE	NAVES	NICOL	SNUDGE	NUDGES	COCHES	OGHAM	OLLAVS	ROOSES
MYOPES	KNAVES	NICOLS	NOMAD	NUDIE	ROCHES	OGHAMS	OLOGY	OOZED
MYRRH	NAVEW	NIDES	NOMADE	NUDIES	OCHRE	OGIVE	OOLOGY	BOOZED
MYRRHS	NAVEWS	SNIDES	NOMADS	NULLA	OCHREA	OGIVES	OLPES	OOZES
NABLA	NAWAB	NIDOR	NOMADY	NULLAH	OCHRED	OGLER	GOLPES	BOOZES
NABLAS	NAWABS	NIDORS	NOMES	NULLAS	OCHRES	OGLERS	OMASA	OPALS
NABOB	NAZIR	NIECE	GNOMES	NURLS	OCHREY	OGLES	OMASAL	COPALS
NABOBS	NAZIRS	NIECES	NOMIC	KNURLS	OCKER	BOGLES	OMBRE	NOPALS
NACHE	NEAFE	NIEVE	ANOMIC	NURRS	COCKER	FOGLES	HOMBRE	OPERA
NACHES	NEAFES	NIEVES	GNOMIC	KNURRS	DOCKER	OGRES	SOMBRE	OPERAS
NACRE	NEAPS	NIFES	NONCE	NURSE	HOCKER	OGRESS	OMBRES	OPINE
NACRES	SNEAPS	KNIFES	NONCES	NURSED	LOCKER	OILED	OMEGA	OPINED
NADIR	NEARS	NIFFS	NONET	NURSE	NURSER	BOILED	OMEGAS	OPINES

OPING	ORTHOS	LOUPED	JOWING	PACTS	PANICK	PASSER	SPEALS	PENCES
COPING	ORVAL	MOUPED	LOWING	EPACTS	PANICS	PASSES	PEANS	PENDS
DOPING	ORVALS	POUPED	MOWING	PADLE	PANIM	PASTA	SPEANS	SPENDS
HOPING	OSHAC	ROUPED	ROWING	PADLES	PANIMS	PASTAS	PEARE	PENED
LOPING	OSHACS	OUPHE	SOWING	PADMA	PANNE	PASTE	PEARES	OPENED
MOPING	OSIER	OUPHES	TOWING	PADMAS	PANNED	PASTED	PEARL	PENIE
OOPING	COSIER	OURIE	VOWING	PADRE	PANNES	PASTEL	PEARLS	PENIES
ROPING	HOSIER	POURIE	WOWING	PADRES	PANTO	PASTER	PEARLY	PENNA
TOPING	NOSIER	OURIER	OWLED	PAEAN	PANTON	PASTES	PEARS	PENNAE
OPIUM	OOSIER	OUSEL	BOWLED	PAEANS	PANTOS	PATCH	SPEARS	PENNAL
OPIUMS	ROSIER	HOUSEL	COWLED	PAEON	PAPAW	PATCHY	PEARST	PENNE
OPTIC	OSIERS	OUSELS	FOWLED	PAEONS	PAPAWS	PATEN	PEASE	PENNED
OPTICS	OSIERY	OUSTS	GOWLED	PAEONY	PAPER	PATENS	PEASED	PENNER
ORACH	OSMIC	JOUSTS	HOWLED	PAGAN	PAPERS	PATENT	PEASES	PENNES
ORACHE	COSMIC	MOUSTS	JOWLED	PAGANS	PAPERY	PATER	PEATS	PERAI
ORALS	OSTIA	ROUSTS	SOWLED	PAGER	PARCH	PATERA	SPEATS	PERAIS
CORALS	OSTIAL	OUTBY	YOWLED	PAGERS	EPARCH	PATERS	PEAZE	PERCE
GORALS	OTARY	OUTBYE	OWLER	PAGLE	PARDI	PATES	PEAZED	PERCED
MORALS	NOTARY	OUTED	BOWLER	PAGLES	PARDIE	SPATES	PEAZES	PERCEN
ORANG	ROTARY	DOUTED	FOWLER	PAGOD	PARED	PATIN	PECAN	PERCES
ORANGE	VOTARY	LOUTED	HOWLER	PAGODA	SPARED	PATINA	PECANS	PERDU
ORANGS	OTHER	POUTED	JOWLER	PAGODS	PAREO	PATINE	PECKE	EPERDU
ORANT	BOTHER	ROUTED	OWLERS	PAGRI	PAREOS	PATINS	PECKED	PERDUE
VORANT	FOTHER	TOUTED	OWLERY	PAGRIS	PARER	PATIO	PECKER	PERDUS
ORANTS	LOTHER	OUTER	OWLET	PAINS	SPARER	PATIOS	PECKES	PERIL
ORATE	MOTHER	COUTER	HOWLET	SPAINS	PARERS	PATTE	PECKS	PERILS
BORATE	POTHER	DOUTER	OWLETS	PAINT	PARES	PATTED	SPECKS	PERIS
LORATE	ROTHER	FOUTER	OWNED	PAINTS	SPARES	PATTEE	PEDAL	PERISH
ORATED	TOTHER	MOUTER	BOWNED	PAINTY	PAREU	PATTEN	PEDALO	PERMS
ORATES	OTHERS	POUTER	DOWNED	PAIRE	PAREUS	PATTER	PEDALS	SPERMS
ORBED	OTTAR	ROUTER	GOWNED	PAIRED	PARGE	PATTES	PEDRO	PERSE
SORBED	COTTAR	SOUTER	LOWNED	PAIRES	SPARGE	PAULS	PEDROS	SPERSE
ORBIT	OTTARS	TOUTER	OWNER	PAISA	PARGED	SPAULS	PEECE	PERSES
ORBITA	OTTER	OUTERS	DOWNER	PAISAS	PARGES	PAUSE	PEECES	PERST
ORBITS	COTTER	OUTRE	OWNERS	PALAY	PARGET	PAUSED	PEELS	SPERST
ORBITY	HOTTER	FOUTRE	OWRES	PALAYS	PARKA	PAUSER	SPEELS	PERVE
ORCIN	JOTTER	OUTRED	HOWRES	PALEA	PARKAS	PAUSES	PEEOY	PERVED
ORCINE	POTTER	OUZEL	POWRES	PALEAE	PARKI	PAVAN	PEEOYS	PERVES
ORCINS	ROTTER	OUZELS	OWRIE	PALED	PARKIN	PAVANE	PEEPE	PESTO
ORDER	TOTTER	OVARY	COWRIE	OPALED	PARKIS	PAVANS	PEEPED	PESTOS
BORDER	OTTERS	COVARY	OWRIER	PALES	PARKS	PAVEN	PEEPER	PETAL
ORDERS	OTTOS	OVATE	OXERS	SPALES	SPARKS	PAVENS	PEEPES	PETALS
OREAD	LOTTOS	BOVATE	BOXERS	PALEST	PARLE	PAVER	PEERS	PETAR
OREADS	POTTOS	OVATED	OXIDE	PALET	PARLED	PAVERS	SPEERS	PETARA
ORGAN	OUBIT	OVATES	OXIDES	PALETS	PARLES	PAVIN	PEEVE	PETARD
ORGANA	WOUBIT	OVENS	OXIME	PALKI	PARLEY	SPAVIN	PEEVED	PETARS
ORGANS	OUBITS	COVENS	OXIMES	PALKIS	PAROL	PAVING	PEEVER	PETARY
ORGIA	OUCHT	OVERS	OXLIP	PALLA	PAROLE	PAVINS	PEEVES	PETER
GORGIA	OUCHTS	COVERS	OXLIPS	PALLAE	PARRY	PAVIS	PEISE	PETERS
ORGIAS	OUGHT	DOVERS	OXTER	PALLAH	SPARRY	PAVISE	PEISED	PETIT
ORGUE	BOUGHT	HOVERS	OXTERS	PALLS	PARSE	PAWAW	PEISES	PETITE
MORGUE	DOUGHT	LOVERS	OYERS	SPALLS	SPARSE	PAWAWS	PEIZE	PETRE
ORGUES	FOUGHT	MOVERS	FOYERS	PAMPA	PARSEC	PAWLS	PEIZED	PETREL
ORIBI	MOUGHT	ROVERS	TOYERS	PAMPAS	PARSED	SPAWLS	PEIZES	PETRES
ORIBIS	NOUGHT	OVERT	OZEKI	PANCE	PARSER	PAWNS	PEKAN	PEWEE
ORIEL	ROUGHT	COVERT	OZEKIS	PANCES	PARSES	SPAWNS	PEKANS	PEWEES
ORIELS	SOUGHT	OVINE	OZONE	PANDA	PARTI	PAYED	PEKOE	PEWIT
ORLOP	OUGHTS	BOVINE	OZONES	PANDAR	PARTIM	SPAYED	PEKOES	PEWITS
ORLOPS	OUIJA	OVIST	PACED	PANDAS	PARTIS	PAYEE	PELLS	PEYSE
ORMER	OUIJAS	OVISTS	SPACED	PANED	PARTS	PAYEES	SPELLS	PEYSED
DORMER	OUNCE	OVOID	PACER	SPANED	SPARTS	PAYER	PELMA	PEYSES
FORMER	BOUNCE	OVOIDS	SPACER	PANEL	PASEO	PAYERS	PELMAS	PHAGE
WORMER	JOUNCE	OVULE	PACERS	PANELS	PASEOS	PEACE	PELTA	PHAGES
ORMERS	POUNCE	OVULES	PACES	PANES	PASHA	PEACED	PELTAE	PHANG
ORPIN	ROUNCE	OWCHE	SPACES	SPANES	PASHAS	PEACES	PELTAS	PHANGS
ORPINE	OUNCES	OWCHES	PACEY	PANGA	PASHM	PEACH	PELTS	UPHANG
ORPINS	OUNDY	OWING	SPACEY	PANGAS	PASHMS	PEACHY	SPELTS	PHARE
ORRIS	WOUNDY	BOWING	PACHA	PANGS	PASSE	PEAKS	PENCE	PHARES
MORRIS	OUPED	COWING	PACHAK	SPANGS	PASSED	SPEAKS	SPENCE	PHASE
ORTHO	COUPED	DOWING	PACHAS	PANIC	PASSEE	PEALS	PENCEL	PHASED

PHASES	PILAWS	PIXIES	PLOATS	POLIOS	POTTOS	PREIF	PRIZER	PSALMS
PHEER	PILED	PIZZA	PLONG	POLKA	POTTY	PREIFE	PRIZES	PSEUD
PHEERE	SPILED	PIZZAS	PLONGD	POLKAS	SPOTTY	PREIFS	PROBE	PSEUDO
PHEERS	PILER	PLACE	PLONGE	POLYP	POUCH	PRENT	PROBED	PSEUDS
PHENE	PILERS	PLACED	PLONGS	POLYPE	POUCHY	SPRENT	PROBES	PSHAW
SPHENE	PILES	PLACER	PLONK	POLYPI	POUKE	PRENTS	PRODS	PSHAWS
PHENES	SPILES	PLACES	PLONKS	POLYPS	POUKES	PRESE	SPRODS	PSORA
PHEON	PILLS	PLACET	PLOOK	POMBE	POULE	PRESES	PROEM	PSORAS
PHEONS	SPILLS	PLACK	UPLOOK	POMBES	POULES	PRESET	PROEMS	PSYCH
PHESE	PILOT	PLACKS	PLOOKS	PONCE	POULP	PREST	PROGS	PSYCHE
PHESED	PILOTS	PLAGE	PLOUK	PONCED	POULPE	UPREST	SPROGS	PSYCHO
PHESES	PILOW	PLAGES	PLOUKS	PONCES	POULPS	PRESTO	PROIN	PSYCHS
PHIAL	PILOWS	PLAID	PLUCK	PONEY	POULT	PRESTS	PROINE	PSYOP
PHIALS	PINAS	UPLAID	PLUCKS	PONEYS	POULTS	PREVE	PROINS	PSYOPS
PHOCA	SPINAS	PLAIDS	PLUCKY	PONGO	POUND	PREVED	PROKE	PUDDY
PHOCAE	PINED	PLAIN	PLUFF	PONGOS	POUNDS	PREVES	PROKED	SPUDDY
PHOCAS	OPINED	PLAINS	PLUFFS	PONGY	POUPE	PRIAL	PROKER	PUDGE
PHONE	SPINED	PLAINT	PLUFFY	SPONGY	POUPED	PRIALS	PROKES	PUDGES
PHONED	PINES	PLAIT	PLUMB	POOFS	POUPES	PRICE	PROLE	PUDOR
PHONES	OPINES	PLAITS	PLUMBS	SPOOFS	POUTS	PRICED	PROLED	PUDORS
PHONEY	SPINES	PLANE	PLUME	POOJA	SPOUTS	PRICER	PROLEG	PUGIL
PHONY	PINGO	PLANED	PLUMED	POOJAH	POUTY	PRICES	PROLER	PUGILS
APHONY	PINGOS	PLANER	PLUMES	POOJAS	SPOUTY	PRICEY	PROLES	PUKER
PHOTO	PINKO	PLANES	PLUMP	POOKA	POWAN	PRICK	PROLL	PUKERS
PHOTON	PINKOS	PLANET	PLUMPS	POOKAS	POWANS	PRICKS	PROLLS	PULER
PHOTOS	PINKS	PLANK	PLUMPY	POOKS	POWER	PRIDE	PROMO	PULERS
PHYLA	SPINKS	PLANKS	PLUNK	SPOOKS	POWERS	PRIDED	PROMOS	PULES
PHYLAE	PINNA	PLANT	PLUNKS	POOLS	POWIN	PRIDES	PRONE	SPULES
PHYLE	PINNAE	PLANTA	PLUSH	SPOOLS	POWINS	PRIEF	PRONER	PULKA
PHYLES	PINNY	PLANTS	PLUSHY	POONS	POWND	PRIEFE	PRONES	PULKAS
PIANO	SPINNY	PLASH	POACH	SPOONS	POWNDS	PRIEFS	PRONG	PULSE
PIANOS	PINON	SPLASH	POACHY	POORT	POWRE	PRIER	SPRONG	PULSED
PICAS	PINONS	PLASHY	POAKA	POORTS	POWRED	PRIERS	PRONGS	PULSES
SPICAS	PINOT	PLASM	POAKAS	POOVE	POWRES	PRIES	PROOF	PULUS
PICKS	PINOTS	PLASMA	POAKE	POOVES	POYNT	PRIEST	PROOFS	OPULUS
SPICKS	PINTA	PLASMS	POAKES	POPPA	POYNTS	PRIGS	PRORE	PUMIE
PICOT	PINTAS	PLAST	PODAL	POPPAS	POYSE	SPRIGS	PRORES	PUMIES
PICOTE	PINTO	YPLAST	APODAL	PORER	POYSED	PRILL	PROSE	PUNCE
PICOTS	PINTOS	PLASTE	PODGE	PORERS	POYSES	PRILLS	PROSED	PUNCES
PICRA	PIOYE	PLATE	PODGES	PORES	PRAAM	PRIMA	PROSER	PUNCH
PICRAS	PIOYES	PLATED	PODIA	SPORES	PRAAMS	PRIMAL	PROSES	PUNCHY
PICUL	PIPAL	PLATEN	PODIAL	PORGE	PRAHU	PRIME	PROUL	PUNKA
PICULS	PIPALS	PLATER	POGGE	PORGED	PRAHUS	PRIMED	PROULS	PUNKAH
PIECE	PIPER	PLATES	POGGES	PORGES	PRANA	PRIMER	PROVE	PUNKAS
APIECE	PIPERS	PLATS	POILU	PORNO	PRANAS	PRIMES	PROVED	PUNKS
PIECED	PIPIT	SPLATS	POILUS	PORNOS	PRANG	PRIMO	PROVEN	SPUNKS
PIECEN	PIPITS	PLAYA	POIND	PORTA	SPRANG	PRIMOS	PROVER	PUNTO
PIECER	PIPUL	PLAYAS	POINDS	PORTAL	PRANGS	PRIMP	PROVES	PUNTOS
PIECES	PIPULS	PLAYS	POINT	PORTAS	PRANK	PRIMPS	PROWL	PUPIL
PIEND	PIQUE	SPLAYS	POINTE	PORTS	PRANKS	PRINK	PROWLS	PUPILS
PIENDS	PIQUED	UPLAYS	POINTS	SPORTS	PRANKY	PRINKS	PROYN	PUREE
PIERS	PIQUES	PLAZA	POINTY	PORTY	PRASE	PRINT	PROYNE	PUREED
PIERST	PIQUET	PLAZAS	POISE	SPORTY	PRASES	SPRINT	PROYNS	PUREES
PIETA	PIRAI	PLEAD	POISED	POSER	PRATE	PRINTS	PRUDE	PURES
PIETAS	PIRAIS	UPLEAD	POISER	POSERS	PRATED	PRION	PRUDES	PUREST
PIGHT	PISTE	PLEADS	POISES	POSES	PRATER	PRIONS	PRUNE	PURGE
SPIGHT	PISTES	PLEAS	POKAL	POSIT	PRATES	PRIOR	PRUNED	SPURGE
YPIGHT	PITCH	PLEASE	POKALS	POSITS	PRATS	PRIORS	PRUNER	PURGED
PIGHTS	PITCHY	PLEAT	POKER	POSSE	SPRATS	PRIORY	PRUNES	PURGER
PIKED	PITON	PLEATS	POKERS	POSSED	PRAWN	PRISE	PRUNT	PURGES
SPIKED	PITONS	PLEON	POKES	POSSER	PRAWNS	EPRISE	PRUNTS	PURIM
PIKER	PITTA	PLEONS	SPOKES	POSSES	PRAYS	UPRISE	PRYER	PURIMS
PIKERS	PITTAS	PLICA	POLAR	POSSET	SPRAYS	PRISED	PRYERS	PURIN
PIKES	PIUMS	PLICAE	POLARS	POTCH	PREED	PRISER	PRYSE	PURINE
SPIKES	OPIUMS	PLICAL	POLER	POTCHE	SPREED	PRISES	PRYSED	PURING
PIKUL	PIVOT	PLIER	POLERS	POTIN	PREEN	PRISM	PRYSES	PURINS
PIKULS	PIVOTS	PLIERS	POLEY	POTING	PREENS	PRISMS	PSALM	PURIS
PILAU	PIXEL	PLINK	POLEYN	POTINS	PREES	PRISMY		PURISM
PILAUS	PIXELS	PLINKS	POLEYS	POTTO	SPREES	PRIZE		PURIST
PILAW	PIXIE	PLOAT	POLIO			PRIZED		PURSE

PURSED
PURSER
PURSES
PURSEW
PUSES
OPUSES
PUSLE
PUSLED
PUSLES
PUTTI
PUTTIE
PUZEL
PUZELS
PYGAL
PYGALS
PYLON
PYLONS
PYRES
SPYRES
QANAT
QANATS
QIBLA
QIBLAS
QUACK
QUACKS
QUADS
SQUADS
QUAFF
QUAFFS
QUAIL
SQUAIL
QUAILS
QUAIR
QUAIRS
QUAKE
QUAKED
QUAKES
QUALM
QUALMS
QUALMY
QUANT
EQUANT
QUANTA
QUANTS
QUARK
QUARKS
QUART
QUARTE
QUARTO
QUARTS
QUARTZ
QUASH
SQUASH
QUATS
SQUATS
QUEAN
QUEANS
QUEEN
QUEENS
QUEER
QUEERS
QUELL
QUELLS
QUEME
QUEMED
QUEMES
QUENA
QUENAS
QUERN
QUERNS

QUEST
QUESTS
QUEUE
QUEUED
QUEUES
QUEYN
QUEYNS
QUICH
QUICHE
QUICK
QUICKS
QUIDS
SQUIDS
QUIET
QUIETS
QUIFF
QUIFFS
QUILL
SQUILL
QUILLS
QUILT
QUILTS
QUINA
QUINAS
QUINE
EQUINE
QUINES
QUINS
QUINSY
QUINT
SQUINT
QUINTA
QUINTE
QUINTS
QUIPO
QUIPOS
QUIPS
EQUIPS
QUIPU
QUIPUS
QUIRE
SQUIRE
QUIRED
QUIRES
QUIRK
QUIRKS
QUIRKY
QUIRT
SQUIRT
QUIRTS
QUIST
QUISTS
QUITE
QUITED
QUITES
QUITS
SQUITS
QUOIF
QUOIFS
QUOIN
QUOINS
QUOIT
QUOITS
QUOLL
QUOLLS
QUONK
QUONKS
QUOTA
QUOTAS

QUOTE
QUOTED
QUOTER
QUOTES
QUOTH
QUOTHA
QUYTE
QUYTED
QUYTES
RABAT
RABATO
RABATS
RABBI
RABBIN
RABBIS
RABBIT
RACED
BRACED
GRACED
TRACED
RACER
BRACER
TRACER
RACERS
RACES
BRACES
GRACES
TRACES
RACHE
ORACHE
RACHES
RACKS
BRACKS
CRACKS
TRACKS
WRACKS
RACON
RACONS
RADAR
RADARS
RADIO
RADIOS
RADON
RADONS
RAFFS
DRAFFS
GRAFFS
RAFTS
CRAFTS
DRAFTS
GRAFTS
KRAFTS
RAGEE
DRAGEE
RAGEES
RAGER
RAGERS
RAGGY
CRAGGY
DRAGGY
RAIDS
BRAIDS
RAIKS
TRAIKS
RAILE
GRAILE
RAILED
RAILER
RAILES
RAILS

BRAILS
DRAILS
FRAILS
GRAILS
TRAILS
RAINE
GRAINE
RAINED
RAINES
RAINS
BRAINS
DRAINS
GRAINS
TRAINS
RAINY
BRAINY
GRAINY
RAIRD
BRAIRD
RAIRDS
RAISE
ARAISE
BRAISE
FRAISE
PRAISE
RAISED
RAISER
RAISES
RAITS
KRAITS
TRAITS
RAJAH
RAJAHS
RAKED
BRAKED
CRAKED
RAKEE
RAKEES
RAKER
RAKERS
RAKERY
RAKES
BRAKES
CRAKES
DRAKES
RAKIS
RAKISH
RALLY
ORALLY
RALLYE
RAMEE
RAMEES
RAMIE
RAMIES
RAMPS
CRAMPS
TRAMPS
RANAS
PRANAS
RANCE
PRANCE
TRANCE
RANCED
RANCEL
RANCES
RANCH
BRANCH
CRANCH
RANCHO
RANDS

BRANDS
GRANDS
RANDY
BRANDY
RANEE
RANEES
RANGE
GRANGE
ORANGE
RANGED
RANGER
RANGES
RANKE
RANKED
RANKER
RANKES
RANKS
BRANKS
CRANKS
FRANKS
PRANKS
RANTS
CRANTS
DRANTS
GRANTS
ORANTS
TRANTS
RAPED
CRAPED
DRAPED
GRAPED
TRAPED
RAPER
DRAPER
RAPERS
RAPES
CRAPES
DRAPES
GRAPES
TRAPES
RAPHE
RAPHES
RAPID
RAPIDS
RASED
ERASED
RASES
BRASES
CRASES
ERASES
PRASES
RASPS
GRASPS
RASSE
WRASSE
RASSES
RATAN
RATANS
RATCH
CRATCH
FRATCH
RATED
CRATED
GRATED
ORATED
PRATED
RATEL
RATELS
RATER
CRATER

FRATER
GRATER
IRATER
PRATER
RATERS
RATES
CRATES
GRATES
ORATES
PRATES
URATES
RATHE
RATHER
RATHS
WRATHS
RATIO
RATION
RATIOS
RATTY
BRATTY
RAVED
BRAVED
CRAVED
GRAVED
RAVEL
GRAVEL
TRAVEL
RAVELS
RAVEN
CRAVEN
GRAVEN
RAVENS
RAVER
BRAVER
CRAVER
GRAVER
RAVERS
RAVES
BRAVES
CRAVES
GRAVES
TRAVES
RAVIN
RAVINE
RAVING
RAVINS
RAWER
BRAWER
DRAWER
RAWLY
BRAWLY
CRAWLY
RAXES
PRAXES
RAYAH
RAYAHS
RAYED
BRAYED
FRAYED
GRAYED
PRAYED
RAYLE
GRAYLE
RAYLED
RAYLES
RAYLET
RAYNE

TRAYNE
RAYNES
RAYON
CRAYON
RAYONS
RAZED
BRAZED
CRAZED
GRAZED
RAZEE
RAZEED
RAZEES
RAZES
BRAZES
CRAZES
GRAZES
RAZOR
RAZORS
REACH
AREACH
BREACH
CREACH
PREACH
REACT
REACTS
READS
AREADS
BREADS
DREADS
OREADS
TREADS
REAKS
BREAKS
CREAKS
FREAKS
WREAKS
REALM
REALMS
REAME
REAMED
REAMER
REAMES
REAMS
BREAMS
CREAMS
DREAMS
REAMY
CREAMY
DREAMY
REARM
REARMS
REARS
DREARS
REAST
BREAST
REASTS
REATA
REATAS
REATE
CREATE
REATES
REAVE
REAVED
REAVER
REAVES
REBEC
REBECK
REBECS
REBEL

REBELS
REBID
REBIDS
REBIT
REBITE
REBUT
REBUTS
RECAL
RECALL
RECALS
RECAP
RECAPS
RECCE
RECCED
RECCES
RECCO
RECCOS
RECIT
RECITE
RECITS
RECKS
DRECKS
TRECKS
WRECKS
RECTA
RECTAL
RECTO
RECTOR
RECTOS
RECUR
RECURE
RECURS
REDAN
REDANS
REDES
AREDES
BREDES
REDIA
UREDIA
REDIAE
REDIP
REDIPS
REECH
BREECH
REECHY
REEDE
REEDED
REEDEN
REEDER
REEDES
REEDS
BREEDS
CREEDS
GREEDS
REEDY
GREEDY
REEKS
BREEKS
CREEKS
REEKY
CREEKY
REELS
CREELS
REENS
GREENS
PREENS
TREENS

REESTY
REEVE
PREEVE
REEVED
REEVES
REFEL
REFELS
REFER
PREFER
REFERS
REFFO
REFFOS
REFIT
REFITS
REGAL
REGALE
REGALS
REGAR
REGARD
REGARS
REGIE
REGIES
REGMA
BREGMA
REGUR
REGURS
REIFS
PREIFS
REIGN
REIGNS
REINS
GREINS
REIRD
REIRDS
REIST
REISTS
REISTY
REIVE
REIVER
REIVES
REJIG
REJIGS
RELAY
RELAYS
RELET
RELETS
RELIC
RELICS
RELICT
RELIE
RELIED
RELIEF
RELIER
RELIES
REMAN
REMAND
REMANS
REMEN
REMENS
REMIT
FREMIT
REMITS
RENAY
RENAYS
RENDS
TRENDS
RENEW
RENEWS
RENEY
RENEYS

RENGA	REWTHS	RIDGEL	CRINES	GRIVET	ROLAGS	GROPER	ROUSED	CRUCKS
RENGAS	**RHEUM**	RIDGES	TRINES	PRIVET	**ROLES**	PROPER	ROUSER	TRUCKS
RENIG	RHEUMS	**RIELS**	URINES	TRIVET	DROLES	ROPERS	ROUSES	**RUDDY**
RENIGS	RHEUMY	ARIELS	**RINGS**	RIVETS	PROLES	ROPERY	**ROUST**	CRUDDY
RENIN	**RHIME**	ORIELS	BRINGS	**RIYAL**	**ROLLS**	**ROPES**	ROUSTS	**RUDER**
RENINS	RHIMES	**RIEVE**	WRINGS	RIYALS	DROLLS	GROPES	**ROUTE**	CRUDER
RENNE	**RHINE**	GRIEVE	**RINKS**	**ROACH**	PROLLS	TROPES	CROUTE	RUDERY
BRENNE	RHINES	PRIEVE	BRINKS	BROACH	TROLLS	**ROQUE**	ROUTED	**RUFFE**
FRENNE	**RHINO**	RIEVER	DRINKS	**ROADS**	**ROMAL**	ROQUES	ROUTER	RUFFED
RENNED	RHINOS	RIEVES	PRINKS	BROADS	ROMALS	ROQUET	ROUTES	RUFFES
RENNES	**RHOMB**	**RIFFS**	**RINSE**	TROADS	**ROMAN**	RORES	**ROUTH**	**RUING**
RENNET	RHOMBI	GRIFFS	RINSED	**ROANS**	ROMANS	CRORES	DROUTH	GRUING
RENTE	**RHOMBS**	**RIFLE**	RINSER	GROANS	**ROMAS**	PRORES	ROUTHS	TRUING
RENTED	**RHONE**	TRIFLE	RINSES	**ROAST**	AROMAS	RORIE	**ROUTS**	RUINGS
RENTER	RHONES	RIFLED	**RIOTS**	ROASTS	GROMAS	RORIER	CROUTS	**RULER**
RENTES	**RHUMB**	RIFLER	GRIOTS	**ROATE**	**ROMPS**	ROSED	GROUTS	RULERS
RENTS	RHUMBA	RIFLES	**RIPED**	ROATED	TROMPS	PROSED	TROUTS	**RUMAL**
PRENTS	RHUMBS	**RIFTE**	GRIPED	ROATES	**RONDE**	**ROSES**	**ROVED**	BRUMAL
REPAY	**RHYME**	RIFTED	**RIPEN**	**ROBED**	RONDEL	BROSES	PROVED	RUMALS
PREPAY	RHYMED	**RIFTS**	RIPENS	PROBED	RONDES	PROSES	**ROVER**	**RUMBA**
REPAYS	RHYMER	DRIFTS	**RIPER**	**ROBES**	RONDO	UROSES	DROVER	RUMBAS
REPEL	RHYMES	GRIFTS	GRIPER	PROBES	RONDOS	**ROSET**	PROVER	**RUMBO**
REPELS	**RHYNE**	**RIFTY**	RIPERS	**ROBIN**	**RONEO**	GROSET	TROVER	RUMBOS
REPLA	RHYNES	DRIFTY	**RIPES**	ROBING	RONEOS	ROSETS	ROVERS	**RUMEN**
REPLAN	**RIALS**	**RIGHT**	CRIPES	ROBINS	**RONES**	**ROSETY**	**ROVES**	CRUMEN
REPLAY	PRIALS	ARIGHT	GRIPES	**ROBLE**	CRONES	**ROSIN**	DROVES	**RUMES**
REPOT	TRIALS	BRIGHT	TRIPES	ROBLES	DRONES	ROSING	GROVES	BRUMES
REPOTS	URIALS	FRIGHT	RIPEST	**ROBOT**	GRONES	ROSINS	PROVES	GRUMES
REPRO	**RIANT**	WRIGHT	**RISEN**	ROBOTS	PRONES	ROSINY	**ROWAN**	**RUMLY**
REPROS	CRIANT	RIGHTO	ARISEN	**ROCKS**	TRONES	**ROSIT**	ROWANS	DRUMLY
RERUN	**RIATA**	**RIGHTS**	**RISER**	BROCKS	**RONTE**	PROSIT	**ROWED**	GRUMLY
RERUNS	RIATAS	RIGID	PRISER	CROCKS	RONTES	ROSITS	CROWED	**RUMMY**
RESAY	**RICED**	FRIGID	RISERS	FROCKS	**RONTS**	**ROSTS**	TROWED	CRUMMY
RESAYS	PRICED	RIGIDS	**RISES**	TROCKS	FRONTS	FROSTS	**ROWEL**	**RUMOR**
RESET	TRICED	**RIGOL**	ARISES	**RODED**	**ROODS**	**ROTAL**	TROWEL	RUMORS
PRESET	**RICER**	RIGOLL	BRISES	ERODED	BROODS	CROTAL	ROWELS	**RUMPS**
RESETS	GRICER	RIGOLS	CRISES	**RODEO**	**ROOFS**	**ROTCH**	**ROWEN**	CRUMPS
RESIN	PRICER	**RIGOR**	FRISES	RODEOS	GROOFS	CROTCH	ROWENS	FRUMPS
RESINS	RICERS	RIGORS	GRISES	**RODES**	PROOFS	**ROTCHE**	**ROWER**	TRUMPS
RESIT	**RICES**	**RILLE**	IRISES	ERODES	**ROOKS**	**ROTOR**	GROWER	**RUNCH**
RESITS	GRICES	GRILLE	KRISES	TRODES	BROOKS	ROTORS	ROWERS	BRUNCH
RESTS	PRICES	RILLED	**RISHI**	**ROGER**	CROOKS	**ROUGE**	**ROWME**	CRUNCH
CRESTS	TRICES	RILLES	RISHIS	DROGER	DROOKS	ROUGED	ROWMES	**RUNED**
PRESTS	**RICEY**	RILLET	**RISKS**	ROGERS	**ROOMS**	ROUGES	**ROWND**	PRUNED
WRESTS	PRICEY	**RILLS**	BRISKS	**ROGUE**	BROOMS	**ROUGH**	ROWNDS	**RUNES**
RETCH	**RICHT**	BRILLS	FRISKS	BROGUE	GROOMS	BROUGH	**ROWTH**	PRUNES
WRETCH	FRICHT	DRILLS	**RISKY**	DROGUE	VROOMS	TROUGH	GROWTH	**RUNTS**
RETES	RICHTS	FRILLS	BRISKY	ROGUED	**ROOMY**	ROUGHS	ROWTHS	BRUNTS
ARETES	**RICIN**	GRILLS	FRISKY	ROGUES	BROOMY	ROUGHT	**ROYAL**	GRUNTS
RETIE	RICING	KRILLS	**RISPS**	**ROILS**	**ROONS**	ROUGHY	ROYALS	PRUNTS
RETIED	RICINS	PRILLS	CRISPS	BROILS	CROONS	**ROULE**	**ROYNE**	**RUPEE**
RETIES	**RICKS**	TRILLS	**RITES**	DROILS	**ROOPS**	ROULES	GROYNE	RUPEES
RETRO	BRICKS	**RIMED**	TRITES	**ROINS**	DROOPS	**ROULS**	ROYNED	**RUPIA**
RETROD	CRICKS	CRIMED	URITES	GROINS	TROOPS	PROULS	ROYNES	RUPIAH
RETROS	ERICKS	GRIMED	WRITES	PROINS	**ROOPY**	**ROUND**	**ROYST**	RUPIAS
REUSE	PRICKS	PRIMED	**RIVAL**	**ROIST**	DROOPY	AROUND	ROYSTS	**RURAL**
REUSED	TRICKS	**RIMER**	RIVALS	ROISTS	**ROOSA**	GROUND	**ROZET**	CRURAL
REUSES	WRICKS	PRIMER	**RIVEL**	**ROKED**	ROOSAS	ROUNDS	ROZETS	RURALS
REVEL	**RIDER**	TRIMER	DRIVEL	BROKED	**ROOSE**	**ROUPS**	**ROZIT**	**RUSES**
REVELS	ARIDER	RIMERS	RIVELS	PROKED	BROOSE	CROUPS	ROZITS	CRUSES
REVET	RIDERS	**RIMES**	**RIVEN**	TROKED	ROOSED	GROUPS	**RUBIN**	DRUSES
BREVET	**RIDES**	CRIMES	DRIVEN	**ROKER**	ROOSES	**ROUPY**	RUBINE	URUSES
REVETS	BRIDES	GRIMES	**RIVER**	BROKER	**ROOST**	CROUPY	RUBINS	**RUSHY**
REVIE	GRIDES	PRIMES	DRIVER	PROKER	ROOSTS	GROUPY	**RUBLE**	BRUSHY
REVIED	IRIDES	**RIMUS**	RIVERS	ROKERS	**ROOTS**	**ROUSE**	RUBLES	**RUSMA**
REVIES	PRIDES	PRIMUS	RIVERY	**ROKES**	WROOTS	AROUSE	**RUCHE**	RUSMAS
REVIEW	**RIDGE**	**RINDS**	**RIVES**	BROKES	**ROPED**	CROUSE	RUCHED	**RUSTS**
REVUE	BRIDGE	GRINDS	DRIVES	PROKES	GROPED	GROUSE	RUCHES	BRUSTS
REVUES	FRIDGE	**RINES**	**RIVET**	TROKES	TROPED	TROUSE	**RUCKS**	CRUSTS
REWTH	RIDGED	BRINES		**ROLAG**	**ROPER**			FRUSTS

TRUSTS	SALEP	SASINS	SCALLS	SCOOP	SCROWS	SEGUES	SERVED	SHARK
RUSTY	SALEPS	SASSE	SCALP	SCOOPS	SCRUB	SEINE	SERVER	SHARKS
CRUSTY	SALET	SASSED	SCALPS	SCOOT	SCRUBS	SEINED	SERVES	SHARN
TRUSTY	SALETS	SASSES	SCAMP	SCOOTS	SCRUM	SEINER	SETON	SHARNS
RUTHS	SALLE	SATIN	SCAMPI	SCOPA	SCRUMP	SEINES	SETONS	SHARNY
TRUTHS	SALLEE	ISATIN	SCAMPS	SCOPAE	SCRUMS	SEISE	SEVEN	SHARP
RUTIN	SALLES	SATING	SCANT	SCOPE	SCUBA	SEISED	SEVENS	SHARPS
RUTINS	SALLET	SATINS	SCANTS	SCOPES	SCUBAS	SEISES	SEVER	SHAVE
RYBAT	SALMI	SATINY	SCANTY	SCORE	SCUDO	SEISM	SEVERE	SHAVED
RYBATS	SALMIS	SATYR	SCAPA	SCORED	ESCUDO	SEISMS	SEVERS	SHAVEN
RYKES	SALON	SATYRA	SCAPAS	SCORER	SCUFF	SEITY	SEVERY	SHAVER
GRYKES	SALONS	SATYRS	SCAPE	SCORES	SCUFFS	ASEITY	SEWEL	SHAVES
RYMME	SALOP	SAUBA	ESCAPE	SCORN	SCUFFY	SEIZE	SEWELS	SHAWL
RYMMED	SALOPS	SAUBAS	SCAPED	SCORNS	SCUFT	SEIZED	SEWEN	SHAWLS
RYMMES	SALSA	SAUCE	SCAPES	SCOTS	SCUFTS	SEIZER	SEWENS	SHAWM
SABER	SALSAS	SAUCED	SCARE	ASCOTS	SCULK	SEIZES	SEWER	SHAWMS
SABERS	SALSE	SAUCER	SCARED	ESCOTS	SCULKS	SELAH	SEWERS	SHAWS
SABIN	SALSES	SAUCES	SCARER	SCOUG	SCULL	SELAHS	SEWIN	PSHAWS
SABINS	SALTO	SAUCH	SCARES	SCOUGS	SCULLE	SELLE	SEWING	SHAYA
SABLE	SALTOS	SAUCHS	SCAREY	SCOUP	SCULLS	SELLER	SEWINS	SHAYAS
USABLE	SALUE	SAUGH	SCARF	SCOUPS	SCULP	SELLES	SEXER	SHCHI
SABLED	SALUED	SAUGHS	SCARFS	SCOUR	SCULPS	SELVA	SEXERS	SHCHIS
SABLES	SALUES	SAULT	SCARP	SCOURS	SCULPT	SELVAS	SEYEN	SHEAF
SABOT	SALVE	SAULTS	ESCARP	SCOUT	SCURF	SEMEN	SEYENS	SHEAFS
SABOTS	SALVED	SAUNA	SCARPS	SCOUTH	SCURFS	SEMENS	SHACK	SHEAFY
SABRA	SALVER	SAUNAS	SCART	SCOUTS	SCURFY	SEMIE	SHACKS	SHEAL
SABRAS	SALVES	SAUNT	SCARTH	SCOWL	SCUSE	SEMIES	SHADE	SHEALS
SABRE	SALVO	SAUNTS	SCARTS	SCOWLS	SCUSED	SENNA	SHADED	SHEAR
SABRED	SALVOR	SAUTE	SCATH	SCOWP	SCUSES	SENNAS	SHADES	SHEARS
SABRES	SALVOS	SAUTED	SCATHE	SCOWPS	SCUTA	SENSE	SHAFT	SHEEL
SACRA	SAMAN	SAUTES	SCATHS	SCRAB	SCUTAL	SENSED	SHAFTS	SHEELS
SACRAL	SAMANS	SAVER	SCATT	SCRABS	SCUTE	SENSES	SHAKE	SHEEN
SADHU	SAMBA	SAVERS	SCATTS	SCRAE	SCUTES	SEPAD	ASHAKE	SHEENS
SADHUS	TSAMBA	SAVEY	SCATTY	SCRAES	SDAYN	SEPADS	SHAKED	SHEENY
SAFES	SAMBAL	SAVEYS	SCAUD	SCRAG	SDAYNS	SEPAL	SHAKEN	SHEEP
SAFEST	SAMBAR	SAVIN	SCAUDS	SCRAGS	SDEIN	SEPALS	SHAKER	SHEEPY
SAGER	SAMBAS	SAVINE	SCAUP	SCRAM	SDEINS	SEPIA	SHAKES	SHEER
USAGER	SAMBO	SAVING	SCAUPS	SCRAMS	SEAME	SEPIAS	SHAKO	SHEERS
SAGES	SAMBOS	SAVINS	SCAUR	SCRAN	SEAMED	SEPOY	SHAKOS	SHEET
USAGES	SAMEL	SAVOR	SCAURS	SCRANS	SEAMEN	SEPOYS	SHALE	SHEETS
SAGEST	SAMELY	SAVORS	SCAURY	SCRAP	SEAMER	SEPTA	SHALED	SHEETY
SAHIB	SAMFU	SAVORY	SCEAT	SCRAPE	SEAMES	SEPTAL	SHALES	SHEIK
SAHIBA	SAMFUS	SAVOY	SCEATT	SCRAPS	SEARE	SERAC	SHALL	SHEIKH
SAHIBS	SAMPI	SAVOYS	SCEND	SCRAT	SEARED	SERACS	SHALLI	SHEIKS
SAICE	SAMPIS	SAWAH	ASCEND	SCRATS	SEARER	SERAI	SHALM	SHELF
SAICES	SANKO	SAWAHS	SCENDS	SCRAW	SEASE	SERAIL	SHALMS	SHELFS
SAICK	SANKOS	SAWER	SCENE	SCRAWL	SEASED	SERAIS	SHAMA	SHELFY
SAICKS	SANSA	SAWERS	SCENED	SCRAWM	SEASES	SERES	SHAMAN	SHELL
SAIDS	SANSAS	SAYED	SCENES	SCRAWS	SEAZE	SEREST	SHAMAS	SHELLS
SAIDST	SAPAN	SAYEDS	SCENT	SCRAY	SEAZED	SERGE	SHAME	SHELLY
SAIGA	SAPANS	SAYER	ASCENT	SCRAYE	SEAZES	SERGES	ASHAME	SHEND
SAIGAS	SAPOR	SAYERS	SCENTS	SCRAYS	SEBUM	SERIF	SHAMED	YSHEND
SAINE	SAPORS	SAYID	SCHMO	SCREE	SEBUMS	SERIFS	SHAMER	SHENDS
SAINED	SAREE	SAYIDS	SCHMOE	SCREED	SECCO	SERIN	SHAMES	SHENT
SAINT	SAREES	SAYON	SCHUL	SCREEN	SECCOS	SERINS	SHAND	YSHENT
SAINTS	SARGE	SAYONS	SCHULS	SCREES	SEDAN	SERON	SHANDS	SHERD
SAITH	SARGES	SCAFF	SCHWA	SCREW	SEDANS	SERONS	SHANDY	SHERDS
SAITHE	SARGO	SCAFFS	SCHWAS	SCREWS	SEDGE	SEROW	SHANK	SHETS
SAITHS	SARGOS	SCAIL	SCION	SCREWY	SEDGED	SEROWS	SHANKS	ASHETS
SAJOU	SARIN	SCAILS	SCIONS	SCRIM	SEDGES	SERRA	SHAPE	SHEVA
SAJOUS	SARINS	SCALA	SCLIM	SCRIMP	SEDUM	SERRAE	SHAPED	SHEVAS
SAKER	SAROD	SCALAE	SCLIMS	SCRIMS	SEDUMS	SERRAN	SHAPEN	SHIEL
SAKERS	SARODS	SCALAR	SCOFF	SCRIP	SEGAR	SERRAS	SHAPER	SHIELD
SAKIA	SARSA	SCALD	SCOFFS	SCRIPS	SEGARS	SERRE	SHAPES	SHIELS
SAKIAS	SARSAS	SCALDS	SCOLD	SCRIPT	SEGNO	SERRED	SHARD	SHIER
SALAD	SARZA	SCALE	SCOLDS	SCROG	SEGNOS	SERRES	SHARDS	ASHIER
SALADE	SARZAS	SCALED	SCONE	SCROGS	SEGOL	SERUM	SHARE	SHIERS
SALADS	SASIN	SCALER	SCONES	SCROW	SEGOLS	SERUMS	SHARED	SHIES
SALAL	SASINE	SCALES	SCOOG	ESCROW	SEGUE	SERVE	SHARER	SHIEST
SALALS		SCALL	SCOOGS	SCROWL	SEGUED		SHARES	SHIFT

SHIFTS	SHROWD	SIRUP	SKIMPS	SLEEPY	SLUSHY	SMOUSE	SNOOL	SONNE
SHIFTY	SHROWS	SIRUPS	SKIMPY	SLEET	SLYPE	SMOUT	SNOOLS	SONNES
SHILL	SHRUB	SISAL	SKINK	SLEETS	SLYPES	SMOUTS	SNOOP	SONNET
SHILLS	SHRUBS	SISALS	SKINKS	SLEETY	SMACK	SMOWT	SNOOPS	SONSE
SHINE	SHRUG	SITAR	SKIRL	SLICE	SMACKS	SMOWTS	SNOOT	SONSES
ASHINE	SHRUGS	SITARS	SKIRLS	SLICED	SMAIK	SNACK	SNOOTS	SOOLE
SHINED	SHTUM	SITHE	SKIRR	SLICER	SMAIKS	SNACKS	SNOOTY	SOOLED
SHINER	SHTUMM	SITHED	SKIRRS	SLICES	SMALL	SNAFU	SNORE	SOOLES
SHINES	SHUCK	SITHEN	SKIRT	SLICK	SMALLS	SNAFUS	SNORED	SOOTE
SHIRE	SHUCKS	SITHES	SKIRTS	SLICKS	SMALM	SNAIL	SNORER	SOOTED
SHIRES	SHUNT	SIVER	SKITE	SLIDE	SMALMS	SNAILS	SNORES	SOOTES
SHIRK	SHUNTS	SIVERS	SKITED	SLIDED	SMALMY	SNAILY	SNORT	SOOTH
SHIRKS	SHYER	SIXER	SKITES	SLIDER	SMALT	SNAKE	SNORTS	SOOTHE
SHIRR	SHYERS	SIXERS	SKIVE	SLIDES	SMALTI	SNAKED	SNORTY	SOOTHS
SHIRRA	SIBYL	SIXTE	SKIVED	SLIME	SMALTO	SNAKES	SNOUT	SOPHA
SHIRRS	SIBYLS	SIXTES	SKIVER	SLIMED	SMALTS	SNARE	SNOUTS	SOPHAS
SHIRT	SIDER	SIXTH	SKIVES	SLIMES	SMARM	SNARED	SNOUTY	SOPOR
SHIRTS	SIDERS	SIXTHS	SKLIM	SLIMS	SMARMS	SNARER	SNOWK	SOPORS
SHIRTY	SIDES	SIZAR	SKLIMS	SLIMSY	SMARMY	SNARES	SNOWKS	SORAS
SHITE	ASIDES	SIZARS	SKOFF	SLING	SMART	SNARK	SNUFF	PSORAS
SHITES	SIDHA	SIZEL	SKOFFS	ISLING	SMARTS	SNARKS	SNUFFS	SORBO
SHIVE	SIDHAS	SIZELS	SKRAN	SLINGS	SMARTY	SNARL	SNUFFY	SORBOS
SHIVER	SIDLE	SIZER	SKRANS	SLINK	SMEAR	SNARLS	SOARE	SORDO
SHIVES	SIDLED	SIZERS	SKRIK	SLINKS	ASMEAR	SNARLY	SOARED	SORDOR
SHLEP	SIDLES	SKAIL	SKRIKS	SLINKY	SMEARS	SNATH	SOARES	SOREE
SHLEPS	SIEGE	SKAILS	SKULK	SLIPE	SMEARY	SNATHE	SOBER	SOREES
SHOAL	SIEGED	SKALD	SKULKS	SLIPES	SMEEK	SNATHS	SOBERS	SOREL
SHOALS	SIEGER	SKALDS	SKULL	SLIVE	SMEEKS	SNEAD	SOCLE	SORELL
SHOALY	SIEGES	SKART	SKULLS	SLIVED	SMELL	SNEADS	SOCLES	SORELS
SHOAT	SIENT	SKARTH	SKUNK	SLIVEN	SMELLS	SNEAK	SOFAR	SORELY
SHOATS	SIENTS	SKARTS	SKUNKS	SLIVER	SMELLY	SNEAKS	SOFARS	SORES
SHOCK	SIETH	SKATE	SKYER	SLIVES	SMELT	SNEAKY	SOFTA	SOREST
SHOCKS	SIETHS	SKATED	SKYERS	SLOAN	SMELTS	SNEAP	SOFTAS	SORGO
SHOER	SIEVE	SKATER	SKYRE	SLOANS	SMILE	SNEAPS	SOGER	SORGOS
SHOERS	SIEVED	SKATES	SKYRED	SLOID	SMILED	SNECK	SOGERS	SORRA
SHOJI	SIEVES	SKATT	SKYRES	SLOIDS	SMILER	SNECKS	SOKEN	SORRAS
SHOJIS	SIGHT	SKATTS	SKYTE	SLOOM	SMILES	SNEER	SOKENS	SOUCE
SHOLA	SIGHTS	SKEAN	SKYTED	SLOOMS	SMILET	SNEERS	SOLAH	SOUCED
SHOLAS	SIGIL	SKEANS	SKYTES	SLOOMY	SMIRK	SNEERY	SOLAHS	SOUCES
SHOOK	SIGILS	SKEAR	SLACK	SLOOP	SMIRKS	SNEES	SOLAN	SOUGH
SHOOKS	SIGMA	SKEARS	SLACKS	SLOOPS	SMIRKY	SNEESH	SOLAND	SOUGHS
SHOOL	SIGMAS	SKEARY	SLADE	SLOOT	SMIRR	SNELL	SOLANO	SOUGHT
SHOOLS	SILEN	SKEER	SLADES	SLOOTS	SMIRRS	SNELLS	SOLANS	SOUND
SHOOT	SILENE	SKEERS	SLAKE	SLOPE	SMIRRY	SNELLY	SOLAR	SOUNDS
SHOOTS	SILENS	SKEERY	ASLAKE	ASLOPE	SMITE	SNICK	SOLARS	SOURS
SHORE	SILENT	SKEET	SLAKED	SLOPED	SMITER	SNICKS	SOLDE	SOURSE
ASHORE	SILER	SKEETS	SLAKES	SLOPES	SMITES	SNIDE	SOLDER	SOUSE
SHORED	SILERS	SKEIN	SLANE	SLOSH	SMITH	SNIDER	SOLDES	SOUSED
SHORER	SILES	SKEINS	SLANES	SLOSHY	SMITHS	SNIDES	SOLEN	SOUSES
SHORES	ESILES	SKELF	SLANG	SLOTH	SMITHY	SNIFF	SOLENS	SOUTH
SHORT	SILVA	SKELFS	SLANGS	SLOTHS	SMOCK	SNIFFS	SOLER	SOUTHS
SHORTS	SILVAE	SKELM	SLANGY	SLOVE	SMOCKS	SNIFFY	SOLERA	SOWAR
SHORTY	SILVAN	SKELMS	SLANT	SLOVEN	SMOKE	SNIFT	SOLERS	SOWARS
SHOTE	SILVAS	SKELP	ASLANT	SLOYD	SMOKED	SNIFTS	SOLID	SOWCE
SHOTES	SIMAR	SKELPS	SLANTS	SLOYDS	SMOKER	SNIFTY	SOLIDI	SOWCED
SHOTT	SIMARS	SKENE	SLATE	SLUBB	SMOKES	SNIPE	SOLIDS	SOWCES
SHOTTS	SINEW	SKENES	SLATED	SLUBBS	SMOKO	SNIPED	SOLUM	SOWER
SHOUT	SINEWS	SKERS	SLATER	SLUBBY	SMOKOS	SNIPER	SOLUMS	SOWERS
SHOUTS	SINEWY	ASKERS	SLATES	SLUIT	SMOLT	SNIPES	SOLVE	SOWFF
SHOVE	SINGE	ESKERS	SLAVE	SLUITS	SMOLTS	SNIRT	SOLVED	SOWFFS
SHOVED	SINGED	SKIER	SLAVED	SLUMP	SMOOR	SNIRTS	SOLVER	SOWLE
SHOVEL	SINGER	SKIERS	SLAVER	SLUMPS	SMOORS	SNOEK	SOLVES	SOWLED
SHOVER	SINGES	SKIES	SLAVES	SLUMPY	SMOOT	SNOEKS	SONAR	SOWLES
SHOVES	SIREN	ESKIES	SLAVEY	SLURB	SMOOTH	SNOKE	SONARS	SOWND
SHRED	SIRENE	SKIFF	SLEEK	SLURBS	SMOOTS	SNOKED	SONCE	SOWNDS
SHREDS	SIRENS	SKIFFS	SLEEKS	SLURP	SMORE	SNOKES	SONCES	SOWNE
SHREW	SIRIH	SKILL	SLEEKY	SLURPS	SMORED	SNOOD	SONDE	SOWNES
SHREWD	SIRIHS	SKILLS	SLEEP	SLUSE	SMORES	SNOODS	SONDES	SOWSE
SHREWS	SIROC	SKILLY	ASLEEP	SLUSES	SMOUS	SNOOK	SONIC	SOWSED
SHROW	SIROCS	SKIMP	SLEEPS	SLUSH	OSMOUS	SNOOKS	SONICS	SOWSES

SOWTH	SPEAR	ASPINE	SPRIGS	STALER	STEDES	STINGS	STOPED	STROWS
SOWTHS	SPEARS	SPINED	SPRIT	STALES	STEED	STINGY	STOPES	STROY
SOYLE	SPEARY	SPINEL	ESPRIT	STALK	STEEDS	STINK	STOPS	STROYS
SOYLED	SPEAT	SPINES	SPRITE	STALKO	STEEDY	STINKS	ESTOPS	STRUM
SOYLES	SPEATS	SPINET	SPRITS	STALKS	STEEK	STINT	STORE	ESTRUM
SPACE	SPECK	SPINK	SPROD	STALKY	STEEKS	STINTS	STORED	STRUMA
SPACED	SPECKS	SPINKS	SPRODS	STALL	STEEL	STINTY	STORER	STRUMS
SPACER	SPECKY	SPIRE	SPROG	STALLS	STEELD	STIPA	STORES	STRUT
SPACES	SPEED	ASPIRE	SPROGS	STAMP	STEELS	STIPAS	STOREY	ASTRUT
SPACEY	SPEEDO	SPIREA	SPRUE	STAMPS	STEELY	STIPE	STORK	STRUTS
SPADE	SPEEDS	SPIRED	SPRUES	STAND	STEEM	STIPEL	STORKS	STUCK
SPADED	SPEEDY	SPIRES	SPRUG	STANDS	ESTEEM	STIPES	STORM	STUCKS
SPADER	SPEEL	SPIRT	SPRUGS	STANE	STEEMS	STIRE	STORMS	STUFF
SPADES	SPEELS	SPIRTS	SPULE	STANED	STEEN	STIRED	STORMY	STUFFS
SPADO	SPEER	SPITE	SPULES	STANES	STEENS	STIRES	STOUN	STUFFY
SPADOS	SPEERS	SPITED	SPUME	STANG	STEEP	STIRK	STOUND	STULL
SPAER	SPEIR	SPITES	SPUMED	STANGS	STEEPS	STIRKS	STOUNS	STULLS
SPAERS	SPEIRS	SPLAT	SPUMES	STANK	STEEPY	STIRP	STOUP	STULM
SPAHI	SPELD	SPLATS	SPUNK	STANKS	STEER	STIRPS	STOUPS	STULMS
SPAHIS	SPELDS	SPLAY	SPUNKS	STAPH	STEERS	STIVE	STOUR	STUMP
SPAIN	SPELK	SPLAYS	SPUNKY	STAPHS	STEERY	STIVED	STOURS	STUMPS
SPAING	SPELKS	SPLIT	SPURN	STARE	STEIL	STIVER	STOURY	STUMPY
SPAINS	SPELL	SPLITS	SPURNE	ASTARE	STEILS	STIVES	STOUT	STUNS
SPALD	SPELLS	SPODE	SPURNS	STARED	STEIN	STOAT	STOUTH	ASTUNS
SPALDS	SPELT	SPODES	SPURT	STARER	STEINS	STOATS	STOUTS	STUNT
SPALE	SPELTS	SPOIL	SPURTS	STARES	STELA	STOCK	STOVE	STUNTS
SPALES	SPEND	SPOILS	SPYAL	STARK	STELAE	STOCKS	STOVED	STUPA
SPALL	SPENDS	SPOILT	SPYALS	STARKS	STELAR	STOCKY	STOVER	STUPAS
SPALLE	SPERM	SPOKE	SPYRE	STARN	STELE	STOEP	STOVES	STUPE
SPALLS	SPERMS	SPOKEN	SPYRES	STARNS	STELES	STOEPS	STOWN	STUPED
SPALT	SPIAL	SPOKES	SQUAB	STARR	STELL	STOIT	STOWND	STUPES
SPALTS	ESPIAL	SPOOF	SQUABS	STARRS	STELLS	STOITS	STRAD	STURT
SPANE	SPIALS	SPOOFS	SQUAD	STARRY	STEME	STOKE	STRADS	STURTS
SPANED	SPICA	SPOOK	SQUADS	START	STEMED	STOKED	STRAE	STYLE
SPANES	SPICAS	SPOOKS	SQUAT	ASTART	STEMES	STOKER	STRAES	STYLED
SPANG	SPICE	SPOOKY	ASQUAT	STARTS	STEND	STOKES	STRAG	STYLES
SPANGS	SPICED	SPOOL	SQUATS	STATE	STENDS	STOLA	STRAGS	STYLET
SPANK	SPICER	SPOOLS	SQUAW	ESTATE	STENT	STOLAS	STRAK	STYLO
SPANKS	SPICES	SPOOM	SQUAWK	STATED	OSTENT	STOLE	STRAKE	STYLOS
SPARE	SPICK	SPOOMS	SQUAWS	STATER	STENTS	STOLED	STRAP	STYME
SPARED	ASPICK	SPOON	SQUEG	STATES	STERE	STOLEN	STRAPS	STYMED
SPARER	SPICKS	SPOONS	SQUEGS	STAVE	STEREO	STOLES	STRAW	STYMES
SPARES	SPICS	SPOONY	SQUIB	STAVED	STERES	STOMP	STRAWN	STYRE
SPARK	ASPICS	SPOOR	SQUIBS	STAVES	STERN	STOMPS	STRAWS	STYRED
SPARKE	SPIDE	SPOORS	SQUID	STEAD	ASTERN	STOND	STRAWY	STYRES
SPARKS	SPIDER	SPORE	SQUIDS	STEADS	STERNS	STONDS	STRAY	SUAVE
SPARS	SPIED	SPORES	SQUIT	STEADY	STICH	STONE	ASTRAY	SUAVER
SPARSE	ESPIED	SPORT	SQUITS	STEAK	STICHS	ASTONE	ESTRAY	SUBAH
SPART	SPIEL	ASPORT	STACK	STEAKS	STICK	STONED	STRAYS	SUBAHS
SPARTH	SPIELS	SPORTS	STACKS	STEAL	STICKS	STONEN	STREP	SUBER
SPARTS	SPIES	SPORTY	STADE	OSTEAL	STICKY	STONER	STREPS	SUBERS
SPASM	ESPIES	SPOSH	STADES	STEALE	STIFF	STONES	STREW	SUCRE
SPASMS	SPIFF	SPOSHY	STAFF	STEALS	STIFFS	STONK	STREWN	SUCRES
SPATE	SPIFFY	SPOUT	STAFFS	STEALT	STILB	STONKS	STREWS	SUDOR
SPATES	SPIKE	ASPOUT	STAGE	STEAM	STILBS	STONN	STRIA	SUDORS
SPAUL	SPIKED	SPOUTS	STAGED	STEAMS	STILE	STONNE	STRIAE	SUEDE
SPAULD	SPIKES	SPOUTY	STAGER	STEAMY	STILED	STONNS	STRID	SUEDED
SPAULS	SPILE	SPRAG	STAGES	STEAN	STILES	STONY	STRIDE	SUEDES
SPAWL	SPILED	SPRAGS	STAGEY	STEANE	STILET	ASTONY	STRIDS	SUGAR
SPAWLS	SPILES	SPRAT	STAIG	STEANS	STILL	STOOK	STRIG	SUGARS
SPAWN	SPILL	SPRATS	STAIGS	STEAR	STILLS	STOOKS	STRIGA	SUGARY
SPAWNS	SPILLS	SPRAY	STAIN	STEARD	STILLY	STOOL	STRIGS	SUING
SPAYD	SPILT	SPRAYS	STAINS	STEARE	STILT	STOOLS	STRIP	SUINGS
SPAYDS	SPILTH	SPRED	STAIR	STEARS	STILTS	STOOP	STRIPE	SUINT
SPEAK	SPINA	SPREDD	STAIRS	STEDD	STILTY	ASTOOP	STRIPS	SUINTS
SPEAKS	SPINAE	SPREDS	STAKE	STEDDE	STIME	STOOPE	STRIPY	SUITE
SPEAL	SPINAL	SPREE	STAKED	STEDDS	STIMED	STOOPS	STROP	SUITED
SPEALS	SPINAR	SPREED	STAKES	STEDDY	STIMES	STOOR	STROPS	SUITES
SPEAN	SPINAS	SPREES	STALE	STEDE	STING	STOORS	STROW	SUJEE
SPEANS	SPINE	SPRIG	STALED	STEDED	STINGO	STOPE	STROWN	SUJEES

SUMAC	SWEAL	SYBOW	ETALON	STARRY	TEAZEL	TENUES	THEMED	THUJA
SUMACH	SWEALS	SYBOWS	TALONS	TARSI	TEAZES	TEPAL	THEMES	THUJAS
SUMACS	SWEAR	SYCEE	TALPA	TARSIA	TEDDY	TEPALS	THEOW	THUMB
SUMMA	SWEARD	SYCEES	TALPAE	TARTS	STEDDY	TEPEE	THEOWS	THUMBS
SUMMAE	SWEARS	SYLPH	TALPAS	STARTS	TEELS	TEPEES	THERE	THUMBY
SUMMAR	SWEAT	SYLPHS	TALUK	TASAR	STEELS	TERAI	THERES	THUMP
SUMMAT	SWEATS	SYLVA	TALUKS	TASARS	TEEMS	TERAIS	THERM	THUMPS
SUMPH	SWEATY	SYLVAE	TAMAL	TASSE	STEEMS	TERCE	THERMS	THYME
SUMPHS	SWEDE	SYLVAN	TAMALE	TASSEL	TEEND	TERCEL	THESE	THYMES
SUPER	SWEDES	SYLVAS	TAMALS	TASSES	TEENDS	TERCES	THESES	TIARA
SUPERB	SWEEL	SYMAR	TAMER	TASSET	TEENE	TERCET	THETA	TIARAS
SUPERS	SWEELS	SYMARS	TAMERS	TASTE	TEENED	TEREK	THETAS	TIBIA
SURAH	SWEEP	SYNCH	TAMES	TASTED	TEENES	TEREKS	THETE	TIBIAE
SURAHS	SWEEPS	SYNCHS	TAMEST	TASTER	TEENS	TERFE	THETES	TIBIAL
SURAT	SWEEPY	SYNOD	TAMIN	TASTES	STEENS	TERFES	THICK	TIBIAS
SURATS	SWEER	SYNODS	TAMINE	TATER	TEENSY	TERNE	THICKO	TICAL
SURED	SWEERT	SYREN	TAMING	STATER	TEERS	ETERNE	THICKS	TICALS
USURED	SWEET	SYRENS	TAMINS	TATERS	STEERS	TERNED	THICKY	TICKS
SURER	SWEETS	SYRUP	TAMIS	TATES	TEETH	TERNES	THIGH	STICKS
USURER	SWEETY	SYRUPS	TAMISE	STATES	TEETHE	TERNS	THIGHS	TICKY
SURES	SWEIR	SYRUPY	TAMPS	TATIE	TEHEE	STERNS	THILL	STICKY
USURES	SWEIRT	SYTHE	STAMPS	TATIES	TEHEED	TERRA	THILLS	TIFFS
SUREST	SWELL	SYTHES	TANGA	TATOU	TEHEES	TERRAE	THING	STIFFS
SURGE	SWELLS	SYVER	TANGAS	TATOUS	TEILS	TERRAS	THINGS	TIGER
SURGED	SWELT	SYVERS	TANGO	TATUS	STEILS	TERSE	THINGY	TIGERS
SURGES	SWELTS	TABLA	TANGOS	STATUS	TEIND	TERSER	THINK	TIGERY
SURRA	SWERF	TABLAS	TANGS	TAUBE	TEINDS	TESLA	THINKS	TIGHT
SURRAS	SWERFS	TABLE	STANGS	TAUBES	TELAE	TESLAS	THIOL	TIGHTS
SUSHI	SWIFT	STABLE	TANKA	TAUNT	STELAE	TESTA	THIOLS	TIGON
SUSHIS	SWIFTS	TABLED	TANKAS	TAUNTS	TELLS	TESTAS	THIRD	TIGONS
SUTOR	SWILL	TABLES	TANKS	TAUPE	STELLS	TESTE	THIRDS	TILDE
SUTORS	SWILLS	TABLET	STANKS	TAUPES	TEMED	TESTED	THIRL	TILDES
SUTRA	SWING	TABOO	TANNA	TAVER	ITEMED	TESTEE	THIRLS	TILED
SUTRAS	ASWING	TABOOS	TANNAH	TAVERN	STEMED	TESTER	THOFT	STILED
SWAGE	SWINGE	TABOR	TANNAS	TAVERS	TEMES	TESTES	THOFTS	TILER
SWAGED	SWINGS	TABORS	TAPER	TAVERT	STEMES	TETRA	THOLE	TILERS
SWAGES	SWINK	TABUN	TAPERS	TAWED	TEMPO	TETRAD	THOLED	TILERY
SWAIN	SWINKS	TABUNS	TAPES	STAWED	TEMPOS	TETRAS	THOLES	TILES
SWAINS	SWIPE	TACHE	ETAPES	TAWER	TEMPT	TEWED	THONG	STILES
SWALE	SWIPED	TACHES	STAPES	TAWERS	TEMPTS	STEWED	THONGS	TILLS
SWALED	SWIPER	TACKS	TAPET	TAWERY	TEMSE	TEWEL	THORN	STILLS
SWALES	SWIPES	STACKS	TAPETA	TAWSE	TEMSED	TEWELS	THORNS	TILLY
SWAMI	SWIPEY	TAFIA	TAPETI	TAWSES	TEMSES	TEWIT	THORNY	STILLY
SWAMIS	SWIRE	TAFIAS	TAPETS	TAXER	TENCH	TEWITS	THORP	TILTH
SWAMP	SWIRES	TAIGA	TAPIR	TAXERS	STENCH	THACK	THORPE	TILTHS
SWAMPS	SWIRL	TAIGAS	TAPIRS	TAXOR	TENDS	THACKS	THORPS	TILTS
SWAMPY	ASWIRL	TAINT	TAPIS	TAXORS	STENDS	THAGI	THOWL	STILTS
SWANK	SWIRLS	TAINTS	TAPIST	TAYRA	TENES	THAGIS	THOWLS	TIMBO
SWANKS	SWIRLY	TAIRA	TAPPA	TAYRAS	CTENES	THANA	THRAW	TIMBOS
SWANKY	SWISH	TAIRAS	TAPPAS	TAZZA	TENET	THANAH	THRAWN	TIMED
SWARD	SWISHY	TAKER	TARED	TAZZAS	TENETS	THANAS	THRAWS	STIMED
USWARD	SWONE	TAKERS	STARED	TEADE	TENIA	THANE	THREE	TIMER
SWARDS	SWONES	TAKES	TARES	TEADES	TENIAE	ETHANE	THREEP	TIMERS
SWARDY	SWOON	STAKES	STARES	TEADS	TENIAS	THANES	THREES	TIMES
SWARF	ASWOON	TAKIN	TARGE	STEADS	TENNE	THANK	THRID	STIMES
SWARFS	SWOONS	TAKING	TARGED	TEAKS	TENNER	THANKS	THRIDS	TIMON
SWARM	SWOOP	TAKINS	TARGES	STEAKS	TENNES	THECA	THRIP	TIMONS
ASWARM	SWOOPS	TALAK	TARGET	TEALS	TENON	THECAE	THRIPS	TINCT
SWARMS	SWORD	TALAKS	TARNS	STEALS	TENONS	THECAL	THROB	TINCTS
SWART	SWORDS	TALAQ	STARNS	TEAMS	TENOR	THEEK	ATHROB	TINEA
SWARTH	SWOUN	TALAQS	TAROC	STEAMS	TENORS	THEEKS	THROBS	TINEAS
SWARTY	SWOUND	TALAR	TAROCS	TEARS	TENSE	THEFT	THROE	TINGE
SWASH	SWOUNE	TALARS	TAROK	STEARS	TENSED	THEFTS	THROED	TINGED
SWASHY	SWOUNS	TALES	TAROKS	TEASE	TENSER	THEGN	THROES	TINGES
SWATH	SYBBE	STALES	TAROT	TEASED	TENSES	THEGNS	THROW	TINGS
SWATHE	SYBBES	TALKS	TAROTS	TEASEL	TENTH	THEIC	THROWE	STINGS
SWATHS	SYBIL	STALKS	TARRE	TEASER	TENTHS	THEICS	THROWN	TINKS
SWATHY	SYBILS	TALMA	TARRED	TEASES	TENTS	THEIR	THROWS	STINKS
SWAYL	SYBOE	TALMAS	TARRES	TEAZE	STENTS	THEIRS	THRUM	TINTS
SWAYLS	SYBOES	TALON	TARRY	TEAZED	TENUE	THEME	THRUMS	STINTS

TINTY	ATONED	TOUSED	STRASS	TROADE	TUBBY	TWIERS	UKASES	UNDAMS
STINTY	STONED	TOUSER	TRAVE	TROADS	STUBBY	TWILL	ULCER	UNDER
TIRED	TONES	TOUSES	TRAVEL	TROAT	TUBER	TWILLS	ULCERS	DUNDER
STIRED	ATONES	TOUTS	TRAVES	TROATS	TUBERS	TWILLY	ULEMA	FUNDER
TIRES	STONES	STOUTS	TRAWL	TROCK	TUCKS	TWILT	ULEMAS	SUNDER
STIRES	TONGA	TOUZE	TRAWLS	TROCKS	STUCKS	TWILTS	ULMIN	UNDERN
TITAN	TONGAS	TOUZED	TRAYS	TRODE	TUFFE	TWINE	ULMINS	UNFIT
TITANS	TONIC	TOUZES	STRAYS	STRODE	TUFFES	TWINED	ULNAR	UNFITS
TITCH	ATONIC	TOWED	TREAD	TRODES	TUFFET	TWINER	ULNARE	UNGET
STITCH	TONICS	STOWED	TREADS	TROKE	TUFFS	TWINES	ULTRA	UNGETS
TITER	TONKS	TOWEL	TREAT	STROKE	STUFFS	TWINK	ULTRAS	UNGOD
TITERS	STONKS	TOWELS	TREATS	TROKED	TUISM	TWINKS	ULYIE	UNGODS
TITHE	TONNE	TOWER	TREATY	TROKES	TUISMS	TWIRE	ULYIES	UNGUM
TITHED	STONNE	TOWERS	TRECK	TROLL	TULIP	TWIRED	ULZIE	UNGUMS
TITHER	TONNES	TOWERY	TRECKS	STROLL	TULIPS	TWIRES	ULZIES	UNHAT
TITHES	TOOLS	TOWSE	TREEN	TROLLS	TULLE	TWIRL	UMBEL	SUNHAT
TITIS	STOOLS	TOWSED	TREENS	TROLLY	TULLES	TWIRLS	UMBELS	UNHATS
OTITIS	TOOTH	TOWSER	TREMA	TROMP	TUMOR	TWIRLY	UMBER	UNIFY
TITLE	TOOTHS	TOWSES	TREMAS	TROMPE	TUMORS	TWIRP	CUMBER	MUNIFY
TITLED	TOOTHY	TOWZE	TREND	TROMPS	TUMPS	TWIRPS	DUMBER	UNION
TITLER	TOOTS	TOWZED	TRENDS	TRONA	STUMPS	TWIST	LUMBER	BUNION
TITLES	TOOTSY	TOWZES	TRENDY	TRONAS	TUMPY	TWISTS	NUMBER	UNIONS
TITRE	TOPED	TOXIN	TRESS	TRONC	STUMPY	TWISTY	UMBERS	UNITE
TITRES	STOPED	TOXINS	STRESS	TRONCS	TUNER	TWITE	UMBERY	DUNITE
TITUP	TOPEE	TOYER	TRESSY	TRONE	TUNERS	TWITES	UMBOS	GUNITE
TITUPS	TOPEES	TOYERS	TREWS	TRONES	TUNIC	TWOER	BUMBOS	MUNITE
TITUPY	TOPEK	TOZIE	STREWS	TROOP	TUNICS	TWOERS	GUMBOS	UNITED
TOAST	TOPEKS	TOZIES	TRIAD	TROOPS	TUPEK	TWYER	JUMBOS	UNITER
TOASTS	TOPER	TRACE	TRIADS	TROPE	TUPEKS	TWYERE	RUMBOS	UNITES
TOASTY	TOPERS	TRACED	TRIAL	TROPED	TUPIK	TWYERS	UMBRA	UNKED
TOAZE	TOPES	TRACER	ATRIAL	TROPES	TUPIKS	TYING	UMBRAE	BUNKED
TOAZED	STOPES	TRACES	TRIALS	TROTH	TUQUE	STYING	UMBRAL	DUNKED
TOAZES	TOPIC	TRACK	TRIBE	TROTHS	TUQUES	TYLER	UMBRAS	FUNKED
TODAY	ATOPIC	TRACKS	TRIBES	TROUT	TURBO	TYLERS	UMBRE	JUNKED
TODAYS	TOPICS	TRACT	TRICE	STROUT	TURBOS	TYPIC	UMBREL	UNKET
TODDE	TOQUE	TRACTS	TRICED	TROUTS	TURBOT	ETYPIC	UMBRES	JUNKET
TODDED	TOQUES	TRADE	TRICES	TROUTY	TURME	TYPTO	UMIAK	SUNKET
TODDES	TORAN	TRADED	TRICK	TROWS	TURMES	TYPTOS	UMIAKS	UNLAW
TOGUE	TORANA	TRADER	TRICKS	STROWS	TUTEE	TYRAN	UMPTY	UNLAWS
TOGUES	TORANS	TRADES	TRICKY	TROYS	TUTEES	TYRANS	HUMPTY	UNLAY
TOILE	TORES	TRADS	TRIDE	STROYS	TUTOR	TYRANT	UNARM	UNLAYS
ETOILE	STORES	STRADS	STRIDE	TRUCE	TUTORS	TYRED	UNARMS	UNLET
TOILED	TORII	TRAGI	TRIER	TRUCES	TUTTI	STYRED	UNBAG	RUNLET
TOILER	TORIIS	TRAGIC	ETRIER	TRUCK	TUTTIS	TYRES	UNBAGS	UNLID
TOILES	TORSE	TRAIK	TRIERS	STRUCK	TWAIN	STYRES	UNBAR	UNLIDS
TOILET	TORSEL	STRAIK	TRIGS	TRUCKS	ATWAIN	TYTHE	UNBARE	UNLIT
TOISE	TORSES	TRAIKS	STRIGS	TRUES	TWAINS	TYTHED	UNBARK	SUNLIT
TOISES	TORSK	TRAIL	TRIKE	TRUEST	TWANG	TYTHES	UNBARS	UNMAN
TOKED	TORSKS	TRAILS	STRIKE	TRULL	TWANGS	UDDER	UNBED	GUNMAN
STOKED	TORSO	TRAIN	TRIKED	TRULLS	TWANGY	DUDDER	SUNBED	UNMANS
TOKEN	TORSOS	TRAINS	TRIKES	TRUMP	TWANK	JUDDER	UNBEDS	UNMEW
TOKENS	TORTE	TRAIT	TRILL	TRUMPS	TWANKS	PUDDER	UNCAP	UNMEWS
TOKES	TORTEN	TRAITS	TRILLO	TRUNK	TWEAK	RUDDER	UNCAPE	UNPAY
ATOKES	TORTES	TRAMP	TRILLS	TRUNKS	TWEAKS	SUDDER	UNCAPS	UNPAYS
STOKES	TOSES	STRAMP	TRINE	TRUST	TWEED	UDDERS	UNCES	UNPEG
TOLAS	PTOSES	TRAMPS	TRINED	TRUSTS	TWEEDS	UGGED	BUNCES	UNPEGS
STOLAS	TOTAL	TRANT	TRINES	TRUSTY	TWEEDY	BUGGED	DUNCES	UNPEN
TOLED	TOTALS	TRANTS	TRIOR	TRUTH	TWEEL	FUGGED	OUNCES	UNPENS
STOLED	TOTEM	TRAPE	TRIORS	TRUTHS	ATWEEL	HUGGED	PUNCES	UNPENT
TOLES	TOTEMS	TRAPED	TRIPE	TRUTHY	TWEELS	JUGGED	UNCLE	UNPIN
STOLES	TOUCH	TRAPES	TRIPES	TRYER	TWEELY	LUGGED	NUNCLE	UNPINS
TOLLS	TOUCHE	TRAPS	STRIPE	TRYERS	TWEER	MUGGED	UNCLED	UNRIG
ATOLLS	TOUCHY	STRAPS	TRIPS	TRYST	TWEERS	PUGGED	UNCLES	RUNRIG
TOMAN	TOUGH	TRASH	STRIPS	TRYSTS	TWEET	RUGGED	UNCLEW	UNRIGS
TOMANS	TOUGHS	TRASHY	TRIST	TSUBA	TWEETS	TUGGED	UNCOS	UNRIP
TONAL	TOUNS	TRASS	TRISTE	TSUBAS	TWERP		BUNCOS	UNRIPE
ATONAL	STOUNS		TRITE	TUART	TWERPS		JUNCOS	UNRIPS
TONDO	TOURS		TRITER	TUARTS	TWICE		UNCUS	UNSAY
TONDOS	STOURS		TRITES	TUATH	TWICER		JUNCUS	UNSAYS
TONED	TOUSE		TROAD	TUATHS	TWIER		UNDAM	UNSET

SUNSET	BURGER	UVULAE	VELDT	VIGORS	VOGIER	WAIFT	WATER	WEIRD
UNSETS	PURGER	UVULAR	VELDTS	VILLA	VOGUE	WAIFTS	WATERS	WEIRDO
UNSEW	URGERS	UVULAS	VENEY	VILLAN	VOGUED	WAINS	WATERY	WEIRDS
UNSEWN	URGES	VADED	VENEYS	VILLAR	VOGUES	SWAINS	WAUFF	WEISE
UNSEWS	GURGES	EVADED	VENGE	VILLAS	VOGUEY	TWAINS	WAUFFS	WEISED
UNTIE	PURGES	VADES	AVENGE	VINCA	VOICE	WAIST	WAUGH	WEISES
AUNTIE	SURGES	EVADES	VENGED	VINCAS	VOICED	WAISTS	WAUGHS	WEIZE
UNTIED	URIAL	VAGUE	VENGER	VINER	VOICER	WAITE	WAUGHT	WEIZED
UNTIES	BURIAL	VAGUED	VENGES	VINERS	VOICES	TWAITE	WAULK	WEIZES
UNTIL	URIALS	VAGUER	VENIN	VINERY	VOIDS	WAITED	WAULKS	WELKE
UNTILE	URINE	VAGUES	VENINS	VINEW	AVOIDS	WAITER	WAURS	WELKED
UNTIN	MURINE	VAILS	VENOM	VINEWS	OVOIDS	WAITES	WAURST	WELKES
MUNTIN	PURINE	AVAILS	VENOMS	VINYL	VOILE	WAITS	WAVER	WELLS
UNTINS	URINED	VAKIL	VENTS	VINYLS	VOILES	AWAITS	WAVERS	DWELLS
UNWIT	URINES	VAKILS	EVENTS	VIOLA	VOLAR	WAIVE	WAVERY	SWELLS
UNWITS	URITE	VALES	VENUE	VIOLAS	VOLARY	WAIVED	WAVEY	SWELTS
UNWON	URITES	AVALES	AVENUE	VIPER	VOLET	WAIVER	WAVEYS	WELTS
UNWONT	URMAN	VALET	VENUES	VIPERS	VOLETS	WAIVES	WAXER	WHACK
UNZIP	URMANS	VALETA	VERGE	VIREO	VOLTE	WAKED	WAXERS	WHACKO
UNZIPS	URNED	VALETE	VERGED	VIREOS	VOLTES	AWAKED	WAYED	WHACKS
UPJET	BURNED	VALETS	VERGER	VIRGA	VOLVA	WAKEN	SWAYED	WHACKY
UPJETS	GURNED	VALIS	VERGES	VIRGAS	VOLVAS	AWAKEN	WAZIR	WHALE
UPLAY	TURNED	VALISE	VERSE	VIRGE	VOLVE	WAKENS	WAZIRS	WHALED
UPLAYS	URSON	VALOR	AVERSE	VIRGER	EVOLVE	WAKER	WEALD	WHALER
UPPED	URSONS	VALORS	VERSED	VIRGES	VOLVED	WAKERS	WEALDS	WHALES
CUPPED	URUBU	VALSE	VERSER	VIRTU	VOLVES	WAKES	WEALS	WHANG
DUPPED	URUBUS	VALSED	VERSES	VIRTUE	VOMER	AWAKES	SWEALS	WHANGS
HUPPED	URVAS	VALSES	VERSET	VIRTUS	VOMERS	WALED	WEAMB	WHARE
PUPPED	MURVAS	VALUE	VERSO	VISED	VOMIT	SWALED	WEAMBS	WHARES
SUPPED	USAGE	VALUED	VERSOS	AVISED	VOMITO	WALER	WEARS	WHARF
TUPPED	USAGER	VALUER	VERST	VISES	VOMITS	WALERS	SWEARS	WHARFS
UPPER	USAGES	VALUES	VERSTS	AVISES	VOTER	WALES	WEARY	WHATS
CUPPER	USERS	VALVE	VERTS	VISIE	VOTERS	DWALES	AWEARY	WHATSO
SUPPER	MUSERS	VALVED	AVERTS	VISIED	VOUCH	SWALES	WEAVE	WHAUP
UPPERS	USHER	VALVES	EVERTS	VISIER	AVOUCH	WALIS	WEAVED	WHAUPS
UPRUN	GUSHER	VAPOR	VERTU	VISIES	VOUGE	WALISE	WEAVER	WHAUR
UPRUNS	HUSHER	VAPORS	VERTUE	VISIT	VOUGES	WALLA	WEAVES	WHAURS
UPSEE	LUSHER	VARAN	VERTUS	VISITE	VOWED	WALLAH	WEBER	WHEAL
UPSEES	MUSHER	VARANS	VERVE	VISITS	AVOWED	WALLAS	WEBERS	WHEALS
UPSET	PUSHER	VAREC	VERVEL	VISNE	VOWEL	WANGS	WECHT	WHEAR
UPSETS	RUSHER	VARECH	VERVEN	VISNES	VOWELS	TWANGS	WECHTS	WHEARE
UPSEY	USHERS	VARECS	VERVES	VISON	VRAIC	WANKS	WEDGE	WHEAT
UPSEYS	USING	VARNA	VERVET	VISONS	VRAICS	SWANKS	WEDGED	WHEATS
UPTAK	BUSING	VARNAS	VESPA	VISOR	VROOM	TWANKS	WEDGES	WHEEL
UPTAKE	FUSING	VARVE	VESPAS	VISORS	VROOMS	WANZE	WEEDS	AWHEEL
UPTAKS	MUSING	VARVED	VESTA	VISTA	VROUW	WANZED	TWEEDS	WHEELS
UPTIE	USNEA	VARVEL	VESTAL	VISTAL	VROUWS	WANZES	WEEDY	WHEELY
UPTIED	USNEAS	VARVES	VESTAS	VISTAS	VULVA	WARDS	TWEEDY	WHEEN
UPTIES	USUAL	VAULT	VETCH	VISTO	VULVAL	AWARDS	WEEKE	WHEENS
URALI	USUALS	VAULTS	KVETCH	VISTOS	VULVAR	SWARDS	WEEKES	WHEFT
OURALI	USURE	VAULTY	VETCHY	VITAL	VULVAS	WARMS	WEELS	WHEFTS
URALIS	USURED	VAUNT	VEXER	AVITAL	WACKE	SWARMS	SWEELS	WHELK
URARI	USURER	AVAUNT	VEXERS	VITALS	WACKES	WARNS	TWEELS	WHELKS
CURARI	USURES	VAUNTS	VEZIR	VITTA	WADDY	AWARNS	WEENY	WHELKY
OURARI	USURP	VAUTE	VEZIRS	VITTAE	SWADDY	WARRE	SWEENY	WHELM
URARIS	USURPS	VAUTED	VIAND	VIVDA	WADER	WARRED	TWEENY	WHELMS
URATE	UTILE	VAWTE	VIANDS	VIVDAS	WADERS	WARREN	WEEPS	WHELP
AURATE	FUTILE	VAWTED	VICAR	VIVER	WAFER	WARREY	SWEEPS	WHELPS
CURATE	RUTILE	VAWTES	VICARS	VIVERS	WAFERS	WARTY	WEEPY	WHERE
URATES	SUTILE	VEALE	VICARY	VIXEN	WAFERY	SWARTY	SWEEPY	WHERES
URBAN	UTTER	VEALES	VIDEO	VIXENS	WAGED	WASHY	WEEST	WHIFF
TURBAN	BUTTER	VEENA	VIDEOS	VIZIR	SWAGED	SWASHY	TWEEST	WHIFFS
URBANE	CUTTER	VEENAS	VIFDA	VIZIRS	WAGER	WASTE	WEETE	WHIFFY
URENA	GUTTER	VEGAN	VIFDAS	VIZOR	WAGERS	WASTED	WEETEN	WHIFT
MURENA	MUTTER	VEGANS	VIGIA	VIZORS	WAGES	WASTEL	WEFTE	WHIFTS
URENAS	NUTTER	VEGIE	VIGIAS	VOCAL	SWAGES	WASTER	WEFTED	WHILE
URGED	PUTTER	VEGIES	VIGIL	VOCALS	WAGON	WASTES	WEFTES	AWHILE
PURGED	RUTTER	VELAR	VIGILS	VODKA	WAGONS	WATCH	WEIGH	WHILED
SURGED	UTTERS	VELARS	VIGOR	VODKAS	WAHOO	AWATCH	WEIGHS	WHILES
URGER	UVULA		VIGORO	VOGIE	WAHOOS	SWATCH	WEIGHT	WHIMS

WHIMSY	WIDOWS	WINZES	WONGAS	**WREAK**	XYLEMS	YEASTY	**YUCCA**	ZINEBS
WHINE	**WIDTH**	**WIPED**	**WOODS**	WREAKE	**XYLOL**	**YENTA**	YUCCAS	**ZINKE**
WHINED	WIDTHS	SWIPED	WOODSY	WREAKS	XYLOLS	YENTAS	**YULAN**	ZINKED
WHINER	**WIELD**	**WIPER**	**WOOER**	**WRECK**	**XYLYL**	**YERBA**	YULANS	ZINKES
WHINES	WIELDS	SWIPER	WOOERS	WRECKS	XYLYLS	YERBAS	**YUPON**	**ZIZEL**
WHIRL	WIELDY	WIPERS	**WOOLD**	**WREST**	**YACCA**	**YESES**	YUPONS	ZIZELS
WHIRLS	**WIGAN**	**WIPES**	WOOLDS	WRESTS	YACCAS	CYESES	**ZABRA**	**ZLOTY**
WHIRR	WIGANS	SWIPES	**WOONS**	**WRICK**	**YACHT**	OYESES	ZABRAS	ZLOTYS
WHIRRS	**WIGHT**	**WIRED**	SWOONS	WRICKS	YACHTS	**YIELD**	**ZAMAN**	**ZOCCO**
WHIRRY	TWIGHT	TWIRED	**WOOSH**	**WRIER**	**YAFFS**	YIELDS	ZAMANG	ZOCCOS
WHISH	WIGHTS	**WIRER**	SWOOSH	OWRIER	NYAFFS	**YLEMS**	ZAMANS	**ZOISM**
WHISHT	**WILLS**	WIRERS	**WORDS**	**WRIES**	**YAGER**	XYLEMS	**ZAMBO**	ZOISMS
WHISK	SWILLS	**WIRES**	SWORDS	WRIEST	YAGERS	**YOBBO**	ZAMBOS	**ZOIST**
WHISKS	TWILLS	SWIRES	**WORLD**	**WRING**	**YAHOO**	YOBBOS	**ZAMIA**	ZOISTS
WHISKY	**WILLY**	TWIRES	WORLDS	WRINGS	YAHOOS	**YODEL**	ZAMIAS	**ZOMBI**
WHIST	TWILLY	**WISES**	**WORSE**	**WRIST**	**YAKKA**	YODELS	ZANJA	ZOMBIE
WHISTS	**WILTS**	WISEST	WORSED	WRISTS	YAKKAS	**YODLE**	ZANJAS	ZOMBIS
WHITE	TWILTS	**WISTS**	WORSEN	WRISTY	**YAMEN**	YODLED	**ZANTE**	**ZONAL**
WHITED	**WINCE**	TWISTS	WORSER	**WRITE**	YAMENS	YODLER	ZANTES	AZONAL
WHITEN	WINCED	**WITCH**	WORSES	WRITER	**YANGS**	YODLES	**ZANZE**	**ZONDA**
WHITER	WINCER	SWITCH	**WORST**	WRITES	KYANGS	**YOGIN**	ZANZES	ZONDAS
WHITES	WINCES	TWITCH	WORSTS	**WROKE**	**YAPOK**	YOGINI	**ZEBEC**	**ZONES**
WHITEY	WINCEY	**WITES**	**WORTH**	YWROKE	YAPOKS	YOGINS	ZEBECK	OZONES
WHOLE	**WINED**	TWITES	WORTHS	WROKEN	**YAPON**	**YOGIS**	ZEBECS	**ZOOEA**
WHOLES	DWINED	**WITHE**	WORTHY	**WRONG**	YAPONS	YOGISM	**ZEBRA**	ZOOEAE
WHOOP	TWINED	WITHED	**WOULD**	AWRONG	**YARFA**	**YOICK**	ZEBRAS	ZOOEAL
WHOOPS	**WINES**	WITHER	WOULDS	WRONGS	YARFAS	YOICKS	**ZEBUB**	ZOOEAS
WHOOT	DWINES	WITHES	**WOUND**	**WROOT**	**YARTA**	**YOJAN**	ZEBUBS	**ZOOID**
WHOOTS	TWINES	**WIZEN**	SWOUND	WROOTS	YARTAS	YOJANA	**ZERDA**	ZOOIDS
WHORE	**WINGE**	WIZENS	WOUNDS	**WURST**	**YARTO**	YOJANS	ZERDAS	**ZORIL**
WHORED	SWINGE	**WODGE**	WOUNDY	WURSTS	YARTOS	**YOKEL**	**ZHOMO**	ZORILS
WHORES	TWINGE	WODGES	**WRACK**	**WUSHU**	**YCLED**	YOKELS	ZHOMOS	**ZORRO**
WHORL	WINGED	**WOKEN**	AWRACK	WUSHUS	CYCLED	**YOUNG**	**ZIBET**	ZORROS
WHORLS	WINGER	AWOKEN	WRACKS	**XEBEC**	**YEALM**	YOUNGS	ZIBETS	**ZUPAN**
WHORT	WINGES	**WOLVE**	**WRAST**	XEBECS	YEALMS	**YOURT**	**ZIGAN**	ZUPANS
WHORTS	**WINGS**	WOLVED	WRASTS	**XENIA**	**YEARD**	YOURTS	ZIGANS	**ZYGON**
WIDEN	SWINGS	WOLVER	**WRATH**	XENIAL	YEARDS	**YOUTH**	**ZIMBI**	ZYGONS
WIDENS	**WINKS**	WOLVES	WRATHS	XENIAS	**YEARN**	YOUTHS	ZIMBIS	**ZYMES**
WIDES	SWINKS	**WOMAN**	WRATHY	**XENON**	YEARNS	YOUTHY	**ZINCO**	AZYMES
WIDEST	TWINKS	WOMANS	**WRAWL**	XENONS	**YEAST**	**YOWIE**	ZINCOS	
WIDOW	**WINZE**	**WONGA**	WRAWLS	**XYLEM**	YEASTS	YOWIES	**ZINEB**	

PART B: 6-letter word hooks
extensible words only

ABATOR	BABYING	HACKERS	WADDLED	**AERIES**	**AGINGS**	WAILING	**ALEXIN**
ABATORS	**ACACIA**	LACKERS	**ADDLES**	FAERIES	PAGINGS	**AIMING**	ALEXINS
ABAYAS	ACACIAS	PACKERS	DADDLES	AERIEST	**AGLETS**	MAIMING	**ALGATE**
KABAYAS	**ACAJOU**	RACKERS	FADDLES	**AEROBE**	EAGLETS	**AIRGAP**	ALGATES
ABDABS	ACAJOUS	TACKERS	PADDLES	AEROBES	HAGLETS	AIRGAPS	**ALIDAD**
HABDABS	**ACANTH**	YACKERS	RADDLES	**AETHER**	**AGNAIL**	**AIRIER**	ALIDADE
ABDUCE	ACANTHA	**ACKNOW**	SADDLES	AETHERS	AGNAILS	HAIRIER	ALIDADS
ABDUCED	ACANTHS	ACKNOWN	WADDLES	**AFFAIR**	**AGNAME**	LAIRIER	**ALIGHT**
ABDUCES	**ACARID**	ACKNOWS	**ADDOOM**	AFFAIRE	AGNAMED	VAIRIER	ALIGHTS
ABDUCT	ACARIDS	**ACMITE**	ADDOOMS	AFFAIRS	AGNAMES	**AIRILY**	**ALIGNS**
ABDUCTS	**ACATER**	ACMITES	**ADDUCE**	**AFFEAR**	**AGNATE**	FAIRILY	MALIGNS
ABELES	ACATERS	**ACQUIT**	ADDUCED	AFFEARD	MAGNATE	**AIRING**	**ALINES**
KABELES	**ACATES**	ACQUITE	ADDUCER	AFFEARE	AGNATES	FAIRING	SALINES
ABELIA	VACATES	ACQUITS	ADDUCES	AFFEARS	**AGNISE**	HAIRING	VALINES
ABELIAS	**ACCEDE**	**ACTING**	**ADDUCT**	**AFFECT**	AGNISED	LAIRING	**ALIPED**
ABJECT	ACCEDED	ACTINGS	ADDUCTS	AFFECTS	AGNISES	PAIRING	TALIPED
ABJECTS	ACCEDER	**ACTION**	**ADHERE**	**AFFEER**	**AGNIZE**	SAIRING	ALIPEDS
ABJURE	ACCEDES	FACTION	ADHERED	AFFEERS	AGNIZED	AIRINGS	**ALISMA**
ABJURED	**ACCEND**	PACTION	ADHERER	**AFFIES**	AGNIZES	**AIRNED**	ALISMAS
ABJURER	ACCENDS	TACTION	ADHERES	BAFFIES	**AGOGIC**	CAIRNED	**ALKALI**
ABJURES	**ACCENT**	ACTIONS	**ADJOIN**	DAFFIES	AGOGICS	**AIRWAY**	ALKALIS
ABLATE	ACCENTS	**ACTIVE**	ADJOINS	TAFFIES	**AGOUTA**	FAIRWAY	**ALKANE**
ABLATED	**ACCEPT**	FACTIVE	ADJOINT	**AFFINE**	AGOUTAS	AIRWAYS	ALKANES
ABLATES	ACCEPTS	**ACTORS**	**ADJURE**	AFFINED	**AGOUTI**	**AJOWAN**	ALKANET
ABLAUT	**ACCITE**	FACTORS	ADJURED	AFFINES	AGOUTIS	AJOWANS	**ALKENE**
ABLAUTS	ACCITED	**ACTUAL**	ADJURES	**AFFIRM**	**AGREGE**	**AKEDAH**	ALKENES
ABLETS	ACCITES	FACTUAL	**ADJUST**	AFFIRMS	AGREGES	AKEDAHS	**ALKYNE**
GABLETS	**ACCLOY**	TACTUAL	ADJUSTS	**AFFORD**	**AGRISE**	**ALALIA**	ALKYNES
TABLETS	ACCLOYS	**ACTURE**	**ADMIRE**	AFFORDS	AGRISED	ALALIAS	**ALLEES**
ABLING	**ACCOIL**	FACTURE	ADMIRED	**AFFRAP**	AGRISES	**ALANGS**	MALLEES
CABLING	ACCOILS	ACTURES	ADMIRER	AFFRAPS	**AGRIZE**	LALANGS	SALLEES
FABLING	**ACCORD**	**ACUITY**	ADMIRES	**AFFRAY**	AGRIZED	**ALARUM**	**ALLEGE**
SABLING	ACCORDS	VACUITY	**ADORER**	AFFRAYS	AGRIZES	ALARUMS	ALLEGED
TABLING	**ACCOST**	**ACUMEN**	ADORERS	**AFFRET**	**AGRYZE**	**ALATED**	ALLEGER
ABOLLA	ACCOSTS	CACUMEN	**ADREAD**	AFFRETS	AGRYZED	PALATED	ALLEGES
ABOLLAE	**ACCREW**	ACUMENS	ADREADS	**AFGHAN**	AGRYZES	**ALBATA**	**ALLELE**
ABOLLAS	ACCREWS	**ACUTES**	**ADSORB**	AFGHANS	**AGUISE**	ALBATAS	ALLELES
ABOUND	**ACCRUE**	ACUTEST	ADSORBS	**AFREET**	AGUISED	**ALBEDO**	**ALLEYS**
ABOUNDS	ACCRUED	**ADAGIO**	**ADVENE**	AFREETS	AGUISES	ALBEDOS	GALLEYS
ABRADE	ACCRUES	ADAGIOS	ADVENED	**AFTERS**	**AGUIZE**	**ALBERT**	VALLEYS
ABRADED	**ACCUSE**	**ADDEEM**	ADVENES	RAFTERS	AGUIZED	HALBERT	**ALLICE**
ABRADES	ACCUSED	ADDEEMS	**ADVENT**	WAFTERS	AGUIZES	ALBERTS	ALLICES
ABRAID	ACCUSER	**ADDEND**	ADVENTS	**AGAMID**	**AHIMSA**	**ALBINO**	**ALLIED**
ABRAIDS	ACCUSES	ADDENDA	**ADVERB**	AGAMIDS	AHIMSAS	ALBINOS	DALLIED
ABRAZO	**ACEDIA**	ADDENDS	ADVERBS	**AGARIC**	**AIDERS**	**ALBITE**	GALLIED
ABRAZOS	ACEDIAS	**ADDERS**	**ADVERT**	AGARICS	RAIDERS	ALBITES	RALLIED
ABREGE	**ACETAL**	GADDERS	ADVERTS	**AGEING**	**AIDING**	**ALBUGO**	SALLIED
ABREGES	ACETALS	LADDERS	**ADVICE**	AGEINGS	LAIDING	ALBUGOS	TALLIED
ABROAD	**ACETYL**	MADDERS	ADVICES	**AGEISM**	MAIDING	**ALCOVE**	**ALLIES**
ABROADS	ACETYLS	PADDERS	**ADVISE**	AGEISMS	RAIDING	ALCOVES	DALLIES
ABRUPT	**ACHAGE**	**ADDICT**	ADVISED	**AGEIST**	**AIGLET**	**ALDOSE**	GALLIES
ABRUPTS	ACHAGES	ADDICTS	ADVISER	AGEISTS	AIGLETS	ALDOSES	RALLIES
ABSEIL	**ACHENE**	**ADDING**	ADVISES	**AGENDA**	**AIKIDO**	**ALDRIN**	SALLIES
ABSEILS	ACHENES	DADDING	**ADWARD**	AGENDAS	AIKIDOS	ALDRINS	TALLIES
ABSENT	**ACHING**	GADDING	ADWARDS	**AGENES**	**AILING**	**ALEGAR**	WALLIES
ABSENTS	BACHING	HADDING	**AEDILE**	SAGENES	BAILING	ALEGARS	**ALLONS**
ABSORB	CACHING	MADDING	AEDILES	**AGGERS**	FAILING	**ALEGGE**	BALLONS
ABSORBS	ACHINGS	PADDING	**AEMULE**	DAGGERS	HAILING	ALEGGED	GALLONS
ABULIA	**ACHKAN**	WADDING	AEMULED	GAGGERS	JAILING	ALEGGES	**ALLOTS**
ABULIAS	ACHKANS	**ADDLED**	AEMULES	JAGGERS	MAILING	**ALERCE**	BALLOTS
ABUSER	**ACKEES**	DADDLED	**AERATE**	LAGGERS	NAILING	ALERCES	TALLOTS
ABUSERS	HACKEES	FADDLED	AERATED	NAGGERS	RAILING	**ALEVIN**	**ALLOWS**
ABVOLT	**ACKERS**	PADDLED	AERATES	SAGGERS	SAILING	ALEVINS	BALLOWS
ABVOLTS	BACKERS	RADDLED	**AERIAL**	TAGGERS	TAILING	**ALEXIA**	CALLOWS
ABYING	DACKERS	SADDLED	AERIALS	YAGGERS	VAILING	ALEXIAS	FALLOWS

GALLOWS	**AMBLES**	**ANANAS**	BANKERS	TANTRUM	ARALIAS	**ARKING**	ARRIVES
HALLOWS	GAMBLES	BANANAS	CANKERS	ANTRUMS	**ARAYSE**	BARKING	**ARROBA**
MALLOWS	HAMBLES	MANANAS	HANKERS	**ANURIA**	ARAYSED	CARKING	ARROBAS
SALLOWS	RAMBLES	**ANANKE**	JANKERS	ANURIAS	ARAYSES	HARKING	**ARROWS**
TALLOWS	WAMBLES	ANANKES	RANKERS	**ANYONE**	**ARBORS**	LARKING	BARROWS
WALLOWS	**AMELIA**	**ANARAK**	TANKERS	ANYONES	HARBORS	MARKING	FARROWS
ALLUDE	AMELIAS	ANARAKS	WANKERS	**ANYWAY**	**ARBOUR**	NARKING	HARROWS
ALLUDED	**AMENDE**	**ANARCH**	YANKERS	ANYWAYS	HARBOUR	PARKING	MARROWS
ALLUDES	AMENDED	ANARCHS	**ANKLED**	**AORIST**	ARBOURS	SARKING	NARROWS
ALLURE	AMENDER	ANARCHY	FANKLED	AORISTS	**ARBUTE**	**ARKITE**	TARROWS
ALLURED	AMENDES	**ANATTA**	RANKLED	**AOUDAD**	ARBUTES	ARKITES	YARROWS
ALLURER	**AMENTA**	ANATTAS	**ANKLES**	AOUDADS	**ARCADE**	**ARKOSE**	**ARROWY**
ALLURES	RAMENTA	**ANATTO**	FANKLES	**APACHE**	ARCADED	ARKOSES	MARROWY
ALMAIN	AMENTAL	ANATTOS	RANKLES	APACHES	ARCADES	**ARMADA**	**ARROYO**
ALMAINS	**AMENTS**	**ANCHOR**	**ANKLET**	**APEDOM**	**ARCHED**	ARMADAS	ARROYOS
ALMOND	LAMENTS	ANCHORS	ANKLETS	APEDOMS	MARCHED	**ARMFUL**	**ARSHIN**
ALMONDS	**AMERCE**	**ANCILE**	**ANLACE**	**APERCU**	PARCHED	HARMFUL	ARSHINE
ALNAGE	AMERCED	ANCILES	ANLACES	APERCUS	**ARCHER**	ARMFULS	ARSHINS
ALNAGER	AMERCES	**ANCOME**	**ANLAGE**	**APHTHA**	MARCHER	**ARMING**	**ARSINE**
ALNAGES	**AMINES**	ANCOMES	ANLAGES	NAPHTHA	ARCHERS	FARMING	ARSINES
ALOGIA	FAMINES	**ANEMIA**	**ANNEAL**	APHTHAE	ARCHERY	HARMING	**ARSONS**
ALOGIAS	GAMINES	ANEMIAS	ANNEALS	**APISMS**	**ARCHES**	WARMING	PARSONS
ALPACA	TAMINES	**ANGELS**	**ANNEXE**	PAPISMS	LARCHES	**ARMLET**	**ARTELS**
ALPACAS	**AMISES**	MANGELS	ANNEXED	**APLITE**	MARCHES	ARMLETS	CARTELS
ALPEEN	CAMISES	**ANGERS**	ANNEXES	APLITES	PARCHES	**ARMOUR**	MARTELS
ALPEENS	KAMISES	BANGERS	**ANNUAL**	**APLOMB**	ARCHEST	ARMOURS	**ARTIER**
ALPINE	TAMISES	DANGERS	ANNUALS	APLOMBS	**ARCHIL**	ARMOURY	TARTIER
ALPINES	**AMMONS**	GANGERS	**ANOINT**	**APNOEA**	ARCHILS	**ARMPIT**	WARTIER
ALSIKE	GAMMONS	HANGERS	ANOINTS	APNOEAS	**ARCHON**	ARMPITS	**ARTIST**
ALSIKES	MAMMONS	MANGERS	**ANOMIE**	**APOGEE**	ARCHONS	**ARMURE**	ARTISTE
ALSOON	**AMOEBA**	RANGERS	ANOMIES	APOGEES	**ARCING**	ARMURES	ARTISTS
ALSOONE	AMOEBAE	**ANGICO**	**ANONYM**	**APOLLO**	FARCING	**ARNICA**	**ASARUM**
ALTERN	AMOEBAS	ANGICOS	ANONYMA	APOLLOS	ARCINGS	ARNICAS	ASARUMS
SALTERN	**AMOMUM**	**ANGINA**	ANONYMS	**APORIA**	**ARCSIN**	**AROINT**	**ASCEND**
ALTERNE	AMOMUMS	ANGINAL	**ANORAK**	APORIAS	ARCSINS	AROINTS	ASCENDS
ALTERS	**AMOOVE**	ANGINAS	ANORAKS	**APOZEM**	**ARCTAN**	**AROLLA**	**ASCENT**
FALTERS	AMOOVED	**ANGLED**	**ANOXIA**	APOZEMS	ARCTANS	AROLLAS	NASCENT
HALTERS	AMOOVES	BANGLED	ANOXIAS	**APPAIR**	**ARCTIC**	**AROUSE**	ASCENTS
PALTERS	**AMORCE**	CANGLED	**ANSATE**	APPAIRS	ARCTICS	CAROUSE	**ASCIAN**
SALTERS	AMORCES	DANGLED	ANSATED	**APPEAL**	**ARDOUR**	AROUSED	ASCIANS
ALTEZA	**AMORET**	FANGLED	**ANSWER**	APPEALS	ARDOURS	AROUSER	**ASCOTS**
ALTEZAS	AMORETS	JANGLED	ANSWERS	**APPEAR**	**AREOLA**	AROUSES	MASCOTS
ALUDEL	**AMOUNT**	MANGLED	**ANTARS**	APPEARS	AREOLAE	**AROYNT**	**ASEITY**
ALUDELS	AMOUNTS	TANGLED	CANTARS	**APPEND**	AREOLAR	AROYNTS	GASEITY
ALUMNA	**AMPERE**	WANGLED	KANTARS	WAPPEND	**AREOLE**	**ARPENT**	**ASHAME**
ALUMNAE	AMPERES	**ANGLER**	**ANTHEM**	APPENDS	AREOLES	PARPENT	ASHAMED
AMADOU	**AMPLER**	DANGLER	ANTHEMS	**APPLES**	**ARGALA**	ARPENTS	ASHAMES
AMADOUS	SAMPLER	JANGLER	**ANTHER**	DAPPLES	ARGALAS	**ARRACK**	**ASHERY**
AMATOL	**AMPULE**	MANGLER	PANTHER	SAPPLES	**ARGALI**	BARRACK	FASHERY
AMATOLS	AMPULES	TANGLER	ANTHERS	**APPORT**	ARGALIS	CARRACK	WASHERY
AMAZON	**AMRITA**	WANGLER	**ANTIAR**	RAPPORT	**ARGAND**	ARRACKS	**ASHIER**
AMAZONS	AMRITAS	ANGLERS	ANTIARS	APPORTS	ARGANDS	**ARRANT**	CASHIER
AMBAGE	**AMTMAN**	**ANGLES**	**ANTICK**	**APPOSE**	**ARGENT**	FARRANT	HASHIER
AMBAGES	AMTMANS	BANGLES	ANTICKE	APPOSED	MARGENT	WARRANT	MASHIER
AMBERS	**AMULET**	CANGLES	**ANTING**	APPOSER	ARGENTS	**ARRAYS**	WASHIER
CAMBERS	AMULETS	DANGLES	BANTING	APPOSES	**ARGHAN**	WARRAYS	**ASHLAR**
JAMBERS	**AMUSER**	FANGLES	CANTING	**APRONS**	ARGHANS	**ARREAR**	ASHLARS
LAMBERS	AMUSERS	JANGLES	DANTING	NAPRONS	**ARGONS**	ARREARS	**ASHLER**
TAMBERS	**AMUSES**	MANGLES	GANTING	**APTOTE**	JARGONS	**ARRECT**	ASHLERS
AMBITS	CAMUSES	TANGLES	KANTING	APTOTES	**ARGUER**	CARRECT	**ASHRAM**
GAMBITS	WAMUSES	WANGLES	PANTING	**ARABIN**	ARGUERS	**ARREST**	ASHRAMA
AMBLED	**AMYLUM**	**ANGORA**	RANTING	CARABIN	**ARGYLE**	ARRESTS	ASHRAMS
GAMBLED	AMYLUMS	ANGORAS	WANTING	ARABINS	ARGYLES	**ARRETS**	**ASKANT**
HAMBLED	**ANADEM**	**ANICUT**	ANTINGS	**ARABLE**	**ARIOSO**	BARRETS	ASKANTS
RAMBLED	ANADEMS	ANICUTS	**ANTLER**	PARABLE	ARIOSOS	GARRETS	**ASKARI**
WAMBLED	**ANALLY**	**ANIMAL**	PANTLER	**ARAISE**	**ARISTA**	**ARRIDE**	ASKARIS
AMBLER	BANALLY	ANIMALS	ANTLERS	ARAISED	ARISTAE	ARRIDED	**ASKERS**
GAMBLER	**ANALOG**	**ANIONS**	**ANTLIA**	ARAISES	ARISTAS	ARRIDES	MASKERS
RAMBLER	ANALOGS	FANIONS	ANTLIAE	**ARALIA**	**ARISTO**	**ARRIVE**	TASKERS
AMBLERS	ANALOGY	**ANKERS**	**ANTRUM**		ARISTOS	ARRIVED	**ASKING**

BASKING	WASTERS	**AUGERS**	**AVOSET**	BADDIES	BALSAMY	**BARRAT**	**BATTLES**
CASKING	**ASTERT**	GAUGERS	AVOSETS	**BADGER**	**BAMBOO**	BARRATS	**BATTUE**
MASKING	ASTERTS	SAUGERS	**AVOURE**	BADGERS	BAMBOOS	**BARREL**	BATTUES
TASKING	**ASTHMA**	**AUGHTS**	AVOURES	**BAETYL**	**BAMMER**	BARRELS	**BAUBLE**
ASLAKE	ASTHMAS	NAUGHTS	**AVOWAL**	BAETYLS	BAMMERS	**BARRET**	BAUBLES
ASLAKED	**ASTONE**	WAUGHTS	AVOWALS	**BAFFLE**	**BAMPOT**	BARRETS	**BAUERA**
ASLAKES	ASTONED	**AUGITE**	**AVOYER**	BAFFLED	BAMPOTS	**BARRIO**	BAUERAS
ASPECT	ASTONES	AUGITES	AVOYERS	BAFFLER	**BANANA**	BARRIOS	**BAWBEE**
ASPECTS	**ASTRAL**	**AUGUST**	**AVULSE**	BAFFLES	BANANAS	**BARROW**	BAWBEES
ASPERS	CASTRAL	AUGUSTE	AVULSED	**BAGFUL**	**BANDAR**	BARROWS	**BAWBLE**
GASPERS	**ASTUTE**	AUGUSTS	AVULSES	BAGFULS	BANDARS	**BARTER**	BAWBLES
JASPERS	ASTUTER	**AUKLET**	**AWAKEN**	**BAGGIT**	**BANDED**	BARTERS	**BAWLER**
RASPERS	**ASYLUM**	AUKLETS	AWAKENS	BAGGITS	ABANDED	**BARTON**	BAWLERS
ASPERSE	ASYLUMS	**AULDER**	**AWARDS**	**BAGNIO**	**BANDIT**	BARTONS	**BAWLEY**
ASPICK	**ATABAL**	CAULDER	VAWARDS	BAGNIOS	BANDITS	**BARYON**	BAWLEYS
ASPICKS	ATABALS	**AUMAIL**	**AWHAPE**	**BAGUIO**	**BANDOG**	BARYONS	**BAXTER**
ASPINE	**ATABEG**	AUMAILS	AWHAPED	BAGUIOS	BANDOGS	**BARYTA**	BAXTERS
ASPINES	ATABEGS	**AUNTER**	AWHAPES	**BAGWIG**	**BANGER**	BARYTAS	**BAYARD**
ASPIRE	**ATABEK**	DAUNTER	**AWHEEL**	BAGWIGS	BANGERS	**BASALT**	BAYARDS
ASPIRED	ATABEKS	GAUNTER	AWHEELS	**BAHADA**	**BANGLE**	BASALTS	**BAZAAR**
ASPIRES	**ATAMAN**	HAUNTER	**AWMRIE**	BAHADAS	BANGLED	BASHAW	BAZAARS
ASPORT	ATAMANS	SAUNTER	AWMRIES	**BAILEE**	BANGLES	BASHAWS	**BEACON**
ASPORTS	**ATAXIA**	TAUNTER	**AWNERS**	BAILEES	**BANIAN**	**BASHED**	BEACONS
ASSAIL	ATAXIAS	VAUNTER	DAWNERS	**BAILER**	BANIANS	ABASHED	**BEADLE**
VASSAIL	**ATOCIA**	AUNTERS	FAWNERS	BAILERS	**BANKER**	**BASHER**	BEADLES
WASSAIL	ATOCIAS	**AUNTIE**	PAWNERS	**BAILEY**	BANKERS	BASHERS	**BEAGLE**
ASSAILS	**ATONED**	JAUNTIE	**AWNIER**	BAILEYS	**BANKET**	**BASHES**	BEAGLED
ASSART	BATONED	AUNTIES	LAWNIER	**BAILIE**	BANKETS	ABASHES	BEAGLER
ASSARTS	**ATONER**	**AURATE**	TAWNIER	BAILIES	**BANNER**	**BASING**	BEAGLES
ASSENT	ATONERS	AURATED	YAWNIER	**BAILLI**	BANNERS	ABASING	**BEAKER**
ASSENTS	**ATRIAL**	AURATES	**AWNING**	BAILLIE	**BANTAM**	**BASKET**	BEAKERS
ASSERT	PATRIAL	**AURIST**	DAWNING	BAILLIS	BANTAMS	BASKETS	**BEAMER**
ASSERTS	**ATRIUM**	AURISTS	FAWNING	**BAILOR**	**BANTER**	**BASNET**	BEAMERS
ASSETS	NATRIUM	**AURORA**	PAWNING	BAILORS	BANTERS	BASNETS	**BEANIE**
BASSETS	**ATTACH**	AURORAE	YAWNING	**BAININ**	**BANYAN**	**BASQUE**	BEANIES
TASSETS	ATTACHE	AURORAL	AWNINGS	BAININS	BANYANS	BASQUED	**BEARER**
ASSIGN	**ATTACK**	AURORAS	**AXILLA**	**BAITER**	**BAOBAB**	BASQUES	BEARERS
ASSIGNS	ATTACKS	**AUTEUR**	MAXILLA	BAITERS	BAOBABS	**BASSES**	**BEATER**
ASSIST	**ATTAIN**	HAUTEUR	AXILLAE	**BAJADA**	**BARBEL**	BASSEST	BEATERS
BASSIST	ATTAINS	AUTEURS	AXILLAR	BAJADAS	BARBELS	**BASSET**	**BEAVER**
ASSISTS	ATTAINT	**AUTHOR**	**AYWORD**	**BAJREE**	**BARBER**	BASSETS	BEAVERS
ASSIZE	**ATTASK**	AUTHORS	NAYWORD	BAJREES	BARBERS	**BASTER**	BEAVERY
ASSIZED	ATTASKS	**AUTISM**	AYWORDS	**BAKING**	**BARBET**	BASTERS	**BEBUNG**
ASSIZER	ATTASKT	AUTISMS	**AZALEA**	BAKINGS	BARBETS	**BASTLE**	BEBUNGS
ASSIZES	**ATTEND**	**AUTUMN**	AZALEAS	**BALATA**	**BARBIE**	BASTLES	**BECALL**
ASSOIL	ATTENDS	AUTUMNS	**AZIONE**	BALATAS	BARBIES	**BATATA**	BECALLS
ASSOILS	**ATTENT**	AUTUMNY	AZIONES	**BALBOA**	**BAREGE**	BATATAS	**BECALM**
ASSORT	ATTENTS	**AVAILE**	**AZOLLA**	BALBOAS	BAREGES	**BATEAU**	BECALMS
ASSORTS	**ATTEST**	AVAILED	AZOLLAS	**BALEEN**	**BARGEE**	BATEAUS	**BECKET**
ASSUME	FATTEST	AVAILES	**AZURES**	BALEENS	BARGEES	BATEAUX	BECKETS
ASSUMED	WATTEST	**AVATAR**	RAZURES	**BALKER**	**BARGES**	**BATHER**	**BECKON**
ASSUMES	ATTESTS	AVATARS	**BAAING**	BALKERS	BARGEST	BATHERS	BECKONS
ASSURE	**ATTIRE**	**AVAUNT**	BAAINGS	**BALLAD**	**BARITE**	**BATING**	**BECOME**
ASSURED	ATTIRED	AVAUNTS	**BABBLE**	BALLADE	BARITES	ABATING	BECOMES
ASSURER	ATTIRES	**AVENGE**	BABBLED	BALLADS	**BARIUM**	**BATLER**	**BECURL**
ASSURES	**ATTONE**	AVENGED	BABBLER	**BALLAN**	BARIUMS	BATLERS	BECURLS
ASTART	ATTONES	AVENGER	BABBLES	BALLANS	**BARKAN**	**BATLET**	**BEDAUB**
ASTARTS	**ATTORN**	AVENGES	**BABIES**	BALLANT	BARKANS	BATLETS	BEDAUBS
ASTERN	ATTORNS	**AVENIR**	BABIEST	**BALLAT**	**BARKEN**	**BATOON**	**BEDAZE**
EASTERN	**ATTRAP**	AVENIRS	**BABLAH**	BALLATS	BARKENS	BATOONS	BEDAZED
PASTERN	ATTRAPS	**AVENUE**	BABLAHS	**BALLET**	**BARKER**	**BATTEL**	BEDAZES
ASTERS	**ATTUNE**	AVENUES	**BABOON**	BALLETS	BARKERS	BATTELS	**BEDBUG**
BASTERS	ATTUNED	**AVIATE**	BABOONS	**BALLON**	**BARLEY**	**BATTEN**	BEDBUGS
CASTERS	ATTUNES	AVIATED	**BABOOS**	BALLONS	BARLEYS	BATTENS	**BEDDER**
FASTERS	**AUBADE**	AVIATES	BABOOSH	**BALLOT**	**BARNEY**	**BATTER**	BEDDERS
LASTERS	AUBADES	**AVISES**	**BACKER**	BALLOTS	BARNEYS	BATTERO	**BEDECK**
MASTERS	**AUCUBA**	MAVISES	BACKERS	**BALLOW**	**BAROCK**	BATTERS	BEDECKS
PASTERS	AUCUBAS	PAVISES	**BACKET**	BALLOWS	BAROCKS	BATTERY	**BEDELL**
RASTERS	**AUDILE**	**AVOCET**	BACKETS	**BALSAM**	**BARQUE**	**BATTLE**	BEDELLS
TASTERS	AUDILES	AVOCETS	**BADDIE**	BALSAMS	BARQUES	BATTLED	**BEDLAM**
						BATTLER	

BEDLAMS	BEHOVES	BENZOLE	BETRAYS	BILIAN	BITTORS	BOBCATS	BONSAI
BEDPAN	BEHOWL	BENZOLS	BETRIM	BILIANS	BITTUR	BOBWIG	BONSAIS
BEDPANS	BEHOWLS	BENZYL	BETRIMS	BILKER	BITTURS	BOBWIGS	BONXIE
BEDRAL	BEIGEL	BENZYLS	BETTED	BILKERS	BIVIUM	BOCAGE	BONXIES
BEDRALS	BEIGELS	BEPELT	ABETTED	BILLET	BIVIUMS	BOCAGES	BOOBOO
BEDROP	BEJADE	BEPELTS	BETTER	BILLETS	BIZONE	BODACH	BOOBOOK
BEDROPS	BEJADED	BEPUFF	ABETTER	BILLIE	BIZONES	BODACHS	BOOBOOS
BEDROPT	BEJADES	BEPUFFS	BETTERS	BILLIES	BLAGUE	BODDLE	BOODIE
BEDUCK	BEJANT	BERATE	BETTOR	BILLON	BLAGUES	BODDLES	BOODIED
BEDUCKS	BEJANTS	BERATED	ABETTOR	BILLONS	BLANCO	BODEGA	BOODIES
BEDUIN	BELACE	BERATES	BETTORS	BILLOW	BLANCOS	BODEGAS	BOODLE
BEDUINS	BELACED	BERLEY	BEURRE	BILLOWS	BLASTS	BODGER	BOODLES
BEDUNG	BELACES	BERLEYS	BEURRES	BILLOWY	OBLASTS	BODGERS	BOOGIE
BEDUNGS	BELATE	BERLIN	BEWAIL	BINDER	BLAZER	BODGIE	BOOGIED
BEDUST	BELATED	BERLINE	BEWAILS	BINDERS	BLAZERS	BODGIES	BOOGIES
BEDUSTS	BELATES	BERLINS	BEWARE	BINDERY	BLAZON	BODICE	BOOKIE
BEEGAH	BELAUD	BERRET	BEWARED	BINGER	BLAZONS	BODICES	BOOKIER
BEEGAHS	BELAUDS	BERRETS	BEWARES	BINGERS	BLENDE	BODING	BOOKIES
BEENAH	BELDAM	BERTHA	BEWEEP	BINGLE	BLENDED	ABODING	BOOMER
BEENAHS	BELDAME	BERTHAS	BEWEEPS	BINGLED	BLENDER	BODINGS	BOOMERS
BEEPER	BELDAMS	BERTHE	BEWRAY	BINGLES	BLENDES	BODKIN	BOORDE
BEEPERS	BELIEF	BERTHED	BEWRAYS	BIOGEN	BLIGHT	BODKINS	BOORDES
BEETLE	BELIEFS	BERTHES	BEYOND	BIOGENS	BLIGHTS	BODRAG	BOOTEE
BEETLED	BELIER	BESEEM	BEYONDS	BIOGENY	BLIGHTY	BODRAGS	BOOTEES
BEETLES	BELIERS	BESEEMS	BEZANT	BIONIC	BLINTZ	BOFFIN	BOOZER
BEFALL	BELLOW	BESIDE	BEZANTS	BIONICS	BLINTZE	BOFFING	BOOZERS
BEFALLS	BELLOWS	BESIDES	BEZOAR	BIOPIC	BLITHE	BOFFINS	BOPPER
BEFANA	BELONG	BESIGH	BEZOARS	BIOPICS	BLITHER	BOGGLE	BOPPERS
BEFANAS	BELONGS	BESIGHS	BEZZLE	BIOTIC	BLONDE	BOGGLED	BORAGE
BEFLUM	BELOVE	BESING	BEZZLED	ABIOTIC	BLONDER	BOGGLER	BORAGES
BEFLUMS	BELOVED	BESINGS	BEZZLES	BIOTIN	BLONDES	BOGGLES	BORANE
BEFOAM	BELOVES	BESMUT	BHAJAN	BIOTINS	BLOTCH	BOGOAK	BORANES
BEFOAMS	BELTER	BESMUTS	BHAJANS	BIRDER	BLOTCHY	BOGOAKS	BORATE
BEFOOL	BELTERS	BESOIN	BHAKTI	BIRDERS	BLOUSE	BOGONG	BORATES
BEFOOLS	BELUGA	BESOINS	BHAKTIS	BIRDIE	BLOUSED	BOGONGS	BORDAR
BEFOUL	BELUGAS	BESORT	BHARAL	BIRDIED	BLOUSES	BOHUNK	BORDARS
BEFOULS	BEMAUL	BESORTS	BHARALS	BIRDIES	BLOWER	BOHUNKS	BORDEL
BEGGAR	BEMAULS	BESPAT	BHINDI	BIREME	BLOWERS	BOILER	BORDELS
BEGGARS	BEMEAN	BESPATE	BHINDIS	BIREMES	BLOWIE	BOILERS	BORDER
BEGGARY	BEMEANS	BESPIT	BHISTI	BIRKIE	BLOWIER	BOILERY	BORDERS
BEGIFT	BEMEANT	BESPITS	BHISTIS	BIRKIES	BLOWIES	BOLDEN	BOREEN
BEGIFTS	BEMETE	BESPOT	BIBBER	BIRLER	BLOWSE	BOLDENS	BOREENS
BEGILD	BEMETED	BESPOTS	BIBBERS	BIRLERS	BLOWSED	BOLERO	BORIDE
BEGILDS	BEMETES	BESTAR	BICARB	BIRSLE	BLOWSES	BOLEROS	BORIDES
BEGIRD	BEMIRE	BESTARS	BICARBS	BIRSLED	BLOWZE	BOLIDE	BORING
BEGIRDS	BEMIRED	BESTIR	BICKER	BIRSLES	BLOWZED	BOLIDES	BORINGS
BEGNAW	BEMIRES	BESTIRS	BICKERS	BISECT	BLOWZES	BOLTER	BORREL
BEGNAWS	BEMOAN	BESTOW	BIDDEN	BISECTS	BLUDGE	BOLTERS	BORRELL
BEGUIN	BEMOANS	BESTOWS	ABIDDEN	BISHOP	BLUDGED	BOMBER	BORROW
BEGUINE	BEMOCK	BESTUD	BIDDER	BISHOPS	BLUDGER	BOMBERS	BORROWS
BEGUINS	BEMOCKS	BESTUDS	BIDDERS	BISMAR	BLUDGES	BONBON	BORSCH
BEGUNK	BEMOIL	BETAKE	BIDENT	BISMARS	BLUDIE	BONBONS	BORSCHT
BEGUNKS	BEMOILS	BETAKEN	BIDENTS	BISQUE	BLUDIER	BONDER	BORZOI
BEHAVE	BEMUSE	BETAKES	BIDING	BISQUES	BLUING	BONDERS	BORZOIS
BEHAVED	BEMUSED	BETEEM	ABIDING	BISTER	BLUINGS	BONDUC	BOSBOK
BEHAVES	BEMUSES	BETEEME	BIDINGS	BISTERS	BLUNGE	BONDUCS	BOSBOKS
BEHEAD	BENAME	BETEEMS	BIFFIN	BISTRE	BLUNGED	BONING	BOSCHE
BEHEADS	BENAMED	BETHEL	BIFFING	BISTRED	BLUNGER	BONINGS	BOSCHES
BEHEST	BENAMES	BETHELS	BIFFINS	BISTRES	BLUNGES	BONISM	BOSKET
BEHESTS	BENDER	BETIDE	BIGGIE	BISTRO	BOATEL	BONISMS	BOSKETS
BEHIND	BENDERS	BETIDED	BIGGIES	BISTROS	BOATELS	BONIST	BOSSES
BEHINDS	BENNET	BETIDES	BIGGIN	BITING	BOATER	EBONIST	BOSSEST
BEHOLD	BENNETS	BETIME	BIGGING	BITINGS	BOATERS	BONISTS	BOSTON
BEHOLDS	BENUMB	BETIMED	BIGGINS	BITTER	BOBBIN	BONITO	BOSTONS
BEHOOF	BENUMBS	BETIMES	BIGWIG	BITTERN	BOBBING	BONITOS	BOTHAN
BEHOOFS	BENZAL	BETISE	BIGWIGS	BITTERS	BOBBINS	BONNET	BOTHANS
BEHOTE	BENZALS	BETISES	BIKING	BITTIE	BOBBLE	BONNETS	BOTHER
BEHOTES	BENZIL	BETOIL	BIKINGS	BITTIER	BOBBLED	BONNIE	BOTHERS
BEHOVE	BENZILS	BETOILS	BIKINI	BITTIES	BOBBLES	BONNIER	BOTHIE
BEHOVED	BENZOL	BETRAY	BIKINIS	BITTOR	BOBCAT	BONNIES	BOTHIES

BOTTLE	BRAIZES	BROGUES	BUGLERS	BURDIES	BUTLERS	CAESARS	CAMLET
BOTTLED	BRANCH	BROKER	BUGLET	BUREAU	BUTLERY	CAFARD	CAMLETS
BOTTLER	BRANCHY	BROKERS	BUGLETS	BUREAUS	BUTTED	CAFARDS	CAMPED
BOTTLES	BRANLE	BROKERY	BUGONG	BUREAUX	CAFILA	SCAMPED
BOTTOM	BRANLES	BROLGA	BUGONGS	BURGEE	BUTTER	CAFILAS	CAMPER
BOTTOMS	BRAVER	BROLGAS	BUKSHI	BURGEES	ABUTTER	CAFTAN	SCAMPER
BOUCHE	BRAVERY	BRONCO	BUKSHIS	BURGER	BUTTERS	CAFTANS	CAMPERS
BOUCHEE	BRAVES	BRONCOS	BULBIL	BURGERS	BUTTERY	CAGOUL	CAMPLE
BOUCHES	BRAVEST	BRONZE	BULBILS	BURGLE	BUTTLE	CAGOULE	CAMPLED
BOUCLE	BRAYED	BRONZED	BULBUL	BURGLED	BUTTLED	CAGOULS	CAMPLES
BOUCLES	ABRAYED	BRONZEN	BULBULS	BURGLES	BUTTLES	CAHIER	CANADA
BOUGET	BRAYER	BRONZES	BULGER	BURGOO	BUTTON	CAHIERS	CANADAS
BOUGETS	BRAYERS	BROOSE	BULGERS	BURGOOS	BUTTONS	CAHOOT	CANAPE
BOUGHT	BRAZEN	BROOSES	BULKER	BURHEL	BUTTONY	CAHOOTS	CANAPES
ABOUGHT	BRAZENS	BROUGH	BULKERS	BURHELS	BUZZER	CAIMAC	CANARD
BOUGHTS	BRAZIL	BROUGHS	BULLER	BURIAL	BUZZERS	CAIMACS	CANARDS
BOUGIE	BRAZILS	BROUGHT	BULLERS	BURIALS	BYGONE	CAIMAN	CANCAN
BOUGIES	BREARE	BROUZE	BULLET	BURITI	BYGONES	CAIMANS	CANCANS
BOULLE	BREARES	BROUZES	BULLETS	BURITIS	BYLINE	CAIQUE	CANCEL
BOULLES	BREAST	BROWSE	BUMBLE	BURKHA	BYLINES	CAIQUES	CANCELS
BOUNCE	ABREAST	BROWSED	BUMBLED	BURKHAS	BYPATH	CAJOLE	CANCER
BOUNCED	BREASTS	BROWSES	BUMBLES	BURLAP	BYPATHS	CAJOLED	CANCERS
BOUNCER	BREATH	BROWST	BUMKIN	BURLAPS	BYROAD	CAJOLES	CANDID
BOUNCES	BREATHE	BROWSTS	BUMKINS	BURLER	BYROADS	CAKING	CANDIDA
BOUNDS	BREATHS	BRUISE	BUMMEL	BURLERS	BYROOM	CAKINGS	CANDIE
ABOUNDS	BREATHY	BRUISED	BUMMELS	BURLEY	BYROOMS	CALCAR	CANDIED
BOURNE	BREESE	BRUISER	BUMMER	BURLEYS	BYSSAL	CALCARS	CANDIES
BOURNES	BREESES	BRUISES	BUMMERS	BURNER	ABYSSAL	CALICO	CANDLE
BOURSE	BREEZE	BRUNET	BUMMLE	BURNERS	BYWORD	CALICOS	CANDLED
BOURSES	BREEZED	BRUNETS	BUMMLED	BURNET	BYWORDS	CALIGO	CANDLES
BOUTON	BREEZES	BUBBLE	BUMMLES	BURNETS	BYWORK	CALIGOS	CANDOR
BOUTONS	BREHON	BUBBLED	BUMPER	BURREL	BYWORKS	CALIPH	CANDORS
BOVATE	BREHONS	BUBBLES	BUMPERS	BURRELL	BYZANT	CALIPHS	CANFUL
OBOVATE	BRENNE	BUCKER	BUNDLE	BURRELS	BYZANTS	CALKER	CANFULS
BOVATES	BRENNES	BUCKERS	BUNDLED	BURROW	CABALA	CALKERS	CANGLE
BOVVER	BRETON	BUCKET	BUNDLES	BURROWS	CABALAS	CALKIN	CANGLED
BOVVERS	BRETONS	BUCKETS	BUNGEE	BURSAR	CABANA	CALKING	CANGLES
BOWFIN	BREVET	BUCKIE	BUNGEES	BURSARS	CABANAS	CALKINS	CANGUE
BOWFINS	BREVETE	BUCKIES	BUNGEY	BURSARY	CABBIE	CALLED	CANGUES
BOWGET	BREVETS	BUCKLE	BUNGEYS	BURTON	CABBIES	SCALLED	CANINE
BOWGETS	BREWER	BUCKLED	BUNGIE	BURTONS	CABRIE	CALLER	CANINES
BOWLER	BREWERS	BUCKLER	BUNGIES	BUSBOY	CABRIES	CALLERS	CANING
BOWLERS	BREWERY	BUCKLES	BUNGLE	BUSBOYS	CABRIT	CALLET	CANINGS
BOWPOT	BRIBER	BUCKRA	BUNGLED	BUSHEL	CABRITS	CALLETS	CANKER
BOWPOTS	BRIBERS	BUCKRAM	BUNGLER	BUSHELS	CACHET	CALLOW	CANKERS
BOWSER	BRIBERY	BUCKRAS	BUNGLES	BUSIES	CACHETS	CALLOWS	CANKERY
BOWSERS	BRIDAL	BUDDLE	BUNION	BUSIEST	CACHOU	CALPAC	CANNED
BOWWOW	BRIDALS	BUDDLED	BUNIONS	BUSING	CACHOUS	CALPACK	SCANNED
BOWWOWS	BRIDGE	BUDDLES	BUNJEE	ABUSING	CACKLE	CALPACS	CANNEL
BOWYER	ABRIDGE	BUDGER	BUNJEES	BUSINGS	CACKLED	CALQUE	CANNELS
BOWYERS	BRIDGED	BUDGERO	BUNJIE	BUSKER	CACKLER	CALQUED	CANNER
BOXCAR	BRIDGES	BUDGERS	BUNJIES	BUSKERS	CACKLES	CALQUES	SCANNER
BOXCARS	BRIDIE	BUDGET	BUNKER	BUSKET	CALTHA	CANNERS
BOXFUL	BRIDIES	BUDGETS	BUNKERS	BUSKETS	CACOON	CALTHAS	CANNERY
BOXFULS	BRIDLE	BUDGIE	BUNKUM	BUSKIN	CACOONS	CALVER	CANNON
BOXING	BRIDLED	BUDGIES	BUNKUMS	BUSKING	CACKLED	CALVERS	CANNONS
BOXINGS	BRIDLER	BUFFER	BUNNIA	BUSKINS	CACOON	CAMBER	CANTAR
BRACER	BRIDLES	BUFFERS	BUNNIAS	BUSTEE	CADDIE	CAMBERS	CANTARS
BRACERS	BRIGUE	BUFFET	BUNTER	BUSTEES	CADDIED	CAMELS	CANTED
BRAIDE	BRIGUED	BUFFETS	BUNTERS	BUSTER	CADDIES	CAMELS	SCANTED
BRAIDED	BRIGUES	BUGGAN	BUNYIP	BUSTERS	SCADDIES	SCAMELS	CANTER
BRAIDER	BROACH	BUGGANE	BUNYIPS	BUSTLE	CADDIS	CAMERA	SCANTER
BRAIDS	ABROACH	BUGGANS	BURBLE	BUSTLED	CADDISH	CAMERAL	CANTERS
ABRAIDS	BROADS	BUGGER	BURBLED	BUSTLER	CADEAU	CAMERAS	CANTLE
BRAIRD	ABROADS	BUGGERS	BURBLES	BUSTLES	CADEAUX	CAMESE	SCANTLE
BRAIRDS	BROCHE	BUGGERY	BURBOT	BUTANE	CADGER	CAMESES	CANTLED
BRAISE	BROCHES	BUGGIN	BURBOTS	BUTANES	CADGERS	CAMION	CANTLES
BRAISED	BROGAN	BUGGING	BURDEN	BUTENE	CADUAC	CAMIONS	CANTLET
BRAISES	BROGANS	BUGGINS	BURDENS	BUTENES	CADUACS	CAMISE	CANTON
BRAIZE	BROGUE	BUGLER	BURDIE	BUTLER	CAESAR	CAMISES	CANTONS

CANTOR	CARPERS	CATKIN	CENTERS	CHANGER	CHICHIS	CHOUSES	CITRIN
CANTORS	CARPET	CATKINS	CENTRE	CHANGES	CHICKS	CHOUTS	CITRINE
CANVAS	CARPETS	CATNAP	CENTRED	CHAPEL	TCHICKS	SCHOUTS	CITRINS
CANVASS	CARRAT	CATNAPS	CENTRES	CHAPELS	CHICLE	CHOWRI	CITRON
CANYON	CARRATS	CATNEP	CENTUM	CHAPES	CHICLES	CHOWRIS	CITRONS
CANYONS	CARREL	CATNEPS	CENTUMS	CHAPESS	CHICON	CHRISM	CIVISM
CAPING	CARRELL	CATNIP	CERATE	CHAPKA	CHICONS	CHRISMS	CIVISMS
SCAPING	CARRELS	CATNIPS	CERATED	CHAPKAS	CHIDER	CHROMA	CLAMBE
CAPITA	CARROT	CATSUP	CERATES	CHARET	CHIDERS	CHROMAS	CLAMBER
CAPITAL	CARROTS	CATSUPS	CEREAL	CHARETS	CHIELD	CHROME	CLAMOR
CAPITAN	CARROTY	CATTED	CEREALS	CHARGE	CHIELDS	CHROMED	CLAMORS
CAPLIN	CARTED	SCATTED	CERIPH	CHARGED	CHIGOE	CHROMES	CLAQUE
CAPLINS	SCARTED	CAUDAL	CERIPHS	CHARGER	CHIGOES	CHROMO	CLAQUES
CAPOTE	CARTEL	ACAUDAL	CERISE	CHARGES	CHIGRE	CHROMOS	CLARET
CAPOTES	CARTELS	CAUDLE	CERISES	CHARTA	CHIGRES	CHUKAR	CLARETS
CAPPER	CARTER	CAUDLED	CERITE	CHARTAS	CHIKOR	CHUKARS	CLAUSE
CAPPERS	CARTERS	CAUDLES	CERITES	CHASER	CHIKORS	CHUKKA	CLAUSES
CAPRIC	CARTES	CAUKER	CERIUM	CHASERS	CHILDE	CHUKKAS	CLAVER
CAPRICE	ECARTES	CAUKERS	CERIUMS	CHASSE	CHILDED	CHUKOR	CLAVERS
CAPRID	CARTON	CAUSER	CERMET	CHASSES	CHILDER	CHUKORS	CLAVES
CAPRIDS	CARTONS	CAUSERS	CERMETS	CHASTE	CHILLI	CHURCH	SCLAVES
CAPSID	CARVEL	CAUSEY	CERNED	CHASTEN	CHILLIS	CHURCHY	CLAVIE
CAPSIDS	CARVELS	CAUSEYS	SCERNED	CHASTER	CHIMER	CHYACK	CLAVIER
CAPTAN	CARVER	CAUTEL	CERNES	CHATON	CHIMERA	CHYACKS	CLAVIES
CAPTANS	CARVERS	CAUTELS	SCERNES	CHATONS	CHIMERE	CHYPRE	CLEANS
CAPTOR	CARVES	CAUTER	CEROON	CHATTA	CHIMERS	CHYPRES	CLEANSE
CAPTORS	SCARVES	CAUTERS	CEROONS	CHATTAS	CHINAR	CICADA	CLEAVE
CARACK	CASBAH	CAUTERY	CERUSE	CHAUFE	CHINARS	CICADAS	CLEAVED
CARACKS	CASBAHS	CAVEAT	CERUSES	CHAUFED	CHINES	CICALA	CLEAVER
CARACT	CASEIN	CAVEATS	CESIUM	CHAUFES	CHINESE	CICALAS	CLEAVES
CARACTS	CASEINS	CAVERN	CESIUMS	CHAUFF	CHINTZ	CICERO	CLEEVE
CARAFE	CASERN	CAVERNS	CESSER	CHAUFFS	CHINTZY	CICEROS	CLEEVES
CARAFES	CASERNE	CAVIAR	CESSERS	CHAUNT	CHISEL	CICUTA	CLEPED
CARBON	CASERNS	CAVIARS	CESTUI	CHAUNTS	CHISELS	CICUTAS	YCLEPED
CARBONS	CASHAW	CAVIARE	CESTUIS	CHEERO	CHITAL	CIERGE	CLERIC
CARBOY	CASHAWS	CAVIER	CESURA	CHEEROS	CHITALS	CIERGES	CLERICS
CARBOYS	CASHEW	CAVIERS	CESURAS	CHEESE	CHITIN	CIGGIE	CLEUCH
CARDER	CASHEWS	CAVING	CESURE	CHEESED	CHITINS	CIGGIES	CLEUCHS
CARDERS	CASING	CAVINGS	CESURES	CHEESES	CHITON	CILICE	CLEUGH
CAREEN	CASINGS	CAVORT	CETANE	CHEMIC	CHITONS	CILICES	CLEUGHS
CAREENS	CASINO	CAVORTS	CETANES	CHEMICS	CHOCHO	CIMIER	CLICHE
CAREER	CASINOS	CAWING	CETYLS	CHENAR	CHOCHOS	CIMIERS	CLICHED
CAREERS	CASKET	CAWINGS	ACETYLS	CHENARS	CHOICE	CINDER	CLICHES
CAREME	CASKETS	CAWKER	CHACMA	CHENET	CHOICER	CINDERS	CLIENT
CAREMES	CASQUE	CAWKERS	CHACMAS	CHENETS	CHOICES	CINDERY	CLIENTS
CARERS	CASQUES	CAYMAN	CHADAR	CHEQUE	CHOKER	CINEMA	CLIFFS
SCARERS	CASSIA	CAYMANS	CHADARS	CHEQUER	CHOKERS	CINEMAS	SCLIFFS
CARIBE	CASSIAS	CAYUSE	CHADOR	CHEQUES	CHOKEY	CINEOL	CLINIC
CARIBES	CASTER	CAYUSES	CHADORS	CHERUB	CHOKEYS	CINEOLE	ACLINIC
CARINA	CASTERS	CEDULA	CHAETA	CHERUBS	CHOLER	CINEOLS	CLINICS
OCARINA	CASTLE	CEDULAS	CHAETAE	CHERUP	CHOLERA	CINQUE	CLIQUE
CARINAS	CASTLED	CELIAC	CHAFER	CHERUPS	CHOLERS	CINQUES	CLIQUES
CARING	CASTLES	CELIACS	CHAFERS	CHESIL	CHOOSE	CIPHER	CLIQUEY
SCARING	CASTOR	CELLAR	CHAGAN	CHESILS	CHOOSER	CIPHERS	CLITIC
CARLOT	CASTORS	CELLARS	CHAGANS	CHEVEN	CHOOSES	CIRCAR	CLITICS
CARLOTS	CASTORY	CEMBRA	CHAISE	CHEVENS	CHOOSEY	CIRCARS	CLOACA
CARNAL	CASUAL	CEMBRAS	CHAISES	CHEVIN	CHOPIN	CIRCLE	CLOACAE
CARNALS	CASUALS	CEMENT	CHAKRA	CHEVINS	CHOPINE	CIRCLED	CLOACAL
CARNET	CATALO	CEMENTA	CHAKRAS	CHEWET	CHOPINS	CIRCLER	CLOCHE
CARNETS	CATALOG	CEMENTS	CHALAN	CHEWETS	CHORAL	CIRCLES	CLOCHES
CARNEY	CATALOS	CENOTE	CHALANS	CHIACK	CHORALE	CIRCLET	CLOQUE
CARNEYS	CATENA	CENOTES	CHALET	CHIACKS	CHORALS	CIRCUS	CLOQUES
CARPAL	CATENAE	CENSER	CHALETS	CHIASM	CHOREA	CIRCUSY	CLOSED
CARPALS	CATENAS	CENSERS	CHANCE	CHIASMA	CHOREAS	CIRQUE	ECLOSED
CARPED	CATERS	CENSOR	CHANCED	CHIASMS	CHOREE	CIRQUES	CLOSER
SCARPED	ACATERS	CENSORS	CHANCEL	CHIBOL	CHOREES	CITHER	CLOSERS
CARPEL	CATGUT	CENTAL	CHANCER	CHIBOLS	CHOUGH	CITHERN	CLOSES
CARPELS	CATGUTS	CENTALS	CHANCES	CHICHA	CHOUGHS	CITHERS	ECLOSES
CARPER	CATION	CENTER	CHANGE	CHICHAS	CHOUSE	CITOLE	CLOSEST
SCARPER	CATIONS		CHANGED	CHICHI	CHOUSED	CITOLES	CLOSET

CLOSETS	COFFEES	COMBLE	CONSUL	CORIUM	COTEAU	SCOWLED	CREATED
CLOTHE	COFFER	COMBLES	CONSULS	CORIUMS	COTEAUX	COWPAT	CREATES
CLOTHED	SCOFFER	COMEDO	CONSULT	CORKER	COTING	COWPATS	CRECHE
CLOTHES	COFFERS	COMEDOS	CONTES	CORKERS	COTINGA	COWPED	CRECHES
CLOUGH	COFFIN	COMFIT	CONTEST	CORKIR	COTISE	SCOWPED	CREDIT
CLOUGHS	COFFING	COMFITS	CONTRA	CORKIRS	COTISED	COWRIE	CREDITS
CLOVER	COFFINS	COMING	CONTRAS	CORNEA	COTISES	SCOWRIE	CREEDS
CLOVERS	COFFLE	COMINGS	CONVEY	CORNEAL	COTTAR	COWRIES	SCREEDS
CLOVERY	COFFLES	COMMER	CONVEYS	CORNEAS	COTTARS	COYOTE	CREESE
CLUSIA	COGGED	COMMERE	CONVOY	CORNED	COTTER	COYOTES	CREESED
CLUSIAS	SCOGGED	COMMERS	CONVOYS	ACORNED	COTTERS	COZIER	CREESES
COAITA	COGGER	COMMIE	COOING	SCORNED	COTTON	COZIERS	CREESH
COAITAS	COGGERS	COMMIES	COOINGS	CORNEL	COTTONS	COZIES	CREESHY
COALER	COGGIE	COMMIT	COOKER	CORNELS	COTTONY	COZIEST	CREMOR
COALERS	COGGIES	COMMITS	COOKERS	CORNER	COTWAL	CRADLE	CREMORS
COARSE	COGGLE	COMMON	COOKERY	SCORNER	COTWALS	CRADLED	CRENEL
COARSEN	COGGLED	COMMONS	COOKIE	CORNERS	COTYLE	CRADLES	CRENELS
COARSER	COGGLES	COMMOT	COOKIES	CORNET	COTYLES	CRAGGY	CREOLE
COATEE	COHERE	COMMOTE	COOLER	CORNETS	COUCAL	SCRAGGY	CREOLES
COATEES	COHERED	COMMOTS	COOLERS	CORNETT	COUCALS	CRAMES	CREPON
COATER	COHERER	COMPEL	COOLIE	CORNUA	COUCHE	CRAMESY	CREPONS
COATERS	COHERES	COMPELS	COOLIES	CORNUAL	COUCHED	CRANCH	CRESOL
COAXER	COHORN	COMPOS	COOLTH	CORONA	COUCHEE	SCRANCH	CRESOLS
COAXERS	COHORNS	COMPOSE	COOLTHS	CORONAE	COUCHES	CRANIA	CRETIC
COBALT	COHORT	COMPOST	COOPED	CORONAL	COUGAR	CRANIAL	CRETICS
COBALTS	COHORTS	COMPOT	SCOOPED	CORONAS	COUGARS	CRANNY	CRETIN
COBBER	COHUNE	COMPOTE	COOPER	COROZO	COULEE	SCRANNY	CRETINS
COBBERS	COHUNES	COMPOTS	SCOOPER	COROZOS	COULEES	CRAPED	CREWED
COBBLE	COIGNE	CONCHA	COOPERS	CORPSE	COUPED	SCRAPED	SCREWED
COBBLED	COIGNED	CONCHAE	COOPERY	CORPSED	SCOUPED	CRAPES	CREWEL
COBBLER	COIGNES	CONCHE	COOSEN	CORPSES	COUPEE	SCRAPES	CREWELS
COBBLES	COINER	CONCHED	COOSENS	CORRAL	COUPEES	CRAPLE	CRIMPS
COBNUT	COINERS	CONCHES	COOSER	CORRALS	COUPER	CRAPLES	SCRIMPS
COBNUTS	COJOIN	CONCUR	COOSERS	CORRIE	COUPERS	CRATCH	CRIMPY
COBURG	COJOINS	CONCURS	COOSIN	CORRIES	COUPLE	SCRATCH	SCRIMPY
COBURGS	SCOLDER	CONDER	COOSINS	CORSES	COUPLED	CRATER	CRINES
COBWEB	COLDER	CONDERS	COPECK	SCORSES	COUPLER	CRATERS	SCRINES
COBWEBS	COLLAR	CONDOM	COPECKS	CORSET	COUPLES	CRATON	CRINGE
COCCID	COLLARD	CONDOMS	COPIER	CORSETS	COUPLET	CRATONS	CRINGED
COCCIDS	COLLARS	CONDOR	COPIERS	CORVEE	COUPON	CRATUR	CRINGER
COCKER	COLLET	CONDORS	COPING	CORVEES	COUPONS	CRATURS	CRINGES
COCKERS	COLLETS	CONFAB	COPINGS	CORVET	COURED	CRAVAT	CRINUM
COCKET	COLLIE	CONFABS	COPITA	CORVETS	SCOURED	CRAVATS	CRINUMS
COCKETS	COLLIED	CONFER	COPITAS	CORVID	COURSE	CRAVEN	CRISTA
COCKLE	COLLIER	CONFERS	COPPER	CORVIDS	SCOURSE	CRAVENS	CRISTAE
COCKLED	COLLIES	CONFIT	COPPERS	CORYMB	COURSED	CRAVER	CRITIC
COCKLES	COLLOP	CONFITS	COPPERY	CORYMBS	COURSER	CRAVERS	CRITICS
COCOON	SCOLLOP	CONGEE	COPPIN	CORYZA	COURSES	CRAWLS	CROCHE
COCOONS	COLLOPS	CONGEED	COPPING	CORYZAS	COUSIN	SCRAWLS	CROCHES
CODDLE	COLOUR	CONGEES	COPPINS	COSECH	COUSINS	CRAWLY	CROCHET
CODDLED	COLOURS	CONGER	COPPLE	COSECHS	COUTER	SCRAWLY	CRONET
CODDLES	COLOURY	CONGERS	COPPLES	COSHER	SCOUTER	CRAYER	CRONETS
CODGER	COLTER	CONGERY	COPULA	COSHERS	COUTERS	CRAYERS	CROSSE
CODGERS	COLTERS	CONGES	SCOPULA	COSHERY	COUTIL	CRAYON	CROSSED
CODING	COLUGO	CONGEST	COPULAR	COSIER	COUTILS	CRAYONS	CROSSER
CODINGS	COLUGOS	CONGOU	COPULAS	COSIERS	COVENT	CREACH	CROSSES
CODIST	COLUMN	CONGOUS	COQUET	COSIES	COVENTS	CREACHS	CROTAL
CODISTS	COLUMNS	CONIMA	COQUETS	COSIEST	COVERT	CREAGH	SCROTAL
CODLIN	COLURE	CONIMAS	CORBAN	COSINE	COVERTS	CREAGHS	CROTALA
CODLING	COLURES	CONINE	CORBANS	COSINES	COVING	CREAKS	CROTALS
CODLINS	COMARB	CONINES	CORBEL	COSMEA	COVINGS	SCREAKS	CROTON
COELOM	COMARBS	CONJEE	CORBELS	COSMEAS	COVYNE	CREAKY	CROTONS
COELOME	COMART	CONJEED	CORBIE	COSSET	COVYNES	SCREAKY	CROUPE
COELOMS	COMARTS	CONJEES	CORBIES	COSSETS	COWAGE	CREAMS	CROUPED
COERCE	COMATE	CONKER	CORDON	COSSIE	COWAGES	SCREAMS	CROUPER
COERCED	COMATES	CONKERS	CORDONS	COSSIES	COWARD	CREASE	CROUPES
COERCES	COMBAT	CONNER	CORERS	COSTAL	COWARDS	CREASED	CROUTE
COEVAL	COMBATS	CONNERS	SCORERS	COSTALS	COWBOY	CREASES	CROUTES
COEVALS	COMBER	CONOID	CORING	COSTER	COWBOYS	CREATE	CRUDES
COFFEE	COMBERS	CONOIDS	SCORING	COSTERS	COWLED	OCREATE	CRUDEST

CRUISE	CUISSES	CURRIES	DACOITS	DANDLED	DAZZLED	DECOCTS	**DEGUST**
CRUISED	**CUITER**	**CURSER**	DACOITY	DANDLER	DAZZLER	**DECODE**	DEGUSTS
CRUISER	CUITERS	CURSERS	**DACTYL**	DANDLES	DAZZLES	DECODED	**DEHORN**
CRUISES	**CULLED**	**CURSOR**	DACTYLS	**DANGER**	**DEACON**	DECODER	DEHORNS
CRUIVE	SCULLED	CURSORS	**DADDLE**	DANGERS	DEACONS	DECODES	**DEHORT**
CRUIVES	**CULLER**	CURSORY	DADDLED	**DANGLE**	**DEADEN**	**DECOKE**	DEHORTS
CRUMEN	SCULLER	**CURTAL**	DADDLES	DANGLED	DEADENS	DECOKED	**DEJECT**
CRUMENS	CULLERS	CURTALS	**DAEDAL**	DANGLER	**DEADER**	DECOKES	DEJECTA
CRUMMY	**CULLET**	**CURVET**	DAEDALE	DANGLES	DEADERS	**DECREE**	DEJECTS
SCRUMMY	CULLETS	CURVETS	**DAEMON**	**DANTON**	**DEAFEN**	DECREED	**DELATE**
CRUMPS	**CULMEN**	**CUSHAT**	DAEMONS	DANTONS	DEAFENS	DECREES	DELATED
SCRUMPS	CULMENS	CUSHATS	**DAFTAR**	**DAPHNE**	**DEALER**	DECREET	DELATES
CRUMPY	**CULTER**	**CUSHAW**	DAFTARS	DAPHNES	DEALERS	**DECREW**	**DELETE**
SCRUMPY	CULTERS	CUSHAWS	**DAFTIE**	**DAPPER**	**DEANER**	DECREWS	DELETED
CRUNCH	**CULVER**	**CUSSER**	DAFTIES	DAPPERS	DEANERY	**DECTET**	DELETES
SCRUNCH	CULVERS	CUSSERS	**DAGABA**	**DAPPLE**	**DEARES**	DECTETS	**DELICE**
CRUNCHY	CULVERT	**CUSTOM**	DAGABAS	DAPPLED	DEAREST	**DEDUCE**	DELICES
CRUSET	**CUMBER**	CUSTOMS	**DAGGER**	DAPPLES	**DEARIE**	DEDUCED	**DELICT**
CRUSETS	SCUMBER	**CUTEST**	DAGGERS	**DARGLE**	DEARIES	DEDUCES	DELICTS
CRUSIE	CUMBERS	ACUTEST	**DAGGLE**	DARGLES	**DEARTH**	**DEDUCT**	**DELUDE**
CRUSIES	**CUMMER**	**CUTLER**	DAGGLED	**DARING**	DEARTHS	DEDUCTS	DELUDED
CRUSTA	SCUMMER	CUTLERS	DAGGLES	DARINGS	**DEASIL**	**DEEJAY**	DELUDER
CRUSTAE	CUMMERS	CUTLERY	**DAGOBA**	**DARKEN**	DEASILS	DEEJAYS	DELUDES
CRUSTAL	**CUMMIN**	**CUTLET**	DAGOBAS	DARKENS	**DEBARK**	**DEEMED**	**DELUGE**
CRYING	CUMMINS	CUTLETS	**DAHLIA**	**DARKEY**	DEBARKS	ADEEMED	DELUGED
SCRYING	**CUNNER**	**CUTTER**	DAHLIAS	DARKEYS	**DEBASE**	**DEEPEN**	DELUGES
CRYINGS	SCUNNER	SCUTTER	**DAIDLE**	**DARKIE**	DEBASED	DEEPENS	**DELVER**
CRYPTO	CUNNERS	CUTTERS	DAIDLED	DARKIES	DEBASER	**DEEPIE**	DELVERS
CRYPTON	**CUPFUL**	**CUTTLE**	DAIDLES	**DARKLE**	DEBASES	DEEPIES	**DEMAIN**
CRYPTOS	CUPFULS	SCUTTLE	**DAIKER**	DARKLED	**DEBATE**	**DEFACE**	DEMAINE
CUBAGE	**CUPOLA**	CUTTLES	DAIKERS	DARKLES	DEBATED	DEFACED	DEMAINS
CUBAGES	CUPOLAR	**CYANIN**	**DAIKON**	**DARNEL**	DEBATER	DEFACER	**DEMAND**
CUBICA	CUPOLAS	CYANINE	DAIKONS	DARNELS	DEBATES	DEFACES	DEMANDS
CUBICAL	**CUPPER**	CYANINS	**DAIMIO**	**DARNER**	**DEBTEE**	**DEFAME**	**DEMARK**
CUBICAS	SCUPPER	**CYATHI**	DAIMIOS	DARNERS	DEBTEES	DEFAMED	DEMARKS
CUBISM	CUPPERS	CYATHIA	**DAIMON**	**DARTER**	**DEBTOR**	DEFAMES	**DEMEAN**
CUBISMS	**CUPULE**	**CYCLER**	DAIMONS	DARTERS	DEBTORS	**DEFAST**	DEMEANE
CUBIST	CUPULES	CYCLERS	**DAINED**	**DARTLE**	**DEBUNK**	DEFASTE	DEMEANS
CUBISTS	**CURARA**	**CYCLIC**	SDAINED	DARTLED	DEBUNKS	**DEFEAT**	**DEMENT**
CUBOID	CURARAS	ACYCLIC	**DAINES**	DARTLES	**DECADE**	DEFEATS	DEMENTI
CUBOIDS	**CURARE**	**CYGNET**	SDAINES	**DARTRE**	DECADES	**DEFECT**	DEMENTS
CUCKOO	CURARES	CYGNETS	**DAKOIT**	DARTRES	**DECAMP**	DEFECTS	**DEMISE**
CUCKOOS	**CURARI**	**CYMBAL**	DAKOITI	**DASHER**	DECAMPS	**DEFEND**	DEMISED
CUDDEN	CURARIS	CYMBALO	DAKOITS	DASHERS	**DECANE**	DEFENDS	DEMISES
CUDDENS	**CURATE**	CYMBALS	**DALLOP**	**DASSIE**	DECANES	**DEFIER**	**DEMIST**
CUDDIE	CURATES	**CYPHER**	DALLOPS	DASSIES	**DECANT**	DEFIERS	DEMISTS
CUDDIES	**CURDLE**	CYPHERS	**DALTON**	**DATING**	DECANTS	**DEFILE**	**DEMODE**
CUDDIN	CURDLED	**CYPRID**	DALTONS	DATINGS	**DECARB**	DEFILED	DEMODED
CUDDINS	CURDLES	CYPRIDS	**DAMAGE**	**DATIVE**	DECARBS	DEFILER	**DEMOTE**
CUDDLE	**CURFEW**	**CYSTID**	DAMAGED	DATIVES	**DECARE**	DEFILES	DEMOTED
SCUDDLE	CURFEWS	CYSTIDS	DAMAGES	**DATURA**	DECARES	**DEFINE**	DEMOTES
CUDDLED	**CURIES**	**CYTASE**	**DAMASK**	DATURAS	**DECCIE**	DEFINED	**DEMURE**
CUDDLES	ECURIES	CYTASES	DAMASKS	**DAUBER**	DECCIES	DEFINER	DEMURED
CUDGEL	**CURIET**	**CYTODE**	**DAMMAR**	DAUBERS	**DECEIT**	DEFINES	DEMURER
CUDGELS	CURIETS	CYTODES	DAMMARS	DAUBERY	DECEITS	**DEFORM**	DEMURES
CUEIST	**CURIOS**	**CZAPKA**	**DAMMER**	**DAUNER**	**DECERN**	DEFORMS	**DENGUE**
CUEISTS	CURIOSA	CZAPKAS	DAMMERS	DAUNERS	DECERNS	**DEFOUL**	DENGUES
CUESTA	**CURIUM**	**DABBER**	**DAMPEN**	**DAUTIE**	**DECIDE**	DEFOULS	**DENIAL**
CUESTAS	CURIUMS	DABBERS	DAMPENS	DAUTIES	DECIDED	**DEFRAY**	DENIALS
CUFFED	**CURLER**	**DABBLE**	**DAMPER**	**DAWDLE**	DECIDER	DEFRAYS	**DENIER**
SCUFFED	CURLERS	DABBLED	DAMPERS	DAWDLED	DECIDES	**DEFUSE**	DENIERS
CUFFIN	**CURLEW**	DABBLER	**DAMSEL**	DAWDLER	**DECIME**	DEFUSED	**DENNET**
CUFFING	CURLEWS	DABBLES	DAMSELS	DAWDLES	DECIMES	DEFUSES	DENNETS
CUFFINS	**CURPEL**	**DACITE**	**DAMSON**	**DAWING**	**DECKER**	**DEFUZE**	**DENOTE**
CUFFLE	CURPELS	DACITES	DAMSONS	ADAWING	DECKERS	DEFUZED	DENOTED
SCUFFLE	**CURRED**	**DACKER**	**DANCER**	**DAWNER**	**DECKLE**	DEFUZES	DENOTES
CUFFLED	SCURRED	DACKERS	DANCERS	DAWNERS	DECKLED	**DEGOUT**	**DENTAL**
CUFFLES	**CURRIE**	**DACOIT**	**DANDER**	**DAWTIE**	DECKLES	DEGOUTS	EDENTAL
CUISSE	CURRIED		DANDERS	DAWTIES	**DECOCT**	**DEGREE**	DENTALS
CUISSER	CURRIER		**DANDLE**	**DAZZLE**		DEGREES	**DENTEL**

DENTELS	DESYNED	DIARCHY	DINGERS	DITHER	DOGGERY	DORIZES	DRAGONS
DENTIL	DESYNES	DIATOM	DINGEY	DITHERS	DOGGIE	DORMER	DRAPER
DENTILS	DETAIL	DIATOMS	DINGEYS	DITHERY	DOGGIER	DORMERS	DRAPERS
DENTIN	DETAILS	DIAXON	DINGLE	DITING	DOGGIES	DORSAL	DRAPERY
DENTINE	DETAIN	DIAXONS	DINGLES	EDITING	DOLLAR	DORSALS	DRAPET
DENTING	DETAINS	DIBBER	DINNER	DITONE	DOLLARS	DORSEL	DRAPETS
DENTINS	DETECT	DIBBERS	DINNERS	DITONES	DOLLOP	DORSELS	DRAUNT
DENUDE	DETECTS	DIBBLE	DINNLE	DITTAY	DOLLOPS	DORSER	DRAUNTS
DENUDED	DETENT	DIBBLED	DINNLED	DITTAYS	DOLMAN	DORSERS	DRAWEE
DENUDES	DETENTE	DIBBLER	DINNLES	DIVERS	DOLMANS	DORTER	DRAWEES
DEODAR	DETENTS	DIBBLES	DIOXAN	DIVERSE	DOLMEN	DORTERS	DRAWER
DEODARS	DETENU	DICAST	DIOXANE	DIVERT	DOLMENS	DOSAGE	DRAWERS
DEPART	DETENUE	DICASTS	DIOXANS	DIVERTS	DOLOUR	DOSAGES	DRAZEL
DEPARTS	DETENUS	DICING	DIOXIN	DIVEST	DOLOURS	DOSSAL	DRAZELS
DEPEND	DETEST	DICINGS	DIOXINS	DIVESTS	DOMAIN	DOSSALS	DREADS
DEPENDS	DETESTS	DICKER	DIPLOE	DIVIDE	DOMAINS	DOSSEL	ADREADS
DEPICT	DETORT	DICKERS	DIPLOES	DIVIDED	DOMETT	DOSSELS	DREARE
DEPICTS	DETORTS	DICKEY	DIPLON	DIVIDER	DOMETTS	DOSSER	DREARER
DEPLOY	DETOUR	DICKEYS	DIPLONS	DIVIDES	DOMINO	DOSSERS	DREARES
DEPLOYS	DETOURS	DICKIE	DIPLONT	DIVINE	DOMINOS	DOSSIL	DREDGE
DEPONE	DEUTON	DICKIER	DIPOLE	DIVINED	DONATE	DOSSILS	DREDGED
DEPONED	DEUTONS	DICKIES	DIPOLES	DIVINER	DONATED	DOTAGE	DREDGER
DEPONES	DEVALL	DIDDER	DIPPER	DIVINES	DONATES	DOTAGES	DREDGES
DEPORT	DEVALLS	DIDDERS	DIPPERS	DIVING	DONGLE	DOTANT	DRIVEL
DEPORTS	DEVEST	DIDDLE	DIRDAM	DIVINGS	DONGLES	DOTANTS	DRIVELS
DEPOSE	DEVESTS	DIDDLED	DIRDAMS	DIZAIN	DONING	DOTARD	DRIVER
DEPOSED	DEVICE	DIDDLER	DIRDUM	DIZAINS	DONINGS	DOTARDS	DRIVERS
DEPOSER	DEVICES	DIDDLES	DIRDUMS	DJEBEL	DONJON	DOTING	DROGER
DEPOSES	DEVISE	DIEDRE	DIRECT	DJEBELS	DONJONS	DOTINGS	DROGERS
DEPUTE	DEVISED	DIEDRES	DIRECTS	DOATER	DONKEY	DOTTLE	DROGUE
DEPUTED	DEVISEE	DIESEL	DIRHAM	DOATERS	DONKEYS	DOTTLED	DROGUES
DEPUTES	DEVISER	DIESELS	DIRHAMS	DOBBER	DONNAT	DOTTLER	DROGUET
DERAIL	DEVISES	DIETER	DIRHEM	DOBBERS	DONNATS	DOTTLES	DROICH
DERAILS	DEVOIR	DIETERS	DIRHEMS	DOBBIE	DONNEE	DOUANE	DROICHS
DERATE	DEVOIRS	DIFFER	DIRIGE	DOBBIES	DONNEES	DOUANES	DROICHY
DERATED	DEVOTE	DIFFERS	DIRIGES	DOBBIN	DONNOT	DOUBLE	DROLES
DERATES	DEVOTED	DIGEST	DIRNDL	DOBBING	DONNOTS	DOUBLED	DROLEST
DERHAM	DEVOTEE	DIGESTS	DIRNDLS	DOBBINS	DONSIE	DOUBLER	DROMON
DERHAMS	DEVOTES	DIGGER	DISARM	DOCENT	DONSIER	DOUBLES	DROMOND
DERIDE	DEVOUR	DIGGERS	DISARMS	DOCENTS	DONZEL	DOUBLET	DROMONS
DERIDED	DEVOURS	DIGLOT	DISBAR	DOCILE	DONZELS	DOUCET	DRONGO
DERIDER	DEVVEL	DIGLOTS	DISBARK	DOCILER	DOOCOT	DOUCETS	DRONGOS
DERIDES	DEVVELS	DIKAST	DISBARS	DOCKEN	DOOCOTS	DOUCHE	DROOME
DERIVE	DEWANI	DIKASTS	DISBUD	DOCKENS	DOODAD	DOUCHED	DROOMES
DERIVED	DEWANIS	DIKTAT	DISBUDS	DOCKER	DOODADS	DOUCHES	DROUTH
DERIVES	DEWITT	DIKTATS	DISCUS	DOCKERS	DOODAH	DOUGHT	DROUTHS
DESALT	DEWITTS	DILATE	DISCUSS	DOCKET	DOODAHS	DOUGHTY	DROUTHY
DESALTS	DEWLAP	DILATED	DISEUR	DOCKETS	DOODLE	DOUSER	DROVER
DESERT	DEWLAPS	DILATER	DISEURS	DOCTOR	DOODLED	DOUSERS	DROVERS
DESERTS	DEWLAPT	DILATES	DISMAL	DOCTORS	DOODLER	DOUTER	DROWSE
DESIGN	DEXTER	DILDOE	DISMALS	DODDER	DOODLES	DOUTERS	DROWSED
DESIGNS	DEXTERS	DILDOES	DISMAN	DODDERS	DOOKET	DOWLNE	DROWSES
DESINE	DHARMA	DILUTE	DISMANS	DODDERY	DOOKETS	DOWLNES	DRUDGE
DESINED	ADHARMA	DILUTED	DISMAY	DODDLE	DOOLIE	DOWLNEY	DRUDGED
DESINES	DHARMAS	DILUTEE	DISMAYD	DODDLES	DOOLIES	DOWNER	DRUDGER
DESIRE	DHARNA	DILUTER	DISMAYL	DODGEM	DOPANT	DOWNERS	DRUDGES
DESIRED	DHARNAS	DILUTES	DISMAYS	DODGEMS	DOPANTS	DOWSER	DRUPEL
DESIRER	DHOOTI	DIMBLE	DISOWN	DODGER	DOPING	DOWSERS	DRUPELS
DESIRES	DHOOTIS	DIMBLES	DISOWNS	DODGERS	DOPINGS	DOWSET	DRYING
DESIST	DHURRA	DIMMER	DISPEL	DODGERY	DOPPER	DOWSETS	DRYINGS
DESISTS	DHURRAS	DIMMERS	DISPELS	DODKIN	DOPPERS	DOYLEY	DUALIN
DESMAN	DIADEM	DIMPLE	DISPLE	DODKINS	DOPPIE	DOYLEYS	DUALINS
DESMANS	DIADEMS	DIMPLED	DISPLED	DODMAN	DOPPIES	DOZING	DUBBIN
DESMID	DIALOG	DIMPLES	DISPLES	DODMANS	DORADO	DOZINGS	DUBBING
DESMIDS	DIALOGS	DIMWIT	DISTIL	DOFFER	DORADOS	DRACHM	DUBBINS
DESORB	DIAPER	DIMWITS	DISTILL	DOFFERS	DORISE	DRACHMA	DUCKER
DESORBS	DIAPERS	DINDLE	DISTILS	DOGATE	DORISED	DRACHMS	DUCKERS
DESPOT	DIAPIR	DINDLED	DISUSE	DOGATES	DORISES	DRAGEE	DUDDER
DESPOTS	DIAPIRS	DINDLES	DISUSED	DOGGER	DORIZE	DRAGEES	DUDDERS
DESYNE	DIARCH	DINGER	DISUSES	DOGGERS	DORIZED	DRAGON	DUDDERY

DUDDIE	DYNAMOS	TEASING	LEDGIER	BEGGARS	GELDERS	EMBANKS	AEMULED
DUDDIER	DYNAST	EASLES	SEDGIER	SEGGARS	MELDERS	EMBARK	EMULES
DUDEEN	DYNASTS	MEASLES	EDGING	EGGCUP	WELDERS	EMBARKS	AEMULES
DUDEENS	DYNASTY	EASTED	HEDGING	EGGCUPS	ELDING	EMBASE	EMULGE
DUDISM	DYNODE	FEASTED	KEDGING	EGGERS	GELDING	EMBASED	EMULGED
DUDISMS	DYNODES	REASTED	WEDGING	LEGGERS	MELDING	EMBASES	EMULGES
DUELLO	DYVOUR	YEASTED	EDGINGS	EGGIER	WELDING	EMBERS	EMUNGE
DUELLOS	DYVOURS	EASTER	EDIBLE	LEGGIER	ELDINGS	MEMBERS	EMUNGED
DUENNA	DYVOURY	FEASTER	EDIBLES	EGGING	ELECTS	EMBLEM	EMUNGES
DUENNAS	DZEREN	EASTERN	EDILES	BEGGING	SELECTS	EMBLEMA	EMURED
DUETTO	DZERENS	EATAGE	AEDILES	LEGGING	ELEGIT	EMBLEMS	DEMURED
DUETTOS	EAGLES	EATAGES	EDITOR	PEGGING	ELEGITS	EMBLIC	EMURES
DUFFEL	BEAGLES	EATCHE	EDITORS	EGGLER	ELENCH	EMBLICS	DEMURES
DUFFELS	TEAGLES	EATCHES	EDUCED	EGGLERS	ELENCHI	EMBOIL	LEMURES
DUFFER	EAGLET	EATERS	DEDUCED	EGGNOG	ELENCHS	EMBOILS	ENABLE
DUFFERS	EAGLETS	BEATERS	REDUCED	EGGNOGS	ELEVEN	EMBOLI	TENABLE
DUFFLE	EAGRES	HEATERS	SEDUCED	EGISES	ELEVENS	EMBOLIC	ENABLED
DUFFLES	MEAGRES	SEATERS	EDUCES	AEGISES	ELEVON	EMBRUE	ENABLER
DUGONG	EANING	EATERY	DEDUCES	EGOISM	ELEVONS	EMBRUED	ENABLES
DUGONGS	BEANING	PEATERY	REDUCES	EGOISMS	ELFING	EMBRUES	ENAMEL
DUGOUT	LEANING	EATHLY	SEDUCES	EGOIST	SELFING	EMBRYO	ENAMELS
DUGOUTS	MEANING	DEATHLY	EDUCTS	EGOISTS	ELFISH	EMBRYON	ENAMOR
DUIKER	PEANING	EATING	DEDUCTS	EGRESS	SELFISH	EMBRYOS	ENAMORS
DUIKERS	SEANING	BEATING	EECHED	NEGRESS	ELICIT	EMERGE	ENCAGE
DUMDUM	WEANING	FEATING	LEECHED	REGRESS	ELICITS	DEMERGE	ENCAGED
DUMDUMS	YEANING	HEATING	REECHED	EGRETS	ELITES	REMERGE	ENCAGES
DUMPER	EARBOB	SEATING	EECHES	REGRETS	PELITES	EMERGED	ENCALM
DUMPERS	EARBOBS	EATINGS	BEECHES	EIGHTH	ELIXIR	EMERGES	ENCALMS
DUMPLE	EARDED	EBBING	KEECHES	EIGHTHS	ELIXIRS	EMESES	ENCAMP
DUMPLED	BEARDED	KEBBING	LEECHES	EIGHTS	ELOIGN	NEMESES	ENCAMPS
DUMPLES	YEARDED	NEBBING	REECHES	HEIGHTS	ELOIGNS	EMESIS	ENCASE
DUNDER	EARFUL	WEBBING	EELIER	WEIGHTS	ELOPER	NEMESIS	ENCASED
DUNDERS	FEARFUL	ECARTE	SEELIER	EIGHTY	ELOPERS	EMETIC	ENCASES
DUNITE	TEARFUL	ECARTES	EERIER	WEIGHTY	ELSHIN	EMETICS	ENCAVE
DUNITES	EARFULS	ECBOLE	BEERIER	EIRACK	ELSHINS	EMETIN	ENCAVED
DUNLIN	EARING	ECBOLES	LEERIER	EIRACKS	ELTCHI	EMETINE	ENCAVES
DUNLINS	BEARING	ECHING	PEERIER	EISELL	ELTCHIS	EMETINS	ENCODE
DUPION	DEARING	EECHING	EFFACE	EISELLS	ELUANT	EMEUTE	ENCODED
DUPIONS	FEARING	LECHING	EFFACED	EITHER	ELUANTS	EMEUTES	ENCODES
DUPLET	GEARING	PECHING	EFFACES	NEITHER	ELUATE	EMIGRE	ENCORE
DUPLETS	HEARING	ECHOER	EFFECT	EJECTA	ELUATES	EMIGRES	ENCORED
DURANT	LEARING	ECHOERS	EFFECTS	DEJECTA	ELUDED	EMMOVE	ENCORES
DURANTS	NEARING	ECLAIR	EFFEIR	EJECTS	DELUDED	EMMOVED	ENCYST
DURBAR	REARING	ECLAIRS	EFFEIRS	DEJECTS	ELUDER	EMMOVES	ENCYSTS
DURBARS	SEARING	ECLOSE	EFFERE	REJECTS	DELUDER	EMOTED	ENDART
DURDUM	TEARING	RECLOSE	EFFERED	ELANCE	ELUDERS	DEMOTED	ENDARTS
DURDUMS	WEARING	ECLOSED	EFFERES	ELANCED	ELUDES	EMOTES	ENDEAR
DURESS	EARINGS	ECLOSES	EFFING	ELANCES	DELUDES	DEMOTES	ENDEARS
DURESSE	EARLAP	ECONUT	JEFFING	ELANET	ELUENT	REMOTES	ENDING
DURGAN	EARLAPS	ECONUTS	REFFING	ELANETS	ELUENTS	EMOVED	BENDING
DURGANS	EARNED	ECTYPE	EFFORT	ELAPSE	ELUTOR	REMOVED	FENDING
DURIAN	LEARNED	ECTYPES	EFFORTS	DELAPSE	ELUTORS	EMOVES	HENDING
DURIANS	YEARNED	ECURIE	EFFRAY	RELAPSE	ELUVIA	REMOVES	LENDING
DURION	EARNER	ECURIES	EFFRAYS	ELAPSED	ELUVIAL	EMPALE	MENDING
DURIONS	EARNERS	ECZEMA	EFFUSE	ELAPSES	ELVERS	EMPALED	PENDING
DURRIE	EARTHS	ECZEMAS	EFFUSED	ELATED	DELVERS	EMPALES	RENDING
DURRIES	DEARTHS	EDDIES	EFFUSES	BELATED	ELYTRA	EMPARE	SENDING
DUSKEN	HEARTHS	NEDDIES	EGALLY	DELATED	ELYTRAL	EMPARED	TENDING
DUSKENS	EARWIG	TEDDIES	LEGALLY	RELATED	EMBACE	EMPARES	VENDING
DUSTED	EARWIGS	EDDISH	REGALLY	VELATED	EMBACES	EMPART	WENDING
ADUSTED	EASELS	REDDISH	EGENCE	ELATER	EMBAIL	EMPARTS	ENDINGS
DUSTER	TEASELS	EDEMAS	REGENCE	RELATER	EMBAILS	EMPIRE	ENDITE
DUSTERS	WEASELS	OEDEMAS	EGENCY	ELATERS	EMBALE	EMPIRES	ENDITED
DUYKER	EASING	EDGERS	REGENCY	ELATES	EMBALED	EMPLOY	ENDITES
DUYKERS	CEASING	HEDGERS	EGESTS	BELATES	EMBALES	EMPLOYS	ENDIVE
DYBBUK	LEASING	KEDGERS	REGESTS	DELATES	EMBALL	EMPUSA	ENDIVES
DYBBUKS	MEASING	LEDGERS	EGGARS	RELATES	EMBALLS	EMPUSAS	ENDUES
DYEING	PEASING	EDGIER		ELCHEE	EMBALM	EMPUSE	VENDUES
DYEINGS	SEASING	HEDGIER		ELCHEES	EMBALMS	EMPUSES	ENDURE
DYNAMO		KEDGIER		ELDERS	EMBANK	EMULED	ENDURED

ENDURER	ENLOCKS	ENTICER	EPOPEES	ESCROWS	ETHNICS	EVZONES	EXPOSER
ENDURES	ENMOVE	ENTICES	EPOSES	ESCUDO	ETHYLS	EXACTS	EXPOSES
ENERVE	ENMOVED	ENTIRE	DEPOSES	ESCUDOS	METHYLS	HEXACTS	EXPUGN
ENERVED	ENMOVES	ENTIRES	REPOSES	ESILES	ETHYNE	EXAMEN	EXPUGNS
ENERVES	ENNEAD	ENTOIL	EPRISE	RESILES	ETHYNES	EXAMENS	EXSECT
ENEWED	ENNEADS	ENTOILS	REPRISE	ESLOIN	ETOILE	EXARCH	EXSECTS
RENEWED	ENNUYE	ENTOMB	EPUISE	ESLOINS	ETOILES	HEXARCH	EXSERT
ENFACE	ENNUYED	ENTOMBS	EPUISEE	ESPADA	ETRIER	EXARCHS	EXSERTS
ENFACED	ENOSES	ENTRAP	EQUANT	ESPADAS	ETRIERS	EXARCHY	EXTANT
ENFACES	KENOSES	ENTRAPS	EQUANTS	ESPIAL	ETTLED	EXCAMB	SEXTANT
ENFANT	ENOSIS	ENTREE	EQUATE	ESPIALS	FETTLED	EXCAMBS	EXTEND
ENFANTS	KENOSIS	ENTREES	EQUATED	ESPRIT	METTLED	EXCEED	EXTENDS
ENFIRE	ENOUGH	ENURES	EQUATES	ESPRITS	NETTLED	EXCEEDS	EXTENT
ENFIRED	ENOUGHS	TENURES	EQUIPE	ESSIVE	PETTLED	EXCEPT	EXTENTS
ENFIRES	ENRACE	ENVIER	EQUIPES	ESSIVES	SETTLED	EXCEPTS	EXTERN
ENFOLD	ENRACED	ENVIERS	ERASER	ESSOIN	ETTLES	EXCIDE	EXTERNE
PENFOLD	ENRACES	ENVIES	ERASERS	ESSOINS	FETTLES	EXCIDED	EXTERNS
TENFOLD	ENRAGE	SENVIES	ERBIUM	ESTATE	KETTLES	EXCIDES	EXTINE
ENFOLDS	ENRAGED	ENVOIS	TERBIUM	GESTATE	METTLES	EXCISE	EXTINES
ENFORM	ENRAGES	RENVOIS	ERBIUMS	RESTATE	NETTLES	EXCISED	EXTIRP
ENFORMS	ENRANK	ENVOYS	ERGATE	TESTATE	PETTLES	EXCISES	EXTIRPS
ENFREE	ENRANKS	LENVOYS	ERGATES	ESTATED	SETTLES	EXCITE	EXTORT
ENFREED	ENRING	RENVOYS	ERIACH	ESTATES	ETYMON	EXCITED	EXTORTS
ENFREES	ENRINGS	ENWALL	ERIACHS	ESTEEM	ETYMONS	EXCITER	EYALET
ENGAGE	ENROBE	ENWALLS	ERINGO	ESTEEMS	EUCAIN	EXCITES	EYALETS
ENGAGED	ENROBED	ENWIND	ERINGOS	ESTERS	EUCAINE	EXCUSE	EYEFUL
ENGAGER	ENROBES	ENWINDS	ERMINE	FESTERS	EUCAINS	EXCUSED	EYEFULS
ENGAGES	ENROLL	ENWOMB	ERMINED	JESTERS	EUCHRE	EXCUSER	EYELET
ENGAOL	ENROLLS	ENWOMBS	ERMINES	NESTERS	EUCHRED	EXCUSES	EYELETS
ENGAOLS	ENROOT	ENWRAP	ERNING	PESTERS	EUCHRES	EXEDRA	EYELID
ENGILD	ENROOTS	ENWRAPS	CERNING	RESTERS	EUGHEN	EXEDRAE	EYELIDS
ENGILDS	ENSEAL	ENZIAN	FERNING	TESTERS	LEUGHEN	EXEMES	EYLIAD
ENGINE	ENSEALS	ENZIANS	GERNING	WESTERS	EUKING	LEXEMES	EYLIADS
ENGINED	ENSEAM	ENZONE	KERNING	ESTRAL	YEUKING	EXEMPT	FABLER
ENGINER	ENSEAMS	ENZONED	TERNING	OESTRAL	EUNUCH	EXEMPTS	FABLERS
ENGINES	ENSEAR	ENZONES	EROTIC	VESTRAL	EUNUCHS	EXHALE	FABRIC
ENGIRD	ENSEARS	ENZYME	XEROTIC	ESTRAY	EUOUAE	EXHALED	FABRICS
ENGIRDS	ENSIGN	ENZYMES	EROTICA	ESTRAYS	EUOUAES	EXHALES	FACADE
ENGLUT	ENSIGNS	EOLITH	EROTICS	ESTRUM	EUPHON	EXHORT	FACADES
ENGLUTS	ENSILE	NEOLITH	ERRAND	OESTRUM	EUPHONS	EXHORTS	FACETE
ENGOBE	PENSILE	EOLITHS	ERRANDS	ESTRUMS	EUPHONY	EXHUME	FACETED
ENGOBES	SENSILE	EONISM	ERRANT	ESTRUS	EUREKA	EXHUMED	FACIAL
ENGORE	TENSILE	PEONISM	ERRANTS	OESTRUS	HEUREKA	EXHUMER	FACIALS
ENGORED	ENSILED	EONISMS	ERRING	ETAGES	EUREKAS	EXHUMES	FACING
ENGORES	ENSILES	EPARCH	HERRING	METAGES	EVEJAR	EXISTS	FACINGS
ENGRAM	ENSOUL	EPARCHS	SERRING	ETALON	EVEJARS	SEXISTS	FACTOR
ENGRAMS	ENSOULS	EPARCHY	ERRINGS	ETALONS	EVERTS	EXOGEN	FACTORS
ENGULF	ENSURE	EPAULE	ERRORS	ETCHED	REVERTS	EXOGENS	FACTORY
ENGULFS	CENSURE	EPAULES	TERRORS	FETCHED	EVINCE	EXONYM	FACTUM
ENHALO	ENSURED	EPAULET	ERYNGO	LETCHED	EVINCED	EXONYMS	FACTUMS
ENHALOS	ENSURER	EPEIRA	ERYNGOS	RETCHED	EVINCES	EXOPOD	FACULA
ENIGMA	ENSURES	EPEIRAS	ESCAPE	ETCHER	EVITES	EXOPODS	FACULAE
ENIGMAS	ENTAIL	EPERDU	ESCAPED	ETCHERS	LEVITES	EXOTIC	FACULAR
ENISLE	VENTAIL	EPERDUE	ESCAPEE	ETCHES	EVOKED	EXOTICA	FADDLE
ENISLED	ENTAILS	EPHEBI	ESCAPER	FETCHES	REVOKED	EXOTICS	FADDLED
ENISLES	ENTAME	EPHEBIC	ESCAPES	KETCHES	EVOKES	EXPAND	FADDLES
ENJAMB	ENTAMED	EPIGON	ESCARP	LETCHES	REVOKES	EXPANDS	FADEUR
ENJAMBS	ENTAMES	EPIGONE	ESCARPS	RETCHES	EVOLUE	EXPECT	FADEURS
ENJOIN	ENTERA	EPIGONI	ESCHAR	VETCHES	EVOLUES	EXPECTS	FADING
ENJOINS	ENTERAL	EPIGONS	ESCHARS	ETHANE	EVOLVE	EXPEND	FADINGS
ENLACE	ENTERS	EPIMER	ESCHEW	METHANE	DEVOLVE	EXPENDS	FAERIE
ENLACED	CENTERS	EPIMERS	ESCHEWS	ETHANES	REVOLVE	EXPERT	FAERIES
ENLACES	RENTERS	EPIZOA	ESCORT	ETHENE	EVOLVED	EXPERTS	FAGGOT
ENLARD	TENTERS	EPIZOAN	ESCORTS	ETHENES	EVOLVES	EXPIRE	FAGGOTS
ENLARDS	VENTERS	EPOCHA	ESCROC	ETHERS	EVOVAE	EXPIRED	FAIBLE
ENLINK	ENTETE	EPOCHAL	ESCROCS	AETHERS	EVOVAES	EXPIRES	FAIBLES
ENLINKS	ENTETEE	EPOCHAS	ESCROL	PETHERS	EVULSE	EXPORT	FAILLE
ENLIST	ENTICE	EPONYM	ESCROLL	TETHERS	EVULSED	EXPORTS	FAILLES
ENLISTS	PENTICE	EPONYMS	ESCROLS	WETHERS	EVULSES	EXPOSE	FAINES
ENLOCK	ENTICED	EPOPEE	ESCROW	ETHNIC	EVZONE	EXPOSED	FAINEST

FAITOR	FAUCET	FESTALS	FILTER	FIZZEN	FODDERS	FORMER	FRICHTS
FAITORS	FAUCETS	FESTER	FILTERS	FIZZENS	FOETOR	FORMERS	FRIDGE
FALCON	FAUTOR	FESTERS	FIMBLE	FIZZER	FOETORS	FORMOL	FRIDGED
FALCONS	FAUTORS	FETICH	FIMBLES	FIZZERS	FOGGER	FORMOLS	FRIDGES
FALLAL	FAVELA	FETICHE	FINALE	FIZZLE	FOGGERS	FORPET	FRIEND
FALLALS	FAVELAS	FETTER	FINALES	FIZZLED	FOGLES	FORPETS	FRIENDS
FALLOW	FAVISM	FETTERS	FINDER	FIZZLES	FOGLESS	FORPIT	FRIEZE
FALLOWS	FAVISMS	FETTLE	FINDERS	FLACON	FOGRAM	FORPITS	FRIEZED
FALSER	FAVOUR	FETTLED	FINEER	FLACONS	FOGRAMS	FORRAY	FRIEZES
FALSERS	FAVOURS	FETTLER	FINEERS	FLAGON	FOIBLE	FORRAYS	FRIGHT
FALSES	FAWNER	FETTLES	FINGAN	FLAGONS	FOIBLES	FORSAY	FRIGHTS
FALSEST	FAWNERS	FEUTRE	FINGANS	FLAMEN	FOISON	FORSAYS	FRIGOT
FALSIE	FEAGUE	FEUTRED	FINGER	FLAMENS	FOISONS	FOSSIL	FRIGOTS
FALSIES	FEAGUED	FEUTRES	FINGERS	FLANGE	FOLDER	FOSSILS	FRIJOL
FALTER	FEAGUES	FEWMET	FINIAL	FLANGED	FOLDERS	FOSSOR	FRIJOLE
FALTERS	FEARED	FEWMETS	FINIALS	FLANGES	FOLIOS	FOSSORS	FRINGE
FAMINE	AFEARED	FEWTER	FINING	FLASER	FOLIOSE	FOSTER	FRINGED
FAMINES	FECULA	FEWTERS	FININGS	FLASERS	FOLLOW	FOSTERS	FRINGES
FANDOM	FECULAS	FIACRE	FINJAN	FLAUNE	FOLLOWS	FOTHER	FRIPON
FANDOMS	FEDORA	FIACRES	FINJANS	FLAUNES	FOMENT	FOTHERS	FRIPONS
FANGLE	FEDORAS	FIANCE	FINNAC	FLAUNT	FOMENTS	FOUGHT	FRISKA
FANGLED	FEEBLE	FIANCEE	FINNACK	FLAUNTS	FONDLE	FOUGHTY	FRISKAS
FANGLES	FEEBLED	FIANCES	FINNACS	FLAUNTY	FONDLED	FOULES	FRIVOL
FANION	FEEBLER	FIASCO	FINNAN	FLAVIN	FONDLER	FOULER	FRIVOLS
FANIONS	FEEBLES	FIASCOS	FINNANS	FLAVINE	FONDLES	FOULEST	FROISE
FANKLE	FEEDER	FIAUNT	FINNER	FLAVINS	FONDUE	FOURTH	FROISES
FANKLED	FEEDERS	FIAUNTS	FINNERS	FLAYER	FONDUES	FOURTHS	FROLIC
FANKLES	FEELER	FIBBER	FIORIN	FLAYERS	FOODIE	FOUSSA	FROLICS
FANNEL	FEELERS	FIBBERS	FIORINS	FLECHE	FOODIES	FOUSSAS	FROWIE
FANNELL	FEERIE	FIBBERY	FIPPLE	FLECHES	FOOTER	FOUTER	FROWIER
FANNELS	FEERIES	FIBRIL	FIPPLES	FLEDGE	FOOTERS	FOUTERS	FROWST
FANNER	FEERIN	FIBRILS	FIRING	FLEDGED	FOOTLE	FOUTRA	FROWSTS
FANNERS	FEERING	FIBRIN	FIRINGS	FLEDGES	FOOTLED	FOUTRAS	FROWSTY
FANTAD	FEERINS	FIBRINS	FIRKIN	FLEECE	FOOTLES	FOUTRE	FRUICT
FANTADS	FELINE	FIBROS	FIRKING	FLEECED	FOOTRA	FOUTRES	FRUICTS
FANTOD	FELINES	FIBROSE	FIRKINS	FLEECER	FOOTRAS	FOWLER	FRYING
FANTODS	FELLAH	FIBULA	FIRLOT	FLEECES	FOOZLE	FOWLERS	FRYINGS
FANTOM	FELLAHS	FIBULAR	FIRLOTS	FLENSE	FOOZLED	FOXING	FUCKER
FANTOMS	FELLER	FIBULAS	FIRMAN	FLENSED	FOOZLER	FOXINGS	FUCKERS
FAQUIR	FELLERS	FICKLE	FIRMANS	FLENSES	FOOZLES	FRAGOR	FUCOID
FAQUIRS	FELLOE	FICKLED	FIRMER	FLEXOR	FORAGE	FRAGORS	FUCOIDS
FARCIN	FELLOES	FICKLER	FIRMERS	FLEXORS	FORAGED	FRAISE	FUDDLE
FARCING	FELLOW	FICKLES	FISCAL	FLIGHT	FORAGER	FRAISED	FUDDLED
FARCINS	FELLOWS	FICTOR	FISCALS	FLIGHTS	FORAGES	FRAISES	FUDDLER
FARDEL	FELTER	FICTORS	FISGIG	FLIGHTY	FORBAD	FRAMER	FUDDLES
FARDELS	FELTERS	FIDDLE	FISGIGS	FLORET	FORBADE	FRAMERS	FUGATO
FARDEN	FEMALE	FIDDLED	FISHER	FLORETS	FORBID	FRAPPE	FUGATOS
FARDENS	FEMALES	FIDDLER	FISHERS	FLORIN	FORBIDS	FRAPPED	FULFIL
FARINA	FEMORA	FIDDLES	FISHERY	FLORINS	FORCAT	FRAPPEE	FULFILS
FARINAS	FEMORAL	FIDDLEY	FISSLE	FLOTEL	FORCATS	FRATCH	FULGOR
FARMER	FENCER	FIDGET	FISSLED	FLOTELS	FORCER	FRATCHY	FULGORS
FARMERS	FENCERS	FIDGETS	FISSLES	FLOUSE	FORCERS	FRATER	FULHAM
FARMERY	FENDER	FIDGETY	FITCHE	FLOUSED	FOREST	FRATERS	FULHAMS
FARREN	FENDERS	FIERCE	FITCHEE	FLOUSES	FORESTS	FRATERY	FULLAM
FARRENS	FENNEC	FIERCER	FITCHES	FLOWER	FORGER	FRAZIL	FULLAMS
FARROW	FENNECS	FIESTA	FITCHET	FLOWERS	FORGERS	FRAZILS	FULLAN
FARROWS	FENNEL	FIESTAS	FITCHEW	FLOWERY	FORGERY	FREETS	FULLANS
FASCIA	FENNELS	FIGURE	FITTER	FLUATE	FORGET	AFREETS	FULLER
FASCIAL	FERREL	FIGURED	FITTERS	FLUATES	FORGETS	FREEZE	FULLERS
FASCIAS	FERRELS	FIGURES	FITTES	FLUENT	FORHOO	FREEZER	FULMAR
FASTEN	FERRET	FILFOT	FITTEST	FLUENTS	FORHOOS	FREEZES	FULMARS
FASTENS	FERRETS	FILFOTS	FIXATE	FLUGEL	FORHOW	FREMIT	FUMADO
FASTER	FERRETY	FILING	FIXATED	FLUGELS	FORHOWS	FREMITS	FUMADOS
FASTERS	FERULA	FILINGS	FIXATES	FLUTER	FORINT	FRENNE	FUMAGE
FATHER	FERULAS	FILLER	FIXING	FLUTERS	FORINTS	FRENNES	FUMAGES
FATHERS	FERULE	FILLERS	FIXINGS	FLYING	FORKER	FRESCO	FUMBLE
FATHOM	FERULES	FILLET	FIXURE	FLYINGS	FORKERS	FRESCOS	FUMBLED
FATHOMS	FESCUE	FILLETS	FIXURES	FLYWAY	FORMAT	FRIAND	FUMBLER
FATTEN	FESCUES	FILLIP	FIZGIG	FLYWAYS	FORMATE	FRIANDE	FUMBLES
FATTENS	FESTAL	FILLIPS	FIZGIGS	FODDER	FORMATS	FRIANDS	FUNDER
						FRICHT	

FUNDERS	**GAITER**	GARCONS	**GAWPER**	GHETTOS	GIRDERS	**GOATEE**	**GOOSEY**
FUNKIA	GAITERS	**GARDEN**	GAWPERS	**GIAOUR**	**GIRDLE**	GOATEED	GOOSEYS
FUNKIAS	**GALAGE**	GARDENS	**GAZEBO**	GIAOURS	GIRDLED	GOATEES	**GOPHER**
FUNNEL	GALAGES	**GARGET**	GAZEBOS	**GIBBER**	GIRDLER	**GOBANG**	GOPHERS
FUNNELS	**GALENA**	GARGETS	**GAZOON**	GIBBERS	GIRDLES	GOBANGS	**GOPURA**
FURANE	GALENAS	**GARGLE**	GAZOONS	**GIBBET**	**GIRKIN**	**GOBBET**	GOPURAM
FURANES	**GALERE**	GARGLED	**GAZUMP**	GIBBETS	GIRKINS	GOBBETS	GOPURAS
FUREUR	GALERES	GARGLES	GAZUMPS	**GIBBON**	**GIRLIE**	**GOBBLE**	**GORGET**
FUREURS	**GALIOT**	**GARIAL**	**GEEZER**	GIBBONS	GIRLIES	GOBBLED	GORGETS
FURFUR	GALIOTS	GARIALS	GEEZERS	**GIBLET**	**GIRNEL**	GOBBLER	**GORGIA**
FURFURS	**GALLET**	**GARJAN**	**GEISHA**	GIBLETS	GIRNELS	GOBBLES	GORGIAS
FUROLE	GALLETS	GARJANS	GEISHAS	**GIDGEE**	**GIRNIE**	**GOBLET**	**GORGIO**
FUROLES	**GALLEY**	**GARLIC**	**GEISTS**	GIDGEES	GIRNIER	GOBLETS	GORGIOS
FURORE	GALLEYS	GARLICS	AGEISTS	**GIDJEE**	**GITANA**	**GOBLIN**	**GORGON**
FURORES	**GALLON**	**GARNER**	**GELADA**	GIDJEES	GITANAS	GOBLINS	GORGONS
FURROW	GALLONS	GARNERS	GELADAS	**GIGGIT**	**GITANO**	**GODDAM**	**GORING**
FURROWS	**GALLOP**	**GARNET**	**GELATI**	GIGGITS	GITANOS	GODDAMN	GORINGS
FURROWY	GALLOPS	GARNETS	GELATIN	**GIGGLE**	**GIVING**	**GODOWN**	**GOSLET**
FUSAIN	**GALLOW**	**GARRAN**	**GELDER**	GIGGLED	GIVINGS	GODOWNS	GOSLETS
FUSAINS	GALLOWS	GARRANS	GELDERS	GIGGLER	**GIZZEN**	**GODSON**	**GOSPEL**
FUSION	**GALOOT**	**GARRET**	**GENDER**	GIGGLES	GIZZENS	GODSONS	GOSPELS
FUSIONS	GALOOTS	GARRETS	GENDERS	**GIGLET**	**GLAIVE**	**GODWIT**	**GOSSAN**
FUSSER	**GALUTH**	**GARRON**	**GENERA**	GIGLETS	GLAIVED	GODWITS	GOSSANS
FUSSERS	GALUTHS	GARRONS	GENERAL	**GIGLOT**	GLAIVES	**GOFFER**	**GOSSIB**
FUSTET	**GAMBET**	**GARROT**	**GENEVA**	GIGLOTS	**GLAMOR**	GOFFERS	GOSSIBS
FUSTETS	GAMBETS	GARROTS	GENEVAS	**GIGOLO**	GLAMORS	**GOGGLE**	**GOSSIP**
FUSTIC	**GAMBIR**	**GARRYA**	**GENNET**	GIGOLOS	**GLANCE**	GOGGLED	GOSSIPS
FUSTICS	GAMBIRS	GARRYAS	GENNETS	**GILCUP**	GLANCED	GOGGLER	GOSSIPY
FUSTOC	**GAMBIT**	**GARTER**	**GENOME**	GILCUPS	GLANCES	GOGGLES	**GOURDE**
FUSTOCS	GAMBITS	GARTERS	GENOMES	**GILDER**	**GLAZER**	**GOGLET**	GOURDES
FUTILE	**GAMBLE**	**GARUDA**	**GENTLE**	GILDERS	GLAZERS	GOGLETS	**GOUTTE**
FUTILER	GAMBLED	GARUDAS	GENTLED	**GILGAI**	**GLEAVE**	**GOITER**	GOUTTES
FUTURE	GAMBLER	**GARVIE**	GENTLER	GILGAIS	GLEAVES	GOITERS	**GOVERN**
FUTURES	GAMBLES	GARVIES	GENTLES	**GILGIE**	**GLEDGE**	**GOITRE**	GOVERNS
FUZZLE	**GAMBOL**	**GASCON**	**GENTOO**	GILGIES	GLEDGED	GOITRED	**GOWFER**
FUZZLED	GAMBOLS	GASCONS	GENTOOS	**GILLET**	GLEDGES	GOITRES	GOWFERS
FUZZLES	**GAMETE**	**GASKET**	**GEODES**	GILLETS	**GLIDER**	**GOLDEN**	**GOWPEN**
FYLFOT	GAMETES	GASKETS	GEODESY	**GILLIE**	GLIDERS	GOLDENS	GOWPENS
FYLFOTS	**GAMINE**	**GASKIN**	**GERBIL**	GILLIED	**GLIOMA**	**GOLFER**	**GOZZAN**
GABBER	GAMINES	GASKINS	GERBILS	GILLIES	GLIOMAS	GOLFERS	GOZZANS
GABBERS	**GAMING**	**GASPER**	**GERENT**	**GILPEY**	**GLOBIN**	**GOLLAN**	**GRABEN**
GABBLE	GAMINGS	GASPERS	GERENTS	GILPEYS	GLOBING	GOLLAND	GRABENS
GABBLED	**GAMMER**	**GATEAU**	**GERMAN**	**GIMBAL**	GLOBINS	GOLLANS	**GRADER**
GABBLER	GAMMERS	GATEAUS	GERMANE	GIMBALS	**GLOIRE**	**GOLLAR**	GRADERS
GABBLES	**GAMMON**	GATEAUX	GERMANS	**GIMLET**	GLOIRES	GOLLARS	**GRADIN**
GABBRO	GAMMONS	**GATHER**	**GERMEN**	GIMLETS	**GLORIA**	**GOLLOP**	GRADINE
GABBROS	**GANDER**	GATHERS	GERMENS	**GIMMAL**	GLORIAS	GOLLOPS	GRADING
GABION	GANDERS	**GATING**	**GERMIN**	GIMMALS	**GLOSSA**	**GOMBRO**	GRADINI
GABIONS	**GANGER**	GATINGS	GERMING	**GIMMER**	GLOSSAE	GOMBROS	GRADINO
GABLET	GANGERS	**GAUCHE**	GERMINS	GIMMERS	GLOSSAL	**GOMOKU**	GRADINS
GABLETS	**GANGUE**	GAUCHER	**GERUND**	**GIMMOR**	GLOSSAS	GOMOKUS	**GRAILE**
GADDER	GANGUES	**GAUCHO**	GERUNDS	GIMMORS	**GLOVER**	**GOMUTI**	GRAILES
GADDERS	**GANNET**	GAUCHOS	**GETTER**	**GINGAL**	GLOVERS	GOMUTIS	**GRAINE**
GADGET	GANNETS	**GAUCIE**	GETTERS	GINGALL	**GLOWER**	**GOMUTO**	GRAINED
GADGETS	**GANOID**	GAUCIER	**GEWGAW**	GINGALS	GLOWERS	GOMUTOS	GRAINER
GADGIE	GANOIDS	**GAUFER**	GEWGAWS	**GINGER**	**GLUTEN**	**GOOBER**	GRAINES
GADGIES	**GANOIN**	GAUFERS	**GEYSER**	GINGERS	GLUTENS	GOOBERS	**GRAITH**
GADOID	GANOINS	**GAUFRE**	GEYSERS	GINGERY	**GLYCIN**	**GOOGLE**	GRAITHS
GADOIDS	**GAOLER**	GAUFRES	**GHARRI**	**GINGLE**	GLYCINE	GOOGLED	**GRAKLE**
GAFFER	GAOLERS	**GAUGER**	GHARRIS	GINGLED	GLYCINS	GOOGLES	GRAKLES
GAFFERS	**GAPING**	GAUGERS	**GHAZAL**	GINGLES	**GLYCOL**	**GOOGOL**	**GRAMAS**
GAGAKU	GAPINGS	**GAUPER**	GHAZALS	**GINNEL**	GLYCOLS	GOOGOLS	GRAMASH
GAGAKUS	**GARAGE**	GAUPERS	**GHAZEL**	GINNELS	**GNAWER**	**GOOLEY**	**GRAMME**
GAGGER	GARAGED	**GAVAGE**	GHAZELS	**GINNER**	GNAWERS	GOOLEYS	GRAMMES
GAGGERS	GARAGES	GAVAGES	**GHERAO**	AGINNER	**GNOMON**	**GOOLIE**	**GRANDE**
GAGGLE	**GARBLE**	**GAVIAL**	GHERAOS	GINNERS	GNOMONS	GOOLIES	GRANDEE
GAGGLED	GARBLED	GAVIALS	**GHESSE**	GINNERY	**GOALIE**	**GOONEY**	GRANDER
GAGGLES	GARBLER	**GAWKER**	GHESSED	**GIPSEN**	GOALIES	GOONEYS	**GRANGE**
GAINER	GARBLES	GAWKERS	GHESSES	GIPSENS	**GOANNA**	**GOOROO**	GRANGER
GAINERS	**GARCON**		**GHETTO**	**GIRDER**	GOANNAS	GOOROOS	GRANGES

GRAPLE	GROCERS	GUISER	GYMBALS	HAIQUES	HANGARS	HARTENS	HEALER
GRAPLES	GROCERY	GUISERS	GYMMAL	HAIRED	HANGED	HASHES	HEALERS
GRAPPA	GROMET	GUISES	GYMMALS	CHAIRED	CHANGED	SHASHES	HEALTH
GRAPPAS	GROMETS	AGUISES	GYNNEY	HAIRST	PHANGED	HASLET	HEALTHS
GRASTE	GROOVE	GUITAR	GYNNEYS	HAIRSTS	WHANGED	HASLETS	HEALTHY
AGRASTE	GROOVED	GUITARS	GYPPIE	HALERS	HANGER	HASSAR	HEARER
GRATER	GROOVES	GUIZER	GYPPIES	THALERS	CHANGER	HASSARS	SHEARER
GRATERS	GROPER	GUIZERS	GYPSUM	WHALERS	HANGERS	HASSLE	HEARERS
GRAVEL	GROPERS	GULDEN	GYPSUMS	HALIDE	HANJAR	HASSLED	HEARSE
GRAVELS	GROSER	GULDENS	GYRATE	HALIDES	KHANJAR	HASSLES	HEARSED
GRAVELY	GROSERS	GULLER	GYRATED	HALING	HANJARS	HASTED	HEARSES
GRAVER	GROSERT	GULLERS	GYRATES	SHALING	HANKED	GHASTED	HEARTH
GRAVERS	GROSET	GULLERY	HABOOB	WHALING	SHANKED	HASTEN	HEARTHS
GRAVES	GROSETS	GULLET	HABOOBS	HALITE	THANKED	CHASTEN	HEASTE
GRAVEST	GROTTO	GULLETS	HACHIS	HALITES	HANKER	HASTENS	HEASTES
GRAYLE	GROTTOS	GULLEY	RHACHIS	HALLAL	THANKER	HATFUL	HEATED
GRAYLES	GROUCH	GULLEYS	HACKED	HALLALI	HANKERS	HATFULS	CHEATED
GRAZER	GROUCHY	GULPER	CHACKED	HALLALS	HANKIE	HATPEG	HEATER
GRAZERS	GROUND	GULPERS	WHACKED	HALLAN	HANKIES	HATPEGS	CHEATER
GREASE	AGROUND	GUMNUT	HACKEE	CHALLAN	HANSEL	HATPIN	THEATER
GREASED	GROUNDS	GUMNUTS	HACKEES	HALLANS	HANSELS	HATPINS	HEATERS
GREASER	GROUSE	GUNITE	HACKER	HALLOA	HANSOM	HATRED	HEATHS
GREASES	GROUSED	GUNITES	WHACKER	HALLOAS	HANSOMS	HATREDS	SHEATHS
GREAVE	GROUSER	GUNNEL	HACKERS	HALLOO	HANTLE	HATTED	HEATHY
GREAVED	GROUSES	GUNNELS	HACKERY	HALLOOS	HANTLES	CHATTED	SHEATHY
GREAVES	GROVEL	GUNNER	HACKLE	HALLOW	HAPPED	HATTER	HEAUME
GREECE	GROVELS	GUNNERA	SHACKLE	SHALLOW	CHAPPED	CHATTER	HEAUMES
GREECES	GROWER	GUNNERS	HACKLED	HALLOWS	WHAPPED	SHATTER	HEAVED
GREESE	GROWERS	GUNNERY	HACKLER	HALOID	HAPPEN	HATTERS	SHEAVED
GREESES	GROWTH	GUNSEL	HACKLES	HALOIDS	HAPPENS	HAUGHT	HEAVEN
GREETE	GROWTHS	GUNSELS	HACKLET	HALSER	HAPTIC	HAUGHTY	HEAVENS
GREETED	GROYNE	GUNTER	HADDIE	HALSERS	HAPTICS	HAULER	HEAVER
GREETES	GROYNES	GUNTERS	HADDIES	HALTER	HARBOR	HAULERS	HEAVERS
GRICER	GRUDGE	GUNYAH	HADING	HALTERS	HARBORS	HAUNTS	HEAVES
GRICERS	GRUDGED	GUNYAHS	SHADING	HALVAH	HARDEN	CHAUNTS	SHEAVES
GRIECE	GRUDGES	GURAMI	HADITH	HALVAHS	HARDENS	HAUYNE	THEAVES
GRIECED	GRUMPH	GURAMIS	HADITHS	HALVER	HAREEM	HAUYNES	HEBONA
GRIECES	GRUMPHS	GURGLE	HADRON	HALVERS	HAREEMS	HAVERS	HEBONAS
GRIEVE	GRYFON	GURGLED	HADRONS	HAMBLE	HARELD	SHAVERS	HECKLE
GRIEVED	GRYFONS	GURGLES	HAEMIN	SHAMBLE	HARELDS	HAVING	HECKLED
GRIEVER	GUANAS	GURJUN	HAEMINS	HAMBLED	HARING	SHAVING	HECKLER
GRIEVES	IGUANAS	GURJUNS	HAFFET	HAMBLES	CHARING	HAVINGS	HECKLES
GRIFFE	GUANIN	GURLET	HAFFETS	HAMING	SHARING	HAWING	HECTIC
GRIFFES	GUANINE	GURLETS	HAFFIT	SHAMING	HARKED	CHAWING	HECTICS
GRIGRI	GUANINS	GURNET	HAFFITS	HAMLET	CHARKED	SHAWING	HECTOR
GRIGRIS	GUBBAH	GURNETS	HAFTED	CHAMLET	SHARKED	THAWING	HECTORS
GRILLE	GUBBAHS	GURNEY	SHAFTED	HAMLETS	HARKEN	HAWKER	HEDDLE
GRILLED	GUDDLE	GURNEYS	HAGBUT	HAMMAL	HARKENS	HAWKERS	HEDDLED
GRILLES	GUDDLED	GURRAH	HAGBUTS	HAMMALS	HARLOT	HAWKEY	HEDDLES
GRILSE	GUDDLES	GURRAHS	HAGDEN	HAMMAM	HARLOTS	HAWKEYS	HEDGER
GRILSES	GUENON	GUSHER	HAGDENS	HAMMAMS	HARMAN	HAWKIE	HEDGERS
GRINGO	GUENONS	GUSHERS	HAGDON	HAMMED	HARMANS	HAWKIES	HEEHAW
GRINGOS	GUFFAW	GUSLAR	HAGDONS	SHAMMED	HARMED	HAWSER	HEEHAWS
GRIPER	GUFFAWS	GUSLARS	HAGGED	WHAMMED	CHARMED	HAWSERS	HEELED
GRIPERS	GUGGLE	GUSSET	SHAGGED	HAMMER	HARMEL	HAYING	SHEELED
GRIPPE	GUGGLED	GUSSETS	HAGGIS	SHAMMER	HARMELS	HAYINGS	WHEELED
GRIPPED	GUGGLES	GUTTER	HAGGISH	HAMMERS	HARMIN	HAYMOW	HEELER
GRIPPER	GUIDER	GUTTERS	HAGGLE	HAMPER	HARMINE	HAYMOWS	WHEELER
GRIPPES	GUIDERS	GUTTLE	HAGGLED	HAMPERS	HARMING	HAYSEL	HEELERS
GRISED	GUIDON	GUTTLED	HAGGLER	HAMZAH	HARMINS	HAYSELS	HEEZED
AGRISED	GUIDONS	GUTTLES	HAGGLES	HAMZAHS	HARPED	HAZARD	PHEEZED
GRISES	GUILER	GUTZER	HAGLET	HANCES	SHARPED	HAZARDS	WHEEZED
AGRISES	GUILERS	GUTZERS	HAGLETS	CHANCES	HARPER	HAZELS	HEEZES
GRISON	GUIMPE	GUYLER	HAIDUK	HANDER	SHARPER	GHAZELS	PHEEZES
GRISONS	GUIMPED	GUYLERS	HAIDUKS	HANDERS	HARPERS	HAZING	WHEEZES
GRIVET	GUIMPES	GUZZLE	HAILER	HANDLE	HARROW	HAZINGS	HEEZIE
GRIVETS	GUINEA	GUZZLED	HAILERS	HANDLED	HARROWS	HEADER	HEEZIES
GRIZES	GUINEAS	GUZZLER	HAINED	HANDLER	HARTAL	HEADERS	HEGIRA
AGRIZES	GUISED	GUZZLES	CHAINED	HANDLES	HARTALS	HEALED	HEGIRAS
GROCER	AGUISED	GYMBAL	HAIQUE	HANGAR	HARTEN	SHEALED	HEIFER

HEIFERS	THERMAE	SHILLED	HOBDAYS	**HOMING**	**HORSON**	**HUMECT**	HUSTLES
HEIGHT	**HERMIT**	**HINDER**	**HOBJOB**	HOMINGS	HORSONS	HUMECTS	**HUZOOR**
AHEIGHT	HERMITS	HINDERS	HOBJOBS	**HONEST**	**HOSIER**	**HUMHUM**	HUZOORS
HEIGHTS	**HERNIA**	**HINGED**	**HOBNOB**	HONESTY	HOSIERS	HUMHUMS	**HYAENA**
HEISTS	HERNIAL	WHINGED	HOBNOBS	**HONEYS**	HOSIERY	**HUMITE**	HYAENAS
THEISTS	HERNIAS	**HINGES**	**HOCKED**	PHONEYS	**HOSTED**	HUMITES	**HYBRID**
HEJIRA	**HEROIC**	WHINGES	CHOCKED	**HONIED**	GHOSTED	**HUMLIE**	HYBRIDS
HEJIRAS	HEROICS	**HIPPED**	SHOCKED	PHONIED	**HOSTEL**	HUMLIES	**HYDRIA**
HELIUM	**HEROIN**	CHIPPED	**HOCKER**	**HONING**	HOSTELS	**HUMMED**	HYDRIAE
HELIUMS	HEROINE	SHIPPED	CHOCKER	PHONING	**HOTBED**	CHUMMED	HYDRIAS
HELLED	HEROINS	WHIPPED	SHOCKER	**HONKER**	HOTBEDS	**HUMMEL**	**HYDYNE**
SHELLED	**HEROON**	**HIPPER**	HOCKERS	HONKERS	**HOTPOT**	HUMMELS	HYDYNES
HELLER	HEROONS	CHIPPER	**HOCKEY**	**HONKIE**	HOTPOTS	**HUMMER**	**HYLISM**
SHELLER	**HETHER**	SHIPPER	HOCKEYS	HONKIES	**HOTTED**	HUMMERS	HYLISMS
HELLERS	THETHER	WHIPPER	**HODDEN**	**HONOUR**	SHOTTED	**HUMMUM**	**HYLIST**
HELMED	WHETHER	**HIPPIE**	HODDENS	HONOURS	**HOTTER**	HUMMUMS	HYLISTS
WHELMED	**HETMAN**	CHIPPIE	**HODDLE**	**HOODOO**	HOTTERS	**HUMOUR**	**HYMNAL**
HELMET	HETMANS	HIPPIER	HODDLED	HOODOOS	**HOTTIE**	HUMOURS	HYMNALS
HELMETS	**HEUCHS**	HIPPIES	HODDLES	**HOOFER**	HOTTIES	**HUMPED**	**HYPATE**
HELPED	SHEUCHS	**HIPPOS**	**HODJAS**	HOOFERS	**HOUDAH**	THUMPED	HYPATES
WHELPED	**HEUGHS**	SHIPPOS	KHODJAS	**HOOKAH**	HOUDAHS	**HUMPEN**	**HYPHEN**
HELPER	SHEUGHS	**HIRING**	**HOEING**	HOOKAHS	**HOUDAN**	HUMPENS	HYPHENS
HELPERS	WHEUGHS	HIRINGS	SHOEING	**HOOKER**	HOUDANS	**HUNGER**	**HYPNIC**
HELVED	**HEWING**	**HIRPLE**	**HOGGED**	HOOKERS	**HOUGHS**	HUNGERS	HYPNICS
SHELVED	CHEWING	HIRPLED	SHOGGED	**HOOKEY**	CHOUGHS	**HUNGRY**	**HYPNUM**
HELVES	SHEWING	HIRPLES	**HOGGER**	HOOKEYS	SHOUGHS	AHUNGRY	HYPNUMS
SHELVES	WHEWING	**HIRSEL**	HOGGERS	**HOOLEY**	**HOUSED**	**HUNKER**	**HYSSOP**
THELVES	HEWINGS	HIRSELS	HOGGERY	HOOLEYS	CHOUSED	HUNKERS	HYSSOPS
HEMINA	**HEXACT**	**HIRSLE**	**HOGGET**	**HOOPED**	**HOUSEL**	**HUNTED**	**IAMBIC**
HEMINAS	HEXACTS	HIRSLED	HOGGETS	WHOOPED	HOUSELS	SHUNTED	IAMBICS
HENNER	**HEXANE**	HIRSLES	**HOGGIN**	**HOOPER**	**HOUSES**	**HUNTER**	**IBICES**
HENNERS	HEXANES	WHISHED	HOGGING	WHOOPER	CHOUSES	CHUNTER	VIBICES
HENNERY	**HEXENE**	**HISHES**	HOGGINS	HOOPERS	**HOVELS**	SHUNTER	**ICHING**
HENNIN	HEXENES	WHISHES	**HOGTIE**	**HOOPOE**	SHOVELS	HUNTERS	MICHING
HENNING	**HEXING**	**HISSED**	HOGTIED	HOOPOES	**HOVERS**	**HURDEN**	NICHING
HENNINS	HEXINGS	WHISSED	HOGTIES	**HOORAH**	SHOVERS	HURDENS	RICHING
HEPTAD	**HEXOSE**	**HISSES**	**HOIDEN**	HOORAHS	**HOVING**	**HURDLE**	**ICICLE**
HEPTADS	HEXOSES	WHISSES	HOIDENS	**HOORAY**	SHOVING	HURDLED	ICICLES
HERALD	**HEYDAY**	**HISTED**	**HOKIER**	HOORAYS	**HOWDAH**	HURDLER	**ICIEST**
HERALDS	HEYDAYS	WHISTED	CHOKIER	**HOOTED**	HOWDAHS	HURDLES	DICIEST
HERBAL	**HICCUP**	**HITHER**	**HOKING**	WHOOTED	**HOWDIE**	**HURLER**	RICIEST
HERBALS	HICCUPS	THITHER	CHOKING	**HOOTER**	HOWDIES	HURLERS	**ICINGS**
HERBAR	HICCUPY	WHITHER	**HOLDER**	HOOTERS	**HOWKER**	**HURLEY**	DICINGS
HERBARS	**HICKEY**	HITHERS	HOLDERS	**HOOVER**	HOWKERS	HURLEYS	**ICKERS**
HERBARY	HICKEYS	**HITTER**	**HOLIES**	HOOVERS	**HOWLER**	**HURRAH**	BICKERS
HERDEN	**HIDAGE**	CHITTER	HOLIEST	**HOPDOG**	HOWLERS	HURRAHS	DICKERS
HERDENS	HIDAGES	WHITTER	**HOLING**	HOPDOGS	**HOWLET**	**HURRAS**	KICKERS
HERDIC	**HIDDEN**	HITTERS	THOLING	**HOPPED**	HOWLETS	DHURRAS	LICKERS
HERDICS	CHIDDEN	**HIVERS**	HOLINGS	CHOPPED	**HOYDEN**	**HURRAY**	NICKERS
HEREAT	SHIDDER	SHIVERS	**HOLISM**	SHOPPED	HOYDENS	HURRAYS	PICKERS
THEREAT	WHIDDER	**HIVING**	WHOLISM	WHOPPED	**HUBBUB**	**HURTER**	RICKERS
WHEREAT	HIDDERS	CHIVING	HOLISMS	**HOPPER**	HUBBUBS	HURTERS	TICKERS
HEREBY	**HIDING**	**HIZZED**	**HOLIST**	CHOPPER	**HUCKLE**	**HURTLE**	WICKERS
THEREBY	CHIDING	WHIZZED	HOLISTS	SHOPPER	CHUCKLE	HURTLED	YICKERS
WHEREBY	HIDINGS	**HIZZES**	**HOLLER**	WHOPPER	HUCKLES	HURTLES	**ICKIER**
HEREIN	**HIGGLE**	PHIZZES	HOLLERS	HOPPERS	**HUDDLE**	**HUSHED**	DICKIER
THEREIN	HIGGLED	WHIZZES	**HOLLOA**	**HOPPLE**	HUDDLED	SHUSHED	PICKIER
WHEREIN	HIGGLER	**HOARSE**	HOLLOAS	HOPPLED	HUDDLES	**HUSHER**	**IDEATE**
HEREOF	HIGGLES	HOARSEN	**HOLLOW**	HOPPLES	**HUFFED**	HUSHERS	IDEATED
THEREOF	**HIGHER**	HOARSER	HOLLOWS	**HORKEY**	CHUFFED	**HUSHES**	IDEATES
WHEREOF	HIGHERS	**HOAXER**	**HOLMIA**	HORKEYS	**HUGGED**	SHUSHES	**IDLING**
HEREON	**HIGHTH**	HOAXERS	HOLMIAS	**HORNED**	CHUGGED	**HUSKER**	HIDLING
THEREON	HIGHTHS	**HOBBIT**	**HOMAGE**	THORNED	**HUMANE**	HUSKERS	KIDLING
WHEREON	**HIJACK**	HOBBITS	HOMAGED	**HORNER**	HUMANER	**HUSSAR**	SIDLING
HERETO	HIJACKS	**HOBBLE**	HOMAGER	HORNERS	**HUMBLE**	HUSSARS	**IFFIER**
THERETO	**HIJRAH**	HOBBLED	HOMAGES	**HORNET**	HUMBLED	**HUSSIF**	MIFFIER
WHERETO	HIJRAHS	HOBBLER	**HOMBRE**	HORNETS	HUMBLER	HUSSIFS	NIFFIER
HERIOT	**HILLED**	HOBBLES	HOMBRES	**HORROR**	HUMBLES	**HUSTLE**	**IGNARO**
HERIOTS	CHILLED	**HOBDAY**	**HOMELY**	HORRORS	**HUMBUG**	HUSTLED	IGNAROS
HERMAE			HOMELYN		HUMBUGS	HUSTLER	**IGNITE**

LIGNITE
IGNITED
IGNITER
IGNITES
IGNORE
SIGNORE
IGNORED
IGNORER
IGNORES
IGUANA
IGUANAS
ILEXES
SILEXES
ILICES
CILICES
ILLIAD
ILLIADS
ILLIPE
ILLIPES
ILLITE
TILLITE
ILLITES
ILLUDE
ILLUDED
ILLUDES
ILLUME
ILLUMED
ILLUMES
ILLUPI
ILLUPIS
IMBARK
IMBARKS
IMBARS
MIMBARS
IMBASE
IMBASED
IMBASES
IMBIBE
IMBIBED
IMBIBER
IMBIBES
IMBOSK
IMBOSKS
IMBRUE
IMBRUED
IMBRUES
IMMASK
IMMASKS
IMMUNE
IMMUNES
IMMURE
IMMURED
IMMURES
IMPACT
IMPACTS
IMPAIR
IMPAIRS
IMPALA
IMPALAS
IMPALE
IMPALED
IMPALES
IMPARK
IMPARKS
IMPARL
IMPARLS
IMPART
IMPARTS
IMPAVE
IMPAVED

IMPAVES
IMPAWN
IMPAWNS
IMPEDE
IMPEDED
IMPEDES
IMPEND
IMPENDS
IMPING
GIMPING
LIMPING
PIMPING
IMPINGE
IMPISH
WIMPISH
IMPLEX
SIMPLEX
IMPONE
IMPONED
IMPONES
IMPORT
IMPORTS
IMPOSE
IMPOSED
IMPOSER
IMPOSES
IMPOST
IMPOSTS
IMPUGN
IMPUGNS
IMPURE
IMPURER
IMPUTE
IMPUTED
IMPUTER
IMPUTES
INANES
INANEST
INCAGE
INCAGED
INCAGES
INCASE
PINCASE
INCASED
INCASES
INCAVE
INCAVED
INCAVES
INCEDE
INCEDED
INCEDES
INCEPT
INCEPTS
INCEST
INCESTS
INCHED
CINCHED
FINCHED
PINCHED
WINCHED
INCHES
CINCHES
FINCHES
LINCHES
PINCHES
WINCHES
INCISE
INCISED
INCISES
INCITE

ZINCITE
INCITED
INCITER
INCITES
INCLIP
INCLIPS
INCOME
INCOMER
INCOMES
INCUSE
INCUSED
INCUSES
INDABA
INDABAS
INDART
INDARTS
INDENE
INDENES
INDENT
INDENTS
INDICT
INDICTS
INDIGO
WINDIGO
INDIGOS
INDITE
INDITED
INDITER
INDITES
INDIUM
INDIUMS
INDOLE
INDOLES
INDOOR
INDOORS
INDUCE
INDUCED
INDUCER
INDUCES
INDUCT
INDUCTS
INDULT
INDULTS
INDUNA
INDUNAS
INFALL
INFALLS
INFAME
INFAMED
INFAMES
INFANT
INFANTA
INFANTE
INFANTS
INFARE
INFARES
INFECT
INFECTS
INFEFT
INFEFTS
INFEST
INFESTS
INFILL
INFILLS
INFLOW
INFLOWS
INFOLD
PINFOLD
INFOLDS
INFORM

INFORMS
INFULA
INFULAE
INFUSE
INFUSED
INFUSER
INFUSES
INGANS
FINGANS
INGATE
INGATES
INGENU
INGENUE
INGENUS
INGEST
INGESTA
INGESTS
INGINE
INGINES
INGLES
BINGLES
DINGLES
GINGLES
JINGLES
KINGLES
LINGLES
MINGLES
PINGLES
SINGLES
TINGLES
INGOES
DINGOES
JINGOES
LINGOES
PINGOES
INGOTS
INGULF
INGULFS
INHALE
INHALED
INHALER
INHALES
INHERE
INHERED
INHERES
INHOOP
INHOOPS
INHUME
INHUMED
INHUMES
INISLE
INISLED
INISLES
INJECT
INJECTS
INJURE
INJURED
INJURER
INJURES
INKERS
JINKERS
SINKERS
TINKERS
WINKERS
INKIER
DINKIER
KINKIER
PINKIER
SINKIER

ZINKIER
INKING
DINKING
FINKING
JINKING
KINKING
LINKING
PINKING
RINKING
SINKING
TINKING
WINKING
ZINKING
INKLED
TINKLED
INKLES
KINKLES
TINKLES
WINKLES
INKPOT
INKPOTS
INLACE
INLACED
INLACES
INLAND
INLANDS
INLIER
INLIERS
INLOCK
INLOCKS
INMATE
INMATES
INNATE
PINNATE
INNERS
DINNERS
FINNERS
GINNERS
PINNERS
SINNERS
TINNERS
WINNERS
INNING
BINNING
DINNING
GINNING
LINNING
PINNING
RINNING
SINNING
TINNING
WINNING
INNINGS
INROAD
INROADS
INSANE
INSANER
INSEAM
INSEAMS
INSECT
INSECTS
INSECTY
INSEEM
INSEEMS
INSERT
INSERTS
INSHIP
KINSHIP
INSHIPS
INSIDE

INSIDER
INSIDES
INSIST
INSISTS
INSOLE
INSOLES
INSOUL
INSOULS
INSPAN
INSPANS
INSTAL
INSTALL
INSTALS
INSTAR
INSTARS
INSTEP
INSTEPS
INSTIL
INSTILL
INSTILS
INSULA
INSULAE
INSULAR
INSULAS
INSULT
INSULTS
INSURE
INSURED
INSURER
INSURES
INTAKE
INTAKES
INTEND
INTENDS
INTENT
INTENTS
INTERN
INTERNE
INTERNS
INTERS
LINTERS
MINTERS
SINTERS
TINTERS
WINTERS
INTIMA
INTIMAE
INTINE
INTINES
INTOMB
INTOMBS
INTONE
INTONED
INTONER
INTONES
INTRON
INTRONS
INTUIT
INTUITS
INTUSE
INTUSES
INULAS
INULASE
INULIN
INULINS
INVADE
INVADED
INVADER
INVADES
INVENT

INVENTS
INVERT
INVERTS
INVEST
INVESTS
INVITE
INVITED
INVITEE
INVITER
INVITES
INVOKE
INVOKED
INVOKES
INWALL
INWALLS
INWARD
INWARDS
INWICK
INWICKS
INWIND
INWINDS
INWORK
INWORKS
INWOVE
INWOVEN
INWRAP
INWRAPS
INYALA
INYALAS
IODATE
IODATES
IODIDE
IODIDES
IODINE
IODINES
IODISE
IODISED
IODISES
IODISM
IODISMS
IODIZE
IODIZED
IODIZES
IOLITE
IOLITES
IONISE
LIONISE
IONISED
IONISER
IONISES
IONIUM
IONIUMS
IONIZE
LIONIZE
IONIZED
IONIZER
IONIZES
IONONE
IONONES
IPECAC
IPECACS
IRADES
TIRADES
IREFUL
DIREFUL
IRENIC
EIRENIC
SIRENIC
IRENICS
IRITIS

MIRITIS
IRKING
DIRKING
FIRKING
KIRKING
LIRKING
YIRKING
IRONER
IRONERS
IRRUPT
IRRUPTS
ISABEL
ISABELS
ISATIN
ISATINE
ISATINS
ISCHIA
ISCHIAL
ISLAND
ISLANDS
ISLING
AISLING
ISOBAR
ISOBARE
ISOBARS
ISOGON
ISOGONS
ISOHEL
ISOHELS
ISOMER
ISOMERE
ISOMERS
ISOPOD
ISOPODS
ISSUED
TISSUED
ISSUER
ISSUERS
ISSUES
TISSUES
ISTLES
MISTLES
ITALIC
ITALICS
ITCHED
BITCHED
DITCHED
HITCHED
MITCHED
PITCHED
WITCHED
ITCHES
AITCHES
BITCHES
DITCHES
FITCHES
HITCHES
MITCHES
PITCHES
TITCHES
WITCHES
IZARDS
LIZARDS
RIZARDS
VIZARDS
WIZARDS
IZZARD
DIZZARD
GIZZARD
IZZARDS

JABBER
JABBERS
JABBLE
JABBLED
JABBLES
JABIRU
JABIRUS
JACANA
JACANAS
JACKAL
JACKALS
JACKET
JACKETS
JAEGER
JAEGERS
JAGGER
JAGGERS
JAGGERY
JAGHIR
JAGHIRE
JAGHIRS
JAGUAR
JAGUARS
JAILER
JAILERS
JAILOR
JAILORS
JAMBEE
JAMBEES
JAMBER
JAMBERS
JAMBOK
SJAMBOK
JAMBOKS
JAMBUL
JAMBULS
JAMJAR
JAMJARS
JAMMER
JAMMERS
JAMPAN
JAMPANI
JAMPANS
JAMPOT
JAMPOTS
JANGLE
JANGLED
JANGLER
JANGLES
JANKER
JANKERS
JARFUL
JARFULS
JARGON
JARGONS
JAROOL
JAROOLS
JARRAH
JARRAHS
JARVEY
JARVEYS
JARVIE
JARVIES
JASPER
JASPERS
JASPERY
JATAKA
JATAKAS
JAUNCE
JAUNCED

JAUNCES
JAUNSE
JAUNSED
JAUNSES
JAWARI
JAWARIS
JAWING
JAWINGS
JEBELS
DJEBELS
JEELIE
JEELIED
JEELIES
JEERER
JEERERS
JEMIMA
JEMIMAS
JENNET
JENNETS
JERBIL
JERBILS
JERBOA
JERBOAS
JEREED
JEREEDS
JERKER
JERKERS
JERKIN
JERKING
JERKINS
JERQUE
JERQUED
JERQUER
JERQUES
JERSEY
JERSEYS
JESSIE
JESSIES
JESTEE
JESTEES
JESTER
JESTERS
JETSAM
JETSAMS
JETSOM
JETSOMS
JETSON
JETSONS
JETTON
JETTONS
JEZAIL
JEZAILS
JIBBAH
DJIBBAH
JIBBAHS
JIBBER
JIBBERS
JIGGER
JIGGERS
JIGGLE
JIGGLED
JIGGLES
JIGJIG
JIGJIGS
JIGSAW
JIGSAWN
JIGSAWS
JILGIE
JILGIES
JILLET

JILLETS
JIMJAM
JIMJAMS
JINGAL
JINGALS
JINGLE
JINGLED
JINGLER
JINGLES
JINGLET
JINKER
JINKERS
JIRBLE
JIRBLED
JIRBLES
JISSOM
JISSOMS
JITNEY
JITNEYS
JITTER
JITTERS
JITTERY
JOANNA
JOANNAS
JOBBER
JOBBERS
JOBBERY
JOCKEY
JOCKEYS
JOGGER
JOGGERS
JOGGLE
JOGGLED
JOGGLES
JOINER
JOINERS
JOINERY
JOJOBA
JOJOBAS
JOLTER
JOLTERS
JORDAN
JORDANS
JOSEPH
JOSEPHS
JOSHER
JOSHERS
JOSKIN
JOSKINS
JOSSER
JOSSERS
JOSTLE
JOSTLED
JOSTLES
JOTTER
JOTTERS
JOTUNN
JOTUNNS
JOUNCE
JOUNCED
JOUNCES
JOURNO
JOURNOS
JOWARI
JOWARIS
JOWLER
JOWLERS
JUBBAH
JUBBAHS
JUDDER

JUDDERS
JUDOGI
JUDOGIS
JUDOKA
JUDOKAS
JUGFUL
JUGFULS
JUGGLE
JUGGLED
JUGGLER
JUGGLES
JUICER
JUICERS
JUJUBE
JUJUBES
JUMART
JUMARTS
JUMBAL
JUMBALS
JUMBIE
JUMBIES
JUMBLE
JUMBLED
JUMBLER
JUMBLES
JUMPER
JUMPERS
JUNGLE
JUNGLES
JUNGLI
JUNGLIS
JUNIOR
JUNIORS
JUNKER
JUNKERS
JUNKET
JUNKETS
JUNKIE
JUNKIER
JUNKIES
JUPATI
JUPATIS
JURANT
JURANTS
JURIST
JURISTS
JUSTLE
JUSTLED
JUSTLES
KABALA
KABALAS
KABAYA
KABAYAS
KABELE
KABELES
KABUKI
KABUKIS
KACCHA
KACCHAS
KAFILA
KAFILAS
KAFTAN
KAFTANS
KAGOOL
KAGOOLS
KAGOUL
KAGOULE
KAGOULS
KAIKAI
KAIKAIS

KAISER
KAISERS
KAKAPO
KAKAPOS
KALIAN
KALIANS
KALIUM
KALIUMS
KALMIA
KALMIAS
KALONG
KALONGS
KALPAK
KALPAKS
KAMALA
KAMALAS
KAMELA
KAMELAS
KAMILA
KAMILAS
KAMSIN
KAMSINS
KANAKA
KANAKAS
KANGHA
KANGHAS
KANTAR
KANTARS
KANTEN
KANTENS
KANTHA
KANTHAS
KAOLIN
KAOLINE
KAOLINS
KARAIT
KARAITS
KARAKA
KARAKAS
KARATE
KARATES
KARITE
KARITES
KARSEY
KARSEYS
KASBAH
KASBAHS
KATANA
KATANAS
KATHAK
KATHAKS
KATION
KATIONS
KEASAR
KEASARS
KEBBIE
KEBBIES
KEBELE
KEBELES
KEBLAH
KEBLAHS
KECKLE
KECKLED
KECKLES
KEDDAH
KEDDAHS
KEDGER
KEDGERS
KEEKER
KEEKERS

KEELER
KEELERS
KEELIE
KEELIES
KEENER
KEENERS
KEEPER
KEEPERS
KEFFEL
KEFFELS
KEKSYE
KEKSYES
KELOID
KELOIDS
KELPER
KELPERS
KELPIE
KELPIES
KELSON
KELSONS
KELTER
SKELTER
KELTERS
KELTIE
KELTIES
KELVIN
KELVINS
KEMPER
KEMPERS
KEMPLE
KEMPLES
KENNEL
KENNELS
KENNER
KENNERS
KENNET
KENNETS
KEPHIR
KEPHIRS
KERMES
KERMESS
KERNEL
KERNELS
KERRIA
KERRIAS
KERSEY
KERSEYS
KETONE
KETONES
KETOSE
KETOSES
KETTLE
KETTLES
KGOTLA
KGOTLAS
KHALAT
KHALATS
KHALIF
KHALIFA
KHALIFS
KHANGA
KHANGAS
KHANUM
KHANUMS
KHARIF
KHARIFS
KHILAT
KHILATS
KHILIM
KHILIMS

KHODJA
KHODJAS
KHURTA
KHURTAS
KIAUGH
KIAUGHS
KIBBLE
KIBBLED
KIBBLES
KIBLAH
KIBLAHS
KICKER
KICKERS
KIDDED
SKIDDED
KIDDER
KIDDERS
KIDDLE
KIDDLES
KIDNAP
KIDNAPS
KIDNEY
KIDNEYS
KIERIE
KIERIES
KIKUYU
KIKUYUS
KILERG
KILERGS
KILLED
SKILLED
KILLER
KILLERS
KILLUT
KILLUTS
KILTER
KILTERS
KILTIE
KILTIES
KIMMER
KIMMERS
KIMONO
OKIMONO
KIMONOS
KINASE
KINASES
KINCOB
KINCOBS
KINDLE
KINDLED
KINDLER
KINDLES
KINEMA
KINEMAS
KINGLE
KINGLES
KINGLET
SKINKED
KINKLE
KINKLES
KINONE
KINONES
KINRED
KINREDS
KIPPED
SKIPPED
KIPPER
SKIPPER

KIPPERS
KIRBEH
KIRBEHS
KIRPAN
KIRPANS
KIRTLE
KIRTLED
KIRTLES
KISMET
KISMETS
KISSER
KISSERS
KITING
SKITING
KITSCH
KITSCHY
KITTEN
KITTENS
KITTENY
KITTLE
SKITTLE
KITTLED
KITTLER
KITTLES
KITTUL
KITTULS
KLAXON
KLAXONS
KLEPHT
KLEPHTS
KLUDGE
KLUDGES
KNAWEL
KNAWELS
KNIGHT
KNIGHTS
KNOWER
KNOWERS
KOBANG
KOBANGS
KOBOLD
KOBOLDS
KONFYT
KONFYTS
KOODOO
KOODOOS
KOOKIE
KOOKIER
KOOLAH
KOOLAHS
KOPECK
KOPECKS
KOPPIE
KOPPIES
KORKIR
KORKIRS
KORORA
KORORAS
KORUNA
KORUNAS
KOSHER
KOSHERS
KOTWAL
KOTWALS
KOULAN
KOULANS
KOWHAI
KOWHAIS
KOWTOW
KOWTOWS

KRAKEN	LADING	LANCERS	LARGESS	PLATTER	GLEAMED	LEFTIE	LETHEE
KRAKENS	LADINGS	LANCES	LARGEST	SLATTER	LEANED	LEFTIES	LETHEES
KREESE	LAGENA	ELANCES	LARIAT	LAUDED	CLEANED	LEGATE	LETTED
KREESED	LAGENAS	GLANCES	LARIATS	BLAUDED	GLEANED	LEGATEE	BLETTED
KREESES	LAGGED	LANCET	LARKER	LAUDER	LEANER	LEGATES	LETTER
KUFIAH	BLAGGED	LANCETS	LARKERS	LAUDERS	CLEANER	LEGATO	LETTERN
KUFIAHS	CLAGGED	LANDAU	LARRUP	LAUNCE	GLEANER	LEGATOR	LETTERS
KUFIYA	FLAGGED	LANDAUS	LARRUPS	LAUNCED	LEANLY	LEGATOS	LETTRE
KUFIYAH	SLAGGED	LANDER	LARUMS	LAUNCES	CLEANLY	LEGEND	LETTRES
KUFIYAS	LAGGEN	BLANDER	ALARUMS	LAUNCH	LEAPER	LEGENDS	LEUCIN
KUMARA	LAGGENS	SLANDER	LASCAR	FLAUNCH	LEAPERS	LEGGED	LEUCINE
KUMARAS	LAGGER	LANDERS	LASCARS	LAUREL	LEARED	ALEGGED	LEUCINS
KUMARI	LAGGERS	LANDES	LASERS	LAURELS	BLEARED	FLEGGED	LEVANT
KUMARIS	LAGGIN	GLANDES	FLASERS	LAVABO	CLEARED	LEGGER	LEVANTS
KUMMEL	LAGGING	LANGER	LASHED	LAVABOS	LEASED	GLEGGER	LEVINS
KUMMELS	LAGGINS	CLANGER	CLASHED	LAVAGE	PLEASED	LEGGERS	ALEVINS
KUNKAR	LAGOON	LANGUE	FLASHED	LAVAGES	LEASER	LEGGES	LEVITE
KUNKARS	LAGOONS	LANGUED	PLASHED	LAVEER	PLEASER	ALEGGES	LEVITES
KUNKUR	LAGUNE	LANGUES	SLASHED	LAVEERS	LEASERS	LEGION	LEXEME
KUNKURS	LAGUNES	LANGUET	LASHER	LAVERS	LEASES	LEGIONS	LEXEMES
KURGAN	LAIDED	LANGUR	FLASHER	CLAVERS	PLEASES	LEGIST	LIABLE
KURGANS	PLAIDED	LANGURS	SLASHER	SLAVERS	LEASOW	LEGISTS	PLIABLE
KURVEY	LAIRED	LANKED	LASHERS	LAVING	LEASOWE	LEGLAN	LIAISE
KURVEYS	GLAIRED	BLANKED	LASHES	SLAVING	LEASOWS	LEGLANS	LIAISED
KWACHA	LAISSE	CLANKED	BLASHES	LAVISH	LEAVED	LEGLEN	LIAISES
KWACHAS	LAISSES	FLANKED	CLASHES	SLAVISH	CLEAVED	LEGLENS	LIBATE
LAAGER	LAKIER	PLANKED	FLASHES	LAVOLT	SLEAVED	LEGLET	LIBATED
LAAGERS	FLAKIER	LANKER	PLASHES	LAVOLTA	LEAVEN	LEGLETS	LIBATES
LABIAL	LAKING	BLANKER	SLASHES	LAVOLTS	LEAVENS	LEGLIN	LIBBED
LABIALS	FLAKING	FLANKER	LASING	LAWING	LEAVES	LEGLINS	GLIBBED
LABLAB	SLAKING	LANKLY	LASINGS	CLAWING	CLEAVES	LEGUME	LIBBER
LABLABS	LALANG	BLANKLY	LASKET	FLAWING	GLEAVES	LEGUMES	GLIBBER
LABOUR	LALANGS	LANNER	LASKETS	LAWINGS	SLEAVES	LEIGER	LIBBERS
LABOURS	LALDIE	PLANNER	LASQUE	LAWYER	LEAZES	LEIGERS	LIBIDO
LABRET	LALDIES	LANNERS	LASQUES	LAWYERS	SLEAZES	LEIPOA	LIBIDOS
LABRETS	LALLAN	LANUGO	LASSES	LAXISM	LEBBEK	LEIPOAS	LIBKEN
LABRID	LALLANS	LANUGOS	CLASSES	LAXISMS	LEBBEKS	LEMING	LIBKENS
LABRIDS	LAMBDA	LAPDOG	GLASSES	LAXIST	LECHER	FLEMING	LICHEE
LACETS	LAMBDAS	LAPDOGS	LASSIE	LAXISTS	LECHERS	LENDER	LICHEES
PLACETS	LAMBER	LAPFUL	LASSIES	LAYERS	LECHERY	BLENDER	LICHEN
LACIER	CLAMBER	LAPFULS	LASTED	FLAYERS	LECHES	SLENDER	LICHENS
GLACIER	LAMBERS	LAPPED	BLASTED	PLAYERS	FLECHES	LENDERS	LICHES
LACING	LAMBERT	CLAPPED	LASTER	SLAYERS	LECHWE	LENGTH	CLICHES
PLACING	LAMBIE	FLAPPED	BLASTER	LAYING	LECHWES	ALENGTH	LICKED
LACINGS	LAMBIES	PLAPPED	PLASTER	ALAYING	LECTIN	LENGTHS	CLICKED
LACKED	LAMENT	SLAPPED	LASTERS	CLAYING	LECTINS	LENGTHY	FLICKED
BLACKED	LAMENTS	LAPPEL	LATENS	FLAYING	LECTOR	LENSES	SLICKED
CLACKED	LAMINA	LAPPELS	PLATENS	PLAYING	ELECTOR	FLENSES	LICKER
SLACKED	LAMINAE	LAPPER	LATEST	SLAYING	LECTORS	LENTIL	CLICKER
LACKER	LAMINAR	CLAPPER	LATESTS	LAYINGS	LEDDEN	LENTILS	FLICKER
BLACKER	LAMING	FLAPPER	LATHEE	LAZIER	LEDDENS	LENTOR	SLICKER
CLACKER	BLAMING	LAPPERS	LATHEES	GLAZIER	LEDGER	LENTORS	LICKERS
FLACKER	FLAMING	LAPPET	LATHER	LAZING	PLEDGER	LENVOY	LICTOR
SLACKER	LAMMED	LAPPETS	BLATHER	BLAZING	SLEDGER	LENVOYS	LICTORS
LACKERS	CLAMMED	LAPPIE	SLATHER	GLAZING	LEDGERS	LEPTON	LIDGER
LACKEY	FLAMMED	LAPPIES	LATHERS	LEADED	LEDGES	LEPTONS	LIDGERS
LACKEYS	SLAMMED	LAPSED	LATHERY	PLEADED	FLEDGES	LESION	LIEGER
LACUNA	LAMMER	ELAPSED	LATRIA	LEADEN	GLEDGES	LESIONS	LIEGERS
LACUNAE	SLAMMER	LAPSES	LATRIAS	LEADENS	PLEDGES	LESSEE	LIERNE
LACUNAL	LAMMERS	ELAPSES	LATRON	LEADER	SLEDGES	LESSEES	LIERNES
LACUNAR	LAMMIE	LAPTOP	LATRONS	PLEADER	LEEING	LESSEN	LIFTED
LADDER	LAMMIES	LAPTOPS	LATTEN	LEADERS	FLEEING	LESSENS	CLIFTED
BLADDER	LAMPAD	LARDER	FLATTEN	LEAGUE	GLEEING	LESSES	LIFTER
CLADDER	LAMPADS	LARDERS	LATTENS	LEAGUED	LEEPED	BLESSES	LIFTERS
GLADDER	LAMPED	LARDON	LATTER	LEAGUER	BLEEPED	LESSON	LIGAND
LADDERS	CLAMPED	LARDONS	BLATTER	LEAGUES	CLEEPED	LESSONS	LIGANDS
LADDERY	LANCED	LARGEN	CLATTER	LEAKER	LEERED	LESSOR	LIGATE
LADDIE	ELANCED	LARGENS	BLATTER	BLEAKER	FLEERED	PLESSOR	LIGATED
GLADDIE	GLANCED	LARGES	FLATTER	LEAKERS	LEEWAY	LESSORS	LIGATES
LADDIES	LANCER			LEAMED	LEEWAYS		LIGGER

LIGGERS
LIGHTS
ALIGHTS
BLIGHTS
FLIGHTS
PLIGHTS
SLIGHTS
LIGNIN
LIGNINS
LIGNUM
LIGNUMS
LIGULA
LIGULAE
LIGULAR
LIGULAS
LIGULE
LIGULES
LIGURE
LIGURES
LIKING
LIKINGS
LIMAIL
LIMAILS
LIMBEC
LIMBECK
LIMBECS
LIMBED
CLIMBED
LIMBER
CLIMBER
LIMBERS
LIMIER
SLIMIER
LIMING
SLIMING
LIMINGS
LIMMER
GLIMMER
SLIMMER
LIMMERS
LIMNER
LIMNERS
LIMPED
FLIMPED
LIMPET
LIMPETS
LINAGE
LINAGES
LINDEN
LINDENS
LINGAM
LINGAMS
LINGEL
LINGELS
LINGER
CLINGER
FLINGER
SLINGER
LINGERS
LINGLE
LINGLES
LINGOT
LINGOTS
LINGUA
LINGUAE
LINGUAL
LINGUAS
LINHAY
LINHAYS
LINING

ALINING
LININGS
LINKED
BLINKED
CLINKED
PLINKED
LINNED
BLINNED
LINNET
LINNETS
LINNEY
LINNEYS
LINSEY
LINSEYS
LINTEL
LINTELS
LINTER
LINTERS
LINTIE
LINTIER
LINTIES
LIONEL
LIONELS
LIONET
LIONETS
LIPASE
LIPASES
LIPIDE
LIPIDES
LIPOID
LIPOIDS
LIPPED
BLIPPED
CLIPPED
FLIPPED
SLIPPED
LIPPEN
LIPPENS
LIPPIE
CLIPPIE
LIPPIER
LIPPIES
LIQUID
LIQUIDS
LIQUOR
LIQUORS
LISPER
LISPERS
LISSES
BLISSES
LISSOM
LISSOME
LISTEL
LISTELS
LISTEN
GLISTEN
LISTENS
LISTER
BLISTER
GLISTER
LISTERS
LINGOT (LITCHI)
LITCHIS
LITHER
BLITHER
SLITHER
LITHES
LITHEST
LITHIA
LITHIAS

LITING
FLITING
LITTER
CLITTER
FLITTER
GLITTER
SLITTER
LITTERS
LITTERY
LITTLE
LITTLER
LITTLES
LIVERS
CLIVERS
OLIVERS
SLIVERS
LIVING
SLIVING
LIVINGS
LIZARD
LIZARDS
LOADEN
LOADENS
LOADER
LOADERS
LOAFER
LOAFERS
LOATHE
LOATHED
LOATHER
LOATHES
LOBATE
GLOBATE
LOBBED
BLOBBED
LOBING
GLOBING
LOBINGS
LOBOSE
GLOBOSE
LOBULE
GLOBULE
LOBULES
LOCALE
LOCALES
LOCATE
LOCATED
LOCATES
LOCHAN
LOCHANS
LOCHIA
LOCHIAL
LOCKED
BLOCKED
CLOCKED
FLOCKED
LOCKER
BLOCKER
CLOCKER
LOCKERS
LOCKET
LOCKETS
LOCULE
LOCULES
LOCUST
LOCUSTA
LOCUSTS
LODGER
LODGERS
LOFTER

LOFTERS
LOGANS
SLOGANS
LOGGAT
LOGGATS
LOGGED
FLOGGED
SLOGGED
LOGGER
CLOGGER
SLOGGER
LOGGERS
LOGGIA
LOGGIAS
LOGIES
ELOGIES
OLOGIES
LOGLOG
LOGLOGS
LOITER
LOITERS
LOLLER
LOLLERS
LOLLOP
LOLLOPS
LOMENT
LOMENTA
LOMENTS
LONELY
ALONELY
LONGAN
LONGANS
LONGED
PLONGED
LONGES
PLONGES
LONGEST
LOOFAH
LOOFAHS
LOOKER
LOOKERS
LOOMED
BLOOMED
GLOOMED
SLOOMED
LOONIE
LOONIER
LOONIES
LOOPED
BLOOPED
LOOPER
BLOOPER
LOOPERS
LOOSEN
LOOSENS
LOOSES
LOOSEST
LOOTER
LOOTERS
LOPERS
ELOPERS
LOPING
ELOPING
SLOPING
LOPPED
CLOPPED
FLOPPED
PLOPPED
SLOPPED

LOPPER
LOPPERS
LOQUAT
LOQUATS
LORCHA
LORCHAS
LORICA
LORICAE
LORIES
GLORIES
LORING
LORINGS
LORIOT
LORIOTS
LOSERS
CLOSERS
LOSING
CLOSING
LOSINGS
LOSSES
FLOSSES
GLOSSES
LOTION
LOTIONS
LOTTED
BLOTTED
CLOTTED
PLOTTED
SLOTTED
LOUDEN
LOUDENS
LOUGHS
CLOUGHS
PLOUGHS
SLOUGHS
LOUNGE
LOUNGED
LOUNGER
LOUNGES
LOURED
CLOURED
FLOURED
LOUSED
BLOUSED
FLOUSED
LOUSES
BLOUSES
FLOUSES
LOUTED
CLOUTED
FLOUTED
GLOUTED
LOUVER
LOUVERS
LOUVRE
LOUVRED
LOUVRES
LOVAGE
LOVAGES
LOVERS
CLOVERS
GLOVERS
PLOVERS
LOVING
GLOVING
LOVINGS
LOWBOY
LOWBOYS
LOWERS
BLOWERS

FLOWERS
GLOWERS
LOWERY
FLOWERY
LOWEST
SLOWEST
LOWING
BLOWING
FLOWING
GLOWING
PLOWING
SLOWING
LOWINGS
CLOWNED
LOWNED
LOWNES
LOWNESS
LOWSES
BLOWSES
LOWSEST
LOZELL
LOZELLS
LUBBER
BLUBBER
SLUBBER
LUBBERS
LUCERN
LUCERNE
LUCERNS
LUCKIE
LUCKIER
LUCKIES
LUCUMA
LUCUMAS
LUCUMO
LUCUMOS
LUFFED
BLUFFED
FLUFFED
PLUFFED
LUGGED
GLUGGED
PLUGGED
SLUGGED
LUGGER
PLUGGER
SLUGGER
LUGGERS
LUGGIE
LUGGIES
LUGING
LUGINGS
LUMBER
CLUMBER
PLUMBER
SLUMBER
LUMBERS
LUMINA
ALUMINA
LUMINAL
LUMINE
LUMINED
LUMINES
LUMMOX
FLUMMOX
LUMPED
CLUMPED
FLUMPED
PLUMPED
SLUMPED

LUMPEN
PLUMPEN
LUMPER
PLUMPER
LUMPERS
LUNATE
LUNATED
LUNGED
BLUNGED
PLUNGED
LUNGES
BLUNGES
PLUNGES
LUNGIE
LUNGIES
LUNKER
BLUNKER
PLUNKER
LUNKERS
LUNTED
BLUNTED
LUNULA
LUNULAR
LUNULAS
LUNULE
LUNULES
LUNYIE
LUNYIES
LUPINE
LUPINES
LURDAN
LURDANE
LURDANS
LURDEN
LURDENS
LURKER
LURKERS
LUSHED
BLUSHED
FLUSHED
SLUSHED
LUSHER
BLUSHER
FLUSHER
PLUSHER
LUSHERS
LUSHES
BLUSHES
FLUSHES
PLUSHES
SLUSHES
LUSHEST
LUSTER
BLUSTER
CLUSTER
FLUSTER
LUSTERS
LUSTRA
LUSTRAL
LUSTRE
LUSTRED
LUSTRES
LUTEAL
GLUTEAL
PLUTEAL
LUTEIN
LUTEINS
LUTERS
FLUTERS
LUTING

ELUTING
FLUTING
LUTINGS
LUTIST
LUTISTS
FLUTIST
FLUTISTS
LUTZES
KLUTZES
LUXATE
LUXATED
LUXATES
LUZERN
LUZERNS
LYCEUM
LYCEUMS
LYCHEE
LYCHEES
LYINGS
FLYINGS
LYNAGE
LYNAGES
LYRATE
LYRATED
LYRISM
LYRISMS
LYRIST
LYRISTS
LYSINE
LYSINES
LYTING
FLYTING
MACACO
MACACOS
MACHAN
MACHANS
MACKLE
MACKLED
MACKLES
MACOYA
MACOYAS
MACRON
MACRONS
MACULA
MACULAE
MACULAR
MACULE
MACULES
MADAME
MADAMED
MADCAP
MADCAPS
MADDEN
MADDENS
MADDER
MADDERS
MADRAS
MADRASA
MAENAD
MAENADS
MAFFIA
MAFFIAS
MAGGOT
MAGGOTS
MAGGOTY
MAGIAN
MAGIANS
MAGILP
MAGILPS
MAGISM
IMAGISM

MAGISMS
MAGNET
MAGNETO
MAGNETS
MAGNUM
MAGNUMS
MAGPIE
MAGPIES
MAGUEY
MAGUEYS
MAHMAL
MAHMALS
MAHOUT
MAHOUTS
MAHSIR
MAHSIRS
MAIDAN
MAIDANS
MAIDEN
MAIDENS
MAIGRE
MAIGRES
MAILER
MAILERS
MAINOR
MAINORS
MAKING
MAKINGS
MALATE
MALATES
MALGRE
MALGRES
MALICE
MALICED
MALICES
MALIGN
MALIGNS
MALKIN
MALKINS
MALLAM
MALLAMS
MALLED
SMALLED
MALLEE
MALLEES
MALLET
MALLETS
MALLOW
MALLOWS
MALMAG
MALMAGS
MALTHA
MALTHAS
MAMMAL
MAMMALS
MAMMEE
MAMMEES
MAMMER
MAMMERS
MAMMET
MAMMETS
MAMMON
MAMMONS
MANAGE
MANAGED
MANAGER
MANAGES
MANANA
MANANAS
MANATI

MANATIS
MANCHE
MANCHES
MANCHET
MANDIR
MANDIRA
MANDIRS
MANDOM
MANDOMS
MANEGE
MANEGED
MANEGES
MANGAL
MANGALS
MANGEL
MANGELS
MANGER
MANGERS
MANGLE
MANGLED
MANGLER
MANGLES
MANIAC
MANIACS
MANILA
MANILAS
MANIOC
MANIOCS
MANITO
MANITOS
MANITOU
MANNER
MANNERS
MANOAO
MANOAOS
MANRED
MANREDS
MANTEL
MANTELS
MANTID
MANTIDS
MANTLE
MANTLED
MANTLES
MANTLET
MANTRA
MANTRAM
MANTRAP
MANTRAS
MANTUA
MANTUAS
MANUAL
MANUALS
MANUKA
MANUKAS
MANURE
MANURED
MANURER
MANURES
MAPPER
MAPPERS
MAPPERY
MARACA
MARACAS
MARAUD
MARAUDS
MARBLE
MARBLED
MARBLER
MARBLES

MARCEL
MARCELS
MARGAY
MARGAYS
MARGIN
MARGINS
MARINA
MARINAS
MARINE
MARINER
MARINES
MARKER
MARKERS
MARKET
MARKETS
MARKKA
MARKKAA
MARKKAS
MARLIN
MARLINE
MARLING
MARLINS
MARMOT
MARMOTS
MAROON
MAROONS
MARQUE
MARQUEE
MARQUES
MARRAM
MARRAMS
MARROW
MARROWS
MARROWY
MARRUM
MARRUMS
MARTED
SMARTED
MARTEL
MARTELS
MARTEN
SMARTEN
MARTENS
MARTIN
MARTING
MARTINI
MARTINS
MARTYR
MARTYRS
MARTYRY
MARVEL
MARVELS
MASCLE
MASCLED
MASCLES
MASCON
MASCONS
MASCOT
MASCOTS
MASHED
SMASHED
MASHER
SMASHER
MASHERS
MASHES
SMASHES
MASHIE
MASHIER
MASHIES
MASJID

MASJIDS
MASKER
MASKERS
MASLIN
MASLINS
MASQUE
MASQUER
MASQUES
MASSED
AMASSED
MASSES
AMASSES
MASSIF
MASSIFS
MASTER
MASTERS
MASTERY
MASTIC
MASTICH
MASTICS
MASULA
MASULAS
MATICO
MATICOS
MATING
AMATING
MATLOW
MATLOWS
MATRIC
MATRICE
MATRICS
MATRON
MATRONS
MATTER
SMATTER
MATTERS
MATTERY
MATTIE
MATTIES
MATURE
MATURED
MATURER
MATURES
MATZAH
MATZAHS
MATZOT
MATZOTH
MAUGRE
MAUGRES
MAULVI
MAULVIS
MAUMET
MAUMETS
MAUVES
MAUVEST
MAUVIN
MAUVINE
MAUVINS
MAWKIN
MAWKINS
MAWMET
MAWMETS
MAXIMA
MAXIMAL
MAXIXE
MAXIXES
MAYDAY
MAYDAYS
MAYHEM
MAYHEMS

MAYING
MAYINGS
MAZARD
MAZARDS
MAZHBI
MAZHBIS
MAZING
AMAZING
MAZOUT
MAZOUTS
MAZUMA
MAZUMAS
MEADOW
MEADOWS
MEADOWY
MEAGRE
MEAGRER
MEAGRES
MEALER
MEALERS
MEALIE
MEALIER
MEALIES
MEANES
MEANEST
MEANIE
MEANIES
MEASLE
MEASLED
MEASLES
MEATHE
MEATHES
MEATHS
SMEATHS
MEAZEL
MEAZELS
MEDDLE
MEDDLED
MEDDLER
MEDDLES
MEDIAL
MEDIALS
MEDIAN
MEDIANS
MEDIANT
MEDICK
MEDICKS
MEDICO
MEDICOS
MEDINA
MEDINAS
MEDIUM
MEDIUMS
MEDLAR
MEDLARS
MEDLEY
MEDLEYS
MEDUSA
MEDUSAE
MEDUSAN
MEDUSAS
MEEKEN
MEEKENS
MEGARA
MEGARAD
MEGASS
MEGASSE
MEGILP
MEGILPS
MEGOHM

MEGOHMS
MEGRIM
MEGRIMS
MEINEY
MEINEYS
MEINIE
MEINIES
MELANO
MELANOS
MELDER
MELDERS
MELLAY
MELLAYS
MELLED
SMELLED
MELLOW
MELLOWS
MELLOWY
MELTED
SMELTED
MELTON
MELTONS
MEMBER
MEMBERS
MEMOIR
MEMOIRS
MENACE
MENACED
MENACER
MENACES
MENAGE
AMENAGE
MENAGES
MENDED
AMENDED
EMENDED
MENDER
AMENDER
MENDERS
MENEER
MENEERS
MENHIR
MENHIRS
MENIAL
MENIALS
MENING
AMENING
OMENING
MENTAL
AMENTAL
OMENTAL
MENTOR
MENTORS
MENTUM
AMENTUM
OMENTUM
MENTUMS
MERCAT
MERCATS
MERCER
MERCERS
MERCERY
MERELL
MERELLS
MERGED
EMERGED
MERGER
MERGERS
MERGES
EMERGES

MERINO
MERINOS
MERISM
MERISMS
MERKIN
MERKINS
MERLIN
MERLING
MERLINS
MERLON
MERLONS
MEROME
MEROMES
MESAIL
MESAILS
MESCAL
MESCALS
MESSAN
MESSANS
MESTEE
MESTEES
METAGE
METAGES
METEOR
METEORS
METHOD
METHODS
METHYL
METHYLS
METICS
EMETICS
METIER
METIERS
METOPE
METOPES
METRIC
METRICS
METTLE
METTLED
METTLES
MEUSES
SMEUSES
MEZAIL
MEZAILS
MEZUZA
MEZUZAH
MGANGA
MGANGAS
MIASMA
MIASMAL
MIASMAS
MICATE
EMICATE
MICATED
MICATES
MICHER
MICHERS
MICKEY
MICKEYS
MICKLE
MICKLES
MICRON
OMICRON
MICRONS
MIDDAY
MIDDAYS
MIDDEN
MIDDENS
MIDDLE
MIDDLED

MIDDLES
MIDGET
MIDGETS
MIDRIB
MIDRIBS
MIDWAY
MIDWAYS
MIGHTS
SMIGHTS
MIGHTST
MIHRAB
MIHRABS
MIKADO
MIKADOS
MIKRON
MIKRONS
MILADI
MILADIS
MILAGE
MILAGES
MILDEN
MILDENS
MILDEW
MILDEWS
MILDEWY
MILERS
SMILERS
MILIEU
MILIEUS
MILIEUX
MILKER
MILKERS
MILLER
MILLERS
MILLET
MILLETS
MILORD
MILORDS
MILSEY
MILSEYS
MILTER
MILTERS
MIMBAR
MIMBARS
MIMOSA
MIMOSAS
MINBAR
MINBARS
MINCER
MINCERS
MINDER
MINDERS
MINGLE
MINGLED
MINGLER
MINGLES
MINIMA
MINIMAL
MINING
MININGS
MINION
MINIONS
MINIUM
MINIUMS
MINNIE
MINNIES
MINNOW
MINNOWS
MINTER
MINTERS

MINUET	MIZZENS	MONGER	MORTAL	MOUTONS	MUMMERY	MUSKLES	NAGARI
MINUETS	MIZZLE	MONGERS	MORTALS	MOVING	MUMMIA	MUSLIN	NAGARIS
MINUTE	MIZZLED	MONGERY	MORTAR	AMOVING	MUMMIAS	MUSLINS	NAGGED
MINUTED	MIZZLES	MONGOL	MORTARS	EMOVING	MUMPER	MUSMON	SNAGGED
MINUTER	MNEMON	MONGOLS	MORULA	MOWING	MUMPERS	MUSMONS	NAGGER
MINUTES	MNEMONS	MONIAL	MORULAR	MOWINGS	MUNDIC	MUSROL	NAGGERS
MINYAN	MOANER	MONIALS	MORULAS	MOYLED	MUNDICS	MUSROLS	NAILED
MINYANS	MOANERS	MONISM	MOSAIC	SMOYLED	MUNITE	MUSSEL	SNAILED
MIRAGE	MOBBIE	MONISMS	MOSAICS	MOYLES	MUNITED	MUSSELS	NAILER
MIRAGES	MOBBIES	MONIST	MOSQUE	SMOYLES	MUNITES	MUSTEE	NAILERS
MIRITI	MOBBLE	MONISTS	MOSQUES	MOZZIE	MUNSHI	MUSTEES	NAILERY
MIRITIS	MOBBLED	MONKEY	MOSSIE	MOZZIES	MUNSHIS	MUSTER	NALLAH
MIRROR	MOBBLES	MONKEYS	MOSSIER	MOZZLE	MUNTIN	MUSTERS	NALLAHS
MIRRORS	MOBILE	MONTEM	MOSSIES	MOZZLES	MUNTING	MUTANT	NAMING
MISAIM	MOBILES	MONTEMS	MOTETT	MUCATE	MUNTINS	MUTANTS	NAMINGS
MISAIMS	MOCKED	MONTRE	MOTETTS	MUCATES	MURAGE	MUTATE	NANDOO
MISCUE	SMOCKED	MONTRES	MOTHER	MUCHEL	MURAGES	MUTATED	NANDOOS
MISCUED	MOCKER	MOOLAH	SMOTHER	MUCHELL	MURDER	MUTATES	NANISM
MISCUES	MOCKERS	MOOLAHS	MOTHERS	MUCHELS	MURDERS	MUTINE	ONANISM
MISERE	MOCKERY	MOONER	MOTHERY	MUCKER	MURENA	MUTINED	NANISMS
MISERES	MOCOCK	MOONERS	MOTILE	MUCKERS	MURENAS	MUTINES	NANKIN
MISFIT	MOCOCKS	MOORED	MOTILES	MUCKLE	MURINE	MUTISM	NANKINS
MISFITS	MOCUCK	SMOORED	MOTION	MUCKLES	MURINES	MUTISMS	NAPALM
MISHAP	MOCUCKS	MOORVA	EMOTION	MUCLUC	MURING	MUTTER	NAPALMS
MISHAPS	MODENA	MOORVAS	MOTIONS	MUCLUCS	EMURING	MUTTERS	NAPKIN
MISHAPT	MODENAS	MOOTED	MOTIVE	MUCOSA	MURLAN	MUTTON	NAPKINS
MISHIT	MODERN	SMOOTED	EMOTIVE	MUCOSAE	MURLANS	MUTTONS	NAPPED
MISHITS	MODERNS	MOOTER	MOTIVED	MUDDLE	MURLIN	MUTTONY	KNAPPED
MISHMI	MODEST	MOOTERS	MOTIVES	MUDDLED	MURLINS	MUTUCA	SNAPPED
MISHMIS	MODESTY	MOOVED	MOTLEY	MUDDLER	MURMUR	MUTUCAS	NAPPER
MISKEN	MODIST	AMOOVED	MOTLEYS	MUDDLES	MURMURS	MUTULE	KNAPPER
MISKENS	MODISTE	MOOVES	MOTMOT	MUESLI	MURRAM	MUTULES	SNAPPER
MISKENT	MODISTS	AMOOVES	MOTMOTS	MUESLIS	MURRAMS	MUTUUM	NAPPERS
MISLAY	MODULE	MOPANE	MOTSER	MUFFIN	MURRAY	MUTUUMS	NAPRON
MISLAYS	MODULES	MOPANES	MOTSERS	MUFFING	MURRAYS	MUZHIK	NAPRONS
MISSAL	MOGGAN	MOPOKE	MOTTLE	MUFFINS	MURREN	MUZHIKS	NARDOO
MISSALS	MOGGANS	MOPOKES	MOTTLED	MUFFLE	MURRENS	MUZZLE	NARDOOS
MISSAY	MOGGIE	MOPPER	MOTTLES	MUFFLED	MURREY	MUZZLED	NARROW
MISSAYS	MOGGIES	MOPPERS	MOTUCA	MUFFLER	MURREYS	MUZZLER	NARROWS
MISSEE	MOHAIR	MOPPET	MOTUCAS	MUFFLES	MURRHA	MUZZLES	NASARD
MISSEEM	MOHAIRS	MOPPETS	MOUJIK	MUFLON	MURRHAS	MYELIN	NASARDS
MISSEEN	MOHAWK	MORALE	MOUJIKS	MUFLONS	MURRIN	MYELINS	NASION
MISSEES	MOHAWKS	MORALES	MOULIN	MUGFUL	MURRINE	MYELON	NASIONS
MISSEL	MOIDER	MORALL	MOULINS	MUGFULS	MURRINS	MYELONS	NASUTE
MISSELS	MOIDERS	MORALLS	MOUNTS	MUGGED	MUSANG	MYGALE	NASUTES
MISSES	MOILED	MORALLY	AMOUNTS	SMUGGED	MUSANGS	MYGALES	NATION
AMISSES	SMOILED	MORASS	MOUSED	MUGGER	MUSCAT	MYOGEN	ENATION
MISSET	MOILER	MORASSY	SMOUSED	SMUGGER	MUSCATS	MYOGENS	NATIONS
MISSETS	MOILERS	MOREEN	MOUSER	MUGGERS	MUSCID	MYOPIA	NATIVE
MISSIS	MOLEST	MOREENS	SMOUSER	MUKLUK	MUSCIDS	MYOPIAS	NATIVES
MISSISH	MOLESTS	MORGAY	MOUSERS	MUKLUKS	MUSCLE	MYOPIC	NATRON
MISTER	MOLINE	MORGAYS	MOUSERY	MULLAH	MUSCLED	MYOPICS	NATRONS
MISTERM	MOLINES	MORGEN	MOUSES	MULLAHS	MUSCLES	MYOSIN	NATTER
MISTERS	MOLLAH	MORGENS	SMOUSES	MULLER	MUSERS	MYOSINS	NATTERS
MISTERY	MOLLAHS	MORGUE	MOUSIE	MULLERS	AMUSERS	MYOTIC	NATTERY
MISTLE	MOLLIE	MORGUES	MOUSIER	MULLET	MUSEUM	MYOTICS	NATURA
MISTLED	MOLLIES	MORION	MOUSIES	MULLETS	MUSEUMS	MYRIAD	NATURAE
MISTLES	MOLOCH	MORIONS	MOUSLE	MULLEY	MUSHER	MYRIADS	NATURAL
MISUSE	MOLOCHS	MORKIN	MOUSLED	MULLEYS	MUSHERS	MYRTLE	NATURE
MISUSED	MOLTEN	MORKINS	MOUSLES	MULMUL	MUSING	MYRTLES	NATURED
MISUSER	YMOLTEN	MORNAY	MOUSME	MULMULS	AMUSING	MYSTIC	NATURES
MISUSES	MOMENT	MORNAYS	MOUSMEE	MULTUM	MUSINGS	MYSTICS	NAUGHT
MITERS	MOMENTA	MOROSE	MOUSMES	MULTUMS	MUSIVE	MZUNGU	NAUGHTS
SMITERS	MOMENTS	MOROSER	MOUSSE	MUMBLE	AMUSIVE	MZUNGUS	NAUGHTY
MITHER	MOMMET	MORPHO	MOUSSES	MUMBLED	MUSKEG	NABBER	NAUSEA
MITHERS	MOMMETS	MORPHOS	MOUTAN	MUMBLER	MUSKEGS	NABBERS	NAUSEAS
MITTEN	MONAUL	MORROW	MOUTANS	MUMBLES	MUSKET	NACKET	NAUTIC
SMITTEN	MONAULS	MORROWS	MOUTER	MUMMER	MUSKETS	NACKETS	NAUTICS
MITTENS	MONETH	MORSEL	MOUTERS	MUMMERS	MUSKLE	NAGANA	NAVAID
MIZZEN	MONETHS	MORSELS	MOUTON			NAGANAS	NAVAIDS

NEAFFE	NEURONE	NIPPERS	NORITES	NULLAHS	OBIISM	LOCULUS	JOINTED
NEAFFES	NEURONS	NIPPLE	NORMAL	NUMBAT	OBIISMS	ODISMS	NOINTED
NEAPED	NEUTER	NIPPLED	NORMALS	NUMBATS	OBJECT	IODISMS	POINTED
SNEAPED	NEUTERS	NIPPLES	NORMAN	NUMBER	OBJECTS	ODISTS	OLDENS
NEARED	NEWELL	NIPTER	NORMANS	NUMBERS	OBJURE	CODISTS	BOLDENS
ANEARED	NEWELLS	NIPTERS	NORSEL	NUMDAH	OBJURED	MODISTS	GOLDENS
UNEARED	NEWING	NIRLIE	NORSELS	NUMDAHS	OBJURES	ODIUMS	OLDEST
NEATEN	ENEWING	NIRLIER	NOSEAN	NUMNAH	OBLAST	SODIUMS	BOLDEST
UNEATEN	NEWTON	NITRYL	NOSEANS	NUMNAHS	OBLASTS	OECIST	COLDEST
NEATENS	NEWTONS	NITRYLS	NOSIES	NUNCIO	OBLATE	OECISTS	GOLDEST
NEBBED	NIACIN	NITWIT	NOSIEST	NUNCIOS	OBLATES	OEDEMA	OLDISH
SNEBBED	NIACINS	NITWITS	NOSING	NUNCLE	OBLIGE	OEDEMAS	COLDISH
NEBBUK	NIBBED	NOBBLE	NOSINGS	NUNCLES	OBLIGED	OEUVRE	GOLDISH
NEBBUKS	SNIBBED	KNOBBLE	NOSTOC	NURHAG	OBLIGEE	OEUVRES	OLEATE
NEBECK	NIBBLE	NOBBLED	NOSTOCS	NURHAGS	OBLIGES	OFFCUT	OLEATES
NEBECKS	NIBBLED	NOBBLER	NOTATE	NURLED	OBLONG	OFFCUTS	OLEFIN
NEBULA	NIBBLER	NOBBLES	NOTATED	KNURLED	OBLONGS	OFFEND	OLEFINE
NEBULAE	NIBBLES	NOBLES	NOTATES	NURSER	OBOIST	OFFENDS	OLEFINS
NEBULAR	NICHER	NOBLEST	NOTICE	NURSERS	OBOISTS	OFFERS	OLFACT
NEBULE	NICHERS	NOCAKE	NOTICED	NURSERY	OBSIGN	COFFERS	OLFACTS
NEBULES	NICKAR	NOCAKES	NOTICES	NURSLE	OBSIGNS	DOFFERS	OLIVER
NECKED	NICKARS	NOCENT	NOTION	NURSLED	OBTAIN	GOFFERS	OLIVERS
SNECKED	NICKED	NOCENTS	NOTIONS	NURSLES	OBTAINS	OFFICE	OLIVES
NECTAR	SNICKED	NOCHEL	NOUGAT	NUTATE	OBTEND	OFFICER	SOLIVES
NECTARS	NICKEL	NOCHELS	NOUGATS	NUTATED	OBTENDS	OFFICES	OLIVET
NECTARY	NICKELS	NOCKED	NOUGHT	NUTATES	OBTEST	OFFING	OLIVETS
NEEDER	NICKER	KNOCKED	NOUGHTS	NUTLET	OBTESTS	BOFFING	OLLAMH
NEEDERS	KNICKER	NOCKET	NOUSLE	NUTLETS	OBTUND	COFFING	OLLAMHS
NEEDLE	SNICKER	NOCKETS	NOUSLED	NUTMEG	OBTUNDS	DOFFING	OMBRES
NEEDLED	NICKERS	NOCTUA	NOUSLES	NUTMEGS	OBTUSE	GOFFING	HOMBRES
NEEDLER	NICKUM	NOCTUAS	NOVENA	NUTRIA	OBTUSER	OFFINGS	SOMBRES
NEEDLES	NICKUMS	NODDED	NOVENAS	NUTRIAS	OBVERT	OFFISH	OMELET
NEEZED	NIDGET	SNODDED	NOVICE	NUTTER	OBVERTS	TOFFISH	OMELETS
SNEEZED	NIDGETS	NODDER	NOVICES	NUTTERS	OCCULT	OFFPUT	OMENTA
NEEZES	NIDING	NODDERS	NOYADE	NUTTERY	OCCULTS	OFFPUTS	LOMENTA
SNEEZES	NIDINGS	NODDLE	NOYADES	NUZZER	OCELOT	OFFSET	MOMENTA
NEGATE	NIELLO	NODDLED	NOZZLE	NUZZERS	OCELOTS	OFFSETS	OMENTAL
NEGATED	NIELLOS	NODDLES	NOZZLES	NUZZLE	OCHERS	OGDOAD	OMERTA
NEGATES	NIFFED	NODULE	NUANCE	SNUZZLE	TOCHERS	OGDOADS	OMERTAS
NEKTON	SNIFFED	NODULED	NUANCED	NUZZLED	OCHREA	OGGINS	OMNIUM
NEKTONS	NIFFER	NODULES	NUANCES	NUZZLES	OCHREAE	HOGGINS	OMNIUMS
NELSON	SNIFFER	NOESES	NUBBED	NYALAS	OCKERS	NOGGINS	ONAGER
NELSONS	NIFFERS	ANOESES	SNUBBED	INYALAS	COCKERS	OGLING	ONAGERS
NEPHEW	NIGGER	NOESIS	NUBBIN	NYANZA	DOCKERS	OGLINGS	ONCOME
NEPHEWS	SNIGGER	ANOESIS	NUBBING	NYANZAS	HOCKERS	OIKIST	ONCOMES
NEREID	NIGGERS	NOETIC	NUBBINS	NYMPHO	LOCKERS	OIKISTS	ONCOST
NEREIDS	NIGGERY	ANOETIC	NUBBLE	NYMPHOS	MOCKERS	OILCAN	ONCOSTS
NERINE	NIGGLE	NOGGIN	KNUBBLE	OAKERS	ROCKERS	OILCANS	ONDINE
NERINES	SNIGGLE	NOGGING	NUBBLED	SOAKERS	SOCKERS	OILERS	ONDINES
NERITE	NIGGLED	NOGGINS	NUBBLES	OARAGE	OCTANE	BOILERS	ONDING
NERITES	NIGGLER	NOINTS	NUBBLY	OARAGES	OCTANES	MOILERS	BONDING
NEROLI	NIGGLES	ANOINTS	KNUBBLY	OARIER	OCTANT	TOILERS	FONDING
NEROLIS	NIGHTS	NOMADE	NUCLEI	HOARIER	OCTANTS	OILERY	PONDING
NERVED	KNIGHTS	NOMADES	NUCLEIN	ROARIER	OCTAVE	BOILERY	ONDINGS
ENERVED	NILGAI	NOMINA	NUCULE	OARING	OCTAVES	OILIER	ONEYER
NERVER	NILGAIS	NOMINAL	NUCULES	HOARING	OCTAVO	ROILIER	MONEYER
NERVERS	NILGAU	NOMISM	NUDGED	ROARING	OCTAVOS	SOILIER	ONEYERS
NERVES	NILGAUS	NOMISMS	SNUDGED	SOARING	OCTETT	OILING	ONEYRE
ENERVES	NIMBLE	NONAGE	NUDGES	OBANGS	OCTETTE	BOILING	ONEYRES
NESTER	NIMBLER	NONAGED	SNUDGES	GOBANGS	OCTETTS	COILING	ONFALL
NESTERS	NIMMER	NONAGES	NUDISM	KOBANGS	OCTROI	FOILING	ONFALLS
NESTLE	NIMMERS	NONANE	NUDISMS	OBDURE	OCTROIS	MOILING	ONFLOW
NESTLED	NINCOM	NONANES	NUDIST	OBDURED	OCTUOR	ROILING	ONFLOWS
NESTLES	NINCOMS	NOODLE	NUDISTS	OBDURES	OCTUORS	SOILING	ONNING
NETFUL	NINCUM	NOODLED	NUGGAR	OBECHE	OCULAR	TOILING	CONNING
NETFULS	NINCUMS	NOODLES	NUGGARS	OBECHES	JOCULAR	OILLET	DONNING
NETTLE	NIPPED	NOOKIE	NUGGET	OBEISM	LOCULAR	OILLETS	FONNING
NETTLED	SNIPPED	NOOKIER	NUGGETS	OBEISMS	VOCULAR	OILNUT	KONNING
NETTLES	NIPPER	NOOKIES	NUGGETY	OBEYER	OCULARS	OILNUTS	RONNING
NEURON	SNIPPER	NORITE	NULLAH	OBEYERS	OCULUS	OINTED	WONNING

ONSIDE	OPIATED	GORGIAS	BOTHERS	OUTAGE	OUTTOPS	OXYMELS	SPALLED
ONSIDES	OPIATES	ORGIAST	FOTHERS	OUTAGES	OUTVIE	OYESES	PALLET
ONUSES	OPPOSE	ORGIES	MOTHERS	OUTBAR	OUTVIED	NOYESES	PALLETS
BONUSES	OPPOSED	PORGIES	POTHERS	OUTBARS	OUTVIES	OYSTER	PALLIA
TONUSES	OPPOSER	ORGONE	ROTHERS	OUTBID	OUTWIN	ROYSTER	PALLIAL
ONWARD	OPPOSES	FORGONE	OTTARS	OUTBIDS	OUTWIND	OYSTERS	PALLOR
ONWARDS	OPPUGN	ORGONES	COTTARS	OUTEAT	OUTWING	OZAENA	PALLORS
ONYCHA	OPPUGNS	ORGUES	OTTAVA	OUTEATS	OUTWINS	OZAENAS	PALMAR
ONYCHAS	OPTANT	MORGUES	OTTAVAS	OUTERS	OUTWIT	PACERS	PALMARY
OOCYTE	OPTANTS	ORIENT	OTTERS	COUTERS	OUTWITH	SPACERS	PALMER
OOCYTES	OPTIMA	ORIENTS	COTTERS	DOUTERS	OUTWITS	PACHAK	PALMERS
OODLES	OPTIMAL	ORIGAN	HOTTERS	FOUTERS	OUVERT	PACHAKS	PALMIE
BOODLES	OPTIME	ORIGANE	JOTTERS	MOUTERS	COUVERT	PACIER	PALMIER
DOODLES	OPTIMES	ORIGANS	POTTERS	POUTERS	OUVERTE	SPACIER	PALMIES
NOODLES	OPTION	ORIGIN	ROTTERS	ROUTERS	OVATES	PACING	PALMIET
POODLES	OPTIONS	ORIGINS	TOTTERS	SOUTERS	BOVATES	SPACING	PALOLO
OOGAMY	OPUSES	ORIOLE	OUBITS	TOUTERS	OVATOR	PACKER	PALOLOS
ZOOGAMY	MOPUSES	ORIOLES	WOUBITS	OUTFIT	OVATORS	PACKERS	PALTER
OOGENY	ORACHE	ORISON	OUCHES	OUTFITS	OVERED	PACKET	PALTERS
ZOOGENY	ORACHES	ORISONS	BOUCHES	OUTFLY	COVERED	PACKETS	PAMPER
OOHING	ORACLE	ORMERS	COUCHES	GOUTFLY	DOVERED	PADANG	PAMPERO
BOOHING	CORACLE	DORMERS	DOUCHES	OUTGUN	HOVERED	PADANGS	PAMPERS
OOIDAL	ORACLED	FORMERS	MOUCHES	OUTGUNS	LOVERED	PADAUK	PANADA
ZOOIDAL	ORACLES	WORMERS	POUCHES	OUTHER	OVERGO	PADAUKS	PANADAS
OOLITE	ORALLY	ORMOLU	TOUCHES	COUTHER	OVERGOT	PADDER	PANAMA
ZOOLITE	MORALLY	ORMOLUS	VOUCHES	MOUTHER	OVERLY	PADDERS	PANAMAS
OOLITES	ORANGE	ORNATE	OUGHLY	POUTHER	LOVERLY	PADDLE	PANDAR
OOLOGY	ORANGER	ORNATER	ROUGHLY	SOUTHER	OVISAC	PADDLED	PANDARS
NOOLOGY	ORANGES	OROGEN	TOUGHLY	OUTHIT	OVISACS	PADDLER	PANDER
ZOOLOGY	ORARIA	OROIDE	OUGHTS	OUTHITS	OWLERS	PADDLES	PANDERS
OOLONG	ORARIAN	OROIDES	BOUGHTS	OUTING	BOWLERS	PADOUK	PANDIT
OOLONGS	ORATES	OROGENY	NOUGHTS	DOUTING	FOWLERS	PADOUKS	PANDITS
OOMIAC	BORATES	ORPHAN	OUGLIE	LOUTING	HOWLERS	PAELLA	PANFUL
OOMIACK	ORATOR	ORPHANS	OUGLIED	POUTING	JOWLERS	PAELLAS	PANFULS
OOMIACS	ORATORS	ORPINE	OUGLIES	ROUTING	OWLETS	PAGING	PANGED
OOMIAK	ORATORY	FORPINE	OULONG	TOUTING	HOWLETS	PAGINGS	SPANGED
OOMIAKS	ORBING	ORPINES	OULONGS	OUTINGS	OWLIER	PAGODA	PANGEN
OOMPAH	SORBING	ORTHOS	OUNCES	OUTJET	LOWLIER	PAGODAS	PANGENE
OOMPAHS	ORBITA	PORTHOS	BOUNCES	OUTJETS	OWLING	PAIDLE	PANGENS
OOPING	ORBITAL	OSCULA	JOUNCES	OUTJUT	BOWLING	PAIDLES	PANICK
COOPING	ORBITAS	OSCULAR	POUNCES	OUTJUTS	COWLING	PAIGLE	PANICKS
HOOPING	ORCEIN	OSCULE	ROUNCES	OUTLAW	FOWLING	PAIGLES	PANICKY
LOOPING	ORCEINS	OSCULES	OUPING	OUTLAWS	GOWLING	PAINED	PANING
MOOPING	ORCHAT	OSIERS	COUPING	OUTLAY	HOWLING	SPAINED	PANISC
POOPING	ORCHATS	COSIERS	LOUPING	OUTLAYS	JOWLING	PAINIM	PANISCS
ROOPING	ORCHEL	HOSIERS	MOUPING	OUTLER	SOWLING	PAINIMS	PANISK
SOOPING	ORCHELS	ROSIERS	POUPING	OUTLERS	YOWLING	PAIOCK	PANISKS
OORIAL	ORCHID	OSIERY	ROUPING	OUTLET	OWNERS	PAIOCKE	PANNED
OORIALS	ORCHIDS	HOSIERY	OURALI	OUTLETS	DOWNERS	PAIOCKS	SPANNED
OORIER	ORCHIL	OSMATE	WOURALI	OUTLIE	OWNING	PAJOCK	PANTER
MOORIER	ORCHILS	OSMATES	OURALIS	OUTLIED	BOWNING	PAJOCKE	PANTERS
OOSIER	ORCINE	OSMIUM	OURARI	OUTLIER	DOWNING	PAJOCKS	PANTON
GOOSIER	PORCINE	OSMIUMS	OURARIS	OUTLIES	GOWNING	PAKEHA	PANTONS
OOZIER	ORCINES	OSMOSE	OUREBI	OUTMAN	LOWNING	PAKEHAS	PANTUN
BOOZIER	ORDAIN	OSMOSED	OUREBIS	OUTMANS	OXGANG	PAKORA	PANTUNS
WOOZIER	ORDAINS	OSMOSES	OURIER	OUTPUT	OXGANGS	PAKORAS	PANZER
OOZILY	ORDEAL	OSMUND	COURIER	OUTPUTS	OXGATE	PALACE	PANZERS
BOOZILY	ORDEALS	OSMUNDA	LOURIER	OUTRAN	OXGATES	PALACES	PAPAIN
WOOZILY	ORDERS	OSMUNDS	OUSELS	OUTRANK	OXHEAD	PALAMA	PAPAINS
OOZING	BORDERS	OSPREY	HOUSELS	OUTRED	OXHEADS	PALAMAE	PAPAYA
BOOZING	ORDURE	OSPREYS	OUSTED	OUTREDS	OXLAND	PALATE	PAPAYAS
OPAQUE	BORDURE	OSSEIN	JOUSTED	OUTRUN	OXLANDS	PALATED	PAPISM
OPAQUED	ORDURES	OSSEINS	MOUSTED	OUTRUNS	OXSLIP	PALATES	PAPISMS
OPAQUER	OREIDE	OSTENT	ROUSTED	OUTSET	OXSLIPS	PALING	PAPIST
OPAQUES	OREIDES	OSTENTS	OUSTER	OUTSETS	OXTAIL	PALINGS	PAPISTS
OPENER	ORGASM	OSTLER	JOUSTER	OUTSIT	OXTAILS	PALKEE	PAPULA
OPENERS	ORGASMS	HOSTLER	ROUSTER	OUTSITS	OXYGEN	PALKEES	PAPULAE
OPHITE	ORGEAT	OSTLERS	OUSTERS	OUTSUM	LOXYGEN	PALLAH	PAPULAR
OPHITES	ORGEATS	OTHERS	OUTACT	OUTSUMS	OXYGENS	PALLAHS	PAPULE
OPIATE	ORGIAS		OUTACTS	OUTTOP	OXYMEL	PALLED	

PAPULES	PARSER	PAUNCHY	PEDLAR	PENSUM	PETHER	PHYLLOS	PILFERS
PARADE	SPARSER	PAUPER	PEDLARS	PENSUMS	PETHERS	PHYSIC	PILFERY
PARADED	PARSERS	PAUPERS	PEDLARY	PENTAD	PETREL	PHYSICS	PILING
PARADES	PARSON	PAUSER	PEELED	PENTADS	PETRELS	PHYSIO	SPILING
PARAGE	PARSONS	PAUSERS	SPEELED	PENTEL	PETROL	PHYSIOS	PILLAR
PARAGES	PARTAN	PAVAGE	PEELER	PENTELS	PETROLS	PHYTON	PILLARS
PARAMO	SPARTAN	PAVAGES	SPEELER	PENULT	PETTER	PHYTONS	PILLAU
PARAMOS	PARTANS	PAVANE	PEELERS	PENULTS	PETTERS	PIAFFE	PILLAUS
PARANG	PARTER	PAVANES	PEENGE	PEOPLE	PETTLE	PIAFFED	PILLED
PARANGS	PARTERS	PAVING	PEENGED	PEOPLED	PETTLED	PIAFFER	SPILLED
PARAPH	PARTON	PAVINGS	PEENGES	PEOPLES	PETTLES	PIAFFES	PILLOW
PARAPHS	PARTONS	PAVINS	PEEPER	PEPLUM	PEWTER	PIAZZA	PILLOWS
PARCEL	PARURE	SPAVINS	PEEPERS	PEPLUMS	PEWTERS	PIAZZAS	PILLOWY
PARCELS	PARURES	PAVIOR	PEEPUL	PEPPER	PEYOTE	PICENE	PILULA
PARDAL	PARVIS	PAVIORS	PEEPULS	PEPPERS	PEYOTES	EPICENE	PILULAR
PARDALE	PARVISE	PAVISE	PEERED	PEPPERY	PEZANT	PICENES	PILULAS
PARDALS	PASCAL	PAVISES	SPEERED	PEPSIN	PEZANTS	PICKER	PILULE
PARDON	PASCALS	PAVONE	PEERIE	PEPSINE	PHALLI	SPICKER	PILULES
PARDONS	PASEAR	PAVONES	PEERIER	PEPSINS	PHALLIC	PICKERS	PIMENT
PARENT	PASEARS	PAWNCE	PEERIES	PEPTIC	PHALLIN	PICKERY	PIMENTO
PARENTS	PASHIM	PAWNCES	PEEVER	PEPTICS	PHANGS	PICKET	PIMENTS
PARERS	PASHIMS	PAWNED	PEEVERS	PERDUE	UPHANGS	PICKETS	PIMPLE
SPARERS	PASSER	SPAWNED	PEEWEE	EPERDUE	PHASIC	PICKLE	PIMPLED
PARGED	PASSERS	PAWNEE	PEEWEES	PERDUES	APHASIC	PICKLED	PIMPLES
SPARGED	PASTEL	PAWNEES	PEEWIT	PERIOD	PHEERE	PICKLER	PINCER
PARGES	PASTELS	PAWNER	PEEWITS	PERIODS	PHEERES	PICKLES	PINCERS
SPARGES	PASTER	SPAWNER	PEINCT	PERKIN	PHEESE	PICNIC	PINDER
PARGET	PASTERN	PAWNERS	PEINCTS	PERKING	PHEESED	PICNICS	PINDERS
PARGETS	PASTERS	PAWPAW	PELAGE	PERKINS	PHEESES	PICOTE	PINGER
PARIAH	PASTIL	PAWPAWS	PELAGES	PERMIT	PHEEZE	PICOTED	PINGERS
PARIAHS	PASTILS	PAYING	PELHAM	PERMITS	PHEEZED	PICOTEE	PINGLE
PARIAL	PASTOR	APAYING	PELHAMS	PERONE	PHEEZES	PIDDLE	PINGLED
PARIALS	PASTORS	SPAYING	PELITE	PERONES	PHENES	PIDDLED	PINGLER
PARING	PATACA	PAYINGS	PELITES	PERRON	SPHENES	PIDDLER	PINGLES
SPARING	PATACAS	PAYNIM	PELLET	PERRONS	PHENIC	PIDDLES	PINIER
PARINGS	PATENT	PAYNIMS	PELLETS	PERSES	SPHENIC	PIDGIN	SPINIER
PARKED	PATENTS	PAYOLA	PELMET	SPERSES	PHENOL	PIDGINS	PINIES
SPARKED	PATERA	PAYOLAS	PELMETS	PERSON	PHENOLS	PIECEN	PINIEST
PARKEE	PATERAE	PEACOD	PELOID	PERSONA	PHENYL	PIECENS	PINING
PARKEES	PATHED	PEACODS	PELOIDS	PERSONS	PHENYLS	PIECER	OPINING
PARKER	SPATHED	PEANED	PELOTA	PERSUE	PHESES	PIECERS	PINION
PARKERS	PATHIC	SPEANED	PELOTAS	PERSUED	APHESES	PIERCE	OPINION
PARKIN	SPATHIC	PEANUT	PELTAS	PERSUES	PHIZOG	PIERCED	PINIONS
PARKING	PATHICS	PEANUTS	PELTAST	PERUKE	PHIZOGS	PIERCER	PINITE
PARKINS	PATINA	PEAPOD	PELTER	PERUKED	PHLEGM	PIERCES	PINITES
PARKIS	PATINAS	PEAPODS	SPELTER	PERUKES	PHLEGMS	PIERID	PINKIE
PARKISH	PATINE	PEARCE	PELTERS	PERUSE	PHLEGMY	PIERIDS	PINKIER
PARKLY	PATINED	PEARCED	PENCEL	PERUSED	PHLOEM	PIFFLE	PINKIES
SPARKLY	PATINES	PEARCES	PENCELS	PERUSER	PHLOEMS	PIFFLED	PINNER
PARLAY	PATROL	PEAVEY	PENCES	PERUSES	PHOBIA	PIFFLER	SPINNER
PARLAYS	PATROLS	PEAVEYS	SPENCES	PESADE	PHOBIAS	PIFFLES	PINNERS
PARLEY	PATRON	PEBBLE	PENCIL	PESADES	PHOEBE	PIGEON	PINNET
PARLEYS	PATRONS	PEBBLED	PENCILS	PESANT	PHOEBES	PIGEONS	SPINNET
PAROLE	PATTED	PEBBLES	PENFUL	PESANTE	PHONEY	PIGGIE	PINNETS
PAROLED	SPATTED	PECKED	PENFULS	PESANTS	PHONEYS	PIGGIER	PINNIE
PAROLEE	PATTEE	SPECKED	PENING	PESETA	PHONIC	PIGGIES	PINNIES
PAROLES	SPATTEE	PECKER	OPENING	PESETAS	APHONIC	PIGGIN	PINOLE
PARPEN	PATTEN	PECKERS	PENNAL	PESEWA	PHONICS	PIGGING	PINOLES
PARPEND	PATTENS	PECTIN	PENNALS	PESEWAS	PHONON	PIGGINS	PINTLE
PARPENS	PATTER	PECTINS	PENNER	PESHWA	PHONONS	PIGHTS	PINTLES
PARPENT	SPATTER	PEDALO	PENNERS	PESHWAS	PHOTIC	SPIGHTS	PIOLET
PARRAL	PATTERN	PEDALOS	PENNON	PESTER	APHOTIC	PIGLET	PIOLETS
PARRALS	PATTERS	PEDANT	PENNONS	PESTERS	PHOTICS	PIGLETS	PIONER
PARREL	PATTLE	PEDANTS	PENSEE	PESTLE	PHOTON	PIGPEN	PIONERS
PARRELS	PATTLES	PEDDER	PENSEES	PESTLED	PHOTONS	PIGPENS	PIONEY
PARROT	PATZER	PEDDERS	PENSEL	PESTLES	PHRASE	PIKING	PIONEYS
PARROTS	PATZERS	PEDDLE	PENSELS	PETARA	PHRASED	SPIKING	PIPAGE
PARROTY	PAUNCE	PEDDLED	PENSIL	PETARAS	PHRASER	PILAFF	PIPAGES
PARSEC	PAUNCES	PEDDLER	PENSILE	PETARD	PHRASES	PILAFFS	PIPING
PARSECS	PAUNCH	PEDDLES	PENSILS	PETARDS	PHYLLO	PILFER	PIPINGS

PIPKIN	PLASTER	**PODIUM**	PONGEES	**POSSES**	POUTERS	PRESETS	**PROTYL**
PIPKINS	**PLATAN**	SPODIUM	**PONGID**	POSSESS	**POWDER**	**PRESTO**	PROTYLE
PIPPIN	PLATANE	**PODLEY**	PONGIDS	**POSSET**	POWDERS	PRESTOS	PROTYLS
PIPPING	PLATANS	PODLEYS	**PONTIE**	POSSETS	POWDERY	**PRESTS**	**PROVEN**
PIPPINS	**PLATEN**	**PODSOL**	PONTIES	**POSSIE**	**POWNEY**	UPRESTS	PROVEND
PIQUET	PLATENS	PODSOLS	**PONTIL**	POSSIES	POWNEYS	**PREWYN**	**PROVER**
PIQUETS	**PLATER**	**PODZOL**	PONTILE	**POSSUM**	**POWNIE**	PREWYNS	PROVERB
PIRANA	PLATERS	PODZOLS	PONTILS	OPOSSUM	POWNIES	**PRICER**	PROVERS
PIRANAS	**PLAYED**	**POETIC**	**PONTON**	POSSUMS	**POWTER**	PRICERS	**PROYNE**
PIRATE	SPLAYED	POETICS	PONTONS	**POSTAL**	POWTERS	**PRIEFE**	PROYNED
PIRATED	**PLAYER**	**POFFLE**	**POODLE**	POSTALS	**POWWOW**	PRIEFES	PROYNES
PIRATES	PLAYERS	POFFLES	POODLES	**POSTER**	POWWOWS	**PRIEST**	**PRUINA**
PIRAYA	**PLEADS**	**POGROM**	**POOGYE**	POSTERN	**POYSON**	PRIESTS	PRUINAS
PIRAYAS	UPLEADS	POGROMS	POOGYEE	POSTERS	POYSONS	**PRIEVE**	**PRUINE**
PIRNIE	**PLEASE**	**POINTE**	POOGYES	**POSTIE**	**PRAISE**	PRIEVED	PRUINES
PIRNIES	PLEASED	POINTED	**POOJAH**	POSTIES	UPRAISE	PRIEVES	**PRUNER**
PISTIL	PLEASER	POINTEL	POOJAHS	**POSTIL**	PRAISED	**PRIMER**	PRUNERS
PISTILS	PLEASES	POINTER	**POOLED**	APOSTIL	PRAISER	PRIMERO	**PRYING**
PISTOL	**PLEDGE**	POINTES	SPOOLED	POSTILS	PRAISES	PRIMERS	PRYINGS
PISTOLE	PLEDGED	**POISER**	**POONAC**	**POTAGE**	**PRANCE**	**PRINCE**	**PSYCHE**
PISTOLS	PLEDGEE	POISERS	POONACS	POTAGES	PRANCED	PRINCED	PSYCHED
PISTON	PLEDGER	**POISON**	**POORER**	**POTASS**	PRANCER	PRINCES	PSYCHES
PISTONS	PLEDGES	POISONS	SPOORER	POTASSA	PRANCES	**PRINTS**	**PSYCHO**
PITARA	PLEDGET	**POLDER**	**POOTER**	**POTCHE**	**PRANCK**	SPRINTS	PSYCHOS
PITARAH	**PLENTY**	POLDERS	POOTERS	POTCHED	PRANCKE	**PRISER**	**PSYWAR**
PITARAS	APLENTY	**POLEYN**	**POPJOY**	POTCHER	PRANCKS	PRISERS	PSYWARS
PITIER	**PLENUM**	POLEYNS	POPJOYS	POTCHES	**PRATED**	**PRISES**	**PTERIA**
PITIERS	PLENUMS	**POLICE**	**POPLAR**	**POTEEN**	UPRATED	UPRISES	APTERIA
PITTED	**PLEUCH**	POLICED	POPLARS	POTEENS	**PRATER**	**PRISON**	**PTERIN**
SPITTED	PLEUCHS	POLICES	**POPLIN**	**POTENT**	PRATERS	PRISONS	PTERINS
PITTEN	**PLEUGH**	**POLING**	POPLINS	POTENTS	**PRATES**	**PRIVET**	**PTISAN**
SPITTEN	PLEUGHS	POLINGS	**POPPER**	**POTFUL**	UPRATES	PRIVETS	PTISANS
PITTER	**PLEURA**	**POLITE**	POPPERS	POTFULS	**PRATIE**	**PRIZER**	**PUBLIC**
SPITTER	PLEURAE	POLITER	**POPPET**	**POTGUN**	PRATIES	PRIZERS	PUBLICS
PITTERS	PLEURAL	**POLLAN**	POPPETS	POTGUNS	**PRAWLE**	**PROBIT**	**PUCKER**
PITURI	**PLEXOR**	POLLANS	**POPPIT**	**POTHER**	PRAWLES	PROBITS	PUCKERS
PITURIS	PLEXORS	**POLLEN**	POPPITS	POTHERS	**PRAYED**	PROBITY	PUCKERY
PIUPIU	**PLIGHT**	POLLENS	**POPPLE**	POTHERY	SPRAYED	**PROFIT**	**PUDDEN**
PIUPIUS	YPLIGHT	POLLENT	POPPLED	**POTION**	**PRAYER**	PROFITS	PUDDENS
PIZZLE	PLIGHTS	**POLLER**	POPPLES	POTIONS	SPRAYER	**PROIGN**	**PUDDER**
PIZZLES	**PLINTH**	POLLERS	**POPRIN**	**POTTED**	PRAYERS	PROIGNS	PUDDERS
PLACER	PLINTHS	**POLYPE**	POPRINS	SPOTTED	**PREACE**	**PROINE**	**PUDDLE**
PLACERS	**PLONGE**	POLYPES	**PORGIE**	**POTTER**	PREACED	PROINED	PUDDLED
PLACET	PLONGED	**POMACE**	PORGIES	SPOTTER	PREACES	PROINES	PUDDLER
PLACETS	PLONGES	POMACES	**PORISM**	POTTERS	**PREACH**	**PROKER**	PUDDLES
PLACIT	**PLOOKS**	**POMADE**	PORISMS	POTTERY	PREACHY	PROKERS	**PUEBLO**
PLACITA	UPLOOKS	POMADED	**PORKER**	**POTTLE**	**PREASE**	**PROLEG**	PUEBLOS
PLACITS	**PLOUGH**	POMADES	PORKERS	POTTLES	PREASED	PROLEGS	**PUFFER**
PLAGUE	PLOUGHS	**POMELO**	**POROSE**	**POUDER**	PREASES	**PROLER**	PUFFERS
PLAGUED	**PLOVER**	POMELOS	POROSES	POUDERS	**PRECIS**	PROLERS	PUFFERY
PLAGUES	PLOVERS	**POMMEL**	**PORTAL**	**POUDRE**	PRECISE	**PROLLS**	**PUFFIN**
PLAGUEY	PLOVERY	POMMELE	PORTALS	POUDRES	**PREEVE**	UPROLLS	PUFFING
PLAICE	**PLUNGE**	POMMELS	**PORTED**	**POUFFE**	PREEVED	**PROMPT**	PUFFINS
PLAICES	PLUNGED	**POMPEY**	SPORTED	POUFFES	PREEVES	PROMPTS	**PUISNE**
PLAINT	PLUNGER	POMPEYS	**PORTER**	**POULPE**	**PREFAB**	**PRONES**	PUISNES
PLAINTS	PLUNGES	**POMPOM**	SPORTER	POULPES	PREFABS	PRONEST	**PULING**
PLANER	**PLURAL**	POMPOMS	PORTERS	**POUNCE**	**PREFER**	**PROPEL**	PULINGS
PLANERS	PLURALS	**POMPON**	**POSADA**	POUNCED	PREFERS	PROPELS	**PULKHA**
PLANET	**PLUTON**	POMPONS	POSADAS	POUNCES	**PREIFE**	**PROPER**	PULKHAS
PLANETS	PLUTONS	**POMROY**	**POSEUR**	POUNCET	PREIFES	PROPERS	**PULLER**
PLANTA	**PLYING**	POMROYS	POSEURS	**POURER**	**PRELIM**	**PROPYL**	PULLERS
PLANTAR	UPLYING	**PONCHO**	**POSHES**	POURERS	PRELIMS	PROPYLA	**PULLET**
PLANTAS	**PNEUMA**	PONCHOS	SPOSHES	**POURIE**	**PREMED**	PROPYLS	PULLETS
PLAQUE	PNEUMAS	**PONDER**	POSHEST	POURIES	PREMEDS	**PROSER**	**PULLEY**
PLAQUES	**POCHAY**	PONDERS	**POSING**	**POUSSE**	**PREMIE**	PROSERS	PULLEYS
PLASHY	POCHAYS	**PONDOK**	POSINGS	POUSSES	PREMIER	**PROTEA**	**PULPER**
SPLASHY	**POCKET**	PONDOKS	**POSNET**	**POUTED**	PREMIES	PROTEAN	PULPERS
PLASMA	POCKETS	**PONGED**	POSNETS	SPOUTED	**PREPAY**	PROTEAS	**PULPIT**
PLASMAS	**PODITE**	SPONGED	**POSSER**	**POUTER**	PREPAYS	**PROTON**	PULPITS
PLASTE	PODITES	**PONGEE**	POSSERS	SPOUTER	**PRESET**	PROTONS	**PULQUE**

PULQUES	**PURRED**	**QUAIGH**	AQUIVER	**RADIAL**	FRAILLY	RANDANS	GRAPING
PULSAR	SPURRED	QUAIGHS	QUIVERS	RADIALE	**RAINED**	**RANDED**	TRAPING
PULSARS	**PURSER**	**QUAILS**	QUIVERY	RADIALS	BRAINED	BRANDED	**RAPIST**
PULTAN	PURSERS	SQUAILS	**QUOIST**	**RADIAN**	DRAINED	**RANDEM**	RAPISTS
PULTANS	**PURSEW**	**QUANGO**	QUOISTS	RADIANS	GRAINED	RANDEMS	**RAPPED**
PULTON	PURSEWS	QUANGOS	**QUOKKA**	RADIANT	TRAINED	**RANDIE**	CRAPPED
PULTONS	**PURSUE**	**QUANTA**	QUOKKAS	**RADIUM**	**RAINES**	RANDIER	DRAPPED
PULTUN	PURSUED	QUANTAL	**QUORUM**	RADIUMS	GRAINES	RANDIES	FRAPPED
PULTUNS	PURSUER	**QUANTS**	QUORUMS	**RADOME**	**RAIRDS**	**RANDOM**	TRAPPED
PULVER	PURSUES	EQUANTS	**QUOTER**	RADOMES	BRAIRDS	RANDOMS	WRAPPED
PULVERS	**PURVEY**	**QUARTE**	QUOTERS	**RADULA**	**RAISED**	**RANDON**	**RAPPEE**
PULVIL	PURVEYS	QUARTER	**QUOTUM**	RADULAE	ARAISED	RANDONS	FRAPPEE
PULVILS	**PUSHER**	QUARTES	QUOTUMS	RADULAR	BRAISED	**RANGED**	RAPPEES
PULWAR	PUSHERS	QUARTET	**QWERTY**	**RAFALE**	FRAISED	PRANGED	**RAPPEL**
PULWARS	**PUSSEL**	**QUARTO**	QWERTYS	RAFALES	PRAISED	**RANGER**	RAPPELS
PUMELO	PUSSELS	QUARTOS	**RABBET**	**RAFFIA**	**RAISER**	GRANGER	**RAPPER**
PUMELOS	**PUTEAL**	**QUARTZ**	DRABBET	RAFFIAS	PRAISER	ORANGER	TRAPPER
PUMICE	PUTEALS	QUARTZY	RABBETS	**RAFFLE**	RAISERS	RANGERS	WRAPPER
PUMICED	**PUTELI**	**QUASAR**	**RABBIN**	RAFFLED	**RAISES**	**RANGES**	RAPPERS
PUMICES	PUTELIS	QUASARS	RABBINS	RAFFLER	ARAISES	GRANGES	**RAPTOR**
PUMMEL	**PUTLOG**	**QUAVER**	**RABBIT**	RAFFLES	BRAISES	ORANGES	RAPTORS
PUMMELS	PUTLOGS	QUAVERS	FRABBIT	**RAFTED**	FRAISES	**RANKED**	**RASCAL**
PUMPER	**PUTTEE**	QUAVERY	RABBITS	CRAFTED	PRAISES	BRANKED	RASCALS
PUMPERS	PUTTEES	**QUEACH**	RABBITY	DRAFTED	**RAISIN**	CRANKED	**RASHED**
PUNCTO	**PUTTER**	QUEACHY	**RABBLE**	GRAFTED	RAISING	FRANKED	BRASHED
PUNCTOS	SPUTTER	**QUEEST**	BRABBLE	**RAFTER**	RAISINS	PRANKED	CRASHED
PUNDIT	PUTTERS	QUEESTS	DRABBLE	DRAFTER	**RAIYAT**	**RANKER**	TRASHED
PUNDITS	**PUTTIE**	**QUELCH**	GRABBLE	GRAFTER	RAIYATS	CRANKER	**RASHER**
PUNKAH	PUTTIED	SQUELCH	PRABBLE	RAFTERS	**RAKING**	FRANKER	BRASHER
PUNKAHS	PUTTIER	**QUELEA**	RABBLED	**RAGEES**	BRAKING	RANKERS	RASHERS
PUNNER	PUTTIES	QUELEAS	RABBLER	DRAGEES	CRAKING	**RANKES**	**RASHES**
PUNNERS	**PUTURE**	**QUETHE**	RABBLES	**RAGGED**	RAKINGS	RANKEST	BRASHES
PUNNET	PUTURES	QUETHES	**RACEME**	BRAGGED	**RALLYE**	**RANKLE**	CRASHES
PUNNETS	**PUZZEL**	**QUICHE**	RACEMED	CRAGGED	RALLYES	CRANKLE	TRASHES
PUNTEE	PUZZELS	QUICHED	RACEMES	DRAGGED	**RAMBLE**	PRANKLE	**RASHEST**
PUNTEES	**PUZZLE**	QUICHES	BRACERS	RAGGEDY	BRAMBLE	RANKLED	**RASING**
PUNTER	PUZZLED	**QUIDAM**	TRACERS	**RAGGEE**	RAMBLED	RANKLES	ERASING
PUNTERS	PUZZLER	QUIDAMS	**RACHES**	RAGGEES	RAMBLER	**RANKLY**	**RASPED**
PUPATE	PUZZLES	**QUIGHT**	BRACHES	**RAGGLE**	RAMBLES	FRANKLY	GRASPED
PUPATED	**PYCNON**	QUIGHTS	ORACHES	DRAGGLE	**RAMCAT**	**RANSEL**	**RASPER**
PUPATES	PYCNONS	**QUILLS**	**RACHIS**	RAGGLED	RAMCATS	RANSELS	GRASPER
PUPPET	**PYEMIA**	SQUILLS	ARACHIS	RAGGLES	**RAMMED**	**RANSOM**	RASPERS
PUPPETS	PYEMIAS	**QUINCE**	**RACING**	**RAGINI**	CRAMMED	TRANSOM	**RASSES**
PURDAH	**PYGARG**	QUINCES	BRACING	RAGINIS	DRAMMED	RANSOMS	BRASSES
PURDAHS	PYGARGS	**QUINIE**	GRACING	**RAGLAN**	**RAMMER**	**RANTED**	FRASSES
PURFLE	**PYONER**	QUINIES	TRACING	RAGLANS	CRAMMER	DRANTED	GRASSES
PURFLED	PYONERS	**QUINOA**	RACINGS	**RAGMAN**	RAMMERS	GRANTED	TRASSES
PURFLES	**PYRENE**	QUINOAS	**RACISM**	RAGMANS	**RAMPED**	TRANTED	WRASSES
PURGER	PYRENES	**QUINOL**	RACISMS	**RAGMEN**	CRAMPED	**RANTER**	**RASTER**
PURGERS	**PYRITE**	QUINOLS	**RACIST**	RAGMENT	TRAMPED	GRANTER	RASTERS
PURGES	PYRITES	**QUINTA**	RACISTS	**RAGOUT**	**RAMPER**	TRANTER	**RASURE**
SPURGES	**PYROPE**	QUINTAL	**RACKED**	RAGOUTS	TRAMPER	RANTERS	RASURES
PURINE	PYROPES	QUINTAN	CRACKED	**RAIDED**	RAMPERS	**RANULA**	ERASURE
PURINES	**PYTHON**	QUINTAS	TRACKED	BRAIDED	**RAMROD**	RANULAS	ERASURES
PURISM	PYTHONS	**QUINTE**	WRACKED	**RAIDER**	RAMRODS	**RANZEL**	**RATBAG**
PURISMS	**PYURIA**	QUINTES	**RACKER**	BRAIDER	**RAMSON**	RANZELS	RATBAGS
PURIST	PYURIAS	QUINTET	CRACKER	RAIDERS	RAMSONS	**RAPERS**	**RATERS**
PURISTS	**QIGONG**	**QUINTS**	TRACKER	**RAIKED**	**RANCED**	DRAPERS	CRATERS
PURLER	QIGONGS	SQUINTS	RACKERS	**RAILED**	PRANCED	**RAPHIA**	FRATERS
PURLERS	**QINTAR**	**QUINZE**	**RACKET**	BRAILED	TRANCED	RAPHIAS	GRATERS
PURLIN	QINTARS	QUINZES	BRACKET	DRAILED	**RANCEL**	**RAPIER**	PRATERS
PURLINE	**QUAERE**	**QUIRED**	RACKETS	TRAILED	RANCELS	CRAPIER	**RATIFY**
PURLING	QUAERED	SQUIRED	RACKETT	**RAILER**	**RANCES**	DRAPIER	GRATIFY
PURLINS	QUAERES	**QUIRES**	RACKETY	FRAILER	PRANCES	GRAPIER	**RATINE**
PURPIE	**QUAGGA**	SQUIRES	**RACOON**	TRAILER	TRANCES	RAPIERS	RATINES
PURPIES	QUAGGAS	**QUIRTS**	RACOONS	RAILERS	**RANCHO**	**RAPINE**	**RATING**
PURPLE	**QUAHOG**	SQUIRTS	**RADDLE**	RAILES	RANCHOS	RAPINES	CRATING
PURPLED	QUAHOGS	**QUITCH**	RADDLED	GRAILES	**RANCOR**	**RAPING**	GRATING
PURPLER	**QUAICH**	SQUITCH	RADDLES	**RAILLY**	RANCORS	CRAPING	ORATING
PURPLES	QUAICHS	**QUIVER**			**RANDAN**	DRAPING	PRATING
							RATINGS

RATION	GRAYLES	**REBUKE**	AREDING	**REFUTE**	**RELINE**	**RENNET**	**RERAIL**
ORATION	RAYLESS	REBUKED	BREDING	REFUTED	RELINED	RENNETS	RERAILS
RATIONS	**RAYLET**	REBUKER	**REDLEG**	REFUTER	RELINES	**RENNIN**	**REREAD**
RATLIN	RAYLETS	REBUKES	REDLEGS	REFUTES	**RELIVE**	RENNING	REREADS
RATLINE	**RAYNES**	**RECALL**	**REDOWA**	**REGAIN**	RELIVED	RENNINS	**RESALE**
RATLING	TRAYNES	RECALLS	REDOWAS	REGAINS	RELIVER	**RENOWN**	RESALES
RATLINS	**RAYONS**	**RECANT**	**REDRAW**	**REGALE**	RELIVES	RENOWNS	**RESCUE**
RATOON	CRAYONS	RECANTS	REDRAWN	GREGALE	**RELOAD**	**RENTAL**	RESCUED
RATOONS	**RAZING**	**RECAST**	REDRAWS	REGALED	RELOADS	TRENTAL	RESCUER
RATTAN	BRAZING	PRECAST	**REDTOP**	REGALES	**RELUCT**	RENTALS	RESCUES
RATTANS	CRAZING	RECASTS	REDTOPS	**REGARD**	RELUCTS	**RENTER**	**RESEAL**
RATTED	GRAZING	**RECEDE**	**REDUCE**	REGARDS	**RELUME**	BRENTER	RESEALS
DRATTED	**RAZURE**	PRECEDE	REDUCED	**REGENT**	RELUMED	RENTERS	**RESEAT**
PRATTED	RAZURES	RECEDED	REDUCER	REGENTS	RELUMES	**RENVOI**	RESEATS
RATTEN	**RAZZIA**	RECEDES	REDUCES	**REGEST**	**REMADE**	RENVOIS	**RESEAU**
RATTENS	RAZZIAS	**RECEPT**	**REDUIT**	REGESTS	REMADES	**RENVOY**	RESEAUS
RATTER	**RAZZLE**	RECEPTS	REDUITS	**REGGAE**	**REMAIN**	RENVOYS	RESEAUX
RATTERS	FRAZZLE	**RECESS**	**REEBOK**	REGGAES	REMAINS	**REOPEN**	**RESECT**
RATTERY	RAZZLES	PRECESS	REEBOKS	**REGIME**	**REMAKE**	REOPENS	RESECTS
RATTLE	**READER**	**RECIPE**	**REEDER**	REGIMEN	REMAKES	**REPACK**	**RESEDA**
BRATTLE	DREADER	RECIPES	BREEDER	REGIMES	**REMAND**	PREPACK	RESEDAS
PRATTLE	TREADER	**RECITE**	REEDERS	**REGINA**	REMANDS	REPACKS	**RESELL**
RATTLED	READERS	RECITED	**REEFER**	REGINAE	**REMARK**	**REPAID**	RESELLS
RATTLER	**REAKED**	RECITER	REEFERS	REGINAL	REMARKS	PREPAID	**RESENT**
RATTLES	CREAKED	RECITES	**REEKIE**	REGINAS	**REMBLE**	**REPAIR**	PRESENT
RATTON	FREAKED	**RECKED**	REEKIER	**REGION**	TREMBLE	REPAIRS	RESENTS
RATTONS	WREAKED	TRECKED	**REELER**	REGIONS	REMBLED	**REPAST**	**RESETS**
RAUCLE	**REAMED**	WRECKED	REELERS	**REGIVE**	REMBLES	REPASTS	PRESETS
RAUCLER	BREAMED	**RECKON**	**REEVED**	REGIVEN	**REMEAD**	**REPAYS**	**RESHIP**
RAUGHT	CREAMED	RECKONS	PREEVED	REGIVES	REMEADS	PREPAYS	RESHIPS
DRAUGHT	DREAMED	**RECOIL**	**REEVES**	**REGLET**	**REMEDE**	**REPEAL**	**RESIDE**
FRAUGHT	**REAMER**	RECOILS	PREEVES	REGLETS	REMEDES	REPEALS	PRESIDE
RAUNCH	CREAMER	**RECORD**	**REFACE**	**REGRET**	**REMEID**	**REPEAT**	RESIDED
BRAUNCH	DREAMER	RECORDS	PREFACE	REGRETS	REMEIDS	REPEATS	RESIDER
CRAUNCH	REAMERS	**RECOUP**	REFACED	**REGULA**	**REMIND**	**REPENT**	RESIDES
RAUNCHY	**REAPER**	RECOUPS	REFACES	REGULAE	REMINDS	REPENTS	**RESIGN**
RAUNGE	REAPERS	**RECTOR**	**REFECT**	REGULAR	**REMISE**	**REPINE**	RESIGNS
RAUNGED	**REARER**	ERECTOR	PREFECT	**REGULO**	PREMISE	REPINED	**RESILE**
RAUNGES	DREARER	RECTORS	REFECTS	REGULOS	REMISED	REPINER	RESILED
RAVAGE	REARERS	RECTORY	**REFERS**	**REHEAR**	REMISES	REPINES	RESILES
RAVAGED	**REASON**	**RECTUM**	PREFERS	REHEARD	**REMISS**	**REPLAN**	**RESIST**
RAVAGER	TREASON	RECTUMS	**REFILL**	REHEARS	PREMISS	REPLANS	RESISTS
RAVAGES	REASONS	**RECULE**	REFILLS	**REHEAT**	**REMITS**	REPLANT	**RESKEW**
RAVELS	**REASTS**	RECULED	**REFINE**	PREHEAT	FREMITS	**REPLAY**	RESKEWS
GRAVELS	BREASTS	RECULES	REFINED	REHEATS	**REMORA**	REPLAYS	**RESKUE**
TRAVELS	**REATES**	**RECURE**	REFINER	**REHEEL**	REMORAS	**REPONE**	RESKUED
RAVENS	CREATES	RECURED	REFINES	REHEELS	**REMOTE**	REPONED	RESKUES
CRAVENS	**REAVER**	RECURES	**REFLAG**	**REINED**	REMOTER	REPONES	**RESOLE**
RAVERS	REAVERS	**RECUSE**	REFLAGS	GREINED	REMOTES	**REPORT**	RESOLED
CRAVERS	**REAVES**	RECUSED	**REFLET**	**REITER**	**REMOVE**	REPORTS	RESOLES
GRAVERS	GREAVES	RECUSES	REFLETS	REITERS	PREMOVE	**REPOSE**	**RESORB**
RAVINE	**REBACK**	RECUSES	**REFLOW**	**REIVER**	REMOVED	REPOSED	RESORBS
RAVINED	REBACKS	**REDACT**	REFLOWS	REIVERS	REMOVER	REPOSES	**RESORT**
RAVINES	**REBATE**	REDACTS	**REFOOT**	**REJECT**	REMOVES	**REPOST**	RESORTS
RAVING	REBATED	**REDDEN**	REFOOTS	REJECTS	**REMUDA**	REPOSTS	**RESTED**
BRAVING	REBATER	REDDENS	**REFORM**	**REJOIN**	REMUDAS	**REPPED**	CRESTED
CRAVING	REBATES	**REDDER**	PREFORM	REJOINS	**RENAME**	PREPPED	PRESTED
GRAVING	**REBECK**	REDDERS	REFORMS	**RELATE**	RENAMED	**REPUGN**	WRESTED
RAVINGS	REBECKS	**REDDLE**	**REFUEL**	PRELATE	RENAMES	REPUGNS	**RESTEM**
RAWEST	**REBIND**	TREDDLE	REFUELS	RELATED	**RENDER**	**REPULP**	RESTEMS
BRAWEST	REBINDS	REDDLED	**REFUGE**	RELATER	RENDERS	REPULPS	**RESTER**
RAWING	**REBITE**	REDDLES	REFUGED	RELATES	**RENEGE**	**REPURE**	WRESTER
DRAWING	REBITES	**REDEAL**	REFUGEE	**RELENT**	RENEGED	REPURED	RESTERS
RAWINGS	**REBOIL**	REDEALS	REFUGES	RELENTS	RENEGER	REPURES	**RESULT**
RAYING	REBOILS	REDEALT	**REFUND**	**RELICT**	RENEGES	**REPUTE**	RESULTS
BRAYING	**REBORE**	**REDEEM**	REFUNDS	RELICTS	**RENNED**	REPUTED	**RESUME**
FRAYING	REBORED	REDEEMS	**REFUSE**	**RELIEF**	GRENNED	REPUTES	RESUMED
GRAYING	REBORES	**REDEYE**	REFUSED	RELIEFS	**RENNES**	**REQUIT**	RESUMES
PRAYING	**REBUFF**	REDEYES	REFUSER	**RELIER**	BRENNES	REQUITE	**RETAIL**
RAYLES	REBUFFS	**REDING**	REFUSES	RELIERS	FRENNES	REQUITS	

RETAILS	**REVESTS**	**RIBOSE**	TRIFLED	RINSERS	DRIVING	BROILED	**ROSACE**
RETAIN	**REVETS**	RIBOSES	**RIFLER**	**RIOTER**	**RIVLIN**	DROILED	ROSACEA
RETAINS	BREVETS	**RICERS**	TRIFLER	RIOTERS	RIVLINS	**ROINED**	ROSACES
RETAKE	**REVEUR**	GRICERS	RIFLERS	**RIPECK**	**RIZARD**	GROINED	**ROSETS**
RETAKEN	REVEURS	PRICERS	**RIFLES**	RIPECKS	RIZARDS	PROINED	GROSETS
RETAKER	**REVIEW**	**RICHEN**	TRIFLES	**RIPERS**	**RIZZAR**	**ROKERS**	**ROSIER**
RETAKES	PREVIEW	RICHENS	**RIFTED**	GRIPERS	RIZZARS	BROKERS	CROSIER
RETAMA	REVIEWS	**RICHES**	DRIFTED	**RIPING**	RIZZART	PROKERS	PROSIER
RETAMAS	**REVILE**	RICHEST	GRIFTED	GRIPING	**RIZZER**	**ROKING**	ROSIERE
RETARD	REVILED	**RICHTS**	**RIGGED**	**RIPPED**	RIZZERS	BROKING	ROSIERS
RETARDS	REVILER	FRICHTS	FRIGGED	DRIPPED	**RIZZOR**	PROKING	**ROSIES**
RETELL	REVILES	**RICIER**	GRIGGED	GRIPPED	RIZZORS	TROKING	ROSIEST
RETELLS	**REVISE**	PRICIER	PRIGGED	TRIPPED	**ROADIE**	**ROLLED**	**ROSILY**
RETENE	PREVISE	**RICING**	TRIGGED	**RIPPER**	ROADIES	DROLLED	PROSILY
RETENES	REVISED	GRICING	**RIGGER**	FRIPPER	**ROAMER**	PROLLED	**ROSING**
RETILE	REVISER	PRICING	FRIGGER	GRIPPER	ROAMERS	TROLLED	PROSING
RETILED	REVISES	TRICING	PRIGGER	TRIPPER	**ROARER**	**ROLLER**	**ROSSER**
RETILES	**REVIVE**	**RICKED**	TRIGGER	RIPPERS	ROARERS	DROLLER	CROSSER
RETINA	REVIVED	BRICKED	RIGGERS	**RIPPLE**	**ROARIE**	PROLLER	GROSSER
RETINAE	REVIVER	CRICKED	**RIGHTO**	ARIPPLE	ROARIER	TROLLER	**ROSSERS**
RETINAL	REVIVES	PRICKED	RIGHTOS	CRIPPLE	**ROATED**	ROLLERS	**ROSTED**
RETINAS	**REVOKE**	TRICKED	**RIGHTS**	GRIPPLE	TROATED	**ROMAGE**	FROSTED
RETIRE	REVOKED	WRICKED	FRIGHTS	TRIPPLE	**ROBALO**	ROMAGES	**ROSTER**
RETIRED	REVOKES	**RICKER**	WRIGHTS	RIPPLED	ROBALOS	**ROMPER**	ROSTERS
RETIREE	**REVOLT**	PRICKER	**RIGLIN**	RIPPLER	**ROBBER**	ROMPERS	**ROSTRA**
RETIRER	REVOLTS	TRICKER	RIGLING	RIPPLES	ROBBERS	**RONDEL**	ROSTRAL
RETIRES	**REWARD**	RICKERS	RIGLINS	RIPPLET	ROBBERY	RONDELS	**ROSULA**
RETOOL	REWARDS	**RICKLE**	**RIGOLL**	**RIPRAP**	**ROBING**	**RONYON**	ROSULAS
RETOOLS	**REWIND**	BRICKLE	RIGOLLS	RIPRAPS	PROBING	RONYONS	**ROTATE**
RETORT	REWINDS	PRICKLE	**RIGOUR**	**RISERS**	ROBINGS	**ROOFED**	ROTATED
RETORTS	**REWIRE**	TRICKLE	RIGOURS	PRISERS	**ROBUST**	PROOFED	ROTATES
RETOUR	REWIRED	RICKLES	**RILLED**	**RISING**	ROBUSTA	**ROOFER**	**ROTCHE**
RETOURS	REWIRES	**RICKLY**	DRILLED	ARISING	**ROCHES**	ROOFERS	**ROTCHES**
RETREE	**REWORD**	PRICKLY	FRILLED	GRISING	BROCHES	**ROOKED**	**ROTGUT**
RETREES	REWORDS	TRICKLY	GRILLED	IRISING	CROCHES	BROOKED	ROTGUTS
RETRIM	**REWORK**	**RIDDER**	PRILLED	KRISING	TROCHES	CROOKED	**ROTHER**
RETRIMS	REWORKS	RIDDERS	TRILLED	PRISING	**ROCHET**	DROOKED	BROTHER
RETTED	**REWRAP**	**RIDDLE**	**RILLES**	RISINGS	CROCHET	**ROOKIE**	ROTHERS
ARETTED	REWRAPS	GRIDDLE	GRILLES	**RISKED**	ROCHETS	ROOKIES	**ROTOLO**
FRETTED	**RHAPHE**	RIDDLED	**RILLET**	BRISKED	**ROCKED**	**ROOMED**	ROTOLOS
RETUND	RHAPHES	RIDDLER	RILLETS	FRISKED	BROCKED	BROOMED	**ROTTAN**
RETUNDS	**RHETOR**	RIDDLES	**RIMERS**	**RISKER**	CROCKED	GROOMED	ROTTANS
RETUNE	RHETORS	**RIDENT**	PRIMERS	BRISKER	FROCKED	VROOMED	**ROTTED**
RETUNED	**RHOMBI**	TRIDENT	TRIMERS	FRISKER	TROCKED	**ROOMER**	TROTTED
RETUNES	RHOMBIC	**RIDGED**	**RIMIER**	RISKERS	**ROCKER**	ROOMERS	**ROTTEN**
RETURF	**RHUMBA**	BRIDGED	GRIMIER	**RISPED**	ROCKERS	**ROOPED**	ROTTENS
RETURFS	RHUMBAS	FRIDGED	**RIMING**	CRISPED	ROCKERY	DROOPED	**ROTTER**
RETURN	**RHYMER**	**RIDGEL**	BRIMING	**RISQUE**	**ROCKET**	TROOPED	TROTTER
RETURNS	RHYMERS	RIDGELS	CRIMING	RISQUES	BROCKET	**ROOSES**	ROTTERS
REURGE	**RHYTHM**	**RIDGES**	GRIMING	**RITTED**	CROCKET	BROOSES	**ROTULA**
REURGED	RHYTHMI	BRIDGES	PRIMING	FRITTED	ROCKETS	**ROOTED**	ROTULAS
REURGES	RHYTHMS	FRIDGES	**RIMMED**	GRITTED	**ROCOCO**	WROOTED	**ROTUND**
REVAMP	**RIBALD**	**RIDGIL**	BRIMMED	**RITTER**	ROCOCOS	**ROOTER**	OROTUND
REVAMPS	RIBALDS	RIDGILS	PRIMMED	CRITTER	**RODDED**	ROOTERS	ROTUNDA
REVEAL	**RIBAND**	**RIDING**	TRIMMED	FRITTER	BRODDED	**ROOTLE**	ROTUNDS
REVEALS	RIBANDS	BRIDING	**RINDED**	GRITTER	PRODDED	ROOTLED	**ROUBLE**
REVERB	**RIBAUD**	GRIDING	BRINDED	RITTERS	**RODENT**	ROOTLES	TROUBLE
PREVERB	RIBAUDS	PRIDING	GRINDED	**RITUAL**	ERODENT	**ROOTLET**	**ROUBLES**
REVERBS	**RIBBED**	RIDINGS	**RINGED**	RITUALS	RODENTS	**ROPERS**	ROUCOU
REVERE	CRIBBED	**RIEVER**	CRINGED	**RIVAGE**	**RODING**	GROPERS	ROUCOUS
REVERED	DRIBBED	GRIEVER	FRINGED	RIVAGES	ERODING	PROPERS	**ROUGHS**
REVERER	**RIBBON**	RIEVERS	WRINGED	**RIVELS**	RODINGS	**ROPING**	BROUGHS
REVERES	RIBBONS	**RIEVES**	**RINGER**	DRIVELS	**ROEMER**	GROPING	TROUGHS
REVERS	RIBBONY	GRIEVES	BRINGER	**RIVERS**	ROEMERS	TROPING	**ROUGHT**
REVERSE	**RIBIBE**	PRIEVES	CRINGER	DRIVERS	**ROGERS**	ROPINGS	BROUGHT
REVERSI	RIBIBES	**RIFFLE**	WRINGER	**RIVETS**	DROGERS	**ROQUET**	DROUGHT
REVERSO	**RIBLET**	RIFFLED	RINGERS	GRIVETS	**ROGUES**	CROQUET	WROUGHT
REVERT	DRIBLET	RIFFLER	**RINKED**	PRIVETS	BROGUES	ROQUETS	**ROUGHY**
REVERTS	TRIBLET	RIFFLES	PRINKED	TRIVETS	DROGUES	**RORTER**	FROUGHY
REVEST	RIBLETS	**RIFLED**	**RINSER**	**RIVING**	**ROILED**	RORTERS	**ROULES**

TROULES	RUBINE	TRUMPED	RYPECK	SALLAL	SANDHIS	SAVAGED	SCERNE
ROUNCE	RUBINES	RUMPLE	RYPECKS	SALLALS	SANGAR	SAVAGER	SCERNED
FROUNCE	RUBRIC	CRUMPLE	RYTHME	SALLEE	SANGARS	SAVAGES	SCERNES
TROUNCE	RUBRICS	FRUMPLE	RYTHMED	SALLEES	SANJAK	SAVANT	SCHELM
ROUNCES	RUCKED	RUMPLED	RYTHMES	SALLET	SANJAKS	SAVANTS	SCHELMS
ROUNDS	TRUCKED	RUMPLES	SABBAT	SALLETS	SANNUP	SAVATE	SCHEME
GROUNDS	RUCKLE	RUNDLE	SABBATS	SALLOW	SANNUPS	SAVATES	SCHEMED
ROUPED	BRUCKLE	TRUNDLE	SACHEM	SALLOWS	SANPAN	SAVINE	SCHEMER
CROUPED	TRUCKLE	RUNDLED	SACHEMS	SALLOWY	SANPANS	SAVINES	SCHEMES
GROUPED	RUCKLED	RUNDLES	SACHET	SALMON	SANSEI	SAVING	SCHISM
TROUPED	RUCKLES	RUNDLET	SACHETS	SALMONS	SANSEIS	SAVINGS	SCHISMA
ROUSED	RUDDER	RUNKLE	SACQUE	SALOON	SANTAL	SAVOUR	SCHISMS
AROUSED	RUDDERS	CRUNKLE	SACQUES	SALOONS	SANTALS	SAVOURS	SCHIST
GROUSED	RUDDLE	RUNKLED	SADDEN	SALOOP	SANTIR	SAVOURY	SCHISTS
ROUSER	RUDDLED	RUNKLES	SADDENS	SALOOPS	SANTIRS	SAVVEY	SCHIZO
AROUSER	RUDDLES	RUNLET	SADDHU	SALTER	SANTON	SAVVEYS	SCHIZOS
GROUSER	RUDELY	RUNLETS	SADDHUS	PSALTER	SANTONS	SAWDER	SCHLEP
ROUSERS	CRUDELY	RUNNEL	SADDLE	SALTERN	SANTUR	SAWDERS	SCHLEPP
ROUSES	RUDERY	RUNNELS	SADDLED	SALTERS	SANTURS	SAWING	SCHLEPS
AROUSES	PRUDERY	RUNNER	SADDLER	SALUKI	SAPELE	SAWINGS	SCHMOE
GROUSES	RUDEST	RUNNERS	SADDLES	SALUKIS	SAPELES	SAWNEY	SCHMOES
TROUSES	CRUDEST	RUNNET	SADISM	SALUTE	SAPOTA	SAWNEYS	SCHOOL
ROUTED	RUDISH	RUNNETS	SADISMS	SALUTED	SAPOTAS	SAWPIT	SCHOOLE
GROUTED	PRUDISH	RUNRIG	SADIST	SALUTER	SAPPAN	SAWPITS	SCHOOLS
ROUTER	RUEING	RUNRIGS	SADISTS	SALUTES	SAPPANS	SAWYER	SCHORL
TROUTER	GRUEING	RUNTED	SAETER	SALVER	SAPPER	SAWYERS	SCHORLS
ROUTERS	TRUEING	BRUNTED	SAETERS	SALVERS	SAPPERS	SAXAUL	SCHOUT
ROUTES	RUEINGS	GRUNTED	SAFARI	SALVIA	SARDEL	SAXAULS	SCHOUTS
CROUTES	RUELLE	PRUNTED	SAFARIS	SALVIAS	SARDELS	SAYING	SCHTIK
ROUTHS	RUELLES	RUNWAY	SAGENE	SALVOR	SARNEY	SAYINGS	SCHTIKS
DROUTHS	RUFFIN	RUNWAYS	SAGENES	SALVORS	SARNEYS	SAYYID	SCHUIT
ROVERS	RUFFING	RUPIAH	SAGGAR	SAMAAN	SARNIE	SAYYIDS	SCHUITS
DROVERS	RUFFINS	RUPIAHS	SAGGARD	SAMAANS	SARNIES	SAZHEN	SCHUYT
PROVERS	RUFFLE	RUSHED	SAGGARS	SAMARA	SARONG	SAZHENS	SCHUYTS
TROVERS	TRUFFLE	BRUSHED	SAGGER	SAMARAS	SARONGS	SCAITH	SCILLA
ROVING	RUFFLED	CRUSHED	SAGGERS	SAMBAL	SARSEN	SCAITHS	SCILLAS
PROVING	RUFFLER	FRUSHED	SAGOIN	SAMBALS	SARSENS	SCALAR	SCIROC
ROVINGS	RUFFLES	RUSHER	SAGOINS	SAMBAR	SARTOR	SCALARS	SCIROCS
ROWELS	RUGGED	RUSHERS	SAGUIN	SAMBARS	SARTORS	SCALER	SCLAFF
TROWELS	DRUGGED	RUSHES	SAGUINS	SAMBAS	SASHAY	SCALERS	SCLAFFS
ROWERS	RUGGER	BRUSHES	SAHIBA	TSAMBAS	SASHAYS	SCAMEL	SCLATE
GROWERS	DRUGGER	CRUSHES	SAHIBAH	SAMBUR	SASINE	SCAMELS	SCLATED
ROWING	RUGGERS	FRUSHES	SAHIBAS	SAMBURS	SASINES	SCAMPI	SCLATES
CROWING	RUINER	RUSSEL	SAIKEI	SAMFOO	SATARA	SCAMPIS	SCLAVE
GROWING	RUINERS	RUSSELS	SAIKEIS	SAMFOOS	SATARAS	SCAPED	SCLAVES
TROWING	RULING	RUSSET	SAILER	SAMIEL	SATEEN	ESCAPED	SCLERA
ROWINGS	RULINGS	RUSSETS	SAILERS	SAMIELS	SATEENS	SCAPES	SCLERAL
ROWTHS	RUMBLE	RUSSETY	SAILOR	SAMITE	SATINS	ESCAPES	SCLERAS
GROWTHS	CRUMBLE	RUSSIA	SAILORS	SAMITES	ISATINS	SCARAB	SCLERE
ROYNED	DRUMBLE	RUSSIAS	SAIQUE	SAMLET	SATIRE	SCARABS	SCLERES
PROYNED	GRUMBLE	RUSTED	SAIQUES	SAMLETS	SATIRES	SCARCE	SCLIFF
ROYNES	RUMBLED	CRUSTED	SAITHE	SAMLOR	SATORI	SCARCER	SCLIFFS
GROYNES	RUMBLER	TRUSTED	SAITHES	SAMLORS	SATORIS	SCARER	SCONCE
PROYNES	RUMBLES	RUSTIC	SAKIEH	SAMOSA	SATRAP	SCARERS	ASCONCE
ROZZER	RUMBLY	RUSTICS	SAKIEHS	SAMOSAS	SATRAPS	SCARPS	SCONCED
ROZZERS	CRUMBLY	RUSTLE	SALAAM	SAMPAN	SATRAPY	ESCARPS	SCONCES
RUBATO	GRUMBLY	RUSTLED	SALAAMS	SAMPANS	SATYRA	SCARRE	SCORER
RUBATOS	RUMKIN	RUSTLER	SALADE	SAMPLE	SATYRAL	SCARRED	SCORERS
RUBBED	RUMKINS	RUSTLES	SALADES	SAMPLED	SATYRAS	SCARRES	SCORIA
DRUBBED	RUMMER	RUSTRE	SALAMI	SAMPLER	SAUCER	SCARTH	SCORIAC
GRUBBED	BRUMMER	RUSTRED	SALAMIS	SAMPLES	SAUCERS	SCARTHS	SCORIAE
RUBBER	DRUMMER	RUSTRES	SALINA	SAMSHU	SAUGER	SCATHE	SCORSE
GRUBBER	GRUMMER	RUTILE	SALINAS	SAMSHUS	SAUGERS	SCATHED	SCORSED
RUBBERS	RUMMERS	RUTILES	SALINE	SANCHO	SAULGE	SCATHES	SCORSER
RUBBERY	RUMOUR	RUTTER	SALINES	SANCHOS	SAULGES	SCAZON	SCORSES
RUBBLE	RUMOURS	RUTTERS	SALIVA	SANDAL	SAULIE	SCAZONS	SCOTER
GRUBBLE	RUMPED	RYOKAN	SALIVAL	SANDALS	SAULIES	SCENDS	SCOTERS
RUBBLES	FRUMPED	RYOKANS	SALIVAS	SANDER	SAUREL	ASCENDS	SCOTIA
RUBIES	CRUMPED		SALLAD	SANDERS	SAURELS	SCENTS	SCOTIAS
RUBIEST	FRUMPED		SALLADS	SANDHI	SAVAGE	ASCENTS	SCOURS

SCOURSE	SCRUZED	SECURED	**SENNIT**	**SETTER**	SHEATHY	**SHOVEL**	SIEGERS
SCOUSE	SCRUZES	SECURER	SENNITS	SETTERS	**SHEAVE**	SHOVELS	**SIENNA**
SCOUSES	**SCRYER**	SECURES	**SENSOR**	**SETTLE**	SHEAVED	**SHOVER**	SIENNAS
SCOUTH	SCRYERS	**SEDATE**	SENSORS	SETTLED	SHEAVES	SHOVERS	**SIERRA**
SCOUTHS	**SCRYNE**	SEDATED	SENSORY	SETTLER	**SHEIKH**	**SHOWER**	SIERRAN
SCOWTH	**SCRYNES**	SEDATER	**SEPHEN**	SETTLES	SHEIKHS	SHOWERS	SIERRAS
SCOWTHS	**SCULLE**	SEDATES	SEPHENS	**SEVERE**	**SHEILA**	SHOWERY	**SIESTA**
SCRAPE	SCULLED	**SEDUCE**	**SEPIUM**	SEVERED	SHEILAS	**SHREEK**	SIESTAS
SCRAPED	SCULLER	SEDUCED	SEPIUMS	SEVERER	**SHEKEL**	SHREEKS	**SIFAKA**
SCRAPER	SCULLES	SEDUCER	**SEPSES**	**SEWAGE**	SHEKELS	**SHREIK**	SIFAKAS
SCRAPES	**SCULPT**	SEDUCES	ASEPSES	SEWAGES	**SHELVE**	SHREIKS	**SIFFLE**
SCRAWL	SCULPTS	**SEEDER**	**SEPSIS**	**SEWING**	SHELVED	**SHRIEK**	SIFFLED
SCRAWLS	**SCUNGE**	SEEDERS	ASEPSIS	SEWINGS	SHELVES	SHRIEKS	SIFFLES
SCRAWLY	SCUNGED	**SEEING**	**SEPTET**	**SEXISM**	**SHENDS**	**SHRIFT**	**SIFTER**
SCRAWM	SCUNGES	SEEINGS	SEPTETS	SEXISMS	YSHENDS	SHRIFTS	SIFTERS
SCRAWMS	**SCYTHE**	**SEEKER**	SEPTETT	**SEXIST**	**SHERIA**	**SHRIKE**	**SIGHER**
SCRAYE	SCYTHED	SEEKERS	**SEPTIC**	SEXISTS	SHERIAS	SHRIKED	SIGHERS
SCRAYES	SCYTHER	**SEEMER**	ASEPTIC	**SEXPOT**	SHERIAT	SHRIKES	**SIGNAL**
SCREAK	SCYTHES	SEEMERS	**SEQUEL**	SEXPOTS	**SHERIF**	**SHRILL**	SIGNALS
SCREAKS	**SDAINE**	**SEESAW**	SEQUELA	**SEXTAN**	SHERIFF	SHRILLS	**SIGNER**
SCREAKY	SDAINED	SEESAWS	SEQUELS	SEXTANS	SHERIFS	SHRILLY	SIGNERS
SCREAM	SDAINES	**SEETHE**	**SEQUIN**	SEXTANT	**SHEUCH**	**SHRIMP**	**SIGNET**
SCREAMS	**SEABED**	SEETHED	SEQUINS	**SEXTET**	SHEUCHS	SHRIMPS	SIGNETS
SCREED	SEABEDS	SEETHER	**SERAIL**	SEXTETS	**SHEUGH**	**SHRINE**	**SIGNOR**
SCREEDS	**SEALCH**	SEETHES	SERAILS	SEXTETT	SHEUGHS	SHRINED	SIGNORA
SCREEN	SEALCHS	**SEGGAR**	**SERANG**	**SEXTON**	**SHEWEL**	SHRINES	SIGNORE
SCREENS	**SEALER**	SEGGARS	SERANGS	SEXTONS	SHEWELS	**SHRINK**	SIGNORI
SCRIBE	SEALERS	**SEGHOL**	**SERAPE**	**SEXUAL**	**SHIELD**	SHRINKS	SIGNORS
ASCRIBE	SEALERY	SEGHOLS	SERAPES	ASEXUAL	SHIELDS	**SHRIVE**	SIGNORY
ESCRIBE	**SEALGH**	**SEICHE**	**SERAPH**	**SHADOW**	**SHIEST**	SHRIVED	**SILAGE**
SCRIBED	SEALGHS	SEICHES	SERAPHS	SHADOWS	ASHIEST	SHRIVEL	SILAGED
SCRIBER	**SEAMER**	**SEINER**	**SERDAB**	SHADOWY	**SHIKAR**	SHRIVEN	SILAGES
SCRIBES	SEAMERS	SEINERS	SERDABS	**SHADUF**	SHIKARI	SHRIVER	**SILANE**
SCRIKE	**SEANCE**	**SEISIN**	**SEREIN**	SHADUFS	SHIKARS	SHRIVES	SILANES
SCRIKED	SEANCES	SEISING	SEREINS	**SHAIKH**	**SHIKSA**	**SHROFF**	**SILENE**
SCRIKES	**SEARAT**	SEISINS	**SERENE**	SHAIKHS	SHIKSAS	SHROFFS	SILENES
SCRIMP	SEARATS	**SEIZER**	SERENED	**SHAIRN**	**SHIKSE**	**SHROUD**	**SILENT**
SCRIMPS	**SEARCE**	SEIZERS	SERENER	SHAIRNS	SHIKSES	SHROUDS	SILENTS
SCRIMPY	SEARCED	**SEIZIN**	SERENES	**SHAKER**	**SHINER**	SHROUDY	**SILICA**
SCRINE	SEARCES	SEIZING	**SERIAL**	SHAKERS	SHINERS	**SHROVE**	SILICAS
SCRINES	**SEASON**	SEIZINS	SERIALS	**SHALLI**	**SHINES**	SHROVED	**SILKEN**
SCRIPT	SEASONS	**SELECT**	**SERING**	SHALLIS	SHINESS	SHROVES	SILKENS
SCRIPTS	**SEATER**	SELECTS	SERINGA	**SHALOT**	**SHINNE**	**SHTCHI**	**SILKIE**
SCRIVE	SEATERS	**SELKIE**	**SERIPH**	SHALOTS	SHINNED	SHTCHIS	SILKIER
SCRIVED	**SEAWAY**	SELKIES	SERIPHS	**SHAMAN**	SHINNES	**SHTETL**	SILKIES
SCRIVES	SEAWAYS	**SELLER**	**SERMON**	SHAMANS	**SHIPPO**	SHTETLS	**SILLER**
SCROBE	**SEBATE**	SELLERS	SERMONS	**SHAMED**	SHIPPON	**SHTICK**	SILLERS
SCROBES	SEBATES	**SEMBLE**	**SEROON**	ASHAMED	SHIPPOS	SHTICKS	**SILVAN**
SCROLL	**SECANT**	SEMBLED	SEROONS	**SHAMER**	**SHIRRA**	**SHTOOK**	SILVANS
ESCROLL	SECANTS	SEMBLES	**SEROSA**	SHAMERS	SHIRRAS	SHTOOKS	**SILVER**
SCROLLS	**SECEDE**	**SEMEME**	SEROSAE	**SHAMES**	**SHIVER**	**SHTUCK**	SILVERN
SCROOP	SECEDED	SEMEMES	SEROSAL	ASHAMES	SHIVERS	SHTUCKS	SILVERS
SCROOPS	SECEDER	**SEMMIT**	SEROSAS	**SHAMOY**	SHIVERY	**SHUFTI**	SILVERY
SCROWL	SECEDES	SEMMITS	**SERRAN**	SHAMOYS	**SHIVOO**	SHUFTIS	**SIMIAN**
SCROWLE	**SECERN**	**SEMPLE**	SERRANS	**SHAPER**	SHIVOOS	**SIALON**	SIMIANS
SCROWLS	SECERNS	SEMPLER	**SERVAL**	SHAPERS	**SHLOCK**	SIALONS	**SIMILE**
SCROWS	**SECKEL**	**SEMSEM**	SERVALS	**SHARER**	SHLOCKS	**SICKEN**	SIMILES
ESCROWS	SECKELS	SEMSEMS	**SERVER**	SHARERS	**SHODER**	SICKENS	**SIMKIN**
SCRUFF	**SECOND**	**SENATE**	SERVERS	**SHARIA**	SHODERS	SICKIE	SIMKINS
SCRUFFS	SECONDE	SENATES	SERVERY	SHARIAS	**SHOFAR**	SICKIES	**SIMMER**
SCRUFFY	SECONDI	**SENDAL**	**SESAME**	SHARIAT	SHOFARS	**SICKLE**	SIMMERS
SCRUMP	SECONDO	SENDALS	SESAMES	**SHAVER**	**SHOGUN**	SICKLED	**SIMNEL**
SCRUMPS	SECONDS	**SENDER**	**SESELI**	SHAVERS	SHOGUNS	SICKLES	SIMNELS
SCRUMPY	**SECRET**	SENDERS	SESELIS	**SHAVIE**	**SHORAN**	**SIDDHA**	**SIMOOM**
SCRUNT	SECRETA	**SENEGA**	**SESTET**	SHAVIES	SHORANS	SIDDHAS	SIMOOMS
SCRUNTS	SECRETE	SENEGAS	SESTETS	**SHAWED**	**SHORER**	**SIDDHI**	**SIMOON**
SCRUNTY	SECRETS	**SENIOR**	SESTETT	PSHAWED	SHORERS	SIDDHIS	SIMOONS
SCRUTO	**SECTOR**	SENIORS	**SESTON**	**SHEATH**	**SHOUGH**	**SIDING**	**SIMORG**
SCRUTOS	SECTORS	**SENNET**	SESTONS	SHEATHE	SHOUGHS	SIDINGS	SIMORGS
SCRUZE	**SECURE**	SENNETS	**SETTEE**	SHEATHS		**SIEGER**	**SIMPAI**

SIMPAIS	SIZZLED	SLEECHY	SMUDGES	SOIGNE	SORELL	SPARRED	SPIRAL
SIMPER	SIZZLER	SLEEVE	SNARER	SOIGNEE	SORELLS	SPARRER	SPIRALS
SIMPERS	SIZZLES	SLEEVED	SNARERS	SOIREE	SORGHO	SPARRES	SPIREA
SIMPLE	SKAITH	SLEEVER	SNASTE	SOIREES	SORGHOS	SPARSE	SPIREAS
SIMPLED	SKAITHS	SLEEVES	SNASTES	SOLACE	SORNER	SPARSER	SPIRED
SIMPLER	SKARTH	SLEIGH	SNATCH	SOLACED	SORNERS	SPARTH	ASPIRED
SIMPLES	SKARTHS	SLEIGHS	SNATCHY	SOLACES	SORREL	SPARTHE	SPIRES
SIMPLEX	SKATER	SLEIGHT	SNATHE	SOLAND	SORRELS	SPARTHS	ASPIRES
SIMURG	SKATERS	SLEUTH	SNATHES	SOLANDS	SORROW	SPATHE	SPIRIC
SIMURGH	SKETCH	SLEUTHS	SNEATH	SOLANO	SORROWS	SPATHED	SPIRICS
SIMURGS	SKETCHY	SLICER	SNEATHS	SOLANOS	SORTER	SPATHES	SPIRIT
SINDON	SKEWER	SLICERS	SNEBBE	SOLDAN	SORTERS	SPAULD	SPIRITS
SINDONS	SKEWERS	SLIDER	SNEBBED	SOLDANS	SORTIE	SPAULDS	SPIRITY
SINGER	SKIDOO	SLIDERS	SNEBBES	SOLDER	SORTIED	SPAVIE	SPITAL
SINGERS	SKIDOOS	SLIGHT	SNEEZE	SOLDERS	SORTIES	SPAVIES	SPITALS
SINGLE	SKIING	SLIGHTS	SNEEZED	SOLERA	SOUARI	SPAVIN	SPLASH
SINGLED	SKIINGS	SLIVER	SNEEZER	SOLERAS	SOUARIS	SPAVINS	SPLASHY
SINGLES	SKIVER	SLIVERS	SNEEZES	SOLITO	SOUPER	SPAYAD	SPLEEN
SINGLET	SKIVERS	SLOGAN	SNIDES	SOLITON	SOUPERS	SPAYADS	SPLEENS
SINKER	SKIVIE	SLOGANS	SNIDEST	SOLIVE	SOUPLE	SPECIE	SPLEENY
SINKERS	SKIVIER	SLOKEN	SNIPER	SOLIVES	SOUPLED	SPECIES	SPLENT
SINNER	SKLATE	SLOKENS	SNIPERS	SOLLAR	SOUPLES	SPEEDO	SPLENTS
SINNERS	SKLATED	SLOUCH	SNIVEL	SOLLARS	SOURCE	SPEEDOS	SPLICE
SINNET	SKLATES	SLOUCHY	SNIVELS	SOLLER	SOURCED	SPENCE	SPLICED
SINNETS	SKLENT	SLOUGH	SNOOZE	SOLLERS	SOURCES	SPENCER	SPLICES
SINTER	ASKLENT	SLOUGHS	SNOOZED	SOLUTE	SOURSE	SPENCES	SPLIFF
SINTERS	SKLENTS	SLOUGHY	SNOOZER	SOLUTES	SOURSES	SPERRE	SPLIFFS
SINTERY	SKLIFF	SLOVEN	SNOOZES	SOLVER	SOUTAR	SPERRED	SPLINE
SIPHON	SKLIFFS	SLOVENS	SNORER	SOLVERS	SOUTARS	SPERRES	SPLINED
SIPHONS	SKREEN	SLUDGE	SNORERS	SOMBRE	SOUTER	SPERSE	SPLINES
SIPPER	SKREENE	SLUDGES	SNUBBE	SOMBRED	SOUTERS	ASPERSE	SPLINT
SIPPERS	SKREENS	SLUICE	SNUBBED	SOMBRER	SOVIET	SPERSED	SPLINTS
SIPPET	SKRIMP	SLUICED	SNUBBER	SOMBRES	SOVIETS	SPERSES	SPLORE
SIPPETS	SKRIMPS	SLUICES	SNUBBES	SOMITE	SOVRAN	SPEWER	SPLORES
SIPPLE	SKRUMP	SMALTO	SNUDGE	SOMITES	SOVRANS	SPEWERS	SPONGE
SIPPLED	SKRUMPS	SMALTOS	SNUDGED	SONANT	SOWING	SPHAER	SPONGED
SIPPLES	SKRYER	SMEATH	SNUDGES	SONANTS	SOWINGS	SPHAERE	SPONGER
SIRCAR	SKRYERS	SMEATHS	SOAKER	SONATA	SOWSSE	SPHAERS	SPONGES
SIRCARS	SKYLAB	SMEETH	SOAKERS	SONATAS	SOWSSED	SPHEAR	SPORTS
SIRDAR	SKYLABS	SMEETHS	SOAPIE	SONERI	SOWSSES	SPHEARE	ASPORTS
SIRDARS	SKYWAY	SMEGMA	SOAPIER	SONERIS	SOWTER	SPHEARS	SPOTTE
SIRENE	SKYWAYS	SMEGMAS	SOAPIES	SONNET	SOWTERS	SPHENE	SPOTTED
SIRENES	SLAIRG	SMEUSE	SOBOLE	SONNETS	SOZZLE	SPHENES	SPOTTER
SIRKAR	SLAIRGS	SMEUSES	SOBOLES	SONSIE	SOZZLED	SPHERE	SPOTTES
SIRKARS	SLAKED	SMIGHT	SOCAGE	SONSIER	SOZZLES	SPHERED	SPOUSE
SIRRAH	ASLAKED	SMIGHTS	SOCAGER	SONTAG	SPACER	SPHERES	ESPOUSE
SIRRAHS	YSLAKED	SMILER	SOCAGES	SONTAGS	SPACERS	SPIALS	SPOUSED
SIRREE	SLAKES	SMILERS	SOCCER	SOOGEE	SPADER	ESPIALS	SPOUSES
SIRREES	ASLAKES	SMILET	SOCCERS	SOOGEED	SPADERS	SPICER	SPRAIN
SISKIN	SLALOM	SMILETS	SOCIAL	SOOGEES	SPAHEE	SPICERS	SPRAINS
SISKINS	SLALOMS	SMITER	ASOCIAL	SOOGIE	SPAHEES	SPICERY	SPRAINT
SISSOO	SLATER	SMITERS	SOCIALS	SOOGIED	SPAING	SPICKS	SPRAWL
SISSOOS	SLATERS	SMOILE	SOCKER	SOOGIES	SPAINGS	ASPICKS	ASPRAWL
SISTER	SLAVER	SMOILED	SOCKERS	SOOJEY	SPALLE	SPIDER	SPRAWLS
SISTERS	SLAVERS	SMOILES	SOCKET	SOOJEYS	SPALLED	SPIDERS	SPRAWLY
SITCOM	SLAVERY	SMOKER	SOCKETS	SOOTHE	SPALLES	SPIDERY	SPREAD
SITCOMS	SLAVEY	SMOKERS	SODAIN	SOOTHED	SPARER	SPIGHT	ASPREAD
SITHEN	SLAVEYS	SMOOTH	SODAINE	SOOTHER	SPARERS	SPIGHTS	SPREADS
SITHENS	SLAYER	SMOOTHE	SODDEN	SOOTHES	SPARES	SPIGOT	SPREDD
SITREP	SLAYERS	SMOOTHS	SODDENS	SOPHIA	SPAREST	SPIGOTS	SPREDDE
SITREPS	SLEAVE	SMOUSE	SODGER	SOPHIAS	SPARGE	SPILTH	SPREDDS
SITTAR	SLEAVED	SMOUSED	SODGERS	SOPITE	SPARGED	SPILTHS	SPRING
SITTARS	SLEAVES	SMOUSER	SODIUM	SOPITED	SPARGER	SPINAR	SPRINGE
SITTER	SLEAZE	SMOUSES	SODIUMS	SOPITES	SPARGES	SPINARS	SPRINGS
SITTERS	SLEAZES	SMOYLE	SOFFIT	SORAGE	SPARID	SPINEL	SPRINGY
SITULA	SLEDGE	SMOYLED	SOFFITS	SORAGES	SPARIDS	SPINELS	SPRINT
SITULAE	SLEDGED	SMOYLES	SOFTEN	SORBET	SPARKE	SPINES	SPRINTS
SIZING	SLEDGER	SMUDGE	SOFTENS	SORBETS	SPARKED	ASPINES	SPRITE
SIZINGS	SLEDGES	SMUDGED	SOFTIE	SORDOR	SPARKES	SPINET	SPRITES
SIZZLE	SLEECH	SMUDGER	SOFTIES	SORDORS	SPARRE	SPINETS	SPRITS

ESPRITS	SQUISHY	STEALED	**STODGE**	**STRAYS**	STRUMAE	**SUDDER**	**SURFER**
SPROUT	**STABLE**	STEALER	STODGED	ESTRAYS	**STRUMS**	SUDDERS	SURFERS
ASPROUT	ASTABLE	STEALES	STODGER	**STREAK**	ESTRUMS	**SUDSER**	**SURING**
SPROUTS	STABLED	**STEALT**	STODGES	STREAKS	**STRUNT**	SUDSERS	USURING
SPRUCE	STABLER	STEALTH	**STOGEY**	STREAKY	STRUNTS	**SUFFER**	**SURREY**
SPRUCED	STABLES	**STEANE**	STOGEYS	**STREAM**	**STUCCO**	SUFFERS	SURREYS
SPRUCER	**STACTE**	STEANED	**STOGIE**	STREAMS	STUCCOS	**SUITOR**	**SURVEW**
SPRUCES	STACTES	STEANES	STOGIES	STREAMY	**STUDIO**	SUITORS	SURVEWE
SPRUIK	**STADDA**	**STEARE**	**STOKER**	**STREEK**	STUDIOS	**SULFUR**	SURVEWS
SPRUIKS	STADDAS	STEARED	STOKERS	STREEKS	**STUMER**	SULFURS	**SURVEY**
SPRUIT	**STADIA**	STEARES	**STOLON**	**STREEL**	STUMERS	**SULLEN**	SURVEYS
SPRUITS	STADIAL	**STEDDE**	STOLONS	STREELS	**STUPID**	SULLENS	**SUSLIK**
SPULYE	STADIAS	STEDDED	**STONED**	**STREET**	STUPIDS	**SULTAN**	SUSLIKS
SPULYED	**STAGER**	STEDDES	ASTONED	STREETS	**STUPOR**	SULTANA	**SUTLER**
SPULYES	STAGERS	**STEEMS**	**STONER**	STREETY	STUPORS	SULTANS	SUTLERS
SPUNGE	STAGERY	ESTEEMS	STONERN	**STRENE**	**STYLAR**	**SUMACH**	SUTLERY
SPUNGES	**STAITH**	**STEEVE**	STONERS	STRENES	ASTYLAR	SUMACHS	**SUTTEE**
SPURGE	STAITHE	STEEVED	**STONES**	**STRICH**	**STYLET**	**SUMMAR**	SUTTEES
SPURGES	STAITHS	STEEVER	ASTONES	ESTRICH	STYLETS	SUMMARY	**SUTTLE**
SPURNE	**STALAG**	STEEVES	**STONNE**	OSTRICH	**STYMIE**	**SUMMAT**	SUTTLED
SPURNED	STALAGS	**STEMME**	STONNED	**STRICT**	STYMIED	SUMMATE	SUTTLES
SPURNER	**STALES**	STEMMED	STONNES	ASTRICT	STYMIES	SUMMATS	**SUTURE**
SPURNES	STALEST	STEMMES	**STOOGE**	**STRIDE**	**SUBACT**	**SUMMER**	SUTURED
SPYING	**STAMEN**	**STENCH**	STOOGED	ASTRIDE	SUBACTS	SUMMERS	SUTURES
ESPYING	STAMENS	STENCHY	STOOGES	STRIDES	**SUBDEW**	SUMMERY	**SVELTE**
SPYINGS	**STANCE**	**STENTS**	**STOOPE**	**STRIFE**	SUBDEWS	**SUMMIT**	SVELTER
SQUAIL	STANCES	OSTENTS	STOOPED	STRIFES	**SUBDUE**	SUMMITS	**SWARDS**
SQUAILS	**STANZA**	**STEPPE**	STOOPER	**STRIFT**	SUBDUED	**SUMMON**	USWARDS
SQUALL	STANZAS	STEPPED	STOOPES	STRIFTS	SUBDUER	SUMMONS	**SWARTH**
SQUALLS	**STANZE**	STEPPER	**STORER**	**STRIGA**	SUBDUES	**SUMPIT**	SWARTHS
SQUALLY	STANZES	STEPPES	STORERS	STRIGAE	**SUBFEU**	SUMPITS	SWARTHY
SQUAMA	**STANZO**	**STEREO**	**STOREY**	**STRIKE**	SUBFEUS	**SUNBED**	**SWARVE**
SQUAMAE	STANZOS	STEREOS	STOREYS	STRIKER	**SUBLET**	SUNBEDS	SWARVED
SQUAME	**STAPLE**	**STEROL**	**STORGE**	STRIKES	SUBLETS	**SUNBOW**	SWARVES
SQUAMES	STAPLED	STEROLS	STORGES	**STRING**	**SUBMIT**	SUNBOWS	**SWATHE**
SQUARE	STAPLER	**STERVE**	**STOUND**	STRINGS	SUBMITS	**SUNDAE**	SWATHED
SQUARED	STAPLES	STERVED	ASTOUND	STRINGY	**SUBORN**	SUNDAES	SWATHES
SQUARER	**STARCH**	STERVES	STOUNDS	**STRIPE**	SUBORNS	**SUNDER**	**SWAYER**
SQUARES	STARCHY	**STEVEN**	**STOUTH**	STRIPED	**SUBSET**	ASUNDER	SWAYERS
SQUASH	**STARER**	STEVENS	STOUTHS	STRIPES	SUBSETS	SUNDERS	**SWEARD**
SQUASHY	STARERS	**STEWER**	**STOVER**	STRIPEY	**SUBTIL**	**SUNDRA**	SWEARDS
SQUAWK	**STARTS**	STEWERS	ESTOVER	**STRIVE**	SUBTILE	SUNDRAS	**SWERVE**
SQUAWKS	ASTARTS	**STIEVE**	STOVERS	STRIVED	**SUBTLE**	**SUNDRI**	SWERVED
SQUAWKY	**STARVE**	STIEVER	**STOWER**	STRIVEN	SUBTLER	SUNDRIS	SWERVER
SQUEAK	STARVED	**STIFLE**	STOWERS	STRIVER	**SUBURB**	**SUNGAR**	SWERVES
SQUEAKS	STARVES	STIFLED	**STOWND**	STRIVES	SUBURBS	SUNGARS	**SWEVEN**
SQUEAKY	**STATED**	STIFLER	STOWNDS	**STROAM**	**SUBWAY**	**SUNHAT**	SWEVENS
SQUEAL	ESTATED	STIFLES	**STOWRE**	STROAMS	SUBWAYS	SUNHATS	**SWINGE**
SQUEALS	**STATER**	**STIGMA**	STOWRES	**STROBE**	**SUCCES**	**SUNKET**	SWINGED
SQUIER	STATERS	STIGMAS	**STRAFE**	STROBES	SUCCESS	SUNKETS	SWINGER
SQUIERS	**STATES**	**STIGME**	STRAFED	**STROKE**	**SUCCOR**	**SUNKIE**	SWINGES
SQUIFF	ESTATES	STIGMES	STRAFES	STROKED	SUCCORS	SUNKIES	**SWIPER**
SQUIFFY	**STATIC**	**STILET**	**STRAFF**	STROKEN	SUCCORY	**SUNRAY**	SWIPERS
SQUILL	ASTATIC	STILETS	STRAFFS	STROKER	**SUCCUS**	SUNRAYS	**SWITCH**
SQUILLS	STATICS	**STIMIE**	**STRAIK**	STROKES	SUCCUSS	**SUNSET**	SWITCHY
SQUINT	**STATOR**	STIMIED	STRAIKS	**STROLL**	**SUCKEN**	SUNSETS	**SWIVEL**
ASQUINT	STATORS	STIMIES	**STRAIN**	STROLLS	SUCKENS	**SUNTAN**	SWIVELS
SQUINTS	**STATUA**	**STINGO**	STRAINS	**STROMB**	**SUCKER**	SUNTANS	**SWIVET**
SQUIRE	STATUAS	STINGOS	STRAINT	STROMBS	SUCKERS	**SUPAWN**	SWIVETS
ESQUIRE	**STATUE**	**STIPEL**	**STRAIT**	**STROND**	**SUCKET**	SUPAWNS	**SWOUND**
SQUIRED	STATUED	STIPELS	STRAITS	STRONDS	SUCKETS	**SUPINE**	SWOUNDS
SQUIRES	STATUES	**STIRRA**	**STRAKE**	**STROOK**	**SUCKLE**	SUPINES	**SWOUNE**
SQUIRM	**STAYER**	STIRRAH	STRAKES	STROOKE	SUCKLED	**SUPPER**	SWOUNED
SQUIRMS	STAYERS	STIRRAS	**STRAMP**	**STROUD**	SUCKLER	SUPPERS	SWOUNES
SQUIRMY	**STAYNE**	**STIRRE**	STRAMPS	STROUDS	SUCKLES	**SUPPLE**	**SWOWND**
SQUIRR	STAYNED	STIRRED	**STRAND**	**STROUP**	**SUDATE**	SUPPLED	SWOWNDS
SQUIRRS	STAYNES	STIRRER	ASTRAND	STROUPS	SUDATED	SUPPLER	**SWOWNE**
SQUIRT	**STAYRE**	STIRRES	STRANDS	**STROUT**	SUDATES	SUPPLES	SWOWNES
SQUIRTS	STAYRES	**STIVER**	**STRATH**	STROUTS	**SUDDEN**	**SURBED**	**SYLVAN**
SQUISH	**STEALE**	STIVERS	STRATHS	**STRUMA**	ASUDDEN	SURBEDS	SYLVANS

SYLVIA	TAIGLES	**TANDEM**	TARSIAS	ATAXIES	**TELLER**	STERNED	**THIRAM**
SYLVIAS	**TAILOR**	TANDEMS	**TARTAN**	**TAXING**	TELLERS	**TERRET**	THIRAMS
SYMBOL	TAILORS	**TANGED**	TARTANA	TAXINGS	**TELSON**	TERRETS	**THIRST**
SYMBOLE	**TAILYE**	STANGED	TARTANE	**TCHICK**	TELSONS	**TERRIT**	ATHIRST
SYMBOLS	TAILYES	**TANGIE**	TARTANS	TCHICKS	**TEMPER**	TERRITS	THIRSTS
SYNDET	**TAIPAN**	TANGIER	**TARTAR**	**TEACUP**	TEMPERA	**TERROR**	THIRSTY
SYNDETS	TAIPANS	TANGIES	TARTARE	TEACUPS	TEMPERS	TERRORS	**THIVEL**
SYNDIC	**TAIVER**	**TANGLE**	TARTARS	**TEAGLE**	**TEMPLE**	**TERTIA**	THIVELS
SYNDICS	TAIVERS	TANGLED	**TARTER**	TEAGLED	STEMPLE	TERTIAL	**THORON**
SYNROC	TAIVERT	TANGLER	STARTER	TEAGLES	TEMPLED	TERTIAN	THORONS
SYNROCS	**TAKAHE**	TANGLES	**TARTLY**	**TEAMED**	TEMPLES	TERTIAS	**THORPE**
SYNTAN	TAKAHEA	**TANGUN**	STARTLY	STEAMED	TEMPLET	**TESTEE**	THORPES
SYNTANS	TAKAHES	TANGUNS	**TASHED**	**TEAMER**	**TENACE**	TESTEES	**THOUGH**
SYPHON	**TAKING**	**TANIST**	STASHED	STEAMER	TENACES	**TESTER**	THOUGHT
SYPHONS	STAKING	TANISTS	**TASHES**	TEAMERS	**TENAIL**	TESTERN	**THOWEL**
SYSTEM	TAKINGS	**TANKER**	STASHES	**TEAPOT**	TENAILS	TESTERS	THOWELS
SYSTEMS	**TALANT**	TANKERS	**TASKER**	TEAPOTS	**TENANT**	**TESTON**	**THRALL**
TABARD	TALANTS	**TANKIA**	TASKERS	**TEAPOY**	TENANTS	TESTONS	THRALLS
TABARDS	**TALBOT**	TANKIAS	**TASLET**	TEAPOYS	**TENDED**	**TETHER**	**THRANG**
TABBED	TALBOTS	**TANNAH**	TASLETS	**TEARER**	STENDED	TETHERS	THRANGS
STABBED	**TALCUM**	TANNAHS	**TASSEL**	TEARERS	**TENDER**	**TETRAD**	**THRAVE**
TABLED	TALCUMS	**TANNER**	TASSELL	**TEASEL**	TENDERS	TETRADS	THRAVES
STABLED	**TALENT**	TANNERS	TASSELS	TEASELS	**TENDON**	**TETRYL**	**THREAD**
TABLES	TALENTS	TANNERY	**TASSET**	**TEASER**	TENDONS	TETRYLS	THREADS
STABLES	**TALION**	**TANNIC**	TASSETS	TEASERS	**TENDRE**	**TETTER**	THREADY
TABLET	TALIONS	STANNIC	**TASSIE**	**TEAZEL**	TENDRES	TETTERS	**THREAP**
TABLETS	**TALKED**	**TANNIN**	TASSIES	TEAZELS	**TENNER**	**TEWART**	THREAPS
TABOUR	STALKED	TANNING	**TASTER**	**TEAZLE**	TENNERS	TEWARTS	**THREAT**
TABOURS	**TALKER**	TANNINS	TASTERS	TEAZLED	**TENOUR**	**TEWHIT**	THREATS
TABRET	STALKER	**TANREC**	**TATAMI**	TEAZLES	TENOURS	TEWHITS	**THREEP**
TABRETS	TALKERS	TANRECS	TATAMIS	**TEBBAD**	**TENREC**	**TEWING**	THREEPS
TABULA	**TALKIE**	**TANTRA**	**TATERS**	TEBBADS	TENRECS	STEWING	**THRENE**
TABULAE	TALKIES	TANTRAS	STATERS	**TECKEL**	**TENSES**	**THAIRM**	THRENES
TABULAR	**TALLAT**	**TAPETA**	**TATLER**	TECKELS	TENSEST	THAIRMS	**THRIFT**
TACKED	TALLATS	**TAPETAL**	TATLERS	**TEDDED**	**TENSON**	**THALER**	THRIFTS
STACKED	**TALLET**	**TAPETI**	**TATTER**	STEDDED	TENSONS	THALERS	THRIFTY
TACKER	TALLETS	TAPETIS	TATTERS	**TEDDER**	**TENSOR**	**THALLI**	**THRILL**
STACKER	**TALLOT**	**TAPIST**	TATTERY	TEDDERS	TENSORS	THALLIC	ATHRILL
TACKERS	TALLOTS	TAPISTS	**TATTIE**	**TEDIUM**	**TENTED**	**THANAH**	THRILLS
TACKET	**TALLOW**	**TAPPED**	TATTIER	TEDIUMS	STENTED	THANAHS	THRILLY
STACKET	TALLOWS	STAPPED	TATTIES	**TEEHEE**	**TENTER**	**THANES**	**THRIST**
TACKETS	TALLOWY	**TAPPER**	**TATTLE**	TEEHEED	TENTERS	ETHANES	THRISTS
TACKETY	**TALONS**	TAPPERS	TATTLED	TEEHEES	**TENTIE**	**THANNA**	THRISTY
TACKLE	ETALONS	**TAPPET**	TATTLER	**TEEMED**	TENTIER	THANNAH	**THRIVE**
TACKLED	**TALWEG**	TAPPETS	TATTLES	STEEMED	**TENURE**	THANNAS	THRIVED
TACKLER	TALWEGS	**TARAND**	**TATTOO**	**TEEMER**	TENURES	**THATCH**	THRIVEN
TACKLES	**TAMALE**	TARANDS	TATTOOS	TEEMERS	**TENZON**	THATCHT	THRIVER
TACTIC	TAMALES	**TARCEL**	**TATTOW**	**TEENED**	TENZONS	**THAWER**	THRIVES
ATACTIC	**TAMANU**	TARCELS	TATTOWS	STEENED	**TEPHRA**	THAWERS	**THROAT**
TACTICS	TAMANUS	**TARGET**	**TATUED**	**TEEPEE**	TEPHRAS	**THEAVE**	THROATS
TAENIA	**TAMARA**	TARGETS	STATUED	TEEPEES	**TERCEL**	THEAVES	THROATY
TAENIAE	TAMARAS	**TARIFF**	**TAUPIE**	**TEERED**	TERCELS	**THEINE**	**THRONE**
TAENIAS	**TAMARI**	TARIFFS	TAUPIES	STEERED	**TERCET**	THEINES	THRONED
TAGGED	TAMARIN	**TARING**	**TAUTEN**	**TEETER**	TERCETS	**THEISM**	THRONES
STAGGED	TAMARIS	STARING	TAUTENS	TEETERS	**TERCIO**	ATHEISM	**THRONG**
TAGGER	**TAMBER**	**TARMAC**	**TAUTOG**	**TEETHE**	TERCIOS	THEISMS	THRONGS
STAGGER	TAMBERS	TARMACS	TAUTOGS	TEETHED	**TEREDO**	**THEIST**	**THROWE**
TAGGERS	**TAMINE**	**TARPAN**	**TAVERN**	TEETHES	TEREDOS	ATHEIST	THROWER
TAGRAG	TAMINES	TARPANS	TAVERNA	**TEGULA**	**TEREFA**	THEISTS	THROWES
TAGRAGS	**TAMING**	**TARPON**	TAVERNS	TEGULAE	TEREFAH	**THENAR**	**THRUST**
TAGUAN	TAMINGS	TARPONS	**TAWING**	TEGULAR	**TERGUM**	THENARS	THRUSTS
TAGUANS	**TAMISE**	**TARRED**	STAWING	**TELEDU**	TERGUMS	**THIBET**	**THULIA**
TAHINA	TAMISES	STARRED	**TAWINGS**	TELEDUS	**TERMER**	THIBETS	THULIAS
TAHINAS	**TAMPED**	**TARROW**	**TAWNEY**	**TELEGA**	TERMERS	**THIBLE**	**THWACK**
TAHINI	STAMPED	TARROWS	TAWNEYS	TELEGAS	**TERMOR**	THIBLES	THWACKS
TAHINIS	**TAMPER**	**TARSAL**	**TAWPIE**	**TELESM**	TERMORS	**THICKO**	**THWART**
TAHSIL	STAMPER	TARSALS	TAWPIES	TELESMS	**TERNAL**	THICKOS	ATHWART
TAHSILS	TAMPERS	**TARSEL**	**TAWTIE**	**TELLAR**	ETERNAL	**THIEVE**	THWARTS
TAIGLE	**TAMPON**	TARSELS	TAWTIER	STELLAR	STERNAL	THIEVED	**THYMOL**
TAIGLED	TAMPONS	**TARSIA**	**TAXIES**	TELLARS	**TERNED**	THIEVES	THYMOLS

THYRSE	TINAJA	TISICK	TOMBACS	TOREROS	TOWMON	TRIGON	TROUSE
THYRSES	TINAJAS	TISICKS	TOMBAK	TOROID	TOWMOND	TRIGONS	TROUSES
TIBIAL	TINCAL	TISSUE	TOMBAKS	TOROIDS	TOWMONS	TRIKES	TROUTS
STIBIAL	TINCALS	TISSUED	TOMBOC	TORPID	TOWMONT	STRIKES	STROUTS
TICKED	TINDAL	TISSUES	TOMBOCS	TORPIDS	TOWNEE	TRILBY	TROVER
STICKED	TINDALS	TITBIT	TOMBOY	TORPOR	TOWNEES	TRILBYS	TROVERS
TICKEN	TINDER	TITBITS	TOMBOYS	TORPORS	TOWNIE	TRIMER	TROWED
TICKENS	TINDERS	TITFER	TOMIUM	TORQUE	TOWNIER	TRIMERS	STROWED
TICKER	TINDERY	TITFERS	TOMIUMS	TORQUED	TOWNIES	TRIODE	TROWEL
STICKER	TINEID	TITHER	TOMPON	TORQUES	TOWSER	TRIODES	TROWELS
TICKERS	TINEIDS	TITHERS	TOMPONS	TORRET	TOWSERS	TRIPES	TRUANT
TICKET	TINFUL	TITIAN	TOMTIT	TORRETS	TOXOID	STRIPES	TRUANTS
TICKETS	TINFULS	TITIANS	TOMTITS	TORSEL	TOXOIDS	TRIPLE	TRUDGE
TICKEY	TINGED	TITLER	TONEME	TORSELS	TOYING	TRIPLED	TRUDGED
TICKEYS	STINGED	TITLERS	TONEMES	TORULA	TOYINGS	TRIPLES	TRUDGEN
TICKLE	ATINGLE	TITOKI	TONGUE	TORULAS	TRACER	TRIPLET	TRUDGER
STICKLE	TINGLED	TITOKIS	TONGUED	TOSHER	TRACERS	TRIPLEX	TRUDGES
TICKLED	TINGLER	TITTER	TONGUES	TOSHERS	TRACERY	TRIPOD	TRUISM
TICKLER	TINGLES	TITTERS	TONIER	TOSSER	TRADER	TRIPODS	TRUISMS
TICKLES	TINKER	TITTLE	TONIES	TOSSERS	TRADERS	TRIPODY	TRYING
TIDBIT	STINKER	TITTLED	ATONIES	TOTARA	TRAIKS	TRISUL	TRYINGS
TIDBITS	TINKERS	TITTLES	STONIER	TOTARAS	STRAIKS	TRISULA	TSAMBA
TIDDLE	TINKLE	TITTUP	TONIEST	TOTTED	TRAINS	TRISULS	TSAMBAS
TIDDLED	TINKLED	TITTUPS	ATONING	STOTTED	STRAINS	TRITES	TSETSE
TIDDLER	TINKLER	TITTUPY	STONING	TOTTER	TRAITS	TRITEST	TSETSES
TIDDLES	TINKLES	TITULE	TONITE	TOTTERS	STRAITS	TRITON	TSOTSI
TIDDLEY	TINNER	TITULED	TONITES	TOTTERY	TRAMPS	TRITONE	TSOTSIS
TIDIES	TINNERS	TITULES	TONKER	TOTTIE	STRAMPS	TRITONS	TUBAGE
TIDIEST	TINNIE	TOCHER	STONKER	TOTTIER	TRANCE	TRIUNE	TUBAGES
TIDING	TINNIER	TOCHERS	TONKERS	TOTTIES	TRANCED	TRIUNES	TUBBED
TIDINGS	TINNIES	TOCSIN	TONLET	TOUCAN	TRANCES	TRIVET	STUBBED
TIERCE	TINPOT	TOCSINS	TONLETS	TOUCANS	TRANSE	TRIVETS	TUBBER
TIERCEL	TINPOTS	TODDLE	TONNAG	TOUCHE	TRANSES	TRIVIA	TUBBERS
TIERCES	TINSEL	TODDLED	TONNAGE	TOUCHED	TRAPAN	TRIVIAL	TUBFUL
TIETAC	TINSELS	TODDLER	TONNAGS	TOUCHER	TRAPANS	TROADE	TUBFULS
TIETACK	TINSEY	TODDLES	TONNES	TOUCHES	TRAPPY	TROADES	TUBING
TIETACS	TINSEYS	TOECAP	STONNES	TOUPEE	STRAPPY	TROCAR	TUBINGS
TIFFED	TINTED	TOECAPS	TONSIL	TOUPEES	TRAUMA	TROCARS	TUBULE
STIFFED	STINTED	TOFFEE	TONSILS	TOUPET	TRAUMAS	TROCHE	TUBULES
TIFFIN	TINTER	TOFFEES	TONSOR	TOUPETS	TRAVEL	TROCHEE	TUCHUN
TIFFING	STINTER	TOGATE	TONSORS	TOURER	TRAVELS	TROCHES	TUCHUNS
TIFFINS	TINTERS	TOGATED	TOOART	TOURERS	TRAYNE	TROGON	TUCKER
TIGLON	TIPPER	TOGGLE	TOOARTS	TOUSER	TRAYNED	TROGONS	TUCKERS
TIGLONS	TIPPERS	TOGGLED	TOOLED	TOUSERS	TRAYNES	TROIKA	TUCKET
TILING	TIPPET	TOGGLES	STOOLED	TOUSLE	TREBLE	TROIKAS	TUCKETS
STILING	TIPPETS	TOILER	TOOLER	TOUSLED	TREBLED	TROKED	TUFFET
TILINGS	TIPPLE	TOILERS	TOOLERS	TOUSLES	TREBLES	STROKED	TUFFETS
TILLED	STIPPLE	TOILES	TOORIE	TOUTER	TREMIE	TROKES	TUFTER
STILLED	TIPPLED	TOILET	TOORIES	STOUTER	TREMIES	STROKES	TUFTERS
TILLER	TIPPLER	TOILETS	TOOTER	TOUTERS	TREMOR	TROLLS	TUGGER
STILLER	TIPPLES	TOISON	TOOTERS	TOUTIE	TREMORS	STROLLS	TUGGERS
TILLERS	TIPTOE	TOISONS	TOOTLE	TOUTIER	TREPAN	TROMPE	TUGRIK
TILTED	TIPTOED	TOKING	TOOTLED	TOUZLE	TREPANG	TROMPES	TUGRIKS
STILTED	TIPTOES	STOKING	TOOTLES	TOUZLED	TREPANS	TROPHI	TUILLE
TILTER	TIPTOP	TOLING	TOPING	TOUZLES	TREVIS	TROPHIC	TUILLES
STILTER	TIPTOPS	TOLINGS	STOPING	TOWAGE	TREVISS	TROPHY	TULBAN
TILTERS	TIPULA	TOLLER	TOPPED	TOWAGES	TRIAGE	ATROPHY	TULBANS
TIMBAL	TIPULAS	TOLLERS	STOPPED	TOWARD	TRIAGES	TROPIC	TULWAR
TIMBALE	TIRADE	TOLSEL	TOPPER	TOWARDS	TRICAR	TROPICS	TULWARS
TIMBALS	TIRADES	TOLSELS	TOPPERS	TOWBAR	TRICARS	TROTYL	TUMBLE
TIMBER	TIRING	TOLSEY	TOPPLE	TOWBARS	TRICKS	TROTYLS	STUMBLE
TIMBERS	STIRING	TOLSEYS	STOPPLE	TOWERS	TRICKSY	TROUGH	TUMBLED
TIMBRE	TIRINGS	TOLTER	TOPPLED	STOWERS	TRICOT	TROUGHS	TUMBLER
TIMBREL	TIRRED	TOLTERS	TOPPLES	TOWHEE	TRICOTS	TROULE	TUMBLES
TIMBRES	STIRRED	TOLUOL	TORANA	TOWHEES	TRIERS	TROULED	TUMOUR
TIMING	TIRRIT	TOLUOLS	TORANAS	TOWING	ETRIERS	TROULES	TUMOURS
STIMING	TIRRITS	TOLZEY	TORERO	STOWING	TRIFLE	TROUPE	TUMPED
TIMINGS	TISANE	TOLZEYS		TOWINGS	TRIFLED	TROUPED	STUMPED
TIMIST	TISANES	TOMBAC			TRIFLER	TROUPER	TUMULT
TIMISTS					TRIFLES	TROUPES	TUMULTS

TUNDRA	TWICER	ULLAGED	UNBOLTS	UNEDGES	UNIQUE	UNPACK	UNSHUT
TUNDRAS	TWICERS	ULLAGES	UNBONE	UNFACT	UNIQUER	UNPACKS	UNSHUTS
TUNDUN	TWIGHT	ULLING	UNBONED	UNFACTS	UNIQUES	UNPICK	UNSNAP
TUNDUNS	TWIGHTS	BULLING	UNBONES	UNFAIR	UNISON	UNPICKS	UNSNAPS
TUNING	TWINER	CULLING	UNBOOT	FUNFAIR	UNISONS	UNPLUG	UNSOUL
TUNINGS	TWINERS	DULLING	UNBOOTS	UNFAIRS	UNITED	UNPLUGS	UNSOULS
TUNNED	TWINGE	FULLING	UNBORN	UNFOLD	MUNITED	UNPOPE	UNSPAR
STUNNED	TWINGED	GULLING	UNBORNE	UNFOLDS	UNITER	UNPOPED	UNSPARS
TUNNEL	TWINGES	HULLING	UNCAGE	UNFOOL	UNITERS	UNPOPES	UNSTEP
TUNNELS	TWITCH	LULLING	UNCAGED	UNFOOLS	UNITES	UNPRAY	UNSTEPS
TUPELO	TWITCHY	MULLING	UNCAGES	UNFORM	DUNITES	UNPRAYS	UNSTOP
TUPELOS	TWYERE	NULLING	UNCAPE	UNFORMS	GUNITES	UNPROP	UNSTOPS
TURACO	TWYERES	PULLING	UNCAPED	UNFURL	MUNITES	UNPROPS	UNSTOW
TURACOS	TYCOON	WULLING	UNCAPES	UNFURLS	UNKING	UNRAKE	UNSTOWS
TURBAN	TYCOONS	ULLINGS	UNCART	UNGEAR	BUNKING	UNRAKED	UNSUIT
TURBAND	TYLOTE	ULOSES	UNCARTS	UNGEARS	DUNKING	UNRAKES	SUNSUIT
TURBANS	TYLOTES	DULOSES	UNCASE	UNGILD	FUNKING	UNREAD	UNSUITS
TURBANT	TYMBAL	ULOSIS	UNCASED	UNGILDS	JUNKING	UNREADY	UNSURE
TURBIT	TYMBALS	DULOSIS	UNCASES	UNGIRD	UNKINGS	UNREEL	UNSURED
TURBITH	TYMPAN	ULSTER	UNCATE	UNGIRT	UNKNIT	UNREELS	UNSURER
TURBITS	TYMPANA	ULSTERS	JUNCATE	UNGIRTH	UNKNITS	UNREIN	UNTACK
TURBOT	TYMPANI	ULTIMA	UNCIAL	UNGLUE	UNKNOT	UNREINS	UNTACKS
TURBOTS	TYMPANO	ULTIMAS	UNCIALS	UNGLUED	UNKNOTS	UNREST	UNTAME
TUREEN	TYMPANS	ULTION	UNCLES	UNGLUES	UNLACE	UNRESTS	UNTAMED
TUREENS	TYMPANY	ULTIONS	NUNCLES	UNGOWN	UNLACED	UNRIGS	UNTAMES
TURGOR	TYPHON	UMBERS	UNCLEW	UNGOWNS	UNLACES	RUNRIGS	UNTEAM
TURGORS	TYPHONS	CUMBERS	UNCLEWS	UNGULA	UNLADE	UNRIPE	UNTEAMS
TURION	TYPING	LUMBERS	UNCLOG	UNGULAE	UNLADED	UNRIPER	UNTENT
TURIONS	TYPINGS	NUMBERS	UNCLOGS	UNGYVE	UNLADEN	UNROBE	UNTENTS
TURKEY	TYPIST	UMBLES	UNCOCK	UNGYVED	UNLADES	UNROBED	UNTENTY
TURKEYS	TYPISTS	BUMBLES	UNCOCKS	UNGYVES	UNLAST	UNROBES	UNTHAW
TURNER	TYRANT	FUMBLES	UNCOIL	UNHAIR	UNLASTE	UNROLL	UNTHAWS
TURNERS	TYRANTS	HUMBLES	UNCOILS	UNHAIRS	UNLEAD	UNROLLS	UNTIES
TURNERY	TYSTIE	JUMBLES	UNCOLT	UNHAND	UNLEADS	UNROOF	AUNTIES
TURNIP	TYSTIES	MUMBLES	UNCOLTS	UNHANDS	UNLESS	UNROOFS	PUNTIES
TURNIPS	UAKARI	NUMBLES	UNCOPE	UNHANDY	SUNLESS	UNROOT	UNTILE
TURRET	OUAKARI	RUMBLES	UNCOPED	UNHANG	UNLIKE	UNROOTS	UNTILED
TURRETS	UAKARIS	TUMBLES	UNCOPES	UNHANGS	SUNLIKE	UNROPE	UNTILES
TURTLE	UBERTY	UMBREL	UNCORD	UNHASP	UNLIKES	UNROPED	UNTINS
TURTLED	PUBERTY	TUMBREL	UNCORDS	UNHASPS	UNLIME	UNROPES	MUNTINS
TURTLER	UBIETY	UMBRELS	UNCORK	UNHATS	UNLIMED	UNRULE	UNTOMB
TURTLES	DUBIETY	UMBRIL	UNCORKS	SUNHATS	UNLIMES	UNRULED	UNTOMBS
TUSCHE	UDDERS	TUMBRIL	UNCOWL	UNHEAD	UNLINE	UNRULES	UNTRIM
TUSCHES	DUDDERS	UMBRILS	UNCOWLS	UNHEADS	UNLINED	UNSAFE	UNTRIMS
TUSKAR	JUDDERS	UMLAUT	UNCURL	UNHEAL	UNLINES	UNSAFER	UNTRUE
TUSKARS	PUDDERS	UMLAUTS	UNCURLS	UNHEALS	UNLINK	UNSEAL	UNTRUER
TUSKER	RUDDERS	UMPIRE	UNDATE	UNHELE	UNLINKS	UNSEALS	UNTUCK
TUSKERS	SUDDERS	UMPIRED	UNDATED	UNHELED	UNLIVE	UNSEAM	UNTUCKS
TUSSAH	UGGING	UMPIRES	UNDEAF	UNHELES	UNLIVED	UNSEAMS	UNTUNE
TUSSAHS	BUGGING	UNABLE	UNDEAFS	UNHELM	UNLIVES	UNSEAT	UNTUNED
TUSSEH	FUGGING	TUNABLE	UNDECK	UNHELMS	UNLOAD	UNSEATS	UNTUNES
TUSSEHS	HUGGING	UNBARE	UNDECKS	UNHIVE	UNLOADS	UNSEEL	UNTURF
TUSSER	JUGGING	UNBARED	UNDERN	UNHIVED	UNLOCK	UNSEELS	UNTURFS
TUSSERS	LUGGING	UNBARES	UNDERNS	UNHIVES	UNLOCKS	UNSEEN	UNTURN
TUSSLE	MUGGING	UNBARK	UNDIES	UNHOOD	UNLORD	UNSEENS	UNTURNS
TUSSLED	PUGGING	UNBARKS	GUNDIES	NUNHOOD	UNLORDS	UNSELF	UNVAIL
TUSSLES	RUGGING	UNBEAR	UNDINE	UNHOODS	UNLOVE	UNSELFS	UNVAILE
TUTSAN	TUGGING	UNBEARS	NUNDINE	UNHOOK	UNLOVED	UNSETS	UNVAILS
TUTSANS	UGLIED	UNBEDS	UNDINES	UNHOOKS	UNLOVES	SUNSETS	UNVEIL
TUXEDO	OUGLIED	SUNBEDS	UNDOCK	UNHOOP	UNMAKE	UNSHED	UNVEILS
TUXEDOS	UGLIES	UNBELT	UNDOCKS	UNHOOPS	UNMAKES	DUNSHED	UNWARE
TUYERE	OUGLIES	SUNBELT	UNDOER	UNHUSK	UNMASK	UNSHIP	UNWARES
TUYERES	UGLIEST	UNBELTS	UNDOERS	UNHUSKS	UNMASKS	GUNSHIP	UNWEAL
TWAITE	ULICON	UNBEND	UNDRAW	UNIONS	UNMOOR	NUNSHIP	UNWEALS
TWAITES	ULICONS	UNBENDS	UNDRAWN	BUNIONS	UNMOORS	UNSHIPS	UNWILL
TWEEZE	ULIKON	UNBIND	UNDRAWS	UNIPED	UNNAIL	UNSHOE	UNWILLS
TWEEZED	ULIKONS	UNBINDS	UNEASE	UNIPEDS	UNNAILS	UNSHOED	UNWIND
TWEEZES	ULLAGE	UNBITT	UNEASES	UNIPOD	UNNEST	UNSHOES	UNWINDS
TWELVE	FULLAGE	UNBITTS	UNEDGE	UNIPODS	DUNNEST	UNSHOT	UNWIRE
TWELVES	SULLAGE	UNBOLT	UNEDGED	UNIPODS	UNNESTS	GUNSHOT	UNWIRED

UNWIRES	UPHURL	UPTILTS	USANCES	VALUER	VENDISS	VERTUE	VIROSES
UNWISE	UPHURLS	UPTOWN	USEFUL	VALUERS	VENDOR	VERTUES	VIRTUE
SUNWISE	UPKEEP	UPTOWNS	MUSEFUL	VALUTA	VENDORS	VERVEL	VIRTUES
UNWISER	UPKEEPS	UPTURN	USHERS	VALUTAS	VENDUE	VERVELS	VISAGE
UNWIVE	UPKNIT	UPTURNS	GUSHERS	VAMOSE	VENDUES	VERVEN	VISAGED
UNWIVED	UPKNITS	UPWAFT	HUSHERS	VAMOSED	VENEER	VERVENS	VISAGES
UNWIVES	UPLAND	UPWAFTS	LUSHERS	VAMOSES	VENEERS	VERVET	VISCIN
UNWORK	UPLANDS	UPWARD	MUSHERS	VAMPER	VENEWE	VERVETS	VISCINS
UNWORKS	UPLEAD	UPWARDS	PUSHERS	VAMPERS	VENEWES	VESICA	VISCUM
UNWOVE	UPLEADS	UPWELL	RUSHERS	VANDAL	VENGED	VESICAE	VISCUMS
UNWOVEN	UPLEAN	UPWELLS	USTION	VANDALS	AVENGED	VESICAL	VISIER
UNWRAP	UPLEANS	UPWIND	USTIONS	VANISH	VENGER	VESPER	VISIERS
UNWRAPS	UPLEANT	UPWINDS	USURER	EVANISH	AVENGER	VESPERS	VISILE
UNYOKE	UPLEAP	URACIL	USURERS	VANNER	VENGERS	VESSEL	VISILES
UNYOKED	UPLEAPS	URACILS	USURES	VANNERS	VENGES	VESSELS	VISING
UNYOKES	UPLEAPT	URALIS	USURESS	VAPOUR	AVENGES	VESTAL	AVISING
UPBEAR	UPLIFT	OURALIS	USWARD	VAPOURS	VENIRE	VESTALS	VISION
UPBEARS	UPLIFTS	URANIN	USWARDS	VAPOURY	VENIRES	VEXING	VISIONS
UPBIND	UPLOCK	URANINS	UTISES	VARECH	VENITE	VEXINGS	VISITE
UPBINDS	UPLOCKS	URANYL	CUTISES	VARECHS	VENITES	VIATOR	VISITED
UPBLOW	UPLOOK	URANYLS	UTMOST	VARIER	VENNEL	AVIATOR	VISITEE
UPBLOWN	UPLOOKS	URARIS	OUTMOST	VARIERS	VENNELS	VIATORS	VISITER
UPBLOWS	UPMAKE	CURARIS	UTMOSTS	VARIES	VENTER	VIBIST	VISITES
UPBOIL	UPMAKER	OURARIS	UTOPIA	OVARIES	EVENTER	VIBISTS	VISUAL
UPBOILS	UPMAKES	URATES	UTOPIAN	VARLET	VENTERS	VIBRIO	VISUALS
UPBRAY	UPPERS	AURATES	UTOPIAS	VARLETS	VENTIL	VIBRIOS	VITRIC
UPBRAYS	CUPPERS	CURATES	UTTERS	VARROA	VENTILS	VICTIM	VITRICS
UPCAST	SUPPERS	URBANE	BUTTERS	VARROAS	VENTRE	VICTIMS	VITTLE
UPCASTS	UPPING	URBANER	CUTTERS	VARVEL	AVENTRE	VICTOR	VITTLES
UPCOIL	CUPPING	URCHIN	GUTTERS	VARVELS	VENTRED	EVICTOR	VIZARD
UPCOILS	DUPPING	URCHINS	MUTTERS	VASSAL	VENTRES	VICTORS	VIZARDS
UPCOME	HUPPING	UREIDE	NUTTERS	VASSALS	VENUES	VICTORY	VIZIER
UPCOMES	PUPPING	UREIDES	PUTTERS	VATFUL	AVENUES	VICUNA	VIZIERS
UPCURL	SUPPING	UREMIA	RUTTERS	VATFULS	VENULE	VICUNAS	VIZSLA
UPCURLS	TUPPING	UREMIAS	VACATE	VAUDOO	VENULES	VIDAME	VIZSLAS
UPDATE	UPPINGS	URENAS	VACATED	VAUDOOS	VERBAL	VIDAMES	VIZZIE
UPDATED	UPRATE	MURENAS	VACATES	VAUNCE	VERBALS	VIELLE	VIZZIED
UPDATES	UPRATED	URETER	VACUUM	VAUNCED	VERDET	VIELLES	VIZZIES
UPDRAG	UPRATES	URETERS	VACUUMS	VAUNCES	VERDETS	VIEWER	VOCULE
UPDRAGS	UPREAR	URGENT	VADING	VAUNTS	VERDIT	VIEWERS	VOCULES
UPDRAW	UPREST	SURGENT	EVADING	AVAUNTS	VERDITS	VIGORO	VOICER
UPDRAWN	UPRESTS	TURGENT	VAGINA	VAWARD	VERGER	VIGOROS	VOICERS
UPDRAWS	UPRISE	URGERS	VAGINAE	VAWARDS	VERGERS	VIGOUR	VOIDED
UPFILL	UPRISEN	BURGERS	VAGINAL	VECTOR	VERISM	VIGOURS	AVOIDED
UPFILLS	UPRISES	PURGERS	VAGINAS	VECTORS	VERISMO	VIHARA	VOIDEE
UPFLOW	UPRIST	URGING	VAGUES	VEGGIE	VERISMS	VIHARAS	VOIDEES
UPFLOWS	UPRISTS	PURGING	VAGUEST	VEGGIES	VERIST	VIKING	VOIDER
UPFURL	UPROAR	SURGING	VAHINE	VELATE	VERISTS	VIKINGS	VOIDERS
UPFURLS	UPROARS	URGINGS	VAHINES	VELATED	VERMIL	VILLAN	VOLANT
UPGANG	UPROLL	URIALS	VAILED	VELETA	VERMILS	VILLANS	VOLANTE
UPGANGS	UPROLLS	BURIALS	AVAILED	VELETAS	VERMILY	VILLANY	VOLLEY
UPGAZE	UPROOT	URINAL	VAKEEL	VELLET	VERMIN	VIMANA	VOLLEYS
UPGAZED	UPROOTS	URINALS	VAKEELS	VELLETS	VERMINS	VIMANAS	VOLOST
UPGAZES	UPSEND	URINES	VALETA	VELLON	VERMINY	VIOLER	VOLOSTS
UPGROW	UPSENDS	MURINES	VALETAS	VELLONS	VERREL	VIOLERS	VOLUME
UPGROWN	UPSHOT	PURINES	VALETE	VELLUM	VERRELS	VIOLET	VOLUMED
UPGROWS	UPSHOTS	URNFUL	VALETED	VELLUMS	VERSAL	VIOLETS	VOLUMES
UPHANG	UPSIDE	URNFULS	VALETES	VELOUR	VERSALS	VIOLIN	VOLUTE
UPHANGS	UPSIDES	URNING	VALINE	VELOURS	VERSER	VIOLINS	EVOLUTE
UPHAUD	UPSTAY	BURNING	VALINES	VELURE	VERSERS	VIRAGO	VOLUTED
UPHAUDS	UPSTAYS	GURNING	VALISE	VELURED	VERSET	VIRAGOS	VOLUTES
UPHEAP	UPSWAY	TURNING	VALISES	VELURES	OVERSET	VIRGER	VOLVED
UPHEAPS	UPSWAYS	URNINGS	VALLAR	VELVET	VERSETS	VIRGERS	EVOLVED
UPHILL	UPTAKE	UROPOD	VALLARY	VELVETS	VERSIN	VIRGIN	VOLVES
UPHILLS	UPTAKEN	UROPODS	VALLEY	VELVETY	VERSINE	VIRGINS	EVOLVES
UPHOLD	UPTAKES	URTICA	VALLEYS	VENDEE	VERSING	VIRION	VOMICA
UPHOLDS	UPTEAR	URTICAS	VALLUM	VENDEES	VERSINS	VIRIONS	VOMICAS
UPHROE	UPTEARS	USAGER	VALLUMS	VENDER	VERTED	VIROID	VOMITO
EUPHROE	UPTILT	USAGERS	VALOUR	VENDERS	AVERTED	VIROIDS	VOMITOS
UPHROES		USANCE	VALOURS	VENDIS	EVERTED	VIROSE	VOODOO

VOODOOS
VOTEEN
VOTEENS
VOUDOU
VOUDOUS
VOULGE
VOULGES
VOWING
AVOWING
VOYAGE
VOYAGED
VOYAGER
VOYAGES
VOYEUR
VOYEURS
VULCAN
VULCANS
VULGAR
VULGARS
WABAIN
WABAINS
WABBLE
WABBLED
WABBLER
WABBLES
WABOOM
WABOOMS
WADDIE
WADDIED
WADDIES
WADDLE
SWADDLE
TWADDLE
WADDLED
WADDLES
WADING
WADINGS
WADMAL
WADMALS
WADMOL
WADMOLL
WADMOLS
WADSET
WADSETS
WADSETT
WAFFLE
WAFFLED
WAFFLES
WAFTER
WAFTERS
WAGGED
SWAGGED
WAGGLE
WAGGLED
WAGGLES
WAGGON
WAGGONS
WAGING
SWAGING
WAHINE
WAHINES
WAILER
WAILERS
WAITED
AWAITED
WAITER
WAITERS
WAITES
TWAITES
WAIVER

WAIVERS
WAKENS
AWAKENS
WAKIKI
WAKIKIS
WAKING
AWAKING
WAKINGS
WALIER
SWALIER
WALIES
WALIEST
WALING
SWALING
WALISE
WALISES
WALKER
WALKERS
WALLAH
WALLAHS
WALLER
WALLERS
WALLET
SWALLET
WALLETS
WALLOP
WALLOPS
WALLOW
SWALLOW
WALLOWS
WALNUT
WALNUTS
WAMBLE
WAMBLED
WAMBLES
WAMPEE
WAMPEES
WAMPUM
WAMPUMS
WANDER
WANDERS
WANDOO
WANDOOS
WANGAN
WANGANS
WANGLE
TWANGLE
WANGLED
WANGLER
WANGLES
WANGUN
WANGUNS
WANING
WANINGS
WANKED
SWANKED
WANKER
SWANKER
WANKERS
WANTER
WANTERS
WANTON
WANTONS
WAPITI
WAPITIS
WAPPED
SWAPPED
WAPPER
SWAPPER
WAPPERS

WARBLE
WARBLED
WARBLER
WARBLES
WARDED
AWARDED
SWARDED
WARDEN
WARDENS
WARDER
WARDERS
WARDOG
WARDOGS
WARMED
SWARMED
WARMER
SWARMER
WARMERS
WARMTH
WARMTHS
WARNED
AWARNED
WARNER
WARNERS
WARPER
WARPERS
WARRAN
WARRAND
WARRANS
WARRANT
WARRAY
WARRAYS
WARREN
WARRENS
WARREY
WARREYS
WARSLE
WARSLED
WARSLES
WASHED
SWASHED
WASHER
SWASHER
WASHERS
WASHERY
WASHES
SWASHES
WASPIE
WASPIER
WASPIES
WASTEL
WASTELS
WASTER
WASTERS
WASTERY
WATTER
SWATTER
WATTLE
TWATTLE
WATTLED
WATTLES
WAUCHT
WAUCHTS
WAUGHT
WAUGHTS
WAVIES
WAVIEST
WAVING
WAVINGS
WAXING

WAXINGS
WAYING
SWAYING
WAYLAY
WAYLAYS
WEAKEN
WEAKENS
WEALTH
WEALTHS
WEALTHY
WEANEL
WEANELS
WEANER
WEANERS
WEAPON
WEAPONS
WEARER
WEARERS
SWEARER
WEARERS
WEASEL
WEASELS
WEAVER
WEAVERS
WEAZEN
WEAZENS
WEDELN
WEDELNS
WEDGIE
WEDGIES
WEEDER
WEEDERS
WEEDERY
WEEING
SWEEING
WEEPER
SWEEPER
WEEPERS
WEEPIE
WEEPIER
WEEPIES
WEETEN
SWEETEN
WEEVER
WEEVERS
WEEVIL
WEEVILS
WEEVILY
WEIGHT
WEIGHTS
WEIGHTY
WEIRDO
WEIRDOS
WELDER
WELDERS
WELDOR
WELDORS
WELKIN
WELKING
WELKINS
WELLED
DWELLED
SWELLED
WELLIE
WELLIES
WELTED
SWELTED
WELTER
SWELTER
WELTERS
WESAND

WESANDS
WESTER
WESTERN
WESTERS
WETHER
WETHERS
WEZAND
WEZANDS
WHACKO
WHACKOS
WHALER
WHALERS
WHALERY
WHARVE
WHARVES
WHEECH
WHEECHS
WHEELS
AWHEELS
WHEEZE
WHEEZED
WHEEZES
WHENCE
WHENCES
WHERES
WHERESO
WHEUGH
WHEUGHS
WHIDAH
WHIDAHS
WHINER
WHINERS
WHINGE
WHINGED
WHINGER
WHINGES
WHISHT
WHISHTS
WHITEN
WHITENS
WHITES
WHITEST
WHITEY
WHITEYS
WHYDAH
WHYDAHS
WICKEN
WICKENS
WICKER
WICKERS
WICKET
WICKETS
WIDDLE
TWIDDLE
WIDDLED
WIDDLES
WIDGET
WIDGETS
WIGEON
WIGEONS
WIGGED
SWIGGED
TWIGGED
WIGGLE
WIGGLED
WIGGLER
WIGGLES
WIGHTS
TWIGHTS
WIGWAG

WIGWAGS
WIGWAM
WIGWAMS
WILDER
WILDERS
WILLED
SWILLED
TWILLED
WILLER
SWILLER
WILLERS
WILLET
WILLETS
WILLEY
WILLEYS
WILLIE
WILLIED
WILLIES
WILLOW
WILLOWS
WILLOWY
WILTED
TWILTED
WIMBLE
WIMBLED
WIMBLES
WIMPLE
WIMPLED
WIMPLES
WINCER
WINCERS
WINCEY
WINCEYS
WINDAC
WINDACS
WINDER
WINDERS
WINDLE
DWINDLE
SWINDLE
WINDLES
WINDOW
WINDOWS
WINERY
SWINERY
WINGED
SWINGED
TWINGED
WINGER
SWINGER
WINGERS
WINGES
SWINGES
TWINGES
WINIER
TWINIER
WINING
DWINING
TWINING
WINKED
SWINKED
TWINKED
WINKER
WINKERS
WINKLE
TWINKLE
WINKLER
WINKLES
WINNER
WINNERS

WINNLE
WINNLES
WINNOW
WINNOWS
WINSEY
WINSEYS
WINTER
TWINTER
WINTERS
WINTERY
WINTLE
WINTLED
WINTLES
WIPERS
SWIPERS
WIPING
SWIPING
WIPINGS
WIRING
TWIRING
WIRINGS
WISARD
WISARDS
WISDOM
WISDOMS
WISENT
WISENTS
WISHED
SWISHED
WISHER
SWISHER
WISHERS
WISHES
SWISHES
WISKET
WISKETS
WISTED
TWISTED
WITGAT
WITGATS
WITHER
SWITHER
WITHERS
WITHIN
WITHING
WITTED
TWITTED
WITTER
TWITTER
WITTERS
WITTOL
WITTOLS
WIVERN
WIVERNS
WIZARD
WIZARDS
WIZIER
WIZIERS
WOBBLE
WOBBLED
WOBBLER
WOBBLES
WOGGLE
WOGGLES
WOLFER
WOLFERS
WOLVER
WOLVERS
WOMBAT
WOMBATS

WOMERA
WOMERAS
WONDER
WONDERS
WONING
WONINGS
WOOBUT
WOOBUTS
WOODIE
WOODIER
WOODIES
WOOFER
WOOFERS
WOOING
WOOINGS
WOONED
SWOONED
WOOSEL
WOOSELL
WOOSELS
WOPPED
SWOPPED
WORDED
SWORDED
WORKER
WORKERS
WORMER
WORMERS
WORMERY
WORRAL
WORRALS
WORREL
WORRELS
WORRIT
WORRITS
WORSEN
WORSENS
WORTLE
WORTLES
WOTTED
SWOTTED
WOUBIT
WOUBITS
WOULDS
WOULDST
WOUNDS
SWOUNDS
WOWSER
WOWSERS
WRAITH
WRAITHS
WRASSE
WRASSES
WRAXLE
WRAXLED
WRAXLES
WREAKE
WREAKED
WREAKER
WREAKES
WREATH
WREATHE
WREATHS
WREATHY
WRETHE
WRETHED
WRETHES
WRIEST
OWRIEST
WRIGHT

WRIGHTS	**XYLOMA**	**YAPOCK**	**YNAMBU**	**YUCKER**	ZARIBAS	ZILLAHS	**ZOOZOO**
WRITER	XYLOMAS	YAPOCKS	YNAMBUS	YUCKERS	**ZARNEC**	**ZIMMER**	ZOOZOOS
WRITERS	**XYLOSE**	**YAPPER**	YODLER	YUMPIE	ZARNECS	ZIMMERS	**ZORINO**
WRITHE	XYLOSES	YAPPERS	YODLERS	YUMPIES	**ZEALOT**	**ZINGEL**	ZORINOS
WRITHED	**XYSTER**	**YARPHA**	**YOGINI**	**YUPPIE**	ZEALOTS	ZINGELS	**ZOSTER**
WRITHEN	XYSTERS	YARPHAS	YOGINIS	YUPPIES	**ZEBECK**	**ZINNIA**	ZOSTERS
WRITHES	**YABBER**	**YARROW**	**YOGISM**	**YWROKE**	ZEBECKS	ZINNIAS	**ZYGOMA**
WROATH	YABBERS	YARROWS	YOGISMS	YWROKEN	**ZEBRAS**	**ZIPPER**	ZYGOMAS
WROATHS	**YABBIE**	**YATTER**	**YOGURT**	**ZABETA**	ZEBRASS	ZIPPERS	**ZYGOSE**
WROKEN	YABBIES	YATTERS	YOGURTS	ZABETAS	**ZELANT**	**ZIRCON**	ZYGOSES
YWROKEN	**YACKER**	**YAUPON**	**YOJANA**	**ZADDIK**	ZELANTS	ZIRCONS	**ZYGOTE**
WUNNER	YACKERS	YAUPONS	YOJANAS	TZADDIK	**ZENANA**	**ZITHER**	ZYGOTES
WUNNERS	**YAFFED**	**YAWPER**	**YOKING**	ZADDIKS	ZENANAS	ZITHERN	**ZYMASE**
WURLEY	NYAFFED	YAWPERS	YOKINGS	**ZAFFER**	**ZENDIK**	ZITHERNS	ZYMASES
WURLEYS	**YAFFLE**	**YELLOW**	YONKER	ZAFFERS	ZENDIKS	ZITHERS	**ZYMITE**
WUTHER	YAFFLES	YELLOWS	YONKERS	**ZAFFRE**	**ZENITH**	**ZODIAC**	AZYMITE
WUTHERS	**YAGGER**	YELLOWY	**YOPPER**	ZAFFRES	ZENITHS	ZODIACS	ZYMITES
WUZZLE	YAGGERS	**YELPER**	YOPPERS	**ZAMANG**	**ZEPHYR**	**ZOMBIE**	**ZYMOME**
WUZZLED	**YAKKER**	YELPERS	**YORKER**	ZAMANGS	ZEPHYRS	ZOMBIES	ZYMOMES
WUZZLES	YAKKERS	**YESTER**	YORKERS	**ZANDER**	**ZONATE**	**ZYTHUM**
WYVERN	**YAMMER**	DYESTER	**YORKIE**	ZANDERS	ZEREBA	ZONATED	ZYTHUMS
WYVERNS	YAMMERS	YESTERN	YORKIES	**ZANIES**	ZEREBAS	**ZONING**
XEROMA	**YANKER**	**YICKER**	**YOWLEY**	ZANIEST	**ZERIBA**	ZONINGS
XEROMAS	YANKERS	YICKERS	YOWLEYS	**ZARAPE**	ZERIBAS	**ZONULA**
XOANON	**YANKIE**	**YIKKER**	**YSHEND**	ZARAPES	**ZEUGMA**	ZONULAR
XOANONS	YANKIES	YIKKERS	YSHENDS	**ZAREBA**	ZEUGMAS	ZONULAS
XYLENE	**YAOURT**	**YMPING**	**YTTRIA**	ZAREBAS	**ZIGZAG**	**ZONULE**
XYLENES	YAOURTS	GYMPING	YTTRIAS	**ZARIBA**	ZIGZAGS	**ZILLAH**	ZONULES
							ZONULET

PART B: 7-letter word hooks
extensible words only

ABACTOR	ABUTTALS	ACQUIRE	ADHARMAS	AFFRONTS	AIRINGS	ALERION
ABACTORS	ABUTTER	ACQUIRED	ADHERER	AGACANT	FAIRINGS	ALERIONS
ABALONE	ABUTTERS	ACQUIRES	ADHERERS	AGACANTE	PAIRINGS	ALEURON
ABALONES	ACADEME	ACQUIST	ADHIBIT	AGAMOID	AIRLESS	ALEURONE
ABANDON	ACADEMES	ACQUISTS	ADHIBITS	AGAMOIDS	HAIRLESS	ALEURONS
ABANDONS	ACALEPH	ACQUITE	ADJOINT	AGELAST	AIRLIFT	ALFALFA
ABATURE	ACALEPHA	ACQUITES	ADJOINTS	AGELASTS	AIRLIFTS	ALFALFAS
ABATURES	ACALEPHE	ACREAGE	ADJOURN	AGELESS	AIRLINE	ALFAQUI
ABDOMEN	ACALEPHS	ACREAGES	ADJOURNS	WAGELESS	HAIRLINE	ALFAQUIS
ABDOMENS	ACANTHA	ACRIDIN	ADJUDGE	AGGRACE	AIRLINER	ALFORJA
ABETTER	ACANTHAS	ACRIDINE	ADJUDGED	AGGRACED	AIRLINES	ALFORJAS
ABETTERS	ACAPNIA	ACRIDINS	ADJUDGES	AGGRACES	AIRMAIL	ALGEBRA
ABETTOR	ACAPNIAS	ACROBAT	ADJUNCT	AGGRADE	AIRMAILS	ALGEBRAS
ABETTORS	ACATOUR	ACROBATS	ADJUNCTS	AGGRADED	AIRPORT	ALGESIA
ABIDING	ACATOURS	ACROGEN	ADMIRAL	AGGRADES	AIRPORTS	ALGESIAS
ABIDINGS	ACCEDER	ACROGENS	ADMIRALS	AGGRATE	AIRSHIP	ALICANT
ABIGAIL	ACCEDERS	ACRONYM	ADMIRER	AGGRATED	AIRSHIPS	ALICANTS
ABIGAILS	ACCIDIE	ACRONYMS	ADMIRERS	AGGRATES	AIRSTOP	ALIDADE
ABILITY	ACCIDIES	ACROTER	ADONISE	AGILITY	AIRSTOPS	ALIDADES
LABILITY	ACCINGE	ACROTERS	ADONISED	VAGILITY	AIRTIME	ALIENEE
ABJOINT	ACCINGED	ACRYLIC	ADONISES	AGINNER	AIRTIMES	ALIENEES
ABJOINTS	ACCINGES	ACRYLICS	ADONIZE	AGINNERS	AIRWARD	ALIENOR
ABJURER	ACCLAIM	ACTINIA	ADONIZED	AGISTER	AIRWARDS	ALIENORS
ABJURERS	ACCLAIMS	ACTINIAE	ADONIZES	MAGISTER	AIRWAVE	ALIFORM
ABLATOR	ACCOAST	ACTINIAN	ADOPTER	AGISTERS	AIRWAVES	PALIFORM
ABLATORS	ACCOASTS	ACTINIAS	ADOPTERS	AGISTOR	AIRWAYS	ALIGNED
ABOULIA	ACCOMPT	ACTINON	ADRENAL	AGISTORS	FAIRWAYS	MALIGNED
ABOULIAS	ACCOMPTS	ACTINONS	ADRENALS	AGITATE	AISLING	ALIMENT
ABREACT	ACCOUNT	ACTIONS	ADULATE	AGITATED	AISLINGS	ALIMENTS
ABREACTS	ACCOUNTS	FACTIONS	RADULATE	AGITATES	AJUTAGE	ALIMONY
ABRIDGE	ACCOURT	PACTIONS	ADULATED	AGITATO	AJUTAGES	PALIMONY
ABRIDGED	ACCOURTS	TACTIONS	ADULATES	AGITATOR	AKVAVIT	ALIPEDS
ABRIDGER	ACCRETE	ACTUATE	ADVANCE	AGNATES	AKVAVITS	TALIPEDS
ABRIDGES	ACCRETED	ACTUATED	TADVANCE	MAGNATES	ALAMEDA	ALIZARI
ABROOKE	ACCRETES	ACTUATES	ADVANCED	AGNOMEN	ALAMEDAS	ALIZARIN
ABROOKED	ACCRUAL	ACTURES	ADVANCES	AGNOMENS	ALAMODE	ALIZARIS
ABROOKES	ACCRUALS	FACTURES	ADVERSE	AGONISE	ALAMODES	ALKALIS
ABSCIND	ACCURSE	ACUMENS	ADVERSER	AGONISED	ALANNAH	ALKALISE
ABSCINDS	ACCURSED	CACUMENS	ADVISER	AGONISES	ALANNAHS	ALKANET
ABSCISE	ACCURSES	ACUSHLA	ADVISERS	AGONIST	ALBERTS	ALKANETS
ABSCISED	ACCUSAL	ACUSHLAS	ADVISOR	AGONISTS	HALBERTS	ALLAYER
ABSCISES	ACCUSALS	ADAMANT	ADVISORS	AGONIZE	ALBUMEN	ALLAYERS
ABSCISS	ACCUSER	ADAMANTS	ADVISORY	AGONIZED	ALBUMENS	ALLEDGE
ABSCISSA	ACCUSERS	ADAPTER	AERATOR	AGONIZES	ALBUMIN	ALLEDGED
ABSCISSE	ACETATE	ADAPTERS	AERATORS	AGRAFFE	ALBUMINS	ALLEDGES
ABSCOND	ACETATES	ADAPTOR	AEROBIC	AGRAFFES	ALCAIDE	ALLEGER
ABSCONDS	ACETONE	ADAPTORS	AEROBICS	AIDANCE	ALCAIDES	ALLEGERS
ABSENCE	ACETONES	ADDLING	AEROSOL	AIDANCES	ALCALDE	ALLEGGE
ABSENCES	ACHARYA	DADDLING	AEROSOLS	AIDLESS	ALCALDES	ALLEGGED
ABSINTH	ACHARYAS	FADDLING	AFFAIRE	MAIDLESS	ALCAYDE	ALLEGGES
ABSINTHE	ACHIEVE	PADDLING	AFFAIRES	AILANTO	ALCAYDES	ALLEGRO
ABSINTHS	ACHIEVED	RADDLING	AFFEARE	AILANTOS	ALCAZAR	ALLEGROS
ABSOLVE	ACHIEVER	SADDLING	AFFEARED	AILERON	ALCAZARS	ALLHEAL
ABSOLVED	ACHIEVES	WADDLING	AFFEARES	AILERONS	ALCHERA	ALLHEALS
ABSOLVER	ACKNOWN	ADDUCER	AFFICHE	AILETTE	ALCHERAS	ALLISES
ABSOLVES	ACKNOWNE	ADDUCERS	AFFICHES	AILETTES	ALCOHOL	GALLISES
ABSTAIN	ACOLYTE	ADENINE	AFFLICT	AILMENT	ALCOHOLS	ALLNESS
ABSTAINS	ACOLYTES	ADENINES	AFFLICTS	BAILMENT	ALCORZA	TALLNESS
ABTHANE	ACOLYTH	ADENOID	AFFOORD	AILMENTS	ALCORZAS	ALLONGE
ABTHANES	ACOLYTHS	ADENOIDS	AFFOORDS	AIRHOLE	ALECOST	ALLONGES
ABUSAGE	ACONITE	ADENOMA	AFFORCE	AIRHOLES	ALECOSTS	ALLONYM
ABUSAGES	TACONITE	ADENOMAS	AFFORCED	AIRIEST	ALEMBIC	ALLONYMS
ABUSION	ACONITES	ADERMIN	AFFORCES	HAIRIEST	ALEMBICS	ALLOWED
ABUSIONS	ACQUEST	ADERMINS	AFFRONT	LAIRIEST	ALEPINE	FALLOWED
ABUTTAL	ACQUESTS	ADHARMA	AFFRONTE	VAIRIEST	ALEPINES	GALLOWED

HALLOWED	AMBIENTS	ANAEMIA	ANILINE	ANTRUMS	APPROVES	ARIETTAS
SALLOWED	AMBLERS	ANAEMIAS	ANILINES	TANTRUMS	APPULSE	ARIETTE
TALLOWED	GAMBLERS	ANAGOGE	ANIMATE	APAGOGE	APPULSES	ARIETTES
WALLOWED	RAMBLERS	ANAGOGES	ANIMATED	APAGOGES	APRAXIA	ARISHES
ALLSEED	AMBLING	ANAGRAM	ANIMATES	APANAGE	APRAXIAS	GARISHES
ALLSEEDS	GAMBLING	ANAGRAMS	ANIMISM	APANAGED	APRICOT	MARISHES
ALLURER	HAMBLING	ANALYSE	ANIMISMS	APANAGES	APRICOTS	PARISHES
ALLURERS	LAMBLING	ANALYSED	ANIMIST	APATITE	AQUAFER	ARMBAND
ALLUVIA	RAMBLING	ANALYSER	ANIMISTS	APATITES	AQUAFERS	ARMBANDS
ALLUVIAL	WAMBLING	ANALYSES	ANISEED	APEHOOD	AQUARIA	ARMHOLE
ALLYING	AMBLINGS	ANALYST	ANISEEDS	APEHOODS	AQUARIAN	ARMHOLES
DALLYING	AMBONES	ANALYSTS	ANNATES	APEPSIA	AQUATIC	ARMIGER
GALLYING	JAMBONES	ANALYZE	TANNATES	APEPSIAS	AQUATICS	ARMIGERO
RALLYING	AMBROID	ANALYZED	ANNATTA	APERIES	AQUAVIT	ARMIGERS
SALLYING	AMBROIDS	ANALYZER	ANNATTAS	NAPERIES	AQUAVITS	ARMILLA
TALLYING	AMENAGE	ANALYZES	ANNATTO	APHAGIA	AQUIFER	ARMILLAE
ALMANAC	AMENAGED	ANAPEST	ANNATTOS	APHAGIAS	AQUIFERS	ARMILLAS
ALMANACS	AMENAGES	ANAPESTS	ANNELID	APHASIA	ARABICA	ARMLESS
ALMIRAH	AMENDER	ANATASE	ANNELIDS	APHASIAC	ARABICAS	HARMLESS
ALMIRAHS	AMENDERS	ANATASES	ANNICUT	APHASIAS	ARABINS	ARMLOCK
ALMONER	AMENTIA	ANCIENT	ANNICUTS	APHELIA	CARABINS	ARMLOCKS
ALMONERS	AMENTIAS	ANCIENTS	ANNULAR	APHELIAN	ARABISE	ARMOIRE
ALNAGER	AMENTUM	ANDANTE	ANNULARS	APHIDES	ARABISED	ARMOIRES
ALNAGERS	RAMENTUM	ANDANTES	ANNULET	RAPHIDES	ARABISES	ARNOTTO
ALODIUM	AMILDAR	ANDIRON	ANNULETS	APHONIA	ARABIZE	ARNOTTOS
ALODIUMS	AMILDARS	ANDIRONS	ANODISE	APHONIAS	ARABIZED	AROUSAL
ALOETIC	AMMETER	ANDROID	ANODISED	APLANAT	ARABIZES	CAROUSAL
ALOETICS	AMMETERS	ANDROIDS	ANODISES	APLANATS	ARANEID	AROUSALS
ALPHORN	AMMIRAL	ANDVILE	ANODIZE	APLASIA	ARANEIDS	AROUSED
ALPHORNS	AMMIRALS	ANDVILES	ANODIZED	APLASIAS	ARAROBA	CAROUSED
ALTERED	AMMONAL	ANELACE	ANODIZES	APOCOPE	ARAROBAS	AROUSER
FALTERED	AMMONALS	ANELACES	ANODYNE	APOCOPES	ARBITER	CAROUSER
HALTERED	AMMONIA	ANEMONE	ANODYNES	APOPLEX	ARBITERS	AROUSERS
PALTERED	AMMONIAC	ANEMONES	ANONYMA	APOPLEXY	ARBLAST	AROUSES
ALTERNE	AMMONIAS	ANEROID	ANONYMAS	APOSTIL	ARBLASTS	CAROUSES
ALTERNES	AMNESIA	ANEROIDS	ANOSMIA	APOSTILS	ARBORET	ARPENTS
ALTESSE	AMNESIAC	ANEURIN	ANOSMIAS	APOSTLE	ARBORETA	PARPENTS
ALTESSES	AMNESIAS	ANEURINS	ANTACID	APOSTLES	ARBORETS	ARRACKS
ALTEZZA	AMNESIC	ANGEKOK	ANTACIDS	APOTHEM	ARBOURS	BARRACKS
ALTEZZAS	AMNESICS	ANGEKOKS	ANTBEAR	APOTHEMS	HARBOURS	CARRACKS
ALTHAEA	AMORISM	ANGELIC	ANTBEARS	APPARAT	ARCHERS	ARRAIGN
ALTHAEAS	AMORISMS	ANGELICA	ANTEFIX	APPARATS	MARCHERS	DARRAIGN
ALTHORN	AMORIST	ANGERED	ANTEFIXA	APPAREL	ARCHING	ARRAIGNS
ALTHORNS	AMORISTS	DANGERED	ANTENNA	APPARELS	MARCHING	ARRANGE
ALUMINA	AMOROSA	ANGIOMA	ANTENNAE	APPEASE	PARCHING	ARRANGED
ALUMINAS	AMOROSAS	ANGIOMAS	ANTENNAL	APPEASED	ARCHIVE	ARRANGER
ALUMIUM	AMOROSO	ANGLERS	ANTENNAS	APPEASES	ARCHIVES	ARRANGES
ALUMIUMS	AMOROSOS	DANGLERS	ANTHERS	APPERIL	ARCHLET	ARRASES
ALUNITE	AMOSITE	JANGLERS	PANTHERS	APPERILL	ARCHLETS	NARRASES
ALUNITES	AMOSITES	MANGLERS	ANTICKE	APPERILS	ARCHWAY	TARRASES
ALVEOLE	AMPHORA	TANGLERS	ANTICKED	APPLAUD	ARCHWAYS	ARRAYED
ALVEOLES	AMPHORAE	WANGLERS	ANTIENT	APPLAUDS	ARCINGS	WARRAYED
ALYSSUM	AMPOULE	ANGLING	ANTIENTS	APPOINT	FARCINGS	ARREEDE
ALYSSUMS	AMPOULES	CANGLING	ANTIGEN	APPOINTS	ARCKING	ARREEDES
AMALGAM	AMPULLA	DANGLING	ANTIGENS	APPORTS	ARCKINGS	ARRIAGE
AMALGAMS	AMPULLAE	FANGLING	ANTILOG	RAPPORTS	ARCUATE	CARRIAGE
AMANITA	AMPUTEE	GANGLING	ANTILOGS	APPOSER	ARCUATED	MARRIAGE
AMANITAS	AMPUTEES	JANGLING	ANTILOGY	APPOSERS	ARDRIGH	ARRIAGES
AMARANT	AMYGDAL	MANGLING	ANTINGS	APPRISE	ARDRIGHS	ARRIERO
AMARANTH	AMYGDALA	TANGLING	BANTINGS	APPRISED	AREFIED	ARRIEROS
AMARANTS	AMYGDALE	WANGLING	CANTINGS	APPRISES	RAREFIED	ARRIVAL
AMASSES	AMYGDALS	ANGLINGS	PANTINGS	APPRIZE	AREFIES	ARRIVALS
CAMASSES	AMYLASE	ANGLIST	WANTINGS	APPRIZED	RAREFIES	ARROWED
AMATEUR	AMYLASES	ANGLISTS	ANTIQUE	APPRIZER	ARGENTS	FARROWED
AMATEURS	AMYLENE	ANGRIES	ANTIQUED	APPRIZES	MARGENTS	HARROWED
AMATION	AMYLENES	ANGRIEST	ANTIQUES	APPROOF	ARGUSES	MARROWED
AMATIONS	AMYLOID	ANGUINE	ANTLERS	APPROOFS	SARGUSES	NARROWED
AMBERED	AMYLOIDS	SANGUINE	PANTLERS	APPROVE	ARGYRIA	TARROWED
CAMBERED		ANGUISH	ANTONYM	APPROVED	ARGYRIAS	ARSENAL
AMBIENT		LANGUISH	ANTONYMS	APPROVER	ARIETTA	ARSENALS

ARSENIC	**ASSEVERS**	**ATOMISE**	AURELIAS	AXOLOTLS	**BAILLIE**	**BANTENG**
ARSENICS	**ASSHOLE**	ATOMISED	**AUREOLA**	**AYWORDS**	BAILLIES	BANTENGS
ARSHEEN	ASSHOLES	ATOMISER	AUREOLAS	NAYWORDS	**BAITING**	**BANTING**
ARSHEENS	**ASSIEGE**	ATOMISES	**AUREOLE**	**AZIMUTH**	BAITINGS	BANTINGS
ARSHINE	ASSIEGED	**ATOMISM**	AUREOLED	AZIMUTHS	**BAKLAVA**	**BAPTISE**
ARSHINES	ASSIEGES	ATOMISMS	AUREOLES	**AZOTISE**	BAKLAVAS	BAPTISED
ARTICLE	**ASSISTS**	**ATOMIST**	**AURICLE**	AZOTISED	**BALADIN**	BAPTISES
PARTICLE	BASSISTS	ATOMISTS	AURICLED	AZOTISES	BALADINE	**BAPTISM**
ARTICLED	**ASSIZER**	**ATOMIZE**	AURICLES	**AZOTIZE**	BALADINS	BAPTISMS
ARTICLES	ASSIZERS	ATOMIZED	**AUSPICE**	AZOTIZED	**BALANCE**	**BAPTIST**
ARTIEST	**ASSUAGE**	ATOMIZER	AUSPICES	AZOTIZES	BALANCED	BAPTISTS
TARTIEST	ASSUAGED	ATOMIZES	**AUSTERE**	**AZULEJO**	BALANCER	**BAPTIZE**
WARTIEST	ASSUAGES	**ATONING**	AUSTERER	AZULEJOS	BALANCES	BAPTIZED
ARTISAN	**ASSURED**	BATONING	**AUTEURS**	**AZURINE**	**BALDRIC**	BAPTIZES
BARTISAN	ASSUREDS	**ATRESIA**	HAUTEURS	AZURINES	BALDRICK	**BARACAN**
PARTISAN	**ASSURER**	ATRESIAS	**AUTOCAR**	**AZURITE**	BALDRICS	BARACANS
ARTISANS	ASSURERS	**ATROPIA**	AUTOCARP	LAZURITE	**BALISTA**	**BARBATE**
ARTISTE	**ASSWAGE**	ATROPIAS	AUTOCARS	AZURITES	BALISTAE	BARBATED
ARTISTES	TASSWAGE	**ATROPIN**	**AUTOCUE**	**AZYMITE**	BALISTAS	**BARBOLA**
ARTLESS	ASSWAGED	ATROPINE	AUTOCUES	AZYMITES	**BALKING**	BARBOLAS
WARTLESS	ASSWAGES	ATROPINS	**AUTOMAT**	**BABASSU**	BALKINGS	**BARBULE**
ARTWORK	**ASTABLE**	**ATTACHE**	AUTOMATA	BABASSUS	**BALLADE**	BARBULES
PARTWORK	TASTABLE	ATTACHED	AUTOMATE	**BABBITT**	BALLADED	**BARCHAN**
ARTWORKS	**ASTATKI**	ATTACHES	AUTOMATS	BABBITTS	BALLADES	BARCHANE
ASCARID	ASTATKIS	**ATTAINT**	**AUTONYM**	**BABBLER**	**BALLANT**	BARCHANS
ASCARIDS	**ASTEISM**	ATTAINTS	TAUTONYM	BABBLERS	BALLANTS	**BARGAIN**
ASCETIC	ASTEISMS	**ATTEMPT**	AUTONYMS	**BABICHE**	**BALLAST**	BARGAINS
ASCETICS	**ASTERIA**	ATTEMPTS	**AUTOVAC**	BABICHES	BALLASTS	**BARGEES**
ASCIDIA	ASTERIAS	**ATTRACT**	AUTOVACS	**BABUCHE**	**BALLING**	BARGEESE
ASCIDIAN	**ASTERID**	ATTRACTS	**AUXETIC**	BABUCHES	BALLINGS	**BARGEST**
ASCRIBE	ASTERIDS	**ATTRIST**	AUXETICS	**BABUDOM**	**BALLIUM**	BARGESTS
ASCRIBED	**ASTHORE**	ATTRISTS	**AVARICE**	BABUDOMS	BALLIUMS	**BARILLA**
ASCRIBES	ASTHORES	**ATTUITE**	AVARICES	**BABUISM**	**BALLOON**	BARILLAS
ASEPTIC	**ASTILBE**	ATTUITED	**AVENGER**	BABUISMS	BALLOONS	**BARKHAN**
ASEPTICS	ASTILBES	ATTUITES	AVENGERS	**BACCARA**	**BALONEY**	BARKHANS
ASHIEST	**ASTOUND**	**AUBERGE**	**AVENTRE**	BACCARAS	BALONEYS	**BARMAID**
HASHIEST	ASTOUNDS	AUBERGES	AVENTRED	BACCARAT	**BAMBINO**	BARMAIDS
MASHIEST	**ASTRICT**	**AUCTION**	AVENTRES	**BACKBIT**	BAMBINOS	**BARMKIN**
WASHIEST	ASTRICTS	AUCTIONS	**AVERAGE**	BACKBITE	**BANDAGE**	BARMKINS
ASHRAMA	**ASTROID**	**AUDIENT**	AVERAGED	**BACKHOE**	BANDAGED	**BAROCCO**
ASHRAMAS	ASTROIDS	AUDIENTS	AVERAGES	BACKHOES	BANDAGES	BAROCCOS
ASINICO	**ATABRIN**	**AUDITOR**	**AVIATOR**	**BACKING**	**BANDANA**	**BARONET**
ASINICOS	ATABRINS	AUDITORS	AVIATORS	BACKINGS	BANDANAS	BARONETS
ASKANCE	**ATAGHAN**	AUDITORY	**AVIETTE**	**BACKLOG**	**BANDEAU**	**BARONNE**
ASKANCED	YATAGHAN	**AUFGABE**	AVIETTES	BACKLOGS	BANDEAUX	BARONNES
ASKANCES	ATAGHANS	AUFGABES	**AVIONIC**	**BACKPAY**	**BANDIES**	**BAROQUE**
ASPERGE	**ATALAYA**	**AUGMENT**	AVIONICS	BACKPAYS	BANDIEST	BAROQUES
ASPERGED	ATALAYAS	AUGMENTS	**AVOCADO**	**BACKSAW**	**BANDING**	**BARRACE**
ASPERGED	**ATAVISM**	**AUGURER**	AVOCADOS	BACKSAWS	ABANDING	BARRACES
ASPERGES	ATAVISMS	AUGURERS	**AWAKING**	**BACKSET**	BANDINGS	**BARRACK**
ASPERSE	**ATEBRIN**	**AUGUSTE**	AWAKINGS	BACKSETS	**BANDOOK**	BARRACKS
ASPERSED	ATEBRINS	AUGUSTER	**AWFULLY**	**BACKSEY**	BANDOOKS	**BARRAGE**
ASPERSES	**ATELIER**	AUGUSTES	LAWFULLY	BACKSEYS	**BANDORA**	BARRAGES
ASPHALT	ATELIERS	**AULDEST**	**AWLBIRD**	**BACLAVA**	BANDORAS	**BARRICO**
ASPHALTS	**ATHANOR**	CAULDEST	AWLBIRDS	BACLAVAS	**BANDORE**	BARRICOS
ASPIRIN	ATHANORS	**AULNAGE**	**AWNIEST**	**BAFFLER**	BANDORES	**BARRIER**
ASPIRING	**ATHEISE**	AULNAGER	LAWNIEST	BAFFLERS	**BANDROL**	BARRIERS
ASPIRINS	ATHEISED	AULNAGES	TAWNIEST	**BAGARRE**	BANDROLS	**BARRING**
ASSAGAI	**ATHEISM**	**AUNTERS**	YAWNIEST	BAGARRES	**BANDURA**	BARRINGS
ASSAGAIS	ATHEISMS	DAUNTERS	**AWNINGS**	**BAGASSE**	BANDURAS	**BARWOOD**
ASSAILS	**ATHEIST**	HAUNTERS	DAWNINGS	BAGASSES	**BANKING**	BARWOODS
VASSAILS	ATHEISTS	SAUNTERS	FAWNINGS	**BAGGAGE**	BANKINGS	**BARYTON**
WASSAILS	**ATHEIZE**	TAUNTERS	YAWNINGS	BAGGAGES	**BANKSIA**	BARYTONE
ASSAULT	ATHEIZED	VAUNTERS	**AXILLAE**	**BAGGING**	BANKSIAS	BARYTONS
ASSAULTS	**ATHEIZE**	**AUNTIES**	MAXILLAE	BAGGINGS	**BANNOCK**	**BASBLEU**
ASSAYER	ATHEIZED	JAUNTIES	**AXILLAR**	**BAGPIPE**	BANNOCKS	BASBLEUS
ASSAYERS	**ATHLETA**	**AUREATE**	AXILLARY	BAGPIPER	**BANQUET**	**BASCULE**
ASSEGAI	ATHLETAS	LAUREATE	**AXINITE**	BAGPIPES	BANQUETS	BASCULES
ASSEGAIS	**ATHLETE**	**AURELIA**	AXINITES	**BAILIFF**	**BANSHEE**	**BASEMEN**
ASSEVER	ATHLETES	AURELIAN	**AXOLOTL**	BAILIFFS	BANSHEES	**BASEMENT**

BASENJI	BEARINGS	BEGORRA	BEPAINTS	BESTREWS	BINOCLE	BLEEPER
BASENJIS	BEASTIE	BEGORRAH	BEPEARL	BESTRID	BINOCLES	BLEEPERS
BASHING	BEASTIES	BEGRIME	BEPEARLS	BESTRIDE	BIOCIDE	BLENDER
ABASHING	BEATING	BEGRIMED	BEPROSE	BETAINE	BIOCIDES	BLENDERS
BASHINGS	BEATINGS	BEGRIMES	BEPROSED	BETAINES	BIOPHOR	BLESBOK
BASHLYK	BEATNIK	BEGUILE	BEPROSES	BETEEME	BIOPHORE	BLESBOKS
BASHLYKS	BEATNIKS	BEGUILED	BEQUEST	BETEEMED	BIOPHORS	BLETHER
BASIDIA	BEAUFET	BEGUILER	BEQUESTS	BETEEMES	BIOTITE	BLETHERS
BASIDIAL	BEAUFETS	BEGUILES	BERCEAU	BETHINK	BIOTITES	BLEWART
BASINET	BEAUFIN	BEGUINE	BERCEAUX	BETHINKS	BIOTYPE	BLEWARTS
BASINETS	BEAUFINS	BEGUINES	BEREAVE	BETHUMB	BIOTYPES	BLINDER
BASOCHE	BEBEERU	BEHIGHT	BEREAVED	BETHUMBS	BIPLANE	BLINDERS
BASOCHES	BEBEERUS	BEHIGHTS	BEREAVEN	BETHUMP	BIPLANES	BLINKER
BASSIST	BECASSE	BEHOOVE	BEREAVES	BETHUMPS	BIRDING	BLINKERS
BASSISTS	BECASSES	BEHOOVED	BERGAMA	BETITLE	BIRDINGS	BLINTZE
BASSOON	BECHARM	BEHOOVES	BERGAMAS	BETITLED	BIRETTA	BLINTZES
BASSOONS	BECHARMS	BEIGNET	BERGYLT	BETITLES	BIRETTAS	BLISTER
BASTARD	BECLOUD	BEIGNETS	BERGYLTS	BETOKEN	BIRLING	BLISTERS
BASTARDS	BECLOUDS	BEJEWEL	BERLINE	BETOKENS	BIRLINGS	BLISTERY
BASTARDY	BEDAWIN	BEJEWELS	BERLINES	BETREAD	BIRLINN	BLITHER
BASTIDE	BEDAWINS	BEKNAVE	BERSERK	BETREADS	BIRLINNS	BLITHERS
BASTIDES	BEDDING	BEKNAVED	BERSERKS	BETROTH	BIRYANI	BLOATER
BASTING	BEDDINGS	BEKNAVES	BESAINT	BETROTHS	BIRYANIS	BLOATERS
BASTINGS	BEDERAL	BELCHER	BESAINTS	BETTERS	BISCUIT	BLOCKER
BASTION	BEDERALS	BELCHERS	BESEEKE	ABETTERS	BISCUITS	BLOCKERS
BASTIONS	BEDEVIL	BELDAME	BESEEKES	BETTING	BISCUITY	BLONDES
BATABLE	BEDEVILS	BELDAMES	BESHAME	ABETTING	BISMUTH	BLONDEST
ABATABLE	BEDIGHT	BELGARD	BESHAMED	BETTINGS	BISMUTHS	BLOOMER
BATHTUB	BEDIGHTS	BELGARDS	BESHAMES	BETTORS	BISTORT	BLOOMERS
BATHTUBS	BEDIZEN	BELIEVE	BESHINE	ABETTORS	BISTORTS	BLOOMERY
BATISTE	BEDIZENS	BELIEVED	BESHINES	BETWEEN	BITTERN	BLOOPER
BATISTES	BEDOUIN	BELIEVER	BESHREW	BETWEENS	BITTERNS	BLOOPERS
BATTERO	BEDOUINS	BELIEVES	BESHREWS	BEWHORE	BITTIES	BLOOSME
BATTEROS	BEDPOST	BELLHOP	BESIEGE	BEWHORED	BITTIEST	BLOOSMED
BATTING	BEDPOSTS	BELLHOPS	BESIEGED	BEWHORES	BITTOCK	BLOOSMES
BATTINGS	BEDRITE	BELOVED	BESIEGER	BEZIQUE	BITTOCKS	BLOSSOM
BATTLER	BEDRITES	BELOVEDS	BESIEGES	BEZIQUES	BITTOUR	BLOSSOMS
BATTLERS	BEDROCK	BELTING	BESLAVE	BHISTEE	BITTOURS	BLOSSOMY
BATTUTA	BEDROCKS	BELTINGS	BESLAVED	BHISTEES	BITUMEN	BLOTTER
BATTUTAS	BEDROOM	BELTWAY	BESLAVER	BIASING	BITUMENS	BLOTTERS
BAUCHLE	BEDROOMS	BELTWAYS	BESLAVES	BIASINGS	BIVALVE	BLOUBOK
BAUCHLED	BEDSIDE	BEMEDAL	BESMEAR	BIBCOCK	BIVALVES	BLOUBOKS
BAUCHLES	BEDSIDES	BEMEDALS	BESMEARS	BIBCOCKS	BIVOUAC	BLOUSON
BAUDRIC	BEDSORE	BEMOUTH	BESPEAK	BIBELOT	BIVOUACS	BLOUSONS
BAUDRICK	BEDSORES	BEMOUTHS	BESPEAKS	BIBELOTS	BLABBER	BLOWGUN
BAUDRICS	BEDTICK	BENCHER	BESPEED	BIBLIST	BLABBERS	BLOWGUNS
BAUXITE	BEDTICKS	BENCHERS	BESPEEDS	BIBLISTS	BLACKEN	BLOWIES
BAUXITES	BEDTIME	BENDING	BESPICE	BICYCLE	BLACKENS	BLOWIEST
BAWCOCK	BEDTIMES	BENDINGS	BESPICED	BICYCLED	BLADDER	BLUBBER
BAWCOCKS	BEDWARD	BENDLET	BESPICES	BICYCLES	BLADDERS	BLUBBERS
BAWDIES	BEDWARDS	BENDLETS	BESPOKE	BIDDING	BLADDERY	BLUCHER
BAWDIEST	BEDWARF	BENEFIC	BESPOKEN	BIDDINGS	BLANKET	BLUCHERS
BAWDKIN	BEDWARFS	BENEFICE	BESPORT	BIDINGS	BLANKETS	BLUDGER
BAWDKINS	BEEFALO	BENEFIT	BESPORTS	ABIDINGS	BLANKETY	BLUDGERS
BAWLING	BEEFALOS	BENEFITS	BESPOUT	BIFOCAL	BLARNEY	BLUECAP
BAWLINGS	BEEHIVE	BENIGHT	BESPOUTS	BIFOCALS	BLARNEYS	BLUECAPS
BAYONET	BEEHIVES	BENIGHTS	BESTAIN	BIGENER	BLASTER	BLUEING
BAYONETS	BEFFANA	BENISON	BESTAINS	BIGENERS	BLASTERS	BLUEINGS
BAZOOKA	BEFFANAS	BENISONS	BESTEAD	BIGHORN	BLATHER	BLUETTE
BAZOOKAS	BEGGING	BENZENE	BESTEADS	BIGHORNS	BLATHERS	BLUETTES
BEADING	BEGGINGS	BENZENES	BESTIAL	BILIMBI	BLATTER	BLUFFER
BEADINGS	BEGHARD	BENZINE	BESTIALS	BILIMBIS	BLATTERS	BLUFFERS
BEAGLER	BEGHARDS	BENZINES	BESTICK	BILLING	BLAUBOK	BLUNDER
BEAGLERS	BEGINNE	BENZOIN	BESTICKS	BILLINGS	BLAUBOKS	BLUNDERS
BEAMING	BEGINNER	BENZOINS	BESTILL	BILLION	BLAWORT	BLUNGER
BEAMINGS	BEGINNES	BENZOLE	BESTILLS	BILLIONS	BLAWORTS	BLUNGERS
BEARDIE	BEGLOOM	BENZOLES	BESTORM	BILTONG	BLEATER	BLUNKER
BEARDIES	BEGLOOMS	BENZOYL	BESTORMS	BILTONGS	BLEATERS	BLUNKERS
BEARING	BEGONIA	BENZOYLS	BESTREW	BINDING	BLEEDER	BLUSHER
ABEARING	BEGONIAS	BEPAINT	BESTREWN	BINDINGS	BLEEDERS	BLUSHERS

BLUSHET	BOOKIEST	BOURDERS	BRAVURAS	BRISURES	BRUMMERS	BRUSHERS	**BULWARK**
BLUSHETS	**BOOKING**	**BOURDON**	**BRAWLER**	**BRITSKA**	**BRUSHER**	BULWARKS
BLUSTER	BOOKINGS	BOURDONS	BRAWLERS	BRITSKAS	BRUSHERS	**BUMBAZE**
BLUSTERS	**BOOKLET**	BOURKHA	**BRAYING**	**BRITTLE**	**BRUSQUE**	BUMBAZED
BLUSTERY	BOOKLETS	BOURKHAS	ABRAYING	BRITTLER	BRUSQUER	BUMBAZES
BOARDER	**BOOKSIE**	**BOURLAW**	**BRAZIER**	BRITTLES	**BRUXISM**	**BUMMOCK**
BOARDERS	BOOKSIER	BOURLAWS	BRAZIERS	**BRITZKA**	BRUXISMS	BUMMOCKS
BOASTER	**BOOMING**	**BOURREE**	**BREADTH**	BRITZKAS	**BUBINGA**	**BUMPKIN**
BOASTERS	BOOMINGS	BOURREES	BREADTHS	**BROADEN**	BUBINGAS	BUMPKINS
BOATING	**BOOSTER**	**BOUTADE**	**BREAKER**	BROADENS	**BUBUKLE**	**BUNDOOK**
BOATINGS	BOOSTERS	BOUTADES	BREAKERS	**BROCADE**	BUBUKLES	BUNDOOKS
BOBSLED	**BOOTLEG**	**BOWHEAD**	**BREATHE**	BROCADED	**BUCCINA**	**BUNGLER**
BOBSLEDS	BOOTLEGS	BOWHEADS	BREATHED	BROCADES	BUCCINAS	BUNGLERS
BOBTAIL	**BORAZON**	**BOWLDER**	BREATHER	**BROCAGE**	**BUCKEEN**	**BUNRAKU**
BOBTAILS	BORAZONS	BOWLDERS	BREATHES	BROCAGES	BUCKEENS	BUNRAKUS
BODIKIN	**BORDURE**	**BOWLINE**	**BRECCIA**	**BROCARD**	**BUCKING**	**BUNTING**
BODIKINS	BORDURES	BOWLINES	BRECCIAS	BROCARDS	BUCKINGS	BUNTINGS
BOGBEAN	**BOREDOM**	**BOWLING**	**BRECHAM**	**BROCHAN**	**BUCKLER**	**BUOYAGE**
BOGBEANS	BOREDOMS	BOWLINGS	BRECHAMS	BROCHANS	BUCKLERS	BUOYAGES
BOGGARD	**BORNITE**	**BOWSHOT**	**BREEDER**	**BROCKET**	**BUCKRAM**	**BURDOCK**
BOGGARDS	BORNITES	BOWSHOTS	BREEDERS	BROCKETS	BUCKRAMS	BURDOCKS
BOGGART	**BORONIA**	**BOXROOM**	**BREVETE**	**BRODKIN**	**BUCKSAW**	**BURETTE**
BOGGARTS	BORONIAS	BOXROOMS	BREVETED	BRODKINS	BUCKSAWS	BURETTES
BOGGLER	**BOROUGH**	**BOXWOOD**	**BREVIER**	**BROIDER**	**BUCOLIC**	**BURGAGE**
BOGGLERS	BOROUGHS	BOXWOODS	BREVIERS	BROIDERS	BUCOLICS	BURGAGES
BOGLAND	**BORSCHT**	**BOYCOTT**	**BREWAGE**	BROIDERY	**BUDDIES**	**BURGEON**
BOGLANDS	BORSCHTS	BOYCOTTS	BREWAGES	**BROILER**	BUDDIEST	BURGEONS
BOGYISM	**BORSTAL**	**BOYHOOD**	**BREWING**	BROILERS	**BUDDING**	**BURGHER**
BOGYISMS	BORSTALL	BOYHOODS	BREWINGS	**BROKAGE**	BUDDINGS	BURGHERS
BOILING	BORSTALS	**BRABBLE**	**BRICKIE**	BROKAGES	**BUDGERO**	**BURGLAR**
BOILINGS	**BORTSCH**	BRABBLED	BRICKIER	**BROKING**	BUDGEROS	BURGLARS
BOLIVAR	BORTSCHT	BRABBLES	BRICKIES	BROKINGS	BUDGEROW	BURGLARY
BOLIVARS	**BOSCAGE**	**BRACHET**	**BRICOLE**	**BROMATE**	**BUFFOON**	**BURNING**
BOLLARD	BOSCAGES	BRACHETS	BRICOLES	BROMATES	BUFFOONS	BURNINGS
BOLLARDS	**BOTARGO**	**BRACKEN**	**BRIDGED**	**BROMIDE**	**BUGABOO**	**BURNOUS**
BOLLOCK	BOTARGOS	BRACKENS	ABRIDGED	BROMIDES	BUGABOOS	BURNOUSE
BOLLOCKS	**BOTCHER**	**BRACKET**	**BRIDGES**	**BROMINE**	**BUGBANE**	**BURRELL**
BOLONEY	BOTCHERS	BRACKETS	ABRIDGES	BROMINES	BUGBANES	BURRELLS
BOLONEYS	BOTCHERY	**BRADAWL**	**BRIDLER**	**BROMMER**	**BUGBEAR**	**BURRHEL**
BOLSHIE	**BOTHOLE**	BRADAWLS	BRIDLERS	BROMMERS	BUGBEARS	BURRHELS
BOLSHIER	BOTHOLES	**BRAIDED**	**BRIDOON**	**BRONCHI**	**BUGGANE**	**BURSTER**
BOLSHIES	**BOTTEGA**	ABRAIDED	BRIDOONS	BRONCHIA	BUGGANES	BURSTERS
BOLSTER	BOTTEGAS	**BRAMBLE**	**BRIGADE**	**BRONCHO**	**BUGGING**	**BURTHEN**
BOLSTERS	**BOTTINE**	BRAMBLES	BRIGADED	BRONCHOS	BUGGINGS	BURTHENS
BOLTING	BOTTINES	**BRANDER**	BRIGADES	**BROODER**	**BUGWORT**	**BURWEED**
BOLTINGS	**BOTTLER**	BRANDERS	**BRIGAND**	BROODERS	BUGWORTS	BURWEEDS
BOMBARD	BOTTLERS	**BRANGLE**	BRIGANDS	**BROOKED**	**BUILDER**	**BUSGIRL**
BOMBARDS	**BOUCHEE**	BRANGLED	**BRIMING**	ABROOKED	BUILDERS	BUSGIRLS
BOMBAST	BOUCHEES	BRANGLES	BRIMINGS	**BROTHEL**	**BUKSHEE**	**BUSHIDO**
BOMBASTS	**BOUDOIR**	**BRANSLE**	**BRIMMER**	BROTHELS	BUKSHEES	BUSHIDOS
BOMBORA	BOUDOIRS	BRANSLES	BRIMMERS	**BROTHER**	**BULGINE**	**BUSHIES**
BOMBORAS	**BOUILLI**	**BRANTLE**	**BRINDLE**	BROTHERS	BULGINES	BUSHIEST
BONANZA	BOUILLIS	BRANTLES	BRINDLED	**BROWNIE**	**BULIMIA**	**BUSKING**
BONANZAS	**BOULDER**	**BRASERO**	BRINDLES	BROWNIER	BULIMIAS	BUSKINGS
BONDAGE	BOULDERS	BRASEROS	**BRINGER**	BROWNIES	**BULIMIC**	**BUSSING**
BONDAGER	**BOULTER**	**BRASHES**	BRINGERS	**BRUCHID**	BULIMICS	BUSSINGS
BONDAGES	BOULTERS	BRASHEST	**BRINJAL**	BRUCHIDS	**BULLACE**	**BUSTARD**
BONDING	**BOUNCER**	**BRASIER**	BRINJALS	**BRUCINE**	BULLACES	BUSTARDS
BONDINGS	BOUNCERS	BRASIERS	**BRIOCHE**	BRUCINES	**BULLBAT**	**BUSTIER**
BONESET	**BOUNDED**	**BRASSET**	BRIOCHES	**BRUCITE**	BULLBATS	BUSTIERS
BONESETS	ABOUNDED	BRASSETS	**BRIQUET**	BRUCITES	**BULLDOG**	**BUSTING**
BONFIRE	**BOUNDEN**	**BRASSIE**	BRIQUETS	**BRUHAHA**	BULLDOGS	BUSTINGS
BONFIRES	YBOUNDEN	BRASSIER	**BRISKEN**	BRUHAHAS	**BULLIES**	**BUSTLER**
BONISTS	**BOUNDER**	BRASSIES	BRISKENS	**BRUISER**	BULLIEST	BUSTLERS
EBONISTS	BOUNDERS	**BRATTLE**	**BRISKET**	BRUISERS	**BULLION**	**BUTANOL**
BONNIES	**BOUQUET**	BRATTLED	BRISKETS	**BRULYIE**	BULLIONS	BUTANOLS
BONNIEST	BOUQUETS	BRATTLES	**BRISTLE**	BRULYIES	**BULLOCK**	**BUTCHER**
BOOBOOK	**BOURBON**	**BRAVADO**	BRISTLED	**BRULZIE**	BULLOCKS	BUTCHERS
BOOBOOKS	BOURBONS	BRAVADOS	BRISTLES	BRULZIES	**BULRUSH**	BUTCHERY
BOOKIES	**BOURDER**	**BRAVURA**	**BRISURE**	**BRUMMER**	BULRUSHY	**BUTCHES**

BUTCHEST	CAISSONS	CAMAIEUX	CANTICOY	CARABINS	CAROUSEL	**CATASTA**
BUTMENT	**CAITIFF**	**CAMARON**	**CANTIER**	**CARACAL**	CAROUSER	CATASTAS
ABUTMENT	CAITIFFS	CAMARONS	SCANTIER	CARACALS	CAROUSES	**CATAWBA**
BUTMENTS	**CAITIVE**	**CAMBISM**	**CANTINA**	**CARACOL**	CAROUSES	CATAWBAS
BUTTERS	CAITIVES	CAMBISMS	CANTINAS	CARACOLE	**CARPARK**	**CATBIRD**
ABUTTERS	**CAJEPUT**	**CAMBIST**	**CANTING**	CARACOLS	CARPARKS	CATBIRDS
BUTTING	CAJEPUTS	CAMBISTS	SCANTING	**CARACUL**	**CARPERS**	**CATBOAT**
ABUTTING	**CAJOLER**	**CAMBIUM**	**CANTINGS**	CARACULS	SCARPERS	CATBOATS
BUTTOCK	CAJOLERS	CAMBIUMS	**CANTION**	**CARAMEL**	**CARPING**	**CATCALL**
BUTTOCKS	CAJOLERY	**CAMBOGE**	CANTIONS	CARAMELS	CARPINGS	CATCALLS
BUVETTE	**CAJUPUT**	CAMBOGES	**CANTLED**	**CARANNA**	**CARPORT**	**CATCHER**
BUVETTES	CAJUPUTS	**CAMBREL**	SCANTLED	CARANNAS	CARPORTS	CATCHERS
BUYABLE	**CALCINE**	CAMBRELS	**CANTLES**	**CARAUNA**	**CARRACK**	**CATCHES**
BUYABLES	CALCINED	**CAMBRIC**	SCANTLES	CARAUNAS	CARRACKS	SCATCHES
BUZZARD	CALCINES	CAMBRICS	**CANTLET**	**CARAVAN**	**CARRACT**	**CATCHUP**
BUZZARDS	**CALCITE**	**CAMELID**	CANTLETS	CARAVANS	CARRACTS	CATCHUPS
BUZZING	CALCITES	CAMELIDS	**CANTRED**	**CARAVEL**	**CARRECT**	CATECHU
BUZZINGS	**CALCIUM**	**CAMELOT**	CANTREDS	CARAVELS	CARRECTS	CATECHUS
BYCOKET	CALCIUMS	CAMELOTS	**CANTREF**	**CARAWAY**	**CARRELL**	**CATELOG**
BYCOKETS	**CALDERA**	**CAMPANA**	CANTREFS	CARAWAYS	CARRELLS	CATELOGS
BYGOING	CALDERAS	CAMPANAS	**CANTRIP**	**CARBIDE**	**CARRIER**	**CATERAN**
BYGOINGS	**CALDRON**	**CAMPERS**	CANTRIPS	CARBIDES	SCARRIER	CATERANS
BYPLACE	CALDRONS	SCAMPERS	**CANZONA**	**CARBINE**	CARRIERS	**CATERER**
BYPLACES	**CALIBER**	**CAMPHOR**	CANZONAS	CARBINES	**CARRION**	CATERERS
BYWONER	CALIBERS	CAMPHORS	**CANZONE**	**CARCAKE**	CARRIONS	**CATHEAD**
BYWONERS	**CALIBRE**	**CAMPING**	CANZONET	CARCAKES	**CARTAGE**	CATHEADS
CABARET	CALIBRED	SCAMPING	**CAPABLE**	**CARCASE**	CARTAGES	**CATHODE**
CABARETS	CALIBRES	**CAMPION**	CAPABLER	CARCASED	**CARTING**	CATHODES
CABBAGE	**CALICHE**	CAMPIONS	**CAPELET**	CARCASES	SCARTING	**CATHOOD**
CABBAGED	CALICHES	**CANAKIN**	CAPELETS	**CARDECU**	**CARTOON**	CATHOODS
CABBAGES	**CALIPEE**	CANAKINS	**CAPELIN**	CARDECUE	CARTOONS	**CATLING**
CABBALA	CALIPEES	**CANASTA**	CAPELINE	CARDECUS	**CARTWAY**	CATLINGS
CABBALAS	**CALIPER**	CANASTAS	CAPELINS	**CARDIAC**	CARTWAYS	**CATMINT**
CABINET	CALIPERS	**CANDELA**	**CAPERER**	CARDIACS	**CARVING**	CATMINTS
CABINETS	**CALIVER**	CANDELAS	CAPERERS	**CARDOON**	CARVINGS	**CATSKIN**
CABLING	CALIVERS	**CANDENT**	**CAPITAL**	CARDOONS	**CASCADE**	CATSKINS
CABLINGS	**CALLANT**	SCANDENT	CAPITALS	**CARIAMA**	CASCADED	**CATSUIT**
CABOOSE	CALLANTS	**CANDIDA**	**CAPITAN**	CARIAMAS	CASCADES	CATSUITS
CABOOSES	**CALLING**	CANDIDAS	CAPITANI	**CARIBOU**	**CASCARA**	**CATTABU**
CACIQUE	CALLINGS	**CANDOCK**	CAPITANO	CARIBOUS	CASCARAS	CATTABUS
CACIQUES	**CALMANT**	CANDOCKS	CAPITANS	**CARIERE**	**CASEMEN**	**CATTALO**
CACKLER	CALMANTS	**CANDOUR**	**CAPORAL**	CARIERES	CASEMENT	CATTALOS
CACKLERS	**CALOMEL**	CANDOURS	CAPORALS	**CARINAS**	**CASERNE**	**CATTERY**
CACODYL	CALOMELS	**CANELLA**	**CAPPING**	OCARINAS	CASERNES	SCATTERY
CACODYLS	**CALORIC**	CANELLAS	CAPPINGS	**CARIOCA**	**CASHIER**	**CATTIER**
CACOLET	CALORICS	**CANIKIN**	**CAPRATE**	CARIOCAS	CASHIERS	SCATTIER
CACOLETS	**CALORIE**	CANIKINS	CAPRATES	**CARIOLE**	**CASSATA**	**CATTIES**
CACUMEN	CALORIES	**CANNACH**	**CAPRICE**	CARIOLES	CASSATAS	CATTIEST
CACUMENS	**CALOTTE**	CANNACHS	CAPRICES	**CARIOUS**	**CASSAVA**	**CATTING**
CADAVER	CALOTTES	**CANNERS**	**CAPSIZE**	SCARIOUS	CASSAVAS	SCATTING
CADAVERS	**CALOYER**	SCANNERS	CAPSIZED	**CARLINE**	**CASSINO**	**CAUDATE**
CADDICE	CALOYERS	**CANNING**	CAPSIZES	CARLINES	CASSINOS	ACAUDATE
CADDICES	**CALPACK**	SCANNING	**CAPSTAN**	**CARLOAD**	**CASSOCK**	ECAUDATE
CADENCE	CALPACKS	**CANNULA**	CAPSTANS	CARLOADS	CASSOCKS	CAUDATED
CADENCED	**CALTRAP**	CANNULAE	**CAPSULE**	**CARLOCK**	**CASSONE**	**CAUDRON**
CADENCES	CALTRAPS	CANNULAS	CAPSULES	CARLOCKS	CASSONES	CAUDRONS
CADENZA	**CALTROP**	**CANTATA**	**CAPTAIN**	**CARMINE**	**CASTING**	**CAULINE**
CADENZAS	CALTROPS	CANTATAS	CAPTAINS	CARMINES	CASTINGS	ACAULINE
CADMIUM	**CALUMBA**	**CANTATE**	**CAPTION**	**CARNAGE**	**CASTOCK**	**CAULKER**
CADMIUMS	CALUMBAS	CANTATES	CAPTIONS	CARNAGES	CASTOCKS	CAULKERS
CAESIUM	**CALUMET**	**CANTDOG**	**CAPTIVE**	**CARNIES**	**CASUIST**	**CAULOME**
CAESIUMS	CALUMETS	CANTDOGS	CAPTIVED	CARNIEST	CASUISTS	CAULOMES
CAESURA	**CALYCLE**	**CANTEEN**	CAPTIVES	**CAROCHE**	**CATALOG**	**CAUSTIC**
CAESURAL	CALYCLED	CANTEENS	**CAPTURE**	CAROCHES	CATALOGS	CAUSTICS
CAESURAS	CALYCLES	**CANTEST**	CAPTURED	**CAROMEL**	**CATALPA**	**CAUTION**
CAFFILA	**CALYPSO**	SCANTEST	CAPTURES	CAROMELS	CATALPAS	CAUTIONS
CAFFILAS	CALYPSOS	**CANTHUS**	**CAPUCHE**	**CAROTIN**	**CATAPAN**	**CAVALLA**
CAGOULE	**CALZONE**	ACANTHUS	CAPUCHES	CAROTINS	CATAPANS	CAVALLAS
CAGOULES	CALZONES	**CANTICO**	**CARABIN**	**CAROUSE**	**CATARRH**	**CAVIARE**
CAISSON	**CAMAIEU**	CANTICOS	CARABINE	CAROUSED	CATARRHS	CAVIARES

CAYENNE	CHADDAR	CHARACT	CHELATE	CHINKIER	CHUCKLED	CLABBERS
CAYENNED	CHADDARS	CHARACTS	CHELATED	CHINKIES	CHUCKLES	CLACHAN
CAYENNES	CHAFFER	CHARADE	CHELATES	CHINOOK	CHUDDAH	CLACHANS
CAZIQUE	CHAFFERS	CHARADES	CHELOID	CHINOOKS	CHUDDAHS	CLACKER
CAZIQUES	CHAFFERY	CHARGER	CHELOIDS	CHINWAG	CHUDDAR	CLACKERS
CEASING	CHAGRIN	CHARGERS	CHEMISE	CHINWAGS	CHUDDARS	CLADDER
CEASINGS	CHAGRINS	CHARIOT	CHEMISES	CHIPPIE	CHUKKER	CLADDERS
CEDILLA	CHALAZA	CHARIOTS	CHEMISM	CHIPPIER	CHUKKERS	CLADISM
CEDILLAS	CHALAZAE	CHARISM	CHEMISMS	CHIPPIES	CHUMLEY	CLADISMS
CEDRATE	CHALAZAS	CHARISMA	CHEMIST	CHIRPER	CHUMLEYS	CLADIST
CEDRATES	CHALDER	CHARISMS	CHEMISTS	CHIRPERS	CHUNDER	CLADISTS
CEILIDH	CHALDERS	CHARLEY	CHEQUER	CHIRRUP	CHUNDERS	CLADODE
CEILIDHS	CHALICE	CHARLEYS	CHEQUERS	CHIRRUPS	CHUNNEL	CLADODES
CEILING	CHALICED	CHARLIE	CHEROOT	CHIRRUPY	CHUNNELS	CLAIMER
CEILINGS	CHALICES	CHARLIES	CHEROOTS	CHITTER	CHUNNER	CLAIMERS
CELADON	CHALLAN	CHARMER	CHERVIL	CHITTERS	CHUNNERS	CLAMBER
CELADONS	CHALLANS	CHARMERS	CHERVILS	CHLORAL	CHUNTER	CLAMBERS
CELESTA	CHALONE	CHARNEL	CHESNUT	CHLORALS	CHUNTERS	CLAMOUR
CELESTAS	CHALONES	CHARNELS	CHESNUTS	CHOBDAR	CHUPATI	CLAMOURS
CELESTE	CHAMADE	CHARPIE	CHESSEL	CHOBDARS	CHUPATIS	CLAMPER
CELESTES	CHAMADES	CHARPIES	CHESSELS	CHOCTAW	CHUTIST	CLAMPERS
CELLIST	CHAMBER	CHARPOY	CHEVRON	CHOCTAWS	CHUTISTS	CLANGER
CELLISTS	CHAMBERS	CHARPOYS	CHEVRONS	CHOICES	CHUTNEY	CLANGERS
CELLULE	CHAMFER	CHARQUI	CHEVRONY	CHOICEST	CHUTNEYS	CLANGOR
CELLULES	CHAMFERS	CHARQUIS	CHEWINK	CHOKIES	CICHLID	CLANGORS
CEMBALO	CHAMISE	CHARTER	CHEWINKS	CHOKIEST	CICHLIDS	CLAPNET
CEMBALOS	CHAMISES	CHARTERS	CHIASMA	CHOLERA	CIELING	CLAPNETS
CENACLE	CHAMISO	CHASING	CHIASMAS	CHOLERAS	CIELINGS	CLAPPER
CENACLES	CHAMISOS	CHASINGS	CHIBOUK	CHOLINE	CILIATE	CLAPPERS
CENSURE	CHAMLET	CHASTEN	CHIBOUKS	CHOLINES	CILIATED	CLARINO
CENSURED	CHAMLETS	CHASTENS	CHICANE	CHONDRE	CINEAST	CLARINOS
CENSURES	CHAMPAC	CHATEAU	CHICANED	CHONDRES	CINEASTE	CLARION
CENTAGE	CHAMPACS	CHATEAUX	CHICANER	CHONDRI	CINEASTS	CLARIONS
CENTAGES	CHAMPAK	CHATTEL	CHICANES	CHONDRIN	CINEOLE	CLARKIA
CENTAUR	CHAMPAKS	CHATTELS	CHICANO	CHOOKIE	CINEOLES	CLARKIAS
CENTAURS	CHANCEL	CHATTER	CHICANOS	CHOOKIES	CINEREA	CLASPER
CENTAURY	CHANCELS	CHATTERS	CHICKEN	CHOOSER	CINEREAL	CLASPERS
CENTAVO	CHANCER	CHAUMER	CHICKENS	CHOOSERS	CINEREAS	CLASSIC
CENTAVOS	CHANCERS	CHAUMERS	CHIDING	CHOPINE	CIPOLIN	CLASSICS
CENTIME	CHANCRE	CHAUNCE	CHIDINGS	CHOPINES	CIPOLINS	CLATTER
CENTIMES	CHANCRES	CHAUNCED	CHIEFER	CHOPPER	CIRCLER	CLATTERS
CENTNER	CHANGER	CHAUNCES	CHIEFERY	CHOPPERS	CIRCLERS	CLAUCHT
CENTNERS	CHANGERS	CHAUNGE	CHIFFON	CHORAGI	CIRCLET	CLAUCHTS
CENTRUM	CHANNEL	CHAUNGED	CHIFFONS	CHORAGIC	CIRCLETS	CLAUGHT
CENTRUMS	CHANNELS	CHAUNGES	CHIGGER	CHORALE	CIRCUIT	CLAUGHTS
CEPHEID	CHANOYU	CHAUVIN	CHIGGERS	CHORALES	CIRCUITS	CLAVATE
CEPHEIDS	CHANOYUS	CHAUVINS	CHIGNON	CHOREGI	CIRCUITY	CLAVATED
CERAMET	CHANSON	CHAYOTE	CHIGNONS	CHOREGIC	CISSIES	CLAVIER
CERAMETS	CHANSONS	CHAYOTES	CHIKARA	CHORINE	CISSIEST	CLAVIERS
CERAMIC	CHANTER	CHEAPEN	CHIKARAS	CHORINES	CISSOID	CLAYPAN
CERAMICS	CHANTERS	CHEAPENS	CHIKHOR	CHORIST	CISSOIDS	CLAYPANS
CERASIN	CHANTEY	CHEAPIE	CHIKHORS	CHORISTS	CISTERN	CLEANER
CERASINS	CHANTEYS	CHEAPIES	CHILIAD	CHORIZO	CISTERNS	CLEANERS
CERESIN	CHANTIE	CHEATER	CHILIADS	CHORIZOS	CISTRON	CLEANSE
CERESINE	CHANTIES	CHEATERS	CHILLER	CHOROID	CISTRONS	CLEANSED
CERESINS	CHANTOR	CHEATERY	SCHILLER	CHOROIDS	CITADEL	CLEANSER
CERNING	CHANTORS	CHECHIA	CHILLERS	CHORTLE	CITADELS	CLEANSES
SCERNING	CHAPATI	CHECHIAS	CHILLUM	CHORTLED	CITHARA	CLEARER
CERUMEN	CHAPATIS	CHECKER	CHILLUMS	CHORTLES	CITHARAS	CLEARERS
CERUMENS	CHAPEAU	CHECKERS	CHIMERA	CHOWDER	CITHERN	CLEAVER
CESSION	CHAPEAUS	CHEEPER	CHIMERAS	CHOWDERS	CITHERNS	CLEAVERS
CESSIONS	CHAPLET	CHEEPERS	CHIMERE	CHRISOM	CITIZEN	CLERUCH
CESSPIT	CHAPLETS	CHEERER	CHIMERES	CHRISOMS	CITIZENS	CLERUCHS
CESSPITS	CHAPPED	CHEERERS	CHIMLEY	CHRONIC	CITRATE	CLERUCHY
CESTODE	SCHAPPED	CHEERIO	CHIMLEYS	CHRONICS	CITRATES	CLICKER
CESTODES	CHAPPIE	CHEERIOS	CHIMNEY	CHRONON	CITRINE	CLICKERS
CESTOID	CHAPPIER	CHEETAH	CHIMNEYS	CHRONONS	CITRINES	CLICKET
CESTOIDS	CHAPPIES	CHEETAHS	CHINDIT	CHUCKIE	CITTERN	CLICKETS
CHABOUK	CHAPTER	CHEKIST	CHINDITS	CHUCKIES	CITTERNS	CLIMATE
CHABOUKS	CHAPTERS	CHEKISTS	CHINKIE	CHUCKLE	CLABBER	CLIMATED

CLIMATES	COBBLERS	COINAGES	**COMMODE**	**CONCEAL**	CONGEALS	CONTENDS
CLIMBER	COBBLERY	**COINING**	COMMODES	CONCEALS	**CONGEST**	**CONTENT**
CLIMBERS	**COCAINE**	COININGS	**COMMOTE**	**CONCEDE**	CONGESTS	CONTENTS
CLINGER	COCAINES	**COITION**	COMMOTES	CONCEDED	**CONGREE**	**CONTEST**
CLINGERS	**COCHLEA**	COITIONS	**COMMOVE**	CONCEDER	CONGREES	CONTESTS
CLINKER	COCHLEAE	**COLIBRI**	COMMOVED	CONCEDES	CONGREET	**CONTEXT**
CLINKERS	COCHLEAR	COLIBRIS	COMMOVES	**CONCEIT**	**CONGRUE**	CONTEXTS
CLIPPER	COCHLEAS	**COLLAGE**	COMMUNE	CONCEITS	CONGRUED	**CONTORT**
CLIPPERS	**COCKADE**	COLLAGEN	COMMUNED	CONCEITY	CONGRUES	CONTORTS
CLIPPIE	COCKADES	COLLAGES	COMMUNES	**CONCENT**	CONIDIA	**CONTOUR**
CLIPPIES	**COCKEYE**	**COLLARD**	**COMMUTE**	CONCENTS	CONIDIAL	CONTOURS
CLITTER	COCKEYED	COLLARDS	COMMUTED	**CONCEPT**	**CONIFER**	**CONTRAS**
CLITTERS	COCKEYES	**COLLATE**	COMMUTER	CONCEPTI	CONIFERS	CONTRAST
CLOBBER	**COCKIES**	COLLATED	COMMUTES	CONCEPTS	**CONIINE**	**CONTROL**
CLOBBERS	COCKIEST	COLLATES	**COMPACT**	**CONCERN**	CONIINES	CONTROLS
CLOCKER	**COCKNEY**	**COLLECT**	COMPACTS	CONCERNS	**CONJECT**	**CONTUND**
CLOCKERS	COCKNEYS	COLLECTS	**COMPAGE**	**CONCERT**	CONJECTS	CONTUNDS
CLOGGER	**COCKPIT**	**COLLEEN**	COMPAGES	CONCERTO	**CONJOIN**	**CONTUSE**
CLOGGERS	COCKPITS	COLLEENS	**COMPARE**	CONCERTS	CONJOINS	CONTUSED
CLOISON	**COCONUT**	**COLLEGE**	COMPARED	**CONCHIE**	CONJOINT	CONTUSES
CLOISONS	COCONUTS	COLLEGER	COMPARES	CONCHIES	**CONJURE**	**CONVENE**
CLOSING	**COCOTTE**	COLLEGES	**COMPART**	**CONCISE**	CONJURED	CONVENED
ECLOSING	COCOTTES	**COLLIDE**	COMPARTS	CONCISED	CONJURER	CONVENER
CLOSINGS	**COCTION**	COLLIDED	**COMPEAR**	CONCISER	CONJURES	CONVENES
CLOSURE	COCTIONS	COLLIDES	COMPEARS	CONCISES	**CONNECT**	**CONVENT**
CLOSURED	**CODEINE**	**COLLIER**	**COMPEER**	**CONCOCT**	CONNECTS	CONVENTS
CLOSURES	CODEINES	COLLIERS	COMPEERS	CONCOCTS	**CONNING**	**CONVERT**
CLOTBUR	**CODICIL**	COLLIERY	**COMPEND**	**CONCORD**	CONNINGS	CONVERTS
CLOTBURS	CODICILS	**COLLING**	COMPENDS	CONCORDS	**CONNIVE**	**CONVICT**
CLOTTER	**CODILLA**	COLLINGS	**COMPERE**	**CONCREW**	CONNIVED	CONVICTS
CLOTTERS	CODILLAS	**COLLOID**	COMPERED	CONCREWS	CONNIVER	**CONVIVE**
CLOTURE	**CODILLE**	COLLOIDS	COMPERES	**CONDEMN**	CONNIVES	CONVIVED
CLOTURED	CODILLES	**COLLOPS**	**COMPETE**	CONDEMNS	**CONNOTE**	CONVIVES
CLOTURES	**CODLING**	SCOLLOPS	COMPETED	**CONDOLE**	CONNOTED	**CONVOKE**
CLOUTER	CODLINGS	**COLLUDE**	COMPETES	CONDOLED	CONNOTES	CONVOKED
CLOUTERS	**COEHORN**	COLLUDED	**COMPILE**	CONDOLES	**CONQUER**	CONVOKES
CLOWDER	COEHORNS	COLLUDER	COMPILED	**CONDONE**	CONQUERS	**COOKOUT**
CLOWDERS	**COELIAC**	COLLUDES	COMPILER	CONDONED	**CONSEIL**	COOKOUTS
CLUDGIE	COELIACS	**COLONEL**	COMPILES	CONDONES	CONSEILS	**COOLANT**
CLUDGIES	**COELOME**	COLONELS	**COMPLIN**	**CONDUCE**	**CONSENT**	COOLANTS
CLUMBER	COELOMES	**COLONIC**	COMPLINE	CONDUCED	CONSENTS	**COONTIE**
CLUMBERS	**COEQUAL**	COLONICS	COMPLINS	CONDUCES	**CONSIGN**	COONTIES
CLUPEID	COEQUALS	**COLUBER**	**COMPLOT**	**CONDUCT**	CONSIGNS	**COOPERS**
CLUPEIDS	**COFFERS**	COLUBERS	COMPLOTS	CONDUCTI	**CONSIST**	SCOOPERS
CLUSTER	**COFFING**	**COLUMEL**	**COMPORT**	CONDUCTS	CONSISTS	**COOPING**
CLUSTERS	SCOFFING	COLUMELS	COMPORTS	**CONDUIT**	**CONSOLE**	SCOOPING
CLUSTERY	**COFFRET**	**COMBINE**	**COMPOSE**	CONDUITS	CONSOLED	**COPAIBA**
CLUTTER	COFFRETS	COMBINED	COMPOSED	**CONDYLE**	CONSOLER	COPAIBAS
CLUTTERS	**COGENCE**	COMBINES	COMPOSER	CONDYLES	CONSOLES	**COPAIVA**
CLYSTER	COGENCES	**COMBING**	COMPOSES	**CONFECT**	**CONSORT**	COPAIVAS
CLYSTERS	**COGENER**	COMBINGS	**COMPOST**	CONFECTS	CONSORTS	**COPEPOD**
COACHEE	COGENERS	**COMBLES**	COMPOSTS	**CONFIDE**	**CONSTER**	COPEPODS
COACHEES	**COGGING**	COMBLESS	**COMPOTE**	CONFIDED	CONSTERS	**COPILOT**
COACHER	SCOGGING	**COMBUST**	COMPOTES	CONFIDER	**CONSULT**	COPILOTS
COACHERS	**COGNATE**	COMBUSTS	**COMPTER**	CONFIDES	CONSULTA	**COPPICE**
COALISE	COGNATES	**COMFORT**	COMPTERS	**CONFINE**	CONSULTS	COPPICED
COALISED	**COGNISE**	COMFORTS	**COMPUTE**	CONFINED	**CONSUME**	COPPICES
COALISES	COGNISED	**COMFREY**	COMPUTED	CONFINER	CONSUMED	**COPULAS**
COALIZE	COGNISES	COMFREYS	**COMPUTER**	CONFINES	CONSUMER	SCOPULAS
COALIZED	**COGNIZE**	**COMIQUE**	COMPUTES	**CONFIRM**	CONSUMES	**COPYISM**
COALIZES	COGNIZED	COMIQUES	**COMRADE**	CONFIRMS	**CONTACT**	COPYISMS
COAMING	COGNIZES	**COMMAND**	COMRADES	**CONFORM**	CONTACTS	**COPYIST**
COAMINGS	**COHABIT**	COMMANDO	**CONACRE**	CONFORMS	**CONTAIN**	COPYISTS
COARSEN	COHABITS	COMMANDS	CONACRED	**CONFUSE**	CONTAINS	**COQUITO**
COARSENS	**COHERER**	**COMMEND**	CONACRES	CONFUSED	**CONTECK**	COQUITOS
COASTER	COHERERS	COMMENDS	**CONARIA**	CONFUSES	CONTECKS	**CORACLE**
COASTERS	**COHIBIT**	**COMMENT**	CONARIAL	**CONFUTE**	**CONTEMN**	CORACLES
COATING	COHIBITS	COMMENTS	**CONCAVE**	CONFUTED	CONTEMNS	**CORANTO**
COATINGS		**COMMERE**	CONCAVED	CONFUTES	**CONTEND**	CORANTOS
COBBLER	**COINAGE**	COMMERES	CONCAVES	**CONGEAL**	**CONTEND**	**CORBEAU**

CORBEAUS	CORSNED	COUNTERS	COWSHED	CREMATES	CROMBIES	CRUSADOS
CORBEIL	CORSNEDS	COUPING	COWSHEDS	CREMONA	CROODLE	CRUSHER
CORBEILS	CORTEGE	SCOUPING	COWSLIP	CREMONAS	CROODLED	CRUSHERS
CORDAGE	CORTEGES	COUPLER	COWSLIPS	CRENATE	CROODLES	CRUSIAN
CORDAGES	CORTILE	COUPLERS	COXCOMB	CRENATED	CROONER	CRUSIANS
CORDIAL	CORTILES	COUPLET	COXCOMBS	CRESSET	CROONERS	CRYINGS
CORDIALS	CORYPHE	COUPLETS	COZENER	CRESSETS	CROPFUL	SCRYINGS
CORDING	CORYPHEE	COUPURE	COZENERS	CRETISM	CROPFULL	CRYOGEN
CORDINGS	CORYPHES	COUPURES	CRABBED	CRETISMS	CROPFULS	CRYOGENS
CORDITE	COSINES	COURAGE	SCRABBED	CREVICE	CROPPER	CRYOGENY
CORDITES	COSINESS	COURAGES	CRACKER	CREVICES	CROPPERS	CRYONIC
CORDOBA	COSMISM	COURANT	CRACKERS	CREWING	CROQUET	CRYONICS
CORDOBAS	ACOSMISM	COURANTE	CRACKLE	SCREWING	CROQUETS	CRYPTON
CORELLA	COSMISMS	COURANTS	CRACKLED	CRIBBLE	CROSIER	CRYPTONS
CORELLAS	COSMIST	COURIER	CRACKLES	CRIBBLED	CROSIERS	CRYSTAL
CORIOUS	ACOSMIST	COURIERS	CRACOWE	CRIBBLES	CROSSES	CRYSTALS
SCORIOUS	COSMISTS	COURING	CRACOWES	CRICKET	CROSSEST	CUBBING
CORKAGE	COSTARD	SCOURING	CRAGGED	CRICKETS	CROTTLE	CUBBINGS
CORKAGES	COSTARDS	COURLAN	SCRAGGED	CRICOID	CROTTLES	CUBHOOD
CORNAGE	COSTATE	COURLANS	CRAMMED	CRICOIDS	CROUPER	CUBHOODS
CORNAGES	ECOSTATE	COURSED	SCRAMMED	CRIMMER	CROUPERS	CUBICLE
CORNERS	COSTATED	SCOURSED	CRAMMER	CRIMMERS	CROUPON	CUBICLES
SCORNERS	COSTEAN	COURSER	CRAMMERS	CRIMPED	CROUPONS	CUCKOLD
CORNETT	COSTEANS	COURSERS	CRAMPET	SCRIMPED	CROUTON	CUCKOLDS
CORNETTI	COSTREL	COURSES	CRAMPETS	CRIMPER	CROUTONS	CUCKOLDY
CORNETTO	COSTRELS	SCOURSES	CRAMPIT	CRIMPERS	CROWDER	CUDBEAR
CORNETTS	COSTUME	COUTERS	CRAMPITS	CRIMPLE	CROWDERS	CUDBEARS
CORNICE	COSTUMED	SCOUTERS	CRAMPON	CRIMPLED	CROWDIE	CUDDLED
CORNICED	COSTUMER	COUTHER	CRAMPONS	CRIMPLES	CROWDIES	SCUDDLED
CORNICES	COSTUMES	SCOUTHER	CRANAGE	CRIMSON	CROWNER	CUDDLES
CORNING	COTERIE	COUTHIE	CRANAGES	CRIMSONS	CROWNERS	SCUDDLES
SCORNING	COTERIES	COUTHIER	CRANIUM	CRINATE	CROWNET	CUDWEED
CORNIST	COTHURN	COUTURE	CRANIUMS	CRINATED	CROWNETS	CUDWEEDS
CORNISTS	COTHURNI	COUTURES	CRANKLE	CRINGER	CROZIER	CUFFING
CORNUTE	COTHURNS	COUVADE	CRANKLED	CRINGERS	CROZIERS	SCUFFING
CORNUTED	COTINGA	COUVADES	CRANKLES	CRINGLE	CRUBEEN	CUFFLED
CORNUTES	COTINGAS	COUVERT	CRANNOG	CRINGLES	CRUBEENS	SCUFFLED
CORNUTO	COTLAND	COUVERTS	CRANNOGS	CRINITE	CRUCIAN	CUFFLES
CORNUTOS	COTLANDS	COVELET	CRAPING	CRINITES	CRUCIANS	SCUFFLES
COROLLA	COTTAGE	COVELETS	SCRAPING	CRINKLE	CRUDDLE	CUISINE
COROLLAS	COTTAGED	COWBANE	CRAPPED	CRINKLED	CRUDDLED	CUISINES
CORONAL	COTTAGER	COWBANES	SCRAPPED	CRINKLES	CRUDDLES	CUISSER
CORONALS	COTTAGES	COWBELL	CRAVING	CRINOID	CRUISER	CUISSERS
CORONER	COTTAGEY	COWBELLS	CRAVINGS	CRINOIDS	CRUISERS	CUITTLE
CORONERS	COTTIER	COWBIRD	CRAWLED	CRIOLLO	CRUISIE	CUITTLED
CORONET	COTTIERS	COWBIRDS	SCRAWLED	CRIOLLOS	CRUISIES	CUITTLES
CORONETS	COTTISE	COWGIRL	CRAWLER	CRIPPLE	CRULLER	CULICID
CORPORA	COTTISED	COWGIRLS	SCRAWLER	CRIPPLED	CRULLERS	CULICIDS
CORPORAL	COTTISES	COWHAGE	CRAWLERS	CRIPPLES	CRUMBLE	CULLERS
CORPORAS	COTTOID	COWHAGES	CRAZIES	CRISPER	CRUMBLED	SCULLERS
CORRADE	COTTOIDS	COWHAND	CRAZIEST	CRISPERS	CRUMBLES	CULLING
CORRADED	COTTOWN	COWHANDS	CREAKED	CRISPIN	CRUMPED	SCULLING
CORRADES	COTTOWNS	COWHEEL	SCREAKED	CRISPING	SCRUMPED	CULLINGS
CORRECT	COUCHEE	COWHEELS	CREAMED	CRISPINS	CRUMPET	CULLION
CORRECTS	COUCHEES	COWHERD	SCREAMED	CRITTER	CRUMPETS	SCULLION
CORRIDA	COUGHER	COWHERDS	CREAMER	CRITTERS	CRUMPLE	CULLIONS
CORRIDAS	COUGHERS	COWHIDE	SCREAMER	CRITTUR	CRUMPLED	CULOTTE
CORRODE	COUGUAR	COWHIDED	CREAMERS	CRITTURS	CRUMPLES	CULOTTES
CORRODED	COUGUARS	COWHIDES	CREAMERY	CROAKER	CRUNCHY	CULPRIT
CORRODES	COULOIR	COWLICK	CREANCE	CROAKERS	SCRUNCHY	CULPRITS
CORRUPT	COULOIRS	COWLICKS	CREANCES	CROCHET	CRUNKLE	CULTISM
CORRUPTS	COULOMB	COWLING	CREATOR	CROCHETS	CRUNKLED	CULTISMS
CORSAGE	COULOMBS	SCOWLING	CREATORS	CROCKET	CRUNKLES	CULTIST
CORSAGES	COULTER	COWLINGS	CREEPER	CROCKETS	CRUPPER	CULTISTS
CORSAIR	COULTERS	COWPING	CREEPERS	CROFTER	CRUPPERS	CULTURE
CORSAIRS	COUNCIL	SCOWPING	CREEPIE	CROFTERS	CRUSADE	CULTURED
CORSIVE	COUNCILS	COWPOKE	CREEPIER	CROMACK	CRUSADED	CULTURES
CORSIVES	COUNSEL	COWPOKES	CREEPIES	CROMACKS	CRUSADER	CULVERT
CORSLET	COUNSELS	COWRIES	CREMATE	CROMBIE	CRUSADES	CULVERTS
CORSLETS	COUNTER	SCOWRIES	CREMATED	CROMBIES	CRUSADO	CUMARIN

CUMARINS	CURTSEYS	CZARDOMS	**DASTARD**	DECEIVED	**DEFINER**	DEMENTIS
CUMBERS	**CURVATE**	**CZARINA**	DASTARDS	DECEIVER	DEFINERS	**DEMERGE**
SCUMBERS	CURVATED	CZARINAS	DASTARDY	DECEIVES	**DEFLATE**	DEMERGED
CUMMERS	**CURVIER**	**CZARISM**	**DASYPOD**	**DECIARE**	DEFLATED	DEMERGER
SCUMMERS	SCURVIER	CZARISMS	DASYPODS	DECIARES	DEFLATER	DEMERGES
CUMQUAT	**CUSHION**	**CZARIST**	**DASYURE**	**DECIBEL**	DEFLATES	**DEMERIT**
CUMQUATS	CUSHIONS	CZARISTS	DASYURES	DECIBELS	**DEFLECT**	DEMERITS
CUMSHAW	CUSHIONY	**DABBLER**	**DATARIA**	**DECIDER**	DEFLECTS	**DEMERSE**
CUMSHAWS	**CUSTARD**	DABBLERS	DATARIAS	DECIDERS	**DEFORCE**	DEMERSED
CUNETTE	CUSTARDS	**DABSTER**	**DAUBING**	**DECIDUA**	DEFORCED	DEMERSES
CUNETTES	**CUSTOCK**	DABSTERS	DAUBINGS	DECIDUAL	DEFORCES	**DEMESNE**
CUNNERS	CUSTOCKS	**DADDOCK**	**DAUNDER**	DECIDUAS	**DEFRAUD**	DEMESNES
SCUNNERS	**CUSTODE**	DADDOCKS	DAUNDERS	**DECIMAL**	DEFRAUDS	**DEMIGOD**
CUNNING	CUSTODES	**DAFFIES**	**DAUNTER**	DECIMALS	**DEFROCK**	DEMIGODS
CUNNINGS	**CUSTREL**	DAFFIEST	DAUNTERS	**DECKING**	DEFROCKS	**DEMIREP**
CUPGALL	CUSTRELS	**DAFFING**	**DAUNTON**	DECKINGS	**DEFROST**	DEMIREPS
CUPGALLS	**CUTAWAY**	DAFFINGS	DAUNTONS	**DECLAIM**	DEFROSTS	**DEMOUNT**
CUPHEAD	CUTAWAYS	**DAGLOCK**	**DAUPHIN**	DECLAIMS	**DEFROZE**	DEMOUNTS
CUPHEADS	**CUTBACK**	DAGLOCKS	DAUPHINE	**DECLARE**	DEFROZEN	**DEMURES**
CUPPERS	CUTBACKS	**DAGWOOD**	DAUPHINS	DECLARED	**DEFUNCT**	DEMUREST
SCUPPERS	**CUTCHES**	DAGWOODS	**DAWCOCK**	DECLARER	DEFUNCTS	**DENDRON**
CUPPING	SCUTCHES	**DAINING**	DAWCOCKS	DECLARES	**DEGRADE**	DENDRONS
CUPPINGS	**CUTICLE**	SDAINING	**DAWDLER**	**DECLASS**	DEGRADED	**DENIZEN**
CUPRITE	CUTICLES	**DAKOITI**	DAWDLERS	DECLASSE	DEGRADES	DENIZENS
CUPRITES	**CUTIKIN**	DAKOITIS	**DAWNING**	**DECLINE**	**DEHISCE**	**DENTATE**
CURACAO	CUTIKINS	**DALLIER**	DAWNINGS	DECLINED	DEHISCED	EDENTATE
CURACAOS	**CUTLINE**	DALLIERS	**DAYMARK**	DECLINES	DEHISCES	DENTATED
CURACOA	CUTLINES	**DAMBROD**	DAYMARKS	**DECODER**	**DEICIDE**	**DENTINE**
CURACOAS	**CUTTERS**	DAMBRODS	**DAYSTAR**	DECODERS	DEICIDES	DENTINES
CURARIS	SCUTTERS	**DAMOSEL**	DAYSTARS	**DECOLOR**	**DEICTIC**	**DENTIST**
CURARISE	**CUTTIES**	DAMOSELS	**DAYTALE**	DECOLORS	DEICTICS	DENTISTS
CURATOR	CUTTIEST	**DAMOZEL**	DAYTALER	**DECORUM**	**DEIFIER**	**DENTURE**
CURATORS	**CUTTING**	DAMOZELS	DAYTALES	DECORUMS	DEIFIERS	DENTURES
CURATORY	CUTTINGS	**DAMPING**	**DAYTIME**	**DECREET**	**DEIGNED**	**DEODAND**
CURCUMA	**CUTTLES**	DAMPINGS	DAYTIMES	DECREETS	SDEIGNED	DEODANDS
CURCUMAS	SCUTTLES	**DANCING**	**DAZZLER**	**DECRIAL**	**DEISEAL**	**DEODATE**
CURETTE	**CUTWORM**	DANCINGS	DAZZLERS	DECRIALS	DEISEALS	DEODATES
CURETTED	CUTWORMS	**DANDIES**	**DEADPAN**	**DECRIER**	**DEJEUNE**	**DEONTIC**
CURETTES	**CUVETTE**	DANDIEST	DEADPANS	DECRIERS	DEJEUNER	DEONTICS
CURLING	CUVETTES	**DANDLER**	**DEALING**	**DECROWN**	DEJEUNES	**DEPAINT**
CURLINGS	**CYANATE**	DANDLERS	DEALINGS	DECROWNS	**DELAINE**	DEPAINTS
CURRACH	CYANATES	**DANELAW**	**DEASIUL**	**DECRYPT**	DELAINES	**DEPECHE**
CURRACHS	**CYANIDE**	DANELAWS	DEASIULS	DECRYPTS	**DELAPSE**	DEPECHES
CURRAGH	CYANIDED	**DANGLER**	**DEASOIL**	**DECUMAN**	DELAPSED	**DEPLANE**
CURRAGHS	CYANIDES	DANGLERS	DEASOILS	DECUMANS	DELAPSES	DEPLANED
CURRANT	**CYANINE**	**DAPHNID**	**DEBACLE**	**DECUPLE**	**DELATOR**	DEPLANES
CURRANTS	CYANINES	DAPHNIDS	DEBACLES	DECUPLED	DELATORS	**DEPLETE**
CURRANTY	**CYANISE**	**DAPSONE**	**DEBASER**	DECUPLES	**DELAYER**	DEPLETED
CURRENT	CYANISED	DAPSONES	DEBASERS	**DECURIA**	DELAYERS	DEPLETES
CURRENTS	CYANISES	**DARIOLE**	**DEBATER**	DECURIAS	**DELIGHT**	**DEPLORE**
CURRIED	**CYANITE**	DARIOLES	DEBATERS	**DECURVE**	DELIGHTS	DEPLORED
SCURRIED	CYANITES	**DARLING**	**DEBBIES**	DECURVED	**DELIMIT**	DEPLORES
CURRIER	**CYANIZE**	DARLINGS	DEBBIEST	DECURVES	DELIMITS	**DEPLUME**
SCURRIER	CYANIZED	**DARNING**	**DEBITOR**	**DEEMING**	**DELIVER**	DEPLUMED
CURRIERS	CYANIZES	DARNINGS	DEBITORS	ADEEMING	DELIVERS	DEPLUMES
CURRIES	**CYCLING**	**DARRAIN**	**DEBOUCH**	**DEERLET**	DELIVERY	**DEPOSAL**
SCURRIES	CYCLINGS	DARRAINE	DEBOUCHE	DEERLETS	**DELOUSE**	DEPOSALS
CURRING	**CYCLIST**	DARRAINS	**DEBRIDE**	**DEFACER**	DELOUSED	**DEPOSER**
SCURRING	CYCLISTS	**DARRAYN**	DEBRIDED	DEFACERS	DELOUSES	DEPOSERS
CURSING	**CYCLOID**	DARRAYNS	DEBRIDES	**DEFAULT**	**DELUDER**	**DEPOSIT**
CURSINGS	CYCLOIDS	**DARSHAN**	**DEBRIEF**	DEFAULTS	DELUDERS	DEPOSITS
CURTAIL	**CYCLONE**	DARSHANS	DEBRIEFS	**DEFENCE**	**DEMAINE**	**DEPRAVE**
CURTAILS	CYCLONES	**DASHEEN**	**DECAGON**	DEFENCED	DEMAINES	DEPRAVED
CURTAIN	**CYMBALO**	DASHEENS	DECAGONS	DEFENCES	**DEMAYNE**	DEPRAVES
CURTAINS	CYMBALOS	**DASHEKI**	**DECAPOD**	**DEFENSE**	DEMAYNES	**DEPRIVE**
CURTANA	**CYPRIAN**	DASHEKIS	DECAPODS	DEFENSES	**DEMEANE**	DEPRIVED
CURTANAS	CYPRIANS	**DASHIKI**	**DECEASE**	**DEFICIT**	DEMEANED	DEPRIVES
CURTAXE	**CYSTOID**	DASHIKIS	DECEASED	DEFICITS	DEMEANES	**DEPSIDE**
CURTAXES	CYSTOIDS		DECEASES	**DEFILER**	**DEMENTI**	DEPSIDES
CURTSEY	**CZARDOM**		**DECEIVE**	DEFILERS	DEMENTIA	**DERAIGN**

DERAIGNS	DEVIANT	DIARIZED	DIMETERS	DISCERNS	DISMAYLS	DISTURB
DERANGE	DEVIANTS	DIARIZES	DIMORPH	DISCERP	DISNEST	DISTURBS
DERANGED	DEVIATE	DIASTER	DIMORPHS	DISCERPS	DISNESTS	DISTYLE
DERANGES	DEVIATED	DIASTERS	DINETTE	DISCIDE	DISOBEY	DISTYLES
DERIDER	DEVIATES	DIBBLER	DINETTES	DISCIDED	DISOBEYS	DISYOKE
DERIDERS	DEVILET	DIBBLERS	DINGBAT	DISCIDES	DISPACE	DISYOKED
DERMOID	DEVILETS	DICHORD	DINGBATS	DISCOER	DISPACED	DISYOKES
DERMOIDS	DEVISAL	DICHORDS	DINGIES	DISCOERS	DISPACES	DITCHER
DERRICK	DEVISALS	DICKIES	DINGIEST	DISCORD	DISPARK	DITCHERS
DERRICKS	DEVISEE	DICKIEST	DINKIES	DISCORDS	DISPARKS	DIURNAL
DESCALE	DEVISEES	DICTATE	DINKIEST	DISCURE	DISPART	DIURNALS
DESCALED	DEVISER	DICTATED	DINMONT	DISCURED	DISPARTS	DIVERGE
DESCALES	DEVISERS	DICTATES	DINMONTS	DISCURES	DISPEND	DIVERGED
DESCANT	DEVISOR	DICTION	DIOCESE	DISDAIN	DISPENDS	DIVERGES
DESCANTS	DEVISORS	DICTIONS	DIOCESES	DISDAINS	DISPLAY	DIVERSE
DESCEND	DEVLING	DIDAKAI	DIOPTER	DISEASE	DISPLAYS	DIVERSED
DESCENDS	DEVLINGS	DIDAKAIS	DIOPTERS	DISEASED	DISPONE	DIVERSES
DESCENT	DEVOICE	DIDAKEI	DIOPTRE	DISEASES	DISPONED	DIVIDER
DESCENTS	DEVOICED	DIDAKEIS	DIOPTRES	DISEDGE	DISPONEE	DIVIDERS
DESERVE	DEVOICES	DIDDLER	DIORAMA	DISEDGED	DISPONER	DIVINER
DESERVED	DEVOLVE	DIDDLERS	DIORAMAS	DISEDGES	DISPONES	DIVINERS
DESERVER	DEVOLVED	DIDICOI	DIORISM	DISEUSE	DISPORT	DIVINES
DESERVES	DEVOLVES	DIDICOIS	DIORISMS	DISEUSES	DISPORTS	DIVINEST
DESIRER	DEVOTEE	DIDICOY	DIORITE	DISFAME	DISPOSE	DIVISOR
DESIRERS	DEVOTEES	DIDICOYS	DIORITES	DISFAMES	DISPOSED	DIVISORS
DESKILL	DEWATER	DIEBACK	DIOXANE	DISFORM	DISPOSER	DIVORCE
DESKILLS	DEWATERS	DIEBACKS	DIOXANES	DISFORMS	DISPOSES	DIVORCED
DESMINE	DEXTRAN	DIEDRAL	DIOXIDE	DISGEST	DISPOST	DIVORCEE
DESMINES	DEXTRANS	DIEDRALS	DIOXIDES	DISGESTS	DISPOSTS	DIVORCER
DESPAIR	DEXTRIN	DIETINE	DIPHONE	DISGOWN	DISPRED	DIVORCES
DESPAIRS	DEXTRINE	DIETINES	DIPHONES	DISGOWNS	DISPREDS	DIVULGE
DESPISE	DEXTRINS	DIETIST	DIPLOID	DISGUST	DISPUTE	DIVULGED
DESPISED	DHARMAS	DIETISTS	DIPLOIDY	DISGUSTS	DISPUTED	DIVULGES
DESPISER	ADHARMAS	DIFFUSE	DIPLOMA	DISHELM	DISPUTER	DIZZARD
DESPISES	DHURRIE	DIFFUSED	DIPLOMAS	DISHELMS	DISPUTES	DIZZARDS
DESPITE	DHURRIES	DIFFUSER	DIPLOMAT	DISHFUL	DISRANK	DIZZIES
DESPITES	DIABASE	DIFFUSES	DIPLONT	DISHFULS	DISRANKS	DIZZIEST
DESPOIL	DIABASES	DIGAMMA	DIPLONTS	DISHING	DISRATE	DJIBBAH
DESPOILS	DIABOLO	DIGAMMAS	DIPNOAN	DISHINGS	DISRATED	DJIBBAHS
DESPOND	DIABOLOS	DIGGING	DIPNOANS	DISHOME	DISRATES	DOATING
DESPONDS	DIADROM	DIGGINGS	DIPPING	DISHOMED	DISROBE	DOATINGS
DESSERT	DIADROMS	DIGITAL	DIPPINGS	DISHOMES	DISROBED	DOCKAGE
DESSERTS	DIAGRAM	DIGITALS	DIPTYCH	DISHORN	DISROBES	DOCKAGES
DESTINE	DIAGRAMS	DIGLYPH	DIPTYCHS	DISHORNS	DISROOT	DOCKING
DESTINED	DIAGRID	DIGLYPHS	DIREMPT	DISJECT	DISROOTS	DOCKINGS
DESTINES	DIAGRIDS	DIGRAPH	DIREMPTS	DISJECTS	DISRUPT	DOCKISE
DESTROY	DIALECT	DIGRAPHS	DIRTIES	DISJOIN	DISRUPTS	DOCKISED
DESTROYS	DIALECTS	DILATER	DIRTIEST	DISJOINS	DISSEAT	DOCKISES
DETENTE	DIALIST	DILATERS	DISABLE	DISJOINT	DISSEATS	DOCKIZE
DETENTES	DIALISTS	DILATOR	DISABLED	DISJUNE	DISSECT	DOCKIZED
DETENUE	DIALLER	DILATORS	DISABLES	DISJUNES	DISSECTS	DOCKIZES
DETENUES	DIALLERS	DILATORY	DISAVOW	DISLEAF	DISSENT	DOCQUET
DETERGE	DIALYSE	DILEMMA	DISAVOWS	DISLEAFS	DISSENTS	DOCQUETS
DETERGED	DIALYSED	DILEMMAS	DISBAND	DISLIKE	DISSERT	DODDIES
DETERGES	DIALYSER	DILLIES	DISBANDS	DISLIKED	DISSERTS	DODDIEST
DETINUE	DIALYSES	DILLIEST	DISBARK	DISLIKEN	DISTAFF	DOGBANE
DETINUES	DIALYZE	DILLING	DISBARKS	DISLIKES	DISTAFFS	DOGBANES
DETRACT	DIALYZED	DILLINGS	DISCAGE	DISLIMB	DISTAIN	DOGBOLT
DETRACTS	DIALYZER	DILUENT	DISCAGED	DISLIMBS	DISTAINS	DOGBOLTS
DETRAIN	DIALYZES	DILUENTS	DISCAGES	DISLIMN	DISTEND	DOGCART
DETRAINS	DIAMOND	DILUTEE	DISCANT	DISLIMNS	DISTENDS	DOGCARTS
DETRUDE	DIAMONDS	DILUTEES	DISCANTS	DISLINK	DISTICH	DOGEATE
DETRUDED	DIAPASE	DILUTER	DISCARD	DISLINKS	DISTICHS	DOGEATES
DETRUDES	DIAPASES	DILUTERS	DISCARDS	DISLOAD	DISTILL	DOGGIES
DEVALUE	DIARISE	DILUTOR	DISCASE	DISLOADS	DISTILLS	DOGGIEST
DEVALUED	DIARISED	DILUTORS	DISCASED	DISMASK	DISTORT	DOGGING
DEVALUES	DIARISES	DILUVIA	DISCASES	DISMASKS	DISTORTS	DOGGINGS
DEVELOP	DIARIST	DILUVIAL	DISCEPT	DISMAST	DISTUNE	DOGGONE
DEVELOPE	DIARISTS	DILUVIAN	DISCEPTS	DISMASTS	DISTUNED	DOGGONED
DEVELOPS	DIARIZE	DIMETER	DISCERN	DISMAYL	DISTUNES	DOGGREL

DOGGRELS	DOULEIAS	DREAREST	DUCHESS	DVANDVAS	EASTING	ECTOZOA
DOGHOLE	DOURINE	DREDGER	DUCHESSE	DVORNIK	FEASTING	ECTOZOAN
DOGHOLES	DOURINES	DREDGERS	DUCKIES	DVORNIKS	REASTING	ECUELLE
DOGSHIP	DOVECOT	DRESSER	DUCKIEST	DWELLER	YEASTING	ECUELLES
DOGSHIPS	DOVECOTE	DRESSERS	DUCKING	DWELLERS	EASTINGS	ECURIES
DOGSKIN	DOVECOTS	DREVILL	DUCKINGS	DWINDLE	EASTLIN	DECURIES
DOGSKINS	DOVEKIE	DREVILLS	DUDGEON	DWINDLED	EASTLING	EDGIEST
DOGTOWN	DOVEKIES	DRIBBER	DUDGEONS	DWINDLES	EASTLINS	HEDGIEST
DOGTOWNS	DOVELET	DRIBBERS	DUDHEEN	DYELINE	EATABLE	KEDGIEST
DOGTROT	DOVELETS	DRIBBLE	DUDHEENS	DYELINES	BEATABLE	LEDGIEST
DOGTROTS	DOWAGER	DRIBBLED	DUELLER	DYESTER	EATABLES	SEDGIEST
DOGVANE	DOWAGERS	DRIBBLER	DUELLERS	DYESTERS	EATINGS	EDGINGS
DOGVANES	DOWDIES	DRIBBLES	DUFFING	DYNAMIC	BEATINGS	HEDGINGS
DOGWOOD	DOWDIEST	DRIBBLET	DUFFINGS	ADYNAMIC	HEATINGS	WEDGINGS
DOGWOODS	DOWNBOW	DRIBLET	DUKEDOM	DYNAMICS	SEATINGS	EDIFICE
DOITKIN	DOWNBOWS	DRIBLETS	DUKEDOMS	DYSODIL	EBAUCHE	EDIFICES
DOITKINS	DOYENNE	DRIFTER	DULCIAN	DYSODILE	EBAUCHES	EDIFIER
DOLLDOM	DOYENNES	DRIFTERS	DULCIANA	DYSODILS	EBBTIDE	EDIFIERS
DOLLDOMS	DOZENTH	DRILLER	DULCIANS	DYSPNEA	EBBTIDES	EDITION
DOLLIER	DOZENTHS	DRILLERS	DULCITE	DYSPNEAL	EBONISE	EDITIONS
DOLLIERS	DRABBER	DRINKER	DULCITES	DYSPNEAS	EBONISED	EDUCATE
DOLPHIN	DRABBERS	DRINKERS	DULCOSE	DYSURIA	EBONISES	EDUCATED
DOLPHINS	DRABBET	DRIZZLE	DULCOSES	DYSURIAS	EBONIST	EDUCATES
DOMICIL	DRABBETS	DRIZZLED	DULLARD	EANLING	EBONISTS	EDUCING
DOMICILE	DRABBLE	DRIZZLES	DULLARDS	WEANLING	EBONITE	DEDUCING
DOMICILS	DRABBLED	DROGHER	DUMAIST	YEANLING	EBONITES	REDUCING
DOMINIE	DRABBLER	DROGHERS	DUMAISTS	EANLINGS	EBONIZED	SEDUCING
DOMINIES	DRABBLES	DROGUET	DUMMIES	EARACHE	EBONIZES	EDUCTOR
DONATOR	DRABLER	DROGUETS	DUMMIEST	EARACHES	EBRIATE	SEDUCTOR
DONATORS	DRABLERS	DROLLER	DUMPBIN	EARDING	EBRIATED	EDUCTORS
DONATORY	DRACHMA	DROLLERY	DUMPBINS	BEARDING	ECBOLIC	EECHING
DONNISM	DRACHMAE	DROMOND	DUMPIES	YEARDING	ECBOLICS	LEECHING
DONNISMS	DRACHMAI	DROMONDS	DUMPIEST	EARDROP	ECHAPPE	REECHING
DONSHIP	DRACHMAS	DROPLET	DUNGEON	EARDROPS	ECHAPPES	EELFARE
DONSHIPS	DRACONE	DROPLETS	DUNGEONS	EARDRUM	ECHELON	EELFARES
DOODLER	DRACONES	DROPPER	DUNNAGE	EARDRUMS	ECHELONS	EELIEST
DOODLERS	DRAFTEE	DROPPERS	DUNNAGES	EARFLAP	ECHIDNA	SEELIEST
DOORMAT	DRAFTEES	DROPPLE	DUNNIES	EARFLAPS	ECHIDNAS	EELPOUT
DOORMATS	DRAFTER	DROPPLES	DUNNIEST	EARINGS	ECHOISE	EELPOUTS
DOORWAY	DRAFTERS	DROSERA	DUNNING	BEARINGS	ECHOISED	EELWORM
DOORWAYS	DRAGGLE	DROSERAS	DUNNINGS	GEARINGS	ECHOISES	EELWORMS
DOPPING	DRAGGLED	DROSTDY	DUNNITE	HEARINGS	ECHOISM	EERIEST
DOPPINGS	DRAGGLES	DROSTDYS	DUNNITES	SEARINGS	ECHOISMS	BEERIEST
DORHAWK	DRAGOON	DROUGHT	DUNNOCK	WEARINGS	ECHOIST	LEERIEST
DORHAWKS	DRAGOONS	DROUGHTS	DUNNOCKS	EARLDOM	ECHOISTS	PEERIEST
DORLACH	DRAINER	DROUGHTY	DUODENA	EARLDOMS	ECHOIZE	EEVNING
DORLACHS	DRAINERS	DROWNER	DUODENAL	EARLESS	ECHOIZED	EEVNINGS
DORMANT	DRAPIER	DROWNERS	DUOTONE	FEARLESS	ECHOIZES	EFFENDI
DORMANTS	DRAPIERS	DRUDGER	DUOTONES	GEARLESS	ECLIPSE	EFFENDIS
DORNICK	DRAPPIE	DRUDGERS	DURABLE	TEARLESS	ECLIPSED	EFFORCE
DORNICKS	DRAPPIES	DRUDGERY	DURABLES	EARLIER	ECLIPSES	EFFORCED
DORTOUR	DRASTIC	DRUGGER	DURAMEN	PEARLIER	ECLOGUE	EFFORCES
DORTOURS	DRASTICS	DRUGGERS	DURAMENS	EARLOCK	ECLOGUES	EFFULGE
DOSSIER	DRAUGHT	DRUGGET	DURANCE	EARLOCKS	ECLOSED	EFFULGED
DOSSIERS	DRAUGHTS	DRUGGETS	DURANCES	EARMARK	ECLOSES	EFFULGES
DOTTLES	DRAUGHTY	DRUMBLE	DURESSE	EARMARKS	RECLOSED	EGALITY
DOTTLEST	DRAWING	DRUMBLED	DURESSES	EARNERS	ECLOSES	LEGALITY
DOTTREL	DRAWINGS	DRUMBLES	DURMAST	LEARNERS	RECLOSES	REGALITY
DOTTRELS	DRAWLER	DRUMLIN	DURMASTS	EARNEST	ECOCIDE	EGENCES
DOUBLER	DRAWLERS	DRUMLINS	DUSTBIN	EARNESTS	ECOCIDES	REGENCES
DOUBLERS	DRAYAGE	DRUMMER	DUSTBINS	EARNING	ECOLOGY	EGGHEAD
DOUBLET	DRAYAGES	DRUMMERS	DUSTING	LEARNING	OECOLOGY	EGGHEADS
DOUBLETS	DREADED	DRYBEAT	ADUSTING	YEARNING	ECORCHE	EGGIEST
DOUBTER	ADREADED	DRYBEATS	DUUMVIR	EARNINGS	ECORCHES	LEGGIEST
DOUBTERS	DREADER	DUALISM	DUUMVIRI	EARPICK	ECOTYPE	EGOTISE
DOUCEUR	DREADERS	DUALISMS	DUUMVIRS	EARPICKS	ECOTYPES	EGOTISED
DOUCEURS	DREAMER	DUALIST	DUVETYN	EARPLUG	ECTHYMA	EGOTISES
DOUCINE	DREAMERS	DUALISTS	DUVETYNE	EARPLUGS	ECTHYMAS	EGOTISM
DOUCINES	DREAMERY	DUBBING	DUVETYNS	EARRING	ECTOPIA	EGOTISMS
DOULEIA	DREARES	DUBBINGS	DVANDVA	EARRINGS	ECTOPIAS	

EGOTIST	ELEVATED	EMBRAIDS	EMPLUMED	**ENDGAME**	**ENGRAVE**	CENSURES
EGOTISTS	ELEVATES	**EMBRAVE**	EMPLUMES	ENDGAMES	ENGRAVED	**ENSWEEP**
EGOTIZE	**ELFHOOD**	EMBRAVED	**EMPOWER**	**ENDINGS**	ENGRAVEN	ENSWEEPS
EGOTIZED	SELFHOOD	EMBRAVES	EMPOWERS	BENDINGS	ENGRAVER	**ENTAILS**
EGOTIZES	ELFHOODS	**EMBREAD**	**EMPRESS**	LENDINGS	ENGRAVES	VENTAILS
EIDETIC	**ELFLAND**	EMBREADS	EMPRESSE	MENDINGS	**ENGUARD**	**ENTAYLE**
EIDETICS	ELFLANDS	**EMBREWE**	**EMPRISE**	SENDINGS	ENGUARDS	VENTAYLE
EIGHTVO	**ELISION**	EMBREWED	EMPRISES	**ENDIRON**	**ENGULPH**	ENTAYLED
EIGHTVOS	ELISIONS	EMBREWES	**EMPTIER**	ENDIRONS	ENGULPHS	ENTAYLES
EILDING	**ELITISM**	**EMBROIL**	EMPTIERS	**ENDOGEN**	**ENHANCE**	**ENTENTE**
EILDINGS	ELITISMS	EMBROILS	**EMPTIES**	ENDOGENS	ENHANCED	ENTENTES
EJECTED	**ELITIST**	**EMBROWN**	EMPTIEST	ENDOGENY	ENHANCES	**ENTERED**
DEJECTED	ELITISTS	EMBROWNS	**EMPTION**	**ENDORSE**	**ENJOYER**	CENTERED
REJECTED	**ELLIPSE**	**EMBRUTE**	EMPTIONS	ENDORSED	ENJOYERS	TENTERED
EJECTOR	ELLIPSES	EMBRUTED	**EMPYEMA**	ENDORSEE	**ENLARGE**	**ENTERER**
REJECTOR	**ELLWAND**	EMBRUTES	EMPYEMAS	ENDORSER	ENLARGED	ENTERERS
EJECTORS	ELLWANDS	**EMBRYON**	**EMULATE**	ENDORSES	ENLARGEN	**ENTERIC**
EKISTIC	**ELMWOOD**	EMBRYONS	EMULATED	**ENDOWER**	ENLARGER	ENTERICS
EKISTICS	ELMWOODS	**EMERALD**	EMULATES	ENDOWERS	ENLARGES	**ENTHRAL**
EKPWELE	**ELOCUTE**	EMERALDS	**EMULING**	**ENDSHIP**	**ENLIGHT**	ENTHRALL
EKPWELES	ELOCUTED	**EMERGED**	AEMULING	ENDSHIPS	PENLIGHT	ENTHRALS
ELAPSED	ELOCUTES	DEMERGED	**EMULSIN**	**ENDURER**	ENLIGHTS	**ENTHUSE**
DELAPSED	**ELOGIST**	REMERGED	EMULSINS	ENDURERS	**ENLIVEN**	ENTHUSED
RELAPSED	ELOGISTS	**EMERGES**	**EMULSOR**	**ENDWISE**	ENLIVENS	ENTHUSES
ELAPSES	**ELOGIUM**	DEMERGES	EMULSORS	BENDWISE	**ENNOBLE**	**ENTICED**
DELAPSES	ELOGIUMS	REMERGES	**EMURING**	**ENERGID**	ENNOBLED	PENTICED
RELAPSES	**ELOINER**	**EMERSED**	DEMURING	ENERGIDS	ENNOBLES	**ENTICER**
ELASTIC	ELOINERS	DEMERSED	**ENABLER**	**ENEWING**	**ENOUNCE**	ENTICERS
GELASTIC	**ELUDERS**	**EMETINE**	ENABLERS	RENEWING	DENOUNCE	**ENTICES**
ELASTICS	DELUDERS	EMETINES	**ENACTOR**	**ENFELON**	RENOUNCE	PENTICES
ELASTIN	**ELUDING**	**EMICATE**	ENACTORS	ENFELONS	ENOUNCED	**ENTITLE**
ELASTINS	DELUDING	EMICATED	**ENAMOUR**	**ENFEOFF**	ENOUNCES	ENTITLED
ELATERS	**ELUSION**	EMICATES	ENAMOURS	ENFEOFFS	**ENPRINT**	ENTITLES
RELATERS	DELUSION	**EMIRATE**	**ENATION**	**ENFOLDS**	ENPRINTS	**ENTOMIC**
ELATING	ELUSIONS	EMIRATES	VENATION	PENFOLDS	**ENQUIRE**	PENTOMIC
BELATING	**ELUSIVE**	**EMITTED**	ENATIONS	**ENFORCE**	ENQUIRED	**ENTOZOA**
DELATING	DELUSIVE	DEMITTED	**ENCHAFE**	RENFORCE	ENQUIRER	ENTOZOAL
RELATING	**ELUSORY**	REMITTED	ENCHAFED	ENFORCED	ENQUIRES	**ENTRAIL**
ELATION	DELUSORY	**EMONGES**	ENCHAFES	ENFORCES	**ENRANGE**	ENTRAILS
DELATION	**ELUTION**	EMONGEST	**ENCHAIN**	**ENFRAME**	ENRANGED	**ENTRAIN**
GELATION	ELUTIONS	**EMOTING**	ENCHAINS	ENFRAMED	ENRANGES	ENTRAINS
RELATION	**ELUVIUM**	DEMOTING	**ENCHANT**	ENFRAMES	**ENRHEUM**	**ENTRANT**
ELATIONS	ELUVIUMS	**EMOTION**	PENCHANT	**ENFROZE**	ENRHEUMS	ENTRANTS
ELATIVE	**EMANATE**	DEMOTION	ENCHANTS	ENFROZEN	**ENROUGH**	**ENTREAT**
RELATIVE	EMANATED	REMOTION	**ENCHARM**	**ENGAGER**	ENROUGHS	ENTREATS
ELATIVES	EMANATES	EMOTIONS	ENCHARMS	ENGAGERS	**ENROUND**	ENTREATY
ELDINGS	**EMBATHE**	**EMOVING**	**ENCHASE**	**ENGINER**	ENROUNDS	**ENTRIES**
GELDINGS	EMBATHED	REMOVING	ENCHASED	ENGINERS	**ENSHELL**	CENTRIES
WELDINGS	EMBATHES	**EMPAIRE**	ENCHASES	ENGINERY	ENSHELLS	GENTRIES
ELECTED	**EMBLAZE**	EMPAIRED	**ENCHEER**	**ENGLOBE**	**ENSLAVE**	SENTRIES
SELECTED	EMBLAZED	EMPAIRES	ENCHEERS	ENGLOBED	ENSLAVED	**ENTRISM**
ELECTOR	EMBLAZES	**EMPANEL**	**ENCLASP**	ENGLOBES	ENSLAVER	CENTRISM
SELECTOR	**EMBLOOM**	EMPANELS	ENCLASPS	**ENGLOOM**	ENSLAVES	ENTRISMS
ELECTORS	EMBLOOMS	**EMPAYRE**	**ENCLAVE**	ENGLOOMS	**ENSNARE**	**ENTRIST**
ELECTRO	**EMBOGUE**	EMPAYRED	ENCLAVED	**ENGORGE**	ENSNARED	CENTRIST
ELECTRON	EMBOGUED	EMPAYRES	ENCLAVES	ENGORGED	ENSNARES	ENTRISTS
ELECTROS	EMBOGUES	**EMPERCE**	**ENCLOSE**	ENGORGES	**ENSNARL**	**ENTRUST**
ELEGIAC	**EMBOSOM**	EMPERCED	ENCLOSED	**ENGRAFF**	ENSNARLS	ENTRUSTS
ELEGIACS	EMBOSOMS	EMPERCES	ENCLOSER	ENGRAFFS	**ENSTAMP**	ENTWINE
ELEGISE	**EMBOUND**	**EMPEROR**	ENCLOSES	**ENGRAFT**	ENSTAMPS	ENTWINED
ELEGISED	EMBOUNDS	EMPERORS	**ENCLOUD**	ENGRAFTS	**ENSTEEP**	ENTWINES
ELEGISES	**EMBOWEL**	**EMPIRIC**	ENCLOUDS	**ENGRAIL**	ENSTEEPS	**ENTWIST**
ELEGIST	EMBOWELS	EMPIRICS	**ENCRUST**	ENGRAILS	**ENSTYLE**	ENTWISTS
ELEGISTS	**EMBOWER**	**EMPLACE**	ENCRUSTS	**ENGRAIN**	ENSTYLED	**ENVAULT**
ELEGIZE	EMBOWERS	EMPLACED	**ENCRYPT**	ENGRAINS	ENSTYLES	ENVAULTS
ELEGIZED	**EMBRACE**	EMPLACES	ENCRYPTS	**ENGRASP**	**ENSURED**	ENVELOP
ELEGIZES	EMBRACED	**EMPLANE**	**ENDEMIC**	ENGRASPS	CENSURED	ENVELOPE
ELEMENT	EMBRACER	EMPLANED	ENDEMICS		**ENSURER**	ENVELOPS
ELEMENTS	EMBRACES	EMPLANES	**ENDERON**		ENSURERS	**ENVENOM**
ELEVATE	**EMBRAID**	**EMPLUME**	ENDERONS		**ENSURES**	ENVENOMS

ENVIRON	EPURATE	ESCROLL	ETHICAL	REVOLVES	EXOMION	EYEBROW
ENVIRONS	DEPURATE	ESCROLLS	ETHICALS	EXACTER	EXOMIONS	EYEBROWS
ENVYING	EPURATED	ESCUAGE	ETIOLIN	EXACTERS	EXORDIA	EYEHOOK
ENVYINGS	EPURATES	ESCUAGES	ETIOLINS	EXACTOR	EXORDIAL	EYEHOOKS
ENWHEEL	EQUATOR	ESLOYNE	ETOURDI	EXACTORS	EXPANSE	EYELIAD
ENWHEELS	EQUATORS	ESLOYNED	ETOURDIE	EXAMINE	EXPANSES	EYELIADS
EOLITHS	EQUINIA	ESLOYNES	ETRENNE	EXAMINED	EXPENSE	EYESORE
NEOLITHS	EQUINIAS	ESPARTO	ETRENNES	EXAMINEE	EXPENSES	EYESORES
EONISMS	ERASION	ESPARTOS	ETTLING	EXAMINER	EXPIATE	FABLIAU
PEONISMS	ERASIONS	ESPOUSE	FETTLING	EXAMINES	EXPIATED	FABLIAUX
EPACRID	ERASURE	ESPOUSED	NETTLING	EXAMPLE	EXPLAIN	FABLING
EPACRIDS	ERASURES	ESPOUSER	PETTLING	EXAMPLED	EXPLAINS	FABLINGS
EPAGOGE	ERATHEM	ESPOUSES	SETTLING	EXAMPLES	EXPLANT	FACONNE
EPAGOGES	ERATHEMS	ESQUIRE	EUCAINE	EXCERPT	EXPLANTS	FACONNES
EPAULET	ERBIUMS	ESQUIRES	EUCAINES	EXCERPTA	EXPLODE	FACTION
EPAULETS	TERBIUMS	ESSAYER	EUCLASE	EXCERPTS	EXPLODED	FACTIONS
EPEIRID	ERECTER	ESSAYERS	EUCLASES	EXCHEAT	EXPLODER	FACTOID
EPEIRIDS	ERECTERS	ESSENCE	EUCRITE	EXCHEATS	EXPLODES	FACTOIDS
EPERGNE	ERECTOR	ESSENCES	EUCRITES	EXCITER	EXPLOIT	FACTURE
EPERGNES	ERECTORS	ESSOYNE	EUGENIC	EXCITERS	EXPLOITS	FACTURES
EPHEDRA	EREMITE	ESSOYNES	EUGENICS	EXCITON	EXPLORE	FADAISE
EPHEDRAS	EREMITES	ESTATED	EUGENOL	EXCITONS	EXPLORED	FADAISES
EPICARP	EREPSIN	GESTATED	EUGENOLS	EXCITOR	EXPLORER	FADDISM
EPICARPS	EREPSINS	RESTATED	EUPHROE	EXCITORS	EXPLORES	FADDISMS
EPICEDE	ERINITE	ESTATES	EUPHROES	EXCLAIM	EXPOSAL	FADDIST
EPICEDES	ERINITES	GESTATES	EUREKAS	EXCLAIMS	EXPOSALS	FADDISTS
EPICENE	ERISTIC	RESTATES	HEUREKAS	EXCLAVE	EXPOSER	FAGGING
EPICENES	MERISTIC	ESTHETE	EUSTYLE	EXCLAVES	EXPOSERS	FAGGINGS
EPICIER	VERISTIC	AESTHETE	EUSTYLES	EXCLUDE	EXPOUND	FAHLORE
EPICIERS	ERMELIN	ESTHETES	EUTEXIA	EXCLUDED	EXPOUNDS	FAHLORES
EPICISM	ERMELINS	ESTIVAL	EUTEXIAS	EXCLUDEE	EXPRESS	FAIENCE
EPICISMS	ERMINED	AESTIVAL	EVACUEE	EXCLUDES	EXPRESSO	FAIENCES
EPICIST	VERMINED	FESTIVAL	EVACUEES	EXCRETE	EXPULSE	FAILING
EPICISTS	ERODENT	ESTOILE	EVANGEL	EXCRETED	EXPULSED	FAILINGS
EPICURE	ERODENTS	ESTOILES	EVANGELS	EXCRETES	EXPULSES	FAILURE
EPICURES	ERODIUM	ESTOVER	EVANGELY	EXCURSE	EXPUNCT	FAILURES
EPIDOTE	ERODIUMS	ESTOVERS	EVASION	EXCURSED	EXPUNCTS	FAIRING
LEPIDOTE	EROSION	ESTRADE	EVASIONS	EXCURSES	EXPUNGE	FAIRINGS
EPIDOTES	EROSIONS	ESTRADES	EVENING	EXCUSAL	EXPUNGED	FAIRWAY
EPIGONE	EROTEMA	ESTREAT	EVENINGS	EXCUSALS	EXPUNGER	FAIRWAYS
EPIGONES	EROTEMAS	ESTREATS	EVENTER	EXCUSER	EXPUNGES	FAITOUR
EPIGRAM	EROTEME	ESTREPE	EVENTERS	EXCUSERS	EXPURGE	FAITOURS
EPIGRAMS	EROTEMES	ESTREPED	EVERTED	EXECUTE	EXPURGED	FALAFEL
EPILATE	EROTICA	ESTREPES	REVERTED	EXECUTED	EXPURGES	FALAFELS
DEPILATE	EROTICAL	ESTROUS	EVICTOR	EXECUTER	EXSCIND	FALBALA
EPILATED	EROTISM	OESTROUS	EVICTORS	EXECUTES	EXSCINDS	FALBALAS
EPILATES	EROTISMS	ESTRUMS	EVIDENT	EXEGETE	EXTERNE	FALCADE
EPISODE	ERRATIC	OESTRUMS	EVIDENTS	EXEGETES	EXTERNES	FALCADES
EPISODES	ERRATICS	ETACISM	EVIRATE	EXEMPLA	EXTRACT	FALCATE
EPISOME	ERRHINE	BETACISM	LEVIRATE	EXEMPLAR	EXTRACTS	FALCATED
EPISOMES	ERRHINES	ETACISMS	EVIRATED	EXEMPLE	EXTRAIT	FALCULA
EPISTLE	ERRINGS	ETAERIO	EVIRATES	EXEMPLES	EXTRAITS	FALCULAS
EPISTLED	HERRINGS	ETAERIOS	EVITATE	EXERGUE	EXTREAT	FALDAGE
EPISTLER	ERUDITE	ETAGERE	LEVITATE	EXERGUES	EXTREATS	FALDAGES
EPISTLES	ERUDITES	ETAGERES	EVITATED	EXHAUST	EXTREME	FALLING
EPITAPH	ESCALOP	ETALAGE	EVITATES	EXHAUSTS	EXTREMER	FALLINGS
EPITAPHS	ESCALOPE	ETALAGES	EVOCATE	EXHEDRA	EXTREMES	FALSISM
EPITHEM	ESCALOPS	ETCHANT	EVOCATED	EXHEDRAE	EXTRUDE	FALSISMS
EPITHEMA	ESCAPEE	ETCHANTS	EVOCATES	EXHIBIT	EXTRUDED	FANATIC
EPITHEMS	ESCAPEES	ETCHING	EVOKING	EXHIBITS	EXTRUDER	FANATICS
EPITHET	ESCAPER	FETCHING	REVOKING	EXHUMER	EXTRUDES	FANCIER
EPITHETS	ESCAPERS	KETCHING	EVOLUTE	EXHUMERS	EXUDATE	FANCIERS
EPITOME	ESCHEAT	LETCHING	EVOLUTED	EXIGENT	EXUDATES	FANCIES
EPITOMES	ESCHEATS	RETCHING	EVOLUTES	EXIGENTS	EXURBIA	FANCIEST
EPIZOAN	ESCOLAR	ETCHINGS	EVOLVED	EXOCARP	EXURBIAS	FANFARE
EPIZOANS	ESCOLARS	ETHANES	DEVOLVED	EXOCARPS	EYEBALL	FANFARED
EPOXIDE	ESCRIBE	METHANES	REVOLVED	EXODERM	EYEBALLS	FANFARES
EPOXIDES	DESCRIBE	ETHANOL	EVOLVES	EXODERMS	EYEBOLT	FANGLES
EPSILON	ESCRIBED	METHANOL	DEVOLVES	EXODIST	EYEBOLTS	FANGLESS
EPSILONS	ESCRIBES	ETHANOLS		EXODISTS		FANNELL

FANNELLS	FEATHERS	**FERRULE**	**FILIATE**	**FIVEPIN**	FLINDERS	**FLYTRAP**
FANNING	**FEATHERY**	**FERRULES**	FILIATED	FIVEPINS	**FLINGER**	FLYTRAPS
FANNINGS	**FEATURE**	**FERTILE**	FILIATES	**FIXTURE**	FLINGERS	**FOAMING**
FANTAIL	FEATURED	FERTILER	**FILIBEG**	FIXTURES	**FLIPPER**	FOAMINGS
FANTAILS	FEATURES	**FERVOUR**	FILIBEGS	**FIZZGIG**	FLIPPERS	**FOGGAGE**
FANTASM	**FECHTER**	FERVOURS	**FILLING**	FIZZGIGS	**FLITTER**	**FOGGAGED**
FANTASMS	FECHTERS	**FESTOON**	FILLINGS	**FIZZING**	**FLITTERN**	FOGGAGES
FANTAST	**FEDARIE**	FESTOONS	**FILMDOM**	FIZZINGS	FLITTERS	**FOGHORN**
FANTASTS	FEDARIES	**FETICHE**	FILMDOMS	**FLACKER**	**FLIVVER**	FOGHORNS
FANTEEG	**FEDAYEE**	FETICHES	**FILMSET**	FLACKERS	FLIVVERS	**FOGYDOM**
FANTEEGS	FEDAYEEN	**FETLOCK**	FILMSETS	**FLACKET**	**FLOATEL**	FOGYDOMS
FANZINE	**FEDERAL**	FETLOCKS	**FIMBRIA**	FLACKETS	FLOATELS	**FOGYISM**
FANZINES	FEDERALS	**FETTLER**	FIMBRIAS	**FLAFFER**	**FLOATER**	FOGYISMS
FARADAY	**FEEBLES**	FETTLERS	**FINAGLE**	FLAFFERS	FLOATERS	**FOILING**
FARADAYS	FEEBLEST	**FEUDING**	FINAGLED	**FLAMFEW**	**FLOORER**	FOILINGS
FARAWAY	**FEEDING**	FEUDINGS	FINAGLES	FLAMFEWS	FLOORERS	**FOISTER**
FARAWAYS	FEEDINGS	**FEUDIST**	**FINANCE**	**FLAMING**	**FLOOSIE**	FOISTERS
FARCEUR	**FEEDLOT**	FEUDISTS	FINANCED	FLAMINGO	FLOOSIES	**FOLACIN**
FARCEURS	FEEDLOTS	**FIANCEE**	FINANCES	**FLANEUR**	**FLOOZIE**	FOLACINS
FARCING	**FEELING**	FIANCEES	**FINBACK**	FLANEURS	FLOOZIES	**FOLDING**
FARCINGS	FEELINGS	**FIBROID**	FINBACKS	**FLANKER**	**FLORIST**	FOLDINGS
FARDAGE	**FEERING**	FIBROIDS	**FINDING**	FLANKERS	FLORISTS	**FOLIAGE**
FARDAGES	FEERINGS	**FIBROIN**	FINDINGS	**FLANNEL**	**FLORUIT**	**FOLIAGED**
FARDING	**FELAFEL**	FIBROINS	**FINDRAM**	FLANNELS	FLORUITS	FOLIAGES
FARDINGS	FELAFELS	**FIBROMA**	FINDRAMS	**FLANNEN**	**FLOTAGE**	**FOLIATE**
FARMING	**FELLATE**	FIBROMAS	**FINESSE**	FLANNENS	FLOTAGES	**FOLIATED**
FARMINGS	FELLATED	**FIBROSE**	FINESSED	**FLAPPER**	**FLOTSAM**	FOLIATES
FARRIER	FELLATES	FIBROSED	FINESSER	FLAPPERS	FLOTSAMS	**FOLIOLE**
FARRIERS	**FELSITE**	FIBROSES	FINESSES	**FLASHER**	**FLOUNCE**	FOLIOLES
FARRIERY	FELSITES	**FIBSTER**	**FINNACK**	FLASHERS	FLOUNCED	**FOLKWAY**
FARRUCA	**FELSPAR**	FIBSTERS	FINNACKS	**FLASHES**	FLOUNCES	FOLKWAYS
FARRUCAS	FELSPARS	**FICKLES**	**FINNOCK**	FLASHEST	**FLOWAGE**	**FONDANT**
FARTHEL	**FELTING**	FICKLEST	FINNOCKS	**FLASKET**	FLOWAGES	FONDANTS
FARTHELS	FELTINGS	**FIDDLER**	**FIREARM**	FLASKETS	**FLUENCE**	**FONDLER**
FASCINE	**FELUCCA**	FIDDLERS	FIREARMS	**FLATLET**	FLUENCES	FONDLERS
FASCINES	FELUCCAS	**FIDDLEY**	**FIREBUG**	FLATLETS	**FLUIDIC**	**FONTLET**
FASCISM	**FELWORT**	FIDDLEYS	FIREBUGS	**FLATTEN**	FLUIDICS	FONTLETS
FASCISMI	FELWORTS	**FIDEISM**	**FIREDOG**	FLATTENS	**FLUNKEY**	**FOOLING**
FASCISMO	**FEMITER**	FIDEISMS	FIREDOGS	**FLATTER**	FLUNKEYS	FOOLINGS
FASCISMS	FEMITERS	**FIELDER**	**FIREPAN**	FLATTERS	**FLUSHER**	**FOOTAGE**
FASCIST	**FENCING**	FIELDERS	FIREPANS	**FLATTERY**	FLUSHERS	FOOTAGES
FASCISTA	FENCINGS	**FIFTEEN**	**FIREPOT**	**FLAUGHT**	**FLUSHES**	**FOOTBAR**
FASCISTI	**FENITAR**	FIFTEENS	FIREPOTS	FLAUGHTS	FLUSHEST	FOOTBARS
FASCISTS	FENITARS	**FIGHTER**	**FIRRING**	**FLAVINE**	**FLUSTER**	**FOOTBOY**
FASHION	**FENLAND**	FIGHTERS	FIRRINGS	FLAVINES	FLUSTERS	FOOTBOYS
FASHIONS	FENLANDS	**FIGMENT**	**FISHEYE**	**FLAVONE**	**FLUSTERY**	**FOOTING**
FASTING	**FEOFFEE**	FIGMENTS	FISHEYES	FLAVONES	**FLUTINA**	FOOTINGS
FASTINGS	FEOFFEES	**FIGWORT**	**FISHGIG**	**FLAVOUR**	FLUTINAS	**FOOTLES**
FATIGUE	**FEOFFER**	FIGWORTS	FISHGIGS	FLAVOURS	**FLUTING**	FOOTLESS
FATIGUED	FEOFFERS	**FILABEG**	**FISHING**	**FLECKER**	FLUTINGS	**FOOTPAD**
FATIGUES	**FEOFFOR**	FILABEGS	FISHINGS	FLECKERS	**FLUTIST**	FOOTPADS
FATLING	FEOFFORS	**FILACER**	**FISSION**	**FLEECER**	FLUTISTS	**FOOTROT**
FATLINGS	**FERLIES**	FILACERS	FISSIONS	FLEECERS	**FLUTTER**	FOOTROTS
FATTIES	FERLIEST	**FILARIA**	**FISSURE**	**FLEERER**	FLUTTERS	**FOOTWAY**
FATTIEST	**FERMATA**	FILARIAL	FISSURED	FLEERERS	**FLUXION**	FOOTWAYS
FAUCHON	FERMATAS	FILARIAS	FISSURES	**FLESHER**	FLUXIONS	**FOOZLER**
FAUCHONS	**FERMENT**	**FILASSE**	**FISTFUL**	FLESHERS	**FLYBANE**	FOOZLERS
FAUNIST	FERMENTS	FILASSES	FISTFULS	**FLETTON**	FLYBANES	**FOPLING**
FAUNISTS	**FERMION**	**FILAZER**	**FISTULA**	FLETTONS	**FLYBELT**	FOPLINGS
FAVRILE	FERMIONS	FILAZERS	FISTULAE	**FLEURET**	FLYBELTS	**FORAGER**
FAVRILES	**FERMIUM**	**FILBERD**	FISTULAR	FLEURETS	**FLYBLOW**	FORAGERS
FAWNING	FERMIUMS	FILBERDS	FISTULAS	**FLEURON**	FLYBLOWS	**FORAYER**
FAWNINGS	**FERNING**	**FILBERT**	**FITCHET**	FLEURONS	**FLYBOAT**	FORAYERS
FAYENCE	FERNINGS	FILBERTS	FITCHETS	**FLEXION**	FLYBOATS	**FORBEAR**
FAYENCES	**FERRATE**	**FILCHER**	**FITCHEW**	FLEXIONS	**FLYBOOK**	FORBEARS
FEARING	FERRATES	FILCHERS	FITCHEWS	**FLEXURE**	FLYBOOKS	**FORBODE**
AFEARING	**FERRITE**	**FILEMOT**	**FITMENT**	FLEXURES	**FLYOVER**	FORBODES
FEASTER	FERRITES	FILEMOTS	FITMENTS	**FLICKER**	FLYOVERS	**FOREARM**
FEASTERS	**FERRUGO**		**FITTING**	FLICKERS	**FLYTING**	FOREARMS
FEATHER	FERRUGOS		FITTINGS	**FLINDER**	FLYTINGS	**FORECAR**

FORECARS	FORTUNES	**FREIGHT**	FUDDLERS	**FUTTOCK**	**GALUMPH**	GAUGINGS
FOREGUT	**FORWARD**	FREIGHTS	**FUELLER**	FUTTOCKS	GALUMPHS	**GAULTER**
FOREGUTS	FORWARDS	**FRESHEN**	FUELLERS	**GABBARD**	**GAMBADO**	GAULTERS
FORELAY	**FORWARN**	FRESHENS	**FUGUIST**	GABBARDS	GAMBADOS	**GAVOTTE**
FORELAYS	FORWARNS	**FRESHER**	FUGUISTS	**GABBART**	**GAMBIER**	GAVOTTES
FORELEG	**FORZATI**	FRESHERS	**FULCRUM**	GABBARTS	GAMBIERS	**GAWKIES**
FORELEGS	SFORZATI	**FRESHES**	FULCRUMS	**GABBLER**	**GAMBIST**	GAWKIEST
FORELIE	**FORZATO**	FRESHEST	**FULGOUR**	GABBLERS	GAMBISTS	**GAZELLE**
FORELIES	SFORZATO	**FRESHET**	FULGOURS	**GABELLE**	**GAMBLER**	GAZELLES
FOREPAW	FORZATOS	FRESHETS	**FULLAGE**	GABELLER	GAMBLERS	**GAZETTE**
FOREPAWS	**FOSSICK**	**FRETSAW**	FULLAGES	GABELLES	**GAMBOGE**	GAZETTED
FORERUN	FOSSICKS	FRETSAWS	**FULMINE**	**GABFEST**	GAMBOGES	GAZETTES
FORERUNS	**FOSSULA**	**FRIANDE**	FULMINED	GABFESTS	**GAMBREL**	**GAZOOKA**
FORESAY	FOSSULAS	FRIANDES	FULMINES	**GADLING**	GAMBRELS	GAZOOKAS
FORESAYS	**FOUDRIE**	**FRIBBLE**	**FULSOME**	GADLINGS	**GAMELAN**	**GEALOUS**
FORESEE	FOUDRIES	FRIBBLED	FULSOMER	**GADROON**	GAMELANS	GEALOUSY
FORESEEN	**FOUETTE**	FRIBBLER	**FUMBLER**	GADROONS	**GAMMOCK**	**GEARING**
FORESEES	FOUETTES	FRIBBLES	FUMBLERS	**GADWALL**	GAMMOCKS	GEARINGS
FORETOP	**FOUGADE**	**FRIGATE**	**FUMETTE**	GADWALLS	**GANGING**	**GEEBUNG**
FORETOPS	FOUGADES	FRIGATES	FUMETTES	**GAFFING**	GANGINGS	GEEBUNGS
FOREVER	**FOULARD**	**FRIGGER**	**FUNDING**	GAFFINGS	**GANGLIA**	**GELATIN**
FOREVERS	FOULARDS	FRIGGERS	FUNDINGS	**GAGSTER**	GANGLIAR	GELATINE
FORFAIR	**FOULDER**	**FRIJOLE**	**FUNERAL**	GAGSTERS	**GANGREL**	GELATINS
FORFAIRN	FOULDERS	FRIJOLES	FUNERALS	**GAHNITE**	GANGRELS	**GELDING**
FORFAIRS	**FOUMART**	**FRIPPER**	**FUNFAIR**	GAHNITES	**GANGWAY**	GELDINGS
FORFEIT	FOUMARTS	FRIPPERS	FUNFAIRS	**GAINING**	GANGWAYS	**GEMMATE**
FORFEITS	**FOUNDER**	FRIPPERY	**FUNICLE**	GAININGS	**GANTLET**	GEMMATED
FORFEND	FOUNDERS	**FRISEUR**	FUNICLES	**GAINSAY**	GANTLETS	GEMMATES
FORFENDS	**FOURGON**	FRISEURS	**FUNNIES**	GAINSAYS	**GARBAGE**	**GEMMULE**
FORGING	FOURGONS	**FRISKER**	FUNNIEST	**GALABEA**	GARBAGES	GEMMULES
FORGINGS	**FOVEOLA**	FRISKERS	**FURCATE**	GALABEAH	**GARBLER**	**GEMSBOK**
FORGIVE	FOVEOLAS	**FRISKET**	FURCATED	GALABEAS	GARBLERS	GEMSBOKS
FORGIVEN	**FOVEOLE**	FRISKETS	**FURCULA**	**GALABIA**	**GARBOIL**	**GENAPPE**
FORGIVES	FOVEOLES	**FRISSON**	FURCULAR	GALABIAH	GARBOILS	GENAPPES
FORHENT	**FOWLING**	FRISSONS	FURCULAS	GALABIAS	**GARDANT**	**GENERAL**
FORHENTS	FOWLINGS	**FRISURE**	**FURFAIR**	**GALANGA**	GARDANTS	GENERALE
FORLANA	**FOXHOLE**	FRISURES	FURFAIRS	GALANGAL	**GARIGUE**	GENERALS
FORLANAS	FOXHOLES	**FRITTER**	**FURIOSO**	GALANGAS	GARIGUES	**GENERIC**
FORLEND	**FOXSHIP**	FRITTERS	FURIOSOS	**GALATEA**	**GARLAND**	GENERICS
FORLENDS	FOXSHIPS	**FRITURE**	**FURLANA**	GALATEAS	GARLANDS	**GENETIC**
FORLESE	**FOXTROT**	FRITURES	FURLANAS	**GALEATE**	**GARMENT**	GENETICS
FORLESES	FOXTROTS	**FRIZZLE**	**FURLONG**	GALEATED	GARMENTS	**GENETTE**
FORLORN	**FRAGILE**	FRIZZLED	FURLONGS	**GALILEE**	**GAROTTE**	GENETTES
FORLORNS	FRAGILER	FRIZZLES	**FURNACE**	GALILEES	GAROTTED	**GENIPAP**
FORMANT	**FRAMING**	**FROGBIT**	FURNACED	**GALIPOT**	GAROTTER	GENIPAPS
FORMANTS	FRAMINGS	FROGBITS	FURNACES	GALIPOTS	GAROTTES	**GENISTA**
FORMATE	**FRANION**	**FROGLET**	**FURRIER**	**GALLANT**	**GARPIKE**	GENISTAS
FORMATED	FRANIONS	FROGLETS	FURRIERS	GALLANTS	GARPIKES	**GENITAL**
FORMATES	**FRAUGHT**	**FRONTAL**	FURRIERY	**GALLATE**	**GARROTE**	GENITALS
FORMING	FRAUGHTS	FRONTALS	**FURRING**	GALLATES	GARROTED	**GENITOR**
FORMINGS	**FRAYING**	**FRONTON**	FURRINGS	**GALLEON**	GARROTES	GENITORS
FORMULA	FRAYINGS	FRONTONS	**FURTHER**	GALLEONS	**GARVOCK**	**GENIZAH**
FORMULAE	**FRAZZLE**	**FROUNCE**	FURTHERS	**GALLIOT**	GARVOCKS	GENIZAHS
FORMULAR	FRAZZLED	FROUNCED	**FURTIVE**	GALLIOTS	**GASAHOL**	**GENTIAN**
FORMULAS	FRAZZLES	FROUNCES	FURTIVER	**GALLISE**	GASAHOLS	GENTIANS
FORPINE	**FRECKLE**	**FROWARD**	**FUSAROL**	GALLISED	**GASOHOL**	**GENTILE**
FORPINED	FRECKLED	FROWARDS	FUSAROLE	GALLISES	GASOHOLS	GENTILES
FORPINES	FRECKLES	**FRUITER**	FUSAROLS	**GALLIUM**	**GASPING**	**GENTLES**
FORSAKE	**FREEBEE**	FRUITERS	**FUSHION**	GALLIUMS	GASPINGS	GENTLEST
FORSAKEN	FREEBEES	FRUITERY	FUSHIONS	**GALLIZE**	**GASSING**	**GEORDIE**
FORSAKES	**FREEBIE**	**FRUMPLE**	**FUSTIAN**	GALLIZED	GASSINGS	GEORDIES
FORSLOE	FREEBIES	FRUMPLED	FUSTIANS	GALLIZES	**GASTRIN**	**GEORGIC**
FORSLOED	**FREEDOM**	FRUMPLES	**FUTCHEL**	**GALLOON**	GASTRINS	GEORGICS
FORSLOES	FREEDOMS	**FRUSTUM**	FUTCHELS	GALLOONS	**GATEWAY**	**GERBERA**
FORSLOW	**FREESIA**	FRUSTUMS	**FUTHARK**	**GALOCHE**	GATEWAYS	GERBERAS
FORSLOWS	FREESIAS	**FUCHSIA**	FUTHARKS	GALOCHED	**GAUDGIE**	**GERENUK**
FORTLET	**FREEWAY**	FUCHSIAS	**FUTHORC**	GALOCHES	GAUDGIES	GERENUKS
FORTLETS	FREEWAYS	**FUCKING**	FUTHORCS	**GALOPIN**	**GAUDIES**	**GERMAIN**
FORTUNE	**FREEZER**	FUCKINGS	**FUTHORK**	GALOPING	GAUDIEST	GERMAINE
FORTUNED	FREEZERS	**FUDDLER**	FUTHORKS	GALOPINS	**GAUGING**	GERMAINS

GESTALT	GLACIERS	GLYPTIC	GOSHAWKS	GRANULE	GRIMACES	GUANINES
GESTALTS	GLADDEN	GLYPTICS	GOSLING	GRANULES	GRINDER	GUARANA
GESTATE	GLADDENS	GNASHER	GOSLINGS	GRAPHIC	GRINDERS	GUARANAS
GESTATED	GLADDIE	GNASHERS	GOSSOON	AGRAPHIC	GRINDERY	GUARDEE
GESTATES	GLADDIES	GNOCCHI	GOSSOONS	GRAPHICS	GRINNER	GUARDEES
GESTURE	GLADDON	GNOCCHIS	GOTHITE	GRAPNEL	GRINNERS	GUAYULE
GESTURED	GLADDONS	GNOMIST	GOTHITES	GRAPNELS	GRIPPER	GUAYULES
GESTURES	GLAIRIN	GNOMISTS	GOUACHE	GRAPPLE	GRIPPERS	GUDGEON
GETAWAY	GLAIRING	GNOSTIC	GOUACHES	GRAPPLED	GRIPPLE	GUDGEONS
GETAWAYS	GLAIRINS	AGNOSTIC	GOUGERE	GRAPPLES	GRIPPLES	GUERDON
GETTING	GLAMOUR	GOBBLER	GOUGERES	GRASPER	GRISING	GUERDONS
GETTINGS	GLAMOURS	GOBBLERS	GOURAMI	GRASPERS	AGRISING	GUEREZA
GHARIAL	GLAZIER	GOBURRA	GOURAMIS	GRASSER	GRISKIN	GUEREZAS
GHARIALS	GLAZIERS	GOBURRAS	GOURMET	GRASSERS	GRISKINS	GUESSER
GHERKIN	GLAZING	GODETIA	GOURMETS	GRASSUM	GRISTLE	GUESSERS
GHERKINS	GLAZINGS	GODETIAS	GOWLAND	GRASSUMS	GRISTLES	GUESTEN
GHILGAI	GLEANER	GODHEAD	GOWLANDS	GRATING	GRITTER	GUESTENS
GHILGAIS	GLEANERS	GODHEADS	GOWNBOY	GRATINGS	GRITTERS	GUICHET
GHILLIE	GLENOID	GODHOOD	GOWNBOYS	GRAUPEL	GRIZZLE	GUICHETS
GHILLIED	GLENOIDS	GODHOODS	GRABBER	GRAUPELS	GRIZZLED	GUIDAGE
GHILLIES	GLIADIN	GODLING	GRABBERS	GRAVING	GRIZZLER	GUIDAGES
GIDDIES	GLIADINE	GODLINGS	GRABBLE	GRAVINGS	GRIZZLES	GUIDING
GIDDIEST	GLIADINS	GODROON	GRABBLED	GRAVURE	GROANER	GUIDINGS
GIGGLER	GLIBBER	GODROONS	GRABBLER	GRAVURES	GROANERS	GUILDER
GIGGLERS	GLIBBERY	GODSEND	GRABBLES	GRAZIER	GROCKLE	GUILDERS
GILBERT	GLIDDER	GODSENDS	GRACKLE	GRAZIERS	GROCKLES	GUIPURE
GILBERTS	GLIDDERY	GODSHIP	GRACKLES	GRAZING	GROGRAM	GUIPURES
GILDING	GLIDING	GODSHIPS	GRADATE	GRAZINGS	GROGRAMS	GUISARD
GILDINGS	GLIDINGS	GODWARD	GRADATED	GREASER	GROMMET	GUISARDS
GILLION	GLIMMER	GODWARDS	GRADATES	GREASERS	GROMMETS	GUISING
GILLIONS	AGLIMMER	GOGGLER	GRADDAN	GREATEN	GROSERT	AGUISING
GILTCUP	GLIMMERS	GOGGLERS	GRADDANS	GREATENS	GROSERTS	GUMBOIL
GILTCUPS	GLIMMERY	GOLDEYE	GRADINE	GRECIAN	GROSSES	GUMBOILS
GIMMICK	GLIMPSE	GOLDEYES	GRADINES	GRECIANS	GROSSEST	GUMBOOT
GIMMICKS	GLIMPSED	GOLFING	GRADUAL	GRECQUE	GROUPER	GUMBOOTS
GIMMICKY	GLIMPSES	GOLFINGS	GRADUALS	GRECQUES	GROUPERS	GUMDROP
GINGALL	GLISTEN	GOLIARD	GRAFTER	GREEING	GROUPIE	GUMDROPS
GINGALLS	GLISTENS	GOLIARDS	GRAFTERS	AGREEING	GROUPIES	GUMMING
GINGHAM	GLISTER	GOLIARDY	GRAINER	GREENER	GROUSER	GUMMINGS
GINGHAMS	GLISTERS	GOLLAND	GRAINERS	GREENERY	GROUSERS	GUMMITE
GINGILI	GLITTER	GOLLANDS	GRAMARY	GREENTH	GROWING	GUMMITES
GINGILIS	AGLITTER	GOMBEEN	GRAMARYE	GREENTHS	GROWINGS	GUMSHOE
GINNERS	GLITTERS	GOMBEENS	GRAMMAR	GREGALE	GROWLER	GUMSHOED
AGINNERS	GLITTERY	GOMERAL	GRAMMARS	GREGALES	GROWLERS	GUMSHOES
GINSENG	GLOBATE	GOMERALS	GRANDAD	GREISEN	GROWLERY	GUNBOAT
GINSENGS	GLOBATED	GOMERIL	GRANDADS	GREISENS	GRUBBER	GUNBOATS
GINSHOP	GLOBOID	GOMERILS	GRANDAM	GREMIAL	GRUBBERS	GUNFIRE
GINSHOPS	GLOBOIDS	GONDOLA	GRANDAMS	GREMIALS	GRUBBLE	GUNFIRES
GIRAFFE	GLOBOSE	GONDOLAS	GRANDEE	GREMLIN	GRUBBLED	GUNNAGE
GIRAFFES	GLOBOSES	GONIDIA	GRANDEES	GREMLINS	GRUBBLES	GUNNAGES
GIRASOL	GLOBULE	GONIDIAL	GRANDMA	GRENADE	GRUMBLE	GUNNERA
GIRASOLE	GLOBULES	GOODIES	GRANDMAS	GRENADES	GRUMBLED	GUNNERAS
GIRASOLS	GLOBULET	GOODIEST	GRANDPA	GREYHEN	GRUMBLER	GUNNING
GIRDING	GLONOIN	GOOSIES	GRANDPAS	GREYHENS	GRUMBLES	GUNNINGS
GIRDINGS	GLONOINS	GOOSIEST	GRANFER	GRIBBLE	GRUMMET	GUNPLAY
GIRDLER	GLOSSER	GOPURAM	GRANFERS	GRIBBLES	GRUMMETS	GUNPLAYS
GIRDLERS	GLOSSERS	GOPURAMS	GRANGER	GRICING	GRUNION	GUNPORT
GIRLOND	GLOZING	GORCOCK	GRANGERS	GRICINGS	GRUNIONS	GUNPORTS
GIRLONDS	GLOZINGS	GORCOCKS	GRANITE	GRIDDLE	GRUNTER	GUNROOM
GIROSOL	GLUCINA	GORCROW	GRANITES	GRIDDLES	GRUNTERS	GUNROOMS
GIROSOLS	GLUCINAS	GORCROWS	GRANNAM	GRIEVER	GRUNTLE	GUNSHIP
GISARME	GLUCOSE	GORILLA	GRANNAMS	GRIEVERS	GRUNTLED	GUNSHIPS
GISARMES	GLUCOSES	GORILLAS	GRANNIE	GRIFFIN	GRUNTLES	GUNSHOT
GITTERN	GLUTTON	GORMAND	GRANNIES	GRIFFINS	GRYPHON	GUNSHOTS
GITTERNS	GLUTTONS	GORMANDS	GRANTEE	GRIFFON	GRYPHONS	GUNWALE
GIZZARD	GLUTTONY	GORSEDD	GRANTEES	GRIFFONS	GRYSBOK	GUNWALES
GIZZARDS	GLYCINE	GORSEDDS	GRANTER	GRIFTER	GRYSBOKS	GURNARD
GLACIAL	GLYCINES	GORSOON	GRANTERS	GRIFTERS	GUANACO	GURNARDS
GLACIALS	GLYCOSE	GORSOONS	GRANTOR	GRIMACE	GUANACOS	GURUDOM
GLACIER	GLYCOSES	GOSHAWK	GRANTORS	GRIMACED	GUANINE	GURUDOMS

GURUISM	HAIRING	HANDJARS	HAROSET	CHAUNTER	HEAVIES	HERBAGE
GURUISMS	CHAIRING	HANDLER	CHAROSET	HAUNTERS	HEAVIEST	HERBAGED
GUTCHER	HAIRPIN	CHANDLER	HAROSETH	HAUTBOY	HEAVING	HERBAGES
GUTCHERS	HAIRPINS	HANDLERS	HAROSETS	HAUTBOYS	SHEAVING	HERBIST
GUTTATE	HALAVAH	HANDLES	HARPERS	HAUTEUR	HEAVINGS	HERBISTS
GUTTATED	HALAVAHS	HANDLESS	SHARPERS	HAUTEURS	HEBENON	HERBLET
GUTTATES	HALBERD	HANDOUT	HARPIES	HAVEOUR	HEBENONS	HERBLETS
GUZZLER	HALBERDS	HANDOUTS	CHARPIES	HAVEOURS	HECKLER	HERDBOY
GUZZLERS	HALBERT	HANDSAW	SHARPIES	HAVEREL	HECKLERS	HERDBOYS
GWINIAD	HALBERTS	HANDSAWS	HARPING	HAVERELS	HECTARE	HERETIC
GWINIADS	HALCYON	HANDSEL	SHARPING	HAVINGS	HECTARES	HERETICS
GWYNIAD	HALCYONS	HANDSELS	HARPINGS	SHAVINGS	HEDGING	HERITOR
GWYNIADS	HALFLIN	HANDSET	HARPIST	HAVIOUR	HEDGINGS	HERITORS
GYMNAST	HALFLING	HANDSETS	HARPISTS	HAVIOURS	HEDONIC	HERLING
GYMNASTS	HALFLINS	HANGDOG	HARPOON	HAWBUCK	HEDONICS	HERLINGS
GYROCAR	HALIBUT	HANGDOGS	HARPOONS	HAWBUCKS	HEELERS	HEROINE
GYROCARS	HALIBUTS	HANGERS	HARRIER	HAWKBIT	WHEELERS	HEROINES
HABITAT	HALIDOM	CHANGERS	HARRIERS	HAWKBITS	HEELING	HEROISE
HABITATS	HALIDOMS	HANGING	HARRIES	HAWKING	SHEELING	HEROISED
HABITUE	HALIMOT	CHANGING	GHARRIES	HAWKINGS	WHEELING	HEROISES
HABITUES	HALIMOTE	PHANGING	HARSHEN	HAYBAND	HEELINGS	HEROISM
HACHURE	HALIMOTS	WHANGING	HARSHENS	HAYBANDS	HEEZING	HEROISMS
HACHURED	HALLALI	HANGINGS	HARSLET	HAYCOCK	PHEEZING	HEROIZE
HACHURES	HALLALIS	HANGOUT	HARSLETS	HAYCOCKS	WHEEZING	HEROIZED
HACKBUT	HALLANS	HANGOUTS	HARVEST	HAYFORK	HEIRDOM	HEROIZES
HACKBUTS	CHALLANS	HANJARS	HARVESTS	HAYFORKS	HEIRDOMS	HERRIED
HACKERS	HALLIAN	KHANJARS	HASSOCK	HAYLOFT	HEISTER	CHERRIED
WHACKERS	HALLIANS	HANKERS	HASSOCKS	HAYLOFTS	HEISTERS	HERRIES
HACKING	HALLING	THANKERS	HASSOCKY	HAYRICK	HELIPAD	CHERRIES
CHACKING	HALLINGS	HANKING	HASTATE	HAYRICKS	HELIPADS	SHERRIES
WHACKING	HALLION	SHANKING	HASTATED	HAYSEED	HELLERS	WHERRIES
HACKINGS	HALLIONS	THANKING	HASTENS	HAYSEEDS	SHELLERS	HERRING
HACKLED	HALLOWS	HANUMAN	CHASTENS	HAYWARD	HELLIER	HERRINGS
SHACKLED	SHALLOWS	HANUMANS	HASTING	HAYWARDS	SHELLIER	HERSALL
HACKLER	HALLWAY	HAPLESS	GHASTING	HAYWIRE	HELLIERS	HERSALLS
HACKLERS	HALLWAYS	CHAPLESS	HASTINGS	HAYWIRES	HELLING	HERSHIP
HACKLES	HALLYON	HAPLOID	HATBAND	HEADING	SHELLING	HERSHIPS
SHACKLES	HALLYONS	HAPLOIDY	HATBANDS	SHEADING	HELLION	HESSIAN
HACKLET	HALOGEN	HAPPIER	HATCHED	HEADINGS	HELLIONS	HESSIANS
HACKLETS	HALOGENS	CHAPPIER	THATCHED	HEADRIG	HELMING	HETAERA
HACKNEY	HALTING	HAPPIES	HATCHEL	HEADRIGS	WHELMING	HETAERAE
HACKNEYS	HALTINGS	CHAPPIES	HATCHELS	HEADSET	HELPING	HETAERAS
HADDOCK	HALYARD	HAPPIEST	HATCHER	HEADSETS	WHELPING	HETAIRA
SHADDOCK	HALYARDS	HAPPING	THATCHER	HEADWAY	HELPINGS	HETAIRAI
HADDOCKS	HAMBLED	CHAPPING	HATCHERS	HEADWAYS	HELVING	HEUREKA
HADROME	SHAMBLED	WHAPPING	HATCHERY	HEALING	SHELVING	HEUREKAS
HADROMES	HAMBLES	HARBOUR	HATCHES	SHEALING	HEMIOLA	HEURISM
HAFFLIN	SHAMBLES	HARBOURS	THATCHES	HEALINGS	HEMIOLAS	HEURISMS
HAFFLINS	HAMLETS	HARDOKE	HATCHET	HEARERS	HEMIONE	HEXAGON
HAFNIUM	CHAMLETS	HARDOKES	HATCHETS	SHEARERS	HEMIONES	HEXAGONS
HAFNIUMS	HAMMERS	HARDTOP	HATCHETY	HEARING	HEMLOCK	HEXAPLA
HAFTING	SHAMMERS	HARDTOPS	HATRACK	HEARINGS	HEMLOCKS	HEXAPLAR
SHAFTING	HAMMING	HARICOT	HATRACKS	SHEARING	HEMPIES	HEXAPLAS
HAGBOLT	SHAMMING	HARICOTS	HATTERS	HEARKEN	HEMPIEST	HEXAPOD
HAGBOLTS	WHAMMING	HARKING	CHATTERS	HEARKENS	HENBANE	HEXAPODS
HAGDOWN	HAMMOCK	CHARKING	SHATTERS	HEARSAY	HENBANES	HEXAPODY
HAGDOWNS	HAMMOCKS	SHARKING	HATTING	HEARSAYS	HENDING	HEYDUCK
HAGGARD	HAMPERS	HARLING	CHATTING	HEARTEN	SHENDING	HEYDUCKS
HAGGARDS	CHAMPERS	HARLINGS	HATTINGS	HEARTENS	HENNIES	HIBACHI
HAGGING	HAMSTER	HARMALA	HATTOCK	HEATERS	HENNIEST	HIBACHIS
SHAGGING	HAMSTERS	HARMALAS	HATTOCKS	CHEATERS	HENPECK	HICATEE
HAGGLER	HANAPER	HARMFUL	HAUBERK	THEATERS	HENPECKS	HICATEES
HAGGLERS	HANAPERS	CHARMFUL	HAUBERKS	HEATHEN	HEPARIN	HIDALGA
HAHNIUM	HANDBAG	HARMINE	HAULAGE	HEATHENS	HEPARINS	HIDALGAS
HAHNIUMS	HANDBAGS	HARMINES	HAULAGES	HEATHER	HEPATIC	HIDALGO
HAINING	HANDCAR	HARMING	HAULIER	HEATHERS	HEPATICS	HIDALGOS
CHAINING	HANDCARS	CHARMING	HAULIERS	HEATHERY	HEPSTER	HIDDERS
HAININGS	HANDFUL	HARMOST	HAUNTED	HEATING	HEPSTERS	SHIDDERS
HAIRCUT	HANDFULS	HARMOSTS	CHAUNTED	CHEATING	HEPTANE	WHIDDERS
HAIRCUTS	HANDJAR	HARMOSTY	HAUNTER	HEATINGS	HEPTANES	HIDEOUT

HIDEOUTS	CHITTERS	**HOMOLOG**	HORNINGS	HUNKIEST	HYPOXIAS	IMAGINER
HIDINGS	WHITTERS	HOMOLOGS	**HORNIST**	**HUNTERS**	**IAMBIST**	IMAGINES
CHIDINGS	**HITTING**	HOMOLOGY	HORNISTS	CHUNTERS	IAMBISTS	**IMAGING**
HIDLING	CHITTING	**HOMONYM**	**HORNITO**	SHUNTERS	**ICEBERG**	IMAGINGS
HIDLINGS	SHITTING	HOMONYMS	HORNITOS	**HUNTING**	ICEBERGS	**IMAGISM**
HIGGLER	**HIZZING**	HOMONYMY	**HORNLET**	SHUNTING	**ICEPACK**	IMAGISMS
HIGGLERS	WHIZZING	**HONEYED**	HORNLETS	HUNTINGS	ICEPACKS	**IMAGIST**
HIGHBOY	**HOARDER**	PHONEYED	**HORSING**	**HURDLER**	**ICHNITE**	IMAGISTS
HIGHBOYS	HOARDERS	**HOODLUM**	HORSINGS	HURDLERS	ICHNITES	**IMAMATE**
HIGHWAY	**HOARSEN**	HOODLUMS	**HOSANNA**	**HURLING**	**ICKIEST**	IMAMATES
HIGHWAYS	HOARSENS	**HOOFROT**	HOSANNAS	HURLINGS	DICKIEST	**IMBATHE**
HILDING	**HOATZIN**	HOOFROTS	**HOSPICE**	**HURRIES**	PICKIEST	IMBATHED
CHILDING	HOATZINS	**HOOKIES**	HOSPICES	DHURRIES	**ICONISE**	IMBATHES
HILDINGS	**HOBBLER**	CHOOKIES	**HOSTAGE**	**HURTLES**	ICONISED	**IMBIBER**
HILLIER	HOBBLERS	HOOKIEST	HOSTAGES	HURTLESS	ICONISES	IMBIBERS
CHILLIER	**HOBNAIL**	**HOOLOCK**	**HOSTING**	**HUSBAND**	**ICONIZE**	**IMBOSOM**
HILLING	HOBNAILS	HOOLOCKS	GHOSTING	HUSBANDS	ICONIZED	IMBOSOMS
CHILLING	**HOBODOM**	**HOOPERS**	HOSTINGS	**HUSHING**	ICONIZES	**IMBOWER**
SHILLING	HOBODOMS	WHOOPERS	**HOSTLER**	SHUSHING	**ICTERIC**	IMBOWERS
HILLOCK	**HOBOISM**	**HOOPING**	HOSTLERS	**HUSKIES**	ICTERICS	**IMBROWN**
HILLOCKS	HOBOISMS	WHOOPING	**HOTHEAD**	HUSKIEST	**ICTUSES**	IMBROWNS
HILLOCKY	**HOCKERS**	**HOOSGOW**	HOTHEADS	**HUSKING**	RICTUSES	**IMBRUTE**
HILLTOP	SHOCKERS	HOOSGOWS	**HOTSHOT**	HUSKINGS	**IDLESSE**	IMBRUTED
HILLTOPS	**HOCKING**	**HOOSHED**	HOTSHOTS	**HUSTLER**	IDLESSES	IMBRUTES
HINDLEG	CHOCKING	WHOOSHED	**HOTTING**	HUSTLERS	**IDOLISE**	**IMBURSE**
HINDLEGS	SHOCKING	**HOOSHES**	HOTTINGS	**HUTMENT**	IDOLISED	IMBURSED
HINNIED	**HOEDOWN**	WHOOSHES	**HOUSING**	HUTMENTS	IDOLISER	IMBURSES
SHINNIED	HOEDOWNS	**HOOTERS**	CHOUSING	**HUTTING**	IDOLISES	**IMITANT**
WHINNIED	**HOGBACK**	SHOOTERS	HOUSINGS	SHUTTING	**IDOLISM**	IMITANTS
HINNIES	HOGBACKS	**HOOTING**	**HOWLING**	HUTTINGS	IDOLISMS	**IMITATE**
SHINNIES	**HOGGING**	SHOOTING	HOWLINGS	**HYACINE**	**IDOLIST**	IMITATED
WHINNIES	SHOGGING	WHOOTING	**HUANACO**	HYACINES	IDOLISTS	IMITATES
HIPPIER	HOGGINGS	**HOPBIND**	HUANACOS	**HYALINE**	**IDOLIZE**	**IMMENSE**
CHIPPIER	**HOGHOOD**	HOPBINDS	**HUCKLES**	HYALINES	IDOLIZED	IMMENSER
WHIPPIER	HOGHOODS	**HOPBINE**	CHUCKLES	**HYALITE**	IDOLIZER	**IMMERGE**
HIPPIES	**HOGWARD**	HOPBINES	**HUFFIER**	HYALITES	IDOLIZES	IMMERGED
CHIPPIES	HOGWARDS	**HOPEFUL**	CHUFFIER	**HYDATID**	**IFFIEST**	IMMERGES
HIPPIEST	**HOGWEED**	HOPEFULS	**HUFFKIN**	HYDATIDS	MIFFIEST	**IMMERSE**
HIPPING	HOGWEEDS	**HOPLITE**	HUFFKINS	**HYDRANT**	NIFFIEST	IMMERSED
CHIPPING	**HOISTER**	HOPLITES	**HUGGING**	HYDRANTH	**IGARAPE**	IMMERSES
SHIPPING	HOISTERS	**HOPPERS**	CHUGGING	HYDRANTS	IGARAPES	**IMPAINT**
WHIPPING	**HOKIEST**	CHOPPERS	**HUITAIN**	**HYDRATE**	**IGNEOUS**	IMPAINTS
HIPPINGS	CHOKIEST	SHOPPERS	HUITAINS	HYDRATED	LIGNEOUS	**IMPANEL**
HIPSTER	**HOLDING**	WHOPPERS	**HUMBLES**	HYDRATES	**IGNITER**	IMPANELS
WHIPSTER	HOLDINGS	**HOPPIER**	HUMBLEST	**HYDRIDE**	IGNITERS	**IMPASSE**
HIPSTERS	**HOLESOM**	CHOPPIER	**HUMDRUM**	HYDRIDES	**IGNITES**	IMPASSES
HIRLING	HOLESOME	SHOPPIER	HUMDRUMS	**HYDROID**	LIGNITES	**IMPASTE**
CHIRLING	**HOLIBUT**	**HOPPING**	**HUMERAL**	HYDROIDS	**IGNOBLE**	IMPASTED
THIRLING	HOLIBUTS	CHOPPING	HUMERALS	**HYDROXY**	IGNOBLED	IMPASTES
WHIRLING	**HOLIDAY**	SHOPPING	**HUMIDOR**	HYDROXYL	IGNOBLER	**IMPASTO**
HIRLINGS	HOLIDAYS	WHOPPING	HUMIDORS	**HYGIENE**	IGNOBLES	IMPASTOS
HIRUDIN	**HOLISMS**	HOPPINGS	**HUMMAUM**	HYGIENES	**IGNORER**	**IMPEARL**
HIRUDINS	WHOLISMS	**HOPSACK**	HUMMAUMS	**HYLDING**	IGNORERS	IMPEARLS
HISHING	**HOLLAND**	HOPSACKS	**HUMMING**	HYLDINGS	**IGNORES**	**IMPERIL**
WHISHING	HOLLANDS	**HORDEIN**	HUMMINGS	**HYLOIST**	SIGNORES	IMPERILS
HISSING	**HOLMIUM**	HORDEINS	CHUMMING	HYLOISTS	**IGUANID**	**IMPINGE**
WHISSING	HOLMIUMS	**HORDOCK**	**HUMMOCK**	**HYMENIA**	IGUANIDS	IMPINGED
HISSINGS	**HOLSTER**	HORDOCKS	HUMMOCKS	HYMENIAL	**IKEBANA**	IMPINGES
HISTING	HOLSTERS	**HORIZON**	HUMMOCKY	**HYMNIST**	IKEBANAS	**IMPLANT**
WHISTING	**HOLYDAM**	HORIZONS	**HUMOGEN**	HYMNISTS	**ILKADAY**	IMPLANTS
HISTONE	HOLYDAME	**HORMONE**	HUMOGENS	**HYPERON**	ILKADAYS	**IMPLATE**
HISTONES	HOLYDAMS	HORMONES	**HUMPIES**	HYPERONS	**ILLAPSE**	IMPLATED
HISTRIO	**HOMAGER**	**HORNBUG**	HUMPIEST	**HYPNONE**	ILLAPSED	IMPLATES
HISTRION	HOMAGERS	HORNBUGS	**HUMPING**	HYPNONES	ILLAPSES	**IMPLEAD**
HISTRIOS	**HOMELYN**	**HORNFUL**	THUMPING	**HYPOGEA**	**ILLITES**	IMPLEADS
HITCHER	HOMELYNS	HORNFULS	**HUNDRED**	HYPOGEAL	TILLITES	**IMPLETE**
HITCHERS	**HOMINID**	**HORNIER**	HUNDREDS	HYPOGEAN	**ILLOGIC**	IMPLETED
HITHERS	HOMINIDS	THORNIER	**HUNKIER**	**HYPONYM**	ILLOGICS	IMPLETES
WHITHERS	**HOMMOCK**	**HORNING**	CHUNKIER	HYPONYMS	**IMAGINE**	**IMPLODE**
HITTERS	HOMMOCKS	THORNING	**HUNKIES**	**HYPOXIA**	IMAGINED	IMPLODED

IMPLODES	INCLOSES	INFORCED	TINNINGS	**INTERIM**	VIRIDIAN	HITCHIER
IMPLORE	**INCLUDE**	INFORCES	WINNINGS	INTERIMS	**IRIDISE**	PITCHIER
IMPLORED	INCLUDED	**INFRACT**	**INNYARD**	**INTERNE**	IRIDISED	**ITCHING**
IMPLORER	INCLUDES	INFRACTS	INNYARDS	INTERNED	IRIDISES	BITCHING
IMPLORES	**INCOMER**	**INFUSER**	**INQILAB**	INTERNEE	**IRIDIUM**	DITCHING
IMPOSER	INCOMERS	INFUSERS	INQILABS	INTERNES	IRIDIUMS	HITCHING
IMPOSERS	**INCONNU**	**INGENER**	**INQUERE**	**INTHRAL**	**IRIDIZE**	MITCHING
IMPOUND	INCONNUE	INGENERS	INQUERED	INTHRALL	IRIDIZED	PITCHING
IMPOUNDS	INCONNUS	**INGENUE**	INQUERES	INTHRALS	IRIDIZES	WITCHING
IMPREGN	**INCRUST**	INGENUES	**INQUEST**	**INTONER**	**IRISATE**	**ITEMISE**
IMPREGNS	INCRUSTS	**INGLOBE**	INQUESTS	INTONERS	IRISATED	ITEMISED
IMPRESA	**INCURVE**	INGLOBED	**INQUIET**	**INTRANT**	IRISATES	ITEMISES
IMPRESAS	INCURVED	INGLOBES	INQUIETS	INTRANTS	**IRKSOME**	**ITEMIZE**
IMPRESE	INCURVES	**INGOING**	**INQUIRE**	**INTREAT**	MIRKSOME	ITEMIZED
IMPRESES	**INDEXER**	INGOINGS	INQUIRED	INTREATS	**IRONING**	ITEMIZES
IMPRESS	INDEXERS	**INGRAFT**	INQUIRER	**INTROIT**	IRONINGS	**ITERATE**
IMPRESSE	**INDICAN**	INGRAFTS	INQUIRES	INTROITS	**IRONISE**	LITERATE
IMPREST	INDICANS	**INGRAIN**	**INSANIE**	**INTRUDE**	IRONISED	ITERATED
IMPRESTS	INDICANT	INGRAINS	INSANIES	INTRUDED	IRONISES	ITERATES
IMPRINT	**INDIGOS**	**INGRATE**	**INSCAPE**	INTRUDER	**IRONIST**	**IVORIST**
IMPRINTS	WINDIGOS	INGRATES	INSCAPES	INTRUDES	IRONISTS	IVORISTS
IMPROVE	**INDITER**	**INGROUP**	**INSCULP**	**INTRUST**	**IRONIZE**	**IVRESSE**
IMPROVED	INDITERS	INGROUPS	INSCULPS	INTRUSTS	IRONIZED	IVRESSES
IMPROVER	**INDORSE**	**INGULPH**	INSCULPT	**INTWINE**	IRONIZES	**IZZARDS**
IMPROVES	INDORSED	INGULPHS	**INSHELL**	INTWINED	**ISAGOGE**	DIZZARDS
IMPULSE	INDORSES	**INHABIT**	INSHELLS	INTWINES	ISAGOGES	GIZZARDS
IMPULSES	**INDRAFT**	INHABITS	**INSHIPS**	**INTWIST**	**ISATINE**	**JACAMAR**
IMPUTER	INDRAFTS	**INHALER**	KINSHIPS	INTWISTS	ISATINES	JACAMARS
IMPUTERS	**INDUCER**	INHALERS	**INSIDER**	**INULASE**	**ISOBARE**	**JACINTH**
INBEING	INDUCERS	**INHAUST**	INSIDERS	INULASES	ISOBARES	JACINTHS
INBEINGS	**INDULGE**	INHAUSTS	**INSIGHT**	**INVADER**	**ISOBASE**	**JACKDAW**
INBREAK	INDULGED	**INHERCE**	INSIGHTS	INVADERS	ISOBASES	JACKDAWS
INBREAKS	INDULGER	INHERCED	**INSIGNE**	**INVALID**	**ISOBATH**	**JACKPOT**
INBREED	INDULGES	INHERCES	INSIGNES	INVALIDS	ISOBATHS	JACKPOTS
INBREEDS	**INDUSIA**	**INHERIT**	**INSINEW**	**INVEIGH**	**ISOCHOR**	**JACKSIE**
INBRING	INDUSIAL	INHERITS	INSINEWS	INVEIGHS	ISOCHORE	JACKSIES
INBRINGS	**INDWELL**	**INHIBIT**	**INSNARE**	**INVERSE**	ISOCHORS	**JACONET**
INBURST	INDWELLS	INHIBITS	INSNARED	INVERSED	**ISODONT**	JACONETS
INBURSTS	**INEARTH**	**INHUMAN**	INSNARES	INVERSES	ISODONTS	**JACUZZI**
INCASES	INEARTHS	INHUMANE	**INSPECT**	**INVITEE**	**ISOGAMY**	JACUZZIS
PINCASES	**INERTIA**	**INITIAL**	INSPECTS	INVITEES	MISOGAMY	**JADEITE**
INCENSE	INERTIAL	INITIALS	**INSPIRE**	**INVITER**	**ISOGRAM**	JADEITES
INCENSED	INERTIAS	**INJOINT**	INSPIRED	INVITERS	ISOGRAMS	**JAGHIRE**
INCENSER	**INFANTA**	INJOINTS	INSPIRER	**INVOICE**	**ISOHYET**	JAGHIRES
INCENSES	INFANTAS	**INJUNCT**	INSPIRES	INVOICED	ISOHYETS	**JALAPIN**
INCHASE	**INFANTE**	**INJURER**	**INSPYRE**	INVOICES	**ISOKONT**	JALAPINS
INCHASED	INFANTED	INJURERS	INSPYRED	**INVOLVE**	ISOKONTS	**JALOUSE**
INCHASES	INFANTES	**INKHORN**	INSPYRES	INVOLVED	**ISOLATE**	JALOUSED
INCHING	**INFARCT**	INKHORNS	**INSTALL**	INVOLVES	ISOLATED	JALOUSES
CINCHING	INFARCTS	**INKIEST**	INSTALLS	**INWEAVE**	ISOLATES	**JAMADAR**
PINCHING	**INFERNO**	DINKIEST	**INSTANT**	INWEAVES	**ISOLINE**	JAMADARS
WINCHING	INFERNOS	KINKIEST	INSTANTS	**IODURET**	ISOLINES	**JAMBEAU**
INCHPIN	**INFIDEL**	PINKIEST	**INSTATE**	IODURETS	**ISOMERE**	JAMBEAUX
LINCHPIN	INFIDELS	SINKIEST	INSTATED	**IONISED**	ISOMERES	**JAMBIER**
INCHPINS	**INFIELD**	ZINKIEST	INSTATES	LIONISED	**ISOSPIN**	JAMBIERS
INCISOR	INFIELDS	**INKLING**	**INSTILL**	**IONISER**	ISOSPINS	**JAMBIYA**
INCISORS	**INFLAME**	TINKLING	INSTILLS	IONISES	**ISOTONE**	JAMBIYAH
INCISORY	INFLAMED	INKLINGS	**INSULIN**	LIONISES	ISOTONES	JAMBIYAS
INCITER	INFLAMER	**INKSPOT**	INSULINS	**IONIZED**	**ISOTOPE**	**JAMBOKS**
INCITERS	INFLAMES	INKSPOTS	**INSURER**	LIONIZED	ISOTOPES	SJAMBOKS
INCITES	**INFLATE**	**INKWELL**	INSURERS	**IONIZER**	**ISOTRON**	**JAMBONE**
ZINCITES	INFLATED	INKWELLS	**INSWING**	IONIZERS	ISOTRONS	JAMBONES
INCLASP	INFLATES	**INLAYER**	INSWINGS	IONIZES	**ISOTYPE**	**JAMBOOL**
INCLASPS	**INFLECT**	INLAYERS	**INTARSI**	LIONIZES	ISOTYPES	JAMBOOLS
INCLINE	INFLECTS	**INNERVE**	INTARSIA	**IONOMER**	**ISSUING**	**JAMDANI**
INCLINED	**INFLICT**	INNERVED	INTARSIO	IONOMERS	TISSUING	JAMDANIS
INCLINES	INFLICTS	INNERVES	**INTEGER**	**IPOMOEA**	**ITACISM**	**JAMPANI**
INCLOSE	**INFOLDS**	**INNINGS**	INTEGERS	IPOMOEAS	ITACISMS	JAMPANIS
INCLOSED	PINFOLDS	PINNINGS	**INTENSE**	**IRIDIAN**	**ITCHIER**	**JANGLER**
INCLOSER	**INFORCE**		INTENSER		BITCHIER	JANGLERS

JANITOR	JIGGING	KACHINAS	KERATINS	KILOBITS	KNAPPLED	LACINIAE
JANITORS	JIGGINGS	KAGOULE	KERMESS	KILOTON	KNAPPLES	LACKERS
JANIZAR	JINGLER	KAGOULES	KERMESSE	KILOTONS	KNEADER	CLACKERS
JANIZARS	JINGLERS	KAINITE	KERNITE	KIMMERS	KNEADERS	FLACKERS
JANIZARY	JINGLET	KAINITES	KERNITES	SKIMMERS	KNEELER	SLACKERS
JANNOCK	JINGLETS	KAJAWAH	KEROGEN	KIMONOS	KNEELERS	LACKING
JANNOCKS	JINJILI	KAJAWAHS	KEROGENS	OKIMONOS	KNEVELL	BLACKING
JANTIES	JINJILIS	KAKODYL	KERYGMA	KINCHIN	KNEVELLS	CLACKING
JANTIEST	JOBBING	KAKODYLS	KERYGMAS	KINCHINS	KNICKER	SLACKING
JARGOON	JOBBINGS	KAMERAD	KESTREL	KINDLER	KNICKERS	LACQUER
JARGOONS	JOGGING	KAMERADS	KESTRELS	KINDLERS	KNIFING	LACQUERS
JARRING	JOGGINGS	KAMICHI	KETCHES	KINDLES	KNIFINGS	LACQUEY
JARRINGS	JOGTROT	KAMICHIS	SKETCHES	KINDLESS	KNITTER	LACQUEYS
JASMINE	JOGTROTS	KAMPONG	KETCHUP	KINDRED	KNITTERS	LACTASE
JASMINES	JOHNNIE	KAMPONGS	KETCHUPS	KINDREDS	KNITTLE	LACTASES
JAUNTIE	JOHNNIES	KAMSEEN	KEYHOLE	KINESES	KNITTLES	LACTATE
JAUNTIER	JOINDER	KAMSEENS	KEYHOLES	AKINESES	KNOBBER	LACTATED
JAUNTIES	JOINDERS	KANTELA	KEYNOTE	KINESIS	KNOBBERS	LACTATES
JAVELIN	JOINING	KANTELAS	KEYNOTED	AKINESIS	KNOBBLE	LACTEAL
JAVELINS	JOININGS	KANTELE	KEYNOTES	KINETIC	KNOBBLED	LACTEALS
JAWBONE	JOINTER	KANTELES	KHADDAR	KINETICS	KNOBBLES	LACTONE
JAWBONED	JOINTERS	KAOLINE	KHADDARS	KINFOLK	KNOCKER	LACTONES
JAWBONES	JOLLIES	KAOLINES	KHALIFA	KINFOLKS	KNOCKERS	LACTOSE
JAWFALL	JOLLIEST	KARAISM	KHALIFAH	KINGCUP	KNOTTER	LACTOSES
JAWFALLS	JONQUIL	KARAISMS	KHALIFAS	KINGCUPS	KNOTTERS	LACUNAR
JAWHOLE	JONQUILS	KARAKUL	KHALIFAT	KINGDOM	KNUBBLE	LACUNARS
JAWHOLES	JOTTING	KARAKULS	KHAMSIN	KINGDOMS	KNUBBLED	LACUNARY
JAYWALK	JOTTINGS	KARTING	KHAMSINS	KINGLES	KNUBBLES	LADANUM
JAYWALKS	JOURNAL	KARTINGS	KHANATE	KINGLESS	KNUCKLE	LADANUMS
JEALOUS	JOURNALS	KASHMIR	KHANATES	KINGLET	KNUCKLED	LADDERS
JEALOUSE	JOURNEY	KASHMIRS	KHANJAR	KINGLETS	KNUCKLES	BLADDERS
JEALOUSY	JOURNEYS	KATHODE	KHANJARS	KINKING	KOFTGAR	CLADDERS
JEEPNEY	JOUSTER	KATHODES	KHEDIVA	SKINKING	KOFTGARI	LADDERY
JEEPNEYS	JOUSTERS	KATORGA	KHEDIVAL	KINLESS	KOFTGARS	BLADDERY
JEERING	JOYANCE	KATORGAS	KHEDIVAS	SKINLESS	KREMLIN	LADDIES
JEERINGS	JOYANCES	KATYDID	KHEDIVE	KINSHIP	KREMLINS	GLADDIES
JELLABA	JUBILEE	KATYDIDS	KHEDIVES	KINSHIPS	KRIMMER	LADRONE
DJELLABA	JUBILEES	KEBBOCK	KHOTBAH	KIPPAGE	KRIMMERS	LADRONES
JELLABAS	JUDOIST	KEBBOCKS	KHOTBAHS	KIPPAGES	KRYPTON	LADYBUG
JEMADAR	JUDOISTS	KEBBUCK	KHOTBEH	KIPPERS	KRYPTONS	LADYBUGS
JEMADARS	JUGGLER	KEBBUCKS	KHOTBEHS	SKIPPERS	KUFFIAH	LADYCOW
JEMIDAR	JUGGLERS	KEELAGE	KHUTBAH	KIPPING	KUFFIAHS	LADYCOWS
JEMIDARS	JUGGLERY	KEELAGES	KHUTBAHS	SKIPPING	KUFFIEH	LADYISM
JEMMIES	JUGULAR	KEELING	KIBITKA	KIRIMON	KUFFIEHS	LADYISMS
JEMMIEST	JUGULARS	KEELINGS	KIBITKAS	KIRIMONS	KUFIYAH	LADYKIN
JEOFAIL	JUMBLER	KEELSON	KIDDIER	KIRKING	KUFIYAHS	LADYKINS
JEOFAILS	JUMBLERS	KEELSONS	KIDDIERS	KIRKINGS	KUMQUAT	LAETARE
JEOPARD	JUMBUCK	KEENING	KIDDING	KIRKTON	KUMQUATS	LAETARES
JEOPARDS	JUMBUCKS	KEENINGS	SKIDDING	KIRKTONS	KURSAAL	LAGGARD
JEOPARDY	JUMELLE	KEEPING	KIDLING	KITCHEN	KURSAALS	LAGGARDS
JERKIES	JUMELLES	KEEPINGS	KIDLINGS	KITCHENS	KYANISE	LAGGING
JERKIEST	JUNCATE	KEEPNET	KIKUMON	KITHARA	KYANISED	BLAGGING
JERKING	JUNCATES	KEEPNETS	KIKUMONS	KITHARAS	KYANISES	CLAGGING
JERKINGS	JUNIPER	KEITLOA	KILLCOW	KITLING	KYANITE	FLAGGING
JERQUER	JUNIPERS	KEITLOAS	KILLCOWS	KITLINGS	KYANITES	SLAGGING
JERQUERS	JUNKIES	KELLAUT	KILLDEE	KITTLED	KYANIZE	LAGGINGS
JESTING	JUNKIEST	KELLAUTS	KILLDEER	SKITTLED	KYANIZED	LAICISE
JESTINGS	JUSSIVE	KELLIES	KILLDEES	KITTLES	KYANIZES	LAICISED
JETFOIL	JUSSIVES	SKELLIES	KILLICK	SKITTLES	LABARUM	LAICISES
JETFOILS	JUSTICE	KELTERS	KILLICKS	KITTLEST	LABARUMS	LAICIZE
JETTIES	JUSTICER	SKELTERS	KILLING	KLAVIER	LABELLA	LAICIZED
JETTIEST	JUSTICES	KEMPING	SKILLING	KLAVIERS	FLABELLA	LAICIZES
JIBBAHS	JUVENAL	KEMPINGS	KILLINGS	KLINKER	GLABELLA	LAIDING
DJIBBAHS	JUVENALS	KENNING	KILLJOY	KLINKERS	LABIATE	PLAIDING
JIBBING	KABBALA	KENNINGS	KILLJOYS	KNACKER	LABIATES	LAIRAGE
JIBBINGS	KABBALAH	KEPPING	KILLOCK	KNACKERS	LABROID	LAIRAGES
JIGAJIG	KABBALAS	SKEPPING	KILLOCKS	KNACKERY	LABROIDS	LAIRIER
JIGAJIGS	KACHERI	KERAMIC	KILOBAR	KNAPPER	LACINGS	GLAIRIER
JIGAJOG	KACHERIS	KERAMICS	KILOBARS	KNAPPERS	PLACINGS	LAIRING
JIGAJOGS	KACHINA	KERATIN	KILOBIT	KNAPPLE	LACINIA	GLAIRING

LAIRISE	LANDLERS	LASHKAR	LAZARETS	LECTURER	BLENDING	SLICKING
LAIRISED	LANEWAY	LASHKARS	LAZIEST	LECTURES	LENDINGS	LICKINGS
LAIRISES	LANEWAYS	LASKETS	GLAZIEST	LECTURN	LENIENT	LIGGING
LAIRIZE	LANGAHA	FLASKETS	LEACHED	LECTURNS	LENIENTS	LIGGINGS
LAIRIZED	LANGAHAS	LASSOCK	BLEACHED	LEDGERS	LENTISK	LIGHTED
LAIRIZES	LANGREL	LASSOCKS	PLEACHED	PLEDGERS	LENTISKS	ALIGHTED
LAKELET	LANGRELS	LASTAGE	LEACHES	SLEDGERS	LEOPARD	BLIGHTED
LAKELETS	LANGUET	LASTAGES	BLEACHES	LEDGIER	LEOPARDS	FLIGHTED
LAKIEST	LANGUETS	LASTERS	PLEACHES	FLEDGIER	LEOTARD	PLIGHTED
FLAKIEST	LANGUOR	BLASTERS	LEADERS	LEECHED	LEOTARDS	SLIGHTED
LALLING	LANGUORS	PLASTERS	PLEADERS	FLEECHED	LEPTOME	LIGHTEN
LALLINGS	LANIARD	LASTING	LEADING	LEECHEE	LEPTOMES	LIGHTENS
LAMBAST	LANIARDS	BLASTING	PLEADING	LEECHEES	LESBIAN	LIGHTER
LAMBASTE	LANKEST	LASTINGS	LEADINGS	LEECHES	LESBIANS	BLIGHTER
LAMBASTS	BLANKEST	LATCHED	LEAFAGE	FLEECHES	LESSORS	PLIGHTER
LAMBERS	LANKING	CLATCHED	LEAFAGES	SLEECHES	PLESSORS	SLIGHTER
CLAMBERS	BLANKING	LATCHES	LEAFBUD	LEEPING	LETCHED	LIGHTERS
LAMBERT	CLANKING	CLATCHES	LEAFBUDS	BLEEPING	FLETCHED	LIGHTLY
LAMBERTS	FLANKING	LATCHET	LEAFLET	CLEEPING	LETCHES	SLIGHTLY
LAMBKIN	PLANKING	LATCHETS	LEAFLETS	SLEEPING	FLETCHES	LIGNAGE
LAMBKINS	LANNERS	LATENCE	LEAGUER	LEERING	LETTERN	LIGNAGES
LAMELLA	PLANNERS	LATENCES	LEAGUERS	FLEERING	LETTERNS	LIGNITE
LAMELLAE	LANOLIN	LATERAL	LEAKAGE	LEERINGS	LETTING	LIGNITES
LAMELLAR	LANOLINE	LATERALS	LEAKAGES	LEEWARD	BLETTING	LIGROIN
LAMETER	LANOLINS	LATHERS	LEAKIER	LEEWARDS	LETTINGS	LIGROINS
LAMETERS	LANTANA	BLATHERS	BLEAKIER	LEFTISM	LETTUCE	LIMACEL
LAMIGER	LANTANAS	SLATHERS	LEAMING	LEFTISMS	LETTUCES	LIMACELS
LAMIGERS	LANTERN	LATHING	GLEAMING	LEFTIST	LEUCINE	LIMACON
LAMINAR	LANTERNS	LATHINGS	LEANEST	LEFTISTS	LEUCINES	LIMACONS
LAMINARY	LANYARD	LATITAT	CLEANEST	LEGATEE	LEUCITE	LIMBECK
LAMITER	LANYARDS	LATITATS	LEANING	LEGATEES	LEUCITES	LIMBECKS
LAMITERS	LAPPERS	LATRINE	CLEANING	LEGATOR	LEUCOMA	LIMBERS
LAMMERS	CLAPPERS	LATRINES	GLEANING	LEGATORS	LEUCOMAS	CLIMBERS
SLAMMERS	FLAPPERS	LATTENS	LEANINGS	LEGGING	LEVATOR	LIMBING
LAMMING	SLAPPERS	FLATTENS	LEARIER	ALEGGING	ELEVATOR	BLIMBING
CLAMMING	LAPPING	LATTICE	BLEARIER	FLEGGING	LEVATORS	CLIMBING
FLAMMING	CLAPPING	LATTICED	LEARING	LEGGINGS	LEVERET	LIMEPIT
SLAMMING	FLAPPING	LATTICES	BLEARING	LEGGISM	LEVERETS	LIMEPITS
LAMMINGS	PLAPPING	LAUDING	CLEARING	LEGGISMS	LEXICON	LIMIEST
LAMPERN	SLAPPING	BLAUDING	LEARNER	LEGHORN	LEXICONS	SLIMIEST
LAMPERNS	LAPPINGS	LAUGHER	LEARNERS	LEGHORNS	LIAISON	LIMITED
LAMPING	LAPSANG	LAUGHERS	LEASERS	LEGISTS	LIAISONS	LIMITEDS
CLAMPING	LAPSANGS	LAUNDER	PLEASERS	ELEGISTS	LIBBARD	LIMITER
LAMPION	LAPSING	LAUNDERS	LEASING	LEGITIM	LIBBARDS	LIMITERS
LAMPIONS	ELAPSING	LAUWINE	PLEASING	LEGITIMS	LIBBING	LIMMERS
LAMPOON	LAPWING	LAUWINES	LEASINGS	LEGROOM	GLIBBING	GLIMMERS
LAMPOONS	LAPWINGS	LAVOLTA	LEASOWE	LEGROOMS	LIBERAL	SLIMMERS
LAMPREY	LAPWORK	LAVOLTAS	LEASOWED	LEGUMIN	LIBERALS	LIMPING
LAMPREYS	LAPWORKS	LAWLAND	LEASOWES	LEGUMINS	LIBRATE	FLIMPING
LAMPUKA	LARDOON	LAWLANDS	LEASURE	LEGWORK	LIBRATED	LIMPINGS
LAMPUKAS	LARDOONS	LAWLESS	PLEASURE	LEGWORKS	LIBRATES	LIMPKIN
LAMPUKI	LARGESS	CLAWLESS	LEASURES	LEIDGER	LICENCE	LIMPKINS
LAMPUKIS	LARGESSE	FLAWLESS	LEATHER	LEIDGERS	LICENCED	LINCHES
LANCHED	LARMIER	LAWSUIT	LEATHERN	LEISLER	LICENCES	CLINCHES
BLANCHED	LARMIERS	LAWSUITS	LEATHERS	LEISLERS	LICENSE	FLINCHES
FLANCHED	LARVATE	LAXATOR	LEATHERY	LEISTER	LICENSED	LINCHET
PLANCHED	LARVATED	LAXATORS	LEAVING	LEISTERS	LICENSEE	LINCHETS
LANCHES	LASAGNA	LAYAWAY	CLEAVING	LEISURE	LICENSER	LINDANE
BLANCHES	LASAGNAS	LAYAWAYS	SLEAVING	LEISURED	LICENSES	LINDANES
FLANCHES	LASAGNE	LAYBACK	LEAVINGS	LEISURES	LICHTER	LINEAGE
PLANCHES	LASAGNES	PLAYBACK	LECTERN	LEKKING	FLICHTER	LINEAGES
LANCING	LASHERS	LAYBACKS	LECTERNS	LEKKINGS	LICHWAY	LINEATE
ELANCING	FLASHERS	LAYETTE	LECTION	LEMMING	LICHWAYS	LINEATED
GLANCING	SLASHERS	LAYETTES	ELECTION	CLEMMING	LICKERS	LINGERS
LANDERS	LASHING	LAYLOCK	FLECTION	LEMMINGS	CLICKERS	CLINGERS
GLANDERS	CLASHING	LAYLOCKS	LECTIONS	LEMPIRA	FLICKERS	FLINGERS
SLANDERS	FLASHING	LAYTIME	LECTORS	LEMPIRAS	SLICKERS	SLINGERS
LANDING	PLASHING	PLAYTIME	ELECTORS	LENDERS	LICKING	LINGIER
LANDINGS	SLASHING	LAYTIMES	LECTURE	LENDING	CLICKING	CLINGIER
LANDLER	LASHINGS	LAZARET	LECTURED		FLICKING	LINGULA

LINGULAE	LITHIUM	CLOGGING	LOUNGERS	SLUGGING	FLUSHIER	MAFFLING
LINGULAR	LITHIUMS	FLOGGING	LOURIER	LUGSAIL	PLUSHIER	MAFFLINS
LINGULAS	LITTERS	SLOGGING	FLOURIER	LUGSAILS	SLUSHIER	MAGENTA
LINKAGE	CLITTERS	LOGGINGS	LOURING	LUGWORM	LUSHING	MAGENTAS
LINKAGES	FLITTERS	LOGICAL	CLOURING	LUGWORMS	BLUSHING	MAGISMS
LINKBOY	GLITTERS	ALOGICAL	FLOURING	PLUMBAGO	FLUSHING	IMAGISMS
LINKBOYS	SLITTERS	LOGLINE	LOURINGS	LUMBAGOS	SLUSHING	MAGNATE
LINKING	LITTERY	LOGLINES	LOUSING	LUMBANG	LUSTERS	MAGNATES
BLINKING	GLITTERY	LOGWOOD	BLOUSING	LUMBANGS	BLUSTERS	MAGNETO
CLINKING	LITTLES	LOGWOODS	FLOUSING	LUMBERS	CLUSTERS	MAGNETON
PLINKING	LITTLEST	LONGBOW	LOUTING	CLUMBERS	FLUSTERS	MAGNETOS
SLINKING	LITTLIN	LONGBOWS	CLOUTING	PLUMBERS	LUSTRUM	MAHATMA
LINNING	LITTLING	LONGING	FLOUTING	SLUMBERS	LUSTRUMS	MAHATMAS
BLINNING	LITTLINS	PLONGING	GLOUTING	LUMMIER	LUTHERN	MAHONIA
LINOCUT	LIVELOD	LONGINGS	LOVERED	PLUMMIER	LUTHERNS	MAHONIAS
LINOCUTS	LIVELODS	LOOBIES	CLOVERED	SLUMMIER	LUTHIER	MAHSEER
LINSANG	LLANERO	LOOBIEST	LOWERED	LUMPERS	LUTHIERS	MAHSEERS
LINSANGS	LLANEROS	LOOFFUL	FLOWERED	CLUMPIER	LUTINGS	MAIDISM
LINSEED	LOADING	LOOFFULS	GLOWERED	GLUMPIER	FLUTINGS	MAIDISMS
LINSEEDS	LOADINGS	LOOKING	LOWINGS	SLUMPIER	LUTISTS	MAILING
LINTIER	LOAFING	LOOKINGS	SLOWINGS	LUMPIER	FLUTISTS	MAILINGS
FLINTIER	LOAFINGS	LOOKOUT	LOWLAND	LUMPING	LYCOPOD	MAILLOT
LINTIES	LOAMING	LOOKOUTS	LOWLANDS	CLUMPING	LYCOPODS	MAILLOTS
LINTIEST	GLOAMING	LOOMING	LOWNESS	FLUMPING	LYDDITE	MAIMING
LIONCEL	LOANING	BLOOMING	SLOWNESS	PLUMPING	LYDDITES	MAIMINGS
LIONCELS	LOANINGS	GLOOMING	LOWNING	SLUMPING	LYMITER	MAINOUR
LIONISE	LOATHER	SLOOMING	CLOWNING	LUMPISH	LYMITERS	MAINOURS
LIONISED	LOATHERS	LOONIES	LOWVELD	GLUMPISH	LYMPHAD	MAINTOP
LIONISES	LOATHES	LOONIEST	LOWVELDS	PLUMPISH	LYMPHADS	MAINTOPS
LIONISM	LOATHEST	LOONING	LOXYGEN	LUMPKIN	LYNCHET	MAISTER
LIONISMS	LOBBING	LOONINGS	LOXYGENS	LUMPKINS	LYNCHETS	MAISTERS
LIONIZE	BLOBBING	LOOPERS	LOZENGE	LUNATIC	LYOPHIL	MAJORAT
LIONIZED	LOBBYER	BLOOPERS	LOZENGED	LUNATICS	LYOPHILE	MAJORATS
LIONIZES	LOBBYERS	LOOPING	LOZENGES	LUNCHER	MACADAM	MALACIA
LIPPIER	LOBELET	BLOOPING	LUBBARD	LUNCHERS	MACADAMS	MALACIAS
SLIPPIER	LOBELETS	LOOPINGS	LUBBARDS	LUNCHES	MACAQUE	MALAISE
LIPPIES	LOBELIA	LOPPING	LUBBERS	CLUNCHES	MACAQUES	MALAISES
CLIPPIES	LOBELIAS	CLOPPING	BLUBBERS	LUNETTE	MACHAIR	MALARIA
LIPPIEST	LOBSTER	FLOPPING	SLUBBERS	LUNETTES	MACHAIRS	MALARIAL
LIPPING	LOBSTERS	PLOPPING	LUCARNE	LUNGFUL	MACHETE	MALARIAN
BLIPPING	LOBULAR	SLOPPING	LUCARNES	LUNGFULS	MACHETES	MALARIAS
CLIPPING	GLOBULAR	LOPPINGS	LUCERNE	LUNGING	MACHINE	MALEATE
FLIPPING	LOBULES	LORDING	LUCERNES	BLUNGING	MACHINED	MALEATES
SLIPPING	GLOBULES	LORDINGS	LUCIFER	PLUNGING	MACHINES	MALEFIC
LIQUATE	LOBWORM	LORDKIN	LUCIFERS	LUNKERS	MACHREE	MALEFICE
LIQUATED	LOBWORMS	LORDKINS	LUCIGEN	BLUNKERS	MACHREES	MALICHO
LIQUATES	LOCKAGE	LORETTE	LUCIGENS	PLUNKERS	MACRAME	MALICHOS
LIQUEUR	BLOCKAGE	LORETTES	LUCKIER	LUNTING	MACRAMES	MALISON
LIQUEURS	LOCKAGES	LORGNON	CLUCKIER	BLUNTING	MACRAMI	MALISONS
LISPING	LOCKERS	LORGNONS	PLUCKIER	LUPULIN	MACRAMIS	MALLARD
LISPINGS	BLOCKERS	LORIMER	LUCKIES	LUPULINE	MADLING	MALLARDS
LISPUND	CLOCKERS	LORIMERS	LUCKIEST	LUPULINS	MADLINGS	MALLING
LISPUNDS	LOCKFUL	LORINER	LUCKILY	LURCHER	MADOQUA	SMALLING
LISTENS	LOCKFULS	LORINERS	PLUCKILY	LURCHERS	MADOQUAS	MALMSEY
GLISTENS	LOCKING	LORRELL	LUDSHIP	LURDANE	MADRASA	MALMSEYS
LISTERS	BLOCKING	LORRELLS	LUDSHIPS	LURDANES	MADRASAH	MALTASE
BLISTERS	CLOCKING	LOSINGS	LUFFING	LURKING	MADRASAS	MALTASES
GLISTERS	FLOCKING	CLOSINGS	BLUFFING	LURKINGS	MADRONA	MALTING
LISTING	LOCKOUT	LOSSIER	FLUFFING	LURRIES	MADRONAS	MALTINGS
LISTINGS	LOCKOUTS	FLOSSIER	PLUFFING	FLURRIES	MADRONO	MALTOSE
LITERAL	LOCKRAM	GLOSSIER	LUGEING	SLURRIES	MADRONOS	MALTOSES
LITERALS	LOCKRAMS	LOTTING	LUGEINGS	LUSHERS	MADWORT	MAMELON
LITHATE	LOCUSTA	BLOTTING	LUGGAGE	BLUSHERS	MADWORTS	MAMELONS
LITHATES	LOCUSTAE	CLOTTING	LUGGAGES	FLUSHERS	MADZOON	MAMILLA
LITHELY	LODGING	PLOTTING	LUGGERS	LUSHEST	MADZOONS	MAMILLAE
BLITHELY	LODGINGS	SLOTTING	LUGGING	FLUSHEST	MAESTRO	MAMILLAR
LITHEST	LOGGERS	LOUNDER	GLUGGING	PLUSHEST	MAESTROS	MAMMOCK
BLITHEST	CLOGGERS	FLOUNDER	PLUGGING	LUSHIER	MAFFICK	MAMMOCKS
LITHITE	SLOGGERS	LOUNDERS			MAFFICKS	MAMMOTH
LITHITES	LOGGING	LOUNGER			MAFFLIN	MAMMOTHS

MANACLE	MANTEAUX	SMARTING	MATZOONS	MEERKATS	MERSIONS	MIDNOONS
MANACLED	MANTEEL	MARTINI	MAULGRE	MEETING	MESHING	MIDRIFF
MANACLES	MANTEELS	MARTINIS	MAULGRES	MEETINGS	MESHINGS	MIDRIFFS
MANAGER	MANTLET	MARTLET	MAUNDER	MEGABAR	MESQUIN	MIDSHIP
MANAGERS	MANTLETS	MARTLETS	MAUNDERS	MEGABARS	MESQUINE	MIDSHIPS
MANAKIN	MANTRAM	MARYBUD	MAUTHER	MEGABIT	MESQUIT	MIDWIFE
MANAKINS	MANTRAMS	MARYBUDS	MAUTHERS	MEGABITS	MESQUITE	MIDWIFED
MANATEE	MANTRAP	MASCARA	MAUVAIS	MEGAFOG	MESQUITS	MIDWIFES
MANATEES	MANTRAPS	MASCARAS	MAUVAISE	MEGAFOGS	MESSAGE	MIDWIVE
MANCHET	MANUMIT	MASHERS	MAUVEIN	MEGARAD	MESSAGED	MIDWIVED
MANCHETS	MANUMITS	SMASHERS	MAUVEINE	MEGARADS	MESSAGES	MIDWIVES
MANDALA	MANURER	MASHIES	MAUVEINS	MEGARON	MESTIZA	MIGRANT
MANDALAS	MANURERS	MASHIEST	MAUVINE	MEGARONS	MESTIZAS	EMIGRANT
MANDATE	MAORMOR	MASHING	MAUVINES	MEGASSE	MESTIZO	MIGRANTS
MANDATED	MAORMORS	SMASHING	MAWSEED	MEGASSES	MESTIZOS	MIGRATE
MANDATES	MAPPIST	MASHINGS	MAWSEEDS	MEGATON	METAMER	EMIGRATE
MANDIOC	MAPPISTS	MASHLAM	MAWTHER	MEGATONS	METAMERE	MIGRATED
MANDIOCA	MARABOU	MASHLAMS	MAWTHERS	MELANGE	METAMERS	MIGRATES
MANDIOCS	MARABOUS	MASHLIM	MAXILLA	MELANGES	METAYER	MILEAGE
MANDIRA	MARABOUT	MASHLIMS	MAXILLAE	MELANIN	METAYERS	MILEAGES
MANDIRAS	MARBLER	MASHLIN	MAXIMIN	MELANINS	METAZOA	MILFOIL
MANDOLA	MARBLERS	MASHLINS	MAXIMINS	MELILOT	METAZOAN	MILFOILS
MANDOLAS	MARCHER	MASHLUM	MAXWELL	MELILOTS	METCAST	MILITAR
MANDORA	MARCHERS	MASHLUMS	MAXWELLS	MELISMA	METCASTS	MILITARY
MANDORAS	MARCHES	MASQUER	MAYPOLE	MELISMAS	METHANE	MILITIA
MANDREL	MARCHESA	MASQUERS	MAYPOLES	MELLING	METHANES	MILITIAS
MANDRELS	MARCHESE	MASSAGE	MAYSTER	SMELLING	METHINK	MILKING
MANDRIL	MARCHESI	MASSAGED	MAYSTERS	MELLITE	METHINKS	MILKINGS
MANDRILL	MARCONI	MASSAGES	MAYWEED	MELLITES	METICAL	MILLDAM
MANDRILS	MARCONIS	MASSEUR	MAYWEEDS	MELODIC	EMETICAL	MILLDAMS
MANGLER	MARDIES	MASSEURS	MAZURKA	MELODICS	METICALS	MILLIME
MANGLERS	MARDIEST	MASSING	MAZURKAS	MELTING	METISSE	MILLIMES
MANGOLD	MAREMMA	AMASSING	MAZZARD	SMELTING	METISSES	MILLING
MANGOLDS	MAREMMAS	MASTABA	MAZZARDS	MELTINGS	METONYM	MILLINGS
MANHOLE	MARGENT	MASTABAS	MEACOCK	MELTITH	METONYMS	MILLION
MANHOLES	MARGENTS	MASTICH	MEACOCKS	MELTITHS	METONYMY	MILLIONS
MANHOOD	MARGOSA	MASTICHS	MEAGRES	MEMENTO	METOPON	MIMMICK
MANHOODS	MARGOSAS	MASTIFF	MEAGREST	MEMENTOS	METOPONS	MIMMICKS
MANHUNT	MARIMBA	MASTIFFS	MEALIES	MENACER	METRIST	MINARET
MANHUNTS	MARIMBAS	MASTOID	MEALIEST	MENACERS	METRISTS	MINARETS
MANIHOC	MARINER	MASTOIDS	MEANDER	MENAGES	MEZUZAH	MINCING
MANIHOCS	MARINERS	MATADOR	MEANDERS	AMENAGES	MEZUZAHS	MINCINGS
MANIKIN	MARKHOR	MATADORE	MEANING	MENDERS	MICATED	MINDING
MANIKINS	MARKHORS	MATADORS	MEANINGS	AMENDERS	EMICATED	MINDINGS
MANILLA	MARKING	MATCHED	MEASURE	MENDING	MICATES	MINDSET
MANILLAS	MARKINGS	SMATCHED	MEASURED	AMENDING	EMICATES	MINDSETS
MANILLE	MARLINE	MATCHER	MEASURER	EMENDING	MICELLA	MINEOLA
MANILLES	MARLINES	MATCHERS	MEASURES	MENDINGS	MICELLAR	MINEOLAS
MANIPLE	MARLING	MATCHES	MECONIN	MENFOLK	MICELLAS	MINERAL
MANIPLES	MARLINGS	SMATCHES	MECONINS	MENFOLKS	MICELLE	MINERALS
MANITOU	MARMITE	MATELOT	MEDALET	MENORAH	MICELLES	MINETTE
MANITOUS	MARMITES	MATELOTE	MEDALETS	MENORAHS	MICHING	MINETTES
MANJACK	MARMOSE	MATELOTS	MEDDLER	MENTHOL	MICHINGS	MINEVER
MANJACKS	MARMOSES	MATINEE	MEDDLERS	MENTHOLS	MICROBE	MINEVERS
MANKIND	MARMOSET	MATINEES	MEDIANT	MENTION	MICROBES	MINGLER
MANKINDS	MARPLOT	MATRICE	MEDIANTS	MENTIONS	MICRONS	MINGLERS
MANNITE	MARPLOTS	MATRICES	MEDIATE	MERCHET	OMICRONS	MINIATE
MANNITES	MARQUEE	MATTERS	MEDIATED	MERCHETS	MICTION	MINIATED
MANNOSE	MARQUEES	SMATTERS	MEDIATES	MERFOLK	EMICTION	MINIATES
MANNOSES	MARQUES	MATTING	MEDICAL	MERFOLKS	MICTIONS	MINICAB
MANPACK	MARQUESS	MATTINGS	MEDICALS	MERGING	MIDDIES	MINICABS
MANPACKS	MARQUIS	MATTOCK	MEDULLA	EMERGING	SMIDDIES	MINICAR
MANRENT	MARQUISE	MATTOCKS	MEDULLAE	MERLING	MIDIRON	MINICARS
MANRENTS	MARRIER	MATTOID	MEDULLAR	MERLINGS	MIDIRONS	MINIKIN
MANSARD	MARRIERS	MATTOIDS	MEDULLAS	MERMAID	MIDLAND	MINIKINS
MANSARDS	MARSHAL	MATURES	MEDUSAN	MERMAIDS	MIDLANDS	MINISUB
MANSION	MARSHALS	MATUREST	MEDUSANS	MERRIES	MIDMOST	MINISUBS
MANSIONS	MARTENS	MATWEED	MEERCAT	MERRIEST	AMIDMOST	MINIVER
MANTEAU	SMARTENS	MATWEEDS	MEERCATS	MERSION	MIDMOSTS	MINIVERS
MANTEAUS	MARTING	MATZOON	MEERKAT	EMERSION	MIDNOON	MINIVET

MINIVETS	MISKNOWN	MISTUNE	MONARDA	MOOTING	MOULDERS	MULATTAS
MINNICK	MISKNOWS	MISTUNED	MONARDAS	SMOOTING	MOUNTED	MULATTO
MINNICKS	MISLEAD	MISTUNES	MONAXON	MOOTINGS	AMOUNTED	MULATTOS
MINNOCK	MISLEADS	MISUSER	MONAXONS	MOOVING	MOUNTER	MULLEIN
MINNOCKS	MISLIKE	MISUSERS	MONDAIN	AMOOVING	MOUNTERS	MULLEINS
MINSTER	MISLIKED	MISWEEN	MONDAINE	MORAINE	MOUNTIE	MULLION
MINSTERS	MISLIKER	MISWEENS	MONDAINS	MORAINES	MOUNTIES	MULLIONS
MINTAGE	MISLIKES	MISWEND	MONEYER	MORCEAU	MOURNER	MULLOCK
MINTAGES	MISLIVE	MISWENDS	MONEYERS	MORCEAUX	MOURNERS	MULLOCKS
MINUEND	MISLIVED	MISWORD	MONGREL	MORDANT	MOUSAKA	MULMULL
MINUENDS	MISLIVES	MISWORDS	MONGRELS	MORDANTS	MOUSAKAS	MULMULLS
MINUTES	MISLUCK	MISYOKE	MONIKER	MORDENT	MOUSERS	MULTURE
MINUTEST	MISLUCKS	MISYOKED	MONIKERS	MORDENTS	SMOUSERS	MULTURED
MINUTIA	MISMAKE	MISYOKES	MONILIA	MORELLO	MOUSIES	MULTURER
MINUTIAE	MISMAKES	MITHERS	MONILIAS	MORELLOS	MOUSIEST	MULTURES
MIRACLE	MISMATE	SMITHERS	MONITOR	MORICHE	MOUSING	MUMBLER
MIRACLES	MISMATED	MITOGEN	MONITORS	MORICHES	SMOUSING	MUMBLERS
MIRADOR	MISMATES	MITOGENS	MONITORY	MORISCO	MOUSINGS	MUMMING
MIRADORS	MISNAME	AMITOSES	MONOCLE	MORISCOS	MOUSMEE	MUMMINGS
MIRBANE	MISNAMED	MITOSIS	MONOCLED	MORLING	MOUSMEES	MUMMOCK
MIRBANES	MISNAMES	AMITOSIS	MONOCLES	MORLINGS	MOUTHER	MUMMOCKS
MIRKIER	MISPLAY	MITOTIC	MONOCOT	MORMAOR	MOUTHERS	MUNCHER
SMIRKIER	MISPLAYS	AMITOTIC	MONOCOTS	MORMAORS	MOVABLE	MUNCHERS
MISCALL	MISRATE	MITZVAH	MONOFIL	MORNING	MOVABLES	MUNDANE
MISCALLS	MISRATED	MITZVAHS	MONOFILS	MORNINGS	MOWBURNS	MUNDANER
MISCAST	MISRATES	MIXTION	MONOMER	MOROCCO	MOWBURNT	MUNNION
MISCASTS	MISREAD	MIXTIONS	MONOMERS	MOROCCOS	MOYLING	MUNNIONS
MISDATE	MISREADS	MIXTURE	MONSOON	MORPHEW	SMOYLING	MUNSTER
MISDATED	MISRULE	MIXTURES	MONSOONS	MORPHEWS	MOZETTA	MUNSTERS
MISDATES	MISRULED	MIZMAZE	MONSTER	MORPHIA	MOZETTAS	MUNTING
MISDEAL	MISRULES	MIZMAZES	MONSTERA	MORPHIAS	MRIDANG	MUNTINGS
MISDEALS	MISSEEM	MOBSTER	MONSTERS	MORRHUA	MRIDANGA	MUNTJAC
MISDEALT	MISSEEMS	MOBSTERS	MONTAGE	MORRHUAS	MRIDANGS	MUNTJACS
MISDEED	MISSEND	MOCHELL	MONTAGES	MORRICE	MUCHELL	MUNTJAK
MISDEEDS	MISSENDS	MOCHELLS	MONTANT	MORRICES	MUCHELLS	MUNTJAKS
MISDEEM	MISSIES	MOCKAGE	MONTANTO	MORRION	MUCIGEN	MUONIUM
MISDEEMS	MISSIEST	MOCKAGES	MONTANTS	MORRIONS	MUCIGENS	MUONIUMS
MISDIET	MISSILE	MOCKING	MONTERO	MORSURE	MUDDIES	MURAENA
MISDIETS	EMISSILE	SMOCKING	MONTEROS	MORSURES	MUDDIEST	MURAENAS
MISDOER	MISSILES	MOCKINGS	MONTURE	MORTICE	MUDDLER	MURGEON
MISDOERS	MISSING	MODICUM	MONTURES	MORTICED	MUDDLERS	MURGEONS
MISDRAW	AMISSING	MODICUMS	MOOCHED	MORTICER	MUDIRIA	MURIATE
MISDRAWN	MISSION	MODISTE	SMOOCHED	MORTICES	MUDIRIAS	MURIATED
MISDRAWS	EMISSION	MODISTES	MOOCHER	MORTISE	MUDLARK	MURIATES
MISEASE	OMISSION	MOELLON	MOOCHERS	AMORTISE	MUDLARKS	MURLAIN
MISEASES	MISSIONS	MOELLONS	MOOCHES	MORTISED	MUDPACK	MURLAINS
MISFALL	MISSIVE	MOFETTE	SMOOCHES	MORTISER	MUDPACKS	MURRAIN
MISFALLS	EMISSIVE	MOFETTES	MOODIES	MORTISES	MUDSCOW	MURRAINS
MISFARE	OMISSIVE	MOIDORE	MOODIEST	MORWONG	MUDSCOWS	MURRION
MISFARED	MISSIVES	MOIDORES	MOOKTAR	MORWONGS	MUDWORT	MURRIONS
MISFARES	MISSTEP	MOILING	MOOKTARS	MOSSIES	MUDWORTS	MURTHER
MISFILE	MISSTEPS	SMOILING	MOONEYE	MOSSIEST	MUEDDIN	MURTHERS
MISFILED	MISSUIT	MOINEAU	MOONEYES	MOTHERS	MUEDDINS	MUSCONE
MISFILES	MISSUITS	MOINEAUS	MOONIES	SMOTHERS	MUEZZIN	MUSCONES
MISFIRE	MISTAKE	MOISTEN	MOONIEST	MOTHERY	MUEZZINS	MUSETTE
MISFIRED	MISTAKEN	MOISTENS	MOONLET	SMOTHERY	MUFFLER	AMUSETTE
MISFIRES	MISTAKES	MOITHER	MOONLETS	MOTIONS	MUFFLERS	MUSETTES
MISFORM	MISTELL	MOITHERS	MOONSET	EMOTIONS	MUGGING	MUSICAL
MISFORMS	MISTELLS	MOLERAT	MOONSETS	MOUCHED	SMUGGING	MUSICALE
MISGIVE	MISTERM	MOLERATS	MOORAGE	SMOUCHED	MUGGINGS	MUSICALS
MISGIVEN	MISTERMS	MOLIMEN	MOORAGES	MOUCHER	MUGSHOT	MUSIMON
MISGIVES	MISTICO	MOLIMENS	MOORHEN	MOUCHERS	MUGSHOTS	MUSIMONS
MISHEAR	MISTICOS	MOLLUSC	MOORHENS	MOUCHES	MUGWORT	MUSKONE
MISHEARD	MISTIME	MOLLUSCS	MOORILL	SMOUCHES	MUGWORTS	MUSKONES
MISHEARS	MISTIMED	MOLLUSK	MOORILLS	MOUFLON	MUGWUMP	MUSTANG
MISHMEE	MISTIMES	MOLLUSKS	MOORING	MOUFLONS	MUGWUMPS	MUSTANGS
MISHMEES	MISTING	MONARCH	SMOORING	MOULAGE	MUKHTAR	MUSTARD
MISJOIN	MISTINGS	MONARCHS	MOORINGS	MOULAGES	MUKHTARS	MUSTARDS
MISJOINS	MISTRAL	MONARCHY	MOORLOG	MOULDER	MULATTA	MUTAGEN
MISKNOW	MISTRALS		MOORLOGS	SMOULDER		MUTAGENS

MUTCHES	NANKEENS	**NEEDLES**	SNICKERS	**NOCKING**	NOTITIAS	**NYMPHAE**
SMUTCHES	**NAPHTHA**	NEEDLESS	**NICKING**	KNOCKING	**NOUMENA**	NYMPHAEA
MUZZLER	NAPHTHAS	**NEEZING**	SNICKING	**NOCTUID**	NOUMENAL	**NYMPHET**
MUZZLERS	**NAPPERS**	SNEEZING	**NICTATE**	NOCTUIDS	**NOURICE**	NYMPHETS
MYALGIA	KNAPPERS	**NEGLECT**	NICTATED	**NOCTULE**	NOURICES	**OAKLING**
MYALGIAS	SNAPPERS	NEGLECTS	NICTATES	NOCTULES	**NOURSLE**	OAKLINGS
MYALISM	**NAPPIER**	**NEGLIGE**	**NIFFERS**	**NOCTURN**	NOURSLED	**OARIEST**
MYALISMS	SNAPPIER	NEGLIGEE	SNIFFERS	NOCTURNE	NOURSLES	HOARIEST
MYCELIA	**NAPPIES**	NEGLIGES	**NIFFIER**	NOCTURNS	**NOUSELL**	ROARIEST
MYCELIAL	NAPPIEST	**NEGROID**	SNIFFIER	**NODDING**	NOUSELLS	**OARWEED**
MYELOMA	**NAPPING**	NEGROIDS	**NIFFING**	SNODDING	**NOVELLA**	OARWEEDS
MYELOMAS	KNAPPING	**NELUMBO**	SNIFFING	NODDINGS	NOVELLAE	**OATCAKE**
MYLODON	SNAPPING	NELUMBOS	**NIFTIER**	**NOGGING**	NOVELLAS	OATCAKES
MYLODONS	**NARGILE**	**NEMESIA**	SNIFTIER	SNOGGING	**NOWHERE**	**OATMEAL**
MYLODONT	NARGILEH	NEMESIAS	**NIGELLA**	NOGGINGS	NOWHERES	OATMEALS
MYNHEER	NARGILES	**NEOLITH**	NIGELLAS	**NOINTED**	**NOYANCE**	**OBELION**
MYNHEERS	**NARRATE**	NEOLITHS	**NIGGARD**	ANOINTED	NOYANCES	OBELIONS
MYOGRAM	NARRATED	**NEONATE**	NIGGARDS	**NOMARCH**	**NUBBIER**	**OBELISE**
MYOGRAMS	NARRATES	NEONATES	**NIGGERS**	NOMARCHS	KNUBBIER	OBELISED
MYOSOTE	**NARTJIE**	**NEPHRON**	SNIGGERS	NOMARCHY	SNUBBIER	OBELISES
MYOSOTES	NARTJIES	NEPHRONS	**NIGGLED**	**NOMBRIL**	**NUBBING**	**OBELISK**
MYOTUBE	**NARWHAL**	**NERVATE**	SNIGGLED	NOMBRILS	SNUBBING	OBELISKS
MYOTUBES	NARWHALS	ENERVATE	**NIGGLER**	**NOMINAL**	**NUBBLED**	**OBELIZE**
MYRBANE	**NASHGAB**	**NERVINE**	SNIGGLER	NOMINALS	KNUBBLED	OBELIZED
MYRBANES	NASHGABS	NERVINES	NIGGLERS	**NOMINEE**	**NUBBLES**	OBELIZES
MYRINGA	**NASTIES**	**NERVING**	**NIGGLES**	NOMINEES	KNUBBLES	**OBLIGEE**
MYRINGAS	NASTIEST	ENERVING	SNIGGLES	**NONAGON**	**NUCLEAR**	OBLIGEES
MYRRHOL	**NATCHES**	**NERVULE**	**NIGHTED**	NONAGONS	NUCLEARY	**OBLIGOR**
MYRRHOLS	SNATCHES	NERVULES	KNIGHTED	**NONETTE**	**NUCLEIN**	OBLIGORS
MYTHISE	**NATIONS**	**NERVURE**	**NIGHTIE**	NONETTES	NUCLEINS	**OBLIQUE**
MYTHISED	ENATIONS	NERVURES	NIGHTIES	**NONETTO**	**NUCLEON**	OBLIQUED
MYTHISES	**NATRIUM**	**NETBALL**	**NIGHTLY**	NONETTOS	NUCLEONS	OBLIQUER
MYTHISM	NATRIUMS	NETBALLS	KNIGHTLY	**NONSUIT**	**NUCLIDE**	OBLIQUES
MYTHISMS	**NATURAL**	**NETSUKE**	**NIOBATE**	NONSUITS	NUCLIDES	**OBSCENE**
MYTHIST	NATURALS	NETSUKES	NIOBATES	**NONUPLE**	**NUDGING**	OBSCENER
MYTHISTS	**NAVARCH**	**NETTING**	**NIOBITE**	NONUPLET	SNUDGING	**OBSCURE**
MYTHIZE	NAVARCHS	NETTINGS	NIOBITES	**NOOKIES**	**NULLING**	OBSCURED
MYTHIZED	NAVARCHY	**NETWORK**	**NIOBIUM**	NOOKIEST	NULLINGS	OBSCURER
MYTHIZES	**NAVARHO**	NETWORKS	NIOBIUMS	**NOONDAY**	**NUMERAL**	OBSCURES
NAARTJE	NAVARHOS	**NEURINE**	**NIPPERS**	NOONDAYS	NUMERALS	**OBSERVE**
NAARTJES	**NAVARIN**	NEURINES	SNIPPERS	**NOONING**	**NUNATAK**	OBSERVED
NACARAT	NAVARINS	**NEURISM**	**NIPPIER**	NOONINGS	NUNATAKS	OBSERVER
NACARATS	**NAVETTE**	ANEURISM	SNIPPIER	**NORIMON**	**NUNDINE**	OBSERVES
NACELLE	NAVETTES	NEURISMS	**NIPPING**	NORIMONS	NUNDINES	**OBTRUDE**
NACELLES	**NAYWARD**	**NEURITE**	SNIPPING	**NORLAND**	**NUNHOOD**	OBTRUDED
NACRITE	NAYWARDS	NEURITES	**NIRVANA**	NORLANDS	NUNHOODS	OBTRUDER
NACRITES	**NAYWORD**	**NEUROMA**	NIRVANAS	**NORTHER**	**NUNSHIP**	OBTRUDES
NAGAPIE	NAYWORDS	NEUROMAS	**NITERIE**	NORTHERN	NUNSHIPS	**OBVERSE**
NAGAPIES	**NEAPING**	**NEURONE**	NITERIES	NORTHERS	**NUPTIAL**	OBVERSES
NAGGIER	SNEAPING	NEURONES	**NITHING**	**NORWARD**	NUPTIALS	**OBVIATE**
KNAGGIER	**NEARING**	**NEUSTON**	NITHINGS	NORWARDS	**NURAGHI**	OBVIATED
SNAGGIER	ANEARING	NEUSTONS	**NITRATE**	**NOSEBAG**	NURAGHIC	OBVIATES
NAGGING	**NEBBICH**	**NEUTRAL**	NITRATED	NOSEBAGS	**NURLING**	**OCARINA**
SNAGGING	NEBBICHS	NEUTRALS	NITRATES	**NOSEGAY**	KNURLING	OCARINAS
NAGMAAL	**NEBBING**	**NEUTRON**	**NITRIDE**	NOSEGAYS	**NURTURE**	**OCCIPUT**
NAGMAALS	SNEBBING	NEUTRONS	NITRIDED	**NOSTRIL**	NURTURED	OCCIPUTS
NAILERY	**NEBBISH**	**NEWCOME**	NITRIDES	NOSTRILS	NURTURER	**OCCLUDE**
SNAILERY	NEBBISHE	NEWCOMER	**NITRILE**	**NOSTRUM**	NURTURES	OCCLUDED
NAILING	**NECKING**	**NEWSBOY**	NITRILES	NOSTRUMS	**NUTCASE**	OCCLUDES
SNAILING	SNECKING	NEWSBOYS	**NITRITE**	**NOTABLE**	NUTCASES	**OCEANID**
NAILINGS	NECKINGS	**NEWSIES**	NITRITES	NOTABLES	**NUTMEAL**	OCEANIDS
NAIVETE	**NECKLET**	NEWSIEST	**NOBBIER**	**NOTAEUM**	NUTMEALS	**OCHERED**
NAIVETES	NECKLETS	**NIBBING**	KNOBBIER	NOTAEUMS	**NUTTING**	TOCHERED
NAMASTE	**NECKTIE**	SNIBBING	SNOBBIER	**NOTCHEL**	NUTTINGS	**OCTAGON**
NAMASTES	NECKTIES	**NIBBLER**	**NOBBLED**	NOTCHELS	**NUZZLED**	OCTAGONS
NANDINE	**NECROSE**	NIBBLERS	KNOBBLED	**NOTELET**	SNUZZLED	**OCTAPLA**
NANDINES	NECROSED	**NIBLICK**	**NOBBLER**	NOTELETS	**NUZZLES**	OCTAPLAS
NANISMS	NECROSES	NIBLICKS	NOBBLERS	**NOTHING**	SNUZZLES	**OCTETTE**
ONANISMS	**NEEDLER**	**NICKERS**	**NOBBLES**	NOTHINGS	**NYLGHAU**	OCTETTES
NANKEEN	NEEDLERS	KNICKERS	KNOBBLES	**NOTITIA**	NYLGHAUS	**OCTOPOD**

OCTOPODS	COLDNESS	**OOSPORE**	ORDINEES	OUAKARIS	**OUTHYRE**	OUTROARS
OCTUPLE	**OLDSTER**	ZOOSPORE	**ORDURES**	**OULAKAN**	OUTHYRED	**OUTROOP**
OCTUPLED	OLDSTERS	OOSPORES	BORDURES	OULAKANS	OUTHYRES	OUTROOPS
OCTUPLES	**OLEARIA**	**OOZIEST**	OREGANO	**OURALIS**	**OUTINGS**	**OUTROOT**
OCTUPLET	OLEARIAS	BOOZIEST	OREGANOS	WOURALIS	POUTINGS	OUTROOTS
OCULATE	**OLEFINE**	WOOZIEST	**OREWEED**	**OURIEST**	ROUTINGS	**OUTROPE**
LOCULATE	OLEFINES	**OPALINE**	OREWEEDS	LOURIEST	**OUTJEST**	OUTROPER
OCULATED	**OLIGIST**	OPALINES	**ORGANZA**	**OURSELF**	OUTJESTS	OUTROPES
OCULIST	OLIGISTS	**OPAQUES**	ORGANZAS	YOURSELF	**OUTJUMP**	**OUTSAIL**
OCULISTS	**OLIVINE**	OPAQUEST	**ORGIAST**	**OUSTERS**	OUTJUMPS	OUTSAILS
ODALISK	OLIVINES	**OPENING**	ORGIASTS	JOUSTERS	**OUTLAND**	**OUTSELL**
ODALISKS	**OLOGIES**	OPENINGS	**ORIFICE**	ROUSTERS	OUTLANDS	OUTSELLS
ODALLER	OOLOGIES	**OPERAND**	ORIFICES	**OUSTING**	**OUTLAST**	**OUTSHOT**
ODALLERS	**OLOROSO**	OPERANDS	**ORIGAMI**	JOUSTING	OUTLASTS	OUTSHOTS
ODDBALL	DOLOROSO	**OPERANT**	ORIGAMIS	MOUSTING	**OUTLEAP**	**OUTSIDE**
ODDBALLS	OLOROSOS	OPERANTS	**ORIGANE**	ROUSTING	OUTLEAPS	OUTSIDER
ODDMENT	**OLYCOOK**	**OPERATE**	ORIGANES	**OUSTITI**	OUTLEAPT	OUTSIDES
ODDMENTS	OLYCOOKS	OPERATED	**OROLOGY**	OUSTITIS	**OUTLIER**	**OUTSIZE**
ODYLISM	**OLYKOEK**	OPERATES	HOROLOGY	**OUTBACK**	OUTLIERS	OUTSIZED
ODYLISMS	OLYKOEKS	**OPINION**	**OROPESA**	OUTBACKS	**OUTLINE**	OUTSIZES
ODYSSEY	**OMENTUM**	OPINIONS	OROPESAS	**OUTBRAG**	OUTLINED	**OUTSOAR**
ODYSSEYS	LOMENTUM	**OPORICE**	**ORPHREY**	OUTBRAGS	OUTLINES	OUTSOARS
OENOMEL	MOMENTUM	OPORICES	ORPHREYS	**OUTBURN**	**OUTLIVE**	**OUTSOLE**
OENOMELS	TOMENTUM	**OPOSSUM**	**ORPINES**	OUTBURNS	OUTLIVED	OUTSOLES
OERSTED	**OMICRON**	OPOSSUMS	FORPINES	OUTBURNT	OUTLIVES	**OUTSPAN**
OERSTEDS	OMICRONS	**OPPIDAN**	**ORRISES**	**OUTCAST**	**OUTLOOK**	OUTSPANS
OESTRUM	**OMITTER**	OPPIDANS	MORRISES	OUTCASTE	OUTLOOKS	**OUTSTAY**
OESTRUMS	OMITTERS	**OPPOSER**	**ORTOLAN**	OUTCASTS	**OUTMODE**	OUTSTAYS
OFFENCE	**OMNIFIC**	OPPOSERS	PORTOLAN	**OUTCOME**	OUTMODED	**OUTSTEP**
OFFENCES	SOMNIFIC	**OPSONIN**	ORTOLANS	OUTCOMES	OUTMODES	OUTSTEPS
OFFENSE	**ONANISM**	OPSONINS	**OSCULUM**	**OUTCROP**	**OUTMOVE**	**OUTTAKE**
OFFENSES	ONANISMS	**OPUNTIA**	OSCULUMS	OUTCROPS	OUTMOVED	OUTTAKEN
OFFERED	**ONANIST**	OPUNTIAS	**OSMIATE**	**OUTDARE**	OUTMOVES	OUTTAKES
COFFERED	ONANISTS	**OPUSCLE**	OSMIATES	OUTDARED	**OUTNAME**	**OUTTALK**
GOFFERED	**ONCOGEN**	OPUSCLES	**OSMOSES**	OUTDARES	OUTNAMED	OUTTALKS
OFFEREE	ONCOGENE	**ORACLES**	COSMOSES	**OUTDATE**	OUTNAMES	**OUTTELL**
OFFEREES	ONCOGENS	CORACLES	KOSMOSES	OUTDATED	**OUTPACE**	OUTTELLS
OFFERER	**ONDATRA**	**ORANGER**	**OSMUNDA**	OUTDATES	OUTPACED	**OUTTURN**
OFFERERS	ONDATRAS	ORANGERY	OSMUNDAS	**OUTDOOR**	OUTPACES	OUTTURNS
OFFEROR	**ONDINGS**	**ORANGES**	**OSSELET**	OUTDOORS	**OUTPART**	**OUTVOTE**
OFFERORS	BONDINGS	ORANGEST	OSSELETS	**OUTDURE**	OUTPARTS	OUTVOTED
OFFICER	**ONENESS**	**ORARIAN**	**OSSETER**	OUTDURED	**OUTPEEP**	OUTVOTER
OFFICERS	DONENESS	ORARIANS	OSSETERS	OUTDURES	OUTPEEPS	OUTVOTES
OFFLOAD	GONENESS	**ORARION**	**OSSICLE**	**OUTEDGE**	**OUTPEER**	**OUTWALK**
OFFLOADS	LONENESS	ORARIONS	OSSICLES	OUTEDGES	OUTPEERS	OUTWALKS
OFFSCUM	**ONEYERS**	**ORARIUM**	**OSTEOMA**	**OUTFACE**	**OUTPLAY**	**OUTWARD**
OFFSCUMS	MONEYERS	ORARIUMS	OSTEOMAS	OUTFACED	OUTPLAYS	OUTWARDS
OFFSIDE	**ONGOING**	**ORATION**	**OSTIOLE**	OUTFACES	**OUTPORT**	**OUTWEAR**
OFFSIDER	ONGOINGS	ORATIONS	OSTIOLES	**OUTFALL**	OUTPORTS	OUTWEARS
OFFSIDES	**ONSTEAD**	**ORATORY**	**OSTLERS**	OUTFALLS	**OUTPOST**	OUTWEARY
OFFTAKE	ONSTEADS	MORATORY	HOSTLERS	**OUTFLOW**	OUTPOSTS	**OUTWEED**
OFFTAKES	**ONYCHIA**	**ORBITAL**	**OTALGIA**	OUTFLOWN	**OUTPOUR**	GOUTWEED
OFTENER	ONYCHIAS	ORBITALS	OTALGIAS	OUTFLOWS	OUTPOURS	OUTWEEDS
SOFTENER	**OOGONIA**	**ORBITER**	**OTARIES**	**OUTFOOT**	**OUTPRAY**	**OUTWEEP**
OILIEST	OOGONIAL	ORBITERS	NOTARIES	OUTFOOTS	OUTPRAYS	OUTWEEPS
ROILIEST	**OOLAKAN**	**ORCHARD**	ROTARIES	**OUTGATE**	**OUTRACE**	**OUTWELL**
SOILIEST	OOLAKANS	ORCHARDS	VOTARIES	OUTGATES	OUTRACED	OUTWELLS
OILSKIN	**OOLITES**	**ORCINOL**	**OTOCYST**	**OUTGIVE**	OUTRACES	**OUTWICK**
OILSKINS	ZOOLITES	ORCINOLS	OTOCYSTS	OUTGIVEN	**OUTRAGE**	OUTWICKS
OINTING	**OOLITIC**	**ORDERED**	**OTOLITH**	OUTGIVES	OUTRAGED	**OUTWIND**
JOINTING	ZOOLITIC	BORDERED	OTOLITHS	**OUTGOER**	OUTRAGES	OUTWINDS
NOINTING	**OOMIACK**	**ORDERER**	**OTTERED**	OUTGOERS	**OUTRANK**	**OUTWING**
POINTING	OOMIACKS	BORDERER	HOTTERED	**OUTGROW**	OUTRANKS	OUTWINGS
OKIMONO	**OOPHYTE**	ORDERERS	POTTERED	OUTGROWN	**OUTRATE**	**OUTWORK**
OKIMONOS	ZOOPHYTE	**ORDINAL**	TOTTERED	OUTGROWS	OUTRATED	OUTWORKS
OLDENED	OOPHYTES	ORDINALS	**OTTOMAN**	**OUTHAUL**	OUTRATES	**OUVRAGE**
BOLDENED	**OORIEST**	**ORDINAR**	OTTOMANS	OUTHAULS	**OUTRIDE**	OUVRAGES
GOLDENED	MOORIEST	ORDINARS	**OUABAIN**	**OUTHIRE**	OUTRIDER	**OUVRIER**
OLDNESS	**OOSIEST**	ORDINARY	OUABAINS	OUTHIRED	OUTRIDES	OUVRIERS
BOLDNESS	GOOSIEST	**ORDINEE**	**OUAKARI**	OUTHIRES	**OUTROAR**	

OVARIES	OVERTLY	PADDINGS	PALMIST	PAPILLA	PARONYMY	PATAGIAL
COVARIES	COVERTLY	PADDLER	PALMISTS	PAPILLAE	PAROTID	PATAMAR
OVATION	OVERTOP	PADDLERS	PALMYRA	PAPILLAR	PAROTIDS	PATAMARS
NOVATION	OVERTOPS	PADDOCK	PALMYRAS	PAPOOSE	PARPANE	PATBALL
OVATIONS	OVERUSE	PADDOCKS	PALOOKA	PAPOOSES	PARPANES	PATBALLS
OVERACT	OVERUSED	PADELLA	PALOOKAS	PAPPIES	PARPEND	PATCHER
OVERACTS	OVERUSES	PADELLAS	PALPATE	PAPPIEST	PARPENDS	PATCHERS
OVERALL	OVICIDE	PADLOCK	PALPATED	PAPRIKA	PARPENT	PATCHERY
COVERALL	OVICIDES	PADLOCKS	PALPATES	PAPRIKAS	PARPENTS	PATELLA
OVERALLS	OVIDUCT	PAENULA	PALSIES	PARABLE	PARQUET	PATELLAE
OVERAWE	OVIDUCTS	PAENULAE	PALSIEST	SPARABLE	PARQUETS	PATELLAR
OVERAWED	OVULATE	PAENULAS	PAMPERO	PARABLED	PARROCK	PATELLAS
OVERAWES	OVULATED	PAEONIC	PAMPEROS	PARABLES	PARROCKS	PATHWAY
OVERBID	OVULATES	PAEONICS	PANACEA	PARACME	PARSING	PATHWAYS
OVERBIDS	OWLIEST	PAGEANT	PANACEAN	PARACMES	PARSINGS	PATIENT
OVERBUY	LOWLIEST	PAGEANTS	PANACEAS	PARADOX	PARSLEY	PATIENTS
OVERBUYS	OXALATE	PAGURID	PANACHE	PARADOXY	PARSLEYS	PATRIAL
OVERDYE	OXALATES	PAGURIDS	PANACHES	PARAFLE	PARSNEP	PATRIALS
OVERDYED	OXAZINE	PAILFUL	PANCAKE	PARAFLES	PARSNEPS	PATRICK
OVERDYES	OXAZINES	PAILFULS	PANCAKED	PARAGON	PARSNIP	PATRICKS
OVEREAT	OXBLOOD	PAILLON	PANCAKES	PARAGONS	PARSNIPS	PATRIOT
OVEREATS	OXBLOODS	PAILLONS	PANDECT	PARANYM	PARTAKE	PATRIOTS
OVEREYE	OXIDANT	PAINING	PANDECTS	PARANYMS	PARTAKEN	PATROON
OVEREYED	OXIDANTS	SPAINING	PANDOOR	PARAPET	PARTAKER	PATROONS
OVEREYES	OXIDASE	PAINTER	PANDOORS	PARAPETS	PARTAKES	PATTERN
OVERGET	OXIDASES	PAINTERS	PANDORA	PARASOL	PARTIAL	PATTERNS
OVERGETS	OXIDATE	PAIOCKE	PANDORAS	PARASOLS	PARTIALS	PATTERS
OVERHIT	OXIDATED	PAIOCKES	PANDORE	PARATHA	PARTING	SPATTERS
OVERHITS	OXIDATES	PAIRIAL	PANDORES	PARATHAS	PARTINGS	PATTING
OVERING	OXIDISE	PAIRIALS	PANDOUR	PARAZOA	PARTITA	SPATTING
COVERING	OXIDISED	PAIRING	PANDOURS	PARAZOAN	PARTITAS	PATULIN
DOVERING	OXIDISER	PAIRINGS	PANDURA	PARBOIL	PARTLET	PATULINS
HOVERING	OXIDISES	PAISANO	PANDURAS	PARBOILS	PARTLETS	PAUSING
OVERJOY	OXIDIZE	PAISANOS	PANGENE	PARCHES	PARTNER	PAUSINGS
OVERJOYS	OXIDIZED	PAISLEY	PANGENES	PARCHESI	PARTNERS	PAVIOUR
OVERLAP	OXIDIZER	PAISLEYS	PANGING	PARDALE	PARTURE	PAVIOURS
OVERLAPS	OXIDIZES	PAJOCKE	SPANGING	PARDALES	PARTURES	PAVLOVA
OVERLAY	OXONIUM	PAJOCKES	PANGRAM	PARDNER	PARVENU	PAVLOVAS
OVERLAYS	OXONIUMS	PAKAPOO	PANGRAMS	PARDNERS	PARVENUS	PAWNERS
OVERLIE	OXYGENS	PAKAPOOS	PANICLE	PAREIRA	PARVISE	SPAWNERS
OVERLIER	LOXYGENS	PAKFONG	PANICLED	PAREIRAS	PARVISES	PAWNING
OVERLIES	OXYTONE	PAKFONGS	PANICLES	PARELLA	PASSADE	SPAWNING
OVERMAN	OXYTONES	PAKTONG	PANNAGE	PARELLAS	PASSADES	PAXIUBA
OVERMANS	OYSTERS	PAKTONGS	PANNAGES	PARELLE	PASSADO	PAXIUBAS
OVERNET	ROYSTERS	PALABRA	PANNICK	PARELLES	PASSADOS	PAYMENT
OVERNETS	OZONISE	PALABRAS	PANNICKS	PARFAIT	PASSAGE	PAYMENTS
OVERPAY	OZONISED	PALADIN	PANNIER	PARFAITS	PASSAGED	PAYROLL
OVERPAYS	OZONISER	PALADINS	PANNIERS	PARGANA	PASSAGES	PAYROLLS
OVERRAN	OZONISES	PALATAL	PANNING	PARGANAS	PASSING	PAYSAGE
OVERRANK	OZONIZE	PALATALS	SPANNING	PARGING	PASSINGS	PAYSAGES
OVERRED	OZONIZED	PALAVER	PANNINGS	SPARGING	PASSION	PEACHER
OVERREDS	OZONIZER	PALAVERS	PANOCHA	PARISON	PASSIONS	PEACHERS
OVERREN	OZONIZES	PALETOT	PANOCHAS	PARISONS	PASSIVE	PEACOCK
OVERRENS	PABULUM	PALETOTS	PANTHER	PARITOR	PASSIVES	PEACOCKS
OVERRUN	PABULUMS	PALETTE	PANTHERS	PARITORS	PASSKEY	PEACOCKY
OVERRUNS	PACHISI	PALETTES	PANTILE	PARKING	PASSKEYS	PEAKING
OVERSEA	PACHISIS	PALFREY	PANTILED	PARKINGS	PASSMEN	SPEAKING
OVERSEAS	PACIEST	PALFREYS	PANTILES	PARKISH	PASSMENT	PEANING
OVERSEE	SPACIEST	PALLING	PANTINE	SPARKISH	PASTERN	SPEANING
OVERSEEN	PACKAGE	SPALLING	PANTINES	PARKWAY	PASTERNS	PEARLER
OVERSEER	PACKAGED	PALLONE	PANTING	PARKWAYS	PASTIES	PEARLERS
OVERSEES	PACKAGER	PALLONES	PANTINGS	PARLING	PASTIEST	PEARLIN
OVERSET	PACKAGES	PALMATE	PANTLER	SPARLING	PASTIME	PEARLING
OVERSETS	PACKING	PALMATED	PANTLERS	PARLOUR	PASTIMES	PEARLINS
OVERSEW	PACKINGS	PALMFUL	PANTOUM	PARLOURS	PASTING	PEASANT
OVERSEWN	PACKWAY	PALMFULS	PANTOUMS	PAROLEE	PASTINGS	PEASANTS
OVERSEWS	PACKWAYS	PALMIES	PAPERER	PAROLEES	PASTURE	PEASANTY
OVERSOW	PACTION	PALMIEST	PAPERERS	PARONYM	PASTURED	PEASCOD
OVERSOWN	PACTIONS	PALMIET	PAPILIO	PARONYMS	PASTURES	PEASCODS
OVERSOWS	PADDING	PALMIETS	PAPILIOS		PATAGIA	PEBRINE

PEBRINES
PECCAVI
PECCAVIS
PECKING
SPECKING
PECKINGS
PECTISE
PECTISED
PECTISES
PECTIZE
PECTIZED
PECTIZES
PECTOSE
PECTOSES
PEDDLER
PEDDLERS
PEDICAB
PEDICABS
PEDICEL
PEDICELS
PEDICLE
PEDICLED
PEDICLES
PEDRAIL
PEDRAILS
PEDRERO
PEDREROS
PEEKABO
PEEKABOO
PEEKABOS
PEELERS
SPEELERS
PEELING
SPEELING
PEELINGS
PEERAGE
PEERAGES
PEERIES
PEERIEST
PEERING
SPEERING
PEGGING
PEGGINGS
PEISHWA
PEISHWAH
PEISHWAS
PELICAN
PELICANS
PELISSE
PELISSES
PELLACH
PELLACHS
PELLACK
PELLACKS
PELLOCK
PELLOCKS
PELORIA
PELORIAS
PELTAST
PELTASTS
PELTERS
SPELTERS
PELTING
PELTINGS
PEMICAN
PEMICANS
PENANCE
PENANCED
PENANCES
PENDANT

PENDANTS
PENDENT
PENDENTS
PENDING
SPENDING
PENFOLD
PENFOLDS
PENGUIN
PENGUINS
PENNANT
PENNANTS
PENNINE
PENNINES
PENSION
PENSIONS
PENTACT
PENTACTS
PENTANE
PENTANES
PENTENE
PENTENES
PENTHIA
PENTHIAS
PENTICE
PENTICED
PENTICES
PENTISE
PENTISED
PENTISES
PENTODE
PENTODES
PENTOSE
PENTOSES
PENUCHE
PENUCHES
PENUCHI
PENUCHIS
PEONAGE
PEONAGES
PEONISM
PEONISMS
PEPSINE
PEPSINES
PEPTIDE
PEPTIDES
PEPTISE
PEPTISED
PEPTISES
PEPTIZE
PEPTIZED
PEPTIZES
PEPTONE
PEPTONES
PERAEON
PERAEONS
PERCALE
PERCALES
PERCEPT
PERCEPTS
PERCHER
PERCHERS
PERDURE
PERDURED
PERDURES
PEREGAL
PEREGALS
PEREIRA
PEREIRAS
PERFECT
PERFECTA

PERFECTI
PERFECTO
PERFECTS
PERFORM
PERFORMS
PERFUME
PERFUMED
PERFUMER
PERFUMES
PERFUSE
PERFUSED
PERFUSES
PERGOLA
PERGOLAS
PERIAPT
PERIAPTS
PERIDIA
PERIDIAL
PERIDOT
PERIDOTE
PERIDOTS
PERIGEE
PERIGEES
PERIGON
PERIGONE
PERIGONS
PERIOST
PERIOSTS
PERIQUE
PERIQUES
PERIWIG
PERIWIGS
PERJURE
PERJURED
PERJURER
PERJURES
PERLITE
PERLITES
PERMUTE
PERMUTED
PERMUTES
PERPEND
PERPENDS
PERPENT
PERPENTS
PERRIER
PERRIERS
PERSICO
PERSICOS
PERSICOT
PERSING
SPERSING
PERSIST
PERSISTS
PERSONA
PERSONAE
PERSONAL
PERSONAS
PERTAIN
PERTAINS
PERTAKE
PERTAKEN
PERTAKES
PERTURB
PERTURBS
PERTUSE
PERTUSED
PERUSAL
PERUSALS
PERUSER

PERUSERS
PERVADE
PERVADED
PERVADES
PERVERT
PERVERTS
PESAUNT
PESAUNTS
PETCOCK
PETCOCKS
PETIOLE
PETIOLED
PETIOLES
PETTIES
PETTIEST
PETTING
SPETTING
PETTINGS
PETUNIA
PETUNIAS
PFENNIG
PFENNIGE
PFENNIGS
PHAEISM
PHAEISMS
PHAETON
PHAETONS
PHALLIN
PHALLINS
PHANTOM
PHANTOMS
PHANTOMY
PHASMID
PHASMIDS
PHEAZAR
PHEAZARS
PHELLEM
PHELLEMS
PHENATE
PHENATES
PHILTER
PHILTERS
PHILTRE
PHILTRES
PHOBISM
PHOBISMS
PHOBIST
PHOBISTS
PHONATE
PHONATED
PHONATES
PHONEME
PHONEMES
PHONIES
APHONIES
PHONIEST
PHOTISM
PHOTISMS
PHRASER
PHRASERS
PIAFFER
PIAFFERS
PIANINO
PIANINOS
PIANISM
PIANISMS
PIANIST
PIANISTE
PIANISTS
PIARIST

APIARIST
PIARISTS
PIASTRE
PIASTRES
PIBROCH
PIBROCHS
PICADOR
PICADORS
PICAMAR
PICAMARS
PICCOLO
PICCOLOS
PICENES
EPICENES
PICKAXE
PICKAXES
PICKEER
PICKEERS
PICKING
PICKINGS
PICKLER
PICKLERS
PICKMAW
PICKMAWS
PICOTEE
PICOTEES
PICQUET
PICQUETS
PICRATE
PICRATES
PICRITE
PICRITES
PICTURE
PICTURED
PICTURES
PIDDLER
PIDDLERS
PIDDOCK
PIDDOCKS
PIDGEON
PIDGEONS
PIEBALD
PIEBALDS
PIERAGE
PIERAGES
PIERCER
PIERCERS
PIERROT
PIERROTS
PIETISM
PIETISMS
PIETIST
PIETISTS
PIFFERO
PIFFEROS
PIFFLER
PIFFLERS
PIGBOAT
PIGBOATS
PIGFEED
PIGFEEDS
PIGGIES
PIGGIEST
PIGGING
PIGGINGS
PIGHTED
SPIGHTED
PIGHTLE
PIGHTLES
PIGLING

PIGLINGS
PIGMEAT
PIGMEATS
PIGMENT
PIGMENTS
PIGSKIN
PIGSKINS
PIGSNEY
PIGSNEYS
PIGSNIE
PIGSNIES
PIGTAIL
PIGTAILS
PIGWEED
PIGWEEDS
PIKELET
SPIKELET
PIKELETS
PILCHER
PILCHERS
PILCORN
PILCORNS
PILCROW
PILCROWS
PILEATE
PILEATED
PILGRIM
PILGRIMS
PILLAGE
SPILLAGE
PILLAGED
PILLAGER
PILLAGES
PILLING
SPILLING
PILLION
PILLIONS
PILLOCK
PILLOCKS
PILSNER
PILSNERS
PIMENTO
PIMENTOS
PINBALL
PINBALLS
PINCASE
PINCASES
PINCHER
PINCHERS
PINDARI
PINDARIS
PINFOLD
PINFOLDS
PINGLER
PINGLERS
PINGUIN
PINGUINS
PINHEAD
PINHEADS
PINHOLE
PINHOLES
PINIEST
SPINIEST
PINIONS
OPINIONS
PINKIES
PINKIEST
PINKING
PINKINGS
PINNACE

PINNACES
PINNATE
PINNATED
PINNERS
SPINNERS
PINNETS
SPINNETS
PINNIES
SPINNIES
PINNING
SPINNING
PINNINGS
PINNOCK
PINNOCKS
PINNULA
PINNULAS
PINNULE
PINNULES
PINOCLE
PINOCLES
PINTADO
PINTADOS
PINTAIL
PINTAILS
PIONEER
PIONEERS
PIONING
PIONINGS
PIPEFUL
PIPEFULS
PIPETTE
PIPETTED
PIPETTES
PIRAGUA
PIRAGUAS
PIRANHA
PIRANHAS
PIRATED
SPIRATED
PIROGUE
PIROGUES
PISCINA
PISCINAE
PISCINAS
PISCINE
PISCINES
PISMIRE
PISMIRES
PISSOIR
PISSOIRS
PISTOLE
PISTOLES
PISTOLET
PITAPAT
PITAPATS
PITARAH
PITARAHS
PITCHER
SPITCHER
PITCHERS
PITFALL
PITFALLS
PITHEAD
PITHEADS
PITTERS
SPITTERS
PITTING
SPITTING
PITTINGS
PITTITE

PITTITES	PLAUDITS	PLUMBERY	POLACRES	**PONIARD**	**POSTEEN**	**POUTHER**
PITUITA	**PLAYBOY**	**PLUMBUM**	**POLARON**	PONIARDS	POSTEENS	POUTHERS
PITUITAS	PLAYBOYS	PLUMBUMS	POLARONS	**PONTAGE**	**POSTERN**	**POUTIER**
PITUITE	**PLAYING**	**PLUMCOT**	**POLECAT**	PONTAGES	POSTERNS	SPOUTIER
PITUITES	SPLAYING	PLUMCOTS	POLECATS	**PONTIFF**	**POSTILS**	**POUTING**
PIVOTER	UPLAYING	**PLUMIST**	**POLEMIC**	PONTIFFS	APOSTILS	SPOUTING
PIVOTERS	**PLAYLET**	PLUMISTS	POLEMICS	**PONTOON**	**POSTING**	POUTINGS
PLACARD	PLAYLETS	**PLUMMET**	**POLENTA**	SPONTOON	POSTINGS	**PRABBLE**
PLACARDS	**PLEADER**	PLUMMETS	POLENTAS	PONTOONS	**POSTURE**	PRABBLES
PLACATE	PLEADERS	**PLUMPEN**	**POLITIC**	**POOFTAH**	POSTURED	**PRACTIC**
PLACATED	**PLEASER**	PLUMPENS	POLITICK	POOFTAHS	POSTURER	PRACTICE
PLACATES	PLEASERS	**PLUMPER**	POLITICO	**POOFTER**	POSTURES	PRACTICK
PLACCAT	**PLECTRE**	PLUMPERS	POLITICS	POOFTERS	**POTABLE**	PRACTICS
PLACCATE	PLECTRES	**PLUMULA**	**POLLACK**	**POOGYEE**	POTABLES	**PRAETOR**
PLACCATS	**PLEDGEE**	PLUMULAE	POLLACKS	POOGYEES	**POTASSA**	PRAETORS
PLACEBO	PLEDGEES	PLUMULAR	**POLLARD**	**POOKING**	POTASSAS	**PRAIRIE**
PLACEBOS	**PLEDGER**	**PLUMULE**	POLLARDS	SPOOKING	**POTCHER**	PRAIRIED
PLACING	PLEDGERS	PLUMULES	**POLLING**	**POOLING**	POTCHERS	PRAIRIES
PLACINGS	**PLEDGET**	**PLUNDER**	POLLINGS	SPOOLING	**POTENCE**	**PRAISED**
PLACKET	PLEDGETS	PLUNDERS	**POLLOCK**	**POPADUM**	POTENCES	UPRAISED
PLACKETS	**PLEDGOR**	**PLUNGER**	POLLOCKS	POPADUMS	**POTHEEN**	**PRAISER**
PLAFOND	PLEDGORS	PLUNGERS	**POLLUTE**	**POPCORN**	POTHEENS	PRAISERS
PLAFONDS	**PLENIPO**	**PLUNKER**	POLLUTED	POPCORNS	**POTHOLE**	**PRAISES**
PLAGIUM	PLENIPOS	PLUNKERS	POLLUTER	**POPEDOM**	POTHOLER	UPRAISES
PLAGIUMS	**PLENIST**	**PLUSAGE**	POLLUTES	POPEDOMS	POTHOLES	**PRALINE**
PLAITER	PLENISTS	PLUSAGES	**POLOIST**	**POPERIN**	**POTHOOK**	PRALINES
PLAITERS	**PLEOPOD**	**PLUSHES**	POLOISTS	POPERINS	POTHOOKS	**PRANCER**
PLANNER	PLEOPODS	PLUSHEST	**POLONIE**	**POPOVER**	**POTICHE**	PRANCERS
PLANNERS	**PLEROMA**	**PLUVIAL**	POLONIES	POPOVERS	POTICHES	**PRANCKE**
PLANTER	PLEROMAS	PLUVIALS	**POLYGAM**	**POPULAR**	**POTOROO**	PRANCKED
PLANTERS	**PLEROME**	**PLYWOOD**	POLYGAMS	POPULARS	POTOROOS	PRANCKES
PLANULA	PLEROMES	PLYWOODS	POLYGAMY	**PORIFER**	**POTTAGE**	**PRANKLE**
PLANULAE	**PLESSOR**	**POACHER**	**POLYGON**	PORIFERS	POTTAGES	PRANKLED
PLANULAR	PLESSORS	POACHERS	POLYGONS	**PORPESS**	**POTTERS**	PRANKLES
PLASHED	**PLEXURE**	**POCHARD**	POLYGONY	PORPESSE	SPOTTERS	**PRATING**
SPLASHED	PLEXURES	POCHARDS	**POLYMER**	**PORRECT**	**POTTIER**	UPRATING
PLASHES	**PLICATE**	**POCHOIR**	POLYMERS	PORRECTS	SPOTTIER	PRATINGS
SPLASHES	PLICATED	POCHOIRS	POLYMERY	**PORRIGO**	**POTTIES**	**PRATTLE**
PLASHET	PLICATES	**POCKARD**	**POLYNIA**	PORRIGOS	POTTIEST	SPRATTLE
PLASHETS	**PLISKIE**	POCKARDS	POLYNIAS	**PORTAGE**	**POTTING**	PRATTLED
PLASMID	PLISKIES	**POCKPIT**	**POLYNYA**	PORTAGES	SPOTTING	PRATTLER
PLASMIDS	**PLODDER**	POCKPITS	POLYNYAS	**PORTEND**	**POUFTAH**	PRATTLES
PLASMIN	PLODDERS	**PODAGRA**	**POLYPOD**	PORTENDS	POUFTAHS	**PRAUNCE**
PLASMINS	**PLONKER**	PODAGRAL	POLYPODS	**PORTENT**	**POUFTER**	PRAUNCED
PLASTER	PLONKERS	PODAGRAS	POLYPODY	PORTENTS	POUFTERS	PRAUNCES
PLASTERS	**PLOOKIE**	**PODESTA**	**POLYZOA**	**PORTERS**	**POULARD**	**PRAWLIN**
PLASTERY	PLOOKIER	PODESTAS	POLYZOAN	SPORTERS	POULARDS	PRAWLINS
PLASTIC	**PLOSION**	**POETISE**	**POMATUM**	**PORTESS**	**POULDER**	**PRAYERS**
APLASTIC	PLOSIONS	POETISED	POMATUMS	PORTESSE	POULDERS	SPRAYERS
PLASTICS	**PLOSIVE**	POETISES	**POMEROY**	**PORTICO**	**POULDRE**	**PRAYING**
PLASTID	PLOSIVES	**POETIZE**	POMEROYS	PORTICOS	POULDRES	SPRAYING
PLASTIDS	**PLOTTER**	POETIZED	**POMFRET**	**PORTIER**	**POULTER**	PRAYINGS
PLATANE	PLOTTERS	POETIZES	POMFRETS	SPORTIER	POULTERS	**PREASSE**
PLATANES	**PLOTTIE**	**POINADO**	**POMPANO**	PORTIERE	**POUNCET**	PREASSED
PLATEAU	PLOTTIES	POINADOS	POMPANOS	**PORTING**	POUNCETS	PREASSES
PLATEAUS	**PLOUKIE**	**POINDER**	**POMPELO**	SPORTING	**POUNDAL**	**PREBEND**
PLATEAUX	PLOUKIER	POINDERS	POMPELOS	**PORTION**	POUNDALS	PREBENDS
PLATINA	**PLOUTER**	**POINTEL**	**POMPION**	PORTIONS	**POUNDER**	**PRECEDE**
PLATINAS	PLOUTERS	POINTELS	POMPIONS	**PORTRAY**	POUNDERS	PRECEDED
PLATING	**PLOWTER**	**POINTER**	**POMPOON**	PORTRAYS	**POURING**	PRECEDES
PLATINGS	PLOWTERS	POINTERS	POMPOONS	**POSAUNE**	POURINGS	**PRECEPT**
PLATOON	**PLUCKER**	**POISSON**	**PONCEAU**	POSAUNES	**POURSEW**	PRECEPTS
PLATOONS	PLUCKERS	POISSONS	PONCEAUS	**POSEUSE**	POURSEWS	**PRECISE**
PLATTED	**PLUGGER**	**POITREL**	PONCEAUX	POSEUSES	**POURSUE**	PRECISED
SPLATTED	PLUGGERS	POITRELS	**PONDAGE**	**POSITON**	POURSUED	PRECISER
PLATTER	**PLUMAGE**	**POKEFUL**	PONDAGES	POSITONS	POURSUES	PRECISES
SPLATTER	PLUMAGED	POKEFULS	**PONGIER**	**POSSUMS**	**POUSSIN**	**PRECOOK**
PLATTERS	PLUMAGES	**POLACCA**	SPONGIER	OPOSSUMS	POUSSINS	PRECOOKS
PLAUDIT	**PLUMBER**	POLACCAS	**PONGING**	**POSTAGE**	**POUTERS**	**PREDATE**
PLAUDITE	PLUMBERS	**POLACRE**	SPONGING	POSTAGES	SPOUTERS	PREDATED

PREDATES	**PRETEND**	PROBANGS	**PROPAGE**	**PROVISO**	**PUPARIA**	PYRAMIDS
PREDIAL	PRETENDS	**PROBATE**	PROPAGED	PROVISOR	PUPARIAL	**PYRETIC**
PREDIALS	**PRETEXT**	PROBATED	PROPAGES	PROVISOS	**PUPUNHA**	APYRETIC
PREDICT	PRETEXTS	PROBATES	**PROPALE**	**PROVOKE**	PUPUNHAS	**PYREXIA**
PREDICTS	**PRETZEL**	**PROBLEM**	PROPALED	PROVOKED	**PURGING**	APYREXIA
PREDOOM	PRETZELS	PROBLEMS	PROPALES	PROVOKER	PURGINGS	PYREXIAL
PREDOOMS	**PREVAIL**	**PROCEED**	**PROPANE**	PROVOKES	**PURITAN**	PYREXIAS
PREEING	PREVAILS	PROCEEDS	PROPANES	**PROVOST**	PURITANS	**PYROGEN**
SPREEING	**PREVENE**	**PROCTOR**	**PROPEND**	PROVOSTS	**PURLIEU**	PYROGENS
PREEMIE	PREVENED	PROCTORS	PROPENDS	**PROWLER**	PURLIEUS	**PYRRHIC**
PREEMIES	PREVENES	**PROCURE**	**PROPENE**	PROWLERS	**PURLINE**	PYRRHICS
PREFACE	**PREVENT**	PROCURED	PROPENES	**PRUNING**	PURLINES	**PYRROLE**
PREFACED	PREVENTS	PROCURER	**PROPHET**	PRUNINGS	**PURLING**	PYRROLES
PREFACES	**PREVERB**	PROCURES	PROPHETS	**PRURIGO**	SPURLING	**PYTHIUM**
PREFADE	PREVERBS	**PRODUCE**	**PROPINE**	PRURIGOS	PURLINGS	PYTHIUMS
PREFADED	**PREVIEW**	PRODUCED	PROPINED	**PSALTER**	**PURLOIN**	**QUACKLE**
PREFADES	PREVIEWS	PRODUCER	PROPINES	PSALTERS	PURLOINS	QUACKLED
PREFECT	**PREVISE**	PRODUCES	**PROPONE**	PSALTERY	**PURPLES**	QUACKLES
PREFECTS	PREVISED	**PRODUCT**	PROPONED	**PSYCHIC**	PURPLEST	**QUADRAT**
PREFORM	PREVISES	PRODUCTS	PROPONES	PSYCHICS	**PURPORT**	QUADRATE
PREFORMS	**PREZZIE**	**PROFANE**	**PROPOSE**	**PTARMIC**	PURPORTS	QUADRATS
PREHEAT	PREZZIES	PROFANED	PROPOSED	PTARMICS	**PURPOSE**	**QUAFFER**
PREHEATS	**PRIBBLE**	PROFANER	PROPOSER	**PTERYLA**	PURPOSED	QUAFFERS
PREHEND	PRIBBLES	PROFANES	PROPOSES	PTERYLAE	PURPOSES	**QUAHAUG**
PREHENDS	**PRICKER**	**PROFFER**	**PRORATE**	**PTYALIN**	**PURPURA**	QUAHAUGS
PRELATE	PRICKERS	PROFFERS	PRORATED	PTYALINS	PURPURAS	**QUAILED**
PRELATES	**PRICKET**	**PROFILE**	PRORATES	**PUCCOON**	**PURPURE**	SQUAILED
PRELECT	PRICKETS	PROFILED	**PROSING**	PUCCOONS	PURPURES	**QUAKING**
PRELECTS	**PRICKLE**	PROFILER	PROSINGS	**PUCELLE**	**PURRING**	QUAKINGS
PRELUDE	PRICKLED	PROFILES	**PROSPER**	PUCELLES	SPURRING	**QUALITY**
PRELUDED	PRICKLES	**PROFUSE**	PROSPERS	**PUDDING**	PURRINGS	EQUALITY
PRELUDES	**PRIGGED**	PROFUSER	**PROTEAS**	SPUDDING	**PURSUAL**	**QUANNET**
PRELUDI	SPRIGGED	**PROGRAM**	PROTEASE	PUDDINGS	PURSUALS	QUANNETS
PRELUDIO	**PRIGGER**	PROGRAMS	**PROTECT**	PUDDINGY	**PURSUER**	**QUANTIC**
PREMIER	PRIGGERS	**PROJECT**	PROTECTS	**PUDDLER**	PURSUERS	QUANTICS
PREMIERE	PRIGGERY	PROJECTS	**PROTEGE**	PUDDLERS	**PURSUIT**	**QUARREL**
PREMIERS	**PRIMAGE**	**PROLATE**	PROTEGEE	**PUDDOCK**	PURSUITS	QUARRELS
PREMISE	PRIMAGES	PROLATED	PROTEGES	PUDDOCKS	**PURVIEW**	**QUARTAN**
PREMISED	**PRIMATE**	PROLATES	**PROTEID**	**PUDENDA**	PURVIEWS	QUARTANS
PREMISES	PRIMATES	**PROLINE**	PROTEIDS	PUDENDAL	**PUSHROD**	**QUARTER**
PREMIUM	**PRIMERO**	PROLINES	**PROTEIN**	**PUFFING**	PUSHRODS	QUARTERN
PREMIUMS	PRIMEROS	**PROLLED**	PROTEINS	PUFFINGS	**PUSTULE**	QUARTERS
PREMOVE	**PRIMEUR**	UPROLLED	**PROTEND**	**PUGGIES**	PUSTULES	**QUARTET**
PREMOVED	PRIMEURS	**PROLLER**	PROTENDS	PUGGIEST	**PUTCHER**	QUARTETS
PREMOVES	**PRIMINE**	PROLLERS	**PROTEST**	**PUGGING**	PUTCHERS	QUARTETT
PREPACK	PRIMINES	**PROLONG**	PROTESTS	PUGGINGS	**PUTCHUK**	**QUARTIC**
PREPACKS	**PRIMING**	PROLONGE	**PROTHYL**	**PUGGREE**	PUTCHUKS	QUARTICS
PREPARE	PRIMINGS	PROLONGS	PROTHYLE	PUGGREES	**PUTLOCK**	**QUASHED**
PREPARED	**PRIMULA**	**PROMISE**	PROTHYLS	**PULDRON**	PUTLOCKS	SQUASHED
PREPARER	PRIMULAS	PROMISED	**PROTIST**	PULDRONS	**PUTTERS**	**QUASHEE**
PREPARES	**PRINCES**	PROMISEE	PROTISTS	**PULSATE**	SPUTTERS	QUASHEES
PREPUCE	PRINCESS	PROMISER	**PROTIUM**	PULSATED	**PUTTIER**	**QUASHES**
PREPUCES	**PRINTED**	PROMISES	PROTIUMS	PULSATES	PUTTIERS	SQUASHES
PREQUEL	SPRINTED	**PROMMER**	**PROTYLE**	**PULTOON**	**PUTTING**	**QUASHIE**
PREQUELS	**PRINTER**	PROMMERS	PROTYLES	PULTOONS	PUTTINGS	QUASHIES
PRESAGE	SPRINTER	**PROMOTE**	**PROULER**	**PULTURE**	**PUTTOCK**	**QUASSIA**
PRESAGED	PRINTERS	PROMOTED	PROULERS	PULTURES	PUTTOCKS	QUASSIAS
PRESAGER	**PRISAGE**	PROMOTER	**PROVAND**	**PUMPION**	**PUZZLER**	**QUAYAGE**
PRESAGES	PRISAGES	PROMOTES	PROVANDS	PUMPIONS	PUZZLERS	QUAYAGES
PRESENT	**PRISING**	**PRONATE**	**PROVEND**	**PUMPKIN**	**PYAEMIA**	**QUELLER**
PRESENTS	UPRISING	PRONATED	PROVENDS	PUMPKINS	PYAEMIAS	QUELLERS
PRESIDE	**PRIVADO**	PRONATES	**PROVERB**	**PUNALUA**	**PYCNITE**	**QUERIST**
PRESIDED	PRIVADOS	**PRONEUR**	PROVERBS	PUNALUAN	PYCNITES	QUERISTS
PRESIDES	**PRIVATE**	PRONEURS	**PROVIDE**	PUNALUAS	**PYEBALD**	**QUESTER**
PRESSER	PRIVATES	**PRONOTA**	PROVIDED	**PUNCHER**	PYEBALDS	QUESTERS
PRESSERS	**PRIVIES**	PRONOTAL	PROVIDER	PUNCHERS	**PYGIDIA**	**QUESTOR**
PRESUME	PRIVIEST	**PRONOUN**	PROVIDES	**PUNNING**	PYGIDIAL	QUESTORS
PRESUMED	**PROBAND**	PRONOUNS	**PROVINE**	PUNNINGS	**PYRALID**	**QUETZAL**
PRESUMER	PROBANDS	**PROOTIC**	PROVINED	**PUNSTER**	PYRALIDS	QUETZALS
PRESUMES	**PROBANG**	PROOTICS	PROVINES	PUNSTERS	**PYRAMID**	**QUEUING**

QUEUINGS	QUOITERS	RAGBOLT	RAMBLERS	RANSACKS	RATPACK	READING
QUEYNIE	RABANNA	RAGBOLTS	RAMBLES	RANSOMS	RATPACKS	AREADING
QUEYNIES	RABANNAS	RAGGIER	BRAMBLES	TRANSOMS	RATTEEN	BREADING
QUIBBLE	RABATTE	CRAGGIER	RAMEKIN	RANTERS	RATTEENS	DREADING
QUIBBLED	RABATTED	DRAGGIER	RAMEKINS	GRANTERS	RATTIER	TREADING
QUIBBLER	RABATTES	RAGGIES	RAMMERS	TRANTERS	BRATTIER	READINGS
QUIBBLES	RABBETS	RAGGIEST	CRAMMERS	RANTING	RATTING	READMIT
QUIBLIN	DRABBETS	RAGGING	RAMMING	DRANTING	PRATTING	READMITS
QUIBLINS	RABBLED	BRAGGING	CRAMMING	GRANTING	RATTINGS	READOPT
QUICKEN	BRABBLED	DRAGGING	DRAMMING	TRANTING	RATTISH	READOPTS
QUICKENS	DRABBLED	RAGGINGS	RAMPAGE	RAPHIDE	BRATTISH	REAGENT
QUICKIE	GRABBLED	RAGGLED	RAMPAGED	RAPHIDES	RATTLED	REAGENTS
QUICKIES	RABBLER	DRAGGLED	RAMPAGES	RAPIERS	BRATTLED	REAKING
QUIDDIT	DRABBLER	RAGGLES	RAMPART	DRAPIERS	PRATTLED	BREAKING
QUIDDITS	GRABBLER	DRAGGLES	RAMPARTS	RAPLOCH	RATTLER	CREAKING
QUIDDITY	RABBLERS	RAGMENT	RAMPERS	RAPLOCHS	PRATTLER	FREAKING
QUIDDLE	RABBLES	FRAGMENT	TRAMPERS	RAPPERS	RATTLERS	WREAKING
QUIDDLED	BRABBLES	RAGMENTS	RAMPICK	TRAPPERS	RATTLES	REALGAR
QUIDDLER	DRABBLES	RAGTIME	RAMPICKS	WRAPPERS	BRATTLES	REALGARS
QUIDDLES	GRABBLES	RAGTIMER	RAMPIKE	RAPPING	PRATTLES	REALIGN
QUIESCE	PRABBLES	RAGTIMES	RAMPIKES	CRAPPING	RATTLIN	REALIGNS
QUIESCED	RABBONI	RAGWEED	RAMPING	DRAPPING	RATTLINE	REALISE
QUIESCES	RABBONIS	RAGWEEDS	CRAMPING	FRAPPING	RATTLING	REALISED
QUIETEN	RACCOON	RAGWORK	TRAMPING	TRAPPING	RATTLINS	REALISER
QUIETENS	RACCOONS	RAGWORKS	RAMPION	WRAPPING	RAVAGER	REALISES
QUIETER	RACEWAY	RAGWORM	RAMPIONS	RAPPINGS	RAVAGERS	REALISM
QUIETERS	RACEWAYS	RAGWORMS	RAMPIRE	RAPPORT	RAVELIN	REALISMS
QUILLAI	RACHIAL	RAGWORT	RAMPIRED	RAPPORTS	RAVELINS	REALIST
QUILLAIA	BRACHIAL	RAGWORTS	RAMPIRES	RAPTURE	RAVENED	REALISTS
QUILLAIS	RACINGS	RAIDING	RANCHED	RAPTURED	CRAVENED	REALIZE
QUILLET	TRACINGS	BRAIDING	BRANCHED	RAPTURES	RAVENER	REALIZED
QUILLETS	RACKERS	RAIKING	CRANCHED	RAREBIT	RAVENERS	REALIZER
QUILLON	CRACKERS	TRAIKING	RANCHER	RAREBITS	RAVINGS	REALIZES
QUILLONS	TRACKERS	RAILERS	BRANCHER	RASCHEL	CRAVINGS	REALLIE
QUILTER	RACKETS	TRAILERS	RANCHERO	RASCHELS	GRAVINGS	REALLIED
QUILTERS	BRACKETS	RAILING	RANCHERS	RASHEST	RAVIOLI	REALLIES
QUINCHE	RACKETT	BRAILING	RANCHES	BRASHEST	RAVIOLIS	REALLOT
QUINCHED	RACKETTS	DRAILING	BRANCHES	RASHING	RAWBONE	REALLOTS
QUINCHES	RACKING	TRAILING	CRANCHES	BRASHING	RAWBONED	REALTIE
QUINIES	CRACKING	RAILINGS	TRANCHES	CRASHING	RAWHEAD	REALTIES
SQUINIES	TRACKING	RAILWAY	RANCING	TRASHING	RAWHEADS	REALTOR
QUININE	WRACKING	RAILWAYS	PRANCING	RASPERS	RAWHIDE	REALTORS
QUININES	RACKINGS	RAIMENT	TRANCING	GRASPERS	RAWHIDES	REAMEND
QUINNAT	RACLOIR	RAIMENTS	RANCOUR	RASPING	RAWINGS	REAMENDS
QUINNATS	RACLOIRS	RAINBOW	RANCOURS	GRASPING	DRAWINGS	REAMERS
QUINONE	RACQUET	RAINBOWS	RANDIES	RASPINGS	RAYLING	CREAMERS
QUINONES	RACQUETS	RAINBOWY	BRANDIES	RASTRUM	GRAYLING	DREAMERS
QUINTAL	RADIANT	RAINIER	RANDIEST	RASTRUMS	RAZZLES	REAMIER
QUINTALS	RADIANTS	BRAINIER	RANDING	RASURES	FRAZZLES	CREAMIER
QUINTET	RADIATE	GRAINIER	BRANDING	ERASURES	REACHED	DREAMIER
QUINTETS	ERADIATE	RAINING	RANGERS	RATAFIA	AREACHED	REAMING
QUINTETT	RADIATED	BRAINING	GRANGERS	RATAFIAS	BREACHED	BREAMING
QUIPPED	RADIATES	DRAINING	RANGING	RATCHES	PREACHED	CREAMING
EQUIPPED	RADICAL	GRAINING	PRANGING	CRATCHES	REACHER	DREAMING
QUIRING	RADICALS	TRAINING	RANKEST	FRATCHES	PREACHER	REARING
SQUIRING	RADICEL	RAISERS	CRANKEST	RATCHET	TREACHER	DREARING
QUIRTED	RADICELS	PRAISERS	FRANKEST	BRATCHET	REACHERS	REARISE
SQUIRTED	RADICLE	RAISING	RANKING	RATCHETS	REACHES	REARISEN
QUITTAL	RADICLES	ARAISING	BRANKING	RATFINK	AREACHES	REARISES
QUITTALS	RAFFISH	BRAISING	CRANKING	RATFINKS	BREACHES	REASONS
QUITTER	DRAFFISH	FRAISING	FRANKING	RATINGS	PREACHES	TREASONS
QUITTERS	RAFFLER	PRAISING	PRANKING	GRATINGS	REACTOR	REASTED
QUITTOR	RAFFLERS	RAISINGS	RANKINGS	PRATINGS	REACTORS	BREASTED
QUITTORS	RAFTERS	RAKSHAS	RANKLED	RATIONS	READAPT	REAVING
QUIZZER	DRAFTERS	RAKSHASA	CRANKLED	ORATIONS	READAPTS	GREAVING
QUIZZERS	GRAFTERS	RALLIER	PRANKLED	RATLINE	READERS	REAWAKE
QUIZZERY	RAFTING	RALLIERS	RANKLES	RATLINES	DREADERS	REAWAKED
QUODLIN	CRAFTING	RAMAKIN	CRANKLES	RATLING	TREADERS	REAWAKEN
QUODLINS	DRAFTING	RAMAKINS	PRANKLES	BRATLING	READIES	REAWAKES
QUOITER	GRAFTING	RAMBLER	RANSACK	RATLINGS	READIEST	REAWOKE

REAWOKEN	RECOWERS	**REEVING**	REGRATER	RELIVERS	REORDERS	**REQUIRE**
REBATER	**RECOYLE**	PREEVING	REGRATES	**REMANET**	**REPACKS**	REQUIRED
REBATERS	RECOYLED	**REFACED**	**REGREDE**	REMANETS	PREPACKS	REQUIRER
REBIRTH	RECOYLES	PREFACED	REGREDED	**REMANIE**	**REPAINT**	REQUIRES
REBIRTHS	**RECRUIT**	**REFACES**	REGREDES	REMANIES	REPAINTS	**REQUITE**
REBLOOM	RECRUITS	PREFACES	**REGREET**	**REMBLAI**	**REPAPER**	REQUITED
REBLOOMS	**RECTION**	**REFECTS**	REGREETS	REMBLAIS	REPAPERS	REQUITER
REBOUND	ERECTION	PREFECTS	**REGRIND**	**REMBLED**	**REPINER**	REQUITES
REBOUNDS	RECTIONS	**REFEREE**	REGRINDS	TREMBLED	REPINERS	**REQUOTE**
REBRACE	**RECTORS**	REFEREED	**REGROUP**	**REMBLES**	**REPIQUE**	REQUOTED
REBRACED	ERECTORS	REFEREES	REGROUPS	TREMBLES	REPIQUED	REQUOTES
REBRACES	**RECUILE**	**REFINER**	**REGULAR**	**REMERGE**	REPIQUES	**REROUTE**
REBUILD	RECUILED	REFINERS	REGULARS	REMERGED	**REPLACE**	REROUTED
REBUILDS	RECUILES	REFINERY	**REHEARS**	REMERGES	REPLACED	REROUTES
REBUKER	**RECURVE**	**REFLATE**	REHEARSE	**REMISED**	REPLACER	**RESCALE**
REBUKERS	RECURVED	REFLATED	**REHEATS**	PREMISED	REPLACES	RESCALED
RECEDED	RECURVES	REFLATES	PREHEATS	**REMISES**	**REPLANT**	RESCALES
PRECEDED	**RECYCLE**	**REFLECT**	**REHOUSE**	PREMISES	REPLANTS	**RESCIND**
RECEDES	RECYCLED	REFLECTS	REHOUSED	**REMNANT**	**REPLETE**	PRESCIND
PRECEDES	RECYCLES	**REFLOAT**	REHOUSES	REMNANTS	REPLETED	RESCINDS
RECEIPT	**REDBACK**	REFLOATS	**REINING**	**REMODEL**	REPLETES	**RESCORE**
RECEIPTS	REDBACKS	**REFORMS**	GREINING	REMODELS	**REPLICA**	RESCORED
RECEIVE	**REDCOAT**	PREFORMS	**REINTER**	**REMORSE**	REPLICAS	RESCORES
RECEIVED	REDCOATS	**REFOUND**	REINTERS	PREMORSE	**REPLIER**	**RESCUER**
RECEIVER	**REDDING**	REFOUNDS	**REISSUE**	REMORSES	REPLIERS	RESCUERS
RECEIVES	REDDINGS	**REFRACT**	REISSUED	**REMOTES**	**REPOINT**	**RESEIZE**
RECENSE	**REDDLED**	REFRACTS	REISSUES	REMOTEST	REPOINTS	RESEIZED
RECENSED	TREDDLED	**REFRAIN**	**REJOICE**	**REMOULD**	**REPOSAL**	RESEIZES
RECENSES	**REDDLES**	REFRAINS	REJOICED	REMOULDS	REPOSALS	**RESENTS**
RECEPTS	TREDDLES	**REFRAME**	REJOICER	**REMOUNT**	**REPOSIT**	PRESENTS
PRECEPTS	**REDNECK**	REFRAMED	REJOICES	REMOUNTS	REPOSITS	**RESERVE**
RECHART	REDNECKS	REFRAMES	**REJONEO**	**REMOVAL**	**REPPING**	PRESERVE
RECHARTS	**REDOUBT**	**REFROZE**	REJONEOS	REMOVALS	PREPPING	RESERVED
RECHATE	REDOUBTS	REFROZEN	**REJOURN**	**REMOVED**	REPPINGS	RESERVES
RECHATES	**REDOUND**	**REFUGEE**	REJOURNS	PREMOVED	**REPRIME**	**RESHAPE**
RECHEAT	REDOUNDS	REFUGEES	**REJUDGE**	**REMOVER**	REPRIMED	RESHAPED
RECHEATS	**REDPOLL**	**REFUSAL**	PREJUDGE	REMOVERS	REPRIMES	RESHAPES
RECHECK	REDPOLLS	REFUSALS	REJUDGED	**REMOVES**	**REPRINT**	**RESIANT**
RECHECKS	**REDRAFT**	**REFUSER**	REJUDGES	PREMOVES	REPRINTS	RESIANTS
RECITAL	REDRAFTS	REFUSERS	**RELACHE**	**REMUAGE**	**REPRISE**	**RESIDED**
RECITALS	**REDRIVE**	**REFUTAL**	RELACHES	REMUAGES	REPRISED	PRESIDED
RECITER	REDRIVEN	REFUTALS	**RELAPSE**	**REMUEUR**	REPRISES	**RESIDER**
RECITERS	REDRIVES	**REFUTER**	RELAPSED	REMUEURS	**REPRIVE**	RESIDERS
RECKING	**REDSKIN**	REFUTERS	RELAPSER	**RENAGUE**	REPRIVED	**RESIDES**
TRECKING	REDSKINS	**REGALES**	RELAPSES	RENAGUED	REPRIVES	PRESIDES
WRECKING	**REDUCER**	GREGALES	**RELATER**	RENAGUES	**REPRIZE**	**RESIDUA**
RECLAIM	REDUCERS	**REGALIA**	RELATERS	**RENDING**	REPRIZED	RESIDUAL
RECLAIMS	**REDWING**	REGALIAN	**RELATES**	TRENDING	REPRIZES	**RESIDUE**
RECLAME	REDWINGS	REGALIAS	PRELATES	**RENEGER**	**REPROOF**	RESIDUES
RECLAMES	**REDWOOD**	**REGATTA**	**RELATOR**	RENEGERS	REPROOFS	**RESINER**
RECLIMB	REDWOODS	REGATTAS	RELATORS	**RENEGUE**	**REPROVE**	RESINERS
RECLIMBS	**REECHED**	**REGENCE**	**RELAXIN**	RENEGUED	REPROVED	**RESOLVE**
RECLINE	BREECHED	REGENCES	RELAXING	RENEGUER	REPROVER	RESOLVED
RECLINED	**REECHES**	**REGIMEN**	RELAXINS	RENEGUES	REPROVES	RESOLVER
RECLINER	BREECHES	REGIMENS	**RELEASE**	**RENEWAL**	**REPRYVE**	RESOLVES
RECLINES	**REECHIE**	REGIMENT	RELEASED	RENEWALS	REPRYVED	**RESOUND**
RECLOSE	REECHIER	**REGMATA**	RELEASEE	**RENEWER**	REPRYVES	RESOUNDS
RECLOSED	**REEDERS**	BREGMATA	RELEASER	RENEWERS	**REPTILE**	**RESPEAK**
RECLOSES	BREEDERS	**REGNANT**	RELEASES	**RENNING**	REPTILES	RESPEAKS
RECLUSE	**REEDIER**	PREGNANT	**RELIEVE**	BRENNING	**REPULSE**	**RESPECT**
RECLUSES	GREEDIER	**REGORGE**	RELIEVED	GRENNING	REPULSED	RESPECTS
RECOUNT	**REEDING**	REGORGED	RELIEVER	RENNINGS	REPULSES	**RESPELL**
RECOUNTS	BREEDING	REGORGES	RELIEVES	**RENTALS**	**REQUERE**	RESPELLS
RECOURE	REEDINGS	**REGRADE**	**RELIEVO**	TRENTALS	REQUERED	**RESPIRE**
RECOURED	**REEFING**	REGRADED	RELIEVOS	**RENTBOY**	REQUERES	RESPIRED
RECOURES	REEFINGS	REGRADES	**RELIGHT**	RENTBOYS	**REQUEST**	RESPIRES
RECOVER	**REEKIER**	**REGRANT**	RELIGHTS	**RENTIER**	REQUESTS	**RESPITE**
RECOVERS	CREEKIER	REGRANTS	**RELIQUE**	RENTIERS	**REQUIEM**	RESPITED
RECOVERY	**REELING**	**REGRATE**	RELIQUES	**REORDER**	REQUIEMS	RESPITES
RECOWER	REELINGS	REGRATED	**RELIVER**	PREORDER		**RESPOKE**

RESPOKEN	RETRAIT	REVIVALS	PRICKETS	FRIGIDER	CRIPPLED	ROBUSTAS
RESPOND	RETRAITE	REVIVER	RICKING	RIGIDLY	TRIPPLED	ROCHETS
RESPONDS	RETRAITS	REVIVERS	BRICKING	FRIGIDLY	RIPPLER	CROCHETS
RESPRAY	RETRAITT	REVIVOR	CRICKING	RIGLING	TRIPPLER	ROCKERY
RESPRAYS	RETRATE	REVIVORS	PRICKING	RIGLINGS	RIPPLERS	CROCKERY
RESTAFF	RETRATED	REVOLVE	TRICKING	RILLING	RIPPLES	ROCKETS
RESTAFFS	RETRATES	REVOLVED	WRICKING	DRILLING	CRIPPLES	BROCKETS
RESTAGE	RETREAD	REVOLVER	RICKLES	FRILLING	GRIPPLES	CROCKETS
RESTAGED	RETREADS	REVOLVES	PRICKLES	GRILLING	TRIPPLES	ROCKIER
RESTAGES	RETREAT	REWEIGH	TRICKLES	PRILLING	RIPPLET	ROCKIERS
RESTART	RETREATS	REWEIGHS	RICKSHA	TRILLING	RIPPLETS	ROCKING
RESTARTS	RETRIAL	REWRITE	RICKSHAS	RIMIEST	RIPTIDE	CROCKING
RESTATE	RETRIALS	REWRITES	RICKSHAW	GRIMIEST	RIPTIDES	FROCKING
RESTATED	RETSINA	REYNARD	RICOTTA	RIMLESS	RISKERS	TROCKING
RESTATES	RETSINAS	REYNARDS	RICOTTAS	BRIMLESS	FRISKERS	ROCKINGS
RESTERS	RETTING	RHABDOM	RIDDLER	RIMMING	RISKFUL	ROCKLAY
WRESTERS	ARETTING	RHABDOMS	RIDDLERS	BRIMMING	FRISKFUL	ROCKLAYS
RESTING	FRETTING	RHENIUM	RIDDLES	PRIMMING	RISKIER	ROCQUET
CRESTING	REUNION	RHENIUMS	GRIDDLES	TRIMMING	FRISKIER	ROCQUETS
PRESTING	REUNIONS	RHIZINE	RIDGING	RINDING	RISKILY	RODDING
WRESTING	REUNITE	RHIZINES	BRIDGING	GRINDING	FRISKILY	BRODDING
RESTINGS	REUNITED	RHIZOID	FRIDGING	RINGBITS	RISKING	PRODDING
RESTOCK	REUNITES	RHIZOIDS	RIDGINGS	RINGERS	BRISKING	RODDINGS
RESTOCKS	REUTTER	RHIZOME	RIDOTTO	BRINGERS	FRISKING	RODENTS
RESTORE	REUTTERS	RHIZOMES	RIDOTTOS	CRINGERS	RISOTTO	ERODENTS
RESTORED	REVALUE	RHODIUM	RIEMPIE	WRINGERS	RISOTTOS	RODEWAY
RESTORER	REVALUED	RHODIUMS	RIEMPIES	RINGGIT	RISPING	RODEWAYS
RESTORES	REVALUES	RHODORA	RIEVERS	RINGGITS	CRISPING	RODSTER
RESTYLE	REVENGE	RHODORAS	RIEVING	RINGING	RISPINGS	RODSTERS
RESTYLED	REVENGED	RHOMBOI	GRIEVING	BRINGING	RISSOLE	ROEBUCK
RESTYLES	REVENGER	RHOMBOID	PRIEVING	CRINGING	RISSOLES	ROEBUCKS
RESUMED	REVENGES	RHUBARB	RIFFLER	FRINGING	RITTERS	ROILING
PRESUMED	REVENUE	RHUBARBS	RIFFLERS	WRINGING	CRITTERS	BROILING
RESUMES	REVENUED	RHUBARBY	RIFLERS	RINGINGS	FRITTERS	DROILING
PRESUMES	REVENUES	RHYMIST	TRIFLERS	RINGLET	GRITTERS	ROINING
RESURGE	REVERBS	RHYMISTS	RIFLING	RINGLETS	RITTING	GROINING
RESURGED	PREVERBS	RHYTHMI	TRIFLING	RINGWAY	FRITTING	PROINING
RESURGES	REVERER	RHYTHMIC	RIFLINGS	RINGWAYS	GRITTING	ROISTER
RETABLE	REVERERS	RHYTINA	RIFTIER	RINKING	RIVERET	ROISTERS
RETABLES	REVERIE	RHYTINAS	DRIFTIER	DRINKING	RIVERETS	ROKELAY
RETAKER	REVERIES	RIBBAND	RIFTING	PRINKING	RIVETER	ROKELAYS
RETAKERS	REVERSE	RIBBANDS	DRIFTING	RINNING	RIVETERS	ROLLERS
RETCHED	REVERSED	RIBBING	GRIFTING	GRINNING	RIVIERA	PROLLERS
WRETCHED	REVERSER	CRIBBING	RIGGALD	RINSING	RIVIERAS	TROLLERS
RETCHES	REVERSES	DRIBBING	RIGGALDS	RINSINGS	RIVIERE	ROLLICK
WRETCHES	REVERSI	RIBBINGS	RIGGERS	RIOTING	RIVIERES	ROLLICKS
RETHINK	REVERSIS	RIBCAGE	FRIGGERS	RIOTINGS	RIVULET	ROLLING
RETHINKS	REVERSO	RIBCAGES	PRIGGERS	RIOTISE	RIVULETS	DROLLING
RETICLE	REVERSOS	RIBIBLE	TRIGGERS	RIOTISES	RIZZART	PROLLING
RETICLES	REVEUSE	RIBIBLES	RIGGING	RIOTIZE	RIZZARTS	TROLLING
RETINOL	REVEUSES	RIBLETS	FRIGGING	RIOTIZES	ROACHED	ROLLINGS
RETINOLS	REVIEWS	DRIBLETS	GRIGGING	RIPIENO	BROACHED	ROLLMOP
RETINUE	PREVIEWS	TRIBLETS	PRIGGING	RIPIENOS	ROACHES	ROLLMOPS
RETINUES	REVILER	RIBSTON	TRIGGING	RIPOSTE	BROACHES	ROLLOCK
RETIRAL	REVILERS	RIBSTONE	RIGGINGS	RIPOSTED	ROADING	ROLLOCKS
RETIRALS	REVISAL	RIBSTONS	RIGGISH	RIPOSTES	ROADINGS	ROMAIKA
RETIREE	REVISALS	RIBWORK	PRIGGISH	RIPPERS	ROADWAY	ROMAIKAS
RETIREES	REVISED	CRIBWORK	RIGHTED	FRIPPERS	BROADWAY	ROMANCE
RETIRER	PREVISED	RIBWORKS	FRIGHTED	GRIPPERS	ROADWAYS	ROMANCED
RETIRERS	REVISER	RIBWORT	RIGHTEN	TRIPPERS	ROARING	ROMANCER
RETITLE	REVISERS	RIBWORTS	BRIGHTEN	RIPPIER	ROARINGS	ROMANCES
RETITLED	REVISES	RICHTED	FRIGHTEN	DRIPPIER	ROASTER	ROMAUNT
RETITLES	PREVISES	FRICHTED	RIGHTENS	GRIPPIER	ROASTERS	ROMAUNTS
RETRACE	TREVISES	RICIEST	RIGHTER	RIPPING	ROATING	ROMNEYA
RETRACED	REVISIT	PRICIEST	BRIGHTER	DRIPPING	TROATING	ROMNEYAS
RETRACES	REVISITS	RICKERS	RIGHTERS	GRIPPING	ROBINIA	RONDEAU
RETRACT	REVISOR	PRICKERS	RIGHTLY	TRIPPING	ROBINIAS	RONDEAUX
RETRACTS	REVISORS	TRICKERS	BRIGHTLY	RIPPLED	ROBOTIC	RONDINO
RETRAIN	REVISORY	RICKETS	RIGIDER		ROBOTICS	RONDINOS
RETRAINS	REVIVAL	CRICKETS			ROBUSTA	RONDURE

RONDURES	FROSTING	GROUTING	RUFFLERS	**RUNKLES**	SADDLERS	SALUTERS
RONTGEN	**ROSTRUM**	TROUTING	**RUFFLES**	CRUNKLES	SADDLERY	**SALVAGE**
RONTGENS	ROSTRUMS	ROUTINGS	TRUFFLES	**RUNNING**	**SAFFIAN**	SALVAGED
ROOFING	**ROTATOR**	**ROWBOAT**	RUGGERS	RUNNINGS	SAFFIANS	SALVAGES
PROOFING	ROTATORS	ROWBOATS	DRUGGERS	**RUNNION**	**SAFFRON**	**SALVETE**
ROOFINGS	ROTATORY	**ROWDIES**	**RUGGING**	TRUNNION	SAFFRONS	SALVETES
ROOINEK	**ROTCHES**	CROWDIES	DRUGGING	RUNNIONS	SAFFRONY	**SALVING**
ROOINEKS	CROTCHES	ROWDIEST	RUGGINGS	**RUPTURE**	**SAFROLE**	SALVINGS
ROOKING	**ROTCHIE**	**ROWINGS**	**RUINATE**	RUPTURED	SAFROLES	**SAMBUCA**
BROOKING	ROTCHIES	GROWINGS	RUINATED	RUPTURES	**SAGENES**	SAMBUCAS
CROOKING	**ROTHERS**	**ROWLOCK**	RUINATES	**RUSALKA**	SAGENESS	**SAMISEN**
DROOKING	BROTHERS	ROWLOCKS	**RUINING**	RUSALKAS	**SAGGARD**	SAMISENS
ROOMFUL	**ROTIFER**	**ROWNDED**	RUININGS	**RUSHERS**	SAGGARDS	**SAMOVAR**
ROOMFULS	ROTIFERS	DROWNDED	**RULLION**	BRUSHERS	**SAGGING**	SAMOVARS
ROOMIER	**ROTTERS**	**ROYALET**	RULLIONS	CRUSHERS	SAGGINGS	**SAMPIRE**
BROOMIER	TROTTERS	ROYALETS	**RULLOCK**	**RUSHIER**	**SAGITTA**	SAMPIRES
ROOMING	**ROTTING**	**ROYNING**	RULLOCKS	BRUSHIER	SAGITTAL	**SAMPLER**
BROOMING	TROTTING	PROYNING	**RUMBLED**	**RUSHING**	SAGITTAS	SAMPLERS
GROOMING	**ROTUNDA**	**ROYSTER**	CRUMBLED	BRUSHING	**SAGOUIN**	SAMPLERY
VROOMING	ROTUNDAS	ROYSTERS	DRUMBLED	CRUSHING	SAGOUINS	**SAMSHOO**
ROOPIER	**ROUBLES**	**ROZELLE**	GRUMBLED	FRUSHING	**SAGUARO**	SAMSHOOS
DROOPIER	TROUBLES	ROZELLES	**RUMBLER**	**RUSTIER**	SAGUAROS	**SANCTUM**
ROOPING	**ROUGHEN**	**RUBBERS**	GRUMBLER	CRUSTIER	**SAHIBAH**	SANCTUMS
DROOPING	ROUGHENS	GRUBBERS	RUMBLERS	TRUSTIER	SAHIBAHS	**SANDBAG**
TROOPING	**ROUGHER**	**RUBBING**	**RUMBLES**	**RUSTILY**	**SAILING**	SANDBAGS
ROOSTER	ROUGHERS	DRUBBING	CRUMBLES	CRUSTILY	SAILINGS	**SANDING**
ROOSTERS	**ROUGHIE**	GRUBBING	DRUMBLES	TRUSTILY	**SAIMIRI**	SANDINGS
ROOTAGE	ROUGHIES	RUBBINGS	GRUMBLES	**RUSTING**	SAIMIRIS	**SANGRIA**
ROOTAGES	**ROULADE**	**RUBBISH**	**RUMMAGE**	BRUSTING	**SAKERET**	SANGRIAS
ROOTIES	ROULADES	RUBBISHY	RUMMAGED	CRUSTING	SAKERETS	**SANICLE**
ROOTIEST	**ROULEAU**	**RUBBLES**	RUMMAGER	TRUSTING	**SAKIYEH**	SANICLES
ROOTING	ROULEAUS	GRUBBLES	RUMMAGES	RUSTINGS	SAKIYEHS	**SANTOUR**
WROOTING	ROULEAUX	**RUBDOWN**	**RUMMERS**	**RUSTLER**	**SAKSAUL**	SANTOURS
ROOTINGS	**ROUMING**	RUBDOWNS	BRUMMERS	RUSTLERS	SAKSAULS	**SAOUARI**
ROOTLES	ROUMINGS	**RUBELLA**	DRUMMERS	**RUSTLES**	**SALAMON**	SAOUARIS
ROOTLESS	**ROUNCES**	RUBELLAN	**RUMMEST**	RUSTLESS	SALAMONS	**SAPAJOU**
ROOTLET	FROUNCES	RUBELLAS	GRUMMEST	**RUTHFUL**	**SALBAND**	SAPAJOUS
ROOTLETS	TROUNCES	**RUBEOLA**	**RUMMIER**	TRUTHFUL	SALBANDS	**SAPHEAD**
ROPEWAY	**ROUNDED**	RUBEOLAS	CRUMMIER	**RUTTING**	**SALCHOW**	SAPHEADS
ROPEWAYS	GROUNDED	**RUBICON**	**RUMMIES**	RUTTINGS	SALCHOWS	**SAPLING**
ROQUETS	**ROUNDEL**	RUBICONS	CRUMMIES	**RYBAULD**	**SALFERN**	SAPLINGS
CROQUETS	ROUNDELS	**RUCHING**	RUMMIEST	RYBAULDS	SALFERNS	**SAPONIN**
RORQUAL	**ROUNDER**	RUCHINGS	**RUMPING**	**RYEPECK**	**SALICET**	SAPONINS
RORQUALS	GROUNDER	**RUCKING**	CRUMPING	RYEPECKS	SALICETA	**SAPPHIC**
ROSACEA	ROUNDERS	TRUCKING	FRUMPING	**SABATON**	SALICETS	SAPPHICS
ROSACEAS	**ROUNDLE**	**RUCKLED**	TRUMPING	SABATONS	**SALICIN**	**SAPROBE**
ROSAKER	ROUNDLES	TRUCKLED	**RUMPLED**	**SABELLA**	SALICINE	SAPROBES
ROSAKERS	ROUNDLET	**RUCKLES**	CRUMPLED	ISABELLA	SALICINS	**SAPSAGO**
ROSALIA	**ROUPIER**	TRUCKLES	FRUMPLED	SABELLAS	**SALIENT**	SAPSAGOS
ROSALIAS	CROUPIER	**RUCTION**	**RUMPLES**	**SABURRA**	SALIENTS	**SAPWOOD**
ROSELLA	**ROUPING**	RUCTIONS	CRUMPLES	SABURRAL	**SALIGOT**	SAPWOODS
ROSELLAS	CROUPING	**RUDDIER**	FRUMPLES	SABURRAS	SALIGOTS	**SARAFAN**
ROSELLE	GROUPING	CRUDDIER	RUMPLESS	**SACCADE**	**SALPIAN**	SARAFANS
ROSELLES	TROUPING	**RUDDIES**	**RUNAWAY**	SACCADES	SALPIANS	**SARANGI**
ROSEOLA	**ROUSERS**	RUDDIEST	RUNAWAYS	**SACCULE**	**SALTANT**	SARANGIS
ROSEOLAS	AROUSERS	**RUDDLED**	**RUNCHES**	SACCULES	SALTANTS	**SARCASM**
ROSETTE	GROUSERS	CRUDDLED	BRUNCHES	**SACKAGE**	**SALTATE**	SARCASMS
ROSETTED	TROUSERS	**RUDDLES**	CRUNCHES	SACKAGES	SALTATED	**SARCODE**
ROSETTES	**ROUSING**	CRUDDLES	**RUNDALE**	**SACKBUT**	SALTATES	SARCODES
ROSIERE	AROUSING	**RUDDOCK**	RUNDALES	SACKBUTS	**SALTERN**	**SARCOID**
ROSIERES	GROUSING	RUDDOCKS	**RUNDLED**	**SACKFUL**	SALTERNS	SARCOIDS
ROSIERS	**ROUSTER**	**RUDERAL**	TRUNDLED	SACKFULS	**SALTERS**	**SARCOMA**
CROSIERS	ROUSTERS	RUDERALS	**RUNDLES**	**SACKING**	PSALTERS	SARCOMAS
ROSIEST	**ROUTERS**	**RUELLIA**	TRUNDLES	SACKINGS	**SALTIER**	**SARDANA**
PROSIEST	TROUTERS	RUELLIAS	**RUNDLET**	**SACRING**	SALTIERS	SARDANAS
ROSOLIO	**ROUTHIE**	**RUFFIAN**	RUNDLETS	SACRINGS	**SALTING**	**SARDINE**
ROSOLIOS	ROUTHIER	RUFFIANS	**RUNDOWN**	**SACRIST**	SALTINGS	SARDINES
ROSSERS	**ROUTINE**	**RUFFLED**	RUNDOWNS	SACRISTS	**SALTIRE**	**SARKFUL**
TROSSERS	ROUTINES	TRUFFLED	**RUNKLED**	SACRISTY	SALTIRES	SARKFULS
ROSTING	**ROUTING**	**RUFFLER**	CRUNKLED	**SADDLER**	**SALUTER**	**SARKING**

SARKINGS	SCALLOP	SCHLOCK	SCOURSES	SCRUPLER	SEASURES	SEMINAR
SARMENT	ESCALLOP	SCHLOCKS	SCOUTER	SCRUPLES	SEATING	SEMINARS
SARMENTA	SCALLOPS	SCHMOCK	SCOUTERS	SCRYING	SEATINGS	SEMINARY
SARMENTS	SCALPEL	SCHMOCKS	SCOWDER	SCRYINGS	SEAWARD	SEMIPED
SARSDEN	SCALPELS	SCHMUCK	SCOWDERS	SCUCHIN	SEAWARDS	SEMIPEDS
SARSDENS	SCALPER	SCHMUCKS	SCOWRER	SCUCHINS	SEAWEED	SEMITAR
SARSNET	SCALPERS	SCHNOOK	SCOWRERS	SCUDDER	SEAWEEDS	SEMITARS
SARSNETS	SCAMBLE	SCHNOOKS	SCOWRIE	SCUDDERS	SECEDER	SENATOR
SASHIMI	SCAMBLED	SCHNORR	SCOWRIES	SCUDDLE	SECEDERS	SENATORS
SASHIMIS	SCAMBLER	SCHNORRS	SCRAICH	SCUDDLED	SECLUDE	SENDING
SATCHEL	SCAMBLES	SCHOLAR	SCRAICHS	SCUDDLES	SECLUDED	SENDINGS
SATCHELS	SCAMPER	SCHOLARS	SCRAIGH	SCUDLER	SECLUDES	SENECIO
SATIATE	SCAMPERS	SCHOOLE	SCRAIGHS	SCUDLERS	SECONDE	SENECIOS
SATIATED	SCAMPIS	SCHOOLED	SCRAPER	SCUFFLE	SECONDED	SENSING
SATIATES	SCAMPISH	SCHOOLES	SCRAPERS	SCUFFLED	SECONDEE	SENSINGS
SATINET	SCANDAL	SCHTICK	SCRAPIE	SCUFFLER	SECONDER	SENSISM
SATINETS	SCANDALS	SCHTICKS	SCRAPIES	SCUFFLES	SECONDES	SENSISMS
SATSUMA	SCANNER	SCHTOOK	SCRATCH	SCULLER	SECRETE	SENSIST
SATSUMAS	SCANNERS	SCHTOOKS	SCRATCHY	SCULLERS	SECRETED	SENSISTS
SATYRAL	SCANTLE	SCHTUCK	SCRAUCH	SCULLERY	SECRETES	SEPIOST
SATYRALS	SCANTLED	SCHTUCKS	SCRAUCHS	SCULPIN	SECTION	SEPIOSTS
SATYRID	SCANTLES	SCIARID	SCRAUGH	SCULPING	SECTIONS	SEPPUKU
SATYRIDS	SCAPING	SCIARIDS	SCRAUGHS	SCULPINS	SECULAR	SEPPUKUS
SAUNTER	ESCAPING	SCIATIC	SCREECH	SCUMBAG	SECULARS	SEPTATE
SAUNTERS	SCAPPLE	SCIATICA	SCREECHY	SCUMBAGS	SECULUM	ASEPTATE
SAURIAN	SCAPPLED	SCIENCE	SCREEVE	SCUMBER	SECULUMS	SEPTETT
SAURIANS	SCAPPLES	SCIENCED	SCREEVED	SCUMBERS	SECURER	SEPTETTE
SAUSAGE	SCAPULA	SCIENCES	SCREEVER	SCUMBLE	SECURERS	SEPTETTS
SAUSAGES	SCAPULAE	SCISSEL	SCREEVES	SCUMBLED	SECURES	SEPTIME
SAUTOIR	SCAPULAR	SCISSELS	SCREICH	SCUMBLES	SECUREST	SEPTIMES
SAUTOIRS	SCAPULAS	SCISSIL	SCREICHS	SCUMMER	SEDATES	SEPTUOR
SAVAGER	SCARLET	SCISSILE	SCREIGH	SCUMMERS	SEDATEST	SEPTUORS
SAVAGERY	SCARLETS	SCISSILS	SCREIGHS	SCUNNER	SEDUCER	SEQUELA
SAVAGES	SCARPED	SCISSOR	SCREWER	SCUNNERS	SEDUCERS	SEQUELAE
SAVAGEST	ESCARPED	SCISSORS	SCREWERS	SCUPPER	SEEDBED	SEQUENT
SAVANNA	SCARPER	SCOFFER	SCRIBED	SCUPPERS	SEEDBEDS	SEQUENTS
SAVANNAH	SCARPERS	SCOFFERS	ASCRIBED	SCURRIL	SEEDING	SEQUOIA
SAVANNAS	SCATOLE	SCOLDER	ESCRIBED	SCURRILE	SEEDINGS	SEQUOIAS
SAVARIN	SCATOLES	SCOLDERS	SCRIBER	SCUTAGE	SEEDLIP	SERENES
SAVARINS	SCATTER	SCOLLOP	SCRIBERS	SCUTAGES	SEEDLIPS	SERENESS
SAVELOY	SCATTERS	SCOLLOPS	SCRIBES	SCUTTER	SEELING	SERENEST
SAVELOYS	SCATTERY	SCOOPER	ASCRIBES	SCUTTERS	SEELINGS	SERFAGE
SAVIOUR	SCAUPER	SCOOPERS	ESCRIBES	SCUTTLE	SEEMING	SERFAGES
SAVIOURS	SCAUPERS	SCOOTER	SCRIECH	SCUTTLED	SEEMINGS	SERFDOM
SAWDUST	SCAVAGE	SCOOTERS	SCRIECHS	SCUTTLER	SEEPAGE	SERFDOMS
SAWDUSTS	SCAVAGER	SCOPULA	SCRIENE	SCUTTLES	SEEPAGES	SERIATE
SAWDUSTY	SCAVAGES	SCOPULAS	SCRIENES	SCYTALE	SEETHER	SERIATED
SAXHORN	SCEDULE	SCORING	SCRIEVE	SCYTALES	SEETHERS	SERIATES
SAXHORNS	SCEDULES	SCORINGS	SCRIEVED	SCYTHER	SEGMENT	SERICIN
SAZERAC	SCENDED	SCORNER	SCRIEVES	SCYTHERS	SEGMENTS	SERICINS
SAZERACS	ASCENDED	SCORNERS	SCROLLS	SDEIGNE	SEINING	SERICON
SCABBLE	SCEPTIC	SCORPER	ESCROLLS	SDEIGNED	SEININGS	SERICONS
SCABBLED	SCEPTICS	SCORPERS	SCROOGE	SDEIGNES	SEISMIC	SERIEMA
SCABBLES	SCEPTRE	SCORPIO	SCROOGED	SEAFOOD	ASEISMIC	SERIEMAS
SCAFFIE	SCEPTRED	SCORPION	SCROOGES	SEAFOODS	SEITIES	SERINGA
SCAFFIES	SCEPTRES	SCORPIOS	SCROTUM	SEAGULL	ASEITIES	SERINGAS
SCAGLIA	SCHAPPE	SCORSER	SCROTUMS	SEAGULLS	SEIZING	SERKALI
SCAGLIAS	SCHAPPED	SCORSERS	SCROUGE	SEALANT	SEIZINGS	SERKALIS
SCALADE	SCHAPPES	SCOTOMA	SCROUGED	SEALANTS	SEIZURE	SERPENT
ESCALADE	SCHEMER	SCOTOMAS	SCROUGER	SEALING	SEIZURES	SERPENTS
SCALADO	SCHEMERS	SCOURER	SCROUGES	SEALINGS	SELFISM	SERPULA
ESCALADO	SCHERZO	SCOURERS	SCROWLE	SEAMARK	SELFISMS	SERPULAE
SCALADOS	SCHERZOS	SCOURGE	SCROWLED	SEAMARKS	SELFIST	SERRATE
SCALDER	SCHISMA	SCOURGED	SCROWLES	SEAPORT	SELFISTS	SERRATED
SCALDERS	SCHISMAS	SCOURGER	SCROYLE	SEAPORTS	SELTZER	SERRATES
SCALIER	SCHLEPP	SCOURGES	SCROYLES	SEARING	SELTZERS	SERUEWE
ESCALIER	SCHLEPPS	SCOURIE	SCRUNCH	SEARINGS	SELVAGE	SERUEWED
SCALING	SCHLEPPY	SCOURIES	SCRUNCHY	SEASIDE	SELVAGED	SERUEWES
SCALINGS	SCHLICH	SCOURSE	SCRUPLE	SEASIDES	SELVAGEE	SERVANT
	SCHLICHS	SCOURSED	SCRUPLED	SEASURE	SELVAGES	SERVANTS

SERVEWE	SHALLOP	SHERIATS	SHORINGS	SIGNIORS	SIRNAMES	SKITTLE
SERVEWED	SHALLOPS	SHERIFF	SHORTEN	SIGNORA	SIROCCO	SKITTLED
SERVEWES	SHALLOT	SHERIFFS	SHORTENS	SIGNORAS	SIROCCOS	SKITTLES
SERVICE	SHALLOTS	SHIATSU	SHORTIE	SIGNORE	SISSIES	SKIVING
SERVICED	SHALLOW	SHIATSUS	SHORTIES	SIGNORES	SISSIEST	SKIVINGS
SERVICES	SHALLOWS	SHICKER	SHOTGUN	SIGNORI	SITDOWN	SKOLLIE
SERVILE	SHALWAR	SHICKERS	SHOTGUNS	SIGNORIA	SITDOWNS	SKOLLIES
SERVILES	SHALWARS	SHICKSA	SHOTTLE	SILENCE	SITFAST	SKREENE
SERVING	SHAMBLE	SHICKSAS	SHOTTLES	SILENCED	SITFASTS	SKREENES
SERVINGS	SHAMBLED	SHIDDER	SHOUTER	SILENCER	SITTING	SKREIGH
SESSION	SHAMBLES	SHIDDERS	SHOUTERS	SILENCES	SITTINGS	SKREIGHS
SESSIONS	SHAMING	SHIFTER	SHOWGHE	SILESIA	SITUATE	SKRIECH
SESTETT	ASHAMING	SHIFTERS	SHOWGHES	SILESIAS	SITUATED	SKRIECHS
SESTETTE	SHAMMER	SHIKARI	SHOWING	SILICLE	SITUATES	SKRIEGH
SESTETTO	SHAMMERS	SHIKARIS	SHOWINGS	SILICLES	SIXAINE	SKRIEGHS
SESTETTS	SHAMPOO	SHIMMER	SHRIEVE	SILICON	SIXAINES	SKUDLER
SESTINA	SHAMPOOS	SHIMMERS	SHRIEVED	SILICONE	SIXTEEN	SKUDLERS
SESTINAS	SHAPING	SHIMMERY	SHRIEVES	SILICONS	SIXTEENS	SKULKER
SESTINE	SHAPINGS	SHINDIG	SHRIGHT	SILIQUA	SIZZLER	SKULKERS
SESTINES	SHARIAT	SHINDIGS	SHRIGHTS	SILIQUAS	SIZZLERS	SKULPIN
SETBACK	SHARIATS	SHINGLE	SHRIVEL	SILIQUE	SJAMBOK	SKULPINS
SETBACKS	SHARING	SHINGLED	SHRIVELS	SILIQUES	SJAMBOKS	SKUMMER
SETTING	SHARINGS	SHINGLER	SHRIVER	SILKIES	SKATING	SKUMMERS
SETTINGS	SHARKER	SHINGLES	SHRIVERS	SILKIEST	SKATINGS	SKUTTLE
SETTLER	SHARKERS	SHIPFUL	SHUCKER	SILLIES	SKATOLE	SKUTTLED
SETTLERS	SHARPEN	SHIPFULS	SHUCKERS	SILLIEST	SKATOLES	SKUTTLES
SETTLOR	SHARPENS	SHIPLAP	SHUDDER	SILLOCK	SKEETER	SKYJACK
SETTLORS	SHARPER	SHIPLAPS	SHUDDERS	SILLOCKS	SKEETERS	SKYJACKS
SETUALE	SHARPERS	SHIPMEN	SHUDDERY	SILURID	SKEGGER	SKYLARK
SETUALES	SHARPIE	SHIPMENT	SHUFFLE	SILURIDS	SKEGGERS	SKYLARKS
SETWALL	SHARPIES	SHIPPEN	SHUFFLED	SIMARRE	SKELDER	SKYLINE
SETWALLS	SHASTER	SHIPPENS	SHUFFLER	SIMARRES	SKELDERS	SKYLINES
SEVENTH	SHASTERS	SHIPPER	SHUFFLES	SIMILOR	SKELLIE	SKYSAIL
SEVENTHS	SHASTRA	SHIPPERS	SHUNTER	SIMILORS	SKELLIED	SKYSAILS
SEVERAL	SHASTRAS	SHIPPON	SHUNTERS	SIMITAR	SKELLIER	SKYWARD
SEVERALS	SHATTER	SHIPPONS	SHUTTER	SIMITARS	SKELLIES	SKYWARDS
SEXFOIL	SHATTERS	SHIRKER	SHUTTERS	SIMPKIN	SKELLUM	SLABBER
SEXFOILS	SHATTERY	SHIRKERS	SHUTTLE	SIMPKINS	SKELLUMS	SLABBERS
SEXTANT	SHAVING	SHITTAH	SHUTTLED	SIMPLER	SKELTER	SLABBERY
SEXTANTS	SHAVINGS	SHITTAHS	SHUTTLES	SIMPLERS	SKELTERS	SLACKEN
SEXTETT	SHAWING	SHITTIM	SHYSTER	SIMPLES	SKEPFUL	SLACKENS
SEXTETTE	PSHAWING	SHITTIMS	SHYSTERS	SIMPLEST	SKEPFULS	SLACKER
SEXTETTS	SHEARER	SHMOOSE	SIAMANG	SIMULAR	SKEPTIC	SLACKERS
SEXTILE	SHEARERS	SHMOOSED	SIAMANGS	SIMULARS	SKEPTICS	SLADANG
SEXTILES	SHEATHE	SHMOOSES	SIAMESE	SIMURGH	SKIDPAN	SLADANGS
SEXTUOR	SHEATHED	SHMOOZE	SIAMESED	SIMURGHS	SKIDPANS	SLAKING
SEXTUORS	SHEATHES	SHMOOZED	SIAMESES	SINCERE	SKIFFLE	ASLAKING
SEYSURE	SHEBANG	SHMOOZES	SIAMEZE	SINCERER	SKIFFLES	SLAMMER
SEYSURES	SHEBANGS	SHOCKER	SIAMEZED	SINDING	SKILLET	SLAMMERS
SFUMATO	SHEBEEN	SHOCKERS	SIAMEZES	SINDINGS	SKILLETS	SLANDER
SFUMATOS	SHEBEENS	SHOEING	SIBLING	SINGING	SKIMMER	ISLANDER
SHABBLE	SHEDDER	SHOEINGS	SIBLINGS	SINGINGS	SKIMMERS	SLANDERS
SHABBLES	SHEDDERS	SHOGGLE	SIBSHIP	SINGLET	SKIMMIA	SLAPPER
SHACKLE	SHEHITA	SHOGGLED	SIBSHIPS	SINGLETS	SKIMMIAS	SLAPPERS
SHACKLED	SHEHITAH	SHOGGLES	SIDEARM	SINGULT	SKINFUL	SLASHER
SHACKLES	SHEHITAS	SHOOGIE	SIDEARMS	SINGULTS	SKINFULS	SLASHERS
SHADING	SHELLAC	SHOOGIED	SIDECAR	SINKAGE	SKINKER	SLATHER
SHADINGS	SHELLACS	SHOOGIES	SIDECARS	SINKAGES	SKINKERS	SLATHERS
SHADOOF	SHELLER	SHOOGLE	SIDEWAY	SINKING	SKINNER	SLATING
SHADOOFS	SHELLERS	SHOOGLED	SIDEWAYS	SINKINGS	SKINNERS	SLATINGS
SHAFTER	SHELTER	SHOOGLES	SIEVERT	SINOPIA	SKIPPER	SLATTER
SHAFTERS	SHELTERS	SHOOTER	SIEVERTS	SINOPIAS	SKIPPERS	SLATTERN
SHAITAN	SHELTERY	SHOOTERS	SIFTING	SINUATE	SKIPPET	SLATTERS
SHAITANS	SHELTIE	SHOPFUL	SIFTINGS	SINUATED	SKIPPETS	SLATTERY
SHAKING	SHELTIES	SHOPFULS	SIGHTER	SIRGANG	SKIRRET	SLEDGER
SHAKINGS	SHERBET	SHOPHAR	SIGHTERS	SIRGANGS	SKIRRETS	SLEDGERS
SHAKUDO	SHERBETS	SHOPHARS	SIGMATE	SIRLOIN	SKIRTER	SLEEKEN
SHAKUDOS	SHEREEF	SHOPPER	SIGMATED	SIRLOINS	SKIRTERS	SLEEKENS
SHALLON	SHEREEFS	SHOPPERS	SIGMATES	SIRNAME	SKITTER	SLEEKER
SHALLONS	SHERIAT	SHORING	SIGNIOR	SIRNAMED	SKITTERS	SLEEKERS

SLEEPER	**SMELTER**	SNIGGLED	SOILINGS	**SORNING**	**SPARTHE**	SPIGNELS
SLEEPERS	SMELTERS	SNIGGLER	**SOILURE**	SORNINGS	SPARTHES	**SPILING**
SLEEPERY	SMELTERY	SNIGGLES	SOILURES	**SOROBAN**	**SPASTIC**	SPILINGS
SLEEVER	**SMICKER**	**SNIPING**	**SOJOURN**	SOROBANS	SPASTICS	**SPILITE**
SLEEVERS	SMICKERS	SNIPINGS	SOJOURNS	**SOROCHE**	**SPATTEE**	SPILITES
SLEIGHT	**SMICKET**	**SNIPPER**	**SOLANUM**	SOROCHES	SPATTEES	**SPILLER**
SLEIGHTS	SMICKETS	SNIPPERS	SOLANUMS	**SORTING**	**SPATTER**	SPILLERS
SLICING	**SMIDGEN**	**SNIPPET**	**SOLDADO**	SORTINGS	SPATTERS	**SPINAGE**
SLICINGS	SMIDGENS	SNIPPETS	SOLDADOS	**SOSSING**	**SPATULA**	SPINAGES
SLICKEN	**SMIDGIN**	SNIPPETY	**SOLDIER**	SOSSINGS	SPATULAR	**SPINDLE**
SLICKENS	SMIDGINS	**SNIRTLE**	SOLDIERS	**SOTTING**	SPATULAS	SPINDLED
SLICKER	**SMILING**	SNIRTLED	SOLDIERY	SOTTINGS	**SPATULE**	SPINDLES
SLICKERS	SMILINGS	SNIRTLES	**SOLICIT**	**SOUBISE**	SPATULES	**SPINNER**
SLIDDER	**SMOKIES**	**SNOOKER**	SOLICITS	SOUBISES	**SPAWNER**	SPINNERS
SLIDDERS	SMOKIEST	SNOOKERS	SOLICITY	**SOUFFLE**	SPAWNERS	SPINNERY
SLIDDERY	**SMOKING**	**SNOOPER**	**SOLIDUM**	SOUFFLES	**SPEAKER**	**SPINNET**
SLIDING	SMOKINGS	SNOOPERS	SOLIDUMS	**SOULDAN**	SPEAKERS	SPINNETS
SLIDINGS	**SMOLDER**	**SNOOZER**	**SOLIPED**	SOULDANS	**SPECIAL**	**SPINNEY**
SLIMMER	SMOLDERS	SNOOZERS	SOLIPEDS	**SOUMING**	ESPECIAL	SPINNEYS
SLIMMERS	**SMOOTHE**	**SNOOZLE**	**SOLITON**	SOUMINGS	SPECIALS	**SPINODE**
SLINGER	SMOOTHED	SNOOZLED	SOLITONS	**SOUNDER**	**SPECKLE**	SPINODES
SLINGERS	SMOOTHEN	SNOOZLES	**SOLOIST**	SOUNDERS	SPECKLED	**SPINOUT**
SLINKER	SMOOTHER	**SNORING**	SOLOISTS	**SOUPCON**	SPECKLES	SPINOUTS
SLINKERS	SMOOTHES	SNORINGS	**SOLVATE**	SOUPCONS	**SPECTER**	**SPINULE**
SLIPPER	**SMOTHER**	**SNORKEL**	SOLVATED	**SOURING**	SPECTERS	SPINULES
SLIPPERS	SMOTHERS	SNORKELS	SOLVATES	SOURINGS	**SPECTRA**	**SPIRAEA**
SLIPPERY	SMOTHERY	**SNORTER**	**SOLVENT**	**SOUROCK**	SPECTRAL	SPIRAEAS
SLIPWAY	**SMOUSER**	SNORTERS	SOLVENTS	SOUROCKS	**SPECTRE**	**SPIRANT**
SLIPWAYS	SMOUSERS	**SNOTTER**	**SOMBRER**	**SOUSING**	SPECTRES	ASPIRANT
SLITHER	**SMUDGER**	SNOTTERS	SOMBRERO	SOUSINGS	**SPECULA**	SPIRANTS
SLITHERS	SMUDGERS	SNOTTERY	**SOMBRES**	**SOUSLIK**	SPECULAR	**SPIREME**
SLITHERY	**SMUGGLE**	**SNOWCAP**	SOMBREST	SOUSLIKS	**SPEEDER**	SPIREMES
SLITTER	SMUGGLED	SNOWCAPS	**SOMEONE**	**SOUTANE**	SPEEDERS	**SPIRING**
SLITTERS	SMUGGLER	**SNUBBER**	SOMEONES	SOUTANES	**SPEELER**	ASPIRING
SLOBBER	SMUGGLES	SNUBBERS	**SOMEWAY**	**SOUTHER**	SPEELERS	**SPIRTLE**
SLOBBERS	**SMYTRIE**	**SNUFFER**	SOMEWAYS	SOUTHERN	**SPELDER**	SPIRTLES
SLOBBERY	SMYTRIES	SNUFFERS	**SONANCE**	SOUTHERS	SPELDERS	**SPITTER**
SLOCKEN	**SNABBLE**	**SNUFFLE**	SONANCES	**SPACING**	**SPELDIN**	SPITTERS
SLOCKENS	SNABBLED	SNUFFLED	**SONDAGE**	SPACINGS	SPELDING	**SPITTLE**
SLOGGER	SNABBLES	SNUFFLER	SONDAGES	**SPADGER**	SPELDINS	SPITTLES
SLOGGERS	**SNAFFLE**	SNUFFLES	**SONDELI**	SPADGERS	**SPELLER**	**SPLENIA**
SLOTTER	SNAFFLED	**SNUGGER**	SONDELIS	**SPAIRGE**	SPELLERS	SPLENIAL
SLOTTERS	SNAFFLES	SNUGGERY	**SONSHIP**	SPAIRGED	**SPELTER**	**SPLODGE**
SLOWING	**SNAPPER**	**SNUGGLE**	SONSHIPS	SPAIRGES	SPELTERS	SPLODGED
SLOWINGS	SNAPPERS	SNUGGLED	**SOOPING**	**SPANCEL**	**SPENCER**	SPLODGES
SLUBBER	**SNARING**	SNUGGLES	SOOPINGS	SPANCELS	SPENCERS	**SPLOTCH**
SLUBBERS	SNARINGS	**SNUZZLE**	**SOOTHER**	**SPANGLE**	**SPENDER**	SPLOTCHY
SLUGGER	**SNARLER**	SNUZZLED	SOOTHERS	SPANGLED	SPENDERS	**SPLURGE**
SLUGGERS	SNARLERS	SNUZZLES	**SOOTHES**	SPANGLER	**SPERSED**	SPLURGED
SLUMBER	**SNEAKER**	**SOAKAGE**	SOOTHEST	SPANGLES	ASPERSED	SPLURGES
SLUMBERS	SNEAKERS	SOAKAGES	**SOPHISM**	SPANGLET	**SPERSES**	**SPODIUM**
SLUMBERY	**SNEERER**	**SOAKING**	SOPHISMS	**SPANIEL**	ASPERSES	SPODIUMS
SLUMMER	SNEERERS	SOAKINGS	**SOPHIST**	SPANIELS	**SPERTHE**	**SPOILER**
SLUMMERS	**SNEEZER**	**SOAPIES**	SOPHISTS	**SPANKER**	SPERTHES	SPOILERS
SMACKER	SNEEZERS	SOAPIEST	**SOPPING**	SPANKERS	**SPHAERE**	**SPONDEE**
SMACKERS	**SNICKER**	**SOARING**	SOPPINGS	**SPANNER**	SPHAERES	SPONDEES
SMARAGD	SNICKERS	SOARINGS	**SOPRANO**	SPANNERS	**SPHEARE**	**SPONDYL**
SMARAGDS	**SNICKET**	**SOBBING**	SOPRANOS	**SPARGER**	SPHEARES	SPONDYLS
SMARTEN	SNICKETS	SOBBINGS	**SORBATE**	SPARGERS	**SPHERIC**	**SPONGER**
SMARTENS	**SNIFFER**	**SOCAGER**	SORBATES	**SPARKLE**	SPHERICS	SPONGERS
SMARTIE	SNIFFERS	SOCAGERS	**SORBENT**	SPARKLED	**SPICATE**	**SPONGIN**
SMARTIES	**SNIFFLE**	**SOCCAGE**	SORBENTS	SPARKLER	SPICATED	SPONGING
SMASHER	SNIFFLED	SOCCAGES	**SORDINE**	SPARKLES	**SPICULA**	SPONGINS
SMASHERS	SNIFFLER	**SOCIATE**	SORDINES	SPARKLET	SPICULAR	**SPONSON**
SMATTER	SNIFFLES	SOCIATES	**SOREDIA**	**SPAROID**	SPICULAS	SPONSONS
SMATTERS	**SNIFTER**	**SOCKEYE**	SOREDIAL	SPAROIDS	**SPICULE**	**SPONSOR**
SMEDDUM	SNIFTERS	SOCKEYES	**SOREHON**	**SPARRER**	SPICULES	SPONSORS
SMEDDUMS	**SNIGGER**	**SOGGING**	SOREHONS	SPARRERS	**SPIELER**	**SPOOFER**
SMELLER	SNIGGERS	SOGGINGS	**SORGHUM**	**SPARROW**	SPIELERS	SPOOFERS
SMELLERS	**SNIGGLE**	**SOILING**	SORGHUMS	SPARROWS	**SPIGNEL**	SPOOFERY

SPOOLER
SPOOLERS
SPOONEY
SPOONEYS
SPOORER
SPOORERS
SPORRAN
SPORRANS
SPORTED
ASPORTED
SPORTER
SPORTERS
SPORULE
SPORULES
SPOTTER
SPOTTERS
SPOUSAL
ESPOUSAL
SPOUSALS
SPOUSED
ESPOUSED
SPOUSES
ESPOUSES
SPOUTER
SPOUTERS
SPRAINT
SPRAINTS
SPRAYER
SPRAYERS
SPREAGH
SPREAGHS
SPREAZE
SPREAZED
SPREAZES
SPREDDE
SPREDDEN
SPREDDES
SPREEZE
SPREEZED
SPREEZES
SPRIGHT
SPRIGHTS
SPRINGE
SPRINGED
SPRINGER
SPRINGES
SPRUCES
SPRUCEST
SPULYIE
SPULYIED
SPULYIES
SPULZIE
SPULZIED
SPULZIES
SPUNKIE
SPUNKIER
SPUNKIES
SPURNER
SPURNERS
SPURRER
SPURRERS
SPURREY
SPURREYS
SPURTLE
SPURTLES
SPUTNIK
SPUTNIKS
SPUTTER
SPUTTERS
SPUTTERY

SQUACCO
SQUACCOS
SQUALOR
SQUALORS
SQUARER
SQUARERS
SQUARES
SQUAREST
SQUEEZE
SQUEEZED
SQUEEZER
SQUEEZES
SQUELCH
SQUELCHY
SQUIDGE
SQUIDGED
SQUIDGES
SQUIRES
ESQUIRES
SQUIRESS
SRADDHA
SRADDHAS
STABBER
STABBERS
STABILE
STABILES
STABLER
STABLERS
STABLES
STABLEST
STACKER
STACKERS
STACKET
STACKETS
STADDLE
STADDLES
STADIAL
STADIALS
STADIUM
STADIUMS
STAFFER
STAFFERS
STAGGER
STAGGERS
STAGING
STAGINGS
STAINER
STAINERS
STAITHE
STAITHES
STALKER
STALKERS
STAMINA
STAMINAL
STAMINAS
STAMMEL
STAMMELS
STAMMER
STAMMERS
STAMPED
STAMPEDE
STAMPEDO
STAMPER
STAMPERS
STANDER
STANDERS
STANIEL
STANIELS
STANNEL
STANNELS

STANYEL
STANYELS
STAPLER
STAPLERS
STAPPLE
STAPPLES
STARDOM
STARDOMS
STARING
STARINGS
STARKEN
STARKENS
STARKER
STARKERS
STARLET
STARLETS
STARNIE
STARNIES
STARTED
ASTARTED
STARTER
STARTERS
STARTLE
STARTLED
STARTLER
STARTLES
STASHIE
STASHIES
STATING
ESTATING
STATION
STATIONS
STATISM
STATISMS
STATIST
STATISTS
STATURE
STATURED
STATURES
STATUTE
STATUTES
STAYING
STAYINGS
STEALER
STEALERS
STEALTH
STEALTHS
STEALTHY
STEAMER
STEAMERS
STEAMIE
STEAMIER
STEAMIES
STEARIN
STEARINE
STEARING
STEARINS
STEEMED
ESTEEMED
STEEPEN
STEEPENS
STEEPER
STEEPERS
STEEPLE
STEEPLED
STEEPLES
STEERER
STEERERS
STEEVES
STEEVEST

STEMBOK
STEMBOKS
STEMLET
STEMLETS
STEMPEL
STEMPELS
STEMPLE
STEMPLES
STEMSON
STEMSONS
STENCIL
STENCILS
STENGAH
STENGAHS
STENTOR
STENTORS
STEPNEY
STEPNEYS
STEPPER
STEPPERS
STEPSON
STEPSONS
STERLET
STERLETS
STERNUM
STERNUMS
STEROID
ASTEROID
STEROIDS
STEWARD
STEWARDS
STEWING
STEWINGS
STEWPAN
STEWPANS
STEWPOT
STEWPOTS
STHENIC
ASTHENIC
STIBBLE
STIBBLER
STIBBLES
STIBINE
STIBINES
STIBIUM
STIBIUMS
STICKER
STICKERS
STICKLE
STICKLED
STICKLER
STICKLES
STICKUP
STICKUPS
STIDDIE
STIDDIED
STIDDIES
STIFFEN
STIFFENS
STIFLER
STIFLERS
STILLER
STILLERS
STILTER
STILTERS
STINGER
STINGERS
STINKER
STINKERS
STINTER

STINTERS
STIPEND
STIPENDS
STIPPLE
STIPPLED
STIPPLER
STIPPLES
STIPULE
STIPULED
STIPULES
STIRRAH
STIRRAHS
STIRRER
STIRRERS
STIRRUP
STIRRUPS
STISHIE
STISHIES
STODGER
STODGERS
STOITER
STOITERS
STOMACH
STOMACHS
STOMACHY
STOMATA
STOMATAL
STONIED
ASTONIED
STONIES
ASTONIES
STONIEST
STONING
ASTONING
STONINGS
STONKER
STONKERS
STOOKER
STOOKERS
STOOLIE
STOOLIES
STOOPER
STOOPERS
STOPING
STOPINGS
STOPPED
ESTOPPED
STOPPER
STOPPERS
STOPPLE
STOPPLED
STOPPLES
STORAGE
STORAGES
STOTTER
STOTTERS
STOUNDS
ASTOUNDS
STOUTEN
STOUTENS
STOVERS
ESTOVERS
STOVING
STOVINGS
STOWAGE
STOWAGES
STOWING
STOWINGS
STRAINT
STRAINTS

STRANGE
ESTRANGE
STRANGER
STRAYED
ESTRAYED
STRAYER
STRAYERS
STRETCH
STRETCHY
STREWER
STREWERS
STRIATE
STRIATED
STRIATES
STRIDOR
STRIDORS
STRIGIL
STRIGILS
STRIKER
STRIKERS
STRIVER
STRIVERS
STRODLE
STRODLED
STRODLES
STROKER
STROKERS
STROOKE
STROOKEN
STROOKES
STROPHE
STROPHES
STROWER
STROWERS
STRUDEL
STRUDELS
STUBBLE
STUBBLED
STUBBLES
STUDDLE
STUDDLES
STUDENT
STUDENTS
STUDIER
STUDIERS
STUFFER
STUFFERS
STUMBLE
STUMBLED
STUMBLER
STUMBLES
STUMMEL
STUMMELS
STUMPER
STUMPERS
STUNNED
ASTUNNED
STUNNER
STUNNERS
STURMER
STURMERS
STUSHIE
STUSHIES
STUTTER
STUTTERS
STYLISE
STYLISED
STYLISES
STYLIST
STYLISTS

STYLITE
STYLITES
STYLIZE
STYLIZED
STYLIZES
STYLOID
STYLOIDS
STYPTIC
STYPTICS
STYRENE
STYRENES
SUASION
SUASIONS
SUBADAR
SUBADARS
SUBATOM
SUBATOMS
SUBBING
SUBBINGS
SUBDEAN
SUBDEANS
SUBDUAL
SUBDUALS
SUBDUCE
SUBDUCED
SUBDUCES
SUBDUCT
SUBDUCTS
SUBDUER
SUBDUERS
SUBEDAR
SUBEDARS
SUBEDIT
SUBEDITS
SUBERIN
SUBERINS
SUBFUSC
SUBFUSCS
SUBFUSK
SUBFUSKS
SUBJECT
SUBJECTS
SUBJOIN
SUBJOINS
SUBLATE
SUBLATED
SUBLATES
SUBLIME
SUBLIMED
SUBLIMER
SUBLIMES
SUBPLOT
SUBPLOTS
SUBSERE
SUBSERES
SUBSIDE
SUBSIDED
SUBSIDES
SUBSIST
SUBSISTS
SUBSOIL
SUBSOILS
SUBSUME
SUBSUMED
SUBSUMES
SUBTACK
SUBTACKS
SUBTEEN
SUBTEENS
SUBTEND

SUBTENDS	SUMMATED	**SURGEON**	**SWEATER**	**SYMBION**	TACHIST	TAMARIND
SUBTEXT	SUMMATES	SURGEONS	SWEATERS	SYMBIONS	TACHISTE	TAMARINS
SUBTEXTS	**SUMMING**	**SURGING**	**SWEENEY**	SYMBIONT	TACHISTS	**TAMARIS**
SUBTILE	SUMMINGS	SURGINGS	SWEENEYS	**SYMBOLE**	**TACHYON**	TAMARISK
SUBTILER	**SUMMIST**	**SURLOIN**	**SWEEPER**	SYMBOLES	TACHYONS	**TAMASHA**
SUBTYPE	SUMMISTS	SURLOINS	SWEEPERS	**SYMITAR**	**TACKERS**	TAMASHAS
SUBTYPES	**SUMPTER**	**SURMISE**	**SWEETEN**	SYMITARE	STACKERS	**TAMBOUR**
SUBUNIT	SUMPTERS	SURMISED	SWEETENS	SYMITARS	**TACKETS**	TAMBOURA
SUBUNITS	**SUNBATH**	SURMISER	**SWEETIE**	**SYMPTOM**	STACKETS	TAMBOURS
SUBVERT	SUNBATHE	SURMISES	SWEETIES	SYMPTOMS	**TACKIES**	**TAMBURA**
SUBVERTS	SUNBATHS	**SURNAME**	**SWELLER**	**SYNAPSE**	TACKIEST	TAMBURAS
SUBZONE	**SUNBEAM**	SURNAMED	SWELLERS	SYNAPSES	**TACKING**	**TAMPERS**
SUBZONES	SUNBEAMS	SURNAMES	**SWELTER**	**SYNAPTE**	STACKING	STAMPERS
SUCCADE	SUNBEAMY	**SURTOUT**	SWELTERS	SYNAPTES	TACKINGS	**TAMPING**
SUCCADES	**SUNBELT**	SURTOUTS	**SWERVER**	**SYNCARP**	**TACKLER**	STAMPING
SUCCEED	SUNBELTS	**SURVEWE**	SWERVERS	SYNCARPS	TACKLERS	TAMPINGS
SUCCEEDS	**SUNBURN**	SURVEWED	**SWIDDEN**	SYNCARPY	**TACTION**	**TAMPION**
SUCCOUR	SUNBURNS	SURVEWES	SWIDDENS	**SYNCOPE**	TACTIONS	TAMPIONS
SUCCOURS	SUNBURNT	**SURVIEW**	**SWIFTER**	SYNCOPES	**TACTISM**	**TANADAR**
SUCCUBA	**SUNDARI**	SURVIEWS	SWIFTERS	**SYNDING**	TACTISMS	TANADARS
SUCCUBAE	SUNDARIS	**SURVIVE**	**SWIGGER**	SYNDINGS	**TADPOLE**	**TANAGER**
SUCCUBAS	**SUNDIAL**	SURVIVED	SWIGGERS	**SYNFUEL**	TADPOLES	TANAGERS
SUCCUMB	SUNDIALS	SURVIVES	**SWILLER**	SYNFUELS	**TAEDIUM**	**TANAGRA**
SUCCUMBS	**SUNDOWN**	**SUSPECT**	SWILLERS	**SYNODAL**	TAEDIUMS	TANAGRAS
SUCKING	SUNDOWNS	SUSPECTS	**SWIMMER**	SYNODALS	**TAFFETA**	**TANGELO**
SUCKINGS	**SUNGLOW**	**SUSPEND**	SWIMMERS	**SYNONYM**	TAFFETAS	TANGELOS
SUCKLER	SUNGLOWS	SUSPENDS	**SWINDGE**	SYNONYMS	**TAGGERS**	**TANGENT**
SUCKLERS	**SUNRISE**	**SUSPENS**	SWINDGED	SYNONYMY	STAGGERS	TANGENTS
SUCRASE	SUNRISES	SUSPENSE	SWINDGES	**SYNOVIA**	**TAGGING**	**TANGHIN**
SUCRASES	**SUNSPOT**	**SUSPIRE**	**SWINDLE**	SYNOVIAL	STAGGING	TANGHINS
SUCRIER	SUNSPOTS	SUSPIRED	SWINDLED	SYNOVIAS	**TAGMEME**	**TANGIES**
SUCRIERS	**SUNSUIT**	SUSPIRES	SWINDLER	**SYRINGA**	TAGMEMES	TANGIEST
SUCROSE	SUNSUITS	**SUSTAIN**	SWINDLES	SYRINGAS	TAILARD	**TANGING**
SUCROSES	**SUNTRAP**	SUSTAINS	**SWINGER**	**SYRINGE**	TAILARDS	STANGING
SUCTION	SUNTRAPS	**SWABBER**	SWINGERS	SYRINGED	**TAILING**	**TANGLER**
SUCTIONS	**SUNWARD**	SWABBERS	**SWINGLE**	SYRINGES	TAILINGS	TANGLERS
SUFFETE	SUNWARDS	**SWADDLE**	SWINGLED	**SYRPHID**	TAILLIE	**TANGRAM**
SUFFETES	**SUPPAWN**	SWADDLED	SWINGLES	SYRPHIDS	TAILLIES	TANGRAMS
SUFFICE	SUPPAWNS	SWADDLER	**SWIPPLE**	**SYSTOLE**	TAILZIE	**TANKAGE**
SUFFICED	**SUPPLES**	SWADDLES	SWIPPLES	ASYSTOLE	TAILZIES	TANKAGES
SUFFICER	SUPPLEST	**SWAGGER**	**SWISHER**	SYSTOLES	**TAKAHEA**	**TANKARD**
SUFFICES	**SUPPORT**	SWAGGERS	SWISHERS	**SYSTYLE**	TAKAHEAS	TANKARDS
SUFFUSE	SUPPORTS	**SWAGGIE**	**SWISHES**	SYSTYLES	**TALAUNT**	**TANKFUL**
SUFFUSED	**SUPPOSE**	SWAGGIES	SWISHEST	TABANID	TALAUNTS	TANKFULS
SUFFUSES	SUPPOSED	**SWALING**	**SWITHER**	TABANIDS	**TALAYOT**	**TANKING**
SUGGEST	SUPPOSER	SWALINGS	SWITHERS	**TABARET**	TALAYOTS	TANKINGS
SUGGESTS	SUPPOSES	**SWALLET**	**SWIZZLE**	TABARETS	**TALIPAT**	**TANLING**
SUICIDE	**SUPREME**	SWALLETS	SWIZZLED	**TABBING**	TALIPATS	TANLINGS
SUICIDES	SUPREMER	**SWALLOW**	SWIZZLES	STABBING	**TALIPED**	**TANNAGE**
SUITING	SUPREMES	SWALLOWS	**SWOBBER**	**TABINET**	TALIPEDS	TANNAGES
SUITINGS	**SUPREMO**	**SWAMPER**	SWOBBERS	TABINETS	**TALIPOT**	**TANNATE**
SULCATE	SUPREMOS	SWAMPERS	**SWOPPER**	**TABLEAU**	TALIPOTS	STANNATE
SULCATED	**SURANCE**	**SWANKER**	SWOPPERS	TABLEAUX	**TALKERS**	TANNATES
SULFATE	SURANCES	SWANKERS	**SWORDER**	**TABLING**	STALKERS	**TANNING**
SULFATED	**SURBASE**	**SWANKEY**	SWORDERS	STABLING	**TALKING**	TANNINGS
SULFATES	SURBASED	SWANKEYS	**SWOTTER**	TABLINGS	STALKING	**TANTARA**
SULKIES	SURBASES	**SWAPPER**	SWOTTERS	**TABLOID**	TALKINGS	TANTARAS
SULKIEST	**SURBATE**	SWAPPERS	**SWOZZLE**	TABLOIDS	**TALLAGE**	**TANTRUM**
SULLAGE	SURBATED	**SWARMER**	SWOZZLES	**TABORER**	STALLAGE	TANTRUMS
SULLAGES	SURBATES	SWARMERS	**SYENITE**	TABORERS	TALLAGED	**TANYARD**
SULPHUR	**SURCOAT**	**SWASHER**	SYENITES	**TABORET**	TALLAGES	TANYARDS
SULPHURS	SURCOATS	SWASHERS	**SYLLABI**	TABORETS	**TALLBOY**	**TAPERER**
SULPHURY	**SURFACE**	**SWATTER**	SYLLABIC	**TABORIN**	TALLBOYS	TAPERERS
SULTANA	SURFACED	SWATTERS	**SYLPHID**	TABORING	**TALLENT**	**TAPIOCA**
SULTANAS	SURFACER	**SWAYING**	SYLPHIDE	TABORINS	TALLENTS	TAPIOCAS
SUMATRA	SURFACES	SWAYINGS	SYLPHIDS	**TABRERE**	**TALLIER**	**TAPPICE**
SUMATRAS	**SURFEIT**	**SWAZZLE**	**SYLVINE**	TABRERES	TALLIERS	TAPPICED
SUMMAND	SURFEITS	SWAZZLES	SYLVINES	**TACHISM**	**TALLITH**	TAPPICES
SUMMANDS	**SURFING**	**SWEARER**	**SYLVITE**	TACHISME	TALLITHS	**TAPPING**
SUMMATE	SURFINGS	SWEARERS	SYLVITES	TACHISMS	**TAMARIN**	STAPPING

TAPPINGS	TEASING	TEREBRAE	THEATER	THUNDERY	TINGLER	TOFFIEST
TAPROOM	TEASINGS	TEREBRAS	THEATERS	THWAITE	TINGLERS	TOHEROA
TAPROOMS	TEATIME	TERGITE	THEATRE	THWAITES	TINHORN	TOHEROAS
TAPROOT	TEATIMES	TERGITES	THEATRES	THYLOSE	TINHORNS	TOILING
TAPROOTS	TECHNIC	TERMITE	THEISMS	THYLOSES	TINKERS	TOILINGS
TAPSTER	TECHNICS	TERMITES	ATHEISMS	THYMINE	STINKERS	TOISECH
TAPSTERS	TEDDIES	TERNING	THEISTS	THYMINES	TINKING	TOISECHS
TARDIES	STEDDIES	STERNING	ATHEISTS	THYROID	STINKING	TOKAMAK
TARDIEST	TEDDING	TERNION	THEORBO	THYROIDS	TINKLER	TOKAMAKS
TARRIER	STEDDING	TERNIONS	THEORBOS	TICKERS	TINKLERS	TOLLAGE
STARRIER	TEEMING	TERPENE	THEOREM	STICKERS	TINNIES	TOLLAGES
TARRIERS	STEEMING	TERPENES	THEOREMS	TICKIES	TINNIEST	TOLLING
TARRIES	TEENAGE	TERRACE	THEORIC	STICKIES	TINNING	TOLLINGS
TARRIEST	TEENAGED	TERRACED	THEORICS	TICKING	TINNINGS	TOLUATE
TARRING	TEENAGER	TERRACES	THERIAC	STICKING	TINTERS	TOLUATES
STARRING	TEENING	TERRAIN	THERIACA	TICKINGS	STINTERS	TOLUENE
TARRINGS	STEENING	TERRAINS	THERIACS	TICKLED	TINTIER	TOLUENES
TARROCK	TEERING	TERRANE	THERMAL	STICKLED	STINTIER	TOMBOLA
TARROCKS	STEERING	TERRANES	THERMALS	TICKLER	TINTING	TOMBOLAS
TARSIER	TEKTITE	TERREEN	THIAMIN	STICKLER	STINTING	TOMBOLO
TARSIERS	TEKTITES	TERREENS	THIAMINE	TICKLERS	TINTINGS	TOMBOLOS
TARTANA	TELECOM	TERRENE	THIAMINS	TICKLES	TINTYPE	TOMFOOL
TARTANAS	TELECOMS	TERRENES	THICKEN	STICKLES	TINTYPES	TOMFOOLS
TARTANE	TELEOST	TERRIER	THICKENS	TIDDIES	TINWARE	TOMPION
TARTANED	TELEOSTS	TERRIERS	THICKET	STIDDIES	TINWARES	TOMPIONS
TARTANES	TELETEX	TERRINE	THICKETS	TIDDIEST	TIPPING	TONDINO
TARTARE	TELETEXT	TERRINES	THICKETY	TIDDLER	TIPPINGS	TONDINOS
TARTARES	TELLING	TERSION	THIGGER	TIDDLERS	TIPPLED	TONIEST
TARTINE	STELLING	TERSIONS	THIGGERS	TIDDLEY	STIPPLED	STONIEST
TARTINES	TELLINGS	TERTIAL	THILLER	TIDDLEYS	TIPPLER	TONIGHT
TARTISH	TELPHER	TERTIALS	THILLERS	TIERCEL	STIPPLER	TONIGHTS
STARTISH	TELPHERS	TERTIAN	THIMBLE	TIERCELS	TIPPLERS	TONKERS
TARTLET	TEMPERA	TERTIANS	THIMBLED	TIETACK	TIPPLES	STONKERS
TARTLETS	TEMPERAS	TESSERA	THIMBLES	TIETACKS	STIPPLES	TONNAGE
TARWEED	TEMPEST	TESSERAE	THINKER	TIFFING	TIPSTER	TONNAGES
TARWEEDS	TEMPESTS	TESSERAL	THINKERS	STIFFING	TIPSTERS	TONNEAU
TASHING	TEMPLES	TESTERN	THINNER	TIFFINGS	TIRASSE	TONNEAUS
STASHING	STEMPLES	TESTERNS	THINNERS	TIGHTEN	TIRASSES	TONNELL
TASKING	TEMPLET	TESTING	THISTLE	TIGHTENS	TIRRING	TONNELLS
TASKINGS	TEMPLETS	TESTINGS	THISTLES	TILAPIA	STIRRING	TONSURE
TASSELL	TEMPTER	TESTOON	THORITE	TILAPIAS	TITCHES	TONSURED
TASSELLS	TEMPTERS	TESTOONS	THORITES	TILLAGE	STITCHES	TONSURES
TASSELLY	TEMPURA	TESTRIL	THORIUM	STILLAGE	TITHING	TONTINE
TASTING	TEMPURAS	TESTRILL	THORIUMS	TILLAGES	TITHINGS	TONTINER
TASTINGS	TENCHES	TESTRILS	THOUGHT	TILLERS	TITLARK	TONTINES
TATTIES	STENCHES	TESTUDO	THOUGHTS	STILLERS	TITLARKS	TOOLBAG
TATTIEST	TENDING	TESTUDOS	THREAVE	TILLIER	TITLING	TOOLBAGS
TATTING	STENDING	TETRACT	THREAVES	STILLIER	TITLINGS	TOOLING
TATTINGS	TENDRIL	TETRACTS	THRIMSA	TILLING	TITRATE	TOOLINGS
TATTLER	TENDRILS	TETRODE	THRIMSAS	STILLING	TITRATED	STOOLING
TATTLERS	TENDRON	TETRODES	THRIVER	TILLINGS	TITRATES	TOOLKIT
TAUNTER	TENDRONS	TEUCHAT	THRIVERS	TILLITE	TITULAR	TOOLKITS
TAUNTERS	TENONER	TEUCHATS	THROMBI	TILLITES	TITULARS	TOOTSIE
TAVERNA	TENONERS	TEXTILE	THROMBIN	TILTERS	TITULARY	TOOTSIES
TAVERNAS	TENSION	TEXTILES	THROWER	STILTERS	TOASTER	TOPARCH
TAWNIES	TENSIONS	TEXTURE	THROWERS	TILTING	TOASTERS	TOPARCHS
TAWNIEST	TENTAGE	TEXTURED	THRUWAY	STILTING	TOASTIE	TOPARCHY
TAXICAB	TENTAGES	TEXTURES	THRUWAYS	TILTINGS	TOASTIES	TOPCOAT
TAXICABS	TENTFUL	THALAMI	THRYMSA	TIMBALE	TOBACCO	TOPCOATS
TAXIWAY	TENTFULS	THALAMIC	THRYMSAS	TIMBALES	TOBACCOS	TOPKNOT
TAXIWAYS	TENTIGO	THALWEG	THUGGEE	TIMBREL	TOCCATA	TOPKNOTS
TEACHER	TENTIGOS	THALWEGS	THUGGEES	TIMBRELS	STOCCATA	TOPLESS
TEACHERS	TENTING	THANAGE	THULITE	TINAMOU	TOCCATAS	STOPLESS
TEAMERS	STENTING	THANAGES	THULITES	TINAMOUS	TODDLER	TOPMAST
STEAMERS	TENTINGS	THANKER	THULIUM	TINCHEL	TODDLERS	TOPMASTS
TEAMING	TEQUILA	THANKERS	THULIUMS	TINCHELS	TOECLIP	TOPONYM
STEAMING	TEQUILAS	THANNAH	THUMPER	TINFOIL	TOECLIPS	TOPONYMS
TEAMINGS	TERBIUM	THANNAHS	THUMPERS	TINFOILS	TOENAIL	TOPONYMY
TEARING	TERBIUMS	THAWING	THUNDER	TINGING	TOENAILS	TOPPERS
STEARING	TEREBRA	THAWINGS	THUNDERS	STINGING	TOFFIES	STOPPERS

TOPPING
STOPPING
TOPPINGS
TOPPLED
STOPPLED
TOPPLES
STOPPLES
TOPSAIL
TOPSAILS
TOPSIDE
TOPSIDES
TOPSPIN
TOPSPINS
TORCHER
TORCHERE
TORCHERS
TORCHON
TORCHONS
TORDION
TORDIONS
TORGOCH
TORGOCHS
TORMENT
TORMENTS
TORMINA
TORMINAL
TORNADE
TORNADES
TORPEDO
TORPEDOS
TORRENT
TORRENTS
TORSADE
TORSADES
TORSION
TORSIONS
TORTURE
TORTURED
TORTURER
TORTURES
TORULIN
TORULINS
TOSHACH
TOSHACHS
TOSSING
TOSSINGS
TOSSPOT
TOSSPOTS
TOTIENT
TOTIENTS
TOTTERS
STOTTERS
TOTTIES
TOTTIEST
TOTTING
STOTTING
TOTTINGS
TOUCHER
TOUCHERS
TOUGHEN
TOUGHENS
TOUGHIE
TOUGHIES
TOURACO
TOURACOS
TOURING
TOURINGS
TOURISM
TOURISMS
TOURIST

TOURISTS
TOURISTY
TOURNEY
TOURNEYS
TOUSING
TOUSINGS
TOWAGES
STOWAGES
TOWINGS
STOWINGS
TOWLINE
TOWLINES
TOWMOND
TOWMONDS
TOWMONT
TOWMONTS
TOWNIES
TOWNIEST
TOWPATH
TOWPATHS
TOWROPE
TOWROPES
TOYSHOP
TOYSHOPS
TRACHEA
TRACHEAE
TRACHEAL
TRACING
TRACINGS
TRACKER
TRACKERS
TRACTOR
TRACTORS
TRADING
TRADINGS
TRADUCE
TRADUCED
TRADUCER
TRADUCES
TRAFFIC
TRAFFICS
TRAGULE
TRAGULES
TRAIKED
STRAIKED
TRAILER
TRAILERS
TRAINED
STRAINED
TRAINEE
TRAINEES
TRAINER
STRAINER
TRAINERS
TRAIPSE
TRAIPSED
TRAIPSES
TRAITOR
TRAITORS
TRAJECT
TRAJECTS
TRAMMEL
STRAMMEL
TRAMMELS
TRAMPED
STRAMPED
TRAMPER
TRAMPERS
TRAMPET
TRAMPETS

TRAMPLE
TRAMPLED
TRAMPLER
TRAMPLES
TRAMWAY
TRAMWAYS
TRANCHE
TRANCHES
TRANCHET
TRANECT
TRANECTS
TRANGAM
TRANGAMS
TRANGLE
STRANGLE
TRANGLES
TRANKUM
TRANKUMS
TRANNIE
TRANNIES
TRANSIT
TRANSITS
TRANSOM
TRANSOMS
TRANTER
TRANTERS
TRAPEZE
TRAPEZED
TRAPEZES
TRAPPED
STRAPPED
TRAPPER
STRAPPER
TRAPPERS
TRASSES
STRASSES
TRAVAIL
TRAVAILS
TRAWLER
TRAWLERS
TRAYBIT
TRAYBITS
TRAYFUL
TRAYFULS
TREACLE
TREACLED
TREACLES
TREADER
TREADERS
TREADLE
TREADLED
TREADLER
TREADLES
TREAGUE
TREAGUES
TREASON
TREASONS
TREATER
TREATERS
TREDDLE
TREDDLED
TREDDLES
TREETOP
TREETOPS
TREFOIL
TREFOILS
TREHALA
TREHALAS
TREILLE
TREILLES

TREKKER
TREKKERS
TREMBLE
ATREMBLE
TREMBLED
TREMBLER
TREMBLES
TREMOLO
TREMOLOS
TRENAIL
TRENAILS
TRENISE
TRENISES
TRENTAL
TRENTALS
TREPANG
TREPANGS
TRESSED
STRESSED
TRESSEL
TRESSELS
TRESSES
STRESSES
TRESTLE
TRESTLES
TREYBIT
TREYBITS
TRIARCH
TRIARCHS
TRIARCHY
TRIATIC
TRIATICS
TRIAXON
TRIAXONS
TRIBADE
TRIBADES
TRIBBLE
TRIBBLES
TRIBLET
TRIBLETS
TRIBUNE
TRIBUNES
TRIBUTE
TRIBUTER
TRIBUTES
TRICKER
TRICKERS
TRICKERY
TRICKLE
STRICKLE
TRICKLED
TRICKLES
TRICKLET
TRICORN
TRICORNE
TRICORNS
TRIDARN
TRIDARNS
TRIDENT
STRIDENT
TRIDENTS
TRIDUUM
TRIDUUMS
TRIFFID
TRIFFIDS
TRIFFIDY
TRIFLER
TRIFLERS
TRIGGED
STRIGGED

TRIGGER
TRIGGERS
TRIGLOT
TRIGLOTS
TRIGRAM
TRIGRAMS
TRIKING
STRIKING
TRILITH
TRILITHS
TRILOBE
TRILOBED
TRILOBES
TRIMMER
TRIMMERS
TRIMTAB
TRIMTABS
TRINDLE
TRINDLED
TRINDLES
TRINGLE
TRINGLES
TRINKET
TRINKETS
TRINKUM
TRINKUMS
TRIOLET
TRIOLETS
TRIONYM
TRIONYMS
TRIPLET
TRIPLETS
TRIPOLI
TRIPOLIS
TRIPPED
STRIPPED
TRIPPER
TRIPPERS
TRIPPERY
TRIPPET
TRIPPETS
TRIPPLE
TRIPPLED
TRIPPLER
TRIPPLES
TRIREME
TRIREMES
TRISECT
TRISECTS
TRISEME
TRISEMES
TRISHAW
TRISHAWS
TRISOME
TRISOMES
TRISULA
TRISULAS
TRITIDE
TRITIDES
TRITIUM
TRITIUMS
TRITONE
TRITONES
TRIUMPH
TRIUMPHS
TRIVIUM
TRIVIUMS
TRIZONE
TRIZONES

TROCHEE
TROCHEES
TROELIE
TROELIES
TROKING
STROKING
TROLLED
STROLLED
TROLLER
STROLLER
TROLLERS
TROLLEY
TROLLEYS
TROLLOP
TROLLOPS
TROLLOPY
TROMINO
TROMINOS
TROMMEL
TROMMELS
TROOLIE
TROOLIES
TROOPER
TROOPERS
TROPHIC
STROPHIC
TROPISM
ATROPISM
TROPISMS
TROPIST
TROPISTS
TROTTER
TROTTERS
TROUBLE
TROUBLED
TROUBLER
TROUBLES
TROUNCE
TROUNCED
TROUNCER
TROUNCES
TROUPER
TROUPERS
TROUTER
TROUTERS
TROWING
STROWING
TRUCAGE
TRUCAGES
TRUCKER
TRUCKERS
TRUCKLE
TRUCKLED
TRUCKLER
TRUCKLES
TRUDGEN
TRUDGENS
TRUDGER
TRUDGERS
TRUFFLE
TRUFFLED
TRUFFLES
TRUMEAU
TRUMEAUX
TRUMPET
STRUMPET
TRUMPETS
TRUNDLE
TRUNDLED
TRUNDLES

TRUSSER
TRUSSERS
TRUSTEE
TRUSTEES
TRUSTER
TRUSTERS
TRYPSIN
TRYPSINS
TRYSAIL
TRYSAILS
TRYSTER
TRYSTERS
TSADDIK
TSADDIKS
TSADDIQ
TSADDIQS
TSARDOM
TSARDOMS
TSARINA
TSARINAS
TSARISM
TSARISMS
TSARIST
TSARISTS
TSIGANE
TSIGANES
TSUNAMI
TSUNAMIS
TUATARA
TUATARAS
TUBBIER
STUBBIER
TUBBING
STUBBING
TUBBINGS
TUBEFUL
TUBEFULS
TUBFAST
TUBFASTS
TUFTING
TUFTINGS
TUGGING
TUGGINGS
TUILYIE
TUILYIED
TUILYIES
TUILZIE
TUILZIED
TUILZIES
TUITION
TUITIONS
TULCHAN
TULCHANS
TUMBLED
STUMBLED
TUMBLER
STUMBLER
TUMBLERS
TUMBLES
STUMBLES
TUMBREL
TUMBRELS
TUMBRIL
TUMBRILS
TUMESCE
TUMESCED
TUMESCES
TUMPING
STUMPING
TUMULAR

TUMULARY	TWATTLER	UDDERED	UNCLOAKS	UNIFIERS	UNQUOTES	UNSTRAP
TUNICIN	TWATTLES	JUDDERED	UNCLOSE	UNIFIES	UNRAVEL	UNSTRAPS
TUNICINS	TWEEDLE	PUDDERED	UNCLOSED	MUNIFIES	UNRAVELS	UNSTRIP
TUNICLE	TWEEDLED	UKELELE	UNCLOSES	UNIFORM	UNREAVE	UNSTRIPS
TUNICLES	TWEEDLES	UKELELES	UNCLOUD	UNIFORMS	UNREAVED	UNSUITS
TUNNAGE	TWEETER	UKULELE	UNCLOUDS	UNIQUES	UNREAVES	SUNSUITS
TUNNAGES	TWEETERS	UKULELES	UNCLOUDY	UNIQUEST	UNREEVE	UNSWEAR
TUNNING	TWELFTH	ULICHON	UNCOVER	UNITING	UNREEVED	UNSWEARS
STUNNING	TWELFTHS	ULICHONS	UNCOVERS	MUNITING	UNREEVES	UNTHINK
TUNNINGS	TWIBILL	ULLAGES	UNCRATE	UNITINGS	UNRIGHT	UNTHINKS
TURACIN	TWIBILLS	FULLAGES	UNCRATED	UNITION	UNRIGHTS	UNTRACE
TURACINS	TWIDDLE	SULLAGES	UNCRATES	MUNITION	UNRIVET	UNTRACED
TURBAND	TWIDDLED	ULLINGS	UNCROWN	PUNITION	UNRIVETS	UNTRACES
TURBANDS	TWIDDLER	CULLINGS	UNCROWNS	UNITIONS	UNROOST	UNTREAD
TURBANT	TWIDDLES	NULLINGS	UNCTION	UNITISE	UNROOSTS	UNTREADS
TURBANTS	TWIGGER	ULULATE	FUNCTION	UNITISED	UNROUND	UNTRUST
TURBINE	TWIGGERS	ULULATED	JUNCTION	UNITISES	UNROUNDS	UNTRUSTS
TURBINED	TWINING	ULULATES	UNCTIONS	UNITIVE	UNSAINT	UNTRUSTY
TURBINES	TWININGS	UMBERED	UNCURSE	PUNITIVE	UNSAINTS	UNTRUTH
TURBITH	TWINKLE	CUMBERED	UNCURSED	UNITIZE	UNSCALE	UNTRUTHS
TURBITHS	TWINKLED	LUMBERED	UNCURSES	UNITIZED	UNSCALED	UNTWINE
TURBOND	TWINKLER	NUMBERED	UNDERDO	UNITIZES	UNSCALES	UNTWINED
TURBONDS	TWINKLES	UMBRAGE	UNDERDOG	UNJOINT	UNSCREW	UNTWINES
TURDION	TWINTER	UMBRAGED	UNDIGHT	UNJOINTS	UNSCREWS	UNTWIST
TURDIONS	TWINTERS	UMBRAGES	UNDIGHTS	UNKNOWN	UNSENSE	UNTWISTS
TURFING	TWIRLER	UMBRELS	UNDINES	UNKNOWNS	UNSENSED	UNTYING
TURFINGS	TWIRLERS	TUMBRELS	NUNDINES	UNLEARN	UNSENSES	UNTYINGS
TURFITE	TWISCAR	UMBRERE	UNDOING	UNLEARNS	UNSHALE	UNVAILE
TURFITES	TWISCARS	UMBRERES	UNDOINGS	UNLEARNT	UNSHALED	UNVAILED
TURMOIL	TWISTER	UMBRILS	UNEARTH	UNLOOSE	UNSHALES	UNVAILES
TURMOILS	TWISTERS	TUMBRILS	UNEARTHS	UNLOOSED	UNSHAPE	UNVISOR
TURNDUN	TWITTEN	UMBROUS	UNEQUAL	UNLOOSEN	UNSHAPED	UNVISORS
TURNDUNS	TWITTENS	CUMBROUS	UNEQUALS	UNLOOSES	UNSHAPEN	UNVOICE
TURNING	TWITTER	UNALIST	UNFAIRS	UNMOULD	UNSHAPES	UNVOICED
TURNINGS	TWITTERS	UNALISTS	FUNFAIRS	UNMOULDS	UNSHELL	UNVOICES
TURNKEY	TWITTERY	UNAWARE	UNFAITH	UNMOUNT	UNSHELLS	UNWARIE
TURNKEYS	TWIZZLE	UNAWARES	UNFAITHS	UNMOUNTS	UNSHIPS	UNWARIER
TURNOFF	TWIZZLED	UNBEGET	UNFROCK	UNNERVE	GUNSHIPS	UNWATER
TURNOFFS	TWIZZLES	UNBEGETS	UNFROCKS	UNNERVED	NUNSHIPS	UNWATERS
TURPETH	TWOSOME	UNBEING	UNFROZE	UNNERVES	UNSHOOT	UNWATERY
TURPETHS	TWOSOMES	UNBEINGS	UNFROZEN	UNNOBLE	UNSHOOTS	UNWEAVE
TURTLER	TYCHISM	UNBELTS	UNGIRTH	UNNOBLED	UNSHOUT	UNWEAVES
TURTLERS	TYCHISMS	SUNBELTS	UNGIRTHS	UNNOBLES	UNSHOUTS	UNWOMAN
TUSSOCK	TYLOPOD	UNBLIND	UNGLOVE	UNORDER	UNSINEW	UNWOMANS
TUSSOCKS	TYLOPODS	UNBLINDS	UNGLOVED	UNORDERS	UNSINEWS	UNWORTH
TUSSOCKY	TYMPANA	UNBLOCK	UNGLOVES	UNPAINT	UNSLING	UNWORTHS
TUSSORE	TYMPANAL	SUNBLOCK	UNGUARD	UNPAINTS	UNSLINGS	UNWORTHY
TUSSORES	TYMPANI	UNBLOCKS	UNGUARDS	UNPANEL	UNSNARL	UNWRITE
TUTANIA	TYMPANIC	UNBOSOM	UNGUENT	UNPANELS	UNSNARLS	UNWRITES
TUTANIAS	TYPHOID	UNBOSOMS	UNGUENTS	UNPAPER	UNSNECK	UPBRAID
TUTELAR	TYPHOIDS	UNBRACE	UNHEART	UNPAPERS	UNSNECKS	UPBRAIDS
TUTELARS	TYPHOON	UNBRACED	UNHEARTS	UNPLACE	UNSPEAK	UPBREAK
TUTELARY	TYPHOONS	UNBRACES	UNHINGE	UNPLACED	UNSPEAKS	UPBREAKS
TUTENAG	TYPICAL	UNBROKE	UNHINGED	UNPLACES	UNSPELL	UPBRING
TUTENAGS	ATYPICAL	UNBROKEN	UNHINGES	UNPLAIT	UNSPELLS	UPBRINGS
TUTWORK	ETYPICAL	UNBUILD	UNHOARD	UNPLAITS	UNSPOKE	UPBROKE
TUTWORKS	TYRANNE	UNBUILDS	UNHOARDS	UNPLUMB	UNSPOKEN	UPBROKEN
TWADDLE	TYRANNED	UNBURNT	UNHOODS	UNPLUMBS	UNSTACK	UPBUILD
TWADDLED	TYRANNES	SUNBURNT	NUNHOODS	UNPLUME	UNSTACKS	UPBUILDS
TWADDLER	TZADDIK	UNCHAIN	UNHORSE	UNPLUMED	UNSTATE	UPBURST
TWADDLES	TZADDIKS	UNCHAINS	UNHORSED	UNPLUMES	UNSTATED	UPBURSTS
TWANGLE	TZADDIQ	UNCHARM	UNHORSES	UNPURSE	UNSTATES	UPCHEER
TWANGLED	TZADDIQS	UNCHARMS	UNHOUSE	UNPURSED	UNSTEEL	UPCHEERS
TWANGLES	UAKARIS	UNCHECK	UNHOUSED	UNPURSES	UNSTEELS	UPCLIMB
TWANKAY	OUAKARIS	UNCHECKS	UNHOUSES	UNQUEEN	UNSTICK	UPCLIMBS
TWANKAYS	UBEROUS	UNCHILD	UNICORN	UNQUEENS	GUNSTICK	UPCLOSE
TWASOME	SUBEROUS	UNCHILDS	UNICORNS	UNQUIET	UNSTICKS	UPCLOSED
TWASOMES	TUBEROUS	UNCLASP	UNIFIED	UNQUIETS	UNSTOCK	UPCLOSES
TWATTLE	UDALLER	UNCLASPS	MUNIFIED	UNQUOTE	GUNSTOCK	UPGOING
TWATTLED	UDALLERS	UNCLOAK	UNIFIER	UNQUOTED	UNSTOCKS	UPGOINGS

UPGRADE	UPVALUE	UTOPIANS	VANILLA	VENDAGES	VERSING	VILIAGO
UPGRADED	UPVALUED	UTOPIAS	VANILLAS	VENERER	VERSINGS	VILIAGOS
UPGRADES	UPVALUES	UTOPIAST	VANNING	VENERERS	VERSION	VILLAGE
UPHEAVE	UPWHIRL	UTOPISM	VANNINGS	VENGERS	AVERSION	VILLAGER
UPHEAVED	UPWHIRLS	UTOPISMS	VANTAGE	AVENGERS	EVERSION	VILLAGES
UPHEAVES	URAEMIA	UTOPIST	VANTAGED	VENGING	VERSIONS	VILLAIN
UPHOARD	URAEMIAS	UTOPISTS	VANTAGES	AVENGING	VERTIGO	VILLAINS
UPHOARDS	URALITE	UTRICLE	VAQUERO	VENISON	VERTIGOS	VILLAINY
UPHOIST	URALITES	UTRICLES	VAQUEROS	VENISONS	VERTING	VILLEIN
UPHOISTS	URANIDE	UTTERED	VAREUSE	VENTAGE	AVERTING	VILLEINS
UPHOORD	URANIDES	BUTTERED	VAREUSES	VENTAGES	EVERTING	VINASSE
UPHOORDS	URANISM	GUTTERED	VARIANT	VENTAIL	VERVAIN	VINASSES
UPHROES	URANISMS	MUTTERED	VARIANTS	AVENTAIL	VERVAINS	VINEGAR
EUPHROES	URANITE	PUTTERED	VARIATE	VENTAILE	VESICLE	VINEGARS
UPLYING	URANITES	UTTERER	VARIATED	VENTAILS	VESICLES	VINEGARY
DUPLYING	URANIUM	MUTTERER	VARIATES	VENTANA	VESSAIL	VINTAGE
UPMAKER	URANIUMS	UTTERERS	VARICES	VENTANAS	VESSAILS	VINTAGED
UPMAKERS	UREDINE	VACANCE	AVARICES	VENTERS	VESTIGE	VINTAGER
UPPINGS	UREDINES	VACANCES	VARIOLA	EVENTERS	VESTIGES	VINTAGES
CUPPINGS	URETHAN	VACATUR	VARIOLAR	VENTIGE	VESTING	VINTNER
UPRAISE	URETHANE	VACATURS	VARIOLAS	VENTIGES	VESTINGS	VINTNERS
UPRAISED	URETHANS	VACCINE	VARIOLE	VENTING	VESTURE	VIOLATE
UPRAISES	URETHRA	VACCINES	OVARIOLE	EVENTING	VESTURED	VIOLATED
UPRIGHT	URETHRAE	VACUATE	VARIOLES	VENTINGS	VESTURER	VIOLATES
UPRIGHTS	URETHRAL	EVACUATE	VARIOUS	VENTRAL	VESTURES	VIOLENT
UPRISAL	URETHRAS	VACUATED	OVARIOUS	VENTRALS	VETCHES	VIOLENTS
UPRISALS	URGENCE	VACUATES	VARMENT	VENTRED	KVETCHES	VIOLIST
UPROUSE	URGENCES	VACUIST	VARMENTS	AVENTRED	VETERAN	VIOLISTS
UPROUSED	URGINGS	VACUISTS	VARMINT	VENTRES	VETERANS	VIOLONE
UPROUSES	PURGINGS	VACUOLE	VARMINTS	AVENTRES	VETIVER	VIOLONES
UPSHOOT	SURGINGS	VACUOLES	VARYING	VENTURE	VETIVERS	VIRANDA
UPSHOOTS	URICASE	VAGRANT	VARYINGS	AVENTURE	VETKOEK	VIRANDAS
UPSILON	URICASES	VAGRANTS	VASCULA	VENTURED	VETKOEKS	VIRANDO
UPSILONS	URIDINE	VAILING	VASCULAR	VENTURER	VETTURA	VIRANDOS
UPSPEAK	URIDINES	AVAILING	VASSAIL	VENTURES	VETTURAS	VIRELAY
UPSPEAKS	URINATE	VAIVODE	VASSAILS	VENTURI	VIADUCT	VIRELAYS
UPSPEAR	URINATED	VAIVODES	VAULTER	VENTURIS	VIADUCTS	VIRETOT
UPSPEARS	URINATES	VALANCE	VAULTERS	VERANDA	VIALFUL	VIRETOTS
UPSPOKE	URNINGS	VALANCED	VAUNTED	VERANDAH	VIALFULS	VIRGATE
UPSPOKEN	BURNINGS	VALANCES	AVAUNTED	VERANDAS	VIATORS	VIRGATES
UPSTAGE	TURNINGS	VALENCE	VAUNTER	VERBENA	AVIATORS	VIRGULE
UPSTAGED	URODELE	VALENCES	VAUNTERS	VERBENAS	VIBRATE	VIRGULES
UPSTAGES	URODELES	VALIANT	VAUNTERY	VERBOSE	VIBRATED	VISCERA
UPSTAIR	UROLITH	VALIANTS	VAURIEN	VERBOSER	VIBRATES	VISCERAL
UPSTAIRS	UROLITHS	VALONEA	VAURIENS	VERDICT	VIBRATO	VISCOSE
UPSTAND	UROLOGY	VALONEAS	VEDALIA	VERDICTS	VIBRATOR	VISCOSES
UPSTANDS	OUROLOGY	VALONIA	VEDALIAS	VERDURE	VIBRATOS	VISIBLE
UPSTARE	UROMERE	VALONIAS	VEDETTE	VERDURED	VICEROY	VISIBLES
UPSTARED	UROMERES	VALUATE	VEDETTES	VERDURES	VICEROYS	VISITEE
UPSTARES	UROSOME	EVALUATE	VEERING	VERISMO	VICIATE	VISITEES
UPSTART	UROSOMES	VALUATED	VEERINGS	VERISMOS	VICIATED	VISITER
UPSTARTS	USHERED	VALUATES	VEGETAL	VERMEIL	VICIATES	VISITERS
UPSURGE	HUSHERED	VALVULA	VEGETALS	VERMEILS	VICOMTE	VISITOR
UPSURGED	USUCAPT	VALVULAE	VEHICLE	VERMELL	VICOMTES	VISITORS
UPSURGES	USUCAPTS	VALVULAR	VEHICLES	VERMELLS	VICTORS	VITAMIN
UPSWARM	USURPER	VALVULE	VEILING	VERNIER	EVICTORS	VITAMINE
UPSWARMS	USURPERS	VALVULES	VEILINGS	VERNIERS	VICTUAL	VITAMINS
UPSWEEP	UTENSIL	VAMOOSE	VEINING	VERONAL	VICTUALS	VITELLI
UPSWEEPS	UTENSILS	VAMOOSED	VEININGS	VERONALS	VIDETTE	VITELLIN
UPSWELL	UTILISE	VAMOOSES	VEINLET	VERRUCA	VIDETTES	VITIATE
UPSWELLS	UTILISED	VAMPING	VEINLETS	VERRUCAE	VIDUAGE	VITIATED
UPSWING	UTILISER	VAMPINGS	VELIGER	VERRUCAS	VIDUAGES	VITIATES
UPSWINGS	UTILISES	VAMPIRE	VELIGERS	VERRUGA	VIEWING	VITRAGE
UPTHROW	UTILITY	VAMPIRED	VELOUTE	VERRUGAS	VIEWINGS	VITRAGES
UPTHROWN	FUTILITY	VAMPIRES	VELOUTES	VERSANT	VIHUELA	VITRAIN
UPTHROWS	UTILIZE	VANDYKE	VENATOR	VERSANTS	VIHUELAS	VITRAINS
UPTRAIN	UTILIZED	VANDYKED	VENATORS	VERSETS	VILAYET	VITREUM
UPTRAINS	UTILIZER	VANDYKES	VENDACE	OVERSETS	VILAYETS	VITREUMS
UPTREND	UTILIZES	VANESSA	VENDACES	VERSINE	VILIACO	VITRINE
UPTRENDS	UTOPIAN	VANESSAS	VENDAGE	VERSINES	VILIACOS	VITRINES

VITRIOL	**WAFTING**	AWANTING	**WASTREL**	WEDLOCKS	WHAIZLES	WHIRLERS
VITRIOLS	WAFTINGS	WANTINGS	WASTRELS	**WEEDIER**	**WHALING**	**WHIRRET**
VOCABLE	**WAFTURE**	**WAPPERS**	**WATCHER**	TWEEDIER	WHALINGS	WHIRRETS
VOCABLES	WAFTURES	SWAPPERS	WATCHERS	**WEEDING**	**WHAMPLE**	**WHIRTLE**
VOCODER	**WAGERER**	**WAPPING**	**WATCHES**	WEEDINGS	WHAMPLES	WHIRTLES
VOCODERS	WAGERERS	SWAPPING	SWATCHES	**WEEKDAY**	**WHANGAM**	**WHISKER**
VOICING	**WAGGING**	**WARATAH**	**WATCHET**	WEEKDAYS	WHANGAMS	WHISKERS
VOICINGS	SWAGGING	WARATAHS	WATCHETS	**WEEKEND**	**WHANGEE**	WHISKERY
VOIDING	**WAGONER**	**WARBLER**	**WATERER**	WEEKENDS	WHANGEES	**WHISKET**
AVOIDING	WAGONERS	WARBLERS	WATERERS	**WEEPERS**	**WHATNOT**	WHISKETS
VOIDINGS	**WAGTAIL**	**WARDING**	**WATTAGE**	SWEEPERS	WHATNOTS	**WHISKEY**
VOITURE	WAGTAILS	AWARDING	WATTAGES	**WEEPIER**	**WHATSIT**	WHISKEYS
VOITURES	**WAILING**	SWARDING	**WATTLED**	SWEEPIER	WHATSITS	**WHISPER**
VOIVODE	WAILINGS	WARDINGS	TWATTLED	**WEEPIES**	**WHEEDLE**	WHISPERS
VOIVODES	**WAINAGE**	**WARDROP**	**WATTLES**	WEEPIEST	WHEEDLED	WHISPERY
VOLANTE	WAINAGES	WARDROPS	TWATTLES	**WEEPING**	WHEEDLER	**WHISTLE**
VOLANTES	**WAINING**	**WARFARE**	**WAULING**	SWEEPING	WHEEDLES	WHISTLED
VOLPINO	SWAINING	WARFARED	WAULINGS	WEEPINGS	**WHEELER**	WHISTLER
VOLPINOS	**WAISTER**	WARFARER	**WAVELET**	**WEETING**	WHEELERS	WHISTLES
VOLTAGE	WAISTERS	WARFARES	WAVELETS	SWEETING	**WHEELIE**	**WHITHER**
VOLTAGES	**WAITING**	**WARHEAD**	**WAVERER**	TWEETING	WHEELIER	WHITHERS
VOLUSPA	AWAITING	WARHEADS	WAVERERS	**WEFTAGE**	WHEELIES	**WHITIES**
VOLUSPAS	WAITINGS	**WARISON**	**WAVESON**	WEFTAGES	**WHEENGE**	WHITIEST
VOLUTED	**WAIVODE**	WARISONS	WAVESONS	**WEIGELA**	WHEENGED	**WHITING**
EVOLUTED	WAIVODES	**WARLING**	**WAWLING**	WEIGELAS	WHEENGES	WHITINGS
VOLUTES	**WAIWODE**	WARLINGS	WAWLINGS	**WEIGHER**	**WHEEPLE**	**WHITLOW**
EVOLUTES	WAIWODES	**WARLOCK**	**WAXBILL**	WEIGHERS	WHEEPLED	WHITLOWS
VOLUTIN	**WAKENED**	WARLOCKS	WAXBILLS	**WEIRDIE**	WHEEPLES	**WHITRET**
VOLUTINS	AWAKENED	**WARLORD**	**WAXWING**	WEIRDIES	**WHEESHT**	WHITRETS
VOLVING	**WAKENER**	WARLORDS	WAXWINGS	**WELCHER**	WHEESHTS	**WHITTAW**
EVOLVING	WAKENERS	**WARMERS**	**WAXWORK**	WELCHERS	**WHEEZLE**	WHITTAWS
VOUCHED	**WAKINGS**	SWARMERS	WAXWORKS	**WELCOME**	WHEEZLED	**WHITTER**
AVOUCHED	AWAKINGS	**WARMING**	**WAYFARE**	WELCOMED	WHEEZLES	WHITTERS
VOUCHEE	**WALIEST**	SWARMING	WAYFARED	WELCOMER	**WHEMMLE**	**WHITTLE**
VOUCHEES	SWALIEST	WARMINGS	WAYFARER	WELCOMES	WHEMMLED	WHITTLED
VOUCHER	**WALKING**	**WARNING**	WAYFARES	**WELDING**	WHEMMLES	WHITTLER
VOUCHERS	WALKINGS	WARNINGS	**WAYMARK**	WELDINGS	**WHERRET**	WHITTLES
VOUCHES	**WALKWAY**	AWARNING	WAYMARKS	**WELFARE**	WHERRETS	**WHIZZER**
AVOUCHES	WALKWAYS	**WARPATH**	**WAYMENT**	WELFARES	**WHETTER**	WHIZZERS
VOYAGER	**WALLABA**	WARPATHS	WAYMENTS	**WELLING**	WHETTERS	**WHOLISM**
VOYAGERS	WALLABAS	**WARPING**	**WAYSIDE**	DWELLING	**WHICKER**	WHOLISMS
VULGATE	**WALLETS**	WARPINGS	WAYSIDES	SWELLING	WHICKERS	**WHOMBLE**
EVULGATE	SWALLETS	**WARRAND**	**WEARERS**	WELLINGS	**WHIDDER**	WHOMBLED
VULGATES	**WALLIES**	WARRANDS	SWEARERS	**WELSHER**	WHIDDERS	WHOMBLES
VULTURE	WALLIEST	**WARRANT**	**WEARIED**	WELSHERS	**WHIFFER**	**WHOMMLE**
VULTURES	**WALLING**	WARRANTS	AWEARIED	**WELTERS**	WHIFFERS	WHOMMLED
VULTURN	WALLINGS	WARRANTY	**WEARIES**	SWELTERS	**WHIFFET**	WHOMMLES
VULTURNS	**WALLOWS**	**WARRIOR**	WEARIEST	**WELTING**	WHIFFETS	**WHOOBUB**
WABBLER	SWALLOWS	WARRIORS	**WEARING**	SWELTING	**WHIFFLE**	WHOOBUBS
WABBLERS	**WALTZER**	**WARSHIP**	SWEARING	**WENCHER**	WHIFFLED	**WHOOPEE**
WABSTER	WALTZERS	WARSHIPS	WEARINGS	WENCHERS	WHIFFLER	WHOOPEES
WABSTERS	**WAMEFUL**	**WARTIER**	**WEASAND**	**WENDIGO**	WHIFFLES	**WHOOPER**
WADDIES	WAMEFULS	SWARTIER	WEASANDS	WENDIGOS	**WHIMPER**	WHOOPERS
SWADDIES	**WANGLED**	**WARTIME**	**WEATHER**	**WERGILD**	WHIMPERS	**WHOPPER**
WADDING	TWANGLED	WARTIMES	WEATHERS	WERGILDS	**WHIMPLE**	WHOPPERS
WADDINGS	**WANGLER**	**WASHERS**	**WEAVING**	**WESTERN**	WHIMPLED	**WHUMMLE**
WADDLED	WANGLERS	SWASHERS	WEAVINGS	WESTERNS	WHIMPLES	WHUMMLED
SWADDLED	**WANGLES**	**WASHIER**	**WEAZAND**	**WESTING**	**WHIMSEY**	WHUMMLES
TWADDLED	TWANGLES	SWASHIER	WEAZANDS	WESTINGS	WHIMSEYS	**WIDDLED**
WADDLES	**WANHOPE**	**WASHING**	**WEBBING**	**WETBACK**	**WHINGER**	TWIDDLED
SWADDLES	WANHOPES	SWASHING	WEBBINGS	WETBACKS	WHINGERS	**WIDDLES**
TWADDLES	**WANIGAN**	WASHINGS	**WEBSTER**	**WETLAND**	**WHINING**	TWIDDLES
WADMAAL	WANIGANS	**WASPIES**	WEBSTERS	WETLANDS	WHININGS	**WIDENER**
WADMAALS	**WANKERS**	WASPIEST	**WEBWORM**	**WHACKER**	**WHIPCAT**	WIDENERS
WADMOLL	SWANKERS	**WASSAIL**	WEBWORMS	WHACKERS	WHIPCATS	**WIDGEON**
WADMOLLS	**WANKING**	WASSAILS	**WEDDING**	**WHAISLE**	**WHIPPER**	WIDGEONS
WADSETT	SWANKING	**WASTAGE**	WEDDINGS	WHAISLED	WHIPPERS	**WIDOWER**
WADSETTS	**WANTAGE**	WASTAGES	**WEDGING**	WHAISLES	**WHIPPET**	WIDOWERS
WAFTAGE	WANTAGES	**WASTING**	WEDGINGS	**WHAIZLE**	WHIPPETS	**WIELDER**
WAFTAGES	**WANTING**	WASTINGS	**WEDLOCK**	WHAIZLED	**WHIRLER**	WIELDERS

WIGGING	WINIEST	WITLOOFS	WORDING	WRINKLE	YELPING	ZEMSTVOS
SWIGGING	TWINIEST	WITTERS	SWORDING	WRINKLED	YELPINGS	ZEOLITE
TWIGGING	WINKING	TWITTERS	WORDINGS	WRINKLES	YESHIVA	ZEOLITES
WIGGINGS	SWINKING	WITTING	WORKING	WRITING	YESHIVAH	ZETETIC
WIGGLER	TWINKING	WITTING	WORKINGS	WRITINGS	YESHIVAS	ZETETICS
WIGGLERS	WINKINGS	WITTINGS	WORKTOP	WRONGER	YIELDER	ZEUXITE
WIGHTED	WINKLER	WITWALL	WORKTOPS	WRONGERS	YIELDERS	ZEUXITES
TWIGHTED	TWINKLER	WITWALLS	WORRIER	WRYBILL	YOGHURT	ZIGANKA
WILDCAT	WINKLERS	WOBBLER	WORRIERS	WRYBILLS	YOGHURTS	ZIGANKAS
WILDCATS	WINKLES	WOBBLERS	WORSHIP	WRYNECK	YOUNGTH	ZILLION
WILDING	TWINKLES	WOIWODE	WORSHIPS	WRYNECKS	YOUNGTHS	ZILLIONS
WILDINGS	WINNING	WOIWODES	WORSTED	XANTHIN	YOUNKER	ZIMOCCA
WILDOAT	TWINNING	WOLFING	WORSTEDS	XANTHINE	YOUNKERS	ZIMOCCAS
WILDOATS	WINNINGS	WOLFINGS	WOSBIRD	XANTHINS	YOWLING	ZINCITE
WILLERS	WINNOCK	WOLFKIN	WOSBIRDS	XERAFIN	YOWLINGS	ZINCITES
SWILLERS	WINNOCKS	WOLFKINS	WOTTING	XERAFINS	YPSILON	ZINCODE
WILLIES	WINSOME	WOLFRAM	SWOTTING	XERASIA	YPSILONS	ZINCODES
TWILLIES	WINSOMER	WOLFRAMS	WOUNDED	XERASIAS	YTTRIUM	ZITHERN
WILLING	WINTERS	WOLVING	SWOUNDED	XYLENOL	YTTRIUMS	ZITHERNS
SWILLING	TWINTERS	WOLVINGS	WOUNDER	XYLENOLS	ZABTIEH	ZOARIUM
TWILLING	WIPEOUT	WOODCUT	WOUNDERS	XYLITOL	ZABTIEHS	ZOARIUMS
WILTING	WIPEOUTS	WOODCUTS	WOURALI	XYLITOLS	ZADDIKS	ZOCCOLO
TWILTING	WIRETAP	WOODIES	WOURALIS	XYLOGEN	TZADDIKS	ZOCCOLOS
WIMBREL	WIRETAPS	WOODIEST	WRANGLE	XYLOGENS	ZAMARRA	ZOISITE
WIMBRELS	WISHERS	WOOLDER	WRANGLED	YACHTER	ZAMARRAS	ZOISITES
WINCING	SWISHERS	WOOLDERS	WRANGLER	YACHTERS	ZAMARRO	ZONULET
WINCINGS	WISHING	WOOLFAT	WRANGLES	YAFFING	ZAMARROS	ZONULETS
WINDAGE	SWISHING	WOOLFATS	WRAPPER	NYAFFING	ZAMOUSE	ZOOLITE
WINDAGES	WISHINGS	WOOLLEN	WRAPPERS	YAKHDAN	ZAMOUSES	ZOOLITES
WINDIGO	WISSING	WOOLLENS	WREAKER	YAKHDANS	ZANELLA	ZOOLITH
WINDIGOS	SWISSING	WOOLSEY	WREAKERS	YAMULKA	ZANELLAS	ZOOLITHS
WINDING	WISTING	WOOLSEYS	WREATHE	YAMULKAS	ZANJERO	ZOONITE
WINDINGS	TWISTING	WOOMERA	WREATHED	YAPSTER	ZANJEROS	ZOONITES
WINDLES	WISTITI	WOOMERAS	WREATHEN	YAPSTERS	ZANYISM	ZOOTYPE
DWINDLES	WISTITIS	WOONING	WREATHER	YARDAGE	ZANYISMS	ZOOTYPES
SWINDLES	WITCHED	SWOONING	WREATHES	YARDAGES	ZAPTIAH	ZORGITE
WINDLESS	SWITCHED	WOORALI	WRECKER	YARDANG	ZAPTIAHS	ZORGITES
WINDOCK	TWITCHED	WOORALIS	WRECKERS	YARDANGS	ZAPTIEH	ZORILLE
WINDOCKS	WITCHEN	WOORARA	WRESTER	YASHMAK	ZAPTIEHS	ZORILLES
WINDORE	WITCHENS	WOORARAS	WRESTERS	YASHMAKS	ZAREEBA	ZORILLO
WINDORES	WITCHES	WOOSELL	WRESTLE	YATAGAN	ZAREEBAS	ZORILLOS
WINDROW	SWITCHES	WOOSELLS	WRESTLED	YATAGANS	ZARNICH	ZYMITES
WINDROWS	TWITCHES	WOOSHED	WRESTLER	YAWNING	ZARNICHS	AZYMITES
WINGERS	WITHERS	SWOOSHED	WRESTLES	YAWNINGS	ZEALANT	ZYMOGEN
SWINGERS	SWITHERS	WOOSHES	WRIGGLE	YEALDON	ZEALANTS	ZYMOGENS
WINGING	WITHIES	SWOOSHES	WRIGGLED	YEALDONS	ZEBRULA	ZYMOTIC
SWINGING	WITHIEST	WOPPING	WRIGGLER	YELLING	ZEBRULAS	ZYMOTICS
TWINGING	WITLING	SWOPPING	WRIGGLES	YELLINGS	ZEBRULE	
WINGLET	WITLINGS	WORDAGE	WRINGER	YELLOCH	ZEBRULES	
WINGLETS	WITLOOF	WORDAGES	WRINGERS	YELLOCHS	ZEMSTVO	

SECTION FIVE

ANAGRAMS

Introduction

This final substantial section contains all valid seven-letter and eight-letter words arranged in alphabetical order of their constituent letters.

Suppose you have the seven letters THORCES on your rack. You are convinced that there must be a valid 7-letter word there. Just arrange the letters in alphabetical order (CEHORST), then look for CEHORST in the following seven-letter lists, where it appears alphabetically ordered between CEHORSS and CEHORSU. You will find that there are six valid anagrams of your seven letters! Perhaps you have the seven letters CORLINE, and you cannot see a valid seven-letter word. Arrange the letters into alphabetical order (CEILNOR) and check the list here. Lo and behold! The list goes from CEILNOP to CEILNOS, confirming that there is no valid anagram of those seven letters.

The same theory applies to eight-letter words. All valid eight-letter words have been reduced to their alphabetically ordered forms, and these have then been arranged themselves into alphabetical order. What anagrams, if any, are there for the eight letters THROUCES? Easy! Put the letters into alphabetical order, check CEHORSTU in the eight-letter list, and find that SCOUTHER and TOUCHERS are both valid words!

The Seven-Letter Anagrams list contains over 25 000 words, and the Eight-Letter list has over 29 000 words. Happy anagram searching!

7-LETTER ANAGRAMS

AAAALTY ATALAYA
AAAABBCL CABBALA
AAAABBKL KABBALA
AAABCCR BACCARA
AAABCIR ARABICA
AAABCLS CABALAS
AAABCLV BACLAVA
AAABCMR CARAMBA
AAABCNR BARACAN
AAABCNS CABANAS
AAABCTW CATAWBA
AAABDGS DAGABAS
AAABDHS BAHADAS
AAABDJS BAJADAS
AAABDNN BANDANA
AAABEGL GALABEA
AAABFLL FALBALA
AAABGIL GALABIA
AAABILX ABAXIAL
AAABKLS KABALAS
AAABKLV BAKLAVA
AAABKSY KABAYAS
AAABLLW WALLABA
AAABLPR PALABRA
AAABLST ALBATAS
ATABALS
BALATAS
AAABMOS ABOMASA
AAABMST MASTABA
AAABNNR RABANNA
AAABNNS BANANAS
AAABORR ARAROBA
AAABRSX ABRAXAS
AAABRSZ BAZAARS
AAABSTT BATATAS
AAACCIS ACACIAS
AAACCLR CARACAL
AAACCRS CASCARA
AAACDLU ACAUDAL
AAACDMM MACADAM
AAACDNS CANADAS
AAACENP PANACEA
AAACGNT AGACANT
AAACHLZ CHALAZA
AAACHNT ACANTHA
AAACHRY ACHARYA
AAACILM MALACIA
AAACIMR CARIAMA
AAACINP ACAPNIA
AAACINR ACARIAN
AAACJMR JACAMAR
AAACJNS JACANAS
AAACLLV CAVALLA
AAACLMN ALMANAC
AAACLPS ALPACAS
AAACLPT CATALPA
AAACLRZ ALCAZAR
AAACMNP CAMPANA
AAACMRS MARACAS
MASCARA
AAACNNR CARANNA
AAACNPT CATAPAN
AAACNRT NACARAT
AAACNRU CARAUNA
AAACNRV CARAVAN
AAACNST CANASTA
AAACNTT CANTATA

AAACPST PATACAS
AAACRWY CARAWAY
AAACSST CASSATA
AAACSSV CASSAVA
AAACSTT CATASTA
AAADELM ALAMEDA
AAADFRY FARADAY
AAADHMR ADHARMA
AAADILX ADAXIAL
AAADIRT DATARIA
AAADJMR JAMADAR
AAADLMN MANDALA
AAADLMW WADMAAL
AAADMNT ADAMANT
AAADMRS ARMADAS
MADRASA
AAADNPS PANADAS
AAADNRS SARDANA
AAADNRT TANADAR
AAAEGLT GALATEA
AAAEGNP APANAGE
AAAEHKT TAKAHEA
AAAEHLT ALTHAEA
AAAEIMN ANAEMIA
AAAELMP PALAMAE
AAAELSZ AZALEAS
AAAENST ANATASE
AAAFFLL ALFALFA
AAAFIRT RATAFIA
AAAFNRS SARAFAN
AAAFRWY FARAWAY
AAAGGLN GALANGA
AAAGHIP APHAGIA
AAAGHLN LANGAHA
AAAGHNT ATAGHAN
AAAGHPR AGRAPHA
AAAGIPT PATAGIA
AAAGISS ASSAGAI
AAAGLMM AMALGAM
AAAGLMN NAGMAAL
AAAGLNS LASAGNA
AAAGLRS ARGALAS
AAAGMMT MAGMATA
AAAGMNR ANAGRAM
AAAGMNS SAGAMAN
AAAGNNS NAGANAS
AAAGNPR PARGANA
AAAGNRT TANAGRA
AAAGNRU GUARANA
AAAGNTY YATAGAN
AAAHHLV HALAVAH
AAAHIPS APHASIA
AAAHJKW KAJAWAH
AAAHLMR HARMALA
AAAHLNN ALANNAH
AAAHMMT MAHATMA
AAAHMRS ASHRAMA
AAAHMST TAMASHA
AAAHPRT PARATHA
AAAHRTW WARATAH
AAAILLS ALALIAS
AAAILMR MALARIA
AAAILPS APLASIA
AAAILRS ARALIAS
AAAILRT TALARIA
AAAIMNT AMANITA
AAAIPRX APRAXIA

AAAIQRU AQUARIA
AAAISTX ATAXIAS
AAAJKST JATAKAS
AAAJMPS PAJAMAS
AAAKKMR MARKKAA
AAAKKNS KANAKAS
AAAKKRS KARAKAS
AAAKLMS KAMALAS
AAAKNRS ANARAKS
AAAKNST KATANAS
AAALLPT PALATAL
AAALMSS SALAAMS
AAALNNT LANTANA
AAALNPT APLANAT
AAALWYY LAYAWAY
AAAMNNS MANANAS
AAAMNPS PANAMAS
AAAMNRT AMARANT
AAAMNSS SAMAANS
AAAMNST ATAMANS
AAAMPRT PATAMAR
AAAMRRZ ZAMARRA
AAAMRSS SAMARAS
AAAMRST TAMARAS
AAANNSV SAVANNA
AAANNTT ANNATTA
AAANRTT TANTARA
TARTANA
AAANSTT ANATTAS
AAAOPRZ PARAZOA
AAAPPRT APPARAT
AAAPPSY PAPAYAS
AAARSST SATARAS
AAARSTV AVATARS
AAARTTU TUATARA
AAARTXY ATARAXY
AABBBOS BAOBABS
AABBCEG CABBAGE
AABBCGY CABBAGY
AABBDGR GABBARD
AABBDHS HABDABS
AABBELT BATABLE
AABBERT BARBATE
AABBGRT GABBART
AABBHLS BABLAHS
AABBLLS LABLABS
AABBLOR BARBOLA
AABBLOS BALBOAS
AABBSST SABBATS
AABBSSU BABASSU
AABCCEL ACCABLE
AABCCER BACCARE
AABCCET BACCATE
AABCCIR BRACCIA
AABCEKR BACKARE
AABCELN BALANCE
AABCELP CAPABLE
PACABLE
AABCEMR MACABRE
AABCERR BARRACE
AABCERT ABREACT
CABARET
AABCHMT AMBATCH
AABCHNR BARCHAN
AABCHOR ABROACH
AABCHSS CASBAHS
AABCILM CAMBIAL

AABCINR CARABIN
AABCIOP COPAIBA
AABCITX TAXICAB
AABCKLY LAYBACK
AABCKPY BACKPAY
AABCKRR BARRACK
AABCKSW BACKSAW
AABCLMU CALUMBA
AABCLSY SCYBALA
AABCMSU SAMBUCA
AABCORT ABACTOR
ACROBAT
AABCOTT CATBOAT
AABCRSS SCARABS
AABCSUU AUCUBAS
AABCTTU CATTABU
AABDDEN ABANDED
AABDDER ABRADED
AABDEFL FADABLE
AABDEGN BANDAGE
AABDEHS ABASHED
AABDEIS DIABASE
AABDELL BALLADE
AABDELT ABLATED
DATABLE
AABDEMN BEADMAN
AABDENU BANDEAU
AABDERS ABRADES
AABDERY ABRAYED
AABDESU AUBADES
AABDGHN HANDBAG
AABDGMO GAMBADO
AABDGNS SANDBAG
AABDGOS DAGOBAS
AABDHMS BADMASH
AABDHNT HATBAND
AABDHNY HAYBAND
AABDHRS BARDASH
AABDIIS BASIDIA
AABDILN BALADIN
AABDIMR BARMAID
AABDINS INDABAS
AABDINT TABANID
AABDIOT BIODATA
AABDIRS ABRAIDS
AABDLLS BALLADS
AABDLMS LAMBDAS
AABDLNS SALBAND
AABDLRW BRADAWL
AABDMNR ARMBAND
AABDNNO ABANDON
AABDNOR BANDORA
AABDNRS BANDARS
AABDNRU BANDURA
AABDORS ABROADS
AABDORV BRAVADO
AABDRST BASTARD
TABARDS
AABDRSU SUBADAR
AABDRSY BAYARDS
AABDSTU DATABUS
AABEELT EATABLE
AABEEMO AMOEBAE
AABEERZ ZAREEBA
AABEFFL AFFABLE
AABEFFN BEFFANA
AABEFGU AUFGABE

AABEFNS BEFANAS	BAAINGS	AABMSSY AMBASSY	AACDEHT CATHEAD
AABEGGG BAGGAGE	AABGINT ABATING	AABNNOZ BONANZA	AACDEII AECIDIA
AABEGGR GARBAGE	AABGRST RATBAGS	AABNNSY BANYANS	AACDEIL ALCAIDE
AABEGLR ALGEBRA	AABHHIS SAHIBAH	AABNOST SABATON	AACDEIN AIDANCE
AABEGMR BERGAMA	AABHHRU BRUHAHA	AABORRS ARROBAS	AACDEIS ACEDIAS
MEGABAR	AABHISS SAHIBAS	AABORST ABATORS	AACDELL ALCALDE
AABEGMS AMBAGES	AABHITT HABITAT	AABORSZ ABRAZOS	AACDELN CANDELA
AABEGRR BAGARRE	AABHJNS BHAJANS	AABOTTY ATTABOY	DECANAL
BARRAGE	AABHKNR BARKHAN	AABQSUU SUBAQUA	AACDELR CALDERA
AABEGSS BAGASSE	AABHKSS KASBAHS	AABRRST BARRATS	AACDELS SCALADE
AABEGST ATABEGS	AABHLRS BHARALS	AABRRSU SABURRA	AACDELY ALCAYDE
AABEGSU ABUSAGE	AABHLTY BATHYAL	AABRRUV BRAVURA	AACDEMY ACADEMY
AABEHLT HATABLE	AABHSSW BASHAWS	AABRSTY BARYTAS	AACDENV ADVANCE
AABEHNT ABTHANE	AABIILX BIAXIAL	AABSSSY SASSABY	AACDENZ CADENZA
AABEHRS EARBASH	AABIJMY JAMBIYA	AABTTTU BATTUTA	AACDEPS SCAPAED
AABEHSS ABASHES	AABIKNS BANKSIA	AACCDES CASCADE	AACDERS ARCADES
AABEIKN IKEBANA	AABILLR BARILLA	SACCADE	AACDERV CADAVER
AABEILM AMABILE	AABILLS LABIALS	AACCDIR CARDIAC	AACDETU CAUDATE
AMIABLE	AABILMN BIMANAL	AACCDIS CICADAS	AACDETV VACATED
AABEILS ABELIAS	AABILMY AMIABLY	AACCDSU CADUACS	AACDEUX CADEAUX
AABEILT LABIATE	AABILOU ABOULIA	AACCEKR CARCAKE	AACDFIR FARADIC
AABEIRS ARABISE	AABILRS BASILAR	AACCELO CLOACAE	AACDFRS CAFARDS
AABEIRZ ARABIZE	AABILST BALISTA	AACCENV VACANCE	AACDHMR DRACHMA
AABEJLL JELLABA	AABILSU ABULIAS	AACCERS CARCASE	AACDHNR HANDCAR
AABEJMU JAMBEAU	AABIMMR MARIMBA	AACCEST SACCATE	AACDHRS CHADARS
AABEKLM MAKABLE	AABINNS BANIANS	AACCHHK KACHCHA	AACDIIS ASCIDIA
AABEKLT TAKABLE	AABINOU OUABAIN	AACCHIR ARCHAIC	AACDILR RADICAL
AABEKST ATABEKS	AABINRS ARABINS	AACCHKS KACCHAS	AACDINT ANTACID
AABELLL LABELLA	AABINRT ATABRIN	AACCHLN CLACHAN	AACDINV VANADIC
AABELLN BALNEAL	AABINST ABSTAIN	AACCHMP CHAMPAC	AACDIOR ACAROID
AABELLO ABOLLAE	AABINSW WABAINS	AACCHMS CHACMAS	AACDIRS ACARIDS
AABELLS SABELLA	AABIPUX PAXIUBA	AACCHNN CANNACH	ASCARID
SALABLE	AABIRSZ ZARIBAS	AACCHRT CHARACT	AACDJKW JACKDAW
AABELMN NAMABLE	AABISTT ABATTIS	AACCILM ACCLAIM	AACDLNO CALANDO
AABELMT TAMABLE	AABKNRS BARKANS	AACCILS CICALAS	AACDLNS SCANDAL
AABELNO ABALONE	AABKOOZ BAZOOKA	AACCIMS CAIMACS	AACDLOR CARLOAD
AABELNR BANALER	AABLLNS BALLANS	AACCIOR CARIOCA	AACDLOS SCALADO
AABELPP PAPABLE	AABLLNT BALLANT	AACCITT ATACTIC	AACDLPR PLACARD
AABELPR PARABLE	AABLLNY BANALLY	AACCKLP CALPACK	AACDMPS MADCAPS
AABELPY PAYABLE	AABLLOS ABOLLAS	AACCKRR CARRACK	AACDNRS CADRANS
AABELRT RATABLE	AABLLPT PATBALL	AACCKRS CARACKS	CANARDS
AABELSS BALASES	AABLLST BALLAST	AACCLLO CLOACAL	AACDOOV AVOCADO
AABELST ABLATES	BALLATS	AACCLLT CATCALL	AACDRSS CSARDAS
ASTABLE	AABLLSY SALABLY	AACCLOP POLACCA	AACDRSZ CZARDAS
AABELSV SAVABLE	AABLLWY WALLABY	AACCLOR CARACOL	AACEEGR ACREAGE
AABELSY SAYABLE	AABLMRU LABARUM	AACCLPS CALPACS	AACEEHR EARACHE
AABELTU TABLEAU	AABLMSS BALSAMS	AACCLPT PLACCAT	AACEEHT CHAETAE
TABULAE	SAMBALS	AACCLRS CALCARS	AACEELN ANELACE
AABELTX TAXABLE	AABLMST LAMBAST	AACCLRU ACCRUAL	AACEENT CATENAE
AABEMNS BASEMAN	AABLMSY ABYSMAL	CARACUL	AACEETT ACETATE
AABEMOS AMOEBAS	BALSAMY	AACCLSU ACCUSAL	AACEFLT FALCATE
AABENRT ANTBEAR	AABLNTT BLATANT	AACCMOS MACACOS	AACEFLU FACULAE
AABENTY ABEYANT	AABLORT ABLATOR	AACCNNS CANCANS	AACEFMN FACEMAN
AABERST ABREAST	AABLOSV LAVABOS	AACCNVY VACANCY	AACEFRS CARAFES
AABERSU BAUERAS	AABLPRU PABULAR	AACCORU CURACAO	AACEGGR AGGRACE
AABERSZ ZAREBAS	AABLRST ARBLAST	CURACOA	AACEGHS ACHAGES
AABERTT RABATTE	AABLRTU TABULAR	AACCOST ACCOAST	AACEGKP PACKAGE
TABARET	AABLRTY RATABLY	AACCOTT TOCCATA	AACEGKS SACKAGE
AABERTU ABATURE	AABLSST BASALTS	AACCRRT CARRACT	AACEGNR CARNAGE
AABESTZ ZABETAS	AABLSSY ABYSSAL	AACCRSS CARCASS	CRANAGE
AABETUX BATEAUX	AABLSTU ABLAUTS	AACCRST CARACTS	AACEGRT CARTAGE
AABFFLY AFFABLY	AABLTTU ABUTTAL	AACDDEL DECADAL	AACEGSV SCAVAGE
AABFILU FABLIAU	AABLTXY TAXABLY	AACDDER ARCADED	AACEHIR ARCHAEI
AABFLRU FABULAR	AABMNOT BOATMAN	AACDDHR CHADDAR	AACEHLP ACALEPH
AABGHNS GABNASH	AABMNST BANTAMS	AACDDIN CANDIDA	AACEHLR ALCHERA
NASHGAB	BATSMAN	AACDEEM ACADEME	AACEHNP PANACHE
AABGHSW BAGWASH	AABMORU MARABOU	AACDEFL FALCADE	AACEHNR ACHARNE
AABGIIL ABIGAIL	AABMRSS SAMBARS	AACDEFS FACADES	AACEHPP APPEACH
AABGINR BARGAIN	AABMRTU TAMBURA	AACDEHM CHAMADE	AACEHPS APACHES
AABGINS ABASING	AABMSST TSAMBAS	AACDEHR CHARADE	AACEHPU CHAPEAU

AACEHRT	TRACHEA
AACEHST	ACHATES
AACEHTT	ATTACHE
AACEHTU	CHATEAU
AACEIMN	ANAEMIC
AACEIMU	CAMAIEU
AACEINR	ACARINE
AACEIRV	AVARICE
	CAVIARE
AACEKNP	PANCAKE
AACEKNS	ASKANCE
AACEKOT	OATCAKE
AACELLN	CANELLA
AACELLS	SACELLA
AACELLT	LACTEAL
AACELMN	MANACLE
AACELMR	CAMERAL
	CARAMEL
AACELMU	MACULAE
AACELNS	ANLACES
AACELNU	LACUNAE
AACELNV	VALANCE
AACELPS	PALACES
AACELPT	PLACATE
AACELRV	CARAVEL
AACELST	ACETALS
	LACTASE
AACELTT	LACTATE
AACELTV	CLAVATE
AACEMMR	MACRAME
AACEMNS	CASEMAN
AACEMNV	CAVEMAN
AACEMPR	PARACME
AACEMQU	MACAQUE
AACEMRS	CAMERAS
AACEMSS	CAMASES
AACENPS	CANAPES
AACENRT	CATERAN
AACENST	CATENAS
AACENTT	CANTATE
AACENTY	CYANATE
AACEORS	ROSACEA
AACEPRT	CAPRATE
AACERSS	CAESARS
AACERST	ACATERS
AACERSU	CAESURA
AACERSZ	SAZERAC
AACERTU	ARCUATE
AACERWY	RACEWAY
AACESTV	CAVEATS
	VACATES
AACETTU	ACTUATE
AACETUV	VACUATE
AACFFIL	CAFFILA
AACFILS	CAFILAS
	FACIALS
	FASCIAL
AACFILU	FAUCIAL
AACFINT	FANATIC
AACFISS	FASCIAS
AACFLLU	FALCULA
AACFLLY	FALLACY
AACFLRU	FACULAR
AACFLTU	FACTUAL
AACFNST	CAFTANS
AACFRRU	FARRUCA
AACGHNS	CHAGANS
AACGILL	GLACIAL
AACGILM	MAGICAL
AACGILS	SCAGLIA
AACGINT	AGNATIC
AACGIRS	AGARICS
AACGIRV	AGRAVIC
AACGLOT	CATALOG
AACGNOU	GUANACO
AACHIKN	KACHINA
AACHIKR	CHIKARA
AACHILR	RACHIAL
AACHIMR	MACHAIR
AACHIMS	CHIASMA
AACHIPS	APHASIC
AACHIPT	CHAPATI
AACHIRS	ARACHIS
AACHIRT	CITHARA
AACHITY	CYATHIA
AACHKMP	CHAMPAK
AACHKNS	ACHKANS
AACHKPS	CHAPKAS
	PACHAKS
AACHKRS	CHAKRAS
AACHKRT	HATRACK
AACHKSW	KWACHAS
AACHLLN	CHALLAN
AACHLNS	CHALANS
AACHLPS	PASCHAL
AACHLST	CALTHAS
AACHLSU	ACUSHLA
AACHMNP	CHAPMAN
AACHMNS	MACHANS
AACHNOP	PANOCHA
AACHNOU	HUANACO
AACHNPX	PANCHAX
AACHNRS	ANARCHS
AACHNRV	NAVARCH
AACHNRY	ANARCHY
AACHNST	ACANTHS
AACHRRT	CATARRH
AACHRST	CHARTAS
AACHRWY	ARCHWAY
AACHSSW	CASHAWS
AACHSTT	CHATTAS
AACIILN	LACINIA
AACIINT	ACTINIA
AACIITV	VIATICA
AACIJLP	JALAPIC
AACIKLR	CLARKIA
AACIKNN	CANAKIN
AACILNR	CRANIAL
AACILNT	ACTINAL
	ALICANT
AACILOS	ASOCIAL
AACILOX	COAXIAL
AACILPS	SPACIAL
AACILPT	CAPITAL
	PLACITA
AACIMMR	MACRAMI
AACIMNS	CAIMANS
	MANIACS
AACIMPR	PICAMAR
AACINNT	CANTINA
AACINOR	CONARIA
	OCARINA
AACINPT	CAPITAN
	CAPTAIN
AACINRS	ARNICAS
	CARINAS
AACINRZ	CZARINA
AACINSS	ASCIANS
AACINST	SATANIC
AACIOPT	TAPIOCA
AACIOPV	COPAIVA
AACIOST	ATOCIAS
	COAITAS
AACIQTU	AQUATIC
AACIRSS	ASCARIS
AACIRST	CARITAS
AACIRSV	CAVIARS
AACISSS	CASSIAS
AACISTT	ASTATIC
AACJKLS	JACKALS
AACJKMN	JACKMAN
	MANJACK
AACJKSS	JACKASS
AACJOSU	ACAJOUS
AACKMNP	MANPACK
	PACKMAN
AACKMRT	AMTRACK
AACKNRS	RANSACK
AACKPRR	CARPARK
AACKPRT	RATPACK
AACKPSZ	CZAPKAS
AACKPWY	PACKWAY
AACKRRS	ARRACKS
AACKSTT	ATTACKS
AACLLNT	CALLANT
AACLLNU	LACUNAL
AACLLOR	CORALLA
AACLLSU	CLAUSAL
AACLLVY	CAVALLY
AACLMNO	COALMAN
AACLMNT	CALMANT
	CLAMANT
AACLMRU	MACULAR
AACLMSU	CALAMUS
AACLNNU	CANNULA
AACLNPY	CLAYPAN
AACLNRS	CARNALS
AACLNRU	LACUNAR
AACLOPR	CAPORAL
AACLOPT	OCTAPLA
AACLORT	CROTALA
AACLORZ	ALCORZA
AACLOST	CATALOS
	COASTAL
AACLOTT	CATTALO
AACLOTV	OCTAVAL
AACLPRS	CARPALS
AACLPRT	CALTRAP
AACLPSS	PASCALS
AACLPSU	PASCUAL
	SCAPULA
AACLRSS	LASCARS
	RASCALS
	SCALARS
AACLRST	CASTRAL
AACLRVY	CAVALRY
AACLSSU	CASUALS
AACLSUV	VASCULA
AACLTTU	TACTUAL
AACMNOR	CAMARON
AACMNRU	ARCANUM
AACMNSY	CAYMANS
AACMORS	SARCOMA
AACMORT	MARCATO
AACMOSY	MACOYAS
AACMRSS	SARCASM
AACMRST	RAMCATS
	TARMACS
AACNNOZ	CANZONA
AACNPST	CAPSTAN
	CAPTANS
	CATNAPS
AACNRST	ARCTANS
	CANTARS
AACNRTU	CURTANA
AACNSSV	CANVASS
AACNSTU	ASCAUNT
AACORST	OSTRACA
AACORTU	ACATOUR
	AUTOCAR
AACOTUV	AUTOVAC
AACRRST	CARRATS
AACRRSU	CURARAS
AACRSTV	CRAVATS
AACRTTT	ATTRACT
AACRTUV	VACATUR
AACRTUY	ACTUARY
AACRTWY	CARTWAY
AACTUWY	CUTAWAY
AADDDEN	ADDENDA
AADDEEL	DAEDALE
AADDEGM	DAMAGED
AADDEIL	ALIDADE
AADDEMM	MADAMED
AADDENP	DEADPAN
AADDEPR	PARADED
AADDEPT	ADAPTED
AADDERS	ADREADS
AADDERW	AWARDED
AADDESX	ADDAXES
AADDGNR	GRADDAN
	GRANDAD
AADDHKR	KHADDAR
AADDHRS	SRADDHA
AADDIIK	DIDAKAI
AADDILS	ALIDADS
AADDNVV	DVANDVA
AADDOSU	AOUDADS
AADDRST	DASTARD
AADDRSW	ADWARDS
AADDSST	STADDAS
AADEEFR	AFEARED
AADEENR	ANEARED
AADEERT	AERATED
AADEFFR	AFFEARD
AADEFGL	FALDAGE
AADEFGP	FARDAGE
AADEFIS	FADAISE
AADEFLU	AEFAULD
AADEFLW	AEFAWLD
AADEGGR	AGGRADE
	GARAGED
AADEGLS	GELADAS
AADEGMN	AGNAMED
	MANAGED
AADEGMR	MEGARAD
AADEGMS	DAMAGES
AADEGNS	AGENDAS
AADEGRT	GRADATE
AADEGRV	RAVAGED
AADEGRY	DRAYAGE
	YARDAGE
AADEGSV	SAVAGED
AADEHKS	AKEDAHS
AADEHMN	HEADMAN
AADEHMS	ASHAMED
AADEHPS	SAPHEAD
AADEHPW	AWHAPED
AADEHRW	RAWHEAD
	WARHEAD

ANAGRAMS: 7-Letter Words

AADEHWY	HEADWAY	AADGLNR	GARLAND	AADLPPU	APPLAUD	AAEFFGR	AGRAFFE
AADEILR	RADIALE	AADGLNS	SLADANG	AADLPRS	PARDALS	AAEFFIR	AFFAIRE
AADEILV	AVAILED	AADGLRU	GRADUAL	AADLRRU	RADULAR	AAEFFLL	FALAFEL
	VEDALIA	AADGMNR	GRANDAM	AADMMRS	DAMMARS	AAEFFNR	FANFARE
AADEINR	ARANEID		GRANDMA	AADMNNS	SANDMAN	AAEFFRS	AFFEARS
AADEINS	NAIADES	AADGMNS	GADSMAN	AADMNOR	MADRONA	AAEFFTT	TAFFETA
AADEIPS	DIAPASE	AADGMRS	SMARAGD		MANDORA	AAEFGTW	WAFTAGE
AADEIRS	ARAISED	AADGNPR	GRANDPA		MONARDA	AAEFLPR	EARFLAP
AADEIRT	RADIATE	AADGNPS	PADANGS		ROADMAN		PARAFLE
	TIARAED	AADGNRS	ARGANDS	AADMNRS	MANSARD	AAEFLRS	RAFALES
AADEITV	AVIATED	AADGNRT	GARDANT	AADMNRY	DRAYMAN	AAEFLSV	FAVELAS
AADEITW	AWAITED	AADGNRY	YARDANG		YARDMAN	AAEFMRT	FERMATA
AADEJMR	JEMADAR	AADGOPR	PODAGRA	AADMNSY	DAYSMAN	AAEFQRU	AQUAFER
AADEKLR	KRAALED	AADGOPS	PAGODAS	AADMNTU	MUTANDA	AAEFRRW	WARFARE
AADEKLS	ASLAKED	AADGRSU	GARUDAS	AADMOQU	MADOQUA	AAEFRWY	WAYFARE
AADEKMR	KAMERAD	AADHILS	DAHLIAS	AADMORT	MATADOR	AAEGGLS	GALAGES
AADELLP	PADELLA	AADHJNR	HANDJAR	AADMOSU	AMADOUS	AAEGGNO	ANAGOGE
AADELLY	ALLAYED	AADHKNY	YAKHDAN	AADMRSU	MARAUDS	AAEGGOP	APAGOGE
AADELMO	ALAMODE	AADHLRY	HALYARD	AADMRSZ	MAZARDS	AAEGGRS	GARAGES
AADELMR	ALARMED	AADHMRS	DHARMAS	AADMRZZ	MAZZARD	AAEGGRT	AGGRATE
AADELMX	MALAXED	AADHNRS	DARSHAN	AADMSYY	MAYDAYS	AAEGGSV	GAVAGES
AADELNR	ADRENAL		DHARNAS	AADNNOT	NOTANDA	AAEGHLU	HAULAGE
AADELNW	DANELAW	AADHNSW	HANDSAW	AADNNRS	RANDANS	AAEGHNT	THANAGE
AADELPR	PARDALE	AADHRSZ	HAZARDS	AADNOPR	PANDORA	AAEGILR	LAIRAGE
AADELPT	PALATED	AADHRWY	HAYWARD	AADNORT	ONDATRA		REGALIA
AADELRU	RADULAE	AADIILR	DIARIAL	AADNORY	ANYROAD	AAEGILS	ALGESIA
AADELRY	ALREADY	AADIINR	DIARIAN	AADNPRS	PANDARS	AAEGINP	NAGAPIE
AADELSS	SALADES	AADIIPS	ASPIDIA	AADNPRU	PANDURA	AAEGINV	VAGINAE
	SALSAED	AADIJMN	JAMDANI	AADNRRW	WARRAND	AAEGINW	WAINAGE
AADELTU	ADULATE	AADIKLY	ILKADAY	AADNRRY	DARRAYN	AAEGIPR	IGARAPE
AADELTY	DAYTALE	AADILLO	ALODIAL	AADNRSS	NASARDS	AAEGIRR	ARRIAGE
AADEMNO	ADENOMA	AADILMR	ADMIRAL	AADNRST	ASTRAND	AAEGISS	ASSEGAI
AADEMNS	ANADEMS		AMILDAR		TARANDS	AAEGITT	AGITATE
	MAENADS	AADILNP	PALADIN	AADNRTY	TANYARD	AAEGJTU	AJUTAGE
AADEMNT	MANDATE	AADILNR	LANIARD	AADNRVW	VANWARD	AAEGKNT	TANKAGE
AADEMSS	AMASSED	AADILPS	APSIDAL	AADNRWY	NAYWARD	AAEGKOS	SOAKAGE
AADENNT	ANDANTE	AADILRS	RADIALS	AADOPRS	PARADOS	AAEGLLR	GLAREAL
AADENRV	VERANDA	AADILRT	TAILARD	AADOPRT	ADAPTOR	AAEGLLT	GALLATE
AADENRW	AWARNED	AADILST	STADIAL	AADOPRX	PARADOX		TALLAGE
AADENST	ANSATED	AADILTV	DATIVAL	AADOPSS	PASSADO	AAEGLMN	GAMELAN
AADENSW	WEASAND	AADILWY	WAYLAID		POSADAS	AAEGLMT	GAMETAL
AADENWZ	WEAZAND	AADIMNR	MANDIRA	AADORWY	ROADWAY	AAEGLNR	ALNAGER
AADEPRS	ASPREAD	AADIMNS	MAIDANS	AADPSSY	SPAYADS	AAEGLNS	ALNAGES
	PARADES	AADIMOR	DIORAMA	AADQRTU	QUADRAT		ANLAGES
AADEPRT	ADAPTER	AADIMOT	DOMATIA	AADRSTU	DATURAS		GALENAS
	READAPT	AADINRR	DARRAIN	AADRSTY	DAYSTAR		LAGENAS
AADEPSS	ESPADAS	AADINRS	RADIANS	AADRSVW	VAWARDS		LASAGNE
	PASSADE	AADINRT	RADIANT	AADRWWY	WAYWARD	AAEGLNU	AULNAGE
AADERRS	ARRASED	AADINRV	VIRANDA	AAEEFFR	AFFEARE	AAEGLOP	APOGEAL
AADERRY	ARRAYED	AADINSV	NAVAIDS	AAEEFGL	LEAFAGE	AAEGLRR	REALGAR
AADERSW	SEAWARD	AADIRRW	AIRWARD	AAEEGKL	LEAKAGE	AAEGLRS	ALEGARS
AADERSY	ARAYSED	AADISST	STADIAS	AAEEGLT	ETALAGE		LAAGERS
AADERTU	AURATED	AADKMRY	DAYMARK		GALEATE	AAEGLST	AGELAST
AADESSY	ASSAYED	AADKMSS	DAMASKS	AAEEGMN	AMENAGE		ALGATES
AADFLTW	TWAFALD	AADKNRT	TANKARD	AAEEGRV	AVERAGE		LASTAGE
AADFNRR	FARRAND	AADKPSU	PADAUKS	AAEEGST	EATAGES	AAEGLSV	LAVAGES
AADFNST	FANTADS	AADKRWW	AWKWARD	AAEEHRT	HETAERA		SALVAGE
AADFRST	DAFTARS	AADLLMR	MALLARD	AAEEINT	TAENIAE	AAEGMNR	MANAGER
AADGGHR	HAGGARD	AADLLNW	LAWLAND	AAEEKRW	REAWAKE	AAEGMNS	AGNAMES
AADGGLR	LAGGARD	AADLLPU	PALUDAL	AAEELMT	MALEATE		MANAGES
AADGGRS	SAGGARD	AADLLSS	SALLADS	AAEELOR	AREOLAE		SAGAMEN
AADGHIL	HIDALGA	AADLMNN	LANDMAN	AAEELRT	LAETARE	AAEGMNT	MAGENTA
AADGIMM	DIGAMMA	AADLMNO	MANDOLA	AAEEMNT	EMANATE		MAGNATE
AADGIMO	AGAMOID	AADLMNU	LADANUM		ENEMATA	AAEGMPR	RAMPAGE
AADGIMR	DIAGRAM	AADLMPS	LAMPADS		MANATEE	AAEGMRT	REGMATA
AADGIMS	AGAMIDS	AADLMSW	WADMALS	AAEEPPS	APPEASE	AAEGMSS	MASSAGE
AADGINW	ADAWING	AADLNRY	LANYARD	AAEEPRT	PATERAE	AAEGNNP	PANNAGE
AADGIOS	ADAGIOS	AADLNSS	SANDALS	AAEERST	AERATES	AAEGNNT	TANNAGE
AADGLLW	GADWALL	AADLNSU	LANDAUS	AAEERTU	AUREATE	AAEGNOP	APOGEAN
AADGLMY	AMYGDAL	AADLNSV	VANDALS	AAEERTX	EXARATE	AAEGNPT	PAGEANT

AAEGNRR	ARRANGE	AAEIPPS	APEPSIA	AAELPTT	TAPETAL	AAERSTU	AURATES
AAEGNRT	TANAGER	AAEIPRR	PAREIRA	AAELPTU	PLATEAU	AAERSTW	AWAREST
AAEGNST	AGNATES	AAEIPRS	SPIRAEA	AAELPTY	APETALY	AAESSTV	SAVATES
AAEGNTV	VANTAGE	AAEIPRT	APTERIA	AAELRTV	LARVATE	AAESSWY	SEAWAYS
AAEGNTW	WANTAGE	AAEIPTT	APATITE	AAELRTZ	LAZARET	AAFFIMS	MAFFIAS
AAEGORS	OARAGES	AAEIRSS	ARAISES	AAELRVY	ALVEARY	AAFFINS	SAFFIAN
AAEGPRR	PARERGA	AAEIRST	ARISTAE	AAELSST	ATLASES	AAFFIRS	AFFAIRS
AAEGPRS	PARAGES		ASTERIA	AAELSTT	SALTATE		RAFFIAS
AAEGPSS	PASSAGE		ATRESIA	AAELSTV	VALETAS	AAFFPRS	AFFRAPS
AAEGPSV	PAVAGES	AAEIRSX	XERASIA	AAELSTZ	ALTEZAS	AAFFRSY	AFFRAYS
AAEGPSY	PAYSAGE	AAEIRTT	ARIETTA	AAELSUX	ASEXUAL	AAFGHNS	AFGHANS
AAEGQUY	QUAYAGE	AAEIRTV	VARIATE	AAELTUV	VALUATE	AAFGORR	FARRAGO
AAEGRRV	RAVAGER	AAEIRVW	AIRWAVE	AAELTVV	VALVATE	AAFHIKL	KHALIFA
AAEGRST	AGRASTE	AAEISTT	SATIATE	AAELTZZ	ALTEZZA	AAFHLWY	HALFWAY
AAEGRSV	RAVAGES	AAEISTV	AVIATES	AAELWWY	WELAWAY	AAFIILR	FILARIA
	SAVAGER	AAEISTX	ATAXIES	AAEMMMR	MAREMMA	AAFIKLS	KAFILAS
AAEGRTT	REGATTA	AAEJNRT	NAARTJE	AAEMMMT	MAMMATE	AAFIKSS	SIFAKAS
AAEGSSU	ASSUAGE	AAEKLMS	KAMELAS	AAEMMOT	OMMATEA	AAFILNT	FANTAIL
	SAUSAGE	AAEKLNS	ALKANES	AAEMNNT	EMANANT	AAFILQU	ALFAQUI
AAEGSSV	AVGASES	AAEKLNT	ALKANET	AAEMNPP	PAMPEAN	AAFINNT	INFANTA
	SAVAGES		KANTELA	AAEMNPS	SPAEMAN	AAFINRS	FARINAS
AAEGSSW	ASSWAGE	AAEKLSS	ASLAKES	AAEMNPT	PEATMAN	AAFIPRT	PARFAIT
AAEGSTU	GATEAUS	AAEKMNW	WAKEMAN	AAEMNRT	RAMENTA	AAFIRSS	SAFARIS
AAEGSTW	WASTAGE	AAEKMRR	EARMARK	AAEMNRU	MURAENA	AAFIRWY	FAIRWAY
AAEGTTW	WATTAGE	AAEKMRS	SEAMARK	AAEMNST	NAMASTE	AAFJLLW	JAWFALL
AAEGTUX	GATEAUX	AAEKNNS	ANANKES	AAEMNTU	MANTEAU	AAFJLOR	ALFORJA
AAEGTWY	GATEWAY	AAEKNSW	AWAKENS	AAEMOTZ	METAZOA	AAFKNST	KAFTANS
	GETAWAY	AAEKPRT	PARTAKE	AAEMQSU	SQUAMAE	AAFLLLS	FALLALS
AAEHHPT	APHTHAE	AAEKRSS	KEASARS	AAEMRST	AMEARST	AAFLLTY	FATALLY
AAEHILP	APHELIA	AAEKRST	KARATES		RETAMAS	AAFLMPR	FRAMPAL
AAEHIRT	HETAIRA	AAELLLM	LAMELLA	AAEMRTU	AMATEUR	AAFLNOR	FORLANA
AAEHKNT	KHANATE	AAELLNZ	ZANELLA	AAEMSSS	AMASSES	AAFLNRU	FURLANA
AAEHKPS	PAKEHAS	AAELLPR	PARELLA	AAENNNT	ANTENNA	AAFLSSY	SALSAFY
AAEHKST	TAKAHES	AAELLPS	PAELLAS	AAENNST	ANNATES	AAFLWYY	FLYAWAY
AAEHLLL	ALLHEAL	AAELLPT	PATELLA	AAENNSZ	ZENANAS	AAFMNRT	RAFTMAN
AAEHLPX	HEXAPLA	AAELLRT	LATERAL	AAENNTT	TANNATE	AAFMNST	FANTASM
AAEHLRT	TREHALA	AAELLRY	ALLAYER	AAENNTV	VENTANA	AAFNRRT	FARRANT
AAEHLTT	ATHLETA	AAELMMT	LEMMATA	AAENOPS	APNOEAS	AAFNSTT	FANTAST
AAEHMSS	ASHAMES	AAELMNT	AMENTAL	AAENOSZ	OZAENAS	AAFNSTY	FANTASY
AAEHMTT	THEMATA	AAELMNU	ALUMNAE	AAENPPR	PARPANE	AAGGILN	GANGLIA
AAEHNPR	HANAPER	AAELMOT	OATMEAL	AAENPST	ANAPEST	AAGGKSU	GAGAKUS
AAEHNSY	HYAENAS	AAELMPT	PALMATE		PEASANT	AAGGMNS	MGANGAS
AAEHPRZ	PHEAZAR	AAELMST	MALATES	AAENPSV	PAVANES	AAGGNOY	ANAGOGY
AAEHPSW	AWHAPES		MALTASE	AAENPSX	PANAXES	AAGGNWY	GANGWAY
AAEHRSY	HEARSAY		TAMALES	AAENPTT	EPATANT	AAGGQSU	QUAGGAS
AAEHSTT	HASTATE	AAELMSX	MALAXES	AAENRRT	NARRATE	AAGGRSS	SAGGARS
AAEILLX	AXILLAE	AAELMSY	AMYLASE	AAENRSS	NARASES	AAGGRST	TAGRAGS
AAEILMN	LAMINAE	AAELNNS	ANNEALS	AAENRST	ANESTRA	AAGHILR	GHARIAL
AAEILMS	AMELIAS	AAELNOV	VALONEA	AAENRTT	TARTANE	AAGHKNS	KANGHAS
	MALAISE	AAELNPT	PLATANE	AAENRTU	NATURAE		KHANGAS
AAEILNO	AEOLIAN	AAELNPU	PAENULA		TAUREAN	AAGHLNT	GNATHAL
AAEILNT	ANTLIAE	AAELNRS	ARSENAL	AAENRTV	TAVERNA	AAGHLOS	GASAHOL
AAEILOR	OLEARIA	AAELNST	SEALANT	AAENRUW	UNAWARE	AAGHLSZ	GHAZALS
AAEILPX	EPAXIAL	AAELNSY	ANALYSE	AAENRUZ	AZUREAN	AAGHMNN	HANGMAN
AAEILRS	AERIALS	AAELNTT	TETANAL	AAENSSU	NAUSEAS	AAGHMNW	WHANGAM
AAEILRU	AURELIA	AAELNTZ	ZEALANT	AAENSSV	VANESSA	AAGHMRS	GRAMASH
AAEILRV	VELARIA	AAELNWY	LANEWAY	AAEORRT	AERATOR	AAGHNRS	ARGHANS
AAEILSS	ALIASES	AAELNYZ	ANALYZE	AAEORRU	AURORAE		HANGARS
AAEILSV	AVAILES	AAELORR	AREOLAR	AAEPPRS	APPEARS	AAGHQUU	QUAHAUG
AAEILSX	ALEXIAS	AAELORU	AUREOLA	AAEPPRT	PARAPET	AAGHSTY	SAGATHY
AAEIMMT	IMAMATE	AAELOTX	OXALATE	AAEPRSS	PASEARS	AAGIKNW	AWAKING
AAEIMNS	AMNESIA	AAELPPR	APPAREL	AAEPRST	PETARAS	AAGIKNZ	ZIGANKA
	ANEMIAS	AAELPPS	APPEALS	AAEPRSZ	ZARAPES	AAGILMY	MYALGIA
AAEIMNT	AMENTIA	AAELPPT	PALPATE	AAEPRTY	PEATARY	AAGILNN	ANGINAL
	ANIMATE	AAELPPU	PAPULAE	AAERRRS	ARREARS	AAGILNP	PAGINAL
AAEIMPY	PYAEMIA	AAELPRS	EARLAPS	AAERRSS	ARRASES	AAGILNS	ANGNAILS
AAEIMRU	URAEMIA	AAELPRT	APTERAL	AAERRTT	TARTARE	AAGILNV	AVALING
AAEIMTV	AMATIVE	AAELPRV	PALAVER	AAERSST	SEARATS		VAGINAL
AAEINNO	AEONIAN	AAELPSS	PALASES	AAERSSY	ARAYSES	AAGILNY	ALAYING
AAEINST	TAENIAS	AAELPST	PALATES		ASSAYER	AAGILOS	ALOGIAS

AAGILOT OTALGIA
AAGILRS ARGALIS
        GARIALS
AAGILSV GAVIALS
AAGILTW WAGTAIL
AAGIMNO ANGIOMA
AAGIMNS MAGIANS
        SIAMANG
AAGIMNT AMATING
AAGIMNZ AMAZING
AAGINNS ANGINAS
AAGINNW WANIGAN
AAGINPY APAYING
AAGINRR ARRAIGN
AAGINRS NAGARIS
        SANGRIA
        SARANGI
AAGINRU GUARANI
AAGINST AGAINST
        GITANAS
AAGINSU IGUANAS
AAGINSV VAGINAS
AAGINSY GAINSAY
AAGIOTT AGITATO
AAGIPRS AIRGAPS
AAGIPRU PIRAGUA
AAGIRRY ARGYRIA
AAGISTT SAGITTA
AAGJNRS GARJANS
AAGJRSU JAGUARS
AAGKOOZ GAZOOKA
AAGKORT KATORGA
AAGLLNS LALANGS
AAGLLNT GALLANT
AAGLMMS MALMAGS
AAGLMNS MANGALS
AAGLNOS ANALOGS
AAGLNOY ANALOGY
AAGLNPS LAPSANG
AAGLNRS RAGLANS
AAGLNRU ANGULAR
AAGLRUU AUGURAL
AAGLSST STALAGS
AAGMMNS MAGSMAN
AAGMMRR GRAMMAR
AAGMMTU GUMMATA
AAGMNNR GRANNAM
AAGMNPR PANGRAM
AAGMNPY PANGAMY
AAGMNRS RAGMANS
AAGMNRT TANGRAM
        TRANGAM
AAGMNSW SWAGMAN
AAGMNSZ ZAMANGS
AAGMOPY APOGAMY
AAGMORS MARGOSA
AAGMOSU AGAMOUS
AAGMRRY GRAMARY
AAGMRSY MARGAYS
AAGNNOS ANGONAS
AAGNNSW WANGANS
AAGNOPR PARAGON
AAGNORS ANGORAS
AAGNORZ ORGANZA
AAGNPRS PARANGS
AAGNRRS GARRANS
AAGNRRY GRANARY
AAGNRSS SANGARS
AAGNRTV VAGRANT
AAGNSTU TAGUANS

AAGOPSS SAPSAGO
AAGORSU SAGUARO
AAGOSTU AGOUTAS
AAGPPRS GRAPPAS
AAGRRSY GARRYAS
AAHHLSV HALVAHS
AAHHMSZ HAMZAHS
AAHHNNT THANNAH
AAHHNPT NAPHTHA
AAHHNST THANAHS
AAHIIMT HIMATIA
AAHIKRT KITHARA
AAHILLL HALLALI
AAHILLN HALLIAN
AAHILMR ALMIRAH
AAHILMT THALAMI
AAHILNT THALIAN
AAHIMNO MAHONIA
AAHIMSS AHIMSAS
AAHINOP APHONIA
AAHINPR PIRANHA
AAHINST SHAITAN
        TAHINAS
AAHIPRS PARIAHS
        RAPHIAS
AAHIPRT PITARAH
AAHIPTZ ZAPTIAH
AAHIRSS SHARIAS
AAHIRST SHARIAT
AAHIRSV VIHARAS
AAHJKNR KHANJAR
AAHJNRS HANJARS
AAHJRRS JARRAHS
AAHKKST KATHAKS
AAHKLRS LASHKAR
AAHKLST KHALATS
AAHKMSY YASHMAK
AAHKNST KANTHAS
AAHKRSS RAKSHAS
AAHLLLS HALLALS
AAHLLNS HALLANS
        NALLAHS
AAHLLOS HALLOAS
AAHLLPS PALLAHS
AAHLLSW WALLAHS
AAHLLWY HALLWAY
AAHLMMS HAMMALS
        MAHMALS
        MASHLAM
AAHLMRS MARSHAL
AAHLMRU HAMULAR
AAHLMST MALTHAS
AAHLNPX PHALANX
AAHLNRW NARWHAL
AAHLPRS PHRASAL
AAHLPST ASPHALT
        TAPLASH
AAHLRSS ASHLARS
AAHLRST HARTALS
AAHLRSW SHALWAR
AAHMMMS HAMMAMS
AAHMMNS MASHMAN
AAHMNNU HANUMAN
AAHMNRS HARMANS
AAHMNSS SHAMANS
AAHMOPR AMPHORA
AAHMQSU QUAMASH
AAHMRSS ASHRAMS
AAHMSST ASTHMAS
AAHMSTZ MATZAHS

AAHNNOS HOSANNA
AAHNNST TANNAHS
        THANNAS
AAHNORT ATHANOR
AAHNORV NAVARHO
AAHNRTX ANTHRAX
AAHNRTY RHATANY
AAHPPRS PARAPHS
AAHPRSY YARPHAS
AAHPRTW WARPATH
AAHPTWY PATHWAY
AAHRSSS HASSARS
AAHRSST SHASTRA
AAHRTTW ATHWART
AAHSSSY SASHAYS
AAIIKKS KAIKAIS
AAIILMR AIRMAIL
AAIILPR PAIRIAL
AAIILPT TILAPIA
AAIILRZ ALIZARI
AAIINNZ ANZIANI
AAIIRVV VIVARIA
AAIJLNP JALAPIN
AAIJMNP JAMPANI
AAIJNRZ JANIZAR
AAIJNST TINAJAS
AAIJRSW JAWARIS
AAIKLLS ALKALIS
AAIKLMS KALMIAS
        KAMILAS
AAIKLNS KALIANS
AAIKMNN MANAKIN
AAIKMNR RAMAKIN
AAIKMOR ROMAIKA
AAIKMRS KARAISM
AAIKNST TANKIAS
AAIKORU OUAKARI
AAIKPPR PAPRIKA
AAIKRSS ASKARIS
AAIKRST KARAITS
AAIKRSU UAKARIS
AAIKSTT ASTATKI
AAIKTVV AKVAVIT
AAILLLP PALLIAL
AAILLMM MAMILLA
AAILLMN MANILLA
AAILLMR ARMILLA
AAILLMX MAXILLA
AAILLNV VANILLA
AAILLPP PAPILLA
AAILLRX AXILLAR
AAILLSV SALIVAL
AAILLUV ALLUVIA
AAILLXY AXIALLY
AAILMMN MAILMAN
AAILMMR AMMIRAL
AAILMMS MIASMAL
AAILMMX MAXIMAL
AAILMNR LAMINAR
        RAILMAN
AAILMNS ALMAINS
        ANIMALS
        MANILAS
AAILMNT MATINAL
AAILMNU ALUMINA
AAILMPS IMPALAS
AAILMRT MARITAL
        MARTIAL
AAILMSS ALISMAS
        SALAMIS

AAILMSU AUMAILS
AAILNOT AILANTO
AAILNOV NOVALIA
        VALONIA
AAILNPS SALPIAN
AAILNPT PLATINA
AAILNRU ULNARIA
AAILNRY LANIARY
AAILNSS SALINAS
AAILNSY INYALAS
AAILNTV VALIANT
AAILORS ROSALIA
AAILORV VARIOLA
AAILPPT APPALTI
AAILPRS PARIALS
AAILPRT PARTIAL
        PATRIAL
AAILPST SPATIAL
AAILPTT TALIPAT
AAILPZZ PALAZZI
AAILRRV ARRIVAL
AAILRST LARIATS
        LATRIAS
AAILRTV TRAVAIL
AAILRWY RAILWAY
AAILSSS ASSAILS
AAILSSV SALIVAS
        SALVIAS
        VASSAIL
AAILSSW WASSAIL
AAILTTT LATITAT
AAIMMNO AMMONIA
AAIMMSS MIASMAS
AAIMNNO OMNIANA
AAIMNOS ANOSMIA
AAIMNOT AMATION
AAIMNRS MARINAS
AAIMNRT TAMARIN
AAIMNST MANATIS
        STAMINA
AAIMNSV VIMANAS
AAIMNTX TAXIMAN
AAIMRST AMRITAS
        TAMARIS
AAIMRSU SAMURAI
AAIMSST STASIMA
AAIMSTT TATAMIS
AAIMSTV ATAVISM
AAIMSUV MAUVAIS
AAINNRU URANIAN
AAINNRV NAVARIN
        NIRVANA
AAINOPS PAISANO
AAINORR ORARIAN
AAINORV OVARIAN
AAINOSX ANOXIAS
AAINPPS PAPAINS
AAINPRS PIRANAS
AAINPST PATINAS
        TAIPANS
AAINRST ANTIARS
        ARTISAN
        TSARINA
AAINRSU ANURIAS
        SAURIAN
AAINRSV SAVARIN
AAINRTV VARIANT
AAINSTT ATTAINS
AAINSTV VANITAS
AAINTTT ATTAINT

AAINTTU	TUTANIA	AALLMPU	AMPULLA
AAIOPRS	APORIAS	AALLNPU	PLANULA
AAIOPRT	ATROPIA	AALLNSY	NASALLY
AAIORSU	SAOUARI	AALLORS	AROLLAS
AAIORTV	AVIATOR	AALLOSZ	AZOLLAS
AAIPPRS	APPAIRS	AALLOTV	LAVOLTA
AAIPPRU	PUPARIA	AALLPPY	PAPALLY
AAIPPTT	PITAPAT	AALLRUY	AURALLY
AAIPRST	PITARAS	AALLRVY	VALLARY
AAIPRSY	PIRAYAS	AALLSTT	TALLATS
AAIPRTT	PARTITA	AALLUVV	VALVULA
AAIPSZZ	PIAZZAS	AALMMMS	MAMMALS
AAIQSSU	QUASSIA	AALMMNO	AMMONAL
AAIQTUV	AQUAVIT	AALMMNT	MALTMAN
AAIRSST	ARISTAS	AALMNOS	SALAMON
	TARSIAS	AALMNOY	ANOMALY
AAIRSTT	STRIATA	AALMNPS	NAPALMS
AAIRSTY	RAIYATS	AALMNSU	MANUALS
AAIRSWY	AIRWAYS	AALMORT	ALAMORT
AAIRSZZ	RAZZIAS	AALMORY	MAYORAL
AAITWXY	TAXIWAY	AALMOST	AMATOLS
AAJJMRS	JAMJARS	AALMPRY	PALMARY
AAJKLWY	JAYWALK		PALMYRA
AAJKMNR	JARKMAN	AALMPSS	PLASMAS
AAJKNSS	SANJAKS	AALMRRU	RAMULAR
AAJMNPS	JAMPANS	AALMRSU	ALARUMS
AAJMNZZ	JAZZMAN	AALMSSU	MASULAS
AAJMORT	MAJORAT	AALMTTU	MULATTA
AAJMPSY	PYJAMAS	AALNNRU	ANNULAR
AAJNNOS	JOANNAS	AALNNSU	ANNUALS
AAJNOSW	AJOWANS	AALNPRT	PLANTAR
AAJNOSY	YOJANAS	AALNPST	PLANTAS
AAJOPSU	SAPAJOU		PLATANS
AAKKLPS	KALPAKS	AALNPUU	PUNALUA
AAKKLRU	KARAKUL	AALNQTU	QUANTAL
AAKKMOT	TOKAMAK	AALNRSU	RANULAS
AAKKMRS	MARKKAS	AALNRTT	LATRANT
AAKKOPS	KAKAPOS	AALNRTU	NATURAL
AAKKSUZ	ZAKUSKA	AALNSST	SANTALS
AAKLMPU	LAMPUKA	AALNSTT	SALTANT
AAKLMRY	MALARKY		TALANTS
AAKLMUY	YAMULKA	AALNSTU	SULTANA
AAKLNOO	OOLAKAN	AALNSTY	ANALYST
AAKLNOU	OULAKAN	AALNTTU	TALAUNT
AAKLOOP	PALOOKA	AALOPPT	APPALTO
AAKLRSU	KURSAAL	AALOPRS	PARASOL
	RUSALKA	AALOPSY	PAYOLAS
AAKLSSU	SAKSAUL	AALOPVV	PAVLOVA
AAKLWWY	WALKWAY	AALOPZZ	PALAZZO
AAKMMNR	MARKMAN	AALORRU	AURORAL
AAKMNSU	MANUKAS	AALORSU	AROUSAL
AAKMOSU	MOUSAKA	AALORTX	LAXATOR
AAKMRSU	KUMARAS	AALOSTT	SALTATO
AAKMRUZ	MAZURKA	AALOSVW	AVOWALS
AAKMRWY	WAYMARK	AALOTTY	TALAYOT
AAKNNTU	NUNATAK	AALPPRU	PAPULAR
AAKNORS	ANORAKS	AALPRRS	PARRALS
AAKNRST	KANTARS	AALPRSW	ASPRAWL
AAKNSST	ASKANTS	AALPRSY	PARLAYS
AAKNTWY	TWANKAY	AALPSTU	SPATULA
AAKOOPP	PAKAPOO	AALRSST	TARSALS
AAKOPRS	PAKORAS	AALRSTU	AUSTRAL
AAKORST	OSTRAKA	AALRSTY	ASTYLAR
AAKPRWY	PARKWAY		SATYRAL
AAKRTUY	AUTARKY	AALSSSV	VASSALS
AAKSSTT	ATTASKS	AALSSTU	ASSAULT
AAKSTTT	ATTASKT	AALSSUX	SAXAULS
AALLLNS	LALLANS	AALSTUV	VALUTAS
AALLLSS	SALLALS	AALSWYY	WAYLAYS
AALLMMS	MALLAMS	AAMMMRY	MAMMARY

AAMMNRT	MANTRAM	AAPRSTT	ATTRAPS
AAMMNST	AMTMANS	AAPRSTY	SATRAPY
AAMMRRS	MARRAMS	AAQRSSU	QUASARS
AAMMRST	RAMSTAM	AARRSTT	TARTARS
AAMMSUZ	MAZUMAS	AARRSWY	WARRAYS
AAMNNOY	ANONYMA	AARSSST	ASSARTS
AAMNOOS	MANOAOS	AARSSTT	ASTARTS
AAMNORS	OARSMAN	AARSSTY	SATYRAS
AAMNOSZ	AMAZONS	AASSTTU	STATUAS
AAMNOTY	ANATOMY	ABBBDEL	BABBLED
AAMNPRT	MANTRAP		BLABBED
	RAMPANT	ABBBELR	BABBLER
AAMNPRY	PARANYM		BLABBER
AAMNPSS	PASSMAN		BRABBLE
	SAMPANS	ABBBELS	BABBLES
AAMNPST	TAPSMAN	ABBBITT	BABBITT
AAMNPTY	TYMPANA	ABBCDER	CRABBED
AAMNRST	ARTSMAN	ABBCDES	SCABBED
	MANTRAS	ABBCEHI	BABICHE
AAMNSTU	MANTUAS	ABBCEHU	BABUCHE
	TAMANUS	ABBCEIS	CABBIES
AAMOORS	AMOROSA	ABBCELR	CLABBER
AAMOPRS	PARAMOS	ABBCELS	SCABBLE
AAMORRZ	ZAMARRO	ABBCIKT	BACKBIT
AAMORSV	SAMOVAR	ABBCIRS	BICARBS
AAMORTY	AMATORY	ABBCOST	BOBCATS
AAMOSSS	SAMOSAS	ABBDDEL	DABBLED
AAMOSTT	STOMATA	ABBDDER	DRABBED
AAMOTTU	AUTOMAT	ABBDEFR	FRABBED
AAMPRRT	RAMPART	ABBDEGL	GABBLED
AAMPSSY	AMPASSY	ABBDEGR	GRABBED
AAMRSST	MATRASS	ABBDEIT	TABBIED
AAMRSSU	ASARUMS	ABBDEJL	JABBLED
AAMRSTU	SUMATRA	ABBDELR	DABBLER
	TRAUMAS		DRABBLE
AAMRTWY	TRAMWAY		RABBLED
AAMSSTU	SATSUMA	ABBDELS	DABBLES
AANNOTT	ANNATTO		SLABBED
AANNPSS	SANPANS	ABBDELW	WABBLED
AANNSYZ	NYANZAS	ABBDERR	DRABBER
AANORST	TORANAS	ABBDERS	DABBERS
AANOSST	SONATAS	ABBDERT	DRABBET
AANOSTT	ANATTOS	ABBDEST	STABBED
AANPPSS	SAPPANS		TEBBADS
AANPRST	PARTANS	ABBDESU	BEDAUBS
	SPARTAN	ABBDESW	SWABBED
	TARPANS	ABBDGIN	DABBING
	TRAPANS	ABBDHIJ	DJIBBAH
AANPSST	PASSANT	ABBDILR	LIBBARD
AANQRTU	QUARTAN	ABBDINR	RIBBAND
AANRRSW	WARRANS	ABBDITY	DABBITY
AANRRTW	WARRANT	ABBDLRU	LUBBARD
AANRSTT	RATTANS	ABBDMOR	BOMBARD
	TANTRAS	ABBDMOU	BABUDOM
	TARTANS	ABBEESW	BAWBEES
AANRUWY	RUNAWAY	ABBEFST	FABBEST
AANSSTV	SAVANTS	ABBEGIR	GABBIER
AANSSTZ	STANZAS	ABBEGLR	GABBLER
AANSTTT	STATANT		GRABBLE
AANSTUV	AVAUNTS	ABBEGLS	GABBLES
AANSWYY	ANYWAYS	ABBEGNO	BOGBEAN
AAOORRW	WOORARA	ABBEGNU	BUGBANE
AAOPSST	POTASSA	ABBEGRR	GRABBER
	SAPOTAS	ABBEGRS	GABBERS
AAORRSU	AURORAS	ABBEGRU	BUGBEAR
AAORRSV	VARROAS	ABBEHLS	SHABBLE
AAORSTT	TOTARAS	ABBEIRS	BARBIES
AAOSTTV	OTTAVAS	ABBEIST	BABIEST
AAPPSWW	PAWPAWS		TABBIES
AAPRSST	SATRAPS	ABBEISY	YABBIES

ABBEJLS	JABBLES	ABCCIMR	CAMBRIC
ABBEJRS	JABBERS	ABCCINU	BUCCINA
ABBELMR	BRAMBLE	ABCCIOR	BORACIC
ABBELNS	SNABBLE		BRACCIO
ABBELPR	PRABBLE	ABCCISU	CUBICAS
ABBELRR	RABBLER	ABCCKOW	BAWCOCK
ABBELRS	BARBELS	ABCCKTU	CUTBACK
	RABBLES	ABCCOOR	BAROCCO
	SLABBER	ABCCOOT	TOBACCO
ABBELRU	BARBULE	ABCCSUU	SUCCUBA
ABBELRW	WABBLER	ABCDDEU	ABDUCED
ABBELSU	BASBLEU	ABCDEEH	BEACHED
	BAUBLES	ABCDEEL	BELACED
ABBELSW	BAWBLES		DEBACLE
	WABBLES	ABCDEHT	BATCHED
ABBELUY	BUYABLE	ABCDEHU	DEBAUCH
ABBEMUZ	BUMBAZE	ABCDEIK	DIEBACK
ABBENRS	NABBERS	ABCDEIN	CABINED
ABBEORS	EARBOBS	ABCDEIP	PEDICAB
ABBERRS	BARBERS	ABCDEIR	CARBIDE
ABBERST	BARBETS	ABCDEKL	BLACKED
	RABBETS	ABCDEKR	REDBACK
	STABBER	ABCDEOR	BROCADE
ABBERSW	SWABBER	ABCDERS	DECARBS
ABBERSY	YABBERS	ABCDERU	CUDBEAR
ABBFIRT	FRABBIT	ABCDESU	ABDUCES
ABBGGIN	GABBING	ABCDHIO	ICHABOD
ABBGHSU	GUBBAHS	ABCDHOR	CHOBDAR
ABBGIJN	JABBING	ABCDHOS	BODACHS
ABBGINN	NABBING	ABCDIIS	DIBASIC
ABBGINR	BARBING	ABCDILR	BALDRIC
ABBGINT	TABBING	ABCDINS	ABSCIND
ABBGINU	BUBINGA	ABCDIRS	SCABRID
ABBGINY	BABYING	ABCDIRT	CATBIRD
ABBGOOU	BUGABOO	ABCDIRU	BAUDRIC
ABBGORS	GABBROS	ABCDISU	SUBACID
ABBHIJS	JIBBAHS	ABCDNOS	ABSCOND
ABBHISY	BABYISH	ABCDOOR	CORDOBA
ABBHJSU	JUBBAHS	ABCDORR	BROCARD
ABBHOOS	BABOOSH	ABCDSTU	ABDUCTS
	HABOOBS	ABCEEHS	BEACHES
ABBHRRU	RHUBARB	ABCEEHU	EBAUCHE
ABBHTTU	BATHTUB	ABCEELS	BELACES
ABBIIMN	BAMBINI	ABCEEMR	EMBRACE
ABBILOR	BILOBAR	ABCEEMS	EMBACES
ABBILOT	BOBTAIL	ABCEENS	ABSENCE
ABBILSU	BUBALIS	ABCEERR	ACERBER
ABBIMNO	BAMBINO		REBRACE
ABBIMSU	BABUISM	ABCEERU	BERCEAU
ABBINOR	RABBONI	ABCEESS	BECASSE
ABBINRS	RABBINS	ABCEESU	BECAUSE
ABBIRST	RABBITS	ABCEGIR	RIBCAGE
ABBIRTY	RABBITY	ABCEGMO	CAMBOGE
ABBKLOU	BLAUBOK	ABCEGOR	BROCAGE
ABBLLTU	BULLBAT	ABCEGOS	BOCAGES
ABBLMRY	BRAMBLY		BOSCAGE
ABBMOOR	BOMBORA	ABCEGSU	CUBAGES
ABBMOOS	BAMBOOS	ABCEHKO	BACKHOE
ABBMOST	BOMBAST	ABCEHLU	BAUCHLE
ABBNOOS	BABOONS	ABCEHMR	BECHARM
ABBORSS	ABSORBS		BRECHAM
ABBQSUY	SQUABBY		CHAMBER
ABCCEIR	ACERBIC		CHAMBRE
	BRECCIA	ABCEHOS	BASOCHE
ABCCEIS	BACCIES	ABCEHRS	BRACHES
	SEBACIC	ABCEHRT	BRACHET
ABCCEOS	BACCOES	ABCEHST	BATCHES
ABCCHII	BACCHII	ABCEILM	ALEMBIC
ABCCHTY	BYCATCH	ABCEILR	CALIBER
ABCCILU	CUBICAL		CALIBRE

ABCEILT	CITABLE	ABCIIOR	CIBORIA
ABCEIMO	AMOEBIC	ABCIIOT	ABIOTIC
ABCEINR	CARBINE	ABCILRS	SCRIBAL
ABCEINT	CABINET	ABCILTU	CUBITAL
ABCEIOR	AEROBIC	ABCIMMS	CAMBISM
ABCEIRS	ASCRIBE	ABCIMMU	CAMBIUM
	CABRIES	ABCIMST	CAMBIST
	CARIBES	ABCINOT	BOTANIC
ABCEISS	ABSCISE	ABCIORR	BARRICO
	SCABIES	ABCIORU	CARIBOU
ABCEITT	TABETIC	ABCIOUV	BIVOUAC
ABCEJST	ABJECTS	ABCIRST	CABRITS
ABCEKLN	BLACKEN	ABCIRTY	BARYTIC
ABCEKLR	BLACKER	ABCISSS	ABSCISS
ABCEKNR	BRACKEN	ABCJOSU	JACOBUS
ABCEKRS	BACKERS	ABCKMRU	BUCKRAM
	REBACKS	ABCKNNO	BANNOCK
ABCEKRT	BRACKET	ABCKORS	BAROCKS
ABCEKST	BACKETS	ABCKOTU	OUTBACK
	BACKSET	ABCKRSU	BUCKRAS
	SETBACK	ABCKSTU	SACKBUT
ABCEKSY	BACKSEY		SUBTACK
ABCEKTW	WETBACK	ABCKSUW	BUCKSAW
ABCELLS	BECALLS	ABCLMNU	CLUBMAN
ABCELLU	BULLACE	ABCLMOY	CYMBALO
ABCELMO	CEMBALO	ABCLMSY	CYMBALS
ABCELMR	CAMBREL	ABCLNOS	BLANCOS
	CLAMBER	ABCLNOY	BALCONY
ABCELMS	BECALMS	ABCLOST	COBALTS
	SCAMBLE	ABCMORS	COMARBS
ABCELOP	PLACEBO	ABCMOST	COMBATS
ABCELOV	VOCABLE		TOMBACS
ABCELPU	BLUECAP	ABCNORS	CARBONS
ABCELPY	BYPLACE		CORBANS
ABCELRU	CURABLE	ABCORSX	BOXCARS
ABCELSU	BASCULE	ABCORSY	CARBOYS
ABCEMRS	CAMBERS	ABCSSTU	SUBACTS
	CEMBRAS	ABDDDEL	BLADDED
ABCEMSX	EXCAMBS	ABDDEEJ	BEJADED
ABCENOS	BEACONS	ABDDEER	BEARDED
ABCENOW	COWBANE		BREADED
ABCENRU	UNBRACE	ABDDEES	DEBASED
ABCEOOS	CABOOSE	ABDDEET	DEBATED
ABCEORU	CORBEAU	ABDDEEZ	BEDAZED
ABCERRS	BRACERS	ABDDEHN	BANDHED
ABCESSS	ABSCESS	ABDDEIN	ABIDDEN
ABCFIKN	FINBACK		BANDIED
ABCFILO	BIFOCAL	ABDDEIR	BRAIDED
ABCFIRS	FABRICS	ABDDEIS	BADDIES
ABCFLOO	COBLOAF	ABDDELR	BLADDER
ABCFNOS	CONFABS	ABDDELU	BLAUDED
ABCGHIN	BACHING	ABDDENR	BRANDED
ABCGHKO	HOGBACK	ABDDEOR	ABORDED
ABCGIKN	BACKING		BOARDED
ABCGILN	CABLING	ABDDERW	BEDWARD
ABCGINR	BRACING	ABDDHIS	BADDISH
ABCGKLO	BACKLOG	ABDDINS	DISBAND
ABCGMSU	SCUMBAG	ABDDLLO	ODDBALL
ABCHIII	HIBACHI	ABDDMOR	DAMBROD
ABCHIMT	BATHMIC	ABDEEGL	BEAGLED
ABCHIOT	COHABIT	ABDEEHO	OBEAHED
ABCHKOU	CHABOUK	ABDEEHS	BEHEADS
ABCHKTU	HACKBUT	ABDEEHT	BEATHED
ABCHKUW	HAWBUCK	ABDEEHV	BEHAVED
ABCHNOR	BROCHAN	ABDEEIR	BEADIER
ABCHNRU	BRAUNCH		BEARDIE
ABCHNRY	BRANCHY	ABDEEJS	BEJADES
ABCIILL	BACILLI	ABDEELM	BELDAME
ABCIIMN	MINICAB		BEMEDAL
ABCIIMS	IAMBICS		EMBALED

ABDEELN ENABLED	BRAIDER	ABDETTU ABUTTED	ABDRUZZ BUZZARD
ABDEELR BEDERAL	BRIARED	ABDGGOR BOGGARD	ABEEELS SEEABLE
BLEARED	RABIDER	ABDGIIN ABIDING	ABEEERV BEREAVE
ABDEELS BEADLES	ABDEIRS BRAISED	ABDGILN BALDING	ABEEFFL EFFABLE
ABDEELT BELATED	DARBIES	ABDGINN BANDING	ABEEFLO BEEFALO
BLEATED	ABDEIRT TRIBADE	ABDGINO ABODING	ABEEFTU BEAUFET
ABDEELY DYEABLE	ABDEIRU DAUBIER	ABDGINR BARDING	ABEEGHR HERBAGE
ABDEEMN BEADMEN	ABDEIRW BAWDIER	BRIGAND	ABEEGHS BEEGAHS
BEDEMAN	ABDEISS BIASSED	ABDGINT DINGBAT	ABEEGLL GABELLE
BENAMED	ABDEIST BASTIDE	ABDGINU DAUBING	ABEEGLR BEAGLER
ABDEEMR AMBERED	ABDEISW BAWDIES	ABDGLNO BOGLAND	ABEEGLS BEAGLES
BREAMED	ABDEJRU ABJURED	ABDGLUY LADYBUG	ABEEGRR GERBERA
EMBREAD	ABDEKLN BLANKED	ABDGNOS BANDOGS	ABEEGRS ABREGES
ABDEEMS EMBASED	ABDEKLU BAULKED	ABDGORS BODRAGS	BAREGES
ABDEEMY EMBAYED	ABDEKNR BRANKED	ABDHHOS DOBHASH	BARGEES
ABDEEMZ BEMAZED	ABDEKNU UNBAKED	ABDHIIT ADHIBIT	ABEEGRU AUBERGE
ABDEERS DEBASER	ABDEKRS DEBARKS	ABDHILS BALDISH	ABEEGRW BREWAGE
SABERED	ABDELMR MARBLED	ABDHMOR RHABDOM	ABEEHMS BESHAME
ABDEERT BERATED	RAMBLED	ABDHMSU BUDMASH	ABEEHMT EMBATHE
BETREAD	ABDELMS BEDLAMS	ABDHNSU HUSBAND	ABEEHNN HENBANE
DEBATER	BELDAMS	ABDHOSY HOBDAYS	ABEEHNS BANSHEE
REBATED	ABDELMW WAMBLED	ABDHRSU BURDASH	BEENAHS
ABDEERW BEWARED	ABDELMY EMBAYLD	RHABDUS	ABEEHNT BENEATH
ABDEERY BERAYED	ABDELNR BLANDER	ABDIKNW BAWDKIN	ABEEHRT BREATHE
ABDEESS DEBASES	ABDELOR LABORED	ABDIKRS DISBARK	ABEEHSV BEHAVES
SEABEDS	ABDELOS ALBEDOS	ABDILOO DIABOLO	ABEEILS BAILEES
ABDEEST BESTEAD	ABDELOT BLOATED	ABDILOR LABROID	ABEEIMR BEAMIER
DEBATES	ABDELOW DOWABLE	ABDILOT TABLOID	ABEEINS BEANIES
ABDEESZ BEDAZES	ABDELPU DUPABLE	ABDILRS BRIDALS	ABEEINT BETAINE
ABDEETT ABETTED	ABDELPY PYEBALD	LABRIDS	ABEEIRT EBRIATE
ABDEFFL BAFFLED	ABDELRR DRABLER	RIBALDS	ABEEIST BEASTIE
ABDEFLU LEAFBUD	ABDELRS BEDRALS	ABDILRW AWLBIRD	ABEEJMS JAMBEES
ABDEFOR FORBADE	ABDELRU DURABLE	ABDILRY RABIDLY	ABEEJRS BAJREES
ABDEFRW BEDWARF	ABDELRW BRAWLED	ABDILUY AUDIBLY	ABEEKLR BLEAKER
ABDEFST BEDFAST	WARBLED	ABDILWY BAWDILY	ABEEKLS KABELES
ABDEGGL BLAGGED	ABDELST BALDEST	ABDIMNR BIRDMAN	ABEEKNT BETAKEN
ABDEGGR BRAGGED	BLASTED	ABDIMOR AMBROID	ABEEKNV BEKNAVE
ABDEGHR BEGHARD	STABLED	ABDINOR INBOARD	ABEEKOP PEEKABO
ABDEGIN BEADING	ABDELSU BELAUDS	ABDINRS RIBANDS	ABEEKPS BESPAKE
ABDEGIR ABRIDGE	ABDELTT BATTLED	ABDINST BANDITS	BESPEAK
BRIGADE	BLATTED	ABDIOSU BADIOUS	ABEEKRR BREAKER
ABDEGLM GAMBLED	ABDEMMO MAMBOED	ABDIPRU UPBRAID	ABEEKRS BEAKERS
ABDEGLN BANGLED	ABDEMNO ABDOMEN	ABDIRRS BRAIRDS	ABEEKST BETAKES
ABDEGLR BELGARD	ABDEMRU RUMBAED	ABDIRSS DISBARS	ABEELLY EYEBALL
GARBLED	ABDENOR BANDORE	ABDIRSU RIBAUDS	ABEELMM EMBLEMA
ABDEGNO BONDAGE	BROADEN	SUBARID	ABEELMS EMBALES
DOGBANE	ABDENOT BATONED	ABDIRTY TRIBADY	ABEELMZ EMBLAZE
ABDEGOS BODEGAS	ABDENOY NAEBODY	ABDKNOO BANDOOK	ABEELNP PLEBEAN
ABDEGRS BADGERS	ABDENPS BEDPANS	ABDLLNY BLANDLY	ABEELNR ENABLER
ABDEHIT HABITED	ABDENRR BRANDER	ABDLLOR BOLLARD	ABEELNS BALEENS
ABDEHLM HAMBLED	ABDENRU UNBARED	ABDLNOR BANDROL	ENABLES
ABDEHLR HALBERD	ABDENRW BRAWNED	ABDLORY BROADLY	ABEELNT TENABLE
ABDEHOW BOWHEAD	ABDENSS BADNESS	ABDLRUY DURABLY	ABEELNU NEBULAE
ABDEHRS BERDASH	ABDENSU SUBDEAN	RYBAULD	ABEELPR BEPEARL
BRASHED	ABDENTU UNBATED	ABDLRYY BYRLADY	ABEELQU EQUABLE
ABDEHRT BREADTH	ABDEOOT TABOOED	ABDLSUU SUBDUAL	ABEELRR BLEARER
ABDEILP BIPEDAL	ABDEORR BOARDER	ABDMNNO BONDMAN	ERRABLE
PIEBALD	BROADER	ABDMRUY MARYBUD	ABEELRT BLEATER
ABDEILR BRAILED	ABDEORT ABORTED	ABDNOOR ONBOARD	RETABLE
RIDABLE	TABORED	ABDNOPR PROBAND	ABEELST BELATES
ABDEILS DISABLE	ABDEOST BOASTED	ABDNOSU ABOUNDS	ABEELSU SUEABLE
ABDEILT LIBATED	ABDEOTU BOUTADE	BAUSOND	ABEELSV BESLAVE
ABDEILU AUDIBLE	ABDEQSU BASQUED	ABDNOYY ANYBODY	ABEEMNS BASEMEN
ABDEIMR EMBRAID	ABDERSS SERDABS	ABDNRTU TURBAND	BEMEANS
ABDEIMS IMBASED	ABDERST DABSTER	ABDOORW BARWOOD	BENAMES
ABDEINR BANDIER	ABDERSU DAUBERS	ABDORRS BORDARS	ABEEMNT BEMEANT
BRAINED	SUBEDAR	ABDORSS ADSORBS	ABEEMRS BEAMERS
ABDEINS BANDIES	ABDERSV ADVERBS	ABDORSY BYROADS	BESMEAR
ABDEINW BEDAWIN	ABDERTY DRYBEAT	ABDRRSU DURBARS	ABEEMRV EMBRAVE
ABDEIRR BARDIER	ABDERUY DAUBERY	ABDRSTU BUSTARD	ABEEMSS EMBASES

ABEEMST	EMBASTE	ABEGMRU UMBRAGE	TRIABLE	ABEKNRS BANKERS
ABEENRV VERBENA	ABEGMST GAMBETS	ABEILSS ABSEILS	BARKENS
ABEEORS AEROBES	ABEGNNT BANTENG	ISABELS	ABEKNST BANKETS
ABEEPST BESPATE	ABEGNOS NOSEBAG	LABISES	ABEKOOR ABROOKE
ABEERRS BEARERS	ABEGNRS BANGERS	ABEILST ALBITES	ABEKPRU UPBREAK
BREARES	GRABENS	ASTILBE	ABEKRRS BARKERS
ABEERRT REBATER	ABEGNSW BEGNAWS	BESTIAL	ABEKSST BASKETS
TABRERE	ABEGORR BEGORRA	LIBATES	ABELLMN BELLMAN
TEREBRA	ABEGORS BORAGES	STABILE	ABELLMS EMBALLS
ABEERST BEATERS	ABEGORX GEARBOX	ABEILSW BEWAILS	ABELLNT NETBALL
BERATES	ABEGOSZ GAZEBOS	ABEILSY BAILEYS	ABELLOS LOSABLE
REBATES	ABEGOTT BOTTEGA	ABEILSZ SIZABLE	ABELLOV LOVABLE
ABEERSV BEAVERS	ABEGOUY BUOYAGE	ABEILVV BIVALVE	VOLABLE
ABEERSW BEWARES	ABEGRST BARGEST	ABEIMNR MIRBANE	ABELLRU RUBELLA
ABEERSZ ZEREBAS	ABEGSTU TUBAGES	ABEIMNT AMBIENT	RULABLE
ABEERTT ABETTER	ABEHILR HIRABLE	ABEIMRR BARMIER	ABELLST BALLETS
ABEERVY BEAVERY	ABEHIMS BEAMISH	ABEIMRS AMBRIES	ABELLTU BULLATE
ABEESST SEBATES	ABEHIMT IMBATHE	ABEIMSS IMBASES	ABELMMR MEMBRAL
ABEESWX BEESWAX	ABEHIRS BEARISH	ABEINOT NIOBATE	ABELMMS EMBALMS
ABEFFIS BAFFIES	ABEHISU BEAUISH	ABEINPT BEPAINT	ABELMNT LAMBENT
ABEFFLR BAFFLER	ABEHITU HABITUE	ABEINRT ATEBRIN	ABELMNU ALBUMEN
ABEFFLS BAFFLES	ABEHITZ ZABTIEH	ABEINST BASINET	ABELMOV MOVABLE
ABEFFOT OFFBEAT	ABEHKLS KEBLAHS	BESAINT	ABELMRR MARBLER
ABEFGIL FILABEG	ABEHKRU HAUBERK	BESTAIN	RAMBLER
ABEFGST GABFEST	ABEHLMS HAMBLES	ABEINTT TABINET	ABELMRS AMBLERS
ABEFILN FINABLE	SHAMBLE	ABEIORS ISOBARE	LAMBERS
ABEFILR FRIABLE	ABEHLNU UNHABLE	ABEIOSS ABIOSES	MARBLES
ABEFILS FAIBLES	ABEHLRS HERBALS	ISOBASE	RAMBLES
ABEFILX FIXABLE	ABEHLRT BLATHER	ABEIOTV OBVIATE	ABELMRT LAMBERT
ABEFINU BEAUFIN	HALBERT	ABEIPST BAPTISE	ABELMSU BEMAULS
ABEFITY BEATIFY	ABEHLSS BLASHES	ABEIPTZ BAPTIZE	ABELMSW WAMBLES
ABEFLLS BEFALLS	ABEHNOS HEBONAS	ABEIRRR BARRIER	ABELMTU MUTABLE
ABEFLLU BALEFUL	ABEHRRS BRASHER	ABEIRRS BRASIER	ABELNOT NOTABLE
ABEFLLY FLYABLE	HERBARS	ABEIRRT ARBITER	ABELNOY BALONEY
ABEFLNU BANEFUL	ABEHRRY HERBARY	RAREBIT	ABELNRS BRANLES
ABEFLNY FLYBANE	ABEHRSS BASHERS	ABEIRRW WARBIER	BRANSLE
ABEFLRS FABLERS	BRASHES	ABEIRRZ BIZARRE	ABELNRT BRANTLE
ABEFMOS BEFOAMS	ABEHRST BATHERS	BRAZIER	ABELNRU NEBULAR
ABEFORR FORBEAR	BERTHAS	ABEIRSS BASSIER	ABELNRY BLARNEY
ABEFPRS PREFABS	BREATHS	BRAISES	ABELNSZ BENZALS
ABEGGIR BAGGIER	ABEHRTY BREATHY	BRASSIE	ABELNTU TUNABLE
ABEGGMO GAMBOGE	ABEIILL BAILLIE	ABEIRST BAITERS	ABELOPR ROPABLE
ABEGGNU BUGGANE	ABEIILS BAILIES	BARITES	ABELOPT POTABLE
ABEGGRS BEGGARS	ABEIJMR JAMBIER	ABEIRSX BRAXIES	ABELORS LABROSE
ABEGGRU BURGAGE	ABEIJNS BASENJI	ABEIRSZ BRAIZES	ABELORT BLOATER
ABEGGRY BEGGARY	ABEIKLL LIKABLE	ZERIBAS	ABELORU RUBEOLA
ABEGHNS SHEBANG	ABEIKLR BALKIER	ABEIRTT BATTIER	ABELORW ROWABLE
ABEGIMN BEAMING	ABEIKLS SKIABLE	BIRETTA	ABELOSS BOLASES
ABEGIMR GAMBIER	ABEIKNR INBREAK	ABEIRTV VIBRATE	ABELOST BOATELS
ABEGIMT MEGABIT	ABEIKNT BEATNIK	ABEIRUX EXURBIA	OBLATES
ABEGINN BEANING	ABEIKRR BARKIER	ABEISSS BIASSES	ABELOSV ABSOLVE
ABEGINO BEGONIA	BRAKIER	ABEISTT BATISTE	ABELPRU PUBERAL
ABEGINR BEARING	ABEILLO LOBELIA	ABEISUV ABUSIVE	ABELQUY EQUABLY
ABEGINT BEATING	ABEILLP PLIABLE	ABEITUX BAUXITE	ABELRRS BARRELS
ABEGINY ABYEING	ABEILLR LIBERAL	ABEJMNO JAMBONE	ABELRRW BRAWLER
ABEGIPP BAGPIPE	ABEILLV LIVABLE	ABEJMNS ENJAMBS	WARBLER
ABEGKOR BROKAGE	ABEILMR BALMIER	ABEJMRS JAMBERS	ABELRSS BRALESS
ABEGLMR GAMBLER	MIRABLE	ABEJMUX JAMBEUX	ABELRST ALBERTS
GAMBREL	REMBLAI	ABEJNOS BANJOES	BATLERS
ABEGLMS GAMBLES	ABEILMS EMBAILS	ABEJNOW JAWBONE	BLASTER
ABEGLNR BRANGLE	LAMBIES	ABEJNST BEJANTS	LABRETS
ABEGLNS BANGLES	ABEILMT LIMBATE	ABEJORS JERBOAS	STABLER
ABEGLOR ALBERGO	TIMBALE	ABEJRRU ABJURER	ABELRSV VERBALS
ABEGLOT GLOBATE	ABEILMX MIXABLE	ABEJRSU ABJURES	ABELRSW BAWLERS
ABEGLRR GARBLER	ABEILMY BEAMILY	ABEKLLY BLEAKLY	WARBLES
ABEGLRS GARBLES	ABEILNP BIPLANE	ABEKLNR BLANKER	ABELRSY BARLEYS
ABEGLST GABLETS	ABEILNS LESBIAN	ABEKLNT BLANKET	ABELRSZ BLAZERS
ABEGLSU BELUGAS	ABEILPT PATIBLE	ABEKLRS BALKERS	ABELRTT BATTLER
BLAGUES	ABEILRS BAILERS	ABEKMNS EMBANKS	BLATTER
ABEGMOR EMBARGO	ABEILRT LIBRATE	ABEKMRS EMBARKS	BRATTLE

ABELRTW BLEWART	ABERRSY BRAYERS	ABGIKNS BAKINGS	ABHIOST ISOBATH
ABELRUZ ZEBRULA	ABERRVY BRAVERY	BASKING	ABHISTU HABITUS
ABELRVY BRAVELY	ABERSSS BRASSES	ABGIKNU BAUKING	ABHKLSY BASHLYK
ABELSST BASTLES	ABERSST BASTERS	ABGILLN BALLING	ABHKORU BOURKHA
STABLES	BESTARS	ABGILMN AMBLING	ABHKRSU BURKHAS
ABELSTT BATLETS	BRASSET	BALMING	KURBASH
BATTELS	BREASTS	BLAMING	ABHMNSU BUSHMAN
BATTLES	ABERSSU ABUSERS	LAMBING	ABHMRSU RHUMBAS
BLATEST	SURBASE	ABGILMS GIMBALS	ABHNOST BOTHANS
TABLETS	ABERSSZ ZEBRASS	ABGILNR BLARING	ABHNSTU SUNBATH
ABELSTU SUBLATE	ABERSTT BATTERS	ABGILNS SABLING	ABHORRS HARBORS
ABELSTY BAETYLS	TABRETS	ABGILNT TABLING	ABHORRU HARBOUR
BEASTLY	ABERSTU ARBUTES	ABGILNW BAWLING	ABHOTUY HAUTBOY
ABELSWY BAWLEYS	SURBATE	ABGILNZ BLAZING	ABHPSTY BYPATHS
ABELTWY BELTWAY	ABERSTV BRAVEST	ABGILOR GARBOIL	ABHRSTU TARBUSH
ABEMMRS BAMMERS	ABERSTW BRAWEST	ABGIMMN BAMMING	ABIIKKT KIBITKA
ABEMNOS AMBONES	WABSTER	ABGIMRS GAMBIRS	ABIILLS BAILLIS
BEMOANS	ABERSTX BAXTERS	ABGIMST GAMBIST	ABIILMU BULIMIA
ABEMNOT BOATMEN	ABERSTY BARYTES	GAMBITS	ABIILNQ INQILAB
ABEMNRY BYREMAN	BETRAYS	ABGINNN BANNING	ABIILNS AIBLINS
MYRBANE	ABERSUU BUREAUS	ABGINNR BARNING	BILIANS
ABEMNST BATSMEN	ABERSWY BEWRAYS	ABGINNT BANTING	ABIILRY BILIARY
ABEMNSU SUNBEAM	ABERTTU ABUTTER	ABGINOS BAGNIOS	ABIILST STIBIAL
ABEMORT BROMATE	ABERTTY BATTERY	GABIONS	ABIILTY ABILITY
ABEMRST TAMBERS	ABERUUX BUREAUX	ABGINOT BOATING	ABIIMST IAMBIST
ABEMSSY EMBASSY	ABESSST BASSEST	ABGINRR BARRING	ABIINNS BAININS
ABENNOR BARONNE	BASSETS	ABGINRS SABRING	ABIINOR ROBINIA
ABENNRS BANNERS	ABESSSY ABYSSES	ABGINRV BRAVING	ABIINRY BIRYANI
ABENORS BORANES	ABESTTU BATTUES	ABGINRY BRAYING	ABIIOSS ABIOSIS
ABENORT BARONET	ABFFGIN BAFFING	ABGINRZ BRAZING	ABIJLNR BRINJAL
REBOANT	ABFFIIL BAILIFF	ABGINSS BASSING	ABIJNOT ABJOINT
ABENORW RAWBONE	ABFFLOU BUFFALO	ABGINST BASTING	ABIJRSU JABIRUS
ABENOTY BAYONET	ABFGILN FABLING	ABGINSU ABUSING	ABIKKSU KABUKIS
ABENQTU BANQUET	ABFGINR BARFING	ABGINTT BATTING	ABIKLMN LAMBKIN
ABENRRU URBANER	ABFGLSU BAGFULS	ABGINTU TABUING	ABIKLOR KILOBAR
ABENRST BANTERS	ABFHLSU BASHFUL	ABGINTY BAYTING	ABIKMNR BARMKIN
ABENRSU UNBARES	ABFIILR BIFILAR	ABGIOPT PIGBOAT	ABIKMRS IMBARKS
UNBEARS	ABFIIMR FIMBRIA	ABGIOSU BAGUIOS	ABIKRST BRITSKA
ABENRSY BARNEYS	ABFILRU FIBULAR	ABGKNOS KOBANGS	ABIKRTZ BRITZKA
ABENRSZ BRAZENS	ABFILSU FIBULAS	ABGKOOS BOGOAKS	ABILLMN BILLMAN
ABENRUX EXURBAN	ABFIMOR FIBROMA	ABGLMNU LUMBANG	ABILLMU BALLIUM
ABENSST ABSENTS	ABFLOTY FLYBOAT	ABGLMOS GAMBOLS	ABILLMY BALMILY
BASNETS	ABFOORT FOOTBAR	ABGLMOU LUMBAGO	ABILLNP PINBALL
ABENSTT BATTENS	ABFSTTU TUBFAST	ABGLMSY GYMBALS	ABILLPY PLIABLY
ABENSTU BUTANES	ABGGGIN BAGGING	ABGLOOT TOOLBAG	ABILLSY SYLLABI
ABENSTZ BEZANTS	ABGGILY BAGGILY	ABGLORS BROLGAS	ABILLTT BATTILL
ABEOOTV OBOVATE	ABGGINN BANGING	ABGLORT RAGBOLT	ABILLWX WAXBILL
ABEOPRS SAPROBE	ABGGINR BARGING	ABGLOSU ALBUGOS	ABILMNU ALBUMIN
ABEOPRT PROBATE	GARBING	ABGLRRU BURGLAR	ABILMST TIMBALS
ABEOQRU BAROQUE	ABGGIST BAGGITS	ABGNOPR PROBANG	ABILNOS ALBINOS
ABEORRS BRASERO	ABGGISW BAGWIGS	ABGNORS BROGANS	ABILNOT BITONAL
ABEORRT ARBORET	ABGGNOS GOBANGS	ABGNOTU GUNBOAT	ABILNOZ BIZONAL
TABORER	ABGGNSU BUGGANS	ABGOORT BOTARGO	ABILNRY BAIRNLY
ABEORST BOASTER	ABGGORT BOGGART	ABGORRU GOBURRA	ABILOPR BIPOLAR
BOATERS	ABGHILN BLAHING	ABGORTU OUTBRAG	PARBOIL
BORATES	ABGHINS BASHING	ABHHKOT KHOTBAH	ABILORS BAILORS
SORBATE	ABGHINT BATHING	ABHHKTU KHUTBAH	ABILORT ORBITAL
ABEORSU AEROBUS	ABGHLOT HAGBOLT	ABHHSUY HUSHABY	ABILOTU OBITUAL
ABEORSV BRAVOES	ABGHLRU BURGHAL	ABHIINT INHABIT	ABILRRY LIBRARY
ABEORSX BORAXES	ABGHOTU ABOUGHT	ABHIKLS KIBLAHS	ABILRSU BURIALS
ABEORSZ BEZOARS	ABGHSTU HAGBUTS	ABHIKST BHAKTIS	RAILBUS
ABEORTT ABETTOR	ABGIILN BAILING	ABHIKTW HAWKBIT	ABILRSZ BRAZILS
BATTERO	ABGIINS BIASING	ABHILNO HOBNAIL	ABIMMRS MIMBARS
TABORET	ABGIINT BAITING	ABHILOS ABOLISH	ABIMNRS MINBARS
ABEOSTV BOVATES	ABGIINZ BAIZING	ABHILTU HALIBUT	ABIMOSS BIOMASS
ABEPRSU UPBEARS	ABGIKLN BALKING	ABHIMRS MIHRABS	ABIMPST BAPTISM
ABEQRSU BARQUES	ABGIKNN BANKING	ABHIMSZ MAZHBIS	ABIMRSS BISMARS
ABEQSSU BASQUES	ABGIKNO BOAKING	ABHINST ABSINTH	ABIMRST IMBRAST
ABERRST BARRETS	ABGIKNR BARKING	ABHIOPS PHOBIAS	ABIMRSU BARIUMS
BARTERS	BRAKING	ABHIORS BOARISH	

```
ABIMRTT TRIMTAB        ABMNSUY YNAMBUS        ACCDORS ACCORDS        ACCENPT PECCANT
ABIMTTY AMBITTY        ABMOOSW WABOOMS        ACCEEHO COACHEE        ACCENRS CANCERS
ABINNSU BUNNIAS        ABMOPST BAMPOTS        ACCEELN CENACLE        ACCENST ACCENTS
ABINOOR BORONIA        ABMORTU TAMBOUR        ACCEENR CREANCE        ACCEOPY CACOEPY
ABINORT TABORIN        ABMOSTU SUBATOM        ACCEERT ACCRETE        ACCEORW CRACOWE
ABINORW RAINBOW        ABMOSTW WOMBATS        ACCEFLU FELUCCA        ACCEPRY PECCARY
ABINOSS BONSAIS        ABMRSSU SAMBURS        ACCEGIN ACCINGE        ACCEPST ACCEPTS
ABINOST BASTION        ABNOORS SOROBAN        ACCEGOS SOCCAGE        ACCERRS SCARCER
        OBTAINS        ABNOORZ BORAZON        ACCEHHI CHECHIA        ACCERRT CARRECT
ABINOSU ABUSION        ABNOOSS BASSOON        ACCEHIL CALICHE        ACCERSU ACCRUES
ABINRTV VIBRANT        ABNOOST BATOONS                CHALICE                ACCURSE
ABIORRS BARRIOS        ABNORST BARTONS        ACCEHIM MACCHIE                ACCUSER
ABIORSS ISOBARS        ABNORSY BARYONS        ACCEHIN CHICANE        ACCERSW ACCREWS
ABIORST ORBITAS        ABNORTY BARYTON        ACCEHLN CHANCEL        ACCESSU ACCUSES
ABIORTV VIBRATO        ABNOSSU BONASUS        ACCEHLO COCHLEA        ACCFIIP PACIFIC
ABIPSTT BAPTIST        ABNOTUY BUOYANT        ACCEHNO CONCHAE        ACCFILY CALCIFY
ABIRTTY TRAYBIT        ABNRSTU TURBANS        ACCEHNR CHANCER        ACCGHIN CACHING
ABISSST BASSIST        ABNRTTU TURBANT                CHANCRE                CHACING
ABJJOOS JOJOBAS        ABNSTYZ BYZANTS        ACCEHNS CHANCES        ACCHHIS CHICHAS
ABJKMOS JAMBOKS        ABOOPSX SOAPBOX        ACCEHNT CATCHEN        ACCHHKU KUCHCHA
        SJAMBOK        ABOORTW ROWBOAT        ACCEHNU CHAUNCE        ACCHIKS CHIACKS
ABJLMOO JAMBOOL        ABORRSU ARBOURS        ACCEHOR CAROCHE        ACCHIMS CHASMIC
ABJLMSU JAMBULS        ABORRSW BARROWS                COACHER        ACCHINO CHICANO
        JUMBALS        ABORSTU OUTBARS        ACCEHOS CHACOES        ACCHIOT CHAOTIC
ABKLLNY BLANKLY                ROBUSTA                COACHES        ACCHIRS SCRAICH
ABKLRUW BULWARK                RUBATOS        ACCEHPU CAPUCHE        ACCHJSU JACCHUS
ABKLSSY SKYLABS                TABOURS        ACCEHRS CREACHS        ACCHKOY HAYCOCK
ABKMNOO BOOKMAN        ABORSTW TOWBARS        ACCEHRT CATCHER        ACCHKSY CHYACKS
ABKMOST TOMBAKS        ABOSTUU AUTOBUS                RECATCH        ACCHLTU CLAUCHT
ABKNRSU UNBARKS        ABPRSTU ABRUPTS        ACCEHST CACHETS        ACCHNRS SCRANCH
ABKNRUU BUNRAKU                UPBRAST                CATCHES        ACCHNRU CRAUNCH
ABLLLUY LULLABY        ABPRSUY UPBRAYS        ACCEHTU CATECHU        ACCHOSU CACHOUS
ABLLNOO BALLOON        ABRRSSU BURSARS        ACCEHXY CACHEXY        ACCHOTW CHOCTAW
ABLLNOS BALLONS        ABRRSUY BURSARY        ACCEIKP ICEPACK        ACCHOUY ACOUCHY
ABLLOPR PROBALL        ABRRTUY TURBARY        ACCEILN CALCINE        ACCHPTU CATCHUP
ABLLORU LOBULAR        ABRSTUU ARBUTUS        ACCEILO COELIAC                UPCATCH
ABLLOST BALLOTS        ABSSUWY SUBWAYS        ACCEILS CALICES        ACCHRRU CURRACH
ABLLOSW BALLOWS        ACCCILY ACYCLIC                CELIACS        ACCHRST SCRATCH
ABLLOTY TALLBOY        ACCDDEE ACCEDED        ACCEILT CALCITE        ACCHRSU SCRAUCH
ABLLRUY BULLARY        ACCDDEI CADDICE        ACCEIMR CERAMIC        ACCIILN ACLINIC
ABLMMOU BUMMALO        ACCDEEN CADENCE                RACEMIC        ACCIINT ACTINIC
ABLMNOU UMBONAL        ACCDEER ACCEDER        ACCEINO COCAINE        ACCIIST ASCITIC
ABLMOOT TOMBOLA        ACCDEES ACCEDES                OCEANIC                SCIATIC
ABLMOPS APLOMBS        ACCDEHK CHACKED        ACCEINV VACCINE        ACCILLU CALCULI
ABLMOSY LAMBOYS        ACCDEHN CHANCED        ACCEIPR CAPRICE        ACCILMO COMICAL
ABLMOVY MOVABLY        ACCDEHO COACHED        ACCEIPS IPECACS        ACCILMU CALCIUM
ABLMPUU PABULUM        ACCDEHT CATCHED        ACCEIPV PECCAVI        ACCILNO CONICAL
ABLMSTY TYMBALS        ACCDEII ACCIDIE        ACCEIQU CACIQUE                LACONIC
ABLMTUY MUTABLY        ACCDEIO ACCOIED        ACCEIRS CARICES        ACCILNY CYNICAL
ABLNOSZ BLAZONS        ACCDEIT ACCITED        ACCEIRT CREATIC        ACCILOR CALORIC
ABLNOTU BUTANOL        ACCDEIU CADUCEI        ACCEIST ACCITES        ACCILOS ACCOILS
ABLNOTY NOTABLY        ACCDEKL CACKLED                ASCETIC                CALICOS
ABLNSTU TULBANS                CLACKED        ACCEKLR CACKLER        ACCILOV VOCALIC
ABLNTUY TUNABLY        ACCDEKO COCKADE                CLACKER        ACCILRU CRUCIAL
ABLOORS ROBALOS        ACCDEKR CRACKED                CRACKLE        ACCILRY ACRYLIC
ABLOORY OBOLARY        ACCDENS ACCENDS        ACCEKLS CACKLES        ACCILSS CLASSIC
ABLOPYY PLAYBOY        ACCDENY CADENCY        ACCEKMO MEACOCK        ACCILST CLASTIC
ABLORST BORSTAL        ACCDEOT COACTED        ACCEKOP PEACOCK        ACCILSU SACCULI
ABLORSU LABOURS        ACCDEOY ACCOYED        ACCEKRR CRACKER        ACCIMOZ ZIMOCCA
ABLORTW BLAWORT        ACCDERU ACCRUED        ACCELLY CALYCLE        ACCINNO CANONIC
ABLORUW BOURLAW                CARDECU        ACCELNO CONCEAL        ACCINOT CANTICO
ABLOSST OBLASTS        ACCDESU ACCUSED        ACCELNS CANCELS        ACCINRU CRUCIAN
ABLOSTT TALBOTS                SUCCADE        ACCELOR CORACLE        ACCIOPR CAPROIC
ABLOSTV ABVOLTS        ACCDFIL FLACCID        ACCELOT CACOLET        ACCIORS SCORIAC
ABLPRSU BURLAPS        ACCDILS SCALDIC        ACCELSU SACCULE        ACCIPRT PRACTIC
ABLPSUY PLAYBUS        ACCDIOT OCTADIC        ACCELSY CALYCES        ACCIRRS CIRCARS
ABLRSWY BYRLAWS        ACCDKNO CANDOCK        ACCEMNU CACUMEN        ACCIRST ARCTICS
ABLRTUU TUBULAR        ACCDKOW DAWCOCK        ACCENOR CONACRE        ACCISTT TACTICS
ABMMNOS MOBSMAN        ACCDLOY ACCOYLD        ACCENOS ASCONCE        ACCISTU CAUSTIC
ABMNSTU NUMBATS                CACODYL        ACCENOV CONCAVE                CICUTAS
```

ACCKLOR	CARLOCK		
ACCKLRY	CRACKLY		
ACCKMOR	CROMACK		
ACCKOSS	CASSOCK		
ACCKOST	CASTOCK		
ACCLOSU	COUCALS		
ACCLOSY	ACCLOYS		
ACCMOPT	ACCOMPT		
	COMPACT		
ACCMRUU	CURCUMA		
ACCNOOR	RACCOON		
ACCNOOS	CACOONS		
ACCNOTT	CONTACT		
ACCNOTU	ACCOUNT		
ACCOQSU	SQUACCO		
ACCORSS	CORCASS		
ACCORTU	ACCOURT		
ACCOSST	ACCOSTS		
ACCRSTU	ACCURST		
ACDDDEI	CADDIED		
ACDDDEL	CLADDED		
ACDDDEU	ADDUCED		
ACDDDKO	DADDOCK		
ACDDEEF	DEFACED		
ACDDEER	CEDARED		
ACDDEES	DECADES		
ACDDEEY	DECAYED		
ACDDEIN	CANDIED		
ACDDEIS	CADDIES		
ACDDEIU	DECIDUA		
ACDDELN	CANDLED		
ACDDELO	CLADODE		
ACDDELR	CLADDER		
	CRADLED		
ACDDELS	SCALDED		
ACDDELU	CAUDLED		
ACDDEMU	DUCDAME		
ACDDEOP	DECAPOD		
ACDDERU	ADDUCER		
ACDDESU	ADDUCES		
	SCAUDED		
ACDDHHU	CHUDDAH		
ACDDHIS	CADDISH		
ACDDHKO	HADDOCK		
ACDDHRU	CHUDDAR		
ACDDIRS	DISCARD		
ACDDIST	ADDICTS		
ACDDKOP	PADDOCK		
ACDDSSY	CADDYSS		
ACDDSTU	ADDUCTS		
ACDEEES	DECEASE		
ACDEEFF	EFFACED		
ACDEEFN	ENFACED		
ACDEEFR	DEFACER		
	REFACED		
ACDEEFS	DEFACES		
ACDEEFT	FACETED		
ACDEEGL	GLACEED		
ACDEEGN	ENCAGED		
ACDEEHL	LEACHED		
ACDEEHP	PEACHED		
ACDEEHR	REACHED		
ACDEEHT	CHEATED		
ACDEEIR	DECIARE		
ACDEEJT	DEJECTA		
ACDEEKR	CREAKED		
ACDEELN	CLEANED		
	ELANCED		
	ENLACED		
ACDEELR	CLEARED		
	CREEDAL	ACDEHMP	CHAMPED
	DECLARE	ACDEHMR	CHARMED
ACDEELS	DESCALE		MARCHED
ACDEELT	CLEATED	ACDEHMS	CHASMED
ACDEELV	CLEAVED	ACDEHMT	MATCHED
ACDEEMN	MENACED	ACDEHNR	ENDARCH
ACDEEMR	AMERCED		RANCHED
	CREAMED	ACDEHNT	CHANTED
	RACEMED	ACDEHOP	POACHED
ACDEENR	ENRACED	ACDEHOR	ROACHED
ACDEENS	DECANES	ACDEHOT	CATHODE
	ENCASED	ACDEHPP	CHAPPED
ACDEENT	ENACTED	ACDEHPR	PARCHED
ACDEENV	ENCAVED	ACDEHPT	PATCHED
	VENDACE	ACDEHPU	CUPHEAD
ACDEEPR	CAPERED	ACDEHRR	CHARRED
	PEARCED	ACDEHRS	CRASHED
	PREACED	ACDEHRT	CHARTED
ACDEEPS	ESCAPED	ACDEHST	SCATHED
ACDEERS	CREASED	ACDEHTT	CHATTED
	DECARES	ACDEHTW	WATCHED
	SEARCED	ACDEHTY	YACHTED
ACDEERT	CATERED	ACDEILL	CEDILLA
	CEDRATE	ACDEILM	CAMELID
	CERATED		CLAIMED
	CREATED		DECIMAL
	REACTED		DECLAIM
ACDEEST	TEDESCA		MALICED
ACDEETU	EDUCATE		MEDICAL
ACDEETX	EXACTED	ACDEILN	INLACED
ACDEFFH	CHAFFED	ACDEILR	DECRIAL
ACDEFHU	CHAUFED		RADICEL
ACDEFIN	FANCIED		RADICLE
ACDEFIR	FARCIED	ACDEILS	SCAILED
ACDEFRS	SCARFED	ACDEILT	CITADEL
ACDEFRT	CRAFTED		DELTAIC
	FRACTED		DIALECT
ACDEGGL	CLAGGED		EDICTAL
ACDEGGR	CRAGGED	ACDEIMT	MICATED
ACDEGHN	CHANGED	ACDEIMY	MEDIACY
	GANCHED	ACDEINO	OCEANID
ACDEGHR	CHARGED	ACDEINR	CAIRNED
ACDEGIN	INCAGED		CARNIED
ACDEGIR	CADGIER	ACDEINS	CANDIES
ACDEGIS	DISCAGE		INCASED
ACDEGKO	DOCKAGE	ACDEINV	INCAVED
ACDEGLN	CANGLED	ACDEINY	CYANIDE
	CLANGED	ACDEIPR	EPACRID
	GLANCED	ACDEIPS	DISPACE
ACDEGNO	CONGAED	ACDEIRR	ACRIDER
	DECAGON		CARRIED
ACDEGNU	UNCAGED	ACDEIRS	CARDIES
ACDEGOR	CARGOED		RADICES
	CORDAGE		SIDECAR
ACDEGRS	CADGERS	ACDEIRU	DECURIA
ACDEHHN	HANCHED	ACDEISS	DISCASE
ACDEHHT	HATCHED	ACDEIST	ACIDEST
ACDEHIN	CHAINED		DACITES
	ECHIDNA	ACDEISV	ADVICES
ACDEHIP	EDAPHIC	ACDEITT	DICTATE
ACDEHIR	CHAIRED	ACDEITY	EDACITY
ACDEHIX	HEXADIC	ACDEJLO	CAJOLED
ACDEHKL	CHALKED	ACDEJNU	JAUNCED
	HACKLED	ACDEKLM	MACKLED
ACDEHKR	CHARKED	ACDEKLN	CLANKED
ACDEHKW	WHACKED	ACDEKLO	CLOAKED
ACDEHLN	LANCHED	ACDEKLS	SLACKED
ACDEHLR	CHALDER	ACDEKLT	TACKLED
ACDEHLS	CLASHED	ACDEKLU	CAULKED
ACDEHLT	LATCHED	ACDEKMS	SMACKED
ACDEKNR	CRANKED		
ACDEKNS	SNACKED		
ACDEKOR	CROAKED		
ACDEKQU	QUACKED		
ACDEKRS	DACKERS		
ACDEKRT	TRACKED		
ACDEKRW	WRACKED		
ACDEKST	STACKED		
ACDELLS	SCALLED		
ACDELMM	CLAMMED		
ACDELMP	CAMPLED		
	CLAMPED		
ACDELMS	MASCLED		
ACDELNO	CELADON		
ACDELNS	CALENDS		
	CANDLES		
ACDELNT	CANTLED		
ACDELNU	LAUNCED		
	UNLACED		
ACDELOR	ORACLED		
ACDELOS	SOLACED		
ACDELOT	LOCATED		
ACDELPP	CLAPPED		
ACDELPS	CLASPED		
	SCALPED		
ACDELQU	CALQUED		
ACDELRS	CRADLES		
	SCALDER		
ACDELRT	CLARTED		
ACDELRU	CAULDER		
ACDELRW	CRAWLED		
ACDELSS	CLASSED		
	DECLASS		
ACDELST	CASTLED		
	SCLATED		
ACDELSU	CAUDLES		
	CEDULAS		
ACDELTT	CLATTED		
ACDELTU	CLAUTED		
ACDEMMR	CRAMMED		
ACDEMNU	DECUMAN		
ACDEMOR	CAROMED		
	COMRADE		
ACDEMPR	CRAMPED		
ACDEMPS	DECAMPS		
	SCAMPED		
ACDENNS	SCANNED		
ACDENNT	CANDENT		
ACDENNU	NUANCED		
ACDENOR	ACORNED		
	DRACONE		
ACDENOS	DEACONS		
ACDENPR	PRANCED		
ACDENPT	PANDECT		
ACDENPU	UNCAPED		
ACDENRS	DANCERS		
ACDENRT	CANTRED		
	TRANCED		
ACDENRU	DURANCE		
	UNRACED		
ACDENRY	ARDENCY		
ACDENSS	ASCENDS		
ACDENST	DECANTS		
	DESCANT		
	SCANTED		
ACDENSU	UNCASED		
ACDENTU	UNACTED		
ACDENUV	VAUNCED		
ACDEOPS	PEACODS		
	PEASCOD		

ACDEOPT	COAPTED	ACDINST	DISCANT
ACDEORR	CORRADE	ACDINSU	SUDANIC
ACDEORS	SARCODE	ACDINSW	WINDACS
ACDEORT	CORDATE	ACDIOPR	PARODIC
	REDCOAT		PICADOR
ACDEOST	COASTED	ACDIORR	CORRIDA
ACDEOUV	COUVADE	ACDIORS	SARCOID
ACDEPPR	CRAPPED	ACDIORT	ARCTOID
ACDEPRS	SCARPED		CAROTID
	SCRAPED	ACDIOST	DACOITS
ACDERRS	CARDERS	ACDIOSZ	ZODIACS
	SCARRED	ACDIOTY	DACOITY
ACDERST	REDACTS	ACDIPRS	CAPRIDS
	SCARTED	ACDIPSS	CAPSIDS
ACDERSU	CRUSADE	ACDIQRU	QUADRIC
	SCAURED	ACDIRST	DRASTIC
ACDERTT	DETRACT	ACDISST	DICASTS
	TRACTED	ACDITUV	VIADUCT
ACDERTU	TRADUCE	ACDJNTU	ADJUNCT
ACDESTT	SCATTED	ACDKLOP	PADLOCK
ACDFIIY	ACIDIFY	ACDKLSY	SKYCLAD
ACDFIOT	FACTOID	ACDKMOO	MOCKADO
ACDGGIN	CADGING	ACDKMPU	MUDPACK
ACDGINN	DANCING	ACDKOPR	POCKARD
ACDGINO	GONADIC	ACDLLOR	COLLARD
ACDGINR	CARDING	ACDLLUY	DUCALLY
ACDGKLO	DAGLOCK	ACDLNOR	CALDRON
ACDGNOT	CANTDOG	ACDLNOT	COTLAND
ACDGORT	DOGCART	ACDLOWY	LADYCOW
ACDHIIL	CHILIAD	ACDLSTY	DACTYLS
ACDHIOP	PHACOID	ACDMMNO	COMMAND
ACDHIRY	DIARCHY	ACDMORZ	CZARDOM
ACDHLOR	CHORDAL	ACDNOOR	CARDOON
	DORLACH	ACDNORS	CANDORS
ACDHMRS	DRACHMS	ACDNORU	CANDOUR
ACDHNOW	COWHAND		CAUDRON
ACDHOOT	CATHOOD	ACDORST	COSTARD
ACDHOPR	POCHARD	ACDORSU	CRUSADO
ACDHORR	ORCHARD	ACDORSW	COWARDS
ACDHORS	CHADORS	ACDRSTU	CUSTARD
ACDHRUY	DUARCHY	ACDRSUU	CARDUUS
ACDHRYY	DYARCHY	ACEEEPS	ESCAPEE
ACDIIIN	INDICIA	ACEEEUV	EVACUEE
ACDIINN	INDICAN	ACEEFFS	EFFACES
ACDIINO	CONIDIA	ACEEFHN	ENCHAFE
ACDIINR	ACRIDIN	ACEEFIN	FAIENCE
ACDIIRS	CIDARIS		FIANCEE
	SCIARID	ACEEFMN	FACEMEN
ACDIIRT	TRIACID	ACEEFNS	ENFACES
	TRIADIC	ACEEFNY	FAYENCE
ACDIITY	ACIDITY	ACEEFPR	PREFACE
ACDIKLS	SKALDIC	ACEEFRS	REFACES
ACDILLO	CODILLA	ACEEGIL	ELEGIAC
ACDILMO	DOMICAL	ACEEGNR	ENGRACE
ACDILMS	CLADISM	ACEEGNS	ENCAGES
ACDILNO	NODICAL	ACEEGNT	CENTAGE
ACDILNU	DULCIAN	ACEEGSU	ESCUAGE
ACDILOP	PLACOID	ACEEHHT	CHEETAH
	PODALIC	ACEEHIP	CHEAPIE
ACDILOR	CORDIAL	ACEEHIT	HICATEE
ACDILPU	PALUDIC		TEACHIE
ACDILST	CLADIST	ACEEHIV	ACHIEVE
ACDILTW	WILDCAT	ACEEHKS	HACKEES
ACDIMMU	CADMIUM	ACEEHLR	RELACHE
ACDIMNO	MANDIOC	ACEEHLS	LEACHES
	MONACID	ACEEHLT	CHELATE
	MONADIC	ACEEHMP	EMPEACH
	NOMADIC	ACEEHMR	MACHREE
ACDIMNY	DYNAMIC	ACEEHMT	MACHETE
ACDINRU	IRACUND	ACEEHNN	ENHANCE

ACEEHNP	CHEAPEN		CASERNE
ACEEHNS	ACHENES		ENRACES
	ENCHASE	ACEENRT	CRENATE
ACEEHOR	OCHREAE	ACEENSS	ENCASES
ACEEHPP	ECHAPPE		SEANCES
ACEEHPR	CHEAPER	ACEENST	CETANES
	PEACHER		TENACES
ACEEHPS	PEACHES	ACEENSV	ENCAVES
ACEEHRR	REACHER	ACEENTU	CUNEATE
ACEEHRS	REACHES	ACEEORS	ACEROSE
ACEEHRT	CHEATER	ACEEORT	OCREATE
	HECTARE	ACEEOST	ACETOSE
	RECHATE		COATEES
	RECHEAT	ACEEOTV	EVOCATE
	TEACHER	ACEEPRR	CAPERER
ACEEHST	EATCHES	ACEEPRS	ESCAPER
	ESCHEAT		PEARCES
	TEACHES		PERCASE
ACEEHTT	THECATE		PREACES
ACEEHTX	EXCHEAT	ACEEPSS	ESCAPES
ACEEILP	CALIPEE	ACEERRS	CAREERS
ACEEIMT	EMICATE	ACEERRT	CATERER
ACEEINR	CINEREA		RETRACE
ACEEINU	EUCAINE		TERRACE
ACEEIRR	CARIERE	ACEERSS	CREASES
ACEEISV	VESICAE		SEARCES
ACEELLN	NACELLE	ACEERST	CERATES
ACEELMP	EMPLACE		CREATES
ACEELMR	RECLAME		ECARTES
ACEELNR	CLEANER		SECRETA
ACEELNS	CLEANSE	ACEERTX	EXACTER
	ELANCES		EXCRETA
	ENLACES	ACEESSS	ASCESES
	SCALENE	ACEESST	ECTASES
ACEELNT	LATENCE	ACEFFHI	AFFICHE
ACEELNV	ENCLAVE	ACEFFHR	CHAFFER
	VALENCE	ACEFFIS	SCAFFIE
ACEELPR	PERCALE	ACEFFOR	AFFORCE
	REPLACE	ACEFFST	AFFECTS
ACEELPT	CAPELET	ACEFHMR	CHAMFER
ACEELRR	CLEARER	ACEFHRS	CHAFERS
ACEELRS	ALERCES	ACEFHSU	CHAUFES
	CEREALS	ACEFILM	MALEFIC
	RESCALE	ACEFILR	FILACER
ACEELRT	TREACLE	ACEFINN	FINANCE
ACEELRU	CAERULE	ACEFINR	FANCIER
ACEELRV	CLEAVER	ACEFINS	FANCIES
ACEELST	CELESTA		FASCINE
ACEELSU	EUCLASE		FIANCES
ACEELSV	CLEAVES	ACEFIRS	FARCIES
ACEELVX	EXCLAVE		FIACRES
ACEEMNR	MENACER	ACEFITV	FACTIVE
ACEEMNS	CASEMEN	ACEFITY	ACETIFY
	MENACES	ACEFKLR	FLACKER
ACEEMNT	CEMENTA	ACEFKLT	FLACKET
ACEEMNV	CAVEMEN	ACEFLRU	CAREFUL
ACEEMRR	CREAMER	ACEFLSU	FECULAS
ACEEMRS	AMERCES	ACEFNNO	FACONNE
	CAREMES	ACEFNRT	CANTREF
	RACEMES	ACEFNRU	FURNACE
ACEEMRT	CERAMET	ACEFOPR	PROFACE
	CREMATE	ACEFORR	FORECAR
	MEERCAT	ACEFOTU	OUTFACE
ACEEMSS	CAMESES	ACEFRRT	REFRACT
ACEEMSZ	ECZEMAS	ACEFRRU	FARCEUR
ACEENNP	PENANCE	ACEFRSU	SURFACE
ACEENNT	CANTEEN	ACEFRTU	FACTURE
ACEENNY	CAYENNE		FURCATE
ACEENOT	ACETONE	ACEFSTU	FAUCETS
ACEENRS	CAREENS	ACEGHLO	GALOCHE

ACEGHNR CHANGER	ACEHINN ENCHAIN	RANCHES	ACEIKSS SEASICK
ACEGHNS CHANGES	ACEHINS INCHASE	ACEHNRT CHANTER	ACEIKST CAKIEST
GANCHES	ACEHINT CHANTIE	TRANCHE	TACKIES
ACEGHNU CHAUNGE	ACEHINY HYACINE	ACEHNST CHASTEN	ACEIKTT TIETACK
ACEGHOU GOUACHE	ACEHIPP CHAPPIE	NATCHES	ACEILLM LIMACEL
ACEGHOW COWHAGE	ACEHIPR CHARPIE	ACEHNTT ETCHANT	MICELLA
ACEGHRR CHARGER	ACEHIPT APHETIC	ACEHNTU UNTEACH	ACEILLS ALLICES
ACEGHRS CHARGES	HEPATIC	ACEHNTY CHANTEY	ACEILLX LEXICAL
CREAGHS	ACEHIRR CHARIER	ACEHOPR POACHER	ACEILMN MELANIC
ACEGHRU GAUCHER	ACEHIRS CAHIERS	ACEHOPS EPOCHAS	ACEILMR CALMIER
ACEGILL ELLAGIC	CASHIER	POACHES	CLAIMER
ACEGILN ANGELIC	ERIACHS	ACEHORS CHOREAS	MIRACLE
ANGLICE	ACEHIRT THERIAC	ORACHES	RECLAIM
ACEGILP PELAGIC	ACEHIRV ARCHIVE	ROACHES	ACEILMS LIMACES
ACEGILR GLACIER	ACEHISS CHAISES	ACEHOSS CHAOSES	MALICES
GRACILE	ACEHIST ACHIEST	ACEHOTY CHAYOTE	ACEILMT CLIMATE
ACEGIMR GRIMACE	AITCHES	ACEHPPS SCHAPPE	METICAL
ACEGIMT GAMETIC	ACEHKLR HACKLER	ACEHPRS EPARCHS	ACEILMX EXCLAIM
ACEGINO COINAGE	ACEHKLS HACKLES	PARCHES	ACEILMY MYCELIA
ACEGINP PEACING	SHACKLE	ACEHPRT CHAPTER	ACEILNP CAPELIN
ACEGINR GRECIAN	ACEHKLT HACKLET	PATCHER	PANICLE
ACEGINS CEASING	ACEHKNY HACKNEY	ACEHPRY EPARCHY	PELICAN
INCAGES	ACEHKRS HACKERS	PREACHY	ACEILNR CARLINE
ACEGINV VEGANIC	ACEHKRW WHACKER	ACEHPSS CHAPESS	ACEILNS ANCILES
ACEGINZ CEAZING	ACEHKRY HACKERY	ACEHPST PATCHES	INLACES
ACEGIRU GAUCIER	ACEHLLP PELLACH	ACEHQUY QUEACHY	SANICLE
ACEGIRW GAWCIER	ACEHLLS SHELLAC	ACEHRRS ARCHERS	ACEILNU CAULINE
ACEGIST CAGIEST	ACEHLMT CHAMLET	ACEHRRT CHARTER	ACEILOR CALORIE
ACEGKLO LOCKAGE	ACEHLMY ALCHEMY	RECHART	CARIOLE
ACEGKLR GRACKLE	ACEHLNN CHANNEL	ACEHRRX XERARCH	COALIER
ACEGKMO MOCKAGE	ACEHLNO CHALONE	ACEHRRY ARCHERY	LORICAE
ACEGKOR CORKAGE	ACEHLNR CHARNEL	ACEHRSS CHASERS	ACEILOS COALISE
ACEGLLO COLLAGE	LARCHEN	CRASHES	ACEILOT ALOETIC
ACEGLNO CONGEAL	ACEHLNS LANCHES	ESCHARS	ACEILOZ COALIZE
ACEGLNR CLANGER	ACEHLOP EPOCHAL	ACEHRST ARCHEST	ACEILPR CALIPER
ACEGLNS CANGLES	ACEHLOR CHOLERA	CHARETS	REPLICA
GLANCES	CHORALE	CHASTER	ACEILPS PLAICES
ACEGLOT CATELOG	ACEHLOS LOACHES	RATCHES	SPECIAL
ACEGLOU CAGOULE	OSCHEAL	ACEHRSU ARCHEUS	ACEILPT PLICATE
ACEGMOP COMPAGE	ACEHLPS CHAPELS	ACEHRSV VARECHS	ACEILRR CERRIAL
ACEGNOR ACROGEN	ACEHLPT CHAPLET	ACEHRSX EXARCHS	ACEILRS CLARIES
CORNAGE	ACEHLPY CHEAPLY	ACEHRSY HYRACES	ECLAIRS
ACEGNOT COGNATE	ACEHLRS LARCHES	ACEHRTT CHATTER	SCALIER
ACEGNSU CANGUES	RASCHEL	RATCHET	ACEILRT ARTICLE
UNCAGES	ACEHLRT ARCHLET	ACEHRTW WATCHER	RECITAL
ACEGORS CARGOES	ACEHLRY CHARLEY	ACEHRTY YACHTER	ACEILRU AURICLE
CORSAGE	ACEHLSS CLASHES	ACEHRXY EXARCHY	ACEILRV CALIVER
SOCAGER	SEALCHS	ACEHSSS CHASSES	CLAVIER
ACEGORU COURAGE	ACEHLST CHALETS	ACEHSST SACHETS	VELARIC
ACEGOSS SOCAGES	LATCHES	SCATHES	ACEILRY CLAYIER
ACEGOSW COWAGES	SATCHEL	ACEHSSW CASHEWS	ACEILSS SALICES
ACEGOTT COTTAGE	ACEHLTT CHATTEL	ACEHSTW WATCHES	ACEILST ASTELIC
ACEGRTU TRUCAGE	LATCHET	ACEHSTX HEXACTS	ELASTIC
ACEGSTU SCUTAGE	ACEHMNP CHAPMEN	ACEHTTU TEUCHAT	LACIEST
ACEHHLT HATCHEL	ACEHMNR ENCHARM	ACEHTTW WATCHET	LATICES
ACEHHNS HANCHES	ACEHMNS MANCHES	ACEIILM CIMELIA	SALICET
ACEHHRT HATCHER	ACEHMNT MANCHET	ACEIILS LAICISE	ACEILSV CLAVIES
ACEHHRU HACHURE	ACEHMRR CHARMER	ACEIILT CILIATE	VESICAL
ACEHHRX HEXARCH	MARCHER	ACEIILZ LAICIZE	ACEILSX CALIXES
ACEHHST HATCHES	ACEHMRS MARCHES	ACEIITV CAITIVE	ACEILTT LATTICE
ACEHHTT HATCHET	MESARCH	VICIATE	TACTILE
ACEHIKR KACHERI	ACEHMRT MATCHER	ACEIJKS JACKSIE	ACEIMNO ENCOMIA
ACEHILL HELICAL	REMATCH	ACEIKMR KERAMIC	ACEIMNP PEMICAN
ACEHILP APHELIC	ACEHMRU CHAUMER	ACEIKNT ANTICKE	ACEIMNR CARMINE
ACEHILR CHARLIE	ACEHMSS SACHEMS	ACEIKOP PAIOCKE	ACEIMNS AMNESIC
ACEHILT ETHICAL	ACEHMST MATCHES	ACEIKPR EARPICK	CINEMAS
ACEHIMN MACHINE	ACEHMTY ECTHYMA	ACEIKPX PICKAXE	ACEIMNT EMICANT
ACEHIMP IMPEACH	ACEHNNT ENCHANT	ACEIKRS EIRACKS	NEMATIC
ACEHIMR CHIMERA	ACEHNRR RANCHER	ACEIKRT TACKIER	ACEIMPR CAMPIER
ACEHIMS CHAMISE	ACEHNRS CHENARS	ACEIKRW WACKIER	ACEIMPY PYAEMIC

ACEIMRT	MATRICE	ACEIRRT	CIRRATE
ACEIMRU	URAEMIC		ERRATIC
ACEIMSS	CAMISES	ACEIRRZ	CRAZIER
ACEIMST	ACMITES	ACEIRST	CRISTAE
	ETACISM		RACIEST
	MICATES		STEARIC
	SEMATIC	ACEIRSU	SAUCIER
ACEIMSU	CAESIUM		URICASE
ACEINNP	PINNACE	ACEIRSV	CARVIES
ACEINNR	CANNIER		CAVIERS
ACEINNS	CANINES		VARICES
	NANCIES		VISCERA
ACEINNT	ANCIENT	ACEIRSZ	CRAZIES
ACEINNY	CYANINE	ACEIRTT	CATTIER
ACEINOP	PAEONIC		CITRATE
ACEINOS	ACINOSE	ACEISSS	ASCESIS
ACEINOT	ACONITE	ACEISST	ASCITES
	ANOETIC		ECTASIS
ACEINPR	CAPRINE	ACEISTT	CATTIES
ACEINPS	INSCAPE		TIETACS
	PINCASE	ACEITTV	CAVETTI
ACEINRR	CARNIER	ACEITTX	EXTATIC
ACEINRS	ARSENIC	ACEITUX	AUXETIC
	CARNIES	ACEJKMN	JACKMEN
	CERASIN	ACEJKOP	PAJOCKE
ACEINRT	CANTIER	ACEJKST	JACKETS
	CERTAIN	ACEJLOR	CAJOLER
	CRINATE	ACEJLOS	CAJOLES
	NACRITE	ACEJNOT	JACONET
ACEINSS	CASEINS	ACEJNOY	JOYANCE
	INCASES	ACEJNSU	JAUNCES
ACEINST	CANIEST	ACEJNTU	JUNCATE
	CINEAST	ACEJPTU	CAJEPUT
ACEINSU	EUCAINS	ACEJRTT	TRAJECT
ACEINSV	INCAVES	ACEKKNR	KNACKER
ACEINSY	CYANISE	ACEKLLP	PELLACK
ACEINTT	NICTATE	ACEKLMS	MACKLES
	TETANIC	ACEKLNR	CRANKLE
ACEINTV	VENATIC	ACEKLNS	SLACKEN
ACEINTX	INEXACT	ACEKLOR	EARLOCK
ACEINTY	CYANITE	ACEKLPT	PLACKET
ACEINYZ	CYANIZE	ACEKLQU	QUACKLE
ACEIOOZ	ZOOECIA	ACEKLRS	CALKERS
ACEIOPT	ECTOPIA		LACKERS
ACEIORS	ORACIES		SLACKER
	SCORIAE	ACEKLRT	TACKLER
ACEIORT	EROTICA	ACEKLRU	CAULKER
ACEIOST	SOCIATE	ACEKLST	TACKLES
ACEIOTX	EXOTICA	ACEKLSY	LACKEYS
ACEIPPR	EPICARP	ACEKMNP	PACKMEN
ACEIPPT	TAPPICE	ACEKMRS	SMACKER
ACEIPRR	CRAPIER	ACEKNOS	NOCAKES
ACEIPRS	EPACRIS	ACEKNPR	PRANCKE
	SCRAPIE	ACEKNRR	CRANKER
	SPACIER	ACEKNRS	CANKERS
ACEIPRT	PARETIC	ACEKNRY	CANKERY
	PICRATE	ACEKNST	NACKETS
ACEIPST	ASEPTIC	ACEKORR	CROAKER
	PACIEST	ACEKPPR	PREPACK
	SPICATE	ACEKPRS	PACKERS
ACEIPSU	AUSPICE		REPACKS
ACEIPSZ	CAPSIZE	ACEKPST	PACKETS
ACEIPTV	CAPTIVE	ACEKRRS	RACKERS
ACEIQRU	ACQUIRE	ACEKRRT	TRACKER
ACEIQSU	CAIQUES	ACEKRSS	SCREAKS
ACEIQTU	ACQUITE	ACEKRST	RACKETS
ACEIQUZ	CAZIQUE		STACKER
ACEIRRR	CARRIER		TACKERS
ACEIRRS	CARRIES	ACEKRSU	CAUKERS
	SCARIER	ACEKRSW	CAWKERS

ACEKRSY	SCREAKY	ACELOPS	ESCALOP
	YACKERS	ACELOPT	POLECAT
ACEKRTT	RACKETT	ACELOQU	COEQUAL
ACEKRTY	RACKETY	ACELORS	COALERS
ACEKSST	CASKETS		ESCOLAR
ACEKSTT	STACKET		ORACLES
	TACKETS	ACELORY	CALOYER
ACEKTTY	TACKETY	ACELOSS	SOLACES
ACELLMO	CALOMEL	ACELOST	ALECOST
ACELLNU	NUCLEAL		LACTOSE
ACELLNY	CLEANLY		LOCATES
ACELLOR	CORELLA		SCATOLE
	OCELLAR		TALCOSE
ACELLOS	LOCALES	ACELOSV	ALCOVES
ACELLOT	COLLATE		COEVALS
ACELLPS	SCALPEL	ACELOTT	CALOTTE
ACELLPY	CLYPEAL	ACELOTU	OCULATE
ACELLRR	CARRELL	ACELOTY	ACOLYTE
ACELLRS	CALLERS		COTYLAE
	CELLARS	ACELOUV	VACUOLE
	RECALLS	ACELPPR	CLAPPER
	SCLERAL	ACELPPS	SCAPPLE
ACELLRY	CLEARLY	ACELPRS	CARPELS
ACELLST	CALLETS		CLASPER
ACELMNO	COALMEN		CRAPLES
ACELMNS	ENCALMS		PARCELS
ACELMOR	CAROMEL		PLACERS
ACELMOT	CAMELOT		SCALPER
ACELMOU	CAULOME	ACELPRT	PLECTRA
	LEUCOMA	ACELPRY	PRELACY
ACELMPR	CLAMPER	ACELPST	PLACETS
ACELMPS	CAMPLES	ACELPSU	CAPSULE
ACELMRS	MARCELS		SPECULA
ACELMRY	CAMELRY	ACELPTY	ECTYPAL
ACELMSS	MASCLES	ACELQRU	LACQUER
	MESCALS	ACELQSU	CALQUES
	SCAMELS		CLAQUES
ACELMST	CALMEST	ACELQUY	LACQUEY
	CAMLETS	ACELRRS	CARRELS
ACELMSU	MACULES	ACELRRU	RAUCLER
ACELMTU	CALUMET	ACELRRW	CRAWLER
ACELNNS	CANNELS	ACELRSS	SCALERS
ACELNNU	UNCLEAN		SCLERAS
ACELNNY	LYNCEAN	ACELRST	CARTELS
ACELNOR	CORNEAL		CLARETS
ACELNOT	LACTONE		SCARLET
ACELNOZ	CALZONE		TARCELS
ACELNPS	ENCLASP	ACELRSU	SECULAR
	SPANCEL	ACELRSV	CALVERS
ACELNPT	CLAPNET		CARVELS
ACELNPU	UNPLACE		CLAVERS
ACELNRS	LANCERS	ACELRTT	CLATTER
	RANCELS	ACELRTY	TREACLY
ACELNRT	CENTRAL	ACELSSS	CLASSES
ACELNRU	LUCARNE		SACLESS
	NUCLEAR	ACELSST	CASTLES
	UNCLEAR		SCLATES
ACELNRY	LARCENY	ACELSSU	CLAUSES
ACELNST	CANTLES	ACELSSV	SCLAVES
	CENTALS	ACELSTU	CAUTELS
	LANCETS		SULCATE
	SCANTLE	ACELSTY	ACETYLS
ACELNSU	CENSUAL		SCYTALE
	LAUNCES	ACELSUX	EXCUSAL
	UNLACES	ACELSXY	CALYXES
	UNSCALE	ACELTUY	ACUTELY
ACELNTT	CANTLET	ACELTXY	EXACTLY
ACELNTY	LATENCY	ACEMMRR	CRAMMER
ACELNVY	VALENCY	ACEMNOR	CREMONA
ACELOPR	POLACRE		ROMANCE

ACEMNOS	ANCOMES		UNCRATE	ACERRSY	CRAYERS		SCARIFY

ACEMNOS ANCOMES
ACEMNPS ENCAMPS
ACEMNSU ACUMENS
ACEMOPR COMPARE
        COMPEAR
ACEMOPS POMACES
ACEMORS AMORCES
ACEMORU MORCEAU
ACEMOSS COSMEAS
ACEMOST COMATES
ACEMOSU MUCOSAE
ACEMPRS CAMPERS
        SCAMPER
ACEMPRT CRAMPET
ACEMPST CAMPEST
ACEMRSS SCREAMS
ACEMRST MERCATS
ACEMRSY CRAMESY
ACEMSSU CAMUSES
ACEMSTT METCAST
ACEMSTU MUCATES
ACENNOS ANCONES
        SONANCE
ACENNOT CONNATE
ACENNOY NOYANCE
ACENNOZ CANZONE
ACENNRS CANNERS
        SCANNER
ACENNRY CANNERY
ACENNST NASCENT
ACENNSU NUANCES
ACENNTY TENANCY
ACENOOR CORONAE
ACENOPT PATONCE
ACENOPU PONCEAU
ACENORS CARNOSE
        COARSEN
        CORNEAS
ACENORT ENACTOR
ACENOSS CASSONE
ACENOST COSTEAN
        OCTANES
ACENOTT ATTONCE
ACENOTV CENTAVO
ACENPRR PRANCER
ACENPRS PRANCES
ACENPRU PRAUNCE
ACENPST CATNEPS
ACENPSU PAUNCES
        UNCAPES
ACENPSW PAWNCES
ACENPTT PENTACT
ACENPTY PATENCY
ACENRSS ANCRESS
        CASERNS
ACENRST CANTERS
        CARNETS
        NECTARS
        RECANTS
        SCANTER
        TANRECS
        TRANCES
ACENRSU SURANCE
ACENRSV CAVERNS
        CRAVENS
ACENRSY CARNEYS
        SCENARY
ACENRSZ ZARNECS
ACENRTT TRANECT
ACENRTU CENTAUR

        UNCRATE
        UNTRACE
ACENRTY ENCRATY
        NECTARY
ACENSST ASCENTS
        SECANTS
        STANCES
ACENSSU UNCASES
        USANCES
ACENSTT CANTEST
ACENSTU NUTCASE
ACENSUV VAUNCES
ACEOOPP APOCOPE
ACEOOTZ ECTOZOA
ACEOPRX EXOCARP
ACEOPST CAPOTES
        SCOPATE
        TOECAPS
ACEOPTU OUTPACE
ACEORRS COARSER
ACEORRT ACROTER
        CREATOR
        REACTOR
ACEORSS ROSACES
ACEORST COASTER
        COATERS
ACEORSU ACEROUS
        CAROUSE
ACEORSX COAXERS
ACEORTU OUTRACE
ACEORTV OVERACT
ACEORTX EXACTOR
ACEOSSU CASEOUS
ACEOSTT COSTATE
ACEOSTU ACETOUS
ACEOSTV AVOCETS
        OCTAVES
ACEOTTV CAVETTO
ACEOTUU AUTOCUE
ACEOTUX COTEAUX
ACEPPRS CAPPERS
ACEPRRS CARPERS
        SCARPER
        SCRAPER
ACEPRSS ESCARPS
        PARSECS
        SCRAPES
        SPACERS
ACEPRST CARPETS
        PRECAST
        SPECTRA
ACEPRSU APERCUS
        SCAUPER
ACEPRTU CAPTURE
ACEPSST ASPECTS
ACEPSTU CUSPATE
        TEACUPS
ACEQRTU RACQUET
ACEQSSU CASQUES
        SACQUES
ACEQSTU ACQUEST
ACERRSS CRASSER
        SCARERS
        SCARRES
ACERRST CARTERS
        CRATERS
        TRACERS
ACERRSU CURARES
ACERRSV CARVERS
        CRAVERS

ACERRSY CRAYERS
ACERRTT RETRACT
ACERRTY TRACERY
ACERRUV VERRUCA
ACERSST ACTRESS
        CASTERS
        RECASTS
ACERSSU ARCUSES
        CAUSERS
        CESURAS
        SAUCERS
        SUCRASE
ACERSSV SCARVES
ACERSSY SCRAYES
ACERSTT SCATTER
ACERSTU ACTURES
        CAUTERS
        CRUSTAE
        CURATES
ACERSTY SECTARY
ACERTTT TETRACT
ACERTTU CURTATE
ACERTTX EXTRACT
ACERTTY CATTERY
ACERTUV CURVATE
ACERTUX CURTAXE
ACERTUY CAUTERY
ACESSTT STACTES
ACESSTU CAESTUS
        CUESTAS
ACESSTY CYTASES
        ECSTASY
ACESSUY CAUSEYS
        CAYUSES
ACESTTU ACUTEST
        SCUTATE
ACESTTY TESTACY
ACESTUY EUSTACY
ACFFHSU CHAUFFS
ACFFIIT CAITIFF
ACFFIKM MAFFICK
ACFFILT AFFLICT
ACFFIRT TRAFFIC
ACFFIRY FARCIFY
ACFFLSS SCLAFFS
ACFGHIN CHAFING
ACFGINR FARCING
ACFGINS FACINGS
ACFHIST CATFISH
ACFHISU FUCHSIA
ACFHLNU FLAUNCH
ACFHNOU FAUCHON
ACFHRTY FRATCHY
ACFIILN FINICAL
ACFIKNN FINNACK
ACFILNO FOLACIN
ACFILRY CLARIFY
ACFILSS FISCALS
ACFIMOR ACIFORM
ACFIMSS FASCISM
ACFINNS FINNACS
ACFINNY INFANCY
ACFINOT FACTION
ACFINRS FARCINS
ACFINRT FRANTIC
        INFARCT
        INFRACT
ACFIOSS FIASCOS
ACFIPRY CAPRIFY
ACFIRSY SACRIFY

        SCARIFY
ACFISST FASCIST
ACFKLSU SACKFUL
ACFLLOY FOCALLY
ACFLNOS FALCONS
        FLACONS
ACFLNSU CANFULS
ACFLOST OLFACTS
ACFLRUU FURCULA
ACFLTTU TACTFUL
ACFLTUY FACULTY
ACFMSTU FACTUMS
ACFNSTU UNFACTS
ACFORST FACTORS
        FORCATS
ACFORTY FACTORY
ACGGINR GRACING
ACGGIOS AGOGICS
ACGGRSY SCRAGGY
ACGHIKN HACKING
ACGHIMO OGHAMIC
ACGHINR ARCHING
        CHAGRIN
        CHARING
ACGHINS ACHINGS
        CASHING
        CHASING
ACGHINT GNATHIC
ACGHINW CHAWING
        CHINWAG
ACGHIOR CHORAGI
ACGHIPR GRAPHIC
ACGHIRS SCRAIGH
ACGHLTU CLAUGHT
ACGHOSU GAUCHOS
ACGHRRU CURRAGH
ACGHRSU SCRAUGH
ACGIILN ALGINIC
ACGIITU AUGITIC
ACGIJKN JACKING
ACGIKLN CALKING
        LACKING
ACGIKNP PACKING
ACGIKNR ARCKING
        CARKING
        CRAKING
        RACKING
ACGIKNS CAKINGS
        CASKING
        SACKING
ACGIKNT TACKING
ACGIKNV VACKING
ACGIKNY YACKING
ACGILLN CALLING
ACGILLO LOGICAL
ACGILMN CALMING
ACGILMY MYALGIC
ACGILNN LANCING
ACGILNO COALING
ACGILNP PLACING
ACGILNS LACINGS
        SCALING
ACGILNT CATLING
ACGILNU GLUCINA
ACGILNV CALVING
ACGILNW CLAWING
ACGILNY CLAYING
ACGILOS CALIGOS
ACGILRS GARLICS
ACGIMMN CAMMING

ACGIMNO	COAMING	ACHILRY	CHARILY
ACGIMNP	CAMPING	ACHILST	CHITALS
ACGIMNU	CAUMING	ACHILSY	CLAYISH
ACGINNN	CANNING	ACHILWY	LICHWAY
ACGINNR	CRANING	ACHIMNO	MANIHOC
	RANCING	ACHIMOS	CHAMISO
ACGINNS	CANINGS		CHAMOIS
ACGINNT	CANTING	ACHIMRS	CHARISM
ACGINOR	ORGANIC	ACHIMSS	CHIASMS
ACGINOS	ANGICOS		SCHISMA
ACGINOT	COATING	ACHIMST	MASTICH
	COTINGA		TACHISM
ACGINOX	COAXING	ACHINNU	UNCHAIN
ACGINPP	CAPPING	ACHINOP	APHONIC
ACGINPR	CARPING	ACHINOY	ONYCHIA
	CRAPING	ACHINPS	SPINACH
ACGINPS	SCAPING	ACHINRS	CHINARS
	SPACING	ACHINRZ	ZARNICH
ACGINRS	ARCINGS	ACHINTX	XANTHIC
	RACINGS	ACHINUV	CHAUVIN
	SACRING	ACHIOPT	APHOTIC
	SCARING	ACHIORT	CHARIOT
ACGINRT	CARTING		HARICOT
	CRATING	ACHIPPS	SAPPHIC
	TRACING	ACHIPST	HAPTICS
ACGINRV	CARVING		PATHICS
	CRAVING		SPATHIC
ACGINRZ	CRAZING	ACHIPTU	CHUPATI
ACGINSS	CASINGS	ACHIPTW	WHIPCAT
ACGINST	ACTINGS	ACHIQRU	CHARQUI
	CASTING	ACHIQSU	QUAICHS
ACGINSU	CAUSING	ACHIRRT	TRIARCH
	SAUCING	ACHIRTU	HAIRCUT
ACGINSV	CAVINGS	ACHIRTY	CHARITY
ACGINSW	CAWINGS	ACHISSS	CHASSIS
ACGINTT	CATTING	ACHISST	SCAITHS
ACGIRST	GASTRIC	ACHISTT	CATTISH
ACGKMMO	GAMMOCK		TACHIST
ACGKORV	GARVOCK	ACHKKSU	CHUKKAS
ACGLLPU	CUPGALL	ACHKMMO	HAMMOCK
ACGLNOR	CLANGOR	ACHKOPS	HOPSACK
ACGLOSU	CAGOULS	ACHKOSS	HASSOCK
ACGNNOR	CRANNOG	ACHKOSW	WHACKOS
ACGNOOT	OCTAGON	ACHKOTT	HATTOCK
ACGNORS	GARCONS	ACHKRSU	CHUKARS
ACGNOSS	GASCONS	ACHKSTW	THWACKS
ACGORRY	GYROCAR	ACHLLOO	ALCOHOL
ACGORSU	COUGARS	ACHLLOR	CHLORAL
ACGORUU	COUGUAR	ACHLMSY	CHLAMYS
ACGSTTU	CATGUTS	ACHLMYY	ALCHYMY
ACHHIRS	RHACHIS	ACHLNOS	LOCHANS
ACHHOST	TOSHACH	ACHLNOY	HALCYON
ACHHTTT	THATCHT	ACHLNTU	TULCHAN
ACHIIKM	KAMICHI		UNLATCH
ACHIILS	ISCHIAL	ACHLOPR	RAPLOCH
ACHIIPS	PACHISI	ACHLOPT	POTLACH
ACHIJKS	HIJACKS	ACHLORS	CHORALS
ACHIJNT	JACINTH		LORCHAS
ACHIKRS	RICKSHA		SCHOLAR
ACHIKRY	HAYRICK	ACHLORT	TROCHAL
ACHIKSS	SHICKSA	ACHLOSW	SALCHOW
ACHILLO	LOCHIAL	ACHLOTY	ACOLYTH
ACHILLP	PHALLIC	ACHLPST	SPLATCH
ACHILLS	CHALLIS	ACHMNOR	MONARCH
ACHILLT	THALLIC		NOMARCH
ACHILMO	MALICHO	ACHMNRU	UNCHARM
ACHILOS	SCHOLIA	ACHMOPR	CAMPHOR
ACHILPS	CALIPHS	ACHMORS	CHROMAS
ACHILRS	ARCHILS	ACHMORZ	MACHZOR
	CARLISH	ACHMOST	STOMACH

ACHMSSU	SUMACHS	ACIKNPY	PANICKY
ACHMSUW	CUMSHAW	ACIKNRS	NICKARS
ACHNNOS	CHANSON	ACIKNST	CATKINS
ACHNORS	ANCHORS		CATSKIN
	ARCHONS	ACIKOPS	PAIOCKS
	RANCHOS	ACIKPRT	PATRICK
ACHNORT	CHANTOR	ACIKPSS	ASPICKS
ACHNOSS	SANCHOS	ACILLMS	MISCALL
ACHNOST	CHATONS	ACILLRY	LYRICAL
ACHNOSY	ONYCHAS	ACILLSS	SCILLAS
ACHNOTY	TACHYON	ACILMNO	LIMACON
ACHNOUY	CHANOYU	ACILMOT	COMITAL
ACHNOVY	ANCHOVY	ACILMPS	PLASMIC
ACHNPSS	SCHNAPS	ACILMSU	MUSICAL
ACHNPUY	PAUNCHY	ACILNNY	CANNILY
ACHNRTY	CHANTRY	ACILNOR	CLARINO
ACHNRUY	RAUNCHY		CLARION
	UNCHARY	ACILNOS	OILCANS
ACHNSTU	CANTHUS	ACILNOZ	CALZONI
	CHAUNTS	ACILNPS	CAPLINS
	STAUNCH		INCLASP
ACHNSTY	SNATCHY	ACILNPY	PLIANCY
ACHOOST	CAHOOTS	ACILNST	TINCALS
ACHOPRT	TOPARCH	ACILNSU	UNCIALS
ACHOPRY	CHARPOY	ACILNTU	LUNATIC
ACHOPSY	POCHAYS	ACILNUV	VINCULA
ACHORST	ORCHATS	ACILOPT	OPTICAL
ACHORSU	AUROCHS		TOPICAL
ACHRSST	SCARTHS	ACILORR	RACLOIR
ACHRSTY	STARCHY	ACILOSS	SOCIALS
ACHRSUU	URACHUS	ACILOST	STOICAL
ACHSSTU	CUSHATS	ACILOTV	VOLATIC
ACHSSUW	CUSHAWS		VOLTAIC
ACHSTUW	WAUCHTS	ACILOTX	TOXICAL
ACHSTUY	CYATHUS	ACILPST	PLACITS
ACIIKNN	CANIKIN		PLASTIC
ACIIKRS	AIRSICK	ACILPSU	SPICULA
ACIILMM	MIMICAL	ACILPTY	TYPICAL
ACIILNR	CLARINI	ACILRSU	URACILS
ACIILNS	SALICIN	ACILRTU	CURTAIL
	SINICAL		TRUCIAL
ACIILNV	VICINAL	ACILRTY	CLARITY
ACIILOV	VILIACO	ACILRYZ	CRAZILY
ACIILRY	CILIARY	ACILSSS	CLASSIS
ACIILSS	SILICAS	ACILSSU	CLUSIAS
ACIILST	ITALICS	ACILSUY	SAUCILY
ACIILTY	LAICITY	ACILTTY	CATTILY
ACIIMMS	MIASMIC		TACITLY
ACIIMNR	MINICAR	ACILTUV	VICTUAL
ACIIMOT	COMITIA	ACIMNOP	CAMPION
ACIIMST	ISMATIC	ACIMNOR	MARCONI
	ITACISM	ACIMNOS	CAMIONS
ACIINNO	ANIONIC		CONIMAS
ACIINNS	NIACINS		MANIOCS
ACIINOS	ASINICO		MASONIC
ACIINOV	AVIONIC	ACIMNRU	CRANIUM
ACIINPS	PISCINA		CUMARIN
ACIINTT	TITANIC	ACIMNTT	CATMINT
ACIIPPR	PRIAPIC	ACIMOOS	OOMIACS
ACIIPRT	PIRATIC	ACIMOPT	POTAMIC
ACIIRST	SATIRIC	ACIMOSS	MOSAICS
ACIIRTT	TRIATIC	ACIMOST	MATICOS
ACIJUZZ	JACUZZI		SOMATIC
ACIKLNS	CALKINS	ACIMOSV	VOMICAS
ACIKMNS	SICKMAN	ACIMPRT	CRAMPIT
ACIKMOO	OOMIACK		PTARMIC
ACIKMPR	RAMPICK	ACIMPRY	PRIMACY
ACIKMPW	PICKMAW	ACIMPSS	SCAMPIS
ACIKNNP	PANNICK		SPASMIC
ACIKNPS	PANICKS	ACIMPST	IMPACTS

ACIMRSS	RACISMS
ACIMRST	MATRICS
ACIMRSZ	CZARISM
ACIMSST	MASTICS
	MISCAST
ACIMSTT	TACTISM
ACINNOT	ACTINON
	CANTION
	CONTAIN
ACINNOZ	CANZONI
ACINNST	STANNIC
ACINNSY	CYANINS
ACINNTU	ANNICUT
ACINOPT	CAPTION
	PACTION
ACINORR	CARRION
ACINORS	SARONIC
ACINORT	CAROTIN
ACINOSS	CAISSON
	CASINOS
	CASSINO
ACINOST	ACTIONS
	CATIONS
ACINOSU	ACINOUS
ACINOTT	TACTION
ACINOTU	AUCTION
	CAUTION
ACINPRT	CANTRIP
ACINPRY	CYPRIAN
ACINPSS	PANISCS
ACINPST	CATNIPS
ACINQTU	QUANTIC
ACINRSS	ARCSINS
ACINRSU	CRUSIAN
ACINRTT	TANTRIC
ACINRTU	CURTAIN
	TURACIN
ACINSTU	ANICUTS
	NAUTICS
ACINSUV	VICUNAS
ACIOPRS	PROSAIC
ACIOPRT	APRICOT
	PAROTIC
	PATRICO
ACIOPST	COPITAS
ACIOPTT	APTOTIC
ACIOPTY	OPACITY
ACIORRS	CORSAIR
ACIORSU	CARIOUS
	CURIOSA
ACIORTT	RICOTTA
ACIOSST	SCOTIAS
ACIOSSV	OVISACS
ACIPRSY	PISCARY
ACIPRVY	PRIVACY
ACIPSST	SPASTIC
ACIPTUY	PAUCITY
ACIQRTU	QUARTIC
ACIQSTU	ACQUIST
	ACQUITS
ACIRRSS	SIRCARS
ACIRRST	TRICARS
ACIRRSU	CURARIS
ACIRSST	RACISTS
	SACRIST
ACIRSSU	CUIRASS
ACIRSTT	ASTRICT
ACIRSTU	URTICAS
ACIRSTW	TWISCAR
ACIRSTY	SATYRIC

ACIRSTZ	CZARIST
ACISSTT	STATICS
ACISSTU	CASUIST
ACISTTU	CATSUIT
ACISTUV	VACUIST
ACITUVY	VACUITY
ACJKKSY	SKYJACK
ACJKNNO	JANNOCK
ACJKOPS	PAJOCKS
ACJKOPT	JACKPOT
ACJLORU	JOCULAR
ACJMNTU	MUNTJAC
ACJPTUU	CAJUPUT
ACKLLOP	POLLACK
ACKLLOY	LAYLOCK
ACKLLSY	SLACKLY
ACKLMNO	LOCKMAN
ACKLMOR	ARMLOCK
	LOCKRAM
ACKLNOU	UNCLOAK
ACKLORW	WARLOCK
ACKLORY	ROCKLAY
ACKLOSS	LASSOCK
ACKMMMO	MAMMOCK
ACKMOTT	MATTOCK
ACKNNOW	ACKNOWN
ACKNOSW	ACKNOWS
ACKNPRS	PRANCKS
ACKNPSU	UNPACKS
ACKNSTU	UNSTACK
	UNTACKS
ACKOPRR	PARROCK
ACKOPSY	YAPOCKS
ACKORRT	TARROCK
ACLLLOY	LOCALLY
ACLLOOR	COROLLA
ACLLOPS	SCALLOP
ACLLORS	COLLARS
ACLLORU	LOCULAR
ACLLOSU	CALLOUS
ACLLOSW	CALLOWS
ACLLOVY	VOCALLY
ACLMNOO	LOCOMAN
ACLMNUY	CALUMNY
ACLMORS	CLAMORS
ACLMORU	CLAMOUR
ACLMSTU	TALCUMS
ACLMSUU	LUCUMAS
ACLMSUY	MASCULY
ACLNOOR	CORONAL
ACLNOOT	COOLANT
ACLNOOV	VOLCANO
ACLNORU	CORNUAL
	COURLAN
ACLNOUV	UNVOCAL
ACLNPSU	UNCLASP
ACLNRTU	TRUNCAL
ACLNSTY	SCANTLY
ACLNSUV	VULCANS
ACLOPRT	CALTROP
	PROCTAL
ACLOPRU	COPULAR
	CUPOLAR
ACLOPSU	COPULAS
	CUPOLAS
	SCOPULA
ACLOPSY	CALYPSO
ACLOPTY	POLYACT
ACLORRS	CORRALS
ACLORST	CARLOTS

	CROTALS
	SCROTAL
ACLORSU	OCULARS
	OSCULAR
ACLORUV	VOCULAR
ACLOSST	COSTALS
ACLOSTU	LOCUSTA
	TALCOUS
ACLOSTW	COTWALS
ACLPRTY	CRYPTAL
ACLPRUU	CUPULAR
ACLRSSW	SCRAWLS
ACLRSSY	CRASSLY
ACLRSTU	CRUSTAL
	CURTALS
ACLRSTY	CRYSTAL
ACLRSWY	SCRAWLY
ACLSSTU	CUTLASS
ACMNOPR	CRAMPON
ACMNOPY	COMPANY
ACMNORS	MACRONS
ACMNORY	ACRONYM
ACMNOSS	MASCONS
ACMNSTU	SANCTUM
ACMOOST	SCOTOMA
ACMOPRT	COMPART
ACMOPSS	COMPASS
ACMOPST	COMPAST
ACMORST	COMARTS
ACMOSST	MASCOTS
ACMOSTU	MOTUCAS
ACMQTUU	CUMQUAT
ACMRSSW	SCRAWMS
ACMSSTU	MUSCATS
ACMSTUU	MUTUCAS
ACMSUUV	VACUUMS
ACNNNOS	CANNONS
ACNNNUY	UNCANNY
ACNNORY	CANONRY
ACNNOST	CANTONS
ACNNOSY	CANYONS
	SONANCY
ACNNRSY	SCRANNY
ACNOOPS	POONACS
ACNOORS	CORONAS
	RACOONS
ACNOORT	CARTOON
	CORANTO
ACNOPSW	SNOWCAP
ACNORRS	RANCORS
ACNORRU	RANCOUR
ACNORST	CANTORS
	CARTONS
	CONTRAS
	CRATONS
ACNORSU	NACROUS
ACNORSY	CRAYONS
ACNORTU	COURANT
ACNOSSZ	SCAZONS
ACNOSTT	OCTANTS
ACNOSTU	CONATUS
	NOCTUAS
	TOUCANS
ACNPRSY	SYNCARP
ACNRRTU	CURRANT
ACNRSTU	UNCARTS
ACNRSUY	UNSCARY
ACNRSWY	SCRAWNY
ACNRTUY	TRUANCY
ACOOPRR	CORPORA

ACOOPSU	OPACOUS
ACOOPTT	TOPCOAT
ACOORTU	TOURACO
ACOOSTV	OCTAVOS
ACOPRRT	CARPORT
ACOPRST	CAPTORS
ACOPSTU	UPCOAST
ACOPSTW	COWPATS
ACORRST	CARROTS
	TROCARS
ACORRTT	TRACTOR
ACORRTU	CURATOR
ACORRTY	CARROTY
ACORSST	CASTORS
ACORSSU	SARCOUS
ACORSTT	COTTARS
ACORSTU	SURCOAT
	TURACOS
ACORSTV	CAVORTS
ACORSTY	CASTORY
ACORSUU	RAUCOUS
ACORSYZ	CORYZAS
ACOSTTU	OUTACTS
	OUTCAST
ACOSUUV	VACUOUS
ACPPRSY	SCRAPPY
ACPSSTU	CATSUPS
	UPCASTS
ACPSTUU	USUCAPT
ACRRSTU	CRATURS
ACRSTTU	TRACTUS
ADDDDEL	DADDLED
ADDDDOR	DODDARD
ADDDEER	DREADED
ADDDEFL	FADDLED
ADDDEGL	GLADDED
ADDDEIL	DAIDLED
ADDDEIS	DADDIES
ADDDEIW	WADDIED
ADDDELN	DANDLED
ADDDELP	PADDLED
ADDDELR	RADDLED
ADDDELS	DADDLES
	SADDLED
ADDDELW	DAWDLED
	WADDLED
ADDDENO	DEODAND
ADDDENS	ADDENDS
ADDDEQU	QUADDED
ADDDGIN	DADDING
ADDDOOS	DOODADS
ADDEEEM	ADEEMED
ADDEEFM	DEFAMED
ADDEEGR	DEGRADE
ADDEEHL	HEALDED
ADDEEHR	ADHERED
ADDEEIR	READIED
ADDEEIT	IDEATED
ADDEEKN	KNEADED
ADDEEKR	DAKERED
ADDEELN	DELENDA
ADDEELP	PLEADED
ADDEELT	DELATED
ADDEELY	DELAYED
ADDEEMN	AMENDED
ADDEEMR	DREAMED
ADDEEMS	ADDEEMS
ADDEENS	DEADENS
ADDEENV	ADVENED
ADDEENY	DENAYED

ADDEEOT DEODATE	ADDELMW DWALMED	ADDGINW DAWDING	ALLEGED
ADDEERR DREADER	ADDELNR DANDLER	WADDING	ADEEGLM GLEAMED
ADDEERS DEADERS	ADDELNS DANDLES	ADDGIOS GADOIDS	ADEEGLN GLEANED
ADDEERT DERATED	ADDELNU UNLADED	ADDGLNO GLADDON	ADEEGLR REGALED
ADDEERY DERAYED	ADDELPP DAPPLED	ADDGMNO GODDAMN	ADEEGLT TEAGLED
YEARDED	ADDELPR PADDLER	ADDGOOS OGDOADS	ADEEGLU LEAGUED
ADDEEST DEADEST	ADDELPS PADDLES	ADDGOOW DAGWOOD	ADEEGMN ENDGAME
SEDATED	ADDELRS LADDERS	ADDGORW GODWARD	MANEGED
STEADED	RADDLES	ADDGOSY DOGDAYS	ADEEGNR ANGERED
ADDEEVW ADVEWED	SADDLER	ADDHINP DAPHNID	DERANGE
ADDEFIR FADDIER	ADDELRT DARTLED	ADDHISS SADDISH	ENRAGED
ADDEFLS FADDLES	ADDELRW DAWDLER	SIDDHAS	GRANDEE
ADDEFLY FADEDLY	DRAWLED	ADDHITY HYDATID	GRENADE
ADDEFNU UNFADED	ADDELRY DREADLY	ADDHOOS DOODAHS	ADEEGNT AGENTED
ADDEFRT DRAFTED	LADDERY	ADDHSSU SADDHUS	NEGATED
ADDEFRU DEFRAUD	ADDELSS SADDLES	ADDIINS DISDAIN	ADEEGNV AVENGED
ADDEFRW DWARFED	ADDELST STADDLE	ADDIKST TSADDIK	VENDAGE
ADDEGGL DAGGLED	ADDELSW DAWDLES	ADDIKSZ ZADDIKS	ADEEGOT DOGEATE
ADDEGGR DRAGGED	SWADDLE	ADDIKTY KATYDID	GOATEED
ADDEGHO GODHEAD	WADDLES	ADDIKTZ TZADDIK	ADEEGRR REGRADE
ADDEGIL GLADDIE	ADDELTW TWADDLE	ADDILMN MIDLAND	ADEEGRS DRAGEES
ADDEGIN DEADING	ADDELYZ DAZEDLY	ADDILNY DANDILY	GREASED
ADDEGJU ADJUDGE	ADDELZZ DAZZLED	ADDILOS DISLOAD	ADEEGRU GUARDEE
ADDEGLN DANGLED	ADDEMMR DRAMMED	ADDIMNO DIAMOND	ADEEGRV GREAVED
GLADDEN	ADDEMMW DWAMMED	ADDIMOR DIADROM	ADEEGRW RAGWEED
ADDEGLR GLADDER	ADDEMNS DEMANDS	ADDIMRS DIRDAMS	WAGERED
ADDEGRS GADDERS	MADDENS	ADDIMSY DISMAYD	ADEEHIR HEADIER
ADDEGRU GUARDED	ADDEMNU MAUNDED	MIDDAYS	ADEEHLR HEDERAL
ADDEHIS HADDIES	ADDEMOP POMADED	ADDINOR ANDROID	ADEEHLS LEASHED
ADDEHKS KEDDAHS	ADDEMRS MADDERS	ADDINRY DIANDRY	SHEALED
ADDEHLN HANDLED	ADDEMST MADDEST	ADDIPRS DISPRAD	ADEEHLX EXHALED
ADDEHOR HOARDED	ADDEMUW DWAUMED	ADDIQST TSADDIQ	ADEEHMN HEADMEN
ADDEHRS SHARDED	ADDENOR ADORNED	ADDIQTZ TZADDIQ	ADEEHNN HENNAED
ADDEIIK DIDAKEI	ADDENOT DONATED	ADDIRZZ DIZZARD	ADEEHNS DASHEEN
ADDEIIS DAISIED	NODATED	ADDLLRU DULLARD	ADEEHNV HAVENED
ADDEILL DALLIED	ADDENOU DUODENA	ADDLOOS SOLDADO	ADEEHPR EPHEDRA
DIALLED	ADDENPU PUDENDA	ADDLTWY TWADDLY	ADEEHRR ADHERER
ADDEILP PLAIDED	ADDENRS DANDERS	ADDMNOS DODMANS	REHEARD
ADDEILR DIEDRAL	ADDENRT DRANTED	ODDSMAN	ADEEHRS ADHERES
DRAILED	ADDENRU DAUNDER	ADDMOOS ADDOOMS	HEADERS
ADDEILS DAIDLES	ADDENSS SADDENS	ADDNNOR DONNARD	HEARSED
LADDIES	ADDENSU ASUDDEN	ADDOORS DORADOS	SHEARED
ADDEILT DILATED	ADDENSY SDAYNED	ADDOPSY DASYPOD	ADEEHRT EARTHED
ADDEIMR ADMIRED	ADDENTU DAUNTED	ADDORST DOTARDS	HEARTED
MARDIED	UNDATED	ADDQSUY SQUADDY	ADEEHRV HAVERED
ADDEIMS DIADEMS	ADDEOPT ADOPTED	ADEEEFY FEDAYEE	ADEEHRX EXHEDRA
ADDEIMX ADMIXED	ADDEORS DEODARS	ADEEEMN DEMEANE	ADEEHST HEADSET
ADDEINO ADENOID	ADDEPPR DRAPPED	ADEEERR ARREEDE	ADEEHSV SHEAVED
ADDEINP PANDIED	ADDEPPS PADDERS	ADEEERX EXEDRAE	ADEEHSY HAYSEED
ADDEINR DANDIER	ADDEPTU UPDATED	ADEEESW SEAWEED	ADEEIJT JADEITE
DRAINED	ADDERSS ADDRESS	ADEEFGU FEAGUED	ADEEILN ALIENED
ADDEINS DANDIES	ADDERST ADDREST	ADEEFHS SHEAFED	DELAINE
SDAINED	ADDERSW SWARDED	ADEEFIR AREFIED	ADEEILR LEADIER
ADDEINU UNAIDED	ADDERSY DRYADES	FEDARIE	ADEEILS AEDILES
ADDEINV INVADED	ADDERTT DRATTED	ADEEFKR FREAKED	DEISEAL
VIDENDA	ADDESST SADDEST	ADEEFLR FEDERAL	ADEEILY EYELIAD
ADDEIOR RADIOED	ADDESTU ADUSTED	ADEEFLT DEFLATE	ADEEIMN DEMAINE
ADDEIOT TOADIED	SUDATED	ADEEFMS DEFAMES	ADEEIMT MEDIATE
ADDEIOV AVOIDED	ADDFHIS FADDISH	ADEEFNS DEAFENS	ADEEINN ADENINE
ADDEIPS PADDIES	ADDFIMS FADDISM	ADEEFPR PREFADE	ADEEINS ANISEED
ADDEIRR ARRIDED	ADDFINY DANDIFY	ADEEFRT DRAFTEE	ADEEIRR READIER
ADDEIRT TARDIED	ADDFIST FADDIST	ADEEFRW WAFERED	ADEEIRS DEARIES
ADDEISV ADVISED	ADDGGIN GADDING	ADEEFST DEAFEST	READIES
ADDEISW WADDIES	ADDGHIN HADDING	DEFASTE	ADEEIRW WEARIED
ADDEITU AUDITED	ADDGIIR DIAGRID	DEFEATS	ADEEISS DISEASE
ADDEJLY JADEDLY	ADDGILN ADDLING	FEASTED	SEASIDE
ADDEJNU UNJADED	ADDGIMN MADDING	ADEEGGH EGGHEAD	ADEEIST IDEATES
ADDEJRU ADJURED	ADDGINO DADOING	ADEEGGL ALEGGED	ADEEITV DEVIATE
ADDEKLR DARKLED	ADDGINP PADDING	ADEEGGN ENGAGED	ADEEJSY DEEJAYS
ADDELLU ALLUDED	ADDGINU DAUDING	ADEEGLL ALLEDGE	ADEEKNR KNEADER

```
          NAKEDER        ADEENNS ENNEADS        ADEFFNY NYAFFED        ADEGGNS SNAGGED
ADEEKNS SNEAKED        ADEENNX ANNEXED        ADEFFQU QUAFFED        ADEGGRS DAGGERS
ADEEKNW WAKENED        ADEENPS SNEAPED        ADEFFST STAFFED        ADEGGRY RAGGEDY
ADEEKRS SKEARED                SPEANED        ADEFFUW WAUFFED        ADEGGST GADGETS
ADEEKRW WREAKED        ADEENRS DEANERS        ADEFGGL FLAGGED                STAGGED
ADEEKTW TWEAKED                ENDEARS        ADEFGLN FANGLED        ADEGGSW SWAGGED
ADEEKWY WEEKDAY        ADEENRU UNEARED                FLANGED        ADEGHIN HEADING
ADEELLS ALLSEED        ADEENRV RAVENED        ADEFGOR FORAGED        ADEGHIR HEADRIG
ADEELLY ALLEYED        ADEENRY DEANERY        ADEFGOT FAGOTED        ADEGHIS HIDAGES
ADEELMP EMPALED                RENAYED        ADEFGOU FOUGADE        ADEGHLU LAUGHED
ADEELMR EMERALD                YEARNED        ADEFGRT GRAFTED        ADEGHMO HOMAGED
ADEELMS MEASLED        ADEENST STEANED        ADEFHIT FAITHED        ADEGHNP PHANGED
ADEELMT MEDALET        ADEENSV ADVENES        ADEFHLS FLASHED        ADEGHNS GNASHED
ADEELMU AEMULED        ADEENTT DENTATE        ADEFHRW WHARFED                HAGDENS
ADEELMY YEALMED        ADEEORS OREADES        ADEFHST SHAFTED        ADEGHNW WHANGED
ADEELNP DEPLANE        ADEEORW OARWEED        ADEFILL FLAILED        ADEGHPR GRAPHED
ADEELNR LEARNED        ADEEPPR PAPERED        ADEFILS DISLEAF        ADEGHST GHASTED
ADEELNS LEADENS        ADEEPRS PREASED        ADEFIMN INFAMED        ADEGHUW WAUGHED
ADEELNT EDENTAL                SPEARED        ADEFIMS DISFAME        ADEGILL GALLIED
        LATENED        ADEEPRT ADEPTER        ADEFINR FRIANDE        ADEGILN ALIGNED
ADEELPR PEARLED                PREDATE        ADEFINT DEFIANT                DEALING
        PLEADER                TAPERED                FAINTED                LEADING
ADEELPS DELAPSE        ADEEPRV DEPRAVE        ADEFIRS FRAISED        ADEGILO GEOIDAL
        ELAPSED                PERVADE        ADEFIST DAFTIES        ADEGILR GLADIER
        PLEASED        ADEEPSS PESADES                FADIEST                GLAIRED
ADEELPT PLEATED        ADEEQRU QUAERED        ADEFITX FIXATED        ADEGILS SILAGED
ADEELRS ARLESED        ADEEQTU EQUATED        ADEFKLN FANKLED        ADEGILT LIGATED
        DEALERS        ADEERRR DREARER                FLANKED                TAIGLED
        LEADERS        ADEERRS DREARES        ADEFKNR FRANKED        ADEGILV GLAIVED
        REDEALS                READERS        ADEFLLN ELFLAND        ADEGINR AREDING
ADEELRT ALERTED                REDSEAR        ADEFLMM FLAMMED                DEARING
        ALTERED                REREADS        ADEFLNN FENLAND                DERAIGN
        REDEALT        ADEERRT RETREAD        ADEFLOT FLOATED                EARDING
        RELATED                TREADER        ADEFLPP FLAPPED                GRADINE
        TREADLE        ADEERRV AVERRED        ADEFLRS FARDELS                GRAINED
ADEELRW LEEWARD        ADEERSS RESEDAS        ADEFLRU DAREFUL                READING
ADEELRX RELAXED        ADEERST DEAREST        ADEFLTT FLATTED        ADEGINS AGNISED
ADEELRY DELAYER                DERATES        ADEFLTU DEFAULT        ADEGINV DEAVING
        LAYERED                ESTRADE                FAULTED                EVADING
        RELAYED                REASTED        ADEFMNU UNFAMED        ADEGINW WINDAGE
ADEELST DELATES                SEDATER        ADEFNRS FARDENS        ADEGINY YEADING
        STEALED                STEARED        ADEFNSU UNDEAFS        ADEGINZ AGNIZED
ADEELSV SLEAVED        ADEERSV ADVERSE        ADEFNUZ UNFAZED        ADEGIOT GODETIA
ADEELSW SWEALED        ADEERSW DRAWEES        ADEFOOS SEAFOOD        ADEGIRS AGRISED
ADEELTV VALETED        ADEERTT ARETTED        ADEFORS FEDORAS        ADEGIRU GAUDIER
        VELATED                TREATED        ADEFORV FAVORED        ADEGIRZ AGRIZED
ADEELTX EXALTED        ADEERTV AVERTED        ADEFORY FEODARY        ADEGIST AGISTED
ADEELTZ TEAZLED                TAVERED                FORAYED        ADEGISU AGUISED
ADEELUV DEVALUE        ADEERTW DEWATER        ADEFPPR FRAPPED                GAUDIES
ADEEMNR AMENDER                TARWEED        ADEFPRR PREFARD        ADEGISV VISAGED
        ENARMED                WATERED        ADEFRRT DRAFTER        ADEGIUV VIDUAGE
        MEANDER        ADEERVW WAVERED                REDRAFT        ADEGIUZ AGUIZED
        REAMEND        ADEESST SEDATES        ADEFRST STRAFED        ADEGJLN JANGLED
        RENAMED        ADEESSY ESSAYED        ADEFRSU FADEURS        ADEGLLU ULLAGED
ADEEMNS AMENDES        ADEESTT ESTATED        ADEFRSW SWARFED        ADEGLMN MANGLED
        DEMEANS        ADEESTU SAUTEED        ADEFRSY DEFRAYS        ADEGLMU GLAUMED
ADEEMNT ENTAMED        ADEESTW SWEATED        ADEFRUY FEUDARY        ADEGLNN ENDLANG
ADEEMNY DEMAYNE        ADEESTY YEASTED        ADEFSTT DAFTEST        ADEGLNR DANGLER
ADEEMOS OEDEMAS        ADEESVY SAVEYED        ADEGGGL GAGGLED                GNARLED
ADEEMPR EMPARED        ADEETUX EXUDATE        ADEGGHL HAGGLED        ADEGLNS DANGLES
        REAMPED        ADEFFFL FLAFFED        ADEGGHS SHAGGED                GLANDES
ADEEMRR DREAMER        ADEFFGR GRAFFED        ADEGGIS GADGIES                SLANGED
        REARMED        ADEFFIN AFFINED        ADEGGIU GAUDGIE        ADEGLNT TANGLED
ADEEMRS REMADES        ADEFFIP PIAFFED                GUIDAGE        ADEGLNU LANGUED
        REMEADS        ADEFFIR DAFFIER        ADEGGLR DRAGGLE        ADEGLNW WANGLED
        SMEARED        ADEFFIS DAFFIES                GARGLED        ADEGLOP GALOPED
ADEEMST STEAMED        ADEFFIX AFFIXED                RAGGLED        ADEGLOT GLOATED
ADEEMSU MEDUSAE        ADEFFLM MAFFLED        ADEGGLS DAGGLES        ADEGLPU PLAGUED
ADEEMSW MAWSEED        ADEFFLR RAFFLED                SLAGGED        ADEGLRS DARGLES
ADEEMTW MATWEED        ADEFFLW WAFFLED        ADEGGLW WAGGLED        ADEGLRU RAGULED
ADEEMWY MAYWEED
```

ADEGLRY	GRADELY	ADEHKNT	THANKED	ADEIJMR	JEMIDAR	ADEIMOW	MIAOWED
ADEGLSS	GLASSED	ADEHKOR	HARDOKE	ADEIKLS	SKAILED	ADEIMPR	DAMPIER
ADEGMNS	GADSMEN	ADEHKOT	KATHODE	ADEIKNS	KANDIES	ADEIMPV	IMPAVED
ADEGMNU	GUDEMAN	ADEHKRS	SHARKED	ADEIKRS	DAIKERS	ADEIMRR	ADMIRER
ADEGNNO	NONAGED	ADEHLLO	HALLOED		DARKIES		MARDIER
ADEGNNU	DUNNAGE	ADEHLNR	HANDLER	ADEIKRT	TRAIKED		MARRIED
ADEGNOP	PONDAGE	ADEHLNS	HANDLES	ADEILLR	DALLIER	ADEIMRS	ADMIRES
ADEGNOR	GROANED		HANDSEL		DIALLER		MARDIES
ADEGNOS	SONDAGE	ADEHLOS	SHOALED		RALLIED		MISREAD
ADEGNOT	TANGOED	ADEHLOT	LOATHED	ADEILLS	DALLIES		SIDEARM
ADEGNOV	DOGVANE	ADEHLPS	PLASHED		DISLEAL	ADEIMRT	READMIT
ADEGNOW	GOWANED	ADEHLRS	HARELDS		LALDIES	ADEIMST	MISDATE
	WAGONED		HERALDS		SALLIED	ADEIMSV	VIDAMES
ADEGNPR	PRANGED	ADEHLSS	HASSLED	ADEILLT	TALLIED	ADEIMSX	ADMIXES
ADEGNPS	SPANGED		SLASHED	ADEILLV	VIALLED	ADEIMTU	TAEDIUM
ADEGNPU	UNPAGED	ADEHLSW	SHAWLED	ADEILLY	IDEALLY	ADEIMTY	DAYTIME
ADEGNRR	GNARRED	ADEHLTY	DEATHLY	ADEILMM	DILEMMA	ADEINNN	NANDINE
	GRANDER	ADEHMMS	SHAMMED	ADEILMP	IMPALED		NANNIED
ADEGNRS	DANGERS	ADEHMMW	WHAMMED		IMPLEAD	ADEINOR	ANEROID
	GANDERS	ADEHMNR	HERDMAN	ADEILMS	MEDIALS	ADEINOS	ADONISE
	GARDENS	ADEHMOR	HADROME		MISDEAL		ANODISE
ADEGNRT	GRANTED	ADEHMRS	DERHAMS		MISLEAD		SODAINE
ADEGNRU	ENGUARD	ADEHMSS	SMASHED	ADEILMU	MIAULED	ADEINOV	NAEVOID
	RAUNGED	ADEHNPS	DAPHNES	ADEILNN	ANNELID	ADEINOX	DIOXANE
ADEGNST	STANGED	ADEHNRS	HANDERS		LINDANE	ADEINOZ	ADONIZE
ADEGNTU	GAUNTED		HARDENS	ADEILNP	PLAINED		ANODIZE
ADEGNTW	TWANGED	ADEHNRU	UNHEARD	ADEILNS	DENIALS	ADEINPR	PARDINE
ADEGNUW	UNWAGED	ADEHNSS	SNASHED		SNAILED	ADEINPS	PANDIES
ADEGNUZ	UNGAZED	ADEHNST	HANDSET	ADEILNU	ALIUNDE		PANSIED
ADEGORW	DOWAGER	ADEHNSU	UNHEADS		UNIDEAL		SPAINED
	WORDAGE	ADEHNTU	HAUNTED	ADEILNV	ANDVILE	ADEINPT	DEPAINT
ADEGOSS	DOSAGES	ADEHOOP	APEHOOD	ADEILOR	DARIOLE		PAINTED
ADEGOST	DOGATES	ADEHOPX	HEXAPOD	ADEILOS	DEASOIL		PATINED
	DOTAGES	ADEHORR	HOARDER	ADEILOU	DOULEIA	ADEINRR	DRAINER
ADEGOTT	TOGATED	ADEHOST	HOASTED	ADEILPP	APPLIED		RANDIER
ADEGOVY	VOYAGED	ADEHOSX	OXHEADS	ADEILPR	PEDRAIL	ADEINRS	RANDIES
ADEGPRS	GRASPED	ADEHPPW	WHAPPED		PREDIAL		SANDIER
	SPADGER	ADEHPRS	PHRASED	ADEILPS	ALIPEDS		SARDINE
	SPARGED		SHARPED		PAIDLES	ADEINRT	DETRAIN
ADEGPRU	UPGRADE	ADEHPST	HEPTADS		PALSIED		TRAINED
ADEGPUZ	UPGAZED		SPATHED	ADEILPT	PLAITED	ADEINRU	UNAIRED
ADEGRRS	GRADERS	ADEHPSW	PSHAWED		TALIPED		URANIDE
	REGARDS	ADEHRRU	HURRAED	ADEILQU	QUAILED	ADEINRV	INVADER
ADEGRSS	GRASSED	ADEHRSS	DASHERS	ADEILRR	LARDIER		RAVINED
ADEGRSU	SUGARED	ADEHRST	DEARTHS	ADEILRS	DERAILS	ADEINSS	SDAINES
ADEGRTY	GYRATED		HARDEST		SIDERAL	ADEINST	DETAINS
	TRAGEDY		HATREDS	ADEILRT	DILATER		INSTEAD
ADEGRUU	AUGURED		THREADS		TRAILED		SAINTED
ADEGRUY	GAUDERY		TRASHED	ADEILRV	VALIDER		SATINED
ADEGRYZ	AGRYZED	ADEHRTW	WRATHED	ADEILRY	READILY		STAINED
ADEGSSU	DEGAUSS	ADEHRTY	HYDRATE	ADEILSS	AIDLESS	ADEINSV	INVADES
ADEHHOT	HOTHEAD		THREADY		DEASILS	ADEINSW	DEWANIS
ADEHIKS	DASHEKI	ADEHSST	STASHED	ADEILST	DETAILS	ADEINTT	TAINTED
ADEHIKV	KHEDIVA	ADEHSSW	SWASHED		DILATES	ADEINTU	AUDIENT
ADEHILN	INHALED	ADEHSTW	SWATHED	ADEILSU	AUDILES	ADEINTV	DEVIANT
ADEHILP	HELIPAD	ADEHSYY	HEYDAYS		DEASIUL	ADEINVV	NAVVIED
ADEHILS	HALIDES	ADEHUZZ	HUZZAED	ADEILSV	DEVISAL	ADEIOPS	ADIPOSE
ADEHILY	HEADILY	ADEIILR	DELIRIA	ADEILSY	DIALYSE	ADEIOPT	OPIATED
ADEHINP	PINHEAD		IRIDEAL		EYLIADS	ADEIORS	ROADIES
ADEHINR	HANDIER	ADEIILS	DAILIES	ADEILYZ	DIALYZE		SOREDIA
ADEHIPP	HAPPIED		LIAISED	ADEIMMR	MERMAID	ADEIORX	EXORDIA
ADEHIPR	RAPHIDE		SEDILIA	ADEIMMS	MISMADE	ADEIOST	IODATES
ADEHIPS	APHIDES	ADEIINR	DENARII	ADEIMNR	ADERMIN		TOADIES
ADEHIPT	PITHEAD	ADEIIPR	PERIDIA		INARMED	ADEIOSX	OXIDASE
ADEHIRR	HARDIER	ADEIIRS	DAIRIES	ADEIMNS	DEMAINS	ADEIOSZ	DIAZOES
	HARRIED		DIARIES		MAIDENS	ADEIOTX	OXIDATE
ADEHIRS	SHADIER		DIARISE		MEDIANS	ADEIOVV	VAIVODE
ADEHIRW	RAWHIDE	ADEIIRZ	DIARIZE		MEDINAS	ADEIOVW	WAIVODE
ADEHIRY	HYDRIAE	ADEIISS	DAISIES	ADEIMNT	MEDIANT	ADEIOWW	WAIWODE
ADEHKNS	SHANKED			ADEIMNU	UNAIMED	ADEIPPR	DRAPPIE

	PREPAID	ADEKNST DANKEST	ADELORU ROULADE	SUDAMEN
ADEIPPU	APPUIED	ADEKNSU UNASKED	ADELOSS ALDOSES	ADEMNSY DAYSMEN
ADEIPRR	DRAPIER	ADEKNSW SWANKED	LASSOED	ADEMNTU UNMATED
	PARRIED	ADEKNUW UNWAKED	ADELOST SALTOED	UNTAMED
	RAPIDER	ADEKNVY VANDYKE	ADELPPP PLAPPED	ADEMOOV AMOOVED
ADEIPRS	ASPIRED	ADEKPRS SPARKED	ADELPPS DAPPLES	ADEMOPS APEDOMS
	DESPAIR	ADEKRST DARKEST	SLAPPED	POMADES
	DIAPERS	STARKED	ADELPRS PEDLARS	ADEMORS RADOMES
	PRAISED	ADEKRSY DARKEYS	ADELPRY PEDLARY	ADEMOSV VAMOSED
ADEIPRT	PARTIED	ADELLMS SMALLED	ADELPST SPALTED	ADEMOSW MEADOWS
	PIRATED	ADELLMU MEDULLA	STAPLED	ADEMOSY SOMEDAY
ADEIPRV	VAPIDER	ADELLNR LANDLER	ADELPSU UPLEADS	ADEMOWY MEADOWY
ADEIPSS	APSIDES	ADELLNW ELLWAND	ADELPSW DEWLAPS	ADEMPRS DAMPERS
ADEIRRS	ARRIDES	ADELLOR ODALLER	SPAWLED	ADEMPRT TRAMPED
	RAIDERS	ADELLOW ALLOWED	ADELPSY SPLAYED	ADEMPSS SPASMED
ADEIRRT	TARDIER	ADELLOY ALLOYED	ADELPTT PLATTED	ADEMPST DAMPEST
	TARRIED	ADELLPS SPALLED	ADELPTW DEWLAPT	STAMPED
ADEIRRV	ARRIVED	ADELLRU ALLURED	ADELRRS LARDERS	ADEMPSW SWAMPED
ADEIRST	ARIDEST	UDALLER	ADELRRU RUDERAL	ADEMRRU EARDRUM
	ASTERID	ADELLST STALLED	ADELRRW DRAWLER	ADEMRST SMARTED
	ASTRIDE	ADELLSU ALLUDES	ADELRSS SARDELS	ADEMRSU REMUDAS
	DIASTER	ALUDELS	ADELRST DARTLES	ADEMRSW SWARMED
	DISRATE	ADELLSV DEVALLS	ADELRSU LAUDERS	ADEMRTU MATURED
	STAIDER	ADELMMS SLAMMED	ADELRSW WARSLED	ADEMSSU ASSUMED
	STAIRED	SMALMED	ADELRSZ DRAZELS	MEDUSAS
	TARDIES	ADELMNN LANDMEN	ADELRTT RATTLED	ADEMTTU MUTATED
	TIRADES	ADELMNR MANDREL	ADELRTW TRAWLED	ADENNOY ANNOYED
ADEIRSU	RESIDUA	ADELMNT MANTLED	ADELRTX DEXTRAL	ANODYNE
ADEIRSV	ADVISER	ADELMOR EARLDOM	ADELRTY LYRATED	ADENNPS SPANNED
	VARDIES	ADELMOS DAMOSEL	ADELRWW WRAWLED	ADENNPT PENDANT
ADEIRTT	ATTIRED	ADELMOZ DAMOZEL	ADELRWX WRAXLED	ADENNST STANDEN
ADEIRTV	TARDIVE	ADELMPS SAMPLED	ADELRZZ DAZZLER	ADENNSU DUENNAS
ADEIRTY	DIETARY	ADELMRS MEDLARS	ADELSST DESALTS	ADENNWY DEWANNY
ADEISSS	DASSIES	ADELMSS DAMSELS	ADELSTT SLATTED	ADENOOP NAPOOED
ADEISST	DISSEAT	ADELNNP PLANNED	ADELSTU AULDEST	ADENOOZ ENDOZOA
	SAIDEST	ADELNNU UNLADEN	SALUTED	ADENOPR APRONED
ADEISSV	ADVISES	ADELNOR LADRONE	ADELSUV AVULSED	OPERAND
ADEISSZ	ASSIZED	ADELNOS LOADENS	ADELSWY SWAYLED	PADRONE
ADEISTU	DAUTIES	ADELNOT TALONED	ADELSZZ DAZZLES	PANDORE
ADEISTV	AVIDEST	ADELNOY YEALDON	ADELTTT TATTLED	ADENOPS DAPSONE
	DATIVES	ADELNPT PLANTED	ADELTTW WATTLED	ADENORT TORNADE
	VISTAED	ADELNRS DARNELS	ADELTUV VAULTED	ADENORU RONDEAU
ADEISTW	DAWTIES	ENLARDS	ADELTUX LUXATED	ADENOST ASTONED
	WAISTED	LANDERS	ADELTWZ WALTZED	DONATES
ADEISVV	SAVVIED	SLANDER	ADEMMRS DAMMERS	ONSTEAD
ADEISWY	SIDEWAY	SNARLED	SMARMED	ADENOSU DOUANES
	WAYSIDE	ADELNRU LAUNDER	ADEMNNS SANDMEN	ADENOSY NOYADES
ADEJMOR	MAJORED	LURDANE	ADEMNNU MUNDANE	ADENOTT NOTATED
ADEJMRU	MUDEJAR	RUNDALE	UNNAMED	ADENOTZ ZONATED
ADEJNSU	JAUNSED	ADELNRY DEARNLY	ADEMNOR ROADMEN	ADENPPR PARPEND
ADEJNTU	JAUNTED	ADELNSS SENDALS	ADEMNOS DAEMONS	ADENPPS APPENDS
ADEJOPR	JEOPARD	ADELNST DENTALS	MASONED	SNAPPED
ADEJRSU	ADJURES	SLANTED	MODENAS	ADENPPW WAPPEND
ADEJSSU	JUDASES	ADELNSU UNLADES	MONADES	ADENPRR PARDNER
ADEKLNP	PLANKED	UNLEADS	NOMADES	ADENPRS PANDERS
ADEKLNR	RANKLED	ADELNTU LUNATED	ADEMNOW WOMANED	ADENPRU UNPARED
ADEKLNS	KALENDS	UNDEALT	ADEMNPS DAMPENS	ADENPRW PRAWNED
ADEKLNY	NAKEDLY	ADELNTW WETLAND	ADEMNRS MANREDS	ADENPST PEDANTS
ADEKLRS	DARKLES	ADELNUW UNLAWED	RANDEMS	PENTADS
ADEKLST	SKLATED	ADELOPR LEOPARD	REMANDS	ADENPSW SPAWNED
	STALKED	PAROLED	ADEMNRU DURAMEN	ADENPSX EXPANDS
ADEKLSY	YSLAKED	ADELOPS DEPOSAL	MANURED	ADENPSY DYSPNEA
ADEKLUW	WAULKED	PEDALOS	MAUNDER	ADENPUV UNPAVED
ADEKMRS	DEMARKS	ADELOPT PLOATED	UNARMED	ADENQTU QUANTED
ADEKNPP	KNAPPED	TADPOLE	ADEMNRY DRAYMEN	ADENRRS DARNERS
ADEKNPR	PRANKED	ADELORS LOADERS	YARDMEN	ERRANDS
ADEKNPS	SPANKED	ORDEALS	ADEMNSS DESMANS	SNARRED
ADEKNRR	KNARRED	RELOADS	MADNESS	ADENRRW REDRAWN
ADEKNRS	DARKENS	ADELORT DELATOR	ADEMNST TANDEMS	ADENRRY REYNARD
ADEKNRU	UNRAKED	LEOTARD	ADEMNSU MEDUSAN	ADENRSS SANDERS

	SARSDEN
ADENRST	ENDARTS
	STANDER
	STARNED
ADENRSU	ASUNDER
	DANSEUR
	DAUNERS
ADENRSW	DAWNERS
	WANDERS
	WARDENS
ADENRSZ	ZANDERS
ADENRTT	TRANTED
ADENRTU	DAUNTER
	NATURED
	UNRATED
	UNTREAD
ADENRTV	VERDANT
ADENRTX	DEXTRAN
ADENRTY	DENTARY
	TRAYNED
	TYRANED
ADENRUY	UNREADY
ADENSSS	SADNESS
ADENSSU	SUNDAES
ADENSSW	WESANDS
ADENSTT	ATTENDS
ADENSTU	SAUNTED
	UNSATED
ADENSTV	ADVENTS
ADENSTY	STAYNED
ADENSUV	UNSAVED
ADENSWY	ENDWAYS
ADENSWZ	WEZANDS
ADENTTU	ATTUNED
	NUTATED
	TAUNTED
ADENTUV	VAUNTED
ADENTUX	UNTAXED
ADENUWY	UNWAYED
ADEOORT	ODORATE
ADEOPPS	APPOSED
	PEAPODS
ADEOPQU	OPAQUED
ADEOPRR	EARDROP
ADEOPRT	ADOPTER
	READOPT
ADEOPRV	VAPORED
ADEOPSS	SPADOES
ADEOPST	PODESTA
ADEORRS	ADORERS
	DROSERA
ADEORRW	ARROWED
ADEORST	DOATERS
	ROASTED
	TORSADE
	TROADES
ADEORSU	AROUSED
ADEORSV	SAVORED
ADEORSW	REDOWAS
ADEORTT	ROTATED
	TROATED
ADEORTU	OUTDARE
ADEORWY	RODEWAY
ADEORYZ	ZEDOARY
ADEOSTT	TOASTED
ADEOTTU	OUTDATE
ADEPPRS	DAPPERS
ADEPPRT	TRAPPED
ADEPPRW	WRAPPED
ADEPPST	STAPPED
ADEPPSW	SWAPPED
ADEPPTU	PUPATED
ADEPPUY	APPUYED
ADEPRRS	DRAPERS
	SPARRED
ADEPRRY	DRAPERY
ADEPRSS	ADPRESS
	SPADERS
	SPREADS
ADEPRST	DEPARTS
	DRAPETS
	PETARDS
ADEPRSY	SPRAYED
ADEPRTT	PRATTED
ADEPRTU	UPRATED
ADEPSTT	SPATTED
ADEPSTU	UPDATES
ADEQRSU	SQUARED
ADERRST	DARTERS
	DARTRES
	RETARDS
	STARRED
ADERRSW	DRAWERS
	REDRAWS
	REWARDS
	WARDERS
ADERSSU	ASSURED
	RUDASES
ADERSSW	SAWDERS
	SWEARDS
ADERSTT	STARTED
	TETRADS
ADERSTV	ADVERTS
	STARVED
ADERSTW	STEWARD
	STRAWED
	WRASTED
ADERSTY	STRAYED
ADERSUY	DASYURE
ADERSVW	DWARVES
	SWARVED
ADERWWY	WEYWARD
ADESSTU	SUDATES
ADESSTW	WADSETS
ADESTTU	STATUED
ADESTTW	SWATTED
	WADSETT
ADFFGIN	DAFFING
ADFFHNO	OFFHAND
ADFFIST	DISTAFF
ADFFLNO	FANFOLD
ADFFLOO	OFFLOAD
ADFFOOR	AFFOORD
ADFFORS	AFFORDS
ADFGGIN	FADGING
ADFGINN	FANDING
ADFGINR	FARDING
ADFGINS	FADINGS
ADFGLLU	GLADFUL
ADFHLNU	HANDFUL
ADFHOOS	SHADOOF
ADFHSSU	SHADUFS
ADFILLU	FLUIDAL
ADFIMNR	FINDRAM
ADFIMNY	DAMNIFY
ADFINRS	FRIANDS
ADFINRT	INDRAFT
ADFIORS	FORSAID
ADFLLYY	LADYFLY
ADFLMOO	DAMFOOL
ADFLNOP	PLAFOND
ADFLORU	FOULARD
ADFMNOS	FANDOMS
ADFMOSU	FUMADOS
ADFNNOT	FONDANT
ADFNOST	FANTODS
ADFOOPT	FOOTPAD
ADFORRW	FORWARD
	FROWARD
ADGGGIN	DAGGING
ADGGHNO	HANGDOG
ADGGILN	GADLING
ADGGILR	RIGGALD
ADGGINN	DANGING
ADGGINO	GOADING
ADGGINR	GRADING
	NIGGARD
ADGGINU	GAUDING
ADGHILO	HIDALGO
ADGHINN	HANDING
ADGHINS	DASHING
	SHADING
ADGHINU	HAUDING
ADGHIPR	DIGRAPH
ADGHIRR	ARDRIGH
ADGHNOS	HAGDONS
ADGHNOW	HAGDOWN
ADGHORW	HOGWARD
ADGHRTU	DRAUGHT
ADGIILN	GLIADIN
	LAIDING
ADGIILT	DIGITAL
ADGIIMN	MAIDING
ADGIINN	DAINING
ADGIINO	GONIDIA
ADGIINR	GRADINI
	RAIDING
ADGIINU	IGUANID
ADGIINW	GWINIAD
ADGIIPY	PYGIDIA
ADGILLN	LADLING
ADGILMN	MADLING
ADGILNN	LANDING
ADGILNO	DIGONAL
	LOADING
ADGILNR	DARLING
	LARDING
ADGILNS	LADINGS
	LIGANDS
ADGILNU	LANGUID
	LAUDING
ADGILOR	GOLIARD
ADGILOS	DIALOGS
ADGILSU	GLADIUS
ADGILUY	GAUDILY
ADGIMMN	DAMMING
ADGIMNN	DAMNING
ADGIMNP	DAMPING
ADGIMNR	MRIDANG
ADGINNR	DARNING
	NARDING
	RANDING
ADGINNS	SANDING
ADGINNT	DANTING
ADGINNW	DAWNING
ADGINOR	ADORING
	GRADINO
	ROADING
ADGINOS	GANOIDS
ADGINOT	DOATING
ADGINPP	DAPPING
ADGINPR	DRAPING
ADGINPS	SPADING
ADGINRR	DARRING
ADGINRS	DARINGS
	GRADINS
ADGINRT	DARTING
	TRADING
ADGINRU	DAURING
ADGINRW	DRAWING
	WARDING
ADGINRY	YARDING
ADGINST	DATINGS
ADGINSW	WADINGS
ADGINTU	DAUTING
ADGINTW	DAWTING
ADGINWY	GWYNIAD
ADGIPRU	PAGURID
ADGIRSU	GUISARD
ADGIRZZ	GIZZARD
ADGLLNO	GOLLAND
ADGLMNO	MANGOLD
ADGLNOO	GONDOLA
ADGLNOR	GOLDARN
ADGLNOW	GOWLAND
ADGLNOY	DAYLONG
ADGLNRY	GRANDLY
ADGLOPS	LAPDOGS
ADGMNOO	GOODMAN
ADGMNOR	GORMAND
ADGNOOR	DRAGOON
	GADROON
ADGNORS	DRAGONS
ADGNORU	AGROUND
ADGNRRU	GURNARD
ADGNRSU	DURGANS
ADGNRUU	UNGUARD
ADGORSW	WARDOGS
ADGPRSU	UPDRAGS
ADHHIRS	HARDISH
ADHHIST	HADITHS
ADHHISW	WHIDAHS
ADHHOSU	HOUDAHS
ADHHOSW	HOWDAHS
ADHHSWY	WHYDAHS
ADHIIKS	DASHIKI
ADHIIMS	MAIDISH
ADHIKNS	DANKISH
ADHIKRS	DARKISH
ADHIKSU	HAIDUKS
ADHILMO	HALIDOM
ADHILNY	HANDILY
ADHILOP	HAPLOID
ADHILOS	HALOIDS
ADHILOY	HOLIDAY
	HYALOID
ADHILRY	HARDILY
ADHILSY	LADYISH
	SHADILY
ADHIMPS	DAMPISH
	PHASMID
ADHIMRS	DIRHAMS
ADHINOT	ANTHOID
ADHINPU	DAUPHIN
ADHINSS	SANDHIS
ADHIRSY	HYDRIAS
ADHJKOS	KHODJAS
ADHKORW	DORHAWK
ADHKOSU	SHAKUDO

ADHLLNO HOLLAND
ADHLMOY HOLYDAM
ADHLMPY LYMPHAD
ADHMNOO HOODMAN
MANHOOD
ADHMNSU NUMDAHS
ADHNNSU UNHANDS
ADHNNUY UNHANDY
ADHNORS HADRONS
ADHNORU UNHOARD
ADHNOSU HOUDANS
ADHNOTU HANDOUT
ADHNRSY SHANDRY
ADHNRTY HYDRANT
ADHNRUY UNHARDY
ADHOORR RHODORA
ADHOPRT HARDTOP
ADHOPRU UPHOARD
ADHOSSW SHADOWS
ADHOSWY SHADOWY
ADHPRSU PURDAHS
ADHPSUU UPHAUDS
ADHRRSU DHURRAS
ADIIILR IRIDIAL
ADIIINR IRIDIAN
ADIIKOS AIKIDOS
ADIIKOT DAKOITI
ADIILLS ILLIADS
ADIILMS MILADIS
MISLAID
ADIILNO LIANOID
ADIILNV INVALID
ADIILOS SIALOID
ADIILST DIALIST
ADIILUV DILUVIA
ADIIMMS MAIDISM
ADIIMOS DAIMIOS
ADIIMPV IMPAVID
ADIIMRU MUDIRIA
ADIIMSS MISSAID
ADIINPR PINDARI
PRIDIAN
ADIINST DISTAIN
ADIINSU INDUSIA
SUIDIAN
ADIINSZ DIZAINS
ADIIPRS DIAPIRS
ADIIPXY PYXIDIA
ADIIRST DIARIST
ADIIRTY ARIDITY
ADIITVY AVIDITY
ADIJMSS MASJIDS
ADIJNOS ADJOINS
ADIJNOT ADJOINT
ADIKLNY LADYKIN
ADIKLOS ODALISK
ADIKLPS KLIPDAS
ADIKMNN MANKIND
ADIKMOS MIKADOS
ADIKMSS DISMASK
ADIKNOS DAIKONS
ADIKNPS KIDNAPS
SKIDPAN
ADIKNRS DISRANK
ADIKOST DAKOITS
ADIKPRS DISPARK
ADIKSST DIKASTS
ADIKSTT DIKTATS
ADILLMM MILLDAM
ADILLSY DISALLY
ADILLVY VALIDLY
ADILMNO MONDIAL
ADILMNR MANDRIL
ADILMNU MAUDLIN
ADILMOP DIPLOMA
ADILMOU ALODIUM
ADILMOY AMYLOID
ADILMPS PLASMID
ADILMSS DISMALS
ADILMSU DUALISM
ADILMSY DISMAYL
LADYISM
ADILNNS INLANDS
ADILNOR ORDINAL
ADILNRS ALDRINS
ADILNRU DIURNAL
ADILNSS ISLANDS
ADILNST TINDALS
ADILNSU DUALINS
SUNDIAL
ADILOOV OVOIDAL
ADILOOZ ZOOIDAL
ADILOPR DIPOLAR
ADILORT DILATOR
ADILOTU OUTLAID
ADILOTW WILDOAT
ADILPRY PYRALID
RAPIDLY
ADILPST PLASTID
ADILPSY DISPLAY
ADILPTU PLAUDIT
ADILPVY VAPIDLY
ADILQSU SQUALID
ADILRSZ LIZARDS
ADILRTY TARDILY
ADILSTU DUALIST
ADILSTY STAIDLY
ADILTUY DUALITY
ADIMNNO MONDAIN
ADIMNOS DAIMONS
DOMAINS
ADIMNRS MANDIRS
ADIMNSS DISMANS
ADIMNST MANTIDS
ADIMOOS ISODOMA
ADIMORR MIRADOR
ADIMOST DIATOMS
MASTOID
ADIMOTT MATTOID
ADIMPRY PYRAMID
ADIMQSU QUIDAMS
ADIMRSS DISARMS
ADIMRSU RADIUMS
ADIMRSW MISDRAW
ADIMRSY MYRIADS
ADIMSSS SADISMS
ADIMSST DISMAST
ADIMSSY DISMAYS
ADIMSTU DUMAIST
STADIUM
ADIMSWY MIDWAYS
ADINNOP DIPNOAN
ADINNOR ANDIRON
ADINNRS INNARDS
ADINNRW INDRAWN
ADINNRY INNYARD
ADINNSU INDUNAS
ADINOOP POINADO
ADINOPP OPPIDAN
ADINOPR PADRONI
PONIARD
ADINOPT PINTADO
ADINORR ORDINAR
ADINORS INROADS
ORDAINS
ADINORV VIRANDO
ADINOSX DIAXONS
DIOXANS
ADINOTX OXIDANT
ADINPST PANDITS
ADINRRT TRIDARN
ADINRST INDARTS
ADINRSU DURIANS
SUNDARI
ADINRSW INWARDS
ADINRTU TRIDUAN
ADINSTT DISTANT
ADINSTU UNSTAID
ADINTTY DITTANY
ADIOPRS SPAROID
ADIOPRT PAROTID
ADIOPRV PRIVADO
ADIORST ASTROID
ADIORSU SAUROID
ADIORSV ADVISOR
ADIORTU AUDITOR
ADIOSVW DISAVOW
ADIPRSS SPARIDS
ADIPRST DISPART
ADIRRSS SIRDARS
ADIRRSZ RIZARDS
ADIRSSU SARDIUS
ADIRSSW WISARDS
ADIRSTY SATYRID
ADIRSUY DYSURIA
ADIRSVZ VIZARDS
ADIRSWZ WIZARDS
ADIRSZZ IZZARDS
ADISSST SADISTS
ADISSYY SAYYIDS
ADISTTY DITTAYS
ADJKOSU JUDOKAS
ADJNORS JORDANS
ADJNORU ADJOURN
ADJSSTU ADJUSTS
ADKKLOY KAKODYL
ADKLMRU MUDLARK
ADKOPSU PADOUKS
ADKRSWY SKYWARD
ADLLMOW WADMOLL
ADLLMOY MODALLY
ADLLNOW LOWLAND
ADLLOPR POLLARD
ADLLOPS DALLOPS
ADLLORS DOLLARS
ADLMNOS ALMONDS
DOLMANS
ADLMORU MODULAR
ADLMOSW WADMOLS
ADLNNOR NORLAND
ADLNOOR LARDOON
ADLNOPU POUNDAL
ADLNORS LARDONS
ADLNORU NODULAR
ADLNOSS SOLANDS
SOLDANS
ADLNOST DALTONS
ADLNOSU SOULDAN
UNLOADS
ADLNOSX OXLANDS
ADLNOSY SYNODAL
ADLNOTU OUTLAND
ADLNPSU UPLANDS
ADLNRSU LURDANS
ADLNRUY LAUNDRY
ADLOPRU POULARD
ADLORRW WARLORD
ADLORSS DORSALS
ADLORSU SUDORAL
ADLOSSS DOSSALS
ADLPSSU SPAULDS
ADMMNOS MANDOMS
ADMMNSU SUMMAND
ADMNOOR MADRONO
ADMNOOW WOODMAN
ADMNOOZ MADZOON
ADMNOQU QUONDAM
ADMNORS RANDOMS
RODSMAN
ADMNORT DORMANT
MORDANT
ADMNOSS DAMSONS
ADMNOSU OSMUNDA
ADMNOSY DYNAMOS
ADMNSTU DUSTMAN
ADMOORT DOORMAT
ADMOPPU POPADUM
ADMORRS RAMRODS
ADMORST STARDOM
TSARDOM
ADMORTW MADWORT
ADMRSTU DURMAST
MUSTARD
ADNNOOS NANDOOS
ADNNOOY NOONDAY
ADNNORS RANDONS
ADNNORT DONNART
ADNNOST DANTONS
DONNATS
ADNNOTU DAUNTON
ADNNRUW UNDRAWN
ADNOOPR PANDOOR
ADNOORS NARDOOS
ADNOORT DONATOR
ODORANT
TORNADO
ADNOOSW WANDOOS
ADNOPRS PARDONS
ADNOPRU PANDOUR
ADNOPRV PROVAND
ADNOPST DOPANTS
ADNORRW NORWARD
ADNORSW ONWARDS
ADNORTU ROTUNDA
ADNORWY NAYWORD
ADNOSTT DOTANTS
ADNOSTU ASTOUND
ADNPRUW UPDRAWN
ADNPSTU UPSTAND
ADNRSST STRANDS
ADNRSSU SUNDRAS
ADNRSTU DRAUNTS
DURANTS
TUNDRAS
ADNRSUW SUNWARD
UNDRAWS
ADNSSTY DYNASTS
ADNSTYY DYNASTY
ADOOPSU APODOUS
ADOOPSW SAPWOOD

ADOORWY	DOORWAY	AEEGILW	WEIGELA	AEEGRRT	GREATER
ADOOSUV	VAUDOOS	AEEGINP	EPIGEAN		REGRATE
ADOPRRW	WARDROP	AEEGINR	REGINAE	AEEGRRW	WAGERER
ADORRSU	ARDOURS	AEEGIPR	PIERAGE	AEEGRSS	GREASES
ADORSTW	TOWARDS	AEEGISS	AEGISES	AEEGRST	ERGATES
ADORSUU	ARDUOUS		ASSIEGE		RESTAGE
ADORSWY	AYWORDS	AEEGJRS	JAEGERS	AEEGRSV	GREAVES
ADORTUW	OUTWARD	AEEGLLR	ALLEGER	AEEGRTU	TREAGUE
ADOUUVX	VAUDOUX	AEEGLLS	ALLEGES	AEEGRUZ	GUEREZA
ADPRSUW	UPDRAWS	AEEGLLZ	GAZELLE	AEEGSSW	SEWAGES
	UPWARDS	AEEGLMN	GLEEMAN	AEEGSTT	GESTATE
ADRSSUW	USWARDS		MELANGE		TAGETES
ADSSTUW	SAWDUST	AEEGLNR	ENLARGE	AEEGTTZ	GAZETTE
AEEEFLR	EELFARE		GENERAL	AEEHHNT	HEATHEN
AEEEGKL	KEELAGE		GLEANER	AEEHHRT	HEATHER
AEEEGLT	LEGATEE	AEEGLNT	ELEGANT	AEEHHST	SHEATHE
AEEEGNT	TEENAGE	AEEGLNV	EVANGEL	AEEHHSW	HEEHAWS
AEEEGPR	PEERAGE	AEEGLPR	PEREGAL	AEEHIPR	HEAPIER
AEEEGPS	SEEPAGE	AEEGLPS	PELAGES	AEEHIRV	HEAVIER
AEEEGRT	ETAGERE	AEEGLRS	GALERES	AEEHIST	ATHEISE
AEEEILN	ALIENEE		REGALES	AEEHISV	HEAVIES
AEEELRS	RELEASE	AEEGLRU	LEAGUER	AEEHITZ	ATHEIZE
AEEELTV	ELEVATE		REGULAE	AEEHKNR	HEARKEN
AEEFFLL	FELAFEL	AEEGLRY	EAGERLY	AEEHKNT	THANKEE
AEEFFNS	NEAFFES	AEEGLSS	AGELESS	AEEHKRU	HEUREKA
AEEFFRS	AFFEERS		ALGESES	AEEHLNT	LETHEAN
AEEFGNT	FANTEEG	AEEGLST	EAGLETS	AEEHLRS	HEALERS
AEEFGRS	SERFAGE		LEGATES	AEEHLRT	LEATHER
AEEFGSU	FEAGUES		TEAGLES	AEEHLRV	HAVEREL
AEEFGTW	WEFTAGE		TELEGAS	AEEHLSS	LEASHES
AEEFHRT	FEATHER	AEEGLSU	LEAGUES	AEEHLST	LATHEES
	TEREFAH	AEEGLSV	GLEAVES	AEEHLSW	AWHEELS
AEEFILR	LEAFIER		SELVAGE	AEEHLSX	EXHALES
AEEFILW	ALEWIFE	AEEGLTU	TEGULAE	AEEHLSY	EYELASH
AEEFIRS	AREFIES	AEEGLTV	VEGETAL	AEEHLTT	ATHLETE
	FAERIES	AEEGMMT	GEMMATE	AEEHMNT	METHANE
	FREESIA		TAGMEME	AEEHMRS	HAREEMS
AEEFLLT	FELLATE	AEEGMNR	GERMANE		MAHSEER
	LEAFLET	AEEGMNS	MANEGES	AEEHMRT	ERATHEM
AEEFLMS	FEMALES		MENAGES		THERMAE
AEEFLRT	REFLATE	AEEGMRR	MEAGRER	AEEHMST	MEATHES
AEEFLRW	WELFARE	AEEGMRS	MEAGRES	AEEHMSU	HEAUMES
AEEFLRY	LEAFERY	AEEGMRU	REMUAGE	AEEHNPT	HEPTANE
AEEFLRZ	ALFEREZ	AEEGMSS	MEGASSE		PHENATE
AEEFLSU	EASEFUL		MESSAGE	AEEHNRS	ARSHEEN
AEEFMNR	ENFRAME	AEEGMST	GAMETES	AEEHNRT	EARTHEN
	FREEMAN		METAGES		HEARTEN
AEEFMRR	REFRAME	AEEGNNP	PANGENE	AEEHNST	ETHANES
AEEFOTV	FOVEATE	AEEGNNR	ENRANGE	AEEHNSV	HEAVENS
AEEFPPR	FRAPPEE	AEEGNOP	PEONAGE	AEEHNSX	HEXANES
AEEFRRT	FERRATE	AEEGNPP	GENAPPE	AEEHNTW	WHEATEN
AEEFRST	AFREETS	AEEGNRS	ENRAGES	AEEHPRS	RESHAPE
	FEASTER	AEEGNRT	GRANTEE		SPHAERE
AEEFRTU	FEATURE		GREATEN		SPHEARE
AEEFRWY	FREEWAY		REAGENT	AEEHPRT	PREHEAT
AEEGGLL	ALLEGGE	AEEGNRU	RENAGUE	AEEHPSS	APHESES
AEEGGLR	GREGALE	AEEGNRV	AVENGER		SPAHEES
AEEGGLS	ALEGGES		ENGRAVE	AEEHPUV	UPHEAVE
AEEGGLT	GATELEG	AEEGNSS	SAGENES	AEEHQSU	QUASHEE
AEEGGNR	ENGAGER		SENEGAS	AEEHRRS	HEARERS
AEEGGNS	ENGAGES	AEEGNST	NEGATES		REHEARS
AEEGGOP	EPAGOGE	AEEGNSV	AVENGES		SHEARER
AEEGGRS	AGREGES		GENEVAS	AEEHRSS	HEARSES
	RAGGEES	AEEGNTT	TENTAGE	AEEHRST	AETHERS
	REGGAES	AEEGNTV	VENTAGE		HEATERS
AEEGHNW	WHANGEE	AEEGOPS	APOGEES		REHEATS
AEEGILL	GALILEE	AEEGOST	GOATEES	AEEHRSV	HEAVERS
AEEGILM	MILEAGE	AEEGPRS	ASPERGE	AEEHRSW	WHEREAS
AEEGILN	LINEAGE		PRESAGE	AEEHRTT	THEATER
AEEGILP	EPIGEAL	AEEGRRS	GREASER		THEATRE

	THEREAT	AEEILRR	EARLIER
AEEHRTV	THREAVE		LEARIER
AEEHRTW	WEATHER	AEEILRS	REALISE
	WHEREAT	AEEILRT	ATELIER
	WREATHE		REALTIE
AEEHSST	HEASTES	AEEILRV	LEAVIER
AEEHSSV	SHEAVES		VEALIER
AEEHSTV	THEAVES	AEEILRZ	REALIZE
AEEIIRS	AIERIES	AEEILTT	AILETTE
AEEIKLR	LEAKIER	AEEILTV	ELATIVE
AEEIKPR	PEAKIER	AEEIMNR	REMANIE
AEEILLR	REALLIE	AEEIMNS	MEANIES
AEEILMR	MEALIER		NEMESIA
AEEILMS	MEALIES	AEEIMNT	MATINEE
AEEILNP	ALEPINE	AEEIMNX	EXAMINE
AEEILNT	LINEATE	AEEIMPR	EMPAIRE
AEEILPT	EPILATE	AEEIMRR	REAMIER
	PILEATE	AEEIMRS	SEAMIER
			SERIEMA
		AEEIMRT	EMIRATE
			MEATIER
		AEEIMSS	MISEASE
			SIAMESE
		AEEIMST	STEAMIE
		AEEIMSZ	SIAMEZE
		AEEIMTT	TEATIME
		AEEINRT	RETINAE
			TRAINEE
		AEEINST	ETESIAN
		AEEINTV	NAIVETE
		AEEINVW	INWEAVE
		AEEIORT	ETAERIO
		AEEIPRR	PEREIRA
		AEEIPRS	APERIES
			EPEIRAS
		AEEIPRT	PEATIER
		AEEIPSV	PEAVIES
		AEEIPTX	EXPIATE
		AEEIRRR	ARRIERE
		AEEIRRS	REARISE
		AEEIRRT	TEARIER
		AEEIRRW	WEARIER
		AEEIRST	AERIEST
			SERIATE
		AEEIRSW	WEARIES
		AEEIRTT	ARIETTE
			ITERATE
		AEEIRTV	EVIRATE
		AEEISST	EASIEST
		AEEISVV	EVASIVE
		AEEITTV	AVIETTE
			EVITATE

ANAGRAMS: 7-Letter Words

```
AEEITUX EUTEXIA        AEELNSW WEANELS        AEEMNSS ENSEAMS        AEEOSUU EUOUAES
AEEIUVX EXUVIAE        AEELNTY ENTAYLE        AEEMNST ENTAMES        AEEOSVV EVOVAES
AEEJKSS JAKESES        AEELOPR PAROLEE                MEANEST        AEEPPRR PAPERER
AEEJMSS JAMESES        AEELORS AREOLES        AEEMNSX EXAMENS                PREPARE
AEEJNST SEJEANT        AEELORU AUREOLE        AEEMORT EROTEMA                REPAPER
AEEJNTU JAUNTEE        AEELOST OLEATES        AEEMOSW AWESOME        AEEPPRS RAPPEES
AEEJRSV EVEJARS        AEELOSW LEASOWE                WAESOME        AEEPRRS REAPERS
AEEKLLT LAKELET        AEELPRR PEARLER        AEEMPRS AMPERES        AEEPRRT TAPERER
AEEKLMN KEELMAN        AEELPRS LEAPERS                EMPARES        AEEPRSS ASPERSE
AEEKLNS ALKENES                PLEASER        AEEMPRT TEMPERA                PARESES
AEEKLNT KANTELE                RELAPSE        AEEMPRY EMPAYRE                PRAESES
AEEKLPS PALKEES                REPEALS        AEEMPSW WAMPEES                PREASES
AEEKLRS LEAKERS        AEELPRT PRELATE        AEEMPTU AMPUTEE                PREASSE
AEEKLSV VAKEELS        AEELPRU PLEURAE        AEEMQRU MARQUEE                SERAPES
AEEKMNS KAMSEEN        AEELPSS ELAPSES        AEEMRRS REAMERS        AEEPRST REPEATS
AEEKMNW WAKEMEN                PLEASES        AEEMRSS SEAMERS        AEEPRSZ SPREAZE
AEEKMRS REMAKES                SAPELES        AEEMRST STEAMER        AEEPRTU EPURATE
AEEKMRT MEERKAT        AEELPSU EPAULES                TEAMERS        AEEPRTY PEATERY
AEEKNNN NANKEEN        AEELPTT PALETTE        AEEMRSU MEASURE        AEEPRTZ TRAPEZE
AEEKNRS SNEAKER                PELTATE        AEEMRTY METAYER        AEEPSSS ASEPSES
AEEKNRT RETAKEN        AEELPTU EPAULET        AEEMSSS SESAMES        AEEPSST PESETAS
AEEKNRW WAKENER        AEELQSU QUELEAS        AEENNOT NEONATE        AEEPSSW PESEWAS
AEEKNSW WEAKENS                SEQUELA        AEENNPT PENNATE        AEEPSTT SEPTATE
AEEKORW REAWOKE        AEELRRT ALERTER                PENTANE                SPATTEE
AEEKPRS PARKEES                RELATER        AEENNRS ENSNARE        AEEPSVY PEAVEYS
        RESPEAK        AEELRSS ARLESES        AEENNRX REANNEX        AEEQRSU QUAERES
        SPEAKER                EARLESS        AEENNST NEATENS        AEEQSTU EQUATES
AEEKPRT PERTAKE                LEASERS        AEENNSX ANNEXES        AEERRRS REARERS
AEEKRRT RETAKER                RESALES        AEENNTU UNEATEN        AEERRSS ERASERS
AEEKRRW WREAKER                RESEALS        AEENOPR PERAEON        AEERRST SERRATE
AEEKRST RETAKES                SEALERS        AEENOSS ANOESES                TEARERS
        SAKERET        AEELRST ELATERS        AEENPST PENATES        AEERRSU ERASURE
AEEKRSU EUREKAS                REALEST                PESANTE        AEERRSV REAVERS
AEEKRSW WREAKES                RELATES        AEENPSW PAWNEES        AEERRSW SWEARER
AEEKSSS ASKESES                STEALER        AEENPSX EXPANSE                WEARERS
AEEKSTW WEAKEST        AEELRSU LEASURE        AEENRRS EARNERS        AEERRTT RETRATE
AEELLLS ALLELES        AEELRSV LAVEERS        AEENRRT TERRANE                RETREAT
AEELLMS MALLEES                REVEALS        AEENRRV RAVENER                TREATER
AEELLOV ALVEOLE                SEVERAL        AEENRSS ENSEARS        AEERRTW WATERER
AEELLPR PARELLE        AEELRSX RELAXES        AEENRST EARNEST        AEERRVW WAVERER
AEELLSS SALLEES        AEELRSY SEALERY                EASTERN        AEERSST RESEATS
AEELMNP EMPANEL        AEELRUV REVALUE                NEAREST                SAETERS
        EMPLANE        AEELSST ALTESSE        AEENRSW WEANERS                SEAREST
AEELMNR REELMAN                STEALES        AEENRTT ENTREAT                SEATERS
AEELMNS ENAMELS                TEASELS                RATTEEN                STEARES
AEELMNT MANTEEL        AEELSSV SLEAVES                TERNATE                TEASERS
AEELMNV VELAMEN        AEELSSW AWELESS        AEENRTV AVENTRE                TESSERA
AEELMNY AMYLENE                WEASELS                NERVATE        AEERSSU RESEAUS
AEELMPS EMPALES        AEELSSZ SLEAZES                VETERAN                SEASURE
AEELMPX EXAMPLE        AEELSTU ELUATES        AEENRUV UNREAVE        AEERSSV ASSEVER
        EXEMPLA                SETUALE        AEENSST ENTASES        AEERSSY ESSAYER
AEELMRS MEALERS        AEELSTV SALVETE                SATEENS        AEERSTT ESTREAT
AEELMRT LAMETER                VALETES                SENATES                RESTATE
AEELMSS MEASLES                VELETAS                STEANES        AEERSTU AUSTERE
AEELMSU AEMULES        AEELSTX LATEXES        AEENSSU UNEASES        AEERSTW SWEATER
AEELMSZ MEAZELS        AEELSTY EYALETS        AEENSSV AVENSES        AEERSUV VAREUSE
AEELMTU EMULATE        AEELSTZ TEAZELS        AEENSSW WAENESS        AEERSUX RESEAUX
AEELNNR LERNEAN                TEAZLES        AEENSTT NEATEST        AEERSVW WEAVERS
AEELNPS ALPEENS        AEELSWY LEEWAYS        AEENSUV AVENUES        AEERTTX EXTREAT
        SPELEAN        AEELTTY LAYETTE        AEENSWZ WEAZENS        AEESSSW SEESAWS
AEELNRR LEARNER        AEELTVW WAVELET        AEENTTV NAVETTE        AEESSTT ESTATES
AEELNRT ALTERNE        AEEMMMS MAMMEES        AEENUVW UNWEAVE        AEESSTX TEXASES
        ENTERAL        AEEMMPY EMPYEMA        AEEOPRT OPERATE        AEESSUX AUXESES
        ETERNAL        AEEMMRT AMMETER        AEEORRS REAROSE        AEESTTT TESTATE
AEELNRW RENEWAL                METAMER        AEEORST ROSEATE        AEFFFLR FLAFFER
AEELNSS ENSEALS        AEEMNNO ANEMONE        AEEORSV OVERSEA        AEFFGIR GIRAFFE
AEELNST ELANETS        AEEMNPS SPAEMEN        AEEORTV OVERATE        AEFFGNR ENGRAFF
        LEANEST        AEEMNPT PEATMEN                OVEREAT        AEFFGRS GAFFERS
AEELNSV ENSLAVE        AEEMNRS RENAMES        AEEORVW OVERAWE        AEFFHST HAFFETS
        LEAVENS        AEEMNRT REMANET                               AEFFINS AFFINES
```

AEFFIPR	PIAFFER
AEFFIPS	PIAFFES
AEFFIST	TAFFIES
AEFFISX	AFFIXES
AEFFKOP	OFFPEAK
AEFFKOT	OFFTAKE
AEFFLLY	FLYLEAF
AEFFLMW	FLAMFEW
AEFFLNS	SNAFFLE
AEFFLRR	RAFFLER
AEFFLRS	RAFFLES
AEFFLRU	FEARFUL
AEFFLSW	WAFFLES
AEFFLSY	YAFFLES
AEFFLTU	FATEFUL
AEFFQRU	QUAFFER
AEFFRST	AFFRETS
	RESTAFF
	STAFFER
AEFFRSY	EFFRAYS
AEFFRSZ	ZAFFERS
	ZAFFRES
AEFFTTY	TAFFETY
AEFGGGO	FOGGAGE
AEFGGMO	MEGAFOG
AEFGGRY	FAGGERY
AEFGILN	FEALING
	FINAGLE
	LEAFING
AEFGILO	FOLIAGE
AEFGILR	FRAGILE
AEFGINR	FEARING
AEFGINT	FEATING
AEFGIRT	FRIGATE
AEFGIRU	REFUGIA
AEFGITU	FATIGUE
AEFGLLU	FULLAGE
AEFGLNS	FANGLES
	FLANGES
AEFGLOT	FLOTAGE
AEFGLOW	FLOWAGE
AEFGLRS	REFLAGS
AEFGLRU	RAGEFUL
AEFGLUZ	GAZEFUL
AEFGMSU	FUMAGES
AEFGNRR	GRANFER
AEFGNRT	ENGRAFT
AEFGOOT	FOOTAGE
AEFGORR	FORAGER
AEFGORS	FORAGES
AEFGORV	FORGAVE
AEFGRRT	GRAFTER
AEFGRSU	GAUFERS
	GAUFRES
AEFHLLS	FELLAHS
AEFHLOR	FAHLORE
AEFHLRS	FLASHER
AEFHLRT	FARTHEL
AEFHLRZ	FAHLERZ
AEFHLSS	FLASHES
AEFHLTU	HATEFUL
AEFHRRT	FARTHER
AEFHRST	FATHERS
	SHAFTER
AEFHRSY	FASHERY
AEFIILT	FILIATE
AEFIIRS	FAIRIES
AEFIJLO	JEOFAIL
AEFIKLR	FLAKIER
AEFILLS	FAILLES
AEFILMN	FEMINAL
	INFLAME
AEFILMR	FLAMIER
AEFILNS	FINALES
AEFILNT	INFLATE
AEFILNU	INFULAE
AEFILNV	FLAVINE
AEFILOT	FOLIATE
AEFILRR	FLARIER
	FRAILER
AEFILRU	FAILURE
AEFILRV	FAVRILE
AEFILRW	FLAWIER
AEFILRX	FLAXIER
AEFILRZ	FILAZER
AEFILSS	FALSIES
	FILASSE
AEFIMNR	FIREMAN
AEFIMNS	FAMINES
	INFAMES
AEFIMOR	FOAMIER
AEFIMRR	FIREARM
AEFIMRS	MISFARE
AEFINNS	FANNIES
AEFINNT	INFANTE
AEFINNZ	FANZINE
AEFINPR	FIREPAN
AEFINRR	REFRAIN
AEFINRS	INFARES
AEFINRT	FAINTER
	FENITAR
AEFINRX	XERAFIN
AEFINST	FAINEST
	NAIFEST
AEFINTX	ANTEFIX
AEFIQRU	AQUIFER
AEFIRRR	FARRIER
AEFIRSS	FRAISES
AEFIRST	FAIREST
AEFIRTT	FATTIER
AEFISST	FIESTAS
AEFISTT	FATTIES
AEFISTX	FIXATES
AEFKLNR	FLANKER
AEFKLNS	FANKLES
AEFKLST	FLASKET
AEFKLUW	WAKEFUL
AEFKNRR	FRANKER
AEFKORS	FORSAKE
AEFLLNN	FANNELL
	FLANNEL
AEFLLOT	FLOATEL
AEFLLSY	FALSELY
AEFLLTT	FLATLET
AEFLLTU	TALEFUL
AEFLLUZ	ZEALFUL
AEFLMNS	FLAMENS
AEFLMOR	FEMORAL
AEFLMUW	WAMEFUL
AEFLMUZ	MAZEFUL
AEFLNNN	FLANNEN
AEFLNNS	FANNELS
AEFLNOV	FLAVONE
AEFLNRS	SALFERN
AEFLNRU	FLANEUR
	FUNERAL
AEFLNSU	FLAUNES
AEFLNTT	FLATTEN
AEFLOOV	FOVEOLA
AEFLORS	LOAFERS
	SAFROLE
AEFLORT	FLOATER
	FLOREAT
	REFLOAT
AEFLORY	FORELAY
AEFLPPR	FLAPPER
AEFLPRS	FELSPAR
AEFLPRY	PALFREY
AEFLRSS	FALSERS
	FLASERS
AEFLRST	FALTERS
AEFLRSU	EARFULS
	FERULAS
	REFUSAL
AEFLRSY	FLAYERS
AEFLRTT	FLATTER
AEFLRTU	REFUTAL
	TEARFUL
AEFLRZZ	FRAZZLE
AEFLSST	FALSEST
	FESTALS
AEFLSTU	FLUATES
	SULFATE
AEFMNOR	FORAMEN
	FOREMAN
AEFMNRT	RAFTMEN
AEFMNRU	FRAENUM
AEFMORR	FOREARM
AEFMORT	FORMATE
AEFMRRS	FARMERS
	FRAMERS
AEFMRRY	FARMERY
AEFNNRS	FANNERS
AEFNNST	ENFANTS
AEFNOPR	PROFANE
AEFNORR	FORERAN
AEFNRRS	FARRENS
AEFNRSS	FARNESS
AEFNRSU	FURANES
	UNSAFER
AEFNRSW	FAWNERS
AEFNSST	FASTENS
	FATNESS
AEFNSTT	FATTENS
AEFOPRW	FOREPAW
AEFORRV	OVERFAR
AEFORRY	FORAYER
AEFORSW	FORESAW
AEFORSY	FORESAY
AEFOSST	FATSOES
AEFOSTU	FEATOUS
AEFRRST	FRATERS
	RAFTERS
AEFRRTY	FRATERY
AEFRSSS	FRASSES
AEFRSST	FASTERS
	STRAFES
AEFRSTW	FRETSAW
	WAFTERS
AEFRTUW	WAFTURE
AEFSSTT	FASTEST
AEFSSUV	FAVUSES
AEFSTTT	FATTEST
AEGGGLS	GAGGLES
AEGGGLU	LUGGAGE
AEGGGRS	GAGGERS
AEGGHLR	HAGGLER
AEGGHLS	HAGGLES
AEGGIJR	JAGGIER
AEGGILN	GEALING
	LIGNAGE
AEGGINR	GEARING
	NAGGIER
AEGGINS	AGEINGS
AEGGIOS	ISAGOGE
AEGGIRR	RAGGIER
AEGGIRS	RAGGIES
	SAGGIER
AEGGIRU	GARIGUE
AEGGISW	SWAGGIE
AEGGJRS	JAGGERS
AEGGJRY	JAGGERY
AEGGLNO	AGELONG
AEGGLNR	GANGREL
AEGGLNS	LAGGENS
AEGGLRS	GARGLES
	LAGGERS
	RAGGLES
AEGGLSW	WAGGLES
AEGGMNY	YEGGMAN
AEGGMSS	EGGMASS
AEGGNNU	GUNNAGE
AEGGNRR	GRANGER
AEGGNRS	GANGERS
	GRANGES
	NAGGERS
AEGGNSU	GANGUES
AEGGRRY	RAGGERY
AEGGRSS	AGGRESS
	SAGGERS
	SEGGARS
AEGGRST	GAGSTER
	GARGETS
	STAGGER
	TAGGERS
AEGGRSU	GAUGERS
AEGGRSW	SWAGGER
AEGGRSY	YAGGERS
AEGGRWY	WAGGERY
AEGGSWW	GEWGAWS
AEGHHIT	AHEIGHT
AEGHIJR	JAGHIRE
AEGHILN	HEALING
AEGHILR	LAIGHER
AEGHINP	HEAPING
AEGHINR	HEARING
AEGHINT	GAHNITE
	HEATING
AEGHINV	HEAVING
AEGHINZ	GENIZAH
AEGHIRS	HEGIRAS
AEGHISS	GEISHAS
AEGHLNO	HALOGEN
AEGHLNT	ALENGTH
AEGHLRU	LAUGHER
AEGHLSS	SEALGHS
AEGHLST	HAGLETS
AEGHLSZ	GHAZELS
AEGHLTW	THALWEG
AEGHMNN	HANGMEN
AEGHMOR	HOMAGER
AEGHMOS	HOMAGES
AEGHMSU	MESHUGA
AEGHNOX	HEXAGON
AEGHNRS	GNASHER
	HANGERS
AEGHNRU	NURAGHE
AEGHNSS	GNASHES
AEGHNST	STENGAH
AEGHOPY	HYPOGEA

AEGHORS	GHERAOS		MEANING
AEGHOST	HOSTAGE	AEGIMNP	PIGMEAN
AEGHPRS	SPREAGH	AEGIMNR	GERMAIN
AEGHPST	HATPEGS		MANGIER
AEGHRST	GATHERS		REAMING
AEGIIMN	IMAGINE	AEGIMNS	ENIGMAS
AEGIKLN	LEAKING		GAMINES
	LINKAGE		MEASING
AEGIKLT	GLAIKET		SEAMING
AEGIKNP	PEAKING	AEGIMNT	MINTAGE
AEGIKNR	REAKING		TEAMING
AEGIKNS	SINKAGE		TEGMINA
AEGIKPP	KIPPAGE	AEGIMOS	IMAGOES
AEGIKPR	GARPIKE	AEGIMPR	EPIGRAM
AEGIKRW	GAWKIER		PRIMAGE
AEGIKSW	GAWKIES	AEGIMPS	MAGPIES
AEGILLL	ILLEGAL	AEGIMPT	PIGMEAT
AEGILLN	NIGELLA	AEGIMRR	ARMIGER
AEGILLP	PILLAGE	AEGIMRS	GISARME
AEGILLS	GALLIES		MAIGRES
	GALLISE		MIRAGES
AEGILLT	TILLAGE	AEGIMRT	MIGRATE
AEGILLU	LIGULAE		RAGTIME
AEGILLV	VILLAGE	AEGIMRU	GAUMIER
AEGILLY	AGILELY	AEGIMRY	IMAGERY
AEGILLZ	GALLIZE	AEGIMSS	AGEISMS
AEGILMN	LEAMING	AEGIMST	GAMIEST
	MEALING		SIGMATE
AEGILMR	GREMIAL	AEGIMSV	MISGAVE
	LAMIGER	AEGINNP	NEAPING
AEGILMS	MILAGES		PEANING
AEGILNN	ANELING	AEGINNR	AGINNER
	EANLING		EARNING
	LEANING		ENGRAIN
	NEALING		GRANNIE
AEGILNP	LEAPING		NEARING
	PEALING	AEGINNS	SEANING
	PLEAING	AEGINNT	ANTEING
AEGILNR	ENGRAIL		ANTIGEN
	LEARING		GENTIAN
	NARGILE	AEGINNU	ANGUINE
	REALIGN		GUANINE
	REGINAL	AEGINNW	WEANING
AEGILNS	LEASING	AEGINNY	YEANING
	LINAGES	AEGINOR	ORIGANE
	SEALING	AEGINOS	AGONIES
AEGILNT	ATINGLE		AGONISE
	ELATING	AEGINOZ	AGONIZE
	GELATIN	AEGINPP	GENIPAP
	GENITAL	AEGINPR	REAPING
AEGILNU	LINGUAE	AEGINPS	PEASING
AEGILNV	LEAVING		SPAEING
AEGILNY	ALEYING		SPINAGE
AEGILOS	GOALIES	AEGINPZ	PEAZING
AEGILOU	EULOGIA	AEGINRR	ANGRIER
AEGILPS	PAIGLES		EARRING
AEGILRR	GLARIER		GRAINER
AEGILRS	GRAILES		RANGIER
AEGILRZ	GLAZIER		REARING
AEGILSS	ALGESIS	AEGINRS	ANGRIES
	SILAGES		EARINGS
AEGILST	AGILEST		ERASING
	AIGLETS		GAINERS
	LIGATES		GRAINES
	TAIGLES		REGAINS
AEGILSV	GLAIVES		REGINAS
AEGILTU	GLUTAEI		SEARING
AEGILTY	EGALITY		SERINGA
AEGIMMR	GAMMIER	AEGINRT	GRANITE
AEGIMNN	AMENING		INGRATE

	TANGIER	AEGLLOT	TOLLAGE
	TEARING	AEGLLRY	ALLERGY
AEGINRV	REAVING		GALLERY
	VINEGAR		LARGELY
AEGINRW	WEARING		REGALLY
AEGINSS	AGNISES	AEGLLST	GALLETS
	SEASING	AEGLLSU	SEAGULL
AEGINST	EASTING		SULLAGE
	EATINGS		ULLAGES
	GAINEST	AEGLLSY	GALLEYS
	GENISTA	AEGLLTU	GLUTEAL
	INGATES	AEGLMNR	MANGLER
	INGESTA	AEGLMNS	MANGELS
	SEATING		MANGLES
	TANGIES	AEGLMOR	GOMERAL
	TEASING	AEGLMOU	MOULAGE
	TSIGANE	AEGLMPU	PLUMAGE
AEGINSU	GUINEAS	AEGLMRS	MALGRES
AEGINSZ	AGNIZES	AEGLMRU	MAULGRE
	SEAZING	AEGLMSY	MYGALES
AEGINTV	VINTAGE	AEGLNOS	ENGAOLS
AEGINTZ	TEAZING	AEGLNOT	TANGELO
AEGINVW	WEAVING	AEGLNPR	GRAPNEL
AEGIORT	GOATIER	AEGLNPS	SPANGLE
AEGIPPR	GAPPIER	AEGLNRS	ANGLERS
AEGIPPS	PIPAGES		LARGENS
AEGIPRR	GRAPIER	AEGLNRT	TANGLER
AEGIPRS	GASPIER		TRANGLE
	PRISAGE	AEGLNRU	GRANULE
	SPAIRGE	AEGLNRW	WANGLER
AEGIRRZ	GRAZIER		WRANGLE
AEGIRSS	AGRISES	AEGLNRY	ANGERLY
	GASSIER	AEGLNSS	GLASSEN
AEGIRST	AGISTER	AEGLNST	LANGEST
	GAITERS		TANGLES
	STAGIER	AEGLNSU	ANGELUS
	STRIGAE		LAGUNES
	TRIAGES		LANGUES
AEGIRSV	GARVIES	AEGLNSW	WANGLES
	GRAVIES	AEGLNSY	LYNAGES
	RIVAGES	AEGLNTT	GANTLET
AEGIRSW	EARWIGS	AEGLNTU	LANGUET
	GAWSIER	AEGLNTW	TWANGLE
AEGIRSZ	AGRIZES	AEGLNUU	UNGULAE
AEGIRTV	VIRGATE	AEGLNUW	GUNWALE
	VITRAGE	AEGLOPR	PERGOLA
AEGIRUZ	GAUZIER	AEGLORS	GAOLERS
AEGISST	AGEISTS	AEGLORT	LEGATOR
	SAGIEST	AEGLOSS	GLOSSAE
AEGISSU	AGUISES	AEGLOST	LEGATOS
AEGISSV	VISAGES	AEGLOSU	GEALOUS
AEGISTU	AUGITES	AEGLOSV	LOVAGES
AEGISTY	GASEITY	AEGLOTV	VOLTAGE
AEGISTZ	GAZIEST	AEGLPPR	GRAPPLE
AEGISUZ	AGUIZES	AEGLPRS	GRAPLES
AEGISYZ	AZYGIES	AEGLPRU	EARPLUG
AEGJLNR	JANGLER		GRAUPEL
AEGJLNS	JANGLES	AEGLPSU	PLAGUES
AEGKKNO	ANGEKOK		PLUSAGE
AEGKLOU	KAGOULE	AEGLPUY	PLAGUEY
AEGKLRS	GRAKLES	AEGLRRU	REGULAR
AEGKMRY	KERYGMA	AEGLRSS	LARGESS
AEGKRSW	GAWKERS	AEGLRST	LARGEST
AEGKSST	GASKETS	AEGLRSV	GRAVELS
AEGLLLY	LEGALLY		VERGLAS
AEGLLNO	ALLONGE	AEGLRSY	ARGYLES
	GALLEON		GRAYLES
AEGLLNR	LANGREL	AEGLRSZ	GLAZERS
AEGLLNS	LEGLANS	AEGLRTU	GAULTER
AEGLLOR	ALLEGRO		TEGULAR

	TRAGULE	AEGNRTU GAUNTER	AEHHRST HEARTHS
AEGLRTY	GREATLY	AEGNSSY GAYNESS	AEHHSSS SHASHES
AEGLRVY	GRAVELY	AEGNSTT GESTANT	AEHHSST SHEATHS
AEGLSSS	GLASSES	AEGNTTU TUTENAG	AEHHSTY SHEATHY
AEGLSSU	SAULGES	AEGOORT ROOTAGE	AEHIILR HAILIER
AEGLSTT	GESTALT	AEGOPPR PROPAGE	AEHIIRR HAIRIER
AEGLSTW	TALWEGS	AEGOPRT PORTAGE	AEHIJRS HEJIRAS
AEGLTUV	VULGATE	AEGOPST POSTAGE	AEHIKNS HANKIES

TRAGULE
AEGLRTY GREATLY   AEGNRTU GAUNTER   AEHHRST HEARTHS   WEARISH
AEGLRVY GRAVELY   AEGNSSY GAYNESS   AEHHSSS SHASHES   AEHIRTW THAWIER
AEGLSSS GLASSES   AEGNSTT GESTANT   AEHHSST SHEATHS   AEHIRWY HAYWIRE
AEGLSSU SAULGES   AEGNTTU TUTENAG   AEHHSTY SHEATHY   AEHISST ASHIEST
AEGLSTT GESTALT   AEGOORT ROOTAGE   AEHIILR HAILIER   SAITHES
AEGLSTW TALWEGS   AEGOPPR PROPAGE   AEHIIRR HAIRIER   STASHIE
AEGLTUV VULGATE   AEGOPRT PORTAGE   AEHIJRS HEJIRAS   TAISHES
AEGLUUY GUAYULE   AEGOPST POSTAGE   AEHIKNS HANKIES   AEHISSV SHAVIES
AEGLUVY VAGUELY   POTAGES   AEHIKRS SHAKIER   AEHISTT ATHEIST
AEGMMNS MAGSMEN   AEGOPTT POTTAGE   AEHIKSS SAKIEHS   STAITHE
AEGMMRS GAMMERS   AEGORRT GARROTE   AEHIKSW HAWKIES   AEHISTZ HAZIEST
        GRAMMES   AEGORSS SORAGES   AEHIKSY SAKIYEH   AEHISVY YESHIVA
AEGMMRU RUMMAGE   AEGORST ORGEATS   AEHILMN HELIMAN   AEHITTW THWAITE
AEGMMSS SMEGMAS   STORAGE   AEHILMO HEMIOLA   AEHJLOW JAWHOLE
AEGMNNO AGNOMEN   AEGORTT GAROTTE   AEHILNR HERNIAL   AEHKNRS HANKERS
AEGMNOR MEGARON   AEGORTU OUTRAGE   INHALER   HARKENS
AEGMNOS MANGOES   AEGORUV OUVRAGE   AEHILNS INHALES   AEHKNRT THANKER
AEGMNOT MAGNETO   AEGORVY VOYAGER   AEHILNY HYALINE   AEHKOSS SHAKOES
        MEGATON   AEGOSSU GASEOUS   AEHILOR AIRHOLE   AEHKRRS SHARKER
        MONTAGE   AEGOSTU OUTAGES   AEHILRS HAILERS   AEHKRSS SHAKERS
AEGMNPY PYGMEAN   AEGOSTW STOWAGE   SHALIER   AEHKRSW HAWKERS
AEGMNRS ENGRAMS   TOWAGES   AEHILRT LATHIER   AEHKSWY HAWKEYS
        GERMANS   AEGOSTX OXGATES   AEHILRU HAULIER   AEHLLOS HALLOES
        MANGERS   AEGOSVY VOYAGES   AEHILSS SHEILAS   AEHLLOV HELLOVA
AEGMNRT GARMENT   AEGOTTU OUTGATE   AEHILST HALITES   AEHLLRS HERSALL
        MARGENT   AEGOTTV GAVOTTE   AEHILSW WHAISLE   AEHLLUV HELLUVA
        RAGMENT   AEGOTUV OUTGAVE   AEHILTT LITHATE   AEHLLYZ HAZELLY
AEGMNST MAGNETS   AEGPRRS GRASPER   AEHILTY HYALITE   AEHLMNO MANHOLE
AEGMNSW SWAGMEN   SPARGER   AEHILUV VIHUELA   AEHLMNY HYMENAL
AEGMNTU AUGMENT   AEGPRRY GRAPERY   AEHILVY HEAVILY   AEHLMOR ARMHOLE
        MUTAGEN   AEGPRSS GASPERS   AEHILWZ WHAIZLE   AEHLMPS PELHAMS
AEGMOOR MOORAGE   SPARGES   AEHIMMR HAMMIER   AEHLMPW WHAMPLE
AEGMORS ROMAGES   AEGPRST PARGETS   AEHIMNR HARMINE   AEHLMRS HARMELS
AEGMOSY GAYSOME   AEGPRSU GAUPERS   AEHIMNS HAEMINS   AEHLMRT THERMAL
AEGMOXY EXOGAMY   AEGPRSW GAWPERS   HEMINAS   AEHLMRU HUMERAL
AEGMRSU MAUGRES   AEGPSSU PEGASUS   AEHIMNY HYMENIA   AEHLMST HAMLETS
        MURAGES   AEGPSTU UPSTAGE   AEHIMPS PHAEISM   AEHLNOS ENHALOS
AEGMSUY MAGUEYS   AEGPSUZ UPGAZES   AEHIMRS MASHIER   AEHLNOT ETHANOL
AEGMSUZ ZEUGMAS   AEGRRSS GRASSER   MISHEAR   AEHLNRT ENTHRAL
AEGNNOS NONAGES   AEGRRST GARRETS   AEHIMST ATHEISM   AEHLNSS HANSELS
AEGNNOT TONNAGE   GARTERS   AEHINPR HEPARIN   AEHLNST HANTLES
AEGNNPS PANGENS   GRATERS   AEHINPS INPHASE   AEHLNSU UNHEALS
AEGNNRT REGNANT   AEGRRSU ARGUERS   AEHINPT PENTHIA   UNLEASH
AEGNNRU GUNNERA   AEGRRSV GRAVERS   AEHINRS ARSHINE   UNSHALE
AEGNNST GANNETS   AEGRRSZ GRAZERS   HERNIAS   AEHLORS SHOALER
AEGNNTT TANGENT   AEGRRUU AUGURER   AEHINRT INEARTH   AEHLORT LOATHER
AEGNNTU TUNNAGE   AEGRRUV GRAVURE   AEHINSS HESSIAN   AEHLOSS ASSHOLE
AEGNOOR OREGANO   VERRUGA   AEHINSV EVANISH   AEHLOST LOATHES
AEGNOPT PONTAGE   AEGRSSS GRASSES   VAHINES   AEHLPRS SPHERAL
AEGNORR GROANER   AEGRSST STAGERS   AEHINSW WAHINES   AEHLPSS HAPLESS
        ORANGER   AEGRSSU ARGUSES   AEHIORR HOARIER   PLASHES
AEGNORS ONAGERS   SAUGERS   AEHIPPR HAPPIER   AEHLPST PLASHET
        ORANGES   USAGERS   AEHIPPS HAPPIES   AEHLPSY SHAPELY
AEGNORW WAGONER   AEGRSTT TARGETS   AEHIPPT EPITAPH   AEHLRSS ASHLERS
AEGNOSY NOSEGAY   AEGRSTV GRAVEST   AEHIPRS HARPIES   HALSERS
AEGNOWY WAYGONE   AEGRSTY GRAYEST   SHARPIE   LASHERS
AEGNPRS ENGRASP   GYRATES   AEHIPSS APHESIS   SLASHER
AEGNPRT TREPANG   STAGERY   AEHIPSW PEISHWA   AEHLRST HALTERS
AEGNRRS GARNERS   AEGRSYZ AGRYZES   AEHIPTZ ZAPTIEH   HARSLET
        RANGERS   AEGSSSU GAUSSES   AEHIQSU HAIQUES   LATHERS
AEGNRRT GRANTER   AEGSTUU AUGUSTE   QUASHIE   SLATHER
        REGRANT   AEGSTUV VAGUEST   AEHIRRR HARRIER   THALERS
AEGNRSS SERANGS   AEGTTTU GUTTATE   AEHIRRS HARRIES   AEHLRSU HAULERS
AEGNRST ARGENTS   AEHHIRS HASHIER   AEHIRSS ARISHES   AEHLRSV HALVERS
        GARNETS   AEHHIST SHEHITA   SHERIAS   AEHLRSW WHALERS
        STRANGE   AEHHLST HEALTHS   AEHIRST HASTIER   AEHLRTY EARTHLY
AEGNRSU RAUNGES   AEHHLTY HEALTHY   SHERIAT   HARTELY
        UNGEARS   AEHHNRS HARSHEN   AEHIRSV ASHIVER   HEARTLY
AEGNRSW GNAWERS   AEHHPRS RHAPHES   AEHIRSW WASHIER   LATHERY
                         AEHHRRS HARSHER   AEHLRWY WHALERY

AEHLSSS	HASSLES		PHRASER	AEIINTX	AXINITE	AEILLRU	RUELLIA
	SLASHES		SHARPER	AEIIPRR	PRAIRIE	AEILLRW	WALLIER
AEHLSST	HASLETS	AEHPRSS	PHRASES	AEIIRRV	RIVIERA	AEILLSS	ALLISES
	HATLESS		SERAPHS		VAIRIER		SALLIES
AEHLSSY	HAYSELS		SHAPERS	AEIIRST	AIRIEST	AEILLST	TALLIES
AEHLSTT	STEALTH		SPHAERS		IRISATE	AEILLSW	WALLIES
AEHLSTW	WEALTHS		SPHEARS	AEIITTV	VITIATE	AEILLUV	ELUVIAL
AEHLTWY	WEALTHY	AEHPRST	SPARTHE	AEIJLNV	JAVELIN	AEILLVX	VEXILLA
AEHMMNS	MASHMEN		TEPHRAS	AEIJLRS	JAILERS	AEILMMN	MAILMEN
AEHMMRS	HAMMERS		THREAPS	AEIJLSZ	JEZAILS	AEILMMS	LAMMIES
	SHAMMER	AEHPRTY	THERAPY	AEIJMMR	JAMMIER		MELISMA
AEHMMSY	MAYHEMS	AEHPSST	SPATHES	AEIJMMS	JEMIMAS	AEILMNN	LINEMAN
AEHMNOR	MENORAH	AEHPSSW	PESHWAS	AEIJMNS	JASMINE		MELANIN
AEHMNOS	HOSEMAN	AEHPSTY	HYPATES	AEIJNRT	JANTIER	AEILMNO	MINEOLA
AEHMNOT	NATHEMO	AEHQSSU	QUASHES		NARTJIE	AEILMNP	IMPANEL
AEHMNOY	HAEMONY	AEHRRSS	RASHERS	AEIJNST	JANTIES		MANIPLE
AEHMNPY	NYMPHAE		SHARERS	AEIJNTU	JAUNTIE	AEILMNR	MANLIER
AEHMNRU	HUMANER	AEHRRTU	URETHRA	AEIJRSV	JARVIES		MARLINE
AEHMNST	ANTHEMS	AEHRSST	RASHEST	AEIJRZZ	JAZZIER		MINERAL
	HETMANS		SHASTER	AEIKLNO	KAOLINE		RAILMEN
AEHMOPT	APOTHEM		TRASHES	AEIKLNR	LANKIER	AEILMNS	ISLEMAN
AEHMPRS	HAMPERS	AEHRSSV	SHAVERS	AEIKLNU	UNALIKE		MENIALS
AEHMPTY	EMPATHY	AEHRSSW	HAWSERS	AEIKLOT	KEITLOA		SEMINAL
AEHMRSS	MARSHES		SWASHER	AEIKLRR	LARKIER	AEILMNT	AILMENT
	MASHERS		WASHERS	AEIKLRS	SERKALI		ALIMENT
	SHAMERS	AEHRSTT	HATTERS	AEIKLRV	KLAVIER	AEILMOR	LOAMIER
	SMASHER		RATHEST	AEIKLRW	WARLIKE	AEILMPR	IMPEARL
AEHMRST	HAMSTER		SHATTER	AEIKLSS	ALSIKES		LEMPIRA
AEHMRTU	MAUTHER		THREATS	AEIKLST	LAKIEST		PALMIER
AEHMRTW	MAWTHER	AEHRSTV	HARVEST		TALKIES	AEILMPS	IMPALES
AEHMSSS	SMASHES		THRAVES	AEIKMMS	MISMAKE		PALMIES
AEHMSST	SMEATHS	AEHRSTW	THAWERS	AEIKMNP	PIKEMAN	AEILMPT	IMPLATE
AEHMUZZ	MEZUZAH		WREATHS	AEIKMNR	MANKIER		PALMIET
AEHNNTU	UNNEATH	AEHRSVW	WHARVES		RAMEKIN	AEILMRR	LARMIER
AEHNNWY	ANYWHEN	AEHRSWY	WASHERY	AEIKMNS	KINEMAS		MARLIER
AEHNOPT	PHAETON	AEHRSXY	HYRAXES	AEIKMPR	RAMPIKE	AEILMRS	MAILERS
	PHONATE	AEHRTUU	HAUTEUR	AEIKMRW	MAWKIER		REALISM
AEHNOPW	WANHOPE	AEHRTWY	WREATHY	AEIKMSS	KAMISES	AEILMRT	LAMITER
AEHNORS	HOARSEN	AEHSSST	STASHES	AEIKMST	MISTAKE		MALTIER
AEHNORT	ANOTHER	AEHSSSW	SWASHES	AEIKNRR	NARKIER	AEILMSS	AIMLESS
AEHNPPS	HAPPENS	AEHSSTW	SWATHES	AEIKNRS	SNAKIER		MESAILS
AEHNPRS	SHARPEN	AEHSTUX	EXHAUST	AEIKNRT	KERATIN		SAMIELS
AEHNPRT	PANTHER	AEIIKNT	KAINITE	AEIKNSS	KINASES		SEISMAL
AEHNPSU	UNSHAPE	AEIILLT	TAILLIE	AEIKNST	INTAKES	AEILMSZ	MEZAILS
AEHNRSS	HARNESS	AEIILNN	ANILINE	AEIKNSY	KYANISE	AEILMTY	LAYTIME
AEHNRST	ANTHERS	AEIILNR	AIRLINE		YANKIES	AEILNNY	INANELY
	HARTENS	AEIILNX	EXILIAN	AEIKNTY	KYANITE	AEILNOP	OPALINE
	THENARS	AEIILRR	LAIRIER	AEIKNYZ	KYANIZE	AEILNOR	AILERON
AEHNRTU	HAUNTER	AEIILRS	LAIRISE	AEIKOST	OAKIEST		ALERION
	UNEARTH		SAILIER	AEIKPRR	PARKIER		ALIENOR
	UNHEART	AEIILRZ	LAIRIZE	AEIKPRW	PAWKIER	AEILNOT	ELATION
	URETHAN	AEIILSS	LIAISES	AEIKQRU	QUAKIER		TOENAIL
AEHNRTX	NARTHEX		SILESIA	AEIKRRS	KERRIAS	AEILNPR	PEARLIN
AEHNSSS	SNASHES	AEIILST	LAITIES		SARKIER		PLAINER
AEHNSST	HASTENS	AEIILTZ	TAILZIE	AEIKRSS	KAISERS		PRALINE
	SNATHES	AEIIMNT	INTIMAE		KARSIES	AEILNPS	ALPINES
	SNEATHS		MINIATE	AEIKRST	ARKITES		SPANIEL
AEHNSSZ	SAZHENS	AEIIMRT	AIRTIME		KARITES		SPLENIA
AEHNSUY	HAUYNES	AEIIMST	AMITIES	AEIKRSZ	KARZIES	AEILNPT	PANTILE
AEHNTTW	WHATTEN		ATIMIES	AEIKSSS	ASKESIS	AEILNPX	EXPLAIN
AEHOORT	TOHEROA	AEIIMTT	IMITATE	AEIKSTT	TAKIEST	AEILNQU	EQUINAL
AEHORRS	HOARSER	AEIINNS	ASININE	AEILLMN	MANILLE	AEILNRS	NAILERS
AEHORST	ASTHORE		INSANIE	AEILLNR	RALLINE	AEILNRT	ENTRAIL
	HAROSET	AEIINQU	EQUINIA	AEILLOV	ALVEOLI		LATRINE
AEHORSX	HOAXERS	AEIINRR	RAINIER	AEILLPR	PALLIER		RATLINE
AEHORUV	HAVEOUR	AEIINRS	SENARII	AEILLPS	ILLAPSE		RELIANT
AEHOSTU	ATHEOUS	AEIINRT	INERTIA	AEILLRR	RALLIER		RETINAL
AEHPPRS	PERHAPS	AEIINST	ISATINE	AEILLRS	RALLIES		TRENAIL
AEHPPSU	UPHEAPS	AEIINSX	SIXAINE	AEILLRT	LITERAL	AEILNRV	RAVELIN
AEHPRRS	HARPERS				TALLIER	AEILNRW	LAWNIER

```
AEILNRX RELAXIN      AEILRVY VIRELAY              MASTIER              NASTIER
AEILNRY INLAYER      AEILRWY WEARILY              MISRATE              RATINES
        NAILERY      AEILSSS LAISSES              SEMITAR              RESIANT
AEILNSS SALINES              LASSIES              SMARTIE              RETAINS
        SILANES      AEILSSU SAULIES      AEIMRSU UREMIAS              RETINAS
AEILNST EASTLIN      AEILSSV VALISES      AEIMRSW AWMRIES              RETINAS
        ELASTIN              VESSAIL      AEIMRTU MURIATE              RETSINA
        ENTAILS      AEILSSW WALISES      AEIMRTW WARTIME              STAINER
        SALIENT      AEILSTU SITULAE      AEIMSSS AMISSES              STARNIE
        SLAINTE      AEILSTV ESTIVAL      AEIMSST ASTEISM              STEARIN
        STANIEL      AEILSTW WALIEST              SAMIEST      AEINRSV AVENIRS
        TENAILS      AEILSTY TAILYES              SAMITES              RAVINES
AEILNSU INSULAE      AEILSTZ LAZIEST              TAMISES      AEINRTT INTREAT
        INULASE      AEILTVY VILAYET      AEIMSSV MASSIVE              ITERANT
AEILNSV ALEVINS      AEILUVX EXUVIAL              MAVISES              NATTIER
        VALINES      AEIMMMS MAMMIES      AEIMSSY MYIASES              NITRATE
AEILNSX ALEXINS      AEIMMNS MISNAME      AEIMSTT MATIEST              TARTINE
AEILNTU ALUNITE      AEIMMRS RAMMIES              MATTIES              TERTIAN
AEILNTV VENTAIL      AEIMMRT MARMITE      AEIMSTZ MAZIEST      AEINRTU RUINATE
AEILNUV UNALIVE      AEIMMST MISMATE              MESTIZA              TAURINE
        UNVAILE              TAMMIES      AEIMSUV AMUSIVE              URANITE
AEILNUW LAUWINE      AEIMMZZ MIZMAZE      AEIMSXX MAXIXES              URINATE
AEILNVY NAIVELY      AEIMNNT MANNITE      AEIMTYZ AZYMITE      AEINRTW TAWNIER
AEILOPR PELORIA      AEIMNOR MORAINE      AEINNNS NANNIES              TINWARE
AEILOPS LEIPOAS      AEIMNOS ANOMIES      AEINNOT ENATION      AEINRUV VAURIEN
AEILORV VARIOLE      AEIMNOU MOINEAU      AEINNPR PANNIER      AEINRUW UNWARIE
AEILOST ISOLATE      AEIMNRR MARINER      AEINNPT PANTINE      AEINRUZ AZURINE
AEILOTV VIOLATE      AEIMNRS MARINES              PINNATE      AEINRVV VERVAIN
AEILPPR APPERIL              REMAINS      AEINNRS INSANER      AEINRWY YAWNIER
        ARIPPLE              SEMINAR              INSNARE      AEINSSS SANSEIS
AEILPPS APPLIES              SIRNAME      AEINNRT ENTRAIN              SASINES
        LAPPIES      AEIMNRT MINARET              TRANNIE      AEINSST ENTASIS
AEILPRS PALSIER              RAIMENT      AEINNRU ANEURIN              NASTIES
        PARLIES      AEIMNRV VERMIAN      AEINNSS SIENNAS              SESTINA
AEILPRT PLAITER      AEIMNSS INSEAMS      AEINNST INANEST              TANSIES
        PLATIER              SAMISEN      AEINNSZ ENZIANS              TISANES
AEILPRV PREVAIL      AEIMNST INMATES      AEINNTT ANTIENT      AEINSSV SAVINES
AEILPSS ESPIALS              MAINEST      AEINOPZ EPIZOAN              VINASSE
        LAPISES              MANTIES      AEINORS ERASION      AEINSTT INSTATE
        LIPASES              TAMINES      AEINORT OTARINE              SATINET
        PALSIES      AEIMNTX TAXIMEN      AEINOSS ANOESIS      AEINSTU AUNTIES
AEILPST APLITES      AEIMNTY AMENITY      AEINOST ATONIES              SINUATE
        PALIEST              ANYTIME      AEINOSV EVASION      AEINSTV NAIVEST
        TALIPES      AEIMNUV MAUVEIN      AEINOSZ AZIONES              NATIVES
AEILPSY PAISLEY              MAUVINE      AEINOXZ OXAZINE              VAINEST
AEILQTU LIQUATE      AEIMOOP IPOMOEA      AEINPPR NAPPIER      AEINSTW AWNIEST
        TEQUILA      AEIMOPR EMPORIA      AEINPPS NAPPIES              TAWNIES
AEILRRS RAILERS      AEIMORR ARMOIRE      AEINPRS RAPINES              WANIEST
        RERAILS      AEIMOST AMOSITE      AEINPRT PAINTER              WANTIES
AEILRRT RETIRAL              ATOMIES              PERTAIN      AEINSTZ ZANIEST
        RETRIAL              ATOMISE              REPAINT      AEINSVV NAVVIES
        TRAILER              OSMIATE      AEINPSS ASPINES      AEINSWY ANYWISE
AEILRSS AIRLESS      AEIMOTZ ATOMIZE              PANSIES      AEINTVY NAIVETY
        SAILERS      AEIMPRR RAMPIRE      AEINPST PANTIES      AEINTXY ANXIETY
        SERAILS      AEIMPRS IMPRESA              PATINES      AEIOPRS SOAPIER
        SERIALS              SAMPIRE              SAPIENT      AEIOPSS SOAPIES
AEILRST REALIST      AEIMPRT PRIMATE              SPINATE      AEIOPST ATOPIES
        RETAILS      AEIMPRV VAMPIRE      AEINPTT PATIENT              OPIATES
        SALTIER      AEIMPSS IMPASSE      AEINPTU PETUNIA      AEIOQSU SEQUOIA
        SALTIRE      AEIMPST IMPASTE      AEINPTY PANEITY      AEIORRR ARRIERO
        SLATIER              PASTIME      AEINQTU ANTIQUE              ROARIER
AEILRSV REVISAL      AEIMPSV IMPAVES              QUINATE      AEIORST OARIEST
AEILRSW SWALIER      AEIMPSW MAPWISE      AEINRRS SIERRAN              OTARIES
        WAILERS      AEIMPSY PYEMIAS              SNARIER      AEIORSV OVARIES
AEILRTT TERTIAL      AEIMRRR MARRIER      AEINRRT RETRAIN      AEIOSTT OSTIATE
AEILRTU URALITE      AEIMRRS MARRIES              TERRAIN              TOASTIE
AEILRTW WALTIER              SIMARRE              TRAINER      AEIOSTZ AZOTISE
AEILRTY IRATELY      AEIMRSS MASSIER      AEINRSS ARSINES      AEIOTZZ AZOTIZE
        REALITY      AEIMRST MAESTRI              SARNIES      AEIPPPR PAPPIER
AEILRVV REVIVAL              MAISTER      AEINRST ANESTRI      AEIPPPS PAPPIES
                                                              AEIPPRS APPRISE
```

	SAPPIER	AEIRSTV TAIVERS	AEKMMNR MARKMEN	AELLPPS LAPPELS
AEIPPRT PERIAPT		VASTIER	AEKMNOS SOKEMAN	AELLPRU PLEURAL
AEIPPRZ APPRIZE		AEIRSTW WAISTER	AEKMNSU UNMAKES	AELLPSS SPALLES
	ZAPPIER	WAITERS	AEKMPRU UPMAKER	AELLPST PALLETS
AEIPPSS PASPIES		WARIEST	AEKMPSU UPMAKES	AELLPTU PLUTEAL
AEIPRRS PARRIES		AEIRSVW WAIVERS	AEKMRRS MARKERS	AELLPTY PLAYLET
	PRAISER	AEIRTTT ATTRITE	REMARKS	AELLQUY EQUALLY
	RAPIERS	TATTIER	AEKMRSS MASKERS	AELLRRU ALLURER
	RASPIER	TITRATE	AEKMRST MARKETS	AELLRST STELLAR
	REPAIRS	AEIRTTV TAIVERT	AEKNNRS ENRANKS	TELLARS
AEIPRSS ASPIRES		AEIRTTW TAWTIER	AEKNNST KANTENS	AELLRSU ALLURES
	PARESIS	AEIRTTX EXTRAIT	AEKNNTU UNTAKEN	LAURELS
	PRAISES	AEIRTUY AUREITY	AEKNPPR KNAPPER	AELLRSW WALLERS
	SPIREAS	AEIRTUZ AZURITE	AEKNPRS SPANKER	AELLRSY RALLYES
AEIPRST PARTIES		AEIRTVY VARIETY	AEKNPSU UNSPEAK	AELLRTY ALERTLY
	PASTIER	AEISSST SIESTAS	AEKNPTU UPTAKEN	ELYTRAL
	PIASTRE	TASSIES	AEKNRRS RANKERS	AELLSST SALLETS
	PIRATES	AEISSSZ ASSIZES	AEKNRSS KRANSES	TASSELL
	PRATIES	AEISSUV SUASIVE	AEKNRST RANKEST	AELLSSW LAWLESS
	TRAIPSE	AEISSUX AUXESIS	STARKEN	AELLSTT TALLEST
AEIPRSU SPURIAE		AEISSVV SAVVIES	TANKERS	TALLETS
	UPRAISE	AEISTTT TATTIES	AEKNRSU UNRAKES	AELLSTW SETWALL
AEIPRSV PARVISE		AEISTTU SITUATE	AEKNRSW SWANKER	SWALLET
AEIPRSW WASPIER		AEISTTV STATIVE	WANKERS	WALLETS
AEIPRTT PARTITE		AEISTTW TWAITES	AEKNRSY YANKERS	AELLSTY STALELY
AEIPRTV PRIVATE		AEISTTY SATIETY	AEKNRSZ KRANZES	AELLSVY VALLEYS
AEIPRTW WIRETAP		AEISTVW WAVIEST	AEKNRVY KNAVERY	AELLTUU ULULATE
AEIPRXY PYREXIA		AEISTWX WAXIEST	AEKNSSU ANKUSES	AELLUVV VALVULE
AEIPSSS ASEPSIS		AEITTTU ATTUITE	AEKNSWY SWANKEY	AELMMNO MAMELON
AEIPSST PASTIES		AEITTTV VITTATE	AEKORRS ROSAKER	AELMMNT MALTMEN
	PATSIES	AEJKMNR JARKMEN	AEKORSS ARKOSES	AELMMOY MYELOMA
	TAPISES	AEJKNRS JANKERS	SOAKERS	AELMMRS LAMMERS
AEIPSSV PASSIVE		AEJLNUV JUVENAL	AEKOTTU OUTTAKE	SLAMMER
	PAVISES	AEJLOSU JALOUSE	AEKPPSU UPSPAKE	AELMMRT TRAMMEL
	SPAVIES	JEALOUS	UPSPEAK	AELMMST STAMMEL
AEIPSSW WASPIES		AEJLOUZ AZULEJO	AEKPRRS PARKERS	AELMMSY MALMSEY
AEIPSTT PATTIES		AEJMMRS JAMMERS	AEKPRSS SPARKES	AELMNOR ALMONER
	TAPETIS	AEJMNZZ JAZZMEN	AEKPSSY PASSKEY	NEMORAL
AEIPSTU TAUPIES		AEJMSST JETSAMS	AEKPSTU UPTAKES	AELMNOS MELANOS
AEIPSTW TAWPIES		AEJMSSY JESSAMY	AEKQSSU SQUEAKS	AELMNOT LOMENTA
AEIPTXY EPITAXY		AEJMSTY MAJESTY	AEKQSUY SQUEAKY	OMENTAL
AEIQRUV AQUIVER		AEJNNOS JOANNES	AEKRRST STARKER	TELAMON
AEIQSSU SAIQUES		AEJNORZ ZANJERO	AEKRSST SKATERS	AELMNPR LAMPERN
AEIRRRT TARRIER		AEJNSST JESSANT	STRAKES	AELMNRU NUMERAL
AEIRRSS ARRISES		AEJNSSU JAUNSES	STREAKS	AELMNST LAMENTS
	RAISERS	AEJPRSS JASPERS	TASKERS	MANTELS
	SIERRAS	AEJPRSY JASPERY	AEKRSSY KARSEYS	MANTLES
AEIRRST ARTSIER		AEJRSVY JARVEYS	AEKRSTY STREAKY	AELMNSU MENSUAL
	TARRIES	AEKKNRS KRAKENS	AEKSSSV KVASSES	AELMNTT MANTLET
	TARSIER	AEKKRSY SKREAKY	AELLMNU LUMENAL	AELMNTU NUTMEAL
AEIRRSV ARRIVES		YAKKERS	AELLMRS SMALLER	AELMOPR PLEROMA
	VARIERS	AEKLLTU KELLAUT	AELLMST MALLETS	AELMOPU AMPOULE
AEIRRTT RATTIER		AEKLNPP KNAPPLE	AELLMSU MALLEUS	AELMOPY MAYPOLE
	RETRAIT	AEKLNPR PRANKLE	AELLMSY MELLAYS	AELMORS MORALES
	TARTIER	AEKLNRS RANKLES	MESALLY	AELMORT MOLERAT
AEIRRTW WARTIER		AEKLNST ANKLETS	AELLMTY METALLY	AELMORV REMOVAL
AEIRRTY RETIARY		ASKLENT	AELLMWX MAXWELL	AELMOST MALTOSE
AEIRSSS SASSIER		LANKEST	AELLNOP PALLONE	AELMOTT MATELOT
AEIRSST SAIREST		AEKLNSW KNAWELS	AELLNOR LLANERO	AELMPRS PALMERS
	SATIRES	AEKLNSY ALKYNES	AELLNOV NOVELLA	SAMPLER
	TIRASSE	AEKLORY ROKELAY	AELLNOY ALONELY	AELMPRT TEMPLAR
AEIRSSU SAURIES		AEKLOST SKATOLE	AELLNPY PENALLY	TRAMPLE
AEIRSSZ ASSIZER		AEKLPRS SPARKLE	AELLNRT ENTRALL	AELMPRY LAMPREY
AEIRSTT ARTIEST		AEKLRRS LARKERS	AELLNSS ALLNESS	AELMPSS SAMPLES
	ARTISTE	AEKLRST STALKER	AELLNSW ENWALLS	AELMPST AMPLEST
	ATTIRES	TALKERS	AELLNTT TALLENT	AELMPSU AMPULES
	IRATEST	AEKLRSW WALKERS	AELLNVY VENALLY	AELMPTU PLUMATE
	STRIATE	AEKLSST LASKETS	AELLORS ROSELLA	AELMRRS MARRELS
	TASTIER	SKLATES	AELLORT REALLOT	AELMRSS ARMLESS
	TERTIAS	AEKLSTU AUKLETS	AELLORV OVERALL	AELMRST ARMLETS

```
                MARTELS        AELOPST APOSTLE        AELRRSU SURREAL                SUMMATE
AELMRSU MAULERS                        PELOTAS        AELRRTT RATTLER        AEMMSTW MAWMETS
AELMRSV MARVELS                AELOPSX EXPOSAL        AELRRTW TRAWLER        AEMNNOS MANNOSE
AELMRTT MARTLET                AELOPTT PALETOT        AELRSST ARTLESS        AEMNNOT MONTANE
AELMSST SAMLETS                AELOPTU OUTLEAP                LASTERS        AEMNNOU NOUMENA
AELMSTU AMULETS                AELORRT REALTOR                SALTERS        AEMNNRS MANNERS
AELNNPR PLANNER                        RELATOR                SLATERS        AEMNNRT MANRENT
AELNNPS PENNALS                AELORSS OARLESS                TARSELS                REMNANT
AELNNPU UNPANEL                        SOLERAS        AELRSSU SAURELS        AEMNNSW NEWSMAN
AELNNRS ENSNARL                AELORST OESTRAL        AELRSSV SALVERS        AEMNNTU UNMEANT
                LANNERS        AELORTV LEVATOR                SERVALS        AEMNOPS MOPANES
AELNNRT LANTERN                AELORTY ROYALET                SLAVERS        AEMNORS ENAMORS
AELNNRU UNLEARN                AELORUU ROULEAU                VERSALS                MOANERS
AELNNST STANNEL                AELORVY OVERLAY        AELRSSW WARSLES                OARSMEN
AELNNTU ANNULET                AELOSSS LASSOES        AELRSSY RAYLESS        AEMNORU ENAMOUR
AELNOOS ALSOONE                AELOSSV SALVOES                SLAYERS                NEUROMA
AELNOPT POLENTA                AELOSSW LEASOWS        AELRSTT RATTLES        AEMNORV OVERMAN
AELNORS ORLEANS                AELOSTV SOLVATE                SLATTER        AEMNORY ROMNEYA
AELNORU ALEURON                AELOSTZ ZEALOTS                STARLET        AEMNOSS MONASES
AELNORV VERONAL                AELOSUZ ZEALOUS                STARTLE        AEMNOST MANTOES
AELNOST ETALONS                AELOSVY SAVELOY                TATLERS        AEMNOTU NOTAEUM
AELNOTV VOLANTE                AELOTTU TOLUATE        AELRSTU SALUTER                OUTNAME
AELNPRS PLANERS                AELOTUV OVULATE        AELRSTV TRAVELS        AEMNPSS PASSMEN
                REPLANS        AELOTVV VOLVATE                VARLETS        AEMNPST ENSTAMP
AELNPRT PANTLER                AELPPRS LAPPERS                VESTRAL                TAPSMEN
                PLANTER                RAPPELS        AELRSTW WASTREL        AEMNPSU PNEUMAS
                REPLANT                SLAPPER        AELRSTY RAYLETS        AEMNPTU PUTAMEN
AELNPRY PLENARY                AELPPRY REAPPLY        AELRSUV VALUERS        AEMNPTY PAYMENT
AELNPSS NAPLESS                AELPPSS SAPPLES        AELRSVV VARVELS        AEMNRRU MANURER
AELNPST PLANETS                AELPPST LAPPETS        AELRSVY SLAVERY        AEMNRST ARTSMEN
                PLATENS                STAPPLE        AELRSWX WRAXLES                MARTENS
AELNPSU UPLEANS                AELPPSU APPULSE        AELRSWY LAWYERS                SARMENT
AELNPTU UPLEANT                        PAPULES        AELRSZZ RAZZLES                SMARTEN
AELNPTX EXPLANT                        UPLEAPS        AELRTTT TARTLET        AEMNRSU MANURES
AELNPTY APLENTY                AELPPTU UPLEAPT                TATTLER                MURENAS
                PENALTY        AELPQSU PLAQUES        AELRTTU TUTELAR                SURNAME
AELNQUU UNEQUAL                AELPRRS PARRELS        AELRTUV VAULTER        AEMNRTU TRUEMAN
AELNRRS SNARLER                AELPRST PALTERS        AELRTWZ WALTZER        AEMNRTV VARMENT
AELNRSS RANSELS                        PLASTER        AELSSST TASSELS        AEMNSSS MESSANS
AELNRST ANTLERS                        PLATERS        AELSSTT LATESTS        AEMNSST STAMENS
                RENTALS                PSALTER                SALTEST        AEMNSSU UNSEAMS
                SALTERN                STAPLER                STALEST        AEMNSTU UNTAMES
                STERNAL        AELPRSU PERUSAL                TASLETS                UNTEAMS
AELNRSZ RANZELS                        SERPULA        AELSSTU SALUTES        AEMNSTY AMNESTY
AELNRTT TRENTAL                AELPRSW PRAWLES                TALUSES        AEMNTWY WAYMENT
AELNRTU NEUTRAL                AELPRSY PARLEYS        AELSSTV VESTALS        AEMOORW WOOMERA
AELNRTV VENTRAL                        PARSLEY        AELSSTW WASTELS        AEMOOST OSTEOMA
AELNRUV UNRAVEL                        PLAYERS        AELSSUV AVULSES        AEMOOSV AMOOVES
AELNSSU SENSUAL                        REPLAYS        AELSSVY SLAVEYS                VAMOOSE
                UNSEALS                SPARELY        AELSSWY WAYLESS        AEMOPPR PAMPERO
AELNSSW AWNLESS                AELPRTT PARTLET        AELSTTT TATTLES        AEMOPSZ APOZEMS
AELNSSX LAXNESS                        PLATTER        AELSTTW WATTLES        AEMORRS REMORAS
AELNSTT LATTENS                        PRATTLE        AELSTTY STATELY                ROAMERS
                TALENTS        AELPRTY PEARTLY                STYLATE        AEMORRV OVERARM
AELNSTU ELUANTS                        PRELATY        AELSTUX LUXATES        AEMORST AMORETS
                UNLASTE                PTERYLA        AELSTWZ WALTZES                MAESTRO
AELNSTV LEVANTS                AELPRUY EPULARY        AELSUVY SUAVELY                OMERTAS
AELNSTY STANYEL                AELPSSS SAPLESS        AELSWZZ SWAZZLE        AEMORSU RAMEOUS
AELNSTZ ZELANTS                AELPSST PASTELS        AELTTTW TWATTLE        AEMORSW WOMERAS
AELNSUW UNWEALS                        STAPLES        AELTTUX TEXTUAL        AEMORSX XEROMAS
AELNTUV ENVAULT                AELPSTT PATTLES        AELTUVV VULVATE        AEMOSST OSMATES
AELOORS AEROSOL                        PELTAST        AEMMMRS MAMMERS        AEMOSSV VAMOSES
                ROSEOLA        AELPSTU PULSATE        AEMMMST MAMMETS        AEMOSTW TWASOME
AELOPPR PROPALE                        PUTEALS        AEMMNOT MOMENTA        AEMOSUZ ZAMOUSE
AELOPPX APOPLEX                        SPATULE        AEMMNTU AMENTUM        AEMOSWY SOMEWAY
AELOPRR PREORAL                AELPUUV UPVALUE        AEMMORS MARMOSE        AEMOTTZ MOZETTA
AELOPRS PAROLES                AELQRRU QUARREL        AEMMRRS RAMMERS        AEMPPRS MAPPERS
                REPOSAL        AELQSSU LASQUES        AEMMRST STAMMER                PAMPERS
AELOPRT PROLATE                        SQUEALS        AEMMRSY YAMMERS        AEMPPRY MAPPERY
AELOPRV OVERLAP                AELQTUZ QUETZAL        AEMMSTU MAUMETS        AEMPRRS RAMPERS
```

AEMPRRT TRAMPER	AENORRT ORNATER	AENRSTW STRAWEN	AEPPRRS RAPPERS
AEMPRST EMPARTS	AENORRV OVERRAN	WANTERS	AEPPRRT TRAPPER
STAMPER	AENORSS REASONS	AENRSTY TRAYNES	AEPPRRW WRAPPER
TAMPERS	AENORST ATONERS	AENRSUW UNSWEAR	AEPPRSS APPRESS
AEMPRSV REVAMPS	SENATOR	UNWARES	SAPPERS
VAMPERS	TREASON	AENRTTU TAUNTER	AEPPRST TAPPERS
AEMPRSW SWAMPER	AENORTV VENATOR	AENRTTY NATTERY	AEPPRSU PAUPERS
AEMPRTT TRAMPET	AENORXY ANOREXY	AENRTUV VAUNTER	UPSPEAR
AEMPRTU TEMPURA	AENOSSS SEASONS	AENRTUW UNWATER	AEPPRSW SWAPPER
AEMPSSU EMPUSAS	AENOSST ASTONES	AENRUWY UNWEARY	WAPPERS
AEMPTTT ATTEMPT	AENOSTT ATTONES	AENSSST ASSENTS	AEPPRSY PREPAYS
AEMPTTU TAPETUM	NOTATES	SNASTES	YAPPERS
AEMQRSU MARQUES	AENOSTU SOUTANE	AENSSTU NASUTES	AEPPSTT TAPPETS
MASQUER	AENOSVW WAVESON	UNSEATS	AEPPSTU PUPATES
AEMQSSU MASQUES	AENOUUV NOUVEAU	AENSSTX SEXTANS	AEPQRTU PARQUET
SQUAMES	AENPPRS NAPPERS	AENSSTY STAYNES	AEPRRRS SPARRER
AEMRRRY REMARRY	PARPENS	AENSSTZ STANZES	AEPRRSS PARSERS
AEMRRST SMARTER	PARSNEP	AENSSWY SAWNEYS	RASPERS
AEMRRSU ARMURES	SNAPPER	AENSSXY SYNAXES	SPARERS
AEMRRSW SWARMER	AENPPRT PARPENT	AENSTTT ATTENTS	SPARRES
WARMERS	AENPPRU UNPAPER	AENSTTU ATTUNES	SPARSER
AEMRRTU ERRATUM	AENPRRT PARTNER	NUTATES	AEPRRST PARTERS
MATURER	AENPRST ARPENTS	TAUTENS	PRATERS
AEMRSST MASTERS	ENTRAPS	TETANUS	AEPRRSU PARURES
STREAMS	PANTERS	UNSTATE	UPREARS
AEMRSSU AMUSERS	PARENTS	AENSTTX SEXTANT	AEPRRSW REWRAPS
MASSEUR	PASTERN	AENSTUX UNTAXES	WARPERS
AEMRSTT MATTERS	PERSANT	AENSTWY TAWNEYS	AEPRRSY PRAYERS
SMATTER	TREPANS	AENTTTU ATTUENT	RESPRAY
AEMRSTU MATURES	AENPRSW ENWRAPS	AEOOPPS PAPOOSE	SPRAYER
STRUMAE	PAWNERS	AEOOPRS OROPESA	AEPRRTU PARTURE
AEMRSTW WARMEST	SPAWNER	AEOPPPS PAPPOSE	RAPTURE
AEMRSTY MASTERY	AENPRSZ PANZERS	AEOPPRS APPOSER	AEPRRTY PETRARY
MAYSTER	AENPRTT PATTERN	AEOPPRV APPROVE	AEPRSSS PASSERS
STREAMY	REPTANT	AEOPPSS APPOSES	AEPRSST PASTERS
AEMRTTY MATTERY	AENPRUV PARVENU	AEOPQRU OPAQUER	REPASTS
AEMRTUU TRUMEAU	AENPSST APTNESS	AEOPQSU OPAQUES	SPAREST
AEMSSSU ASSUMES	PATNESS	AEOPRRT PRAETOR	AEPRSSU PAUSERS
AEMSSUW WAMUSES	PESANTS	PRORATE	AEPRSSY PESSARY
AEMSSYZ ZYMASES	AENPSSY SYNAPSE	AEOPRST ESPARTO	AEPRSTT PATTERS
AEMSTTU MUTATES	AENPSTT PATENTS	PROTEAS	SPATTER
AEMSTUV MAUVEST	PATTENS	SEAPORT	TAPSTER
AENNNOS NONANES	AENPSTU PEANUTS	AEOPRTT PORTATE	AEPRSTU PASTURE
AENNNPT PENNANT	PESAUNT	AEOPRVY OVERPAY	UPRATES
AENNOPS PANNOSE	AENPSTW STEWPAN	AEOPRWY ROPEWAY	UPSTARE
AENNOSS NOSEANS	AENPSTY SYNAPTE	AEOPSSS PSOASES	UPTEARS
AENNOSV NOVENAS	AENPSTZ PEZANTS	AEOPSTT APTOTES	AEPRSTY YAPSTER
AENNOSY ANYONES	AENQSTU EQUANTS	TEAPOTS	AEPRSTZ PATZERS
AENNOTU TONNEAU	AENRRSS SERRANS	AEOPSTY TEAPOYS	AEPRSWY YAWPERS
AENNPRS SPANNER	SNARERS	AEOPSTZ TOPAZES	AEPRSYY SPRAYEY
AENNQTU QUANNET	AENRRST ERRANTS	AEOQRTU EQUATOR	AEPRTXY APTERYX
AENNRST TANNERS	RANTERS	QUORATE	AEPSSTU PETASUS
AENNRSV VANNERS	AENRRSW WARNERS	AEOQRUV VAQUERO	AEPSTTU UPSTATE
AENNRTT ENTRANT	WARRENS	AEOQSUU AQUEOUS	AEPSZZZ PZAZZES
AENNRTV VERNANT	AENRRTT TRANTER	AEORRRS ROARERS	AEQRRSU SQUARER
AENNRTY TANNERY	AENRRTY TERNARY	AEORRST ROASTER	AEQRRTU QUARTER
TYRANNE	AENRSSS SARSENS	AEORRSU AROUSER	AEQRSSU SQUARES
AENNSSW WANNESS	AENRSST SARSNET	AEORSSS SAROSES	AEQRSTU QUARTES
AENNSTT TANNEST	TRANSES	SEROSAS	AEQRSUV QUAVERS
TENANTS	AENRSSW ANSWERS	AEORSSU AROUSES	AEQRTTU QUARTET
AENNSTW WANNEST	RAWNESS	AEORSTT ROTATES	AEQRUVY QUAVERY
AENOOTZ ENTOZOA	AENRSSY SARNEYS	TOASTER	AERRSST ARRESTS
AENOPPR PROPANE	AENRSTT NATTERS	AEORSUV AVOURES	RASTERS
AENOPRS PERSONA	RATTENS	AEORSVW OVERSAW	STARERS
AENOPRT OPERANT	AENRSTU AUNTERS	AEORSVY AVOYERS	AERRSSU ASSURER
PRONATE	NATURES	AEORTTU OUTRATE	RASURES
PROTEAN	SAUNTER	AEORTUW OUTWEAR	AERRSTT RATTERS
AENOPSU POSAUNE	AENRSTV SERVANT	AEORTVX OVERTAX	RESTART
AENOPSV PAVONES	TAVERNS	AEOSSTV AVOSETS	STARTER
AENOPSW WEAPONS	VERSANT	AEOSTTU OUTEATS	AERRSTY STRAYER

AERRSUZ	RAZURES	AFGGGIN	FAGGING
AERRSWY	WARREYS	AFGGINN	FANGING
AERRTTY	RATTERY	AFGGOST	FAGGOTS
AERSSST	ASSERTS	AFGHHIS	HAGFISH
	TRASSES	AFGHINS	FASHING
AERSSSU	ASSURES	AFGHINT	HAFTING
	SARUSES	AFGHIRS	GARFISH
AERSSSW	WRASSES	AFGHLSU	GASHFUL
AERSSTT	ASTERTS	AFGHLTU	FLAUGHT
	STARETS	AFGHRTU	FRAUGHT
	STATERS	AFGIIKN	FAIKING
	TASTERS	AFGIILN	FAILING
AERSSTV	STARVES	AFGIINN	FAINING
AERSSTW	WASTERS	AFGIINR	FAIRING
AERSSTY	ESTRAYS	AFGIINT	FIATING
	STAYERS	AFGIINW	WAIFING
	STAYRES	AFGIKLN	FLAKING
AERSSUV	VARUSES	AFGILLN	FALLING
AERSSVW	SWARVES	AFGILMN	FLAMING
AERSSWY	SAWYERS	AFGILNO	FOALING
	SWAYERS		LOAFING
AERSTTT	STRETTA	AFGILNR	FLARING
	TARTEST	AFGILNS	FALSING
	TATTERS	AFGILNT	FATLING
AERSTTU	ASTUTER	AFGILNU	GAINFUL
	STATURE	AFGILNW	FLAWING
AERSTTW	SWATTER	AFGILNY	ANGLIFY
	TEWARTS		FLAYING
AERSTTY	YATTERS	AFGILRU	FIGURAL
AERSTTZ	STARETZ	AFGIMNO	FOAMING
AERSTUU	AUTEURS	AFGIMNR	FARMING
AERSTUY	ESTUARY		FRAMING
AERSTWY	WASTERY	AFGIMNY	MAGNIFY
AERTTTY	TATTERY	AFGINNN	FANNING
AERTTUV	VETTURA	AFGINNW	FAWNING
AESSSTT	TASSETS	AFGINNY	FAYNING
AESSTTT	ATTESTS	AFGINRR	FARRING
AESSTTU	STATUES	AFGINRS	FARSING
AESSTTV	VASTEST	AFGINRT	FARTING
AESSTUV	SUAVEST		INGRAFT
AESSTUY	EUSTASY		RAFTING
AESSVVY	SAVVEYS	AFGINRY	FRAYING
AESTTTU	STATUTE	AFGINST	FASTING
	TAUTEST	AFGINTT	FATTING
AESTTTW	WATTEST	AFGINTW	WAFTING
AFFFGIN	FAFFING	AFGIOTT	FAGOTTI
AFFGGIN	GAFFING	AFGIRTY	GRATIFY
AFFGINN	NAFFING	AFGKNOP	PAKFONG
AFFGINW	WAFFING	AFGKORT	KOFTGAR
AFFGINY	AFFYING	AFGLLUY	FUGALLY
	YAFFING	AFGLNOS	FLAGONS
AFFGSUW	GUFFAWS	AFGLRYY	GRAYFLY
AFFHIKU	KUFFIAH	AFGMNOR	FROGMAN
AFFHILN	HAFFLIN	AFGMORS	FOGRAMS
AFFHIRS	RAFFISH	AFGOOTT	FAGOTTO
AFFHIST	HAFFITS	AFGORRS	FRAGORS
AFFILMN	MAFFLIN	AFGOSTU	FUGATOS
AFFILPS	PILAFFS	AFHIIRS	FAIRISH
AFFILSY	FALSIFY	AFHIKLS	KHALIFS
AFFIMRS	AFFIRMS	AFHIKRS	KHARIFS
AFFIMST	MASTIFF	AFHIKSU	KUFIAHS
AFFINRU	FUNFAIR	AFHIKUY	KUFIYAH
	RUFFIAN	AFHILLN	HALFLIN
AFFINTY	TIFFANY	AFHILSS	FALSISH
AFFIORR	FORFAIR	AFHIMNU	HAFNIUM
AFFIRRU	FURFAIR	AFHINOS	FASHION
AFFIRST	TARIFFS	AFHINTU	UNFAITH
AFFNORS	SAFFRON	AFHISST	FASTISH
AFFNORT	AFFRONT	AFHISTT	FATTISH
AFFRSST	STRAFFS		

AFHKORY	HAYFORK	AFKLRSU	SARKFUL
AFHKRTU	FUTHARK	AFLLMPU	PALMFUL
AFHLMRU	HARMFUL	AFLLMSU	FULLAMS
AFHLMSU	FULHAMS	AFLLNOS	ONFALLS
AFHLOOS	LOOFAHS	AFLLNSU	FULLANS
AFHLOTY	HAYLOFT	AFLLOOY	ALOOFLY
AFHLSTU	HATFULS	AFLLOSW	FALLOWS
AFHMOST	FATHOMS	AFLLOTU	OUTFALL
AFHOOPT	POOFTAH	AFLLPSU	LAPFULS
AFHOPTU	POUFTAH	AFLLPUY	PLAYFUL
AFHORSS	SHOFARS	AFLLUWY	AWFULLY
AFIILNS	FINIALS	AFLMNOU	MOANFUL
AFIILRT	AIRLIFT	AFLMORU	FORMULA
AFIILRY	FAIRILY	AFLMORW	WOLFRAM
AFIIMOS	MAFIOSI	AFLMOST	FLOTSAM
AFIJNNS	FINJANS	AFLMRSU	ARMFULS
AFIKNRT	RATFINK		FULMARS
AFIKNSU	FUNKIAS	AFLMSTU	MASTFUL
AFIKRSS	FRISKAS	AFLMSUU	FAMULUS
AFIKSUY	KUFIYAS	AFLNORT	FRONTAL
AFILLMS	MISFALL	AFLNOTT	FLOTANT
AFILLNS	INFALLS	AFLNPSU	PANFULS
AFILLNY	FINALLY	AFLNRTU	RUNFLAT
AFILLPT	PITFALL	AFLNSTU	FLAUNTS
AFILLPU	PAILFUL	AFLNTUY	FLAUNTY
AFILLRY	FRAILLY	AFLOOTW	WOOLFAT
AFILLUV	FLUVIAL	AFLORSU	FUSAROL
	VIALFUL	AFLORUV	FLAVOUR
AFILLUW	WAILFUL	AFLORWW	WARWOLF
AFILMOR	ALIFORM	AFLOSSU	FOSSULA
AFILMOY	FOAMILY	AFLPRTY	FLYTRAP
AFILMPY	AMPLIFY	AFLRTUY	TRAYFUL
AFILMSS	FALSISM	AFLSTUV	VATFULS
AFILNPU	PAINFUL	AFLSWYY	FLYWAYS
AFILNSV	FLAVINS	AFMNOOT	FOOTMAN
AFILNTU	FLUTINA	AFMNORT	FORMANT
AFILNTY	FAINTLY	AFMNOST	FANTOMS
AFILQUY	QUALIFY	AFMNRSU	SURFMAN
AFILRRY	FRIARLY	AFMNRTU	TURFMAN
AFILRSZ	FRAZILS	AFMOOSS	SAMFOOS
AFILRTY	FRAILTY	AFMORST	FARMOST
AFILSSY	SALSIFY		FORMATS
AFILSTU	FISTULA	AFMORTU	FOUMART
AFILSTY	FALSITY	AFMOSTT	AFTMOST
AFIMNRS	FIRMANS	AFMOSTU	SFUMATO
AFIMOOS	MAFIOSO	AFNORRW	FORWARN
AFIMORV	AVIFORM	AFNSSTU	SUNFAST
AFIMSSS	MASSIFS	AFOOPPR	APPROOF
AFIMSSV	FAVISMS	AFOORST	FOOTRAS
AFINNNS	FINNANS	AFOORTZ	FORZATO
AFINNOR	FRANION	AFOOTWY	FOOTWAY
AFINNOS	FANIONS	AFORRSW	FARROWS
AFINNST	INFANTS	AFORRSY	FORRAYS
AFINRSU	UNFAIRS	AFORSSY	FORSAYS
AFINSSU	FUSAINS	AFORSTU	FAUTORS
AFINSTU	FAUNIST		FOUTRAS
	FIAUNTS	AFORSUV	FAVOURS
	FUSTIAN	AFOSSSU	FOUSSAS
	INFAUST	AFOSTUU	FATUOUS
AFIORST	FAITORS	AFPSTUW	UPWAFTS
AFIORTU	FAITOUR	AGGGGIN	GAGGING
AFIORTZ	FORZATI	AGGGHIN	HAGGING
AFIQRSU	FAQUIRS	AGGGIJN	JAGGING
AFISSTT	SITFAST	AGGGILN	LAGGING
AFISSTY	SATISFY	AGGGIMN	MAGGING
AFITTUY	FATUITY	AGGGINN	GANGING
AFJLRSU	JARFULS		NAGGING
AFKLNRY	FRANKLY	AGGGINR	RAGGING
AFKLNTU	TANKFUL	AGGGINS	SAGGING
AFKLOWY	FOLKWAY	AGGGINT	TAGGING

AGGGGINU	GAUGING	AGHHIWY	HIGHWAY	AGHLOOS	GASOHOL		JIGSAWN
AGGGINW	WAGGING	AGHHOSW	HOGWASH	AGHLOSU	GOULASH	AGIJNZZ	JAZZING
AGGGINZ	ZAGGING	AGHHTUY	HAUGHTY	AGHLSTU	GALUTHS	AGIJSSW	JIGSAWS
AGGHHIS	HAGGISH	AGHIILN	HAILING	AGHLSTY	GHASTLY	AGIKKNY	YAKKING
AGGHIIL	GHILGAI	AGHIINN	HAINING	AGHNNSU	UNHANGS	AGIKLNN	LANKING
AGGHIMN	GINGHAM	AGHIINR	HAIRING	AGHNOTU	HANGOUT	AGIKLNO	OAKLING
AGGHINN	HANGING	AGHIJRS	JAGHIRS	AGHNPSU	UPHANGS	AGIKLNR	LARKING
AGGHINS	GASHING	AGHIKNN	HANKING	AGHNRST	THRANGS	AGIKLNS	SLAKING
AGGHISW	WAGGISH	AGHIKNR	HARKING	AGHNRSU	NURHAGS	AGIKLNT	TALKING
AGGIIJJ	JIGAJIG	AGHIKNS	SHAKING	AGHNRUY	AHUNGRY	AGIKLNW	WALKING
AGGIILS	GILGAIS	AGHIKNW	HAWKING	AGHNSTU	NAUGHTS	AGIKMNR	MARKING
AGGIIMN	IMAGING	AGHIKSU	KIAUGHS	AGHNSUY	GUNYAHS	AGIKMNS	MAKINGS
AGGIINN	GAINING	AGHILLN	HALLING	AGHNTUY	NAUGHTY		MASKING
AGGIJJO	JIGAJOG	AGHILNO	HALOING	AGHOQSU	QUAHOGS	AGIKNNR	NARKING
AGGIKNW	GAWKING	AGHILNR	HARLING	AGHPTUY	PAUGHTY		RANKING
AGGILLN	GALLING	AGHILNS	HALSING	AGHRRSU	GURRAHS	AGIKNNS	SNAKING
	GINGALL		LASHING	AGHRSTY	GYTRASH	AGIKNNT	KANTING
AGGILNN	ANGLING		SHALING	AGHSTUW	WAUGHTS		TANKING
AGGILNO	GAOLING	AGHILNT	HALTING	AGIIJLN	JAILING	AGIKNNU	UNAKING
	GOALING		LATHING	AGIIKLN	LAIKING	AGIKNNW	WANKING
AGGILNR	GLARING	AGHILNU	HAULING	AGIIKLT	GLAIKIT	AGIKNNY	YANKING
AGGILNS	GINGALS	AGHILNV	HALVING	AGIIKNP	PAIKING	AGIKNOS	SOAKING
	LAGGINS	AGHILNW	WHALING	AGIIKNR	RAIKING	AGIKNOY	KAYOING
AGGILNZ	GLAZING	AGHILRS	LARGISH	AGIILMN	MAILING		OKAYING
AGGILOS	LOGGIAS	AGHILRT	ALRIGHT	AGIILNN	ALINING	AGIKNPR	PARKING
AGGIMMN	GAMMING	AGHILST	ALIGHTS		NAILING	AGIKNQU	QUAKING
AGGIMNS	GAMINGS	AGHIMMN	HAMMING	AGIILNR	GLAIRIN	AGIKNRS	RAKINGS
AGGIMNU	GAUMING	AGHIMNR	HARMING		LAIRING		SARKING
AGGINNP	PANGING	AGHIMNS	MASHING		RAILING	AGIKNRT	KARTING
AGGINNR	RANGING		SHAMING	AGIILNS	AISLING	AGIKNSS	GASKINS
AGGINNT	GANTING	AGHIMNW	HAWMING		NILGAIS	AGIKNST	SKATING
	TANGING	AGHIMPS	GAMPISH		SAILING		STAKING
AGGINNW	GNAWING	AGHINNT	TANGHIN	AGIILNT	TAILING		TAKINGS
AGGINPP	GAPPING	AGHINOR	HOARING	AGIILNV	VAILING		TASKING
AGGINPR	GRAPING	AGHINOX	HOAXING	AGIILNW	WAILING	AGIKNSW	WAKINGS
	PARGING	AGHINPP	HAPPING	AGIILOV	VILIAGO	AGIKNUW	WAUKING
AGGINPS	GAPINGS	AGHINPR	HARPING	AGIILPT	PIGTAIL	AGILLLN	LALLING
	GASPING	AGHINPS	HASPING	AGIILTY	AGILITY	AGILLMN	MALLING
	PAGINGS		PASHING	AGIIMMN	MAIMING	AGILLMU	GALLIUM
AGGINPU	GAUPING		PHASING	AGIIMMS	IMAGISM	AGILLNP	PALLING
AGGINPW	GAWPING		SHAPING	AGIIMNN	MAINING	AGILLNU	LINGUAL
AGGINRR	GARRING	AGHINPT	PATHING	AGIIMOR	ORIGAMI		LINGULA
AGGINRS	SIRGANG	AGHINRS	GARNISH	AGIIMST	IMAGIST	AGILLNW	WALLING
AGGINRT	GRATING		RASHING	AGIINNP	PAINING	AGILLNY	ALLYING
	TARGING		SHARING	AGIINNR	AIRNING	AGILLOR	GORILLA
AGGINRU	ARGUING	AGHINRU	NURAGHI		INGRAIN	AGILLOT	GALLIOT
AGGINRV	GRAVING	AGHINSS	SASHING		RAINING	AGILLRU	LIGULAR
AGGINRY	GRAYING	AGHINST	HASTING	AGIINNS	SAINING	AGILLSU	LIGULAS
AGGINRZ	GRAZING		TASHING	AGIINNW	WAINING		LUGSAIL
AGGINSS	GASSING	AGHINSU	ANGUISH	AGIINPR	PAIRING	AGILMMN	LAMMING
AGGINST	GASTING		HAUSING	AGIINRS	AIRINGS	AGILMMS	GIMMALS
	GATINGS	AGHINSV	HAVINGS		ARISING	AGILMNO	LOAMING
	STAGING		SHAVING		RAGINIS	AGILMNP	LAMPING
AGGINSW	SWAGING	AGHINSW	HAWSING		RAISING		PALMING
AGGINUV	VAGUING		SHAWING		SAIRING	AGILMNR	MARLING
AGGIORS	GORGIAS		WASHING	AGIINRT	AIRTING	AGILMNS	LINGAMS
AGGISWW	WIGWAGS	AGHINSY	HAYINGS		RAITING		MALIGNS
AGGISZZ	ZIGZAGS	AGHINSZ	HAZINGS	AGIINSV	AVISING	AGILMNT	MALTING
AGGLOST	LOGGATS	AGHINTT	HATTING		VISAING	AGILMNU	MAULING
AGGMNOS	MOGGANS		TATHING	AGIINTW	WAITING	AGILMOS	GLIOMAS
AGGMORR	GROGRAM	AGHINTW	THAWING	AGIINTX	TAXIING	AGILMPS	MAGILPS
AGGMOST	MAGGOTS	AGHIOST	GOATISH	AGIINVV	VIVAING	AGILMPU	PLAGIUM
AGGMOTY	MAGGOTY	AGHIPSW	PIGWASH	AGIINNW	WAIVING	AGILNNO	LOANING
AGGNOSW	WAGGONS	AGHIQSU	QUAIGHS	AGIINVZ	AVIZING	AGILNNP	PLANING
AGGNOSX	OXGANGS	AGHIRRS	GHARRIS	AGIJLNS	JINGALS	AGILNNR	LARNING
AGGNPSU	UPGANGS	AGHIRST	GRAITHS	AGIJMMN	JAMMING	AGILNNS	LINSANG
AGGNRSU	NUGGARS	AGHIRSU	GUARISH	AGIJNPP	JAPPING	AGILNNT	TANLING
AGGPRSY	PYGARGS	AGHKOSW	GOSHAWK	AGIJNPU	JAUPING	AGILNOP	GALOPIN
AGHHIMN	HIGHMAN	AGHLMPU	GALUMPH	AGIJNRR	JARRING	AGILNOT	ANTILOG
AGHHINS	HASHING	AGHLNUY	NYLGHAU	AGIJNSW	JAWINGS	AGILNOV	LOAVING

AGILNPP	LAPPING	AGIMORU	GOURAMI
	PALPING	AGIMOSY	ISOGAMY
AGILNPR	PARLING	AGIMRRT	TRIGRAM
AGILNPS	LAPSING	AGIMRSU	GURAMIS
	PALINGS	AGIMRTY	TRIGAMY
	SAPLING	AGIMSST	STIGMAS
AGILNPT	PLATING	AGIMSWW	WIGWAMS
AGILNPW	LAPWING	AGINNNP	PANNING
AGILNPY	PLAYING	AGINNNT	TANNING
AGILNRT	RATLING	AGINNNV	VANNING
AGILNRW	WARLING	AGINNNW	WANNING
AGILNRY	ANGRILY	AGINNOS	GANOINS
	NARGILY	AGINNOT	ATONING
	RAYLING	AGINNPP	NAPPING
AGILNSS	LASINGS	AGINNPS	SPANING
	SIGNALS	AGINNPT	PANTING
AGILNST	ANGLIST	AGINNPW	PAWNING
	LASTING	AGINNRS	SNARING
	SALTING	AGINNRT	RANTING
	SLATING	AGINNRW	WARNING
	STALING	AGINNRY	YARNING
AGILNSU	LINGUAS	AGINNST	ANTINGS
	NILGAUS		STANING
	SALUING	AGINNSU	GUANINS
AGILNSV	SALVING	AGINNSW	AWNINGS
	SLAVING		WANINGS
	VALSING	AGINNTW	WANTING
AGILNSW	LAWINGS	AGINNWY	YAWNING
	SWALING	AGINNWZ	WANZING
AGILNSY	LAYINGS	AGINNYZ	ZANYING
	SLAYING	AGINOOO	OOGONIA
AGILNTY	GIANTLY	AGINOPS	SOAPING
AGILNUV	VALUING	AGINORR	ROARING
AGILNUW	WAULING	AGINORS	IGNAROS
AGILNVV	VALVING		ORIGANS
AGILNWW	WAWLING		SIGNORA
AGILNWY	YAWLING		SOARING
AGILOPT	GALIPOT	AGINORT	ORATING
AGILORS	GIRASOL		ROATING
	GLORIAS	AGINOSS	SAGOINS
AGILOST	GALIOTS	AGINOST	AGONIST
	SALIGOT		GITANOS
AGILRSS	SLAIRGS	AGINOSU	SAGOUIN
AGILSTY	STAGILY	AGINOTV	OVATING
AGIMMNR	RAMMING	AGINOTZ	TOAZING
AGIMMSS	MAGISMS	AGINOVW	AVOWING
AGIMNNN	MANNING	AGINPPP	PAPPING
AGIMNNO	MOANING	AGINPPR	RAPPING
AGIMNNR	RINGMAN	AGINPPS	SAPPING
AGIMNNS	NAMINGS	AGINPPT	TAPPING
AGIMNOR	ROAMING	AGINPPW	WAPPING
AGIMNOT	MOATING	AGINPPY	YAPPING
AGIMNOV	AMOVING	AGINPPZ	ZAPPING
AGIMNPP	MAPPING	AGINPRS	PARINGS
AGIMNPR	RAMPING		PARSING
AGIMNPT	TAMPING		RASPING
AGIMNPV	VAMPING		SPARING
AGIMNRR	MARRING	AGINPRT	PARTING
AGIMNRS	MARGINS		PRATING
AGIMNRT	MARTING		TRAPING
	MIGRANT	AGINPRW	WARPING
AGIMNRW	WARMING	AGINPRY	PRAYING
AGIMNRY	MYRINGA	AGINPSS	PASSING
AGIMNSS	MASSING		SPAINGS
AGIMNST	MASTING	AGINPST	PASTING
	TAMINGS	AGINPSU	PAUSING
AGIMNSU	AMUSING	AGINPSV	PAVINGS
AGIMNSY	MAYINGS	AGINPSY	PAYINGS
AGIMNTT	MATTING		SPAYING
AGIMORS	ISOGRAM	AGINPTT	PATTING

AGINPWY	YAWPING	AGLLOSS	GLOSSAL
AGINRRT	TARRING	AGLLOSW	GALLOWS
AGINRRW	WARRING	AGLLOTT	GLOTTAL
AGINRST	GASTRIN	AGLLRYY	GYRALLY
	RATINGS	AGLMMSY	GYMMALS
	STARING	AGLMOPY	POLYGAM
AGINRSV	RAVINGS	AGLMORS	GLAMORS
AGINRSW	RAWINGS	AGLMORU	GLAMOUR
AGINRSY	SIGNARY	AGLNNOS	LONGANS
	SYRINGA	AGLNOOS	LAGOONS
AGINRTT	RATTING	AGLNORU	LANGUOR
AGINRTY	GIANTRY	AGLNOSS	SLOGANS
AGINRUW	WAURING	AGLNOST	ALONGST
AGINRVY	VARYING	AGLNOSU	LANUGOS
AGINRWY	RINGWAY	AGLNPSY	SPANGLY
AGINRZZ	RAZZING	AGLNPUY	GUNPLAY
AGINSSS	ASSIGNS	AGLNRSU	LANGURS
AGINSSU	SAGUINS	AGLNTUY	GAUNTLY
AGINSSV	SAVINGS	AGLOOPY	APOLOGY
AGINSSW	SAWINGS	AGLOOST	GALOOTS
AGINSSY	SAYINGS	AGLOSSS	GLOSSAS
AGINSTT	STATING	AGLOSUV	VALGOUS
	TASTING	AGLRSSU	GUSLARS
AGINSTU	SAUTING	AGLRSUU	ARGULUS
AGINSTV	STAVING	AGLRSUV	VULGARS
AGINSTW	STAWING	AGMMNOS	GAMMONS
	TAWINGS	AGMMNSU	MAGNUMS
	WASTING	AGMMORY	MYOGRAM
AGINSTX	TAXINGS	AGMNNOS	SONGMAN
AGINSTY	STAYING	AGMNNOW	GOWNMAN
AGINSVW	WAVINGS	AGMNORU	ORGANUM
AGINSWX	WAXINGS	AGMNOST	AMONGST
AGINSWY	SWAYING	AGMNSSU	MUSANGS
AGINTTT	TATTING	AGMNSTU	MUSTANG
AGINTTU	TATUING	AGMNSTY	GYMNAST
	TAUTING	AGMNSYY	SYNGAMY
AGINTTV	VATTING	AGMOOYZ	ZOOGAMY
AGINTTW	TAWTING	AGMOPRR	PROGRAM
AGINTUV	VAUTING	AGMOPRU	GOPURAM
AGINTVW	VAWTING	AGMORRW	RAGWORM
AGINTXY	TAXYING	AGMORSS	ORGASMS
AGINTYZ	TZIGANY	AGMORSY	MORGAYS
AGINVYZ	AVYZING	AGMOSYZ	ZYGOMAS
AGINWWX	WAXWING	AGMPRSU	GRAMPUS
AGIORST	AGISTOR	AGMPSUZ	GAZUMPS
	ORGIAST	AGMRSSU	GRASSUM
AGIORSU	GIAOURS	AGNNNOO	NONAGON
AGIORSV	VIRAGOS	AGNNOOR	ORGANON
AGIOSTU	AGOUTIS	AGNNOST	TONNAGS
AGIRSTU	GUITARS	AGNNSTU	TANGUNS
AGIRTVY	GRAVITY	AGNNSUW	WANGUNS
AGISTTW	WITGATS	AGNOOSZ	GAZOONS
AGISTUV	VAGITUS	AGNOQSU	QUANGOS
AGJLRUU	JUGULAR	AGNORRS	GARRONS
AGJNOOR	JARGOON	AGNORRT	GRANTOR
AGJNORS	JARGONS	AGNORSS	SARONGS
AGKLNOS	KALONGS	AGNOSSS	GOSSANS
AGKLOOS	KAGOOLS	AGNOSST	SONTAGS
AGKLOST	KGOTLAS	AGNOSTU	NOUGATS
AGKLOSU	KAGOULS	AGNOSZZ	GOZZANS
AGKMNOP	KAMPONG	AGNRSSU	SUNGARS
AGKNOPT	PAKTONG	AGNRTUY	GAUNTRY
AGKNRSU	KURGANS	AGOPRSU	GOPURAS
AGKORRW	RAGWORK	AGORRST	GARROTS
AGLLNOO	GALLOON	AGORRTW	RAGWORT
AGLLNOS	GALLONS	AGORSTU	RAGOUTS
	GOLLANS	AGOSTTU	TAUTOGS
AGLLOPS	GALLOPS	AGOSUYZ	AZYGOUS
AGLLORS	GOLLARS	AGSSTUU	AUGUSTS
		AHHHISS	HASHISH

AHHIJRS HIJRAHS	AHIMPSW WAMPISH	AHLMNSY HYMNALS	AIIILMT MILITIA
AHHIKSS SHAIKHS	AHIMRSS MAHSIRS	AHLMNUY HUMANLY	AIIILNT INITIAL
AHHIKSW HAWKISH	AHIMRST THAIRMS	AHLMOOS MOOLAHS	AIIIMRS SAIMIRI
AHHIMNU HAHNIUM	THIRAMS	AHLMORU HUMORAL	AIIKKSW WAKIKIS
AHHIPRS RHAPHIS	THRIMSA	AHLMSUU HAMULUS	AIIKMMS SKIMMIA
AHHISTT SHITTAH	AHIMTUZ AZIMUTH	AHLNOPR ALPHORN	AIIKMNN MANIKIN
AHHKOOS HOOKAHS	AHIMTVZ MITZVAH	AHLNORT ALTHORN	AIIKRTT TRAIKIT
AHHLRSY HARSHLY	AHINNSW WANNISH	AHLORST HARLOTS	AIILLLP LAPILLI
AHHOORS HOORAHS	AHINNTX XANTHIN	AHLOSST SHALOTS	AIILLMN LIMINAL
AHHOPRS SHOPHAR	AHINORT ORTHIAN	AHLOSTU OUTLASH	AIILLMS LIMAILS
AHHRRSU HURRAHS	AHINOTZ HOATZIN	AHLOTUU OUTHAUL	AIILLNV VILLAIN
AHIIKRS SHIKARI	AHINPST HATPINS	AHLPRSY SHARPLY	AIILLQU QUILLAI
AHIILPS SILPHIA	AHINRSS ARSHINS	AHLPRUY HYPURAL	AIILMMN MINIMAL
AHIILST LITHIAS	SHAIRNS	AHLPSSY SPLASHY	AIILMNO MONILIA
AHIIMNT THIAMIN	AHINRST TARNISH	AHMMMOT MAMMOTH	AIILMRS SIMILAR
AHIIMSS SASHIMI	AHINRSU UNHAIRS	AHMMMUU HUMMAUM	AIILMRT MILITAR
AHIINPR HAIRPIN	AHINRSV VARNISH	AHMNNSU NUMNAHS	AIILMRY MILIARY
AHIINST TAHINIS	AHINRTY RHYTINA	AHMNNTU MANHUNT	AIILNOS LIAISON
AHIINTU HUITAIN	AHINSTU INHAUST	AHMNNUU UNHUMAN	AIILNPT PINTAIL
AHIIPRS AIRSHIP	AHIOPSS SOPHIAS	AHMNOPS SHOPMAN	AIILNPU NAUPLII
AHIKLRS LARKISH	AHIOPXY HYPOXIA	AHMNOPT PHANTOM	AIILNTU NAUTILI
AHIKLST KHILATS	AHIORUV HAVIOUR	AHMNORY HARMONY	AIILNTY ANILITY
AHIKLSY SHAKILY	AHIPRST HARPIST	AHMNOSS HANSOMS	AIILOPP PAPILIO
AHIKMNS KHAMSIN	AHIPRSU RUPIAHS	AHMNOSW SHOWMAN	AIILORV RAVIOLI
AHIKMRS KASHMIR	AHIPRSW WARSHIP	AHMNRYY HYMNARY	AIILQSU SILIQUA
AHIKMSW MAWKISH	AHIPSSW WASPISH	AHMOOPS OOMPAHS	AIILRTV TRIVIAL
AHIKNSS SNAKISH	AHIRRSS SHIRRAS	SHAMPOO	VITRAIL
AHIKNSV KNAVISH	SIRRAHS	AHMOOSS SAMSHOO	AIIMMNS ANIMISM
AHIKOSW KOWHAIS	AHIRRST STIRRAH	AHMORRU MORRHUA	AIIMMNX MAXIMIN
AHIKPRS PARKISH	AHIRSST HAIRSTS	AHMORST HARMOST	AIIMMSS MISAIMS
AHIKRSS SHIKARS	AHIRSTT ATHIRST	AHMOSSY SHAMOYS	AIIMNOR AMORINI
AHIKSSS SHIKSAS	RATTISH	AHMOSTU MAHOUTS	AIIMNPS PAINIMS
AHIKSST SKAITHS	TARTISH	AHMOSWY HAYMOWS	PIANISM
AHILLNO HALLION	AHIRSTW TRISHAW	AHMOTTZ MATZOTH	AIIMNPT IMPAINT
AHILLNP PHALLIN	WRAITHS	AHMRRSU MURRHAS	TIMPANI
AHILLRT ATHRILL	AHISSTT STAITHS	AHMRSTW WARMTHS	AIIMNRT MARTINI
AHILLSS SHALLIS	AHISSTU SHIATSU	AHMRSTY THRYMSA	AIIMNSS SIMIANS
AHILLSZ ZILLAHS	THIASUS	AHMSSSU SAMSHUS	AIIMNST ANIMIST
AHILLTT TALLITH	AHISSTW WHATSIS	AHNOOPR HARPOON	AIIMNTT IMITANT
AHILMMS MASHLIM	AHISTTW WHATSIT	AHNOPRS ORPHANS	AIIMNTU MINUTIA
AHILMMY HAMMILY	AHITTWW WHITTAW	AHNORSS SHORANS	AIIMNTV VITAMIN
AHILMNS MASHLIN	AHJOOPS POOJAHS	AHNORSX SAXHORN	AIIMPRS IMPAIRS
AHILMOS HOLMIAS	AHKLOOS KOOLAHS	AHNOTTW WHATNOT	AIIMPSS SIMPAIS
AHILMOT HALIMOT	AHKLPSU PULKHAS	AHNPPUU PUPUNHA	AIIMRST SIMITAR
AHILMSU ALUMISH	AHKMNSU KHANUMS	AHNPPUY UNHAPPY	AIIMSSY MYIASIS
AHILNPS PLANISH	AHKMORR MARKHOR	AHNPRXY PHARYNX	AIINNOP PIANINO
AHILNRS SHRINAL	AHKMOSW MOHAWKS	AHNPSSU UNHASPS	AIINNSZ ZINNIAS
AHILNRT INTHRAL	AHKMRTU MUKHTAR	AHNSSTU SUNHATS	AIINNTY INANITY
AHILNSY LINHAYS	AHKNPSU PUNKAHS	AHNSTUW UNTHAWS	AIINOPS SINOPIA
AHILORY HOARILY	AHKRSST SKARTHS	AHNSTUY UNHASTY	AIINOTT NOTITIA
AHILPPS SHIPLAP	AHKRSTU KHURTAS	AHOORSY HOORAYS	AIINPRS ASPIRIN
AHILPPY HAPPILY	AHLLMOS MOLLAHS	AHOPRTY ATROPHY	AIINPST PIANIST
AHILPSY APISHLY	OLLAMHS	AHOPTTW TOWPATH	AIINRSS RAISINS
AHILSST SALTISH	AHLLMSU MULLAHS	AHORRSW HARROWS	AIINRST INTARSI
TAHSILS	AHLLNOS SHALLON	AHORSTT THROATS	AIINRTV VITRAIN
AHILSSV SLAVISH	AHLLNOY HALLYON	AHORSTU AUTHORS	AIINSST ISATINS
AHILSTU HALITUS	AHLLNSU NULLAHS	AHORSTW WROATHS	AIINSTT TITIANS
THULIAS	AHLLOOS HALLOOS	AHORTTY THROATY	AIIPRST PIARIST
AHILSTY HASTILY	HOLLOAS	AHPRRTY PHRATRY	AIIPSTW WAPITIS
AHIMMRS RAMMISH	AHLLOPS SHALLOP	AHPRSST SPARTHS	AIIPTTU PITUITA
AHIMNNS MANNISH	AHLLOST SHALLOT	AHPSXYY ASPHYXY	AIJJMMS JIMJAMS
AHIMNNU INHUMAN	AHLLOSW HALLOWS	AHQSSUY SQUASHY	AIJLORS JAILORS
AHIMNPS SHIPMAN	SHALLOW	AHRRSUY HURRAYS	AIJLYZZ JAZZILY
AHIMNRS HARMINS	AHLLOTY LOATHLY	AHRSSSU HUSSARS	AIJNORT JANITOR
AHIMOPR MORPHIA	AHLLPSU PHALLUS	AHRSSTT STRATHS	AIJORSW JOWARIS
AHIMORS MOHAIRS	AHLLPYY APHYLLY	AHRSSTW SWARTHS	AIJPSTU JUPATIS
AHIMPSS MISHAPS	AHLLRST THRALLS	AHRSTTW THWARTS	AIKKSUZ ZAKUSKI
PASHIMS	AHLLSTU THALLUS	AHRSTWY SWARTHY	AIKLMMN MILKMAN
AHIMPST MISHAPT	AHLMMSU MASHLUM	AHRTUWY THRUWAY	AIKLMNN LINKMAN
AHIMPSV VAMPISH	AHLMNPY NYMPHAL	AHSSSTU TUSSAHS	AIKLMNS MALKINS

AIKLMPU	LAMPUKI	AILNNPU	PINNULA	AILSTUW	LAWSUIT	AINNSTU	UNSAINT
AIKLMSU	KALIUMS	AILNNSU	UNNAILS	AILTTTY	TATTILY	AINNTUY	ANNUITY
AIKLNOS	KAOLINS		UNSLAIN	AIMMMSU	MUMMIAS	AINOOPR	PRONAOI
AIKLNSY	SNAKILY	AILNOPY	POLYNIA	AIMMMUX	MAXIMUM	AINOORR	ORARION
AIKLPWY	PAWKILY	AILNOSS	SIALONS	AIMMNTU	MANUMIT	AINOORT	ORATION
AIKLRTT	TITLARK	AILNOST	TALIONS	AIMMORS	AMORISM	AINOOTV	OVATION
AIKLSSU	SALUKIS	AILNOTU	OUTLAIN	AIMMOSS	MIMOSAS	AINOPPT	APPOINT
AIKLSSY	SKYSAIL	AILNPRW	PRAWLIN	AIMMOST	ATOMISM	AINOPRS	PARISON
AIKMMSS	IMMASKS	AILNPST	PLAINTS	AIMNNOS	MANSION		SOPRANI
AIKMNNS	KINSMAN	AILNPSX	SALPINX		ONANISM	AINOPRT	ATROPIN
AIKMNSS	KAMSINS	AILNPTU	NUPTIAL	AIMNNSS	NANISMS	AINOPSS	PASSION
AIKMNSW	MAWKINS		PATULIN	AIMNNSY	MINYANS	AINOPTU	OPUNTIA
AIKMOOS	OOMIAKS		UNPLAIT	AIMNOOR	AMORINO		UTOPIAN
AIKMPRS	IMPARKS	AILNPTY	INAPTLY	AIMNOPR	RAMPION	AINOQSU	QUINOAS
AIKMRSU	KUMARIS		PTYALIN	AIMNOPT	MAINTOP	AINORST	AROINTS
AIKNNNS	NANKINS	AILNQTU	QUINTAL		TAMPION		RATIONS
AIKNNPS	NAPKINS	AILNRST	RATLINS		TIMPANO	AINORSW	WARISON
AIKNOST	KATIONS	AILNRSU	INSULAR	AIMNORS	MAINORS	AINORTX	TRIAXON
AIKNPRS	KIRPANS		URINALS	AIMNORT	TORMINA	AINOSSU	SANIOUS
	PARKINS	AILNRTT	RATTLIN	AIMNORU	MAINOUR		SUASION
AIKNPSS	PANISKS	AILNSST	INSTALS	AIMNOST	MANITOS	AINOSTT	STATION
AIKORST	TROIKAS	AILNSSU	INSULAS		STAMNOI	AINOSUX	ANXIOUS
AIKRRSS	SIRKARS	AILNSSV	SILVANS	AIMNOTU	MANITOU	AINOSVY	SYNOVIA
AIKRSST	STRAIKS	AILNSTU	UNALIST		TINAMOU	AINPPRS	PARSNIP
AILLMNU	LUMINAL	AILNSTY	NASTILY	AIMNPSW	IMPAWNS	AINPQTU	PIQUANT
AILLMOT	MAILLOT		SAINTLY	AIMNPSY	PAYNIMS	AINPRSS	SPINARS
AILLMPU	PALLIUM	AILNSUV	UNVAILS	AIMNPTY	TYMPANI		SPRAINS
AILLNNO	LANOLIN	AILNTTY	NATTILY	AIMNRRU	MURRAIN	AINPRST	SPIRANT
AILLNOP	PAILLON	AILNTUV	UNVITAL	AIMNRST	MARTINS		SPRAINT
AILLNPY	PLAINLY	AILOORS	OORIALS	AIMNRSU	URANISM	AINPRSU	PRUINAS
AILLNST	INSTALL	AILOORW	WOORALI	AIMNRTU	NATRIUM	AINPRSW	INWRAPS
AILLNSV	VILLANS	AILOPST	APOSTIL	AIMNRTV	VARMINT	AINPRTU	PURITAN
AILLNSW	INWALLS		TOPSAIL	AIMNRUU	URANIUM		UPTRAIN
AILLNVY	VILLANY	AILOPSY	SOAPILY	AIMNSTT	MATTINS	AINPSST	PTISANS
AILLPRS	PILLARS	AILOPTT	TALIPOT	AIMNSTU	TSUNAMI	AINPSSV	SPAVINS
AILLPRU	PILULAR	AILOPTV	PIVOTAL	AIMNSUV	MAUVINS	AINQRST	QINTARS
AILLPSU	PILLAUS	AILOQTU	ALIQUOT	AIMNSYZ	ZANYISM	AINQRUY	QUINARY
	PILULAS	AILORSS	SAILORS	AIMOPST	IMPASTO	AINQSTU	ASQUINT
AILLPUV	PLUVIAL	AILORST	TAILORS	AIMOPSY	MYOPIAS		QUINTAS
AILLRSU	ARILLUS	AILORSU	OURALIS	AIMORRU	ORARIUM	AINRRTY	TRINARY
AILLSTY	SALTILY	AILORUW	WOURALI	AIMORST	AMORIST	AINRRUY	URINARY
AILLTVY	VITALLY	AILORUX	UXORIAL	AIMORUZ	ZOARIUM	AINRSST	INSTARS
AILLTWW	WITWALL	AILORVY	OLIVARY	AIMOSTT	ATOMIST		SANTIRS
AILMMOR	IMMORAL	AILOSSS	ASSOILS	AIMPPSS	PAPISMS		STRAINS
AILMMSY	MYALISM	AILOSTU	OUTSAIL	AIMPPST	MAPPIST	AINRSTT	STRAINT
AILMMUU	ALUMIUM	AILOSTX	OXTAILS	AIMPRRY	PRIMARY		TRANSIT
AILMNNO	NOMINAL	AILPRSS	SPIRALS	AIMPRST	ARMPITS	AINRSTU	NUTRIAS
AILMNOP	LAMPION	AILPRSU	PARULIS		IMPARTS	AINRTUY	UNITARY
AILMNOS	MALISON		UPRISAL	AIMPRSY	PYRAMIS	AINSSTT	TANISTS
	MONIALS	AILPRSY	PYRALIS	AIMQRSU	MARQUIS	AINSSTU	ISSUANT
	SOMNIAL	AILPSST	PASTILS	AIMRSST	TSARISM		SUSTAIN
AILMNOY	ALIMONY		SPITALS	AIMRSTY	MAISTRY	AINSSXY	SYNAXIS
AILMNPS	PLASMIN	AILPSTU	TIPULAS		SYMITAR	AINTTVY	TANTIVY
AILMNPT	IMPLANT	AILPSWY	SLIPWAY	AIMSSSY	MISSAYS	AIOORSS	ARIOSOS
AILMNRS	MARLINS	AILQSSU	SQUAILS	AIMSSTT	STATISM	AIOPRRT	AIRPORT
AILMNRU	MURLAIN	AILQTTU	QUITTAL	AIMSSTU	AUTISMS		PARITOR
AILMNSS	MASLINS	AILQTUY	QUALITY	AINNNST	TANNINS	AIOPRST	AIRSTOP
AILMOPT	OPTIMAL	AILRRVY	RIVALRY	AINNOPS	SAPONIN		PAROTIS
AILMOST	SOMITAL	AILRSTT	STARLIT	AINNOSS	NASIONS	AIOPRSV	PAVIORS
AILMPRS	IMPARLS	AILRSTU	RITUALS	AINNOST	ANOINTS	AIOPRTT	PATRIOT
AILMPRU	PRIMULA		TRISULA		NATIONS	AIOPRTY	TOPIARY
AILMPST	PALMIST	AILRSTY	TRYSAIL		ONANIST	AIOPRUV	PAVIOUR
AILMPSY	MISPLAY	AILRTTU	TITULAR	AINNPSS	INSPANS	AIOPSTU	UTOPIAS
AILMRST	MISTRAL	AILRTUV	VIRTUAL	AINNPTU	UNPAINT	AIORRRW	WARRIOR
AILMRSU	SIMULAR		VITULAR	AINNQTU	QUINNAT	AIORRSU	OURARIS
AILMSSS	MISSALS	AILSSTX	LAXISTS		QUINTAN	AIORRTT	TRAITOR
AILMSSX	LAXISMS	AILSSUV	VISUALS	AINNRSU	URANINS	AIORRTX	ORATRIX
AILMSSY	MISLAYS	AILSSVY	SYLVIAS	AINNRTT	INTRANT	AIORSST	AORISTS
AILMSTU	ULTIMAS	AILSSVZ	VIZSLAS	AINNRTU	URINANT		ARISTOS
AILMSUV	MAULVIS	AILSTTY	TASTILY	AINNSTT	INSTANT		SATORIS

AIORSSU	SOUARIS	ALLLOYY	LOYALLY	ALNOOPR	POLARON		MURRAMS
AIORSTU	SAUTOIR	ALLMNOP	POLLMAN	ALNOOPT	PLATOON	AMMRSUY	SUMMARY
AIORSTV	TRAVOIS	ALLMNOT	TOLLMAN	ALNOORT	ORTOLAN	AMMSSTU	SUMMATS
	VIATORS	ALLMNOY	ALLONYM	ALNOOSS	SALOONS	AMNNOOX	MONAXON
AIORSTY	OSTIARY	ALLMORS	MORALLS		SOLANOS	AMNNORS	NORMANS
AIORSUV	SAVIOUR	ALLMORY	MORALLY	ALNOPPY	PANOPLY	AMNNOSW	SNOWMAN
	VARIOUS	ALLMOSS	SLALOMS	ALNOPSS	SPONSAL	AMNNOSY	ANONYMS
AIPPRRS	RIPRAPS	ALLMOSW	MALLOWS	ALNOPYY	POLYNYA	AMNNOTT	MONTANT
AIPPSST	PAPISTS	ALLMPUU	PLUMULA	ALNORST	LATRONS	AMNNOTY	ANTONYM
AIPRSST	RAPISTS	ALLMSUV	VALLUMS	ALNORUY	UNROYAL	AMNNOUW	UNWOMAN
AIPRSTU	UPSTAIR	ALLNOPS	POLLANS	ALNORUZ	ZONULAR	AMNOOPP	POMPANO
AIPRSUY	PYURIAS	ALLNRUU	LUNULAR	ALNOSUZ	ZONULAS	AMNOORS	MAROONS
AIPRTVY	PRAVITY	ALLNSTY	SLANTLY	ALNPRUY	PLANURY	AMNOOTT	OTTOMAN
AIPSSTT	TAPISTS	ALLNSUU	LUNULAS	ALNPSTU	PULTANS	AMNOOTZ	MATZOON
AIPSSTW	SAWPITS	ALLNTUU	ULULANT	ALNPTUY	UNAPTLY	AMNOPRT	PORTMAN
AIRRSST	STIRRAS	ALLOOPS	APOLLOS	ALNPTXY	PLANXTY	AMNOPRY	PARONYM
AIRRSZZ	RIZZARS		PALOLOS	ALNRSUY	URANYLS	AMNOPST	POSTMAN
AIRRTZZ	RIZZART	ALLOOTX	AXOLOTL	ALNSSTU	SULTANS		TAMPONS
AIRSSSU	RUSSIAS	ALLOPRS	PALLORS	ALNSSVY	SYLVANS		TOPSMAN
AIRSSTT	ARTISTS	ALLOPRY	PAYROLL	ALNSTUW	WALNUTS	AMNOPTU	PANTOUM
	SITTARS	ALLOPSW	WALLOPS	ALNSUUU	UNUSUAL	AMNOPTY	TYMPANO
	STRAITS	ALLORSS	SOLLARS	ALOOPSS	SALOOPS	AMNORSS	RAMSONS
	TSARIST	ALLORYY	ROYALLY	ALOOPYZ	POLYZOA		RANSOMS
AIRSSTU	AURISTS	ALLOSSW	SALLOWS	ALOORRS	SORORAL	AMNORST	MATRONS
AIRSTTT	ATTRIST	ALLOSTT	TALLOTS	ALOPPRS	POPLARS		TRANSOM
AIRSTTY	YTTRIAS	ALLOSTV	LAVOLTS	ALOPPRU	POPULAR	AMNORSY	MASONRY
AIRSTVY	VARSITY	ALLOSTW	TALLOWS	ALOPPRY	PROPYLA		MORNAYS
AIRTUVX	VITRAUX	ALLOSWW	SWALLOW	ALOPPST	LAPTOPS	AMNORTU	ROMAUNT
AISSSST	ASSISTS		WALLOWS	ALOPRRU	PARLOUR	AMNOSST	STAMNOS
AISSTTT	STATIST	ALLOSWY	SALLOWY	ALOPRST	PATROLS	AMNOSTU	AMOUNTS
AISTTVY	VASTITY	ALLOTTY	TOTALLY		PORTALS		MOUTANS
AISTUVY	SUAVITY	ALLOTWY	TALLOWY	ALOPRSU	PARLOUS		OUTMANS
AJKMNNU	JUNKMAN	ALLOTYY	LOYALTY	ALOPSST	POSTALS	AMNOTUY	AUTONYM
AJKMNTU	MUNTJAK	ALLPRSU	PLURALS	ALOPSSU	SPOUSAL	AMNPSTY	TYMPANS
AJLLRUY	JURALLY	ALLQSSU	SQUALLS	ALOPSUV	VOLUSPA	AMNPTYY	TYMPANY
AJLNORU	JOURNAL	ALLQSUY	SQUALLY	ALOPTUY	OUTPLAY	AMNQTUU	QUANTUM
AJLOORS	JAROOLS	ALLRRUY	RURALLY	ALOQRRU	RORQUAL	AMNRRUY	UNMARRY
AJLOPPY	JALOPPY	ALLRSTU	LUSTRAL	ALOQRSU	SQUALOR	AMNRSTU	ANTRUMS
AJMNRUY	JURYMAN	ALLSUUY	USUALLY	ALOQSTU	LOQUATS		UNSMART
AJMOPST	JAMPOTS	ALMMSUY	AMYLUMS	ALORRST	ROSTRAL	AMNRTTU	TANTRUM
AJMRSTU	JUMARTS	ALMNNUY	UNMANLY	ALORRSW	WORRALS	AMNSTTU	MUTANTS
AJNRSTU	JURANTS	ALMNOOP	LAMPOON	ALORSSU	ROSULAS	AMNSTUU	AUTUMNS
AKKLRSY	SKYLARK	ALMNOOT	TOOLMAN	ALORSSV	SALVORS	AMNTUUY	AUTUMNY
AKKNRSU	KUNKARS	ALMNOOW	WOOLMAN	ALORSTU	ROTULAS	AMOOORS	AMOROSO
AKKOQSU	QUOKKAS	ALMNORS	NORMALS		TORULAS	AMOOPRT	TAPROOM
AKLNOSU	KOULANS	ALMNORU	UNMORAL	ALORSUV	VALOURS	AMOORSU	AMOROUS
AKLNOSX	KLAXONS	ALMNORY	ALMONRY	ALORTYY	ROYALTY	AMOORSV	MOORVAS
AKLOPRW	LAPWORK	ALMNOSS	SALMONS	ALOSTTU	OUTLAST	AMOPSTT	TOPMAST
AKLOSTW	KOTWALS	ALMNOSU	MONAULS	ALOSTUW	OUTLAWS	AMORRST	MORTARS
AKLOTTU	OUTTALK		SOLANUM	ALOSTUY	OUTLAYS	AMORRSU	ARMOURS
AKLOTUW	OUTWALK	ALMNOWY	WOMANLY	ALPRRSU	LARRUPS	AMORRSW	MARROWS
AKLPRSY	SPARKLY	ALMNRSU	MURLANS	ALPRSSU	PULSARS	AMORRUY	ARMOURY
AKLRSTY	STARKLY	ALMNSUU	ALUMNUS	ALPRSSW	SPRAWLS	AMORRWY	MARROWY
AKMNORW	WORKMAN	ALMOPRT	MARPLOT	ALPRSUU	PURSUAL	AMORSST	MATROSS
AKMNRTU	TRANKUM	ALMORRU	MORULAR	ALPRSUW	PULWARS		STROAMS
AKMNSSU	UNMASKS	ALMORSS	SAMLORS	ALPRSWY	SPRAWLY	AMORSSY	MORASSY
AKMOORT	MOOKTAR	ALMORST	MORTALS	ALRSTTY	STARTLY	AMOSTUZ	MAZOUTS
AKMQTUU	KUMQUAT	ALMORSU	MORULAS	ALRSTUU	SUTURAL	AMOSUYZ	AZYMOUS
AKNORSU	KORUNAS	ALMOSST	SMALTOS	ALRSTUW	TULWARS	AMPRSST	STRAMPS
AKNORSY	RYOKANS	ALMOSTW	MATLOWS	AMMMNOS	MAMMONS	AMPRSUW	UPSWARM
AKNORTU	OUTRANK	ALMOSXY	XYLOMAS	AMMMOSU	AMOMUMS	AMRRSTU	RASTRUM
AKOOPRT	PARTOOK	ALMOTTU	MULATTO	AMMNOOR	MOORMAN	AMRRSTY	MARTYRS
AKOORRS	KORORAS	ALMRSTY	SMARTLY	AMMNOOT	MOOTMAN	AMRRSUY	MURRAYS
AKOOSTU	ATOKOUS	ALMRSUU	RAMULUS	AMMNRUY	NUMMARY	AMRRTYY	MARTYRY
AKORRTW	ARTWORK	ALMRTUU	TUMULAR	AMMOORR	MAORMOR	AMRSTTU	STRATUM
AKORWWX	WAXWORK	ALMSSUY	ALYSSUM		MORMAOR	ANNOOSX	XOANONS
AKQSSUW	SQUAWKS		ASYLUMS	AMMOPTU	POMATUM	ANNOPRS	NAPRONS
AKQSUWY	SQUAWKY	ALMSTUU	UMLAUTS	AMMORST	MARMOTS	ANNOPST	PANTONS
AKRSSTU	TUSKARS	ALNNRSU	UNSNARL	AMMPSUW	WAMPUMS	ANNOPTY	POYNANT
AKSSWYY	SKYWAYS	ALNNSUU	ANNULUS	AMMRRSU	MARRUMS	ANNORST	NATRONS

ANNOSST	SANTONS	AOPRRTY	PARROTY
	SONANTS		PORTRAY
ANNOSTW	WANTONS	AOPRSST	ASPORTS
ANNOTTY	TANTONY		PASTORS
ANNPSSU	SANNUPS	AOPRSTU	ASPROUT
	UNSNAPS	AOPRSUV	VAPOURS
ANNPSTU	PANTUNS	AOPRTTU	OUTPART
ANNRTYY	TYRANNY	AOPRTUY	OUTPRAY
ANNSSTU	SUNTANS	AOPRUVY	VAPOURY
ANNSSTY	SYNTANS	AOPSSTU	PASSOUT
ANOOPRS	PRONAOS	AOPSTUY	AUTOPSY
	SOPRANO	AOQRSTU	QUARTOS
ANOOPRT	PATROON	AORRSST	SARTORS
	PRONOTA	AORRSTW	TARROWS
ANOORST	RATOONS	AORRSWY	SOWARRY
ANOORTT	ARNOTTO		YARROWS
ANOPRRS	SPORRAN	AORSSST	ASSORTS
ANOPRSS	PARSONS	AORSSTT	STATORS
ANOPRST	PARTONS	AORSSTU	SOUTARS
	PATRONS	AORSSUV	SAVOURS
	TARPONS	AORSSUY	OSSUARY
ANOPRTV	PROVANT		SUASORY
ANOPSTT	OPTANTS	AORSTUY	YAOURTS
ANOPSTU	OUTSPAN	AORSUVY	SAVOURY
ANOPSUY	YAUPONS	AORTUVY	AVOUTRY
ANORRSW	NARROWS	AOSTTTW	TATTOWS
ANORSSV	SOVRANS	AOSTTUY	OUTSTAY
ANORSTT	ATTORNS	APPRRUU	PURPURA
	RATTONS	APPRSTY	STRAPPY
	ROTTANS	APPRSUY	PAPYRUS
ANORSTU	ROUSANT	APRSSSU	SURPASS
	SANTOUR	APRSSWY	PSYWARS
ANORSTY	AROYNTS	APRSTTU	UPSTART
ANORSUU	ANUROUS	APRSTTY	TAPSTRY
	URANOUS	APSSTUY	UPSTAYS
ANORWWY	WAYWORN	APSSUWY	UPSWAYS
ANOSSTZ	STANZOS	AQRTUYZ	QUARTZY
ANPPSUW	SUPPAWN	AQSTTUY	SQUATTY
ANPRSSU	UNSPARS	ARSSTTU	STRATUS
ANPRSTU	SUNTRAP	BBBDELO	BLOBBED
	UNSTRAP		BOBBLED
ANPRSUW	UNWRAPS	BBBDELU	BLUBBED
ANPRSUY	UNPRAYS		BUBBLED
ANPSSUW	SUPAWNS	BBBEIOS	BOBBIES
ANRSSTU	SANTURS	BBBEIRS	BIBBERS
ANRSSUY	SUNRAYS	BBBEISU	BUBBIES
ANRSTTU	TRUANTS	BBBELOS	BOBBLES
ANRSTTY	TYRANTS	BBBELRU	BLUBBER
ANRSUWY	RUNWAYS	BBBELSU	BUBBLES
ANSSTTU	TUTSANS	BBBEORY	BOBBERY
AOOPPRS	APROPOS	BBBGIIN	BIBBING
AOOPRTT	TAPROOT	BBBGINO	BOBBING
AOORRST	ORATORS	BBBHIOS	BOBBISH
AOORRSY	ARROYOS	BBBHSUU	HUBBUBS
AOORRTT	ROTATOR	BBBINOS	BOBBINS
AOORRTU	OUTROAR	BBCCIKO	BIBCOCK
AOORRTY	ORATORY	BBCDEHU	CHUBBED
AOORSTT	TOOARTS	BBCDEIR	CRIBBED
AOORSTU	OUTSOAR	BBCDELO	COBBLED
AOORSTV	OVATORS	BBCDELU	CLUBBED
AOOSTTT	TATTOOS	BBCEHIN	NEBBICH
AOOSTUZ	AZOTOUS	BBCEILR	CRIBBLE
AOOTXYZ	ZOOTAXY	BBCEIOR	COBBIER
AOPPPSU	PAPPOUS	BBCEISU	CUBBIES
AOPPRRT	RAPPORT	BBCEKKO	KEBBOCK
AOPPRST	APPORTS	BBCEKKU	KEBBUCK
AOPRRST	PARROTS	BBCELOR	CLOBBER
	RAPTORS		COBBLER
AOPRRSU	UPROARS	BBCELOS	COBBLES
AOPRRSW	SPARROW	BBCEORS	COBBERS

BBCEOSW	COBWEBS	BBEGIRS	GIBBERS
BBCGINO	COBBING	BBEGIST	GIBBETS
BBCGINU	CUBBING	BBEGLOR	GOBBLER
BBCHISU	CUBBISH	BBEGLOS	GOBBLES
BBCINOU	BUBONIC	BBEGLRU	GRUBBLE
BBCRSUY	SCRUBBY	BBEGNSU	BEBUNGS
BBDDEIL	DIBBLED	BBEGOST	GOBBETS
BBDDEIR	DRIBBED	BBEGRRU	GRUBBER
BBDDERU	DRUBBED	BBEHINS	NEBBISH
BBDEEIR	DEBBIER	BBEHIOS	HOBBIES
BBDEEIS	DEBBIES	BBEHISU	HUBBIES
BBDEEIT	EBBTIDE	BBEHLOR	HOBBLER
BBDEELP	PEBBLED	BBEHLOS	HOBBLES
BBDEENS	SNEBBED	BBEHMTU	BETHUMB
BBDEFLU	FLUBBED	BBEIILR	RIBIBLE
BBDEGIL	GLIBBED	BBEIIMR	IMBIBER
BBDEGLO	GOBBLED	BBEIIMS	IMBIBES
BBDEGRU	GRUBBED	BBEIIRR	RIBBIER
BBDEGSU	BEDBUGS	BBEIIRS	RIBIBES
BBDEHLO	HOBBLED	BBEIJRS	JIBBERS
BBDEIIM	IMBIBED	BBEIKLS	KIBBLES
BBDEIKL	KIBBLED	BBEILNR	NIBBLER
BBDEILN	NIBBLED	BBEILNS	NIBBLES
BBDEILO	BILOBED	BBEILOS	BILBOES
	LOBBIED		LOBBIES
BBDEILR	DIBBLER	BBEILOT	BIBELOT
	DRIBBLE	BBEILPR	PRIBBLE
BBDEILS	DIBBLES	BBEILQU	QUIBBLE
BBDEINS	SNIBBED	BBEILRS	LIBBERS
BBDEIOS	DOBBIES	BBEILRT	TRIBBLE
BBDEIRR	DRIBBER	BBEILST	STIBBLE
BBDEIRS	DIBBERS	BBEILSY	YIBBLES
BBDEKNO	KNOBBED	BBEIMOS	MOBBIES
BBDELMO	MOBBLED	BBEINOR	NOBBIER
BBDELMU	BUMBLED	BBEINRU	NUBBIER
BBDELNO	NOBBLED	BBEIOOS	BOOBIES
BBDELNU	NUBBLED	BBEIRRS	BRIBERS
BBDELOS	BOBSLED	BBEIRRY	BRIBERY
BBDELOW	WOBBLED	BBEIRTU	TUBBIER
BBDELRU	BURBLED	BBEISSU	BUSBIES
BBDELSU	SLUBBED	BBEJORS	JOBBERS
BBDENSU	SNUBBED	BBEJORY	JOBBERY
BBDEORS	DOBBERS	BBEKLNO	KNOBBLE
BBDEOSW	SWOBBED	BBEKLNU	KNUBBLE
BBDESTU	STUBBED	BBEKLOS	BLESBOK
BBDGIIN	DIBBING	BBEKLUU	BUBUKLE
BBDGINO	DOBBING	BBEKNOR	KNOBBER
BBDGINU	DUBBING	BBEKNSU	NEBBUKS
BBDILRY	DRIBBLY	BBELMOS	MOBBLES
BBDINOS	DOBBINS	BBELMSU	BUMBLES
BBDINSU	DUBBINS	BBELNOR	NOBBLER
BBDKSUY	DYBBUKS	BBELNOS	NOBBLES
BBEEERU	BEBEERU	BBELNSU	NUBBLES
BBEEIKS	KEBBIES	BBELORS	SLOBBER
BBEEIRW	WEBBIER	BBELORW	WOBBLER
BBEEKLS	LEBBEKS	BBELORY	LOBBYER
BBEELPS	PEBBLES	BBELOSW	WOBBLES
BBEELSS	EBBLESS	BBELRSU	BURBLES
BBEENSS	SNEBBES		LUBBERS
BBEFILR	FRIBBLE		RUBBLES
BBEFIRS	FIBBERS		SLUBBER
BBEFIRU	FUBBIER	BBELSTU	STUBBLE
BBEFIRY	FIBBERY	BBEMNSU	BENUMBS
BBEFRUY	FUBBERY	BBEMORS	BOMBERS
BBEGIKN	KEBBING	BBENOTW	BOWBENT
BBEGILR	GLIBBER	BBENRSU	SNUBBER
	GRIBBLE	BBENSSU	SNUBBES
BBEGINN	NEBBING	BBEOOSY	YOBBOES
BBEGINW	WEBBING	BBEORRS	ROBBERS
BBEGIOS	GIBBOSE	BBEORRY	ROBBERY

BBEORSW SWOBBER	BCDEEHN BENCHED	BCEHOSS BOSCHES	BCGIKNU BUCKING
BBERRSU RUBBERS	BCDEEIL DECIBEL	BCEHOST BOTCHES	BCGIMNO COMBING
BBERRUY RUBBERY	BCDEEKS BEDECKS	BCEHOSU BOUCHES	BCGINNU BUNCING
BBERSTU TUBBERS	BCDEHIR BIRCHED	BCEHRSU CHERUBS	BCGINRU CURBING
BBFGIIN FIBBING	BCDEHIT BITCHED	BCEHRTU BUTCHER	BCGORSU COBURGS
BBFGINO FOBBING	BCDEHNU BUNCHED	BCEHSTU BUTCHES	BCHIIOT COHIBIT
BBFGINU FUBBING	BCDEHOT BOTCHED	BCEIIKR BRICKIE	BCHIKOU CHIBOUK
BBGGIIN GIBBING	BCDEHOU DEBOUCH	BCEIISV VIBICES	BCHIKSU BUCKISH
BBGIIJN JIBBING	BCDEIIO BIOCIDE	BCEIKLM LIMBECK	BCHILOS CHIBOLS
BBGIILN LIBBING	BCDEIKR BRICKED	BCEIKLR BRICKLE	BCHIMOR RHOMBIC
BBGIINN NIBBING	BCDEIKT BEDTICK	BCEIKNR BRICKEN	BCHINOR BRONCHI
BBGIINR BRIBING	BCDEILM CLIMBED	BCEIKRS BICKERS	BCHIOPR PIBROCH
RIBBING	BCDEILO DOCIBLE	BCEIKST BESTICK	BCHLOTY BLOTCHY
BBGIJNO JOBBING	BCDEIOS BODICES	BCEIKSU BUCKIES	BCHNOOR BRONCHO
BBGILNO LOBBING	BCDEIRS SCRIBED	BCEILMO EMBOLIC	BCHORST BORSCHT
BBGILNU BULBING	BCDEKLO BLOCKED	BCEILMR CLIMBER	BORTSCH
BBGIMNO BOMBING	BCDEKLU BUCKLED	RECLIMB	BCIIKLN NIBLICK
MOBBING	BCDEKOR BEDROCK	BCEILMS EMBLICS	BCIILMU BULIMIC
BBGINNU NUBBING	BROCKED	LIMBECS	BCIILOR COLIBRI
BBGINOO BOOBING	BCDEKSU BEDUCKS	BCEILNO BINOCLE	BCIINOS BIONICS
BBGINOR ROBBING	BCDELOU BECLOUD	BCEILOR BRICOLE	BCIINOT BIONTIC
BBGINOS GIBBONS	BCDEMOR CROMBED	CORBEIL	BCIIOPS BIOPICS
SOBBING	BCDEMRU CRUMBED	BCEIMNO COMBINE	BCIISTU BISCUIT
BBGINRU RUBBING	BCDENOU BOUNCED	BCEIMOR COMBIER	BCIKNOS KINCOBS
BBGINSU GUBBINS	BUNCOED	CROMBIE	BCIKORT BROCKIT
SUBBING	BCDEORU COURBED	MICROBE	BCIKOTT BITTOCK
BBGINTU TUBBING	BCDESUU SUBDUCE	BCEINOZ BENZOIC	BCILMPU PLUMBIC
BBGIOSU GIBBOUS	BCDHIOR BICHORD	BCEINRU BRUCINE	UPCLIMB
BBGIOSW BOBWIGS	BCDHIRU BRUCHID	BCEIORS CORBIES	BCILPSU PUBLICS
BBHHIOS HOBBISH	BCDHOOU CUBHOOD	BCEIRRS SCRIBER	BCIMSSU CUBISMS
BBHIMOS MOBBISH	BCDIORW COWBIRD	BCEIRSS SCRIBES	BCINORU RUBICON
BBHIOST HOBBITS	BCDIOSU CUBOIDS	BCEIRSU SUBERIC	BCINSUU INCUBUS
BBHIOSY YOBBISH	BCDKORU BURDOCK	BCEIRTU BRUCITE	BCIOORT ROBOTIC
BBHIRSU RUBBISH	BCDNOSU BONDUCS	BCEISST BISECTS	BCIORST STROBIC
BBHISTU TUBBISH	BCDSTUU SUBDUCT	BCEJOST OBJECTS	BCIOSTY SYBOTIC
BBHJOOS HOBJOBS	BCEEEHN BEECHEN	BCEJSTU SUBJECT	BCIRRSU RUBRICS
BBHNOOS HOBNOBS	BCEEEHS BEECHES	BCEKLOR BLOCKER	BCIRTUY BUTYRIC
BBHOOUW WHOOBUB	BESEECH	BCEKLRU BRUCKLE	BCISSTU CUBISTS
BBHRSUY SHRUBBY	BCEEFIN BENEFIC	BUCKLER	BCISTUU CUBITUS
BBIIILM BILIMBI	BCEEGIR ICEBERG	BCEKLSU BUCKLES	BCJKMUU JUMBUCK
BBIILST BIBLIST	BCEEHIP EPHEBIC	BCEKMOS BEMOCKS	BCKLLOO BOLLOCK
BBIKTUZ KIBBUTZ	BCEEHLR BELCHER	BCEKNOS BECKONS	BCKLLOU BULLOCK
BBILLSU BULBILS	BCEEHLS BELCHES	BCEKORT BROCKET	BCKLNOU UNBLOCK
BBILNOY NOBBILY	BCEEHNR BENCHER	BCEKORU ROEBUCK	BCKMMOU BUMMOCK
BBINNSU NUBBINS	BCEEHNS BENCHES	BCEKOSU BUCKOES	BCKMOSU BUCKSOM
BBINORS RIBBONS	BCEEHOS OBECHES	BCEKOTY BYCOKET	BCKOTTU BUTTOCK
BBINORY RIBBONY	BCEEHOU BOUCHEE	BCEKRSU BUCKERS	BCLMOOU COULOMB
BBKLNOY KNOBBLY	BCEEIPS BESPICE	BCEKSTU BESTUCK	BCLMRUY CRUMBLY
BBKLNUY KNUBBLY	BCEEIRS ESCRIBE	BUCKETS	BCLOOSU COLOBUS
BBKLOOU BLOUBOK	BCEEKNS NEBECKS	BCELLOW COWBELL	BCLORTU CLOTBUR
BBKOOOO BOOBOOK	BCEEKNU BUCKEEN	BCELMNU CLUBMEN	BCMOOST TOMBOCS
BBKOOSS BOSBOKS	BCEEKRS REBECKS	BCELMOS COMBLES	BCMORSY CORYMBS
BBLLSUU BULBULS	BCEEKST BECKETS	BCELMRU CLUMBER	BCMOSTU COMBUST
BBLOSUU BULBOUS	BCEEKSZ ZEBECKS	CRUMBLE	BCNOORS BRONCOS
BBLSTUY STUBBLY	BCEELOS ECBOLES	BCELMSU SCUMBLE	BCNOSTU COBNUTS
BBNNOOS BONBONS	BCEEMOS BECOMES	BCELORS CORBELS	BCOOSWY COWBOYS
BBNOORU BOURBON	BCEENOS OBSCENE	BCELORU COLUBER	BCOOTTY BOYCOTT
BBOOOOS BOOBOOS	BCEENRU CRUBEEN	BCELOSU BOUCLES	BDDDELU BUDDLED
BBORSTU BURBOTS	BCEFIIS SEBIFIC	BCELRSU BECURLS	BDDDEOR BRODDED
BBOSSUY BUSBOYS	BCEGIKN BECKING	BCELSSU CUBLESS	BDDEEES SEEDBED
BBRSSUU SUBURBS	BCEHINR BIRCHEN	BCEMNTU CUMBENT	BDDEEEW BEDEWED
BCCEILO ECBOLIC	BCEHINT BENTHIC	BCEMORS COMBERS	BDDEEIR DEBRIDE
BCCEILU CUBICLE	BCEHIOR BRIOCHE	BCEMRSU CUMBERS	BDDEEIS BEDSIDE
BCCEILY BICYCLE	BCEHIRS BIRCHES	SCUMBER	BDDEEIT BETIDED
BCCILOU BUCOLIC	BCEHIST BITCHES	BCENORU BOUNCER	DEBITED
BCCINOO OBCONIC	BCEHITW BEWITCH	BCENOSU BOUNCES	BDDEELN BLENDED
BCCISUU SUCCUBI	BCEHLRU BLUCHER	BCEORSS SCROBES	BDDEERS BEDDERS
BCCMOOX COXCOMB	BCEHNSU BUNCHES	BCEORSU OBSCURE	BDDEGIN BEDDING
BCCMSUU SUCCUMB	BCEHORS BROCHES	BCFSSUU SUBFUSC	BDDEGIR BRIDGED
BCDEEHL BELCHED	BCEHORT BOTCHER	BCGIKNO BOCKING	BDDEGLU BLUDGED

BDDEIIR BIRDIED
BDDEIIS BIDDIES
BDDEILN BLINDED
BDDEILR BRIDLED
BDDEILU BUILDED
BDDEINR BRINDED
BDDEIOO BOODIED
BDDEIRS BIDDERS
BDDEIRU BUDDIER
BDDEISU BUDDIES
BDDELNU BUNDLED
BDDELOO BLOODED
BDDELOS BODDLES
BDDELOU DOUBLED
BDDELSU BUDDLES
BDDENOU BOUNDED
BDDEOOR BROODED
BDDEORU OBDURED
BDDEOTU DOUBTED
BDDESUU SUBDUED
BDDGIIN BIDDING
BDDGINU BUDDING
BDDISSU DISBUDS
BDEEEFL FEEBLED
BDEEELL DELEBLE
BDEEELP BLEEPED
BDEEELR BLEEDER
BDEEELT BEETLED
BDEEEMN BEDEMEN
BDEEEMT BEMETED
BDEEEPS BESPEED
BDEEERR BREEDER
        BREERED
BDEEERZ BREEZED
BDEEEST DEBTEES
BDEEFIR BRIEFED
        DEBRIEF
BDEEGOR BEGORED
BDEEHOV BEHOVED
BDEEHRT BERTHED
BDEEIKN BEINKED
BDEEILL BELLIED
        DELIBLE
BDEEILS EDIBLES
BDEEILV BEDEVIL
BDEEIMR BEMIRED
BDEEIMT BEDTIME
        BETIMED
BDEEINR BENDIER
        INBREED
BDEEINZ BEDIZEN
BDEEIRR BERRIED
        BRIERED
BDEEIRS DERBIES
BDEEIRT BEDRITE
BDEEISS BESIDES
BDEEIST BETIDES
BDEEIVV BEVVIED
BDEEJLS DJEBELS
BDEEKMO KEMBOED
BDEEKRU REBUKED
BDEELLS BEDELLS
BDEELMR REMBLED
BDEELMS SEMBLED
BDEELNR BLENDER
BDEELNS BLENDES
BDEELNT BENDLET
BDEELOV BELOVED
BDEELOW ELBOWED
BDEELRT TREBLED

BDEELSS BLESSED
BDEELTT BLETTED
BDEELZZ BEZZLED
BDEEMOW EMBOWED
BDEEMOX EMBOXED
BDEEMRU EMBRUED
        UMBERED
BDEEMSU BEMUSED
BDEENOR ENROBED
BDEENPR PREBEND
BDEENRS BENDERS
BDEEORR REBORED
BDEEORS BEDSORE
        SOBERED
BDEEORW BOWERED
BDEEOSX SEEDBOX
BDEERUW BURWEED
BDEFFLU BLUFFED
BDEFILR FILBERD
BDEFLMU FUMBLED
BDEFLOU BODEFUL
BDEFOOR FORBODE
BDEGGLO BOGGLED
BDEGGOR BROGGED
BDEGHIT BEDIGHT
BDEGILN BINGLED
BDEGILO OBLIGED
BDEGILS BEGILDS
BDEGINN BENDING
BDEGINO BOINGED
BDEGINR BREDING
BDEGIOO BOOGIED
BDEGIOS BODGIES
BDEGIOT BIGOTED
BDEGIRS BEGIRDS
        BRIDGES
BDEGIRU BRIGUED
BDEGISU BUDGIES
BDEGLNU BLUNGED
        BUNGLED
BDEGLRU BLUDGER
        BURGLED
BDEGLSU BLUDGES
BDEGNSU BEDUNGS
BDEGORS BODGERS
BDEGORU BUDGERO
BDEGRSU BUDGERS
BDEGSTU BUDGETS
BDEHINS BEHINDS
BDEHLMU HUMBLED
BDEHLOS BEHOLDS
BDEHLSU BLUSHED
BDEHMTU THUMBED
BDEHORY HERDBOY
BDEHOST HOTBEDS
BDEHRSU BRUSHED
BDEIIRS BIRDIES
        BRIDIES
BDEIIVV BIVVIED
BDEIJLR JIRBLED
BDEIKLN BLINKED
BDEIKMO KIMBOED
BDEIKNO BOINKED
BDEIKRS BRISKED
BDEILLU BULLIED
BDEILMS DIMBLES
BDEILMW WIMBLED
BDEILNN BLINNED
BDEILNR BLINDER
        BRINDLE

BDEILOP LOBIPED
BDEILOR BROILED
BDEILOS BOLIDES
BDEILPP BLIPPED
BDEILRR BRIDLER
BDEILRS BIRSLED
        BRIDLES
BDEILRT DRIBLET
BDEILRU BLUDIER
        BUILDER
        REBUILD
BDEILTZ BLITZED
BDEIMMR BRIMMED
BDEIMNR BIRDMEN
BDEIMOR BROMIDE
BDEIMRU IMBRUED
BDEIMTU BITUMED
BDEINOR INORBED
BDEINOU BEDOUIN
BDEINRS BINDERS
        REBINDS
BDEINRY BINDERY
BDEINST BIDENTS
BDEINSU BEDUINS
BDEIOOS BOODIES
BDEIORR BROIDER
BDEIORS BORIDES
        DISROBE
BDEIORT DEBITOR
        ORBITED
BDEIORV OVERBID
BDEIORZ ZEBROID
BDEIOSY DISOBEY
BDEIRRS BIRDERS
BDEIRST BESTRID
        BISTRED
BDEIRSU BRUISED
        BURDIES
BDEIRTU BRUITED
BDEISSU SUBSIDE
BDEISTU BUISTED
        SUBEDIT
BDEITUY DUBIETY
BDEJLMU JUMBLED
BDEJORU OBJURED
BDEKLNU BLUNKED
BDEKNOU BUNKOED
BDEKNSU DEBUNKS
BDEKOOR BROOKED
BDELMMU BUMMLED
        MUMBLED
BDELMOO BLOOMED
BDELMPU PLUMBED
BDELMRU DRUMBLE
        RUMBLED
BDELMTU TUMBLED
BDELNOR BLONDER
BDELNOS BLONDES
        BOLDENS
BDELNRU BLUNDER
BDELNSU BUNDLES
BDELNTU BLUNTED
BDELOOP BLOOPED
BDELOOS BOODLES
BDELORS BORDELS
BDELORU BOULDER
        DOUBLER
BDELORW BOWLDER
BDELOST BOLDEST
BDELOSU BLOUSED

        DOUBLES
BDELOSW BLOWSED
BDELOTT BLOTTED
        BOTTLED
BDELOTU BOULTED
        DOUBLET
BDELOWZ BLOWZED
BDELRRU BLURRED
BDELRTU BLURTED
BDELSSU BUDLESS
BDELSTU BUSTLED
BDELSWY LEWDSBY
BDELTTU BUTTLED
BDEMNNO BONDMEN
BDEMNOU EMBOUND
BDEMOOR BEDROOM
        BOREDOM
        BROOMED
BDEMOOS BOSOMED
BDEMORS SOMBRED
BDEMSTU DUMBEST
BDENNOU BOUNDEN
        UNBONED
BDENNSU UNBENDS
BDENORS BONDERS
BDENORU BOUNDER
        REBOUND
        UNROBED
BDENORW BROWNED
BDENORZ BRONZED
BDENOST OBTENDS
BDENOSY BEYONDS
BDENOUW UNBOWED
BDENOUX UNBOXED
BDENRSU BURDENS
BDENRTU BRUNTED
BDENSSU SUNBEDS
BDENSTU SUBTEND
BDENSUY SEBUNDY
BDEOORR BROODER
BDEOORS BOORDES
BDEOOST BOOSTED
BDEOPRS BEDROPS
BDEOPRT BEDROPT
BDEOPST BEDPOST
BDEORRS BORDERS
BDEORRU BORDURE
        BOURDER
BDEORSS DESORBS
BDEORST DEBTORS
BDEORSU OBDURES
BDEORSW BROWSED
BDEORTU DOUBTER
        OBTRUDE
        OUTBRED
        REDOUBT
BDERSSU SURBEDS
BDERSTU BURSTED
BDERSUU SUBDUER
BDERSUY RUDESBY
BDESSTU BEDUSTS
        BESTUDS
BDESSUU SUBDUES
BDESSUW SUBDEWS
BDFIIOR FIBROID
BDFIISU FIDIBUS
BDFIORS FORBIDS
BDGGINO BODGING
BDGGINU BUDGING
BDGIINN BINDING

BDGIINR	BIRDING
	BRIDING
BDGIINS	BIDINGS
BDGIIOO	GOBIOID
BDGILOO	GLOBOID
BDGIMNU	DUMBING
BDGINNO	BONDING
BDGINNU	BUNDING
BDGINOS	BODINGS
BDGINOY	BODYING
BDGLLOU	BULLDOG
BDGLOOT	DOGBOLT
BDHIINS	BHINDIS
BDHINOP	HOPBIND
BDHIOSU	BUSHIDO
BDHIRSY	HYBRIDS
BDHMOOO	HOBODOM
BDHOOOY	BOYHOOD
BDIIKNO	BODIKIN
BDIILMS	DISLIMB
BDIILOS	LIBIDOS
BDIIMRS	MIDRIBS
BDIISTT	TIDBITS
BDIKNOR	BRODKIN
BDIKNOS	BODKINS
BDILLNY	BLINDLY
BDILNNU	UNBLIND
BDILNUU	UNBUILD
BDILPUU	UPBUILD
BDILRUY	BUIRDLY
BDILTUY	DIBUTYL
BDIMNPU	DUMPBIN
BDINNSU	UNBINDS
BDINOOR	BRIDOON
BDINPSU	UPBINDS
BDINSTU	DUSTBIN
BDIOOOV	OBOVOID
BDIOORU	BOUDOIR
BDIORSW	WOSBIRD
BDIOSSY	BYSSOID
BDIOSTU	OUTBIDS
BDIOSUU	DUBIOUS
BDIRSTU	DISTURB
BDISSUY	SUBSIDY
BDKLOOS	KOBOLDS
BDKNOOU	BUNDOOK
BDLOOOX	OXBLOOD
BDNNOUU	UNBOUND
BDNOORU	BOURDON
BDNOOWW	DOWNBOW
BDNOPUU	UPBOUND
BDNORTU	TURBOND
BDNORUW	RUBDOWN
BDNOSTU	OBTUNDS
BDOOOWX	BOXWOOD
BDORSWY	BYWORDS
BEEEEFR	FREEBEE
BEEEEKS	BESEEKE
BEEEEMT	BETEEME
BEEEFIR	BEEFIER
	FREEBIE
BEEEFLR	FEEBLER
BEEEFLS	FEEBLES
BEEEGIS	BESIEGE
BEEEGRR	BERGERE
BEEEHIV	BEEHIVE
BEEEHNS	SHEBEEN
BEEEILV	BELIEVE
BEEEIRR	BEERIER
BEEEJLW	BEJEWEL
BEEEKLS	KEBELES
BEEELPR	BLEEPER
BEEELST	BEETLES
BEEEMOS	BEESOME
BEEEMRW	EMBREWE
BEEEMSS	BESEEMS
BEEEMST	BEMETES
	BETEEMS
BEEENNZ	BENZENE
BEEENTW	BETWEEN
BEEEPRS	BEEPERS
BEEEPSW	BEWEEPS
BEEERSS	BREESES
BEEERSZ	BREEZES
BEEERTV	BREVETE
BEEFGIN	BEEFING
BEEFILR	FEBRILE
BEEFILS	BELIEFS
BEEFINT	BENEFIT
BEEFIRR	BRIEFER
BEEFNRU	FUNEBRE
BEEGGNU	GEEBUNG
BEEGILL	LEGIBLE
BEEGILO	OBLIGEE
BEEGILS	BEIGELS
BEEGILU	BEGUILE
BEEGIMR	BEGRIME
BEEGINN	BEGINNE
BEEGINP	BEEPING
BEEGINR	BIGENER
BEEGINT	BEETING
	BEIGNET
BEEGINU	BEGUINE
BEEGLNO	ENGLOBE
BEEGMNO	GOMBEEN
BEEGMOU	EMBOGUE
BEEGNOS	ENGOBES
BEEGNSU	BUNGEES
BEEGNTU	UNBEGET
BEEGRSU	BURGEES
BEEHINS	BESHINE
BEEHIRR	HERBIER
BEEHIST	BHISTEE
BEEHKSU	BUKSHEE
BEEHLRT	BLETHER
	HERBLET
BEEHLST	BETHELS
BEEHNNO	HEBENON
BEEHNOS	BESHONE
BEEHOOV	BEHOOVE
BEEHOPS	EPHEBOS
	PHOEBES
BEEHORS	HERBOSE
BEEHORW	BEWHORE
BEEHOST	BEHOTES
BEEHOSV	BEHOVES
BEEHPSU	EPHEBUS
BEEHRST	BERTHES
	SHERBET
BEEHRSW	BESHREW
BEEHRTY	THEREBY
BEEHRWY	WHEREBY
BEEHSST	BEHESTS
BEEHSTY	BHEESTY
BEEIJLU	JUBILEE
BEEILLS	BELLIES
BEEILNR	BERLINE
BEEILOS	OBELISE
BEEILOZ	OBELIZE
BEEILRS	BELIERS
BEEILTT	BETITLE
BEEIMRS	BEMIRES
	BIREMES
BEEIMST	BETIMES
BEEINNS	BENNIES
BEEINNZ	BENZINE
BEEINOS	EBONIES
	EBONISE
BEEINOT	EBONITE
BEEINOZ	EBONIZE
BEEINPR	PEBRINE
BEEINRT	BENTIER
BEEINRZ	ZEBRINE
BEEIORS	EBRIOSE
BEEIQUZ	BEZIQUE
BEEIRRS	BERRIES
BEEIRRV	BREVIER
BEEIRST	REBITES
BEEIRTY	EBRIETY
BEEISST	BETISES
BEEISTT	BETTIES
BEEISVV	BEVVIES
BEEJNSU	BUNJEES
BEEKNOT	BETOKEN
BEEKOPS	BESPOKE
BEEKORS	REEBOKS
BEEKRRS	BERSERK
BEEKRRU	REBUKER
BEEKRSU	REBUKES
BEELLMN	BELLMEN
BEELLOT	LOBELET
BEELMMS	EMBLEMS
BEELMOW	EMBOWEL
BEELMRS	REMBLES
BEELMRT	TREMBLE
BEELMSS	SEMBLES
BEELNNO	ENNOBLE
BEELNOZ	BENZOLE
BEELNSU	NEBULES
BEELOSV	BELOVES
BEELOTY	EYEBOLT
BEELPST	BEPELTS
BEELRST	BELTERS
	TREBLES
BEELRSY	BERLEYS
BEELRUZ	ZEBRULE
BEELSSS	BLESSES
BEELSZZ	BEZZLES
BEELTTU	BLUETTE
BEEMMRS	MEMBERS
BEEMNPT	BENEMPT
BEEMNRY	BYREMEN
BEEMORW	EMBOWER
BEEMOSS	MEBOSES
BEEMOSX	EMBOXES
BEEMRRU	UMBRERE
BEEMRSU	EMBRUES
BEEMRTU	EMBRUTE
BEEMSSU	BEMUSES
BEENNRS	BRENNES
BEENNST	BENNETS
BEENORS	BOREENS
	ENROBES
BEENOST	BONESET
BEENRRT	BRENTER
BEENSTU	BUTENES
	SUBTEEN
BEEOOST	BOOTEES
BEEOPRS	BEPROSE
BEEORRS	REBORES
	SOBERER
BEEORRU	BOURREE
BEEORSV	OBSERVE
	OBVERSE
	VERBOSE
BEEORSY	OBEYERS
BEEORWY	EYEBROW
BEEOSST	OBESEST
BEEPRRV	PREVERB
BEEQSTU	BEQUEST
BEERRST	BERRETS
BEERRSU	BEURRES
BEERRSV	REVERBS
BEERRSW	BREWERS
BEERRWY	BREWERY
BEERSSU	REBUSES
	SUBSERE
BEERSTT	BETTERS
BEERSTV	BREVETS
BEERSTW	BESTREW
	WEBSTER
BEERTTU	BURETTE
BEESSTU	BUSTEES
BEETTUV	BUVETTE
BEFFLRU	BLUFFER
BEFFPSU	BEPUFFS
BEFFRSU	BUFFERS
	REBUFFS
BEFFSTU	BUFFETS
BEFGIIL	FILIBEG
BEFGIRU	FIREBUG
BEFGIST	BEGIFTS
BEFHOOS	BEHOOFS
BEFILMS	FIMBLES
BEFILOS	FOIBLES
BEFILPY	PLEBIFY
BEFILRT	FILBERT
BEFILRY	BRIEFLY
BEFILSU	FUSIBLE
BEFINOR	BONFIRE
BEFIORS	FIBROSE
BEFIRST	FIBSTER
BEFIRSU	FUBSIER
BEFLLTY	FLYBELT
BEFLMRU	FUMBLER
BEFLMSU	BEFLUMS
	FUMBLES
BEFLOOS	BEFOOLS
BEFLOSU	BEFOULS
BEFLTUU	TUBEFUL
BEFOORR	FORBORE
BEFSSUU	SUBFEUS
BEGGGIN	BEGGING
BEGGIIS	BIGGIES
BEGGINO	BEGOING
BEGGIOR	BOGGIER
BEGGIST	BIGGEST
BEGGISU	BUGGIES
BEGGLOR	BOGGLER
BEGGLOS	BOGGLES
BEGGRSU	BUGGERS
BEGGRUY	BUGGERY
BEGHHIT	BEHIGHT
BEGHINT	BENIGHT
BEGHISS	BESIGHS
BEGHITT	BETIGHT
BEGHRRU	BURGHER
BEGIILR	BILGIER
BEGIINN	INBEING
BEGIKMN	KEMBING

BEGILLN	BELLING		
BEGILLY	LEGIBLY		
BEGILNO	IGNOBLE		
	INGLOBE		
BEGILNS	BINGLES		
BEGILNT	BELTING		
BEGILNU	BLUEING		
	BULGINE		
BEGILNY	BELYING		
BEGILOS	OBLIGES		
BEGILRS	GERBILS		
BEGILRT	GILBERT		
BEGILRU	BULGIER		
BEGILST	GIBLETS		
BEGINNU	UNBEING		
BEGINOS	BIOGENS		
BEGINOY	BIOGENY		
	OBEYING		
BEGINRR	BRINGER		
BEGINRS	BINGERS		
BEGINRW	BREWING		
BEGINSS	BESINGS		
	BIGNESS		
BEGINST	BESTING		
BEGINSU	BEGUINS		
	BUNGIES		
BEGINTT	BETTING		
BEGIOOS	BOOGIES		
BEGIOSU	BOUGIES		
BEGIRSU	BRIGUES		
	RUGBIES		
BEGISSU	GIBUSES		
BEGKMOS	GEMSBOK		
BEGKNSU	BEGUNKS		
BEGLLOU	GLOBULE		
BEGLMOO	BEGLOOM		
BEGLMRU	GRUMBLE		
BEGLNOS	BELONGS		
BEGLNRU	BLUNGER		
	BUNGLER		
BEGLNSU	BLUNGES		
	BUNGLES		
BEGLOOS	GLOBOSE		
BEGLOOT	BOOTLEG		
BEGLOST	GOBLETS		
BEGLOSU	GLEBOUS		
BEGLRSU	BUGLERS		
	BULGERS		
	BURGLES		
BEGLRTY	BERGYLT		
BEGLSTU	BUGLETS		
BEGNNUU	UNBEGUN		
BEGNORU	BURGEON		
BEGNOSY	BYGONES		
BEGNOTU	UNBEGOT		
BEGNSUY	BUNGEYS		
BEGOORS	GOOBERS		
BEGORSU	BROGUES		
BEGOSTU	BOUGETS		
BEGOSTW	BOWGETS		
BEGRRSU	BURGERS		
BEGRSSU	BURGESS		
BEHHKOT	KHOTBEH		
BEHIITX	EXHIBIT		
BEHIKNT	BETHINK		
BEHIKRS	KIRBEHS		
BEHILMS	BLEMISH		
BEHILMT	THIMBLE		
BEHILOS	BOLSHIE		
BEHILRT	BLITHER		
BEHILST	THIBLES		
BEHILSU	HELIBUS		
BEHINOP	HOPBINE		
BEHIOST	BOTHIES		
BEHIOTW	HOWBEIT		
BEHIRRT	REBIRTH		
BEHIRST	HERBIST		
BEHIRSU	BUSHIER		
BEHISSU	BUSHIES		
BEHISTT	THIBETS		
BEHLLOP	BELLHOP		
BEHLMOW	WHOMBLE		
BEHLMRU	HUMBLER		
BEHLMSU	HUMBLES		
BEHLOOT	BOTHOLE		
BEHLORT	BROTHEL		
BEHLOSW	BEHOWLS		
BEHLRRU	BURRHEL		
BEHLRSU	BLUSHER		
	BURHELS		
BEHLSSU	BLUSHES		
	BUSHELS		
BEHLSTU	BLUSHET		
BEHMNSU	BUSHMEN		
BEHMORS	HOMBRES		
BEHMOTU	BEMOUTH		
BEHMPTU	BETHUMP		
BEHNORS	BREHONS		
BEHNOST	BENTHOS		
BEHNRTU	BURTHEN		
BEHOORT	THEORBO		
BEHORRT	BROTHER		
BEHORST	BOSHTER		
	BOTHERS		
BEHORSU	HERBOUS		
BEHORTT	BETROTH		
BEHRRSU	BRUSHER		
BEHRSSU	BRUSHES		
BEIIKLR	RIBLIKE		
BEIIKRS	BIRKIES		
BEIILLS	BILLIES		
BEIILRS	RISIBLE		
BEIILSV	VISIBLE		
BEIINOT	NIOBITE		
BEIINRR	BRINIER		
BEIINST	STIBINE		
BEIIOTT	BIOTITE		
BEIIRRS	BIRSIER		
BEIIRST	BITSIER		
BEIIRTT	BITTIER		
BEIISTT	BITTIES		
BEIISVV	BIVVIES		
BEIJLRS	JERBILS		
	JIRBLES		
BEIJMSU	JUMBIES		
BEIJNSU	BUNJIES		
BEIKLNR	BLINKER		
BEIKLNS	LIBKENS		
BEIKLOS	OBELISK		
BEIKLRS	BILKERS		
BEIKLRU	BULKIER		
BEIKNRS	BRISKEN		
BEIKOOR	BOOKIER		
BEIKOOS	BOOKIES		
	BOOKSIE		
BEIKORS	BOSKIER		
BEIKRRS	BRISKER		
BEIKRST	BRISKET		
BEILLMN	BILLMEN		
BEILLRU	BULLIER		
BEILLST	BESTILL		
	BILLETS		
BEILLSU	BULLIES		
BEILMNR	NIMBLER		
BEILMOR	EMBROIL		
BEILMOS	BEMOILS		
	EMBOILS		
	MOBILES		
BEILMRS	LIMBERS		
BEILMRT	TIMBREL		
BEILMRW	WIMBREL		
BEILMSU	SUBLIME		
BEILMSW	WIMBLES		
BEILNOO	OBELION		
BEILNOW	BOWLINE		
BEILNRS	BERLINS		
BEILNSY	BYLINES		
BEILNSZ	BENZILS		
BEILNTZ	BLINTZE		
BEILOOR	LOOBIER		
BEILOOS	LOOBIES		
BEILOQU	OBLIQUE		
BEILORR	BROILER		
BEILORS	BOILERS		
	REBOILS		
BEILORT	TRILOBE		
BEILORW	BLOWIER		
BEILORY	BOILERY		
BEILOST	BETOILS		
BEILOSW	BLOWIES		
BEILOSX	BOLIXES		
BEILRRS	BIRLERS		
BEILRRU	BURLIER		
BEILRSS	BIRSLES		
	RIBLESS		
BEILRST	BLISTER		
	BRISTLE		
	RIBLETS		
BEILRTT	BRITTLE		
	TRIBLET		
BEILRTU	REBUILT		
BEILRTY	LIBERTY		
BEILRUY	BRULYIE		
BEILRUZ	BRULZIE		
BEILSSS	BLISSES		
BEILSTU	BLUIEST		
	SUBTILE		
BEILSTW	BLEWITS		
BEILSTZ	BLITZES		
BEIMMRR	BRIMMER		
BEIMNOR	BROMINE		
BEIMNTU	BITUMEN		
BEIMORW	IMBOWER		
BEIMOSS	OBEISMS		
BEIMOSZ	ZOMBIES		
BEIMPRU	BUMPIER		
BEIMRST	BETRIMS		
	TIMBERS		
	TIMBRES		
BEIMRSU	ERBIUMS		
	IMBRUES		
	IMBURSE		
BEIMRTU	IMBRUTE		
	TERBIUM		
BEINNOR	BONNIER		
BEINNOS	BENISON		
	BONNIES		
BEINNOZ	BENZOIN		
BEINNSU	BUNNIES		
BEINOOS	BOONIES		
BEINORT	BORNITE		
BEINORW	BROWNIE		
BEINOSS	BESOINS		
BEINOST	BONIEST		
	EBONIST		
BEINOSX	BONXIES		
BEINOSZ	BIZONES		
BEINOTT	BOTTINE		
BEINRSU	RUBINES		
	SUBERIN		
BEINRSY	BYRNIES		
BEINRTT	BITTERN		
BEINRTU	BUNTIER		
	TRIBUNE		
	TURBINE		
BEINSSY	BYSSINE		
BEIOORZ	BOOZIER		
BEIOOST	BOOTIES		
BEIOPTY	BIOTYPE		
BEIORRT	ORBITER		
BEIORSS	BOSSIER		
	RIBOSES		
BEIORST	ORBIEST		
BEIORSU	BOUSIER		
	OUREBIS		
BEIOSSU	SOUBISE		
BEIOSTT	BOTTIES		
BEIOSTX	BOXIEST		
BEIOSTY	OBESITY		
BEIPSST	BESPITS		
BEIPSSU	PUBISES		
BEIQRTU	BRIQUET		
BEIQSSU	BISQUES		
BEIRRRU	BURRIER		
BEIRRSU	BRISURE		
	BRUISER		
BEIRSST	BESTIRS		
	BISTERS		
	BISTRES		
BEIRSSU	BRUISES		
BEIRSTT	BITTERS		
BEIRSTU	BUSTIER		
	RUBIEST		
BEIRTTU	TRIBUTE		
BEIRTTY	TREYBIT		
BEIRTVY	BREVITY		
BEIRUZZ	BUZZIER		
BEISSTU	BUSIEST		
BEISTTU	BUTTIES		
BEITTWX	BETWIXT		
BEJJSUU	JUJUBES		
BEJLMRU	JUMBLER		
BEJLMSU	JUMBLES		
BEJLOSS	JOBLESS		
BEJORSU	OBJURES		
BEKLNRU	BLUNKER		
BEKLOOT	BOOKLET		
BEKLRSU	BULKERS		
BEKMNOO	BOOKMEN		
BEKMOST	STEMBOK		
BEKNNOW	BEKNOWN		
BEKNORS	BONKERS		
BEKNORU	UNBROKE		
BEKNRSU	BUNKERS		
BEKOPRU	UPBROKE		
BEKORRS	BROKERS		
BEKORRY	BROKERY		
BEKOSST	BOSKETS		
BEKRSSU	BUSKERS		
BEKSSTU	BUSKETS		

BELLORR BORRELL	BUSTLER	BEORSST BESORTS	BGGINOY BYGOING
BELLOSU BOULLES	BUTLERS	SORBETS	BGGINSU BUGGINS
LOBULES	SUBTLER	STROBES	BGGNOOS BOGONGS
SOLUBLE	BELRSUY BURLEYS	BEORSSU BOURSES	BGGNOSU BUGONGS
BELLOSW BELLOWS	BELRTUY BUTLERY	BEORSSW BOWSERS	BGHHIOY HIGHBOY
BELLOUV VOLUBLE	BELSSTU BUSTLES	BROWSES	BGHILST BLIGHTS
BELLRRU BURRELL	SUBLETS	BEORSTT BETTORS	BGHILTY BLIGHTY
BELLRSU BULLERS	BELSTTU BUTTLES	BEORSTU OBTUSER	BGHINOO BOOHING
BELLSTU BULLETS	BELSTUU TUBULES	BEORSTV OBVERTS	HOBOING
BELMMOO EMBLOOM	BEMMNOS MOBSMEN	BEORSUU UBEROUS	BGHINOR BIGHORN
BELMMRU MUMBLER	BEMMOOS EMBOSOM	BEORSUZ BROUZES	BGHINSU BUSHING
BELMMSU BUMMELS	BEMMORR BROMMER	SUBZERO	BGHMSUU HUMBUGS
BUMMLES	BEMMRRU BRUMMER	BEORSVV BOVVERS	BGHNORU HORNBUG
MUMBLES	BEMMRSU BUMMERS	BEORSWY BOWYERS	BGHOORU BOROUGH
BELMNOU NELUMBO	BEMNORW EMBROWN	BEORUVY OVERBUY	BGHORSU BROUGHS
BELMNSU NUMBLES	BEMNORY EMBRYON	BEOSSST BOSSEST	BGHORTU BROUGHT
BELMOOR BLOOMER	BEMNOST ENTOMBS	BEOSSTT OBTESTS	BGHOSTU BOUGHTS
REBLOOM	BEMNOSU UMBONES	BEOSSTW BESTOWS	BGIIKLN BILKING
BELMOOS BLOOSME	BEMNOSW ENWOMBS	BEPRRTU PERTURB	BGIIKNS BIKINGS
BELMOPR PROBLEM	BEMNPTY BYNEMPT	BEPRTUY PUBERTY	BGIILLN BILLING
BELMORT TEMBLOR	BEMNRSU NUMBERS	BEPSTUY SUBTYPE	BGIILMN LIMBING
BELMOSU EMBOLUS	BEMNSTU NUMBEST	BEQRSUU BRUSQUE	BGIILNO BOILING
BELMOSY SYMBOLE	BEMNTTU BUTMENT	BERRSTU BURSTER	BGIILNR BIRLING
BELMPRU PLUMBER	BEMOORS BOOMERS	BERSSTU BUSTERS	BGIILNS SIBLING
BELMRRU RUMBLER	BEMORRS SOMBRER	BERSTTU BUTTERS	BGIIMNR BRIMING
BELMRSU LUMBERS	BEMORSS SOMBRES	BERSTUV SUBVERT	BGIIMNU IMBUING
RUMBLES	BEMORST BESTORM	BERSUZZ BUZZERS	BGIINNN BINNING
SLUMBER	MOBSTER	BERTTUY BUTTERY	BGIINNR BRINING
UMBRELS	BEMORSU UMBROSE	BESSSTU SUBSETS	INBRING
BELMRTU TUMBLER	BEMORSY EMBRYOS	BESTTUX SUBTEXT	BGIINRT RINGBIT
TUMBREL	BEMORUX BUXOMER	BFFGIIN BIFFING	BGIINST BITINGS
BELMRTY TREMBLY	BEMORWW WEBWORM	BFFGINO BOFFING	BGIINTT BITTING
BELMSTU STUMBLE	BEMOTUY MYOTUBE	BFFGINU BUFFING	BGIKLNU BULKING
TUMBLES	BEMPRSU BUMPERS	BFFIINS BIFFINS	BGIKNNO BONKING
BELNNOU UNNOBLE	BEMSSTU BESMUTS	BFFINOS BOFFINS	BGIKNNU BUNKING
BELNNTU UNBLENT	BEMSSUU SUBSUME	BFFLLUY BLUFFLY	BGIKNOO BOOKING
BELNOOY BOLONEY	BENNORU UNBORNE	BFFNOOU BUFFOON	BGIKNOR BROKING
BELNOST NOBLEST	BENNORW NEWBORN	BFGIORT FROGBIT	BGIKNRU BURKING
BELNOSZ BENZOLS	BENNORZ BRONZEN	BFHILSU LUBFISH	BGIKNSU BUSKING
BELNOYZ BENZOYL	BENNOST BONNETS	BFHIRSU FURBISH	BGILLNO BOLLING
BELNRTU BLUNTER	BENNOSU UNBONES	BFHISTU TUBFISH	BGILLNU BULLING
BELNSSU UNBLESS	BENOPRU UPBORNE	BFIILRS FIBRILS	BGILMNO MOBLING
BELNSTU SUNBELT	BENORRW BROWNER	BFIINOR FIBROIN	BGILMOU GUMBOIL
UNBELTS	BENORST BRETONS	BFIINRS FIBRINS	BGILNOS GLOBINS
UNBLEST	SORBENT	BFILMRU BRIMFUL	GOBLINS
BELNSYZ BENZYLS	BENORSU BOURNES	BFINOSW BOWFINS	LOBINGS
BELOOPR BLOOPER	UNROBES	BFIORSU FIBROUS	BGILNOT BILTONG
BELOORS BOLEROS	BENORSZ BRONZES	BFIRTUY BRUTIFY	BOLTING
BELOOSS SOBOLES	BENORTY RENTBOY	BFKLOOU BOOKFUL	BGILNOW BLOWING
BELOPSU PUEBLOS	BENORWY BYWONER	BFKLOOY FLYBOOK	BOWLING
BELORST BOLSTER	BENOSSU BONUSES	BFKSSUU SUBFUSK	BGILNOY IGNOBLY
BOLTERS	BENOSUX UNBOXES	BFLLOWY BLOWFLY	BGILNRU BURLING
LOBSTER	BENOSUZ SUBZONE	FLYBLOW	BGILNSU BLUINGS
BELORSU ROUBLES	BENOSWY NEWSBOY	BFLOSUX BOXFULS	BGILOOR OBLIGOR
BELORSW BLOWERS	BENRRSU BURNERS	BFLSTUU TUBFULS	BGILOOY BIOLOGY
BOWLERS	BENRSTU BRUNETS	BFOOOTY FOOTBOY	BGILRSU BUSGIRL
BELORSY SOBERLY	BUNTERS	BGGGIIN BIGGING	BGIMMNU BUMMING
BELORTT BLOTTER	BURNETS	BGGGINO BOGGING	BGIMNNU NUMBING
BOTTLER	BURSTEN	BGGGINU BUGGING	BGIMNOO BOOMING
BELORTU BOULTER	BEOORSS BROOSES	BGGHIIS BIGGISH	BGIMNOT TOMBING
TROUBLE	BEOORST BOOSTER	BGGIILN BILGING	BGIMNOW WOMBING
BELOSSU BLOUSES	BEOORSZ BOOZERS	BGGIINN BINGING	BGIMNPU BUMPING
BOLUSES	BEOPPRS BOPPERS	BGGIINS BIGGINS	BGIMOSY BOGYISM
BELOSSW BLOWSES	BEOPRRV PROVERB	BGGIISW BIGWIGS	BGINNOS BONINGS
BELOSTT BOTTLES	BEOPRST BESPORT	BGGILNO GLOBING	BGINNOU BOUNING
BELOSTU BOLETUS	BEOPSST BESPOTS	BGGILNU BUGLING	BGINNOW BOWNING
BELOSWZ BLOWZES	BEOPSTU BESPOUT	BULGING	BGINNRU BURNING
BELRRSU BURLERS	BEOQSUY OBSEQUY	BGGINNO BONGING	BGINNTU BUNTING
BURRELS	BEOQTUU BOUQUET	BGGINNU BUNGING	BGINOOS BOOSING
BELRSTU BLUSTER	BEORRSS RESORBS	BGGINOU BOUGING	BGINOOT BOOTING

BGINOOZ BOOZING	BIILLNO BILLION	BIOORSZ BORZOIS	BPRSTUU UPBURST
BGINOPP BOPPING	BIILLOU BOUILLI	BIOOSST OBOISTS	CCCDIOO COCCOID
BGINOPR PROBING	BIILLTW TWIBILL	BIOOSUV OBVIOUS	CCCDIOS COCCIDS
BGINORS BORINGS	BIILNNR BIRLINN	BIOPRST PROBITS	CCCNOOT CONCOCT
ROBINGS	BIILNQU QUIBLIN	BIOPRTY PROBITY	CCDEEER RECCEED
SORBING	BIILOSU BILIOUS	BIORRTW RIBWORT	CCDEEHK CHECKED
BGINOSS BOSSING	BIILSVY VISIBLY	BIORSST BISTROS	CCDEEIO ECOCIDE
OBSIGNS	BIIMNOU NIOBIUM	BIORSTT BISTORT	CCDEEIR RECCIED
BGINOSU BOUSING	BIIMNSU MINIBUS	BITTORS	CCDEEIS DECCIES
BGINOSW BOWSING	MINISUB	BIORSUU RUBIOUS	CCDEEKL CLECKED
BGINOSX BOXINGS	BIIMOSS OBIISMS	BIORTTU BITTOUR	CCDEENO CONCEDE
BGINOTT BOTTING	BIIMSTU STIBIUM	BIOSTUW WOUBITS	CCDEENY DECENCY
BGINOUY BUOYING	BIIMSUV BIVIUMS	BIRSTTU BITTURS	CCDEEOR COERCED
BGINPRU BURPING	BIINOST BIOTINS	TURBITS	CCDEESU SUCCEED
UPBRING	BIIORSV VIBRIOS	BISSSTU SUBSIST	CCDEHIL CLICHED
BGINRRU BURRING	BIIOSUV BIVIOUS	BJNOORU BONJOUR	CCDEHIN CINCHED
BGINRTU BRUTING	BIIRSTU BURITIS	BKMNSUU BUNKUMS	CCDEHKO CHOCKED
BGINRUY BURYING	BIISSTV VIBISTS	BKNORSY SKYBORN	CCDEHKU CHUCKED
RUBYING	BIISTTT TITBITS	BKORSWY BYWORKS	CCDEHNO CONCHED
BGINSSU BUSINGS	BIJNOSU SUBJOIN	BLLNTUY BLUNTLY	CCDEHOU COUCHED
BUSSING	BIKLLUY BULKILY	BLLOSUU LOBULUS	CCDEIIT DEICTIC
BGINSTU BUSTING	BIKLNOY LINKBOY	BLLOUVY VOLUBLY	CCDEIKL CLICKED
TUBINGS	BIKLRSY BRISKLY	BLMMPUU PLUMBUM	CCDEIKR CRICKED
BGINSUY BUSYING	BIKMNPU BUMPKIN	BLMNPUU UNPLUMB	CCDEILR CIRCLED
BGINTTU BUTTING	BIKMNSU BUMKINS	BLNNOUW UNBLOWN	CCDEIMO COMEDIC
BGINUZZ BUZZING	BIKMOSS IMBOSKS	BLNOOSU BLOUSON	CCDEIOS CODICES
BGIORTY BIGOTRY	BIKNSSU BUSKINS	BLNOPUW UPBLOWN	CCDEKLO CLOCKED
BGIOSSS GOSSIBS	BIKORRW RIBWORK	BLNOSTU UNBOLTS	COCKLED
BGKORSY GRYSBOK	BILLNOS BILLONS	BLOOOTX TOOLBOX	CCDEKLU CLUCKED
BGLMRUY GRUMBLY	BILLNOU BULLION	BLOOQUY OBLOQUY	CCDEKOR CROCKED
BGLNOOS OBLONGS	BILLOOY LOOBILY	BLOOSWY LOWBOYS	CCDELOU OCCLUDE
BGLNOOW LONGBOW	BILLOSW BILLOWS	BLOPSTU SUBPLOT	CCDENOS SCONCED
BGLNOUW BLOWGUN	BILLOUV VOLUBIL	BLOPSUW UPBLOWS	CCDENOU CONDUCE
BGLOOSU GLOBOUS	BILLOWY BILLOWY	BMNOOSU UNBOSOM	CCDEOST DECOCTS
BGLOSSU BUGLOSS	BILLRWY WRYBILL	BMNORUW MOWBURN	CCDHIIL CICHLID
BGMOORS GOMBROS	BILMNOR NOMBRIL	BMNOSTU UNTOMBS	CCDIILO CODICIL
BGMOOTU GUMBOOT	BILMOSU LIMBOUS	BMOOORX BOXROOM	CCDIILU CULICID
BGNOOWY GOWNBOY	BILMRSU UMBRILS	BMOORSY BYROOMS	CCDIIOR CRICOID
BGOORSU BURGOOS	BILMRTU TUMBRIL	BMOOSTT BOTTOMS	CCDILOY CYCLOID
BGORTUW BUGWORT	BILMSUU BULIMUS	BMOOSTY TOMBOYS	CCDKLOU CUCKOLD
BHIIINT INHIBIT	BILNNOY BONNILY	BMORSST STROMBS	CCDNOOR CONCORD
BHIINRS BRINISH	BILNTUU UNBUILT	BMORSUU BRUMOUS	CCDNOTU CONDUCT
BHIIPSS SIBSHIP	BILOOYZ BOOZILY	UMBROUS	CCEEGNO COGENCE
BHIISST BHISTIS	BILOPSU UPBOILS	BNNRSUU SUNBURN	CCEEHKR CHECKER
BHIKOOS BOOKISH	BILOSSU SUBSOIL	BNNRTUU UNBURNT	RECHECK
BHIKSSU BUKSHIS	BILOSSY BOSSILY	BNOOSST BOSTONS	CCEEHOR ECORCHE
BHILLSU BULLISH	BILPTUU UPBUILT	BNOOSTU BOUTONS	CCEEHOU COUCHEE
BHILOTU HOLIBUT	BILRSTY BRISTLY	UNBOOTS	CCEEHRS CRECHES
BHILPSU PUBLISH	TRILBYS	BNOOTTY BOTTONY	SCREECH
BHIMOOR RHOMBOI	BILRTUY TILBURY	BNORSSU SUBORNS	CCEEILN LICENCE
BHIMOOS HOBOISM	BIMMOOS IMBOSOM	BNORSTU BURTONS	CCEEINR ECCRINE
BHIMOPS PHOBISM	BIMNORS MISBORN	BNORSUU BURNOUS	CCEEINS SCIENCE
BHIMORT THROMBI	BIMNORW IMBROWN	BNORTUU OUTBURN	CCEEIRS RECCIES
BHIMSTU BISMUTH	BIMNOSS BONISMS	BNOSSUW SUNBOWS	CCEEIRV CREVICE
BHINRSU BURNISH	BIMNOST INTOMBS	BNOSTTU BUTTONS	CCEEKOY COCKEYE
BHIOOPR BIOPHOR	BIMNOSU OMNIBUS	BNOTTUY BUTTONY	CCEELRY RECYCLE
BHIOORS BOORISH	BIMNOSY SYMBION	BOOPSTW BOWPOTS	CCEENRY RECENCY
BHIOPSS BISHOPS	BIMRSUX BRUXISM	BOORRSW BORROWS	CCEEORS COERCES
BHIOPST PHOBIST	BIMSSSU SUBMISS	BOOSTUW WOOBUTS	CCEERSY SECRECY
BHIOSWZ SHOWBIZ	BIMSSTU SUBMITS	BOOSWWW BOWWOWS	CCEFNOT CONFECT
BHIRSTU BRUTISH	BINNOSU BUNIONS	BORRSUW BURROWS	CCEGNOY COGENCY
BHIRTTU TURBITH	BINOORS BONSOIR	BORSSTW BROWSTS	CCEHHIS CHICHES
BHKNOSU BOHUNKS	BINOOST BONITOS	BORSTTU TURBOTS	CCEHIKN CHICKEN
BHLRSUU BULRUSH	BINOOSU NIOBOUS	BORSTXY BOSTRYX	CCEHIKU CHUCKIE
BHMOORS RHOMBOS	BINORST RIBSTON		CCEHILS CHICLES
BHMORSU RHOMBUS	BINOSST BONISTS		CLICHES
BHMUUZZ HUMBUZZ	BINPSUY BUNYIPS		CCEHIMS CHEMICS
BHOOSTW BOWSHOT	BINRSTU INBURST		CCEHINO CONCHIE
BIIIKNS BIKINIS	BINSTTU UNBITTS		CCEHINS CINCHES
BIIKLOT KILOBIT	BINSTUU SUBUNIT		CCEHINT TECHNIC

CCEHIOR CHOICER	CCENORT CONCERT	CCKOOSU CUCKOOS	CDDHIOR DICHORD
CCEHIOS CHOICES	CCENORW CONCREW	CCKOSTU CUSTOCK	CDDIIIO DIDICOI
CCEHIRS SCREICH	CCENOSS SCONCES	CCLMSUU MUCLUCS	CDDIIOS DISCOID
SCRIECH	CCEOOTT COCOTTE	CCLOOOZ ZOCCOLO	CDDIIOY DIDICOY
CCEHIST CHICEST	CCEOPRT PERCOCT	CCLOPSY CYCLOPS	CDDIIRU DRUIDIC
HECTICS	CCEORRT CORRECT	CCLOSTU OCCULTS	CDDIKOP PIDDOCK
CCEHKLU CHUCKLE	CCEORSS ESCROCS	CCMOOOR MOROCCO	CDDINSU CUDDINS
CCEHKNU UNCHECK	SOCCERS	CCNOOOS COCOONS	CDDIORS DISCORD
CCEHKOR CHOCKER	CCEOSSU SUCCOSE	CCNOOPU PUCCOON	CDDKOPU PUDDOCK
CCEHLOS CLOCHES	CCESSSU SUCCESS	CCNOOTU COCONUT	CDDKORU RUDDOCK
CCEHLRU CLERUCH	CCFIRUY CRUCIFY	CCNOPUY CONCUPY	CDEEEFL FLEECED
CCEHLSU CLEUCHS	CCFLOSU FLOCCUS	CCNORSU CONCURS	CDEEEFN DEFENCE
CULCHES	CCGHINO GNOCCHI	CCNOSSU CONCUSS	CDEEEHK CHEEKED
CCEHNOS CONCHES	CCGIINS SICCING	CCOOORS ROCOCOS	CDEEEHL LEECHED
CCEHORS CROCHES	CCGIKNO COCKING	CCORSSU SUCCORS	CDEEEHP CHEEPED
CCEHORT CROCHET	CCGILNY CYCLING	CCORSUU SUCCOUR	DEPECHE
CCEHOSS COSECHS	CCGKOOR GORCOCK	CCORSUY SUCCORY	CDEEEHR CHEERED
CCEHOSU COUCHES	CCHHIIS CHICHIS	CCOSSTU STUCCOS	REECHED
CCEHRSU CURCHES	CCHHIIT ICHTHIC	CCOSSUU SUCCOUS	CDEEEHS CHEESED
CCEHSTU CUTCHES	CCHHILS SCHLICH	CCSSSUU SUCCUSS	CDEEEIP EPICEDE
CCEIILS CILICES	CCHHOOS CHOCHOS	CDDDEEI DECIDED	CDEEEIV DECEIVE
ICICLES	CCHHRUY CHURCHY	CDDDEEO DECODED	CDEEEJT EJECTED
CCEIIMS CIMICES	CCHIIST STICHIC	CDDDEEU DEDUCED	CDEEEKL CLEEKED
CCEIIRT ICTERIC	CCHIKST SCHTICK	CDDDELO CLODDED	CDEEELP CLEEPED
CCEIKLR CLICKER	TCHICKS	CODDLED	CDEEELT ELECTED
CCEIKLT CLICKET	CCHILOR CHLORIC	CDDDELU CUDDLED	CDEEEPR PRECEDE
CCEIKOR COCKIER	CCHIMOR CHROMIC	CDDDESU SCUDDED	CDEEERS CREESED
CCEIKOS COCKIES	CCHINOR CHRONIC	CDDEEER DECREED	DECREES
CCEIKRT CRICKET	CCHINOS CHICONS	RECEDED	RECEDES
CCEIKRY CRICKEY	CCHINSU SCUCHIN	CDDEEES SECEDED	SECEDER
CCEILOT COCTILE	CCHIORY CHICORY	CDDEEII DEICIDE	CDEEERT DECREET
CCEILRR CIRCLER	CCHIOTW COWITCH	CDDEEIN INCEDED	ERECTED
CCEILRS CIRCLES	CCHIPSU HICCUPS	CDDEEIR DECIDER	CDEEESS SECEDES
CLERICS	CCHIPSY PSYCHIC	DECRIED	CDEEESX EXCEEDS
CCEILRT CIRCLET	CCHIPUY HICCUPY	CDDEEIS DECIDES	CDEEFHT FETCHED
CCEILSU CULICES	CCHIRST SCRITCH	CDDEEIX EXCIDED	CDEEFII EDIFICE
CCEILSY CYLICES	CCHKLOS SCHLOCK	CDDEEKL DECKLED	CDEEFKL FLECKED
CCEILTU CUTICLE	CCHKMOS SCHMOCK	CDDEEKO DECKOED	CDEEFLT DEFLECT
CCEIMNO MECONIC	CCHKMSU SCHMUCK	DECOKED	CDEEFOR DEFORCE
CCEIMOT COMETIC	CCHKOSY COCKSHY	CDDEENO ENCODED	CDEEFST DEFECTS
CCEIMST SMECTIC	CCHKSTU SCHTUCK	CDDEENS DESCEND	CDEEGIR GRIECED
CCEINOR CORNICE	CCHNRSU SCRUNCH	SCENDED	CDEEGNO CONGEED
CCEINOS CONCISE	CCHNRUY CRUNCHY	CDDEEOR DECODER	CDEEHIP CEPHEID
CCEINOT CONCEIT	CCIIILS SILICIC	CDDEEOS DECODES	CDEEHIS DEHISCE
CCEINRT CENTRIC	CCIILNS CLINICS	CDDEEOY DECOYED	CDEEHIV CHEVIED
CCEIOPP COPPICE	CCIILST CLITICS	CDDEERU REDUCED	CDEEHKL HECKLED
CCEIOPT ECTOPIC	CCIINPS PICNICS	CDDEESU DEDUCES	CDEEHLT LETCHED
CCEIORS CICEROS	CCIIRST CRITICS	SEDUCED	CDEEHLW WELCHED
CCEIORT ORECTIC	CCIIRTU CIRCUIT	CDDEEUW CUDWEED	CDEEHMS SCHEMED
CCEIOSS CISCOES	CCIISTY SICCITY	CDDEHIL CHILDED	CDEEHNW WENCHED
CCEIPST SCEPTIC	CCIKLOW COWLICK	CDDEHIN CHIDDEN	CDEEHOR COHERED
CCEIRST CRETICS	CCIKLOY COCKILY	CDDEHIT DICHTED	OCHERED
CCEJNOT CONJECT	COLICKY	DITCHED	CDEEHPR PERCHED
CCEKLOR CLOCKER	CCIKOPT COCKPIT	CDDEHNU DUNCHED	CDEEHRT RETCHED
CCEKLOS COCKLES	CCILNOO COLONIC	CDDEHOU DOUCHED	CDEEHRU EUCHRED
CCEKNOT CONTECK	CCILNOU COUNCIL	CDDEIIS DISCIDE	CDEEHST CHESTED
CCEKNOY COCKNEY	CCILOOP PICCOLO	CDDEINU INDUCED	CDEEIIT EIDETIC
CCEKOPS COPECKS	CCILSTY CYCLIST	CDDEISU CUDDIES	CDEEILN DECLINE
CCEKOPT PETCOCK	CCIMOTY MYCOTIC	CDDELOS CODDLES	CDEEILP PEDICEL
CCEKORS COCKERS	CCINOOT COCTION	SCOLDED	PEDICLE
CCEKORT CROCKET	CCINORY CRYONIC	CDDELOU CLOUDED	CDEEILS DELICES
CCEKOST COCKETS	CCINOTV CONVICT	CDDELRU CRUDDLE	CDEEIMN ENDEMIC
CCELLOT COLLECT	CCIOORS SIROCCO	CURDLED	CDEEIMS DECIMES
CCELNOY CYCLONE	CCIOPTU OCCIPUT	CDDELSU CUDDLES	CDEEINO CODEINE
CCELNUY LUCENCY	CCIORSS SCIROCS	SCUDDLE	CDEEINR CEDRINE
CCELRSY CYCLERS	CCIPRTY CRYPTIC	CDDENSU CUDDENS	CDEEINS INCEDES
CCENNOR CONCERN	CCIRSUY CIRCUSY	CDDEORW CROWDED	CDEEINT ENTICED
CCENNOT CONCENT	CCKMOOS MOCOCKS	CDDERSU SCUDDER	CDEEINV EVINCED
CONNECT	CCKMOSU MOCUCKS	CDDESTU DEDUCTS	CDEEIOS DIOCESE
CCENOPT CONCEPT	CCKNOSU UNCOCKS	CDDGINO CODDING	CDEEIOV DEVOICE

CDEEIPR	PIERCED		
CDEEIPT	PEDETIC		
CDEEIRR	DECRIER		
CDEEIRS	DECRIES		
CDEEIRT	RECITED		
CDEEIST	DECEITS		
CDEEISV	DEVICES		
CDEEISX	EXCIDES		
	EXCISED		
CDEEITV	EVICTED		
CDEEITX	EXCITED		
CDEEJNO	CONJEED		
CDEEJST	DEJECTS		
CDEEKKL	KECKLED		
CDEEKLR	CLERKED		
CDEEKLS	DECKLES		
CDEEKNR	REDNECK		
CDEEKNS	SNECKED		
CDEEKOS	DECOKES		
CDEEKPS	SPECKED		
CDEEKRS	DECKERS		
CDEEKRT	TRECKED		
CDEEKRW	WRECKED		
CDEELMM	CLEMMED		
CDEELOS	ECLOSED		
CDEELPU	DECUPLE		
CDEELPY	YCLEPED		
CDEELRU	RECULED		
	ULCERED		
CDEELSU	SCEDULE		
	SECLUDE		
CDEELUX	EXCLUDE		
CDEENOR	ENCORED		
CDEENOS	ENCODES		
	SECONDE		
CDEENOZ	COZENED		
CDEENRS	DECERNS		
	SCERNED		
CDEENRT	CENTRED		
	CREDENT		
CDEENST	DESCENT		
	SCENTED		
CDEEOOY	COOEYED		
CDEEOPR	COPERED		
	PROCEED		
CDEEORV	COVERED		
CDEEORW	COWERED		
CDEEOST	CESTODE		
	TEDESCO		
CDEEOTV	COVETED		
CDEERRU	RECURED		
	REDUCER		
CDEERSS	SCREEDS		
CDEERST	CRESTED		
CDEERSU	RECUSED		
	REDUCES		
	RESCUED		
	SECURED		
	SEDUCER		
CDEERSW	DECREWS		
	SCREWED		
CDEERTU	ERUCTED		
CDEERUV	DECURVE		
CDEESSU	SEDUCES		
CDEESSY	ECDYSES		
CDEESTT	DECTETS		
	DETECTS		
CDEESUX	EXCUSED		
CDEFFHU	CHUFFED		
CDEFFIL	CLIFFED		
CDEFFLU	CUFFLED		
CDEFFOS	SCOFFED		
CDEFFSU	SCUFFED		
CDEFHIL	FILCHED		
CDEFHIN	FINCHED		
CDEFIIT	DEFICIT		
CDEFIKL	FICKLED		
	FLICKED		
CDEFILT	CLIFTED		
CDEFINO	CONFIDE		
CDEFKLO	FLOCKED		
CDEFKOR	DEFROCK		
	FROCKED		
CDEFNTU	DEFUNCT		
CDEFOSU	FOCUSED		
CDEFRTU	FRUCTED		
CDEFSUU	FUCUSED		
CDEGGHU	CHUGGED		
CDEGGLO	CLOGGED		
	COGGLED		
CDEGGOS	SCOGGED		
CDEGGSU	SCUGGED		
CDEGHLU	GULCHED		
CDEGHOU	COUGHED		
CDEGIKN	DECKING		
CDEGILU	CLUDGIE		
CDEGINO	COIGNED		
CDEGINR	CRINGED		
CDEGINU	EDUCING		
CDEGIOR	ERGODIC		
CDEGLSU	CUDGELS		
CDEGNSU	SCUNGED		
CDEGOOS	SCOOGED		
CDEGORS	CODGERS		
CDEGOSU	SCOUGED		
CDEHHIL	HILCHED		
CDEHHIT	HITCHED		
CDEHHNU	HUNCHED		
CDEHHOT	HOTCHED		
CDEHHTU	HUTCHED		
CDEHIIL	CEILIDH		
CDEHIIV	CHIVIED		
CDEHIKN	CHINKED		
CDEHIKO	HOICKED		
CDEHIKR	CHIRKED		
CDEHIKT	THICKED		
CDEHILL	CHILLED		
CDEHILO	CHELOID		
	HELCOID		
CDEHILP	DELPHIC		
CDEHILR	CHILDER		
	CHIRLED		
CDEHILS	CHIELDS		
CDEHILT	LICHTED		
CDEHIMR	CHIRMED		
CDEHIMT	MITCHED		
CDEHINO	HEDONIC		
CDEHINP	PINCHED		
CDEHINW	WINCHED		
CDEHIOR	CHOIRED		
CDEHIOW	COWHIDE		
CDEHIPP	CHIPPED		
CDEHIPR	CHIRPED		
CDEHIPT	PITCHED		
CDEHIQU	QUICHED		
CDEHIRR	CHIRRED		
CDEHIRS	CHIDERS		
	HERDICS		
CDEHIRT	CHIRTED		
	DITCHER		
		RICHTED	
		CDEHIST DITCHES	
		CDEHISU DUCHIES	
		CDEHITT CHITTED	
		CDEHITW WITCHED	
		CDEHIVV CHIVVED	
		CDEHKOS SHOCKED	
		CDEHKSU SHUCKED	
		CDEHKUY HEYDUCK	
		CDEHLMU MULCHED	
		CDEHLNU LUNCHED	
		CDEHLNY LYNCHED	
		CDEHLOT CLOTHED	
		CDEHLRU LURCHED	
		CDEHMMU CHUMMED	
		CDEHMNU MUNCHED	
		CDEHMOO MOOCHED	
		CDEHMOP CHOMPED	
		CDEHMOR CHROMED	
		CDEHMOU MOUCHED	
		CDEHNOR CHONDRE	
		CDEHNOT NOTCHED	
		CDEHNPU PUNCHED	
		CDEHNRU CHUNDER	
		CHURNED	
		CDEHNSU DUNCHES	
		CDEHNSY SYNCHED	
		CDEHOPP CHOPPED	
		CDEHOPT POTCHED	
		CDEHOPU POUCHED	
		CDEHORT TORCHED	
		CDEHORW CHOWDER	
		COWHERD	
		CDEHOSU CHOUSED	
		DOUCHES	
		HOCUSED	
		CDEHOSW COWSHED	
		CDEHOTU TOUCHED	
		CDEHOUV VOUCHED	
		CDEHPSY PSYCHED	
		CDEHRRU CHURRED	
		CDEHRSU CRUSHED	
		CDEHSSU DUCHESS	
		CDEHSTU DUTCHES	
		CDEHSTY SCYTHED	
		CDEIIKR DICKIER	
		CDEIIKS DICKIES	
		CDEIIMR DIMERIC	
		CDEIINS INCISED	
		INDICES	
		CDEIINT IDENTIC	
		INCITED	
		CDEIIOR ERICOID	
		CDEIIOV OVICIDE	
		CDEIIRT DICTIER	
		CDEIIST DEISTIC	
		DICIEST	
		CDEIISU SUICIDE	
		CDEIJST DISJECT	
		CDEIKLN CLINKED	
		CDEIKLP PICKLED	
		CDEIKLS SICKLED	
		SLICKED	
		CDEIKLT TICKLED	
		CDEIKMS MEDICKS	
		CDEIKNS DICKENS	
		SNICKED	
		CDEIKNZ ZINCKED	
		CDEIKOS DOCKISE	
		CDEIKOY YOICKED	
			CDEIKOZ DOCKIZE
			CDEIKPR PRICKED
			CDEIKRR DERRICK
			CDEIKRS DICKERS
			SCRIKED
			CDEIKRT TRICKED
			CDEIKRU DUCKIER
			CDEIKRW WRICKED
			CDEIKST STICKED
			CDEIKSU DUCKIES
			CDEIKSY DICKEYS
			CDEILLO CODILLE
			COLLIDE
			COLLIED
			CDEILLU CULLIED
			CDEILMO MELODIC
			CDEILNU INCLUDE
			NUCLIDE
			CDEILOO OCELOID
			CDEILOP POLICED
			CDEILOR DOCILER
			CDEILPP CLIPPED
			CDEILPS SPLICED
			CDEILPU CLUPEID
			CDEILRU LUCIDER
			CDEILST DELICTS
			CDEILSU SLUICED
			CDEILTU DUCTILE
			DULCITE
			CDEIMNO DEMONIC
			CDEIMOR DORMICE
			CDEIMOS MEDICOS
			CDEIMOT DEMOTIC
			CDEIMPR CRIMPED
			CDEIMPU PUMICED
			CDEIMSU MISCUED
			CDEINOS SECONDI
			CDEINOT CTENOID
			DEONTIC
			NOTICED
			CDEINOU DOUCINE
			CDEINOZ ZINCODE
			CDEINPR PRINCED
			CDEINRS CINDERS
			DISCERN
			RESCIND
			CDEINRU INDUCER
			CDEINRY CINDERY
			CDEINSU INCUDES
			INCUSED
			INDUCES
			CDEINSX EXSCIND
			CDEINTT TINCTED
			CDEIOPR PERCOID
			CDEIOPT PICOTED
			CDEIORS DISCOER
			CDEIORT CORDITE
			CDEIORV DIVORCE
			CDEIORW CROWDIE
			CDEIOST CESTOID
			COTISED
			CDEIPRS CRISPED
			DISCERP
			CDEIPRT PREDICT
			CDEIPST DEPICTS
			DISCEPT
			CDEIRRU CURDIER
			CURRIED
			CDEIRST CREDITS
			DIRECTS

CDEIRSU	CRUISED		CORSNED	CDHINOR	CHONDRI	CEEEHKS	KEECHES
	DISCURE		SCORNED	CDHIOOR	CHOROID	CEEEHLS	ELCHEES
CDEIRSV	SCRIVED	CDENORW	CROWNED		OCHROID		LEECHES
CDEIRTV	VERDICT		DECROWN	CDHIORS	DROICHS	CEEEHNR	ENCHEER
CDEISST	DISSECT	CDENOSS	SECONDS		ORCHIDS	CEEEHPR	CHEEPER
CDEISSY	ECDYSIS	CDENOST	DOCENTS	CDHIORY	DROICHY	CEEEHRR	CHEERER
CDEITUX	EXCUDIT	CDENOTU	COUNTED	CDHIPTY	DIPTYCH	CEEEHRS	REECHES
CDEJNOU	JOUNCED	CDENPUY	PUDENCY	CDHKOOR	HORDOCK	CEEEHSS	CHEESES
CDEKKNO	KNOCKED	CDENRUU	UNCURED	CDIIIOT	IDIOTIC	CEEEINP	EPICENE
CDEKLNO	CLONKED	CDENRUY	DUNCERY	CDIIJRU	JURIDIC	CEEEIPR	CREEPIE
CDEKLNU	CLUNKED	CDEOOPP	COPEPOD	CDIILLY	IDYLLIC	CEEEIRV	RECEIVE
CDEKLOW	WEDLOCK	CDEOOPS	SCOOPED	CDIILMO	DOMICIL	CEEELLU	ECUELLE
CDEKLPU	PLUCKED	CDEOORR	CORRODE	CDIINOR	CRINOID	CEEELPY	YCLEEPE
CDEKLRU	RUCKLED	CDEOORV	VOCODER	CDIINOT	DICTION	CEEELST	CELESTE
CDEKLSU	SCULKED	CDEOOST	SCOOTED	CDIINOZ	ZINCOID	CEEELSV	CLEEVES
	SUCKLED	CDEOOTV	DOVECOT	CDIINST	INDICTS	CEEEMPR	EMPERCE
CDEKMOS	SMOCKED	CDEOPPR	CROPPED	CDIIOSS	CISSOID	CEEENRS	RECENSE
CDEKNOS	DOCKENS	CDEOPRS	CORPSED	CDIIOTY	IDIOTCY	CEEENSS	ESSENCE
CDEKNRU	DRUCKEN	CDEOPRU	CROUPED	CDIKNOR	DORNICK	CEEEPRR	CREEPER
CDEKNSU	UNDECKS		PRODUCE	CDIKNOW	WINDOCK	CEEERRT	ERECTER
CDEKOOR	CROOKED	CDEOPSU	SCOUPED	CDILLOO	COLLOID	CEEERSS	CREESES
CDEKORS	DOCKERS	CDEOPSW	SCOWPED	CDILLUY	LUCIDLY	CEEERST	SECRETE
CDEKORT	TROCKED	CDEOQTU	DOCQUET	CDILNOS	CODLINS	CEEERSV	SCREEVE
CDEKOST	DOCKETS	CDEORRS	RECORDS	CDILOTU	DULOTIC	CEEERTX	EXCRETE
	STOCKED	CDEORRW	CROWDER	CDIMMOU	MODICUM	CEEETUX	EXECUTE
CDEKRSU	DUCKERS	CDEORSS	CROSSED	CDIMNOO	MONODIC	CEEFFNO	OFFENCE
CDEKRTU	TRUCKED		SCORSED	CDIMNSU	MUNDICS	CEEFFOR	EFFORCE
CDELLOU	COLLUDE	CDEORSU	COURSED	CDIMOSU	MUSCOID	CEEFFOS	COFFEES
CDELLSU	SCULLED		SCOURED	CDIMSSU	MUSCIDS	CEEFFST	EFFECTS
CDELMPU	CLUMPED		SOURCED	CDINOOS	CONOIDS	CEEFHIR	CHIEFER
CDELMSU	MUSCLED	CDEORSW	SCOWDER	CDINOOT	ODONTIC	CEEFHIT	FETICHE
CDELMTU	MULCTED	CDEORTU	COURTED	CDINOSY	SYNODIC		FITCHEE
CDELNOO	CONDOLE		EDUCTOR	CDINOTU	CONDUIT	CEEFHLS	FLECHES
CDELNOU	ENCLOUD	CDEORUU	DOUCEUR		NOCTUID	CEEFHRT	FECHTER
CDELNOW	CLOWNED	CDEOSSU	ESCUDOS	CDINSSY	SYNDICS	CEEFHST	FETCHES
CDELNOY	CONDYLE	CDEOSTU	CUSTODE	CDINSTU	INDUCTS	CEEFINV	VENEFIC
CDELOOR	COLORED		DOUCEST	CDIOOTT	COTTOID	CEEFIRR	FIERCER
	CROODLE		DOUCETS	CDIORSV	CORVIDS	CEEFKLR	FLECKER
	DECOLOR		SCOUTED	CDIOSST	CODISTS		FRECKLE
CDELOPP	CLOPPED	CDEOSTY	CYTODES	CDIOSTY	CYSTOID	CEEFLNU	FLUENCE
CDELOPU	COUPLED	CDEPRSU	SPRUCED	CDIOTUV	OVIDUCT	CEEFLRT	REFLECT
CDELORS	SCOLDER	CDEPRTY	DECRYPT	CDIPRSY	CYPRIDS	CEEFNNS	FENNECS
CDELORU	CLOURED	CDERRSU	SCURRED	CDIRSUY	DYSURIC	CEEFNOR	ENFORCE
CDELORW	CLOWDER	CDERSTU	CRUDEST	CDIRTUY	CRUDITY	CEEFNRS	FENCERS
CDELOST	COLDEST		CRUSTED	CDISSSU	DISCUSS	CEEFPRT	PERFECT
CDELOSU	DULCOSE	CDERSUZ	SCRUZED	CDISSTY	CYSTIDS		PREFECT
CDELOSW	SCOWLED	CDFHIOS	CODFISH	CDKNNOU	DUNNOCK	CEEFRST	REFECTS
CDELOTT	CLOTTED	CDFIILU	FLUIDIC	CDKNOSU	UNDOCKS	CEEFSSU	FESCUES
CDELOTU	CLOUTED	CDFILUY	DULCIFY	CDLNOUU	UNCLOUD	CEEGHIN	EECHING
CDELOUY	DOUCELY	CDFIOOT	OCTOFID	CDLOOPY	LYCOPOD	CEEGINR	CREEING
CDELPSU	SCULPED	CDFIOSU	FUCOIDS	CDMNOOS	CONDOMS		ENERGIC
CDELRSU	CURDLES	CDGHIIN	CHIDING	CDMOSUW	MUDSCOW		GENERIC
	SCUDLER	CDGIINO	GONIDIC	CDNNOTU	CONTUND	CEEGINT	GENETIC
CDELRUY	CRUDELY	CDGIINS	DICINGS	CDNOORS	CONDORS	CEEGINU	EUGENIC
CDEMMNO	COMMEND		DISCING		CORDONS	CEEGIRS	CIERGES
CDEMMOO	COMMODE	CDGIINT	DICTING	CDNORSU	UNCORDS		GRIECES
CDEMMSU	SCUMMED	CDGIKNO	DOCKING	CDOOOPT	OCTOPOD	CEEGKOS	GECKOES
CDEMNNO	CONDEMN	CDGIKNU	DUCKING	CDOOOST	DOOCOTS	CEEGLLO	COLLEGE
CDEMNOP	COMPEND	CDGILNO	CODLING	CDOORRY	CORRODY	CEEGLNT	NEGLECT
CDEMOOS	COMEDOS	CDGINNO	CONDIGN	CDOORST	DOCTORS	CEEGLOU	ECLOGUE
CDEMOPT	COMPTED	CDGINOR	CORDING	CDOOTUW	WOODCUT	CEEGNOR	COGENER
CDEMORU	DECORUM	CDGINOS	CODINGS	CDOPRTU	PRODUCT		CONGREE
CDEMPRU	CRUMPED	CDGINRU	CURDING	CDOSTUY	CUSTODY	CEEGNOS	CONGEES
CDENNOO	CONDONE	CDGINTU	DUCTING	CEEEEHL	LEECHEE	CEEGNRU	URGENCE
CDENNOT	CONTEND	CDHIIMO	DOCHMII	CEEEFLR	FLEECER	CEEGNRY	REGENCY
CDENOOR	CROONED	CDHIINT	CHINDIT	CEEEFLS	FLEECES	CEEGORT	CORTEGE
CDENOOS	SECONDO	CDHIIST	DISTICH	CEEEGNR	REGENCE	CEEGQRU	GRECQUE
CDENOPU	POUNCED	CDHILLY	CHILDLY	CEEEGNS	EGENCES	CEEHHSW	WHEECHS
	UNCOPED	CDHILNU	UNCHILD	CEEEGRS	GREECES	CEEHILN	ELENCHI
CDENORS	CONDERS	CDHILOS	COLDISH	CEEEHIR	REECHIE	CEEHILS	HELICES

	LICHEES	CEEIKPR	PICKEER	CEEKPRS	PECKERS	CEEOPTY	ECOTYPE
CEEHILV	VEHICLE	CEEILLM	MICELLE	CEEKPRY	RYEPECK	CEEORRS	RESCORE
CEEHIMR	CHIMERE	CEEILNO	CINEOLE	CEEKRRW	WRECKER	CEEORRT	ERECTOR
CEEHIMS	CHEMISE	CEEILNR	RECLINE	CEELLLU	CELLULE	CEEORRU	RECOURE
CEEHINR	INHERCE	CEEILNS	LICENSE	CEELLNO	COLLEEN	CEEORRV	RECOVER
CEEHINS	CHINESE		SELENIC	CEELLPU	PUCELLE	CEEORRW	RECOWER
CEEHIOR	CHEERIO		SILENCE	CEELMNT	CLEMENT	CEEORSU	CEREOUS
CEEHIOS	ECHOISE	CEEILNU	LEUCINE	CEELMOO	COELOME	CEEORSV	CORVEES
CEEHIOZ	ECHOIZE	CEEILPS	ECLIPSE	CEELMOT	TELECOM	CEEOTTT	OCTETTE
CEEHIRT	ETHERIC	CEEILRT	RETICLE	CEELMOW	WELCOME	CEEPPRT	PERCEPT
	HERETIC		TIERCEL	CEELNOS	ENCLOSE		PRECEPT
	TECHIER	CEEILRU	RECUILE	CEELNPS	PENCELS	CEEPPRU	PREPUCE
CEEHIRW	CHEWIER	CEEILST	SECTILE	CEELNRS	CRENELS	CEEPRSS	PRECESS
CEEHISS	SEICHES	CEEILSV	VESICLE	CEELNRT	LECTERN	CEEPRST	RECEPTS
CEEHISV	CHEVIES	CEEILTU	LEUCITE	CEELNRU	LUCERNE		RESPECT
CEEHKLR	HECKLER	CEEIMNT	CENTIME	CEELORS	CREOLES		SCEPTRE
CEEHKLS	HECKLES	CEEIMRS	MERCIES		RECLOSE		SPECTER
CEEHKNP	HENPECK	CEEIMST	EMETICS	CEELORT	ELECTOR		SPECTRE
CEEHKST	KETCHES	CEEINNS	INCENSE		ELECTRO	CEEPRTX	EXCERPT
CEEHLNO	ECHELON	CEEINOS	SENECIO	CEELORY	RECOYLE	CEEPSTX	EXCEPTS
CEEHLNS	ELENCHS	CEEINPR	PERCINE	CEELOSS	ECLOSES		EXPECTS
CEEHLNU	LEUCHEN	CEEINPS	PICENES	CEELOSU	COULEES	CEEPSTY	ECTYPES
CEEHLOW	COWHEEL		PIECENS	CEELOTU	ELOCUTE	CEERRSU	RECURES
CEEHLRS	LECHERS	CEEINPT	PENTICE	CEELOTV	COVELET		RESCUER
CEEHLRW	WELCHER	CEEINRS	CERESIN	CEELPRT	PLECTRE		SECURER
CEEHLRY	CHEERLY		SCRIENE		PRELECT	CEERRSW	SCREWER
	LECHERY		SINCERE	CEELRSS	SCLERES	CEERRUV	RECURVE
CEEHLSS	CHESSEL	CEEINRT	ENTERIC	CEELRST	TERCELS	CEERSSS	CESSERS
CEEHLST	LETCHES		ENTICER	CEELRSU	RECLUSE		CRESSES
CEEHLSW	LECHWES	CEEINRV	CERVINE		RECULES	CEERSST	CRESSET
	WELCHES	CEEINST	ENTICES	CEELRSW	CREWELS		RESECTS
CEEHLSY	LYCHEES	CEEINSV	EVINCES	CEELRTU	LECTURE		SECRETS
	SLEECHY	CEEIOPT	PICOTEE	CEELRTY	ERECTLY	CEERSSU	CERUSES
CEEHMRS	SCHEMER	CEEIORT	COTERIE	CEELSST	SELECTS		CESURES
CEEHMRT	MERCHET	CEEIPRR	CREPIER	CEELTTU	LETTUCE		RECUSES
CEEHMSS	SCHEMES		PIERCER	CEEMMOR	COMMERE		RESCUES
CEEHNPU	PENUCHE	CEEIPRS	PIECERS	CEEMNOW	NEWCOME		SECURES
CEEHNRW	WENCHER		PIERCES	CEEMNRU	CERUMEN	CEERSTT	TERCETS
CEEHNST	CHENETS		PRECISE	CEEMNST	CEMENTS	CEERSUX	EXCURSE
	TENCHES		RECIPES	CEEMOPR	COMPEER		EXCUSER
CEEHNSV	CHEVENS	CEEIPRT	RECEIPT		COMPERE	CEERTTU	CURETTE
CEEHNSW	WENCHES	CEEIPRU	EPICURE	CEEMOPT	COMPETE	CEESSTX	EXSECTS
	WHENCES	CEEIPSS	SPECIES	CEEMRRS	MERCERS	CEESSUX	EXCUSES
CEEHORR	COHERER	CEEIPST	PECTISE	CEEMRRY	MERCERY	CEETTUV	CUVETTE
CEEHORS	CHEEROS	CEEIPTZ	PECTIZE		REMERCY	CEFFIOR	OFFICER
	CHOREES	CEEIQSU	QUIESCE	CEEMRST	CERMETS	CEFFIOS	OFFICES
	COHERES	CEEIRRT	RECITER	CEEMSTU	TUMESCE	CEFFISU	SUFFICE
	ECHOERS	CEEIRSS	CERISES	CEEMSTY	MYCETES	CEFFLOS	COFFLES
CEEHORT	TROCHEE	CEEIRST	CERITES	CEENNOU	ENOUNCE	CEFFLSU	CUFFLES
CEEHOUV	VOUCHEE		RECITES	CEENNOV	CONVENE		SCUFFLE
CEEHPRR	PERCHER		TIERCES	CEENNRT	CENTNER	CEFFORS	COFFERS
CEEHPRS	PERCHES	CEEIRSU	ECURIES	CEENOPT	POTENCE		SCOFFER
CEEHPRU	UPCHEER	CEEIRSV	SCRIEVE	CEENORS	ENCORES	CEFFORT	COFFRET
CEEHQRU	CHEQUER		SERVICE		NECROSE	CEFGINN	FENCING
CEEHQSU	CHEQUES	CEEIRTU	EUCRITE	CEENORZ	COZENER	CEFHILR	FILCHER
CEEHQUY	QUEECHY	CEEIRTX	EXCITER	CEENOST	CENOTES	CEFHILS	FILCHES
CEEHRST	ETCHERS	CEEISSX	EXCISES	CEENPRS	SPENCER	CEFHILY	CHIEFLY
	RETCHES	CEEISTX	EXCITES	CEENPSS	SPENCES	CEFHINS	FINCHES
CEEHRSU	EUCHRES	CEEITTZ	ZETETIC	CEENRSS	CENSERS	CEFHIRY	CHIEFRY
CEEHRSY	CREESHY	CEEJNOS	CONJEES		SCERNES	CEFHIST	FITCHES
CEEHRTU	TEUCHER	CEEJORT	EJECTOR		SCREENS	CEFHITT	FITCHET
CEEHSSS	CHESSES	CEEJRST	REJECTS		SECERNS	CEFHITW	FITCHEW
CEEHSSW	ESCHEWS	CEEKKLS	KECKLES	CEENRST	CENTERS	CEFHLTU	FUTCHEL
CEEHSTV	VETCHES	CEEKKSS	KECKSES		CENTRES	CEFIILT	FICTILE
CEEHSTW	CHEWETS	CEEKLNT	NECKLET		TENRECS	CEFIIOR	ORIFICE
CEEIINR	EIRENIC	CEEKLPS	SPECKLE	CEENRSU	CENSURE	CEFIITV	FICTIVE
CEEIIPR	EPICIER	CEEKLSS	SECKELS	CEENRSY	SCENERY	CEFIKLR	FICKLER
CEEIJOR	REJOICE	CEEKLST	TECKELS	CEENTTU	CUNETTE		FLICKER
CEEIKLT	CLEEKIT	CEEKOSS	COKESES	CEEOPST	PECTOSE	CEFIKLS	FICKLES
CEEIKNT	NECKTIE	CEEKOSY	SOCKEYE	CEEOPSU	COUPEES	CEFILNT	INFLECT

CEFILNU FUNICLE
CEFILRU LUCIFER
CEFIMOR COMFIER
CEFIMRY MERCIFY
CEFINNO CONFINE
CEFINOR CONIFER
        INFORCE
CEFINST INFECTS
CEFIPSY SPECIFY
CEFIRSS SFERICS
CEFIRTY CERTIFY
        RECTIFY
CEFKLOT FETLOCK
CEFKLRY FRECKLY
CEFKRSU FUCKERS
CEFLNOU FLOUNCE
CEFLNUY FLUENCY
CEFMORY COMFREY
CEFNORS CONFERS
CEFNORU FROUNCE
CEFNOSS CONFESS
CEFNOST CONFEST
CEFNOSU CONFUSE
CEFNOTU CONFUTE
CEFOPRS FORCEPS
CEFORRS FORCERS
CEFORRT CROFTER
CEFORSS FRESCOS
CEFOSSU FOCUSES
CEFRSUW CURFEWS
CEFSSUU FUCUSES
CEGGHIR CHIGGER
CEGGIIS CIGGIES
CEGGIKN GECKING
CEGGIOR GEORGIC
CEGGIOS COGGIES
CEGGLOR CLOGGER
CEGGLOS COGGLES
CEGGORS COGGERS
CEGGPSU EGGCUPS
CEGHILN LECHING
CEGHINO ECHOING
CEGHINP PECHING
CEGHINT ETCHING
CEGHINW CHEWING
CEGHIOR CHOREGI
CEGHIOS CHIGOES
CEGHIRS CHIGRES
        SCREIGH
CEGHITU GUICHET
CEGHLSU CLEUGHS
        GULCHES
CEGHORU COUGHER
CEGHRTU GUTCHER
CEGIILN CEILING
        CIELING
CEGIINP PIECING
CEGIKKN KECKING
CEGIKNN NECKING
CEGIKNP PECKING
CEGIKNR RECKING
CEGIKRU GUCKIER
CEGILNP CLEPING
CEGILNR CLINGER
        CRINGLE
CEGILNU CLUEING
        LUCIGEN
CEGILNW CLEWING
CEGILNY GLYCINE
CEGIMNU MUCIGEN

CEGINNR CERNING
CEGINNS CENSING
        SCENING
CEGINOS COGNISE
        COIGNES
CEGINOZ COGNIZE
CEGINPR CREPING
        PERCING
CEGINRR CRINGER
CEGINRS CRINGES
CEGINRW CREWING
CEGINSS CESSING
CEGIRRS GRICERS
CEGKLOR GROCKLE
CEGLOOY ECOLOGY
CEGLOSU GLUCOSE
CEGLOSY GLYCOSE
CEGNNOO ONCOGEN
CEGNORS CONGERS
CEGNORU CONGRUE
CEGNORY CONGERY
        CRYOGEN
CEGNOST CONGEST
CEGNRUY URGENCY
CEGNSSU SCUNGES
CEGNSTY CYGNETS
CEGOORS SCROOGE
CEGORRS GROCERS
CEGORRY GROCERY
CEGORSU SCOURGE
        SCROUGE
CEHHILS HILCHES
CEHHIRS CHERISH
        SHRIECH
CEHHIRT HITCHER
CEHHIST HITCHES
CEHHNSU HUNCHES
CEHHOOS HOOCHES
CEHHOST HOTCHES
        SHOCHET
CEHHSSU SHEUCHS
CEHHSTU HUTCHES
CEHIIKN CHINKIE
CEHIINR HIRCINE
CEHIINS NICEISH
CEHIINT ICHNITE
CEHIIPP CHIPPIE
CEHIIRT ITCHIER
        TICHIER
CEHIISV CHIVIES
CEHIKNT KITCHEN
        THICKEN
CEHIKNW CHEWINK
CEHIKOO CHOOKIE
CEHIKOR CHOKIER
CEHIKOS CHOKIES
CEHIKPS PECKISH
CEHIKRS SHICKER
        SKRIECH
CEHIKRT THICKER
CEHIKRW WHICKER
CEHIKST CHEKIST
CEHIKSY HICKEYS
CEHIKTT THICKET
CEHILLR CHILLER
CEHILMY CHIMLEY
CEHILNO CHOLINE
CEHILNS LICHENS
        LINCHES
CEHILNT LINCHET

        TINCHEL
CEHILPR PILCHER
CEHILPS PILCHES
CEHILRT LICHTER
CEHILRV CHERVIL
CEHILSS CHESILS
        CHISELS
CEHILST ELTCHIS
CEHILSZ ZILCHES
CEHILTY LECYTHI
CEHIMMS CHEMISM
CEHIMNY CHIMNEY
CEHIMOR MORICHE
CEHIMOS ECHOISM
CEHIMRS CHIMERS
        MICHERS
CEHIMRT THERMIC
CEHIMST CHEMIST
        MITCHES
CEHINOP CHOPINE
        PHOCINE
CEHINOR CHORINE
CEHINOT HENOTIC
CEHINOX CHOENIX
CEHINPR NEPHRIC
        PHRENIC
        PINCHER
CEHINPS PINCHES
        SPHENIC
CEHINPU PENUCHI
CEHINQU QUINCHE
CEHINRS NICHERS
        RICHENS
CEHINRT CITHERN
CEHINST ETHNICS
        STHENIC
CEHINSU ECHINUS
CEHINSV CHEVINS
CEHINSW WINCHES
CEHINTW WITCHEN
CEHIOPS HOSPICE
CEHIOPT POTICHE
CEHIORS HEROICS
CEHIORT ROTCHIE
        THEORIC
CEHIOST ECHOIST
        TOISECH
CEHIOTU COUTHIE
CEHIPPR CHIPPER
CEHIPRR CHIRPER
CEHIPRS CERIPHS
        CIPHERS
        SPHERIC
CEHIPRT PITCHER
CEHIPST PITCHES
CEHIQSU QUICHES
CEHIRRT RICHTER
CEHIRST CITHERS
        ESTRICH
        RICHEST
CEHIRSU CUSHIER
CEHIRSZ SCHERZI
CEHIRTT CHITTER
CEHISSU CUISHES
CEHISTT TITCHES
CEHISTW WITCHES
CEHKKRU CHUKKER
CEHKLMO HEMLOCK
CEHKLSU HUCKLES
CEHKORS CHOKERS

        HOCKERS
        SHOCKER
CEHKOSY CHOKEYS
        HOCKEYS
CEHKPTU KETCHUP
CEHKRSU SHUCKER
CEHKSTU KUTCHES
CEHKSTY SKETCHY
CEHLLMO MOCHELL
CEHLLMU MUCHELL
CEHLLNS SCHNELL
CEHLLOY YELLOCH
CEHLMSS SCHELMS
CEHLMSU MUCHELS
        MULCHES
CEHLMSZ SCHMELZ
CEHLMUY CHUMLEY
CEHLNNU CHUNNEL
CEHLNOS NOCHELS
CEHLNOT NOTCHEL
CEHLNRU LUNCHER
CEHLNSU LUNCHES
CEHLNSY LYNCHES
CEHLNTY LYNCHET
CEHLOOS SCHOOLE
CEHLORS CHOLERS
        ORCHELS
CEHLORT CHORTLE
CEHLOST CLOTHES
CEHLPPS SCHLEPP
CEHLPSS SCHLEPS
CEHLPSU PLEUCHS
CEHLQSU SQUELCH
CEHLRRU LURCHER
CEHLRSU LURCHES
CEHMNRU MUNCHER
CEHMNSU MUNCHES
CEHMOOR MOOCHER
CEHMOOS MOOCHES
CEHMORS CHROMES
CEHMORU MOUCHER
CEHMOSS SCHMOES
CEHMOSU MOUCHES
CEHMSTU HUMECTS
        MUTCHES
CEHNNRU CHUNNER
CEHNOOR COEHORN
CEHNORV CHEVRON
CEHNOST NOTCHES
CEHNOSU COHUNES
CEHNPRU PUNCHER
        UNPERCH
CEHNPSU PUNCHES
CEHNRSU RUNCHES
CEHNRTU CHUNTER
CEHNSTU CHESNUT
CEHNSTY STENCHY
CEHNSUU EUNUCHS
CEHNTUY CHUTNEY
CEHOOPS POOCHES
CEHOORS CHOOSER
        SOROCHE
CEHOORT CHEROOT
CEHOOSS CHOOSES
CEHOOSY CHOOSEY
CEHOPPR CHOPPER
CEHOPRS PORCHES
CEHOPRT POTCHER
CEHOPRY CORYPHE
CEHOPST POTCHES

```
CEHOPSU POUCHES              CRINITE      CEIKPRY PICKERY     CEIMNOR INCOMER
CEHORRT TORCHER              INCITER      CEIKPST PICKETS     CEIMNOS INCOMES
CEHORSS COSHERS              NERITIC              SKEPTIC             MESONIC
CEHORST HECTORS      CEIINRZ ZINCIER      CEIKQRU QUICKER     CEIMNOT ENTOMIC
        ROCHETS      CEIINSS ICINESS      CEIKRRS RICKERS             TONEMIC
        ROTCHES              INCISES      CEIKRRT TRICKER     CEIMNRS CREMSIN
        TOCHERS      CEIINST INCITES      CEIKRSS SCRIKES             MINCERS
        TORCHES      CEIINSU CUISINE      CEIKRST RICKETS     CEIMNRU NUMERIC
        TROCHES      CEIINTZ CITIZEN              STICKER     CEIMNYZ ENZYMIC
CEHORSU CHOREUS              ZINCITE              TICKERS     CEIMOOR COOMIER
CEHORSY COSHERY      CEIIOPZ EPIZOIC      CEIKRSW WICKERS     CEIMOPT METOPIC
CEHORSZ SCHERZO      CEIIPPR PIPERIC      CEIKRSY YICKERS     CEIMOQU COMIQUE
CEHORTU COUTHER      CEIIPRR PRICIER      CEIKRTY RICKETY     CEIMORR MORRICE
        RETOUCH      CEIIPRS SPICIER      CEIKRUY YUCKIER     CEIMORT MORTICE
        TOUCHER      CEIIPRT PICRITE      CEIKSST SICKEST     CEIMOTT TOTEMIC
CEHORTW WOTCHER      CEIIPST EPICIST      CEIKSTT TICKETS     CEIMOTV VICOMTE
CEHORUV VOUCHER      CEIIRSS CISSIER      CEIKSTW WICKETS     CEIMPRR CRIMPER
CEHOSSU CHOUSES      CEIIRST ERISTIC      CEIKSTY TICKEYS     CEIMPRS SPERMIC
        HOCUSES              RICIEST      CEILLNO LIONCEL     CEIMPSU PUMICES
CEHOSTU TOUCHES      CEIIRSU CRUISIE     CEILLNU NUCELLI     CEIMRST CRETISM
CEHOSUV VOUCHES      CEIISSS CISSIES      CEILLOR COLLIER             METRICS
CEHPRSU CHERUPS      CEIISVV CIVVIES      CEILLOS COLLIES     CEIMRSU CERIUMS
CEHPRSY CHYPRES      CEIJNST INJECTS      CEILLST CELLIST             MURICES
        CYPHERS      CEIJRSU JUICERS      CEILLSU CULLIES     CEIMSSU CESIUMS
CEHPRTU PUTCHER      CEIJSTU JUSTICE      CEILMOP COMPILE             MISCUES
CEHPSSY PSYCHES      CEIKKNR KNICKER              POLEMIC     CEINNOS CONINES
CEHQSTU QUETSCH      CEIKKRS KICKERS      CEILMPR CRIMPLE     CEINNOV CONNIVE
CEHRRSU CRUSHER      CEIKLMS MICKLES      CEILNNU NUCLEIN     CEINOOT COONTIE
CEHRSSU CRUSHES      CEIKLNR CLINKER      CEILNOP PINOCLE     CEINOPR PERICON
CEHRSTT STRETCH              CRINKLE      CEILNOS CINEOLS             PORCINE
CEHRSTY SCYTHER      CEIKLNS NICKELS              CONSEIL     CEINOPT ENTOPIC
CEHSSTU TUSCHES              SLICKEN              INCLOSE             NEPOTIC
CEHSSTY SCYTHES      CEIKLPR PICKLER      CEILNOT LECTION     CEINORR CORNIER
CEIIJRU JUICIER              PRICKLE      CEILNOX LEXICON     CEINORS COINERS
CEIIKLS SICLIKE      CEIKLPS PICKLES      CEILNPS PENCILS             CRINOSE
CEIIKMS MICKIES      CEIKLRS LICKERS              SPLENIC             CRONIES
CEIIKNT KINETIC              RICKLES      CEILNST CLIENTS             ORCEINS
CEIIKPR PICKIER              SLICKER              LECTINS             ORCINES
CEIIKQU QUICKIE      CEIKLRT TICKLER              STENCIL             SERICON
CEIIKSS SICKIES              TRICKLE      CEILNSU LEUCINS     CEINORT RECTION
CEIIKST EKISTIC      CEIKLRU LUCKIER      CEILNTU CUTLINE     CEINORU NOURICE
        ICKIEST      CEIKLSS SICKLES              TUNICLE     CEINORV CORVINE
        TICKIES      CEIKLST STICKLE      CEILOOS COOLIES     CEINORY ORIENCY
CEIIKSW WICKIES              TICKLES      CEILOPR PELORIC     CEINOSS CESSION
CEIILLS SILICLE      CEIKLSU LUCKIES      CEILOPS POLICES             COSINES
CEIILNN INCLINE      CEIKLSY KYLICES      CEILOPT TOECLIP     CEINOST NOTICES
CEIILPP CLIPPIE      CEIKMNS SICKMEN      CEILORS RECOILS             SECTION
CEIILPT PELITIC      CEIKMRS SMICKER      CEILORT CORTILE     CEINOSV NOVICES
CEIILST ELICITS      CEIKMRU MUCKIER      CEILORU URCEOLI     CEINOTT ENTOTIC
CEIILTV LEVITIC      CEIKMST SMICKET      CEILOSS OSSICLE             TONETIC
CEIIMMT MIMETIC      CEIKMSY MICKEYS      CEILOST CITOLES     CEINOTX EXCITON
CEIIMNR CRIMINE      CEIKNOS CONKIES      CEILPPR CLIPPER     CEINOUV UNVOICE
CEIIMNS MENISCI      CEIKNOT KENOTIC              CRIPPLE     CEINOVV CONVIVE
CEIIMOT MEIOTIC      CEIKNQU QUICKEN      CEILPSS SPLICES     CEINPRS PINCERS
CEIIMPR EMPIRIC      CEIKNRS NICKERS      CEILPSU SPICULE             PRINCES
CEIIMPS EPICISM              SNICKER      CEILQSU CLIQUES     CEINPRY CYPRINE
CEIIMRS CIMIERS      CEIKNSS SICKENS      CEILQUY CLIQUEY     CEINPST INCEPTS
CEIIMSS SEISMIC      CEIKNST SNICKET      CEILRRU CURLIER             INSPECT
CEIIMTT TITMICE              TICKENS      CEILRSS SLICERS             PECTINS
CEIINNO CONIINE      CEIKNSW WICKENS      CEILRST RELICTS             PEINCTS
        INCONIE      CEIKOOS COOKIES      CEILRSV CLIVERS     CEINPTY PYCNITE
CEIINOR ONEIRIC      CEIKOPR POCKIER      CEILRSY CLERISY     CEINQSU CINQUES
CEIINOS ICONISE      CEIKORR CORKIER      CEILRTT CLITTER             QUINCES
CEIINOV INVOICE              ROCKIER      CEILRTU UTRICLE     CEINRRU CURNIER
CEIINOZ ICONIZE      CEIKOST COKIEST      CEILSSS SCISSEL     CEINRSS SCRINES
CEIINPS PISCINE      CEIKPRR PRICKER      CEILSSU SLUICES     CEINRST CISTERN
CEIINRS IRENICS      CEIKPRS PICKERS      CEILTTU CUITTLE             CRETINS
        SERICIN              RIPECKS      CEIMMOS COMMIES     CEINRSV CRIVENS
        SIRENIC              SPICKER      CEIMMRR CRIMMER     CEINRSW WINCERS
CEIINRT CITRINE      CEIKPRT PRICKET      CEIMNNO MECONIN     CEINRTT CITTERN
```

CEINRUV	INCURVE	CEIRSSV	SCRIVES
CEINSST	INCESTS	CEIRSTT	TRISECT
	INSECTS	CEIRSTU	CUITERS
CEINSSU	INCUSES		CURIETS
CEINSTY	INSECTY		ICTERUS
CEINSWY	WINCEYS	CEIRSTW	TWICERS
CEINTTX	EXTINCT	CEIRSUV	CRUIVES
CEINVVY	VIVENCY		CURSIVE
CEIOOPR	OPORICE	CEIRTTU	CUTTIER
CEIOPPS	COPPIES	CEIRTTX	TECTRIX
CEIOPRS	COPIERS	CEISSSU	CUISSES
	COPSIER	CEISSTU	CESTUIS
	PERSICO		CUEISTS
CEIOPST	POETICS		CUTISES
CEIOPSU	PICEOUS		ICTUSES
CEIORRS	CIRROSE	CEISTTU	CUTTIES
	CORRIES	CEJKOSY	JOCKEYS
	CROSIER	CEJNORU	CONJURE
CEIORRU	COURIER	CEJNOSU	JOUNCES
CEIORRZ	CROZIER		JUNCOES
CEIORSS	COSIERS	CEJOPRT	PROJECT
CEIORST	EROTICS	CEKKLNU	KNUCKLE
	TERCIOS	CEKKNOR	KNOCKER
CEIORSU	SCOURIE	CEKKOPS	KOPECKS
CEIORSV	CORSIVE	CEKLLOP	PELLOCK
	VOICERS	CEKLLRY	CLERKLY
CEIORSW	COWRIES	CEKLMNO	LOCKMEN
	SCOWRIE	CEKLMSU	MUCKLES
CEIORSZ	COZIERS	CEKLNOS	ENLOCKS
CEIORTT	COTTIER		SLOCKEN
CEIORTV	EVICTOR	CEKLNRU	CRUNKLE
CEIORTX	EXCITOR	CEKLORS	LOCKERS
	XEROTIC	CEKLOST	LOCKETS
CEIORVY	VICEROY	CEKLPRU	PLUCKER
CEIOSSS	COSSIES	CEKLRSU	RUCKLES
CEIOSST	COSIEST		SUCKLER
	COTISES	CEKLRTU	TRUCKLE
	OECISTS	CEKLSSU	SUCKLES
CEIOSSV	VISCOSE	CEKMORS	MOCKERS
CEIOSTT	COTTISE	CEKMORY	MOCKERY
CEIOSTV	COSTIVE	CEKMRSU	MUCKERS
CEIOSTX	COXIEST	CEKNNSU	UNSNECK
	EXOTICS	CEKNOOV	CONVOKE
CEIOSTY	SOCIETY	CEKNORR	CRONKER
CEIOSTZ	COZIEST	CEKNORS	CONKERS
CEIPPST	PEPTICS		RECKONS
CEIPQTU	PICQUET	CEKNOST	NOCKETS
CEIPRRS	CRISPER	CEKNRWY	WRYNECK
	PRICERS	CEKNSSU	SUCKENS
CEIPRSS	SPICERS	CEKOOPR	PRECOOK
CEIPRST	TRICEPS	CEKOOPW	COWPOKE
CEIPRSY	SPICERY	CEKOORR	CROOKER
CEIPRTU	CUPRITE	CEKOORS	COOKERS
	PICTURE	CEKOORY	COOKERY
CEIPRTY	PYRETIC	CEKOPST	POCKETS
CEIPRXY	PYREXIC	CEKORRS	CORKERS
CEIPSSS	SCEPSIS		ROCKERS
CEIPSST	CESSPIT	CEKORRY	ROCKERY
CEIQRSU	CIRQUES	CEKORSS	SOCKERS
CEIRRRU	CURRIER	CEKORST	RESTOCK
CEIRRSU	CRUISER		ROCKETS
	CURRIES	CEKOSST	SOCKETS
	SUCRIER	CEKPRSU	PUCKERS
CEIRRTT	CRITTER	CEKPRSY	RYPECKS
CEIRRTU	RECRUIT	CEKPRUY	PUCKERY
CEIRRTX	RECTRIX	CEKRRTU	TRUCKER
CEIRRUV	CURVIER	CEKRSSU	SUCKERS
CEIRSSU	CRUISES	CEKRSTU	TUCKERS
	CRUSIES	CEKRSUY	YUCKERS
	CUISSER	CEKSSTU	SUCKETS

CEKSTTU	TUCKETS	CELOSTY	COTYLES
CELLMOU	COLUMEL	CELOSUV	VOCULES
CELLNOO	COLONEL	CELOTTU	CULOTTE
CELLORS	ESCROLL	CELPRSU	CURPELS
CELLOST	COLLETS		SCRUPLE
CELLOSU	LOCULES	CELPSUU	CUPULES
	OCELLUS	CELPSUY	CLYPEUS
CELLOSY	CLOSELY	CELRRSU	CURLERS
CELLRRU	CRULLER	CELRSTU	CLUSTER
CELLRSU	CRUELLS		CULTERS
	CULLERS		CUSTREL
	SCULLER		CUTLERS
CELLRUY	CRUELLY		RELUCTS
CELLSSU	SCULLES	CELRSTY	CLYSTER
CELLSTU	CULLETS	CELRSUV	CULVERS
CELMNOO	LOCOMEN	CELRSUW	CURLEWS
	MONOCLE	CELRTTU	CLUTTER
CELMNSU	CULMENS	CELRTUU	CULTURE
CELMOOS	COELOMS	CELRTUV	CULVERT
CELMOPS	COMPELS	CELRTUY	CRUELTY
CELMOPX	COMPLEX		CUTLERY
CELMPRU	CRUMPLE	CELSTTU	CUTLETS
CELMSSU	MUSCLES		CUTTLES
CELMSUU	SECULUM		SCUTTLE
CELMSUY	LYCEUMS	CEMMNOT	COMMENT
CELNNOU	NUCLEON	CEMMNOU	COMMUNE
CELNNSU	NUNCLES	CEMMOOT	COMMOTE
CELNOOS	COLONES	CEMMOOV	COMMOVE
	CONSOLE	CEMMORS	COMMERS
CELNORS	CORNELS	CEMMOTU	COMMUTE
CELNOSU	COUNSEL	CEMMRSU	CUMMERS
	UNCLOSE		SCUMMER
CELNOTU	NOCTULE	CEMNNOT	CONTEMN
CELNRSU	LUCERNS	CEMNOOP	COMPONE
CELNRTU	LECTURN	CEMNOOS	ONCOMES
CELNSUU	NUCLEUS	CEMNOOY	ECONOMY
	NUCULES	CEMNOSU	CONSUME
CELNSUW	UNCLEWS		MUSCONE
CELOORS	COOLERS	CEMNRSU	CRUMENS
CELOOST	COOLEST	CEMNRTU	CENTRUM
	OCELOTS	CEMNSTU	CENTUMS
CELOPPS	COPPLES	CEMOOPS	COMPOSE
CELOPRU	COUPLER	CEMOOPT	COMPOTE
CELOPSU	COUPLES	CEMOOTU	OUTCOME
	OPUSCLE	CEMOPRT	COMPTER
	UPCLOSE	CEMOPSU	UPCOMES
CELOPTU	COUPLET	CEMOPTU	COMPUTE
	OCTUPLE	CEMORRS	CREMORS
CELOQSU	CLOQUES	CEMOSSU	COMUSES
CELORSS	CLOSERS		MUSCOSE
	CRESOLS	CEMOSSY	MYCOSES
	ESCROLS	CEMOSTU	COSTUME
CELORST	COLTERS	CEMPRRU	CRUMPER
	CORSLET	CEMPRTU	CRUMPET
	COSTREL	CEMRRUY	MERCURY
	LECTORS	CEMRSTU	RECTUMS
CELORSU	CLOSURE	CEMSSUU	MUCUSES
	COLURES	CENNOOT	CONNOTE
CELORSV	CLOVERS	CENNORS	CONNERS
CELORSW	SCROWLE	CENNOST	CONSENT
CELORSY	SCROYLE		NOCENTS
CELORTT	CLOTTER	CENNOTT	CONTENT
	CROTTLE	CENNOTV	CONVENT
CELORTU	CLOTURE	CENNRSU	CUNNERS
	CLOUTER		SCUNNER
	COULTER	CENOORR	CORONER
CELORVY	CLOVERY		CROONER
CELOSST	CLOSEST	CENOORS	CEROONS
	CLOSETS	CENOORT	CORONET
CELOSSU	OSCULES	CENOOSS	COOSENS

```
CENOPRS CREPONS                SCOURER    CFIIMNO OMNIFIC    CGIINNZ ZINCING
CENOPSU POUNCES        CEORRSW SCOWRER    CFIINOT FICTION    CGIINOV VOICING
        UNCOPES        CEORRSY SORCERY    CFIINYZ ZINCIFY    CGIINPR PRICING
CENOPSY SYNCOPE        CEORRTY RECTORY    CFIIOSS OSSIFIC    CGIINPS SPICING
CENOPTU POUNCET        CEORSSS CROSSES    CFIKNNO FINNOCK    CGIINRT TRICING
CENOPTY POTENCY                SCORSES    CFIKOSS FOSSICK    CGIKLNO CLOKING
CENOQRU CONQUER        CEORSST CORSETS    CFILORS FROLICS            LOCKING
CENORRS CORNERS                COSTERS    CFILORU FLUORIC    CGIKMNO MOCKING
        SCORNER                ESCORTS    CFIMNOR CONFIRM    CGIKMNU MUCKING
CENORRW CROWNER                SCOTERS    CFIMOST COMFITS    CGIKNNO CONKING
CENORSS CENSORS                SECTORS    CFINOST CONFITS            NOCKING
CENORST CONSTER        CEORSSU COURSES    CFIORST FICTORS    CGIKNOO COOKING
        CORNETS                SCOURSE    CFIORSY SCORIFY    CGIKNOR CORKING
        CRONETS                SOURCES    CFIRSTU FRUICTS            ROCKING
CENORSU ROUNCES                SUCROSE    CFISSTU FUSTICS    CGIKNOS SOCKING
CENORTT CORNETT        CEORSSW ESCROWS    CFKLLOU LOCKFUL    CGIKNOY YOCKING
CENORTU CORNUTE        CEORSTT COTTERS    CFKNORU UNFROCK    CGIKNPU KINGCUP
        COUNTER        CEORSTU COUTERS    CFKOTTU FUTTOCK    CGIKNRU RUCKING
        RECOUNT                CROUTES    CFLMRUU FULCRUM    CGIKNSU SUCKING
        TROUNCE                SCOUTER    CFLNORY CORNFLY    CGIKNTU TUCKING
CENORTV CONVERT        CEORSTV CORVETS    CFLNOUX CONFLUX    CGIKNUY YUCKING
CENORTW CROWNET                COVERTS    CFLOPRU CROPFUL    CGILLNO COLLING
CENORUV UNCOVER                VECTORS    CFLPSUU CUPFULS    CGILLNU CULLING
CENOSSY COYNESS        CEORTUU COUTURE    CFMNOOR CONFORM    CGILMNU CULMING
CENOSTT CONTEST        CEORTUV COUVERT    CFMOORT COMFORT    CGILNNO CLONING
CENOSTU CONTUSE        CEOSSST COSSETS    CFOSSTU FUSTOCS    CGILNNU UNCLING
        ECONUTS        CEOSSSU SCOUSES    CFOSSUU FUSCOUS    CGILNOO COOLING
CENOSTV COVENTS        CEOSSSY SYCOSES    CGGGINO COGGING    CGILNOS CLOSING
CENOSVY CONVEYS        CEOSTTT OCTETTS    CGGIINR GRICING    CGILNOT COLTING
        COVYNES        CEOSTTU CUTTOES    CGGORSY SCROGGY    CGILNOW COWLING
CENOTTX CONTEXT        CEPPRRU CRUPPER    CGHHOSU CHOUGHS    CGILNOY CLOYING
CENPRTY ENCRYPT        CEPPRSU CUPPERS    CGHIIMN CHIMING    CGILNPY CLYPING
CENPTUX EXPUNCT                SCUPPER            MICHING    CGILNRU CURLING
CENRRTU CURRENT        CEPRRSU SPRUCER    CGHIINN CHINING    CGILNSY GLYCINS
CENRSSY SCRYNES        CEPRSTU PERCUSS            INCHING    CGILORW COWGIRL
CENRSTU ENCRUST                SPRUCES            NICHING    CGILOTT GLOTTIC
CENRSUU UNCURSE        CEPRSSY CYPRESS    CGHIINR RICHING    CGILPSU GILCUPS
CENRSUW UNSCREW        CEPRSTY SCEPTRY    CGHIINT ITCHING    CGILPTU GILTCUP
CENRTUY CENTURY        CEPSSTU SUSPECT    CGHIINV CHIVING    CGILPTY GLYPTIC
CENSSTY ENCYSTS        CERRSSU CURSERS    CGHIKNO CHOKING    CGIMNOO COOMING
CEOOPRS COOPERS        CERRSSY SCRYERS            HOCKING    CGIMNOR CROMING
        SCOOPER        CERSSSU CUSSERS    CGHILPY GLYPHIC    CGIMNOS COMINGS
CEOOPRY COOPERY        CERSSTU CRUSETS    CGHINNO CHIGNON    CGINNNO CONNING
CEOORSS COOSERS        CERSSUZ SCRUZES    CGHINOR OCHRING    CGINNNU CUNNING
CEOORST SCOOTER        CERSTTU CURTEST    CGHINOS COSHING    CGINNOP PONCING
CEOOSTY COYOTES                CUTTERS    CGHINRU RUCHING    CGINNOR CORNING
        OOCYTES                SCUTTER    CGHINSU CHUSING    CGINNOS CONSIGN
CEOPPRR CROPPER        CERSTUV CURVETS    CGHIOSY GOYISCH    CGINNSY SYNCING
CEOPPRS COPPERS        CERSTUY CURTSEY    CGHLOSU CLOUGHS    CGINOOP COOPING
CEOPPRY COPPERY        CFFGINO COFFING    CGHOORT TORGOCH    CGINOOS COOINGS
CEOPRRS SCORPER        CFFGINU CUFFING    CGHORUY GROUCHY    CGINOPP COPPING
CEOPRRT PORRECT        CFFHINO CHIFFON    CGIIJNU JUICING    CGINOPS COPINGS
CEOPRRU CROUPER        CFFILSS SCLIFFS    CGIIKKN KICKING            COPSING
        PROCURE        CFFINOS COFFINS    CGIIKLN LICKING    CGINOPU COUPING
CEOPRSS CORPSES        CFFINSU CUFFINS    CGIIKMM GIMMICK    CGINOPW COWPING
        PROCESS        CFFMOSU OFFSCUM    CGIIKNN NICKING    CGINOPY COPYING
CEOPRSU COUPERS        CFFOSTU OFFCUTS    CGIIKNP PICKING    CGINORS SCORING
        CROUPES        CFFRSSU SCRUFFS    CGIIKNR RICKING    CGINORU COURING
        RECOUPS        CFFRSUY SCRUFFY    CGIIKNS SICKING    CGINORW CROWING
CEOPRTT PROTECT        CFGIINO COIFING    CGIIKNT TICKING    CGINOST COSTING
CEOPRUU COUPURE        CFGIKNU FUCKING    CGIIKNW WICKING            GNOSTIC
CEOQRTU CROQUET        CFGINOR FORCING    CGIILLO ILLOGIC    CGINOSU SOUCING
        ROCQUET        CFHIMYY CHYMIFY    CGIILNO COILING    CGINOSV COVINGS
CEOQSTU COQUETS        CFHIOSW COWFISH    CGIILNP CLIPING    CGINOSW SOWCING
CEORRSS CROSSER        CFHIRST FRICHTS    CGIILNS SLICING    CGINPPU CUPPING
        RECROSS        CFHORTU FUTHORC    CGIIMNN MINCING    CGINRRU CURRING
        SCORERS        CFIIIMR MIRIFIC    CGIIMNR CRIMING    CGINRSU CURSING
        SCORSER        CFIIIVV VIVIFIC    CGIINNO COINING    CGINRSY CRYINGS
CEORRST RECTORS        CFIIKNY FINICKY    CGIINNR CRINING            SCRYING
CEORRSU COURSER        CFIILNT INFLICT    CGIINNW WINCING    CGINRUV CURVING
```

CGINSSU	CUSSING	CHIOSST	STICHOS
	SCUSING	CHIOSSZ	SCHIZOS
CGINTTU	CUTTING	CHIPRRU	CHIRRUP
CGIOOOS	GIOCOSO	CHIPRRY	PYRRHIC
CGIOTYZ	ZYGOTIC	CHIPSSY	PHYSICS
CGLLOSY	GLYCOLS	CHIQSTU	SQUITCH
CGLNOSU	UNCLOGS	CHIRRSU	CURRISH
CGLOOSU	COLUGOS	CHIRSTY	CHRISTY
CGNOOSU	CONGOUS	CHISSST	SCHISTS
CGOORRW	GORCROW	CHISSTU	SCHUITS
CHHIKOR	CHIKHOR	CHISTTU	CHUTIST
CHHINOR	RHONCHI	CHISTWY	SWITCHY
CHHINTU	UNHITCH	CHITTWY	TWITCHY
CHHIRST	SHRITCH	CHKLOOO	HOOLOCK
CHHISST	SHTCHIS	CHKLOSS	SHLOCKS
CHHISTY	ICHTHYS	CHKMMOO	HOMMOCK
CHHRTTU	THRUTCH	CHKMMOU	HUMMOCK
CHIIKNN	KINCHIN	CHKNOOS	SCHNOOK
CHIIKSS	SICKISH	CHKOOST	SCHTOOK
CHIILLS	CHILLIS	CHKORSU	CHUKORS
CHIILST	LITCHIS	CHKPTUU	PUTCHUK
CHIIMSU	ISCHIUM	CHKSSTU	SHTUCKS
CHIINNP	INCHPIN	CHLMOOS	MOLOCHS
CHIINST	CHITINS	CHLOOSS	SCHOOLS
CHIIOPT	OPHITIC	CHLOOST	COOLTHS
CHIIOST	STICHOI	CHLOPST	SPLOTCH
CHIKLLO	HILLOCK	CHLORSS	SCHORLS
CHIKLTY	THICKLY	CHLORTY	CHOLTRY
CHIKNOO	CHINOOK	CHLOSSS	SCHLOSS
CHIKORS	CHIKORS	CHLOSUY	SLOUCHY
CHIKORY	HICKORY	CHMOORS	CHROMOS
CHIKOST	THICKOS	CHMOOST	SCHTOOM
CHIKPSU	PUCKISH	CHMOSUY	CHYMOUS
CHIKSST	SCHTIKS	CHNNOOR	CHRONON
	SHTICKS	CHNNOSU	NONSUCH
CHIKSTY	KITSCHY	CHNOOPS	PONCHOS
CHILLMU	CHILLUM	CHNOORS	COHORNS
CHILLTY	LICHTLY	CHNOORT	TORCHON
CHILNOU	ULICHON	CHNORRS	SCHNORR
CHILNSY	LYCHNIS	CHNORTU	COTHURN
CHILOOS	COOLISH	CHNOTUU	UNCOUTH
CHILORS	ORCHILS	CHNSTUU	TUCHUNS
CHILOST	COLTISH	CHOORST	COHORTS
CHILSTU	CULTISH	CHOORSU	OCHROUS
CHIMNPY	NYMPHIC	CHOPSSY	PSYCHOS
CHIMOPR	MORPHIC	CHORSTU	TROCHUS
CHIMORS	CHRISOM	CHOSSTU	SCHOUTS
CHIMRRY	MYRRHIC		SCOUTHS
CHIMRSS	CHRISMS	CHOSSTW	SCOWTHS
CHIMSSS	SCHISMS	CHPSSUY	SCYPHUS
CHIMSTY	TYCHISM	CHRRSUU	CHURRUS
CHINOOR	CHORION	CHSSTUY	SCHUYTS
CHINOPS	CHOPINS	CIIILLT	ILLICIT
	PHONICS	CIIILNV	INCIVIL
CHINOST	CHITONS	CIIIMNR	CRIMINI
CHINOSU	CUSHION	CIIINPT	INCIPIT
CHINPSY	HYPNICS	CIIKKLL	KILLICK
CHINQSU	SQUINCH	CIIKMMM	MIMMICK
CHINRSU	URCHINS	CIIKMNN	MINNICK
CHINTUW	UNWITCH	CIIKNSW	INWICKS
CHINTYZ	CHINTZY	CIIKNTU	CUTIKIN
CHIOOPR	POCHOIR	CIIKSST	TISICKS
CHIOORS	ISOCHOR	CIIKSTT	STICKIT
CHIOORZ	CHORIZO	CIILLTY	LICITLY
CHIOPRT	TROPHIC	CIILLVY	CIVILLY
CHIOPST	PHOTICS	CIILNOP	CIPOLIN
CHIOPXY	HYPOXIC	CIILNOS	SILICON
CHIORST	CHORIST	CIILNPS	INCLIPS
	OSTRICH	CIILNUV	UNCIVIL
CHIORSW	CHOWRIS	CIILOOT	OOLITIC

CIILOPT	POLITIC	CILNOXY	XYLONIC
CIILOST	COLITIS	CILNPSU	INSCULP
	SOLICIT		SCULPIN
CIILPSY	SPICILY	CILNPTU	UNCLIPT
CIILSSS	SCISSIL	CILNSTU	LINCTUS
CIIMMRY	MIMICRY	CILOOPT	COPILOT
CIIMNNO	NIMONIC	CILOORU	COULOIR
CIIMNOT	MICTION	CILOOSS	COLOSSI
CIIMOST	MISTICO	CILOOST	SCIOLTO
	SOMITIC	CILOPRW	PILCROW
CIIMOTT	MITOTIC	CILOPRY	PYLORIC
CIIMOTV	MOTIVIC	CILOPSU	UPCOILS
CIIMSSV	CIVISMS	CILOPSW	COWSLIP
CIIMSTV	VICTIMS	CILORST	LICTORS
CIINNTU	TUNICIN	CILOSTU	COUTILS
CIINOOT	COITION		OCULIST
CIINOPS	PSIONIC	CILPRSY	CRISPLY
CIINORS	INCISOR	CILPRTU	CULPRIT
CIINPRS	CRISPIN	CILRRSU	SCURRIL
CIINQTU	QUINTIC	CILRSUU	SURCULI
CIINRST	CITRINS	CILSTTU	CULTIST
CIINSSV	VISCINS	CIMMNSU	CUMMINS
CIINTUY	UNICITY	CIMMOSS	COSMISM
CIIORST	SORITIC	CIMMOST	COMMITS
CIIOSUV	VICIOUS	CIMNNOS	NINCOMS
CIIPRSS	SPIRICS	CIMNNSU	NINCUMS
CIIPRTY	PYRITIC	CIMNOOR	MORONIC
CIIRSTV	VITRICS		OMICRON
CIIRTVX	VICTRIX	CIMNORS	CRIMSON
CIJNNOO	CONJOIN		MICRONS
CIJNNTU	INJUNCT	CIMNRSU	CRINUMS
CIJNOOS	COJOINS	CIMOORS	MORISCO
CIKKLLO	KILLOCK	CIMOOST	OSMOTIC
CIKLLOP	PILLOCK	CIMOPSY	COPYISM
CIKLLOR	ROLLICK		MISCOPY
CIKLLOS	SILLOCK		MYOPICS
CIKLLOW	KILLCOW	CIMORSU	CORIUMS
CIKLLSY	SLICKLY	CIMOSST	COSMIST
CIKLLUY	LUCKILY		SITCOMS
CIKLMSU	MISLUCK	CIMOSSY	MYCOSIS
CIKLMSY	SMICKLY	CIMOSTY	MYOTICS
CIKLNOS	INLOCKS	CIMOTYZ	ZYMOTIC
CIKLNRY	CRINKLY	CIMPRSS	SCRIMPS
CIKLORY	ROCKILY	CIMPRSY	SCRIMPY
CIKLPRY	PRICKLY	CIMRSSU	CRISSUM
CIKLQUY	QUICKLY	CIMRSUU	CURIUMS
CIKLRTY	TRICKLY	CIMSSTY	MYSTICS
CIKLSTU	LUSTICK	CIMSSUV	VISCUMS
CIKMNNO	MINNOCK	CINNNOU	INCONNU
CIKMNSU	NICKUMS	CINNORU	UNICORN
CIKNNOP	PINNOCK	CINNOSU	NUNCIOS
CIKNNOW	WINNOCK	CINNOTU	UNCTION
CIKNPSU	UNPICKS	CINNSUU	UNCINUS
CIKNSTU	UNSTICK	CINOOPS	OPSONIC
CIKOPPT	POCKPIT	CINOORS	CORONIS
CIKORRS	CORKIRS	CINOOSS	COOSINS
CIKOTUW	OUTWICK	CINOPPS	COPPINS
CIKPSTU	STICKUP	CINOPRX	PRINCOX
CIKRSTY	TRICKSY	CINORRT	TRICORN
CILLNOU	CULLION	CINORSS	INCROSS
CILLOOR	CRIOLLO	CINORST	CISTRON
CILLOPY	POLLICY		CITRONS
CILMNOP	COMPLIN		CORNIST
CILMSTU	CULTISM	CINORSZ	ZIRCONS
CILNOOR	ORCINOL	CINORTU	RUCTION
CILNOOS	CLOISON	CINOSST	CONSIST
CILNOPR	PILCORN		TOCSINS
CILNOSU	ULICONS	CINOSSU	COUSINS
	UNCOILS	CINOSTU	SUCTION
CILNOTU	LINOCUT	CINOSUZ	ZINCOUS

CINRSTU INCRUST	CLORSSY CROSSLY	DDDEELS SLEDDED	DDEEFUZ DEFUZED
CIOOPRS SCORPIO	CLORTUY COURTLY	DDDEELU DELUDED	DDEEGGL GLEDGED
CIOOPRT PORTICO	CLOSSTU LOCUSTS	DDDEEMO DEMODED	DDEEGIN DEEDING
PROOTIC	CLPRSUU UPCURLS	DDDEENS SNEDDED	DEIGNED
CIOOPSU COPIOUS	CLPSSTU SCULPTS	DDDEENU DENUDED	DDEEGIS DISEDGE
CIOOQTU COQUITO	CMMNOOS COMMONS	DDDEERU UDDERED	DDEEGLP PLEDGED
CIOORST OCTROIS	CMMOOST COMMOTS	DDDEEST STEDDED	DDEEGLS SLEDGED
CIOORSU CORIOUS	CMMRSUY SCRUMMY	DDDEFIL FIDDLED	DDEEGLU DELUGED
CIOPRST TROPICS	CMNOOOT MONOCOT	DDDEFLU FUDDLED	DDEEGNU UNEDGED
CIOPSTY COPYIST	CMNOOPY COMPONY	DDDEGII GIDDIED	DDEEGRR DREDGER
CIOQRSU CROQUIS	CMNPTUU PUNCTUM	DDDEGLU GUDDLED	DDEEGRS DREDGES
CIORRSU CIRROUS	CMOOPRT COMPORT	DDDEGRU DRUDGED	DDEEHLS HEDDLES
CIORSSS SCISSOR	CMOOPST COMPOST	DDDEHIW WHIDDED	DDEEHNU DUDHEEN
CIORSTT TRICOTS	COMPOTS	DDDEHLO HODDLED	DDEEHRS SHEDDER
CIORSTU CITROUS	CMOORSU CORMOUS	DDDEHLU HUDDLED	DDEEILS SLEIDED
CIORSTV VICTORS	CMOOSTY SCOTOMY	DDDEHTU THUDDED	DDEEILW WIELDED
CIORSUU CURIOUS	CMORSTU SCROTUM	DDDEIIK KIDDIED	DDEEILY DEEDILY
CIORTVY VICTORY	CMORTUW CUTWORM	DDDEIIV DIVIDED	YIELDED
CIOSSSY SYCOSIS	CMOSSTU CUSTOMS	DDDEIKS SKIDDED	DDEEIMP IMPEDED
CIOSSUV VISCOUS	CMPRSSU SCRUMPS	DDDEILM MIDDLED	DDEEIMS DEMISED
CIPRSST SCRIPTS	CMPRSUY SCRUMPY	DDDEILN DINDLED	MISDEED
CIPRSSU PRUSSIC	CNNOPSY PYCNONS	DDDEILP PIDDLED	DDEEINS DESINED
CIPRTTY TRYPTIC	CNNORTU NOCTURN	DDDEILR DIDDLER	NEDDIES
CIPSTTY STYPTIC	CNNORUW UNCROWN	RIDDLED	SDEINED
CIRRTTU CRITTUR	CNOOPPR POPCORN	DDDEILS DIDDLES	DDEEINT ENDITED
CIRSSTU RUSTICS	CNOOPRU CROUPON	DDDEILT TIDDLED	TEINDED
CIRTUVY CURVITY	CNOOPSU COUPONS	DDDEILW WIDDLED	DDEEINW INDEWED
CISSTUY CYTISUS	SOUPCON	DDDEIMU MUDDIED	WIDENED
CJNORUY CONJURY	CNOORST CONSORT	DDDEIOR DODDIER	DDEEINX INDEXED
CKLLMOU MULLOCK	CROTONS	DDDEIOS DODDIES	DDEEINZ DIZENED
CKLLOOP POLLOCK	CNOORTT CONTORT	DDDEIRS DIDDERS	DDEEIOV VIDEOED
CKLLOOR ROLLOCK	CNOORTU CONTOUR	DDDEIRU DUDDIER	DDEEIPR PREDIED
CKLLORU RULLOCK	CORNUTO	RUDDIED	DDEEIPS DEPSIDE
CKLNOSU UNLOCKS	CROUTON	DDDELMU MUDDLED	DDEEIRR DERIDER
CKLNUUY UNLUCKY	CNOOSST NOSTOCS	DDDELNO NODDLED	REDDIER
CKLOOOY OLYCOOK	ONCOSTS	DDDELOO DOODLED	RIDERED
CKLOORW ROWLOCK	CNOOSTT COTTONS	DDDELOP PLODDED	DDEEIRS DERIDES
CKLOOTU LOCKOUT	CNOOSTY TYCOONS	DDDELOS DODDLES	DESIRED
CKLOPSU UPLOCKS	CNOOSUU NOCUOUS	DDDELOT TODDLED	DIEDRES
CKLOPTU PUTLOCK	CNOOSVY CONVOYS	DDDELPU PUDDLED	RESIDED
CKMMMOU MUMMOCK	CNOOTTW COTTOWN	DDDELRU RUDDLED	DDEEIRV DERIVED
CKNORSU UNCORKS	CNOOTTY COTTONY	DDDENOS SNODDED	DDEEIRW WEIRDED
CKNOSTU UNSTOCK	CNOPRTY CRYPTON	DDDEOPR PRODDED	DDEEIST DEIDEST
CKNSTUU UNSTUCK	CNOPSTU PUNCTOS	DDDEOQU QUODDED	TEDDIES
UNTUCKS	CNORSSU UNCROSS	DDDEORS DODDERS	DDEEISV DEVISED
CKOOOTU COOKOUT	CNORSSY SYNROCS	DDDEORY DODDERY	DDEEKKO DEKKOED
CKOORSU SOUROCK	CNORTUY COUNTRY	DDDEPSU SPUDDED	DDEELLU DUELLED
CKOPTTU PUTTOCK	CNRSSTU SCRUNTS	DDDERSU DUDDERS	DDEELLW DWELLED
CKOSSTU TUSSOCK	CNRSTUY SCRUNTY	DDDERUY DUDDERY	DDEELMR MEDDLER
CLLMOSU MOLLUSC	COOORSZ COROZOS	DDDESTU STUDDED	DDEELMS MEDDLES
CLLOOPS COLLOPS	COOPRRT PROCTOR	DDDGINO DODDING	DDEELNO OLDENED
SCOLLOP	COOPRSS SCROOPS	DDEEEIR DEEDIER	DDEELNS LEDDENS
CLLORSS SCROLLS	COOPRTU OUTCROP	DDEEELN NEEDLED	DDEELPR PEDDLER
CLLOSUU LOCULUS	COOPSTU OCTOPUS	DDEEELT DELETED	DDEELPS PEDDLES
CLMNOSU COLUMNS	COORSTU OCTUORS	DDEEEMN EMENDED	SPELDED
CLMOOPT COMPLOT	COORSUU ROUCOUS	DDEEENT TEENDED	DDEELRS REDDLES
CLMOPTU PLUMCOT	COOSTTY OTOCYST	DDEEENW ENDEWED	DDEELRT TREDDLE
CLMOSUU LUCUMOS	COPRRTU CORRUPT	DDEEEPS SPEEDED	DDEELRU DELUDER
OSCULUM	COPRSTY CRYPTOS	DDEEEST DEEDEST	DDEELSU DELUDES
CLMSUUU CUMULUS	COPRSUU CUPROUS	STEEDED	DDEEMOT DEMOTED
CLNOORT CONTROL	CORRSSU CURSORS	DDEEESX DESEXED	DDEEMRU DEMURED
CLNOOSS CONSOLS	CORRSUY CURSORY	DDEEFGL FLEDGED	DDEENOP DEPONED
CLNOSSU CONSULS	CORSSTU SCRUTOS	DDEEFII DEIFIED	DDEENOT DENOTED
CLNOSTU CONSULT	DDDEEIL DIDDLED	EDIFIED	DDEENOW ENDOWED
UNCOLTS	DDDEEGR DREDGED	DDEEFIL DEFILED	DDEENOZ DOZENED
CLNOSUW UNCOWLS	DDDEEHL HEDDLED	FIELDED	DDEENPS DEPENDS
CLNRSUU UNCURLS	DDDEEIR DERIDED	DDEEFIN DEFINED	DDEENRS REDDENS
CLOORSU COLOURS	DDDEELM MEDDLED	DDEEFLU DEEDFUL	DDEENRT TRENDED
CLOORUY COLOURY	DDDEELP PEDDLED	DDEEFNS DEFENDS	DDEENRU ENDURED
CLORSSW SCROWLS	DDDEELR REDDLED	DDEEFSU DEFUSED	DDEENST STENDED

DDEENSU	DENUDES	DDEHNRU HUNDRED	DDEINST DISTEND	DDENOSW SOWNDED

DDEENSU DENUDES
       DUDEENS
DDEENSY DESYNED
DDEEOPS DEPOSED
DDEEORR ORDERED
DDEEORV DOVERED
DDEEORW DOWERED
DDEEOTV DEVOTED
DDEEPRS PEDDERS
       SPREDDE
DDEEPTU DEPUTED
DDEERRS REDDERS
DDEERSS DRESSED
DDEERST REDDEST
       TEDDERS
DDEERTU DETRUDE
DDEESST STEDDES
DDEETTU DUETTED
DDEFGIR FRIDGED
DDEFILR FIDDLER
DDEFILS FIDDLES
DDEFILY FIDDLEY
DDEFIRT DRIFTED
DDEFLNO FONDLED
DDEFLOO FLOODED
DDEFLRU FUDDLER
DDEFLSU FUDDLES
DDEFNOR FRONDED
DDEFNOU FOUNDED
DDEFORS FODDERS
DDEGGRU DRUGGED
       GRUDGED
DDEGHIT DIGHTED
DDEGIIR GIDDIER
DDEGIIS GIDDIES
DDEGILR GIRDLED
       GLIDDER
       GRIDDLE
DDEGIMO DEMIGOD
DDEGINR GRINDED
       REDDING
DDEGINT TEDDING
DDEGINW WEDDING
DDEGINY EDDYING
DDEGIOR DODGIER
DDEGLSU GUDDLES
DDEGMOS DODGEMS
DDEGMSU SMUDGED
DDEGNOS GODSEND
DDEGNOU DUDGEON
DDEGNSU SNUDGED
DDEGORS DODGERS
       GORSEDD
DDEGORY DODGERY
DDEGOSS GODDESS
DDEGOST STODGED
DDEGRRU DRUDGER
DDEGRSU DRUDGES
DDEGRTU TRUDGED
DDEHIRS HIDDERS
       REDDISH
       SHIDDER
DDEHIRT THIRDED
DDEHIRW WHIDDER
DDEHIRY HYDRIDE
DDEHLOS HODDLES
DDEHLRU HURDLED
DDEHLSU HUDDLES
DDEHNOS HODDENS
DDEHNOU HOUNDED

DDEHNRU HUNDRED
DDEHNSU DUNSHED
DDEHRSU SHUDDER
DDEHRSY SHREDDY
DDEIIKR KIDDIER
DDEIIKS KIDDIES
DDEIIMS MIDDIES
DDEIINT INDITED
DDEIINV DIVINED
DDEIIOS IODIDES
       IODISED
DDEIIOX DIOXIDE
DDEIIOZ IODIZED
DDEIIRT DIRTIED
       TIDDIER
DDEIIRV DIVIDER
DDEIIST STIDDIE
       TIDDIES
DDEIISV DIVIDES
DDEIISW WIDDIES
DDEIITT DITTIED
DDEIIVV DIVVIED
DDEIIZZ DIZZIED
DDEIKLN KINDLED
DDEIKLS KIDDLES
DDEIKNR KINDRED
DDEIKRS KIDDERS
DDEILLO DOLLIED
DDEILLR DRILLED
DDEILLU ILLUDED
DDEILMP DIMPLED
DDEILMS MIDDLES
DDEILNN DINNLED
DDEILNS DINDLES
       SLIDDEN
DDEILNW DWINDLE
DDEILOR DROILED
DDEILOS DILDOES
DDEILOT DELTOID
DDEILPR PIDDLER
DDEILPS DISPLED
       PIDDLES
DDEILPU DUPLIED
DDEILQU QUIDDLE
DDEILRR RIDDLER
DDEILRS RIDDLES
       SLIDDER
DDEILRT TIDDLER
DDEILST TIDDLES
DDEILSW WIDDLES
DDEILTU DILUTED
DDEILTW TWIDDLE
DDEILTY LYDDITE
       TIDDLEY
DDEIMMU DUMMIED
DDEIMNS MIDDENS
DDEIMNU MUEDDIN
DDEIMOO MOODIED
DDEIMOR DERMOID
DDEIMOS DESMOID
DDEIMRU MUDDIER
DDEIMSS DESMIDS
DDEIMST MIDDEST
DDEIMSU DEDIMUS
       MUDDIES
DDEINOP POINDED
DDEINOS NODDIES
DDEINOT DENTOID
DDEINPS DISPEND
DDEINRU UNDRIED

DDEINST DISTEND
DDEINSW SWIDDEN
DDEIOPR PODDIER
DDEIORS DORISED
       SODDIER
DDEIORV OVERDID
DDEIORW DOWDIER
DDEIORZ DORIZED
DDEIOST TODDIES
DDEIOSW DOWDIES
DDEIOTT DITTOED
DDEIOWW WIDOWED
DDEIPPR DRIPPED
DDEIPRS DISPRED
DDEIPSU PUDDIES
DDEIRRS RIDDERS
DDEIRRU RUDDIER
DDEIRSU RUDDIES
DDEISSU DISUSED
DDEISTU STUDIED
DDEJRSU JUDDERS
DDEKMOU DUKEDOM
DDEKOOR DROOKED
DDEKORU DROUKED
DDELLOR DROLLED
DDELMOU MOULDED
DDELMPU DUMPLED
DDELMRU MUDDLER
DDELMSU MUDDLES
DDELNOO NOODLED
DDELNOS NODDLES
DDELNOU LOUNDED
       NODULED
DDELNOW LOWNDED
DDELNRU RUNDLED
DDELOOR DOODLER
       DROOLED
DDELOOS DOODLES
DDELOOW WOOLDED
DDELOPR PLODDER
DDELORT TODDLER
DDELORW WORLDED
DDELOST TODDLES
DDELOTT DOTTLED
DDELPRU PUDDLER
DDELPSU PUDDLES
DDELRSU RUDDLES
DDELSTU STUDDLE
DDEMMRU DRUMMED
DDEMMSU SMEDDUM
DDEMNOS ODDSMEN
DDEMNOT ODDMENT
DDEMNOU MOUNDED
DDENNOR DENDRON
       DONNERD
DDENOOS SNOODED
DDENOPS DESPOND
DDENOPU POUNDED
DDENOPW POWNDED
DDENORS NODDERS
DDENORT TRODDEN
DDENORU REDOUND
       ROUNDED
       UNDERDO
DDENORW DROWNED
       ROWNDED
       WONDRED
DDENOSS ODDNESS
       SODDENS
DDENOSU SOUNDED

DDENOSW SOWNDED
DDENOSY DYNODES
DDENOUW WOUNDED
DDENPSU PUDDENS
DDENRSU DUNDERS
DDENSTU STUDDEN
DDEOOPR DROOPED
DDEOORU ODOURED
DDEOORW REDWOOD
DDEOPPR DROPPED
DDEORSW DROWSED
       SWORDED
DDEPRSS SPREDDS
DDEPRSU PUDDERS
DDERRSU RUDDERS
DDERSSU SUDDERS
DDGGINO DODGING
       GODDING
DDGHINO HODDING
DDGHOOO GODHOOD
DDGIIKN KIDDING
DDGIILY GIDDILY
DDGIINR RIDDING
DDGIMNU MUDDING
DDGINNO NODDING
DDGINOP PODDING
DDGINOR RODDING
DDGINOS SODDING
DDGINOT TODDING
DDGINPU PUDDING
DDGINRU RUDDING
DDGINUW WUDDING
DDGOOOW DOGWOOD
DDHIISS SIDDHIS
DDHIKSU KIDDUSH
DDHIORY HYDROID
DDIILOP DIPLOID
DDIIQTU QUIDDIT
DDIKNOS DODKINS
DDILMUY MUDDILY
DDILNRS DIRNDLS
DDILOSY DYSODIL
DDILOWY DOWDILY
DDILRUY RUDDILY
DDILTWY TWIDDLY
DDIMRSU DIRDUMS
DDIMSSU DUDISMS
DDINOST SNODDIT
DDIORTU TURDOID
DDLLMOO DOLLDOM
DDMMSUU DUMDUMS
DDMNOOR DROMOND
DDMRSUU DURDUMS
DDORSTY DROSTDY
DEEEEHT TEEHEED
DEEEEMX EXEEMED
DEEEFFR EFFERED
DEEEFLR FLEERED
DEEEFLT FLEETED
DEEEFNR ENFREED
DEEEFNS DEFENSE
DEEEFRS FEEDERS
DEEEFRV FEVERED
DEEEGKL GLEEKED
DEEEGLP PLEDGEE
DEEEGLT GLEETED
DEEEGMR DEMERGE
       EMERGED
DEEEGNP PEENGED
DEEEGNR GREENED

	RENEGED
DEEEGRR	REGREDE
DEEEGRS	DEGREES
DEEEGRT	DETERGE
	GREETED
DEEEGST	EGESTED
DEEEHKT	THEEKED
DEEEHLS	SHEELED
DEEEHLW	WHEEDLE
	WHEELED
DEEEHNS	SHEENED
DEEEHPS	PHEESED
DEEEHPZ	PHEEZED
DEEEHRS	SHEERED
DEEEHST	SEETHED
	SHEETED
DEEEHTT	TEETHED
DEEEHWZ	WHEEZED
DEEEIJL	JEELIED
DEEEIMR	EMERIED
DEEEINR	NEEDIER
DEEEIPS	DEEPIES
DEEEIRR	REEDIER
DEEEIRS	SEEDIER
DEEEIRW	WEEDIER
DEEEISV	DEVISEE
DEEEJNU	DEJEUNE
DEEEJRS	JEREEDS
DEEEKLN	KNEELED
DEEEKLS	SLEEKED
DEEEKMS	SMEEKED
DEEEKNW	WEEKEND
DEEEKRS	KREESED
	SKEERED
DEEELMS	MESELED
DEEELNR	NEEDLER
DEEELNS	NEEDLES
DEEELPS	SPEELED
DEEELPT	DEPLETE
DEEELRT	DEERLET
DEEELRV	LEVERED
DEEELST	DELETES
	SLEETED
	STEELED
DEEELSV	SLEEVED
DEEELSW	SWEELED
DEEELTW	TWEEDLE
	TWEELED
DEEELTX	TELEXED
DEEEMMW	EMMEWED
DEEEMNS	DEMESNE
DEEEMNW	ENMEWED
DEEEMRS	DEMERSE
	EMERSED
	REDEEMS
	REMEDES
DEEEMRT	METERED
DEEEMST	STEEMED
DEEENPR	PREENED
DEEENPS	DEEPENS
DEEENQU	QUEENED
DEEENRS	NEEDERS
	SERENED
	SNEERED
DEEENRT	ENTERED
DEEENRV	ENERVED
DEEENRW	RENEWED
DEEENRY	RENEYED
DEEENST	STEENED
DEEENSV	VENDEES
DEEENSW	ENSEWED
DEEENSZ	SNEEZED
DEEENTT	DETENTE
DEEENTU	DETENUE
DEEEORW	OREWEED
DEEEOTV	DEVOTEE
DEEEPRS	SPEEDER
	SPEERED
DEEEPRT	PETERED
DEEEPRU	EPERDUE
DEEEPRV	PREEVED
DEEEPSS	PEDESES
DEEEPST	DEEPEST
	STEEPED
DEEEQRU	QUEERED
DEEERRS	REEDERS
DEEERRV	REVERED
DEEERSS	SEEDERS
DEEERST	REESTED
	STEERED
DEEERSV	DESERVE
	SEVERED
DEEERSW	SEWERED
	SWEERED
	WEEDERS
DEEERSY	REDEYES
DEEERTV	EVERTED
DEEERTW	TWEERED
DEEERTX	EXERTED
DEEERWY	WEEDERY
DEEESSX	DESEXES
DEEESTV	STEEVED
DEEESTW	SWEETED
DEEETTV	VEDETTE
DEEETTW	TWEETED
DEEETWZ	TWEEZED
DEEFFFO	FEOFFED
DEEFFIN	EFFENDI
DEEFFOR	OFFERED
DEEFFSU	EFFUSED
DEEFGGL	FLEGGED
DEEFGIN	FEEDING
	FEIGNED
DEEFGIP	PIGFEED
DEEFGLS	FLEDGES
DEEFGRU	REFUGED
DEEFHLS	FLESHED
	SHELFED
DEEFHLU	HEEDFUL
DEEFHRS	FRESHED
DEEFIIR	DEIFIER
	EDIFIER
	REIFIED
DEEFIIS	DEIFIES
	EDIFIES
DEEFILN	ENFILED
DEEFILR	DEFILER
	FERLIED
	FIELDER
DEEFILS	DEFILES
DEEFINR	DEFINER
	ENFIRED
	FENDIER
	REFINED
DEEFINS	DEFINES
DEEFINT	FEINTED
DEEFINX	ENFIXED
DEEFIRR	FERRIED
DEEFIRS	DEFIERS
DEEFIRT	FETIDER
DEEFIRZ	FRIEZED
DEEFLLU	FUELLED
DEEFLNS	FLENSED
DEEFLNU	NEEDFUL
DEEFLOT	FEEDLOT
DEEFLTT	FETTLED
DEEFMOR	FREEDOM
DEEFNRS	FENDERS
DEEFNUU	UNFEUED
DEEFORV	OVERFED
DEEFORZ	DEFROZE
DEEFRSU	REFUSED
DEEFRSW	SWERFED
DEEFRTT	FRETTED
DEEFRTU	FEUTRED
	REFUTED
DEEFSSU	DEFUSES
DEEFSTT	DEFTEST
DEEFSUZ	DEFUZES
DEEGGIS	GIDGEES
DEEGGLS	GLEDGES
DEEGHIN	HEEDING
	NEIGHED
DEEGHIR	HEDGIER
DEEGHIW	WEIGHED
DEEGHOW	HOGWEED
DEEGHRS	HEDGERS
DEEGHSS	GHESSED
DEEGIJS	GIDJEES
DEEGIKR	KEDGIER
DEEGILN	DELEING
DEEGILR	GELIDER
	LEDGIER
	LEIDGER
DEEGIMN	DEEMING
DEEGINN	ENGINED
	NEEDING
DEEGINR	DREEING
	ENERGID
	GREINED
	REEDING
	REIGNED
DEEGINS	SDEIGNE
	SEEDING
DEEGINV	DEEVING
DEEGINW	WEEDING
DEEGINY	YEEDING
DEEGIOR	GEORDIE
DEEGIPW	PIGWEED
DEEGIRS	SEDGIER
DEEGIRV	DIVERGE
	GRIEVED
DEEGIST	EDGIEST
DEEGISW	WEDGIES
DEEGJRU	REJUDGE
DEEGKRS	KEDGERS
DEEGLMU	EMULGED
DEEGLNS	LEGENDS
DEEGLNT	GENTLED
	GLENTED
DEEGLOY	GOLDEYE
DEEGLPR	PLEDGER
DEEGLPS	PLEDGES
DEEGLPT	PLEDGET
DEEGLRS	GELDERS
	LEDGERS
	REDLEGS
	SLEDGER
DEEGLSS	SLEDGES
DEEGLSU	DELUGES
DEEGMNU	EMUNGED
	GUDEMEN
DEEGNNO	ENDOGEN
DEEGNNR	GRENNED
DEEGNOR	ENGORED
DEEGNRS	GENDERS
DEEGNSU	DENGUES
	UNEDGES
DEEGOOS	SOOGEED
DEEGORR	ROGERED
DEEGOSY	GEODESY
DEEGOTU	OUTEDGE
DEEGRRU	REURGED
DEEGSSU	GUESSED
DEEGSTU	GUESTED
DEEHIKV	KHEDIVE
DEEHILS	SHIELED
DEEHILT	LETHIED
DEEHINR	INHERED
DEEHIRR	HERRIED
DEEHIST	HEISTED
DEEHITV	THIEVED
DEEHKLW	WHELKED
DEEHLLO	HELLOED
DEEHLLS	SHELLED
DEEHLMW	WHELMED
DEEHLNU	UNHELED
DEEHLOV	HOVELED
DEEHLPW	WHELPED
DEEHLSV	SHELVED
DEEHLSW	WELSHED
DEEHMNR	HERDMEN
DEEHMNS	MENSHED
DEEHMRU	RHEUMED
DEEHMUX	EXHUMED
DEEHNOY	HONEYED
DEEHNPR	PREHEND
DEEHNRS	HERDENS
DEEHNUY	UNHEEDY
DEEHORV	HOVERED
DEEHPRS	SPHERED
DEEHRSS	HERDESS
DEEHRSU	USHERED
DEEHRSW	SHREWED
DEEHRTW	WRETHED
DEEHTTW	WHETTED
DEEIINT	DIETINE
DEEIIPR	EPEIRID
DEEIIRW	WEIRDIE
DEEIIST	DEITIES
DEEIJLL	JELLIED
DEEIKLL	KILLDEE
DEEIKLN	LIKENED
DEEIKNS	ENSKIED
DEEIKOV	DOVEKIE
DEEILNO	ELOINED
DEEILNR	RELINED
DEEILNS	ENISLED
	ENSILED
	LINSEED
DEEILNV	LIVENED
DEEILNY	DYELINE
	NEEDILY
DEEILPR	REPLIED
DEEILPS	SEEDLIP
	SPIELED
DEEILRS	RESILED
DEEILRT	RETILED
DEEILRV	DELIVER
	RELIVED

REVILED	DEEIPSS DESPISE	DEELNSW WEDELNS	DEENOST DENOTES
DEEILRW WIELDER	PEDESIS	DEELNSY DENSELY	DEENPPR PERPEND
DEEILRY YIELDER	DEEIPST DESPITE	DEELNTT NETTLED	DEENPRS SPENDER
DEEILSS DIESELS	DEEIQRU QUERIED	DEELOPP PEOPLED	DEENPRT PRETEND
IDLESSE	DEEIQTU QUIETED	DEELOPR DEPLORE	DEENPSX EXPENDS
DEEILSY EYELIDS	DEEIRRS DERRIES	DEELOPV DEVELOP	DEENRRS RENDERS
SEEDILY	DESIRER	DEELOPX EXPLODE	DEENRRU ENDURER
DEEILTU DILUTEE	RESIDER	DEELORS RESOLED	DEENRSS REDNESS
DEEILTV DEVILET	SERRIED	DEELORU URODELE	SENDERS
DEEIMMS MISDEEM	DEEIRRT RETIRED	DEELORV LOVERED	DEENRST STERNED
DEEIMMW IMMEWED	RETRIED	DEELORW LOWERED	TENDERS
DEEIMNR ERMINED	TIREDER	DEELOSU DELOUSE	TENDRES
DEEIMNS DESMINE	DEEIRRV REDRIVE	DEELOTV DOVELET	DEENRSU ENDURES
DEEIMNT DEMENTI	RIVERED	DEELOVV DEVOLVE	ENSURED
DEEIMPR DEMIREP	DEEIRRW REWIRED	EVOLVED	DEENRSV VENDERS
DEEIMPS IMPEDES	WEIRDER	DEELPRS SPELDER	DEENRSZ DZERENS
SEMIPED	DEEIRSS DESIRES	DEELPRU PRELUDE	DEENRTU DENTURE
DEEIMPT EMPTIED	RESIDES	DEELPST PESTLED	RETUNED
DEEIMRS REMEIDS	DEEIRST DIETERS	DEELPTT PETTLED	DEENRTV VENTRED
REMISED	REISTED	DEELRRU RULERED	DEENSST DENSEST
DEEIMRT DEMERIT	DEEIRSU RESIDUE	DEELRSU ELUDERS	DEENSSY DESYNES
DIMETER	UREIDES	DEELRSV DELVERS	DEENSTT DETENTS
MERITED	DEEIRSV DERIVES	DEELRSW WELDERS	STENTED
MITERED	DEVISER	DEELRUV VELURED	DEENSTU DETENUS
DEEIMSS DEMISES	DIVERSE	DEELSTT SETTLED	DEENSTX EXTENDS
DEEIMTT EMITTED	REVISED	DEELSTU TELEDUS	DEENSUV VENDUES
DEEINNP PENNIED	DEEIRTU ERUDITE	DEELSTW LEWDEST	DEENSUW UNSEWED
DEEINNS INDENES	DEEIRTV RIVETED	SWELTED	DEENSUX UNSEXED
DEEINNT DENTINE	DEEIRVV REVIVED	DEELSUV EVULSED	DEENUVX UNVEXED
DEEINNU ENNUIED	DEEISSU DISEUSE	DEELSVV DEVVELS	DEEOPRR PEDRERO
DEEINNZ DENIZEN	DEEISSV DEVISES	DEELTUX EXULTED	DEEOPRS DEPOSER
DEEINOR ORDINEE	DEEISTT TEDIEST	DEELVXY VEXEDLY	REPOSED
DEEINPR REPINED	DEEISTW DEWIEST	DEEMMOV EMMOVED	DEEOPRW POWERED
RIPENED	DEEISTX EXISTED	DEEMMST STEMMED	DEEOPSS DEPOSES
DEEINRR DERNIER	DEEITTV VIDETTE	DEEMNOV ENMOVED	SPEEDOS
DEEINRS DENIERS	DEEJNOY ENJOYED	VENOMED	DEEOPSX EXPOSED
NEREIDS	DEEJQRU JERQUED	DEEMNOY MONEYED	PODEXES
RESINED	DEEKKRT TREKKED	DEEMNRS MENDERS	DEEORRR ORDERER
DEEINRU UREDINE	DEEKLLN KNELLED	DEEMNST DEMENTS	REORDER
DEEINRW WIDENER	DEEKLPS SKELPED	DEEMNTU UNMETED	DEEORRS REREDOS
DEEINRX INDEXER	DEEKLRS SKELDER	DEEMNUW UNMEWED	DEEORRV OVERRED
DEEINSS DESINES	DEEKNOT TOKENED	DEEMORS EMERODS	REDROVE
DEEINST DESTINE	DEEKORV REVOKED	DEEMORV REMOVED	DEEORST OERSTED
ENDITES	DEEKPPS SKEPPED	DEEMORX EXODERM	ROSETED
STEINED	DEEKPRU PERUKED	DEEMOSS DEMOSES	TEREDOS
DEEINSV ENDIVES	DEEKRRS SKERRED	DEEMOST DEMOTES	DEEORTT OTTERED
DEEINSW ENDWISE	DEEKRSU RESKUED	DEEMOSY MOSEYED	TETRODE
SINEWED	DEELLMS SMELLED	DEEMPRS PREMEDS	DEEORTW TOWERED
DEEINSX INDEXES	DEELLNS SNELLED	DEEMPTT TEMPTED	DEEORTX OXTERED
DEEINTT DINETTE	DEELLPS SPELLED	DEEMRRU DEMURER	DEEORTZ ROZETED
DEEINTU DETINUE	DEELLQU QUELLED	DEEMRSU DEMURES	DEEORUV OVERDUE
DEEINTV EVIDENT	DEELLRU DUELLER	RESUMED	DEEORVY OVERDYE
DEEINVW VINEWED	DEELLRW DWELLER	DEENNOR ENDERON	DEEOSTV DEVOTES
DEEINVX INVEXED	DEELLRY ELDERLY	DEENNOS DONNEES	DEEOTUW OUTWEED
DEEINWZ WIZENED	DEELLST STELLED	DEENNOT TENONED	DEEPPPR PREPPED
DEEIOPS EPISODE	DEELLSW SWELLED	DEENNOY DOYENNE	DEEPPST STEPPED
POESIED	DEELMNO LEMONED	DEENNOZ ENZONED	DEEPRRS SPERRED
DEEIOPT EPIDOTE	DEELMOR REMODEL	DEENNPT PENDENT	DEEPRRU PERDURE
DEEIOPX EPOXIDE	DEELMPT TEMPLED	DEENNST DENNETS	REPURED
DEEIORS OREIDES	DEELMPU DEPLUME	STENNED	DEEPRSS DEPRESS
OSIERED	DEELMRS MELDERS	DEENNTZ TENDENZ	PRESSED
DEEIOSV VOIDEES	DEELMRU RELUMED	DEENNUY ENNUYED	SPERSED
DEEIPPT PEPTIDE	DEELMST SMELTED	DEENOOR RONEOED	DEEPRST PRESTED
DEEIPRS PREDIES	DEELMSY MEDLEYS	DEENOPR REPONED	DEEPRSU PERDUES
PRESIDE	DEELMTT METTLED	DEENOPS DEPONES	PERSUED
SPEIRED	DEELNRS LENDERS	SPONDEE	PERUSED
DEEIPRT TEPIDER	SLENDER	DEENOPT PENTODE	SUPERED
DEEIPRV DEPRIVE	DEELNSS ENDLESS	DEENORS ENDORSE	DEEPRTU ERUPTED
PRIEVED	DEELNST DENTELS	DEENORT ERODENT	REPUTED
DEEIPRX EXPIRED	NESTLED	DEENORW ENDOWER	DEEPSTU DEPUTES

DEEQSTU QUESTED	DEFIIMS FIDEISM	DEFMORS DEFORMS	DEGHINN HENDING
DEERRSS DRESSER	DEFIIMW MIDWIFE	SERFDOM	DEGHINR HERDING
REDRESS	DEFIINU UNIFIED	DEFMPRU FRUMPED	DEGHINT NIGHTED
DEERRUV VERDURE	DEFIINX INFIXED	DEFNOOR FORDONE	DEGHINW WHINGED
DEERSSS DRESSES	DEFIKLS FLISKED	DEFNORT FRONTED	DEGHIOT HOGTIED
DEERSST DESERTS	DEFIKRS FRISKED	DEFNORU FOUNDER	DEGHIPT PIGHTED
DESSERT	DEFILLO FOLLIED	REFOUND	DEGHIRT GIRTHED
TRESSED	DEFILLR FRILLED	DEFNORW FROWNED	RIGHTED
DEERSSU DURESSE	DEFILMP FLIMPED	DEFNOST FONDEST	DEGHIST SIGHTED
DEERSTV STERVED	DEFILNR FLINDER	DEFNOSU FONDUES	DEGHITW WIGHTED
VERDETS	DEFILNU UNFILDE	DEFNRSU FUNDERS	DEGHLOO DOGHOLE
DEERSTW STREWED	UNFILED	REFUNDS	DEGHLPU GULPHED
WRESTED	DEFILOO FOLIOED	DEFOOPR PROOFED	DEGHNOT THONGED
DEERSTX DEXTERS	DEFILPP FLIPPED	DEFOOPS SPOOFED	DEGHORR DROGHER
DEERSTY DYESTER	DEFILRT FLIRTED	DEFOORS FORDOES	DEGHORU ROUGHED
DEERSVW SWERVED	TRIFLED	DEFORST DEFROST	DEGHOST GHOSTED
DEERTTU UTTERED	DEFILRU DIREFUL	FROSTED	DEGHOSU SOUGHED
DEERTUX EXTRUDE	DEFILSS FISSLED	DEGGGIL GIGGLED	DEGIILL GILLIED
DEESSTT DETESTS	DEFILST STIFLED	DEGGGIR GRIGGED	DEGIILN EILDING
DEESSTV DEVESTS	DEFILTT FLITTED	DEGGGLO GOGGLED	ELIDING
DEESTTT STETTED	DEFILXY FIXEDLY	DEGGGLU GLUGGED	DEGIINR DINGIER
DEFFFLU FLUFFED	DEFILZZ FIZZLED	GUGGLED	DEGIINS DINGIES
DEFFHIW WHIFFED	DEFIMOR DEIFORM	DEGGGOR GROGGED	DEGIINT DIETING
DEFFHOU HOUFFED	DEFINRS FINDERS	DEGGHIL HIGGLED	EDITING
DEFFHOW HOWFFED	FRIENDS	DEGGHIN HEDGING	IGNITED
DEFFIKS SKIFFED	DEFINRU UNFIRED	DEGGHIW WHIGGED	DEGIIPS GIPSIED
DEFFILP PIFFLED	DEFINST SNIFTED	DEGGHOS SHOGGED	DEGIIRR RIDGIER
DEFFILR RIFFLED	DEFINSU INFUSED	DEGGIJL JIGGLED	RIGIDER
DEFFILS SIFFLED	DEFINSY DENSIFY	DEGGIKN KEDGING	DEGIIRS DIRIGES
DEFFINS SNIFFED	DEFINUX UNFIXED	DEGGILN GELDING	DEGIJLN JINGLED
DEFFIOS OFFSIDE	DEFINUY UNDEIFY	GINGLED	DEGIKLO GODLIKE
DEFFIRS DIFFERS	DEFIOOS FOODIES	NIGGLED	DEGILLR GRILLED
DEFFIST STIFFED	DEFIOQU QUOIFED	DEGGILW WIGGLED	DEGILLU GULLIED
DEFFISU DIFFUSE	DEFIORU FOUDRIE	DEGGINS EDGINGS	DEGILLY GELIDLY
DEFFKOS SKOFFED	DEFIOST FOISTED	SNIGGED	DEGILMN MEDLING
DEFFLMU MUFFLED	DEFIPRY PERFIDY	DEGGINW WEDGING	MELDING
DEFFLPU PLUFFED	DEFIRRT DRIFTER	DEGGIOR DOGGIER	MINGLED
DEFFLRU RUFFLED	DEFIRST FRISTED	DEGGIOS DOGGIES	DEGILNN LENDING
DEFFLSU DUFFELS	DEFIRTT FRITTED	DEGGIPR PRIGGED	DEGILNO GLENOID
DUFFLES	DEFIRTU FRUITED	DEGGIRS DIGGERS	DEGILNP PINGLED
DEFFNOR FORFEND	DEFIRZZ FRIZZED	DEGGIRT TRIGGED	DEGILNS DINGLES
DEFFNOS OFFENDS	DEFISTU FEUDIST	DEGGISW SWIGGED	ELDINGS
DEFFNSU SNUFFED	DEFISTW SWIFTED	DEGGITW TWIGGED	ENGILDS
DEFFORS DOFFERS	DEFKLNU FLUNKED	DEGGJLO JOGGLED	SINGLED
DEFFOSW SOWFFED	DEFLLOU DOLEFUL	DEGGJLU JUGGLED	DEGILNT GLINTED
DEFFRSU DUFFERS	DEFLLUW DEWFULL	DEGGKSU SKUGGED	TINGLED
DEFFSTU DUFFEST	DEFLMPU FLUMPED	DEGGLOO GOOGLED	DEGILNU ELUDING
STUFFED	DEFLNOO ONEFOLD	DEGGLOR DOGGREL	INDULGE
DEFGGIR FRIGGED	DEFLNOP PENFOLD	DEGGLOS SLOGGED	DEGILNV DELVING
DEFGGLO FLOGGED	DEFLNOR FONDLER	DEGGLOT TOGGLED	DEVLING
DEFGGOR FROGGED	FORLEND	DEGGLPU PLUGGED	DEGILNW WELDING
DEFGINN FENDING	DEFLNOS ENFOLDS	DEGGLRU GURGLED	DEGILOR GLORIED
DEFGINR FRINGED	FONDLES	DEGGLSU SLUGGED	GODLIER
DEFGINU FEUDING	DEFLNOT TENFOLD	DEGGMSU SMUGGED	GOLDIER
DEFGINY DEFYING	DEFLNRU DERNFUL	DEGGNOO DOGGONE	DEGILOU OUGLIED
DEFGIOR FIREDOG	DEFLOOR FLOORED	DEGGNOS SNOGGED	DEGILRR GIRDLER
DEFGIRS FRIDGES	DEFLOOT FOOTLED	DEGGNOU GUDGEON	DEGILRS GILDERS
DEFGIRT GRIFTED	DEFLOOZ FOOZLED	DEGGNSU SNUGGED	GIRDLES
DEFGIRU FIGURED	DEFLOPP FLOPPED	DEGGOPR PROGGED	GLIDERS
DEFGIST FIDGETS	DEFLORS FOLDERS	DEGGORS DOGGERS	GRISLED
DEFGITY FIDGETY	DEFLORU FLOURED	DEGGORT TROGGED	LIDGERS
DEFGRTU GRUFTED	FOULDER	DEGGORY DOGGERY	RIDGELS
DEFHIRS REDFISH	DEFLOSU DEFOULS	DEGGOSS DOGGESS	DEGILRU GUILDER
DEFHIST SHIFTED	FLOUSED	DEGGRRU DRUGGER	DEGILRW WERGILD
DEFHLOO ELFHOOD	DEFLOTU FLOUTED	DEGGRSU GRUDGES	DEGILUV DIVULGE
DEFHLSU FLUSHED	DEFLPRU PURFLED	DEGGRTU DRUGGET	DEGIMNN MENDING
DEFHORT FROTHED	DEFLRRU FLURRED	DEGHHOU HOUGHED	DEGIMNS SMIDGEN
DEFHRSU FRUSHED	DEFLRUU DUREFUL	DEGHILN HINDLEG	DEGIMPU GUIMPED
DEFIILN INFIDEL	DEFLUZZ FUZZLED	DEGHILT DELIGHT	DEGIMST MIDGETS
INFIELD	DEFMNUU UNFUMED	LIGHTED	DEGINNN DENNING

DEGINNP	PENDING	DEGLOPR	PLEDGOR
DEGINNR	GRINNED	DEGLOPS	SPLODGE
	RENDING	DEGLORS	LODGERS
DEGINNS	ENDINGS	DEGLORW	GROWLED
	SENDING	DEGLOSS	GLOSSED
DEGINNT	DENTING		GODLESS
	TENDING	DEGLOST	GOLDEST
DEGINNU	ENDUING	DEGLOTU	GLOUTED
DEGINNV	VENDING	DEGLSSU	SLUDGES
DEGINNW	WENDING	DEGLTTU	GLUTTED
DEGINNY	DENYING		GUTTLED
DEGINOP	PIDGEON	DEGLUZZ	GUZZLED
DEGINOR	ERODING	DEGMNOO	GOODMEN
	GROINED	DEGMOOR	GROOMED
	IGNORED	DEGMRSU	SMUDGER
	NEGROID	DEGMSSU	SMUDGES
	REDOING	DEGNNOU	DUNGEON
DEGINOS	DINGOES	DEGNOPR	PRONGED
DEGINOW	WENDIGO	DEGNOPS	SPONGED
	WIDGEON	DEGNORU	GUERDON
DEGINRR	GRINDER		UNDERGO
	REGRIND		UNGORED
DEGINRS	DINGERS	DEGNORW	WRONGED
	ENGIRDS	DEGNOTU	TONGUED
DEGINRU	DUNGIER	DEGNRSU	GERUNDS
DEGINRW	REDWING	DEGNRTU	GRUNTED
	WRINGED		TRUDGEN
DEGINRY	YERDING	DEGNRUU	UNURGED
DEGINSS	DESIGNS	DEGNSSU	SNUDGES
DEGINST	NIDGETS	DEGNUVY	UNGYVED
	STEDING	DEGOORV	GROOVED
	STINGED	DEGOOST	STOOGED
DEGINSU	GUNDIES	DEGOPRU	GROUPED
	SUEDING	DEGORRS	DROGERS
DEGINSW	SWINDGE	DEGORSS	GROSSED
	SWINGED		SODGERS
DEGINSY	DINGEYS	DEGORST	STODGER
	DYEINGS	DEGORSU	DROGUES
DEGINTW	TWINGED		GOURDES
DEGINUX	EXUDING		GROUSED
DEGIOOR	GOODIER	DEGORTU	DROGUET
DEGIOOS	GOODIES		GROUTED
	SOOGIED	DEGOSST	STODGES
DEGIOPR	PODGIER	DEGOSTU	DEGOUTS
DEGIORT	GOITRED	DEGOSTW	GOWDEST
DEGIPPR	GRIPPED	DEGRRTU	TRUDGER
DEGIPRU	PUDGIER	DEGRSTU	TRUDGES
DEGIPSY	GYPSIED	DEGSSTU	DEGUSTS
DEGIQSU	SQUIDGE	DEHHISW	WHISHED
DEGIRRS	GIRDERS	DEHHMPU	HUMPHED
DEGIRRU	DURGIER	DEHHOOS	HOOSHED
DEGIRSS	DIGRESS	DEHHSSU	SHUSHED
DEGIRSU	GUIDERS	DEHIINN	HINNIED
DEGIRTT	GRITTED	DEHIIPS	PIEDISH
DEGISST	DIGESTS	DEHIIRS	DISHIER
	DISGEST	DEHIKRS	SHIRKED
DEGISTU	GIUSTED		SHRIKED
DEGISTW	WIDGETS	DEHIKSW	WHISKED
DEGKLSU	KLUDGES	DEHILLO	HILLOED
DEGLMMO	GLOMMED	DEHILLS	SHILLED
DEGLMOO	GLOOMED	DEHILMS	DISHELM
DEGLNNO	ENDLONG	DEHILNP	DELPHIN
DEGLNOP	PLONGED	DEHILPR	HIRPLED
DEGLNOS	DONGLES	DEHILRS	HIRSLED
	GOLDENS	DEHILRT	THIRLED
DEGLNOU	LOUNGED	DEHILRW	WHIRLED
DEGLNPU	PLUNGED	DEHILSS	SHIELDS
DEGLNSU	GULDENS	DEHILTY	DIETHYL
DEGLNUU	UNGLUED	DEHIMMW	WHIMMED
	UNGULED	DEHIMNU	INHUMED

DEHIMOR	HEIRDOM		THRONED
DEHIMOS	DISHOME	DEHNOSU	UNSHOED
DEHIMOT	ETHMOID	DEHNOSY	HOYDENS
DEHIMRS	DIRHEMS	DEHNOTZ	DOZENTH
DEHIMRU	HUMIDER	DEHNRSU	HURDENS
DEHIMST	SMITHED	DEHNRTU	THUNDER
DEHINNS	SHINNED	DEHNSSU	DUNSHES
DEHINNT	THINNED		SNUSHED
DEHINOP	DIPHONE	DEHNSSY	YSHENDS
	PHONIED	DEHNSTU	SHUNTED
DEHINOR	HORDEIN	DEHNSYY	HYDYNES
DEHINOS	HOIDENS	DEHOOPT	PHOTOED
DEHINPS	ENDSHIP	DEHOOPW	WHOOPED
DEHINRS	HINDERS	DEHOOST	SOOTHED
	SHRINED	DEHOOSW	WOOSHED
DEHINRU	UNHIRED	DEHOOTT	TOOTHED
DEHINUV	UNHIVED	DEHOOTW	WHOOTED
DEHIORT	THEROID	DEHOPPS	SHOPPED
DEHIOST	HOISTED	DEHOPPW	WHOPPED
DEHIOSU	HIDEOUS	DEHORSS	SHODERS
DEHIOSV	DOVEISH	DEHORST	DEHORTS
DEHIOSW	HOWDIES		SHORTED
DEHIOTU	HIDEOUT	DEHORSV	SHROVED
DEHIPPS	SHIPPED	DEHORSW	SHROWED
DEHIPPW	WHIPPED	DEHORTT	TROTHED
DEHIRRS	SHIRRED	DEHORTW	WORTHED
DEHIRRU	DHURRIE	DEHOSTT	SHOTTED
	HURRIED	DEHOSTU	SHOUTED
DEHIRRW	WHIRRED		SOUTHED
DEHIRST	DITHERS	DEHOSTW	SOWTHED
	SHIRTED	DEIIIRS	IRIDISE
DEHIRSU	HURDIES	DEIIIRZ	IRIDIZE
DEHIRSV	DERVISH	DEIIJMM	JIMMIED
	SHRIVED	DEIIKLS	DISLIKE
DEHIRTV	THRIVED	DEIIKNR	DINKIER
DEHIRTW	WRITHED	DEIIKNS	DINKIES
DEHIRTY	DITHERY	DEIIKST	DIKIEST
DEHISSW	SWISHED	DEIILLR	DILLIER
	WHISSED	DEIILLS	DILLIES
DEHISTW	WHISTED	DEIILLW	WILLIED
DEHISVV	SHIVVED	DEIILMP	IMPLIED
DEHIWZZ	WHIZZED	DEIILMT	DELIMIT
DEHLLOO	HOLLOED		LIMITED
DEHLLOU	HULLOED	DEIILNS	INISLED
DEHLMSU	MULSHED	DEIILOS	DOILIES
DEHLOOS	SHOOLED		IDOLISE
DEHLOPP	HOPPLED	DEIILOZ	IDOLIZE
DEHLORS	HOLDERS	DEIILPS	LIPIDES
DEHLORW	WHORLED	DEIILRV	LIVIDER
DEHLOSS	SLOSHED	DEIIMMX	IMMIXED
DEHLOST	SLOTHED	DEIIMNO	DOMINIE
DEHLRRU	HURDLER	DEIIMRT	TIMIDER
DEHLRSU	HURDLES	DEIIMST	MISDIET
DEHLRTU	HURTLED		STIMIED
DEHLSSU	SLUSHED	DEIIMVW	MIDWIVE
DEHLSTU	HUSTLED	DEIINOS	IODINES
DEHMNOO	HOODMEN		IONISED
DEHMORU	HUMORED	DEIINOT	EDITION
DEHMOST	METHODS		TENIOID
DEHMOTU	MOUTHED	DEIINOZ	IONIZED
DEHMPTU	THUMPED	DEIINRR	RINDIER
DEHMRTY	RYTHMED	DEIINRS	INSIDER
DEHNNSU	SHUNNED	DEIINRT	INDITER
DEHNOOR	HONORED		NITRIDE
DEHNOOW	HOEDOWN	DEIINRU	URIDINE
DEHNOPU	UNHOPED	DEIINRV	DIVINER
DEHNORS	DEHORNS	DEIINRW	WINDIER
DEHNORT	NORTHED	DEIINSS	INSIDES
	THONDER	DEIINST	INDITES
	THORNED		TINEIDS

DEIINSV	DIVINES	DEILLOV	LIVELOD
DEIINTV	INVITED	DEILLPR	PRILLED
DEIIORT	DIORITE	DEILLPS	SPILLED
DEIIORV	IVORIED	DEILLQU	QUILLED
DEIIOSS	IODISES	DEILLRR	DRILLER
DEIIOSX	OXIDISE	DEILLRT	TRILLED
DEIIOSZ	IODIZES	DEILLRU	DULLIER
DEIIOXZ	OXIDIZE	DEILLRV	DREVILL
DEIIPPR	DIPPIER	DEILLSS	LIDLESS
DEIIPRS	PIERIDS	DEILLST	STILLED
DEIIPRT	RIPTIDE	DEILLSU	ILLUDES
DEIIRRT	DIRTIER		SULLIED
DEIIRST	DIRTIES	DEILLSW	SWILLED
DEIIRTT	TRITIDE	DEILLTW	TWILLED
DEIIRVV	VIVIDER	DEILMMP	PLIMMED
DEIIRZZ	DIZZIER	DEILMMS	SLIMMED
DEIISTT	DIETIST	DEILMNS	MILDENS
	DITTIES	DEILMNU	LUMINED
	TIDIEST		UNLIMED
DEIISTV	VISITED	DEILMOP	IMPLODE
DEIISVV	DIVVIES	DEILMOS	SMOILED
DEIISZZ	DIZZIES	DEILMOY	MYELOID
DEIIVZZ	VIZZIED	DEILMPP	PIMPLED
DEIJLLO	JOLLIED	DEILMPS	DIMPLES
DEIJNOR	JOINDER		SIMPLED
DEIJNOT	JOINTED	DEILMPW	WIMPLED
DEIJNRU	INJURED	DEILMST	MILDEST
DEIJNSU	DISJUNE		MISTLED
DEIJOST	JOISTED	DEILMSW	MILDEWS
DEIJTTU	JUTTIED	DEILMWY	MILDEWY
DEIKKNS	SKINKED	DEILMXY	MIXEDLY
DEIKLLS	DESKILL	DEILMZZ	MIZZLED
	SKILLED	DEILNNS	DINNLES
DEIKLNP	PLINKED		LINDENS
DEIKLNR	KINDLER	DEILNNU	UNLINED
DEIKLNS	KINDLES	DEILNOO	EIDOLON
DEIKLNT	TINKLED	DEILNOS	INDOLES
DEIKLOR	RODLIKE		SONDELI
DEIKLOS	KELOIDS	DEILNOT	LENTOID
DEIKLRS	SKIRLED	DEILNOU	UNOILED
DEIKLRT	KIRTLED	DEILNPP	NIPPLED
DEIKLTT	KITTLED	DEILNPS	SPELDIN
DEIKMMS	SKIMMED		SPINDLE
DEIKMPS	SKIMPED		SPLINED
DEIKMRS	SMIRKED	DEILNRT	TENDRIL
DEIKNNS	SKINNED		TRINDLE
DEIKNOV	INVOKED	DEILNST	DENTILS
DEIKNPR	PRINKED	DEILNSW	SWINDLE
DEIKNRR	DRINKER		WINDLES
DEIKNRS	KINREDS	DEILNSY	SNIDELY
	REDSKIN	DEILNTU	DILUENT
DEIKNST	DINKEST		UNTILED
	KINDEST	DEILNTW	INDWELT
DEIKNSW	SWINKED		WINTLED
DEIKNSY	KIDNEYS	DEILNUV	UNLIVED
DEIKNSZ	ZENDIKS	DEILOOS	DOOLIES
DEIKNTT	KNITTED	DEILOPS	DESPOIL
DEIKNTW	TWINKED		DIPLOES
DEIKOSY	DISYOKE		DIPOLES
DEIKPPS	SKIPPED		PELOIDS
DEIKQRU	QUIRKED		SOLIPED
DEIKRRS	SKIRRED		SPOILED
DEIKRST	SKIRTED	DEILOPT	PILOTED
DEIKRSU	DUIKERS	DEILORS	SOLDIER
	DUSKIER		SOLIDER
DEIKSTY	DYKIEST	DEILORT	DOILTER
DEILLMU	ILLUMED	DEILOSY	DOYLIES
DEILLNW	INDWELL	DEILOTU	OUTLIED
DEILLOR	DOLLIER	DEILPPR	RIPPLED
DEILLOS	DOLLIES	DEILPPS	SIPPLED

	SLIPPED	DEIMPRT	DIREMPT
DEILPPT	TIPPLED	DEIMPRU	DUMPIER
DEILPPU	UPPILED		UMPIRED
DEILPRT	TRIPLED	DEIMPSU	DUMPIES
DEILPRU	PRELUDI	DEIMPTU	IMPUTED
DEILPSS	DISPELS	DEIMRRS	SMIRRED
	DISPLES	DEIMRSW	MISDREW
DEILPSU	DUPLIES	DEIMRUU	UREDIUM
DEILPTY	TEPIDLY	DEIMSST	DEMISTS
DEILQTU	QUILTED	DEIMSSU	MISUSED
DEILRRU	LURIDER	DEIMSTT	SMITTED
DEILRSS	SLIDERS	DEIMSTU	MUISTED
DEILRSV	DRIVELS		TEDIUMS
DEILRSW	SWIRLED	DEIMSTY	STYMIED
	WILDERS	DEINNNU	NUNDINE
DEILRTU	DILUTER	DEINNOO	ONIONED
DEILRTW	TWIRLED	DEINNOP	PINNOED
DEILRVY	DEVILRY	DEINNOR	ENDIRON
DEILRWY	WEIRDLY	DEINNOS	ONDINES
DEILRWZ	WRIZLED	DEINNOT	INTONED
DEILRZZ	DRIZZLE		NOINTED
DEILSTT	STILTED	DEINNRS	DINNERS
DEILSTU	DILUTES	DEINNRU	DUNNIER
DEILSTW	WILDEST		INURNED
DEILSTY	DISTYLE	DEINNST	DENTINS
DEILSZZ	SIZZLED		INDENTS
DEILTTT	TITTLED		INTENDS
DEILTTU	TITULED	DEINNSU	DUNNIES
DEILTTW	TWILTED		UNDINES
DEIMMMU	MUMMIED	DEINNSW	ENWINDS
DEIMMOT	TOMMIED	DEINNTU	DUNNITE
DEIMMPR	PRIMMED	DEINNTW	TWINNED
DEIMMRS	DIMMERS	DEINOPR	POINDER
DEIMMRT	TRIMMED		PROINED
DEIMMRU	DUMMIER	DEINOPS	DISPONE
	IMMURED		SPINODE
DEIMMST	DIMMEST	DEINOPT	POINTED
DEIMMSU	DUMMIES	DEINOQU	QUOINED
	MEDIUMS	DEINORR	DRONIER
DEIMNNU	MINUEND	DEINORS	DONSIER
DEIMNOP	IMPONED		INDORSE
DEIMNOS	MISDONE		ROSINED
DEIMNPS	IMPENDS		SORDINE
DEIMNRS	MINDERS	DEINORU	DOURINE
	REMINDS		OUNDIER
DEIMNRU	UNRIMED	DEINORW	DOWNIER
DEIMNSS	DIMNESS		WINDORE
	MISSEND	DEINOSS	ONSIDES
DEIMNST	MINDSET	DEINOST	DITONES
DEIMNSW	MISWEND		STONIED
DEIMNTU	MINUTED	DEINPPS	SNIPPED
	MUNITED	DEINPRS	PINDERS
	MUTINED	DEINPRT	PRINTED
DEIMNUX	UNMIXED	DEINPST	STIPEND
DEIMOOR	DOOMIER	DEINPSU	UNIPEDS
	MOIDORE		UNSPIDE
	MOODIER		UNSPIED
DEIMOOS	MOODIES	DEINPUW	UNWIPED
DEIMOPS	IMPOSED	DEINRST	TINDERS
DEIMORS	MISDOER	DEINRSU	INSURED
	MOIDERS	DEINRSW	REWINDS
DEIMORU	ERODIUM		WINDERS
DEIMOSS	MISDOES	DEINRTT	TRIDENT
DEIMOST	DOMIEST	DEINRTU	INTRUDE
	MODISTE		TURDINE
	MOISTED		UNTIRED
DEIMOTT	OMITTED		UNTRIDE
DEIMOTV	MOTIVED		UNTRIED
	VOMITED	DEINRTX	DEXTRIN
DEIMPPR	PRIMPED	DEINRTY	TINDERY

DEINRUW	UNWIRED
DEINSST	DISNEST
	DISSENT
	SNIDEST
DEINSSV	VENDISS
DEINSSW	WINDSES
DEINSTT	DENTIST
	DISTENT
	STINTED
DEINSTU	DISTUNE
	DUNITES
DEINSTY	DENSITY
	DESTINY
DEINSUZ	UNSIZED
DEINUVW	UNWIVED
DEIOORS	OROIDES
DEIOORW	WOODIER
DEIOOST	OSTEOID
DEIOOSW	WOODIES
DEIOOVV	VOIVODE
DEIOOWW	WOIWODE
DEIOPPP	POPPIED
DEIOPPS	DOPPIES
DEIOPRS	PERIODS
DEIOPRT	DIOPTER
	DIOPTRE
	PERIDOT
	PROTEID
DEIOPRV	PROVIDE
DEIOPSS	DISPOSE
DEIOPST	DEPOSIT
	DOPIEST
	PODITES
	POSITED
	SOPITED
	TOPSIDE
DEIOPSV	VESPOID
DEIOPTT	TIPTOED
DEIOPTV	PIVOTED
DEIOQTU	QUOITED
DEIORRT	DORTIER
DEIORRW	ROWDIER
	WORDIER
	WORRIED
DEIORSS	DORISES
	DOSSIER
DEIORST	EDITORS
	ROISTED
	ROSITED
	SORTIED
	STEROID
	STORIED
	TRIODES
DEIORSV	DEVISOR
	DEVOIRS
	VISORED
	VOIDERS
DEIORSW	DOWRIES
	ROWDIES
	WEIRDOS
DEIORSZ	DORIZES
DEIORTT	DOTTIER
DEIORTU	ETOURDI
	IODURET
	OUTRIDE
DEIORTZ	ROZITED
DEIORVZ	VIZORED
DEIORWW	WIDOWER
DEIOSTT	DOTIEST
	STOITED
DEIOSTU	OUTSIDE
	TEDIOUS
DEIOSTV	DOVIEST
DEIOSTW	DOWIEST
DEIOSTX	EXODIST
DEIOSTZ	DOZIEST
DEIOSUV	DEVIOUS
DEIOTUV	OUTVIED
DEIPPPU	PUPPIED
DEIPPQU	QUIPPED
DEIPPRS	DIPPERS
DEIPPRT	TRIPPED
DEIPPSU	DUPPIES
DEIPRSS	SPIDERS
DEIPRST	SPIRTED
	STRIPED
DEIPRSU	PUDSIER
	SIRUPED
DEIPRSY	SPIDERY
DEIPSSU	UPSIDES
DEIPSTT	SPITTED
DEIPSTU	DISPUTE
DEIPSXY	PYXIDES
DEIPTTU	PUTTIED
	TITUPED
DEIQRSU	SQUIRED
DEIQRTU	QUIRTED
DEIQTTU	QUITTED
DEIQUZZ	QUIZZED
DEIRRST	STIRRED
DEIRRSU	DRUSIER
	DURRIES
DEIRRSV	DRIVERS
DEIRRUX	DRUXIER
DEIRSST	DISSERT
	STRIDES
DEIRSSU	DISEURS
	SUDSIER
DEIRSTU	DUSTIER
	REDUITS
	STUDIER
DEIRSTV	DIVERTS
	STRIVED
	VERDITS
DEISSST	DESISTS
DEISSSU	DISUSES
DEISSTU	STUDIES
	TISSUED
DEISSTV	DIVESTS
DEISTTW	DEWITTS
	TWISTED
DEITTTW	TWITTED
DEJLOST	JOSTLED
DEJLSTU	JUSTLED
DEJOSTU	JOUSTED
DEKKLSU	SKULKED
DEKKNSU	SKUNKED
DEKLLNO	KNOLLED
DEKLNOP	PLONKED
DEKLNPU	PLUNKED
DEKLNRU	KNURLED
	RUNKLED
DEKLRSU	SKUDLER
DEKNNRU	DRUNKEN
DEKNOOS	SNOOKED
DEKNOQU	QUONKED
DEKNOSW	SNOWKED
DEKNOSY	DONKEYS
DEKNOTT	KNOTTED
DEKNOTU	KNOUTED
DEKNOUY	UNYOKED
DEKNPSU	SPUNKED
DEKNRRU	DRUNKER
DEKNRTU	TRUNKED
DEKNSSU	DUSKENS
DEKOOPS	SPOOKED
DEKOOST	DOOKETS
	STOOKED
DEKOOTW	KOTOWED
DEKOPST	DESKTOP
DEKORST	STROKED
DEKOSSU	KUDOSES
DEKRSUY	DUYKERS
DEKSSTU	DUSKEST
DELLOOW	WOOLLED
DELLOPR	PROLLED
	REDPOLL
DELLORR	DROLLER
DELLORT	TROLLED
DELLOSU	DUELLOS
DELLOVW	LOWVELD
DELLSTU	DULLEST
DELMMSU	SLUMMED
DELMNOS	DOLMENS
DELMOOS	SLOOMED
DELMOOW	ELMWOOD
DELMORS	SMOLDER
DELMORU	MOULDER
	REMOULD
DELMOSU	MODULES
	MOUSLED
DELMOSY	SMOYLED
DELMOTT	MOTTLED
DELMOTU	MOULTED
DELMOUV	VOLUMED
DELMPPU	PLUMPED
DELMPRU	RUMPLED
DELMPSU	DUMPLES
	SLUMPED
DELMUZZ	MUZZLED
DELNOOS	NOODLES
	SNOOLED
DELNORS	RONDELS
DELNORT	ENTROLD
DELNORU	LOUNDER
	ROUNDEL
	ROUNDLE
DELNOSS	OLDNESS
DELNOSU	LOUDENS
	NODULES
	NOUSLED
DELNOSW	DOWLNES
DELNOSZ	DONZELS
DELNOTY	NOTEDLY
DELNOUV	UNLOVED
DELNOWY	DOWLNEY
DELNPRU	PLUNDER
DELNRSU	LURDENS
	NURSLED
	RUNDLES
DELNRTU	RUNDLET
	TRUNDLE
DELNRUU	UNRULED
DELNSSU	DULNESS
DELNUWY	UNWELDY
DELNUZZ	NUZZLED
DELOOPP	PLEOPOD
DELOOPS	POODLES
	SPOOLED
DELOORT	ROOTLED
DELOORW	WOOLDER
DELOOST	STOOLED
DELOOTT	TOOTLED
DELOPPP	PLOPPED
	POPPLED
DELOPPR	DROPPLE
DELOPPS	SLOPPED
DELOPPT	TOPPLED
DELOPRS	POLDERS
DELOPRT	DROPLET
DELOPRU	POULDER
	POULDRE
	PROULED
DELOPRW	PROWLED
DELOPSU	SOUPLED
DELOPSY	DEPLOYS
	PODLEYS
DELOPTT	PLOTTED
DELORRY	ORDERLY
DELORSS	DORSELS
	RODLESS
	SOLDERS
DELORST	DROLEST
	OLDSTER
	STRODLE
DELORSW	WELDORS
DELORSY	YODLERS
DELORTT	DOTTLER
	DOTTREL
DELORTU	TROULED
DELORUV	LOUVRED
DELOSSS	DOSSELS
DELOSSU	DULOSES
DELOSTT	DOTTLES
	SLOTTED
DELOSTU	LOUDEST
	TOUSLED
DELOSYY	DOYLEYS
DELOSZZ	SOZZLED
DELOTUV	VOLUTED
DELOTUZ	TOUZLED
DELPPRU	PURPLED
DELPPSU	SUPPLED
DELPRSU	DRUPELS
	SLURPED
DELPSSU	PLUSSED
DELPSTU	DUPLETS
DELPSUY	SPULYED
DELPUZZ	PUZZLED
DELRRSU	SLURRED
DELRSTU	LUSTRED
	RUSTLED
	STRUDEL
DELRTTU	TURTLED
DELSSTU	TUSSLED
DELSTTU	SUTTLED
DELUWZZ	WUZZLED
DEMMRRU	DRUMMER
DEMMSTU	STUMMED
DEMNOOR	MORENDO
DEMNOOW	WOODMEN
DEMNORS	MODERNS
	RODSMEN
DEMNORT	MORDENT
DEMNORU	MOURNED
DEMNORY	DEMONRY
DEMNOST	ENDMOST
DEMNOTU	DEMOUNT
	MOUNTED
DEMNOUV	UNMOVED

DEMNSTU	DUSTMEN		SOUNDER		DROWSES	DFLOTWY	TWYFOLD
DEMOOPP	POPEDOM		UNDOERS	DEORSTT	DETORTS	DFNNOUU	UNFOUND
DEMOOPR	PREDOOM	DENORSV	VENDORS	DEORSTU	DETOURS	DFNORUY	FOUNDRY
DEMOOPS	SPOOMED	DENORSW	DOWNERS		DOUREST	DGGGIIN	DIGGING
DEMOORS	DROOMES		WONDERS		DOUTERS	DGGGINO	DOGGING
	SMOORED	DENORUW	REWOUND		OUTREDS	DGGHIOS	DOGGISH
DEMOORT	MOTORED		WOUNDER		ROUSTED	DGGIILN	GILDING
DEMOORV	VROOMED	DENOSTT	SNOTTED	DEORSTW	STROWED		GLIDING
DEMOOSS	OSMOSED	DENOSTU	DEUTONS		WORSTED	DGGIINN	DINGING
DEMOOST	SMOOTED		SNOUTED	DEORSTY	DESTROY	DGGIINR	GIRDING
DEMOOTT	MOTTOED	DENOSUW	SWOUNED		ROYSTED		GRIDING
DEMOOTU	OUTMODE	DENPRSU	SPURNED		STROYED		RIDGING
DEMOPST	STOMPED	DENPRTU	PRUDENT	DEORSUV	DEVOURS	DGGIINU	GUIDING
DEMORRS	DORMERS		PRUNTED	DEORTTT	TROTTED	DGGIJNU	JUDGING
DEMORRU	RUMORED		UPTREND	DEORTTU	TUTORED	DGGILNO	GODLING
DEMORST	STORMED	DENPSSU	SUSPEND	DEORTUU	OUTDURE		LODGING
DEMOSSU	SMOUSED		UPSENDS	DEOSSSW	SOWSSED	DGGINNO	DONGING
DEMOSTT	DOMETTS	DENRSSU	SUNDERS	DEOSSTW	DOWSETS	DGGINNU	DUNGING
DEMOSTU	MOUSTED		UNDRESS	DEOSSYY	ODYSSEY		NUDGING
	SMOUTED	DENRSSY	DRYNESS	DEOSTTT	STOTTED	DGGINRY	GRYDING
DEMOSTY	MODESTY	DENRSTU	RETUNDS	DEOSTTU	DUETTOS	DGGNOSU	DUGONGS
DEMPRSU	DUMPERS		UNDREST		TESTUDO	DGHHOOO	HOGHOOD
DEMPRTU	TRUMPED	DENRSUU	UNSURED	DEOSTTW	SWOTTED	DGHIILN	HIDLING
DEMPSTU	STUMPED	DENSSTY	SYNDETS	DEOSTUU	DUTEOUS		HILDING
DEMRRSU	MURDERS	DENSTTU	STUDENT	DEOSTUX	TUXEDOS	DGHIINS	DISHING
	SMURRED		STUNTED	DEPRRSU	SPURRED		HIDINGS
DEMSTTU	SMUTTED	DENTUVY	DUVETYN	DEPRRUY	PRUDERY		SHINDIG
DENNORT	DONNERT	DEOOPPS	OPPOSED	DEPRSTU	SPURTED	DGHILNO	HOLDING
	TENDRON	DEOOPRS	SPOORED	DEPRSUU	PURSUED	DGHILNY	HYLDING
DENNORU	ENROUND	DEOOPRT	TORPEDO		USURPED	DGHILOS	GOLDISH
DENNOST	STONNED		TROOPED	DEPRSUY	SYRUPED	DGHILPY	DIGLYPH
	TENDONS	DEOOPST	STOOPED	DERRSTU	RUSTRED	DGHINOO	HOODING
DENNOTU	UNNOTED	DEOOPSW	SWOOPED	DERSSSU	SUDSERS	DGHINOR	HORDING
	UNTONED	DEOOPSX	EXOPODS	DERSSTU	DUSTERS	DGHINSU	DUSHING
DENNOUW	ENWOUND	DEOORST	ROOSTED		TRUSSED	DGHINTU	UNDIGHT
	UNOWNED	DEOORTU	OUTRODE	DERSTTU	STURTED	DGHIOOS	GOODISH
DENNOUZ	UNZONED	DEOORTW	WROOTED		TRUSTED	DGHIOPS	DOGSHIP
DENNRSU	UNDERNS	DEOOSTU	OUTDOES	DERSTTY	TRYSTED		GODSHIP
DENNSTU	DUNNEST	DEOPPPR	PROPPED	DERSTUU	SUTURED	DGHOOPS	HOPDOGS
	STUNNED	DEOPPQU	QUOPPED	DFFGINO	DOFFING	DGHORTU	DROUGHT
DENNTUU	UNTUNED	DEOPPRR	DROPPER	DFFGINU	DUFFING	DGHOTUY	DOUGHTY
DENOOPS	SNOOPED	DEOPPRS	DOPPERS	DFFIIMR	MIDRIFF	DGIIINV	DIVIING
	SPOONED	DEOPPST	STOPPED	DFFIIRT	TRIFFID	DGIIKLN	KIDLING
DENOOST	SNOOTED	DEOPPSW	SWOPPED	DFFIMOR	DIFFORM	DGIIKNN	DINKING
	STOODEN	DEOPRRU	PROUDER	DFFLOOU	FOODFUL		KINDING
DENOOSW	SWOONED	DEOPRST	DEPORTS	DFGGIIN	FIDGING	DGIIKNR	DIRKING
DENOOSZ	SNOOZED		REDTOPS	DFGGINU	FUDGING	DGIIKNS	DISKING
DENOOTU	DUOTONE		SPORTED	DFGHIOS	DOGFISH	DGIILLN	DILLING
	OUTDONE	DEOPRSU	POUDERS	DFGIINN	FINDING	DGIILNO	LOIDING
DENOOUW	UNWOOED		POUDRES	DFGIINY	DIGNIFY	DGIILNR	DIRLING
DENOPPR	PROPEND	DEOPRSW	POWDERS	DFGILNO	FOLDING	DGIILNS	SIDLING
DENOPPU	UNPOPED	DEOPRTU	TROUPED	DFGINNO	FONDING		SLIDING
DENOPRS	PONDERS	DEOPRWY	POWDERY	DFGINNU	FUNDING	DGIILNW	WILDING
	RESPOND	DEOPSST	DESPOTS	DFGINOR	FORDING	DGIILRS	RIDGILS
DENOPRT	PORTEND	DEOPSSU	SPOUSED	DFGINOU	FUNGOID	DGIILRY	RIGIDLY
	PROTEND	DEOPSTT	SPOTTED	DFGMOOY	FOGYDOM	DGIIMMN	DIMMING
DENOPRU	POUNDER	DEOPSTU	SPOUTED	DFHILSU	DISHFUL	DGIIMNN	MINDING
	UNROPED	DEOPTTY	TYPTOED	DFILMMO	FILMDOM	DGIIMNS	SMIDGIN
DENOPRV	PROVEND	DEOQRTU	TORQUED	DFILMNU	MINDFUL	DGIIMOS	SIGMOID
DENOPRY	PROYNED	DEORRSS	DORSERS	DFILNOP	PINFOLD	DGIINNN	DINNING
DENOPSU	UNPOSED	DEORRST	DORTERS	DFILNOS	INFOLDS	DGIINNR	RINDING
DENOPTY	POYNTED		RODSTER	DFILOSX	SIXFOLD	DGIINNS	NIDINGS
DENOPUX	EXPOUND	DEORRSU	ORDURES	DFILOTW	TWIFOLD		SINDING
DENORRU	RONDURE	DEORRSV	DROVERS	DFILTUU	DUTIFUL	DGIINNT	DINTING
	ROUNDER	DEORRSW	REWORDS	DFIMNUY	MUNDIFY		TINDING
	UNORDER		SWORDER	DFIMORS	DISFORM	DGIINNU	INDUING
DENORRW	DROWNER	DEORSSS	DOSSERS	DFLMOOU	DOOMFUL	DGIINNW	DWINING
DENORST	RODENTS		DROSSES	DFLNOSU	UNFOLDS		WINDING
	SNORTED	DEORSSU	DOUSERS	DFLOOTW	TWOFOLD	DGIINOS	INDIGOS
DENORSU	RESOUND	DEORSSW	DOWSERS	DFLOPRY	DROPFLY	DGIINOV	VOIDING

DGIINOW WINDIGO	DGIOPRY PRODIGY	DHORXYY HYDROXY	DILSTUY DUSTILY
DGIINPP DIPPING	DGIOSTW GODWITS	DIIIMRU IRIDIUM	DIMMOST MIDMOST
DGIINPR PRIDING	DGIQSUY SQUIDGY	DIIIMSV DIVISIM	DIMNNOO MIDNOON
DGIINPS PIDGINS	DGISSTU DISGUST	DIIINPS INSIPID	DIMNNOS DONNISM
DGIINPU PINGUID	DGLNOUY UNGODLY	DIIJNOS DISJOIN	DIMNNOT DINMONT
DGIINRS RIDINGS	DGLOOOW LOGWOOD	DIIKLNS DISLINK	DIMNOOS DOMINOS
DGIINRT DIRTING	DGLOPSY SPLODGY	DIIKNOT DOITKIN	DIMNOPU IMPOUND
DGIINRV DRIVING	DGLOSYY DYSLOGY	DIILLST DISTILL	DIMNSSU NUDISMS
DGIINRY YIRDING	DGMOPRU GUMDROP	DIILMNS DISLIMN	DIMOPSU SPODIUM
DGIINSS SIDINGS	DGMORUU GURUDOM	DIILMOO MODIOLI	DIMORSW MISWORD
DGIINST TIDINGS	DGNOOOR GODROON	DIILMOS IDOLISM	DIMOSST MODISTS
DGIINSV DIVINGS	DGNOORS DRONGOS	DIILMTY TIMIDLY	DIMOSSU SODIUMS
DGIINTT DITTING	DGNOOSS GODSONS	DIILNWY WINDILY	DIMOSSW WISDOMS
DGIINTY DIGNITY	DGNOOSW GODOWNS	DIILOPS LIPOIDS	DIMRTUU TRIDUUM
TIDYING	DGNOOTW DOGTOWN	DIILOST IDOLIST	DIMRUUV DUUMVIR
DGIIORT TIGROID	DGNORSU GROUNDS	DIILQSU LIQUIDS	DINNOOR RONDINO
DGIJOSU JUDOGIS	DGOORTT DOGTROT	DIILRSU SILURID	DINNOOT TONDINO
DGIKMNO KINGDOM	DGOSTUU DUGOUTS	DIILRTY DIRTILY	DINNOSS SINDONS
DGIKNNU DUNKING	DHIILNS HIDLINS	DIILSST DISTILS	DINNOUW INWOUND
DGIKNNY KYNDING	DHIILOT LITHOID	DIILVVY VIVIDLY	DINNSUW UNWINDS
DGIKNOO DOOKING	DHIILSW WILDISH	DIILYZZ DIZZILY	DINOORS INDOORS
DGIKNOS DOGSKIN	DHIIMMS DIMMISH	DIIMNOR MIDIRON	SORDINO
DGIKNSU DUSKING	DHIIMNO HOMINID	DIIMNSU INDIUMS	DINOORT TORDION
DGILLNO DOLLING	DHIIMPS MIDSHIP	DIIMORS DIORISM	DINOOST ISODONT
DGILLNU DULLING	DHIINRU HIRUDIN	DIIMOSS IODISMS	DINOPSU DUPIONS
DGILLOY GODLILY	DHIIOPX XIPHOID	DIIMSSS DISMISS	UNIPODS
DGILMNO MOLDING	DHIIORZ RHIZOID	DIIMSTW DIMWITS	DINORSU DURIONS
DGILNOR GIRLOND	DHIIOST HISTOID	DIIMSUV VIDIMUS	DINORTU TURDION
LORDING	DHIKSSU DUSKISH	DIINNOT TONDINI	DINORWW WINDROW
DGILNOY YODLING	DHILLOS DOLLISH	DIINNSW INWINDS	DINOSSW DISOWNS
DGILNSU UNGILDS	DHILLSU DULLISH	DIINORS SORDINI	DINOSTW SITDOWN
DGILNYY DYINGLY	DHILMUY HUMIDLY	DIINOSX DIOXINS	DINOSWW WINDOWS
DGILOST DIGLOTS	DHILNOP DOLPHIN	DIIOPRS SPIROID	DINOTUW OUTWIND
DGILRUY GUILDRY	DHILOST DOLTISH	DIIORSV DIVISOR	DINPSTU PUNDITS
DGIMNOO DOOMING	DHILOSU LOUDISH	VIROIDS	DINPSUW UPWINDS
DGIMNPU DUMPING	DHILPSU LUDSHIP	DIITUVY VIDUITY	DINRSSU SUNDRIS
DGIMOPY PYGMOID	DHILPSY SYLPHID	DIJOSTU JUDOIST	DINSSTU NUDISTS
DGINNNO DONNING	DHILRTY THIRDLY	DIKLNOR LORDKIN	DIOOPSS ISOPODS
DGINNNU DUNNING	DHIMOPR DIMORPH	DIKLSUY DUSKILY	DIOORST DISROOT
DGINNOP PONDING	DHIMORU HUMIDOR	DIKNORV DVORNIK	TOROIDS
DGINNOR DRONING	RHODIUM	DIKOORT DROOKIT	DIOORTT RIDOTTO
DGINNOS DONINGS	DHIMPSU DUMPISH	DIKOOSS SKIDOOS	DIOOSTX TOXOIDS
ONDINGS	DHINNOS DONNISH	DIKORTU DROUKIT	DIOPRST DISPORT
DGINNOU UNDOING	DHINNSU DUNNISH	DILLOSY SOLIDLY	TORPIDS
DGINNOW DOWNING	DHINOPS DONSHIP	DILLRUY LURIDLY	TRIPODS
DGINNSY SYNDING	DHINOPY HYPNOID	DILMNRU DRUMLIN	DIOPRTY TRIPODY
DGINNTU DUNTING	DHINORS DISHORN	DILMOOY MOODILY	DIOPSST DISPOST
TUNDING	DRONISH	DILMORS MILORDS	DIORRST STRIDOR
DGINNUY UNDYING	DHIOOST DHOOTIS	DILMOST MISTOLD	DIORSTT DISTORT
DGINOOW WOODING	DHIOPTY TYPHOID	DILMOSU SOLIDUM	DIOSSTU STUDIOS
DGINOPP DOPPING	DHIORSW WORDISH	DILMOSY ODYLISM	DIOSUUV VIDUOUS
DGINOPS DOPINGS	DHIORTY THYROID	DILMTUY TUMIDLY	DIPRSTU DISRUPT
PONGIDS	DHIPRSU PRUDISH	DILNNSU DUNLINS	DIPSSTU STUPIDS
DGINORR DORRING	DHIPRSY SYRPHID	DILNOOS OODLINS	DIRSTUY SURDITY
DGINORS RODINGS	DHKORSY DROSHKY	DILNOPS DIPLONS	DJNNOOS DONJONS
DGINORT DORTING	DHLMOOU HOODLUM	DILNOPT DIPLONT	DKNNRUU UNDRUNK
DGINORW WORDING	DHLOPSU UPHOLDS	DILNOQU QUODLIN	DKNOOPS PONDOKS
DGINOSS DOSSING	DHMMRUU HUMDRUM	DILNORT INTROLD	DKOOOOS KOODOOS
DGINOST DOTINGS	DHMNOYY HYMNODY	DILNOSU UNSOLID	DKOOOSZ ODZOOKS
DGINOSU DOUSING	DHNNOOU NUNHOOD	DILNPSU LISPUND	DLLOOPS DOLLOPS
GUIDONS	DHNOOSU UNHOODS	DILNPSY SPINDLY	DLLORWY WORLDLY
DGINOSW DISGOWN	DHOOOOS HOODOOS	DILNSTU INDULTS	DLMNOOY MYLODON
DOWSING	DHOOPRU UPHOORD	DILORTU DILUTOR	DLMNOUU UNMOULD
DGINOSZ DOZINGS	DHOORSU RHODOUS	DILORWY ROWDILY	DLMOSUU MODULUS
DGINOTT DOTTING	DHOPRSU PUSHROD	WORDILY	DLNOPRU PULDRON
DGINOTU DOUTING	DHORSSU SHROUDS	DILOSSS DOSSILS	DLNOPSY SPONDYL
DGINPPU DUPPING	DHORSTU DROUTHS	DILOSSU DULOSIS	DLNORSU UNLORDS
DGINRSU UNGIRDS	DHORSUY HYDROUS	SOLIDUS	DLNORUY ROUNDLY
DGINRSY DRYINGS	SHROUDY	DILOSTY STYLOID	DLNOSUY SOUNDLY
DGINSTU DUSTING	DHORTUY DROUTHY	DILRYZZ DRIZZLY	DLOOPPY POLYPOD

DLOOPSS	PODSOLS	EEEGLNT	GENTEEL	EEEKLNR	KNEELER	EEENRSZ	SNEEZER

```
DLOOPSS  PODSOLS     EEEGLNT  GENTEEL     EEEKLNR  KNEELER     EEENRSZ  SNEEZER
DLOOPSZ  PODZOLS     EEEGMRR  REMERGE     EEEKLNS  SLEEKEN     EEENRTV  EVENTER
DLOOPTY  TYLOPOD     EEEGMRS  EMERGES     EEEKLPW  EKPWELE     EEENRTX  EXTERNE
DLOOPUY  DUOPOLY     EEEGNPR  EPERGNE     EEEKLRS  KEELERS     EEENRUV  REVENUE
DLOOPWY  PLYWOOD     EEEGNPS  PEENGES              SLEEKER              UNREEVE
DLOORSU  DOLOURS     EEEGNRR  GREENER     EEEKMNS  MEEKENS     EEENSSZ  SNEEZES
DLOOSTU  OUTSOLD              RENEGER     EEEKMST  MEEKEST     EEENSTV  EVENEST
DLOOTTU  OUTTOLD     EEEGNRS  RENEGES     EEEKNPT  KEEPNET     EEENSTW  SWEETEN
DLOPRUY  PROUDLY     EEEGNRU  RENEGUE     EEEKNRS  KEENERS     EEENSTX  EXTENSE
DLOSTUW  WOULDST     EEEGNRV  REVENGE              SKREENE     EEENSVW  VENEWES
DMNOORS  DROMONS     EEEGNSS  GENESES     EEEKNST  KEENEST     EEENSWY  SWEENEY
DMNOOTW  TOWMOND     EEEGNTT  GENETTE     EEEKPRS  KEEPERS     EEEOPPS  EPOPEES
DMNOSSU  OSMUNDS     EEEGRRT  REGREET     EEEKRSS  KREESES     EEEORSV  OVERSEE
DMORTUW  MUDWORT     EEEGRSS  GREESES              SEEKERS     EEEORSY  EYESORE
DNNOOST  DONNOTS     EEEGRST  GREETES     EEEKRST  SKEETER     EEEORVY  OVEREYE
DNNORUU  UNROUND     EEEGRSZ  GEEZERS     EEELMNR  REELMEN     EEEPPRS  PEEPERS
DNNORUW  RUNDOWN     EEEGRUX  EXERGUE     EEELMNT  ELEMENT     EEEPRSS  PEERESS
DNNOSUU  UNSOUND     EEEHILW  WHEELIE     EEELMPX  EXEMPLE     EEEPRST  ESTREPE
DNNOSUW  SUNDOWN     EEEHISZ  HEEZIES     EEELMSX  LEXEMES              STEEPER
DNNOUUW  UNWOUND     EEEHLNW  ENWHEEL     EEELNST  STELENE     EEEPRSV  PEEVERS
DNNRTUU  TURNDUN     EEEHLPW  WHEEPLE     EEELNSV  ELEVENS              PREEVES
DNNSTUU  TUNDUNS     EEEHLRS  HEELERS     EEELPRS  PEELERS     EEEPRSW  SWEEPER
DNOORTU  OROTUND              REHEELS              SLEEPER              WEEPERS
DNOPUUW  UPWOUND     EEEHLRW  WHEELER              SPEELER     EEEPRSZ  SPREEZE
DNORSST  STRONDS     EEEHLST  LETHEES     EEELPRT  REPLETE     EEEQRRU  QUEERER
DNORSTU  ROTUNDS     EEEHLWZ  WHEEZLE     EEELPST  STEEPLE              REQUERE
DNOSSTU  STOUNDS     EEEHNST  ETHENES     EEELRRS  REELERS     EEEQSUZ  SQUEEZE
DNOSSTW  STOWNDS     EEEHNSX  HEXENES     EEELRSV  SLEEVER     EEERRRV  REVERER
DNOSSUW  SWOUNDS     EEEHPRS  PHEERES     EEELRTV  LEVERET     EEERRST  RETREES
DNOSSWW  SWOWNDS     EEEHPSS  PHEESES     EEELSSS  LESSEES              STEERER
DOOOOSV  VOODOOS     EEEHPSZ  PHEEZES     EEELSST  TELESES     EEERRSV  RESERVE
DOOORSU  ODOROUS     EEEHRRS  SHEERER     EEELSSV  SLEEVES              REVERES
DOOORTU  OUTDOOR     EEEHRST  SEETHER     EEELSSY  EYELESS              REVERSE
DOOPRSU  UROPODS     EEEHSST  SEETHES     EEELSTX  TELEXES              SEVERER
DOOPRSY  PROSODY     EEEHSTT  ESTHETE     EEELSTY  EYELETS     EEERSSS  SEERESS
DOOPSTU  UPSTOOD              TEETHES     EEELTTX  TELETEX     EEERSTT  TEETERS
DOORRSS  SORDORS     EEEHSWZ  WHEEZES     EEEMMSS  MESEEMS     EEERSTV  STEEVER
DOORRTU  DORTOUR     EEEIJLS  JEELIES              SEMEMES     EEERSTW  SWEETER
DOOSUUV  VOUDOUS     EEEIKLS  KEELIES     EEEMNRS  MENEERS     EEERSUV  REVEUSE
DORSSTU  STROUDS     EEEIKRR  REEKIER     EEEMNSS  NEMESES     EEERSUW  SERUEWE
DORSUVY  DYVOURS     EEEILRR  LEERIER     EEEMORT  EROTEME     EEERSVW  SERVEWE
DORUVYY  DYVOURY     EEEILRS  SEELIER     EEEMRSS  SEEMERS              WEEVERS
EEEEFRR  REFEREE     EEEILRV  RELIEVE     EEEMRST  TEEMERS     EEERTTW  TWEETER
EEEEGTX  EXEGETE     EEEILST  EELIEST     EEEMRTX  EXTREME     EEESSTT  SETTEES
EEEEHST  TEEHEES     EEEIMNS  ENEMIES     EEEMSST  ESTEEMS              TESTEES
EEEENTT  ENTETEE     EEEIMNT  EMETINE              MESTEES     EEESSTV  STEEVES
EEEEPST  TEEPEES     EEEIMPR  PREEMIE     EEEMSTT  MEETEST     EEESTWZ  TWEEZES
EEEEPSW  PEEWEES     EEEIMRS  EMERIES     EEEMSTU  EMEUTES     EEFFFNO  ENFEOFF
EEEFFFO  FEOFFEE     EEEIMRT  EREMITE     EEENNPT  PENTENE     EEFFFOR  FEOFFER
EEEFFOR  OFFEREE     EEEINRT  TEENIER     EEENNRT  ETRENNE     EEFFGLU  EFFULGE
EEEFFRS  EFFERES     EEEINRW  WEENIER     EEENNTT  ENTENTE     EEFFINT  FIFTEEN
EEEFGRU  REFUGEE     EEEIPRR  PEERIER     EEENPRT  TERPENE     EEFFIRS  EFFEIRS
EEEFHRS  SHEREEF     EEEIPRS  PEERIES     EEENPRV  PREVENE     EEFFKLS  KEFFELS
EEEFIRS  FEERIES              SEEPIER     EEENPSS  PENSEES     EEFFNOS  OFFENSE
EEEFLRR  FLEERER     EEEIPRW  WEEPIER     EEENPST  ENSTEEP     EEFFORR  OFFERER
EEEFLRS  FEELERS     EEEIPSU  EPUISEE              STEEPEN     EEFFOST  TOFFEES
EEEFLRT  FLEETER     EEEIPSW  WEEPIES     EEENPSW  ENSWEEP     EEFFSSU  EFFUSES
EEEFMNR  FREEMEN     EEEIRRT  RETIREE     EEENPSX  EXPENSE     EEFFSTU  SUFFETE
EEEFNRS  ENFREES     EEEIRRV  REVERIE     EEENRRS  SERENER     EEFGILN  FEELING
EEEFORS  FORESEE     EEEIRST  EERIEST              SNEERER              FLEEING
EEEFRRS  REEFERS     EEEIRSV  VEERIES     EEENRRT  ENTERER     EEFGINR  FEERING
EEEFRRZ  FREEZER     EEEIRSZ  RESEIZE              TERREEN              FREEING
EEEFRSZ  FREEZES     EEEISTW  SWEETIE              TERRENE              REEFING
EEEGHNW  WHEENGE     EEEJNPY  JEEPNEY     EEENRRV  VENERER     EEFGINS  FEESING
EEEGILS  ELEGIES     EEEJPRS  JEEPERS     EEENRRW  RENEWER     EEFGINZ  FEEZING
         ELEGISE     EEEJRRS  JEERERS     EEENRSS  SERENES     EEFGLLU  GLEEFUL
EEEGILZ  ELEGIZE     EEEJSST  JESTEES     EEENRST  ENTREES     EEFGLOR  FORELEG
EEEGINP  EPIGENE     EEEKKRS  KEEKERS              RETENES     EEFGRSU  REFUGES
EEEGIPR  PERIGEE     EEEKLLU  UKELELE     EEENRSV  ENERVES     EEFHIRS  HEIFERS
EEEGLMN  GLEEMEN     EEEKLMN  KEELMEN              VENEERS     EEFHIRT  HEFTIER
```

EEFHISY	FISHEYE
EEFHLNS	ENFLESH
EEFHLRS	FLESHER
	HERSELF
EEFHLSS	FLESHES
EEFHNRS	FRESHEN
EEFHORT	THEREOF
EEFHORW	WHEREOF
EEFHRRS	FRESHER
	REFRESH
EEFHRSS	FRESHES
EEFHRST	FRESHET
EEFIIRR	FIERIER
EEFIIRS	REIFIES
EEFILLS	FELLIES
EEFILLX	FLEXILE
EEFILNO	OLEFINE
EEFILNS	FELINES
EEFILOR	FORELIE
EEFILRR	FERLIER
EEFILRS	FERLIES
	RELIEFS
EEFILRT	FERTILE
EEFILST	FELSITE
	LEFTIES
	LIEFEST
EEFIMNR	FIREMEN
EEFIMRT	FEMITER
EEFINNR	FENNIER
EEFINRR	FERNIER
	REFINER
EEFINRS	ENFIRES
	FEERINS
	FINEERS
	REFINES
EEFINRT	FEINTER
EEFINSS	FINESSE
EEFINSX	ENFIXES
EEFIPRS	PREIFES
	PRIEFES
EEFIRRS	FERRIES
EEFIRRT	FERRITE
EEFIRSZ	FRIEZES
EEFISTV	FESTIVE
EEFLLOS	FELLOES
EEFLLRS	FELLERS
EEFLLRU	FUELLER
EEFLLST	FELLEST
EEFLLTY	FLEETLY
EEFLMTU	TEEMFUL
EEFLNNO	ENFELON
EEFLNNS	FENNELS
EEFLNOS	ONESELF
EEFLNSS	FLENSES
EEFLOOV	FOVEOLE
EEFLORS	FORLESE
EEFLRRS	FERRELS
EEFLRRU	FERRULE
EEFLRST	FELTERS
	REFLETS
EEFLRSU	FERULES
	REFUELS
EEFLRTT	FETTLER
EEFLRTU	FLEURET
EEFLRUX	FLEXURE
EEFLSTT	FETTLES
EEFLSUY	EYEFULS
EEFMNOR	FOREMEN
EEFMNRT	FERMENT
EEFMOTT	MOFETTE

EEFMPRU	PERFUME
EEFMSTW	FEWMETS
EEFMTTU	FUMETTE
EEFNNRS	FRENNES
EEFNORT	OFTENER
EEFNORZ	ENFROZE
EEFNRRY	FERNERY
EEFNRTV	FERVENT
EEFNSSW	FEWNESS
EEFORRV	FOREVER
EEFORRZ	REFROZE
EEFOTTU	FOUETTE
EEFPRRS	PREFERS
EEFPRSU	PERFUSE
EEFRRST	FERRETS
EEFRRSU	REFUSER
EEFRRTU	REFUTER
EEFRRTY	FERRETY
EEFRSST	FESTERS
EEFRSSU	REFUSES
EEFRSTT	FETTERS
EEFRSTU	FEUTRES
	REFUTES
EEFRSTW	FEWTERS
EEFSSTU	FETUSES
EEGGGLR	GLEGGER
EEGGHTU	THUGGEE
EEGGILN	GLEEING
	NEGLIGE
EEGGILR	LEGGIER
EEGGINR	GREEING
EEGGIPS	PEGGIES
EEGGIST	EGGIEST
EEGGISV	VEGGIES
EEGGKRS	SKEGGER
EEGGLRS	EGGLERS
	LEGGERS
EEGGMNY	YEGGMEN
EEGGNOR	ENGORGE
EEGGNOY	GEOGENY
EEGGORR	REGORGE
EEGGORU	GOUGERE
EEGGPRU	PUGGREE
EEGHILN	HEELING
EEGHINT	THEEING
EEGHINY	HYGIENE
EEGHINZ	HEEZING
EEGHIRW	REWEIGH
	WEIGHER
EEGHLNU	LEUGHEN
EEGHNRT	GREENTH
EEGHNRY	GREYHEN
EEGHRTU	TEUGHER
EEGHSSS	GHESSES
EEGIIRS	GRIESIE
EEGIJLN	JEELING
EEGIJNR	JEERING
EEGIKKN	KEEKING
EEGIKLN	KEELING
EEGIKNN	KEENING
	KNEEING
EEGIKNP	KEEPING
	PEEKING
EEGIKNR	REEKING
EEGIKNS	SEEKING
EEGILNP	LEEPING
	PEELING
EEGILNR	LEERING
	REELING
EEGILNS	LEESING

	SEELING
EEGILNT	GENTILE
EEGILOS	ELOGIES
EEGILRS	LEIGERS
	LIEGERS
EEGILRV	VELIGER
EEGILST	ELEGIST
	ELEGITS
EEGIMMR	GEMMIER
	IMMERGE
EEGIMNR	MEERING
	REGIMEN
EEGIMNS	SEEMING
EEGIMNT	MEETING
	TEEMING
EEGIMNX	EXEMING
EEGIMRS	EMIGRES
	REGIMES
	REMIGES
EEGINNP	PEENING
EEGINNR	ENGINER
	INGENER
EEGINNS	ENGINES
	NEESING
	SNEEING
EEGINNT	TEENING
EEGINNU	GENUINE
	INGENUE
EEGINNV	EEVNING
	EVENING
EEGINNW	ENEWING
	WEENING
EEGINNZ	NEEZING
EEGINOP	EPIGONE
EEGINOS	SOIGNEE
EEGINPP	PEEPING
EEGINPR	PEERING
	PREEING
EEGINPS	SEEPING
EEGINPV	PEEVING
EEGINPW	WEEPING
EEGINRS	GREISEN
EEGINRT	GENTIER
	INTEGER
	TEERING
	TREEING
EEGINRV	REEVING
	REGIVEN
	VEERING
EEGINSS	GENESIS
	SEEINGS
EEGINSW	SEEWING
	SWEEING
EEGINTV	VENTIGE
EEGINTW	WEETING
EEGINTX	EXIGENT
EEGIOST	EGOTISE
	GOETIES
EEGIOTZ	EGOTIZE
EEGIRRV	GRIEVER
EEGIRSS	SIEGERS
EEGIRSV	GRIEVES
	REGIVES
EEGIRTT	TERGITE
EEGISTV	VESTIGE
EEGKNOR	KEROGEN
EEGKNRU	GERENUK
EEGLLNS	LEGLENS
EEGLLSS	LEGLESS
EEGLLST	LEGLETS

EEGLMMU	GEMMULE
EEGLMSU	EMULGES
	LEGUMES
EEGLNOR	ERELONG
EEGLNOU	EUGENOL
EEGLNOZ	LOZENGE
EEGLNRT	GENTLER
EEGLNRY	GREENLY
EEGLNST	GENTLES
	LENGEST
EEGLRST	REGLETS
EEGLRTY	TELERGY
EEGMMRY	GEMMERY
EEGMNOS	EMONGES
	GENOMES
EEGMNRS	GERMENS
EEGMNST	SEGMENT
EEGMNSU	EMUNGES
EEGMRRS	MERGERS
EEGNNST	GENNETS
EEGNOPS	PONGEES
EEGNORS	ENGORES
	NEGROES
EEGNOSX	EXOGENS
EEGNPUX	EXPUNGE
EEGNRSS	NEGRESS
EEGNRST	GERENTS
	REGENTS
EEGNRSV	VENGERS
EEGNSSU	GENUSES
	NEGUSES
EEGNSTU	GUESTEN
EEGOOPY	POOGYEE
EEGOOSS	SOOGEES
EEGOPRT	PROTEGE
EEGORTV	OVERGET
EEGOSSS	GESSOES
EEGPRUX	EXPURGE
EEGRRSS	REGRESS
EEGRRST	REGRETS
EEGRRSU	RESURGE
	REURGES
EEGRRSV	VERGERS
EEGRSST	REGESTS
EEGRSSU	GUESSER
EEGRSSY	GEYSERS
EEGRSTT	GETTERS
EEGRSTU	GESTURE
EEGRSTY	GREYEST
EEGSSSU	GUESSES
EEHHRTT	THETHER
EEHHRTW	WHETHER
EEHHSTW	WHEESHT
EEHILLR	HELLIER
EEHILMN	HELIMEN
EEHILPS	EPHELIS
EEHILRS	LEISHER
EEHILST	SHELTIE
EEHILSX	HELIXES
EEHIMMS	MISHMEE
EEHIMNO	HEMIONE
EEHIMPR	HEMPIER
EEHIMPS	HEMPIES
EEHIMPT	EPITHEM
EEHIMRS	MESHIER
EEHINNR	HENNIER
EEHINNS	HENNIES
EEHINOR	HEROINE
EEHINRR	ERRHINE
EEHINRS	HENRIES

	INHERES		WHOEVER
EEHINRT	NEITHER	EEHOSST	ETHOSES
	THEREIN	EEHOSSX	HEXOSES
EEHINRW	WHEREIN	EEHOSTW	TOWHEES
EEHINST	THEINES	EEHPPST	HEPPEST
EEHIORS	HEROISE	EEHPRSS	SPHERES
EEHIORZ	HEROIZE	EEHPRST	HEPSTER
EEHIPRT	PRITHEE		PETHERS
EEHIPSV	PEEVISH		SPERTHE
EEHIPTT	EPITHET		THREEPS
EEHIRRS	HERRIES	EEHPRTY	PRYTHEE
EEHIRSS	HEIRESS	EEHQSTU	QUETHES
	HERISSE	EEHRRSW	WERSHER
EEHIRST	HEISTER	EEHRRTW	WHERRET
EEHIRSV	SHRIEVE	EEHRSTT	TETHERS
EEHIRTW	THEWIER	EEHRSTW	WETHERS
EEHIRWY	WHEYIER		WRETHES
EEHISTV	THIEVES	EEHRSTZ	HERTZES
EEHKLOY	KEYHOLE	EEHRTTW	WHETTER
EEHKLSS	SHEKELS	EEHRVWY	WHYEVER
EEHKOOY	EYEHOOK	EEIIKRS	KIERIES
EEHKRSS	SHREEKS	EEIILRV	VEILIER
EEHLLMP	PHELLEM	EEIIMNS	MEINIES
EEHLLNS	ENSHELL	EEIIMPR	RIEMPIE
EEHLLOS	HELLOES	EEIIMRT	EMERITI
EEHLLRS	HELLERS	EEIIMST	ITEMISE
	SHELLER	EEIIMTZ	ITEMIZE
EEHLMMW	WHEMMLE	EEIINRT	ERINITE
EEHLMST	HELMETS		NITERIE
EEHLNSU	UNHELES	EEIINRV	VEINIER
EEHLPRS	HELPERS	EEIINTV	INVITEE
EEHLPRT	TELPHER	EEIIPST	PIETIES
EEHLPSS	PLESHES	EEIIRRV	RIVIERE
EEHLRST	SHELTER	EEIIRVW	VIEWIER
EEHLRSW	WELSHER	EEIISST	SEITIES
EEHLRSY	SHEERLY	EEIISTV	VISITEE
EEHLSSU	HUELESS	EEIJKRR	JERKIER
EEHLSSV	SHELVES	EEIJKRS	JERKIES
EEHLSSW	SHEWELS	EEIJLLS	JELLIES
	WELSHES	EEIJMMR	JEMMIER
EEHLSTV	THELVES	EEIJMMS	JEMMIES
EEHMNOP	PHONEME	EEIJNNS	JENNIES
EEHMNOS	HOSEMEN	EEIJRRS	JERRIES
EEHMNRU	ENRHEUM	EEIJRTT	JETTIER
EEHMNRY	MYNHEER	EEIJSSS	JESSIES
EEHMNSS	MENSHES	EEIJSTT	JETTIES
EEHMORT	THEOREM	EEIKLLS	KELLIES
EEHMRUX	EXHUMER		SKELLIE
EEHMSST	SMEETHS	EEIKLPS	KELPIES
EEHMSUX	EXHUMES	EEIKLPT	PIKELET
EEHNNRS	HENNERS	EEIKLSS	SELKIES
EEHNNRY	HENNERY	EEIKLST	KELTIES
EEHNOPT	POTHEEN		SLEEKIT
EEHNORT	THEREON	EEIKMNP	PIKEMEN
EEHNORW	NOWHERE	EEIKNRT	KERNITE
	WHEREON	EEIKNSS	ENSKIES
EEHNPSS	SEPHENS		KINESES
	SPHENES	EEIKPRR	PERKIER
EEHNPSW	NEPHEWS	EEIKPRS	PESKIER
EEHNRST	THRENES	EEIKRSY	SKIEYER
EEHNSTU	ENTHUSE	EEIKSTT	STEEKIT
EEHNSTV	SEVENTH	EEIKTTT	TEKTITE
EEHNSTY	ETHYNES	EEILLMT	MELLITE
EEHOOPW	WHOOPEE	EEILLNS	NELLIES
EEHOPRU	EUPHROE	EEILLPS	ELLIPSE
EEHORSU	REHOUSE	EEILLRS	LEISLER
EEHORSW	WHERESO	EEILLRT	TREILLE
EEHORTT	THERETO	EEILLRV	EVILLER
EEHORTW	WHERETO	EEILLSS	EISELLS
EEHORVW	HOWEVER	EEILLST	TELLIES

EEILLSV	VIELLES		MISSEEM
EEILLSW	WELLIES	EEIMNNO	NOMINEE
EEILMNN	LINEMEN	EEIMNNT	EMINENT
EEILMNR	ERMELIN	EEIMNOS	SEMEION
EEILMNS	ISLEMEN	EEIMNRS	ERMINES
EEILMPT	IMPLETE	EEIMNRV	MINEVER
EEILMRV	VERMEIL	EEIMNSS	INSEEMS
EEILMST	ELMIEST		MISSEEN
EEILNNO	LEONINE		NEMESIS
EEILNNT	LENIENT		SIEMENS
EEILNNV	ENLIVEN	EEIMNST	EMETINS
EEILNOR	ELOINER	EEIMNSW	MISWEEN
EEILNPS	PENSILE	EEIMNSY	MEINEYS
EEILNRS	LIERNES	EEIMNTT	MINETTE
	RELINES	EEIMOPS	EPISOME
EEILNSS	ENISLES	EEIMOPT	EPITOME
	ENSILES	EEIMORS	ISOMERE
	SENSILE	EEIMOSS	MEIOSES
	SILENES	EEIMOTV	EMOTIVE
EEILNST	TENSILE	EEIMPRR	PREMIER
EEILNTT	ENTITLE		REPRIME
EEILNTV	VEINLET	EEIMPRS	EMPIRES
EEILOPT	PETIOLE		EMPRISE
EEILORT	TROELIE		EPIMERS
EEILORV	OVERLIE		IMPRESE
	RELIEVO		PREMIES
EEILOST	ESTOILE		PREMISE
	ETOILES		SPIREME
EEILOTZ	ZEOLITE	EEIMPRT	EMPTIER
EEILPRR	REPLIER	EEIMPST	EMPTIES
EEILPRS	REPLIES		SEPTIME
	SPIELER	EEIMQRU	REQUIEM
EEILPRT	PERLITE	EEIMRRR	MERRIER
	REPTILE	EEIMRRS	MERRIES
EEILPRU	PUERILE	EEIMRRT	TRIREME
EEILPSS	PELISSE	EEIMRSS	MESSIER
EEILPST	EPISTLE		MISERES
	PELITES		REMISES
EEILQRU	RELIQUE	EEIMRST	METIERS
EEILRRS	RELIERS		TREMIES
EEILRRV	RELIVER		TRISEME
	REVILER	EEIMRTT	TERMITE
EEILRSS	RESILES	EEIMSSS	MISSEES
EEILRST	LEISTER		SEMISES
	RETILES	EEIMSST	METISSE
	STERILE	EEINNNP	PENNINE
EEILRSU	LEISURE	EEINNPS	PENNIES
EEILRSV	RELIVES	EEINNRS	NERINES
	REVILES	EEINNRT	INTERNE
	SERVILE	EEINNRU	NEURINE
EEILRTT	RETITLE	EEINNRV	ENRIVEN
EEILSSS	SESELIS		INNERVE
	SESSILE		NERVINE
EEILSST	TELESIS	EEINNRW	WENNIER
	TIELESS	EEINNST	INTENSE
EEILSSU	ILEUSES	EEINNTW	ENTWINE
EEILSSW	LEWISES	EEINOPR	PEREION
EEILSSX	LEXISES		PIONEER
	SILEXES	EEINOPS	PEONIES
EEILSTV	LEVITES	EEINPPS	PEPSINE
	LIEVEST	EEINPRR	REPINER
EEILSTX	SEXTILE	EEINPRS	EREPSIN
EEILSUV	ELUSIVE		REPINES
EEILSVW	WEEVILS	EEINPRT	INEPTER
EEILSZZ	LEZZIES	EEINPRZ	PRENZIE
EEILTTX	TEXTILE	EEINPSS	PENISES
EEILVWY	WEEVILY	EEINPST	PENTISE
EEIMMNS	IMMENSE	EEINPSV	PENSIVE
EEIMMRS	IMMERSE		VESPINE
EEIMMSS	MIMESES	EEINQRU	ENQUIRE

```
          INQUERE                QUERIES    EEKLSTT KETTLES    EELNPSY SPLEENY
EEINQTU QUIETEN    EEIQRTU QUIETER          EEKMNOS SOKEMEN    EELNQUY QUEENLY
EEINQUY QUEYNIE           REQUITE           EEKMPRS KEMPERS    EELNRST RELENTS
EEINRRS RESINER    EEIRRRT RETIRER          EEKMRSS KERMESS    EELNRSU UNREELS
EEINRRT INERTER           TERRIER           EEKNNRS KENNERS    EELNRTT LETTERN
        REINTER    EEIRRSS SERRIES          EEKNNST KENNETS    EELNRUV NERVULE
        RENTIER           SIRREES           EEKNOSS KENOSES    EELNSSS LESSENS
        TERRINE    EEIRRST ETRIERS          EEKNOST KETONES    EELNSST NESTLES
EEINRRV NERVIER           REITERS           EEKNOTY KEYNOTE    EELNSSU UNSEELS
        VERNIER           RESTIER           EEKNRSS SKREENS    EELNSTT NETTLES
EEINRSS SEINERS           RETIRES           EEKNSTU NETSUKE    EELNSTU ELUENTS
        SEREINS           RETRIES           EEKOPRS RESPOKE            UNSTEEL
        SIRENES           TERRIES           EEKORSV REVOKES    EELNSTY ENSTYLE
EEINRST ENTIRES    EEIRRSV REIVERS          EEKOSSS SEKOSES            TENSELY
        ENTRIES           REVERSI           EEKOSST KETOSES    EELNSUV VENULES
        NERITES           REVISER           EEKPPSU UPKEEPS    EELNSXY XYLENES
        TRENISE           RIEVERS           EEKPRSU PERUKES    EELNTTU LUNETTE
EEINRSV ENVIERS    EEIRRSW REWIRES          EEKRSST STREEKS    EELOPPS PEOPLES
        INVERSE    EEIRRTV RIVERET          EEKRSSU RESKUES    EELOPRS ELOPERS
        VENIRES           RIVETER           EEKRSSW RESKEWS            LEPROSE
        VERSINE    EEIRRTW REWRITE                  SKEWERS    EELOPRX EXPLORE
EEINRSW NEWSIER    EEIRRVV REVIVER          EEKRSSY KERSEYS    EELOPSS ELOPSES
EEINRTT NETTIER    EEIRSSU REISSUE          EEKSSTW SKEWEST    EELOPTU EELPOUT
        TENTIER    EEIRSSV IVRESSE          EELLMRS MERELLS    EELORSS RESOLES
EEINRTU NEURITE           REVISES                  SMELLER    EELORSV RESOLVE
        RETINUE    EEIRSSZ SEIZERS          EELLMRV VERMELL    EELORTT LORETTE
        REUNITE    EEIRSTT TESTIER          EELLNOV NOVELLE    EELORVV REVOLVE
        UTERINE    EEIRSTU SUBTIER          EELLNRS SNELLER    EELOSSS LOESSES
EEINSST SESTINE    EEIRSTV RESTIVE          EELLNSW NEWELLS    EELOSST OSSELET
EEINSSV SENVIES           SIEVERT           EELLORS ROSELLE            TELOSES
EEINSSW NEWSIES           STIEVER           EELLORZ ROZELLE    EELOSTT TELEOST
EEINSTV TENSIVE           VERIEST           EELLPRS RESPELL    EELOSUV EVOLUES
        VENITES    EEIRSTW STEWIER                  SPELLER    EELOSVV EVOLVES
EEINSTX EXTINES    EEIRSTZ ZESTIER          EELLPST PELLETS    EELOTUV EVOLUTE
        SIXTEEN    EEIRSUZ SEIZURE          EELLQRU QUELLER            VELOUTE
EEINSTY SYENITE    EEIRSVV REVIVES          EELLRSS RESELLS    EELPPRX PERPLEX
EEIOPSS POESIES    EEIRSVW REVIEWS                  SELLERS    EELPPSU PEEPULS
EEIOPST POETISE           VIEWERS           EELLRST RETELLS    EELPQRU PREQUEL
EEIOPSX EPOXIES    EEIRTVV VETIVER                  TELLERS    EELPRST PELTERS
EEIOPTZ POETIZE    EEISSSV ESSIVES          EELLRSU RUELLES            PETRELS
EEIORRS ROSIERE    EEISSTX SEXIEST          EELLRSW SWELLER            RESPELT
EEIORSS SOIREES    EEISTVX VITEXES          EELLSTV VELLETS            SPELTER
EEIORSV EROSIVE    EEITUXZ ZEUXITE          EELMMOP POMMELE    EELPRSU REPULSE
EEIOSST ISOETES    EEJKRRS JERKERS          EELMMPU EMPLUME    EELPRSY SLEEPRY
EEIPPPR PEPPIER    EEJLLMU JUMELLE          EELMNOO OENOMEL            YELPERS
EEIPPST PEPTISE    EEJLRWY JEWELRY          EELMOPR PLEROME    EELPRTZ PRETZEL
EEIPPTT PIPETTE    EEJNNST JENNETS          EELMOPT LEPTOME    EELPRUX PLEXURE
EEIPPTZ PEPTIZE    EEJNOOR REJONEO          EELMORW EELWORM    EELPRVY REPLEVY
EEIPQRU PERIQUE    EEJNORS REJONES          EELMOST OMELETS    EELPSST PESTLES
        REPIQUE    EEJNORY ENJOYER          EELMPRS SEMPLER    EELPSTT PETTLES
EEIPQSU EQUIPES    EEJPRRU PERJURE          EELMPST PELMETS    EELPSTY STEEPLY
EEIPRRR PERRIER    EEJQRRU JERQUER                  STEMPEL    EELPSUX EXPULSE
EEIPRRS PERRIES    EEJQRSU JERQUES                  STEMPLE    EELQRUY QUEERLY
        REPRISE    EEJRSST JESTERS                  TEMPLES    EELQSSU SEQUELS
        RESPIRE    EEJRSSY JERSEYS          EELMPTT TEMPLET    EELRRSV VERRELS
EEIPRRV REPRIVE    EEKKOTV VETKOEK          EELMRST SMELTER    EELRRVY REVELRY
EEIPRRZ REPRIZE    EEKKRRT TREKKER          EELMRSU LEMURES    EELRSST STREELS
EEIPRST RESPITE    EEKKSSY KEKSYES                  RELUMES            TRESSEL
EEIPRSV PREVISE    EEKLLNV KNEVELL          EELMSST TELESMS    EELRSSU RULESSE
        PRIEVES    EEKLLSY SLEEKLY          EELMSTT METTLES    EELRSTT LETTERS
EEIPRSW SPEWIER    EEKLLUU UKULELE                  STEMLET            LETTRES
EEIPRSX EXPIRES    EEKLMPS KEMPLES          EELNNSV VENNELS            SETTLER
        PREXIES    EEKLNNS KENNELS          EELNOPV ENVELOP            STERLET
EEIPRTT PETTIER    EEKLNOS KEELSON          EELNOSV ELEVONS            TRESTLE
EEIPRVW PREVIEW    EEKLNRS KERNELS          EELNOSY ESLOYNE    EELRSTV SVELTER
EEIPRZZ PREZZIE    EEKLPRS KELPERS          EELNOTT NOTELET    EELRSTW SWELTER
EEIPSTT PETTIES    EEKLRST KELTERS          EELNOTU TOLUENE            WELTERS
EEIPSTW PEEWITS            KESTREL          EELNPSS PENSELS            WRESTLE
EEIQRRU REQUIRE            SKELTER                  SPLEENS    EELRSTY RESTYLE
EEIQRSU ESQUIRE    EEKLSSY KEYLESS          EELNPST PENTELS            TERSELY
```

```
EELRSTZ SELTZER        EENNOTY NEOTENY                UNSEXES      EEPSTTU PUTTEES
EELRSUV VELURES        EENNPRS PENNERS        EENSSVW SWEVENS      EEQRRUY EQUERRY
EELRSVV VERVELS        EENNQUU UNQUEEN        EENSTTX EXTENTS      EEQRSTU QUESTER
EELSSSU USELESS        EENNRST RENNETS        EENSTTY TEENTSY              REQUEST
EELSSSV VESSELS                TENNERS        EENSTUW UNSWEET      EEQSSTU QUEESTS
EELSSSX SEXLESS        EENNRUV UNNERVE        EENSTVY SEVENTY      EEQSUYZ SQUEEZY
EELSSTT SETTLES        EENNSST SENNETS        EEOOPRS OPEROSE      EERRSST RESTERS
EELSSUV EVULSES        EENNSSU UNSEENS        EEOOPTU OUTPEEP      EERRSSV SERVERS
EELSTUY EUSTYLE                UNSENSE        EEOPRRV REPROVE              VERSERS
EELSTVV VELVETS        EENNSSW NEWNESS        EEOPRSS REPOSES      EERRSTT TERRETS
EELSTVW TWELVES        EENOPPR PROPENE        EEOPRSX EXPOSER      EERRSTU URETERS
EELSTWY SWEETLY        EENOPPT PEPTONE        EEOPRTT TREETOP      EERRSTV REVERTS
EELTVVY VELVETY        EENOPRS OPENERS        EEOPRTU OUTPEER      EERRSTW STREWER
EEMMNOT MEMENTO                PERONES        EEOPSSS SPEOSES              WRESTER
EEMMORS MEROMES                REOPENS        EEOPSST POETESS      EERRSUV REVEURS
EEMMOSU MOUSMEE                REPONES        EEOPSSU ESPOUSE      EERRSVW SWERVER
EEMMOSV EMMOVES        EENOPST OPENEST                POSEUSE      EERRSVY SERVERY
EEMMSSS SEMSEMS                PENTOSE        EEOPSSX EXPOSES      EERRTTU REUTTER
EEMMSST STEMMES                POSTEEN        EEOPSTU TOUPEES              UTTERER
EEMNNOV ENVENOM                POTEENS        EEOPSTY PEYOTES      EERRTTY RETTERY
EEMNNSW NEWSMEN        EENORRV OVERREN        EEOPTUW OUTWEEP      EERSSST TRESSES
EEMNOOS SOMEONE        EENORSY ONEYERS        EEOQRTU REQUOTE      EERSSTT SETTERS
EEMNOOY MOONEYE                ONEYRES        EEORRST RESTORE              STREETS
EEMNORS MOREENS        EENORTV OVERNET        EEORRSV REVERSO              TERSEST
EEMNORV OVERMEN        EENOSSY ESSOYNE        EEORRTU REROUTE              TESTERS
EEMNORY MONEYER                NOYESES        EEORRTW REWROTE      EERSSTV REVESTS
EEMNOST TEMENOS        EENOSTV VENTOSE        EEORSST OSSETER              STERVES
        TONEMES                VOTEENS                STEREOS              VERSETS
EEMNOSV ENMOVES        EENOSTW TOWNEES        EEORSSX SOREXES      EERSSTW STEWERS
EEMNPTU UMPTEEN        EENOSVZ EVZONES                XEROSES              WESTERS
EEMNRTU TRUEMEN        EENPPRT PERPENT        EEORSTT ROSETTE      EERSSTX EXSERTS
EEMNSYZ ENZYMES        EENPRST PRESENT        EEORSTV ESTOVER      EERSSUY SEYSURE
EEMOOSW WOESOME                REPENTS                OVERSET      EERSSVW SWERVES
EEMOPRR EMPEROR                SERPENT        EEORSTX XEROTES      EERSTTT STRETTE
EEMOPRT TEMPORE        EENPRSY PYRENES        EEORSTY ESOTERY              TETTERS
EEMOPRV PREMOVE        EENPRTV PREVENT        EEORSUV OEUVRES      EERSTTU TRUSTEE
EEMOPRW EMPOWER        EENPSTU PUNTEES                OVERUSE      EERSTTY STREETY
EEMOPST METOPES        EENPSTW ENSWEPT        EEORSVW OVERSEW      EERSTUV VERSUTE
EEMORRS REMORSE        EENPSTY STEPNEY        EEORTUV OUVERTE              VERTUES
        ROEMERS        EENQSTU SEQUENT        EEPPPRS PEPPERS              VESTURE
EEMORRT REMOTER        EENRRST RENTERS        EEPPPRY PEPPERY      EERSTUY TUYERES
EEMORRU UROMERE                STERNER        EEPPRST STEPPER      EERSTVV VERVETS
EEMORRV REMOVER        EENRRSU ENSURER        EEPPSST STEPPES      EERSTWY TWYERES
EEMORST METEORS        EENRRSV NERVERS        EEPPSUW UPSWEEP      EERSUVW SURVEWE
        REMOTES        EENRRUV NERVURE        EEPPSUY EUPEPSY      EERTTUX TEXTURE
EEMORSV REMOVES        EENRSST NESTERS        EEPRRSS PRESSER      EESSSTT SESTETS
EEMPRRT PRETERM                RESENTS                REPRESS              TSETSES
EEMPRSS EMPRESS                STRENES                SPERRES      EESSTTT SESTETT
EEMPRST TEMPERS        EENRSSU ENSURES        EEPRRSU PERUSER      EESSTTU SUTTEES
EEMPRSU PRESUME        EENRSTT TENTERS                REPURES      EESSTTX SEXTETS
        SUPREME                TESTERN        EEPRRTV PERVERT      EESSTTY STEYEST
EEMPRTT TEMPTER        EENRSTU NEUTERS        EEPRRVY REPRYVE      EESTTTW WETTEST
EEMPRTU PERMUTE                RETUNES        EEPRSSS PRESSES      EESTTTX SEXTETT
EEMPSSU EMPUSES                TENURES                SPERSES      EFFFIRU FUFFIER
EEMPSTT TEMPEST                TUREENS        EEPRSST PESTERS      EFFFOOR FEOFFOR
EEMPSTX EXEMPTS        EENRSTV VENTERS                PRESETS      EFFGIJN JEFFING
EEMRRST TERMERS                VENTRES        EEPRSSU PERSUES      EFFGINR REFFING
EEMRRUU REMUEUR        EENRSTW WESTERN                PERUSES      EFFGIRS GRIFFES
EEMRSST RESTEMS        EENRSTX EXTERNS        EEPRSSV VESPERS      EFFGORS GOFFERS
EEMRSSU RESUMES        EENRSTY STYRENE        EEPRSSW SPEWERS      EFFGRRU GRUFFER
EEMRSUX MUREXES                YESTERN        EEPRSSX EXPRESS      EFFHIKU KUFFIEH
EEMSSSU SMEUSES        EENRSVV VERVENS        EEPRSTT PERTEST      EFFHILW WHIFFLE
EEMSSTU MUSTEES        EENRTUV VENTURE                PETTERS      EFFHIRS SHERIFF
EEMSTTU MUSETTE        EENSSST SETNESS        EEPRSTU PERTUSE      EFFHIRU HUFFIER
EENNORT ENTERON        EENSSSY SYNESES                REPUTES      EFFHIRW WHIFFER
        TENONER        EENSSTT TENSEST        EEPRSTW PEWTERS      EFFHITW WHIFFET
EENNORU NEURONE        EENSSTV STEVENS        EEPRSTX EXPERTS      EFFHLSU SHUFFLE
EENNOSS ONENESS        EENSSTW WETNESS        EEPRTTX PRETEXT      EFFIIJS JIFFIES
EENNOSZ ENZONES        EENSSUV VENUSES        EEPSSTT SEPTETS      EFFIIMR MIFFIER
EENNOTT NONETTE        EENSSUX NEXUSES        EEPSTTT SEPTETT      EFFIINR NIFFIER
```

EFFIIST	FIFTIES	EFGIORV FORGIVE	EFIKNRU FUNKIER	EFINSSU INFUSES
	IFFIEST	EFGIRRT GRIFTER	EFIKORR FORKIER	EFINSUX UNFIXES
EFFIKLS	SKIFFLE	EFGIRSU FIGURES	EFIKRRS FRISKER	EFINSZZ FIZZENS
EFFILLU	LIFEFUL	EFGLLSU FLUGELS	EFIKRST FRISKET	EFIOOPR POOFIER
EFFILNS	SNIFFLE	EFGLNSU ENGULFS	EFILLMS MISFELL	EFIOORR ROOFIER
EFFILPR	PIFFLER	EFGLNTU FULGENT	EFILLOO FOLIOLE	EFIOORT FOOTIER
EFFILPS	PIFFLES	EFGLORS GOLFERS	EFILLOS FOLLIES	EFIOORW WOOFIER
EFFILRR	RIFFLER	EFGLORT FROGLET	EFILLRS FILLERS	EFIOPRR PORIFER
EFFILRS	RIFFLES	EFGLOSS FOGLESS		REFILLS	EFIOPRT FIREPOT
EFFILRY	FIREFLY	EFGMNOR FROGMEN	EFILLST FILLETS	EFIORRT ROTIFER
EFFILSS	SIFFLES	EFGNOOR FORGONE	EFILLUW WILEFUL	EFIORRW FROWIER
EFFINRS	NIFFERS	EFGOORS FORGOES	EFILMNU FULMINE	EFIORSS FROISES
	SNIFFER	EFGORRS FORGERS	EFILMOT FILEMOT	EFIORST FOISTER
EFFIINST	INFEFTS	EFGORRU FERRUGO	EFILMSS SELFISM		FORTIES
	STIFFEN	EFGORRY FORGERY	EFILMST FILMSET	EFIOSST SOFTIES
EFFIOPR	PIFFERO	EFGORST FORGETS		LEFTISM	EFIOSTX FOXIEST
EFFIORT	FORFEIT	EFGORSW GOWFERS	EFILNOS OLEFINS	EFIOSTZ FOZIEST
	TOFFIER	EFGORTU FOREGUT	EFILNOX FLEXION	EFIPPRR FRIPPER
EFFIOST	TOFFIES	EFHIINS FINEISH	EFILNSS FINLESS	EFIPRTY PETRIFY
EFFIPRU	PUFFIER	EFHIIRS FISHIER	EFILOOS FLOOSIE	EFIRRRU FURRIER
EFFIRST	RESTIFF	EFHIJSW JEWFISH		FOLIOSE	EFIRRSU FRISEUR
	STIFFER	EFHILMS FLEMISH	EFILOOZ FLOOZIE		FRISURE
EFFLMRU	MUFFLER		HIMSELF	EFILOPR PROFILE		SURFIER
EFFLMSU	MUFFLES	EFHILSS SELFISH	EFILORR FLORIER	EFIRRTT FRITTER
EFFLNSU	SNUFFLE	EFHINNS FENNISH	EFILORT LOFTIER	EFIRRTU FRITURE
EFFLOPS	POFFLES	EFHIRSS FISHERS		TREFOIL		FRUITER
EFFLOSU	SOUFFLE		SERFISH	EFILOSX SEXFOIL		TURFIER
EFFLRRU	RUFFLER		SHERIFS	EFILPPR FLIPPER	EFIRRTY TERRIFY
EFFLRSU	RUFFLES	EFHIRST SHIFTER	EFILPPS FIPPLES	EFIRRUZ FURZIER
EFFLRTU	FRETFUL	EFHIRSY FISHERY	EFILPPU PIPEFUL	EFIRSST SIFTERS
	TRUFFLE	EFHISUW HUSWIFE	EFILPRS PILFERS		STRIFES
EFFNRSU	SNUFFER	EFHLLPU HELPFUL	EFILPRY PILFERY	EFIRSSU FISSURE
EFFNRUU	UNRUFFE	EFHLLSY FLESHLY	EFILQUY LIQUEFY		FUSSIER
EFFOORR	OFFEROR	EFHLNSU UNFLESH	EFILRRS RIFLERS	EFIRSTT FITTERS
EFFOPRR	PROFFER	EFHLOOX FOXHOLE	EFILRRT TRIFLER		TITFERS
EFFOPSU	POUFFES	EFHLOPU HOPEFUL	EFILRST FILTERS	EFIRSTU FUSTIER
EFFORST	EFFORTS	EFHLOSS FLOSHES		LIFTERS		SURFEIT
EFFOSST	OFFSETS	EFHLRSU FLUSHER		STIFLER	EFIRSTW SWIFTER
EFFPRSU	PUFFERS	EFHLRSY FRESHLY		TRIFLES	EFIRSUX FIXURES
EFFPRUY	PUFFERY	EFHLSSU FLUSHES	EFILRTT FLITTER	EFIRSVY VERSIFY
EFFRSSU	SUFFERS	EFHLSTY THYSELF	EFILRTU FLUTIER	EFIRSZZ FIZZERS
EFFRSTU	STUFFER	EFHLTTW TWELFTH		FUTILER		FRIZZES
EFFSSUU	SUFFUSE	EFHNORT FORHENT	EFILRVV FLIVVER	EFIRTTU TUFTIER
EFFSTTU	TUFFETS	EFHOORS HOOFERS	EFILRZZ FRIZZLE		TURFITE
EFGGIOR	FOGGIER	EFHORST FOTHERS	EFILSSS FISSLES	EFIRTUV FURTIVE
EFGGIRR	FRIGGER	EFHRRTU FURTHER	EFILSST SELFIST	EFIRTUX FIXTURE
EFGGIRU	FUGGIER	EFHRSSU FRUSHES		STIFLES	EFIRUZZ FUZZIER
EFGGIRY	FIGGERY	EFIIKST FIKIEST	EFILSTT LEFTIST	EFISTTT FITTEST
EFGGORS	FOGGERS	EFIILLS FILLIES	EFILSTU FLUIEST	EFISTTY TESTIFY
EFGHINT	HEFTING	EFIILMR FILMIER	EFILSZZ FIZZLES	EFJLSTU JESTFUL
EFGHIRT	FIGHTER	EFIILMS MISFILE	EFILUVX FLUXIVE	EFKLMNO MENFOLK
	FREIGHT	EFIILRT FITLIER	EFIMMRU FERMIUM	EFKLMOR MERFOLK
EFGILLN	FELLING	EFIILRY FIERILY	EFIMNOR FERMION	EFKLNUY FLUNKEY
EFGILMN	FLEMING	EFIILSS FISSILE	EFIMNTT FITMENT	EFKLOPU POKEFUL
EFGILNR	FLINGER	EFIIMRS MISFIRE	EFIMOST FOMITES	EFKLPSU SKEPFUL
EFGILNS	SELFING	EFIINNR FINNIER	EFIMRRS FIRMERS	EFKORRS FORKERS
EFGILNT	FELTING	EFIINPV FIVEPIN	EFIMRST FIRMEST	EFLLOST FLOTELS
EFGILNX	FLEXING	EFIINRT NIFTIER		FREMITS	EFLLOSW FELLOWS
EFGILNY	FLEYING	EFIINRU UNIFIER	EFIMSTU FUMIEST	EFLLRSU FULLERS
EFGILRU	GULFIER	EFIINSU UNIFIES	EFIMTTU FUMETTI	EFLLSTU FULLEST
EFGIMNT	FIGMENT	EFIINSX INFIXES	EFINNOR INFERNO	EFLMOSU FULSOME
EFGINNP	PFENNIG	EFIIRRR FIRRIER	EFINNRS FINNERS	EFLMPRU FRUMPLE
EFGINNR	FERNING	EFIIRRT RIFTIER	EFINNRU FUNNIER	EFLMSUU MUSEFUL
EFGINOR	FOREIGN	EFIIRST FISTIER	EFINNSU FUNNIES	EFLNNSU FUNNELS
EFGINRS	FINGERS	EFIIRZZ FIZZIER	EFINOPR FORPINE	EFLNORT FORLENT
	FRINGES	EFIISSV FISSIVE	EFINRST SNIFTER	EFLNORU FLEURON
EFGINRU	GUNFIRE	EFIJLLY JELLIFY	EFINRSU INFUSER	EFLNORY FELONRY
EFGINTT	FETTING	EFIJLOR FRIJOLE	EFINRUY REUNIFY	EFLNOTT FLETTON
EFGINTW	WEFTING	EFIJLOT JETFOIL	EFINSST FITNESS		FONTLET
EFGIOOR	GOOFIER	EFIKLRU FLUKIER		INFESTS	EFLNPSU PENFULS

EFLNSSU	FULNESS, UNSELFS
EFLNSTU	FLUENTS, NETFULS
EFLNSUY	SYNFUEL
EFLNTTU	TENTFUL
EFLNTUU	TUNEFUL
EFLOORR	FLOORER, FORLORE
EFLOORS	FORSLOE
EFLOORY	FOOLERY
EFLOORZ	FOOZLER
EFLOOST	FOOTLES
EFLOOSZ	FOOZLES
EFLORST	FLORETS, LOFTERS
EFLORSU	FUROLES, OURSELF
EFLORSW	FLOWERS, FOWLERS, REFLOWS, WOLFERS
EFLORSX	FLEXORS
EFLORTT	FORTLET
EFLORTW	FELWORT
EFLORVY	FLYOVER, OVERFLY
EFLORWW	WERWOLF
EFLORWY	FLOWERY
EFLOSSS	FLOSSES
EFLOSSU	FLOUSES
EFLOSTU	FOULEST
EFLOTUW	OUTFLEW
EFLPRSU	PURFLES
EFLPRUY	PREYFUL
EFLPSTU	PESTFUL
EFLRSTU	FLUSTER, FLUTERS, RESTFUL
EFLRTTU	FLUTTER
EFLSTUZ	ZESTFUL
EFLSUZZ	FUZZLES
EFMNOOT	FOOTMEN
EFMNORS	ENFORMS
EFMNOST	FOMENTS
EFMNRSU	SURFMEN
EFMNRTU	TURFMEN
EFMOORZ	ZOEFORM
EFMOPRR	PERFORM, PREFORM
EFMOPRT	POMFRET
EFMORRS	FORMERS, REFORMS
EFMOTTU	FUMETTO
EFMPRUY	PERFUMY
EFMRTUY	FURMETY
EFNNORT	FORNENT
EFNNOTU	UNOFTEN
EFNOOST	FESTOON
EFNORRU	FORERUN
EFNORTU	FORTUNE
EFNORTW	FORWENT
EFNORUZ	UNFROZE
EFNOSST	SOFTENS
EFOOPRR	REPROOF
EFOOPRS	SPOOFER
EFOOPRT	FORETOP, POOFTER
EFOORRS	ROOFERS
EFOORST	FOETORS, FOOTERS, REFOOTS
EFOORSW	WOOFERS
EFOPPRY	FOPPERY
EFOPRSS	PROFESS
EFOPRST	FORPETS
EFOPRSU	PROFUSE
EFOPRTU	POUFTER
EFOPRTY	TORPEFY
EFORRSU	FERROUS, FURORES
EFORRTY	TORREFY
EFORRUV	FERVOUR
EFORSST	FORESTS, FOSTERS
EFORSSU	FOURSES
EFORSTU	FOUTERS, FOUTRES
EFOSSTT	SOFTEST
EFOSTWW	WOWFEST
EFPRTUY	PUTREFY
EFPSTUY	STUPEFY
EFRRSSU	SURFERS
EFRRSTU	RETURFS
EFRRSUU	FUREURS
EFRSSSU	FUSSERS
EFRSTTU	TUFTERS
EFRSTUU	FUTURES
EFSSTTU	FUSTETS
EGGGILN	LEGGING
EGGGILR	GIGGLER
EGGGILS	GIGGLES
EGGGINP	PEGGING
EGGGLOR	GOGGLER
EGGGLOS	GOGGLES
EGGGLSU	GUGGLES
EGGGNOS	EGGNOGS
EGGHILR	HIGGLER
EGGHILS	HIGGLES
EGGHINP	PEGHING
EGGHIRT	THIGGER
EGGHLOS	SHOGGLE
EGGHORS	HOGGERS
EGGHORY	HOGGERY
EGGHOST	HOGGETS
EGGIILS	GILGIES
EGGIINS	SIEGING
EGGIIPR	PIGGIER
EGGIIPS	PIGGIES
EGGIJLS	JIGGLES
EGGIJRS	JIGGERS
EGGILLN	GELLING
EGGILMS	LEGGISM
EGGILNN	LENGING
EGGILNR	NIGGLER, NIGGLES, SNIGGLE
EGGILNU	LUGEING
EGGILNY	GLEYING
EGGILRS	LIGGERS
EGGILRW	WIGGLER, WRIGGLE
EGGILST	GIGLETS
EGGILSU	LUGGIES
EGGILSW	WIGGLES
EGGIMMN	GEMMING
EGGIMMN	MENGING
EGGIMNR	GERMING, MERGING
EGGIMOS	MOGGIES
EGGIMRU	MUGGIER
EGGINNR	GERNING
EGGINNS	GINSENG
EGGINNV	VENGING
EGGINRS	GINGERS, NIGGERS, SNIGGER
EGGINRU	GRUEING, GUNGIER
EGGINRV	VERGING
EGGINRW	GREWING
EGGINRY	GINGERY, GREYING, NIGGERY
EGGINSS	GESSING
EGGINTT	GETTING
EGGINTW	TWIGGEN
EGGIORS	SOGGIER
EGGIPRR	PRIGGER
EGGIPRU	PUGGIER
EGGIPRY	PIGGERY
EGGIPSU	PUGGIES
EGGIRRS	RIGGERS
EGGIRRT	TRIGGER
EGGIRRU	RUGGIER
EGGIRSW	SWIGGER
EGGIRTW	TWIGGER
EGGIRUV	VUGGIER
EGGIRWY	WIGGERY
EGGJLOS	JOGGLES
EGGJLRU	JUGGLER
EGGJLSU	JUGGLES
EGGJORS	JOGGERS
EGGLMSU	SMUGGLE
EGGLNSU	SNUGGLE
EGGLOOS	GOOGLES
EGGLOOY	GEOLOGY
EGGLORS	LOGGERS, SLOGGER
EGGLOST	GOGLETS, TOGGLES
EGGLOSW	WOGGLES
EGGLPRU	PLUGGER
EGGLRSU	GURGLES, LUGGERS, SLUGGER
EGGMRSU	MUGGERS, SMUGGER
EGGNOOY	GEOGONY
EGGNRSU	SNUGGER
EGGNSTU	NUGGETS
EGGNTUY	NUGGETY
EGGORRY	GREGORY
EGGORST	GORGETS
EGGORTY	TOGGERY
EGGPRUY	PUGGERY
EGGRRSU	RUGGERS
EGGRSTU	TUGGERS
EGGSSTU	SUGGEST
EGHHIMN	HIGHMEN
EGHHIRS	HIGHERS
EGHHIST	EIGHTHS, HEIGHTS, HIGHEST
EGHHOSW	SHOWGHE
EGHHSSU	SHEUGHS
EGHHSUW	WHEUGHS
EGHIILL	GHILLIE
EGHIINR	HEIRING
EGHIINT	NIGHTIE
EGHIINV	INVEIGH
EGHIKNR	GHERKIN
EGHIKRS	SKREIGH, SKRIEGH
EGHILLN	HELLING
EGHILMN	HELMING
EGHILNP	HELPING
EGHILNR	HERLING
EGHILNS	SHINGLE
EGHILNT	ENLIGHT, LIGHTEN
EGHILNV	HELVING
EGHILPT	PIGHTLE
EGHILRT	LIGHTER, RELIGHT
EGHILSS	SLEIGHS
EGHILST	SLEIGHT
EGHIMMN	HEMMING
EGHIMNS	MESHING
EGHIMNT	THEMING
EGHIMPT	EMPIGHT
EGHINNN	HENNING
EGHINNT	HENTING
EGHINNU	UNHINGE
EGHINOS	SHOEING
EGHINPS	HESPING, PHESING
EGHINRR	HERRING
EGHINRT	RIGHTEN
EGHINRW	WHINGER
EGHINRY	HERYING
EGHINST	NIGHEST
EGHINSW	HEWINGS, SHEWING, WHINGES
EGHINSX	HEXINGS
EGHINTT	TIGHTEN
EGHINWW	WHEWING
EGHIOOS	SHOOGIE
EGHIORS	OGREISH
EGHIORU	ROUGHIE
EGHIOST	HOGTIES
EGHIOTT	GOTHITE
EGHIOTU	TOUGHIE
EGHIOTV	EIGHTVO
EGHIRRT	RIGHTER
EGHIRSS	SIGHERS
EGHIRST	SIGHTER
EGHIRSU	GUSHIER
EGHIRSY	GREYISH
EGHIRTT	TIGHTER
EGHISTW	WEIGHTS
EGHITWY	WEIGHTY
EGHLMPS	PHLEGMS
EGHLMPY	PHLEGMY
EGHLNOR	LEGHORN
EGHLNPU	ENGULPH
EGHLNST	LENGTHS
EGHLNTY	LENGTHY
EGHLOOS	SHOOGLE
EGHLOSS	SEGHOLS
EGHLPSU	PLEUGHS
EGHMMOS	MEGOHMS
EGHMNOU	HUMOGEN
EGHMOSU	GUMSHOE
EGHNORU	ENROUGH, ROUGHEN
EGHNOSU	ENOUGHS
EGHNOTU	TOUGHEN

EGHNRSU	HUNGERS	EGIKLNW	WELKING
EGHOPRS	GOPHERS	EGIKLRS	KILERGS
EGHORRU	ROUGHER	EGIKMNP	KEMPING
EGHORTU	TOUGHER	EGIKNNN	KENNING
EGHOSTT	GHETTOS	EGIKNNR	KERNING
EGHOSUU	HUGEOUS	EGIKNNT	KENTING
EGHRSSU	GUSHERS	EGIKNOV	EVOKING
EGHRTUY	THEURGY	EGIKNPP	KEPPING
EGIIJLS	JILGIES	EGIKNPR	PERKING
EGIILLS	GILLIES	EGIKNRV	KERVING
EGIILMT	LEGITIM	EGIKNRY	YERKING
EGIILNR	LEIRING	EGIKNST	KESTING
	LINGIER	EGIKNSW	SKEWING
EGIILNS	SEILING	EGIKNSY	YESKING
EGIILNT	LIGNITE	EGIKNUY	YEUKING
EGIILNV	VEILING	EGILLMN	MELLING
EGIILNX	EXILING	EGILLNO	LOGLINE
EGIILPS	GILPIES	EGILLNS	LEGLINS
EGIILRS	GIRLIES		LINGELS
EGIIMNN	MEINING		LINGLES
EGIIMNP	IMPINGE		SELLING
EGIIMNR	MINGIER	EGILLNT	TELLING
EGIIMNT	ITEMING	EGILLNW	WELLING
EGIIMNV	MIEVING	EGILLNY	YELLING
EGIIMPS	PIGMIES	EGILLOS	GOLLIES
EGIIMRR	GRIMIER	EGILLRS	GRILLES
EGIIMSV	MISGIVE	EGILLST	GILLETS
EGIINNP	PEINING	EGILLSU	GULLIES
EGIINNR	REINING		LIGULES
EGIINNS	INGINES	EGILMMN	LEMMING
	INSIGNE	EGILMMR	GLIMMER
	SEINING	EGILMNR	GREMLIN
EGIINNV	VEINING		MERLING
EGIINOP	EPIGONI		MINGLER
EGIINPS	PEISING	EGILMNS	MINGLES
	PIGSNIE	EGILMNT	MELTING
EGIINPZ	PEIZING	EGILMNU	EMULING
EGIINRR	GIRNIER		LEGUMIN
EGIINRT	IGNITER	EGILMNW	MEWLING
	TIERING	EGILMNY	YELMING
	TIGRINE	EGILMOR	GOMERIL
EGIINRV	REIVING	EGILMOS	SEMILOG
	RIEVING	EGILMOU	ELOGIUM
EGIINRW	WEIRING	EGILMPS	GLIMPSE
	WINGIER		MEGILPS
EGIINRZ	ZINGIER	EGILMST	GIMLETS
EGIINSS	SEISING	EGILNNS	GINNELS
EGIINST	IGNITES	EGILNOP	ELOPING
EGIINSV	SIEVING	EGILNOS	ELOIGNS
	VISEING		LEGIONS
EGIINSW	WEISING		LINGOES
EGIINSZ	SEIZING	EGILNOT	LENTIGO
EGIINTV	EVITING	EGILNPP	LEPPING
EGIINTX	EXITING	EGILNPR	PINGLER
EGIINVW	VIEWING	EGILNPS	PINGLES
EGIINWZ	WEIZING		SPIGNEL
EGIIPPS	GIPPIES	EGILNPT	PELTING
EGIIPRW	PERIWIG	EGILNPY	YELPING
EGIIPSS	GIPSIES	EGILNRS	GIRNELS
EGIJKNR	JERKING		LINGERS
EGIJLLN	JELLING		SLINGER
EGIJLNR	JINGLER	EGILNRT	RINGLET
EGIJLNS	JINGLES		TINGLER
EGIJLNT	JINGLET		TRINGLE
EGIJNOS	JINGOES	EGILNRY	RELYING
EGIJNST	JESTING	EGILNSS	SINGLES
EGIJNTT	JETTING	EGILNST	GLISTEN
EGIKKLN	LEKKING		LESTING
EGIKLNS	KINGLES		SINGLET
EGIKLNT	KINGLET		TINGLES

EGILNSU	LUNGIES		MISGOES
	SLUEING	EGIMOST	EGOTISM
EGILNSW	SLEWING	EGIMPSU	GUIMPES
	SWINGLE	EGIMPSY	PYGMIES
EGILNSZ	ZINGELS	EGIMSST	STIGMES
EGILNTT	ETTLING	EGINNNP	PENNING
	LETTING	EGINNNR	RENNING
EGILNTU	ELUTING	EGINNNY	YENNING
EGILNTW	WELTING	EGINNOP	OPENING
	WINGLET	EGINNPU	PENGUIN
EGILNVY	LEVYING	EGINNRR	GRINNER
EGILOOS	GOOLIES	EGINNRS	ENRINGS
	OLOGIES		GINNERS
EGILORS	GLOIRES	EGINNRT	RENTING
	GLORIES		RINGENT
EGILOSS	GLIOSES		TERNING
EGILOST	ELOGIST	EGINNRU	ENURING
EGILOSU	OUGLIES	EGINNRV	NERVING
EGILPPR	GRIPPLE	EGINNRY	GINNERY
EGILPST	PIGLETS		RENYING
EGILPSY	GILPEYS	EGINNSS	ENSIGNS
EGILRRU	GURLIER		SENSING
EGILRSS	GRILSES	EGINNST	NESTING
EGILRST	GLISTER		SENTING
	GRISTLE		TENSING
EGILRSU	GUILERS	EGINNSU	ENSUING
	LIGURES		GUNNIES
	LURGIES		INGENUS
EGILRSY	GREISLY	EGINNSW	NEWSING
	GRIESLY	EGINNSY	GYNNIES
	GRISELY	EGINNTT	NETTING
EGILRTT	GLITTER		TENTING
EGILRTY	TIGERLY	EGINNTV	VENTING
EGILRUV	VIRGULE	EGINNVY	ENVYING
EGILRZZ	GRIZZLE	EGINOPR	PERIGON
EGILSST	LEGISTS		PONGIER
EGILSSW	WIGLESS	EGINOPS	EPIGONS
EGILSTU	GLUIEST		PIGEONS
	UGLIEST		PINGOES
EGILSTZ	GLITZES	EGINORR	IGNORER
EGIMMRR	GRIMMER	EGINORS	ERINGOS
EGIMMRS	GIMMERS		IGNORES
	MEGRIMS		REGIONS
EGIMMRU	GUMMIER		SIGNORE
EGIMMTU	GUMMITE	EGINORT	GENITOR
EGIMNNN	NEMNING	EGINORV	OVERING
EGIMNNO	OMENING	EGINORZ	ZEROING
EGIMNNR	RINGMEN	EGINOSU	IGNEOUS
EGIMNNS	MENSING	EGINOSW	INGOWES
EGIMNOS	MISGONE		WIGEONS
EGIMNOT	EMOTING	EGINOSY	ISOGENY
	MITOGEN	EGINOTT	TENTIGO
EGIMNOV	EMOVING	EGINOTV	VETOING
EGIMNOW	MEOWING	EGINPPP	PEPPING
EGIMNPR	IMPREGN	EGINPPR	REPPING
	PERMING	EGINPPS	PIGPENS
EGIMNPT	PIGMENT	EGINPRS	PERSING
	TEMPING		PINGERS
EGIMNQU	QUEMING		SPRINGE
EGIMNRS	GERMINS	EGINPRU	PUERING
EGIMNRT	METRING	EGINPRV	PERVING
	TERMING		PREVING
EGIMNRU	EMURING	EGINPRY	PREYING
EGIMNSS	MESSING	EGINPSS	GIPSENS
EGIMNST	STEMING	EGINPSU	SPUEING
	TEMSING	EGINPSW	SPEWING
EGIMNSU	MEUSING	EGINPSY	ESPYING
EGIMNSW	MEWSING		PEYSING
EGIMORR	GORMIER		PIGSNEY
EGIMOSS	EGOISMS	EGINPTT	PETTING

EGINPYY	EPIGYNY		
EGINQUU	QUEUING		
EGINRRS	ERRINGS		
	RINGERS		
	SERRING		
EGINRRW	WRINGER		
EGINRSS	INGRESS		
	RESIGNS		
	SIGNERS		
	SINGERS		
EGINRST	RESTING		
	STINGER		
EGINRSU	REUSING		
	RUEINGS		
	SIGNEUR		
EGINRSV	SERVING		
	VERSING		
EGINRSW	SWINGER		
	WINGERS		
EGINRSY	SYRINGE		
EGINRTT	GITTERN		
	RETTING		
EGINRTU	TRUEING		
EGINRTV	VERTING		
EGINRTY	RETYING		
EGINRVV	REVVING		
EGINRVY	REVYING		
EGINSST	INGESTS		
	SIGNETS		
EGINSSW	SEWINGS		
	SWINGES		
EGINSTT	SETTING		
	TESTING		
EGINSTU	GUNITES		
EGINSTV	VESTING		
EGINSTW	STEWING		
	TWINGES		
	WESTING		
EGINSVX	VEXINGS		
EGINSZZ	GIZZENS		
EGINTTV	VETTING		
EGINTTW	WETTING		
EGIOOPR	GOOPIER		
EGIOORS	GOOSIER		
EGIOOSS	GOOSIES		
	SOOGIES		
EGIOOST	GOOIEST		
EGIOPRS	PORGIES		
	SERPIGO		
EGIOPRU	GROUPIE		
	PIROGUE		
EGIORRS	GORSIER		
EGIORST	GOITERS		
	GOITRES		
	GORIEST		
EGIORTU	GOUTIER		
EGIORTV	VERTIGO		
EGIORTZ	ZORGITE		
EGIORUV	VOGUIER		
EGIOSST	EGOISTS		
	STOGIES		
EGIOSTT	EGOTIST		
EGIOSTV	VOGIEST		
EGIOTUV	OUTGIVE		
EGIPPRR	GRIPPER		
EGIPPRS	GRIPPES		
EGIPPSU	GUPPIES		
EGIPPSY	GYPPIES		
EGIPRRS	GRIPERS		
EGIPRUU	GUIPURE		

EGIPSSY	GYPSIES
EGIRRSU	GURRIES
	SURGIER
EGIRRSV	VIRGERS
EGIRRTT	GRITTER
EGIRSST	TIGRESS
EGIRSSU	GUISERS
EGIRSTU	GUSTIER
	GUTSIER
EGIRSTV	GRIVETS
EGIRSUZ	GUIZERS
EGISTTU	GUTTIES
EGJLNSU	JUNGLES
EGKLORW	LEGWORK
EGKMSSU	MUSKEGS
EGLLRSU	GULLERS
EGLLRUY	GULLERY
EGLLSTU	GULLETS
EGLLSUY	GULLEYS
EGLMMRU	GLUMMER
EGLMNOO	ENGLOOM
EGLMNOR	MONGREL
EGLMOOR	LEGROOM
EGLNNSU	GUNNELS
EGLNOOY	NEOLOGY
EGLNOPS	PLONGES
EGLNORU	LOUNGER
EGLNOST	LONGEST
EGLNOSU	LOUNGES
EGLNOUV	UNGLOVE
EGLNOXY	LOXYGEN
	XYLOGEN
EGLNOYZ	LOZENGY
EGLNPRU	PLUNGER
EGLNPSU	PLUNGES
EGLNRTU	GRUNTLE
EGLNSSU	GUNSELS
EGLNSTU	ENGLUTS
	GLUTENS
EGLNSUU	UNGLUES
EGLOOSY	GOOLEYS
EGLOPRS	PROLEGS
EGLOPSS	GOSPELS
EGLORRW	GROWLER
EGLORSS	GLOSSER
EGLORSU	REGULOS
EGLORSV	GLOVERS
	GROVELS
EGLORSW	GLOWERS
EGLOSSS	GLOSSES
EGLOSST	GOSLETS
EGLOSUV	VOULGES
EGLPRSU	GULPERS
	SPLURGE
EGLRSTU	GURLETS
EGLRSUU	REGULUS
EGLRSUY	GUYLERS
EGLRSYY	GRYSELY
	GRYSELY
EGLRUZZ	GUZZLER
EGLSSTU	GUTLESS
EGLSTTU	GUTTLES
EGLSTUU	GLUTEUS
EGLSUZZ	GUZZLES
EGMMORT	GROMMET
EGMMRRU	GRUMMER
EGMMRTU	GRUMMET
EGMNNOS	SONGMEN
EGMNNOW	GOWNMEN
EGMNORS	MONGERS

	MORGENS
EGMNORU	MURGEON
EGMNORY	MONGERY
EGMNOST	EMONGST
EGMNOSY	MYOGENS
EGMNOYZ	ZYMOGEN
EGMNSTU	NUTMEGS
EGMORST	GROMETS
EGMORSU	GRUMOSE
	MORGUES
EGMORTU	GOURMET
EGMRSTU	TERGUMS
EGNNORT	RONTGEN
EGNNOSU	GUENONS
EGNNPTU	PUNGENT
EGNNRSU	GUNNERS
EGNNRUY	GUNNERY
EGNNSYY	GYNNEYS
EGNNTUU	UNGUENT
EGNOOPS	PONGOES
EGNOORS	ORGONES
	OROGENS
EGNOORY	OROGENY
EGNOOST	GENTOOS
EGNOOSY	GOONEYS
EGNOOTU	OUTGONE
EGNOOYZ	ZOOGENY
EGNOPRS	SPONGER
EGNOPRY	PROGENY
	PYROGEN
EGNOPSS	SPONGES
EGNOPSW	GOWPENS
EGNORRW	WRONGER
EGNORSS	ENGROSS
EGNORSU	SURGEON
EGNORSV	GOVERNS
EGNORSY	ERYNGOS
	GROYNES
EGNORUY	YOUNGER
EGNOSTU	TONGUES
EGNOSXY	OXYGENS
EGNPRSU	REPUGNS
EGNPSSU	SPUNGES
EGNPSUX	EXPUGNS
EGNRRTU	GRUNTER
EGNRSTU	GUNTERS
	GURNETS
	SURGENT
EGNRSUY	GURNEYS
EGNRSYY	SYNERGY
EGNRTTU	GRUTTEN
	TURGENT
EGNSUVY	UNGYVES
EGOOPSY	POOGYES
EGOORSV	GROOVES
EGOORSY	GOOSERY
EGOORTU	OUTGOER
EGOORTV	OVERGOT
EGOOSST	STOOGES
EGOOSSY	GOOSEYS
EGOOSTU	OUTGOES
EGOPRRS	GROPERS
EGOPRRU	GROUPER
	REGROUP
EGORRSS	GROSERS
	GROSSER
EGORRST	GROSERT
EGORRSU	GROUSER
EGORRSW	GROWERS
EGORRUY	ROGUERY

EGORSSS	GROSSES
EGORSST	GROSETS
	STORGES
EGORSSU	GROUSES
EGORTUW	OUTGREW
EGOSSTY	STOGEYS
EGOSSYZ	ZYGOSES
EGOSTTU	GOUTTES
EGOSTYZ	ZYGOTES
EGPRRSU	PURGERS
EGPRSSU	SPURGES
EGPRSUU	UPSURGE
EGRRSUY	SURGERY
EGRSSUY	GYRUSES
EGRSTTU	GUTTERS
EGRSTUZ	GUTZERS
EGSSSTU	GUSSETS
EHHIKSS	SHEIKHS
EHHILLS	HELLISH
EHHIPRS	HERSHIP
EHHIRST	HITHERS
EHHIRSU	HUSHIER
EHHIRTT	THITHER
EHHIRTW	WHITHER
EHHISSW	WHEYISH
EHHISWY	WHEYISH
EHHNPSY	HYPHENS
EHHOOSS	HOOSHES
EHHORTT	THOTHER
EHHRSSU	HUSHERS
EHHSSSU	SHUSHES
EHIILLR	HILLIER
EHIILTT	LITHITE
EHIINNS	HINNIES
EHIINRS	SHINIER
EHIINRT	INHERIT
EHIINRW	WHINIER
EHIINRZ	RHIZINE
EHIIPPR	HIPPIER
EHIIPPS	HIPPIES
EHIIPRT	PITHIER
EHIIRST	HIRSTIE
EHIIRTW	WHITIER
	WITHIER
EHIISST	STISHIE
EHIISTW	WHITIES
	WITHIES
EHIJNNO	JOHNNIE
EHIKLRU	HULKIER
EHIKMNT	METHINK
EHIKNOS	HONKIES
EHIKNRS	KERNISH
EHIKNRT	RETHINK
	THINKER
EHIKNRU	HUNKIER
EHIKNSS	KNISHES
EHIKNSU	HUNKIES
EHIKOOR	HOOKIER
EHIKOOS	HOOKIES
EHIKOST	HOKIEST
EHIKPRS	KEPHIRS
EHIKRRS	SHIRKER
EHIKRSS	SHREIKS
	SHRIEKS
	SHRIKES
EHIKRSU	HUSKIER
EHIKRSW	WHISKER
EHIKSSS	SHIKSES
EHIKSSU	HUSKIES
EHIKSTW	WHISKET

EHIKSWY	WHISKEY	EHIMTYZ	MYTHIZE
EHILLMN	HILLMEN	EHINNNS	HENNINS
EHILLNO	HELLION	EHINNRT	THINNER
EHILLNS	INSHELL	EHINNSS	SHINNES
EHILLOS	HILLOES	EHINNSW	WENNISH
	HOLLIES	EHINOPR	PHONIER
EHILLRS	RELLISH	EHINOPS	PHONIES
EHILLRT	THILLER	EHINOPX	PHOENIX
EHILLRU	HULLIER	EHINORR	HORNIER
EHILLTY	LITHELY	EHINORS	HEROINS
EHILMPW	WHIMPLE		INSHORE
EHILMSU	HELIUMS	EHINOST	HISTONE
	HUMLIES	EHINOSU	HEINOUS
EHILMTT	MELTITH	EHINPPS	SHIPPEN
EHILMUW	UMWHILE	EHINRSS	SHINERS
EHILNOP	PINHOLE		SHRINES
EHILNOT	NEOLITH	EHINRSV	SHRIVEN
EHILNPS	PLENISH	EHINRSW	WHINERS
EHILNSS	ELSHINS	EHINRTV	THRIVEN
EHILOOR	HOOLIER	EHINRTW	WRITHEN
EHILOPT	HOPLITE	EHINRTZ	ZITHERN
EHILOSS	ISOHELS	EHINSSS	SHINESS
EHILOST	EOLITHS	EHINSST	SITHENS
	HOLIEST	EHINSTW	WHITENS
	HOSTILE	EHINSTZ	ZENITHS
EHILPRS	HIRPLES	EHINSUV	UNHIVES
EHILPRT	PHILTER	EHIOPPR	HOPPIER
	PHILTRE	EHIOPST	ETHIOPS
EHILRRW	WHIRLER		OPHITES
EHILRSS	HIRSELS	EHIORRS	HORSIER
	HIRSLES	EHIORRT	HERITOR
EHILRST	SLITHER	EHIORSS	HOSIERS
EHILRSU	HURLIES	EHIORST	HERIOTS
	LUSHIER		HOISTER
EHILRSV	SHRIVEL		SHORTIE
EHILRTU	LUTHIER		TOSHIER
EHILRTW	WHIRTLE	EHIORSW	SHOWIER
EHILSSS	SLISHES	EHIORSY	HOSIERY
EHILSTT	LISTETH	EHIORTT	THORITE
	LITHEST	EHIORTU	OUTHIRE
	THISTLE		ROUTHIE
EHILSTV	THIVELS	EHIORTV	OVERHIT
EHILSTW	WHISTLE	EHIOSTT	HOTTIES
EHILTTU	THULITE	EHIOSTY	ISOHYET
EHILTTW	WHITTLE	EHIPPRS	SHIPPER
EHILTWY	WHITELY	EHIPPRW	WHIPPER
EHIMMRS	SHIMMER	EHIPPST	HIPPEST
EHIMNPS	SHIPMEN	EHIPPTW	WHIPPET
EHIMNRS	MENHIRS	EHIPRSS	RESHIPS
EHIMNRU	RHENIUM		SERIPHS
EHIMNSU	INHUMES	EHIPRST	HIPSTER
EHIMNTY	THYMINE	EHIPRSU	PUSHIER
EHIMORS	HEROISM	EHIPRSW	WHISPER
	MOREISH	EHIPSTT	PETTISH
EHIMORT	MOITHER	EHIPSZZ	PHIZZES
	MOTHIER	EHIRRSS	SHERRIS
EHIMORZ	RHIZOME	EHIRRSU	HURRIES
EHIMOST	HOMIEST		RUSHIER
EHIMPRU	HUMPIER	EHIRRSV	SHRIVER
EHIMPRW	WHIMPER	EHIRRTV	THRIVER
EHIMPSU	HUMPIES	EHIRRTW	WHIRRET
EHIMRST	HERMITS	EHIRSSV	SHIVERS
	MITHERS		SHRIVES
EHIMRSU	HEURISM	EHIRSSW	SWISHER
	MUSHIER		WISHERS
EHIMRTY	THYMIER	EHIRSTT	HITTERS
EHIMSST	THEISMS		TITHERS
EHIMSTU	HUMITES	EHIRSTU	HIRSUTE
EHIMSTY	MYTHISE	EHIRSTV	THRIVES
EHIMSWY	WHIMSEY	EHIRSTW	SWITHER

	WITHERS	EHLRSSU	LUSHERS
	WRITHES	EHLRSTU	HURTLES
EHIRSTZ	ZITHERS		HUSTLER
EHIRSVY	SHIVERY	EHLRSUY	HURLEYS
EHIRTTW	WHITRET	EHLSSSU	SLUSHES
	WHITTER	EHLSSTT	SHTETLS
EHIRWZZ	WHIZZER	EHLSSTU	HUSTLES
EHISSSU	HUSSIES		LUSHEST
EHISSSW	SWISHES		SLEUTHS
	WHISSES	EHLSTTU	SHUTTLE
EHISSTT	THEISTS	EHMMRSU	HUMMERS
EHISSTU	STUSHIE	EHMNOOR	HORMONE
EHISTTW	TEWHITS		MOORHEN
	WETTISH	EHMNOPS	SHOPMEN
	WHITEST	EHMNOST	MONETHS
EHISTWY	WHITEYS	EHMNOSW	SHOWMEN
EHISUZZ	HUZZIES	EHMNPSU	HUMPENS
EHISWZZ	WHIZZES	EHMNPTY	NYMPHET
EHJOPSS	JOSEPHS	EHMNTTU	HUTMENT
EHJORSS	JOSHERS	EHMOOSS	SHMOOSE
EHKLNOS	LOKSHEN	EHMOOST	SMOOTHE
EHKLPST	KLEPHTS	EHMOOSW	SOMEHOW
EHKNORS	HONKERS	EHMOOSZ	SHMOOZE
EHKNRSU	HUNKERS	EHMOPRW	MORPHEW
	HUNKSES	EHMORST	MOTHERS
EHKOORS	HOOKERS		SMOTHER
EHKOOSY	HOOKEYS		THERMOS
EHKORSS	KOSHERS	EHMORTU	MOUTHER
EHKORSW	HOWKERS	EHMORTY	MOTHERY
EHKORSY	HORKEYS	EHMOSWY	SOMEWHY
EHKRSSU	HUSKERS	EHMPRTU	THUMPER
EHLLNSU	UNSHELL	EHMRRSY	RHYMERS
EHLLOOS	HOLLOES	EHMRRTU	MURTHER
EHLLORS	HOLLERS	EHMRSSU	MUSHERS
EHLLOSU	HULLOES	EHMRSTY	RYTHMES
EHLMMOW	WHOMMLE	EHMRSUU	HUMERUS
EHLMMSU	HUMMELS	EHMSSUU	HUMUSES
EHLMMUW	WHUMMLE	EHNNOPR	NEPHRON
EHLMNOT	MENTHOL	EHNNOPY	HYPNONE
EHLMNOY	HOMELYN	EHNNSTU	UNSHENT
EHLMNSU	UNHELMS	EHNNSUW	UNSHEWN
EHLMOOS	HOLESOM	EHNOORS	HEROONS
EHLMOPS	PHLOEMS		ONSHORE
EHLMSSU	MULSHES		SOREHON
EHLMSTY	METHYLS	EHNOPRY	HYPERON
EHLNOPS	PHENOLS	EHNOPSU	EUPHONS
EHLNORT	HORNLET	EHNOPSY	PHONEYS
EHLNPSY	PHENYLS	EHNOPUY	EUPHONY
EHLNRTU	LUTHERN	EHNORRS	HORNERS
EHLNTTY	TENTHLY	EHNORRT	HORRENT
EHLOOPT	POTHOLE		NORTHER
EHLOOSY	HOOLEYS	EHNORRY	HERONRY
EHLOPPS	HOPPLES	EHNORST	HORNETS
EHLOPSX	PHLOXES		SHORTEN
EHLORST	HOLSTER		THRENOS
	HOSTLER		THRONES
EHLORSW	HOWLERS	EHNORSU	UNHORSE
EHLORTY	HELOTRY	EHNOSST	HOTNESS
EHLOSSS	SLOSHES	EHNOSSU	UNSHOES
EHLOSST	HOSTELS	EHNOSTT	SHOTTEN
EHLOSSU	HOUSELS	EHNOSTY	HONESTY
EHLOSSV	SHOVELS	EHNOSUU	UNHOUSE
EHLOSTT	LOTHEST	EHNPRSY	PHRENSY
	SHOTTLE	EHNRSTU	HUNTERS
EHLOSTW	HOWLETS		SHUNTER
	THOWELS		UNHERST
EHLOSTY	THYLOSE	EHNRTWY	WRYTHEN
EHLPRSU	PLUSHER	EHNSSSU	SNUSHES
EHLPSSU	PLUSHES	EHNSSSY	SHYNESS
EHLRRSU	HURLERS	EHOOOPS	HOOPOES

EHOOPRS	HOOPERS	EIIKNPS PINKIES	UTILIZE	UNITISE
EHOOPRW	WHOOPER	EIIKNRS SINKIER	EIILTXY EXILITY	EIINSTV INVITES
EHOOPTY	OOPHYTE	EIIKNRZ ZINKIER	EIIMMSS MIMESIS	VINIEST
EHOORST	HOOTERS	EIIKNSS KINESIS	EIIMMST MISTIME	EIINSTW WINIEST
	SHOOTER	EIIKNST INKIEST	EIIMMSX IMMIXES	EIINTUV UNITIVE
	SOOTHER	EIIKPRS SPIKIER	EIIMNNS MINNIES	EIINTUZ UNITIZE
EHOORSV	HOOVERS	EIIKPSS PISKIES	EIIMNPR PRIMINE	EIIORST RIOTISE
EHOOSST	SOOTHES	EIIKRRS RISKIER	EIIMNRT INTERIM	EIIORSV IVORIES
EHOOSSW	WOOSHES	EIIKRSV SKIVIER	MINTIER	EIIORTZ RIOTIZE
EHOPPRS	HOPPERS	EIIKSTT KITTIES	TERMINI	EIIOSTZ ZOISITE
	SHOPPER	EIILLMM MILLIME	EIIMNRV MINIVER	EIIPPPR PIPPIER
EHOPPRT	PROPHET	EIILLMT LIMELIT	EIIMNST MINIEST	EIIPPRR RIPPIER
EHOPPRW	WHOPPER	EIILLNV VILLEIN	EIIMNTV MINIVET	EIIPPRT TIPPIER
EHOPRRY	ORPHREY	EIILLPS ILLIPES	EIIMNTY NIMIETY	EIIPPRZ ZIPPIER
EHOPRST	POTHERS	EIILLRS SILLIER	EIIMOSS MEIOSIS	EIIPPST PIPIEST
	STROPHE	EIILLRT TILLIER	EIIMPRS PISMIRE	EIIPPSY YIPPIES
	THORPES	EIILLSS SILLIES	PRIMSIE	EIIPRRS SPIRIER
EHOPRSU	UPHROES	EIILLST ILLITES	EIIMPRW WIMPIER	EIIPRRV PRIVIER
EHOPRTU	POUTHER	EIILLSW WILLIES	EIIMPST PIETISM	EIIPRST PITIERS
EHOPRTY	POTHERY	EIILLTT TILLITE	EIIMPTY IMPIETY	TIPSIER
EHOPRUY	EUPHORY	EIILLTV VITELLI	EIIMRSS MISSIER	EIIPRSV PRIVIES
EHOPSSS	SPOSHES	EIILMNV MILVINE	EIIMRST MIRIEST	EIIPRSW SWIPIER
EHOPSST	POSHEST	EIILMPR IMPERIL	MISTIER	WISPIER
EHORRSS	SHORERS	EIILMPS IMPLIES	RIMIEST	EIIPSTT PIETIST
EHORRST	RHETORS	EIILMPT LIMEPIT	EIIMSSS MISSIES	EIIPTTT PITTITE
	ROTHERS	EIILMRR MIRLIER	EIIMSST ISMIEST	EIIPTTU PITUITE
	SHORTER	EIILMRS MILREIS	STIMIES	EIIRRTZ RITZIER
EHORRTW	THROWER	EIILMRT LIMITER	EIIMSSV MISSIVE	EIIRSSS SISSIER
EHORSST	TOSHERS	EIILMSS MISSILE	EIIMSTT MITIEST	EIIRSSV VISIERS
EHORSSV	SHOVERS	SIMILES	EIIMSTX MIXIEST	EIIRSTV REVISIT
	SHROVES	EIILMST ELITISM	EIINNNS NINNIES	STIVIER
EHORSSW	SHOWERS	LIMIEST	EIINNPS PINNIES	VISITER
EHORSTT	HOTTERS	LIMITES	EIINNQU QUININE	EIIRSTW WIRIEST
EHORSTU	SHOUTER	EIILMSU MILIEUS	EIINNRT TINNIER	EIIRSVZ VIZIERS
	SOUTHER	EIILMSV MISLIVE	EIINNST INTINES	EIIRSWZ WIZIERS
EHORSTW	THROWES	EIILMUX MILIEUX	TINNIES	EIIRTTW WITTIER
EHORSTX	EXHORTS	EIILNNS LINNIES	EIINNSW INSINEW	EIISSSS SISSIES
EHORSWY	SHOWERY	EIILNOS ELISION	EIINNTV INVENIT	EIISSTV VISITES
EHORTUY	OUTHYRE	ISOLINE	EIINNTW INTWINE	EIISSTX SIXTIES
EHOSSST	HOSTESS	LIONISE	EIINOPR RIPIENO	EIISSTZ SIZIEST
EHOSTTT	HOTTEST	EIILNOT ETIOLIN	EIINOPS PIONIES	EIISTTT TITTIES
EHOTTTW	WOTTETH	EIILNOV OLIVINE	EIINORS IONISER	EIISTUV UVEITIS
EHPRSSU	PUSHERS	EIILNOZ LIONIZE	IRONIES	EIISTZZ TIZZIES
EHPRSYZ	ZEPHYRS	EIILNPS SPLENII	IRONISE	EIISVZZ VIZZIES
EHPRTTU	TURPETH	EIILNRR NIRLIER	NOISIER	EIJKNPR PERJINK
EHPRTUW	UPTHREW	EIILNRS INLIERS	EIINORZ IONIZER	PREJINK
EHRRSSU	RUSHERS	EIILNRT LINTIER	IRONIZE	EIJKNRS JERKINS
EHRRSTU	HURTERS	NITRILE	EIINOSS IONISES	JINKERS
EHRSSTY	SHYSTER	EIILNSS INISLES	EIINOSZ IONIZES	EIJKNRU JUNKIER
	THYRSES	EIILNST INLIEST	EIINPPR NIPPIER	EIJKNSU JUNKIES
EHRSTTU	SHUTTER	LINIEST	EIINPRS INSPIRE	EIJKOST JOKIEST
EHRSTTW	STREWTH	LINTIES	PIRNIES	EIJLLNY INJELLY
EHRSTUW	WUTHERS	EIILORR ROILIER	SNIPIER	EIJLLOR JOLLIER
EHRSTUY	TUSHERY	EIILORS SOILIER	SPINIER	EIJLLOS JOLLIES
EHRTTTY	THRETTY	EIILORV RILIEVO	EIINPST PINIEST	EIJLLST JILLETS
EHSSSTU	TUSSEHS	EIILOST IOLITES	PINITES	EIJLORT JOLTIER
EIIILRV	RILIEVI	OILIEST	EIINQRU INQUIRE	EIJMPRU JUMPIER
EIIILST	ILEITIS	EIILPPR LIPPIER	EIINQSU QUINIES	EIJMPST JIMPEST
EIIINPR	RIPIENI	EIILPPS LIPPIES	EIINQTU INQUIET	EIJNNOS ENJOINS
EIIJMMS	JIMMIES	EIILPST SPILITE	EIINRTT NITRITE	EIJNORS JOINERS
EIIJMPR	JIMPIER	EIILQSU SILIQUE	NITTIER	REJOINS
EIIKKNR	KINKIER	EIILRST SILTIER	TINTIER	EIJNORT JOINTER
EIIKLMR	MILKIER	EIILRSX ELIXIRS	EIINRTV INVITER	EIJNORY JOINERY
EIIKLMS	MISLIKE	EIILSSV VISILES	VITRINE	EIJNOST JONTIES
EIIKLPS	PLISKIE	EIILSTT ELITIST	EIINRTW TWINIER	EIJNPRU JUNIPER
EIIKLRS	SILKIER	EIILSTU UTILISE	EIINSSS SEISINS	EIJNRRU INJURER
EIIKLSS	SILKIES	EIILSTW WILIEST	EIINSSZ SEIZINS	EIJNRSU INJURES
EIIKLST	KILTIES	EIILTUY TUILYIE	EIINSTT SITTINE	EIJNSTY JITNEYS
EIIKMRR	MIRKIER	EIILTUZ TUILZIE	TINIEST	EIJRSTT JITTERS
EIIKNPR	PINKIER		EIINSTU UNITIES	EIJRTTY JITTERY

EIJSSUV	JUSSIVE	EIKNOSS	KENOSIS
EIJSTTU	JUTTIES	EIKNOSV	INVOKES
EIKKLNR	KLINKER	EIKNPRS	PERKINS
EIKKLNS	KINKLES	EIKNPST	PINKEST
EIKKNRS	SKINKER	EIKNPSU	SPUNKIE
EIKKOOR	KOOKIER	EIKNRSS	SINKERS
EIKKRSY	YIKKERS	EIKNRST	SKINTER
EIKKRUY	YUKKIER		STINKER
EIKLLNW	INKWELL		TINKERS
EIKLLOS	SKOLLIE	EIKNRSW	WINKERS
EIKLLRS	KILLERS	EIKNRTT	KNITTER
EIKLLST	SKILLET		TRINKET
EIKLMMN	MILKMEN	EIKNSSU	SUNKIES
EIKLMNN	LINKMEN	EIKNSTT	KITTENS
EIKLMNR	KREMLIN	EIKNTTY	KITTENY
EIKLMRS	MILKERS	EIKOORS	ROOKIES
EIKLNNS	ENLINKS	EIKOPPS	KOPPIES
EIKLNRS	SLINKER	EIKOPRR	PORKIER
EIKLNRT	TINKLER	EIKOPST	POKIEST
EIKLNRW	WINKLER	EIKORST	ROKIEST
	WRINKLE	EIKORSY	YORKIES
EIKLNSS	KINLESS	EIKOSST	KETOSIS
	SILKENS	EIKPPRS	KIPPERS
EIKLNST	LENTISK		SKIPPER
	TINKLES	EIKPPST	SKIPPET
EIKLNSU	SUNLIKE	EIKPSSS	SKEPSIS
	UNLIKES	EIKRRSS	RISKERS
EIKLNSV	KELVINS	EIKRRST	SKIRRET
EIKLNSW	WELKINS		SKIRTER
	WINKLES		STRIKER
EIKLNSY	SKYLINE	EIKRSSS	KISSERS
EIKLNTT	KNITTLE	EIKRSST	STRIKES
EIKLNTW	TWINKLE	EIKRSSV	SKIVERS
EIKLOOP	PLOOKIE	EIKRSTT	SKITTER
EIKLOPU	PLOUKIE	EIKRSTU	TURKIES
EIKLORY	YOLKIER		TUSKIER
EIKLPRY	PERKILY	EIKSSTW	WISKETS
EIKLPSY	PESKILY	EIKSSTY	SKYIEST
EIKLRST	KILTERS	EIKSTUY	YUKIEST
	KIRTLES	EILLLOS	LOLLIES
EIKLRSU	SULKIER	EILLMNU	MULLEIN
EIKLRTT	KITTLER	EILLMOS	MOLLIES
EIKLSSU	SULKIES	EILLMOT	MELILOT
EIKLSTT	KITTLES	EILLMOU	MOUILLE
	SKITTLE	EILLMRS	MILLERS
EIKMMRR	KRIMMER	EILLMST	MILLETS
EIKMMRS	KIMMERS		MISTELL
	SKIMMER	EILLMSU	ILLUMES
EIKMNNS	KINSMEN	EILLNNP	PENNILL
EIKMNOR	MONIKER	EILLNOS	LIONELS
EIKMNRS	MERKINS		NIELLOS
EIKMNSS	MISKENS	EILLNSS	ILLNESS
EIKMNST	MISKENT	EILLNST	LENTILS
EIKMNSW	MISKNEW		LINTELS
EIKMORS	IRKSOME	EILLOPS	POLLIES
	SMOKIER	EILLORW	LOWLIER
EIKMOSS	SMOKIES	EILLORZ	ZORILLE
EIKMOSY	MISYOKE	EILLOST	OILLETS
EIKMRRU	MURKIER	EILLOSV	VILLOSE
EIKMRSS	KIRMESS	EILLOSW	WOLLIES
EIKMRST	MIRKEST	EILLPRS	SPILLER
EIKMRSU	MUSKIER	EILLPSS	LIPLESS
EIKMSST	KISMETS	EILLPSU	PILULES
EIKNNOS	KINONES	EILLQTU	QUILLET
EIKNNRS	SKINNER	EILLRSS	SILLERS
EIKNOOR	NOOKIER	EILLRST	RILLETS
	ROOINEK		STILLER
EIKNOOS	NOOKIES		TILLERS
EIKNOPS	PINKOES		TRELLIS
EIKNORW	WONKIER	EILLRSW	SWILLER

	WILLERS	EILNOOR	LOONIER
EILLRTT	LITTLER	EILNOOS	LOONIES
EILLSST	LISTELS	EILNOOV	VIOLONE
EILLSSU	SULLIES	EILNOPP	PLENIPO
EILLSTT	LITTLES	EILNOPR	PROLINE
EILLSTU	TUILLES	EILNOPS	EPSILON
EILLSTW	WILLEST		PINOLES
	WILLETS	EILNOPT	POINTEL
EILLSWY	WILLEYS		PONTILE
EILMMNO	MOLIMEN	EILNORR	LORINER
EILMMRS	LIMMERS	EILNORS	NEROLIS
	SLIMMER	EILNORT	RETINOL
EILMMRU	LUMMIER	EILNOSS	ESLOINS
EILMNOS	MOLINES		INSOLES
EILMNRS	LIMNERS		LESIONS
	MERLINS		LIONESS
EILMNSS	SIMNELS	EILNOST	ENTOILS
EILMNSU	EMULSIN		LIONETS
	LUMINES	EILNOSU	ELUSION
	UNLIMES	EILNOTU	ELUTION
EILMNSY	MYELINS		OUTLINE
EILMOOS	MOOLIES	EILNOTV	VIOLENT
EILMOPR	IMPLORE	EILNOTW	TOWLINE
EILMORR	LORIMER	EILNOVV	INVOLVE
EILMORS	MOILERS	EILNPPS	LIPPENS
EILMORT	MOTLIER		NIPPLES
EILMOSS	LIMOSES	EILNPRS	PILSNER
	LISSOME	EILNPRU	PURLINE
	SMOILES	EILNPSS	PENSILS
EILMOST	MOTILES		SPINELS
EILMPPS	PIMPLES		SPLINES
EILMPPU	PLUMPIE	EILNPST	PINTLES
EILMPRS	PRELIMS		PLENIST
	SIMPLER	EILNPSU	LUPINES
EILMPRU	LUMPIER		SPINULE
	PLUMIER	EILNPTY	INEPTLY
EILMPRY	PRIMELY	EILNPUV	VULPINE
EILMPSS	SIMPLES	EILNRST	LINTERS
EILMPST	LIMPEST		SNIRTLE
	LIMPETS	EILNRSV	SILVERN
EILMPSU	IMPULSE	EILNRTY	INERTLY
EILMPSW	WIMPLES	EILNSSS	SINLESS
EILMPSX	SIMPLEX	EILNSST	ENLISTS
EILMPTY	EMPTILY		LISTENS
EILMRRU	MURLIER		SILENTS
EILMRRY	MERRILY		TINSELS
EILMRSS	RIMLESS	EILNSSU	INSULSE
	SMILERS		SILENUS
EILMRST	MILTERS	EILNSSV	SNIVELS
EILMRSU	MISRULE	EILNSSY	LINSEYS
EILMRSV	VERMILS		LYSINES
EILMRSY	MISERLY	EILNSTU	LUTEINS
EILMRTY	LYMITER		UNTILES
EILMRVY	VERMILY		UTENSIL
EILMSSS	MISSELS	EILNSTV	VENTILS
EILMSST	MISTLES	EILNSTW	WESTLIN
	SMILETS		WINTLES
EILMSSU	MUESLIS	EILNSUV	UNLIVES
EILMSSY	MESSILY		UNVEILS
	MILSEYS	EILNSUY	LUNYIES
EILMSTT	SMITTLE	EILNSVY	SYLVINE
EILMSTZ	MILTZES	EILNVXY	VIXENLY
EILMSZZ	MIZZLES	EILOOPR	LOOPIER
EILMUUV	ELUVIUM	EILOORS	ORIOLES
EILNNPU	PINNULE	EILOORT	TROOLIE
EILNNST	LINNETS	EILOOST	OOLITES
EILNNSU	UNLINES		OSTIOLE
EILNNSW	WINNLES		STOOLIE
EILNNSY	LINNEYS	EILOOTZ	ZOOLITE
EILNOOP	POLONIE	EILOPRS	SLOPIER

	SPOILER
EILOPRT	POITREL
	POLITER
EILOPST	PIOLETS
	PISTOLE
EILOPSU	PILEOUS
EILOPSV	PLOSIVE
EILOPTT	PLOTTIE
EILOPTX	EXPLOIT
EILORRS	LORRIES
EILORRU	LOURIER
EILORSS	LORISES
	LOSSIER
	RISSOLE
EILORST	LOITERS
	TOILERS
EILORSU	LOUSIER
	SOILURE
EILORSV	OLIVERS
	VIOLERS
EILORTT	TORTILE
	TRIOLET
EILORTU	OUTLIER
EILOSSV	SOLIVES
EILOSTT	LITOTES
	TOILETS
EILOSTU	OUTLIES
EILOSTV	OLIVETS
	VIOLETS
EILOSTW	OWLIEST
EILOTUV	OUTLIVE
EILPPRR	RIPPLER
EILPPRS	RIPPLES
	SLIPPER
EILPPRT	RIPPLET
	TIPPLER
	TRIPPLE
EILPPRU	PULPIER
EILPPSS	PIPLESS
	SIPPLES
EILPPST	STIPPLE
	TIPPLES
EILPPSW	SWIPPLE
EILPRSS	LISPERS
EILPRST	SPIRTLE
	TRIPLES
EILPRTT	TRIPLET
EILPRTX	TRIPLEX
EILPRUU	PURLIEU
EILPSST	STIPELS
EILPSTT	SPITTLE
EILPSTU	PULIEST
	PUTELIS
	STIPULE
EILPSUY	SPULYIE
EILPSUZ	SPULZIE
EILPSZZ	PIZZLES
EILPTTY	PETTILY
EILQRTU	QUILTER
EILQRUU	LIQUEUR
EILQTUY	QUIETLY
EILRRSU	LURRIES
	SURLIER
EILRRTW	TWIRLER
EILRSST	LISTERS
EILRSSV	SILVERS
	SLIVERS
EILRSTT	LITTERS
	SLITTER
	STILTER
	TESTRIL
	TILTERS
	TITLERS
EILRSTU	LUSTIER
	RULIEST
	RUTILES
EILRSUW	WURLIES
EILRSVY	SILVERY
EILRSZZ	SIZZLER
EILRTTY	LITTERY
	TRITELY
EILRTUV	RIVULET
EILSSTT	STILETS
EILSSTY	STYLISE
EILSSVW	SWIVELS
EILSSZZ	SIZZLES
EILSTTT	TITTLES
EILSTTU	TITULES
EILSTTV	VITTLES
EILSTTY	STYLITE
	TESTILY
EILSTVY	SYLVITE
EILSTYZ	STYLIZE
EILSWZZ	SWIZZLE
EILTWZZ	TWIZZLE
EIMMMOS	MOMMIES
EIMMMST	MIMMEST
EIMMMSU	MUMMIES
EIMMNRS	NIMMERS
EIMMNSU	IMMUNES
EIMMOPS	POMMIES
EIMMORS	MEMOIRS
EIMMOST	TOMMIES
EIMMPRR	PRIMMER
EIMMPRU	PREMIUM
EIMMRRT	TRIMMER
EIMMRRU	RUMMIER
EIMMRSS	MERISMS
	SIMMERS
EIMMRST	MISTERM
EIMMRSU	IMMURES
	MUMSIER
	RUMMIES
EIMMRSW	SWIMMER
EIMMRSZ	ZIMMERS
EIMMRUY	YUMMIER
EIMMSST	SEMMITS
EIMMSTU	TUMMIES
EIMMSTZ	TZIMMES
EIMNNOT	MENTION
EIMNOOR	IONOMER
	MOONIER
EIMNOOS	MOONIES
	NOISOME
EIMNOOT	EMOTION
EIMNOOX	EXOMION
EIMNOPS	IMPONES
	PEONISM
EIMNOPT	EMPTION
	PIMENTO
EIMNORS	MERINOS
	MERSION
EIMNOSS	EONISMS
EIMNOST	MOISTEN
EIMNOSW	WINSOME
EIMNOTU	MOUNTIE
EIMNOTY	OMNEITY
	OMNIETY
EIMNPST	PIMENTS
EIMNPTU	PINETUM
EIMNQSU	MESQUIN
EIMNRRU	MURRINE
EIMNRST	ENTRISM
	MINSTER
	MINTERS
EIMNRSU	MURINES
	NEURISM
EIMNRSV	VERMINS
EIMNRTU	MINUTER
EIMNRVY	VERMINY
EIMNSSS	SENSISM
EIMNSST	MISSENT
EIMNSSU	MINUSES
EIMNSTT	MITTENS
	SMITTEN
EIMNSTU	MINUETS
	MINUTES
	MISTUNE
	MUNITES
	MUTINES
EIMNSTW	MISWENT
EIMNSZZ	MIZZENS
EIMNUZZ	MUEZZIN
EIMOORR	MOORIER
	ROOMIER
EIMOPPR	MOPPIER
	POMPIER
EIMOPRR	PRIMERO
EIMOPRS	IMPOSER
	PROMISE
EIMOPRV	IMPROVE
EIMOPSS	IMPOSES
	MOPSIES
EIMOPST	MOPIEST
	OPTIMES
EIMORRW	WORMIER
EIMORSS	ISOMERS
	MOSSIER
EIMORST	EROTISM
	MOISTER
	MORTISE
	TRISOME
EIMORSU	MOUSIER
EIMORSV	VERISMO
EIMORTT	MOTTIER
	OMITTER
EIMOSSS	MOSSIES
EIMOSST	MITOSES
	SOMITES
EIMOSSU	MOUSIES
EIMOSTT	MOTIEST
	TITMOSE
EIMOSTU	TIMEOUS
EIMOSTV	MOTIVES
EIMOSTZ	MESTIZO
EIMOSZZ	MOZZIES
EIMPRRS	PRIMERS
EIMPRRU	IMPURER
	PRIMEUR
EIMPRSS	IMPRESS
	PREMISS
	SIMPERS
EIMPRST	IMPREST
	PERMITS
EIMPRSU	SPUMIER
	UMPIRES
EIMPRTU	IMPUTER
EIMPSST	MISSTEP
EIMPSSU	SEPIUMS
EIMPSTU	IMPETUS
	IMPUTES
EIMPSUY	YUMPIES
EIMQSTU	MESQUIT
EIMRRST	RETRIMS
	TRIMERS
EIMRRSU	MURRIES
EIMRSST	MISTERS
	SMITERS
EIMRSSU	MISUSER
	MUSSIER
	SURMISE
EIMRSSV	VERISMS
EIMRSTT	METRIST
EIMRSTU	MUSTIER
EIMRSTY	MISTERY
	SMYTRIE
EIMRTUV	VITREUM
EIMRTUX	MIXTURE
EIMRUZZ	MUZZIER
EIMSSST	MISSETS
EIMSSSU	MISUSES
EIMSSSX	SEXISMS
EIMSSTY	STYMIES
EIMSTYZ	ZYMITES
EINNNOS	NONNIES
EINNNRS	RENNINS
EINNOOS	IONONES
EINNOPS	PENSION
EINNOQU	QUINONE
EINNORT	INTONER
	TERNION
EINNORU	NOUNIER
	REUNION
EINNORV	ENVIRON
EINNOSS	SONNIES
EINNOST	INTONES
	TENSION
EINNOSV	VENISON
EINNOTT	NONETTI
	TONTINE
EINNOVW	INWOVEN
EINNPRS	PINNERS
	SPINNER
EINNPRT	ENPRINT
EINNPST	PINNETS
	SPINNET
	TENPINS
EINNPSY	SPINNEY
EINNRRU	RUNNIER
EINNRSS	SINNERS
EINNRST	INTERNS
	TINNERS
EINNRSU	SUNNIER
	UNREINS
	UNRISEN
EINNRSW	WINNERS
EINNRTV	VINTNER
EINNRUV	UNRIVEN
EINNSST	SENNITS
	SINNETS
EINNSSY	SINSYNE
EINNSTT	INTENTS
EINNSTU	TUNNIES
EINNSTV	INVENTS
EINNSUW	UNSINEW
EINNTUW	UNTWINE
EINOOPZ	EPIZOON
EINOORS	EROSION
EINOOST	ISOTONE

EINOOSZ	OZONISE
EINOOTZ	ZOONITE
EINOOZZ	OZONIZE
EINOPPR	POPERIN
	PROPINE
EINOPRS	ORPINES
	PIONERS
	PROINES
EINOPRT	POINTER
	PROTEIN
	PTERION
	REPOINT
EINOPRV	PROVINE
EINOPSS	SPINOSE
EINOPST	POINTES
	PONTIES
EINOPSW	POWNIES
EINOPSY	PIONEYS
EINOQUX	EQUINOX
EINORRS	IRONERS
EINORSS	ORNISES
	SENIORS
	SONERIS
	SONSIER
EINORST	NORITES
	ORIENTS
	STONIER
	TERSION
	TRIONES
EINORSV	RENVOIS
	VERSION
EINORSW	SNOWIER
EINORTT	TRITONE
EINORTU	ROUTINE
EINORTW	TOWNIER
EINORTZ	TRIZONE
EINOSSS	ESSOINS
	OSSEINS
	SESSION
EINOSST	NOSIEST
	SONTIES
	STONIES
EINOSSU	SINUOSE
EINOSTT	TONIEST
	TONITES
EINOSTW	TOWNIES
EINOSUV	ENVIOUS
	NIVEOUS
	VEINOUS
EINOTTT	TOTIENT
EINPPRS	NIPPERS
	SNIPPER
EINPPSS	PEPSINS
EINPPST	SNIPPET
EINPRRT	PRINTER
	REPRINT
EINPRRU	UNRIPER
EINPRSS	SNIPERS
EINPRST	NIPTERS
	PTERINS
EINPRSU	PRUINES
	PURINES
	UPRISEN
EINPRSY	INSPYRE
EINPSST	INSTEPS
	SPINETS
EINPSSU	PUISNES
	SUPINES
EINPSTT	SPITTEN
EINPSTU	PUNIEST

	PUNTIES
EINPTTY	TINTYPE
EINQRUU	UNIQUER
EINQRUY	ENQUIRY
EINQSSU	SEQUINS
EINQSTU	INQUEST
	QUINTES
EINQSUU	UNIQUES
EINQSUZ	QUINZES
EINQTTU	QUINTET
EINQTUU	UNQUIET
EINRRSS	RINSERS
EINRRSU	INSURER
	RUINERS
EINRRTU	RUNTIER
EINRSST	INSERTS
	SINTERS
EINRSSU	INSURES
	SUNRISE
EINRSSV	VERSINS
EINRSTT	ENTRIST
	STINTER
	TINTERS
EINRSTU	TRIUNES
	UNITERS
EINRSTV	INVERTS
	STRIVEN
EINRSTW	TWINERS
	WINTERS
EINRSTY	SINTERY
EINRSUW	UNWIRES
	UNWISER
EINRSVW	WIVERNS
EINRSWY	SWINERY
EINRTTU	NUTTIER
EINRTTW	TWINTER
	WRITTEN
EINRTUV	UNRIVET
	VENTURI
EINRTUW	UNWRITE
EINRTWY	WINTERY
EINSSST	SENSIST
EINSSSU	NISUSES
	SINUSES
EINSSSY	SYNESIS
EINSSTU	INTUSES
EINSSTV	INVESTS
EINSSTW	WISENTS
	WITNESS
EINSSTY	TINSEYS
EINSSUW	SUNWISE
EINSSWY	WINSEYS
EINSTTU	TUNIEST
EINSTTW	ENTWIST
EINSTTY	TENSITY
EINSUVW	UNWIVES
EINTTTW	TWITTEN
EINTTUY	TENUITY
EIOOPRR	ROOPIER
EIOOPRV	POOVIER
EIOOPST	ISOTOPE
EIOORRT	ROOTIER
EIOORST	OORIEST
	ROOTIES
	SOOTIER
	TOORIES
EIOORWZ	WOOZIER
EIOOSST	OOSIEST
EIOOSTT	TOOTSIE
EIOOSTZ	OOZIEST

EIOPPPS	POPPIES
EIOPPRS	SOPPIER
EIOPPSS	POPSIES
EIOPRRS	PROSIER
EIOPRRT	PIERROT
	PORTIER
EIOPRRU	ROUPIER
EIOPRSS	POISERS
EIOPRST	PERIOST
	PORIEST
	REPOSIT
	RIPOSTE
	ROPIEST
EIOPRSU	POURIES
	SOUPIER
EIOPRSX	PROXIES
EIOPRTT	POTTIER
EIOPRTU	POUTIER
EIOPRTV	PIVOTER
EIOPSSS	POSSIES
EIOPSST	POSTIES
	SEPIOST
	SOPITES
EIOPSTT	POTTIES
	TIPTOES
EIOPSTU	PITEOUS
EIOPSTX	POXIEST
EIOPSTY	ISOTYPE
EIOPSZZ	POZZIES
EIOPTUW	WIPEOUT
EIOQRTU	QUOITER
EIORRRS	SORRIER
EIORRRT	RORTIER
EIORRRW	WORRIER
EIORRSS	ORRISES
	ROSIERS
EIORRST	RIOTERS
	ROISTER
	RORIEST
EIORRSV	REVISOR
EIORRSW	WORRIES
EIORRUV	OUVRIER
EIORRVV	REVIVOR
EIORSST	ROSIEST
	SORITES
	SORTIES
	STORIES
	TOSSIER
EIORSSU	SERIOUS
EIORSSV	VIROSES
EIORSSX	XEROSIS
EIORSTT	STOITER
EIORSTU	OURIEST
	TOUSIER
EIORSTV	TORSIVE
EIORSTW	OWRIEST
	TOWSIER
EIORTTT	TOTTIER
EIORTTU	TOUTIER
EIORTTV	TORTIVE
	VIRETOT
EIORTUV	VOITURE
EIOSSTV	SOVIETS
	STOVIES
EIOSTTT	TOTTIES
EIOSTTU	TOUSTIE
EIOSTTW	TOWIEST
EIOSTUV	OUTVIES
EIOSTUZ	OUTSIZE
EIPPPSU	PUPPIES

EIPPRRS	RIPPERS
EIPPRRT	TRIPPER
EIPPRSS	SIPPERS
EIPPRST	TIPPERS
EIPPRSU	PURPIES
EIPPRSZ	ZIPPERS
EIPPRTT	TRIPPET
EIPPSST	SIPPETS
EIPPSTT	TIPPETS
EIPPSUY	YUPPIES
EIPQSTU	PIQUETS
EIPRRSS	PRISERS
EIPRRSU	PURSIER
EIPRRSZ	PRIZERS
EIPRRTU	PURTIER
EIPRRTY	TRIPERY
EIPRRUV	UPRIVER
EIPRSST	ESPRITS
	PERSIST
	PRIESTS
	SITREPS
	SPRITES
	STIRPES
	STRIPES
	TRIPSES
EIPRSSU	SUSPIRE
	UPRISES
EIPRSSW	SWIPERS
EIPRSTT	PITTERS
	SPITTER
	TIPSTER
EIPRSTU	PERITUS
	PUIREST
EIPRSTV	PRIVETS
EIPRSTX	EXTIRPS
EIPRSTY	PYRITES
	STRIPEY
EIPRSUU	EURIPUS
EIPRTTU	PUTTIER
EIPRUVW	PURVIEW
EIPSSSU	PUSSIES
EIPSSTZ	SPITZES
EIPSTTU	PUTTIES
EIQRSSU	RISQUES
	SQUIERS
	SQUIRES
EIQRSTU	QUERIST
	REQUITS
EIQRSUV	QUIVERS
EIQRTTU	QUITTER
EIQRUVY	QUIVERY
EIQRUZZ	QUIZZER
EIQSTUU	QUIETUS
EIQSUZZ	QUIZZES
EIRRRST	STIRRER
EIRRSST	STIRRES
EIRRSTT	RITTERS
	TERRITS
EIRRSTU	RUSTIER
EIRRSTV	STRIVER
EIRRSTW	WRITERS
EIRRSZZ	RIZZERS
EIRRTTU	RUTTIER
EIRSSST	RESISTS
	SISTERS
EIRSSSU	ISSUERS
	RISUSES
EIRSSTT	SITTERS
EIRSSTV	STIVERS
	STRIVES

	TREVISS	EKMNOSU	MUSKONE	ELLOPRR	PROLLER	ELMSTUU	MUTULES
	VERISTS	EKMNOSY	MONKEYS	ELLOPRS	POLLERS	ELMSUZZ	MUZZLES
EIRSSUU	USURIES	EKMNPTU	UNKEMPT	ELLOPTU	POLLUTE	ELNNOPU	NONUPLE
EIRSSUV	VIRUSES	EKMOOPS	MOPOKES	ELLORRS	ROLLERS	ELNNOSS	NELSONS
EIRSTTT	STRETTI	EKMORSS	SMOKERS	ELLORRT	TROLLER	ELNNRSU	RUNNELS
	TITTERS	EKMRSTU	MURKEST	ELLORSS	SOLLERS	ELNNSTU	TUNNELS
	TRITEST	EKMSSTU	MUSKETS		SORELLS	ELNOOSS	LOOSENS
EIRSTTU	TERTIUS	EKNNOST	NEKTONS	ELLORST	TOLLERS	ELNOOSU	UNLOOSE
EIRSTTV	TRIVETS	EKNOORS	SNOOKER	ELLORTY	TROLLEY	ELNOOSZ	SNOOZLE
EIRSTTW	TWISTER	EKNOPSU	UNSPOKE	ELLORVY	LOVERLY	ELNOPRU	PLEURON
	WITTERS	EKNORST	STONKER	ELLOSST	TOLSELS	ELNOPRY	PRONELY
EIRSTUV	VIRTUES		STROKEN	ELLOSTU	OUTSELL	ELNOPST	LEPTONS
EIRSUVV	SURVIVE		TONKERS	ELLOSVY	VOLLEYS	ELNOPSY	POLEYNS
EIRSUVW	SURVIEW	EKNORSW	KNOWERS	ELLOSWY	YELLOWS	ELNOPTU	OPULENT
EIRTTTW	TWITTER	EKNORSY	YONKERS	ELLOTTU	OUTTELL	ELNORSS	NORSELS
EISSSTU	TISSUES	EKNORTT	KNOTTER	ELLOTUW	OUTWELL	ELNORST	LENTORS
EISSSTW	SWITSES	EKNORTW	NETWORK	ELLOVWY	VOWELLY	ELNORSU	NOURSLE
EISSSTX	SEXISTS	EKNORUY	YOUNKER	ELLOWYY	YELLOWY	ELNORTY	ELYTRON
EISSTTY	TYSTIES	EKNORWY	YWROKEN	ELLPRSU	PULLERS	ELNOSSS	LESSONS
EISSTUV	TUSSIVE	EKNOSUY	UNYOKES	ELLPSTU	PULLETS		SONLESS
EISSTVW	SWIVETS	EKNRTUY	TURNKEY	ELLPSUW	UPSWELL	ELNOSST	TELSONS
EISSWZZ	SWIZZES	EKNSSTU	SUNKETS		UPWELLS	ELNOSSU	ENSOULS
EISTTTU	TUTTIES	EKOOPRT	PERTOOK	ELLPSUY	PULLEYS		NOUSLES
EJJMNUU	JEJUNUM	EKOOPRV	PROVOKE	ELMMOPS	POMMELS	ELNOSSV	SLOVENS
EJKMNNU	JUNKMEN	EKOORRY	ROOKERY	ELMMORT	TROMMEL	ELNOSSW	LOWNESS
EJKNRSU	JUNKERS	EKOORST	STOOKER	ELMMPSU	PUMMELS	ELNOSTT	TONLETS
EJKNSTU	JUNKETS		STROOKE	ELMMPTU	PLUMMET	ELNOSTU	LENTOUS
EJKOORY	JOOKERY	EKOPPSU	UPSPOKE	ELMMRSU	SLUMMER	ELNOSTV	SOLVENT
EJKORUY	JOUKERY	EKOPRRS	PORKERS	ELMMSTU	STUMMEL	ELNOSUV	UNLOVES
EJLORST	JOLTERS		PROKERS	ELMNOOT	MOONLET	ELNOSUZ	ZONULES
EJLORSW	JOWLERS	EKORRST	STROKER		TOOLMEN	ELNOSVY	LENVOYS
EJLOSST	JOSTLES	EKORRSW	REWORKS	ELMNOOW	WOOLMEN	ELNOSZZ	NOZZLES
EJLOSSY	JOYLESS		WORKERS	ELMNORS	MERLONS	ELNOTUZ	ZONULET
EJLSSTU	JUSTLES	EKORRSY	YORKERS	ELMNOST	LOMENTS	ELNOTVY	NOVELTY
EJMNRUY	JURYMEN	EKORSST	STOKERS		MELTONS	ELNPSST	SPLENTS
EJMOSST	JETSOMS	EKPPSUU	SEPPUKU	ELMNOSY	MYELONS	ELNPSTU	PENULTS
EJMPRSU	JUMPERS	EKPRSSY	KRYPSES	ELMNOTU	MOULTEN	ELNRSSU	NURSLES
EJNORRU	REJOURN	EKRRSSY	SKRYERS	ELMNOTY	YMOLTEN	ELNRSTU	RUNLETS
EJNORUY	JOURNEY	EKRSSTU	TUSKERS	ELMNPPU	PLUMPEN	ELNRSTY	STERNLY
EJNOSST	JETSONS	EKRSTUY	TURKEYS	ELMNPSU	PLENUMS	ELNRSUU	UNRULES
EJNOSTT	JETTONS	EKRSUVY	KURVEYS	ELMNPUU	UNPLUME	ELNRSUZ	LUZERNS
EJOORVY	OVERJOY	ELLLORR	LORRELL	ELMOOPP	POMPELO	ELNSSSU	SUNLESS
EJOOSSY	SOOJEYS	ELLLORS	LOLLERS	ELMOOPS	POMELOS	ELNSSSY	SLYNESS
EJORSSS	JOSSERS	ELLLOSZ	LOZELLS	ELMOORT	TREMOLO	ELNSTTU	NUTLETS
EJORSTT	JOTTERS	ELLMNOO	MOELLON	ELMOPRY	POLYMER	ELNSUZZ	NUZZLES
EJORSTU	JOUSTER	ELLMNOP	POLLMEN	ELMOPSU	PLUMOSE		SNUZZLE
EJOSTTU	OUTJEST	ELLMNOT	TOLLMEN		PUMELOS	ELOOPRS	LOOPERS
	OUTJETS	ELLMOOR	MORELLO	ELMOPSY	EMPLOYS		SPOOLER
EJPRRUY	PERJURY	ELLMOSW	MELLOWS	ELMORSS	MORSELS	ELOORST	LOOTERS
EJSSTTU	JUSTEST	ELLMOWY	MELLOWY	ELMORSU	EMULSOR		RETOOLS
EKKLOOY	OLYKOEK	ELLMPUU	PLUMULE	ELMOSST	MOLESTS		ROOTLES
EKKLRSU	SKULKER	ELLMRSU	MULLERS	ELMOSSU	MOUSLES		TOOLERS
EKLLMSU	SKELLUM	ELLMSTU	MULLETS	ELMOSSY	SMOYLES	ELOORTT	ROOTLET
EKLMMSU	KUMMELS	ELLMSUV	VELLUMS	ELMOSTT	MOTTLES	ELOOSST	LOOSEST
EKLMSSU	MUSKLES	ELLMSUY	MULLEYS	ELMOSTY	MOTLEYS		LOTOSES
EKLNOPR	PLONKER	ELLNNOT	TONNELL	ELMOSUU	EMULOUS	ELOOSSW	WOOSELS
EKLNORS	SNORKEL	ELLNOOW	WOOLLEN	ELMOSUV	VOLUMES	ELOOSTT	TOOTLES
EKLNOSS	KELSONS	ELLNOPS	POLLENS	ELMOSXY	OXYMELS	ELOOSTU	OUTSOLE
	SLOKENS	ELLNOPT	POLLENT	ELMOSZZ	MOZZLES	ELOOSWY	WOOLSEY
EKLNPRU	PLUNKER	ELLNORS	ENROLLS	ELMPPRU	PLUMPER	ELOPPPS	POPPLES
EKLNRSU	LUNKERS	ELLNOSU	NOUSELL	ELMPPSU	PEPLUMS	ELOPPRS	LOPPERS
	RUNKLES	ELLNOSV	VELLONS	ELMPRSU	LUMPERS		PROPELS
EKLNSST	SKLENTS	ELLNOSW	SWOLLEN		RUMPLES	ELOPPST	STOPPLE
EKLOORS	LOOKERS	ELLNOXY	XYLENOL	ELMPRUY	PLUMERY		TOPPLES
EKLRRSU	LURKERS	ELLNPSU	UNSPELL	ELMRSTY	MYRTLES	ELOPPSU	POULPES
EKLSTTU	SKUTTLE	ELLNSSU	SULLENS	ELMRTUU	MULTURE	ELOPPSY	POLYPES
EKLSTUZ	KLUTZES	ELLNSUU	LUNULES	ELMRTUY	ELYTRUM	ELOPRRS	PROLERS
EKMMRSU	SKUMMER	ELLOOSW	WOOSELL	ELMRUZZ	MUZZLER	ELOPRRU	PROULER
EKMNORW	WORKMEN	ELLOOSY	LOOSELY	ELMSSSU	MUSSELS	ELOPRRW	PROWLER
EKMNORY	MONKERY				SUMLESS	ELOPRRY	PYRROLE

```
ELOPRSS PLESSOR     ELPRSTU SPURTLE             MONSTER     ENNORSW RENOWNS
        SPLORES     ELPRSUV PULVERS             MONTRES     ENNORTU NEUTRON
ELOPRST PETROLS     ELPRTUU PULTURE     EMNORTT TORMENT     ENNOSST SONNETS
ELOPRSU LEPROUS     ELPRUZZ PUZZLER     EMNORTU MONTURE             STONNES
       ·PELORUS     ELPSSSU PLUSSES             MOUNTER             TENSONS
        PERLOUS             PUSSELS             REMOUNT     ENNOSSW NOWNESS
        SPORULE     ELPSSU  LUPUSES     EMNOSST STEMSON     ENNOSTU NEUSTON
ELOPRSV PLOVERS     ELPSSUY SPULYES     EMNOSTU UNSMOTE     ENNOSTW NEWTONS
ELOPRSX PLEXORS     ELPSTUU PLUTEUS     EMNOSTY ETYMONS     ENNOSTZ TENZONS
ELOPRSY LEPROSY             PUSTULE     EMNOSXY EXONYMS     ENNOUVW UNWOVEN
ELOPRTT PLOTTER     ELPSUZZ PUZZELS     EMNPSSU PENSUMS     ENNPRSU PUNNERS
ELOPRTU PLOUTER             PUZZLES     EMNRRSU MURRENS     ENNPSTU PUNNETS
        POULTER     ELRRSTU RUSTLER     EMNRSTU MUNSTER             UNSPENT
ELOPRTW PLOWTER     ELRRTTU TURTLER             STERNUM     ENNRRSU RUNNERS
ELOPRTY PROTYLE     ELRSSSU RUSSELS     EMOOPRT PROMOTE     ENNRSTU RUNNETS
ELOPRVY OVERPLY     ELRSSTU LUSTERS     EMOOPRY POMEROY             STUNNER
        PLOVERY             LUSTRES     EMOORRS MOROSER     ENNRSUW WUNNERS
ELOPSST TOPLESS             RESULTS             ROOMERS     ENNSSTU UNNESTS
ELOPSSU SOUPLES             RUSTLES     EMOORST MOOTERS     ENNSTTU UNTENTS
ELOPSTT POTTLES             SUTLERS     EMOORSU UROSOME     ENNSTUU UNTUNES
ELOPSTU TUPELOS             ULSTERS     EMOOSSS OSMOSES     ENNTTUY UNTENTY
ELORRSS SORRELS     ELRSTTU TURTLES     EMOOSTT MOOTEST     ENOOPPR PROPONE
ELORRSW WORRELS     ELRSTTY TETRYLS             MOTTOES     ENOOPRS SNOOPER
ELORSSS LESSORS     ELRSTUY SUTLERY             TOOMEST     ENOOPSY SPOONEY
ELORSST OSTLERS     ELRSTWY SWELTRY     EMOOSTW TWOSOME     ENOORSS SEROONS
        STEROLS     ELRSUWY WURLEYS     EMOOSTY MYOSOTE     ENOORST ENROOTS
        TORSELS     ELRTTUY UTTERLY             TOYSOME     ENOORSU ONEROUS
ELORSSV SOLVERS     ELRTUUV VULTURE     EMOOTUV OUTMOVE     ENOORSZ SNOOZER
ELORSTT SETTLOR     ELSSSTU TUSSLES     EMOPPRS MOPPERS     ENOOSST SOONEST
        SLOTTER     ELSSTTU SUTTLES     EMOPPST MOPPETS     ENOOSSZ SNOOZES
        TOLTERS     ELSSTTY STYLETS     EMOPPSY POMPEYS     ENOOSTT TESTOON
ELORSTU ELUTORS     ELSSTYY SYSTYLE     EMOPRRS ROMPERS     ENOOSTU UNSOOTE
        OUTLERS     ELSUWZZ WUZZLES     EMOPRST TROMPES     ENOOTXY OXYTONE
        TROULES     EMMMOST MOMMETS     EMOPRSU SUPREMO     ENOPPSU UNPOPES
ELORSTV REVOLTS     EMMMRSU MUMMERS     EMOPSSU MOPUSES     ENOPRRS PERRONS
ELORSTW TROWELS     EMMMRUY MUMMERY     EMOPSSY MYOPSES     ENOPRRU PRONEUR
        WORTLES     EMMNNOS MNEMONS     EMOQSSU MOSQUES     ENOPRSS PERSONS
ELORSUV LOUVERS             MOORMEN     EMORRST TERMORS     ENOPRST POSTERN
        LOUVRES     EMMNOOR MONOMER             TREMORS             PRONEST
        VELOURS             MOORMEN     EMORRSU MORSURE     ENOPRSU UNROPES
ELORSUY ELUSORY     EMMNOOT MOOTMEN     EMORRSW WORMERS     ENOPRSY PROYNES
ELORSVW WOLVERS     EMMNOST MOMENTS     EMORRWY WORMERY             PYONERS
ELORTTY LOTTERY             MONTEMS     EMORSST MOTSERS     ENOPRTT PORTENT
ELORTVY OVERTLY     EMMNOTU OMENTUM     EMORSSU MOUSERS     ENOPRTY ENTROPY
ELOSSTU LOTUSES     EMMNOTY METONYM             SMOUSER     ENOPSST POSNETS
        SOLUTES     EMMNSTU MENTUMS     EMORSTU MOUTERS             STEPSON
        TOUSLES     EMMOPRR PROMMER             OESTRUM     ENOPSTT POTENTS
ELOSSTW LOWSEST     EMMOSSU MOUSMES     EMORSUY MOUSERY     ENOPSWY POWNEYS
        SLOWEST     EMMOSYZ ZYMOMES     EMOSSSU MOUSSES     ENOQTUU UNQUOTE
ELOSSTY SYSTOLE     EMMPRSU MUMPERS             SMOUSES     ENORRSS SNORERS
        TOLSEYS     EMMRRSU RUMMERS     EMOSSYZ ZYMOSES             SORNERS
        TYLOSES     EMMRSSU SUMMERS     EMOSTTT MOTETTS     ENORRST SNORTER
ELOSSXY XYLOSES     EMMRSTU RUMMEST     EMOSTVZ ZEMSTVO     ENORRTT TORRENT
ELOSSZZ SOZZLES     EMMRSUY SUMMERY     EMPPRSU PUMPERS     ENORRUV OVERRUN
ELOSTTU OUTLETS     EMMSSUU MUSEUMS     EMPRSTU STUMPER     ENORSSS SENSORS
ELOSTTY TYLOTES     EMNNOOR MONERON             SUMPTER     ENORSST STONERS
ELOSTUU LUTEOUS     EMNNOSW SNOWMEN     EMPRTTU TRUMPET             TENSORS
ELOSTUV VOLUTES     EMNOOPT METOPON     EMRRSTU STURMER     ENORSSW WORSENS
ELOSTUZ TOUZLES     EMNOORS MOONERS     EMRRSUY MURREYS     ENORSSY SENSORY
ELOSTYZ TOLZEYS     EMNOORT MONTERO     EMRSSTU ESTRUMS     ENORSTT ROTTENS
ELOSWYY YOWLEYS     EMNOOSS MONOSES             MUSTERS             SNOTTER
ELOSWZZ SWOZZLE     EMNOOST MOONSET             STUMERS             STENTOR
ELPPRRU PURPLER     EMNOOSY NOYSOME     EMRSTTU MUTTERS     ENORSTU TENOURS
ELPPRSU PULPERS     EMNOOTY ENOMOTY     EMRSTYY MYSTERY             TONSURE
        PURPLES     EMNOPRT PORTMEN     EMSSSTY SYSTEMS     ENORSTY TYRONES
        REPULPS     EMNOPST POSTMEN     ENNNOPS PENNONS     ENORSUV NERVOUS
        SUPPLER             TOPSMEN     ENNNRUY NUNNERY     ENORSUW UNSWORE
ELPPSSU SUPPLES     EMNOPSY EPONYMS     ENNOOTT NONETTO     ENORSVY RENVOYS
ELPQSUU PULQUES     EMNORRU MOURNER     ENNORST STONERN     ENORTUW UNWROTE
ELPRRSU PURLERS     EMNORSS SERMONS     ENNORSU NEURONS     ENORTUY TOURNEY
                    EMNORST MENTORS
```

```
ENOSSST  SESTONS
ENOSSTT  OSTENTS
         TESTONS
ENOSSTU  OUTNESS
         TONUSES
ENOSSTW  TWONESS
ENOSSTX  SEXTONS
ENOSSUW  SWOUNES
ENOSSWW  SWOWNES
ENOSTTU  STOUTEN
ENOSTUU  TENUOUS
ENOTTUW  OUTWENT
ENPRRSU  PRUNERS
         SPURNER
ENPRSSU  SPURNES
ENPRSTU  PUNSTER
         PUNTERS
ENPRSUU  UNPURSE
ENPRSWY  PREWYNS
ENPSSSU  SUSPENS
ENPSSTU  UNSTEPS
ENPSTTU  STUPENT
ENPSTUW  UNSWEPT
ENRRSSU  NURSERS
ENRRSTU  RETURNS
         TURNERS
ENRRSUU  UNSURER
ENRRSUY  NURSERY
ENRRTUU  NURTURE
         UNTRUER
ENRRTUY  TURNERY
ENRSSTU  UNRESTS
ENRSSWY  WRYNESS
ENRSTTU  ENTRUST
         NUTTERS
ENRSUZZ  NUZZERS
ENRSVWY  WYVERNS
ENRTTUY  NUTTERY
ENSSSTU  SUNSETS
EOOOPRS  OOSPORE
EOOPPRS  OPPOSER
         PROPOSE
EOOPPRV  POPOVER
EOOPPSS  OPPOSES
EOOPRRS  SPOORER
EOOPRRT  TROOPER
EOOPRSS  POROSES
EOOPRST  POOREST
         POOTERS
         STOOPER
EOOPRTU  OUTROPE
EOOPRTV  OVERTOP
EOOPRTW  TOWROPE
EOOPRVY  POOVERY
EOOPRYZ  ZOOPERY
EOOPSST  STOOPES
EOOPTYZ  ZOOTYPE
EOORRST  ROOSTER
         ROOTERS
         TOREROS
EOORSSS  SOROSES
EOORSTT  TOOTERS
EOORSVW  OVERSOW
EOORTUW  OUTWORE
EOOSSSU  OSSEOUS
EOOSTWZ  WOOTZES
EOOTTUV  OUTVOTE
EOPPPRS  POPPERS
EOPPPST  POPPETS
EOPPRRS  PROPERS
         PROSPER
EOPPRSS  OPPRESS
         PORPESS
EOPPRST  STOPPER
         TOPPERS
EOPPRSU  PURPOSE
EOPPRSW  SWOPPER
EOPPRSY  PYROPES
         YOPPERS
EOPPSSU  SUPPOSE
EOPRRSS  PRESSOR
         PROSERS
EOPRRST  PORTERS
         REPORTS
         SPORTER
EOPRRSU  POURERS
EOPRRSV  PROVERS
EOPRRTU  TROUPER
EOPRSSS  POSSERS
EOPRSST  PORTESS
         POSTERS
         PRESTOS
         REPOSTS
EOPRSSU  POSEURS
         SOUPERS
EOPRSSW  PROWESS
EOPRSSY  OSPREYS
         PYROSES
EOPRSTT  POTTERS
         PROTEST
         SPOTTER
EOPRSTU  PETROUS
         POSTURE
         POUTERS
         PROTEUS
         SEPTUOR
         SPOUTER
         TROUPES
EOPRSTW  POWTERS
         PROWEST
EOPRSTX  EXPORTS
EOPRSUU  POURSUE
         UPROUSE
EOPRSUW  POURSEW
EOPRTTY  POTTERY
EOPRTUY  EUTROPY
EOPRTVY  POVERTY
EOPSSSS  POSSESS
EOPSSST  POSSETS
EOPSSSU  POUSSES
         SPOUSES
EOPSSTT  SPOTTES
EOPSSTX  SEXPOTS
EOPSTTU  OUTSTEP
         TOUPETS
EOPSTTW  STEWPOT
EOPTTUW  OUTWEPT
EOQRSTU  QUESTOR
         QUOTERS
         ROQUETS
         TORQUES
EORRRST  RORTERS
         TERRORS
EORRSSS  ROSSERS
EORRSST  RESORTS
         ROSTERS
         SORTERS
         STORERS
EORRSSU  ROUSERS
EORRSTT  RETORTS
         ROTTERS
         TORRETS
EORRSTU  RETOURS
         ROUSTER
         ROUTERS
         TOURERS
EORRSTV  TROVERS
EORRSTW  STROWER
EORRSTY  ROYSTER
EORRSZZ  ROZZERS
EORRTTT  TROTTER
EORRTTU  TORTURE
         TROUTER
EORSSST  TOSSERS
EORSSSU  SOURSES
EORSSTU  ESTROUS
         OESTRUS
         OUSTERS
         SOUREST
         SOUTERS
         TOUSERS
         TROUSES
         TUSSORE
EORSSTV  STOVERS
EORSSTW  SOWTERS
         STOWERS
         STOWRES
         TOWSERS
EORSSTY  OYSTERS
         STOREYS
EORSSTZ  ZOSTERS
EORSSWW  WOWSERS
EORSTTT  STOTTER
         STRETTO
         TOTTERS
EORSTTU  STOUTER
         TOUTERS
EORSTTW  SWOTTER
EORSTTX  EXTORTS
EORSTTY  ROSETTY
EORSTUX  SEXTUOR
EORSUVY  VOYEURS
EORTTTY  TOTTERY
EOSSSSW  SOWSSES
EOSSTTU  OUTSETS
EOSTTTW  WOTTEST
EPPPSTU  PUPPETS
EPPRRTU  PRERUPT
EPPRRUU  PURPURE
EPPRSSU  SUPPERS
EPPSTUW  UPSWEPT
EPRRRSU  SPURRER
EPRRSSU  PURSERS
EPRRSUU  PURSUER
         USURPER
EPRRSUY  SPURREY
EPRRTUU  RUPTURE
EPRSSTU  UPRESTS
EPRSSTY  SPRYEST
EPRSSUU  PURSUES
EPRSSUW  PURSEWS
EPRSTTU  PUTTERS
         SPUTTER
EPRSTUU  PUTURES
EPRSUVY  PURVEYS
EQRSTWY  QWERTYS
ERRSSTU  RUSTRES
         TRUSSER
ERRSSUU  USURERS
ERRSSUY  SURREYS
ERRSTTU  RUTTERS
         TRUSTER
         TURRETS
ERRSTTY  TRYSTER
ERSSSTU  RUSSETS
         TRUSSES
         TUSSERS
ERSSSUU  USURESS
ERSSTTU  TUTRESS
ERSSTUU  SUTURES
ERSSTUY  RUSSETY
ERSSTXY  XYSTERS
ERSSUVW  SURVEWS
ERSSUVY  SURVEYS
ERSTTTU  STUTTER
FFFGINU  FUFFING
FFGGINO  GOFFING
FFGHINU  HUFFING
FFGIIMN  MIFFING
FFGIINN  NIFFING
FFGIINR  GRIFFIN
FFGIINT  TIFFING
FFGILNU  LUFFING
FFGIMNU  MUFFING
FFGINOR  GRIFFON
FFGINOS  OFFINGS
FFGINPU  PUFFING
FFGINRU  RUFFING
FFGLRUY  GRUFFLY
FFHHISU  HUFFISH
FFHIISY  FISHIFY
FFHIKNU  HUFFKIN
FFHILSU  FISHFUL
FFHILTY  FIFTHLY
FFHILUY  HUFFILY
FFHIOST  TOFFISH
FFHORSS  SHROFFS
FFIINST  TIFFINS
FFIISUZ  ZIFFIUS
FFIKLSS  SKLIFFS
FFILLSU  FULFILS
FFILOST  FILFOTS
FFILOUZ  ZUFFOLI
FFILPSS  SPLIFFS
FFILPUY  PUFFILY
FFILRTY  FRITFLY
FFILSTU  FISTFUL
FFILSTY  STIFFLY
FFIMNSU  MUFFINS
FFINOPT  PONTIFF
FFINPSU  PUFFINS
FFINRSU  RUFFINS
FFIORTY  FORTIFY
FFIOSST  SOFFITS
FFIQSUY  SQUIFFY
FFIRTUY  FRUTIFY
FFLLOOU  LOOFFUL
FFLOOUZ  ZUFFOLO
FFLOSTY  FYLFOTS
FFNORTU  TURNOFF
FFOPSTU  OFFPUTS
FFRRSUU  FURFURS
FGGGIIN  FIGGING
FGGGINO  FOGGING
FGGGINU  FUGGING
FGGHIIS  FISHGIG
FGGIINT  GIFTING
FGGIISS  FISGIGS
FGGIISZ  FIZGIGS
FGGIIZZ  FIZZGIG
```

FGGILNO	GOLFING	FGIMNOR	FORMING	FIIIKNN	FINIKIN	PROFITS
FGGILNU	FUGLING	FGIMOSY	FOGYISM	FIIKNRS	FIRKINS	FIOPSTX POSTFIX
	GULFING	FGINNNO	FONNING	FIIKNYZ	ZINKIFY	FIORSUU FURIOUS
FGGILOY	FOGGILY	FGINNNU	FUNNING	FIILLMO	MILFOIL	FIOSTTU OUTFITS
FGGINOO	GOOFING	FGINNOY	FOYNING	FIILLNS	INFILLS	FIRSSTT STRIFTS
FGGINOR	FORGING	FGINOOR	ROOFING	FIILLPS	FILLIPS	FKLORUW WORKFUL
FGGINOW	GOWFING	FGINOOT	FOOTING	FIILNOT	TINFOIL	FKNOSTY KONFYTS
FGHIINS	FISHING	FGINORT	FORTING	FIILPTU	PITIFUL	FKOOORS FORSOOK
FGHILST	FLIGHTS	FGINOST	SOFTING	FIIMSST	MISFITS	FLLOOSW FOLLOWS
FGHILSU	SIGHFUL	FGINOSW	SOWFING	FIINORS	FIORINS	FLLOPTU PLOTFUL
FGHILTY	FLIGHTY	FGINOSX	FOXINGS	FIINOSS	FISSION	TOPFULL
FGHIMNU	HUMFING	FGINRRU	FURRING	FIINRTY	NITRIFY	FLLOSUU SOULFUL
FGHINOO	HOOFING	FGINRSU	SURFING	FIIPSTY	TIPSIFY	FLLOUWY WOFULLY
FGHINOU	HOUFING	FGINRSY	FRYINGS	FIIRTVY	VITRIFY	FLLSTUU LUSTFUL
FGHINOW	HOWFING	FGINRTU	TURFING	FIJLLOY	JOLLIFY	FLMMOUX FLUMMOX
FGHIOSY	FOGYISH	FGINSSU	FUSSING	FIJSTUY	JUSTIFY	FLMNOOU MOUFLON
FGHIRST	FRIGHTS	FGINSTU	FUSTING	FIKKLNO	KINFOLK	FLMNOOS MUFLONS
FGHNOOR	FOGHORN	FGINTTU	TUFTING	FIKLLSU	SKILFUL	FLMOOOT TOMFOOL
FGHORUY	FROUGHY	FGINUZZ	FUZZING	FIKLNOW	WOLFKIN	FLMOORS FORMOLS
FGHOTUY	FOUGHTY	FGIORST	FRIGOTS	FIKLNSU	SKINFUL	FLMOORU ROOMFUL
FGIIKNN	FINKING	FGIORTW	FIGWORT	FIKLRSU	RISKFUL	FLNOORF FORLORN
	KNIFING	FGISTUU	FUGUIST	FIKNNOS	FINNSKO	FLNOOSU UNFOOLS
FGIIKNR	FIRKING	FGJLSUU	JUGFULS	FILLMOY	MOLLIFY	FLNOOSW ONFLOWS
FGIIKNS	FISKING	FGLLNUU	LUNGFUL	FILLNUY	NULLIFY	FLNRSUU UNFURLS
FGIILLN	FILLING	FGLMSUU	MUGFULS	FILLOTU	TOILFUL	URNFULS
FGIILMN	FILMING	FGLNORU	FURLONG	FILLOTY	LOFTILY	FLOORSW FORSLOW
FGIILNO	FOILING	FGLNOSU	SONGFUL	FILLPSU	UPFILLS	FLOOTUW OUTFLOW
FGIILNR	RIFLING	FGLNPUU	UPFLUNG	FILLSTU	LISTFUL	FLOPSTU POTFULS
FGIILNS	FILINGS	FGLOOUY	UFOLOGY	FILMNOO	MONOFIL	FLOPSUW UPFLOWS
FGIILNT	FLITING	FGLORSU	FULGORS	FILMSTU	MISTFUL	FLOSUUV FULVOUS
	LIFTING	FGLORUU	FULGOUR	FILNNUY	FUNNILY	FLPRSUU UPFURLS
FGIILNX	FLIXING	FGLOTUY	GOUTFLY	FILNORS	FLORINS	FLRSSUU SULFURS
FGIILNY	LIGNIFY	FGLSTUU	GUSTFUL	FILNOSW	INFLOWS	FMNORSU UNFORMS
FGIIMNR	FIRMING	FGNOORU	FOURGON	FILNOUX	FLUXION	FMRSTUU FRUSTUM
FGIINNO	FOINING	FGNORSY	GRYFONS	FILNSTU	TINFULS	FNNNUUY UNFUNNY
FGIINNS	FININGS	FGNOSUU	FUNGOUS	FILNTUY	UNFITLY	FNNOORT FRONTON
FGIINRR	FIRRING	FHIILMS	FILMISH	FILOOTW	WITLOOF	FNOORRW FORWORN
FGIINRS	FIRINGS	FHIINPS	PINFISH	FILORST	FIRLOTS	FNOORSU UNROOFS
FGIINRT	RIFTING	FHILLSU	FULLISH		FLORIST	FNOPRTU UPFRONT
FGIINRY	NIGRIFY	FHILOOS	FOOLISH	FILORSV	FRIVOLS	FNRSTUU UNTURFS
FGIINRZ	FRIZING	FHILOSW	WOLFISH	FILORTU	FLORUIT	FNSTTUU UNSTUFT
FGIINST	FISTING	FHILPSU	SHIPFUL	FILORTY	TRIFOLY	FOOORTT FOOTROT
	SIFTING	FHILPTU	PITHFUL	FILOSSS	FOSSILS	FOOOTTU OUTFOOT
FGIINSX	FIXINGS	FHILSUW	WISHFUL	FILPPUY	PULPIFY	FOORSSS FOSSORS
FGIINSY	SIGNIFY	FHINOSU	FUSHION	FILPSTU	UPLIFTS	FOORTTX FOXTROT
FGIINTT	FITTING	FHINRSU	FURNISH	FILRSTY	FIRSTLY	FORRSUW FURROWS
	TIFTING	FHIOOST	OOFTISH	FILRYZZ	FRIZZLY	FORRUWY FURROWY
FGIINZZ	FIZZING	FHIOPPS	FOPPISH	FILSSUY	FUSSILY	FORSSTW FROWSTS
FGIKLNU	FLUKING	FHIOPSX	FOXSHIP	FILSTTU	FLUTIST	FORSTWY FROWSTY
FGIKNNU	FUNKING	FHIORRY	HORRIFY	FILSTUW	WISTFUL	GGGGIIN GIGGING
FGIKNOR	FORKING	FHIOSST	SOFTISH	FILSTUY	FUSTILY	GGGHINO HOGGING
FGILLNU	FULLING	FHIPPSU	PUPFISH	FILSTWY	SWIFTLY	GGGHINU HUGGING
FGILNOO	FOOLING	FHIRSST	SHRIFTS	FILUYZZ	FUZZILY	GGGIIJN JIGGING
	LOOFING	FHIRSTT	THRIFTS	FIMMMUY	MUMMIFY	GGGIILN LIGGING
FGILNOP	FOPLING	FHIRTTY	THRIFTY	FIMMORS	MISFORM	GGGIINP PIGGING
FGILNOT	LOFTING	FHIRTUY	THURIFY	FIMNORS	INFORMS	GGGIINR RIGGING
FGILNOU	FOULING	FHISSSU	HUSSIFS	FIMNORU	UNIFORM	GGGIINT TIGGING
FGILNOW	FLOWING	FHISSTU	SHUFTIS	FIMOORV	OVIFORM	GGGIINW WIGGING
	FOWLING	FHKORTU	FUTHORK	FIMORRT	TRIFORM	GGGIINZ ZIGGING
	WOLFING	FHLNORU	HORNFUL	FIMORTY	MORTIFY	GGGIIST GIGGITS
FGILNOY	FOYLING	FHLNSUU	UNFLUSH	FIMRTUY	FRUMITY	GGGIJNO JOGGING
FGILNPY	FLYPING	FHLOPSU	SHOPFUL	FIMSTYY	MYSTIFY	GGGIJNU JUGGING
FGILNRU	FURLING	FHLPSUU	PUSHFUL	FINOOSS	FOISONS	GGGILNO LOGGING
FGILNSU	INGULFS	FHLRTUU	HURTFUL	FINOPRS	FRIPONS	GGGILNU LUGGING
FGILNSY	FLYINGS		RUTHFUL	FINOPTY	PONTIFY	GGGIMNU MUGGING
FGILNTU	FLUTING	FHOOORS	FORHOOS	FINORSS	FRISSON	GGGINNO GONGING
FGILNTY	FLYTING	FHOOORT	HOOFROT	FINORST	FORINTS	NOGGING
FGILNUX	FLUXING	FHOOOTT	HOTFOOT	FINOSSU	FUSIONS	GGGINOR GORGING
FGILOOY	GOOFILY	FHOORSW	FORHOWS	FIOORSU	FURIOSO	GGGINOS SOGGING
FGILORY	GLORIFY	FHORSTU	FOURTHS	FIOPRST	FORPITS	GGGINOT TOGGING

GGGINOU	GOUGING	GGIMNSU	MUGGINS	GHIKNOO	HOOKING	GHIORST	RIGHTOS
GGGINPU	PUGGING	GGINNNU	GUNNING	GHIKNOW	HOWKING	GHIORSU	ROGUISH
GGGINRU	RUGGING	GGINNOO	ONGOING	GHIKNST	KNIGHTS	GHIOSUV	VOGUISH
GGGINTU	TUGGING	GGINNOP	PONGING	GHIKNSU	HUSKING	GHIPRST	SPRIGHT
GGHHIIN	HIGHING	GGINNOR	GRONING	GHIKNTY	KYTHING	GHIPRTU	UPRIGHT
GGHHIOS	HOGGISH	GGINNOS	NOGGINS	GHILLNU	HULLING	GHIPSST	SPIGHTS
GGHIIJS	JIGGISH	GGINNOW	GOWNING	GHILLSU	GULLISH	GHIPTTU	UPTIGHT
GGHIINN	HINGING	GGINNRU	GURNING	GHILLTY	LIGHTLY	GHIQSTU	QUIGHTS
	NIGHING	GGINOOS	GOOSING	GHILNOS	HOLINGS	GHIRSTW	WRIGHTS
GGHIINS	SIGHING	GGINOPR	GROPING		LONGISH	GHISTTW	TWIGHTS
GGHIIPS	PIGGISH		PORGING	GHILNOT	THOLING	GHLMOOO	HOMOLOG
GGHIIRS	RIGGISH	GGINOPU	UPGOING	GHILNOW	HOWLING	GHLOOSY	SHOOGLY
GGHIITT	THIGGIT	GGINOQS	QIGONGS	GHILNPU	INGULPH	GHLOPSU	PLOUGHS
GGHIMSU	MUGGISH	GGINORS	GORINGS	GHILNRU	HURLING	GHLORUY	ROUGHLY
GGHINNO	HONGING		GRINGOS	GHILNSU	LUSHING	GHLOSSU	SLOUGHS
GGHINOS	HOGGINS	GGINORU	ROGUING	GHILNSY	SHINGLY	GHLOSTY	GHOSTLY
GGHINSU	GUSHING		ROUGING	GHILNTY	NIGHTLY	GHLOSUY	SLOUGHY
GGHIPSU	PUGGISH	GGINORW	GROWING	GHILPST	PLIGHTS	GHLOTUY	TOUGHLY
GGHLOSY	SHOGGLY	GGINOUV	VOGUING	GHILPTY	YPLIGHT	GHMORSU	SORGHUM
GGIIILN	GINGILI	GGINPPY	GYPPING	GHILRTY	RIGHTLY	GHMOSTU	MUGSHOT
GGIIJJS	JIGJIGS	GGINPRU	PURGING	GHILSST	SLIGHTS	GHMPRSU	GRUMPHS
GGIIKNN	KINGING	GGINRSU	SURGING	GHILSTY	SIGHTLY	GHNOPRY	GRYPHON
GGIILLN	GILLING		URGINGS	GHILTTY	TIGHTLY	GHNORST	THRONGS
GGIILNP	PIGLING	GGINSTU	GUSTING	GHILTWY	WIGHTLY	GHNORUU	UNROUGH
GGIILNR	RIGLING	GGINTTU	GUTTING	GHIMMNU	HUMMING	GHNOSSU	SHOGUNS
GGIILNU	GUILING	GGIOORS	GORGIOS	GHIMNNY	HYMNING	GHNOSTU	GUNSHOT
GGIIMMN	MINGING	GGIPRSY	SPRIGGY	GHIMNOS	GNOMISH		NOUGHTS
GGIIMNP	GIMPING	GGLLOOS	LOGLOGS		HOMINGS		SHOTGUN
GGIIMNR	GRIMING	GGLOOOS	GOOGOLS	GHIMNPU	HUMPING	GHNOTUY	YOUNGTH
GGIINNN	GINNING	GGNOORS	GORGONS	GHIMNRY	RHYMING	GHOOOSW	HOOSGOW
GGIINNO	INGOING	GHHHIIS	HIGHISH	GHIMNSU	MUSHING	GHOORSS	SORGHOS
GGIINNP	PINGING	GHHHIST	HIGHTHS	GHIMRSU	SIMURGH	GHORSTU	TROUGHS
GGIINNR	GIRNING	GHHIIIN	HISHING	GHIMSST	SMIGHTS	GHORSTW	GROWTHS
	RINGING	GHHINSU	HUSHING	GHIMSTT	MIGHTST	GHORTUW	WROUGHT
GGIINNS	SIGNING	GHHIRST	SHRIGHT	GHINNOP	PHONING	GHORTUY	YOGHURT
	SINGING	GHHORTU	THROUGH	GHINNOR	HORNING	GHOSTUU	OUTGUSH
GGIINNT	TINGING	GHHOSSU	SHOUGHS	GHINNOS	NOSHING	GIIINRS	IRISING
GGIINNW	WINGING	GHHOTTU	THOUGHT	GHINNOT	NOTHING	GIIJKNN	JINKING
GGIINNZ	ZINGING	GHIIKNO	HOIKING	GHINNTU	HUNTING	GIIJLNT	JILTING
GGIINPR	GRIPING	GHIIKNT	KITHING	GHINOOP	HOOPING	GIIJNNO	JOINING
GGIINPS	PIGGINS	GHIILLN	HILLING	GHINOOS	SHOOING	GIIJNNX	JINXING
GGIINRS	GRISING	GHIILNR	HIRLING	GHINOOT	HOOTING	GIIKKNN	KINKING
GGIINRT	GIRTING	GHIILNT	HILTING	GHINOOV	HOOVING	GIIKKNR	KIRKING
	RINGGIT		LITHING	GHINOPP	HOPPING	GIIKLLN	KILLING
GGIINSU	GUISING	GHIILNW	WHILING	GHINOPS	GINSHOP	GIIKLMN	MILKING
GGIINSV	GIVINGS	GHIILRS	GIRLISH		POSHING	GIIKLNN	INKLING
GGIIRRS	GRIGRIS	GHIINNS	SHINING	GHINORS	HORSING		KILNING
GGIJNSU	JUGGINS	GHIINNT	HINTING		SHORING		LINKING
GGILLNU	GULLING		NITHING	GHINORW	WHORING	GIIKLNR	LIRKING
GGILNNO	LONGING	GHIINNW	WHINING	GHINOST	HOSTING	GIIKLNS	LIKINGS
GGILNNU	LUNGING	GHIINOS	HOISING		TOSHING		SILKING
GGILNOS	GOSLING	GHIINPP	HIPPING	GHINOSU	HOUSING	GIIKLNT	KILTING
	OGLINGS	GHIINPS	PISHING	GHINOSV	SHOVING		KITLING
GGILNOV	GLOVING	GHIINPT	PITHING	GHINOSW	SHOWING	GIIKNNP	PINKING
GGILNOW	GLOWING	GHIINRS	HIRINGS	GHINOTT	HOTTING	GIIKNNR	RINKING
	GOWLING	GHIINSS	HISSING		TONIGHT	GIIKNNS	SINKING
GGILNOZ	GLOZING	GHIINST	HISTING	GHINOTU	THOUING	GIIKNNT	TINKING
GGILNPU	GULPING		INSIGHT	GHINPPU	HUPPING	GIIKNNV	KNIVING
GGILNRU	GURLING		SHITING	GHINPPY	HYPPING	GIIKNNW	WINKING
GGILNSU	LUGINGS		SITHING	GHINPSU	GUNSHIP	GIIKNNZ	ZINKING
GGILNUY	GUYLING	GHIINSW	WISHING		PUSHING	GIIKNPP	KIPPING
	UGLYING	GHIINTT	HITTING	GHINRSU	RUSHING	GIIKNPS	PIGSKIN
GGILOOS	GIGOLOS		TITHING	GHINRTU	HURTING		SPIKING
GGILOST	GIGLOTS	GHIINTW	WHITING		UNGIRTH	GIIKNRS	GIRKINS
GGILOSY	SOGGILY		WITHING		UNRIGHT		GRISKIN
GGILRWY	WRIGGLY	GHIINZZ	HIZZING	GHINSTU	TUSHING		KRISING
GGIMMNU	GUMMING	GHIIRST	TIGRISH		UNSIGHT		RISKING
GGIMNOR	GORMING	GHIJNOS	JOSHING	GHINTTU	HUTTING	GIIKNRT	TRIKING
GGIMNPU	GUMPING	GHIKLNU	HULKING	GHINTTY	TYTHING	GIIKNRY	YIRKING
GGIMNPY	GYMPING	GHIKNNO	HONKING	GHIOPSZ	PHIZOGS	GIIKNSS	KISSING

	SKIINGS	GIINNOP OPINING	GIJLLNO JOLLING	POOLING
GIIKNST	KISTING	PIONING	GIJLNOT JOLTING	GILNOOS LOOSING
	SKITING	GIINNOR IRONING	GIJLNOU JOULING	SOLOING
GIIKNSV	SKIVING	ROINING	GIJLNOW JOWLING	SOOLING
	VIKINGS	GIINNOS NOISING	GIJLNSU JUNGLIS	GILNOOT LOOTING
GIIKNTT	KITTING	GIINNOT OINTING	GIJMNPU JUMPING	TOOLING
GIILLLN	LILLING	GIINNPP NIPPING	GIJNOTT JOTTING	GILNOPP LOPPING
GIILLMN	MILLING	GIINNPS SNIPING	GIJNSTU JUSTING	GILNOPR PROLING
GIILLNN	NILLING	GIINNPU PINGUIN	GIJNTTU JUTTING	GILNOPS POLINGS
GIILLNO	GILLION	GIINNRS RINSING	GIKKNNO KONKING	SLOPING
GIILLNP	PILLING	GIINNRT TRINING	GIKKNOO KOOKING	GILNOPT POLTING
GIILLNR	RILLING	GIINNRU INURING	GIKKNOY YOKKING	GILNOPU LOUPING
GIILLNT	LILTING	RUINING	GIKLNOO LOOKING	GILNOPW PLOWING
	TILLING	URINING	GIKLNOP POLKING	GILNORS LORINGS
GIILLNW	WILLING	GIINNSW INSWING	GIKLNRU LURKING	GILNORU LOURING
GIILMNN	LIMNING	GIINNTT TINTING	GIKLNSU LUSKING	GILNOSS LOSINGS
GIILMNO	MOILING	GIINNTU UNITING	SULKING	GILNOST LINGOTS
GIILMNP	LIMPING	GIINNTV VINTING	GIKMNOS SMOKING	TIGLONS
GIILMNS	LIMINGS	GIINNTW TWINING	GIKMNSU MUSKING	TOLINGS
	SLIMING	GIINOPS POISING	GIKNNNO KONNING	GILNOSU LOUSING
	SMILING	GIINORS ORIGINS	GIKNNOP PONKING	GILNOSV LOVINGS
GIILMNT	MILTING	SIGNIOR	GIKNNOS SNOKING	SOLVING
GIILMPR	PILGRIM	SIGNORI	GIKNNOT TONKING	GILNOSW LOWINGS
GIILMRY	GRIMILY	GIINORT RIOTING	GIKNNOW KNOWING	LOWSING
GIILNNN	LINNING	GIINOSY YOGINIS	GIKNNSU UNKINGS	SLOWING
GIILNNR	NIRLING	GIINPPP PIPPING	GIKNOOP POOKING	SOWLING
GIILNNS	LIGNINS	GIINPPR RIPPING	GIKNOOR ROOKING	GILNOTT LOTTING
	LININGS	GIINPPS PIPINGS	GIKNOPR PROKING	GILNOTU LOUTING
GIILNNY	INLYING	SIPPING	GIKNOPU POUKING	GILNOTW LOWTING
GIILNOR	LIGROIN	GIINPPT TIPPING	GIKNORT TROKING	GILNOVV VOLVING
	ROILING	GIINPPY YIPPING	GIKNORW WORKING	GILNOVW WOLVING
GIILNOS	SILOING	GIINPPZ ZIPPING	GIKNORY YORKING	GILNOWY YOWLING
	SOILING	GIINPQU PIQUING	GIKNOST STOKING	GILNPPU PULPING
GIILNOT	TOILING	GIINPRS PRISING	GIKNOSY YOKINGS	GILNPRU PURLING
GIILNPP	LIPPING	RISPING	GIKNOUY YOUKING	GILNPSU PLUSING
GIILNPS	LISPING	SPIRING	GIKNRSY SKRYING	PULINGS
	SPILING	GIINPRZ PRIZING	SKYRING	PULSING
GIILNRS	RIGLINS	GIINPSS PISSING	GIKNSTU TUSKING	PUSLING
GIILNRT	TIRLING	GIINPST SPITING	GIKNSTY SKYTING	GILNPUY UPLYING
GIILNST	LISTING	GIINPSW SWIPING	GIKRSTU TUGRIKS	GILNRSU RULINGS
	SILTING	WIPINGS	GILLLNO LOLLING	GILNSTU LUSTING
	STILING	WISPING	GILLLNU LULLING	LUTINGS
	TILINGS	GIINPTT PITTING	GILLMNU MULLING	SINGULT
GIILNSV	LIVINGS	GIINPTY PITYING	GILLNNU NULLING	GILNSTY STYLING
	SLIVING	GIINQRU QUIRING	GILLNOP POLLING	GILNVYY VYINGLY
GIILNTT	TILTING	GIINQTU QUITING	GILLNOR ROLLING	GILOORS GIROSOL
	TITLING	GIINRRS SIRRING	GILLNOT TOLLING	GILORTT TRIGLOT
GIILNTW	WILTING	GIINRRT TIRRING	GILLNPU PULLING	GILORTY TRILOGY
	WITLING	GIINRSS RISINGS	GILLNSU ULLINGS	GILOSTT GLOTTIS
GIILOSS	GLIOSIS	GIINRST STIRING	GILLNUW WULLING	GILRSTY GRISTLY
GIILOST	OLIGIST	TIRINGS	GILLNYY LYINGLY	GILRTUY LITURGY
GIILRST	STRIGIL	GIINRSV VIRGINS	GILLORS RIGOLLS	GILRYZZ GRIZZLY
GIIMMNN	NIMMING	GIINRSW WIRINGS	GILMNOO LOOMING	GIMMMNU MUMMING
GIIMMNR	RIMMING	GIINRTT RITTING	MOOLING	GIMMNPU MUMPING
GIIMNNS	MININGS	GIINRTW TWIRING	GILMNOR MORLING	GIMMNRY RYMMING
GIIMNNT	MINTING	WRITING	GILMNOT MOLTING	GIMMNSU SUMMING
GIIMNPP	PIMPING	GIINSST SISTING	GILMNOY MOYLING	GIMMNUV VUMMING
GIIMNPR	PRIMING	GIINSSU ISSUING	GILMNPU LUMPING	GIMMORS GIMMORS
GIIMNRT	MITRING	GIINSSW WISSING	PLUMING	GIMNNOO MOONING
GIIMNSS	MISSING	GIINSSZ SIZINGS	GILMNRU MURLING	GIMNNOR MORNING
GIIMNST	MISTING	GIINSTT SITTING	GILMNSU LIGNUMS	GIMNNTU MUNTING
	SMITING	GIINSTU SUITING	GILNNOO GLONOIN	GIMNOOP MOOPING
	STIMING	GIINSTV STIVING	LOONING	GIMNOOR MOORING
	TIMINGS	GIINSTW WISTING	GILNNOU LOUNING	ROOMING
GIINNNP	PINNING	GIINTTT TITTING	GILNNOW LOWNING	GIMNOOS SOOMING
GIINNNR	RINNING	GIINTTW WITTING	GILNNRU NURLING	GIMNOOT MOOTING
GIINNNS	INNINGS	GIINZZZ ZIZZING	GILNNSU UNSLING	TOOMING
	SINNING	GIJKNNU JUNKING	GILNNTU LUNTING	GIMNOOV MOOVING
GIINNNT	TINNING	GIJKNOO JOOKING	GILNNUV VULNING	GIMNOOZ ZOOMING
GIINNNW	WINNING	GIJKNOU JOUKING	GILNOOP LOOPING	GIMNOPP MOPPING

GIMNOPR	ROMPING	GINOPPW WOPPING		SPRINGY	GNNORYY GYRONNY
GIMNOPU	MOUPING	GINOPRS PROIGNS	GINPSSY SPYINGS	GNNOSUW UNGOWNS
GIMNOPY	YOMPING		PROSING	GINPSTU STUPING	GNNRUUW UNWRUNG
GIMNORS	SMORING		ROPINGS	GINPSTY TYPINGS	GNOOORS GORSOON
GIMNORU	ROUMING	GINOPRT PORTING	GINPSUW UPSWING	GNOOOSS GOSSOON
GIMNORW	WORMING		TROPING	GINPTTU PUTTING	GNOOOYZ ZOOGONY
GIMNOSS	MOSSING	GINOPRU INGROUP	GINPTUY UPTYING	GNOORST TROGONS
GIMNOST	GNOMIST		POURING	GINQTUY QUYTING	GNOPPSU OPPUGNS
GIMNOSU	MOUSING		ROUPING	GINRRSU RUNRIGS	GNOPRTU GUNPORT
	SOUMING	GINOPRV PROVING	GINRSST STRINGS	GNOPRUW UPGROWN
GIMNOSW	MOWINGS	GINOPRW POWRING	GINRSTU RUSTING	GNOPSTU POTGUNS
	SOWMING	GINOPSS POSINGS	GINRSTY STRINGY	GNOSTUU OUTGUNS
GIMNPPU	PUMPING		POSSING		STYRING	GOOOORS GOOROOS
GIMNPRU	RUMPING	GINOPST POSTING		TRYINGS	GOORSTT GROTTOS
GIMNPSU	IMPUGNS		STOPING	GINRSUU USURING	GOORTUW OUTGROW
	SPUMING	GINOPSY POYSING	GINRTTU RUTTING	GOPRSUW UPGROWS
GIMNPTU	TUMPING	GINOPTT POTTING	GINSSSU SUSSING	GORRSTU TURGORS
GIMNSSU	MUSINGS	GINOPTU POUTING	GINTTTU TUTTING	GORSTTU ROTGUTS
	MUSSING	GINOQTU QUOTING	GIOOPRR PORRIGO	GORSTUY YOGURTS
GIMNSTU	MUSTING	GINORRV VORRING	GIOORSV VIGOROS	HHIIPPS HIPPISH
GIMNSTY	STYMING	GINORSS GRISONS	GIOPRRU PRURIGO	HHIISTW WHITISH
GIMORSS	SIMORGS		INGROSS	GIOPSSS GOSSIPS	HHIMRTY RHYTHMI
GIMOSSY	YOGISMS		SIGNORS	GIOPSST SPIGOTS	HHINORS HORNISH
GIMOSTU	GOMUTIS	GINORST ROSTING	GIOPSSY GOSSIPY	HHIORSW WHORISH
GIMRSSU	SIMURGS		SORTING	GIORRSU RIGOURS	HHIOSTT HOTTISH
GIMRSUU	GURUISM		STORING	GIORSUV VIGOURS	HHISSTW WHISHTS
GINNNOO	NOONING		TRIGONS	GIOSSYZ ZYGOSIS	HHMMSUU HUMHUMS
GINNNOR	RONNING	GINORSU ROUSING	GISWWYY WYSIWYG	HHMRSTY RHYTHMS
GINNNOW	WONNING		SOURING	GJNOOSU GOUJONS	HHOOSTT HOTSHOT
GINNNPU	PUNNING	GINORSV ROVINGS	GJNRSUU GURJUNS	HIIJKNS HIJINKS
GINNNRU	RUNNING	GINORSW ROWINGS	GJOORTT JOGTROT	HIIKLMS KHILIMS
GINNNSU	SUNNING		WORSING	GKMOOSU GOMOKUS	HIIKNPS KINSHIP
GINNNTU	TUNNING	GINORSY ROSYING	GLLOOPS GOLLOPS		PINKISH
GINNOOS	NOOSING		SIGNORY	GLMNOOS MONGOLS	HIILMTU LITHIUM
GINNOOW	WOONING	GINORTT ROTTING	GLMOOOR MOORLOG	HIILPST SHILPIT
GINNOPS	SPONGIN	GINORTU ROUTING	GLMOOYY MYOLOGY	HIILPTY PITHILY
GINNOPY	PONYING		TOURING	GLMORUW LUGWORM	HIILRTT TRILITH
GINNORS	SNORING	GINORTW ROWTING	GLNNOOR LORGNON	HIIMMSS MISHMIS
	SORNING		TROWING	GLNNSUU UNSLUNG	HIIMPSW WIMPISH
GINNORU	GRUNION	GINOSSS SOSSING	GLNOOOS OOLONGS	HIIMSSS MISSISH
GINNORW	INGROWN	GINOSST STINGOS	GLNOOOY NOOLOGY	HIIMSST MISHITS
GINNORY	ROYNING		TOSSING	GLNOOPR PROLONG	HIIMSTT SHITTIM
GINNOSS	NOSINGS	GINOSSU SOUSING	GLNOOPY POLYGON	HIINORS ROINISH
GINNOST	STONING	GINOSSW SOWINGS	GLNOOSU OULONGS	HIINPSS INSHIPS
GINNOSW	SNOWING		SOWSING	GLNORWY WRONGLY	HIINSSW SWINISH
	WONINGS	GINOSTT SOTTING	GLNOSUW SUNGLOW	HIIOPRZ RHIZOPI
GINNOSZ	ZONINGS	GINOSTU OUSTING	GLNOTTU GLUTTON	HIIORST HISTRIO
GINNOTW	WONTING		OUTINGS	GLNOUYY YOUNGLY	HIKLSSU LUSKISH
GINNPRU	PRUNING		TOUSING	GLNPSUU UNPLUGS	HIKLSUY HUSKILY
GINNPTU	PUNTING	GINOSTV STOVING	GLOOORY OROLOGY	HIKMNOS MONKISH
GINNRSU	NURSING	GINOSTW STOWING	GLOOOTY OTOLOGY	HIKMRSU MURKISH
	URNINGS		TOWINGS	GLOOOYZ ZOOLOGY	HIKMSUZ MUZHIKS
GINNRTU	TURNING		TOWSING	GLOORUY UROLOGY	HIKNNOR INKHORN
GINNSTU	TUNINGS	GINOSTY TOYINGS	GLOPSTU PUTLOGS	HIKNNTU UNTHINK
GINNTTU	NUTTING	GINOTTT TOTTING	GLORSSY GROSSLY	HIKNRSS SHRINKS
GINNTUY	UNTYING	GINOTTU TOUTING	GLPRSUY SPLURGY	HIKOORS ROOKISH
GINOOPP	POOPING	GINOTTW TOWTING	GMMOSUU GUMMOUS	HILLOPT HILLTOP
GINOOPR	ROOPING		WOTTING	GMMPUUW MUGWUMP	HILLOPY LYOPHIL
GINOOPS	SOOPING	GINOTUW OUTWING	GMNNOOS GNOMONS	HILLPSU UPHILLS
GINOOPT	POOTING	GINOTUZ TOUZING	GMNOORU GUNROOM	HILLRSS SHRILLS
GINOORS	ROOSING	GINOTWZ TOWZING	GMNOORW MORWONG	HILLRST THRILLS
GINOORT	ROOTING	GINPPPU PUPPING	GMNSTUU GUMNUTS	HILLRSY SHRILLY
GINOOSS	ISOGONS	GINPPSU SUPPING	GMNSUUZ MZUNGUS	HILLRTY THRILLY
GINOOST	SOOTING		UPPINGS	GMOOPRS POGROMS	HILMMOU HOLMIUM
GINOOSW	WOOINGS	GINPPTU TUPPING	GMOOSTU GOMUTOS	HILMOPS LOMPISH
GINOOTT	TOOTING	GINPRRU PURRING	GMORSUU GRUMOUS		PHLOMIS
GINOPPP	POPPING	GINPRSS SPRINGS	GMORTUW MUGWORT	HILMOSS HOLISMS
GINOPPS	SOPPING	GINPRSU PURSING	GMPSSUY GYPSUMS	HILMOSW WHOLISM
GINOPPT	TOPPING	GINPRSY PRYINGS	GMRUYYZ ZYMURGY	HILMPSU LUMPISH
GINOPPU	POUPING		PRYSING	GNNORUW UNGROWN	HILMSSY HYLISMS

HILMSUY MUSHILY	HIQSSUY SQUISHY	IIISTTW WISTITI	IINOSUV INVIOUS
HILMTUU THULIUM	HIRSSTT THIRSTS	IIJMNOS MISJOIN	IINOTTU TUITION
HILNNTY NINTHLY	THRISTS	IIJNNOT INJOINT	IINPPPS PIPPINS
HILNPST PLINTHS	HIRSTTU RUTTISH	IIKLLMY MILKILY	IINQRUY INQUIRY
HILOOTT OTOLITH	HIRSTTY THIRSTY	IIKLLSY SILKILY	IINRTTY TRINITY
HILOOTZ ZOOLITH	THRISTY	IIKLMNP LIMPKIN	IINSSST INSISTS
HILORTU UROLITH	HKKLOOZ KOLKHOZ	IIKLNOS OILSKIN	IINSTTU INTUITS
HILOSST HOLISTS	HKNOOSU UNHOOKS	IIKLPSY SPIKILY	IINSTTW INTWIST
HILOSSW SLOWISH	HKNSSUU UNHUSKS	IIKLRSY RISKILY	NITWITS
HILOSTU LOUTISH	HKOOOPT POTHOOK	IIKMNOR KIRIMON	IIOPRSS PISSOIR
HILOSTY HYLOIST	HKOOSST SHTOOKS	IIKMNPS SIMPKIN	IIORSSV VIROSIS
HILOSVW WOLVISH	HLLOOSW HOLLOWS	IIKMNSS SIMKINS	IIORSTV IVORIST
HILOSWY SHOWILY	HLLOPSY PHYLLOS	IIKNPPS PIPKINS	VISITOR
HILOTWW WHITLOW	HLMNOTY MONTHLY	IIKNSSS SISKINS	IIOSTTU OUSTITI
HILPRUW UPWHIRL	HLMNPYY NYMPHLY	IIKOSST OIKISTS	IIPPSUU PIUPIUS
HILPSST SPILTHS	HLMORRY MYRRHOL	IIKOSTT TITOKIS	IIPRSST SPIRITS
HILSSTY HYLISTS	HLMOSTY THYMOLS	IILLLSY SILLILY	TRIPSIS
STYLISH	HLOOSTY SOOTHLY	IILLMNO MILLION	IIPRSTU PITURIS
HILSTTY THISTLY	HLOPRTY PROTHYL	IILLMSY SLIMILY	IIPRSTY SPIRITY
HILSTXY SIXTHLY	HLORSTY SHORTLY	IILLNOP PILLION	IIPRTVY PRIVITY
HIMMPSU MUMPISH	HLOTUYY YOUTHLY	IILLNOZ ZILLION	IIRRSTT TIRRITS
HIMMRSU RUMMISH	HLPRSUU SULPHUR	IILLNST INSTILL	IJKLLOY KILLJOY
HIMMSTY MYTHISM	UPHURLS	IILLNTT LITTLIN	IJKMOSU MOUJIKS
HIMNOOS MOONISH	HMMMSUU HUMMUMS	IILLPSU ILLUPIS	IJKNOSS JOSKINS
HIMNSSU MUNSHIS	HMMNOOY HOMONYM	IILMNOS LIONISM	IJLLLOQ JOLLILY
HIMNSTY HYMNIST	HMMRTUY THRUMMY	IILMORS SIMILOR	IJLLOTY JOLLITY
HIMOORS MOORISH	HMNOPSY NYMPHOS	IILMOSS LIMOSIS	IJLMPUY JUMPILY
HIMOPRS ROMPISH	HMNOPYY HYPONYM	IILMSTU STIMULI	IJLNOQU JONQUIL
HIMOPSS SOPHISM	HMNPSUY HYPNUMS	IILMSTY MISTILY	IJLNOTY JOINTLY
HIMOPST PHOTISM	HMOOPRS MORPHOS	IILNNSU INSULIN	IJMOSSS JISSOMS
HIMORTU THORIUM	HMOOSST SMOOTHS	INULINS	IJNNOTU UNJOINT
HIMOTTY TIMOTHY	HMORSUU HUMOURS	IILNORS SIRLOIN	IJNORSU JUNIORS
HIMPRSS SHRIMPS	HMSTUYZ ZYTHUMS	IILNOSV VIOLINS	IJRSSTU JURISTS
HIMPRTU TRIUMPH	HNNOOPS PHONONS	IILNOSY NOISILY	IKKMNOU KIKUMON
HIMPTUY PYTHIUM	HNNORSU UNSHORN	IILNPUV PULVINI	IKKNORT KIRKTON
HIMRSTY RHYMIST	HNNOSUW UNSHOWN	IILNRSV RIVLINS	IKKORRS KORKIRS
HIMSSTU ISTHMUS	HNOOPST PHOTONS	IILNSST INSTILS	IKKSUUY KIKUYUS
HIMSTTY MYTHIST	HNOOPTY TYPHOON	IILOPRT TRIPOLI	IKLLSTU KILLUTS
HINNNSU NUNNISH	HNOORSS HORSONS	IILORTV VITRIOL	IKLLSUY SULKILY
HINNORT TINHORN	HNOORST THORONS	IILOSTV VIOLIST	IKLMNPU LUMPKIN
HINNOST TONNISH	HNOORSU HONOURS	IILPRVY PRIVILY	IKLMOSY SMOKILY
HINNPSU NUNSHIP	HNOOSTU UNSHOOT	IILPSST PISTILS	IKLMRUY MURKILY
HINOOPS INHOOPS	HNOPSSY SYPHONS	IILPSTY TIPSILY	IKLMSUY MUSKILY
HINOORT HORNITO	HNOPSTY PHYTONS	IILTTUY UTILITY	IKLNNSU UNLINKS
HINOORZ HORIZON	PYTHONS	IILTTWY WITTILY	IKLNOOS SKOLION
HINOOST INSOOTH	TYPHONS	IIMMMNU MINIMUM	IKLNOOT KILOTON
HINOPPS SHIPPON	HNORTUW UNWORTH	IIMMNSU MINIMUS	IKLNOSU ULIKONS
HINOPSS SIPHONS	HNOSTUU UNSHOUT	MINIUMS	IKLNPSU SKULPIN
SONSHIP	HNRTTUU UNTRUTH	IIMNNOS MINIONS	IKLNRWY WRINKLY
HINORST HORNIST	HNSSTUU UNSHUTS	IIMNOSS MISSION	IKLOOTT TOOLKIT
HINORSU NOURISH	HOOPRST PORTHOS	IIMNOSU IONIUMS	IKLOSSU SOUSLIK
HINORSY ROYNISH	HOOPSTT HOTPOTS	NIMIOUS	IKLSSSU SUSLIKS
HINOSSW SNOWISH	HOOPSTU UPSHOOT	IIMNOTX MIXTION	IKLSTTU KITTULS
HINOSTW TOWNISH	HOOPSTY TOYSHOP	IIMNPRT IMPRINT	IKMNOOO OKIMONO
HINPSSU UNSHIPS	HOORRRS HORRORS	IIMOPSU IMPIOUS	IKMNOOS KIMONOS
HINPTUW UNWHIPT	HOORRST ORTHROS	IIMOSST MITOSIS	IKMNORS MIKRONS
HINRSTU RUNTISH	HOORSUZ HUZOORS	IIMOSSU SIMIOUS	MORKINS
HIOOPRS POORISH	HOOSTTU OUTSHOT	IIMRTTU TRITIUM	IKMNOSW MISKNOW
HIOOSSV SHIVOOS	HOPRTUW UPTHROW	IIMRTUV TRIVIUM	IKMNPPU PUMPKIN
HIOPPSS SHIPPOS	HOPSSSY HYSSOPS	IIMSSTT TIMISTS	IKMNRSU RUMKINS
HIOPRSW WORSHIP	HOPSSTU UPSHOTS	IIMSSTU MISSUIT	IKMNRTU TRINKUM
HIOPSST SOPHIST	HOPSTUY TYPHOUS	IINNOOP OPINION	IKMOOST MISTOOK
HIOPSSY PHYSIOS	HORSTUU OUTRUSH	IINNOPS PINIONS	IKMOSSU KOUMISS
HIOPSTU UPHOIST	HOSSTTU STOUTHS	IINNOTU UNITION	IKMPRSS SKRIMPS
HIORSSU SOURISH	HRSSTTU THRUSTS	IINOPSS ISOSPIN	IKNNPTU UNPINKT
HIORSTY HISTORY	HRSSTUY THYRSUS	SINOPIS	IKNNSTU UNKNITS
HIOSSTT SOTTISH	IIIJJLN JINJILI	IINORST IRONIST	IKNOOST ISOKONT
HIOSTTU OUTHITS	IIIKMNN MINIKIN	IINORSV VIRIONS	IKNOPST INKPOTS
HIOTTUW OUTWITH	IIIMRST MIRITIS	IINORTT INTROIT	INKSPOT
WITHOUT		IINOSSV VISIONS	IKNORSW INWORKS

IKNPSTU	SPUTNIK	ILOORTY	OLITORY
	UPKNITS	ILOOSST	SOLOIST
IKPRSSU	SPRUIKS	ILOOSTY	SOOTILY
IKPRSSY	KRYPSIS	ILOOWYZ	WOOZILY
ILLLOWY	LOWLILY	ILOPPSY	SOPPILY
ILLMNOU	MULLION	ILOPRSY	PROSILY
ILLMOOR	MOORILL	ILOPSST	PISTOLS
ILLMPUY	LUMPILY		POSTILS
ILLMSUU	LIMULUS	ILOPSSX	OXSLIPS
ILLNOQU	QUILLON	ILOPSTT	SPOTLIT
ILLNORU	RULLION	ILOPSUY	PIOUSLY
ILLNPUU	LUPULIN	ILOQRSU	LIQUORS
ILLNSUW	UNWILLS	ILORRSY	SORRILY
ILLNTUY	NULLITY	ILOSSTY	TOSSILY
ILLOORZ	ZORILLO		TYLOSIS
ILLOPRY	PILLORY	ILOSTTW	WITTOLS
ILLOPSW	PILLOWS	ILPPSTU	PULPITS
ILLOPWY	PILLOWY	ILPSTTU	UPTILTS
ILLOSUV	VILLOUS	ILRSSTU	TRISULS
ILLOSUY	LOUSILY	ILRSSTY	LYRISTS
ILLOSWW	WILLOWS	ILRSTUY	RUSTILY
ILLOTXY	XYLITOL	ILSSTTU	LUTISTS
ILLOWWY	WILLOWY	ILSSTTY	STYLIST
ILLPPUY	PULPILY	IMMNOSS	MONISMS
ILLPSUV	PULVILS		NOMISMS
ILLQSSU	SQUILLS	IMMNOSU	MUSIMON
ILLRSUY	SURLILY		OMNIUMS
ILLSTUY	LUSTILY	IMMNOUU	MUONIUM
ILMMRUY	RUMMILY	IMMOOSS	SIMOOMS
ILMMSUU	MIMULUS	IMMOPTU	OPTIMUM
ILMNOOT	MOONLIT	IMMOSSU	OSMIUMS
ILMNOSU	MOULINS	IMMOSTU	TOMIUMS
ILMNRSU	MURLINS	IMMSSTU	MUTISMS
ILMNSSU	MUSLINS		SUMMIST
ILMOORY	ROOMILY		SUMMITS
ILMOOSS	MOLOSSI	IMNNNOU	MUNNION
ILMORTU	TURMOIL	IMNNOOR	NORIMON
ILMOSTY	MOISTLY	IMNNOSW	MINNOWS
ILMPSTU	PLUMIST	IMNNSTU	MUNTINS
ILMRSSY	LYRISMS	IMNOOPP	POMPION
ILMUYZZ	MUZZILY	IMNOOPT	TOMPION
ILNNSUY	SUNNILY	IMNOORR	MORRION
ILNOOPS	PLOSION	IMNOORS	MORIONS
ILNOOPV	VOLPINO	IMNOORT	MONITOR
ILNOOST	LOTIONS		TROMINO
	SOLITON	IMNOOSS	MONOSIS
ILNOPPS	POPLINS		SIMOONS
ILNOPRU	PURLOIN	IMNOOST	MOTIONS
ILNOPST	PONTILS	IMNOOSU	OMINOUS
ILNOPSU	UPSILON	IMNOOSY	ISONOMY
ILNOPSY	YPSILON	IMNOOUX	OXONIUM
ILNOQSU	QUINOLS	IMNOPPU	PUMPION
ILNORST	NOSTRIL	IMNORRU	MURRION
ILNORSU	SURLOIN	IMNORTY	TRIONYM
ILNORTU	TORULIN	IMNOSST	MONISTS
ILNOSST	TONSILS	IMNOSSY	MYOSINS
ILNOSSU	INSOULS	IMNOSVY	VISNOMY
ILNOSTU	OILNUTS	IMNRRSU	MURRINS
	ULTIONS	IMNRSTU	UNTRIMS
ILNOSTY	STONILY	IMOOPRX	PROXIMO
ILNOSWY	SNOWILY	IMOOSSS	OSMOSIS
ILNOTUV	VOLUTIN	IMOOSSU	OSMIOUS
ILNPRSU	PURLINS	IMOOSTV	VOMITOS
ILNPSST	SPLINTS	IMOPRSS	PORISMS
ILNPSTU	UNSPILT	IMOPRST	IMPORTS
ILNRSTY	NITRYLS		TROPISM
ILNSSTU	INSULTS	IMOPRTU	PROTIUM
ILOOORS	ROSOLIO	IMOPSST	IMPOSTS
ILOOPST	POLOIST	IMOPSTU	UTOPISM
ILOORST	LORIOTS	IMORRRS	MIRRORS

IMORSTU	TOURISM		TROPIST
IMORSTY	TRISOMY	IOPSTTU	UTOPIST
IMOSSYZ	ZYMOSIS	IOQRTTU	QUITTOR
IMOSTTT	TOMTITS	IOQSSTU	QUOISTS
IMPRSSU	PURISMS	IORRSTW	WORRITS
IMPSSTU	SUMPITS	IORRSZZ	RIZZORS
IMQRSSU	SQUIRMS	IORRTTX	TORTRIX
IMQRSUY	SQUIRMY	IORSSTU	SUITORS
IMRSSTU	SISTRUM	IORSTTU	TOURIST
	TRISMUS	IOSSSTT	TSOTSIS
	TRUISMS	IOSSTTU	OUTSITS
IMRTTUY	YTTRIUM	IOSTTUW	OUTWITS
INNNORU	RUNNION	IPRRSTU	IRRUPTS
INNOOPS	OPSONIN		STIRRUP
INNOOST	NOTIONS	IPRSSTU	PURISTS
INNORST	INTRONS		SPRUITS
INNOSSU	UNISONS		UPRISTS
INNOSTU	NONSUIT	IPRSTUU	PURSUIT
INNOSWW	WINNOWS	IPSSSTY	STYPSIS
INNQSUY	SQUINNY	IPSSTTY	TYPISTS
INOOPRT	PORTION	IPSTTTU	TITTUPS
INOOPSS	POISONS	IPTTTUY	TITTUPY
	POISSON	IQRRSSU	SQUIRRS
INOOPST	OPTIONS	IQRSSTU	SQUIRTS
	POSITON	JMOPTUU	OUTJUMP
	POTIONS	JNNOSTU	JOTUNNS
INOORSS	ORISONS	JNOORSU	JOURNOS
INOORST	ISOTRON		SOJOURN
	TORSION	JOOPPSY	POPJOYS
INOORSZ	ZORINOS	JOSTTUU	OUTJUTS
INOOSST	TOISONS	KKLMSUU	MUKLUKS
INOOSUX	NOXIOUS	KKNRSUU	KUNKURS
INOPPRS	POPRINS	KLLMOSU	MOLLUSK
INOPPST	TOPSPIN	KLOOOTU	LOOKOUT
INOPRSS	PRISONS		OUTLOOK
INOPSST	PISTONS	KLOOPSU	UPLOOKS
INOPSSU	POUSSIN	KMPRSSU	SKRUMPS
	SPINOUS	KNNNOUW	UNKNOWN
INOPSTT	TINPOTS	KNNOSTU	UNKNOTS
INOPSTU	SPINOUT	KNOOPTT	TOPKNOT
INORSTT	TRITONS	KNOPRTY	KRYPTON
INORSTU	NITROUS	KNORSUW	UNWORKS
	TURIONS	KOOOTTU	OUTTOOK
INORSUU	RUINOUS	KOOPRTW	WORKTOP
	URINOUS	KOORTUW	OUTWORK
INORSUV	UNVISOR	KOOSTWW	KOWTOWS
INOSSTU	USTIONS	KORTTUW	TUTWORK
INOSSUU	SINUOUS	LLLMMUU	MULMULL
INOSTUW	OUTWINS	LLLOOPS	LOLLOPS
INPRSST	SPRINTS	LLMMSUU	MULMULS
INPRSTU	TURNIPS	LLMOOPR	ROLLMOP
	UNSTRIP	LLMPPUY	PLUMPLY
INPRSTY	TRYPSIN	LLNORSU	UNROLLS
INQSSTU	SQUINTS	LLOOPRT	TROLLOP
INRSTTU	INTRUST	LLOOSTU	TOLUOLS
INSSTUU	SUNSUIT	LLOPRSU	UPROLLS
	UNSUITS	LLORSST	STROLLS
INSTTUW	UNTWIST	LMMSTUU	MULTUMS
INTTUWY	UNWITTY	LMOORSU	ORMOLUS
IOOPRSS	POROSIS	LMOOSTY	TOYLSOM
IOOPRSV	PROVISO	LMOPSUU	PLUMOUS
IOOPSTY	ISOTOPY	LMORSSU	MUSROLS
IOORSSS	SOROSIS	LMRSTUU	LUSTRUM
IOORSTT	RISOTTO	LMSTTUU	TUMULTS
IOORSTU	RIOTOUS	LMSTUUU	TUMULUS
IOOSSSS	SISSOOS	LNNOPSU	NONPLUS
IOPPPST	POPPITS	LNOOPTU	PULTOON
IOPPSTT	TIPTOPS	LNOOSST	STOLONS
IOPRSSY	PYROSIS	LNOPSTU	PLUTONS
IOPRSTT	PROTIST		PULTONS

LNOSSUU	UNSOULS	MNOOOYZ	ZOONOMY	MOSSTUU	OUTSUMS	NRSTTUU	UNTRUST
LNPSTUU	PULTUNS	MNOOPPS	POMPONS	NNNSUUY	UNSUNNY	OOOOPRT	POTOROO
LNRTUUV	VULTURN	MNOOPST	TOMPONS	NNOOOPT	PONTOON	OOOOSZZ	ZOOZOOS
LNRTUUY	UNTRULY	MNOOPTY	TOPONYM	NNOOPRU	PRONOUN	OOOPRTU	OUTROOP
LOOOORS	OLOROSO	MNOORSU	UNMOORS	NNOOPSS	SPONSON	OOORTTU	OUTROOT
LOOOORST	ROTOLOS	MNOOSTU	MOUTONS	NNOOPST	PONTONS	OOPRRST	TORPORS
LOOSSTV	VOLOSTS	MNOOSTW	TOWMONS	NNOORSY	RONYONS	OOPRSTU	PORTOUS
LOPPRSY	PROPYLS	MNOOSUY	ONYMOUS	NNORSUW	UNSWORN		UPROOTS
LOPPSUU	PULPOUS	MNOOTTW	TOWMONT	NNOSSUY	UNSONSY	OOPRSTV	PROVOST
LOPPSUY	POLYPUS	MNORSTU	NOSTRUM	NNOSTYY	SYNTONY	OOPRTTU	OUTPORT
LOPRSTY	PROTYLS	MNOSTTU	MUTTONS	NNRSTUU	UNTURNS	OOPRTUU	OUTPOUR
LOPRSUY	PYLORUS	MNOTTUY	MUTTONY	NOOPRSS	SPONSOR	OOPSSTT	TOSSPOT
LOPRTUY	POULTRY	MOOOTYZ	ZOOTOMY	NOOPRST	PROTONS	OOPSTTU	OUTPOST
LORSTTY	TROTYLS	MOOPPSU	POMPOUS	NOOPSSY	POYSONS		OUTTOPS
LORSTUU	TORULUS	MOOPRSY	POMROYS	NOORSST	TONSORS	OOPSWWW	POWWOWS
LOSTTUY	STOUTLY	MOOPSSU	OPOSSUM	NOORSTU	UNROOST	OORRSSW	SORROWS
LPRSSUU	SURPLUS	MOOPSTT	TOPMOST		UNROOTS	OORSTUU	ROUTOUS
MMNOSSU	MUSMONS	MOORRSW	MORROWS	NOORTUW	OUTWORN	OPPRRTU	PURPORT
	SUMMONS	MOOSTTU	OUTMOST	NOPPRSU	UNPROPS	OPPRSTU	SUPPORT
MMOOPPS	POMPOMS	MOPPRST	PROMPTS	NOPSSTU	SUNSPOT	OPPRSTY	STROPPY
MMOOSTT	MOTMOTS	MOPSSSU	POSSUMS		UNSTOPS	OPPRSUY	PYROPUS
MMOPSTY	SYMPTOM	MOPSSUU	SPUMOUS	NOPSTUW	UPTOWNS	OPRSSTU	SPROUTS
MMRRSUU	MURMURS	MOQRSUU	QUORUMS	NORSTUU	OUTRUNS		STROUPS
MMSTUUU	MUTUUMS	MOQSTUU	QUOTUMS	NORTTUU	OUTTURN		STUPORS
MNNOOOS	MONSOON	MORRSTU	ROSTRUM	NOSSTUW	UNSTOWS	OPSTTUU	OUTPUTS
MNNOSYY	SYNONYM	MORRSUU	RUMOURS	NPRSTUU	UPTURNS	ORSSTTU	STROUTS
MNNOTUU	UNMOUNT	MORSTUU	TUMOURS	NRSSTTU	STRUNTS	ORSSUUU	USUROUS
MNOOOPP	POMPOON	MOSSTTU	UTMOSTS	NRSSTUU	UNTRUSS	ORSTTUU	SURTOUT

8-LETTER ANAGRAMS

AAAACCRR	CARACARA
AAAACJRR	JARARACA
AAAACNRS	ANASARCA
AAAADMTV	AMADAVAT
AAAADTVV	AVADAVAT
AAAAHJMR	MAHARAJA
AAAAIMPR	ARAPAIMA
AAAAIRTX	ATARAXIA
AAAAJKRR	JARARAKA
AAAAKKMT	TAKAMAKA
AAAAKKNT	KATAKANA
AAAALSTY	ATALAYAS
AAAAMMTT	MATAMATA
AAAARRSS	SASARARA
AAABBCLS	CABBALAS
AAABBELT	ABATABLE
AAABBHKL	KABBALAH
AAABBILT	ABBATIAL
AAABBKLS	KABBALAS
AAABCCRS	BACCARAS
AAABCCRT	BACCARAT
AAABCHLS	CALABASH
AAABCHMU	MACAHUBA
AAABCINT	ANABATIC
AAABCIRS	ARABICAS
AAABCLSV	BACLAVAS
AAABCNRR	BARRACAN
	BARRANCA
AAABCNRS	BARACANS
AAABCNRU	CARNAUBA
AAABCPRY	CAPYBARA
AAABCSTW	CATAWBAS
AAABDEST	DATABASE
AAABDKNT	DATABANK
AAABDNNN	BANDANNA
AAABDNNS	BANDANAS
AAABDNRS	SARABAND
AAABDNRT	ABRADANT
AAABEGHL	GALABEAH
AAABEGLL	GALLABEA
AAABEGLS	GALABEAS
AAABEHNR	HABANERA
AAABEHRT	BARATHEA
AAABEMPR	PARABEMA
AAABENSS	ANABASES
AAABFLLS	FALBALAS
AAABGHIL	GALABIAH
AAABGILL	GALLABIA
AAABGILS	GALABIAS
AAABGILY	GALABIYA
AAABGLOR	ALGAROBA
AAABGRTU	RUTABAGA
AAABILTT	BATTALIA
AAABINSS	ANABASIS
AAABIPSS	PIASSABA
AAABKLSV	BAKLAVAS
AAABKPSS	BAASSKAP
AAABLLSW	WALLABAS
AAABLOPR	PARABOLA
AAABLPRS	PALABRAS
AAABMSST	MASTABAS
AAABNNRS	RABANNAS
AAABORRS	ARAROBAS
AAACCEPR	CARAPACE
AAACCIMM	CAIMACAM
AAACCLRS	CARACALS
AAACCRSS	CASCARAS

AAAACCRTT	CATARACT
AAACDEIM	ACADEMIA
AAACDEQU	AQUACADE
AAACDETU	ACAUDATE
AAACDILR	CALDARIA
AAACDINR	ACARIDAN
AAACDKLY	LACKADAY
AAACDMMS	MACADAMS
AAACDNNO	ANACONDA
AAACDNRS	SANDARAC
AAACDOTV	ADVOCAAT
AAACEGNT	AGACANTE
AAACEGTU	AGUACATE
AAACEHLP	ACALEPHA
AAACEHLZ	CHALAZAE
AAACELNT	ANALECTA
AAACELST	CATALASE
AAACENNP	PANACEAN
AAACENPS	PANACEAS
AAACGINT	CAATINGA
AAACGLSW	SCALAWAG
AAACGMNP	CAMPAGNA
AAACHIPS	APHASIAC
AAACHLNR	ANARCHAL
AAACHLSZ	CHALAZAS
AAACHNST	ACANTHAS
AAACHRSY	ACHARYAS
AAACILMN	MANIACAL
AAACILMS	MALACIAS
AAACILSY	CALISAYA
AAACIMRS	CARIAMAS
AAACINPS	ACAPNIAS
AAACINTV	CAVATINA
AAACIPSU	SAPUCAIA
AAACIRRS	SACRARIA
AAACIRTX	ATARAXIC
AAACJMRS	JACAMARS
AAACKMRT	TAMARACK
AAACLLSV	CAVALLAS
AAACLMNS	ALMANACS
AAACLMRY	CALAMARY
AAACLPST	CATALPAS
AAACLRST	ALCATRAS
AAACLRSZ	ALCAZARS
AAACMNPS	CAMPANAS
AAACMRSS	MASCARAS
AAACMRSU	AMARACUS
AAACNNRS	CARANNAS
AAACNPST	CATAPANS
AAACNRST	NACARATS
AAACNRSU	CARAUNAS
AAACNRSV	CARAVANS
AAACNSST	CANASTAS
AAACNSTT	CANTATAS
AAACRRWY	CARRAWAY
AAACRSWY	CARAWAYS
AAACSSST	CASSATAS
AAACSSSV	CASSAVAS
AAACSSTT	CATASTAS
AAACSTWY	CASTAWAY
AAADEGNP	APANAGED
AAADELMS	ALAMEDAS
	SALAAMED
AAADENTV	VANADATE
AAADEPRT	TAPADERA
AAADFRSY	FARADAYS
AAADGLMY	AMYGDALA

AAADHMRS	ADHARMAS
	MADRASAH
AAADHNRT	THANADAR
AAADIILR	RADIALIA
AAADILRU	ADULARIA
AAADIMNY	ADYNAMIA
AAADIRST	DATARIAS
AAADJMRS	JAMADARS
AAADKLMN	KALAMDAN
AAADKRRV	AARDVARK
AAADLMNQ	QALAMDAN
AAADLMNS	MANDALAS
AAADLMSW	WADMAALS
AAADMNST	ADAMANTS
AAADMNTU	TAMANDUA
AAADMRSS	MADRASAS
	MADRASSA
AAADNRSS	SARDANAS
AAADNRST	TANADARS
AAAEGISS	ASSEGAAI
AAAEGLMX	MALAXAGE
AAAEGLRT	ALTARAGE
AAAEGLST	GALATEAS
AAAEGNPP	APPANAGE
AAAEGNPS	APANAGES
AAAEGRST	GASTRAEA
AAAEHKST	TAKAHEAS
AAAEHLST	ALTHAEAS
AAAEHMNT	ANATHEMA
AAAEHNPS	ANAPHASE
AAAEIMNS	ANAEMIAS
AAAEKKRT	KARATEKA
AAAELMPT	PALAMATE
AAAELMTX	MALAXATE
AAAELRTV	LAVATERA
AAAENNSS	ANANASES
AAAENOPR	PARANOEA
AAAENPRV	PARAVANE
AAAENPST	ANAPAEST
AAAENSST	ANATASES
AAAERTWY	TEARAWAY
AAAFFLLS	ALFALFAS
AAAFINST	FANTASIA
AAAFINUV	AVIFAUNA
AAAFIRST	RATAFIAS
AAAFNRSS	SAFRANAS
AAAFRSWY	FARAWAYS
AAAGGLLN	GALANGAL
AAAGGLNS	GALANGAS
AAAGGLOP	GALAPAGO
AAAGHIPR	AGRAPHIA
AAAGHIPS	APHAGIAS
AAAGHLNS	LANGAHAS
AAAGHNST	ATAGHANS
AAAGHNTY	YATAGHAN
AAAGILPT	PATAGIAL
AAAGILRT	ALIGARTA
AAAGINRR	AGRARIAN
AAAGISSS	ASSAGAIS
AAAGLMMS	AMALGAMS
AAAGLMNS	NAGMAALS
AAAGLMST	STALAGMA
AAAGLNSS	LASAGNAS
AAAGLRRW	WARRAGAL
AAAGLRST	ASTRAGAL
AAAGMNRS	ANAGRAMS
AAAGMPRR	PARAGRAM

AAAGNOPR	ARAPONGA
AAAGNPRS	PARASANG
	PARGANAS
AAAGNPRU	ARAPUNGA
AAAGNPRU	ARAPUNGA
AAAGNRST	TANAGRAS
AAAGNRSU	GUARANAS
AAAGNSTY	YATAGANS
AAAHHLSV	HALAVAHS
AAAHIMNR	MAHARANI
AAAHIMNS	SHAMIANA
AAAHIMRT	HAMARTIA
AAAHINPR	RAPHANIA
AAAHIPSS	APHASIAS
AAAHJKSW	KAJAWAHS
AAAHKMNS	KHANSAMA
AAAHKRSS	RAKSHASA
AAAHLMRS	HARMALAS
AAAHLNNS	ALANNAHS
AAAHMMST	MAHATMAS
AAAHMNRT	AMARANTH
AAAHMRSS	ASHRAMAS
AAAHMSST	TAMASHAS
AAAHNNSV	SAVANNAH
AAAHNOPR	ANAPHORA
AAAHNSTY	ATHANASY
AAAHPRST	PARATHAS
AAAHRSTW	WARATAHS
AAAHTTWY	THATAWAY
AAAIINPR	APIARIAN
AAAIKKMM	KAIMAKAM
AAAILLMR	MALARIAL
AAAILLPT	PALATIAL
AAAILMNR	MALARIAN
AAAILMRS	MALARIAS
AAAILMSV	MALVASIA
AAAILNRU	AULARIAN
AAAILPRV	PARAVAIL
AAAILPSS	APLASIAS
AAAILRST	SALARIAT
AAAIMMST	MIASMATA
AAAIMNST	AMANITAS
AAAINNRR	RANARIAN
AAAINOPR	PARANOIA
AAAINQRU	AQUARIAN
AAAIPRSX	APRAXIAS
AAAIPSSV	PIASSAVA
AAAKKTZZ	KAZATZKA
AAAKMNRS	NAMASKAR
AAAKOSWY	SOAKAWAY
AAALLPRX	PARALLAX
AAALLPST	PALATALS
AAALNNPT	PLATANNA
AAALNNST	LANTANAS
AAALNPRT	RATAPLAN
AAALNPST	APLANATS
AAALNRTT	TARLATAN
AAALPRST	SATRAPAL
AAALSWYY	LAYAWAYS
AAAMNOPR	PANORAMA
AAAMNRST	AMARANTS
AAAMOTTU	AUTOMATA
AAAMPRST	PATAMARS
AAAMRRSZ	ZAMARRAS
AAAMRTTU	TRAUMATA
AAAMRTZZ	RAZMATAZ
AAANNSSV	SAVANNAS
AAANNSTT	ANNATTAS

AAANOPRZ PARAZOAN	AABCEILM AMICABLE	AABCRSTT ABSTRACT	AABDKNNS SANDBANK
AAANORSY SAYONARA	AABCEIMN AMBIANCE	AABCSTTU CATTABUS	AABDLLRY BALLADRY
AAANPRTV PARAVANT	AABCEINR CARABINE	AABDDEGN BANDAGED	AABDLLUY LAUDABLY
AAANQTUU AQUANAUT	AABCEIRT BACTERIA	AABDDEHN HEADBAND	AABDLMNU LABDANUM
AAANRSTT TANTARAS	AABCEKLM CLAMBAKE	AABDDEIR ABRAIDED	AABDLMNY DAMNABLY
TARANTAS	AABCEKLR LACEBARK	AABDDELL BALLADED	AABDLNPT PLATBAND
TARTANAS	AABCELLP PLACABLE	AABDDENR BRANDADE	AABDLNSS SALBANDS
AAAORSWY SOARAWAY	AABCELLR CABALLER	AABDDLNS BADLANDS	AABDLORR LARBOARD
AAAPPRST APPARATS	AABCELLS SCALABLE	AABDDMOR DAMBOARD	AABDLORY ADORABLY
AAAPQRTU PARAQUAT	AABCELNR BALANCER	AABDEEHL BEHEADAL	AABDLRSW BRADAWLS
AAARSTTU TUATARAS	BARNACLE	AABDEELR READABLE	AABDMNNS BANDSMAN
AABBCDEG CABBAGED	AABCELNS BALANCES	AABDEELT DATEABLE	AABDMNNY BANDYMAN
AABBCDKN BACKBAND	AABCELOR ALBACORE	DEALBATE	AABDMNRS ARMBANDS
AABBCDRS SCABBARD	AABCELPR CAPABLER	AABDEELV EVADABLE	AABDNNOS ABANDONS
AABBCEGS CABBAGES	AABCELRT BRACTEAL	AABDEERY BAYADERE	AABDNNTU ABUNDANT
AABBCEIS ABBACIES	AABCELWY CABLEWAY	AABDEGIN BADINAGE	AABDNORS BANDORAS
AABBCEKR BAREBACK	AABCEMRV VAMBRACE	AABDEGLR GRADABLE	AABDNRRY BARNYARD
AABBCINR BARBICAN	AABCENYY ABEYANCY	AABDEGNS BANDAGES	AABDNRSU BANDURAS
AABBCIRR BARBARIC	AABCEORT BOATRACE	AABDEHHI DAHABIEH	AABDORSV BRAVADOS
AABBCIST SABBATIC	AABCERRS BARRACES	AABDEHKR HARDBAKE	AABDORWY BROADWAY
AABBCORS BARBASCO	AABCERST ABREACTS	AABDEHMR HARDBEAM	AABDRRSS BRASSARD
AABBDERT BARBATED	CABARETS	AABDEILN BALADINE	AABDRSST BASTARDS
AABBDGRS GABBARDS	AABCESSU ABACUSES	AABDEIOU ABOIDEAU	AABDRSSU SUBADARS
AABBEELR BEARABLE	AABCFIIL BIFACIAL	AABDEIRS ARABISED	AABDRSTY BASTARDY
AABBEELT BEATABLE	AABCFKLL BACKFALL	AABDEIRZ ARABIZED	AABEEGKR BREAKAGE
AABBEILL BAILABLE	AABCFKLT FLATBACK	AABDEISS DIABASES	AABEEGNT ABNEGATE
AABBEKLN BANKABLE	AABCFKST FASTBACK	AABDEJLL DJELLABA	AABEEHLL HEALABLE
AABBELLM BLAMABLE	AABCHILR BRACHIAL	AABDEJNX BANJAXED	AABEEHLT HATEABLE
AABBELLS BASEBALL	AABCHINR BRANCHIA	AABDEKRY DAYBREAK	AABEEKLM MAKEABLE
AABBELRY BEARABLY	AABCHKLS BACKLASH	AABDELLS BALLADES	AABEEKLT TAKEABLE
AABBEORT BAREBOAT	AABCHKRS SHABRACK	AABDELLU LAUDABLE	AABEEKMT BAKEMEAT
AABBGRST GABBARTS	AABCHKSW BACKWASH	AABDELMN DAMNABLE	MAKEBATE
AABBHKSU BABUSHKA	AABCHLOO COOLABAH	AABDELMS BALSAMED	AABEEKRW BAKEWARE
AABBIILL BILABIAL	AABCHNRS BARCHANS	AABDELOR ADORABLE	AABEELLS LEASABLE
AABBILRT BARBITAL	AABCIILS BASILICA	AABDELPR PARABLED	SALEABLE
AABBLLMY BLAMABLY	AABCIKLT TAILBACK	AABDELPT BALDPATE	AABEELMN AMENABLE
AABBLORS BARBOLAS	AABCILLR BACILLAR	AABDELRS BASELARD	NAMEABLE
AABBLSSU SUBBASAL	AABCILMS BALSAMIC	AABDELRT TRADABLE	AABEELMT TAMEABLE
AABBMMOZ ZAMBOMBA	CABALISM	AABDELRW DRAWABLE	AABEELRS ERASABLE
AABBSSSU BABASSUS	AABCILMY AMICABLY	AABDELRY READABLY	AABEELRT RATEABLE
AABCCCHI BACCHIAC	AABCILNN CANNIBAL	AABDEMNS BEADSMAN	AABEELRW WEARABLE
AABCCEHK BACKACHE	AABCILNO ANABOLIC	AABDENTU UNABATED	AABEELST EATABLES
AABCCELS CASCABEL	AABCILST BASALTIC	AABDENUX BANDEAUX	AABEEMPR ABAMPERE
AABCCERT BRACCATE	CABALIST	AABDENVW WAVEBAND	AABEENOR ANAEROBE
AABCCHIS BISCACHA	AABCINNN CANNABIN	AABDEORS SEABOARD	AABEERRT ABERRATE
AABCCHIZ BIZCACHA	AABCINNR CINNABAR	AABDERRT TABERDAR	AABEERSZ ZAREEBAS
AABCCHKT BACKCHAT	AABCINNS CANNABIS	AABDERRW BEARWARD	AABEERTT TRABEATE
AABCCHNT BACCHANT	AABCINRS CARABINS	AABDERTT RABATTED	AABEFFNS BEFFANAS
AABCCINN CANNABIC	AABCINSU BANAUSIC	AABDERTV VARTABED	AABEFGSU AUFGABES
AABCCKKP BACKPACK	AABCIOPS COPAIBAS	AABDERWY WAYBREAD	AABEFLLL FLABELLA
AABCCKLP BLACKCAP	AABCIRSS BRASSICA	AABDFHLN FAHLBAND	AABEFLMU FLAMBEAU
AABCCKLW CLAWBACK	AABCISSS ABSCISSA	AABDGHNS HANDBAGS	AABEGGGS BAGGAGES
AABCCMOT CATACOMB	AABCISTX TAXICABS	AABDGINN ABANDING	AABEGGRS GARBAGES
AABCDEIN ABIDANCE	AABCKLPY PLAYBACK	AABDGINR ABRADING	AABEGHIL GALABIEH
AABCDEIT ABDICATE	AABCKLSY LAYBACKS	AABDGMOS GAMBADOS	AABEGHLN HANGABLE
AABCDELL CABALLED	AABCKPSY BACKPAYS	AABDGNOV VAGABOND	AABEGHNR BERGHAAN
AABCDELN BALANCED	AABCKRRS BARRACKS	AABDGNSS SANDBAGS	AABEGILN GAINABLE
AABCDHKN BACKHAND	AABCKSSW BACKSAWS	AABDGORR GARBOARD	AABEGINR ABEARING
AABCDHKR HARDBACK	AABCKSWY SWAYBACK	AABDGOTU GADABOUT	AABEGLLL GLABELLA
AABCDIIS DIABASIC	AABCLLLO COALBALL	AABDHLLN HANDBALL	AABEGLLS ALGEBRAS
AABCDINT ABDICANT	AABCLLPY PLACABLY	AABDHNST HATBANDS	AABEGLRT GLABRATE
AABCDKRW BACKWARD	AABCLMSU CALUMBAS	AABDHNSY HAYBANDS	AABEGLRU ARGUABLE
DRAWBACK	AABCLNUU CUNABULA	AABDHRSU SUBAHDAR	AABEGMNR BARGEMAN
AABCDKRY BACKYARD	AABCLOOR COOLABAR	AABDIILS BASIDIAL	AABEGMNY MANGABEY
AABCDNRR BRANCARD	AABCLRRY CARBARYL	AABDILLN BALLADIN	AABEGMRS BERGAMAS
AABCEENY ABEYANCE	AABCMSSU SAMBUCAS	AABDILNS BALADINS	MEGABARS
AABCEERS SCARABEE	AABCNORR BARRANCO	AABDIMNR MADBRAIN	AABEGMRT BREGMATA
AABCEERT ACERBATE	AABCORST ABACTORS	AABDIMRS BARMAIDS	AABEGNOR BARONAGE
AABCEGOT CABOTAGE	ACROBATS	AABDINNR RAINBAND	AABEGORT ABROGATE
AABCEHNR BARCHANE	AABCOSTT CATBOATS	AABDINST TABANIDS	AABEGOST SABOTAGE

AABEGRRS	BAGARRES	
	BARRAGES	
AABEGSSS	BAGASSES	
AABEGSSU	ABUSAGES	
AABEHIRR	HERBARIA	
AABEHKLS	SHAKABLE	
AABEHLOT	OATHABLE	
AABEHLPS	SHAPABLE	
AABEHLPT	ALPHABET	
AABEHLRW	WARHABLE	
AABEHLSW	WASHABLE	
AABEHNST	ABTHANES	
AABEIKNS	IKEBANAS	
AABEILLM	MAILABLE	
AABEILLS	ISABELLA	
	SAILABLE	
AABEILNR	INARABLE	
AABEILRS	RAISABLE	
AABEILRV	VARIABLE	
AABEILST	BALISTAE	
	LABIATES	
	SATIABLE	
AABEILTV	ABLATIVE	
AABEINOZ	ZABAIONE	
AABEINRT	RABATINE	
AABEINST	BASANITE	
AABEIOTU	ABOITEAU	
AABEIRSS	ARABISES	
AABEIRSV	ABRASIVE	
AABEIRSZ	ARABIZES	
AABEJLLS	JELLABAS	
AABEJMUX	JAMBEAUX	
AABEJNSX	BANJAXES	
AABEKLLT	TALKABLE	
AABEKLLW	WALKABLE	
AABEKMNR	BRAKEMAN	
AABEKPRR	PARBREAK	
AABEKRRS	BARESARK	
AABELLNO	LOANABLE	
AABELLPP	PALPABLE	
AABELLPS	LAPSABLE	
AABELLPY	PLAYABLE	
AABELLSS	SABELLAS	
AABELLSV	SALVABLE	
AABELLSY	SALEABLY	
AABELLUV	VALUABLE	
AABELMNY	AMENABLY	
AABELMST	BLASTEMA	
	LAMBASTE	
AABELMSU	AMUSABLE	
AABELMTU	AMBULATE	
AABELNNT	TANNABLE	
AABELNOS	ABALONES	
AABELNPS	ANABLEPS	
AABELNPT	PANTABLE	
AABELNRY	BALNEARY	
AABELNST	BANALEST	
AABELOPR	PARABOLE	
AABELORR	ARBOREAL	
AABELOSV	LAVABOES	
AABELOVW	AVOWABLE	
AABELPRS	PARABLES	
	SPARABLE	
AABELPSS	PASSABLE	
AABELRST	ARBALEST	
AABELRTY	BETRAYAL	
	RATEABLY	
AABELSTT	STATABLE	
	TASTABLE	
AABELTTU	TABULATE	
AABELTUX	TABLEAUX	
AABENRRT	ABERRANT	
AABENRST	ANTBEARS	
	RATSBANE	
AABEORRT	ARBORETA	
AABEORST	RABATOES	
AABERSTT	RABATTES	
	TABARETS	
AABERSTU	ABATURES	
AABESZZZ	BAZAZZES	
AABFILUX	FABLIAUX	
AABFLOTT	FALTBOAT	
	FLATBOAT	
AABGGNOT	TABOGGAN	
AABGGRRT	BRAGGART	
AABGHINS	ABASHING	
AABGHNSS	NASHGABS	
AABGIILS	ABIGAILS	
AABGILNT	ABLATING	
AABGINRS	BARGAINS	
AABGINRY	ABRAYING	
AABGIRST	BARGAIST	
AABGLLRY	BALLYRAG	
AABGLMNU	GALBANUM	
AABGLRUY	ARGUABLY	
AABGMORR	BAROGRAM	
AABGNORZ	GARBANZO	
AABHHISS	SAHIBAHS	
AABHHORU	BROUHAHA	
AABHHRSU	BRUHAHAS	
AABHIINU	BAUHINIA	
AABHIJMY	JAMBIYAH	
AABHILTU	HABITUAL	
AABHINST	HABITANS	
AABHINTT	HABITANT	
AABHIRST	TABASHIR	
AABHISTT	HABITATS	
AABHKRNS	BARKHANS	
AABHNOTU	AUTOBAHN	
AABHQSSU	SQUABASH	
AABHRRSU	SURBAHAR	
AABIJMSY	JAMBIYAS	
AABIKNSS	BANKSIAS	
AABILLLY	LABIALLY	
AABILLRS	BARILLAS	
AABILLST	BALLISTA	
AABILMNS	BAILSMAN	
AABILNNU	BIANNUAL	
AABILNOR	BARONIAL	
AABILNOT	ABLATION	
AABILNRU	BINAURAL	
AABILNTY	BANALITY	
AABILOSU	ABOULIAS	
AABILOTT	BOATTAIL	
AABILRRT	ARBITRAL	
AABILRST	ARBALIST	
AABILRVY	VARIABLY	
AABILSST	BALISTAS	
AABIMMRS	MARIMBAS	
AABIMNNO	BONAMANI	
AABIMNRU	MANUBRIA	
AABIMORS	AMBROSIA	
AABINNPR	BRAINPAN	
AABINORS	ABRASION	
AABINOSU	OUABAINS	
AABINRST	ATABRINS	
	BARTISAN	
AABINRTZ	BARTIZAN	
AABINSST	ABSTAINS	
AABIORRS	SORBARIA	
AABIORTT	ABATTOIR	
AABIOSSY	BIOASSAY	
AABIPSUX	PAXIUBAS	
AABIRTUY	RUBAIYAT	
AABJLMNO	JAMBOLAN	
AABKLLPR	BALLPARK	
AABKMNNS	BANKSMAN	
AABKOOSZ	BAZOOKAS	
AABLLMOR	BALMORAL	
AABLLNST	BALLANTS	
AABLLPPY	PALPABLY	
AABLLPST	PATBALLS	
AABLLSST	BALLASTS	
AABLLSTU	BLASTULA	
AABLLUVY	VALUABLY	
AABLMNOR	ABNORMAL	
AABLMNTU	AMBULANT	
AABLMRSU	LABARUMS	
AABLMSST	LAMBASTS	
AABLNTTT	BLATTANT	
AABLORST	ABLATORS	
AABLOTUY	LAYABOUT	
AABLPSSY	PASSABLY	
AABLRRSU	SABURRAL	
AABLRSST	ARBLASTS	
AABLSTTU	ABUTTALS	
AABMMOSU	ABOMASUM	
AABMNNOO	BONAMANO	
AABMNOTW	BATWOMAN	
AABMNRTU	RAMBUTAN	
AABMORSU	MARABOUS	
AABMORTU	MARABOUT	
	TAMBOURA	
AABMOSSU	ABOMASUS	
AABMRSTU	TAMBURAS	
AABNNOST	ABSONANT	
AABNNOSZ	BONANZAS	
AABNOSST	SABATONS	
AABORRRT	BARRATOR	
AABORSTT	BAROSTAT	
AABRRRTY	BARRATRY	
AABRRSST	BRASSART	
AABRRSSU	SABURRAS	
AABRRSUV	BRAVURAS	
AABSTTTU	BATTUTAS	
AACCCDIS	SACCADIC	
AACCCHHU	CACHUCHA	
AACCCRUY	ACCURACY	
AACCDDES	CASCADED	
AACCDEIM	ACADEMIC	
AACCDELO	ACCOLADE	
AACCDENU	CADUCEAN	
AACCDERS	CARCASED	
AACCDESS	CASCADES	
	SACCADES	
AACCDIRS	CARDIACS	
AACCDOVY	ADVOCACY	
AACCEELT	CALCEATE	
AACCEENT	CETACEAN	
AACCEGOR	ACCORAGE	
AACCEGRU	CARUCAGE	
AACCEHIX	CACHEXIA	
AACCEIRR	CERCARIA	
AACCEKRS	CARCAKES	
AACCELOR	CARACOLE	
AACCELPT	PLACCATE	
AACCENRT	CARCANET	
AACCENSV	VACANCES	
AACCERSS	CARCASES	
AACCERTU	ACCURATE	
		CARUCATE
AACCFGOO		CACAFOGO
AACCFILR		FARCICAL
AACCGILT		GALACTIC
AACCHILL		CAILLACH
AACCHILP		PACHALIC
AACCHINR		ANARCHIC
		CHARACIN
AACCHISV		VISCACHA
AACCHIVZ		VIZCACHA
AACCHLNS		CLACHANS
AACCHLOR		CHARCOAL
AACCHLOT		CACHALOT
AACCHLRS		CLARSACH
AACCHMNO		COACHMAN
AACCHMPS		CHAMPACS
AACCHNNS		CANNACHS
AACCHNOR		CORANACH
AACCHRST		CHARACTS
AACCIINV		VACCINIA
AACCIIST		SCIATICA
AACCILMS		ACCLAIMS
AACCILNV		VACCINAL
AACCILRU		ACICULAR
AACCILTT		TACTICAL
AACCIORS		CARIOCAS
AACCIORU		CARIACOU
AACCIPTY		CAPACITY
AACCIRTY		CARYATIC
AACCJKRW		CRACKJAW
AACCJORU		CARCAJOU
		CARJACOU
AACCKLPS		CALPACKS
AACCKORT		COATRACK
AACCKRRS		CARRACKS
AACCLLRU		CALCULAR
AACCLLST		CATCALLS
AACCLMNY		CLAMANCY
AACCLOPS		POLACCAS
AACCLORS		CARACOLS
AACCLPRS		CALCSPAR
AACCLPST		PLACCATS
AACCLRSU		ACCRUALS
		CARACULS
		SACCULAR
AACCLSSU		ACCUSALS
AACCORSU		CURACAOS
		CURACOAS
AACCOSST		ACCOASTS
AACCOSTT		STACCATO
		STOCCATA
		TOCCATAS
AACCRRST		CARRACTS
AACDDEIL		DAEDALIC
AACDDENV		ADVANCED
AACDDETU		CAUDATED
AACDDHRS		CHADDARS
AACDDINS		CANDIDAS
AACDEEHH		HEADACHE
AACDEEHR		AREACHED
		HEADRACE
AACDEEHS		HEADCASE
AACDEELS		ESCALADE
AACDEEMS		ACADEMES
AACDEEPS		ESCAPADE
AACDEEST		ESTACADE
AACDEETU		ECAUDATE
AACDEFHR		HARDFACE
AACDEFLS		FALCADES
AACDEFLT		FALCATED

AACDEGGR	AGGRACED	AACDIINS	ASCIDIAN
AACDEGKP	PACKAGED	AACDILLP	PALLADIC
AACDEGMR	DECAGRAM	AACDILMT	DALMATIC
AACDEHHY	HEADACHY	AACDILNO	DIACONAL
AACDEHIN	HACIENDA	AACDILNR	CARDINAL
AACDEHLN	CHALANED	AACDILNU	DULCIANA
AACDEHLP	CEPHALAD	AACDILOZ	ZODIACAL
AACDEHMR	DRACHMAE	AACDILRR	RAILCARD
AACDEHMS	CHAMADES	AACDILRS	RADICALS
AACDEHRS	CHARADES	AACDIMNO	MANDIOCA
AACDEHRT	CATHEDRA	AACDIMNY	ADYNAMIC
AACDEHST	CATHEADS	AACDIMOS	CAMISADO
AACDEHTT	ATTACHED	AACDIMRS	CAMISARD
AACDEILS	ALCAIDES	AACDIMRT	DRAMATIC
	SIDALCEA	AACDINRT	RADICANT
AACDEIMN	MAENADIC		TRIDACNA
AACDEIMS	CAMISADE	AACDINRY	RADIANCY
AACDEINR	CANARIED	AACDINST	ANTACIDS
	RADIANCE	AACDIOTU	AUTACOID
AACDEINS	AIDANCES	AACDIRSS	ASCARIDS
AACDEIRT	RADICATE	AACDIRTY	CARYATID
AACDEJNT	ADJACENT	AACDITUY	AUDACITY
AACDEKNP	PANCAKED	AACDJKSW	JACKDAWS
AACDEKNS	ASKANCED	AACDJQRU	JACQUARD
AACDEKTT	ATTACKED	AACDKLLN	LACKLAND
AACDELLS	ALCALDES	AACDLNSS	SCANDALS
AACDELMN	MANACLED	AACDLORS	CARLOADS
AACDELNR	CALENDAR	AACDLORT	CARTLOAD
	LANDRACE	AACDLOSS	SCALADOS
AACDELNS	CANDELAS	AACDLPRS	PLACARDS
AACDELNV	VALANCED	AACDLRTY	DACTYLAR
AACDELOS	ESCALADO	AACDMMOR	CARDAMOM
AACDELPT	PLACATED	AACDMMRU	CARDAMUM
AACDELRS	CALDERAS	AACDMNNO	MANCANDO
AACDELSS	SCALADES	AACDMNOR	CARDAMON
AACDELSY	ALCAYDES	AACDOOSV	AVOCADOS
AACDELTT	LACTATED	AACDORRT	CARTROAD
AACDELTV	CLAVATED	AACEEFIT	FACETIAE
AACDENSV	ADVANCES	AACEEFLP	PALEFACE
	CANVASED	AACEEGIR	ACIERAGE
AACDENSZ	CADENZAS		AGACERIE
AACDENTU	ADUNCATE	AACEEGLR	CLEARAGE
AACDENTV	TADVANCE	AACEEGLV	CLEAVAGE
AACDEOPS	ESCAPADO	AACEEGRS	ACREAGES
AACDEOTU	AUTOCADE	AACEEHLP	ACALEPHE
AACDEOVT	ADVOCATE	AACEEHLT	LEACHATE
AACDEQUY	ADEQUACY	AACEEHRS	AREACHES
AACDERST	CADASTRE		EARACHES
AACDERSV	CADAVERS	AACEEHRT	TRACHEAE
AACDERTU	ARCUATED	AACEEIMT	EMACIATE
AACDETTU	ACTUATED	AACEEINN	ENCAENIA
AACDETUV	VACUATED	AACEEIRT	ACIERATE
AACDGINR	ARCADING	AACEEKRT	CARETAKE
	CARANGID	AACEELNS	ANELACES
	CARDIGAN	AACEELRT	LACERATE
AACDHHKR	HARDHACK	AACEELST	ESCALATE
AACDHIIS	DICHASIA	AACEELTU	ACULEATE
AACDHILR	DIARCHAL	AACEEMRT	MACERATE
AACDHIMR	DRACHMAI		RACEMATE
AACDHINP	HANDICAP	AACEEMST	CASEMATE
AACDHINR	ARACHNID	AACEENTT	CATENATE
AACDHKRT	HARDTACK	AACEEPSS	SEASCAPE
AACDHLNP	HANDCLAP	AACEERTV	ACERVATE
AACDHLOT	CATHODAL	AACEESST	ACETATES
AACDHLRY	CHARLADY	AACEETUV	EVACUATE
AACDHMMR	DRAMMACH	AACEETVX	EXCAVATE
AACDHMRS	DRACHMAS	AACEFFIN	AFFIANCE
AACDHNRS	HANDCARS	AACEFHLP	HALFPACE
AACDHPRS	CRASHPAD	AACEFIST	FASCIATE
AACDIINR	CNIDARIA	AACEFRST	SEACRAFT

AACEFRSX	CARFAXES	AACEINRS	CANARIES
AACEFRTT	ARTEFACT	AACEINRT	CARINATE
AACEGGRS	AGGRACES	AACEINRV	VARIANCE
AACEGHNT	CHANTAGE	AACEINST	ESTANCIA
AACEGILN	ANGELICA	AACEIPPS	PAPACIES
AACEGILT	GLACIATE	AACEIPRS	AIRSPACE
AACEGINR	CANAIGRE	AACEIPRT	APRICATE
AACEGIOP	APOGAEIC	AACEIPSS	CAPIASES
AACEGIRR	CARRIAGE	AACEIPTT	APATETIC
AACEGIRV	VICARAGE		CAPITATE
AACEGKPR	PACKAGER	AACEIRSV	AVARICES
AACEGKPS	PACKAGES		CAVIARES
AACEGKRT	TRACKAGE	AACEIRTV	VICARATE
AACEGKSS	SACKAGES	AACEITTV	ACTIVATE
AACEGLNY	LANCEGAY		CAVITATE
AACEGNRS	CARNAGES	AACEJLTU	JACULATE
	CRANAGES	AACEKKLW	CAKEWALK
AACEGRST	CARTAGES	AACEKNPS	PANCAKES
AACEGRSV	SCAVAGER	AACEKNSS	ASKANCES
AACEGSSV	SCAVAGES	AACEKOST	OATCAKES
AACEHILL	HELIACAL	AACEKRTT	ATTACKER
AACEHILN	ACHENIAL	AACELLMR	MARCELLA
AACEHIMR	CHIMAERA	AACELLNS	CANELLAS
AACEHIMT	HAEMATIC	AACELLOT	ALLOCATE
AACEHIRS	ARCHAISE	AACELLST	CASTELLA
AACEHIRT	THERIACA		LACTEALS
AACEHIRZ	ARCHAIZE	AACELMNP	PLACEMAN
AACEHLNT	CALANTHE	AACELMNS	MANACLES
AACEHLPS	ACALEPHS	AACELMRS	CARAMELS
AACEHLRS	ALCHERAS	AACELMTU	MACULATE
AACEHLRT	TRACHEAL	AACELNNU	CANNULAE
AACEHLSS	CALASHES	AACELNOR	LECANORA
AACEHLST	ALCAHEST	AACELNPR	PARLANCE
AACEHMNP	CAMPHANE	AACELNPT	PLACENTA
AACEHMRS	MARCHESA	AACELNRT	LACERANT
AACEHMSS	CAMASHES	AACELNRY	ARCANELY
AACEHMST	SCHEMATA	AACELNST	ANALECTS
AACEHNPS	PANACHES	AACELNSV	VALANCES
AACEHPSU	CHAPEAUS	AACELNTU	LACUNATE
AACEHRSS	CHARASES	AACELOST	CATALOES
AACEHRSU	ARCHAEUS	AACELOSU	ACAULOSE
AACEHRTT	REATTACH	AACELPST	PLACATES
AACEHSTT	ATTACHES	AACELPSU	SCAPULAE
AACEHTUX	CHATEAUX	AACELRSU	CAESURAL
AACEIILN	LACINIAE	AACELRSV	CARAVELS
AACEIINT	ACTINIAE	AACELRWY	CLEARWAY
AACEIIRV	CAVIARIE	AACELSST	LACTASES
AACEIKMT	KAMACITE	AACELSTT	LACTATES
AACEILLM	CAMELLIA	AACELSTY	CATALYSE
AACEILLN	ALLIANCE	AACELTYZ	CATALYZE
	CANAILLE	AACEMMRS	MACRAMES
AACEILMN	ANALCIME	AACEMNPS	SPACEMAN
	CALAMINE	AACEMNST	CAMSTANE
AACEILMT	CALAMITE	AACEMPRS	PARACMES
AACEILNS	CANALISE	AACEMQSU	MACAQUES
AACEILNT	ANALCITE	AACEMRSS	MASSACRE
	LAITANCE	AACEMSSS	CAMASSES
AACEILNU	ACAULINE	AACENOTU	OCEANAUT
AACEILNV	VALIANCE	AACENPRS	PANCREAS
AACEILNZ	CANALIZE	AACENPST	PASTANCE
AACEILOP	ALOPECIA	AACENPSU	SAUCEPAN
AACEILRT	TAILRACE	AACENRST	CANASTER
AACEILRV	CAVALIER		CATERANS
AACEILST	SALICETA	AACENRTT	REACTANT
AACEIMNS	AMNESIAC	AACENRTY	CATENARY
AACEIMRS	MACARISE	AACENRVZ	CZAREVNA
	MESARAIC	AACENSSV	CANVASES
AACEIMRZ	MACARIZE	AACENSTT	CANTATES
AACEIMTT	CATAMITE	AACENSTY	CYANATES
AACEIMUX	CAMAIEUX	AACENTUV	EVACUANT

AACEOPRT CAPROATE
AACEORSS ROSACEAS
AACEORSU ARACEOUS
AACEOSST SEACOAST
AACEPRST CAPRATES
AACERSSU CAESURAS
AACERSSZ SAZERACS
AACERSTT CASTRATE
AACERSWY RACEWAYS
AACERTTT TRACTATE
AACESSSV CAVASSES
AACESSTT SCEATTAS
AACESTTU ACTUATES
AACESTUV VACUATES
AACESUWY CAUSEWAY
AACFFILS CAFFILAS
AACFGRST CRAGFAST
AACFHMST CAMSHAFT
AACFILLY FACIALLY
AACFILOS FASCIOLA
AACFINST FANATICS
AACFIRRT AIRCRAFT
AACFIRTT ARTIFACT
AACFISST FASCISTA
AACFJKLP FLAPJACK
AACFLLSU FALCULAS
AACFRRSU FARRUCAS
AACGGINO ANAGOGIC
AACGGIOP APAGOGIC
AACGHIPR AGRAPHIC
AACGHIRR CHIRAGRA
AACGHLLO AGALLOCH
AACGHOPZ GAZPACHO
AACGHORU GUACHARO
AACGIIMN MAGICIAN
AACGILLO ALOGICAL
AACGILLS GLACIALS
AACGILLU ALGUACIL
AACGILNO ANALOGIC
AACGILNV GALVANIC
AACGILOX COXALGIA
AACGILRT TRAGICAL
AACGILSS SCAGLIAS
AACGIMMT MAGMATIC
AACGIMNN MANGANIC
AACGIMNP CAMPAIGN
        PANGAMIC
AACGIMRR MARGARIC
AACGIMUU GUAIACUM
AACGINPS SCAPAING
AACGINTV VACATING
AACGISTY SAGACITY
AACGLMOU GLAUCOMA
AACGLOST CATALOGS
AACGMNRS CRAGSMAN
AACGNOSU GUANACOS
AACGNRVY VAGRANCY
AACHHIKR KACHAHRI
AACHHTWY HATCHWAY
AACHIIMR MARIACHI
AACHIKNR CHINKARA
AACHIKNS KACHINAS
AACHIKRS CHIKARAS
AACHILLP CALIPHAL
AACHILLR RACHILLA
AACHILMS CHAMISAL
AACHILMT THALAMIC
AACHILNP CHAPLAIN
AACHILPS CALIPASH
AACHILRV ARCHIVAL

AACHIMNP CHINAMPA
AACHIMNR CHAIRMAN
AACHIMNS SHAMANIC
AACHIMNT MATACHIN
AACHIMRR ARMCHAIR
AACHIMRS ARCHAISM
        CHARISMA
        MACHAIRS
AACHIMSS CHIASMAS
AACHIMST CATHISMA
AACHINNT ACANTHIN
AACHINRT CANTHARI
AACHINSW CHAINSAW
AACHIPST CHAPATIS
AACHIPTT CHAPATTI
AACHIRST ARCHAIST
        CITHARAS
AACHIRTX TAXIARCH
AACHKMPS CHAMPAKS
AACHKPSS SCHAPSKA
AACHKRST HATRACKS
AACHKSTY HAYSTACK
AACHLLNS CHALLANS
AACHLMNO MONACHAL
AACHLMOS CHLOASMA
AACHLSSU ACUSHLAS
AACHMMNR MARCHMAN
AACHMNNR RANCHMAN
AACHMNTW WATCHMAN
AACHMNUY NAUMACHY
AACHMORT ACHROMAT
        TRACHOMA
AACHMPRT CHAMPART
AACHMPRY PHARMACY
AACHNOPS PANOCHAS
AACHNOSU HUANACOS
AACHNPRS SARPANCH
AACHNRSV NAVARCHS
AACHNRVY NAVARCHY
AACHNSTU ACANTHUS
AACHOPPR APPROACH
AACHORTU RACAHOUT
AACHOTTU TACAHOUT
AACHRRST CATARRHS
AACHRSWY ARCHWAYS
AACHRTUY AUTARCHY
AACIILMN ANIMALIC
AACIILMO MAIOLICA
AACIILRT IATRICAL
AACIILRV VICARIAL
AACIINNT ACTINIAN
AACIINPR PICARIAN
AACIINPT CAPITANI
AACIINST ACTINIAS
AACIJLMO MAJOLICA
AACIJNOP JAPONICA
AACIKLRS CLARKIAS
AACIKMNW MACKINAW
AACIKNNS CANAKINS
AACIKRTU AUTARKIC
AACILLMR LACRIMAL
AACILLMT CLIMATAL
AACILLPY APICALLY
AACILLRY RACIALLY
AACILMNT CALAMINT
        CLAIMANT
AACILMOR ACROMIAL
AACILMOT ATOMICAL
AACILMTY CALAMITY
AACILNOR CONARIAL

AACILNRV CARNIVAL
AACILNST ALICANTS
AACILNTT TANTALIC
AACILNTU NAUTICAL
AACILNTY ANALYTIC
AACILNUV NAVICULA
AACILNVY VALIANCY
AACILPRU PIACULAR
AACILPST APLASTIC
        CAPITALS
AACILPSZ CAPSIZAL
AACILPTU CAPITULA
AACILPTY ATYPICAL
AACILQRU ACQUIRAL
AACILRTY ALACRITY
AACILRUU AURICULA
AACILSTT STATICAL
AACILSTY SALACITY
AACIMMNO AMMONIAC
AACIMMRS MACARISM
        MACRAMIS
        MARASMIC
AACIMNOR MACARONI
        MAROCAIN
AACIMNOT ANATOMIC
AACIMORT AROMATIC
AACIMPRS PICAMARS
AACINNST CANTINAS
AACINOPR PARANOIC
AACINOPT CAPITANO
        PACATION
AACINORS OCARINAS
AACINORT RAINCOAT
AACINOTV VACATION
AACINPST CAPITANS
        CAPTAINS
AACINPTY CAPITAYN
AACINQTU ACQUAINT
AACINRST ARCANIST
AACINRSZ CZARINAS
AACINSTZ STANZAIC
AACIOPST TAPIOCAS
AACIOPSV COPAIVAS
AACIPRST SATRAPIC
AACIPRTY RAPACITY
AACIQSTU AQUATICS
AACIRRTT TARTARIC
AACIRSTT CASTRATI
AACIRTZZ CZARITZA
AACJKLPS SLAPJACK
AACJKMNS MANJACKS
AACJKOOR JACKAROO
AACKKNPS KNAPSACK
AACKLNPS KNAPSCAL
AACKLOWY LOCKAWAY
AACKMNPS MANPACKS
AACKMNRT TRACKMAN
AACKMNST TACKSMAN
AACKMRST AMTRACKS
AACKNRSS RANSACKS
AACKORWY ROCKAWAY
AACKPRRS CARPARKS
AACKPRST RATPACKS
AACKPSWY PACKWAYS
AACKRTWY TRACKWAY
AACLLMRY LACRYMAL
AACLLNRY CARNALLY
AACLLNST CALLANTS
AACLLRSY RASCALLY
AACLLSUU CLAUSULA

AACLLSUY CASUALLY
        CAUSALLY
AACLLTUY ACTUALLY
AACLMNNS CLANSMAN
AACLMNSS CLASSMAN
AACLMNST CALMANTS
AACLMRRU MACRURAL
AACLNNOT CANTONAL
AACLNNSU CANNULAS
AACLNOTT OCTANTAL
AACLNPSY CLAYPANS
AACLNRSU LACUNARS
AACLNRUY LACUNARY
AACLNTVY VACANTLY
AACLOOPT TAPACOLO
AACLOPRS CAPORALS
AACLOPST OCTAPLAS
AACLOPTU TAPACULO
AACLORRU ORACULAR
AACLORSU CAROUSAL
AACLORSZ ALCORZAS
AACLORUV VACUOLAR
AACLOSTT CATTALOS
AACLPPRT CLAPTRAP
AACLPRST CALTRAPS
AACLPRSU CAPSULAR
        SCAPULAR
AACLPRTY CALYPTRA
AACLPSSU SCAPULAS
AACLPTTU CATAPULT
AACLRSTU CLAUSTRA
AACLRSUV VASCULAR
AACLSTTY CATALYST
AACLSTUY CASUALTY
AACMNOOR MACAROON
AACMNORS CAMARONS
        MASCARON
AACMNPRY RAMPANCY
AACMORSS SARCOMAS
AACMRSSS SARCASMS
AACNNOSZ CANZONAS
AACNOTTY CATATONY
AACNPSST CAPSTANS
AACNRSTT TRANSACT
AACNRSTU CURTANAS
AACOORTX TOXOCARA
AACOPRSU ACARPOUS
AACOPRTU AUTOCARP
AACORRTV VARACTOR
AACORSTT CASTRATO
AACORSTU ACATOURS
        AUTOCARS
AACORTTU ACTUATOR
        AUTOCRAT
AACOSTUV AUTOVACS
AACRSTTT ATTRACTS
AACRSTUV VACATURS
AACRSTWY CARTWAYS
AACSTUWY CUTAWAYS
AADDDEER ADREADED
AADDDERW ADWARDED
AADDDGNR GRANDDAD
AADDEGGR AGGRADED
AADDEGRT GRADATED
AADDEHHR HARDHEAD
AADDEHLN HEADLAND
AADDEHMN HANDMADE
AADDEHRZ HAZARDED
AADDEILN DEDALIAN
AADDEILS ALIDADES

AADDEIRT RADIATED	AADEGILT GLADIATE	AADEIPPR APPAIRED	AADERRWY WARRAYED
AADDEKMS DAMASKED	AADEGINR AREADING	AADEIPRS PARADISE	AADERSST ASSARTED
AADDELTU ADULATED	DRAINAGE	AADEIPSS DIAPASES	AADERSSW SEAWARDS
AADDEMNT MANDATED	GARDENIA	AADEIPSU DIAPAUSE	AADERSTT ASTARTED
AADDEMRU MARAUDED	AADEGINT INDAGATE	AADEIPTV ADAPTIVE	AADERSTW EASTWARD
AADDEMRY DAYDREAM	AADEGITT AGITATED	AADEIRST DATARIES	AADFGNNO FANDANGO
AADDENPR PANDARED	AADEGITV DIVAGATE	RADIATES	AADFGRSU SAUFGARD
AADDENPS DEADPANS	AADEGJTU ADJUTAGE	AADEIRTV VARIATED	AADFHNST HANDFAST
AADDGNRS GRADDANS	AADEGLLT TALLAGED	AADEISST DIASTASE	AADFIMRS FARADISM
GRANDADS	AADEGLMN MAGDALEN	AADEISTT SATIATED	AADFINRU UNAFRAID
AADDGNRU GRADUAND	AADEGLMY AMYGDALE	AADEITVW VIEWDATA	AADFLLLN LANDFALL
AADDHHRS SHRADDHA	AADEGLNS SELADANG	AADEJMPY PYJAMAED	AADFLORW AARDWOLF
AADDHIMN HANDMAID	AADEGLSV SALVAGED	AADEJMRS JEMADARS	AADFLOTX TOADFLAX
AADDHKRS KHADDARS	AADEGMPR RAMPAGED	AADEJNNP JAPANNED	AADFLOWY FOLDAWAY
AADDHRSS SRADDHAS	AADEGMRS MEGARADS	AADEKLNR KALENDAR	AADFMRRY FARMYARD
AADDIIKS DIDAKAIS	AADEGMSS MASSAGED	AADEKMNR MANDRAKE	AADGGHRS HAGGARDS
AADDILNO DIANODAL	AADEGNRR ARRANGED	AADEKMRS KAMERADS	AADGGIMN DAMAGING
AADDKMMO MOKADDAM	AADEGNTV VANTAGED	AADEKNST ASKANTED	AADGGLNN GANGLAND
AADDLLNY LANDLADY	AADEGPSS PASSAGED	AADEKSTT ATTASKED	AADGGLRS LAGGARDS
AADDLNRW LANDWARD	AADEGRST GRADATES	AADELLPP APPALLED	AADGGRSS SAGGARDS
AADDLNRY YARDLAND	AADEGRSV SAVEGARD	AADELLPS PADELLAS	AADGGRST STAGGARD
AADDMMQU MUQADDAM	AADEGRSY DRAYAGES	AADELLRT DATALLER	AADGHILS HIDALGAS
AADDNRST STANDARD	YARDAGES	AADELLWY WELLADAY	AADGHIPR DIAGRAPH
AADDNRWY YARDWAND	AADEGRTU GRADUATE	AADELMNR ALDERMAN	AADGHRTU HATGUARD
AADDNSVV DVANDVAS	AADEGSSU ASSUAGED	MALANDER	AADGIINS GAINSAID
AADDRSST DASTARDS	AADEGSSW ASSWAGED	AADELMNS DALESMAN	AADGILLR GAILLARD
AADDRSTY DASTARDY	AADEHHOR HOARHEAD	LEADSMAN	GALLIARD
AADEEFFR AFFEARED	AADEHILR HEADRAIL	AADELMOS ALAMODES	AADGILMR MADRIGAL
AADEEGHR HEADGEAR	AADEHIRR DIARRHEA	AADELMPT PALMATED	AADGILNO DIAGONAL
AADEEGLR LAAGERED	AADEHKMR HEADMARK	AADELMRU ALARUMED	GONADIAL
AADEEGLT GALEATED	AADEHLLL HALALLED	AADELMYZ AMAZEDLY	AADGILNS SALADING
AADEEGMN AMENAGED	AADEHLLO HALLOAED	AADELNRS ADRENALS	AADGIMMN MADAMING
ENDAMAGE	AADEHLMP HEADLAMP	AADELNST EASTLAND	AADGIMMS DIGAMMAS
AADEEGRV AVERAGED	AADEHLNR ANHEDRAL	AADELNSW DANELAWS	AADGIMNR MRIDANGA
AADEEHMT MEATHEAD	AADEHLRS ASHLARED	AADELNSY ANALYSED	AADGIMOS AGAMOIDS
AADEEIRT ERADIATE	AADEHMNS HEADSMAN	AADELNYZ ANALYZED	AADGIMPR PARADIGM
AADEEIRW AWEARIED	AADEHMST MASTHEAD	AADELPPT PALPATED	AADGIMRS DIAGRAMS
AADEEKNW AWAKENED	AADEHNRV VERANDAH	AADELPRS PARDALES	AADGIMRT GRADATIM
AADEEKRW REAWAKED	AADEHPPR PARAPHED	AADELPRY PARLAYED	AADGINPR PARADING
AADEELNN ANNEALED	AADEHPSS SAPHEADS	AADELRTU RADULATE	AADGINRU GUARDIAN
AADEELPP APPEALED	AADEHRRW HARDWARE	AADELRTV LARVATED	AADGINRR DARRAIGN
AADEELTV ALVEATED	AADEHRSS HARASSED	AADELRTY DAYTALER	AADGINRW AWARDING
AADEEMNT EMANATED	AADEHRSW RAWHEADS	AADELSTT SALTATED	AADGIQRU QUADRIGA
AADEEMRR DEMERARA	WARHEADS	AADELSTU ADULATES	AADGLLSW GADWALLS
AADEENTT ANTEDATE	AADEHSSY SASHAYED	AADELSTY DAYTALES	AADGLMOR MALGRADO
AADEEPPR APPEARED	AADEHSTT HASTATED	AADELTUV VALUATED	AADGLMSY AMYGDALS
AADEEPPS APPEASED	AADEHSWY HEADWAYS	AADEMNOS ADENOMAS	AADGLNRS GARLANDS
AADEEPRS PASEARED	AADEIIKK KAIKAIED	AADEMNPS SPADEMAN	AADGLNSS SLADANGS
AADEEQTU ADEQUATE	AADEILMS MALADIES	AADEMNST MANDATES	AADGLOPR PODAGRAL
AADEFFLT AFFLATED	AADEILMU AUMAILED	AADEMNUZ UNAMAZED	AADGLRSU GRADUALS
AADEFFNR FANFARED	AADEILNT DENTALIA	AADEMORT MATADORE	AADGMNOR DRAGOMAN
AADEFFRY AFFRAYED	AADEILPR PRAEDIAL	AADEMRRU MARAUDER	AADGMNOS GOADSMAN
AADEFGLS FALDAGES	AADEILPS PALISADE	AADEMRSS MADRASES	AADGMNRS DRAGSMAN
AADEFGRS FARDAGES	AADEILPT LAPIDATE	AADEMSSS ADMASSES	GRANDAMS
AADEFHLT FLATHEAD	AADEILRS SALARIED	AADENNST ANDANTES	GRANDMAS
AADEFHST HEADFAST	AADEILSS ASSAILED	AADENNRT NARRATED	AADGMRSS SMARAGDS
AADEFIRS FARADISE	AADEILSV VEDALIAS	AADENRRW WARRANED	AADGNNQU QUANDANG
SAFARIED	AADEILTV VALIDATE	AADENRSV VERANDAS	AADGNPPS GRANDPAS
AADEFIRZ FARADIZE	AADEIMNN AMANDINE	AADENRTT TARTANED	AADGNRST GARDANTS
AADEFISS FADAISES	AADEIMNP PANDEMIA	AADENSSW WEASANDS	AADGNRSY YARDANGS
AADEFLLR FALDERAL	AADEIMNR MARINADE	AADENSWZ WEAZANDS	AADGNRTU GUARDANT
AADEFLRY DEFRAYAL	AADEIMNT ANIMATED	AADENTUV AVAUNTED	AADGNRUV VANGUARD
AADEFLTT FALDETTA	DIAMANTE	AADEOPRT TAPADERO	AADGOPRS PODAGRAS
AADEFRRW WARFARED	AADEIMPZ DIAZEPAM	AADEOPST ADESPOTA	AADGORRU GURDWARA
AADEFRWY WAYFARED	AADEIMRV MARAVEDI	AADEORRT AERODART	AADHHIPS PADISHAH
AADEGGRS AGGRADES	AADEIMST DIASTEMA	AADEPRST ADAPTERS	AADHIINP APHIDIAN
AADEGGRT AGGRATED	AADEINRR DARRAINE	READAPTS	AADHILLR HALLIARD
AADEGGRU GUARDAGE	AADEINRS ARANEIDS	AADEPSSS PASSADES	AADHILNR HANDRAIL
AADEGHLN DANELAGH	AADEINRT DENTARIA	AADEQRTU QUADRATE	AADHILRV HAVILDAR
AADEGILL DIALLAGE	AADEINTT ATTAINED	AADERRRW REARWARD	

```
AADHINRR HARRIDAN     AADKLMNR LANDMARK     AAEEGRSV AVERAGES     AAEFLRTW FLATWARE
AADHJNRS HANDJARS     AADKLNPR PARKLAND     AAEEGRTW WATERAGE     AAEFMRST FERMATAS
AADHKNSY YAKHDANS     AADKLRTU TALUKDAR     AAEEHIRT HETAERIA     AAEFQRSU AQUAFERS
AADHLMOY DALMAHOY     AADKMNRS DARKMANS     AAEEHPRT HEARTPEA     AAEFRRRW WARFARER
AADHLNPY HANDPLAY     AADKMRSY DAYMARKS     AAEEHRST HETAERAS     AAEFRRSW WARFARES
AADHLNSW WASHLAND     AADKNRST TANKARDS     AAEEHRTW WHEATEAR     AAEFRRWY WAYFARER
AADHLRSY HALYARDS     AADKORWY WORKADAY     AAEEHRWY HEREAWAY     AAEFRSWY WAYFARES
AADHMNNY HANDYMAN     AADKPRRW PARKWARD     AAEEILNT ALIENATE     AAEGGINR GRAINAGE
AADHMNOU OMADHAUN     AADLLMRS MALLARDS     AAEEINTT TAENIATE     AAEGGIOT AGIOTAGE
AADHNRSS DARSHANS     AADLLNSW LAWLANDS     AAEEJMNP JAMPANEE     AAEGGLNR LANGRAGE
AADHNSSW HANDSAWS     AADLMNNS LANDSMAN     AAEEKLTW LATEWAKE     AAEGGLNU LANGUAGE
AADHNSTT HATSTAND     AADLMNOR MANDORLA     AAEEKMNS NAMESAKE     AAEGGNOS ANAGOGES
AADHRRTW THRAWARD     AADLMNOS MANDOLAS     AAEEKNRW REAWAKEN     AAEGGNOW WAGONAGE
AADHRRYZ HAZARDRY     AADLMNSS LANDMASS     AAEEKPRT PARAKEET     AAEGGNRY GARGANEY
AADHRSWY HAYWARDS     AADLMNSU LADANUMS     AAEEKQSU SEAQUAKE     AAEGGOPR PARAGOGE
AADIJMNS JAMDANIS     AADLMNUU LAUDANUM     AAEEKRSW REAWAKES     AAEGGOPS APAGOGES
AADIKLLO ALKALOID     AADLNOPR PARLANDO     AAEELLLM LAMELLAE     AAEGGRST AGGRATES
AADIKLLR KILLADAR     AADLNOST SALTANDO     AAEELLMT MALLEATE     AAEGHLNP PHALANGE
AADIKLRY KAILYARD     AADLNRSY LANYARDS     AAEELLPT PATELLAE     AAEGHLSU HAULAGES
AADIKLSY ILKADAYS     AADLORST LOADSTAR     AAEELMST MALEATES     AAEGHMRX HEXAGRAM
AADIKMNS DAMASKIN     AADLORTU ADULATOR     AAEELNNR ANNEALER     AAEGHMSS GAMASHES
AADILLLO ALLODIAL     AADLPPSU APPLAUDS              LERNAEAN     AAEGHNRU HARANGUE
AADILLNR LANDRAIL     AADMMNOW MADWOMAN     AAEELNPS SEAPLANE     AAEGHNST THANAGES
AADILLPR PALLIARD     AADMMNSU MANDAMUS              SPELAEAN     AAEGHOPY HYPOGAEA
AADILLRS SILLADAR     AADMNORS MADRONAS     AAEELNPU PAENULAE     AAEGILLT ALLIGATE
AADILLRY RADIALLY              MANDORAS     AAEELORT AREOLATE     AAEGILNP PELAGIAN
AADILMNN MAINLAND              MONARDAS     AAEELRST LAETARES     AAEGILNR REGALIAN
AADILMNO DOMAINAL              ROADSMAN     AAEELRTU LAUREATE     AAEGILNT AGENTIAL
         DOMANIAL     AADMNORT MANDATOR     AAEELSST ELASTASE              ALGINATE
AADILMNP PLAIDMAN     AADMNRSS MANSARDS     AAEELTUV EVALUATE     AAEGILRS GASALIER
AADILMRS ADMIRALS     AADMOPPP PAPPADOM     AAEEMNST EMANATES              LAIRAGES
         AMILDARS     AADMOQSU MADOQUAS              MANATEES              REGALIAS
AADILNOR ORDALIAN     AADMORST MATADORS     AAEEMPRS PARAMESE     AAEGILSS ALGESIAS
AADILNPR PRANDIAL     AADMRSZZ MAZZARDS     AAEENNNT ANTENNAE     AAEGILSX GALAXIES
AADILNPS PALADINS     AADNOPRS PANDORAS     AAEENPRT PARANETE     AAEGIMNO EGOMANIA
AADILNRS LANIARDS     AADNORST ONDATRAS     AAEENRRS ARRASENE     AAEGIMNS MAGNESIA
AADILNTT DILATANT     AADNORTY DONATARY     AAEENRST ARSENATE     AAEGIMNZ MAGAZINE
AADILOPS PALISADO     AADNOSUV VANADOUS              SERENATA     AAEGIMRR MARRIAGE
AADILORR RAILROAD     AADNOSWY NOWADAYS     AAEENSTU NAUSEATE     AAEGIMRT GEMATRIA
AADILPRS PARDALIS     AADNPRSU PANDURAS     AAEEPPRR APPEARER              MARITAGE
AADILPRY LAPIDARY     AADNQRSU QUADRANS              RAPPAREE     AAEGINNR ANEARING
AADILRRS RISALDAR     AADNQRTU QUADRANT              REAPPEAR     AAEGINPS NAGAPIES
AADILRST TAILARDS     AADNQRUY QUANDARY     AAEEPPSS APPEASES              PAGANISE
AADILSST STADIALS     AADNRRSW WARRANDS     AAEEPRST ASPERATE     AAEGINPT PAGINATE
AADIMNNR MANDARIN     AADNRRSY DARRAYNS              SEPARATE     AAEGINPZ PAGANIZE
AADIMNRS MANDIRAS     AADNRSTY TANYARDS     AAEEPSTT ASEPTATE     AAEGINRS ANGARIES
AADIMNRT TAMARIND     AADNRSWY NAYWARDS     AAEERRWW REWAREWA     AAEGINRT AERATING
AADIMNRY DAIRYMAN     AADOPPRR PARADROP     AAEERSTT STEARATE     AAEGINST SAGINATE
         MAINYARD     AADOPRST ADAPTORS     AAEERSWX EARWAXES     AAEGINSW WAINAGES
AADIMNRZ ZAMINDAR     AADOPRXY PARADOXY     AAEFFGRS AGRAFFES     AAEGINTV NAVIGATE
AADIMNSS DAMASSIN     AADOPSSS PASSADOS     AAEFFGST STAFFAGE              VAGINATE
AADIMNSU SUDAMINA     AADOPSUY PADUASOY     AAEFFIRS AFFAIRES     AAEGIPRS IGARAPES
AADIMNUV VANADIUM     AADORSWY ROADWAYS     AAEFFLLS FALAFELS     AAEGIPRU PERIAGUA
AADIMORS DIORAMAS     AADQRSTU QUADRATS     AAEFFLPR PARAFFLE     AAEGIRRS ARRIAGES
AADIMSTZ SAMIZDAT     AADRSSTY DAYSTARS     AAEFFNRS FANFARES     AAEGIRSV VAGARIES
AADINNOT ADNATION     AAEEHHRT HETAERAE     AAEFFSTT TAFFETAS     AAEGISSS ASSEGAIS
AADINOPR PARANOID     AAEEFFRS AFFEARES     AAEFGHRW WHARFAGE     AAEGISTT AGITATES
AADINOPS DIAPASON     AAEEFGLS LEAFAGES     AAEFGINR AFEARING     AAEGIVWY GIVEAWAY
AADINOPT ADAPTION     AAEEFRRS SEAFARER     AAEFGITT FATIGATE     AAEGJSTU AJUTAGES
AADINRRS DARRAINS     AAEEGILN ALIENAGE     AAEFGLLL FLAGELLA     AAEGKNST TANKAGES
AADINRRW AIRDRAWN     AAEEGILP EPIGAEAL     AAEFGLOT FLOATAGE     AAEGKOSS SOAKAGES
AADINRST RADIANTS     AAEEGINP EPIGAEAN     AAEFGRTU FRAUTAGE     AAEGLLMS SMALLAGE
AADINRSV VIRANDAS     AAEEGKLS LEAKAGES     AAEFGSTW WAFTAGES     AAEGLLPR PELLAGRA
AADIOPRS DIASPORA     AAEEGLLN ENALLAGE     AAEFILTY FAYALITE     AAEGLLSS GALLEASS
AADIORRT RADIATOR     AAEEGLST ETALAGES     AAEFIMRR AIRFRAME     AAEGLLST GALLATES
AADIPSUY UPADAISY     AAEEGMNS AMENAGES     AAEFINNT FAINEANT              STALLAGE
AADIRRSW AIRWARDS     AAEEGMPR AMPERAGE     AAEFINTX ANTEFIXA              TALLAGES
AADIRRSY DISARRAY     AAEEGMTY METAYAGE     AAEFLMTT FLATMATE     AAEGLLTU GLUTAEAL
AADJNTTU ADJUTANT     AAEEGNRS SANGAREE     AAEFLPRS EARFLAPS     AAEGLMNS GAMELANS
AADJNTUV ADJUVANT     AAEEGRST STEARAGE              PARAFLES     AAEGLMNV GAVELMAN
```

AAEGLNOU	ANALOGUE		HAEMATIN	AAEILPRT	PARIETAL	AAEKNPRT	PARTAKEN
AAEGLNPT	PLANTAGE	AAEHINPT	APHANITE	AAEILPST	STAPELIA	AAEKPRRT	PARTAKER
AAEGLNRS	ALNAGERS	AAEHINST	ASTHENIA	AAEILRRT	ARTERIAL	AAEKPRST	PARTAKES
AAEGLNRU	AULNAGER	AAEHIPST	APATHIES	AAEILRSS	SALARIES	AAEKSSSV	KAVASSES
AAEGLNSS	LASAGNES	AAEHKLST	ALKAHEST	AAEILRSU	AURELIAS		VAKASSES
AAEGLNSU	AULNAGES	AAEHKMRY	HAYMAKER	AAEILRTV	VARIETAL	AAELLLMR	LAMELLAR
AAEGLNTU	ANGULATE	AAEHKNST	KHANATES	AAEILSTV	AESTIVAL	AAELLLPR	PARALLEL
AAEGLOSV	AASVOGEL	AAEHLLLS	ALLHEALS		SALIVATE	AAELLMPU	AMPULLAE
AAEGLRRS	REALGARS	AAEHLMSY	SEALYHAM	AAEILSTX	SAXATILE	AAELLNPU	PLANULAE
	RESALGAR	AAEHLMTU	HAMULATE	AAEILTVX	LAXATIVE	AAELLNSZ	ZANELLAS
AAEGLRRW	WARRAGLE	AAEHLNTX	EXHALANT	AAEIMMST	IMAMATES	AAELLORV	ALVEOLAR
AAEGLRST	AGRESTAL	AAEHLPRX	HEXAPLAR	AAEIMNOT	METANOIA	AAELLPRS	PARELLAS
AAEGLRTY	LEGATARY	AAEHLPSX	HEXAPLAS	AAEIMNPR	PEARMAIN	AAELLPRT	PATELLAR
AAEGLSST	AGELASTS	AAEHLPUV	UPHEAVAL	AAEIMNPT	IMPANATE	AAELLPST	PATELLAS
	LASTAGES	AAEHLRST	TREHALAS	AAEIMNRT	MARINATE	AAELLRST	LATERALS
AAEGLSSV	SALVAGES	AAEHLRTT	THEATRAL	AAEIMNRZ	MAZARINE	AAELLRSY	ALLAYERS
AAEGLSVY	SAVAGELY	AAEHLSTT	ATHLETAS	AAEIMNSS	AMNESIAS	AAELLUVV	VALVULAE
AAEGLTUV	VAULTAGE	AAEHMNPY	NYMPHAEA	AAEIMNST	AMENTIAS	AAELLWWY	WELLAWAY
AAEGMMNR	ENGRAMMA	AAEHMNRS	SHAREMAN		ANIMATES	AAELLWYY	ALLEYWAY
AAEGMNPY	PYGMAEAN		SHEARMAN	AAEIMOPR	PAROEMIA	AAELMMNO	MELANOMA
AAEGMNRS	MANAGERS	AAEHMNRT	EARTHMAN	AAEIMOTX	TOXAEMIA	AAELMMTU	MALAMUTE
AAEGMNRV	GRAVAMEN	AAEHMOPR	AMPHORAE	AAEIMPSY	PYAEMIAS	AAELMNOT	MALONATE
AAEGMNST	MAGENTAS	AAEHMORT	ATHEROMA	AAEIMRSU	URAEMIAS	AAELMNPT	PLATEMAN
	MAGNATES	AAEHNPRS	HANAPERS	AAEIMSUV	MAUVAISE	AAELMNRT	MATERNAL
AAEGMORR	AEROGRAM	AAEHNPST	PHEASANT	AAEINNTT	ANTENATI	AAELMNSS	SALESMAN
AAEGMORS	SAGAMORE	AAEHNPSY	SYNAPHEA	AAEINORT	AERATION	AAELMNST	TALESMAN
AAEGMPRS	RAMPAGES	AAEHNTTX	XANTHATE	AAEINORX	ANOREXIA	AAELMNSW	WEALSMAN
AAEGMPRU	RAMPAUGE	AAEHPRSZ	PHEAZARS	AAEINPRS	PANARIES	AAELMNSY	SEAMANLY
AAEGMRRV	MARGRAVE	AAEHRRSS	HARASSER	AAEINRST	ANTISERA	AAELMOST	OATMEALS
AAEGMRRY	GRAMARYE	AAEHRSSS	HARASSES		ARTESIAN	AAELMPRT	MALAPERT
AAEGMSSS	MASSAGES	AAEHRSSY	HEARSAYS		RESINATA	AAELMPRX	EXAMPLAR
AAEGMTTW	MEGAWATT	AAEHRTWX	EARTHWAX	AAEINRTT	REATTAIN	AAELMPSS	LAMPASES
AAEGNNOP	NEOPAGAN	AAEIIKNS	AKINESIA	AAEINRTU	INAURATE		LAMPASSE
AAEGNNPS	PANNAGES	AAEIIMRV	VIRAEMIA	AAEINSTT	ASTATINE	AAELMPST	PLATEASM
AAEGNNST	TANNAGES	AAEIIPRS	APIARIES		SANITATE	AAELMPTV	VAMPLATE
AAEGNPST	PAGEANTS	AAEIIRSV	AVIARIES		TANAISTE	AAELMPTY	PLAYMATE
AAEGNRRR	ARRANGER	AAEIKKMZ	KAMIKAZE	AAEINSTV	SANATIVE	AAELMRSY	LAMASERY
AAEGNRRS	ARRANGES	AAEIKLLN	ALKALINE	AAEINTTT	TITANATE	AAELMRTT	MALTREAT
AAEGNRST	STARAGEN	AAEIKLLS	ALKALIES	AAEIPPRS	APPRAISE	AAELMSST	MALTASES
	TANAGERS		ALKALISE	AAEIPPSS	APEPSIAS	AAELMSSY	AMYLASES
AAEGNRTU	RUNAGATE	AAEIKLLZ	ALKALIZE	AAEIPRRS	PAREIRAS	AAELNNNT	ANTENNAL
AAEGNSTT	STAGNATE	AAEIKMRR	KRAMERIA	AAEIPRSS	SPIRAEAS	AAELNNOT	NEONATAL
AAEGNSTV	VANTAGES	AAEILLLU	ALLELUIA	AAEIPRST	ASPIRATE	AAELNNTU	ANNULATE
AAEGNSTW	WANTAGES	AAEILLMM	MAMILLAE		PARASITE	AAELNOSS	SEASONAL
AAEGNTUV	VAUNTAGE	AAEILLMR	ARMILLAE		SEPTARIA	AAELNOSV	VALONEAS
AAEGORRT	ARROGATE	AAEILLMX	MAXILLAE	AAEIPRTT	PATRIATE	AAELNPRS	PRENASAL
AAEGORTT	AEGROTAT	AAEILLPP	PAPILLAE	AAEIPRTZ	TRAPEZIA	AAELNPRT	PARENTAL
AAEGPPRW	WRAPPAGE	AAEILLPT	PALLIATE	AAEIPRXY	APYREXIA		PATERNAL
AAEGPSSS	PASSAGES	AAEILLRT	ARILLATE	AAEIPSTT	APATITES		PRENATAL
AAEGPSSY	PAYSAGES	AAEILLRY	AERIALLY	AAEIRRRT	TERRARIA	AAELNPRW	WARPLANE
AAEGQSUY	QUAYAGES	AAEILLTT	TALLIATE	AAEIRSST	ASTERIAS	AAELNPST	PLATANES
AAEGRRSV	RAVAGERS	AAEILLTV	ALLATIVE		ATRESIAS		PLEASANT
AAEGRSTT	REGATTAS	AAEILMNT	ALAIMENT	AAEIRSSX	XERASIAS	AAELNPSU	PAENULAS
AAEGRSVY	SAVAGERY		LAMINATE	AAEIRSTT	ARIETTAS	AAELNRSS	ARSENALS
AAEGSSSU	ASSUAGES	AAEILMNV	VELAMINA		ARISTATE	AAELNRSY	ANALYSER
	SAUSAGES	AAEILMRT	MATERIAL	AAEIRSTV	VARIATES	AAELNRTT	ALTERANT
AAEGSSSW	ASSWAGES	AAEILMSS	MALAISES	AAEIRSVW	AIRWAVES		ALTERNAT
AAEGSSTV	SAVAGEST	AAEILNNS	ANNALISE	AAEIRTTZ	ZARATITE	AAELNRTX	RELAXANT
AAEGSSTW	TASSWAGE	AAEILNNZ	ANNALIZE	AAEISSTT	SATIATES	AAELNRYZ	ANALYZER
	WASTAGES	AAEILNPR	AIRPLANE	AAEITTVX	TAXATIVE	AAELNSST	SEALANTS
AAEGSTTW	WATTAGES	AAEILNPT	PALATINE	AAEJNNPR	JAPANNER	AAELNSSV	ENVASSAL
AAEGSTWY	GATEWAYS	AAEILNRU	AURELIAN	AAEJNRST	NAARTJES	AAELNSSY	ANALYSES
	GETAWAYS	AAEILNRV	VALERIAN	AAEJNRTZ	JAZERANT	AAELNSTZ	ZEALANTS
AAEHIIRT	HETAIRAI	AAEILNSS	NASALISE	AAEJRSSW	SWARAJES	AAELNSWY	LANEWAYS
	HETAIRIA	AAEILNSZ	NASALIZE	AAEKLMRY	MALARKEY	AAELNSYZ	ANALYZES
AAEHILMN	HIELAMAN	AAEILNTT	ANTLIATE	AAEKLNRS	LARNAKES	AAELORSU	AUREOLAS
AAEHILNP	APHELIAN	AAEILNTV	AVENTAIL	AAEKLNST	ALKANETS	AAELORTY	ALEATORY
AAEHILNT	ANTHELIA	AAEILORS	OLEARIAS		KANTELAS	AAELOSTX	OXALATES
AAEHILPR	PARHELIA	AAEILPPS	PAPALISE	AAEKMRRS	EARMARKS	AAELPPRS	APPARELS
AAEHIMNT	ANTHEMIA	AAEILPPZ	PAPALIZE	AAEKMRSS	SEAMARKS	AAELPPST	PALPATES

```
AAELPPSU APPLAUSE    AAEORTTV ROTAVATE    AAGGNSWY GANGWAYS    AAGINNTW AWANTING
AAELPRST PALESTRA    AAEPPRST PARAPETS    AAGHHINS SHANGHAI    AAGINPPY APPAYING
AAELPRSV PALAVERS    AAEPPSTT APPESTAT    AAGHILNN HANGNAIL    AAGINPRU PAGURIAN
AAELPRSY PARALYSE    AAEPSWXX PAXWAXES    AAGHILPY HYPALGIA    AAGINRRS ARRAIGNS
AAELPRTT TETRAPLA    AAEPSZZZ PAZAZZES    AAGHILRS GHARIALS    AAGINRRY ARRAYING
AAELPRYZ PARALYZE    AAERRSST TARRASES             HARIGALS    AAGINRSS SANGRIAS
AAELPSTU PLATEAUS    AAERRSTT TARTARES    AAGHIMNS ASHAMING             SARANGIS
AAELPSTV PALSTAVE    AAERRTTT TARTRATE    AAGHIMRT TAGHAIRM    AAGINRSY ARAYSING
AAELPTUV VAPULATE    AAERSSSY ASSAYERS    AAGHINPS PAGANISH    AAGINSST ASSIGNAT
AAELPTUX PLATEAUX    AAERSTTU SATURATE    AAGHINPW AWHAPING    AAGINSSU GAUSSIAN
AAELRSTZ LAZARETS    AAERTWWY WATERWAY    AAGHIPRR AIRGRAPH    AAGINSSY ASSAYING
AAELRTUV VELATURA    AAFFILRT TAFFRAIL    AAGHIRSV VAGARISH             GAINSAYS
AAELRUZZ ZARZUELA    AAFFINPR PARAFFIN    AAGHKMNY GYMKHANA    AAGIORTT AGITATOR
AAELRWYY WAYLAYER    AAFFINSS SAFFIANS    AAGHLNPY ANAGLYPH    AAGIPRSU PIRAGUAS
AAELSSTT SALTATES    AAFFLPST PALSTAFF    AAGHLOSS GASAHOLS    AAGIRRSY ARGYRIAS
AAELSTUV VALUATES    AAFFLSTU AFFLATUS    AAGHMNOY MAHOGANY    AAGIRSTV GRAVITAS
AAELSTZZ ALTEZZAS    AAFFNNOR FANFARON    AAGHMNSW WHANGAMS             STRAVAIG
AAEMMMRS MAREMMAS    AAFGILNO GOLFIANA    AAGHNOPR AGRAPHON    AAGISSTT SAGITTAS
AAEMMNRT ARMAMENT    AAFGLLNU LANGLAUF    AAGHOPPR APOGRAPH    AAGKNOOR KANGAROO
AAEMMSTT STEMMATA    AAFGLNRT FLAGRANT    AAGHQSUU QUAHAUGS    AAGKOOSZ GAZOOKAS
AAEMNOTZ METAZOAN    AAFGNRRT FRAGRANT    AAGHRRTU ARRAUGHT    AAGKORST KATORGAS
AAEMNPRS SPEARMAN    AAFHHIKL KHALIFAH    AAGIILMN IMAGINAL    AAGLLMOY ALLOGAMY
AAEMNPRT PARAMENT    AAFHIKLS KHALIFAS    AAGIILNV AVAILING    AAGLLNOO LAGOONAL
AAEMNRST SARMENTA    AAFHIKLT KHALIFAT    AAGIIMST ASTIGMIA    AAGLLNRY LARYNGAL
         SEMANTRA             KHILAFAT    AAGIINRS ARAISING    AAGLLNST GALLANTS
AAEMNRSU MURAENAS    AAFHIRST AIRSHAFT    AAGIINTV AVIATING    AAGLLOPY POLYGALA
AAEMNRTT ATRAMENT    AAFHRSUU HAUSFRAU    AAGIINTW AWAITING    AAGLMNSS GLASSMAN
AAEMNRTW WATERMAN    AAFIILLM FAMILIAL    AAGIKLNO KAOLIANG    AAGLNNOO ANALOGON
AAEMNSST NAMASTES    AAFIILLR FILARIAL    AAGIKLNR KRAALING    AAGLNPSS LAPSANGS
AAEMNSTU MANTEAUS    AAFIILMR FAMILIAR    AAGIKLNS ASLAKING    AAGLNQUU AQUALUNG
AAEMNTUX MANTEAUX    AAFIILRS FILARIAS    AAGIKMRS SKIAGRAM    AAGLNRRU GRANULAR
AAEMORTT TERATOMA    AAFIINST FISTIANA    AAGIKNSW AWAKINGS    AAGLOPRY PARALOGY
AAEMOSTT STEATOMA    AAFIKLLY ALKALIFY    AAGIKNSZ ZIGANKAS    AAGLRRUW WARRAGUL
AAEMOTTU AUTOMATE    AAFILLNR RAINFALL    AAGILLNY ALLAYING    AAGLRSTU GASTRULA
AAEMPPSS PAMPASES    AAFILLUV AVAILFUL    AAGILLSS GALLIASS    AAGMMRRS GRAMMARS
AAEMPTTU AMPUTATE    AAFILMST FATALISM    AAGILLTV GALLIVAT    AAGMNNOR NANOGRAM
AAEMQSTU SQUAMATE    AAFILNST FANTAILS    AAGILLUZ ALGUAZIL    AAGMNNRS GRANNAMS
AAEMRRTU ARMATURE    AAFILOPR PARAFOIL    AAGILMNO MAGNOLIA    AAGMNOPZ ZAMPOGNA
AAEMRSTU AMATEURS    AAFILQSU ALFAQUIS    AAGILMNR ALARMING    AAGMNORT MARTAGON
AAEMRTTU MATURATE    AAFILSTT FATALIST             MARGINAL    AAGMNPRS PANGRAMS
AAENNNST ANTENNAS    AAFILTTY FATALITY    AAGILMNX MALAXING    AAGMNRST TANGRAMS
AAENNOTT ANNOTATE    AAFIMNOR FORAMINA    AAGILMOT GLIOMATA             TRANGAMS
AAENNSTT STANNATE    AAFINNRS SAFRANIN    AAGILMSY MYALGIAS    AAGMNRTU ARMGAUNT
         TANNATES    AAFINNST INFANTAS    AAGILNOT GALTONIA    AAGMNSSW SWAGSMAN
AAENNSTU NAUSEANT    AAFINRRW WARFARIN    AAGILNPT PALATING    AAGMNSTY SYNTAGMA
AAENNSTV VENTANAS    AAFINSTU FAUSTIAN    AAGILNRR LARRIGAN    AAGMORSS MARGOSAS
AAENORRU AUROREAN    AAFIPRST PARFAITS    AAGILNSS SALSAING    AAGMOTUY AUTOGAMY
AAENORST ANOESTRA    AAFIRSWY FAIRWAYS    AAGILNUV VAGINULA    AAGMRRST MATGRASS
AAENORSU ARANEOUS    AAFJLLSW JAWFALLS    AAGILOOP APOLOGIA    AAGNNSTT STAGNANT
AAENORTU AERONAUT    AAFJLORS ALFORJAS    AAGILOST OTALGIAS    AAGNOPRS PARAGONS
AAENOSST ASSONATE    AAFLLPRT PRATFALL    AAGILPRY PLAGIARY    AAGNOPRT TRAGOPAN
AAENPPRS PARPANES    AAFLLPST SPATFALL    AAGILRRW WARRIGAL    AAGNORRT ARROGANT
AAENPPRT APPARENT    AAFLMORV LAVAFORM    AAGILSTT SAGITTAL             TARRAGON
         TRAPPEAN    AAFLNORS FORLANAS    AAGILSTW WAGTAILS    AAGNORSZ ORGANZAS
AAENPRTY PRYTANEA    AAFLNOTT FLOATANT    AAGIMMRR MARIGRAM    AAGNORTU ARGONAUT
AAENPSST ANAPESTS    AAFLNRSU FURLANAS    AAGIMNNO AGNOMINA    AAGNRSTV VAGRANTS
         PEASANTS    AAFLSTWY FLATWAYS    AAGIMNOS ANGIOMAS    AAGNRTUY GUARANTY
AAENPSTT ANTEPAST    AAFMNRST RAFTSMAN    AAGIMNPS PAGANISM    AAGNRTYZ ZYGANTRA
AAENPSTY PEASANTY    AAFMNSST FANTASMS    AAGIMNRR MARGARIN    AAGOPSSS SAPSAGOS
AAENRRSS NARRASES    AAFNPPRT FRAPPANT    AAGIMNSS AMASSING    AAGORSSS SARGASSO
AAENRRST NARRATES    AAFNSSTT FANTASTS             SIAMANGS    AAGORSSU SAGUAROS
AAENRSTT TARTANES    AAGGGINR GARAGING    AAGIMNSY GYMNASIA    AAGRSSTU SASTRUGA
AAENRSTV TAVERNAS    AAGGILNR GANGLIAR    AAGIMPTU PATAGIUM    AAGRSTUZ ZASTRUGA
         TSAREVNA    AAGGIMNN MANAGING    AAGIMSSV SAVAGISM    AAHHNNST THANNAHS
AAENRSUW UNAWARES    AAGGIMNR MARAGING    AAGIMSTT STIGMATA    AAHHNPST NAPHTHAS
AAENSSSV VANESSAS    AAGGINRV RAVAGING    AAGINNOT AGNATION    AAHIIKRT TARAKIHI
AAENTTTT ATTENTAT    AAGGINSV SAVAGING    AAGINNRW AWARNING    AAHIJPRS RAJASHIP
AAEOPSTT APOSTATE    AAGGITTW GIGAWATT    AAGINNSW WANIGANS    AAHIKLPS PASHALIK
AAEORRST AERATORS    AAGGLLLY LALLYGAG    AAGINNSY SYNANGIA    AAHIKRST KITHARAS
AAEORSTT AEROSTAT    AAGGMNNS GANGSMAN    AAGINNTV VAGINANT    AAHILLLS HALLALIS
```

AAHILLNS	HALLIANS	AAIIRTVX	AVIATRIX	AAILNSSY	ANALYSIS	AAINRSSV	SAVARINS
AAHILMNR	HARMALIN	AAIJLLQU	QUILLAJA	AAILNSTV	VALIANTS	AAINRSTV	VARIANTS
AAHILMRS	ALMIRAHS	AAIJLNPS	JALAPINS	AAILNSTY	NASALITY	AAINRSTY	SANITARY
AAHILNNT	INHALANT	AAIJMNPS	JAMPANIS	AAILNTTT	LATITANT	AAINSSSS	ASSASSIN
AAHILNOT	HALATION	AAIJNRSZ	JANIZARS	AAILNTTY	NATALITY	AAINSTTT	ANTISTAT
AAHILPSY	PHYSALIA	AAIJNRYZ	JANIZARY	AAILORRS	RASORIAL		ATTAINTS
AAHIMNOS	MAHONIAS	AAIKKNOS	SKOKIAAN	AAILORRV	VARIOLAR	AAINSTTU	TUTANIAS
AAHIMNPS	PASHMINA	AAIKLNST	NASTALIK	AAILORSS	ROSALIAS	AAINSTTY	SATANITY
AAHINOPS	APHONIAS	AAIKMNNS	MANAKINS	AAILORSV	VARIOLAS	AAIOPRRT	TROPARIA
AAHINPRS	PIRANHAS	AAIKMNRS	RAMAKINS	AAILPPRU	PUPARIAL	AAIOPRST	ATROPIAS
AAHINRTU	HAURIANT	AAIKMNST	ANTIMASK	AAILPPST	PAPALIST	AAIOPRSU	PAROUSIA
AAHINSST	SHAITANS	AAIKMORS	ROMAIKAS	AAILPRST	PARTIALS	AAIOPSTU	AUTOPSIA
AAHIPRST	PITARAHS	AAIKMRSS	KARAISMS		PATRIALS	AAIORSSU	SAOUARIS
AAHIPSTZ	ZAPTIAHS	AAIKMRST	TAMARISK		TRIAPSAL	AAIORSTV	AVIATORS
AAHIPSXY	ASPHYXIA	AAIKORSU	OUAKARIS	AAILPSTT	TALIPATS	AAIPPSTT	PITAPATS
AAHIRSST	SHARIATS	AAIKPPRS	PAPRIKAS	AAILRRSV	ARRIVALS	AAIPRSSX	SPARAXIS
AAHJKNRS	KHANJARS	AAIKSSTT	ASTATKIS	AAILRSTV	TRAVAILS	AAIPRSTT	PARTITAS
AAHKLLMR	HALLMARK	AAIKSSTV	SVASTIKA	AAILRSVY	SALIVARY	AAIQRSTU	AQUARIST
AAHKLRSS	LASHKARS	AAIKSSTW	SWASTIKA	AAILRSWY	RAILWAYS	AAIQSSSU	QUASSIAS
AAHKMOTW	TOMAHAWK	AAIKSTVV	AKVAVITS	AAILSSSV	VASSAILS	AAIQSTUV	AQUAVITS
AAHKMSSY	YASHMAKS	AAILLLUV	ALLUVIAL	AAILSSSW	WASSAILS	AAIRSSTT	TSARITSA
AAHLLLOO	HALLALOO	AAILLMMM	MAMMILLA	AAILSSTY	STAYSAIL	AAIRSTWY	STAIRWAY
AAHLLOPT	ALLOPATH	AAILLMMR	MAMILLAR	AAILSTTT	LATITATS	AAISTWXY	TAXIWAYS
AAHLLSWY	HALLWAYS	AAILLMNS	MANILLAS	AAIMMNOS	AMMONIAS	AAJKLSWY	JAYWALKS
AAHLMMSS	MASHLAMS	AAILLMNT	MANTILLA	AAIMMNST	MAINMAST	AAJMMORR	MARJORAM
AAHLMOOS	MASOOLAH	AAILLMNY	ANIMALLY	AAIMMRSU	SAMARIUM	AAJMORST	MAJORATS
AAHLMRSS	MARSHALS	AAILLMRS	ARMILLAS	AAIMNORT	ANIMATOR	AAJOPSSU	SAPAJOUS
AAHLMSTU	THALAMUS	AAILLNOV	VALLONIA		MONTARIA	AAKKLRSU	KARAKULS
AAHLNRSW	NARWHALS	AAILLNSV	VANILLAS		TAMANOIR	AAKKMOST	TOKAMAKS
AAHLPSST	ASPHALTS	AAILLPPR	PAPILLAR	AAIMNORW	AIRWOMAN	AAKLMPSU	LAMPUKAS
AAHLRSSW	SHALWARS	AAILLRRY	ARILLARY	AAIMNOSS	ANOSMIAS	AAKLMRUY	YARMULKA
AAHMNNSU	HANUMANS	AAILLRXY	AXILLARY	AAIMNOST	AMATIONS	AAKLMSUY	YAMULKAS
AAHMNORT	MARATHON	AAILMMRS	ALARMISM	AAIMNPRZ	MARZIPAN	AAKLNOOS	OOLAKANS
AAHMNOST	HOASTMAN		AMMIRALS	AAIMNPTU	PUTAMINA	AAKLNOSU	OULAKANS
AAHMNOTX	XANTHOMA	AAILMNNT	LAMANTIN	AAIMNRRT	TRIMARAN	AAKLOOPS	PALOOKAS
AAHMNPST	PHANTASM	AAILMNOP	PALAMINO	AAIMNRRU	RANARIUM	AAKLPRTY	KALYPTRA
AAHMRSST	STRAMASH	AAILMNOR	MANORIAL	AAIMNRST	TAMARINS	AAKLRSSU	KURSAALS
AAHNNOSS	HOSANNAS		MORAINAL	AAIMNSST	MANTISSA		RUSALKAS
AAHNORST	ATHANORS	AAILMNOX	MONAXIAL		SATANISM	AAKLSSSU	SAKSAULS
AAHNORSV	NAVARHOS	AAILMNPS	PANISLAM		STAMINAS	AAKLSWWY	WALKWAYS
AAHNPSTY	PHANTASY	AAILMNRU	MANURIAL	AAIMNSTU	AMIANTUS	AAKMMNRS	MARKSMAN
AAHOPRTU	AUTOHARP	AAILMNRY	LAMINARY	AAIMNSTY	MAINSTAY	AAKMOSSU	MOUSAKAS
AAHPRSTW	WARPATHS	AAILMNST	STAMINAL	AAIMOPRS	MARIPOSA		MOUSSAKA
AAHPSTWY	PATHWAYS		TALISMAN	AAIMPRST	PASTRAMI	AAKMRSUZ	MAZURKAS
AAHRRTTW	THRAWART	AAILMNSU	ALUMINAS	AAIMPRSU	MARSUPIA	AAKMRSWY	WAYMARKS
AAHRSSST	SHASTRAS	AAILMNSV	NAVALISM	AAIMQRUU	AQUARIUM	AAKNNSTU	NUNATAKS
AAIIILMR	MILIARIA	AAILMOPT	LIPOMATA	AAIMRRSY	MISARRAY	AAKNSTWY	TWANKAYS
AAIIKKNN	KINAKINA	AAILMORR	ARMORIAL	AAIMSSTV	ATAVISMS	AAKOOPPS	PAKAPOOS
AAIILLQU	QUILLAIA	AAILMPPS	PAPALISM	AAINNOPV	PAVONIAN	AAKPRSWY	PARKWAYS
AAIILMNS	MAINSAIL	AAILMPRT	PRIMATAL	AAINNOST	SONATINA	AALLLSTY	LAYSTALL
AAIILMRS	AIRMAILS	AAILMRST	ALARMIST	AAINNOTT	NATATION	AALLMNST	STALLMAN
AAIILNRZ	ALIZARIN		ALASTRIM	AAINNRSV	NAVARINS	AALLMNTY	TALLYMAN
AAIILNUX	UNIAXIAL	AAILMTTU	ULTIMATA		NIRVANAS	AALLMNUY	MANUALLY
AAIILPRR	RIPARIAL	AAILNNOT	NATIONAL	AAINNRTU	NUTARIAN	AALLNNUY	ANNUALLY
AAIILPRS	PAIRIALS	AAILNNPT	PLAINANT	AAINNSST	NAISSANT	AALLNPRU	PLANULAR
AAIILPST	TILAPIAS		PLANTAIN	AAINNSSY	SANNYASI	AALLOORW	WALLAROO
AAIILRSZ	ALIZARIS	AAILNNRU	LUNARIAN	AAINOPSS	PAISANOS	AALLORSU	ALLOSAUR
AAIILRTX	TRIAXIAL	AAILNNST	ANNALIST	AAINORRS	ORARIANS	AALLOSTV	LAVOLTAS
AAIILRUX	AUXILIAR		SANTALIN		ROSARIAN	AALLPRST	PLASTRAL
AAIIMNNT	MAINTAIN	AAILNOPS	SALOPIAN	AAINOTTX	TAXATION	AALLRUVV	VALVULAR
AAIIMNPX	PANMIXIA	AAILNOPT	TALAPOIN	AAINPRST	ASPIRANT	AALMMNOS	AMMONALS
AAIINOTV	AVIATION	AAILNORT	NOTARIAL		PARTISAN	AALMNORT	MATRONAL
AAIINPRR	RIPARIAN		RATIONAL	AAINPRTZ	PARTIZAN	AALMNORU	MONAURAL
AAIINPZZ	PIAZZIAN	AAILNOST	AILANTOS	AAINQRTU	QUATRAIN	AALMNOSS	SALAMONS
AAIINRST	INTARSIA	AAILNOSV	VALONIAS	AAINQTTU	AQUATINT	AALMNPTY	TYMPANAL
AAIIOPST	APOSITIA	AAILNOTV	LAVATION	AAINRRSS	SARRASIN	AALMNTTU	TANTALUM
AAIIORTZ	ZOIATRIA	AAILNPRU	PLANURIA	AAINRRSZ	SARRAZIN	AALMNTUU	AUTUMNAL
AAIIPRST	APIARIST	AAILNPSS	SALPIANS	AAINRSST	ARTISANS	AALMOOSS	MASSOOLA
AAIIRSTV	AVIARIST	AAILNPST	PLATINAS		TSARINAS	AALMOPSX	AXOPLASM
AAIIRSTW	WISTARIA	AAILNQTU	ALIQUANT	AAINRSSU	SAURIANS	AALMOSTT	STOMATAL

AALMPPSU	PASPALUM	AAOPSSST	POTASSAS
AALMPRSY	PALMYRAS	AAOPSSTY	APOSTASY
AALMPSTY	PLATYSMA	AAORSSTT	STAROSTA
AALMQSUU	SQUAMULA	AAORSUVV	VAVASOUR
AALMSTTU	MULATTAS	AAORSVVY	VAVASORY
AALNNOPT	PANTALON	AAOSTWWY	STOWAWAY
AALNNPUU	PUNALUAN	AARSTTUY	STATUARY
AALNNRSU	ANNULARS	ABBBDEEL	BEDABBLE
AALNNTUU	LUNANAUT	ABBBDELR	BRABBLED
AALNOPRT	PATRONAL	ABBBEILR	BABBLIER
AALNPSUU	PUNALUAS	ABBBELRS	BABBLERS
AALNRRTY	ARRANTLY		BLABBERS
AALNRSTU	NATURALS		BRABBLES
AALNSSTT	SALTANTS	ABBBGILN	BABBLING
AALNSSTU	SULTANAS		BLABBING
AALNSSTY	ANALYSTS	ABBBISTT	BABBITTS
AALNSTTU	TALAUNTS	ABBCDELS	SCABBLED
	TANTALUS	ABBCDERS	SCRABBED
AALOPPRV	APPROVAL	ABBCDKNO	BACKBOND
AALOPRSS	PARASOLS	ABBCEERU	BARBECUE
AALOPRST	PASTORAL	ABBCEGIR	CRIBBAGE
AALOPSVV	PAVLOVAS	ABBCEHIS	BABICHES
AALORSSU	AROUSALS	ABBCEHOU	BABOUCHE
AALORSTX	LAXATORS	ABBCEHSU	BABUCHES
AALORTUV	VALUATOR	ABBCEHTU	BATHCUBE
AALORTVY	LAVATORY	ABBCEIKT	BACKBITE
AALOSTTY	TALAYOTS	ABBCEILR	BARBICEL
AALPRSTU	PASTURAL	ABBCEIRR	CRABBIER
	SPATULAR	ABBCEIRS	SCABBIER
AALPSSTU	SPATULAS	ABBCEKLU	BLUEBACK
AALRRTTY	TARTARLY	ABBCEKNO	BACKBONE
AALRSSTY	SATYRALS	ABBCEKNU	BUCKBEAN
AALRSSVY	VASSALRY	ABBCELLU	CLUBABLE
AALRSTTW	STALWART	ABBCELRS	CLABBERS
AALRSTUY	SALUTARY		SCRABBLE
AALSSSTU	ASSAULTS	ABBCELRU	CURBABLE
AAMMNPRS	RAMPSMAN	ABBCELSS	SCABBLES
AAMMNRST	MANTRAMS	ABBCGINR	CRABBING
AAMMOTXY	MYXOMATA	ABBCGINS	SCABBING
AAMMRSSU	MARASMUS	ABBCGIOR	GABBROIC
AAMNNOSY	ANONYMAS	ABBCIILL	BIBLICAL
AAMNPRST	MANTRAPS	ABBCIINR	RABBINIC
AAMNPRSY	PARANYMS	ABBCIKRT	BRICKBAT
AAMNQSUW	SQUAWMAN	ABBCILRY	CRABBILY
AAMOORSS	AMOROSAS	ABBCKLOY	BLACKBOY
AAMOPRRU	PARAMOUR	ABBDDEEL	BEDDABLE
AAMORRRU	PARAMOUR	ABBDDEEU	BEDAUBED
AAMORRSZ	ZAMARROS	ABBDDEIL	BIDDABLE
AAMORSSV	SAMOVARS	ABBDDELR	DRABBLED
AAMORSTT	STROMATA	ABBDEEJR	JABBERED
AAMOSTTU	AUTOMATS	ABBDEERR	BARBERED
AAMPPRST	RAMPARTS	ABBDEERT	RABBETED
AAMRSSST	SMARTASS	ABBDEERY	YABBERED
AAMRSSTU	SUMATRAS	ABBDEGLR	GRABBLED
AAMRSTWY	TRAMWAYS	ABBDEIRR	DRABBIER
AAMSSSTU	SATSUMAS	ABBDEIRT	RABBITED
AANNOSST	ASSONANT	ABBDELMO	BABELDOM
AANNOSTT	ANNATTOS	ABBDELNS	SNABBLED
AANNRSTY	STANNARY	ABBDELRR	DRABBLER
AANOOPPX	OPOPANAX	ABBDELRS	DABBLERS
AANOOPRZ	PARAZOON		DRABBLES
AANOPRTY	ANATROPY	ABBDEMUZ	BUMBAZED
AANORRRT	NARRATOR	ABBDENRU	UNBARBED
AANORSTY	SANATORY	ABBDEORS	ABSORBED
AANORTTY	NATATORY	ABBDEQSU	SQUABBED
AANQRSTU	QUARTANS	ABBDERRS	DRABBERS
AANRRSTW	WARRANTS	ABBDERST	DRABBEST
AANRRTWY	WARRANTY		DRABBETS
AANRSTTU	SATURANT	ABBDFOOY	BABYFOOD
AANRSUWY	RUNAWAYS	ABBDGILN	DABBLING
AAOORRSW	WOORARAS		

ABBDGINR	DRABBING	ABBGILNU	BAUBLING
ABBDGIOR	GABBROID	ABBGILNW	WABBLING
ABBDHIJS	DJIBBAHS	ABBGINST	STABBING
ABBDHIRS	DRABBISH	ABBGINSU	BUBINGAS
ABBDHIRT	BIRDBATH	ABBGINSW	SWABBING
ABBDHOOY	BABYHOOD	ABBGINTY	TABBYING
ABBDILNO	BAILBOND	ABBGOOSU	BUGABOOS
ABBDILRS	LIBBARDS	ABBHIIMS	BIMBASHI
ABBDINRS	RIBBANDS	ABBHILSY	SHABBILY
ABBDLRSU	LUBBARDS	ABBHRRSU	RHUBARBS
ABBDMORS	BOMBARDS	ABBHRRUY	RHUBARBY
ABBDMOSU	BABUDOMS	ABBHSTTU	BATHTUBS
ABBEEINR	BEARBINE	ABBIINOT	BIBATION
ABBEEJRR	JABBERER	ABBILLOT	BOATBILL
ABBEEJRS	BEJABERS	ABBILLSU	SILLABUB
ABBEENOR	BAREBONE	ABBILOST	BIOBLAST
ABBEERTT	BARBETTE		BOBTAILS
ABBEESSS	ABBESSES	ABBIMNOS	BAMBINOS
ABBEFILR	FLABBIER	ABBIMSSU	BABUISMS
ABBEGIST	GABBIEST	ABBINORS	RABBONIS
ABBEGLRR	GRABBLER	ABBIRRTY	RABBITRY
ABBEGLRS	GABBLERS	ABBIRSUU	SUBURBIA
	GRABBLES	ABBKLOSU	BLAUBOKS
ABBEGNOS	BOGBEANS	ABBLLLOW	BLOWBALL
ABBEGNSU	BUGBANES	ABBLLSTU	BULLBATS
ABBEGRRS	GRABBERS	ABBLLSUY	SYLLABUB
ABBEGRSU	BUGBEARS	ABBLOPRY	PROBABLY
ABBEHILS	BABELISH	ABBMOORS	BOMBORAS
ABBEHIRS	SHABBIER	ABBMOSST	BOMBASTS
ABBEHLSS	SHABBLES	ABBNRSUU	SUBURBAN
ABBEHORT	BATHROBE	ABBOSSTY	BOBSTAYS
ABBEILMS	BABELISM	ABCCDEHO	CABOCHED
ABBEILNU	BUBALINE	ABCCDHIK	DABCHICK
ABBEILOT	BILOBATE	ABCCEEHN	BECHANCE
ABBEILRS	SLABBIER	ABCCEELP	PECCABLE
ABBEILRW	WABBLIER	ABCCEEOR	CABOCEER
ABBEILST	BISTABLE	ABCCEILY	CELIBACY
ABBEINTT	TABBINET	ABCCEIRS	BRECCIAS
ABBEIRRT	RABBITER	ABCCEIRT	BACTERIC
ABBEKLOO	BOOKABLE	ABCCESUU	SUCCUBAE
ABBELMRS	BRAMBLES	ABCCHISU	BACCHIUS
ABBELNSS	SNABBLES	ABCCHNOO	CABOCHON
ABBELOPR	PROBABLE	ABCCIKKK	KICKBACK
ABBELORU	BELABOUR	ABCCIKKP	PICKBACK
ABBELPRS	PRABBLES	ABCCIKOR	ABRICOCK
ABBELQSU	SQUABBLE	ABCCILOR	CARBOLIC
ABBELRRS	RABBLERS	ABCCILOT	COBALTIC
ABBELRSS	SLABBERS	ABCCIMRS	CAMBRICS
ABBELRSU	BARBULES	ABCCINOR	CARBONIC
ABBELRSW	WABBLERS	ABCCINSU	BUCCINAS
ABBELRSY	SLABBERY	ABCCIORS	ASCORBIC
ABBELSSU	BASBLEUS	ABCCKLLO	BALLCOCK
ABBELSUY	BUYABLES	ABCCKLOX	CLACKBOX
ABBEMOOR	AEROBOMB	ABCCKOOT	COCKBOAT
ABBEMOSX	BOMBAXES	ABCCKOSW	BAWCOCKS
ABBEMSUZ	BUMBAZES	ABCCKRTU	BUCKCART
ABBEORRS	ABSORBER	ABCCKSTU	CUTBACKS
	REABSORB	ABCCOORS	BAROCCOS
ABBEORTW	BROWBEAT	ABCCOOST	TOBACCOS
ABBEQRSU	SQUABBER	ABCCSSUU	SUCCUBAS
ABBERRRY	BARBERRY	ABCDDEER	DECARBED
ABBERRYY	BAYBERRY	ABCDDEOR	BROCADED
ABBERSST	STABBERS	ABCDDETU	ABDUCTED
ABBERSSW	SWABBERS	ABCDEEFK	FEEDBACK
ABBFGINR	FRABBING	ABCDEEHL	BLEACHED
ABBGGILN	GABBLING	ABCDEEHR	BERDACHE
ABBGGINR	GRABBING		BREACHED
ABBGIJLN	JABBLING	ABCDEEJT	ABJECTED
ABBGILNR	RABBLING	ABCDEEKR	REBACKED
ABBGILNS	SLABBING	ABCDEELL	BECALLED

ABCDEELM	BECALMED	ABCEEHLS	BLEACHES
ABCDEELS	DEBACLES	ABCEEHRS	BREACHES
ABCDEELU	EDUCABLE	ABCEEHSU	EBAUCHES
ABCDEEMR	CAMBERED	ABCEEILT	CELIBATE
	EMBRACED	ABCEEIMN	AMBIENCE
ABCDEEMX	EXCAMBED	ABCEELRR	CEREBRAL
ABCDEENO	BEACONED	ABCEELRT	BRACELET
ABCDEERR	REBRACED	ABCEEMRR	EMBRACER
ABCDEETU	ABDUCTEE	ABCEEMRS	EMBRACES
ABCDEGIR	BIRDCAGE	ABCEENSS	ABSENCES
	CAGEBIRD	ABCEERRS	REBRACES
ABCDEHLN	BLANCHED	ABCEERST	ACERBEST
ABCDEHLU	BAUCHLED	ABCEERUX	BERCEAUX
ABCDEHNR	BRANCHED	ABCEESSS	BECASSES
ABCDEHOR	BROACHED	ABCEFIIT	BEATIFIC
ABCDEHOS	CABOSHED	ABCEFIKR	BACKFIRE
ABCDEIIT	DIABETIC	ABCEFINO	BONIFACE
ABCDEIKS	BACKSIDE	ABCEGHIN	BEACHING
	DIEBACKS	ABCEGILN	BELACING
ABCDEILR	CALIBRED	ABCEGIMN	EMBACING
ABCDEIPS	PEDICABS	ABCEGIRS	RIBCAGES
ABCDEIRS	ASCRIBED	ABCEGKLL	BLACKLEG
	CARBIDES	ABCEGKLO	BLOCKAGE
ABCDEISS	ABSCISED	ABCEGKOR	BROCKAGE
ABCDEKLO	BLOCKADE	ABCEGMOS	CAMBOGES
ABCDEKLV	BACKVELD	ABCEGNOR	BONGRACE
ABCDEKNU	UNBACKED	ABCEGORS	BROCAGES
ABCDEKRS	REDBACKS	ABCEGOSS	BOSCAGES
ABCDELMS	SCAMBLED	ABCEHITT	BATHETIC
ABCDELNO	BLANCOED	ABCEHKOS	BACKHOES
ABCDELOO	CABOODLE	ABCEHKTW	BETHWACK
ABCDEMOT	COMBATED	ABCEHLNS	BLANCHES
ABCDENRU	UNBRACED	ABCEHLOR	BACHELOR
ABCDENTU	ABDUCENT	ABCEHLSU	BAUCHLES
ABCDEORS	BROCADES		CHASUBLE
ABCDERSU	CUDBEARS	ABCEHMOT	HECATOMB
ABCDESTU	SUBACTED	ABCEHMRS	BECHARMS
ABCDGINU	ABDUCING		BRECHAMS
ABCDHKLO	HOLDBACK		CHAMBERS
ABCDHORS	CHOBDARS	ABCEHNRR	BRANCHER
ABCDIILO	BIOCIDAL	ABCEHNRS	BRANCHES
	DIABOLIC	ABCEHOPU	PABOUCHE
ABCDIIMY	CYMBIDIA	ABCEHORR	BROACHER
ABCDIIRT	TRIBADIC	ABCEHORS	BROACHES
ABCDIKLR	BALDRICK	ABCEHORU	BAROUCHE
ABCDIKLS	BACKSLID	ABCEHOSS	BASOCHES
ABCDIKRU	BAUDRICK	ABCEHRST	BRACHETS
ABCDILLR	BIRDCALL	ABCEHRTT	BRATCHET
ABCDILOU	CUBOIDAL	ABCEIKKL	KICKABLE
ABCDILRS	BALDRICS	ABCEIKLR	CRABLIKE
ABCDINSS	ABSCINDS	ABCEILLR	CRIBELLA
ABCDIRST	CATBIRDS	ABCEILLT	BALLETIC
ABCDIRSU	BAUDRICS	ABCEILMS	ALEMBICS
	SUBACRID	ABCEILNN	BINNACLE
ABCDKNOW	BACKDOWN	ABCEILNU	BACULINE
ABCDKOPR	BACKDROP	ABCEILOR	ALBICORE
ABCDKORW	BACKWORD		CABRIOLE
ABCDLLNU	CLUBLAND	ABCEILOS	SOCIABLE
ABCDNOSS	ABSCONDS	ABCEILRS	CALIBERS
ABCDOORS	CORDOBAS		CALIBRES
ABCDOPRU	CUPBOARD	ABCEILTT	BITTACLE
ABCDORRS	BROCARDS	ABCEILTU	BACULITE
ABCDORTU	ABDUCTOR	ABCEIMST	BETACISM
ABCDORUY	OBDURACY	ABCEINOO	COENOBIA
ABCEEEFK	BEEFCAKE	ABCEINRS	CARBINES
ABCEEFNT	BENEFACT	ABCEINST	CABINETS
ABCEEHIR	BEACHIER	ABCEINTU	INCUBATE
ABCEEHLM	BECHAMEL	ABCEIORS	AEROBICS
ABCEEHLN	ALEBENCH	ABCEIORT	BORACITE
ABCEEHLR	BLEACHER	ABCEIRRT	CRIBRATE

ABCEIRSS	ASCRIBES	ABCHILMO	CHOLIAMB
ABCEIRSW	CRABWISE	ABCHILOO	COOLIBAH
ABCEIRTT	BRATTICE	ABCHIMOR	CHORIAMB
ABCEIRTY	ACERBITY	ABCHINOR	BRONCHIA
ABCEISSS	ABSCISES	ABCHIOOR	BORACHIO
	ABSCISSE	ABCHIOST	COHABITS
ABCEISST	ASBESTIC	ABCHIRRT	TRIBRACH
ABCEJLTY	ABJECTLY	ABCHKLOT	HACKBOLT
ABCEKLMO	MOCKABLE	ABCHKMPU	HUMPBACK
ABCEKLNS	BLACKENS	ABCHKOOP	CHAPBOOK
ABCEKLOO	COOKABLE	ABCHKOSU	CHABOUKS
ABCEKLPU	PALEBUCK	ABCHKSTU	HACKBUTS
ABCEKLST	BLACKEST	ABCHKSUW	HAWBUCKS
ABCEKNRS	BRACKENS	ABCHMOTX	MATCHBOX
ABCEKOOS	BOOKCASE	ABCHNORS	BROCHANS
	CASEBOOK	ABCIIMNS	MINICABS
ABCEKRST	BRACKETS	ABCIINOT	CIBATION
ABCEKSST	BACKSETS	ABCIINSS	ABSCISIN
	SETBACKS	ABCIIORS	ISOBARIC
ABCEKSSY	BACKSEYS	ABCIIRST	TRIBASIC
ABCEKSTW	WETBACKS	ABCIISTY	BASICITY
ABCELLPU	CULPABLE	ABCIITUX	BAUXITIC
ABCELLSU	BUCELLAS	ABCIKLST	BACKLIST
	BULLACES	ABCIKNPS	BACKSPIN
ABCELMNY	LAMBENCY	ABCILLRU	LUBRICAL
ABCELMOS	CEMBALOS	ABCILLSU	BACILLUS
ABCELMRS	CAMBRELS	ABCILLSY	SYLLABIC
	CLAMBERS	ABCILNPU	PUBLICAN
	SCAMBLER	ABCILOOR	COOLIBAR
	SCRAMBLE	ABCILOSY	SOCIABLY
ABCELMSS	SCAMBLES	ABCILRRU	RUBRICAL
ABCELNOT	BALCONET	ABCIMSSS	CAMBISMS
ABCELNUU	NUBECULA	ABCIMMSU	CAMBIUMS
ABCELOOT	BOOTLACE	ABCIMORR	MICROBAR
ABCELOPS	PLACEBOS	ABCIMRTU	UMBRATIC
ABCELORT	BROCATEL	ABCIMSST	CAMBISTS
ABCELOST	OBSTACLE	ABCINORU	CONURBIA
ABCELOSV	VOCABLES	ABCINRVY	VIBRANCY
ABCELOTU	BLUECOAT	ABCIORRS	BARRICOS
ABCELPSU	BLUECAPS	ABCIORSU	CARIBOUS
ABCELPSY	BYPLACES	ABCIOSSU	SCABIOUS
ABCELRSW	BESCRAWL	ABCIOSUV	BIVOUACS
ABCELRTT	BRACTLET	ABCIRSTT	ABSTRICT
ABCELSSU	BASCULES	ABCJKOOT	JACKBOOT
ABCEMORS	CRAMBOES	ABCKKORW	BACKWORK
ABCENOSW	COWBANES	ABCKLLOS	BALLOCKS
ABCENOUY	BUOYANCE	ABCKLOPT	BLACKTOP
ABCENRSU	UNBRACES	ABCKLOSW	SLOWBACK
ABCENTUX	EXCUBANT	ABCKLOTU	BLACKOUT
ABCEOOSS	CABOOSES	ABCKMOOR	BACKROOM
ABCEORSU	CORBEAUS	ABCKMORR	BROCKRAM
ABCERRTU	CARBURET	ABCKMOST	BACKMOST
ABCERTUU	CUBATURE	ABCKMRSU	BUCKRAMS
ABCESTUU	SUBACUTE	ABCKNNOS	BANNOCKS
ABCFIKLL	BACKFILL	ABCKNRTU	TURNBACK
ABCFIKNS	FINBACKS	ABCKOORU	BUCKAROO
ABCFILOS	BIFOCALS	ABCKOPST	BACKSTOP
ABCFKOST	SOFTBACK	ABCKORUY	BUCKAYRO
ABCGGIMO	GAMBOGIC	ABCKOSTU	OUTBACKS
ABCGHINT	BATCHING	ABCKSSTU	SACKBUTS
ABCGHKOS	HOGBACKS		SUBTACKS
ABCGIINN	CABINING	ABCKSSUW	BUCKSAWS
ABCGIKLN	BLACKING	ABCLLPUY	CULPABLY
ABCGIKNS	BACKINGS	ABCLMOSY	CYMBALOS
ABCGILNS	CABLINGS	ABCLMSUY	SCYBALUM
ABCGKLOS	BACKLOGS	ABCLNORY	CARBONYL
ABCGMSSU	SCUMBAGS	ABCLORXY	CARBOXYL
ABCHHIIS	HIBACHIS	ABCLSSSU	SUBCLASS
ABCHIKLS	BLACKISH	ABCLSUUU	SUBUCULA
ABCHIKRS	BRACKISH	ABCMOORT	MOBOCRAT

```
ABCNNORU CONURBAN            DIABETES              BRIGADES     ABDEISTW BAWDIEST
ABCNORTY CORYBANT   ABDEEITU BEAUTIED    ABDEGLNR BRANGLED     ABDEITTU DUBITATE
ABCNOUYY BUOYANCY   ABDEEJMN ENJAMBED    ABDEGLOT GLOBATED     ABDEJNOW JAWBONED
ABCORRSS CROSSBAR   ABDEEKMN EMBANKED    ABDEGLRS BELGARDS     ABDEKLSW SKEWBALD
ABCORRTU TURBOCAR   ABDEEKMR BEDMAKER    ABDEGLRY BADGERLY     ABDEKNNU UNBANKED
ABCORSSU SCABROUS            EMBARKED    ABDEGMRU UMBRAGED     ABDEKNRU UNBARKED
ABCOSSTU SUBCOSTA   ABDEEKNR BARKENED    ABDEGNOR BONDAGER     ABDEKOOR ABROOKED
ABCOSTTU COTTABUS            BEDARKEN    ABDEGNOS BONDAGES     ABDEKORY KEYBOARD
ABCRSTTU SUBTRACT   ABDEEKNV BEKNAVED             DOGBANES     ABDELLOT BALLOTED
ABDDDEEM BEMADDED   ABDEELLL LABELLED    ABDEGOPR PEGBOARD     ABDELMNU UNBLAMED
ABDDEEEH BEHEADED   ABDEELLM EMBALLED    ABDEGRSU SUBGRADE     ABDELNOR BANDEROL
ABDDEEGG DEBAGGED   ABDEELLW WELDABLE    ABDEHILL BILLHEAD     ABDELNOZ BLAZONED
ABDDEEGR BADGERED   ABDEELMM EMBALMED    ABDEHILS DISHABLE     ABDELNRY BYLANDER
ABDDEEHS BEDASHED   ABDEELMS BELDAMES    ABDEHIMT IMBATHED     ABDELNSS BALDNESS
ABDDEEKR DEBARKED            BEMEDALS    ABDEHINS BANISHED     ABDELNST BLANDEST
ABDDEELU BELAUDED   ABDEELMU BEMAULED    ABDEHITU HABITUDE     ABDELORU LABOURED
ABDDEERR DEBARRED   ABDEELMZ EMBLAZED    ABDEHKLU BULKHEAD     ABDELOSV ABSOLVED
ABDDEEST BEDSTEAD   ABDEELNT BANDELET    ABDEHLLN HANDBELL     ABDELPSY PYEBALDS
         BESTADDE   ABDEELRS BEDERALS    ABDEHLLU BULLHEAD     ABDELRRS DRABLERS
ABDDEGIR ABRIDGED   ABDEELSV BESLAVED    ABDEHLMS SHAMBLED     ABDELRSU DURABLES
         BRIGADED   ABDEELTT BATTELED    ABDEHLOT BOLTHEAD     ABDELRTT BRATTLED
ABDDEHMO HEBDOMAD            TABLETED    ABDEHLRS HALBERDS     ABDELSTU SUBLATED
ABDDEHOY HOBDAYED   ABDEELZZ BEDAZZLE    ABDEHMRU RHUMBAED     ABDEMNNS BANDSMEN
ABDDEILS DISABLED   ABDEEMNO BEMOANED    ABDEHMSU AMBUSHED     ABDEMNNY BANDYMEN
ABDDEILU BUDDLEIA   ABDEEMNS BEADSMEN    ABDEHNTU UNBATHED     ABDEMNOS ABDOMENS
ABDDEINR BRANDIED            BEDESMAN    ABDEHORR ABHORRED     ABDEMRTU DRUMBEAT
         RIBANDED   ABDEEMRR EMBARRED             HARBORED              UMBRATED
ABDDEIRR BRAIRDED   ABDEEMRS EMBREADS    ABDEHOSW BESHADOW     ABDENOOT BATOONED
ABDDELRS BLADDERS   ABDEEMRV EMBRAVED             BOWHEADS     ABDENORS BANDORES
ABDDELRY BLADDERY   ABDEENNR BANNERED    ABDEHRST BREADTHS              BROADENS
ABDDENNU UNBANDED   ABDEENNT BANTERED    ABDEIIRT DIATRIBE     ABDENORW RAWBONED
ABDDENOU ABOUNDED   ABDEENRZ BRAZENED    ABDEIKMR IMBARKED     ABDENORY BONEYARD
ABDDEORS ADSORBED   ABDEENST ABSENTED    ABDEIKNU BAUDEKIN     ABDENOTW DOWNBEAT
ABDDERSW BEDWARDS   ABDEENTT BATTENED    ABDEILMN MANDIBLE     ABDENRRS BRANDERS
ABDDGILN BLADDING   ABDEEPRS BESPREAD    ABDEILNR BILANDER     ABDENRRU UNBARRED
ABDDHIOR RHABDOID   ABDEEPTT BEPATTED    ABDEILNT BIDENTAL     ABDENRSS DRABNESS
ABDDILMO LAMBDOID   ABDEERRT BARTERED    ABDEILNY DENIABLY     ABDENRST BANDSTER
ABDDILRY LADYBIRD   ABDEERSS DEBASERS    ABDEILOV VOIDABLE     ABDENRTU BREADNUT
ABDDIMNO BONDMAID   ABDEERST BETREADS    ABDEILPS PIEBALDS              TURBANED
ABDDINSS DISBANDS            BREASTED    ABDEILRT LIBRATED     ABDENSSU SUBDEANS
ABDDLLOS ODDBALLS            DEBATERS    ABDEILRV DRIVABLE     ABDENTTU DEBUTANT
ABDDMORS DAMBRODS   ABDEERTT BATTERED    ABDEILRY DIABLERY     ABDEOPRT PROBATED
ABDEEEFN BEDEAFEN            DRABETTE    ABDEILSS DISABLES     ABDEORRS BOARDERS
ABDEEEMN BEMEANED   ABDEERTY BETRAYED    ABDEILTU DUTIABLE     ABDEORRU ARBOURED
ABDEEERV BEAVERED   ABDEERWY BEWRAYED    ABDEIMNR BRIDEMAN     ABDEORRW WARDROBE
         BEREAVED   ABDEESST BASSETED    ABDEIMOO AMOEBOID     ABDEORST BROADEST
ABDEEFIT TABEFIED            BESTEADS    ABDEIMOR AMBEROID     ABDEORTU OBDURATE
ABDEEFLM FLAMBEED   ABDEFLLO FOLDABLE    ABDEIMRR IMBARRED              TABOURED
ABDEEFMO BEFOAMED   ABDEFLNU FUNDABLE    ABDEIMRS EMBRAIDS     ABDEOSTU BOUTADES
ABDEEGGL BEDAGGLE            UNFABLED    ABDEINOR DEBONAIR     ABDEPRUY UPBRAYED
ABDEEGGR BEGGARED   ABDEFLOR FORDABLE    ABDEINOT OBTAINED     ABDEPSSY BYPASSED
ABDEEGHR HERBAGED   ABDEFLSU LEAFBUDS    ABDEINRS BRANDIES     ABDERRSU ABSURDER
ABDEEGNW BEGNAWED   ABDEFNRU FABURDEN             BRANDISE     ABDERSST DABSTERS
ABDEEGRU BEDEGUAR   ABDEFRSW BEDWARFS    ABDEINST BANDIEST     ABDERSSU SUBEDARS
ABDEEHMS BESHAMED   ABDEGGIL DIGGABLE    ABDEINSU UNBIASED              SURBASED
ABDEEHMT EMBATHED   ABDEGGNU UNBAGGED    ABDEINSW BEDAWINS     ABDERSTU SURBATED
ABDEEHNO BONEHEAD   ABDEGHRS BEGHARDS    ABDEINTU UNBAITED     ABDERSTW BEDSTRAW
ABDEEHRT BREATHED   ABDEGIJN BEJADING    ABDEIOTV OBVIATED     ABDERSTY DRYBEATS
ABDEEHSS BEDASHES   ABDEGILN BLINDAGE    ABDEIPST BAPTISED     ABDFLOOT FOLDBOAT
ABDEEHST BETHESDA   ABDEGILU GUIDABLE    ABDEIPTZ BAPTIZED     ABDGGORS BOGGARDS
ABDEEHTT BEHATTED   ABDEGIMT GAMBITED    ABDEIRST BANDIEST     ABDGHINN BANDHING
ABDEEILM EMBAILED   ABDEGINO GABIONED             BRAIDEST     ABDGHINR HANGBIRD
ABDEEILN DENIABLE   ABDEGINR BEARDING             BRAIDEST     ABDGIINR BRAIDING
ABDEEILR RIDEABLE            BREADING             RABIDEST     ABDGIINS ABIDINGS
ABDEEILS ABSEILED   ABDEGINS BEADINGS             TRIBADES     ABDGILNR BARDLING
ABDEEILT DELIBATE            DEBASING    ABDEIRSW BAWDRIES     ABDGILNU BLAUDING
ABDEEILW BEWAILED   ABDEGINT DEBATING             DAWBRIES     ABDGIMRU GUIMBARD
ABDEEIRS BEARDIES   ABDEGINZ BEDAZING    ABDEIRTV VIBRATED     ABDGINNR BRANDING
ABDEEIRT EBRIATED   ABDEGIRR ABRIDGER    ABDEISST BASTIDES     ABDGINNS BANDINGS
ABDEEIST BEADIEST   ABDEGIRS ABRIDGES    ABDEISSU DISABUSE     ABDGINNY BANDYING
                                         ABDEISTU DAUBIEST
```

ABDGINOR	ABORDING	ABEEEERRT	TEREBRAE	ABEEISTU	BEAUTIES	ABEEORST	REBATOES
	BOARDING	ABEEERSV	BEREAVES	ABEEITUX	BEAUXITE	ABEEORTV	OVERBEAT
ABDGINRS	BRIGANDS	ABEEFFTU	BEAUFFET	ABEEJMOR	JAMBOREE	ABEEPRRY	PEABERRY
ABDGINST	DINGBATS	ABEEFILS	FEASIBLE	ABEEKLOT	KEELBOAT	ABEERRRT	BARTERER
ABDGINSU	DAUBINGS	ABEEFIST	TABEFIES	ABEEKLST	BLEAKEST	ABEERRST	REBATERS
ABDGLNOS	BOGLANDS	ABEEFLLL	FELLABLE	ABEEKMNR	BRAKEMEN		TABRERES
ABDGLOOR	LOGBOARD	ABEEFLLN	BEFALLEN		EMBANKER		TEREBRAS
ABDGLSUY	LADYBUGS	ABEEFLOS	BEEFALOS	ABEEKNSV	BEKNAVES	ABEERRSY	SEABERRY
ABDHHSSU	SHADBUSH	ABEEFORR	FOREBEAR	ABEEKOOP	PEEKABOO	ABEERRTT	BARRETTE
ABDHIIST	ADHIBITS	ABEEFSTU	BEAUFETS	ABEEKOPS	PEEKABOS	ABEERRTV	VERTEBRA
	DISHABIT	ABEEGHRS	HERBAGES	ABEEKPSS	BESPEAKS	ABEERRTY	BETRAYER
ABDHILLN	HANDBILL	ABEEGHRT	BERTHAGE	ABEEKRRS	BREAKERS		TEABERRY
ABDHILNS	BLANDISH	ABEEGINR	BAREGINE	ABEEKRST	BESTREAK	ABEERSTT	ABETTERS
ABDHINRS	BRANDISH		BERGENIA	ABEELLLS	SELLABLE	ABEERSTU	SUBERATE
ABDHIORS	BROADISH	ABEEGIRV	VERBIAGE	ABEELLLT	TELLABLE	ABEESZZZ	BEZAZZES
ABDHIPRS	BARDSHIP	ABEEGLLR	GABELLER	ABEELLOT	BALLOTEE	ABEFFLRS	BAFFLERS
ABDHIRTY	BIRTHDAY	ABEEGLLS	GABELLES	ABEELLOV	LOVEABLE	ABEFGILS	FILABEGS
ABDHKNOO	HANDBOOK	ABEEGLRS	BEAGLERS	ABEELLSY	EYEBALLS	ABEFGLLR	BERGFALL
ABDHLORW	BLOWHARD	ABEEGLTT	GETTABLE	ABEELLTT	LETTABLE	ABEFGSST	GABFESTS
ABDHMORS	RHABDOMS	ABEEGMNR	BARGEMEN	ABEELMMR	EMBALMER	ABEFHILS	FISHABLE
ABDHMOTU	BADMOUTH	ABEEGMTY	MEGABYTE		EMMARBLE	ABEFHOOT	HOOFBEAT
ABDHNSSU	HUSBANDS	ABEEGOSZ	GAZEBOES	ABEELMOV	MOVEABLE	ABEFILLL	FALLIBLE
ABDIILLR	BILLIARD	ABEEGRRS	GERBERAS	ABEELMPR	PREAMBLE	ABEFILLM	FILMABLE
ABDIIMNR	MIDBRAIN	ABEEGRST	ABSTERGE	ABEELMRT	ATREMBLE	ABEFILLR	FIREBALL
ABDIIMSU	BASIDIUM	ABEEGRSU	AUBERGES	ABEELMSS	ASSEMBLE	ABEFILLT	LIFTABLE
ABDIINOS	OBSIDIAN	ABEEGRSW	BREWAGES		BEAMLESS	ABEFILOT	LIFEBOAT
ABDIINTT	BANDITTI	ABEEGTTU	BAGUETTE	ABEELMSZ	EMBLAZES	ABEFILRS	BARFLIES
ABDIIRTY	RABIDITY	ABEEHILR	HIREABLE	ABEELMTT	EMBATTLE	ABEFILSU	FABULISE
ABDIKLNR	BLINKARD	ABEEHINT	THEBAINE	ABEELNOP	BEANPOLE	ABEFILSY	FEASIBLY
ABDIKNSW	BAWDKINS	ABEEHLLP	HELPABLE		OPENABLE	ABEFILUZ	FABULIZE
ABDIKRSS	DISBARKS	ABEEHLLR	BEERHALL	ABEELNRS	ENABLERS	ABEFINSU	BEAUFINS
ABDILOOS	DIABOLOS		HAREBELL	ABEELNRT	RENTABLE	ABEFIRRT	FIREBRAT
ABDILORS	LABROIDS	ABEEHLSV	BEHALVES	ABEELNTU	TUNEABLE	ABEFITUY	BEAUTIFY
ABDILOST	BLASTOID	ABEEHMSS	BESHAMES	ABEELOPR	OPERABLE	ABEFLLMU	BLAMEFUL
	TABLOIDS	ABEEHMST	EMBATHES		ROPEABLE	ABEFLLTU	TABLEFUL
ABDILRRY	RIBALDRY	ABEEHNNS	HENBANES	ABEELOPS	POSEABLE	ABEFLMOR	FORMABLE
ABDILRSW	AWLBIRDS	ABEEHNPP	BEHAPPEN	ABEELORX	EXORABLE	ABEFLNRU	FUNEBRAL
ABDILRZZ	BLIZZARD	ABEEHNSS	BANSHEES	ABEELPRS	BEPEARLS	ABEFLNSY	FLYBANES
ABDIMORS	AMBROIDS	ABEEHNTT	HEBETANT	ABEELRST	BLEAREST	ABEFOORT	BAREFOOT
ABDINOTY	ANTIBODY	ABEEHQTU	BEQUEATH		BLEATERS	ABEFORRS	FORBEARS
ABDINRTY	BANDITRY	ABEEHRRT	BREATHER		RETABLES	ABEGGHLU	HUGGABLE
ABDIPRSU	UPBRAIDS	ABEEHRST	BREATHES	ABEELRSU	REUSABLE	ABEGGILN	BEAGLING
ABDIRRUY	RIBAUDRY		HARTBEES	ABEELRSV	BESLAVER	ABEGGIST	BAGGIEST
ABDKLNOO	BOOKLAND	ABEEIKLL	LIKEABLE	ABEELRTT	BATTELER	ABEGGLRY	BEGGARLY
ABDKNOOS	BANDOOKS	ABEEIKLR	BLEAKIER	ABEELRTU	BATELEUR	ABEGGMOS	GAMBOGES
ABDLLNOS	SLOBLAND	ABEEIKRS	BAKERIES		BLEUATRE	ABEGGNSU	BUGGANES
ABDLLORS	BOLLARDS	ABEEILLR	RELIABLE	ABEELSSS	BASELESS	ABEGGRSU	BURGAGES
ABDLNORS	BANDROLS	ABEEILLV	LEVIABLE	ABEELSST	BATELESS	ABEGHILP	PHILABEG
ABDLRSUY	ABSURDLY		LIVEABLE	ABEELSSU	SUBLEASE	ABEGHILL	ALBERGHI
	RYBAULDS	ABEEILMS	BELAMIES	ABEELSSV	BESLAVES	ABEGHINO	OBEAHING
ABDLSSUU	SUBDUALS	ABEEILNP	PLEBEIAN	ABEELSTT	TESTABLE	ABEGHINT	BEATHING
ABDLSTUU	SUBADULT	ABEEILNU	BANLIEUE	ABEEMMNR	MEMBRANE	ABEGHINV	BEHAVING
ABDMNNOS	BONDSMAN	ABEEILNV	ENVIABLE	ABEEMMRU	BUMMAREE	ABEGHNSS	SHEBANGS
ABDMNOUW	MAWBOUND	ABEEILPX	EXPIABLE	ABEEMNOR	BEMOANER	ABEGHORR	BEGORRAH
ABDMOOPR	MOPBOARD	ABEEILRR	BLEARIER	ABEEMNST	BASEMENT	ABEGHRRY	HAGBERRY
ABDMRSUY	MARYBUDS	ABEEILRT	LIBERATE	ABEEMNTT	ABETMENT	ABEGHRST	BARGHEST
ABDNOPRS	PROBANDS	ABEEILSV	EVASIBLE		BATEMENT	ABEGIIMS	BIGAMIES
ABDNORUY	BOUNDARY	ABEEILSZ	SEIZABLE	ABEEMRSS	BESMEARS	ABEGIKNR	BREAKING
ABDNRSTU	TURBANDS		SIZEABLE	ABEEMRSV	EMBRAVES	ABEGIKNT	BETAKING
ABDOORSW	BARWOODS	ABEEILTV	EVITABLE	ABEENNRT	BANNERET	ABEGILMN	EMBALING
ABDOORTU	OUTBOARD	ABEEILVW	VIEWABLE	ABEENNRU	EBURNEAN	ABEGILNN	ENABLING
ABDOOSSW	BASSWOOD	ABEEIMRT	AMBERITE	ABEENNTU	UNBEATEN	ABEGILNR	BLEARING
ABDRSSTU	BUSTARDS	ABEEIMST	BEAMIEST	ABEENORS	SEABORNE	ABEGILNS	SINGABLE
ABDRSUZZ	BUZZARDS	ABEEINST	BETAINES	ABEENOTZ	BENZOATE	ABEGILNT	BELATING
ABEEEGRS	BARGEESE	ABEEINTY	AYENBITE	ABEENRRR	BARRENER		BLEATING
ABEEEGRV	BEVERAGE	ABEEIPRS	BEPRAISE	ABEENRRT	BANTERER		TANGIBLE
ABEEEHTT	HEBETATE	ABEEIRTT	BATTERIE	ABEENRSS	BARENESS	ABEGILNY	BELAYING
ABEEENRT	TENEBRAE	ABEEIRTV	BREVIATE	ABEENRSV	VERBENAS	ABEGILOT	OBLIGATE
ABEEENRV	BEREAVEN	ABEEISST	BEASTIES	ABEENSSS	BASENESS	ABEGIMNN	BENAMING
ABEEENST	ABSENTEE	ABEEISSV	ABESSIVE	ABEEORRV	OVERBEAR	ABEGIMNR	BREAMING

ABEGIMNS	BEAMINGS
	EMBASING
ABEGIMNY	EMBAYING
ABEGIMRS	GAMBIERS
ABEGIMST	MEGABITS
ABEGIMUX	GIAMBEUX
ABEGINOR	ABORIGEN
ABEGINOS	BEGONIAS
ABEGINRS	BEARINGS
	SABERING
ABEGINRT	BERATING
	REBATING
ABEGINRW	BEWARING
ABEGINRY	BERAYING
ABEGINST	BEATINGS
ABEGINTT	ABETTING
ABEGINTW	WINGBEAT
ABEGIOSS	BIOGASES
ABEGIPPR	BAGPIPER
ABEGIPPS	BAGPIPES
ABEGKORS	BROKAGES
	GROSBEAK
ABEGLLLU	GULLABLE
ABEGLLOR	BARGELLO
ABEGLMRS	GAMBLERS
	GAMBRELS
ABEGLNRS	BRANGLES
ABEGLRRS	GARBLERS
ABEGLRUU	BLAGUEUR
ABEGLSTU	GUSTABLE
ABEGMNOS	GAMBESON
ABEGMORT	BERGAMOT
ABEGMRSU	UMBRAGES
ABEGNNST	BANTENGS
ABEGNOSS	NOSEBAGS
ABEGNRST	BANGSTER
ABEGNRTU	BURGANET
ABEGNSTU	SUBAGENT
ABEGOORS	BARGOOSE
ABEGOSTT	BOTTEGAS
ABEGOSUY	BUOYAGES
ABEGRRUV	BURGRAVE
ABEGRSST	BARGESTS
ABEGSSTU	SUBSTAGE
ABEHILLR	HAIRBELL
ABEHILNR	HIBERNAL
ABEHILRS	BLASHIER
ABEHILTT	TITHABLE
ABEHIMOS	OBEAHISM
ABEHIMST	IMBATHES
ABEHINSS	BANISHES
ABEHINST	ABSINTHE
ABEHIOPU	EUPHOBIA
ABEHIORV	BEHAVIOR
ABEHIRRS	BRASHIER
ABEHISTU	HABITUES
ABEHISTZ	ZABTIEHS
ABEHKLLW	HAWKBELL
ABEHKNOR	HORNBEAK
ABEHKRSU	HAUBERKS
ABEHLLRT	BETHRALL
ABEHLMMU	HUMMABLE
ABEHLMSS	SHAMBLES
ABEHLNOT	BENTHOAL
ABEHLOTY	HYLOBATE
ABEHLRST	BLATHERS
	HALBERTS
ABEHLSSS	BASHLESS
ABEHMNOR	HORNBEAM
ABEHMOOR	REHOBOAM

ABEHMSSU	AMBUSHES
ABEHNSTU	SUNBATHE
ABEHORRR	ABHORRER
ABEHORST	BATHORSE
ABEHOSST	BATHOSES
ABEHOSTX	HATBOXES
ABEHOSXY	HAYBOXES
ABEHRSST	BRASHEST
ABEIILLS	BAILLIES
ABEIILMT	IMITABLE
ABEIILNN	BIENNIAL
ABEIILNV	INVIABLE
ABEIILPT	PITIABLE
ABEIILRR	LIBRAIRE
ABEIILRS	BISERIAL
ABEIILST	ALBITISE
	SIBILATE
ABEIILTV	VITIABLE
ABEIILTZ	ALBITIZE
ABEIINRR	BRAINIER
ABEIINRS	BINARIES
ABEIJLTU	JUBILATE
ABEIJMNN	BENJAMIN
ABEIJMRS	JAMBIERS
ABEIJNSS	BASENJIS
ABEIKLLN	BALKLINE
ABEIKLNS	BLANKIES
ABEIKLSS	KISSABLE
ABEIKLST	BALKIEST
ABEIKNRR	BRANKIER
ABEIKNRS	BEARSKIN
	INBREAKS
ABEIKNST	BEATNIKS
ABEIKRST	BARKIEST
	BRAKIEST
	BREASKIT
ABEILLLT	TILLABLE
ABEILLLW	WILLABLE
ABEILLMM	LIMBMEAL
ABEILLOS	ISOLABLE
	LOBELIAS
ABEILLOV	VIOLABLE
ABEILLQU	LIQUABLE
ABEILLRS	LIBERALS
ABEILLRY	BERYLLIA
	RELIABLY
ABEILLST	BASTILLE
ABEILLTT	TILTABLE
ABEILMNS	BAILSMEN
ABEILMNT	BAILMENT
ABEILMOR	BROMELIA
ABEILMRR	MARBLIER
ABEILMRS	REMBLAIS
ABEILMRW	WAMBLIER
ABEILMSS	MISSABLE
ABEILMST	BALMIEST
	TIMBALES
ABEILNNW	WINNABLE
ABEILNOP	OPINABLE
ABEILNPS	BIPLANES
ABEILNPT	PINTABLE
ABEILNRS	RINSABLE
ABEILNRU	RUINABLE
ABEILNSS	ALBINESS
	LESBIANS
ABEILNST	INSTABLE
ABEILNTV	BIVALENT
ABEILNUV	UNVIABLE
ABEILNVY	ENVIABLY
ABEILPRT	PARTIBLE

ABEILPRZ	PRIZABLE
ABEILPSS	PASSIBLE
ABEILPST	EPIBLAST
ABEILRRU	REBURIAL
ABEILRRW	BRAWLIER
ABEILRST	LIBRATES
ABEILRTW	WRITABLE
ABEILSST	ASTILBES
	BESTIALS
	STABILES
ABEILSSU	ISSUABLE
	SUASIBLE
ABEILSTU	SUITABLE
ABEILSTY	BEASTILY
ABEILSUX	BISEXUAL
ABEILSVV	BIVALVES
ABEIMNRS	MIRBANES
ABEIMNST	AMBIENTS
ABEIMRST	BARMIEST
ABEIMRSU	AUMBRIES
ABEIMRTV	AMBIVERT
	VERBATIM
ABEIMSSU	IAMBUSES
ABEINNOZ	BEZONIAN
ABEINNRR	BRANNIER
ABEINNRU	INURBANE
ABEINORR	AIRBORNE
ABEINORS	BARONIES
ABEINORT	BARITONE
	OBTAINER
ABEINOST	BOTANIES
	BOTANISE
	NIOBATES
	OBEISANT
ABEINOTZ	BOTANIZE
ABEINPST	BEPAINTS
ABEINQSU	BASQUINE
ABEINRRW	BRAWNIER
ABEINRST	ATEBRINS
	BANISTER
ABEINRSU	ANBURIES
	URBANISE
ABEINRTU	URBANITE
ABEINRUZ	URBANIZE
ABEINSST	BASINETS
	BASSINET
	BESAINTS
	BESTAINS
ABEINSSU	UNBIASES
ABEINSTT	TABINETS
ABEINTTU	INTUBATE
ABEIORSS	ISOBARES
ABEIORST	SABOTIER
ABEIORTV	ABORTIVE
ABEIOSSS	ISOBASES
ABEIOSTV	OBVIATES
ABEIPSST	BAPTISES
ABEIPSTZ	BAPTIZES
ABEIRRRS	BARRIERS
ABEIRRSS	BRASIERS
	BRASSIER
ABEIRRST	ARBITERS
	RAREBITS
ABEIRRSZ	BRAZIERS
ABEIRRTT	BRATTIER
ABEIRRVY	BREVIARY
ABEIRSSS	BRASSIES
ABEIRSTT	BIRETTAS
ABEIRSTV	VIBRATES
ABEIRSTW	WARBIEST

ABEIRSTY	BESTIARY
	SYBARITE
ABEIRSUX	EXURBIAS
ABEIRTTY	YTTERBIA
ABEISSST	BASSIEST
ABEISSTT	BATISTES
ABEISTTT	BATTIEST
ABEISTUX	BAUXITES
ABEISZZZ	BIZAZZES
ABEITTTU	TITUBATE
ABEJKLOU	KABELJOU
ABEJMNOS	JAMBONES
ABEJMOOR	JEROBOAM
ABEJNOSW	JAWBONES
ABEJOOSW	JAWBOOES
ABEJRRSU	ABJURERS
ABEKLMOS	SMOKABLE
ABEKLNOW	KNOWABLE
ABEKLNST	BLANKEST
	BLANKETS
ABEKLNTY	BLANKETY
ABEKLORW	WORKABLE
ABEKLRSS	BARKLESS
ABEKMNNS	BANKSMEN
ABEKNSSY	SNEAKSBY
ABEKOORS	ABROOKES
ABEKORTU	OUTBREAK
ABEKPRSU	UPBREAKS
ABEKRSTY	BASKETRY
ABELLLMU	LABELLUM
ABELLLOR	ROLLABLE
ABELLLOT	TOLLABLE
ABELLLSY	SYLLABLE
ABELLMOR	OMBRELLA
ABELLMRU	UMBELLAR
	UMBRELLA
ABELLNOT	BALLONET
ABELLNRU	RUBELLAN
ABELLNST	NETBALLS
ABELLOSV	SOLVABLE
ABELLOTU	LOBULATE
ABELLRSU	RUBELLAS
ABELLRVY	VERBALLY
ABELMNNO	NOBLEMAN
ABELMNOZ	EMBLAZON
ABELMNST	SEMBLANT
ABELMNSU	ALBUMENS
ABELMOOT	MOOTABLE
ABELMOSV	MOVABLES
ABELMOVY	MOVEABLY
ABELMPTU	PLUMBATE
ABELMRRS	MARBLERS
	RAMBLERS
ABELMRST	LAMBERTS
ABELMSSY	ASSEMBLY
ABELNNOR	BANNEROL
ABELNNRU	RUNNABLE
ABELNORZ	BLAZONER
ABELNOST	NEOBLAST
	NOTABLES
ABELNOSY	BALONEYS
ABELNQTU	BLANQUET
ABELNRSS	BRANSLES
ABELNRST	BRANTLES
ABELNRSY	BLARNEYS
ABELNRUY	URBANELY
ABELNRYZ	BRAZENLY
ABELNSTU	UNSTABLE
ABELNSTY	ABSENTLY
ABELNSUU	UNUSABLE

ABELOPRT PORTABLE	TABORETS	BIASSING	ABGORRSU GOBURRAS
ABELOPRU POURABLE	ABEORSTU SABOTEUR	ABGIINST BAITINGS	ABGORSTU OUTBRAGS
ABELOPRV PROVABLE	ABEORTTU OBTURATE	ABGIJNRU ABJURING	ABHHKOST KHOTBAHS
ABELOPST POTABLES	TABOURET	ABGIKLNN BLANKING	ABHHKSTU KHUTBAHS
ABELOQTU QUOTABLE	ABEORTUV OUTBRAVE	ABGIKLNS BALKINGS	ABHHRSTU HATBRUSH
ABELORRU LABOURER	ABEOSSST ASBESTOS	ABGIKLNU BAULKING	ABHIINRS BRAINISH
ABELORST BLOATERS	ABEOSTUV SUBOVATE	ABGIKNNR BRANKING	ABHIINST INHABITS
SORTABLE	ABEPRRTU ABRUPTER	ABGIKNNS BANKINGS	ABHIIORZ RHIZOBIA
STORABLE	ABEPSSSY BYPASSES	ABGILLMN LAMBLING	ABHIKLOR KOHLRABI
ABELORSU RUBEOLAS	ABEQRSUU ARQUEBUS	ABGILLNS BALLINGS	ABHIKSTW HAWKBITS
ABELORSV ABSOLVER	ABERRTYY TAYBERRY	ABGILMNR MARBLING	ABHILLPT PITHBALL
ABELOSSU SABULOSE	ABERRWXY WAXBERRY	RAMBLING	ABHILNOS HOBNAILS
ABELOSSV ABSOLVES	ABERSSST BRASSETS	ABGILMNS AMBLINGS	ABHILNOT BIATHLON
ABELOSTU ABSOLUTE	ABERSSSU SURBASES	ABGILMNW WAMBLING	ABHILSST STABLISH
ABELOSTW BESTOWAL	ABERSSTU ABSTRUSE	ABGILNNT BANTLING	ABHILSTU HALIBUTS
ABELPRTU PUBERTAL	SURBATES	ABGILNOR LABORING	ABHIMMST BATHMISM
ABELQSUU SUBEQUAL	ABERSSTW WABSTERS	ABGILNOT BLOATING	ABHINSST ABSINTHS
ABELRRSW BRAWLERS	ABERSTTU ABUTTERS	OBLIGANT	ABHIOSST ISOBATHS
WARBLERS	ABERTTUY BUTYRATE	ABGILNRT BRATLING	ABHIOSTU HAUTBOIS
ABELRRTU BARRULET	ABFFGILN BAFFLING	ABGILNRW BRAWLING	ABHIRSTT BRATTISH
ABELRSST BLASTERS	ABFFIILS BAILIFFS	WARBLING	ABHKLSSY BASHLYKS
STABLERS	ABFFLLPU PUFFBALL	ABGILNST BLASTING	ABHKLSUW BUSHWALK
ABELRSSY LABRYSES	ABFFNOTU BOUFFANT	STABLING	ABHKORSU BOURKHAS
ABELRSTT BATTLERS	ABFGILNS FABLINGS	TABLINGS	KOURBASH
BLATTERS	ABFGLLOO GOOFBALL	ABGILNSW BAWLINGS	ABHLLMOT MOTHBALL
BRATTLES	ABFGORUU FAUBOURG	ABGILNTT BATTLING	ABHLLOOY BALLYHOO
ABELRSTU BALUSTER	ABFHIIST BAITFISH	BLATTING	ABHLPSUY SUBPHYLA
ABELRSTW BLEWARTS	ABFHILLS FISHBALL	ABGILNTY TANGIBLY	ABHMNOTY BOTHYMAN
ABELRSUZ ZEBRULAS	ABFHIORS BOARFISH	ABGILORS GARBOILS	ABHMNSUU SUBHUMAN
ABELRTTU BURLETTA	ABFIILLR FIBRILLA	ABGIMMNO MAMBOING	ABHMOORT BATHROOM
REBUTTAL	ABFIIMRS FIMBRIAS	ABGIMNRU RUMBAING	ABHNSSTU SUNBATHS
ABELSSTT STABLEST	ABFILLLY FALLIBLY	ABGIMOSU BIGAMOUS	ABHOORST TARBOOSH
ABELSSTU SUBLATES	ABFILNSU BASINFUL	SUBIMAGO	ABHORRSU HARBOURS
ABELSTUU SUBULATE	ABFILSTU FABULIST	ABGIMSST GAMBISTS	ABHORSTU TARBOUSH
ABELSTWY BELTWAYS	ABFIMORS FIBROMAS	ABGINNOT BATONING	ABHOSTUY HAUTBOYS
ABELTTUU TUBULATE	ABFJORSU FRABJOUS	ABGINNRU UNBARING	ABIIINRY BIRIYANI
ABEMMNOO MOONBEAM	ABFKLLOR KORFBALL	ABGINNRX BANXRING	ABIIKKST KIBITKAS
ABEMNOTU UMBONATE	ABFLLOOT FOOTBALL	ABGINNST BANTINGS	ABIIKLSS BASILISK
ABEMNOTW BATWOMEN	ABFLLOST SOFTBALL	ABGINOOT TABOOING	ABIILLMR MILLIBAR
ABEMNPRU PENUMBRA	ABFLOSTU BOASTFUL	ABGINORT ABORTING	ABIILLTY LABILITY
ABEMNRSY MYRBANES	ABFLOSTY FLYBOATS	TABORING	ABIILMNO BINOMIAL
ABEMNSSU SUNBEAMS	ABFLOSUU FABULOUS	ABGINOST BOASTING	ABIILMNS ALBINISM
ABEMNSUY SUNBEAMY	ABFNORTU TURBOFAN	BOATINGS	ABIILMSU BULIMIAS
ABEMNTTU ABUTMENT	ABFOORST FOOTBARS	BOSTANGI	ABIILNOT LIBATION
ABEMORRS EMBRASOR	ABFSSTTU TUBFASTS	ABGINRRS BARRINGS	ABIILNQS INQILABS
ABEMORST BROMATES	ABGGGILN BLAGGING	ABGINRST BRASTING	ABIILNST SIBILANT
ABEMORSU AMBEROUS	ABGGGINR BRAGGING	ABGINSST BASTINGS	ABIILPTY PITIABLY
ABEMORTZ BAROMETZ	ABGGGINS BAGGINGS	ABGINSTT BATTINGS	ABIIMNOT AMBITION
ABENNORS BARONNES	ABGGIJNN JINGBANG	ABGINSTW BATSWING	ABIIMSST IAMBISTS
ABENOPSU SUBPOENA	ABGGILMN GAMBLING	ABGINTTU ABUTTING	ABIINORS ROBINIAS
ABENORSS BARONESS	ABGGILNR GARBLING	ABGIOPST PIGBOATS	ABIINRSY BIRYANIS
ABENORST BARONETS	ABGGNOOT TOBOGGAN	ABGLLLOY GLOBALLY	ABIIRSSV VIBRISSA
ABENORTT BETATRON	ABGGORST BOGGARTS	ABGLLORU GLOBULAR	ABIJLNRS BRINJALS
ABENORTV BEVATRON	ABGHHILL HIGHBALL	ABGLLRUY BULLYRAG	ABIJLNTU JUBILANT
ABENORTY BARYTONE	ABGHIINT HABITING	ABGLMNSU LUMBANGS	ABIJNOOT JOBATION
ABENOSTY BAYONETS	ABGHILMN HAMBLING	ABGLMOPU PLUMBAGO	ABIJNOST ABJOINTS
ABENQSTU BANQUETS	ABGHINRS BRASHING	ABGLMOSU LUMBAGOS	BANJOIST
ABENRRYZ BRAZENRY	ABGHINSS BASHINGS	ABGLNOOT LONGBOAT	ABIKLMNS LAMBKINS
ABENRSTU UNBRASTE	ABGHIOPR BIOGRAPH	ABGLNOUW BUNGALOW	LAMBSKIN
URBANEST	ABGHLOST HAGBOLTS	ABGLOOST TOOLBAGS	ABIKLNRY BYRLAKIN
ABEOPRSS SAPROBES	ABGHMORU BROUGHAM	ABGLOOTY BATOLOGY	ABIKLORS KILOBARS
ABEOPRST PROBATES	ABGIILNR BRAILING	ABGLORST RAGBOLTS	ABIKMNNR BRINKMAN
ABEOQRSU BAROQUES	ABGIILNS SAIBLING	ABGLORSU GLABROUS	ABIKMNRS BARMKINS
ABEORRSS BRASEROS	ABGIILNT LIBATING	ABGLRSSU BURGLARS	ABIKNORR IRONBARK
ABEORRST ARBORETS	ABGIIMNS IMBASING	ABGLRRUY BURGLARY	ABIKRSST BRITSKAS
TABORERS	ABGIIMST BIGAMIST	ABGMNOOR GAMBROON	ABIKRSTZ BRITZKAS
ABEORSST BOASTERS	ABGIINNR BRAINING	ABGNOPRS PROBANGS	BRITZKA
SORBATES	ABGIINOR ABORIGIN	ABGNORSU OSNABURG	ABILLLPY PLAYBILL
ABEORSTT ABETTORS	ABGIINRS BRAISING	ABGNOSTU GUNBOATS	ABILLMSU BALLIUMS
BATTEROS	ABGIINSS BIASINGS	ABGOORST BOTARGOS	ABILLNPS PINBALLS

Code	Word(s)
ABILLOVY	VIOLABLY
ABILLRTY	TRIBALLY
ABILLSWX	WAXBILLS
ABILMNOU	OLIBANUM
ABILMNSU	ALBUMINS
ABILMOPS	BIOPLASM
ABILNOOT	LOBATION
	OBLATION
ABILNORU	UNILOBAR
ABILNOTU	ABLUTION
	ABUTILON
ABILNRTU	TRIBUNAL
	TURBINAL
ABILOPRS	PARBOILS
ABILOPST	BIOPLAST
ABILORST	ORBITALS
	STROBILA
ABILORSV	BOLIVARS
ABILORTY	LIBATORY
ABILPSSY	PASSIBLY
ABILRSSY	BRASSILY
ABILRSUV	SUBVIRAL
ABILSSUY	ISSUABLY
ABILSTUY	SUITABLY
ABIMMNOO	MAINBOOM
ABIMNOSU	BIMANOUS
ABIMNRTU	TAMBURIN
ABIMPSST	BAPTISMS
ABIMRSST	STRABISM
ABIMRSTT	TRIMTABS
ABINOORS	BORONIAS
ABINOORT	ABORTION
ABINORST	TABORINS
ABINORSW	RAINBOWS
ABINORTU	TABOURIN
ABINORWY	RAINBOWY
ABINOSST	BASTIONS
ABINOSSU	ABUSIONS
ABINOSTT	BOTANIST
ABINRTUY	URBANITY
ABINTTTU	TITUBANT
ABIOPRSU	BIPAROUS
ABIOPSTU	SUBTOPIA
ABIORRST	ARBORIST
ABIORRTV	VIBRATOR
ABIORSTV	VIBRATOS
ABIORTUY	OBITUARY
ABIPSSTT	BAPTISTS
ABIRRSTU	AIRBURST
ABIRSSUZ	SUBSIZAR
ABIRSTTY	TRAYBITS
ABISSSST	BASSISTS
ABJKMOSS	SJAMBOKS
ABJLMOOS	JAMBOOLS
ABKKMOOR	BOOKMARK
ABKLLNOR	BANKROLL
ABKLOOPY	PLAYBOOK
ABKLRSUW	BULWARKS
ABKNPRTU	BANKRUPT
ABKNRSUU	BUNRAKUS
ABKOORTW	WORKBOAT
ABKOOSTT	KOTTABOS
ABLLMOPW	BLOWLAMP
ABLLNOOS	BALLOONS
ABLLNOSW	SNOWBALL
ABLLORST	BORSTALL
ABLLOSTY	TALLBOYS
ABLLRTUY	BRUTALLY
ABLLSSUY	SYLLABUS
ABLMNRUU	ALBURNUM
	LABURNUM
ABLMOOST	TOMBOLAS
ABLMOSTY	MYOBLAST
ABLMPSUU	PABULUMS
ABLNORYZ	BLAZONRY
ABLNOSTU	BUTANOLS
ABLNOSUZ	SUBZONAL
ABLNRSUU	SUBLUNAR
ABLNSUUY	UNUSABLY
ABLOORTY	OBLATORY
ABLOOSTT	BOOTLAST
ABLOOSTZ	ZOOBLAST
ABLOPRVY	PROVABLY
ABLOPSUU	PABULOUS
ABLOPSYY	PLAYBOYS
ABLOQTUY	QUOTABLY
ABLORSST	BORSTALS
ABLORSSU	SUBSOLAR
ABLORSTW	BLAWORTS
ABLORSUW	BOURLAWS
ABLOSSUU	SABULOUS
ABLOSTTU	SUBTOTAL
ABLPRTUY	ABRUPTLY
ABMNTTUY	BUTTYMAN
ABMORSTU	TAMBOURS
ABMOSSTU	SUBATOMS
ABNOORRT	ROBORANT
ABNOORSB	SOROBANS
ABNOORSZ	BORAZONS
ABNOOSSS	BASSOONS
ABNORSTY	BARYTONS
ABNORTUU	RUNABOUT
ABNOSSSU	BONASSUS
ABNRSTTU	TURBANTS
ABOORRSU	ARBOROUS
ABOORSTW	ROWBOATS
ABORSSTU	ROBUSTAS
ACCCDIIO	COCCIDIA
ACCCENPY	PECCANCY
ACCCFIIL	CALCIFIC
ACCCHILO	COLCHICA
ACCCIIPR	CAPRICCI
ACCCILLY	CYCLICAL
ACCCIOPU	CAPUCCIO
ACCDDEEN	ACCENDED
	CADENCED
ACCDDEIS	CADDICES
ACCDDEOR	ACCORDED
ACCDDIIT	DIDACTIC
ACCDEENS	CADENCES
ACCDEENT	ACCENTED
ACCDEEPT	ACCEPTED
ACCDEERS	ACCEDERS
ACCDEERT	ACCRETED
ACCDEERU	CARDECUE
ACCDEERW	ACCREWED
ACCDEESS	ACCESSED
ACCDEGIN	ACCEDING
	ACCINGED
ACCDEHIK	CHIACKED
ACCDEHIL	CHALICED
ACCDEHIN	CHICANED
ACCDEHKY	CHYACKED
ACCDEHLT	CLATCHED
ACCDEHNR	CRANCHED
ACCDEHNU	CHAUNCED
ACCDEIIS	ACCIDIES
ACCDEILN	CALCINED
ACCDEILU	CAUDICLE
ACCDEILY	DELICACY
ACCDEINT	ACCIDENT
ACCDEIRT	ACCREDIT
ACCDEISU	CAUDICES
ACCDEKLR	CRACKLED
ACCDEKOS	COCKADES
ACCDELLY	CALYCLED
ACCDELOY	ACCLOYED
ACCDENOR	CONACRED
ACCDENOV	CONCAVED
ACCDEORR	ACCORDER
ACCDEOST	ACCOSTED
ACCDERSU	ACCURSED
	CARDECUS
ACCDESSU	SUCCADES
ACCDESUU	CADUCEUS
	CAUCUSED
ACCDGHOO	COACHDOG
ACCDHIIR	DIARCHIC
ACCDHIMO	DOCHMIAC
ACCDHIOT	CATHODIC
ACCDHLOR	CLOCHARD
ACCDIIST	DICASTIC
ACCDIITY	DICACITY
ACCDILOY	CALYCOID
ACCDILTY	DACTYLIC
ACCDINOR	CANCROID
	DRACONIC
ACCDIOOR	CORACOID
ACCDIORS	SARCODIC
ACCDIOST	STICCADO
ACCDITUY	CADUCITY
ACCDKNOS	CANDOCKS
ACCDKOSW	DAWCOCKS
ACCDLOSY	CACODYLS
ACCDOOST	STOCCADO
ACCDOOXY	CACODOXY
ACCDOSUU	CADUCOUS
ACCEEHIT	HICCATEE
ACCEEHLO	COCHLEAE
ACCEEHOS	COACHEES
ACCEEHRT	CETERACH
ACCEEHST	SEECATCH
ACCEEILR	CELERIAC
ACCEEILS	ECCLESIA
ACCEEKLN	NECKLACE
ACCEELNR	CLARENCE
ACCEELNS	CENACLES
ACCEELOS	COALESCE
ACCEENNS	NASCENCE
ACCEENPR	CREPANCE
ACCEENRS	CREANCES
ACCEENST	ACESCENT
ACCEEORT	CROCEATE
ACCEEPRT	ACCEPTER
ACCEERST	ACCRETES
ACCEESSS	ACCESSES
ACCEFFIY	EFFICACY
ACCEFILS	FASCICLE
ACCEFLSU	FELUCCAS
ACCEGINS	ACCINGES
ACCEGOSS	SOCCAGES
ACCEHHIS	CHECHIAS
ACCEHHKO	CHECHAKO
ACCEHILM	ALCHEMIC
	CHEMICAL
ACCEHILP	CEPHALIC
ACCEHILS	CALICHES
	CHALICES
ACCEHILT	HECTICAL
ACCEHIMN	MECHANIC
ACCEHINO	ANECHOIC
ACCEHINR	CHANCIER
	CHICANER
ACCEHINS	CHICANES
ACCEHIOS	COACHIES
ACCEHIRT	CATCHIER
ACCEHLNS	CHANCELS
ACCEHLOR	COCHLEAR
ACCEHLOS	COCHLEAS
ACCEHLOT	CATECHOL
ACCEHLST	CLATCHES
ACCEHMNO	COACHMEN
ACCEHNNO	CHACONNE
ACCEHNNY	CYNANCHE
ACCEHNOR	CHARNECO
	ENCROACH
ACCEHNOT	CONCHATE
ACCEHNRS	CHANCERS
	CHANCRES
	CRANCHES
ACCEHNSU	CHAUNCES
ACCEHORS	CAROCHES
	COACHERS
ACCEHPSU	CAPUCHES
ACCEHRST	CATCHERS
	CRATCHES
ACCEHSST	SCATCHES
ACCEHSTU	CATECHUS
ACCEIKPS	ICEPACKS
ACCEILLN	CANCELLI
ACCEILLR	CLERICAL
ACCEILLU	CAULICLE
ACCEILLV	CLAVICLE
ACCEILNS	CALCINES
	SCENICAL
ACCEILNT	CANTICLE
ACCEILNV	CLAVECIN
ACCEILNY	CALYCINE
ACCEILOS	CALICOES
	COELIACS
ACCEILRV	CERVICAL
ACCEILST	CALCITES
ACCEIMOS	OCCAMIES
ACCEIMRS	CERAMICS
ACCEINNR	CANCRINE
ACCEINOS	COCAINES
ACCEINSV	VACCINES
ACCEINTU	CUNEATIC
ACCEIOTV	COACTIVE
ACCEIPRS	CAPRICES
ACCEIPRT	PRACTICE
ACCEIPSV	PECCAVIS
ACCEIQSU	CACIQUES
ACCEIRRR	RICERCAR
ACCEIRSU	CURACIES
ACCEIRTU	CRUCIATE
ACCEISST	ASCETICS
ACCEISTT	ECSTATIC
ACCEKLNR	CRACKNEL
ACCEKLRS	CACKLERS
	CLACKERS
	CRACKLES
ACCEKMOS	MEACOCKS
ACCEKOPS	PEACOCKS
ACCEKOPY	PEACOCKY
ACCEKRRS	CRACKERS
ACCELLSY	CALYCLES
ACCELLUY	CALYCULE
ACCELMNY	CYCLAMEN
ACCELNOS	CONCEALS

ACCELNOV CONCLAVE	ACCHRRSU CURRACHS	ACCNOSTT CONTACTS	ACDEEESS DECEASES
ACCELNRU CARUNCLE	ACCHRSSU SCRAUCHS	ACCNOSTU ACCOUNTS	ACDEEFFT AFFECTED
ACCELORS CORACLES	ACCHRSTY SCRATCHY	ACCOQSSU SQUACCOS	ACDEEFHN ENCHAFED
ACCELOST CACOLETS	ACCIIIOT OITICICA	ACCORRTY CARRYCOT	ACDEEFIL CALEFIED
ACCELRSY SCARCELY	ACCIILLN CLINICAL	ACCORSTU ACCOURTS	ACDEEFIN DEFIANCE
ACCELSSU SACCULES	ACCIILMT CLIMATIC	ACDDDEIT ADDICTED	ACDEEFPR PREFACED
ACCELWYY CYCLEWAY	ACCIILRT CRITICAL	ACDDDETU ADDUCTED	ACDEEFRS DEFACERS
ACCEMNSU CACUMENS	ACCIIMNN CINNAMIC	ACDDDKOS DADDOCKS	FRESCADE
ACCENNSY NASCENCY	ACCIINNO ANICONIC	ACDDEEES DECEASED	ACDEEFRY FEDERACY
ACCENORR CORNACRE	ACCIINNP PICCANIN	ACDDEEHT DETACHED	ACDEEGLY DELEGACY
ACCENORS CONACRES	ACCIINOT ACONITIC	ACDDEEIT DEDICATE	ACDEEGNR ENGRACED
ACCENORT ACCENTOR	ACCIIPST PASTICCI	ACDDEEKR DACKERED	ACDEEHIV ACHIEVED
ACCENOST COSECANT	ACCIIRTX CICATRIX	ACDDEELR DECLARED	ACDEEHLP PLEACHED
ACCENOSU CONCAUSE	ACCIJKMR JIMCRACK	ACDDEELS DESCALED	ACDEEHLT CHELATED
ACCENOSV CONCAVES	ACCIKLOT COCKTAIL	ACDDEEMP DECAMPED	ACDEEHMR DEMARCHE
ACCEOPRT ACCEPTOR	ACCIKNST CANSTICK	ACDDEENR CREDENDA	ACDEEHNN ENHANCED
ACCEOPTU OCCUPATE	ACCIKOPR APRICOCK	ACDDEENS ASCENDED	ACDEEHNR ENARCHED
ACCEORSS ARCCOSES	ACCIKPRT PRACTICK	ACDDEENT DECADENT	ACDEEHNS ENCASHED
ACCEORST ECTOSARC	ACCILMOS COSMICAL	DECANTED	ENCHASED
ACCEORSW CRACOWES	ACCILMOX CACOMIXL	ACDDEERT REDACTED	ACDEEHPR PREACHED
ACCEORTU ACCOUTRE	ACCILMSU CALCIUMS	ACDDEETU EDUCATED	ACDEEHRS SEARCHED
ACCEOSSS SACCOSES	ACCILNOT CICLATON	ACDDEGIS DISCAGED	ACDEEHSS CHASSEED
ACCERRST CARRECTS	ACCILNOV VOLCANIC	ACDDEIIL DEICIDAL	ACDEEHST DETACHES
ACCERSST SCARCEST	ACCILNUV VULCANIC	ACDDEIIM MEDICAID	ACDEEIIP EPICEDIA
ACCERSSU ACCURSES	ACCILORS CALORICS	ACDDEILU DECIDUAL	ACDEEILT DELICATE
ACCURSERS	ACCILORT CORTICAL	ACDDEINR CANDIDER	ACDEEIMR MEDICARE
ACCESSTU CACTUSES	ACCILPRY CAPRYLIC	RIDDANCE	ACDEEIMT DECIMATE
ACCESSUU CAUCUSES	ACCILRRU CIRCULAR	ACDDEINT DEDICANT	EMICATED
ACCFHLTY CATCHFLY	ACCILRSY ACRYLICS	ACDDEINY CYANIDED	MEDICATE
ACCFIILT LACTIFIC	ACCILSSS CLASSICS	ACDDEIPS DISPACED	ACDEEINN DECENNIA
ACCGHIKN CHACKING	ACCIMNOS MOCCASIN	ACDDEISS CADDISES	ENNEADIC
ACCGHINN CHANCING	ACCIMNTU CANTICUM	DISCASED	ACDEEINR DERACINE
ACCGHINO COACHING	ACCIMORU COUMARIC	ACDDEISU DECIDUAS	ACDEEINU AUDIENCE
ACCGHINT CATCHING	ACCIMOSZ ZIMOCCAS	ACDDEITT DICTATED	ACDEEINV DEVIANCE
ACCGHIOR CHORAGIC	ACCIMPSU CAPSICUM	ACDDEKLO DEADLOCK	ACDEEIPS DISPEACE
ACCGIINT ACCITING	ACCINOOS OCCASION	ACDDEKOR RADDOCKE	ACDEEIRS DECIARES
ACCGIKLN CACKLING	ACCINOOT COACTION	ACDDELOS CLADODES	ACDEEJKT JACKETED
CLACKING	ACCINORT NARCOTIC	ACDDELRS CLADDERS	ACDEEKLR LACKERED
ACCGIKMR GIMCRACK	ACCINORV CAVICORN	ACDDENTU ADDUCENT	ACDEEKLY LACKEYED
ACCGIKNR CRACKING	ACCINOST CANTICOS	ACDDEOPS DECAPODS	ACDEEKNR CANKERED
ACCGINOT COACTING	ACCINOTY CANTICOY	ACDDEORR CORRADED	ACDEEKPR REPACKED
ACCGINOY ACCOYING	CYANOTIC	ACDDEORW COWARDED	ACDEEKPT PACKETED
ACCGINRU ACCRUING	ACCINRSU CRUCIANS	ACDDERSU ADDUCERS	ACDEEKRS SCREAKED
ACCGINSU ACCUSING	ACCIOPST SPICCATO	CRUSADED	ACDEEKRT RACKETED
ACCGLOOY CACOLOGY	ACCIORST ACROSTIC	ACDDERTU TRADUCED	ACDEELLR CELLARED
ACCHHITT CHITCHAT	ACCIORSY ISOCRACY	ACDDGILN CLADDING	RECALLED
ACCHHMOS CAMSHOCH	ACCIOSTT STICCATO	ACDDGINU ADDUCING	ACDEELMN ENCALMED
ACCHIIRT RACHITIC	ACCIOSTU ACOUSTIC	ACDDGINY CADDYING	ACDEELMP EMPLACED
ACCHIIST CHIASTIC	ACCIPRST PRACTICS	ACDDHHSU CHUDDAHS	ACDEELNR CALENDER
ACCHILNO CHALONIC	ACCIRSTY SCARCITY	ACDDHIIO DIADOCHI	ENCRADLE
ACCHILOR ORICHALC	ACCISSTU CAUSTICS	ACDDHIMR DIDRACHM	ACDEELNS CLEANSED
ACCHILOT CATHOLIC	ACCKKRSU RUCKSACK	ACDDHKOS HADDOCKS	ACDEELNT LANCETED
ACCHINNO CINCHONA	ACCKLORS CARLOCKS	SHADDOCK	ACDEELNV ENCLAVED
ACCHINOS CHICANOS	ACCKMMRU CRUMMACK	ACDDHRSU CHUDDARS	ACDEELPR REPLACED
ACCHINPU CAPUCHIN	ACCKMORS CROMACKS	ACDDIIOR CARDIOID	ACDEELRR DECLARER
ACCHIORT THORACIC	ACCKOOOT COCKATOO	ACDDILNY CANDIDLY	ACDEELRS DECLARES
TROCHAIC	ACCKOPRT CRACKPOT	ACDDILTY DIDACTYL	RESCALED
ACCHIRRT CARRITCH	ACCKOSSS CASSOCKS	ACDDINNU UNCANDID	ACDEELRT CLARETED
ACCHIRSS SCRAICHS	ACCKOSST CASTOCKS	ACDDINSY DISCANDY	DECRETAL
ACCHKLOR CHARLOCK	ACCLLOSU OCCLUSAL	ACDDIRSS DISCARDS	TREACLED
ACCHKOSY HAYCOCKS	ACCLLSUU CALCULUS	ACDDKLNO DOCKLAND	ACDEELRV CALVERED
ACCHLOOT CACHOLOT	ACCLSSUU SACCULUS	ACDDKOPS PADDOCKS	CLAVERED
ACCHLSTU CLAUCHTS	ACCMOPST ACCOMPTS	ACDDKORY DOCKYARD	ACDEELSS DECLASSE
ACCHMORS CASCHROM	COMPACTS	ACDDORTU ADDUCTOR	DESCALES
ACCHNNUY UNCHANCY	ACCMOSTU ACCUSTOM	ACDEEEFT DEFECATE	ACDEEMNP ENCAMPED
ACCHNOOR CORONACH	ACCMRSUU CURCUMAS	ACDEEEKS SEEDCAKE	ACDEEMRS SCREAMED
ACCHNOTU COUCHANT	ACCNOORS RACCOONS	ACDEEENR CAREENED	ACDEEMRT CREMATED
ACCHORTU CARTOUCH	ACCNOOTU COCOANUT	ACDEEENT ANTECEDE	ACDEENNP PENANCED
ACCHOSTW CHOCTAWS	ACCNOPTU OCCUPANT	ACDEEERR CAREERED	ACDEENNT TENDANCE
ACCHPSTU CATCHUPS	ACCNORTT CONTRACT	ACDEEERS DECREASE	ACDEENNY CAYENNED

ACDEENOT ANECDOTE	ACDEHILT DITHECAL	ACDEILMX CLIMAXED	ACDELMOR CLAMORED
ACDEENRS ASCENDER	ACDEHIMN MACHINED	ACDEILNP PANICLED	ACDELMSU MUSCADEL
REASCEND	ACDEHIMS SCHIEDAM	ACDEILOS COALISED	ACDELNOO CANOODLE
ACDEENRT CANTERED	ACDEHINR INARCHED	ACDEILOZ COALIZED	ACDELNOR COLANDER
CRENATED	ACDEHINS ECHIDNAS	ACDEILPR PLACIDER	ACDELNOS CELADONS
DECANTER	INCHASED	ACDEILPS DISPLACE	ACDELNPU UNPLACED
NECTARED	ACDEHIRS RACHIDES	ACDEILPT PLICATED	ACDELNRY CALENDRY
RECANTED	ACDEHIRT THRIDACE	ACDEILRS DECRIALS	ACDELNST SCANTLED
ACDEENRV CAVERNED	TRACHEID	RADICELS	ACDELNSU UNSCALED
CRAVENED	ACDEHIST SCAITHED	RADICLES	ACDELOPT CLODPATE
ACDEENRY CARNEYED	ACDEHISU CHIAUSED	ACDEILRT ARTICLED	ACDELOPU CUPOLAED
ACDEENRZ CREDENZA	ACDEHKLO HEADLOCK	ACDEILRU AURICLED	ACDELORV OVERCLAD
ACDEENSV VENDACES	ACDEHKLS SHACKLED	RADICULE	ACDELOTU OCULATED
ACDEENTT DANCETTE	ACDEHKNU UNHACKED	ACDEILST CITADELS	ACDELPPS SCAPPLED
ACDEEOPS PEASECOD	ACDEHKOV HAVOCKED	DIALECTS	ACDELRSS SCALDERS
ACDEEORT DECORATE	ACDEHKRU ARCHDUKE	ACDEILTT LATTICED	ACDELRSW SCRAWLED
ACDEEOTV EVOCATED	ACDEHKTW THWACKED	ACDEIMNO COMEDIAN	ACDELRSY SACREDLY
ACDEEPPR RECAPPED	ACDEHLNP PLANCHED	DAEMONIC	ACDELSTU CAULDEST
ACDEEPRS ESCARPED	ACDEHLNR CHANDLER	DEMONIAC	SULCATED
ACDEEPRT CARPETED	ACDEHLNU LAUNCHED	ACDEIMNP PANDEMIC	ACDEMMRS SCRAMMED
ACDEEPST ASPECTED	ACDEHLRS CHALDERS	ACDEIMPT IMPACTED	ACDEMNOR ROMANCED
ACDEERRS SCAREDER	ACDEHMST SMATCHED	ACDEIMST DERMATIC	ACDEMNSU DECUMANS
ACDEERRT RETRACED	ACDEHNOR ANCHORED	ACDEINNR CRANNIED	ACDEMOPR COMPARED
TERRACED	RONDACHE	ACDEINOP CANOPIED	ACDEMORS COMRADES
ACDEERSS CARESSED	ACDEHNPU PAUNCHED	ACDEINOS DIOCESAN	ACDEMORT DEMOCRAT
ACDEERST CEDRATES	ACDEHNRU RAUNCHED	OCEANIDS	ACDEMRSW SCRAWMED
ACDEESTU EDUCATES	ACDEHNST SNATCHED	ACDEINOV VOIDANCE	ACDEMUUV VACUUMED
ACDEESUX CAUDEXES	STANCHED	ACDEINPT PEDANTIC	ACDENNNO CANNONED
ACDEESUY CAUSEYED	ACDEHNSU UNCASHED	PENTADIC	ACDENNOR ORDNANCE
ACDEFFHU CHAUFFED	ACDEHNTU CHAUNTED	ACDEINRR RANCIDER	ACDENNOT CANTONED
ACDEFFLS SCLAFFED	ACDEHOPY POCHAYED	ACDEINRT CRINATED	ACDENNST SCANDENT
ACDEFFOR AFFORCED	ACDEHORR HARDCORE	DICENTRA	ACDENOPR ENDOCARP
ACDEFGIN DEFACING	ACDEHORT CHORDATE	ACDEINST DISTANCE	ACDENORS DRACONES
ACDEFHLN FLANCHED	ACDEHORW COWHEARD	ACDEINSY CYANIDES	ENDOSARC
ACDEFIIL DEIFICAL	ACDEHOST CATHODES	CYANISED	ACDENORT CARTONED
ACDEFIIP PACIFIED	ACDEHOUV AVOUCHED	ACDEINTT NICTATED	ACDENORY CRAYONED
ACDEFILR FRICADEL	ACDEHPPS SCHAPPED	ACDEINVY DEVIANCY	DEACONRY
ACDEFINN FINANCED	ACDEHPRU UPCHEARD	ACDEINYZ CYANIZED	ACDENOSY CYANOSED
ACDEFLOT OLFACTED	ACDEHPST DESPATCH	ACDEIOPS DIASCOPE	ACDENOTU OUTDANCE
ACDEFNRU FURNACED	ACDEHPSU CUPHEADS	ACDEIORS IDOCRASE	ACDENPPU UNCAPPED
ACDEFORT FACTORED	ACDEHQTU QUATCHED	ACDEIORT CERATOID	ACDENPRU PRAUNCED
ACDEFOTU OUTFACED	ACDEHRST STARCHED	ACDEIORV COVARIED	ACDENPST PANDECTS
ACDEFRSU SURFACED	ACDEHTUW WAUCHTED	ACDEIOSS ACIDOSES	ACDENRST CANTREDS
ACDEFRTU FURCATED	ACDEIILS LAICISED	ACDEIOSU EDACIOUS	ACDENRSU DURANCES
ACDEGGRS SCRAGGED	ACDEIILT CILIATED	ACDEIPPT TAPPICED	ACDENRTU UNCARTED
ACDEGHLO GALOCHED	ACDEIILZ LAICIZED	ACDEIPRS EPACRIDS	UNCRATED
ACDEGHNU CHAUNGED	ACDEIIMU AECIDIUM	ACDEIPSS DISPACES	UNDERACT
GAUNCHED	ACDEIINR ACRIDINE	SPADICES	UNTRACED
ACDEGIIL ALGICIDE	ACDEIINS SCIAENID	ACDEIPST SPICATED	ACDENRVY VERDANCY
ACDEGIKM MAGICKED	ACDEIINT ACTINIDE	ACDEIPSZ CAPSIZED	ACDENSST DESCANTS
ACDEGIMR DECIGRAM	DIACTINE	ACDEIPTV CAPTIVED	ACDENSUU UNCAUSED
GRIMACED	INDICATE	ACDEIQRU ACQUIRED	ACDENTTY DANCETTY
ACDEGINU GUIDANCE	ACDEIINU INDUCIAE	ACDEIRSS SIDECARS	ACDEOPRU CROUPADE
ACDEGINY DECAYING	ACDEIITV CAVITIED	ACDEIRST ACRIDEST	ACDEOPSS PEASCODS
ACDEGIRS DISGRACE	VATICIDE	ACDEIRSU DECURIAS	ACDEOPTT CAPOTTED
ACDEGISS DISCAGES	VICIATED	ACDEIRTT TETRACID	ACDEOPTU OUTPACED
ACDEGIST CADGIEST	ACDEIJNU JAUNDICE	TETRADIC	ACDEORRS CORRADES
ACDEGKOS DOCKAGES	ACDEIKNP PANICKED	ACDEISSS DISCASES	ACDEORRT REDACTOR
ACDEGLOU CLOUDAGE	ACDEIKNT ANTICKED	ACDEISTT DICTATES	ACDEORSS SARCODES
ACDEGNOS DECAGONS	ACDEILLM MEDALLIC	ACDEKLNR CRANKLED	ACDEORST REDCOATS
ACDEGNRU UNGRACED	ACDEILLN DECLINAL	ACDEKLQU QUACKLED	ACDEORSU CAROUSED
ACDEGORS CORDAGES	ACDEILLS CEDILLAS	ACDEKNPR PRANCKED	ACDEORTU EDUCATOR
ACDEGOTT COTTAGED	ACDEILLV CAVILLED	ACDEKNPU UNPACKED	OUTRACED
ACDEHHIN HAINCHED	ACDEILMO CAMELOID	ACDEKNRU UNRACKED	ACDEORTV CAVORTED
ACDEHHNU HAUNCHED	ACDEILMS CAMELIDS	ACDEKNTU UNTACKED	ACDEOSTT COSTATED
ACDEHHRU HACHURED	DECIMALS	ACDEKOST STOCKADE	ACDEOSUV COUVADES
ACDEHHTT THATCHED	DECLAIMS	ACDELLNU UNCALLED	ACDEOTTU OUTACTED
ACDEHIIP APHICIDE	MEDICALS	ACDELLOR CAROLLED	ACDEPPRS SCRAPPED
ACDEHIJK HIJACKED	ACDEILMT CLIMATED	COLLARED	ACDEPRTU CAPTURED
ACDEHILR HERALDIC	MALEDICT	ACDELLOT COLLATED	ACDEQTUU AQUEDUCT

ACDERRSU	CRUSADER	ACDIIRST	CARDITIS	ACDNORSU	CANDOURS	ACEEHLSS	LACHESES
ACDERRTU	TRADUCER	ACDIIRTY	ACRIDITY		CAUDRONS	ACEEHLST	CHELATES
ACDERSSU	CRUSADES	ACDIISST	SADISTIC	ACDNOSTW	DOWNCAST	ACEEHLTV	CHEVALET
ACDERSTT	DETRACTS	ACDIKMOO	COOKMAID	ACDNOSUU	ADUNCOUS	ACEEHMNP	CAMPHENE
	SCRATTED	ACDIKRRY	RICKYARD	ACDOOPTY	OCTAPODY	ACEEHMNR	MENARCHE
ACDERSTU	TRADUCES	ACDILLOS	CODILLAS	ACDOORST	OSTRACOD	ACEEHMRS	CASHMERE
ACDERTUV	CURVATED	ACDILLOU	CAUDILLO		SCORDATO		MACHREES
ACDFFHNU	HANDCUFF		LODICULA	ACDOPRST	POSTCARD		MARCHESE
ACDFFIRT	DIFFRACT	ACDILLPY	PLACIDLY	ACDORRWY	COWARDRY	ACEEHMST	MACHETES
ACDFFLOS	SCAFFOLD	ACDILMOR	DROMICAL	ACDORSST	COSTARDS	ACEEHNNS	ENHANCES
ACDFIILU	FIDUCIAL	ACDILMSS	CLADISMS	ACDORSSU	CRUSADOS	ACEEHNPS	CHEAPENS
ACDFILOU	FUCOIDAL	ACDILNOO	CONOIDAL	ACDRSSTU	CUSTARDS	ACEEHNRS	ENARCHES
ACDFIOST	FACTOIDS	ACDILNOS	SCALDINO	ACEEEFRR	CAREFREE	ACEEHNRV	REVANCHE
ACDGIILO	DIALOGIC	ACDILNSU	DULCIANS	ACEEEGLN	ELEGANCE	ACEEHNSS	ENCASHES
ACDGILNN	CANDLING	ACDILNSY	SYNDICAL	ACEEEGRS	CARGEESE	ACEEHORT	OCHREATE
ACDGILNR	CRADLING	ACDILNUU	NUDICAUL	ACEEEIPR	EARPIECE	ACEEHPPS	ECHAPPES
ACDGILNS	SCALDING	ACDILOPY	POLYACID	ACEEEKNT	NECKATEE	ACEEHPRR	PREACHER
ACDGILNU	CAUDLING	ACDILORS	CORDIALS	ACEEELMR	CAMELEER	ACEEHPRS	PEACHERS
ACDGIMOT	DOGMATIC	ACDILOUV	OVIDUCAL	ACEEENRS	ENCREASE		PREACHES
ACDGINNS	DANCINGS	ACDILPSU	CUSPIDAL	ACEEENSV	EVANESCE	ACEEHPRT	ETHERCAP
ACDGINNY	CANDYING	ACDILSST	CLADISTS	ACEEEPSS	ESCAPEES	ACEEHPST	CHEAPEST
ACDGINSU	SCAUDING	ACDILSTW	WILDCATS	ACEEERRT	RECREATE	ACEEHQSU	QUEACHES
ACDGIOPR	PODAGRIC	ACDIMMSU	CADMIUMS	ACEEERTX	EXECRATE	ACEEHRRS	REACHERS
ACDGKLOS	DAGLOCKS	ACDIMNOO	MONOACID	ACEEESUV	EVACUEES		RESEARCH
ACDGNOST	CANTDOGS	ACDIMNOS	MANDIOCS	ACEEFFIN	CAFFEINE	ACEEHRRT	TREACHER
ACDGORST	DOGCARTS	ACDIMNSU	MUSCADIN	ACEEFFRT	AFFECTER	ACEEHRSS	SEARCHES
ACDHIILS	CHILIADS		SCANDIUM	ACEEFHNS	ENCHAFES	ACEEHRST	CHEATERS
ACDHIKOR	CHOKIDAR	ACDIMNSY	DYNAMICS	ACEEFILM	MALEFICE		HECTARES
ACDHILPR	PILCHARD	ACDIMOSY	DOCIMASY	ACEEFILS	CALEFIES		RECHATES
ACDHILPS	CLAPDISH	ACDINOPS	SPONDAIC	ACEEFINS	FAIENCES		RECHEATS
ACDHINOR	HADRONIC	ACDINORS	SARDONIC		FIANCEES		TEACHERS
	RHODANIC	ACDINORT	TORNADIC	ACEEFKOR	ECOFREAK	ACEEHRTT	CATHETER
ACDHINRY	DINARCHY	ACDINORW	CORDWAIN	ACEEFLPU	PEACEFUL	ACEEHRTY	CHEATERY
ACDHINSW	SANDWICH	ACDINSST	DISCANTS	ACEEFLSS	FACELESS	ACEEHSST	ESCHEATS
ACDHIOPS	SCAPHOID	ACDINSTY	DYNASTIC	ACEEFNSY	FAYENCES	ACEEHSTX	CATHEXES
ACDHIORY	HYRACOID	ACDINTUY	ADUNCITY	ACEEFPRS	PREFACES		EXCHEATS
ACDHIPST	DISPATCH	ACDIOPRS	PICADORS	ACEEFPRT	PERFECTA	ACEEIKNP	PEACENIK
ACDHLNOR	CHALDRON		SPORADIC		PRAEFECT	ACEEIKRR	CREAKIER
	CHLORDAN	ACDIORRS	CORRIDAS	ACEEFRSU	FARCEUSE	ACEEILMN	CAMELINE
	CHONDRAL	ACDIORSS	SARCOIDS	ACEEGHNR	ENCHARGE	ACEEILMT	EMETICAL
ACDHLORS	DORLACHS	ACDIORTT	DICTATOR	ACEEGHNX	EXCHANGE	ACEEILNP	CAPELINE
ACDHMORU	MOUCHARD	ACDIPRST	ADSCRIPT	ACEEGHRR	RECHARGE	ACEEILNR	CINEREAL
ACDHNORW	CHAWDRON	ACDIRSST	DRASTICS	ACEEGILS	ELEGIACS		RELIANCE
ACDHNOSW	COWHANDS	ACDIRSTT	DISTRACT		LEGACIES	ACEEILNS	SALIENCE
ACDHOOST	CATHOODS	ACDISTUV	VIADUCTS	ACEEGINS	AGENCIES	ACEEILPS	CALIPEES
ACDHOPRS	POCHARDS	ACDJNSTU	ADJUNCTS	ACEEGKNR	NECKGEAR		ESPECIAL
ACDHORRS	ORCHARDS	ACDKLOPS	PADLOCKS	ACEEGKRW	WRECKAGE	ACEEILRS	ESCALIER
ACDHORSW	SHOWCARD	ACDKMMOR	DRAMMOCK	ACEEGLNY	ELEGANCY	ACEEILRV	RECEIVAL
ACDHORSY	DYSCHROA	ACDKMPSU	MUDPACKS	ACEEGLPU	PUCELAGE	ACEEIMOT	ACOEMETI
ACDIIIPR	DIAPIRIC	ACDKOPRS	POCKARDS	ACEEGNOZ	COZENAGE	ACEEIMRR	CREAMIER
ACDIIJLU	JUDICIAL	ACDLLORS	COLLARDS	ACEEGNRS	ENGRACES		REARMICE
ACDIILMS	DISCLAIM	ACDLNNOR	CORNLAND	ACEEGNRY	REAGENCY	ACEEIMRS	RACEMISE
ACDIILNO	CONIDIAL	ACDLNOPR	CROPLAND	ACEEGNST	CENTAGES	ACEEIMRT	CEMITARE
ACDIILNS	SCALDINI	ACDLNORS	CALDRONS	ACEEGNSV	SCAVENGE	ACEEIMRZ	RACEMIZE
ACDIILSU	SUICIDAL	ACDLNORU	CAULDRON	ACEEGORR	RACEGOER	ACEEIMST	EMICATES
ACDIILTY	CALIDITY	ACDLNORY	CONDYLAR	ACEEGORV	COVERAGE	ACEEINPS	SAPIENCE
	DIALYTIC	ACDLNOST	COTLANDS	ACEEGSSU	ESCUAGES	ACEEINPT	PATIENCE
ACDIIMNO	DAIMONIC	ACDLOORT	DOCTORAL	ACEEHHST	CHEETAHS	ACEEINRS	CINEREAS
ACDIIMOR	DIORAMIC	ACDLORWY	COWARDLY	ACEEHILR	LEACHIER		INCREASE
ACDIIMOT	DIATOMIC	ACDLOSWY	LADYCOWS	ACEEHINT	ECHINATE		RESIANCE
ACDIIMSU	ASCIDIUM	ACDMMNOO	COMMANDO	ACEEHIPR	PEACHIER	ACEEINRT	CENTIARE
ACDIINNS	INDICANS	ACDMMNOS	COMMANDS	ACEEHIPS	CHEAPIES		CREATINE
ACDIINNT	INDICANT	ACDMNORY	DORMANCY	ACEEHIPT	PETECHIA		INCREATE
ACDIINOP	PINACOID		MORDANCY	ACEEHIRV	ACHIEVER		ITERANCE
ACDIINOT	ACTINOID	ACDMOOPR	MACROPOD	ACEEHIST	HICATEES	ACEEINST	CINEASTE
	DIATONIC	ACDMORSZ	CZARDOMS	ACEEHISV	ACHIEVES	ACEEINSU	EUCAINES
ACDIINPY	PYCNIDIA	ACDNOORR	RONCADOR	ACEEHITV	ATCHIEVE	ACEEINTV	ENACTIVE
ACDIINRS	ACRIDINS	ACDNOORS	CARDOONS	ACEEHKTT	HACKETTE	ACEEINTX	EXITANCE
ACDIIOSS	ACIDOSIS	ACDNOORV	CORDOVAN	ACEEHLPS	PLEACHES		
ACDIIRSS	SCIARIDS	ACDNOOTU	DUCATOON	ACEEHLRS	RELACHES		

ACEEIPST	SPECIATE		CREMATES	ACEFILRS	FILACERS	ACEGILNN	CLEANING
ACEEIRRS	CARIERES		MEERCATS	ACEFINNS	FINANCES		ELANCING
	CREASIER	ACEENNPS	PENANCES	ACEFINRS	FANCIERS		ENLACING
ACEEIRSU	CAUSERIE	ACEENNRT	ENTRANCE	ACEFINRX	CARNIFEX	ACEGILNR	CLEARING
ACEEIRSW	WISEACRE	ACEENNST	CANTEENS	ACEFINSS	FASCINES	ACEGILNT	CLEATING
ACEEIRTV	CREATIVE	ACEENNSY	CAYENNES	ACEFINST	FANCIEST	ACEGILNV	CLEAVING
	REACTIVE	ACEENORT	CAROTENE	ACEFIOSS	FIASCOES	ACEGILOS	CALIGOES
ACEEISTV	VESICATE	ACEENOST	ACETONES	ACEFIRRT	CRAFTIER	ACEGILRS	GLACIERS
ACEEKLMR	MACKEREL	ACEENPRR	PARCENER	ACEFIRTT	TRIFECTA	ACEGILRV	CLAVIGER
ACEEKLRW	EELWRACK	ACEENPRT	PERCEANT	ACEFIRTY	FERACITY	ACEGILSS	GLACISES
ACEEKMPT	EMPACKET	ACEENRRT	RECANTER	ACEFKLRS	FLACKERS	ACEGILST	GELASTIC
ACEEKNRW	NECKWEAR		RECREANT	ACEFKLST	FLACKETS	ACEGIMMT	TAGMEMIC
ACEEKRRT	RACKETER	ACEENRSS	CASERNES	ACEFLLSS	CALFLESS	ACEGIMNN	MENACING
ACEELLNS	NACELLES	ACEENRST	REASCENT	ACEFLMNO	FLAMENCO	ACEGIMNR	AMERCING
ACEELLNT	LANCELET		SARCENET	ACEFLNOR	FALCONER		CREAMING
ACEELLOT	OCELLATE	ACEENRTU	ENACTURE	ACEFLNOT	CONFLATE	ACEGIMNT	MAGNETIC
ACEELLPT	CAPELLET		UNCREATE		FALCONET	ACEGIMOX	EXOGAMIC
ACEELLRR	CELLARER	ACEEORST	CREASOTE	ACEFLORS	ALFRESCO	ACEGIMRS	GRIMACES
ACEELLRT	CELLARET	ACEEOSTT	ECOSTATE	ACEFLRTU	FULCRATE	ACEGINNO	CANOEING
ACEELMNO	CAMELEON	ACEEOSTV	EVOCATES	ACEFMNOO	MOONFACE	ACEGINNR	ENRACING
ACEELMNP	PLACEMEN	ACEEPRRS	CAPERERS	ACEFNNOS	FACONNES	ACEGINNS	ENCASING
ACEELMPS	EMPLACES	ACEEPRSS	ESCAPERS	ACEFNORV	CONFERVA	ACEGINNT	ENACTING
ACEELMRS	RECLAMES	ACEEPRTT	ETTERCAP	ACEFNPRT	PENCRAFT	ACEGINNV	ENCAVING
	SCLEREMA	ACEEPRTU	PERACUTE	ACEFNRST	CANTREFS	ACEGINOS	COINAGES
ACEELNPT	PENTACLE	ACEEPRTX	EXCERPTA	ACEFNRSU	FURNACES	ACEGINPR	CAPERING
ACEELNRR	LARCENER	ACEEPSSU	AUCEPSES	ACEFOOPT	FOOTPACE		PEARCING
ACEELNRS	CLEANERS	ACEEPSTT	SPECTATE	ACEFOPST	POSTFACE		PREACING
	CLEANSER	ACEERRST	CATERERS	ACEFORRS	FORECARS	ACEGINPS	ESCAPING
ACEELNRU	CERULEAN		RETRACES	ACEFORST	FORECAST	ACEGINRS	CREASING
ACEELNSS	CLEANSES		TERRACES	ACEFORSX	CARFOXES		GRECIANS
ACEELNST	CLEANEST	ACEERRSU	ECRASEUR	ACEFOSTU	OUTFACES		SEARCING
	LATENCES	ACEERRTU	CREATURE	ACEFRRST	REFRACTS	ACEGINRT	CATERING
ACEELNSU	NUCLEASE	ACEERRUV	VERRUCAE	ACEFRRSU	FARCEURS		CITRANGE
ACEELNSV	ENCLAVES	ACEERRSS	CARESSES		SURFACER		CREATING
	VALENCES	ACEERSST	CATERESS	ACEFRRTU	FRACTURE		REACTING
ACEELNTT	TENTACLE		CERASTES	ACEFRSSU	SURFACES	ACEGINSS	CAGINESS
ACEELNTU	NUCLEATE	ACEERSSU	SURCEASE	ACEFRSTU	FACTURES		CEASINGS
ACEELOPS	ESCALOPE	ACEERSSV	CREVASSE	ACEGGILN	CAGELING	ACEGINTX	EXACTING
ACEELORS	ESCAROLE	ACEERSTU	SECATEUR		GLACEING	ACEGIOTT	COGITATE
ACEELORT	RELOCATE	ACEERSTX	EXACTERS	ACEGGILR	CLAGGIER	ACEGIPRS	SPAGERIC
ACEELPRR	REPLACER	ACEERTTU	ERUCTATE	ACEGGINN	ENCAGING	ACEGIRST	AGRESTIC
ACEELPRS	PERCALES	ACEESSST	ECSTASES	ACEGGIOP	EPAGOGIC	ACEGISTU	GAUCIEST
	REPLACES	ACEESSTT	CASSETTE	ACEGGIRR	CRAGGIER	ACEGISTW	GAWCIEST
ACEELPST	CAPELETS	ACEESTTX	EXACTEST	ACEGHILN	LEACHING	ACEGKLOS	LOCKAGES
ACEELPTU	PECULATE	ACEFFGIN	EFFACING	ACEGHILT	LICHGATE	ACEGKLOV	GAVELOCK
ACEELPTY	CLYPEATE	ACEFFHIR	CHAFFIER	ACEGHINP	PEACHING	ACEGKLRS	GRACKLES
ACEELRRS	CLEARERS	ACEFFHIS	AFFICHES	ACEGHINR	REACHING	ACEGKMOS	MOCKAGES
ACEELRSS	CARELESS	ACEFFHRS	CHAFFERS	ACEGHINT	CHEATING	ACEGKORS	CORKAGES
	RESCALES	ACEFFHRU	CHAUFFER		TEACHING	ACEGKORW	CAGEWORK
ACEELRST	CLEAREST	ACEFFHRY	CHAFFERY	ACEGHLOS	GALOCHES	ACEGKRTU	TRUCKAGE
	SCELERAT	ACEFFIMS	CAFFEISM	ACEGHLRS	SCHLAGER	ACEGLLNO	COLLAGEN
	TREACLES	ACEFFISS	SCAFFIES	ACEGHLTY	LYCHGATE	ACEGLLOS	COLLAGES
ACEELRSV	CLEAVERS	ACEFFORS	AFFORCES	ACEGHMMU	CHUMMAGE	ACEGLNOS	CONGEALS
ACEELRTT	RACLETTE	ACEFGINN	ENFACING	ACEGHMOR	ECHOGRAM	ACEGLNRS	CLANGERS
ACEELRTU	ULCERATE	ACEFGINR	REFACING		GRAMOCHE	ACEGLOST	CATELOGS
ACEELRTV	CERVELAT	ACEFGINT	FACETING	ACEGHNRS	CHANGERS	ACEGLOSU	CAGOULES
ACEELSST	CELESTAS	ACEFGLRU	GRACEFUL	ACEGHNRU	UNCHARGE	ACEGMNOY	GEOMANCY
ACEELSSU	EUCLASES	ACEFHIKS	FISHCAKE	ACEGHNSU	CHAUNGES	ACEGMNRS	CRAGSMEN
ACEELSTT	TELECAST	ACEFHLNS	FLANCHES		GAUNCHES	ACEGMOPS	COMPAGES
ACEELSVX	EXCLAVES	ACEFHMRS	CHAMFERS	ACEGHOSU	GOUACHES	ACEGMORS	SCARMOGE
ACEEMNOT	MECONATE	ACEFHORU	FAROUCHE	ACEGHOSW	COWHAGES	ACEGMRRY	GRAMERCY
ACEEMNPS	SPACEMEN	ACEFHRST	FRATCHES	ACEGHRRS	CHARGERS	ACEGNNOY	CYANOGEN
ACEEMNRS	MENACERS	ACEFIIPR	PACIFIER	ACEGHRTU	RECAUGHT	ACEGNNTY	TANGENCY
ACEEMNST	CASEMENT	ACEFIIPS	PACIFIES	ACEGHSTU	GAUCHEST	ACEGNORS	ACROGENS
ACEEMORS	RACEMOSE	ACEFIIRT	ARTIFICE	ACEGIIMP	EPIGAMIC		CORNAGES
ACEEMORV	OVERCAME	ACEFILLY	FACILELY	ACEGIINV	VICINAGE	ACEGNOST	COGNATES
ACEEMRRS	CREAMERS	ACEFILOP	EPIFOCAL	ACEGIKNR	CREAKING	ACEGNSSY	CAGYNESS
	SCREAMER	ACEFILOS	FASCIOLE	ACEGILLO	COLLEGIA	ACEGOORS	CARGOOSE
ACEEMRRY	CREAMERY		FOCALISE	ACEGILLR	ALLERGIC	ACEGOPRY	GEOCARPY
ACEEMRST	CERAMETS	ACEFILOZ	FOCALIZE	ACEGILMU	MUCILAGE	ACEGORSS	CORSAGES

	SOCAGERS	ACEHINSY HYACINES	ACEHLRST ARCHLETS	ACEHPRTY PATCHERY
ACEGORST	ESCARGOT	SYNECHIA	ACEHLRSY CHARLEYS	PETCHARY
ACEGORSU	COURAGES	ACEHIOPR POACHIER	ACEHLRTU ARCHLUTE	ACEHQSTU QUATCHES
ACEGORTT	COTTAGER	ACEHIOST TOISEACH	TRAUCHLE	ACEHRRST CHARTERS
ACEGORTY	CATEGORY	ACEHIPPR CHAPPIER	ACEHLSSS CASHLESS	RECHARTS
ACEGOSTT	COTTAGES	ACEHIPPS CHAPPIES	ACEHLSST SATCHELS	STARCHER
ACEGOTTY	COTTAGEY	ACEHIPRS CHARPIES	ACEHLSTT CHATTELS	ACEHRRTT TETRARCH
ACEGRSTU	TRUCAGES	PARCHESI	LATCHETS	ACEHRSST STARCHES
ACEGSSTU	SCUTAGES	SERAPHIC	ACEHLSTY CHASTELY	ACEHRSSU CHASSEUR
ACEHHINS	HAINCHES	ACEHIPRT CHAPITER	ACEHMMNR MARCHMEN	ACEHRSTT CHATTERS
ACEHHIRR	HIERARCH	PATCHIER	ACEHMMNR RANCHMEN	RATCHETS
ACEHHIST	SHECHITA	PHREATIC	ACEHMNRS ENCHARMS	ACEHRSTW WATCHERS
ACEHHLST	HATCHELS	ACEHIPST HEPATICS	ACEHMNRT MERCHANT	ACEHRSTY YACHTERS
ACEHHLSU	SHAUCHLE	PASTICHE	ACEHMNSS CHESSMAN	ACEHRTTY TRACHYTE
ACEHHMNN	HENCHMAN	ACEHIPTT PATHETIC	ACEHMNST MANCHETS	ACEHSSSU CHAUSSES
ACEHHNRT	ETHNARCH	ACEHIPTW WHITECAP	ACEHMNTW WATCHMEN	ACEHSSST CHASTEST
ACEHHNSU	HAUNCHES	ACEHIRSS CASHIERS	ACEHMORT CHROMATE	ACEHSSTW SWATCHES
ACEHHPRT	HEPTARCH	RACHISES	ACEHMPRS CHAMPERS	ACEHSTTU CATHETUS
ACEHHRST	HATCHERS	ACEHIRST CHARIEST	ACEHMRRS CHARMERS	TEUCHATS
ACEHHRSU	HACHURES	THERIACS	MARCHERS	ACEHSTTW WATCHETS
ACEHHRTT	THATCHER	ACEHIRSU EUCHARIS	ACEHMRST MATCHERS	ACEHTTUZ ZUCHETTA
ACEHHRTY	HATCHERY	ACEHIRSV ARCHIVES	ACEHMRSU CHAUMERS	ACEIILMN LIMACINE
	THEARCHY	ACEHIRSW ARCHWISE	ACEHMSST SMATCHES	ACEIILNR IRENICAL
ACEHHSTT	HATCHETS	ACEHIRTT CHATTIER	ACEHMSTU MUSTACHE	ACEIILNS SALICINE
	THATCHES	THEATRIC	ACEHMSTY ECTHYMAS	SILICANE
ACEHHTTY	HATCHETY	ACEHISST CHASTISE	ACEHNNOP PANCHEON	ACEIILSS LAICISES
ACEHIIMS	ISCHEMIA	TAISCHES	ACEHNNPT PENCHANT	ACEIILST SILICATE
ACEHIIRT	HIERATIC	ACEHISSU CHIAUSES	ACEHNNST ENCHANTS	ACEIILSZ LAICIZES
ACEHIJKR	HIJACKER	ACEHISTT CHATTIES	ACEHNOPR CANEPHOR	ACEIIMRV VIRAEMIC
ACEHIKLP	KEPHALIC	TACHISTE	CHAPERON	ACEIIMSS ASEISMIC
ACEHIKLR	CHALKIER	ACEHISTX CATHEXIS	ACEHNOPT CENOTAPH	ACEIIMTU MAIEUTIC
	HACKLIER	ACEHKLOV HAVELOCK	ACEHNORR RANCHERO	ACEIINPS PISCINAE
ACEHIKLW	LICHWAKE	ACEHKLPR KREPLACH	ACEHNORT ANCHORET	ACEIINRS RIANCIES
ACEHIKRS	KACHERIS	ACEHKLRS HACKLERS	ACEHNPRT PENTARCH	ACEIINST CANITIES
ACEHIKRW	WHACKIER	ACEHKLSS SHACKLES	ACEHNPRU UNPREACH	ACEIINTV INACTIVE
ACEHILLT	HELLICAT	ACEHKLST HACKLETS	ACEHNPSU PAUNCHES	ACEIINTZ ANTICIZE
ACEHILMN	INCHMEAL	ACEHKLTY LATCHKEY	ACEHNRRS RANCHERS	ACEIIPRS PIRACIES
ACEHILMP	IMPLEACH	ACEHKNSY HACKNEYS	ACEHNRSS ARCHNESS	ACEIIRRT CRITERIA
ACEHILMS	CAMELISH	ACEHKOSW WHACKOES	ACEHNRST CHANTERS	ACEIIRSV VICARIES
ACEHILNT	CHAINLET	ACEHKOTU TUCKAHOE	SNATCHER	ACEIISTU ACUITIES
	ETHNICAL	ACEHKRSW WHACKERS	STANCHER	ACEIISTV CAITIVES
ACEHILOR	HALICORE	ACEHKRTW THWACKER	TRANCHES	CAVITIES
	HEROICAL	ACEHLLMO MALLECHO	ACEHNRSU RAUNCHES	VICIATES
ACEHILPR	PARHELIC	ACEHLLOR ORCHELLA	ACEHNRTT TRANCHET	ACEIITTV VITICETA
ACEHILRS	CHARLIES	ACEHLLPS PELLACHS	ACEHNRTU CHAUNTER	ACEIJKSS JACKSIES
ACEHILST	ETHICALS	ACEHLLSS SHELLACS	ACEHNSST CHASTENS	ACEIJMST MAJESTIC
ACEHILTT	ATHLETIC	ACEHLLSU HALLUCES	SNATCHES	ACEIJNRR JERRICAN
	THETICAL	ACEHLMOT CHAMELOT	STANCHES	ACEIKKNR KNACKIER
ACEHIMNP	CAMPHINE	ACEHLMST CHAMLETS	ACEHNSTT ETCHANTS	ACEIKLRT TALCKIER
ACEHIMNR	CHAIRMEN	ACEHLNNS CHANNELS	ACEHNSTU NAUTCHES	ACEIKLRY CREAKILY
ACEHIMNS	MACHINES	ACEHLNOS CHALONES	UNCHASTE	ACEIKMNN NICKNAME
ACEHIMNU	ACHENIUM	ACEHLNOU EULACHON	ACEHNSTY CHANTEYS	ACEIKMRS KERAMICS
ACEHIMPR	CAMPHIRE	ACEHLNPS PLANCHES	ACEHOPRR REPROACH	ACEIKMRV MAVERICK
ACEHIMPT	EMPATHIC	ACEHLNPT PLANCHET	ACEHOPRS POACHERS	ACEIKNRR CRANKIER
	EMPHATIC	ACEHLNRS CHARNELS	ACEHORRS HORSECAR	ACEIKOPS PAIOCKES
ACEHIMRS	CHASMIER	ACEHLNRU LAUNCHER	ACEHORRV OVERARCH	ACEIKORR CROAKIER
	CHIMERAS	ACEHLNST STANCHEL	ACEHORST CHAROSET	ACEIKPRS EARPICKS
	MARCHESI	ACEHLNSU LAUNCHES	THORACES	ACEIKPSX PICKAXES
ACEHIMRT	RHEMATIC	ACEHLORS CHOLERAS	ACEHORTT THEOCRAT	ACEIKRRV VRAICKER
ACEHIMSS	CHAMISES	CHORALES	ACEHORTU OUTREACH	ACEIKSTT TACKIEST
ACEHIMST	MISTEACH	ACEHLORT CHELATOR	ACEHOSSW SHOWCASE	TIETACKS
	TACHISME	CHLORATE	ACEHOSTU CATHOUSE	ACEIKSTW WACKIEST
ACEHIMTT	THEMATIC	TROCHLEA	SOUTACHE	ACEILLLT CLITELLA
ACEHINNS	ENCHAINS	ACEHLORU LEACHOUR	ACEHOSTY CHAYOTES	ACEILLMR MICELLAR
ACEHINOT	INCHOATE	ACEHLOST ESCHALOT	ACEHOSUV AVOUCHES	MILLRACE
ACEHINRS	INARCHES	ACEHLPRT CHAPTREL	ACEHPPSS CHAPPESS	ACEILLMS LIMACELS
ACEHINRV	VACHERIN	ACEHLPRY CHAPELRY	SCHAPPES	MICELLAS
ACEHINSS	INCHASES	ACEHLPSS CHAPLESS	ACEHPRST CHAPTERS	ACEILLMT METALLIC
ACEHINST	ASTHENIC	ACEHLPST CHAPLETS	PATCHERS	ACEILLMY MYCELIAL
	CHANTIES	ACEHLRSS RASCHELS	ACEHPRSU PURCHASE	ACEILLNT CLIENTAL

ACEILLOP CALLIOPE
ACEILLOR ROCAILLE
ACEILLOS LOCALISE
ACEILLOT TEOCALLI
ACEILLOZ LOCALIZE
ACEILLPR CALLIPER
ACEILLPS ALLSPICE
ACEILLPY EPICALLY
ACEILLRV CAVILLER
ACEILMMO CAMOMILE
ACEILMMR CLAMMIER
ACEILMNN CLINAMEN
ACEILMNP MANCIPLE
ACEILMNS MESCALIN
ACEILMOS CAMISOLE
ACEILMPS MISPLACE
ACEILMPT PELMATIC
ACEILMRS CLAIMERS
      MIRACLES
      RECLAIMS
ACEILMRT METRICAL
ACEILMST CALMIEST
      CLEMATIS
      CLIMATES
      METICALS
ACEILMSU MUSICALE
ACEILMSX CLIMAXES
      EXCLAIMS
ACEILMTU AMULETIC
ACEILNNP PANNICLE
      PINNACLE
ACEILNNR ENCRINAL
ACEILNOR ACROLEIN
      CREOLIAN
      LONICERA
ACEILNPS CAPELINS
      PANICLES
      PELICANS
ACEILNPT ICEPLANT
      PECTINAL
      PLANETIC
ACEILNRS CARLINES
ACEILNRT CLARINET
ACEILNSS SANICLES
ACEILNSU AESCULIN
      LUNACIES
ACEILNSY SALIENCY
ACEILOPR CAPRIOLE
ACEILOPT POETICAL
ACEILORR CARRIOLE
ACEILORS CALORIES
      CARIOLES
ACEILORT EROTICAL
      LORICATE
ACEILOSS COALISES
ACEILOST ALOETICS
      COALIEST
      SOCIETAL
ACEILOSV VOCALISE
ACEILOSZ COALIZES
ACEILOTV LOCATIVE
ACEILOVZ VOCALIZE
ACEILPPY PIPECLAY
ACEILPRS CALIPERS
      REPLICAS
      SPIRACLE
ACEILPRT PARTICLE
      PRELATIC
ACEILPRU PECULIAR
ACEILPSS SPECIALS

ACEILPST PLICATES
ACEILPTY ETYPICAL
ACEILPXY EPICALYX
ACEILRRT CLARTIER
ACEILRRW CRAWLIER
ACEILRSS CLASSIER
ACEILRST ALTRICES
      ARTICLES
      RECITALS
      SELICTAR
ACEILRSU AURICLES
ACEILRSV CALIVERS
      CLAVIERS
      VISCERAL
ACEILRTT TRACTILE
ACEILRTV VERTICAL
ACEILRTY LITERACY
ACEILSST ELASTICS
      SALICETS
      SCALIEST
ACEILSTT LATTICES
ACEILSTY CLAYIEST
ACEILSUV VESICULA
ACEILTVY ACTIVELY
ACEIMMNP PEMMICAN
ACEIMMOS SEMICOMA
ACEIMMRS RACEMISM
ACEIMNOR CORAMINE
ACEIMNPS PEMICANS
ACEIMNRS CARMINES
ACEIMNRU MANICURE
ACEIMNSS AMNESICS
ACEIMNST SEMANTIC
ACEIMNSU SEMUNCIA
ACEIMNSY SYCAMINE
ACEIMOPT POEMATIC
ACEIMOTX TOXAEMIC
ACEIMOTZ METAZOIC
ACEIMPRR CRAMPIER
      MERICARP
ACEIMPSS ESCAPISM
ACEIMPST CAMPIEST
      CAMPSITE
ACEIMPTU PUMICATE
ACEIMRST CERAMIST
      MATRICES
ACEIMRTT TREMATIC
ACEIMRTU MURICATE
ACEIMSST ETACISMS
ACEIMSSU CAESIUMS
ACEINNOS CANONISE
ACEINNOT ENACTION
ACEINNOZ CANONIZE
ACEINNPS PINNACES
ACEINNRS CRANNIES
ACEINNST ANCIENTS
      CANNIEST
      INSTANCE
ACEINNSU NUISANCE
ACEINNSY CYANINES
ACEINNTU UNCINATE
ACEINOPR APOCRINE
      CAPONIER
      PROCAINE
ACEINOPS CANOPIES
      CAPONISE
      PAEONICS
ACEINOPZ CAPONIZE
ACEINORS SCENARIO
ACEINORT ANORETIC

      CREATION
      REACTION
ACEINORV VERONICA
ACEINORX ANOREXIC
ACEINOST ACONITES
      CANOEIST
ACEINOTT TACONITE
ACEINOTV CONATIVE
      INVOCATE
ACEINOTX EXACTION
ACEINPSS INSCAPES
      PINCASES
ACEINPTT PITTANCE
ACEINPUY PICAYUNE
ACEINRRU CURARINE
ACEINRRY CINERARY
ACEINRSS ARSENICS
      CERASINS
      RACINESS
ACEINRST CANISTER
      CARNIEST
      NACRITES
      SCANTIER
ACEINRTT INTERACT
ACEINRTV NAVICERT
ACEINRTX XERANTIC
ACEINRVY VICENARY
ACEINSST CINEASTS
      SCANTIES
ACEINSSU ISSUANCE
ACEINSSY CYANISES
ACEINSTT CANTIEST
      NICTATES
ACEINSTV CISTVAEN
      VESICANT
ACEINSTY CYANITES
ACEINSYZ CYANIZES
ACEINTTU TUNICATE
ACEINTTX EXCITANT
ACEINTTY TENACITY
ACEINTUV UNACTIVE
ACEIOPRT OPERATIC
ACEIOPST ECTOPIAS
ACEIORSV COVARIES
      VARICOSE
ACEIOSST SOCIATES
ACEIOSSU CAESIOUS
ACEIOSTT OSCITATE
ACEIOTVV VOCATIVE
ACEIPPRR PERICARP
ACEIPPRS EPICARPS
ACEIPPST TAPPICES
ACEIPRRS PERISARC
ACEIPRSS SCRAPIES
ACEIPRST CRAPIEST
      CRISPATE
      PICRATES
      PRACTISE
ACEIPRTV PRACTIVE
ACEIPRTY APYRETIC
ACEIPSST ASEPTICS
      ESCAPIST
      SPACIEST
ACEIPSSU AUSPICES
ACEIPSSZ CAPSIZES
ACEIPSTV CAPTIVES
ACEIQRSU ACQUIRES
ACEIQSTU ACQUITES
ACEIQSUZ CAZIQUES
ACEIRRRS CARRIERS

      SCARRIER
ACEIRRST ERRATICS
ACEIRRSU CURARISE
ACEIRRSW AIRSCREW
ACEIRRTT RETRAICT
ACEIRRTX CREATRIX
ACEIRRTY RETIRACY
ACEIRRUZ CURARIZE
ACEIRSST SCARIEST
ACEIRSSU SCAURIES
      URICASES
ACEIRSSV VICARESS
ACEIRSTT CITRATES
      CRISTATE
      SCATTIER
ACEIRSTU SURICATE
ACEIRSTZ CRAZIEST
ACEIRTTU URTICATE
ACEIRTTV TRACTIVE
ACEIRTUV CURATIVE
ACEIRTVY VERACITY
ACEISSST CASSISES
ACEISSST ECSTASIS
ACEISSSU SAUCISSE
ACEISSTU SAUCIEST
ACEISTTT CATTIEST
ACEISTTU EUSTATIC
ACEISTUX AUXETICS
ACEJKOOR JACKEROO
ACEJKOPS PAJOCKES
ACEJLORS CAJOLERS
ACEJLORY CAJOLERY
ACEJMRST SCRAMJET
ACEJNNOO JONCANOE
ACEJNOST JACONETS
ACEJNOSY JOYANCES
ACEJNRRY JERRYCAN
ACEJNSTU JUNCATES
ACEJPSTU CAJEPUTS
ACEJRSTT TRAJECTS
ACEKKNRS KNACKERS
ACEKKNRY KNACKERY
ACEKLLPS PELLACKS
ACEKLNRS CRANKLES
ACEKLNSS SLACKENS
ACEKLNTU UNTACKLE
ACEKLORS EARLOCKS
ACEKLORV LAVEROCK
ACEKLPRS SPRACKLE
ACEKLPST PLACKETS
ACEKLQSU QUACKLES
ACEKLRSS SLACKERS
ACEKLRST TACKLERS
ACEKLRSU CAULKERS
ACEKLSSS SACKLESS
ACEKLSST SLACKEST
ACEKMNRT TRACKMEN
ACEKMNST TACKSMEN
ACEKMRSS SMACKERS
ACEKNNOW ACKNOWNE
ACEKNPRS PRANCKES
ACEKNPRU UNPACKER
ACEKNRST CRANKEST
ACEKOORT CARETOOK
ACEKOORW COOKWARE
ACEKORRS CROAKERS
ACEKORRV OVERRACK
ACEKPPRS PREPACKS
ACEKPSSY SKYSCAPE
ACEKQRUY QUACKERY

```
ACEKRRST TRACKERS      ACELOPSS ESCALOPS      ACENNOSS CANONESS      ACEORSST COARSEST
ACEKRRTY RACKETRY      ACELOPST POLECATS               SONANCES               COASTERS
ACEKRSST STACKERS      ACELOPTU COPULATE      ACENNOSU SONUANCE      ACEORSSU CAROUSES
ACEKRSTT RACKETTS      ACELOPTY CALOTYPE      ACENNOSY NOYANCES      ACEORSTT SECTATOR
ACEKSSTT STACKETS      ACELOQSU COEQUALS      ACENNOTV COVENANT      ACEORSTU OUTRACES
ACEKSSUW WAESUCKS      ACELORRT RECTORAL      ACENNOTZ CANZONET      ACEORSTV OVERACTS
ACELLLRU CELLULAR      ACELORSS ESCOLARS      ACENNPRY PERNANCY               OVERCAST
ACELLMOS CALOMELS               LACROSSE      ACENNRSS SCANNERS      ACEORSTX EXACTORS
ACELLMSU SACELLUM      ACELORST SECTORAL      ACENNSUY SEACUNNY      ACEORTUY EUCARYOT
ACELLNRU NUCELLAR      ACELORSU CAROUSEL      ACENOORT CORONATE      ACEOSTTU OUTCASTE
ACELLOPS COLLAPSE      ACELORSY CALOYERS      ACENOOTZ ECTOZOAN      ACEOSTUU AUTOCUES
         ESCALLOP               COARSELY      ACENOPRT PORTANCE      ACEPRRSS SCARPERS
ACELLORR CAROLLER      ACELORTU COLATURE      ACENOPST CAPSTONE               SCRAPERS
ACELLORS CORELLAS      ACELOSST ALECOSTS      ACENOPSU PONCEAUS      ACEPRSSU CARPUSES
ACELLORV COVERALL               COATLESS      ACENOPUX PONCEAUX               SCAUPERS
         OVERCALL               LACTOSES      ACENOQTU COTQUEAN      ACEPRSTU CAPTURES
ACELLORW CALLOWER               SCATOLES      ACENORRW CAREWORN               PRESCUTA
ACELLOST COLLATES      ACELOSTT CALOTTES      ACENORSS COARSENS      ACEPSTTY TYPECAST
ACELLOTU LOCULATE      ACELOSTU LACTEOUS               NARCOSES      ACEQRSTU RACQUETS
ACELLPSS SCALPELS               LOCUSTAE      ACENORST ANCESTOR      ACEQSSTU ACQUESTS
ACELLRRS CARRELLS               OSCULATE               ENACTORS      ACERRSTT RETRACTS
ACELLRTY RECTALLY      ACELOSTY ACOLYTES               SARCONET      ACERRSUV VERRUCAS
ACELLSSU CALLUSES      ACELOSUV VACUOLES               SORTANCE      ACERSSST CRASSEST
ACELLSSW CLAWLESS      ACELPPRS CLAPPERS      ACENORSU CARNEOUS      ACERSSSU SUCRASES
ACELLSTU SCUTELLA               SCRAPPLE               NACREOUS      ACERSSTT SCATTERS
ACELLTWY CETYWALL      ACELPPSS SCAPPLES      ACENORTT CONTRATE      ACERSTTT TETRACTS
ACELMMOU MAMELUCO      ACELPRSS CLASPERS      ACENORTU COURANTE      ACERSTTU CRUSTATE
ACELMNNS CLANSMEN               SCALPERS               OUTRANCE      ACERSTTX EXTRACTS
ACELMNOR AMELCORN      ACELPRST SCEPTRAL      ACENORUY EUCARYON      ACERSTTY SCATTERY
ACELMNRU CRUMENAL               SPECTRAL      ACENOSSS CASSONES      ACERSTUX CURTAXES
ACELMNSS CALMNESS      ACELPRSU SPECULAR      ACENOSST COSTEANS      ACFFGHIN CHAFFING
         CLASSMEN      ACELPSSU CAPSULES      ACENOSSV CAVESSON      ACFFHNOR CHAFFRON
ACELMOPT COMPLEAT      ACELPTUU CUPULATE      ACENOSSY CYANOSES      ACFFIILO OFFICIAL
ACELMORS CAROMELS      ACELPTUY EUCALYPT      ACENOSTT CONSTATE      ACFFIIST CAITIFFS
         SCLEROMA      ACELQRSU LACQUERS      ACENOSTV CENTAVOS      ACFFIKMS MAFFICKS
ACELMORY CLAYMORE      ACELQRUU CLAQUEUR      ACENOTTU TOUCANET      ACFFILNU FANCIFUL
ACELMOST CAMELOTS      ACELQSUY LACQUEYS      ACENPRRS PRANCERS      ACFFILST AFFLICTS
         MOLECAST      ACELRRSW CRAWLERS      ACENPRSU ENCARPUS      ACFFIRST TRAFFICS
ACELMOSU CAULOMES               SCRAWLER               PRAUNCES      ACFFLOSW SCOFFLAW
         LEUCOMAS      ACELRSSS SCARLESS      ACENPSTT PENTACTS      ACFGHINU CHAUFING
         MACULOSE      ACELRSST SCARLETS      ACENPTTU PUNCTATE      ACFGIIMN MAGNIFIC
ACELMPRS CLAMPERS      ACELRSSU SECULARS      ACENRSST CRANTSES      ACFGIIPR CAPRIFIG
ACELMPSY ECLAMPSY      ACELRSTT CLATTERS      ACENRSSU SURANCES      ACFGINNY FANCYING
ACELMSSU LACMUSES               SCRATTLE      ACENRSTT TRANECTS      ACFGINRS FARCINGS
ACELMSTU CALUMETS      ACELRSTU RAUCLEST               TRANSECT               SCARFING
         MUSCATEL      ACELRTTU CULTRATE      ACENRSTU CENTAURS      ACFGINRT CRAFTING
ACELMSUU SAECULUM      ACELSSTT TACTLESS               RECUSANT               FRACTING
ACELMTUU CUMULATE      ACELSSTY SCYTALES               UNCRATES      ACFGITUY FUGACITY
ACELNNRS SCRANNEL      ACELSSUX EXCUSALS               UNTRACES      ACFGKNOP PACKFONG
ACELNOST LACTONES      ACEMMOTY MYCETOMA      ACENRSTY ANCESTRY      ACFHHINW HAWFINCH
ACELNOSU LACUNOSE      ACEMMRRS CRAMMERS      ACENRTTU TRUNCATE      ACFHILNO FALCHION
ACELNOSZ CALZONES      ACEMNORR ROMANCER      ACENRTUY CENTAURY      ACFHILNU FAULCHIN
ACELNOTV COVALENT      ACEMNORS CREMONAS               CYANURET      ACFHILOS COALFISH
ACELNOVY CONVEYAL               ROMANCES      ACENSSTT SCANTEST      ACFHINOU FAUCHION
ACELNPSS ENCLASPS      ACEMNOST CAMSTONE      ACENSSTU NUTCASES      ACFHIRSS SCARFISH
         SPANCELS      ACEMNRUY NUMERACY      ACENSSTW NEWSCAST      ACFHIRSW CRAWFISH
ACELNPST CLAPNETS      ACEMNSSU MANCUSES      ACEOOPPS APOCOPES      ACFHIRSY CRAYFISH
ACELNPSU UNPLACES      ACEMOOST COMATOSE      ACEOOPSU POACEOUS      ACFHISSU FUCHSIAS
ACELNRSU LUCARNES      ACEMOPRS COMPARES      ACEOORTV OVERCOAT      ACFHLMRU CHARMFUL
ACELNRUY NUCLEARY               COMPEARS      ACEOPPRS COPPERAS      ACFHLTUW WATCHFUL
ACELNRVY CRAVENLY               MESOCARP      ACEOPRRT RECAPTOR      ACFHMNOR CHAMFRON
ACELNSST SCANTLES      ACEMORRT CREMATOR      ACEOPRSX EXOCARPS      ACFHNOSU FAUCHONS
ACELNSSU UNSCALES      ACEMORSY SYCAMORE      ACEOPRTT ATTERCOP      ACFIILST FISTICAL
ACELNSTT CANTLETS      ACEMORTY COMETARY      ACEOPSTU OUTPACES      ACFIILSV SALVIFIC
ACELOPPU POPULACE      ACEMORUX MORCEAUX      ACEORRST ACROTERS      ACFIILTY FACILITY
ACELOPRS PARCLOSE      ACEMPRSS SCAMPERS               CREATORS      ACFIIMPS PACIFISM
         POLACRES      ACEMPRST CRAMPETS               REACTORS      ACFIIMSS FASCISMI
ACELOPRT PECTORAL      ACEMPSSU CAMPUSES      ACEORRSU CAROUSER      ACFIIPST PACIFIST
ACELOPRU OPERCULA      ACEMSSTT METCASTS      ACEORRTT RETROACT      ACFIISST FASCISTI
                       ACENNNOU ANNOUNCE      ACEORRVW OVERCRAW      ACFIKLNS CALFSKIN
```

ACFIKNNS	FINNACKS	ACGHINPR	PARCHING
ACFILNOR	FORNICAL	ACGHINPT	NIGHTCAP
ACFILNOS	FOLACINS		PATCHING
ACFILORT	TRIFOCAL	ACGHINRR	CHARRING
ACFILRTY	CRAFTILY	ACGHINRS	CHAGRINS
ACFILSSY	CLASSIFY		CRASHING
ACFIMNRU	FRANCIUM	ACGHINRT	CHARTING
ACFIMOSS	FASCISMO	ACGHINRU	CHURINGA
ACFIMSSS	FASCISMS		NURAGHIC
ACFINORT	FRACTION	ACGHINSS	CHASINGS
ACFINOST	FACTIONS	ACGHINST	SCATHING
ACFINRST	INFARCTS	ACGHINSW	CHINWAGS
	INFRACTS	ACGHINTT	CHATTING
ACFINSTY	SANCTIFY	ACGHINTW	WATCHING
ACFIOSTU	FACTIOUS	ACGHINTY	YACHTING
ACFIRTUY	FURACITY	ACGHIPRS	GRAPHICS
ACFISSST	FASCISTS	ACGHIQTU	ACQUIGHT
ACFKLORS	FORSLACK	ACGHIRSS	SCRAIGHS
ACFKLOST	LOCKFAST	ACGHLLOR	GRALLOCH
ACFKLRUW	WRACKFUL	ACGHLSTU	CLAUGHTS
ACFKLSSU	SACKFULS	ACGHNTUU	UNCAUGHT
ACFKOSTT	FATSTOCK	ACGHORSU	CHORAGUS
ACFLMNOO	MOONCALF	ACGHPTUU	UPCAUGHT
ACFLNORY	FALCONRY	ACGHRRSU	CURRAGHS
ACFLOOPS	FOOLSCAP	ACGHRSSU	SCRAUGHS
ACFLORSU	SCROFULA	ACGIILMN	CLAIMING
ACFLRRUU	FURCULAR		MALICING
ACFLRSUU	FURCULAS	ACGIILNN	INLACING
ACFMOTTU	FACTOTUM	ACGIILNO	LOGICIAN
ACGGGILN	CLAGGING	ACGIILNS	SCAILING
ACGGHINN	CHANGING	ACGIIMNT	MICATING
	GANCHING	ACGIIMOS	ISOGAMIC
ACGGHINR	CHARGING	ACGIIMST	SIGMATIC
ACGGIINN	INCAGING	ACGIINNS	INCASING
ACGGIINT	GIGANTIC	ACGIINNV	INCAVING
ACGGIIOS	ISAGOGIC	ACGIINRT	GRANITIC
ACGGILNN	CANGLING	ACGIIPRS	SPAGIRIC
	CLANGING	ACGIJJKO	JICKAJOG
	GLANCING	ACGIJLNO	CAJOLING
ACGGINNO	CONGAING	ACGIJNNU	JAUNCING
ACGGINNU	UNCAGING	ACGIKLMN	MACKLING
ACGGINOR	CARGOING	ACGIKLNN	CLANKING
ACGGIOOR	CORAGGIO	ACGIKLNO	CLOAKING
ACGGLNOU	GLUCAGON	ACGIKLNS	SLACKING
ACGGLRSY	SCRAGGLY	ACGIKLNT	TACKLING
ACGHHIJK	HIGHJACK	ACGIKLNU	CAULKING
ACGHHINN	HANCHING	ACGIKLRY	GARLICKY
ACGHHINT	HATCHING	ACGIKMNS	SMACKING
ACGHIINN	CHAINING	ACGIKNNR	CRANKING
ACGHIINR	CHAIRING	ACGIKNNS	SNACKING
ACGHIKLN	CHALKING	ACGIKNOR	CROAKING
	HACKLING	ACGIKNPS	PACKINGS
ACGHIKNR	CHARKING	ACGIKNQU	QUACKING
ACGHIKNS	HACKINGS	ACGIKNRS	ARCKINGS
ACGHIKNW	WHACKING		RACKINGS
ACGHILNN	LANCHING	ACGIKNRT	TRACKING
ACGHILNS	CLASHING	ACGIKNRW	WRACKING
ACGHILNT	LATCHING	ACGIKNSS	SACKINGS
ACGHILNU	LAUCHING	ACGIKNST	STACKING
ACGHILOR	OLIGARCH		TACKINGS
ACGHIMNP	CHAMPING	ACGIKPRS	GRIPSACK
ACGHIMNR	CHARMING	ACGILLNS	CALLINGS
	MARCHING	ACGILMMN	CLAMMING
ACGHIMNT	MATCHING	ACGILMNP	CAMPLING
ACGHINNR	RANCHING		CLAMPING
ACGHINNT	CHANTING	ACGILNNT	CANTLING
ACGHINNU	UNACHING	ACGILNNU	LAUNCING
ACGHINOP	POACHING		UNLACING
ACGHINOR	ROACHING	ACGILNOR	ORACLING
ACGHINPP	CHAPPING	ACGILNOS	SOLACING

ACGILNOT	LOCATING	ACGLOSUU	GLAUCOUS
ACGILNPP	CLAPPING	ACGNNOOT	CONTANGO
ACGILNPS	CLASPING	ACGNNORS	CRANNOGS
	PLACINGS	ACGNOOST	OCTAGONS
	SCALPING	ACGORRSY	GYROCARS
ACGILNQU	CALQUING	ACGORSSW	COWGRASS
ACGILNRT	CLARTING	ACGORSUU	COUGUARS
ACGILNRW	CRAWLING	ACGPPSUU	SCUPPAUG
ACGILNSS	CLASSING	ACHHILPT	PHTHALIC
	SCALINGS	ACHHINTW	WHINCHAT
ACGILNST	CASTLING	ACHHINTY	HYACINTH
	CATLINGS	ACHHIPPR	HIPPARCH
	SCLATING	ACHHLMOS	MASHLOCH
ACGILNSU	GLUCINAS	ACHHLNOR	RHONCHAL
ACGILNTT	CLATTING	ACHHLPRY	PHYLARCH
ACGILNTU	CLAUTING	ACHHLSUY	SHAUCHLY
ACGILRSU	SURGICAL	ACHHNTTU	NUTHATCH
ACGIMMNR	CRAMMING		UNTHATCH
ACGIMNOR	CAROMING	ACHHOSST	TOSHACHS
ACGIMNOS	COAMINGS	ACHHPTUZ	CHUTZPAH
ACGIMNPR	CRAMPING	ACHIIKMS	KAMICHIS
ACGIMNPS	SCAMPING	ACHIILMS	CHILIASM
ACGIMNSY	GYMNASIC	ACHIILST	CHILIAST
	SYNGAMIC	ACHIINRT	TRICHINA
ACGIMORS	ORGASMIC	ACHIIPSS	PACHISIS
ACGINNNS	SCANNING	ACHIIRST	RACHITIS
ACGINNNU	NUANCING	ACHIIRSU	ISCHURIA
ACGINNPR	PRANCING	ACHIJKPW	WHIPJACK
ACGINNPU	UNCAPING	ACHIJNST	JACINTHS
ACGINNRT	TRANCING	ACHIKKNS	KNACKISH
ACGINNRU	UNCARING	ACHIKKSW	KICKSHAW
ACGINNRY	CARNYING	ACHIKLLW	HICKWALL
ACGINNST	CANTINGS	ACHIKLPT	CHALKPIT
	SCANTING	ACHIKNOP	PACHINKO
ACGINNSU	UNCASING	ACHIKRSS	RICKSHAS
ACGINNUV	VAUNCING	ACHIKRSW	RICKSHAW
ACGINOPT	COAPTING	ACHIKRSY	HAYRICKS
ACGINORY	CONGIARY	ACHIKSSS	SHICKSAS
ACGINOST	AGNOSTIC	ACHILLOR	ORCHILLA
	COASTING	ACHILLRT	CLITHRAL
	COATINGS	ACHILMOP	OMPHALIC
	COTINGAS	ACHILMOS	MALICHOS
ACGINPPR	CRAPPING	ACHILMRS	CHRISMAL
ACGINPPS	CAPPINGS	ACHILMTY	MYTHICAL
ACGINPRS	CARPINGS	ACHILNNS	CLANNISH
	SCARPING	ACHILNOO	HOOLICAN
	SCRAPING	ACHILNOS	LICHANOS
ACGINPSS	SPACINGS	ACHILNPS	CLANSHIP
ACGINRRS	SCARRING	ACHILOPR	RHOPALIC
ACGINRRY	CARRYING	ACHILOPS	SOPHICAL
ACGINRSS	SACRINGS	ACHILORT	ACROLITH
ACGINRST	SCARTING	ACHILPSY	PHYSICAL
	TRACINGS	ACHILPTY	PATCHILY
ACGINRSU	SCAURING	ACHILRUY	CHYLURIA
ACGINRSV	CARVINGS	ACHILRVY	CHIVALRY
	CRAVINGS	ACHILSWY	LICHWAYS
ACGINRTT	TRACTING	ACHIMMOS	MACHISMO
ACGINSST	CASTINGS	ACHIMMST	MISMATCH
ACGINSTT	SCATTING	ACHIMNNW	WINCHMAN
ACGIOORS	GRACIOSO	ACHIMNOP	CHAMPION
ACGIORST	ORGASTIC	ACHIMNOR	CHOIRMAN
ACGIORSU	GRACIOUS		HARMONIC
ACGIPRSY	SPAGYRIC	ACHIMNOS	MANIHOCS
ACGJLNOU	CONJUGAL	ACHIMNPT	PITCHMAN
ACGKMMOS	GAMMOCKS	ACHIMOPR	AMPHORIC
ACGKORSV	GARVOCKS	ACHIMOSS	CHAMISOS
ACGLLPSU	CUPGALLS		ISOCHASM
ACGLMOUU	COAGULUM	ACHIMPSS	SCAMPISH
ACGLNORS	CLANGORS	ACHIMRSS	CHARISMS
ACGLNORU	CLANGOUR	ACHIMRST	CHARTISM

ACHIMSSS	SCHISMAS	ACHNRSYY	SYNARCHY
ACHIMSST	MASTICHS	ACHNRTUY	CHAUNTRY
	TACHISMS	ACHOPRST	TOPARCHS
ACHIMSSU	CHIASMUS	ACHOPRSY	CHARPOYS
ACHIMTUY	CYATHIUM	ACHOPRTY	TOPARCHY
ACHINNOP	PANCHION	ACHOTTUW	OUTWATCH
ACHINNSU	UNCHAINS	ACHRSTTU	STRAUCHT
ACHINOPR	PAROCHIN	ACIIILMN	INIMICAL
ACHINORT	ANORTHIC	ACIIILNV	CIVILIAN
ACHINOSY	ONYCHIAS	ACIIKNNN	CANNIKIN
ACHINOTZ	HOACTZIN	ACIIKNNS	CANIKINS
ACHINRSZ	ZARNICHS	ACIIKPRT	PAITRICK
ACHINSUV	CHAUVINS	ACIILLSU	SILICULA
ACHIORSS	COARSISH	ACIILLTV	VILLATIC
ACHIORST	CHARIOTS	ACIILMNR	CRIMINAL
	HARICOTS	ACIILNOR	IRONICAL
ACHIPPSS	SAPPHICS	ACIILNOT	TALIONIC
ACHIPRRT	PARRITCH	ACIILNPT	PLATINIC
ACHIPSTU	CHUPATIS	ACIILNSS	SALICINS
ACHIPSTW	WHIPCATS	ACIILOSV	VILIACOS
ACHIPTTU	CHUPATTI	ACIILRTT	TRITICAL
ACHIQRSU	CHARQUIS	ACIILRTU	URALITIC
ACHIRRST	TRIARCHS	ACIILSST	SILASTIC
ACHIRRTY	TRIARCHY	ACIILSTV	SILVATIC
ACHIRSTT	CHARTIST	ACIIMNOR	MORAINIC
	STRAICHT	ACIIMNOS	SIMONIAC
ACHIRSTU	HAIRCUTS	ACIIMNOT	AMNIOTIC
ACHISSTT	TACHISTS	ACIIMNRS	MINICARS
ACHISTTY	CHASTITY	ACIIMNST	ACTINISM
ACHKMMOS	HAMMOCKS	ACIIMNSU	MUSICIAN
ACHKMORS	SHAMROCK	ACIIMNTU	ACTINIUM
ACHKNOOT	CANTHOOK	ACIIMNTY	IMITANCY
ACHKOPSS	HOPSACKS		INTIMACY
ACHKOSSS	HASSOCKS		MINACITY
ACHKOSSY	HASSOCKY	ACIIMOST	IOTACISM
ACHKOSTT	HATTOCKS	ACIIMOTT	AMITOTIC
ACHLLOOS	ALCOHOLS	ACIIMPRT	PRIMATIC
ACHLLORS	CHLORALS	ACIIMPRV	VAMPIRIC
ACHLLORY	CHORALLY	ACIIMRST	SCIMITAR
ACHLMSTZ	SCHMALTZ	ACIIMRTU	MURIATIC
ACHLNOOU	OULACHON	ACIIMSST	ITACISMS
ACHLNOSY	HALCYONS	ACIIMSTV	ACTIVISM
ACHLNSTU	TULCHANS	ACIIMTUV	VIATICUM
ACHLNSTY	STANCHLY	ACIINNOT	INACTION
ACHLOPRS	RAPLOCHS		NICOTIAN
ACHLOPRT	CALTHROP	ACIINNQU	CINQUAIN
ACHLOPRY	POLYARCH	ACIINNTT	INCITANT
ACHLOPTT	POTLATCH	ACIINNTY	CANINITY
ACHLCRSS	SCHOLARS	ACIINOPT	OPTICIAN
ACHLOSSW	SALCHOWS	ACIINORZ	ZIRCONIA
ACHLOSTY	ACOLYTHS	ACIINOSS	ASINICOS
ACHMNORS	MONARCHS	ACIINOSV	AVIONICS
	NOMARCHS	ACIINOTT	CITATION
ACHMNORY	MONARCHY	ACIINPSS	PISCINAS
	NOMARCHY	ACIINRSS	NARCISSI
ACHMNRSU	UNCHARMS	ACIINRTU	URANITIC
ACHMNRTU	TRUCHMAN	ACIIORST	AORISTIC
ACHMOPRS	CAMPHORS	ACIIORTV	VICTORIA
ACHMORTU	OUTMARCH	ACIIPPST	PAPISTIC
ACHMOSST	STOMACHS	ACIIRSTT	ARTISTIC
ACHMOSTY	STOMACHY		TRIATICS
ACHMOTTU	OUTMATCH	ACIISTTU	AUTISTIC
ACHMSSUW	CUMSHAWS	ACIISTTV	ACTIVIST
ACHNNORU	UNANCHOR	ACIITTVY	ACTIVITY
ACHNNOSS	CHANSONS	ACIITVVY	VIVACITY
ACHNORST	CHANTORS	ACIJKKPS	SKIPJACK
ACHNOSTY	TACHYONS	ACIJKSTW	STICKJAW
ACHNOSUY	CHANOYUS	ACIJSUZZ	JACUZZIS
ACHNPPSS	SCHNAPPS	ACIKLMST	MALSTICK
ACHNRSTU	UNSTARCH	ACIKLNRY	CRANKILY

ACIKLORY	CROAKILY	ACIMNORS	MARCONIS
ACIKMOOS	OOMIACKS	ACIMNORT	ROMANTIC
ACIKMPRS	RAMPICKS	ACIMNORU	CONARIUM
ACIKMPST	MAPSTICK		COUMARIN
ACIKMPSW	PICKMAWS	ACIMNORY	ACRIMONY
ACIKNNPS	PANNICKS	ACIMNOSS	MOCASSIN
ACIKNSST	CATSKINS	ACIMNOST	MONASTIC
ACIKPRST	PATRICKS	ACIMNOTU	ACONITUM
ACILLLOP	POLLICAL	ACIMNPTY	TYMPANIC
ACILLMMY	CLAMMILY	ACIMNRSU	CRANIUMS
ACILLMOS	LOCALISM		CUMARINS
ACILLMSS	MISCALLS	ACIMNSTT	CATMINTS
ACILLNOO	COLONIAL	ACIMORST	ACROTISM
ACILLNOR	CARILLON	ACIMORSY	CRAMOISY
ACILLNOS	SCALLION	ACIMOSST	ACOSMIST
ACILLOQU	COQUILLA		MASSICOT
ACILLORT	CLITORAL	ACIMOSTT	MASTICOT
ACILLORY	COLLYRIA		STOMATIC
ACILLOST	LOCALIST	ACIMPRST	CRAMPITS
ACILLOSY	SOCIALLY		PTARMICS
ACILLOTY	LOCALITY	ACIMRRSY	MISCARRY
ACILMNOP	COMPLAIN	ACIMRSSZ	CZARISMS
ACILMNOS	LACONISM	ACIMSSST	MISCASTS
	LIMACONS	ACIMSSTT	TACTISMS
ACILMOOS	SCOLIOMA	ACINNOOT	CONATION
ACILMOPR	PROCLAIM	ACINNORR	NARICORN
ACILMOPT	COMPITAL	ACINNOSS	SCANSION
ACILMOSV	VOCALISM	ACINNOST	ACTINONS
ACILMPTU	PLACITUM		CANONIST
ACILMSSU	MUSICALS		CANTIONS
ACILMSTY	MYSTICAL		CONTAINS
ACILMTUY	ULTIMACY		SANCTION
ACILNOOT	COLATION	ACINNOTU	CONTINUA
	LOCATION	ACINNRTY	TYRANNIC
ACILNOOV	VOCALION	ACINNSTU	ANNICUTS
ACILNOPS	SALPICON	ACINNSTY	INSTANCY
ACILNOPT	PLATONIC	ACINOOPR	PICAROON
ACILNORS	CLARINOS	ACINOOTV	VOCATION
	CLARIONS	ACINOPPT	PANOPTIC
ACILNORT	CONTRAIL	ACINOPRS	PARSONIC
ACILNOSU	UNSOCIAL	ACINOPST	CAPTIONS
ACILNOUV	UNIVOCAL		PACTIONS
ACILNPSS	INCLASPS	ACINORRS	CARRIONS
ACILNRSU	CISLUNAR	ACINORRT	CONTRAIR
ACILNRUY	CULINARY	ACINORSS	NARCOSIS
ACILNSTU	LUNATICS	ACINORST	CANTORIS
	SULTANIC		CAROTINS
ACILNSTY	SCANTILY	ACINORTT	TRACTION
ACILOPRT	TROPICAL	ACINOSSS	CAISSONS
ACILORRS	RACLOIRS		CASSINOS
ACILORRV	CORRIVAL	ACINOSSY	CYANOSIS
ACILORST	CALORIST	ACINOSTT	OSCITANT
ACILORTV	VORTICAL		TACTIONS
ACILOSTV	VOCALIST	ACINOSTU	ANTICOUS
ACILOTVY	VOCALITY		AUCTIONS
ACILPRSU	SPICULAR		CAUTIONS
ACILPRTU	PICTURAL	ACINOSTW	WAINSCOT
ACILPSST	PLASTICS	ACINOSWX	COXSWAIN
ACILPSSU	SPICULAS	ACINOTTX	TOXICANT
ACILRSTU	CURTAILS	ACINPQUY	PIQUANCY
	RUSTICAL	ACINPRST	CANTRIPS
ACILRTUV	CULTIVAR	ACINPRSY	CYPRIANS
	CURVITAL	ACINPSTY	SYNAPTIC
ACILSTUV	VICTUALS	ACINQSTU	QUANTICS
ACILSTVY	SYLVATIC	ACINRSSU	CRUSIANS
ACIMMOSS	ACOSMISM	ACINRSTU	CURTAINS
ACIMMTUY	CYMATIUM		SATURNIC
ACIMNNNO	CINNAMON		TURACINS
ACIMNOOR	ACROMION	ACINRTTU	TACITURN
ACIMNOPS	CAMPIONS		URTICANT

```
ACINSTTY SANCTITY
         SCANTITY
ACINSTYY SYNCYTIA
ACIOOPST SCOTOPIA
ACIOOTYZ ZOOCYTIA
ACIOPRST APRICOTS
         PISCATOR
ACIOPRTT PROTATIC
ACIOPRTY POTICARY
ACIOPSST POTASSIC
ACIOPSSU SPACIOUS
ACIOPSTU CAPTIOUS
ACIOPTTU AUTOPTIC
ACIORRSS CORSAIRS
ACIORSSU SCARIOUS
ACIORSTT RICOTTAS
ACIORTTY ATROCITY
         CITATORY
ACIORTVY VORACITY
ACIOSTUU CAUTIOUS
ACIPRRUU PIRARUCU
ACIPSSST SPASTICS
ACIQRSTU QUARTICS
ACIQSSTU ACQUISTS
ACIRRTTX TRACTRIX
ACIRRTUX CURATRIX
ACIRSSST SACRISTS
ACIRSSTT ASTRICTS
ACIRSSTW TWISCARS
ACIRSSTY SACRISTY
ACIRSSTZ CZARISTS
ACISSSTU CASUISTS
ACISSTTU CATSUITS
ACISSTUV VACUISTS
ACISTTUY ASTUCITY
ACJKKSSY SKYJACKS
ACJKNNOS JANNOCKS
ACJKOPST JACKPOTS
ACJMNSTU MUNTJACS
ACJPSTUU CAJUPUTS
ACKKMOPR POCKMARK
ACKKORRW RACKWORK
ACKLLOPS POLLACKS
ACKLLOSY LAYLOCKS
ACKLLPSU SKULLCAP
ACKLMNOS LOCKSMAN
ACKLMORS ARMLOCKS
         LOCKRAMS
ACKLNOSU UNCLOAKS
ACKLOOSW WOOLSACK
ACKLORSW WARLOCKS
ACKLORSY ROCKLAYS
ACKLOSSS LASSOCKS
ACKMMMOS MAMMOCKS
ACKMNOST STOCKMAN
ACKMNRTU TRUCKMAN
ACKMOSTT MATTOCKS
ACKNSSTU UNSTACKS
ACKOPRRS PARROCKS
ACKORRST TARROCKS
ACLLMNOU COLUMNAL
ACLLMORU CORALLUM
ACLLOORS COROLLAS
ACLLOORT COLLATOR
ACLLOOSS COLOSSAL
ACLLOPSS SCALLOPS
ACLLORUY OCULARLY
ACLLRTUU CULTURAL
ACLMMNOU COMMUNAL
ACLMNOOO COOLAMON

ACLMNORU COLUMNAR
ACLMNORY NORMALCY
ACLMORSU CLAMOURS
ACLMORTU CROTALUM
ACLMPRSU SCALPRUM
ACLMRSUU MUSCULAR
ACLMSUUV VASCULUM
ACLNOORS CORONALS
ACLNOORT COLORANT
ACLNOOST COOLANTS
ACLNOPSY SYNCOPAL
ACLNORSU CONSULAR
         COURLANS
ACLNOSTU CONSULTA
         OSCULANT
ACLNPSSU UNCLASPS
ACLNPTUU PUNCTUAL
ACLNSSUY UNCLASSY
ACLOOPRR CORPORAL
ACLOPRST CALTROPS
ACLOPRXY XYLOCARP
ACLOPSSU SCOPULAS
ACLOPSSY CALYPSOS
ACLOPSUU OPUSCULA
ACLORRTU TORCULAR
ACLOSSTU OUTCLASS
ACLRSSTY CRYSTALS
ACMMNOSY SCAMMONY
ACMMNOYY MYOMANCY
ACMNOOPR MONOCARP
ACMNOORR CROMORNA
ACMNOORT MONOCRAT
ACMNOOYZ ZOOMANCY
ACMNOPRS CRAMPONS
ACMNORSY ACRONYMS
ACMNSSTU SANCTUMS
ACMOOSST SCOTOMAS
ACMOPRST COMPARTS
ACMORSTY COSTMARY
ACMQSTUU CUMQUATS
ACNNNORY CANNONRY
ACNNOSTT CONSTANT
ACNOOORT OCTAROON
ACNOORRY CORONARY
ACNOORST CARTOONS
         CORANTOS
         OSTRACON
ACNOORSU CANOROUS
ACNOORTY OCTONARY
ACNOPSSW SNOWCAPS
ACNORRSU RANCOURS
ACNORRTY CONTRARY
ACNORSTT CONTRAST
ACNORSTU COURANTS
ACNORTTU TURNCOAT
ACNORTUY NOCTUARY
ACNPRSSY SYNCARPS
ACNPRSSU SPRAUNCY
ACNPRSSY SYNCARPY
ACNRRSTU CURRANTS
ACNRRTUY CURRANTY
ACOOPRRS CORPORAS
ACOOPSTT TOPCOATS
ACOORSTU TOURACOS
ACOPRRST CARPORTS
ACOPRRTT PROTRACT
ACORRSTT TRACTORS
ACORRSTU CURATORS
ACORRTUY CURATORY
ACORSSTU SURCOATS

ACORSSUW CURASSOW
ACORSSWY CROSSWAY
ACORSTTY CRYOSTAT
ACOSSTTU OUTCASTS
ACPSSTUU USUCAPTS
ADDDEEEM ADDEEMED
ADDDEEEN DEADENED
ADDDEEGR DEGRADED
ADDDEEIM DIADEMED
ADDDEELR LADDERED
ADDDEEMN DEMANDED
         MADDENED
ADDDEENR DANDERED
         REDDENDA
ADDDEENS SADDENED
ADDDEEPS SEPADDED
ADDDEGJU ADJUDGED
ADDDELSW SWADDLED
ADDDELTW TWADDLED
ADDDEMNU ADDENDUM
ADDDEMOO ADDOOMED
ADDDENOS DEODANDS
ADDDENRU DEUDDARN
ADDDEORS ADDORSED
ADDDGILN DADDLING
ADDEEEFN DEAFENED
ADDEEEFT DEFEATED
ADDEEEJY DEEJAYED
ADDEEELN LEADENED
ADDEEEMN DEMEANED
ADDEEENR DEADENER
         ENDEARED
ADDEEFIL DEFILADE
ADDEEFIM MADEFIED
ADDEEFLT DEFLATED
ADDEEFNU UNDEAFED
ADDEEFPR PREFADED
ADDEEFRY DEFRAYED
ADDEEFTT DEFATTED
ADDEEGLL ALLEDGED
ADDEEGLN DANEGELD
ADDEEGNR DANGERED
         DERANGED
         GARDENED
ADDEEGRR REGARDED
         REGRADED
ADDEEGRS DEGRADES
ADDEEGSS DEGASSED
ADDEEHLR HERALDED
ADDEEHLY ALDEHYDE
ADDEEHNR HARDENED
ADDEEHNU UNHEADED
ADDEEHRT THREADED
ADDEEIKR DAIKERED
ADDEEILN DEADLINE
ADDEEILR DEADLIER
         DERAILED
ADDEEILT DETAILED
ADDEEIMT MEDIATED
ADDEEINT DETAINED
ADDEEIPR DIAPERED
ADDEEISS DISEASED
ADDEEIST STEADIED
ADDEEITV DEVIATED
ADDEEKMR DEMARKED
ADDEEKNR DARKENED
ADDEELLM MEDALLED
ADDEELLP PEDALLED
ADDEELLV DEVALLED
ADDEELNO LOADENED

ADDEELNP DEPLANED
ADDEELNR ENLARDED
ADDEELNU UNLEADED
ADDEELOR RELOADED
ADDEELPS DELAPSED
ADDEELRT TREADLED
ADDEELST DESALTED
ADDEELUV DEVALUED
ADDEEMNN DEMANNED
ADDEEMNP DAMPENED
ADDEEMNR DAMNEDER
         DEMANDER
         REMANDED
ADDEENPP APPENDED
ADDEENPR PANDERED
ADDEENPX EXPANDED
ADDEENRR DARNEDER
ADDEENRT ENDARTED
ADDEENRU DAUNERED
ADDEENRW DAWNERED
         WANDERED
         WARDENED
ADDEENSS DEADNESS
ADDEENTT ATTENDED
         DENTATED
ADDEENTU DENUDATE
ADDEEOST DEODATES
ADDEEPRT DEPARTED
         PREDATED
ADDEEPRV DEPRAVED
         PERVADED
ADDEERRS DREADERS
ADDEERRT RETARDED
ADDEERRW REWARDED
         WARDERED
ADDEERSW SAWDERED
ADDEERTV ADVERTED
ADDEFFOR AFFORDED
ADDEFIIL LADIFIED
ADDEFILY LADYFIED
ADDEFIST FADDIEST
ADDEFLRU DREADFUL
ADDEFRSU DEFRAUDS
ADDEGGLR DRAGGLED
ADDEGHOS GODHEADS
ADDEGILS GLADDIES
ADDEGINR DREADING
ADDEGIRS DISGRADE
ADDEGJSU ADJUDGES
ADDEGLNS GLADDENS
ADDEGLST GLADDEST
ADDEGNRU UNGRADED
ADDEGPRU UPGRADED
ADDEHHIN HINDHEAD
ADDEHILR DIHEDRAL
ADDEHMRU DRUMHEAD
ADDEHNNU UNHANDED
ADDEHNSU UNDASHED
         UNSHADED
ADDEHORW HEADWORD
ADDEHOSW SHADOWED
ADDEHRTY HYDRATED
ADDEIIKS DIDAKEIS
ADDEIIRS DIARISED
ADDEIIRZ DIARIZED
ADDEIITV ADDITIVE
ADDEIJNO ADJOINED
ADDEILNS ISLANDED
ADDEILRS DIEDRALS
ADDEILSY DIALYSED
```

ADDEILYZ DIALYZED	ADDGILNP PADDLING	ADEEELNS ENSEALED	ADEEGLLT GALLETED
ADDEIMOS SODAMIDE	ADDGILNR RADDLING	ADEEELNV LEAVENED	ADEEGLNO ENGAOLED
ADDEIMRS DISARMED	ADDGILNS SADDLING	ADEEELPR REPEALED	ADEEGLNR ENLARGED
MISDREAD	ADDGILNW DAWDLING	ADEEELRS RELEASED	LARGENED
ADDEIMST MISDATED	WADDLING	RESEALED	ADEEGLNT DANEGELT
ADDEIMSY DISMAYED	ADDGINPS PADDINGS	ADEEELRV LAVEERED	ADEEGLSV SELVAGED
ADDEIMTT ADMITTED	ADDGINQU QUADDING	REVEALED	ADEEGMMT GEMMATED
ADDEINOR ORDAINED	ADDGINSW WADDINGS	ADEEELST TEASELED	ADEEGMNR GENDARME
ADDEINOS ADENOIDS	ADDGINWY WADDYING	ADEEELSW WEASELED	ADEEGMNS ENDGAMES
ADONISED	ADDGLNOS GLADDONS	ADEEELTV ELEVATED	ADEEGMNY MEGADYNE
ANODISED	ADDGOOSW DAGWOODS	ADEEELTZ TEAZELED	ADEEGMOP MEGAPODE
ADDEINOZ ADONIZED	ADDGORSW GODWARDS	ADEEEMNS DEMEANES	ADEEGMSS MESSAGED
ANODIZED	ADDHHLNO HANDHOLD	ENSEAMED	ADEEGNNR ENDANGER
ADDEINRT INDARTED	ADDHIMOO MAIDHOOD	ADEEEMNT EMENDATE	ENRANGED
ADDEINST DANDIEST	ADDHINPS DAPHNIDS	ADEEEMRU EMERAUDE	ADEEGNNV VENDANGE
ADDEIOPR PARODIED	ADDHINRW HINDWARD	ADEEENNT NEATENED	ADEEGNOR RENEGADO
ADDEIORS ROADSIDE	ADDHINSY DANDYISH	ADEEENRS ENSEARED	ADEEGNRR GARDENER
ADDEIOTX OXIDATED	ADDHIOTY HYDATOID	SERENADE	GARNERED
ADDEIPPR DIDAPPER	ADDHISTY HYDATIDS	ADEEENTT ATTENDEE	ADEEGNRS DERANGES
ADDEIPRS DISPREAD	ADDHLOOY LADYHOOD	EDENTATE	GRANDEES
ADDEIPSS DIPSADES	ADDHOORW HARDWOOD	ADEEENWZ WEAZENED	GRENADES
ADDEIRST DISRATED	ADDIIKMZ ZADDIKIM	ADEEEPRT REPEATED	ADEEGNRU DUNGAREE
ADDEIRSW SIDEWARD	ADDIILUV DIVIDUAL	ADEEERRS ARREEDES	RENAGUED
ADDEIRVZ VIZARDED	ADDIINOT ADDITION	ADEEERST RESEATED	UNGEARED
ADDEISSU DISSUADE	ADDIINSS DISDAINS	ADEEESSW SEAWEEDS	ADEEGNRV ENGRAVED
ADDEISSW SWADDIES	ADDIINTV DIVIDANT	SEESAWED	ADEEGNSS AGEDNESS
ADDEJSTU ADJUSTED	ADDIKSST TSADDIKS	ADEEFFIR EFFRAIDE	ADEEGNSV VENDAGES
ADDEKNVY VANDYKED	ADDIKSTY KATYDIDS	ADEEFHOR FOREHEAD	ADEEGORT DEROGATE
ADDELLOR DOLLARED	ADDIKSTZ TZADDIKS	ADEEFHRT FATHERED	ADEEGOST DOGEATES
ADDELMOS DOLMADES	ADDILMNS MIDLANDS	ADEEFILN ENFILADE	ADEEGOTW GOATWEED
ADDELNOU DUODENAL	ADDILNNW LANDWIND	ADEEFIMS MADEFIES	ADEEGPRS ASPERGED
UNLOADED	ADDILOSS DISLOADS	ADEEFINR FREDAINE	PRESAGED
ADDELNPU PUDENDAL	ADDIMNOS DIAMONDS	ADEEFIOR FOEDARIE	ADEEGPRT PARGETED
ADDELNRS DANDLERS	ADDIMNSY DANDYISM	ADEEFIRR RAREFIED	ADEEGRRR REGARDER
ADDELNSU UNSADDLE	ADDIMORS DIADROMS	ADEEFIRS FEDARIES	ADEEGRRS REGRADES
ADDELPRS PADDLERS	ADDINNOR ORDINAND	ADEEFIRY REAEDIFY	ADEEGRRT GARRETED
ADDELRSS SADDLERS	ADDINORS ANDROIDS	ADEEFLLT FELLATED	GARTERED
ADDELRST STRADDLE	DISADORN	ADEEFLOR FREELOAD	REGRATED
ADDELRSW DAWDLERS	ADDINQUY QUIDDANY	ADEEFLRR DEFERRAL	ADEEGRRU REDARGUE
SWADDLER	ADDINRWW WINDWARD	ADEEFLRS FEDERALS	ADEEGRSS DRESSAGE
ADDELRSY SADDLERY	ADDIQSST TSADDIQS	ADEEFLRT DEFLATER	ADEEGRST RESTAGED
ADDELRTW TWADDLER	ADDIQSTZ TZADDIQS	FALTERED	ADEEGRSU GUARDEES
ADDELSST STADDLES	ADDIRSZZ DIZZARDS	REFLATED	ADEEGRSW RAGWEEDS
ADDELSSW SWADDLES	ADDKNRRU DRUNKARD	ADEEFLSS FADELESS	ADEEGRTT TARGETED
ADDELSTW TWADDLES	ADDLLNOR LANDLORD	ADEEFLST DEFLATES	ADEEGSSS DEGASSES
ADDEMMNU UNDAMMED	ADDLLRSU DULLARDS	ADEEFMNR ENFRAMED	ADEEGSTT GESTATED
ADDEMNNU UNDAMNED	ADDLNNOW DOWNLAND	FREEDMAN	ADEEGSWY EDGEWAYS
ADDEMNPU UNDAMPED	ADDLNOOW WOODLAND	ADEEFMRR REFRAMED	ADEEGTTZ GAZETTED
ADDENNOT DANTONED	ADDLNORS LANDDROS	ADEEFNRU UNFEARED	ADEEHHRS REHASHED
ADDENOPR PARDONED	ADDLOOSS SOLDADOS	ADEEFNSS DEAFNESS	ADEEHHST SHEATHED
ADDENORU UNADORED	ADDMOOSY DOOMSDAY	ADEEFNST FASTENED	ADEEHILN HEADLINE
ADDENPRU UNDRAPED	ADDNOPWY PANDOWDY	ADEEFNTT FATTENED	ADEEHILS DEISHEAL
ADDENRST STRANDED	ADDNORWW DOWNWARD	ADEEFORR FOREREAD	ADEEHIRT DEATHIER
ADDENRSU DAUNDERS	ADDOORWW WOODWARD	ADEEFORT FOREDATE	ADEEHISS EADISHES
ADDENRTU DRAUNTED	ADDOORWY WOODYARD	ADEEFPRS PREFADES	ADEEHIST ATHEISED
UNTRADED	ADDOPSSY DASYPODS	ADEEFRRT RAFTERED	HEADIEST
ADDENRUW UNWARDED	ADEEEFFR AFFEERED	ADEEFRRY DEFRAYER	ADEEHISV ADHESIVE
ADDEORTU OUTDARED	ADEEEFNY FEDAYEEN	FEDERARY	ADEEHITZ ATHEIZED
ADDEOTTU OUTDATED	ADEEEFRT FEDERATE	ADEEFRST DRAFTEES	ADEEHKNR HANKERED
ADDEPRSU SUPERADD	ADEEEGLT DELEGATE	ADEEFRTU FEATURED	HARKENED
ADDFFILO DAFFODIL	ADEEEGNR RENEGADE	ADEEGGHS EGGHEADS	ADEEHKWW HAWKWEED
ADDFFINR DANDRIFF	ADEEEGNT TEENAGED	ADEEGGLL ALLEGGED	ADEEHLNO ENHALOED
ADDFFNRU DANDRUFF	ADEEEGPS GAPESEED	ADEEGGRR RAGGEDER	ADEEHLNR REHANDLE
ADDFGILN FADDLING	ADEEEGRS DEGREASE	ADEEGHOR GHERAOED	ADEEHLNU UNHEALED
ADDFIMSS FADDISMS	ADEEEHHW HEEHAWED	ADEEGHRT GATHERED	ADEEHLRS ASHLERED
ADDFISST FADDISTS	ADEEEHRT REHEATED	ADEEGIMN ADEEMING	ADEEHLRT HALTERED
ADDGGILN GLADDING	ADEEEHRX EXHEDRAE	ADEEGINR REGAINED	LATHERED
ADDGIILN DAIDLING	ADEEEHSY EYESHADE	ADEEGIRS DISAGREE	ADEEHLSS HEADLESS
ADDGIIRS DIAGRIDS	ADEEEINT DETAINEE	ADEEGISS ASSIEGED	ADEEHMMR HAMMERED
ADDGILNN DANDLING	ADEEEKNW WEAKENED	ADEEGLLS ALLEDGES	ADEEHMNN MENHADEN

ADEEHMNS	HEADSMEN
ADEEHMNT	ANTHEMED
ADEEHMPR	HAMPERED
ADEEHNOT	HEADNOTE
ADEEHNPP	HAPPENED
ADEEHNRR	HARDENER
ADEEHNRT	ADHERENT
	HARTENED
	THREADEN
ADEEHNSS	DASHEENS
ADEEHNST	HASTENED
ADEEHNTU	UNHEATED
ADEEHOPR	HEADROPE
ADEEHORS	SOREHEAD
ADEEHORV	OVERHEAD
ADEEHPPU	UPHEAPED
ADEEHPRS	EPHEDRAS
	RESHAPED
ADEEHPUV	UPHEAVED
ADEEHRRS	ADHERERS
	REDSHARE
ADEEHRRT	THREADER
ADEEHRST	HEADREST
ADEEHRSW	WASHERED
ADEEHRTT	HATTERED
	THREATED
ADEEHRTW	WREATHED
ADEEHSST	HEADSETS
ADEEHSSY	HAYSEEDS
ADEEIILS	IDEALISE
ADEEIILZ	IDEALIZE
ADEEIITV	IDEATIVE
ADEEIJMR	JEREMIAD
ADEEIJRS	JADERIES
ADEEIJST	JADEITES
ADEEILLO	OEILLADE
ADEEILLR	REALLIED
ADEEILMN	ENDEMIAL
ADEEILMR	REMEDIAL
ADEEILMV	MEDIEVAL
ADEEILNS	DELAINES
ADEEILNT	ENTAILED
	LINEATED
ADEEILPR	PEDALIER
ADEEILPT	DEPILATE
	EPILATED
	PILEATED
ADEEILRR	DERAILER
	RERAILED
ADEEILRS	REALISED
	SIDEREAL
ADEEILRT	RETAILED
ADEEILRZ	REALIZED
ADEEILSS	DEISEALS
	IDEALESS
ADEEILST	LEADIEST
ADEEILSV	DISLEAVE
ADEEILSY	EYELIADS
ADEEIMNR	REMAINED
ADEEIMNS	DEMAINES
	INSEAMED
ADEEIMNT	DEMENTIA
ADEEIMNX	EXAMINED
ADEEIMPR	EMPAIRED
ADEEIMRR	DREAMIER
ADEEIMRS	MADERISE
ADEEIMRT	DIAMETER
	REMEDIAT
ADEEIMRZ	MADERIZE
ADEEIMSS	SIAMESED
ADEEIMST	MEDIATES
ADEEIMSZ	SIAMEZED
ADEEIMTT	MEDITATE
ADEEINNS	ADENINES
	ANDESINE
ADEEINPR	PINDAREE
ADEEINPT	DIAPENTE
	NEAPTIDE
ADEEINRS	ARSENIDE
	DENARIES
	DRAISENE
	NEARSIDE
ADEEINRT	DETAINER
	RETAINED
ADEEINSS	ANISEEDS
ADEEINST	ANDESITE
ADEEIPRR	REPAIRED
ADEEIPTX	EXPIATED
ADEEIRRR	DREARIER
ADEEIRST	READIEST
	SERIATED
	STEADIER
ADEEIRSV	READVISE
ADEEIRTT	ITERATED
ADEEIRTV	DERIVATE
	EVIRATED
	TAIVERED
ADEEISSS	DISEASES
	SEASIDES
ADEEISST	STEADIES
ADEEISSV	ADESSIVE
ADEEISTV	DEVIATES
	SEDATIVE
ADEEITTV	EVITATED
ADEEKMRR	REMARKED
ADEEKMRT	MARKETED
ADEEKNNR	ENRANKED
ADEEKNPW	KNAPWEED
ADEEKNRS	KNEADERS
ADEEKNST	NAKEDEST
ADEEKQSU	SQUEAKED
ADEEKRST	STREAKED
ADEEKSWY	WEEKDAYS
ADEELLLP	LAPELLED
ADEELLMT	METALLED
ADEELLMU	MEDULLAE
ADEELLNP	PANELLED
ADEELLNW	ENWALLED
ADEELLNY	LEADENLY
ADEELLPR	PEDALLER
	PREDELLA
ADEELLPT	PALLETED
	PETALLED
ADEELLQU	EQUALLED
ADEELLRS	SARDELLE
ADEELLRT	TELLARED
ADEELLRV	RAVELLED
ADEELLSS	ALLSEEDS
	LEADLESS
ADEELLTY	ELATEDLY
ADEELMNO	LEMONADE
ADEELMNP	EMPLANED
ADEELMNR	ALDERMEN
ADEELMNS	DALESMEN
	EMENDALS
	LEADSMEN
ADEELMNT	LAMENTED
ADEELMOS	SOMEDEAL
ADEELMPX	EXAMPLED
ADEELMRS	DEMERSAL
	EMERALDS
ADEELMST	MEDALETS
ADEELMTU	EMULATED
ADEELNNU	UNANELED
ADEELNOR	OLEANDER
ADEELNPS	DEPLANES
ADEELNPU	UPLEANED
ADEELNRT	ANTLERED
ADEELNRV	LAVENDER
ADEELNSU	UNLEASED
	UNSEALED
ADEELNSV	ENSLAVED
ADEELNTT	TALENTED
ADEELNTU	UNELATED
ADEELNTV	LEVANTED
ADEELNTY	ENTAYLED
ADEELOPS	PEDALOES
ADEELORU	AUREOLED
ADEELORV	OVERLADE
ADEELOST	DESOLATE
ADEELOSW	LEASOWED
ADEELPPR	LAPPERED
ADEELPPT	LAPPETED
ADEELPPU	UPLEAPED
ADEELPRS	PLEADERS
	RELAPSED
ADEELPRT	PALTERED
ADEELPRY	PARLEYED
	REPLAYED
ADEELPSS	DELAPSES
ADEELPST	PEDESTAL
ADEELPTY	PEDATELY
ADEELQSU	SQUEALED
ADEELRRR	LARDERER
ADEELRRT	TREADLER
ADEELRST	TREADLES
ADEELRSV	SLAVERED
ADEELRSW	LEEWARDS
ADEELRSY	DELAYERS
ADEELRUV	REVALUED
ADEELSST	DATELESS
ADEELSTY	SEDATELY
ADEELSUV	DEVALUES
ADEEMMMR	MAMMERED
ADEEMMRY	YAMMERED
ADEEMMSS	MESDAMES
ADEEMMXY	MYXEDEMA
ADEEMNNR	MANNERED
	REMANNED
ADEEMNOR	DEMEANOR
	ENAMORED
ADEEMNOT	NEMATODE
ADEEMNPS	SPADEMEN
ADEEMNRS	AMENDERS
	MEANDERS
	REAMENDS
ADEEMNSS	SEEDSMAN
ADEEMNST	STAMENED
ADEEMNSU	UNSEAMED
ADEEMNSY	DEMAYNES
ADEEMNTU	UNTEAMED
ADEEMNTW	METEWAND
ADEEMORS	SEADROME
ADEEMORT	MODERATE
ADEEMPPR	PAMPERED
ADEEMPRT	EMPARTED
	TAMPERED
ADEEMPRV	REVAMPED
ADEEMPRY	EMPAYRED
ADEEMPST	STAMPEDE
	STEPDAME
ADEEMRRS	DREAMERS
ADEEMRRY	DREAMERY
ADEEMRST	MASTERED
	STREAMED
ADEEMRSU	MEASURED
ADEEMRTT	MATTERED
ADEEMRTY	METEYARD
ADEEMSSW	MAWSEEDS
ADEEMSTW	MATWEEDS
ADEEMSWY	MAYWEEDS
ADEENNRS	ENSNARED
ADEENNRU	UNEARNED
ADEENNTT	TENANTED
ADEENNUW	UNWEANED
ADEENNUY	UNYEANED
ADEENOPW	WEAPONED
ADEENORS	REASONED
ADEENORY	AERODYNE
ADEENOSS	SEASONED
ADEENOTT	DENOTATE
	DETONATE
ADEENPRT	PARENTED
ADEENPRU	UNREAPED
ADEENPRX	EXPANDER
ADEENPTT	PATENTED
	PATTENED
ADEENRRW	WANDERER
ADEENRSS	DEARNESS
ADEENRSU	UNDERSEA
ADEENRSW	ANSWERED
ADEENRTT	ATTENDER
	NATTERED
	RATTENED
ADEENRTU	DENATURE
ADEENRTV	AVENTRED
ADEENRUV	UNREAVED
ADEENSST	ASSENTED
ADEENSSU	DANSEUSE
ADEENSTU	UNSEATED
ADEENTTU	TAUTENED
ADEENTTV	VENDETTA
ADEEOPRR	PADERERO
ADEEOPRT	OPERATED
ADEEORRV	OVERREAD
ADEEORSW	OARWEEDS
ADEEORVW	OVERAWED
ADEEPPRR	DAPPERER
	PREPARED
ADEEPPRW	WAPPERED
ADEEPPRS	SPREADER
ADEEPRRT	DEPARTER
ADEEPRRU	UPREARED
ADEEPRSS	ASPERSED
	PREASSED
	REPASSED
ADEEPRST	PREDATES
	REPASTED
	TRAPESED
ADEEPRSU	PERSUADE
ADEEPRSV	DEPRAVES
	PERVADES
ADEEPRSW	PERSWADE
ADEEPRSZ	SPREAZED
ADEEPRTT	PATTERED
ADEEPRTU	DEPURATE
	EPURATED
ADEEPRTZ	TRAPEZED
ADEEPSST	STAPEDES
ADEEPSTT	ADEPTEST

ADEEPSWY SPEEDWAY	ADEFILMN INFLAMED	ADEGHIRS GARISHED	ADEGIOST GODETIAS
ADEEQRTU DETRAQUE	ADEFILNR FILANDER	HEADRIGS	ADEGIPRS SPAIRGED
ADEEQRUV QUAVERED	ADEFILNT INFLATED	ADEGHIRT GRAITHED	ADEGIRWY RIDGEWAY
ADEERRRT RETARDER	ADEFILOR FORELAID	ADEGHLNO HEADLONG	ADEGISSU DISUSAGE
ADEERRRW REREWARD	ADEFILOT FOLIATED	ADEGHLOS GALOSHED	ADEGISTU GAUDIEST
REWARDER	ADEFILSS DISLEAFS	ADEGHNNU UNHANGED	ADEGISUV VIDUAGES
ADEERRST ARRESTED	ADEFILSY LADYFIES	ADEGHNRT THRANGED	ADEGJNOR JARGONED
DREAREST	ADEFIMPR FIREDAMP	ADEGHOOP PAGEHOOD	ADEGKLOY DEKALOGY
RETREADS	ADEFIMRS MISFARED	ADEGHORT GOATHERD	ADEGLLNU GLANDULE
SERRATED	ADEFIMSS DISFAMES	ADEGHRTU DAUGHTER	UNGALLED
TREADERS	ADEFINNT INFANTED	ADEGHTUW WAUGHTED	ADEGLLOP GALLOPED
ADEERRSV ADVERSER	ADEFINRS FRIANDES	ADEGIILN GLIADINE	ADEGLLOR GOLLARED
ADEERRTT RETRATED	ADEFINRU UNFAIRED	ADEGIIMN IMAGINED	ADEGLLOW GALLOWED
ADEERRTW REDWATER	ADEFINYZ DENAZIFY	ADEGIIMS DIGAMIES	ADEGLMOR GLAMORED
ADEERRWY WARREYED	ADEFIORS FORESAID	ADEGIINT IDEATING	ADEGLMOS GLADSOME
ADEERSST ASSERTED	ADEFLLLU LADLEFUL	ADEGIITT DIGITATE	ADEGLMPU PLUMAGED
ESTRADES	ADEFLLNS ELFLANDS	ADEGIJSW JIGSAWED	ADEGLMUY AMYGDULE
ADEERSTT ASTERTED	ADEFLLOW FALLOWED	ADEGIKNN KNEADING	ADEGLNOY GONDELAY
RESTATED	ADEFLLUY FEUDALLY	ADEGIKNR DAKERING	ADEGLNPS SPANGLED
ADEERSTW DEWATERS	ADEFLMRU DREAMFUL	ADEGILLO GLADIOLE	ADEGLNRS DANGLERS
TARWEEDS	ADEFLNNS FENLANDS	ADEGILLP PILLAGED	GLANDERS
WASTERED	ADEFLNOR FORELAND	ADEGILLR GRILLADE	ADEGLNRW WRANGLED
ADEERSTY ESTRAYED	ADEFLNRU DEARNFUL	ADEGILLS GALLISED	ADEGLNSS GLADNESS
ADEERTTT TATTERED	ADEFLNTU FLAUNTED	ADEGILLZ GALLIZED	ADEGLNTW TWANGLED
ADEERTTY YATTERED	ADEFLNUU UNFEUDAL	ADEGILMN MALIGNED	ADEGLNUZ UNGLAZED
ADEERTWW WARTWEED	ADEFLNUW UNFLAWED	ADEGILNO GALENOID	ADEGLOPP GALOPPED
ADEERVYY EVERYDAY	ADEFLORT DEFLATOR	ADEGILNP PLEADING	ADEGLPPR GRAPPLED
ADEESSSS ASSESSED	ADEFLPRS FELDSPAR	ADEGILNR DEARLING	ADEGMMNO GAMMONED
ADEESSTT SEDATEST	ADEFLPSU SPADEFUL	DRAGLINE	ADEGMMRU RUMMAGED
ADEESTTT ATTESTED	ADEFLRTU TRADEFUL	ADEGILNS DEALINGS	ADEGMNOS GOADSMEN
ADEESTUX EXUDATES	ADEFLRTW LEFTWARD	LEADINGS	ADEGMNOY ENDOGAMY
ADEESVVY SAVVEYED	ADEFLRZZ FRAZZLED	ADEGILNT DELATING	ADEGMNRS DRAGSMEN
ADEFFGUW GUFFAWED	ADEFLSTU DEFAULTS	ADEGILNY DELAYING	ADEGMORS ORGASMED
ADEFFIMR AFFIRMED	SULFATED	ADEGILOS GOLIASED	ADEGMPUZ GAZUMPED
ADEFFIRR DRAFFIER	ADEFMNRU UNFRAMED	ADEGILOU DIALOGUE	ADEGNNOR ANDROGEN
ADEFFIRT TARIFFED	ADEFMORT FORMATED	ADEGILRS SLAIRGED	DRAGONNE
ADEFFIST DAFFIEST	ADEFMOSU FAMOUSED	ADEGILSS GLISSADE	ADEGNNPU UNPANGED
ADEFFLNS SNAFFLED	FUMADOES	ADEGILST GLADIEST	ADEGNNSU DUNNAGES
ADEFFRST STRAFFED	ADEFNNNU UNFANNED	ADEGILSV DISGAVEL	ADEGNOPS PONDAGES
ADEFGGGO FOGGAGED	ADEFNOPR PROFANED	ADEGIMNN AMENDING	ADEGNOPU POUNDAGE
ADEFGGOT FAGGOTED	ADEFNSST DAFTNESS	ADEGIMNR DREAMING	ADEGNORT DRAGONET
ADEFGIIS GASIFIED	ADEFOOSS SEAFOODS	MARGINED	ADEGNOSS SONDAGES
ADEFGILN FINAGLED	ADEFORRR FORRADER	ADEGIMOR IDEOGRAM	ADEGNOSV DOGVANES
ADEFGILO FOLIAGED	ADEFORRW FARROWED	ADEGIMRT MIGRATED	ADEGNPUY PYENGADU
ADEFGILS GADFLIES	FOREWARD	ADEGIMST SIGMATED	ADEGNRRU GRANDEUR
GASFIELD	ADEFORRY FORRAYED	ADEGINNV ADVENING	ADEGNRST GRANDEST
ADEFGIMN DEFAMING	ADEFORUV FAVOURED	ADEGINNY DENAYING	ADEGNRSU ENGUARDS
ADEFGIRT DRIFTAGE	ADEFPTUW UPWAFTED	ADEGINOR ORGANDIE	ADEGNRUU UNARGUED
ADEFGIRU ARGUFIED	ADEFRRST DRAFTERS	ADEGINOS AGONISED	ADEGNRUZ UNGRAZED
ADEFGITU FATIGUED	REDRAFTS	DIAGNOSE	ADEGOORY GOODYEAR
ADEFGLOT GATEFOLD	ADEFSSTT STEDFAST	ADEGINOZ AGONIZED	ADEGOPPR PROPAGED
ADEFGLRU FELDGRAU	ADEGGIRR DRAGGIER	ADEGINPU ANGUIPED	ADEGOPRR PROGRADE
ADEFGNOR FRONDAGE	ADEGGISU GAUDGIES	ADEGINRR DREARING	ADEGORRT GARROTED
ADEFGOSU FOUGADES	GUIDAGES	ADEGINRS DERAIGNS	ADEGORST GOADSTER
ADEFHILS DEALFISH	ADEGGJLY JAGGEDLY	GRADINES	ADEGORSW DOWAGERS
ADEFHILY HAYFIELD	ADEGGLRS DRAGGLES	READINGS	WORDAGES
ADEFHIMS FAMISHED	ADEGGLRY RAGGEDLY	ADEGINRT DERATING	ADEGORTT GAROTTED
ADEFHKOR FORKHEAD	ADEGGMOY DEMAGOGY	GRADIENT	ADEGORTU OUTRAGED
ADEFHLTU DEATHFUL	ADEGGNOW WAGGONED	TREADING	RAGOUTED
ADEFHMOT FATHOMED	ADEGGNUU UNGAUGED	ADEGINRY DERAYING	ADEGPRSS SPADGERS
ADEFHNOR FOREHAND	ADEGGOPY PEDAGOGY	READYING	ADEGPRSU UPGRADES
ADEFHOST SOFTHEAD	ADEGGPRS SPRAGGED	YEARDING	ADEGPSTU UPSTAGED
ADEFIILR AIRFIELD	ADEGGRTY GADGETRY	ADEGINSS ASSIGNED	ADEGRRST DRAGSTER
ADEFIILS LADIFIES	ADEGHHOS HOGSHEAD	ADEGINST SEDATING	ADEGRSSU GRADUSES
SALIFIED	ADEGHILN HEALDING	STEADING	ADEGTTTU GUTTATED
ADEFIILT FILIATED	ADEGHILT ALIGHTED	ADEGINSW WINDAGES	ADEHHIPR RHAPHIDE
ADEFIIMR RAMIFIED	ADEGHINR ADHERING	ADEGINTV VINTAGED	ADEHHIPS HEADSHIP
ADEFIINS SANIFIED	HEADRING	ADEGINVW ADVEWING	ADEHHNTU HEADHUNT
ADEFIIRT RATIFIED	ADEGHINS HEADINGS	ADEGINYZ ZYGAENID	ADEHHOOR HOORAHED
ADEFIIRU AURIFIED	SHEADING	ADEGIORT ERGATOID	ADEHHOST HOTHEADS

ADEHHRRU HURRAHED	ADEHMOOR HEADROOM	VITIATED	DEASOILS
ADEHHRST THRASHED	ADEHMORS HADROMES	ADEIITUV AUDITIVE	ADEILOST DIASTOLE
ADEHIITZ THIAZIDE	ADEHMORW HOMEWARD	ADEIJMRS JEMIDARS	ISOLATED
ADEHIKLV KHEDIVAL	ADEHMOST HEADMOST	ADEIKLLO KELOIDAL	SODALITE
ADEHIKNS SKINHEAD	ADEHMOSU MADHOUSE	ADEIKLLP PIKADELL	SOLIDATE
ADEHIKSS DASHEKIS	ADEHMOSY SHAMOYED	ADEIKLLY LADYLIKE	ADEILOSU DOULEIAS
ADEHIKST SKAITHED	ADEHNOPR ORPHANED	ADEIKLSW SIDEWALK	ADEILOTT DATOLITE
ADEHIKSV KHEDIVAS	ADEHNOPT PHONATED	ADEIKMMS IMMASKED	ADEILOTV DOVETAIL
ADEHILLP PHIALLED	ADEHNORV HANDOVER	ADEIKMPR IMPARKED	VIOLATED
PILLHEAD	OVERHAND	ADEIKMRT TIDEMARK	ADEILPPP PEDIPALP
ADEHILNR HARDLINE	ADEHNPSU UNHASPED	ADEIKNSY KYANISED	ADEILPRS PEDRAILS
ADEHILNU UNHAILED	UNSHAPED	ADEIKNYZ KYANIZED	PREDIALS
ADEHILPS HELIPADS	ADEHNPTU UNPATHED	ADEIKORT KERATOID	ADEILPRT DIPTERAL
ADEHILSV LAVISHED	ADEHNRSS HARDNESS	ADEIKRST STRAIKED	TRIPEDAL
ADEHILSW WHAISLED	ADEHNRSU UNSHARED	ADEILLMY MEDIALLY	ADEILPRU EPIDURAL
ADEHILWZ WHAIZLED	ADEHNRSW SWANHERD	ADEILLNU UNALLIED	ADEILPRV DEPRIVAL
ADEHIMRS MISHEARD	ADEHNRTU UNTHREAD	ADEILLNW INWALLED	ADEILPSS DESPISAL
ADEHIMRY HYDREMIA	ADEHNSST HANDSETS	ADEILLOR ARILLODE	ADEILPST TALIPEDS
ADEHINOP DIAPHONE	ADEHNSSU UNSASHED	ADEILLPR PALLIDER	ADEILPTU PLAUDITE
ADEHINOS ADHESION	ADEHNSUV UNSHAVED	ADEILLPS ILLAPSED	ADEILQSU SQUAILED
ADEHINPS DEANSHIP	ADEHNSUW UNWASHED	SPADILLE	ADEILQTU LIQUATED
PINHEADS	ADEHNTTU UNHATTED	ADEILLRS DALLIERS	ADEILRRY DREARILY
ADEHINPU DAUPHINE	ADEHNTUW UNTHAWED	DIALLERS	ADEILRST DILATERS
ADEHINRU UNHAIRED	ADEHOOPS APEHOODS	ADEILLRV RIVALLED	LARDIEST
ADEHINSS SHANDIES	ADEHOORW HAREWOOD	ADEILMMS DILEMMAS	ADEILRSU RESIDUAL
ADEHINST HANDIEST	ADEHOORY HOORAYED	ADEILMNP PLAIDMEN	ADEILRSY DIALYSER
ADEHINSV VANISHED	ADEHOPRS RHAPSODE	ADEILMNU UNMAILED	ADEILRTT DETRITAL
ADEHIOTT ATHETOID	ADEHOPST POTASHED	ADEILMNY MAIDENLY	ADEILRTY DIELYTRA
ADEHIPRS RAPHIDES	ADEHOPSX HEXAPODS	ADEILMOS DAMOISEL	ADEILRVY VARIEDLY
ADEHIPST PITHEADS	ADEHOPXY HEXAPODY	ADEILMPP PALMIPED	ADEILRYZ DIALYZER
ADEHIRSS RADISHES	ADEHORRS HOARDERS	ADEILMPR IMPARLED	ADEILSSU DEASIULS
ADEHIRST HAIRSTED	ADEHORRW HARROWED	ADEILMPS IMPLEADS	ADEILSSV DEVISALS
HARDIEST	ADEHORSW SHADOWER	MISPLEAD	ADEILSSY DIALYSES
ADEHIRSV RAVISHED	ADEHORTT THROATED	ADEILMPT IMPLATED	ADEILSTV VALIDEST
ADEHIRSW RAWHIDES	ADEHORTU AUTHORED	ADEILMRY DREAMILY	ADEILSTY DIASTYLE
ADEHIRVW HIVEWARD	ADEHQSSU SQUASHED	ADEILMSS MAIDLESS	STEADILY
ADEHISST SHADIEST	ADEHRRUY HURRAYED	MISDEALS	ADEILSUV DISVALUE
ADEHJLOT JOLTHEAD	ADEHRSTY HYDRATES	MISLEADS	ADEILSXY DYSLEXIA
ADEHKLNU LUNKHEAD	ADEHRTTW THWARTED	ADEILMST MISDEALT	ADEILSYZ DIALYZES
ADEHKNRS REDSHANK	ADEIILMN LIMNAEID	ADEILMSY DYSMELIA	ADEILTTU ALTITUDE
ADEHKNSU UNSHAKED	ADEIILMS IDEALISM	ADEILNNR INLANDER	LATITUDE
ADEHKORS HARDOKES	MILADIES	ADEILNNS ANNELIDS	ADEIMMNS MISNAMED
ADEHKORW HEADWORK	ADEIILPR PERIDIAL	LINDANES	ADEIMMNU UNMAIMED
ADEHKOST KATHODES	ADEIILRS LAIRISED	ADEILNNU UNNAILED	ADEIMMRS MERMAIDS
ADEHLLOO HALLOOED	ADEIILRZ LAIRIZED	ADEILNOP PALINODE	ADEIMMST MISMATED
HOLLOAED	ADEIILST IDEALIST	ADEILNOS NODALISE	ADEIMNNO DEMONIAN
ADEHLLOW HALLOWED	ADEIILTV DILATIVE	ADEILNOT DELATION	MONDAINE
ADEHLLRT THRALLED	ADEIILTY IDEALITY	ADEILNOZ NODALIZE	ADEIMNOP DOPAMINE
ADEHLLRW HELLWARD	ADEIIMMS MISAIMED	ADEILNPT PANTILED	ADEIMNOS NOMADIES
ADEHLMNO HOMELAND	ADEIIMNR MERIDIAN	ADEILNPU PALUDINE	NOMADISE
ADEHLMOY HOLYDAME	ADEIIMNT MINIATED	ADEILNRS ISLANDER	ADEIMNOT DOMINATE
ADEHLNRS HANDLERS	ADEIIMPR IMPAIRED	ADEILNSU UNSAILED	NEMATOID
ADEHLNSS HANDLESS	ADEIIMTT IMITATED	ADEILNSV ANDVILES	ADEIMNOZ NOMADIZE
HANDSELS	ADEIINNS SANIDINE	ADEILNTU UNTAILED	ADEIMNPW IMPAWNED
ADEHLNST SHETLAND	ADEIINOT IDEATION	ADEILNTV DIVALENT	ADEIMNRR MANRIDER
ADEHLNSU UNHALSED	TAENIOID	ADEILNUV UNVAILED	ADEIMNRS ADERMINS
UNLASHED	ADEIINRS DRAISINE	ADEILOPS EPISODAL	SIRNAMED
UNSHALED	ADEIINRT DAINTIER	OPALISED	ADEIMNRY DAIRYMEN
ADEHLOPS ASPHODEL	ADEIINRU UREDINIA	SEPALOID	ADEIMNRZ ZEMINDAR
PHOLADES	ADEIINST ADENITIS	ADEILOPT PETALOID	ADEIMNSS SIDESMAN
ADEHLPSS SPLASHED	DAINTIES	ADEILOPZ OPALIZED	ADEIMNST MEDIANTS
ADEHLRRY HERALDRY	ADEIINUV INDUVIAE	ADEILOQU ODALIQUE	ADEIMNSU MAUNDIES
ADEHMNNY HANDYMEN	ADEIIPRR PERRADII	ADEILORS DARIOLES	ADEIMNSY DYNAMISE
ADEHMNOS HANDSOME	PRAIRIED	SOLIDARE	ADEIMNTY DYNAMITE
ADEHMNOT METHADON	ADEIIPRS PRESIDIA	SOREDIAL	ADEIMNYZ DYNAMIZE
THANEDOM	ADEIIPST STAPEDII	ADEILORT IDOLATER	ADEIMORR AIRDROME
ADEHMNRS HERDSMAN	ADEIIRSS DIARISES	TAILORED	ADEIMORT MEDIATOR
ADEHMNRU UNHARMED	ADEIIRST IRISATED	ADEILORV OVERLAID	ADEIMOSS SESAMOID
ADEHMNSU UNSHAMED	ADEIIRSZ DIARIZES	ADEILORX EXORDIAL	ADEIMOST ATOMISED
ADEHMOOP OOMPAHED	ADEIITTV TIDIVATE	ADEILOSS ASSOILED	ADEIMOTZ ATOMIZED

ADEIMPRR	RAMPIRED		RUINATED	ADEJOPRY	JEOPARDY	ADELNSTU	UNSALTED
ADEIMPRT	IMPARTED		URINATED	ADEJRSTU	ADJUSTER	ADELNSTW	WETLANDS
ADEIMPRV	VAMPIRED	ADEINRUV	UNVARIED		READJUST	ADELNTUU	UNDULATE
ADEIMPST	DAMPIEST	ADEINRVY	VINEYARD	ADEKLMRY	MARKEDLY	ADELNUUV	UNVALUED
	IMPASTED	ADEINSST	SANDIEST	ADEKLNPP	KNAPPLED	ADELNUZZ	UNDAZZLE
ADEIMRRS	ADMIRERS	ADEINSSW	WINDASES	ADEKLNPR	PRANKLED	ADELOORV	OVERLOAD
	DISARMER	ADEINSTT	INSTATED	ADEKLNSU	UNSLAKED	ADELOOWW	WOODWALE
ADEIMRSS	MISREADS	ADEINSTU	AUDIENTS	ADEKLPRS	SPARKLED	ADELOPPR	PROPALED
	SIDEARMS		SINUATED	ADEKMNRU	UNMARKED	ADELOPRS	LEOPARDS
ADEIMRST	MARDIEST	ADEINSTV	DEVIANTS	ADEKMNSU	UNMASKED	ADELOPRT	PROLATED
	MISRATED	ADEINSTY	DESYATIN	ADEKMORS	DARKSOME	ADELOPSS	DEPOSALS
	READMITS	ADEIOPRS	DIASPORE	ADEKNNSS	DANKNESS	ADELOPST	TADPOLES
ADEIMRTU	MURIATED		PARODIES	ADEKNRSS	DARKNESS	ADELOPSU	PALUDOSE
ADEIMSST	MISDATES	ADEIOPRV	OVERPAID	ADEKNSVY	VANDYKES	ADELOPSY	SEPALODY
ADEIMSTU	TAEDIUMS	ADEIOPST	DIOPTASE	ADEKQSUW	SQUAWKED	ADELOPTY	PETALODY
ADEIMSTY	DAYTIMES	ADEIOPTV	ADOPTIVE	ADELLMOR	MORALLED	ADELORRV	OVERLARD
ADEINNNS	NANDINES	ADEIORRT	ADROITER	ADELLMOS	SLALOMED	ADELORSS	ROADLESS
ADEINNOT	ANOINTED	ADEIORST	ASTEROID	ADELLMRU	MEDULLAR	ADELORST	DELATORS
	ANTINODE	ADEIORTT	TERATOID	ADELLMSU	MEDULLAS		LEOTARDS
ADEINNPT	PINNATED	ADEIORTV	DEVIATOR	ADELLNNU	ANNULLED		LODESTAR
ADEINNPU	UNPAINED	ADEIOSSX	OXIDASES	ADELLNPS	SPENDALL	ADELORSU	ROULADES
ADEINNRS	INSNARED	ADEIOSTX	OXIDATES	ADELLNRS	LANDLERS	ADELOSSW	DOWLASES
ADEINNRZ	RENDZINA	ADEIOSTZ	AZOTISED	ADELLNSS	LANDLESS	ADELOSTV	SOLVATED
ADEINNSU	UNSAINED	ADEIOSVV	VAIVODES	ADELLNSW	ELLWANDS	ADELOTUV	OVULATED
ADEINNSX	DISANNEX	ADEIOSVW	WAIVODES		WALLSEND	ADELOTUW	OUTLAWED
ADEINNTU	INUNDATE	ADEIOSWW	WAIWODES	ADELLNUW	UNWALLED	ADELOVWY	AVOWEDLY
ADEINOPT	ANTIPODE	ADEIOTZZ	AZOTIZED	ADELLOPW	WALLOPED	ADELPPRY	DAPPERLY
ADEINORR	ORDAINER	ADEIPPRS	APPRISED	ADELLORS	ODALLERS	ADELPRRU	LARRUPED
	REORDAIN		DRAPPIES	ADELLOSW	SALLOWED	ADELPRSW	SPRAWLED
ADEINORS	ANEROIDS	ADEIPPRZ	APPRIZED	ADELLOTT	ALLOTTED	ADELPRTT	PRATTLED
	DONARIES	ADEIPRRS	DRAPIERS		TOTALLED	ADELPSTT	SPLATTED
ADEINORT	AROINTED	ADEIPRSS	DESPAIRS	ADELLOTV	LAVOLTED	ADELPSTU	PULSATED
	DERATION	ADEIPRST	RAPIDEST	ADELLOTW	TALLOWED	ADELPUUV	UPVALUED
	ORDINATE		SPIRATED	ADELLOWW	WALLOWED	ADELRRSU	RUDERALS
	RATIONED		TRAIPSED	ADELLQSU	SQUALLED	ADELRRSW	DRAWLERS
ADEINORU	DOUANIER	ADEIPRSU	UPRAISED	ADELLRSU	UDALLERS	ADELRRTU	ULTRARED
ADEINOSS	ADONISES	ADEIPRTU	EUPATRID	ADELLTUU	UMLAUTED	ADELRSTT	STARTLED
	ANODISES	ADEIPSTV	VAPIDEST	ADELMNNS	LANDSMEN	ADELRSZZ	DAZZLERS
ADEINOST	ASTONIED	ADEIPTTU	APTITUDE	ADELMNOS	LODESMAN	ADELRTUY	ADULTERY
	SEDATION	ADEIQRRU	QUARRIED	ADELMNRS	MANDRELS	ADELSTTY	STATEDLY
ADEINOSX	DIOXANES	ADEIQSUY	QUAYSIDE	ADELMORS	EARLDOMS	ADELTTTW	TWATTLED
ADEINOSZ	ADONIZES	ADEIRRSW	SWARDIER	ADELMOSS	DAMOSELS	ADEMMNOW	MADWOMEN
	ANODIZES	ADEIRRTW	TAWDRIER	ADELMOSZ	DAMOZELS	ADEMMSTU	SUMMATED
ADEINOTT	ANTIDOTE	ADEIRRWW	WIREDRAW	ADELMOTU	MODULATE	ADEMNNNU	UNMANNED
	TETANOID	ADEIRRZZ	RIZZARED	ADELMPRT	TRAMPLED	ADEMNNOU	UNMOANED
ADEINOTV	DONATIVE	ADEIRSST	ASTERIDS	ADELMRRU	DEMURRAL	ADEMNNRU	MUNDANER
ADEINPPX	APPENDIX		DIASTERS	ADELMSUY	AMUSEDLY		UNDERMAN
ADEINPRS	SPRAINED		DISASTER	ADELMTUU	UMLAUTED	ADEMNOOR	MAROONED
ADEINPRT	DIPTERAN		DISRATES	ADELNNNU	UNNANELD	ADEMNOPR	POMANDER
ADEINPRU	UNPAIRED	ADEIRSSU	RADIUSES	ADELNNOT	LENTANDO	ADEMNOPT	TAMPONED
	UNREPAID		SUDARIES	ADELNOPR	PONDERAL	ADEMNORS	RANSOMED
ADEINPST	DEPAINTS	ADEIRSSV	ADVISERS	ADELNORS	LADRONES		ROADSMEN
ADEINPSV	SPAVINED	ADEIRSTT	STRAITED		SOLANDER	ADEMNOTU	AMOUNTED
ADEINQTU	ANTIQUED		STRIATED	ADELNORU	UNLOADER		OUTNAMED
ADEINRRS	DRAINERS		TARDIEST		URODELAN	ADEMNPSS	DAMPNESS
	SERRANID	ADEIRSTW	TAWDRIES	ADELNORV	OVERLAND	ADEMNRRU	UNDERARM
ADEINRSS	ARIDNESS	ADEIRTTT	TITRATED		RONDAVEL		UNMARRED
	SARDINES	ADEIRVWY	DRIVEWAY	ADELNOSY	YEALDONS	ADEMNRSU	DURAMENS
ADEINRST	DETRAINS	ADEISSST	ASSISTED	ADELNPRS	SPANDREL		MAUNDERS
	RANDIEST		DISSEATS	ADELNPRU	PENDULAR		SURNAMED
	STRAINED	ADEISSTT	DISTASTE		UNDERLAP	ADEMNRTU	UNDREAMT
ADEINRSU	DENARIUS		STAIDEST		UPLANDER	ADEMNRUW	UNWARMED
	UNRAISED	ADEISSWY	SIDEWAYS	ADELNPRY	PANDERLY	ADEMNSSU	MEDUSANS
	URANIDES		WAYSIDES	ADELNPSY	DYSPNEAL	ADEMNSUU	UNAMUSED
ADEINRSV	INVADERS	ADEISTTU	SITUATED	ADELNRSS	SLANDERS	ADEMOORT	MODERATO
	SANDIVER	ADEITTTU	ATTITUDE	ADELNRSU	LAUNDERS	ADEMOOST	STOMODEA
ADEINRSY	SYNEDRIA		ATTUITED		LURDANES	ADEMOOSV	VAMOOSED
ADEINRTT	NITRATED	ADEJLOSU	JALOUSED		RUNDALES	ADEMOPST	STAMPEDO
ADEINRTU	DATURINE	ADEJMRRU	JUMARRED	ADELNRTY	ARDENTLY	ADEMORRT	MORTARED
	INDURATE	ADEJOPRS	JEOPARDS	ADELNRUY	UNDERLAY	ADEMORRU	ARMOURED

ADEMORRW	MARROWED	ADEOPPRV	APPROVED	ADFIORSV	DISFAVOR	ADGILLNY DALLYING
ADEMORST	STROAMED	ADEOPRRS	EARDROPS	ADFKLLNO	FOLKLAND	ADGILMNS MADLINGS
ADEMPRST	STRAMPED	ADEOPRRT	PARROTED	ADFLLNOW	DOWNFALL	ADGILMNW DWALMING
ADEMRRSU	EARDRUMS		PREDATOR	ADFLMNOR	LANDFORM	ADGILMOR MARIGOLD
ADEMRRTY	MARTYRED		PRORATED	ADFLMNOY	MANYFOLD	ADGILNNS LANDINGS
ADENNNTU	UNTANNED	ADEOPRRU	UPROARED	ADFLMOPR	FRAMPOLD	SANDLING
ADENNOSY	ANODYNES	ADEOPRST	ADOPTERS	ADFLNOPS	PLAFONDS	ADGILNNU UNLADING
ADENNOTU	UNATONED		ASPORTED	ADFLOOWY	FLOODWAY	ADGILNOS LOADINGS
ADENNOTW	WANTONED		READOPTS	ADFLORSU	FOULARDS	ADGILNPP DAPPLING
ADENNPST	PENDANTS	ADEOPRTT	TETRAPOD	ADFNNOST	FONDANTS	ADGILNRS DARLINGS
ADENNRRU	UNDERRAN	ADEOPRUV	VAPOURED	ADFNOORZ	FORZANDO	ADGILNRT DARTLING
ADENNRTY	TYRANNED	ADEOPSST	PODESTAS	ADFOOPST	FOOTPADS	ADGILNRW DRAWLING
ADENNRUW	UNWARNED	ADEOPSTT	DESPOTAT	ADFORRSW	FORWARDS	ADGILNRY DARINGLY
ADENNSTU	ASTUNNED		POSTDATE		FROWARDS	ADGILNZZ DAZZLING
ADENNTUW	UNWANTED	ADEORRSS	DROSERAS	ADGGGILN	DAGGLING	ADGILOPR PRODIGAL
ADENOOPS	EPANODOS	ADEORRST	ROADSTER	ADGGGINR	DRAGGING	ADGILORS GOLIARDS
ADENOORT	RATOONED	ADEORRTW	TARROWED	ADGGHNOS	HANGDOGS	ADGILORY GOLIARDY
ADENOORW	WANDEROO	ADEORRVW	OVERDRAW	ADGGILNN	DANGLING	GYROIDAL
ADENOPRR	PARDONER	ADEORSST	ASSORTED	ADGGILNS	GADLINGS	ADGIMMNR DRAMMING
ADENOPRS	OPERANDS		TORSADES	ADGGILRS	RIGGALDS	ADGIMMNW DWAMMING
	PANDORES	ADEORSTU	OUTDARES	ADGGINRS	NIGGARDS	ADGIMMNU MAUNDING
ADENOPRT	PRONATED	ADEORSTX	EXTRADOS	ADGGINRU	GUARDING	ADGIMNOP POMADING
ADENOPRX	EXPANDOR	ADEORSUV	SAVOURED	ADGGLRSU	SLUGGARD	ADGIMNPS DAMPINGS
ADENOPSS	DAPSONES	ADEORSWY	RODEWAYS	ADGHHILN	HIGHLAND	ADGIMNRS MRIDANGS
	SPADONES	ADEORTTU	OUTRATED	ADGHHIOR	HIGHROAD	ADGIMNRY MARDYING
ADENOPSU	UNSOAPED	ADEOSSTT	ASSOTTED	ADGHILNN	HANDLING	ADGIMNUW DWAUMING
ADENOPSY	DYSPNOEA	ADEOSTTU	OUTDATES	ADGHILOS	HIDALGOS	ADGIMOSU DIGAMOUS
ADENORRW	NARROWED	ADEOTTTW	TATTOWED	ADGHILPY	DIAGLYPH	ADGINNOR ADORNING
ADENORST	TORNADES	ADEPPRST	STRAPPED	ADGHILTY	DAYLIGHT	ADGINNOT DONATING
ADENORTT	ATTORNED	ADEPRRTU	RAPTURED	ADGHINOR	HOARDING	ADGINNPY PANDYING
ADENORTY	AROYNTED	ADEPRSTU	PASTURED	ADGHINPR	HANDGRIP	ADGINNRS DARNINGS
ADENORUX	RONDEAUX		UPSTARED	ADGHINSS	SHADINGS	ADGINNRT DRANTING
ADENOSST	ONSTEADS	ADEPSTUY	UPSTAYED	ADGHIPRS	DIGRAPHS	ADGINNSS SANDINGS
ADENOTUY	AUTODYNE	ADEPSUWY	UPSWAYED	ADGHIRRS	ARDRIGHS	ADGINNST STANDING
ADENOUVW	UNAVOWED	ADEQSTTU	SQUATTED	ADGHITTW	TIGHTWAD	ADGINNSW DAWNINGS
ADENPPRS	PARPENDS	ADERRSSW	WARDRESS	ADGHLNNO	LONGHAND	ADGINNSY SDAYNING
ADENPPSU	UNSAPPED	ADERRSST	REDSTART	ADGHNOSW	HAGDOWNS	ADGINNTU DAUNTING
ADENPPTU	UNTAPPED	ADERSSSU	ASSUREDS	ADGHOOPR	ODOGRAPH	ADGINOOP POIGNADO
ADENPRRS	PARDNERS	ADERSSTW	STEWARDS	ADGHORSW	HOGWARDS	ADGINOOR RIGADOON
ADENPRSU	UNSPARED	ADERSSUY	DASYURES	ADGHPSYY	DYSPHAGY	ADGINOPT ADOPTING
ADENPRTU	DEPURANT	ADERSTTU	STATURED	ADGHRSTU	DRAUGHTS	ADGINORS ROADINGS
ADENPRTY	PEDANTRY	ADERSTUX	SURTAXED	ADGHRTUY	DRAUGHTY	ADGINOST DOATINGS
ADENPRUW	UNWARPED	ADERSTWW	WESTWARD	ADGIILLN	DIALLING	ADGINOTY TOADYING
ADENPRUY	UNDERPAY	ADESSTTW	WADSETTS	ADGIILLO	GLADIOLI	ADGINPPR DRAPPING
	UNPRAYED	ADFFGIIR	GIRAFFID	ADGIILNO	GONIDIAL	ADGINPTU UPDATING
ADENPSSY	DYSPNEAS	ADFFGINS	DAFFINGS	ADGIILNP	PLAIDING	ADGINRST TRADINGS
ADENQRSU	SQUANDER	ADFFHIRS	DRAFFISH	ADGIILNR	DRAILING	ADGINRSW DRAWINGS
ADENRRSY	REYNARDS	ADFFISST	DISTAFFS	ADGIILNS	GLIADINS	SWARDING
ADENRRTU	UNTARRED	ADFFLOOS	OFFLOADS	ADGIILNT	DILATING	WARDINGS
ADENRRWY	WARDENRY	ADFFLRUU	FRAUDFUL	ADGIILPY	PYGIDIAL	ADGINRTY TARDYING
ADENRSSS	SARSDENS	ADFFOORS	AFFOORDS	ADGIILST	DIGITALS	ADGINSTU ADUSTING
ADENRSST	STANDERS	ADFGINNU	UNFADING	ADGIILTY	ALGIDITY	SUDATING
ADENRSSU	DANSEURS	ADFGINRS	FARDINGS	ADGIIMNR	ADMIRING	ADGINSWY GWYNIADS
ADENRSTU	DAUNTERS	ADFGINRT	DRAFTING	ADGIIMNX	ADMIXING	ADGIPRSU PAGURIDS
	TRANSUDE	ADFGINRW	DWARFING	ADGIIMST	DIGAMIST	ADGIRSSU GUISARDS
	UNTREADS	ADFHIOST	TOADFISH	ADGIINNR	DRAINING	ADGIRSZZ GIZZARDS
ADENRSTX	DEXTRANS	ADFHIRSW	DWARFISH	ADGIINNS	SDAINING	ADGKOOSZ GADZOOKS
ADENRSUY	UNDERSAY	ADFHLNSU	HANDFULS	ADGIINNV	INVADING	ADGLLNOS GOLLANDS
ADENRTTU	TRUANTED	ADFHLOST	HOLDFAST	ADGIINNY	DIGYNIAN	ADGLMNOS MANGOLDS
ADENRTTY	TYRANTED	ADFHOOSS	SHADOOFS	ADGIINOR	RADIOING	ADGLNOOS GONDOLAS
ADENRUWY	UNDERWAY	ADFIILPY	LAPIDIFY	ADGIINOV	AVOIDING	ADGLNOSW GOWLANDS
ADENSTTU	UNSTATED	ADFILLLN	LANDFILL	ADGIINRR	ARRIDING	ADGLOORY GARDYLOO
	UNTASTED	ADFILLMN	FILMLAND	ADGIINRY	DAIRYING	ADGMNORS GORMANDS
ADENSTUW	UNWASTED	ADFILLNW	WINDFALL	ADGIINSU	IGUANIDS	ADGMNORU GOURMAND
ADENSTUY	UNSTAYED	ADFILMNO	MANIFOLD	ADGIINSV	ADVISING	ADGNNOQU QUANDONG
	UNSTEADY	ADFIMNRS	FINDRAMS	ADGIINSW	GWINIADS	ADGNNORS GRANDSON
ADENSUWY	UNSWAYED	ADFIMORY	FAIRYDOM	ADGIINTU	AUDITING	ADGNNRYY GYNANDRY
ADEOOPSS	APODOSES	ADFIMRSW	DWARFISM	ADGIJNRU	ADJURING	ADGNOORS DRAGOONS
ADEOORRT	TOREADOR	ADFINORZ	FORZANDI	ADGIKLNR	DARKLING	GADROONS
ADEOOTTT	TATTOOED	ADFINRST	INDRAFTS	ADGILLNU	ALLUDING	ADGNRRSU GURNARDS

ADGNRSUU UNGUARDS	INDUVIAL	ADILNOOV VINDALOO	ADINOPRS PONIARDS
ADGOOPRS GOSPODAR	ADIILOPP DIPLOPIA	ADILNOPY PALINODY	ADINOPST PINTADOS
ADGORTUU OUTGUARD	ADIILSST DIALISTS	ADILNORS ORDINALS	ADINORRS ORDINARS
ADHHIPRS HARDSHIP	ADIILSSY DIALYSIS	ADILNOTY NODALITY	ADINORRY ORDINARY
ADHHNRTY HYDRANTH	ADIILTVY VALIDITY	ADILNPRS SPANDRIL	ADINORST INTRADOS
ADHIIKSS DASHIKIS	ADIIMMSS MAIDISMS	ADILNPST DISPLANT	ADINORSU DINOSAUR
ADHIINOP OPHIDIAN	ADIIMPSU ASPIDIUM	ADILNRSU DIURNALS	ADINORSV VIRANDOS
ADHIINRW WHINIARD	ADIIMRSU MUDIRIAS	ADILNRWY INWARDLY	ADINORTU DURATION
ADHILLMO HOLLIDAM	ADIINNOT NIDATION	ADILNSSU SUNDIALS	ADINOSTU SUDATION
ADHILLOP PHALLOID	ADIINOTU AUDITION	ADILNSSW WINDLASS	ADINOSTX OXIDANTS
ADHILLOT THALLOID	ADIINPRS PINDARIS	ADILOORT TOROIDAL	ADINRRST TRIDARNS
ADHILMOO HOMALOID	ADIINNST DISTRAIN	ADILOPRT TRIPODAL	ADINRSSU SUNDARIS
ADHILMOS HALIDOMS	ADIINSST DISTAINS	ADILOPSS DISPOSAL	ADINRUVZ UNVIZARD
ADHILNST HANDLIST	ADIIOPRS SPORIDIA	ADILOQSU SQUALOID	ADIOOPSS APODOSIS
ADHILOPY HAPLOIDY	ADIIOPRT TAPIROID	ADILORST DILATORS	ADIOPRSS SPAROIDS
ADHILOSY HOLIDAYS	ADIIORST TARSIOID	ADILORSY SOLIDARY	ADIOPRST PARODIST
ADHILPSY LADYSHIP	ADIIPRTU TRIPUDIA	ADILORTY ADROITLY	PAROTIDS
ADHIMNOS ADMONISH	ADIIPRTY RAPIDITY	DILATORY	ADIOPRSV PRIVADOS
ADHIMNOU HUMANOID	ADIIPSTY SAPIDITY	IDOLATRY	ADIOPRTY PODIATRY
ADHIMOPP AMPHIPOD	ADIIPTVY VAPIDITY	ADILOSTW WILDOATS	ADIOPSTY DYSTOPIA
ADHIMPSS PHASMIDS	ADIIRSST DIARISTS	ADILOSTY SODALITY	ADIORRTT TRADITOR
ADHIMRTY MYRIADTH	ADIIRSTT DISTRAIT	ADILPPSY DISAPPLY	ADIORSST ASTROIDS
ADHINPSU DAUPHINS	TRIADIST	ADILPRSY PYRALIDS	ADIORSTU AUDITORS
ADHINRWY WHINYARD	ADIJNOST ADJOINTS	ADILPSST PLASTIDS	ADIORSVY ADVISORY
ADHINSST STANDISH	ADIKKRRW KIRKWARD	ADILPSSY DISPLAYS	ADIORTUY AUDITORY
ADHINSSY SANDYISH	ADIKKRRY KIRKYARD	ADILPSTU PLAUDITS	ADIOSSVW DISAVOWS
ADHINSTU DIANTHUS	ADIKLNPS LANDSKIP	ADILRTWY TAWDRILY	ADIPRRTU PURTRAID
ADHIOSTY TOADYISH	ADIKLNSY LADYKINS	ADILRWYZ WIZARDLY	ADIPRSST DISPARTS
ADHIPRSW WARDSHIP	ADIKLOSS ODALISKS	ADILSSTU DUALISTS	ADIRRWYZ WIZARDRY
ADHIPRSY SHIPYARD	ADIKMNNS MANKINDS	ADIMMNOO AMMONOID	ADIRSSTY SATYRIDS
ADHIPSTY DISPATHY	ADIKMSSS DISMASKS	ADIMMNOS MONADISM	ADIRSSUY DYSURIAS
ADHIRTWW WITHDRAW	ADIKNNNU DUNNAKIN	NOMADISM	ADJNORSU ADJOURNS
ADHKNORW HANDWORK	ADIKNNST INKSTAND	ADIMMNSY DYNAMISM	ADJORSTU ADJUSTOR
ADHKORSW DORHAWKS	ADIKNPSS SKIDPANS	ADIMMOST AMIDMOST	ADKKLOSY KAKODYLS
ADHKOSSU SHAKUDOS	ADIKNRSS DISRANKS	ADIMMOTU DOMATIUM	ADKLMRSU MUDLARKS
ADHLLNOS HOLLANDS	ADIKNRST STINKARD	ADIMNNOS MONDAINS	ADKLOORW WORKLOAD
ADHLMORT THRALDOM	ADIKPRSS DISPARKS	ADIMNNOT DOMINANT	ADKMOORR DARKROOM
ADHLMOSY HOLYDAMS	ADILLLPY PALLIDLY	ADIMNOOR MAINDOOR	ADKNORTU OUTDRANK
ADHLMPSY LYMPHADS	ADILLMMS MILLDAMS	ADIMNOST DONATISM	ADKNRSTU STUNKARD
ADHLNORW WALDHORN	ADILLMNR MANDRILL	SAINTDOM	ADKRSSWY SKYWARDS
ADHMNOOS MANHOODS	ADILLMOU ALLODIUM	ADIMNRSW MISDRAWN	ADLLMOSW WADMOLLS
ADHNNOOR HONORAND	ADILLMOV VILLADOM	ADIMNRSY MISANDRY	ADLLNOSW LOWLANDS
ADHNORSU UNHOARDS	ADILLMSY DISMALLY	ADIMNSTY DYNAMIST	ADLLOPRS POLLARDS
ADHNOSTU HANDOUTS	ADILLNPS LANDSLIP	ADIMOPRY MYRIAPOD	ADLLORSY DORSALLY
THOUSAND	ADILLOPS SPADILLO	ADIMOPSY SYMPODIA	ADLMNOOR MOORLAND
ADHNOSUW UNSHADOW	ADILLOSW DISALLOW	ADIMORRS MIRADORS	ADLMNORY RANDOMLY
ADHNRSTY HYDRANTS	ADILLOSY DISLOYAL	ADIMOSST MASTOIDS	ADLMNOSS MOSSLAND
ADHOOPRS HOSPODAR	ADILLRWY WILLYARD	ADIMOSTT MATTOIDS	ADLMOORU MALODOUR
ADHOORRS RHODORAS	ADILLSTY DISTALLY	ADIMOSTY TOADYISM	ADLMOPRW MOLDWARP
ADHOORSW ROADSHOW	ADILMMOS MODALISM	ADIMPRSY PYRAMIDS	ADLMOPSY PSALMODY
ADHOORYZ HYDROZOA	ADILMNNO MANDOLIN	ADIMRSSW MISDRAWS	ADLNNORS NORLANDS
ADHOPRST HARDTOPS	ADILMNOS SALMONID	ADIMRSUU SUDARIUM	ADLNNOTW TOWNLAND
ADHOPRSU UPHOARDS	ADILMNRS MANDRILS	ADIMSSST DISMASTS	ADLNNTUU UNDULANT
ADHOPRSY RHAPSODY	ADILMOOR MODIOLAR	ADIMSSTU DUMAISTS	ADLNOORS LARDOONS
ADHORSTU TOADRUSH	ADILMOPS DIPLOMAS	STADIUMS	ADLNOPRT PORTLAND
ADHPSTYY DYSPATHY	ADILMOPT DIPLOMAT	ADINNNTU INUNDANT	ADLNOPRU PAULDRON
ADIIINRV VIRIDIAN	ADILMOPY OLYMPIAD	ADINNOOT DONATION	ADLNOPSU POUNDALS
ADIIIQRU DAIQUIRI	ADILMORU ORDALIUM	NOTATION	ADLNORWY ONWARDLY
ADIIKLMM MILKMAID	ADILMOST MODALIST	ADINNOPS DIPNOANS	ADLNOSSU SOULDANS
ADIIKLST TAILSKID	ADILMOSU ALODIUMS	ADINNORS ANDIRONS	ADLNOSSY SYNODALS
ADIIKNOP PINAKOID	ADILMOSY AMYLOIDS	ADINNORT ORDINANT	ADLNOSTU OUTLANDS
ADIIKOST DAKOITIS	ADILMOTY MODALITY	ADINNOTU NUDATION	ADLOORWW WOOLWARD
ADIILLMR MILLIARD	ADILMPSS PLASMIDS	ADINNRSY INNYARDS	ADLOPRSU POULARDS
ADIILLNY IDYLLIAN	ADILMPSU PALUDISM	ADINOOPS ISOPODAN	ADLOPSUU PALUDOUS
ADIILLUV DILUVIAL	ADILMSSU DUALISMS	POINADOS	ADLOQSUW OLDSQUAW
ADIILNOT DILATION	ADILMSSY DISMAYLS	ADINOOPT ADOPTION	ADLORRSW WARLORDS
ADIILNSU INDUSIAL	LADYISMS	ADINOORT TANDOORI	ADLORTWY TOWARDLY
ADIILNSV INVALIDS	ADILNNNU NUNDINAL	ADINOOTT DOTATION	ADLPRUWY UPWARDLY
ADIILNTY DAINTILY	ADILNNSU DISANNUL	ADINOPPS OPPIDANS	
ADIILNUV DILUVIAN	ADILNOOR DOORNAIL	ADINOPRR RAINDROP	

ADMMNOOS	DOOMSMAN	
ADMMNSSU	SUMMANDS	
ADMMNTUU	MUTANDUM	
ADMNNORY	MONANDRY	
ADMNNOTU	NOTANDUM	
ADMNOOOT	ODONTOMA	
ADMNOORS	MADRONOS	
ADMNOOST	MASTODON	
ADMNOOSW	WOODSMAN	
ADMNOOSZ	MADZOONS	
ADMNORST	DORMANTS	
	MORDANTS	
ADMNORSW	SWORDMAN	
ADMNOSSU	OSMUNDAS	
ADMOORST	DOORMATS	
ADMOPPPU	POPPADUM	
ADMOPPSU	POPADUMS	
ADMORSST	STARDOMS	
	TSARDOMS	
ADMORSTW	MADWORTS	
ADMRSSTU	DURMASTS	
	MUSTARDS	
ADNNOOSY	NOONDAYS	
ADNNORTY	DYNATRON	
ADNNOSTU	DAUNTONS	
ADNOOPRS	PANDOORS	
	SPADROON	
ADNOOQRU	QUADROON	
ADNOORST	DONATORS	
ADNOORTY	DONATORY	
ADNOOSVW	ADVOWSON	
ADNOPRSU	PANDOURS	
ADNOPRSV	PROVANDS	
ADNOQRSU	SQUADRON	
ADNORRSW	NORWARDS	
ADNORSTU	ROTUNDAS	
ADNORSTW	SANDWORT	
ADNORSWY	NAYWORDS	
ADNORSXY	SARDONYX	
ADNORTUW	UNTOWARD	
ADNORWWY	WANWORDY	
ADNOSSTU	ASTOUNDS	
ADNOSTTU	OUTSTAND	
ADNPSSTU	UPSTANDS	
ADNRSSUW	SUNWARDS	
ADOOPRSU	SAUROPOD	
ADOOPSSW	SAPWOODS	
ADOORSWY	DOORWAYS	
ADOPRRSW	WARDROPS	
ADOPRSSW	PASSWORD	
ADORRSTU	DARTROUS	
ADORSTUW	OUTWARDS	
ADORSTUY	SUDATORY	
ADORTUVY	ADVOUTRY	
ADPRRTUY	PURTRAYD	
ADSSSTUW	SAWDUSTS	
ADSSTUWY	SAWDUSTY	
AEEEELRS	RELEASEE	
AEEEFLRS	EELFARES	
AEEEFRTY	AFTEREYE	
AEEEGKLS	KEELAGES	
AEEEGLLS	LEGALESE	
AEEEGLNR	GENERALE	
AEEEGLRT	EGLATERE	
	REGELATE	
	RELEGATE	
AEEEGLRV	LEVERAGE	
AEEEGLST	LEGATEES	
AEEEGLSV	SELVAGEE	
AEEEGNRT	GENERATE	

	RENEGATE	
	TEENAGER	
AEEEGPRS	PEERAGES	
AEEEGPSS	SEEPAGES	
AEEEGRST	ETAGERES	
	STEERAGE	
AEEEGRSW	SEWERAGE	
AEEEGTTV	VEGETATE	
AEEEHLRT	ETHEREAL	
AEEEHMPR	EPHEMERA	
AEEEHNRS	ENHEARSE	
AEEEHRRS	REHEARSE	
AEEEHRRT	REHEATER	
AEEEHSTT	AESTHETE	
AEEEILNS	ALIENEES	
AEEEIMNX	EXAMINEE	
AEEEIRST	EATERIES	
AEEEJNTT	JEANETTE	
AEEEKKPS	KEEPSAKE	
AEEEKMSS	KAMEESES	
AEEEKMSZ	KAMEEZES	
AEEEKNRW	WEAKENER	
AEEELLST	TELESALE	
AEEELNRV	VENEREAL	
AEEELNST	SELENATE	
AEEELPRR	REPEALER	
AEEELQSU	SEQUELAE	
AEEELRRS	RELEASER	
AEEELRRV	REVEALER	
AEEELRSS	RELEASES	
AEEELRST	TEASELER	
AEEELRSW	WEASELER	
AEEELSTV	ELEVATES	
AEEEMMRT	METAMERE	
AEEEMNST	EASEMENT	
AEEEMPRS	PERMEASE	
AEEEMPRT	PERMEATE	
AEEENNRV	VENEREAN	
AEEENPTT	PATENTEE	
AEEENRST	SERENATE	
AEEENRTT	ENTERATE	
AEEENRTV	ENERVATE	
	VENERATE	
AEEEPRRT	REPARTEE	
	REPEATER	
AEEEPSTW	SWEETPEA	
AEEERRST	ARRESTEE	
AEEERSST	TESSERAE	
AEEFFLLS	FELAFELS	
AEEFFLRT	TAFFEREL	
AEEFFNRT	AFFERENT	
AEEFGILR	FILAGREE	
AEEFGIRR	FERRIAGE	
AEEFGIRS	FEGARIES	
AEEFGLSU	FUSELAGE	
AEEFGNST	FANTEEGS	
AEEFGRSS	SERFAGES	
AEEFGSTW	WEFTAGES	
AEEFHIRS	SHEAFIER	
AEEFHRST	FEATHERS	
AEEFHRTY	FEATHERY	
AEEFIKRR	FREAKIER	
AEEFIKRS	FAKERIES	
AEEFIKRW	WAKERIFE	
AEEFILNR	FLANERIE	
AEEFILRS	SERAFILE	
AEEFILRT	FRAILTEE	
AEEFILST	FEALTIES	
	LEAFIEST	

AEEFIPSW	SPAEWIFE	
AEEFIRRS	RAREFIES	
AEEFIRSS	FREESIAS	
AEEFISST	SAFETIES	
AEEFKMNT	FAKEMENT	
AEEFKOPR	FOREPEAK	
AEEFLLMR	FEMERALL	
AEEFLLMT	FLAMELET	
AEEFLLNV	EVENFALL	
AEEFLLRW	FAREWELL	
AEEFLLSS	LEAFLESS	
AEEFLLST	FELLATES	
	LEAFLETS	
AEEFLMOS	FLEASOME	
AEEFLMSS	FAMELESS	
AEEFLNRU	FUNEREAL	
AEEFLORV	OVERLEAF	
AEEFLRRR	REFERRAL	
AEEFLRSS	FEARLESS	
AEEFLRST	REFLATES	
AEEFLRSW	WELFARES	
AEEFMNOR	FOREMEAN	
	FORENAME	
AEEFMNRS	ENFRAMES	
AEEFMORS	FEARSOME	
AEEFMRRS	REFRAMES	
AEEFMRTY	FEMETARY	
AEEFNRST	FASTENER	
	FENESTRA	
AEEFNRTT	FATTENER	
AEEFNSSS	SAFENESS	
AEEFOSTU	FEATEOUS	
AEEFRRST	FERRATES	
AEEFRSST	FEASTERS	
AEEFRSTU	FEATURES	
AEEFRSWY	FREEWAYS	
AEEFTTUV	FAUVETTE	
AEEGGHIW	WEIGHAGE	
AEEGGINR	AGREEING	
AEEGGIRV	AGGRIEVE	
AEEGGLLS	ALLEGGES	
AEEGGLOU	AEGLOGUE	
AEEGGLRS	GREGALES	
AEEGGNNR	GANGRENE	
AEEGGNOS	GASOGENE	
AEEGGNOZ	GAZOGENE	
AEEGGNRS	ENGAGERS	
AEEGGOPS	EPAGOGES	
AEEGGPRU	PUGGAREE	
AEEGHIRT	HERITAGE	
AEEGHLOT	HELOTAGE	
AEEGHLRW	RAGWHEEL	
AEEGHMPR	GRAPHEME	
AEEGHNRS	SHAGREEN	
AEEGHNSW	WHANGEES	
AEEGHRRT	GATHERER	
	REGATHER	
AEEGIINR	AEGIRINE	
AEEGIIRT	AEGIRITE	
AEEGIIST	GAIETIES	
AEEGILLS	GALILEES	
	LEGALISE	
AEEGILLZ	LEGALIZE	
AEEGILMN	LIEGEMAN	
AEEGILMR	GLEAMIER	
AEEGILMS	MILEAGES	
AEEGILNR	ALGERINE	
AEEGILNS	ENSILAGE	
	LINEAGES	
AEEGILNT	GALENITE	

	GELATINE	
	LEGATINE	
AEEGILNV	INVEAGLE	
AEEGILPR	PERIGEAL	
AEEGILRS	GASELIER	
AEEGILST	ELEGIAST	
AEEGILSW	WEIGELAS	
AEEGILTV	LEVIGATE	
AEEGIMNR	GERMAINE	
AEEGIMNT	GEMINATE	
AEEGIMRS	GAMESIER	
AEEGIMRT	EMIGRATE	
	REMIGATE	
AEEGINPR	PERIGEAN	
AEEGINRR	REGAINER	
AEEGINRS	GESNERIA	
AEEGINRZ	RAZEEING	
AEEGINSS	ASSIGNEE	
AEEGINST	SAGENITE	
AEEGINSV	ENVISAGE	
AEEGINTV	NEGATIVE	
AEEGINTX	EXIGEANT	
AEEGIPQU	EQUIPAGE	
AEEGIPRS	PIERAGES	
AEEGIRRS	GREASIER	
AEEGIRTT	AIGRETTE	
AEEGISSS	ASSIEGES	
AEEGLLNR	ALLERGEN	
AEEGLLRS	ALLEGERS	
AEEGLLSZ	GAZELLES	
AEEGLMNS	MELANGES	
AEEGLMNV	GAVELMEN	
AEEGLMRT	TELEGRAM	
AEEGLMRY	MEAGRELY	
AEEGLNNR	ENLARGEN	
AEEGLNNT	ENTANGLE	
AEEGLNOS	GASOLENE	
AEEGLNOT	ELONGATE	
AEEGLNRR	ENLARGER	
AEEGLNRS	ENLARGES	
	GENERALS	
	GLEANERS	
AEEGLNSV	EVANGELS	
AEEGLNVY	EVANGELY	
AEEGLOST	SEGOLATE	
AEEGLPRS	PEREGALS	
AEEGLRSS	EELGRASS	
	GEARLESS	
	LARGESSE	
AEEGLRSU	LEAGUERS	
AEEGLRTU	REGULATE	
AEEGLRUX	EXERGUAL	
AEEGLSST	GATELESS	
AEEGLSSV	SELVAGES	
AEEGLSSW	WAGELESS	
AEEGLSSY	EYEGLASS	
AEEGLSTV	VEGETALS	
AEEGLTTU	TUTELAGE	
AEEGLTUV	EVULGATE	
AEEGMMOS	GAMESOME	
AEEGMMST	GEMMATES	
	TAGMEMES	
AEEGMNOR	ARGEMONE	
AEEGMNRS	AGREMENS	
AEEGMNRT	AGREMENT	
AEEGMNSS	GAMENESS	
	MAGNESES	
AEEGMNTZ	GAZEMENT	
AEEGMOST	SOMEGATE	
AEEGMRST	GAMESTER	

```
         MEAGREST     AEEHIPTT HEPATITE     AEEHNSST ANTHESES     AEEILQSU EQUALISE
AEEGMRSU REMUAGES     AEEHIPTZ APHETIZE     AEEHNSTU UNEATHES     AEEILQUX EXEQUIAL
AEEGMSSS MEGASSES              HEPATIZE     AEEHNSTW ENSWATHE     AEEILQUZ EQUALIZE
         MESSAGES     AEEHIRRS HEARSIER     AEEHORRV OVERHEAR     AEEILRRS REALISER
AEEGMSSU MESSUAGE     AEEHIRRT EARTHIER     AEEHORSS SEAHORSE     AEEILRRT RETAILER
AEEGNNNO ENNEAGON              HEARTIER              SEASHORE     AEEILRRZ REALIZER
AEEGNNPS PANGENES     AEEHIRSS ASHERIES     AEEHORTV OVERHEAT     AEEILRSS REALISES
AEEGNNRS ENRANGES     AEEHIRST HEARTIES     AEEHPRRS REPHRASE     AEEILRST ATELIERS
AEEGNNRT GENERANT     AEEHIRSV SHIVAREE     AEEHPRSS RESHAPES              EARLIEST
AEEGNNRU ENRAUNGE     AEEHISST ATHEISES              SPHAERES              LEARIEST
AEEGNNRV ENGRAVEN              ESTHESIA              SPHEARES              REALTIES
AEEGNOPS PEONAGES     AEEHISTT ATHETISE     AEEHPRST PREHEATS     AEEILRSV VELARISE
AEEGNPPS GENAPPES              HESITATE              SPREATHE     AEEILRSY YEARLIES
AEEGNRRT ETRANGER     AEEHISTV HEAVIEST     AEEHPSUV UPHEAVES     AEEILRSZ REALIZES
AEEGNRRV ENGRAVER     AEEHISTZ ATHEIZES     AEEHQSSU QUASHEES              SLEAZIER
AEEGNRST ESTRANGE     AEEHITTZ ATHETIZE     AEEHRRSS SHEARERS     AEEILRTT LATERITE
         GRANTEES     AEEHKLLR RAKEHELL     AEEHRRTU URETHRAE              LITERATE
         GREATENS     AEEHKLLU KEELHAUL     AEEHRRTW WREATHER     AEEILRTV LEVIRATE
         REAGENTS     AEEHKNRS HEARKENS     AEEHRSTT THEATERS              RELATIVE
         SEGREANT     AEEHKRSU HEUREKAS              THEATRES     AEEILRVW LIVEWARE
         SERGEANT     AEEHLLSS SEASHELL     AEEHRSTV THREAVES              REVIEWAL
         STERNAGE     AEEHLMNW WHEELMAN     AEEHRSTW WEATHERS     AEEILRVZ VELARIZE
AEEGNRSU RENAGUES     AEEHLMNY HYMENEAL              WREATHES     AEEILSST ASTELIES
AEEGNRSV AVENGERS     AEEHLMOS HEALSOME     AEEHRTVW WHATEVER     AEEILSTT AILETTES
         ENGRAVES     AEEHLMPT HELPMATE     AEEIIMRT METAIRIE     AEEILSTV ELATIVES
AEEGNRTU GAUNTREE     AEEHLNOS ENHALOES     AEEIISST ASEITIES              LEAVIEST
AEEGNSSS SAGENESS     AEEHLNPT ELEPHANT     AEEIKKLW LIKEWAKE              VEALIEST
AEEGNSTT TENTAGES     AEEHLNRT LEATHERN     AEEIKLRW WEAKLIER     AEEILSVW ALEWIVES
AEEGNSTV VENTAGES     AEEHLNSS HALENESS     AEEIKLST LEAKIEST     AEEILTTV LEVITATE
AEEGNTTV VEGETANT     AEEHLNVY HEAVENLY     AEEIKLVW WAVELIKE     AEEIMMNT MEANTIME
AEEGOPRV OVERPAGE     AEEHLORS ARSEHOLE     AEEIKMMR MERIMAKE     AEEIMNRS REMANIES
AEEGOPSS SAPEGOES     AEEHLORV OVERHALE     AEEIKNRS SNEAKIER     AEEIMNRX EXAMINER
AEEGORVV OVERGAVE     AEEHLPST PLEASETH     AEEIKNRT ANKERITE     AEEIMNSS NEMESIAS
AEEGOSTX GEOTAXES     AEEHLPTT TELEPATH              KREATINE     AEEIMNST MATINEES
AEEGPRRS ASPERGER     AEEHLRST HALTERES     AEEIKNSS AKINESES              SEMINATE
         PRESAGER              LEATHERS     AEEIKPST PEAKIEST     AEEIMNSX EXAMINES
AEEGPRRT PARGETER     AEEHLRSV HAVERELS     AEEIKRRS RAKERIES     AEEIMNUV MAUVEINE
AEEGPRSS ASPERGES     AEEHLRTT HEARTLET              SKEARIER     AEEIMPRS EMPAIRES
         PRESAGES     AEEHLRTY LEATHERY     AEEILLNT TENAILLE     AEEIMRRS SMEARIER
AEEGRRRT REGRATER     AEEHLSST HATELESS     AEEILLRS REALLIES     AEEIMRSS SERIEMAS
AEEGRRSS GREASERS     AEEHLSTT ATHLETES     AEEILLST LEALTIES     AEEIMRST EMIRATES
AEEGRRST REGRATES     AEEHLTTY ETHYLATE     AEEILMMN MELAMINE              REAMIEST
AEEGRRSW WAGERERS     AEEHMMRR HAMMERER     AEEILMNT MELANITE              STEAMIER
AEEGRSST RESTAGES     AEEHMNNY HYMENEAN     AEEILMRS ALMERIES     AEEIMRTV VIAMETER
AEEGRSTT GREATEST     AEEHMNRS SHAREMEN              MEASLIER     AEEIMSSS MISEASES
AEEGRSTU TREAGUES              SHEARMEN     AEEILMRT EREMITAL              SIAMESES
AEEGRSTW STREWAGE     AEEHMNRT EARTHMEN              MATERIEL     AEEIMSST SEAMIEST
AEEGRSUZ GUEREZAS     AEEHMNST METHANES              REALTIME              STEAMIES
AEEGSSTT GESTATES     AEEHMNTX EXANTHEM     AEEILMST MEALIEST     AEEIMSSZ SIAMEZES
AEEGSTTZ GAZETTES     AEEHMPSS EMPHASES     AEEILMSV MALVESIE     AEEIMSTT ESTIMATE
AEEHHHSS HASHEESH     AEEHMRSS MAHSEERS     AEEILNPR PERINEAL              ETATISME
AEEHHIRT HEATHIER     AEEHMRST ERATHEMS     AEEILNPS ALEPINES              MEATIEST
AEEHHNST ENSHEATH     AEEHMRTY ERYTHEMA              PENALISE              TEATIMES
         HEATHENS     AEEHMSST MATHESES              SEPALINE     AEEIMSTW TEAMWISE
AEEHHOOP PAHOEHOE     AEEHMTUX EXHUMATE     AEEILNPT PETALINE     AEEINNRS ANSERINE
AEEHHRSS REHASHES     AEEHNNSS SNEESHAN              TAPELINE     AEEINOPS PAEONIES
AEEHHRST HEATHERS     AEEHNNTX XANTHENE     AEEILNPZ PENALIZE     AEEINPRS NAPERIES
AEEHHRTY HEATHERY     AEEHNOPR EARPHONE     AEEILNRT ELATERIN     AEEINPRT APERIENT
AEEHHSST SHEATHES     AEEHNPST HEPTANES              ENTAILER     AEEINPTT PIANETTE
AEEHIKRS SHIKAREE              PHENATES              TREENAIL     AEEINRRS REARISEN
AEEHILNP ELAPHINE              STEPHANE     AEEILNTV ELVANITE     AEEINRRT RETAINER
AEEHILRS SHIRALEE     AEEHNRSS ARSHEENS              VENTAILE     AEEINRSS SENARIES
AEEHILRT ETHERIAL     AEEHNRST HASTENER     AEEILORT AEROLITE     AEEINRST ARSENITE
AEEHIMPT EPITHEMA              HEARTENS     AEEILOTT ETIOLATE              RESINATE
AEEHIMTT HEMATITE     AEEHNRSU UNHEARSE     AEEILPRR PEARLIER              STEARINE
AEEHINRS INHEARSE     AEEHNRTT HATERENT     AEEILPRS ESPALIER              TRAINEES
AEEHINRT ATHERINE              THREATEN              PEARLIES     AEEINRSU UNEASIER
AEEHIPST APHETISE     AEEHNRTU URETHANE     AEEILPRT PEARLITE     AEEINSSS EASINESS
         HEAPIEST     AEEHNRTW WREATHEN     AEEILPST EPILATES     AEEINSSV VAINESSE
         HEPATISE     AEEHNRWY ANYWHERE     AEEILPSW PALEWISE     AEEINSTT ANISETTE
```

```
                  TETANIES      AEEKNPSU SNEAKEUP      AEELNRSW RENEWALS      AEEMNPRT PETERMAN
                  TETANISE      AEEKNPSW NEWSPEAK      AEELNRTV LEVANTER      AEEMNPRY EMPYREAN
AEEINSTV NAIVETES AEEKNRSS SNEAKERS               RELEVANT      AEEMNPTV PAVEMENT
AEEINSVW INWEAVES AEEKNRSW WAKENERS      AEELNRTX EXTERNAL      AEEMNRST REMANETS
AEEINTTZ TETANIZE AEEKNSSW WEAKNESS      AEELNSST LATENESS      AEEMNRSW MENSWEAR
AEEIOOPP EPOPOEIA AEEKORRV OVERRAKE      AEELNSSV ENSLAVES      AEEMNRTU NUMERATE
AEEIORST ETAERIOS AEEKORST KERATOSE               VANELESS      AEEMNRTV AVERMENT
AEEIPPSS APEPSIES          KREASOTE      AEELNSTY ENTAYLES      AEEMNRTW WATERMEN
AEEIPPST APPETISE AEEKORTV OVERTAKE      AEELNTUV EVENTUAL      AEEMNRUV MANEUVER
AEEIPPSU EUPEPSIA          TAKEOVER      AEELNTVY VENTAYLE      AEEMNSSS SAMENESS
AEEIPPTT APPETITE AEEKPRSS RESPEAKS      AEELOPRS PAROLEES      AEEMNSST TAMENESS
AEEIPPTZ APPETIZE          SPEAKERS      AEELOPRV OVERLEAP      AEEMNSTU MANSUETE
AEEIPRRR REPAIRER AEEKPRST PERTAKES      AEELORRS RELEASOR      AEEMORST EROTEMAS
AEEIPRRS PEREIRAS AEEKQRSU SQUEAKER      AEELORST OLEASTER      AEEMPPRR PAMPERER
         SPEARIER AEEKRRST RETAKERS      AEELORSU AUREOLES      AEEMPPRT TAMPERER
AEEIPRST PETARIES          STREAKER      AEELORTT TOLERATE      AEEMPRST TEMPERAS
AEEIPRTV PERVIATE AEEKRRSW WREAKERS      AEELORTV ELEVATOR      AEEMPRSY EMPAYRES
AEEIPSST EPITASES AEEKRSST SAKERETS      AEELOSSW LEASOWES      AEEMPRTT ATTEMPER
AEEIPSTT PEATIEST AEELLLTT TELLTALE      AEELOTTT TEETOTAL      AEEMPSTU AMPUTEES
AEEIPSTX EXPIATES AEELLMMS MAMSELLE      AEELPRRS PEARLERS      AEEMQRRU REMARQUE
AEEIQRSU QUEASIER AEELLNOV NOVELLAE               RELAPSER      AEEMQRSU MARQUEES
AEEIQRUZ QUEAZIER AEELLOSV ALVEOLES      AEELPRRT PALTERER      AEEMQTTU MAQUETTE
AEEIQSTU EQUISETA AEELLOTT ALLOTTEE      AEELPRSS PLEASERS      AEEMRRST STREAMER
AEEIRRSS REARISES AEELLPRS PARELLES               RELAPSES      AEEMRRSU MEASURER
AEEIRRST ARTERIES AEELLPTT PLATELET      AEELPRST PRELATES      AEEMRSST MASSETER
         REASTIER AEELLRRT TERRELLA      AEELPRSU PLEASURE               SEAMSTER
AEEIRRTT RETRAITE AEELLSST SATELLES               SERPULAE               STEAMERS
AEEIRRTW WATERIER          TESSELLA      AEELPRSV VESPERAL      AEEMRSSU MEASURES
AEEIRSST SERIATES AEELLSSZ ZEALLESS      AEELPRTY PTERYLAE               REASSUME
AEEIRSTT ARIETTES AEELLSTT STELLATE      AEELPSST SPATLESE      AEEMRSTT TEAMSTER
         ITERATES AEELLSWY WEASELLY               TAPELESS      AEEMRSTY METAYERS
         TEARIEST AEELLTVV VALVELET      AEELPSTT PALETTES      AEEMSSSU MASSEUSE
         TREATIES AEELMMTU MALEMUTE      AEELPSTU EPAULETS      AEEMSSTU MEATUSES
         TREATISE AEELMNPS EMPANELS      AEELPSTV SEPTLEVA      AEEMSTTU AMUSETTE
AEEIRSTV EVIRATES          EMPLANES      AEELQRSU SQUEALER      AEENNOST NEONATES
AEEIRSTW SWEATIER          ENSAMPLE      AEELRRST RELATERS      AEENNPST PENTANES
         TAWERIES AEELMNPT PLATEMEN      AEELRRSV REVERSAL      AEENNRSS ENSNARES
         WEARIEST AEELMNSS LAMENESS               SLAVERER               NEARNESS
AEEIRSTY YEASTIER          MANELESS      AEELRRTU URETERAL      AEENNRTU ENAUNTER
AEEIRSVV AVERSIVE          NAMELESS      AEELRSST STEALERS      AEENNRTV REVENANT
AEEISSTX EXTASIES          SALESMEN               TEARLESS      AEENNRUX ANNEXURE
AEEISTTT ETATISTE AEELMNST MANTEELS               TESSERAL      AEENNSSS SANENESS
         STEATITE          TALESMEN      AEELRSSU LEASURES      AEENNSST NEATNESS
AEEISTTV AVIETTES AEELMNSW WEALSMEN      AEELRSSV SEVERALS      AEENOPRS PERAEONS
         ESTIVATE AEELMNSY AMYLENES      AEELRSSW WARELESS               PERSONAE
         EVITATES AEELMNTT MANTELET      AEELRSTT ALERTEST      AEENORRS REASONER
AEEISTUX EUTAXIES AEELMNTV LAVEMENT      AEELRSTU RESALUTE      AEENORSS SEASONER
         EUTEXIAS AEELMOTT MATELOTE      AEELRSTY EASTERLY      AEENORST RESONATE
AEEITTUX EUTAXITE AEELMPRX EXEMPLAR      AEELRSUV REVALUES      AEENORTV OVERNEAT
AEEITUVX EXUVIATE AEELMPRY EMPYREAL      AEELRSVY AVERSELY               RENOVATE
AEEJLNPT JETPLANE AEELMPSX EXAMPLES      AEELSSST ALTESSES      AEENORVW OVENWARE
AEEJLOSU JEALOUSE AEELMPTT PALMETTE               SATELESS      AEENOTTU OUTEATEN
AEEJNRST SERJEANT          TEMPLATE               SEATLESS      AEENPPTT APPETENT
AEEJOPRT PEJORATE AEELMRST LAMETERS      AEELSSTU SETUALES      AEENPQTU PETANQUE
AEEKKLWY LYKEWAKE AEELMSSS SEAMLESS      AEELSSTV SALVETES      AEENPSSX EXPANSES
AEEKKPSY KEEPSAKY AEELMSST MATELESS      AEELSSVW WAVELESS      AEENRRRW WARRENER
AEEKLLST LAKELETS          MEATLESS      AEELSTTY LAYETTES      AEENRRSS RARENESS
         SKELETAL          TAMELESS      AEELSTVW WAVELETS      AEENRRST TERRANES
AEEKLMRT TELEMARK AEELMSTU EMULATES      AEEMMNRS MERESMAN      AEENRRSV RAVENERS
AEEKLMSS MAKELESS AEELNNRT LANNERET      AEEMMNTZ MAZEMENT      AEENRRSW ANSWERER
AEEKLNST KANTELES AEELNNSS LEANNESS      AEEMMPSY EMPYEMAS               REANSWER
AEEKLSSW WAKELESS AEELNOPR PERONEAL      AEEMMRST AMMETERS      AEENRRTV TAVERNER
AEEKLSTY EYESTALK AEELNOPT ANTELOPE               METAMERS      AEENRSSS SEARNESS
AEEKMNSS KAMSEENS AEELNORU ALEURONE      AEEMMSST MESSMATE      AEENRSST ASSENTER
AEEKMRRR REMARKER AEELNPPS SPALPEEN      AEEMNNOS ANEMONES               EARNESTS
AEEKMRRT MARKETER AEELNPSS PALENESS      AEEMNNRT REMANENT               SARSENET
AEEKMRST MEERKATS AEELNRRS LEARNERS      AEEMNNSS MEANNESS      AEENRSSX XERANSES
AEEKNNNS NANKEENS AEELNRSS REALNESS      AEEMNORV OVERNAME      AEENRSTT ENTREATS
AEEKNORW REAWOKEN AEELNRST ALTERNES      AEEMNORZ ARMOZEEN               RATTEENS
AEEKNPRT PERTAKEN AEELNRSV ENSLAVER      AEEMNPRS SPEARMEN      AEENRSTV AVENTRES
```

	VETERANS	AEESSSSS ASSESSES	AEFHIKRS FREAKISH	AEFILSTU FISTULAE
AEENRSUV	UNREAVES	AEFFFLRS FLAFFERS	AEFHIKSW WEAKFISH	AEFILSTV FESTIVAL
AEENRTTV	ANTEVERT	AEFFGIRS GIRAFFES	AEFHILLN FELLAHIN	AEFILSTW FLATWISE
AEENRTTX	EXTERNAT	AEFFGNRS ENGRAFFS	AEFHILOR FORHAILE	FLAWIEST
AEENRTTY	ENTREATY	AEFFGRSU SUFFRAGE	AEFHILOX HEXAFOIL	AEFILSTX FLAXIEST
AEENRTUV	AVENTURE	AEFFHIKY KAFFIYEH	AEFHILRS FLASHIER	AEFILTUU FAUTEUIL
AEENSTTV	NAVETTES	AEFFILUV EFFLUVIA	AEFHIMSS FAMISHES	AEFIMMMR MAMMIFER
AEENSUVW	UNWEAVES	AEFFIMRR AFFIRMER	AEFHLMSU SHAMEFUL	AEFIMNST MANIFEST
AEEOPRRT	PATERERO	REAFFIRM	AEFHLORS FAHLORES	AEFIMNOR AERIFORM
	PERORATE	AEFFIPRS PIAFFERS	AEFHLRSS FLASHERS	AEFIMORT FORMIATE
AEEOPRST	OPERATES	AEFFKLRU FREAKFUL	AEFHLRST FARTHELS	AEFIMOST FOAMIEST
	PROTEASE	AEFFKOST OFFTAKES	AEFHLRTY FATHERLY	AEFIMRRS FIREARMS
AEEOPRTT	OPERETTA	AEFFLMSW FLAMFEWS	AEFHLSST FLASHEST	AEFIMRRW FIRMWARE
AEEORRSU	REAROUSE	AEFFLNSS SNAFFLES	AEFHMNRS FRESHMAN	AEFIMRSS MISFARES
AEEORRSW	SOWARREE	AEFFLNTU AFFLUENT	AEFHNRSW FERNSHAW	AEFINNRS FAINNESS
AEEORRTV	OVERRATE	AEFFLRRS RAFFLERS	AEFHRSST SHAFTERS	AEFINNST INFANTES
AEEORRVW	OVERWEAR	AEFFLSTU FEASTFUL	AEFHRSTT FARTHEST	AEFINNSZ FANZINES
AEEORRVY	OVERYEAR	SUFFLATE	AEFIILMS FAMILIES	AEFINOPR PINAFORE
AEEORSSV	OVERSEAS	AEFFLSUX AFFLUXES	AEFIILNS FINALISE	AEFINORS FARINOSE
AEEORSTV	OVEREATS	AEFFMRSU EARMUFFS	AEFIILNZ FINALIZE	AEFINPRS FIREPANS
AEEORSVW	OVERAWES	AEFFNORT AFFRONTE	AEFIILSS SALIFIES	AEFINRRS REFRAINS
AEEPPRRR	PREPARER	AEFFORST AFFOREST	AEFIILST FILIATES	AEFINRRU UNFAIRER
AEEPPRRS	PAPERERS	AEFFQRSU QUAFFERS	AEFIIMNS INFAMIES	AEFINRRZ FRANZIER
	PREPARES	AEFFRSST RESTAFFS	INFAMISE	AEFINRSS FAIRNESS
	REPAPERS	STAFFERS	AEFIIMNZ INFAMIZE	SANSERIF
AEEPRRRT	PARTERRE	AEFGGGOS FOGGAGES	AEFIIMRS RAMIFIES	AEFINRST FENITARS
AEEPRRST	TAPERERS	AEFGGILR FLAGGIER	AEFIINRT FAINTIER	AEFINRSX XERAFINS
AEEPRRTT	PATTERER	AEFGGINU FEAGUING	AEFIINSS SANIFIES	AEFIRRRY FARRIERY
AEEPRRTU	APERTURE	AEFGGMOS MEGAFOGS	AEFIINST FAINITES	AEFIRRST FRATRIES
AEEPRSSS	ASPERSES	AEFGHINR HANGFIRE	AEFIIPRT APERITIF	AEFIRTUX FIXATURE
	PREASSES	AEFGHINS SHEAFING	AEFIIRRS FRIARIES	AEFISTTT FATTIEST
	REPASSES	AEFGHOSS FOGASHES	AEFIIRRT RATIFIER	AEFKLMRY FLYMAKER
AEEPRSST	TRAPESES	AEFGHTTU FUGHETTA	AEFIIRST RATIFIES	AEFKLNRS FLANKERS
AEEPRSSZ	SPREAZES	AEFGIIRS GASIFIER	AEFIIRSU AURIFIES	AEFKLRUW WREAKFUL
AEEPRSTU	EPURATES	AEFGIISS GASIFIES	AEFIITVX FIXATIVE	AEFKLSST FLASKETS
	SUPERATE	AEFGIKNR FREAKING	AEFIJLOS JEOFAILS	AEFKLSTT TALKFEST
AEEPRSTZ	TRAPEZES	AEFGILNS FINAGLES	AEFIKLST FLAKIEST	AEFKNORS FORSAKEN
AEEPSSTT	SPATTEES	AEFGILOS FOLIAGES	AEFIKMRR FIREMARK	AEFKNRST FRANKEST
AEEQRRUV	QUAVERER	AEFGILRR FRAGILER	AEFIKRUW WAUKRIFE	AEFKOPRS FORSPEAK
AEERRRST	ARRESTER	AEFGIMTU FUMIGATE	AEFILLOT FELLATIO	AEFKORSS FORSAKES
	REARREST	AEFGINRW WAFERING	AEFILMNR INFLAMER	AEFLLMMU FLAMMULE
AEERRSST	ASSERTER	AEFGINRY AREFYING	RIFLEMAN	AEFLLNNS FANNELLS
	REASSERT	AEFGINST FEASTING	AEFILMNS FLAMINES	FLANNELS
	SERRATES	AEFGINTU FANTIGUE	INFLAMES	AEFLLNNU UNFALLEN
	TERRASES	AEFGIRST FRIGATES	MISFALNE	AEFLLORV OVERFALL
AEERRSSU	ERASURES	AEFGIRSU ARGUFIES	AEFILMNT FILAMENT	AEFLLORW FALLOWER
	REASSURE	FRUITAGE	AEFILMST FLAMIEST	AEFLLOST FLOATELS
AEERRSSW	SWEARERS	AEFGISTU FATIGUES	AEFILMSY MAYFLIES	AEFLLPRT PRATFELL
AEERRSTT	RETRATES	AEFGLLOP FLAGPOLE	AEFILMTY FEMALITY	AEFLLPTU PLATEFUL
	RETREATS	AEFGLLSU FULLAGES	AEFILNNR INFERNAL	AEFLLRUW AWFULLER
	TREATERS	AEFGLMNU FUGLEMAN	AEFILNOR FORELAIN	AEFLLRUX FLEXURAL
AEERRSTU	AUSTERER	AEFGLNSS FANGLESS	AEFILNOT OLEFIANT	AEFLLSSW FLAWLESS
	TREASURE	AEFGLORW GAREFOWL	AEFILNPS LIFESPAN	AEFLLSTT FLATLETS
AEERRSTV	TRAVERSE	AEFGLOST FLOTAGES	AEFILNRU FRAULEIN	AEFLLSTY FESTALLY
AEERRSTW	WATERERS	AEFGLOSW FLOWAGES	AEFILNST INFLATES	AEFLMNOT MATFELON
AEERRSVW	WAVERERS	AEFGLRTU GRATEFUL	AEFILNSV FLAVINES	AEFLMORU FORMULAE
AEERSSSS	REASSESS	AEFGMNOR FORGEMAN	AEFILOOR AEROFOIL	FUMAROLE
AEERSSSU	SEASURES	AEFGMNRT FRAGMENT	AEFILORS FORESAIL	AEFLMOSS FOAMLESS
AEERSSSV	ASSEVERS	AEFGNNOT FONTANGE	AEFILORT FLOATIER	AEFLMPRR FRAMPLER
AEERSSSY	ESSAYERS	AEFGNORT FRONTAGE	AEFILOST FOLIATES	AEFLMSUW WAMEFULS
AEERSSTT	ESTREATS	AEFGNRRS GRANFERS	AEFILRST FLARIEST	AEFLNNNS FLANNENS
	RESTATES	AEFGNRST ENGRAFTS	FRAILEST	AEFLNNOT FONTANEL
AEERSSTW	SWEATERS	AEFGOOPT FOOTPAGE	AEFILRSU FAILURES	AEFLNOPR FOREPLAN
AEERSSTZ	ERSATZES	AEFGOORT FOOTGEAR	AEFILRSV FAVRILES	AEFLNOPT PANTOFLE
AEERSSUU	URAEUSES	AEFGOOST FOOTAGES	AEFILRSZ FILAZERS	AEFLNORS FARNESOL
AEERSSUV	VAREUSES	AEFGORRS FORAGERS	AEFILRTT FILTRATE	AEFLNOSV FLAVONES
AEERSTTT	ATTESTER	AEFGORTT FROTTAGE	AEFILRTU FAULTIER	AEFLNRSS SALFERNS
AEERSTTX	EXTREATS	AEFGOSSU FOUGASSE	FILATURE	
AEERTTTZ	TERZETTA	AEFGRRST GRAFTERS	AEFILRUW WEARIFUL	
AEERVWYY	EVERYWAY		AEFILSSS FILASSES	

AEFLNRSU	FLANEURS	AEGGHMSU	MESHUGGA
	FUNERALS	AEGGHOPY	GEOPHAGY
AEFLNRTU	FLAUNTER	AEGGHORU	ROUGHAGE
AEFLNSST	FLATNESS	AEGGIJST	JAGGIEST
AEFLNSTT	FLATTENS	AEGGIKNR	KNAGGIER
AEFLNSUY	UNSAFELY	AEGGILLN	ALLEGING
AEFLOOSV	FOVEOLAS	AEGGILLR	GRILLAGE
AEFLOPRY	FOREPLAY	AEGGILMN	GLEAMING
AEFLORSS	SAFROLES	AEGGILNN	GLEANING
AEFLORST	FLOATERS	AEGGILNR	GANGLIER
	FORESTAL		REGALING
	REFLOATS	AEGGILNS	LIGNAGES
AEFLORSU	FUSAROLE	AEGGILNT	TEAGLING
AEFLORSY	FORELAYS	AEGGILNU	LEAGUING
AEFLOSTT	FALSETTO	AEGGILRS	SLAGGIER
AEFLPPRS	FLAPPERS	AEGGILRW	WAGGLIER
AEFLPPRY	FLYPAPER	AEGGIMNN	MANEGING
AEFLPRSS	FELSPARS	AEGGIMRT	GREGATIM
AEFLPRSY	PALFREYS	AEGGINNR	ANGERING
AEFLPSUU	PAUSEFUL		ENRAGING
AEFLRSSU	REFUSALS	AEGGINNT	AGENTING
AEFLRSTT	FATTRELS		NEGATING
	FLATTERS	AEGGINNV	AVENGING
AEFLRSTU	REFUTALS	AEGGINRS	GEARINGS
AEFLRSZZ	FRAZZLES		GREASING
AEFLRTTY	FLATTERY		SNAGGIER
AEFLSSTU	FLATUSES	AEGGINRV	GREAVING
	SULFATES	AEGGINRW	WAGERING
AEFLSTTT	FLATTEST	AEGGINST	NAGGIEST
AEFLSTTU	TASTEFUL	AEGGIOPR	ARPEGGIO
AEFLSTUW	WASTEFUL		GEROPIGA
AEFMNRRY	FERRYMAN	AEGGIOSS	ISAGOGES
AEFMNRST	RAFTSMEN	AEGGIQRU	QUAGGIER
AEFMORRS	FOREARMS	AEGGIRRU	GARRIGUE
AEFMORST	FOREMAST	AEGGIRST	RAGGIEST
	FORMATES	AEGGIRSU	GARIGUES
AEFMORVW	WAVEFORM	AEGGIRWY	EARWIGGY
AEFMOSSU	FAMOUSES	AEGGISST	SAGGIEST
AEFNNSTU	UNFASTEN	AEGGISSW	SWAGGIES
AEFNOPRR	PROFANER	AEGGLNRS	GANGRELS
AEFNOPRS	PROFANES	AEGGLORY	GARGOYLE
AEFNORRW	FOREWARN	AEGGLRST	STRAGGLE
AEFNRRST	TRANSFER	AEGGMMNS	GANGSMEN
AEFNRRUY	FUNERARY	AEGGMORR	ERGOGRAM
AEFNSSST	FASTNESS	AEGGMORT	MORTGAGE
AEFNSSTU	UNSAFEST	AEGGNNSU	GUNNAGES
AEFNSTUY	UNSAFETY	AEGGNORV	OVERGANG
AEFOORTW	FOOTWEAR	AEGGNORW	WAGGONER
AEFOPRRT	FOREPART	AEGGNRRS	GRANGERS
AEFOPRST	FOREPAST	AEGGNRST	GANGSTER
AEFOPRSW	FOREPAWS	AEGGOPRU	GROUPAGE
AEFORRSW	FORSWEAR	AEGGRSST	GAGSTERS
AEFORRSY	FORAYERS		STAGGERS
AEFORRUV	FAVOURER	AEGGRSSW	SWAGGERS
AEFORRWY	FORWEARY	AEGHIJRS	JAGHIRES
AEFORSSY	FORESAYS	AEGHILLS	SHIGELLA
AEFORSTW	FORWASTE	AEGHILMT	MEGALITH
	SOFTWARE	AEGHILNR	NARGHILE
AEFORSTY	FORESTAY		NARGILEH
AEFOSTUU	FEATUOUS	AEGHILNS	HEALINGS
AEFOSTUV	VOUTSAFE		LEASHING
AEFPRSST	PRESSFAT		SHEALING
AEFRSSTW	FRETSAWS	AEGHILNT	ATHELING
AEFRSTUW	WAFTURES	AEGHILNX	EXHALING
AEGGGILN	ALEGGING	AEGHILRT	LITHARGE
AEGGGINN	ENGAGING		THIRLAGE
AEGGGLSU	LUGGAGES	AEGHILRU	LAUGHIER
AEGGHIRS	SHAGGIER	AEGHILST	LAIGHEST
AEGGHISS	HAGGISES	AEGHIMPS	MAGESHIP
AEGGHLRS	HAGGLERS	AEGHINNT	NAETHING

AEGHINNV	HAVENING	AEGIKNSS	SINKAGES
AEGHINRS	HEARINGS	AEGIKNTW	TWEAKING
	HEARSING	AEGIKPPS	KIPPAGES
	SHEARING	AEGIKPRS	GARPIKES
AEGHINRT	EARTHING	AEGIKSTW	GAWKIEST
	HEARTING	AEGILLMS	LEGALISM
AEGHINRV	HAVERING	AEGILLNS	NIGELLAS
AEGHINST	GAHNITES	AEGILLNU	LINGULAE
	HEATINGS	AEGILLNY	GENIALLY
AEGHINSV	HEAVINGS	AEGILLPR	PILLAGER
	SHEAVING	AEGILLPS	PILLAGES
AEGHINSZ	GENIZAHS		SPILLAGE
AEGHINTT	GNATHITE	AEGILLRU	GUERILLA
AEGHIOPS	ESOPHAGI	AEGILLRV	VILLAGER
AEGHIPPR	EPIGRAPH	AEGILLSS	GALLISES
AEGHIPRT	GRAPHITE	AEGILLST	LEGALIST
AEGHIRRS	GHARRIES		STILLAGE
AEGHIRSS	GARISHES		TILLAGES
AEGHLNOS	HALOGENS	AEGILLSV	VILLAGES
AEGHLOPY	HYPOGEAL	AEGILLSZ	GALLIZES
AEGHLOSS	GALOSHES	AEGILLTU	LIGULATE
AEGHLOTX	HEXAGLOT	AEGILLTY	LEGALITY
AEGHLRSU	LAUGHERS	AEGILMMR	AGLIMMER
AEGHLRTU	LAUGHTER		LAMMIGER
AEGHLRTY	LETHARGY	AEGILMNP	EMPALING
AEGHLSTW	THALWEGS	AEGILMNR	GERMINAL
AEGHMNOP	PHENOGAM		MALIGNER
AEGHMOPT	APOTHEGM		MALINGER
AEGHMORS	HOMAGERS	AEGILMNS	MEASLING
AEGHNNST	HANGNEST	AEGILMNT	LIGAMENT
AEGHNOPT	HEPTAGON	AEGILMNU	AEMULING
	PATHOGEN	AEGILMNY	YEALMING
AEGHNOPY	HYPOGEAN	AEGILMRS	GREMIALS
AEGHNORV	HANGOVER		LAMIGERS
	OVERHANG		REGALISM
AEGHNOSX	HEXAGONS	AEGILMRX	LEXIGRAM
AEGHNPSW	SPANGHEW	AEGILNNR	LEARNING
AEGHNRSS	GNASHERS	AEGILNNS	EANLINGS
AEGHNSST	STENGAHS		LEANINGS
AEGHOPPY	APOPHYGE	AEGILNNT	GANTLINE
AEGHOPXY	EXOPHAGY		LATENING
AEGHORST	SHORTAGE	AEGILNNU	UNGENIAL
AEGHOSST	HOSTAGES	AEGILNNW	WEANLING
AEGHPRSS	SPREAGHS	AEGILNNY	YEANLING
AEGHPRTU	UPGATHER	AEGILNOR	GERANIOL
AEGIILLU	AIGUILLE		REGIONAL
AEGIILMR	REMIGIAL	AEGILNOS	GASOLINE
AEGIILLN	ALIENING	AEGILNOT	GELATION
AEGIILNR	GAINLIER		LEGATION
AEGIILRR	GLAIRIER	AEGILNPR	PEARLING
AEGIILTT	LITIGATE	AEGILNPS	ELAPSING
AEGIIMNR	IMAGINER		PLEASING
	MIGRAINE	AEGILNPT	PLEATING
AEGIIMNS	IMAGINES	AEGILNRR	GNARLIER
AEGIIMTT	MITIGATE	AEGILNRS	ARLESING
AEGIINNR	ARGININE		ENGRAILS
AEGIINRR	GRAINIER		NARGILES
AEGIIRRT	IRRIGATE		REALIGNS
AEGIISTV	VESTIGIA		SANGLIER
AEGIJLNR	JANGLIER		SLANGIER
AEGIKLNS	LINKAGES	AEGILNRT	ALERTING
AEGIKLNW	WEAKLING		ALTERING
AEGIKMNR	REMAKING		INTEGRAL
AEGIKNNS	SNEAKING		RELATING
AEGIKNNW	WAKENING		TANGLIER
AEGIKNOY	KAYOEING		TRIANGLE
AEGIKNPS	SPEAKING	AEGILNRX	RELAXING
AEGIKNRS	SKEARING	AEGILNRY	LAYERING
AEGIKNRT	RETAKING		RELAYING
AEGIKNRW	WREAKING		YEARLING

AEGILNSS GAINLESS
         GLASSINE
         LEASINGS
         SEALINGS
AEGILNST EASTLING
         GELATINS
         GENITALS
         STEALING
AEGILNSV LEAVINGS
         SLEAVING
AEGILNSW SWEALING
AEGILNTV VALETING
AEGILNTX EXALTING
AEGILNTZ TEAZLING
AEGILNUV VAGINULE
AEGILOPS SPOILAGE
AEGILOPT PILOTAGE
AEGILORS GASOLIER
         GIRASOLE
         SERAGLIO
AEGILOSS GOLIASES
AEGILOST OTALGIES
AEGILPPS SLIPPAGE
AEGILPPU PUPILAGE
AEGILPRU PLAGUIER
AEGILRRU GLAURIER
AEGILRSS GLASSIER
AEGILRST GLARIEST
         REGALIST
AEGILRSY GREASILY
AEGILRSZ GLAZIERS
AEGILRTT AGLITTER
AEGILRTU LIGATURE
AEGILRTY REGALITY
AEGILSTZ GLAZIEST
AEGIMMST GAMMIEST
AEGIMNNR ENARMING
         RENAMING
AEGIMNNS MEANINGS
AEGIMNNT ENTAMING
AEGIMNPR EMPARING
AEGIMNRR REARMING
AEGIMNRS GERMAINS
         SMEARING
AEGIMNRT EMIGRANT
AEGIMNRU GERANIUM
AEGIMNST MANGIEST
         MINTAGES
         STEAMING
         TEAMINGS
AEGIMNSV VEGANISM
AEGIMOOS OOGAMIES
AEGIMORR ARMIGERO
AEGIMORS GORAMIES
AEGIMORW WAGMOIRE
AEGIMPRS EPIGRAMS
         PRIMAGES
AEGIMPRU UMPIRAGE
AEGIMPST PIGMEATS
AEGIMQRU QUAGMIRE
AEGIMRRS ARMIGERS
AEGIMRRT RAGTIMER
AEGIMRSS GISARMES
AEGIMRST MAGISTER
         MIGRATES
         RAGTIMES
         STERIGMA
AEGIMSST SIGMATES
AEGIMSSU MISUSAGE
AEGIMSTU GAUMIEST

AEGINNNX ANNEXING
AEGINNOT NEGATION
AEGINNPS SNEAPING
         SPEANING
AEGINNRS AGINNERS
         EARNINGS
         ENGRAINS
         GRANNIES
AEGINNRV RAVENING
AEGINNRY RENAYING
         YEARNING
AEGINNST ANTIGENS
         GENTIANS
         STEANING
AEGINNSU GUANINES
         SANGUINE
AEGINORS IGNAROES
         ORGANISE
         ORIGANES
AEGINORZ ORGANIZE
AEGINOSS AGONISES
AEGINOSZ AGONIZES
AEGINPPR PAPERING
AEGINPPS GENIPAPS
AEGINPRS PREASING
         SPEARING
AEGINPRT TAPERING
AEGINPRY REPAYING
AEGINPSS SPINAGES
AEGINQTU EQUATING
AEGINRRS EARRINGS
         GRAINERS
AEGINRRV AVERRING
AEGINRSS REASSIGN
         SEARINGS
         SERINGAS
AEGINRST ANGRIEST
         ASTRINGE
         GANISTER
         GANTRIES
         GRANITES
         INGRATES
         RANGIEST
         REASTING
         STEARING
AEGINRSV VINEGARS
AEGINRSW SWEARING
         WEARINGS
AEGINRSY RESAYING
AEGINRTT ARETTING
         TREATING
AEGINRTV AVERTING
         TAVERING
         VINTAGER
AEGINRTW TWANGIER
         WATERING
AEGINRVW WAVERING
AEGINRVY VINEGARY
AEGINRWY WEARYING
AEGINSST EASTINGS
         GENISTAS
         GIANTESS
         SEATINGS
         TEASINGS
         TSIGANES
AEGINSSY ESSAYING
AEGINSTT ESTATING
         TANGIEST
AEGINSTU SAUTEING
AEGINSTV VINTAGES

AEGINSTW SWEATING
AEGINSTY YEASTING
AEGINSVW WEAVINGS
AEGINSVY SAVEYING
AEGIOPRR PROGERIA
AEGIORSS ARGOSIES
AEGIORSV VIRAGOES
AEGIOSTT GOATIEST
AEGIOSTU AGOUTIES
AEGIOSTX GEOTAXIS
AEGIPPST GAPPIEST
AEGIPRSS PRISAGES
         SPAIRGES
AEGIPRST GRAPIEST
AEGIPRTY PTERYGIA
AEGIPSST GASPIEST
AEGIQRSU SQUIRAGE
AEGIRRSS GRASSIER
AEGIRRSU SUGARIER
AEGIRRSZ GRAZIERS
AEGIRRTY ARGYRITE
         GERIATRY
AEGIRSST AGISTERS
AEGIRSTT STRIGATE
AEGIRSTV VIRGATES
         VITRAGES
AEGIRSUU AUGURIES
AEGISSST GASSIEST
AEGISSTT STAGIEST
AEGISSTW GAWSIEST
AEGISTUZ GAUZIEST
AEGJLNRS JANGLERS
AEGJLTUU JUGULATE
AEGKKKNO ANGEKKOK
AEGKKNOS ANGEKOKS
AEGKLOSU KAGOULES
AEGKMNRU GUNMAKER
AEGKMRSY KERYGMAS
AEGLLLMU GLUMELLA
AEGLLNOS ALLONGES
         GALLEONS
AEGLLNOV LONGEVAL
AEGLLNPS LANGSPEL
AEGLLNRS LANGRELS
AEGLLOPR GALLOPER
AEGLLORS ALLEGROS
AEGLLORV OVERGALL
AEGLLORY ALLEGORY
AEGLLOSS GOALLESS
AEGLLOST TOLLAGES
AEGLLOTT TOLLGATE
AEGLLRVY GRAVELLY
AEGLLSSU GALLUSES
         SEAGULLS
         SULLAGES
AEGLMNNO MANGONEL
AEGLMNRS MANGLERS
AEGLMNSS GLASSMEN
AEGLMNTU GUNMETAL
AEGLMORS GOMERALS
AEGLMOSU MOULAGES
AEGLMOTV MEGAVOLT
AEGLMPSU PLUMAGES
AEGLMRSU MAULGRES
AEGLMSSU GAUMLESS
AEGLNNPT PLANGENT
AEGLNNTU UNTANGLE
AEGLNOPT GANTLOPE
AEGLNORY YEARLONG
AEGLNOST TANGELOS

AEGLNPRS GRAPNELS
         SPANGLER
         SPRANGLE
AEGLNPSS PANGLESS
         SPANGLES
AEGLNPST SPANGLET
AEGLNRRW WRANGLER
AEGLNRST STRANGLE
         TANGLERS
         TRANGLES
AEGLNRSU GRANULES
AEGLNRSW WANGLERS
         WRANGLES
AEGLNRSY LARYNGES
AEGLNRUY GUNLAYER
AEGLNSTT GANTLETS
AEGLNSTU LANGUETS
AEGLNSTW TWANGLES
AEGLNSUW GUNWALES
AEGLNTTU GAUNTLET
AEGLNTUU UNGULATE
AEGLOOOZ ZOOGLOEA
AEGLOOPU APOLOGUE
AEGLOORY AEROLOGY
AEGLOPRS PERGOLAS
AEGLORST LEGATORS
AEGLORSU GLAREOUS
AEGLORTU OUTGLARE
AEGLORTW WATERLOG
AEGLORTY GEOLATRY
AEGLOSSW GALOWSES
AEGLOSTV VOLTAGES
AEGLOSUY GEALOUSY
AEGLPPRS GRAPPLES
AEGLPRSU EARPLUGS
         GRAUPELS
AEGLPSSU PLUSAGES
         PLUSSAGE
AEGLRRSU REGULARS
AEGLRRUV VULGARER
AEGLRSTU GAULTERS
         GESTURAL
         TRAGULES
AEGLRTUY ARGUTELY
AEGLSSTT GESTALTS
AEGLSSUV VALGUSES
AEGLSTUU GLUTAEUS
AEGLSTUV VULGATES
AEGLSUUY GUAYULES
AEGMMNOR GAMMONER
AEGMMRRU RUMMAGER
AEGMMRSU RUMMAGES
AEGMNNOS AGNOMENS
AEGMNNOT MAGNETON
AEGMNORS MEGARONS
AEGMNORV MANGROVE
AEGMNOST MAGNETOS
         MEGATONS
         MONTAGES
AEGMNOSX MAGNOXES
AEGMNOXY XENOGAMY
AEGMNRST GARMENTS
         MARGENTS
         RAGMENTS
AEGMNRTU ARGUMENT
AEGMNSSW SWAGSMEN
AEGMNSTU AUGMENTS
         MUTAGENS
AEGMOORS MOORAGES
AEGMOPRW GAPEWORM

AEGMORSS	GOSSAMER	AEGRSTUU	AUGUSTER	AEHIMPSS	EMPHASIS
AEGMPSTU	STUMPAGE	AEGSSTUU	AUGUSTES		MISSHAPE
AEGNNOPT	PENTAGON	AEGSTTTU	GUTTATES		PHAEISMS
AEGNNORT	NEGATRON	AEHHHIST	SHEHITAH	AEHIMPST	MATESHIP
AEGNNOST	TONNAGES	AEHHHIMTW	HAMEWITH		SHIPMATE
AEGNNPRT	PREGNANT	AEHHIPSW	PEISHWAH	AEHIMRRS	MARSHIER
AEGNNRSS	GUNNERAS	AEHHISST	HASHIEST	AEHIMRSS	MARISHES
AEGNNRTY	GANNETRY		SHEHITAS		MISHEARS
AEGNNSTT	TANGENTS	AEHHISVY	YESHIVAH	AEHIMSST	ATHEISMS
AEGNNSTU	TUNNAGES	AEHHLNTU	UNHEALTH		MASHIEST
AEGNOORS	OREGANOS	AEHHNRSS	HARSHENS		MATHESIS
AEGNOPRR	PARERGON	AEHHNRSW	HERNSHAW	AEHINNSS	SHANNIES
AEGNOPST	PONTAGES	AEHHORST	HAROSETH	AEHINNTX	XANTHEIN
AEGNORRS	GROANERS	AEHHRRST	THRASHER		XANTHINE
AEGNORRY	ORANGERY	AEHHRSST	HARSHEST	AEHINOPS	APHONIES
AEGNORST	ORANGEST		THRASHES	AEHINOPU	EUPHONIA
	RAGSTONE	AEHIIKLR	HAIRLIKE	AEHINPRS	HEPARINS
AEGNORSW	WAGONERS	AEHIIKRT	TERAKIHI		PARISHEN
AEGNORTT	TETRAGON	AEHIIKST	SHIITAKE		SERAPHIN
AEGNORTY	NEGATORY	AEHIILMO	HEMIOLIA	AEHINPRT	PERIANTH
AEGNORUV	VARGUENO	AEHIILNR	HAIRLINE	AEHINPST	PENTHIAS
AEGNOSSY	NOSEGAYS	AEHIILST	HAILIEST		THESPIAN
AEGNOTUY	AUTOGENY	AEHIIMNT	THIAMINE	AEHINRRS	SHARNIER
AEGNPRSS	ENGRASPS	AEHIIMOP	HEMIOPIA	AEHINRSS	ARSHINES
AEGNPRST	TREPANGS	AEHIINNT	IANTHINE	AEHINRST	INEARTHS
AEGNPRYY	PANEGYRY	AEHIIRST	HAIRIEST	AEHINRSV	ENRAVISH
AEGNRRST	GRANTERS	AEHIKNSS	SNEAKISH		VANISHER
	REGRANTS	AEHIKSST	SHAKIEST	AEHINRTU	HAURIENT
	STRANGER	AEHIKSSY	SAKIYEHS	AEHINRTW	TARWHINE
AEGNRSTU	STRAUNGE	AEHILLNT	THALLINE	AEHINSSS	HESSIANS
AEGNSSST	GASTNESS	AEHILMNY	HYMENIAL	AEHINSST	ANTHESIS
AEGNSTTU	GAUNTEST	AEHILMOS	HEMIOLAS		SHANTIES
	TUTENAGS	AEHILMOT	HALIMOTE	AEHINSSV	VANISHES
AEGOORST	ROOTAGES	AEHILMSW	LIMEWASH	AEHINSSZ	HAZINESS
AEGOORSV	VORAGOES	AEHILNOP	APHELION	AEHINSTT	HESITANT
AEGOOSWY	WAYGOOSE	AEHILNRS	INHALERS	AEHINSTW	INSWATHE
AEGOPPRS	PROPAGES	AEHILNSY	HYALINES	AEHINTTT	ANTITHET
AEGOPPST	STOPPAGE	AEHILNTX	ANTHELIX	AEHIOPRS	APHORISE
AEGOPPSU	SUPPEAGO	AEHILNTZ	ZENITHAL	AEHIOPRU	EUPHORIA
AEGOPRST	PORTAGES	AEHILORS	AIRHOLES	AEHIOPRZ	APHORIZE
AEGOPRTU	PORTAGUE		SHOALIER	AEHIORRV	OVERHAIR
AEGOPSST	POSTAGES	AEHILORT	AEROLITH	AEHIORST	HOARIEST
AEGOPSSU	SPOUSAGE		LOATHIER	AEHIORTU	THIOUREA
AEGOPSTT	POTTAGES	AEHILPRS	PLASHIER	AEHIPPRS	PAPISHER
AEGORRRT	REGRATOR	AEHILRSS	HAIRLESS		SAPPHIRE
AEGORRST	GARROTES	AEHILRSU	HAULIERS	AEHIPPSS	PAPISHES
AEGORRTT	GAROTTER	AEHILRSV	LAVISHER	AEHIPPST	EPITAPHS
	GARROTTE		SHRIEVAL		HAPPIEST
AEGORSST	STORAGES	AEHILRTY	HEARTILY		PEATSHIP
AEGORSTT	GAROTTES	AEHILSST	SHALIEST	AEHIPRRS	PHRASIER
AEGORSTU	OUTRAGES	AEHILSSV	LAVISHES	AEHIPRRT	RATHRIPE
AEGORSUV	OUVRAGES	AEHILSSW	WHAISLES	AEHIPRSS	PARISHES
AEGORSVY	VOYAGERS	AEHILSTT	LATHIEST		SHARPIES
AEGORTTU	TUTORAGE		LITHATES	AEHIPRTT	THREAPIT
AEGORUVY	VOYAGEUR	AEHILSTY	HYALITES	AEHIPSSW	PEISHWAS
AEGOSSTW	STOWAGES	AEHILSUV	VIHUELAS	AEHIPSTZ	ZAPTIEHS
AEGOSTTU	OUTGATES	AEHILSWZ	WHAIZLES	AEHIQSSU	QUASHIES
AEGOSTTV	GAVOTTES	AEHIMMSS	SHAMMIES	AEHIRRRS	HARRIERS
AEGPRRSS	GRASPERS	AEHIMMST	HAMMIEST	AEHIRRSS	ARRISHES
	SPARGERS	AEHIMNNU	INHUMANE	AEHIRRST	TRASHIER
AEGPSSTU	UPSTAGES	AEHIMNRS	HARMINES	AEHIRRSV	RAVISHER
AEGPSSUU	GAUPUSES		SHIREMAN	AEHIRRTW	WRATHIER
AEGPSSUW	GAWPUSES	AEHIMNSS	SHAMISEN	AEHIRSST	SHERIATS
AEGQRTUU	TRUQUAGE	AEHIMNSU	HUMANISE	AEHIRSSV	RAVISHES
AEGRRSSS	GRASSERS	AEHIMNTU	INHUMATE	AEHIRSSW	SWASHIER
AEGRRSUU	AUGURERS	AEHIMNUZ	HUMANIZE	AEHIRSTW	SWATHIER
AEGRRSUV	GRAVURES	AEHIMPRS	SAMPHIRE		WATERISH
	VERRUGAS		SERAPHIM	AEHIRSTY	HYSTERIA
AEGRSSSU	SARGUSES	AEHIMPRT	TERAPHIM	AEHIRSWY	HAYWIRES
AEGRSTTY	STRATEGY	AEHIMPRX	XERAPHIM	AEHISSST	STASHIES
				AEHISSSW	SIWASHES
				AEHISSSY	ESSAYISH
				AEHISSTT	ATHEISTS
					HASTIEST
					STAITHES
				AEHISSTU	HIATUSES
				AEHISSTW	WASHIEST
				AEHISSVY	YESHIVAS
				AEHISTTW	THAWIEST
					THWAITES
				AEHJLOSW	JAWHOLES
				AEHJNNOS	JOHANNES
				AEHKMOPW	MOPEHAWK
				AEHKNNSU	UNSHAKEN
				AEHKNRST	THANKERS
				AEHKNSWW	NEWSHAWK
				AEHKRRSS	SHARKERS
				AEHLLLTY	LETHALLY
				AEHLLMOP	LAMPHOLE
				AEHLLNRT	ENTHRALL
				AEHLLRSS	HERSALLS
				AEHLMMNS	HELMSMAN
				AEHLMNOS	MANHOLES
				AEHLMNOT	METHANOL
				AEHLMNUY	HUMANELY
				AEHLMORS	ARMHOLES
				AEHLMPPT	PAMPHLET
				AEHLMPSW	WHAMPLES
				AEHLMRSS	HARMLESS
				AEHLMRST	THERMALS
				AEHLMRSU	HUMERALS
				AEHLNOST	ETHANOLS
				AEHLNPRS	SHRAPNEL
				AEHLNPTY	ENTHALPY
				AEHLNRST	ENTHRALS
				AEHLNSST	NATHLESS
				AEHLNSSU	UNLASHES
					UNSHALES
				AEHLNSTY	NAYTHLES
				AEHLNTUZ	HAZELNUT
				AEHLOPRT	PLETHORA
				AEHLORST	LOATHERS
				AEHLORSY	HOARSELY
				AEHLORUV	OVERHAUL
				AEHLOSSS	ASSHOLES
				AEHLOSST	SHOALEST
				AEHLOSTT	LOATHEST
				AEHLPPRT	THRAPPLE
				AEHLPRSS	SPLASHER
				AEHLPSSS	SPLASHES
				AEHLPSST	PATHLESS
					PLASHETS
				AEHLPSTU	SULPHATE
				AEHLPSTY	STAPHYLE
				AEHLRRTU	URETHRAL
				AEHLRSSS	SLASHERS
				AEHLRSST	HARSLETS
					SLATHERS
				AEHLSSTT	STEALTHS
				AEHLSSTW	THAWLESS
				AEHLSTTY	STEALTHY
				AEHMMRSS	SHAMMERS
				AEHMNNPY	NYMPHEAN
				AEHMNOPR	MORPHEAN
				AEHMNORS	HORSEMAN
					MENORAHS
					SHOREMAN
				AEHMNOST	HOASTMEN
				AEHMNOSU	HOUSEMAN
				AEHMNPRU	PREHUMAN

AEHMNSTU HUMANEST	AEIIINTT INITIATE	AEIIPRZZ PIZZERIA	AEIKRSST ASTERISK
AEHMOPRT METAPHOR	AEIIIRRT RETIARII	AEIIPSST EPITASIS	SARKIEST
AEHMOPST APOTHEMS	AEIIKLNT KALINITE	AEIIRRST RARITIES	AEILLLMO MALLEOLI
AEHMOSTW SOMEWHAT	AEIIKNRS KAISERIN	AEIIRRSV RIVIERAS	AEILLLNY LINEALLY
AEHMPRST HAMPSTER	AEIIKNSS AKINESIS	AEIIRRTT IRRITATE	AEILLMNS MANILLES
AEHMRSSS SMASHERS	AEIIKNST KAINITES	AEIIRSSS SIRIASES	AEILLMSY MESIALLY
AEHMRSST HAMSTERS	AEIIKRTY TERIYAKI	AEIIRSST IRISATES	AEILLNNO LANOLINE
AEHMRSTU MAUTHERS	AEIILLMR MILLIARE	SATIRISE	AEILLNNS NAINSELL
AEHMRSTW MAWTHERS	AEIILLRS RAILLIES	AEIIRSTV VAIRIEST	AEILLNNU UNLINEAL
AEHMSSSU SHAMUSES	AEIILLST TAILLIES	AEIIRSTW WISTERIA	AEILLNOP APOLLINE
AEHMSTTY AMETHYST	AEIILLTV ILLATIVE	AEIIRSTZ SATIRIZE	AEILLNOR ALLERION
AEHMSUZZ MEZUZAHS	AEIILMNN MAINLINE	AEIIRSVV VIVARIES	AEILLNPS SPLENIAL
AEHNNPRU NENUPHAR	AEIILMNS ALIENISM	AEIIRTTT TRITIATE	AEILLNQU QUINELLA
AEHNNPSU UNSHAPEN	AEIILMPR IMPERIAL	AEIIRTVZ VIZIRATE	AEILLNRY LINEARLY
AEHNNSUV UNSHAVEN	AEIILMTT MILITATE	AEIISTTV VITIATES	AEILLNSS SENSILLA
AEHNNSUW UNWASHEN	AEIILNNS ANILINES	AEIITTTV TITIVATE	AEILLNVY VENIALLY
AEHNOOPT HANEPOOT	AEIILNQU AQUILINE	AEIITTVV VITATIVE	AEILLOTV VOLATILE
AEHNOPRT HAPTERON	AEIILNRR AIRLINER	AEIJKNSS JANSKIES	AEILLPPR APPERILL
AEHNOPST PHAETONS	AEIILNRS AIRLINES	AEIJLNSV JAVELINS	AEILLPSS ILLAPSES
PHONATES	SNAILIER	AEIJLOPS JALOPIES	AEILLPST PALLIEST
STANHOPE	AEIILNRT INERTIAL	AEIJLOSU JALOUSIE	PASTILLE
AEHNOPSW WANHOPES	AEIILNST ALIENIST	AEIJMMST JAMMIEST	AEILLPSV LIPSALVE
AEHNOPXY XENOPHYA	LITANIES	AEIJMNSS JASMINES	AEILLQTU TEQUILLA
AEHNOQTU HAQUETON	AEIILPRT LIPARITE	AEIJNRST NARTJIES	AEILLRRS RALLIERS
AEHNORSS HOARSENS	AEIILRSS LAIRISES	AEIJNRTU JAUNTIER	AEILLRRY RAILLERY
AEHNPRSS SHARPENS	AEIILRST LAIRIEST	AEIJNSTT JANTIEST	AEILLRSS RAILLESS
AEHNPRST PANTHERS	AEIILRSV RIVALISE	AEIJNSTU JAUNTIES	AEILLRST LITERALS
AEHNPSSU UNSHAPES	AEIILRSZ LAIRIZES	AEIJORST JAROSITE	TALLIERS
AEHNRSSS RASHNESS	AEIILRTT LITERATI	AEIJPSSS JASPISES	AEILLRSU RUELLIAS
AEHNRSTU HAUNTERS	AEIILRVZ RIVALIZE	AEIJSTZZ JAZZIEST	AEILLRSY SERIALLY
UNEARTHS	AEIILSSS SILESIAS	AEIKKLLW LIKEWALK	AEILLRTU TAILLEUR
UNHEARTS	AEIILSST SAILIEST	AEIKKLPR PARKLIKE	AEILLSSS SAILLESS
URETHANS	AEIILSTV VITALISE	AEIKKMNO KAKIEMON	AEILLSST TAILLESS
AEHNSSTT THATNESS	AEIILSTX LAXITIES	AEIKLLSS KILLASES	AEILLSTW WALLIEST
AEHNSSTW WHATNESS	AEIILSTZ TAILZIES	AEIKLNNP PANNIKEL	AEILLSUV ALLUSIVE
AEHNSTUW UNSWATHE	AEIILTVZ VITALIZE	AEIKLNOS KAOLINES	AEILLSYZ SLEAZILY
AEHOORST TOHEROAS	AEIIMMRT MARITIME	AEIKLNSS SEALSKIN	AEILLTUZ LAZULITE
AEHOPPRS PROPHASE	AEIIMMSX MAXIMISE	AEIKLNST LANKIEST	AEILMMNS MELANISM
AEHOPRSS PHAROSES	AEIIMMXZ MAXIMIZE	AEIKLNSW SWANLIKE	AEILMMNT IMMANTLE
AEHOPSST PATHOSES	AEIIMNST MINIATES	AEIKLNSY SNEAKILY	AEILMMNY IMMANELY
POTASHES	AEIIMNTT INTIMATE	AEIKLOST KEITLOAS	AEILMMOR MEMORIAL
SPATHOSE	AEIIMNTU MINUTIAE	AEIKLPSS KALPISES	AEILMMOT IMMOLATE
AEHOPSTT HEATSPOT	AEIIMNTV VITAMINE	AEIKLRSS SERKALIS	AEILMMRS SMALMIER
AEHORRSV OVERRASH	AEIIMRST AIRTIMES	AEIKLRST LARKIEST	AEILMMRT TRILEMMA
AEHORSST ASTHORES	SERIATIM	STALKIER	AEILMMSS MELISMAS
HAROSETS	AEIIMSTT IMITATES	STARLIKE	AEILMNNO MINNEOLA
HOARSEST	AEIINNRS SIRENIAN	AEIKLRSV KLAVIERS	AEILMNNP IMPANNEL
AEHORSTT RHEOSTAT	AEIINNSS INSANIES	AEIKLSSS SAIKLESS	AEILMNNS LINESMAN
AEHORSTX THORAXES	AEIINNTV INNATIVE	AEIKMMSS MISMAKES	MELANINS
AEHORSUV HAVEOURS	AEIINPRT PAINTIER	AEIKMNRS RAMEKINS	AEILMNOS MINEOLAS
AEHORSVW OVERWASH	AEIINPST PIANISTE	AEIKMNST MANKIEST	SEMOLINA
AEHORSWY HORSEWAY	AEIINQSU EQUINIAS	MISTAKEN	AEILMNPS IMPANELS
AEHPRRSS PHRASERS	AEIINRRV RIVERAIN	AEIKMPRS RAMPIKES	MANIPLES
SHARPERS	AEIINRSS AIRINESS	AEIKMPSS MISSPEAK	AEILMNRS MARLINES
AEHPRSST SHARPEST	AEIINRST INERTIAS	AEIKMSST MISTAKES	MINERALS
SPARTHES	RAINIEST	AEIKMSTW MAWKIEST	AEILMNRT TERMINAL
AEHPRSUX HARUSPEX	AEIINRSY YERSINIA	AEIKNPRR PRANKIER	AEILMNRU LEMURIAN
AEHPRSUY EUPHRASY	AEIINSST ISATINES	AEIKNRST KERATINS	AEILMNSS ISLESMAN
AEHQRSSU SQUASHER	SANITIES	NARKIEST	AEILMNST AILMENTS
AEHQSSSU SQUASHES	SANITISE	AEIKNRSW SWANKIER	ALIMENTS
AEHRRSTU URETHRAS	AEIINSSX SIXAINES	AEIKNRTW KNITWEAR	MANLIEST
AEHRRSTY TRASHERY	AEIINSTV VANITIES	AEIKNSST SNAKIEST	AEILMOPR PROEMIAL
AEHRRTTW THWARTER	AEIINSTX AXINITES	AEIKNSSW SWANKIES	AEILMORS MORALISE
AEHRSSST SHASTERS	AEIINSTZ SANITIZE	AEIKNSSY KYANISES	AEILMORZ MORALIZE
AEHRSSSW SWASHERS	AEIINSVV INVASIVE	AEIKNSTV KISTVAEN	AEILMOST LOAMIEST
AEHRSSTT SHATTERS	AEIINTTT TITANITE	AEIKNSTY KYANITES	AEILMPRS IMPEARLS
AEHRSSTV HARVESTS	AEIINTTU UINTAITE	AEIKNSYZ KYANIZES	LEMPIRAS
AEHRSTTY SHATTERY	AEIIPRRS PRAIRIES	AEIKPRST PARKIEST	AEILMPRV PRIMEVAL
AEHRSTUU HAUTEURS	AEIIPRST PARITIES	AEIKPSTW PAWKIEST	AEILMPST IMPLATES
AEHSSTUX EXHAUSTS	AEIIPRSW PAIRWISE	AEIKQSTU QUAKIEST	PALMIEST

```
          PALMIETS        AEILNSTW LAWNIEST        AEILRSVV REVIVALS        AEIMPRRS RAMPIRES
          PETALISM        AEILNSUV UNVAILES        AEILRSVY VIRELAYS        AEIMPRRT IMPARTER
          SEPTIMAL        AEILNSUW LAUWINES        AEILRTTY ALTERITY        AEIMPRSS IMPRESAS
AEILMPTY  PLAYTIME        AEILNSUY UNEASILY        AEILRTUZ LAZURITE                 SAMPIRES
AEILMQRU  QUALMIER        AEILNTVY NATIVELY        AEILRTVV TRIVALVE        AEIMPRST PRIMATES
AEILMRRS  LARMIERS                 VENALITY        AEILSSSV VESSAILS        AEIMPRSV VAMPIRES
AEILMRSS  REALISMS        AEILNUVV UNIVALVE        AEILSSTT SALTIEST        AEIMPRSW SWAMPIER
AEILMRST  LAMITERS        AEILOORV OVARIOLE                 SLATIEST        AEIMPRTU APTERIUM
          MARLIEST        AEILOPPT OPPILATE        AEILSSTW SWALIEST        AEIMPSSS IMPASSES
AEILMRSY  SMEARILY        AEILOPRS PELORIAS        AEILSTTW WALTIEST        AEIMPSST IMPASTES
AEILMRTT  REMITTAL                 POLARISE        AEILSTVY VILAYETS                 PASTIMES
AEILMRUV  VELARIUM        AEILOPRT EPILATOR        AEIMMNNT IMMANENT        AEIMQRSU MARQUISE
AEILMSSX  SMILAXES                 PETIOLAR        AEIMMNOT AMMONITE        AEIMRRRS MARRIERS
AEILMSTT  MALTIEST        AEILOPRZ POLARIZE        AEIMMNSS MISNAMES        AEIMRRSS SIMARRES
          SMALTITE        AEILOPST SPOLIATE        AEIMMPRS SPAMMIER        AEIMRRST ASTERISM
AEILMSTU  SIMULATE        AEILORSS SOLARISE        AEIMMPST PSAMMITE                 MAISTERS
AEILMSTY  LAYTIMES        AEILORST SOTERIAL        AEIMMRRS SMARMIER                 MISRATES
          STEAMILY        AEILORSV OVERSAIL        AEIMMRST MARMITES                 SEMITARS
AEILMTTU  MUTILATE                 VALORISE        AEIMMRTU IMMATURE                 SMARTIES
          ULTIMATE                 VARIOLES        AEIMMSST MISMATES        AEIMRSSY EMISSARY
AEILNNOS  SOLANINE                 VOLARIES        AEIMMSZZ MIZMAZES        AEIMRSTT MISTREAT
AEILNNRT  INTERNAL        AEILORSY ROYALISE        AEIMNNOT NOMINATE                 TERATISM
AEILNNSY  INSANELY        AEILORSZ SOLARIZE        AEIMNNRS REINSMAN        AEIMRSTU MURIATES
AEILNNTY  INNATELY        AEILORTT LITERATO        AEIMNNST MANNITES                 SEMITAUR
AEILNOPS  OPALINES        AEILORVZ VALORIZE        AEIMNOPT PTOMAINE        AEIMRSTW WARTIMES
AEILNOPT  ANTIPOLE        AEILORYZ ROYALIZE        AEIMNORS MORAINES        AEIMRSTX MATRIXES
AEILNOPU  POULAINE        AEILOSST ISOLATES        AEIMNORW AIRWOMEN        AEIMRSTY SYMITARE
AEILNORS  AILERONS        AEILOSSX OXALISES        AEIMNORZ ARMOZINE        AEIMRSWW SWIMWEAR
          ALERIONS        AEILOSTT TOTALISE        AEIMNOSU MOINEAUS        AEIMSSST ASTEISMS
          ALIENORS        AEILOSTV VIOLATES        AEIMNOSW WOMANISE                 MASSIEST
AEILNORT  ORIENTAL        AEILOTTV VOLITATE        AEIMNOTZ MONAZITE        AEIMSSTT MASTIEST
          RELATION        AEILOTTZ TOTALIZE        AEIMNOWZ WOMANIZE                 MISSTATE
AEILNORV  OVERLAIN        AEILPPQU APPLIQUE        AEIMNPRT TRIPEMAN        AEIMSSTZ MESTIZAS
AEILNOST  ELATIONS        AEILPPRS APPERILS        AEIMNQRU RAMEQUIN        AEIMSTYZ AZYMITES
          INSOLATE        AEILPPTU PUPILATE        AEIMNRRS MARINERS        AEIMTTUV MUTATIVE
          TOENAILS        AEILPRRS REPRISAL        AEIMNRRV RIVERMAN        AEINNNOX ANNEXION
AEILNOTT  TONALITE        AEILPRRT PALTRIER        AEIMNRSS SEMINARS        AEINNOPV PAVONINE
AEILNPRS  PEARLINS        AEILPRST PILASTER                 SIRNAMES        AEINNORS RAISONNE
          PRALINES                 PLAISTER        AEIMNRST MINARETS        AEINNORT INORNATE
AEILNPRT  TRIPLANE                 PLAITERS                 RAIMENTS        AEINNOST ENATIONS
AEILNPSS  PAINLESS        AEILPRSV PREVAILS        AEIMNRSU ANEURISM        AEINNOTT INTONATE
          SPANIELS        AEILPRSW SLIPWARE        AEIMNRSY SEMINARY        AEINNOTV INNOVATE
AEILNPST  PANTILES        AEILPRXY PYREXIAL        AEIMNRTT MARTINET                 VENATION
          PLAINEST        AEILPSST PALSIEST        AEIMNRTU RUMINATE        AEINNPRS PANNIERS
AEILNPSX  EXPLAINS        AEILPSSY PAISLEYS        AEIMNRTW WARIMENT        AEINNPST PANTINES
AEILNRRS  SNARLIER        AEILPSTT PLATIEST        AEIMNRTY TYRAMINE        AEINNRRT INERRANT
AEILNRSS  RAINLESS        AEILPSTY PTYALISE        AEIMNSSS SAMISENS        AEINNRSS INSNARES
AEILNRST  ENTRAILS        AEILPSUV PLAUSIVE        AEIMNSST MANTISES        AEINNRST ENTRAINS
          LATRINES        AEILPTYZ PTYALIZE        AEIMNSSU ANIMUSES                 TRANNIES
          RATLINES        AEILQRSU SQUAILER        AEIMNSSZ MAZINESS        AEINNRSU ANEURINS
          TRENAILS                 REQUITAL        AEIMNSUV MAUVEINS                 UNARISEN
AEILNRSU  LUNARIES        AEILQRTU QUARTILE                 MAUVINES        AEINNRSW SWANNIER
AEILNRSV  RAVELINS        AEILQSTU LIQUATES        AEIMNTTU MATUTINE        AEINNSST INSANEST
AEILNRSX  RELAXINS                 TEQUILAS        AEIMNTVZ VIZAMENT        AEINNSSV VAINNESS
AEILNRSY  INLAYERS        AEILQSUY QUEASILY        AEIMOOPS IPOMOEAS        AEINNSTT ANTIENTS
          SNAILERY        AEILQTUY EQUALITY        AEIMOPSX APOMIXES                 STANNITE
AEILNRTT  RATTLINE        AEILRRST RETIRALS        AEIMOPTT OPTIMATE        AEINNTUV UNNATIVE
AEILNRTU  RETINULA                 RETRIALS        AEIMORRS ARMOIRES        AEINOPPT ANTIPOPE
          TENURIAL                 TRAILERS                 ARMORIES        AEINOPRT ATROPINE
AEILNRTV  INTERVAL        AEILRRSU RURALISE        AEIMORST AMORTISE        AEINOPST SAPONITE
AEILNRTY  INTERLAY        AEILRRTY LITERARY                 ATOMISER        AEINOPSZ EPIZOANS
AEILNSST  EASTLINS        AEILRRUZ RURALIZE        AEIMORTT AMORETTI        AEINOPTZ TOPAZINE
          ELASTINS        AEILRSST REALISTS        AEIMORTZ AMORTIZE        AEINOQTU EQUATION
          SALIENTS                 SALTIERS                 ATOMIZER        AEINORRT ANTERIOR
          STANIELS                 SALTIRES        AEIMOSST AMITOSES        AEINORRW IRONWARE
AEILNSSU  INULASES                 SLAISTER                 AMOSITES        AEINORSS ERASIONS
AEILNSSZ  LAZINESS        AEILRSSV REVISALS                 ATOMISES        AEINORST ANOESTRI
AEILNSTU  ALUNITES                 RIVALESS                 OSMIATES                 ARSONITE
          INSULATE        AEILRSTT TERTIALS        AEIMOSTZ ATOMIZES                 NOTARIES
AEILNSTV  VENTAILS        AEILRSTU URALITES        AEIMOTTV MOTIVATE                 NOTARISE
```

	ROSINATE
AEINORSV	AVERSION
AEINORTT	TENTORIA
AEINORTZ	NOTARIZE
AEINOSST	ASSIENTO
	ASTONIES
AEINOSSV	EVASIONS
AEINOSSX	SAXONIES
AEINOSTV	STOVAINE
AEINOSTX	SAXONITE
AEINOSXZ	OXAZINES
AEINOTVX	VEXATION
AEINPPRS	SNAPPIER
AEINPPST	NAPPIEST
AEINPRRT	TERRAPIN
AEINPRRU	UNREPAIR
AEINPRST	PAINTERS
	PANTRIES
	PERTAINS
	PINASTER
	REPAINTS
AEINPRSU	UNPRAISE
AEINPRTT	TRIPTANE
AEINPRTU	PAINTURE
AEINPRTX	EXPIRANT
AEINPSTT	PATIENTS
AEINPSTU	PETUNIAS
	SUPINATE
AEINPSTY	EPINASTY
AEINPTTY	ANTITYPE
AEINQRTU	QUAINTER
	QUANTISE
AEINQTTU	EQUITANT
AEINQTUZ	QUANTIZE
AEINRRST	RESTRAIN
	RETRAINS
	STRAINER
	TERRAINS
	TRAINERS
	TRANSIRE
AEINRRTV	VERATRIN
AEINRRTW	INTERWAR
AEINRRUW	UNWARIER
AEINRSST	RESIANTS
	RETSINAS
	SNARIEST
	STAINERS
	STARNIES
	STEARINS
AEINRSSU	SENARIUS
AEINRSSW	WARINESS
AEINRSSX	XERANSIS
AEINRSTT	INTREATS
	NITRATES
	STRAITEN
	TARTINES
	TERTIANS
AEINRSTU	RUINATES
	URANITES
	URINATES
AEINRSTW	TINWARES
AEINRSUV	VAURIENS
AEINRSUZ	AZURINES
	SUZERAIN
AEINRSVV	VERVAINS
AEINRSZZ	SNAZZIER
AEINRTTU	TAINTURE
AEINSSST	SAINTESS
	SESTINAS
AEINSSSV	VINASSES
AEINSSTT	INSTATES
	NASTIEST
	SATINETS
AEINSSVW	WAVINESS
AEINSSWX	WAXINESS
AEINSTTT	NATTIEST
AEINSTTV	TASTEVIN
AEINSTTW	TAWNIEST
AEINSTWY	YAWNIEST
AEINSUVV	VESUVIAN
AEINTTUU	AUTUNITE
AEIOPPST	APPOSITE
AEIOPRRT	PRIORATE
AEIOPRSV	VAPORISE
AEIOPRTX	EXPIATOR
AEIOPRVZ	VAPORIZE
AEIOPSST	SOAPIEST
AEIOPTTV	OPTATIVE
AEIOQSSU	SEQUOIAS
AEIORRRS	ARRIEROS
AEIORRSS	ROSARIES
AEIORRST	ROARIEST
	ROTARIES
AEIORSSV	SAVORIES
AEIORSTV	VOTARIES
AEIORSVW	AVOWRIES
AEIORTTV	ROTATIVE
AEIOSSTT	TOASTIES
AEIOSSTZ	AZOTISES
AEIOSTZZ	AZOTIZES
AEIPPPST	PAPPIEST
AEIPPRRT	TRAPPIER
AEIPPRRZ	APPRIZER
AEIPPRSS	APPRISES
AEIPPRST	PERIAPTS
AEIPPRSZ	APPRIZES
AEIPPSST	SAPPIEST
AEIPPSTZ	ZAPPIEST
AEIPQRTU	PRATIQUE
AEIPRRSS	PRAISERS
AEIPRRSY	SPRAYIER
AEIPRSST	PASTRIES
	PIASTRES
	RASPIEST
	TRAIPSES
AEIPRSSU	UPRAISES
AEIPRSSV	PARVISES
AEIPRSTV	PRIVATES
AEIPRSTW	WIRETAPS
AEIPRSTY	ASPERITY
AEIPRSVY	VESPIARY
AEIPRSXY	PYREXIAS
AEIPSSST	PASTISES
AEIPSSSV	PASSIVES
AEIPSSTT	PASTIEST
AEIPSSTW	WASPIEST
AEIPSZZZ	PIZAZZES
AEIPTTUV	PUTATIVE
AEIQRRRU	QUARRIER
AEIQRRSU	QUARRIES
AEIQRRTU	QUARTIER
AEIRRRST	STARRIER
	TARRIERS
AEIRRSST	TARSIERS
AEIRRSSY	SISERARY
AEIRRSTT	RETRAITS
	STRAITER
	TARRIEST
AEIRRSTW	STRAWIER
	SWARTIER
AEIRRTTT	RETRAITT
AEIRRTTY	TERTIARY
AEIRRVWY	RIVERWAY
AEIRSSST	TIRASSES
AEIRSSSZ	ASSIZERS
AEIRSSTT	ARTISTES
	ARTSIEST
	STRIATES
AEIRSSTV	TRAVISES
AEIRSSTW	WAISTERS
	WAITRESS
	WASTRIES
AEIRSTTT	RATTIEST
	TARTIEST
	TITRATES
AEIRSTTW	WARTIEST
AEIRSTTX	EXTRAITS
AEIRSTUZ	AZURITES
AEIRSTVY	VESTIARY
AEIRSWWY	WAYWISER
AEISSSST	SASSIEST
AEISSSTW	TISWASES
AEISSSTY	ESSAYIST
AEISSTTT	TASTIEST
AEISSTTU	SITUATES
AEISSTTV	VASTIEST
AEISSTWZ	TIZWASES
AEISTTTT	TATTIEST
AEISTTTU	ATTUITES
AEISTTTW	TAWTIEST
AEJLNSUV	JUVENALS
AEJLOSSU	JALOUSES
AEJLOSUY	JEALOUSY
AEJLOSUZ	AZULEJOS
AEJNORSZ	ZANJEROS
AEKKLLWY	LYKEWALK
AEKKMNOO	KAKEMONO
AEKKOSSS	SAKKOSES
AEKLLSTU	KELLAUTS
AEKLMRUW	LUKEWARM
AEKLMRUY	YARMULKE
AEKLNNSS	LANKNESS
AEKLNOSY	ANKYLOSE
AEKLNPPS	KNAPPLES
AEKLNPRS	PRANKLES
AEKLOPTY	KALOTYPE
AEKLORSW	SALEWORK
AEKLORSY	ROKELAYS
AEKLORTV	OVERTALK
AEKLOSST	SKATOLES
	STALKOES
AEKLPRRS	SPARKLER
AEKLPRSS	SPARKLES
AEKLPRST	SPARKLET
AEKLRSST	STALKERS
AEKMMNRS	MARKSMEN
AEKMMNSU	UNMASKER
AEKMOPRT	TOPMAKER
AEKMORTW	TEAMWORK
AEKMPRRV	VERKRAMP
AEKMPRSU	UPMAKERS
AEKNNRSS	RANKNESS
AEKNORRV	OVERRANK
AEKNORUY	EUKARYON
AEKNOTTU	OUTTAKEN
AEKNPPRS	KNAPPERS
AEKNPRSS	SPANKERS
AEKNPSSU	UNSPEAKS
AEKNRSST	STARKENS
AEKNRSSW	SWANKERS
AEKNRSTZ	KRANTZES
AEKNSSTW	SWANKEST
AEKNSSWY	SWANKEYS
AEKOPSTU	OUTSPEAK
AEKORRSS	ROSAKERS
AEKORRWW	WORKWEAR
AEKORSSS	KAROSSES
AEKORSTV	OVERTASK
AEKORTUY	EUKARYOT
AEKOSTTU	OUTTAKES
AEKPPSSU	UPSPEAKS
AEKPSSSY	PASSKEYS
AEKQRSUW	SQUAWKER
AEKRRSST	STARKERS
AEKRSSTT	STARKEST
AELLLORY	LOYALLER
AELLLRTU	TELLURAL
AELLLSUV	VULSELLA
AELLMNOZ	MANZELLO
AELLMNST	STALLMEN
AELLMNTY	MENTALLY
	TALLYMEN
AELLMORR	MORALLER
AELLMORT	MARTELLO
AELLMOTY	TOMALLEY
AELLMPUU	PLUMULAE
AELLMRSY	MERSALYL
AELLMSST	SMALLEST
AELLMSWX	MAXWELLS
AELLNOPS	PALLONES
AELLNOPV	VOLPLANE
AELLNORS	LLANEROS
AELLNOSV	NOVELLAS
AELLNOWW	ENWALLOW
AELLNPRU	PRUNELLA
AELLNPSS	PLANLESS
AELLNPTT	PLANTLET
AELLNPTU	PLANTULE
AELLNRUY	UNREALLY
AELLNRVY	VERNALLY
AELLNSST	TALLNESS
AELLNSTT	TALLENTS
AELLNTTY	LATENTLY
AELLNTUU	LUNULATE
AELLOPRS	REPOSALL
AELLOPRW	WALLOPER
AELLORRY	ROYALLER
AELLORSS	ROSELLAS
AELLORST	REALLOTS
AELLORSV	OVERALLS
AELLORSW	SALLOWER
AELLORWW	WALLOWER
AELLOSUV	ALVEOLUS
AELLPSTY	PLAYLETS
AELLQRSU	SQUALLER
AELLRRSU	ALLURERS
AELLRRTY	RETRALLY
AELLRTTY	LATTERLY
AELLRTVY	TREVALLY
AELLRWYY	LAWYERLY
AELLSSST	SALTLESS
	TASSELLS
AELLSSTW	SETWALLS
	SWALLETS
AELLSSTY	TASSELLY
AELLSTUU	ULULATES
AELLSUVV	VALVULES
AELLSUXY	SEXUALLY
AELMMNOS	MAMELONS

ANAGRAMS: 8-Letter Words

AELMMOSY	MYELOMAS	AELNORTT	TETRONAL
AELMMRSS	SLAMMERS		TOLERANT
AELMMRST	STRAMMEL	AELNORTU	OUTLEARN
	TRAMMELS	AELNORTY	ORNATELY
AELMMSST	STAMMELS	AELNOSTV	VOLANTES
AELMMSSY	MALMSEYS	AELNPRST	PANTLERS
AELMNNOU	NOUMENAL		PLANTERS
AELMNNRY	MANNERLY		REPLANTS
AELMNNTU	UNMANTLE	AELNPRSU	PURSLANE
AELMNOPS	NEOPLASM		SUPERNAL
	PLEONASM	AELNPRTY	PLENARTY
AELMNORS	ALMONERS	AELNPSSS	SPANLESS
AELMNOST	SALMONET	AELNPSSU	SPANSULE
AELMNOSU	MELANOUS	AELNPSTX	EXPLANTS
AELMNOYY	YEOMANLY	AELNPTTU	PETULANT
AELMNPRS	LAMPERNS	AELNPTTY	PATENTLY
AELMNRSU	MENSURAL	AELNQSUU	UNEQUALS
	NUMERALS	AELNRRSS	SNARLERS
AELMNSTT	MANTLETS	AELNRRTY	ERRANTLY
AELMNSTU	NUTMEALS	AELNRRUV	NERVULAR
AELMOOPT	OMOPLATE	AELNRSST	SALTERNS
AELMOPRR	PREMOLAR	AELNRSTT	SLATTERN
AELMOPRS	PLEROMAS		TRENTALS
AELMOPRT	PROMETAL	AELNRSTU	NEUTRALS
	TEMPORAL	AELNRSTV	VENTRALS
AELMOPSU	AMPOULES	AELNRSUV	UNRAVELS
AELMOPSX	EXOPLASM	AELNRSVY	SYLVANER
AELMOPSY	MAYPOLES	AELNRSXY	LARYNXES
	PLAYSOME	AELNRUWY	UNWARELY
AELMOPTT	PALMETTO	AELNSSST	SALTNESS
AELMORST	MOLERATS	AELNSSTY	STANYELS
AELMORSU	RAMULOSE	AELNSTUV	ENVAULTS
AELMORSV	REMOVALS	AELNSUUX	UNSEXUAL
AELMORTU	EMULATOR	AELNTTUX	EXULTANT
AELMOSSS	MOLASSES	AELOOPRZ	ZOOPERAL
AELMOSST	MALTOSES	AELOORSS	AEROSOLS
AELMOSTT	MATELOTS		ROSEOLAS
AELMOSTY	ATMOLYSE	AELOORTZ	ZOOLATER
AELMOTYZ	ATMOLYZE	AELOPPRS	PROLAPSE
AELMPRRT	TRAMPLER		PROPALES
AELMPRSS	SAMPLERS		SAPROPEL
AELMPRST	TRAMPLES	AELOPPSU	PAPULOSE
AELMPRSY	LAMPREYS	AELOPPTU	POPULATE
	SAMPLERY	AELOPPXY	APOPLEXY
AELMQSUU	SQUAMULE	AELOPQUY	OPAQUELY
AELMRSTT	MALTSTER	AELOPRRV	REPROVAL
	MARTLETS	AELOPRSS	REPOSALS
AELMRSTY	MASTERLY	AELOPRST	PETROSAL
AELMRTUY	MATURELY		PROLATES
AELMSSST	MASTLESS	AELOPRSU	LEAPROUS
AELNNNPU	UNPANNEL	AELOPRSV	OVERLAPS
AELNNOOP	NAPOLEON	AELOPRVY	OVERPLAY
AELNNOOX	NALOXONE	AELOPSSS	SOAPLESS
AELNNORU	NEURONAL	AELOPSST	APOSTLES
AELNNOSU	ANNULOSE	AELOPSSU	ESPOUSAL
AELNNPRS	PLANNERS		SEPALOUS
AELNNPSU	UNPANELS	AELOPSSX	EXPOSALS
AELNNRSS	ENSNARLS	AELOPSTT	PALETOTS
AELNNRST	LANTERNS	AELOPSTU	OUTLEAPS
AELNNRSU	UNLEARNS		PETALOUS
AELNNRTU	UNLEARNT	AELOPTTU	OUTLEAPT
AELNNSST	STANNELS	AELORRST	REALTORS
AELNNSTU	ANNULETS		RELATORS
AELNOOTZ	ENTOZOAL	AELORSTU	ROSULATE
AELNOPRS	PERSONAL	AELORSTV	LEVATORS
AELNOPST	LAPSTONE	AELORSTY	ROYALETS
	PLEONAST	AELORSUU	ROULEAUS
	POLENTAS	AELORSVY	OVERLAYS
AELNORSU	ALEURONS	AELORTTV	VARLETTO
AELNORSV	VERONALS	AELORTYZ	ZEALOTRY

AELORUUX	ROULEAUX	AEMMNRRY	MERRYMAN
AELOSSTV	SOLVATES	AEMMNRTU	RAMENTUM
AELOSSTY	ASYSTOLE	AEMMORSS	MARMOSES
AELOSSVY	SAVELOYS	AEMMORST	MARMOSET
AELOSTTU	TOLUATES	AEMMRSST	STAMMERS
AELOSTUV	OVULATES	AEMMRTUY	MAUMETRY
AELOSTUY	AUTOLYSE	AEMMRTWY	MAWMETRY
AELOTUUV	OUTVALUE	AEMMSSTU	SUMMATES
AELOTUYZ	AUTOLYZE	AEMMSSUW	WAMMUSES
AELPPRSS	SLAPPERS	AEMNNOPW	PENWOMAN
AELPPSST	STAPPLES	AEMNNORT	ORNAMENT
AELPPSSU	APPULSES	AEMNNOSS	MANNOSES
AELPRRSW	SPRAWLER	AEMNNRST	MANRENTS
AELPRRTT	PRATTLER		REMNANTS
AELPRSST	PLASTERS	AEMNOORR	MAROONER
	PSALTERS	AEMNOORT	ANTEROOM
	STAPLERS	AEMNOORY	AERONOMY
AELPRSSU	PERUSALS	AEMNOOTZ	METAZOON
AELPRSSY	PARSLEYS	AEMNOPRS	PROSEMAN
	SPARSELY	AEMNOPRT	EMPATRON
AELPRSTT	PARTLETS	AEMNOPRW	MANPOWER
	PLATTERS	AEMNORRS	RANSOMER
	PRATTLES	AEMNORST	MONSTERA
	SPLATTER		STOREMAN
	SPRATTLE	AEMNORSU	ENAMOURS
AELPRSTU	APLUSTRE		NEUROMAS
AELPRSTY	PLASTERY	AEMNORSV	OVERMANS
	PSALTERY		OVERSMAN
AELPSSSS	PASSLESS	AEMNORSY	ROMNEYAS
AELPSSSU	LAPSUSES	AEMNORTT	MARTENOT
AELPSSTT	PELTASTS	AEMNORTU	ROUTEMAN
AELPSSTU	PULSATES	AEMNORTY	MONETARY
	SPATULES	AEMNORYY	YEOMANRY
AELPSUUV	UPVALUES	AEMNOSTU	NOTAEUMS
AELQRRSU	QUARRELS		OUTNAMES
AELQRSUY	SQUARELY		SEAMOUNT
AELQSTTU	SQUATTLE	AEMNPRSS	PRESSMAN
AELQSTUZ	QUETZALS	AEMNPRSU	SUPERMAN
AELRRSTT	RATTLERS	AEMNPSST	ENSTAMPS
	STARTLER		PASSMENT
AELRRSTW	TRAWLERS	AEMNPSTY	PAYMENTS
AELRRTVY	VARLETRY	AEMNQSUW	SQUAWMEN
AELRSSST	STARLESS	AEMNRRSU	MANURERS
AELRSSTT	SLATTERS	AEMNRRUY	NUMERARY
	STARLETS	AEMNRSST	SARMENTS
	STARTLES		SMARTENS
AELRSSTU	SALUTERS	AEMNRSSU	SURNAMES
AELRSSTW	WARTLESS	AEMNRSSW	WARMNESS
	WASTRELS	AEMNRSTU	ANESTRUM
AELRSSUW	WALRUSES		MENSTRUA
AELRSTTT	TARTLETS		TRANSUME
	TATTLERS	AEMNRSTV	VARMENTS
AELRSTTU	LUSTRATE	AEMNRSTW	TRANSMEW
	TUTELARS		TREWSMAN
AELRSTTY	SLATTERY	AEMNRSUY	ANEURYSM
AELRSTUV	VAULTERS	AEMNSTWY	WAYMENTS
	VESTURAL	AEMOOPST	POMATOES
AELRSTWZ	WALTZERS	AEMOORSW	WOOMERAS
AELRSUVY	SURVEYAL	AEMOORTT	AMORETTO
AELRTTTW	TWATTLER	AEMOOSST	MAESTOSO
AELRTTUX	TEXTURAL		OSTEOMAS
AELRTTUY	TUTELARY	AEMOOSSV	VAMOOSES
AELSSSTU	SALTUSES	AEMOOSTT	TOMATOES
AELSSSTY	STAYLESS	AEMOOSTU	AUTOSOME
AELSSWZZ	SWAZZLES	AEMOPPRS	PAMPEROS
AELSTTTW	TWATTLES	AEMOPRTW	POMWATER
AELSTTUY	ASTUTELY		TAPEWORM
AEMMMOTU	OMMATEUM	AEMOQSSU	SQUAMOSE
AEMMMRTY	MAMMETRY	AEMORRRU	ARMOURER
AEMMNPRS	RAMPSMEN	AEMORRST	REARMOST

AEMORRSY	ROSEMARY	AENORSTV	VENATORS
AEMORSSS	MORASSES	AENORSUV	RAVENOUS
AEMORSST	MAESTROS	AENORTTX	TETRAXON
AEMORSSY	MAYORESS	AENORTTY	ATTORNEY
AEMORSTV	OVERMAST	AENOSSTU	SOUTANES
AEMORSVW	OVERSWAM	AENOSSTZ	STANZOES
AEMORTTU	TAUTOMER	AENOSSUU	NAUSEOUS
AEMOSSTT	EASTMOST	AENOSSVW	WAVESONS
AEMOSSTW	TWASOMES	AENPPRSS	PARSNEPS
AEMOSSUZ	ZAMOUSES		SNAPPERS
AEMOSSWY	SOMEWAYS	AENPPRST	PARPENTS
AEMOSTTZ	MOZETTAS	AENPPRSU	UNPAPERS
AEMOTTZZ	MOZZETTA	AENPRRST	PARTNERS
AEMPRRST	TRAMPERS	AENPRSST	PASTERNS
AEMPRRSY	SPERMARY	AENPRSSW	SPAWNERS
AEMPRSST	STAMPERS	AENPRSTT	PATTERNS
AEMPRSSW	SWAMPERS		TRANSEPT
AEMPRSTT	TRAMPETS	AENPRSTU	PERSAUNT
AEMPRSTU	TEMPURAS	AENPRSUV	PARVENUS
	UPSTREAM	AENPSSSY	SYNAPSES
AEMPSSUW	MAWPUSES	AENPSSTU	PESAUNTS
	WAMPUSES	AENPSSTW	STEWPANS
AEMPSTTT	ATTEMPTS	AENPSSTY	SYNAPTES
AEMQRSSU	MARQUESS	AENPSSTZ	SPETSNAZ
	MASQUERS	AENPSTZZ	SPETZNAZ
AEMRRSSW	SWARMERS	AENQRRTU	QUARTERN
AEMRRTUV	VERATRUM	AENQSTTU	QUESTANT
AEMRSSSU	MASSEURS	AENRRRTY	ERRANTRY
AEMRSSTT	MATTRESS	AENRRSTT	TRANTERS
	SMARTEST	AENRSSST	SARSNETS
	SMATTERS	AENRSSTT	TARTNESS
AEMRSSTY	MAYSTERS	AENRSSTU	ANESTRUS
AEMRSTTU	MATUREST		SAUNTERS
	TESTAMUR	AENRSSTV	SERVANTS
AEMRTUUX	TRUMEAUX		VERSANTS
AEMSTTTU	TESTATUM	AENRSSUW	UNSWEARS
AENNNPST	PENNANTS	AENRSTTU	TAUNTERS
AENNNTTU	UNTENANT	AENRSTUV	VAUNTERS
AENNOPRT	PATRONNE	AENRSTUW	UNWATERS
AENNOPST	PENTOSAN	AENRSTWY	STERNWAY
AENNOPUW	UNWEAPON	AENRTUVY	VAUNTERY
AENNORST	RESONANT	AENRTUWY	UNWATERY
AENNORSU	UNREASON	AENSSSTV	VASTNESS
AENNORTW	WANTONER	AENSSSTW	WASTNESS
AENNORVY	NOVENARY	AENSSTTU	TAUTNESS
AENNOSSU	UNSEASON		UNSTATES
AENNOSTU	TONNEAUS	AENSSTTX	SEXTANTS
AENNPRSS	SPANNERS	AENSSTXY	SYNTAXES
AENNPSSU	PANNUSES	AEOOPPPS	PAPPOOSE
AENNQSTU	QUANNETS	AEOOPPSS	PAPOOSES
AENNRSTT	ENTRANTS	AEOOPRRT	OPERATOR
AENNRSTY	TYRANNES	AEOOPRSS	OROPESAS
AENNRSWY	SWANNERY	AEOOPSTT	POTATOES
AENNRTTY	TENANTRY	AEOORRST	SORORATE
AENOOPST	TEASPOON	AEOORTTT	TATTOOER
AENOORRT	RATOONER	AEOORTTV	ROTOVATE
AENOPPRS	PROPANES	AEOPPRRV	APPROVER
AENOPRSS	PERSONAS	AEOPPRSS	APPOSERS
	RESPONSA	AEOPPRSV	APPROVES
AENOPRST	OPERANTS	AEOPQRTU	PAROQUET
	PRONATES	AEOPQSTU	OPAQUEST
AENOPRTT	PATENTOR	AEOPRRRT	PARROTER
AENOPRWY	WEAPONRY		PRORATES
AENOPSSU	POSAUNES	AEOPRRTV	OVERPART
AENORRRW	NARROWER	AEOPRRUV	VAPOURER
AENORRST	ANTRORSE	AEOPRRVW	WRAPOVER
AENORSST	ASSENTOR	AEOPRSST	ESPARTOS
	SENATORS		PORTASES
	TREASONS		PROTASES
AENORSTT	ORNATEST		

	SEAPORTS	AEQRTTTU	QUARTETT
AEOPRSSU	ASPEROUS	AERRSSSU	ASSURERS
AEOPRSSV	OVERPASS	AERRSSTT	RESTARTS
AEOPRSST	PROSTATE		STARTERS
AEOPRSTU	APTEROUS	AERRSSTU	SERRATUS
AEOPRSTV	OVERPAST	AERRSSTY	STRAYERS
AEOPRSVY	OVERPAYS	AERRSTUY	TREASURY
AEOPRSWY	ROPEWAYS	AERSSSST	STRASSES
AEOPSSTT	POTASSES	AERSSSTY	SATYRESS
AEOPTTUY	AUTOTYPE	AERSSTTU	STATURES
AEOQRSTU	EQUATORS	AERSSTTW	SWATTERS
	QUAESTOR	AERSSTUX	SURTAXES
AEOQRSUV	VAQUEROS	AERSSTXY	STYRAXES
AEOQRTTU	TORQUATE	AERSTTUV	VETTURAS
AEOQRTUZ	QUATORZE	AERSTTVY	TRAVESTY
AEORRRST	ARRESTOR	AERTTUXY	TEXTUARY
AEORRSST	ASSERTOR	AESSTTTU	ASTUTEST
	ORATRESS		STATUTES
	ROASTERS	AFFFFINN	NIFFNAFF
AEORRSSU	AROUSERS	AFFFGILN	FLAFFING
AEORRSST	ROSTRATE	AFFGGINR	GRAFFING
AEORRTUV	AVOUTRER	AFFGGINS	GAFFINGS
AEORRTZZ	TERRAZZO	AFFGHIRT	AFFRIGHT
AEORSSSS	ASSESSOR	AFFGIINP	PIAFFING
AEORSSTT	STRATOSE	AFFGIINX	AFFIXING
	TOASTERS	AFFGIIRT	GRAFFITI
AEORSSTV	VOTARESS	AFFGILMN	MAFFLING
AEORSSTX	STORAXES	AFFGILNR	RAFFLING
AEORSTTT	ATTESTOR	AFFGILNW	NWAFFLING
	TESTATOR	AFFGIMRS	MISGRAFF
AEORSTTU	OUTRATES	AFFGINNY	NYAFFING
	OUTSTARE	AFFGINQU	QUAFFING
AEORSTUW	OUTSWEAR	AFFGINST	STAFFING
	OUTWEARS	AFFGINUW	WAUFFING
AEORSTVY	OVERSTAY	AFFGIORT	GRAFFITO
AEORSUVW	WAVEROUS	AFFHIKSU	KUFFIAHS
AEORSVWY	OVERSWAY	AFFHILNS	HAFFLINS
AEORTUWY	OUTWEARY	AFFHILST	FLATFISH
AEORTVXY	VEXATORY	AFFHILTU	FAITHFUL
AEPPPSSU	PAPPUSES	AFFIINTY	AFFINITY
AEPPRRST	STRAPPER	AFFILMNS	MAFFLINS
	TRAPPERS	AFFILSUX	SUFFIXAL
AEPPRRSW	WRAPPERS	AFFIMSST	MASTIFFS
AEPPRSSU	UPSPEARS	AFFINORR	FORFAIRN
AEPPRSSW	SWAPPERS	AFFINOSU	AFFUSION
AEPQRSTU	PARQUETS	AFFINRSU	FUNFAIRS
AEPRRRSS	SPARRERS		RUFFIANS
AEPRRSSY	RESPRAYS	AFFIORRS	FORFAIRS
	SPRAYERS	AFFIPSTT	TIPSTAFF
AEPRRSTU	PARTURES	AFFIRRSU	FURFAIRS
	RAPTURES	AFFLLOOT	FOOTFALL
AEPRSSST	SPARSEST	AFFLLTUU	FAULTFUL
	TRESPASS	AFFLOOOT	FOALFOOT
AEPRSSTT	SPATTERS	AFFLORTU	FORFAULT
	TAPSTERS	AFFLRRUU	FURFURAL
AEPRSSTU	PASTURES	AFFNORSS	SAFFRONS
	UPSTARES	AFFNORST	AFFRONTS
AEPRSSTY	YAPSTERS	AFFNORSY	SAFFRONY
AEPRSTTU	STUPRATE	AFFNRRUU	FURFURAN
AEPRSTTY	TAPESTRY	AFGGGILN	FLAGGING
AEPRSTUX	SUPERTAX	AFGGGINS	FAGGINGS
AEPRTUVY	PYRUVATE	AFGGILNN	FANGLING
AEPSSSSU	PASSUSES		FLANGING
AEQRRSSU	SQUARERS	AFGGINOR	FORAGING
AEQRRSTU	QUARTERS	AFGGINOT	FAGOTING
AEQRSSTU	SQUAREST	AFGGINRT	GRAFTING
AEQRSTTU	QUARTETS	AFGHIINT	FAITHING
	SQUATTER	AFGHILLN	HALFLING
AEQRSTUZ	QUARTZES	AFGHILNS	FLASHING
		AFGHILNT	FANLIGHT

```
AFGHILPS FLAGSHIP
AFGHINRT FARTHING
AFGHINRW WHARFING
AFGHINST SHAFTING
AFGHIOST GOATFISH
AFGHLLUU LAUGHFUL
AFGHLSTU FLAUGHTS
         GHASTFUL
AFGHRSTU FRAUGHTS
AFGIILLN FLAILING
AFGIILNS FAILINGS
AFGIIMNN INFAMING
AFGIINNT FAINTING
AFGIINRS FAIRINGS
         FRAISING
AFGIINTX FIXATING
AFGIKLNN FANKLING
         FLANKING
AFGIKNNR FRANKING
AFGIKORT KOFTGARI
AFGILLNS FALLINGS
AFGILLNT FLATLING
AFGILMMN FLAMMING
AFGILMNO FLAMINGO
AFGILNOS LOAFINGS
AFGILNOT FLOATING
AFGILNPP FLAPPING
AFGILNST FATLINGS
AFGILNTT FLATTING
AFGILNTU FAULTING
AFGILORW GAIRFOWL
AFGILSSY GLASSIFY
AFGIMNOS FOAMINGS
AFGIMNRS FARMINGS
         FRAMINGS
AFGIMNTU FUMIGANT
AFGIMORS GASIFORM
AFGIMRST MISGRAFT
AFGINNNS FANNINGS
AFGINNSW FAWNINGS
AFGINORV FAVORING
AFGINORY FORAYING
AFGINPPR FRAPPING
AFGINRST INGRAFTS
         STRAFING
AFGINRSW SWARFING
AFGINRSY FRAYINGS
AFGINRTU FIGURANT
AFGINSST FASTINGS
AFGINSTW WAFTINGS
AFGINSUY SANGUIFY
AFGKNOPS PAKFONGS
AFGKORST KOFTGARS
AFGLLNOT FLATLONG
AFGLLRUU FULGURAL
AFGLLRUY FRUGALLY
AFGLLSSU GLASSFUL
AFGLLSTU GASTFULL
AFGLNNOO GONFALON
AFGLNORU GROANFUL
AFGLNOUW WAGONFUL
AFGNNNOO GONFANON
AFGOORTZ ZOOGRAFT
AFHIILRS FRAILISH
AFHIIMST MISFAITH
AFHIINST FAINTISH
AFHIKSUY KUFIYAHS
AFHILLNS FLANNILS
AFHILLSW WALLFISH
AFHILLSY FLASHILY
```


```
AFHILSTT FLATTISH
AFHIMNST MANSHIFT
AFHIMNSU HAFNIUMS
AFHINOSS FASHIONS
AFHINSTU UNFAITHS
AFHIOSSU FASHIOUS
AFHIRSST STARFISH
AFHKLNTU THANKFUL
AFHKORSX FOXSHARK
AFHKORSY HAYFORKS
AFHKRSTU FUTHARKS
AFHLLOTU LOATHFUL
AFHLOSTU OUTFLASH
AFHLOSTY HAYLOFTS
AFHLRTUW WRATHFUL
AFHNOOST FANTOOSH
AFHOOPST POOFTAHS
AFHOOPTT FOOTPATH
AFHOPSTU POUFTAHS
AFIIKMRS FAKIRISM
AFIILLLY FILIALLY
AFIILLNU UNFILIAL
AFIILMMS FAMILISM
AFIILMNS FINALISM
AFIILNRU UNIFILAR
AFIILNST FINALIST
AFIILNTY FINALITY
AFIILRST AIRLIFTS
AFIIMRSY FAIRYISM
AFIINNOS SAINFOIN
         SINFONIA
AFIINOTX FIXATION
AFIIORRT TRIFORIA
AFIKLNNR FRANKLIN
AFIKLORT FORKTAIL
AFIKNRST RATFINKS
AFILLLOT FLOTILLA
AFILLMSS MISFALLS
AFILLNPU PLAINFUL
AFILLPST PITFALLS
AFILLPSU PAILFULS
AFILLSUV VIALFULS
AFILLTUY FAULTILY
AFILMNOR FORMALIN
         INFORMAL
AFILMOPR PALIFORM
AFILMSSS FALSISMS
AFILNORT FLATIRON
         INFLATOR
AFILNPPT FLIPPANT
AFILNRUY UNFAIRLY
AFILNSTU FLUTINAS
         INFLATUS
AFILORTY FILATORY
AFILRSTU FISTULAR
AFILSSTU FISTULAS
AFILSTTU FLAUTIST
AFIMMNOR MANIFORM
AFIMMORR RAMIFORM
AFIMNOPR NAPIFORM
AFIMNORR RANIFORM
AFIMNORT NATIFORM
AFIMNOSU INFAMOUS
AFIMORRU AURIFORM
AFIMORRV VARIFORM
AFIMORSV VASIFORM
AFINNORS FRANIONS
AFINNOTU FOUNTAIN
AFINNRTY INFANTRY
AFINOPSY SAPONIFY
```


```
AFINOQTU QUANTIFY
AFINRSTX TRANSFIX
AFINSSTU FAUNISTS
         FUSTIANS
AFIORSTU FAITOURS
AFIORSTZ SFORZATI
AFIRSTTY STRATIFY
AFISSSTT SITFASTS
AFKLNOTU OUTFLANK
AFKLNPRU PRANKFUL
AFKLNSTU TANKFULS
AFKLOSWY FOLKWAYS
AFKLRSSU SARKFULS
AFKMOORT FOOTMARK
AFLLLORY FLORALLY
AFLLLUWY LAWFULLY
AFLLMNUY MANFULLY
AFLLMORY FORMALLY
AFLLMPSU PALMFULS
AFLLNOSW SNOWFALL
AFLLNUUW UNLAWFUL
AFLLOSTU OUTFALLS
AFLLRTUY ARTFULLY
AFLLSTUW WASTFULL
AFLMNORU UNFORMAL
AFLMOPRT PLATFORM
AFLMORRU FORMULAR
AFLMORSU FORMULAS
AFLMORSW WOLFRAMS
AFLMORTU FOULMART
AFLMORTW FLATWORM
AFLMOSST FLOTSAMS
AFLMOSUY FAMOUSLY
AFLNOPRU APRONFUL
AFLNORST FRONTALS
AFLNRTUU UNARTFUL
AFLNTUUV VAUNTFUL
AFLNTUUY UNFAULTY
AFLOOSTW WOOLFATS
AFLORSSU FUSAROLS
AFLORSUV FLAVOURS
AFLOSSSU FOSSULAS
AFLOSTUU FLATUOUS
AFLPRSTY FLYTRAPS
AFLRSTTU STARTFUL
AFLRSTUY TRAYFULS
AFMNNORT FRONTMAN
AFMNORST FORMANTS
AFMOOPRR PROFORMA
AFMORSTU FOUMARTS
AFMORTUY FUMATORY
AFMOSSTU SFUMATOS
AFNORRSW FORWARNS
AFOOPPRS APPROOFS
AFOOPRRT RATPROOF
AFOORSTZ FORZATOS
         SFORZATO
AFOOSTWY FOOTWAYS
AFORSTTW FORSWATT
AFOSSTUU FASTUOUS
AGGGGILN GAGGLING
AGGGHILN HAGGLING
AGGGHINS SHAGGING
AGGGILNN GANGLING
AGGGILNR GARGLING
         RAGGLING
AGGGILNS LAGGINGS
         SLAGGING
AGGGILNW WAGGLING
AGGGINNS GANGINGS
```


```
                  SNAGGING
AGGGINRS RAGGINGS
AGGGINSS SAGGINGS
AGGGINST STAGGING
AGGGINSU GAUGINGS
AGGGINSW SWAGGING
AGGGIYZZ ZIGZAGGY
AGGHIILS GHILGAIS
AGGHILNU LAUGHING
AGGHILST GASLIGHT
AGGHILSY SHAGGILY
AGGHIMNO HOMAGING
AGGHIMNS GINGHAMS
AGGHINNP PHANGING
AGGHINNS GNASHING
         HANGINGS
AGGHINNW WHANGING
AGGHINPR GRAPHING
AGGHINST GHASTING
AGGHINUW WAUGHING
AGGIIJJS JIGAJIGS
AGGIILNN ALIGNING
AGGIILNR GLAIRING
AGGIILNS SILAGING
AGGIILNT LIGATING
         TAIGLING
AGGIILNV GINGIVAL
AGGIIMNS IMAGINGS
AGGIINNR GRAINING
AGGIINNS AGNISING
         GAININGS
AGGIINNZ AGNIZING
AGGIINRS AGRISING
AGGIINRZ AGRIZING
AGGIINST AGISTING
AGGIINSU AGUISING
AGGIINUZ AGUIZING
AGGIJJOS JIGAJOGS
AGGIJLNN JANGLING
AGGILLNS GINGALLS
AGGILLNU ULLAGING
AGGILLNY GALLYING
AGGILMNN MANGLING
AGGILMNO GLOAMING
AGGILMNU GLAUMING
AGGILNNO GANGLION
AGGILNNR GNARLING
AGGILNNS ANGLINGS
         SLANGING
AGGILNNT GNATLING
         TANGLING
AGGILNNW WANGLING
AGGILNOP GALOPING
AGGILNOT GLOATING
         GOATLING
AGGILNPU PLAGUING
AGGILNPY GAPINGLY
AGGILNRY GRAYLING
         RAGINGLY
AGGILNSS GLASSING
AGGILNSZ GLAZINGS
AGGINNOR GROANING
AGGINNOT TANGOING
AGGINNOW WAGONING
AGGINNPR PRANGING
AGGINNPS SPANGING
AGGINNRR GNARRING
AGGINNRT GRANTING
AGGINNRU RAUNGING
AGGINNST STANGING
```

Key	Word	Key	Word	Key	Word	Key	Word
AGGINNTU	GAUNTING	AGHINNTY	ANYTHING		TRAILING	AGIKNOST	GOATSKIN
AGGINNTW	TWANGING	AGHINOST	HOASTING	AGIILNRV	VIRGINAL	AGIKNPRS	PARKINGS
AGGINOVY	VOYAGING	AGHINPPW	WHAPPING	AGIILNSS	AISLINGS		SPARKING
AGGINPRS	GRASPING	AGHINPPY	HAPPYING		SAILINGS	AGIKNPTU	UPTAKING
	SPARGING	AGHINPRS	HARPINGS	AGIILNST	TAILINGS	AGIKNQSU	QUAKINGS
AGGINPSS	GASPINGS		PHRASING	AGIILNSW	WAILINGS	AGIKNRSS	SARKINGS
AGGINPUZ	UPGAZING		SHARPING	AGIILNTT	LITIGANT	AGIKNRST	KARTINGS
AGGINRSS	GRASSING	AGHINPSS	SHAPINGS	AGIILNTV	VIGILANT		STARKING
	SIRGANGS	AGHINPSW	PSHAWING	AGIILOSV	VILIAGOS	AGIKNSST	SKATINGS
AGGINRST	GRATINGS	AGHINQSU	QUASHING	AGIILPST	PIGTAILS		TASKINGS
AGGINRSU	SUGARING	AGHINRRU	HURRAING	AGIILTVY	VAGILITY	AGILLLNS	LALLINGS
AGGINRSV	GRAVINGS	AGHINRRY	HARRYING	AGIIMMNS	MAIMINGS	AGILLMNS	SMALLING
AGGINRSZ	GRAZINGS	AGHINRSS	SHARINGS	AGIIMMSS	IMAGISMS	AGILLMNU	MULLIGAN
AGGINRTY	GYRATING	AGHINRST	TRASHING	AGIIMNNR	INARMING	AGILLMNY	MALIGNLY
AGGINRUU	AUGURING	AGHINRTW	THRAWING	AGIIMNOW	MIAOWING	AGILLMSU	GALLIUMS
AGGINRYZ	AGRYZING		WRATHING	AGIIMNPV	IMPAVING	AGILLNOW	ALLOWING
AGGINSSS	GASSINGS	AGHINSST	HASTINGS	AGIIMNSS	AMISSING	AGILLNOY	ALLOYING
AGGINSST	STAGINGS		STASHING	AGIIMNST	GIANTISM	AGILLNPS	SPALLING
AGGIRTUZ	ZIGGURAT	AGHINSSV	SHAVINGS	AGIIMNTT	MITIGANT	AGILLNRU	ALLURING
AGGLLLOY	LOLLYGAG	AGHINSSW	SWASHING	AGIIMORS	ORIGAMIS		LINGULAR
AGGLLOOY	ALGOLOGY		WASHINGS	AGIIMSST	IMAGISTS	AGILLNRY	NARGILLY
AGGLMOOR	LOGOGRAM	AGHINSTT	HATTINGS	AGIINNPS	SPAINING		RALLYING
AGGLOORY	AGROLOGY	AGHINSTW	SWATHING	AGIINNPT	PAINTING	AGILLNST	STALLING
AGGLRSTY	STRAGGLY		THAWINGS	AGIINNRS	INGRAINS	AGILLNSU	LINGULAS
AGGMORRS	GROGRAMS	AGHINUZZ	HUZZAING	AGIINNRT	TRAINING	AGILLNSW	WALLINGS
AGGNUWZZ	ZUGZWANG	AGHIPRRT	TRIGRAPH	AGIINNRV	RAVINING	AGILLNSY	SALLYING
AGHHIILT	HIGHTAIL	AGHIRSTT	STRAIGHT	AGIINNST	SAINTING		SIGNALLY
AGHHISWY	HIGHWAYS	AGHISSTW	SIGHTSAW		SATINING		SLANGILY
AGHHLOTU	ALTHOUGH	AGHKOSSW	GOSHAWKS		STAINING	AGILLNTY	TALLYING
AGHIILNN	INHALING	AGHLLMPU	GALLUMPH	AGIINNSW	SWAINING	AGILLOOR	GILLAROO
AGHIINNS	HAININGS	AGHLMOOR	HOLOGRAM	AGIINNTT	TAINTING	AGILLOPT	GALLIPOT
AGHIIRTT	AIRTIGHT	AGHLMPSU	GALUMPHS	AGIINOPT	OPIATING	AGILLORS	GORILLAS
AGHIJNRT	NIGHTJAR	AGHLNOSU	SHOGUNAL	AGIINORS	SIGNORIA	AGILLOST	GALLIOTS
AGHIKNNS	SHANKING	AGHLNSUY	NYLGHAUS	AGIINPRS	ASPIRING	AGILLPRY	PLAYGIRL
AGHIKNNT	THANKING	AGHLOOSS	GASOHOLS		PAIRINGS	AGILLPUY	PLAGUILY
AGHIKNRS	SHARKING	AGHMMOOY	HOMOGAMY		PRAISING	AGILLSSU	LUGSAILS
AGHIKNSS	SHAKINGS	AGHMOOPY	OMOPHAGY	AGIINPRT	PIRATING	AGILLSSY	GLASSILY
AGHIKNSW	HAWKINGS	AGHMOPRY	MYOGRAPH	AGIINRRV	ARRIVING	AGILMMNS	LAMMINGS
AGHILLNO	HALLOING	AGHNNSTU	SHANTUNG	AGIINRSS	RAISINGS		SLAMMING
AGHILLNS	HALLINGS	AGHNOORS	SHAGROON	AGIINRTT	ATTIRING		SMALMING
AGHILLNT	ALLNIGHT	AGHNORST	STAGHORN	AGIINSSZ	ASSIZING	AGILMNNT	MANTLING
AGHILMTY	ALMIGHTY	AGHNOSTU	HANGOUTS	AGIINSTV	VISTAING	AGILMNPS	SAMPLING
AGHILNOO	HOOLIGAN	AGHNPRSY	SYNGRAPH	AGIINSTW	WAITINGS	AGILMNQU	QUALMING
AGHILNOS	SHOALING	AGHNTTUU	UNTAUGHT	AGIISSTV	VISAGIST	AGILMNRS	MARLINGS
AGHILNOT	LOATHING	AGHOPSSW	SWAGSHOP	AGIJMNOR	MAJORING	AGILMNST	MALTINGS
AGHILNPS	PLASHING	AGHRSTTU	STRAUGHT	AGIJNNSU	JAUNSING	AGILMOPR	LIPOGRAM
AGHILNRS	HARLINGS	AGIIILNS	LIAISING	AGIJNNTU	JAUNTING	AGILMORS	ALGORISM
	RINGHALS	AGIIINNS	INSIGNIA	AGIJNRRS	JARRINGS	AGILMPSU	PLAGIUMS
AGHILNRY	NARGHILY	AGIIKLNS	SKAILING	AGIKLMOR	KILOGRAM	AGILNNNP	PLANNING
AGHILNSS	HASSLING	AGIIKNRT	TRAIKING	AGIKLNNP	PLANKING	AGILNNOP	PANGOLIN
	LASHINGS	AGIILLOV	VILLAGIO	AGIKLNNR	RANKLING	AGILNNOS	LOANINGS
	SLANGISH		VILLIAGO	AGIKLNOS	OAKLINGS	AGILNNPT	PLANTING
	SLASHING	AGIILMNP	IMPALING	AGIKLNST	SKLATING	AGILNNRS	SNARLING
AGHILNST	HALTINGS	AGIILMNS	MAILINGS		STALKING	AGILNNSS	LINSANGS
	LATHINGS	AGIILMNU	MIAULING		TALKINGS	AGILNNST	SLANTING
AGHILNSU	LANGUISH	AGIILNNP	PLAINING	AGIKLNSW	WALKINGS		TANLINGS
AGHILNSW	SHAWLING	AGIILNNS	NAILINGS	AGIKLNTY	TAKINGLY	AGILNNUW	UNLAWING
	WHALINGS		SNAILING	AGIKLNUW	WAULKING	AGILNNUY	UNGAINLY
AGHILRSY	GARISHLY	AGIILNNU	INGUINAL	AGIKMNNU	UNMAKING		UNLAYING
AGHILRTY	GRAITHLY	AGIILNNY	INLAYING	AGIKMNPU	UPMAKING	AGILNOOO	OOGONIAL
AGHILSUY	AGUISHLY	AGIILNOR	ORIGINAL	AGIKMNRS	MARKINGS	AGILNOOS	ISOGONAL
AGHIMMNS	SHAMMING	AGIILNOT	INTAGLIO	AGIKNNPP	KNAPPING	AGILNOPR	PAROLING
AGHIMMNW	WHAMMING		LIGATION	AGIKNNPR	PRANKING	AGILNOPS	GALOPINS
AGHIMNSS	MASHINGS		TAGLIONI	AGIKNNPS	SPANKING	AGILNOPT	PLOATING
	SMASHING	AGIILNOX	GLOXINIA	AGIKNNRR	KNARRING	AGILNORT	TRIGONAL
AGHIMNTY	THINGAMY	AGIILNPT	PLAITING	AGIKNNRS	RANKINGS	AGILNOSS	GLOSSINA
AGHIMPRU	GRAPHIUM	AGIILNQU	QUAILING	AGIKNNRU	UNRAKING		LASSOING
AGHINNSS	SNASHING	AGIILNRS	GLAIRINS	AGIKNNST	TANKINGS	AGILNOST	ANTILOGS
AGHINNST	TANGHINS		RAILINGS	AGIKNNSW	SWANKING		SALTOING
AGHINNTU	HAUNTING	AGIILNRT	RINGTAIL	AGIKNOSS	SOAKINGS	AGILNOTY	ANTILOGY

```
AGILNPPP PLAPPING
AGILNPPS LAPPINGS
         SLAPPING
AGILNPPY APPLYING
AGILNPRS SPARLING
         SPRINGAL
AGILNPSS SAPLINGS
AGILNPST PLATINGS
         SPALTING
         STAPLING
AGILNPSW LAPWINGS
         SPAWLING
AGILNPSY PALSYING
         SPLAYING
AGILNPTT PLATTING
AGILNPUY UPLAYING
AGILNRST RATLINGS
         STARLING
AGILNRSU SINGULAR
AGILNRSW WARLINGS
         WARSLING
AGILNRTT RATTLING
AGILNRTW TRAWLING
AGILNRVY RAVINGLY
AGILNRWW WRAWLING
AGILNRWX WRAXLING
AGILNSST ANGLISTS
         LASTINGS
         SALTINGS
         SLATINGS
AGILNSSV SALVINGS
AGILNSSW SWALINGS
AGILNSTT SLATTING
AGILNSTU SALUTING
AGILNSUV AVULSING
AGILNSUW WAULINGS
AGILNSVY SAVINGLY
AGILNSWW WAWLINGS
AGILNSWY SWAYLING
AGILNTTT TATTLING
AGILNTTW WATTLING
AGILNTUV VAULTING
AGILNTUX LUXATING
AGILNTWZ WALTZING
AGILOORS GLORIOSA
AGILOOXY AXIOLOGY
AGILOPST GALIPOTS
AGILORSS GIRASOLS
AGILOSST SALIGOTS
AGILSYYZ SYZYGIAL
AGIMMNRS SMARMING
AGIMMOSY MISOGAMY
AGIMNNOS MASONING
AGIMNNOW WOMANING
AGIMNNRU MANURING
         UNARMING
AGIMNNTU UNTAMING
AGIMNOOV AMOOVING
AGIMNORS ORGANISM
AGIMNORU ORIGANUM
AGIMNORY AGRIMONY
AGIMNOSV VAMOSING
AGIMNPRT TRAMPING
AGIMNPSS SPASMING
AGIMNPST STAMPING
         TAMPINGS
AGIMNPSV VAMPINGS
AGIMNPSW SWAMPING
AGIMNRRY MARRYING
AGIMNRST MIGRANTS

         SMARTING
AGIMNRSW SWARMING
         WARMINGS
AGIMNRSY MYRINGAS
AGIMNRTU MATURING
AGIMNSSU ASSUMING
AGIMNSTT MATTINGS
AGIMNTTU MUTATING
AGIMORRT MIGRATOR
AGIMORSS ISOGRAMS
AGIMORSU GOURAMIS
AGIMQRUY QUAGMIRY
AGIMRRST TRIGRAMS
AGINNNVY NANNYING
AGINNNOY ANNOYING
AGINNNPS PANNINGS
         SPANNING
AGINNNST TANNINGS
AGINNNSV VANNINGS
AGINNOOP NAPOOING
AGINNOPR APRONING
AGINNOPT POIGNANT
AGINNORT IGNORANT
AGINNOST ASTONING
AGINNOTT NOTATING
AGINNPPS SNAPPING
AGINNPRW PRAWNING
AGINNPST PANTINGS
AGINNPSW SPAWNING
         WINGSPAN
AGINNPUY UNPAYING
AGINNQTU QUANTING
AGINNRRS SNARRING
AGINNRSS SNARINGS
AGINNRST STARNING
AGINNRTT TRANTING
AGINNRTU NATURING
AGINNRTY TRAYNING
         TYRANING
AGINNSTU SAUNTING
         UNSATING
AGINNSTW WANTINGS
AGINNSTY STAYNING
AGINNSUY UNSAYING
AGINNSWY YAWNINGS
AGINNTTU ATTUNING
         NUTATING
         TAUNTING
AGINNTUV VAUNTING
AGINNTUX UNTAXING
AGINNVVY NAVVYING
AGINOORT ROGATION
AGINOPPS APPOSING
AGINOPQU OPAQUING
AGINOPRV VAPORING
AGINORRS GARRISON
         ROARINGS
AGINORRW ARROWING
AGINORSS ASSIGNOR
         SIGNORAS
         SOARINGS
AGINORST ORGANIST
         ROASTING
AGINORSU AROUSING
AGINORSV SAVORING
AGINORTT ROTATING
         TROATING
AGINORTV GRAVITON
AGINORTY GYRATION

         ORGANITY
AGINOSST AGONISTS
AGINOSSU SAGOUINS
AGINOSTT TANGOIST
         TOASTING
AGINPPRS RAPPINGS
AGINPPRT TRAPPING
AGINPPRW WRAPPING
AGINPPST STAPPING
         TAPPINGS
AGINPPSW SWAPPING
AGINPPTU PUPATING
AGINPPUY APPUYING
AGINPRRS SPARRING
AGINPRRY PARRYING
AGINPRSS PARSINGS
         RASPINGS
AGINPRST PARTINGS
         PRATINGS
AGINPRSW WARPINGS
AGINPRSY PRAYINGS
         SPRAYING
AGINPRTT PRATTING
AGINPRTU UPRATING
AGINPRTY PARTYING
AGINPSSS PASSINGS
AGINPSST PASTINGS
AGINPSSU PAUSINGS
AGINPSTT SPATTING
AGINQRSU SQUARING
AGINRRST STARRING
         TARRINGS
AGINRRTY TARRYING
AGINRSST GASTRINS
         STARINGS
AGINRSSU ASSURING
AGINRSSY SYRINGAS
AGINRSTT RATTINGS
         STARTING
AGINRSTV STARVING
AGINRSTW STRAWING
         WRASTING
AGINRSTY STRAYING
AGINRSVW SWARVING
AGINRSVY VARYINGS
AGINRSWY RINGWAYS
AGINSSTT TASTINGS
AGINSSTW WASTINGS
AGINSSTY STAYINGS
AGINSSWY SWAYINGS
AGINSTTT TATTINGS
AGINSTTW SWATTING
AGINSVVY SAVVYING
AGINSWWX WAXWINGS
AGIOORSU ORAGIOUS
AGIOORSZ GRAZIOSO
AGIOORTU AUTOGIRO
AGIOPPRT AGITPROP
AGIORRTT GRATTOIR
AGIORSST AGISTORS
         ORGIASTS
AGIRSSTU SASTRUGI
AGIRSTUZ ZASTRUGI
AGIRTTUY GRATUITY
AGJLRSUU JUGULARS
AGJNOORS JARGOONS
AGKMMORY KYMOGRAM
AGKMNOPS KAMPONGS
AGKNOPST PAKTONGS
AGKORRSW RAGWORKS

AGLLLNOW LONGWALL
AGLLMOPW GLOWLAMP
AGLLNOOS GALLOONS
AGLLRUVY VULGARLY
AGLMOOTY ATMOLOGY
AGLMOPSY POLYGAMS
AGLMOPYY POLYGAMY
AGLMORSU GLAMOURS
AGLNORSU LANGUORS
AGLNOSST GLASNOST
AGLNOSWY LONGWAYS
AGLNPSUY GUNPLAYS
AGLNRUUV UNVULGAR
AGLNSSSU SUNGLASS
AGLNSTUY YGLAUNST
AGLOOPST GOALPOST
AGLOOTUY AUTOLOGY
AGLOPRSS LOPGRASS
AGLORSSY GLOSSARY
AGLPSSSY SPYGLASS
AGLRTTUU GUTTURAL
AGLSTUUY AUGUSTLY
AGMMNOOR MONOGRAM
         NOMOGRAM
AGMMNOOY MONOGAMY
AGMMOORT TOMOGRAM
AGMMORSY MYOGRAMS
AGMNNOSW GOWNSMAN
AGMNOOPR PORNOMAG
AGMNOORY AGRONOMY
AGMNORST ANGSTROM
AGMNSSTU MUSTANGS
AGMNSSTY GYMNASTS
AGMOOOSU OOGAMOUS
AGMOOPRY POROGAMY
AGMOPRRS PROGRAMS
AGMOPRSU GOPURAMS
AGMORRSW RAGWORMS
AGMRSSSU GRASSUMS
AGNNNOOS NONAGONS
AGNNOOPT POONTANG
AGNNOQTU QUANTONG
AGNORRST GRANTORS
AGNORTUY NUGATORY
AGNPPRSU UPSPRANG
AGOORRTY ROGATORY
AGOORTUY AUTOGYRO
AGORRSST GROSSART
         ROTGRASS
AGORRSTW RAGWORTS
AGORRTYY GYRATORY
AGORSTTY GYROSTAT
AHHIKLSS SHASHLIK
AHHILNPT PHTHALIN
AHHILOST HAILSHOT
AHHILPSW WHIPLASH
AHHIMMSS MISHMASH
AHHIMNSU HAHNIUMS
AHHIPRSS SHARPISH
AHHISSTT SHITTAHS
AHHLMRTY RHYTHMAL
AHHLNOPT NAPHTHOL
AHHMPRRU HARRUMPH
AHHNORTW HAWTHORN
AHHOPRSS SHOPHARS
AHHOPSTU APHTHOUS
AHIIKRSS SHIKARIS
AHIILNPS PLAINISH
AHIILOST HALIOTIS
AHIILRTY HILARITY
```

AHIIMNOT	HIMATION	AHIORSTV	TOVARISH
AHIIMNST	ISTHMIAN	AHIORSUV	HAVIOURS
	THIAMINS	AHIOSTWY	HOISTWAY
AHIIMSSS	SASHIMIS	AHIPPSST	SAPPHIST
AHIINPRS	HAIRPINS	AHIPRSST	HARPISTS
AHIINPST	ANTISHIP	AHIPRSSW	WARSHIPS
AHIINSST	SAINTISH	AHIQRSSU	SQUARISH
AHIINSSW	SWAINISH	AHIRRSST	STIRRAHS
AHIINSTU	HUITAINS	AHIRSSTT	STARTISH
AHIIOPST	HOSPITIA	AHIRSSTW	TRISHAWS
AHIIPRSS	AIRSHIPS	AHISSSTU	SHIATSUS
AHIKLNRS	RINKHALS	AHISSTTW	WHATSITS
AHIKLRSY	RAKISHLY	AHISTTWW	WHITTAWS
AHIKMNSS	KHAMSINS	AHKMORRS	MARKHORS
AHIKMRSS	KASHMIRS	AHKMRSTU	MUKHTARS
AHIKNPRS	PRANKISH	AHLLNOOS	SHALLOON
AHIKPRSS	SPARKISH	AHLLNOSS	SHALLONS
AHILLMPS	PHALLISM	AHLLNOSY	HALLYONS
AHILLMSS	SMALLISH	AHLLNOUW	UNHALLOW
AHILLMTU	THALLIUM	AHLLOPSS	SHALLOPS
AHILLNOS	HALLIONS	AHLLOSST	SHALLOTS
AHILLNPS	PHALLINS	AHLLOSSW	SHALLOWS
AHILLNRT	INTHRALL	AHLLOSTU	THALLOUS
AHILLNTW	WANTHILL	AHLLPRYY	PHYLLARY
AHILLSTT	TALLITHS	AHLMMOPY	LYMPHOMA
AHILLSVY	LAVISHLY	AHLMMSSU	MASHLUMS
AHILMMSS	MASHLIMS	AHLMNOOR	HORMONAL
AHILMNSS	MASHLINS	AHLMOOPS	OMPHALOS
AHILMOPT	PHILAMOT	AHLMOPTY	POLYMATH
AHILMOST	HALIMOTS	AHLNNORT	LANTHORN
AHILMQSU	QUALMISH	AHLNOPRS	ALPHORNS
AHILNOPS	SIPHONAL	AHLNORST	ALTHORNS
AHILNOPT	OLIPHANT	AHLORRTY	HARLOTRY
AHILNORT	HORNTAIL	AHLOSTUU	OUTHAULS
AHILNRST	INTHRALS	AHLRSTUY	LATHYRUS
AHILOPST	HOSPITAL	AHLRTTWY	THWARTLY
AHILOSTU	HALITOUS	AHMMMOST	MAMMOTHS
AHILPPSS	SHIPLAPS	AHMMMSUU	HUMMAUMS
AHILPSSY	PHYSALIS	AHMNNSTU	HUNTSMAN
AHILRSTY	TRASHILY		MANHUNTS
AHILRTWY	WRATHILY	AHMNOPST	PHANTOMS
AHIMMNSU	HUMANISM	AHMNOPTY	PHANTOMY
AHIMMORZ	MAHZORIM	AHMOOPSS	SHAMPOOS
AHIMMOSV	MOSHAVIM	AHMOORSW	WASHROOM
AHIMNOST	HOISTMAN	AHMOOSSS	SAMSHOOS
AHIMNOSW	WOMANISH	AHMORRSU	MORRHUAS
AHIMNSTU	HUMANIST	AHMORSST	HARMOSTS
AHIMNTUY	HUMANITY	AHMORSTY	HARMOSTY
AHIMOPRS	APHORISM	AHMPSTYY	SYMPATHY
	MORPHIAS	AHMQSSUU	MUSQUASH
AHIMOPST	OPSIMATH	AHMRSSTY	THRYMSAS
AHIMPPSS	SAPPHISM	AHNNSTYY	SYNANTHY
AHIMRSST	THRIMSAS	AHNOOPRS	HARPOONS
AHIMSTUZ	AZIMUTHS	AHNOOPSU	APHONOUS
AHIMSTVZ	MITZVAHS	AHNOORRY	HONORARY
AHINNNSY	NANNYISH	AHNOPPSW	PAWNSHOP
AHINNOPT	ANTIPHON	AHNOPPSY	PANSOPHY
AHINNSTX	XANTHINS	AHNOPSST	SNAPSHOT
AHINOPRU	OPHIURAN	AHNORSSX	SAXHORNS
AHINORST	TRAHISON	AHNORTWW	WANWORTH
AHINOSST	ASTONISH	AHNOSTTW	WHATNOTS
AHINOSTZ	HOATZINS	AHNOSTUX	XANTHOUS
AHINPPSS	SNAPPISH	AHNPPSUU	PUPUNHAS
AHINPRST	TRANSHIP	AHOOPTYZ	ZOOPATHY
AHINQSUV	VANQUISH	AHOOSSTY	SOOTHSAY
AHINRSTY	RHYTINAS	AHOPSTTW	TOWPATHS
AHINSSTU	INHAUSTS	AHOPSTUW	SOUTHPAW
AHIOOPPT	PHOTOPIA	AHOSSTUY	SOUTHSAY
AHIOPRST	APHORIST	AHRSTUWY	THRUWAYS
AHIOPSXY	HYPOXIAS		

AIIILLVX	LIXIVIAL	AIIMOPSX	APOMIXIS
AIIILMST	MILITIAS	AIIMORTT	IMITATOR
AIIILNST	INITIALS		TIMARIOT
AIIILRVZ	VIZIRIAL	AIIMOSST	AMITOSIS
AIIIMRSS	SAIMIRIS	AIIMPPRS	PRIAPISM
AIIIRSSS	SIRIASIS	AIIMPRTY	IMPARITY
AIIJKMOT	KOMITAJI	AIIMRSST	SIMITARS
AIIJNRTX	JANITRIX	AIIMRUVV	VIVARIUM
AIIKKSUY	SUKIYAKI	AIIMSSTT	MASTITIS
AIIKLLST	SILKTAIL	AIINNOPS	PIANINOS
AIIKLNRR	LARRIKIN	AIINNOSV	INVASION
AIIKMMSS	SKIMMIAS	AIINNQTU	QUINTAIN
AIIKMNNN	MANNIKIN	AIINNSTY	INSANITY
AIIKMNNS	MANIKINS	AIINOOSV	AVOISION
AIIKNNNP	PANNIKIN	AIINOPSS	SINOPIAS
AIILLLMT	MILLTAIL	AIINORST	INTARSIO
AIILLMRY	MILLIARY	AIINORTT	TRITONIA
AIILLNNV	VANILLIN	AIINOSTT	NOTITIAS
AIILLNOP	POLLINIA	AIINPRSS	ASPIRINS
AIILLNOT	ILLATION	AIINPSST	PIANISTS
AIILLNSV	VILLAINS	AIINRRTT	IRRITANT
AIILLNVY	VILLAINY	AIINRSTV	VITRAINS
AIILLPRS	SLIPRAIL	AIINSTTV	NATIVIST
	SPIRILLA		VISITANT
AIILLQSU	QUILLAIS	AIINTTVY	NATIVITY
AIILLWWW	WILLIWAW	AIIORRST	SARTORII
AIILMNOS	MONILIAS	AIIORSTT	AORTITIS
AIILMNOT	LIMATION	AIIORSTV	OVARITIS
	MILTONIA	AIIORTTV	VITIATOR
AIILMNPS	ALPINISM	AIIPRRST	AIRSTRIP
AIILMNPT	PALMITIN	AIIPRSST	PIARISTS
AIILMNTT	MILITANT	AIIPRVVY	VIVIPARY
AIILMPUV	IMPLUVIA	AIIPSTTU	PITUITAS
AIILMRST	MISTRIAL	AIIRSSTT	SATIRIST
	TRIALISM	AIISSSTY	SYSSITIA
AIILMRTY	LIMITARY	AIJKKNOU	KINKAJOU
	MILITARY	AIJLLOOR	JILLAROO
AIILMSTV	VITALISM	AIJLLOVY	JOVIALLY
AIILNOPV	PAVILION	AIJLNTUY	JAUNTILY
AIILNOSS	LIAISONS	AIJMORTY	MAJORITY
AIILNOSV	VISIONAL	AIJNNRTU	INJURANT
AIILNPST	ALPINIST	AIJNOPPY	POPINJAY
	PINTAILS	AIJNORST	JANITORS
AIILNSTY	SALINITY	AIKKNOTY	KANTIKOY
AIILOPPS	PAPILIOS	AIKKRTUZ	ZIKKURAT
AIILORSV	RAVIOLIS	AIKLLMRR	RILLMARK
AIILQSSU	SILIQUAS	AIKLMPSU	LAMPUKIS
AIILRSTT	TRIALIST	AIKLMPTU	KALUMPIT
AIILRTTY	TRIALITY	AIKLNPST	LANTSKIP
AIILRTVY	RIVALITY	AIKLOTTW	KILOWATT
AIILSTTV	VITALIST	AIKLRSTT	TITLARKS
AIILTTVY	VITALITY	AIKLSSSY	SKYSAILS
AIIMMNNY	MINYANIM	AIKMMNOO	MAKIMONO
AIIMMNSS	ANIMISMS	AIKMORSS	KOMISSAR
AIIMMNSX	MAXIMINS	AIKNNOOS	NAINSOOK
AIIMMNTY	IMMANITY	AIKNORST	SKIATRON
AIIMMSTX	MAXIMIST	AIKNOSTT	STOTINKA
AIIMNNOS	INSOMNIA	AIKRSSTY	SATYRISK
AIIMNPSS	PIANISMS	AILLLNOO	LINALOOL
	SINAPISM	AILLMMSY	SMALMILY
AIIMNPST	IMPAINTS	AILLMNQU	QUILLMAN
AIIMNPSX	PANMIXIS	AILLMOST	MAILLOTS
AIIMNRST	MARTINIS		MISALLOT
AIIMNSST	ANIMISTS	AILLMOTY	MOLALITY
	SAINTISM	AILLMPRY	PRIMALLY
	SAMNITIS	AILLMUUV	ALLUVIUM
AIIMNSTT	IMITANTS	AILLNNOS	LANOLINS
AIIMNSTV	NATIVISM	AILLNOPP	PAPILLON
	VITAMINS	AILLNOPS	PAILLONS
AIIMNTTU	TITANIUM	AILLNOST	STALLION

Letters	Word(s)
AILLNOSU	ALLUSION
AILLNOUV	ALLUVION
AILLNPTY	PLIANTLY
AILLNSST	INSTALLS
AILLORSY	SAILORLY
AILLORTT	LITTORAL
	TORTILLA
AILLOSTY	LOYALIST
AILLPPSU	SUPPLIAL
AILLPRSY	SPIRALLY
AILLPRTY	PALTRILY
AILLPSUV	PLUVIALS
AILLPSWY	SPILLWAY
AILLRSTY	RALLYIST
AILLRTUY	RITUALLY
AILLRTWY	WILLYART
AILLSTWW	WITWALLS
AILLSUVY	VISUALLY
AILMMNOO	MONOMIAL
AILMMNUU	ALUMINUM
AILMMORS	MORALISM
AILMMORT	IMMORTAL
AILMMRSY	SMARMILY
AILMMSSY	MYALISMS
AILMMSUU	ALUMIUMS
AILMNNOS	NOMINALS
AILMNNOT	MANNITOL
AILMNNTU	LUMINANT
AILMNOOP	PALOMINO
AILMNOOR	MONORAIL
AILMNOOS	MOONSAIL
AILMNOOT	MOTIONAL
AILMNOPR	PROLAMIN
AILMNOPS	LAMPIONS
AILMNOPY	PALIMONY
AILMNORT	TORMINAL
AILMNOSS	MALISONS
AILMNPSS	PLASMINS
AILMNPST	IMPLANTS
AILMNPTU	PLATINUM
AILMNRSU	MURLAINS
AILMNRUY	LUMINARY
AILMNSTU	SIMULANT
AILMOORT	MOTORAIL
	MOTORIAL
AILMOPRX	PROXIMAL
AILMORSS	SOLARISM
AILMORST	MORALIST
AILMORSU	SOLARIUM
AILMORSY	ROYALISM
AILMORTY	MOLARITY
	MORALITY
AILMOSTU	SOLATIUM
AILMOSTV	VOLTAISM
AILMPPSY	MISAPPLY
AILMPRSU	PRIMULAS
AILMPSST	PALMISTS
	PSALMIST
AILMPSSY	MISPLAYS
AILMPSTY	PTYALISM
AILMRRSU	RURALISM
AILMRSST	MISTRALS
AILMRSSU	SIMULARS
	SURMISAL
AILMRSTU	ALTRUISM
	MURALIST
	ULTRAISM
AILNNOOT	NOTIONAL
AILNNOSU	UNISONAL
AILNNOTU	LUNATION
AILNNPSU	PINNULAS
AILNNPTU	UNPLIANT
AILNNSTU	INSULANT
AILNOOPT	OPTIONAL
AILNOOST	SOLATION
AILNOPRU	UNIPOLAR
AILNOPSY	POLYNIAS
AILNORTZ	TRIZONAL
AILNOSSS	SASSOLIN
AILNOSUV	AVULSION
AILNOSVY	SYNOVIAL
AILNOTTV	VOLITANT
AILNOTTY	TONALITY
AILNOTUX	LUXATION
AILNPPSY	SNAPPILY
AILNPRSU	PURSLAIN
AILNPRSW	PRAWLINS
AILNPRUV	PULVINAR
AILNPSTU	NUPTIALS
	PATULINS
	UNPLAITS
AILNPSTY	PTYALINS
AILNPSUU	NAUPLIUS
AILNPTTU	TULIPANT
AILNQRTU	TRANQUIL
AILNQSTU	QUINTALS
AILNQTUY	QUAINTLY
AILNRSTT	RATTLINS
AILNRSTU	LUNARIST
AILNRTTU	RUTILANT
AILNRUWY	UNWARILY
AILNSSTU	STUNSAIL
	UNALISTS
AILNSTTU	LUTANIST
AILNSTUU	NAUTILUS
AILOOPRT	TROOPIAL
AILOORRS	SORORIAL
AILOORST	ISOLATOR
AILOORSW	WOORALIS
AILOORTV	VIOLATOR
AILOPRRV	PROVIRAL
AILOPRTU	TROUPIAL
AILOPRTY	POLARITY
AILOPRUY	POLYURIA
AILOPSST	APOSTILS
	TOPSAILS
AILOPSTT	TALIPOTS
AILORSST	SOLARIST
AILORSTU	SUTORIAL
AILORSTY	ROYALIST
	SOLITARY
AILORSUW	WOURALIS
AILORTTU	TUTORIAL
AILORTUV	OUTRIVAL
AILOSSTU	OUTSAILS
AILOTTTY	TOTALITY
AILPPRUY	PUPILARY
AILPRSSU	UPRISALS
AILPRSTU	STIPULAR
AILPSSWY	SLIPWAYS
AILPSTUY	PLAYSUIT
AILQSTTU	QUITTALS
AILRRSTU	RURALIST
AILRRSTY	STARRILY
AILRRTUY	RURALITY
AILRSSTU	TRISULAS
AILRSSTY	TRYSAILS
AILRSTTU	ALTRUIST
	TITULARS
	ULTRAIST
AILRSTTY	STRAITLY
AILRSUVV	SURVIVAL
AILRTTUY	TITULARY
AILSSTUW	LAWSUITS
AIMMMNOU	AMMONIUM
AIMMNORT	MORTMAIN
AIMMNSTU	MANUMITS
AIMMORSS	AMORISMS
AIMMOSST	ATOMISMS
	SOMATISM
AIMMOSSU	MIASMOUS
AIMMRRSY	MISMARRY
AIMMRSUU	MASURIUM
AIMNNOSS	MANSIONS
	ONANISMS
AIMNNOTU	MOUNTAIN
AIMNNOTY	ANTIMONY
	ANTINOMY
AIMNNRTU	RUMINANT
AIMNOOOZ	ZOONOMIA
AIMNOPRS	RAMPIONS
AIMNOPST	MAINTOPS
	TAMPIONS
AIMNOQRU	MAROQUIN
AIMNORSU	MAINOURS
AIMNORTY	MINATORY
AIMNOSST	STASIMON
AIMNOSTU	MANITOUS
	TINAMOUS
AIMNOTTU	MUTATION
AIMNPRYY	PAYNIMRY
AIMNPSTU	SUMPITAN
AIMNRRSU	MURRAINS
AIMNRSSU	URANISMS
AIMNRSTT	TRANSMIT
AIMNRSTU	NATRIUMS
	NATURISM
AIMNRSTV	VARMINTS
AIMNRSUU	URANIUMS
AIMNSSTU	TSUNAMIS
AIMNSSYZ	ZANYISMS
AIMOPRSS	PROSAISM
AIMOPRST	ATROPISM
AIMOPSST	IMPASTOS
AIMOPSSY	SYMPOSIA
AIMORRST	ARMORIST
AIMORRSU	ORARIUMS
	ROSARIUM
AIMORRUV	VARIORUM
AIMORSST	AMORISTS
AIMORSSU	OSSARIUM
AIMORSUZ	ZOARIUMS
AIMOSSTT	ATOMISTS
	SOMATIST
AIMPPRUU	PUPARIUM
AIMPPSST	MAPPISTS
AIMPRSTY	PARTYISM
AIMRSSST	TSARISMS
AIMRSSTY	SYMITARS
AIMRSTTU	STRIATUM
AIMRTTUY	MATURITY
AIMSSSTT	STATISMS
AINNNOST	SANTONIN
AINNOOTT	NOTATION
AINNOOTV	NOVATION
AINNOOTZ	ZONATION
AINNOPSS	SAPONINS
AINNOSST	ONANISTS
AINNOTTU	NUTATION
AINNPSTU	UNPAINTS
AINNQSTU	QUINNATS
AINNRSTT	INTRANTS
AINNRSTU	INSURANT
AINNRSTY	TYRANNIS
AINNSSTT	INSTANTS
AINNSSTU	UNSAINTS
AINOOPTT	POTATION
AINOORRS	ORARIONS
AINOORST	ORATIONS
AINOORTT	ROTATION
AINOOSTT	OSTINATO
AINOOSTV	OVATIONS
AINOOTTV	OTTAVINO
AINOPPRT	PARPOINT
AINOPPST	APPOINTS
AINOPPTU	PUPATION
AINOPRSS	PARISONS
AINOPRST	ATROPINS
AINOPRTV	PROVIANT
AINOPSSS	PASSIONS
AINOPSTU	OPUNTIAS
	UTOPIANS
AINOQRSU	NARQUOIS
AINORRSW	WARRISON
AINORRTU	URINATOR
AINORSST	ARSONIST
AINORSSW	WARISONS
AINORSTT	STRONTIA
AINORSTU	SUTORIAN
AINORSTX	TRIAXONS
AINORTVY	VANITORY
AINOSSSU	SUASIONS
AINOSSTT	STATIONS
AINOSSVY	SYNOVIAS
AINOSTTU	TITANOUS
AINPPRSS	PARSNIPS
AINPPRTT	TRIPPANT
AINPRSST	SPIRANTS
	SPRAINTS
AINPRSTU	PURITANS
	UPTRAINS
AINPSSSY	SYNAPSIS
AINPSSTU	PUISSANT
AINQTTUY	QUANTITY
AINRSSTT	STRAINTS
	TRANSITS
AINRSTTU	NATURIST
AINRSTTY	TANISTRY
AINSSSTU	SUSTAINS
AIOOORRT	ORATORIO
AIOORSUV	OVARIOUS
AIOPRRST	AIRPORTS
	PARITORS
AIOPRRTT	PORTRAIT
AIOPRSST	AIRSTOPS
	PROSAIST
	PROTASIS
AIOPRSTT	PATRIOTS
AIOPRSUV	PAVIOURS
AIOPSTTU	UTOPIAST
AIORRRSW	WARRIORS
AIORRSTT	TRAITORS
AIORRSTV	VARISTOR
AIORRTWY	RYOTWARI
AIORSSTU	SAUTOIRS
AIORSSUV	SAVIOURS
AIORSTTV	VOTARIST
AIORSTUV	VIRTUOSA
AIOSSSTY	ISOSTASY
AIPPRSTY	PAPISTRY

AIPRSSTU	UPSTAIRS	ALNRRTUU	NURTURAL
AIPRSSTY	SPARSITY	ALOOPPRS	PROPOSAL
AIRRSTTY	ARTISTRY	ALOOPRTU	UPROOTAL
AIRRSTZZ	RIZZARTS	ALOORSUV	VALOROUS
AIRSSSTT	TSARISTS	ALOORTYZ	ZOOLATRY
AIRSSTTT	ATTRISTS	ALOPPRSU	POPULARS
AISSSTTT	STATISTS	ALOPPRYY	POLYPARY
AJKMNSTU	MUNTJAKS	ALOPPSSU	SUPPOSAL
AJKNNOOU	JUNKANOO	ALOPPSUU	PAPULOUS
AJLNORSU	JOURNALS	ALOPRRSU	PARLOURS
AJMRSTUY	JURYMAST		SPORULAR
AJORRTUY	JURATORY	ALOPRSTT	PORTLAST
AKKLRSSY	SKYLARKS	ALOPRSTU	POSTURAL
AKLNNOPT	PLANKTON		PULSATOR
AKLOPRSW	LAPWORKS	ALOPRSTY	PASTORLY
AKLOSTTU	OUTTALKS	ALOPSSSU	SPOUSALS
AKLOSTUW	OUTWALKS	ALOPSSUV	VOLUSPAS
AKLPRRSU	LARKSPUR	ALOPSTUU	PATULOUS
AKMMNOOR	MONOMARK	ALOPSTUY	OUTPLAYS
AKMNRSTU	TRANKUMS	ALOQRRSU	RORQUALS
AKMOORST	MOOKTARS	ALOQRSSU	SQUALORS
AKMOPRST	POSTMARK	ALORRSUY	SURROYAL
AKMQSTUU	KUMQUATS	ALORSUVY	SAVOURLY
AKNOORST	OSTRAKON	ALORTUWY	OUTLAWRY
AKNOPSTW	SWANKPOT	ALOSSTTU	OUTLASTS
AKNORSTU	OUTRANKS	ALPPSTUY	PLATYPUS
AKOPRRTW	PARTWORK	ALPRSSUU	PURSUALS
AKORRSTW	ARTWORKS	ALPRSTUU	PUSTULAR
AKORSWWX	WAXWORKS	AMMNOORT	MOTORMAN
ALLLPRUY	PLURALLY	AMMNPTUY	TYMPANUM
ALLMNORY	NORMALLY	AMMOORRS	MAORMORS
ALLMNOSY	ALLONYMS		MORMAORS
ALLMOPSX	SMALLPOX	AMMOPSTU	POMATUMS
ALLMORTY	MORTALLY	AMNNOOSX	MONAXONS
ALLMOUWY	MULLOWAY	AMNNOOTT	MONTANTO
ALLMPRUU	PLUMULAR	AMNNORSW	MANSWORN
ALLMTUUY	MUTUALLY	AMNNORSY	MANSONRY
ALLNORSS	LASSLORN	AMNNOSTT	MONTANTS
ALLOOSTX	AXOLOTLS	AMNNOSTW	TOWNSMAN
ALLOPRSY	PAYROLLS	AMNNOSTY	ANTONYMS
ALLORTWW	WALLWORT	AMNNOSUW	UNWOMANS
ALLOSSWW	SWALLOWS	AMNNOTTU	MOUNTANT
ALLRUUVY	UVULARLY	AMNNPSTU	PUNTSMAN
ALMMNRUU	NUMMULAR	AMNNSTTU	STUNTMAN
ALMMORTW	MALTWORM	AMNOOPPS	POMPANOS
ALMNOOPS	LAMPOONS	AMNOOSTT	OTTOMANS
ALMNORTY	MATRONLY	AMNOORST	MATZOONS
ALMNOSSU	SOLANUMS	AMNOOTUY	AUTONOMY
ALMOOPRY	PLAYROOM	AMNOOTWY	TOYWOMAN
ALMOPPST	LAMPPOST	AMNOOTXY	TAXONOMY
ALMOPRST	MARPLOTS	AMNOPRSY	PARONYMS
ALMORSUU	RAMULOUS	AMNOPRYY	PARONYMY
ALMOSTTU	MULATTOS	AMNOPSTU	PANTOUMS
ALMRTUUY	TUMULARY	AMNORSST	TRANSOMS
ALMSSSUY	ALYSSUMS	AMNORSTU	ROMAUNTS
ALNNOOPR	NONPOLAR	AMNOSTUY	AUTONYMS
ALNNOTWY	WANTONLY	AMNOTTUY	TAUTONYM
ALNNRSSU	UNSNARLS	AMNRSTTU	TANTRUMS
ALNOOPRS	POLARONS	AMOOORSS	AMOROSOS
ALNOOPRT	PORTOLAN	AMOOPRST	TAPROOMS
	PRONOTAL	AMOORRTY	MORATORY
ALNOOPST	PLATOONS	AMOORSTZ	SMORZATO
ALNOOPXY	POLYAXON	AMOORTWY	MOTORWAY
ALNOOPYZ	POLYZOAN	AMOOSSTU	ASTOMOUS
ALNOORST	ORTOLANS	AMOOTTUY	AUTOTOMY
ALNOPRST	PLASTRON	AMOPRSXY	PAROXYSM
ALNOPRTU	PORTULAN	AMOPSSTT	TOPMASTS
ALNOPSYY	POLYNYAS	AMOQSSUU	SQUAMOUS
ALNORRWY	NARROWLY	AMORRTUY	MORTUARY
ALNPPSTU	SUPPLANT	AMORSTTU	OUTSMART

AMORTTUY	MUTATORY	BBCEILRS	CRIBBLES
AMPRSSUW	UPSWARMS		SCRIBBLE
AMRRSSTU	RASTRUMS	BBCEIOST	COBBIEST
ANNOORST	SONORANT	BBCEKKOS	KEBBOCKS
ANNOSSTU	STANNOUS	BBCEKKSU	KEBBUCKS
ANOOPRRT	PRONATOR	BBCEKLUU	BLUEBUCK
ANOOPRSS	SOPRANOS	BBCELORS	CLOBBERS
ANOOPRST	PATROONS		COBBLERS
ANOORSTT	ARNOTTOS	BBCELORY	COBBLERY
ANOORSUU	ANOUROUS	BBCEMNOU	BUNCOMBE
ANOPRRSS	SPORRANS	BBCERRSU	SCRUBBER
ANOPRTTU	TRAPUNTO	BBCGIINR	CRIBBING
ANOPSSTU	OUTSPANS	BBCGILNO	COBBLING
ANOQRSSU	SQUARSON	BBCGILNU	CLUBBING
ANORSSTU	SANTOURS	BBCGINSU	CUBBINGS
ANORSTVY	SOVRANTY	BBCHILSU	CLUBBISH
ANPSSUW	SUPPAWNS	BBCHKOOS	BOSCHBOK
ANPRSSTU	SUNTRAPS	BBCILMSU	CLUBBISM
	UNSTRAPS	BBCILRSY	SCRIBBLY
ANPRSTUU	PURSUANT	BBCILSTU	CLUBBIST
ANRRTTUY	TRUANTRY	BBDDEEMO	DEMOBBED
ANRSSTYY	SYNASTRY	BBDDEILR	DRIBBLED
AOOOPRTZ	PROTOZOA	BBDDENUU	UNDUBBED
AOOPPRSY	APOSPORY	BBDEEGIR	GIBBERED
AOOPRSSU	SAPOROUS	BBDEEGIT	GIBBETED
AOOPRSTT	TAPROOTS	BBDEEIJR	JIBBERED
AOOPRSTU	ATROPOUS	BBDEEIST	DEBBIEST
AOOPRSTW	SOAPWORT		EBBTIDES
AOOPRSUV	VAPOROUS	BBDEEMNU	BENUMBED
AOOPRTTY	POTATORY	BBDEENUW	UNWEBBED
AOORRSTT	ROTATORS	BBDEEOPP	BEBOPPED
AOORRSTU	OUTROARS	BBDEERRU	RUBBERED
AOORRTTY	ROTATORY	BBDEERSU	SUBBREED
AOORSSTU	OUTSOARS	BBDEFILR	FRIBBLED
AOORSSUV	SAVOROUS	BBDEGLRU	GRUBBLED
AOPPRRST	RAPPORTS	BBDEHORT	THROBBED
AOPPRSST	PASSPORT	BBDEHRSU	SHRUBBED
AOPRRRTY	PARROTRY	BBDEILLN	BELLBIND
AOPRRSSW	SPARROWS	BBDEILQU	QUIBBLED
AOPRRSTY	PORTRAYS	BBDEILRR	DRIBBLER
AOPRRTUY	POURTRAY	BBDEILRS	DIBBLERS
AOPRSSTT	STARSPOT		DRIBBLES
AOPRSTTU	OUTPARTS	BBDEILRT	DRIBBLET
AOPRSTTY	PYROSTAT	BBDEILRU	BLUEBIRD
AOPRSTUY	OUTPRAYS	BBDEINOR	RIBBONED
AORRSTTW	STARWORT	BBDEINRU	UNRIBBED
AORRTTWW	WARTWORT	BBDEIQSU	SQUIBBED
AORSSTTU	STRATOUS	BBDEIRRS	DRIBBERS
AORSSTTY	STAROSTY	BBDEKLNO	KNOBBLED
AOSSTTUY	OUTSTAYS	BBDEKLNU	KNUBBLED
APPRRSUU	PURPURAS	BBDELOSS	BOBSLEDS
APRSSTTU	UPSTARTS	BBDELSTU	STUBBLED
BBBCEOWY	COBWEBBY	BBDENRUU	UNRUBBED
BBBDEEOR	BEROBBED	BBDGIILN	DIBBLING
BBBEILRU	BUBBLIER	BBDGIINR	DRIBBING
BBBEILSU	BUBBLIES	BBDGINRU	DRUBBING
BBBEINOT	BOBBINET	BBDGINSU	DUBBINGS
BBBELRSU	BLUBBERS	BBDOSUYY	BUSYBODY
BBBGILNO	BLOBBING	BBEEERSU	BEBEERUS
	BOBBLING	BBEEHINS	NEBBISHE
BBBGILNU	BLUBBING	BBEEHLOW	BOBWHEEL
	BUBBLING	BBEEIIRR	BERIBERI
BBBHNOOY	HOBNOBBY	BBEEILPR	PEBBLIER
BBBHOOUU	HUBBUBOO		PLEBBIER
BBCCIKOS	BIBCOCKS	BBEEIRRS	BERBERIS
BBCDEILR	CRIBBLED	BBEEISTW	WEBBIEST
BBCDERSU	SCRUBBED	BBEELLLU	BLUEBELL
BBCDIMOY	BOMBYCID	BBEFILRR	FRIBBLER
BBCEHINS	NEBBICHS	BBEFILRS	FRIBBLES
BBCEHIRU	CHUBBIER	BBEFISTU	FUBBIEST

BBEGIIST	GIBBSITE	BBGIILLN	NIBBLING
BBEGILNP	PEBBLING	BBGIINNS	SNIBBING
BBEGILRS	GRIBBLES	BBGIINRS	RIBBINGS
BBEGILRY	GLIBBERY	BBGIJNOS	JOBBINGS
BBEGILST	GLIBBEST	BBGILMNO	MOBBLING
BBEGINNS	SNEBBING	BBGILMNU	BUMBLING
BBEGINSW	WEBBINGS	BBGILNNO	NOBBLING
BBEGIRRU	GRUBBIER	BBGILNNU	NUBBLING
BBEGLORS	GOBBLERS	BBGILNOW	WOBBLING
BBEGLRSU	GRUBBLES	BBGILNOY	LOBBYING
BBEGRRSU	GRUBBERS	BBGILNRU	BURBLING
BBEHLORS	HOBBLERS	BBGILNSU	SLUBBING
BBEHMSTU	BETHUMBS	BBGINNSU	SNUBBING
BBEIILRS	RIBIBLES	BBGINOSS	SOBBINGS
BBEIIMRS	IMBIBERS	BBGINOSW	SWOBBING
BBEIIRST	RIBBIEST	BBGINRSU	RUBBINGS
BBEIKNOR	KNOBBIER	BBGINSSU	SUBBINGS
BBEIKNRU	KNUBBIER	BBGINSTU	STUBBING
BBEILLNO	BONIBELL		TUBBINGS
BBEILNRS	NIBBLERS	BBHIMOSY	HOBBYISM
BBEILNRU	NUBBLIER	BBHINOSS	SNOBBISH
BBEILORS	SLOBBIER	BBHINSSU	SNUBBISH
BBEILORW	WOBBLIER	BBHIOOSY	BOOBYISH
BBEILOST	BIBELOTS	BBHIORTY	HOBBITRY
BBEILOSW	WOBBLIES	BBHIOSTY	HOBBYIST
BBEILPRS	PRIBBLES	BBHIRSUY	RUBBISHY
BBEILQRU	QUIBBLER	BBHOOSUW	WHOOBUBS
BBEILQSU	QUIBBLES	BBHRSSUU	SUBSHRUB
BBEILNRU	RUBBLIER	BBIIILMS	BILIMBIS
BBEILRRY	BILBERRY	BBIILSST	BIBLISTS
BBEILRST	STIBBLER	BBIKLLOO	BILLBOOK
	TRIBBLES	BBIKLNOO	BOBOLINK
BBEILRSU	SLUBBIER	BBILLOYY	BILLYBOY
BBEILSST	STIBBLES	BBILOSTY	LOBBYIST
BBEIMOST	BOMBSITE	BBILOSUU	BIBULOUS
BBEIMRSU	BRUMBIES	BBIMNOSS	SNOBBISM
BBEINORS	SNOBBIER	BBIMOOSY	BOOBYISM
BBEINOST	NOBBIEST	BBINORRY	RIBBONRY
BBEINRSU	SNUBBIER	BBKLOOSU	BLOUBOKS
BBEINSTU	NUBBIEST	BBKOOOOS	BOOBOOKS
BBEIRSTU	STUBBIER	BBNOORSU	BOURBONS
	SUBTRIBE	BBNORSTU	STUBBORN
BBEISSTU	STUBBIES	BCCDEILY	BICYCLED
BBEISTTU	TUBBIEST	BCCDHIKO	DOBCHICK
BBEKLNOS	KNOBBLES	BCCDIKOR	COCKBIRD
BBEKLNSU	KNUBBLES	BCCEEIRR	CEREBRIC
BBEKLOSS	BLESBOKS	BCCEHIRU	CHERUBIC
BBEKLSUU	BUBUKLES	BCCEIIIS	CICISBEI
BBEKNOOT	BONTEBOK	BCCEIILO	LIBECCIO
BBEKNORS	KNOBBERS	BCCEIIOS	CICISBEO
BBELLRUY	LUBBERLY	BCCEILOS	ECBOLICS
BBELNORS	NOBBLERS	BCCEILRU	CRUCIBLE
BBELORSS	SLOBBERS	BCCEILSU	CUBICLES
BBELORSW	WOBBLERS	BCCEILSY	BICYCLES
BBELORSY	LOBBYERS	BCCEMRUU	CUCUMBER
	SLOBBERY	BCCIIMOR	MICROBIC
BBELRSSU	SLUBBERS	BCCILMOU	COLUMBIC
BBELSSTU	STUBBLES	BCCILOOR	BROCCOLI
BBENORSY	SNOBBERY	BCCILOSU	BUCOLICS
BBENRSSU	SNUBBERS	BCCIRTUU	CUCURBIT
BBEORSSW	SWOBBERS	BCCMOOSX	COXCOMBS
BBFGILNU	FLUBBING	BCCMSSUU	SUCCUMBS
BBGGIILN	GLIBBING	BCCSSUUU	SUCCUBUS
BBGGILNO	GOBBLING	BCDDEEEK	BEDECKED
BBGGINRU	GRUBBING	BCDDEEKU	BEDUCKED
BBGHILNO	HOBBLING	BCDDEHIL	CHILDBED
BBGIIIMN	IMBIBING	BCDDESUU	SUBDUCED
BBGIIJNS	JIBBINGS	BCDEEEHR	BREECHED
BBGIIKLN	KIBBLING	BCDEEEHLN	BLENCHED
BBGIILMN	BLIMBING	BCDEEHNR	BEDRENCH

BCDEEHOU	DEBOUCHE	BCEEMNRU	ENCUMBER
BCDEEIKR	BICKERED	BCEEMRRU	CEREBRUM
BCDEEILR	CREDIBLE		CUMBERER
BCDEEILS	DECIBELS	BCEENORS	OBSCENER
BCDEEILU	EDUCIBLE	BCEENRSU	CRUBEENS
BCDEEINT	BENEDICT	BCEERSTU	SUBERECT
BCDEEIPS	BESPICED	BCEFFIIR	FEBRIFIC
BCDEEIRS	DESCRIBE	BCEFILOR	FORCIBLE
	ESCRIBED	BCEGHILN	BELCHING
BCDEEIST	BISECTED	BCEGHINN	BENCHING
BCDEEJOT	OBJECTED	BCEGIINO	BIOGENIC
BCDEEKMO	BEMOCKED	BCEGIMNO	BECOMING
BCDEEKNO	BECKONED	BCEGLNOO	CONGLOBE
BCDEEKTU	BUCKETED	BCEHIIRT	BITCHIER
BCDEELRU	BECURLED	BCEHIMRS	BESMIRCH
BCDEEMRU	CUMBERED	BCEHIMRU	CHERUBIM
BCDEEORV	BEDCOVER	BCEHINRU	BUNCHIER
BCDEEOTT	OBTECTED		CHERUBIN
BCDEHINS	DISBENCH	BCEHIORS	BRIOCHES
BCDEHLOT	BLOTCHED	BCEHIORT	BOTCHIER
BCDEHOOR	BROOCHED	BCEHIRST	BRITCHES
BCDEIIOS	BIOCIDES	BCEHIRTY	BITCHERY
BCDEIITU	DECUBITI	BCEHLOST	BLOTCHES
BCDEIKRR	REDBRICK	BCEHLRSU	BLUCHERS
BCDEIKST	BEDTICKS	BCEHMSTU	BESMUTCH
BCDEILRY	CREDIBLY	BCEHNRSU	BRUNCHES
BCDEIMNO	COMBINED	BCEHOORS	BROOCHES
BCDEKORS	BEDROCKS	BCEHORRU	BROCHURE
BCDEKOSS	BEDSOCKS	BCEHORSS	BORSCHES
BCDELMRU	CRUMBLED	BCEHORST	BOTCHERS
BCDELMSU	SCUMBLED	BCEHORTY	BOTCHERY
BCDELOSU	BECLOUDS	BCEHRSTU	BUTCHERS
BCDEMNOU	UNCOMBED	BCEHRTUY	BUTCHERY
BCDENRUU	UNCURBED	BCEHSTTU	BUTCHEST
BCDEORSU	OBSCURED	BCEIIKLN	ICEBLINK
BCDESSUU	SUBDUCES	BCEIIKRR	BRICKIER
BCDHIRSU	BRUCHIDS	BCEIIKRS	BRICKIES
BCDHOOSU	CUBHOODS	BCEIILMS	MISCIBLE
BCDIIMOR	BROMIDIC	BCEIILNV	VINCIBLE
BCDIIPSU	BICUSPID	BCEIIMRS	IMBRICES
BCDIKLLU	DUCKBILL	BCEIINRS	INSCRIBE
BCDILMOY	MOLYBDIC	BCEIKLMS	LIMBECKS
BCDINRUU	RUBICUND	BCEIKLOO	BOOKLICE
BCDIORSW	COWBIRDS	BCEIKLOR	BOCKLIER
BCDKORSU	BURDOCKS	BCEIKSST	BESTICKS
BCDSSTUU	SUBDUCTS	BCEILMRS	CLIMBERS
BCEEEFIN	BENEFICE		RECLIMBS
BCEEEFKN	NECKBEEF	BCEILNOS	BINOCLES
BCEEEHRS	BREECHES	BCEILNRU	RUNCIBLE
BCEEENRS	BESCREEN	BCEILORS	BRICOLES
BCEEERSU	BERCEUSE		CORBEILS
BCEEFILN	FENCIBLE	BCEILOTU	TUBICOLE
BCEEGIRS	ICEBERGS	BCEILPRU	REPUBLIC
BCEEHKSU	BUCKSHEE	BCEIMNOS	COMBINES
BCEEHLNS	BLENCHES	BCEIMORS	CROMBIES
BCEEHLRS	BELCHERS		MICROBES
BCEEHNRS	BENCHERS	BCEIMOST	COMBIEST
BCEEHNRU	UNBREECH	BCEIMOSW	COMBWISE
BCEEHOSU	BOUCHEES	BCEIMRRU	CRUMBIER
BCEEIILM	IMBECILE	BCEINORU	BOUNCIER
BCEEINOT	CENOBITE	BCEINOVX	BICONVEX
BCEEIOSX	ICEBOXES	BCEINRSU	BRUCINES
BCEEIPSS	BESPICES	BCEIOOPS	BIOSCOPE
	BICEPSES	BCEIORRS	CRIBROSE
BCEEIRSS	ESCRIBES	BCEIORST	BISECTOR
BCEEIRTT	BRETTICE	BCEIRRSS	SCRIBERS
BCEEKNSU	BUCKEENS	BCEIRSTU	BRUCITES
BCEELLOT	BELLCOTE	BCEJOORT	OBJECTOR
BCEELOOR	BORECOLE	BCEJSSTU	SUBJECTS
BCEELRTU	TUBERCLE	BCEKLNOT	BLONCKET

BCEKLNUU UNBUCKLE	BCIKOSTT BITTOCKS	DISROBED	BDEEHLNO BEHOLDEN
BCEKLORS BLOCKERS	BCILLPUY PUBLICLY	BDDEISSU SUBSIDED	BDEEHLOR BEHOLDER
BCEKLRSU BUCKLERS	BCILMOSY SYMBOLIC	BDDEISTU BUDDIEST	BDEEHLOW BEHOWLED
BCEKMSTU STEMBUCK	BCILMPSU UPCLIMBS	BDDELMRU DRUMBLED	BDEEHOOV BEHOOVED
BCEKOORU BUCKEROO	BCILNOUY BOUNCILY	BDDENOTU OBTUNDED	BDEEHORT BOTHERED
BCEKORST BROCKETS	BCINORSU RUBICONS	BDDEORTU OBTRUDED	BDEEHORW BEWHORED
BCEKORSU ROEBUCKS	BCINOSSU SUBSONIC	BDDGIINS BIDDINGS	BDEEHOSS DEBOSHES
BCEKOSTY BYCOKETS	BCINOSTU SUBTONIC	BDDGILNU BUDDLING	BDEEIILN INEDIBLE
BCELLOSW COWBELLS	BCINOSUU INCUBOUS	BDDGINOR BRODDING	BDEEIILR BIELDIER
BCELMOSS COMBLESS	BCIOORST ROBOTICS	BDDGINSU BUDDINGS	BDEEIIPT BEPITIED
BCELMRSU CLUMBERS	BCIORSST CROSSBIT	BDDGOOSY DOGSBODY	BDEEIKRS KERBSIDE
CRUMBLES	BCJKMSUU JUMBUCKS	BDDHIIRY DIHYBRID	BDEEIKSS BEKISSED
BCELMSSU SCUMBLES	BCKLLOOS BOLLOCKS	BDDINOOW WOODBIND	BDEEILLL LIBELLED
BCELORSU COLUBERS	BCKLLOSU BULLOCKS	BDDINPUU PUDIBUND	BDEEILLT BILLETED
BCELORTU CLOTEBUR	BCKLNOSU SUNBLOCK	BDEEEEMS BESEEMED	BDEEILLU ELUDIBLE
BCELRSSU CURBLESS	UNBLOCKS	BDEEEEMT BETEEMED	BDEEILMO BEMOILED
BCEMRSSU SCUMBERS	BCKMMOSU BUMMOCKS	BDEEEGIS BESIEGED	EMBOILED
BCENORSU BOUNCERS	BCKOOOPY COPYBOOK	BDEEEGMM BEGEMMED	BDEEILMR LIMBERED
BCEORRSU OBSCURER	BCKOSTTU BUTTOCKS	BDEEEGNO EDGEBONE	BDEEILNV VENDIBLE
BCEORRWY COWBERRY	BCLMOORU CLUBROOM	BDEEEGRU BUDGEREE	BDEEILOR REBOILED
BCEORSSU OBSCURES	BCLMOOSU COULOMBS	BDEEEHTU HEBETUDE	BDEEILOS OBELISED
BCFIIMOR MORBIFIC	BCLOORTU CLUBROOT	BDEEEILV BELIEVED	BDEEILOT BETOILED
BCFIIORT FIBROTIC	BCLORSTU CLOTBURS	BDEEEINS BENISEED	BDEEILOZ OBELIZED
BCFILORY FORCIBLY	BCMORSUU CUMBROUS	BDEEELLR REBELLED	BDEEILRW BEWILDER
BCFIMORU CUBIFORM	BCMOSSTU COMBUSTS	BDEEELLV BEVELLED	BDEEILSV BEDEVILS
BCFSSSUU SUBFUSCS	BCOORSSW CROSSBOW	BDEEELMM EMBLEMED	BDEEILTT BETITLED
BCGHIINR BIRCHING	BCOOSTTY BOYCOTTS	BDEEELPT BEPELTED	BDEEIMNR BRIDEMEN
BCGHIINT BITCHING	BCORSTTU OBSTRUCT	BDEEELRS BLEEDERS	BDEEIMOS EMBODIES
BCGHINNU BUNCHING	BDDDEEEM EMBEDDED	BDEEELUW BLUEWEED	BDEEIMRT TIMBERED
BCGHINOT BOTCHING	BDDDEEIM IMBEDDED	BDEEEMMR MEMBERED	BDEEIMST BEDTIMES
BCGHINTU BUTCHING	BDDDEEIR DEBRIDED	BDEEEMNS BEDESMEN	BDEEIMSU EMBUSIED
BCGIIKNR BRICKING	BDDDEEMU BEMUDDED	BDEEEMRW EMBREWED	BDEEINOS EBONISED
BCGIILMN CLIMBING	BDDDENNU UNBEDDED	BDEEENTT BENETTED	BDEEINOT OBEDIENT
BCGIINRS SCRIBING	BDDDENUU UNBUDDED	BDEEEPSS BESPEEDS	BDEEINOZ EBONIZED
BCGIKLNO BLOCKING	BDDEEELL DEBELLED	BDEEERRS BREEDERS	BDEEINRS INBREEDS
BCGIKLNU BUCKLING	BDDEEESS SEEDBEDS	BDEEERRV REVERBED	BDEEINST BENDIEST
BCGIKNSU BUCKINGS	BDDEEFLU BEFUDDLE	BDEEERTT BETTERED	BDEEINSW BENDWISE
BCGIMNOR CROMBING	BDDEEGGU DEBUGGED	BDEEERTV BREVETED	BDEEINSZ BEDIZENS
BCGIMNOS COMBINGS	BDDEEGIL BEGILDED	BDEEETTW BEWETTED	BDEEIORU BOUDERIE
BCGIMNRU CRUMBING	BDDEEGIR BEGIRDED	BDEEFFPU BEPUFFED	BDEEIRRU REBURIED
BCGINNOU BOUNCING	BDDEEGNU BEDUNGED	BDEEFFRU BUFFERED	BDEEIRST BEDRITES
BUNCOING	BDDEEGTU BUDGETED	REBUFFED	BESTRIDE
BCGINORU COURBING	BDDEEHOS DEBOSHED	BDEEFFTU BUFFETED	BDEEKNRU BUNKERED
BCHIILTY BITCHILY	BDDEEIMM BEDIMMED	BDEEFGGO BEFOGGED	BDEELLOW BELLOWED
BCHIIOST COHIBITS	BDDEEIMO EMBODIED	BDEEFGIT BEGIFTED	BOWELLED
BCHIISSU HIBISCUS	BDDEEINR REBIDDEN	BDEEFILR BELFRIED	BDEELLRU BULLERED
BCHIKLOS BLOCKISH	BDDEEINT INDEBTED	BDEEFINR BEFRIEND	BDEELMNO EMBOLDEN
BCHIKOSU CHIBOUKS	BDDEEINW BINDWEED	BDEEFIRS DEBRIEFS	BDEELMOR REBELDOM
BCHIOORY CHOIRBOY	BDDEEIRS BIRDSEED	BDEEFIRU RUBEFIED	BDEELMPU BEPLUMED
BCHIOPRS PIBROCHS	DEBRIDES	BDEEFITT BEFITTED	BDEELMRT TREMBLED
BCHKNORU BUCKHORN	BDDEEISS BEDSIDES	BDEEFLOO BEFOOLED	BDEELMRU LUMBERED
BCHKOSTU BUCKSHOT	BDDEEKNU DEBUNKED	BDEEFLOU BEFOULED	BDEELNNO ENNOBLED
BCHNOORS BRONCHOS	BDDEELMU BEMUDDLE	BDEEFOOR FOREBODE	BDEELNRS BLENDERS
BCHNORSU BRONCHUS	BDDEELNO BOLDENED	BDEEFSSU SUBFEUED	BDEELNST BENDLETS
BCHORSST BORSCHTS	BDDEENNU UNBENDED	BDEEGGIW BEWIGGED	BDEELNTU UNBELTED
BCHORSTT BORTSCHT	BDDEENOT OBTENDED	BDEEGGMO EMBOGGED	BDEELORU REDOUBLE
BCIIILMU UMBILICI	BDDEENRU BURDENED	BDEEGGNU UNBEGGED	BDEELORW BOWLERED
BCIIKLNS NIBLICKS	BDDEEORR BORDERED	BDEEGGRU BEGRUDGE	BDEELOSU BESOULED
BCIILMRU LUMBRICI	BDDEEORS DESORBED	BUGGERED	BDEELOSV BELOVEDS
BCIILMSU BULIMICS	BDDEESSU DEBUSSED	BDEEGHIS BESIGHED	BDEELRTU BUTLERED
BCIILORS COLIBRIS	BDDEESTU BEDUSTED	BDEEGILN BLEEDING	BDEEMNOT BODEMENT
BCIIMNOO BIONOMIC	BDDEESUW SUBDEWED	BDEEGILU BEGUILED	ENTOMBED
BCIIMORU CIBORIUM	BDDEGINS BEDDINGS	BDEEGIMR BEGRIMED	BDEEMNOW ENWOMBED
BCIIMRSS SCRIBISM	BDDEIIMO IMBODIED	BDEEGINR BREEDING	BDEEMNRU NUMBERED
BCIINORV VIBRONIC	BDDEILNR BRINDLED	BDEEGINW BEDEWING	BDEEMORR EMBORDER
BCIISSTU BISCUITS	BDDEILOO BLOODIED	BDEEGINY BEDYEING	BDEEMOSS EMBOSSED
BCIISTUY BISCUITY	BDDEINNU UNBIDDEN	BDEEGKNU BEGUNKED	BDEEMPRU BUMPERED
BCIKKNSU BUCKSKIN	BDDEINOU UNBODIED	BDEEGLNO BELONGED	BDEEMRTU EMBRUTED
BCIKLOOT BOOTLICK	BDDEINRU UNDERBID	ENGLOBED	BDEEMSSU EMBUSSED
BCIKORRW CRIBWORK	BDDEIORS DISROBED	BDEEGMOU EMBOGUED	BDEENNOT BONNETED

BDEENOUY UNOBEYED	BDEILORT TRILOBED	BDENNOUY YBOUNDEN	BDIKNORS BRODKINS
BDEENPRS PREBENDS	BDEILORV LOVEBIRD	BDENNRUU UNBURDEN	BDILLOOY BLOODILY
BDEEOPRS BEPROSED	BDEILOSS BODILESS	UNBURNED	BDILMORY MORBIDLY
BDEEOPRW BEPOWDER	BDEILOSW DISBOWEL	BDENOOTU UNBOOTED	BDILNNSU UNBLINDS
BDEEORRR BORDERER	BDEILRRS BRIDLERS	BDENOOTW BENTWOOD	BDILNOWW WINDBLOW
BDEEORRS RESORBED	BDEILRST BRISTLED	BDENORSU BOUNDERS	BDILNPRU PURBLIND
BDEEORSS BEDSORES	DRIBLETS	REBOUNDS	BDILNSUU UNBUILDS
BDEEORST BESORTED	BDEILRSU BUILDERS	SUBORNED	BDILPSUU UPBUILDS
BESTRODE	REBUILDS	BDENOTTU BUTTONED	BDILRTUY TURBIDLY
BDEEORSV OBSERVED	BDEILSTU BLUDIEST	BDENRSUU UNBRUSED	BDIMNORU MORIBUND
BDEEORTU OUTBREED	BDEIMNOT INTOMBED	BDENRUUY UNDERBUY	BDIMNPSU DUMPBINS
BDEEORTV OBVERTED	BDEIMNSU NIMBUSED	BDENSSTU SUBTENDS	BDIMOOSS DISBOSOM
BDEEOSSS OBSESSED	BDEIMNUU UNIMBUED	BDEOORRS BROODERS	BDIMOSTU MISDOUBT
BDEEOSST BETOSSED	BDEIMORR IMBORDER	BDEOORRW BORROWED	BDINNRUW WINDBURN
BDEEOSTT BESOTTED	BDEIMORS BROMIDES	BDEOOTUX OUTBOXED	BDINOORS BRIDOONS
OBTESTED	BDEIMOSS IMBOSSED	BDEOPSST BEDPOSTS	BDINRTUU UNTURBID
BDEEOSTW BESTOWED	BDEIMRSU IMBURSED	BDEORRSU BORDURES	BDINSSTU DUSTBINS
BDEERSUW BURWEEDS	BDEIMRTU IMBRUTED	BOURDERS	BDIOORSU BOUDOIRS
BDEERTTU BUTTERED	BDEINOOS NOBODIES	SUBORDER	BDIOORTY BOTRYOID
REBUTTED	BDEINOOW WOODBINE	BDEORRTU OBTRUDER	BDIORSSW WOSBIRDS
BDEESSSU DEBUSSES	BDEINOSU BEDOUINS	BDEORRUW BURROWED	BDIRSSTU DISTURBS
BDEFIIRU RUBIFIED	BDEINRSU BURNSIDE	BDEORSTU DOUBTERS	BDKNOOOR DOORKNOB
BDEFILRS FILBERDS	BDEINRTU TURBINED	OBTRUDES	BDKNOOSU BUNDOOKS
BDEFINRR FERNBIRD	UNDERBIT	REDOUBTS	BDKOOORW WORDBOOK
BDEFIORS FIBROSED	BDEINRUU UNBURIED	BDERSSUU SUBDUERS	BDKOORWY BODYWORK
BDEFOORS FORBODES	BDEINTTU UNBITTED	BDERSTUU SUBTRUDE	BDLLSTUU BULLDUST
BDEGHILT BLIGHTED	BDEIOORR BROODIER	BDFGNOOU FOGBOUND	BDLNOOOU DOUBLOON
BDEGHIRT BEDRIGHT	BDEIORRS BROIDERS	BDFIIORS FIBROIDS	BDLNOOUY UNBLOODY
BDEGHIST BEDIGHTS	BDEIORRY BROIDERY	BDFILLLO BILLFOLD	BDLNOOWN BLOWDOWN
BDEGIINT BETIDING	BDEIORSS DISROBES	BDFINORU UNFORBID	BDLOOOSX OXBLOODS
DEBITING	BDEIORST DEBITORS	BDFINRUU FURIBUND	BDMOORRS SMORBROD
BDEGILNN BLENDING	BDEIORSV OVERBIDS	BDFLOTUU DOUBTFUL	BDNNOOTU BUNODONT
BDEGILNO IGNOBLED	BDEIOSSY DISOBEYS	BDGGIINR BRIDGING	BDNOORSU BOURDONS
INGLOBED	BDEIOSUX SUBOXIDE	BDGGILNU BLUDGING	BDNOOSWW DOWNBOWS
BDEGINNS BENDINGS	BDEIRSSU DISBURSE	BDGIILNN BLINDING	BDNOOTUU OUTBOUND
BDEGINOS OBSIGNED	BDEISSSU SUBSIDES	BDGIILNR BRIDLING	BDNORSTU TURBONDS
BDEGLMRU GRUMBLED	BDEISSTU SUBEDITS	BDGIILNU BUILDING	BDNORSUW RUBDOWNS
BDEGLRSU BLUDGERS	BDEKNOOU UNBOOKED	BDGIINNS BINDINGS	BDOOOSWX BOXWOODS
BDEGORRY DOGBERRY	BDELLOOR BORDELLO	BDGIINRS BIRDINGS	BEEEEFLN ENFEEBLE
BDEGORSU BUDGEROS	DOORBELL	BDGIINRW BIRDWING	BEEEEFRS FREEBEES
BDEGORUW BUDGEROW	BDELLOUZ BULLDOZE	BDGILNNU BUNDLING	BEEEEKSS BESEEKES
BDEHIKOS KIBOSHED	BDELMOOS BLOOSMED	BDGILNOO BLOODING	BEEEEMST BETEEMES
BDEHILMT THIMBLED	BDELMRSU DRUMBLES	BDGILNOU DOUBLING	BEEEENNT TEREBENE
BDEHIOPS BISHOPED	BDELMRUU DELUBRUM	BDGILOOS GLOBOIDS	BEEEENRZ EBENEZER
BDEHKOSY KYBOSHED	BDELMSTU STUMBLED	BDGINNOS BONDINGS	BEEEFIRS FREEBIES
BDEHLMOW WHOMBLED	BDELNNOU UNNOBLED	BDGINNOU BOUNDING	BEEEFIST BEEFIEST
BDEHLSUV BUSHVELD	BDELNNUU UNBUNDLE	UNBODING	BEEEFLSS FEBLESSE
BDEHORSY HERDBOYS	BDELNOSS BOLDNESS	BDGINOOR BROODING	BEEEFLST FEEBLEST
BDEIIKTZ KIBITZED	BDELNOST BLONDEST	BDGINOOY BOODYING	BEEEGILN BELEEING
BDEIILRU BLUIDIER	BDELNOTU UNBOLTED	BDGINORS SONGBIRD	BEEEGINS BESEEING
BDEIILTY DEBILITY	BDELNOUU UNDOUBLE	BDGINORU OBDURING	BEEEGIRS BESIEGER
BDEIIMOS IMBODIES	BDELNOUW UNBLOWED	BDGINOTU DOUBTING	BEEEGISS BESIEGES
BDEIKMOS IMBOSKED	BDELNRSU BLUNDERS	BDGINSUU SUBDUING	BEEEGRTT BEGETTER
BDEIKNOR BRODEKIN	BDELOORV OVERBOLD	BDGLLOSU BULLDOGS	BEEEHIST BHEESTIE
BDEIKNSU BUSKINED	BDELORSU BOULDERS	BDGLOOST DOGBOLTS	BEEEHISV BEEHIVES
BDEILLMU BDELLIUM	DOUBLERS	BDGNRUUY BURGUNDY	BEEEHLRT HERBELET
BDEILLOW BILLOWED	BDELORSW BOWLDERS	BDHIIPRW WHIPBIRD	BEEEHLWW WEBWHEEL
BDEILMSU SUBLIMED	BDELORTU TROUBLED	BDHIMOOR RHOMBOID	BEEEHNSS SHEBEENS
BDEILNOU UNILOBED	BDELOSST BESTSOLD	BDHIMORT BIRTHDOM	BEEEILLL LIBELLEE
BDEILNOY BODYLINE	BDELOSTU DOUBLETS	BDHINOPS HOPBINDS	BEEEILRV BELIEVER
BDEILNRS BLINDERS	BDELPSUU SUBDUPLE	BDHIORST BIRDSHOT	BEEEILSV BELIEVES
BRINDLES	BDEMNNOS BONDSMEN	BDHIOSSU BUSHIDOS	BEEEINST EBENISTE
BDEILNRU UNBRIDLE	BDEMNOSU EMBOUNDS	BDHMOOOS HOBODOMS	BEEEIRRZ BREEZIER
BDEILNST BLINDEST	BDEMNOTU UNTOMBED	BDHNRSUU UNSHRUBD	BEEEIRST BEERIEST
BDEILNVY VENDIBLY	BDEMNSSU DUMBNESS	BDHOOOSY BOYHOODS	BEEEJLSW BEJEWELS
BDEILOOR BLOODIER	BDEMOORS BEDROOMS	BDIIINRS BRINDISI	BEEELLRR REBELLER
BDEILOOS BLOODIES	BOREDOMS	BDIIKNOS BODIKINS	BEEELLRT BELLETER
BDEILOPU UPBOILED	BDEMOOSY SOMEBODY	BDIILMSS DISLIMBS	BEEELLRV BEVELLER
BDEILOQU OBLIQUED	BDEMOOTT BOTTOMED	BDIILOQU OBLIQUID	BEEELMNS ENSEMBLE
	BDEMSSUU SUBSUMED	BDIIMRUU RUBIDIUM	BEEELMRS RESEMBLE

BEEEELMSY	BESEEMLY		
BEEEELMZZ	EMBEZZLE		
BEEEELPRS	BLEEPERS		
BEEEEMMRR	REMEMBER		
BEEEEMNSU	UNBESEEM		
BEEEEMRSW	EMBREWES		
BEEEENNSZ	BENZENES		
BEEEENSST	SEBESTEN		
BEEEENSTW	BETWEENS		
BEEEPPPR	BEPEPPER		
BEEEPRST	BEPESTER		
BEEERSST	BRETESSE		
BEEERSTT	BESETTER		
BEEESSST	TSESSEBE		
BEEFFLMU	BEMUFFLE		
BEEFGILN	FEEBLING		
BEEFGINR	BEFRINGE		
BEEFHILS	FEEBLISH		
BEEFILLT	LIFEBELT		
BEEFILLX	FLEXIBLE		
BEEFILNU	UNBELIEF		
BEEFILRS	BELFRIES		
BEEFINST	BENEFITS		
BEEFIRST	BRIEFEST		
BEEFIRSU	RUBEFIES		
BEEFLORW	BEFLOWER		
BEEFNORR	FREEBORN		
BEEFNRTU	UNBEREFT		
BEEGGNSU	GEEBUNGS		
BEEGHLMR	BERGMEHL		
BEEGIILL	ELIGIBLE		
BEEGIILX	EXIGIBLE		
BEEGILLR	GERBILLE		
BEEGILNP	BLEEPING		
BEEGILNT	BEETLING		
BEEGILOS	OBLIGEES		
BEEGILRU	BEGUILER		
BEEGILSU	BEGUILES		
BEEGIMNT	BEMETING		
BEEGIMRS	BEGRIMES		
BEEGINNR	BEGINNER		
	BENIGNER		
BEEGINNS	BEGINNES		
BEEGINRR	BREERING		
BEEGINRS	BIGENERS		
BEEGINRZ	BREEZING		
BEEGINST	BEIGNETS		
BEEGINSU	BEGUINES		
BEEGINSW	BEESWING		
BEEGKLUY	KEYBUGLE		
BEEGLNOR	BELONGER		
BEEGLNOS	ENGLOBES		
BEEGMNOS	GOMBEENS		
BEEGMOSU	EMBOGUES		
BEEGMRSU	SUBMERGE		
BEEGNOOW	WOBEGONE		
BEEGNOTT	BEGOTTEN		
BEEGNSTU	UNBEGETS		
BEEHHMOT	BEHEMOTH		
BEEHINSS	BESHINES		
	NEBISHES		
BEEHIRST	HERBIEST		
BEEHISST	BHISTEES		
BEEHKSSU	BUKSHEES		
BEEHLOOR	BOREHOLE		
BEEHLOVY	BEHOVELY		
BEEHLRSS	HERBLESS		
BEEHLRST	BLETHERS		
	HERBLETS		
BEEHNNOS	HEBENONS		
BEEHNRRT	BRETHREN	BEELLSST	BESTSELL
BEEHOOSV	BEHOOVES	BEELMMOP	BEPOMMEL
BEEHORSW	BEWHORES	BEELMNNO	NOBLEMEN
BEEHRSST	SHERBETS	BEELMOSW	EMBOWELS
BEEHRSSW	BESHREWS	BEELMRRT	TREMBLER
BEEIILNZ	ZIBELINE	BEELMRRU	LUMBERER
BEEIINOS	EBIONISE	BEELMRST	TREMBLES
BEEIINOZ	EBIONIZE	BEELNNOS	ENNOBLES
BEEIINRT	BENITIER	BEELNOSS	BONELESS
BEEIIPST	BEPITIES		NOBLESSE
BEEIIRRR	BRIERIER	BEELNOSU	BLUENOSE
BEEIISTU	UBIETIES	BEELNOSZ	BENZOLES
BEEIJLSU	JUBILEES	BEELNSSU	BLUENESS
BEEIJSTU	BEJESUIT	BEELNTUY	BUTYLENE
BEEIKSSS	BEKISSES	BEELOOST	OBSOLETE
BEEILLLR	LIBELLER	BEELOQRU	BRELOQUE
BEEILLNO	LOBELINE	BEELORVW	OVERBLEW
BEEILLTT	BELITTLE	BEELOSTW	STEELBOW
BEEILMOS	EMBOLIES	BEELOSTY	EYEBOLTS
BEEILMPR	PERIBLEM	BEELPRUV	BUPLEVER
BEEILNNS	BLENNIES	BEELRSSV	VERBLESS
BEEILNRS	BERLINES	BEELRSUZ	ZEBRULES
BEEILNSS	SENSIBLE	BEELSSTU	TUBELESS
BEEILNST	STILBENE	BEELSTTU	BLUETTES
	TENSIBLE	BEEMNRRU	NUMBERER
BEEILNSU	NEBULISE		RENUMBER
BEEILNUZ	NEBULIZE	BEEMOPRT	OBTEMPER
BEEILOSS	OBELISES	BEEMORSS	EMBOSSER
BEEILOSZ	OBELIZES	BEEMORSW	EMBOWERS
BEEILOTV	LOVEBITE	BEEMOSSS	EMBOSSES
BEEILRRT	TERRIBLE	BEEMQSUU	EMBUSQUE
BEEILRSU	BLUESIER	BEEMRRSU	UMBRERES
BEEILRYZ	BREEZILY	BEEMRSSU	SUBMERSE
BEEILSTT	BETITLES	BEEMRSTU	EMBRUTES
BEEIMRRU	UMBRIERE	BEEMRTTU	UMBRETTE
BEEIMRTT	EMBITTER	BEEMRTUZ	ZERUMBET
BEEIMSSU	EMBUSIES	BEEMSSSU	EMBUSSES
BEEINNSS	BEINNESS	BEENORTU	BOUNTREE
BEEINNSZ	BENZINES	BEENOSST	BONESETS
BEEINORT	TENEBRIO	BEENPRST	BESPRENT
BEEINOSS	EBONISES	BEENRSTT	BRENTEST
BEEINOST	BETONIES	BEENRSTW	BESTREWN
	EBONITES	BEENRTTU	BRUNETTE
BEEINOSZ	EBONIZES	BEENSSTU	SUBTEENS
BEEINPRS	PEBRINES		SUBTENSE
BEEINRSS	NEBRISES	BEEOORRT	BOORTREE
BEEINRTT	REBITTEN	BEEOORRV	OVERBORE
BEEINSTT	BENTIEST	BEEOORTT	BEETROOT
BEEIOQSU	OBSEQUIE		BOOTTREE
BEEIORSS	SOBERISE	BEEOPRSS	BEPROSES
BEEIORSW	BOWERIES	BEEORRSU	BOURREES
BEEIORSZ	SOBERIZE	BEEORRSV	OBSERVER
BEEIORTV	OVERBITE		VERBOSER
BEEIQSUZ	BEZIQUES	BEEORRTU	BOURTREE
BEEIRRSU	REBURIES	BEEORSST	SOBEREST
BEEIRRSV	BREVIERS	BEEORSSU	SUBEROSE
BEEIRRTT	BITTERER	BEEORSSV	OBSERVES
BEEIRSSU	SUBERISE		OBVERSES
BEEIRSSW	BREWISES	BEEORSTU	TUBEROSE
BEEIRSTU	UBERTIES	BEEORSTW	BESTOWER
BEEIRSUZ	SUBERIZE	BEEORSWY	EYEBROWS
BEEKMOPR	PEMBROKE	BEEOSSSS	OBSESSES
BEEKNOPS	BESPOKEN	BEEOSSST	BETOSSES
BEEKNOST	BETOKENS	BEEPRRSU	SUPERBER
	STEENBOK	BEEPRRSV	PREVERBS
BEEKRRSS	BERSERKS	BEEPRSTY	PRESBYTE
BEEKRRSU	REBUKERS	BEEQSSTU	BEQUESTS
BEELLORW	BELLOWER	BEERRSTW	BREWSTER
	REBELLOW	BEERRTTU	REBUTTER
BEELLOST	LOBELETS	BEERSSSU	SUBSERES

BEERSSTW	BESTREWS
	WEBSTERS
BEERSSUV	SUBSERVE
	SUBVERSE
BEERSTTU	BURETTES
BEESTTUV	BUVETTES
BEFFLRSU	BLUFFERS
BEFFLSTU	BLUFFEST
BEFGIILL	FILLIBEG
BEFGIILS	FILIBEGS
BEFGIINR	BRIEFING
BEFGIRSU	FIREBUGS
BEFHILSU	BLUEFISH
BEFHIRSU	BUSHFIRE
BEFIIRSU	RUBIFIES
BEFILLXY	FLEXIBLY
BEFILMOR	FORELIMB
BEFILOST	BOTFLIES
BEFILRST	FILBERTS
BEFINORS	BONFIRES
BEFIORSS	FIBROSES
BEFIORTT	FOREBITT
BEFIRSST	FIBSTERS
BEFISSTU	FUBSIEST
BEFLLLUY	BELLYFUL
BEFLLSTY	FLYBELTS
BEFLMRSU	FUMBLERS
BEFLORUW	FURBELOW
BEFLSTUU	TUBEFULS
BEFNOORR	FORBORNE
BEFNOSSY	FYNBOSES
BEFORRXY	FOXBERRY
BEGGGINS	BEGGINGS
BEGGIINN	BINGEING
BEGGIOST	BOGGIEST
BEGGLORS	BOGGLERS
BEGGOOOS	GOOSEGOB
BEGHHIST	BEHIGHTS
BEGHIILP	PHILIBEG
BEGHILRT	BLIGHTER
	THERBLIG
BEGHINOR	NEIGHBOR
BEGHINOT	BEHOTING
BEGHINOV	BEHOVING
BEGHINRT	BERTHING
	BRIGHTEN
BEGHINST	BENIGHTS
BEGHIRRT	BRIGHTER
BEGHNOTU	BOUGHTEN
BEGHOSTU	BESOUGHT
BEGHOSUU	BUGHOUSE
BEGHRRSU	BURGHERS
BEGIIISS	SIGISBEI
BEGIILLY	ELIGIBLY
BEGIILST	BILGIEST
BEGIIMNR	BEMIRING
BEGIIMNT	BETIMING
BEGIINNS	INBEINGS
BEGIINRT	REBITING
BEGIINRZ	ZINGIBER
BEGIIOSS	SIGISBEO
BEGIKMNO	KEMBOING
BEGIKNRU	REBUKING
BEGILLLU	GULLIBLE
BEGILLNU	BULLGINE
BEGILLNY	BELLYING
BEGILMNR	REMBLING
BEGILMNS	SEMBLING
BEGILNNY	BENIGNLY
BEGILNOR	IGNOBLER

```
BEGILNOS IGNOBLES        BEHIOOPR BIOPHORE        BEIKNRSS BRISKENS        BEIMPSTU BUMPIEST
         INGLOBES        BEHIRRST REBIRTHS        BEIKOORS BOOKSIER        BEIMRSSU IMBURSES
BEGILNOV BELOVING        BEHIRRSU BRUSHIER        BEIKOORT BROOKITE        BEIMRSTU IMBRUTES
BEGILNOW ELBOWING        BEHIRSST HERBISTS        BEIKOOST BOOKIEST                 RESUBMIT
BEGILNRT TREBLING        BEHIRSSU HUBRISES        BEIKOSST BOSKIEST                 TERBIUMS
BEGILNSS BLESSING        BEHIRSSY HYBRISES        BEIKRSST BRISKEST        BEINNOSS BENISONS
         GLIBNESS        BEHISSTU BUSHIEST                 BRISKETS                 BONINESS
BEGILNST BELTINGS        BEHKOSSY KYBOSHES        BEILLMSS LIMBLESS        BEINNOST BONNIEST
BEGILNSU BLUEINGS        BEHLLOOT BOLTHOLE        BEILLMSU SEMIBULL        BEINNOSZ BENZOINS
         BULGINES        BEHLLOOW BLOWHOLE        BEILLNTU BULLETIN        BEINNRYZ ZEBRINNY
BEGILNTT BLETTING        BEHLLOPS BELLHOPS        BEILLORS BROLLIES        BEINORRW BROWNIER
BEGILNUW BLUEWING        BEHLLPSU BELLPUSH        BEILLOSX BOLLIXES        BEINORRZ BRONZIER
BEGILNZZ BEZZLING        BEHLMOSW WHOMBLES        BEILLSST BESTILLS        BEINORST BORNITES
BEGILRST GILBERTS        BEHLMSTU HUMBLEST        BEILLSTU BULLIEST                 RIBSTONE
BEGILSTU BULGIEST        BEHLOOPY HYPOBOLE        BEILMMOS EMBOLISM        BEINORSW BROWNIES
BEGIMNOW EMBOWING                 LYOPHOBE        BEILMNOU NOBELIUM        BEINORSY BRYONIES
BEGIMNOX EMBOXING        BEHLOOST BOTHOLES        BEILMNRU UNLIMBER        BEINORTZ BRONZITE
BEGIMNRU EMBRUING        BEHLORST BROTHELS        BEILMNST NIMBLEST        BEINOSST EBONISTS
         UMBERING        BEHLOSSU SLOEBUSH        BEILMNUU NEBULIUM        BEINOSSX BOXINESS
BEGIMNSU BEMUSING        BEHLRRSU BURRHELS        BEILMOOR BLOOMIER        BEINOSTT BOTTINES
BEGIMOST MISBEGOT        BEHLRSSU BLUSHERS        BEILMORS EMBROILS        BEINOSTU BOUNTIES
BEGIMOSY BOGEYISM        BEHLSSTU BLUSHETS        BEILMPTU PLUMBITE        BEINRRSY NISBERRY
BEGINNNR BRENNING        BEHMNOTY BOTHYMEN        BEILMRRU RUMBLIER        BEINRSSU SUBERINS
BEGINNNU UNBENIGN        BEHMOSTU BEMOUTHS        BEILMRSS BRIMLESS        BEINRSTT BITTERNS
BEGINNOR ENROBING        BEHMPSTU BETHUMPS        BEILMRST TIMBRELS        BEINRSTU TRIBUNES
         RINGBONE        BEHNNOUY HONEYBUN        BEILMRSU SUBLIMER                 TURBINES
BEGINNSU UNBEINGS        BEHNRSTU BURTHENS        BEILMRSW WIMBRELS        BEINRSUU UNBURIES
BEGINOOS BESOGNIO        BEHOOOST BOOTHOSE        BEILMSSU SUBLIMES        BEINSSSU BUSINESS
BEGINORR REBORING        BEHOORST THEORBOS        BEILNNTU BUNTLINE        BEINSTTU BUNTIEST
BEGINORS SOBERING        BEHOOSUY HOUSEBOY        BEILNOOS OBELIONS        BEIOORST ROBOTISE
BEGINORW BOWERING        BEHORRST BROTHERS        BEILNOPS BONSPIEL        BEIOORTZ ROBOTIZE
BEGINRRS BRINGERS        BEHORSST BETROTHS        BEILNOSW BOWLINES        BEIOOSSV OVIBOSES
BEGINRRY BERRYING        BEHRRSSU BRUSHERS        BEILNSSY SENSIBLY        BEIOOSSZ BOOZIEST
BEGINRSW BREWINGS        BEIIKRTZ KIBITZER        BEILNSTZ BLINTZES        BEIOPSTY BIOTYPES
BEGINSTT BETTINGS        BEIIKSTZ KIBITZES        BEILOORV OVERBOIL        BEIOQTUU BOUTIQUE
BEGKMOSS GEMSBOKS        BEIILMMO IMMOBILE        BEILOOST LOOBIEST        BEIORRST ORBITERS
BEGLLOSU GLOBULES        BEIILMOS MOBILISE        BEILOPPW BLOWPIPE        BEIORRSU BOURSIER
BEGLLOTU GLOBULET        BEIILMOZ MOBILIZE        BEILOPSS POSSIBLE        BEIORRTU ROBURITE
BEGLMOOS BEGLOOMS        BEIILMSU BULIMIES        BEILOQRU OBLIQUER        BEIORSTY SOBRIETY
BEGLMRRU GRUMBLER        BEIILNRS RINSIBLE        BEILOQSU OBLIQUES        BEIOSSST BOSSIEST
BEGLMRSU GRUMBLES        BEIILOPR PERIBOLI        BEILORRS BROILERS        BEIOSSTU SOUBISES
BEGLNOUW BLUEGOWN        BEIILRST TRILBIES        BEILORST STROBILE        BEIOSSTU BOUSIEST
BEGLNRSU BLUNGERS        BEIILRTT LIBRETTI                 TRILOBES        BEIOTTZZ BOZZETTI
         BUNGLERS        BEIILRUZ BRUILZIE        BEILORSW BLOWSIER        BEIQRSTU BRIQUETS
BEGLOOSS GLOBOSES        BEIILSSV VISIBLES        BEILORTT BLOTTIER        BEIRRSSU BRISURES
BEGLOOST BOOTLEGS        BEIILSTT STILBITE                 LIBRETTO                 BRUISERS
BEGLRSTY BERGYLTS        BEIIMNNR RENMINBI        BEILORWZ BLOWZIER        BEIRRSTU BURRIEST
BEGNOORU BOURGEON        BEIIMNOS EBIONISM        BEILOSTW BLOWIEST        BEIRRTTU TRIBUTER
BEGNORSU BURGEONS        BEIIMRTT IMBITTER        BEILRRTT BRITTLER        BEIRSSTU BUSTIERS
BEGNORTU BURGONET        BEIINORS BRIONIES        BEILRRTY TERRIBLY        BEIRSTTU TRIBUTES
BEGNSSUU SUBGENUS        BEIINOST NIOBITES        BEILRSST BLISTERS        BEIRSTTY TREYBITS
BEHHKOST KHOTBEHS        BEIINRST BRINIEST                 BRISTLES        BEISSTTU BUSTIEST
BEHIISTX EXHIBITS        BEIINSST STIBINES        BEILRSTT BRITTLES        BEISTUZZ BUZZIEST
BEHIKNST BETHINKS        BEIINSTT STIBNITE                 TRIBLETS        BEJKOOST JESTBOOK
BEHIKOSS KIBOSHES        BEIIOPSS BIOPSIES        BEILRSTU BURLIEST        BEJLMRSU JUMBLERS
BEHILLOS SHOEBILL        BEIIORST ORBITIES                 SUBTILER        BEKLNORY BROKENLY
BEHILLTY BLITHELY        BEIIOSTT BIOTITES        BEILRSTY BLISTERY        BEKLNRSU BLUNKERS
BEHILMRW WHIMBREL        BEIIRSST BIRSIEST        BEILRSUY BRULYIES        BEKLOOOR BOOKLORE
BEHILMST THIMBLES        BEIISSTT BITSIEST        BEILRSUZ BRULZIES        BEKLOORT BROOKLET
BEHILNPY BIPHENYL        BEIISTTT BITTIEST        BEILRTTY BITTERLY        BEKLOOSS BOOKLESS
BEHILORR HORRIBLE        BEIJLMRU JUMBLIER        BEILSTTU SUBTITLE        BEKLOOST BOOKLETS
BEHILORS BOLSHIER        BEIJMOSU JUMBOISE        BEIMMRRS BRIMMERS        BEKLORUV OVERBULK
BEHILOSS BOLSHIES        BEIJMOUZ JUMBOIZE        BEIMNORS BROMINES        BEKMOOPS SPEKBOOM
BEHILRST BLITHERS        BEIJNORW BIJWONER        BEIMNSSU NIMBUSES        BEKMOSST STEMBOKS
BEHILRTU THURIBLE        BEIKLNRS BLINKERS        BEIMNSTU BITUMENS        BEKNNORU UNBROKEN
BEHILSTT BLITHEST        BEIKLOSS OBELISKS        BEIMOORR BROOMIER        BEKNOOOT NOTEBOOK
BEHIMNOO BONHOMIE        BEIKLOTY KILOBYTE        BEIMOORS RIBOSOME        BEKNOPRU UPBROKEN
BEHIMRTU THUMBIER        BEIKLSTU BULKIEST        BEIMORSW IMBOWERS        BEKOOORV OVERBOOK
BEHINOPS HOPBINES        BEIKMNNR BRINKMEN        BEIMORTY BIOMETRY        BEKOORST BOOKREST
BEHINOSW WISHBONE        BEIKNRRY INKBERRY        BEIMOSSS IMBOSSES        BEKOORTU OUTBROKE
```

BEKOOTTX	TEXTBOOK	BEMOSTUX	BUXOMEST
BELLMORT	MORTBELL	BEMOSTUY	MYOTUBES
BELLMORU	UMBRELLO	BEMSSSUU	SUBSUMES
BELLMRUY	LUMBERLY	BENNNOTU	UNBONNET
BELLNTUY	TUNBELLY	BENNOOTU	BOUTONNE
BELLORTW	BELLWORT	BENORRSU	SUBORNER
BELLRRSU	BURRELLS	BENORRUV	OVERBURN
BELMMOOS	EMBLOOMS	BENORSST	SORBENTS
BELMMRSU	MUMBLERS	BENORSTU	RUBSTONE
BELMNOSU	NELUMBOS	BENORSTW	BESTROWN
BELMOORS	BLOOMERS		BROWNEST
	REBLOOMS	BENORSTY	RENTBOYS
BELMOORY	BLOOMERY	BENORSUU	BURNOUSE
BELMOOSS	BLOOSMES	BENORSWY	BYWONERS
BELMOPRS	PROBLEMS	BENORTTU	REBUTTON
BELMORSY	SOMBRELY	BENOSSUZ	SUBZONES
BELMORUW	RUMBELOW	BENOSSWY	NEWSBOYS
BELMOSST	TOMBLESS	BENSSSUY	BUSYNESS
BELMOSSY	SYMBOLES	BEOORRRW	BORROWER
BELMPRSU	PLUMBERS	BEOORRVW	OVERBROW
BELMPRUY	PLUMBERY	BEOORSST	BOOSTERS
BELMRRSU	RUMBLERS	BEOORSTY	BOTRYOSE
BELMRRUY	MULBERRY	BEOOSTUX	OUTBOXES
BELMRSSU	SLUMBERS	BEOOTTZZ	BOZZETTO
BELMRSTU	STUMBLER	BEOPRRSV	PROVERBS
	TUMBLERS	BEOPRSST	BESPORTS
	TUMBRELS	BEOPSSTU	BESPOUTS
BELMRSUY	SLUMBERY	BEOQSTUU	BOUQUETS
BELMSSTU	STUMBLES	BEORRSTU	ROBUSTER
BELNNOSU	UNNOBLES	BEORSSSU	SORBUSES
BELNOOSY	BOLONEYS	BEORSSUU	SUBEROUS
BELNOSUU	NEBULOUS	BEORSTUU	TUBEROUS
BELNOSYZ	BENZOYLS	BEORSUVY	OVERBUSY
BELNSSTU	SUNBELTS		OVERBUYS
BELNSTTU	BLUNTEST	BEOSSTTU	OBTUSEST
BELNSTUU	UNSUBTLE	BEPRRSTU	PERTURBS
BELOOPRS	BLOOPERS	BEPSSTUY	SUBTYPES
BELOORVW	OVERBLOW	BEQRRSUU	BRUSQUER
BELOOSST	BOOTLESS	BERRSSTU	BURSTERS
BELOOTUV	OBVOLUTE	BERRSTUU	SURREBUT
BELORRTU	TROUBLER	BERSSTTU	BUTTRESS
BELORSST	BOLSTERS	BERSSTUV	SUBVERST
	LOBSTERS		SUBVERTS
BELORSSW	BROWLESS	BESSSSUY	BYSSUSES
BELORSTT	BLOTTERS	BESSTTUX	SUBTEXTS
	BOTTLERS	BFFGILNU	BLUFFING
BELORSTU	BOULTERS	BFFNOOSU	BUFFOONS
	TROUBLES	BFFNOSUX	SNUFFBOX
BELOSTUY	OBTUSELY	BFGILMNU	FUMBLING
BELPRSUY	SUPERBLY	BFGIORST	FROGBITS
BELRSSTU	BLUSTERS	BFGLLORU	BULLFROG
	BUSTLERS	BFHLLSUU	BLUSHFUL
BELRSTUY	BLUSTERY	BFIINORS	FIBROINS
BELSSTTU	SUBTLEST	BFIIORSS	FIBROSIS
BELSSTUY	SUBSTYLE	BFILLSSU	BLISSFUL
BELSTTUY	SUBTLETY	BFIMNORU	NUBIFORM
BEMMOOSS	EMBOSOMS	BFIMORTU	TUBIFORM
BEMMORRS	BROMMERS	BFINORYZ	BRONZIFY
BEMMRRSU	BRUMMERS	BFIORSTT	FROSTBIT
BEMNOORT	TROMBONE	BFKLOOSY	FLYBOOKS
BEMNORSW	EMBROWNS	BFKSSSUU	SUBFUSKS
BEMNORSY	EMBRYONS	BFLLOSWY	FLYBLOWS
BEMNSTTU	BUTMENTS	BFLOORSU	SUBFLOOR
BEMNTTUY	BUTTYMEN	BFOOOSTY	FOOTBOYS
BEMOORRS	SOMBRERO	BGGGILNO	BOGGLING
BEMORSST	BESTORMS	BGGGINOR	BROGGING
	MOBSTERS	BGGGINSU	BUGGINGS
	SOMBREST	BGGIILNN	BINGLING
BEMORSSU	MORBUSES	BGGIILNO	OBLIGING
BEMORSWW	WEBWORMS	BGGIILNY	GIBINGLY

BGGIINNO	BOINGING	BGILNOSU	BLOUSING
BGGIINNR	BRINGING	BGILNOSW	BOWLINGS
BGGIINRU	BRIGUING	BGILNOTT	BLOTTING
BGGILNNU	BLUNGING		BOTTLING
	BUNGLING	BGILNOTU	BOULTING
BGGILNRU	BURGLING	BGILNRRU	BLURRING
BGGINOOT	TOBOGGIN	BGILNRTU	BLURTING
BGGINOSY	BYGOINGS	BGILNSTU	BUSTLING
BGHHIORW	HIGHBROW	BGILNTTU	BUTTLING
BGHHIOSY	HIGHBOYS	BGILOORS	OBLIGORS
BGHILMNU	HUMBLING	BGILRSSU	BUSGIRLS
BGHILNSU	BLUSHING	BGIMNOOR	BROOMING
BGHILRTY	BRIGHTLY	BGIMNOOS	BOOMINGS
BGHIMNTU	THUMBING		BOSOMING
BGHINORS	BIGHORNS	BGIMNORS	SOMBRING
BGHINRSU	BRUSHING	BGIMOSSY	BOGYISMS
BGHNORSU	HORNBUGS	BGINNNOU	UNBONING
BGHNOTUU	UNBOUGHT	BGINNORU	UNROBING
BGHOOPTU	BOUGHPOT	BGINNORW	BROWNING
BGHOORSU	BOROUGHS	BGINNORZ	BRONZING
BGIIJLNR	JIRBLING	BGINNOUX	UNBOXING
BGIIKLNN	BLINKING	BGINNRSU	BURNINGS
BGIIKMNO	KIMBOING	BGINNRTU	BRUNTING
BGIIKNNO	BOINKING	BGINNSTU	BUNTINGS
BGIIKNRS	BRISKING	BGINOOST	BOOSTING
BGIILLNS	BILLINGS	BGINORSW	BROWSING
BGIILMNW	WIMBLING	BGINPRSU	UPBRINGS
BGIILNNN	BLINNING	BGINRSTU	BRUSTING
BGIILNOR	BROILING		BURSTING
BGIILNOS	BOILINGS	BGINSSSU	BUSSINGS
BGIILNPP	BLIPPING	BGINSSTU	BUSTINGS
BGIILNRS	BIRLINGS	BGINSUZZ	BUZZINGS
	BIRSLING	BGKNOOOS	SONGBOOK
	BRISLING	BGKORSSY	GRYSBOKS
BGIILNSS	SIBLINGS	BGLNOOSW	LONGBOWS
BGIILNTZ	BLITZING	BGLNOSUW	BLOWGUNS
BGIIMMNR	BRIMMING	BGLOORXY	GLORYBOX
BGIIMNRS	BRIMINGS	BGLOORYY	BRYOLOGY
BGIIMNRU	IMBRUING	BGMOOSTU	GUMBOOTS
BGIINNOR	INORBING	BGNOOSWY	GOWNBOYS
BGIINNRS	INBRINGS	BGOPRSUU	SUBGROUP
BGIINORT	ORBITING	BGORSTUW	BUGWORTS
BGIINRST	RINGBITS	BHIIINST	INHIBITS
BGIINRSU	BRUISING	BHIIKRSS	BRISKISH
BGIINRTU	BRUITING	BHIILMPS	BLIMPISH
BGIINSTU	BUISTING	BHIIMRST	MISBIRTH
BGIINVVY	BIVVYING	BHIIOPRT	PROHIBIT
BGIJLMNU	JUMBLING	BHIIPSSS	SIBSHIPS
BGIJNORU	OBJURING	BHIKLLOO	BILLHOOK
BGIKLNNU	BLUNKING	BHILLNOR	HORNBILL
BGIKNNOU	BUNKOING	BHILLSTU	BULLSHIT
BGIKNOOR	BROOKING	BHILNSTU	BLUNTISH
BGIKNOOS	BOOKINGS	BHILORRY	HORRIBLY
BGIKNORS	BROKINGS	BHILOSTU	HOLIBUTS
BGIKNSSU	BUSKINGS	BHILOSYY	BOYISHLY
BGILLNOU	GLOBULIN	BHIMNORT	THROMBIN
BGILLNUY	BULLYING	BHIMOOPR	BIOMORPH
BGILMMNU	BUMMLING	BHIMOOSS	HOBOISMS
	MUMBLING	BHIMOPSS	PHOBISMS
BGILMNOO	BLOOMING	BHIMSSTU	BISMUTHS
BGILMNPU	PLUMBING	BHINOPSU	UNBISHOP
BGILMNRU	RUMBLING	BHINORSW	BROWNISH
BGILMNTU	TUMBLING	BHIOOPRS	BIOPHORS
BGILMORY	GORBLIMY	BHIOPSST	PHOBISTS
BGILMOSU	GUMBOILS	BHIRSTTU	TURBITHS
BGILNNOS	SNOBLING	BHKNOOOR	HORNBOOK
BGILNNTU	BLUNTING	BHKOOOPS	BOOKSHOP
BGILNOOP	BLOOPING	BHLOOOTT	TOLBOOTH
BGILNOST	BILTONGS	BHLRSUUY	BULRUSHY
	BOLTINGS	BHMOPTTU	THUMBPOT

BHMORSTU	THROMBUS
BHOOSSTW	BOWSHOTS
BIIKLOST	KILOBITS
BIIKNOOT	BOOTIKIN
BIILLMOR	MORBILLI
BIILLNOS	BILLIONS
BIILLOSU	BOUILLIS
BIILLSTW	TWIBILLS
BIILMOTY	MOBILITY
BIILNNRS	BIRLINNS
BIILNOOV	OBLIVION
BIILNOTY	NOBILITY
BIILNQSU	QUIBLINS
BIILNTUY	NUBILITY
BIILORST	STROBILI
BIILOSSU	SIBILOUS
BIIMMOSZ	ZOMBIISM
BIIMNOSU	NIOBIUMS
BIIMNSSU	MINISUBS
BIIMSSTU	STIBIUMS
BIINRSTU	BURINIST
BIIQTUUY	UBIQUITY
BIIRSSTU	BURSITIS
BIJNOSSU	SUBJOINS
BIKLNOSY	LINKBOYS
BIKMNPSU	BUMPKINS
BIKOOUUZ	BOUZOUKI
BIKORRSW	RIBWORKS
BILLMSUY	BULLYISM
BILLNOOU	BOUILLON
BILLNOSU	BULLIONS
BILLRSWY	WRYBILLS
BILLSTUY	SUBTILLY
BILMMPSU	PLUMBISM
BILMNORS	NOMBRILS
BILMOSTU	BOTULISM
BILMRSTU	TUMBRILS
BILNOSUU	NUBILOUS
BILOORST	SORBITOL
BILOPSSY	POSSIBLY
BILORSST	BRISTOLS
BILOSSSU	SUBSOILS
BILSSTTU	SUBTLIST
BILSTTUY	SUBTILTY
BIMMOOSS	IMBOSOMS
BIMNORSW	IMBROWNS
BIMNOSSY	SYMBIONS
BIMNOSTY	SYMBIONT
BIMNRUUV	VIBURNUM
BIMOSSTY	SYBOTISM
BIMRSSUX	BRUXISMS
BINOORST	ISOBRONT
BINORSST	RIBSTONS
BINRSSTU	INBURSTS
BINSSTUU	SUBUNITS
BIOPRRSU	SUBPRIOR
BIOPRSTW	BOWSPRIT
BIORRSTW	RIBWORTS
BIORSSTT	BISTORTS
BIORSTTU	BITTOURS
BIORSTUY	BISTOURY
BIOSTTUY	OBTUSITY
BIRSSTTU	SUBTRIST
BISSSSTU	SUBSISTS
BKKOOORW	BOOKWORK
	WORKBOOK
BKMOOORW	BOOKWORM
BKMOORUZ	ZOMBORUK
BLLLLOOY	LOBLOLLY
BLMMPSUU	PLUMBUMS

BLMNPSUU	UNPLUMBS
BLMOOOST	TOMBOLOS
BLMOOOTY	LOBOTOMY
BLMOORSW	LOBWORMS
BLMOOSSS	BLOSSOMS
BLMOOSSY	BLOSSOMY
BLMOPSUU	PLUMBOUS
BLNOOSSU	BLOUSONS
BLOOSSTY	SLYBOOTS
BLOPSSTU	SUBPLOTS
BLORSTUY	ROBUSTLY
BLOSTUUU	TUBULOUS
BMNOOSSU	UNBOSOMS
BMNORSUW	MOWBURNS
BMNORTUW	MOWBURNT
BMOOORSX	BOXROOMS
BMOORSSU	SOMBROUS
BMORSSTU	STROMBUS
BNNOTTUU	UNBUTTON
BNNRSSUU	SUNBURNS
BNNRSTUU	SUNBURNT
BNOOOSUY	SONOBUOY
BNOORTUW	BROWNOUT
BNORRUUW	UNBURROW
BNORSTUU	OUTBURNS
BNORTTUU	OUTBURNT
BNRSSTUU	SUNBURST
BORSTTUU	OUTBURST
BPRSSTUU	UPBURSTS
CCCDIILY	DICYCLIC
CCCEEILT	ECLECTIC
CCCEGOSY	COCCYGES
CCCEIIRT	ECCRITIC
CCCEILNY	ENCYCLIC
CCCEILUY	EUCYCLIC
CCCHIORY	CHICCORY
CCCIINSU	SUCCINIC
CCCILNOY	CYCLONIC
CCCILOPY	CYCLOPIC
CCCINSTU	SUCCINCT
CCCIOORS	SCIROCCO
CCCNOOST	CONCOCTS
CCDDEENO	CONCEDED
CCDDEEOT	DECOCTED
CCDDELOU	OCCLUDED
CCDDENOU	CONDUCED
CCDEEENR	CREDENCE
CCDEEHLN	CLENCHED
CCDEEILN	LICENCED
CCDEEINS	SCIENCED
CCDEEIOS	ECOCIDES
CCDEEKOR	COCKERED
CCDEEKOY	COCKEYED
CCDEELRY	RECYCLED
CCDEENOR	CONCEDER
CCDEENOS	CONCEDES
CCDEESSU	SUCCEEDS
CCDEHHRU	CHURCHED
CCDEHIKT	TCHICKED
CCDEHILN	CLINCHED
CCDEHIPU	HICCUPED
CCDEHKLU	CHUCKLED
CCDEHLTU	CLUTCHED
	DECLUTCH
CCDEHNRU	CRUNCHED
CCDEHORS	SCORCHED
CCDEHORT	CROTCHED
CCDEHORU	CROUCHED
CCDEHOST	SCOTCHED
CCDEHRTU	CRUTCHED

CCDEHSTU	SCUTCHED
CCDEIINO	COINCIDE
CCDEIIST	DEICTICS
CCDEILOS	SCOLECID
CCDEINOR	CORNICED
CCDEINOS	CONCISED
CCDEINOT	OCCIDENT
CCDEIOPP	COPPICED
CCDEIOPU	OCCUPIED
CCDEKNOU	UNCOCKED
CCDELNOU	CONCLUDE
CCDELOSU	OCCLUDES
CCDELOTU	OCCULTED
CCDENOOO	COCOONED
CCDENOSU	CONDUCES
CCDEORRU	OCCURRED
CCDEORSU	SUCCORED
CCDEOSTU	STUCCOED
CCDHIIKP	DIPCHICK
CCDHIILO	CICHLOID
CCDHIILS	CICHLIDS
CCDHIIOR	DICHROIC
CCDHINOO	CONCHOID
CCDIILOS	CODICILS
CCDIILSU	CULICIDS
CCDIINOO	CONOIDIC
CCDIINOS	SCINCOID
CCDIINST	DISCINCT
CCDIIORS	CRICOIDS
CCDIIORT	DICROTIC
CCDILOSY	CYCLOIDS
CCDINOTU	CONDUCTI
CCDKLOSU	CUCKOLDS
CCDKLOUY	CUCKOLDY
CCDKOOOW	WOODCOCK
CCDNOORS	CONCORDS
CCDNOSTU	CONDUCTS
CCEEELMN	CLEMENCE
CCEEGINR	RECCEING
CCEEGNOS	COGENCES
CCEEHIKR	CHECKIER
CCEEHINZ	ZECCHINE
CCEEHKRS	CHECKERS
	RECHECKS
CCEEHLNS	CLENCHES
CCEEHORS	ECORCHES
CCEEHOSU	COUCHEES
CCEEHRSY	SCREECHY
CCEEIILS	CICELIES
CCEEIIST	CECITIES
CCEEILNR	ENCIRCLE
CCEEILNS	LICENCES
CCEEILNT	ELENCTIC
CCEEILPY	EPICYCLE
CCEEILRT	ELECTRIC
CCEEIMNU	ECUMENIC
CCEEINOR	CICERONE
CCEEINOV	CONCEIVE
CCEEINSS	SCIENCES
CCEEIORV	COERCIVE
CCEEIPSS	SPECCIES
CCEEIRSS	ECCRISES
CCEEIRSV	CRESCIVE
	CREVICES
CCEEITTU	EUTECTIC
CCEEKLOR	COCKEREL
CCEEKOSY	COCKEYES
CCEELMNY	CLEMENCY
CCEELOSS	SCOLECES
CCEELRSY	RECYCLES

CCEEMMNO	COMMENCE
CCEEMMOR	COMMERCE
CCEEMOPS	COMPESCE
CCEENNOS	ENSCONCE
CCEENORT	CONCRETE
CCEENRST	CRESCENT
CCEERSSU	CERCUSES
CCEFIIPS	SPECIFIC
CCEFIRRU	CRUCIFER
CCEFLLOU	FLOCCULE
CCEFLOOS	FLOCCOSE
CCEFNOST	CONFECTS
CCEGHIKN	CHECKING
CCEGHIOR	CHOREGIC
CCEGIKLN	CLECKING
CCEGILOO	ECOLOGIC
CCEGILRY	GLYCERIC
CCEGINOR	COERCING
CCEGINRY	RECCYING
CCEGNOOS	COGNOSCE
CCEHHINS	CHINCHES
CCEHHRSU	CHURCHES
CCEHIIMR	CHIMERIC
CCEHIIMS	ISCHEMIC
CCEHIINZ	ZECCHINI
CCEHIKNS	CHICKENS
CCEHIKSU	CHUCKIES
CCEHILNR	CLINCHER
CCEHILNS	CLINCHES
CCEHILOR	CHOLERIC
CCEHILOY	CHOICELY
CCEHINOR	CORNICHE
	ENCHORIC
CCEHINOS	CONCHIES
CCEHINOZ	ZECCHINO
CCEHINST	TECHNICS
CCEHIORT	RICOCHET
CCEHIOST	CHOICEST
CCEHIRSS	SCREICHS
	SCRIECHS
CCEHKLSU	CHUCKLES
CCEHKNSU	UNCHECKS
CCEHLMOR	CROMLECH
CCEHLNNU	UNCLENCH
CCEHLNSU	CLUNCHES
CCEHLRSU	CLERUCHS
CCEHLRUY	CLERUCHY
CCEHLSTU	CLUTCHES
	CULTCHES
CCEHNRSU	CRUNCHES
CCEHORRS	SCORCHER
CCEHORSS	SCORCHES
CCEHORST	CROCHETS
	CROTCHES
CCEHORSU	CROUCHES
CCEHORTT	CROTCHET
CCEHOSST	SCOTCHES
CCEHRSTU	CRUTCHES
	SCUTCHER
CCEHRTUY	CUTCHERY
CCEHSSTU	SCUTCHES
CCEIIKLN	NICKELIC
CCEIILNT	ENCLITIC
CCEIILNU	CULICINE
CCEIILOR	LICORICE
CCEIILPT	ECLIPTIC
CCEIILST	SCILICET
CCEIILTU	LEUCITIC
CCEIINNR	ENCRINIC
CCEIINOR	CICERONI

CCEIIRRT CIRCITER	CCENORSW CONCREWS	CCILNOOS COLONICS	CDDEEKNU UNDECKED
CCEIIRSS ECCRISIS	CCENORTY CORNETCY	CCILNOSU COUNCILS	CDDEEKOT DOCKETED
CCEIIRST ICTERICS	CCENRRUY CURRENCY	CCILOOPS PICCOLOS	CDDEEKUW DUCKWEED
CCEIIRTT RECTITIC	CCEOOORR COROCORE	CCILORUU CURCULIO	CDDEELPU DECUPLED
CCEIIRTU EUCRITIC	CCEOORSU CROCEOUS	CCILOSSY CYCLOSIS	CDDEELSU SECLUDED
CCEIKLRS CLICKERS	CCEOOSTT COCOTTES	CCILSSTY CYCLISTS	CDDEELUX EXCLUDED
CCEIKLRU CLUCKIER	CCEOPRUY REOCCUPY	CCIMNSUU SUCCINUM	CDDEELUY DEUCEDLY
CCEIKLST CLICKETS	CCEORRST CORRECTS	CCINOOST COCTIONS	CDDEENOS SECONDED
CCEIKORS COCKSIER	CCEORRSU CROCUSES	CCINOPRT PROCINCT	CDDEENSS DESCENDS
CCEIKOST COCKIEST	CCEORSTU STUCCOER	CCINOPSY SYNCOPIC	CDDEEORR RECORDED
CCEIKRST CRICKETS	CCESSSUU CUSCUSES	CCINORSY CRYONICS	CDDEEORS DECODERS
CCEILMOO COELOMIC	CCFIINOR CORNIFIC	CCINOSTV CONVICTS	CDDEERUV DECURVED
CCEILMOP COMPLICE	CCFIIRUX CRUCIFIX	CCIOOPST SCOTOPIC	CDDEESUW CUDWEEDS
CCEILNOR CORNICLE	CCFILLOU FLOCCULI	CCIOORSS SIROCCOS	CDDEFIIO CODIFIED
CCEILNUY UNICYCLE	CCFILNOT CONFLICT	CCIOOTXY OXYTOCIC	CDDEFINO CONFIDED
CCEILOSS SCOLICES	CCFKLOOT COCKLOFT	CCIOPSTU OCCIPUTS	CDDEGIIN DECIDING
CCEILRRS CIRCLERS	CCFLOOOO LOCOFOCO	CCIRSSUY CIRCUSSY	CDDEGINO DECODING
CCEILRRU CURRICLE	CCGHHIOU HICCOUGH	CCJNNOTU CONJUNCT	CDDEGINU DEDUCING
CCEILRST CIRCLETS	CCGHIINN CINCHING	CCKKLMUU MUCKLUCK	CDDEHIOW COWHIDED
CCEILRTY TRICYCLE	CCGHIKNO CHOCKING	CCKMMORU CRUMMOCK	CDDEIINT INDICTED
CCEILRUU CURLICUE	CCGHIKNU CHUCKING	CCKMOOOR MOORCOCK	CDDEIISS DISCIDES
CCEILSTU CUTICLES	CCGHINNO CONCHING	CCKNORTU TURNCOCK	CDDEIKOS DOCKISED
CCEIMNOO ECONOMIC	CCGHINOS GNOCCHIS	CCKOPRSU COCKSPUR	CDDEIKOZ DOCKIZED
CCEIMOST COSMETIC	CCGHINOU COUCHING	CCKOSSTU CUSTOCKS	CDDEILLO COLLIDED
CCEIMRRU MERCURIC	CCGIIKLN CLICKING	CCLLOTUY OCCULTLY	CDDEILNU INCLUDED
CCEINNOS INSCONCE	CCGIIKNR CRICKING	CCLMOOPU COCOPLUM	CDDEILOR CLODDIER
CCEINNOV CONVINCE	CCGIILNR CIRCLING	CCLNOOOR CONCOLOR	CDDEILRU CUDDLIER
CCEINOOR COERCION	CCGIKLNO CLOCKING	CCLOOOSZ ZOCCOLOS	CDDEINTU INDUCTED
CCEINOPT CONCEPTI	COCKLING	CCLOORSU OCCLUSOR	CDDEIORV DIVORCED
CCEINORS CONCISER	CCGIKLNU CLUCKING	CCMOOORS MOROCCOS	CDDEIRRU CRUDDIER
CORNICES	CCGIKNOR CROCKING	CCNOOPSU PUCCOONS	CDDEIRSU DISCURED
CCEINORT NECROTIC	CCGILLOY GLYCOLIC	CCNOORSU CONCOURS	CDDEKNOU UNDOCKED
CCEINOSS CONCISES	CCGILNOY GLYCONIC	CCNOOSTU COCONUTS	CDDELLOU COLLUDED
CCEINOST CONCEITS	CCGILNSY CYCLINGS	CCOOOORR COROCORO	CDDELNOO CONDOLED
CCEINOTT CONCETTI	CCGILOSU GLUCOSIC	CCOOSSUU COUSCOUS	CDDELOOR CROODLED
TECTONIC	CCGINNOS SCONCING	CCOOTTUU TUCOTUCO	CDDELRSU CRUDDLES
CCEINOTY CONCEITY	CCGKOORS GORCOCKS	CCORSSTU CROSSCUT	CDDELSSU SCUDDLES
CCEINPRT PRECINCT	CCHHILSS SCHLICHS	CCORSSUU SUCCOURS	CDDEMNOU DUNCEDOM
CCEINRTU CINCTURE	CCHHINOT CHTHONIC	CCOTTUUU TUCUTUCO	CDDENNOO CONDONED
CCEINSTY SYNECTIC	CCHHLRUY CHURCHLY	CCRSUUUU SURUCUCU	CDDENOOR CORDONED
CCEIOORT CROCOITE	CCHHNRUU UNCHURCH	CDDDEETU DEDUCTED	CDDENORU UNCORDED
CCEIOOTZ ECTOZOIC	CCHIINUZ ZUCCHINI	CDDDEIIS DISCIDED	CDDEOORR CORRODED
CCEIOPPS COPPICES	CCHIIORT ORCHITIC	CDDDELRU CRUDDLED	CDDEOORT DOCTORED
CCEIOPRT ECTROPIC	CCHIKMPU CHIPMUCK	CDDDELSU SCUDDLED	CDDEOPRU PRODUCED
CCEIOPRU OCCUPIER	CCHIKSST SCHTICKS	CDDDIIIO DIDDICOI	CDDERSSU SCUDDERS
CCEIOPSU OCCUPIES	CCHINORS CHRONICS	CDDDIIOY DIDDICOY	CDDGHILO GODCHILD
CCEIORST CORTICES	CCHINOSU SCUCHION	CDDEEEEX EXCEEDED	CDDGILNO CLODDING
CCEIPSST SCEPTICS	CCHINSSU SCUCHINS	CDDEEEFN DEFENCED	CODDLING
CCEIRSSU CIRCUSES	CCHIPSSY PSYCHICS	CDDEEEFT DEFECTED	CDDGILNU CUDDLING
CCEJNOST CONJECTS	CCHKLOSS SCHLOCKS	CDDEEEIV DECEIVED	CDDGINSU SCUDDING
CCEKLORS CLOCKERS	CCHKMOSS SCHMOCKS	CDDEEEJT DEJECTED	CDDHIIRY DIHYDRIC
CCEKNOST CONTECKS	CCHKMSSU SCHMUCKS	CDDEEENR DECERNED	CDDHILOS CLODDISH
CCEKNOSY COCKNEYS	CCHKOOST COCKSHOT	CDDEEENT DECEDENT	CDDHIORS DICHORDS
CCEKOPST PETCOCKS	CCHKOPTU PUTCHOCK	CDDEEEPR PRECEDED	CDDIIIOS DIDICOIS
CCEKORRY CROCKERY	CCHKOSTU COCKSHUT	CDDEEERS SCREEDED	CDDIIOSY DIDICOYS
CCEKORST CROCKETS	CCHKSSTU SCHTUCKS	CDDEEERW DECREWED	CDDIISTY DYTISCID
CCEKORSU COCKSURE	CCHLNTUU UNCLUTCH	CDDEEETT DETECTED	CDDIKOPS PIDDOCKS
CCELLOST COLLECTS	CCHNRSUY SCRUNCHY	CDDEEFOR DEFORCED	CDDIORSS DISCORDS
CCELMOPT COMPLECT	CCIIKNPY PICNICKY	CDDEEHIS DEHISCED	CDDKOPSU PUDDOCKS
CCELNOSY CYCLONES	CCIIMNSY CYNICISM	CDDEEHNR DRENCHED	CDDKORSU RUDDOCKS
CCELOPSY CYCLOPES	CCIINNSU CICINNUS	CDDEEIIS DEICIDES	CDDMMOUU MOCUDDUM
CCELOSSY CYCLOSES	CCIINORZ ZIRCONIC	CDDEEIKR DICKERED	CDEEEFFT EFFECTED
CCELSSUY CYCLUSES	CCIIRSTU CIRCUITS	CDDEEILN DECLINED	CDEEEFHL FLEECHED
CCENNORS CONCERNS	CCIIRTUY CIRCUITY	CDDEEILP PEDICLED	CDEEEFNS DEFENCES
CCENNOST CONCENTS	CCIKKLOP LOCKPICK	CDDEEIOV DEVOICED	CDEEEFRT REFECTED
CONNECTS	PICKLOCK	CDDEEIPT DEPICTED	CDEEEHHW WHEECHED
CCENOORT CONCERTO	CCIKLOSW COWLICKS	CDDEEIRS DECIDERS	CDEEEHLR LECHERED
CCENOOTT CONCETTO	CCIKNOPR PRINCOCK	DESCRIED	CDEEEHMS SMEECHED
CCENOPST CONCEPTS	CCIKOPRS CROPSICK	CDDEEIRT CREDITED	CDEEEHPS DEPECHES
CCENORST CONCERTS	CCIKOPST COCKPITS	DIRECTED	SPEECHED

CDEEEHRS	CREESHED		DECIPHER	CDEEINPR	PINCERED	CDEENNTU	UNDECENT
CDEEEHST	TEDESCHE	CDEEHIPS	CEPHEIDS	CDEEINPS	DISPENCE	CDEENNTY	TENDENCY
CDEEEHSW	ESCHEWED	CDEEHIRR	CHERRIED	CDEEINPT	DEPEINCT	CDEENOOS	COOSENED
CDEEEINP	PIECENED		DREICHER		INCEPTED	CDEENORR	CORNERED
CDEEEINV	EVIDENCE	CDEEHISS	DEHISCES		PEINCTED	CDEENORS	CENSORED
CDEEEIPS	EPICEDES	CDEEHIST	TEDESCHI		PENTICED		NECROSED
CDEEEIRV	DECEIVER	CDEEHITW	ITCHWEED	CDEEINTV	INVECTED		SECONDER
	RECEIVED	CDEEHKST	SKETCHED	CDEEIORV	DIVORCEE	CDEENORT	CENTRODE
CDEEEISV	DECEIVES	CDEEHKTV	KVETCHED	CDEEIOSS	DIOCESES	CDEENOSS	SECONDES
CDEEEJRT	REJECTED	CDEEHLMO	LEECHDOM	CDEEIOSV	DEVOICES	CDEENOVX	CONVEXED
CDEEEKNW	NECKWEED	CDEEHLQU	QUELCHED	CDEEIPRS	PRECISED	CDEENOVY	CONVEYED
CDEEELLX	EXCELLED	CDEEHLSU	SCHEDULE	CDEEIPRT	DECREPIT	CDEENPRU	PRUDENCE
CDEEELST	DESELECT	CDEEHMTU	HUMECTED		DEPICTER	CDEENRSU	CENSURED
	SELECTED	CDEEHNQU	QUENCHED	CDEEIPRU	PEDICURE	CDEENRUV	VERECUND
CDEEELUX	EXCLUDEE	CDEEHNRR	DRENCHER	CDEEIPST	PECTISED	CDEENSST	DESCENTS
CDEEEMNT	CEMENTED	CDEEHNRS	DRENCHES	CDEEIPTZ	PECTIZED	CDEENSSU	CENSUSED
CDEEEMPR	EMPERCED	CDEEHNRT	TRENCHED	CDEEIQSU	QUIESCED	CDEENSTY	ENCYSTED
CDEEENNT	TENDENCE	CDEEHNRW	WRENCHED	CDEEIRRS	DECRIERS	CDEEOOPR	COOPERED
CDEEENOS	SECONDEE	CDEEHNST	STENCHED	CDEEIRRT	DIRECTER	CDEEOOTV	DOVECOTE
CDEEENRS	RECENSED	CDEEHNUW	UNCHEWED		REDIRECT	CDEEOPPR	COPPERED
	SCREENED	CDEEHORS	COSHERED	CDEEIRSS	DESCRIES	CDEEOPRS	PROCEEDS
	SECERNED	CDEEHORT	HECTORED	CDEEIRST	DISCREET	CDEEOPRU	RECOUPED
CDEEENRT	CENTERED		TOCHERED		DISCRETE	CDEEORRR	RECORDER
	DECENTER	CDEEHPRU	CHERUPED	CDEEIRSU	DECURIES	CDEEORRS	RESCORED
CDEEEPRS	PRECEDES	CDEEHPRY	CYPHERED	CDEEIRSV	DESCRIVE	CDEEORRU	RECOURED
CDEEEPTX	EXCEPTED	CDEEHQTU	QUETCHED		SCRIEVED	CDEEORST	CORSETED
	EXPECTED	CDEEHRTW	WRETCHED		SERVICED		ESCORTED
CDEEERRS	SCREEDER	CDEEHSSU	DUCHESSE	CDEEIRTU	CUITERED		SECTORED
CDEEERSS	RECESSED	CDEEIILT	ELICITED	CDEEJKOY	JOCKEYED	CDEEORTT	DETECTOR
	SECEDERS	CDEEIIMN	MEDICINE	CDEEKLNO	ENLOCKED	CDEEORTV	CORVETED
CDEEERST	DECREETS	CDEEIIMP	EPIDEMIC	CDEEKLPS	SPECKLED		VECTORED
	RESECTED	CDEEIINT	INDICTEE	CDEEKMRU	MUCKERED	CDEEOSST	CESTODES
	SECRETED	CDEEIIST	EIDETICS	CDEEKNOR	RECKONED		COSSETED
CDEEERSV	SCREEVED	CDEEIISV	DECISIVE	CDEEKNRS	REDNECKS	CDEEOSTT	ESCOTTED
CDEEERTX	EXCRETED	CDEEIITT	DIETETIC	CDEEKNRU	UNRECKED	CDEEPRST	SCEPTRED
CDEEESTX	EXSECTED	CDEEIJNT	INJECTED	CDEEKOPT	POCKETED	CDEERRRU	RECURRED
CDEEETUX	EXECUTED	CDEEIJOR	REJOICED	CDEEKORT	ROCKETED	CDEERRSU	REDUCERS
CDEEFFOR	COFFERED	CDEEIKMY	MICKEYED	CDEEKORW	ROCKWEED	CDEERRUV	RECURVED
	EFFORCED	CDEEIKNR	NICKERED	CDEEKOST	SOCKETED	CDEERSSU	SEDUCERS
CDEEFHLN	FLENCHED	CDEEIKNS	SICKENED	CDEEKPRU	PUCKERED	CDEERSUV	DECURVES
CDEEFHLT	FLETCHED	CDEEIKNV	INVECKED	CDEEKRSU	SUCKERED	CDEERSUX	EXCURSED
CDEEFIIS	EDIFICES	CDEEIKPT	PICKETED	CDEEKRTU	TUCKERED	CDEERTTU	CURETTED
CDEEFIIT	FETICIDE	CDEEIKRW	WICKEDER	CDEELLPU	CUPELLED	CDEERTUV	CURVETED
CDEEFINT	INFECTED		WICKERED	CDEELMOW	WELCOMED	CDEFFINO	COFFINED
CDEEFKLR	FRECKLED	CDEEIKRY	YICKERED	CDEELNOS	ENCLOSED	CDEFFISU	SUFFICED
CDEEFKOR	FOREDECK	CDEEIKTT	TICKETED	CDEELNPU	PEDUNCLE	CDEFFLSU	SCUFFLED
CDEEFLST	DEFLECTS	CDEEILNP	PENDICLE	CDEELNTY	DECENTLY	CDEFHILN	FLINCHED
CDEEFNNU	UNFENCED	CDEEILNR	RECLINED	CDEELNUW	UNCLEWED	CDEFHIMO	CHIEFDOM
CDEEFNOR	ENFORCED	CDEEILNS	DECLINES	CDEELOPU	DECOUPLE	CDEFHIRT	FRICHTED
CDEEFORS	DEFORCES		LICENSED	CDEELORS	RECLOSED	CDEFIIIL	FILICIDE
	FRESCOED		SILENCED	CDEELORV	CLOVERED	CDEFIIIT	CITIFIED
CDEEFORT	DEFECTOR	CDEEILNT	DENTICLE	CDEELORY	RECOYLED	CDEFIIOR	CODIFIER
CDEEGIIR	REGICIDE	CDEEILNU	NUCLEIDE	CDEELOST	CLOSETED	CDEFIIOS	CODIFIES
CDEEGINO	GENOCIDE	CDEEILOR	RECOILED	CDEELOTU	ELOCUTED	CDEFIIST	DEFICITS
CDEEGINR	RECEDING	CDEEILPS	ECLIPSED	CDEELPRU	PRECLUDE	CDEFINNO	CONFINED
CDEEGINS	SECEDING		PEDICELS	CDEELPSU	DECUPLES	CDEFINNU	INFECUND
CDEEGIOS	GEODESIC		PEDICLES	CDEELRTU	LECTURED	CDEFINOR	CONFIDER
CDEEGIOT	GEODETIC	CDEEILRS	SCLEREID		RELUCTED		INFORCED
CDEEGNOR	CONGREED	CDEEILRT	DERELICT	CDEELSSU	SCEDULES	CDEFINOS	CONFIDES
CDEEHHSU	SHEUCHED	CDEEILRU	RECUILED		SECLUDES	CDEFINOX	CONFIXED
CDEEHHTT	THETCHED	CDEEIMNR	ENDERMIC	CDEELSUX	EXCLUDES	CDEFKORS	DEFROCKS
CDEEHILN	LICHENED	CDEEIMNS	ENDEMICS	CDEEMOPR	COMPERED	CDEFLNOU	FLOUNCED
CDEEHILP	CHELIPED	CDEEIMOR	MEDIOCRE	CDEEMOPT	COMPETED	CDEFLORY	FORCEDLY
CDEEHINR	ENRICHED	CDEEIMOS	COMEDIES	CDEEMORT	ECTODERM	CDEFNORU	FROUNCED
	INHERCED	CDEEIMPR	PREMEDIC	CDEEMSTU	TUMESCED		UNFORCED
	NICHERED	CDEEIMRS	MISCREED	CDEENNOS	CONDENSE	CDEFNOSU	CONFUSED
	RICHENED	CDEEIMRV	DECEMVIR	CDEENNOU	DENOUNCE	CDEFNOTU	CONFUTED
CDEEHIOS	ECHOISED	CDEEINNS	INCENSED		ENOUNCED	CDEFNSTU	DEFUNCTS
CDEEHIOZ	ECHOIZED	CDEEINNT	INDECENT	CDEENNOV	CONVENED	CDEFOSSU	FOCUSSED
CDEEHIPR	CIPHERED	CDEEINOS	CODEINES	CDEENNPY	PENDENCY	CDEGHORU	GROUCHED

Code	Word
CDEGHRTU	GRUTCHED
CDEGIINN	INCEDING
CDEGIINX	EXCIDING
CDEGIKNO	DECKOING
	DECOKING
CDEGIKNS	DECKINGS
CDEGILSU	CLUDGIES
CDEGINNO	ENCODING
CDEGINNS	SCENDING
CDEGINOS	COGNISED
CDEGINOY	DECOYING
CDEGINOZ	COGNIZED
CDEGINRU	REDUCING
CDEGINRY	DECRYING
CDEGINSU	SEDUCING
CDEGINSY	DYSGENIC
CDEGNORU	CONGRUED
CDEGOORS	SCROOGED
CDEGORSU	SCOURGED
	SCROUGED
CDEGORSW	SCROWDGE
CDEHIILO	HELICOID
CDEHIILS	CEILIDHS
CDEHIIMO	HOMICIDE
CDEHIINO	ECHINOID
CDEHIIVV	CHIVVIED
CDEHIKOS	HOICKSED
CDEHIKRW	HERDWICK
CDEHILMR	MERCHILD
CDEHILNR	CHILDREN
CDEHILOR	CHLORIDE
CDEHILOS	CHELOIDS
CDEHILRT	ELDRITCH
CDEHIMOT	METHODIC
CDEHIMRS	SMIRCHED
CDEHINNR	INDRENCH
CDEHINOS	HEDONICS
CDEHINQU	QUINCHED
CDEHINST	SNITCHED
CDEHIOOR	OCHIDORE
CDEHIOSW	COWHIDES
CDEHIOTY	THEODICY
CDEHIQTU	QUITCHED
CDEHIRST	DITCHERS
CDEHISTT	STITCHED
CDEHISTW	SWITCHED
CDEHITTW	TWITCHED
CDEHKLSU	SHELDUCK
CDEHKSUY	HEYDUCKS
CDEHLOOS	DESCHOOL
	SCHOOLED
CDEHLORT	CHORTLED
CDEHLOSU	SLOUCHED
CDEHMOOS	SMOOCHED
CDEHMOSU	SMOUCHED
CDEHMSTU	SMUTCHED
CDEHNORS	CHONDRES
CDEHNRSU	CHUNDERS
CDEHOORR	RHEOCORD
CDEHORSU	CHORUSED
CDEHORSW	CHOWDERS
	COWHERDS
CDEHOSSU	HOCUSSED
CDEHOSSW	COWSHEDS
CDEHSSSU	SCHUSSED
CDEIIILS	SILICIDE
CDEIIIMT	MITICIDE
CDEIIIOS	IDIOCIES
CDEIIIRV	VIRICIDE
CDEIIITV	VITICIDE
CDEIIKLS	SICKLIED
CDEIIKMM	MIMICKED
CDEIIKNR	CIDERKIN
CDEIIKNW	INWICKED
CDEIIKRS	DRICKSIE
CDEIIKRT	DICKTIER
CDEIIKST	DICKIEST
	STICKIED
CDEIILMO	DOMICILE
CDEIILNN	INCLINED
CDEIILNO	INDOCILE
CDEIILOT	IDIOLECT
CDEIILPS	DISCIPLE
CDEIILPU	PULICIDE
CDEIILRU	RIDICULE
CDEIIMOS	DIOECISM
CDEIIMRT	DIMETRIC
CDEIINNT	INCIDENT
CDEIINOS	DECISION
	ICONISED
CDEIINOV	INVOICED
CDEIINOZ	ICONIZED
CDEIINRT	INDIRECT
CDEIIOPR	PERIODIC
CDEIIOPS	EPISODIC
CDEIIOPT	EPIDOTIC
CDEIIOSV	OVICIDES
CDEIIPRR	CIRRIPED
CDEIIRTU	DIURETIC
CDEIIRUV	VIRUCIDE
CDEIISSU	SUICIDES
CDEIISTT	DICTIEST
CDEIJNOO	COJOINED
CDEIJSST	DISJECTS
CDEIKLNO	INLOCKED
CDEIKLNR	CRINKLED
CDEIKLNU	UNLICKED
CDEIKLOS	SIDELOCK
CDEIKLPR	PRICKLED
CDEIKLRT	TRICKLED
CDEIKLST	STICKLED
CDEIKLWY	WICKEDLY
CDEIKMSU	MUSICKED
CDEIKNPU	UNPICKED
CDEIKNTU	TUNICKED
CDEIKOSS	DOCKISES
CDEIKOSY	YOICKSED
CDEIKOSZ	DOCKIZES
CDEIKRRS	DERRICKS
CDEIKSTU	DUCKIEST
CDEILLOS	CODILLES
	COLLIDES
CDEILLOU	LODICULE
CDEILLPU	PELLUCID
CDEILMMS	SCLIMMED
CDEILMOP	COMPILED
	COMPLIED
CDEILMOS	MELODICS
CDEILMPR	CRIMPLED
CDEILMRU	DULCIMER
CDEILMSY	DYSMELIC
CDEILNOS	INCLOSED
CDEILNOU	UNCOILED
CDEILNRY	CYLINDER
CDEILNSU	INCLUDES
	NUCLIDES
CDEILOOW	WOODLICE
CDEILOPU	CLUPEOID
	UPCOILED
CDEILORS	SCLEROID
CDEILORU	CLOUDIER
CDEILORV	COVERLID
CDEILOSS	DISCLOSE
CDEILOST	DOCILEST
CDEILPPR	CRIPPLED
CDEILPSU	CLUPEIDS
CDEILRTY	DIRECTLY
CDEILSTU	DULCITES
	LUCIDEST
CDEILSXY	DYSLEXIC
CDEILTTU	CUITTLED
CDEIMMOX	COMMIXED
CDEIMOOW	WOODMICE
CDEIMORT	MORTICED
CDEIMOST	DOMESTIC
CDEIMPRS	SCRIMPED
CDEINNOU	UNCOINED
CDEINNOV	CONNIVED
CDEINOOS	COOSINED
CDEINOOZ	ENDOZOIC
CDEINORR	CORDINER
CDEINORS	CONSIDER
CDEINORT	CENTROID
	DOCTRINE
CDEINORU	DECURION
CDEINOST	DEONTICS
CDEINOSU	DOUCINES
CDEINOSZ	ZINCODES
CDEINOTU	EDUCTION
CDEINOUV	UNVOICED
CDEINOVV	CONNIVED
CDEINPRS	PRESCIND
CDEINPRU	UNPRICED
CDEINPSY	DYSPNEIC
CDEINRRU	INCURRED
CDEINRSS	DISCERNS
	RESCINDS
CDEINRSU	INDUCERS
CDEINRUV	INCURVED
CDEINSSX	EXSCINDS
CDEINSTY	SYNDETIC
CDEIOORS	CORODIES
CDEIOPRT	DEPICTOR
CDEIOPST	DESPOTIC
CDEIORRT	CREDITOR
	DIRECTOR
CDEIORRV	DIVORCER
CDEIORSS	DISCOERS
CDEIORST	CORDITES
CDEIORSU	DISCOURE
CDEIORSV	DISCOVER
	DIVORCES
CDEIORSW	CROWDIES
CDEIORSY	DECISORY
CDEIORTU	OUTCRIED
CDEIOSST	CESTOIDS
CDEIOSTT	COTTISED
CDEIPRSS	DISCERPS
CDEIPRST	PREDICTS
	SCRIPTED
CDEIPRSY	CYPRIDES
CDEIPRTU	PICTURED
CDEIPSST	DISCEPTS
CDEIRRSU	SCURRIED
CDEIRSSU	DISCURES
CDEIRSTU	CRUDITES
	CURDIEST
	CURTSIED
CDEIRSTV	VERDICTS
CDEISSST	DISSECTS
CDEISSSU	DISCUSES
CDEJNORU	CONJURED
CDEKKLNU	KNUCKLED
CDEKLMOR	CLERKDOM
CDEKLMOU	DUCKMOLE
CDEKLNOU	UNLOCKED
CDEKLNRU	CRUNKLED
CDEKLOPU	UPLOCKED
CDEKLORY	YELDROCK
CDEKLOSW	WEDLOCKS
CDEKLRTU	TRUCKLED
CDEKNOOU	UNCOOKED
CDEKNOOV	CONVOKED
CDEKNORU	UNCORKED
CDEKNSUU	UNSUCKED
CDEKNTUU	UNTUCKED
CDELLNUU	UNCULLED
CDELLOOP	CLODPOLE
CDELLORS	SCROLLED
CDELLORU	COLLUDER
CDELLOSU	COLLUDES
CDELLOTU	CLOUDLET
CDELMNOO	MONOCLED
CDELMNOU	COLUMNED
CDELMPRU	CRUMPLED
CDELNOOS	CONDOLES
	CONSOLED
CDELNOSS	COLDNESS
CDELNOSU	ENCLOUDS
	UNCLOSED
CDELNOSY	CONDYLES
	SECONDLY
CDELNOTU	UNCOLTED
CDELNOUW	UNCOWLED
CDELNRUU	UNCURLED
CDELOORS	CROODLES
	DECOLORS
CDELOORU	COLOURED
	DECOLOUR
CDELOPSU	UPCLOSED
CDELOPTU	OCTUPLED
CDELORSS	CORDLESS
	SCOLDERS
CDELORSU	CLOSURED
CDELORSW	CLOWDERS
	SCROWLED
CDELORTU	CLOTURED
CDELOSSU	DULCOSES
CDELOSTU	LOCUSTED
CDELPRSU	SCRUPLED
CDELPRUU	UPCURLED
CDELPSTU	SCULPTED
CDELRSSU	SCUDLERS
CDELRSUY	CURSEDLY
CDELRTUU	CULTURED
CDELSSTU	DUCTLESS
CDELSTTU	SCUTTLED
CDEMMNOO	COMMONED
CDEMMNOS	COMMENDS
CDEMMNOU	COMMUNED
CDEMMOOS	COMMODES
CDEMMOOV	COMMOVED
CDEMMOTU	COMMUTED
CDEMMRSU	SCRUMMED
CDEMNNOS	CONDEMNS
CDEMNOOW	COMEDOWN
CDEMNOPS	COMPENDS
CDEMNOSU	CONSUMED
CDEMNOTU	DOCUMENT
CDEMNSUU	SECUNDUM

Key	Word
CDEMOOPS	COMPOSED
CDEMOPTU	COMPUTED
CDEMORSU	DECORUMS
CDEMOSTU	COSTUMED
	CUSTOMED
CDEMPRSU	SCRUMPED
CDENNOOS	CONDONES
CDENNOOT	CONNOTED
CDENNOST	CONTENDS
CDENNOUY	UNCOYNED
CDENOORT	CREODONT
CDENOOST	SECODONT
CDENOOTT	COTTONED
CDENOOVY	CONVOYED
CDENORSS	CORSNEDS
CDENORSW	DECROWNS
CDENORTU	CORNUTED
	TROUNCED
CDENOSTU	CONTUSED
CDENRSUU	UNCURSED
CDENRTUU	UNDERCUT
CDEOOPPS	COPEPODS
CDEOOPRS	SCROOPED
CDEOOPST	POSTCODE
CDEOORRS	CORRODES
CDEOORSU	DECOROUS
CDEOORSV	VOCODERS
CDEOOSTV	DOVECOTS
CDEOPRRU	PROCURED
	PRODUCER
CDEOPRSU	PRODUCES
CDEOQSTU	DOCQUETS
CDEORRSW	CROWDERS
CDEORSST	DOCTRESS
CDEORSSU	SCOURSED
CDEORSSW	SCOWDERS
CDEORSTU	EDUCTORS
	SEDUCTOR
CDEORSUU	DOUCEURS
CDEOSSTU	CUSTODES
CDEPRSTY	DECRYPTS
CDEPRUUV	UPCURVED
CDERSTTU	DESTRUCT
CDFIILSU	FLUIDICS
CDFIKORS	DISFROCK
CDFNNOOU	CONFOUND
CDGHIILN	CHILDING
CDGHIINS	CHIDINGS
CDGHIINT	DICHTING
	DITCHING
CDGHINNU	DUNCHING
CDGHINOU	DOUCHING
CDGIINNU	INDUCING
CDGIKLNU	DUCKLING
CDGIKLOR	GRIDLOCK
CDGIKNOS	DOCKINGS
CDGIKNSU	DUCKINGS
CDGILNOS	CODLINGS
	SCOLDING
CDGILNOU	CLOUDING
CDGILNRU	CURDLING
CDGINORS	CORDINGS
CDGINORW	CROWDING
CDHHIILS	CHILDISH
CDHIILTW	TWICHILD
CDHIINST	CHINDITS
CDHIIOOR	CHORIOID
CDHIIORT	HIDROTIC
	TRICHOID
CDHIIOSZ	SCHIZOID
CDHIISST	DISTICHS
CDHILNSU	UNCHILDS
CDHILOOS	DOLICHOS
CDHIMOSU	DOCHMIUS
CDHINNOR	CHONDRIN
CDHIOOPW	WOODCHIP
CDHIOORS	CHOROIDS
CDHIOORT	TROCHOID
CDHIOPRW	WHIPCORD
CDHIOPRY	HYDROPIC
CDHIOPSY	PSYCHOID
CDHIORRT	TRICHORD
CDHIOSUV	DISVOUCH
CDHIPSTY	DIPTYCHS
CDHKOORS	HORDOCKS
CDHLOOPY	COPYHOLD
CDHNORSU	CHONDRUS
CDHOORRU	UROCHORD
CDIIIMNU	·INDICIUM
CDIIIORT	DIORITIC
CDIILMOS	DOMICILS
CDIILOTY	DOCILITY
CDIILTUY	LUCIDITY
CDIIMNOU	CONIDIUM
	ONCIDIUM
CDIINOOS	ISODICON
	ONISCOID
CDIINORS	CRINOIDS
CDIINOST	DICTIONS
CDIINSTT	DISTINCT
CDIIOORS	SORICOID
CDIIOPRT	DIOPTRIC
CDIIORSU	SCIUROID
CDIIOSSS	CISSOIDS
CDIIPTUY	CUPIDITY
	PUDICITY
CDIIRSTT	DISTRICT
CDIJNSTU	DISJUNCT
CDIKKNOW	KICKDOWN
CDIKNORS	DORNICKS
CDIKNOSW	WINDOCKS
CDILLOOS	COLLOIDS
CDILLOTU	DULCITOL
CDILLOUY	CLOUDILY
CDILOOPS	PODSOLIC
CDILOORT	LORDOTIC
CDILOOTY	COTYLOID
CDILOSST	DISCLOST
CDIMMOSU	MODICUMS
CDIMOORT	MICRODOT
CDINNQUU	QUIDNUNC
CDINOOOR	CORONOID
CDINORSW	DISCROWN
CDINORTU	INDUCTOR
CDINOSTU	CONDUITS
	DISCOUNT
	NOCTUIDS
CDIOOPRS	PROSODIC
CDIOORRR	CORRIDOR
CDIOOSTT	COTTOIDS
CDIOPRSU	CUSPIDOR
CDIOSSTY	CYSTOIDS
CDIOSTUV	OVIDUCTS
CDJLNOUY	JOCUNDLY
CDKMMORU	DRUMMOCK
CDKNNOSU	DUNNOCKS
CDKOOORW	CORKWOOD
CDLLLOOP	CLODPOLL
CDLNOSUU	UNCLOUDS
CDLNOUUY	UNCLOUDY
CDLOOOTW	COLTWOOD
CDLOOPSY	LYCOPODS
CDLOORTY	DOCTORLY
CDLOOSTU	OUTSCOLD
CDMNOOPU	COMPOUND
CDMNORUU	CORUNDUM
CDMOSSUW	MUDSCOWS
CDNNOOOT	CONODONT
CDNNOSTU	CONTUNDS
CDOOOPST	OCTOPODS
CDOORRUY	CORDUROY
CDOOSTUW	WOODCUTS
CDOPRSTU	PRODUCTS
CEEEEHLS	LEECHEES
CEEEEPRS	PRECEESE
CEEEFFIR	EFFIERCE
CEEEFFRT	EFFECTER
CEEEFHLS	FLEECHES
CEEEFILR	FLEECIER
CEEEFINR	ENFIERCE
CEEEFLRS	FLEECERS
CEEEFNOR	CONFEREE
CEEEGIMN	EMCEEING
CEEEGINS	EGENCIES
CEEEGINX	EXIGENCE
CEEEGITX	EXEGETIC
CEEEGMNR	MERGENCE
CEEEGNRS	REGENCES
CEEEHIKR	CHEEKIER
CEEEHIRR	CHEERIER
	REECHIER
CEEEHIRS	CHEESIER
CEEEHLRV	CHEVEREL
CEEEHLSS	SLEECHES
CEEEHMSS	SMEECHES
CEEEHNNP	PENNEECH
CEEEHNRS	ENCHEERS
CEEEHPRS	CHEEPERS
CEEEHPSS	SPEECHES
CEEEHRRS	CHEERERS
CEEEHRSS	CREESHES
	SECESHER
CEEEHRVY	CHEVERYE
CEEEHSSS	SECESHES
CEEEIJTV	EJECTIVE
CEEEIKRR	CREEKIER
CEEEILNN	LENIENCE
CEEEILNS	LICENSEE
CEEEILNT	TELECINE
CEEEILRS	CELERIES
CEEEILRT	ERECTILE
CEEEILTV	CLEVEITE
	ELECTIVE
CEEEIMNN	EMINENCE
CEEEIMPR	EMPIERCE
CEEEIMRR	REREMICE
CEEEINNT	ENCEINTE
CEEEINPR	PIECENER
CEEEINPS	EPICENES
CEEEINRS	CERESINE
CEEEINSS	ESNECIES
CEEEIPRR	CREEPIER
CEEEIPRS	CREEPIES
CEEEIPRV	PERCEIVE
CEEEIRRV	RECEIVER
CEEEIRSV	RECEIVES
CEEEIRSX	EXERCISE
CEEEIRTV	ERECTIVE
CEEEJRRT	REJECTER
CEEEKNNP	PENNEECK
CEEELLSU	ECUELLES
CEEELRRV	CLEVERER
CEEELRST	RESELECT
CEEELRTT	ELECTRET
	TERCELET
CEEELSST	CELESTES
CEEEMNRT	CEREMENT
CEEEMPRS	EMPERCES
CEEEMRTY	CEMETERY
CEEENNPT	TENPENCE
CEEENNST	SENTENCE
CEEENPRS	PRESENCE
CEEENPRT	PRETENCE
CEEENQSU	SEQUENCE
CEEENRRS	SCREENER
CEEENRRT	RECENTER
	RECENTRE
CEEENRSS	RECENSES
CEEENSSS	ESSENCES
CEEENSST	CENTESES
CEEEPRRS	CREEPERS
CEEEPRTX	EXPECTER
CEEERRST	ERECTERS
CEEERRSV	SCREEVER
CEEERRSS	RECESSES
CEEERSST	SECRETES
	SESTERCE
CEEERSSV	SCREEVES
CEEERSTX	EXCRETES
CEEERTUX	EXECUTER
CEEESSSX	EXCESSES
CEEESTUX	EXECUTES
CEEFFNOS	OFFENCES
CEEFFORS	EFFORCES
CEEFFORT	EFFECTOR
CEEFGILN	FLEECING
CEEFHIKR	KERCHIEF
CEEFHIRY	CHIEFERY
CEEFHISS	CHIEFESS
CEEFHIST	CHIEFEST
	FETICHES
CEEFHLNS	FLENCHES
CEEFHLRT	FLETCHER
CEEFHLRU	CHEERFUL
CEEFHLST	FLETCHES
CEEFHRST	FECHTERS
CEEFIINT	INFICETE
CEEFILRY	FIERCELY
CEEFINPP	FIPPENCE
CEEFINRT	FRENETIC
CEEFIPRT	PERFECTI
CEEFIRST	FIERCEST
CEEFKLRS	FLECKERS
	FRECKLES
CEEFKLSS	FECKLESS
CEEFLNOR	FLORENCE
CEEFLNSU	FLUENCES
CEEFLNTU	FECULENT
CEEFLRST	REFLECTS
CEEFNORR	CONFRERE
	RENFORCE
CEEFNORS	ENFORCES
CEEFNRVY	FERVENCY
CEEFOPRR	PERFORCE
CEEFOPRT	PERFECTO
CEEFORRS	FRESCOER
CEEFORSS	FRESCOES
CEEFORTW	CROWFEET
CEEFPRST	PERFECTS
	PREFECTS

CEEGHIKN	CHEEKING	CEEHIOSZ	ECHOIZES
CEEGHILN	LEECHING	CEEHIPRT	HERPETIC
CEEGHINP	CHEEPING	CEEHIQRU	CHEQUIER
CEEGHINR	CHEERING	CEEHIRRR	CHERRIER
	REECHING	CEEHIRRS	CHERRIES
CEEGHINS	CHEESING	CEEHIRRT	CHERTIER
CEEGIJNT	EJECTING	CEEHIRSS	RICHESSE
CEEGIKLN	CLEEKING	CEEHIRST	CHESTIER
CEEGILNP	CLEEPING		HERETICS
CEEGILNT	ELECTING	CEEHIRTT	TETCHIER
CEEGILOT	ECLOGITE	CEEHIRTU	HEURETIC
CEEGILRS	CLERGIES	CEEHIRTV	VETCHIER
CEEGILRT	TELERGIC	CEEHISTT	ESTHETIC
CEEGIMNS	MISCEGEN		TECHIEST
CEEGINOO	COOEEING	CEEHISTW	CHEWIEST
CEEGINOR	EROGENIC	CEEHKLRS	HECKLERS
CEEGINPR	CREEPING	CEEHKNPS	HENPECKS
CEEGINRS	CREESING	CEEHKRST	SKETCHER
	GENERICS	CEEHKRTV	KVETCHER
CEEGINRT	ERECTING	CEEHKSST	SKETCHES
	GENTRICE	CEEHKSTV	KVETCHES
CEEGINST	GENETICS	CEEHLNOS	ECHELONS
CEEGINSU	EUGENICS	CEEHLNOT	ENCLOTHE
CEEGINXY	EXIGENCY	CEEHLNPU	PENUCHLE
CEEGIORX	EXOERGIC	CEEHLNSU	ELENCHUS
CEEGLLOR	COLLEGER	CEEHLORT	RECLOTHE
CEEGLLOS	COLLEGES	CEEHLOSS	ECHOLESS
CEEGLNST	NEGLECTS	CEEHLOSW	COWHEELS
CEEGLOSU	ECLOGUES	CEEHLQSU	QUELCHES
CEEGMMOR	COMMERGE	CEEHLRSW	WELCHERS
CEEGNNOO	ONCOGENE	CEEHLSSS	CHESSELS
CEEGNNOR	CONGENER	CEEHMNSS	CHESSMEN
CEEGNNPU	PUNGENCE		MENSCHES
CEEGNORS	COGENERS	CEEHMORT	COMETHER
	CONGREES	CEEHMRSS	SCHEMERS
CEEGNORT	CONGREET	CEEHMRST	MERCHETS
CEEGNORV	CONVERGE	CEEHNNOW	NOWHENCE
CEEGNOTY	ECTOGENY	CEEHNNRT	ENTRENCH
CEEGNRSU	URGENCES	CEEHNORT	COHERENT
CEEGNRVY	VERGENCY	CEEHNORV	CHEVERON
CEEGORST	CORTEGES	CEEHNPSU	PENUCHES
CEEGQRSU	GRECQUES	CEEHNQRU	QUENCHER
CEEHHMNN	HENCHMEN	CEEHNQSU	QUENCHES
CEEHHSTT	THETCHES	CEEHNRRT	RETRENCH
CEEHIIST	ETHICISE		TRENCHER
CEEHIITZ	ETHICIZE	CEEHNRST	TRENCHES
CEEHIKLY	CHEEKILY	CEEHNRSW	WENCHERS
CEEHIKNW	CHEEWINK		WRENCHES
CEEHILLN	CHENILLE	CEEHNSST	STENCHES
CEEHILLV	CHEVILLE	CEEHOPRY	CORYPHEE
CEEHILRT	TELECHIR	CEEHOPTT	POCHETTE
CEEHILRV	CHEVERIL	CEEHORRS	COHERERS
CEEHILRW	CLERIHEW		COSHERER
CEEHILRY	CHEERILY	CEEHORRT	HECTORER
CEEHILSV	VEHICLES		TORCHERE
CEEHILSW	SWELCHIE	CEEHORSS	ORCHESES
CEEHIMMS	CHEMMIES	CEEHORST	TROCHEES
CEEHIMRS	CHIMERES	CEEHOSUV	VOUCHEES
CEEHIMRT	HERMETIC	CEEHPRRS	PERCHERS
CEEHIMSS	CHEMISES	CEEHPRSU	UPCHEERS
CEEHINPR	ENCIPHER	CEEHPSST	SPETCHES
CEEHINPT	PHENETIC	CEEHQRSU	CHEQUERS
CEEHINRS	ENRICHES	CEEHQSTU	QUETCHES
	INHERCES	CEEHRSTW	WRETCHES
CEEHINST	SITHENCE	CEEHRTTU	TEUCHTER
CEEHINSX	CHENIXES	CEEHSTTU	TEUCHEST
CEEHINTT	ENTHETIC	CEEIIMPR	EPIMERIC
CEEHIORS	CHEERIOS	CEEIIMRT	EREMITIC
CEEHIOSS	ECHOISES	CEEIINRT	ICTERINE
CEEHIOSV	COHESIVE	CEEIINST	NICETIES

CEEIINVV	EVINCIVE	CEEINORX	EXOCRINE
CEEIIPRS	EPICIERS	CEEINOSS	SENECIOS
CEEIIRST	SERICITE	CEEINOST	SEICENTO
CEEIJNOT	EJECTION	CEEINOTV	EVECTION
CEEIJORR	REJOICER	CEEINPRT	PRENTICE
CEEIJORS	REJOICES	CEEINPST	PECTINES
CEEIJRUV	VERJUICE		PENTICES
CEEIKKSS	KECKSIES	CEEINPSX	SIXPENCE
CEEIKLNN	NECKLINE	CEEINRRS	SINCERER
CEEIKLPR	PICKEREL	CEEINRSS	CERESINS
CEEIKNRS	SICKENER		SCRIENES
CEEIKNST	NECKTIES	CEEINRST	CENTRIES
CEEIKPRS	PICKEERS		ENTERICS
	SPECKIER		ENTICERS
CEEIKPRT	PICKETER		SCIENTER
CEEILLLP	PELLICLE		SECRETIN
CEEILLMS	MICELLES	CEEINRSU	INSECURE
CEEILLNT	LENTICEL		SINECURE
	LENTICLE	CEEINRTT	RETICENT
CEEILMOR	COMELIER	CEEINRTU	CEINTURE
CEEILMPS	SEMPLICE		ENURETIC
CEEILNNT	CENTINEL	CEEINSST	CENTESIS
CEEILNNY	LENIENCY	CEEIOPPR	PERICOPE
CEEILNOS	CINEOLES	CEEIOPPS	EPISCOPE
CEEILNOT	COTELINE	CEEIOPST	ECTOPIES
	ELECTION		PICOTEES
CEEILNOV	VIOLENCE	CEEIORST	COTERIES
CEEILNRR	RECLINER		ESOTERIC
CEEILNRS	LICENSER	CEEIORSX	EXORCISE
	RECLINES	CEEIORTT	EROTETIC
	SILENCER	CEEIORTX	EXOTERIC
CEEILNRU	CERULEIN	CEEIORXZ	EXORCIZE
CEEILNRV	VERNICLE	CEEIOSTV	COVETISE
CEEILNSS	ENCLISES	CEEIPPRT	PRECEPIT
	LICENSES	CEEIPPTU	EUPEPTIC
	SILENCES	CEEIPRRS	PIERCERS
CEEILNSU	LEUCINES		PRECISER
CEEILORR	RECOILER	CEEIPRSS	PRECISES
CEEILOSS	SOLECISE	CEEIPRST	CREPIEST
CEEILOSZ	SOLECIZE		RECEIPTS
CEEILPSS	ECLIPSES	CEEIPRSU	EPICURES
CEEILQSU	LIQUESCE	CEEIPSST	PECTISES
CEEILRST	RETICLES	CEEIPSTZ	PECTIZES
	SCLERITE	CEEIQSSU	QUIESCES
	TIERCELS	CEEIRRSS	CERRISES
CEEILRSU	CISELEUR		CRESSIER
	CISELURE	CEEIRRST	RECITERS
	RECUILES	CEEIRRSW	SCREWIER
CEEILRSV	VERSICLE	CEEIRRTU	URETERIC
CEEILRTU	RETICULE	CEEIRSSV	SCRIEVES
CEEILRTY	CELERITY		SERVICES
CEEILSSV	CLEVISES	CEEIRSTU	CERUSITE
	VESICLES		CUTESIER
CEEILSTT	TELESTIC		EUCRITES
	TESTICLE	CEEIRSTV	VERTICES
CEEILSTU	LEUCITES	CEEIRSTX	EXCITERS
CEEIMMRS	MESMERIC	CEEIRSVX	CERVIXES
CEEIMNNY	EMINENCY	CEEISSST	CITESSES
CEEIMNPS	SPECIMEN	CEEISTTZ	ZETETICS
CEEIMNST	CENTIMES	CEEISUVX	EXCUSIVE
CEEIMORT	METEORIC	CEEJKOTT	JOCKETTE
CEEINNOT	NEOTENIC	CEEJORRT	REJECTOR
CEEINNRS	INCENSER	CEEJORST	EJECTORS
CEEINNRT	INCENTRE	CEEKKNPS	KENSPECK
CEEINNSS	INCENSES	CEEKLNST	NECKLETS
	NICENESS	CEEKLPSS	SPECKLES
CEEINNST	NESCIENT	CEEKLRSS	CLERKESS
CEEINORT	ERECTION		RECKLESS
	NEOTERIC	CEEKNORR	RECKONER
CEEINORV	OVERNICE	CEEKNRSU	SUCKENER

CEEKORRT ROCKETER	CEENNORV CONVENER	SUFFICER	CEFNOSTU CONFUTES
CEEKOSSY SOCKEYES	CEENNOSU ENOUNCES	CEFFISSU SUFFICES	CEFORRST CROFTERS
CEEKPRSY RYEPECKS	CEENNOSV CONVENES	CEFFLORU FORCEFUL	CEFORSTU FRUCTOSE
CEEKRRSW WRECKERS	CEENNRST CENTNERS	CEFFLRSU SCUFFLER	CEFOSSSU FOCUSSES
CEELLLSU CELLULES	CEENOPST POTENCES	CEFFLSSU SCUFFLES	CEGGHIRS CHIGGERS
CEELLMOU MOLECULE	CEENOPTW TWOPENCE	CEFFORSS SCOFFERS	CEGGILOO GEOLOGIC
CEELLNOS COLLEENS	CEENORSS NECROSES	CEFFORST COFFRETS	CEGGILOR CLOGGIER
CEELLNOU NUCLEOLE	CEENORSV CONSERVE	CEFGHINT FECHTING	COGGLIER
CEELLORT RECOLLET	CONVERSE	FETCHING	CEGGILRS SCRIGGLE
CEELLPSU PUCELLES	CEENORSZ COZENERS	CEFGIKLN FLECKING	CEGGINNO CONGEING
CEELLRRU CRUELLER	CEENORTT TRECENTO	CEFGINNS FENCINGS	CEGGINOO GEOGONIC
CEELLRVY CLEVERLY	CEENORVY CONVEYER	CEFGLNUY FULGENCY	CEGGIORS GEORGICS
CEELLSSU CLUELESS	RECONVEY	CEFHIIMS MISCHIEF	SCROGGIE
CEELMOOS COELOMES	CEENOSVX CONVEXES	CEFHILNR FLINCHER	CEGGLNOY GLYCOGEN
CEELMOPT COMPLETE	CEENPPTU TUPPENCE	CEFHILNS FLINCHES	CEGGLORS CLOGGERS
CEELMORW WELCOMER	CEENPRSS SPENCERS	CEFHILRS FILCHERS	CEGHHINT HECHTING
CEELMOST TELECOMS	CEENPSSU SUSPENCE	CEFHILRT FLICHTER	CEGHIINY HYGIENIC
CEELMOSW WELCOMES	CEENRSSU CENSURES	CEFHILST FLITCHES	CEGHIKLN HECKLING
CEELMRTU ELECTRUM	CEENRSTU UNSECRET	CEFHINSU FUCHSINE	CEGHIKNT KETCHING
CEELNNOP PENONCEL	CEENSSSU CENSUSES	CEFHISTT FITCHETS	CEGHILNT LETCHING
CEELNNOT CENTONEL	CEENSTTU CUNETTES	CEFHISTU FUCHSITE	CEGHILNW WELCHING
CEELNOPU OPULENCE	CEEOORRW ORECROWE	CEFHISTW FITCHEWS	CEGHILST GLITCHES
CEELNORS ENCLOSER	CEEOORST CREOSOTE	CEFHLSSY FLYSCHES	CEGHIMNS SCHEMING
CEELNORT ELECTRON	CEEOPRRT RECEPTOR	CEFHLSTU CHESTFUL	CEGHINNW WENCHING
CEELNORU ENCOLURE	CEEOPRTX EXCEPTOR	FUTCHELS	CEGHINOR COHERING
CEELNOSS ENCLOSES	CEEOPSST PECTOSES	CEFIIIST CITIFIES	OCHERING
CEELNPTU CENTUPLE	CEEOPSTY ECOTYPES	CEFIILRT CLIFTIER	CEGHINPR PERCHING
CEELNRST LECTERNS	CEEOQTTU COQUETTE	CEFIILST FELSITIC	CEGHINRT RETCHING
CEELNRSU LUCERNES	CEEORRSS SORCERER	CEFIILTY FELICITY	CEGHINRU EUCHRING
CEELNRTU RELUCENT	CEEORRST ERECTORS	CEFIIOPR OPIFICER	CEGHINST ETCHINGS
CEELNRTY RECENTLY	CEEORRSU RECOURES	CEFIIORS ORIFICES	CEGHINVY CHEVYING
CEELNSTU ESCULENT	RECOURSE	CEFIIPRT PETRIFIC	CEGHIRSS SCREIGHS
CEELORSS CORELESS	RESOURCE	CEFIIRRT FERRITIC	CEGHIRTU THEURGIC
RECLOSES	CEEORRSV RECOVERS	TERRIFIC	CEGHISTU GUICHETS
SCLEROSE	CEEORRSW RECOWERS	CEFIKLOR FIRELOCK	CEGHMRUY CHEMURGY
CEELORST CORSELET	CEEORRVY RECOVERY	CEFIKLRS FLICKERS	CEGHNORS GROSCHEN
ELECTORS	CEEORSTX CORTEXES	CEFIKLST FICKLEST	CEGHORSU CHOREGUS
ELECTROS	CEEORTTV CORVETTE	CEFILLLO FOLLICLE	COUGHERS
SELECTOR	CEEORTUX EXECUTOR	CEFILMRU CRIMEFUL	GROUCHES
CEELORSY RECOYLES	CEEOSTTT OCTETTES	MERCIFUL	CEGHRSTU GRUTCHES
CEELORTV COVERLET	CEEPPRST PERCEPTS	CEFILNOT FLECTION	GUTCHERS
CEELOSSU COLEUSES	PRECEPTS	CEFILNST INFLECTS	CEGIILNR CLINGIER
CEELOSTU ELOCUTES	CEEPPRSU PREPUCES	CEFILNSU FUNICLES	CEGIILNS CEILINGS
CEELOSTV COVELETS	CEEPRRSU PRECURSE	CEFILOUV VOICEFUL	CIELINGS
CEELPRST PLECTRES	CEEPRSST RESPECTS	CEFILRSU LUCIFERS	CEGIILNT GENTILIC
PRELECTS	SCEPTRES	CEFIMOST COMFIEST	CEGIILOP EPILOGIC
CEELRRTU LECTURER	SPECTERS	CEFINNOR CONFINER	CEGIILOS LOGICISE
CEELRSST LECTRESS	SPECTRES	CEFINNOS CONFINES	CEGIILOZ LOGICIZE
CEELRSSU CURELESS	CEEPRSTX EXCERPTS	CEFINORS CONIFERS	CEGIINNT ENTICING
RECLUSES	CEERRSST RECTRESS	FORENSIC	CEGIINNV EVINCING
CEELRSTU LECTURES	CEERRSSU RESCUERS	FORINSEC	CEGIINPR PIERCING
CEELRSTY SECRETLY	SECURERS	INFORCES	CEGIINRT RECITING
CEELRSUY SECURELY	CEERRSSW SCREWERS	CEFINORT INFECTOR	CEGIINSS GNEISSIC
CEELSTTU LETTUCES	CEERRSUV RECURVES	CEFINOSX CONFIXES	CEGIINSX EXCISING
CEEMMNTU CEMENTUM	CEERRTUZ CREUTZER	CEFINOTT CONFETTI	CEGIINTV EVICTING
CEEMMORS COMMERES	CEERSSST CRESSETS	CEFIOPRS FORCIPES	CEGIINTX EXCITING
CEEMNORR CREMORNE	CEERSSTU SECUREST	CEFIORTY FEROCITY	CEGIIOST EGOISTIC
CEEMNORW NEWCOMER	CEERSSUX EXCURSES	CEFIRRSU SCURFIER	CEGIJLOU LOGJUICE
CEEMNORY CEREMONY	EXCUSERS	CEFIRSTU FRUTICES	CEGIKKLN KECKLING
CEEMNOYZ COENZYME	CEERSTTU CURETTES	CEFKLLOS ELFLOCKS	CEGIKLNR CLERKING
CEEMNRSU CERUMENS	CEERTUXY EXECUTRY	CEFKLOOR FORELOCK	RECKLING
CEEMOORV OVERCOME	CEESSSTU CESTUSES	CEFKLOST FETLOCKS	CEGIKNNS NECKINGS
CEEMOORW OWRECOME	CEESTTUV CUVETTES	CEFKLRUW WRECKFUL	SNECKING
CEEMOPRS COMPEERS	CEFFHIRU CHUFFIER	CEFLLOSU FLOSCULE	CEGIKNPS PECKINGS
COMPERES	CEFFIILR CLIFFIER	CEFLNOSU FLOUNCES	SPECKING
CEEMOPST COMPETES	CEFFIORS OFFICERS	CEFLNRUU FURUNCLE	CEGIKNRT TRECKING
CEEMOSSS COSMESES	CEFFIORU COIFFEUR	CEFLNSTU SCENTFUL	CEGIKNRW WRECKING
CEEMSSTU TUMESCES	COIFFURE	CEFMORSY COMFREYS	CEGIKSTU GUCKIEST
CEENNORT CRETONNE	CEFFIRSU SCUFFIER	CEFNORSU FROUNCES	CEGILMMN CLEMMING
CEENNORU RENOUNCE		CEFNOSSU CONFUSES	CEGILNOO NEOLOGIC

CEGILNOS ECLOSING	CEHHOOST HOOTCHES	CEHILPTY PHYLETIC	RICHTEST
CEGILNRS CLINGERS	CEHHOPTY HYPOTHEC	CEHILRSV CHERVILS	STITCHER
CRINGLES	CEHIIKNR CHINKIER	CEHILSTT LICHTEST	CEHIRSTY HYSTERIC
CEGILNRU RECULING	CEHIIKNS CHINKIES	CEHILSTW SWITCHEL	CEHIRTTW TWITCHER
ULCERING	CEHIILLR CHILLIER	CEHILTTY TETCHILY	CEHIRTWY WITCHERY
CEGILNRY GLYCERIN	CEHIILLS CHILLIES	CEHIMMRU CHUMMIER	CEHISSTT STITCHES
CEGILNSU LUCIGENS	CEHIILMO HEMIOLIC	CEHIMMSS CHEMISMS	CEHISSTU CUSHIEST
CEGILNSY GLYCINES	CEHIILNO LICHENIN	CEHIMMSU CHUMMIES	CEHISSTW SWITCHES
CEGILNTU CULTIGEN	CEHIILNT LECITHIN	CEHIMNNW WINCHMEN	CEHISSUW SUCHWISE
CEGIMNOY MYOGENIC	CEHIILOT EOLITHIC	CEHIMNOP PHONEMIC	CEHISTTW TWITCHES
CEGIMNSU MUCIGENS	CEHIIMOP HEMIOPIC	CEHIMNOR CHOIRMEN	CEHKKRSU CHUKKERS
CEGIMNUY GYNECIUM	CEHIIMOS ISOCHEIM	CEHIMNPT PITCHMEN	CEHKLLOS SKELLOCH
CEGINNOR ENCORING	ISOCHIME	CEHIMNSY CHIMNEYS	CEHKLMOS HEMLOCKS
CEGINNOZ COZENING	CEHIIMPT MEPHITIC	CEHIMORS MORICHES	CEHKORSS SHOCKERS
CEGINNRS SCERNING	CEHIIMST ETHICISM	CEHIMORT CHROMITE	CEHKPSTU KETCHUPS
CEGINNRT CENTRING	CEHIINST ICHNITES	TRICHOME	CEHKRSSU SHUCKERS
CEGINNST SCENTING	CEHIIPPR CHIPPIER	CEHIMOSS ECHOISMS	CEHKRSTU HUCKSTER
CEGINNSY ENSIGNCY	CEHIIPPS CHIPPIES	CEHIMRSS SMIRCHES	CEHLLMOS MOCHELLS
CEGINOOP GEOPONIC	CEHIIPRR CHIRPIER	CEHIMSST CHEMISTS	CEHLLMSU MUCHELLS
CEGINOOR OROGENIC	CEHIIPRT PITCHIER	CEHINNRT INTRENCH	SCHELLUM
CEGINOOY COOEYING	TRICHITE	CEHINOOS COHESION	CEHLLOSY YELLOCHS
CEGINOOZ ZOOGENIC	CEHIISTT CHITTIES	CEHINOPS CHOPINES	CEHLLOUY LOUCHELY
CEGINOPR COPERING	ETHICIST	CEHINOPT PHONETIC	CEHLMNOU HOMUNCLE
CEGINOPY PYOGENIC	ITCHIEST	CEHINOPU EUPHONIC	CEHLMSUY CHUMLEYS
CEGINORT GERONTIC	THEISTIC	CEHINORS CHORINES	CEHLNNOU LUNCHEON
CEGINORV COVERING	TICHIEST	CEHINORT NOTCHIER	CEHLNNSU CHUNNELS
CEGINORW COWERING	CEHIISVV CHIVVIES	CEHINORU UNHEROIC	CEHLNOST NOTCHELS
CEGINOSS COGNISES	CEHIKLPT KLEPHTIC	CEHINOSY HYOSCINE	CEHLNOTU UNCLOTHE
CEGINOSZ COGNIZES	CEHIKLRS CLERKISH	CEHINOTY ONYCHITE	CEHLNRSU LUNCHERS
CEGINOTV COVETING	CEHIKLSU SUCHLIKE	CEHINPRS PINCHERS	CEHLNSTY LYNCHETS
CEGINRRS CRINGERS	CEHIKMOS HOMESICK	CEHINPRU PUNCHIER	CEHLOOSS SCHOOLES
CEGINRRU RECURING	CEHIKNRU CHUNKIER	UNCIPHER	CEHLORST CHORTLES
CEGINRST CRESTING	CEHIKNST KITCHENS	CEHINPSU PENUCHIS	CEHLORSU SLOUCHER
CEGINRSU RECUSING	KNITCHES	CEHINQSU QUINCHES	CEHLORTY HECTORLY
RESCUING	THICKENS	CEHINRSS RICHNESS	CEHLOSSU SLOUCHES
SCUNGIER	CEHIKNSW CHEWINKS	CEHINRST CHRISTEN	CEHLOSTU SELCOUTH
SECURING	CEHIKOOS CHOOKIES	CITHERNS	CEHLPPSS SCHLEPPS
CEGINRSW SCREWING	CEHIKOSS HOICKSES	SNITCHER	CEHLPPSY SCHLEPPY
CEGINRSY SYNERGIC	CEHIKOST CHOKIEST	CEHINRTU RUTHENIC	CEHLQSUY SQUELCHY
CEGINRTU ERUCTING	THICKOES	CEHINSST SNITCHES	CEHLRRSU LURCHERS
CEGINSUX EXCUSING	CEHIKRSS KIRSCHES	CEHINSTW WITCHENS	CEHLSTUY LECYTHUS
CEGIRSTU SCUTIGER	SHICKERS	CEHINSTZ CHINTZES	CEHMNRSU MUNCHERS
CEGKLORS GROCKLES	SKRIECHS	CEHIOORS CHOOSIER	CEHMNRTU TRUCHMEN
CEGLLOOU COLLOGUE	CEHIKRSW WHICKERS	ISOCHORE	CEHMNSSU MUCHNESS
CEGLLORY GLYCEROL	CEHIKSST CHEKISTS	CEHIOPPR CHOPPIER	CEHMOORS MOOCHERS
CEGLLRYY GLYCERYL	KITSCHES	CEHIOPRS SOPHERIC	CEHMOOSS SMOOCHES
CEGLNOTY COGENTLY	CEHIKSTT THICKEST	CEHIOPRU EUPHORIC	CEHMOOSZ SCHMOOZE
CEGLOOOY OECOLOGY	THICKETS	POUCHIER	CEHMORSU MOUCHERS
CEGLOOTY CETOLOGY	THICKSET	CEHIOPSS HOSPICES	CEHMORUV OVERMUCH
CEGLOSSU GLUCOSES	CEHIKTTY THICKETY	CEHIOPST POSTICHE	CEHMOSSU SMOUCHES
CEGLOSSY GLYCOSES	CEHILLRS CHILLERS	POTICHES	CEHMSSTU SMUTCHES
CEGMNNOO COGNOMEN	SCHILLER	CEHIORRT RHETORIC	CEHNNNOU NUNCHEON
CEGNNOOS ONCOGENS	CEHILLST CHILLEST	CEHIORSS CHORISES	CEHNNOPU PUNCHEON
CEGNNPUY PUNGENCY	CEHILMMS SCHIMMEL	ORCHESIS	CEHNNOSU NONESUCH
CEGNOOTY GONOCYTE	CEHILMSY CHIMLEYS	ORCHISES	UNCHOSEN
CEGNORSS CONGRESS	CEHILMTY METHYLIC	CEHIORST ROTCHIES	CEHNNRSU CHUNNERS
CEGNORSU CONGRUES	CEHILNOP PHENOLIC	THEORICS	CEHNOORS COEHORNS
SCROUNGE	PINOCHLE	CEHIORSW CHOWRIES	SCHOONER
CEGNORSY CRYOGENS	CEHILNOR CHLORINE	CEHIORTT TROCHITE	CEHNORSV CHEVRONS
CEGNORYY CRYOGENY	CEHILNOS CHOLINES	CEHIORTU COUTHIER	CEHNORTU CHOUNTER
CEGNOSST CONGESTS	CEHILNPY PHENYLIC	TOUCHIER	CEHNORVY CHEVRONY
CEGOORSS SCROOGES	CEHILNSS CHINLESS	CEHIOSST ECHOISTS	CEHNPRSU PUNCHERS
CEGORRSU SCOURGER	CEHILNST LINCHETS	TOISECHS	CEHNRSTU CHUNTERS
SCROUGER	TINCHELS	CEHIPRRS CHIRPERS	CEHNSSSU SUCHNESS
CEGORSSU SCOURGES	CEHILORT CHLORITE	CEHIPRSS SPHERICS	CEHNSSTU CHESNUTS
SCROUGES	CLOTHIER	CEHIPRST PITCHERS	CEHNSTTU CHESTNUT
CEHHIIRT HITCHIER	CEHILORY HEROICLY	SPITCHER	CEHNSTUY CHUTNEYS
CEHHINPY HYPHENIC	CEHILPRS PILCHERS	CEHIQSTU QUITCHES	CEHOOORZ ZOOCHORE
CEHHIRST HITCHERS		CEHIRSST STRICHES	CEHOORSS CHOOSERS
CEHHNORU HURCHEON		CEHIRSTT CHITTERS	SOROCHES

Letters	Words
CEHOORST	CHEROOTS
CEHOORSU	OCHEROUS
	OCHREOUS
CEHOOSUW	COWHOUSE
CEHOPPRS	CHOPPERS
CEHOPPRY	PROPHECY
CEHOPRST	POTCHERS
CEHOPRSY	CORYPHES
CEHORRST	TORCHERS
CEHORSSU	CHORUSES
CEHORSSZ	SCHERZOS
CEHORSTU	SCOUTHER
	TOUCHERS
CEHORSTW	SCOWTHER
CEHORSUV	VOUCHERS
CEHOSSSU	HOCUSSES
CEHOSTTU	COUTHEST
CEHOTTUZ	ZUCHETTO
CEHPRSTU	PUTCHERS
CEHPSSTU	PUTSCHES
CEHRRSSU	CRUSHERS
CEHRSSTY	SCYTHERS
CEHRSTTY	STRETCHY
CEHSSSSU	SCHUSSES
CEIIILSV	CIVILISE
CEIIILVZ	CIVILIZE
CEIIIMNT	CIMINITE
CEIIINSS	SINICISE
CEIIINSV	INCISIVE
CEIIINSZ	SINICIZE
CEIIJSTU	JUICIEST
CEIIKLMR	LIMERICK
CEIIKLRS	SICKLIER
CEIIKLRT	TICKLIER
CEIIKLSS	SICKLIES
CEIIKMMR	MIMICKER
CEIIKNRZ	ZINCKIER
CEIIKNSS	KINESICS
CEIIKNST	KINETICS
CEIIKPST	PICKIEST
CEIIKQSU	QUICKIES
CEIIKRRT	TRICKIER
CEIIKRST	STICKIER
CEIIKSST	EKISTICS
	STICKIES
CEIILLMT	MELLITIC
CEIILLOP	POLLICIE
CEIILLPT	ELLIPTIC
CEIILLSS	SILICLES
CEIILLSU	SILICULE
CEIILMNT	LIMNETIC
CEIILMOT	CIMOLITE
CEIILNNS	INCLINES
CEIILNOS	ISOCLINE
	SILICONE
CEIILNQU	CLINIQUE
CEIILNSS	ENCLISIS
CEIILOPP	EPIPLOIC
	EPIPOLIC
CEIILOPS	POLICIES
CEIILORT	ELICITOR
CEIILOTZ	ZEOLITIC
CEIILPPS	CLIPPIES
CEIILPRT	PERLITIC
CEIILPRU	PIRLICUE
CEIILPTX	EXPLICIT
CEIILPTY	PYELITIC
CEIILQRU	CLIQUIER
CEIILRSU	SLUICIER
CEIILRTV	VERTICIL
CEIILSSS	SCISSILE
CEIIMNOT	EMICTION
CEIIMOPT	EPITOMIC
CEIIMORS	ISOMERIC
CEIIMOST	COMITIES
	SEMIOTIC
CEIIMPRR	CRIMPIER
CEIIMPRS	EMPIRICS
CEIIMPSS	EPICISMS
CEIIMRRT	TRIMERIC
CEIIMRST	MERISTIC
	TRISEMIC
CEIINNOP	NEPIONIC
CEIINNOR	IRENICON
CEIINNOS	CONIINES
	OSCININE
CEIINNOT	NICOTINE
CEIINNRT	INTRINCE
CEIINNST	INSCIENT
CEIINOPS	EPINOSIC
CEIINOPT	EPITONIC
CEIINORS	RECISION
	SORICINE
CEIINOSS	ICONISES
CEIINOSV	INVOICES
CEIINOSX	EXCISION
CEIINOSZ	ICONIZES
CEIINOTV	EVICTION
CEIINPSS	PISCINES
CEIINRSS	SERICINS
CEIINRST	CITRINES
	CRINITES
	INCITERS
CEIINRSU	INCISURE
	SCIURINE
CEIINSSU	CUISINES
CEIINSTU	CUTINISE
CEIINSTY	CYTISINE
	SYENITIC
CEIINSTZ	CITIZENS
	ZINCIEST
	ZINCITES
CEIINTUZ	CUTINIZE
CEIIOPRS	IRISCOPE
CEIIOPRT	PERIOTIC
CEIIOPTT	PICOTITE
CEIIOSTV	SOVIETIC
CEIIPRRS	CRISPIER
CEIIPRST	PICRITES
	PRICIEST
CEIIPSST	EPICISTS
	SPICIEST
CEIIQRTU	CRITIQUE
CEIIRSSU	CRUISIES
CEIIRSTT	RECTITIS
CEIIRSTV	VERISTIC
CEIISSST	CISSIEST
CEIISTVV	VIVISECT
CEIJNORT	INJECTOR
CEIJNOUV	CUNJEVOI
CEIJRSTU	JUSTICER
CEIJSSTU	JUSTICES
CEIKKNRS	KNICKERS
CEIKKRRS	SKERRICK
CEIKLNPS	SPICKNEL
CEIKLNRS	CLINKERS
	CRINKLES
CEIKLNSS	SLICKENS
CEIKLOSV	LOVESICK
CEIKLPRS	PICKLERS
	PRICKLES
CEIKLPRU	PLUCKIER
CEIKLRSS	SLICKERS
CEIKLRST	STICKLER
	STRICKLE
	TICKLERS
	TRICKLES
CEIKLRSY	SICKERLY
CEIKLRTT	TRICKLET
CEIKLSST	SLICKEST
	STICKLES
CEIKLSTU	LUCKIEST
CEIKMNOR	MONICKER
CEIKMOPT	IMPOCKET
CEIKMORS	OCKERISM
CEIKMRSS	SMICKERS
CEIKMRSU	MUSICKER
CEIKMSST	SMICKETS
CEIKMSTU	MUCKIEST
CEIKNNSU	INSUCKEN
CEIKNQSU	QUICKENS
CEIKNRSS	SNICKERS
CEIKNRST	STRICKEN
CEIKNRSU	UNSICKER
CEIKNSSS	SICKNESS
CEIKNSST	SNICKETS
CEIKOPST	POCKIEST
CEIKORRS	ROCKIERS
CEIKORST	CORKIEST
	ROCKIEST
	STOCKIER
CEIKOSSY	YOICKSES
CEIKPRRS	PRICKERS
CEIKPRST	PRICKETS
CEIKPSST	SKEPTICS
	SPICKEST
CEIKQSTU	QUICKEST
	QUICKSET
CEIKRRST	TRICKERS
CEIKRRTY	TRICKERY
CEIKRSST	STICKERS
CEIKRTTY	RICKETTY
CEIKSTUY	YUCKIEST
CEILLNOS	LIONCELS
CEILLNOU	NUCLEOLI
CEILLOPS	POLLICES
CEILLOQU	COQUILLE
CEILLORS	COLLIERS
	ORSELLIC
CEILLORY	COLLIERY
CEILLOTU	COUTILLE
CEILLRTU	TELLURIC
CEILLSST	CELLISTS
CEILLSSU	CULLISES
CEILMMUY	MYCELIUM
CEILMNOP	COMPLINE
CEILMNOT	MONTICLE
CEILMOPR	COMPILER
	COMPLIER
CEILMOPS	COMPILES
	COMPLIES
	POLEMICS
CEILMOSS	SOLECISM
CEILMOSU	COLISEUM
CEILMPRS	CRIMPLES
CEILMPRU	CLUMPIER
CEILMPUU	PECULIUM
CEILMRSU	CLUMSIER
CEILMTUU	LUTECIUM
CEILNNOT	CONTLINE
CEILNNSU	NUCLEINS
CEILNNSY	SYNCLINE
CEILNOOS	COLONIES
	COLONISE
	ECLOSION
CEILNOOZ	COLONIZE
CEILNOPR	PERCOLIN
CEILNOPS	PINOCLES
CEILNOPT	LEPTONIC
CEILNORS	INCLOSER
	LICENSOR
CEILNOSS	CONSEILS
	INCLOSES
CEILNOST	LECTIONS
CEILNOSX	LEXICONS
CEILNPRY	PRINCELY
CEILNRTU	LINCTURE
CEILNRUV	CULVERIN
CEILNSST	STENCILS
CEILNSTU	CUTLINES
	TUNICLES
CEILNSUU	UNSLUICE
CEILOPRT	PETROLIC
CEILOPRV	PROCLIVE
CEILOPST	TOECLIPS
CEILOPTU	EPULOTIC
	POULTICE
CEILOPTY	EPICOTYL
CEILORST	CLOISTER
	COISTREL
	CORTILES
	COSTLIER
	CREOLIST
CEILORTT	CLOTTIER
CEILORTY	CRYOLITE
CEILOSSS	OSSICLES
CEILOSST	SOLECIST
	SOLSTICE
CEILOSSU	COULISSE
CEILOTVY	VELOCITY
CEILPPRS	CLIPPERS
	CRIPPLES
CEILPRSU	SURPLICE
CEILPRUU	PURLICUE
CEILPSSU	SPICULES
CEILRRSU	SCURRILE
CEILRSTT	CLITTERS
CEILRSTU	CURLIEST
	UTRICLES
CEILSSSS	SCISSELS
CEILSTTU	CUITTLES
CEIMMNNO	MNEMONIC
CEIMMNOU	ENCOMIUM
	MECONIUM
CEIMMORT	RECOMMIT
CEIMMOSX	COMMIXES
CEIMMRRS	CRIMMERS
CEIMMRRU	CRUMMIER
CEIMMRSU	CRUMMIES
	SCUMMIER
CEIMMRSY	MERYCISM
CEIMNNOO	ENCOMION
CEIMNNOS	MECONINS
CEIMNNOY	NEOMYCIN
CEIMNOPT	PENTOMIC
CEIMNORS	CREMOSIN
	INCOMERS
	SERMONIC
CEIMNORT	INTERCOM

Key	Word(s)
CEIMNRST	CENTRISM
CEIMNSSU	MENISCUS
CEIMOOST	COOMIEST
CEIMOOUZ	ZOOECIUM
CEIMOPRS	COMPRISE
CEIMOQSU	COMIQUES
CEIMORRS	MORRICES
CEIMORRT	MORTICER
CEIMORST	MORTICES
CEIMORSX	EXORCISM
CEIMORSY	ISOCRYME
CEIMORTY	EMICTORY
CEIMOSSS	COSMESIS
CEIMOSTV	VICOMTES
CEIMPRRS	CRIMPERS
CEIMPRRU	CRUMPIER
CEIMRRSU	SCRIMURE
CEIMRRTU	TURMERIC
CEIMRSST	CRETISMS
CEIMSSTY	SYSTEMIC
CEINNNOT	INNOCENT
CEINNNOU	INCONNUE
CEINNORS	INCENSOR
CEINNORV	CONNIVER
CEINNOSV	CONNIVES
CEINNOTU	CONTINUE
CEINOOST	COONTIES
CEINOOTZ	ENTOZOIC
	ENZOOTIC
CEINOPPR	CORNPIPE
CEINOPRS	CONSPIRE
	INCORPSE
CEINOPRT	INCEPTOR
CEINOPRV	PROVINCE
CEINOPTT	ENTOPTIC
CEINOPTU	UNPOETIC
CEINORRS	RESORCIN
CEINORRT	TRICORNE
CEINORSS	NECROSIS
	SERICONS
CEINORST	CORNIEST
	RECTIONS
CEINORSU	NOURICES
	ROUNCIES
CEINORTT	CONTRITE
	CORNETTI
CEINORTU	NEUROTIC
CEINORTV	CONTRIVE
CEINOSSS	CESSIONS
	COSINESS
CEINOSST	SECTIONS
CEINOSSX	COXINESS
CEINOSTT	CENTOIST
	STENOTIC
CEINOSTU	COUNTIES
CEINOSTX	EXCITONS
CEINOSTY	CYTOSINE
CEINOSUV	UNVOICES
CEINOSVV	CONVIVES
CEINPRSS	PRINCESS
CEINPSST	INSPECTS
CEINPSTY	PYCNITES
CEINRSST	CISTERNS
CEINRSTT	CENTRIST
	CITTERNS
CEINRSTU	CURNIEST
CEINRSUV	INCURVES
CEINRSVV	CRIVVENS
CEINRTTU	INTERCUT
	TINCTURE
CEIOOPRS	OPORICES
CEIOOTUV	OUTVOICE
CEIOOTXX	EXOTOXIC
CEIOPPRS	CROPPIES
CEIOPPSY	EPISCOPY
CEIOPRRU	CROUPIER
CEIOPRSS	PERSICOS
CEIOPRST	PERSICOT
CEIOPRSU	PRECIOUS
CEIOPRTU	EUTROPIC
	OUTPRICE
CEIOPSST	COPSIEST
CEIOPSSU	SPECIOUS
CEIORRSS	CROSIERS
CEIORRSU	COURIERS
CEIORRSZ	CROZIERS
CEIORRTU	COURTIER
CEIORRUZ	CRUZEIRO
CEIORSSU	SCOURIES
CEIORSSV	CORSIVES
CEIORSSW	SCOWRIES
CEIORSSX	SIXSCORE
CEIORSTT	COTTIERS
CEIORSTU	CITREOUS
	OUTCRIES
CEIORSTV	EVICTORS
	VORTICES
CEIORSTX	EXCITORS
	EXORCIST
CEIORSVY	VICEROYS
CEIORTTU	TOREUTIC
CEIOSSSV	VISCOSES
CEIOSSTT	COTTISES
CEIOSSTU	COITUSES
CEIPQSTU	PICQUETS
CEIPRRSS	CRISPERS
CEIPRRST	RESCRIPT
CEIPRSST	CRISPEST
CEIPRSTU	CREPITUS
	CUPRITES
	PICTURES
	PIECRUST
CEIPSSST	CESSPITS
CEIRRRSU	CURRIERS
	SCURRIER
CEIRRSSU	CRUISERS
	SCURRIES
	SUCRIERS
CEIRRSTT	CRITTERS
	RESTRICT
	STRICTER
CEIRRSTU	CRUSTIER
	RECRUITS
CEIRRSUV	SCURVIER
CEIRSSSU	CUISSERS
	SCISSURE
CEIRSSTT	TRISECTS
CEIRSSTU	CITRUSES
	CURTSIES
	RICTUSES
CEIRSSTV	VICTRESS
CEIRSSUV	SCURVIES
CEIRSTTU	TUTRICES
CEIRSTUV	CURVIEST
CEIRSTUY	SECURITY
CEISSSTU	CISTUSES
CEISTTTU	CUTTIEST
CEJLOOSY	JOCOSELY
CEJNORRU	CONJURER
CEJNORSU	CONJURES
CEJNRTUU	JUNCTURE
CEJNSSUU	JUNCUSES
CEJOPRST	PROJECTS
CEKKLNSU	KNUCKLES
CEKKNORS	KNOCKERS
CEKLLOOV	LOVELOCK
CEKLLOPS	PELLOCKS
CEKLLSSU	LUCKLESS
CEKLMNOS	LOCKSMEN
CEKLNOSS	SLOCKENS
CEKLNOST	STENLOCK
CEKLNRSU	CRUNKLES
CEKLOPST	LOCKSTEP
CEKLPRSU	PLUCKERS
CEKLRRTU	TRUCKLER
CEKLRSSU	SUCKLERS
CEKLRSTU	TRUCKLES
CEKMNOST	STOCKMEN
CEKMNRTU	TRUCKMEN
CEKNNSSU	UNSNECKS
CEKNOOSV	CONVOKES
CEKNOPST	PENSTOCK
CEKNORST	CRONKEST
CEKNORTU	COKERNUT
CEKNOSTU	UNSOCKET
CEKNRSTU	STRUCKEN
CEKNRSWY	WRYNECKS
CEKOOPRS	PRECOOKS
CEKOOPSW	COWPOKES
CEKOORST	CROOKEST
CEKOPRST	SPROCKET
CEKORRTY	ROCKETRY
CEKORSST	RESTOCKS
CEKRRSTU	TRUCKERS
CEKRSSUU	RUCKUSES
CELLMOSU	COLUMELS
CELLNOOS	COLONELS
CELLNSUU	NUCELLUS
CELLNTUU	LUCULENT
CELLOOQU	COLLOQUE
CELLORSS	ESCROLLS
CELLOSSY	CLOYLESS
CELLRRSU	CRULLERS
CELLRSSU	SCULLERS
CELLRSUY	SCULLERY
CELMNOOS	MONOCLES
CELMNOTY	CLOYMENT
CELMNOUY	UNCOMELY
CELMNTUU	MUCULENT
CELMOOOT	LOCOMOTE
CELMOOSY	CLOYSOME
CELMOPSU	COMPULSE
CELMOPSY	SYMPLOCE
CELMOSUU	CUMULOSE
CELMPRSU	CRUMPLES
CELMPRTU	PLECTRUM
CELMPSUU	SPECULUM
CELMSSUU	SECULUMS
CELNNOSU	NUCLEONS
CELNNOTY	NOCENTLY
CELNNOUV	UNCLOVEN
CELNOORS	CONSOLER
CELNOORU	ENCOLOUR
CELNOOSS	CONSOLES
	COOLNESS
CELNOOVV	CONVOLVE
CELNOPRT	PLECTRON
CELNOPUU	UNCOUPLE
CELNORTW	CROWNLET
CELNORWY	CLOWNERY
CELNOSSU	CLONUSES
	COUNSELS
	UNCLOSES
CELNOSTU	NOCTULES
CELNOSUV	CONVULSE
CELNOSVY	SOLVENCY
CELNOVXY	CONVEXLY
CELNPTUU	PUNCTULE
CELNRSTU	LECTURNS
CELOOPSS	CESSPOOL
CELOORRU	COLOURER
CELOORVY	OVERCLOY
CELOPRSU	COUPLERS
CELOPSSU	OPUSCLES
	UPCLOSES
CELOPSTU	COUPLETS
	OCTUPLES
CELOPSUU	OPUSCULE
CELOPTTU	OCTUPLET
CELORSST	CORSLETS
	COSTRELS
	CROSSLET
CELORSSU	CLOSURES
	SCLEROUS
CELORSSW	SCROWLES
CELORSSY	SCROYLES
CELORSTT	CLOTTERS
	CROTTLES
CELORSTU	CLOTURES
	CLOUTERS
	COULTERS
CELORSTY	COYSTREL
CELORSUU	ULCEROUS
	URCEOLUS
CELORSUY	CROUSELY
CELORTTU	COURTLET
CELORTVY	COVERTLY
CELOSTTU	CULOTTES
CELPRRSU	SCRUPLER
CELPRSSU	SCRUPLES
CELPRSUY	SPRUCELY
CELRSSTU	CLUSTERS
	CUSTRELS
CELRSSTY	CLYSTERS
CELRSTTU	CLUTTERS
	SCUTTLER
CELRSTUU	CULTURES
CELRSTUV	CULVERTS
CELRSTUY	CLUSTERY
CELSSTTU	SCUTTLES
CELSSTUU	CULTUSES
CEMMNOOR	COMMONER
CEMMNOOS	CONSOMME
CEMMNOOY	COMMONEY
CEMMNOST	COMMENTS
CEMMNOSU	COMMUNES
CEMMOOST	COMMOTES
CEMMOOSV	COMMOVES
CEMMORTU	COMMUTER
CEMMOSTU	COMMUTES
CEMMRSSU	SCUMMERS
CEMMNOST	CONTEMNS
CEMNOORR	CROMORNE
CEMNOOTY	MONOCYTE
CEMNOPTT	CONTEMPT
CEMNORSU	CONSUMER
	MUCRONES
CEMNOSSU	CONSUMES
	MUSCONES
CEMNRSTU	CENTRUMS

CEMOOPRS	COMPOSER	CEOPPRRS	CROPPERS	CFIINORT	FRICTION	CGHIKNOS	SHOCKING

CEMOOPRS COMPOSER
CEMOOPSS COMPOSES
CEMOOPST COMPOTES
CEMOORSY SYCOMORE
CEMOOSSS COSMOSES
CEMOOSTU OUTCOMES
CEMOPRSS COMPRESS
CEMOPRST COMPTERS
CEMOPRTU COMPUTER
CEMOPSTU COMPUTES
CEMORSSU CORMUSES
CEMORSTU COSTUMER
  CUSTOMER
CEMOSSTU COSTUMES
CEMPRSTU CRUMPEST
  CRUMPETS
  SPECTRUM
CENNOORV CONVENOR
CENNOOST CONNOTES
CENNORTU NOCTURNE
CENNOSST CONSENTS
CENNOSTT CONTENTS
CENNOSTV CONVENTS
CENNRRSU SCUNNERS
CENOOOTZ ECTOZOON
CENOORRS CORONERS
  CROONERS
CENOORST CORONETS
CENOORSU CORNEOUS
CENOORTT CORNETTO
CENOORVY CONVEYOR
CENOPRSY NECROPSY
CENOPSSY SYNCOPES
CENOPSTU POUNCETS
CENOQRSU CONQUERS
CENOQSTU CONQUEST
CENORRSS SCORNERS
CENORRSW CROWNERS
CENORRTU TROUNCER
CENORSST CONSTERS
CENORSTT CORNETTS
CENORSTU CONSTRUE
  CORNUTES
  COUNTERS
  RECOUNTS
  TROUNCES
CENORSTV CONVERTS
CENORSTW CROWNETS
CENORSUU CERNUOUS
CENORSUV UNCOVERS
CENORSUY CYNOSURE
CENOSSTT CONTESTS
CENOSSTU CONTUSES
  COUNTESS
CENOSTTX CONTEXTS
CENPRSWX ENCRYPTS
CENPRTUU PUNCTURE
CENPSTUX EXPUNCTS
CENRRSTU CURRENTS
CENRSSTU CURTNESS
  ENCRUSTS
CENRSSUU UNCURSES
CENRSSUW UNSCREWS
CEOOOPST OTOSCOPE
CEOOPRRV OVERCROP
CEOOPRSS SCOOPERS
CEOOPSWX COWPOXES
CEOORRVW OVERCROW
CEOORSST SCOOTERS
CEOOSTUV COVETOUS

CEOPPRRS CROPPERS
CEOPPRST PROSPECT
CEOPRRRU PROCURER
CEOPRRSS SCORPERS
CEOPRRST PORRECTS
CEOPRRSU CROUPERS
  PROCURES
CEOPRSTT PROTECTS
CEOPRSTW SCREWTOP
CEOPRSUU COUPURES
  CUPREOUS
CEOQRSTU CROQUETS
  ROCQUETS
CEOQRTUY COQUETRY
CEORRSSS SCORSERS
CEORRSSU COURSERS
  CURSORES
  SCOURERS
CEORRSSW SCOWRERS
CEORRSTY CORSETRY
CEORSSST CROSSEST
CEORSSSU SCOURSES
  SUCROSES
CEORSSTU SCOUTERS
CEORSSUV CORVUSES
CEORSTUU COUTURES
CEORSTUV COUVERTS
CEORSTUY COURTESY
CEOSSSTU COSTUSES
CEPPRRSU CRUPPERS
CEPPRSSU SCUPPERS
CEPPRTUU UPPERCUT
CEPRSSTU SPRUCEST
CEPRSSUY CYPRUSES
CEPRSTTU CUTPURSE
CEPSSSTU SUSPECTS
CERSSSUU CURSUSES
  RUSCUSES
CERSSTTU SCUTTERS
CERSSTUY CURTSEYS
CERSSUUX EXCURSUS
CFFGILNU CUFFLING
CFFGINOS SCOFFING
CFFGINSU SCUFFING
CFFHINOS CHIFFONS
CFFIRTUY FRUCTIFY
CFFMOSSU OFFSCUMS
CFGHIILN FILCHING
CFGIIKLN FICKLING
  FLICKING
CFGIKLNO FLOCKING
CFGIKNOR FROCKING
CFGIKNSU FUCKINGS
CFGINORT CROFTING
CFGINOSU FOCUSING
CFHIINOO FINOCHIO
CFHIIORR HORRIFIC
CFHIMOSS SCOMFISH
CFHIMSSU SCUMFISH
CFHLOPUU POUCHFUL
CFHORSTU FUTHORCS
CFIIILSY SILICIFY
CFIIKNYZ ZINCKIFY
CFIILNST INFLICTS
CFIILNUU FUNICULI
CFIILOPR PROLIFIC
CFIILPSU PULSIFIC
CFIIMORT MORTIFIC
CFIINOPT PONTIFIC

CFIINORT FRICTION
CFIINOST FICTIONS
CFIKLSTU STICKFUL
CFIKNNOS FINNOCKS
CFIKOSSS FOSSICKS
CFIKPSTU PUCKFIST
CFILMOOR COLIFORM
CFIMNOOR CONIFORM
CFIMNORS CONFIRMS
CFIMNORU UNCIFORM
CFINNOTU FUNCTION
CFKKLOOR FOLKROCK
CFKLLOSU LOCKFULS
CFKNORSU UNFROCKS
CFKOSTTU FUTTOCKS
CFLLOPRU CROPFULL
CFLMRSUU FULCRUMS
CFLNOORT CORNLOFT
CFLNORSU SCORNFUL
CFLOOPSU SCOOPFUL
CFLOPRSU CROPFULS
CFMNOORS CONFORMS
CFMOORST COMFORTS
CFNNOORT CONFRONT
CFOOORTW CROWFOOT
CFRSTUUU USUFRUCT
CGGGHINU CHUGGING
CGGGILNO CLOGGING
  COGGLING
CGGGINOS SCOGGING
CGGGINSU SCUGGING
CGGHILNU GULCHING
CGGHINOU COUGHING
CGGIILNN CLINGING
CGGIINNO COIGNING
CGGIINNR CRINGING
CGGIINRS GRICINGS
CGGILRSY SCRIGGLY
CGGINNSU SCUNGING
CGGINOOS SCOOGING
CGGINOSU SCOUGING
CGHHIILN HILCHING
CGHHIINT HITCHING
CGHHINNU HUNCHING
CGHHINOT HOTCHING
CGHHINTU HUTCHING
CGHIIKNN CHINKING
CGHIIKNO HOICKING
CGHIIKNR CHIRKING
CGHIIKNT THICKING
CGHIILLN CHILLING
CGHIILNR CHIRLING
CGHIILNT LICHTING
CGHIIMNR CHIRMING
CGHIIMNS MICHINGS
CGHIIMNT MITCHING
CGHIINNP PINCHING
CGHIINNW WINCHING
CGHIINOR CHOIRING
CGHIINPP CHIPPING
CGHIINPR CHIRPING
CGHIINPT PITCHING
CGHIINQU QUICHING
CGHIINRR CHIRRING
CGHIINRT CHIRTING
  RICHTING
CGHIINTT CHITTING
CGHIINTW WITCHING
CGHIINVV CHIVVING
CGHIINVY CHIVYING

CGHIKNOS SHOCKING
CGHIKNSU SHUCKING
CGHILMNU MULCHING
CGHILNNU LUNCHING
CGHILNNY LYNCHING
CGHILNOT CLOTHING
CGHILNRU LURCHING
CGHIMMNU CHUMMING
CGHIMNNU MUNCHING
CGHIMNOO MOOCHING
CGHIMNOP CHOMPING
CGHIMNOR CHROMING
CGHIMNOU MOUCHING
CGHIMPSY SPHYGMIC
CGHINNOS CHIGNONS
CGHINNOT NOTCHING
CGHINNPU PUNCHING
CGHINNRU CHURNING
CGHINNSY SYNCHING
CGHINOOS CHOOSING
CGHINOPP CHOPPING
CGHINOPT POTCHING
CGHINOPU POUCHING
CGHINORT TORCHING
CGHINOSU CHOUSING
  HOCUSING
CGHINOTU TOUCHING
CGHINOUV VOUCHING
CGHINPSY PSYCHING
CGHINPTU PINCHGUT
CGHINRRU CHURRING
CGHINRSU CRUSHING
  RUCHINGS
CGHINSTY SCYTHING
CGHNOOSU SOUCHONG
CGHOORST TORGOCHS
CGIIILNT LIGNITIC
CGIIINNS INCISING
CGIIINNT INCITING
CGIIKLNN CLINKING
CGIIKLNP PICKLING
CGIIKLNS LICKINGS
  SLICKING
CGIIKLNT TICKLING
CGIIKMMS GIMMICKS
CGIIKMMY GIMMICKY
CGIIKNNS SNICKING
CGIIKNNZ ZINCKING
CGIIKNOY YOICKING
CGIIKNPR PRICKING
CGIIKNPS PICKINGS
CGIIKNRS SCRIKING
CGIIKNRT TRICKING
CGIIKNRW WRICKING
CGIIKNST STICKING
  TICKINGS
CGIILLOS ILLOGICS
CGIILNOP POLICING
CGIILNPP CLIPPING
CGIILNPS SPLICING
CGIILNSS SLICINGS
CGIILNSU SLUICING
CGIILOST LOGISTIC
CGIILRTU LITURGIC
CGIIMNNO INCOMING
CGIIMNNS MINCINGS
CGIIMNPR CRIMPING
CGIIMNPU PUMICING
CGIIMNSU MISCUING
CGIINNOS COININGS

CGIINNOT NOTICING	UNCOPING	CHIKNNOP PHINNOCK	CHNORSTU COTHURNS
CGIINNPR PRINCING	CGINNORS SCORNING	CHIKNOOS CHINOOKS	CHOOORYZ ZOOCHORY
CGIINNSU INCUSING	CGINNORW CROWNING	CHIKOPTY KYPHOTIC	CHORSTTU SHORTCUT
CGIINNSW WINCINGS	CGINNOSS CONSIGNS	CHIKORST TROCHISK	CIIIKNTU CUITIKIN
CGIINNTT TINCTING	CGINNOTU COUNTING	CHIKOSST STOCKISH	CIIILMPT IMPLICIT
CGIINOOS ISOGONIC	CGINOOPS SCOOPING	CHIKPSYY PHYSICKY	CIIILMSU SILICIUM
CGIINOPT PICOTING	CGINOOST SCOOTING	CHILLMSU CHILLUMS	CIIILPST SPILITIC
CGIINORT TRIGONIC	CGINOOTV COGNOVIT	CHILLOOT OILCLOTH	CIIILSTV CIVILIST
CGIINOST COTISING	CGINOPPR CROPPING	CHILMOPS COMPLISH	CIIILTVY CIVILITY
CGIINOSV VOICINGS	CGINOPRS CORPSING	CHILMOSU SCHOLIUM	CIIIMNSV INCIVISM
CGIINPRS CRISPING	CGINOPRU CROUPING	CHILNNPY LYNCHPIN	CIIINNOS INCISION
CGIINRSU CRUISING	CGINOPSU SCOUPING	CHILNOOS SCHOLION	CIIINTVY VICINITY
CGIINRSV SCRIVING	CGINOPSW SCOWPING	CHILNOSU ULICHONS	CIIJRSTU JURISTIC
CGIJNNOU JOUNCING	CGINORSS CROSSING	CHILNOSW CLOWNISH	CIIKKLLS KILLICKS
CGIKKNNO KNOCKING	SCORINGS	CHILOOOZ HOLOZOIC	CIIKLLSY SICKLILY
CGIKLNNO CLONKING	SCORSING	CHILOOPT HOLOPTIC	CIIKLOPT POLITICK
CGIKLNNU CLUNKING	CGINORSU COURSING	CHILOSYY COYISHLY	CIIKLPST LIPSTICK
CGIKLNOR ROCKLING	SCOURING	CHILOTUY TOUCHILY	CIIKLRTY TRICKILY
CGIKLNPU PLUCKING	SOURCING	CHIMMORU CHROMIUM	CIIKLSTY STICKILY
CGIKLNRU RUCKLING	CGINORTU COURTING	CHIMNOOR HORMONIC	CIIKMMMS MIMMICKS
CGIKLNSU SCULKING	CGINOSTU SCOUTING	CHIMNOSU INSOMUCH	CIIKMNNS MINNICKS
SUCKLING	CGINPPSU CUPPINGS	CHIMNOUY ONYCHIUM	CIIKNOOT COOTIKIN
CGIKMNOS MOCKINGS	CGINPRSU SPRUCING	CHIMOORU MOUCHOIR	CIIKNSTU CUTIKINS
SMOCKING	CGINRRSU SCURRING	CHIMORSS CHRISOMS	CIILLNOP POLLINIC
CGIKNOOR CROOKING	CGINRSSU CURSINGS	CHIMORST CHRISTOM	CIILMOPY IMPOLICY
CGIKNORS ROCKINGS	CGINRSSY SCRYINGS	CHIMPSSY PSYCHISM	CIILMOSS SCIOLISM
CGIKNORT TROCKING	CGINRSTU CRUSTING	CHIMSSTY TYCHISMS	CIILMQSU CLIQUISM
CGIKNORW CORKWING	CGINRSUZ SCRUZING	CHINOORT ORTHICON	CIILMRSY LYRICISM
CGIKNOST STOCKING	CGINSTTU CUTTINGS	CHINOPTY HYPNOTIC	CIILNOPS CIPOLINS
CGIKNPSU KINGCUPS	CGKNOSTU GUNSTOCK	PYTHONIC	CIILNOSS SILICONS
CGIKNRTU TRUCKING	CGLLOSYY GLYCOSYL	TYPHONIC	CIILOOPT POLITICO
CGIKNSSU SUCKINGS	CGLMOOYY MYCOLOGY	CHINORTU COTHURNI	CIILOOTZ ZOOLITIC
CGIKNSTU GUNSTICK	CGLNOOOY ONCOLOGY	CHINOSSU CUSHIONS	CIILOPPT POPLITIC
CGILLNOS COLLINGS	CGLOOOTY TOCOLOGY	CHINOSTZ SCHIZONT	CIILOPST POLITICS
CGILLNOY COLLYING	CGLOOTYY CYTOLOGY	CHINOSUY CUSHIONY	PSILOTIC
CGILLNSU CULLINGS	CGMNNOOR MONGCORN	CHINSTTU UNSTITCH	CIILORST CLITORIS
SCULLING	CGMNNORU MUNGCORN	CHIOOPPT PHOTOPIC	COISTRIL
CGILLNUY CULLYING	CGOORRSW GORCROWS	CHIOOPRS POCHOIRS	CIILOSST SCIOLIST
CGILMNPU CLUMPING	CHHIIKST THICKISH	CHIOORSS ISOCHORS	SOLICITS
CGILMNSU MUSCLING	CHHIILTY HITCHILY	CHIOORSU ICHOROUS	CIILOSTY SOLICITY
CGILMNTU MULCTING	CHHIIPST PHTHISIC	CHIOORSZ CHORIZOS	CIILOSVV SLIVOVIC
CGILMNUU CINGULUM	CHHIKORS CHIKHORS	CHIOORTT ORTHOTIC	CIILRSTY LYRICIST
GLUCINUM	CHHILRSU CHURLISH	CHIOPRST STROPHIC	CIILRTUU UTRICULI
CGILNNOW CLOWNING	CHHIMRTY RHYTHMIC	CHIOPSTY HYPOCIST	CIILSSSS SCISSILS
CGILNOOR COLORING	CHHNORSU RHONCHUS	CHIORSSS CROSSISH	CIIMNOOS ISONOMIC
CGILNOOY COOINGLY	CHHOOPTT HOTCHPOT	CHIORSST CHORISTS	CIIMNOST MICTIONS
CGILNOPP CLOPPING	CHIIKLST TICKLISH	CHIPRRSU CHIRRUPS	MONISTIC
CGILNOPU COUPLING	CHIIKNNS KINCHINS	CHIPRRSY PYRRHICS	NOMISTIC
CGILNORU CLOURING	CHIIKRST TRICKISH	CHIPRRUY CHIRRUPY	CIIMORST TRISOMIC
CGILNOSS CLOSINGS	CHIILLLY CHILLILY	CHIPRTTY TRIPTYCH	CIIMOSST MISTICOS
CGILNOSW COWLINGS	CHIILMSY HYLICISM	CHIPSSTY PSYCHIST	STOICISM
SCOWLING	CHIILNNP LINCHPIN	CHIRRSSU SCIRRHUS	CIIMOSTY MYOSITIC
CGILNOTT CLOTTING	CHIILOST HOLISTIC	CHISSTTU CHUTISTS	CIIMRSTY MYRISTIC
CGILNOTU CLOUTING	CHIILPRY CHIRPILY	CHKLOOOS HOOLOCKS	CIINNSTT INSTINCT
CGILNPSU SCULPING	CHIILQSU CLIQUISH	CHKMMOOS HOMMOCKS	CIINNSTU TUNICINS
CGILNRSU CURLINGS	CHIILSTY HYLICIST	CHKMMOSU HUMMOCKS	CIINOOST COITIONS
CGILOORU UROLOGIC	CHIIMPPU PICHURIM	CHKMMOUY HUMMOCKY	ISOTONIC
CGILORSW COWGIRLS	CHIINNPS INCHPINS	CHKNOOSS SCHNOOKS	CIINOOTZ ZOONITIC
CGILPSTU GILTCUPS	CHIINOPS SIPHONIC	CHKNORSU CORNHUSK	CIINOPSU OPINICUS
CGILPSTY GLYPTICS	CHIINORT ORNITHIC	CHKOOOPS COOKSHOP	CIINORSS INCISORS
CGIMMNSU SCUMMING	CHIIORSS CHORISIS	CHKOOSST SCHTOOKS	CIINORSY INCISORY
CGIMNNOO GNOMONIC	CHIIORST HISTORIC	CHKPSTUU PUTCHUKS	CIINOSSS SCISSION
ONCOMING	ORCHITIS	CHLNOOOP COLOPHON	CIINOTTY TONICITY
CGIMNOPT COMPTING	CHIIPPRU HIPPURIC	CHLOORSU CHLOROUS	CIINPRSS CRISPINS
CGIMNPRU CRUMPING	CHIIRSTT TRISTICH	CHLOPSTY SPLOTCHY	CIINPSTU SINCIPUT
CGIMRRUY MICRURGY	CHIKLLOS HILLOCKS	CHLORTUY CHOULTRY	CIIOOPST ISOTOPIC
CGINNNOS CONNINGS	CHIKLLOY HILLOCKY	CHMNORRU CRUMHORN	CIIOPRST PORISTIC
CGINNNSU CUNNINGS	CHIKMNPU CHIPMUNK	CHNNOORS CHRONONS	CIIOQTUX QUIXOTIC
CGINNOOR CROONING	CHIKMNTU MUTCHKIN	CHNOORST TORCHONS	CIIORRWW WIRRICOW
CGINNOPU POUNCING		CHNORRSS SCHNORRS	CIIOTTXY TOXICITY

Letters	Word	Letters	Word	Letters	Word	Letters	Word
CIIPRRTU	PRURITIC	CILPSSTU	SCULPSIT	CKLOOOSY	OLYCOOKS	DDDEEENP	DEPENDED
CIIPRSTU	PURISTIC	CILRSTTY	STRICTLY	CKLOORSW	ROWLOCKS	DDDEEENR	REDDENED
CIIRSTTU	TRUISTIC	CILRSTUY	CRUSTILY	CKLOOSTU	LOCKOUTS	DDDEEENU	UNDEEDED
CIISSTTY	CYSTITIS	CILRSUVY	SCURVILY	CKLOPSTU	PUTLOCKS	DDDEEFOR	FODDERED
CIJNNOOS	CONJOINS	CILSSTTU	CULTISTS	CKMMMOSU	MUMMOCKS	DDDEEGIS	DISEDGED
CIJNNOOT	CONJOINT	CIMMOSSS	COSMISMS	CKMOOOOR	COOKROOM	DDDEEHRS	SHREDDED
CIJNNOTU	JUNCTION	CIMNOOOZ	ZOONOMIC	CKNOSSTU	UNSTOCKS	DDDEEIST	STEDDIED
CIJNNSTU	INJUNCTS	CIMNOORS	OMICRONS	CKNRSTUU	UNSTRUCK	DDDEEJRU	JUDDERED
CIJOOSTY	JOCOSITY	CIMNOORU	CORONIUM	CKOOOSTU	COOKOUTS	DDDEELRT	TREDDLED
CIKKLLOS	KILLOCKS	CIMNOPRT	COMPRINT	CKOORSSU	SOUROCKS	DDDEENOR	REDDENDO
CIKLLOPR	KILLCROP	CIMNORSS	CRIMSONS	CKOPSTTU	PUTTOCKS	DDDEENOS	SODDENED
CIKLLOPS	PILLOCKS	CIMNORSY	CRONYISM	CKOSSSTU	TUSSOCKS	DDDEENUW	UNWEDDED
CIKLLORS	ROLLICKS	CIMNOSTU	MISCOUNT	CKOSSTUY	TUSSOCKY	DDDEEORR	DODDERER
CIKLLOSS	SILLOCKS	CIMNOSUY	SYCONIUM	CLLLOOPT	CLOTPOLL	DDDEEPRU	PUDDERED
CIKLLOSW	KILLCOWS	CIMOOOTZ	ZOOTOMIC	CLLMOSSU	MOLLUSCS	DDDEERTU	DETRUDED
CIKLLPUY	PLUCKILY	CIMOORSS	MORISCOS	CLLOOPSS	SCOLLOPS	DDDEGNOU	UNGODDED
CIKLMSSU	MISLUCKS	CIMOPSSY	COPYISMS	CLLOOQUY	COLLOQUY	DDDEHIRT	THRIDDED
CIKLNOST	LINSTOCK	CIMOSSST	COSMISTS	CLMMNOOY	COMMONLY	DDDEIINV	DIVIDEND
CIKLOSTY	STOCKILY	CIMOSTUU	MUTICOUS	CLMOOOTY	COLOTOMY	DDDEIIST	STIDDIED
CIKMNNOS	MINNOCKS	CIMOSTUY	MUCOSITY	CLMOOPST	COMPLOTS	DDDEILNU	UNLIDDED
CIKMOORS	SICKROOM	CIMOSTYZ	ZYMOTICS	CLMOPSTU	PLUMCOTS	DDDEILNW	DWINDLED
CIKMOPST	MOPSTICK	CINNNOSU	INCONNUS	CLMOSSUU	OSCULUMS	DDDEILQU	QUIDDLED
CIKNNOPS	PINNOCKS	CINNOOSS	SCOINSON	CLNOORST	CONTROLS	DDDEILRS	DIDDLERS
CIKNNOSW	WINNOCKS	CINNOOST	SCONTION	CLNOORTU	CONTROUL	DDDEILTW	TWIDDLED
CIKNSSTU	UNSTICKS	CINNOOTU	CONTINUO		COUNTROL	DDDEIMOS	DISMODED
CIKOPPST	POCKPITS	CINNORSU	UNICORNS	CLNOSSTU	CONSULTS	DDDEINOR	DENDROID
CIKOSSTT	STOCKIST	CINNOSTU	UNCTIONS	CLNOSTUY	UNCOSTLY	DDDEINRU	UNDERDID
CIKOSTUW	OUTWICKS	CINNOSTY	SYNTONIC	CLOOOPRT	PROTOCOL	DDDEIOST	DODDIEST
CIKPSSTU	STICKUPS	CINNQUUX	QUINCUNX	CLOORTUY	LOCUTORY	DDDEIQSU	SQUIDDED
CILLMSUY	CLUMSILY	CINOOPRS	SCORPION	CLOOSSSU	COLOSSUS	DDDEISTU	DUDDIEST
	CULLYISM	CINOOPRT	PROTONIC	CLOPRSTU	SCULPTOR	DDDENORW	DROWNDED
CILLNOOT	COTILLON	CINOOSUV	COVINOUS	CLRSSUUU	SURCULUS	DDDGIILN	DIDDLING
CILLNORS	INSCROLL	CINOOTXY	OXYTOCIN	CMMNNOOU	UNCOMMON	DDDIIOOR	DORIDOID
CILLNOSU	CULLIONS	CINOPSTY	SYNOPTIC	CMNOOOST	MONOCOTS	DDEEEEMR	REDEEMED
	SCULLION	CINORRST	TRICORNS	CMNOOOTY	ONCOTOMY	DDEEEENP	DEEPENED
CILLOOOT	OCOTILLO	CINORSST	CISTRONS	CMNOORRW	CORNWORM	DDEEEFLX	DEFLEXED
CILLOORS	CRIOLLOS		CORNISTS	CMNOPSTU	CONSUMPT	DDEEEFNR	DEFENDER
CILMNOPS	COMPLINS	CINORSTT	CONTRIST	CMOOPRST	COMPORTS	DDEEEFRR	DEFERRED
CILMNOPU	PULMONIC	CINORSTU	RUCTIONS	CMOOPSST	COMPOSTS	DDEEEGLR	LEDGERED
CILMNOUU	INOCULUM	CINORSUY	COUSINRY	CMORSSTU	SCROTUMS	DDEEEGMR	DEMERGED
CILMNUUV	VINCULUM	CINOSSST	CONSISTS	CMORSTUW	CUTWORMS	DDEEEGNR	DEGENDER
CILMOPSY	OLYMPICS	CINOSSTU	SUCTIONS	CNNOOORT	CONTORNO		GENDERED
CILMPRSY	SCRIMPLY	CINOSTUV	VISCOUNT	CNNORSTU	NOCTURNS	DDEEEGRR	REGREDED
CILMPSUU	SPICULUM	CINRSSTU	INCRUSTS	CNNORSUW	UNCROWNS	DDEEEGRT	DETERGED
CILMSSTU	CULTISMS	CINRSTTU	INSTRUCT	CNOOOORT	OCTOROON	DDEEEHLW	WHEEDLED
CILNOORS	ORCINOLS	CINRSTUY	SCRUTINY	CNOOPPRS	POPCORNS	DDEEEHNU	UNHEEDED
CILNOORU	UNICOLOR	CIOOPRSS	SCORPIOS	CNOOPRSU	CROUPONS	DDEEEIMR	REMEDIED
CILNOOSS	CLOISONS	CIOOPRST	PORTICOS	CNOOPSSU	SOUPCONS	DDEEEIST	DEEDIEST
CILNOOST	COLONIST		PROOTICS	CNOORRTY	CRYOTRON		STEEDIED
CILNOOTU	LOCUTION	CIOOPTYZ	ZOOTYPIC	CNOORSST	CONSORTS	DDEEELLV	DEVELLED
CILNOPRS	PILCORNS	CIOOQSTU	COQUITOS	CNOORSTT	CONTORTS	DDEEELNW	WEDELNED
CILNOSTU	LINOCUTS	CIOORRWW	WORRICOW	CNOORSTU	CONTOURS	DDEEELPT	DEPLETED
CILNOSUY	COUSINLY	CIOORSSU	SCORIOUS		CORNUTOS	DDEEELSS	DEEDLESS
CILNPSSU	INSCULPS	CIOPSSTY	COPYISTS		CROUTONS	DDEEELTW	TWEEDLED
	SCULPINS	CIORRSTU	CURSITOR		OUTSCORN	DDEEEMNT	DEMENTED
CILNPSTU	INSCULPT	CIORSSSS	SCISSORS	CNOOSTTW	COTTOWNS	DDEEEMRS	DEMERSED
CILOOPST	COPILOTS	CIPPRRUU	PURPURIC	CNOPRSTY	CRYPTONS	DDEEENNU	UNNEEDED
CILOOPYZ	POLYZOIC	CIPSSTTY	STYPTICS	CNOSTTUU	UNCTUOUS	DDEEENPX	EXPENDED
CILOORRT	TRICOLOR	CIRRSTTU	CRITTURS	COOOPSYZ	ZOOSCOPY	DDEEENRR	RENDERED
CILOORST	CORTISOL	CJNOORRU	CONJUROR	COOPRRST	PROCTORS	DDEEENRT	TENDERED
CILOORSU	COULOIRS	CJOOORSU	JOCOROUS	COOPRSTU	OUTCROPS	DDEEENSU	UNSEEDED
CILOOSSU	SCIOLOUS	CJRSUUUU	SUCURUJU	COOPRSUU	CROUPOUS	DDEEENTX	EXTENDED
CILOPPRY	PROPYLIC	CKKNOOTU	KNOCKOUT	COOPRSUY	UROSCOPY	DDEEENUW	UNWEEDED
CILOPRSW	PILCROWS	CKKOORRW	ROCKWORK	COORRWWY	WORRYCOW	DDEEERRT	DETERRED
CILOPSSW	COWSLIPS	CKLLMOSU	MULLOCKS	COORSSTU	OUTCROSS	DDEEERST	DESERTED
CILORSTY	COYSTRIL	CKLLOOPS	POLLOCKS	COOSSTTY	OTOCYSTS	DDEEERSV	DESERVED
CILOSSTU	OCULISTS	CKLLORSU	RULLOCKS	COPRRSTU	CORRUPTS	DDEEESTT	DETESTED
CILOSSTY	SYSTOLIC	CKLMMOSU	SLUMMOCK	DDDDEEIR	DIDDERED	DDEEESTV	DEVESTED
CILOSSUU	LUSCIOUS			DDDDEEOR	DODDERED	DDEEFFIR	DIFFERED
CILPRSTU	CULPRITS			DDDEEEFN	DEFENDED	DDEEFFNO	OFFENDED

DDEEFGIT	FIDGETED	DDEELLOY	YODELLED	DDEGILRS	GRIDDLES	DDEILNRU	UNRIDDLE
DDEEFINR	FRIENDED	DDEELMPU	DEPLUMED	DDEGILRY	GLIDDERY	DDEILNSW	DWINDLES
DDEEFINU	UNDEFIDE	DDEELMRS	MEDDLERS	DDEGILST	GLIDDEST		SWINDLED
	UNDEFIED	DDEELNOU	LOUDENED	DDEGILUV	DIVULGED	DDEILOPS	DISPLODE
DDEEFLNO	ENFOLDED	DDEELOPR	DEPLORED	DDEGIMOS	DEMIGODS	DDEILOSY	DYSODILE
DDEEFLOU	DEFOULED		POLDERED	DDEGINNS	SNEDDING	DDEILPRS	PIDDLERS
DDEEFMOR	DEFORMED	DDEELOPX	EXPLODED	DDEGINNU	DENUDING	DDEILPRU	PUDDLIER
DDEEFNRU	REFUNDED	DDEELOPY	DEPLOYED	DDEGINRS	REDDINGS	DDEILQRU	QUIDDLER
	UNDERFED	DDEELORS	SOLDERED	DDEGINRU	UNGIRDED	DDEILQSU	QUIDDLES
DDEEFORR	FODDERER	DDEELOSU	DELOUSED	DDEGINST	STEDDING	DDEILRRS	RIDDLERS
DDEEGGOR	DOGGEDER	DDEELOVV	DEVOLVED	DDEGINSW	SWINDGED	DDEILRSS	SLIDDERS
DDEEGHNU	UNHEDGED	DDEELPRS	PEDDLERS		WEDDINGS	DDEILRST	STRIDDLE
DDEEGILN	ENGILDED	DDEELPRU	PRELUDED	DDEGINUU	UNGUIDED		TIDDLERS
DDEEGINR	ENRIDGED	DDEELRST	TREDDLES	DDEGIOST	DODGIEST	DDEILRSY	SLIDDERY
DDEEGINS	DESIGNED	DDEELRSU	DELUDERS	DDEGIQSU	SQUIDGED	DDEILRTW	TWIDDLER
	SDEIGNED	DDEEMNOR	ENDODERM	DDEGLOPS	SPLODGED	DDEILRZZ	DRIZZLED
DDEEGIRV	DIVERGED	DDEEMRRU	DEMURRED	DDEGNORU	GROUNDED	DDEILSTW	TWIDDLES
DDEEGISS	DISEDGES		MURDERED		UNDERDOG	DDEILSTY	LYDDITES
DDEEGIST	DIGESTED	DDEENNOR	DONNERED	DDEGNOSS	GODSENDS		TIDDLEYS
DDEEGJRU	REJUDGED	DDEENNOY	ENDODYNE	DDEGNOSU	DUDGEONS	DDEIMMNU	UNDIMMED
DDEEGLNO	GOLDENED	DDEENNTU	UNTENDED	DDEGORSS	GORSEDDS	DDEIMNNU	UNMINDED
DDEEGMMU	DEGUMMED	DDEENOPR	PERDENDO	DDEGRRSU	DRUDGERS	DDEIMNSU	MUEDDINS
DDEEGOPS	GODSPEED		PONDERED	DDEGRRUY	DRUDGERY	DDEIMNUV	VIDENDUM
DDEEGRRS	DREDGERS	DDEENOPW	PONDWEED	DDEHILNY	HIDDENLY	DDEIMORS	DERMOIDS
DDEEGSTU	DEGUSTED	DDEENORS	ENDORSED	DDEHILOO	IDLEHOOD	DDEIMOSU	MEDUSOID
DDEEHILS	SHIELDED	DDEENORW	WONDERED	DDEHIMOS	DISHOMED	DDEIMSTU	MUDDIEST
DDEEHINR	HINDERED	DDEENOSS	ENDOSSED	DDEHINNU	UNHIDDEN	DDEINNRU	UNRIDDEN
DDEEHIRT	DITHERED	DDEENPRS	SPREDDEN	DDEHINOR	DIHEDRON	DDEINNTU	UNDINTED
DDEEHISS	EDDISHES	DDEENRSU	SUNDERED	DDEHIORS	SHODDIER	DDEINOPS	DISPONED
DDEEHNOR	DEHORNED	DDEENRTU	RETUNDED	DDEHIOSS	SHODDIES	DDEINORS	INDORSED
DDEEHNSU	DUDHEENS	DDEEOPRT	DEPORTED	DDEHIRSS	SHIDDERS	DDEINOSW	DISENDOW
DDEEHORT	DEHORTED	DDEEOPRW	POWDERED	DDEHIRSW	WHIDDERS		DISOWNED
DDEEHRRS	SHREDDER	DDEEORRW	REWORDED	DDEHIRSY	HYDRIDES	DDEINOWW	WINDOWED
DDEEHRSS	SHEDDERS	DDEEORTT	DETORTED	DDEHNOOU	UNHOODED	DDEINPPU	UNDIPPED
DDEEIINT	INEDITED	DDEEORTU	DETOURED	DDEHNPUU	UPHUDDEN	DDEINPSS	DISPENDS
DDEEIIRV	REDIVIDE	DDEEOORV	DEVOURED	DDEHNRSU	HUNDREDS	DDEINRST	STRIDDEN
DDEEILLV	DEVILLED	DDEEORVY	OVERDYED	DDEHOOOO	HOODOOED	DDEINRTU	INTRUDED
DDEEILMN	MILDENED	DDEEPRRU	PERDURED	DDEHOOSW	WOODSHED	DDEINSST	DISTENDS
DDEEILMW	MILDEWED	DDEEPRSS	SPREDDES	DDEHORSU	SHROUDED	DDEINSSW	SWIDDENS
DDEEILRW	WILDERED	DDEERRUV	VERDURED	DDEHRSSU	SHUDDERS	DDEINSTU	DISTUNED
DDEEIMNP	IMPENDED	DDEERSTU	DETRUDES	DDEHRSUY	SHUDDERY	DDEIOPRS	DROPSIED
DDEEIMNR	REMINDED	DDEERTUX	EXTRUDED	DDEIIIRS	IRIDISED	DDEIOPRV	PROVIDED
DDEEIMOR	MOIDERED	DDEFFISU	DIFFUSED	DDEIIIRZ	IRIDIZED	DDEIOPSS	DISPOSED
DDEEIMSS	MISDEEDS	DDEFIIIN	NIDIFIED	DDEIIKLS	DISLIKED	DDEIOPST	PODDIEST
DDEEIMST	DEMISTED	DDEFIILM	MIDFIELD	DDEIIKRS	KIDDIERS	DDEIORRS	DISORDER
DDEEIMTT	DEMITTED	DDEFIILR	FIDDLIER	DDEIILNR	DIELDRIN		SORDIDER
DDEEINNR	DINNERED	DDEFIIMO	MODIFIED	DDEIILOS	IDOLISED	DDEIOSST	SODDIEST
DDEEINNT	INDENTED	DDEFIIMW	MIDWIFED	DDEIILOZ	IDOLIZED	DDEIOSTW	DOWDIEST
	INTENDED	DDEFILNO	INFOLDED	DDEIILRT	TIDDLIER	DDEIPRSS	DISPREDS
DDEEINRT	DENDRITE	DDEFILRS	FIDDLERS	DDEIILST	TIDDLIES	DDEIPRSU	SPUDDIER
DDEEINST	DESTINED	DDEFILSY	FIDDLEYS	DDEIIMSS	SMIDDIES	DDEIPSTU	DISPUTED
DDEEINTU	UNEDITED	DDEFLNOU	UNFOLDED	DDEIIMVW	MIDWIVED	DDEIRSSU	DRUIDESS
DDEEIOPR	PERIODED	DDEFLRSU	FUDDLERS	DDEIINRT	NITRIDED	DDEIRSTU	RUDDIEST
DDEEIPPR	REDIPPED	DDEFLRUU	UDDERFUL	DDEIINTU	UNTIDIED		STURDIED
DDEEIPRS	PRESIDED	DDEFNNUU	UNFUNDED	DDEIIOPS	DIOPSIDE	DDEKMOSU	DUKEDOMS
DDEEIPRV	DEPRIVED	DDEGGINR	DREDGING		DIPODIES	DDELLNUU	UNDULLED
DDEEIPSS	DEPSIDES	DDEGGLOY	DOGGEDLY	DDEIIOST	ODDITIES	DDELMRSU	MUDDLERS
	DESPISED	DDEGGNOO	DOGGONED	DDEIIOSX	DIOXIDES	DDELNORU	UNLORDED
DDEEIRRS	DERIDERS	DDEGHILN	HEDDLING		OXIDISED	DDELNRTU	TRUNDLED
DDEEIRST	REDDIEST	DDEGHINS	SHEDDING	DDEIIOXZ	OXIDIZED	DDELNSUY	SUDDENLY
DDEEIRSV	DIVERSED	DDEGIINR	DERIDING	DDEIIRSV	DIVIDERS	DDELOORS	DOODLERS
DDEEIRTV	DIVERTED	DDEGIIST	GIDDIEST	DDEIISST	STIDDIES	DDELOPRS	PLODDERS
DDEEISST	DESISTED	DDEGILMN	MEDDLING	DDEIISTT	TIDDIEST	DDELORST	STRODDLE
	STEDDIES	DDEGILNP	PEDDLING	DDEIKNRS	KINDREDS		STRODLED
DDEEISTV	DIVESTED	DDEGILNR	REDDLING	DDEIKOSY	DISYOKED		TODDLERS
DDEEITTW	DEWITTED	DDEGILNS	SLEDDING	DDEILMOP	IMPLODED	DDELOSYY	DYSODYLE
DDEEJLLO	JODELLED	DDEGILNU	DELUDING	DDEILMOV	DEVILDOM	DDELPRSU	PUDDLERS
DDEEKNSU	DUSKENED		INDULGED	DDEILNPS	SPINDLED	DDELSSTU	STUDDLES
DDEELLMO	MODELLED		UNGILDED		SPLENDID	DDEMMSSU	SMEDDUMS
DDEELLOW	DOWELLED	DDEGILOS	DISLODGE	DDEILNRT	TRINDLED	DDEMNOOU	UNDOOMED

DDEMNOST	ODDMENTS	DDIINOPU	DUPONDII	DEEEHLRW	WHEEDLER
DDEMNOUU	DUODENUM	DDIIQSTU	QUIDDITS	DEEEHLSS	HEEDLESS
DDEMNPUU	PUDENDUM	DDIIQTUY	QUIDDITY	DEEEHLSW	WHEEDLES
DDEMOOTU	OUTMODED	DDILORSY	SORDIDLY	DEEEHLWZ	WHEEZLED
DDENNORS	DENDRONS	DDILOSSY	DYSODILS	DEEEHMMS	EMMESHED
DDENNOSU	UNSODDEN	DDIMOSUY	DIDYMOUS	DEEEHMNS	ENMESHED
DDENOOUW	UNWOODED	DDIMOSWY	DOWDYISM	DEEEHRTT	TETHERED
DDENOPSS	DESPONDS	DDINNOWW	DOWNWIND	DEEEILNR	NEEDLIER
DDENORSU	REDOUNDS	DDINOOOT	ODONTOID	DEEEILNS	SELENIDE
DDENORTU	ROTUNDED	DDINOOWW	WOODWIND	DEEEILRV	RELIEVED
DDENORUW	UNWORDED	DDLLMOOS	DOLLDOMS	DEEEILTV	DELETIVE
DDENOSTU	STOUNDED	DDLMORSU	DOLDRUMS	DEEEILVW	WEEVILED
DDENOSTW	STOWNDED	DDMNOORS	DROMONDS	DEEEIMNS	INSEEMED
DDENOSUW	SWOUNDED	DDOORWWY	ROWDYDOW	DEEEIMRS	REMEDIES
DDENSTUY	SUDDENTY	DDORSSTY	DROSTDYS	DEEEINRR	REINDEER
DDEOOOOV	VOODOOED	DEEEEFRR	REFEREED	DEEEINST	NEEDIEST
DDEOORSW	REDWOODS	DEEEEFRZ	DEFREEZE	DEEEINSX	ENDEIXES
DDEOORWW	ROWDEDOW	DEEEEGKR	KEDGEREE	DEEEINTV	EVENTIDE
DDEOOUUV	VOUDOUED	DEEEEHLR	REHEELED	DEEEIPRS	SPEEDIER
DDEORTUU	OUTDURED	DEEEEKMN	MEEKENED	DEEEIPTX	EXPEDITE
DDFGIILN	FIDDLING	DEEEELTY	EYELETED	DEEEIRRR	DERRIERE
DDFGILNU	FUDDLING	DEEEEMMS	MESEEMED	DEEEIRRS	DIERESES
DDFIIOSU	FIDDIOUS	DEEEEMRR	REDEEMER	DEEEIRST	REEDIEST
DDFMNOUU	DUMFOUND	DEEEEMST	ESTEEMED	DEEEIRSZ	RESEIZED
DDGGIINY	GIDDYING	DEEEENRV	VENEERED	DEEEIRTW	TWEEDIER
DDGGILNU	GUDDLING	DEEEERTT	TEETERED	DEEEIRVW	REVIEWED
DDGGINRU	DRUDGING	DEEEFFIR	EFFEIRED	DEEEISST	SEEDIEST
DDGHIINW	WHIDDING	DEEEFINR	FINEERED		STEEDIES
DDGHILNO	HODDLING		REDEFINE	DEEEISSV	DEVISEES
DDGHILNU	HUDDLING	DEEEFIPT	TEPEFIED	DEEEISTW	WEEDIEST
DDGHINTU	THUDDING	DEEEFIRW	FIREWEED	DEEEJLLW	JEWELLED
DDGHOOOS	GODHOODS	DEEEFLLR	REFELLED	DEEEJNRU	DEJEUNER
DDGIIINV	DIVIDING	DEEEFLPT	DEEPFELT	DEEEJNSU	DEJEUNES
DDGIIKNS	SKIDDING	DEEEFLRT	FELTERED	DEEEKNSW	WEEKENDS
DDGIIKNY	KIDDYING	DEEEFLRX	REFLEXED	DEEEKOPW	POKEWEED
DDGIILMN	MIDDLING	DEEEFLSX	DEFLEXES	DEEEKRST	STREEKED
DDGIILNP	PIDDLING	DEEEFMNR	FREEDMEN	DEEEKRSW	RESKEWED
DDGIILNR	RIDDLING	DEEEFNRT	DEFERENT		SKEWERED
DDGIILNT	TIDDLING	DEEEFNSS	DEFENSES	DEEELLLV	LEVELLED
DDGIILNW	WIDDLING	DEEEFNST	ENFESTED	DEEELLNT	DENTELLE
DDGILMNU	MUDDLING	DEEEFORV	OVERFEED	DEEELLNV	NEVELLED
DDGILNNO	NODDLING	DEEEFRRR	DEFERRER	DEEELLNW	NEWELLED
DDGILNOO	DOODLING		REFERRED	DEEELLPR	REPELLED
DDGILNOP	PLODDING	DEEEFRRT	FERRETED	DEEELLPT	PELLETED
DDGILNOT	TODDLING	DEEEFRST	FESTERED	DEEELLPX	EXPELLED
DDGILNPU	PUDDLING	DEEEFRTT	FETTERED	DEEELLRT	TELLERED
DDGILNRU	RUDDLING	DEEEFRTW	FEWTERED	DEEELLRV	REVELLED
DDGIMNUY	MUDDYING	DEEEGHNW	WHEENGED	DEEELMOS	SOMEDELE
DDGIMRSU	DRUDGISM	DEEEGILS	ELEGISED	DEEELNPU	UNPEELED
DDGINNOS	NODDINGS	DEEEGILZ	ELEGIZED	DEEELNRS	NEEDLERS
	SNODDING	DEEEGIPR	PEDIGREE	DEEELNRT	RELENTED
DDGINOPR	PRODDING	DEEEGIRR	GREEDIER	DEEELNRU	UNREELED
DDGINOQU	QUODDING	DEEEGISS	DIEGESES	DEEELNSS	LESSENED
DDGINORS	RODDINGS	DEEEGISW	EDGEWISE		NEEDLESS
DDGINPSU	PUDDINGS	DEEEGLPS	PLEDGEES		SELDSEEN
	SPUDDING	DEEEGLSS	EDGELESS	DEEELNSU	UNSEELED
DDGINPUY	PUDDINGY	DEEEGLSV	SELVEDGE	DEEELOPV	DEVELOPE
DDGINRUY	RUDDYING	DEEEGMRR	DEMERGER	DEEELPRT	PELTERED
DDGINSTU	STUDDING		REMERGED		REPLETED
DDGOOOSW	DOGWOODS	DEEEGMRS	DEMERGES	DEEELPST	DEPLETES
DDHILOSY	SHODDILY	DEEEGNNR	ENGENDER		STEEPLED
DDHIORSY	HYDROIDS	DEEEGNRU	RENEGUED	DEEELRSS	REDELESS
DDHIOSWY	DOWDYISH	DEEEGNRV	REVENGED	DEEELRST	DEERLETS
DDHLLOOO	DOLLHOOD	DEEEGQSU	SQUEEDGE		STREELED
DDIIIIVV	DIVIDIVI	DEEEGRRS	REGREDES	DEEELRTT	LETTERED
DDIILOPY	DIPLOIDY	DEEEGRST	DETERGES	DEEELRTW	WELTERED
DDIIMMUY	DIDYMIUM	DEEEGRTT	GETTERED	DEEELSSS	SEEDLESS
DDIIMRSU	DRUIDISM	DEEEHKRS	SHREEKED	DEEELSSW	WEEDLESS
	SIDDURIM	DEEEHLMT	HELMETED	DEEELSTW	TWEEDLES
		DEEEHLPW	WHEEPLED	DEEELTVV	VELVETED

DEEEMNNT	NEEDMENT
DEEEMNSS	DEMESNES
	SEEDSMEN
DEEEMPRT	TEMPERED
DEEEMPTX	EXEMPTED
DEEEMRSS	DEMERSES
DEEEMRST	DEEMSTER
DEEENNRT	ENTENDER
DEEENNUW	UNWEENED
DEEENOPR	REOPENED
DEEENORS	ENDORSEE
DEEENPRT	REPENTED
	REPETEND
DEEENPRU	UNPEERED
DEEENPRV	PREVENED
DEEENPRX	EXPENDER
DEEENPSS	DEEPNESS
DEEENRRR	RENDERER
DEEENRRT	TENDERER
DEEENRRV	REVEREND
DEEENRST	RESENTED
DEEENRTT	TENTERED
DEEENRTU	NEUTERED
DEEENRTX	EXTENDER
DEEENRUV	REVENUED
	UNREEVED
DEEENSSS	SEEDNESS
DEEENSTT	DETENTES
DEEENSTU	DETENUES
DEEENSTX	DENTEXES
DEEENSUV	VENDEUSE
DEEEOPRR	PEDERERO
DEEEOPRT	DEPORTEE
DEEEORST	STEREOED
DEEEORSW	OREWEEDS
DEEEORVY	OVEREYED
DEEEOSTV	DEVOTEES
DEEEPPPR	PEPPERED
DEEEPRSS	SPEEDERS
DEEEPRST	ESTREPED
	PESTERED
DEEEPRSZ	SPREEZED
DEEEPRTX	EXPERTED
DEEEQRRU	REQUERED
DEEEQSUZ	SQUEEZED
DEEERRRV	VERDERER
DEEERRST	DESERTER
DEEERRSV	DESERVER
	RESERVED
	REVERSED
DEEERRTV	REVERTED
DEEERSSV	DESERVES
DEEERSTT	RESETTED
	SETTERED
	STREETED
DEEERSTV	REVESTED
DEEERSTW	WESTERED
DEEERSTX	EXSERTED
DEEERSUW	SERUEWED
DEEERSVW	SERVEWED
DEEERTTT	TETTERED
DEEERTTV	REVETTED
DEEESTTU	SUEDETTE
DEEESTTV	VEDETTES
DEEFFGLU	EFFULGED
DEEFFGOR	GOFFERED
DEEFFINR	NIFFERED
DEEFFINS	EFFENDIS
DEEFFINT	INFEFTED
DEEFFNOR	OFFENDER

	REOFFEND		REJIGGED	DEEGIRST	DIGESTER	DEEHLNPU	UNHELPED
DEEFFRSU	SUFFERED	DEEGGINR	GINGERED		ESTRIDGE	DEEHLORV	OVERHELD
DEEFGILR	FLEDGIER		NIGGERED	DEEGIRSU	GUDESIRE		VERDELHO
DEEFGINR	FINGERED		RENIGGED	DEEGIRSV	DIVERGES	DEEHLPPS	SHLEPPED
DEEFGINS	FEEDINGS	DEEGGIRR	DREGGIER	DEEGISST	SEDGIEST	DEEHLSTU	SLEUTHED
DEEFGIPS	PIGFEEDS	DEEGGLOR	DOGGEREL	DEEGJPRU	PREJUDGE	DEEHMNRS	HERDSMEN
DEEFGIUW	GUDEWIFE	DEEGGNOR	ENGORGED	DEEGJRSU	REJUDGES	DEEHMORT	MOTHERED
DEEFGLNU	ENGULFED	DEEGGNPU	UNPEGGED	DEEGLLRU	GRUELLED	DEEHNOPY	PHONEYED
DEEFHIMU	HUMEFIED	DEEGGORR	REGORGED	DEEGLLUY	GULLEYED	DEEHNORR	DEERHORN
DEEFHINT	HINDFEET	DEEGGRRU	RUGGEDER	DEEGLNOR	GOLDENER		DEHORNER
DEEFHLOR	FREEHOLD	DEEGGQSU	SQUEGGED	DEEGLNOU	ENGOULED	DEEHNORT	DETHRONE
DEEFHLRS	FELDSHER	DEEGHHIR	HIGHERED	DEEGLNOZ	LOZENGED		THRENODE
DEEFHORT	FOTHERED	DEEGHHSU	SHEUGHED	DEEGLNRY	LEGENDRY	DEEHNPRS	PREHENDS
DEEFIILN	FEDELINI	DEEGHHUW	WHEUGHED	DEEGLOPR	PLEDGEOR	DEEHNSTU	ENTHUSED
	LENIFIED	DEEGHILS	SLEIGHED	DEEGLOPS	DOGSLEEP	DEEHOORV	HOOVERED
DEEFIINT	DEFINITE	DEEGHIST	HEDGIEST	DEEGLORW	GLOWERED	DEEHOPRT	POTHERED
DEEFIIRS	DEIFIERS	DEEGHITW	WEIGHTED	DEEGLOSY	GOLDEYES	DEEHORRT	DEHORTER
	EDIFIERS	DEEGHNRU	HUNGERED	DEEGLPRS	PLEDGERS	DEEHORSU	REHOUSED
	FIRESIDE	DEEGHOPR	GOPHERED	DEEGLPST	PLEDGETS	DEEHORSW	SHOWERED
DEEFIIRV	VERIFIED	DEEGHOPS	SHEEPDOG	DEEGLRSS	SLEDGERS	DEEHORTT	HOTTERED
DEEFILLR	REFILLED	DEEGHORW	HEDGEROW	DEEGMNRU	DUNGMERE	DEEHORTX	EXHORTED
DEEFILLT	FILLETED	DEEGHOSW	HOGWEEDS	DEEGNNOS	ENDOGENS	DEEHRRSW	SHREWDER
DEEFILMS	MEDFLIES	DEEGHOTT	DOGTEETH	DEEGNNOY	ENDOGENY	DEEHRTUW	WUTHERED
DEEFILNX	INFLEXED	DEEGIINN	INDIGENE	DEEGNORV	GOVERNED	DEEIILRV	LIVERIED
DEEFILPR	PILFERED	DEEGIISS	DIEGESIS	DEEGNPRU	REPUGNED	DEEIILRW	WIELDIER
DEEFILRS	DEFILERS	DEEGIKST	KEDGIEST	DEEGNPUX	EXPUNGED	DEEIIMRS	DIMERISE
	FIELDERS	DEEGILMO	LIEGEDOM		EXPUNGED	DEEIIMRZ	DIMERIZE
DEEFILRT	FILTERED	DEEGILMP	IMPLEDGE	DEEGOSTU	OUTEDGES	DEEIIMST	ITEMISED
DEEFIMTU	TUMEFIED	DEEGILMT	GIMLETED	DEEGOTUW	GOUTWEED	DEEIIMTZ	ITEMIZED
DEEFINNR	INFERRED	DEEGILNN	NEEDLING	DEEGPRUX	EXPURGED	DEEIINST	DIETINES
DEEFINRS	DEFINERS	DEEGILNO	ELOIGNED	DEEGRRSU	RESURGED	DEEIINSX	ENDEIXIS
DEEFINRZ	FRENZIED		LEGIONED	DEEGRSTU	GESTURED	DEEIIPRS	EPEIRIDS
DEEFINSS	FINESSED	DEEGILNR	ENGIRDLE	DEEGRTTU	GUTTERED	DEEIIRSS	DIERESIS
DEEFINST	FENDIEST		LINGERED	DEEGSSTU	GUSSETED	DEEIIRST	SIDERITE
	INFESTED		REEDLING	DEEHHIRT	HITHERED	DEEIIRSV	DERISIVE
DEEFIORS	FORESIDE	DEEGILNS	SEEDLING	DEEHHNPY	HYPHENED	DEEIIRSW	WEIRDIES
DEEFIORT	FOETIDER	DEEGILNT	DELETING	DEEHHPRS	SHEPHERD	DEEIISSS	DISSEISE
DEEFIPRX	PREFIXED	DEEGILRS	LEIDGERS	DEEHHRST	THRESHED	DEEIISSW	SIDEWISE
DEEFIRRV	FERVIDER	DEEGILRW	WEREGILD	DEEHHRSU	HUSHERED	DEEIISSZ	DISSEIZE
DEEFIRTT	REFITTED	DEEGILRY	GREEDILY	DEEHIKRS	SHREIKED	DEEIJNNO	ENJOINED
DEEFISTT	FETIDEST	DEEGILST	GELIDEST		SHRIEKED	DEEIJNOR	REJOINED
DEEFLLNU	UNFELLED		LEDGIEST	DEEHIKSV	KHEDIVES	DEEIJRTT	JITTERED
DEEFLNOR	FORELEND	DEEGIMMR	IMMERGED	DEEHILNS	ENSHIELD	DEEIKKRY	YIKKERED
DEEFLNSU	UNSELFED	DEEGIMNN	EMENDING	DEEHILRS	RELISHED	DEEIKLLR	KILLDEER
DEEFLNTU	DEFLUENT	DEEGIMRU	DEMIURGE		SHIELDER	DEEIKLLS	KILLDEES
DEEFLORW	DEFLOWER	DEEGINNR	ENRINGED	DEEHILSV	DISHEVEL		SKELLIED
	FLOWERED	DEEGINNS	ENSIGNED	DEEHIMMS	IMMESHED	DEEIKLNN	ENKINDLE
	REFLOWED	DEEGINNT	TEENDING	DEEHIMNS	INMESHED		ENLINKED
DEEFLOST	FEEDLOTS	DEEGINNW	ENDEWING	DEEHIMRT	MITHERED	DEEIKLNR	REKINDLE
DEEFLPSU	SPEEDFUL	DEEGINOP	PIGEONED	DEEHINRR	HINDERER	DEEIKLNS	SILKENED
DEEFLRUX	REFLUXED	DEEGINPS	SPEEDING	DEEHINRS	DRISHEEN	DEEIKLSW	SILKWEED
DEEFMNOR	ENFORMED	DEEGINRS	DESIGNER	DEEHINST	DISTHENE	DEEIKNRS	DEERSKIN
DEEFMNOT	FOMENTED		ENERGIDS	DEEHINTW	WHITENED	DEEIKNRT	TINKERED
DEEFMORR	DEFORMER		REDESIGN	DEEHIORS	HEROISED	DEEIKNTT	KITTENED
	REFORMED		REEDINGS	DEEHIORZ	HEROIZED	DEEIKOSV	DOVEKIES
DEEFMORS	FREEDOMS		RESIGNED	DEEHIPRS	HESPERID	DEEIKPPR	KIPPERED
DEEFMPRU	PERFUMED	DEEGINSS	DINGESES		PERISHED	DEEIKRSU	DUKERIES
DEEFNORZ	DEFROZEN		EDGINESS	DEEHIRRS	REDSHIRE	DEEIKRSV	SKIVERED
DEEFNOST	SOFTENED		SDEIGNES	DEEHIRRT	DITHERER	DEEIKSTT	DISKETTE
DEEFNRRU	REFUNDER		SEEDINGS	DEEHIRSV	SHIVERED	DEEILLMP	IMPELLED
DEEFNSST	DEFTNESS	DEEGINST	INGESTED		SHRIEVED		MILLEPED
DEEFOORT	REFOOTED		SIGNETED	DEEHIRTW	WITHERED	DEEILLNO	NIELLOED
DEEFORST	DEFOREST		STEEDING	DEEHIRTY	HEREDITY	DEEILLOR	ORIELLED
	FORESTED	DEEGINSW	WEEDINGS	DEEHKNOS	KEESHOND	DEEILLPR	PERILLED
	FOSTERED	DEEGINSX	DESEXING	DEEHKNRU	HUNKERED	DEEILLRT	TILLERED
DEEFPRSU	PERFUSED	DEEGINZZ	GIZZENED	DEEHLLOR	HOLLERED		TREDILLE
DEEFRRTU	RETURFED	DEEGIORS	GEORDIES	DEEHLLOV	HOVELLED	DEEILLRV	RIVELLED
DEEGGHHO	HEDGEHOG	DEEGIOST	EGOTISED	DEEHLMMW	WHEMMLED	DEEILLWY	WILLEYED
DEEGGHIP	HEDGEPIG	DEEGIOTZ	EGOTIZED	DEEHLMNU	UNHELMED	DEEILMOS	MELODIES
DEEGGIJR	JIGGERED	DEEGIPSW	PIGWEEDS	DEEHLMSW	WELDMESH		MELODISE

Letters	Word
DEEILMOZ	MELODIZE
DEEILMPT	IMPLETED
DEEILNOS	ESLOINED
DEEILNOT	DELETION
	ENTOILED
DEEILNPP	LIPPENED
DEEILNRU	UNDERLIE
DEEILNSS	IDLENESS
	LINSEEDS
DEEILNST	ENLISTED
	LINTSEED
	LISTENED
DEEILNSY	DYELINES
DEEILNTT	ENTITLED
DEEILNUV	UNVEILED
DEEILOPT	LEPIDOTE
	PETIOLED
DEEILORT	DOLERITE
	LOITERED
DEEILOTT	TOILETED
DEEILPSS	SEEDLIPS
DEEILPST	EPISTLED
DEEILPSU	EPULIDES
DEEILPSY	SPEEDILY
DEEILRSU	LEISURED
DEEILRSV	DELIVERS
	DESILVER
	SILVERED
	SLIVERED
DEEILRSW	WIELDERS
DEEILRSY	YIELDERS
DEEILRTT	LITTERED
	RETITLED
DEEILRVY	DELIVERY
DEEILSSS	IDLESSES
DEEILSST	TIDELESS
DEEILSSV	DEVILESS
DEEILSTU	DILUTEES
DEEILSTV	DEVILETS
DEEILSUV	DELUSIVE
DEEILTUY	YULETIDE
DEEIMMNS	ENDEMISM
DEEIMMRS	IMMERSED
	SIMMERED
DEEIMMSS	MISDEEMS
DEEIMNOR	DOMINEER
DEEIMNOS	DEMONISE
DEEIMNOZ	DEMONIZE
DEEIMNPT	PEDIMENT
DEEIMNRR	REMINDER
DEEIMNRV	VERMINED
DEEIMNSS	DESMINES
	SIDESMEN
DEEIMNST	DEMENTIS
	SEDIMENT
DEEIMNTT	MITTENED
DEEIMOST	TEDISOME
DEEIMPRR	PERIDERM
	REPRIMED
DEEIMPRS	DEMIREPS
	PREMISED
	SIMPERED
DEEIMPRX	PREMIXED
DEEIMPSS	SEMIPEDS
DEEIMRSS	DERMISES
DEEIMRST	DEMERITS
	DEMISTER
	DIMETERS
	MISTERED
DEEIMRTT	REMITTED
DEEIMSSU	MEDIUSES
DEEINNRS	SINNERED
DEEINNRT	INDENTER
	INTENDER
	INTERNED
DEEINNRU	UNREINED
DEEINNRV	INNERVED
DEEINNST	DENTINES
	DESINENT
DEEINNSZ	DENIZENS
DEEINNTV	INVENTED
DEEINNTW	ENTWINED
DEEINNUV	UNENVIED
DEEINOPS	DISPONEE
DEEINORS	ORDINEES
DEEINORT	ORIENTED
DEEINPPR	NIPPERED
DEEINPSS	DISPENSE
	PIEDNESS
DEEINPST	PENTISED
DEEINPSU	UNESPIED
DEEINQRU	ENQUIRED
	INQUERED
DEEINRRT	INTERRED
	TRENDIER
DEEINRRV	REDRIVEN
DEEINRST	INSERTED
	RESIDENT
	SINTERED
	TRENDIES
DEEINRSU	UREDINES
DEEINRSV	INVERSED
DEEINRSW	WIDENERS
DEEINRSX	INDEXERS
DEEINRTU	REUNITED
DEEINRTV	INVERTED
DEEINRTW	WINTERED
DEEINRTX	DEXTRINE
DEEINSST	DESTINES
DEEINSSV	VENDISES
DEEINSSW	DEWINESS
	WIDENESS
DEEINSTT	DINETTES
DEEINSTU	DETINUES
DEEINSTV	EVIDENTS
	INVESTED
DEEINSUZ	UNSEIZED
DEEINTUV	DUVETINE
DEEINUVW	UNVIEWED
DEEIOPRT	PERIDOTE
DEEIOPRX	PEROXIDE
DEEIOPSS	EPISODES
DEEIOPST	EPIDOTES
	POETISED
DEEIOPSX	EPOXIDES
DEEIOPTZ	POETIZED
DEEIORRV	OVERRIDE
DEEIORSV	OVERSIDE
DEEIORTU	ETOURDIE
DEEIOTVX	VIDEOTEX
DEEIPPQU	EQUIPPED
DEEIPPRZ	ZIPPERED
DEEIPPST	PEPTIDES
	PEPTISED
DEEIPPTT	PIPETTED
DEEIPPTZ	PEPTIZED
DEEIPQRU	REPIQUED
DEEIPQTU	PIQUETED
DEEIPRRS	REPRISED
	RESPIRED
DEEIPRRT	TREPIDER
DEEIPRRV	REPRIVED
DEEIPRRZ	REPRIZED
DEEIPRSS	DESPISER
	DISPERSE
	PRESIDES
DEEIPRST	PRIESTED
	RESPITED
DEEIPRSU	DUPERIES
DEEIPRSV	DEPRIVES
	PREVISED
DEEIPRTT	PITTERED
DEEIPRTX	EXTIRPED
DEEIPSSS	DESPISES
DEEIPSST	DESPITES
DEEIPSTT	TEPIDEST
DEEIPSTU	DEPUTIES
	DEPUTISE
DEEIPTUZ	DEPUTIZE
DEEIQRRU	REQUIRED
DEEIQRTU	REQUITED
DEEIQRUV	QUIVERED
DEEIQTUU	QUIETUDE
DEEIRRSS	DERRISES
	DESIRERS
	DRESSIER
	RESIDERS
DEEIRRST	DESTRIER
DEEIRRSU	RUDERIES
DEEIRRSV	REDRIVES
DEEIRRTV	VERDITER
DEEIRRWW	WIREDREW
DEEIRRZZ	RIZZERED
DEEIRSST	EDITRESS
	RESISTED
	SISTERED
DEEIRSSU	DIURESES
	REISSUED
	RESIDUES
DEEIRSSV	DEVISERS
	DISSERVE
	DISSEVER
	DIVERSES
DEEIRSTT	TIREDEST
DEEIRSTU	ERUDITES
	SURETIED
DEEIRSTW	WEIRDEST
DEEIRTTT	TITTERED
DEEIRTTV	RIVETTED
DEEIRTTW	WITTERED
DEEISSSU	DISEUSES
DEEISTTV	VIDETTES
DEEJKNTU	JUNKETED
DEEJPRRU	PERJURED
DEEJPTTU	UPJETTED
DEEKLNOS	SLOKENED
DEEKLNST	SKLENTED
DEEKLRSS	SKELDERS
DEEKMNOY	MONKEYED
DEEKNNNU	UNKENNED
DEEKNOTW	KNOTWEED
DEEKNOTY	KEYNOTED
DEEKORRW	REWORKED
DEEKRUVY	KURVEYED
DEELLMOR	MODELLER
DEELLMOW	MELLOWED
DEELLNOP	POLLENED
DEELLNOR	ENROLLED
DEELLORW	ROWELLED
DEELLORY	YODELLER
DEELLOTW	TOWELLED
DEELLOTX	EXTOLLED
DEELLOVV	VOWELLED
DEELLOVY	VOLLEYED
DEELLOWY	YELLOWED
DEELLPUW	UPWELLED
DEELLRSU	DUELLERS
DEELLRSW	DWELLERS
DEELLSSW	WELDLESS
DEELLSUX	DUXELLES
DEELMMPU	EMPLUMED
DEELMNOO	MELODEON
DEELMNOS	LODESMEN
DEELMNTU	UNMELTED
DEELMNTW	WELDMENT
DEELMOOS	DOLESOME
DEELMOPR	EMPOLDER
DEELMOPY	EMPLOYED
DEELMORS	REMODELS
DEELMOST	MOLESTED
DEELMOSU	DUELSOME
DEELMPSU	DEPLUMES
DEELMRUY	DEMURELY
DEELNOOS	LOOSENED
DEELNORT	REDOLENT
DEELNORV	OVERLEND
DEELNOSS	LESSONED
DEELNOSU	ENSOULED
DEELNOSY	ESLOYNED
DEELNPRS	RESPLEND
DEELNRTU	UNDERLET
DEELNRTY	TENDERLY
DEELNSSW	LEWDNESS
DEELNSTY	ENSTYLED
DEELOORT	RETOOLED
DEELOPPR	LOPPERED
DEELOPRS	DEPLORES
DEELOPRX	EXPLODER
	EXPLORED
DEELOPRY	REDEPLOY
DEELOPSV	DEVELOPS
DEELOPSX	EXPLODES
DEELORRS	SOLDERER
DEELORSU	URODELES
DEELORSV	RESOLVED
DEELORTT	DOTTEREL
	TOLTERED
DEELORTV	REVOLTED
DEELORTY	DELETORY
DEELORUV	LOUVERED
DEELORVV	REVOLVED
DEELOSSU	DELOUSES
DEELOSTV	DOVELETS
DEELOSVV	DEVOLVES
DEELOTUV	EVOLUTED
DEELPPRU	REPULPED
DEELPRSS	SPELDERS
DEELPRSU	PRELUDES
	REPULSED
DEELPRTU	DRUPELET
DEELPRUV	PULVERED
DEELPSUX	DUPLEXES
	EXPULSED
DEELPTTY	PETTEDLY
DEELRSTU	LUSTERED
	RESULTED
	ULSTERED
DEELRSTW	LEWDSTER
	WRESTLED

DEELRSTY RESTYLED	DEENRRTU RETURNED	DEERRTTU TURRETED	DEFIILNS INFIDELS
DEEMMORS MESODERM	DEENRSSU RUDENESS	DEERRTUX EXTRUDER	INFIELDS
DEEMMRRU DUMMERER	DEENRSTU DENTURES	DEERSSST DESSERTS	DEFIILRW WILDFIRE
DEEMMRSU SUMMERED	SEDERUNT	STRESSED	DEFIILSU FLUIDISE
DEEMNNRU UNDERMEN	UNDERSET	DEERSSSU DURESSES	DEFIILTY FIDELITY
DEEMNNTU TENENDUM	UNDESERT	DEERSSTU RUSSETED	DEFIILUZ FLUIDIZE
DEEMNOOS MOONSEED	DEENRSUU UNDERUSE	DEERSSTY DYESTERS	DEFIIMNO OMNIFIED
DEEMNOQU QUEENDOM	DEENRSUV UNVERSED	DEERSSUV SUVERSED	DEFIIMNU MUNIFIED
DEEMNORR MODERNER	DEENRTUV VENTURED	DEERSTUV VESTURED	DEFIIMOR MODIFIER
DEEMNORS SERMONED	DEENSSSY SYNDESES	DEERSTUX EXTRUDES	DEFIIMOS MODIFIES
DEEMNORT ENTODERM	DEENSTTU UNTESTED	DEERSUVW SURVEWED	DEFIIMRS MISFIRED
DEEMNOSS DEMONESS	DEENTTUW UNWETTED	DEERSUVY SURVEYED	DEFIIMSS FIDEISMS
ENMOSSED	DEENTUVY DUVETYNE	DEERTTUX TEXTURED	DEFIIMSW MIDWIFES
DEEMNOUY EUDEMONY	DEEOORRV OVERDOER	DEFFHILW WHIFFLED	DEFIINOT NOTIFIED
DEEMOORT ODOMETER	OVERRODE	DEFFHLSU SHUFFLED	DEFIINTU FINITUDE
DEEMOPPY POMPEYED	DEEOORSV OVERDOES	DEFFHORS SHROFFED	DEFIINTY IDENTIFY
DEEMOPRV PREMOVED	OVERDOSE	DEFFILNS SNIFFLED	DEFIIOSS OSSIFIED
DEEMOPST DEEPMOST	DEEOPPST ESTOPPED	DEFFILOV FIVEFOLD	DEFIIOTV VIDEOFIT
DEEMOQRU QUEERDOM	DEEOPRRR PREORDER	DEFFIORS OFFSIDER	DEFIIPRU PURIFIED
DEEMORST MODESTER	DEEOPRRS PEDREROS	DEFFIOSS OFFSIDES	DEFIIPSS FISSIPED
DEEMORSX EXODERMS	DEEOPRRT REPORTED	DEFFIRSU DIFFUSER	DEFIIPTY TYPIFIED
DEEMORTU MOUTERED	DEEOPRRV REPROVED	DEFFISSU DIFFUSES	DEFIIRRT DRIFTIER
UDOMETER	DEEOPRSS DEPOSERS	DEFFISUX SUFFIXED	DEFILLNU UNFILLED
DEEMPRST DEMPSTER	DEEOPRSS POSTERED	DEFFLNSU SNUFFLED	DEFILLPU UPFILLED
DEEMPRSU PRESUMED	REEDSTOP	DEFFLRTU TRUFFLED	DEFILMNU FULMINED
DEEMPRTU PERMUTED	REPOSTED	DEFFNORS FORFENDS	UNFILMED
DEEMRRRU DEMURRER	DEEOPRTT POTTERED	DEFFSSUU SUFFUSED	DEFILNNO NINEFOLD
MURDERER	REPOTTED	DEFFSTUY DYESTUFF	DEFILNRS FLINDERS
DEEMRSTU DEMUREST	DEEOPRTW POWTERED	DEFGGILN FLEDGING	DEFILNRU UNRIFLED
MUSTERED	DEEOPRTX EXPORTED	DEFGHILT FLIGHTED	URNFIELD
DEEMRTTU MUTTERED	DEEOPRUZ DOUZEPER	DEFGHIRT FRIGHTED	DEFILNRY FRIENDLY
DEEMSSTY SYSTEMED	DEEOPSST POSSETED	DEFGIILN DEFILING	DEFILOPR PROFILED
DEENNNOP PENNONED	DEEOPSSU ESPOUSED	FIELDING	DEFILORR FLORIDER
DEENNNPU UNPENNED	DEEOQRTU REQUOTED	DEFGIILU UGLIFIED	DEFILORU FLUORIDE
DEENNOPT DEPONENT	ROQUETED	DEFGIINN DEFINING	DEFILOTU OUTFIELD
DEENNOPU UNOPENED	DEEORRRS ORDERERS	DEFGIINY DEIFYING	DEFILPRU PRIDEFUL
DEENNORS ENDERONS	REORDERS	EDIFYING	DEFILPTU UPLIFTED
DEENNORW RENOWNED	DEEORRRV VERDEROR	DEFGIIRR FRIGIDER	DEFILRRU FLURRIED
DEENNOSS DONENESS	DEEORRST RESORTED	DEFGILNU INGULFED	DEFILRVY FERVIDLY
DEENNOST SONNETED	RESTORED	DEFGILTY GIFTEDLY	DEFILRZZ FRIZZLED
DEENNOSY DOYENNES	ROSTERED	DEFGINSU DEFUSING	DEFIMNOR INFORMED
DEENNPST PENDENTS	DEEORRSV OVERREDS	FEUDINGS	DEFIMORY REMODIFY
DEENNRTU UNTENDER	DEEORRTT RETORTED	DEFGINTU UNGIFTED	DEFIMRRU DRUMFIRE
DEENNRUV UNNERVED	DEEORRTU REROUTED	DEFGINUZ DEFUZING	DEFINNRU REINFUND
DEENNSSU NUDENESS	RETOURED	DEFGIOOW GOODWIFE	UNFRIEND
UNSENSED	DEEORRUV DEVOURER	DEFGIORS FIREDOGS	DEFINOPR FORPINED
DEENNSTU UNNESTED	DEEORRVW OVERDREW	DEFGJORU FORJUDGE	DEFINORW FOREWIND
DEENNTTU UNNETTED	DEEORSST OERSTEDS	DEFGNORU UNFORGED	DEFINSTU UNSIFTED
UNTENTED	DEEORSTT ROSETTED	DEFGOOSX DOGFOXES	DEFINTTU UNFITTED
DEENNTUV UNVENTED	TETRODES	DEFHIIMU HUMIFIED	DEFIOORW FIREWOOD
DEENOORT ENROOTED	DEEORSTX DEXTROSE	DEFHIINS FIENDISH	DEFIOPRT PROFITED
DEENOORV OVERDONE	DEEORSTY STOREYED	FINISHED	DEFIORSU FOUDRIES
DEENOPRR PONDERER	DEEORSUV OVERUSED	DEFHILLO LIFEHOLD	DEFIOTXY DETOXIFY
DEENOPSS SPONDEES	DEEORSVY OVERDYES	DEFHILSS DISFLESH	DEFIRRST DRIFTERS
DEENOPST PENTODES	DEEORTTT TOTTERED	DEFHINSU UNFISHED	DEFIRSSU FISSURED
DEENORRS ENDORSER	DEEORTTX EXTORTED	DEFHIOOW WIFEHOOD	DEFISSTU FEUDISTS
DEENORRW WONDERER	DEEORTUV DEVOUTER	DEFHLOOS ELFHOODS	DEFKLORY FORKEDLY
DEENORSS ENDORSES	DEEOSSUX EXODUSES	SELFHOOD	DEFLLOOR FOLDEROL
DEENORST ERODENTS	DEEOSTUW OUTWEEDS	DEFHLOSU FLOUSHED	DEFLLOOW FOLLOWED
DEENORSW ENDOWERS	DEEOSTUX TUXEDOES	DEFHOOOR FORHOOED	DEFLMPRU FRUMPLED
WORSENED	DEEPPRSU SUPPERED	DEFHOORS SERFHOOD	DEFLNOOU UNFOOLED
DEENORTU DEUTERON	DEEPRRSU PERDURES	DEFHOORW FORHOWED	DEFLNOPS PENFOLDS
DEENOSSS ENDOSSES	DEEPRRVY REPRYVED	DEFIIILV VILIFIED	DEFLNORS FONDLERS
DEENOSST STENOSED	DEEPRSTU PERTUSED	DEFIIIMN MINIFIED	FORLENDS
DEENPPRS PERPENDS	DEEPRSUW PURSEWED	DEFIIINS NIDIFIES	DEFLNORU FLOUNDER
DEENPRSS SPENDERS	DEEPRSUY PSEUDERY	DEFIIIVV VIVIFIED	UNFOLDER
DEENPRST PRETENDS	DEEPRTTU PUTTERED	DEFIILLN INFILLED	DEFLNRUU UNFURLED
DEENRRSU ENDURERS	DEEPRUVY PURVEYED	DEFIILLP FILLIPED	DEFLNSSU FUNDLESS
SUNDERER	DEERRSSS DRESSERS	DEFIILLW WILDLIFE	DEFLOORS FORSLOED
	DEERRSUV VERDURES	DEFIILMS MISFILED	DEFLOORT FORETOLD

DEFLOORV	OVERFOLD
DEFLOOSS	FOODLESS
DEFLOPUW	UPFLOWED
DEFLORSU	FOULDERS
DEFLPRUU	UPFURLED
DEFLRSUU	SULFURED
DEFMNORU	UNFORMED
DEFMOOOR	FOREDOOM
DEFMORSS	SERFDOMS
DEFNNORT	FRONDENT
DEFNNOSS	FONDNESS
DEFNOORS	FRONDOSE
DEFNOORU	UNROOFED
DEFNOORV	OVERFOND
DEFNOOTU	UNFOOTED
DEFNOPRS	FORSPEND
DEFNORRU	FRONDEUR
DEFNORSU	FOUNDERS
	REFOUNDS
DEFNORTU	FORTUNED
DEFNOSSW	DOWFNESS
DEFNRRUU	UNDERFUR
	UNFURRED
DEFNRTUU	UNTURFED
DEFOORRW	FOREWORD
DEFOOTUX	OUTFOXED
DEFORRUW	FURROWED
DEFORSST	DEFROSTS
DEFORSTW	FROWSTED
DEGGGIIT	GIGGITED
DEGGGILN	GLEDGING
DEGGHINS	HEDGINGS
DEGGHLOS	SHOGGLED
DEGGHRSU	SHRUGGED
DEGGIINN	DEIGNING
DEGGILNP	PLEDGING
DEGGILNS	GELDINGS
	SLEDGING
	SNIGGLED
DEGGILNU	DELUGING
DEGGILRW	WRIGGLED
DEGGINNU	UNEDGING
DEGGINRU	UNRIGGED
DEGGINSW	WEDGINGS
DEGGINUW	UNWIGGED
DEGGIORS	DISGORGE
DEGGIOST	DOGGIEST
DEGGIPRS	SPRIGGED
DEGGIRST	STRIGGED
DEGGLMSU	SMUGGLED
DEGGLNSU	SNUGGLED
DEGGLORS	DOGGRELS
DEGGLRUY	RUGGEDLY
DEGGNORU	UNGORGED
DEGGNOSU	GUDGEONS
DEGGRRSU	DRUGGERS
DEGGRSTU	DRUGGETS
DEGHIILL	GHILLIED
DEGHIINS	DINGHIES
DEGHIKNT	KNIGHTED
DEGHILNS	HINDLEGS
	SHINGLED
DEGHILOU	OUGHLIED
DEGHILPT	PLIGHTED
DEGHILST	DELIGHTS
	SLIGHTED
DEGHINNS	SHENDING
DEGHINNU	UNHINGED
DEGHIOOS	SHOOGIED
DEGHIOPS	DOGESHIP

DEGHIORU	DOUGHIER
DEGHIPST	DESPIGHT
	SPIGHTED
DEGHIQTU	QUIGHTED
DEGHITTW	TWIGHTED
DEGHLNOR	HORNGELD
DEGHLOOS	DOGHOLES
	GOLOSHED
	SHOOGLED
DEGHLOPU	PLOUGHED
DEGHLOSU	SLOUGHED
DEGHMOSU	GUMSHOED
DEGHMPRU	GRUMPHED
DEGHNORT	THRONGED
DEGHNORY	HYDROGEN
DEGHORRS	DROGHERS
DEGHPSUU	UPGUSHED
DEGIIIRS	RIGIDISE
DEGIIIRZ	RIGIDIZE
DEGIIIST	DIGITISE
DEGIIITZ	DIGITIZE
DEGIILNR	GRIDELIN
DEGIILNS	EILDINGS
	SIDELING
DEGIILNT	DILIGENT
DEGIILNV	DEVILING
DEGIILNW	WIELDING
DEGIILNY	YIELDING
DEGIILTY	GELIDITY
DEGIIMNP	IMPEDING
	IMPINGED
DEGIIMNS	DEMISING
DEGIIMSU	MISGUIDE
DEGIINNR	NIDERING
DEGIINNS	DESINING
	SDEINING
DEGIINNT	ENDITING
	INDIGENT
	TEINDING
DEGIINNW	INDEWING
	WIDENING
DEGIINNX	INDEXING
DEGIINNZ	DIZENING
DEGIINOS	INDIGOES
DEGIINOV	VIDEOING
DEGIINRS	DESIRING
	RESIDING
	RINGSIDE
DEGIINRT	DIRIGENT
DEGIINRV	DERIVING
	VIRGINED
DEGIINRW	WEIRDING
DEGIINST	DINGIEST
	INDIGEST
DEGIINSV	DEVISING
DEGIIRST	RIDGIEST
	RIGIDEST
DEGIISSU	DISGUISE
DEGIJMSU	MISJUDGE
DEGIKKNO	DEKKOING
DEGIKLNU	DUKELING
DEGIKNNU	UNKINGED
DEGILLNU	DUELLING
DEGILLNW	DWELLING
DEGILMPS	GLIMPSED
DEGILNNO	OLDENING
DEGILNNS	LENDINGS
DEGILNOP	DIPLOGEN
DEGILNOS	GLENOIDS
	SIDELONG

DEGILNPS	SPELDING
DEGILNRU	INDULGER
DEGILNRY	YELDRING
DEGILNSU	INDULGES
DEGILNSV	DEVLINGS
DEGILNSW	SWINGLED
	WELDINGS
DEGILNWY	WINGEDLY
DEGILOOR	GOODLIER
DEGILOOY	IDEOLOGY
DEGILOST	GODLIEST
	GOLDIEST
DEGILOSZ	GOLDSIZE
DEGILPSU	PULSIDGE
DEGILRRS	GIRDLERS
DEGILRSU	GUILDERS
	SLUDGIER
DEGILRSW	WERGILDS
DEGILRZZ	GRIZZLED
DEGILSUV	DIVULGES
DEGIMNNS	MENDINGS
DEGIMNOS	SMIDGEON
DEGIMNOT	DEMOTING
DEGIMNPU	IMPUGNED
DEGIMNRU	DEMURING
DEGIMNSS	SMIDGENS
DEGIMOOT	GOODTIME
DEGIMOOY	GEOMYOID
DEGIMRSU	SMUDGIER
DEGINNNU	UNENDING
DEGINNOP	DEPONING
DEGINNOT	DENOTING
DEGINNOW	ENDOWING
DEGINNOZ	DOZENING
DEGINNPS	SPENDING
DEGINNRT	TRENDING
DEGINNRU	ENDURING
	UNRINGED
DEGINNSS	SENDINGS
DEGINNST	STENDING
DEGINNSU	UNSIGNED
DEGINNSY	DESYNING
DEGINNTU	UNTINGED
DEGINNUW	UNWINGED
DEGINOPR	PROIGNED
DEGINOPS	DEPOSING
	DISPONGE
	PIDGEONS
DEGINORR	ORDERING
DEGINORS	NEGROIDS
DEGINORU	GUERIDON
DEGINORV	DOVERING
DEGINORW	DOWERING
DEGINOSW	WENDIGOS
	WIDGEONS
DEGINOTV	DEVOTING
DEGINPRS	SPRINGED
DEGINPRY	PREDYING
DEGINPSU	DISPUNGE
DEGINPTU	DEPUTING
DEGINRRS	GRINDERS
	REGRINDS
DEGINRRY	GRINDERY
DEGINRSS	DRESSING
DEGINRST	STRINGED
DEGINRSW	REDWINGS
DEGINRSY	SYNERGID
	SYRINGED
DEGINSSU	DINGUSES
DEGINSSW	SWINDGES

DEGINSTU	DUNGIEST
DEGINTTU	DUETTING
DEGIOORS	GOODSIRE
DEGIOOST	GOODIEST
DEGIOPRR	PORRIDGE
DEGIOPSS	GOSSIPED
DEGIOPST	PODGIEST
DEGIORRU	GOURDIER
DEGIORST	STODGIER
DEGIPSTU	PUDGIEST
DEGIQSSU	SQUIDGES
DEGIRSTU	DURGIEST
DEGISSST	DISGESTS
DEGJMNTU	JUDGMENT
DEGLLNOY	GOLDENLY
DEGLLOOP	GOLLOPED
DEGLLOSS	GOLDLESS
DEGLMNOT	LODGMENT
DEGLMOOY	DEMOLOGY
DEGLNOUV	UNGLOVED
DEGLNRTU	GRUNTLED
DEGLOOPY	PEDOLOGY
DEGLOOUU	DUOLOGUE
DEGLOPRS	PLEDGORS
DEGLOPSS	SPLODGES
DEGLPRSU	SPLURGED
DEGMMNUU	UNGUMMED
DEGMRSSU	SMUDGERS
DEGNNORU	GROUNDEN
DEGNNOSU	DUNGEONS
DEGNNOUW	UNGOWNED
DEGNOORS	DRONGOES
DEGNOOSS	GOODNESS
DEGNOOST	STEGODON
DEGNOPPU	OPPUGNED
DEGNORRU	GROUNDER
	REGROUND
DEGNORSU	GUERDONS
DEGNORTU	TRUDGEON
DEGNORUU	UNROUGED
DEGNORYY	GYRODYNE
DEGNPRUU	UNPURGED
DEGNRSTU	TRUDGENS
DEGORSST	STODGERS
DEGORSTU	DROGUETS
DEGPRSUU	UPSURGED
DEGRRSTU	TRUDGERS
DEHHILTW	WITHHELD
DEHHISTW	WHISHTED
DEHHMRTY	RHYTHMED
DEHHOOSW	WHOOSHED
DEHIILLS	HILLSIDE
DEHIILLW	WHILLIED
DEHIILSV	DEVILISH
DEHIIMMS	SHIMMIED
DEHIIMNS	MINISHED
DEHIIMRU	MUDIRIEH
DEHIIMST	DITHEISM
	SMITHIED
DEHIINNS	SHINNIED
DEHIINNW	WHINNIED
DEHIINSS	SHINDIES
DEHIIRRW	WHIRRIED
DEHIIRST	DISHERIT
DEHIISST	DISHIEST
DEHIISTT	DITHEIST
	STITHIED
DEHIJMNO	DEMIJOHN
DEHIKMOS	SHEIKDOM
DEHIKPSU	DUKESHIP

DEHILLOP PHELLOID	DEHMMRTU THRUMMED	DEIIMMRS DIMERISM	DEIISSTT DIETISTS
DEHILLRS SHRILLED	DEHMNOOY HOMODYNE	DEIIMMST MISTIMED	DEIISTVV VIVIDEST
DEHILLRT THRILLED	DEHMNRUY UNRHYMED	DEIIMMTT IMMITTED	DEIISTZZ DIZZIEST
DEHILMOS DEMOLISH	DEHMOORW WHOREDOM	DEIIMNOS DOMINIES	DEIJNORS JOINDERS
DEHILMPW WHIMPLED	DEHMOOSS SHMOOSED	DEIIMNRT DIRIMENT	DEIJNSSU DISJUNES
DEHILMSS DISHELMS	DEHMOOST SMOOTHED	DEIIMNTU MUTINIED	DEIKKLNO KLONDIKE
DEHILMTY DIMETHYL	DEHMOOSZ SHMOOZED	DEIIMPRU PERIDIUM	DEIKLLSS DESKILLS
DEHILNOR INHOLDER	DEHMOPRY HYPODERM	DEIIMSST MISDIETS	DEIKLMMS SKLIMMED
DEHILNPY DIPHENYL	DEHMORUU HUMOURED	DEIIMSTT TIMIDEST	DEIKLMNU UNMILKED
DEHILOOR HELIODOR	DEHNNTUU UNHUNTED	DEIIMSVW MIDWIVES	DEIKLNNU UNLINKED
DEHILOOS DHOOLIES	DEHNOOPU UNHOOPED	DEIINNOP PINIONED	DEIKLNRS KINDLERS
DEHILOPS POLISHED	DEHNOORU HONOURED	DEIINNPP PINNIPED	DEIKLNRW WRINKLED
DEHILPSU SULPHIDE	DEHNOOSW HOEDOWNS	DEIINNTW INTWINED	DEIKLNSS KINDLESS
DEHILPSY SYLPHIDE	DEHNOPSY SYPHONED	DEIINNUV UNDIVINE	DEIKLNTW TWINKLED
DEHILRTW WRITHLED	DEHNORSU ENSHROUD	DEIINORS DERISION	DEIKLSTT SKITTLED
DEHILSTW WHISTLED	UNHORSED	IRONISED	DEIKMOSY MISYOKED
DEHILTTW WHITTLED	DEHNORSY ENHYDROS	RESINOID	DEIKMPRS SKRIMPED
DEHIMNOS HEDONISM	DEHNORTY THRENODY	DEIINORZ IRONIZED	DEIKNNPU UNPINKED
DEHIMORS HEIRDOMS	DEHNOSTZ DOZENTHS	DEIINOST EDITIONS	DEIKNNRU UNKINDER
DEHIMOSS DISHOMES	DEHNOSUU UNHOUSED	SEDITION	DEIKNNSS KINDNESS
DEHIMPRS SHRIMPED	DEHNRSTU THUNDERS	DEIINOSV VISIONED	DEIKNORV OVERKIND
DEHIMPSY DEMYSHIP	DEHNRTUY THUNDERY	DEIINPPW WINDPIPE	DEIKNORW INWORKED
DEHIMSTU HUMIDEST	DEHOOOPP POPEHOOD	DEIINPRS INSPIRED	DEIKNRRS DRINKERS
DEHIMSTY MYTHISED	DEHOOPRT THEROPOD	DEIINPRT INTREPID	DEIKNRSS REDSKINS
DEHIMTYZ MYTHIZED	DEHOOSSW SWOOSHED	DEIINPRY PYRIDINE	DEIKNSSU UNKISSED
DEHINOOP INHOOPED	DEHOPRST POTSHERD	DEIINPTU UNPITIED	DEIKORSS DROSKIES
DEHINOPR NEPHROID	DEHORRST REDSHORT	DEIINQRU INQUIRED	DEIKOSSY DISYOKES
DEHINOPS DIPHONES	DEHORTUY OUTHYRED	DEIINQSU QUINSIED	DEIKPRSU SPRUIKED
SIPHONED	DEHOSSTU STOUSHED	SQUINIED	DEIKRRSU SKURRIED
SPHENOID	DEHPRSSU SPRUSHED	DEIINRSS INDRISES	DEIKSSTU DUSKIEST
DEHINORS HORDEINS	DEHPRSUU UPRUSHED	INSIDERS	DEILLMNU UNMILLED
DEHINOST HEDONIST	DEHRSTTU THRUSTED	DEIINRST DISINTER	DEILLNSW INDWELLS
DEHINPSS ENDSHIPS	DEIIIMST DIMITIES	INDITERS	DEILLNTU UNTILLED
DEHINPSU PUNISHED	DEIIINSV DIVINISE	NITRIDES	DEILLNUW UNWILLED
DEHINSUW UNWISHED	DEIIINVZ DIVINIZE	RINDIEST	DEILLOOV LIVELOOD
DEHIOOVW WIVEHOOD	DEIIIRSS IRIDISES	DEIINRSU DISINURE	DEILLOPW PILLOWED
DEHIOPRS SPHEROID	DEIIIRSZ IRIDIZES	URIDINES	DEILLORR LORDLIER
DEHIOPRT TROPHIED	DEIIIRTV VIRIDITE	DEIINRSV DIVINERS	DEILLORS DOLLIERS
DEHIORRR HORRIDER	DEIIISVV DIVISIVE	DEIINRTU UNTIDIER	DEILLOSV LIVELODS
DEHIORSS DISHORSE	DEIIKLMS MISLIKED	DEIINSST INSISTED	DEILLOWW WILLOWED
HIDROSES	DEIIKLNR KINDLIER	TIDINESS	DEILLRRS DRILLERS
DEHIORTU OUTHIRED	DEIIKLNS DISLIKEN	DEIINSTU DISUNITE	DEILLRSV DREVILLS
DEHIORTW WORTHIED	DEIIKLNV DEVILKIN	NUDITIES	DEILLSTU DUELLIST
DEHIORTY THYREOID	DEIIKLSS DISLIKES	UNITISED	DULLIEST
DEHIOSSU DISHOUSE	DEIIKNST DINKIEST	UNTIDIES	DEILMNOO MELODION
DEHIOSTU HIDEOUTS	DEIILLMP MILLIPED	DEIINSTV DIVINEST	DEILMNSS MILDNESS
DEHIPSSU PSEUDISH	DEIILLMT TIDEMILL	DEIINSTW WINDIEST	MINDLESS
DEHIQSSU SQUISHED	DEIILLST DILLIEST	DEIINTTU INTUITED	DEILMNSU MUSLINED
DEHIRRSU DHURRIES	DEIILMPR DIMPLIER	DEIINTTY IDENTITY	DEILMOOT DOLOMITE
DEHIRSTT THIRSTED	DEIILMRU DELIRIUM	DEIINTUZ UNITIZED	DEILMOPR IMPLORED
THRISTED	DEIILMST DELIMITS	DEIIOPRS PRESIDIO	IMPOLDER
DEHIRTWW WITHDREW	LIMITEDS	DEIIOPRT DIPTEROI	DEILMOPS IMPLODES
DEHKLNOU ELKHOUND	DEIILMSV DEVILISM	DEIIOPZZ PEZIZOID	DEILMORU LEMUROID
DEHKNOOU UNHOOKED	MISLIVED	DEIIORST DIORITES	MOULDIER
DEHLLOOW HOLLOWED	DEIILNNU INDULINE	DEIIORSX OXIDISER	DEILMOST MELODIST
DEHLLOPY PHYLLODE	DEIILNOS LIONISED	DEIIORTX TRIOXIDE	DEILMOSU EMULSOID
DEHLMMOW WHOMMLED	DEIILNOZ LIONIZED	DEIIORTY IODYRITE	DEILMPPU PLUMIPED
DEHLMMUW WHUMMLED	DEIILNPV VILIPEND	DEIIORXZ OXIDIZER	DEILMPSU DISPLUME
DEHLMORY HYDROMEL	DEIILNVY DIVINELY	DEIIOSSX OXIDISES	DEILMPTU MULTIPED
DEHLOORV HOLDOVER	DEIILORS IDOLISER	DEIIOSXZ OXIDIZES	DEILMRRU DRUMLIER
OVERHOLD	DEIILORZ IDOLIZER	DEIIPPRR DRIPPIER	DEILMRSU MISRULED
DEHLOOSS HOODLESS	DEIILOSS IDOLISES	DEIIPPST DIPPIEST	DEILMSSY DEMISSLY
DEHLOPRU UPHOLDER	DEIILOSZ IDOLIZES	DEIIPRST RIPTIDES	DEILNNOT INDOLENT
DEHLOPSS SPLOSHED	DEIILPRT TRIPLIED	SPIRITED	DEILNOOS SOLENOID
DEHLORSU SHOULDER	DEIILRST REDISTIL	DEIIPRSZ DISPRIZE	DEILNORS DISENROL
DEHLPRUU UPHURLED	DEIILSTU UTILISED	DEIIPTTY TEPIDITY	DEILNOSS SONDELIS
DEHLRRSU HURDLERS	DEIILSTV LIVIDEST	DEIIQSTU DISQUIET	DEILNOSU DELUSION
DEHLRSWY SHREWDLY	DEIILTUY TUILYIED	DEIIRSSU DIURESIS	INSOULED
DEHLSTTU SHUTTLED	DEIILTUZ TUILZIED	DEIIRSTT DIRTIEST	UNSOILED
	UTILIZED	TRITIDES	DEILNOTU OUTLINED

```
DEILNOVV INVOLVED     DEIMNOST DEMONIST              SOURDINE              WORDIEST
DEILNPRS SPELDRIN     DEIMNOTW DOWNTIME     DEINORSW WINDORES     DEIORSWW WIDOWERS
DEILNPRU UNDERLIP     DEIMNPRU UNPRIMED              WINDROSE     DEIORTUV OUTDRIVE
DEILNPSS SPELDINS     DEIMNPSS MISSPEND     DEINORTT INTORTED     DEIOSSTU OUTSIDES
         SPINDLES     DEIMNPTU IMPUDENT     DEINORVW OVERWIND     DEIOSSTX EXODISTS
DEILNPST SPLINTED     DEIMNRTU RUDIMENT     DEINOSST DONSIEST     DEIOSTTT DOTTIEST
DEILNRSS RINDLESS     DEIMNSSS MISSENDS     DEINOSSV VOIDNESS     DEIOSTUZ OUTSIZED
DEILNRST SNIRTLED     DEIMNSST MINDSETS     DEINOSSZ DOZINESS     DEIPPRST STRIPPED
         TENDRILS     DEIMNSSU UNMISSED     DEINOSTU OUNDIEST     DEIPRRTU IRRUPTED
         TRINDLES     DEIMNSSW MISWENDS     DEINOSTW DOWNIEST              PUTRIDER
DEILNRSW SWINDLER     DEIMNSTU MISTUNED     DEINOTTU DUETTINO     DEIPRSSU DISPURSE
DEILNSSV VILDNESS     DEIMOORS MOIDORES     DEINPPRU UNRIPPED              SUSPIRED
DEILNSSW SWINDLES     DEIMOOSS SODOMIES     DEINPPUZ UNZIPPED     DEIPRSTU DISPUTER
         WILDNESS              SODOMISE     DEINPRST SPRINTED              STUPIDER
         WINDLESS     DEIMOOST DOOMIEST     DEINPRSY INSPYRED     DEIPSSTU DISPUTES
DEILNSTU DILUENTS              MOODIEST     DEINPRTU TURNIPED              PUDSIEST
         INSULTED              SODOMITE     DEINPRUZ UNPRIZED     DEIPTTTU TITTUPED
         UNLISTED     DEIMOOSZ SODOMIZE     DEINPSST STIPENDS     DEIQRRSU SQUIRRED
DEILNTTU UNTITLED     DEIMOPRS PROMISED     DEINQSTU SQUINTED     DEIQRSTU SQUIRTED
DEILNTUY UNITEDLY     DEIMOPRT IMPORTED     DEINRRTU INTRUDER     DEIRRSTU STURDIER
DEILNUWY UNWIELDY     DEIMOPRV IMPROVED     DEINRRSU SUNDRIES     DEIRSSST DISSERTS
DEILOOPS POOLSIDE     DEIMORRR MIRRORED     DEINRSTT STRIDENT              DISTRESS
DEILOPPY POLYPIDE     DEIMORRS MISORDER              TRIDENTS     DEIRSSTU DIESTRUS
DEILOPRU PRELUDIO              MORRISED     DEINRSTU INTRUDES              DRUSIEST
DEILOPSS DESPOILS     DEIMORSS MISDOERS     DEINRSTX DEXTRINS              STUDIERS
         SOLIPEDS     DEIMORST MORTISED     DEINRTUW UNDERWIT              STURDIES
DEILOQRU LIQUORED     DEIMORSU DIMEROUS     DEINSSST DISNESTS     DEIRSSUY DYSURIES
DEILORSS SOLDIERS              ERODIUMS              DISSENTS     DEIRSTTU DETRITUS
DEILORST STOLIDER              SOREDIUM     DEINSSSY SYNDESIS     DEIRSTUX DRUXIEST
DEILORSU SOULDIER     DEIMORUX EXORDIUM     DEINSSTT DENTISTS     DEIRSUVV SURVIVED
DEILORSY SOLDIERY     DEIMOSST MODISTES     DEINSSTU DISTUNES     DEISSSTU SUDSIEST
DEILOSST SOLIDEST     DEIMOSTT DEMOTIST     DEINSTUU UNSUITED     DEISSTTU DUSTIEST
DEILOSSV DISSOLVE     DEIMPRST DIREMPTS     DEINTTUW UNWITTED     DEISTTTU DUETTIST
DEILOSTT DOILTEST     DEIMPSTU DUMPIEST     DEIOOPRR DROOPIER     DEJLOOOR JORDELOO
DEILOSTU SOLITUDE     DEIMQRSU SQUIRMED     DEIOORSW WOODSIER     DEJOOPPY POPJOYED
DEILOTUV OUTLIVED     DEIMRSSU SURMISED     DEIOOSTW WOODIEST     DEKKLNOY KLONDYKE
DEILPPRT TRIPPLED     DEIMRSUU RESIDUUM     DEIOOSVV VOIVODES     DEKLNOOU UNLOOKED
DEILPPST STIPPLED     DEINNNOU INNUENDO     DEIOOSWW WOIWODES     DEKLOOPU UPLOOKED
DEILPPSU SUPPLIED     DEINNNPU UNPINNED     DEIOPRRV PROVIDER     DEKLRSSU SKUDLERS
DEILPPTU PULPITED     DEINNNSU NUNDINES     DEIOPRSS DISPOSER     DEKLSTTU SKUTTLED
DEILPSTT SPLITTED     DEINNNTU UNTINNED              DROPSIES     DEKMPRSU SKRUMPED
DEILPSTU STIPULED     DEINNOOT NOONTIDE     DEIOPRST DIOPTERS     DEKNORUW UNWORKED
DEILPSUY SPULYIED     DEINNORS ENDIRONS              DIOPTRES     DEKNRSTU DRUNKEST
DEILPSUZ SPULZIED     DEINNORU UNIRONED              DIPTEROS     DEKNRSUY UNDERSKY
DEILPTTU UPTILTED     DEINNOWW WINNOWED              PERIDOTS     DEKNSSSU DUSKNESS
DEILRSTU DILUTERS     DEINNPRU UNDERPIN              PROTEIDS     DEKOOPRV PROVOKED
         LURIDEST     DEINNRUU UNINURED              RIPOSTED     DEKOOTWW KOWTOWED
DEILRSVY DIVERSLY     DEINNRUV UNDRIVEN     DEIOPRSV DISPROVE     DELLLOOP LOLLOPED
DEILRSZZ DRIZZLES     DEINNSTU DUNNIEST              PROVIDES     DELLMOSW SWELLDOM
DEILRTVY DEVILTRY              DUNNITES     DEIOPRSW DROPWISE     DELLNOPU UNPOLLED
DEILSSTY DISTYLES     DEINNTUW UNTWINED     DEIOPSSS DISPOSES     DELLNORU UNROLLED
         STYLISED     DEINOOPS POISONED     DEIOPSST DEPOSITS     DELLNORW ROWNDELL
DEILSTUY SEDULITY     DEINOOSZ OZONISED              TOPSIDES     DELLNPUU UNPULLED
DEILSTYZ STYLIZED     DEINOOTV DEVOTION     DEIORRRT TORRIDER     DELLNSSU DULLNESS
DEILSWZZ SWIZZLED     DEINOOZZ OZONIZED     DEIORRSS DROSSIER     DELLOPRS REDPOLLS
DEILTWZZ TWIZZLED     DEINOPPR PROPINED     DEIORRSW DROWSIER     DELLOPRU UPROLLED
DEIMMNOS DEMONISM     DEINOPPW DOWNPIPE     DEIORRSY DERISORY     DELLOPTU POLLUTED
DEIMMOST IMMODEST     DEINOPRS DISPONER     DEIORRTU OUTRIDER     DELLORRY DROLLERY
DEIMMPST MISDEMPT              POINDERS     DEIORRTW WORRITED     DELLORSS LORDLESS
DEIMMSTU DUMMIEST              PRISONED     DEIORRZZ RIZZORED     DELLORST DROLLEST
DEIMNNOS MISDONNE     DEINOPRV PROVINED     DEIORSSS DOSSIERS              STROLLED
DEIMNNOU UNMONIED     DEINOPRY PYRENOID     DEIORSST STEROIDS     DELLOSVW LOWVELDS
DEIMNNSU MINUENDS     DEINOPSS DISPONES     DEIORSSU DESIROUS     DELLOTUW OUTDWELL
DEIMNOOS DOMINOES              SPINODES     DEIORSSV DEVISORS     DELMNOOV NOVELDOM
         MONODIES     DEINOPSU UNPOISED     DEIORSTT DORTIEST     DELMNORY MODERNLY
DEIMNOOT DEMOTION     DEINOPTW DEWPOINT     DEIORSTU IODURETS     DELMNOSU UNSELDOM
         MOTIONED     DEINORSS INDORSES              OUTRIDES     DELMNOTW MELTDOWN
DEIMNOOX MONOXIDE              SORDINES              OUTSIDER     DELMNPUU PENDULUM
DEIMNOPT PIEDMONT     DEINORST DRONIEST              SUITORED              UNPLUMED
DEIMNORT DORMIENT     DEINORSU DOURINES     DEIORSTW ROWDIEST     DELMOOSW ELMWOODS
```

DELMORSS	SMOLDERS	DEMOOPRS	PREDOOMS	DEOOPRST	DOORSTEP
DELMORSU	MOULDERS	DEMOOPRT	PROMOTED		TORPEDOS
	REMOULDS	DEMOORST	DOOMSTER	DEOOPRTU	UPROOTED
	SMOULDER	DEMOORSU	DORMOUSE	DEOOPWWW	POWWOWED
DELMOSTY	MODESTLY	DEMOORTY	ODOMETRY	DEOORRSW	SORROWED
DELMRTUU	MULTURED	DEMOOSTU	OUTMODES	DEOORRVW	OVERWORD
DELMTTUU	TUMULTED	DEMOOTUV	OUTMOVED	DEOORRWW	OWREWORD
DELNOOSU	NODULOSE	DEMOPPRT	PROMPTED	DEOORTUV	OUTDROVE
	UNLOOSED	DEMOPSSU	POSSUMED	DEOOTTUV	OUTVOTED
DELNOOSZ	SNOOZLED	DEMORRUU	RUMOURED	DEOPPRRS	DROPPERS
DELNOOWY	WOODENLY	DENNNSUU	UNSUNNED	DEOPPRST	STROPPED
DELNOPPU	UNLOPPED	DENNOOOZ	ENDOZOON	DEOPPRSU	PURPOSED
DELNOPRS	SPLENDOR	DENNORST	TENDRONS	DEOPPSSU	SUPPOSED
DELNORSU	LOUNDERS	DENNORSU	ENROUNDS	DEOPRRTU	PROTRUDE
	NOURSLED	DENNOTUW	UNWONTED	DEOPRSTU	POSTURED
	ROUNDELS	DENNPRUU	UNPRUNED		PROUDEST
	ROUNDLES	DENNRRUU	UNDERRUN		SPROUTED
	UNSOLDER	DENNRTUU	UNTURNED	DEOPRSUU	POURSUED
DELNORTU	ROUNDLET	DENOOOVW	OVENWOOD		UPROUSED
DELNORYY	YONDERLY	DENOOPPR	PROPONED	DEORRSST	RODSTERS
DELNOSSU	LOUDNESS	DENOOPRS	PRODNOSE	DEORRSSW	SWORDERS
DELNOSUU	UNDULOSE	DENOOPSY	POYSONED	DEORRTTU	TORTURED
	UNSOULED	DENOORTU	UNROOTED	DEORSSTW	WORSTEDS
DELNOSUV	UNSOLVED	DENOOSSW	WOODNESS	DEORSSTY	DESTROYS
DELNPRSU	PLUNDERS	DENOOSTU	DUOTONES	DEORSTTU	STROUTED
DELNRSTU	RUNDLETS	DENOPPRS	PROPENDS	DEORSTUU	OUTDURES
	TRUNDLES	DENOPRSS	RESPONDS	DEORSTUV	OVERDUST
DELNSUZZ	SNUZZLED	DENOPRST	PORTENDS	DEORSTUX	DEXTROUS
DELOOPPS	PLEOPODS		PROTENDS	DEOSSSYY	ODYSSEYS
DELOORRV	OVERLORD	DENOPRSU	POUNDERS	DEOSSTTU	TESTUDOS
DELOORSS	LORDOSES	DENOPRSV	PROVENDS	DEPPSSYY	DYSPEPSY
DELOORSV	OVERSOLD	DENOPRUV	UNPROVED	DEPRRTUU	RUPTURED
DELOORSW	WOOLDERS	DENOPSTU	OUTSPEND	DEQRSUUY	SURQUEDY
DELOORTY	ROOTEDLY		UNPOSTED	DERSTTTU	STRUTTED
DELOOSSW	WOODLESS	DENOPSTW	STEWPOND	DFFGINSU	DUFFINGS
DELOPPRS	DROPPLES	DENOPSUX	EXPOUNDS	DFFIILUY	FLUIDIFY
DELOPPST	STOPPLED	DENOQTUU	UNQUOTED	DFFIIMRS	MIDRIFFS
DELOPRST	DROPLETS	DENORRSU	RONDURES	DFFIIRST	TRIFFIDS
DELOPRSU	POULDERS		ROUNDERS	DFFIIRTY	TRIFFIDY
	POULDRES		UNORDERS	DFFLOORU	FOURFOLD
DELOPSTU	POSTLUDE	DENORRSW	DROWNERS	DFFOORUW	WOODRUFF
DELORSST	OLDSTERS	DENORRTU	ROTUNDER	DFGGHIOT	DOGFIGHT
	STRODLES	DENORRUU	ROUNDURE	DFGGIINR	FRIDGING
DELORSSW	WORDLESS	DENORSSU	DOURNESS	DFGHILOS	GOLDFISH
DELORSTT	DOTTRELS		RESOUNDS	DFGIIIRY	RIGIDIFY
DELORSUY	DELUSORY		SOUNDERS	DFGIILRY	FRIGIDLY
DELOSSUU	SEDULOUS	DENORSTU	ROUNDEST	DFGIINNS	FINDINGS
DELOSTTT	DOTTLEST		TONSURED	DFGIINRT	DRIFTING
DELOTTUW	OUTDWELT		UNSORTED	DFGILNNO	FONDLING
DELOTUVY	DEVOUTLY	DENORSUU	UNROUSED	DFGILNOO	FLOODING
DELRSSTU	STRUDELS		UNSOURED	DFGILNOS	FOLDINGS
DELSSSTU	DUSTLESS	DENORSUW	WOUNDERS	DFGINNOU	FOUNDING
DEMMNOOO	MONOMODE	DENORTTU	UNROTTED	DFGINNSU	FUNDINGS
DEMMNOOS	DOOMSMEN	DENORTUW	UNDERTOW	DFGINOOR	FORDOING
DEMMNOSU	SUMMONED	DENOSSTU	SOUNDEST	DFGMOOSY	FOGYDOMS
DEMMNSUU	UNSUMMED	DENOSTUW	UNSTOWED	DFHIIMUY	HUMIDIFY
DEMMRRSU	DRUMMERS	DENOTUUV	UNDEVOUT	DFHILSSU	DISHFULS
DEMMRRUU	MURMURED	DENPRSTU	UPTRENDS	DFHIMRSU	DRUMFISH
DEMMRSTU	STRUMMED	DENPRSUU	UNPURSED	DFHINOOT	HINDFOOT
DEMNOOOP	MONOPODE	DENPRTUU	UPTURNED	DFHLOOOT	FOOTHOLD
DEMNOORU	UNMOORED	DENPSSSU	SUSPENDS	DFHNOOUX	FOXHOUND
DEMNOOSW	WOODSMEN	DENRRTTU	NURTURED	DFIIINVY	DIVINIFY
DEMNORST	MORDENTS	DENRSTTU	STRUNTED	DFIILMTU	MULTIFID
DEMNORSW	SWORDMEN	DENSSTTU	STUDENTS	DFIILOSY	SOLIDIFY
DEMNORSY	SYNDROME	DENSTUVY	DUVETYNS	DFIILTUY	FLUIDITY
DEMNORUW	UNWORMED	DEOOORSW	ROSEWOOD	DFIINPRT	DRIFTPIN
DEMNOSTU	DEMOUNTS	DEOOOSWW	WOODWOSE	DFIKNOOS	SKINFOOD
	MUDSTONE	DEOOPPRS	PROPOSED	DFILLOOT	FLOODLIT
DEMOOPPS	POPEDOMS	DEOOPPRT	PTEROPOD	DFILLORY	FLORIDLY
DEMOOPRR	PRODROME	DEOOPRRV	PROVEDOR	DFILMMOS	FILMDOMS

DFILNOPS	PINFOLDS
DFIMOOOR	IODOFORM
DFIMORSS	DISFORMS
DFINRSUW	WINDSURF
DFIOOPRS	DISPROOF
DFLNOOWW	DOWNFLOW
DFNOOPRU	PROFOUND
DFOOOSTW	SOFTWOOD
DGGGIINS	DIGGINGS
DGGGINOS	DOGGINGS
DGGGINRU	DRUGGING
	GRUDGING
DGGHIINT	DIGHTING
DGGIILNR	GIRDLING
	RIDGLING
DGGIILNS	GILDINGS
	GLIDINGS
DGGIINNR	GRINDING
DGGIINNW	WINGDING
DGGIINRS	GIRDINGS
	RIDGINGS
DGGIINSU	GUIDINGS
DGGILNOS	GODLINGS
	LODGINGS
DGGIMNSU	SMUDGING
DGGINNSU	SNUDGING
DGGINOST	STODGING
DGGINRTU	TRUDGING
DGGIRSTU	DRUGGIST
DGHHOOOS	HOGHOODS
DGHIILNS	HIDLINGS
	HILDINGS
DGHIIMNT	MIDNIGHT
DGHIIMST	MISDIGHT
DGHIINPS	SPHINGID
DGHIINRT	THIRDING
DGHIINSS	DISHINGS
	SHINDIGS
DGHIISST	DISSIGHT
DGHIKNOO	KINGHOOD
DGHILNOS	HOLDINGS
DGHILNRU	HURDLING
DGHILNSY	HYLDINGS
DGHILOOR	GIRLHOOD
DGHILPSY	DIGLYPHS
DGHINNOU	HOUNDING
DGHINNSU	DUNSHING
DGHINSTU	UNDIGHTS
DGHIOPSS	DOGSHIPS
	GODSHIPS
DGHNOTUU	DOUGHNUT
DGHOOOTT	DOGTOOTH
DGHORSTU	DROUGHTS
DGHORTUY	DROUGHTY
DGIIIMRS	DIRIGISM
DGIIINNT	INDITING
DGIIINNV	DIVINING
DGIIINOS	IODISING
DGIIINOZ	IODIZING
DGIIIRTY	RIGIDITY
DGIIKLNN	KINDLING
DGIIKLNS	KIDLINGS
DGIIKNNR	DRINKING
DGIILLNR	DRILLING
DGIILLNS	DILLINGS
DGIILLNU	ILLUDING
DGIILLOU	LIGULOID
DGIILMNP	DIMPLING
DGIILNNN	DINNLING
DGIILNOR	DROILING

DGIILNOS	DISLOIGN
DGIILNPS	DISPLING
DGIILNSS	SLIDINGS
DGIILNSW	WILDINGS
DGIILNTU	DILUTING
DGIIMNNS	MINDINGS
DGIIMNOS	MISDOING
DGIIMNOU	GONIDIUM
DGIIMNSS	SMIDGINS
DGIIMPUY	PYGIDIUM
DGIINNOP	POINDING
DGIINNRW	WINDRING
DGIINNSS	SINDINGS
DGIINNSW	WINDINGS
DGIINORR	GRIDIRON
DGIINORS	DORISING
DGIINORZ	DORIZING
DGIINOSV	VOIDINGS
DGIINOSW	WINDIGOS
DGIINOTT	DITTOING
DGIINOWW	WIDOWING
DGIINPPR	DRIPPING
DGIINPPS	DIPPINGS
DGIINRST	STRIDING
DGIINRTY	DIRTYING
DGIINSSU	DISUSING
DGIINTTY	DITTYING
DGIINVVY	DIVVYING
DGIINYZZ	DIZZYING
DGIKLOOY	KIDOLOGY
DGIKMNOS	KINGDOMS
DGIKNOOR	DROOKING
DGIKNOOW	KINGWOOD
DGIKNORU	DROUKING
DGIKNOSS	DOGSKINS
DGILLNOR	DROLLING
	LORDLING
DGILLNOY	DOLLYING
DGILLOOW	GOODWILL
DGILMNOU	MOULDING
DGILMNPU	DUMPLING
DGILMSUY	SMUDGILY
DGILNNOO	NOODLING
DGILNNOU	LOUNDING
DGILNNOW	LOWNDING
DGILNOOR	DROOLING
DGILNOOW	WOOLDING
DGILNORS	GIRLONDS
	LORDINGS
DGILNORY	YOLDRING
DGILNPUY	DUPLYING
DGILOOTW	GILTWOOD
DGILOSTY	STODGILY
DGILRTUY	TURGIDLY
DGIMMNRU	DRUMMING
DGIMMNUY	DUMMYING
DGIMNNOU	MOUNDING
DGIMNOOY	MOODYING
DGINNNSU	DUNNINGS
DGINNOOS	SNOODING
DGINNOPU	POUNDING
DGINNOPW	POWNDING
DGINNORU	ROUNDING
DGINNORW	DROWNING
	ROWNDING
DGINNOSU	SOUNDING
	UNDOINGS
DGINNOSW	SOWNDING
DGINNOUW	WOUNDING
DGINNSSY	SYNDINGS

DGINOOPR	DROOPING
DGINOOPS	SPONGOID
DGINOOTU	OUTDOING
DGINOPPR	DROPPING
DGINOPPS	DOPPINGS
DGINORSW	DROWSING
	SWORDING
	WORDINGS
DGINOSSW	DISGOWNS
DGINOSUY	DIGYNOUS
DGINSTUY	STUDYING
DGISSSTU	DISGUSTS
DGLOOOPY	PODOLOGY
DGLOOOSW	LOGWOODS
DGLOOOSY	DOSOLOGY
DGLOOOXY	DOXOLOGY
DGMOPRSU	GUMDROPS
DGMOPSYY	GYPSYDOM
DGMORSUU	GURUDOMS
DGNNORUU	UNGROUND
DGNOOORS	GODROONS
DGNOOSTW	DOGTOWNS
DGNOOTYZ	ZYGODONT
DGOORSTT	DOGTROTS
DHHILOTW	WITHHOLD
DHIIMNNS	DIMINISH
DHIIIOST	HISTIOID
	IDIOTISH
DHIILOSS	SOLIDISH
DHIIMNOO	HOMINOID
DHIIMNOS	HOMINIDS
DHIIMPSS	MIDSHIPS
DHIIMTUY	HUMIDITY
DHIINPSW	WINDSHIP
DHIINRSU	HIRUDINS
DHIINTWW	WITHWIND
DHIIOPRU	OPHIURID
DHIIORSS	HIDROSIS
DHIIORSZ	RHIZOIDS
DHIKNOOW	HOODWINK
DHIKORSY	HYDROSKI
DHILLNOW	DOWNHILL
DHILLOPY	PHYLLOID
DHILLORS	DROLLISH
DHILLOST	TOLLDISH
DHILMOPY	LYMPHOID
DHILMOSY	MODISHLY
DHILNOPS	DOLPHINS
DHILOPRS	LORDSHIP
DHILOPSS	SLIPSHOD
DHILORRY	HORRIDLY
DHILPSSU	LUDSHIPS
DHILPSSY	SYLPHIDS
DHIMNOST	HINDMOST
DHIMNOSU	UNMODISH
DHIMOOOY	OMOHYOID
DHIMOOSS	MISSHOOD
DHIMOPPY	HIPPYDOM
DHIMOPRS	DIMORPHS
DHIMORSU	HUMIDORS
	RHODIUMS
DHINOORS	DISHONOR
DHINOPSS	DONSHIPS
DHINORSS	DISHORNS
DHINORSU	ROUNDISH
DHIOOPRZ	RHIZOPOD
DHIOOPSU	PROUDISH
DHIOPSTY	TYPHOIDS
DHIORSTY	THYROIDS
	THYRSOID

DHIORSWY	ROWDYISH
DHIPRSSY	SYRPHIDS
DHJOPRSU	JODHPURS
DHKMNOOO	MONKHOOD
DHLLOPYY	PHYLLODY
DHLMOOSU	HOODLUMS
DHLOOORT	ROOTHOLD
DHLORXYY	HYDROXYL
DHLOSSTU	SHOULDST
DHMMRSUU	HUMDRUMS
DHMNOOOT	HOMODONT
DHMORTUY	DRYMOUTH
DHNNOOSU	NUNHOODS
DHNORSUU	UNSHROUD
DHNORSUW	DOWNRUSH
DHOOOPRT	ORTHOPOD
DHOOORTX	ORTHODOX
DHOOPRSU	UPHOORDS
DHOPRSSU	PUSHRODS
DHOPRSYY	HYDROPSY
DIIILLQU	ILLIQUID
DIIILTVY	LIVIDITY
DIIIMOST	IDIOTISM
DIIIMRSU	IRIDIUMS
DIIIMTTY	TIMIDITY
DIIINOSV	DIVISION
DIIINTVY	DIVINITY
DIIIPRST	DISPIRIT
DIIIRTVY	VIRIDITY
DIIITVVY	VIVIDITY
DIIJNOSS	DISJOINS
DIIJNOST	DISJOINT
DIIKLLNY	KINDLILY
DIIKLNSS	DISLINKS
DIIKNOST	DOITKINS
DIILLMNR	MILLRIND
DIILLMNW	WINDMILL
DIILLMPY	LIMPIDLY
DIILLQUY	LIQUIDLY
DIILLSST	DISTILLS
DIILLSTY	IDYLLIST
DIILMNSS	DISLIMNS
DIILMOSS	IDOLISMS
	SOLIDISM
DIILMOTY	MYTILOID
DIILMUUV	DILUVIUM
DIILNOTU	DILUTION
DIILNOUV	DILUVION
DIILNOXY	XYLOIDIN
DIILNTUY	UNTIDILY
DIILOPRT	TRIPLOID
DIILOPSY	YPSILOID
DIILORSU	SILUROID
DIILOSST	IDOLISTS
	SOLIDIST
DIILOSTY	SOLIDITY
DIILQSUU	LIQUIDUS
DIILRSSU	SILURIDS
DIIMNNOO	DOMINION
DIIMNNSU	UNDINISM
DIIMNORS	MIDIRONS
DIIMNSUU	INDUSIUM
DIIMOPRS	PRISMOID
DIIMORSS	DIORISMS
DIIMPUXY	PYXIDIUM
DIIMRUUV	DUUMVIRI
DIIMTTUY	TUMIDITY
DIINNOSU	DISUNION
DIINNOSU	SINUSOID
DIINSTUY	DISUNITY

DIIOPRTY	PITYROID
DIIORSSV	DIVISORS
DIJOSSTU	JUDOISTS
DIKLMOOW	MILKWOOD
DIKLNNUY	UNKINDLY
DIKLNORS	LORDKINS
DIKLRUUU	DURUKULI
DIKNORSV	DVORNIKS
DIKNORTU	OUTDRINK
DIKOOSTU	DITOKOUS
DILLMNOP	MILLPOND
DILLOSTY	STOLIDLY
DILMNOOS	SMILODON
DILMNORW	LINDWORM
DILMNRSU	DRUMLINS
DILMOOSU	MODIOLUS
DILMOSSU	SOLIDUMS
DILMOSSY	ODYLISMS
DILNOPST	DIPLONTS
DILNOPSU	LISPOUND
DILNOQSU	QUODLINS
DILNOUWY	WOUNDILY
DILNPSSU	LISPUNDS
DILOOPPY	POLYPOID
DILOOPPY	DROOPILY
DILOORSS	LORDOSIS
DILOOSUY	ODIOUSLY
DILOOTUV	VOLUTOID
DILOPRTY	TORPIDLY
DILORSTU	DILUTORS
DILORSWY	DROWSILY
DILOSSTY	STYLOIDS
DILPRTUY	PUTRIDLY
DILPSTUY	STUPIDLY
DILRSTUY	STURDILY
DIMMNORY	MYRMIDON
DIMMOOSU	ISODOMUM
DIMMOSST	MIDMOSTS
DIMNNOOS	MIDNOONS
DIMNNOSS	DONNISMS
DIMNNOST	DINMONTS
DIMNOOOS	ISODOMON
DIMNOOST	MONODIST
DIMNOPSU	IMPOUNDS
DIMNOSTU	DISMOUNT
DIMNOSUW	UNWISDOM
DIMOOPRR	PRODROMI
DIMOOPRY	MYRIOPOD
DIMOORTW	MODIWORT
DIMOPRSU	MISPROUD
DIMOPSSU	SPODIUMS
DIMORSSW	MISWORDS
DIMORSWY	ROWDYISM
DIMOSTUY	DUMOSITY
DIMRSTUU	TRIDUUMS
DIMRSUUV	DUUMVIRS
DINNOORS	RONDINOS
DINNOOST	TONDINOS
DINOOORW	IRONWOOD
DINOOPSU	DIPNOOUS
DINOORST	TORDIONS
DINOORSU	NIDOROUS
DINOOSST	ISODONTS
DINOOSTT	ODONTIST
DINOOSTY	NODOSITY
DINORSTU	STURNOID
	TURDIONS
DINORSWW	WINDROWS
DINOSSTW	SITDOWNS
DINOSTUW	OUTWINDS

Letters	Word
DINPRTUY	PUNDITRY
DINRSTUY	INDUSTRY
DIOOPRRT	PRODITOR
DIOOPRRV	PROVIDOR
DIOORSST	DISROOTS
DIOORSTT	RIDOTTOS
DIOPRSST	DISPORTS
DIOPSSST	DISPOSTS
DIORRSST	STRIDORS
DIORSSTT	DISTORTS
DIOSSTUU	STUDIOUS
DIPRSSTU	DISRUPTS
DIRSSTTU	DISTRUST
DKNORTUU	OUTDRUNK
DKOOORWW	WOODWORK
DKORSTUW	STUDWORK
DLLNORUY	UNLORDLY
DLMNOOSY	MYLODONS
DLMNOOTY	MYLODONT
DLMNOSUU	UNMOULDS
DLMORSUY	SMOULDRY
DLNOOPRU	POULDRON
DLNOOSUU	NODULOUS
DLNOPRSU	PULDRONS
DLNOPSSY	SPONDYLS
DLNORTUY	ROTUNDLY
DLNOSUUU	UNDULOUS
DLOOOORS	DOLOROSO
DLOOORSU	DOLOROUS
DLOOPPSY	POLYPODS
DLOOPPUW	PULPWOOD
DLOOPPYY	POLYPODY
DLOOPSTY	TYLOPODS
DLOOPSWY	PLYWOODS
DMNNOOOT	MONODONT
DMNOOSTW	DOWNMOST
	TOWMONDS
DMOOORWW	WOODWORM
	WORMWOOD
DMOPPPUU	PUPPODUM
DMOPPPUY	PUPPYDOM
DMORSTUW	MUDWORTS
DNNOOPRU	PUNDONOR
DNNORSUU	UNROUNDS
DNNORSUW	RUNDOWNS
DNNORTUW	DOWNTURN
DNNOSSUW	SUNDOWNS
DNNRSTUU	TURNDUNS
DNOOPPRU	PROPOUND
DNOOPRSW	SNOWDROP
DNOOPRUW	DOWNPOUR
DNOORSUW	WONDROUS
DNOOSTWW	STOWDOWN
DNOOTUUW	OUTWOUND
DNORRSUU	SURROUND
DNORSSUY	UNDROSSY
DOOOPRST	DOORPOST
	DOORSTOP
DOOORSTU	OUTDOORS
DOOOSTTU	OUTSTOOD
DOOPSWWY	POWSOWDY
DOORRSTU	DORTOURS
DOORRSTUU	ORDUROUS
DOORSSUU	SUDOROUS
EEEEFNRZ	ENFREEZE
EEEEFRRS	REFEREES
EEEEFRRZ	REFREEZE
EEEEGGRR	GREEGREE
EEEEGQSU	SQUEEGEE
EEEEGSSX	EXEGESES
EEEEGSTX	EXEGETES
EEEELLPX	EXPELLEE
EEEELMST	TELESEME
EEEENNRV	VENEERER
EEEEPPSW	PEESWEEP
EEEEPRRV	REPREEVE
EEEEPTTW	PEETWEET
EEEFFFOS	FEOFFEES
EEEFFLOR	FOREFEEL
EEEFFLTY	EFFETELY
EEEFFNRT	EFFERENT
EEEFFORS	OFFEREES
EEEFFORT	FOREFEET
EEEFFRVW	FEVERFEW
EEEFGRSU	REFUGEES
EEEFHRSS	SHEREEFS
EEEFIPRR	REPRIEFE
EEEFIPST	TEPEFIES
EEEFIRRT	FREETIER
EEEFLRRS	FLEERERS
EEEFLRSX	REFLEXES
EEEFLSST	FEETLESS
EEEFLSTT	FLEETEST
EEEFNNPY	PENNYFEE
EEEFNORS	FORESEEN
EEEFNRRT	REFERENT
EEEFNRSS	FREENESS
EEEFNRTT	ENFETTER
EEEFNRUZ	UNFREEZE
EEEFORRV	OVERFREE
EEEFORSS	FORESEES
EEEFRRRT	FERRETER
EEEFRRSZ	FREEZERS
EEEGGILN	NEGLIGEE
EEEGGIRS	EGGERIES
EEEGHINT	EIGHTEEN
	TEHEEING
EEEGHNSW	WHEENGES
EEEGILMN	LIEGEMEN
EEEGILNV	ENVEIGLE
	LEVEEING
EEEGILPS	ESPIEGLE
EEEGILRT	GLEETIER
EEEGILSS	ELEGISES
EEEGILSZ	ELEGIZES
EEEGIMNX	EXEEMING
EEEGINNR	ENGINEER
EEEGINRR	GREENIER
EEEGINRS	ENERGIES
	ENERGISE
EEEGINRV	ENGRIEVE
EEEGINRZ	ENERGIZE
EEEGIPRS	PERIGEES
EEEGISSX	EXEGESIS
EEEGISTV	EGESTIVE
EEEGITVV	VEGETIVE
EEEGLMOS	GLEESOME
EEEGLNRT	GREENLET
EEEGMNRT	EMERGENT
EEEGMORT	GEOMETER
EEEGMRRS	REMERGES
EEEGNNRS	SENGREEN
EEEGNPRS	EPERGNES
EEEGNRRS	RENEGERS
EEEGNRRU	RENEGUER
EEEGNRRV	REVENGER
EEEGNRRY	GREENERY
EEEGNRST	GREENEST
EEEGNRSU	RENEGUES
EEEGNRSV	REVENGES
EEEGNSTT	GENETTES
EEEGOPRT	PROTEGEE
EEEGRRST	REGREETS
EEEGRSSS	EGRESSES
EEEGRSUX	EXERGUES
EEEHILRW	EREWHILE
	WHEELIER
EEEHILSW	WHEELIES
EEEHINRS	SHEENIER
EEEHINSS	SHEENIES
EEEHIPRS	SHEEPIER
EEEHIRSS	HERESIES
EEEHIRST	ETHERISE
	SHEETIER
EEEHIRTZ	ETHERIZE
EEEHIRWZ	WHEEZIER
EEEHKLNO	KNEEHOLE
EEEHLMNW	WHEELMEN
EEEHLMPT	HELPMEET
EEEHLNSW	ENWHEELS
EEEHLNTV	ELEVENTH
EEEHLNTY	ETHYLENE
EEEHLNXY	HEXYLENE
EEEHLOPW	WEEPHOLE
EEEHLPSW	WHEEPLES
EEEHLRSW	WHEELERS
EEEHLSWZ	WHEEZLES
EEEHMMSS	EMMESHES
EEEHMNSS	ENMESHES
EEEHMNTV	VEHEMENT
EEEHMRSS	HERSEEMS
EEEHNNPT	NEPENTHE
EEEHNNQU	HENEQUEN
EEEHNPRS	ENSPHERE
EEEHNRSS	HERENESS
EEEHNRVW	WHENEVER
EEEHNSSS	SNEESHES
EEEHPRST	SPREETHE
EEEHRRVW	WHEREVER
EEEHRSST	SEETHERS
	SHEEREST
EEEHSSST	ESTHESES
EEEHSSTT	ESTHETES
EEEIKLMS	MISLEEKE
EEEIKLRS	SKEELIER
	SLEEKIER
EEEIKLSW	WEEKLIES
EEEIKRRS	SKEERIER
EEEIKRST	REEKIEST
EEEILLRV	REVEILLE
EEEILMRS	SEEMLIER
EEEILNNO	EOLIENNE
EEEILNPR	PELERINE
EEEILNRY	EYELINER
EEEILNST	SELENITE
EEEILPRS	SLEEPIER
EEEILRRV	RELIEVER
EEEILRST	LEERIEST
	SLEETIER
	STEELIER
EEEILRSV	RELIEVES
EEEILRSZ	SLEEZIER
EEEILSST	SEELIEST
EEEILSSW	ELSEWISE
EEEILSTV	TELEVISE
EEEILTVW	TELEVIEW
EEEIMNRU	MEUNIERE
EEEIMNST	EMETINES
EEEIMPRR	PREMIERE
EEEIMPRS	EMPERIES
	EMPERISE
	PREEMIES
EEEIMPRZ	EMPERIZE
EEEIMRRS	MISERERE
EEEIMRST	EREMITES
EEEIMRTT	REMITTEE
EEEINNNT	NINETEEN
EEEINNRT	INTERNEE
EEEINQTU	QUEENITE
EEEINRRS	SNEERIER
EEEINRSS	EERINESS
EEEINRST	ETERNISE
	TEENSIER
EEEINRSV	VENERIES
EEEINRSZ	SNEEZIER
EEEINRTT	REINETTE
	TEENTIER
EEEINRTZ	ETERNIZE
EEEINSSW	SWEENIES
EEEINSTT	TEENIEST
EEEINSTW	TWEENIES
	WEENIEST
EEEINTUX	EUXENITE
EEEIPRRV	REPRIEVE
EEEIPRST	PEERIEST
	STEEPIER
EEEIPRSW	SWEEPIER
EEEIPSST	SEEPIEST
EEEIPSTW	WEEPIEST
EEEIQSUX	EXEQUIES
EEEIRRST	REESTIER
	RETIREES
EEEIRRSV	REREVISE
	REVERIES
EEEIRRTV	RETRIEVE
EEEIRRVW	REVIEWER
EEEIRSST	STEERIES
EEEIRSSV	SEVERIES
EEEIRSSZ	RESEIZES
EEEIRTVX	EXERTIVE
EEEISSTW	SWEETIES
EEEJLLRW	JEWELLER
EEEJNPSY	JEEPNEYS
EEEKLLSU	UKELELES
EEEKLNNR	ENKERNEL
EEEKLNRS	KNEELERS
EEEKLNSS	SLEEKENS
EEEKLPSW	EKPWELES
EEEKLRSS	SLEEKERS
EEEKLSST	SLEEKEST
EEEKMNSS	MEEKNESS
EEEKMRSS	KERMESSE
EEEKNNSS	KEENNESS
EEEKNORS	KEROSENE
EEEKNORV	OVERKNEE
EEEKNPST	KEEPNETS
EEEKNRSS	SKREENES
EEEKOPRV	OVERKEEP
EEEKRSST	SKEETERS
EEELLLRV	LEVELLER
EEELLLSW	SEWELLEL
EEELLNQU	QUENELLE
EEELLPRR	REPELLER
EEELLRRT	RETELLER
EEELLRRV	REVELLER
EEELMNST	ELEMENTS
EEELMOPP	EMPEOPLE
EEELMOPY	EMPLOYEE
EEELMOTT	OMELETTE
EEELMPSX	EXEMPLES

Key	Word
EEELMRTU	MULETEER
EEELMSSS	SEEMLESS
EEELMSST	TEEMLESS
EEELNOPV	ENVELOPE
EEELNOSV	NOVELESE
EEELNQTU	QUEENLET
EEELNRSW	NEWSREEL
EEELNRSY	SERENELY
EEELNRTV	NERVELET
EEELOPPR	REPEOPLE
EEELORST	SLOETREE
EEELPRSS	PEERLESS
	SLEEPERS
	SPEELERS
EEELPRST	REPLETES
EEELPRSY	SLEEPERY
EEELPSST	STEEPLES
EEELRRTT	LETTERER
EEELRSST	TREELESS
EEELRSSV	SLEEVERS
EEELRSTT	RESETTLE
EEELRSTV	LEVERETS
	VERSELET
EEELRSVY	SEVERELY
EEELRTVV	VELVERET
EEELSSTW	WEETLESS
EEELSTVY	STEEVELY
EEELTTTX	TELETEXT
EEEMMNRS	MERESMEN
EEEMMRUZ	MEZEREUM
EEEMNNTT	TENEMENT
EEEMNORZ	MEZEREON
EEEMNPRT	PETERMEN
EEEMNRST	ENTREMES
EEEMNSST	MEETNESS
EEEMORRV	EVERMORE
EEEMORST	EROTEMES
	STEREOME
EEEMORTV	OVERTEEM
EEEMPRRT	TEMPERER
EEEMPRSS	EMPRESSE
EEEMPSSY	EMPYESES
EEEMRRTX	EXTREMER
EEEMRSST	SEMESTER
EEEMRSTX	EXTREMES
EEENNOPR	NEOPRENE
EEENNPST	PENTENES
EEENNRST	ETRENNES
EEENNRUV	UNEVENER
EEENNSSV	EVENNESS
EEENNSTT	ENTENTES
EEENOPRR	REOPENER
EEENORSV	OVERSEEN
EEENORVW	OVERWEEN
EEENORVY	EVERYONE
EEENPPRS	PREPENSE
EEENPRRT	REPENTER
EEENPRST	PRETENSE
	TERPENES
EEENPRSV	PREVENES
EEENPSST	ENSTEEPS
	STEEPENS
EEENPSSW	ENSWEEPS
EEENPSSX	EXPENSES
EEENRRSS	SNEERERS
EEENRRST	ENTERERS
	RESENTER
	TERREENS
	TERRENES
EEENRRSV	RENVERSE
	VENERERS
EEENRRSW	RENEWERS
EEENRRTU	RETURNEE
EEENRRTV	REVERENT
EEENRSSS	SERENESS
EEENRSST	SERENEST
EEENRSSU	ENURESES
EEENRSSZ	SNEEZERS
EEENRSTV	EVENTERS
EEENRSTX	EXTERNES
EEENRSTY	YESTREEN
EEENRSUV	REVENUES
	UNREEVES
EEENRSTW	SWEETENS
	TWEENESS
EEENSSWY	SWEENEYS
EEEOPRRV	OVERPEER
EEEORRSV	OVERSEER
EEEORSST	EROTESES
EEEORSSV	OVERSEES
EEEORSSY	EYESORES
EEEORSVY	OVEREYES
EEEPPPRR	PEPPERER
EEEPPRST	PESTERER
EEEPPRSU	REPERUSE
EEEPRRSV	PERVERSE
	PRESERVE
EEEPRRTW	PEWTERER
EEEPRRST	ESTREPES
	STEEPERS
EEEPRRSW	SWEEPERS
EEEPRRSZ	SPREEZES
EEEPSSTT	STEEPEST
EEEPSTTT	SEPTETTE
EEEQRRSU	REQUERES
EEEQRRUV	VERQUERE
EEEQRSTU	QUEEREST
EEEQRSUZ	SQUEEZER
EEEQSSUZ	SQUEEZES
EEERRRSV	REVERERS
	REVERSER
EEERRSST	STEERERS
EEERRSSV	RESERVES
	REVERSES
EEERRSTT	RESETTER
EEERRSTV	SEVEREST
EEERRSUV	REVEUSES
EEERRSUW	SERUEWES
EEERRSVW	SERVEWES
EEERRSTW	TWEETERS
EEERSTWZ	TWEEZERS
EEESSSTT	SESTETTE
EEESSTTV	STEEVEST
EEESSTTW	SWEETEST
EEESTTTX	SEXTETTE
EEFFFGLU	GEFUFFLE
EEFFFKLU	KEFUFFLE
EEFFFNOS	ENFEOFFS
EEFFFORS	FEOFFERS
EEFFGIIS	EFFIGIES
EEFFGINR	EFFERING
EEFFGIRR	GREFFIER
EEFFGLSU	EFFULGES
EEFFHIKY	KEFFIYEH
EEFFINST	FIFTEENS
EEFFISUV	EFFUSIVE
EEFFLNTU	EFFLUENT
EEFFLORT	FOREFELT
EEFFLSUX	EFFLUXES
EEFFNOSS	OFFENSES
EEFFORRS	OFFERERS
EEFFORSX	FORFEXES
EEFFRRSU	SUFFERER
EEFFSSTU	SUFFETES
EEFGIILR	FILIGREE
EEFGILNR	FLEERING
EEFGILNS	FEELINGS
EEFGILNT	FLEETING
EEFGINNP	PFENNIGE
EEFGINRR	REFRINGE
EEFGINRS	FEERINGS
	REEFINGS
EEFGINRV	FEVERING
EEFGINRZ	FREEZING
EEFGIRRU	REFIGURE
EEFGLMNU	FUGLEMEN
EEFGLNRY	GREENFLY
EEFGLNUV	VENGEFUL
EEFGLORS	FORELEGS
EEFGMNOR	FORGEMEN
EEFGNOOR	FOREGONE
EEFGOORR	FOREGOER
EEFGOORS	FOREGOES
EEFHILRS	FLESHIER
	SHELFIER
EEFHIMSU	HUMEFIES
EEFHIRSV	FEVERISH
EEFHISST	FETISHES
EEFHISSY	FISHEYES
EEFHISTT	HEFTIEST
EEFHLLWY	FLYWHEEL
EEFHLMOT	HOMEFELT
EEFHLRSS	FLESHERS
EEFHMNRS	FRESHMEN
EEFHMORR	HEREFROM
EEFHNORT	FOREHENT
EEFHNRSS	FRESHENS
EEFHORRT	THEREFOR
EEFHORRW	WHEREFOR
EEFHORSW	FORESHEW
EEFHRRSS	FRESHERS
EEFHRSST	FRESHEST
	FRESHETS
EEFIIKLL	LIFELIKE
EEFIIKRS	FIKERIES
EEFIILMT	LIFETIME
EEFIILNS	LENIFIES
EEFIILRW	WIFELIER
EEFIIMNN	FEMININE
EEFIIMNS	FEMINISE
EEFIIMNZ	FEMINIZE
EEFIINRS	FINERIES
EEFIIRRT	FREITIER
EEFIIRRV	VERIFIER
EEFIIRST	FEISTIER
	FERITIES
	FIERIEST
EEFIIRSV	VERIFIES
EEFIKNNP	PENKNIFE
EEFILLMT	TELEFILM
EEFILLSS	LIFELESS
EEFILMNR	RIFLEMEN
EEFILMOS	LIFESOME
EEFILMST	FISTMELE
EEFILNOS	FELONIES
	OLEFINES
EEFILNSS	FINELESS
EEFILNUV	NIEVEFUL
EEFILORS	FORELIES
EEFILPRR	PILFERER
EEFILRRT	FERTILER
EEFILRSS	FIRELESS
EEFILRST	FERLIEST
EEFILRSU	FUSILEER
EEFILSST	FELSITES
EEFILSSW	WIFELESS
EEFIMORT	FORETIME
EEFIMRST	FEMITERS
EEFIMSTU	TUMEFIES
EEFINNSS	FINENESS
EEFINNST	FENNIEST
EEFINORV	OVERFINE
EEFINRRS	REFINERS
EEFINRRY	REFINERY
EEFINRSS	FINESSER
	RIFENESS
EEFINRST	FERNIEST
EEFINRSU	REINFUSE
EEFINRSZ	FRENZIES
EEFINSSS	FINESSES
EEFINSTT	FEINTEST
EEFIORRV	OVERFIRE
EEFIORSX	ORIFEXES
EEFIPRSX	PREFIXES
EEFIRRST	FERRITES
EEFIRRTT	FRETTIER
EEFIRSTT	FRISETTE
EEFIRSTY	ESTERIFY
EEFKNORW	FOREKNEW
EEFLLNSS	FELLNESS
EEFLLORT	FORETELL
EEFLLORV	OVERFELL
EEFLLRSU	FUELLERS
EEFLLRXY	REFLEXLY
EEFLLSSS	SELFLESS
EEFLMNSU	MENSEFUL
EEFLMORU	FUMEROLE
EEFLNNOS	ENFELONS
EEFLNORT	FORELENT
EEFLNORW	ENFLOWER
EEFLNOST	FELSTONE
EEFLNRTU	REFLUENT
EEFLNSSS	SELFNESS
EEFLNSSU	SENSEFUL
EEFLNTUV	EVENTFUL
EEFLOOSV	FOVEOLES
EEFLOPTT	POLTFEET
EEFLORRW	FLOWERER
	REFLOWER
EEFLORSS	FORLESES
EEFLORTW	FLOWERET
EEFLORVW	OVERFLEW
EEFLORWW	WEREWOLF
EEFLOSUX	FLEXUOSE
EEFLRRSU	FERRULES
EEFLRSTT	FETTLERS
EEFLRSTU	FLEURETS
EEFLRSUX	FLEXURES
	REFLUXES
EEFMNORT	FOMENTER
EEFMNRRY	FERRYMEN
EEFMNRST	FERMENTS
EEFMORRR	REFORMER
EEFMOSTT	MOFETTES
EEFMPRRU	PERFUMER
EEFMPRSU	PERFUMES
EEFMSTTU	FUMETTES
EEFNNORS	ENFROSEN
EEFNNORZ	ENFROZEN
EEFNORRZ	REFROZEN

Pattern	Words
EEFNORST	ENFOREST / SOFTENER
EEFNORTU	FOURTEEN
EEFNORTW	FOREWENT
EEFNOSTT	OFTENEST
EEFNQRTU	FREQUENT
EEFNRTTU	UNFETTER
EEFORRST	FORESTER / FOSTERER
EEFORRSU	FERREOUS
EEFORSTV	FOREVERS
EEFORRTY	FERETORY
EEFORSUV	FEVEROUS
EEFOSSTT	FOSSETTE
EEFOSSTU	FOETUSES
EEFOSTTU	FOUETTES
EEFPRSSU	PERFUSES
EEFRRSSU	REFUSERS
EEFRRSTU	REFUTERS
EEGGGLST	GLEGGEST
EEGGHLLS	EGGSHELL
EEGGHLOR	HOGGEREL
EEGGHMSU	MESHUGGE
EEGGHSTU	THUGGEES
EEGGIJRR	REJIGGER
EEGGIKLN	GLEEKING
EEGGILNR	LEGERING
EEGGILNS	NEGLIGES
EEGGILNT	GLEETING
EEGGILST	LEGGIEST
EEGGIMNR	EMERGING
EEGGINNP	PEENGING
EEGGINNR	GREENING / RENEGING
EEGGINRS	GREESING
EEGGINRT	GREETING
EEGGINST	EGESTING
EEGGINSU	SEGUEING
EEGGKRSS	SKEGGERS
EEGGLOOR	GEOLOGER
EEGGNORS	ENGORGES
EEGGORRS	REGORGES
EEGGORSU	GOUGERES
EEGGPRRS	PREGGERS
EEGGPRSU	PUGGREES
EEGGQRSU	SQUEGGER
EEGHHINT	HEIGHTEN
EEGHIIST	EIGHTIES
EEGHIKNT	THEEKING
EEGHIKRS	SKEIGHER
EEGHILNS	HEELINGS / SHEELING
EEGHILNW	WHEELING
EEGHINNS	SHEENING
EEGHINPS	PHEESING
EEGHINPT	PHENGITE
EEGHINPZ	PHEEZING
EEGHINRS	GREENISH / SHEERING
EEGHINST	SEETHING / SHEETING
EEGHINSY	HYGIENES
EEGHINTT	TEETHING
EEGHINWZ	WHEEZING
EEGHIOTT	GOETHITE
EEGHIRSW	REWEIGHS / WEIGHERS
EEGHISST	SIGHTSEE
EEGHISTY	EYESIGHT
EEGHLNNT	LENGTHEN
EEGHMNOY	HEGEMONY
EEGHNNRU	ENHUNGER
EEGHNOOP	GEOPHONE
EEGHNOPS	PHOSGENE
EEGHNOPY	HYPOGENE
EEGHNRST	GREENTHS
EEGHNRSY	GREYHENS
EEGHNSSU	HUGENESS
EEGHOPTY	GEOPHYTE
EEGHORTT	TOGETHER
EEGHOSTT	GHETTOES
EEGHSTTU	TEUGHEST
EEGIILNR	LINGERIE
EEGIILNV	INVEIGLE
EEGIIMNS	GEMINIES
EEGIINTV	GENITIVE
EEGIIOST	EGOITIES
EEGIJLNY	JEELYING
EEGIJNRS	JEERINGS
EEGIKLNN	KNEELING
EEGIKLNS	KEELINGS / SLEEKING
EEGIKLOT	EKLOGITE
EEGIKMNS	SMEEKING
EEGIKNNS	KEENINGS
EEGIKNPS	KEEPINGS
EEGIKNRS	KREESING / SKEERING
EEGIKNST	STEEKING
EEGILNOR	ELOIGNER
EEGILNPS	PEELINGS / SLEEPING / SPEELING
EEGILNRR	LINGERER
EEGILNRS	LEERINGS / REELINGS
EEGILNRU	REGULINE
EEGILNRV	LEVERING
EEGILNSS	SEELINGS
EEGILNST	GENTILES / SLEETING / STEELING
EEGILNSV	SLEEVING
EEGILNSW	SWEELING
EEGILNTW	TWEELING
EEGILNTX	TELEXING
EEGILOPU	EPILOGUE
EEGILOSS	GELOSIES
EEGILOSU	EULOGIES / EULOGISE
EEGILOUZ	EULOGIZE
EEGILQSU	SQUILGEE
EEGILRSU	REGULISE
EEGILRSV	VELIGERS
EEGILRTV	VERLIGTE
EEGILRTY	LEGERITY
EEGILRUZ	REGULIZE
EEGILSST	ELEGISTS
EEGIMMNW	EMMEWING
EEGIMMRS	IMMERGES
EEGIMMST	GEMMIEST
EEGIMNNS	MENINGES
EEGIMNNW	ENMEWING
EEGIMNRS	REGIMENS
EEGIMNRT	METERING / REGIMENT
EEGIMNRU	MERINGUE
EEGIMNRY	EMERYING
EEGIMNSS	SEEMINGS
EEGIMNST	MEETINGS / STEEMING
EEGIMNSU	EUGENISM
EEGINNPR	PREENING
EEGINNQU	QUEENING
EEGINNRS	ENGINERS / INGENERS / SERENING / SNEERING
EEGINNRT	ENTERING
EEGINNRV	ENERVING
EEGINNRW	RENEWING
EEGINNRY	ENGINERY / RENEYING
EEGINNST	STEENING
EEGINNSU	INGENUES / UNSEEING
EEGINNSV	EVNINGS / EVENINGS
EEGINNSW	ENSEWING
EEGINNSZ	SNEEZING
EEGINNTV	EVENTING
EEGINOOS	OOGENIES
EEGINOPR	PERIGONE
EEGINOPS	EPIGONES
EEGINORR	ERIGERON
EEGINORS	ERINGOES
EEGINORV	VIROGENE
EEGINOST	EGESTION
EEGINPRS	SPEERING / SPREEING
EEGINPRT	PETERING
EEGINPRU	PUREEING
EEGINPRV	PREEVING
EEGINPST	STEEPING
EEGINPSW	SWEEPING / WEEPINGS
EEGINQRU	QUEERING
EEGINQUU	QUEUEING
EEGINRRS	RESIGNER
EEGINRRV	REVERING
EEGINRSS	GREISENS
EEGINRST	GENTRIES / INTEGERS / REESTING / STEERING / STREIGNE
EEGINRSU	SEIGNEUR
EEGINRSV	SEVERING / VEERINGS
EEGINRSW	SEWERING
EEGINRTU	GENITURE
EEGINRTV	EVERTING
EEGINRTW	TWEERING
EEGINRTX	EXERTING / GENETRIX
EEGINSSS	GNEISSES
EEGINSSU	GENIUSES
EEGINSTT	GENTIEST
EEGINSTU	EUGENIST
EEGINSTV	STEEVING / VENTIGES
EEGINSTW	SWEETING
EEGINSTX	EXIGENTS
EEGINTTV	VIGNETTE
EEGINTTW	TWEETING
EEGINTUX	TEGUEXIN
EEGINTWZ	TWEEZING
EEGIOPSU	EPIGEOUS
EEGIORST	ERGOTISE
EEGIORTZ	ERGOTIZE
EEGIORVV	OVERGIVE
EEGIOSST	EGOTISES
EEGIOSTZ	EGOTIZES
EEGIPRST	PRESTIGE
EEGIRRST	REGISTER
EEGIRRSV	GRIEVERS
EEGIRSTT	GRISETTE / TERGITES
EEGISSTV	VESTIGES
EEGJORSU	GOUJEERS
EEGKNORS	KEROGENS
EEGKNRSU	GERENUKS
EEGLMMSU	GEMMULES
EEGLMNOP	EMPLONGE
EEGLMNTU	EMULGENT
EEGLMOSS	GLOSSEME
EEGLNNTU	UNGENTLE
EEGLNOPY	POLYGENE
EEGLNOSU	EUGENOLS
EEGLNOSZ	LOZENGES
EEGLNOTY	TELEGONY
EEGLNSTT	GENTLEST
EEGMMOSU	GEMMEOUS
EEGMNOST	EMONGEST / GEMSTONE
EEGMNSST	SEGMENTS
EEGMNTTU	TEGUMENT
EEGMORSU	GRUESOME
EEGMORTY	GEOMETRY
EEGNNORT	ROENTGEN
EEGNNOSS	GONENESS
EEGNNOSV	EVENSONG
EEGNOORV	ENGROOVE / OVERGONE
EEGNOPTY	GENOTYPE
EEGNORST	ESTROGEN
EEGNORSU	GENEROUS
EEGNORSY	ERYNGOES
EEGNPRUX	EXPUNGER
EEGNPSUX	EXPUNGES
EEGNRSSY	GREYNESS
EEGNRSUY	GUERNSEY
EEGNSSTU	GUESTENS
EEGOOPSY	POOGYEES
EEGOORSV	OVERGOES
EEGOPRST	PROTEGES
EEGORRST	OSTREGER
EEGORRVW	OVERGREW
EEGORSSS	OGRESSES
EEGORSTU	UROSTEGE
EEGORSTV	OVERGETS
EEGPRSUX	EXPURGES
EEGRRSSU	RESURGES
EEGRSSSU	GUESSERS
EEGRSSTU	GESTURES
EEHHIPSS	SHEEPISH
EEHHIRTW	HEREWITH
EEHHLRST	THRESHEL
EEHHRRST	THRESHER
EEHHRSST	THRESHES
EEHHSSTW	WHEESHTS
EEHIIKLV	HIVELIKE
EEHIKLMO	HOMELIKE
EEHIKLRW	WHELKIER
EEHIKRRS	SHRIEKER
EEHILLMS	SHLEMIEL
EEHILLNP	HELPLINE
EEHILLRS	HELLIERS / SHELLIER
EEHILMOR	HOMELIER

EEHILNOP	NEOPHILE	EEHKLOSY	KEYHOLES	EEHRSSSU	RHESUSES	EEIKLLRY	KYRIELLE
EEHILORT	HOTELIER	EEHKOOSY	EYEHOOKS		USHERESS	EEIKLLSS	SKELLIES
EEHILOSS	HELIOSES	EEHLLMPS	PHELLEMS	EEHRSSTW	WERSHEST	EEIKLNSS	LIKENESS
EEHILRSS	HEIRLESS	EEHLLMSS	HELMLESS	EEHRSTTW	WHETTERS	EEIKLORS	ROSELIKE
	RELISHES	EEHLLNSS	ENSHELLS	EEIIKLLR	LIKELIER	EEIKLORT	LORIKEET
EEHILRSV	SHELVIER	EEHLLORV	HOVELLER	EEIIKLPP	PIPELIKE	EEIKLPST	PIKELETS
EEHILSST	LEISHEST	EEHLLPSS	HELPLESS	EEIIKLSW	LIKEWISE		SPIKELET
	SHELTIES	EEHLLRSS	SHELLERS	EEIILLMM	MILLIEME	EEIKLRST	TRISKELE
EEHILSSV	HIVELESS	EEHLMMNS	HELMSMEN	EEIILLMT	MELILITE	EEIKMRSS	KERMISES
EEHILWYZ	WHEEZILY	EEHLMMSW	WHEMMLES	EEIILLOP	EOLIPILE	EEIKNORS	KEROSINE
EEHIMMSS	HIMSEEMS	EEHLMOOS	HOLESOME	EEIILLRV	LIVELIER	EEIKNRST	KERNITES
	IMMESHES	EEHLMOSS	HOMELESS	EEIILMNT	ILMENITE	EEIKOQUV	EQUIVOKE
	MISHMEES	EEHLNOTT	TELETHON		MELINITE	EEIKPPRR	KIPPERER
EEHIMNOS	HEMIONES	EEHLOPSS	HOPELESS	EEIILMRT	TIMELIER	EEIKPRST	PERKIEST
EEHIMNRS	SHIREMEN	EEHLORST	HOSTELER	EEIILMSS	EMISSILE	EEIKPSST	PESKIEST
EEHIMNSS	INMESHES	EEHLORSV	SHOVELER	EEIILNPP	PIPELINE	EEIKRRSS	SKERRIES
EEHIMPRS	EMPERISH	EEHLOSSS	SHOELESS	EEIILNST	LENITIES	EEIKSSTY	SKIEYEST
EEHIMPST	EPITHEMS	EEHLPRST	TELPHERS	EEIILNTV	LENITIVE	EEIKSTTT	TEKTITES
	HEMPIEST	EEHLPRSU	SPHERULE	EEIILORS	OILERIES	EEILLMPR	IMPELLER
EEHIMQUV	VEHMIQUE	EEHLRSST	SHELTERS	EEIILRST	TILERIES	EEILLMRS	SMELLIER
EEHIMRST	ERETHISM	EEHLRSSW	WELSHERS	EEIILRSV	LIVERIES	EEILLMRU	REILLUME
	ETHERISM	EEHLRSTY	SHELTERY	EEIILSTV	LEVITIES	EEILLMST	MELLITES
EEHIMRTT	THERMITE	EEHLSSTW	THEWLESS		VEILIEST	EEILLNOR	LONELIER
EEHIMSST	MESHIEST	EEHMMOPR	MORPHEME	EEIILSTW	LEWISITE	EEILLNSY	SENILELY
EEHINNQU	HENEQUIN	EEHMMORT	OHMMETER	EEIIMMTT	MIMETITE	EEILLNVV	VENVILLE
EEHINNRS	ENSHRINE	EEHMNOOS	MOONSHEE	EEIIMNOT	MEIONITE	EEILLORS	ORSEILLE
EEHINNRT	INHERENT	EEHMNOPS	PHONEMES	EEIIMNST	ENMITIES	EEILLORV	LOVELIER
EEHINNSS	SNEESHIN	EEHMNORS	HORSEMEN	EEIIMOST	MOIETIES	EEILLOSV	LOVELIES
EEHINNST	HENNIEST		SHOREMEN	EEIIMPRS	RIEMPIES	EEILLPSS	ELLIPSES
EEHINORS	HEROINES	EEHMNOSU	HOUSEMEN	EEIIMRSS	MISERIES	EEILLPSY	SLEEPILY
EEHINORT	ETHERION	EEHMNOSW	SOMEWHEN	EEIIMSST	ITEMISES	EEILLRSS	LEISLERS
EEHINPRS	INSPHERE	EEHMNRSU	ENRHEUMS	EEIIMSSV	EMISSIVE	EEILLRST	TREILLES
EEHINPRT	NEPHRITE	EEHMNRSY	MYNHEERS	EEIIMSTZ	ITEMIZES	EEILLSSV	VEILLESS
	PREHNITE	EEHMOORT	RHEOTOME	EEIINNST	NINETIES	EEILLSTV	EVILLEST
	TREPHINE	EEHMOOSS	HOMEOSES	EEIINORT	ERIONITE	EEILLTVY	VELLEITY
EEHINRRS	ERRHINES	EEHMORST	THEOREMS	EEIINPPR	PIPERINE	EEILLVWY	WEEVILLY
EEHINRTT	THIRTEEN	EEHMORVW	WHOMEVER	EEIINPRS	PINERIES	EEILMNNS	LINESMEN
EEHINRTW	WHITENER	EEHMRSUX	EXHUMERS	EEIINPRV	VIPERINE	EEILMNNU	ENLUMINE
EEHIOPPS	HOSEPIPE	EEHMSSTY	METHYSES	EEIINRRV	RIVERINE	EEILMNOP	PEMOLINE
EEHIORSS	HEROISES	EEHNNORT	ENTHRONE	EEIINRSS	RESINISE	EEILMNRS	ERMELINS
EEHIORST	ISOTHERE	EEHNNPPU	UNHEPPEN	EEIINRST	ERINITES	EEILMNRU	LEMURINE
	THEORIES	EEHNNSSS	NESHNESS		NITERIES		RELUMINE
	THEORISE	EEHNNSTU	UNNETHES	EEIINRSV	VINERIES	EEILMNSS	ISLESMEN
EEHIORSZ	HEROIZES	EEHNOPRU	HEREUPON	EEIINRSW	WINERIES	EEILMNSU	SELENIUM
EEHIORTZ	THEORIZE	EEHNOPST	POSHTEEN	EEIINRSZ	RESINIZE		SEMILUNE
EEHIPPST	PSEPHITE		POTHEENS	EEIINRTT	INTERTIE	EEILMOPS	POLEMISE
EEHIPPTY	EPIPHYTE	EEHNOPTY	HYPNOTEE		RETINITE	EEILMOPZ	POLEMIZE
EEHIPRRS	PERISHER		NEOPHYTE	EEIINSSV	INESSIVE	EEILMORT	MOTELIER
	SPHERIER	EEHNORST	HONESTER	EEIINSTT	ENTITIES	EEILMOST	MESOLITE
EEHIPRSS	PERISHES	EEHNORSW	HERONSEW	EEIINSTV	INVITEES		MISLETOE
EEHIPRST	TREESHIP		NOWHERES		VEINIEST	EEILMPST	IMPLETES
EEHIPRTT	PERTHITE	EEHNORTU	HEREUNTO	EEIIORSS	OSIERIES	EEILMPSX	IMPLEXES
	TEPHRITE	EEHNORTV	OVERHENT	EEIIPRSX	EXPIRIES	EEILMRST	TERMLIES
	THREEPIT	EEHNPRSU	UNSPHERE	EEIIPRTT	EPITRITE	EEILMRSV	VERMEILS
EEHIPSST	STEEPISH	EEHNRTTU	UNTETHER	EEIIQSTU	EQUITIES	EEILMSST	TIMELESS
EEHIPSTT	EPITHETS	EEHNSSTU	ENTHUSES	EEIIQTUV	QUIETIVE	EEILMSUV	EMULSIVE
EEHIPSUU	EUPHUISE	EEHNSSTV	SEVENTHS	EEIIRRST	REISTIER	EEILNNST	LENIENTS
EEHIPUUZ	EUPHUIZE	EEHOOPRS	OOSPHERE	EEIIRRSV	RIVIERES		SENTINEL
EEHIQRSU	QUEERISH	EEHOOPSW	WHOOPEES	EEIIRRTV	TIRRIVEE	EEILNNSV	ENLIVENS
EEHIRRSS	SHERRIES	EEHOORSV	OVERSHOE	EEIIRRTY	VERITIES	EEILNNSW	ENLIVENS
EEHIRRSW	WHERRIES	EEHOPRSU	EUPHROES	EEIISSTV	VISITEES	EEILNOPR	LEPORINE
EEHIRSST	HEISTERS	EEHOORTX	EXHORTER	EEIISTVW	VIEWIEST	EEILNORS	ELOINERS
EEHIRSSV	SHRIEVES	EEHORSSU	REHOUSES	EEIJKRST	JERKIEST	EEILNOST	NOSELITE
EEHIRSSX	RHEXISES	EEHORSVW	WHOSEVER	EEIJLNNU	JULIENNE	EEILNOSV	NOVELISE
EEHIRSTT	ETHERIST	EEHORTTU	THEREOUT	EEIJLNRT	JETLINER	EEILNOVZ	NOVELIZE
EEHIRTVY	THIEVERY	EEHORTUW	WHEREOUT	EEIJLNUV	JUVENILE	EEILNPPZ	ZEPPELIN
EEHISSST	ESTHESIS	EEHPRSST	HEPSTERS	EEIJMMST	JEMMIEST	EEILNPRS	PILSENER
EEHISSTW	SWEETISH		SPERTHES	EEIJNNOR	ENJOINER	EEILNPRU	PERILUNE
EEHISTTW	THEWIEST	EEHPRSTU	SUPERHET	EEIJSTTT	JETTIEST	EEILNPRV	REPLEVIN
EEHISTWY	WHEYIEST	EEHRRSTW	WHERRETS	EEIKLLRS	SKELLIER	EEILNPST	PLENTIES
						EEILNRSS	REINLESS

EEILNRST	LISTENER	EEIMNORS	EMERSION		WENNIEST	EEINSTTW	TENTWISE
	SILENTER	EEIMNORT	TIMONEER	EEINOPPR	PEPERINO		TWENTIES
EEILNRTY	ENTIRELY	EEIMNORV	VOMERINE		PEPERONI	EEINSTTX	EXISTENT
	LIENTERY	EEIMNOST	MONETISE	EEINOPRS	ISOPRENE	EEIOPPRS	EPISPORE
EEILNRUV	UNVEILER		SEMITONE		PIONEERS		POPERIES
EEILNSSV	EVILNESS	EEIMNOTX	XENOTIME	EEINORRT	REORIENT	EEIOPRRS	ROPERIES
	VILENESS	EEIMNOTZ	MONETIZE	EEINORSS	ESSOINER	EEIOPRRT	PORTIERE
EEILNSTT	ENTITLES	EEIMNPRT	TRIPEMEN	EEINORST	SEROTINE	EEIOPRRV	OVERRIPE
EEILNSTV	VEINLETS	EEIMNPRU	PERINEUM	EEINORSV	EVERSION	EEIOPRST	POETRIES
EEILOPRS	PELORIES	EEIMNPST	SEPIMENT	EEINORTT	TENORITE	EEIOPSST	POETISES
EEILOPST	PETIOLES	EEIMNQSU	MESQUINE	EEINORTX	EXERTION	EEIOPSTZ	POETIZES
EEILORRT	LOITERER	EEIMNRRT	TERMINER	EEINOSST	ESSONITE	EEIORRRS	ORRERIES
EEILORRV	OVERLIER	EEIMNRRV	RIVERMEN	EEINOSTT	NOISETTE	EEIORRSS	ROSERIES
EEILORRW	LOWERIER	EEIMNRSV	MINEVERS		TEOSINTE		ROSIERES
EEILORST	LITEROSE	EEIMNRTU	MUTINEER	EEINPPSS	PEPSINES	EEIORRTV	OVERTIRE
	TROELIES	EEIMNRTV	VIREMENT	EEINPRRS	REPINERS	EEIORRTW	TOWERIER
EEILORSV	OVERLIES	EEIMNSSW	MISWEENS	EEINPRSS	EREPSINS	EEIORRTX	EXTERIOR
	RELIEVOS	EEIMNSTT	MINETTES		RIPENESS	EEIORRUV	OUVRIERE
	VOLERIES	EEIMOPRS	PROMISEE	EEINPRSU	PENURIES	EEIORSST	EROTESIS
EEILORSW	OWLERIES		REIMPOSE		RESUPINE	EEIORSSX	OREXISES
EEILORVV	OVERLIVE	EEIMOPSS	EPISOMES	EEINPRTX	INEXPERT	EEIORSVW	OVERWISE
	OVERVEIL	EEIMOPST	EPITOMES	EEINPSST	PENTISES	EEIORSVZ	OVERSIZE
EEILOSST	ESTOILES		EPSOMITE	EEINPSTT	INEPTEST	EEIORVVW	OVERVIEW
EEILOSTW	OWELTIES	EEIMORSS	ISOMERES		SPINETTE	EEIORVWW	WIREWOVE
EEILOSTZ	ZEOLITES	EEIMORST	TIRESOME	EEINQRRU	ENQUIRER	EEIPPPRR	PREPPIER
EEILOSVW	VOWELISE	EEIMORTV	OVERTIME	EEINQRSU	ENQUIRES	EEIPPPRS	PREPPIES
EEILOTTT	TOILETTE	EEIMORTX	OXIMETER		INQUERES	EEIPPPST	PEPPIEST
EEILOVWZ	VOWELIZE	EEIMOSSW	SOMEWISE		SQUIREEN	EEIPPRRS	PERSPIRE
EEILPPSS	PIPELESS	EEIMOSSX	EXOMISES	EEINQSTU	QUIETENS	EEIPPRRT	PERIPETY
EEILPPSY	EPILEPSY	EEIMPPRS	EPISPERM	EEINQSUY	QUEYNIES	EEIPPSST	PEPTISES
EEILPRRS	REPLIERS	EEIMPRRS	PREMIERS	EEINRRSS	RESINERS	EEIPPSTT	PIPETTES
EEILPRSS	SPIELERS		REPRIMES	EEINRRST	INSERTER	EEIPPSTZ	PEPTIZES
EEILPRST	EPISTLER		SIMPERER		REINSERT	EEIPQRSU	PERIQUES
	PELTRIES	EEIMPRSS	EMPRISES		REINTERS		REPIQUES
	PERLITES		IMPRESES		RENTIERS	EEIPRRRS	PERRIERS
	REPTILES		IMPRESSE		TERRINES	EEIPRRSS	REPRISES
EEILPSSS	PELISSES		MESPRISE	EEINRRSU	REINSURE		RESPIRES
EEILPSST	EPISTLES		PREMISES	EEINRRSV	VERNIERS	EEIPRRSV	REPRIVES
EEILPSSU	EPULISES		SPIREMES	EEINRRTV	INVERTER	EEIPRRSZ	REPRIZES
EEILPSSV	PELVISES	EEIMPRST	EMPTIERS	EEINRRTX	INTERREX	EEIPRRTT	PRETERIT
EEILPSTY	EPISTYLE	EEIMPRSX	PREMIXES	EEINRSST	INTERESS		PRETTIER
EEILQRSU	RELIQUES	EEIMPRSZ	MESPRIZE		SENTRIES	EEIPRSST	RESPITES
EEILRRSV	RELIVERS	EEIMPSST	SEPTIMES		TRENISES	EEIPRSSV	PREVISES
	REVILERS	EEIMPSSY	EMPYESIS	EEINRSSU	ENURESIS	EEIPRSTT	PRETTIES
EEILRSST	LEISTERS	EEIMPSTT	EMPTIEST	EEINRSSV	INVERSES	EEIPRSTY	PERSEITY
	RITELESS	EEIMQRSU	REQUIEMS		VERSINES	EEIPRSVW	PREVIEWS
	TIRELESS	EEIMQSTU	MESQUITE	EEINRSTT	INERTEST	EEIPRSZZ	PREZZIES
EEILRSSU	LEISURES	EEIMRRST	MERRIEST		INTEREST	EEIPRTUV	ERUPTIVE
EEILRSSV	SERVILES		TRIREMES		STERNITE	EEIPSSSS	SPEISSES
EEILRSSW	WIRELESS	EEIMRRTT	REMITTER	EEINRSTU	ESURIENT	EEIPSSTW	SPEWIEST
EEILRSTT	RETITLES		TRIMETER		NEURITES		STEPWISE
EEILSSTW	WITELESS	EEIMRSST	TRISEMES		RETINUES	EEIPSTTT	PETTIEST
EEILSSVW	VIEWLESS	EEIMRSSV	VERMISES		REUNITES	EEIQRRRU	REQUIRER
EEILSTTX	TEXTILES	EEIMRSTT	TERMITES	EEINRSTV	NERVIEST	EEIQRRSU	REQUIRES
EEILSTVY	STIEVELY	EEIMRSTU	EMERITUS		REINVEST	EEIQRRTU	REQUITER
EEIMMNRS	IMMENSER	EEIMRTTY	TEMERITY		SERVIENT	EEIQRRUV	VERQUIRE
EEIMMORS	MEMORIES	EEIMSSST	MESSIEST		SIRVENTE	EEIQRSSU	ESQUIRES
	MEMORISE		METISSES	EEINRSTX	INTERSEX	EEIQRSTU	QUIETERS
EEIMMORZ	MEMORIZE	EEINNNPS	PENNINES	EEINRSTY	SERENITY		REQUITES
EEIMMOST	SOMETIME	EEINNPTT	PENITENT	EEINRSUV	UNIVERSE	EEIQRSTW	QWERTIES
EEIMMRSS	IMMERSES	EEINNRST	INTENSER	EEINRTTY	ENTIRETY	EEIQRTUY	QUEERITY
EEIMMRST	MERISTEM		INTERNES		ETERNITY	EEIQSSSU	ESQUISSE
	MIMESTER	EEINNRSU	NEURINES	EEINSSST	SESTINES	EEIQSTTU	QUIETEST
	MISMETRE	EEINNRSV	INNERVES	EEINSSSW	WISENESS	EEIRRRST	RETIRERS
EEIMMRSU	EUMERISM		NERVINES	EEINSSSX	SEXINESS		TERRIERS
EEIMMSSS	MISSEEMS	EEINNRTT	RENITENT	EEINSSTW	NEWSIEST	EEIRRSST	TRESSIER
EEIMNNOS	NOMINEES	EEINNRUX	XENURINE	EEINSSTX	SIXTEENS	EEIRRSSV	REVERSIS
EEIMNNRS	REINSMEN	EEINNSST	TENNISES	EEINSSTY	SYENITES		REVISERS
EEIMNOPS	EPISEMON	EEINNSTT	SENTIENT	EEINSTTT	NETTIEST	EEIRRSTV	REVERIST
		EEINNSTW	ENTWINES		TENTIEST		RIVERETS

	RIVETERS		SPELLERS
EEIRRSTW	REWRITES	EELLQRSU	QUELLERS
EEIRRSVV	REVIVERS	EELLRSSU	RULELESS
EEIRRTTT	TITTERER	EELLRSSW	SWELLERS
EEIRSSSU	REISSUES	EELLSSTW	SWELLEST
EEIRSSSV	IVRESSES	EELMMPSU	EMPLUMES
EEIRSSTT	RESTIEST	EELMMPUX	EXEMPLUM
EEIRSSTU	SURETIES	EELMNOOS	LONESOME
EEIRSSTV	SIEVERTS		OENOMELS
	TREVISES	EELMNORS	SOLEMNER
	VESTRIES	EELMNSUY	UNSEEMLY
EEIRSSUZ	SEIZURES	EELMNTTU	TEMULENT
EEIRSTVV	VETIVERS	EELMNTUY	UNMEETLY
EEIRSTVY	SEVERITY	EELMOOSV	LOVESOME
EEIRTTTZ	TERZETTI	EELMOPRS	PLEROMES
EEISSTTT	TESTIEST	EELMOPRY	EMPLOYER
EEISSTTU	SUETIEST	EELMOPST	LEPTOMES
EEISSTTV	STIEVEST	EELMOPSY	POLYSEME
EEISSTTW	STEWIEST	EELMORST	MOLESTER
EEISSTTZ	ZESTIEST	EELMORSW	EELWORMS
EEISTTTX	TETTIXES	EELMORTY	MOTLEYER
EEISTUXZ	ZEUXITES		REMOTELY
EEJJLNUY	JEJUNELY	EELMOSSV	MOVELESS
EEJKMOOS	JOKESOME	EELMOTVW	TWELVEMO
EEJLLMSU	JUMELLES	EELMPPRU	EMPURPLE
EEJLPSTU	PULSEJET	EELMPSST	SEMPLEST
EEJNOORS	REJONEOS		STEMPELS
EEJNORSY	ENJOYERS		STEMPLES
EEJPRRRU	PERJURER	EELMPSTT	TEMPLETS
EEJPRRSU	PERJURES	EELMRRTU	MURRELET
EEJQRRSU	JERQUERS	EELMRSST	SMELTERS
EEKKOSTV	VETKOEKS		TERMLESS
EEKKRRST	TREKKERS	EELMRSTY	SMELTERY
EEKLLNRY	KERNELLY	EELMRTUX	LUXMETER
EEKLLNSV	KNEVELLS	EELMSSST	STEMLESS
EEKLLSUU	UKULELES	EELMSSTT	STEMLETS
EEKLNNNU	UNKENNEL	EELNNOSS	LONENESS
EEKLNOSS	KEELSONS	EELNNUVY	UNEVENLY
EEKLNOST	SKELETON	EELNOORS	LOOSENER
EEKLNOSV	VELSKOEN	EELNOPPU	UNPEOPLE
EEKLRSST	KESTRELS	EELNOPRT	PETRONEL
	SKELTERS	EELNOPSV	ENVELOPS
EEKNOPRS	RESPOKEN	EELNOPTY	POLYTENE
EEKNOSTY	KEYNOTES	EELNOQTU	ELOQUENT
	KEYSTONE	EELNORST	ENTRESOL
EEKNSSTU	NETSUKES	EELNORTT	TELETRON
EEKOORST	KREOSOTE	EELNORTV	OVERLENT
EEKOPRTV	OVERKEPT	EELNOSSS	NOSELESS
EEKORSTV	OVERKEST		SOLENESS
EEKRRTUZ	KREUTZER	EELNOSST	NOTELESS
EELLMORW	MELLOWER		TONELESS
EELLMPTU	PLUMELET	EELNOSSU	SELENOUS
EELLMRSS	SMELLERS	EELNOSSY	ESLOYNES
EELLMRSV	VERMELLS	EELNOSSZ	ZONELESS
EELLNORR	ENROLLER	EELNOSTT	NOTELETS
EELLNOUV	NOUVELLE	EELNOSTU	TOLUENES
EELLNPRU	PRUNELLE	EELNOTVV	EVOLVENT
EELLNRSU	SULLENER	EELNRSTT	LETTERNS
EELLNSST	SNELLEST	EELNRSUV	NERVULES
EELLNSTU	ENTELLUS	EELNSSTU	TUNELESS
EELLOPSS	ELLOPSES		UNSTEELS
EELLORSS	ROSELLES	EELNSSTY	ENSTYLES
EELLORST	SOLLERET	EELNSSUV	UNSELVES
EELLORSV	OVERSELL	EELNSTTU	LUNETTES
EELLORSZ	ROZELLES		UNSETTLE
EELLORTX	EXTOLLER	EELOPPSS	PEPLOSES
EELLORWY	YELLOWER	EELOPPST	ESTOPPEL
EELLOSSV	LOVELESS	EELOPRRX	EXPLORER
EELLOSUV	LEVULOSE	EELOPRSX	EXPLORES
EELLPRSS	RESPELLS	EELOPSTU	EELPOUTS
	OUTSLEEP	EEMOORRV	MOREOVER
EELOQRUY	REQUOYLE	EEMOORTT	ROOMETTE
EELORRSV	RESOLVER	EEMOOSSX	EXOSMOSE
EELORRTV	REVOLTER	EEMOPRRS	EMPERORS
EELORRUV	OVERRULE		PREMORSE
EELORRVV	REVOLVER	EEMOPRSV	PREMOVES
EELORSSS	ROSELESS	EEMOPRSW	EMPOWERS
EELORSSV	RESOLVES	EEMOQTTU	MOQUETTE
EELORSTT	LORETTES	EEMORRSS	REMORSES
EELORSTU	RESOLUTE	EEMORRSU	UROMERES
EELORSVV	REVOLVES	EEMORRSV	REMOVERS
EELORTTU	ROULETTE	EEMORRTU	MOUTERER
EELORTUV	REVOLUTE		OUTREMER
EELOSSST	OSSELETS	EEMORSST	SOMERSET
EELOSSSU	SOLEUSES	EEMORSTT	REMOTEST
EELOSSTT	TELEOSTS	EEMORSTU	TEMEROUS
EELOSSTV	VOTELESS	EEMOTTTU	TEETOTUM
EELOSTTX	SEXTOLET	EEMPRRSU	PRESUMER
EELOSTUV	EVOLUTES		SUPREMER
	VELOUTES	EEMPRSST	SEMPSTER
EELPPSSU	PEPLUSES	EEMPRSSU	PRESUMES
EELPPSTU	SEPTUPLE		SUPREMES
EELPQRSU	PREQUELS	EEMPRSTT	TEMPTERS
EELPRSST	SPELTERS	EEMPRSTU	PERMUTES
EELPRSSU	REPULSES	EEMPSSTT	TEMPESTS
EELPRSTZ	PRETZELS	EEMPSSTY	EMPTYSES
EELPRSUX	PLEXURES	EEMRRSTU	MUSTERER
EELPRTXY	EXPERTLY	EEMRRSUU	REMUEURS
EELPSSUX	EXPULSES	EEMRRTTU	MUTTERER
	PLEXUSES	EEMSSTTU	MUSETTES
EELPSTUX	SEXTUPLE	EENNNOSS	NONSENSE
EELRRSTW	WRESTLER	EENNNPTY	TENPENNY
EELRSSST	RESTLESS	EENNOORT	ROTENONE
	TRESSELS	EENNOPSS	OPENNESS
EELRSSTT	SETTLERS	EENNOPTX	EXPONENT
	STERLETS	EENNORRW	RENOWNER
	TRESTLES	EENNORST	TENONERS
EELRSSTW	SWELTERS	EENNORSU	NEURONES
	WRESTLES	EENNOSTT	NONETTES
EELRSSTY	RESTYLES	EENNQSUU	UNQUEENS
	TYRELESS	EENNRSUV	UNNERVES
EELRSSTZ	SELTZERS	EENNSSSU	UNSENSES
EELRSTWY	WESTERLY	EENNSSTX	NEXTNESS
EELSSTTV	SVELTEST	EENOORST	ROESTONE
EELSSTUY	EUSTYLES	EENOORTV	OVERTONE
EEMMNOOP	MENOPOME	EENOPPRS	PROPENES
EEMMNOST	MEMENTOS		PROPENSE
EEMMNOTV	MOVEMENT	EENOPPST	PEPTONES
EEMMNRRY	MERRYMEN	EENOPRSS	RESPONSE
EEMMOORS	MEROSOME	EENOPRST	PROTENSE
EEMMOSSU	MOUSMEES	EENOPRSU	PERONEUS
EEMMNOPW	PENWOMEN	EENOPRTT	ENTREPOT
EEMMNOSV	ENVENOMS	EENOPRXY	PYROXENE
EEMNOOSS	SOMEONES	EENOPSST	PENTOSES
EEMNOOSY	MOONEYES		POSTEONS
EEMNOPRS	PROSEMEN	EENORRSV	OVERRENS
EEMNORRS	SERMONER	EENORRTT	ROTTENER
EEMNORST	SERMONET	EENORSSS	SORENESS
	STOREMEN	EENORSSU	NEUROSES
EEMNORSU	MOUNSEER	EENORSTT	ONSETTER
EEMNORSV	OVERSMEN	EENORSTV	OVERNETS
EEMNORSY	MONEYERS	EENORSTX	EXTENSOR
EEMNORTU	ROUTEMEN	EENORSVW	OVERSEWN
EEMNPPRS	PRESSMEN	EENORTVW	OVERWENT
EEMNPRSU	SUPERMEN	EENOSSST	STENOSES
EEMNPRTU	UNTEMPER	EENOSSSY	ESSOYNES
EEMNRSTW	TREWSMEN	EENPPRST	PERPENTS
EEMNSSTU	MUTENESS	EENPRSST	PERTNESS
	TENESMUS		PRESENTS
EEMNSTTV	VESTMENT		SERPENTS

EENPRSSU PURENESS	EEPRRSSS PRESSERS	EFFIPSTU PUFFIEST	EFGINRSU GUNFIRES
EENPRSTT STREPENT	EEPRRSSU PERUSERS	EFFIQRSU SQUIFFER	REFUSING
EENPRSTV PREVENTS	PRESSURE	EFFIRSTU STUFFIER	EFGINRSW SWERFING
EENPSSSU SUSPENSE	EEPRRSTV PERVERTS	EFFISSTT STIFFEST	EFGINRTT FRETTING
EENPSSTY STEPNEYS	EEPRRSVY REPRYVES	EFFISSUX SUFFIXES	EFGINRTU FEUTRING
EENPSTTU PETUNTSE	EEPRSTTU UPSETTER	EFFLMNUU UNMUFFLE	REFUTING
EENPTTUZ PETUNTZE	EEPRSTTX PRETEXTS	EFFLMRSU MUFFLERS	EFGINRTY GENTRIFY
EENQSSTU SEQUENTS	EEPSSTTT SEPTETTS	EFFLNRSU SNUFFLER	EFGIOOST GOOFIEST
EENRRSSU ENSURERS	EEQRSSTU QUESTERS	EFFLNRUU UNRUFFLE	EFGIOPTT PETTIFOG
EENRRSTV RENVERST	REQUESTS	EFFLNSSU SNUFFLES	EFGIORSV FORGIVES
EENRRSUV NERVURES	EERRSSTU TRESSURE	EFFLOSSU SOUFFLES	EFGIRRST GRIFTERS
EENRRTUV VENTURER	EERRSSTW STREWERS	EFFLRRSU RUFFLERS	EFGLOOVX FOXGLOVE
EENRSSSU SURENESS	WRESTERS	EFFLRSTU TRUFFLES	EFGLORST FROGLETS
EENRSSTT STERNEST	EERRSSVW SWERVERS	EFFNRSSU SNUFFERS	EFGLRSUU SURGEFUL
TESTERNS	EERRSTTU REUTTERS	EFFOOORT FOREFOOT	EFGLSSTU SLUGFEST
EENRSSTU TRUENESS	UTTERERS	EFFOORRS OFFERORS	EFGNOSST SONGFEST
EENRSSTW WESTERNS	EERRSTUV VESTURER	EFFOPRRS PROFFERS	EFGNSSUU FUNGUSES
EENRSSTY STYRENES	EERRSTVY REVESTRY	EFFORRUV OVERRUFF	EFGORRSU FERRUGOS
EENRSTUV VENTURES	EERRSUVY RESURVEY	EFFRSSTU STUFFERS	EFGORSTU FOREGUTS
EEOOPRSX EXOSPORE	EERSSSST STRESSES	EFFSSSUU SUFFUSES	EFHHIRSS FRESHISH
EEOOPRTZ ZOETROPE	EERSSSTU ESTRUSES	EFGGGILN FLEGGING	EFHIILRT FILTHIER
EEOORRVW OVERWORE	EERSSSUY SEYSURES	EFGGIINN FEIGNING	EFHIILST TILEFISH
EEOPPRSS PORPESSE	EERSSTTU TRUSTEES	EFGGILOS SOLFEGGI	EFHIIMSU HUMIFIES
EEOPPSTU OUTPEEPS	EERSSTUV VESTURES	EFGGINRU REFUGING	EFHIINRS FINISHER
EEOPRRRT REPORTER	EERSSUVW SURVEWES	EFGGIORR FROGGIER	EFHIINSS FINISHES
EEOPRRRV REPROVER	EERSTTTU UTTEREST	EFGGIOST FOGGIEST	EFHIIPPS PIPEFISH
EEOPRRSU REPOSURE	EERSTTUX TEXTURES	EFGGIRRS FRIGGERS	EFHIIPRS FIRESHIP
EEOPRRSV REPROVES	EESSSTTT SESTETTS	EFGGISTU FUGGIEST	EFHIIRST SHIFTIER
EEOPRRTT POTTERER	EESSTTTX SEXTETTS	EFGGORRY FROGGERY	EFHIISST FISHIEST
EEOPRRTX EXPORTER	EFFFGINO FEOFFING	EFGHILNS FLESHING	EFHILRSU FLUSHIER
EEOPRSSS ESPRESSO	EFFFILRU FLUFFIER	SHELFING	EFHIOOOR FORHOOIE
EEOPRSST PORTESSE	EFFFISTU FUFFIEST	EFGHINRS FRESHING	EFHIOPRS FORESHIP
EEOPRSSU ESPOUSER	EFFFOORS FEOFFORS	EFGHINRT FRIGHTEN	EFHIORRT FROTHIER
REPOUSSE	EFFGILRU GRIEFFUL	EFGHIRST FIGHTERS	EFHIORSS ROSEFISH
EEOPRSSX EXPOSERS	EFFGINOR OFFERING	FREIGHTS	EFHIORSV OVERFISH
EXPRESSO	EFFGINSU EFFUSING	EFGHNOTU FOUGHTEN	EFHIORTT FORTIETH
EEOPRSTT TREETOPS	EFFGRSTU GRUFFEST	EFGIILNU FIGULINE	EFHIPRSS SERFSHIP
EEOPRSTU OUTPEERS	EFFHIIRW WHIFFIER	EFGIILSU UGLIFIES	EFHIPRSU FURPHIES
EEOPRSTV OVERSTEP	EFFHIISW FISHWIFE	EFGIIMNS MISFEIGN	EFHIRRTU THURIFER
EEOPRSTY SEROTYPE	EFFHIITT FIFTIETH	EFGIINNR ENFIRING	EFHIRSST SHIFTERS
EEOPRSUX EXPOSURE	EFFHIKSU KUFFIEHS	INFRINGE	EFHISSTU SHUFTIES
EEOPSSSU ESPOUSES	EFFHIKUY KUFFIYEH	REFINING	EFHKLNOU FUNKHOLE
POSEUSES	EFFHILRW WHIFFLER	EFGIINNT FEINTING	EFHLLLSU SHELLFUL
EEOPSTUW OUTWEEPS	EFFHILSW WHIFFLES	EFGIINNX ENFIXING	EFHLNORS HORNFELS
EEOQRSTU REQUOTES	EFFHIRSS SHERIFFS	EFGIINRR FRINGIER	EFHLOORS HOOFLESS
EEOQRTTU ROQUETTE	EFFHIRSW WHIFFERS	EFGIINRU FIGURINE	EFHLOOSX FOXHOLES
EEORRRST RESORTER	EFFHISTU HUFFIEST	EFGIINRY REIFYING	EFHLOPSU HOPEFULS
RESTORER	EFFHISTW WHIFFETS	EFGIINRZ FRIEZING	EFHLORSY HORSEFLY
RETRORSE	EFFHLRSU SHUFFLER	EFGIITUV FUGITIVE	EFHLOSSU FLOUSHES
EEORRRTT RETORTER	EFFHLSSU SHUFFLES	EFGIKNOR FOREKING	EFHLOSUU HOUSEFUL
EEORRSST RESTORES	EFFHOORS OFFSHORE	EFGILLNO LIFELONG	EFHLRSSU FLUSHERS
EEORRSSV REVERSOS	EFFIIMST MIFFIEST	EFGILLNU FUELLING	EFHLSSTU FLUSHEST
EEORRSTU REROUTES	EFFIINRS SNIFFIER	EFGILLUU GUILEFUL	EFHLSTTW TWELFTHS
EEORRSTX EXTRORSE	EFFIINSS IFFINESS	EFGILMOR FILMGOER	EFHNORST FORHENTS
EEORRTTT TOTTERER	EFFIINST NIFFIEST	EFGILNNS FLENSING	EFHOORSW FORESHOW
EEORRTUV OVERTURE	EFFIIPRS SPIFFIER	EFGILNOR FLORIGEN	EFHORRTY FROTHERY
TROUVERE	EFFIKLSS SKIFFLES	EFGILNRS FLINGERS	EFHRRSTU FURTHERS
EEORRSST OSSETERS	EFFILNRS SNIFFLER	EFGILNRY FERLYING	EFHRSTTU FURTHEST
EEORSSTT ROSETTES	EFFILNSS SNIFFLES	EFGILNST FELTINGS	EFIIILRV VILIFIER
EEORSSTV ESTOVERS	EFFILORT FORELIFT	EFGILNTT FETTLING	EFIIILSV VILIFIES
OVERSETS	EFFILPRS PIFFLERS	EFGILSTU GULFIEST	EFIIIMNS MINIFIES
EEORSSUV OVERUSES	EFFILPRU PLUFFIER	EFGIMNST FIGMENTS	EFIIINNT INFINITE
EEORSSVW OVERSEWS	EFFILRRS RIFFLERS	EFGIMRUU REFUGIUM	EFIIIRVV VIVIFIER
EEORSTVX VORTEXES	EFFINOSU EFFUSION	EFGINNNP PFENNING	EFIIISTX FIXITIES
EEORTTTZ TERZETTO	EFFINRSS SNIFFERS	EFGINNPS PFENNIGS	EFIIISVV VIVIFIES
EEOSSSVW VOWESSÉS	EFFINRSU SNUFFIER	EFGINNRS FERNINGS	EFIIKLRS FLISKIER
EEOSSTTT SESTETTO	EFFINSST STIFFENS	EFGINORV FORGIVEN	EFIIKRRS FRISKIER
EEPPRSST STEPPERS	EFFIOPRS PIFFEROS	EFGINORW FOREWING	EFIILLRR FRILLIER
EEPPSSUW UPSWEEPS	EFFIORST FORFEITS	EFGINPUY PINGUEFY	EFIILLRS FRILLIES
EEPQRRUU PERRUQUE	EFFIOSTT TOFFIEST	EFGINRRY FERRYING	EFIILMRS FLIMSIER

Code	Word(s)
EFIILMSS	FLIMSIES / MISFILES
EFIILMST	FILMIEST
EFIILNRT	FLINTIER / INFILTER
EFIILNTY	FELINITY / FINITELY
EFIILOQU	FILIOQUE
EFIILRRT	FLIRTIER
EFIILRSU	FUSILIER
EFIILSTT	FITLIEST
EFIIMMNS	FEMINISM
EFIIMNOS	FISNOMIE / OMNIFIES
EFIIMNRR	INFIRMER
EFIIMNST	FEMINIST
EFIIMNSU	MUNIFIES
EFIIMNTY	FEMINITY
EFIIMRSS	MISFIRES
EFIINNST	FINNIEST
EFIINORR	INFERIOR
EFIINORT	NOTIFIER
EFIINOST	NOTIFIES
EFIINPSV	FIVEPINS
EFIINPSX	SPINIFEX
EFIINRST	SNIFTIER
EFIINRSU	UNIFIERS
EFIINRSY	RESINIFY
EFIINSTT	NIFTIEST
EFIINSUV	INFUSIVE
EFIIOSSS	OSSIFIES
EFIIPRRU	PURIFIER
EFIIPRST	SPITFIRE
EFIIPRSU	PURIFIES
EFIIPRTY	TYPIFIER
EFIIPSTY	TYPIFIES
EFIIRRST	FIRRIEST
EFIIRRTU	FRUITIER
EFIIRRZZ	FRIZZIER
EFIIRSTT	RIFTIEST
EFIIRTUV	FRUITIVE
EFIIRVVY	REVIVIFY
EFIISSTT	FISTIEST
EFIISTZZ	FIZZIEST
EFIJLORS	FRIJOLES
EFIJLOST	JETFOILS
EFIKLNSU	FLUNKIES
EFIKLORS	FOLKSIER
EFIKLSTU	FLUKIEST
EFIKNNOS	FINNESKO
EFIKNORS	FORESKIN
EFIKNRSU	REFUSNIK
EFIKNSTU	FUNKIEST
EFIKORRW	FIREWORK
EFIKORST	FORKIEST
EFIKRRSS	FRISKERS
EFIKRSST	FRISKETS
EFILLLNU	FLUELLIN
EFILLMSU	SMILEFUL
EFILLOOS	FOLIOLES
EFILLORV	OVERFILL
EFILLRUY	IREFULLY
EFILLSTY	STELLIFY
EFILLTUY	FUTILELY
EFILMNSU	FULMINES
EFILMOST	FILEMOTS
EFILMRSS	FIRMLESS
EFILMSSS	SELFISMS
EFILMSST	FILMSETS / LEFTISMS
EFILMSUY	EMULSIFY
EFILNNTU	INFLUENT
EFILNORU	FLUORINE
EFILNOSU	NOISEFUL
EFILNOSX	FLEXIONS
EFILNRTT	FLITTERN
EFILNSUX	INFLUXES
EFILNUWY	UNWIFELY
EFILOOSS	FLOOSIES
EFILOOSZ	FLOOZIES
EFILOPPR	FLOPPIER
EFILOPRR	PROFILER
EFILOPRS	PROFILES
EFILORRU	FLOURIER
EFILORSS	FLOSSIER
EFILORST	FLORIEST / TREFOILS
EFILORTU	FLUORITE
EFILOSSX	SEXFOILS
EFILOSTT	LOFTIEST
EFILOSTU	OUTFLIES
EFILPPRS	FLIPPERS
EFILPPST	FLIPPEST
EFILPPSU	PIPEFULS
EFILPRTU	UPLIFTER
EFILPSTU	SPITEFUL
EFILRRST	TRIFLERS
EFILRRSU	FLURRIES
EFILRSST	RIFTLESS / STIFLERS
EFILRSTT	FLITTERS
EFILRSTW	FEWTRILS
EFILRSVV	FLIVVERS
EFILRSZZ	FRIZZLES
EFILRTTU	FRUITLET
EFILSSST	SELFISTS
EFILSSTT	LEFTISTS
EFILSTTU	FLUTIEST / FUTILEST
EFILSTTW	SWIFTLET
EFIMMRSU	FERMIUMS
EFIMNORR	INFORMER / REINFORM / RENIFORM
EFIMNORS	ENSIFORM / FERMIONS
EFIMNRSS	FIRMNESS
EFIMNSTT	FITMENTS
EFIMORRT	RETIFORM
EFIMORRW	FIREWORM
EFIMOSTT	OFTTIMES
EFIMPRRU	FRUMPIER
EFIMRSTU	FREMITUS
EFINNORS	INFERNOS
EFINNSTU	FUNNIEST
EFINOPRS	FORPINES
EFINOPTX	PONTIFEX
EFINORRT	FRONTIER
EFINORSU	REFUSION
EFINORSX	FORNIXES
EFINOSSX	FOXINESS
EFINOSSZ	FOZINESS
EFINRSST	SNIFTERS
EFINRSSU	INFUSERS
EFINRTTU	UNFITTER
EFIOOPST	POOFIEST
EFIOORST	ROOFIEST
EFIOOSTT	FOOTIEST
EFIOOSTW	WOOFIEST
EFIOPRRS	PORIFERS
EFIOPRRT	PROFITER
EFIOPRST	FIREPOTS
EFIORRST	FROSTIER / ROTIFERS
EFIORRSW	FROWSIER
EFIORRTT	RETROFIT
EFIORRWZ	FROWZIER
EFIORSST	FOISTERS
EFIORSTW	FROWIEST
EFIPPRRS	FRIPPERS
EFIPPRRY	FRIPPERY
EFIPRRUY	REPURIFY
EFIPRTTY	PRETTIFY
EFIRRRSU	FURRIERS
EFIRRRUY	FURRIERY
EFIRRSSU	FRISEURS / FRISURES
EFIRRSTT	FRITTERS
EFIRRSTU	FRITURES / FRUITERS / FURRIEST
EFIRRTUV	FURTIVER
EFIRRTUY	FRUITERY
EFIRSSSU	FISSURES
EFIRSSTU	SURFEITS / SURFIEST
EFIRSSTW	SWIFTERS
EFIRSTTU	TURFIEST / TURFITES
EFIRSTUX	FIXTURES
EFIRSTUZ	FURZIEST
EFISSSTU	FUSSIEST
EFISSTTU	FUSTIEST
EFISSTTW	SWIFTEST
EFISTTTU	TUFTIEST
EFISTUZZ	FUZZIEST
EFKLLOOR	FOLKLORE
EFKLMNOS	MENFOLKS
EFKLMORS	MERFOLKS
EFKLNSUY	FLUNKEYS
EFKLOPSU	POKEFULS
EFKLORUW	FLUEWORK
EFKLPSSU	SKEPFULS
EFKNOORW	FOREKNOW
EFKOOPRS	FORSPOKE
EFKORRTW	FRETWORK
EFLLLOOW	WOOLFELL
EFLLLOWY	FELLOWLY
EFLLLPSU	SPELLFUL
EFLLNSSU	FULLNESS
EFLLNTUY	FLUENTLY
EFLLOORW	FOLLOWER
EFLLORUV	OVERFULL
EFLLOUWY	WOEFULLY
EFLLRUUY	RUEFULLY
EFLLSUUY	USEFULLY
EFLMMRUY	FLUMMERY
EFLMORRY	FORMERLY
EFLMORSS	FORMLESS
EFLMORSU	FULSOMER
EFLMPRSU	FRUMPLES
EFLNOOSU	FELONOUS
EFLNORSU	FLEURONS
EFLNORTT	FRONTLET
EFLNOSSU	FOULNESS
EFLNOSTT	FLETTONS / FONTLETS
EFLNSSUY	SYNFUELS
EFLNSTTU	TENTFULS
EFLNSUUU	UNUSEFUL
EFLOORRS	FLOORERS
EFLOORSS	FORSLOES / ROOFLESS
EFLOORSW	FORESLOW
EFLOORSZ	FOOZLERS
EFLOORTU	FOOTRULE
EFLOORVW	OVERFLOW
EFLOOSST	FOOTLESS
EFLOPRUW	POWERFUL
EFLORSTT	FORTLETS
EFLORSTW	FELWORTS
EFLORSUY	YOURSELF
EFLORSVY	FLYOVERS
EFLOSUUX	FLEXUOUS
EFLPRSSU	PRESSFUL
EFLPRSUU	PURSEFUL
EFLRSSTU	FLUSTERS
EFLRSTTU	FLUTTERS
EFLRSTUU	FRUSTULE
EFLRSTUY	FLUSTERY
EFMNNORT	FRONTMEN
EFMNORTY	FROMENTY
EFMNRTUY	FRUMENTY / FURMENTY
EFMOORST	FOREMOST
EFMOORSU	FOURSOME
EFMOPRRS	PERFORMS / PREFORMS
EFMOPRST	POMFRETS
EFNNOOOR	FORENOON
EFNNORST	FORNENST
EFNNORUZ	UNFROZEN
EFNOOOTT	FOOTNOTE
EFNOOPRT	PENTROOF
EFNOOSST	EFTSOONS / FESTOONS
EFNOPRST	FORSPENT
EFNORRST	RENFORST
EFNORRSU	FORERUNS
EFNORSTU	FORTUNES
EFNOSSST	SOFTNESS
EFOOORST	FOOTSORE
EFOOPRRS	REPROOFS
EFOOPRSS	SPOOFERS
EFOOPRST	FORETOPS / POOFTERS
EFOOPRSY	SPOOFERY
EFOOPSTT	FOOTSTEP
EFOORRSW	FORSWORE
EFOORRST	FOOTREST
EFOOSTUX	OUTFOXES
EFOPRRSU	PROFUSER
EFOPRSTU	POUFTERS
EFORRSST	FORTRESS
EFORRSTW	FROWSTER
EFORRSTY	FORESTRY
EFORRSUV	FERVOURS
EFORRTTU	FROTTEUR
EFORSSTT	FOSTRESS
EGGGIILR	GIGGLIER
EGGGILNS	LEGGINGS
EGGGILOR	GOGGLIER
EGGGILRS	GIGGLERS
EGGGINPS	PEGGINGS
EGGGIORR	GROGGIER
EGGGLORS	GOGGLERS
EGGGNNOR	RONGGENG
EGGGOOOS	GOOSEGOG
EGGGORRY	GROGGERY
EGGHIINN	NEIGHING

EGGHIINW	WEIGHING	EGGLORUY	GURGOYLE
EGGHILRS	HIGGLERS	EGGLPRSU	PLUGGERS
EGGHINSS	GHESSING	EGGLRSSU	SLUGGERS
EGGHIRST	THIGGERS	EGGLRSTU	STRUGGLE
EGGHLOSS	SHOGGLES	EGGMNTUY	NUTMEGGY
EGGHRTUY	THUGGERY	EGGMSSTU	SMUGGEST
EGGIILNR	NIGGLIER	EGGNOOST	GEOGNOST
EGGIILRW	WIGGLIER	EGGNOOSY	GEOGNOSY
EGGIINNN	ENGINING	EGGNORST	GONGSTER
EGGIINNR	GREINING	EGGNRSUY	SNUGGERY
	REIGNING	EGGNSSTU	SNUGGEST
EGGIINNS	SINGEING	EGGOORSU	GORGEOUS
EGGIINNW	WINGEING	EGGSSSTU	SUGGESTS
EGGIINRV	GRIEVING	EGHHILTY	EIGHTHLY
	REGIVING	EGHHINSS	HIGHNESS
EGGIIPST	PIGGIEST	EGHHOSSW	SHOWGHES
EGGIIRTW	TWIGGIER	EGHIILLS	GHILLIES
EGGIKNOS	GINGKOES	EGHIILNR	HIRELING
	GINKGOES	EGHIILNS	SHEILING
EGGILLNY	GINGELLY		SHIELING
EGGILMNU	EMULGING	EGHIIMRT	MIGHTIER
EGGILMSS	LEGGISMS	EGHIINNR	INHERING
EGGILNNO	LONGEING	EGHIINRT	THINGIER
EGGILNNT	GENTLING	EGHIINST	HEISTING
	GLENTING		NIGHTIES
EGGILNNU	LUNGEING		THINGIES
EGGILNRS	NIGGLERS	EGHIINSV	INVEIGHS
	SNIGGLER	EGHIINTV	THIEVING
EGGILNRY	GINGERLY	EGHIIRST	TIGERISH
EGGILNSS	SNIGGLES	EGHIKNRS	GHERKINS
EGGILNSU	LUGEINGS	EGHIKRSS	SKREIGHS
EGGILOOS	GOOGLIES		SKRIEGHS
EGGILQSU	SQUIGGLE	EGHILLNO	HELLOING
EGGILRRW	WRIGGLER	EGHILLNS	SHELLING
EGGILRSW	WIGGLERS	EGHILMNW	WHELMING
	WRIGGLES	EGHILNNU	UNHELING
EGGIMNNU	EMUNGING	EGHILNOV	HOVELING
EGGIMORS	SMOGGIER	EGHILNPS	HELPINGS
EGGIMSTU	MUGGIEST	EGHILNPT	PENLIGHT
EGGINNNR	GRENNING	EGHILNPW	WHELPING
EGGINNOR	ENGORING	EGHILNRS	HERLINGS
EGGINNSS	GINSENGS		SHINGLER
EGGINORR	GORGERIN	EGHILNSS	SHINGLES
	ROGERING	EGHILNST	ENLIGHTS
EGGINRRU	GRUNGIER		LIGHTENS
	REURGING	EGHILNSV	SHELVING
EGGINRSS	GRESSING	EGHILNSW	WELSHING
	SNIGGERS	EGHILNUW	GLUHWEIN
EGGINSSU	GUESSING	EGHILORT	REGOLITH
EGGINSTT	GETTINGS	EGHILOSU	OUGHLIES
EGGINSTU	GUESTING	EGHILPRT	PLIGHTER
	GUNGIEST	EGHILPST	PIGHTLES
EGGIOSST	SOGGIEST	EGHILRST	LIGHTERS
EGGIPRRS	PRIGGERS		RELIGHTS
EGGIPRRY	PRIGGERY		SLIGHTER
EGGIPSTU	PUGGIEST	EGHILSST	SLEIGHTS
EGGIRRST	TRIGGERS	EGHILSTT	LIGHTEST
EGGIRSSW	SWIGGERS	EGHIMNNS	MENSHING
EGGIRSTT	TRIGGEST	EGHIMNSS	MESHINGS
EGGIRSTU	RUGGIEST	EGHIMNUX	EXHUMING
	STUGGIER	EGHIMPRU	GRUMPHIE
EGGISTW	TWIGGERS	EGHIMSTT	MIGHTEST
EGGISTUV	VUGGIEST	EGHINNOY	HONEYING
EGGJLRSU	JUGGLERS	EGHINNSS	NIGHNESS
EGGJLRUY	JUGGLERY	EGHINNST	SENNIGHT
EGGLMOOY	GEMOLOGY	EGHINNSU	UNHINGES
EGGLMRSU	SMUGGLER	EGHINORT	THROEING
EGGLMSSU	SMUGGLES	EGHINORV	HOVERING
EGGLNSSU	SNUGGLES	EGHINOSS	SHOEINGS
EGGLORSS	SLOGGERS	EGHINOST	HISTOGEN
EGHINOSU	GINHOUSE	EGIILNNU	LINGUINE
EGHINPRS	SPHERING	EGIILNNV	LIVENING
EGHINPSS	SPHINGES	EGIILNOR	RELIGION
EGHINQTU	QUETHING	EGIILNPS	SPIELING
EGHINRRS	HERRINGS	EGIILNRS	RESILING
EGHINRRU	HUNGRIER	EGIILNRT	GIRTLINE
EGHINRRY	HERRYING		RETILING
EGHINRST	RIGHTENS		TINGLIER
EGHINRSU	USHERING		TIRELING
EGHINRSW	SHREWING	EGIILNRV	RELIVING
	WHINGERS		REVILING
EGHINRTW	WRETHING	EGIILNST	LIGNITES
EGHINSTT	SHETTING		LINGIEST
	TIGHTENS	EGIILNSV	VEILINGS
EGHINTTW	WHETTING	EGIILNSW	WISELING
EGHIOOSS	SHOOGIES	EGIILRRS	GRISLIER
EGHIOPSU	PISHOGUE	EGIILRTU	GUILTIER
EGHIORST	GHOSTIER	EGIILRTZ	GLITZIER
EGHIORSU	ROUGHIES	EGIIMMNW	IMMEWING
EGHIOSTT	GOTHITES	EGIIMNNU	INGENIUM
EGHIOSTU	TOUGHIES	EGIIMNOS	IGNOMIES
EGHIOSTV	EIGHTVOS	EGIIMNPS	IMPINGES
EGHIOTUW	OUTWEIGH	EGIIMNRS	REMISING
EGHIQRTU	REQUIGHT	EGIIMNRT	MERITING
EGHIRRST	RIGHTERS		MITERING
EGHIRRUY	HIERURGY	EGIIMNST	MINGIEST
EGHIRSST	SIGHTERS	EGIIMNSV	MISGIVEN
EGHIRSTT	RIGHTEST	EGIIMNTT	EMITTING
	STREIGHT	EGIIMOPT	IMPETIGO
EGHISSTU	GUSHIEST	EGIIMORR	GRIMOIRE
EGHISTTT	TIGHTEST	EGIIMRST	GRIMIEST
EGHLMNOP	PHLEGMON		TIGERISM
EGHLNORS	LEGHORNS	EGIIMSSV	MISGIVES
EGHLNPSU	ENGULPHS	EGIINNPR	REPINING
EGHLNRUY	HUNGERLY		RIPENING
EGHLOOOR	HOROLOGE	EGIINNRS	RESINING
EGHLOORY	RHEOLOGY	EGIINNSS	INSIGNES
EGHLOOSS	GOLOSHES		SEININGS
	SHOOGLES	EGIINNST	STEINING
EGHLOOTY	ETHOLOGY	EGIINNSV	VEININGS
	THEOLOGY	EGIINNSW	SINEWING
EGHLOPRU	PLOUGHER	EGIINNVW	VINEWING
EGHMNOOY	HOMOGENY	EGIINNWZ	WIZENING
EGHMNOSU	HUMOGENS	EGIINOPR	PEIGNOIR
EGHMOPUY	HYPOGEUM	EGIINORS	SEIGNIOR
EGHMOSSU	GUMSHOES	EGIINPRS	SPEIRING
EGHNOOPT	PHOTOGEN	EGIINPRV	PRIEVING
EGHNOOTY	THEOGONY	EGIINPRX	EXPIRING
EGHNORSU	ENROUGHS	EGIINPSS	PIGSNIES
	ROUGHENS	EGIINQTU	QUIETING
EGHNORUV	OVERHUNG	EGIINRRT	RETIRING
EGHNOSTU	TOUGHENS	EGIINRRW	REWIRING
EGHNRSTT	STRENGTH	EGIINRST	GIRNIEST
EGHOOOSW	HOOSEGOW		IGNITERS
EGHORRSU	ROUGHERS		REISTING
EGHORRTW	REGROWTH		STINGIER
EGHORSTU	ROUGHEST		STRIGINE
EGHOSTTU	TOUGHEST	EGIINRSU	SIGNIEUR
EGHPSSUU	UPGUSHES	EGIINRSV	REVISING
EGIIINSV	VISIEING	EGIINRSW	RINGWISE
EGIIJLNR	JINGLIER	EGIINRTU	INTRIGUE
EGIIKLLO	KILLOGIE	EGIINRTV	RIVETING
EGIIKLNN	LIKENING	EGIINRTX	GENITRIX
EGIIKLNR	KINGLIER	EGIINRVV	REVIVING
EGIILMMN	IMMINGLE	EGIINSSZ	SEIZINGS
EGIILMST	LEGITIMS	EGIINSTW	WINGIEST
EGIILNNO	ELOINING	EGIINSTX	EXISTING
EGIILNNR	RELINING	EGIINSTZ	ZINGIEST
EGIILNNS	ENISLING	EGIINSVW	VIEWINGS
	ENSILING	EGIIPPRR	GRIPPIER

EGIIPRSW	PERIWIGS
EGIIPSST	PIGSTIES
EGIIRRTT	GRITTIER
EGIITUXY	EXIGUITY
EGIJKNRS	JERKINGS
EGIJLLNY	JELLYING
EGIJLNRS	JINGLERS
EGIJLNRU	JUNGLIER
EGIJLNST	JINGLETS
EGIJNNOY	ENJOYING
EGIJNQRU	JERQUING
EGIJNSST	JESTINGS
EGIKKLNS	LEKKINGS
EGIKKNRT	TREKKING
EGIKLLNN	KNELLING
EGIKLNPS	SKELPING
EGIKLNSS	KINGLESS
EGIKLNST	KINGLETS
EGIKMNPS	KEMPINGS
EGIKNNNS	KENNINGS
EGIKNNOT	TOKENING
EGIKNNSY	ENSKYING
EGIKNORV	OVERKING
	REVOKING
EGIKNPPS	SKEPPING
EGIKNRRS	SKERRING
EGIKNRSU	RESKUING
EGILLMNS	SMELLING
EGILLNNS	SNELLING
EGILLNOS	LOGLINES
EGILLNOV	LIVELONG
EGILLNPS	SPELLING
EGILLNQU	QUELLING
EGILLNST	STELLING
	TELLINGS
EGILLNSW	SWELLING
	WELLINGS
EGILLNSY	YELLINGS
EGILLNTU	GLUTELIN
EGILLOOR	GLORIOLE
EGILMMNS	LEMMINGS
EGILMMRS	GLIMMERS
EGILMMRY	GLIMMERY
EGILMNNO	LEMONING
EGILMNPU	IMPLUNGE
EGILMNRS	GREMLINS
	MERLINGS
	MINGLERS
EGILMNRU	RELUMING
EGILMNST	MELTINGS
	SMELTING
EGILMNSU	LEGUMINS
EGILMOOR	GLOOMIER
EGILMORS	GOMERILS
EGILMOSU	ELOGIUMS
EGILMOUU	EULOGIUM
EGILMPRU	GLUMPIER
EGILMPSS	GLIMPSES
EGILNNST	NESTLING
EGILNNTT	NETTLING
EGILNOPP	PEOPLING
	POPELING
EGILNORS	RESOLING
EGILNORW	LOWERING
EGILNOSU	LIGNEOUS
EGILNOSW	LONGWISE
EGILNOVV	EVOLVING
EGILNPRS	PINGLERS
	SPERLING
	SPRINGLE

EGILNPRY	REPLYING
EGILNPSS	SPIGNELS
EGILNPST	PELTINGS
	PESTLING
EGILNPSY	YELPINGS
EGILNPTT	PETTLING
EGILNRRU	RULERING
EGILNRRY	ERRINGLY
EGILNRSS	RINGLESS
	SLINGERS
EGILNRST	LINGSTER
	RINGLETS
	STERLING
	TINGLERS
	TRINGLES
EGILNRSW	NEWSGIRL
EGILNRUV	VELURING
EGILNSSS	SIGNLESS
EGILNSST	GLISTENS
	SINGLETS
EGILNSSU	UGLINESS
EGILNSSW	SWINGLES
	WINGLESS
EGILNSTT	LETTINGS
	SETTLING
EGILNSTW	SWELTING
	WINGLETS
EGILNSUV	EVULSING
EGILNTUX	EXULTING
EGILNVXY	VEXINGLY
EGILOOOS	OOLOGIES
EGILOOSU	ISOLOGUE
EGILOOTY	ETIOLOGY
EGILORRW	GROWLIER
EGILORSS	GLOSSIER
EGILOSSS	GLOSSIES
EGILOSST	ELOGISTS
EGILOSTU	EULOGIST
EGILPPRS	GRIPPLES
EGILRRZZ	GRIZZLER
EGILRSST	GLISTERS
	GRISTLES
EGILRSTT	GLITTERS
EGILRSTU	GURLIEST
EGILRSUV	VIRGULES
EGILRSZZ	GRIZZLES
EGILRTTY	GLITTERY
EGIMMNOV	EMMOVING
EGIMMNST	STEMMING
EGIMMRST	GRIMMEST
EGIMMSTU	GUMMIEST
	GUMMITES
EGIMNNNO	MIGNONNE
EGIMNNOV	ENMOVING
	VENOMING
EGIMNNUW	UNMEWING
EGIMNORS	NEGROISM
EGIMNORV	REMOVING
EGIMNOST	MITOGENS
EGIMNOSU	GEMINOUS
EGIMNOSY	MOSEYING
EGIMNPRS	IMPREGNS
EGIMNPRU	IMPUGNER
EGIMNPST	PIGMENTS
EGIMNPTT	TEMPTING
EGIMNPTY	EMPTYING
EGIMNRSS	GRIMNESS
EGIMNRSU	RESUMING
EGIMNRUY	ERYNGIUM
EGIMORST	ERGOTISM

	GORMIEST
EGIMOSST	EGOTISMS
EGIMOSTW	TWIGSOME
EGIMPRRU	GRUMPIER
EGINNNOT	TENONING
EGINNNOZ	ENZONING
EGINNNRS	RENNINGS
EGINNNST	STENNING
EGINNNUY	ENNUYING
EGINNOOR	RONEOING
EGINNOPR	REPONING
EGINNOPS	OPENINGS
EGINNORT	NITROGEN
EGINNORV	VIGNERON
EGINNPSU	PENGUINS
EGINNRRS	GRINNERS
EGINNRRU	UNERRING
EGINNRST	STERNING
EGINNRSU	ENSURING
EGINNRTU	RETUNING
EGINNRTV	VENTRING
EGINNSSS	SENSINGS
EGINNSTT	NETTINGS
	STENTING
	TENTINGS
EGINNSTV	VENTINGS
EGINNSUW	UNSEWING
EGINNSUX	UNSEXING
EGINNSVY	ENVYINGS
EGINOORV	INGROOVE
EGINOPRS	PERIGONS
	REPOSING
	SPONGIER
EGINOPRW	POWERING
EGINOPRY	PIGEONRY
EGINOPST	PONGIEST
EGINOPSX	EXPOSING
EGINOPSY	POESYING
EGINORRS	IGNORERS
EGINORSS	SIGNORES
EGINORST	GENITORS
	ROSETING
EGINORSY	SEIGNORY
EGINORTT	OTTERING
EGINORTU	OUTREIGN
	ROUTEING
EGINORTW	TOWERING
EGINORTX	OXTERING
EGINORTZ	ROZETING
EGINORVW	OVERWING
EGINOSTT	TENTIGOS
EGINOTUV	OUTGIVEN
EGINPPPR	PREPPING
EGINPPRS	REPPINGS
EGINPPST	STEPPING
EGINPRRS	SPERRING
	SPRINGER
EGINPRRU	REPURING
EGINPRSS	PRESSING
	SPERSING
	SPRINGES
EGINPRST	PRESTING
EGINPRSU	PERSUING
	PERUSING
	SUPERING
EGINPRTU	ERUPTING
	REPUTING
EGINPRYY	PERIGYNY
EGINPSSY	PIGSNEYS
EGINPSTT	PETTINGS

	SPETTING
EGINQRUY	QUERYING
EGINQSTU	QUESTING
EGINQSUU	QUEUINGS
EGINRRST	RESTRING
	RINGSTER
	STRINGER
EGINRRSW	WRINGERS
EGINRRSY	SERRYING
EGINRRTY	RETRYING
EGINRSST	RESTINGS
	STINGERS
	TRESSING
	TRIGNESS
EGINRSSV	SERVINGS
	VERSINGS
EGINRSSW	SWINGERS
EGINRSSY	SYRINGES
EGINRSTT	GITTERNS
EGINRSTV	STERVING
EGINRSTW	STREWING
	WRESTING
EGINRSVW	SWERVING
EGINRTTU	UTTERING
EGINSSTT	SETTINGS
	TESTINGS
EGINSSTV	VESTINGS
EGINSSTW	STEWINGS
	WESTINGS
EGINSTTT	STETTING
EGIOOPST	GOOPIEST
EGIOORRV	GROOVIER
EGIOOSST	GOOSIEST
EGIOPRSU	GROUPIES
	PIROGUES
EGIOPRTU	PORTIGUE
EGIORRTT	GROTTIER
EGIORRTU	GROUTIER
EGIORSST	GORSIEST
	STRIGOSE
EGIORSSU	GRISEOUS
EGIORSTU	GOUSTIER
EGIORSTV	VERTIGOS
EGIORSTY	OYSTRIGE
EGIORSTZ	ZORGITES
EGIORSUV	GRIEVOUS
EGIOSSTT	EGOTISTS
EGIOSTTU	GOUTIEST
EGIOSTUV	OUTGIVES
	VOGUIEST
EGIOSUUX	EXIGUOUS
EGIPPRRS	GRIPPERS
EGIPRSUU	GUIPURES
EGIRRSTT	GRITTERS
EGIRRSTY	REGISTRY
EGIRSSTU	SURGIEST
EGIRSTTT	GRITTEST
EGISSTTU	GUSTIEST
	GUTSIEST
EGISSYYZ	SYZYGIES
EGJLNORU	JONGLEUR
EGJLNOTU	JELUTONG
EGKLORSW	LEGWORKS
EGLLMORW	GROMWELL
EGLLOOPY	PELOLOGY
EGLMMSTU	GLUMMEST
EGLMNOOS	ENGLOOMS
	LONGSOME
EGLMNOOY	MENOLOGY
EGLMNORS	MONGRELS

Key	Word
EGLMNSSU	GLUMNESS
EGLMOORS	LEGROOMS
EGLMOPRU	PROMULGE
EGLMORSS	GORMLESS
EGLNNOOR	LONGERON
EGLNNOSS	LONGNESS
EGLNNTUY	UNGENTLY
EGLNOOOY	OENOLOGY
EGLNOOPR	PROLONGE
EGLNOOPY	PENOLOGY
EGLNOORV	OVERLONG
EGLNOPYY	POLYGENY
EGLNORSU	LOUNGERS
EGLNORUU	LONGUEUR
EGLNOSSS	SONGLESS
EGLNOSUV	UNGLOVES
EGLNOSXY	LOXYGENS
	XYLOGENS
EGLNPRSU	PLUNGERS
EGLNRSTU	GRUNTLES
EGLNRTUY	URGENTLY
EGLOOORY	OREOLOGY
EGLOOPRU	PROLOGUE
EGLOOPTY	LOGOTYPE
EGLOORSY	SEROLOGY
EGLOOSXY	SEXOLOGY
EGLOPRTU	GROUPLET
EGLORRSW	GROWLERS
EGLORRWY	GROWLERY
EGLORSSS	GLOSSERS
EGLORSUU	RUGULOSE
EGLORSUY	RUGOSELY
EGLPRSSU	SPLURGES
EGLRSUZZ	GUZZLERS
EGLSSUUV	VULGUSES
EGMMORST	GROMMETS
EGMMOSSU	GUMMOSES
EGMMRSTU	GRUMMEST
	GRUMMETS
EGMNNOOY	MONOGENY
	NOMOGENY
EGMNNOSW	GOWNSMEN
EGMNOOOS	MONGOOSE
EGMNOORY	MEROGONY
EGMNOOSU	MUNGOOSE
EGMNORSU	MURGEONS
EGMNOSYZ	ZYMOGENS
EGMNRSSU	GRUMNESS
EGMNSSSU	SMUGNESS
EGMORSTU	GOURMETS
EGNNOOTY	ONTOGENY
EGNNORST	RONTGENS
EGNNOSTU	GUNSTONE
EGNNOTTU	UNGOTTEN
EGNNSSSU	SNUGNESS
EGNNSTTU	TUNGSTEN
EGNNSTUU	UNGUENTS
EGNOOORV	GOVERNOR
EGNOPPRU	OPPUGNER
EGNOPRSS	SPONGERS
EGNOPRSY	PYROGENS
EGNORRST	STRONGER
EGNORRSW	WRONGERS
EGNORSST	SONGSTER
EGNORSSU	SURGEONS
EGNORSTU	STURGEON
EGNORSTW	WRONGEST
EGNOSTUY	YOUNGEST
EGNRRSTU	GRUNTERS
	RESTRUNG
EGOOPRRU	PROROGUE
EGOORRVW	OVERGROW
EGOORSTT	GROTTOES
EGOORSTU	OUTGOERS
EGOPRRSS	PROGRESS
EGOPRRSU	GROUPERS
	REGROUPS
EGOPSSUY	GYPSEOUS
EGORRSST	GROSERTS
EGORRSSU	GROUSERS
EGORSSST	GROSSEST
EGPRSSUU	UPSURGES
EHHIIPRS	HEIRSHIP
EHHIISTV	THIEVISH
EHHILMNT	HELMINTH
EHHIOPRS	HEROSHIP
EHHIORTT	HITHERTO
EHHIPRSS	HERSHIPS
EHHIPSST	PHTHISES
EHHIRSSW	SHREWISH
EHHIRSTW	WHITHERS
EHHISSTU	HUSHIEST
EHHNOORS	SHOEHORN
EHHOOPST	THEOSOPH
EHHOOSSW	WHOOSHES
EHHOOSTU	HOTHOUSE
EHHORSTU	SHOUTHER
EHHRSSTU	THRUSHES
EHIIKLPT	PITHLIKE
EHIIKLPW	WHIPLIKE
EHIIKSSW	WHISKIES
EHIILLST	HILLIEST
EHIILLSW	WHILLIES
EHIILMOS	HOMILIES
EHIILOSS	HELIOSIS
EHIILRSV	LIVERISH
EHIILSTT	LITHITES
EHIIMMRW	WHIMMIER
EHIIMMSS	SHIMMIES
EHIIMPST	MEPHITIS
EHIIMRSW	WHIMSIER
EHIIMSST	SMITHIES
EHIIMSSW	WHIMSIES
EHIINNOS	INHESION
EHIINNQU	HENIQUIN
EHIINNRS	INSHRINE
EHIINNRW	WHINNIER
EHIINNSS	SHINNIES
EHIINNSW	WHINNIES
EHIINRRT	HIRRIENT
EHIINRST	INHERITS
EHIINRSZ	RHIZINES
EHIINSST	SHINIEST
	SHINTIES
EHIINSTW	WHINIEST
EHIINSVX	VIXENISH
EHIIPPRW	WHIPPIER
EHIIPPST	HIPPIEST
EHIIPRSV	VIPERISH
EHIIPSTT	PITHIEST
EHIIRRST	SHIRTIER
EHIIRRSW	WHIRRIES
EHIIRRTX	HERITRIX
EHIIRSSU	HUISSIER
EHIIRSSW	SWISHIER
EHIIRSTT	SHITTIER
	THIRTIES
EHIISSST	STISHIES
EHIISSTT	STITHIES
EHIISTTW	WHITIEST
	WITHIEST
EHIISTTX	SIXTIETH
EHIJNNOS	JOHNNIES
EHIKLOSY	YOKELISH
EHIKLOTY	LEKYTHOI
EHIKLSTU	HULKIEST
EHIKMNST	METHINKS
EHIKNRRS	SHRINKER
EHIKNRST	RETHINKS
	THINKERS
EHIKNSTU	HUNKIEST
EHIKOOST	HOOKIEST
EHIKOPRS	POKERISH
EHIKRRSS	SHIRKERS
EHIKRSSW	WHISKERS
EHIKRSWY	WHISKERY
EHIKSSTU	HUSKIEST
EHIKSSTW	WHISKETS
EHIKSSWY	WHISKEYS
EHILLLMO	MOLEHILL
EHILLMOY	HOMELILY
EHILLNOS	HELLIONS
EHILLNSS	INSHELLS
EHILLOPY	LYOPHILE
EHILLPTY	PHYLLITE
EHILLRRS	SHRILLER
EHILLRRT	THRILLER
EHILLRST	THILLERS
EHILLRTY	LITHERLY
EHILLSSW	SWELLISH
EHILLSTU	HULLIEST
EHILMOOR	HEIRLOOM
EHILMOST	HELOTISM
EHILMPSW	WHIMPLES
EHILMPSY	SYMPHILE
EHILMQUU	UMQUHILE
EHILMSTT	MELTITHS
EHILNOOP	OENOPHIL
EHILNOPS	PINHOLES
EHILNORU	UNHOLIER
EHILNOSS	HOLINESS
EHILNOST	NEOLITHS
EHILNOSV	NOVELISH
EHILNOTX	XENOLITH
EHILNPSY	SYLPHINE
EHILOOPZ	ZOOPHILE
EHILOOST	HOOLIEST
EHILOPRS	PILHORSE
	POLISHER
EHILOPRT	HELIPORT
EHILOPSS	POLISHES
EHILOPST	HELISTOP
	HOPLITES
	ISOPLETH
EHILORSS	SLOSHIER
EHILORTY	RHYOLITE
EHILPRST	PHILTERS
	PHILTRES
EHILPRSU	PLUSHIER
EHILPSSS	SHIPLESS
EHILPSST	PITHLESS
	THLIPSES
EHILPSTU	SULPHITE
EHILRRSW	WHIRLERS
EHILRSST	SLITHERS
	THRISSEL
EHILRSSU	SLUSHIER
EHILRSSV	SHRIVELS
EHILRSTT	THRISTLE
EHILRSTU	LUTHIERS
EHILRSTW	WHIRTLES
	WHISTLER
EHILRSTY	SLITHERY
EHILRTTW	WHITTLER
EHILRTTY	TRIETHYL
EHILSSTT	THISTLES
EHILSSTU	LUSHIEST
EHILSSTW	WHISTLES
EHILSTTU	THULITES
EHILSTTW	WHITTLES
EHIMMNUY	HYMENIUM
EHIMMRSS	SHIMMERS
EHIMMRSY	SHIMMERY
EHIMNOPR	MORPHINE
EHIMNORT	THERMION
EHIMNOST	HOISTMEN
EHIMNOSU	HEMIONUS
EHIMNOTT	MONTEITH
EHIMNPRS	PHRENISM
EHIMNPST	SHIPMENT
EHIMNRRU	MURRHINE
EHIMNRRY	MYRRHINE
EHIMNRSU	RHENIUMS
EHIMNSTY	THYMINES
EHIMOOSS	HOMEOSIS
EHIMOOST	SMOOTHIE
EHIMOPRS	SOPHERIM
EHIMOPSS	PHIMOSES
EHIMORSS	HEROISMS
EHIMORST	ISOTHERM
	MOITHERS
EHIMORSZ	RHIZOMES
EHIMORTU	MOUTHIER
EHIMOSTT	MOTHIEST
EHIMPPSS	PSEPHISM
EHIMPRRS	SHRIMPER
EHIMPRSU	MURPHIES
EHIMPRSW	WHIMPERS
EHIMPSTU	HUMPIEST
	HUMPTIES
	TUMPHIES
EHIMPSUU	EUPHUISM
EHIMPTTU	UMPTIETH
EHIMRSST	SMITHERS
EHIMRSSU	HEURISMS
EHIMRSTY	SMITHERY
EHIMSSTU	MUSHIEST
EHIMSSTY	METHYSIS
	MYTHISES
EHIMSSWY	WHIMSEYS
EHIMSTTY	THYMIEST
EHIMSTYZ	MYTHIZES
EHINNRST	THINNERS
EHINNSST	THINNESS
EHINNSSU	SUNSHINE
EHINNSTT	THINNEST
EHINOPPR	HORNPIPE
EHINOPRT	TRIPHONE
EHINOPST	PHONIEST
	SIPHONET
EHINORRT	THORNIER
EHINORSS	HERISSON
EHINORST	HORNIEST
EHINOSST	HISTONES
EHINOSTU	OUTSHINE
EHINPPSS	SHIPPENS
EHINPRSU	PUNISHER
EHINPSSU	PUNISHES

Key	Word	Key	Word	Key	Word	Key	Word
EHINPSSX	SPHINXES	EHLMMSUW	WHUMMLES	EHNOOSTU	OUTSHONE	EIIKLNRS	SLINKIER
EHINRSSU	INRUSHES	EHLMNOST	MENTHOLS	EHNOPRSY	HYPERONS	EIIKLNRT	TINKLIER
EHINRSTZ	ZITHERNS	EHLMNOSY	HOMELYNS	EHNOPSSS	POSHNESS	EIIKLPSS	PLISKIES
EHINSSST	THISNESS	EHLMNOUY	UNHOMELY	EHNOPSSY	HYPNOSES	EIIKLRTT	KITTLIER
EHINSSUW	UNWISHES	EHLMORTY	MOTHERLY	EHNORRST	NORTHERS	EIIKLSST	SILKIEST
EHIOORTT	TOOTHIER	EHLNNOPU	UNHOLPEN	EHNORSST	SHORTENS	EIIKMPRS	SKIMPIER
EHIOOSST	STOOSHIE	EHLNOPSU	SULPHONE	EHNORSSU	ONRUSHES	EIIKMRRS	SMIRKIER
EHIOPPPS	POPESHIP	EHLNORSS	HORNLESS		UNHORSES	EIIKMRST	MIRKIEST
EHIOPPRS	SHOPPIER	EHLNORST	HORNLETS	EHNORSTT	THORNSET	EIIKNNRS	SKINNIER
EHIOPPST	HOPPIEST	EHLNOSTY	HONESTLY	EHNORSTU	SOUTHERN	EIIKNNSS	INKINESS
	POETSHIP	EHLNRSTU	LUTHERNS	EHNOSSUU	UNHOUSES	EIIKNPST	PINKIEST
EHIOPRST	TROPHIES	EHLNSSSU	LUSHNESS	EHNOSTUU	NUTHOUSE	EIIKNSST	SINKIEST
EHIORRST	HERITORS		SHUNLESS	EHNRSSTU	HUNTRESS	EIIKNSTZ	ZINKIEST
EHIORRTU	ROUTHIER	EHLOOPRT	PORTHOLE		SHUNTERS	EIIKPSST	SPIKIEST
EHIORRTW	WORTHIER		POTHOLER	EHNSSSTU	THUSNESS	EIIKQRRU	QUIRKIER
EHIORSST	HOISTERS	EHLOOPST	POTHOLES	EHOOPRSW	WHOOPERS	EIIKRSST	RISKIEST
	HORSIEST	EHLOOPTY	HOLOTYPE	EHOOPRTY	ORTHOEPY	EIIKSSTV	SKIVIEST
	HOSTRIES	EHLOPPRT	THROPPLE	EHOOPSTU	HOUSETOP	EIIKSSVV	SKIVVIES
	SHORTIES	EHLOPRTY	PROTHYLE		POTHOUSE	EIILLLVY	LIVELILY
EHIORSTT	THEORIST	EHLOPSSS	SPLOSHES	EHOOPSTY	OOPHYTES	EIILLMMS	MILLIMES
	THORITES	EHLORSST	HOLSTERS	EHOOPTYZ	ZOOPHYTE	EIILLMNR	MILLINER
EHIORSTU	OUTHIRES		HOSTLERS	EHOORSST	ORTHOSES	EIILLMNS	SLIMLINE
EHIORSTV	OVERHITS	EHLORSTT	THROSTLE		SHOOTERS	EIILLMNU	ILLUMINE
EHIORSTW	WORTHIES	EHLORSTY	HOSTELRY		SOOTHERS	EIILLNST	NIELLIST
EHIORTUY	YOUTHIER	EHLORTTT	THROTTLE	EHOORSTV	OVERSHOT	EIILLNSU	SUILLINE
EHIORTWZ	HOWITZER	EHLOSSTT	SHOTTLES	EHOOSSSW	SWOOSHES	EIILLNSV	VILLEINS
EHIOSSTT	TOSHIEST	EHLOSSTW	THOWLESS	EHOOSSTT	SOOTHEST	EIILLNTV	VITELLIN
EHIOSSTW	SHOWIEST	EHLOSSTY	THYLOSES	EHOOSTUU	OUTHOUSE	EIILLPSS	ELLIPSIS
EHIOSSTY	ISOHYETS	EHLPSSTU	PLUSHEST	EHOPPRSS	SHOPPERS	EIILLRST	STILLIER
EHIPPRSS	SHIPPERS	EHLRSSTU	HURTLESS	EHOPPRST	PROPHETS	EIILLSST	SILLIEST
EHIPPRSW	WHIPPERS		HUSTLERS	EHOPPRSW	WHOPPERS	EIILLSTT	TILLIEST
EHIPPSSU	HIPPUSES		RUTHLESS	EHOPPRSY	PROPHESY		TILLITES
EHIPPSTW	WHIPPETS	EHLSSTTU	SHUTTLES	EHOPRRSY	ORPHREYS	EIILLSTW	TWILLIES
EHIPQSUY	PHYSIQUE	EHMMRRTU	THRUMMER	EHOPRSST	STROPHES	EIILLSUV	ILLUSIVE
EHIPRSST	HIPSTERS	EHMMSSUU	HUMMUSES	EHOPRSTU	POUTHERS	EIILMNNT	LINIMENT
	THRIPSES	EHMNNSTU	HUNTSMEN	EHOPRSTY	TROPHESY	EIILMNOT	LIMONITE
EHIPRSSW	WHISPERS	EHMNOORS	HORMONES	EHOPRTUY	EUTROPHY	EIILMNSS	LIMINESS
EHIPRSTW	WHIPSTER		MOORHENS	EHOPSSTY	PHYTOSES	EIILMOPT	IMPOLITE
EHIPRSWY	WHISPERY	EHMNOOST	SMOOTHEN	EHORRSTW	THROWERS	EIILMPPR	PIMPLIER
EHIPSSTU	PUSHIEST	EHMNOOTY	THEONOMY	EHORSSTT	SHORTEST	EIILMPRS	IMPERILS
EHIPSTUU	EUPHUIST	EHMNOPSU	HOMESPUN	EHORSSTU	SHOUTERS	EIILMPST	LIMEPITS
EHIQSSSU	SQUISHES	EHMNPSTY	NYMPHETS		SOUTHERS	EIILMRSS	SLIMSIER
EHIRRSSV	SHRIVERS	EHMNSTTU	HUTMENTS	EHORSTUY	OUTHYRES	EIILMRST	LIMITERS
EHIRRSTT	THIRSTER	EHMOOOTZ	ZOOTHOME	EHOSSSTU	STOUSHES		MIRLIEST
EHIRRSTV	THRIVERS	EHMOOPTY	HOMOTYPE	EHPRSSSU	SPRUSHES	EIILMRZZ	MIZZLIER
EHIRRSTW	WHIRRETS	EHMOORST	SMOOTHER	EHPRSSUU	UPRUSHES	EIILMSSS	MISSILES
EHIRRTTU	TRUTHIER	EHMOOSSS	SHMOOSES	EHPRSTTU	TURPETHS	EIILMSST	ELITISMS
EHIRSSSW	SWISHERS	EHMOOSST	SMOOTHES	EHPSSTUY	TYPHUSES		SLIMIEST
EHIRSSTU	RUSHIEST	EHMOOSSZ	SHMOOZES	EHRRSTTU	THRUSTER	EIILMSSV	MISLIVES
EHIRSSTW	SWITHERS	EHMOPRSW	MORPHEWS	EHRSSSTY	SHYSTERS	EIILMSTT	MISTITLE
EHIRSTTW	WHITRETS	EHMORSST	SMOTHERS	EHRSSTTU	SHUTTERS	EIILMSTY	MYELITIS
	WHITSTER	EHMORSTU	MOUTHERS	EIIILMSS	SIMILISE	EIILNNOT	LENITION
	WHITTERS	EHMORSTY	SMOTHERY	EIIILMSZ	SIMILIZE	EIILNOSS	ELISIONS
EHIRSWZZ	WHIZZERS	EHMORTUV	VERMOUTH	EIIILPPR	LIRIPIPE		ISOLINES
EHIRTTTW	WHITTRET	EHMOSSTY	MYTHOSES	EIIIMMNS	MINIMISE		LIONISES
EHISSSTU	STUSHIES	EHMOTUZZ	MEZUZOTH	EIIIMMNZ	MINIMIZE		OILINESS
EHISSSTW	SWISHEST	EHMPRSTU	THUMPERS	EIIIRRTV	TIRRIVIE	EIILNOST	ETIOLINS
EHISSTUW	THUSWISE	EHMRRSTU	MURTHERS	EIIIRSST	IRITISES	EIILNOSV	OLIVINES
EHISSUVW	HUSWIVES	EHMRTUYY	EURYTHMY	EIIJKNRT	JIRKINET	EIILNOSZ	LIONIZES
EHKLOSTY	LEKYTHOS	EHMSSTUY	MYTHUSES	EIIJMPST	JIMPIEST	EIILNOTT	TOILINET
EHKMOORW	HOMEWORK		THYMUSES	EIIJNRSU	INJURIES	EIILNQTU	QUINTILE
EHKMORSU	HUMORESK	EHNNOPRS	NEPHRONS	EIIKKLLM	MILKLIKE	EIILNRST	NIRLIEST
EHKNNRSU	SHRUNKEN	EHNNOPSY	HYPNONES	EIIKKNST	KINKIEST		NITRILES
EHKOPSSY	KYPHOSES	EHNNORRT	NORTHERN	EIIKLLMN	LIMEKILN	EIILNSSW	WILINESS
EHLLMOPY	PHYLLOME	EHNNORTU	UNTHRONE	EIIKLLRS	SKILLIER	EIILNSTT	LINTIEST
EHLLNSSU	UNSHELLS	EHNNOSTU	UNHONEST	EIIKLLSS	SKILLIES	EIILNSTY	SENILITY
EHLLNSTU	NUTSHELL	EHNOOPTY	HONEYPOT	EIIKLMRS	MISLIKER	EIILNSVY	SYLVIINE
EHLLOOOP	LOOPHOLE	EHNOORRU	HONOURER	EIIKLMSS	MISLIKES	EIILNTTU	INTITULE
EHLLOORW	HOLLOWER	EHNOORSS	SOREHONS	EIIKLMST	MILKIEST	EIILNTUV	VITULINE
EHLMMOSW	WHOMMLES	EHNOORSW	WHORESON	EIIKLNPS	SPELIKIN	EIILOPST	PISOLITE

POLITIES	EIIMSSTT MISTIEST	EIIPRSST SPIRIEST	EIKLSSTT SKITTLES
EIILORST ROILIEST	EIINNNPS NINEPINS	EIIPRSTT RISPETTI	EIKLSSTU SULKIEST
EIILORTT TROILITE	EIINNOSU UNIONISE	EIIPRSTU PURITIES	EIKLSTTT KITTLEST
EIILOSST SOILIEST	EIINNOSV ENVISION	EIIPRSTV PRIVIEST	EIKMMORS MIRKSOME
EIILOTVV VOLITIVE	EIINNOUZ UNIONIZE	EIIPRSTY PYRITISE	EIKMMRRS KRIMMERS
EIILPPRR RIPPLIER	EIINNRTV INVERTIN	EIIPRSVV SPIVVIER	EIKMMRSS SKIMMERS
EIILPPRS SLIPPIER	EIINNSST TININESS	EIIPRTYZ PYRITIZE	EIKMNORS MONIKERS
EIILPPST LIPPIEST	EIINNSSW INSINEWS	EIIPSSTT PIETISTS	EIKMNOST TOKENISM
EIILPRST TRIPLIES	EIINNSTT TINNIEST	STIPITES	EIKMNOSU MOUSEKIN
EIILPRSU PLURISIE	EIINNSTW INTWINES	TIPSIEST	EIKMOPSS MISSPOKE
EIILPSST PITILESS	EIINOPRS RIPIENOS	EIIPSSTW SWIPIEST	EIKMOSST SMOKIEST
SPILITES	EIINOPRT POINTIER	WISPIEST	EIKMOSSY MISYOKES
EIILPSTY PYELITIS	EIINOPST SINOPITE	EIIPSTTT PITTITES	EIKMRSTU MURKIEST
EIILPSUZ SPUILZIE	EIINOPTT PETITION	EIIPSTTU PITUITES	EIKMSSSU KUMISSES
EIILQSSU SILIQUES	EIINORRT INTERIOR	EIIQSTTU QUIETIST	EIKMSSTU MUSKIEST
EIILRRSW SWIRLIER	EIINORSS IONISERS	EIIRRSTW WRISTIER	EIKNNOST INKSTONE
EIILRRTW TWIRLIER	IRONISES	EIIRSSTV REVISITS	EIKNNPSS PINKNESS
EIILRSTT STILTIER	EIINORSV REVISION	VISITERS	EIKNNRSS SKINNERS
EIILRSTU UTILISER	VISIONER	EIIRSTTU UTERITIS	EIKNOORS ROOINEKS
EIILRTUZ UTILIZER	EIINORSZ IONIZERS	EIIRSTTW TWISTIER	EIKNOOST NOOKIEST
EIILSSTT ELITISTS	IRONIZES	EIIRSTTZ RITZIEST	EIKNORTT KNOTTIER
SILTIEST	EIINOSST NOISIEST	EIISSSST SISSIEST	EIKNOSTW WONKIEST
EIILSSTU ULITISES	EIINOSTV NOVITIES	EIISSTTV STIVIEST	EIKNPRSU SPUNKIER
UTILISES	EIINPPRS SNIPPIER	EIISTTTW WITTIEST	EIKNPRTU TURNPIKE
EIILSTUY TUILYIES	EIINPPST NIPPIEST	EIJJNTUY JEJUNITY	EIKNPSSU SPUNKIES
EIILSTUZ TUILZIES	EIINPRRS INSPIRER	EIJKNSTU JUNKIEST	EIKNRSST STINKERS
UTILIZES	EIINPRSS INSPIRES	EIJLLOST JOLLIEST	EIKNRSTT KNITTERS
EIIMMNNT IMMINENT	EIINPRST PRISTINE	EIJLOSTT JOLTIEST	TRINKETS
MINIMENT	EIINPSST SNIPIEST	EIJMNPSS JIMPNESS	EIKNSSSU UNKISSES
EIIMMNSU IMMUNISE	SPINIEST	EIJMPSTU JUMPIEST	EIKNSSTT SKINTEST
EIIMMNUZ IMMUNIZE	EIINPTUV PUNITIVE	EIJNORST JOINTERS	EIKOOPRS SPOOKIER
EIIMMPRU IMPERIUM	EIINQRRU INQUIRER	EIJNORTU JOINTURE	EIKOPPRW PIPEWORK
EIIMMRSW SWIMMIER	EIINQRSU INQUIRES	EIJNOSTT JETTISON	EIKOPRST PORKIEST
EIIMMSSS SEISMISM	EIINQSSU QUINSIES	EIJNPRSU JUNIPERS	EIKOPRSV OVERSKIP
EIIMMSST MISTIMES	SQUINIES	EIJNRRSU INJURERS	EIKORRWW WIREWORK
EIIMNOPT PIMIENTO	EIINQSTU INQUIETS	EIJSSSUV JUSSIVES	EIKPPRRS SKIPPERS
EIIMNORT MINORITE	EIINQTUY EQUINITY	EIKKLNRS KLINKERS	EIKPPSST SKIPPETS
EIIMNOSS EMISSION	INEQUITY	EIKKNRSS SKINKERS	EIKPRRSU SPRUIKER
SIMONIES	EIINRRTW WINTRIER	EIKKOOST KOOKIEST	EIKRRSST SKIRRETS
EIIMNOSV VISNOMIE	EIINRSST SINISTER	EIKKSTUY YUKKIEST	SKIRTERS
EIIMNOTV MONITIVE	EIINRSSW WIRINESS	EIKLLMSS MILKLESS	STRIKERS
EIIMNPRS PRIMINES	EIINRSTT NITRITES	EIKLLNSW INKWELLS	EIKRRSSU SKURRIES
EIIMNRSS MIRINESS	STINTIER	EIKLLNUY UNLIKELY	EIKRSSTT SKITTERS
EIIMNRST INTERIMS	EIINRSTU NEURITIS	EIKLLORV OVERKILL	EIKRSSTU TURKISES
MINISTER	EIINRSTV INVITERS	EIKLLOSS SKOLLIES	EIKSSTTU TUSKIEST
EIIMNRSV MINIVERS	VINTRIES	EIKLLSSS SKILLESS	EILLLOVY LOVELILY
EIIMNRTT INTERMIT	VITRINES	EIKLLSST SKILLETS	EILLLPUV PULVILLE
EIIMNRTX INTERMIX	EIINSSSZ SIZINESS	EIKLMNOS MOLESKIN	EILLMNOU LINOLEUM
EIIMNSTT MINTIEST	EIINSSTU UNITISES	EIKLMNRS KREMLINS	EILLMNQU QUILLMEN
EIIMNSTU MUTINIES	EIINSTTT NITTIEST	EIKLNOOR OERLIKON	EILLMNSU MULLEINS
EIIMNSTV MINIVETS	TINTIEST	EIKLNOSW SNOWLIKE	EILLMOPS PLIMSOLE
EIIMOPRX MIREPOIX	EIINSTTW TWINIEST	EIKLNPRS SPRINKLE	EILLMOST MELILOTS
EIIMOPST OPTIMISE	EIINSTUZ UNITIZES	EIKLNRRU KNURLIER	EILLMPSS MISSPELL
EIIMOPTZ OPTIMIZE	EIIOPRRS PRIORIES	EIKLNRSS SLINKERS	PSELLISM
EIIMOSSV OMISSIVE	EIIOPSTV POSITIVE	EIKLNRST LINKSTER	EILLMPTU MULTIPLE
EIIMOSTY MOYITIES	EIIORRST RIOTRIES	STRINKLE	EILLMSST MISTELLS
EIIMOSUX EXIMIOUS	EIIORSST RIOTISES	TINKLERS	EILLMUVX VEXILLUM
EIIMOTVV VOMITIVE	EIIORSTZ RIOTIZES	EIKLNRSW WINKLERS	EILLNOPY EPYLLION
EIIMPRSS MISPRISE	EIIOSSTT OSTEITIS	WRINKLES	EILLNOST STELLION
PISMIRES	OTITISES	EIKLNRTW TWINKLER	EILLNOTU LUTEOLIN
EIIMPRSZ MISPRIZE	EIIOSSTZ ZOISITES	EIKLNSSS SKINLESS	EILLNPUU LUPULINE
EIIMPSST PIETISMS	EIIOTTTV TOTITIVE	EIKLNSST LENTISKS	EILLNSTY SILENTLY
EIIMPSTW WIMPIEST	EIIPPPST PIPPIEST	EIKLNSSY SKYLINES	TINSELLY
EIIMQSTU QUIETISM	EIIPPRRS RIPPIERS	EIKLNSTT KNITTLES	EILLNSVY SNIVELLY
EIIMRRSW SMIRRIER	EIIPPSTT TIPPIEST	EIKLNSTW TWINKLES	EILLNUVY UNLIVELY
EIIMRSTT METRITIS	EIIPPSTZ ZIPPIEST	EIKLOOPR PLOOKIER	EILLOORW WOOLLIER
EIIMRSTW MISWRITE	EIIPRRSS PRISSIER	EIKLOORT ROOTLIKE	EILLOOSW WOOLLIES
EIIMSSSS MISSISES	EIIPRRST STRIPIER	EIKLOPRU PLOUKIER	EILLOPTY POLITELY
EIIMSSST MISSIEST		EIKLOPRW PILEWORK	EILLORST TRILLOES
EIIMSSSV MISSIVES		EIKLOSTY YOLKIEST	TROLLIES

EILLORSZ	ZORILLES	EILNOPPY	POLYPINE	EILORSSU	SOILURES	EIMMNORS	MISNOMER
EILLOSSS	SOILLESS	EILNOPRS	PROLINES	EILORSTT	TRIOLETS	EIMMOPRU	EMPORIUM
EILLOSST	TOILLESS	EILNOPSS	EPSILONS	EILORSTU	LOURIEST	EIMMOPST	METOPISM
EILLOSTW	LOWLIEST	EILNOPST	POINTELS		OUTLIERS	EIMMOSTT	TOTEMISM
EILLPRSS	SPILLERS	EILNOPTU	UNPOLITE	EILORSZZ	SOZZLIER	EIMMPRST	PRIMMEST
EILLQSTU	QUILLETS	EILNORRS	LORINERS	EILORTTY	TOILETRY	EIMMPRSU	PREMIUMS
EILLRSST	STILLERS	EILNORRT	RITORNEL	EILOSSST	LOSSIEST	EIMMRRST	TRIMMERS
EILLRSSW	SWILLERS	EILNORST	RETINOLS	EILOSSTU	LOUSIEST	EIMMRSST	MISTERMS
EILLRSTT	TESTRILL	EILNORTT	TROTLINE	EILOSTTT	STILETTO	EIMMRSSW	SWIMMERS
EILLRSVY	SILVERLY	EILNOSSU	ELUSIONS	EILOSTUV	OUTLIVES	EIMMRSTT	TRIMMEST
EILLSSST	LISTLESS	EILNOSSW	LEWISSON		SOLUTIVE	EIMMRSTU	RUMMIEST
EILLSSTT	STILLEST	EILNOSTU	ELUTIONS	EILPPRRS	RIPPLERS	EIMMSSTU	MUMSIEST
EILLSTTT	LITTLEST		OUTLINES	EILPPRRT	TRIPPLER	EIMMSTUY	YUMMIEST
EILLSTUV	VITELLUS	EILNOSTV	NOVELIST	EILPPRSS	SLIPPERS	EIMNOPPT	IMPONENT
EILMMNOS	MOLIMENS		VIOLENTS	EILPPRST	RIPPLETS	EIMNNOST	MENTIONS
EILMMPRU	PLUMMIER	EILNOSTW	TOWLINES		STIPPLER	EIMNNOTT	OINTMENT
EILMMRSS	SLIMMERS	EILNOSUV	EVULSION		TIPPLERS	EIMNNOUY	EUONYMIN
EILMMRSU	SLUMMIER	EILNOSVV	INVOLVES		TRIPPLES	EIMNOOPS	EMPOISON
EILMMSST	SLIMMEST	EILNOTUV	INVOLUTE	EILPPRSU	PERIPLUS	EIMNOORS	IONOMERS
EILMMSTU	LUMMIEST	EILNOTXY	XYLONITE		SUPPLIER		MOONRISE
EILMNOSU	EMULSION	EILNOTYZ	ZYLONITE	EILPPRSY	SLIPPERY	EIMNOORT	REMOTION
EILMNOSV	NOVELISM	EILNPRSS	PILSNERS	EILPPRTU	PULPITER	EIMNOORV	OMNIVORE
EILMNOTU	MOULINET	EILNPRST	SPLINTER	EILPPSST	STIPPLES	EIMNOOSS	MONOSIES
EILMNOTY	MYLONITE	EILNPRSU	PURLINES	EILPPSSU	SUPPLIES	EIMNOOST	EMOTIONS
EILMNPSU	SPLENIUM	EILNPSST	PLENISTS	EILPPSSW	SWIPPLES		MOONIEST
EILMNRST	MINSTREL	EILNPSSU	SPINULES	EILPPSTU	PULPIEST	EIMNOOSX	EXOMIONS
EILMNSSS	SLIMNESS		SPLENIUS	EILPRSST	SPIRTLES	EIMNOPRT	ORPIMENT
EILMNSSU	EMULSINS	EILNPSUY	SUPINELY	EILPRSTT	SPLITTER	EIMNOPSS	PEONISMS
EILMNSTU	MUSLINET	EILNQUUY	UNIQUELY		TRIPLETS	EIMNOPST	EMPTIONS
EILMNTUY	MINUTELY	EILNRRUU	UNRULIER	EILPRSTY	PRIESTLY		NEPOTISM
	UNTIMELY	EILNRSST	SNIRTLES		SPRITELY		PIMENTOS
EILMOOPS	LIPOSOME	EILNRSTU	INSULTER	EILPRSUU	PURLIEUS	EIMNOPTT	IMPOTENT
EILMOORS	SLOOMIER		LUSTRINE	EILPRSUY	PLEURISY	EIMNORSS	MERSIONS
EILMOOST	TOILSOME	EILNRSTY	TINSELRY	EILPRTTY	PRETTILY		MINORESS
EILMOPRR	IMPLORER	EILNRTUV	VIRULENT	EILPSSTT	SPITTLES	EIMNORSU	MONSIEUR
EILMOPRS	IMPLORES	EILNRTWY	WINTERLY	EILPSSTU	STIPULES	EIMNORSW	WINSOMER
	PELORISM	EILNSSTT	TINTLESS	EILPSSUY	SPULYIES	EIMNORTY	ENORMITY
EILMOPST	POLEMIST	EILNSSTU	UTENSILS	EILPSSUZ	SPULZIES	EIMNOSST	MOISTENS
EILMORRS	LORIMERS	EILNSSVY	SYLVINES	EILQRRSU	SQUIRREL	EIMNOSTU	MOUNTIES
EILMOSTT	MOTLIEST	EILNSTTU	LUTENIST	EILQRSTU	QUILTERS	EIMNPRSS	PRIMNESS
EILMPPRU	IMPURPLE	EILNSUWY	UNWISELY	EILQRSUU	LIQUEURS	EIMNPSST	MISSPENT
EILMPRSS	SIMPLERS	EILOOPRR	POORLIER	EILQRSUY	SQUIRELY	EIMNRSST	ENTRISMS
EILMPRSU	SLUMPIER	EILOOPST	LOOPIEST	EILQSTUU	LUSTIQUE		MINSTERS
EILMPRUY	IMPURELY	EILOOPTZ	ZOPILOTE	EILRRSSU	SLURRIES		TRIMNESS
EILMPSST	MISSPELT	EILOORST	TROOLIES	EILRRSTU	SULTRIER	EIMNRSSU	NEURISMS
	SIMPLEST	EILOORTV	OVERTOIL	EILRRTWY	TWIRLERS	EIMNRSTU	TERMINUS
EILMPSSU	IMPULSES	EILOOSST	OSTIOLES	EILRRTWY	WRITERLY	EIMNRSTY	ENTRYISM
EILMPSTU	LUMPIEST		STOOLIES	EILRSSST	STIRLESS		MISENTRY
	PLUMIEST	EILOOSTZ	ZOOLITES	EILRSSTT	SLITTERS	EIMNSSSS	SENSISMS
EILMRSSU	MISRULES	EILOPPPR	POPPLIER		STILTERS	EIMNSSSU	SENSUISM
EILMRSSY	REMISSLY	EILOPPRS	SLOPPIER		TESTRILS	EIMNSSTU	MISTUNES
EILMRSTU	MURLIEST	EILOPPTY	POLYPITE	EILRSSTU	SURLIEST	EIMNSTTU	MINUTEST
EILMRSTY	LYMITERS	EILOPRRT	PORTLIER	EILRSSTY	SISTERLY	EIMNSUZZ	MUEZZINS
EILMSSTU	LITMUSES	EILOPRSS	SPOILERS	EILRSSZZ	SIZZLERS	EIMOORST	MOORIEST
EILMSUUV	ELUVIUMS	EILOPRST	POITRELS	EILRSTTU	SURTITLE		MOTORISE
EILMTTUU	LUTETIUM	EILOPRSU	PERILOUS	EILRSTTW	WRISTLET		ROOMIEST
EILMTTUY	MULTEITY	EILOPRSV	OVERSLIP	EILRSTTZ	STRELITZ	EIMOORTZ	MOTORIZE
EILNNOST	INSOLENT	EILOPRTW	PILEWORT	EILRSTUV	RIVULETS	EIMOPPRR	IMPROPER
EILNNOSW	SNOWLINE	EILOPSSS	PSILOSES	EILRSUUX	LUXURIES	EIMOPPST	MOPPIEST
EILNNOTV	VINOLENT	EILOPSST	PISTOLES	EILSSSTY	STYLISES	EIMOPRRS	PRIMEROS
EILNNPSU	PINNULES		PTILOSES	EILSSTTU	LUSTIEST		PRIMROSE
EILNNTTY	INTENTLY		SLOPIEST	EILSSTTY	STYLITES		PROMISER
EILNOOPP	EPIPLOON	EILOPSSV	PLOSIVES	EILSSTUU	LITUUSES	EIMOPRRT	IMPORTER
EILNOOPS	POLONIES	EILOPSTT	PISTOLET	EILSSTVY	SYLVITES		REIMPORT
	POLONISE		PLOTTIES	EILSSTYZ	STYLIZES	EIMOPRRV	IMPROVER
EILNOOPZ	POLONIZE		POLITEST	EILSSWZZ	SWIZZLES	EIMOPRSS	IMPOSERS
EILNOOST	LOONIEST	EILOPSTX	EXPLOITS	EILSTWZZ	TWIZZLES		PROMISES
	OILSTONE	EILOPSUV	PLUVIOSE	EIMMMNOT	IMMOMENT	EIMOPRST	IMPOSTER
EILNOOSV	VIOLONES	EILORRTU	ULTERIOR	EIMMNNOT	MONIMENT	EIMOPRSV	IMPROVES
EILNOPPS	PLENIPOS	EILORSSS	RISSOLES	EIMMNNTU	MUNIMENT	EIMOPRUU	EUROPIUM

EIMOPSTY	PEYOTISM	EINNPSST	SPINNETS
EIMOQSTU	MISQUOTE	EINNPSSU	PUNINESS
EIMORRSS	MORRISES	EINNPSSY	SPINNEYS
EIMORRST	MORTISER	EINNPSXY	SIXPENNY
	STORMIER	EINNRSTU	RUNNIEST
EIMORRTT	REMITTOR		STURNINE
EIMORSST	EROTISMS	EINNRSTV	VINTNERS
	MORTISES	EINNRTTU	NUTRIENT
	TRISOMES	EINNSSTU	SUNNIEST
EIMORSSV	VERISMOS	EINNSSUW	UNSINEWS
EIMORSTT	OMITTERS	EINNSTUW	UNTWINES
EIMORSTU	MOISTURE	EINOOPRS	POISONER
EIMORSTW	MISWROTE		SPOONIER
	WORMIEST	EINOOPSS	SPOONIES
EIMORSTY	ISOMETRY	EINOORSS	EROSIONS
EIMORSVW	OVERSWIM	EINOORST	SNOOTIER
EIMOSSST	MOSSIEST	EINOORSZ	OZONISER
EIMOSSTT	MOISTEST	EINOORZZ	OZONIZER
EIMOSSTU	MOUSIEST	EINOOSST	ISOTONES
EIMOSSTZ	MESTIZOS	EINOOSSZ	OOZINESS
EIMOSTTT	MOTTIEST		OZONISES
	TOTEMIST	EINOOSTZ	ZOONITES
EIMOSTTU	TITMOUSE	EINOOSZZ	OZONIZES
EIMPRRSU	PRIMEURS	EINOOTXX	EXOTOXIN
EIMPRSST	IMPRESTS	EINOPPRS	POPERINS
EIMPRSSU	PRIMUSES		PROPINES
EIMPRSTU	IMPUREST	EINOPRRS	PRISONER
	IMPUTERS	EINOPRSS	PORINESS
	STUMPIER		PRESSION
EIMPSSST	MISSTEPS		ROPINESS
EIMPSSTU	SPUMIEST	EINOPRST	POINTERS
	STUMPIES		PROTEINS
EIMPSSTY	EMPTYSIS		REPOINTS
EIMQSSTU	MESQUITS	EINOPRSU	PRUINOSE
EIMQSTUY	MYSTIQUE	EINOPRSV	OVERSPIN
EIMRRRSU	SMURRIER		PROVINES
EIMRRSSU	SURMISER	EINOPRTU	ERUPTION
EIMRSSST	MISTRESS	EINOPSTT	NEPOTIST
EIMRSSSU	MISUSERS	EINOQSTU	QUESTION
	SURMISES	EINOQTTU	QUOTIENT
EIMRSSTT	METRISTS	EINORRST	INTRORSE
EIMRSSTY	SMYTRIES		SNORTIER
EIMRSSUU	MIURUSES	EINORRTV	INVERTOR
EIMRSTTU	SMUTTIER	EINORSSS	ROSINESS
EIMRSTUV	VITREUMS	EINORSST	TERSIONS
EIMRSTUX	MIXTURES	EINORSSU	NEUROSIS
EIMSSSSU	MISSUSES		RESINOUS
EIMSSSTU	MUSSIEST	EINORSSV	VERSIONS
EIMSSTTU	MUSTIEST	EINORSTT	SNOTTIER
EIMSTUZZ	MUZZIEST		TENORIST
EINNOPSS	PENSIONS		TRITONES
EINNOQSU	QUINONES	EINORSTU	ROUTINES
EINNORST	INTONERS		SNOUTIER
	TERNIONS	EINORSTV	INVESTOR
EINNORSU	REUNIONS	EINORSTY	TYROSINE
EINNORSV	ENVIRONS	EINORSTZ	TRIZONES
EINNORTT	TONTINER	EINORSUV	SOUVENIR
EINNORTU	NEUTRINO	EINORTTU	RITENUTO
EINNORTV	INVENTOR	EINOSSSS	SESSIONS
	NOVERINT	EINOSSST	SONSIEST
EINNORWW	WINNOWER		STENOSIS
EINNOSSS	NOSINESS	EINOSSTT	SNOTTIES
EINNOSST	TENSIONS		STONIEST
EINNOSSV	VENISONS	EINOSSTW	SNOWIEST
EINNOSTT	TINSTONE	EINOSTTT	TOTIENTS
	TONTINES	EINOSTTW	TOWNIEST
EINNOSTU	NOUNIEST	EINOSTUU	TENUIOUS
EINNPRSS	SPINNERS	EINOSTVY	VENOSITY
EINNPRST	ENPRINTS	EINPPRSS	SNIPPERS
EINNPRSY	SPINNERY	EINPPSST	SNIPPETS

EINPPSTY	SNIPPETY		SPORTIVE
EINPRRST	PRINTERS	EIOPRSUV	PERVIOUS
	REPRINTS		PREVIOUS
	SPRINTER		VIPEROUS
EINPRRTU	PRURIENT	EIOPRTTT	TRIPTOTE
EINPRSST	SPINSTER	EIOPRTTY	PETITORY
EINPRSSY	INSPYRES	EIOPRTUZ	OUTPRIZE
EINPRSTU	UNPRIEST	EIOPSSST	SEPIOSTS
	UNRIPEST	EIOPSSTU	SOUPIEST
EINPRTTU	INPUTTER	EIOPSSTY	ISOTYPES
EINPSTTX	SPINTEXT	EIOPSTTT	POTTIEST
EINPSTTY	TINTYPES	EIOPSTTU	POUTIEST
EINQRSTU	SQUINTER	EIOPSTTY	PEYOTIST
EINQSSTU	INQUESTS	EIOPSTUW	WIPEOUTS
EINQSTTU	QUINTETS	EIOQRSTU	QUOITERS
EINQSTUU	UNIQUEST	EIORRRST	ERRORIST
	UNQUIETS	EIORRRSW	WORRIERS
EINQTTTU	QUINTETT	EIORRRTU	ROTURIER
EINRRSSU	INSURERS	EIORRSST	RESISTOR
EINRSSST	INSTRESS		ROISTERS
EINRSSSU	SUNRISES		SORRIEST
EINRSSTT	ENTRISTS	EIORRSSV	REVISORS
	STINTERS	EIORRSTT	RORTIEST
EINRSSXY	SYRINXES	EIORRSTU	STOURIER
EINRSTTU	RUNTIEST	EIORRSTV	SERVITOR
EINRSTTW	TWINTERS	EIORRSUV	OUVRIERS
EINRSTTY	ENTRYIST	EIORRSVV	REVIVORS
EINRSTUV	UNRIVETS	EIORRSVY	REVISORY
	VENTURIS	EIORRTTU	TROUTIER
EINRSTUW	UNWRITES	EIORSSTT	STOITERS
EINRTUUV	UNVIRTUE	EIORSSTY	SEROSITY
EINSSSST	SENSISTS	EIORSTTU	TUTORISE
EINSSSTU	SENSUIST	EIORSTTV	VIRETOTS
EINSSTTW	ENTWISTS	EIORSTUV	VIRTUOSE
EINSSTUW	UNWISEST		VITREOUS
EINSSTUX	UNSEXIST		VOITURES
EINSSTXY	SYNTEXIS	EIORTTUZ	TUTORIZE
EINSTTTU	NUTTIEST	EIOSSSTT	TOSSIEST
EINSTTTW	TWITTENS	EIOSSTTU	TOUSIEST
EIOOPPRS	PORPOISE	EIOSSTTW	TOWSIEST
EIOOPPST	OPPOSITE	EIOSSTUZ	OUTSIZES
EIOOPRST	PORTOISE	EIOSTTTT	TOTTIEST
	ROOPIEST	EIOSTTTU	TOUTIEST
EIOOPSST	ISOTOPES	EIPPRRST	STRIPPER
EIOOPSTV	POOVIEST		TRIPPERS
EIOORRSS	SORORISE	EIPPRRTY	TRIPPERY
EIOORRSZ	SORORIZE	EIPPRSTT	TRIPPETS
EIOORSTT	ROOTIEST	EIPQRSTU	QUIPSTER
	TORTOISE	EIPRRRSU	SPURRIER
EIOOSSTT	SOOTIEST	EIPRRSSU	SPURRIES
	TOOTSIES		SURPRISE
EIOOSTWZ	WOOZIEST	EIPRRSTZ	SPRITZER
EIOPPRTW	PIPEWORT	EIPRSSST	PERSISTS
EIOPPSST	SOPPIEST	EIPRSSSU	SUSPIRES
EIOPRRSS	PRIORESS	EIPRSSTT	SPITTERS
EIOPRRST	PIERROTS		TIPSTERS
	SPORTIER	EIPRSSTU	PURSIEST
EIOPRRSU	SUPERIOR	EIPRSTTU	PURTIEST
EIOPRRTV	OVERTRIP		PUTTIERS
EIOPRSST	PERIOSTS	EIPRSUVW	PURVIEWS
	PROSIEST	EIPRSVVY	SPIVVERY
	REPOSITS	EIPSSTXY	PTYXISES
	RIPOSTES	EIQRRSTU	SQUIRTER
	TRIPOSES	EIQRSSSU	SQUIRESS
EIOPRSTT	PORTIEST	EIQRSSTU	QUERISTS
	RISPETTO	EIQRSTTU	QUITTERS
	SPOTTIER	EIQSSUZZ	QUIZZERS
EIOPRSTU	ROUPIEST	EIQRUYZZ	QUIZZERY
	SPOUTIER	EIRRRSST	STIRRERS
EIOPRSTV	PIVOTERS	EIRRSSTV	STRIVERS

Code	Word	Code	Word
EIRRSTTU	TRUSTIER	ELLMNOSY	SOLEMNLY
EIRSSSTU	SUITRESS	ELLMNOTY	MOLTENLY
EIRSSTTU	RUSTIEST	ELLMNPUY	LUMPENLY
	TRUSTIES	ELLMOORS	MORELLOS
EIRSSTTW	TWISTERS	ELLMPSUU	PLUMULES
EIRSSUVV	SURVIVES	ELLNNOST	TONNELLS
EIRSSUVW	SURVIEWS	ELLNNSSU	NULLNESS
EIRSTTTU	RUTTIEST	ELLNOORV	LOVELORN
EIRSTTTW	TWITTERS	ELLNOOSW	WOOLLENS
EIRSTTUX	TUTRIXES	ELLNOPRU	PRUNELLO
EIRTTTWY	TWITTERY	ELLNOSSU	NOUSELLS
EIRTTUWZ	WURTZITE	ELLNOSVY	SLOVENLY
EISSSSTU	TUSSISES	ELLNOSXY	XYLENOLS
EJLOPSTU	PULSOJET	ELLNOUVY	UNLOVELY
EJMOPRUV	OVERJUMP	ELLNPSSU	UNSPELLS
EJNORRSU	REJOURNS	ELLOOSSW	WOOSELLS
EJNORSUY	JOURNEYS	ELLOPRRS	PROLLERS
EJNRSTUU	UNJUSTER	ELLOPRST	POLLSTER
EJNSSSTU	JUSTNESS	ELLOPRTU	POLLUTER
EJOORSVY	OVERJOYS	ELLOPRUV	PULLOVER
EJORSSTU	JOUSTERS	ELLOPSST	PLOTLESS
EJOSSTTU	OUTJESTS	ELLOPSTU	POLLUTES
EKKLOOSY	OLYKOEKS	ELLORRST	STROLLER
EKKLRSSU	SKULKERS		TROLLERS
EKKMORSY	KROMESKY	ELLORSTY	TROLLEYS
EKLLMSSU	SKELLUMS	ELLOSSSU	SOULLESS
EKLLOSSY	KYLLOSES	ELLOSSTU	OUTSELLS
EKLNOOOR	ONLOOKER	ELLOSTTU	OUTTELLS
EKLNOPRS	PLONKERS	ELLOSTUW	OUTSWELL
EKLNORSS	SNORKELS		OUTWELLS
EKLNOSST	KNOTLESS	ELLPSSUW	UPSWELLS
EKLNPRSU	PLUNKERS	ELLSSSTU	LUSTLESS
EKLOOORV	OVERLOOK	ELMMNOTU	LOMENTUM
EKLOOPSW	SLOWPOKE	ELMMNOTY	MOMENTLY
EKLORSSW	WORKLESS	ELMMORST	TROMMELS
EKLSSSTU	TUSKLESS	ELMMOSUX	LUMMOXES
EKLSSTTU	SKUTTLES	ELMMPSTU	PLUMMETS
EKMMORSU	MURKSOME	ELMMRSSU	SLUMMERS
EKMMRSSU	SKUMMERS	ELMMRSTU	STRUMMEL
EKMNOSSU	MUSKONES	ELMMRSUY	SUMMERLY
EKMOORSW	WORKSOME	ELMMSSTU	STUMMELS
EKMOOSSS	KOSMOSES	ELMNNOSU	UNSOLEMN
EKMRSTUY	MUSKETRY	ELMNOOOP	MONOPOLE
EKNNOPSU	UNSPOKEN	ELMNOOSS	MOONLESS
EKNOORSS	SNOOKERS	ELMNOOST	MOONLETS
EKNOORST	STROOKEN	ELMNOPSU	PULMONES
EKNOPPSU	UPSPOKEN	ELMNPPSU	PLUMPENS
EKNORSST	STONKERS	ELMNPSUU	UNPLUMES
EKNORSTT	KNOTTERS	ELMNUUZZ	UNMUZZLE
EKNORSTW	NETWORKS	ELMOOPPS	POMPELOS
EKNORSUY	YOUNKERS	ELMOOPSY	POLYSOME
EKNRSTUY	TURNKEYS	ELMOORST	TREMOLOS
EKOOORTV	OVERTOOK	ELMOORSY	MOROSELY
EKOOPRRV	PROVOKER	ELMOOSSY	LYSOSOME
EKOOPRRW	ROPEWORK	ELMOPRSY	POLYMERS
EKOOPRSV	PROVOKES	ELMOPRTY	METOPRYL
EKOOPRSY	SPOOKERY	ELMOPRRY	POLYMERY
EKOOPSTU	OUTSPOKE	ELMOPSYY	POLYSEMY
EKOORRVW	OVERWORK	ELMORSSU	EMULSORS
EKOORSST	STOOKERS	ELMOSYYZ	LYSOZYME
	STROOKES	ELMPPRSU	PLUMPERS
EKOPRSTU	UPSTROKE	ELMPPSTU	PLUMPEST
EKORRSST	STROKERS	ELMPRSSU	RUMPLESS
EKORRUVY	KURVEYOR	ELMRRTUU	MULTURER
EKORSSTU	KURTOSES	ELMRSTUU	MULTURES
EKPPSSUU	SEPPUKUS	ELMRSUZZ	MUZZLERS
ELLLMOWY	MELLOWLY	ELNNOOSU	UNLOOSEN
ELLLNSUY	SULLENLY	ELNNOPTU	NONUPLET
ELLLORRS	LORRELLS	ELNOOSST	SOLONETS
ELLMNOOS	MOELLONS	ELNOOSSU	UNLOOSES

Code	Word	Code	Word
ELNOOSSZ	SNOOZLES	EMMNNOTU	MONUMENT
ELNOOSTZ	SOLONETZ	EMMNOORS	MONOMERS
ELNOPTTY	POTENTLY	EMMNOORT	MOTORMEN
ELNORSSU	NOURSLES	EMMNORSU	SUMMONER
ELNORSTU	TURNSOLE	EMMNOSTY	METONYMS
ELNORSVY	SLOVENRY	EMMNOTTU	TOMENTUM
ELNORTTY	ROTTENLY	EMMNOTYY	METONYMY
ELNOSSSW	SLOWNESS	EMMOOORS	ROOMSOME
	SNOWLESS	EMMOPRRS	PROMMERS
ELNOSSTV	SOLVENTS	EMMOPTTY	POMMETTY
ELNOSSTW	WONTLESS	EMMRRRUU	MURMURER
ELNOSTUZ	ZONULETS		REMURMUR
ELNPPSUU	UNSUPPLE	EMMRSTYY	SYMMETRY
ELNPRTUU	PURULENT	EMNNNOOU	NOUMENON
ELNSSUZZ	SNUZZLES	EMNNOOOT	MONOTONE
ELOOPRSS	SPOOLERS	EMNNOSTW	TOWNSMEN
ELOOPRUW	OWERLOUP	EMNNPSTU	PUNTSMEN
ELOOPSSS	SESSPOOL	EMNNSTTU	STUNTMEN
ELOORSST	ROOTLESS	EMNOOPST	METOPONS
ELOORSTT	ROOTLETS	EMNOOPTY	MONOTYPE
ELOORSTU	TORULOSE	EMNOORST	MESOTRON
ELOORSUV	OVERSOUL		MONTEROS
ELOOSSST	SOOTLESS	EMNOORSU	ENORMOUS
ELOOSSTU	OUTSOLES		NEMOROUS
ELOOSSWY	WOOLSEYS	EMNOORSW	NEWSROOM
ELOPPRRY	PROPERLY	EMNOORTY	NOOMETRY
ELOPPSST	STOPPLES	EMNOOSST	MOONSETS
ELOPRRSU	PROULERS	EMNOOSUV	VENOMOUS
ELOPRRSW	PROWLERS	EMNOOTTY	TENOTOMY
ELOPRRSY	PYRROLES	EMNOOTUV	OUTVENOM
ELOPRRTY	PORTERLY	EMNOOTWY	TOYWOMEN
ELOPRSSS	PLESSORS	EMNORRSU	MOURNERS
ELOPRSSU	SPORULES	EMNORSST	MONSTERS
ELOPRSTT	PLOTTERS	EMNORSTT	SORTMENT
ELOPRSTU	PLOUTERS		TORMENTS
	POULTERS	EMNORSTU	MONTURES
ELOPRSTW	PLOWTERS		MOUNTERS
ELOPRSTY	PROSTYLE		REMOUNTS
	PROTYLES	EMNORSUU	NUMEROUS
ELOPRSUV	OVERPLUS	EMNOSSST	STEMSONS
ELOPRSYY	PYROLYSE	EMNOSUUY	EUONYMUS
ELOPRXYY	PYROXYLE	EMNRSSTU	MUNSTERS
ELOPRYYZ	PYROLYZE		STERNUMS
ELOPSSST	SPOTLESS	EMOOPRRT	PROMOTER
	STOPLESS	EMOOPRST	PROMOTES
ELOPSSUU	OPULUSES	EMOOPRSY	POMEROYS
ELOPSTTU	OUTSLEPT		PYROSOME
ELORSSTT	SETTLORS	EMOOPRSZ	ZOOSPERM
	SLOTTERS	EMOOPSSU	ESPUMOSO
ELORSTUY	SOUTERLY	EMOORSST	MOROSEST
	UROSTYLE	EMOORSSU	UROSOMES
ELORTTTU	TROUTLET	EMOORTYZ	ZOOMETRY
ELOSSSTY	SYSTOLES	EMOOSSTW	TWOSOMES
ELOSSWZZ	SWOZZLES	EMOOSSTY	MYOSOTES
ELPPRSTU	PURPLEST	EMOOSTUV	OUTMOVES
ELPPSSTU	SUPPLEST	EMOPPRRT	PROMPTER
ELPRSSSU	SPURLESS	EMOPRSSU	SPERMOUS
ELPRSSTU	SPURTLES		SUPREMOS
ELPRSTTU	SPLUTTER	EMORRRUU	RUMOURER
ELPRSTUU	PULTURES	EMORRSSU	MORSURES
ELPRSUZZ	PUZZLERS	EMORSSSU	SMOUSERS
ELPSSTUU	PUSTULES	EMORSSTU	OESTRUMS
ELRRSSTU	RUSTLERS		STRUMOSE
ELRRSTTU	TURTLERS	EMORSUVW	OVERSWUM
ELRSSSTU	RUSTLESS	EMOSSTTW	WESTMOST
ELRSTTUY	SLUTTERY	EMOSSTVZ	ZEMSTVOS
ELRSTUUV	VULTURES	EMPRRTUY	TRUMPERY
ELSSSTUY	STYLUSES	EMPRSSTU	STUMPERS
ELSSSTYY	SYSTYLES		SUMPTERS
EMMMNOTU	MOMENTUM	EMPRSSUU	RUMPUSES

EMPRSTTU STRUMPET
TRUMPETS
EMRRSSTU STURMERS
ENNOOORT TENOROON
ENNOOOTZ ENTOZOON
ENNOOPPT OPPONENT
ENNOOSTT NONETTOS
ENNOPRSU UNPERSON
ENNOPRUV UNPROVEN
ENNOPTWY TWOPENNY
ENNORSST STERNSON
ENNORSTU NEUTRONS
ENNORSTY SONNETRY
ENNORTTU UNROTTEN
ENNOSSTU NEUSTONS
SUNSTONE
ENNPPTUY TUPPENNY
ENNRSSTU STUNNERS
ENOOOSSZ ZOONOSES
ENOOPPRS PROPONES
ENOOPPST POSTPONE
ENOOPRSS POORNESS
SNOOPERS
ENOOPSSY SPOONEYS
ENOOPSTT POTSTONE
ENOORRVW OVERWORN
ENOORSSZ SNOOZERS
ENOORSVW OVERSOWN
ENOOSSTT TESTOONS
ENOOSTXY OXYTONES
ENOPPRRU UNPROPER
ENOPRRSU PRONEURS
ENOPRSST POSTERNS
ENOPRSTT PORTENTS
ENOPSSST STEPSONS
ENOPSSSY SYNOPSES
ENOPSTTU OUTSPENT
ENOQSTUU UNQUOTES
ENORRSST SNORTERS
ENORRSTT TORRENTS
ENORRSUV OVERRUNS
ENORRTUU TOURNURE
ENORRTUV OVERTURN
TURNOVER
ENORSSSU SOURNESS
ENORSSTT SNOTTERS
STENTORS
ENORSSTU TONSURES
ENORSTTU STENTOUR
ENORSTTY SNOTTERY
ENORSTUV VENTROUS
ENORSTUY TOURNEYS
ENOSSSUU SENSUOUS
ENOSSTTU STOUTENS
ENPRRSSU SPURNERS
ENPRSSSY SPRYNESS
ENPRSSTU PUNSTERS
ENPRSSUU UNPURSES
ENPRTTUY UNPRETTY
ENRRRTUU NURTURER
ENRRSTUU NURTURES
ENRRSTTU ENTRUSTS
ENRSSTUU UNSUREST
ENRSTTUU UNTRUEST
EOOOPRSS OOSPORES
SOPOROSE
EOOOPRSZ ZOOSPORE
EOOOPRTZ ZOOTROPE
EOOPPRRS PROPOSER
EOOPPRSS OPPOSERS

PROPOSES
EOOPPRSV POPOVERS
EOOPRRSS SPOORERS
EOOPRRST TROOPERS
EOOPRRTU OUTROPER
UPROOTER
EOOPRSST STOOPERS
EOOPRSTU OUTROPES
PORTEOUS
EOOPRSTV OVERPOST
OVERTOPS
EOOPRSTW TOWROPES
EOOPRTUW OUTPOWER
EOOPSTYZ ZOOTYPES
EOORRRSW SORROWER
EOORRSST ROOSTERS
EOORRSTU OESTROUS
EOORSSVW OVERSOWS
EOORSTUW OUTSWORE
EOORTTUV OUTVOTER
EOOSTTUV OUTVOTES
EOPPRRSS PROSPERS
EOPPRRTY PROPERTY
EOPPRSST STOPPERS
EOPPRSSU PURPOSES
SUPPOSER
EOPPSSSU SUPPOSES
EOPRRSST PORTRESS
SPORTERS
EOPRRSTU POSTURER
TROUPERS
EOPRRUVY PURVEYOR
EOPRSSTT PROTESTS
SPOTTERS
EOPRSSTU POSTURES
SEPTUORS
SPOUTERS
EOPRSSUU POURSUES
UPROUSES
EOPRSSUW POURSEWS
EOPSSTTU OUTSTEPS
EOPSSTTW STEWPOTS
EOQRSSTU QUESTORS
EORRRTTU TORTURER
EORRSSST STRESSOR
TROSSERS
EORRSSTU ROUSTERS
TROUSERS
EORRSSTW STROWERS
TROWSERS
EORRSSTY ROYSTERS
EORRSTTT TROTTERS
EORRSTTU TORTURES
TROUTERS
EORRSUVY SURVEYOR
EORRTUUV TROUVEUR
EORSSSTU TUSSORES
EORSSTTT STOTTERS
EORSSTTU TUTORESS
EORSSTTW SWOTTERS
EORSSTUX SEXTUORS
EORSTTUW OUTWREST
EORSTUUV VERTUOUS
EOSSSTXY XYSTOSES
EOSSTTTU STOUTEST
EPPPRTUY PUPPETRY
EPPRRSUU PURPURES
EPPRSSSU SUPPRESS
EPRRRSSU SPURRERS

EPRRSSUU PURSUERS
USURPERS
EPRRSSUY SPURREYS
EPRRSTUU RUPTURES
EPRSSTTU SPUTTERS
EPRSTTUY SPUTTERY
EQRRTUUU TRUQUEUR
ERRSSSTU TRUSSERS
ERRSSTTU TRUSTERS
ERRSSTTY TRYSTERS
ERRSTTTU STRUTTER
ERSSTTTU STUTTERS
ESSSTUXY XYSTUSES
FFFGILNU FLUFFING
FFFMOOTU FOOTMUFF
FFGGIILN GLIFFING
FFGHIINW WHIFFING
FFGHINOU HOUFFING
FFGHINOW HOWFFING
FFGHIRSU GRUFFISH
FFGIIKNS SKIFFING
FFGIILNP PIFFLING
FFGIILNR RIFFLING
FFGIILNS SIFFLING
FFGIINNS SNIFFING
FFGIINPS SPIFFING
FFGIINRS GRIFFINS
FFGIINST STIFFING
TIFFINGS
FFGIKNOS SKOFFING
FFGILMNU MUFFLING
FFGILNPU PLUFFING
FFGILNRU RUFFLING
FFGINNSU SNUFFING
FFGINORS GRIFFONS
FFGINOSW SOWFFING
FFGINPSU PUFFINGS
FFGINSTU STUFFING
FFHIISST STIFFISH
FFHIISTY FIFTYISH
FFHIKNSU HUFFKINS
FFHIOPSS SPOFFISH
FFHOOOST OFFSHOOT
FFIILMOR FILIFORM
FFIILNSY SNIFFILY
FFIILNTY FLINTIFY
FFIINOOS SOFFIONI
FFIKLRSU FRISKFUL
FFILLOPP FLIPFLOP
FFILLTUY FITFULLY
FFILRTUU FRUITFUL
FFILSSTU FISTFULS
FFILSTUY STUFFILY
FFIMORSU FUSIFORM
FFINOPRT OFFPRINT
FFINOPST PONTIFFS
FFLLOOSU LOOFFULS
FFLMNOOU MOUFFLON
FFLNOTUU FOUNTFUL
FFLORRUU FURFUROL
FFNORSTU TURNOFFS
FFNSTUUY UNSTUFFY
FGGGIINR FRIGGING
FGGGILNO FLOGGING
FGGGINOR FROGGING
FGGHIINT FIGHTING
FGGHIISS FISHGIGS
FGGHINTU GUNFIGHT
FGGIILLN FLINGING
FGGIINNR FRINGING

FGGIINRT GRIFTING
FGGIINRU FIGURING
FGGIISZZ FIZZGIGS
FGGILNOR FROGLING
FGGILNOS GOLFINGS
FGGINOOR FORGOING
FGGINORS FORGINGS
FGHIIKNS KINGFISH
FGHIINSS FISHINGS
FGHIINST SHIFTING
FGHILLTU LIGHTFUL
FGHILMTU MIGHTFUL
FGHILNSU FLUSHING
FGHILRTU RIGHTFUL
FGHINORT FROTHING
FGHINRSU FRUSHING
FGHIOTTU OUTFIGHT
FGHLORUU FURLOUGH
FGHNOORS FOGHORNS
FGHNOTUU UNFOUGHT
FGIIINNX INFIXING
FGIIKLNS FLISKING
FGIIKNNS KNIFINGS
FGIIKNRS FRISKING
FGIILLNR FRILLING
FGIILLNS FILLINGS
FGIILMNP FLIMPING
FGIILNOO FOLIOING
FGIILNOS FOILINGS
FGIILNPP FLIPPING
FGIILNRS RIFLINGS
FGIILNRT FLIRTING
TRIFLING
FGIILNSS FISSLING
FGIILNST STIFLING
FGIILNTT FLITTING
FGIILNZZ FIZZLING
FGIINNST SNIFTING
FGIINNSU INFUSING
FGIINNUX UNFIXING
FGIINNUY UNIFYING
FGIINOQU QUOIFING
FGIINOST FOISTING
FGIINRRS FIRRINGS
FGIINRST FRISTING
FGIINRTT FRITTING
FGIINRTU FRUITING
FGIINRZZ FRIZZING
FGIINSST SIFTINGS
FGIINSTT FITTINGS
FGIINSTW SWIFTING
FGIINSZZ FIZZINGS
FGIIRSTU FIGURIST
FGIKLNNU FLUNKING
FGILLNOW WOLFING
FGILLNOY FOLLYING
FGILMNPU PLUMPING
FGILNNTU GUNFLINT
FGILNOOR FLOORING
FGILNOOS FOOLINGS
FGILNOOT FOOTLING
FGILNOOZ FOOZLING
FGILNOPP FLOPPING
FGILNOPS FOPLINGS
FGILNORU FLOURING
FGILNOST SOFTLING
FGILNOSU FLOUSING
FGILNOSW FOWLINGS
WOLFINGS
FGILNOTU FLOUTING

OUTFLING	FIILLMSY FLIMSILY	FLNOOTUW OUTFLOWN	GGHIINRT GIRTHING
FGILNPRU PURFLING	FIILLMTU MULTIFIL	FLOOOPTT POLTFOOT	RIGHTING
FGILNRRU FLURRING	FIILLNTY FLINTILY	FLOOPTTY TOPLOFTY	GGHIINST SIGHTING
FGILNSTU FLUTINGS	FIILMNRY INFIRMLY	FLOORSSW FORSLOWS	GGHIINTW WIGHTING
FGILNSTY FLYTINGS	FIILMOPR PILIFORM	FLOOSTUW OUTFLOWS	GGHIIPRS PRIGGISH
FGILNUZZ FUZZLING	FIILMPSY SIMPLIFY	FLOPRSTU SPORTFUL	GGHILNPU GULPHING
FGIMNORS FORMINGS	FIILNOST TINFOILS	FLORTTUU TROUTFUL	GGHILSSU SLUGGISH
FGIMNPRU FRUMPING	FIILTTUY FUTILITY	FLRSTTUU TRUSTFUL	GGHIMSTU THUGGISM
FGIMOSSY FOGYISMS	FIIMOPRS PISIFORM	FMRSSTUU FRUSTUMS	GGHINORU ROUGHING
FGINNORT FRONTING	FIIMOSTY MOISTIFY	FNNOOORT FRONTOON	GGHINOST GHOSTING
FGINNORW FROWNING	FIINNOSU INFUSION	FNNOORST FRONTONS	GGHINOSU SOUGHING
FGINOOPR PROOFING	FIINORTU FRUITION	FNOOORTW FOOTWORN	GGHINOTY HOGTYING
FGINOOPS SPOOFING	FIINOSSS FISSIONS	FNOOPRSU SUNPROOF	GGIIILNS GINGILIS
FGINOORS ROOFINGS	FIINTUXY UNFIXITY	FNOORRSW FROSWORN	GGIIINNT IGNITING
FGINOOST FOOTINGS	FIIQUYZZ QUIZZIFY	FNOORTUW OUTFROWN	GGIIJLNN JINGLING
FGINORST FROSTING	FIKKLNOS KINFOLKS	FOOOPSTT FOOTPOST	GGIIKLNN KINGLING
FGINRRSU FURRINGS	KINSFOLK	FOOORSTT FOOTROTS	GGIILLNR GRILLING
FGINRSSU SURFINGS	FIKLNOSW WOLFKINS	FOOOSTTU OUTFOOTS	GGIILLNY GILLYING
FGINRSTU TURFINGS	FIKLNSSU SKINFULS	FOORSTTX FOXTROTS	GGIILMNN MINGLING
FGINSTTU TUFTINGS	FIKNORSW FORSWINK	GGGGIILN GIGGLING	GGIILMNY GINGLYMI
FGIORSTW FIGWORTS	FILLLUWY WILFULLY	GGGGIINR GRIGGING	GGIILNNP PINGLING
FGISSTUU FUGUISTS	FILLNUUW UNWILFUL	GGGGILNO GOGGLING	GGIILNNS SINGLING
FGLLMOOU GLOOMFUL	FILLOPPY FLOPPILY	GGGGILNU GLUGGING	SLINGING
FGLLNSUU LUNGFULS	FILLOPSU SPOILFUL	GUGGLING	GGIILNNT GLINTING
FGLNORSU FURLONGS	FILMNOOS MONOFILS	GGGGINOR GROGGING	TINGLING
FGLNORUW WRONGFUL	FILMOPRS SLIPFORM	GGGHIILN HIGGLING	GGIILNPS PIGLINGS
FGLOOOST FOOTSLOG	FILMORRY LYRIFORM	GGGHIINT THIGGING	GGIILNRS RIGLINGS
FGLORSUU FULGOURS	FILMOSSU MOFUSSIL	GGGHIINW WHIGGING	GGIIMNOS MISGOING
FGNOORSU FOURGONS	FILNOSUX FLUXIONS	GGGHINOS HOGGINGS	GGIIMNPU GUIMPING
FGNOORTU UNFORGOT	FILOOSTW WITLOOFS	SHOGGING	GGIIMPRS PRIGGISM
FHHOORST SHOFROTH	FILORSST FLORISTS	GGGIIJLN JIGGLING	GGIINNNR GRINNING
FHIIKLMS MILKFISH	FILORSTU FLORUITS	GGGIIJNS JIGGINGS	GGIINNOR GROINING
FHIIKNSS FISHSKIN	FILORSTY FROSTILY	GGGIILNN GINGLING	IGNORING
FHIILLTY FILTHILY	FILRSTTU TRISTFUL	NIGGLING	GGIINNOS INGOINGS
FHIILRST FLIRTISH	FILSSTTU FLUTISTS	GGGIILNS LIGGINGS	GGIINNRS RINGINGS
FHIILSTY SHIFTILY	FILSTTUY STULTIFY	GGGIILNW WIGGLING	GGIINNRW WRINGING
FHIKLLLO HILLFOLK	FIMMNOOR OMNIFORM	GGGIINNS SNIGGING	GGIINNSS SINGINGS
FHIKMNOS MONKFISH	FIMMORRU MURIFORM	GGGIINPR PRIGGING	GGIINNST STINGING
FHIKNORT FORTHINK	FIMMORSS MISFORMS	GGGIIPNS PIGGINGS	GGIINNSW SWINGING
FHILLOOT FOOTHILL	FIMNORSU UNIFORMS	GGGIINRS RIGGINGS	GGIINNTW TWINGING
FHILMPSU LUMPFISH	FIMOPRRY PYRIFORM	GGGIINRT TRIGGING	GGIINNUV UNGIVING
FHILMRTU MIRTHFUL	FIMORTUY FUMITORY	GGGIINSW SWIGGING	GGIINPPR GRIPPING
FHILORSU FLOURISH	FIMOSTUY FUMOSITY	GGGIINTW TWIGGING	GGIINPSY GIPSYING
FHILORTY FROTHILY	FIMRSTUU FUTURISM	GGGIJLNO JOGGLING	GGIINRST RINGGITS
FHILPSSU SHIPFULS	FINORSSS FRISSONS	GGGIJLNU JUGGLING	GGIINRTT GRITTING
FHIMPRSU FRUMPISH	FINORSUY INFUSORY	GGGIJNOS JOGGINGS	GGIINSTU GIUSTING
FHINOSSU FUSHIONS	FIOORSSU FURIOSOS	GGGIKNSU SKUGGING	GGIIRRSS GRISGRIS
FHINRTTU UNTHRIFT	FIORTTUY FORTUITY	GGGILNOO GOOGLING	GGILLNUY GULLYING
FHIOOPTT PHOTOFIT	FIRSTTUU FUTURIST	GGGILNOS LOGGINGS	GGILLOOW GOLLIWOG
FHIOPSSX FOXSHIPS	FIRTTUUY FUTURITY	SLOGGING	GGILMNNO GLOMMING
FHIORSTY FORTYISH	FJLLOUYY JOYFULLY	GGGILNOT TOGGLING	GGILMNOO GLOOMING
FHKORSTU FUTHORKS	FJLNOUUY UNJOYFUL	GGGILNPU PLUGGING	GGILNNOP PLONGING
FHLLLOTU LOTHFULL	FKKLOORW WORKFOLK	GGGILNRU GURGLING	GGILNNOS LONGINGS
FHLLOSTU SLOTHFUL	FKKOORTW KOFTWORK	GGGILNSU SLUGGING	GGILNNOU LOUNGING
FHLMOTUU MOUTHFUL	FKLMOOOT FOLKMOOT	GGGIMNSU MUGGINGS	GGILNNPU PLUNGING
FHLNORSU HORNFULS	FKLNRTUU TRUNKFUL	SMUGGING	GGILNNUU UNGLUING
FHLOOSTU SOOTHFUL	FKMOORRW FORMWORK	GGGINNOS NOGGINGS	GGILNORW GROWLING
FHLOOTTU TOOTHFUL	FKNORSUW FORSWUNK	SNOGGING	GGILNORY GLORYING
FHLOPSSU SHOPFULS	FKOOORTW FOOTWORK	GGGINNSU SNUGGING	GGILNOSS GLOSSING
FHLORTTU TROTHFUL	FLLOOPUW UPFOLLOW	GGGINOPR PROGGING	GOSLINGS
FHLORTUW WORTHFUL	FLLRSTUY STRYFULL	GGGINORT TROGGING	GGILNOSZ GLOZINGS
FHLORTUY FOURTHLY	FLMNOOSU MOUFLONS	GGGINOSS SOGGINGS	GGILNOTU GLOUTING
FHLOSTUU OUTFLUSH	FLMNORUU MOURNFUL	GGGINPSU PUGGINGS	GGILNTTU GLUTTING
FHLOTUUY YOUTHFUL	FLMOOORW MOORFOWL	GGGINRSU RUGGINGS	GUTTLING
FHLRTTUU TRUTHFUL	FLMOOOST TOMFOOLS	GGGINSTU TUGGINGS	GGILNUZZ GUZZLING
FHOOORST FORSOOTH	FLMOORSU ROOMFULS	GGHHIINT HIGHTING	GGILQSUY SQUIGGLY
HOOFROTS	FLMORSTU STORMFUL	GGHHINOU HOUGHING	GGIMMNSU GUMMINGS
FIIINNTY INFINITY	FLNOOPSU SPOONFUL	GGHIILNT LIGHTING	GGIMNOOR GROOMING
FIIKLRSY FRISKILY	FLNOORRS FORLORNS	GGHIINPT PIGHTING	GGINNNSU GUNNINGS
FIILLMOS MILFOILS	FLNOOSTU SNOOTFUL		GGINNOOS ONGOINGS

GGINNOPR PRONGING	GHIINRTV THRIVING	GHINOPSS GINSHOPS	GIIKKNNS SKINKING
GGINNOPS SPONGING	GHIINRTW WRITHING	GHINORSS HORSINGS	GIIKKNRS KIRKINGS
GGINNORW WRONGING	GHIINSSS HISSINGS	SHORINGS	GIIKLLNS KILLINGS
GGINNOSS SINGSONG	GHIINSST INSIGHTS	GHINORST SHORTING	SKILLING
GGINNOTU TONGUING	GHIINSSW SWISHING	GHINORSV SHROVING	GIIKLMNS MILKINGS
GGINNRTU GRUNTING	WHISSING	GHINORSW SHROWING	GIIKLNNP PLINKING
GGINNUVY UNGYVING	WISHINGS	GHINORTT TROTHING	GIIKLNNS INKLINGS
GGINOORV GROOVING	GHIINSTT SHITTING	GHINORTW INGROWTH	SLINKING
GGINOOST STOOGING	TITHINGS	THROWING	GIIKLNNT TINKLING
GGINOOTU OUTGOING	GHIINSTW WHISTING	WORTHING	GIIKLNRS SKIRLING
GGINOPRS PROGGINS	WHITINGS	GHINOSST HOSTINGS	GIIKLNST KITLINGS
GGINOPRU GROUPING	GHIINSVV SHIVVING	GHINOSSU HOUSINGS	GIIKLNTT KITTLING
GGINOPSU UPGOINGS	GHIINWZZ WHIZZING	GHINOSSW SHOWINGS	GIIKMMNS SKIMMING
GGINORSS GROSSING	GHIIORSV VIGORISH	GHINOSTT SHOTTING	GIIKMNPS SKIMPING
GGINORSU GROUSING	GHIIRSTT RIGHTIST	TONIGHTS	GIIKMNRS SMIRKING
GGINORSW GROWINGS	GHIKLNTY KNIGHTLY	GHINOSTU SHOUTING	GIIKNNNS SKINNING
GGINORTU GROUTING	GHIKLSTY SKYLIGHT	SOUTHING	GIIKNNOV INVOKING
GGINPRSU PURGINGS	GHIKNNTU UNKNIGHT	GHINOSTW SOWTHING	GIIKNNPR PRINKING
GGINPSYY GYPSYING	GHIKNSSU HUSKINGS	GHINOSUY YOUNGISH	GIIKNNPS PINKINGS
GGINRSSU SURGINGS	GHILLNOO HOLLOING	GHINOTTU OUTNIGHT	GIIKNNSS SINKINGS
GGLLOOWY GOLLYWOG	GHILLNOU HULLOING	GHINPSSU GUNSHIPS	GIIKNNST STINKING
GHHIILST LIGHTISH	GHILLSTY SLIGHTLY	GHINRRUY HURRYING	GIIKNNSW SWINKING
GHHIINSW WHISHING	GHILMNSU MULSHING	GHINRSTU UNGIRTHS	WINKINGS
GHHIISTT TIGHTISH	GHILMPSU GLUMPISH	UNRIGHTS	GIIKNNTT KNITTING
GHHILOSU GHOULISH	GHILNOOS SHOOLING	GHINSSTU HUSTINGS	GIIKNNTW TWINKING
GHHIMNPU HUMPHING	GHILNOPP HOPPLING	GHINSTTU HUTTINGS	GIIKNPPS SKIPPING
GHHIMOST HIGHMOST	GHILNOPS LONGSHIP	SHUTTING	GIIKNPSS PIGSKINS
GHHINOOS HOOSHING	GHILNOPY HOPINGLY	GHIORTTU OUTRIGHT	GIIKNQRU QUIRKING
GHHINSSU SHUSHING	GHILNOSS SLOSHING	GHIOSTTU OUTSIGHT	GIIKNRRS SKIRRING
GHHIORSU ROUGHISH	GHILNOST SLOTHING	GHIPRSST SPRIGHTS	GIIKNRSS GRISKINS
GHHIOSTU TOUGHISH	GHILNOSU HOUSLING	GHIPRSTU UPRIGHTS	GIIKNRST SKIRTING
GHHIRSST SHRIGHTS	GHILNOSW HOWLINGS	GHIPRSUU GURUSHIP	STRIKING
GHHOORTU THOROUGH	GHILNPSU INGULPHS	GHLMOOOS HOMOLOGS	GIIKNSSV SKIVINGS
GHHOSTTU THOUGHTS	GHILNRSU HURLINGS	GHLMOOOY HOMOLOGY	GIILLMNS MILLINGS
GHIIJNOS JINGOISH	GHILNRTU HURTLING	GHLNNOOR LONGHORN	GIILLMNU ILLUMING
GHIIKNNT THINKING	GHILNRUY HUNGRILY	GHLNOORU HOURLONG	GIILLNOS GILLIONS
GHIIKNPS KINGSHIP	GHILNSSU SLUSHING	GHLNORSU SLUGHORN	GIILLNPR PRILLING
GHIIKNRS SHIRKING	GHILNSTU HUSTLING	GHLNOTYY YONGTHLY	GIILLNPS SPILLING
SHRIKING	SUNLIGHT	GHLOOORY HOROLOGY	GIILLNQU QUILLING
GHIIKNSW WHISKING	GHILORSW SHOWGIRL	GHLORTUU TURLOUGH	GIILLNRT TRILLING
GHIILLNO HILLOING	GHILPRTY TRIGLYPH	GHMORSSU SORGHUMS	GIILLNST STILLING
GHIILLNS SHILLING	GHIMMNSU HUMMINGS	GHMOSSTU MUGSHOTS	TILLINGS
GHIILMST MISLIGHT	GHIMNOPU GUMPHION	GHMPSSUY SPHYGMUS	GIILLNSW SWILLING
GHIILMTY MIGHTILY	GHIMNORU HUMORING	GHNOPRSY GRYPHONS	GIILLNTT LITTLING
GHIILNPR HIRPLING	GHIMNOTU MOUTHING	GHNOPYYY HYPOGYNY	GIILLNTW TWILLING
GHIILNRS HIRLINGS	GHIMNPTU THUMPING	GHNOSSTU GUNSHOTS	GIILLNWY WILLYING
HIRSLING	GHIMNRTY RYTHMING	SHOTGUNS	GIILLOPW POLLIWIG
GHIILNRT THIRLING	GHIMNSTU GUNSMITH	GHNOSTUU UNSOUGHT	GIILLPSW PIGSWILL
GHIILNRW WHIRLING	GHIMRSSU SIMURGHS	GHNOSTUY YOUNGTHS	GIILLTUY GUILTILY
GHIILNST TINGLISH	GHINNNSU SHUNNING	GHOOOSSW HOOSGOWS	GIILMMNP PLIMMING
GHIILNTW WHITLING	GHINNOOR HONORING	GHOORTUY YOGHOURT	GIILMMNS SLIMMING
GHIILTTW TWILIGHT	GHINNOPY PHONYING	GHOPRTUW UPGROWTH	GIILMNNU LUMINING
GHIIMMNW WHIMMING	GHINNORS HORNINGS	GHORSTUY YOGHURTS	UNLIMING
GHIIMNNU INHUMING	GHINNORT NORTHING	GIIILMNT LIMITING	GIILMNOS SMOILING
GHIIMNST SMITHING	THORNING	GIIILNNS INISLING	GIILMNPS LIMPINGS
GHIINNNS SHINNING	THRONING	GIIILNNU LINGUINI	SIMPLING
GHIINNNT THINNING	GHINNOST NOTHINGS	GIIILOTV VITILIGO	GIILMNPW WIMPLING
GHIINNNY HINNYING	GHINNSSU SNUSHING	GIIIMMNX IMMIXING	GIILMNPY IMPLYING
GHIINNRS SHRINING	GHINNSTU HUNTINGS	GIIINNOS IONISING	GIILMNSS SMILINGS
GHIINNST NITHINGS	SHUNTING	GIIINNOT IGNITION	GIILMNST MISTLING
GHIINNSW WHININGS	GHINOOPT PHOTOING	GIIINNOZ IONIZING	GIILMNZZ MIZZLING
GHIINNUV UNHIVING	GHINOOPW WHOOPING	GIIINNTV INVITING	GIILMPRS PILGRIMS
GHIINOST HOISTING	GHINOOST SHOOTING	GIIINSTV VISITING	GIILMPSU PUGILISM
GHIINPPS HIPPINGS	SOOTHING	GIIJMMNY JIMMYING	GIILNNNU UNLINING
SHIPPING	GHINOOSW WOOSHING	GIIJMNOS JINGOISM	GIILNNPP NIPPLING
GHIINPPW WHIPPING	GHINOOTT TOOTHING	GIIJNNOS JOININGS	GIILNNPS SPLINING
GHIINRRS SHIRRING	GHINOOTW WHOOTING	GIIJNNOT JOINTING	GIILNNTU UNTILING
GHIINRRW WHIRRING	GHINOPPS HOPPINGS	GIIJNNRU INJURING	GIILNNTW TWINLING
GHIINRST SHIRTING	SHOPPING	GIIJNOST JINGOIST	WINTLING
GHIINRSV SHRIVING	GHINOPPW WHOPPING	JOISTING	GIILNNUV UNLIVING

Letters	Words
GIILNOPS	SPOILING
GIILNOPT	PILOTING
GIILNORS	LIGROINS
GIILNOSS	SOILINGS
GIILNOST	TOILINGS
GIILNPPR	RIPPLING
GIILNPPS	SIPPLING
	SLIPPING
GIILNPPT	TIPPLING
GIILNPRS	SPIRLING
GIILNPRT	TRIPLING
GIILNPSS	LISPINGS
	SPILINGS
GIILNQSU	QUISLING
GIILNQTU	QUILTING
GIILNRSW	SWIRLING
GIILNRTW	TWIRLING
GIILNRVY	VIRGINLY
GIILNSST	LISTINGS
GIILNSTT	SLITTING
	STILTING
	TILTINGS
	TITLINGS
GIILNSTU	LINGUIST
GIILNSTW	WITLINGS
GIILNSTY	STINGILY
GIILNSZZ	SIZZLING
GIILNTTT	TITTLING
GIILNTTU	TITULING
GIILNTTW	TWILTING
GIILOSST	OLIGISTS
GIILPSTU	PUGILIST
GIILRSST	STRIGILS
GIIMMNPR	PRIMMING
GIIMMNRT	TRIMMING
GIIMMNRU	IMMURING
GIIMMNSW	SWIMMING
GIIMMNOP	IMPONING
GIIMMNOY	IGNOMINY
GIIMMNTU	MINUTING
	MUNITING
	MUTINING
GIIMNOPS	IMPOSING
GIIMNOST	MOISTING
GIIMNOTT	OMITTING
GIIMNOTV	MOTIVING
	VOMITING
GIIMNPPR	PRIMPING
GIIMNPRS	PRIMINGS
GIIMNPRU	UMPIRING
GIIMNPTU	IMPUTING
GIIMNRRS	SMIRRING
GIIMNSST	MISTINGS
GIIMNSSU	MISUSING
GIIMNSSW	SWINGISM
GIIMNSTT	SMITTING
GIIMNSTU	MUISTING
GIIMNSTY	STIMYING
GIIMORRS	RIGORISM
GIINNNOO	ONIONING
GIINNNOT	INTONING
	NOINTING
GIINNNPS	PINNINGS
	SPINNING
GIINNNRU	INURNING
GIINNNST	TINNINGS
GIINNNSW	WINNINGS
GIINNNTW	TWINNING
GIINNOPR	PROINING
GIINNOPS	PIONINGS
GIINNOPT	POINTING
GIINNOQU	QUOINING
GIINNORS	IRONINGS
	ROSINING
GIINNORT	IGNITRON
GIINNPPS	SNIPPING
GIINNPSS	SNIPINGS
GIINNPSU	PINGUINS
GIINNRSS	RINSINGS
GIINNRSU	INSURING
	RUININGS
GIINNRTU	UNTIRING
GIINNRUW	UNWIRING
GIINNSSW	INSWINGS
GIINNSTT	STINTING
	TINTINGS
GIINNSTU	UNITINGS
GIINNSTW	TWININGS
GIINNUVW	UNWIVING
GIINOPST	POSITING
	SOPITING
GIINOPTV	PIVOTING
GIINOQTU	QUOITING
GIINORSS	SIGNIORS
GIINORST	RIOTINGS
	ROISTING
	ROSITING
GIINORSV	VISORING
GIINORTZ	ROZITING
GIINORVZ	VIZORING
GIINOSTT	STOITING
GIINPPQU	QUIPPING
GIINPPRT	TRIPPING
GIINPPST	TIPPINGS
GIINPRSS	RISPINGS
GIINPRST	SPIRTING
	STRIPING
GIINPRSU	SIRUPING
	UPRISING
GIINPSTT	PITTINGS
	SPITTING
GIINPTTU	TITUPING
GIINQRSU	SQUIRING
GIINQRTU	QUIRTING
GIINQTTU	QUITTING
GIINQUZZ	QUIZZING
GIINRRST	STIRRING
GIINRSTV	STRIVING
GIINRSTW	WRITINGS
GIINSSSW	SWISSING
GIINSSTT	SITTINGS
GIINSSTU	SUITINGS
	TISSUING
GIINSTTW	TWISTING
	WITTINGS
GIINTTTW	TWITTING
GIIORRST	RIGORIST
GIIPRSTZ	SPRITZIG
GIJKLNOY	JOKINGLY
GIJLLNOY	JOLLYING
GIJLNOST	JOSTLING
GIJLNSTU	JUSTLING
GIJNOSTT	JOTTINGS
GIJNOSTU	JOUSTING
GIJNTTUY	JUTTYING
GIKKLNSU	SKULKING
GIKKNNSU	SKUNKING
GIKLLNNO	KNOLLING
GIKLNNOP	PLONKING
GIKLNNPU	PLUNKING
GIKLNNRU	KNURLING
	RUNKLING
GIKLNNUY	UNKINGLY
GIKLNOOS	LOOKINGS
GIKLNOPR	PORKLING
GIKLNRSU	LURKINGS
GIKMNOSS	SMOKINGS
GIKNNOOS	SNOOKING
GIKNNOQU	QUONKING
GIKNNOSW	SNOWKING
GIKNNOTT	KNOTTING
GIKNNOTU	KNOUTING
GIKNNOUY	UNYOKING
GIKNNPSU	SPUNKING
GIKNNRTU	TRUNKING
GIKNOOPS	SPOOKING
GIKNOOST	STOOKING
GIKNOOTW	KOTOWING
GIKNOPST	KINGPOST
GIKNORRW	RINGWORK
GIKNORST	STROKING
GIKNORSW	WORKINGS
GILLMOOY	GLOOMILY
GILLNNSU	NULLINGS
GILLNOPR	PROLLING
GILLNOPS	POLLINGS
GILLNORS	ROLLINGS
GILLNORT	TROLLING
GILLNOST	TOLLINGS
GILLNOSY	LOSINGLY
GILLNOVY	LOVINGLY
GILLNPUY	PULINGLY
GILLNSUY	SULLYING
GILLOOPW	POLLIWOG
GILLOPSS	LIPGLOSS
GILLOPWY	POLLYWIG
GILLORVY	GILLYVOR
GILLOSSY	GLOSSILY
GILMMNSU	SLUMMING
GILMNOOS	SLOOMING
GILMNOPY	MOPINGLY
GILMNORS	MORLINGS
GILMNORT	MORTLING
GILMNOSS	MOSLINGS
GILMNOSU	MOUSLING
GILMNOSY	SMOYLING
GILMNOTT	MOTTLING
GILMNOTU	MOULTING
GILMNOUV	VOLUMING
GILMNOVY	MOVINGLY
GILMNPPU	PLUMPING
GILMNPRU	RUMPLING
GILMNPSU	SLUMPING
GILMNSUY	MUSINGLY
GILMNUZZ	MUZZLING
GILMOOSY	MISOLOGY
GILMPRUY	GRUMPILY
GILNNOOS	GLONOINS
	LOONINGS
	SNOOLING
GILNNOSU	NOUSLING
GILNNOTW	TOWNLING
GILNNOUV	UNLOVING
GILNNRSU	NURSLING
GILNNSSU	UNSLINGS
GILNNUZZ	NUZZLING
GILNOOPS	LOOPINGS
	SPOOLING
GILNOORT	ROOTLING
GILNOOST	STOOLING
	TOOLINGS
GILNOOTT	TOOTLING
GILNOOVY	VINOLOGY
GILNOOWY	WOOINGLY
GILNOPPP	PLOPPING
	POPPLING
GILNOPPS	LOPPINGS
	SLOPPING
GILNOPPT	TOPPLING
GILNOPRU	PROULING
GILNOPRW	PROWLING
GILNOPSU	SOUPLING
GILNOPSY	POSINGLY
	SPONGILY
GILNOPTT	PLOTTING
GILNORSU	LOURINGS
GILNORTU	TROULING
GILNORVY	ROVINGLY
GILNOSSW	SLOWINGS
GILNOSTT	SLOTTING
GILNOSTU	TOUSLING
GILNOSVW	WOLVINGS
GILNOSWY	YOWLINGS
GILNOSZZ	SOZZLING
GILNOTUY	OUTLYING
GILNOTUZ	TOUZLING
GILNPPRU	PURPLING
GILNPPSU	SUPPLING
GILNPRSU	PURLINGS
	SLURPING
	SPURLING
GILNPRYY	PRYINGLY
GILNPSSU	PLUSSING
GILNRRSU	SLURRING
GILNRSTU	LUSTRING
	RUSTLING
GILNRTTU	TURTLING
GILNRTYY	TRYINGLY
GILNSSTU	SINGULTS
	TUSSLING
GILNSTTU	SUTTLING
GILNTUUY	UNGUILTY
GILNUWZZ	WUZZLING
GILOOORS	ROSOGLIO
GILOOOST	OOLOGIST
GILOORSS	GIROSOLS
GILOORSU	GLORIOUS
GILOORVY	VIROLOGY
GILOOSSS	ISOGLOSS
GILOOSTY	SITOLOGY
GILORSTT	TRIGLOTS
GILOSTUY	GULOSITY
GIMMMNSU	MUMMINGS
GIMMMNUY	MUMMYING
GIMMNOTY	TOMMYING
GIMMNSSU	SUMMINGS
GIMMNSTU	STUMMING
GIMMOSSU	GUMMOSIS
GIMNNORS	MORNINGS
GIMNNORU	MOURNING
GIMNNOTU	MOUNTING
GIMNNOUV	UNMOVING
GIMNNSTU	MUNTINGS
GIMNOOOU	OOGONIUM
GIMNOOPS	SPOOMING
GIMNOORS	MOORINGS
	SMOORING
GIMNOORT	MOTORING

GIMNOORV VROOMING	GINOPPQU QUOPPING	GIOPRSTU GROUPIST	HIIKSSTT SKITTISH
GIMNOOSS OSMOSING	GINOPPSS SOPPINGS	GIORSTUY RUGOSITY	HIILMMSS SLIMMISH
GIMNOOST MOOTINGS	GINOPPST STOPPING	GJOORSTT JOGTROTS	HIILMOST HOMILIST
SMOOTING	TOPPINGS	GKLOOOTY TOKOLOGY	HIILMPSU SILPHIUM
GIMNOPST STOMPING	GINOPPSW SWOPPING	GLLOOPTY POLYGLOT	HIILMPSY IMPISHLY
GIMNOPTU GUMPTION	GINOPRSS PROSINGS	GLLOOPWY POLLYWOG	HIILMSTU LITHIUMS
GIMNORRU RUMORING	GINOPRST SPORTING	GLLOOXYY XYLOLOGY	HIILMSWY WHIMSILY
GIMNORRW RINGWORM	GINOPRSU INGROUPS	GLMNOOOT MONOGLOT	HIILMTUY HUMILITY
GIMNORST STORMING	POURINGS	GLMNOOOY MONOLOGY	HIILPSST THLIPSIS
GIMNORSU ROUMINGS	GINOPRTU TROUPING	NOMOLOGY	HIILPSSY SYPHILIS
GIMNOSST GNOMISTS	GINOPSST POSTINGS	GLMOOOPY POMOLOGY	HIILRSTT TRILITHS
GIMNOSSU MOUSINGS	SIGNPOST	GLMOOORS MOORLOGS	HIILSSTT STILTISH
SMOUSING	STOPINGS	GLMOOYYZ ZYMOLOGY	HIIMNSTT TINSMITH
SOUMINGS	GINOPSSU SPOUSING	GLMORSUW LUGWORMS	HIIMOPSS PHIMOSIS
GIMNOSTU MOUSTING	GINOPSTT SPOTTING	GLNNOORS LORGNONS	HIIMSSTT SHITTIMS
SMOUTING	GINOPSTU POUTINGS	GLNOOOSY NOSOLOGY	HIINORST HISTRION
GIMNOSYY MISOGYNY	SPOUTING	GLNOOOTY ONTOLOGY	HIINPSTW TWINSHIP
GIMNPRTU TRUMPING	GINOPTTY TYPTOING	GLNOOPRS PROLONGS	HIIORSST HISTRIOS
GIMNPSTU STUMPING	GINORRWY WORRYING	GLNOOPSY POLYGONS	HIIPPQSU QUIPPISH
GIMNRRSU SMURRING	GINORSST SORTINGS	GLNOOPYY POLYGONY	HIKNNORS INKHORNS
GIMNSTTU SMUTTING	GINORSSU SOURINGS	GLNOPYYY POLYGYNY	HIKNNSTU UNTHINKS
GIMNSTYY STYMYING	GINORSTU ROUSTING	GLNORSTY STRONGLY	HIKNOTTU OUTTHINK
GIMPSSYY GYPSYISM	ROUTINGS	GLNORTUW LUNGWORT	HIKOOPSS SPOOKISH
GIMRSSUU GURUISMS	TOURINGS	GLNOSSUW SUNGLOWS	HIKOPSSY KYPHOSIS
GINNNOOS NOONINGS	GINORSTW STROWING	GLNOSTTU GLUTTONS	HILLMSUY MULISHLY
GINNNOST STONNING	WORSTING	GLNOTTUY GLUTTONY	HILLNOUY UNHOLILY
GINNNPSU PUNNINGS	GINORSTY ROYSTING	GLOOOPSY POSOLOGY	HILLOPST HILLTOPS
GINNNRSU RUNNINGS	STORYING	GLOOOPTY OPTOLOGY	HILMMOSU HOLMIUMS
GINNNSTU STUNNING	STROYING	TOPOLOGY	HILMNOOT MONOLITH
TUNNINGS	GINORTTT TROTTING	GLOOORUY OUROLOGY	HILMOOPT PHILOMOT
GINNNTUU UNTUNING	GINORTTU TROUTING	GLOOPSSY GOSSYPOL	HILMOPSY MOPISHLY
GINNOOPS SNOOPING	TUTORING	GLOOPTYY TYPOLOGY	HILMOSSW WHOLISMS
SPOONING	GINOSSSS SOSSINGS	GLOORSUU ORGULOUS	HILMPPSU PLUMPISH
GINNOOST SNOOTING	GINOSSST TOSSINGS	GMMPSUUW MUGWUMPS	HILMPSYY SYMPHILY
GINNOOSW SWOONING	GINOSSSU SOUSINGS	GMNNOOOY MONOGONY	HILMSTUU THULIUMS
GINNOOSZ SNOOZING	GINOSSSW SOWSSING	GMNNOOYY MONOGYNY	HILNOPSU UNPOLISH
GINNOPPU UNPOPING	GINOSSTT SOTTINGS	GMNOORSU GUNROOMS	HILNOSTY TONISHLY
GINNOPRU UNROPING	GINOSSTU TOUSINGS	GMNOORSW MORWONGS	HILOOPYZ ZOOPHILY
GINNOPRY PROYNING	GINOSSTV STOVINGS	GMORSTUW MUGWORTS	HILOOSTT OTOLITHS
GINNOPSS SPONGINS	GINOSSTW STOWINGS	GNNPRSUU UNSPRUNG	HILOOSTZ ZOOLITHS
SPONSING	GINOSTTT STOTTING	GNNRSTUU UNSTRUNG	HILOPPSY POPISHLY
GINNOPSY PYONINGS	TOTTINGS	GNOOORSS GORSOONS	HILORSTU UROLITHS
GINNOPTY POYNTING	GINOSTTW SWOTTING	GNOOOSSS GOSSOONS	HILORTWY WORTHILY
GINNORSS SNORINGS	GINOSTUW OUTSWING	GNOORSUW WRONGOUS	HILOSSTY HYLOISTS
SORNINGS	OUTWINGS	GNOORTUW OUTGROWN	THYLOSIS
GINNORST SNORTING	GINOTUVY OUTVYING	GNOPRSTU GUNPORTS	HILOSTWW WHITLOWS
GINNORSU GRUNIONS	GINPPPUY PUPPYING	GNPPRSUU UPSPRUNG	HILOSTYY TOYISHLY
GINNOSST STONINGS	GINPPRSU UPSPRING	GOORSTUW OUTGROWS	HILPPRSU PURPLISH
GINNOSTT SNOTTING	GINPPRRSU PURRINGS	GOORTTUW GOUTWORT	HILPPSUY UPPISHLY
GINNOSTU SNOUTING	SPURRING	HHIINNST THINNISH	HILPRSUW UPWHIRLS
STOUNING	GINPRSTU SPURTING	HHIIPSST PHTHISIS	HILSSTTU SLUTTISH
GINNOSTY STONYING	GINPRSUU PURSUING	HHILPSSY SYLPHISH	HIMMOPRU PHORMIUM
GINNOSUW SWOUNING	USURPING	HHIMNPSY NYMPHISH	HIMMSSTY MYTHISMS
GINNPRSU PRUNINGS	GINPRSUY SYRUPING	HHIMPSSU SUMPHISH	HIMNOPRX PHORMINX
SPURNING	GINPSSUW UPSWINGS	HHINOOSW NOHOWISH	HIMNOPSY PHISNOMY
GINNRSTU TURNINGS	GINPSTTU PUTTINGS	HHIORSST SHORTISH	HIMNSSTY HYMNISTS
UNSTRING	GINPTTUY PUTTYING	HHKKSSUU KHUSKHUS	HIMOOPRS ISOMORPH
GINNSTTU NUTTINGS	GINRSSTU RUSTINGS	HHMRSTUY RHYTHMUS	HIMOPRWW WHIPWORM
STUNTING	TRUSSING	HHOOPPRS PHOSPHOR	HIMOPSSS SOPHISMS
GINNSTUY UNTYINGS	GINRSTTU RUTTINGS	HHOOSSTT HOTSHOTS	HIMOPSST PHOTISMS
GINOOPPS OPPOSING	STURTING	HIIILMNS NIHILISM	HIMORSTU HUMORIST
GINOOPRS SPOORING	TRUSTING	HIIILNST NIHILIST	THORIUMS
GINOOPRT TROOPING	GINRSTTY TRYSTING	HIIILNTY NIHILITY	HIMOTTVZ MITZVOTH
GINOOPSS SOOPINGS	GINRSTUU SUTURING	HIINNRST RHINITIS	HIMPRSTU TRIUMPHS
GINOOPST STOOPING	GIOOPRRS PORRIGOS	HIIKMNST MISTHINK	HIMPSTUY PYTHIUMS
GINOOPSW SWOOPING	GIOORRSU RIGOROUS	HIIKMRSS SKIRMISH	HIMRSSTY RHYMISTS
GINOORST ROOSTING	GIOORSTU GOITROUS	HIIKNNSS KINSHIPS	HIMSSTTY MYTHISTS
ROOTINGS	GIOORSUV VIGOROUS	HIIKOPRS PIROSHKI	HINNORST TINHORNS
GINOORTW WROOTING	GIOPRRSU PRURIGOS	HIIKOPRZ PIROZHKI	HINNPSSU NUNSHIPS
GINOPPPR PROPPING	GIOPRSSY GOSSIPRY	HIIKQRSU QUIRKISH	HINNSSUY SUNSHINY

HINOORST HORNITOS	IIIKMNNS MINIKINS	IIMNNOOT MONITION	IKMNPPSU PUMPKINS
HINOORSZ HORIZONS	IIIKMNSS MINISKIS	IIMNNOSU UNIONISM	IKMNRSTU TRINKUMS
HINOPPSS SHIPPONS	IIILLMNP MINIPILL	IIMNNOTU MUNITION	IKNNRSTU TURNSKIN
HINOPSSS SONSHIPS	IIILLMNU ILLINIUM	IIMNOOSS OMISSION	IKNOOPRT PINKROOT
HINOPSSY HYPNOSIS	IIILLNOS ILLISION	IIMNOPRS IMPRISON	IKNOORRW IRONWORK
HINOPSTW TOWNSHIP	IIILMRSV VIRILISM	IIMNOPST MISPOINT	IKNOOSST ISOKONTS
HINORSST HORNISTS	IIILMUVX LIXIVIUM	IIMNORTT INTROMIT	IKNOPSST INKSPOTS
HINORTXY THYROXIN	IIILRTVY VIRILITY	IIMNORTY MINORITY	IKNOPSTW TOWNSKIP
HIOOPRTT POORTITH	IIIMMMNS MINIMISM	IIMNOSSS MISSIONS	IKNPSSTU SPUTNIKS
HIOORSST ORTHOSIS	IIIMMNST INTIMISM	IIMNOSST SIMONIST	IKORSSTU KURTOSIS
HIOOSSTT SHOOTIST	MINIMIST	IIMNOSTX MIXTIONS	IKORSTTU OUTSKIRT
HIOPRSSW WORSHIPS	IIIMMPRS IMPRIMIS	IIMNPRST IMPRINTS	ILLLMOPS PLIMSOLL
HIOPRSUZ RHIZOPUS	IIIMNSTT INTIMIST	MISPRINT	ILLLMPPU PULPMILL
HIOPSSST SOPHISTS	IIIMNTTY INTIMITY	IIMNPTUY IMPUNITY	ILLLOOPP LOLLIPOP
HIOPSSTU UPHOISTS	IIINORRS IRRISION	IIMNRSTY MINISTRY	ILLMNOSU MULLIONS
HIOPSSTY PHYTOSIS	IIINPRST INSPIRIT	IIMOPSTT OPTIMIST	ILLMOORS MOORILLS
HIORRSSY SORRYISH	IIINQTUY INIQUITY	IIMOSSTY MYOSITIS	ILLMOPRW PILLWORM
HIOSSTTU STOUTISH	IIINSSTU SINUITIS	IIMOTTVY MOTIVITY	ILLMPTUY MULTIPLY
HIPPPSUY PUPPYISH	IIIOSTTI OUISTITI	IIMPRTUY IMPURITY	ILLNOQSU QUILLONS
HKMNORRU KRUMHORN	IIISSTTW WISTITIS	IIMRRTUV TRIUMVIR	ILLNORSU RULLIONS
HKNOORRW HORNWORK	IIJJMNSS MISJOINS	IIMRSTTU TRITIUMS	ILLNPSUU LUPULINS
HKOOOPST POTHOOKS	IIJNNOST INJOINTS	IIMRSTUV TRIVIUMS	ILLOOPRW POORWILL
HKOOPRSW WORKSHOP	IIKLLNOS SKILLION	IIMSSSTU MISSUITS	ILLOORSZ ZORILLOS
HLLLOOWY HOLLOWLY	IIKLMNPS LIMPKINS	IIMSSTUW SWIMSUIT	ILLOPPSS SLIPSLOP
HLLMNOOU MONOHULL	IIKLMPSY SKIMPILY	IINNOOPS OPINIONS	ILLOPPSY SLOPPILY
HLLOPPRY PROPHYLL	IIKLNOSS OILSKINS	IINNOPTU PUNITION	ILLOPRTW PILLWORT
HLMOOSTY SMOOTHLY	IIKMNORS KIRIMONS	IINNOSTU INUSTION	ILLOPRXY PROLIXLY
HLMORRSY MYRRHOLS	IIKMNPSS SIMPKINS	UNIONIST	ILLORSUY ILLUSORY
HLNOOPPY POLYPHON	IIKNOSTT STOTINKI	UNITIONS	ILLOSTXY XYLITOLS
HLOPRSTY PROTHYLS	IILLLPUV PULVILLI	IINNPSST TINSNIPS	ILLOTTWY WITTOLLY
HLPRSSUU SULPHURS	IILLMNOS MILLIONS	IINNSTTU TINNITUS	ILLRSTUY SULTRILY
HLPRSUUY SULPHURY	IILLMRTU TRILLIUM	IINOOPST POSITION	ILMNOOPS POLONISM
HMMNOOSY HOMONYMS	IILLNOOR ORILLION	IINOPSSS ISOSPINS	ILMNOOPU POLONIUM
HMMNOOYY HOMONYMY	IILLNOPS PILLIONS	IINORSST IRONISTS	ILMNOSUU LUMINOUS
HMMOORSU MUSHROOM	IILLNORT TRILLION	IINORSTT INTROITS	ILMOPPSU POPULISM
HMMRSTUU HUMSTRUM	IILLNOST STILLION	IINOSTTU TUITIONS	ILMORSTU TURMOILS
HMNOOOST MOONSHOT	IILLNOSU ILLUSION	IINOSTVY VINOSITY	ILMORSTY STORMILY
HMNOOOTY HOMOTONY	IILLNOSZ ZILLIONS	IINRTTUY TRIUNITY	ILMOSTUV VOLUMIST
HMNOORRW HORNWORM	IILLNSST INSTILLS	IINSSTTW TWISTINS	ILMOSTUY TIMOUSLY
HMNOOSTU UNSMOOTH	IILLNSTT LITTLINS	IIOOPSTV OVIPOSIT	ILMPPTUU PULPITUM
HMNOPSYY HYPONYMS	IILLOPUV PULVILIO	IIOOSTTY OTIOSITY	ILMPSSTU PLUMISTS
SYMPHONY	IILMMPSS SIMPLISM	IIOPRRTY PRIORITY	ILMPSTUY STUMPILY
HMOOOPRZ ZOOMORPH	IILMMSUU SIMULIUM	IIOPRSSS PISSOIRS	ILMSSTUU STIMULUS
HMOOORSW SHOWROOM	IILMNORT MIRLITON	IIORRRSY IRRISORY	ILMSTTUY SMUTTILY
HMOOPTYY HOMOTYPY	IILMNOSS LIONISMS	IIORSSTV IVORISTS	ILNOOPSS PLOSIONS
HMOORSUU HUMOROUS	IILMNSTU LUMINIST	VISITORS	ILNOOPSV VOLPINOS
HNOOOOPR OOPHORON	IILMORSS SIMILORS	IIORSTUV VIRTUOSI	ILNOOPSY SPOONILY
HNOOPRSW SHOPWORN	IILMORST TROILISM	IIOSSTTU OUSTITIS	ILNOOSST SOLITONS
HNOOPSTY TYPHOONS	IILMOTTY MOTILITY	IIPRSSTU SPIRITUS	ILNOOSTU SOLUTION
HNOORRTW HORNWORT	IILMPSST SIMPLIST	IJKLLOSY KILLJOYS	ILNOOTUV VOLUTION
HNOORSTU SOUTHRON	IILMRSSY MISSILRY	IJLNOQSU JONQUILS	ILNOPRSU PURLOINS
HNOOSSTU UNSHOOTS	IILNNOOT NOLITION	IJNNOSTU UNJOINTS	ILNOPSSU UPSILONS
HNOPRTUW UPTHROWN	IILNNSSU INSULINS	IKKLNORW LINKWORK	ILNOPSSW SNOWSLIP
HNORSTUW UNWORTHS	IILNOOST INOSITOL	IKKLNOSY KOLINSKY	ILNOPSSY YPSILONS
HNORTUWY UNWORTHY	IILNOOTV VOLITION	IKKMNOSU KIKUMONS	ILNOPSTU UNSPOILT
HNOSSTUU UNSHOUTS	IILNORSS SIRLOINS	IKKNORST KIRKTONS	ILNORSST NOSTRILS
HNRSTTUU UNTRUTHS	IILOOPPR LIRIPOOP	IKKNORTW KIRKTOWN	ILNORSSU SURLOINS
HOOOSTTU OUTSHOOT	IILOPRST TRIPOLIS	IKLLOOTV KILOVOLT	ILNORSTU TORULINS
HOOPPSTY PHOTOPSY	IILOPSSS PSILOSIS	IKLLOSSY KYLLOSIS	ILNORTXY NITROXYL
HOOPRRST PORTHORS	IILOPSST PTILOSIS	IKLMNPSU LUMPKINS	ILNOSSTW STOWLINS
HOOPSSTU UPSHOOTS	IILOPSTY PILOSITY	IKLMORSW SILKWORM	ILNOSTTY SNOTTILY
HOOPSSTY TOYSHOPS	IILORSTT TROILIST	IKLMORTW MILKWORT	ILNOSTUV VOLUTINS
HOORTTUW OUTWORTH	IILORSTV VITRIOLS	IKLNOOST KILOTONS	ILNPSUUV PULVINUS
HOOSSTTU OUTSHOTS	IILOSSTV VIOLISTS	IKLNPSSU SKULPINS	ILOOORSS ROSOLIOS
HOPPRRYY PORPHYRY	IILRSSTU SILURIST	IKLOOPSY SPOOKILY	ILOOPPRS PROPOLIS
HOPRRSUY PYRRHOUS	IILSTUUV UVULITIS	IKLOOSTT TOOLKITS	ILOOPSST POLOISTS
HOPRSTUW UPTHROWS	IILSTUVV VULVITIS	IKLOSSSU SOUSLIKS	ILOORSTU RISOLUTO
HPRSTTUU UPTHRUST	IIMMNTUY IMMUNITY	IKMNNOSW MISKNOWN	ILOOSSST SOLOISTS
IIIJJLNS JINJILIS	IIMMOPST OPTIMISM	IKMNOOOS OKIMONOS	ILOPPSTU POPULIST
IIIKLNPS SPILIKIN	IIMMSTTU MITTIMUS	IKMNOSSW MISKNOWS	ILOPRSTY SPORTILY

ILOPSTTY	SPOTTILY		SPONSION	IOQRTUXY	QUIXOTRY	MMOPSSTY	SYMPTOMS
ILOPSUUV	PLUVIOUS	INNOOPSU	UNPOISON	IORRSUVV	SURVIVOR	MNNOOOSS	MONSOONS
ILOQRTUU	LOQUITUR	INNOORST	NOTORNIS	IORSSTTU	TOURISTS	MNNOOOTY	MONOTONY
ILPPRTUY	PULPITRY	INNOPRSU	UNPRISON	IORSSUUU	USURIOUS	MNNOSSYY	SYNONYMS
ILRSTTUY	TRUSTILY	INNOSSTU	NONSUITS	IORSTTUY	TOURISTY	MNNOSTUU	UNMOUNTS
ILRSTUUX	LUXURIST	INOOOSSZ	ZOONOSIS		YTTRIOUS	MNNOSYYY	SYNONYMY
ILSSSTTY	STYLISTS	INOOOTXZ	ZOOTOXIN	IORSTUUV	VIRTUOUS	MNOOOPPS	POMPOONS
IMMNOSSU	MUSIMONS	INOOPRST	PORTIONS	IPRRSSTU	STIRRUPS	MNOOORTW	MOONWORT
IMMNOSUU	MUONIUMS		POSITRON	IPRRSTUU	PRURITUS	MNOOORXY	OXYMORON
IMMOORTU	MOTORIUM		SORPTION	IPRSSTUU	PURSUITS	MNOOPRTU	PRONOTUM
IMMRSTUY	SUMMITRY	INOOPSSS	POISSONS	JLNSTUUY	UNJUSTLY	MNOOPSTY	TOPONYMS
IMMSSSTU	SUMMISTS	INOOPSST	POSITONS	JLOOSUYY	JOYOUSLY	MNOOPTYY	TOPONYMY
IMNNNOSU	MUNNIONS	INOOPSTT	SPITTOON	JMOPSTUU	OUTJUMPS	MNOOSTTW	TOWMONTS
IMNNOORS	NORIMONS	INOOPTTU	OUTPOINT	JNNOORRU	NONJUROR	MNORSSTU	NOSTRUMS
IMNNOOTT	MONOTINT	INOORSST	ISOTRONS	JNOORSSU	SOJOURNS	MNORSTUU	SURMOUNT
IMNNOSUU	NUMINOUS		TORSIONS	JNOOSUUY	UNJOYOUS	MOOOPRRT	PROMOTOR
IMNOOPPS	POMPIONS	INOORSTY	SONORITY	KKNOORTW	KNOTWORK	MOOORRTW	TOMORROW
IMNOOPST	TOMPIONS	INOPPSST	TOPSPINS	KKOOSSUU	KOUSKOUS	MOOPSSSU	OPOSSUMS
IMNOOPSU	OPSONIUM	INOPRTUY	PUNITORY	KLLMNSUU	NUMSKULL	MOORRSUU	RUMOROUS
IMNOORRS	MORRIONS	INOPSSSU	POUSSINS	KLLMOSSU	MOLLUSKS	MOORSTUU	TUMOROUS
IMNOORST	MONITORS	INOPSSSY	SYNOPSIS	KLNORSTY	KLYSTRON	MORRSSTU	ROSTRUMS
	TROMINOS	INOPSSTU	SPINOUTS	KLOOORWW	WOOLWORK	MORSSTUU	STRUMOUS
IMNOORTY	MONITORY	INORSSUV	UNVISORS	KLOOOSTU	LOOKOUTS	NNOOOPST	PONTOONS
IMNOORVY	OMNIVORY	INPPRRUU	PURPURIN		OUTLOOKS		SPONTOON
IMNOOSUX	OXONIUMS	INPRSSTU	UNSTRIPS	KLOOPRSW	SLOPWORK	NNOOPRSU	PRONOUNS
IMNOPPSU	PUMPIONS	INPRSSTY	TRYPSINS	KMOOORRW	WORKROOM	NNOOPSSS	SPONSONS
IMNORRSU	MURRIONS	INPRSTTU	TURNSPIT	KNNNOSUW	UNKNOWNS	NOOOPPRS	PROSOPON
IMNORSTY	TRIONYMS	INRSSTTU	INTRUSTS	KNOOPSTT	TOPKNOTS	NOOORSSS	SONOROUS
IMNOSTUU	MUTINOUS	INSSSTUU	SUNSUITS	KNOPRSTY	KRYPTONS	NOOPRSSS	SPONSORS
IMNRSTUU	UNTRUISM	INSSTTUW	UNTWISTS	KOOPRSTW	WORKTOPS	NOORSSTU	UNROOSTS
IMOOPRRS	PROMISOR	IOOPRRSV	PROVISOR	KOORSTUW	OUTWORKS	NOORSTUW	OUTSWORN
IMOOPRST	IMPOSTOR	IOOPRSSV	PROVISOS	KORSTTUW	TUTWORKS	NOPSSSTU	SUNSPOTS
IMOOQSTU	MOSQUITO	IOOPRSSY	ISOSPORY	LLLMMSUU	MULMULLS	NORSTTUU	OUTTURNS
IMOORSTT	MOTORIST	IOOPRSTY	ISOTROPY	LLMOOPRS	ROLLMOPS	NRSSTTUU	UNTRUSTS
IMOORSTU	SUMOTORI		POROSITY	LLOOPRST	TROLLOPS	NRSTTUUY	UNTRUSTY
	TIMOROUS	IOORRSTY	SORORITY	LLOOPRTY	TROLLOPY	OOOOPRST	POTOROOS
IMOORSTY	MOROSITY	IOORRTTT	TROTTOIR	LLOSUUVV	VOLVULUS	OOOPRSSU	SOPOROUS
IMOORTVY	VOMITORY	IOORSSTT	RISOTTOS	LMNOOOPY	MONOPOLY	OOOPRSTU	OUTROOPS
IMOOSSTY	MYOSOTIS	IOORSSUV	VOUSSOIR	LMNOOPYY	POLYONYM	OOORSTTU	OUTROOTS
IMOPRRSY	PRIMROSY	IOORSTTU	TORTIOUS	LMOOOORT	TOOLROOM	OOPRSSTV	PROVOSTS
IMOPRSST	TROPISMS	IOORSTUV	VIRTUOSO	LMOOPSYY	POLYSOMY	OOPRSTTU	OUTPORTS
IMOPRSTU	PROTIUMS	IOORSUUX	UXORIOUS	LMOOSSSU	MOLOSSUS		OUTSPORT
IMOPSSTU	UTOPISMS	IOOSSTTU	STOTIOUS	LMOPPRTY	PROMPTLY	OOPRSTUU	OUTPOURS
IMORSSTU	TOURISMS	IOPRRSUV	PROVIRUS	LMRSSTUU	LUSTRUMS	OOPSSSTT	TOSSPOTS
IMORSTTU	TUTORISM	IOPRSSTT	PROTISTS	LNOOOPRT	POLTROON	OOPSSTTU	OUTPOSTS
IMPPPSUY	PUPPYISM		TROPISTS	LNOOOPYZ	POLYZOON	OORSTTUU	TORTUOUS
IMRSSTTU	MISTRUST	IOPRSSUU	SPURIOUS	LNOOPPRY	PROPYLON	OPPRRSTU	PURPORTS
IMRSSTTY	MISTRYST	IOPRSTTU	OUTSTRIP	LNOOPSTU	PULTOONS	OPPRSSTU	SUPPORTS
IMRSTTUY	YTTRIUMS	IOPRSTUU	POURSUIT	LNRSTUUV	VULTURNS	OPRSSSUU	SOURPUSS
INNNORSU	RUNNIONS	IOPRSTUY	PYRITOUS	LOOOORSS	OLOROSOS	ORSSTTUU	SURTOUTS
INNNORTU	TRUNNION	IOPRSUVX	POXVIRUS	LOOPPSUU	POPULOUS	RRSSSUUU	SUSURRUS
INNNOSTY	SYNTONIN	IOPSSTTU	UTOPISTS	LOOPPSUY	POLYPOUS		
INNOOPSS	OPSONINS	IOQRSTTU	QUITTORS	LORSSTUU	LUSTROUS		